LANGENSCHEIDT
STANDARD DICTIONARIES

# LANGENSCHEIDT'S
# STANDARD
# TURKISH DICTIONARY

*First Part*

## Turkish-English

by
RESUHİ AKDİKMEN

Assistant Lexicographer
EKREM UZBAY

# LANGENSCHEIDT

# Contents

### İçindekiler

# Foreword

This Turkish-English part of the dictionary includes all words of common Turkish, which are in practical use today.

The base of the vocabulary is colloquial Turkish; in addition all such areas as engineering, medicine, business, botany, chemistry etc., marked by special symbols or abbreviations, have been given due attention.

The pronunciation of Turkish head-words, which present difficulties with respect to long vowels and stress, has been given following the respective head-word in a simplified manner.

This dictionary contains modern, newly-coined and old (not obsolete) words; care has been taken that all entries are still in common use.

# Önsöz

Sözlüğün Türkçe-İngilizce olan bu kısmı, Türk dilinin günün pratik gereksinimi için gerekli sözcükleri içine almış bulunmaktadır. Türkçe konuşma dili esas olarak alınmış, bunun yanısıra teknik, tıp, ticaret, botanik, kimya v.s. gibi bir çok dallarına da özel sembol ve kısaltmalarıyle geniş ölçüde yer verilmiştir.

Özellikle hecelerinin uzatılması ve vurgulanmasında güçlük çekilen sözcüklerin okunuşu oldukça basit bir şekilde ilgili sözcükten sonra köşeli parantez içinde gösterilmiştir. Sözcüklerin değişik anlamları da, birbirlerine karıştırılmamaları ve kolayca görülüp anlaşılması için numaralandırılmıştır.

Sözlükte en yeni Türkçe sözcükler ile eski gibi görünmesine rağmen hâlâ kullanılan sözcükler de bulunmaktadır. Bunun yanısıra, Türk dilinin en çok kullanılan deyim ve atasözleri de sözlüğe alınmıştır.

Özellikle Türkçe'den İngilizce'ye çevirilerde büyük bir gereksinimi karşılayacak olan bu sözlüğü sunmaktan kıvanç duymaktayız.

# Using the Dictionary
## Sözlüğün Kullanımı

**1.** The tilde (~) replaces the head-word, example:
**vadeli** ...: ~ hesap = vadeli hesap.

**2.** The short hyphen (-) preceding declension and conjugation suffixes replaces the head-word and indicates the writing in one word; example:
**vade** ...: -si gelmek = vadesi gelmek.

**3.** The *-i* case of Turkish nouns and adjectives is, if necessary, given in an abbreviated form; example:
**vahşet,** -ti
**vakıf,** -kfı

**4.** The present tense (geniş zaman) of a Turkish verb is indicated by means of the suffix of the third person; example:
**varmak,** (-ır) = varır
**yanmak,** (-ar) = yanar

**5.** A long vowel of a head-word is marked by a line placed on top of the respective vowel, which is seperately given in brackets; example:
**vahşi** [ī]
**yani** [ā]
**suret,** -ti [ū]

**6.** The character of the syllable, whether short, long or stressed, is indicated by the following symbols [.], [-], [x]; example:
**vanilya** [.x.] (= all syllables are short, the second syllable is stressed).
**viran** [--] (= both syllables are long).

**7.** Phrases and proverbs are registered following the different meanings of the head-word.

**8.** A voiceless consonant at the end of a verbal root becomes voiced when a suffix beginning with a vowel is added. This change is indicated in this way:
**git-mek** (-der) = gider.

# Symbols – Semboller

| | | |
|---|---|---|
| F | colloquial language | konuşma dili |
| P | provincialism | taşra dili |
| † | obsolete | eski |
| ⚔ | rare, little used | az kullanılan |
| ⚘ | botany | botanik, bitkibilim |
| ⊕ | mechanics | mekanik |
| ⚒ | mining | madencilik |
| ✕ | military term | askeri terim |
| ⚓ | nautical term | denizcilik terimi |
| ✝ | commercial term | ticari terim |
| ⛟ | railway, railroad | demiryolu |
| ✈ | aviation | havacılık |
| ✆ | postal affairs | postacılık |
| ♪ | musical term | müzik terimi |
| ◬ | architecture | mimarlık |
| ⚡ | electrical engineering | elektrik mühendisliği |
| ⚖ | jurisprudence | hukuk |
| Å | mathematics | matematik |
| | agriculture | ziraat, tarım |
| ♋ | chemistry | kimya |
| ⚕ | medicine | tıp |
| < | | kelimenin aslı |

# Abbreviations – Kısaltmalar

| | | |
|---|---|---|
| a. | also | keza |
| abbr. | abbreviation | kısaltma |
| abl. | ablative | -den hali |
| acc. | accusative | -i hali |
| adj. | adjective | sıfat |
| adv. | adverb | zarf |
| Am. | Americanism | Amerikan dili |
| anat. | anatomy | anatomi, yapıbilim |
| ast. | astronomy | astronomi, gökbilim |
| b-de | biri(si)nde | |
| b-den | biri(si)nden | |
| b-i | biri(si) | |
| biol. | biology | biyoloji, dirimbilim |
| b-le | biri(si)yle | |
| b-ne | biri(si)ne | |
| b-ni | biri(si)ni | |
| b-nin | biri(si)nin | |
| b.s. | bad sense | kötü anlamda |
| bş | bir şey | |
| bşde | bir şeyde | |
| bşden | bir şeyden | |

| | | |
|---|---|---|
| bşe | bir şeye | |
| bşi | bir şeyi | |
| bşin | bir şeyin | |
| bşle | bir şeyle | |
| caus. | causative | ettirgen |
| co. | comical | komik |
| comp. | comparative | üstünlük derecesi |
| contp. | contemptuously | aşağılayıcı olarak |
| dat. | dative | -e hali |
| eccl. | ecclesiastical | dini |
| emph. | emphatic form | kuvvetlendirilmiş |
| etc. | et cetera | ve saire |
| etm. | etmek | |
| euph. | euphemism | edebikelâm, örtmece |
| fig. | figuratively | mecazi olarak |
| gen. | genitive | -in hali |
| geogr. | geography | coğrafya |
| geol. | geology | jeoloji, yerbilim |
| geom. | geometry | geometri |
| gr. | grammar | gramer, dilbilgisi |
| hist. | history | tarih |
| hunt. | hunting | avcılık |
| ichth | ichthyology | balıklar bilimi |
| inf. | infinitive | mastar, eylemlik |
| int. | interjection | ünlem |
| iro. | ironically | alaylı |
| isl. | Islamic | İslami |
| k-de | kendi(si)nde | |
| k-den | kendi(si)nden | |
| k-le | kendi(si)yle | |
| k-ne | kendi(si)ne | |
| k-ni | kendi(si)ni | |
| k-nin | kendi(si)nin | |
| lit. | literary | edebi, yazınsal |
| loc. | locative | -de hali |
| log. | logic | mantık |
| metall. | metallurgy | metalurji, metalbilim |
| meteor. | meteorology | meteoroloji, havabilgisi |
| mf. | men's forename | erkek ismi |
| mot. | motoring | otomobilcilik |
| myth. | mythology | mitoloji, efsanebilim |
| neol. | neologism | yeni kelime |
| olm. | olmak | |
| o.s. | oneself | kendi(si); kendi kendine |
| paint. | painting | ressamlık |
| parl. | parliamentary term | parlamento terimi |
| part. | particularly | özellikle |
| pass. | passive | edilgen |
| pharm. | pharmacy | eczacılık |
| phls. | philosophy | felsefe |
| phot. | photography | fotoğrafçılık |
| phys. | physics | fizik |
| physiol. | physiology | fizyoloji |
| pl. | plural | çoğul |
| poet. | poetry; poetic | şiir sanatı; şiirsel |
| pol. | politics | siyaset |
| poss. | possessive | iyelik zamiri veya eki |
| pr. n. | proper noun | özel isim |

| pro. | proverb | atasözü |
|------|---------|---------|
| pron. | pronoun | zamir |
| psych. | psychology | psikoloji, ruhbilim |
| refl. | reflexive | dönüşlü fiil |
| s. | see | bakınız |
| sl. | slang | argo |
| s.o. | someone | biri(si) |
| s.th. | something | bir şey |
| sup. | superlative | enüstünlük derecesi |
| syn. | synonym | eşanlam |
| tel. | telegraphy | telgrafçılık |
| teleph. | telephony | telefonculuk |
| thea. | theatre | tiyatro |
| typ. | typography | basımcılık |
| univ. | university | üniversite |
| v.b. | ve benzeri | |
| vet. | veterinary medicine | veterinerlik |
| vn. | verbal noun | isim-fiil |
| wf. | women's forename | kadın ismi |
| zo. | zoology | zooloji, hayvanbilim |

# Numerical Expressions
## Sayısal İfadeler

### Asıl Sayılar
### Cardinal Numbers

0 sıfır *nought, zero*
1 bir *one*
2 iki *two*
3 üç *three*
4 dört *four*
5 beş *five*
6 altı *six*
7 yedi *seven*
8 sekiz *eight*
9 dokuz *nine*
10 on *ten*
11 on bir *eleven*
12 on iki *twelve*
13 on üç *thirteen*
14 on dört *fourteen*
15 on beş *fifteen*
16 on altı *sixteen*
17 on yedi *seventeen*
18 on sekiz *eighteen*
19 on dokuz *nineteen*
20 yirmi *twenty*
21 yirmi bir *twenty-one*
22 yirmi iki *twenty-two*
30 otuz *thirty*
31 otuz bir *thirty-one*
40 kırk *forty*

41 kırk bir *forty-one*
50 elli *fifty*
51 elli bir *fifty-one*
60 altmış *sixty*
61 altmış bir *sixty-one*
70 yetmiş *seventy*
71 yetmiş bir *seventy-one*
80 seksen *eighty*
81 seksen bir *eighty-one*
90 doksan *ninety*
91 doksan bir *ninety-one*
100 yüz *a/one hundred*
101 yüz bir *hundred and one*
200 iki yüz *two hundred*
300 üç yüz *three hundred*
572 beş yüz yetmiş iki *five hundred and seventy-two*
1000 bin *a/one thousand*
1066 bin altmış altı *ten sixty-six*
1971 bin dokuz yüz yetmiş bir *nineteen seventy-one*
2000 iki bin *two thousand*
1 000 000 bir milyon *a/one million*
2 000 000 iki milyon *two million*
1 000 000 000 bir milyar *a/one milliard. Am. billion.*

## Sıra Sayıları
## Ordinal Numbers

1 birinci *first*
2. ikinci *second*
3. üçüncü *third*
4. dördüncü *fourth*
5. beşinci *fifth*
6. altıncı *sixth*
7. yedinci *seventh*
8. sekizinci *eighth*
9. dokuzuncu *ninth*
10. onuncu *tenth*
11. on birinci *eleventh*
12. on ikinci *twelfth*
13. on üçüncü *thirteenth*
14. on dördüncü *fourteenth*
15. on beşinci *fifteenth*
16. on altıncı *sixteenth*
17. on yedinci *seventeenth*
18. on sekizinci *eighteenth*
19. on dokuzuncu *nineteenth*
20. yirminci *twentieth*
21. yirmi birinci *twenty-first*
22. yirmi ikinci *twenty-second*
23. yirmi üçüncü *twenty-third*
30. otuzuncu *thirtieth*
31. otuz birinci *thirty-first*

40. kırkıncı *fortieth*
41. kırk birinci *forty-first*
50. ellinci *fiftieth*
51. elli birinci *fifty-first*
60. altmışıncı *sixtieth*
61. altmış birinci *sixty-first*
70. yetmişinci *seventieth*
71. yetmiş birinci *seventy-first*
80. sekseninci *eightieth*
81. seksen birinci *eighty-first*
90. doksanıncı *ninetieth*
91. doksan birinci *ninety-first*
100. yüzüncü *a/one hundredth*
101. yüz birinci *hundred and first*
200. iki yüzüncü *two hundredth*
300. üç yüzüncü *three hundredth*
572. beş yüz yetmiş ikinci *five hundred and seventy-second*
1000. bininci *a/one thousandth*
1950. bin dokuz yüz ellinci *nineteen hundred and fiftieth*
2000. iki bininci *two thousandth*
1 000 000. bir milyonuncu *a/one millionth*
2 000 000. iki milyonuncu *two millionth*

# A

**A 1.** X = alay; **2.** *phys.* = amper.

**a¹** [ā] *int.* O!, Oh!, Ah!, Ha!

**a²** [ā] *iro.* nonsense!, certainly not!

**a³** [ā] *pers. connective in various archaic compounds. e.g.* lebalep, peyapey, *etc.*

**a⁴** [ā], e *(after 2nd person conditional, imperative with impatient tone)* alsana! there, take it!; baksana! look here!; söylesenize! tell, then!

**a⁵** *(emphatic, confirms a statement)* olur a! these things happen!; söyledik a! we told you!

**-a** *(dative suffix)* to, towards, for.

**A.A.** *abbr. for* Anatolia News Agency.

**aa, aah** F no!, impossible!, not at all!, not a bit of it!

**ab, -bı** [-] † water.

**aba 1.** coarse woolen material; **2.** coat *or* cloak made of such material; ~ altından değnek göstermek *fig.* to threaten with soft words, to use an iron hand in a velvet glove; ~ gibi coarse and thick *(material);* ~ kebe rough and old clothes, tatters; -nın kadri yağmurda belli olur *pro.* you appreciate the value of s.th. when its necessity arises; *(b-ne)* -yı yakmak to fall desperately in love with s.o., to be gone on s.o.

**abacı** maker *or* seller of aba.

**abadi** [- - -] kind of valuable yellow glazed paper, Manila paper.

**abajur** lampshade.

**abalı 1.** wearing coarse woolen garments *(s.* aba); **2.** *fig.* weak, poor, wretched; vur -ya! hit him when he's down!

**abandone** *sports:* concession; ~ etm. to concede defeat.

**abani** [- - -] **1.** a fine cotton material embroidered with yellow silk; **2.** made of this cloth.

**abanmak 1.** to lean forward, to push forward with one's weight; **2.** *sl. b-ne* to live at s.o.'s expense.

**abanoz 1.** ebony; **2.** made of ebony; ~ ağacı ebony-tree; ~ gibi **1.** black as ebony; **2.** very hard; ~ kesilmek *fig.* to become as hard as ebony; ~ yürekli hardhearted.

**abartı** exaggeration.

**abartıcı** a person who exaggerates; boaster.

**abartma** exaggeration, overstatement.

**abartmak** to exaggerate.

**Abaza** Abkhasia(n).

**Abazaca** Abkhasian (language).

**abazan** *sl.* **1.** hungry, craving; **2.** starved for sex.

**Abbas** *mf.;* ~ yolcudur duramaz *said of s.o. who must leave.*

**Abbasi** [ . - - ] Abbaside.

**ABD** *(abbr. for* Amerika Birleşik Devletleri) U.S.A.

**abe** P Hey!

**abes 1.** silly, stupid, useless, vain; **2.** unreasonable; nonsense, absurdity; ~ kaçmak to be improper; -le uğraşmak to exert o.s. in vain, to fool around.

**abıhayat, -tı** [- . - .] **1.** water of life; **2.** elixer; ~ içmiş *fig.* healthy and young-looking; long-lived.

**abıru** [-.-] hono(u)r, glory, pride; ~ dökmek to abase o.s., to implore humbly.

**abi** *(sl. for* ağabey) older brother.

**abide** monument, memorial, edifice.

**abideleşmek** *fig.* to be memorialized, to become an hono(u)red symbol.

**abidevi** [-...] monumental.

**abis** *geogr.* abyss.

**abit, -bdi 1.** † servant; **2.** *fig.* slave; **3.** God's creature, human being.

**âbit, -di** devotee; worshipper.

**abla** [x .] **1.** older sister; **2.** F Miss!

**ablak** round, chubby-faced.

**ablatya** [. x .] large fishing net.

**abli** [x .] ↓ vang, gaff-balancer rope on a trisail; -yı bırakmak *(or* kaçırmak) *fig.* to become confused, to lose one's bearings.

**abluka** [. x .] blockade; ~ bölgesi blockade zone; ~ etm. *or* -ya almak to blockade; -dan kurtarmak to free s.o. *or* s.th. from blockade; -yı kaldırmak to raise a blockade; -yı yarmak to run a blockade.

**abone 1.** subscriber; **2.** subscription; **3.** subscription fee; ~ bedeli subscription fee; ~ fiyatı price; ~ olm. *(bşe)* to subscribe (to), to become a subscriber (to); ~ şeraiti (or şartları) terms of subscription; ~ ücreti = ~ bedeli; ~yi kesmek to cancel a subscription.

**abonman 1.** subscription; **2.** season ticket (or pass).

**aborda** [. x .] ↓ alongside; ~ etm. to come up alongside (a dock, pier, another ship, etc.).

**abraş 1.** speckled, dappled, piebald (horse); **2.** having colo(u)rless spots (face, leaf); **3.** leprous.

**abraşlamak** to become spotted.

**abse** s. apse.

**absorbe** absorbed; ~ etm. -i to absorb.

**abstrakt,** -tı s. abstre.

**abstre** abstract; ~ sayı A abstract number.

**abuk sabuk 1.** incoherent, nonsensical; **2.** inconsiderate, rash; ~ insan illogical, incoherent person; ~ konuşmak to talk nonsense, to talk incoherently.

**abullabut** sl. **1.** boorish; **2.** dunce.

**abullabutluk** sl. boorishness, stupidity.

**abur cubur 1.** all sorts of food; **2.** haphazard, confused, incongruous; ~ yemek to eat greedily (without regard to kind or quality).

**abus** [ū] unfriendly, cross-looking, grim, frowning.

**acaba 1.** (in a question) I wonder (if); ~ gitsem mi? I wonder if I should go?; ~ sonu ne olacak? I wonder what the outcome is going to be?; **2.** (showing disbelief) Indeed!, I wonder!

**acaip,** -bi [. -.] **1.** acaibisebaiâlem the Seven Wonders of the World; **2.** s. acayip.

**acar 1.** clever, cunning; enterprising; **2.** fearless, bold; **3.** new.

**acayip,** -bi **1.** strange, peculiar, curious; **2.** How strange!, Odd!; (b-nin) acayibine gitmek to find s.th. strange.

**acele 1.** hurry, haste; **2.** urgent (telegram, etc.); **3.** hurriedly, hastily; ~ etm. to hasten, to be in a hurry, to hurry up; ~ ile in a hurry, hastily; ~ işe şeytan karışır pro. haste makes waste; haste is the Devil's work; -si yok there is no hurry; -ye boğmak (bşi) to use haste to cloud or confuse an issue; -ye gelmek to be done hastily and carelessly; -ye getirmek **1.** to profit from s.o.'s need for quick action; **2.** to do s.th. sloppily and hastily.

**aceleci** hustler, impatient person; always on the go.

**aceleleştirmek** -i to hasten, to speed s.th. up.

**Acem** a Persian; ~ gömleği type of shirt, overall; ~ kılıcı two-edged sword; ~ kılıcı gibi two-faced, double dealing; ~ mübalağası excessive exaggeration.

**Acemce** Persian (language).

**acemi 1.** untrained, inexperienced, raw; **2.** recruit, beginner; ~ çaylak F tyro, clumsy person; ~ er X raw recruit; ~ oğlanı hist. conscript boy (selected to be raised as a Janissary); ~ öğretmeye vaktim yok I won't argue with s.o. who doesn't know what he's talking about, I have no time to argue with fools; ~ şansı beginner's luck.

**acemilik** inexperience, lack of experience; ~ çekmek to suffer from inexperience.

**Acemistan** F Persia, Iran.

**acenta, acente** [. x .] **1.** agent, representative; **2.** agency.

**acentalık, acentelik** agency; ~ etm. to represent.

**acep** F s. acaba.

**aceze** pl. of âciz the destitute, the needy.

**acı 1.** bitter, acrid; **2.** hot, peppery; **3.** sharp (taste, smell or flavour); **4.** painful; **5.** pitiful, pitiable; **6.** pain, ache; **7.** hurtful, biting (words); ~ ~ bağırmak to cry out in pain; ~ bir teessürle haber almak to regret to learn; ~ çekmek to suffer, to feel pain; ~ çiğdem ♀ meadow saffron; ~ damkoruğu ♀ bitter houseleek; ~ dil reproach, bitter words; ~ dülek s. acıhıyar; ~ göl salt lake; ~ görmüş undergone suffering; ~ ılgın ♀ bitter tamarisk; ~ kahve coffee made without sugar; ~ kahve içmek fig. to invite s.o. to one's home; ~ kök quassia; ~ manyak bitter manioc; ~ marul dandelion; ~ patlıcanı kırağı çalmaz pro. (lit. frost doesn't touch bitter eggplants) ill weeds grow apace, only valuable things get lost; ~ söylemek to tell the painful truth bluntly; ~ soğuk bitter cold; ~ su bitter, brackish water; ~ su sabunu hard water soap; ~ süt otu ♀ bitter milkwort; ~ yitimi ☧ pain killer, analgesia; -sı tepemden çıktı I nearly passed out from pain; -sı yüreğine çıkmak (bşin) to be overcome with grief; -sını çekmek to pay the consequence for; -sını çıkarmak to get revenge for, to get back at s.o. for s.th.; -sını koymamak s. acısını çıkarmak.

**acıağaç** -cı ♀ bitter wood, quassia.

**acıbadem** bitter almond; ~ kurabiyesi almond cooky.

**acıbakla** ♀ white horsebean.

**acıelma** ♀ colocynth, bitter apple.

**acıhıyar** ♀ **1.** bitter cucumber, colocynth;

**2.** squirting cucumber.

**acık 1.** grief, sorrow, tragedy; **2.** mourning.

**acıklı** sorrowful, pathetic, tragic, touching; sentimental.

**acıklılık** mournfulness, grief.

**acıkmak** to feel (or become) hungry; karnım acıktı I'm hungry.

**acıkmış** hungry.

**acılanmak, acılaşmak 1.** to become bitter, rancid, sour or hot; **2.** to become sorry or regretful.

**acılı 1.** spicy, having a bitter taste; **2.** grieved, mourning.

**acılık** degree of bitterness, spiciness, etc.

**acıma** vn. of acımak pity, compassion.

**acımak 1.** to hurt, to feel pain, to ache; **2.** (b-ne) to feel sorry for, to take pity on; **3.** to become bitter, to turn rancid (butter, oil, etc.); **4.** to begrudge; paraya acıyor he can't bring himself to spend the money.

**acımasız** cruel, merciless, pitiless.

**acımış** rancid.

**acımsı, acımtırak** somewhat bitter.

**acınacak** pitiable, heart-rending; regrettable.

**acındırmak** to arouse compassion for o.s.

**acınmak** -e to be pitied; to become sorry for, to feel pity for.

**acırak** s. acımsı.

**acırga** ♣ horseradish.

**acısız 1.** painless; **2.** not bitter, without pepper, etc.

**acıtmak 1.** to hurt, to cause pain; **2.** to make s.th. bitter, etc.; to make s.th. go sour.

**acıyonca** ♣ bitter clover (leaves used in certain medicines).

**acibe** [î] strange thing, curiosity.

**âcil 1.** critical, urgent, requiring immediate attention; **2.** swift; **3.** transitory, fleeting.

**âcilen** without delay; urgently.

**aciz, -czi 1.** inability; **2.** helplessness; **3.** ♂♂ insolvency; ~ kemiği s. sağrı kemiği.

**âciz** weak, incapable, impotent, helpless; ~ kalmak -den to be incapable of, to be unable to.

**âcizane** humbly, modestly.

**acul, -lü** always in a hurry, very impatient.

**acun** ast. cosmos, universe.

**acunsal** ast. cosmic, universal.

**acur 1.** ♣ hairy cucumber; **2.** = ajur.

**acuze** [û] hag; shrew, vixen.

**acyo** [x .] agio, premium.

**acyocu** dealer in agiotage.

**acyoculuk** agiotage.

**aç, -cı 1.** hungry; **2.** destitute; **3.** greedy, insatiable; **4.** (b-şe) hungry (for); ~ ~ ile yatınca arada dilenci doğar when two hungry people marry a beggar is born; ~ -ına on a hungry stomach; ~ ayı oynamaz pro. (lit. hungry bears won't dance) if you want s.o. to work you must feed him adequately, a discontented man won't work well; ~ bırakmak (or koymak) to starve (a person), to let s.o. go hungry, to fail to feed; ~ bîilâç starving, utterly destitute; ~ çıplak hungry and naked, destitute; ~ doyurmak to feed the poor (or hungry); ~ durmak to go without food, to do without food; ~ gezmektense tok ölmek yeğdir pro. it is better to die full than to live hungry; ~ kalmak **1.** not to eat, to go hungry, to be left hungry; **2.** to be poor; ~ karnına on an empty stomach; ~ kurt aslana saldırır pro. (lit. a hungry wolf will attack lions.) hunger makes a person desperate; ~ kurt gibi fig. like a hungry wolf, with overwhelming greed or ambition; ~ susuz without food and water; ~ tavuk k-ni arpa ambarında sanır pro. (lit. a hungry chicken thinks it's in the barley barn.) wishful thinking; acından ölmek to starve to death.

**açacak 1.** opener; **2.** key; **3.** pencil sharpener.

**açalya** [. x .] ♣ azalea.

**açan 1.** opener; **2.** anat. extensor, tensor.

**açar 1.** key; **2.** aperitif; **3.** appetizer.

**açgözlü** greedy, covetous, avaricious.

**açgözlülük** greed; ~ etm. to act greedily.

**açı 1.** Å angle; **2.** point of view; ~ uzaklığı ast. visual angle.

**açıcı 1.** opener; **2.** relieving; **3.** customs inspector.

**açık 1.** open, not closed; **2.** uncovered; naked, bare; **3.** clear, unoccupied, empty (space); **4.** lucid, easy to understand; **5.** unhidden, not secret, in the open; **6.** clear; **7.** light (colour); **8.** obscene; **9.** audible; **10.** blank; **11.** clear, cloudless, fine; **12.** frank(ly), open(ly); **13.** gap; **14.** unobstructed, free; **15.** open for business; **16.** defenseless, unprotected (city); **14.** not enclosed; **15.** vacancy: **16.** deficit, shortage; **17.** outskirts; **18.** open sea; Marmara açıklarında offshore in the Marmara; Yeşilköy açıklarında off Yeşilköy; ~ ~ openly, frankly; ~ ~ konuşmak to have a heart-to-heart talk, to talk frankly and freely; ~ ağızlı imbecile, stupid; ~ alınlı fig. with clear conscience; ~ arazi open country; ~ artırma sale by public auction; ~ ateş X direct fire; ~ baş 1. bare-headed, bald; 2. *fig.* immoral; ~ bono *a. fig.* blank check; ~ bono vermek to give (a person) a blank check; ~ bulundurmak (*or* tutmak) to keep open, to keep free; ~ ciro blank endorsement, general endorsement; ~ deniz high seas; ~ denize çıkmak to enter the high seas; ~ doru light chestnut (*horse*); ~ durmak to stand aside, not to interfere; ~ eksiltme public bidding for a contract; ~ elli open-handed, generous; ~ fikirli broad-minded, liberal; ~ gel! *sl.* 1. Stand away!; 2. Come on, out with it!; ~ gelmek *sl.* to stay away, not to come near; ~ hava 1. clear weather; 2. open air, the outdoors; fresh air; ~ hava tiyatrosu (sineması) open air theatre (cinema); ~ hava toplantısı public protest meeting; ~ hece open syllable; ~ imza signature at the bottom of a blank piece of paper (*given to s.o. who can be trusted*); ~ kalmak to stay open; ~ kalpli open-hearted, guileless; ~ kanat X open wing; ~ kapı open door; ~ kapı bırakmak to leave the door open (*for further opportunities*); ~ kapı siyaseti open-door policy; ~ konuşmak to talk frankly; ~ kredi open credit, blank credit; ~ liman 1. unprotected port; 2. free port; 3. port subject to bad weather conditions; ~ maaş half pay (*given to an official who has been temporarily removed from office*); ~ mavi light-blue; ~ mektup open letter; ~ mevzi X exposed position; ~ mukavele open agreement; ~ ordugâh bivouac; ~ oturum panel discussion; ~ oy open vote; ~ öz tok söz *fig.* pure and honest; ~ saçık indecent, immodest, obscene; ~ saçık gezmek to move about too freely, too openly (*of a woman*); ~ saçık yayın pornography; ~ seçik distinct, clear; ~ söylemek to speak openly, to speak frankly, to speak without leaving anything unclear; ~ şehir X open city; ~ şehir ilân etm. to declare to be an open city; ~ teşekkür public acknowledgement, public thanks; ~ vermek 1. to show a deficit; 2. to lay o.s. open to criticism; ~ vicdanla with free conscience; ~ yer vacancy; ~ yürekle without concealing anything, without deception; ~ yürekli sincere, openhearted; ~ yüzlü fair-faced, with an honest face, undeceitful; ~ zincir serisi *?*, aliphatic molecular structure; (açığa): ~ çıkarmak 1. to remove (*or* fire) from a government office; 2. to bring out into the open; ~

çıkmak 1. to be removed from office; 2. to become known, to be revealed; ~ satış public sale; ~ vermek (*or* vurmak) to reveal, to disclose; ~ vurmak to become apparent; açığı çıkmak to have a deficit; açığı kapatmak 1. to get rid of a deficit; 2. to close a gap; açıklar livası *co.* brigade of the unemployed; (açıkta): 1. in the open air, outdoors, exposed; 2. in the offing, offshore; 3. unemployed; ~ bırakmak 1. to leave s.o. without home *or* employment; 2. to leave s.th. out in the open; 3. to leave out, to exclude (*a person from a privilege*); ~ kalmak 1. to be without home *or* employment; 2. to be exposed to the elements; 3. to be left out (*of a generally provided benefit*); 4. to be left outside; ~ olm. *s.* ~ kalmak; ~ yatmak to camp out; (açıktan): 1. from a distance; 2. additional, extra; 3. without having worked for it; ~ açığa openly, frankly, publicly; ~ para kazanmak to get a windfall, to get an unearned and unexpected addition to one's income; ~ satış short sale; ~ tayin edilmek (*or* atanmak) to be transferred from outside an organization, *etc.*

**açıkça** [. x .] openly, without concealment, clearly; -sı in plain words, in short, frankly speaking, to tell the truth.

**açıkçı** short seller, bear (*on the Stock Market*).

**açıkgöz(lü)** 1. sharp, cunning, clever; 2. trickster.

**açıkgöz(lü)lük** slyness, cunning, trickery; ~ etm. to be shrewd, to jump at an opportunity.

**açıklama** 1. explanation, statement; 2. disclosure; 3. announcement; commentary.

**açıklamak** 1. to explain; 2. to disclose, to reveal; 3. to announce, to make public.

**açıklayıcı** explanatory.

**açıklı**: ~ koyulu with light and dark colo(u)rs.

**açıklık** 1. being open, free *or* clear; 2. opening, aperture; 3. nakedness, nudity, indeceny; 4. lightness (*of colour*); 5. degree of articulation *or* comprehensibility; 6. space, gap, distance, open space; 7. *ast.* azimuth.

**açıkmeşrep**, -bi overfree, licentious.

**açıksözlü** frank, outspoken.

**açılama** *cinema:* shooting a scene from several angles.

**açılır kapanır** collapsible, folding; ~ geçit roadway barrier; ~ köprü drawbridge; swing bridge.

**açılış 1.** opening; **2.** inaguration; ~ töreni opening ceremony.

**açılma 1.** X deployment; **2.** = açılış.

**açılmadık** unopened; örtüsü ~ sırlar deep secrets; yakası ~ küfürler heavy curses; yakası ~ usuller completely untried methods.

**açılmak 1.** *pass. of* açmak; **2.** to open, to open up; **3.** to become clear, to improve *(of the weather, etc.)*; **4.** to open out *(-e* into); **5.** to bloom; **6.** to become relaxed, to be at ease; **7.** *(b-ne)* to confide (in *s.o.)*; **8.** to become wider, etc.; **9.** to become vacant, empty, etc.; **10.** to cheer up; **11.** to cast off, to set sail, to put to sea; açılıp saçılmak to be immodestly dressed.

**açıölçer** protractor.

**açısal** angular.

**açış** opening, inaguration.

**açkı 1.** burnishing; **2.** smith's tool for widening a hole; **3.** key.

**açkıcı 1.** polisher; burnisher; **2.** key maker.

**açkılamak** to polish; to burnish.

**açkılı** polished, glossy.

**açlık 1.** hunger; **2.** famine; **3.** poverty; ~ grevi hunger strike; -tan kırılmak to be starving, to be dying of hunger; -tan nefesi kokmak to be poverty-stricken.

**açma 1.** opening; **2.** clearing; **3.** kind of pastry.

**açmak 1.** to open; **2.** to construct and open *(a road, etc.)*; **3.** to draw aside, to lift *(a covering, etc.)*; **4.** to open out, to unfold; **5.** to set *(a sail)*; **6.** to unfurl *(a flag)*; **7.** to uncover; **8.** to roll out; **9.** to undo, to untie *(a knot, etc.)*; **10.** to unlock; **11.** to turn on *(switch, light, radio, etc.)*; **12.** to widen *(the space between)*; **13.** to explain fully; **14.** to begin, to open *(a meeting, a conversation, etc.)*; **15.** to disclose; **16.** to make lighter *(colour)*; **17.** to suit, to go well with; **18.** to whet, to sharpen *(one's appetite)*; **19.** to open *(flower)*; **20.** to clear up *(weather)*; açtı ağzını yumdu gözünü he became angry and started cursing wildly, he spoke without reflection.

**açmaz 1.** will not open; **2.** secretive; **3.** difficult position, impasse, dilemma; **4.** *chess:* pin; -a düşmek *(or* gelmek) to fall into an impasse; -a getirmek to dupe, to entrap, to deceive.

**açmazlık 1.** difficulty; **2.** secrecy.

**ad¹,** -dı **1.** name; **2.** first name; **3.** reputation, fame; ~ almak to become well-

-known; ~ koymak *(or* vermek) to name, to give a name *(-e* to); ~ takmak to nickname, to give a nickname *(-e* to); (adı): ~ batası *(or* batsın)! damn!, (may he) be damned!; ~ batmak to become unknown, to pass into oblivion; ~ belirsiz unknown, obscure; ~ bile okunamamak to be a nobody, to be insignificant; ~ bozulmak to lose one's reputation; ~ çıkmak **1.** to get a bad name, to become notorious; **2.** to become noted; ~ geçen above mentioned, the aforesaid; ~ sanı one's name and reputation; ~ şimdi dilime gelmiyor I can't remember his name for the moment; ~ üstünde its name makes everything clear; adını çıkarmak to discredit, to bring into discredit; adını koymak co. set the price *(-in* of); adını vermek **1.** *fig.* to broadcast, to advertise, to spread around; **2.** to name *s.o. or* s.th.; adıyle sanıyle s. adlı sanlı.

**ad²,** -ddı estimation, esteeming, deeming, considering, s. a. addetmek.

**ada 1.** island; **2.** ward of town, etc.; **3.** lot, plot of land; city block; ~ gibi very large *(ship)*.

**adabalığı,** -nı zo. tench.

**adabımuaşeret,** -ti [- - . . - . .] etiquette, rules of good behavio(u)r.

**adacık** islet.

**adaçayı,** -nı ♀ garden sage; ~ tütsüsü **1.** fumigation with garden sage; **2.** inhaling the vapo(u)rs of garden sage.

**adadiyoz** sl. shabby, ragged.

**adak 1.** vow; **2.** votive offering.

**Adalardenizi** s. Ege denizi.

**adale** anat. muscle.

**adaleli** muscular.

**adalet,** -ti [ . - . ] **1.** justice; **2.** the courts; **3.** equity; fairness; righteousness; ♀ Bakanı Minister of Justice; ♀ Bakanlığı Ministry of Justice; ♀ Divanı the International Court of Justice; -in pençesi *fig.* the long arm of the Law.

**adaletli** just, fair.

**adaletsiz** unjust, unfair.

**adaletsizlik** injustice.

**adalı** islander.

**Adalı** Aegean islander.

**adalı** [i] muscular.

**adam 1.** man; **2.** human being; **3.** person, individual; **4.** a brave, capable, good, etc. person; **5.** man-servant, employee, worker; **6.** minion; **7.** partisan; **8.** agent; **9.** all, everyone; **10.** P husband, man; ~ başına per person, apiece, each; ~ boyu a man's height; ~ etm. **1.** to make a man of; **2.** to raise well; **3.** to turn into s.th.

useful or good, to set s.th. in order; ~ evlâdı well-bred, a person of good family; ~ gibi 1. manly, like a man; 2. correctly, properly; ~ içine gitmek (or çıkmak) to mix with important people; ~ kaldırmak 🕱 to kidnap, to abduct; ~ öldürme 🕱 homicide, manslaughter; ~ sarrafı a good judge of character; ~ sen de!, come off it!, don't worry!; ~ sırasına geçmek (or girmek) to become an important person; ~ yerine koymak to count as important or of consequence; -dan saymak not to disregard; s. ~ yerine koymak.

**adamak** 1. to devote, to vow, to promise; 2. to dedicate o.s. (-e to); -la mal tükenmez pro. it costs nothing to make a promise.

**adamakıllı** 1. proper, duly, as required; 2. thorough(ly).

**adamcağız** 1. good fellow; 2. poor chap.

**adamlık** humanness, humanity.

**adamsendecilik** indifference, callousness.

**adamsız** 1. alone, without help; 2. without servants; ~ kalmak to be without servants or help.

**adamsızlık** 1. lack of good help or servants; 2. lack of protection.

**adap, -bı** (pl. of edep) 1. regular customs; 2. accepted ways; ~ erkân customary practice or observance; adaba aykırı contrary to rules of accepted ways; adabı umumiye public morals.

**adaptasyon** 1. adaptation (of a play, novel, etc.); 2. an adapted work.

**adapte** adapted (novel or play); ~ etm. to adapt, to make an adaptation.

**adasoğanı**, -nı ♀ squill, sea onion.

**adaş** namesake, person sharing the same proper name.

**adatavşanı**, -nı European rabbit, cony.

**aday** candidate, nominee; ~ adayı candidate for nomination.

**adaylık** candidacy.

**adçekme** 1. drawing of lots; 2. drawing straws.

**addetmek** [x ..] to count, to enumerate; to esteem.

**adem** 1. non-existance, nothingness; 2. lack, absence; -i emniyet insecurity; -i kabiliyet inability; -i tecavüz nonaggression.

**Âdem** pr. n. Adam; ~ elması Adam's apple; ~ evladı (or oğlu) man, mankind, human being.

**Aden** pr. n. Eden; cenneti ~ the garden of Eden; paradise.

**adese** 1. lens; 2. lenticel.

**adet** 1. number; 2. unit.

**âdet, -ti** 1. custom, practice; 2. habit; 3. menstrual period; ~ bezi (or bağı) hygenic pad; ~ budur en sonra gelir bezme ekâbir custom preceeds all; ~ çıkarmak to start a new custom; ~ edinmek to form a habit (-i of); ~ görmek to menstruate; ~ üzere according to custom; ~ yerini bulsun diye for the sake of custom; -ten kesilmek to reach menopause.

**adeta** [x . -] 1. nearly, almost; 2. simply, merely; 3. rather, sort of; ~! walk! (riding command).

**adetçe** in number.

**adıl** pronoun.

**adım** 1. step; 2. pace; 3. fig. step; ~ açmak to increase the pace; ~ ~ step by step; ~ atmak to take the first step, to begin; ~ başın(d)a 1. at every step; 2. everywhere; ~ uydurmak to follow the example (-e of).

**adımlamak** 1. to pace off; 2. to measure by pacing.

**adımlık** pace, distance; üç ~ a distance of three paces.

**adi** [ - - ] 1. customary, usual; 2. ordinary, common; 3. vulgar, base, low, mean, ornery; ~ adım ✕ break step; ~ hisse senedi common stock; ~ iflas 🕱 non-fraudulent bankruptcy; ~ itiraz 🕱 simple objection; ~ mektup ordinary letter; ~ suç ordinary crime; ~ şirket (or ortaklık) 🕱 unincorporated association.

**adilik** vulgarity, baseness.

**âdil** just, dealing justly.

**âdilâne** [- . - .] justly, equitably.

**adlandırma** 1. naming; 2. classification.

**adlandırmak** 1. to name; 2. to rate, to classify.

**adlanmak** 1. to be named; 2. to become famous, to get a bad reputation.

**adlı** 1. with the name of; named; 2. famous; ~ sanlı well-known, famous, celebrated.

**adlî** [î] judicial, legal; ~ hata legal error; ~ sicil record of previous convictions; ~ subay provost marshal; ~ tıp forensic medicine; ~ yıl court year.

**adliye** 1. (administration of) justice; court system; 2. courthouse; ♀ Vekâleti s. Adalet Bakanlığı; ~ mahkemeleri 🕱 ordinary courts of justice; ~ sarayı courthouse; -nin pençesi s. adaletin pençesi.

**adliyeci** specialist in judical affairs; a legal authority.

**adrenalin** adrenalin.

**adres** address; ~ rehberi directory, address book; ~ sahibi addressee.

**Adriyatik (Denizi)** pr. n. Adriatic (Sea).

**adsız 1.** nameless; **2.** unknown, obscure.
**adsızparmak** ring finger.
**aerodinamik 1.** aerodynamics; **2.** aerodynamic; ~ biçim streamlined.
**af,** -ffı **1.** pardon, forgiving, forgiveness; **2.** amnesty; **3.** exemption; **4.** discharge of obligation, etc.; **5.** liquidation of a debt; ~ dilemek to beg pardon, to apologize; affı umumi s. umumi af.
**afacan** rascal, urchin, wild or restless child.
**afakan** boredom; -lar basmak to be severely depressed.
**afaki** [- - -] **1.** objective; **2.** superficial.
**afal 1.** stupid; **2.** startled; ~ ~ bakmak **1.** to look stupidly; **2.** to look startled.
**afallamak, afallaşmak** to be amazed, to be taken aback, to be disconcerted, to be bewildered.
**aferin** [ā] [x . .] congratulations!, bravo!, well done!, very good!; ~ almak to receive hono(u)rable mention.
**afet,** -ti **1.** calamity, disaster, catastrophe; **2.** F bewitching person; **3.** ₮ tissue damage; ~ gibi very beautiful *(woman).*
**afetzede** victim of a disaster.
**affetmek** [ X . . ] **1.** to pardon, to excuse, to forgive; **2.** to exempt (-den from); **3.** to release *(from an obligation, etc.)*; affedersiniz! I beg your pardon!, excuse me!
**affolunmaz** inexcusable, unpardonable.
**Afgan** pr. n. Afghan.
**Afganistan** pr. n. Afghanistan.
**Afganlı** pr. n. Afghani, from Afghanistan.
**afif** [ . - ] chaste, uncorrupted.
**afili** sl. swaggering, showy.
**afiş** poster, placard, bill.
**afişe etmek** to make a public spectacle (-i of).
**afiyet,** -ti [ā] **1.** good health, well-being; **2.** appetite; ~(ler) olsun! I hope you enjoy it, good appetite! *(said when offering food to s.o.).*
**afiyetlemek** to wish s.o. a good appetite.
**aforoz** excommunication; ~ etm. **1.** to excommunicate; **2.** fig. to put on ice, to relegate to the background.
**aforozlamak** s. aforoz etm.
**aforozlu 1.** excommunicated; **2.** fig. shelved.
**Afrika** pr. n. Africa.
**Afrikalı** pr. n. African.
**afsun** [ū] spell, charm, incantation.
**afsuncu** spellmaster, charmer, magic user.
**afsunculuk** spell-weaving, witchcraft, sorcery.

**afsunlamak** to bewitch, to charm, to enchant.
**afsunlu** charmed, enchanted, bewitched.
**afyon 1.** opium; **2.** 2 Karahisar *city in Western Anatolia;* ~ ruhu tincture of opium.
**afyonkeş** opium addict.
**afyonkeşlik** opium addiction.
**afyonlu** *(a. fig.)* containing opium.
**agâh 1.** informed, aware; **2.** vigilant, on guard; ~ etm. to put on guard, to inform, to make aware.
**agrandisman** phot. enlargement.
**agrandisör** phot. enlarger.
**agreman** agreement.
**agu** *term of endearment used towards babies;* ~ bebek darling child.
**agucuk** s. agu.
**agulamak** to make baby-like noises.
**ağ 1.** net *(a. fig.)*; **2.** tailoring gore, gusset; **3.** network; **4.** *(spider's)* web; -lar the nets *(behind the goal in soccer).*
**ağa 1.** lord, master, chief, boss, landowner; **2.** = -bey; **3.** Mister *(used after a proper name when addressing an old and/or illiterate person).*
**ağababa 1.** *familiar term used to address an old man;* **2.** grandfather ,oldest man in the family.
**ağabey** [ābi] **1.** older brother; **2.** *familiar term of respect used to address any male somewhat older than o.s.*
**ağaç,** -cı **1.** tree; **2.** shrub; **3.** timber, wood; **4.** wooden support, pillar, piece, part, etc.; **5.** wooden; ~ çivi peg; ~ kabuğu bark; ~ kaplama wooden wainscoting; ~ kova wooden bucket; ~ kovuğu hollow of a tree; ~ kurdu wood borer; ~ olmak sl. to stand and wait a long time; ~ oyma wood carving; ~ sıpa wood(en) horse; ~ tıpa wooden dowel, peg, stopper; ~ tokmak wooden hammer; ~ yaş iken eğilir pro. you cannot teach an old dog new tricks.
**ağacbıtı,** -nı zo. termite.
**ağaccileği,** -ni ₮ raspberry.
**ağackakan** zo. woodpecker.
**ağackavunu,** -nu ₮ citron.
**ağaçlamak 1.** to afforest, to plant trees in an area; **2.** to cover with timber.
**ağaçlı** having trees, wooded.
**ağaçlık 1.** clump of trees; **2.** woods; -lı wooded, forested.
**ağalanmak** to lord it over, to become overweening.
**ağalık 1.** being an ağa; **2.** generosity, nobility; **3.** pride, conceit; **4.** territory of an ağa.

**ağarmak 1.** to get bleached, to whiten; **2.** to become visible in the distance; **3.** to dawn.

**ağartı 1.** barely visible shadow in the darkness; **2.** milk product.

**ağartmak 1.** to make s.th. become grey, pale, white, etc.; **2.** to bleach, to blanch.

**ağda 1.** semi-solid sweet, syrup; **2.** epilating wax; ~ kullanmak (or yapıştırmak) to use ağda to remove hair from the skin.

**ağdalanmak, ağdalaşmak 1.** to become thick, to begin to thicken; **2.** fig. to become heavy, slow, cumbersome, pompous.

**ağdalı 1.** thick as a syrup; **2.** fig. heavy, pompous, bombastic.

**ağı** poison, venom.

**ağıl 1.** pen, sheep fold; **2.** halo.

**ağılamak** to poison.

**ağıllanmak 1.** to be put in a pen or fold; **2.** to be surrounded by a halo (moon).

**ağım** instep.

**ağımlı** high in the instep.

**ağır 1.** heavy; **2.** heavy, difficult (work); **3.** significant; **4.** weighty; **5.** difficult, troublesome; **6.** serious, grave (sickness); **7.** difficult to digest, rich, heavy (food); **8.** unfavo(u)rable, unhealthy (climate); **9.** unpleasant, disagreeable; **10.** offensive, painful; **10.** slow, indolent; **11.** slowly-moving; **12.** stuffy; smelly; **13.** valuable, precious; ~ ~ **1.** slowly; **2.** (to weigh) at the very most; ~ almak (bir işi) to work slowly; ~ basmak **1.** to have influence; **2.** (b-ni) to give nightmares (to), to oppress; **3.** to be heavy; **4.** to be important, to have priority; ~ canlı phlegmatic, lazy, inactive; ~ ceza ⅋ major punishment; ~ ceza işleri ⅋ indictable offenses; ~ ceza mahkemesi ⅋ criminal court for major cases; ~ davranmak **1.** to react slowly; **2.** to move slowly; ~ ezgi, fıstıki makam F **1.** slowly and surely; **2.** ponderously; ~ gelmek **1.** to be difficult to bear; **2.** to offend, to hurt; **3.** to be difficult to digest; ~ hapis imprisonment for five years or more; ~ hastalık heavy illness, serious disease; ~ hava **1.** unwholesome climate; **2.** slow or sad melody; **3.** kind of slow folk dance; ~ hıyanet ⅋ high treason; ~ ihmal (or kusur) ⅋ gross negligence; ~ iş hard work; ~ işitmek (a fig.) to be hard of hearing; ~ kazan geç kaynar pro. important things take time; ~ makineli tüfek X heavy machine gun; ~ ol! **1.** slow down!, take it easy!, calm down! **2.** get serious!; ~ oturmak fig. to behave with

dignity, to be costly; ~ sanayi heavy industry; ~ satmak (k-ni) to emphasize one's own importance; ~ sıklet boxing: heavy weight; ~ söz harsh words; ~ takımdan F distinguished, aristocratic: ~ tutmak fig. to be unwilling (to do): ~ yaralı seriously wounded, gravely injured.

**ağırayak** pregnant, with child; about to give birth.

**ağırbaşlı 1.** prudent; **2.** deserving; **3.** sedate, staid; **4.** respectable; **5.** virtuous (woman or girl).

**ağırkanlı 1.** slow, lazy, indolent; **2.** numbed, insensate.

**ağırküre** barysphere.

**ağırlamak 1.** to slacken, to slow down; **2.** to treat (a guest) well, to show hospitality.

**ağırlaşmak 1.** to become heavy; **2.** to become important; **3.** to become serious (illness); **4.** to slow down; **5.** to spoil (food); **6.** to get harder, to become more difficult.

**ağırlaştırmak** caus. of ağırlaşmak; ağırlaştıran sebepler (or nedenler) ⅋ grievous circumstances.

**ağırlık 1.** weight, heaviness; **2.** significance, importance; **3.** prudence; **4.** respectability; **5.** difficulty; **6.** slowness (of motion or action); **7.** indigestibility; **8.** oppressiveness (of the weather); **9.** drowsiness, lethargy; **10.** burden, responsibility; **11.** severity (of a disease); **12.** baggage, luggage; **13.** X munitions, supplies; **14.** nightmare; **15.** dowry; ~ merkezi phys. center of gravity; ağırlığınca altın değmek to be worth its weight in gold; üzerime ~ bastı **1.** I had a nightmare; **2.** I felt sleepy; **3.** I felt uncomfortable.

**ağırşak 1.** disk; **2.** bobbin; **3.** round and/or swollen thing; ~ kemiği kneecap.

**ağıt 1.** dirge, funeral song; **2.** wailing, lamentation; ~ yakmak to lament for the dead, to wail.

**ağız, -ğzı 1.** mouth; **2.** snout, muzzle; **3.** bill, beak; **4.** nozzle; **5.** opening; **6.** entrance; **7.** beginning; **8.** outlet; **9.** first thick milk (at birth); **10.** edge, blade (of a knife, etc.); **11.** crossing point, corner (of roads); **12.** local style (of music); **13.** accent; **14.** dialect; **15.** ♪ key; **16.** time; **17.** mst pl. (-lar) gossip; **18.** flattery; **19.** rim, brink; ~ açmak **1.** to open one's mouth; **2.** to gape with astonishment; ~ açmamak **1.** not to open one's mouth; **2.** to stay without saying a word; ~ ağıza dolu completely full; ~ ağıza vermek to whisper privately; ~ aramak (or yoklamak) 1. to get opinions; 2. to learn intentions; ~ armonikası harmonica; ~ atmak to brag, to boast; ~ dalaşı bickering, quarrel; ~ değiştirmek 1. ♪ to change key; 2. to change one's tune; ~ dolusu 1. mouthful; 2. at the top of one's voice; ~ dolusu küfür unrestrained swearing; ~ etm. 1. to speak out freely; 2. to try to persuade; 3. to make boastful speeches; ~ kavafı troublesome chatterbox, one who overinsists with much talking; ~ kavgası = ~ dalaşı; ~ sakızı *fig.* endless chatter; ~ suyu saliva, spittle; ~ şakası joke; ~ tadı *fig.* enjoyment, pleasure, harmony; ~ tadı ile 1. with enjoyment; 2. enjoying the flavo(u)r; -dan kapmak 1. to elicit a secret; 2. to overhear; -dan kulağa söylemek to whisper; -dan sakız avlamak *fig.* to sound out (*a person's opinion);* -larda bir parmak bal olm. to be talked about; (**ağza**): ~ alınmaz 1. uneatable; 2. unspeakable, obscene, very vulgar; ~ almak to mention; ~ düşmek to be talked about, to be a subject of common gossip; (**ağzı**): ~ açık 1. startled; 2. stupid, idiotic; 3. open, without a cover; ~ bir all telling the same story; ~ bozuk foulmouthed; vituperative; ~ büyük boastful, bragging; ~ gevşek chatterbox; indiscreet; ~ havada 1. proud; 2. exorbitant; 3. thoughtless, negligent; ~ ile aslan tuttuğunu söylemek to be an unbearable chatterbox; ~ ile kuş tutmak to be very capable; ~ örtülü küp covered clay pitcher; ~ pis foulmouthed; ~ sıkı untalkative, secretive; ~ sulandı his mouth watered; ~ süt kokuyor *fig.* he's still wet behind the ears; ~ teneke kaplı *fig.* his mouth is insensitive to hot food, *etc.;* ~ var dili yok close mouthed; ~ varmak (*bşi söylemeğe)* to bring o.s. to say; (**ağzına**): ~ bakmak (*b-nin)* 1. to hang on s.o.'s words; 2. to wait to see what s.o. will say; 3. to act according to s.o.'s instruction; ~ bir parmak bal çalmak 1. to put off with sweet words; 2. to speak with tongue in cheek; ~ kedi ciğere bakar gibi bakıp dinlemek (*b-nin)* to hang on s.o.'s every word (*like a cat with its eye on a piece of liver);* ~ layık delicious; first-class; (**ağzında**): ~ bakla ıslanmaz (*or* baklayı ~ ıslatmaz) he can't keep a secret; ~ gevelemek (*lakırdıyı, sözü lafı)* to beat around the bush; (**ağzından**): ~ baklayı çıkarmak to say what's really on one's mind, to let the cat out of the

bag; ~ çıkanı kulağı işitmemek *fig.* not to even hear what he's saying, to speak without listening to himself; (**ağzını**): ~ açmak 1. to begin to speak; 2. to begin to swear; ~ aramak (*or* yoklamak) to collect opinions; ~ bıçak açmıyor uncommunicative; ~ bozmak to start to swear; ~ havaya (*or* poyraza) açmak to be cut out, to be left out, to be left empty-handed; ~ hayra aç! speak no evil!; ~ kapamak 1. to shut up; 2. to pay not to talk; 3. to cover up, to conceal; ~ öpeyim (*or* seveyim)! well-said!; ~ silmek 1. to wipe one's mouth; 2. to shut up; ~ tıkamak 1. to stop up the mouth; 2. to keep one from speaking; ~ tutmak 1. to keep one's piece; 2. to avoid saying s.th. bad; ~ yormak to waste time talking; (**ağzının**): ~ içine bakmak (*b-nin)* to hang on *s.o.'s* every word; ~ suyu akıyor he wants s.th. very badly, his mouth is watering; ~ suyunu akıtmak to make one's mouth water; ~ tadını almak (*bşden)* to have a bad experience; ~ tadını bilmek to know what one likes; to be a gourmet; ~ tadını bozmak to spoil the enjoyment (-*in* of); ağzınızdan çıkanı kulaklarınız işitsin! mind what you say!; ağzınızı değiştiriniz! I won't have that!; ağzınızı düzeltiniz! I won't listen to that kind of talk; ağzınla kuş tutsan bile nafile! even if you do the impossible, it's useless!

**ağızbirliği**, -ni agreement on what is to be said.

**ağızboşluğu**, -nu mouth cavity.

**ağızlık** 1. cigarette holder; 2. mouthpiece (*of a pipe, instrument, etc.);* 3. muzzle; 4. cover of leaves (*over a basket of fruit);* 5. circle of stones at the top of a well; 6. funnel.

**ağızsız** submissive, docile.

**ağkepçe** landing net

**ağlamak** 1. to cry, to weep; 2. to grieve; 3. to complain, to whine; 4. (*sap in trees)* to rise, to flow; ağlamayan çocuğa meme vermezler *pro* (*lit.* the baby who doesn't cry isn't fed) the squeaking wheel gets the grease.

**ağlama(k)lı** tearful, ready to cry.

**ağlaşmak** 1. to weep together; 2. to cry continuously.

**ağnam** [. -] flocks; ~ vergisi 🐑 sheep tax.

**ağrı** 1. ache, pain; 2. travail.

**Ağrıdağı**, -nı *pr. n.* Mount Ararat.

**ağrı(k)lı** diseased; painful.

**ağrımak** to ache, to hurt.

ağrısız painless; without pain.
ağsı *biol.* netlike.
ağtabaka retina.
ağucuk *s.* agucuk.
ağustos August; ~ gülü ⚘ dog-rose; -ta suya girse balta kesmez buz olur *pro.* he's very unlucky, he's always unfortunate.
ağustosböceği, -ni *zo.* cicada.
ağyar [ . - ] others, strangers.
ağzıpek discreet, rather silent.
ah 1. Ah!, Oh!, Alas!; 2. sigh, groan; 3. complaint; 4. curse; ~ almak to be cursed for one's cruelty; ~ çekmek to sigh; -a gelmek (*or* uğramak) 1. = ~ almak; 2. to suffer retribution; -ı çıkmak (*for one's curse*) to take effect; -ı yerde kalmamak to have one's curse take effect; -ı tutuyor (*b-ne*) for one's curse to be realized (*against another*).
aha P here, there.
ahali [ . - . ] 1. inhabitant(s); 2. population; 3. public; ~ mübadelesi exchange of populations.
âhar † different.
ahbap, -bı 1. acquaintance; friend; 2. My friend! (*used to attract the attention of a person*); ~ çavuşlar *co.* inseparable friends, pals.
ahbaplaşmak 1. to become friendly; 2. to chum up to.
ahbaplık friendship, acquaintance.
ahçı 1. cook; 2. proprietor of a small restaurant; 3. *hist. title of a janissary chief;* ~ baltası cleaver; ~ dükkânı low-class restaurant; ~ kadın female cook; ~ yamağı cook's assistance, kitchen boy.
ahçılık 1. cooking; 2. profession of being a cook; ~ etm. to work as a cook.
ahdetmek [ x . . ] to swear an oath, to undertake, to promise o.s.
ahenk, -gi [ â ] 1. ♪ harmony; 2. concord, accord; 3. musical gathering (*of oriental music*); 4. *gr.* agreement; ~ kaidesi vowel harmony (*in Turkish phonetics*); ~ tahtası sounding board (*on a stringed instrument*).
ahenkli [ â ] 1. ♪ in tune; 2. in unison; 3. good-natured.
ahenksiz [ â ] 1. ♪ out of tune; 2. inharmonious, discordant.
aheste slow; calm.
ahfeş: -in keçisi gibi ne söyleseler başını sallar he agrees with everything that s.o. says.
ahım şahım 1. beautiful, bright; 2. *fig.* conspicuous .
ahır stable, shed, barn; ~ gibi filthy and

confused (*place*); -a çekmek to lead to stable; -a çevirmek to mess up.
âhir last; final; latter; ~ vakit last days of one's life.
ahiren [ î ] † 1. lastly; 2. recently.
ahit, -hdi 1. vow, resolution; 2. agreement, pact, treaty; contract; 3. period, era.
ahitleşmek to enter into solemn agreement.
ahiz, -hzi † 1. receiving; 2. reception; ~ kabiliyeti reception sensitivity.
ahize receiver.
ahkâm (*pl. of* hüküm) judgements; dispositions; laws; inferences; ~ çıkarmak to draw arbitrary conclusions, to put forward obsurd suppositions; ~ kesmek to make judgements without restraint; ahkâmı cezaiye (kanunu) † Criminal Law; ahkâmı şahsiye ⚘ personal statute.
ahlak, -kı (*pl. of* hulk) 1. morals; 2. *phls.* ethics; 3. character; ~ düşkünlüğü moral lapse; ~ hocalığı etm. to be a teacher of ethics; ~ âdap ⚘ good morals.
ahlakçı 1. moralist; 2. teacher of ethics.
ahlaki [ î ] moral, ethical; pertaining to morals; ~ zabıta Morals Squad (*police*).
ahlaklı of good conduct, decent.
ahlaksız 1. immoral; 2. unethical; 3. amoral, asocial.
ahlamak to sigh, to moan.
ahlat, -tı ⚘ wild pear; ~ ağa boor, fool; -ın (*or* armudun) iyisini ayı yer *pro.* (*lit. the best pears are eaten by bears*) the best things fall to those who don't deserve them.
ahmak fool, idiot; ~ ıslatan F fine drizzle.
ahret, -ti the next world, the future life; ~ evi the other world; ~ suali sormak (*b-ne*) F to ask endless questions, to cross-examine; -i boylamak *sl.* to kick the bucket; -te on parmağım yakasında olacak I'll get even if it's in the next world.
ahretlik 1. adopted girl; 2. otherworldly.
ahşap, -bı 1. wooden; 2. made of wood.
ahtapot, -tu 1. *zo.* octopus; 2. ♣ polyp, cancerous ulcer; 3. *sl.* parasite, sponger.
ahu [ - - ] *zo.* gazelle.
ahubaba 1. ghost; 2. talkative old man.
ahududu, -nu ⚘ raspberry.
ahval, -li [ . - ] 1. conditions, circumstances; 2. incidents, affairs, events, occurrences; ahvali şahsiye ⚘ personal circumstances.
aidat, -tı [ - . - ] subscription, membership fee; contribution; allowance.
aile 1. family; 2. F wife; 3. grouping of people; 4. grouping by language, cul-

ture, etc.; **5.** animal or plant grouping; ~ efradı members of a family; ~ malları family property; ~ reisi head of the family; ~ sofrası family table; ~ terbiyesi *fig.* well-bred.

**ailevi** [- · · -] regarding the family, domestic.

**ait,** -di **1.** concerning, relating to; belonging to, pertaining to; **2.** descended from.

**ajan 1.** (political) agent; **2.** (commercial) agent, representative; **3.** political representative.

**ajanda** date book, engagement calendar.

**ajans 1.** press agency; **2.** press release; **3.** branch office (*of a bank*); ~ bülteni news bulletin.

**ajur 1.** mesh, hemstitch; **2.** embroidery frame.

**ajurlu 1.** with an embroidered edge; **2.** embroidered (*stocking*).

**ak,** -kı **1.** white; **2.** clear, unspotted; **3.** white spot; ~ akçe kara gün içindir *pro.* save for a rainy day; ~ arap white Arabian (*horse*); ~ babaya dönmek to become entirely white; ~ bıyık *fig.* advanced in years, old; ~ düşmek (*saça, sakala*) gradually to become grey or white (*hair, beard*); ~ pak **1.** completely clean; **2.** aged; ~ yüz ile successfully and hono(u)rably; -ı karayı seçememek to be unable to tell black from white, to have no intelligence at all.

**akabinde** immediately after.

**akademi 1.** academy; **2.** picture made from a live nude model.

**akademik 1.** academic; **2.** in the form of an academy.

**akademisyen** member of an academy.

**akağaç** (white) birch.

**akaju** acajou.

**akala** a hybrid cotton developed in Turkey.

**akamet,** -ti [· - ·] **1.** sterility; **2.** failure; -e uğramak to fail.

**akanyıldız** *ast.* meteor.

**akar[1]** [ · - ] rental property, real estate.

**akar[2]** flowing, fluid, liquid; ~ amber **1.** ♀ amber-tree; **2.** liquid ambergis; **3.** solution of musk; -ı (yok), kokarı yok! F completely blameless!

**akarat,** -tı, **akaret,** -ti [ · - ·] property rented out and bringing income.

**akarsu 1.** *geogr.* flowing stream; **2.** watercourse; **3.** single strand pearl or diamond necklace; ~ pis tutmaz *pro.* water under the bridge.

**akaryakıt,** -tı fuel oil.

**akasma** ♀ white bryony.

**akasya** [ . x . ] ♀ **1.** acacia; **2.** locust.

**akbaba** *zo.* vulture.

**akbasma** ♂ cataract.

**akbenek** white speck in the eye.

**akciğer** lung(s).

**akça** rather white; ~ pakça pretty fair or attractive (*woman*); ~ completely clean.

**akçaağaç,** -cı ♀ maple.

**akçakavak** ♀ white poplar.

**akçayel** southeast wind.

**akçe 1.** money; **2.** *hist.* a small silver coin; ~ düşkünü greedy, stingy; ~ etmez worthless; ~ farkı premium, agio; ~ ile bohça ile *fig.* by bribery; ~ kesmek *fig.* to be very rich.

**Akdeniz** *pr. n.* the Mediterranean.

**akdetmek** [x . .] **1.** to conclude (*a contract*); **2.** to hold (*a meeting, session, etc.*); **3.** to negotiate (*a loan*).

**akdiken** ♀ buckthorn.

**akgözlü** *fig.* mean, low, common.

**akgünlük** incense.

**akgürgen** ♀ white alder.

**akı** *phys.* flux, flow.

**akıbet,** -ti **1.** end, consequence, result, outcome; **2.** destiny, fate; **3.** eventuality; -ini tayin etm. to determine the fate of s.th.

**akıcı 1.** fluid, liquid; **2.** fluent; ~ ünsüz liquid consonant.

**akıcılık** fluency.

**akıl,** -klı **1.** reason, intellect, mind; **2.** intelligence; **3.** idea, thought, sense; **4.** *iro.* bright idea; **5.** recollection, remembrance; **6.** wisdom, discretion; ~ almak to get opinions; ~ almaz unbelieveable; ~ bu ya! *iro.* what a story!; ~ danışmak (*b-ne*) to consult *s.o.*; ~ etm. (*bşi*) to think of, to dream up; ~ fikir complete attention; ~ fikir dağıtmak (*or* bırakmamak) to distract totally; ~ hastalıkları mental disorders; ~ hocası **1.** one who gives good advice; **2.** *iro.* one who gives pretentious, pointless, etc. advice; ~ kârı olmamak to be unreasonable (to do); ~ kumkuması (*or* kutusu) trusty adviser, mine of wisdom; ~ melakâtı mental facilities; ~ öğrenmek **1.** to get good advice; **2.** *iro.* to be given useless advice; ~ öğretmek (*b-ne*) **1.** to give good advice; **2.** *iro.* to give pointless, useless advice; **3.** to put idea into *s.o.*'s head; ~ satmak *iro.* to give useless advice; ~ sormak to inquire, to consult; ~ var, izan (*or* yakın *or* mantık) var **1.** with a little bit of intelligence one can understand it; **2.** *iro.* why don't you wise up?; ~ yaşta değil baştadır *pro.* intelligence does not depend on age; ~ zayıflığı mental deficiency; (akla): ~ hayale sığmayan unthinkable, unimaginable; ~ sığmak to be evident, to be obvious; ~ yakın plausible, reasonable; (aklı): ~ almak *(bşi)* 1. to understand. to grasp; 2. to believe; ~ başına gelmek 1. to come to one's senses; 2. to come to; ~ başında sensible, rational; ~ başından gitmek to be overwhelmed, to be beside o.s.; ~ çalık 1. light-minded, frivolous; 2. crazy, out of one's head; ~ durmak to be perplexed, to be dumbfounded; ~ ermek *(bşe)* to understand *s.th.;* ~ kesmek to decide, to judge; ~ kıt *(or* kısa) half-witted; ~ oynamak 1. to be crazy; 2. to go insane; ~ sıra *iro.* as one hopes, as one believes; ~ sonradan geldi 1. it later occured to him; 2. he was too wise too late; ~ tepesinden yukarı thoughtless, foolish, absent-minded; ~ yatmak *(bşe)* 1. to understand, to grasp; 2. to be convinced; 3. to find reasonable; ~ zıvanasından çıkmış görünüyor he seems to be out of his head; aklı başına yar ise if he knows what's good for him; (aklına): ~ gelmek 1. to come to one's mind; 2. to recall; ~ getirmek to recollect, to call to mind; ~ koymak 1. to make up one's mind, to be determined; 2. to suggest; 3. not to forget; ~ sığdırmak 1. to comprehend; 2. to make s.o. understand; (aklını): ~ başına almak *(or* toplamak) 1. to come to one's senses; 2. to sober up; 3. to think better of; ~ çelmek *(or* değiştirmek) to change one's mind; ~ çelmek *(b-nin)* 1. to mislead; 2. to put *s.o.* off doing.

**akılcı** 1. rationalistic; 2. rationalist.

**akılcılık** *phls.* rationalism.

**akıldışı,** -nı irrational.

**akıldişi,** -ni wisdom tooth.

**akıllanmak** 1. to become wiser; 2. to have learned one's lesson.

**akıllı** 1. intelligent, reasonable, wise; 2. clever, shrewed; ~ davranmak to act wisely; ~ geçinmek to pass for a wise man.

**akılsız** stupid; unreasonable; ~ başın zahmetini ayak çeker *pro.* little wit in the head makes much work for the feet.

**akılsızlık** 1. stupidity; 2. foolishness.

**akım** 1. current; 2. trend, movement.

**akın** 1. sudden rush; 2. X (roving) expedition. raid; 3. *(air)* attack; 4. run *(of fish);* ~ ~ wave after wave, surging; ~ etm. 1. to raid, attack and pillage; 2. to surge *(of a crowd);* ~ halinde *s.* ~ ~.

**akıncı** 1. raider; 2. plunderer; 3. *sports:*

forward; 4. enterprising, energetic.

**akıntı** 1. current, flow; 2. stream; 3. **?** flux; 4. gradient, fall, descent; -ya kapılmak to get caught in the current; -ya kürek çekmek 1. to row upstream; 2. to waste one's efforts.

**akış** 1. flow, current, course; 2. ⊕ outlet, outfall.

**akışkan** fluid.

**akide** [î] 1. dogma; 2. confession of faith, creed; 3. (şekeri) sugar candy; -yi bozmak 1. to apostatize; 2. *fig.* to stray from the true path.

**akik** *geol.* agate.

**akim** [î] 1. sterile; 2. unsuccessful, ineffective, in vain; ~ bırakmak to thwart, to frustrate; ~ kalmak to be unsuccessful, to be thwarted.

**akis,** -ksi 1. reflection; 2. ⅄ inversion; 3. *log.* conversion; 4. echo; 5. reaction; 6. reversion.

**akit,** -kdi 1. closing, conclusion; 2. marriage contract; 3. undertaking *(of a loan);* 4. agreement, contract, treaty, arrangement; ~ yapma va'di 🕮 preliminary agreement; akdi nikâh etm. *s.* nikâh kıymak.

**akitleşmek** to conclude *(a contract, etc.).*

**akkarınca** termite, white ant.

**akkavak** ♧ white poplar.

**akkefal** *zo.* bleak.

**akkor** ∅, *phys.* 1. incandescent; 2. incandescence.

**aklamak** 1. to clear one's hono(u)r, to clear s.o. of responsibility; 2. to make white.

**aklan** *geogr.* slope, slant.

**aklen** [x .] rational.

**aklı** white-spotted; ~ karalı 1. pepper-and-salt; 2. spotted.

**aklıselim** [î] commonsense.

**aklî** [î] 1. intellectual; 2. mental, rational; ~ denge mental balance; ~ melekât mental faculties.

**akliye** 1. mental illnesses; 2. psychiatric clinic; 3. *phls.* rationalism; ~ hekimi psychiatrist.

**akmak,** (-ar) 1. to flow; 2. to leak; 3. to be shed *(blood);* 4. to run *(faucet, water);* 5. F to slip away; 6. to unravel *(textile).* 7. to fall *(shooting star);* akacak kan damarda kalmaz *pro.* one can't escape fate; akan sular durur it broaches no argument; akmazsa da damlar *pro.* anything is better than nothing; akmış çorap laddered stocking; akmış kumaş frayed.

**akmaz** 1. stagnant, stale; 2. standing water.

**akordeon 1.** accordion; **2.** accordion pleats.

**akort, -du 1.** ♪ accord; **2.** ♪ being in key; akordu bozuk *fig.* out of tune, out of key, inharmonious.

**akortçu** (piano) tuner.

**akortlamak** (*or* akort etm.) to tune (*a musical instrument*).

**akraba 1.** relative(s); **2.** related.

**akrabalık** kinship, affinity.

**akran** [. -] equal, peer, match; kendi akranıyle with one's match or equal.

**akreditif** † letter of credit.

**akrep, -bi 1.** *zo.* scorpion; **2.** hour hand (*of a clock*); **3.** ♌ *ast.* Scorpio.

**akrobasi 1.** acrobatics; **2.** stunt flying.

**akrobat, -tı 1.** acrobat; **2.** stunt flier.

**akrobatlık 1.** acrobatics; **2.** stunt flying.

**akropol, -lü 1.** acropolis; **2.** ♌ *pr. n.* The Acropolis (*in Athens*).

**aksak 1.** lame, limping; **2.** crippled; ♌ Timur Tamerlane.

**aksakal 1.** old, aged; **2.** village elder; ~ karasakal *fig.* the high and the low; -dan yok sakala gelmek to become very aged.

**aksaklık 1.** lameness, limp; **2.** lopsidedness; **2.** flaw, defect, disturbance, trouble; ~ göstermek not to work right, to run wrong.

**aksamak 1.** to be lame; to limp; **2.** *fig.* not to work right, to run wrong, to develop a hitch.

**aksan** accent, stress.

**akse 1.** ₹ fit, attack; **2.** *biol.* reflex.

**akselator** ⊕ accelerator, gas pedal.

**akseptans** † acceptance.

**aksesuar 1.** accessory; **2.** stage prop.

**aksetmek** [x . .] **1.** to be reflected; **2.** to echo; **3.** to reverberate; **4.** to resound; **5.** to come to one's ear, knowledge or attention.

**aksırık** sneeze; ~ tozu sneezing powder; -lı tıksırıklı **1.** sneezing and coughing; **2.** *fig.* old and in bad health.

**aksırmak** to sneeze.

**aksi 1.** opposite, contrary, opposed; **2.** disagreeable, unpleasant; **3.** adverse, untoward; ~ akıntı countercurrent; ~ gibi F unfortunately; ~ halde otherwise; ~ mütalâa (*or* fikir) contrary opinion; ~ olarak on the contrary; ~ takdirde otherwise; ~ tesadüf **1.** mischance; **2.** unluckily; işlerim aksi gidiyor I'm having a run of bad luck.

**aksilik 1.** bad luck, misfortune; **2.** unpleasantness, disagreeableness; **3.** crossness, bad temper, obstinacy; ~ etm. to

be obstinate; to raise difficulties.

**aksiseda** [. . . -] echo, reflection; ~ vermek to give an echo, to reverberate.

**aksitesir** [. . - -] reaction, opposite effect.

**aksiyom** axiom.

**aksiyon 1.** share; **2.** activity, occupation, business; **3.** stage business.

**aksiyoner** shareholder.

**aksöğüt, -dü** ♀ white willow.

**aksu** *s.* akbasma.

**aksülamel** reaction, counter-effect.

**aksülümen** ♏ sublimate.

**akşam 1.** evening; **2.** in the evening; **3.** last night; **4.** the sunset hour, the time of the evening prayer; ~ demez sabah demez **1.** all day long; **2.** he comes at any time of day or night, considerate; ~ etm. to finish up the day; ~ ezanı **1.** evening prayer-call; **2.** evening time; ~ gazetesi evening newspaper; ~ olm. to become evening; ~ (*or* -ki) yediğini sabah unutmak to become exceedingly forgetful; ~ yemeği the evening meal, dinner; -a doğru (*or* karşı) towards evening; -dan kalmış (*or* kalma) hung over; -dan sonra merhaba *fig.* to say s.th. too late and thus uselessly; -lar hayrolsun! good evening!

**akşamcı 1.** one who spends all his evenings drinking; **2.** night-worker; **3.** one whose turn of duty falls in the evening; **4.** night student.

**akşamcılık** habit of drinking every evening.

**akşamgüneşi, -ni 1.** setting sun; **2.** yellowish-pink; **3.** autumn of one's years; ~ gibi rapidly vanishing.

**akşamki** of the evening, in the evening.

**akşamlamak 1.** to stay until evening; **2.** to spend the evening in a place.

**akşamleyin** in the evening.

**akşamlı sabahlı** all the time, morning and evening.

**akşamlık** intended for evening use.

**Akşamyıldızı, -nı** evening star, Venus.

**aktar** haberdasher, mercer; ~ dükkânı haberdasher's shop, mercery.

**aktarma 1.** *vn.* of aktarmak; **2.** transfer; **3.** transfer, change (*of trains. etc.*): **4.** quotation, plagiarism; **5.** plowing a field for the first or second time; **6.** *sports:* pass; ~ bileti transfer ticket; ~ eşyası transit goods; ~ etm. **1.** to carry over, to transfer; **2.** to transpose, to shift (*into another form*); **3.** *s.* aktarmak; ~ limanı transit port; ~ merkezi (*or* yeri) ✗ transfer point; ~ yapmak to change (*trains, etc.*).

**aktarmak 1.** to transfer; to move; **2.** to

transship; **3.** to carry over; **4.** to quote *(a passage from another book, etc.);* **5.** ✎ to bring into disorder; **6.** to reassign; **7.** to reload; **8.** to review; **9.** to transmit, to convey; **10.** *sports:* to pass; **11.** to retile *(a roof);* **12.** to plow *(new ground);* **13.** ✿ to transplant.

**aktarmalı** having a connection *(flight, etc.);* ~ bilet transfer ticket.

**aktavşan** zo. jerboa.

**aktif 1.** active; **2.** ✝ assets; **3.** effective.

**aktör** actor.

**aktris** actress.

**aktüalite 1.** the news of the day; **2.** popular subject; **3.** *(film)* newsreel; ~ filmi newsreel; ~ haline gelmek to become a subject for popular discussion.

**aktüel** actual; present; current.

**akupliman** ⊕ coupling, clutch.

**akustik** acoustic(s).

**akü, akümülatör** storage battery.

**akvam** [. -] *pl. of* kavim; ⚲ Cemiyeti *hist.* League of Nations.

**akvaryum** aquarium.

**akyuvar** *biol.* white blood corpuscle.

**akzambak** ✿ Madonna lily.

**al¹ 1.** scarlet, crimson, vermillion, red; **2.** chestnut *(horse);* **3.** bright red; **4.** rouge; **5.** ✿ eryspelas; ~ at sorrel *(horse);* ~ basmak (loğusayı) ✿ to suffer puerperal fever; ~ kanlar içinde revan *(or puyan)* in a pool of blood; alı alına moru moruna **1.** all flushed in the face; **2.** out of breath; allar giymek to rejoice.

**al²** deceit, intrigue.

**âl, -li 1.** family, dynasty; **2.** high-born; âli Osman Ottoman Dynasty.

**ala 1.** colo(u)rful; **2.** light brown; **3.** *s.* alabalık; ~ kaz white-cheeked goose.

**âlâ** first-rate, excellent, very good.

**alabalık** zo. trout.

**alabanda** [. . x .] **1.** bulwarks; **2.** broadside; **3.** *sl.* obtrusive; ~ etm. **1.** to put the helm hard over; **2.** to tip over; ~ vermek *(b-ne)* to give *s.o.* a real scolding; ~ yemek to get a real scolding.

**alabildiğine** maximum, extremely, the most possible; ~ şişman bir adam an incredibly fat man.

**alabora** ⬇ capsizing, overturn; ~ etm. ⬇ to overturn; ~ olm. to capsize, to turn over.

**alaca 1.** *s.* ala; **2.** bad temper(ed); **3.** *kinds of variegated cloth;* ~ at piebald *(horse);* ~ bulaca **1.** loud (coloured); **2.** incongruously colo(u)red; ~ dostluk insincere friendship; ~ gre speckled sandstone; ~

karanlık twilight; ~ karga zo. **1.** jackdaw; **2.** rook; **3.** magpie; ~ kargaya borçlu up to his ears in debt; -sı içinde crafty, deceitful, fraudulent.

**alacadoğan** zo. peregrine falcon.

**alacak 1.** ✎ claim, demand; **2.** credit; ~ davası ✎ personal action; ~ olan receiver; ~ senedi promissory note, debenture; alacağı olsun! he'll pay for this! I'll show him; alacağım elli lira I've got fifty liras coming.

**alacaklı** creditor; ~ bakiye credit balance; ~ taraf credit side.

**alacalanmak 1.** to become colo(u)rful *or* spotted; **2.** to blush.

**alacalı** *s.* ala **1.;** ~ bulacalı loud (colour); ~ kuntaşı *s.* alaca gre.

**alacalık 1.** motleyness; **2.** *fig.* deceit; ~ etm. to be deceitful.

**alaçam** ✿ spruce.

**aladoğan** *s.* alacadoğan.

**alafranga** [. . x .] in the European style; ~ musiki European music; ~ tuvalet Western style toilet.

**alafrangacı** follower of European custom.

**alafrangacılık** preference for European styles.

**alafrangalaşmak** to adopt Western ways.

**alafrangalık** European mode of living.

**alagarson** boyish bob.

**alageyik** zo. fallow deer.

**alaimisema** [. - . . . -] rainbow.

**alaka 1.** interest; **2.** affection; **3.** relation; **4.** claim; **5.** ⚿ affinity; ~ göstermek to show interest; to take an interest *(-e* in): ~ uyandırmak to arouse interest; ~ verici captivating, fascinating; -sı var there is a connection; he has an interest; -sını kesmek to terminate one's association, to break off relations *(ile* with).

**alakadar** [. - . -] **1.** connected; concerned; **2.** interested; **3.** responsible; ~ etm. -i **1.** to interest *(ile* in); **2.** to concern; ~ olm. **1.** to be interested *(ile* in); **2.** to be concerned *(ile* with).

**alakalanmak 1.** to be interested *(ile* in); **2.** to be enamored *(ile* of, with).

**alakalı 1.** interested; **2.** enamored; **3.** authoritative; standard; **4.** associated; **5.** participating, participant.

**alakarga** zo. **1.** spotted crow; **2.** jackdaw; **3.** magpie; **4.** jay.

**alakasız 1.** disinterested, indifferent; **2.** uninteresting; **3.** not related.

**alakasızlık 1.** indifference; **2.** lack of interest.

**alako(y)mak** *s.* alıko(y)mak.

**Alaman** *s.* Alman.

**alamana** [ . . x . ] ↓ **1.** lugger; **2.** large trawnet.

**alamet,** -ti **1.** sign, mark, symbol; **2.** *a.* ✕ badge; **3.** monstrous, enormous, *(anything conspicuous by its size);* -i farika **1.** trademark; **2.** ↓ emblem.

**alan 1.** *phys.* field; **2.** A area; **3.** *phls.* field, sphere, domain; **4.** (public) square; **5.** plain, space; **6.** airport.

**alan talan** F in complete confusion; ~ etm. to mess up.

**alarga** [ . x . ] **1.** ↓ open sea; **2.** F stand off!, keep away!; ~ durmak *sl.* to keep off, to keep away; ~ etm. **1.** to enter the high seas; **2.** *sl.* to keep one's distance; -da anchored offshore.

**alarm 1.** alarm; **2.** state of emergency; ~ işareti **1.** warning sign; **2.** ✕ warning signal.

**alaşağı** etm. **1.** to pull down; **2.** to overthrow, to depose.

**alaşım** alloy.

**alaturka** [ . . x . ] in the Turkish style: ~ 1270'te in 1270 *(old calendar);* ~ müzik Turkish music; ~ yemek Turkish *(or* Oriental) cousine or style of cooking.

**alaturkacı** F **1.** partisan of Turkish style *(esp. old Turkish music);* **2.** performer or singer of Turkish music.

**alavere** [ . . x . ] **1.** complete confusion; **2.** passing or throwing about *(from hand to hand);* **3.** coal chute; ~ dalavere dirty tricks; ~ tulumbası suction pump.

**alay 1.** procession; **2.** ✕ regiment. squadron, group; **3.** large quantity, all of *(a group);* **4.** solemnity; **5.** mockery, sarcasm. teasing; ~ ~ row upon row, in large crowds; ~ etme! don't mock!; ~ etm. *(b-le)* to make fun (of), to mock; ~ geçmek *sl. s.* ~ etm; ~ malay F the whole outfit; -a almak F to deride, to ridicule, to mock; -ında olm. *(bşin)* not to take *s.th.* seriously, to take *s.th.* as a joke.

**alaycı 1.** mocking, sarcastic, ironic; **2.** mocker.

**alayiş** [ - - .] pomp, show.

**alaylı 1.** ✕ from the ranks: **2.** *fig.* uneducated, unschooled; **3.** mocking; **4.** ceremonious.

**alaz** flame.

**alazlanmak 1.** to be singed; **2.** to get red areas on the skin.

**albastı** ⚇ puerperal fever.

**albatr** alabaster.

**albatros** albatross.

**albay 1.** ✕ colonel; **2.** ↓ captain.

**albeni** charm, attractiveness.

**albüm** album.

**albümin** albumen.

**alçacık** [ x . . ] very low.

**alçak 1.** low; **2.** vile, mean, low, base, abject; **3.** cowardly; ~ basınç low pressure; ~ gönüllü humble, modest, unpretentious; ~ gönüllülük modesty, humility.

**alçakça 1.** rather low; **2.** [ . x . ] shamefully, viciously.

**alçaklık 1.** lowness; **2.** shamefulness, vileness; ~ etm. to behave viciously.

**alçalma 1.** decline, descent; **2.** ebb tide; **3.** degradation.

**alçalmak 1.** to become low; to decline; to go down; **2.** to descend, to lose altitute; **3.** to degrade o.s.; to lose esteem.

**alçaltıcı** degrading.

**alçarak** somewhat low.

**alçı** gypsum. plaster of Paris; ~ kalıbı plaster mo(u)ld; -ya koymak to put in a plaster cast.

**alçıtaşı,** -nı *geol.* gypsum, parget.

**aldaç** trick. ruse.

**aldanç** easily fooled.

**aldangıç** trick, cheat.

**aldanmak 1.** to be deceived. to be taken in: **2.** to be mistaken, to be wrong.

**aldatıcı** deceptive. misleading.

**aldatılmak** to be deceived.

**aldatma** deception, deceiving.

**aldatmaca** deception, trick.

**aldatmak 1.** to deceive, to dupe, to cheat; **2.** to mislead; **3.** to mislead s.o. by appearance; **4.** to be unfaithful *(-i* to).

**aldırış** attention, care; ~ etmemek not to mind, not to pay any attention *(-e* to).

**aldırışsız** indifferent.

**aldırmak 1.** *caus. of* almak; **2.** to mind, to take notice *(-e* of), to pay attention *(-e* to); aldırmamak *s.* aldırış etmemek.

**alegori** allegory.

**alelacayip** very peculiar, odd.

**alelacele** hastily, in a big hurry.

**alelade** ordinary, usual, normal.

**alelhesap** as an advance *(payment),* on account.

**alelumum** in general, generally.

**alelusul** as a formality.

**alem 1.** flag, banner; **2.** peak *(of a minaret);* **3.** † proper name.

**âlem 1.** world, universe; **2.** realm; **3.** condition. state (of); **4.** field, sphere; **5.** the world of people, the public; **6.** revel, orgy; ~ yapmak to have a wild party; -i var mı? is it really proper?

**alemdar** [ . . -] **1.** standard-bearer; **2.** *fig.* leader.

**âlemşümul, -lü** [ᵘ] worldwide, universal; ~ **bir şöhret** a worldwide fame.

**alenen** [x ..] openly, publicly.

**alengirli** *sl.* showy.

**aleni** [ī] open, public; ~ **müzayede** *s.* açık artırma; ~ **satış** public sale.

**aleniyet, -ti** publicity.

**alerji** 𝔅 allergy.

**alerjik** 𝔅 allergic.

**alert, -ti** alert, alarm.

**alesta** [. x .] **1.** ready!, stand by!; **2.** *sl.* ready; **3.** *sl.* right away, right now; ~ **beklemek** to stand by.

**alet, -ti** [ā] **1.** tool, instrument, implement, device; **2.** apparatus, machine; **3.** *fig.* tool, means, instrument, agent; **4.** *anat.* organ; ~ **edevat** tools, implements; ~ **etm** *(b-ni)* to make a tool of *s.o.;* ~ olm. to be an istrument *(-e* to), to be a tool *(-e* to), to lend o.s. *(-e* to), to stooge *(-e* for); -li jimnastik apparatus gymnastics.

**alev 1.** flame; **2.** pennant *(on a lance);* **3.** ♀ *wf.;* ~ **almak 1.** to catch fire; **2.** *fig.* to flare up, to blaze up, to flame out, to flare out; ~ **cihazı** ✕ flame thrower; ~ **kesilmek** to blaze up, to flame out; ~ **saçağı** *(or* bacayı) sardı things have gone too far, danger has gone beyond control; -lere yem olm. to fall a victim to the flames.

**Alevi** [. . -] partisan of the Caliph Ali; Shiite.

**Alevilik** Shiism.

**alevlendirmek 1.** to make *(the fire)* flame up; **2.** *fig.* to inflame, to incite, to exacerbate.

**alevlenmek 1.** to flare, to blaze up; **2.** *fig.* to flame up, to flare up, to flame out; **3.** to glisten.

**alevli 1.** flaming, in flames; **2.** *fig.* violent, furious.

**aleyh** against; -inde, -ine against him; -inde bulunmak to talk against, to backbite, to run down; -te olm. to be in opposition.

**aleyhtar** opponent.

**aleyhtarlık** opposition.

**aleykümselam** peace be upon you *(said in reply to the greeting* selamünaleyküm).

**alfabe 1.** alphabet; **2.** primer; **3.** *fig.* the ABC (of).

**alfabetik** alphabetical; ~ **sıra** alphabetical order.

**algı** perception; sensation; impression.

**algılama** perception, comprehension.

**algılamak** to perceive, to comprehend.

**alıcı 1.** buyer, customer, purchaser; **2.** ⊕ receiver, recipient; **3.** movie camera; **4.** the Angel of Death *(Azrail);* ~ **gözüyle bakmak** to look meticulously; ~ **kuş** bird of prey; ~ **radyo makinesi** radio receiver, radio set; ~ **verici 1.** one who takes back a present he has given; **2.** ⊕ two-way radio.

**alık** clumsy, stupid, imbecile, silly; ~ ~ stupidly.

**alıklaşmak** to be astounded, to be taken aback.

**alıklık** stupidity, imbecility.

**alıko(y)mak 1.** to hold s.o. in a place; **2.** to keep back, to detain, to restrain, to prevent *(-den* from); **3.** to set aside, to reserve.

**alım 1.** taking; **2.** purchase, buying; **3.** attractiveness; ~ **satım** trade, business; purchase and sale.

**alımlı** attractive, charming; ~ **çalımlı** eye-cathing, charming.

**alımsız** unattractive.

**alın, -lnı 1.** forehead, brow; **2.** ✗ face; ~ **akı** hono(u)r, integrity; ~ **çatmak** to frown, to scowl; ~ **damarı** shame; ~ **damarı çatlamak** to lose all sense of shame; ~ **karası** shame, disgrace; ~ **teri** *fig.* effort, work, labo(u)r; ~ **teri dökmek** *fig.* to toil, to sweat (over), to struggle; ~ **teri ile kazanmak** to turn an honest penny; -dan ter boşanmak *fig.* to sweat blood; alnı açık alkblameless, irreproachable; alnı davul derisi *fig.* unabashed, shameless; alnında yazılmış olm. to be one's fate, to be destined; alnını karışlarım! **1.** I'll show you!; **2.** I dare you!; alnını karışlayayım! he is no threat; alnının akı ile hono(u)rably, with no shadow of blame, without a blemish.

**alındı** receipt.

**alındılı** registered *(mail).*

**alıngan** touchy, irascible, choleric, testy.

**alınganlık** touchiness, testiness.

**alınlı 1.** having a forehead; **2.** *fig.* saucy, cheeky, *Am. sl.* fresh.

**alınlık 1.** ornament worn on the forehead; **2.** facade, frontal.

**alınmak 1.** *pass. of* almak; **2.** to take offence *(-e, -den* at), to resent.

**alıntı** quotation; ~ **yapmak** to quote.

**alınyazısı, -nı** *fig.* destiny, ordinance, predestination.

**alış 1.** taking, receiving; **2.** purchase, buying; ~ **fiyatı** purchase price; ~ **valfı** inlet valve.

**alışagelmek** to be accustomed *(-e* to).

**alışık** accustomed *(-e* to), used *(-e* to).

**alışıklık 1.** habit; **2.** familiarity.
**alışılmış** ordinary, usual, accustomed.
**alışkan** accustomed *(-e* to), used *(-e* to).
**alışkanlık 1.** habit; **2.** force of habit; **3.** familiarity.
**alışkı** habit, practice, usage.
**alışkın** *s.* alışık.
**alışmak 1.** to get used *(-e* to), to get accustomed *(-e* to); to become familiar *(-e* with); **2.** to accustom o.s. *(-e* to); **3.** to come to fit; **4.** to become addicted *(-e* to); **5.** P to catch fire.
**alıştırma 1.** exercise; **2.** training.
**alıştırmak 1.** to accustom *(-e* to), to familiarize; **2.** to domesticate, to tame; to train; **3.** to allow s.o. to become addicted *(-e* to); **4.** ⊕ to break in, to make s.th. work smoothly; **5.** to set on fire; *b-ne* alıştırarak haber vermek to break the news gently to *s.o.*
**alışveriş 1.** shopping; buying and selling, trade, business, commerce; **2.** *fig.* dealings, relations: ~ yapmak **1.** to shop. to go :hopping; **2.** *(b-le)* to do business with *s.o.;* **-i** olmamak *(b-le)* to avoid contact with *s.o.,* not to have anything to do with *s.o.;* **-ten** dönmek to return from shopping; dostlar **-te** görsün! for the sake of appearances.
**Ali** *mf.;* ~ paşa vergisi *iro.* a present which is taken back; **-nin** külahını Veli'ye Veli'nin külahını Ali'ye giydirmek F to rob Peter to pay Paul.
**âli †  1.** high, exalted, sublime; **2.** ♀ *mf.;* zatı âliniz your worship, you; ismi âliniz nedir? what is your name?
**âlicenap,** **-bı** noble-hearted, magnanimous.
**âlicenaplık** magnanimity.
**alicengiz oyunu** F a dirty trick.
**alikıran başkesen** F bully, despot.
**alim** all-knowing, omniscient.
**âlim 1.** scholar; **2.** wise, learned.
**alimallah!** by God!
**âlimlik 1.** scholarship; **2.** erudition.
**alivre †** short *(sale).*
**alize** trade wind.
**alkali** ⚗ alkali.
**alkaloit** ⚗ alkaloid.
**alkım** *meteor.* rainbow.
**alkış** applause, clapping; ~ tufanı flood of applause; ~ tutmak **1.** to clap *(-e* for); **2.** to cheer.
**alkışçı** *contp.* **1.** applauder; **2.** flatterer, toady.
**alkışlamak** to clap *(-i* for),·to acclaim, to applaud.
**alkışlanmak** *pass.* of alkışlamak to be

clapped, to be greeted with applause; ayakta ~ to be given a standing ovation.
**alkol,** **-lü** alcohol.
**alkolik** alcoholic.
**alkolizm** alcoholism.
**alkollü 1.** alcoholic, spirituous, intoxicating; **2.** drunk; **3.** while drunk.
**alkolsuz** non-alcoholic, soft *(drink).*
**Allah** [. -] **1.** God; **2.** o God!; **3.** how wonderful!, really!; ~ acısın! may God have pity on him!; ~ afiyet versin! may God give you success!; ~ ~ **1.** good Lord!, goodness gracious!; **2.** Turkish battle cry; ~ aşkına! **1.** for God's sake!, for heaven's sake!; **2.** how wonderful!; ~ bağışlasın God bless him; ~ belâsını versin! damn him!; ~ bilir! God knows!; ~ bir kapıyı kaparsa, başka kapıyı açar *pro.* when one door shuts, another opens; ~ canını alsın! God damn you!; ~ cezanı vermesin *(or* ~ cezanı versin) God damn you; ~ dağına göre kar verir *pro.* God tempers the wind to the shorn lamb; ~ derim! all I can say is 'o God'; ~ esirgesin! God forbid!; ~ göstermesin! God forbid!; ~ hakkı için! in God's name; ~ (seni) inandırsın... take it from me that..., take my word...; ~ korusun! God forbid!; ~ layığını versin! damn you *(or* him)!; ~ müstahakını versin! *s.* ~ layığını versin; ~ ömürler versin! may God give you a long life!; ~ rahatlık versin! good night!; ~ rahmet eylesin! may God have mercy on him; ~ rahmetine kavuşmak to meet one's Maker, to die; ~ versin! **1.** may God help you!; **2.** may you enjoy it!; **(Allaha)** ~ ısmarladık good-bye; ~ şükür! thank God!; Allahı(nı) seversen for God's sake; **(Allahın):** ~ belası nuisance, pest, trial; ~ cezası damn, damned; ~ günü every darn day; ~ ondurmadığını, Peygamber sopa ile kovar *pro.* misfortunes never come singly; ~ tembeli bone-lazy; **(Allahtan): 1.** luckily, fortunately; **2.** from birth: ~ bulsun! let God punish him!; ~ korkmaz cruel, unmerciful, ruthless; ~ umut kesilmez while there is life there is hope.
**Allahlık 1.** harmless, simpleton, simple man; **2.** left to God, unpredictable.
**Allahsız 1.** atheist; **2.** *fig.* unmerciful, merciless.
**Allahuekber** [. - . . .] God is almighty.
**allak 1.** untrustworthy, fickle; **2.** deceitful.
**allak bullak 1.** topsy-turvy, pell-mell; **2.** in great confusion; ~ etm. **1.** to make a mess *(-i* of), to upset; **2.** *fig.* to confuse, to bewilder.

**allame** † 1. scholar, learned man; 2. learned.

**allasan** [. - .] [. x .] = Allahı seversen.

**allegretto** ♪ allegretto.

**allegro** ♪ allegro.

**allem kallem** tricks, dodges; **allem etti, kallem etti** he tried all sorts of wiles.

**allı pullu** spangled, showily dressed.

**allık** 1. redness; 2. rouge.

**almaç** teleph. recevier.

**almak,** (-ır) 1. to take; 2. to get, to obtain, to procure; 3. to buy; 4. to receive; to accept; 5. to steal; 6. to marry (a girl); 7. to take along, to call for; 8. to hold, to contain, to take; 9. to capture, to conquer; 10. to take in, to shorten (a dress); 11. to pluck out, to remove, to take away; 12. to clean, to sweep, to dust; 13. to have, to take (a bath); 14. to lead; 15. to drink; to smoke; 16. to last, to take (a period of time); 17. to swallow, to take (medicine); 18. to cover, to travel (a distance); 19. to catch (cold, fire); 20. to employ, to hire, to take on; 21. to move; 22. to sense, to smell, to hear; 23. to put on, to throw over o.s. (garment); 24. to take (water); 25. to carry away, to destroy (flood); 26. to overwelm, to sweep through (smoke, fear); 27. to begin all at once (rain); **al birini vur ötekine** tarred with the same brush; **alıp satmak** to trade, to commerce; **alıp vermek** 1. to exchange, to trade; 2. to have one's heart beat wildly; 3. to dwell on a matter; **alıp yürüdü** it has made headway.

**Alman** German; ~ **hükümeti** German government.

**almanak** almanac.

**Almanca** [. x .] German, the German language; ~ **gramer** German grammar; ~ **öğretmeni** teacher of German; ~ **sözlü bir film** a film in German; **bunun -sı nedir?** what does it mean in German?

**almangümüşü** German silver, albata.

**Almanya** [. x .] pr. n. Germany.

**Almanyalı** German; from Germany.

**alo!** [x .] (telefon) hello!

**Alp, Alpler** pr. n. the Alps.

**alpaka** zo. alpaca.

**alpyıldızı** ❅ edelweiss.

**alt,** -tı 1. bottom, underside, lower part; 2. buttocks, rump, bottom; 3. continuation, the rest; 4. the farther; 5. the lower, inferior; 6. (altına, altında) under, beneath, below; ~ **alta** one under the other; ~ **alta üst üste** rough-and-tumble; ~ **alta üst üste boğuşma** rough-and-tumble fight; ~ **aşağı vurmak** to cast down, to

overthrow, to conquer; ~ **başından** from the very bottom (of); ~ **etm.** to beat, to defeat, to overwhelm; ~ **kat** 1. downstairs; 2. first (or ground) floor; ~ **olm.** to be defeated, to be overcome (-e by); ~ **taraf** the lower part; the underside; ~ **tarafı çıkmaz sokak** F this business is a blind alley; ~ **yazı** footnote, postscript; **-ı alay, üstü kalay** gaudy, showy, tawdry; **-ı çizilmiş kelime** underlined word; **-ı kaval, üstü şişhane** odd-looking; (**altına**): ~ **almak** to throw s.o. down; ~ **etm.** (or koyvermek or kaçırmak) to wet or soil one's clothes a little; **-ında kalmak** to have no retort. to be unable to reply; **-ından girip üstünden çıkmak** to squander, to blow, to blue, to play ducks and drakes with (money); **-ını üstüne getirmek** 1. to turn upside down; 2. to search high and low; **altta kalanın canı çıksın!** woe to the vanquished!, vae victis!, the devil take the hindmost!; **altta kalmak** to be defeated, to be beaten, to lose.

**altbilinç** psych. the subconscious.

**altçene** the lower jaw.

**altderi** anat. corium, derma.

**alternatif** 1. alternative; 2. alternate; ~ **akım** ⚡ alternating current.

**alternatör** generator, alternator.

**altes** his highness, her highness.

**altgeçit** underpass.

**altı** six; ~ **köşe(li)** 1. six-cornered; 2. ⚔ hexagon; ~ **okka etm.** (b-ni) to carry s.o. by having people lift his arms and legs; **-da bir** one sixth; **-nı çizmek** fig. to underline.

**altıgen** ⚔ hexagon.

**altılı** 1. cards: six; 2. ♪ sextet, sextette.

**altın** 1. gold; 2. gold coin; 3. golden; ~ **adını bakır etm.** fig. to degrade o.s., to disgrace o.s.; ~ **anahtar** fig. money; ~ **anahtar her kapıyı açar** money talks; ~ **babası** moneybags, well-heeled; ~ **bilezik** 1. gold bracelet; 2. fig. a skill one can use to support o.s.; ~ **çağı** golden age; ~ **kaplama** 1. gold-plating; 2. gold-plated; ~ **kesmek** to be coining (or minting) money, to make pots of money; ~ **kıymetli** ⚖ gold clause; ~ **pas tutmaz** pro. a good character cannot be harmed by slander; ~ **sarısı** golden blond; ~ **varak** gold-leaf; ~ **yıldönümü** golden anniversary (or wedding); ~ **yumurtlayan tavuk** person with a generous income.

**altınbaş** 1. gold-headed; 2. ⚘ muskmelon, cantaloupe; ~ **kefal** zo. golden mullet.

**altıncı**[1] sixth.

**altıncı**[2] goldsmith.

**altınlamak** to gild; to ornament with gold.

**Altınordu** *pr. n. hist.* Golden Horde.

**altınsuyu,** -nu ♔ aqua regia.

**altıntop,** -pu ♥ grapefruit.

**altıparmak** 1. six-fingered; having six toes; 2. *zo.* large bonito.

**altıpatlar** six-shooter, revolver.

**altışar** six each, six apiece; ~ ~ six by six.

**altız** sextuplet.

**altlık** 1. support, base; 2. pad, coaster.

**altmış** sixty.

**altmışaltı** sixty-six *(a card game)*; -ya bağlamak *sl.* to put s.o. off with promises.

**altmışıncı** sixtieth.

**altmışlık** 1. containing sixty; 2. sixty years old, sexagenarian.

**alto** [x .] ♪ 1. viola; 2. alto; 3. alto saxophone.

**altşube** subbranch.

**altulaşım** underground transportation.

**altuni** [. - -] golden, gold colo(u)red.

**altüst,** -tü topsy-turvy, upside down; ~ etm 1. to turn topsy-turvy, to mess up, to turn upside down, to upset; 2. to damage, to ruin, to wreck; ~ olm. *pass. of* ~ etm.

**altyapı** 1. substructure; 2. infrastructure.

**altyazı** subtitle.

**aluvyon** alluvium.

**alüfte** 1. promiscuous *(woman)*; 2. prostitute, whore.

**alümin** ♔ alumina, alumin.

**alüminyum** aluminium, *Am.* aluminum.

**alyans** wedding ring.

**alyuvar** *anat.* erythrocyte.

**am** *sl.* cunt, pussy, vulva.

**ama** [x .] 1. but, still, yet; 2. above all; absolutely; 3. truly, really; -sı maması yok! there are no buts about it!, but me no buts!; amma da yaptın ha! *a. iro.* how can it be!, not really!.

**âmâ** blind.

**amaç** aim, goal, target, object, objective, purpose, end; ~ gütmek to pursue a goal; amacına ulaşmak to attain one's object.

**amaçlamak** to aim (-i at), to intend, to purpose.

**amaçlı** purposeful.

**amaçsız** purposeless, aimless.

**amade** [- - .] ready, prepared (-e for); emre ~ olm. to be ready; to be at s.o.'s disposal.

**amal,** -li [- -] † *pl. of* amel works, deeds, actions; amali erbaa † *s.* dört işlem.

**aman** [. -] 1. oh!, mercy!, help!; 2. please; 3. for goodness sake; 4. heavens!, my!; 5. mercy; ~ Allah çağırmak *fig.* to be much distressed; ~ aralık vermemek not

to give any respite; ~ dedirtmek *(b-ne)* to make *s.o.* give up, to make *s.o.* yield; ~ demek *(or* dilemek) to ask for mercy; to surrender; ~ vermek to grant one his life, to spare one's life; -a gelmek to come to terms, to give in, to give up and submit; -a getirmek *s.* ~ dedirtmek; -ı zamanı yok there is no trying to get out of it, you must; -ını tüketmek to exhaust.

**amanın** F oh my!, what now!

**amansız** 1. merciless; 2. inexorable, cruel; 3. incurable *(disease).*

**amatör** amateur.

**amazon** 1. amazon; 2. equestrienne.

**ambalaj** 1. packing, wrapping; 2. package; ~ kâğıdı wrapping paper; ~ yapmak to pack, to wrap up.

**ambalajlamak** to pack, to wrap up.

**ambale olm.** to be overwhelmed and confused.

**ambar** 1. granary; grain silo; 2. warehouse, storehouse, magazine; 3. express company, trucking firm; 4. hold *(of a ship)*; ~ ağzı ↓ hatchway; ~ kapağı ↓ hatch (cover); ~ memuru storekeeper, warehouse official.

**ambarcı** 1. trucker, express agent; 2. *s.* ambar memuru.

**ambargo** [. x .] embargo; ~ koymak to impose an embargo (-e on); -yu kaldırmak to lift the embargo.

**ambarlama** storage.

**amber** 1. ambergris; 2. *s.* akar amber.

**amberbalığı,** -nı *zo.* sperm whale, cachalot.

**amberbaris** [. . - .] ♥ barberry.

**amberçiçeği,** -ni ♥ musk-mallow.

**amboli** embolism.

**ambülans** ambulance.

**amca** [x .] 1. (paternal) uncle; 2. sir *(polite form of address to an older man)*; ~ kızı girl cousin; ~ oğlu male cousin.

**amcalık** 1. unclehood; 2. step uncle; ~ etm. to be avuncular (-e towards), to act like an uncle.

**amcazade** cousin.

**amel** 1. act, action, deed, work; 2. performance, practice; 3. diarrhea; ~ olm. to have diarrhea.

**amele** worker, workman; ~ çavuşu foreman.

**amelebaşı,** -nı foreman.

**amelelik** workmanship.

**ameli** practical, applied.

**amelimanda** disabled, retired; invalid.

**ameliyat,** -tı 1. practice, performance; 2. ℞ surgical operation; ~ etm. ℞ to operate (-i on); ~ olm. to be operated on, to have an operation.

**ameliyathane** [. . . . . .] operating room (*or* theatre).

**ameliye** process, procedure, operation.

**amenna!** [- x -] **1.** we believe!; **2.** admitted!, agreed!; ~ demek F to admit, to accept, to agree.

**amentü** [ā] I believe; credo.

**Amerika 1.** *pr. n.* America; **2.** *sl.* well-heeled, rich, rolling in money; ~ Birleşik Devletleri the United States of America, U.S.A.

**Amerikalı 1.** American; **2.** an American.

**amerikalılaşmak** to become Americanized.

**amerikalılaştırmak** to Americanize.

**Amerikan 1.** American; **2.** an American; ~ bar bar: ~ fıstığı ♀ peanut; ~ şekeri fine ground sugar.

**amerikanbezi**, -ni unbleached calico.

**amfi** amphitheatre, lecture room.

**amfibi** amphibian.

**amfiteatr** *s.* amfi.

**amigo** cheerleader.

**amil** factor, agent, motive, reason, cause; doing, active.

**amin** [ā] amen.

**amip**, -bi *zo.* ameba, amoeba.

**amipli** amebic; ~ dizanteri ⚕ amebic dysentery.

**amir 1.** commander; **2.** superior, chief; ~ hükümler ᴎ imperative provisions.

**amiral**, -li admiral; ~ gemisi flagship.

**amirallik** admiralship, admiralty.

**amirane** [- . - .] ﻻ **1.** imperiously, commandingly; **2.** imperious *(action)*.

**amirlik 1.** authority, superiority in rank; **2.** air of authority; ~ taslamak to behave arrogantly.

**amit** ⚗ amide.

**amiyane 1.** colloquial; **2.** common, ordinary.

**amma** *s.* ama.

**amme 1.** the public; **2.** public, general; ~ davası ᴎ public prosecution; ~ hizmeti public service; ~ menfaati ᴎ public interest; ~ nizamı public policy.

**amonyak** ⚗ ammonia (water).

**amonyum** ⚗ ammonium; ~ karbonatı salt of hartshorn.

**amorti 1.** *lottery:* the smallest prize; **2.** redemption of a bond issue; ~ etm. to amortize. to redeem, to pay off.

**amortisman 1.** amortization; **2.** the redemption of a bond; ~ akcesi depreciation fund; ~ sandığı sinking-fund.

**amortisör** ⊕ **1.** shock absorber; **2.** damper.

**amper** ⚡ ampere.

**amperaj** amperage.

**ampermetre, amperölçer** ⚡ ammeter.

**ampersaat**, -ti ampere-hour.

**ampirik** empirical.

**amplifikasyon** ⊕ amplification.

**amplifikatör** ⊕ amplifier.

**ampul**, -lü **1.** ⚡ electric bulb; **2.** ¶ ampule; **3.** *sl.* boob.

**amudi** [ū, ī] vertical, perpendicular.

**amudufıkari** [. - . - .] backbone, spinal column.

**amut**, -du [ū] perpendicular; amuda kalkmak to do a hand stand.

**amyant**, -tı asbestos.

**an** [ā] **1.** moment, instant; **2.** boundary *(between fields)*.

**ana 1.** mother; **2.** mother animal, dam; **3.** protector, patroness; **4.** principle, main, basic, fundamental; **5.** † capital, stock; principal; ~ akçe principal; ~ baba parents, father and mother; ~ baba bir (kardeş) having the same father and mother; ~ baba eline bakar he depends on his parents for his support; ~ baba evladı beloved child; ~ baba günü pandemonium, tumult; ~ baba sevgisi parental love; ~ defter ledger; ~ demiryolu main railway; ~ direk ⬇ lower mast; ~ fikir central theme; ~ hat main (*or* truck) line; ~ hatlar the main lines, the outline; ~ kısmı kindergarten; nursery-school; ~ kucağı *fig.* mother's bosom; ~ kuzusu **1.** very small baby. dear child; **2.** sissy, milksop, mollycoddle; ~ makinesi incubator; ~ mesele main subject; ~ sermaye original capital; ~ ses *phys.* keynote; ~ şaft ⊕ cardan shaft; ~ tem ♪ main theme; -dan doğduğuna pişman olm. *fig.* to be sorry to have been born, to feel very miserable; -dan doğma **1.** stark naked; **2.** from birth; congenital; -m babam! *sl.* oh dear!, oh my!; -mdan emdiğim süt burnumdan fitil fitil geldi I went through extreme hardship; -n yerinde kadın the woman as old as your mother; -sı danası F his mother and the rest of the family, the whole bunch; -sına bak kızını al, kenarına bak bezini al *pro.* what is bred in the bone will never come out of the flesh. the sack is known by the sample; -sını satayım! I don't care two hoots!, I don't give a damn!; -sının ak sütü gibi helal (olsun)! you are welcome to it!; -sının çocuğu like mother like child; -sının gözü *sl.* sly ,cunning. tricky, shifty: -sının ipini pazara çıkarmış *fig.* wicked, vicious; -sının körpe kuzusu mother's darling (*or* pet); -sının nikâhını istemek *fig.* to charge s.o. an arm and a leg, to make s.o. pay through the nose.

**anacık** darling mother.

**anaç 1.** matured *(animal)*; **2.** fruit-bearing, mature *(tree)*; **3.** experienced, shrewd; **4.** tough, huge.

**anadil** parent language.

**anadili** mother tongue, native language.

**Anadolu** *pr. n.* Anatolia; ~ Ajansı *pr. n.* Anatolian Agency; ~ yakası Anatolian quarter.

**Anadolulu 1.** an Anatolian; **2.** Anatolian.

**anaerki** matriarchy.

**anaerkil** matriarchal.

**anafor 1.** eddy, countercurrent, back current; **2.** *sl.* illicit gain, windfall; -a konmak *sl.* to get s.th. for nothing; ~ *(or* -dan) gelmek *(b-ne) sl.* to fall into one's lap, to come easily.

**anaforcu** *sl.* **1.** freeloader, parasite, sponger; **2.** opportunist, cheater.

**anaforculuk** *sl.* **1.** freeloading; **2.** cheating.

**anaforlamak** *sl.* to pinch, to swipe, to steal.

**anahtar 1.** key; **2.** spanner, *Am.* wrench; **3.** ♪ switch; **4.** clef; ~ deliği keyhole; ~ uydurmak to match up a key *(to a lock).*

**anahtarcı 1.** locksmith; **2.** *sl.* thief who picks locks.

**anahtarlık** key ring *(or* holder).

**anakara** continent.

**analı** having a mother; ~ kuzu kınalı kuzu *fig.* a child whose mother is alive is clean and well cared for; iki ~ kuzu *fig.* two-job man, dual wage-earner.

**analık 1.** maternity, motherhood; **2.** stepmother, adoptive mother; **3.** maternal love; **4.** motherliness; ~ etm. *(b-ne)* to be a mother to s.o.

**analitik** analytical; ~ geometri analytical geometry.

**analiz** analysis; ~ etm. to analyse.

**analizlemek** ⌃ to analyse.

**anamal** capital.

**anamalcı 1.** capitalist; **2.** capitalistic.

**anamalcılık** capitalism.

**ananas** pineapple.

**anane** tradition; -siyle anlatmak *fig.* to tell in detail.

**ananeperest,** -ti traditionalist.

**ananeperestlik** traditionalism.

**ananet,** -ti ♀ sexual impotence.

**ananevi** [î] traditional.

**anaokulu** kindergarten, infant school, nursery school.

**anapara** capital.

**anarşi** anarchy.

**anarşist,** -ti anarchist.

**anarşizm** anarchism.

**anason 1.** aniseed; **2.** anise; -lu containing aniseed.

**anatomi** anatomy.

**anatomik** anatomical.

**anavatan** *s.* anayurt.

**anayasa** constitution.

**anayasal** constitutional.

**anayol** main *(or* trunk) road.

**anayön** cardinal point *(of the compass).*

**anayurt,** -du mother country, homeland.

**anbean** [â, â] with every moment, gradually.

**anca** [x .]: ~ beraber kanca beraber we will stick together through thick and thin.

**ancak** [x .] **1.** only, solely, merely; **2.** hardly, just, barely; **3.** but, however, on the other hand; **4.** not until, only.

**ançüez** anchovy.

**andaç** souvenir, gift, keepsake, memento.

**andavallı** *sl.* imbecile, idiot, fool, simpleton.

**andetmek** [x . .] to swear, to take an oath.

**andırışma 1.** resembling; **2.** ambiguity.

**andırmak 1.** to resemble, . to be reminiscent *(-i* of); **2.** to bring to mind.

**andızotu** ⌀ elecampane.

**andiçmek** [x . .] to take an oath, to swear.

**andilya** [. x .] ⌀ endive.

**ane** [â] pubic bone; ~ biti *zo.* crab-louse.

**anekdot,** -tu anecdote.

**anestezi** ♀ anesthesia.

**angaje 1.** occupied, reserved; **2.** hired, employed, engaged; **3.** tied *(-e* to), bound *(-e* to); ~ etm. to employ, to engage.

**angajman** engagement, employment, undertaking; ~ yapmak to reach a formal agreement *(ile* with).

**angarya, angarye** [. x .] **1.** forced labo(u)r, corvée; **2.** angary; **3.** drudgery.

**angı** memory.

**angın** famous.

**angıt 1.** *zo.* ruddy, sheldrake; **2.** *sl.* fool, idiot.

**Anglikan** *pr. n.* Anglican.

**Anglosakson** *pr. n.* Anglo-Saxon.

**angudi** [î] ruddy.

**angut** *s.* angıt.

**anı** memory.

**anık** apt *(-e* to), ready *(-e* to), inclined *(-e* to.

**anılmak** *pass.* of anmak to be remembered, to be mentioned.

**anımsamak** to remember, to recall.

**anırmak** to bray.

**anıt,** -tı monument.

**anıtkabir,** -bri **1.** mausoleum; **2.** ♀ *pr. n.* tomb of Atatürk in Ankara.

**anıtmezar** mausoleum.

anıtsal monumental.
anız stubble.
ani [î] 1. sudden, instantaneous, unexpected; 2. suddenly, all of a sudden.
aniden suddenly, all of a sudden.
anjin angina.
Anka 1. *pr. n.* phoenix; 2. *sl.* well-heeled, moneybags; ~ gibi nonexistent.
ankesman paying in, collection *(of payment)*.
ankesör public call-office, coin telephone.
anket, -ti questionnaire, (opinion) poll, public survey; ~ yapmak to take a poll.
anketçi pollster.
anlak *psych.* intelligence.
anlam 1. meaning, sense; 2. connotation; -ına gelmek to mean, to amount (to).
anlamak 1. to understand, to comprehend, to conceive; 2. to find out; 3. *(bşden)* to know about *s.th.*, to have knowledge of *s.th.*; 4. to deduce; to realize; 5. *(bşden) sl.* to appreciate *s.th.*, to enjoy *s.th.*; 6. *sl.* to try, to sample *(a delicacy)*; anladımsa, Arap olayım! it is all Greek to me, I am unable to make head or tail of it!; Anlayana sivrisinek saz, anlamayana davul zurna az *pro.* a word is enough to the wise.
anlambilim semantics.
anlamdaş 1. synonymous; 2. synonym.
anlamdaşlık synonymy, synonymity.
anlamlandırmak to explain.
anlamlı meaningful, expressive.
anlamsal semantic.
anlamsız meaningless.
anlamsızlık meaninglessness.
anlaşamamazlık 1. disagreement, conflict; 2. misunderstanding.
anlaşılmak *pass. of* anlamak to be understood; anlaşılan... it appears that...
anlaşılmaz incomprehensible, unintelligible.
anlaşma 1. agreement, understanding; pact, treaty; -ya varmak to come to an agreement.
anlaşmak 1. to understand each other; 2. to come to (or reach) an agreement.
anlaşmalı arranged by agreement.
anlaşmazlık 1. disagreement, conflict, incompatibility; 2. misunderstanding.
anlatı narration.
anlatım expression, exposition.
anlatımlı expressive.
anlatmak *caus. of* anlamak 1. to explain, to expound; 2. to narrate, to relate, to tell; 3. to describe; 4. to show *s.o.*, to learn *s.o.*
anlayış 1. understanding, comprehension;

2. intelligence, perceptiveness; 3. sympathy; 4. mind, intellect; ~ göstermek to be tolerant (-e towards).
anlayışlı 1. understanding; 2. intelligent.
anlayışsız 1. insensitivite, inconsiderate; 2. lacking in understanding.
anma 1. remembrance; 2. commemoration; ~ töreni commemorative ceremony.
anmak 1. to call to mind, to remember, to think (-i of); 2. to commemorate; 3. to call, to name, to distinguish.
anmalık keepsake, souvenir.
anne [x .] mother; ~ olm. to become a mother; -ler günü Mother's Day.
anneanne grandmother.
anneciğim! mum!, mummy!
annelik motherhood; ~ etm. *(b-ne)* to be a mother to *s.o.*
anofel *zo.* anopheles.
anonim 1. anonymous; 2. incorporated; ~ şirket joint-stock company.
anons announcement; ~ etm. to announce; to page *(in a hotel, etc.)*.
anorak anorak.
anormal abnormal.
anormalleşmek to become abnormal.
anormallik abnormality.
anot anode.
ansefalit, -ti 𝔶 encephalitis.
ansızın suddenly, all of a sudden, without warning.
ansiklopedi encyclopedia.
ansiklopedik encyclopedic.
ant, -dı 1. oath, vow; 2. resolution; ~ içmek to take an oath, to swear; ~ vermek to importune *s.o.* with pleading oaths; andını bozmak to break one's oath.
antant, -tı agreement; ~ kalmak to come to an agreement.
antarktik Antarctic.
anten aerial, antenna *(a. zo.)*.
antepfıstığı, -nı pistachio.
antet, -ti letterhead.
antibiyotik antibiotic.
antidemokratik antidemocratic.
antifeding *radio:* antifading.
antifriz ⊕ antifreeze.
antika [. x .] 1. antique; 2. F queer, funny, eccentric; 3. hemstitch.
antikacı antique-dealer.
antikalık 1. antiquity; 2. F queerness, eccentricity.
antikite antiquity; -ler antiques.
antikor *biol.* antibody.
antilop *zo.* antelope.
antimon 𝅘 antimony.
antipati antipathy.
antipatik antipathetic; ~ bulmak to dis-

like.

**antiseptik** *ƀ* antiseptic.

**antişambr** antechamber.

**antitez** antithesis.

**antitoksin** *biol.* antitoxin.

**antlaşma** pact, treaty.

**antlaşmak** to come to a solemn agreement.

**antlı** under oath, sworn.

**antoloji** anthology.

**antrakt** intermission, interval.

**antrasit**, -ti anthracite.

**antre** entrance, doorway, vestibule.

**antrenman** *sports:* training, exercise, work-out; ~ yapmak to work out, to exercise, to go into training.

**antrenör** *sports:* trainer, coach.

**antrepo** bonded warehouse, entrepôt.

**antropoloji** anthropology.

**antrparantez** parenthetically, in parenthesis.

**anudane** [. - - .] stubborn(ly), obstinate(ly).

**anus** [x . .] *anat.* anus.

**aort**, -tu *anat.* aorta.

**apaçık** [x . .] as plain as the nose on one's face, clear, evident.

**apak** [x .] snow-white, pure white, all white.

**apandis** *anat.* appendix.

**apandisit**, -ti *anat.* appendicitis; ~ olm. to suffer from appendicitis.

**apansız** [x . .], **apansızın** [. x . .] at the drop of a hat, suddenly, all of a sudden, out of the blue.

**aparmak 1.** to carry away; **2.** *sl.* to make off (-i with).

**apartman** block of flats, apartment house; ~ dairesi flat, apartment.

**apar topar** posthaste, pell-mell, headlong, helter-skelter.

**apaşikâr** as plain as the nose on one's face.

**apaydın** [x . .] very bright, well lit.

**apayrı** [x . .] as different as chalk and cheese, as like as chalk to cheese, completely different.

**apaz 1.** cupped hand; **2.** handful.

**aperitif** apéritif, appetizer.

**apış** the inner sides of the thighs; ~ açmak to straddle; ~ arası the space between the thighs.

**apışık** holding its tail between its legs.

**apışıklık** gore, gusset.

**apışmak 1.** to spread its legs apart and collapse *(animal)*; **2.** *fig.* to give up, to stand helpless; apışıp kalmak to be nonplussed.

**apiko** [. x .] **1.** ⬇ apeak; **2.** *sl.* alert, ready, quick; **3.** *sl.* handsome, spruce, smart.

**apikoluk** *sl.* spruceness.

**aplik**, -ği wall lamp (or fixture).

**aplikasyon 1.** appliqué; **2.** *surv.* staking out.

**aplike** = aplikasyon.

**apolet**, -ti epaulet.

**apostrof** apostrophe.

**apre 1.** size, finish; **2.** sizing.

**apse** *ƀ* abscess.

**apşak 1.** bowlegged; **2.** sluggish; fagged out.

**aptal** silly, stupid, fool, simpleton; ~ oğlu ~ fucker.

**aptalca 1.** stupid *(act)*; **2.** stupidly.

**aptallaşmak 1.** to become stupid; **2.** *fig.* to be taken aback.

**aptallık** stupidity, foolishness.

**aptes 1.** ritual ablution; **2.** feces; ~ almak to perform an ablution; ~ bozacağı gelmek to be taken short; ~ bozmak to relieve nature, to go to the toilet; ~ etm. = ~ bozmak; ~ vermek *fig.* to scold, to reprimand; -i kaçtı he ceased to need to go to the toilet; -i olm. (or gelmek) to be taken short.

**apteshane** [. . - .] toilet, water closet, latrine.

**aptessiz** canonically unclean; ~ yere basmamak *fig.* to be very strict in one's religious practices.

**apul apul** waddlingly.

**ar**[1] are *(100 m²)*.

**ar**[2] [ā] shame; ~ damarı sense of shame; ~ etm. to be ashamed.

**ara 1.** distance; **2.** interval; gap; **3.** relation; **4.** break *(in a game)*; intermission; interlude; **5.** space, spacing; **6.** intermediate, intermediary; **7.** time; **8.** arasına, arasında between; among; ~ bozmak to destroy the friendship (between); ~ bulmak to reconcile, to mediate; ~ hattı diving (or parting) line; ~ imtihanı intermediate examination; ~ seçimi by-election; ~ sıra sometimes, now and then, from time to time, occasionally; ~ vermek *(bşe)* to take a break, to stop doing *s.th.* for a while, to pause; (arada) between; among; ~ bir from time to time, seldom, rarely; ~ gitmek to pass unnoticed; ~ kalmak to be mixed up in an affair; ~ kaynamak to pass unnoticed; ~ sırada s. ~ sıra; (aradan): ~ çıkarmak to remove; ~ çıkmak not to interfere; görüşmeyeli ~ uzun zaman geçti long time no see; (araları): ~ açıktır they are at odds, they are at loggerheads; ~ açıldı they are on bad terms; ~ bozuldu they are on strained terms; ~ iyileşti they became reconciled; ~ soğudu. a coolness has arisen in their friendship; ~ şekerrenk their relations are strained; ~ yağ bal they are on good terms, they stand well with each other; -nda dağlar kadar fark olm. to be as different as black and white, to be as different as chalk and cheese; -nda kan olm. to have a blood feud (between); -ndan kara kedi geçmek *fig.* to be cross with each other, to bear resentment against each other; -ından su sızmaz *fig.* they are on intimate terms with each other; -nı açmak to create a rift (between); -nı bulmak to reconcile; -nı düzeltmek to reconcile; (arası): ~ geçmeden without delay; ~ soğumak *(bşin)* to lose *its* importance with the passage of time; -nı bulmak to reconcile; (araya): ~ girmek to meddle, to interfere; ~ gitmek 1. to go to waste; 2. F to be lost in the confusion; ~ koymak *(b-ni)* to ask *s.o.* to mediate, to put in *s.o.* as intermediary.

**âra** [ā] † *pl. of* rey 1. votes; 2. opinions.

**araba** 1. car, automobile; 2. cart, carriage; 3. cartload, wagonload; truckload; ~ devrilince yol gösteren çok olur *pro.* it is easy to be wise after the event; ~ vapuru car ferry, ferry-boat; ~ yolu carriageway; -sını düze çıkarmak *fig.* to overcome difficulties, to put matters straight; -yı çekmek *sl.* to piss off, to clear out, to beat it, to scram.

**arabacı** 1. driver; coachman; 2. cartwright.

**arabalık** 1. coach-house, cart shed; 2. carload, wagonload; truckload; 3. garage.

**arabesk** arabesque.

**Arabi** [ī] 1. Arabic, Arabian; 2. Arabic, the Arabic language.

**Arabistan** *pr. n.* Arabia; ~ çölü the Arabian desert.

**arabozan** mischief-maker.

**arabozanlık** mischief-making.

**arabozucu** mischief-maker.

**arabozuculuk** mischief-making.

**arabulma** mediation, reconciliation.

**arabulucu** mediator, peacemaker, go-between.

**arabuluculuk** mediation, intervention; ~ etm. to mediate.

**aracı** 1. go-between, mediator; 2. middleman.

**aracılık** mediation, intervention; ~ etm. to mediate.

**araç** 1. means; 2. tool, implement; 3. vehicle.

**araçlı** indirect.

**araçsız** direct.

**Araf** [- -] *isl. myth.* purgatory.

**arakçı** *sl.* pilferer, thief.

**arakçılık** *sl.* pilferage, theft.

**arakesit,** -ti Å intersection.

**arakıye** [. - . .] 1. a soft felt cap; 2. a small oboe-like instrument.

**araklamak** *sl.* to pilfer, to pinch, to filch, to walk off (-*i* with), to swipe, to nick, to nip.

**aralamak** 1. to leave ajar *(door)*; 2. to open out, to space; 3. to separate.

**aralanmak** 1. *pass. of* aralamak; 2. *sl.* to piss off, to toddle off.

**aralık** 1. space, interval, gap, opening; 2. time, moment, interval; 3. ajar *(door)*; 4. corridor; passageway; 5. toilet, loo; ~ ~ now and then, occasionally; ~ ayı December; ~ bırakmak 1. to leave ajar *(door)*; 2. to leave a space; ~ etm. to leave ajar, to open part way; ~ hattı dividing (*or* parting) line; ~ vermeden uninterruptedly, on and on; ~ vermek to take a break, to pause, to halt.

**aralıklı** 1. spaced, having intervals; 2. at intervals, on and off.

**aralıksız** 1. continuous; 2. continuously, on end, on and on.

**arama** *vn. of* aramak search, exploration; ~ tarama body search; police search; ~ yapmak to search.

**aramak** 1. to look (-*i* for), to hunt (-*i* for), to seek; 2. to search; 3. to miss, to long (-*i* for); 4. F to look for trouble; 5. to ask (-*i* for), to demand; 6. to drop in on; ara ki bulasın! you can never find it!; arama! it is too much to expect; Arayan belasını da bulur, Mevlasını da *pro.* he that seeks finds.

**aranjman** ♪ arrangement.

**aranmak** 1. *pass. of* aramak; 2. to be in demand, to be sought after; 3. to be missed; 4. to search one's own clothes and pockets; 5. F to look for trouble.

**Arap,** -bı 1. Arab; 2. Arabian; 3. F Negro; ~ aklı primitive thought; ~ Birliği *pr. n.* Arabic League; ~ uyandı F we have learned our lesson.

**Arapça** the Arabic language, Arabic.

**arapsabunu,** -nu soft soap.

**arapsaçı,** -nı 1. fuzzy hair; 2. *fig.* tangled affair, mess; -na döndürmek to confound.

**arapzamkı,** -nı gum arabic.

**ararot,** -tu ♧ arrowroot (starch).

**Arasat,** -tı [. . -] *isl. myth.* the place of the Doomsday.

**arasız** continuously, on end, on and on.
**arasöz** digression.
**araştırıcı 1.** researcher, investigator; **2.** inquisitive, curious; **3.** investigative.
**araştırma** investigation, research.
**araştırmacı** researcher.
**araştırmak** to research, to investigate, to explore; to search.
**aratümce** *gr.* parenthetical clause.
**arayıcı 1.** seeker; searcher; searching; **2.** customs inspector; **3.** *ast.* finder.
**araz** symptoms.
**arazi [. - -]** land; estate(s); ~ açmak to clear land; ~ olm. *sl.* to take to one's heels, to beat it; ~ sahibi landowner; ~ vergisi land tax; -ye uymak *sl.* to lay low.
**arazi** accidental, extrinsic.
**arbede** tumult, riot, uproar, brawl.
**arbitraj** arbitrage.
**arda 1.** (marking) stake; **2.** lathe chisel.
**ardala 1.** camel bell; **2.** pillion, cushion.
**ardıç, -cı** ♀ juniper.
**ardıçkuşu, -nu** *zo.* fieldfare.
**ardıl 1.** consecutive; **2.** successor.
**ardın ardın** backwards.
**ardınca** behind, following, shortly afterwards.
**ardışık** Ⱥ consecutive.
**ardiye 1.** warehouse; **2.** storage rent.
**arduvaz** slate.
**arena** arena.
**argaç, -cı** woof, weft.
**argaçlamak** to weave.
**argalı** argal(i).
**argın** tired, weak, feeble.
**argınlık** weakness, feebleness.
**argo [x .]** 1. slang, cant; **2.** argot, jargon.
**arı¹** *zo.* bee; ~ beyi queen bee; ~ gibi busy as a bee; ~ kovanı **1.** beehive; **2.** ♀ foxglove; ~ kovanı gibi işlemek to hum with people; ~ sürüsü swarm of bees.
**arı²** **1.** pure; **2.** clean; **3.** innocent; ~ su pure water.
**arıcı** beekeeper, apiarist.
**arıcılık** beekeeping, apiculture.
**arık 1.** lean, thin; **2.** lean *(meat).*
**arıkuşu, -nu** *zo.* bee eater.
**arılamak** to absolve.
**arılaşmak** to become pure.
**arılaştırmak** to purify.
**arılık 1.** purity; **2.** innocence; **3.** cleanliness.
**arındırmak** to purify.
**arınmak** to be purified.
**arısütü, -nü** royal jelly.
**arış 1.** warp; **2.** pole *(of a car).*
**arıtımevi** refinery.
**arıtmak 1.** to refine; **2.** to purify, to clean.

**arız** happening; ~ olm. to happen, to occur, to befall (-*e* to).
**arıza 1.** breakdown, defect, failure, obstruction; **2.** unevenness, roughness; **3.** ♪ accidental; ~ yapmak to break down.
**arızalanmak** to break down.
**arızalı** out of order, defective.
**arızi 1.** accidental, casual; **2.** temporary.
**Ari [ă]** Aryan.
**ari 1.** free (-*den* of); **2.** lacking; **3.** naked, bare.
**arif 1.** wise, knowing, sagacious; **2.** ♀ *mf.*
**arifane** wisely.
**arife** eve.
**aristokrasi** aristocracy.
**aristokrat, -tı 1.** aristocrat; **2.** aristocratic.
**aristokratlık** aristocracy.
**aritmetik 1.** arithmetic; **2.** arithmetical.
**ariyet, -ti [ă]** on loan, lent; ~ almak to borrow; ~ vermek to lend.
**ariyeten** as a loan.
**arizamik [. - . -]** thoroughly.
**Arjantin** *pr. n.* Argentina.
**Arjantinli** an Argentine; Argentinean.
**ark, -kı** irrigation trench, canal; ~ lambası arc-lamp.
**arka 1.** the back; **2.** back part, rear, reverse; **3.** buttocks, rump, fanny; **4.** hind, back, posterior; **5.** *fig.* backer, supporter; pull, influence; **6.** sequel; **7.** arkasına, arkasında behind; ~ -ya one after the other; ~ -ya vermek to back each other, to join forces; ~ -ya beş gün five days in succession, five days running; ~ çantası knapsack, rucksack; ~ çıkmak (*b-ne*) to back *s.o.* up; ~ kapı back door; ~ plan background; ~ sokak back street; ~ taraf back side, reverse; ~ üstü yatmak to lie on one's back; ~ vermek to lean one's back (-*e* against); ~ yüz back side, reverse; -da bırakmak to leave behind, to outstrip; to outdistance; -da kalanlar the bereaved; -da kalmak **1.** to stay behind; to be outdistanced; **2.** *fig.* to be overshadowed; -dan **1.** from behind, in the back; behind the back; **2.** afterwards; -dan -ya under the counter, secretively; -dan söylemek to backbite; (**arkası**): ~ gelmedi it didn't last (*or* continue); ~ kesilmek to run out, to peter out; ~ sıra right after, on one's heels; ~ var to be continued; ~ yere gelmemek not to be defeated; ~ yufka! there is not much to follow!; -na düşmek **1.** to follow up (*a matter*); **2.** to follow, to dog, to tail *s.o.*; -nı almak to bring to an end; -nı bırakmamak to follow up, to stick to; -nı dayamak (*b-ne*) to build (*or* rely) on *s.o.*; -nı getireme-

dim I was unable to carry through it; -nı kesmek to stop, to cut off; -nı vermek 1. to lean one's back (-e against); 2. fig. to rely (or build) (-e on).

arkadaş friend, companion; ~ olm. to become friends; -ını soyle, kim olduğunu söyleyeyim pro. men are known by the company they keep, birds of a feather flock together.

arkadaşlık friendship; ~ etm. 1. to accompany; 2. to be a friend (ile of).

arkaik archaic.

arkalamak 1. to hoist s.th. onto one's back; 2. fig. to back up, to protect, to support.

arkalanmak 1. pass. of arkalamak; 2. to rely (or count or depend) on.

arkalı fig. having a backing, having a friend at court.

arkalık 1. a sleeveless jacket; 2. back (of a chair); 3. porter's back pad; 4. carrier (of a bicycle).

arkeolog archeologist.

arkeoloji archeology; ~ müzesi archeological museum.

arkeolojik archeological.

arklı arc...; ~ lamba arc-lamp.

arktik Arctic; ~ kuşak geogr. Arctic Zone.

arlanmak to feel ashamed.

arma [x .] 1. coat of arms, armorial bearings; 2. ↓ rigging; 3. sl. jewellery; ~ donatmak ↓ to rig a ship; ~ soymak ↓ to unrig a ship.

armador ↓ rigger.

armağan 1. present, gift; 2. prize, award; ~ etm. to present (-e to).

armatör shipowner.

armatur 1. armature; 2. condenser plate.

armoni ♪ harmony.

armonik(a) 1. harmonica, mouth organ; 2. accordion.

armoz ↓ seam, joint.

armudi [ū, ī] pear-shaped.

armut, -du 1. ♦ pear; 2. sl. blockhead; ~ piş, ağzıma düş demek to expect things to fall into one's lap without doing anything; armudun sapı var, üzümün çöpü var demek fig. there is no garden without its weed.

armuz ↓ seam, joint.

Arnavut, -du Albanian; ~ biberi red pepper.

arnavutciğeri, -ni fried liver.

Arnavutça Albanian (language).

arnavutkaldırımı rough cobblestone pavement.

Arnavutluk 1. the character of an Albanian; 2. pr. n. Albania.

arozöz sprinkler, watering truck.

arpa ♦ barley; ~ boyu very short distance; ~ boyu kadar gitmek to show little progress; ~ ektim, darı çıktı fig. I did not get what I expected.

arpacı[1] seller of barley; ~ kumrusu gibi düşünmek to be in a brownstudy.

arpacı[2] sl. thief, pilferer.

arpacık 1. ♥ sty; 2. front sight (of a gun).

arpalık 1. barley field; 2. barley bin; 3. fig. sinecure; 4. = başmaklık.

arsa building-ground, building-site, vacant lot.

arsenik ↗ arsenic.

arsıulusal international.

arsız 1. saucy, cheeky, impudent, insolent, shameless; 2. vigorous (plant).

arsızlanmak to act shamelessly, to be saucy.

arsızlık impudence, insolence; ~ etm. to behave shamelessly.

arslan s. aslan.

arş[1]: ~! ✕ march!

arş[2] 1. isl. myth. the highest heaven; 2. trolley pole.

arşe violin bow.

arşın yard, cubit (a former Turkish unit of length, 60-70 cm.).

arşınlamak 1. to measure by the yard; 2. to stride through.

arşıdük, -kü archduke.

arşidüşes archduchess.

arşiv archives.

art, -dı 1. back, rear, behind; hind; 2. squel; ~ arda one after another; ~ düşünce hidden intent; ~ niyet s. ~ düşünce; ardı arası kesilmeden uninterruptedly; ardı ardına one after another, continually; ardı arkası gelmeyen endless, never-ending; ardı kesilmek to run out; ardı sıra 1. (along) behind; 2. immediately after; ardına düşmek 1. to follow in the steps of; 2. to follow up, to tail, to pursue; ardına kadar açık wide open (door, window); ardına koymamak fig. to revenge o.s. (on); ardınca behind; ardında gezmek (or dolaşmak) to run after; ardını almak to complete; ardını bırakmamak to follow up, to stick to; artta kalmak 1. to remain (or stay) behind, to be left behind; 2. to survive.

artağan exceptionally fruitful.

artakalan remainder.

artakalmak to be left over, to remain.

artan remaining, left over.

artçı ✕ rear guard.

artdamak hard palate.

arter artery.

artezyen artesian well.

**artı** Ḁ plus.

**artık 1.** left (over), remaining; **2.** remainder, remnant, residue, leavings; **3.** extra, superfluous, redundant; **4.** now, well then; **5.** finally; from now on; **6.** (with negative) any more; ~ başlayalım! let's start!; '~ mal göz çıkarmaz pro. a little extra does no harm.

**artıkgün** ast. leap(-year) day.

**artıklık** superabundancy.

**artıkyıl** ast. leap year.

**artırım** economy, saving, frugality.

**artırma 1.** auction; **2.** saving, economizing.

**artırmak 1.** to increase, to expand, to add (to), to augment, to step up; **2.** to save, to economize (money); **3.** to overbid (at an auction); **4.** to go too far.

**artış** increase, augmentation, mark-up.

**artist, -ti 1.** artist; **2.** actor, actress.

**artistik** artistic; ~ patinaj artistic skating.

**artkafa** back of the head, occiput.

**artmak,** (-ar) **1.** to increase, to go up (price); **2.** to remain, to be left over.

**artsız arasız** uninterrupted, perpetual.

**aruz** [ū] prosody.

**arya** [x .] ♪ aria.

**arz¹** the earth.

**arz² 1.** width; **2.** latitude; ~ dairesi parallel of latitude.

**arz³** presentation, representation, demonstration; petition; ~ etm. **1.** to present; **2.** to show; **3.** to offer; ~ ve talep supply and demand; arzı hürmet(ler) (ederim) yours faithfully; arzı veda etm. (b-ne) to bid farewell to s.o., to say good-bye to s.o.

**arzi¹** earthly.

**arzi²** aeogr. terrestrial.

**arzu** [ū] wish, desire, longing; ~ etm. to wish (-i for), to want; to desire, to long (-i for); ~ üzerine on request; kalmak -sundadır he wishes to stay.

**arzuhal, -li** [. . -] petition.

**arzuhalci** scrivener.

**arzukeş** desirous.

**arzulamak** to desire, to wish (-i for), to long (-i for), to want.

**arzulu** s. arzukeş.

**as¹** zo. ermine, stoat.

**as² 1.** cards: ace; **2.** ace, champion.

**as-** sub-

**asa** scepter, stick, baton, staff.

**asabi 1.** nervous, irritable, on edge; **2.** neural.

**asabileşmek** to get nervous.

**asabilik** nervousness, irritability.

**asabiye 1.** nervous diseases; **2.** neurology, neuropathology.

**asabiyeci** nerve specialist, neurologist.

**asabiyet, -ti** nervousness, irritability; -e kapılmak to get nervous.

**asal** basic, fundamental; ~ sayı Ḁ prime (or odd) number.

**asalak 1.** ♀, zo. parasite; **2.** fig. hanger-on, sponger, parasite.

**asalaklık 1.** parasitism; **2.** fig. freeloading, sponging.

**asalet, -ti** [. - .] **1.** nobility, nobleness; **2.** definitive appointment.

**asaleten** [. - . .] acting as principal.

**asaletli** [. - . .] noble.

**asamble** assembly.

**asansör** lift, Am. elevator.

**asansörcü** liftman, liftboy.

**asap, -bı** anat. nerves; ~ bozukluğu nervous upset; ~ cümlesi anat. nervous system; asabı bozulmak to get nervous; asabına dokunmak to get on one's nerves.

**asar** [ā] † pl. of eser monuments, works.

**asarıatika** antiquities, ancient monuments.

**asayiş** [- - .] repose, public peace (or security).

**asayişsiz** troubled, insecure, unsafe.

**asbaşkan** vice-president, deputy chief.

**asbest, -ti** geol. asbestos.

**aselbent** storax.

**asepsi** asepsis.

**asetat, -tı** acetate.

**asetilen** ⚗ acetylene.

**aseton** acetone.

**asfalt, -tı 1.** asphalt; **2.** asphalt highway, paved road.

**asfaltlamak** to asphalt.

**asgari** [ī] minimum, least, smallest; ~ fiyat minimum price; ~ ücret minimum wage.

**ashap, -bı** [. -] † pl. of sahip possessors, masters.

**ası¹:** -da olm. (or kalmak) to be in the air, to hang in the balance, to be in suspense.

**ası²** profit, benefit.

**asık 1.** sulky; **2.** hanging; ~ suratlı (or yüzlü) sulky, sullen, grouchy.

**asıl 1.** (the) original; **2.** origin; **3.** truth, reality; basis; **4.** actual, true; real, essential; **5.** main, the most important; **6.** actually, essentially; ~ maksatları their main purpose; ~ sayılar gr. cardinal numbers; (aslı): ~ astarı yok it is unfounded, it is not true; ~ çıkmak to prove to be true; ~ faslı yok there is no truth in it; ~ nesli bellisiz whose origin is unknown; ~ var it is true; ~ yok nesli yok s. ~ astarı yok; bu söylentinin ~ yok this rumo(u)r is not true.

**asılı** hanging, suspended.

**asılmak** 1. *pass. of* asmak; 2. to be hanged; 3. to insist; 4. to pull hard; 5. *(b-ne)* to pester *s.o.*, to bother *s.o.*

**asılsız** unfounded, groundless *(news, rumour).*

**asılsızlık** groundlessness.

**asılzade** [. . - .] 1. nobleman, aristocrat, peer; 2. *sl.* pander, pimp, procurer.

**asılzadelik** nobility, peerage.

**asıntı** 1. delay; 2. pestering, bothering; -da kalmak to hang in the air; -ya bırakmak to delay, to postpone.

**asır**, -srı 1. century; 2. era, epoch, age, time, period.

**asırlık** a century old.

**asi** [î] 1. rebellious, refractory; 2. rebel, insurgent.

**aside** [î] dish made of okra with ground meat and flour.

**asil** 1. noble, aristocrat; 2. hono(u)rable, praiseworthy, noble *(action)*; 3. permanent *(official)*; 4. ᴕᴕ principal; ~ kan blue blood.

**asileşmek** to rebel, to be unruly.

**asilik** 1. rebelliousness; 2. rebellion.

**asillik** nobility, blue blood.

**asistan** 1. assistant; 2. assistant doctor.

**asistanlık** assistantship.

**asit**, -di ᴕ acid.

**asitli** containing acid.

**asker** 1. soldier; troops; 2. military service; 3. militant, valiant; 4. *sl.* tin, dough; ~ kaçağı deserter; ~ olm. to join the army; -den kaçmak to desert; -e alınmak to be drafted; -e çağırmak to draft, to call up; -e çağrılmak to be called up, to be drafted; -e gitmek to go into the army.

**askerce** soldierly, military.

**askeri** military; ~ bando military band; ~ fabrika war *(ar armament)* factory; ~ hastane military hospital; ~ inzibat military police *(or policeman)*; ~ lise cadets school; ~ mahkeme military court, court-martial; ~ mıntıka military zone; ~ müze military museum; ~ öğrenci cadet; ~ zabıta military police.

**askerileşmek** to become militarized.

**askerileştirmek** to militarize.

**askerlik** military service; ~ şubesi local draft office, recruiting office; ~ yoklaması roll call.

**askı** 1. hook, hanger; 2. braces, *Am.* suspenders; 3. coat rack; 4. ᴕ sling; 5. the posting *(of an announcement)*; 6. necklace *or* gold chain; -da bırakmak to leave in the air, to shelve; -da kalmak to hang in the balance, to remain in suspense; -ya almak 1. to prop up temporarily

*(house)*; 2. to lift by lines from other ships; -ya çıkarmak to post *(the banns).*

**asla** [x -] never, by no means, in no way.

**aslan¹** 1. *zo.* lion; 2. *fig.* plucky person, brave man; ~ ağzında olm. *fig.* to be very hard to get; ~ gibi 1. like a lion *(person)*; 2. healthy, in the pink; ~ payı the lion's share; ~ terbiyecisi lion-tamer; ~ yürekli *fig.* lion-hearted; -ım! my lad!

**aslan²** *s.* aslen.

**Aslan³** *ast.* Leo.

**aslanağzı**, -nı ᴕ snapdragon.

**aslen** fundamentally, essentially, basically, originally.

**asli** [î] fundamental, essential, original, principal; ~ adet cardinal number; ~ maaş basic salary; ~ nüsha original text; ~ vazife principal duty.

**asliye:** ~ mahkemesi ᴕᴕ court of first instance.

**asma¹** ᴕ 1. vine; 2. grapevine; ~ kütüğü vine stock; ~ yaprağı vine leaf.

**asma²** 1. hanging, suspended; 2. suspension; ~ kat mezzanine; ~ kilit padlock; ~ köprü suspension bridge; ~ saat wall clock.

**asmabahçe** hanging garden.

**asmak**, (-ar) 1. to hang up *(-e on)*, to suspend; 2. to hang *(a person)*; 3. *sl.* to play truant *(or* hooky), to skip, to cut *(school)*; 4. *sl.* to neglect; 5. *sl.* to skip out *(-i on)*; 6. *sl.* to refuse to pay back *(a debt)*; asıp kesmek to play the tyrant; astığı astık kestiği kestik what he says goes.

**asmakabağı**, -nı ᴕ long edible squash .

**aspiratör** 1. exhaust *(or* suction) fan; 2. ᴕ aspirator.

**aspirin** aspirin.

**asri** modern, up-to-date.

**asrileşmek** to be modernized.

**asrilik** modernity.

**assubay** X noncommissioned officer.

**aşşuur** subconscious.

**ast**, -tı 1. X sub, under; 2. subordinate.

**astar** 1. lining; 2. priming, undercoat *(before painting)*; 3. caulking; ~ boyası undercoat, priming; -ı yüzünden pahalı it costs more than it is worth.

**astarlamak** 1. to line *(a garment)*; 2. to prime.

**asteğmen** X second lieutenant.

**astım** ᴕ asthma.

**astigmat** ᴕ astigmatic.

**astragan** astrakhan.

**astroloji** astrology.

**astronomi** astronomy.

**astronomik** astronomical; ~ fiyat astronomical price.

**astronot** astronaut.

**asude** [ū] calm, quiet, tranquil.

**asuman** [ā, ā] sky, the heavens.

**Asya** pr. n. Asia.

**Asyalı** pr. n. Asiatic.

**aş** cooked food; ~ deliye kalıyor the person who does not get involved in an argument profits; ~ kabı X mess tin, Am. mess kit; -ta (or çorbada) tuzu bulunmak (b-nin) to make a contribution, however small.

**aşağı** 1. bottom, the lower part; 2. lower; 3. inferior, low; 4. common, mean, commonplace; 5. down, downstairs; ~ atmak to pay no attention (to), to disregard; ~ görmek to look down (-i on), to despise; ~ kalmak to fall short (-den of); ~ mal inferior goods; ~ yukarı more or less, about, approximately; -daki below; -dan almak to ingratiate o.s.; Mehmet ~ Mehmet yukarı it is 'Mehmet' all the time, nothing but 'Mehmet'.

**aşağılamak** to run down, to lower, to degrade, to denigrate.

**aşağılık** 1. coarse, vulgar; 2. vulgarity; ~ duygusu (or kompleksi) inferiority complex.

**aşama** 1. degree, rank, level, position, grade; 2. stage, step.

**aşarî** [- - -] † Å decimal.

**aşçı** s. ahçı.

**aşçılık** s. ahçılık.

**aşevi**, -ni 1. restaurant; 2. soup kitchen; 3. temporary kitchen.

**aşhane** [. - .] s. aşevi.

**aşı** 1. vaccine; 2. vaccination, inoculation; 3. budding, grafting; 4. scion, graft, bud; ~ kâğıdı certificate of vaccination; ~ olm. to be inoculated; ~ yapmak 1. to inoculate, to vaccinate; 2. to graft, to bud.

**aşıboyası**, -nı 1. red ocher; 2. brick red.

**aşıcı** 1. vaccinator; 2. grafter (of trees).

**aşık** anat. astragalus, talus, anklebone, hucklebone; ~ atmak 1. to play knucklebones; 2. fig. to vie, to compete (ile with); aşığı bey (or çift or cuk) oturuyor he is having everything smoothly.

**âşık** 1. in love (-e with); 2. lover, suitor; 3. bard, troubadour; 4. absent-minded person; ~ olm. to fall in love (-e with); -lısı lover (of), devotee.

**âşıkane** 1. amorously; 2. amorous (act).

**âşıktaş** sweetheart.

**aşılamak** 1. to inoculate (a. fig.), to vaccinate; 2. to bud, to graft; 3. to infect; 4. fig. to inculcate, to instill, to inoculate

(ideas) (-e in).

**aşındırmak** 1. to abrade, to wear away; 2. ⌃ to corrode; 3. fig. to frequent (a place).

**aşınma** 1. corrosion; 2. wear and tear; 3. erosion.

**aşınmak** 1. to wear away, to be corroded, to be abraded, to be eroded; 2. to depreciate.

**aşırı** 1. extreme, excessive; 2. extremely, excessively; 3. beyond, over; 4. every other; ~ gitmek to exceed the limit, to go beyond bounds, to overshoot the mark; ~ solcu extreme leftist; gün ~ every other day.

**aşırıdoyma** ⌃ supersaturation.

**aşırıduyu** hyperesthesia.

**aşırılık** excessiveness.

**aşırma** 1. vn. of aşırmak; 2. theft, pilfering; 3. stolen, pilfered; 4. P bucket; ~ kayış (drive) belt.

**aşırmak** 1. (bir yerden) to pass over (a place); 2. F to swipe, to nick, to nip, to pinch; 3. sl. to get rid (of); 4. to plagiarize.

**aşifte** [ā] loose woman.

**aşikâr** [ā] clear, evident, manifest, open.

**aşina** [ā, ā] 1. familiar, well-known; 2. acquaintance; 3. knowing, acquainted (-e with).

**aşinalık** acquaintance, intimacy; ~ etm. to bow, to greet by a gesture.

**aşiret**, -ti [ī] tribe.

**aşk**, -kı love, passion; ~ etm. to land, to inflict (a blow); -a gelmek to go into a rapture, to be enraptured; aşkınıza! to your health!

**aşkın** 1. more than, over, beyond; 2. excessive; işi başından -dır he is up to his ears in work; yaşı elliyi -dır he is over fifty.

**aşkolsun!** 1. bravo!, well done!; 2. shame on you!

**aşlamak** to mix hot water with (cold water).

**aşlık** 1. provisions; 2. wheat.

**aşmak**, (-ar) 1. to pass (over), to go (beyond); 2. to exceed, to surpass; 3. to cover (a mare); 4. sl. to slip away, to sneak away.

**aşna fişne** sl. secret love affair.

**aşure** [ū] pudding made with cereals, sugar and raisins.

**aşüfte** [ā] s. aşifte.

**at**, -tı zo. horse; ~ başı beraber (or bir) neck and neck; ~ çalındıktan sonra ahırın kapısını kapamak to lock the stable door after the horse has been stolen; ~

hırsızı rustler; ~ koşusu (or yarışı) horse--racing; ♀ Meydanı pr. n. Hippodrome; -a binmek to ride a horse; -ı alan Üsküdar'ı geçmek to miss the bus (or boat); -ı eşkin, kılıcı keskin fig. he is powerful.

**ata** 1. father; 2. ancestor; 3. ♀ pr. n. abbr. for Atatürk; -lardan kalma ancestral.

**atacılık** biol. atavism, reversion.

**ataerki,** -ni patriarchy.

**ataerkil** patriarchal.

**atak** 1. rash, reckless, boastful (person); 2. football: attack.

**ataklık** rashness.

**atalanı,** -nı hippodrome.

**atalet,** -ti [. - .] 1. laziness, lassitude; 2. unemployment; 3. phys. inertia; ~ kanunu phys. principle of inertia.

**atalık** fatherliness.

**atamak** to appoint (-e to).

**ataman** ataman, hetman.

**atanmak** to be appointed (-e to).

**atardamar** anat. artery.

**atasözü,** -nü proverb.

**ataşe** attaché.

**Atatürk** pr. n. founder and first president of the Turkish Republic.

**Atatürkçü** pr. n. Kemalist.

**Atatürkçülük** pr. n. Kemalism.

**atavik** atavistic.

**atçı** horse breeder.

**atçılık** horse breeding.

**ateh** dotage, senility; ~ getirmek to dote.

**ateizm** atheism.

**atelye** 1. workshop; 2. studio, atelier.

**aterina** [. . x .] zo. silversides, atherine.

**ateş** 1. fire; 2. ♀ temperature, fever; 3. vehemence, fervo(u)r, zeal, ardo(u)r; 4. fig. vivacity, exuberance; 5. ✕ gunfire; artillery fire; 6. a light (for a cigarette); 7. danger; catastrophe; ~ açmak ✕ to open fire (-e on); ~ almak 1. to catch (or take) fire; 2. ✕ to be fired (gun); 3. to be alarmed; ~ etm. ✕ to fire (-e on), to shoot (-e at); ~ gibi 1. piping hot; 2. agile, intelligent; ~ gibi yanmak to run a temperature; ~ hattı (or boyu) ✕ firing line; ~ kesilmek fig. to become industrious and active; ~ kesmek to cease fire; ~ koymak to set on fire; ~ olmayan yerden duman çıkmaz pro. there is no smoke without fire, where there is smoke there is fire; ~ pahasına very expensive; ~ püskürmek fig. to spit fire (-e at), to go up in the air; ~ vermek to set on fire, to burn; ~ e körükle gitmek fig. to add fuel to the flames; -e vermek 1. to set fire (-i to); 2. to panic, to upset; 3. to ravage, to devastate (a country); -i başına vur-

mak to blow one's top; -i çıkmak (or yükselmek) to run a temperature; -le oynamak to play with fire (or edged tools); -ler içinde feverish; -ten gömlek ordeal.

**ateşbalığı,** -nı sardine.

**ateşböceği,** -ni zo. firefly, glowworm.

**ateşçi** fireman, stoker.

**ateşkes** cease-fire, armistice, truce.

**ateşleme** ✍ ignition.

**ateşlemek** 1. to set fire (-i to), to ignite, to light; 2. fig. to provoke, to incite.

**ateşlendirmek** 1. to enliven; 2. to stir up, to aggravate (trouble).

**ateşlenmek** 1. pass. of ateşlemek; 2. to run a temperature; 3. fig. to get angry.

**ateşli** 1. ♀ feverish; 2. fig. fiery; 3. fig. fervent, vivacious; 4. ✕ fire...; ~ silah firearm.

**ateşlik** 1. firepan; 2. fit for burning.

**atfen** [x .] 1. ascribed (-e to); 2. based (-e on).

**atfetmek** [x . .] 1. to attribute (-e to), to ascribe (-e to), to impute (-e to); 2. to direct, to turn (-e to) (one's glance).

**atıcı** 1. marksman; 2. fig. fibber.

**atıcılık** 1. marksmanship; 2. fig. mendacity, fibbing.

**atıf,** -tfı attribution.

**atıfet,** -ti [ⁱ] affection, sympathy.

**atık** small churn.

**atıl** 1. lazy; 2. idle; 3. phys. inert.

**atılgan** 1. dashing, bold, plucky; 2. enterprising.

**atılganlık** 1. audacity, boldness; 2. enterprise.

**atılım, atılış** 1. advance, progress; 2. sports: attack.

**atılmak** 1. pass. of atmak; 2. to attack, to go (-e at); 3. sl. to butt in, to cut in; 4. to begin, to go (-e into).

**atım** range (of a gun).

**atımlık** the quantity of powder for one charge; iki ~ barut two charges of powder.

**atış** 1. throwing; 2. firing, shooting; 3. beating (of the heart); ~ menzili range.

**atışmak** 1. (b-le) to quarrel with s.o., to have a tiff with s.o.; 2. to try to make up (-e with); 3. to indulge in poetic repartee.

**atıştırmak** 1. caus. of atışmak; 2. to bolt, to gobble (food); 3. to drizzle, to spit (rain, snow).

**ati** the future; -deki in the future.

**atik**[1] alert, agile.

**atik**[2], -kı ancient.

**Atina** pr. n. Athens.

**Atinalı** pr. n. an Athenian.

atkafalı dumb, stupid.
atkestanesi, -ni [. . - .] ♀ horse chestnut.
atkı 1. shawl, stole; 2. weft, woof; 3. shoe strap; 4. pitchfork; 5. lintel.
atkılamak to weave the woof in.
atkuyruğu, -nu 1. ♀ mare's-tail; 2. pony-tail.
atlama jump; ~ taşı steppingstone; ~ taşı yapmak fig. to use as a steppingstone.
atlamak 1. to jump; 2. to jump down (-den from), to leap (-den from); 3. to jump (-e into) (a taxi); 4. to skip, to miss, to leave out: 5. journalism: to miss a scoop; 6. to be misled, to be mistaken (-de in); 7. sl. to screw, to stuff, to fuck.
atlambaç leapfrog.
atlanmak 1. pass. of atlamak; 2. to mount a horse; 3. to get a horse.
Atlantik pr. n. Atlantic.
atlas 1. atlas, map book; 2. anat. atlas; 3. satin.
atlasçiçeği, -ni ♀ cactus.
atlatmak caus. of atlamak 1. to make s.o. jump; 2. to overcome, to weather (crisis, danger, etc.); 3. to put off, to get rid of (a person).
atlayış leap.
atlet, -ti 1. athlete; 2. muscular, well-developed; 3. (a. ~ fanilası) undershirt, vest.
atletik athletic.
atletizm athletics.
atlı rider, horseman; mounted on horse-back; ~ araba horse cart, wagon.
atlıkarınca merry-go-round, carousel, roundabout.
atmaca zo. sparrow-hawk.
atmak, (-ar) 1. to throw; 2. to drop; 3. to send away; 4. to put out, to extend; 5. to fire (a gun, a shot); 6. to postpone, to put off; 7. to throw on ,to put on (a garment); 8. to impute, to throw (-e on), to put (-e on) (blame); 9. to expel s.o. (-den from); 10. to discard, to throw away; 11. to reject, to expel; 12. to blow up, to demolish; 13. F to lie, to fib; 14. F to drink; 15. to fluff (cotton); 16. to split crack, to come loose; 17. to pulsate, to beat, to throb (heart, artery); 18. to send, to post (letter); 19. to let out (cry, scream); 20 to abandon, to give up; 21. sl. to perform (a dance); 22. sl. to sing (a song); 23. to land (a blow); 24. to write (one's signature, the date); at martini Debre'li Hasan! don't try to pull my leg!; atıp tutmak (or savurmak) 1. to run down; 2. to talk big, to boast; atma Recep, din kardeşiyiz! don't try to pull my

leg!; attığı tırnak olamamak (b-nin) fig. can't hold a candle to s.o.
atmasyon sl. 1. lie; 2. false, made up.
atmasyoncu sl. 1. liar; 2. mendacious.
atmasyonculuk sl. lying, mendacity.
atmosfer atmosphere.
atol, -lü atoll.
atom atom; ~ bombası atomic bomb, A--bomb, sl. nuke; ~ çağı atomic age; ~ çe-kirdeği (atomic) nucleus; ~ enerjisi or -lar arası enerjisi atomic energy.
atomal atomic.
atraksiyon number in a floor show, fea-ture.
atsineği, -ni zo. horsefly, forest fly.
av 1. hunt(ing), chase; shooting; fishing; 2. game, prey; catch (fish); 3. fig. vic-tim, prey; ~ alayı X fighter wing (or group); ~ aramak to look for game; ~ köpeği hound, hunting dog; ~ kuşu 1. fowling hawk; 2. game bird; ~ takımı hunting equipment; ~ tüfeği fowling--piece, shotgun; -a giden avlanır pro. the biter is sometimes bit.
avadan ✹ set of tools.
avadanlık 1. set of tools; 2. sl. cock and bollocks.
aval¹, -li 1. endorsement of a bill of ex-change by a third party; 2. endorser.
aval² sl. half-witted, stupid.
aval aval sl. stupidly.
avam [. -] pl. of amme common people, lower classes; ♀ Kamarası pr. n. the House of Commons.
avanak sl. gullible, simpleton.
avanaklık sl. gullibility.
avans advance (of money), earnest-(-money); ~ almak to get an advance; ~ vermek to advance money.
avanta [. x .] sl. illicit profit; -dan for noth-ing, gratis.
avantacı sl. freeloader, sponger, bum.
avantacılık sl. freeloading.
avantaj advantange, profit, gain.
avara [. x .] ↓ shoving off; ~ etm. to shove off; ~ kolu ⊕ switch lever.
avare vagabond, good-for-nothing, out of work.
avarız [. - .] pl. of arıza roughness.
avarya [. x .] ↓ average.
avaz [. -] shout, cry; ~ ~ bağırmak or -ı çıktığı kadar bağırmak to shout at the top of one's voice.
avcı 1. hunter, huntsman; 2. X rifleman, skirmisher; ~ uçağı fighter; ~ zağarı 1. hound; 2. fig. hanger-on.
avcılık 1. hunting, huntsmanship, shoot-ing; 2. fig. woman-chasing.

**avdet,** -ti return; ~ etm. to return.
**avene** accomplices, gang.
**avgın** drainhole *(in a wall).*
**avisto** [. x .] ↑ at sight.
**avize** [î] chandelier.
**avizeağacı,** -nı ♀ yucca.
**avizo** [. x .] ⚓ dispatch boat.
**avlak** hunting ground.
**avlamak 1.** to hunt, to shoot; **2.** *fig.* to dupe, to deceive.
**avlanmak 1.** *pass. of* avlamak; **2.** to go hunting.
**avlu** court(yard).
**Avrasya** *pr. n.* Eurasia.
**avrat,** -ti *contp., sl. or* ᴾ **1.** woman; **2.** wife.
**avret,** -ti private parts, genitals.
**Avrupa** [. x .] *pr. n.* Europe.
**Avrupai** European (style).
**Avrupalı** European.
**Avrupalılaşmak** to become Europeanized.
**avt, avut** *football:* out.
**avuç,** -cu **1.** the hollow of the hand; ~ handful; ~ açmak to beg, to cadge; ~ ~ **1.** handful to each; **2.** by the handful, lavishly; ~ dolusu plenty of, a lot of; ~ dolusu para tutmak to cost an arm and a leg; ~ içi kadar **1.** skimpy; **2.** narrow *(place)*; avucu gidişmek *(or* kaşınmak) *fig.* to anticipate getting money; avucuna saymak to pay in hand *(cash)*; avucunu yalamak to be left empty-handed; avucunun içi gibi bilmek to know like the back of one's hand; avucunun içindedir *fig.* he is at her command.
**avuçlamak 1.** to grasp; **2.** to take by handfuls.
**avukat,** -ti lawyer, solicitor, advocate, barrister.
**avukatlık 1.** advocacy, barristership; **2.** *fig.* unnecessary defence.
**avunç** consolation, comfort.
**avundurmak** to console, to comfort.
**avunmak 1.** to be consoled *(ile* with), to be cheered up; **2.** to be preoccupied *(ile* with); **3.** to be bred, to become pregnant *(animal).*
**avuntu** consolation.
**avurt,** -du pouch of the cheek; ~ etm. to put on airs; ~ kesmek to give *o.s.* airs; ~ satmak *(or* şişirmek) to brag, to talk big; ~ zavurt etm. **1.** *s.* ~ satmak; **2.** to threaten *(or* browbeat) others; avurdu avurduna göçmek to have sunken cheeks.
**avurtlamak** *s.* avurt etm.
**Avustralya** [. . x .] *pr. n.* Australia.
**Avustralyalı** [. . x .] **1.** Australian; **2.** an Australian.
**Avusturya** [. . x .] *pr. n.* Austria.

**Avusturyalı** [. . x . .] **1.** Austrian; **2.** an Austrian.
**avut** *s.* avt.
**avutmak 1.** to soothe, to distract; to delude, to quieten; **2.** to console, to comfort; **3.** to attract and amuse.
**ay¹ 1.** moon; crescent; **2.** month *(of the year)*; ~ aydını *(or* aydınlığı) moonlight; ~ dede the moon; ~ ışığı moonlight; ~ modülü moon module; ~ parçası a beauty; ~ tutulması lunar eclipse; ~ yıldız star and crescent *(Turkish emblem)*; -da yılda bir once in a blue moon; -ın on dördü full moon; -ın on dördü gibi very beautiful *(woman).*
**ay² 1.** oh!; **2.** ouch!
**aya** palm of the hand.
**ayak 1.** foot; **2.** leg; **3.** pedestal, base, footing; **4.** outlet *(of a lake)*; **5.** step; **6.** treadle *(of a sewing machine)*; **7.** shaft *(of a loom)*; **8.** tributary; **9.** pace, gait; **10.** rhyme; **11.** foot *(measure)*; ~ atmak **1.** to go for the first time; **2.** to take a step; ~ ~ üstüne atmak to cross one's legs; ~ bağı hindrance, impediment; ~ basmak **1.** *(bir yere)* to set foot in *(or* on) somewhere; **2.** to arrive *(-e* at, in), to enter; ~ bileği **1.** ankle; **2.** *anat.* tarsus; ~ değiştirmek to get into step by changing one's foot *(in marching)*; ~ diremek to put one's foot down, to insist; ~ işi errands and small deals; ~ kirası messenger's tip; ~ parmakları toes; ~ patırdısı tramping of feet; ~ uydurmak **1.** to fall in step; to keep in step *(-e* with); **2.** *fig.* to keep pace *(-e* with); ~ üstü in haste, without sitting down; ayağa fırlamak to jump to one's feet; ayağa kaldırmak to incite, to stir up to rebellion; ayağa kalkmak **1.** to stand up, to rise to one's feet; **2.** to get excited, to be aroused; **3.** to get about, to get round, to go about; (ayağına): ~ çabuk swift of foot; ~ çağırmak to call into one's presence; ~ kadar gelmek to condescend to visit *s.o.*; ~ gitmek to visit personally *(as an act of deference)*; ~ karası inmek to be on one's last legs; (ayağını): ~ çabuk tut! shake a leg!; ~ çelmek to trip up; ~ denk almak to watch one's step, to keep one's eyes skinned; ~ kaydırmak to cut the ground from under *s.o.*'s feet; ~ öpeyim! I beg *(or* implore) you!; ~ vurmak *(ayakkabı)* to pinch, to chafe one's foot; ~ yorganına göre uzatmak *pro.* to cut one's coat according to one's cloth; -nın tozu ile having just arrived; ayakta **1.** standing, on one's feet; **2.** *fig.* excited, aroused; **3.** ♀

ambulatory; ayakta durmak to stand; ayakta kalmak 1. to be left without a seat; 2. to remain standing; to have lasted; ayakta tedavi ∯ ambulatory treatment; ayakta uyumak to be dead on one's feet.

**ayakaltı,** -nı much frequented place; -nda dolaşmak to get under foot, to be in the way.

**ayakkabı,** -yı shoe; footwear.

**ayakkabıcı 1.** shoemaker; **2.** shoe-dealer.

**ayakkabıcılık 1.** shoemaking; **2.** shoe trade.

**ayaklamak** to measure by pacing.

**ayaklanma** rebellion, mutiny, revolt.

**ayaklanmak 1.** *pass. of* ayaklamak; **2.** to rebel, to revolt; **3.** to begin to walk *(child).*

**ayaklı** footed, legged; ~ canavar naughty child; ~ kütüphane *fig.* very learned person.

**ayaklık 1.** pedal, treadle; **2.** stilts; **3.** place to step on.

**ayaktakımı,** -nı rabble, mob.

**ayakteri,** -ni tip given to a messenger.

**ayaktopu,** -nu football, soccer.

**ayakucu,** -nu **1.** foot *(of a bed)*; **2.** tiptoe.

**ayakyolu,** -nu toilet, water closet, loo.

**ayan** [. -] clear, evident, plain, manifest; ~ beyan very clear.

**âyan** [- -] **1.** notables; **2.** senators; ~ meclisi the senate.

**ayar 1.** standard *(of time)*; **2.** adjustment for accuracy *(watch)*: **3.** adjustment, set-up *(machine)*; **4.** fineness; karats *(gold, silver)*; **5.** *fig.* quality, character *(person)*; ~ etm. to adjust, to fix, to regulate, to set; -ı bozuk **1.** out of order; **2.** *fig.* of bad character.

**ayarlamak 1.** to adjust, to fix, to regulate, to set; **2.** to arrange, to put in order; **3.** to test, to assay, to gauge.

**ayarlı 1.** regulated *(clock)*; **2.** of standard fineness; ~ bomba time bomb.

**ayarsız 1.** out of adjustment; **2.** unassayed; below standard; **3.** *fig.* unbalanced *(person)*.

**ayartmak** to lead astray, to seduce, to tempt, to entice, to pervert.

**Ayasofya** [. . x .] *pr. n.* Hagia Sophia.

**ayaz 1.** dry cold, nip in the air; frostiness; **2.** cold, frosty *(air, night)*; ~ almak to get nothing; ~ kesmek *fig.* to be exposed to the cold for a long time; ~ olm. to be frosty; ~ paşa kola çıkmış *(or* kol geziyor*)* F Jack Frost is going the rounds, it is freezing weather; -a kalmak *s.* ~ almak; -a çekmek to turn cold *(weather).*

**ayazlamak 1.** to become clear and cold *(weather)*; **2.** to become cold in the

freeze; **3.** *sl.* to wait in vain.

**ayazlanmak** to be cooled.

**ayazma** [. x .] *eccl.* sacred spring.

**aybaşı,** -nı menstruation, menses, the curse.

**ayçiçeği,** -nı ♀ sunflower; ~ yağı vegetable oil, sunflower oil.

**aydın 1.** well lighted; **2.** lucid, clear; **3.** intellectual, enlightened person; **4.** *(in expressions)* joyous, happy.

**aydınlanmak 1.** to brighten up, to become luminous; **2.** to be enlightened, to become informed *(on a subject)*; **3.** to become clear.

**aydınlatıcı 1.** illuminating; **2.** informative, enlightening.

**aydınlatmak 1.** to illuminate, to illumine; **2.** to clarify, to explain; **3.** to enlighten.

**aydınlık 1.** light; **2.** bright, luminous; **3.** clear, brilliant; **4.** luminousness; **5.** clarity; **6.** light shaft.

**ayet,** -ti [- .] verse of the Koran.

**aygın:** ~ baygın **1.** languid; **2.** languishing *(-e* for); **3.** languidly.

**aygır 1.** stallion; **2.** *fig.* lout.

**aygıt,** -tı **1.** apparatus, instrument, device; tool; **2.** *biol.* system.

**ayı 1.** *zo.* bear; **2.** *fig.* jerk; ~ gibi bearish; -ya dayı demek *fig.* to cajole *s.o.*; -ya kaval çalmak to try in vain to explain *s.th.* to a blockhead.

**ayıbalığı,** -nı *zo.* seal.

**ayıcı 1.** bear leader; **2.** *fig.* rude, rough, coarse.

**ayık 1.** sober; **2.** *fig.* wide-awake, alert.

**ayıklamak 1.** to pick over, to clean off, to sort, to select; **2.** to shell *(peas, beans)*; ayıkla pirincin taşını! *fig.* that is a fine *(or* pretty*)* kettle of fish!

**ayıklanma** *biol.* selection.

**ayılmak 1.** to sober up; **2.** to come to, to come round; **3.** to come to one's senses, to see the light; ~ bayılmak *fig.* to be wild *(-e* about), to be nuts *(-e* about, over).

**ayıltmak** to sober up.

**ayıp,** -bı **1.** shame, disgrace; **2.** shameful, disgraceful; **3.** defect, fault; **4.** shame on you!; ~ etm. *(or* yapmak) to behave shamefully; -tır söylemesi if you will excuse my French.

**ayıplamak** to condemn, to censure, to blame, to vilify.

**ayıplı** faulty, defective.

**ayıpsız** intact, free from defects.

**ayırım** discrimination; ~ yapmak to discriminate.

**ayırmak 1.** to separate, to part, to sever *(-den* from); **2.** to select, to pick, to choose; **3.** to discriminate (between); **4.** to distinguish (*-den* from); **5.** to divide, to sunder; **6.** to set apart; **7.** to save, to spare, to reserve (*-e* for); **8.** to isolate (*-den* from).

**ayırt etm.** to distinguish, to discriminate, to discern (*-den* from).

**ayin** [i] **1.** rite; **2.** ceremony; **ayini ruhani** church worship.

**aykırı 1.** contrary; **2.** contrary (*-e* to), against, in violation of; **3.** diverging, divergent; ~ düşmek to be contrary (*-e* to), to be incongruous (*-e* with); ~ olm. to be contrary, to be opposite (*-e* to).

**aykırılaşmak** to become contrary.

**aykırılık** incongruity; difference, disagreement.

**aylak** idle, unemployed; ~ ~ dolaşmak to fool around (*or* about).

**aylakçı** casual labo(u)rer.

**aylaklık** idleness, unemployment.

**aylık 1.** monthly; **2.** monthly salary (*or* pay); **3.** ... months old (*baby*); **4.** lasting ... months; **5.** enough for ... months; ~ almak to be on salary; ~ bağlamak (*b-ne*) to put *s.o.* on salary.

**aylıkçı** salaried employee.

**aylıklı** salaried.

**aymak** to come to, to awake.

**aymaz** unaware.

**ayn 1.** exact copy, counterpart; **2.** ṣṣ thing, ' res; **3.** *s.* aynı.

**ayna 1.** mirror, looking glass; **2.** telescope; **3.** ↓ sextant; **4.** panel (*of a door*); **5.** blade (*of an oar*); **6.** kneecap (*of a horse*); **7.** *sl.* perfect; ~ gibi **1.** mirror-like, lustrous; **2.** glassy (*water*).

**aynacı 1.** maker of mirrors; **2.** *fig.* trickster.

**aynalı 1.** having a mirror; **2.** *sl.* beautiful; ~ dolap wardrobe fitted with mirrors.

**Aynaroz** *pr. n.* Mount Athos.

**aynasız 1.** *sl.* bad, unpleasant; **2.** *sl.* policeman, pig, cop, bobby.

**aynen** [x .] exactly, likewise, textually.

**aynı** the same, identical; ~ kapıya (*or* yola) çıkmak to amount (*or* come) to the same thing; ~ şekilde in the same way, likewise; ~ şey it makes no difference; ~ zamanda at the same time, simultaneously; meanwhile.

**aynılık** sameness, identity.

**aynıyle** without any change, as it is.

**ayni** in kind; ~ kıymet ṣṣ real value.

**ayniyat,** -tı goods. property, belongings.

**ayniyet,** -ti identity.

**ayol** [x .] well!, hey!, you!

**ayraç** *gr.* bracket, paranthesis; paranthe-

ses.

**ayran 1.** *a drink made of yogurt and water*; **2.** buttermilk; ~ ağızlı (*or* budalası *or* delisi) F stupid, simpleton; ~ı kabarmak *sl.* **1.** to fly off the handle; **2.** to be sexually aroused; ~ım ekşi diyen olmaz *pro.* nobody confesses to the shortcomings of his own work.

**ayrı 1.** different, distinct; **2.** separate, apart; **3.** exceptional; ~ ~ **1.** separate, distinct; **2.** individual; **3.** one by one, separately; ~ gayrı bilmemek to have all things in common; ~ koymak to put aside; ~ seçi olm. to withdraw one's property. to divide out; ~ seçi yapmak to discriminate; ~ tutmak to discriminate (between); -sı gayrısı olmamak **1.** = ~ gavrı bilmemek; **2.** to make no discriminations.

**ayrıbasım** offprint, reprint.

**ayrıca** [x . .] **1.** separately; **2.** specially; **3.** besides, also, moreover, furthermore, in addition.

**ayrıcalı 1.** privileged; **2.** exceptional.

**ayrıcalık** privilege.

**ayrıcalıklı** privileged.

**ayrıcinsten** heterogeneous.

**ayrık 1.** separated; **2.** exceptional; **3.** *log.* disjunctive.

**ayrıkotu,** -nu ❦ couch grass.

**ayrılanmak 1.** to separate out; **2.** to be isolated.

**ayrılaşmak** to become outstanding.

**ayrılık 1.** separateness; **2.** separation, rupture; **3.** difference; **4.** deviation; **5.** ṣṣ legal separation; ~ davası ṣṣ action for legal separation.

**ayrılmak 1.** *pass. of* ayırmak; **2.** to part, to separate from one another; **3.** to split, to crack, to open up; **4.** to leave, to depart (*-den* from); **5.** to split (*-e* into); **6.** ṣṣ to divorce.

**ayrım 1.** difference; **2.** differentiation; **3.** section, part, chapter; **4.** *cinema:* sequence.

**ayrımlı 1.** different; **2.** divided into sections.

**ayrıntı** detail; -lar details.

**ayrıntılı** detailed, in details.

**ayrışık 1.** decomposed; **2.** different, various.

**ayrışım** ❦ decomposition.

**ayrışmak** ❦ to be decomposed.

**ayrıştırmak** ❦ to decompose, to analyze.

**ayrıt,** -tı ⚠ edge.

**aysar** moonstruck.

**aysberg,** -ki iceberg.

**Ayşe** *wf.*; ♀ kadın fasulyesi French (*or* string *or* green) bean.
**ayva** ♀ quince; ~ tüyü fuzz on a youth's cheek; -yı yemek *sl.* to be in the soup, to be in hot (*or* deep) waters.
**ayvalık** quince orchard.
**ayvaz 1.** footman; **2.** ⚓ hospital aide on a ship; ~ kasap her bir hesap it makes no difference.
**ayyaş** drunkard, toper, sot.
**ayyaşlık** dipsomania, drunkenness.
**ayyuk,** -ku [ū] the highest point of the sky; -a çıkarmak *fig.* to praise to the skies, to vaunt; -a çıkmak **1.** to be very loud (*sound*); **2.** to be widely known (*event*).
**az 1.** little, small (*amount*); **2.** few; **3.** seldom, rarely; **4.** less (-*den* than); ~ ~ little by little, gradually; ~ buçuk **1.** scanty, hardly enough; **2.** somewhat, a little; ~ bulmak to consider insufficient; ~ buz şey değil! F it is no small matter!; ~ çok more or less; ~ daha almost, nearly; ~ gelmek not to be enough; ~ görmek to find insufficient; ~ kaldı (*or* kalsın) almost, nearly, all but; ~ maz F more or less; ~ olsun öz olsun! let it be little but good!; ~ tamah çok ziyan getirir *pro.* grasp all, lose all; -a çoğa bakmamak to be satisfied with what one gets; -ı çoğa tutmak *fig.* to take the will for the deed.
**aza** [- -] **1.** member, participant; **2.** *anat.* limbs, organs.
**azade** [- - .] **1.** free, untrammeled; **2.** free, released (-*den* from); **3.** ♀ *pr. n. wf.*
**azalmak** to lessen, to diminish, to be reduced, to be decreased.
**azaltmak** to lessen, to diminish, to reduce, to decrease, to lower.
**âzam** † greatest, largest.
**azamet,** -ti **1.** greatness, grandeur, majesty; **2.** *fig.* conceit, arrogance.
**azametlenmek** to give *o.s.* airs.
**azametli 1.** grand, great, august; **2.** *fig.* conceited, haughty, arrogant.
**azami** [ī] maximum, greatest, utmost; ~ fiyat maximum price; ~ hızla at full (*or* top) speed; ~ sürat top speed.
**azap,** -bı [. -] pain, torment, torture; ~ çekmek to suffer torments; ~ vermek to torment.
**azar** reprimand, reproach, scolding; ~ işitmek to get it in the neck, to be scolded.
**azar azar** little by little.
**azarlamak** to scold, to reproach, to reprimand, to rebuke, to give what-for.
**azat,** -dı [. -] **1.** emancipation, liberation, setting free; **2.** dismissal (*from school*);

~ etm. **1.** to set free, to free; **2.** to dismiss (*from school*).
**azatlamak** *s.* azat etm.
**azca** rather little (*or* few).
**azcık** *s.* azıcık.
**azdırmak 1.** to irritate, to inflame; **2.** to tease; **3.** to excite sexually; **4.** to spoil, to indulge (*a child*); **5.** to lead astray, to corrupt.
**Azeri** [ā] Azerbaijani.
**azgelişmiş** underdeveloped; ~ ülke underdeveloped country.
**azgın 1.** wild, mad, furious; fierce, ferocious; **2.** tender, sensitive (*skin*); **3.** naughty, mischievous (*child*); **4.** oversexed; **5.** in heat, in rut (*animal*).
**azgınlaşmak 1.** to get wild; **2.** to become oversexed, to become lecherous.
**azgınlık 1.** wildness, fierceness; **2.** naughtiness (*in a child*).
**azı** *a.* -dişi molar tooth.
**azıcık 1.** very small (*amount*); **2.** just a little bit; **3.** for a moment; ~ aşım kaygısız başım! it is good to live simply.
**azıdişi,** -ni *s.* azı.
**azık 1.** provisions; **2.** food.
**azıklanmak** to provide *o.s.* with provisions.
**azıklık 1.** provisions; **2.** nosebag.
**azılı** ferocious, wild, savage, inhuman.
**azım,** -zmı † *s.* kemik.
**azımsamak 1.** to consider too little; **2.** to underestimate, to undervalue.
**azınlık** minority; -ta kalmak to be in the minority.
**azışmak** to grow vehement, to intensify.
**azıtmak 1.** to get wild, to get out of control; **2.** to drive away; **3.** to make worse, to aggravate, to exacerbate.
**azil,** -zli dismissal, removal.
**azim,** -zmi determination, resolution; -le resolutely.
**azim 1.** great, immense, vast; **2.** powerful, glorious.
**azimet,** -ti [ī] departure; ~ etm. to set out on a journey.
**azimkâr** resolute, determined.
**azimli** *s.* azimkâr.
**aziz** [ī] **1.** dear, beloved, precious; **2.** saint; **3.** ♀ [x .] *mf.*
**azizlik 1.** sainthood; **2.** *fig.* practical joke, trick; ~ etm. to play a trick (-*e* on).
**azletmek** [x . .] to dismiss from office, to fire.
**azlık 1.** scarcity; **2.** *s.* azınlık.
**azlolunmak** to be fired, to be dismissed.
**azma 1.** *vn. of* azmak; **2.** hybrid, half-bred.
**azmak¹ 1.** dry well (*or* pit); **2.** puddle; **3.**

ditch.

**azmak²** **1.** to get wild, to romp, to become unmanageable; **2.** to get rough (sea); **3.** to be on heat, to rut; **4.** to get inflamed (wound); **5.** to be of mixed blood; **6.** to be in flood (river).

**azman 1.** overgrown, enormous; **2.** heavy log; **3.** s. azma 2.; adam -ı giant, hulk.

**azmetmek** [x . .] to resolve (-e upon), to persevere.

**aznavur:** ~ gibi terror-inspiring, fierce-faced.

**azot,** -tu ♏ nitrogen.

**azotik** nitrous; ~ asit nitric acid.

**azotlamak** ♏ to nitrify, to nitrogenize.

**azotlu** nitrogenous.

**Azrail** [. - -] isl. myth. Azrael; -e bir can borcu ölm. fig. **1.** to free o.s. from debt; **2.** to resign o.s. to one's eventual death; -in elinden kurtulmak to be saved from death.

# B

**B 1.** ♪ = baso; **2.** = bor; **3.** = Bay.
**baba 1.** father; **2.** forefathers; **3.** abbot;
**4.** benefactor; **5.** venerable man; elderly
man; **6.** head of a religious order; **7.** ⚓
bollard; bitt; **8.** newel post; **9.** knob;
-larım my forefathers; -larımı ayağa kaldırma! *fig.* don't infuriate me!; -m mezardan kalksa never!; -na rahmet! bravo!, well done!, bless your father!; -sı
tutmak **1.** to fly into a rage; **2.** to have an
epileptic fit; -sına rahmet okumak *fig.* to
have bad intentions toward; -sının hayrı-
na without following one's selfish interest, just for love, in a disinterested
manner; -sının oğlu like father like son.
**babaanne** paternal grandmother, father's
mother.
**babacan** good-natured, fatherly *(man)*.
**babacanlaşmak** to behave in a fatherly
way.
**babaç 1.** big *(turkey, cock or other fowl)*;
**2.** swaggering.
**babaçko** F strong; imposing *(woman)*.
**babafingo** ⚓ topgallant.
**babalanmak** s. babası tutmak 1.
**babalı 1.** having a father; **2.** epileptic; **3.**
irascible, irritable.
**babalık 1.** fatherhood, paternity; **2.** stepfather; **3.** father-in-law; **4.** adoptive father; **5.** F simple old man; ~ etm. to act
as a father (-e to); ~ fırın has işler! *iro.*
a father's oven produces good bread
*(said regarding a young man who spends
his father's money)*.
**babayani** [. . - .] **1.** fatherly; **2.** unpretentious, free and easy, plain, simple.
**babayiğit,** -di brave, virile; brave lad,
strong fellow.
**Babıâli** [- . - .] **1.** *pr. n. hist.* the Sublime
Porte; **2.** *name of a quarter in Istanbul
where many publishing houses are
found.*
**Babil** [ā] *pr. n.* Babylon, Babel.
**baca 1.** chimney; flue; ⚓ funnel; **2.** skylight; smoke hole; **3.** (mine) shaft; ~ başı
stone mantelpiece; -sı tütmez olm. *fig.* to
be destitute *(or impoverished or impecu-
nious or left without resources)*.

**bacak 1.** leg; shank; **2.** *cards:* jack,
knave; ~ ~ üstüne atmak to cross one's
legs, to sit with one's legs crossed; ~
kadar tiny, shorty, knee-high; ~ kadar
boy **1.** smallness; **2.** insignificance; ~
kadar boyuyla *iro.* so small and pretentious.
**bacaklı 1.** ... legged; **2.** long-legged; **3.** †
Dutch ducat; ~ yazı large, plain and
clear handwriting.
**bacaksız 1.** without legs; **2.** short-legged,
dwarfish; **3.** *iro.* urchin, brat.
**bacanak** brother-in-law *(husband of one's
wife's sister)*.
**bacı 1.** negro nurse; **2.** F (elder) sister; **3.**
F wife.
**baç,** çı *hist.* **1.** tribute; tax; **2.** toll.
**badana** whitewash, limewash; ~ etm. (*or*
vurmak) to whitewash.
**badanacı** whitewasher.
**badanalamak** s. badana etm.
**badanalı 1.** whitewashed; **2.** over made-up
*(woman)*.
**badaşmak** s. bağdaşmak.
**badem** [ā] almond; ~ ezmesi almond
paste, marchpane, marzipan; ~ şekeri
sugared almonds.
**bademcik** [ā] *anat.* tonsil.
**bademlik** [ā] almond orchard.
**bademyağı** [ā] almond oil.
**badi** *zo.* duck; ~ ~ bacak short-legged;
~ ~ yürümek to waddle.
**badik 1.** duck; gosling; **2.** *sl.* short, tiny.
**badiklemek** s. badi badi yürümek.
**badire** [ā] unexpected calamity, unforeseen danger.
**badya** [x .] tub; a wooden *or* glass vessel.
**bagaj 1.** luggage, baggage; **2.** *mot.* trunk,
boot; ~ dairesi luggage office.
**bağ¹ 1.** vineyard; **2.** garden, orchard; ~
bozmak to harvest grapes; ~ budamak to
prune a vineyard; ~ kütüğü vine stock.
**bağ² 1.** tie, cord, string, lace; bandage; **2.**
⚓ knot; **3.** bunch; bundle; **4.** bond, connection, link; affection; **5.** impediment,
restraint; **6.** *gr.* conjunction; **7.** *anat.*
ligament.
**bağa 1.** tortoise-shell; **2.** tumo(u)r; ~

gözlük horn-rimmed spectacles.

**bağbozumu,** -nu **1.** vintage; **2.** autumn, fall.

**bağcı** viticulturalist; grape grower.

**bağcık** cord, string, strap.

**bağcılık** viniculture, viticulture.

**bağdadi** [. - -] *(walls or ceiling)* made of lath and plaster.

**bağdalamak** to trip (up).

**bağdamak 1.** to intertwine; **2.** to deadlock.

**bağdaş** sitting cross-legged; ~ **kurmak** to sit cross-legged.

**bağdaşmak 1.** to suit, to agree, to get along *(ile* with); **2.** to choose one's partner *(in children's games)*; **3.** † to embrace one another; **4.** ℙ to sit cross-legged.

**Bağdat,** -dı *pr. n.* Baghdad; ~ **haraboldu** *co.* I am hungry; **Bağdadı tamir etm.** *co.* to eat one's meal.

**bağı** spell, charm.

**bağıcı 1.** sorcerer, sorceress, witch, magician; **2.** attractive; **3.** seductive; **4.** seducer.

**bağıl** *phys.* relative.

**bağıldak, bağırdak** the strap with which a baby is kept safe in its cradle.

**bağım** dependence.

**bağımlaşma** interdependence.

**bağımlı** dependent (-e on).

**bağımlılık** dependence.

**bağımsız** independent.

**bağımsızlaşmak** to become independent, to gain one's independence.

**bağımsızlık** independence.

**bağıntı** relation(ship) *(-e* to).

**bağır,** -ğrı **1.** breast, bosom; **2.** heart; **3.** liver, lungs; **4.** middle part *(of an archery bow);* saddle *(of a mountain);* ~ **yeleği** jacket worn under armo(u)r; **(bağrı):** ~ **açık** with one's shirt opened; ~ **çökük** hollow-chested; ~ **yanık** *fig.* heartsick, distressed; -**na basmak 1.** to embrace, to fondle, to hug; **2.** to shelter, to protect, to sponsor; -**na taş basmak** *fig.* to bear suffering with great patience, to suffer patiently.

**bağır bağır bağırmak** *s.* **bar bar bağırmak.**

**bağırlar** *anat.* viscera.

**bağırış** shouting, clamo(u)r.

**bağırmak** to shout, to yell, to cry out: **bağırıp çağırmak** to clamo(u)r, to make a fuss, to make a lot of noise.

**bağırsak** *s.* **barsak.**

**bağırtı** shout, yell, outcry.

**bağış** gift, donation, grant.

**bağışlama** ☾ donation.

**bağışlamak 1.** to donate, to give gratis; **2.** to forgive, to pardon; **3.** to spare.

**bağlaç** *gr.* conjunction.

**bağlaçlı** having a conjunction; ~ **yantümce** subordinate clause.

**bağlama 1.** *vn. of* **bağlamak; 2.** folk instrument with three double strings and a long neck; **3.** tied, bound; **4.** ⊕ coupling, connecting; **5.** ⚑ crossbar; ~ **borusu** connecting tube; ~ **limanı** home port, port of registry.

**bağlamacı 1.** a person who makes or sells a **bağlama; 2.** a person who plays a **bağlama.**

**bağlamak 1.** to tie, to fasten, to bind; to connect; **2.** to chain, to tie up, to fetter; **3.** to bandage; **4.** to wrap up; to make a knot, to tie; **5.** to conclude, to finish *(speech, etc.);* **6.** to make secure, to settle *(by contract, etc.);* **7.** to appropriate, to assign *(salary, etc.);* to invest *(capital),* to engage, to lock up in *(money):* **8.** to hinder, to obstruct, to paralyze, to frustrate; **9.** to form *(skin, crust, etc.);* **10.** to form *(seeds, head, fruit);* **11.** to bind by a charm or spell.

**bağlan** *zo.* ruddy shelduck.

**bağlanış** ⊕ connecting, coupling.

**bağlanmak** *pass. of* **bağlamak 1.** to be tied *(-e* to); to be obliged *(-e* to); **2.** to be dedicated *(-e* to); **3.** *fig.* to undertake; to engage or commit one's self.

**bağlantı 1.** tie, connection; **2.** liaison; **3.** ⊕ connecting.

**bağlaşık** allied.

**bağlaşmak 1.** to agree, to come to terms, to unite; **2.** to harmonize; **3.** to form an alliance *(ile* with); **4.** to be at one, to be agreed.

**bağlayıcı 1.** connective, connecting; **2.** binding, in force.

**bağlı 1.** bound *(-e* to), tied *(-e* to), chained, fastened, attached *(-e* to), connected *(-e* with); **2.** dependent *(-e* on); **3.** having ties, strings, *etc.;* **4.** faithful, devoted *(-e* to); **5.** closed, locked; **6.** made impotent.

**bağlılık 1.** devotion, attachment, loyalty, faithfulness, affection; **2.** dependence; **3.** solidarity; ~ **akçesi** forfeit.

**bağnaz** fanatical, bigoted.

**bağnazlık** fanaticism, bigotry.

**bağrışma** outcry, shout, yell, scream, shriek.

**bağrışmak 1.** to cry out together, to yell at each other; **2.** to scold each other noisily.

**bahadır** [. - .] brave, gallant, valiant; hero, champion.

**bahane** [. - .] pretext, excuse; ~ **etm.** to plead, to use as an excuse.

**bahar¹ 1.** spring; **2.** flowers, blossoms; **3.**

*fig.* youth, the prime *(of life)*; ♀ Bayramı the Spring Festival *(1st May)*; ～ noktası *ast.* spring equinox.

**bahar²** spice.

**baharat,** -tı [. - -] spices.

**baharatçı** [. - - .] spice-seller.

**baharlı** spiced, aromatic, spicy.

**bahçe** garden; park; ～ mimarisi landscape gardening.

**bahçe-sokak** *neol.* street with a garden.

**bahçeci** (landscape) gardener.

**bahçecilik** horticulture, gardening.

**bahçeli** having a garden *or* gardens; ～ evler garden city.

**bahçelik 1.** full of gardens; **2.** garden-plot.

**bahçıvan** gardener; ～ kovası watering can; ～ takımları gardener's tools.

**bahçıvanlık** gardenig; horticulture.

**bahis,** -hsi **1.** subject, topic; **2.** bet, wager; **3.** ✂ inquiry, search, investigation; **4.** ✂ discussion, argument, dispute, debate; ～ açmak to bring up *(a subject)*; ～ konusu theme, subject of discussion; ～ koymak to bet, to wager; ～ tutuşmak *or* bahse girişmek to wager, to bet; bahsi geçen aforementioned, above-mentioned; bahsi müşterek pools.

**bahri** *zo.* kingfisher.

**bahri** maritime, naval, nautical; ～ imparatorluk maritime predominance.

**bahriye 1.** navy; **2.** *zo.* turtle; ～ feriki *hist.* vice-admiral.

**bahriyeli** sailor; naval officer.

**bahsetmek** [x . .] *-den* **1.** to treat *(of a subject)*, to talk (about), to mention, to speak of; **2.** to wager, to bet; **3.** ✂ to discuss.

**bahşetmek** [x . .] to give, to endow, to grant.

**bahşiş 1.** tip, bakhshish; **2.** ✂ present, gift; ～ atın dişine bakılmaz *pro.* never look a gift horse in the mouth; ～ vermek to tip.

**baht,** -tı **1.** luck, fortune, destiny; **2.** good fortune, good luck; ～ işi a matter of luck, a turn of fortune; ～ yıldızı lucky star; -ı açık lucky, fortunate; -ı kara unlucky, unfortunate; -ın gür olsun! good luck!

**bahtiyar** [. . .] lucky, fortunate; happy.

**bahtsız** unfortunate, unlucky, ill-starred.

**bahusus** [- . .] especially.

**baka** *s.* beka.

**bakadurmak, bakakalmak** *s.* bakmak.

**bakalit,** -ti Bakelite.

**bakalorya** bachelor's degree.

**bakan** minister, state secretary; -lar kurulu cabinet, council of ministers.

**bakanlık** ministry.

**bakara** baccarat.

**bakarkör 1.** *a blind person whose eyes appear normal, part.* stone-blind; **2.** *fig.* innattentive, careless, absent-minded.

**bakaya** †, *pl. of* bakıye **1.** remnants; **2.** arrears, outstanding taxes; **3.** ✗ deserter.

**bakı** *geogr.* exposure.

**bakıcı 1.** attendant, guard; nurse; **2.** soothsayer, fortuneteller.

**bakılmak** to be attended to, to be looked after, to be taken care of.

**bakım 1.** care, attention, upkeep; **2.** point of view, viewpoint; **3.** glance, look; ～ evi nursing home, dispensary, polyclinic; bir -dan *(or* -a) in one respect; bu -dan from this point of view.

**bakımından** from the point of view (of).

**bakımsız** neglected, unkempt, disorderly.

**bakıncak** the back sight of a gun.

**bakındı** [x . .] *int.* just look!, gee!

**bakınmak 1.** to look about, to look around; **2.** to be examined *(medically)* (by).

**bakır 1.** copper; **2.** of copper, copper...; **3.** copper utensil; ～ çalmak to be contaminated with verdigris *(food)*; ～ pası verdigris.

**bakırcak** copper vessel.

**bakırcı** coppersmith.

**bakış** glance, look; view; care.

**bakışık** symmetrical.

**bakışım** symmetry.

**bakışımlı** symmetric.

**bakışımsız** asymmetric.

**bakışımsızlık** asymmetry.

**bakışmak** to look at one another.

**baki** [- -] **1.** permanent, everlasting, enduring; **2.** ♀ remainder; **3.** still valid, not yet ended; **4.** remaining; remnant, surplus; **5.** ♀ *pr. n. (Turkish poet in 16th century.)*

**bâki** rain cloud; raining.

**bakir** [ᵃ] virginal, untouched; ～ orman virgin forest; ～ toprak virgin soil.

**bakire** [ᵃ] virgin, girl, maiden.

**bakiye 1.** remainder, remnant, residue; **2.** † arrears *(of a debt),* balance.

**bakkal 1.** grocer; **2.** grocery.

**bakkaliye 1.** groceries; **2.** grocery shop.

**bakkam 1.** logwood; **2.** fading colo(u)r; ～ boya **1.** = bakkam 2; **2.** *fig.* spurious, false.

**bakla¹** ♀ broad-bean, horsebean; ～ atmak *(or* dökmek) to throw beans *(for fortune-telling),* to tell fortunes by beans; ～ kadar big, large *(louse, flea, etc.)*; -yı ağızdan çıkarmak *fig.* to spill the beans, to let the cat out of the bag; -yı ağzında ıslatmaz *fig.* he is an indiscreet talker, he is a chatterbox.

**bakla²** chain link.

**baklaçiçeği,** -ni a dirty yellowish white colo(u)r.

**baklagiller** ⚥ leguminous plants.

**baklakırı,** -nı dappled gray.

**baklava** *sweet pastry made of flake pastry, nuts, and honey;* ~ biçimi diamond-shaped.

**bakliyat,** -tı [. . -] pulses *(peas, beans, etc.).*

**bakmak,** (-ar) **1.** to look *(-e* at), to pay attention *(-e* to), to consider; **2.** to face, to front *(-e* towards); **3.** to examine, to investigate, to look into; **4.** to look for; **5.** to take care *(-e* of), to look after, to see to, to tend; **6.** to treat; **7.** to be in charge (of); **8.** to depend (on); **9.** to be dependent (on); **10.** to verge *(on another colour);* **11.** to serve *(waiter);* **bakadurmak** to stare at constantly, to keep looking (at); **bakakalmak** to stand in astonishment; **bakalım** *(or* bakayım) **1.** let's see; we'll see; **2.** well now!, oh!; **bakar mısın(ız)?** hey!, I say!; **bakarsın** possibly, perhaps; **bakıp durmak** *s.* bakadurmak; **baksan(ız)a!** hey!, look here!, I say!, listen to me!

**bakraç,** -cı copper bucket.

**bakteri** bacterium.

**bakteriyoloji** bacteriology.

**bal,** -lı **1.** honey; **2.** ⚥ nectar; ~ alacak çiçeği bulmak *(or* bilmek) *fig.* to know which side one's bread is buttered; ~ başı the purest honey; ~ dök de yala! *fig.* spick-and-span; ~ gibi **1.** honey-sweet; like honey; **2.** in spite of it all, very well; **3.** all the more; ~ sağmak to take honey *(from the hive);* ~ tutan parmağını yalar *pro. (lit.* one who touches honey licks his finger) one who has *s.th.* to do with a big deal will get some profit out of it.

**bala** ⚥ child, babe.

**balaban 1.** husky *(person),* great, huge; **2.** tame bear; **3.** large drum.

**balabankuşu,** -nu *zo.* bittern.

**balabanlaşmak** to become very large.

**balad** ballad.

**balak** young animal, cub, *part.* buffalo calf.

**balalayka** balalaika.

**balans** balance; ~ ayarı *mot.* wheel balance.

**balansuvar** *(koltuğu)* rocking-chair.

**balar** shingle, joist, rafter, beam.

**balarısı,** -nı *zo.* (honey)bee.

**balast,** -tı ballast.

**balastlamak** to ballast.

**balata** *mot.* brake lining.

**balayı** honeymoon; ~ seyahati honeymoon trip.

**balcı** dealer in honey.

**balcılık** apiculture.

**balcak** guard of a sword hilt.

**balçık** clay, mud; ~ hurması crushed dates.

**baldır** *anat.* calf; back of the shank; ~ bacak meydanda showing her bare legs; ~ kemiği tibia, shinbone.

**baldırak** lower part of a trouser leg.

**baldıran** ⚥ poison hemlock.

**baldırıçıplak** rowdy, rough, ruffian.

**baldırıkara** ⚥ maidenhair fern.

**baldırsokan** stable fly.

**baldız** sister-in-law *(sister of the wife).*

**bale** ballet.

**balerin** ballerina.

**balet,** -ti ballet.

**balgam** mucus, phlegm; ~ atmak *fig.* to drop a malicious hint; ~ çıkarmak *(or* sökmek) to expectorate.

**balgamtaşı,** -nı meerschaum.

**balık 1.** fish; **2.** ♀ *ast.* Pisces, the Fishes; ~ ağı fishing-net; ~ avı fishing; ~ avlamak to fish; ~ baştan kokar *pro. (lit.* the fish begins to stink at the head) corruption starts at the top; ~ kavaga çıkınca *(or* çıktığı zaman) *fig.* never; ~ nefesi spermaceti; ~ oltası fishing line; ~ pazarı fish market; ~ pulu fish scale; ~ tutmak to fish, to angle; ~ yumurtası hard roe, spawn; ~ yuvası spawn place; balığa çıkmak to go out fishing; balığın belkemiğini bulmak *fig.* to discover.

**balıkadam** skin diver.

**balıkçı 1.** fisherman; **2.** fish pedlar, fish-monger; ~ yaka turtle-neck, pole-neck.

**balıkçıl 1.** piscivorous; **2.** *zo.* heron, egret, bittern.

**balıkçılık** fishery, fishing.

**balıkçın** *zo.* tern.

**balıketi,** -ni **balıketinde, balıketli** plump, matronly.

**balıkhane** [. . - .] central establishment for the marketing and taxation of fish.

**balıklama 1.** *vn. of* balıklamak; **2.** header; **3.** headlong; ~ atlamak to take a header.

**balıklamak** to writhe in agony.

**balıklava** good fishing ground.

**balıklı** abounding in fish.

**balıksırtı,** -nı **1.** camber, ridge; **2.** ridged, hogbacked *(road, roof).*

**balıkyağı,** -nı **1.** fish oil; **2.** cod-liver oil.

**baliğ** [ā] **1.** adolescent; adult; **2.** perfect, mature; ~ olm. *-e* to amount to, to reach.

**balina** [. x .] **1.** whale; **2.** whalebone.

**balinagiller** whales, dolphins.

**balistik** ballistics.

**balkabağı,** -nı **1.** ♀ winter squash; **2.** *fig.* blockhead, brainless.

**balkan** thickly wooded mountain rage; ♀ Yarımadası the Balkan Peninsula.

**Balkanlar** the Balkans.

**Balkar** Balkar.

**Balkarca** the Balkar dialect of Turkish.

**balkon** balcony.

**ballandırmak** *fig.* to praise extravagantly, to make one's mouth water (for).

**ballanmak 1.** to become covered with honey, to become thick like honey; **2.** *fig.* to ripen; to get ripe and sweet *(fruit).*

**ballı** honeyed, containing honey.

**ballıbaba** ♀ dead-nettle.

**ballıbasra** an insect pest on figs.

**balmumu,** -nu wax; ~ müzesi waxworks; ~ yapıştırmak *fig.* to mark, to notice and remember *(words).*

**balo** [x .] ball, dance; ~ vermek to give a ball.

**balon** balloon; ~ uçurmak *fig.* to fly a kite.

**baloz** low-class cabaret.

**balotaj** *pol.* ballotage.

**balözü,** -nü nectar.

**balsıra** honeydew; mildew.

**balta** axe, *Am.* ax, hatchet; ~ asmak *fig.* to pester, to annoy; to blackmail; ~ değmemiş *(or* girmemiş *or* görmemiş) orman virgin *(or* untouched) forest; ~ ile girişiyor *fig.* he is like a bull in a china shop; ~ ile yontulmuş *fig.* unpolished, uncouth, rough; ~ olm. *(b-ne) fig.* to pester, to keep on at s.o., to harass; -yı kapıya asmak *fig.* to be tiresome, to bore; -yı taşa vurmak *fig.* to put one's foot in it, to blunder.

**baltabaş** ⚓ straight-stemmed.

**baltaburun 1.** *s.* baltabaş; **2.** *sl.* hooknosed.

**baltacı 1.** maker *or* seller of axes; **2.** woodcutter; **3.** fireman equipped with an axe; **4.** *hist.* halberdier attached to the sultan's palace.

**baltalama 1.** *vn. of* baltalamak; **2.** *part.* sabotage; -dan gitmek **1.** to act violently; **2.** to pronounce words barbarously.

**baltalamak 1.** to cut down with an axe, to hew down; to cut away; **2.** *fig.* to sabotage, to paralyze, to torpedo, to block.

**baltalı 1.** furnished with an axe; armed with a halberd; **2.** = gammalı.

**baltalık 1.** district in which the inhabitants of a village have the right of woodcutting; **2.** coppice, copse.

**Baltık** the Baltic; ~ Denizi the Baltic sea; ~ devletleri the Baltic countries.

**balya** [x .] bale, packet; ~ bezi pack-cloth;

~ yapmak to bale, to make into bales.

**balyemez** *hist.* long-range battering gun.

**balyos** *hist.* Bailo.

**balyoz** sledge-hammer; ~ gibi very heavy.

**bambaşka** [x . .] utterly *(or* quite) different.

**bambu** ♀ bamboo.

**bamburuk;** -larını sökmek to maul, to batter.

**bamteli,** -ni **1.** bass-string; **2.** imperial; **3.** *fig.* vital point, sore spot; -ne basmak *(or* dokunmak) -in *fig.* to tread on s.o.'s corns.

**bamya** [x .] ♀ gumbo, okra; ~ tarlası *sl.* churchyard, cemetery.

**bana** (to) me; ~ bak(sana)! look here!, hey!; ~ bakma! don't count on me!. never mind what I do!; ~ gelince as to me, for me; ~ göre hava hoş! F it is all the same to me, it makes no difference to me; ~ kalırsa as far as I am concerned; ~ mısın dememek *fig.* to be thick-skinned; to have no effect, to show no reaction (to).

**bandaj** bandage; -lı bandaged.

**bandıra** [x . .] flag, colo(u)rs.

**bandıralı** having a flag; sailing under the colo(u)rs of.

**bandırmak** *s.* banmak.

**bando** [x .] ♪ band.

**bandrol,** -lü revenue stamp.

**bangır bangır** sobbingly, at the top of one's voice; ~ ağlamak = hüngür hüngür ağlamak; ~ bağırmak to shout loudly, to bawl.

**bangırdamak** *s.* bangır bangır bağırmak.

**bangoboz** *sl.* fool, idiot, simpleton.

**bani 1.** builder, constructor; **2.** founder.

**bank 1.** = banka; **2.** bench *(in a public place).*

**banka** [x .] bank.

**bankacı 1.** banker; **2.** bank clerk.

**bankacılık** banking.

**bankalık** bankable.

**banker 1.** banker; stockbroker; **2.** *fig.* immensely rich person.

**banket,** -ti hard shoulder *(of a road).*

**banknot,** -tu banknote, paper money.

**bankiz** ice field, ice pack.

**banko** [x .] **1.** bench; **2.** counter; **3.** *int. gambling:* bank!

**banliyö** suburb; ~ treni suburban train, commuter's train.

**banmak** to dip (-e into).

**banotu,** -nu ♀ henbane.

**bant,** -dı **1.** band. tape; **2.** ribbon; **3.** *radio:* wave-band; **4.** *billiards:* cushion; ~ izole ✂ insulating tape.

**banyo** [x .] 1. bath; 2. bathroom; 3. bathtub; 4. spa; 5. *phot.* developer; ~ etm. to develop *(film)*; ~ yapmak to take (or have) a bath; to bathe.

**bap,** -bı [ā] 1. = kapı 2. section, chapter; 3. theme, subject; bu -ta on this matter; in this respect; in this connection.

**bar¹** *name of a folk dance in Eastern Anatolia.*

**bar²** 1. dirt, tarnish; 2. fur *(on the tongue).*

**bar³** bar, night club.

**bar bar:** ~ bağırmak to shout at the top of one's voice.

**baraj** 1. dam; 2. ✕ barrage; 3. *football:* wall; -ı aşmak to pass *(the examination)*; ~ ateşi ✕ barrage, curtain-fire.

**barak** 1. † plush; long-piled cloth; 2. P long-haired dog.

**baraka** [. x .] hut, shed.

**barbakan** barbican.

**barbar** barbarian; barbarous.

**barbarizm** barbarism.

**barbarlık** barbarism, brutality.

**barbunya** [. x .] 1. *zo.* red mullet; 2. ♀ a kind of bean.

**barbut,** -tu a kind of dice game.

**barda** [x .] cooper's adze.

**bardacık** a fresh fig.

**bardak** 1. glass, goblet, cup, mug; 2. P jug, pitcher.

**bardakerliği,** -ni egg-plum, greengage.

**barem** 1. classification of salaries; 2. ready reckoner; ~ cetveli fixed schedule of salaries; ~ kanunu law regulating official salaries.

**barfiks** *sports:* horizontal bar.

**bargam** fish of the bass family.

**barhana** 1. impractically large mansion; 2. baggage, luggage, movables; ~ gibi colossal *(house).*

**barı** P garden wall, fence.

**barınak** 1. shelter, refuge, hiding-place; 2. home.

**barınmak** 1. to take refuge (or shelter) in; 2. to get along.

**barış** peace; reconciliation; ~ görüş olm. to become reconciled, to make peace *(ile* with).

**barışçı(l)** peace-loving, pacific, peaceable.

**barışık** reconciled, at peace.

**barışıklık** mutual peace, reconciliation.

**barışmak** to make peace *(ile* with), to become reconciled.

**barışsever** pacifistic, peace-loving.

**barıştırmak** to reconcile, to conciliate.

**bari** [ā] at least, for once.

**barikat,** -tı barricade; -la kapatmak to barricade, to block or defend with a barri-

cade.

**barikatlamak** *s.* barikatla kapatmak.

**barisfer** barysphere.

**bariton** ♪ baritone.

**bariz** prominent, manifest, glaring; clear, obvious.

**bark,** -kı house, home, dwelling.

**barka** [x .] ♨ barge.

**barklanmak** to have a household, to set up house.

**barko** [x .] ♨ bark, barque.

**barlam** *zo.* hake.

**barmen** barman, bartender.

**baro** [x .] bar, the body of lawyers.

**barok** baroque.

**barometre** barometer.

**baron** baron.

**barparalel** parallel bars.

**barsak** intestine, bowel, gut, entrail.

**barsakçı** intestine-dealer.

**barsam** *zo.* sting fish.

**barudi** [. - -] slate-colo(u)red.

**barut,** -du (or -tu) gunpowder; ~ ambarı (or deposu) gunpowder store; ~ gibi 1. irascible; 2. too hot or sour; ~ hakkı powder charge; ~ kesilmek (or olm.) *fig.* to fly into a rage.

**baruthane** [. . - .] 1. powder mill; 2. powder magazine.

**barutluk** 1. powder flask (or horn); 2. powder magazine.

**baryum** barium.

**basamak** 1. step, stair; 2. tread, round; 3. running board; 4. ⚭ order, degree: ~ yapmak *fig.* to use as a stepping-stone.

**basarık** 1. treadle; pedal; 2. bolt *(of a gate).*

**basbayağı** [x . .] 1. quite common(ly), ordinary; 2. simply, just; without hesitation.

**bası** printing, impression.

**basıcı** printer.

**basık** 1. low; 2. flat; 3. compressed; pressed down.

**basılı** printed.

**basılış** printing, impression.

**basım** printing, impression.

**basımcı** printer.

**basımevi,** -ni printing house, press.

**basın** press, newspapers *(syn.* matbuat); ~ ataşesi press attaché; ~ toplantısı press conference.

**basınç,** -cı *phys.* pressure *(syn.* tazyik).

**basiret,** -ti [ī] prudence, understanding, insight, discernment; caution, circumspection, care, attention; -i bağlanmak to become blind *(to a danger).*

**basiretkâr, basiretli** prudent, sagacious;

cautious, circumspect.
**basiretsiz** imprudent.
**basit,** -ti **1.** simple, easy, plain, elementary; **2.** common, ordinary.
**basitleşmek** to be simplified, to become simple.
**basitleştirmek** to simplify, to make simple.
**basitlik** simplicity, simpleness.
**basketbol,** -lü basketball.
**baskı 1.** press; **2.** constraint, restraint, oppression; **3.** stamp; **4.** printing; **5.** edition; **6.** hem; **7.** circulation *(of a newspaper)*; ~ altında under pressure *(or discipline)*; ~ altında tutmak *a.* ✕ to suppress, to oppress.
**baskılık** paper-weight.
**baskın 1.** raid, sudden attack; **2.** unexpected visit; **3.** overpowering, superior; **4.** heavy, oppressing; ~ çıkmak to get the upper hand *(-den* over), to be superior *(-e* to); ~ vermek to be attacked, to be raided; ~ yapmak to raid, to swoop down *(-e* on).
**baskıncı** raider.
**baskül** weigh-bridge; scales, weighing machine.
**basma 1.** *vn. of* basmak; **2.** printed goods; printed matter; **3.** printed cotton, calico; **4.** a card game; **5.** *geol.* transgression.
**basmak,** (-ar) **1.** to tread *(-e* on), to stand *(-e* on); **2.** to press *(-e* on); to weigh down; **3.** to set (the foot on); **4.** to enter *(upon a year or age)*; **5.** to impress, to stamp; to print; to coin; **6.** to swoop down (on), to overwhelm, to overpower; to raid, to surprise; to flood; **7.** to crowd in; **8.** to set in *(darkness, pain, cold)*; **9.** to bring down *(a blow)*; to let out *(cry)*; **10.** to settle, to sag; **11.** to sit *(on eggs)*; **12.** *a.* basıp gitmek *sl.* to go off, to go away, to walk off; **13.** *sl.* = faka basmak.
**basmakalıp,** -bı **1.** trite, cliché, conventional; **2.** pressure-molded; **3.** stereotyped.
**basso** [x .] ♪ bass.
**bastarda** [. x .] **1.** *hist.* bastard; **2.** *hist.* flag-ship; **3.** foremast.
**bastı** vegetable stew.
**bastıbacak 1.** shortlegged, bandylegged, knock-kneed; **2.** gamin, urchin, squat.
**bastırmak** *caus. of* basmak **1.** to have printed, to publish; **2.** to suppress, to crush, to extinguish; **3.** to appease, to satisfy, to stay *(hunger)*; **4.** to hem; **5.** to surpass; **6.** to quell, to force down *(rebellion)*; **7.** to set in, to settle in, to close in *(cold, etc.)*; **8.** = baskın çıkmak;

**9.** to go unannounced, to take *s.o.* unawares; **10.** to drown out *(a sound)*; **11.** to hide, to hush up *(scandal, etc.)*; **12.** ↓ to splice.
**bastika** ↓ a hole in a spar.
**baston 1.** (walking-)stick, cane; **2.** ↓ jib-boom; ~ yutmuş gibi as stiff as a poker.
**basur** [- -] ⚕ piles, hemorrhoids; ~ memesi hemorrhoidal swelling.
**bâsübadelmevt,** -ti [- . - . .] resurrection.
**baş 1.** head; **2.** chief, head, leader; warden; **3.** beginning, commencement; first, initial; **4.** summit, top; **5.** knob; **6.** bulb *(of a plant)*; cyme; **7.** ↓ prow, bow, fore-part; **8.** lump *(of cheese, crude sugar, etc.)*; **9.** head *(of cattle, etc.)*; **10.** skein, hank *(of silk, etc.)*; **11.** river head. spring; **12.** main, chief, principal; **13.** † agio, premium on bills; **14.** *wrestling:* first class; **15.** end, extremity; ~ ağrısı **1.** headache; **2.** *fig.* trouble, nuisance; ~ aşağı gelmek *(or* gitmek) to go steadily down; ~ -a **1.** face to face, privately; **2.** together, tête-à-tête; ~ -a vermek to have a tête-à-tête, to collaborate, to put their heads together; ~ belası trial, pest, nuisance, trouble-maker; ~ edememek *(b-le)* to be unable to cope with *s.o.*; ~ göstermek to appear, to arise; to break out *(revolt, etc.)*; ~ göz yarmak to cause havoc; ~ kaldırmak to rebel *(-e* against); ~ kaldırmamak to keep one's nose to the grindstone; ~ kaldırtmamak *fig.* to suppress; ~ kesmek to bow; ~ korkusu fear for one's life; ~ sallamak to nod, to agree (with); ~ tacı **1.** crown; **2.** a greatly respected and loved person; ~ taraf beginning, commencement; ~ üstüne! with pleasure!; ~ vurmak **1.** to apply *(-e* to), to consult; **2.** to bite *(fish)*; **(başı):** ~ açık **1.** bare-headed; **2.** obvious, evident, clear; ~ açılmak to go bald, to get thin on top *(hair)*; ~ bağlı married, betrothed; ~ bozuk **1.** civilian; **2.** irregular; ~ sert hard-headed, obstinate; başımla beraber with pleasure, gladly, willingly; başın(ız) sağ olsun! may your life be spared; **(başına):** ~ belâ kesilmek to pester, to annoy; ~ buyruk independent; ~ çıkmak to plague, to become a trial *(-in* to); ~ devlet kuşu konmak to have a stroke of great luck; ~ dikilmek to stand over *s.o.*, to supervise; ~ gün doğmak to have unhoped-for luck; ~ hal gelmek to be in great trouble, to get into hot water; başıma hal geldiği takdirde in case *s.th.* happens to me; ~ kakmak to rub it in, to cast *s.th.* in one's teeth; ~ teller takınmak to

be overjoyed; (başından): ~ atmak to get rid (-i of); ~ geçmek to happen to s.o., to go through, to undergo; ~ savmak (or savuşturmak) to turn away, to get rid (-i of); (başını): ~ dik tutmak to hold one's head high; ~ ezmek *fig.* to crush; ~ gözünü yarmak 1. to handle roughly; 2. to speak badly, to murder *(language, etc.)*; ~ ortaya koymak to challenge death, to risk one's life; ~ sallamak to nod, to a-gree (with); ~ taşa vurmak to repent greatly, to regret; (baştan): 1. from the beginning; 2. again, once more; ~ aşağı from top to bottom, from head to foot, from end to end, throughout; ~ aşmak to be too much for s.o.; ~ atmak to get rid (of); ~ çıkarmak to tempt, to lead astray, to corrupt, to seduce; ~ çıkmak to be led astray, to be corrupted.

başabaş 1. only just enough; 2. ↑ at par.

başak 1. ear *(of grain)*, spike; 2. gleanings; ~ bağlamak (or tutmak) to come into ear; ~ etm. to glean.

Başak *ast.* Virgo.

başakçı gleaner.

başaklı 1. with gleanings left; 2. eared, in ear.

başaltı, -nı 1. *wrestling:* second class; 2. steerage.

başarı success; accomplishment; ~ elde etm. to have success, to succeed; ~ göstermek to show success; -lar dilemek to wish success.

başarılı successful.

başarısız unsuccessful.

başarısızlık failure.

bşsarmak to succeed (-i in), to accomplish, to achieve.

başasistan chief intern *(in a hospital).*

başat dominant.

başatlık dominance, dominancy.

başbakan prime minister, premier.

başbakanlık prime ministry, premiership.

başbuğ ✹ commander-in-chief.

başçavuş ✕ sergeant-major.

başçı 1. foreman; 2. seller of cooked sheep's heads.

başgedikli ✕ sergeant-major.

başgöz ~ etm. to marry; ~ olm. to marry.

başhakem chief referee.

başhekim head doctor *(in a hospital).*

başıboş 1. untied, free, independent; 2. untamed; 3. uncared-for, neglected *(child)*; ~ bırakmak to allow s.o. to run wild, to leave uncontrolled; ~ kalmak to run wild; to be independent.

başıkabak 1. bald; 2. bare-headed.

başka 1. other, another, different (from);

2. except, apart (-den from), other (-den than); ~ ~ 1. separately, one by one; 2. different; -ları others, the other people; -sı another, someone else.

başkaca 1. somewhat different; 2. besides, furthermore, moreover, otherwise.

başkalamak to alter, to change, to vary.

başkalaşım metamorphism.

başkalaşmak 1. to change, to grow different, to alter; 2. to metamorphose.

başkalık 1. difference; 2. alteration, change, diversity.

başkan president; chief; chairman.

başkanlık presidency; chairmanship; ~ etm. to preside.

başkâtip, -bi head clerk.

başkent capital.

başkomutan commander-in-chief.

başkomutanlık supreme military command.

başkonsolos consul general.

başkonsolosluk consulate general.

başkumandan commander-in-chief.

başlamak to begin, to start, to commence.

başlangıç, -cı 1. beginning, start, commencement; 2. preface, foreword; ~ noktası starting point.

başlanmak 1. *pass. of* başlamak; 2. to cyme, to bulb *(plant).*

başlıbaşına separate, independent, in itself; independently, by himself, on one's own.

başlıca main, principal, chief.

başlık 1. cowl, cap, headgear; crown; helmet; head-harness; 2. capital *(of a column);* 3. truss; 4. title; headline; crosshead, heading *(of a column);* 5. war head *(of a torpedo);* 6. heading, superscription; 7. caption *(of a page);* 8. ⊕ hub, nave *(of a wheel);* 9. headship, presidency; 10. money paid by the bridegroom to the bride's family; 11. hood; ~ atmak to write a headline.

başmak shoe; slipper.

başmakale [.. - .] editorial, leading article, leader.

başmakçı 1. shoemaker; 2. person in charge of shoes that are taken off at the door of a mosque.

başmaklık *hist.* fief conferred on the royal women of the sultan's family.

başmuharrir editor, editorial writer.

başmüddeiumumi attorney general.

başmüfettiş chief inspector.

başmühendis chief engineer.

başmüşavir [. . - .] chief counsellor, chief advisor.

başoyuncu co-star, featured actor *or* actress.

**başöğretmen** (school) principal.

**başörtü(sü)** head-scarf, kerchief.

**başparmak 1.** thumb; **2.** big toe.

**başpehlivan** wrestling champion.

**başpiskopos** archbishop.

**başpiskoposluk** archbishopric.

**başrol** lead, leading role.

**başsağı, başsağlığı** condolence; **başsağı** (or başsağıları or başsağlığı) dilemek to offer one's condolences.

**başsavcı** attorney-general.

**başsız 1.** headless; **2.** having no chief.

**başsızlık 1.** lack of government; **2.** anarchy.

**başşehir, -hri** capital.

**baştanbaşa** entirely; from first to last.

**baştankara** zo. great titmouse.

**baştarda** s. bastarda.

**başucu, -nu 1.** head end (of a bed); **2.** ast. zenith; -mda at my bedside; -na dikilmek fig. to afflict incessantly.

**başvekâlet, -ti** s. başbakanlık.

**başvekil** s. başbakan.

**başyaver** [. - .] first aide-de-camp.

**başyazar** editor, editorial writer.

**başyazı** editorial, leader, leading article.

**başyazman** head clerk.

**batak 1.** bog, marsh, swamp; **2.** marshy, boggy, swampy; **3.** floundering, unstable, unsound; **4.** pond; tank for immersion.

**batakçı 1.** fraudulent borrower; bankrupt; **2.** swindler, cheat, crook.

**batakhane** [. - . .] **1.** gambling den; **2.** den of thieves; **3.** sl. joint.

**bataklık** bog, marsh, swamp, fen, moor.

**batar** P = zatürrie.

**batarya** [. x .] **1.** ♪ & ✕ battery; **2.** ↓ the guns of one deck.

**bateri** battery.

**baterist** drummer (in a jazz band).

**batı 1.** west; western; **2.** west wind; **3.** West, Occident; Western, Occidental; ～ Avrupa(sı) western Europe.

**batıcı 1.** stinging, pricking, hurting; **2.** Westernizer.

**batık 1.** sunk(en), hollow; **2.** submerged (submarine); **3.** wrecked, ruined.

**batıl** superstitous, vain, false, useless, non-valid; ～ itikat superstition.

**batılı** Western(er), Occidental.

**batılılaşmak** to westernize, to adopt European practices.

**batın, -tnı 1.** abdomen; **2.** gestation; **3.** generation; bir -da at a birth.

**batırmak 1.** to sink, to submerge; **2.** to plunge, to dip; to ruin; **3.** to stick (into). to prick; **4.** to lose (capital, etc.); **5.** to

speak ill (of), to decry, to run down; **6.** to dirty.

**bati** [ī] ✎ slow; slothful, lazy.

**batma** vn. of batmak part. breakdown, collapse.

**batmak,** (-ar) **1.** to sink (-e into), to go to the bottom; to be plunged (into); **2.** to set (sun, etc.); **3.** to be lost sight (of); **4.** to go bankrupt, to be ruined; **5.** to penetrate; **6.** to hurt. to prick, to sting; **7.** to dirty; **8.** to get on the nerves (of), to irk; **9.** to be lost (money), to perish, to go to pieces; **10.** ↓ to run aground, to founder; **11.** to pass out of existence; bata çıka dragging o.s. along; battı balık yan gider in for a penny, in for a pound.

**batman** batman.

**batri** ♪ percussion instruments, drums.

**batonsale** breadstick.

**battal 1.** useless. worthless; void, non--valid. abrogated, canceled; obsolete, out of use; **2.** over-size, large and clumsy; ～ etm. **1.** to cancel, to render null and void; **2.** to abrogate, to abolish, to do away with.

**battaniye** [. - . .] blanket.

**batur** brave; hero.

**bavul** suitcase, trunk.

**Bavyera** [. x .] pr. n. ✎ Bavaria.

**Bavyeralı** Bavarian.

**bay 1.** gentleman; **2.** Mr., Sir; **3.** P rich.

**bayağı 1.** ordinary, common, plain; **2.** mean, vulgar, banal, rough, coarse; **3.** quite, simply; ～ gün weekday.

**bayağıkesir** common fraction.

**bayağılaşmak** to become vulgar.

**bayan 1.** lady, madame; **2.** Mrs., Miss; -lar, baylar! ladies and gentlemen!

**bayat, -tı 1.** stale. not fresh; **2.** trite, old, insipid, out-of-date.

**bayatlamak** to get stale.

**baygın 1.** faint, languid; **2.** fainted, unconscious; **3.** amorous; **4.** drooping (plant); **5.** heavy (smell).

**baygınlık** faintness, swoon, fainting.

**bayılmak 1.** to faint, to swoon; **2.** to fall for, to tumble for. to be enraptured (by); **3.** sl. to shell out (money); **4.** to droop (plant); gülmekten ～ to roll in the aisles; susuzluktan ～ to die of thirst.

**bayıltmak 1.** to make faint; **2.** ⚕ to narcotize, to anesthetize.

**bayındır** prosperous, developed, cultivated.

**bayındırlık** prosperity, development, public works; 2 Bakanlığı Ministry of Public Works.

**bayır 1.** slope; ascent; **2.** hill; ～ aşağı

downhill.

**bayi,** -ii **1.** vendor, seller; **2.** supplier, outlet.

**baykuş** zo. owl.

**bayrak** flag, standard, colo(u)rs; ~ açmak **1.** to unfurl a flag; **2.** to recruit volunteers; **3.** to revolt; -ları açmak to become abusive and insolent; -ları indirmek to lower (or dip) the flag; -ları yarıya indirmek to fly the flag at half-mast.

**bayraktar** standard (or flag) bearer.

**bayram** religious festival, Bayram; holiday; festival, festivity; ~ etm. (or yapmak) fig. to feast, to be very delighted; ~ haftasını mangal tahtası anlamak to misunderstand completely; ~ tatili festive holiday; -ınız kutlu olsun! happy Bayram!, happy feast!; -dan -a fig. once in a blue moon, on occasion.

**bayramlaşmak** to exchange greetings at a holiday, to celebrate the Bairam together.

**bayramlık 1.** fit for a festival; **2.** present given on a festival; **3.** one's best dress, festive dress.

**baytar** veterinary surgeon, veterinarian.

**baz** ⌐ base.

**bazal** ⌐ basic.

**bazalt** basalt.

**bazan, bazen** [- .] [x .] sometimes, now and then.

**bazı 1.** some, a few, certain; some of; **2.** = bazen; -larınca for some people.

**bazilika 1.** basilica; **2.** royal palace.

**bazlama(ç)** flat bread baked on an iron sheet.

**bazu** s. pazı[2].

**bazubent** s. pazıbent.

**bazuka** [. x .] X bazooka.

**be!** F hi!, I say!, hey!; ~, çocuk! hey, you! (to a child).

**bebe** P baby.

**bebecik** little baby, little darling.

**bebek 1.** baby; **2.** doll; **3.** anat. pupil (of the eye); ~ beklemek to expect a baby, to be pregnant; ~ karyolası cot, crib.

**bebeklik** babyhood; infancy; ~ etm. to be childish.

**beberuhi** dwarfish man.

**becayiş** [â] exchange of posts between two officials.

**becelleşmek** to argue, to quarrel.

**beceri** skill, dexterity, adroitness.

**becerik** ↖ skill.

**becerikli** skillful, adroit, resourceful, capable, clever.

**beceriklilik** skill, adroitness, dexterity.

**beceriksiz** clumsy, incapable, maladroit, unskillful.

**beceriksizlik** clumsiness, unskillfulness, incapability.

**becermek 1.** to do skillfully, to carry out successfully, to manage cleverly; **2.** iro. to spoil, to ruin, to make a mess (of); **3.** fig. to rape.

**bed 1.** bad, ill, evil; **2.** ugly, unseemly.

**bedahet,** -ti [â] **1.** obviousness; **2.** improvisation.

**bedava** [x . .] gratis, for nothing, free; -dan ucuz dirt-cheap.

**bedavacı** F freeloader, sponger, bum.

**bedavet,** -ti [â] nomad life, nomadism.

**bedbaht,** -tı unfortunate, unhappy, unlucky, miserable.

**bedbahtlık** unhappiness.

**bedbin** [î] pessimistic.

**bedbinlik** pessimism.

**beddua** curse, malediction, imprecation; ~ etm. to curse, to put a curse (-e on); -sını almak to be an object of malediction.

**bedel 1.** equivalent (-e of); **2.** value, worth; price; **3.** substitute (-e for); in lieu of, in exchange for; **4.** = bedeli nakdî; -i nakdî ☼ sum paid for exemption from military service; ~ vermek to pay the government a fee (in lieu of regular military service).

**bedelsiz** free, without charge.

**beden 1.** body; **2.** trunk; **3.** wall (of a castle); **4.** size; ~ eğitimi physical education (or training).

**bedenen** physically.

**bedeni** bodily, corporal, physical, somatic.

**bedesten** covered market (for the sale of valuable goods).

**bedevi** [î] **1.** Bedouin; **2.** nomadic.

**bedhah** malevolent, malicious.

**bedihi** [i, î] self-evident, obvious.

**bedii 1.** esthetic; **2.** rhetorical.

**bedir,** -dri (a. bedri tam) full moon.

**bedmest,** -ti intoxicated.

**bednam** [â] ill-famed, notorious.

**begüm** begum.

**beğence** commendatory preface.

**beğendi** a dish of aubergines; mashed eggplant.

**beğeni** affinity, taste, zest, gusto.

**beğenmek 1.** to like, to admire; to approve (-i of); **2.** to choose; to prefer.

**beğenmezlik** disapproval.

**beha** s. paha.

**behemehal,** -li [. x . .] in any case, whatever happens, for sure, absolutely.

**beher** to each, for each, per; -ine per person or piece.

**behey** *int.* hey!, o!

**behimi** [i, i] animal *(feelings)*, bestial, brutish.

**behre** lot, share, portion, part.

**beis**, -e'si harm; ~ görmemek to see no harm in it; ~ yok never mind!, no harm!, no matter!

**bej** beige.

**bek¹**, -ki *soccer:* back.

**bek²**, -ki gas burner.

**beka** [ā] permanence, eternalness; sequel; lasting; ~ bulmak to last, to be permanent.

**bekar** ♪ the natural sign.

**bekâr** 1. unmarried, bachelor, single; 2. grass widower.

**bekâret**, -ti 1. virginity, maidenhood; 2. hymen, maidenhead; 3. *fig.* purity; -ten almak to deflower.

**bekârlık** bachelorhood, celibacy; ~ sultanlıktır *fig.* a bachelor is as comfortable and independent as a sovereign.

**bekas** *zo.* woodcock.

**bekçi** (night )watchman; sentry, guard; lookout; ~ köpeği watchdog.

**bekçilik** *etm.* to stand guard.

**bekhent**, -di *tennis:* backhand stroke.

**bekleme** waiting; ~ odası *(or* salonu) waiting room.

**beklemek** 1. to wait (-i for), to await, to hope (-i for), to look (-i for); 2. to expect (-i from); 3. to watch (-i over), to attend, to guard.

**beklen(il)mek** to be expected.

**beklenmedik** unexpected, unforeseen.

**bekletmek** 1. to cause to wait; 2. to delay, to postpone.

**bekri** toper, sot, tippler; ♀ Mustafa *sl.* name of a famous drunkard, hero of many anecdotes.

**Bektaşi** [ā] dervish of the Bektashi order; ~ sırrı F unfathomable secret.

**bektaşiüzümü**, -nü ♀ gooseberry.

**bel¹** 1. waist; 2. loins; the small of the back; 3. mountain pass, defile, notch; 4. ♀ midship body; 5. semen, spunk, come, sperm; ~ bağlamak to rely (-e on), to trust; ~ bölgesi *anat.* lumbar region; ~ gevşekliği ♀ incontinence; ~ vermek to bulge, to sag; -I çökmek to become hump-backed.

**bel²** spade; digging fork.

**bel³**: ~ ~ bakmak to stare (-e at), to goggle (-e at).

**bel⁴** mark, sign.

**bela** trouble, misfortune, calamity, evil, curse; ~ aramak to trail one's coat, to look for trouble; ~ çıkarmak to stir up

trouble, to make a scene; -lar mübareki the last straw; -sını bulmak to get one's deserts; to get into trouble; -sını çekmek to suffer for, to pay for; -ya çatmak *(or* girmek *or* uğramak) to run into trouble; -yı satın almak to invite trouble.

**belagat** -ti 1. eloquence; 2. rhetoric.

**belahat**, -ti foolishness, stupidity, idiocy.

**belalı** 1. troublesome, calamitous, tiresome; 2. quarrelsome, brawling; 3. bully, pimp.

**Belçika** *pr. n.* Belgium.

**Belçikalı** Belgian.

**belde** city, town.

**beledi** 1. municipal, urban; 2. local; town-made; 3. a kind of locally-made cotton material.

**belediye** municipality; ~ meclisi town council; ~ reisi mayor; ~ seçimi municipal election.

**belediyeci** municipal officer.

**belermek** to stare *(eyes)*, to be wide open.

**beleş** *sl.* gratis, for nothing, free (of charge).

**beleşçi** *sl.* freeloader, sponger, bum, hanger-on.

**belge** document, certificate; ~ almak to be expelled from school, to flunk out.

**belgelemek** to document; to confirm, to prove.

**belgeli** 1. confirmed, proved; 2. dismissed *(from school)*.

**belgesel** documentary; ~ film documentary film.

**belgin** clear.

**belgisiz** *gr.* indefinite; ~ adıl indefinite pronoun; ~ sıfat nonrestrictive adjective.

**beliğ** [i] eloquent.

**belirgin** clear, evident, prominent, manifest.

**belirginlik** clarity.

**belirlemek** to determine, to fix.

**belirleyici** characteristic, diagnostic.

**belirli** determined, definite, precise, specific.

**belirmek** 1. to appear, to become visible, to come into sight; 2. = belermek.

**belirsiz** 1. indefinite, undetermined, unknown, uncertain; 2. imperceptible.

**belirteç** *gr.* adverb.

**belirten** *gr.* modifier, defining word.

**belirti** symptom; sign, symbol.

**belirtmek** *caus. of* belirmek to state, to make clear, to expound; to determine.

**beliyye** trouble, evil, calamity, affliction.

**belkemiği**, -ni 1. backbone, spine; 2. *fig.* pillar, fundamental part.

**belki** [x .] perhaps, maybe.

**belladon 1.** ♀ deadly nightshade; **2.** *pharm.* belladonna, atropine.

**bellek** memory.

**belleme 1.** *vn. of* bellemek; **2.** horse-blanket, numnah.

**bellemek 1.** to commit to memory, to learn by heart, to memorize; **2.** to suppose, to think; **3.** to dig with a spade, to spade.

**belleten** bulletin, notice.

**belletici** tutor.

**belli 1.** evident, clear, obvious, known; visible; **2.** certain, definite; ~ başlı **1.** clear, definite, proper; **2.** eminent, notable, well-known; main, chief; ~ belirsiz hardly visible; ~ etm. **1.** to make clear; **2.** to show; to be unable to hide; ~ günler certain days.

**belsoğukluğu,** -nu ♀ gonorrhea, *sl.* clap.

**bembeyaz** [x . .] snow-white, pure white.

**bemol.** -lü ♪ flat; ml ~ E flat.

**ben¹** I, me.

**ben² 1.** mole; beauty-spot, birthmark; **2.** bait, lure.

**bence** [x .] in my opinion, as to me, as for me.

**bencil** selfish; ~ olm. to be selfish.

**bencileyin** like me.

**bencillik** egotism; ~ etm. to be selfish.

**bende¹** *abl. of* ben¹.

**bende²** ⚔ slave; servant; bondsman; -nlz your humble servant, I.

**benek** spot, speck, freckle; ~ ~ speckled; ~ sakal imperial.

**benekli** spotted, speckled.

**beni¹** *acc. of* ben¹.

**beni²** ⚔ the sons of; ~ İsrail children of Israel, the Jews; ~ nevi mankind.

**benim¹** [. x] *gen. of* ben¹ my; mine; ~ için for me; ~ var I have.

**benim²** [x .] I am, it is I.

**benimki** mine.

**benimsemek** to adopt, to appropriate to *o.s.*, to make one's own, to identify *o.s.* with, to welcome.

**beniz,** -nzi colo(u)r of the face; benzi atmak to blanch, to grow (*or* turn) pale; benzi bozuk pale.

**benli** spotted, freckled.

**benlik 1.** egotism; **2.** personality, ego; **3.** conceit; ~ davasında olm. to be self-assertive; ~ sahibi kimse conceited person; benliğinden çıkmak to change one's personality.

**bent,** -di **1.** dam, dike, dyke, weir, barrage, aqueduct; **2.** reservoir; **3.** paragraph; article; **4.** † newspaper article; **5.** stanza (*in a poem*).

**benzemek** to resemble, to be like, to look like, to seem like, to look as if.

**benzer** similar, like; resembling; -i yok unique.

**benzerlik** similarity, resemblance.

**benzeşmek** to resemble each other.

**benzetmek** *caus. of* benzemek **1.** to liken (*-e* to); **2.** to compare (*-e* with); **3.** to mistake (*-e* for), to mix up (*-e* with); **4.** *iro.* to ruin, to bust, to smash, to wreck; **5.** F to thrash, to wallop.

**benzeyiş** resemblance.

**benzin** petrol, *Am.* gasoline; benzine; ~ borusu petrol pipe; ~ deposu petrol tank; ~ istasyonu petrol station, filling station; ~ pompası pump feeding petrol into carburetor.

**beraat,** -tı [ā] acquittal, innocence, non-guilt; ~ etm. to be acquitted; ~ ettirmek to acquit.

**beraber** [ā] **1.** together; **2.** equal; level, abreast, even, in a line; ~ kalmak to be in company with; ~ olm. **1.** to be together (*ile* with); **2.** to be on the same level (*ile* with); -e kalmak to draw, to tie; -inde together, with one; bununla ~ nevertheless, however, still, yet; ... olmakla ~ **1.** (al)though; **2.** ... as well as..., both ... and...

**beraberlik** [ā] **1.** draw, tie; **2.** unity, cooperation, solidarity; ~ golü equalising goal.

**beraet** *s.* beraat.

**berat,** -tı patent, warrant; ♀ Gecesi (*or* Kandili) *Moslem feast, celebrating the night of the revelation of his mission to Mohammed.*

**berbat,** -dı **1.** ruined, spoilt, injured; **2.** filthy, soiled, dirty; dreadful, disgusting; ~ etm. **1.** to spoil, to ruin, to corrupt, to make a mess of, to mess up; **2.** to dirty, to soil; ~ olm. *pass. of* ~ etm.

**berber** barber; hairdresser.

**Berberi** *pr. n.* a Berber.

**berdevam** [ā] going on, continuing.

**berduş** vagabond, tramp, vagrant.

**bere¹** beret.

**bere²** bruise; dent.

**bereket,** -ti **1.** blessing; **2.** abundance, plenty; fruitfulness; **3.** fortunately, luckily; **4.** P rain; ~ versin! fortunately!, luckily! ,thank God!; God bless you!, thank you!

**bereketli** fruitful; fertile; abundant; blessed.

**bereketsiz** infertile; unfruitful; scanty; bringing no good luck.

**berelemek** to bruise; to dent, to batter, to cause bruises (*-i* on).

**bereli** bruised; dented, battered.

**berhane** impractically large mansion, rambling house.

**berhava** blown up; ~ etm. to blow up; ~ olm. 1. to explode; 2. to go for nothing.

**berhayat** [. . -] living, alive.

**berhudar** [ā] happy, prosperous, successful; ~ ol! God bless you!, thank you!

**beri** 1. the near side, this side, hither, here, hithermost; 2. -den since; -de on this side.

**beriki** the nearest, the nearer one; the last mentioned; this one.

**berjer** easy chair.

**berk** hard, firm, strong, solid, tight, fast.

**bermuda** Bermuda shorts.

**bermutat**, -dı· [ū, ā] as usual.

**berrak**, -kı or -ğı clear, limpid, transparent.

**bertaraf** aside, apart, out of the way; ~ etm. to put aside, to do away (with), to get rid (of), to remove.

**berzah** 1. geogr. isthmus, neck of land; 2. fig. precipice, chasm, abyss.

**besbedava** [x . - .] dirt cheap.

**besbelli** [x . .] emph. of belli.

**besbeter** [x . .] emph. of beter.

**besi** 1. nourishing, nutrition; 2. fattening, feeding up; 3. prop, shim; -ye çekmek to fatten (an animal).

**besici** fattener (of livestock).

**besili** fat(ted), well-fed, fleshy, plump.

**besin** nutriment, nourishment, food.

**besleme** 1. vn. of beslemek; 2. foster-child; 3. ⊕ feed(ing); 4. ⊕ base, support.

**beslemek** 1. to feed, to nourish; 2. to fatten (animal); 3. to support, to keep, to maintain; 4. to rear (animal); 5. to bear (grudge, etc.), to nourish (hope, etc.); 6. ⊕ to prop, to shim up, to reinforce; 7. ⊕ to feed.

**besleyici** nutritious, nourishing, nutritive.

**besmele** the formula bismillahirrahmanirrahim; ~ çekmek (or okumak) to pronounce this formula.

**besmelesiz** sl. bastard; good-for-nothing.

**beste** musical composition, tune, melody.

**besteci, bestekâr** composer.

**bestelemek** to compose, to set to music.

**beş** five; ~ aşağı ~ yukarı close bargaining; ~ aşağı ~ yukarı aynı almost the same; ~ duyu the five senses; ~ kardeş(ler) co. slap; ~ para etmez worthless, rubbishy; ~ parasız broke, penniless, skint; ~ vakit namaz the complete schedule of daily prayers; -i bir yerde ornamental coin worth five Turkish gold pounds; -te bir one fifth.

**beşbıyık** ♀ medlar.

**beşer**[1] five each, five apiece.

**beşer**[2] man, mankind.

**beşeri** human; ~ coğrafya anthropogeography.

**beşeriyet**, -ti 1. human nature; 2. humanity, mankind.

**beşgen** ⅍ pentagon.

**beşibirlik** = beşi bir yerde.

**beşik** cradle (a. fig.); ~ kertme nişanlı (or ~ kertiği or ~ kertmesi) engaged to one another while yet in the cradle.

**beşinci** fifth.

**beşiz** quintuplets.

**beşizli** fivefold.

**beşlemek** to quintuple; to raise its quantity to five.

**beşli** 1. fivefold; 2. ♪ quintain; 3. card games: the five.

**beşlik** 1. five-kurush piece; 2. perception to five.

**beşpençe** zo. starfish.

**beşuş** smiling; cheerful; merry.

**beşyüz** five hundred.

**beşyüzlük** 1. five-hundréd lira bill; 2. containing five hundred.

**bet**, -ti face; ~ beniz colo(u)r of the face; -i benzi atmak to go pale from fear; -i bereketi olmamak to grow scarce, to run out.

**beter** (a. daha beter) worse; -in -i var nothing so bad but might have been worse.

**betimlemek** to describe.

**beton** concrete.

**betonarme** reinforced concrete.

**bevil**, -vli urine.

**bevliye** urology.

**bevliyeci** urologist.

**bey** 1. gentleman, sir; Mr., bey (used after the first name); 2. chief, head, ruler, master, prince; 3. husband; 4. notable, country gentleman; 5. card games: ace; ~ baba father.

**beyan** [ā] 1. declaration, expression; 2. gr. explanation; 3. clearness, distinctness; ~ etm. to declare, to announce, to express; -da bulunmak to give an explanation, to deliver a speech.

**beyanat**, -tı [. - -] (pl. of beyan) statement, declaration; -ta bulunmak or ~ yapmak to make a statement.

**beyanname** [ā, ā] written statement, declaration; † manifest.

**beyarı** s. arıbeyi.

**beyaz** 1. white; 2. fair copy; 3. fair-skinned; ~ etm. to make a fair copy (of); ~ harp war of nerves; ♀ Saray pr. n. the White House (in Washington); -a çekmek to make a fair copy (of).

**beyazımsı, beyazımtırak** whitish.

**beyazlatmak** to whiten, to bleach.

**beyazlık** whiteness.

**beyazperde 1.** movie screen; **2.** the cinema.

**beyazpeynir** white cheese.

**beyefendi** sir; Mr. *(after name)*.

**beygir 1.** horse; packhorse, cart horse; **2.** gelding; ~ gibi clumsy, stupid, awkward.

**beygirgücü,** -nü horsepower.

**beyhude** [ü] in vain; useless, vain; ~ yere in vain, uselessly.

**beyin,** -yni **1.** brain; **2.** intelligence, brains; mind; ~ sarsıntısı *ϙ* concussion of the brains; ~ sektesi *ϙ* cerebral apoplexy; ~ tavası brain fritters, fried brain, baked brains; ~ yıkamak to brainwash; beyni atmak to fly off the handle, to fly into a rage; beyninden vurulmuşa dönmek to be greatly upset.

**beyincik** *anat.* cerebellum.

**beyinli 1.** ... brained, having brains; **2.** intelligent, sensible.

**beyinsiz** *fig.* brainless, stupid.

**beyit,** -yti **1.** verse, couplet, distich; **2.** † house.

**beyiye** commission.

**beylerbeyi,** -ni *hist.* governer-general.

**beylik 1.** title or status of bey; **2.** state-owned; **3.** commonplace, conventional, trite; **4.** principality, district governed by a bey; **5.** thin, small soldier's blanket; ~ lakırdı cliché; ~ satmak to give o.s. airs.

**beynamaz** person who does not perform the canonical prayers.

**beynelmilel** international.

**beynelmilelcilik** internationalism.

**beynelmileliyet,** -ti international character.

**beysbol** baseball.

**beyyine** *bᴬ* proof, evidence, argument.

**beyzi** [ī] oval, ellipse; elliptical.

**bez¹** cloth, duster, dustcloth, diaper; canvas; -den bebek **1.** rag doll; **2.** *fig.* lazy, useless person; o taraflarda -i yok *fig.* he has nothing to do with that.

**bez²** *anat.* gland.

**bezdirmek** *caus. of* bezmek to disgust, to sicken, to weary, to annoy, to plague.

**beze 1.** gland; **2.** lump of dough.

**bezek** ornament; decoration.

**bezekci 1.** decorator; **2.** lady's maid.

**bezelye** [. x .] *ϙ* pea(s).

**bezemek** to adorn, to deck, to embellish.

**bezen** *contp.* ornament, embellishment.

**bezenmek 1.** to decorate o.s.; **2.** to be ornamented.

**bezesten** *s.* bedesten.

**bezgin** disgusted, wearied; depressed, discouraged.

**bezginlik** weariness, lethargy.

**bezik** bezique.

**bezir,** -ri zri **1.** flaxseed; **2.** *(yağı)* linseed oil.

**bezirgân 1.** greedy merchant *(part. Jewish)*; **2.** merchant.

**bezm** banquet; feast.

**bezmek** *(bşden)* to get tired of *s.th.*, to become disgusted with *s.th.*, to become sick of *s.th.*

**bıcıl 1.** *anat.* knucklebones; **2.** game of dice.

**bıçak** knife; ~ ağzı the sharp edge of a knife; ~ altına yatmak to go under the knife; ~ çekmek to draw a knife (-e on); ~ bıçağa gelmek to be at daggers drawn *(ile* with); ~ kemiğe dayanmak *fig.* to become unbearable, to reach the limit; ~ sırtı kadar fark a hairbreadth's difference; ~ yarası onulur, dil yarası onulmaz words cut more than swords; ~ yemek to get knifed.; bıçağın ağzında olm. *fig.* to be on a razor's edge.

**bıçakçı** cutler, dealer in knives.

**bıçaklamak** to stab, to knife.

**bıçkı** two-handed saw, bucksaw, cross-cut saw.

**bıçkıcı** sawyer.

**bıçkın** F rascal, rowdy, bully, vagabond.

**bıdık** short and tubby.

**bıkkın** bored, tired, disgusted.

**bıkkınlık** disgust, boredom.

**bıkmak** *(bşden)* to tire of *s.th.*, to get bored with *s.th.*, to grow tired of *s.th.*

**bıktırıcı** tiresome, irksome, annoying, boring.

**bıldır** (< *bir yıldır*) **1.** last year; **2.** a year ago.

**bıldırcın 1.** *zo.* quail; **2.** *sl.* plump little woman.

**bıllık bıllık** buxom, roundish, plump.

**bıngıl bıngıl 1.** = bıllık bıllık; **2.** well nourished, fat.

**bıngıldak** *anat.* fontanel.

**bıngıldamak** to quiver like jelly.

**bırakmak,** (-ır, *ᴬ* -ar) **1.** to leave; to quit, to abandon; to desert; **2.** to let, to allow, to permit, to tolerate; **3.** to put down *(or* aside), to lay down; **4.** to put off, to postpone, to defer, to adjourn; **5.** to give up, to relinquish *(habit)*; **6.** to grow *(beard)*; **7.** to let off, to let go, to release, to set free, to liberate, to emancipate; **8.** *(karı)* to divorce; **9.** to fail *(in an examination)*; **10.** to entrust, to confide; to deposit; **11.** to assign (-e to), to transfer, to bequeath;

**12.** to come unstuck, to come away (from) **13.** to yield, to bring *(profit)*.

**bıyık 1.** moustache, *Am.* mustache; **2.** *zo.* whiskers; **3.** tendril; ~ altından gülmek to laugh up one's sleeve; ~ bırakmak to grow a moustache; ~ burmak **1.** to twist the moustache; **2.** *fig.* to swagger, to put on airs.

**bıyıklı** having a moustache, moustached.

**bızdık** nipper.

**b:zır** *anat.* clitoris.

**biat,** -tı homage; ~ etm. to do *(or* pay) homage *(-e* to).

**biber 1.** pepper; **2.** paprika; ~ dolması stuffed peppers; ~ ekmek to pepper; ~ tanesi peppercorn; ~ turşusu pickled green pepper.

**biberiye** ♀ rosemary.

**biberli** peppery, peppered.

**biberlik** pepper pot, pepperbox, pepper shaker.

**biberon** feeding bottle.

**biblo** knicknack, trinket, curio.

**bicare** [î, â] poor, wretched, pitiable, helpless.

**biçerbağlar** reaper, binder, harvester.

**biçerdöver** combine(-harvester), reaper--thresher.

**biçim 1.** shape, form; manner, way; **2.** elegant form, well-proportioned shape; **3.** *tailoring:* cut; **4.** harvest; ~ almak to take shape; -e sokmak *(or* ~ vermek) to shape; bu ne ~ iş? this is odd!, what's this?

**biçimlendirmek** to shape, to put into a form.

**biçimlenmek** to take shape *(or* form).

**biçimli** shapely, well-shaped, trim, well--cut.

**biçimsel** formal.

**biçimsiz 1.** ill-shaped, ugly; **2.** unlovely; ~ haber F bad news.

**biçki** cutting out *(clothes);* ~ dikiş yurdu tailoring school.

**biçme 1.** *vn. of* biçmek; **2.** ▲ prism.

**biçmek 1.** to cut; to cut out *(or* up); **2.** to reap, to mow; **3.** to assess, to fix *(price).*

**bidayet,** -ti [â] beginning, commencement.

**bide** bidet.

**bidon** can, drum, barrel.

**biftek** beefsteak, steak.

**bigâne** stranger *(-e* to), detached *(-e* from).

**biudi** hair curler.

**bihaber** unaware *(-den* of), ignorant *(-den* of).

**bihakkın 1.** rightly; **2.** truly, fully.

**bıkarbonat,** -tı ☊ bicarbonate.

**bikes** [î] friendless, destitute; orphan.

**bikini** bikini.

**bikir,** -kri virginity, maidenhood; bikrini izale etm. *(bir kızın)* to deflower.

**bilahara** later, afterwards.

**bilaistisna** without exception.

**bilakaydüşart,** -tı unconditionally.

**bilakis** [x . .] on the contrary.

**bilanço** [. x .] balance (sheet).

**bilardo** [. x .] billiards.

**bilâvasıta** [. - - .] directly.

**bilbedahe** [â] ⚡ extempore, extemporane-ously.

**bilcümle** all, entire; in all; totally, entirely.

**bildik 1.** known; **2.** acquaintance; bildiğinden şaşmamak to get one's own way; bildiğini okumak to go one's own way; bildiğini yapmak to do what one wants.

**bildirge 1.** report; **2.** tax report.

**bildiri** communiqué.

**bildirim** declaration; announcement, notice.

**bildirmek** *caus. of* bilmek to notify, to make known *(-e* to), to communicate, to inform.

**bile 1.** even; **2.** † together; **3.** *s.* bilye.

**bileği** whetstone, grindstone, hone.

**bileğitaşı** whetstone.

**bilek 1.** wrist; **2.** pastern *(in an animal);* ~ kuvveti brute force *(or* strength); ~ saati wrist watch; bileğine güvenmek to rely on one's fists.

**bilemek** to sharpen, to whet, to grind.

**bileşik 1.** composed; **2.** ⚛ compound; ~ faiz compound interest; ~ kesir compound fraction; ~ sözcük compound word.

**bileşim** ⚛ composition.

**bileşke** resultant.

**bileşmek** ⚛ to be compounded *(ile* with), to combine.

**bilet,** -ti ticket; ~ gişesi ticket window *(or* office), box office, ticket booth.

**biletçi** conductor, ticket collector, ticket man.

**bileyici** knife-grinder.

**bilezik 1.** bracelet; **2.** *sl.* handcuffs, nippers; **3.** ⊕ metal ring.

**bilfarz** [x .] supposing; supposedly.

**bilfiil** [x . .] in fact, actually.

**bilge** learned; wise.

**bilgi 1.** knowledge; learning; **2.** (branch of) science; **3.** information; ~ edinmek to be informed, to get information.

**bilgiç 1.** pedant(ic); **2.** † sage.

**bilgili** learned; well-informed.

**bilgin** scholar, savant; scientist, learned man, expert.

**bilgisayar** computer.
**bilgisiz** ignorant.
**bilgisizlik** ignorance.
**bilhassa** [x . .] especially, in particular, particularly; ~ ve ~ above all.
**bilim** science; knowledge, learning.
**bilimkurgu** science fiction.
**bilimsel** scientific.
**bilinç** the conscious.
**bilinçaltı,** -nı the subconscious.
**bilinçdışı,** -nı the unconscious.
**bilinçlendirmek** to make s.o. conscious of s.th.
**bilinçli** conscious.
**bilinçsiz** unconscious.
**bilinmek** to be known.
**bilirkişi** expert; ~ raporu expertise.
**billah, billahi** [x . .] by God!
**billur** 1. crystal; 2. rock crystal; 3. cut glass.
**billuriye** cut-glass ware.
**billurlaş(tır)mak** to crystallize.
**biimece** riddle, enigma; puzzle.
**bilmedik** [x . .] unknown.
**bilmek,** (-ir) 1. to know; to be aware (or informed); 2. to understand; 3. to consider, to deem; to suppose, to think, to believe; 4. to learn; to hear; to guess; to recognize; 5. to hold responsible; 6. to appreciate, to value; to experience; 7. to be able to *inf.*; görebilmek to be able to see; çörmeyebilmek to be unable to see; bile bile on purpose, intentionally, wittingly.
**bilmemezlik** ignorance; -ten gelmek to feign ignorance, to act innocent, to pretend not to know.
**bilmez** ignorant.
**bilmisil** in a like manner.
**bilmukabele** [ā] in return, in retaliation, in reciprocation.
**bilumum** [x . .] on the whole, in general; all.
**bilvasıta** [x - . .] indirectly.
**bilvesile** [. . - .] taking this opportunity, profiting by the occasion.
**bilya, bilye** [x .] 1. marble; 2. ⊕ ball.
**bilyon** a thousand million. *Am.* billion.
**bin¹** thousand; ~ bir 1. one thousand and one; 2. *fig.* innumerable. a great many; ~ can ile with heart and soul; ~ dereden su getirmek to beat about the bush; ~ kalıba girmek to change permanently; ~ pişman olm. to regret greatly; ~ tarakta bezi var he has too many irons in the fire; ~ yaşa(sın)! may you live a thousand years!. long live!; -de bir scarcely, once in a blue moon; -i bir para(ya) 1.

dirt-cheap; 2. worthless; 3. abundant, numberless, countless; -in yarısı beşyüz *fig.* a penny for your thoughts!; -lerce thousands of.
**bin²** ◊ son of.
**bina** [ā] 1. building, edifice, structure; construction; 2. chapter on indeclinable words in Arabic grammar; 3. *gr.* voice; ~ etm. 1. to build, to construct; 2. to base (upon).
**binaen** [ā] in consequence (of), on account (of), based (on); buna ~ consequently, therefore, hereupon.
**binaenaleyh** [. - . . .] [. x . . .] = buna binaen.
**binbaşı** ✕ major; commander; squadron leader.
**bindallı** purple velvet embroidered with silver thread.
**bindirme** *vn. of* bindirmek *part.* 1. ✕ loading, shipping; 2. ⊕ overlapping; joint; ~ iskelesi port of embarkation.
**bindirmek** *caus. of* binmek 1. to cause to mount; to load; 2. to collide (-e with), to run (-e into), to ram; 3. to add on; 4. ⊕ to overlap.
**binek** saddle beast, mount (*horse*); ~ atı saddle horse.
**biner** a thousand each; ~ ~ by thousands.
**bingözotu,** -nu ♀ scammony.
**binici** rider, horseman; equestrian.
**binicilik** horsemanship, horse-riding; ~ müsabakası equestrian contest.
**bininci** the thousandth.
**biniş** 1. act of riding; 2. ancient ceremonial riding dress; 3. long cloak worn by certain dignitaries.
**binişmek** 1. to get out of line (*muscles*); 2. to get on the same vehicle.
**binlik** 1. a thousand-lira note; 2. large bottle holding 1000 drams.
**binme** *vn. of* binmek; ~ iskelesi boarding pier.
**binmek,** (-er) 1. to mount, to embark. to board, to get on, to go on (*a train, etc.*); 2. to ride (*a horse, a bircycle, etc.*); 3. to overlap; 4. to be added (-e to); 5. to rise, to increase (*price*); bindiği dalı kesmek to cut (*or* slit) one's (own) throat.
**biperva** [ī, ā] 1. intrepid, fearless, daredevil; 2. fearlessly.
**bir** 1. one; a, an; 2. unique; 3. the same, equal, alike; 4. once; 5. mere, only; merely; just; 6. so, in such a way; günün -inde one day; ~ ağızdan in unison. with one voice; ~ an evvel as soon as possible; ~ arada 1. all together; 2. at the same time; ~ araya gelmek to come together;

**birleştirme**

to clash; ~ aşağı ~ yukarı dolaşmak to walk up and down; ~ avazı yerde ~ avazı gökte *fig.* to shout with all one's might; ~ ayağı çukurda olm. to have one foot in the grave; ~ baltaya sap olm. *fig.* to find a job, to be employed; ~ bardak suda fırtına koparmak *fig.* to raise a tempest in a teapot; ~ cihetten in a way, in one way; ~ çırpıda without interruption, at once; ~ çiçekle bahar (*or* yaz) olmaz *pro.* one swallow does not make a summer; ~ çift söz a word or two; ~ çifte (*kayık, sandal*) rowing-boat; ~ daha 1. once more, once again; 2. one more; ~ de also, in addition, furthermore; ~ dediğini iki etmemek (*b-nin*) to dance attendance on *s.o.*, to be at *s.o.*'s beck and call; ~ deri ~ kemik only skin and bones, a bag of bones; ~ düziye continuously, incessantly; ~ elin nesi var, iki elin sesi var *pro.* united we stand, divided we fall; ~ hoş olm. 1. to feel embarrassed; 2. to feel sad; ~ hoşluğu olm. to be out of sorts; ~ içim su 1. a gulp of water; 2. very pretty (*woman*); ~ iki one or two, very few; ~ kafada of the same opinion; ~ kalemde in one go; ~ kapıya çıkmak to come to the same thing; ~ kulağından girip öbür kulağından çıkmak to go in at one ear and out at the other; ~ miktar a little, some; ~ nice a good many; ~ parça 1. a little, a bit; 2. one piece, a whole; ~ şey değil! not at all!, you are welcome!; ~ şeyler something, several things; ~ şeyler olm. to become strange; to put on airs; ~ tahtası eksik olm. *fig.* to have a screw loose; ~ tarafa koymak 1. to save, to put aside (*or* away), to lay aside (*or* by); 2. to overlook, to disregard; ~ taşla iki kuş vurmak *fig.* to kill two birds with one stone; ~ tesadüf eseri by chance; ~ türlü 1. somehow, in one way or another; 2. in no way; 3. just as bad; ~ vakit a one time; ~ varmış ~ yokmuş once upon a time; ~ yana aside from, apart from; ~ yastığa baş koymak to be husband and wife; ~ yiyip bin şükretmek to call o.s. happy, to be very thankful; -e on katmak to exaggerate too much; -e geldi it is one o'clock; -e kadar by one o'clock, till one o'clock.

**bira** [x .] beer; ~ fabrikası brewery; ~ mayası barm. yeast.

**biracı** brewer.

**birader** [ª] 1. brother; 2. fellow; hey you!; 3. Mason.

**birahane** [. . - .] beer-house.

**biraz** [x .] a little, some, somewhat; ~ son-

ra soon after, after a short while.

**birazcık** [x . .] a little bit.

**birazdan** [x . .] a little later, after a while; in a little while.

**bir(i)biri**, -ni one another, each other; ~ ardınca one after the other; -ne düşürmek to set persons by the ears, to play one person off against another, to set at loggerheads, to set at odds; -ne girmek 1. to start quarrelling; 2. to be stirred up.

**birçok** [x .] many, a lot (of); ~ kimse(ler) many people; -ları = ~ kimseler.

**birden** 1. suddenly; 2. at a time, in one lot; together.

**birdenbire** [. x . .] suddenly, all of a sudden, out of the blue.

**birdirbir oynamak** to play leapfrog.

**birebir** most effective (*remedy*).

**birer** one each, one apiece; ~ ~ one by one, singly.

**birey** individual.

**bireysel** individual.

**biri** someone, somebody, one person; one of them.

**biricik** unique, sole, the only.

**birikim** accumulation, buildup.

**birikinti** accumulation, heap, mass, assemblage.

**birikmek** to come together, to accumulate, to assemble, to collect, to form a puddle.

**biriktirmek** 1. to gather, to pile up, to assemble, to accumulate, to amass; 2. to save up (*money*); 3. to collect; 4. ⊕ to store up.

**birim** unit; -ler A units.

**birinci** 1. the first; 2. first-class; 3. champion; ~ elden † at first hand; ~ gelmek to be best; ~ mevki first class (*in a train, bus*), cabin class (*on a ship*).

**birincil** primary.

**birkaç**, -çı a few, some, several; ~ kitap a few books; -ı some of them.

**birkaçıncı** umpteenth.

**birle** [x .] 1. † with; 2. = gibi.

**birleşik** united, joint; ♀ Amerika Devletleri United States of America; ~ oturum joint meeting; ~ sözcük compound word.

**birleşme** *vn. of* birleşmek *part.* 1. *biol.*, ♀ copulation; 2. ♋ combination; 3. ♋ fusion, amalgamation, merger; ~ noktası (point of) intersection; ~ parçası extension.

**birleşmek** 1. to unite, to merge, to join together; 2. to meet; 3. to agree; 4. to converge; Birleşmiş Milletler *pr. n.* United Nations.

**birleştirici** uniting, unifying.

**birleştirme** *vn. of* birleştirmek; ~ çizgisi

hyphen.

**birleştirmek** to unite, to connect, to put together, to merge, to join.

**birli 1.** *cards:* ace; **2.** *dominoes:* the one.

**birlik 1.** unity, oneness; accord; **2.** sameness; equality; similarity; identity; **3.** union; association; corporation; **4.** ✗ unit; **5.** ♪ semibreve.

**birlikli** common, joint.

**birlikte** together, in company.

**birsam** [ā] hallucination.

**birtakım** some, a certain number of, a quantity ~ kimseler some people.

**bis!** da capo!, encore!

**bisiklet**, -ti bicycle, cycle, bike; ~ yolu cycle track; -e binmek to bicycle, to cycle, to bike, to ride a bicycle.

**bisikletçi** bicyclist, cyclist.

**bisküvi, bisküvit**, -ti biscuit, cracker.

**bismillah** in the name of God; ~ demek *fig.* to start an undertaking by invoking the name of God.

**bisturi** lancet.

**bit**, -ti louse; ~ sirkesi nit; -i kanlanmak *fig.* to become well off (*or* lousy).

**bitap**, -bı [- -] exhausted, feeble; ~ düşmek to get exhausted.

**bitaraf** [ī] neutral; impartial.

**bitaraflık** [ī] neutrality.

**bitek** ↓ fertile.

**biteksiz** ↓ infertile.

**bitevi** [x . .], **biteviye** [x . . .] **1.** continuously, incessantly, monotonously, uninterruptedly; **2.** all of a piece, whole, complete.

**bitey** flora.

**bitik** exhausted, worn out, broken down.

**bitim** end(ing).

**bitirim 1.** *vn. of* bitirmek; **2.** *sl.* smart, topping, appealing; **3.** *sl.* gambling-den.

**bitirmek 1.** to finish, to complete, to terminate, to bring to an end; to eat up; **2.** to accomplish; **3.** to exhaust, to use up; to kill; to destroy.

**bitirmiş** F experienced, versed in all vices; cunning.

**bitiş** end.

**bitişik 1.** touching, neighbo(u)ring, contiguous, adjacent, joining; attached; **2.** next door.

**bitişmek** to join, to grow together, to become contiguous; to adhere.

**bitiştirmek** to join, to unite, to attach.

**bitki** plant.

**bitkimsi** plant-like, phytoid.

**bitkin** exhausted, worn out, dead tired; ~ düşmek to collapse from exhaustion.

**bitkinlik** exhaustion, fatigue.

**bitkisel** vegetal, vegetable; ~ yaşam life without consciousness.

**bitlemek 1.** to delouse, to clear of lice; **2.** *sl.* to angle for a quarrel.

**bitlenmek 1.** to be infested with lice, to get lice, to become lousy; **2.** to clear o.s. of lice.

**bitli** lousy, infested with lice.

**bitmek[1] 1.** to end, to come to an end, to finish, to terminate; to be settled, to be completed; **2.** to be all gone; to be exhausted; **3.** to be ruined (*or* destroyed); **4.** to fall for, to tumble for; bitmedi to be continued; bitmez tükenmez infinite, endless, vast, never ending.

**bitmek[2]** to grow, to sprout.

**bitnik** beatnik.

**bitpazarı**, -nı flea ma:ket, rag-fair.

**bittabi** [x . .] of course, sure, naturally, certainly.

**bitter** [x .] **1.** a kind of bitter beer; **2.** bitter chocolate.

**bityeniği** -nı *fig.* catch, s.th. fishy.

**biyografi** biography.

**biyokimya** biochemistry.

**biyoloji** biology.

**biyopsi** biopsy.

**biyoşimi** biochemistry.

**biz[1]** we; ~ -e by ourselves, without outsiders.

**biz[2]** awl.

**Bizans** *pr. n.* Byzantium.

**Bizanslı** *pr. n.* Byzantine.

**bizar** [- -] tired; weary, disgusted, sick (of); ~ olm. to be disgusted (-*den* of).

**bizatihi** [ā] [. x . .] in himself, in itself, of itself, by itself.

**bizce** according to us, in our opinion.

**bizden 1.** *abl. of* biz 1 & 2; **2.** *sl.* sly, cunning, crafty, wily.

**bizim** *gen. of* biz 1 our; ours; ~ için for us.

**bizimki 1.** ours; **2.** my wife, my husband.

**bizon** *zo.* bison.

**bizzat** [x .] in person, personally.

**blok 1.** block; **2.** writing pad; **3.** *pol.* bloc.

**blokaj 1.** blockage, blocking; **2.** covering.

**bloke** blocked; stopped; ~ etm. to close, to stop; ~ hesap blocked account.

**blokhavs** [x .] **1.** blockhouse; **2.** ✗ bunker, pillbox.

**bloklaşmak** to form a bloc.

**bloknot**, -tu [x .] writing pad, memorandum block.

**boküs** blockade.

**blont**, -du blond(e), fair.

**blöf** bluff; ~ yapmak to bluff.

**blöfçü** bluffer.

**blucin** (blue) jeans.

**blum** a card game.

**bluz** blouse.

**Bn.** = bayan.

**boa 1.** *(yılanı) zo.* boa; **2.** feather-boa.

**bobin 1.** *phys.* reel, spool, bobbin; **2.** ≯ coil; **3.** *phot.* roll of film, spool.

**bobinaj** winding.

**bobstil** dandy; snob.

**boca [x .] 1.** ↓ lee (side); **2.** turning over, tilting, canting over; ~ etm. **1.** ↓ to bear away to leeward; **2.** to cant over, to tilt, to turn over.

**bocalamak 1.** ↓ to veer, to bear away; **2.** to falter, to vacillate, to reel, to stagger, to get confused.

**bocurgat,** -tı capstan, crab.

**bodoslama 1.** ↓ stempost; sternpost; **2.** *sl.* nose.

**bodrum** cellar, dungeon; ~ katı basement.

**bodur** dumpy, squat; dwarf.

**boğa 1.** bull; **2.** *ast.* Taurus; ~ güreşçisi toreador; ~ güreşi *(or* dövüşü) bullfight.

**boğaca** *s.* poğaça.

**boğak** ≯ angina.

**boğası** thin twill used for linings.

**boğaz 1.** throat; gullet, esophagus; **2.** neck *(of a bottle, etc.)*; **3.** mountain pass, defile; **4.** strait; **5.** ♀ = Boğaziçi; **6.** mouth of a river; **7.** board, food, maintenance; **8.** a mouth to feed; eating, food; appetite; **9.** sore throat; ~ açılmak to develop an appetite, to become hungry; ~ -a düşmek to be at each other's throat, to be at daggers drawn; ~ derdine düşmek to struggle for a living; ~ olm. to have a sore throat; ~ tokluğuna çalışmak to work in return for food; -ına dizilmek to stick in one's throat; -ına düşkün gourmet, gastronome, glutton, gourmand; -ına kadar up to one's neck; -ına kadar tok full; -ından geçmemek to stick in one's throat; -ını çıkarmak to earn just enough for one's food; -ını yırtmak to shout at the top of one's voice.

**Boğaziçi,** -ni *pr. n.* the Bosphorus.

**boğazkesen** defensive fortress commanding a strait, *part.* Rumeli Hisarı *(on the Bosphorus).*

**boğazlamak** to cut the throat of, to strangle, to slaughter.

**Boğazlar** *pr. n.* the straits *(Bosphorus and Dardanelles);* ~ Rejimi control of the straits.

**boğazlaşmak 1.** to cut each other's throats; **2.** *fig.* to fight violently.

**boğazlı** gluttonous.

**boğmaca** ≯ whooping-cough, pertussis, croup.

**boğmak¹ 1.** to strangle, to choke; **2.** to suffocate; **3.** to drown; **4.** to overwhelm (with), to swamp (with); **5.** to constrict by binding; **6.** to conceal *(under a flood of words, jokes, etc.).*

**boğmak²** node, joint, articulation.

**boğucu** sultry, suffocating; ~ gaz poisongas; ~ sıcak oppressive heat, stifling heat.

**boğuk** hoarse, raucous; muffled; ~ ~ hoarsely; with a muffled sound; ~ sesli hoarse-voiced.

**boğulmak** *pass. of* boğmak **1.** to become hoarse *(voice);* **2.** *mot.* to be flooded; **3.** *sl.* to be fleeced.

**boğum 1.** ♀ knot, joint, node; **2.** internode; **3.** *anat.* ganglion.

**boğuntu 1.** profiteering, swindling, cheating. duping; **2.** oppression, suffocation; ~ yeri *sl.* gambling-den; -ya getirmek to swindle money out of s.o.

**boğuşma** scramble, romp, scuffle, fray.

**boğuşmak 1.** to fly at one another's throats, to be at each other's throats; **2.** to romp, to scruffle, to scramble.

**bohça 1.** wrapping cloth; bundle; **2.** small bale of fine tobacco; **3.** *sl.* buttocks, ass, arse; ~ etm. to wrap up in a bundle; -sını bağlamak to pack up one's belongings; -sını koltuğuna vermek *fig.* to give s.o. the sack, to fire.

**bohçacı** woman pedlar of small draperies.

**bohçalamak** to wrap up in a bundle.

**bohem** bohemian.

**bok,** -ku *sl.* **1.** shit, crap; excrement, dung, ordure, feces; **2.** rubbish, dirt; worthless, shit; ~ atmak *sl.* to throw dirt (-e on), to slander, to defame, to blacken, to calumniate; ~ etm. *sl.* to spoil; ~ püsür *sl.* **1.** rubbish, nonsense; **2.** details; -u çıktı *sl.* it has come to light.

**boklamak** *sl.* **1.** to shit, to crap; **2.** to ruin, to louse up, to spoil, to mismanage; **3.** to soil, to befoul; **4.** to besmirch, to calumniate, to defame, to blacken.

**bokluca bülbül 1.** *zo.* wren; **2.** a pert *(or* saucy) child.

**bokluk** *sl.* **1.** dunghill; **2.** filthy place, dump; **3.** state of disorder, bad state.

**boks** boxing; ~ maçı boxing-match; ~ yapmak to box.

**boksör** boxer.

**boktan** *sl.* made of rubbish, useless, worthless.

**bol¹ 1.** wide, loose; loose-fitting; **2.** abundant, copious, ample; ~ ağızdan *(or* keseden *or* pacadan) atıp tutmak to scatter promises around, to make extravagant promises; ~ biçmek *fig.* to estimate lavishly; ~ ~ abundantly, amply, generously; ~ doğramak **1.** to squander, to blow *(money)*; **2.** to be lavish in promises; ~ keseden generously.

**bol², -lü [ - ]** bowle, fruit punch, claret cup.

**bol³ [-]** bowls.

**bolca 1.** fairly abundant, rather amply; **2.** somewhat wide.

**boliçe [. x .]** Jewish woman.

**bollanmak, bollaşmak 1.** to become wide *(or* loose), to widen; **2.** to become abundant *(or* copious).

**bollatmak, bollaştırmak 1.** to widen; **2.** to make abundant *(or* plentiful).

**bolluk 1.** wideness, looseness; **2.** abundance, plenty; **3.** plenteous *(country)*.

**Bolşevik** Bolshevik.

**Bolşeviklik** Bolshevism.

**Bolşevist, -ti, Bolşevistlik** *s.* Bolşevik(lik).

**Bolşevizm** *s.* Bolşeviklik.

**bom 1.** *int.* boom!, bang!; **2.** *sl.* lie, humbug; ~ atmak *sl.* to lie.

**bomba [x .] 1.** bomb; **2.** barrel; **3.** bomb-shaped metal container; ~ atmak to throw *(or* drop) bomb(s); ~ gibi F in the pink, in good condition.

**bombacı [x . .] 1.** bombardier; **2.** bomb-maker; **3.** bomber.

**bombalamak** to bomb.

**bombardıman** bombardment, bombing; ~ etm. to shell, to bombard; ~ uçağı bomber.

**bombasalan** mortar.

**bombe** arch.

**bombok** *sl.* utterly spoiled, very bad, quite useless.

**bomboş [x .]** quite empty.

**bomcu** *sl.* liar.

**bon:** ~ şans! good luck!

**bonbon** candy, bonbon, sweet-meat.

**boncuk 1.** bead; **2.** F Negro, Negress; ~ gibi beady *(eyes)*; ~ illeti 𝔽 infantile convulsions; fit; ~ mavisi turquoise blue.

**bone 1.** bonnet, lady's hat; **2.** bathing cap.

**bonfile** sirloin steak.

**bonjur!** good morning!

**bonmarşe** department store.

**bono [x .]** bond, bill; cheque; -nun vadesi geldi the bill is due.

**bonservis** testimonial, certificate of good service, written character.

**bora [x .] 1.** tempest, hurrican, gale, squall, storm; **2.** *sl.* violent scolding; ~ patlatmak *sl.* to break out in a fury, to storm.

**borak** barren, sterile *(land)*.

**boraks** borax.

**borani [ᵃ]** dish of stewed and fried vegetables with yogurt.

**borazan 1.** trumpet; **2.** trumpeter; ~ başı first trumpeter; ~ çalmak **1.** to trumpet, to play a trumpet; **2.** *fig.* to let everybody know.

**borcetmek [x . .]** to get into debt, to become indebted.

**borç, -cu 1.** debt; loan; **2.** obligation, duty; **3.** debit; ~ almak to borrow *(money)*; ~ gırtlağa çıkmak *(or* paçadan akmak) *fig.* to be head over heels in debt, to be over head and ears in debt; ~ harç getting money by hook or by crook; ~ vermek to lend; borca girmek to get into debt; borcunu kapatmak to settle one's debt.

**borçlanmak** to get into debt, to become indebted *(-e* to).

**borçlu 1.** debtor; **2.** indebted, under obligation *(-e* to).

**borda [x .] 1.** board, broadside, ship's side; **2.** beam; **3.** *sl.* = yan.

**bordalamak** to board.

**bordro [x .]** payroll; docket; list, register, roll.

**bordür** bordure, border; edging; frame.

**bornoz, bornuz [x .]** bath-robe.

**borsa [x .] 1.** (stock) exchange, bourse; ~ acentesi stockbroker; ~ rayici exchange rate; ~ oyunu speculation.

**borsacı** stock-broker, speculator.

**boru 1.** tube, pipe; **2.** trumpet; horn; **3.** speaking trumpet; phonograph horn; **4.** *sl.* nonsense, idle tale, empty talk; **5.** *sl.* boaster, vain; ~ çalmak **1.** to sound a trumpet; **2.** to hoot, to honk *(car)*; ~ değil bu! *sl.* that's no small matter!; ~ su ötmek *fig.* to be the «big noise», to have a say in, to wear the trousers.

**borucu 1.** trumpeter; **2.** maker *or* seller of pipes, tubes, horns *or* trumpets; **3.** leader of the pump squad of a fire brigade.

**borucuk** *anat.* tubule, tubulus.

**boruçiçeği, -ni ¾** downy thornapple; morning-glory.

**borumsu** *biol.* tubiform.

**boruyolu, -nu** pipeline.

**Bosna [x .]** *pr. n.* Bosnia; ~ Saray = Saraybosna.

**bostan 1.** market garden, truck garden, vegetable garden, truck farm; **2.** melon; watermelon; **3.** melon field; ~ dolabı noria, irrigation water-wheel; ~ korkuluğu **1.** scarecrow; **2.** *fig.* a mere puppet.

**bostancı 1.** market gardener; **2.** *hist.* member of the Imperial guard; ~ başı commander of the Sultan's bodyguards.

**boş 1.** empty, empty-handed; blank; hollow; **2.** uninhabited; **3.** vacant (post); **4.** free (seat); **5.** futile, frivolous, unfounded; **6.** ignorant, superficial (person); **7.** unoccupied; unemployed, out of work, idle; **8.** neutral (gear); **9.** loose, slack (rope); **10.** not in use (machine); **11.** unsown, uncultivated (land); **12.** divorced (woman); **13.** typ. space; ~ atıp dolu tutmak fig. to hit the mark at a venture, to make a lucky shot, to draw a bow at a venture; ~ bulunmak to be taken unawares; ~ çıkmak (lottery) to hit a blank; ~ dönmek to come back empty-handed; ~ durmak to be unoccupied, to idle; ~ düşmek (or olmak) to be considered as divorced; ~ gezenin boş kalfası co. do-nothing, idler, loafer; ~ gezmek to loaf, to laze, to wander about idly; to be unemployed; ~ kafalı silly, empty-headed; ~ vermek sl. not to give a damn, to pay no attention; ~ yere **1.** in vain: **2.** groundlessly; s. a. boşta, boşuboşuna, boşuna; -a çıkmak to fall flat, to fall to the ground (hope, etc.); -a gitmek to go for nothing, to come to nothing, to be to no end.

**boşalım** discharge, release.

**boşalmak 1.** to be emptied; to empty itself, to run out; **2.** to become free, to become vacant; **3.** to get loose (animal); **4.** to unwind itself, to be unwound (rope); **5.** to be discharged (gun).

**boşaltım** biol. excretion; ~ aygıtı excretory organ.

**boşaltmak** caus. of boşalmak **1.** to empty, to pour (out); **2.** to evacuate; to vacate, to move out (house); **3.** to discharge (gun); **4.** to unload, to discharge (cargo, ship); **5.** to land, to disembark (troops); **6.** to unbosom o.s.; **7.** to vomit, to bring up.

**boşamak** to divorce, to repudiate (one's wife).

**boşanma** divorce(ment); ~ davası ʊ̈ʊ divorce case (or suit).

**boşanmak 1.** to be divorced (-den from); **2.** to be loosed, to be set at large; to break loose; **3.** to pelt down, to teem (rain, etc.); **4.** to burst forth (tears, blood); **5.** to rush out; **6.** to pour out one's heart.

**boşanmış** divorced.

**boşatmak** to make a wife be divorced.

**boşboğaz** garrulous, indiscreet, blab.

**boşboğazlık** indiscretion, idle talk; ~ etm. to talk indiscreetly, to blab.

**boşlamak** sl. **1.** to ignore, to neglect; to

let alone; **2.** to let go.

**boşluk 1.** emptiness; **2.** blank; cavity; **3.** vacuum.

**Boşnak,** -kı Bosnian.

**Boşnakça** Bosnian (language).

**boşta 1.** unemployed, non-employed, idle; **2.** mot. in neutral gear, not in gear; ~ kalmak (or oturmak) to be unemployed, to loaf.

**boşuboşuna** in vain, uselessly; ~ gayretler vain efforts.

**boşuna** in vain, for nothing, uselessly.

**bot[1],** -tu boat, dinghy.

**bot[2],** -tu boot.

**botanik 1.** botany; **2.** botanic(al).

**botanikçi** botanist.

**boy[1]** clan, tribe; ~ beyi chieftain of a clan.

**boy[2] 1.** height; stature; **2.** length; **3.** size; **4.** edge (of a road), bank (of a river); **5.** phot. full-length; ~ almak (or atmak) to grow in height; to shoot up; ~ aptesti ritual bathing of the body; ~ aynası cheval-glass, full-length mirror; ~ ~ assorted, of various sizes; of various qualities; ~ göstermek to cut (or dash) a figure, to show o.s. off; ~ ölçüşmek to compete (ile with); ~ satmak to put on airs; ~ vermek **1.** to be above one's head (water); **2.** to grow taller; -a çekmek to shoot up (child); -dan -a all over, from end to end; -u beraber as tall as himself; -u bosu yerinde tall and well made; -u devrilsin! may he die!; -unun ölçüsünü almak fig. to get one's deserts; to be disappointed (by s.o.'s indifference).

**boya 1.** paint; **2.** dye; colo(u)r; **3.** make-up; **4.** fig. varnish; ~ atmak to fade; ~ tabancası spray-gun; air brush; ~ tutmak **1.** to take paint (wood, etc.); **2.** to take a dye (fabric); ~ vurmak to paint; -sı atmak to fade.

**boyacı 1.** shoeblack, shoeshine boy; **2.** housepainter; dyer; **3.** dealer in paints; ~ küpü dyer's vat; ~ küpü değil ya hemen daldırıp çıkarasın! it is not so easy as all that!

**boyahane** [. . - .] dye-house, dyer's shop.

**boyalamak** to cover with paint.

**boyalı 1.** painted; dyed; colo(u)red; **2.** made-up (woman).

**boyama 1.** action of painting; **2.** painted, colo(u)red; dyed; **3.** colo(u)red handkerchief.

**boyamak** to paint, to dye, to colo(u)r.

**boyanmak 1.** pass. of boyamak **2.** to make up, to put on make-up.

**boyarmadde** ʌ̃ pigment, colo(u)ring matter, dye.

**boyasız 1.** unpainted; **2.** undyed, uncolo(u)red; unpolished *(shoe);* **3.** without make-up *(woman).*

**boyca 1.** as regards height; **2.** lengthwise, longitudinally; ~ akran olm. to be of the same height; ~ evlat a practically grown--up child; ~ günaha girmek to go deep into sin; ~ kefil olm. to vouch fully.

**boydaş 1.** of the same height, equal in stature; **2.** equal, peer.

**boykot,** -tu boycott; ~ etm. to boycott.

**boykotaj** boycott.

**boykotçu** boycotter.

**boylam** *ast.* longitude.

**boylamak 1.** traverse lengthwise; **2.** *(bir yeri)* to end up (in), to land up (in); **3.** to measure the length *or* height (of); **4.** to fall prone *(upon the ground);* **5.** to escape, to run away.

**boylanmak 1.** to grow in height, to become taller *or* longer; **2.** to go on, to walk on; **3.** *pass. of* boylamak.

**boyler** boiler.

**boylu 1.** tall, high; long; **2.** of high stature; ~ boslu tall and well-built, handsome; ~ boyuna *(or* boyunca) **1.** at full length; **2.** from end to end.

**boynuz 1.** horn, antler; **2.** horn, trumpet; **3.** cupping horn; **4.** antenna *(of insects, etc.);* ~ taktırmak *sl.* to cuckold; ~ vurmak to gore.

**boynuzlamak 1.** to gore; **2.** *sl.* to cuckold.

**boynuzlanmak 1.** to grow horns, to become horned; **2.** to be gored; **3.** *sl.* to be cuckold.

**boynuzlu 1.** horned; **2.** *sl.* cuckold *(man).*

**boynuzsuz** hornless, polled; ~ koyun *fig.* harmless person.

**boyotu,** -nu *♀* cumin.

**boyskavt,** -tı boy scout.

**boysuz** short, not tall.

**boyun,** -ynu **1.** neck; **2.** *geogr.* pass, defile; **3.** *fig.* responsibility; ~ borcu honorary obligation, binding duty; ~ çeviren *zo.* wryneck; ~ eğmek to submit; to humiliate o.s.; ~ kesmek to bow the head; ~ vermek to surrender; to submit; **(boynu):** ~ altında kalsın! may he die!; ~ kıldan ince *fig.* ready to accept any decision; -na almak to take upon o.s.; -na atmak to put the blame (on); -na atılmak to fall on s.o.'s neck; -na binmek to pester, to dun; -nu vurmak to behead, to decapitate.

**boyuna 1.** lengthwise; longitudinally; **2.** [x . .] incessantly, continually.

**boyunbağı,** -nı necktie.

**boyunca 1.** along; **2.** lengthwise; **3.** throughout, during.

**boyunduruk 1.** yoke *(a. fig.);* **2.** *wrestling:* headlock; ~ altına almak *(or* boyunduruğa vurmak) to put under the yoke, to enslave.

**boyut,** -tu dimension.

**boz 1.** grey; roan; **2.** rough, waste, uncultivated *(land).*

**boza** boza *(drink made of fermented millet);* ~ gibi thick *(liquid).*

**bozacı** maker *or* seller of boza.

**bozarmak 1.** to turn pale; **2.** to become grey.

**bozca 1.** greyish; **2.** uncultivated soil.

**bozdoğan 1.** *zo.* merlin; **2.** *(a.* bozdağan) iron war-mace.

**bozdurmak 1.** *caus. of* bozmak; **2.** to change *(money),* to get change for.

**bozgun 1.** rout, defeat; **2.** routed, defeated; ~ vermek *(or* -a uğramak) to get clobbered, to be routed; -a uğratmak to clobber, to rout, to defeat.

**bozguncu** defeatist.

**bozgunculuk** defeatism.

**bozkır** steppe, wold.

**bozkurt,** -du grey wolf.

**bozma 1.** *vn. of* bozmak; **2.** made out (-den of); **3.** pervert, proselyte; **4.** descendant of mixed blood; **5.** *ʤ* cassation, abrogation, quashing.

**bozmacı** second-hand dealer, junk dealer.

**bozmak,** (-ar) **1.** to spoil, to ruin, to destroy; **2.** to change *(money);* **3.** to upset *(stomach, plans, etc.);* **4.** to undo, to disintegrate; **5.** to take to pieces, to take down *(tent),* to demolish, to scrap; **6.** to disturb *(peace);* **7.** to disorganize; **8.** to defeat, to clobber, to rout *(enemy);* **9.** to deform; to taint, to make putrid; **10.** to adulterate; to deprave, to corrupt; to cause to wither; **11.** to erase, to cross out, to deface, to obliterate; **12.** to break *(oath, custom),* to cancel *(agreement);* **13.** *ʤ* to quash *(by cassation);* **14.** to deflower, to violate; **15.** to disconcert; to embarrass, to humiliate; **16.** to break, to change for the worse *(weather);* **17.** to be crazy *(about),* to be wild *(about).*

**bozrak** grayish, greyish.

**bozuk 1.** destroyed, spoilt, broken; gone bad; **2.** out of order, out of repair; **3.** depraved, bad, corrupt; **4.** bad *(weather);* **5.** (small) change; ~ çalmak to be in a bad mood; ~ para small change; ~ para gibi harcamak to use a person in a demeaning way.

**bozukdüzen 1.** irregular, disordered; **2.** unsettled conditions.

**bozukluk 1.** vice; defeat; **2.** small change, coins.

**bozulmak 1.** *pass. of* bozmak; **2.** to be spoilt, to be destroyed, to become tainted (*or* putrid); **3.** to become corrupt (*or* depraved); to wither; to become thin and sallow; **4.** to break down (*car, etc.*); **5.** to look vexed, to resent, to be humiliated, to be disconcerted; **6.** to go bad (*meat, etc.*); bozulmaz denge *phys.* indifferent (*or* neutral) equilibrium; bozulup kalmak to be discomfited.

**bozum 1.** *sl.* discomfiture, humiliation, embarrassment; **2.** *sl.* pecuniary embarrassment, going broke; ~ etm *sl.* to embarrass; ~ havası *sl.* atmosphere of embarrassment; ~ olm. *sl.* to be embarrassed, to lose face, to be discomfited.

**bozumca** a kind of lizard.

**bozunma** ⚛ disintegration, decomposition.

**bozunmak** ⚛ to disintegrate, to decompose.

**bozuntu 1.** discomfiture, embarrassment; **2.** F caricature (of), mere parody (of); **3.** scrap, refuse; -ya vermemek to keep up appearances.

**bozuşmak** to break with one another, to fall out (*ile* with).

**bozuşuk** on unfriendly terms, on bad terms.

**böbrek** *anat.* kidney; ~ iltihabı nephritis.

**böbürlenmek** to boast, to be arrogant, to strut, to brag, to be puffed up.

**böcek 1.** *zo.* insect; **2.** bug, beetle; worm; **3.** louse; **4.** lobster; crayfish; **5.** *hist.* detectivite; ~ zehirl pesticide.

**böcekçil** *biol.* insectivorous.

**böcekkabuğu**, -nu greenish blue with a metallic luster.

**böceklenmek** to become infested with vermin, to get buggy.

**böğür**, -ğrü **1.** side, flank (*of the body*); **2.** side-piece of a saddle frame.

**böğürmek** to bellow, to low; to moo.

**böğürtlen 1.** 🌿 blackberry, bramble; **2.** *sl.* = kusmuk.

**böğürtü** bellow, roar; moo.

**bölen** ⚛ divisor.

**bölge 1.** zone, district, region; **2.** section; part; line of division.

**bölgeci** regionalist.

**bölgesel** regional.

**bölme 1.** *vn. of* bölmek; **2.** partition, dividing wall; **3.** ⚛ division; **4.** compartment; **5.** ⚓ bulkhead.

**bölmek 1.** to separate; to cut up; **2.** ⚛ to divide (-e into).

**bölmeli** partitioned.

**bölü** ⚛ divided by.

**bölücü 1.** ⚛ divider; **2.** separationist, intriguer, plotter.

**bölücülük** divisive behavio(u)r.

**bölük 1.** ✕ company; squadron; **2.** ⚛ order, place; **3.** part, division, subdivision; compartment; **4.** body, group (*of men*); **5.** one of two braids of hair; **6.** *hist.* detachment, squad; ~ ~ in groups; ~ komutanı ✕ captain; ~ pörçük in bits.

**bölüm 1.** ⚛ quotient, dividing; **2.** portion, slice, division, chapter, part, episode, section.

**bölümlemek** to classify, to sort out.

**bölünebilme** ⚛ divisibility.

**bölünen** ⚛ dividend.

**bölünme 1.** *vn. of* bölünmek; **2.** *biol.* division.

**bölünmek** to be divided (-e into), to be separated.

**bölünmez** indivisible.

**bölüntü** part, section.

**bölüşmek** to divide up, to share out.

**bölüştürme** division, distribution.

**bön** naive, silly, imbecile, simple; bakmak to stare foolishly.

**bönlük** naiveté, imbecility, foolishness.

**börek** pastry, pie.

**börekçi** maker *or* seller of börek.

**börtmek** to boil slightly.

**börülce** 🌿 cowpea, black-eyed bean.

**böyle** so, thus, in this way; such; ~ iken (*or* ise de) anyhow, while this is so, notwithstanding the circumstances; bundan ~ henceforth; bunlar kim ~? who on earth are they?; nereden (nereye) ~? where are you coming from? (where are you going?)

**böylece** [x . .] thus, in this way.

**böylelikle** [. . x .] = böylece.

**böylesi** the like, such a one, this kind.

**brakisefal**, -li brachycephalic.

**branda** [x .] sailor's hammock; ~ bezi canvas.

**branş** branch, department, field of work.

**bravo!** *int.* bravo!, well done!

**bre!** *int.* P **1.** you!, hey!, you chap!, fellow! **2.** oh!, ah!, gee!

**Brezilya** [. x .] **1.** *pr. n.* Brazil; **2.** ♀ brazilwood; ~ kestanesi brazil-nut.

**brıçka** [x .] buggy.

**briç**, -ci *cards:* bridge.

**brifing** briefing.

**brik**[1], -gi ⚓ brig.

**brik**[2], -ki a horse carriage.

**briket**, -ti briquette.

**briyantin** brilliantine, pomade.

**broderi** embroidery.

broderili embroidered.
brokar brocade.
brom 1. ⚗ bromine; 2. ♃ brome grass.
bromür ⚗ bromide.
bronş *anat.* bronchus.
bronşçuk *anat.* bronchiole.
bronşit, -ti bronchitis.
bronz bronze; ~ tel bronze wire.
broş brooch.
broşür brochure, pamphlet.
bröve pilot's licence; testimonial, certificate.
Brüksel *pr. n.* Brussels; ~ lahanası Brussels sprouts.
brülör burner, combustion unit.
brüt gross.
bu this; ~ arada 1. meanwhile, in the meantime; 2. among other things, in passing; ~ aralıkta at this moment *(or instant)*; ~ cihetten in this respect; from this point of view; ~ cümleden as an instance of this ~ defa this time; and now; ~ gece tonight; ~ gibi like this, such, of this kind; ~ ne perhiz bu ne lahana turşusu! *fig.* what a contrast!, how inconsistent!; ~ sabah (akşam) this morning (evening); ~ sefer *s.* ~ defa; ~ yakınlarda 1. recently; 2. in the near future; 3. hereabouts; -nda bir iş var there is s.th. fishy in it, there is a catch in it; -ndan başka besides, moreover, furthermore, in addition; -ndan böyle from now on, henceforth; -ndan dolayı *(or* ötürü*)* because of this, for this reason, therefore, that is why; -ndan iyisi sağlık *(or* can sağlığı*)* this is the best; -ndan sonra *(or* böyle*)* 1. henceforth, from now on, in future, from today; 2. after this.
bucak 1. corner, nook; 2. *pol.* sub-district *(syn.* nahiye); ~ ~ here and there, high and low; dünyanın dört bucağına to the four corners of the earth; yurdun her bucağında all over the country.
bucurgat *s.* bocurgat.
buç end, limit.
buçuk half *(after numerals)*; dört ~ 1. four and a half; 2. it is half past four.
buçuklu having halves *or* fractions.
budak 1. knot *(in timber)*, burr; 2. twig, branch; ~ özü young shoot.
budaklanmak to become knotty; to send forth shoots; dallanıp ~ *fig.* to become complicated.
budaklı knotty, gnarled.
budala 1. silly, imbecile; foolish; 2. crazy (about), wild (about), mad (about).
budalalık 1. stupidity, foolishness; 2. madness, craze.

budamak 1. to prune, to lop, to trim; 2. *fig.* to diminish, to decrease, to lessen.
budanmak 1. *pass. of* budamak; 2. to apply o.s. assiduously to s.th.
Budist, -ti Buddhist.
Budizm Buddhism.
budun nation, people.
budunlararası international.
bugün [x .] today; ~ yarın soon, at any time; -den from today; -den tezi yok right away; -e ~ don't forget that; unquestionably, sure enough; -ler these days: -lerde nowadays, in these days; -ün işini yarına bırakma never put off until tomorrow what you can do today.
bugünkü [x ..] of today, today's; ~ günde 1. today; 2. under present conditions; ~ tavuk yarınki kazdan iyidir a bird in the hand is worth two in the bush.
bugünlük [x ..] for today; ~ yarınlık that may happen any moment.
buğday wheat; ~ benizli darkskinned.
buğdaygiller ♃ gramineae, poaceae.
buğdaypası, -nı wheat rust.
buğu 1. vapo(u)r, steam, fog, mist; 2. moisture, dew.
buğuevi, -ni fumigating station.
buğulamak to steam up, to mist up.
buğulanmak 1. *pass. of* buğulamak; 2. to be steamed up, to mist over.
buğulu steamed up, fogged.
buhar steam, vapo(ur); ~ gemisi steamship; ~ kazanı boiler; ~ makinesi steam engine.
buharlaşma evaporation.
buharlaşmak to evaporate, to vapo(u)rize.
buharlaştırmak to vapo(u)rize.
buharlı steamy, vaporous.
buhran [ᵃ] crisis; mali ~ financial crisis.
buhranlı critical, stressful.
buhur [. -] incense, fumigatory.
buhurdan(lık) = buhurluk.
buhurlamak to fumigate with incense, to cense.
buhurluk 1. censer; 2. incense box.
buhurumeryem ♃ cyclamen.
buji *mot.* spark plug.
bukadar [x ..] 1. this much, that much, so many; 2. that's all; bin ~ yıl önce a thousand odd years ago; -ı da fazla! enough's enough!
bukağı fetter; hobble.
bukağılamak to fetter.
bukağılı fettered.
bukalemun *zo.* & *fig.* chameleon.
buket, -ti bouquet, bunch of flowers.
bukle lock, curl of hair.
bukleli curly.

**bulak** P spring, fountain, river-head.

**bulama 1.** *vn. of* bulamak; **2.** grape-juice *(boiled down to the consistency of honey).*

**bulamaç,** -cı thick soup *(made with flour, butter and sugar).*

**bulamak 1.** to roll *(in flour);* to besmear, to bedaub *(-e* with); to smear *(-e* on); **2.** to dirty.

**bulandırıcı 1.** causing nausea; **2.** agitator, instigator.

**bulandırmak 1.** to render turbid *(or* muddy), to muddy, to roil; **2.** to turn *(the stomach).*

**bulanık** turbid, roily; cloudy, overcast; dim; ~ hava overcast *(or* cloudy) weather; ~ suda balık avlamak *fig.* to fish in troubled waters.

**bulanıklık** turbidity; dimness.

**bulanmak 1.** *pass. of* bulamak; **2.** to become cloudy; to become turpid; **3.** to be stirred, to be upset, to get confused; **4.** to be dimmed; **5.** to become bloodshot *(or* opaque) *(eye);* midesi ~ to become nauseated.

**bulantı 1.** nausea, queasiness; **2.** turbidity.

**bulaşıcı** infectious, contagious.

**bulaşık 1.** smeared, soiled, bedaubed; tainted; **2.** contagious, infected *(disease);* **3.** dirty dishes, dirty kitchen utensils; **4.** *sl.* saucy, pert *(person);* **5.** irregular; ~ bezi dish-cloth; ~ deniz dangerous waters; ~ makinesi dishwasher; ~ suyu dishwater; ~ suyu gibi wishywashy *(soup, tea, etc.).*

**bulaşıkçı** dishwasher.

**bulaşkan 1.** sticky, adhesive; **2.** combative *(person).*

**bulaşmak 1.** to become dirty, to be smeared; **2.** to soil, to become smeared *(-e* on), to get sticky; **3.** to be spread by contagion, to communicate itself *(-e* to) *(disease);* **4.** to be involved *(-e* in), to interfere *(-e* in); **5.** to molest, to pester, to annoy; **6.** to take in hand *(work).*

**bulaştırmak 1.** to smear, to stick on, to dirty; **2.** to spread, to infect *(disease);* **3.** to involve *(-e* in).

**buldok** bulldog.

**buldozer** bulldozer.

**Bulgaristan [. x . .], Bulgarya [. x .]** *pr. n.* Bulgaria.

**bulgu 1.** finding, discovery; **2.** invention; **3.** diagnosis.

**bulgur** boiled and pounded wheat; ~ pilavı dish of boiled pounded wheat.

**bulmaca** crossword puzzle.

**bulmak,** (-ur) **1.** to find; **2.** to discover; to

invent; **3.** to hit, to reach; **4.** to meet (with); **5.** to find *(fault)* *(-e* with), to blame *(-e* on); **6.** to amount to *(a sum);* **7.** to recall; buldu da bunadı he always wishes for more; bulup buluşturmak to be adroit in providing; bulup çıkarmak to find out.

**buluğ** puberty; -a ermek to reach puberty.

**bulundurmak** *caus. of* bulunmak to make available, to provide, to have present, to have waiting, to keep in stock.

**bulunmak 1.** *pass. or refl. of* bulmak; **2.** to be found, to be discovered; **3.** to be present, to exist, to be; **4.** to take part *(-de* in), to be present *(-de* at), to participate *(-de* in).

**bulunmaz** unobtainable; rare, choice; ~ Hint kumaşı *fig.* rarity, a very rare thing; bu, bulunmaz Hint kumaşı değil ya! it is not certainly a rarity!

**buluntu 1.** a rare find; **2.** foundling.

**buluş 1.** invention; discovery; finding; **2.** idea, original thought.

**buluşma** meeting, rendezvous; ~ yeri rendezvous, meeting place.

**buluşmak** to meet, to rendezvous, to come together.

**bulut,** -tu **1.** cloud; **2.** *sl.* pissed as a newt, as drunk as a lord; ~ gibi (sarhoş) = bulut **2;** -tan nem almak *(or* kapmak) *fig.* to be very touchy *(or* suspicious).

**bulutlanmak** to become cloudy.

**bulutlu 1.** cloudy, overcast; **2.** opaque, turbid.

**bulutsu** *ast.* nebular, nebulous.

**bulvar** boulevard.

**bumbar 1.** sausage casing; **2.** sausage *(made of rice and meat stuffed in a large gut);* **3.** weatherstripping.

**bumbulanık [x . . .]** quite turbid.

**bumburuşuk [x . . .]** very creased, wrinkled all over.

**bunak** dotard.

**bunaklık** dotage.

**bunalım 1.** crisis; **2.** depression, stupefaction.

**bunalmak 1.** to be stupefied, to be suffocated *(-den* with); **2.** to be depressed *(or* bored).

**bunaltıcı 1.** sultry, stupefying, suffocating, oppressive, stifling; **2.** depressing, boring.

**bunaltmak 1.** to stupefy, to stifle, to oppress; **2.** to depress, to bore.

**bunama** dotage.

**bunamak** to dote, to be in one's dotage.

**bunca [x .]** this much, so much; ~ zaman for such a long time.

**bunda** *loc. of* bu.

**bundan** *abl. of* bu; ~ başka besides, moreover, furthermore, in addition; ~ böyle henceforth; ~ dolayı therefore, that is why, thereof; ~ ötürü s. ~ dolayı; ~ sonra 1. after this; 2. from now on, henceforth.

**bunlar** *pl. of* bu these.

**bunsuz** without this.

**bunu** *acc. of* bu.

**bunun** *gen. of* bu; ~ için therefore, that is why; ~ üzerine thereupon; -la beraber (*or* birlikte) nevertheless.

**bura** this place, this spot; ~ adamları the men of this place; -da here; -dan from here, hence; -sı neresi? what place is this?; -ya to this spot, here, hither.

**burağan** *meteor.* whirlwind.

**buralı** native of this place.

**buram buram** in whirls (*snow*), in clouds (*smoke*), in great quantities (*smell*, *sweat*); ~ duman çıkıyor it is steaming; ~ kokmak to smell very much; ~ terlemek to sweat profusely; ~ tütmek to smoke in clouds.

**buran** *s.* burağan.

**buranı** *s.* boranı.

**burcu burcu** fragrantly, smelling sweetly.

**burç, -cu** 1. tower; bastion; 2. sign of the zodiac; 3. ♀ mistletoe.

**burçak** ♀ common vetch.

**burçin, burçun** hind.

**burgacık** [x . .] *s.* kargacık.

**burgaç, -cı** whirlpool.

**burgu** 1. auger, gimlet, drill; 2. corkscrew; ~ yapmak 🕂 to go into a spin.

**burgulamak** to drill, to bore.

**burjuva** bourgeois.

**burjuvazi** bourgeoisie.

**burkmak** to sprain, to wrench; to twist.

**burkulma** sprain, wrench.

**burkulmak** to be sprained, to be wrenched.

**burma** [x .] 1. *vn. of* burmak; 2. screwed, twisted, spiral; screw, convolution; 3. castrated by twisting; 4. cock, tap, faucet; 5. P bracelet; 6. gripe of colic; 7. *s.* sarığı burma.

**burmak** 1. to twist, to screw; to wring; 2. to castrate; 3. to gripe (*bowels*); 4. (*ağzını*) to cause an acrid feeling in the mouth; bura bura sıkmak to wring out.

**burnaz** hawk-nosed, large-nosed.

**burs** scholarship, bursary; ~ öğrencisi scholar, bursar.

**bursiye** = burs öğrencisi.

**buruk** 1. acrid, astringent, puckery; 2. sprained, twisted; 3. oversensitive, touchy (*person*).

**burukluk** 1. pungency, acridity; 2. resentment, being upset.

**burulmak** 1. *pass. of* burmak; 2. to writhe; 3. (*bşe*) to resent *s.th.*, to take offence at *s.th.*

**burum burum:** ~ burulmak to gripe repeatedly.

**burun** (*acc.:* burunu; *poss. suffix* burnu) 1. nose; 2. bill, beak; 3. tip; 4. *geogr.* promontory, cape, headland, point; 5. *fig.* arrogance, pride; ~ boşluğu nasal cavity; ~ buruna gelmek to run into; ~ burmak to turn one's nose up (-*e* at); ~ deliği nostril; ~ kıvırmak to turn one's nose up (-*e* at), to sniff (-*e* at); ~ maskesi muzzle; ~ silmek to blow one's nose, to wipe one's nose; (burnu): ~ bile kanamadan *fig.* with (*or* in) a whole skin; ~ büyük *fig.* conceited, arrogant; ~ havada *fig.* nose-in-the-air; ~ havada olm. to be on one's high horse; ~ kırılmak to eat humble pie, to be humiliated; -na girmek *fig.* to come too close (-*in* to); -nda tütmek *fig.* to long for; -ndan düşen bin parça olur he is very sulky; -ndan düşmüş the spit and image of, the dead spit of; -ndan (fitil fitil) gelmek *fig.* to be spoiled completely, to do penance for; -ndan kıl aldırmamak to be untouchable; to be very conceited and unapproachable; -dan solumak to go up in the air; -nu çekmek 1. to sniff; 2. *fig.* to be the loser, to go without, to be bereft of; -nu sokmak to poke one's nose (-*e* into), to meddle (-*e* in), to snoop (-*e* into); -nu sürtmek to eat humble pie; -nun dibinde right under one's (very) nose; -nun dikine (*or* doğrusuna) gitmek to follow one's nose; -nun direği kırılmak *fig.* to be suffocated by bad smell; -nun doğrusundan ayrılmamak to follow one's nose; -nun ucunu görememek *fig. sl.* to be pissed as a newt, to be as drunk as a lord.

**burunduruk** barnacle.

**burunlu** 1. ... nosed; ... pointed; 2. *fig.* proud, snooty.

**burunluk** nose-ring (*of a bull*); iron toe-cap (*of a boot*).

**burunsalık** muzzle.

**buruntu** colic.

**buruşmak** 1. to wrinkle, to crease, to pucker up, to crumple; 2. to have the teeth set on edge.

**buruşturmak** to crease, to wrinkle, to pucker, to crumple, to contort, to ruffle.

**buruşuk** wrinkled, puckered, crumpled, ruffled, contorted, shrivelled.

**buruşukluk** pucker, crease, wrinkle.

**buse** [ū] kiss.

**but,** -du thigh, rump, the buttocks.

**butik** boutique.

**butlan** [ª] invalidity, nullity, voidness; ~ davası ़़ action for nullity, action for voidance.

.**buut,** -u'du 1. dimension; 2. distance.

**buymak** 1. to freeze to death; 2. to freeze, to be chilled to the bone.

**buyot,** -tu hot-water bottle.

**buyruk** order, command, decree; başına ~ olm. to be one's own master (or man).

**buyrultu** 1. order, decree; 2. mandate, rescript.

**buyurmak** 1. to order, to decree; 2. to command, to rule; 3. to come, to enter, to pass; 4. to take, to have, to eat, to drink; 5. to say, to utter; 6. to be so kind as to, to condescend (to *inf.*), to deign; buyurun cenaze namazına! we are done for!

**buy(u)run(uz)!** 1. please!; 2. come in!; 3. sıt down!; 4. help yourself!

**buz** 1. ice; 2. frozen, very cold; ~ bağlamak to ice up, to freeze; ~ gibi 1. icy, ice-cold; 2. regular, good and proper; 3. fat and firm (*meat*); ~ kesilmek 1. to freeze; 2. *fig.* to be stunned, to stand aghast (at); ~ kesmek *fig.* to freeze, to feel very cold; ~ tutmak to ice up, to ice over, to freeze; ~ üstüne yazı yazmak *fig.* to write in (or on) water, to build on sand.

**buzağı** calf; fawn.

**buzağılamak** to calve.

**buzdağı,** -nı iceberg.

**buzdolabı,** -nı refrigerator, fridge, ice-box.

**buzhane** [ª] 1. ice house; ice factory; 2. cold storage plant.

**buzkıran** ice-breaker.

**buzlanmak** to ice up (or over), to get icy.

**buzlu** 1. iced, icy; 2. dulled, clouded; 3. frosted, ground (*glass*).

**buzlucam** frosted (or ground) glass.

**buzluk** 1. = buzhane; 2. ice-box; ice cube tray.

**buzul** glacier; ~ devri glacial period, ice age.

**buzullaşma** glaciation.

**bücür** squat, short, dwarf, stocky.

**büfe** 1. sideboard; 2. buffet, refreshment stall, bar.

**büfeci** barkeeper.

**büfecilik** barkeeping.

**büğe, büğelek** gadfly.

**bühtan** [ª] calumny, slander; ~ etm. (b-ne) to slander, to calumniate.

**büklüm** 1. twist, curl, fold, coil; 2. *anat.* plica; 3. bend; ~ ~ curly, in curls.

**bükme** 1. *vn. of* bükmek; 2. cord, braid, (twisted) thread, twine.

**bükmek** 1. to bend; 2. to twist, to curl, to contort; 3. to fold; 4. to spin; to twine; 5. to flex (*muscle*).

**Bükreş** *pr. n.* Bucharest.

**bükük** twisted, bent, curved.

**bükülgen** flexible.

**bükülme** bending, curvature.

**bükülmek** 1. *pass. of* bükmek; 2. to twist, to curl; to bend; to fold.

**bükülü** bent, twisted, crooked,. curled, spun.

**büküm** curl, twine, twist, bend, torsion, fold.

**bükünmek** to writhe (*with pain*).

**büküntü** 1. bend, fold, twist; 2. colic; 3. hem.

**bülbül** nightingale; ~ dişi a kind of fine needlework; ~ gibi fluently; ~ gibi oku-mak to read fluently; ~ kesilmek to spill the beans.

**bülent,** -di 1. high, elevated; 2. tall, lofty; 3. ़ *mf.*

**bülten** bulletin.

**bülüğ** *s.* buluğ.

**bünye** 1. structure (*a. gr.*), constitution; 2. edifice, building; 3. construction (*of a building*).

**bürç,** -cü *s.* burç.

**bürcük** curl of hair.

**bürgü** kerchief, scarf; veil; woman's cloak.

**bürhan** [ª] 1. indisputable argument; 2. evidence, proof.

**büro** [x .] bureau, office; ~ şefi head clerk.

**bürokrasi** bureaucracy, red tape.

**bürülü** wrapped, enfolded, enveloped.

**bürüm** 1. roll, fold; 2. ़ involucre.

**bürümcek** anything wrapped up like a cocoon.

**bürümcük** 1. raw silk gauze; 2. ़ involucel.

**bürümeden** superficially.

**bürümek** 1. to wrap. to enfold; 2. to cover up, to clothe, to infest, to invade, to fill; gözünü kan ~ to see red.

**bürünmek** *pass. or refl. of* bürümek to wrap o.s. up (-e in), to be clothed (-e in); to wrap around o.s.; to be filled (-e with).

**büsbütün** [x ..] altogether, quite, com-nletely, wholly.

**büst,** -tü bust; portrait.

**bütan** butane.

**bütçe** budget; ~ yılı budget year.

**bütün** 1. whole, entire, complete, total;

all; 2. undivided, unbroken; 3. altogether, wholly; 4. ∧ sum, total; ~ ~ = büsbütün.

**bütünleme** *vn. of* bütünlemek; ~ sınavı make-up examination.

**bütünlemek** 1. to complete; to complement; to make up, to supplement; 2. to mend, to repair.

**bütünlemeli** having a make-up examination.

**bütünler** supplementary; ~ açı ∧ supplementary angle.

**bütünlük** entirety, universality, fullness, wholeness; ~ harbi ↖ total war.

**büve(lek)** *zo.* gadfly; ~ sokmuşa dönmek *fig.* to rage as if stung.

**büvet**, -ti refreshment stall.

**büyü** magic, spell, incantation, sorcery, charm; ~ bozmak to break a spell; ~ yapmak to cast a spell (-*e* over), to put a spell (-*e* on), to practice sorcery.

**büyücek** somewhat large.

**büyücü** sorcerer, witch, magician.

**büyücülük** sorcery; witchcraft.

**büyük** 1. big, large; 2. great, high; 3. important, serious, major; 4. elder, older, senior, eldest; ~ aptes feces; ~ atardamar aorta; ≗ çarşı *pr. n.* Grand Bazaar; ~ çizgi dash; ~ harf capital (letter); ~ laf etm. to talk big; ≗ Millet Meclisi *pr. n.* the Grand National Assembly; ~ ölçüde on a large scale; ~ söylemek to dogmatize, to talk big, to boast.

**büyükana, büyükanne** grandmother.

**büyükamiral**, -li full admiral, Admiral of the Fleet.

**Büyükayı** *ast.* Big Dipper, Ursa Major.

**büyükbaba** grandfather.

**büyükbaş** cattle.

**büyükelçi** ambassador.

**büyükelçilik** embassy.

**büyüklü küçüklü** everybody, old and young.

**büyüklük** 1. greatness, largeness; seniority; 2. gravity, importance; 3. size; ~ göstermek to act nobly; ~ taslamak to put on airs.

**büyüksemek** to overrate, to enlarge; to exaggerate.

**büyülemek** to bewitch (*a. fig.*); to charm, to fascinate.

**büyülenme** fascination.

**büyültme** *phot.* blow-up, enlargement.

**büyültmek** 1. to lengthen, to prolong, to extend; 2. *phot.* to enlarge, to blow up; 3. to enlarge.

**büyülü** bewitched, charmed, enchanted, magic.

**büyüme** growing up, development.

**büyümek** 1. to grow (up); 2. to prosper, to thrive; 3. to become large: büyümüş de küçülmüş precocious (*child*).

**büyüteç** magnifying glass.

**büyütme** 1. *vn. of* büyütmek; 2. foster child; 3. *phot.* blow-up, enlargement.

**büyütmek** *caus. of* büyümek 1. to bring up (*child*), to rear, to raise; 2. to exaggerate; to magnify; 3. to enlarge.

**büzgü** smocking, shirr, gather, pucker.

**büzgülü** smocked, shirred, gathered.

**büzme** 1. *vn. of* büzmek; 2. drawn together.

**büzmek** to gather, to constrict, to pucker.

**büzük** 1. contracted, puckered, constricted; 2. *sl.* asshole, arsehole, anus; 3.' *sl.* courage.

**büzülmek** 1. *pass. of* büzmek; 2. to shrink, to shrivel up; 3. to crouch, to cower; büzülüp oturmak to sit shyly; ezile büzüle cap in hand.

# C

**caba** [x .] **1.** free (of charge), gratis, without payment; **2.** thrown into the bargain, over and above, on (the) top of it.

**cabacı** [x . .] F sponger, parasite, toady.

**cabadan** [x . .] for nothing, gratis, gratuitously, free (of charge).

**cacık** a dish consisting of chopped cucumber, garlic and dill in yoghurt.

**cadaloz** a spiteful old hag; nagging woman, shrew.

**cadde** main road, street, avenue; -yi tutmak **1.** sl. to clear out; **2.** to close off the street.

**cadı 1.** ghost, spectre, vampire; **2.** witch; **3.** old and ugly woman, hag; ~ kazanı den of intrigue.

**cafcaf** F **1.** ostentatious, showy talk; **2.** pompousness, showiness.

**cafcaflı** pompous, showy.

**cahil** [â] **1.** ignorant; **2.** uneducated, illiterate; **3.** untaught; inexperienced; fig. greenhorn, beginner; **4.** not knowing, ignorant (of).

**cahillik** [â] **1.** ignorance; **2.** a stupid act; **3.** inexperience; youth; ~ etm. to act foolishly.

**caiz** [â] lawful, permitted; admissible, permissible, allowable, valid.

**caize** [â] **1.** hist. reward, present (given to a poet for a laudatory poem); **2.** mark, tick; **3.** pl. quotation-marks, inverted commas.

**caka** [x .] sl. brag, boast; ostentation, swagger; ~ satmak sl. to show off, to boast, to brag, to swagger.

**cakacı** [x . .] sl. boaster, braggart, swaggerer, bounder.

**cakalı** [x . .] sl. boastful; showy, ostentatious, swaggering.

**câli** [- -] artificial, affected; false, not genuine; insincere.

**cam 1.** glass; **2.** of glass; **3.** window (pane); **4.** phot. plate; **5.** optical lens; ~ takmak **1.** to glaze, to install panes; **2.** to replace lenses.

**camadan 1.** double-breasted velvet waistcoat; **2.** ↓ reef.

**cambaz 1.** rope-dancer, tight-rope walker, acrobat; roughrider, circus rider; **2.** horse dealer; **3.** sly, cunning, crafty, wily, juggler, trick rider, swindler.

**cambazhane** [. . - .] **1.** circus; **2.** variety theatre.

**camcı** glazier.

**camcılık** glaziery.

**camekân 1.** shop-window, show-case; **2.** glass cupboard; **3.** greenhouse, hothouse; **4.** dressing room of a Turkish bath; **5.** sl. specs.

**camgöbeği,** -ni glass-green.

**camgöz 1.** zo. tope, shark; **2.** fig. greedy, insatiable, avaricious, stingy, miser; **3.** one who has a glass eye.

**camız** zo. water buffalo.

**cami** -ii (a. frequently -si) mosque; ~ yıkılmış ama mihrap yerinde fig. there may be snow on the roof but there is still fire in the furnace.

**camia** [- . .] **1.** community, body, group; **2.** phys. collector.

**camlamak** to cover with glass.

**camlık 1.** glassed-in place; **2.** small greenhouse, hotbed, hothouse.

**camyünü,** -nü fiberglass, glass wool.

**can 1.** soul; **2.** life; **3.** vitality, energy, zeal, vigo(u)r; **4.** darling, love; **5.** person, individual; **6.** intimate friend, confidant; **7.** a member of an order. eccl. a. friar; **8.** dear, sympathetic; ~ acısı acute pain; ~ acısıyle with fear of death; ~ acıtmak ta pain (or hurt) a person. to cause a person pain; to oppress; ~ alacak yer (or nokta) **1.** tender spot, the most sensitive spot; **2.** central point (or issue). key (of); ~ atmak (bşe) to desire passionately, to crave; ~ beslemek to feed o.s. well; ~ çekişme death-struggle, being in the throes of death; ~ damarı vital point; ~ dostu a very close friend, dear friend; ~ düşmanı deadly enemy, mortal enemy; ~ evi **1.** the seat of life (heart, pit of stomach); **2.** the vital spot. sensitive point; ~ korkusu fear of death; fig. mortal dread; ~ kulağıyle dinlemek to be all ears, to listen intently (-i to); ~ pazarı a matter of life and death; ~ sıkıntısı 1. boredom, tediousness, ennui, vexation: 2. oppression, anguish, anxiety; ~ vermek 1. to die, to perish; 2. fig. to desire passionately; 3. to grant spiritual strength; 4. to resusciate again, to give life again (-e to); ~ yakmak 1. to do violence to, to violate; 2. to torture, to torment; 3. to cause great injure, to hurt; -a ~ katmak 1. to enhance the joy of life, to refresh, to increase the vitality; 2. to invigorate, to strengthen; 3. to intensify; -a yakın lovable, amiable, sympathetic(ally), likable; aggreable; (canı): ~ ağzına gelmek to be half-dead (from anxiety, fear), to be frightened to death; ~ çekmek to desire, to crave for, to long for; ~ çıkmak 1. to die; 2. to be killed, to perish; 3. fig. to get very tired; 4. fig. to be worn out (clothes); ~ pek tenacious of life, tough, stout; ~ sıkılmak 1. to feel angry, to feel vexed (by); 2. to be restless; 3. to be bored (-e by); to be annoyed; ~ yanmak 1. to suffer (-den from); 2. to be deeply sad (or grieved) (at, about); canım 1. my darling!; 2. my dear; canıma minnet! 1. what more could I want!, so much the better; 2. I do it with great pleasure; (canına): ~ kıymak 1. to kill without mercy; 2. to commit suicide; canla başla with heart and soul.

**canan** [- -] beloved, sweetheart.

**canavar** 1. wild beast, brute, monster; 2. fig. brutish person; 3. co. young scamp (or rascal), little unruly devil; 4. ⚡ dragon; ~ düdüğü (warning) siren; ~ ruhlu brutal, inhuman.

**canavarlık** savagery, ferocity.

**canciğer** 1. intimate friendship, very close relation: ~ kuzu sarması fig. inseperable friend, intimate friend.

**candan** 1. sincere, wholehearted, hearty, cordial; 2. sincerely, wholeheartedyl.

**caneriği,** -ni green plum.

**canfes** taffeta.

**cangıl cungul** 1. tinkle, clink; 2. ding-dong.

**canhıraş** heart-reading, harrowing, bitter.

**cani** [- -] criminal, murderer.

**cankurtaran** 1. life-saving remedy; 2. life-saver; 3. a. ~ filikası life-boat; 4. a. ~ arabası ambulance; ~ yeleği life-belt; ~ yok mu! help!

**canlandırmak** caus. of canlanmak 1. to invigorate. to animate; 2. thea. to (im)personate. to perform.-

**canlanmak** 1. to revive; 2. to come to life; 3. to become active (or lively).

**canlı** 1. alive, living; 2. lively, active; 3.

vigorous, powerful; 4. living creature, living being; 5. (in compounds) fond of, mad after, bent on; ~ bebek fig. charming, lovely: nice, Am. cute; ~ canavar naughty and mischievous, urchin; ~ cenaze wan and worn-out person; ~ yayın live broadcast.

**canlılık** liveliness, vigo(u)r.

**cansız** 1. lifeless, dead, inanimate; 2. feeble, weak; F lame; 3. stagnant (market conditions): 4. dull, spiritless; 5. listless; ~ düşmek to become poor in health.

**cansiperane** self-sacrificing (act).

**capcanlı** vivacious, brisk.

**car¹** woman's shawl (or cloak).

**car²** P cry, wail.

**car car** noisily.

**carcar** F chatterbox.

**carcur** P catridge clip.

**carı** [- -] 1. flowing, running; 2. ✝ current; 3. usual, customary; 4. valid; effective; ~ fiyat current price; ~ hesap current account.

**cariye** [- - .] female slave; concubine.

**cartadak!** [x . .] bang!

**cascavlak** [x . .] 1. stark naked; 2. bald--headed; ~ etm. to plunder, to empty; ~ kalmak fig. to be in low water, to be on the rocks.

**casus** [ā] 1. spy; 2. agent.

**casuslamak** [- . . . .] to spy, to explore.

**casusluk** [ā] espionage, spying.

**cavalacoz** sl. worthless.

**cavlak** 1. naked. nude, bare; 2. bald (-headed), hairless, featherless; cavlağı çekmek sl. to peg out.

**caydırmak** caus. of caymak to dissuade s.o. from s.th.. to cause to renounce, to make s.o. change his purpose.

**cayır cayır** furiously. fiercely: willy-nilly: ~ yanmak to burn in full blaze, to be ablaze; ~ yırtılmak to get torn in rags completely.

**cayırdamak** to creak, to rattle; to grate (voice).

**cayırtı** creak. rattle, crash; yell, roar, shout: -yı basmak (or koparmak) to start shouting furiously.

**caymak** to retire from an undertaking, to back out to change one's mind, to renounce (-den from), to give up.

**caz** jazz: jazz band.

**cazırdamak** 1. to crackle (fire); 2. fig. to sound off.

**cazibe** [ā] 1. attractive power, gravitation. the force of gravity; 2. charm, attraction, appeal.

**cazibeli** [- . . .] charming, attractive.

**cazip** attractive, attracting; alluring, appealing.

**cazzadak** whizzing, hissing.

**cebbar** [ā] 1. violent, brutal; despotic, tyrannical; tyrant; 2. F capable *(woman).*

**cebellezi** [. x . .] *sl.* pinch, swipe.

**Cebelitarık,** -kı [ā] Gibraltar.

**ceberut,** -tu [ū] 1. omnipotence of God; 2. arrogance, haughtiness, presumption; 3. tyranny; 4. despotic, tyrannical, tyrant.

**cebir,** -bri 1. force, compulsion, violence; 2. A algebra.

**cebire** [. - .] splint.

**Cebrail** [. - -] the Archangel Gabriel.

**cebren** [x .] by force.

**cebretmek** [x . .] 1. to force, to enforce *(part. legal),* to compel, to urge; 2. to impose upon forcibly.

**cebri** 1. forcible, violent, compulsory, forced; 2. A algebraic; ~ tedbirler violent measures; ~ yürüyüş X forced march.

**cebrinefis,** -fsi [. . x .] self-victory, self--control, self-restraint.

**cefa** [ā] 1. ill-treatment, cruelty, severity, tormenting; *fig.* vexation; 2. pain, suffering; ~ çekmek to suffer, to be subject to suffering; ~ etm. to ill-treat, to abuse, to torment, to inflict pain *(-e on).*

**cefakâr** long-suffering.

**cehalet,** -ti [ā] ignorance, inexperience.

**cehdetmek** [x . .] to exert o.s., to strive, to struggle.

**cehennem** hell, inferno *(a. fig.);* ~ azabı hellish torture; ~ ol! go to hell!, clear out!; ~ zebanisi demon, brute, devil.

**cehennemlik** 1. worthy of hell, deserving hell; 2. furnace, stokehole *(of a Turkish bath).*

**cehennemtaşı,** -nı silver nitrate.

**cehre** spindle, spool, reel.

**cehri** ¾ 1. dyer's weed, yellow weed; buckthorn.

**ceht,** -di effort, endeavo(u)r; strain; zeal, eagerness, enthusiasm.

**ceket,** -ti jacket, sports coat, jacket of a suit.

**ceketatay** morning coat.

**celal,** -li 1. glory, majesty of God; 2. ♀ *mf.*

**celallenmek** to get into a rage.

**celbe** net bag used by hunters.

**celbetmek** [x . .] 1. to attract, to pull, to draw; 2. to summon, to cite; X to call up, Am. to draft, to induct; 3. to give rise to, to call forth, to cause.

**celep,** -bi cattle-dealer, drover.

**cellat,** -dı 1. executioner; 2. *fig.* cruel, pitiless, unmerciless.

**celp,** -bi ♋ summons; 2. attraction; 3. X call(ing) up, Am. draft, induction.

**celpname** [ā] ♋ summons, written citation.

**celse** 1. session; 2. ♋ hearing, sitting; -yi açmak to open the session.

**cemaat,** -ti [. - .] 1. congregation, group, community at divine service; 2. religious community; 3. crowd; -e uymak to conform.

**cemal,** -li 1. beauty, grace; 2. perfection (of God).

**cem'an** altogether; ~ yekûn sum total, in all.

**cemetmek** [x . .] 1. to collect, to gather, to bring together; 2. A to add up.

**cemi,** -m'i 1. collecting, bringing together; 2. A sum, addition, total; 3. *gr.* plural.

**cemile** [ī] kindness, friendliness, courtesy, attentiveness, compliment.

**cemilekâr** [ī] kind, obliging, amiable, loveable.

**cemiyet,** -ti 1. society; association; 2. social gathering; 3. union, assembly; 4. ceremony, party, wedding.

**cemiyetli** 1. full of people, crowded; 2. significant, expressive, meaningful, comprehensive.

**cemre** 1. † glowing ashes; 2. increase of warmth in February *(a short-time before beginning of spring).*

**cenabet,** -ti [ā] 1. ritual impurity, uncleanliness; 2. ritually impure *(person);* 3. *fig.* nauseous, foul, disgusting; nasty, unpleasant.

**cenah** [ā] wing *(a. X, ♠, pol. & sports).*

**cenap,** -bı [ā] 1. high personality; excellency, majesty; 2. ♀ [x .] *mf.;* Cenabı Hak God, Lord; Sefir Cenapları His Excellency the Ambassador.

**cenaze** [ā] 1. corpse, (dead) body; 2. funeral; ~ alayı funeral procession.

**cendere** 1. (roller) press, cylinder, mangle; press, screw; 2. narrow pass, defile, valley; -ye koymak *(or* sokmak*) fig.* give a person a hard time, to put under pressure, to torture.

**Cenevizli** a Genoese.

**Cenevre** [. x .] Geneva.

**cengâver** 1. warlike, heroic; 2. brave, courageous.

**cengâverlik** heroism.

**cengel** jungle.

**Cengiz** *pr. n.* 1. Genghis Khan; 2. *mf.*

**cenin** [ī] f(o)etus, embryo; cenini sakıt 1. abortive fruit; 2. miscarriage, abortion.

**cenk,** -gi fight, battle, combat; war; ~ etm. to fight, to struggle: to make war.

**cenkleşmek** to fight; to quarrel.

**cennet,** -ti **1.** † garden, park; **2.** paradise, heaven *(a. fig.)*; ~ gibi heavenly; ~ öküzü simpleton, good-hearted but simple person.

**cenneikuşu,** -nu bird of paradise.

**cennetli** late, deceased, defunct, blessed, happy.

**cennetlik 1.** pious, religious, faithful, believing; deserving of heaven; **2.** defunct.

**Cenova** [x . .] Genoa.

**centilmen (adam)** gentleman.

**centilmence** gentlemanlike; in a gentlemanly way.

**cenii.menlik** gentlemanliness; gentle behavio(u)r.

**cenubi** [. - -] southern, south...

**cenup,** -bu **1.** south; **2.** south...; ♀ Amerika(sı) South America; ♀ Kutbu South Pole; cenubu garbi southwest..., south-western; cenubu şarki south-east, south-eastern.

**cep,** -bi **1.** pocket; **2.** ✕ pocket, break-through; ~ harçlığı pocket money; ~ saati pocket watch; ~ sözlüğü pocket dictionary; cebi boş (or delik) **1.** beggar; **2.** penniless, broke; cebi para görmek to ea.n money.

**cephane** [â] **1.** ammunition, munitions; **2.** † powder magazine; **3.** *sl.* opium.

**cephanelik** [â] ammunition depot, store; arsenal.

**cephe 1.** front(side), facade; **2:** ✕ front-line; **3.** *fig.* side, face; ~ almak to turn against, to take sides (-e against).

**cepken** short embroidered jacket.

**cepkitabı,** -nı pocketbook.

**cer,** -rri pulling, dragging; ~ atelyesi railway repair shop.

**cerahat,** -ti [. - .] matter, pus; ~ bağlamak (or toplamak) to suppurate.

**cerahatlanmak** [. - . . .] to suppurate.

**cerahatlı** [. - . .] suppurating.

**cerbeze 1.** eloquence, quick-wittedness; **2.** ability to win one's way into favo(u)r.

**cerbezeli** convincing.

**ceremo** *s.* cerime.

**cereyan** [â] **1.** flowing, stream; **2.** ≠ current; **3.** course; **4.** movement, trend; **5.** draught; ~ etm. **1.** to flow, to run, to pass; **2.** to take place, to happen, to occur.

**cerh 1.** wounding, hurt, injury; **2.** refutation, confutation; ~ etm. **1.** to wound, to injure; **2.** to refute, to disprove.

**ceride** [î] † **1.** newspaper, journal; **2.** diary; daybook, account book; **3.** register.

**cerime** [î] **1.** penalty; **2.** ♂♂ fine; -sini çekmek to pay the penalty of...

**Cermen** *hist.* Teuton.

**cerrah** [â] **1.** surgeon; **2.** † dresser of wounds.

**cerrahi** [â] surgical; ~ müdahale operation.

**cerrahlık** surgery.

**cerrar** [â] obtrusive beggar.

**cerretmek** [x . .] **1.** to pull through, to drag.

**cesamet,** -ti [â] **1.** size, largeness, bulkiness; *(absolute)* greatness.

**cesametli** huge, bulky.

**cesaret,** -ti [â] **1.** courage, daring, boldness; **2.** audacity, daredevilry, impudence; ~ almak to summon up courage, to take heart; ~ bulmak to become bold (or impudent or audacious); ~ etm. to venture, to dare.

**cesaretlenmek** [â] **1.** to take courage, to summon up courage; **2.** to become bold (or impudent).

**cesaretli** [â] **1.** courageous, brave, bold, daring; **2.** audacious, impudent.

**ceset,** -di [â] **1.** (dead) body, corpse; **2.** † body.

**ceste ceste** little by little, gradually; by instalments; piece by piece, bit by bit.

**cesur** = cesaretli.

**cet,** -ddi **1.** grandfather; **2.** ancestor, forefather.

**cetvel 1.** (tahtası) ruler; **2.** scale; **3.** printed form, blank form, list, roll, register, record, schedule; **4.** *typ.* writing frame; **5.** watering canal, trench.

**cevaben** [â] in reply (-e to).

**cevabi** [. - -] replying; ~ nota reply note; ~ ziyaret return visit.

**cevahir** [â] *(pl. of* cevher) precious stone, gem, jewels, jcwel(le)ry; ~ yumurtlıyor *iro.* he speaks wisely and well.

**cevap,** -bı answer, reply; return *(a. fig.)*; ♂♂ defence; ~ vermek -e to answer, to reply, to return; ~ ziyareti return visit.

**cevaplandırmak** to answer.

**cevaplı 1.** having an answer; **2.** with reply coupon; **3.** reply-paid *(telegram)*.

**cevapsız** unanswered; without a reply; ~ bırakmak to leave unanswered; to refuse to reply; *fig.* to keep silent.

**cevaz** [â] **1.** admissibility; lawfulness; **2.** permission; ~ görmek to be judged as permissible; ~ vermek to allow, to permit.

**cevelân 1.** circulation *(a. ♥)*; **2.** walk, stroll, drive round *(a town, etc.)*; ~ etm. to circle, to revolve, to rotate, to circulate.

**cevher 1.** *biol.* substance, matter; **2.** *phls.*

essence, substance; 3. nature; 4. talent, abiliity; 5. precious stone, gem; 6. ✗ ore; -ini tüketmek to be at one's wits' end.

**cevherli** 1. gifted, talented; 2. set with jewels.

**cevir,** -vri maltreatment, cruelty, tormenting.

**ceviz** 1. ✿ walnut; 2. (ağacı) walnut-tree; 3. walnut...; ~ içi 1. kernel; 2. shelled walnuts; ~ kabuğu walnut shell; ~ kabuğu doldurmaz *fig.* ridiculous, very unimportant, insignificant, slight.

**cevretmek** [x . .] *(b-ne)* to torment, to torture.

**cevval,** -li [ā] living, alive, lively, brisk, active, quick.

**ceylan** *zo.* gazelle, antelope; ~ bakışlı having alluring eyes.

**ceza** [ā] punishment, penalty; fine; ~ almak to be punished; to be fined; ~ çekmek to serve a sentence *(-den* for), to complete one's sentence, to serve one's time; ~ görmek to be fined; to be punished; ~ kanunu criminal code; ~ sahası *sports:* penalty area ~ vermek 1. to punish; to fine; 2. ♉ to pay a fine; ~ vuruşu *sports:* penalty kick; ~ yemek to be fined; to be punished; -sını bulmak to get one's due punishment; -sını çekmek 1. to do penance (for), to atone (for), to be fined for; 2. to serve a sentence.

**cezaen** [ā] † as a punishment.

**cezaevi,** -ni prison.

**cezalandırmak** [. - . . .] to punish.

**cezalanmak** [. - . .] to be punished.

**Cezayir** *pr. n.* 1. Algiers; 2. Algeria; ~ dayısı military governor of Algeria; ~ dayısı *(or* kadısı) gibi kurulmak *co.* to strike an attitude.

**cezbe** (mystical) ecstacy, rapture.

**cezbetmek** [x . .] 1. to draw, to attract, to draw to one, *fig.* to take hold of; 2. *fig.* to charm, to fascinate, to infatuate; 3. to absorb, to suck up.

**cezir,** -zri 1. ✿, ✿, *gr.* root; 2. ✿ radical; 3. ebb (tide); ~ hareketi ebb.

**cezmetmek** [x . .] 1. † to amputate; 2. to decide, to determine, to resolve.

**cezp,** -bi 1. attraction; 2. charm, grace, allurement; 3. suction.

**cezri** 1. radical, fundamental, basic(ally); 2. ✿ basic element.

**cezve** pot *(for making Turkish coffee).*

**cezvit** *s.* cizvit.

**cıcık:** cıcığı çıkmış worn-out, in pieces, old; cıcığını çıkarmak to make useless and wear out, to damage by use.

**cıgara** [x . .] P cigarette; ~ böreği *a kind of* long, thin pastry; ~ içmek to smoke cigarette; ~ kâğıdı gibi filmy, flimsy; ~ tablası ashtray.

**cılız** meagre, lean, feeble, weak, thin, undersized, puny, delicate.

**cılk** 1. rotten *(egg);* 2. purulent, inflamed, festering *(wound);* ~ çıkmak 1. to be addled, to be spoiled; 2. *fig.* to turn out to be a washout, to come to naught *(affair).*

**cılkava** *fur made of pieces from the neck of wolves or foxes.*

**cımbız** 1. (a pair of) tweezers; 2. nap, pile *(cloth);* 3. *fig.* bitter words.

**cırboğa** 1. *zo.* jerboa; 2. *fig.* meagre, weak child.

**cırcır** annoying chatterbox; babbler; gossip.

**cırcırböceği,** -ni cricket; cicada.

**cırlak** 1. creaking, screechy, shrill, squeaking, chirping; 2. = cırcırböceği; 3. *zo.* cricket.

**cırıt!** harsh!, screeching sound.

**cırtlak** 1. = cırlak; 2. braggart, boaster.

**cırtlamak** to make a screeching sound.

**cıva** [x .] mercury, quicksilver; ~ gibi *fig.* very restless.

**cıvadra** [. x .] ↓ bowsprit.

**cıvata** [. x .] 1. bolt, screw; 2. ↓ ring bolt; ~ anahtarı spanner.

**cıvık** 1. greasy, soft, runny, wet, sticky; 2. *fig.* importunate, obtrusive, impertinent.

**cıvıklanmak** 1. to become wet *(or* sticky); 2. to get impudent.

**cıvıl cıvıl** 1. twittering; 2. peeping *(chick).*

**cıvıldamak** 1. to twitter, to chirp; 2. to peep.

**cıvıltı** twittering, chirping sound.

**cıvımak** 1. to become wet *(or* sticky); 2. *fig.* to become insipid *(or* tiresome); 3. *sl.* to become impertinent *(or* obtrusive).

**cıyak cıyak** with a shrill voice *(cry).*

**cıyaklamak** to cry with a shrill voice.

**cıyırdamak** to make a creaking sound when torn *(paper, cloth, etc.).*

**cıyırtı** sound as of cloth tearing.

**cız** 1. *baby's language:* fire; 2. sizzling noise; ~ etm. to make a sizzking noise; to have a pang.

**cızbız** grilled meat *(part.* köfte).

**cızık** 1. = çizgi; 2. grieves; ~ ~ bağırmak to shout with the fear of death *(mice).*

**cızıktırmak** F to scribble, to scrawl, to smear.

**cızır cızır** 1. with a sizzling noise; 2. with a creaking noise *(glass);* 3. with a scratching noise *(feather).*

**cızırdamak 1.** to sizzle; **2.** to creak; **3.** to scratch.

**cızırtı** sizzling (or creaking) noise.

**cızlamak 1.** = cızırdamak; **2.** = cız etm.

**cibilli** [. . -] natural, innate, inborn.

**cibilliyet,** -ti disposition, nature, temperament, character.

**cibilliyetsiz 1.** common, unprincipled; **2.** avaricious, stingy, mean, niggardly, ignoble.

**cibinlik** mosquito-net.

**cibre** [x .] husks of grapes, residue of fruits after pressing.

**cici** baby's language: good, pretty, nice; toy, plaything; ~ bey a proper man; -m! my darling!, my sweet!, my dear!; -m pilicim! my sweet darling!

**cicianne** grandma.

**cici bici** nice, sweet, Am. cute.

**cicili bicili** gaudy, glaringly ornamented, dressed up glaringly.

**cicim** light carpet woven on a hand loom.

**cicoz** sl. **1.** not at hand, not present, nothing left; **2.** away!, gone!, off!.

**cicozlamak** sl. to beat it, to go away at once.

**cidal,** -li [ā] **1.** fight, combat, battle; **2.** quarrel, dispute, argument, discussion.

**cidar** anat., phys. wall, inner side, inside.

**cidden** [x .] **1.** seriously; **2.** really, truly, actually, in fact; **3.** very, exceedingly, extremely, greatly.

**ciddi 1.** serious, earnest; **2.** true, real, actual; **3.** sincere, upright, trustworthy, reliable; ~ mi söylüyorsun? are you serious?; -ye almak to take s.th. seriously.

**ciddileşmek 1.** to become serious, to become aggravate; **2.** to become threatening.

**ciddilik** seriousness.

**ciddiyet,** -ti seriousness.

**cif** † abbr. for coast, insurance and freight.

**cife** [¹] **1.** carrion, carcass; **2.** fig. nauseous, disgusting; nasty.

**cıgara** s. cıgara.

**ciğer 1.** lung(s); **2.** liver; **3.** vitals, essential parts as heart, lungs and liver; **4.** internal parts; **5.** courage; **6.** darling; **7.** = ~ takımı; -i beş para etmez a bad egg. a worthless fellow, despicable; -i yanmak (or sızlamak) to feel great compassion (-e for); to suffer greatly (-den from); -im! my darling!

**ciğerci** seller of liver and lungs.

**ciğerpare** [ā] darling.

**cihad** [ā] holy war.

**cihan** [ā] world, universe; ~ harbi world

war.

**cihangir** [. - -] **1.** world conqueror; **2.** ♀ mf.

**cihanşümul** [ā, ū] worldwide, global, mondial; ~ şöhretli world-renowned, world-famed, universally known.

**cihar** [ā] dice: four; -du four and two; -üse four and three; -üyek four and one.

**cihaz** [ā] **1.** = çeyiz; **2.** ♠, phys. apparatus, equipment; **3.** biol. organs, system.

**cihazlamak** [. - . .] to equip, to provide, to supply (ile with).

**cihazlandırmak** [. - . . .] = cihazlamak.

**cihazlanmak** [. - . .] pass. of cihazlamak.

**cihet,** -ti **1.** side, direction, quarter; **2.** aspect, point of view, viewpoint, respect, regard, consideration; **3.** cause, on grounds of, based on; **4.** modality; ...diği cihetle because, since, in view of, considering.

**cila 1.** shellac, lacquer, varnish; polish; **2.** fig. whitewash, varnish; ~ etm. = cilalamak; ~ sürmek (or vurmak) to polish, to burnish, to varnish, to lacquer.

**cilacı** varnisher, finisher.

**cilalamak** to polish, to varnish, to shine, to finish.

**cilalı** polished, varnished, finished; shining.

**cilasız** unpolished, unvarnished, unfinished.

**cilasun:** ~ gibi tall and handsome, brave, mighty.

**cilbent,** -di **1.** † large pocket-book, portfolio; **2.** † set of surgical instruments; **3.** ♦ letter-file; **4.** large folder (for drawing, etc.).

**cildiye 1.** dermatology; **2.** skin disease.

**cildiyeci** dermatologist.

**cilt,** -di **1.** skin; **2.** binding, cover (of a book); **3.** volume, tome; ~ hastalığı skin disease.

**ciltçi** bookbinder.

**ciltlemek** to bind (a book).

**ciltevi,** -ni bindery.

**ciltli** bound (book).

**ciltsiz** unbound, in paper cover, stitched.

**cilve 1.** grace, coquetry, charm; **2.** appearance; manifestation, attestation.

**cilvelenmek** to coquet, to flirt.

**cilveleşmek** to flirt with each other; **2.** to tease mutually, to chaff reciprocally.

**cilveli** graceful; coquettish, flirtatious.

**cim** a letter of the old alphabet; ~ karnında bir nokta a matter of no importance.

**cima,** -aı [ā] **1.** sexual intercourse, coition; **2.** ♀ copulation, fecundation; ~ etm.

to have (sexual) intercourse with.

**cimbakuka** [..x.] thin and ugly, puny: gnomish, gnomelike.

**cimcime 1.** small and delicious watermelon; **2.** small and sweet.

**cimnastik 1.** gymnastics; **2.** practise.

**cimnastikhane** [...-.] **1.** gym(nasium); **2.** gymnastics hall.

**cimri** niggardly, stingy, mean, miserly, parsimonious.

**cimrileşmek** to become stingy.

**cimrilik** stinginess.

**cin**[1] gin.

**cin**[2], -nni *(wicked)* genie, demon, spirit, evil; ~ fikirli clever and crafty; ~ tutmak to lose one's mind, to go mad; ~ yavrusu mischievous. little child, imp, urchin; -ler(i) başına çıkmak *(or* toplanmak *or* üşüşmek) *fig.* to get furious *(or* violent); -ler *(or* in cin *or* ecinniler) top *(or* cirit) oynuyor to be completely deserted.

**cinai** [.--] criminal.

**cinas** [ā] **1.** play on words, pun; **2.** personal remark, suggestiveness; equivocal allusion.

**cinaslı** [ā] suggestive; personal.

**cinayet**, -ti [ā] crime, murder; ~ işlemek to commit murder.

**cingil** a stalk of a bunch of grapes.

**cingöz** = cin fikirli.

**cinli** haunted.

**cinmısırı**, -nı popcorn.

**cinnet**, -ti insanity, madness; ~ getirmek to lose one's mind, to go mad, to become insane.

**cinni** = cin[2].

**cins 1.** ♀, *zo.* race, species, genus; **2.** sex; **3.** *gr.* gender; **4.** category, group, kind, type, sort; **5.** thoroughbred, breed *(horse);* first-class; ~ ~ of various kinds, various; ~ ismi *gr.* common noun.

**cinsel, cinsi 1.** sexual; **2.** generic.

**cinsellik** sexuality.

**cinsiyet**, -ti **1.** sex; **2.** sexuality.

**cinslik** sex; sexuality.

**cinsliksiz** asexual.

**cip** [ī] jeep.

**ciranta** [.x.] ✝ endorser, indorser.

**cirim**, -rmi **1.** *(inanimate)* body; **2.** size, largeness, extention, expansion, dimension, volume; kendi cirmi kadar on his strength of.

**cirit**, -di **1.** javelin, dart *(without head);* **2.** the game of jereed: **3.** speer, javelin; ~ atma javelin-throw(ing); ~ oynamak **1.** to organize a jereed game; **2.** *fig.* to move around freely.

**ciro** [x.] ✝ endorsement, transfer note; ~

etm. to endorse; to transfer.

**cisim**, -smi **1.** body, substance; **2.** material thing, matter, object.

**cisimcik 1.** corpuscle; **2.** particle, atom.

**cisimlenmek** to take a material form.

**cismani** [.--] **1.** corporeal; material; **2.** *eccl.* wordly; ~ ceza corporal punishment; ~ zarar δ's *(grievous)* bodily harm.

**cismen** [x.] bodily, material; in size.

**civan** [ā] **1.** young, youthful, juvenile; **2.** handsome young man.

**civankaşı**, -nı *embroidery:* zigzag ornamentation.

**civanmert**, -di [ā] brave, noble(minded), generous, knightly.

**civanperçemi**, -ni [ā] ♀ yarrow.

**civar** [ā] **1.** neighbo(u)rhood, vicinity, surroundings, environs; **2.** neighbo(u)ring; -ında **1.** near; **2.** about. approximately.

**civciv 1.** chick(en); **2.** twitter, chirp.

**civcivli 1.** hen; **2.** animated, merry, gay, funny; **3.** lively, crowded, busy, intensive.

**civelek 1.** lively, fresh, playful, vivacious; **2.** *hist.* young man in·the service of the Janissaries; **3.** agricultural labo(u)r, farm hand, day-labo(u)rer.

**civeleklik** liveliness, vivacity.

**cizvit**, -ti **1.** Jesuit, Jesuitic(al); **2.** *fig.* instigator, agitator, tricky, sly.

**cizye** *hist.* poll tax.

**coğrafi** geographical.

**coğrafya** [.x.] geography.

**coğrafyacı** [.x..] **1.** geographer; **2.** F geography teacher.

**cokey** [x.] jockey.

**cokeylik** work of a jockey.

**conta** [x.] ⊕ joint, packing, seal, gasket.

**cop**, -pu **1.** thick stick *(with round head);* **2.** *(rubber)* truncheon, *Am.* club, F billy, nightstick.

**coplamak** to beat s.o. with a nightstick, to truncheon.

**corum** shoal, flow together; balık -u shoal of fish.

**coşku** enthusiasm, strong excitement.

**coşkulu** enthusiastic.

**coşkun 1.** fiery, lively, ebullient, exuberant, boiling over, enthusiastic; **2.** agitated, animated; **3.** overflown its banks *(river);* **4.** very vehement, very violent, very strong, very heavy *(wind, rain).*

**coşkunluk** enthusiasm; overflowing.

**coşmak 1.** to be(come) fiery *(or* enthusiastic), to boil over; **2.** to turn out to be a strong movement *(sea);* **3.** to overflow its bank, to rise *(river);* **4.** to become violent *(wind).*

coşturmak to inspire, to fill with enthu- siasm, to excite, to stimulate, to incite.

cömert, -di 1. liberal, generous, munifi- cent 2. fruitful.

cömertleşmek to become generous.

cömertlik generosity, munificence.

cönk, -kü 1. ship, vessel; 2. anthology, collection of poems, collection of various essays.

cudam pitiful simpleton, stupid blunderer, clumsy fool.

cuma Friday.

cumartesi, -ni or -yi Saturday.

cumba [x .] 1. bay-window, bay-stor(e)y; 2. lattice-window.

cumbadak [x . .] 1. int. plop!, splash!; 2. head over heels; very sudden, abrupt.

cumbalak somersault.

cumbul cumbul 1. gurgling; gargling (water); 2. rumbling, resounding; 3. too watery, diluted (food).

cumbuldamak 1. to make a plopping sound, to make a gurgling sound (water); 2. to rumble, to resound; 3. to plop, to flop, to thud.

cumburlop! int. plop!

cumburtu 1. gurgle, gargle (water); 2. flop, plop, thud.

cumhur [. -] 1. the mass of the people, the public, populace; 2. dervish hymn.

cumhurbaşkanı, -nı president of a republic.

cumhuriyet, -ti [. - . .] 1. republic; 2. sl. † a paper bank-note; 2 Bayramı celebration of being a republic (October 28-30 th.); ~ Senatosu (Turkish) Senate.

cumhuriyetçi [. - . . .] republican.

cumhurluk republic.

cunda [x .] ↓ end of a gaff, peak.

cunta pol. junta.

cuntacı pol. member of a junta.

cup! plop!, splash!

cuppadak s. cumbadak.

cura 1. two or three-stringed bağlama; 2. a small, shrill-voiced hawk; 3. sl. the last drag on a cigarette.

curcuna [.x .] 1. noisy dance in a drunken revel, carousal; 2. noisy confusion, con- fused medley; -ya çevirmek (or döndür- mek or vermek) (bir yeri) to fill with noise and fuss, to raise an uproar (in a place); -ya kalkmak 1. to behave frolic- some; 2. to start a quarrel.

curnal 1. denunciation; 2. report of an in- former; ~ etm. (or vermek) to denounce, to inform against, to report (-e to).

curnalcı denouncer, informer, police-spy.

curnata an onrush of quail.

cuşiş exuberance.

cüce dwarf.

cücelik 1. dwarfish growth; 2. dwarfish- ness.

cücük 1. † sweet, tender, tasty; 2. heart of an onion; 3. tuft of beard, imperial.

cücüklenmek to sprout.

cüda [ā] far, distant, remote, separate(d): ~ düşmek to get separated (-den from): to long for.

cühela pl. of. cahil, ignorant people.

cülus accession (to the throne); ~ etm. to access (to the throne).

cümbür cemaat the whole kit and caboo- dle.

cümbüş 1. (music, dance) pleasure, en- joyment, carousal; 2. kind of mandolin or guitar with a metal body; ~ etm. (or yapmak) to carouse, to revel, to enjoy, to divert, to amuse (with music).

cümle 1. all (of them), total, whole; 2. biol. system; 3. gr. phrase, sentence, clause; 4. ۾ group; 5. ۿ periodical system; ~ kapısı main door; -miz all of us, we all; -si all of; bu -den for example, for in- stance.

cümlecik gr. clause.

cümleten all together.

cümudiye [ū] glacier; iceberg.

cünha [ā] crime, serious offence.

cünun [ū] insanity.

cünüp, -nbü, -mbü canonically unclean (from sexual act).

cüppe robe (with full sleeves and long skirts); ~ gibi long and loose (garment).

cüret, -ti 1. courage, boldness, daring, daredevilry, audacity; 2. contp. boldness, impudence, insolence; F sauciness; ~ etm. 1. to venture, to dare, to take the liberty of doing; 2. contp. to have the impudence.

cüretkâr, cüretli 1. courageous, brave, audacious, daring; 2. bold, impudent, insolent.

cüretkârlık 1. boldness, bravery; 2. inso- lence.

cüretsiz timid.

cüruf [ū] slag, dross, scoria.

cürüm, -rmü crime, felony, offence; ~ iş- lemek to commit a crime; cürmümeşhut halinde ஜ caught in the act, in flagrante delicto; cürmümeşhut yapmak to set a trap for, to lay a trap to catch s.o. red- -handed.

cüsse 1. body (build, figure); 2. big, strong body.

cüsseli big-bodied; huge.

cüz, -z'ü 1. part, section; 2. a thirtieth

part of the Koran; **3.** *(book)* number, single volume, fascicle *(print work).*
**cüzam** [ª] 🜊 leprosy.
**cüzamlı** [ª] 🜊 leprous; leper.

**cüzdan** [ª] **1.** wallet; **2.** account-book; *(bank)* pass-book; **3.** portfolio.
**cüzl 1.** very few, very little, trifling; **2.** partial.

# Ç

**çaba** zeal, eagerness, exertion; effort; ~ göstermek to work hard.

**çabalamak 1.** to strive, to struggle, to do one's best, to flounder; **2.** to exert o.s., to try, to put forth effort.

**çabalanmak** to flounder with one's arms and legs.

**çabucacık** [x . . .], **çabucak** [x . .] quickly, in all haste, immediately, forthwith.

**çabuk 1.** quick, fast, swift, hasty, agile; **2.** quickly, soon; ~ ~ quickly; ~ olm. **1.** to hurry, to make haste; **2.** to be finished; ~ parlayan ~ söner *pro.* what flares up fast dies down fast.

**çabuklaşmak** to accelerate, to hasten, to speed up.

**çabuklaştırılmak** to get accelerated, to be speeded up.

**çabuklaştırma** speeding up.

**çabuklaştırmak** to speed up, to expedite, to hasten.

**çabukluk** speed, haste; quickness, fastness, rapidity, promptness.

**çaça 1.** (*balığı*) zo. sprat; **2.** old and experienced sailor; **3.** the cha-cha; **4.** *sl.* madam (*brothel-keeper*).

**çaçaron** F talkative, garrulous, chatterbox.

**çaçaronluk** being a chatterbox.

**çadır** tent; ~ bezi tent canvas; ~ kurmak to pitch a tent.

**çadırcı** tentmaker.

**çadırcılık** tentmaking.

**çadırçiçeği,** -ni ♀ bindwind.

**çadıruşağı,** -nı ♀ gum ammoniacum.

**çağ 1.** time, date; **2.** age, period, epoch; **3.** the right time (*for s.th.*); ~ açmak to open a period; ~ dışı olm. to be dropped from the roll of military reserves because of old age.

**çağında** in the period (of), at the age (of).

**çağanak 1.** castanet; **2.** small gypsy tambourine.

**çağanoz** zo. crab; ~ gibi crooked and humpbacked (*man*).

**Çağatay** Jagatai, Chagatai.

**Çağatayca** the Jagatai language.

**çağcıl** modern, up-to-date.

**çağcılık** modernism.

**çağcıllaşmak** to become modern.

**çağcıllaştırmak** to modernize.

**çağdaş** contemporary.

**çağdaşlaşmak** to become contemporary.

**çağdaşlık** being contemporary.

**çağdışı 1.** anachronistic; **2.** not of draft age.

**çağıl çağıl** with a babbling, murmuring or crashing sound (*water*).

**çağıldamak** to bable, to barble, to murmur, to dabble.

**çağıltı** the babbling sound, the burbling sound, the murmur of running water.

**çağırıcı** person sent to invite or summon s.o.

**çağırış** way of calling, inviting or summoning.

**çağırma** calling, inviting.

**çağırmak 1.** to call; to invite (-*e* to); **2.** to shout, to call out, to cry; **3.** X to call up; *parl.* to convoke; to convene; to sing.

**çağırtı** call, shout.

**çağırtkan 1.** decoy bird; **2.** decoy whistle.

**çağırtmaç** town crier.

**çağırtmak 1.** to have s.o. called; **2.** to have s.o. sing.

**çağla** green almond eaten in the shell; ~ yeşili almond green.

**çağlamak** to burble, to murmur, to rustle, to roar, to splash, to crash (*falling water*).

**çağlar** *s.* çağlayan.

**çağlayan** cascade, small waterfall.

**çağlayık** bubbling spring; hot spring.

**çağmak** (*sun*) to beat down (-*e* on).

**çağrı 1.** invitation, summons, citation, convocation, request (*to accession*); **2.** interjection; **3.** *gr.* vocative; **4.** X call.

**çağrıcı** summoner.

**çağrılı** invited (*person*).

**çağrılık** invitation (card).

**çağrılmak** to be invited, to be called.

**çağrım** the reach of a voice.

**çağrışım** psych. association.

**çağrışımcılık** psych. associationism.

**çağrışmak 1.** to cry out together, to shout

together; **2.** ✲ to sing in unison; **3.** to call (out)to one another.

**çakal 1.** *zo.* jackal; **2.** *sl.* helpless, weak; **3.** *sl.* cunning, crafty, wily; **4.** *sl.* shady person, underhanded person.

**çakaleriği,** -ni ✣ sloe, wild plum; unripe plum.

**çakaloz** *hist.* a swivel gun.

**çakar** dragnet for catching mackerel; ~ almaz **1.** lighter; **2.** *sl.* pistol that won't fire; **3.** useless, good for nothing.

**çakı** pocketknife; ~ gibi lively, active, alert, quick by the hands.

**çakıl 1.** pebble; **2.** gravel, grit; ~ döşemek **1.** to pave with pebbles; **2.** to gravel; ~ taşı rounded pebble.

**çakıldak 1.** mill clapper; **2.** rattle; **3.** chatterbox, babbler; **4.** ball of dried dung hanging on an animal's tail.

**çakıldamak** to rattle, to rustle, to clatter.

**çakıldatmak** to rattle, to shake s.th. noisily.

**çakılı** fixed, nailed (-*e* to).

**çakıllı** pebbly.

**çakıllık 1.** place paved with pebbles; **2.** gravel pit.

**çakılmak 1.** to be driven into place *(nail, peg);* **2.** to be pegged down, to be nailed down.

**çakıltı** rattle, rustle, clatter.

**çakım, çakın 1.** lightning; **2.** spark.

**çakır¹ 1.** greyish blue, bluish; **2.** = çakırdoğan.

**çakır²** † wine.

**çakır³:** ~ çukur **1.** uneven, rough, bumpy; *fig.* stumbling; **2.** rattling noise.

**çakırdiken** ✣ burdock, burr.

**çakırdoğan** *zo.* goshawk.

**çakırkanat** *zo.* teal.

**çakırkeyf** F half-tipsy, slightly-tipsy, mellow, *Am.* happy.

**çakırpençe 1.** having a hawk-like grip; **2.** greedy, avaricious, stingy, mean.

**çakışmak 1.** ✲ to fit into one another; **2.** to beat *(or* strike) one after *(or* upon) another; **3.** to compete in impromptu verse; **4.** A to be congruent.

**çakıştırmak 1.** *caus. of* çakışmak; **2.** to drink, to carouse, to tipple.

**çakma 1.** *vn. of* çakmak; **2.** nailed on; **3.** embossed; **4.** mo(u)ld for embossing.

**çakmak¹ 1.** flash of fire; **2.** steel for striking on a flint; **3.** (cigarette, pocket) lighter.

**çakmak² 1.** to drive in s.th. with blows; **2.** to nail on; **3.** to bind, to tie up; **4.** to palm off s.th. on s.o.; **5.** *sl.* to strike, to hit; **6.** *sl.* to cotton on, to get the notion

*(or* idea), to percieve, to grasp; **7.** *sl.* to know (-*den* about); **8.** to flash (up) *(lightning);* **9.** *sl.* to drink, to booze; **10.** *sl.* to fail *(an examination, a subject).* to be 'ploughed' *(in an examination), Am.* to flunk; **11.** to snap (at) all of a sudden; **12.** to fire (off), to discharge.

**çakmakçı** repairer *or* maker of lighters.

**çakmaklı** flintlock gun.

**çakmaklık** lighter *(fluid).*

**çakmaktaşı 1.** *geol.* flint; **2.** artificial flint.

**çakşır 1.** *(long, wide)* trousers *(with light leather boots at the ankles);* **2.** shank feather.

**çakşırlı** with feathered shanks *(pigeon).*

**çaktırılmak** to be nailed down.

**çaktırmak** to have (a nail) hammered down.

**çalak** swift, nimble.

**çalakalem:** ~ yazmak to write in haste *or* without deliberation, to scribble down.

**çalakaşık:** ~ yemek F to tuck in.

**çalakürek:** ~ çekmek to row with all one's might.

**Çalap,** -bı God.

**çalapaça** dragging s.o. along by force.

**çalar 1.** alarm, striking mechanism *(of a clock);* **2.** equipped with an alarm mechanism *(clock);* ~ saat **1.** alarm clock; **2.** repeater; **3.** musical clock.

**çalçene** chatterbox, babler, gossip.

**çaldırmak 1.** *caus. of* çalmak; **2.** to lose by theft.

**çalgı 1.** music; **2.** musical instrument; **3.** orchestra, band; ~ çağanak with music and noise; ~ çaldırmak to have s.o. *or* a band play musical instrument(s); ~ çalmak **1.** to play a musical instrument; **2.** to play music.

**çalgıcı 1.** musician, instrumentalist; **2.** producer *or* seller of musical instruments.

**çalgıcılık** being a professional musician.

**çalgıcıotu,** -nu ✣ hedge mustard.

**çalgıç** plectrum.

**çalgılı** offering entertainment *(restaurant, etc.),* with music.

**çalı 1.** bush, shrub; **2.** underwood. scrub, *Am.* brush; thicket; ~ çırpı brushwood; sticks and twigs.

**çalıfasulyesi,** -ni climbing kidney-beans.

**çalık 1.** oblique. crooked: **2.** cut slanting *(cloth);* **3.** restive *(animal);* **4.** faded *(cloth. etc.);* **5.** whose name is struck off the roll; **6.** pock-marked; **7.** pock-mark; **8.** mange; **9.** deranged in the mind.

**çalıkkavak** ✣ a kind of poplar whose branches are used in wickerwork.

çalıkuşu, -nu 1. zo. goldcrest kinglet; 2. zo. wren; 3. fig. inconstant, fickle, unstable; 4. fig. lively.

çalılık thicket; brushwood.

çalım 1. † blow, stroke; 2. edge (sabre); 3. swagger, boasting, big talk; 4. soccer: adroit movements; ~ etm. (or satmak) to behave arrogantly, to boast; -ına getirmek fig. to find a favo(u)rable time or position to achieve or obtain.

çalımlamak soccer: adroitly to keep the ball from.

çalımlanmak 1. to swagger; 2. soccer: to be kept away from the ball.

çalımlı 1. pompous; 2. ⚓ narrow-built and with a high bow.

çalınmak pass. of çalmak.

çalıntı 1. stolen goods; 2. plagiarized matter, plagiarism.

çalışkan industrious, hard-working, diligent, studious.

çalışkanlık diligence.

çalışma work; study; ⚚ Bakanlığı Ministry of Labo(u)r; ~ müsaadesi working permit.

çalışmak 1. to try, to strive; 2. to be in the employ of, to work for; 3. to be in activity; to run (machine); 4. to exert o.s.; 5. to study; çalışıp çabalamak to do one's best, to try hard.

çalıştırıcı trainer, coach.

çalıştırılmak to get run.

çalıştırmak 1. to operate, to use; 2. to make run, to make work; 3. to employ; 4. to tutor; 5. sl. to make fun of; 6. sl. to shell out (money).

çalkağı cotton gin.

çalka(la)mak 1. to rinse, to wash off (or up or out); 2. to shake, to jog; 3. to stir up; 4. to beat, to whip (egg); 5. to churn (milk); 6. to disturb and addle (an egg of a brooding hen); 7. to winnow (corn, grain); süt, çocuğu çalka(la)dı milk turned the baby's stomach.

çalka(la)nmak 1. pass. of çalka(la)mak; 2. to be shaked; 3. to be rough (sea); 4. to be talked about everywhere; 5. to be tossed around; 6. to shake o.s.

çalkantı 1. violent shock; 2. remaining chaff; 3. ⚕ diarrh(o)ea, vomitting; 4. strong internal excitement; 5. wave (sea); 6. beaten eggs.

çalkar 1. † anything that upsets the stomach; 2. cotton gin; 3. ⚕ laxative, purgative.

çalma 1. vn. of çalmak; 2. stolen; 3. beaten up, shaken; 4. a turban; 5. chiseled (metal object).

çalmak, (-ar) 1. to hit, to strike, to knock on, to give a blow to 2. to add, to mix in; 3. to make (yoghurt); 4. to spread (butter, honey, etc.); 5. to steal, to take away (-den from); 6. to spoil, to taint; 7. to play (a musical instrument); 8. to chase, to engrave (a design on a metal); 9. to cut on the bias; 10. to sweep hard; 11. to taste of, to have a flavo(u)r of, to tend to resemble; 12. to ring, to toll, to strike ,to put in action (clock, bell); 13. to strike (the hour); 14. to knock (at the door); bunu al da başına çal! iro. may it do you no good!; çalmadan oynamak 1. to be very lively and happy; 2. to be always ready (to do s.th.), to be officious; çalıp çırpmak to steal whatever is in sight.

çalpara 1. castanet; 2. zo. lady crab; 3. ⊕ guide-box.

çalyaka seizing by the collar; ~ etm. to collar s.o.

çam 1. ♀ pine; fir; 2. any of several types of tall tree with thin sharp leaves that do not drop off in winter, found esp. in colder parts of the world; ~ devirmek F to blunder, to drop a brick, to put one's foot in it; ~ yarması gibi enormous, giant (person).

çamaşır 1. linen, underwear, underclothing; 2. laundry; 3. washing; ~ değiş(tir)mek to change one's underwear; ~ dolabı dresser; ~ ipeği silk embroidery thread; ~ ipi clothesline; ~ makinesi washing machine; ~ yıkamak to wash clothes, to do the laundry.

çamaşırcı washerwoman; laundryman; laundress.

çamaşırevi, -ni, çamaşırhane [. - - - .] laundry room, washhouse.

çamaşırlık 1. = çamaşırevi; 2. suitable material for underwear manufacturing.

çamca roach (small fresh-water fish).

çamcak wooden dipper.

çamfıstığı, -nı pine nut, pine kernel.

çamlık pine grove.

çamsakızı, -nı 1. pine resin; 2. fig. (a ~ gibi) importunate, obtrusive, troublesome, bothersome, annoying (person); ~ çoban armağanı small present.

çamuka [. x .] kind of sardine, sand smelt.

çamur 1. mud, mire; 2. argillaceous earth; 3. dirth, filth; 4. mortar, plaster; 5. mixture of clay; 6. sl. brazen, impertinent, obtrusive; ~ atmak 1. to sling mud (-e at); 2. fig. to calumniate, to defame; a. 🜨 to slander; ~ etm. to dirty; fig. to soil; ~ olm. to get muddy; -a bulaşmak F to be down on one's luck; -a yatmak *sl.* 1. to default on a debt; 2. not to keep a promise.

**çamurcuk** a small carp.

**çamurcun** *zo.* teal.

**çamurlamak** 1. to smear with mud; 2. *fig.* to defame, to calumniate.

**çamurlanmak** to get muddy.

**çamurlaşmak** 1. to turn into mud; 2. to become aggressive, to begin to pick a quarrel.

**çamurlatmak** to have s.th. plastered with mud.

**çamurlu** 1. muddy, miry; 2. dirty; ~ yer marsh, slough.

**çamurluk** 1. mudguard, *Am.* fender; 2. running-board, foot-board; 3. trough; 4. muddy place; 5. gaiter, legging; 6. waterproof boots; 7. footscraper; 8. metal fittings.

**çan** bell, church bell; ~ çalmak 1. to ring a bell; 2. *fig.* to trumpet, to noise abroad; 3. to ring; ~ kulesi belfry, bell tower; -ına ot tıkamak *fig.* to put a spoke in one's wheel.

**çanak** 1. earthenware pot; 2. ⚛ calyx; ~ ağızlı 1. having a large mouth; 2. *fig.* blabbermouth; ~ çömlek eartenware pots; ~ tutmak to ask for (trouble); ~ yalamak to flatter; ~ yalayıcı parasite, sponger; toady, sycophant.

**çanakçı** potter; seller of pottery.

**çanakçılık** making *or* selling eartenware.

**Çanakkale Boğazı** *pr. n.* the Dardanelles, the Hellespont.

**çanaklık** 1. depository; 2. ⚓ masthead.

**çanaksı** *biol.* calyciform.

**çanakyaprağı,** -nı sepal.

**çancı** 1. maker *or* seller of bells; 2. bell ringer.

**çançan** F loud and stupid idle talk, twaddle.

**çançiçeği,** -ni ⚛ bellflower.

**çangal** branch, limb.

**çangallı** having branches.

**çangıl çungul** with a clattering and crashing sound.

**çangırdamak** to clang, to clatter, to jangle.

**çangırtı** clattering (*or* crashing) sound.

**çanıltı** the clanging of a bell.

**çanta** [x.] 1. bag; 2 handbag; 3. briefcase; 4. purse; 5. knapsack; 6. suitcase; -da keklik *fig.* in hand, in the bag; already gained.

**çap,** -pı 1. ⚗ diameter; 2. *a.* ✕ caliber, bore; 3. size, largeness, scale, extent, volume; 4. quality, worth; 5. plan show-

ing the size and boundaries of a plot; -tan düşmek to go downhill, to decline, to be undersized.

**çapa** [x.] 1. hoe, mattock; 2. ⚓ anchor; 3. bilge plank.

**çapacı** 1. hoer; 2. maker *or* seller of hoes.

**çapaçul** F disorderly, slovenly, untidy.

**çapaçulluk** untidiness.

**çapak** 1. dried rheum round the eye, crust; 2. wire edge, burr; fin, beard (*of a casting*).

**çapaklanmak** to become gummy (*eye*).

**çapaklı** 1. crusty, having dried rheum round the eye; 2. with fins *or* burrs (*from casting*); 3. *print.* having a flaw in the casting (*letter*).

**çapalamak** to hoe up.

**çapanoğlu,** -nu unpleasent *or* difficult situation that might appear, a hidden difficulty.

**çapar** 1. a kind of boat used in the Black Sea; 2. spotted, mottled; 3. albino; 4. *hist.* mounted courier.

**çaparı** trawl, trotline.

**çaparız** F 1. obstacle; 2. inverted, reversed, upside down, untoward, adverse, inconvenient; 3. ⚓ being athwarthawse.

**çapçak** 1. wooden bowl; 2. open barrel.

**çapkın** 1. † swift (*horse*); 2. † vagabond, vagrant, tramp; 3. womanizer, philanderer, casanova; 4. young scamp (*or* rascal); 5. sensual, greedy, covetous (*look*).

**çapkınlaşmak** to turn into a skirt-chaser.

**çapkınlık** profligacy; debauchery.

**çapla** cold chisel.

**çaplamak** to gauge, to measure the diam eter of, to calibrate.

**çaplı** 1. having a diameter (of); calibered; 2. large sized, of large caliber; 3. F husky, strapping.

**çapmak** 1. to run. to trot, to gallop; 2. to ride (*horse*) fast; 3. to raid, to pillage.

**çaprak** saddle-cloth.

**çapraşık** 1. complicated, tangled, intricate; 2. crosswise.

**çapraşıklaşmak** to get confused and chaotic.

**çapraşıklık** confusion, chaos.

**çapraşmak** 1. to get complicated; 2. to cross each other.

**çapraz** 1. crossing, transverse, crosswise; 2. diagonal; 3 saw set, saw file; 4. *tailoring:* double-breasted; 5. *wrestling:* a clinch; ~ kelime bulmacası crossword puzzle.

**çaprazlama** 1. diagonally; 2. chiasmus.

**çaprazlamak** to cross obliquely, to put

crosswise (-e to).

**çaprazlaşmak** to become confused and involved.

**çaprazlık** being in crosswise arrangement.

**çaprazölçer** set gauge (for saw teeth).

**çapul** raid, sack, loot, pillage; booty, spoil.

**çapulcu** looter, marauder, pillager.

**çaput**, -tu P 1. rag; 2. coarse cloth.

**çar** czar, tsar.

**çarçabuk** [x . .] as quick as lightning, with lightning speed, very quickly.

**çarçur** dissipation, waste, squandering; ~ etm. to throw out of the window (money), to squander; ~ olm. to be squandered.

**çardak** arbo(u)r, hut, pergola.

**çare** [ā] means, way; solution; remedy, medicament, cure; help; ~ aramak to look for a remedy; -sine bakmak to settle, to see (to); bundan başka çare yok there is no other way out, this is the only thing to do.

**çaresiz** [ā] 1. helpless, poor; 2. unalterable, irrevocable, imperious, commanding; 3. willy-nilly.

**çaresizlik** helplessness, lack of means; poverty.

**çareviç** [x . .] czarevitch, tsarevitch.

**çarık** 1. rural footwear, rawhide sandal; 2. brake-shoe, brake-block; 3. sl. wallet; ~ çürük s. çürük ~.

**çarıklı** 1. wearing rawhide sandals; 2. fig. rural, rustic; ~ diplomat (or erkânıharp) a sly rustic, a wily rustic.

**çarice** czarina, tsarine.

**çark**, -kı 1. wheel (of a machine); 2. wheelwork, gear(ing); 3. disk, plate; 4. X wheel, pivoting manoeuvre; 5. fate, destiny; 6. firmament; 7. ↓ paddle wheel; 8. fly-wheel; ~ etm. 1. X to turn; 2. to change one's resoluteness (a. fig.); -a vermek (or çektirmek) to put (a blade) to the grindstone; -ı bozulmak fig. to have one's affairs upset, to meet misfortune; -ına etm. (or okumak) F to bungle; to ruin one.

**çarkçı** 1. machinist, engine operator; 2. knife-grinder. 3. ↓ engineer, mechanic.

**çarkçılık** 1. ↓ occupation of an engineer; 2. knife-grinding.

**çarkıfelek** 1. sky, heaven; 2. moonlight; 3. destiny, fate; 4. pinwheel; 5. ♀ passion flower.

**çarlık** czardom, tsardom.

**çarliston** charleston (dance).

**çarmıh, çarm'k** cross (for crucifying); çarm'ha germek to crucify.

**çarmık** ↓ shrouds.

**çarnanar** [- - -] willy-nilly.

**çarpan** A multiplier.

**çarpanbalığı**, -nı zo. greater weever.

**çarpı** 1. whitewash; 2. A ...times, multiplied by.

**çarpık** oblique, crooked, distorted, bent; slanting; ~ bacaklı bow-legged; ~ çurpuk crooked and oblique; deformed.

**çarpılan** A multiplicand.

**çarpılma** 1. being hit, collison; 2. becoming crooked.

**çarpılmak** 1. pass. of çarpmak; 2. to take s.th. ill (or amiss), to take offence at, to resent; cezaya ~ to be punished.

**çarpım** A product; ~ tablosu multiplication table.

**çarpınma** 1. convulsion, spasm; 2. a struggle to find a way to get s.th. done.

**çarpınmak** 1. fig. to struggle, to try every possible means; to exert o.s.; 2. to move agitatedly.

**çarpıntı** 1. violent beating (or palpitation) of the heart; 2. strong excitement.

**çarpışık** 1. collided; 2. irregular.

**çarpışma** 1. fight, combat, battle; 2. collision, clash.

**çarpışmak** 1. to collide, to strike one another; 2. to fight; 3. to be in conflict.

**çarpıtmak** to distort (a face), to wrench.

**çarpma** 1. impact, shock (a. X); 2. stroke, blow; 3. A multiplication; 4. embossed; 5. s.th. produced by beating; 6. stolen.

**çarpmak**, (-ar) 1. to strike, to knock against; 2. to throw (at); 3. to strike, to smite, to paralyze, to distort (evil spirit); 4. sl. to steal cleverly; 5. A to multiply; 6. to affect violently (sun, disease); 7. to go one's head (wine); 8. to beat, to palpitate (heart); 9. to slam (a door); 10. to collide with.

**çarptırmak** 1. to make (two things) collide; 2. to have one's pocket picked.

**çarşaf** 1. sheet of a bed; 2. veiled dress (formerly worn by Turkish women in public); ~ gibi as calm as a millpond, calm (sea); ~ kadar very large (said for s.th. supposed to be small).

**çarşaflamak** to fasten a sheet.

**çarşaflanmak** to have a cover fastened on it.

**çarşaflı** wearing a veiled dress.

**çarşamba** Wednesday; ~ karısı hag, hell-cat; ~ pazarı gibi a place in disorder and confusion.

**çarşı** shopping district, permanent market, bazaar, street with shops; ~ pazar dolaşmak to go on a shopping expedition; -ya çıkarmak to (put on the) market; -ya gitmek to go shopping.

**çarşılı** tradesman.

**çaşıt** spy.

**çaşıtlamak** to spy.

**çat,** -tı *int.* crash!, bang!; ~ kapı unexpectedly there was a knock at the door; ~ orda ~ burda, ~ kapı arkasında now here now there *(said for s.o. or s.th. always in a different place)*; ~ pat 1. abrupt, disjointed; 2. very little; now and then, rarely.

**çatadak** [x . .] with a sudden cracking noise.

**çatak** 1. valley; 2. *fig.* complicated, intricate; 3. twins, double *(fruits)*; 4. nagging, quarrelsome.

**çatal** 1. forked, bifurcated; 2. fork; 3. bifurcation; 4. *fig.* dilemma; 5. horns, antlers *(deer)*; 6. difficult, hard, complicated, intricate; 7. having a double meaning *(word)*; ~ görmek 1. to squint; 2. *fig.* to make a mistake; ~ tırnaklı cloven hoofed.

**çatalağız,** -ğzı delta *(river)*.

**çatallanmak** to bifurcate, to fork.

**çatallaşmak** 1. ↖ = çatallanmak; 2. to get complicated; 3. to become cracked *(voice)*.

**çatallı** 1. forked, bifurcated; 2. badly arranged, difficult to survey, complicated; 3. *gr.* disjunctive; 4. cracked *(voice)*.

**çatana** [. x .] ↓ small steam boat.

**çatapat,** -tı small toy explosive that goes off when stepped on.

**çatı** 1. roof; 2. framework of a roof; 3. attic; 4. *anat.* pubis; 5. *gr.* voice; ~ katı *(or* arası *or* altı) attic, penthouse.

**çatık** 1. frowning, sulky, stern *(face)*; 2. stacked *(rifles)*; ~ kaşlı beetle-browed, frowning.

**çatır çatır** 1. with a cracking *(or* crashing*)* noise; with a crackling and snapping noise *(fire)*; with a creaking *(or* popping*)* noise *(wood, bones)*; 2. by force; like it or not; 3. fluently, easily.

**çatırdamak** 1. to crackle, to snap; to creak, to pop; 2. to chatter *(teeth)*.

**çatırtı** crackle, snap; clattering, chattering.

**çatışık** contradictory, clashing.

**çatışma** 1. ✕ skirmish; 2. dispute; argument; 3. *psych.* state of conflict.

**çatışmak** 1. to clash, to collide *(ile* with*)*; 2. to contradict, to clash, to be in conflict *(ideas)*; 3. to have a quarrel; 4. *(dogs, camels)* to mate; 5. to coincide *(ile* with*)* *(time)*.

**çatkı** 1. stack of rifles; 2. cloth headband; 3. frame, skeleton; 4. basting.

**çatkın** 1. = çatık; 2. favo(u)rite, protégé.

**çatlak** 1. split, slit, fissured; 2. crack, fissure, crevice; 3. chapped *(hand)*; 4. cracked *(voice)*; 5. *fig.* cracked, not all there; 6. *fig.* mad, crazy.

**çatlaklık** 1. crack; 2. *fig.* craziness.

**çatlamak** 1. to crack, to split; 2. to chap *(hand)*; 3. to burst with impatience; 4. to die from overeating *(or* exhaustion*)*.

**çatlatmak** 1. to split, to crack; 2. F to drive crazy.

**çatma** 1. *vn.* of çatmak; 2. framework of a building; 3. ठँ picking a quarrel.

**çatmak,** (-ar) 1. to stack *(arms)*; 2. to fit together; 3. to baste *(or* tack*)* together; 4. to tie; 5. to load *(on* an animal*)*; 6. to inveigh *(-e* against*)*, to lash out *(-e* against, at*)*; 7. to collide *(-e* with*)*, to knock *(-e* against*)*, to bump up *(-e* against*)*; 8. to meet *(with* trouble*)*, to come up *(a-gainst* a difficulty*)*; 9. to win favo(u)r of s.o.

**çatra patra** [x . x .] incorrectly and brokenly *(speaking a language)*.

**çavdar** ❦ rye; ~ ekmeği rye-bread.

**çavdarmahmuzu,** -nu ❦ rye ergot.

**çavlan** waterfall.

**çavlı** young untrained hawk.

**çavuş** 1. ✕ sergeant; 2. guard; 3. herald, messenger.

**çavuşkuşu,** -nu *zo.* hoopoe.

**çavuşüzümü,** -nü ❦ sweet-water.

**çay**[1] 1. tea; 2. tea plant; 3. tea party, reception; ~ demlemek to steep *(tea)*.

**çay**[2] brook, rivulet, creek, stream; -ı görmeden paçaları sıvamak to count one's chickens before they are hatched.

**çaycı** 1. seller of tea; tea merchant; 2. keeper of a teahouse; 3. drinker of tea.

**çaydanlık** teapot, teakettle.

**çayevi,** -ni teahouse.

**çayhane** [. . -] teahouse.

**çayır** 1. meadow; pasture; 2. pasture grass; green *(or* fresh*)* fodder; -a çıkarmak to pasture, to graze.

**çayırkuşu,** -nu *zo.* skylark.

**çayırlanmak** to graze, to pasture.

**çayırlık** meadowland, pasture.

**çayırotu,** -nu ❦ 1. grass; fodder; 2. timothy grass.

**çaylak** 1. *zo.* kite; 2. *fig.* green, tiro, fledgling.

**çeç,** -ci heap of winnowed grain.

**cece** *zo.* tsetse fly.

**çedik** morocco slipper; ~ pabuç lady's house slippers.

çehre 1. face, countenance; 2. aspect, appearance; 3. sour face; ~ asmak (or etm. or çatmak) to pull a long face; ~ zügürdü ugly-faced.

çek, -ki cheque, Am. check; ~ defteri chequebook; ~ yazmak to make out a cheque.

Çek, -ki Czech.

Çekçe Czech.

çekçek small four-wheeled handcart.

çekecek shoehorn.

çekek ⚓ slip.

çekememezlik envy, jealousy.

çeki a weight of 250 kilos; ~ taşı a stone weight of 230 kilos; ~ taşı gibi panderous; -ye gelmez 1. it is too heavy; it is unbearable; 2. it is disorderly, it is untidy.

çekici fig. attractive, charming.

çekicilik fig. attractiveness, charm.

çekiç, -ci 1. hammer; 2. anat. malleus; ~ atma throwing the hammer.

çekiçhane [â] steamhammer shop of a factory.

çekiçkemiği, -ni anat. hammer, malleus.

çekiçlemek to hammer.

çekidüzen tidiness, orderliness; ~ vermek to tidy up, to put in order.

çekik 1. slanting (eyes); 2. drawn out; 3. drawn in; ~ gözlü slit-eyed.

çekiliş drawing (in a lottery).

çekilmek 1. pass. of çekmek; 2. to withdraw, to draw back, to recede; 3. to retreat; 4. to resign; 5. (oyundan) to give up; 6. to flex (muscle); çekil oradan! F clear out of there!

çekilmez unbearable, intolerable, unendurable.

çekim 1. phys. attraction; 2. gr. inflection, declination, conjugation; 3. cinema: shot, take; 4. sl. sniff (of snuff); ~ eki gr. termination.

çekimlemek 1. gr. to inflect, to decline, to conjugate; 2. phys. to attract.

çekimli 1. attractive, graceful; 2. gr. inflectional.

çekimser 1. abstaining; 2. uncommitted.

çekimserlik abstention.

çekince 1. drawback; 2. risk.

çekingen timid, shy, hesitant, bashful.

çekingenlik timidity, shyness.

çekinik biol. recessive.

çekinmek 1. to beware (-den of), to refrain (-den from), to recoil (-den from), to hesitate to do, to be timid; 2. to put on (eye make-up).

çekinti hesitation.

çekirdek 1. pip, seed, stone (of a fruit); 2.

nucleus; 3. nuclear; 4. kernel (a. fig.); ~ kahve coffee beans; -ten yetişme trained from the cradle.

çekirdeklenmek to from seeds, to seed.

çekirdeksel phys. nuclear.

çekirdeksiz seedless.

çekirge 1. zo. grasshopper, locust; 2. cricket.

çekişme argument, quarrel.

çekişmek 1. to argue, to quarrel, to dispute; 2. to pull in opposite directions; 3. to draw mutually (knife); 4. to try hard (as a group); çekişe çekişe pazarlık etm. to haggle.

çekişmeli 1. contentious; 2. hard, difficult.

çekiştirmek 1. caus. of çekişmek; 2. to back bite, to run down.

çekme 1. vn. of çekmek; 2. drawer, tilt; 3. overalls; 4. shapely, well-shaped; 5. plucked (instrument); 6. stunted (tree); 7. chinning-up (an exercise); ~ demir rolled iron; ~ halatı tow rope; ~ taşıtı recovery vehicle.

çekmece 1. drawer; tilt; 2. coffer.

çekmek, (-er) 1. to pull; 2. to draw, to haul, to drag, to tug; 3. to hoist (flag); 4. to pull on (boots, trousers); 5. to drive, to move (car); 6. ⚓ to tow; 7. to draw (knife, gun); 8. to extract, to pull out (tooth); 9. to draw (magnet); 10. to attract, to charm, to fascinate; 11. to absorb; 12. to bear, to suspend (weight, load); 13. to bear, to pay for, to stand (expense); 14. to bear, to endure, to put up with, to go through, to suffer, to undergo (experience, sorrow, pain); 15. to breathe in; to suck in; to sniff; 16. to withdraw, to draw out (money); 17. to withdraw, to draw back (troops); 18. to suck up, to pump out (liquid); 19. to distill; 20. to draw (chimney); 21. to draw (line); 22. to extend, to lengthen; 23. to build (fence, wall); to stretch out, to hang (curtain); 24. to lay (cable); 25. to stretch (wire, rope); 26. to weigh; 27. to draw (lots); 28. to copy; 29. to prepare, to draw up (protest, policy); 30. to send (telegram); 31. to photograph, to take (photograph); 32. to grind (coffee); 33. (b-ne) to resemble s o., to take after s.o.; 34. to shrink (cloth); 35. to paint, to give (a coat of paint); 36. gr. to conjugate (verb); 37. sl. to drink. to wet one's whistle; 38. to give (a banquet); çek (or çek arabanı!) sl. clear out!, beat it!, hop it!; çekip çekiştirmek to backbite, to run down; çekip çevirmek to manage; çekip çıkarmak to pull (or pluck) out;

çekip gitmek to go away; çekip uzatma prolixity.

çekmekat, -tı penthouse.

Çekoslovak, -kı *pr. n.* Czechoslovakian.

Çekoslovakya *pr. n.* Czechoslovakia.

çekül plumb line.

çelebi 1. educated, well-bred; 2. gentleman; 3. † prince; 4. *title given to men of certain religious orders.*

çelenç *sports:* challenge.

çelenk, -gi wreath; garland; ~ koymak to lay a wreath.

çelik¹ steel; ~ gibi as tough as a leather.

çelik² 1. short piece of tapered wood; 2. cat *(in tipcat);* 3. cutting; 4. ⚓ marlinespike; carling.

çelikçomak tipcat.

çelikhane [ā] steel works, steel foundry.

çelikleşmek 1. to become steel; 2. to become as tough as a leather.

çelim stature, form, shape.

çelimsiz puny, misshapen, scraggy, frail.

çelişik contradictory.

çelişki contradiction.

çelişmek *(bşle)* to be in contradiction with *s.th.*

çelme 1. *vn. of* çelmek; 2. tripping; ~ atmak *(or* takmak) to trip up.

çelmek 1. to cut on the bias; 2. to divert, to change another's course; 3. to wipe out, to negate, to void; 4. (aklını *or* zihnini) to pervert, to dissuade, to talk s.o. into doing s.th., to seduce; 5. to be in contradiction (with).

çelmelemek *(b-ni)* to trip *s.o.* with one's foot.

çeltik rice in the husk.

çember 1. ⚭ circle; 2. hoop; rim; 3. child's hoop; barrel hoop; 4. strap; 5. hoop-shaped; 6. *basketball:* basket, hoop; 7. ✗ encirclement; ~ çevirmek to trundle *(or* roll) a hoop; ~ içine almak ✗ to encircle; ~ sakal round trimmed beard.

çemberlemek 1. to hoop, to strap; 2. ✗ to encircle, to surround.

çemberli strapped; hooped.

çemen ♣ cumin.

çemre(le)mek 1. to tuck up *(one's garments, sleeves, etc.);* 2. to squeeze the end of s.th. together.

çemrenmek to roll up one's sleeves *(a. fig.).*

çene 1. chin; 2. jaw; 3. jaw bone; 4. *fig.* garrulity, talkativeness; ~ çalmak to chat, to natter, to chatter; ~ kavafı talkative; ~ sakızı *fig.* a saying that is always in one's mouth; ~ yarışı talkfest; -n pırtı! shut up!; -si atmak to drop one's

jaw in dying, to die; -si düşük chatter-box, garrulous, chatty; -ye kuvvet by dint of talking.

çenebaz talkative, garrulous.

çenebazlık talkativeness.

çenek 1. ✿, *zo.* valve; 2. *anat.* mandible.

çeneli *fig.* talkative, chatty.

çengel hook; ~ takmak to get one's claws *(-e* into), to be a nuisance *(-e* to).

çengellemek to hook.

çengellenmek 1. *pass. of* çengellemek; 2. to be hung on a hook.

çengelli hooked.

çengelliiğne safety pin.

çengelsakızı, -nı chewing gum *(made from the juice of cardoon).*

çengi dancing girl.

çenk, -gi primitive harp

çentik 1. notch; nick; 2. notched; nicked; 3. incisure.

çent'klemek to notch; to nick.

çentikli notched; nicked.

çentmek 1. to notch; to nick; 2. to chop up *(onions).*

çepçevre [x..], çepeçevre [.x..] all a-round.

çepel 1. muddy, dirty, foul; 2. gloomy, dull, disagreeable; 3. rubbish.

çeper 1. bamboo fence; 2. immoral; 3. *biol.* membrane.

çepiç year-old goat.

çepken *s.* cepken.

çerçeve 1. frame; 2. sash, window frame; 3. rim *(of glasses);* 4. shaft *(of a loom);* 5. parallel bars; 6. *fig.* framework.

çerçeveci picture-framer.

çerçevelemek to frame, to put in a frame.

çerçi sundries pedlar.

çerçöp 1. twigs; 2. sweepings, rubbish; 3. odds and ends.

çerden çöpten flimsy, jerry-built.

çerez 1. tidbits, nuts, snack; 2. appetizers, hors d'oeuvres.

çerezci seller of appetizers *(or* tidbits).

çerezlenmek 1. to eat appetizers; 2. *fig.* to take advantage of opportunities.

çerge makeshift *(or* gypsy's) tent.

çeri † troops, army.

çeribaşı † 1. gypsy chief; 2. commander of troops.

Çerkez *pr. n.* Circassian; ~ tavuğu chicken with walnut.

çerviş 1. inferior cooking fat; 2. the juicy part of a cooked dish.

çeşit, -di 1. kind, sort, variety *(a. biol.);* 2. assortment; 3. † sample; ~ ~ assorted; ~ düzmek *(or* yapmak) to buy various sorts of a thing.

**çeşitleme** ♪ variation.
**çeşitlemek** to increase the variety of.
**çeşitli** different, various, assorted.
**çeşitlilik** variety, diversity.
**çeşme** fountain.
**çeşni 1.** taste, flavo(u)r; **2.** sample, specimen; **3.** enjoyment, special flavo(u)r; -sine bakmak *(bşin)* to taste s.th., to test the flavo(u)r of s.th.
**çeşnilemek** to make palatable *(or* tasty).
**çeşnilik** seasoning.
**çete [x .]** band of rebels, guerrillas *or* brigands; ~ harbi guerrilla warfare; ~ reisi guerrilla leader.
**çeteci [x . .]** guerrilla, brigand, marauder.
**çetecilik** brigandage, marauding.
**çetele [x . .]** tally (stick); ~ tutmak to keep tally.
**çetin 1.** hard, difficult, harsh; **2.** perverse, intractable; ~ ceviz *fig.* hard *(or* tough) nut to crack.
**çetinleşmek** to get difficult; to become intractable.
**çetrefil 1.** confused, complicated; **2.** bad, incorrect, ungrammatical *(language).*
**çetrefilleşmek** to get complicated.
**çevgen 1.** polo stick; **2.** polo.
**çevik** nimble, agile, swift.
**çeviklik** agility, nimbleness.
**çeviren** translator.
**çevirgeç** *phys.* commutator.
**çeviri** translation.
**çevirici** translator.
**çevirim** filming.
**çevirme 1.** *vn. of* çevirmek; **2.** translation; translating; **3.** translated; **4.** meat roasted on a spit; **5.** ✕ encirclement.
**çevirmek 1.** to turn; **2.** to rotate, to turn; **3.** to translate *(-e* into); **4.** to return, to reject, or refuse, to turn down *(offer, etc.);* **5.** to manage; **6.** to interpret, to explain *(another's words);* **7.** to turn inside out *(garment);* **8.** to surround, to enclose; **9.** to pull *(a trick);* çevir kazı yanmasın F turn cat in pan.
**çevirmen** translator.
**çevre 1.** surroundings; **2.** circumference; contour, circuit, periphery; **3.** environment, milieu; **4.** embroidered handkerchief.
**çevrelemek** to encircle, to surround, to enclose; to circumscribe.
**çevren** *ast.* horizon.
**çevresel** environmental.
**çevri 1.** *geogr.* whirlwind; whirlpool; **2.** forced interpretation.
**çevrik 1.** turned (around); **2.** surrounded; **3.** whirlpool; whirlwind; waterspout.

**çevrili 1.** bordered, surrounded; **2.** facing, turned towards.
**çevrilmek** *pass. or refl. of* çevirmek.
**çevrim** period, cycle.
**çevrimsel** ⌢ cyclic, periodic.
**çevrinti 1.** rotation, eddy, whirl; **2.** whirlpool; whirlwind.
**çevriyazı,** -yı *gr.* transcription, transliteration.
**ceyiz** trousseau; ~ cemen complete trousseau; ~ düzmek to prepare a trousseau.
**çeyrek 1.** quarter, one fourth; **2.** quarter *(of an hour).*
**çıban** boil, furuncle, abscess; pustule; ~ başı **1.** head of a boil; **2.** *fig.* delicate matter; ~ işlemek to ooze pus *(boil);* -ın başını koparmak *fig.* to bring matters to a head.
**çıdam** patience.
**çıfıt 1.** *contp.* Jew; **2.** *fig.* miser, stingy; **3.** *fig.* tricky.
**çığ** avalanche; ~ gibi büyümek *fig.* to snowball.
**çığa** *(balığı)* *zo.* sturgeon.
**çığıltı** confused noise of animal cries.
**çığır,** -ğrı **1.** track left by an avalanche; **2.** path; track, rut; **3.** *fig.* epoch; ~ açmak to mark a new epoch, to break new *(or* fresh) ground; çığrından çıkmak to go off the rails.
**çığırtkan 1.** = çağırtkan; **2.** barker, tout.
**çığlık** cry, scream, shriek; ~ atmak *(or* basmak *or* koparmak) to shriek, to scream.
**çıkagelmek** to appear suddenly, to burst in.
**çıkar** interest, profit, advantage; ~ sağlamak to exploit, to profit by; ~ yol **1.** way out; **2.** *fig.* solution to a difficulty; -ına bakmak to look after number one; -ının nerede olduğunu bilmek to know which side one's bread is buttered.
**çıkarcı** opportunist, exploiter.
**çıkarcılık** opportunism, avarice.
**çıkarma 1.** A subtraction; **2.** ✕ landing.
**çıkarmak 1.** to take out, to get out, to bring out, to push out, to expel, to send out; **2.** to extract, to remove, to take out *(stain);* **3.** to take out, to obtain, to procure *(patent);* **4.** to publish; **5.** to omit, to strike out; **6.** to export; **7.** A to subtract; **8.** to land, to unload; **9.** *(telefonda)* to get through; **10.** *(b-ni)* to place s.o.; **11.** to vomit, to throw up *(food);* **12.** to take off *(garment);* **13.** to deduce, to derive; **14.** to make out, to decipher; **15.** to take it out *(-den* on), to vent one's anger *(-den* on); **16.** to cause, to be the source of; **17.**

to offer, to serve; çıkarıp atmak to throw off *(garment)*; sizi çıkaramadım I can't place you.

**çıkarsama** *log.* inference.

**çıkartma** sticker, decal.

**çıkartmak** *caus. of* çıkarmak.

**çıkı** P small bundle.

**çıkık 1.** dislocated, out of joint *(bone)*; **2.** dislocation; **3.** projecting, protruding.

**çıkıkçı** bonesetter.

**çıkın** knotted bundle.

**çıkıntı 1.** projecting *(or* salient) part; **2.** marginal note.

**çıkış 1.** exit; **2.** ✕ sortie, sally; **3.** *races:* start, **4.** scolding; ~ imtihanı leaving *(or* final) examination; ~ vizesi *pol.* exit visa.

**çıkışlı** graduate *(of a school)*.

**çıkışma** reprimand, rebuke.

**çıkışmak 1.** *(b-ne)* to scold *s.o.,* to rebuke *s.o.,* to chide *s.o.,* to inveigh against *s.o.;* **2.** to be enough, to suffice *(money)*.

**çıkma 1.** *vn. of* çıkmak; **2.** projection; promontory; **3.** marginal note; **4.** come out; appeared; **5.** separated *(from a group)*.

**çıkmak,** (-ar) **1.** to come out, to go out, to emerge; **2.** to move out *(of a house)*, to vacate; **3.** to graduate *(-den* from); **4.** to withdraw *(-den* from), to leave, to quit; **5.** to be made *(or* produced) *(-den* from); **6.** to depart *(-den* from), to leave; **7.** to be subtracted *(-den* from), **8.** to turn out to be, to prove, to come true; **9.** to go up, to climb, to ascend, to step on (-*e* to); **10.** to come off; **11.** to break out *(war, fire, etc.)*; **12.** to fall to one's lot; **13.** to cost, to amount (to); **14.** to lead (-*e* to) *(street)*; **15.** to set *(or* start) off; **16.** to run, to come out *(colour)*; **17.** to be dislocated *(limb)*; **18.** to get about *(rumour)*; **19.** to rise, to come out *(sun, moon)*; **20.** to appear, to become visible; **21.** to be published, to come out, to appear *(book)*; **22.** to come out, to be removed *(stain)*; **23.** to be audible; to be detectible; **24.** to come on the market, to become available, to appear; **25.** to sprout; **26.** to be over *(month, season)*; **27.** to go up, to increase *(fever, prices)*; **28.** to be issued *(order, law)*; **29.** to be announced *(promotion)*; **30.** to appear *(before the court)*; **31.** to apply in person *(to a high official)*; **32.** to go out *(ile* with), to date; **33.** to go to the toilet; **34.** *sl.* to fork out, to pay up *(money)*; çıkmadık canda ümit vardır *pro.* while there is life, there is hope.

**çıkmaz 1.** blind alley, dead-end street,

impasse; **2.** *fig.* dilemma, deadlock; ~ ayın son çarşambası F Greek calends; -a sokmak *(b-ni)* to place *s.o.* in a dilemma.

**çıkra** thick scrub.

**çıkrık 1.** windlass; **2.** spinning wheel *(or* jenny); **3.** sheave, pulley wheel.

**çılbır 1.** dish of poached eggs with yogurt; **2.** leading rein.

**çıldırasıya** madly, passionately.

**çıldır çıldır** brightly; ~ bakmak to look with bright and shining eyes; ~ yan mak to burn brightly.

**çıldırmak 1.** to go mad, to lose one's wits, to go off one's head; **2.** *fig. (için)* to be nuts (over), to be wild (obut).

**çıldırtmak** to drive crazy.

**çılgın** mad, insane, crazy, raving, frenzied.

**çılgınca** madly; ~ eğlenmek F to whoop it up.

**çılgınlık** madness, frenzy, craziness.

**çıma** [x .] ⚓ hawser, rope's end.

**çımacı** [x . .] quayside hand.

**çımkırık** bird's feces.

**çın** true, real.

**çınar** *(ağacı)* ✿ plane tree.

**çın çın:** ~ ötmek to make a continuous ringing sound.

**çıngar** *sl.* row, quarrel, brawl; ~ çıkarmak *sl.* to make a scene, to kick up *(or* make) a row.

**çıngıl** a bunch of undeveloped grapes.

**çıngırak 1.** small bell; **2.** rattle; çıngırağı çekmek *sl.* to kick the bucket, to die.

**çıngıraklıyılan** *zo.* rattlesnake.

**çıngır çıngır** with a rattling sound.

**çıngırdak 1.** = çıngırak; **2.** rattle.

**çıngırdamak** to ring, to tinkle.

**çıngırtı** tinkle.

**çınlamak 1.** to give out a tinkling sound; **2.** to ring *(ear)*; **3.** to echo.

**çıpıldak** naked.

**çıplak 1.** naked, nude; bare; **2.** *fig.* destitute, needy; ~ gözle with the naked eye.

**çıplaklık** nakedness, nudity.

**çıra** [x .] pitch-pine.

**çırak** apprentice; ~ çıkarmak *(or* etm.) to free *(an apprentice)* to work on his own.

**çıraklık 1.** apprenticeship; **2.** apprentice's fee; ~ etm. to work as an apprentice.

**çıralı** resinous.

**çıramoz** torch-holder *(for attracting fish by night)*.

**çırçıplak** [x . .] stark naked, in the altogether, in one's birthday suit.

**çırçır 1.** cotton gin; **2.** trickling spring; **3.** *s.* cırcırböceği.

**çırçırbalığı,** -nı *zo.* wrasse.

çırılçıp:ldak [. x . . .], çırılçıplak [. x . .] s. çırcıplak.

çırpı 1. chip, clipping, shaving; 2. chalk line; ~ ipi 1. carpenter's chalk line; 2. mason's leveling line; ~ vurmak to mark a straight line with the chalk line; -ya getirmek to line up.

çırpınma struggle, fluttering.

çırpınmak 1. to flutter, to struggle; 2. to be all in a fluster; 3. to struggle desperately.

çırpıntı 1. flurry; 2. slight agitation (of the sea).

çırpıntılı slightly agitated (sea).

çırpışmak to flutter (birds).

çırpıştırmak 1. to tap, to beat lightly; 2. F to do superficially.

çırpmak (-ar) 1. to beat, to strike, to tap, to pat; 2. to beat (carpet); 3. to clap (hands); 4. to flutter (wings); 5. to rinse (laundry); 6. tq full (cloth); 7. to trim, to clip; 8. fig. to steal, to pilfer; 9. to stir; to beat (food).

çırt, -tı irrigation pump powered by an animal.

çıt, -tı crack, cracking sound; ~ çıkmamak to be dead silent; ~ yok there is a dead silence.

çıta [x .] lath.

çıtçıt snap fastener, press-stud, popper.

çıtı pıtı F dainty.

çıtır çıtır with a crackling sound; ~ etm. to crackle.

çıtırdamak to crackle.

çıtır pıtır prattling, babbling sweetly.

çıtırtı crackle.

çıtkırıldım 1. fragile, overdelicate; 2. fig. dandy, sissified, effeminate.

çıtlamak to crackle.

çıtlatmak 1. to crack; 2. fig. to drop a hint.

çıtpıt, -tı percussion cap (which goes off when trodden on).

çıvgar auxiliary animal (for ploughing).

çıyan 1. zo. centipede; 2. fig. disgusting blond person.

çızıktırmak F to dash off, to knock off, to tear off.

çiçek 1. flower, blossom; 2. ♀ smallpox, variola; 3. fig. fickle and tricky person; 4. ⚘ flowers; ~ açmak to blossom, to bloom, to come into flower; ~ aşısı vaccination; ~ çıkarmak (or dökmek) ♀ to have smallpox; ~ gibi açılmak to blossom; ~ tozu pollen; çiçeği burnunda brand new, very fresh.

çiçekbozuğu, -nu 1. pockmark; 2. pock-marked.

çiçekçi florist.

çiçekçilik floriculture, floristry.

çiçeklemek 1. to plant with flowers; 2. to decorate with flowers.

çiçeklenmek to flower, to blossom, to come into flower.

çiçekli flowered, in bloom.

çiçeklik 1. (flower) vase; flower stand; 2. flower bed; 3. flower garden; 4. greenhouse; 5. ♀ receptacle.

çiçeksimek ⚘ to effloresce.

çiçeksiz without flowers.

çift, -ti 1. pair, couple; double; 2. duplicate; 3. pincers; ~ camlı pencere double-glazed window; ~ ~ by (or in) pairs; ~ çubuk farming implements; ~ koşmak to harness to a plough (horses ,etc.); ~ meclis sistemi pol. two-chamber system; ~ priz ⚡ two-pin plug; ~ sürmek to plough, Am. to plow.

çiftçi farmer, agriculturalist.

çiftçilik agriculture, farming.

çifte 1. double, paired; 2. kick (of a horse); 3. shotgun, double-barreled gun; 4. double-oared boat; ~ atmak to kick (horse, etc.); ~ dikiş sl. repeater (in a class); ~ kumrular fig. two inseparable chums; ~ şamdan two-branched candlestick.

çiftehane [. . - .] pairing cage (for birds).

çifteker bicycle.

çiftelemek to kick.

çifter çifter in pairs.

çiftetelli a kind of solo folk dance.

çiftleşmek 1. to become a pair; 2. to mate.

çiftleştirmek 1. to make a pair; 2. to mate (two animals).

çiftlik farm, plantation.

çiftsayı ⚶ even number.

çiğ¹ 1. raw, uncooked; 2. green, crude, fresh, soft (person); 3. crude, unfitting (word, act); 4. crude (colour); 5. P immature, unripe (fruit); uncultivated (land); ~ kaçmak fig. to be crude; ~ yemedim ki karnım ağrısın! fig. I have done nothing that I should be blamed!

çiğ² dew.

çiğde ⚘ jujube (tree).

çiğdem ⚘ crocus, meadow saffron.

çiğindirik shoulder yoke.

çiğit cotton seed.

çiğlik 1. rawness; 2. fig. crudeness.

çiğnemek 1. to chew; 2. to run over (a person in car accident); 3. to trample down, to tread under foot; 4. fig. to violate (rule, law).

çiklet, -ti chewing-gum.

çikolata [. . x .] chocolate.

çil¹ zo. hazel grouse; ~ yavrusu gibi dağılmak to scatter like a covey of partridges.

**çil²** 1. freckle; 2. spot *(on a mirror)*; 3. freckled, speckled; 4. root hair; 5. bright, shiny *(coin)*.

**çile¹** 1. hank, skein; 2. bowstring.

**çile²** ordeal, trial, sufferance; ~ çekmek *(or* çıkarmak *or* doldurmak) to pass through a severe trial, to suffer greatly; -den çıkarmak to infuriate, to exasperate; -den çıkmak to lose one's temper.

**çilecilik** asceticism.

**çilek** ⚘ strawberry (plant).

**çilekeş** 1. long-suffering; 2. religious ascetic; 3. ascetical.

**çileli** 1. suffering, enduring; 2. full of suffering.

**çilemek** to sing *(nightingale)*.

**çilenti** drizzle.

**çilingir** 1. locksmith; 2. *sl.* lockbreaker, burglar; ~ sofrası F small table with raki and light snacks.

**çilingirlik** locksmithery.

**çillenmek** to become freckled *(or* speckled).

**çilli** freckled, speckled.

**çim** lawn, garden grass.

**çimbali, çimbalo** ♪ cymbal.

**çimdik** 1. pinch; 2. a pinch (of); 3. *fig.* an unfriendly remark; ~ atmak *(or* basmak) to pinch.

**çimdiklemek** 1. to pinch; 2. to crumble.

**çimen** 1. wild grass; 2. = çemen.

**çimenlik** 1. grassy; 2. meadow, lawn.

**çimento** [ . x .] cement.

**çimentolamak** to cement.

**çimlemek** to plant with grass.

**çimlendirmek** to grass over.

**çimlenmek** 1. to sprout, to germinate; 2. to become grassy; 3. *co.* to get pickings.

**çimmek** to duck under water, to dip down *(in water)*.

**Cin** *pr. n.* China.

**Çinakop,** -pu *zo.* young of the bluefish.

**Çince** *pr. n.* Chinese, the Chinese language.

**çinçilya** *zo.* chinchilla.

**Çingene¹** [x . .] *pr. n.* Gypsy; the Gypsies; ~ borçları petty debts; ~ çergesi 1. Gypsy tent; 2. dump; ~ düğünü 1. Gypsy wedding; 2. *fig.* riotous and disorderly assembly.

**çingene²** *fig.* miser, stingy person.

**Çingenece** *pr. n.* the Romany language.

**çingeneleşmek** to pinch pennies.

**çingenelik** 1. miserliness, stinginess; 2. paltriness, shabbiness; 3. vagabondage.

**çingenepalamudu,** -nu *zo.* the young of the

bonito.

**Çin Halk Cumhuriyeti** *pr. n.* People's Republic of China.

**çini** 1. tile, encaustic *(or* glazed) tile; 2. tile, tiled; 3. porcelain, china; ~ döşemek to tile; ~ mürekkebi India ink.

**çinici** maker of tiles.

**çinicilik** the art of tile-making.

**çinili** tiled.

**çinko** [x .] 1. zinc; zinc sheet; 2. zincograph; 3. payoff *(in a lotto game)*.

**çinkograf** zincographer.

**çinkografi** zincography.

**Çinli** *pr. n.* 1. Chinese; 2. a Chinese.

**çintan, çintaniye, çintiyan** wide trousers worn by peasant women.

**çipil** 1. gummy, bleary, dirty *(eye)*; bleary-eyed; 2. = çepel.

**çipo** [x .] ⚓ anchor stock.

**çipura** [. x.] *zo.* gilt-head bream.

**çiriş** paste, glue; size.

**çirişlemek** to smear with paste.

**çirişli** pasted; pasty, gluey; sized.

**çirişotu,** -nu ⚘ asphodel.

**çirkef** 1. filthy *(or* foul) water; 2. *fig.* disgusting, loathsome *(person)*.

**çirkin** 1. ugly; 2. unseemly, unbecoming, ugly, shameful.

**çirkinleşmek** to get ugly.

**çirkinlik** ugliness.

**çirkinsemek** to consider ugly.

**çiroz** 1. salted and dried thin mackerel; 2. *fig.* a bag of bones.

**çis** ⚘ manna.

**çise** drizzle.

**çiselemek** to drizzle, to spit.

**çisenti** drizzle.

**çiskin** 1. wet by a drizzle; 2. drizzle.

**çiş** urine, pee, peepee; ~ etm. to pee; -i gelmek to want to pee.

**çişik** leveret, bunny.

**çit,** -ti 1. hedge; fence; 2. chintz; 3. kerchief.

**çitari** *zo.* salpa.

**çiti** rubbing, scrubbing *(laundry)*.

**çit(ile)mek** to rub together *(clothes)*.

**çitili** rubbed, scrubbed *(laundry)*.

**çitişmek** 1. to interlace; 2. to occlude well *(teeth)*.

**çitlembik** ⚘ nettle tree berry; ~ gibi small and dark *(girl)*.

**çitlemek** 1. to hedge, to fence; 2. to crack between one's teeth *(dried seeds)*.

**çitmik** 1. *s.* çıngıl; 2. a pinch.

**çitsarmaşığı,** -nı ⚘ convolvulus, bindweed, corn lily.

**çivi** 1. nail; 2. pin, peg; 3. tubercle, stud, knob; ~ çakmak to drive in nails; ~ -yi söker *pro.* set a thief to catch a thief, an old poacher makes the best keeper: ~ dişi canine tooth; ~ gibi 1. healthy, strong; 2. stiff with cold *(finger)*; ~ kesmek F to freeze, to feel very cold.

çivici 1. seller of nails; 2. *sports:* smasher.

çividi [.--] *(mavi)* indigo blue.

çivileme 1. *vn. of* çivilemek; 2. feet-first jump; 3. *sports:* smash.

çivilemek 1. to nail; 2. *fig.* F to stab.

çivilenmek 1. *pass. of* çivilemek; 2. *fig. (bir yere)* to be rooted (to *a spot*).

çivili 1. nailed; 2. having nails.

çivit, -di indigo, blue dye; ~ mavisi indigo

çivitlemek 1. to dye with indigo; 2. to blue *(laundry).*

çivitli blued *(laundry).*

çivitotu, -nu ♥ 1. indigo plant; 2. woad.

çıvıyazısı, -nı cuneiform writing.

çiy dew; ~ düşmek (*or* yağmak) to fall *(dew).*

çiyli dewry.

çizecek scriber.

çizelge chart.

çizem diagram, plan; outline.

çizemsel diagrammatic, schematic.

çizge diagram, curve, graph.

çizgi 1. Å line; 2. stripe; striation; 3. scratch, mark, scar; 4. dash; 5. part *(in a person's hair)*; ~ cekmek (*or* çizmek) to draw a line; ~ ~ striped; ~ hakemi *sports:* linesman; ~ resim drawing.

çizgilemek to mark with lines, to lineate.

çizgili 1. ruled, marked with lines; 2. striped, striated; 3. scratched; ~ cek ↑ crossed cheque; ~ kâğıt ruled paper.

çizgilik straightedge.

çizgisiz unlined; unstriped; unmarked; ~ kâğıt plain-paper.

çizi 1. = çizgi; 2. furrow.

çizik 1. = çizgi; 2. = çizili.

çizikli lined.

çiziktirmek to scrawl.

çizili 1. ruled, lined; 2. scratched, marked; 3. drawn, delineated; 4. cancelled, crossed out; 5. *(altı)* underlined.

çizim Å construction.

çizinti 1. scratch; 2. part crossed off.

çizme 1. *vn. of* çizmek; 2. high (*or* top) boot; -den yukarı çıkmak to be over-wise.

çizmeci bootmaker.

çizmek, (-er) 1. to draw; to mark; to score; 2. to sketch, to draw; 3. to cross out, to strike off, to cancel; 4. to scarify, to scratch.

çizmeli booted.

çoban 1. shepherd, herdsman; 2. *fig.* rustic, boor; ~ armağanı çam sakızı *pro.* a

shepherd's present is pine resin *(expression of modesty, in giving a present)*; ~ itikadı simple and firm faith; ~ köpeği sheep dog.

çobanaldatan *zo.* goatsucker, nightjar.

çobanlama *lit.* pastoral.

çobanlık etm. to shepherd.

Çobanyıldızı, -nı *ast.* Venus.

çocuğumsu childish.

çocuk 1. child, infant; 2. childish; ~ aldırmak ♀ to have an abortion; ~ arabası pram, *Am.* baby carriage; ~ bahçesi 1. children's playground; 2. playpen; ~ bakımevi day nursery, crèche; ~ bezi nappy, *Am.* diaper; ~ büyütmek to bring up children; ~ canlısı fond of children; ~ dili child's language; ~ doğurmak to give birth to a child, to bear a child; ~ doktoru pediatrician; ~ düşürme ♀ abortion, miscarriage; ~ düşürmek ♀ to abort, to miscarry; ♀ Esirgeme Kurumu Society for the Protection of Children; ~ felci infantile paralysis, polio; ~ gibi childish(ly); childlike; ~ mahkemesi ♂ juvenile court; ~ odası nursery; ~ oyuncağı 1. toy; 2. *fig.* child's play, pushover; ~ yuvası nursery school; ~ zammı child allowance; -tan al haberi! *pro.* a child will tell the truth!

çocukbilim pedology, paidology.

çocukbilimci pedologist, paidologist.

çocukça 1. childish *(act)*; 2. childishly.

çocukcağız poor little child.

çocuklaşmak to become childish; to act childishly.

çocukluk 1. childhood; 2. childishness; folly; ~ etm. to act childishly.

çocuksu childish.

çoğalmak to increase, to multiply.

çoğaltım reproduction, copying.

çoğaltmak 1. to increase, to augment; 2. to reproduce.

çoğu, -nu 1. most (of); 2. mostly, usually; ~ zaman usually.

çoğul *gr.* plural; ~ ekleri plural endings.

çoğulcu pluralists.

çoğullaştırmak *gr.* to pluralize.

çoğulluk plural form.

çoğun(ca) often.

çoğunluk majority.

çoğunlukla 1. with a majority of votes; 2. usually.

çok 1. many, much; 2. often, long *(time)*; 3. too; too much; too many; too long; 4. very; ~ çocuklu having many children; ~ ~ at (the) most; ~ defa often; ~ fazla far too much; ~ geçmeden soon, before long; ~ gelmek 1. to be too much (-e for);

**2.** to become unbearable; ~ görmek **1.** to consider to be too much; **2.** to begrudge; ~ olm. to go too far, to overstep the limit; ~ şey! how strange!; ~ şükür! thank God!; ~ taraflı ☾☽ multilateral; ~ yaşa! long live!, hurrah!; çoğa kalmaz (or varmaz or varmadan) before long, soon; çoğa oturmak (or varmak) to cost dearly.

**çoka** [x .] s. çığa balığı.

**çokal** plate armo(u)r, coat of mail.

**çokayaklılar** zo. myriapoda.

**çokbiçimli** polymorphic.

**çokbilmiş 1.** cunning, sly; **2.** precocious.

**çokça** a good many, somewhat abundant.

**çokçuluk** phls. pluralism.

**çokdüzlemli** ⚹ polyhedral.

**çokevli** polygamous.

**çokevlilik** polygamy.

**çokfazlı** phys. polyphasal.

**çokgen** ⚹ polygon.

**çokkarılı** polygynous.

**çokkocalı** polyandrous.

**çoklu 1.** abundance; **2.** majority; **3.** often; mostly.

**çoktanrıcılık** polytheism.

**çoktanrılı** polytheist.

**çokterimli** ⚹ polynomial.

**çokyüzlü** ⚹ **1.** polyhedral; **2.** polyhedron.

**çolak** with one arm; crippled in one hand.

**çolpa** clumsy, uncouth.

**çoluk çocuk 1.** wife and children, household, family; **2.** (pack of) children; çoluk çocuğa karışmak to get married and have children.

**çomak 1.** cudgel, truncheon; short thick stick; **2.** stick, bat (in tipcat).

**çomar 1.** mastiff, large watchdog; **2.** sl. old tavern-keeper; **3.** P hornless sheep.

**çopra 1.** backbone (of a fish); **2.** impenetrable scrub.

**çoprabalığı,** -nı zo. loach.

**çopur 1.** pock-marked; **2.** pockmarks.

**çopurina** zo. picarel.

**çor 1.** illness, disease; **2.** P murrain, anthrax.

**çorak 1.** arid, barren; **2.** brackish, bitter (water); **3.** saltpeter bed; **4.** an impervious kind of clay.

**çoraklaşmak** to become arid.

**çoraklaştırmak** to make arid (or barren), to destroy the fertility of (land).

**çoraklık 1.** aridity, barrenness (of land); **2.** brackishness (of water).

**çorap** sock, stocking, hose; ~ kaçmak to ladder, Am. to run (stocking); ~ örmek **1.** to knit stockings; **2.** fig. to plot (against s.o.), to get s.o. into trouble; ~ sökü-ğü gibi fig. in rapid succession, easily

and quickly; ~ şişi knitting needle.

**çorapçı** hosier.

**çorapçılık** the hosiery business.

**çorba 1.** soup; **2.** fig. mess; ~ içmek to eat soup; ~ etm. fig. to make a mess (of); ~ gibi fig. in a mess, confused; ~ kaşığı tablespoon; -da tuzu bulunmak fig. to participate in a small way; -ya dönmek fig. to become a mess.

**çorbacı 1.** maker or seller of soup; **2.** the form of address used by sailors when addressing the ship's owner; **3.** Christian notable in Turkish towns; **4.** sl. boss.

**çorbalık** suitable for making soup.

**çotira** zo. triggerfish.

**çotra** [x .] flat wooden bottle.

**çotuk 1.** tree stump; **2.** stock of a vine.

**çöğür 1.** lute; **2.** seedling.

**çökek 1.** hollow, low spot; **2.** bog.

**çökelek 1.** cheese made of curds; **2.** ☾ precipitate.

**çökelmek** ☾ to precipitate, to settle.

**çökelti** ☾ s. çökelek 2.

**çökeltmek** ☾ to precipitate.

**çökertme 1.** vn. of çökertmek; **2.** a kind of fishing-net; **3.** ✕ break-through.

**çökertmek 1.** to make kneel down (camel); **2.** to cause to collapse.

**çökkün 1.** collapsed, broken down; **2.** psych. depressed.

**çökkünlük** breakdown; depression.

**çökmek,** (-er) **1.** to collapse, to fall in (or down); to break down; to give way; **2.** to sit down suddenly; **3.** to come down (fog, smoke); **4.** to fall (darkness); **5.** (diz) to kneel; **6.** to cave in, to become sunk and hollow; **7.** to settle, to precipitate; **8.** to descend on one (sorrow); **9.** to be prostrated (by age or fatigue), to break down.

**çökük 1.** collapsed, fallen in; **2.** caved in, sunken (in); **3.** prostrated (by age).

**çöküntü 1.** debris, wreckage; **2.** deposit, sediment; **3.** depression; subsidence (of land).

**çöküş** collapse, fall (a. fig.).

**çöküşmek** to sit down together; to gather.

**çöl** desert; wasteland, wilderness.

**çölfaresi,** -ni zo. jerboa.

**çöllük 1.** desert tract of country; **2.** arid, barren.

**çömelmek** to squat down.

**çömez 1.** boy who works in return for board and lodging; **2.** fig. follower, disciple.

**çömlek** earthen pot; ~ hesabı fig. calculation of an illiterate person; crude scheme.

# çömlekçi

**çömlekçi** potter; ~ çamuru potter's clay.
**çömlekçilik** pottery.
**çöp,** -pü **1.** straw, chip; **2.** matchstick; **3.** stalk, peduncle *(of a fruit)*; **4.** rubbish, litter, trash, garbage, sweepings; ~ arabası garbage truck; ~ atlamaz *fig.* meticulous, punctilious; ~ dökmek to tip, to dump *(rubbish)*; ~ dökmek yasaktır no rubbish to be tipped here; ~ gibi skinny; ~ tenekesi garbage can, dustbin, litterbin; -ten direk *fig.* unsound undertaking.
**çöpçatan** matchmaker.
**çöpçatanlık** matchmaking.
**çöpçü 1.** dustman, street sweeper, scavenger; **2.** garbage collector.
**çöpçülük** garbage collecting.
**çöpleme** ♀ bear's foot.
**çöplenmek 1.** to pick up scraps for a meal; **2.** *fig.* to get pickings.
**çöplüce bülbül** *zo.* wren.
**çöplük** tip, dump *(a. fig.)*; ~ horozu *fig.* debauchee, profligate.
**çöpsüz 1.** free from rubbish; **2.** seedless.
**çörek 1.** cookie; **2.** disc.
**çöreklenmek 1.** to coil itself up *(snake)*; **2.** to settle down and stay.
**çöre(k)otu,** -nu ♀ black cumin, seeds of Nigella sativa.
**çöven 1.** ♀ soapwort; **2.** polo (stick).
**çözelti** ⚗ solution.
**çözgü** warp.
**çözgün 1.** untied, unfastened; **2.** dissolved, dispersed; gone.
**çözme 1.** *vn.* of çözmek; **2.** a kind of cotton sheeting.
**çözmek,** (-er) **1.** to untie, to unfasten; **2.** to unbutton; **3.** to solve *(problem)*; **4.** to unravel, to disentagle, to undo *(knot)*; **5.** ⚗ to dissolve.
**çözücü** solvent.
**çözük 1.** untied, loose; **2.** unraveled.
**çözülmek 1.** *pass.* of çözmek; **2.** to thaw *(ice)*; **3.** to be scattered, to lose its unity; **4.** to become feeble, to lose its strength; **5.** ✕ to withdraw; to become routed *(or* scattered); **6.** *sl.* to run away.
**çözülüm 1.** ✕ disengagement; rout; **2.** *psych.* dissociation.
**çözüm** solution.
**çözümleme** analysis.
**çözümlemek** to analyze.
**çözümsel** analytic(al).
**çözünmek** ⚗ to dissolve; to decompose.
**çözünüm** *psych.* dissociation.
**çözüşme** ⚗ dissociation.
**çözüşmek** ⚗ to dissociate.
**çubuk 1.** rod, bar; **2.** staff, wand; **3.** shoot, twig; sapling; **4.** cigarette holder; **5.**

stripe, rib *(in cloth)*; **6.** ⚓ upper mast; çubuğu tellendirmek *fig.* to take it easy.
**çubuklamak** to beat *(carpet)*.
**çubuklu 1.** barred; **2.** striped, ribbed *(cloth)*.
**çuha** broadcloth.
**çuhaçiçeği,** -ni ♀ cowslip.
**çuhçuh** choo-choo *(train)*.
**çukur 1.** pit, hole, hollow, ditch; dent; cavity; **2.** concave; depressed; low; **3.** dimple; **4.** cesspool; **5.** *fig.* grave; **6.** *sl.* buttocks; ~ açmak to dig a pit; ~ gözlü hollow-eyed; ~ tabak soup-plate; -unu kazmak *(b-nin) fig.* to plot against *s.o.*
**çukurlaşmak** to become hollowed *(or* bowl-shaped); to be dented.
**çukurlatmak 1.** to pit; **2.** to depress, to make concave.
**çukurlu** pitted; dented.
**çukurluk 1.** concavity, hollowness; **2.** pit, hole.
**çul 1.** haircloth; **2.** horsecloth; **3.** clothes; ~ çuval haircloth sack; ~ çürütmek *fig.* to sit a long time *(guest)*; ~ tutmaz spendthrift, shiftless; -u tutmak to grow rich.
**çulha** weaver.
**çulhakuşu,** -nu *zo.* penduline titmouse.
**çullamak** to furnish *(or* cover) with a horsecloth.
**çullanmak 1.** *pass.* of çullamak; **2.** *(b-ne)* to jump on *s.o.*; **3.** *(b-ne) fig.* to pester *s.o.*, to bother *s.o.*
**çulluk** *zo.* woodcock.
**Çulpan** *ast. s.* Çobanyıldızı.
**çulsuz** *fig.* penniless, skint.
**çultar** quilted saddle-cloth.
**çurçur** (balığı) *s.* çırçır (balığı).
**çuval 1.** sack; **2.** *sl.* fat *(person)*; ~ gibi loose, untidy *(clothes)*.
**çuvaldız** packing needle.
**çuvallamak 1.** to bag, to put in sacks; **2.** *sl.* to fail the class, to flunk.
**çük** penis.
**çünkı** *s.* çünkü.
**çünkü** [x .] because.
**çürük 1.** rotten, spoilt, decayed; **2.** unstable; **3.** unfounded; untenable; **4.** bruise, discolo(u)ration, black-and-blue spot; **5.** rotten, bad *(egg)*; **6.** carious *(tooth)*; **7.** disabled *(soldier)*; ~ çarık worn out, useless; ~ gaz ⊕ exhaust fumes; çürüğe çıkarmak to discard as useless; **2.** ✕ to invalid out *(soldier)*.
**çürükçül** saprophyte.
**çürüklük 1.** rottenness, putrefaction; **2.** garbage dump; **3.** *fig.* graveyard.
**çürümek 1.** to rot, to decay, to putrify; **2.**

to be refuted, to be disproved *(claim, etc.)*; **3.** to be bruised *(or* discoloured); **4.** to become worn out *(or* unsound) *(material)*; **5.** to become infirm *(because of aging)*.

**çürütmek** *caus. of* çürümek, *part.* **1.** to make decay; **2.** to refute, to disprove *(one's argument)*; **3.** to season, to age *(meat)*.

**çüş 1.** whoa!; **2.** *sl.* you fool!, you ass!

# D

**da 1.** also, too; **2.** and; **3.** but; **4.** in, at, on, upon; **5.** within, in; **6.** in the possession of, with; **7.** having, of; **8.** denominator *(in fractions).*

**-da** *particle forming the locative case; s.a.* -de, -ta, -te.

**da** [ā] † illness, disease.

**dadanmak 1.** *(bşe) mst contp.* to acquire a taste for *s.th.*; **2.** *(bir yere)* to frequent, to visit *(a place)* frequently.

**dadaş** P **1.** brother; **2.** pal, comrade; **3.** youth, youngster.

**dadı** nurse(maid), nanny.

**dafi, -ii** [ā] ⚔ **1.** that repels, wards off; **2.** God.

**dağ¹ 1.** stigma, brand; **2.** ⚕ cautery, cauterization, mark; **3.** branding iron; ~ basmak to brand, to cauterize.

**dağ² 1.** mountain; **2.** mound, heap; **3.** wild; ~ adamı **1.** mountaineer, highlander; **2.** boor; ~ başı **1.** summit, mountain top; **2.** wilds, remote place; ~ deviren a bull in a china shop; ~ eteği foothills, hillside, skirts of a mountain; ~ harbi mountain warfare; ~ silsilesi mountain range; ~ taş all around, as far as the eye can see, ~ yürümezse, abdal yürür if the mountain will not come to Mohammed, Mohammed must go to the mountain; -a çıkmak to take to the hills; -a kaldırmak to kidnap, to elope (with); -lara taşlara! may such a thing be far from us!; aralarında -lar kadar fark var they are as different as chalk and cheese.

**dağarcık 1.** leather sack *(or* pouch); **2.** *fig.* knowledge.

**dağcı** alpinist, mountaineer, mountain climber.

**dağcılık** mountaineering, mountain climbing.

**dağdağa** tumult, turmoil.

**dağdağalı** tumultuous.

**dağılım 1.** dissociation; **2.** dispersion; **3.** distribution.

**dağılış 1.** dispersal; **2.** fall, collapse.

**dağılmak 1.** to scatter; to disperse, to separate; **2.** to spread, to be disseminated *(rumours);* **3.** to dissolve; to fall to

pieces; **4.** to become untidy; **5.** to be distributed.

**dağınık 1.** untidy; disorganized; **2.** scattered, dispersed.

**dağınıklık** untidiness; dispersion.

**dağıtıcı 1.** deliverer, deliveryman; distributor; **2.** divisive.

**dağıtıcılık** delivery; distribution.

**dağıtım** distribution; delivery.

**dağıtımevi, -ni** distributor.

**dağıtmak 1.** to scatter, to disperse; **2.** to distribute, to deliver, to serve out; **3.** to mess up, to disorder *(room, etc.);* **4.** to break into pieces; **5.** to dissolve, to annul *(parliament, business, etc.);* **6.** *(k-ni)* to go to pieces; **7.** to divert, to distract *(attention).*

**dağkeçisi** *zo.* chamois.

**dağlamak 1.** to brand; to cauterize, to sear; **2.** to burn, to scorch *(sun, wind);* **3.** *fig.* to grieve, to afflict, to take to heart.

**dağlı¹ 1.** branded; **2.** scarred; **3.** hurt to the quick, sore.

**dağlı² 1.** mountaineer, highlander; **2.** *cards:* king; **3.** unmannerly, uncouth, discourteous, unmannered.

**dağlıç** a kind of stump-tailed sheep.

**dağlık** mountainous, hilly.

**dağsıçanı, -nı** marmot.

**daha 1.** more *(-den* than), further; and, plus; **2.** still, so far, yet; **3.** only; ~ neler! how absurd!; -sı var that is not all, to be continued; bir ~ once more.

**dahdah** gee-gee.

**dahi** also, too, even.

**dâhi** genius.

**dahil 1.** inside, the interior; **2.** including; included; ~ etm. to include; to insert; ~ olm. to be included, to join, to participate *(-e* in).

**dahilen** inwardly, internally.

**dahili** internal, inner; ~ deniz inland sea; ~ harp civil war; ~ işler internal affairs, domestic affairs; ~ merkez hypocentrum; ~ nizamname ⚙ internal regulations; *pol.* standing orders.

**dahiliye** [ā] **1.** home *(or* internal) affairs;

**2.** internal diseases; **3.** = Dahiliye Vekâleti; **4.** department of buildings and grounds; ♀ Vekâleti *(or* Nezareti) Ministry of the Interior.

**dâhiyane** [- . - .] ingenious, brilliant.

**dahletmek** [x . .] to interfere *(-e* with), to meddle *(-e* in); to blame.

**daima** [- . .] always, continually, perpetually.

**daimi** [- . -] constant, permanent, perpetual; ~ encümen standing comittee; ~ kadro permanent staff.

**daimilik** [ā] permanency.

**dair** [ā] concerning, about, relating *(-e* to).

**daire** [ā] **1.** circle; circumference; **2.** office, department; **3.** limit, range; **4.** flat, apartments; **5.** ♪ tambourine.

**dairesel** circular.

**dairevi** [- . . -] circular.

**dakik,** -ki [ī] **1.** punctual, time-minded, exact, particular, thorough, painstaking; **2.** fine, subtle.

**dakika, dakka** minute; -sı -sına punctually, to the very minute; -sında at once, instantly.

**daktilo** [x . .] **1.** typewriting; **2.** typist *(person)*; **3.** *a.* ~ makinesi typewriter; ~ etm. to type; ~ ile yazılmış typewritten, typed.

**daktilograf** typist.

**daktilografi** typewriting, typing.

**daktiloskopi** fingerprinting.

**dal¹ 1.** branch, bough, twig; **2.** *fig.* branch, subdivision, ramification; ~ budak salmak **1.** to shoot out branches; **2.** *fig.* to spread, to become wide-spread; ~ gibi slender, graceful; -dan -a atlamak *fig.* to jump from one thing to the other, to ramble; -dan -a konan *fig.* fickle, inconstant.

**dal² 1.** back; shoulder; -ına basmak *(b-nin)* to tread on *s.o.*'s corns *(or* toes); -ına binmek *(b-nin)* to pester *s.o.*, to put pressure on *s.o.*

**dal³** naked, bare.

**dalak 1.** spleen; milt; **2.** honeycomb.

**dalalet,** -ti heresy, deviation, aberration; -e düşmek to deviate, to go astray.

**dalamak 1.** to bite; **2.** to prick, to sting; to burn, to sear; to scratch; to chafe.

**dalaş** dogfight, brawl, row.

**dalaşmak 1.** to fight savagely *(dogs)*; **2.** *fig.* to wrangle.

**dalavere** [. . x .] F trick, intrigue, swindle, deception, deceit; ~ çevirmek to intrigue, to plot; -li iş sharp practice.

**dalavereci** trickster, intriguer, sharper, swindler.

**dalbastı** big and fine in quality *(cherry)*.

**dalburun** nosy, inquisitive.

**daldırma 1.** *vn. of* daldırmak; **2.** layered *(branch)*; layer.

**daldırmak** *caus. of* dalmak **1.** to layer *(a shoot)*; **2.** to plunge *(-e* into), to dip *(-e* into); **3.** *fig.* to disparage.

**dalga 1.** wave, ripple; undulation, corrugation; **2.** watering *(on silk)*; **3.** wave *(of hair)*; **4.** ∳ wave; **5.** *sl.* distraction; **6.** *sl.* trick, intrigue; **7.** *sl.* dope; ~ boyu *phys.* wavelength; ~ ~ **1.** in waves; **2.** wavy *(hair)*; **3.** striped. in light and dark *(colours)*; ~ geçmek *sl.* **1.** to woolgather; **2.** *(b-le)* to make fun of *s.o.*, to make mock of *s.o.*

**dalgacı 1.** F woolgatherer; **2.** *sl.* trickster, swindler; ~ Mahmut F dodger.

**dalgakıran** breakwater, mole.

**dalgalanmak 1.** to wave, to surge, to billow, to undulate; **2.** to fluctuate *(prices)*; **3.** to get rough *(sea)*; **4.** to become uneven *(dye)*; **5.** to get watered *(silk)*; **6.** ⊕ to get corrugated *(metal sheet)*.

**dalgalı 1.** rough *(sea)*; undulated; **2.** wavy *(hair)*; **3.** corrugated *(metal)*; **4.** watered *(silk)*.

**dalgıç,** -cı **1.** diver; **2.** *zo.* grebe; ~ elbisesi diving suit *(or* dress).

**dalgın 1.** absent-minded, contemplative, abstracted, plunged in thought, preoccupied; **2.** unconscious *(sick person)*, comatose.

**dalgınlık 1.** absent-mindedness, abstractedness, preoccupation, reverie.

**dalkavuk** toady, bootlicker, hanger-on, leech, lickspittle; sycophant, parasite.

**dalkavukluk** flattery, toadyism, fawning; sycophancy; ~ etm. to toady, to fawn, to truckle, to cringe.

**dalkılıç** with naked sword.

**dallandırmak 1.** to cause to ramify; **2.** to complicate, to render difficult; **3.** to exaggerate.

**dallanmak 1.** to shoot out branches, to branch out, to ramify, to become branched; **2.** to spread, to become complicated.

**dallı 1.** branched, ramified; **2.** ornamented with branches; ~ budaklı **1.** ramified; **2.** *fig.* complicated, intricate, knotty.

**dalmak,** (-ar) **1.** to dive, to plunge *(-e* into); **2.** to be intent *(-e* on); **3.** to burst *(-e* into), to blow *(-e* into), to plunge *(-e* into); **4.** to be lost in thought; **5.** to become absorbed *(-e* in); **6.** to drop off, to doze off; to become unconscious *(sick person)*; dala çıka F sinking or rising, with the greatest difficulty.

**daltaban 1.** barefooted; **2.** *fig.* destitute, wretched; **3.** *fig.* contemptible *(person).*

**dalya** dahlia.

**dalyan** fishing weir; ~ gibi well-built, well set-up.

**dalyarak** *sl.* booby, boob.

**dam**[1] **1.** roof; **2.** outhouse; roofed shed; **3.** stable; **4.** P house; **5.** *sl.* jail, stir, cooler; ~ altı loft, attic, garret; -dan düşer gibi out of the blue, out of a clear (blue) sky.

**dam**[2] **1.** lady partner *(in dance)*; **2.** *cards:* queen.

**dama [x .] 1.** game of draughts, *Am.* game of checkers; **2.** *draughts:* king; ~ tahtası draughtboard, *Am.* checkerboard; ~ taşı **1.** *draughts:* man; **2.** *fig.* one who is often reassigned.

**damacana** demijohn, large bottle.

**damak** palate.

**damaklı** having a palate.

**damaksıl** palatal.

**damalı** chequered, *Am.* checkered.

**damar 1.** *biol.* vein, blood-vessel; **2.** *anat.* vessel, vas; **3.** *geol.* seam; **4.** ♀ vein; **5.** ✗ vein, streak; lode; **6.** *fig.* obstinacy, wil(l)fulness; **7.** *fig.* temper, nature, disposition; **8.** *fig.* streak; ~ sertliği ♥ arteriosclerosis; ~ tıkanıklığı embolism; -ına basmak *(b-nin)* to touch *one's* sore spot, to tread on *s.o.'s* corns; -ını bulmak to find the weak spot *(in a person).*

**damarlı 1.** veined, veiny; **2.** vascular; **3.** *fig.* obstinate.

**damarsız 1.** having no veins; **2.** *fig.* docile, biddable.

**damasko [. x .]** damask.

**damat,** -dı son-in-law; bridegroom.

**damdazlak [x . .]** completely bald.

**damga 1.** stamp, mark; hallmark; **2.** (rubber-)stamp; **3.** *fig.* stain, stigma; ~ basmak to stamp; ~ pulu revenue stamp; ~ resmi stamp duty; ~ vurmak to stamp.

**damgalamak 1.** to stamp; **2.** *fig.* to brand, to stigmatize.

**damgalanmak 1.** *pass of* damgalamak; **2.** *fig.* to be branded, to be stigmatized.

**damgalı 1.** stamped, marked; **2.** *fig.* branded, stigmatized.

**damıtık** distilled.

**damıtmak** to distil(l).

**damız** stable.

**damızlık 1.** animal kept for breeding; **2.** yeast, ferment.

**damla 1.** drop; ♥ drops; **2.** bit; **3.** medicine dropper; **4.** paralytic stroke; **5.** gout; ~ drop by drop, little by little, bit by bit; ~ inmek *(b-ne)* to have a stroke.

**damlalık 1.** ♥ dropper; **2.** eavestrough; **3.** dripstone.

**damlamak 1.** to drip, to tricle; **2.** *sl.* to turn up, to show up; damlaya damlaya göl olur *pro.* many a little makes a mickle.

**damlatmak** to drip, to pour out drop by drop; to distil(l).

**damlayakut,** -tu fine kind of ruby.

**damperli kamyon** dump-truck.

**damping** dumping; ~ yapmak to dump.

**-dan**[1] **1.** from; (out) of; due to, because of; since; **2.** than; **3.** through, by way of, via, by.

**-dan**[2] [ä] case of, receptacle of.

**-dan**[3] [ä] who knows.

**dan dun!** bang! bang!

**dana** calf; ~ eti veal; -lar gibi bağırmak to bawl, to shout blue murder; -nın kuyruğu kopacak! *fig.* the crucial moment will come.

**danaburnu,** -nu *zo.* mole cricket.

**dandini [x . .] 1.** *expression used when dandling a baby;* **2.** in a mess, untidy; ~ bebek childish person.

**dangalak** F blockhead, boor, dumb, loutish.

**dangalaklık** F idiocy, stupidity.

**dangıl dungul** boorish; ~ konuşmak to drivel.

**danış** consultation; conversation.

**danışık 1.** = danış; **2.** mutual agreement.

**danışıklı** sham, prearranged; ~ dövüş *fig.* **1.** sham fight; **2.** put-up job.

**danışma** information; inquiry; ~ bürosu information office.

**danışmak** *(bşi b-ne)* **1.** to consult *s.o.* about *s.th.;* **2.** to confer (about), to discuss.

**danışman** adviser, consultant, counselor.

**Danıştay** Council of State.

**Danimarka [. . x .]** *pr. n.* Denmark.

**Danimarkalı** Dane; Danish.

**daniska [. x .]** F the best, the finest; -sı *(bşin) sl.* the best of *s.th.;* o, işin -sını bilir he knows this from A to Z, he knows the A to Z of this.

**dank:** beynine *(or* kafasına) ~ demek *(or* etmek) to dawn (upon).

**dans** dance; ~ etm. to dance; ~ salonu ballroom.

**dansör** dancer *(man).*

**dansöz** dancer *(woman),* belly-dancer, danseuse.

**dantel(a)** lace(-work).

**dantelli** ornamented with lace.

**dapdaracık [x . . .]** *emph. of* dar(acık) very narrow *(or* tight).

**dar 1.** narrow; tight; **2.** scanty, scant; **3.** *fig.* straits, difficulty; **4.** *fig.* with difficulty, barely, only just; ~ açı Ậ acute angle; ~ boğaz *fig.* bottle-neck; ~ hat narrow-gauge line; ~ kafalı narrow-minded; ~ yetişmek to cut it fine; -a boğmak **1.** to take advantage of s.o.'s difficulties; **2.** to rush, to bring pressure (on); -da bulunmak (*or* kalmak) to be in financial straits.

**dâr** dwelling place, house, habitation.

**-dar** [ā] that has, possesses, holds.

**dara** [x .] tare; -sını almak to deduct the tare (-*ın* of).

**daraban** [. . -] throbbing, palpitation; pulsation.

**daracık** *emph.* of **dar** rather narrow (*or* tight).

**daradar** barely, very narrowly, only just.

**darağacı**, -nı gallows.

**daralmak 1.** to narrow, to become narrow (*or* tight); to shrink; **2.** to become scanty; to become restricted (*or* difficult); vaktimiz daraldı we are pushed for time.

**daraltmak** to narrow, to make narrower, to take in (*dress*), to reduce.

**darbe** blow, stroke; bir ~ indirmek to strike; hükümet -si coup d'état.

**darbelemek** *mst fig.* to sabotage.

**darbetmek** [x . .] **1.** to strike, to hit; **2.** to coin (*money*); **3.** to pulsate, to throb, to palpitate.

**darbevari** [. . - -] ✗ abrupt.

**darbımesel** proverb; ~ kabilinden proverbial.

**darbuka** [. x .] clay drum.

**dardağan** in utter confusion.

**dardarına** very narrowly, barely, only just.

**dargın** angry, irritated, cross, sulky.

**dargınlık** anger, irritability, sulk.

**darı** ✿ **1.** millet; **2.** P corn, maize; -sı başınıza! may your turn come next!, may you follow suit!.

**darılgan** easily offended (*or* hurt), huffy.

**darılmak 1.** to be offended (-*e* with), to take offence (-*e* at), to get cross (-*e* with), to get sulky (-*e* with); **2.** to resent; **3.** to scold; darılmaca yok! no offence!

**darıltmak** to give offence (-*i* to), to offend.

**darlaşmak 1.** to narrow; **2.** to become tight; **3.** to be limited, to be in straits.

**darlaştırmak 1.** to narrow, to make narrow; **2.** to restrict.

**darlatmak** *s.* darlaştırmak.

**darlık 1.** narrowness; **2.** *fig.* poverty, need, destitution.

**darmadağan, darmadağın** in utter confusion, in a terrible mess.

**darp**, -bı **1.** blow; **2.** coining (*money*); **3.** ♪ stroke; **4.** Ậ multiplication.

**darphane** mint.

**darülaceze** [- . . .‿.] poorhouse, hospice, workhouse.

**darülfünun** [- . . -] † university.

**darülharb** [- . .] the countries outside the dominion of Islam.

**Darüşşafaka** [- . . . .] *pr. n. name of a school for orphans in Istanbul.*

**dasnik** *sl.* pimp.

**-daş** *suffix implying fellowship or participation:* dindaş coreligionist.

**daülfil** [- . . -] ☤ elephantiasis.

**daülkelp**, -bi [ā] ☤ rabies, hydrophobia.

**daülrakıs**, -ksı [- . . .] ☤ St. Vitus's dance.

**daüssıla** [- . . .] homesickness, nostalgia.

**dava 1.** suit, lawsuit, action, case; **2.** trial; **3.** claim; assertion, allegation; complaint; **4.** thesis, preposition; matter, cause, problem, question; **5.** Ậ theorem; problem; ~ başı main argument; ~ eden ♋ plaintiff, claimant; litigant; ~ edilen ♋ defendant; litigant; ~ etm. (*b-ni*) to sue for *s.o.*, to bring *s.o.* to court, to go to law against *s.o.*; ~ vekili lawyer, attorney, barrister.

**davacı** ♋ plaintiff, claimant; litigant.

**davalı** ♋ **1.** defendant; **2.** litigant; **3.** contested, in dispute.

**davar 1.** sheep *or* goat; **2.** sheep *or* goats.

**davet**, -ti [ā] **1.** invitation; **2.** party, feast; **3.** ♋ summons; **4.** ✝ convocation; **5.** call; request; ~ etm. **1.** to invite, to call, to summon; to convoke; **2.** to provoke; **3.** to request; ~ yapmak to give a party, to feast.

**davetiye** [ā] **1.** invitation card; **2.** ♋ summons, citation.

**davetli** invited (guest).

**davetname** invitation card.

**davetsiz** uninvited; gatecrasher.

**davlumbaz 1.** paddlebox; **2.** chimney hood; ~ kılıklı *fig.* dressed up to the nines, dolled up.

**davranış** behavio(u)r, attitude.

**davranmak 1.** to behave, to act; **2.** to take action, to set about, to bestir o.s.; **3.** to make (for), to reach (for); **4.** to take pains.

**davudi** [- - -] bass (*voice*).

**davul** drum; ~ çalmak (*or* dövmek) **1.** to beat the drum; **2.** *fig.* to trumpet, to noise abroad; ~ gibi swollen; ~ zurna drum and pipe, with pomp; -un sesi uzaktan hoş gelir *pro.* distance lends enchantment.

**davulcu** drummer.

**Davut,** -du *pr. n.* **1.** David; **2.** *mf.*

**dayak 1.** beating, hiding, cudgeling, thrashing; **2.** ⊕ prop, support, shore; ~ atmak *(b-ne)* to give *s.o.* a beating *(or* hiding *or* thrashing); ~ kaçkını one who deserves a beating; ~ yemek to get a hiding *(or* beating *or* thrashing).

**dayaklık 1.** deserving a beating; **2.** ⊕ suitable as a prop.

**dayalı 1.** leaning (-e against); **2.** propped up, shored; ~ döşeli furnished *(house)*.

**dayamak 1.** to lean (-e against), to rest (-e on); to base (-e on); to hold (-e against); to draw up (-e against); **2.** to shore up, to prop up, to support; **3.** to present immediately; **4.** to thrust resolutely, to fling offensively; **5.** *s.* döşemek.

**dayanak 1.** (noktası) ✕ base; **2.** support; **3.** *phls.* substratum.

**dayanıklı** strong, resistant, lasting, enduring.

**dayanıksız** weak, not lasting, not resistant.

**dayanıksızlık** weakness.

**dayanılmaz 1.** irresistable; **2.** unbearable.

**dayanışma** solidarity.

**dayanışmak** to act with solidarity.

**dayanmak 1.** ⚹ *pass. of* dayamak; **2.** to lean (-e against, on); to push, to press (-e against, on); **3.** to rest, to be based (-e on, upon); **4.** to rely (-e on, upon), to be backed (by); to confide, to trust (-e in); **5.** to resist, to hold out; **6.** to endure, to last; **7.** to bear, to tolerate, to endure, to put up (-e with), to support; **8.** (bir yere) to reach, to arrive (-e in, at), to get (-e to); **9.** to step (-e on); **10.** to set about s.th. energetically; **11.** to go a long way, to last, to be enough; **12.** to arrive at the door (of); **13.** to be drawn up (-e against).

**dayatmak 1.** *caus. of* dayamak; **2.** to insist (on).

**dayı 1.** maternal uncle; **2.** *sl.* policeman, pig, cop; **3.** protector; **4.** pull, protection; **5.** *hist.* dey; -sı dümende he has a friend at court, he has friends in high places.

**dayızade** [. - .] cousin.

**daz 1.** bald(-headed); **2.** bare *(country)*.

**dazara dazar, dazıra dazır** in a great hurry, speedily.

**dazlak 1.** bald; **2.** bare, barren *(country)*; ~ kafalı bald-headed.

**dazlaklık** baldness.

**de** *s.* da; ...se ~ even if, although.

**-de** *s. a.* -de, ta, -te.

**debagat,** -ti [. - .] **1.** the trade of a tanner; **2.** tanning.

**debarkman** ✕ disembarkation.

**debboy** depot.

**debdebe** splendo(u)r, pomp, display.

**debdebeli** splendid, magnificent, resplendent, showy.

**debelenmek 1.** to thrash about, to kick about, to fidget about, to flounder; **2.** *fig.* to struggle desperately.

**debriyaj** ⊕ clutch; ~ pedalı clutch pedal.

**dede 1.** grandfather; **2.** ancestor, forefather; **3.** old man; **4.** sheikh.

**Dedeağaç,** -cı *pr. n.* Alexandroupolis.

**dedik** (one's) word, promise, what one says; dediği ~ olm. *(b-nin)* to abide by what one says, to be an obstinate fellow.

**dedikodu** gossip, tittle-tattle; backbiting; ~ etm. (*or* yapmak) to gossip; to backbite.

**dedikoducu** gossip, gossiper, backbiter.

**dedikodulu** gossipy *(news)*.

**dedirgin** unsettled, troubled, stirred up.

**def 1.** *s.* tef; **2.** *s.* defi.

**defa** time, turn; -larca again and again, repeatedly ,time after time; birkaç ~ on several occasions; çok ~ often.

**defalık:** bu ~ for this time.

**defetmek** [x . .] **1.** to repel, to repulse, to drive away, to push back, to rebuff; **2.** to expel, to eject, to dismiss; **3.** *phys.* to repel.

**defi,** -f'i **1.** repulsion, driving away; **2.** *phys.* repulsion; **3.** ⚔ defence; **4.** ⚹ refutation; defi bela kabilinden F so as to ward off an evil; defi hacet etm. to go to the toilet; defi tabii bowel movement, stool.

**defile** fashion show.

**defin,** -fni interment, burial.

**define** [¹] **1.** buried treasure; treasure; treasure-trove; **2.** *fig.* unexpected wealth.

**defineci** [. - .] treasure-seeker.

**deflasyon** deflation.

**defne** [x .] ⚘ bay-tree, laurel.

**defnetmek** [x . .] *(bir yere)* to bury, to inter.

**defo** flaw.

**defolmak** [x . .] to piss off, to clear out, to go away, to blow; defoll off with you!, piss off!

**defolu** flawed.

**defter 1.** notebook, exercise book, copybook; **2.** register, inventory; **3.** (account) book; **4.** -ler the rolls; **5.** list, catalogue; ~ açmak to open a subscription list; ~ tutmak to keep the books; -e geçirmek to enter in the book; defteri âmal *isl. myth.* list of an individual's good and bad acts; defteri kebir ledger.

**defterdar** [ᵃ] **1.** accountant; **2.** *hist.* minister of finance.

**değer 1.** value, worth; **2.** price; ~ biçmek to evaluate, to assess, to assay, to appraise; ~ vermek to esteem, to appreciate, to respect.

**değerbilir** appreciative.

**değerbilmez** inapprecive.

**değerlemek** to esteem highly, to respect.

**değerlendirmek 1.** to appraise, to evaluate, to assess; **2.** to estimate; **3.** to utilize, to turn to (good) account, to put to good use.

**değerlenmek 1.** *pass. of* değerlemek; **2.** to appreciate, to increase in value.

**değerli 1.** valuable, precious; **2.** worthy, talented; **3.** estimable.

**değersiz** worthless, valueless.

**değersizlik** worthlessness.

**değil 1.** not; **2.** no; **3.** not only, let alone; **4.** not caring.

**değin** until, till; bugüne ~ until today, up to now.

**değinmek** to touch (-e on).

**değirmen 1.** mill; **2.** grinder, grinding machine; **3.** *sl.* watch.

**değirmenci** miller, millwright.

**değirmentaşı** millstone.

**değirmi 1.** round, circular; **2.** square *(cloth).*

**değiş** exchange; ~ (*or* ~ tokuş) etm. *(bşi bşle)* to exchange *s.th.* for *s.th.*, to barter *s.th.* for *s.th.*

**değişen** changeable; ~ hareket (*or* devim) *phys.* irregular motion.

**değişici** changeable.

**değişik 1.** different, changed; **2.** novel, original; **3.** varied; **4.** exchanged, substituted.

**değişiklik 1.** difference; **2.** change, variation, amendment, alteration; ~ olsun diye for a change.

**değişim** variation.

**değişken 1.** changeable, changeful, mutable; **2.** Å variable.

**değişkenlik** changeableness, changefulness, mutability.

**değişkin** modified.

**değişmek 1.** to change, to alter, to vary, to be replaced; **2.** to substitute; **3.** to exchange, to barter *(ile* for).

**değişmez** unchangeable, invariable; constant, stable.

**değiştirgeç** converter; transformer.

**değiştirmek 1.** to change, to alter, to shift, to modify; **2.** to exchange *(ile* for).

**değme 1.** contact, touch; **2.** every, any.

**değmede** [x . .] unlikely.

**değmek,** (-er) **1.** to touch; **2.** to reach, to hit,

to attain; **3.** to be worth, to be worth-while; **4.** (yüreğine *or* içine) to take to heart, to affect.

**değnek 1.** stick, rod, cane, wand; **2.** thrashing, hiding; ~ yemek to get the cane.

**değneklemek** to cane, to give the cane.

**deh!** giddap!; ~ deyip salıvermek F to kick out.

**deha** [ā] genius, sagacity; ~ sahibi ingenious.

**dehakâr** [. - -] ingenious.

**dehalet,** -ti [ā] submission.

**-de hali** *gr.* locative.

**dehlemek 1.** to urge on, to drive on *(animal);* **2.** F to send s.o. packing, to fire, to oust, to give s.o. the sack.

**dehlenmek 1.** to be urged on *(animal);* **2.** F to be fired, to get the sack.

**dehlíz 1.** corridor, entrance-hall; **2.** *anat.* ear-passage; vestibule.

**dehşet,** -ti **1.** terror, horror, awe, dread; **2.** marvel(l)ous; **3.** wow!, well, I'm blowed!: ~ saçmak to · horrify, to terrorize.

**dehşetli 1.** terrible, dreadful, horrible, awful; **2.** marvel(l)ous, formidable, tremendous.

**dejenere** degenerate; ~ etm. to make degenerate; ~ olm. to degenerate.

**dejenereleşmek** to degenerate.

**dek** until, as far as.

**dekagram** Å decagram.

**dekalitre** Å decaliter.

**dekametre** Å decameter.

**dekan** dean *(of a faculty).*

**dekanlık 1.** deanship; **2.** dean's office.

**dekar** measure of land *(0.247 acres).*

**dekatlon** *sports:* decathlon.

**deklanşör** *phot.* trigger, shutter release button.

**dekolte 1.** low-neck, low-cut, decolleté; **2.** licentious, indecent, immodest; ~ konuşmak *fig.* not to mince matters.

**dekont,** -tu statement of account, deduction.

**dekor** décor, setting; scenery.

**dekorasyon** decoration.

**dekoratif** decorative.

**dekoratör** decorator.

**dekorcu** (set) designer.

**dekovil** narrow-gauge railroad.

**dekupaj** *film:* scenario, *Am.* script.

**delalet,** -ti **1.** guidance; **2.** indication; denotation; signification; **3.** mediation; ~ etm. **1.** to guide (-e to); **2.** to show, to indicate, to denote; ... -iyle through, by the agency of; care of (c/o).

**deldirmek** to have s.th. bored.

**delegosyon** delegation.

**delege** delegate, representative.

**delgeç** punch.

**delgi** drill, gimlet.

**deli** 1. mad, insane, lunatic, crazy; 2. whimsical, eccentric; 3. foolish, inconsiderate; rash, foolhardy; ~ alacası motley, variegated; ~ baş obstinate, wil(l)-ful; ~ çıkmak 1. to go mad; 2. *fig.* to fly into a rage, to blow one's top; ~ divane crazy (about); nuts (over); ~ etm. to drive one out of one's wits, to drive s.o. mad; ~ gibi like mad, madly; ~ ırmak torrential river; ~ olm. 1. to be crazy (-*e* about), to be wild (-*e* about), to be nuts (-*e* over); 2. to fly into a rage; ~ saçması tommy-rot; ~ pazarı in a pickle; -ye dönmek to throw one's hat in the air.

**delibozuk** unbalanced, fitful; inconstant.

**delice** 1. somewhat mad, crazy; 2. madly, crazily; 3. crazy, mad *(act)*; 4. wild *(plant)*; 5. (otu) ♀ darnel, rye grass; ergoted rye.

**delicesine** 1. madly, crazily; 2. passionately *(love)*.

**delidolu** indiscreet, inconsiderate, thoughtless, rash, reckless.

**deliduman** reckless, daredevil, foolhardy.

**delifişek** unbalanced, flippant, flighty, giddy.

**delik** 1. hole, opening, orifice; 2. pierced, bored; 3. *anat.* foramen; 4. *sl.* prison, cooler, stir, clink, choky; ~ açmak to hole, to bore, to pierce; ~ deşik full of holes; ~ deşik etm. to riddle;·deliğe girmek *sl.* to go to clink; deliğe tıkamak *sl.* tö put into clink, to jug.

**delikanlı** youth, young man, youngster.

**delikanlılık** youth; ·youthfulness.

**delikli** 1. holey; 2. sieve, skimmer, strainer.

**delikliler** *zo.* foraminifera.

**deliksiz** 1. without a hole; 2. *fig.* sound *(sleep)*; ~ çıkarmak *fig.* to carry out faultlessly.

**delil** [ı] 1. ♣ proof, evidence; 2. guide; 3. indication, sign; ~ göstermek to adduce proofs.

**delilenmek** to become mad, to behave madly, to act crazily.

**deli'lik** 1. madness, insanity; mania; 2. folly, foolishness, eccentricity.

**delinmek** 1. *pass. of* delmek; 2. to be holed *(or* perforated); to become worn through; to burst; 3. to be pierced; 4. to get a puncture, to be punctured.

**deliorman** a vast and dense forest.

**deliotu** ♀ alyssum, madwort.

**delirmek** to go mad, to become insane.

**delirtmek** to drive mad.

**delişmen** madcap, spoiled, over-impulsive, flighty, giddy.

**delişmenlik** impulsiveness, giddiness.

**delk**, -ki *phys.* friction.

**delme** 1. *vn. of* delmek; 2. bored, pierced, perforated, punched; 3. P waistcoat; ~ kudreti ✗ penetrating power.

**delmek**, (-er) to hole, to pierce, to bore, to break through *(a.* ✗*)*; delip geçmek to pierce through, to penetrate.

**delta** *geogr.* delta.

**deltakası** *anat.* deltoid muscle.

**dem¹** blood, hemorrhage; ~ dökmek to menstruate.

**dem²** 1. breath; gust, blast; 2. time, moment, instant; 3. alcoholic drink; 4. sip, draught; ~ çekmek 1. *(of birds)* to warble; 2. *co.* to drink; ~ tutmak ♪ to accompany music; ~ vurmak (*bşden*) to talk at random about s.th.

**dem³** steeping; ~ çekmek to steep *(tea)*; -i çok well steeped, strong *(tea)*.

**demagog** demagogue.

**demagoji** demagogy.

**deme** 1. *vn. of* demek; 2. meaning; -m o ~ değil that is not what I mean, that is not my meaning.

**demeç** statement; speech; -te bulunmak to make a statement.

**demek¹** 1. to say (-*e* to); 2. to tell, to mention *(-e* to); 3. to think, to be of the opinion; 4. to call, to name; 5. to mean; deme yahu! you don't say so!; oh, don't!; dememek not to pay attention, not to heed; demeye kalmamak no sooner than, as soon as; derken 1. while saying; 2. while trying to, when intending to; 3. just at that moment; then; desene, desenize F that means, that is to say, then; deyip geçmek to underrate, to underestimate; diyecek yok (*bşe*) it's fine, it's OK.

**demek²**, **demek ki** so, thus, in this case, therefore, that means (to say).

**demet**, -ti 1. bunch, bouquet *(flowers)*; 2. bundle, faggot; 3. sheaf *(of grain)*; wisp; 4. *phys.* bundle *(of rays)*; 5. ♀ corymb; ~ ~ in bunches, in sheaves.

**demetlemek** to bunch, to sheaf.

**demevi** [ı] full-blooded; sanguine.

**demin** [x .] just now, a second ago.

**demincek** [x . .] *emph. of* demin.

**deminden** [x . .] = demin.

**deminki** [x . .] foregoing, of a second ago.

**demir** 1. iron; 2. anchor; 3. iron part of anything; 4. made of iron; 5. heelplate;

**6.** irons, fetters; **7.** grille (of a window); **8.** bar (of a door); **9.** ♀ mf.; ~ almak **1.** ⚓ to weigh anchor; **2.** F to go away, to hop it; ~ atmak **1.** ⚓ to let go (or drop or cast) the anchor, to anchor; **2.** fig. to overstay one's welcome; ~ gibi **1.** strong, ironlike; **2.** very cold; ~ kırı iron grey (horse); ~ kırıntısı scrap iron; ~ leblebi fig. tough (or hard) nut to crack; ~ resmi anchorage; ~ taramak ⚓ to drag the anchor; ~ tavında dövülür pro. strike while the iron is hot; -de yatmak ⚓ to lie at anchor; -e vurmak to fetter, to chain.

**demirbaş 1.** furnishings, inventory, fixtures; **2.** old timer, fixture (person); **3.** inflexible; obstinate.

**demirci** blacksmith,   iron-monger, Am. hardware dealer; ~ ocağı smithy, forge.

**demircilik 1.** ironworking; **2.** hardware business.

**demirhane** [ā] ironworks, iron-foundry.

**demirhindi 1.** ♀ tamarind; **2.** sl. stingy, mean, niggardly.

**demiri** iron-grey.

**demirkapan** magnet.

**Demirkazık** North Star, Polaris, Polestar.

**demirlemek 1.** to bolt and bar (door); **2.** ⚓ to anchor.

**demirli 1.** ⚓ anchored, at anchor; **2.** ferriferous, containing iron; **3.** bolted; chained; **4.** barred.

**demirlibeton** reinforced concrete.

**demirpası,** -nı iron rust (colour).

**demirperde** pol. Iron Curtain.

**demiryeri,** -ni berth, anchorage, moorage.

**demiryol** s. demiryolu.

**demiryolcu** railwayman.

**demiryolculuk** railwaymanship.

**demiryolu,** -nu railway, railroad.

**demlemek** to steep, to brew (tea).

**demlendirmek** s. demlemek.

**demlenmek 1.** to be steeped (tea); **2.** co. to carouse, to imbibe.

**demli** well steeped, strong (tea).

**demlik** teapot.

**demode** outmoded, out-of-date, old-fashioned, démodé.

**demografi** demography.

**demokrasi** democracy.

**demokrat,** -tı democrat(ic); ♀ Parti Democrat Party.

**demokratik** democratic.

**demokratlaşmak** to become democratic.

**demokratlık** democracy.

**demontabl** ⊕ demountable.

**demontaj** ⊕ disassembly, dismantlement.

**demonte** disassembly, dismantlement; ~

⌐tm. to disassemble, to dismantle.

**-den** s.a. -dan, -tan, -ten.

**denaet,** -ti [ā] baseness, cowardice, meanness, vileness.

**denaetkâr** mean, vile.

**denden** ditto mark.

**denek 1.** † proved, tried; **2.** psych. subject (of an experiment).

**denektaşı,** -nı touch-stone.

**deneme 1.** trial, test, experiment; **2.** essay.

**denemeci** essayist.

**denemek 1.** to test, to try, to experiment; to attempt; **2.** to tempt.

**denenmek** pass. of denemek.

**denet 1.** control, supervision; **2.** inspection; audit; **3.** trial projection (of a finished film).

**denetçi** controller, supervisor; inspector, auditor.

**denetim 1.** control, supervision; **2.** inspection; auditing.

**denetlemek** to check, to oversee, to supervise, to control.

**deney** ⌐, phys. test, experiment.

**deneyim** experimentation.

**deneykap** ⌐ test tube.

**deneysel** experimental; empirical.

**deneyselcilik** experimentalism; empiricism.

**deneyüstü** phls. transcendental.

**denge** balance, equilibrium.

**dengelemek** to balance, to equilibrate, to stabilize.

**dengeli** balanced; stable, stabilized.

**dengesiz** unbalanced, out of balance; unstable.

**-den hali** gr. ablative.

**deni** [ī] ⚑ base, despicable, vile.

**denilmek** pass. of demek **1.** to be said; **2.** to be called, to be named; denilen so-called, would-be.

**deniz 1.** sea; ocean; **2.** maritime, marine, naval, nautical; **3.** waves; high sea; swell; **4.** fig. expanse, tract; ~ baskını high tide; tidal wave, tsunami; ~ birliği naval unit; ~ buzulu ice floe; ~ feneri lighthouse; ~ kurdu fig. old salt, sea dog; ~ kuvvetleri naval forces; ~ mili nautical (or sea) mile; ~ sigortası maritime insurance; ~ subayı naval officer; ~ tutmak (b-ni) to get seasick; ~ üssü naval base; ~ yolları maritime lines; -de balık fig. a bird in the bush; -de kum, onda para he is lousy with money, he has got pots of money; -den bir avuç su çibi like a drop in the bucket (or ocean); -den çıkmış balığa dönmek to feel like a fish out of water; -e düşen yılana sarılır pro.

a drowning man will clutch at a straw.
**denizaltı,** -nı 1. submarine; 2. submerged;
3. deep-sea *(current)*.
**denizaltıcı** submariner.
**denizanası** *zo.* jellyfish, medusa.
**denizaşırı** overseas.
**denizatı,** -nı *zo.* seahorse.
**denizayısı,** -nı *zo.* manatee, sea cow.
**denizbilim** *geogr.* oceanography.
**denizcöceği** *zo.* shrimp.
**denizci** seaman, sailor.
**denizcilik** 1. navigation, sailing; 2. seamanship.
**denizçakısı,** -nı *zo.* razor clam.
**denizçulluğu,** -nu *zo.* sanderling.
**denizdantell,** -ni *zo.* millepore.
**denizel** *geogr.* marine; naval.
**denizgergedanı,** -nı *zo.* narwhal.
**deniziğnesi,** -ni *zo.* European pipefish.
**denizineği,** -ni *zo.* sea cow.
**denizkaplumbağası,** -nı *zo.* sea turtle.
**denizkestanesi,** -ni *zo.* sea urchin.
**denizkırlangıcı,** -nı *zo.* tern.
**denizkızı,** -nı *myth.* mermaid, siren, nixie, nymph.
**denizkulağı,** -nı lagoon.
**denizsel** *geogr.* maritime.
**denizyıldızı,** -nı starfish.
**denk,** -gi 1. bale; 2. in equilibrium, equal, balanced; 3. suitable; match; 4. ♣ equivalent; 5. counterpoise; trim; ~ etm. 1. to balance, to equilibrate; 2. ♨ to trim *(a boat)*; ~ gelmek to balance, to be in equipoise; to be suitable, to be timely; dengiyle karşılamak to retaliate, to pay s.o. in his own *(or* the same) coin, to reciprocate.
**denklem** ♣ equation.
**denklemek** 1. to make up in bales, to tie up; 2. to balance.
**denkleşmek** to become well balanced, to be in equilibrium.
**denkleştirmek** 1. to bring into balance, to equalize; 2. to find, to put together *(money)*.
**denli** tractable, tactful; ~ densiz söz söylemek to talk out of turn, to speak offhandedly.
**denmek** *pass. of* demek.
**densiz** tactless, lacking in manners.
**densizleşmek** to become tactless.
**densizlik** tactlessness.
**denyo** *sl.* fool, ass, idiot.
**deontoloji** deontology.
**depar** flying start.
**deplasman:** ~ maçı away match.
**depo** [x .] 1. depot; 2. store, warehouse; ~ etm. to store.

**depocu** warehouseman; stockman.
**depolamak** to store.
**depozit(o)** deposit, security.
**deppoy** *s.* debboy.
**deprem** earthquake; ~ bölgesi seismic zone.
**deprembilim** seismology.
**depremyazar** seismograph.
**depresyon** *psych.* depression.
**depreşmek** to move, to rise, to reappear.
**depreştirmek** to stir, to reawaken; to renew.
**derakap** [x . .] instantly, immediately afterwards.
**derayman** derailment; ~ etm. to derail *(train)*.
**derbeder** 1. vagrant, tramp, vagabond; 2. untidy, slovenly, disorderly, irregular.
**derbederlik** vagrancy, vagabondage.
**derbent,** -di defile, pass.
**dercetmek** [x . .] to insert, to include.
**derç,** -ci insertion, inclusion.
**derdetmek** [x . .] to grieve.
**dere** 1. brook, runnel, rivulet, stream, creek; 2. valley; ~ tepe up hill and down dale; ~ tepe demeyip over hedge and ditch; -den tepeden konuşmak to have a chitchat, to have a small talk.
**derebeyi,** -ni 1. feudal lord; 2. *fig.* bully, tyrant.
**derebeylik** 1. local despotate; 2. feudalism.
**derece** 1. degree, grade; 2. stage, step, stair, rank; 3. F thermometer; 4. so... *(that)*; ~ ~ by degrees, gradually.
**derecelenmek** to become graded.
**dereceli** graded.
**dereke** ♘ low stratum.
**dereotu,** -nu ♣ dill.
**dergâh** dervish convent.
**dergi** magazine, periodical, review.
**derhal** [x .] at once, immediately, right away.
**deri** 1. skin, hide; 2. leather; 3. peel, rind; -sine sığmaz *fig.* he is too big for his boots; -sini yüzmek 1. to skin, to flay; 2. *fig.* to strip, to rob; 3. to torture to death.
**derialtı,** -nı *anat.* subcutaneous.
**deribilim** dermatology.
**derici** leather dealer.
**dericilik** leather trade.
**derilenmek** to heal up *(wound)*.
**derin** 1. deep; depth; 2. profound; ~ ~ deeply, soundly *(sleep)*; ~ ~ dalmak to be plunged in thought; ~ ~ düşünmek to be in a brown study; ~ saygılarımı sunarım yours faithfully, very truly yours.
**derinlemesine, derinliğine** in depth, deeply.

**derinleşmek 1.** to deepen, to get deep; **2.** to specialize (*-de* in); **3.** to fade away with distance (*sound*).

**derinleştirmek** to deepen (*a. fig.*).

**derinlik 1.** depth; deepness; depths; **2.** profundity; **3.** *phot.* depth of focus.

**derişik** concentrated.

**derk, -ki** ⚹ comprehension.

**derkenar** [ã] marginal note, postscript.

**derleme 1.** compilation, miscellany; **2.** collected, selected; **3.** anthology.

**derlemek** to compile, to collect, to gather; ~ toplamak to tidy up, *Am.* to straighten up, to put in order, to clear away.

**derlenmek 1.** *pass. of* derlemek; **2.** to compose o.s., to pull o.s. together; derle-nip toplanmak **1.** to pull o.s. together, to compose o.s.; **2.** to get ready.

**derleyici** compiler; anthologist.

**derli toplu** tidy, in order; well coordinated.

**derman** [ã] **1.** strength, energy, power; **2.** remedy, cure, medicine; ~ aramak to seek a remedy; ~ bulmak to find a remedy (*-e* for); ~ olm. to be a remedy, to cure (*-e* for); -ım yok I am bushed.

**dermansız** [ã] **1.** exhausted, feeble, weak, bushed; **2.** incurable, irremediable.

**dermansızlaşmak** to get feeble.

**dermansızlık 1.** exhaustion, feebleness; **2.** incurability, debility.

**derme 1.** *vn. of* dermek; **2.** collection; **3.** gathered, compiled, collected; ~ çatma **1.** hastily put up, jerry-built; **2.** scraps, odds and ends.

**dermek** to pick (*flower*), to gather, to compile, to pick up.

**dermeyan** [ã] ⚹ in the midst, under discussion; ~ etm. to put forward.

**dernek** association, club, society.

**derpiş etm.** [ı] to put forward, to consider, to bear in mind, to take into consideration.

**ders 1.** lesson, class, lecture; **2.** warning, example, moral; ~ almak **1.** to take lessons (*-den* from); **2.** to learn a lesson (*-den* by); **3.** to take warning (*-den* from); ~ anlatmak to give a lesson, to teach, to lecture; ~ çalışmak to study; ~ kitabı textbook, schoolbook; ~ odası classroom; -i asmak to cut a class, to skip class; bu sana ~ olsun let this be a warning to you.

**dershane** [ã] **1.** classroom, schoolroom; **2.** private institute offering specialized courses.

**dert, -di 1.** pain, suffering, disease, illness, malady; **2.** trouble, sorrow, grief, cares, worries, affliction, woe; annoyance, grievance; **3.** tumo(u)r, boil; ~ çekmek to

suffer; ~ dökmek to unbosom o.s.; ~ ortağı confidant, fellow-sufferer; ~ yanmak *fig.* to unbosom o.s.; derde girmek to get into trouble, to get into hot water; derdine düşmek (*bşin*) to be quite taken up with *s.th.*; derdini dökmek to unbosom o.s., to air one's grievances.

**dertlenmek** to be pained (by), to be sorry (because of), to have troubles.

**dertleşmek** to have a heart-to-heart talk (*ile* with).

**dertli 1.** pained; sorrowful, wretched; **2.** aggrieved, complaining; **3.** troubled.

**dertop:** ~ etm. to gather together; ~ olm. to roll into a ball.

**dertsiz** untroubled, free from trouble.

**derttaş** confidant.

**deruhte etm.** to undertake, to take upon o.s.

**derun** [û] ⚹ inside, interior; mind, soul, heart.

**deruni** [. - -] ⚹ **1.** internal, inner; **2.** cordial, sincere.

**derviş 1.** dervish; **2.** *fig.* humble, contented, tolerant; -in fikri ne ise, zikri de odur he has a bee in his bonnet; sabreden ~ muradına ermiş everything comes to him who waits.

**dervişmeşrep, -bı** unconventional; tolerant, modest.

**derya** [ã] **1.** sea, ocean; **2.** *fig.* very learned man.

**desen 1.** design; ornament; **2.** drawing.

**desenli** figured.

**desigram** decigram.

**desilitre** deciliter.

**desimetre** decimeter.

**desinatör** stylist.

**desise** [ı] trick, intrigue, device, plot; ~ çevirmek to plot, to intrigue, to trick.

**despot, -tu** despot(ic).

**despothane** office and residence of a despot.

**despotluk** despotism.

**dessas** [ã] trickster, intriguer.

**destan** [ã] **1.** story, legend, epic; **2.** ballad, song; ~ olm. *contp.* to become very famous.

**destanlaşmak** to become legendary.

**destar** [ã] turban.

**deste 1.** bunch, bouquet; packet; wisp; **2.** a quire of paper; **3.** handle, hilt; ~ başı choice specimen put on the top of a package of goods; ~ ~ in bunches; in packets; by dozens.

**destek 1.** support; **2.** prop; beam; **3.** ⚓ crutch; **4.** ✗ reinforcement; ~ vurmak to put a prop (*-e* to), to prop up, to shore up.

**desteklemek** 1. to support, to prop, to shore up; 2. to root for *(a team)*.

**destekli** supported, propped up.

**destelemek** to bundle (up).

**destroyer** [. x .] destroyer.

**destur** [ü] 1. permission; leave; 2. *int.* by your leave!, make way!, gangway!

**desturun** [x . .] begging your pardon!

**deşarj** discharge; ~ olm. 1. . to be discharged; 2. *fig.* to unbosom o.s.

**deşelemek** to scratch up.

**deşik** 1. pierced, burst open; 2. hole; 3. *s.* delik deşik.

**deşilmek** 1. *pass. of* deşmek; 2. to be lanced, to open.

**deşmek** 1. to lance *(boil)*; 2. *fig.* to open up, to rake up *(a painful subjcet)*; 3. to dig up, to dig into.

**detay** detail.

**detektif** detective.

**detektör** ♪ detector.

**deterjan** detergent.

**determinant** A determinant.

**determinizm** determinism.

**dev** 1. ogre; demon, fiend, devil; 2. giant; gigantic; ~ gibi gigantic, huge, enormous.

**deva** [ā] remedy, cure, medicine.

**devali** [. - -] ⚕ varicose.

**devalüasyon** devaluation.

**devam** [ā] 1. continuation, permanence; 2. duration; 3. attendance, frequenting; 4. constancy, assiduity; 5. *int.* go on!; ~ etm. 1. to go on, to last; to continue, to keep on; to carry on, to go on (-e with); 2. to attend, to follow *(classes)*; 3. to extend (-*den*, -e *kadar* from, to); 4. to persevere; ~ eden on-going; -ı var to be continued.

**devamlı** [ā] 1. continuous, lasting, steady, unbroken, uninterrupted; 2. constant, assiduous; regular; ~ sulh continuous peace.

**devamlılık** continuity; assiduousness.

**devamsız** 1. discontinuous; 2. inconstant; 3. irregular *(in attendance)*.

**devamsızlık** discontinuity; absenteeism.

**devasa** [. - -] ⚒ gigantic, giant-like.

**devaynası**, -nı convex *(or* magnifying) mirror.

**deve** zo. camel; ~ gibi huge and awkward; ~ kini *fig.* deep-seated ranco(u)r; ~ olm. F to disappear *(money, etc.)*; ~ yapmak co. to embezzle; ~ yürekli coward; -de kulak a drop in the bucket *(or* ocean).

**devebağırtan** *fig.* steep and stony road.

**deveci** 1. camel driver, cameleer; 2. camel owner.

**devedikeni** ♀ thistle.

**devekuşu**, -nu zo. ostrich.

**develope** etm. *phot.* to develop.

**deveran** [ā] 1. rotation, circulation; 2. revolution; ~ etm. to circulate, to rotate.

**deveranıdem** blood circulation.

**devetabanı**, nı ♀ philodendron, monstera.

**devetımarı**, -nı *fig.* superficial.

**devetüyü** 1. camel hair; 2. camel colo(u)red.

**devim** *biol., phys.* movement, motion, flux.

**devingen** mobile, dynamic, active.

**devinim** movement, motion, action.

**devinmek** to move.

**devir**, -vri 1. period, epoch, era; 2. cycle, rotation; 3. circuit, circumference, periphery; 4. tour, turn, revolution; 5. transfer, turning over; devri âlem seyahati globe-trotting.

**devirli** periodic.

**devirmek** 1. to overturn, to knock down, to turn over; 2. to overthrow, to throw down; 3. to upset. to capsize; 4. to tilt to one side; 5. to drink down, to toss off, to drink to the dregs 6. to read from cover to cover *(a book)*.

**devlet**, -ti 1. state; government; power; 2. prosperity, success, good luck; ~ adamı statesman; ~ başkanı president; ~ hazinesi state treasury, Exchequer; ~ hizmeti government *(or* public *or* civil) service; ~ kuşu windfall, unexpected good luck; ~ memuru civil servant. government official: ~ reisi head of state: ~ tahvili state bond; -le! good luck to you!

**devletçe** on the part of the government.

**devletçi** partisan of state control, favo(u)ring state control, etatist.

**devletçilik** etatism, state control.

**devletleştirmek** to nationalize, to collectivize.

**devralmak** to take over.

**devran** [ā] 1. time, age, epoch; 2. fate, wheel of fortune; ~ sürmek to live happily in prosperity.

**devre** 1. period; term, epoch; 2. session *(of Parliament)*; 3. cycle; 4. ♪ circuit; 5. *sports:* half time.

**devren** [x .] as a sublet, as a sublease, by cession. by continuation of the present contract: ~ kiralık subletting.

**devretmek** [x . .] 1. to turn over, to transfer (-e to); 2. to sublet.

**devri** 1. rotatory; 2. ♫, A periodic(al), cyclical.

**devrik 1.** folded, turned over; **2.** inverted *(sentence)* **3.** overthrown; ~ yaka turn--down collar.

**devrilmek 1.** *pass. of* devirmek; **2.** to be overturned; to capsize; to be overthrown *(government)*.

**devrim 1.** revolution; reform; **2.** folding; curve, bend.

**devrimci** revolutionary, revolutionist.

**devrimcilik** revolutionism.

**devrisi** = ertesi.

**devriye 1.** anniversary; **2.** beat, patrol, police round; ~ arabası patrol car; ~ gezmek to go the rounds, to walk the beat, to patrol.

**devşirmek 1.** to collect, to pick, to gather; **2.** to fold, to roll up.

**devvar** [ā] revolving, rotating; ~ köprü swing-bridge.

**deyim** idiom, phrase, expression.

**deyiş 1.** way of speaking; **2.** a kind of folk song; poem; **3.** expression; statement, report.

**deyyus** [ū] pander, cuckold.

**dezenfekte** disinfected; ~ etm. to disinfect.

**dılı,** -l'ı **1.** *geom.* side; **2.** *anat.* rib.

**dımdızlak** [x . .] **1.** naked, bare, nude; **2.** destitute; empty-handed; **3.** *sl.* stony--broke.

**dırdır** grumbling; nagging; ~ etm. to nag, to grumble.

**dırdırcı** nag, nagger, grumbler, carper.

**dırdırlanmak** to murmur, to babble, to grouch, to mutter to o.s.

**dırıltı 1.** grumbling, snarling; **2.** squabble; ~ çıkarmak to cause a squabble.

**dırlanmak** to complain, to talk annoyingly, to gripe.

**dırlaşmak** to squabble in undertones.

**dış 1.** outside, exterior; **2.** outer space; **3.** external, outer; **4.** foreign; **5.** *geom.* circumscribed; ~ haberler foreign news: ~ hat **1.** external line: **2.** international line *(a. teleph.)*; ~ kapının dış mandalı *fig.* a very distant relative; ~ lastik *mot.* tyre, *Am.* tire, casing; ~ taraf outside: ~ ticaret foreign trade .

**dışadönük** *psych.* extrovert.

**dışalım** importation.

**dışarı 1.** out; outside, exterior; **2.** outdoor; out of doors; **3.** provinces; the country; **4.** abroad. foreign lands; ~ gitmek **1.** to go out; **2.** to go abroad; -da outside; abroad; -dan from the outside; from a-broad; -ya abroad; towards the outside.

**dışbükey** convex.

**dışderi 1.** ectoderm; **2.** ♀ exodermis.

**dışık** ♈ scoria.

**dışişleri,** -ni *pol.* foreign *(or external)* affairs; ♀ Bakanlığı Ministry of Foreign Affairs.

**dışkı** feces.

**dışkılık** cloaca.

**dışmerkez** *geol.* epicenter.

**dışmerkezli** *geom.* eccentric.

**dışplazma** *biol.* ectoplasm.

**dışsatım** exportation.

**dız** buzz, hum, whizz; ~ etm. to buzz, to hum, to whizz.

**dızdız 1.** = dız; **2.** *sl.* swindling, trickery.

**dızlanmak** to keep on humming to o.s.

**diba** [- -] brocade; silk tissue.

**dibek** large stone *or* wooden mortar; ~ kahvesi coffee ground in a mortar.

**Dicle** *pr. n.* Tigris.

**didaktik 1.** didactic; **2.** didactics.

**didik** teased out, pulled to shreds; ~ ~ etm. **1.** *s.* didiklemek; **2.** to pull to pieces; ~ ~ doğramak to shred, to cut to shreds.

**didiklemek 1.** to tear to pieces; **2.** to pick into fibers and shreds; **3.** to put in disorder.

**didinmek 1.** to toil, to wear o.s. out; **2.** to fret.

**didişmek** to scrap, to scuffle, to quarrel, to bicker *(ile* with).

**diferansiyel** *mot.* differential gear.

**difteri** diphtheria.

**diftong** *gr.* diphthong.

**diğer 1.** other, another; different; **2.** next, succeeding; ~ taraftan on the other hand.

**dik 1.** perpendicular; **2.** upright, straight, stiff; **3.** steep; **4.** fixed, intent, penetrating *(look);* **5.** *geom.* right; **6.** obstinate, contrary; ~ açı ⅄ right angle; ~ aşağı straight down; ~ başlı pig-headed, obstinate; ~ ~ bakmak to stare (-e at), to glare (-e at), to gaze (-e at), to look daggers; ~ ~ cevap vermek to retort, to answer back; ~ dörtgen ⅄ rectangle; ~ kafalı pig-headed, obstinate, cussed; ~ üçgen *geom.* right triangle; -ine dalan uçak dive-bomber; -ine gitmek *(b-nin)* to do just the opposite of what one is asked for; to be pig-headed; -ine tıraş **1.** shaving against the grain; **2.** F utterly boring talk.

**diken 1.** thorn; spine; **2.** sting; **3.** thornbush; **4.** *fig.* obstacle, hindrance; ~ üstünde olmak *fig.* to be on tenterhooks.

**dikence** *zo.* stickleback.

**dikendudu,** -nu ♀ blackberry.

**dikenli** thorny, prickly; ~ tel barbed wire.

**dikensi** spinoid, spinelike.

**dikensiz** without thorns; spineless; ~ gül olmaz there is no rose without a thorn.

**dikey** *geom.* vertical, perpendicular.
**dikici 1.** cobbler, shoe-repairer; **2.** tailor:
**dikili 1.** sewn; stitched; **2.** planted, set; **3.** erected, set up.
**dikilitaş** obelisk.
**dikilmek 1.** *pass. of* dikmek; **2.** to stand stiff, to post o.s., to plant o.s.; **3.** to become erect *(penis)*.
**dikim** *vn. of* dikmek sewing; planting; ~ evi (*or* yurdu) sewing workshop; ~ zamanı planting time.
**dikimhane** [ā] = dikim evi.
**dikine** vertically, upright.
**dikiş** *vn. of* dikmek *part.* **1.** sewing. stitching; seam; **2.** *anat.* suture: **3.** gulp: ~ dikmek to sew; ~ iğnesi sewing needle; ~ kaynağı ⊕ welding seam; ~ kutusu sewing box; ~ makinesi sewing machine; ~ yeri **1.** seam; **2.** ✶ stitch scars.
**dikişçi** seamstress, dressmaker.
**dikişli** sewed, stitched; spliced.
**dikişsiz** seamless.
**dikit** *geol.* stalagmite.
**dikiz** *sl.* peeping, look; ~ aynası rear view mirror; ~ etm. (*or* geçmek) to peep.
**dikizci** *sl.* peeping Tom, voyeur.
**dikizlemek** *sl.* to peep.
**dikkat, -ti 1.** attention, care; **2.** take care!, look out!; ~ çekmek to attract attention, to call attention (-*e* to); ~ etm. **1.** to pay attention (-*e* to), to note, to notice, to mind; **2.** to be careful (-*e* with); ~ kesilmek to be all ears; -*e* almak to take note (-*i* of). to take into consideration; -*e* şayan note-worthy, remarkable; -*i* çekmek to attract attention.
**dikkatle** carefully, with care.
**dikkatli** attentive, careful, painstaking; -*ce* carefully, attentively.
**dikkatsiz** careless, inattentive; thoughtless.
**dikkatsizlik** carelessness, inattentiveness; thoughtlessness.
**diklenmek, dikleşmek 1.** to become steep; **2.** to get stubborn; **3.** to stand erect.
**dikme 1.** *vn. of* dikmek; **2.** *geom.* perpendicular; **3.** seedling; **4.** derrick; prop; **5.** pole, post.
**dikmek,** (-*er*) **1.** to sew; to stitch; **2.** to set up, to erect; **3.** to plant; **4.** to stare, to fix *(eyes)*; **5.** to prick up *(ears)*; **6.** to drain, to drink off; **7.** to station *(a guard)*; **8.** to build, to construct, to put up; **9.** to set down *(a ball)* for play.
**diksiyon** diction; intonation.
**dikta** dictate.
**diktafon** dictaphone.
**diktatör** dictator.

**diktatörlük** dictatorship.
**dikte** dictation; ~ etm. **1.** to dictate *(letter)*; **2.** *fig.* to dictate to, to force (up)on *(order)*.
**dil 1.** tongue; **2.** language; dialect; **3.** *geogr.* promontory, spit; **4.** ⊕ bolt *(of a lock)*; **5.** ⊕ tenon *(of a mortise)*; **6.** ⬇ sheave *(of a block or pulley)*; **7.** index *(of a balance)*; **8.** reed *(of a wind instrument)*; **9.** ✕ prisoner of war captured for interrogation; ~ çıkarmak to put one's tongue out; ~ dalaşı quarrel; ~ dökmek to talk s.o. round (*or* over); ♀ Devrimi Language Reform; ~ sürçmesi slip of the tongue; ♀. Tarih ve Coğrafya Fakültesi *pr. n.* the College of Languages, History and Geography; ~ uzatmak to assail (with), to malign, to defame; -*e* (*or* -*lere*) düşmek to become a subject of common talk, to be on everyone's tongue; -*e* düşürmek to set tongues (*or* chins *or* beards) wagging; -*e* getirmek **1.** to cause to talk; **2.** to express, to give utterance to; -*e* kolay easier said than done; -*e* vermek to divulge, to denounce; -*i* çözülmek to find one's tongue; -*i* dolaşmak to mumble, to stumble; -*i* ensesinden çekilsin! may his tongue be pulled out; -*i* kayıyor he is making a slip of the tongue; -*i* tutuk tongue-tied; -*i* uzun impudent, insolent; -*imin ucunda* on the tip of my tongue; -*inde* tüy bitmek to talk till one is blue in the face; -*inden* düşürmemek to keep on and on (-*i* about); -*ine* dolamak to keep on and on (-*i* about); -*ini* kesmek to shut up; to silence; -*ini* tutmak to hold one's tongue (*or* peace); -*ini* yutmak to have lost one's tongue; -*inin* altında bir bakla (*or* şey) var there is s.th. he hasn't come out with yet; -*inin* ucunda olm. to have s.th. on the tip of one's tongue; -*lerde* dolaşmak to be the subject of common gossip.
**dilak** *anat.* clitoris.
**dilaltı, -nı 1.** sublingual, hypoglossal; **2.** pip *(in fowls)*.
**dilbalığı, -nı** *zo.* sole.
**dilbasan** ✶ spatula.
**dilbaz** [ā] eloquent.
**dilber** beautiful, beloved.
**dilberdudağı, -nı** a kind of Turkish pastry.
**dilbilgisi, -ni** grammar.
**dilbilim** linguistics.
**dilci** linguist.
**dilcik 1.** ⚘ ligula; **2.** = dilak; **3.** = kurbağacık **4.** ⚘ pip *(of fowl)*; **5.** P uvula.
**dilek 1.** wish, desire; **2.** request, petition, demand; ~ kipleri *gr.* optatives; ~ şart

**kİpi** *gr.* conditional optative; -te bulun-mak to make a wish.

**dilekçe** petition, formal request.

**dilekçi** petitioner.

**dilemek 1.** to wish (for), to desire, to long (for); **2.** to ask (for), to beg, to request; özür ~ to ask pardon, to apologize.

**dilenci** beggar, cadger; ~ değneğine dön-mek to become a bag of bones; ~ vapuru steamer that stops at every port of call; -ye hıyar vermişler de, eğri diye beğenme-miş beggars can't be choosers.

**dilencilik** begging, beggary, mendicancy.

**dilenmek 1.** *pass. of* dilemek; **2.** to beg, to cadge; **3.** to ask (for), to plead (for).

**dilhâh** ✕ heart's desire, beloved object.

**di'li:** ~ geçmiş zaman *gr.* past tense.

**dilim 1.** slice; strip; **2.** leaf (*of a radiator*); ~ ~ in slices, in strips.

**dilimlemek** to cut into slices, to slice.

**dilinim** *geol.* cleavage.

**dillemek** ✕ **1.** to touch *or* lick with the tongue; **2.** *fig.* to backbite, to censure.

**dillenmek 1.** *pass. of* dillemek **2.** to loosen one's tongue, to begin to talk; **3.** to be-come chatty; **4.** to be on everyone's tongue.

**dilleşmek** to chat.

**dilli 1.** ... tongued; **2.** bolted; sheaved; **3.** *fig.* talkative, chatty.

**dillidüdük 1.** talkative, chatterbox, wind-bag; **2.** reed whistle.

**dilmek** to slice, to cut into slices.

**dilsel** lingual, linguistic.

**dilsiz 1.** dumb, mute; **2.** *fig.* docile, easy-going; ~ kaval German flute.

**dilsizlik** dumbness.

**dimağ** brain, mind; intelligence.

**dimağce** *anat.* cerebellum.

**dimağı [. - -]** cerebral.

**dimdik [x .]** *emph. of* dik *part.* bolt up-right, erect, stiff.

**din¹** *phys.* dyne.

**din²** religion; belief, faith; creed; -i bir uğruna for the sake of Islam; -i bütün religious; hay -ine yandığım! the cursed!, damned!

**dinamik** dynamic(s).

**dinamit** dynamite.

**dinamitlemek** to dynamite.

**dinamizm** dynamism.

**dinamo** dynamo.

**dinar** dinar.

**dincelmek** to become vigorous, to recover one's strength.

**dinci [- .]** clerical.

**dincierki** theocracy.

**dinç 1.** vigorous, robust; **2.** calm, untrou-bled.

**dinçleşmek** to become robust.

**dinçleştirmek** to strengthen, to invigorate.

**dinçlik** vigo(u)r, vivacity, robustness.

**dindar [- -]** religious, pious, devout, godly, god-fearing.

**dindarlık** religiousness, devotion, piety, godliness.

**dindaş [¹]** coreligionist.

**dindışı** secular, temporal, civil.

**dindirmek** to stop (*pain, etc.*); to slake (*thirst*).

**dineri [. x .]** diamonds.

**dingil** ⊕ axle, axletree.

**dingildemek 1.** to rattle, to wooble; to sway; **2.** to tremble (*with fear*).

**dingin 1.** calm; **2.** ⸜ inactive; **3.** inactive (*volcano*); **4.** exhausted, bushed.

**dinginleşmek** to calm down, to get calm.

**dinginlik** calm, quietness.

**dini [- -]** religious; pertaining to religion; ~ ayin divine service; ~ nikâh ecclesias-tical wedding.

**dinleme** *vn. of* dinlemek *part.* ausculta-tion; ~ aleti ⸙ stethoscope; ~ hizmeti ✕ listening service.

**dinlemek 1.** to listen (-i to), to hear; **2.** to pay attention (-i to); to obey, to conform (-i to); **3.** to auscultate.

**dinlence 1.** restful thing; **2.** holiday, vaca-tion.

**dinlendirici** relaxing.

**dinlendirmek 1.** to (let) rest; **2.** to leave (*a field*) fallow; **3.** to set aside; **4.** to put out (*fire, light, etc.*).

**dinlenme** rest, relaxation; ~ kampı holiday camp; ~ yeri resort, vacation place; road house; ~ yurdu recreation home.

**dinlenmek 1.** *pass. of* dinlemek; **2.** to rest, to relax; **3.** to be set aside (*wine, etc.*).

**dinletmek** *caus. of* dinlemek to have s.o. listen *or* obey; **k-ni** ~ to make o.s. heard.

**dinleyici** listener; -ler audience.

**dinmek,** (-er) to stop, to cease, to leave off (*rain, etc.*); to die down, to get better, to calm down, to pass off (*pain*).

**dinöncesi** prereligion, preanimism.

**dinsel** religious, pertaining to religion.

**dinsiz [- .] 1.** irreligious, ungodly, impious, unbelieving, atheistic; **2.** cruel, tyrant; -in hakkından imansız gelir *pro.* set a thief to catch a thief, take hair of dog that bit you, an old poacher makes the best keep-er.

**dinsizlik 1.** irreligion, atheism; **2.** cruelty.

**dip, -bi 1.** bottom; foot, lowest part; **2.** the far end, back; ~ göstermek (*or* sömür-mek) to drink to the dregs; dibinden bu-

**damak 1.** to cut from the bottom; **2.** to nip in the bud; **dibine darı ekmek** to use up, to finish off.

**dipçik** butt *(of a rifle)*.

**dipçiklemek** to club with a rifle butt.

**dipdiri** [x . .] **1.** full of life, energetic, active; **2.** shapely; **3.** fresh.

**dipkoçanı,** -nı stub, counterfoil.

**diplemek** *sl.* to flunk, to fail *(in school)*.

**diploma** [. x .] diploma, certificate; degree.

**diplomalı** graduate; qualified.

**diplomasız 1.** having no diploma; **2.** without a licence.

**diplomasi** diplomacy.

**diplomat,** -tı diplomat.

**diplomatik** diplomatic.

**dipnot** footnote.

**dipsiz 1.** bottomless; **2.** *fig.* unfounded, false; **3.** unfathomable; **~ kile boş ambar 1.** he spends everything he gets; **2.** it will never be of any use; **~ testi** *fig.* spendthrift, squanderer.

**dirayet,** -ti [ā] **1.** ability; **2.** skillfulness; **3.** perception, discernment.

**dirayetli 1.** capable, effective; **2.** skillful; **3.** perceptive.

**dirayetsiz 1.** incapable; **2.** unskilled; **3.** imperceptive.

**direk 1.** pole, post; **2.** mast; **3.** beam, rafter; **4.** column, pillar; **5.** *football:* goalpost, crossbar; **6.** *fig.* pillar, mainstay; **~ ~ bağırmak** to shout at the top of one's voice; **ailenin direği** mainstay of the family.

**direksiyon 1.** steering-wheel; **2.** *fig.* guidance; **~ boşluğu** play in the steering; **-da** at the wheel; **-u idare etm.** to steer, to drive; **-u kırmak** to swerve.

**direkt,** -ti **1.** direct, nonstop; **2.** directly.

**direktif** directive, instruction, order.

**direktör** director; principal.

**direktörlük** directorship.

**diremek 1.** to support, to hold up, to sustain; **2.** to resist.

**diren** pitchfork.

**direnç** *phys.* resistance.

**dirençli 1.** resistant; **2.** tough.

**dirençsiz** having low resistance.

**dirençsizlik** low resistance.

**direnek** *neol.* X bulwark.

**direngen** stubborn, obstinate.

**direngenlik** obstinacy.

**direniş 1.** resistance, opposition; **2.** boycott.

**direnme 1.** resistance; **2.** persistence.

**direnmek 1.** to insist (-de on); **2.** to resist, to hold out; **3.** to put one's foot down.

**direşken** persistent, determined, insistent.

**direşmek** P **1.** to persevere; to be determined; **2.** to resist.

**diretmek** to put one's foot down, to insist (-de on), to show obstinacy.

**direy** fauna.

**dirgen** *s.* diren.

**dirhem** drachma; **k-ni ~ ~ satmak** to make a great show of reluctance.

**diri 1.** alive, living; **2.** vigorous, lively, energetic; **3.** fresh; **4.** undercooked; rare.

**diriksel** animal, physiological.

**dirilik 1.** life, liveliness; **2.** freshness.

**diriliş** revival, invigoration; resurgence.

**dirilmek 1.** to come (or return) to life; **2.** to be revived, to gain fresh vigo(u)r.

**diriltmek** to revive, to bring to life.

**dirim** life.

**dirlik 1.** peace, peaceful coexistence; **2.** affluence; **~ düzenlik** harmony in social relations, peace; **~ vermemek** *(b-ne)* to give *s.o.* no rest.

**dirliksiz** cantankerous, cross.

**dirsek 1.** elbow; **2.** bend, turn *(in a line, road or river)*; **3.** *(pipe)* elbow; **4.** ↓ prop; **~ çevirmek** *(b-ne)* *fig.* to drop *s.o.* socially, to throw *s.o.* over; **~ çürütmek** to study long and hard.

**dirseklemek** to elbow.

**disiplin** discipline.

**disiplinli** disciplined.

**disiplinsiz** undisciplined.

**disk,** -ki **1.** *sports:* discus; **2.** record; **3.** ⊕ disk; **~ atma** throw the discus.

**diskalifiye** disqualified; **~ etm.** to disqualify; **~ olm.** to be disqualified.

**diskotek,** -ği **1.** discotheque; **2.** collection of recorded music.

**dispanser** dispensary.

**distribütör** ≠ distributor.

**diş 1.** tooth; **2.** tusk; **3.** tooth *(of a saw, comb)*; **4.** cog *(of a wheel)*; **5.** ward *(of a key)*; **6.** thread *(of a screw)*; **7.** clove *(of garlic)*; **8.** head *(of cloves)*; **9.** *sl.* dope, hashish; **~ ağrısı** toothache; **~ bakımı** dental care; **~ bilemek** *(b-ne)* to watch for a change to take revenge on *s.o.*; **~ çekmek** to extract *(or pull out)* a tooth; **~ çektirmek** to have a tooth extracted *(or pulled out)*; **~ çıkarmak** to cut a tooth, to teethe; **~ doldurmak** to fill *(or stop)* a tooth; **~ fırçası** toothbrush; **~ geçirmek** *fig.* to be able to influence *(a powerful person)*; **~ gıcırdatmak** *fig.* to gnash one's teeth; **~ göstermek** *fig.* to snow one's teeth; **~ hekimi** dentist; **~ hekimliği** dentistry; **~ kamaştırmak** to set one's teeth on edge; **~ kemiği** dentine;

~ kovuğu cavity; ~ macunu toothpaste; ~ pası tartar, scale; ~ siniri dental nerve; ~ tababeti dentistry; ~ tabibi dentist; -e dokunur worthwhile; -inden tırnağından artırmak to pinch and scrape, to scrimp and save; -ine göre within one's power; -ini sıkmak to grit one's teeth, to endure, to bare; -ini tırnağına takmak to work tooth and nail, to try every means.

**dişbudak** ♥ ash tree.

**dişçi 1.** dentist; **2.** *sl.* one who robs graves for gold teeth.

**dişçilik** dentistry.

**dişeti,** -ni gum.

**dişi 1.** female, she; **2.** woman; **3.** feminine; **4.** ⊕ female; **5.** malleable *(metal)*; ~ anahtar hollow key; ~ kopça an eye for a hook.

**dişil 1.** female; **2.** *gr.* feminine.

**dişileşmek** to become feminine.

**dişilik** feminine gender, female sex.

**dişiorgan** ♥ pistil.

**dişlek** bucktoothed, having protruding teeth.

**dişlemek 1.** to bite, to nibble, to gnaw; **2.** ⊕ to tooth, to serrate.

**dişli 1.** toothed, serrated; notched, jagged; cogged; **2.** ⊕ cogwheel, gear; **3.** sprocket; **4.** *fig.* formidable, influential; ~ tırnaklı red in tooth and claw, very aggressive and fierce.

**dişsel** dental.

**dişsiz 1.** toothless; **2.** unserrated.

**ditmek,** (-er) **1.** to card, to tease *(cotton, wool)*; **2.** to shred.

**divan** [- -] **1.** sofa, divan, couch; **2.** collection of stamps; **3.** *pol.* council of state; ~ durmak to stand in a respectful position with hands folded in front; 2 Edebiyatı classical Ottoman poetry; dıvanı haysiyet, haysiyet dıvanı court of hono(u)r.

**divane** [- - .] crazy, mad, insane; -si olm. *(bşin)* to be nuts over *s.th.*, to be wild about *s.th.*

**divanelik** craziness.

**divanhane** [- - - .] large hall.

**divanıharp,** -bi court-martial, military court.

**divik** *zo.* termite, white ant.

**divit,** -ti a pen-case with an inkholder, ink--and-pen case.

**diyabet,** -ti diabetes.

**diyafram** *anat., phys., phot.* diaphragm.

**diyagram 1.** graph; **2.** diagram.

**diyakoz** [. x .] deacon.

**diyalekt** dialect.

**diyalektik** dialectic(s).

**diyalog** dialogue.

**diyanet,** -ti [ā] **1.** piety, devoutness; **2.** religion; ~ işleri religious affairs.

**diyanetkâr, diyanetli** [ā] religious, pious.

**diyani** [. - -] religious; ~ tesis ♂ religious foundation.

**diyapazon** diapason, tuning fork.

**diyar** [ā] country, land.

**diye** (< diyerek) **1.** so that; lest; **2.** because; **3.** by saying; **4.** on the assumption that; by mistake; **5.** named, called.

**diyecek** s.th. to say; diyeceği olmamak to have no objection; to have nothing to say.

**diyet[1],** -ti diet.

**diyet[2],** -ti blood money, wergeld.

**Diyet[3],** -ti Diet.

**diyez** ♪ sharp.

**diz 1.** knee; **2.** lap; ~ boyu knee-deep, up to the knees; ~ çökmek to kneel (down); ~ çöktürmek **1.** to make s.o. kneel down; **2.** to bring s.o. to his knees; ~ kırmak **1.** to bend one's knees; **2.** to curtsy; ~ üstü on one's knees, kneeling; -e gelmek to fall on one's knees; to give up, to surrender; -e getirmek *(b-ni)* to bring *s.o.* to heel; -ini dövmek *fig.* to repent bitterly; -inin bağı çözüldü *fig.* he is on his last legs.

**dizanteri** ♀ dysentery.

**dizbağı,** -nı garter; ~ nişanı the Order of the Garter.

**dizbarko** [. x .] ♂ unloading *(of a ship)*.

**dizdirmek 1.** to have s.th. typeset; **2.** to have things strung on a cord; **3.** to have things arranged in order.

**dize** line *(of poetry)*.

**dizel** diesel engine.

**dizgi** composition, typesetting.

**dizgici** typesetter, compositor.

**dizgin** rein, bridle; ~ vurmak to bridle; -ini çekmek *(or* kısmak*) fig.* to keep a tight rein (on); -leri ele almak to take the reins; -leri ele vermek *(or* başkasına kaptırmak*) fig.* to let another take the reins; -leri salıvermek *fig.* to give the reins (to); -lerini toplamak to rein in, to check off.

**dizginlemek 1.** to bridle *(a horse)*; **2.** *fig.* to restrain.

**dizginsiz** *fig.* uncontrolled, unbridled.

**dizi 1.** string *(of beads)*; **2.** line, row; **3.** series; **4.** ♪ scale; **5.** ♫ progression; series; **6.** ✕ file *(of soldiers)*; ~ kol nizamında in single *(or* Indian*)* file.

**dizici** *typ.* typesetter, compositor.

**dizili 1.** strung *(beads)*; **2.** *typ.* set.

**diziliş** arrangement.

**dizilmek 1.** to be arranged (-e in); **2.** to be

strung (-e on); **3.** to line up; **4.** *typ.* to be set.

**dizim** typesetting, composition.

**dizin** index.

**dizkapağı,** -nı kneecap; ~ kemiği *anat.* kneepan, kneecap, patella.

**dizlik 1.** knee-guard; **2.** knee-breeches.

**dizmek 1.** to line up, to arrange in a row; **2.** to string *(beads)*; **3.** *typ.* to set.

**dizmen** typesetter, compositor.

**do** ♪ **1.** do, doh; **2.** C.

**doanahtarı** ♪ key of C.

**dobra dobra** [x . x .] bluntly, frankly.

**doçent,** -ti lecturer, assistant professor, associate professor.

**doçentlik** associate professorship, lecturership.

**doğa** nature.

**doğacı** animist.

**doğal** natural; ~ ayıklanma natural selection; ~ bilimler the natural sciences; ~ kaynaklar natural resources; ~ olarak naturally.

**doğallık** naturalness.

**doğan** *zo.* falcon.

**doğaötesi,** -ni **1.** metaphysics; **2.** metaphysical.

**doğarlık** birth-rate.

**doğaüstü,** -nü supernatural.

**doğma 1.** *vn.* of doğmak; **2.** born; ~ büyüme İstanbullu born and bred in İstanbul.

**doğmak,** (-ar) **1.** to be born; **2.** *ast.* to rise *(sun, moon)*; **3.** to emerge, to appear, to arise; **4.** *(b-ne)* to occor to *s.o.*; doğduğu yer birthplace; doğduğuna pişman tired of life, miserable, unhappy; içime doğdu I felt it in my bones.

**doğmalık** congenital.

**doğram** slice; ~ ~ in slices.

**doğrama 1.** *vn.* of doğramak; **2.** woodwork, joinery.

**doğramacı** joiner, carpenter.

**doğramacılık** joinery.

**doğramak** to cut into pieces *(or* slices); to carve, to chop to bits.

**doğru 1.** straight; **2.** true; **3.** suitable, proper; **4.** honest, good *(person)*; **5.** correct, accurate; **6.** the truth; **7.** ⅄ line; **8.** truly, correctly; **9.** straight, directly; **10.** towards, in the direction of; **11.** toward, near the time of; **12.** that's true!; **13** F correct answer *(in a test)*; ~ akım ⚡ direct current; ~ bulmak to approve (-i of), to see fit; ~ çıkmak to come true, to prove to be right; ~ durmak **1.** to stand straignt; **2.** to sit still, to keep quiet; ~ dürüst F **1.** properly; **2.** genuine, proper, real; ~ orantılı ⅄ directly proportional;

~ oturmak to sit still, to behave o.s.; -dan -ya directly.

**doğruca** [x . .] **1.** more or less right; **2.** straight, directly.

**doğrucu** truthful, veracious.

**doğrulamak** to verify, to confirm, to corroborate.

**doğrulmak 1.** to straighten out; to be straightened; to become erect *(or* straight); **2.** to sit up; **3.** to be righted; to be put right; **4.** F to be earned; **5.** to direct *o.s.* (-e towards), to head (-e for).

**doğrultmak 1.** to straighten, to put straight; **2.** to correct; **3.** to aim, to point (-e at), to direct; **4.** F to get, to take in *(money)*.

**doğrultu** direction.

**doğruluk 1.** truth; honesty, uprightness; **2.** straightness; ~ kâğıdı certificate of conduct.

**doğrusal** linear.

**doğrusu** the truth of the matter; to speak honestly, to be quite frank about it; -nu isterseniz to tell the truth; daha ~ as a matter of fact, to be more exact.

**doğu 1.** east; **2.** eastern; **3.** the East, the Orient; the eastern provinces of Turkey; **4.** *ast.* equinoctial sunrise point; ~ Afrika(sı) East Africa.

**doğulu 1.** easterner; **2.** Oriental.

**doğum 1.** birth; **2.** year of birth; **3.** = doğarlık; **4.** confinement; **5.** delivery, parturition; ~ günü birthday; ~ hali nascent condition; ~ kontrol hapı the pill, contraceptive pill; ~ kontrolu birth control; ~ kütüğü birth-register; ~ sancısı **1.** labo(u)r pain; **2.** *fig.* birth pangs; ~ yapmak to give birth to a child, to bear.

**doğumevi,** -ni maternity hospital.

**doğumlu** born in such and such a year; 1940 -lar born in 1940.

**doğumsal** natal.

**doğurgan** prolific, fecund.

**doğurganlık** prolificacy, fecundity.

**doğurmak 1.** to give birth (to), to bear; **2.** *fig.* to give birth to, to cause, to bring about, to bring forth.

**doğurtmak** to assist *(a mother)* at childbirth.

**doğuş 1.** birth; **2.** *ast.* rise; **3.** emergence; -tan innate; from birth; congenital.

**dok,** -ku ⚓ dock, wharf.

**doka** *s.* duka.

**doksan** ninety.

**doksanar** ninety each.

**doksanıncı** ninetieth.

**doksanlık 1.** containing ninety; **2.** ninety years old.

**doktor 1.** doctor, physician; **2.** person with a doctorate; ~ çıkmak (or olm.) **1.** to become a doctor; **2.** to take one's degree.

**doktora 1.** doctorate; **2.** doctoral examination; ~ talebesi postgraduate; ~ tezi thesis.

**doktorluk 1.** = doktora; **2.** profession of a doctor; ~ etm. to work as a doctor.

**doktrin** doctrine.

**doku** *anat.* tissue.

**dokubilim** histology.

**dokuma 1.** *vn. of* dokumak; **2.** woven; **3.** textile; **4.** cotton cloth; ~ makinesi loom.

**dokumacı** weaver; textile worker.

**dokumacılık** textile industry.

**dokumak 1.** to weave; **2.** to knock down (*fruit from a tree*).

**dokunaklı** touching, moving, biting, harmful, harsh, insinuating.

**dokundurmak 1.** to make s.th.   touch another thing; **2.** to hint (about).

**dokunmak 1.** *pass. of* dokumak; **2.** to touch, to make contact (*-e* with); **3.** to take in one's hand, to touch; **4.** to disturb, to upset, to meddle (*-e* with); **5.** to take and use; **6.** to disagree (*-e* with), to upset (*one's health*); **7.** to affect; **8.** to move, to cut (*or* touch) s.o. to the quick; **9.** to touch (*-e* on), to deal (*-e* with).

**dokunulmazlık** *pol.* immunity.

**dokunum** *biol.* sense of touch.

**dokurcun 1.** stack of hay *or* grain; **2.** a game played with nine small stones.

**dokuz** nine; ~ doğurmak *fig.* to sweat blood, to be on pins and needles; ~ düğüm altında under lock and key; ~ yorgan eskitmek *fig.* to have a very long life.

**dokuzar** nine each.

**dokuzlamak** to increase to nine.

**dokuzlu 1.** containing nine; **2.** *cards:* the nine; **3.** made up of nine-line stanzas.

**dokuztaş** a game played with nine small stones.

**dokuzuncu** ninth.

**doküman** document; ~ fotoğraf documentary photograph.

**dokümanter** documentary; ~ film documentary film.

**dolak** puttee.

**dolam 1.** one turn of any coiled thing; **2.** enough for a turn.

**dolama 1.** *vn. of* dolamak; **2.** dolman; **3.** whitlow, felon.

**dolamak 1.** to twist, to wind (*-e* on); **2.** to wrap around (*one's arms*).

**dolambaç 1.** curve, bend; **2.** *anat.* labyrinth; **3.** = dolambaçlı.

**dolambaçlı 1.** sinuous, winding, meandering; **2.** *fig.* tangled, involved, intricate; ~ yollardan gitmek *fig.* to prevaricate, to shuffle, to dodge.

**dolamık** trap, snare, net.

**dolan** deception, deceit.

**dolandırıcı** swindler, embezzler, deceiver, cheat.

**dolandırıcılık** swindle, fraud, deceit.

**dolandırılmak** to be swindled.

**dolandırmak 1.** = dolaştırmak; **2.** to cheat, to swindle, to defraud, to deceive.

**dolanmak 1.** *pass. of* dolamak; **2.** to be wrapped (*-e* around); **3.** to be wound on (*-e* to); **4.** to hang about (*or* around), to wander about, to rove, to roam about.

**dolap, -bı 1.** cupboard; wardrobe; **2.** water wheel; **3.** treadmill; **4.** Ferris wheel; merry-go-round; **5.** stall in the Covered Market in İstanbul; **6.** ♪ musical box; **7.** *fig.* plot, trick, intrigue; ~ çevirmek *fig.* to pull a trick, to set a trap.

**dolar** dollar.

**dolaşık 1.** roundabout, indirect, meandering, sinuous (*road, way*); **2.** confused tortuous, tangled, intricate (*matter*); ~ yol detour, roundabout way.

**dolaşıklık 1.** entanglement, intricateness, crookedness; **2.** indirectness; **3.** tortuosity.

**dolaşıksız 1.** direct; **2.** directly.

**dolaşım** *biol.* circulation.

**dolaşlı** winding; twining; *fig.* having obstacles.

**dolaşmak 1.** to stroll, to wander, to walk around; **2.** to go the long way round, to make a roundabout way; **3.** to be indirect (*road*); **4.** to get tangled (*hair, thread*); **5.** to go around, to get around (*rumour, news*); **6.** to patrol (*soldier*); **7.** to go on the beat (*police*); **8.** to get about, to wander around (*a place*).

**dolaştırmak** *caus. of* dolaşmak *part.* **1.** to take s.o. for a walk, to make s.o. go around; to show s.o. around; **2.** to wind (*or* tangle) s.th. around s.th. else.

**dolay 1.** vicinity, environment, surroundings; **2.** suburbs, outskirts; **3.** turn, bend (*in a road*).

**dolayı 1.** = dolay; **2.** because of, due to, on account of, thanks to, owing to; **3.** as, because; bundan ~ therefore, that's why, for that reason.

**dolayısıyle** [. . . - .] **1.** consequently, so; **2.** because of, on account of, owing to, due to.

**dolaylı** *neol.* **1.** indirect; **2.** indirectly; ~ tümleç *gr.* indirect object.

**dolaysız 1.** direct; **2.** directly.

**doldurma 1.** loading, filling; **2.** *phys.* charging; ~ makinesi charging machine.

**doldurmak 1.** to fill (up), to stuff; **2.** to complete (*sum or period of time*); **3.** to charge (*a battery*); **4.** to load (*firearm*); **5.** to fill out, to fill in (*a printed form*); **6.** (*b-ni*) to turn s.o. against s.o. else.

**doldurtmak** to have s.th. filled (out).

**dolgu 1.** act of filling (*out*); **2.** filling, stopping; ~ yapmak to fill, to stop; ~ yaptırmak to have a tooth filled (*or stopped*).

**dolgun 1.** full, filled, stuffed; **2.** plump, buxom; **3.** high (*salary*); **4.** abundantly endowed (*with information or knowledge*); ~ maaşlı high salaried; ~ mide full stomach; ~ yüzlü round-faced.

**dolgunlaşmak** to get plump.

**dolgunluk 1.** fullness; **2.** plumpness.

**dolma 1.** *vn. of* dolmak; **2.** filled up, reclaimed (*land*); **3.** stuffed (*food*); **4.** *sl.* lie, tall story, humbug; ~ yutmak *sl.* to be duped, to be humbugged; ~ yutturmak *sl.* to dupe, to humbug, to hoax.

**dolmak,** (-ar) **1.** to get full, to become full, to be filled; **2.** to be packed (*ile* with); **3.** to expire (*term, period*); **4.** *fig.* to be ready to burst (*from anger*), to be exasperated.

**dolmakalem** fountain-pen.

**dolmuş 1.** jitney, shared-taxi, collective-taxi, dolmush (*a taxi which only starts when it is filled up with passengers*); **2.** full, filled, stuffed.

**dolmuşçu** driver of a shared-taxi.

**dolmuşçuluk** driving a shared-taxi.

**dolu¹ 1.** full, filled; **2.** abounding in, teeming (*ile* with), alive (*ile* with); **3.** loaded (*gun*); **4.** charged (*battery*); **5.** solid; **6.** oversensitive; **7.** a glass (*containing a drink*); **8.** *fig.* about to blow up (*with anger*); ~ ~ plentifully, in abundance; ~ tüfek *fig.* choleric person.

**dolu²** hail; ~ tanesi hailstone; ~ yağıyor it is hailing.

**doludizgin** at full speed, galloping, at a full gallop.

**doluk** goatskin bottle.

**doluluk** fullness, plenitude.

**dolunay** full moon.

**doluşmak** to crowd (*into a place*).

**domalan** ⚓ truffle.

**domalıç** humped; bulging; bulbous; protruding.

**domalika** [. . x .] shellac.

**domalmak 1.** to bulge out, to stand out, to rise; **2.** to squat down in a humped position.

**domaniç** *s.* domalıç.

**domaran** *s.* domalan.

**domates** [. x .] ⚓ tomato; ~ suyu tomato juice.

**dombalan** *s.* domalan.

**dombay** *zo.* water buffalo.

**dombaz** *s.* tombaz.

**domino 1.** dominoes (*game*); **2.** domino (*costume*).

**domuz 1.** *zo.* pig, hog, swine; **2.** *fig.* obstinate; spiteful, malicious; **3.** you fink!, you swine!; ~ derisi pigskin; ~ eti pork; ~ gibi F **1.** vicious(ly); **2.** for certain; ~ yağı lard; ~ yavrusu pig; bu ~ karı *sl.* this swine broad.

**domuzayağı,** -nı wormer used for with drawing the charge from a gun.

**domuzdamı** gallery of a mine supported by wooden props.

**domuzlan** *zo.* bombardier beetle.

**domuzlaşmak** to become malicious.

**domuzluk 1.** viciousness; **2.** water wheel casing.

**don¹ 1.** pair of drawers, underpants; **2.** coat, colo(u)r (*of a horse*); -una etm. (*or* kaçırmak) to wet *or* soil one's underwear; -una yapmak **1.** to wet *or* soil one's underwear (*child*); **2.** *fig.* to shake in one's shoes.

**don²** frost, freeze; ~ çözülmek to thaw; ~ tutmak to freeze.

**donakalmak,** (-ır) to stand aghast (at), to be petrified with horror *or* astonishment.

**donamak** to decorate, to embellish, to adorn.

**donanım** ⚓ rigging, tackle.

**donanma 1.** *vn. of* donanmak; **2.** fleet, navy, naval force; **3.** fireworks; flags and bunting; **2.** illumination; ~ fişeği rocket, skyrocket.

**donanmak 1.** to dress up; **2.** to be decorated; **3.** to be equipped; **2.** to be illuminated.

**donatan** rigger.

**donatım 1.** equipping; **2.** equipment, outfit; **3.** ✗ procurement of ordnance; **2.** incidental details.

**donatımcı** progman, property man.

**donatmak 1.** to dress up; **2.** to ornament, to deck out, to illuminate, to decorate; **3.** ⚓ to equip (*a ship*); to rig; **4.** to set lavishly (*table*); **5.** *sl.* to insult, to abuse, to swear (at).

**dondurma 1.** *vn. of* dondurmak; **2.** ice-cream; **3.** (made) frozen, solidified.

**dondurmacı** ice-cream vendor, ice-cream seller; maker of ice-cream.

**dondurmak** to freeze (*a. fig.*).

**dondurucu** freezing; cold, chilling.

**dondurulmuş 1.** frozen; **2.** fixed.

**Donkişotluk** quixotism, quixotry.

**donma** freezing; ~ noktası freezing point.

**donmak,** (-ar) **1.** to freeze; **2.** to freeze to death; **3.** to freeze, to feel very cold; **4.** to set, to harden, to solidify (concrete, etc.); **5.** to freeze, to remain motionless.

**donsuz** fig. destitute, needy; vagabond.

**donuk** matt, dull, lusterless, lifeless.

**donuklaşmak** to be dull, to be lifeless.

**donukluk** dimness, dullness.

**donyağı, -nı 1.** tallow; **2.** fig. cold fish, disagreeable person; donyağıyle pekmez fig. incompatible.

**.dopdolu** [x . .] chockful, full up.

**doru** chestnut (horse).

**doruk 1.** summit, peak, apex, top; **2.** fig. zenith; ~ çizgisi watershed, water parting.

**doruklamak** to brim, to fill to the brim.

**dosa** ↓ gangplank.

**dosdoğru** [x - .] emph. of doğru straight ahead; perfectly correct.

**dost, -tu 1.** friend; comrade, confidant, intimate; **2.** friendly; **3.** lover; mistress; ~ devlet friendly state; ~ düşman friend and foe, everybody; ~ edinmek **1.** to make friends (with); **2.** to take a lover or a mistress; ~ kara günde belli olur pro. a friend in need is a friend indeed; ~ olm. to become friends; -a düşmana karşı in front of everybody; in the eyes of everybody, publicly; -lar başına! may the same befall all my friends!; -lar başından ırak! I wouldn't wish such a thing on my friends!

**dostane** [ā] friendly.

**dostça** = dostane.

**dostluk** friendship; ~ etm. (or göstermek) to be friends (-e with); ~ kurmak to make friends (ile with).

**dosya** [x .] **1.** file, dossier; **2.** file folder.

**dosyalamak** to file, to put in a file.

**dosyalanmak** pass. of dosyalamak to be filed.

**dosye** s. dosya.

**doyasıya** to one's heart's content, to repletion, as much as one can.

**doygun 1.** satiated; **2.** saturated.

**doygunluk 1.** satiation; **2.** saturation.

**doyma** saturation (a. ?).

**doymak 1.** to eat one's fill, to be full up, to be satiated; **2.** (bşe) to be satisfied with s.th.; **3.** ? to be saturated (-e with); doya doya to one's heart's content, to repletion.

**doymaz** greedy, insatiable.

**doymazlık** greed, insatiability.

**doymuş** ? saturated.

**doyum** satiety, satisfaction; buna ~ olmaz one never gets tired of this, one cannot have enough of it.

**doyumluk** enough to satisfy.

**doyurmak 1.** to fill up, to satisfy, to satiate, to allay one's hunger; **2.** ? to saturate.

**doyurucu 1.** satisfying, filling (food); **2.** fig. convincing, persuasive.

**doz** ? dose; -unu kaçırmak to overdo, to go too far.

**dozer** bulldozer.

**dökme 1.** vn. of dökmek; **2.** poured; **3.** cast (metal); **4.** spilled, scattered; **5.** † in bulk; ~ demir cast iron.

**dökmeci** foundryman, founder.

**dökmecilik** foundry work.

**dökmehane** [ā] foundry.

**dökmek** (-er) **1.** to pour (out); **2.** to spill; **3.** to throw out; **4.** to scatter; **5.** to shed; **6.** to cast; **7.** to empty; **8.** to let (one's hair) hang freely; **9.** to pour out (one's troubles); **10.** to fail, to flunk (students in a class); **11.** to have (spots, freckles) break out on one's skin; **12.** (kâğıda) to write down, to commit to paper.

**döktürmek 1.** caus. of dökmek; **2.** sl. to do a swell job.

**dökük 1.** nicely hanging (cloth); **2.** loose, free (hair); **3.** F shabby, seedy.

**döküksaçık 1.** rough, untidy (hair); **2.** shabby, ragged.

**dökülmek 1.** pass. of dökmek; **2.** to go out in large numbers (people); **3.** to disintegrate; **4.** to drape, to drop off; **5.** to get ragged; **6.** sl. to be dead tired, to be bushed. to be worn out; **7.** to be miserable; dökülüp saçılmak **1.** to unburden o.s. to unbosom o.s., to make a clean breast of it; **2.** to blow, to blue, to squander (money).

**döküm 1.** casting, cast; **2.** dropping; **3.** enumeration (of an account); **4.** inventory; **5.** ⚕ addition; **6.** mo(u)lting; shedding; **7.** sl. ugly (woman); **8.** sl. sloppily dressed; ~ kalıbı casting mo(u)ld.

**dökümcü** foundryman.

**dökümcülük** foundry work.

**dökümevi, dökümhane** [ā] ⊕ foundry, ironworks.

**dökümlü** well-fitting (clothing).

**dökünmek** refl. of dökmek part. to throw over o.s. (water, etc.).

**döküntü 1.** remains, remnants, leavings, debris, remainder; **2.** stragglers; **3.** skin eruption, exanthema; **4.** drifters; **5.** reef (of rock); ~ erler ✕ stragglers.

**döl 1.** seed, germ, semen, sperm; **2.** young, offspring, issue, new generation; **3.** new plant, seedling; **4.** descendants, posterity; **5.** generation; **6.** race, stock, origin; ~ döş children, family, descendants, progeny; ~ tutmak to become pregnant *(animal)*; ~ vermek to give birth, to bring forth young, to reproduce.

**döllemek** *biol.* to inseminate, to make pregnant, to fertilize, to fecundate.

**döllenme** insemination, fecundation, fertilization.

**döllenmek** *pass. of* döllemek to be inseminated, to be fertilized, to be fecundated.

**dölüt** *biol.* fetus.

**dölyatağı,** -nı *anat.* uterus, womb.

**dölyolu,** -nu *anat.* vagina.

**döndürmek 1.** to turn round, to reverse, to rotate, to spin; **2.** to send back; **3.** to drive s.o. *(wild, crazy)*; **4.** to fail, to flunk *(a student)*; **5.** to pull *(a. trick)*.

**döneç** *phys.* rotor.

**dönek** fickle, untrustworthy, inconstant, changeable.

**döneklik** fickleness, inconstancy; ~ etm. to go back on one's word.

**dönem 1.** period *(of time)*, era; **2.** *parl.* term; **3.** school term; **4.** *boxing:* round; ~ sonu sınavları end-of-term examinations.

**dönemeç** bend, curve *(in a road)*.

**dönemeçli** winding, curved *(road)*.

**dönence 1.** *ast.* tropic; **2.** turning point.

**döner** turning, revolving; ~ kapı revolving door; ~ kebap pressed lamb roasted on a large vertical spit; ~ koltuk swivel chair; ~ merdiven spiral stairs; ~ sermaye revolving fund, circulating capital.

**döngel** ♀ medlar.

**döngü** circle *(s. kısır döngü)*.

**dönme 1.** *vn. of* dönmek; **2.** converted to Islam; ~ dolap **1.** Ferris wheel, big wheel; **2.** revolving cupboard.

**dönmek,** (-er) **1.** to turn, to revolve, to rotate, to spin; **2.** to return, to go back, to come back; **3.** to turn (-e towards); **4.** to turn (-e into), to become; **5.** to fail; **6.** to be converted *(to another religion)*; **7.** to change *(weather, etc.)*; **8.** to be going on *(s.th. tricky)*; **9.** to swerve *(from a course)*; **10.** *(sözünden)* to break *(one's promise)*, to go back on one's word; **11.** *(kararından)* to change one's mind; döne döne çıkmak to ascend in a spiral; dönüp dolaşıp in the long run, after all; dönüp dolaşmak to walk back and forth.

**dönük 1.** turned (-e to, towards), facing;

**2.** aimed (-e at), addressed (-e to).

**dönüm 1.** a land measure of about 920 m²; **2.** turning, returning; **3.** rotating, revolving; **4.** (round) trip; ~ noktası turning point.

**dönüş 1.** turning; **2.** return(ing); **3.** *sports:* pivoting turn.

**dönüşlü** *gr.* reflective.

**dönüşmek 1.** to change (-e into), to turn (-e into), to be transformed (-e into); **2.** to mutate.

**dönüştürmek 1.** to change (-e into), to transform (-e into); **2.** to cause a mutation (in).

**dönüşüm 1.** transformation; **2.** metaplasia.

**döpiyes** two-piece.

**dörder** four each; ~ ~ by fours.

**dördüncü** fourth; ~ zaman *geol.* Quaternary.

**dördüz** quadruplet.

**dört,** -dü four; ~ ayak üstüne düşmek to land on one's feet, to fall on one's feet; ~ başı mamur *fig.* in perfect condition, prosperous, flourishing; ~ bucakta everywhere, high and low; ~ duvar arasında kalmak to be shut in; ~ elle sarılmak **1.** *(bir işe)* to stick heart and soul (-e at), to be wrapped up (-e in); **2.** *(b-ne)* to cling to s.o.; ~ gözle beklemek to wait eargerly (-i for), to look forward (-i to); ~ işlem ♣ the four operations.

**dörtayak 1.** quadruped; **2.** on all fours.

**dörtcihar** [ā] *dice:* double four.

**dörtgen** ♣ quadrangle, quadrilateral.

**dörtkenar** *s.* dörtgen.

**dörtlemek** to quadruplicate.

**dörtlü 1.** *cards:* four; **2.** quartet.

**dörtlük 1.** ♪ quarter note; **2.** quatrain; **3.** *ast.* quarter *(of the sky)*; ~ es ♪ crotchet-rest.

**dörtnal** gallop.

**dörtnala** at a gallop, galloping.

**dörtyol** crossroads; ~ ağzı crossroads, junction, intersection.

**döş 1.** breast, bosom; **2.** brisket, breast.

**döşek** mattress, bed; ~ esiri olm. to be bedridden, to be confined to bed, *Am.* to be bedfast.

**döşeli 1.** furnished; **2.** floored, laid; dayalı ~ completely furnished *(house)*.

**döşeme 1.** floor(ing), pavement; **2.** furniture; **3.** upholstery; covering.

**döşemeci 1.** upholsterer; **2.** furniture dealer.

**döşemecilik 1.** upholstery; **2.** furniture trade.

**döşemek 1.** to spread, to lay down; **2.** to floor, to pave; **3.** to furnish, to upholster;

**dayayıp** ~ to furnish completely *(house)*.

**döşenmek 1.** *pass. of* döşemek; **2.** *(b-ne)* to scold *s.o.*; **3.** *(bş. hakkında)* to write a diatribe against *s.th.*; **4.** F to take to one's bed, to be bedridden.

**döşeyici** installer; fitter; plumber; electrician.

**dövdürmek** to have s.o. beaten.

**döven** threshing sled; flail.

**döviz 1.** foreign currency, foreign exchange; **2.** motto, slogan, device; **3.** placard; ~ kontrolu exchange control.

**dövme 1.** *vn. of* dövmek; **2.** tattoo; **3.** forging; **4.** wrought *(iron)*; **5.** dehusked wheat.

**dövmek,** (-er) **1.** to beat, to flog, to thrash; **2.** to thresh *(grain)*; **3.** to hammer, to forge *(hot metal)*; **4.** to beat *(laundry)*; **5.** to pound to a powder, to crush up; **6.** to beat *(eggs)*; **7.** to tamp, to pound down; **8.** to shell, to bombard; **9.** to beat, to pound *(waves, rain)*.

**dövülgen** ⊕ malleable.

**dövülgenlik** ⊕ malleability.

**dövülmek** *pass. of* dövmek *part.* to be beaten, to be pounded, to be threshed, to be forged.

**dövünmek 1.** to beat o.s., to beat one's breast; **2.** *fig.* to lament, to be frantic with sorrow.

**dövüş 1.** beating; **2.** fight, brawl, scuffle.

**dövüşçü** fighter.

**dövüşken** bellicose, combative, belligerent.

**dövüşkenlik** bellicosity, pugnacity.

**dövüşmek 1.** to fight, to struggle; **2.** to clash *(armed forces)*; **3.** to box.

**dövüştürmek** to pit *(fighters, animals)* against each other.

**drahmi** drachma.

**drahoma** [x . .] dowry.

**draje 1.** sugar-coated pill; **2.** chocolate-coated nuts.

**dram 1.** *thea.* drama; **2.** tragedy, tragic event.

**dramatik 1.** dramatic; **2.** tragic.

**drenaj** drainage.

**dresuvar** sideboard.

**dretnot,** -tu dreadnought.

**dua** [ā] prayer, blessing; ~ etm. to pray, to bless; -sını almak *(b-nin)* to have the blessing of *s.o.*

**duacı** well-wisher.

**duayen** doyen.

**duba** [x .] pontoon, barge; ~ **gibi** paunchy, very fat.

**dubara** [. - .] **1.** *dice:* double deuce; **2.** *sl.* trick, fraud.

**dubaracı** *sl.* trickster, cheat.

**dublaj** dubbing; ~ yapmak to dub.

**duble 1.** double *(spirits, beer)*; **2.** lining *(of a garment)*; **3.** slip, underdress; ~ etm. to line *(a garment)*.

**dubleks** duplex *(house)*.

**dublör** stunt-man.

**duçar** [- -] subject (-e to), afflicted (-e with), exposed (-e to); ~ olm. to be subject (-e to), to be exposed (-e to), to be afflicted (-e with).

**dudak** lip; ~ boyası lipstick; ~ bükmek to curl one's lip; ~ dudağa lip to lip; ~ sarkıtmak to hang the lip, to sulk; dudağı yarık hare-lipped; dudağını ısırmak to bite one's lip.

**dudaksıl** labial.

**dudu 1.** old Armenian woman; **2.** *title given to women*; **3.** = ~ kuşu; ~ gibi konuşmak to prattle, to chat; ~ kuşu parrot.

**duhul,** -lü [. -] **1.** entering, entrance; **2.** penetration; **3.** 🜊 a man's consummating the sexual act; ~ hakkı 🜊 right of free entrance; ~ imtihanı † entrance examination.

**duhuliye** [. - .] **1.** entrance fee; **2.** import duty.

**duka** [x .] **1.** † duke; **2.** ducat.

**dul** [ū] **1.** widow; widower; **2.** widowed; ~ kalmak to be widowed; ~ karı enciği F chatterer.

**dulavratotu,** -nu 🜂 burdock.

**duman 1.** smoke; fumes; **2.** mist, fog, haze; **3.** F bad, hopeless *(condition)*; **4.** *sl.* hashish, dope; ~ attırmak *sl.* to intimidate: ~ çökmek to settle down *(smoke or mist)*; ~ etm. *sl.* **1.** to spoil, to break up; **2.** to clobber, to defeat; ~ olm. *sl.* to be very bad *(situation)*; -a boğmak to smoke up; -ı üstünde *fig.* very fresh, brand new.

**dumanlamak 1.** to smoke up, to fill with smoke; **2.** to smoke, to cure; **3.** *(kafayı)* to get fuddled.

**dumanlanmak 1.** *pass. of* dumanlamak; **2.** to get smoky; **3.** to become cloudy *(eyes)*; **4.** to get confused *(mind)*, to get fuddled; **5.** to be smoked, to be cured.

**dumanlı 1.** smoky; fumy; **2.** misty, foggy; **3.** *(kafası)* tipsy, fuddled.

**dumansız** smokeless.

**dumdum** dumdum bullet.

**dumur** [. -] atrophy; -a uğramak to be atrophied.

**dun** [ū] 🜂 lower, inferior.

**dupduru** crystal clear.

**duraç**[1], -cı *zo.* francolin.

**duraç**[2], -cı base, pedestal *(of a statute)*.

**durağan** fixed, stable.

**durağanlık** stability.

**durak 1.** stop; **2.** halt, pause, break; **3.** tonic note; **4.** caesura.

**durakı** ✻ nectarine.

**duraklama 1.** pause; **2.** hesitation; **3.** ✕ standstill.

**duraklamak 1.** to stop, to pause, to halt; **2.** to hesitate.

**duraklı** *phys.* stationary.

**duraksama** hesitation.

**duraksamak** to hesitate.

**dural** *phls.* static, unchanging.

**duralama** hesitation, pause.

**duralamak 1.** to pause, to halt, to come to a stop; **2.** to hesitate.

**durdinlen** pause, halt, break; ~ yok there is no time for a break.

**durdurmak** to stop, to halt, to bring to a halt.

**durgun 1.** calm, quiet, still; **2.** stagnant, stationary; **3.** subdued, withdrawn; ~ su standing (*or* stagnant) water.

**durgunlaşmak 1.** to get calm, to calm down; **2.** to become dull, to become torpid.

**durgunluk 1.** calmness; **2.** dullness, heaviness; **3.** stagnation, standstill.

**durmak, (-ur) 1.** to stop, to cease; **2.** to last, to endure, to continue to exist; **3.** to stand; to lie; **4.** to be, to remain (*at a place*); **5.** to exist as a possession, to (still) have; **6.** to suit, to go, to appear, to look; **7.** to behave (*in a specified way*); **8.** (*bir nokta üzerinde*) to dwell on (*a subject*): dur(un)! wait!, stop!; dur! kimdir o? ✕ stop! who goes there?; durakalmak to be taken aback; duracak yer standing-place; durmaksızın *or* durmadan continuously, on end; durmuş oturmuş staid, sedate; durup dururken **1.** suddenly, out, of the blue; **2.** with no reason, without provocation.

**duru** clear, limpid.

**durulama** *vn. of* durulamak rinsing; ~ suyu rinse water; ~ tesisatı purification plant.

**durulamak** to rinse.

**durulaşmak** to become clear (*or* transparent).

**durulmak 1.** to become clear and limpid; **2.** to settle down, to quiet down, to calm down.

**duruluk** clearness, limpidity.

**durum 1.** state, condition, situation, circumstances, position, occasion; **2.** behavio(u)r, attitude.

**duruş 1.** rest, stop; **2.** posture, attitude.

**duruşma** ⛌ trial, hearing (*of a case*).

**duruşmak** to confront one another.

**duş 1.** shower, shower-bath; **2.** shower nozzle; ~ yapmak to have (*or* take) a shower.

**dut, -tu, -du 1.** mulberry; **2.** *sl.* tipsy, pissed; ~ gibi olm. *sl.* **1.** to be pissed, to be as drunk as a lord: **2.** to be greatly a-shamed; ~ yemiş bülbüle benzemek (*or* dönmek) to be tongue-tied, to become sad and taciturn.

**duvak 1.** bridal veil; **2.** large stone lid (*for covering a cistern*); ~ düşkünü young widow; duvağına doymamak to be widowed *or* die while still young (*bride*).

**duvaklı** veiled.

**duvar 1.** wall; **2.** barrier (*between two people*); **3.** *sports:* blocking, defensive barrier; ~ gibi stone-deaf, as deaf as a post; ~ kâğıdı wallpaper; ~ örmek to put up a wall; ~ resmi fresco; ~ saati wall clock; -a yazıyorum! *fig.* mark my words!

**duvarcı 1.** bricklayer; stonemason; **2.** *sl.* burglar.

**duvarcılık** bricklaying; stonemasonry.

**duy** ✄ socket.

**duyar** sensible, sensitive.

**duyarga** *zo.* antenna.

**duyarlı** sensitive.

**duyarlık** sensitiveness; sensitivity.

**duygu 1.** feeling, attitude; **2.** emotion; **3.** sensation, sense; perception; **4.** impression; **5.** sentiment.

**duygudaş** sympathizer.

**duygudaşlık** sympathy.

**duygulamak** to affect, to touch, to move.

**duygulandırmak** to move, to affect, to touch.

**duygulanmak** to be affected, to be touched, to be moved.

**duygulu 1.** sensitive; **2.** impressionable, emotional.

**duygululuk** sensitivity.

**duygun** sensitive.

**duygunluk** sensitivity.

**duygusal 1.** emotional; **2.** romantic, sentimental.

**duygusuz** unfeeling, hardhearted, callous, insensitive, apathetic.

**duygusuzluk** insensitivity, heartlessness.

**duymak, (-ar) 1.** to hear; **2.** to get word of, to learn; **3.** to be aware of; **4.** to feel, to sense, to perceive, to experience; **5.** to have the sensation of; **6.** to feel (*pride, pleasure, etc.*).

**duyu** sense.

**duyulmak** *pass. of* duymak.

**duyum** sensation; ~ eşlği *psych*. threshold of consciousness.

**duyumölçer** esthesiometer.

**duyumsal** sensorial.

**duyurmak** *caus. of* duymak *part.* to announce,· *(b-ne bşi)* to let *s.o.* hear *(or* learn) *s. th.*

**duyuru** announcement; notification.

**duyusal** sensorial.

**duyuş** 1. hearing; 2. perception; 3. impression, feeling.

**duziko** F raki.

**dübeş** *dice:* fives.

**dübür** ⚔ the hinder part of anything; F the buttocks; *sl.* the anus, ass, arse.

**düçar** [ª] *s.* duçar.

**düdük** 1. whistle, pipe, flute, hooter; 2. *sl.* stupid, empty-headed, brainless; ~ gibi kalmak to be left entirely alone; ~ makarnası 1. macaroni; 2. *sl.* silly, dull, imbecile; düdüğü çalmak 1. to succeed; 2. *fig.* to become happy; -le beraber *football:* with the whistle.

**düdüklemek** *sl.* to screw, to stuff.

**düdüklü** having a whistle; ~ tencere pressure cooker.

**düello** duel; ~ etm. to duel.

**düet** ♪ duet.

**düğme** 1. button; 2. ⚡ switch; 3. bud.

**düğmeci** maker *or* seller of buttons.

**düğmelemek** to button up.

**düğmeli** buttoned.

**düğüm** 1. *a.* ⚓, *phys*. knot, bow; 2. *fig.* knotty problem; 3. *lit.* climax; 4. *phys.* node; ~ atmak to knot, to tie in a knot; ~ istasyonu railway junction; ~ noktası *fig.* crucial (*or* vital) point; ~ olm. to get knotted.

**düğümlemek** to knot, to tie in a knot.

**düğümlenmek** *pass. of* düğümlemek, *part.* to get tangled.

**düğümlü** knotted.

**düğün** 1. wedding feast; 2. circumcision feast; ~ bayram etm. *fig.* to be as happy as the day is long, to be as happy as a sandboy; ~ dernek, hep bir örnek F it's always the same old thing; ~ yapmak to hold a wedding.

**düğünçiçeği,** -ni ⚘ buttercup.

**dük,** -kü duke; ♀ dö Windsor duke of Windsor.

**dükkân** 1. shop; 2. *sl.* gambling house; ~ açmak to open shop, to set up business.

**dükkâncı** shopkeeper.

**düldül** *sl.* 1. nag, broken-down horse; 2. lizzie, jalopy, crate.

**dülger** carpenter; builder.

**dülgerbalığı,** -nı *zo.* John Dory, dory.

**dülgerlik** carpentry.

**dümbelek** 1. tabor, timbal; 2. *sl.* idiot.

**dümbelekçi** drummer.

**dümdar** [ª] ✗ rear guard; ~ muharebeleri rear guard action.

**dümdüz** [x .] 1. perfectly smooth, quite level; 2. straight -ahead; 3. *sl.* simple, plain *(person).*

**dümen** 1. rudder, helm; 2. *sl.* trick, humbug; 3. *fig.* control, administration; ~ çevirmek F to play tricks, to humbug; ~ erbaşı steersman; ~ kırmak ⚓ to veer; ~ kolu rudder bar; ~ kullanmak 1. ·to steer; 2. *fig.* to be on one's guard; ~ neferi *fig.* the last *or* laziest *(person);* ~ suyundan gitmek *(b-nin)* to follow in *s.o.'s* wake; ~ tutmak to steer; ~ yapmak *sl.* to trick, to deceive, to cheat; ~ yekesi ⚓ tiller; -i eğri *co.* walking sideways; -i kırmak *sl.* to slip away, to clear out, to beat it, to make off.

**dümenci** 1. helmsman, steersman; 2. *sl.* the last *or* laziest *(student);* 3. *sl.* trickster, cheat.

**dümencilik** 1. steering; 2. *sl.* the tail end; being the last; 3. *sl.* trickiness.

**dün** 1. yesterday; 2. the past; ~ akşam last night, yesterday evening; ~ bir, bugün iki it is still too soon; ~ değil evvelki gün the day before yesterday.

**dünden** 1. from yesterday; 2. eagerly; ~ bugüne in a short time, overnight; ~ hazır eager; ~ ölmüş listless, without zest; ~ teşnedir *fig.* he is over-eager.

**dünkü** 1. yesterday's, of yesterday; 2. *fig.* raw, inexperienced, green, tiro; ~ çocuk greenhorn, tyro.

**dünür** 1. the father-in-law *or* mother-in-law of one's child; 2. = dünürsü; ~ gezmek to search for a suitable bride for·a suitor.

**dünürcü** woman sent out to see about a prospective bride.

**dünürsü, dünüş** the mother-in-law of a woman's child.

**dünya** 1. world, earth; 2. universe; 3. everyone, people; ~ âlem F everyone, all the world; ~ başına yıkılmak *fig.* to be very miserable; ~ durdukça for ever and ever; ~ evine girmek to get married; ~ harbi world-war; ~ kadar a world of, loads of, pots of; ~ şampiyonu *sports:* world champion; ~ yıkılsa umurunda olmamak not to give a damn; -da never in this world; -dan elini eteğini çekmek to go *(or* retire) into one's shell; -nın dört bucağı the four corners of the earth; -ya gelmek to be born, to come into the world; -ya getirmek to give birth to, to bring into the world; -ya gözlerini kapamak to die, to pass away, to pass on; -ya kazık çakmak (or kakmak) fig. to live to a ripe old age; -yayı tozpembe görmek to see the world through rose-colo(u)red spectacles.

**dünyevi** worldly.

**düpedüz** [x . .] 1. openly; 2. sheer, absolute, downright, utter.

**dürbün** 1. binoculars, field glasses; 2. small telescope.

**dürmek** to roll up, to fold.

**dürtmek** 1. to prod, to goad, to nudge; 2. fig. to incite, to stir up, to provoke, to urge on, to instigate.

**dürlü** psych. impulse, compulsion, drive.

**dürtüklemek** to nudge.

**dürtüşmek** to push (or prod) one another.

**dürülmek** pass. of dürmek.

**dürüm** roll, fold, pleat.

**dürüm** dürüm in rolls.

**dürüst**, -tü 1. honest, straightforward; 2. fig. flawless.

**dürüstlük** honesty.

**dürüşt**, -tü harsh, coarse, severe, brutal.

**Dürzi** pr. n. Druse.

**dürzü** sl. scoundrel.

**düse** [- .] dice: double three.

**düstur** [ü] 1. norm; rule; 2. code of laws; 3. ?, A̧ formula; 4. principle.

**düş** 1. dream; 2. aspiration, hope; ~ görmek to have a dream; ~ kırıklığı disappointment; ~ kurmak to daydream.

**düşes** duchess.

**düşeş** 1. dice: double six; 2. fig. windfall; bargain.

**düşey** A̧ perpendicular, vertical.

**düşgelmek** to chance (-e on), to come across, to come (-e upon).

**düşkün** 1. addicted (-e to), given (-e to), devetod (-e to); 2. deeply devoted (-e to), wrapped up (-e in); 3. down-and-out, who has seen better days; 4. worn-out, washed-out; 5. unchaste, fallen, loose (woman).

**düşkünleşmek** 1. to come down in the world, to fall upon hard times; 2. (of women) to go on (or walk) the streets.

**düşkünlük** 1. poverty, decay; 2. excessive addiction.

**düşman** enemy, foe, adversary; ~ ağzı calumny; ~ olm. to beocme an enemy (-e of).

**düşmanca** in a hostile manner.

**düşmanlık** enmity, hostility, animosity.

**düşme** 1. vn. of düşmek; 2. phys. fall.

**düşmek**, (-er) 1. to fall; 2. to drop, to go down, to decrease, to fall; 3. to subtract; to deduct; 4. to be born dead (fetus); 5. to fall (-e into) (doubt, worry, trouble); 6. to get (tired, weak); 7. to suit, to match, to go (-e with); 8. to be up (-e to), to lie within one's responsibility; 9. to lie (in a direction); 10. to fall (on a certain day); 11. to fall to one's lot; 12. to come (-e to) by chance; 13. to be left out (-den of), to be omitted, to be skipped; 14. to wind up (-e in), to end up (-e in), to land up (-e in) (prison, court, hospital); 15. to drop (in value); 16. to fall (government, fort); 17. (birbirine) to be set by the ears; 18. to drop (fever); düş önüme! come along with me!; düşe kalka struggling along, with difficulty; düşenin dostu olmaz pro. laugh, the whole world will laugh with you; cry, and you will cry alone; düşüp kalkmak (b-le) to live with s.o., to live together, to shack up with s.o.

**düşsel** oneiric.

**düşük** 1. fallen, drooping; 2. low (price, quality); 3. unchaste, fallen, loose (woman); 4. gr. misconstrued (sentence); 5. ? miscarriage, abortion; ~ etek fig. slipshod, sloppy (woman).

**düşüm** fall, decline.

**düşümdeşlik** phls. coincidence.

**düşün** thought.

**düşünce** 1. thought; 2. idea, opinion, reflection; 3. anxiety, worry; -ye dalmak to be lost in thought.

**düşünceleme** phls. ideation.

**düşünceli** 1. thoughtful, considerate; 2. worried, anxious, depressed; 3. pensive, lost in thought.

**düşüncesiz** 1. thoughtless, inconsiderate, tactless; careless; 2. unworried; carefree.

**düşüncesizlik** thoughtlessness, tactlessness. inconsiderateness.

**düşündürmek** caus. of düşünmek.

**düşündürücü** thought-provoking.

**düşünme** 1. thinking, thought; 2. phls. introspection.

**düşünmece** problem, brain-twister, Am. quiz.

**düşünmek** 1. to think (-i of); 2. to consider, to think (-i about), to ponder (üzerinde over); 3. to worry (-i about); 4. to remember; düşünüp taşınmak to consider at length, to mull over.

**düşünülmek** pass. of düşünmek.

**düşünür** thinker, intellectual.

**düşünüş** mentality, way of thinking, reflection.

**düşürmek** caus. of düşmek part. 1. to drop, to let fall, to bring down; 2. to reduce; 3. to miscarry, to abort (child); 4. to pass (from the body); 5. to get at a bargain; 6. to overthrow, to bring down (goverment); 7. (birbirine) to set at loggerheads, to play one person off against another.

**düşüş** 1. fal, falling; 2. decrease.

**düşüt** aborted fetus.

**düt** toot.

**düttürü** [x . .] 1. oddly dressed; 2. odd or tight dress.

**düve** zo. heifer.

**düven** threshing sled; ~ sürmek to thresh.

**düyun** [ū] pl. debts.

**düz** 1. smooth, even; flat, level; 2. straight; 3. simple, plain; without ornament, plain-colo(u)red; 4. level area, plain; ~ tümleç gr. direct object.

**düzayak** 1. without stairs, on one floor; 2. on a level with the street.

**düzce** [x .] fairly smooth (or level); -si frankly, to tell the truth.

**düzelmek** 1. to be put in order, to be arranged; 2. to improve, to get better; 3. to straighten out; 4. to get well, to get about.

**düzeltici** 1. corrective; 2. proofreader.

**düzelticilik** proofreading.

**düzeltme** vn. of düzeltmek part. 1. proofreading; 2. correction: 3. reform; ~ işareti circumflex.

**düzeltmek** caus. of düzelmek 1. to smooth, to make smooth; to straighten; 2. to put in order, to repair; 3. to correct; 4. to proofread.

**düzeltmen** proofreader.

**düzem** ♫ formula, recipe.

**düzen** 1. order, harmony, regularity, orderliness; arrangement; 2. the social order, the system; 3. ♪ tuning; 4. fig. trick, swindle; ~ kurmak fig. to set a trap, to prepare a trick, to resort to deception; ~ vermek (or -e koymak or -e sokmak) to put in order, to tidy up.

**düzenbaz**, **düzenci** trickster, cheat, humbug.

**düzenek** 1. plan; 2. mechanism.

**düzengeç** phys. regulator.

**düzenleme** vn. of düzenlemek arrangement; preparation.

**düzenlemek** 1. to put in order; 2. to arrange, to hold (a meeting); to prepare.

**düzenlenmek** pass. of düzenlemek.

**düzenli** 1. tidy, orderly, in order; 2. fig. systematic.

**düzenlilik** orderliness, tidiness.

**düzensiz** 1. out of order, untidy, disorderly, tumultuous; 2. fig. unsystematic.

**düzensizlik** disorder, untidiness.

**düzenteker** phys. flywheel.

**düzey** 1. level; 2. rank; 3. contour line.

**düzgün**[1] 1. smooth, level; 2. orderly, well-arranged, tidy; 3. correct; 4. ♣ regular; 5. smoothly, regularly.

**düzgün**[2] a liquid make-up for the face.

**düzgünlük** order, regularity, smoothness.

**düzgüsel** phls. normative.

**düzgüsüz** phls. abnormal.'

**düzine** 1. dozen; 2. dozens of, lots of.

**düzlem** ♣ plane; ~ geometri plane geometry.

**düzlemek** 1. to smooth, to level, to flatten; 2. to mill, to machine.

**düzlemküre** planisphere.

**düzleşmek** to become smooth (or level or straight).

**düzletmek** to smooth, to flatten.

**düzlük** 1. smoothness, flatness, levelness; 2. evenness, uniformity; 3. plainness; 4. level (or flat) place, plain.

**düzme** 1. vn. of düzmek; 2. false, fake; forged.

**düzmece** = düzme 2.

**düzmeci** forger, faker, cheat.

**düzmecilik** forgery; deception, deceit.

**düzmek**, (-er) 1. to arrange, to compose; to prepare; 2. to invent, to fabricate (a story); 3. to forge, to counterfeit; 4. sl. to rape; düzüp koşmak to arrange, to compose.

**düztaban** 1. flat-footed; 2. fig. ill-omened, Jonah; 3. flatfoot; 4. rabbet plane.

**düztabanlık** flat-footedness.

**düzülmek** 1. pass. of düzmek; 2. s. yola ~.

**düzyazı** prose.

# E

**e 1.** *(in request or question)* well, all right; **2.** then; **3.** *s. a* (4); **4.** now then, now; **5.** oh! *(surprise)*.

**-e** *(ending of dat)*.

**-e halı** *gr.* dative *(case)*.

**ebat** [ā] **1.** dimensions; **2.** size.

**ebe 1.** midwife; **2.** it *(in children's games):* ~ hekim obstetrician; -nin örekesi F pack of nonsense.

**ebeden** [x . .] **1.** ever, eternally; **2.** *(followed by negative verb)* never.

**ebedi** eternal, without end, never-ending.

**ebediyen** [î] [. . x .] **1.** eternally, for ever, in perpetuity; **2.** *(in negative sentences)* not at all, by no means.

**ebediyet,** -ti eternity.

**ebegümeci,** -ni ♀ mallow.

**ebekuşağı,** -nı rainbow.

**ebet** eternity without end.

**ebeveyn** parents.

**ebleh** stupid, foolish, silly; imbecile.

**ebonit,** -ti ebonite.

**ebru** [ū] **1.** marbling *(of variegated paper);* marbled *(paper);* **2.** watering *(of fabrics).*

**ebrulamak** [. - . .] **1.** to marble *(paper);* **2.** to water *(a fabric).*

**ecdat** [. - ] ancestors.

**ece** queen.

**ecel 1.** ठ appointed term; **2.** death, decease, appointed hour of death; ~ teri dökmek to be in mortal fear, to be in a cold sweat, to be in fear and trembling; -i gelmek to have one's fated time of death arrive; -ine susamak to be fool hardy, to be daredevil; -iyle ölmek to die a natural death; eceli kaza accidental death.

**ecinli, ecinni** P = cin².

**ecir,** -cri **1.** reward, recompense; **2.** pay, wage, remuneration; ~ sabır dilemek to condole (with).

**eciş bücüş 1.** out of shape, crooked, distorted; contorted; **2.** eccentric, odd, unusual; **3.** wizened *(person).*

**ecnebi 1.** foreigner, stranger, alien; foreign, strange; ~ matbuat (-ı) foreign press.

**ecza,** -aı [ā] **1.** parts; **2.** Å submultiple; **3.** drugs, medicines, chemicals; **4.** *phot.* developer; **5.** in paper cover, unbound.

**eczacı** [ā] chemist, druggist, pharmacist.

**eczacılık** [ā] pharmacy *(profession).*

**eczalı** [ā] prepared with chemicals; containing chemicals; ~ pamuk medical cotton.

**eczane** [ā] pharmacy, chemist's shop, drugstore.

**eda** [ā] **1.** payment; **2.** execution, fulfil(l)-ment, performance; **3.** behavio(u)r, conduct, manner, style, tone, affectation; **4.** arrogance, insolence; **5.** representation, articulation; ~ etm. **1.** to fulfil(l), to perform *(a duty);* **2.** to articulate *(word or letter);* **3.** to represent; **4.** to pay *(a debt).*

**edalı** [ā] **1.** having an air; **2.** charming, gracious; **3.** arrogant, affected, pretended.

**edat,** -tı [ā] **1.** instrument, implement; **2.** *gr.* particle, preposition.

**edebi** literary.

**edebikelâm** euphemism.

**edebiyat,** -tı [ā] literature; ~ dekoru rhetorical ornamentation; ♀ Fakültesi Faculty of Arts, the College of Literature and Arts; ~ yapmak to use a pompous language.

**edebiyatçı** [ā] man of letters, literary man, writer.

**edep,** -bi **1.** good breeding, good manners, politeness, respect, modesty; rule custom; **2.** = ayıp; ~ erkân good manners; etiquette; ~ yeri private parts, genitals; edebini takınmak to behave o.s., to be polite; -tir söylemesi P excuse the expression.

**edepli** well-behaved, well-mannered, with good manners.

**edepsiz** ill-mannered, rude, shameless, insolent.

**eder** price.

**edevat,** -tı [ā] **1.** tools, instruments, implements; **2.** *gr.* particles; ~ deposu tools store.

edibane [. - - .] 1. = edepli; 2. in a literary manner; worthy of a literary man.

edilgen *gr.* passive; ~ fiil *gr.* passive.

edilmek *pass. of* etmek.

edinmek to get, to have, to procure, to acquire.

edip [¹] man of letters, literary man, writer; 2. = edepli.

Edirne *pr. n.* Edirne, Adrianople.

editör 1. publisher; 2. editor.

efe¹ 1. elder brother; 2. brave chap, courageous lad; 3. guer(r)illa, irregular; 4. village hero, swashbuckling village dandy.

efe² ⁴ effect.

efekt, -ti ⊕ effect.

efektif cash,˙ ready money.

efelik swagger, dash: ~ satmak *(or* yapmak) to swagger, to strut, to boast.

efendi [. x .] 1. *title given to literate people, members of the Clergy, Ottoman princes, army officers up to major;* 2. master; Mr. *(after the first name);* 3. *pej.* strange, odd, peculiar *(person);* 4. *(a.* -den*)* gentleman; ~ adam gentleman.

efendim 1. yes? *(as an answer to a call);* 2. I beg your pardon?; 3. sir; ma'am; 4. added to a sentence for politeness.

Efes Ephesus.

Efgan(istan) *s.* Afgan(istan).

efkâr *(pl. of* fikir*)* 1. thoughts, ideas, opinions; 2. intentions; 3. worry, anxiety; ~ dağıtmak to cheer o.s. up.

efkârıumumiye public opinion.

efkârlanmak F to become wistfully sad.

efkârlı worried, anxious.

Eflâtun [ū] *pr. n.* Plato.

eflâtun [ū] *(renkli)* lilac-colo(u)red.

efor effort, exertion.

efrat, -dı [ā] *(pl. of* fert*)* 1. individuals, people; 2. X private soldiers. the ranks, rank and file; 3. members.

efsane [ā] 1. legend; fable, tale, myth; 2. *pej.* idle tale.

efsanevi [ā] legendary.

efsun charm, spell, enchantment.

eften püften flimsy.

Ege Aegean Sea; ~ Denizi Aegean Sea; ~ havzası Aegean territory.

ege master guardian.

egemen sovereign, dominant.

egemenlik sovereignty, dominance.

egoist egoist, selfish.

egoistlik egoism, selfishness.

egoizm egoism, selfishness.

egosantrizm egocentricity.

egzama [x . .] eczema.

egzersiz exercise, practice.

egzistansialist, -ti existentialist.

egzos, egzost, -tu ⊕ exhaust; ~ borusu exhaust pipe; ~ gazı exhaust gas.

egzotik exotic.

eğe¹ file.

eğe² *anat.* rib.

eğelemek to file.

eğer [x .] 1. if, whether; when; 2. *s.* eyer.

eğik 1. Ⱥ oblique; 2. inclined, sloping down.

eğilim tendency, inclination, affinity; ~ göstermek to show tendency *(-e* to*)*.

eğilme Ⱥ, *phys.* inclination, dip.

eğilmek 1. *pass. of* eğmek; 2. to bend; to incline; to curve; to warp; 3. to bow (down), to stoop; 4. to submit, to yield; 5. to get down to *(a job);* eğilip bükülmek to wind.

eğim 1. slope, declivity; 2. Ⱥ dip, grade, gradient.

eğin, -ğni back, shoulders; eğne binmek *fig.* to bully, to tyrannize.

eğinç, -ci tumo(u)r.

eğinik leaning, inclined.

eğinim inclination, tendency, affinity.

eğinti filings.

eğirmek to spin.

eğirmen spindle, distaff.

eğitbilim pedagogy.

eğitici 1. pedagogue; 2. educational, instructive.

eğitim education, training, instruction.

eğitimci educator, educationalist, pedagogue.

eğitimli educated, trained, instructed.

eğitmek 1. to educate; 2. to train, to break in.

eğitmen educator; instructor.

eğitsel educational.

eğlemek 1. to retard, to delay, to hold back; 2. to amuse.

eğlence 1. diversion, amusement, enjoyment, entertainment, fun; 2. butt of derision, laughing-stock, joke; 3. entertaining party: ~ yeri pleasure ground, amusement park, recreation ground.

eğlenceli amusing, diverting, entertaining.

eğlencelik 1. titbits, tidbits; 2. *fig.* laughing-stock.

eğlendirmek to entertatain, to amuse, to divert.

eğlenmek 1. to be amused, to amuse o.s., to enjoy o.s., to have a good time; 2. *(b-le)* to make fun of s.o., to joke with s.o., to make a mock of s.o., to ridicule; 3. to while away, to loaf.

eğlenti blow-out, amusement, feast, party. entertainment.

**eğmek** to bend, to incline, to curve, to bow.

**eğre** saddlecloth.

**eğrelti, eğreltiotu,** -nu ♀ fern, bracken.

**eğreti 1.** artificial, false: **2.** borrowed; **3.** provisional, temporary, makeshift; ~ almak *(bşi b-den)* to borrow; ~ ata binen tez iner *pro.* he who rides a borrowed horse must soon dismount; ~ oturmak to sit on the edge of *s.th.*

**eğri 1.** crooked, bent, curved; **2.** oblique, slanting, inclined, awry, askew; **3.** ⅄ curve, bend, angle; **4.** perverse, wrong, unjust, untrue; **5.** ↓ rib; ~ bakmak **1.** to look at *s.th.* slantwise; **2.** to leer (*-e* at); ~ gitmek *fig.* to deviate, to go wrong; ~ oturmak to sit informally; ~ söylemek **1.** to say maliciously; **2.** to fib, to tell fibs.

**eğribacak** bow-legged, bandy-legged, knock-kneed.

**eğribüğrü** [- . . . .] **1.** bent and crooked, contorted, twisted, gnarled, devious; **2.** pitiful, pitiable, miserable.

**eğrili** ⅄ curvilinear.

**eğrilik 1.** crookedness; curvature; **2.** dishonesty; **3.** obliquity, slope, incline; **4.** ⅄ bend(ing).

**eğrilmek** to become bent, to incline, to arch, to slope, to bow.

**eğriltmek** to make crooked, to bend, to twist.

**eh** *int.* well, all right, come on, enough.

**ehemmiyet,** -ti importance, significance; ~ vermek *(bşe)* to attach importance to *s.th.;* -le kaydetmek to render prominently, to emphasize; -le rica etm. to entreat, to beseech, to implore, to adjure.

**ehemmiyetli** important, significant.

**ehemmiyetsiz** unimportant, insignificant.

**ehil,** -hli **1.** community, people; **2.** competent; **3.** gifted, talented; **4.** husband; wife; spouse; **5.** possessor, owner, proprietor; ehli olm. *(bşin)* to be endowed with *s.th.,* to be versed in *s.th.*

**ehli** tame, domestic(ated).

**ehlibeyt,** -ti the Prophet's family.

**ehlihibre** *(sg. or pl.)* expert.

**ehliislam** Muslim(s).

**ehlikeyf** self-indulgent, pleasure-seeking.

**ehlileştirmek** to tame.

**Ehlisalip,** -bi *hist.* Crusaders; ~ Seferleri *hist.* Crusades.

**ehlivukuf** *s.* ehlihibre.

**ehliyet,** -ti **1.** capacity, competence, efficiency; **2.** (= ~ vesikası) driving license, driver's license; ~ sahibi expert, specialist; ehliyeti fenniye vesikası certificate of qualification, certificate of compe-

tence.

**ehliyetli 1.** able, capable; gifted, talented; **2.** competent, qualified; **3.** licensed.

**ehliyetname** [â] **1.** driving license, driver's license; **2.** certificate of competence, certificate of qualification.

**ehram** [â] **1.** the Pyramids; **2.** Pyramid.

**ehven 1.** cheap(est), inexpensive; **2.** the better; ehveni şer the lesser of two evils.

**ejder, ejderha** [â] dragon.

**ek,** -ki **1.** addition; appendix; **2.** extension; **3.** supplement; **4.** seam, scar, knot *(tree);* **5.** wing; **6.** join(t); **7.** *gr.* inflexion-ending; **8.** *gr.* suffix, affix, prefix; ~ pük odds and ends, bits and pieces; ~ yeri seam, scar; body joint; -ini belli etmemek *fig.* to cover up, to dissimulate, to dissemble.

**ekâbir** the great; important people; VIP's, F bigwig, big shot, big pot.

**ekalliyet,** -ti minority; -ler hukuku ⚖ Law of Minorities; -te kalmak to be in the minority.

**ekber 1.** greatest, very great, highest; **2.** older, oldest.

**ekici** sower.

**ekili** sown, planted *(field).*

**ekim 1.** sowing, planting; **2.** *(ayı)* October.

**ekin 1.** crops, growing grain; **2.** culture, civilization; ~ biçmek to reap, to harvest.

**ekinci 1.** sower; cultivator; **2.** farmer.

**ekip,** -pi team *(a. sport),* crew, gang, company.

**eklem** *anat.* joint, articulation.

**eklemek 1.** to add, to join; **2.** to lengthen; **3.** to put together, to compose, to compound, to assemble; **4.** to combine, to merge, to consolidate, to fuse; **5.** *sl.* to knock down, to fell.

**eklenmek** to be joined (*-e* to), to be added (*-e* to).

**eklenti 1.** *gr.* suffix; **2.** annex.

**ekler¹** *biol.* annexa.

**ekler²** zip fastener, zip(per).

**ekli** pieced, put together; ~ püklü patchy.

**ekmek¹ 1.** to sow; **2.** to till, to cultivate *(field);* **3.** to scatter, to sprinkle, to spread; **4.** *sl.* to squander, to blue, to blow *(money);* **5.** *sl.* to pass, to overtake, to outstrip; **6.** *sl.* to put s.o. off, to get rid of s.o.

**ekmek² 1.** bread; **2.** bread and butter, bread-winning, living, livelihood; **3.** food; **4.** job; ~ çiğne(n)meden yutulmaz *pro.* you have to chew the bread to swallow it; ~ kabuğu crust of a loaf; ~ kapısı *fig.* the place where one works for one's living; ~ ufağı breadcrumb; ekmeği di-

zinde *fig.* submissive, servile, ungrateful; ekmeğine yağ sürmek *fig.* to play into s.o.'s. hands.
**ekmekçi 1.** baker; **2.** bakery.
**ekmeklik 1.** breadbasket; **2.** suitable for bread making; **3.** *sl.* simpleton, dupe, fool, easy victim, easy mark.
**ekoloji** ecology.
**ekonomi** economy; 2 Bakanlığı Ministry of Economy; ~ politik political economy.
**ekonomik** economic(al); ~ coğrafya economic geography.
**ekose** plaid, tartan.
**ekran 1.** screen; **2.** *phot.* filter.
**eksantrik** eccentric; ~ mili ⊕ eccentric rod.
**ekselans** Excellency.
**eksen 1.** axis; **2.** axle.
**ekser¹** large nail, spike; -i oynamış *fig.* mad, nuts.
**ekser² [x . .], ekseri [x . .]** majority, the greater part; ekser(i) ahvalde mostly, generally; ekserisi usually.
**ekseriya [x . .]** generally, mostly, usually, often.
**ekseriyet,** -ti majority; -le generally, usually, mostly.
**eksi** A minus; yedi ~ üç seven minus three.
**eksibe** sand dunes.
**eksik 1.** missing, lacking, absent, defect, wanting; **2.** less (than); **3.** deficient, incomplete, defective, imperfect; **4.** deficit; ~ etmemek to keep always in stock, always to have, never to omit; ~ gedik small necessities, deficiencies; ~ gelmek to be insufficient; ~ olma(-yın)! thank you very much!; ~ olsun! no, thank you!; ~ olmamak always to turn up, always to be available; eksiğini tamamlamak to fill the gap, to make good a deficiency, to complement, to supplement.
**eksiklik 1.** deficiency, defectiveness; lack, absence; **2.** shortcoming, defect, fault.
**eksiksiz 1.** complete, perfect; **2.** permanent; **3.** without defect, faultless.
**eksilmek 1.** to decrease, to lessen, to diminish, to dwindle; **2.** to be absent, to disappear.
**eksiltme** bid, tender.
**eksiltmek** to diminish, to reduce, to lessen, to decrease.
**eksiz 1.** seamless (*a.* ⊕); **2.** *gr.* without a suffix.
**ekskavatör** excavator, steam shovel.
**eksos** *s.* egzos(t).
**eksper** expert, valuer.
**ekspres** express train *or* steamer.

**ekstra [x .]** extra, first quality; ~ ~ the very best, best of all.
**ekşi 1.** sour, acid, tart; **2.** *fig.* sour-faced, unfriendly; ~ surat long (*or* surly *or* sullen) face; -ye çalmak to taste sour.
**ekşilik 1.** sourness, acidity, tartness; **2.** *fig.* unfriendliness.
**ekşimek 1.** to (become) sour, to turn sour; **2.** to ferment; **3.** *sl.* to be disgraced, to fall into disgrace, to be disconcerted; **4.** to be upset (*stomach*); **5.** to become cross (*or* disagreeable).
**ekşimik** a kind of soft cheese.
**ekşimsi, ekşimtırak** sourish.
**ekşitmek** to sour; *part. sl.* to compromise.
**ekvator** equator.
**el¹ 1.** hand; **2.** forefoot; **3.** grip, handle; **4.** handful; **5.** help, assistance, aid; **6.** handwriting; **7.** possession; **8.** shot, discharge (*of a fire-arm*); **9.** hand, deal (*of cards*); **10.** power; ~ açmak to beg (for), to go begging; ~ altında handy, on hand, available, ready; ~ altından under the counter, underhandedly, secretly; ~ arabası **1.** wheel-barrow, hand-cart, push-cart; **2.** *sl. school:* wank; ~ atmak (*bşe*) **1.** to lay hands (on), to seize, to usurp; **2.** to attempt, to undertake, to take over, to assume; **3.** to intervene, to interfere; ~ çekmek (*bşden*) to withdraw, to give up, to relinquish, to leave off, to desist (from); ~ koymak (*bşe*) **1.** to take s.th. in hand; **2.** to seize, monopolize, to confiscate; ~ ulağı **1.** messenger boy; **2.** helper, assistant; ~ uzatmak **1.** to stretch out the hand, to reach (for); **2.** (*b-ne*) *fig.* to help s.o. (out), to give (*or* lend) s.o. a hand; ~ yazısı **1.** handwriting; **2.** manuscript; -de bulunmak to be available, to be at s.o.'s disposal; -de etm. **1.** to get hold of, to obtain, to get, to secure, to achieve, to attain; **2.** to win s.o. over; -den **1.** by oneself, in person; **2.** by hand, by a messenger; -den ağıza yaşamak to live from hand to mouth; -den çıkarmak to sell, to dispose (of), to get rid (of); -den düşme secondhand; -den -e from hand to hand; -den geçirmek **1.** to review, to go over, to examine, to look through; **2.** to overhaul; -den gelmek **1.** to be able to do, to be within one's capabilities; **2.** *sl.* to fork out, to tip, to pay up; -e geçirmek **1.** to get hold (of), to obtain, to secure; **2.** to conquer; -e vermek to hand over, to give away, to betray, to put the finger on; -i açık open-handed, generous, liberal; -i ağır **1.** heavy-handed, slow; **2.** heavy-fisted, strong-fisted; -i

ayağı tutmak to be alive and kicking, to be in the pink (of health); -ı bayraklı quarrelsome, insolent, shrew, virago, scold, vixen; -ı çabuk adroit, nimble- -fingered; -ı dar(-da) hard up; -ı hafif light-handed; -ı maşalı shrew, virago, scold, vixen, termagant, amazon; -ı sıkı close-fisted; -ı uzun light-fingered; -ı varmamak not to have the heart (to do s.th.); -ı yatkın deft, handy; -ı yüzü düzgün presentable; -inde in the hands of, in s.o.'s hands; -inde bulunmak 1. to be at s.o.'s disposal; 2. to be owned (by); -inden tutmak *fig.* 1. to help (out); 2. to patronize, to protect; -ine bakmak 1. to depend (-*in* on), to be dependent (-*in* on), to be supported (-*in* by); 2. to look at s.o.'s hands to see what has been brought; -ine geçmek 1. to earn, to get; 2. to meet, to come across; 3. to find; -ine su dökemez (*b-nin*) can't hold a candle to s.o.; -ini çabuk tutmak to hurry up; -ini kolunu bağlamak (*b-nin*) to tie (*or* bind) s.o. hand and foot; -ini veren kolunu alamaz (*b-ne*) give him an inch and he'll take a yard; -ini yüzünü yıkamak (*bşden*) to wash one's hands of s.th.; -ler yukarı! hands up!; -leri yanına gelmek to die; -lerinizden öperim I kiss your hands.

**el[2]** 1. land, country; 2. people; 3. stranger, alien; 4. others; ~ ağzıyle çorba yemek to slander s.o.; ~ gün = elalem; ~ kapısı a stranger's house; ~ kapısında çalışmak to work in another's house; ~ oğlu = elalem; -e güne karşı in the eyes of everybody.

**ela** hazel (eyes).

**elado etm** *sl.* to snatch away.

**elalem** people, all the world, everybody, strangers; -e kepaze olm. to become the laughing-stock of people.

**elaman** 1. ⚒ mercy, pardon; 2. enough!, I am fed up!

**el'an** [ā] now, at present; still, yet.

**elastik(i)** elastic.

**elastikiyet** elasticity.

**elbet,** -ti [x .], **elbette** [x . .] *or* [. x .] certainly, decidedly, surely.

**elbirliği** co-operation.

**elbise** 1. clothes, clothing, garments; 2. dress, suit (*of clothes*); ~ askısı coat-hanger.

**elçi** envoy; ambassador.

**elçilik** embassy; legation.

**eldiven** glove.

**elebaşı** 1. *contp.* ringleader; 2. captain (*in a game*).

**elek** sieve; -ten geçirmek to sift (*a. fig*).

**elektrifikasyon** electrification.

**elektrik** 1. electricity; 2. † electric; ~ akımı electric current; ~ düğmesi switch; ~ fabrikası (electric) power station.

**elektrikçi** electrician.

**elektrikleştirmek** 1. to electrify; 2. to inspire, to thrill.

**elektrikli** electric; live (*wire*); ~ koltuk (*or* sandalye) electric chair.

**elektrokardiyografi** electrocardiography.

**elektromanyetik** electromagnetic.

**elektromıknatıs** electromagnet.

**elektron** electron.

**elektronik** electronic(s); ~ beyin computer.

**elem** pain, suffering; sorrow, care; illness, ailment; affliction, grief; ~ çekmek to suffer.

**eleman** 1. element, part, component; 2. personnel, staff member, performer, worker; 3. ∮ battery cell.

**elemanter** elementary.

**eleme** 1. *vn.* of elemek; 2. sifted, sieved; selected; 3. elimination; ~ imtihanı (*or* sınavı) preliminary examination.

**elemek** 1. to sift, to sieve; 2. *fig.* to eliminate, to select, to pick out; 3. to wind into hanks (*yarn*).

**element** element.

**elemli** painful, grievous, sorrowful.

**Elen** 1. Hellene; 2. Greek, Hellenic.

**elenika:** -sını bilmek (*bşin*) to have s.th. at one's fingertips.

**eleştiri** criticism.

**eleştirici** 1. critic; 2. critical.

**eleştirim** criticism.

**eleştirimci** critic.

**eleştirme** criticism.

**eleştirmek** to criticize.

**eleştirmen** critic.

**elfatiha** *name of the opening chapter of the Koran.*

**elhamdülillah** [. x . .] ⚒ Thank God!

**elhasıl** in short, in brief, to sum up.

**elif** *name of the first letter of the Arabic alphabet;* -i -ine exactly, just, sharply; -i görse mertek (*or* direk) sanır he knows not a «B» from a bull's foot.

**elifba, elifbe** the Arabic alphabet.

**elim** painful, grievous, deplorable, sorrowful

**elinsaf!** have a heart!, be reasonable!

**elişi** 1. handicraft, manual labo(u)r; 2. hand-made.

**elkitabı** handbook, manual.

**elleme** 1. *vn.* of ellemek; 2. *part.* hand-picked charcoal.

**ellemek** to handle, to feel with the hand.

**emmek**

to touch with the hand.

**elleşmek** *(b-le)* **1.** to push and shove; **2.** to shake hands; **3.** to try one another's strength by hand grips; **4.** to come to blows *(or* grips); **5.** to disturb, to trouble, to molest, to annoy, to bother.

**elli**[1] ...handed; having hands.

**elli**[2] fifty; ~ altı **1.** fifty-six; **2.** *sl.* slap; a beating; ~ dirhem otuz *sl.* pissed, pickled.

**ellilik 1.** a banknote for fifty liras; **2.** quinquagenarian, fifty years old.

**ellinci** fiftieth.

**ellişer** fifty each; fifty at a time.

**elma** ♀ apple; ~ ağacı apple tree; ~ kürk *fur made of the cheek pieces of fox skin;* ~ şarabı cider; ~ şekeri candied apple.

**elmacık** cheekbone, zygomatic bone.

**elmalık** apple orchard.

**elmas 1.** diamond; **2.** diamond glass cutter; **3.** diamond...; **4.** precious, beloved.

**elmascı** seller *or* cutter of diamonds, diamond-merchant.

**elmasiye** [ā] fruit jelly.

**elmastıraş 1.** diamond glass cutter; **2.** cut glass, cut diamond; **3.** diamond-cutter.

**eloğlu,** -nu stranger.

**elti** sister-in-law *(relationship between the wives of two brothers).*

**eltopu,** -nu *sports:* handball.

**elulağı,** -nı helper.

**elveda,** -aı [ā] farewell, good-bye ;~ etm. to say good-bye, to bid farewell.

**elverişli 1.** sufficient; **2.** profitable; **3.** suitable, convenient, useful, well-adapted, handy.

**elverişsiz** unsuitable, inconvenient.

**elverişsizlik** inconvenience, unsuitability.

**elvermek 1.** to suffice, to be enough; **2.** to be suitable, to be convenient.

**elyaf** fibres, *Am.* fibers.

**elyevm** ✕ today, at the present time.

**elzem** indispensable, imperative, essential, most necessary.

**em'a** entrails, bowels, intestines.

**emanet,** -ti [ā] **1.** a trust, deposit, anything entrusted to s.o.; **2.** *hist.* government office; **3.** left luggage office, *Am.* baggage room; ~ almak to take over; ~ etm. to entrust, to commit (-e to).

**emanetçi** [ā] depositary, trustee.

**emaneten** [ā] on deposit; as a trust, for safekeeping.

**emare** [ā] ✕ sign, mark, token, indication; clue; ❨ circumstantial evidence.

**emaret,** -ti *hist.* emirate; chieftainship, leadership.

**emaye 1.** enameled; **2.** glazed.

**embriyon** *anat.* embryo.

**embube** [ū] tube, canal.

**emcik** P teat; nipple.

**emece** *s.* imece.

**emek 1.** work, labo(u)r; **2.** trouble, pains, fatigue; ~ çekmek *or* vermek to labo(u)r, to take great pains; emeği geçmek to contribute efforts.

**emekbirliği,** -ni co-operation.

**emekçi 1.** worker, labo(u)rer; **2.** proletarian.

**emeklemek 1.** to crawl *(or* creep) on all fours; **2.** to attempt, to try *(as a beginner);* emekliye emekliye with great difficulty.

**emekli 1.** retired; pensioner; **2.** = emektar; **3.** ✕ troublesome, hard, laborious; **4.** inactive *(sportsman);* -ye ayırmak to pension off, to retire; -ye ayrılmak to retire, to be pensioned off.

**emeklilik** retirement.

**emeksiz** effortless, easy, free from labo(u)r.

**emektar** [ā] old and faithful; veteran.

**emektarlık** [ā] loyal service, loyalty.

**emel** longing, desire, wish, coveting, ambition, ideal; ~ beslemek *(or* edinmek) to long (for), to aspire (to, after).

**emeroit,** -ti hemorrhoid.

**emilmek** *pass. of* emmek.

**emin** [ī] **1.** safe, secure; **2.** sure, certain; firm, strong; **3.** trustworthy; **4.** steward, custodian, trustee; **5.** *hist.* superintendent; **6.** God; **7.** ♀ [x .] *mf.;* ~ olm. to be sure (-den of), to be confident (-den of).

**emir**[1], -mri **1.** order, command; decree; **2.** ✕ matter, business; event, case; **3.** *(kipi) gr.* imperative (mood); ~ neferi *(or* eri) ✕ orderly, batman; emre amade *(or* müheyya) ready, at one's service *(or* disposal); emrinde olm. to be at s.o.'s disposal *(or* command); emri ahire kadar until further notice.

**emir**[2] emir, chief, prince, leader, ruler, commander.

**emirber** ✕ orderly, batman.

**emirlik** emirate.

**emirname** [ā] written command, decree.

**emisyon 1.** ✝ issue; **2.** transmission.

**emişkamış olm.** F to be familiar, to be intimate.

**emlak,** -ki *(pl. of* mülk) lands, possessions, real estate; ~ alım vergisi purchase tax on real estate; ~ komisyoncusu estate agent; ~ vergisi property tax.

**emme** *vn. of* emmek; ~ tulumba suction pump.

**emmek 1.** to suck; **2.** to absorb; **3.** *sl.* to

swindle money out of s.o.

**emniyet,** -ti **1.** security, safety; **2.** confidence, belief; **3.** reliance; **4.** safety-catch; **5.** the police, the law; ~ **altına almak** to secure, to make safe, to ensure; ~ **edilir** reliable, dependable, trustworthy; ~ **etm. 1.** to trust; **2.** to entrust; ~ **kemeri** safety belt; ~ **supabı** ⊕ safety valve, bypass valve.

**emniyetli 1.** safe; **2.** reliable, trustworthy.

**emniyetsiz 1.** unsafe, insecure; **2.** distrustful, untrustworthy.

**emniyetsizlik** lack of confidence, untrustworthiness.

**emperyalist** *pol.* **1.** imperialist; **2.** imperialistic.

**emperyalizm** *pol.* imperialism.

**empresyonizm** impressionism.

**empoze** imposition; ~ **etm.** to force (up)on, to impose.

**emprime** print fabric.

**emretmek** [x . .] to order, to command.

**emrihak,** -kkı **1.** God's will; **2.** *euph.* death; ~ **vaki olm.** to die, to pass away.

**emrivaki,** -ii [ā] fait accompli, accomplished fact.

**emriyevmi** ✕ order of the day.

**emsal,** -li [ā] **1.** similars, equals; **2.** peer, compeer; **3.** precedent; **4.** Ⅺ coefficient; -i **bulunmaz** (*or* **görülmedik**) matchless, incomparable, unprecedented, unparalleled; -i **misillû** in the same way.

**emsalsiz** [ā] peerless, unequalled, matchless.

**emtia** (*pl. of* **meta**) ⚔ goods, merchandise, wares.

**emval,** -li [ā] (*pl. of* **mal**) goods, property.

**emzik 1.** baby's bottle, feeding bottle; **2.** nipple, teat; **3.** (a. ~ **memesi**) dummy, *Am.* pacifier; **4.** P. spout; **5.** P cigarette-holder.

**emzirmek** to suckle, to nurse, to breast-feed.

**en¹** width, breadth; -i **boyu bir** as wide as it is long; -i **sonu** *or* -**inde sonunda** in the end, at last, eventually; -**ine boyuna 1.** tall and well-built, husky, hefty, huge; **2.** in length and breadth; **3.** fully, completely, thoroughly.

**en²** most (*superlative*); ~ **az(dan)** at least; ~ **başta** at the very beginning; ~ **birinci** first of all; ~ **çok 1.** mostly; **2.** at (the) most, at the outside; **3.** at the latest; ~ **güzel** most beautiful; ~ **mühim bir mesele** most important matter; ~ **önce** first of all; ~ **sonra** finally; ~ **yüksek** maximum.

**en'am** [ā] **1.** *pl. of* **nimet**; **2.** Koran anthology.

**enaniyet,** -ti [ā] ⚔ self-centredness.

**enayi** *sl.* sucker, fool, idiot, gullible; ~ **dümbeleği** a prize idiot.

**enayilik** foolishness, gullibility.

**encam** [ā] ⚔ end, conclusion, result, extremity, termination; -i **kâr** † finally, at the end.

**encek, encik** pup, cub, whelp.

**encümen** council, committee, commission.

**endaht,** -tı **1.** † a throwing; **2.** a firing, discharge (*of a firearm*); ~ **etm. 1.** † to throw; **2.** to fire, to shoot, to discharge.

**endam** [ā] shape, figure, body, stature; ~ **aynası** full-length mirror.

**endamlı** [ā] shapely, well-proportioned, graceful.

**endaze** [ā] **1.** measure; proportion; **2.** † linear measure (= 0,65 m.); -ye **vurmak 1.** to measure; **2.** *fig.* to calculate, to consider.

**ender** (*comp. of* **nadir**) very rare; rarely.

**enderun** [ū] ⚔ gynaeceum, women's apartments of a palace.

**enderuni** [ū, i] ⚔ inner, interior.

**endişe** [i] **1.** anxiety, perplexity, care, disquietude; **2.** worry, fear, suspicion; thought; ~ **etm.** to worry, to be anxious.

**endişelenmek** [i] to become anxious, to be troubled, to feel anxiety (-*den* about); to be thoughtful.

**endişeli** [. - . .] thoughtful, anxious, troubled, worried.

**endişesiz** [. - . .] carefree, unworried, calm.

**endüstri** industry.

**endüstrileştirmek** to industrialize.

**enek** P castrated.

**enemek** to castrate.

**enerji** energy; ~ **santralı** power station (*or* plant); -**nin sakımı** *phys.* preservation of energy.

**enerjik** energetic.

**enfarktüs** ⚕ heart attack.

**enfes** (*comp. of* **nefis**) delightful, delicious, excellent, wonderful.

**enfiye** snuff; ~ **çekmek** to snuff, to take snuff; ~ **kutusu** sunuff-box.

**enflasyon** inflation.

**enfüsi** [i] subjective.

**engebe** unevenness of ground; broken ground, rough country.

**engebeli** *geogr.* steep and broken, uneven, rough.

**engebesiz** even, smooth.

**engel** obstacle, difficulty, hindrance, handicap; ~ **imtihanı** second check; ~ **olm.** to hinder, to prevent.

**engellemek** to hinder, to hamper, to prevent.

**engelli:** ~ koşu (or yarış) 1. hurdles; 2. steeple-chase.

**engerek** zo. adder, viper.

**engin** 1. vast, boundless, open, wide; 2. the high sea, the open sea ,offing; 3. ordinary, common, low; cheap; 4. base, mean; ~ deniz the high seas, the open sea; -lere dalmak to brood, to ponder, to pore (over).

**enginar** ♀ artichoke.

**enginlik** vastness, vastitude, wideness.

**engizisyon** the Inquisition.

**enik** P whelp, cub, puppy.

**enikonu** quite, thoroughly, fully, at length.

**enine** [x . .] in width, breadthwise, crosswise, transversally.

**enişte** [x . .] husband of an aunt or sister, brother-in-law, uncle.

**enjeksiyon** injection.

**enjektör** injector.

**enkaz** ruins; debris; wreck(age).

**enlem** parallel, line of latitude.

**enli** wide, broad.

**enlilik** breadth, width.

**enmuzec,** -ci ✎ model, sample.

**ense** 1. back of the neck, nape; 2. sl. buttocks, bottom, rump; ~ kökü nape of the neck; ~ yapmak sl. to goof off; -si kalın 1. willful, obstinate, stiff-necked; 2. well-to-do, prosperous, well-off, well--heeled; -sinde boza pişirmek (b-nin) sl. to drive hard, to over-tire and torment; -sinden gitmek to follow close (upon); -sine binmek (b-nin) to persecute s.o., to tyrannize s.o.

**enselemek** sl. to nick.

**ensiz** narrow.

**ensizlik** narrowness.

**enstantane** snapshot.

**enstitü** institute.

**enstrüman** instrument.

**ensülin** insulin.

**entari** [ā] 1. loose robe; 2. dress.

**entbent** F confused, disconcerted, perplexed; ~ olm. to be taken aback.

**entelektüel** intellectual.

**entegrasyon** integration.

**enteresan** interesting.

**enternasyonal** 1. international; 2. pol. International.

**enterne etm.** to intern.

**enterüptör** ⊕ interruptor.

**entipüften** sl. flimsy.

**entrika** [. x .] intrigue, trick; ~ çevirmek to intrigue, to scheme.

**entrikacı** schemer, trickster.

**enüstünlük** gr. superlative degree.

**envanter** 1. inventory; 2. stock-taking.

**envestisman** investment.

**epeski** [x . .] very old, ancient.

**epey** a good many, a good deal of; pretty well, fairly; ~ zaman long time.

**epeyce** pretty well, fairly.

**epher** anat. aorta.

**epidemi** epidemic.

**epik** epic(al).

**epkem** † dumb, mute, silent.·

**er¹** =erken; ~ veya geç = ergeç.

**er²** 1. man, male; 2. ✗ private; 3. brave man; 4. capable man, able man; 5. P husband; ~ oğlu ~ hero, brave man; -e gitmek (or varmak) P to marry a man; -e vermek to give in marriage.

**eramil** [ā] pl. ✎ widows.

**erat,** -tı ✗ privates, recruits.

**erbap,** -bı [ā] expert, specialist.

**erbaş** ✗ non-commisioned officer.

**erdem** virtue.

**erdemli** virtuous.

**erdemsizlik** lack of virtue.·

**erdirmek** caus. of ermek to cause to reach or attain.

**erek** aim, end, goal.

**ereklik** phil. finality.

**erenler** 1. those who have arrived at the divine truth; 2. mode of address among dervishes.

**ergeç** sooner or later.

**ergen** 1. marriageable; 2. unmarried, single, celibate; ~ olm. to be old enough to marry.

**ergenlik** 1. singleness, bachelorhood; 2. youthful acne; ~ dişi wisdom-tooth.

**ergime** fusion.

**ergimek** to melt.

**ergin** 1. mature, adult, ripe; 2. ♫ major.

**erginleşmek** to mature.

**erginlik** maturity, puberty; ♫ majority.

**erguvan** [ā] ♀ 1. judas-tree, redbud; 2. purple.

**erguvani** [. . - -] purple.

**erik** ♀ plum.

**eril** gr. masculine.

**erim¹** † reach, range.

**erim²:** ~ ~ erimek to pine away.

**erimek** 1. to melt, to fuse, to dissolve; to pass away; 2. to wear out (textiles); 3. to pine away; 4. to be greatly embarrassed.

**erirlik** ♒ solubility.

**erişmek** 1. (bşe) to arrive, to attain, to reach; 2. to mature, to reach the age of marriage; 3. to come.

**erişte** vermicelli.

**eritmek 1.** to melt, to dissolve; **2.** to squander *(money)*.

**eriyik** ♫ solution.

**erk** power, faculty; authority.

**erkân** *(pl. of* rükün) **1.** great men, high officials, pillars of the state; **2.** generals; **3.** rules of conduct, way, method; -ı harp X general staff.

**erkeç** *zo.* he-goat, billy-goat.

**erkek 1.** man, male; **2.** manly, courageous, virile, honest and true; **3.** P husband; **4.** good, hard *(metal)*; **5.** ⊕ male; ~ berberi men's hairdresser, barber; ~ dul widower; ~ kopça hook for an eye.

**erkekçe** manly; manfully.

**erkeklik 1.** masculinity; manliness; courage; **2.** sexual potency, virility.

**erkeksi** tomboyish, masculine; ~ kadın amazon, mannish woman.

**erkeksiz 1.** without husband; **2.** alone, lonely *(woman)*.

**erken** early.

**erkence** rather early, a little early, somewhat early.

**erkenci** early riser, early comer.

**erkenden** early.

**erkin 1.** free, independent; **2.** ♀ *mf.*

**erklik** power.

**erlik 1.** manliness, bravery, courage; **2.** soldiership.

**ermek** (-lr) **1.** to attain; to reach; **2.** to ripen, to mature; **3.** to come of age; **4.** to reach spiritual perfection.

**Ermeni** Armenian; ~ gelini gibi kırıtmak **1.** to hang back; **2.** to be affected, to attitudinize.

**Ermenice** Armenian (language).

**Ermenistan** *pr. n.* Armenia.

**ermiş** saint, holy person.

**eroin** heroin, junk.

**eroinman** junky, junkie.

**erozyon** erosion.

**ersiz** without husband.

**ertak!** *sl.* let's go!

**erte** the next, the following *(s.a.* ertesi).

**ertelemek** to postpone, to defer, to adjourn, to put off.

**ertesi** the next, the following; ~ gün the next day, the following day; ~ sene the next year, the following year, the year after.

**ervah** spirits, souls; -ına yuf olsun! damn him!

**erzak** [â] *(pl. of* rızk) provisions, food.

**erzats** ersatz, substitute.

**es** ♪ rest; ~ geçmek *sl.* to disregard.

**esame** [â] *hist.* muster roll *(or* roster) of the Janissaries.

**esameli** [â] **1.** registered in esame; **2.** previousy convicted; **3.** notorious, ill-famed.

**esami** [. - -] *(†. pl. of* isim); ~ üzerine yoklama X roll-call; -si okunmamak *fig.* to be disregarded, to be of no consequence.

**esans** essence, perfume.

**esaret 1.** slavery; captivity; **2.** yoke.

**esas 1.** foundation, base, basis; **2.** basic, fundamental, principle, essential; **3.** true state; **4.** ♫ base; ~ itibariyle in principle, as a matter of fact, essentially, basically; ~ nokta main roint; ~ sermaye (original) stock, capital deposit.

**esasen** [â] [. x .] **1.** fundamentally, in principle, essentially; **2.** anyhow.

**esasi** [. - -] fundamental, essential, basic *(a.* ♫).

**esaslı** [â] **1.** based, founded; **2.** fundamental, main; **3.** real, true, sure, reliable; **4.** sound, solid, concrete; ~ bir noktaya dokunmak to hit the mark; ~ malumat thorough information.

**esassız** [â] baseless, unfounded, groundless.

**esatir** [. - -] *pl.* legends, myths, tales, stories.

**esatirî** [. - - -] mythological.

**esbab**, -bı [â] **1.** *(†. pl. of* sebep) causes, reasons; -ı mucibe 𝓈𝓈 motives.

**esef** regret; ~ etm. to be sorry, to pity, to feel regret (for); -e şayan regretable, deplorable.

**esefle** regretfully, deplorably.

**esefli** regretable, deplorable.

**eselemek:** ~ beselemek to leave no stone unturned, to leave nothing undone.

**esen** hearty healthy, robust, sound; ~ kal(-ınız) so long!

**esenlik** health, soundness, welfare.

**eser 1.** work (of art); **2.** trace, sign, mark; **3.** remains, monuments; ~ sahibi author.

**esermek:** ~ besermek to bring about laboriously.

**esham** [â] *(pl. of* sehim) share, bonds, securities; ~ ve tahvilât borsası stock exchange.

**esinlenmek** to be inspired (-den by).

**esinti** breeze.

**esintili** breezy.

**esir** [î] **1.** captive, prisoner of war; **2.** slave; **3.** infatuated with, gone on; ~ almaca prisoners' bas~; ~ almak to take prisoner; ~ düşmek *(or* olm.) *(b-ne)* to be taken prisoner; ~ etm. to enslave, to take prisoner; ~ kampı prison(ers') camp; ~ ticareti slave trade.

**esir** ether, aether.

**esirci** slave trader.

**esircilik** slave trade.

**esirgemek 1.** to protect (*-den* from), to spare; **2.** to grudge; to withhold (*-den* from); Allah esirgesin! may God protect us!, God forbid!

**esirlik** captivity; slavery.

**eski 1.** old, ancient; **2.** former, ex-; **3.** worn out, old; **4.** second-hand; **5.** out of date; **6.** chronic (*disease*); ~ çamlar bardak oldu (*or* kürek olmuş) *fig.* a lot of water has flowed (*or* passed *or* gone) under the bridge; ~ defterleri karıştırmak to rake over the ashes, to rake up the past; ~ göz ağrısı an old flame; ~ hamam, eski tas the same old thing, just the same as ever; ~ hayratı berbat etmek to make s.th. worse by trying to improve it; ~ kafalı old fogy; ~ kurt old hand; ~ püskü old and tattered things, castoffs, junk; ~ toprak *fig.* old-timer; ~ zaman(-lar) **1.** antiquity; **2.** olden times, the past; -si gibi as of old, as before.

**eskici 1.** oldclothes man, ragman; **2.** shoe--repairer, cobbler.

**eskiçağ** prehistoric period.

**eskiden** formerly, in the past, in old days; ~ kalma handed down, passed down.

**eskiler 1.** the ancients; **2.** castoffs.

**eskileşmek 1.** to go out (of date); **2.** to wear out.

**eskilik** oldness.

**eskime** *vn. of* eskimek; ~ ve aşınma ✕ natural attrition, wear and tear.

**eskimek 1.** = eskileşmek; **2.** to become chronic; **3.** to become grey-headed.

**Eskimo** [. x .] Eskimo.

**eskişehirtaşı**, -nı meerschaum.

**eskitmek** to wear out, to wear up.

**eskiz** draft, sketch, model.

**eskrim** fencing; ~ meçi foil.

**eskrimci** fencer.

**esmek 1.** to blow (*wind*); **2.** *fig.* to come into the mind of s.o., to occur to s.o.; esip savurmak F **1.** to brag, to boast, to show off, to talk big; **2.** to rage, to storm and bluster.

**esmer** brunette, swarthy, dark complexioned; ~ güzeli dark brown beauty, dark complexioned belle.

**esmerleşmek** to tan, to get brown.

**esna** [ā] ✕ moment, instant, time, course, interval; harb -sında during the war; ~ -da at that time, meanwhile; -da while; -sında in the course of, during.

**esnaf** [ā] (*pl. of* sınıf) **1.** trades, guilds; **2.** tradesmen, artisans; **3.** *sl.* prostitute, whore, bitch, tart.

**esnek 1.** elastic, flexible; **2.** ambiguous.

**esneklik** elasticity, flexibility.

**esnemek 1.** to yawn, to gape; **2.** to bulge, to bend, to give (*board, etc.*); **3.** to stretch (*material*).

**esnetmek** *caus. of* esnemek *a.* to vex, to annoy, to bore.

**espri** wisecrack, witticism, wit; ~ yapmak to wisecrack.

**esprili** witty.

**esrar** [ā] (†, *pl. of* sır) **1.** secrets; mysteries; **2.** hashish; ~ kumkuması (*or* kutusu *or* küpü) secretive *or* mysterious person, a locked door; ~ çekmek to smoke hashish; to take drugs; ~ tekkesi opium den.

**esrarengiz** [. - . -] mysterious.

**esrarlı** [ā] **1.** = esrarkeş; **2.** mysterious.

**esrarkeş** [ā] hashish addict; doper.

**esselamünaleyküm** = selamünaleyküm.

**estağfurullah** [. x . . .] **1.** ✕ God forbid!; **2.** don't mention it!, not at all!

**estek:** ~ köstek etm. *or* ~ etm. köstek etm. to make all sorts of excuses to get out of doing s.th.

**ester**[1] ✕ mule.

**ester**[2] ✕ ester.

**estetik 1.** esthetics; **2.** esthetic.

**esvap** clothes; garment; dress; suit.

**eş 1.** one of a pair, mate, fellow; **2.** husband; wife; partner; **3.** a similar thing, match; ~ dost friends and acquaintances; ~ tutmak to choose a partner; -i görülmedik peerless, matchless, unique.

**eşanlam** synonym.

**eşanlamlı** synonymous.

**eşarp**, -pı scarf; stole, sash.

**eşcinsel** homosexual.

**eşdeğer** equivalence.

**eşdeğerli** equivalent.

**eşek 1.** donkey, ass; **2.** jackass, boor; ~ başı *fig.* superior without authority; ~ başı mısın? why don't you use your authority?; ~ herif jackass; ~ kadar oldu *sl.* he is big enough to know what's what; ~ sudan gelinceye kadar dövmek to tan s.o.'s hide, to beat the hell out of s.o., to beat to a pulp; ~ şakası practical joke, horseplay; eşeğe ters bindirmek *fig.* to pillory, to brand, to denounce, to show s.o. up.

**eşekarısı**, -nı *zo.* wasp, hornet.

**eşekçe(sine)** coarsely; stupidly.

**eşekhıyarı**, -nı *s.* acıhıyar.

**eşeksırtı**, -nı gable roof.

**eşeksineği**, -ni *zo.* horsefly, gadfly.

**eşekzeytini**, -ni a kind of large olive.

**eşelemek** (bşi) **1.** to scrape, to scratch; **2.** *fig.* to stir up, to rake up, to rummage, to hunt (for).

eşey sex.

eşeysel sexual.

eşhas [ā] (pl. of şahıs) persons; characters (in a play).

eşik 1. threshold, doorstep; 2. bridge (of a violine, etc.); 3. fig. verge, brink; eşiğine gelmek (b-nin) 1. to petition; 2. to molest, to pester; eşliğini aşındırmak (b-nin) to frequent constantly.

eşinmek to scratch, to paw.

eşit 1. equal, eqivalent, match; the same; 2. A equals.

eşitlik equality.

eşkâl, -li [. -] 1. features and appearance, .description 2. shapes, figures.

eşkenar A equilateral.

eşkıya [ā] (pl. of şaki) 1. brigands; 2. brigand, thug, bandit; ~ yatağı 1. den of robbers, hide-out; 2. accomplice.

eşleme 1. pairing; 2. cinema; synchronization.

eşlemek 1. to pair, to match; 2. to synchronize.

eşleşmek 1. to be partners (in a game); 2. (animals) to mate with each other.

eşlik 1. partnership; 2. ♪ accompaniment; ~ etm. to accompany.

eşmek 1. to dig lightly; to scratch up the ground; 2. to search and investigate.

eşofman 1. tracksuit; 2. warming up.

eşeğlu eşek sl. silly ass, louse.

eşraf [ā] (pl. of şerif) notables (of a town, etc.).

eşref (comp. of şerif) ✣ most noble; ~ saati propitious moment, opportune time.

eşsesli homonym.

eşsiz 1. matchless, peerless, unique; 2. unpaired.

eşya [ā] (pl. of şey) 1. things, objects; 2. furniture; luggage; belongings; goods.

eşyalı furnished.

eşyasız unfurnished.

eşzamanlı isochronal.

et, -ti 1. meat; 2. flesh; 3. pulp (of a fruit); 4. skin; ~ bağlamak 1. to close up, to heal up (wound); 2. to put on weight, to get fat; ~ but (or can) tutmak to put on weight, to get stout; ~ suyu 1. meat broth, bouillon; 2. gravy; ~ tırnaktan ayrılmaz pro. blood is thicker than water; ~ yığını fig. fleshy; -i budu yerinde or -ine dolgun plump, buxom, roly-poly, matronly.

etabli settled, naturalized.

etajer dresser, whatnot; shelves, bookcase.

etap sports: lag, stage; distance between

laps.

etcil biol. carnivorous.

etek 1. skirt; 2. foot (of a mountain), hillside; 3. fringe; 4. private parts, genital area; ~ dolusu or ~ ~ loads of, plenty of, in abundance; ~ öpmek fig. to flatter, to toady; ~ silkmek (bşden) to dissociate o.s. from s.th.; eteği belinde industrious, diligent (woman); eteği düşük slovenly, sloppy, slipshod (woman); -leri tutuşmak to be exceedingly alarmed; -leri zil (or ıslık) çalıyor he is up in the air, he is walking on air.

eteklemek 1. to kiss s.o.'s skirt; 2. to flatter.

eteklik 1. skirt, frock; 2. material for a skirt.

etelemek: ~ betelemek to treat unfriendly.

eter ☾ ether.

etıbba [ā] (pl. of tabip) doctors.

Eti Hittite.

etiket, -ti 1. label, ticket; 2. etiquette.

etiketlemek to label.

etilen ethylene.

etimoloji etymology.

etkafalı blockhead, dumb, dizzy, thick-headed.

etken 1. agent, factor; 2. effective; 3. gr. active.

etki 1. effect, influence; 2. impression, impact.

etkilemek to affect, to influence.

etkili effective, influential, effectual.

etkin active, effective.

etkinlik 1. activity; 2. efficiency, effectiveness.

etlenmek to grow fat.

etli 1. fleshy, plump; 2. pulpy, fleshy (fruit); 3. meaty; ~ butlu plump, buxom; ~ kemikli corporeal; ~ yemek meaty dish; -ye sütlüye karışmamak to mind one's own business, to avoid getting involved.

etmek (eder) 1. to do, to make; 2. to be worth, to be of value; 3. to come to, to amount to; 4. to act, to behave; 5. to live, to be alive, to exist; 6. to reach; 7. to deprive (or rob) of; 8. to do s.th. to s.o.; 9. to urinate or to defecate; eden bulur one pays for what one does; ettiğini yanına bırakmamak not to let s.o. get away with s.th., to get revenge on s.o.

etmen factor.

etnik ethnic.

etoburlar zo. carnivorous animals.

etol, -lü stole.

etraf [ā] (pl. of taraf) 1. sides, ends; 2. surroundings; 3. relatives; 4. directions, regions; **5.** -ına, -ında around; **6.** -ında concerning, with regard to, in respect of; -a haber vermek to trumpet (forth), to noise abroad; -ını almak (or çevirmek or sarmak) to surround, to encircle; -iyle detailed, in detail; -ta in the neighbo(u)r-hood, in the vicinity, around; -tan from all around, from all directions.

**etraflı(ca)** detailed, in detail, fully.

**atsineği,** -ni zo. blowfly.

**etsiz 1.** without meat; fleshless; **2.** thin, weak, puny.

**ettahiyat,** -tı [. . . .] nameof a certain Muslim canticle.

**ettirgen** gr. causative (verb).

**ettirmek** to cause to do.

**etüt,** -dü **1.** study, essay, research; **2.** ♪ preliminary study; **3.** study hall.

**etüv 1.** 🔥 drying-out cupboard; **2.** sterilizer.

**etyaran** whitlow.

**Etyopi, Etyopya** [. x .] pr. n. Ethiopia.

**ev 1.** house, dwelling; **2.** home, household; **3.** office, institution; **4.** fig. family, clan; ~ açmak to seᵗ up house; ~ bark house and home, household; ~ bark sahibi family man; ~ ekmeği homemade bread; ~ eşyası furniture, effects; ~ halkı household, family; ~ hanımı hostess; ~ idaresi housekeeping; ~ işletmek to run a brothel; ~ işi housework; ~ kadını housewife; ~ kadınlığı housewifery; ~ sahibi **1.** host; **2.** landlord; ~ tutmak to rent a house; ~ yıkmak to break up a home; -de kalmış fig. on the shelf; -lere şenlik! happiness to homes!, joy to houses!

**evani** [. - .] pl. 🔥 pots, dishes, vessels.

**evce, evcek** with the whole family.

**evci 1.** homebody; **2.** weekly boarder.

**evcil** domesticated, tame.

**evcilik:** ~ oynamak to play mothers and fathers.

**evcilleştirmek** to domesticate, to tame.

**evcimen, evciment,** -di home-lover, domesticated.

**evedi** s. ivedi.

**evelemek** s. gevelemek.

**evemek** to hasten, to hurry.

**evermek** P to marry off, to give in marriage.

**evet,** -ti yes, certainly; ~ efendim! yes!, sure!, certainly!; ~ efendimci yes-man; ~ efendim, sepet efendim, güzel efendim demek to say amen.

**evetlemek** to say 'yes', to okay.

**evham** [ª] (pl. of vehim) delusions, apprehensions, illusions; -a kapılmak to become suspicious, to be hypochondriac.

**evhamlı** [ª] hypochondriac, suspicious.

**evirmek** to change, to alter; evire çevire thoroughly, soundly; ~ çevirmek **1.** to turn s.th. over and over; **2.** fig. to turn s.th. over in one's mind.

**eviye** (pl. of via) anat. vessels.

**evkaf** (pl. of vakıf) **1.** pious foundations; estates in mortmain; **2.** the government department in control of estates in mortmain.

**evla** 🔥 best, most suitable, preferable, better (than).

**evladiyelik** heirloom.

**evlat,** -di [ª] (pl. of velet) **1.** child, son, daughter; **2.** children, descendants; ~ acısı grief for one's deceased child; ~ canlısı very fond of his or her children; ~ edinmek to adopt a child; ~ sevgisi love for one's children.

**evlatlık 1.** adopted child; **2.** foster child; -tan ret (or çıkarma) disownment.

**evlek 1.** furrow (in a field); **2.** a quarter of dönüm; **3.** sl. a ten-lira note; **4.** water-channel, drainage ditch.

**evlendirmek** caus. of evlenmek to marry (off), to give in marriage.

**evlenme** vn. of evlenmek marriage; ~ dairesi registry office; ~ kâğıdı 🔥 marriage certificate (or lines).

**evlenmek** to marry; to get married.

**evleviyet,** -ti 🔥 preference; -le all the more, so much the sooner.

**evli** married; ~ hayat married life; ~ kadın married woman.

**evlilik** marriage; ~ birliği 🔥 conjugal community.

**evliya** [ª] (pl. of veli) saint; ~ gibi saintly, gentle.

**evrak,** -kı [ª] **1.** †, 🌿 leaves; **2.** documents, papers; ~ çantası brief-case, portfolio; ~ kalemi record office, registry; ~ memuru registrar; -ı müsbite document of proof.

**evre** phase.

**evren 1.** universe; **2.** cosmos; **3.** environment; **4.** time; **5.** great.

**evrensel** universal.

**evrim** evolution.

**evrimsel** evolutionary.

**evsaf** [ª] (pl. of vasıf) 🔥 qualities, qualifications; birinci -ta askerler highly qualified soldiers.

**evvel 1.** first; ago; before, earlier, of old; initial; **2.** the first part, the beginning; ~ emirde first of all; ~ zaman içinde once upon a time; bundan ~ before this, previously; iki sene -sine nazaran compared to (or in comparison with) the time two years ago.

**evvela** [x . .] firstly, first of all, to begin with.

**evvelce** formerly, previously.

**evvelden** previously; formerly, beforehand; ~ sezmek to foresee, to anticipate.

**evvel** 1. in the old days; 2. the previous.

**evveliyat,** -tı [ā] antecedents, first stages, first principles,' beginnings.

**evvelki, evvelsi** 1. the previous; 2. the (year, month, week) before last; ~ gün the day before yesterday; ~ sene the year before last.

**evza** [ā] (pl. of vazı) ⚹ 1. gestures; 2. acts, conduct, behavio(u)r; 3. position, postures.

**ey** 1. o!; 2. now see here!; 3. so?, so what?

**eyalet,** -ti [ā] province; state.

**eyer** saddle; ~ takımı saddle and harness; ~ takmak (or vurmak) to put a saddle on, to saddle.

**eyerci** saddler.

**eyerlemek** to saddle.

**eyerli** saddled.

**eyersiz** unsaddled; bareback.

**eylem** 1. action, deed; 2. operation; 3. verb; ~ tümcesi gr. verbal sentence; -e geçmek to put into operation.

**eylemci** activist.

**eylemcilik** activism.

**eylemek** s. etmek.

**eylül,** -lü september.

**eytam** [ā] (pl. of yetim) ⚹ orphans.

**eyvah** [ā] alas!; ~ çekmek to sigh; -lar olsun! alas!, what a pity!

**eyvallah** [x . -] 1. thank you!, thanks!; 2. good bye!; 3. all right!; ~ demek to agree, to accept; ~ etm. 1. to comply with s.o.'s wish; 2. to flatter, to adulate; -ı olmamak (b-ne) to be obliged to no one.

**eyyam** [ā] (pl. of yevm) 1. time, period; 2. better days, prosperous days; 3. power, influence; 4. ⚓ favo(u)rable wind; ~ efendisi (or ağası or reisi) opportunist, timeserver; ~ görmüş (or sürmüş) who has seen better days; ~ ola! ⚓ may wind and weather be favo(u)rable to you!; -ı bahur dog-days.

**eza** [ā] annoyance, vexation; pain, torment, torture.

**ezan** [ā] call to prayer.

**ezani** [. - -]: ~ saat the hour as reckoned from sunset.

**ezber** 1. by heart; 2. memorization; lesson to be memorized.

**ezberci** who learns parrot fashion.

**ezberden** 1. by heart; 2. without knowing; ~ okumak to recite by heart.

**ezbere** 1. by heart; 2. superficially; ~ iş görmek to act without due knowledge, to do s.th. superficially.

**ezberlemek** to learn by heart, to memorize, to commit to memory.

**ezcümle** [x . .] 1. among other things; for instance, for example; 2. in short; 3. especially, particularly.

**ezel** ⚹ past eternity; -denberi from eternity, all along.

**ezeli** without beginning, eternal; ~ ve ebedi eternal; without beginning or end.

**ezeliyet,** -ti past eternity.

**ezgi** 1. ♪ tune, note, melody; 2. fig. style, tempo; 3. worry, anxiety.

**ezgin** = ezik.

**ezici** crushing, overwhelming.

**ezik** 1. crushed, squashed; 2. worried, anxious; 3. bruise.

**eziklik** 1. worry; depression; 2. feeling of hunger.

**ezilmek** 1. pass. of ezmek to be crushed, to be oppressed; 2. (with mide, yürek or iç) to have a sinking feeling; ezildi büzüldü 1. he was embarrassed; 2. he felt a great deal of pain, he was racked with pain.

**eziyet,** -ti injury, pain, torture, torment; hurt, fatigue, suffering; cruelty, ill-treatment; ~ çekmek to suffer fatigue; ~ etm. (or vermek) to torment, to torture, to cause pain.

**eziyetci** tormentor, torturer.

**eziyetli** fatiguing, painful, tiring, vexatious.

**eziyetsiz** easy, untroublesome.

**ezkaza** [. . .] by chance, accidentally.

**ezme** 1. vn. of ezmek; 2. purée, paste.

**ezmek,** (-er) 1. to crush, to pound, to powder, to bruise, to squash, to mash; 2. to trample down, to tread down; 3. to over-exert, to over-strain, to suppress; 4. to overcome, to overpower, to overwhelm (enemy); 5. to run over; 6. F to dissipate (money); 7. to melt, to dissolve (sugar); 8. fig. sport: to trounce; ezip suyunu iç! it is absolutely worthless!

**Ezrail** s. Azrail.

# F

**fa** ♪ fa.

**faal, -li** [. -] **1.** active, industrious; **2.** serviceable.

**faaliyet, -ti** [. - . .] **1.** activity, energy; **2.** serviceableness; ~ göstermek to function; ~ sahası **1.** scope, field of activity; **2.** † line of business; -e geçmek **1.** to begin to operate; **2.** to take action.

**faanahtarı, -nı** ♪ bass clef.

**fabrika** [x . .] factory, mill, plant, works; ~ işi machine made; ~ mamulatı manufactured (or factory-made) goods or article; ~ tesisatı manufacturing plant.

**fabrikacı** manufacturer, factory owner, industrialist.

**fabrikacılık 1.** factory ownership; **2.** industrial production; **3.** manufacture.

**fabrikator, fabrikatör** s. fabrikacı.

**facia** [- . .] **1.** calamity, disaster, catastrophe; **2.** drama, tragedy.

**facialı** [- . . .] tragic, terrible, disastrous, catastrophic.

**facianüvis** [- . . . -] † dramatist, tragedian.

**faça** [x .] **1.** ⬩ a ship's facing the wind with the topsail aback; **2.** sl. mug, face; **3.** sl. the bottommost card, the card at the bottom of a pack; **4.** sl. clothing, clothes, dress; -sını almak (aşağıya) sl. to ridicule, to make fun (-in of).

**façeta** [. x .] facet.

**façuna** [. x .] ⬩ the serving or whipping (of a rope).

**fağfur 1.** ancient title of the Emperor of China; **2.** porcelain.

**fahim, -hmi** great, grand, illustrious, glorious.

**fahime** intelligence; understanding.

**fahiş** [ā] **1.** excessive, exorbitant; **2.** ⬩ obscene, immoral.,

**fahişe** [ā] prostitute, whore, harlot, sl. bitch, tart.

**fahrenhayt, -tı** Fahrenheit.

**fahri 1.** honorary; **2.** Fahri [x .] mf.; **3.** voluntary, volunteer.

**faide** s. fayda.

**faik, -kı** [ā] **1.** superior; **2.** ⬩ outstanding, excellent; **3.** ♀ mf.

**faikıyet, -ti** [ā] superiority.

**fail** [ā] **1.** agent, author; **2.** perpetrator, author (of a crime); **3.** biol. effective; **4.** gr. subject; -i muhtar free agent, independent.

**failiyet, -ti** [ā] **1.** ⬩ effect, effectiveness; **2.** efficiency, activity.

**faiz** [ā] interest; ~ fiyatı (or nispeti) rate of interest; ~ yürütmek to calculate interest; -e ~ yürütülmesi calculation of compound interest; -e vermek (or yatırmak) to lend at interest; -i işlemek (bşin) to yield interest, to bear interest; -i mürekkep (or birleşik ~) compound interest.

**faizci** [ā] usurer, moneylender.

**faizcilik** [ā] usury.

**faizli** [ā] interest-bearing, at interest.

**faizsiz** [ā] interest-free.

**fak, -kı** P snare, trap; -a basmak to be duped.

**fakat, -tı** [x .] but, however, only, merely.

**fakfon** German silver.

**fakih 1.** Moslem jurist; **2.** [faki] learned man.

**fakir** [i] **1.** poor, pauper, needy, destitute; beggar; **2.** † your humble servant; ~ düşmek to become poor; ~ fukara the poor.

**fakirhane** [. - - .] **1.** poorhouse; **2.** my house.

**fakirleşmek** to become poor.

**fakirlik** poverty.

**faksimile** facsimile.

**faktör** factor.

**fakülte** faculty (of a university).

**fakülteli** university student.

**fal, -lı** [ā] **1.** fortune; omen, augury; **2.** fortune-telling, soothsaying; ~ açmak (or atmak) to tell fortunes; ~ çıktı the prophecy was fulfilled; ~ taşı a pebble or bean from which an omen is taken; ~ tutmak to have one's fortune told; -a bakmak s. ~ açmak.

**falaka** [x . .] bastinado; -ya çekmek to bastinado.

**falan** F **1.** so and so, such and such; **2.** and so on; **3.** and such like; about, approximately; ~ festekiz (or feşmekan or fıstık or filan) mst iro. = falan 2.

**falanca** F = falan 1.

**falanıncı** F the nth, the umpteenth.

**falbala** furbelow.

**falcı** fortune-teller.

**falcılık** fortune-telling.

**falçete** [. x .] curved shoemaker's knife.

**falez** precipice.

**falihayır** [- . . .] good omen.

**falname** [-↙ .] oracular book used in fortune-telling.

**falso** [x .] 1. ♪ discord, dissonance, false note; 2. *fig.* blunder, false step, slip; 3. *billiards:* side, *Am.* English; ~ basmak (or etm.) to blunder, to make a slip, F to put one's foot in it; ~ vermek 1. = ~ etm.; 2. billiards: to put English on.

**falsolu** 1. discordant, dissonant; 2. awkward, clumsy, maladroit; 3. *billiards:* with English on.

**familya** [. x .] 1. *a.* ♀, geol., biol. family; 2. ⚒ wife.

**fanatik** fanatic.

**fanatizm** fanaticism.

**fanfan** 1. slur; 2. unintelligible (*chatter*).

**fani** [ⁱ] transitory, perishable; mortal.

**fanila** [. x .] 1. flannel; 2. undershirt, vest.

**fantastik** fantastic.

**fantaziye** [. x . .] phantasy, fancy, imagination.

**fantezi** 1. ♪ fantasia; 2. fancy, de luxe, pompous; 3. fancy, imagination; ~ yelek fanciful waistcoat.

**fanus** [ā] 1. lantern; lamp-glass; 2. † lighthouse.

**fanya** [x .] wide-meshed part of a fishnet.

**far** 1. *mot.* headlight; 2. eye-shadow.

**faraş** dustpan.

**faraza** [x . .] supposing that..., assuming.

**farazi** [ⁱ] hypothetical.

**faraziye** hypothesis, supposition, assumption; ~ yürütmek to make supposition.

**farbala** *s.* falbala.

**fare** [ā] zo. mouse; rat; ~ kapanı mouse-trap; ~ zehiri rat poison.

**farfara** empty-headed, braggart; windbag.

**farfaralık** idle brag, frivolity.

**farımak** 1. to grow old; 2. to weaken; 2. to wear out.

**fariğ** [ā] ⚒ 1. unemployed, non-employed; 2. exempt (-den from), free (-den from); 3. ♿ transferer, assignor.

**farik,** -kı [ā] ⚒ distinguishing, separating, distinctive.

**farika** [- . .] 1. typical, distinguishing; 2. ♬ characteristic.

**Farisi** [- . -] the Persian language; Persian.

**fariza** sacred duty, obligation.

**fark,** -kı 1. difference, distinction; 2. discrimination; 3. disparity; ~ etm. 1. to notice, to perceive; to realize, to discriminate, to distinguish, to discern; 2. to differ, to change; 3. to matter; to make a difference; ~ gözetmek to discriminate; -ına varmak (bşin) to become aware of *s.th.*, to notice *s.th.*, to perceive *s.th.*; -ında olm. (bşin) to be aware of *s.th.*, to notice *s.th.*; -ında olmamak (bşin) to be unaware of *s.th.*

**farklanmak** 1. to differentiate; 2. to rise (*price*).

**farklı** 1. different, changed; 2. better; dearer; ~ farksız hardly distinguishable; ~ tutmak to discriminate, to differentiate.

**farklılık** difference.

**farksız** indistinguishable, without difference, same, equal.

**farmakoloji** pharmacology.

**farmason** 1. freemason; 2. F irreligious, ungodly, atheist; ~ locası freemasons' lodge.

**farmasonluk** freemasonry.

**Fars** Persian.

**Farsça** Persian (language).

**fart¹,** -tı ⚒ excess, overdoing, exaggeration.

**fart²,** -tı: ~ furt brag; empty threats.

**farta** [x .]: fartafurtasız F tactless, inconsiderate; awkward, clumsy; -sı furtası olmamak to speak inconsiderately.

**farz** 1. ⚒ supposition, hypothesis; 2. *eccl.* precept; ~ etm. to suppose, to assume, to imagine; farzedelim ki... let us suppose, supposing...

**farzımuhal,** -li [. . . -] supposing the impossible that...; ~ olarak as a possible example.

**Fas** *pr. n.* 1. Morocco; 2. Fez.

**fasafiso** [. . x .] *sl.* trash, twaddle, prattle, nonsense.

**fasahat,** -ti [. - .] correctness, purity, cleanness, clearness (of speech), eloquence.

**fasarya** [. x .] *sl.* 1. = fasafiso; 2. coquetry, coquettishness.

**fasıl¹,** -slı 1. division, chapter, section; 2. solution; 3. † season; 4. *a concert program all in the same* makam; 5. *thea.* act; 6. gossip; slander.

**fasıl²** ⚒ separating, dividing.

**fasıla** 1. separation; 2. interval, interruption; ~ vermek to interrupt, to break.

**fasılasız** continuous, uninterrupted, unceasing.

**fasih** [ⁱ] correct and clear (speech); eloquent, fluent, lucid.

**fasikül** fascicle, section (of a book).

**fasile** [ⁱ] ♀, zo. family.

**fasit,** -di 1. vicious, wicked, evil, corrupt;

**2.** perverse; ~ **daire** vicious circle.

**faska** [x'.] wrapper cloth (for babies).

**fasletmek** [x . .] **1.** to separate; **2.** to divide; **3.** to decide; **4.** to gossip, to malign, to traduce.

**fason 1.** fashion, style, cutting; ⊕ trimming, bordering.

**fasulye** [x .] ⚘ bean; **taze** ~ string beans.

**faşır faşır** in gushes.

**faşist** Fascist.

**faşizm** Fascism.

**fatih** conqueror, victor.

**fatiha** the opening chapter of the Koran; ~ **okumak 1.** to recite the fatiha; **2.** fig. (bşe) to give up hope.

**fatura** invoice; ~ **düzenlemek** to invoice; ~ **kesmek** to make out an invoice.

**faturalamak** to write an invoice for.

**faul** sports: faul.

**favori 1.** whiskers, side-burns; **2.** favorite.

**fayans** tile.

**fayda** use, profit, advantage; **-sı dokunmak** (bşin) to come in handy, to come in useful, to be of help.

**faydalanmak** to profit (-den by), to make use (-den of), to utilize, to benefit (-den from).

**faydalı** useful, profitable, advantageous; ~ **malumat 1.** useful information; **2.** informative knowledge.

**faydasız** useless, unprofitable, in vain.

**fayrap** [x .] ⚓ fire up!; ~ **etm. 1.** ⚓ to get up steam; **2.** fig. to speed up.

**fayton** phaeton.

**faytoncu** coachman.

**faz** [ā] phys. phase; ~ **kalemi** circuit-tester.

**fazilet,** -ti [. - ] virtue, grace; merit, superiority.

**faziletli** virtuous, excellent.

**fazla 1.** excessive; superfluous; **2.** remainder; **3.** more (than); **4.** too (much); very much; too many; **5.** a lot; plenty; ~ **gecikmek** to be overdue, to be too late; ~ **olarak** besides, moreover, furthermore; ~ **olm. 1.** to be superfluous, to be too much; **2.** to go too far; ~ **tazyik** ⊕ over-pressure; **-siyle** abundantly, amply.

**fazlalaşmak** to increase.

**fazlalık 1.** excess; **2.** abundance; **3.** surplus.

**fecaat,** -ti [. - .] calamity, tragedy, catastrophe.

**feci,** -ii [i] painful, tragic, terrible, catastrophic.

**fecir,** -cri dawn.

**feda,** -ai [ā] sacrifice; ransom; ~ **etm.** to sacrifice; ~ **olm.** (pass. of ~ **etm.**) to be

sacrificed; ~ **olsun!** let it be sacrificed!

**fedai** [. - -] **1.** bodyguard, bouncer; **2.** patriot.

**fedakâr** [. - -] self-sacrificing, devoted, loyal.

**fedakârlık** [. - - .] **1.** self-sacrifice, devotion; **2.** great difficulties and expense.

**federal** federal.

**federasyon** federation, association.

**federatif** federative.

**federe** federate; ~ **devlet** ⚘ federal state; canton.

**feding** radio: fading.

**fehamet,** -ti [ā] highness.

**fehim,** -hmi comprehension, understanding.

**fehmetmek** [x . .] to understand, to comprehend.

**fehva** [ā] ⚘ tenor, import, meaning, sense.

**fek,** -kki ⚘ **1.** severing, detaching, separation; **2.** solving (a difficulty); **3.** ⚘ redemption.

**fekketmek** [x . .] ⚘ **1.** to sever, to detach, to separate; to break open; **2.** to undo, to raise.

**fekül** fecula.

**felah 1.** prosperity, happiness; **2.** deliverance.

**felaket,** -ti disaster, catastrophe, calamity; ~ **haberi** bad news; **-e uğramak** to have a disaster.

**felaketli 1.** disastrous, fatal, sinister, ominous, calamitous; **2.** = felaketzede.

**felaketzede** victim (of a disaster).

**felc,** -ci ⚕ paralysis; **çocuk felci** infantile paralysis; **felce uğramak** to be paralysed (a. fig.).

**felçli** paralytic, paralyzed.

**feldmareşal,** -li [x . . .] ✕ field marshal.

**felek 1.** firmament, heavens; **2.** fate, destiny; **3.** the universe; **feleğin çemberinden geçmiş** gone through the mill: **-ten kâm almak** fig. to have a very good time.

**Felemenk,** -gi [x . .] pr. n. Holland, the Netherlands.

**Felemenkli** pr. n. Dutch; Dutchman.

**felfelek** a kind of small butterfly.

**fellah 1.** fellah, Egyptian farmer; **2.** F Negro.

**fellek fellek** or **fellik fellik** running hither and thither: ~ **aramak** to search high and low (-i for).

**felsefe** philosophy; ~ **yapmak** (or **yürütmek**) to philosophize.

**felsefi** philosophical.

**feminist,** -ti feminist.

**fen,** -nni **1.** natural sciences; **2.** technics, art; ~ **fakültesi** faculty of science; ~ **he-**

yeti technical commission; -ni harp † the art of war.

fena 1. bad, unpleasant; evil; 2. ill, sick; 3. awful, terrible, miserable; 4. extremely, terribly; ~ değil! not bad!; ~ etm. 1. to treat badly, to ill-treat; 2. to do evil; 3. to make s.o. feel sick; ~ halde badly, extremely; ~ muamele ill-treatment; ~ olm. 1. to feel sick; 2. to be upset; ~ puan bad mark; -sına gitmek (b-nin) to be exasperated; -ya çekmek (or almak) to take s.th. amiss (or ill); -ya sarmak (or varmak) to get worse, to take a turn for the worse.

fena ٭ death, extinction, annihilation.

fenalaşmak 1. to get worse, to deteriorate; 2. to turn faint; 3. to become more serious.

fenalaştırmak to worsen, to make worse.

fenalık 1. evil, badness; injury, harm; 2. fainting; ~ etm. (or yapmak) 1. to do evil; 2. (b-ne) to harm s.o.; ~ geçirmek to feel faint.

fenci 1. scientist; 2. F science teacher.

fener 1. lantern; street-lamp; 2. lighthouse; 3. coffee tray with handle on top; 4. ⊕ pinion (of a shaft); ~ alayı torchlight procession; ~ resmi lighthouse dues.

fenerbalığı, -nı angler.

fenik pfennig (unit of German money).

Fenike pr. n. Phoenicia.

fenlenmiş F early-ripe, precocious (girl).

fenni scientific, technical, expert; ~ terimler technical terms.

fenol, -lü phenol.

fenomen phenomenon.

fent, -di trick, ruse; feint.

feodal feudal.

feodalite feudalism.

fer 1. brightness, radiance, lustre, Am. luster, brilliancy; 2. vividness.

ferace [. - .] a kind of overall (formerly worn by Turkish women).

feragat, -ti [. - .] 1. self-sacrifice, abnegation; 2. ٥٥ renunciation, abandonment (of a right), cession, waiver; abdication; ~ etm. to renounce, to give up, to abandon, to cede; to abdicate (-den from); ~ göstermek to show self-denial, to act altruistically; ~ sahibi altruistic, unselfish.

feragatname [. - - . -] certificate of renunciation.

ferağ [ā] 1. cession (of property), transfer; 2. † leisure, rest, withdrawing from work; ~ etm. to cede, to withdraw (-den from).

ferah 1. spacious, open, roomy, wide; 2.

joy, pleasure, cheerfulness, gladness; ~ ~ 1. easily, abundantly, amply; 2. at least; içi ~ cheerful, in a good humo(u)r; -a çıkmak to feel relieved.

ferahi [. - -] 1. hist. gorget; 2. crescent-shaped metal collar plate formerly worn by police guards.

ferahlamak 1. to become spacious or airy; to clear up; 2. to become cheerful, to feel relieved.

ferahlık 1. spaciousness, airiness; 2. cheerfulness; relief.

feraset, -ti [ā] 1. † horsemanship; 2. sagacity, intuition; understanding, intelligence.

ferasetli [ā] perceptive.

ferç, -ci vulva.

ferda [ā] ٭ 1. the morrow, the next day; 2. the future; eternity; 3. the Day of Judgement.

ferdasız [ā] fig. hopeless.

ferde ٭ bale.

ferdi 1. individual; 2. personal; ~ teşebbüs individual enterprise.

ferdiyet, -ti individuality.

ferdiyetçi individualist.

ferdiyetçilik individualism.

fere P chick of a game bird; chicken.

feri, -r'i 1. branch, subdivision; 2. accessory circumstance, particular point, detail, item.

fer'i derived, secondary; subordinate; accessory.

feribot, -tu [x . .] train or car ferry, ferryboat.

ferih [ı] ٭ cheerful, merry; ~ fahur in abundance; in comfort.

ferik 1. pullet; 2. kind of apple.

ferik † ✕ Divisional General.

ferma [ā] pointing, setting; ~ etm. (or durmak) to point, to set (hound).

ferman [ā] 1. firman, imperial edict; 2. ٭ command, order, decree; ~ dinlememek to ignore the law.

fermejüp, -pü snap-fastener, press-stud, popper.

fermene [. x .] short embroidered vest.

fermetür, fermuar zip-fastener, zip(per).

ferraş ٭ 1. mosque sweeper; 2. carpet-layer, servant.

fersah parasang (5 ½ km); ~ ~ greatly, very far.

fersiz lusterless, dull, dim.

fersude [ū] ٭ worn out, old, ragged.

ferş ٭ laying, spreading; ~ etm. to lay down, to spread out (carpets).

ferşiyat, -tı [ā] the laying (of rails, pipes, etc.).

**fert,** -di **1.** person, individual; **2.** ♀ particular specimen.

**fertçi** individualist.

**fertçilik** individualism.

**fertik [x .]:** fertiği çekmek (or kırmak) sl. **1.** to run away, to make off; **2.** ⚔ to peg out.

**fertiklemek** sl. = fertiği çekmek.

**feryat,** -dı [ā] **1.** cry, wail, scream, yell, shriek; **2.** fig. complaint; ~ etm. **1.** to lament, to cry out, to wail, to yell, to scream, to shriek; **2.** to complain.

**ferz** chess: queen.

**fes** fez; ~ ibiği fez tassel.

**fesat,** -dı [ā] **1.** depravity, corruption, malice, intrigue, duplicity, mischief; **2.** mischievous, intriguer; **3.** ⚔ sedition, disturbance, disorder; **4.** pol. unrest; **5.** rebellion, revolt; **6.** ⚙ plot, conspiracy; ~ başı ring-leader, main plotter (or intriguer); ~ çıkarmak to cause trouble, to plot mischief, to conspire; ~ kumkuması (or kutusu) mischief-maker, conspirator; ~ tohumu saçmak to sow the seeds of intrigue: fesada vermek to plot, to conspire.

**fesatçı** insurgent, conspirator, rebel, instigator, agitator, mischief-maker.

**feshetmek [x . .]** **1.** to annul, to cancel, to abolish, to rescind, to revoke; **2.** to dissolve (parliament).

**fesih,** -shi **1.** abolition, cancellation, annulment; **2.** dissolution.

**fesrengi,** -ni deep red.

**festekiz** s. falan.

**festival,** -li **1.** festival; **2.** sl. fiasco, utter failure.

**fesuphanallah [. . - . -]** oh my God!

**feşafeş** ⚔ swish, a rustling noise.

**feşmekan** s. falan.

**fetha 1.** anat. opening, orifice; **2.** vowel sign for a, e in Arabic script.

**fethetmek [x . .]** to conquer.

**fethimeyyit,** -ti autopsy.

**fetih,** -thi conquest.

**fetihçi 1.** ⚔ = fatih; **2.** imperialist(ic).

**fetiş** fetish.

**fettan [ā]** tempting, seductive, alluring; ~ civelek good-for-nothing.

**fetva [ā]** eccl. decision (on religious matter given by a mufti); ~ vermek **1.** to deliver a fetva; **2.** co to express an opinion.

**fevç,** -ci crowd, a stream of people, a flow of people; ~ ~ (or fevçafevç) in streams, in crowds.

**feveran [ā] 1.** boiling, effervescence; **2.**

flying into a temper, flaring up, rage; **3.** excitement; **4.** eruption (volcano); ~ etm. to boil over with anger, to flare up, to fly off the handle.

**fevk,** -kı top, upper part, superior to.

**fevkalade [x . - .]** **1.** extraordinary, unusual; **2.** unusually, exceptionally, exceedingly, excessively; **3.** wonderful, excellent; ~ ağır over-weight; ~ delege special delegate; ~ haller exceptional circumstances; ~ nüsha special edition.

**fevkalbeşer [x . . .]** superhuman.

**fevkattabia** supernatural.

**fevren [x .]** promptly, at once; impulsively, hastily.

**fevri 1.** speedy, sudden; **2.** impulsive.

**fevt,** -ti ⚔ **1.** irreparable loss; going by; **2.** death; ~ etm. to let slip, to miss, to lose; ~ olm. **1.** pass. of ~ etm.; **2.** to die.

**fevz** ⚔ success, victory, triumph.

**feyezan [ā] 1.** overflowing, flood, inundation; **2.** ⚔ abundance.

**feyizli** abundant; prosperous; bountiful, productive.

**feylesof** philosopher.

**feyyaz [ā]** ⚔ **1.** munificent, generous; **2.** overflowing, abounding, flourishing.

**feyz 1.** abundance; prosperity; bountifulness, fertility; **2.** enlightenment; **3.** bounteous gift; ~ almak **1.** fig. to make headway, to get ahead; **2.** to be enlightened (-den by), to learn (-den from); ~ bulmak = ~ almak **1.**

**feza [ā]** space, universe.

**fezahat,** -ti vulgarity, meanness.

**fezleke 1.** summary; **2.** police report.

**fıçı** cask, barrel; tub; ~ balığı salted fish in barrels; ~ birası draught beer, Am. draft beer; ~ gibi corpulent, squat.

**fıçıcı** cooper.

**fıçılamak** to barrel, to put in a barrel.

**fıkara** s. fukara.

**fıkı** s. sıkı fıkı.

**fıkıh,** -khı Muslim canonical jurisprudence.

**fıkır fıkır 1.** with a bubbling noise; **2.** coquettish.

**fıkırdak 1.** coquettish; **2.** restless, fidget.

**fıkırdamak 1.** to boil up, to bubble; **2.** to behave coquettishly; to giggle.

**fıkra 1.** anecdote; **2.** short column (in a newspaper); **3.** paragraph; passage; **4.** anat. vertebra; ~ başı new paragraph.

**fıkracı 1.** anecdotist; **2.** columnist.

**fıldır fıldır** rolling (eyes).

**fındık** hazel-nut, filbert; ~ altını **1.** name of a gold coin; **2.** fig. small and valuable thing; ~ kabuğunu doldurmaz trifling, unimportant; nonsensical; ~ kurdu gibi tiny and roly-poly *(woman).*

**fındıkçı 1.** seller of nuts; **2.** F flirtatious woman.

**fındıkfaresi,** -ni common house-mouse.

**fındıkkıran** nutcrackers.

**fındıkkurdu,** -nu nut maggot.

**fır** whirr; ~ ~ = fırıl fırıl.

**Fırat,** -tı *pr. n.* the Euphrates.

**fırça 1.** brush; **2.** paint-brush; ~ çekmek *sl.* to dress down.

**fırçalamak** to brush, to dust.

**fırdolayı** [x . . .] all around; round about.

**fırdöndü 1.** swivel; **2.** ⊕ lathe carrier; **3.** gambler's top; **4.** *fig.* inconstant, fickle, changeable.

**fırıl fırıl** whirling, around and around.

**fırıldak 1.** ventilator; **2.** weathercock; **3.** spinning-top; whirligig; **4.** windmill *(child's toy);* **5.** *fig.* intrigue, deception, trick, ruse; ~ çevirmek to intrigue, to be up to some mischief.

**fırılda(n)mak** to spin around.

**fırın 1.** oven; **2.** bakery; **3.** kiln; **4.** furnace.

**fırıncı** baker.

**fırınlamak** ⊕ to kiln-dry.

**fırınlanmış** ⊕ kiln-dried.

**fırka 1.** *pol.* party; **2.** ✕ division; ↓ squadron; **3.** group.

**fırlak** protruding, sticking out, overhanging.

**fırlama** *sl.* bastard; brat.

**fırlamak 1.** to fly off, to fly out; to leap up; **2.** to rush; **3.** to protrude, to stick out, to overhang; **4.** *fig.* to scar, to sky-rocket *(price).*

**fırlatmak** *caus. of* fırlamak *part. to* hurl, to shoot, to throw, to fling, to cast.

**fırsat,** -tı opportunity, chance; occasion; ~ bu ~! this is my (your, his) chance!; ~ düşkünü opportunist; -ı ganimet bilmek to seize the opportunity; -ı kaçırmak to miss the opportunity; -tan istifade taking advantage of an opportunity.

**fırsatçı** opportunist.

**fırt fırt** continually, incessantly, unremittingly.

**fırtına 1.** gale, storm, tempest; **2.** *fig.* vehemence, violence; ~ kopmak **1.** to break suddenly *(storm);* **2.** *fig.* to break out in noisy arguments; -ya tutulmak to be caught in a storm.

**fırtınalı** stormy *(a. fig.).*

**fıs:** ~ geçmek to whisper.

**fısı fıs** in whispers, in a whisper.

**fısıl fısıl** = fıs fıs.

**fısıldamak** to whisper.

**fısıltı** whisper.

**fısır fısır** with a crackling noise, with a hissing noise.

**fıskıye** jet of water, fountain.

**fıslamak 1.** to whisper; **2.** to tip the wink, to tip off.

**fıstık[1]** pistachio nut; ground nut; peanut; ~ çamı ♀ pine; ~ gibi F **1.** buxom, plump, stout; **2.** as pretty as a picture.

**fıstık[2]** *emph. of* falan *or* filan.

**fıstıki** [i] pistachio green, light green; ~ makam *co.* slowly, unhurriedly, ponderously.

**fış fış** *or* fışıl fışıl *or* fışır fışır **1.** with a rustling noise *(silk clothes);* **2.** with a splashing noise *(water).*

**f şırdamak** to gurgle, to rustle.

**fışkı** horse dung; manure.

**fışkılamak** to dung *(horse).*

**fışkılık** dunghill.

**fışkırmak 1.** to gush out, to spurt out, to squirt forth, to jet; **2.** to spring up *(plant).*

**fışkırtmak** to spurt, to splash.

**fıta 1.** skiff; **2.** = futa.

**fıtık** hernia, rupture; ~ bağı ♀ truss; ~ olm. **1.** to get a hernia; **2.** *sl.* to become irritated.

**fıtır** the ending of a religious fast.

**fıtnat,** -tı natural intelligence.

**fıtrat,** -tı **1.** † creation; **2.** nature, constitution.

**fıtraten** [x . .] by nature, naturally; by birth, congenitally.

**fıtri** [i] **1.** natural, innate, congenital; **2.** *phls.* native.

**fiber** fibreboard, *Am.* fiberboard.

**fiberglas** fibreglass, *Am.* fiberglass.

**fidan** young plant; sapling; ~ boylu tall and slender; ~ gibi slim *(girl).*

**fidanlık** nursery.

**fide** [x .] seedling plant.

**fidelemek** to plant out seedlings.

**fidelik** nursery bed.

**fidye, fidyeinecat,** -tı [â] ransom.

**fifre** [x .] fife.

**figan** [â] wail, lamentation; ~ etm. to lament.

**figür** figure.

**figüran** extra, supernumerary; *thea.* super.

**fiğ** ♀ vetch.

**fihrist,** -ti index; catalogue, list.

**fiil,** -li **1.** act, action, deed; **2.** ⚚, *phls.* activity; **3.** *gr.* verb; -e gelmek **1.** to be carried out; **2.** to become a fact; -e getirmek to carry out, to execute; -i bozuk immoral; -i şeni indecent assault; -i teşemmüs sunstroke.

**fiilen** 1. actually, really; 2. *st.* in act; 3. *pol.* de facto.

**fiili** 1. actual, real; 2. de facto; 3. acting; 4. *gr.* verbal; ~ hizmet active service.

**fiiliyat**, -tı [ā] 1. *pl.* acts, deeds; 2. practice; -ta in practice, de facto.

**fikir**, -krı thought, idea; opinion, mind; ~ adamı intellectual, savant, thinker; ~ edinmek to have an idea; to form an opinion (about); ~ işçisi white-collar worker; ~ vermek to give an idea (about); ~ yürütmek to opine; fikre getirmek to recall; fikri dağınık distracted, absent-minded; fikrince in one's opinion; fikrinde tutmak to keep (*or* bear) in mind; fikrine koymak 1. to make up one's mind (about); 2. to put into the mind of; fikri sabit; sabit fikir fixed idea, fixation.

**fikirli** 1. having ideas; 2. rich in ideas, intelligent, thoughtful.

**fikirsiz** 1. lacking in ideas; 2. thoughtless, heedless.

**fikren** [x .] in ideas, in thought, intellectually.

**fikri** mental, intellectual.

**fikriyat**, -tı [ā] 1. intellectual aspects (*of a matter*); 2. ideology.

**fikstür** *sport:* fixture.

**fil** 1. elephant; 2. *chess:* bishop; ~ gibi greedy, voracious; huge, enormous.

**filan** *s.* falan; ~ fıstık and so on, this and that, and so forth.

**filanca** *s.* falanca.

**filandra** *s.* flandra.

**filanıncı** *s.* falanıncı.

**filarmonik** philharmonic; ~ orkestra(sı) philharmonic orchestra.

**fildekos** lisle.

**fildişi**, -nı ivory.

**file** 1. net (*or* string) bag; 2. netting; 3. hair-net.

**fileto** [x .] fillet; loin.

**filhakika** [x . - .] in fact, actually, truly, in truth.

**Filibe** *pr. n.* Philippopolis, Plovdiv.

**filibit**, -tı ℞ phlebitis.

**filigran** watermark (*in paper*).

**filika** [. x .] ⚓ life-boat, ship's boat.

**filinta** [. x .] carbine, short gun; ~ gibi handsome.

**Filipinler** *pr. n.* Philippines.

**Filistin** [. x .] *pr. n.* Palestine.

**Filistinli** [. x . .] Palestinian.

**filiz** 1. tendril, young shoot, bud, sprout, scion; 2. *min.* ore; ~ gibi slender.

**filizi** bright green.

**filizlenmek** 1. to sprout, to send forth shoots, to shoot; 2. *fig.* to burgeon.

**film** 1. film (*for a camera*); 2. film, movie; ~ çekmek 1. to film; 2. to X-ray; ~ çevirmek 1. to make a movie, to film; 2. *sl.* to swagger, to show off; ~ koparmak *sl.* to talk rubbish; ~ makinesi movie camera; ~ oynatmak so show; ~ yıldızı film star; -e çekmek to film; -ini almak 1. to film; 2. to X-ray.

**filo** [x .] 1. fleet; squadron; 2. ⚓ reef sails!

**filoloji** philology.

**filotilla** [. . x .] flotilla.

**filozof** 1. philosopher; 2. *fig.* philosophical.

**filozofi** philosophy.

**filozofluk** the quality of a philosopher; being a philosopher; *part. co.* indifference.

**filtraj** filtering; ~ tesisatı purification plant.

**filtre** [x .] filter, sieve; ~ etm. to filter.

**filvaki** [x - .] in fact, actually.

**Fin** *pr. n.* Finn; Finnish; ~ hamamı sauna.

**final**, -li 1. *sports:* final; 2. ♪ finale; -e kalmak *sports:* to go on to the finals.

**finalist**, -tı *sports:* finalist.

**finance** finance; ~ etm. to finance.

**finansman** financing.

**fincan** 1. cup; 2. ⚡ porcelain insulator; ~ tabağı saucer; ~ zarfı metal cup holder.

**fingir fingir** coquettishly.

**fingirdek** coquettish, frivolous.

**fingirdemek** to behave coquettishly, to coquet.

**finiş** *sport:* finish.

**fink**: ~ atmak (*or* atıp gezmek) F to saunter about and enjoy o.s., to flirt around, to gallivant.

**Finlandiya** [. x . .] *pr. n.* Finland.

**fino** [x .] pet (*or* lap) dog.

**firak**, -kı [. -] seperation.

**fıraklı** sad, meloncholy.

**firar** [ā] 1. flight; ✗ desertion; ~ etm. 1. to run away, to flee; 2. ✗ to desert.

**firari** [. - -] 1. fugitive, runaway; 2. ✗ deserter.

**firavun** 1. Pharaoh; 2. *fig.* haughty, despotical (*person*).

**fire** [x .] *st.* loss, decrease, diminution; wastage; shrinkage; ~ vermek to suffer wastage; to diminish; to shrink.

**firigo** *sl.* disagreeable, unpleasant (*person*).

**firik** P roasted unripe wheat.

**firkat**, -tı separation, absence.

**firkateyn** ⚓ frigate.

**firkete** [. x .] hair-pin.

**firketelemek** [. x . . .] to pin up (*one's hair*).

**firma** [x .] 1. firm; 2. trade name.

**firuze** [ū] turquoise.

**fisebilillah** [- . - . -] (*lit.* in the way of God) expecting nothing in return.

**fiske** 1. flick, flip (*with the finger*); 2. pinch; 3. pimple; ~ vurmak = fiskelemek.

**fiskelemek** to give a flip (to), to flick.

**fisket**, -ti boatswain's pipe; whistle.

**fiskos** whispering; gossip.

**fistan** 1. dress, petticoat, skirt; 2. kilt.

**fisto** [x .] decorative scalloped ribbon.

**fistül** fistula.

**fiş** 1. slip of paper, card; 2. ⚡ plug; 3. form; 4. chip, receipt; 5. counter (*games*): ~ açmak to prepare a file card.

**fişek** 1. cartridge; 2. rocket; 3. roll of coins; 4. fireworks; ~ atmak 1. to fire (*or* let fly) a rocket; 2. *sl.* to put the cat among the pigeons; 3. *sl.* to have sexual relations (-e with); ~ gibi quickly, speedily; ~ gibi girmek to burst in, to blow in.

**fişekçi** 1. cartridge-maker; 2. pyrotechnist.

**fişekhane** [ā] cartridge factory.

**fişeklik** cartridge belt; bandolier; ammunition pouch; cartridge box.

**fişlemek** 1. to prepare an index card (-i on); 2. (*the police*) to open a file (-i on).

**fit¹** -ti instigation; incitement; ~ çıkarmak (*or* vermek) to instigate, to incite.

**fit²**, -ti 1. ready; consenting; 2. (*bşe*) *sl.* quits; ~ olm. *sl.* to be quits, to settle for.

**fit³** -ti [ī] ⊕ feed.

**fitçi** agitator, instigator, intriguer.

**fitil** 1. wick; 2. ⚡ seton, tent; 3. ✕ fuse; 4. piping; 5. a kind of card game; ~ (gibi) as drunk as a lord; ~ vermek to infuriate, to exasperate, to incite, to stir up; -i almak to flare up, to become alarmed.

**fitillemek** 1. to light (*the fuse of a mine*); 2. to attach a fuse *or* wick to; 3. = fitil vermek.

**fitlemek** to instigate, to excite, to incite, to denounce, to set one person against another.

**fitne** 1. instigation; mischief-making; 2. † sedition, disorder, rebellion; 3. = fitneci; ~ basmak (*or* kopmak) to break out (*unrest*); ~ etm. 1. to incite, to intrigue; 2. to revolt; ~ fücur dangerous agitator; ~ kumkuması dangerous intriguer; ~ sokmak (*or* koymak) to set people at loggerheads, to set s.o. against s.o.; ~ vermek 1. to mislead, to lead astray; 2. to make a mischievous suggestion.

**fitneci** intriguer, agitator.

**fitnelemek** to calomniate, to inform (on), to denounce, to peach, to betray.

**fitre** alms (*given at the close of Ramadan*).

**fitret**, -ti ✕ interregnum.

**fiyaka** [. x .] *sl.* showing off, ostentation, swagger, swank, pretension; ~ satmak *sl.* to show off, to swank, to swagger; -yı bozmak to ridicule s.o.'s swagger.

**fiyakacı** *sl.* swank, swaggerer.

**fiyakalı** *sl.* showy, nobby, ostentatious.

**fiyasko** fiasco, washout, failure; ~ vermek to end in fiasco.

**fiyat**, -tı price; ~ bıçmak to estimate a price (-e for); ~ farkı price difference; ~ indirimi reduction; ~ kırmak to reduce the price, to discount; ~ koymak to fix price (-e of); ~ vermek to quote a price (-e for).

**fiyatlanmak** to get expensive, to go up in price.

**fiyatlı** expensive, dear, costly.

**fiyonga** [. x .], **fiyonk** 1. bow tie; 2. bowknot, bow.

**fiyort**, -du fiord.

**fizik** 1. physics; 2. physical; ~ tedavisi physiotherapy.

**fizikçi** physicist.

**fiziki** physical.

**fizikötesi**, -ni 1. metaphysics; 2. metaphysical.

**fiziksel** physical.

**fizyoloji** physiology.

**fizyolojik** physiological.

**fizyonomi** physiognomy.

**flama** 1. pennant, streamer, colo(u)rs, banners; 2. stadia (*or* surveyor's) rod.

**flamingo**, **flamankuşu**, -nu *zo.* flamingo.

**flandra** [x .] 1. ⚓ pennant; 2. *zo.* red bandfish.

**flaş** *phot.* 1. flash; 2. flash bulb.

**flavta** [x .] † flute.

**flebit**, -ti ⚕ phlebitis.

**flok**, -ku ⚓ jibsail.

**Floransa** [. x .] *pr. n.* Florence.

**floresan** fluorescent; ~ lamba fluorescent lamp.

**florin** florin, guilder.

**floş** 1. floss silk; 2. *cards:* flush.

**flöre** *fencing:* foil.

**flört**, -tü 1. flirtation; 2. girl (*or* boy) friend; ~ etm. to flirt.

**flû** *phot.* blurred, weak.

**flüorışı** fluorescence.

**flüt**, -tü flute.

**flütçü** flutist, flautist.

**fob** † f.o.b., free on board.

**fobi** [x .] phobia.

**fodra** [x .] lining, padding.

**fodul** vain, presumptuous.

**foga** [x .] † fire!; ~ etm. to fire.

**fok,** -ku zo. seal.

**fokurdamak** to boil up, to bubble.

**fokur fokur** boiling up, bubbling noisily.

**fokurtu** bubbling sound.

**foküs** focus.

**fol** nest egg.

**folklor,** -ru [x .] folklore; folk dancing.

**folkon** ⬦ frame-liner, timber-band (of a wooden ship).

**folluk** nesting-box.

**folya** [x .] zo. eagle ray.

**fon** 1. fund, asset; 2. paint. background colo(u)r; 3. thea. décor, setting; ~ müziği background music, accompaniment.

**fonda** [x .] ⬦ let go the anchor!; ~ etm. to let go the anchor.

**fondan** fondant; ~ çikolata vanilla chocolate.

**fondo** [x .] † stock; bond; funds.

**fonem** gr. phoneme.

**fonetik** 1. phonetics; 2. phonetic.

**fonksiyon** function.

**fonograf** phonograph.

**fonojenik** phonogenic.

**font,** -tu cast (or pig) iron.

**fora** ⬦ open it!, unfurl (the sail)!; ~ etm. 1. ⬦ to open, to unfurl; 2. sl. to pull off (bşi s.th.).

**foravelâ** [. . x .] †, ⬦ to make sail.

**form** form; -a girmek sports: to get into shape; -unda olm. sports: to be in (good) form.

**forma** [x .] 1. forme, folio; 2. uniform; 3. form; 4. colo(u)rs (of a sporting club); 5. football: shirt; ~ ~ in parts.

**formalist,** -ti formalist.

**formalite** formality; red tape; ~ düşkünü formalist; ~ gereği as a matter of form.

**formasyon** 1. formation; 2. training education.

**formika** formica.

**formsuz** sports: out of form, off form.

**formül** 1. a. Ⓐ, ⧖ formula; 2. = formüler.

**formüle:** ~ etm. to formulate.

**formüler** formulary.

**foroz** haul (of fish).

**fors** 1. ⬦ admiral's flag at the main; personal flag flown on a ship; 2. flag (or pennant) of office; 3. F power, esteem, influence, prestige; -u olm. F to have influence.

**forsa** [x .] 1. galley slave; 2. typ. pressure.

**forseps** ⚕ forceps.

**forslu** influential, powerful.

**forsmajör** force majeure; compulsion.

**forum** forum.

**forvet,** -ti sports: forward.

**fos** sl. rotten, putrid, bad, false, shaky, groundless; ~ dalga sl. malice, treachery.

**fosfat,** -tı phosphate.

**fosfor** phosphorus.

**fosforışı** phosphorescence.

**fosforlu** phosphorous; phosphoric.

**fosil** fossil.

**foslamak** sl. to fail, to be upset, to turn up bad or false.

**fosseptik** cesspool, cesspit.

**fosur fosur** in puffs.

**fota** [x .] cask (for making wine).

**fotin** s. potin.

**foto** 1. photo; 2. photographer; ~ muhabiri newspaper photographer.

**fotografi, fotografya** [. . x .] photography.

**fotoğraf** 1. photograph; 2. photography; ~ çekmek to take a photograph, to photograph; ~ makinesi camera; -ını çektirmek to have one's photograph taken.

**fotoğrafçı** 1. photographer; 2. photographer's studio.

**fotoğrafçılık** photography.

**fotoğrafhane** [. . . - .] photographer's studio.

**fotojenik** photogenic.

**fotokopi** photocopy, photostat (copy), Xerox; ~ makinesi photocopier, photostat.

**fotometre** photometer.

**fotomontaj** photomontage.

**fotoroman** photo-story.

**fotosentez** photosynthesis.

**foya** [x .] 1. foil (for setting off a gem); 2. fig. eyewash, fraud; ~ vermek fig. to give o.s. away; -sı bozuk 1. deceitful, fraudulent; 2. charlatan, quack, mountebank; -sı meydana (or ortaya) çıkmak to give the show away.

**fötr** felt; ~ şapka felt hat.

**fragman** fragment ; cinema: trailer.

**frak,** -kı tail-coat, tails.

**francala** [x . .] white bread; roll.

**frank,** -gı franc.

**Fransa** [x .] pr. n. France.

**Fransız** 1. French; 2. Frenchman.

**Fransızca** French (language).

**frapan** striking, flamboyant.

**frekans** frequency.

**fren** brake; ~ ayarı brake adjusment; ~ balatası brake lining; ~ çubuğu brake rod; ~ pedalı brake pedal; ~ tutmadı the brakes failed to grip; ~ yapmak to brake.

**frenci** brake(s)man.

**frengi** [x .] syphilis, pox.

**Frenk,** -gi European.

**frenkarpası,** -nı pearl barley.

**frenkasması,** -nı Virginia creeper.

frenkeriği, -ni greengage plum.
frenkgömleği, -ni shirt.
frenksalatası, -nı rampion.
frenküzümü, -nü red currant.
frenlemek 1. to brake; 2. *fig.* to moderate, to check.
frensiz 1. brakeless; 2. *fig.* unrestrained (*person*).
freze [x .] milling cutter; ~ etm. to mill.
frezeci workman skilled in milling.
frigorifik frigorific, refrigerated.
frijider refrigerator, ice-box.
frikik *football:* free kick.
friksiyon friction, massage.
fuar [. x] fair, exposition.
fuaye *thea.* foyer.
fuhşiyat, -tı [ã] prostitution; obscenities, immoralities; -a tahrik ☾☽ soliciting.
fuhuş, -hşu prostitution.
fukara [. . -] 1. the poor; 2. poor, destitute, needy, pauper; 3. dervish.
fukaralık poverty, destitution.
fukaraperver charitable; benevolent.
ful, -lü ♀ 1. broad bean; 2. syringa.
fular cravat.
fulya [x .] ♀ jonquil.
funda [x .] 1. thicket, shrub; 2. ♀ heath; ~ toprağı humus of heath.
fundalık scrub, underwood, brush.
funya [x .] primer.
furgon luggage-van, freight-car.
furş fork of a bicycle.
furta *s.* farta.

furun *s.* fırın.
furya [x .] rush; glut.
fus *biol.* lobe.
futa [x .] 1. loin-cloth; 2. = fıtaı 3. = fota.
futbol, -lu football, soccer; ~ bahsimüştereki football-pools; ~ maçı football match; ~ meraklısı football fan.
futbolcu footballer.
fuzulen [. - .] superfluously; without right; unjustly.
fuzuli [. - -] 1. unnecessary, needless, superfluous; 2. officious; 3. excessive; 4. unnecessarily; ~ gayretkeş over-zealous; ~ tasarruflar ☾☽ dispositions (*or* contracts) made without authority.
fücceten [x . .] suddenly; ~ ölmek to die a sudden death.
füme smoked; ~ etm. to smoke.
fümuvar smoking room.
füniküler suspension railway, (aerial) cableway.
fürce 1. *anat.* fissure; 2. ⚲ breach, gap; 3. ⚲ leisure.
füsun [ü] charm, enchantment, spell, magic.
fütuhat, -tı [. - -] victories; conquests.
fütuhatçı [. - -.] conqueror; imperialist.
fütur [. -] languor; abatement; ~ getirmek to get tired (of), to lose zeal.
fütursuz [. - .] 1. indifferent; 2. undeterred.
füze [x .] rocket, missile.
füzen charcoal pencil (*or* drawing).

# G

gabardin gabardine.

gabari loading gauge.

gabavet, -ti [. - .] stupidity, obtuseness.

gabi thick-headed, stupid, obtuse.

gabilik s. gabavet.

gabin ʊ̌ʊ̌ fraud, cheating (on a sale).

gabro gabbro.

gabya [x .] ⚓ topmast, topsail.

gacırdamak to creak.

gacır gucur producing a continuous creaking noise.

gaco sl. woman; sweetheart; ~ eskisi sl. English pound.

gaddar [. -] cruel, perfidious, tyrant.

gaddare [. - .] a heavy double-edged scimitar.

gaddarlık cruelty, perfidy, tyranny.

gadir, -dri 1. cruelty; 2. injustice; tyranny.

gadolinyum ⚗ gadolinium.

gadretmek [x .] (b-ne) 1. to do wrong to s.o., to treat unjustly towards s.o.; 2. to treat cruelly towards s.o.

gaf blunder, gaffe, faux pas; ~ yapmak to blunder.

gafçı blunderer.

gafil [ā] unaware (-den of); careless, inattentive, unmindful; ~ avlamak to catch unawares, to take by surprise; ~ bulunmak (or olm.) to take no heed.

gaflet, -ti heedlessness, carelessness; -e düşmek to be careless, to act heedlessly.

gafleten unawares, inadvertently.

gaga 1. beak, bill; 2. sl. mouth, trap; ~ burun hook-nosed, aquiline; ~ -ya vermek to bill and coo; -sından yakalamak fig. to catch by the nose; kapa -nı! sl. shut your trap!

gagalamak 1. to peck; 2. fig. to scorn, to rebuke.

gagalaşmak 1. to peck one another; 2. to bill and coo.

gagalı beaked.

gâh s. kâh.

gaile [ā] trouble, anxiety, worry, difficulty.

gaileli 1. troubled, worried; 2. troublesome.

gailesiz 1. untroubled; 2. trouble-free, carefree.

gailesizlik untroubledness.

gaip, -bi [ā] 1. absent, invisible; missing, lost; 2. the invisible world; -ten haber vermek to foretell, to divine.

gaiplik [ā] ʊ̌ʊ̌ disappearance; ~ kararı ʊ̌ʊ̌ declaration of death.

gaita [- . .] feces.

gak! caw! (of a crow).

gaklamak to caw.

Gal pr. n. Wales.

gala [x .] 1. gala, première; 2. state dinner; ~ gecesi gala night.

galat, -tı error, mistake; galatı hilkat freak of nature, monster.

galatıhis, -ssi illusion.

galatımeşhur commonly accepted error (in language).

galdır guldur with an uneven, heavy, rolling gait.

galebe 1. victory; 2. supremacy, predominance; ~ çalmak to conquer, to overwhelm; ~ etm. 1. to get the upper hand; 2. to overcome, to overwhelm.

galen geol. galena.

galeri 1. gallery; 2. art gallery; 3. gallery, working drift; 4. thea. gallery, balcony; 5. showroom (or display lot) (for automobiles, etc.).

galeta [. x .] bread stick, rusk; ~ tozu bread crumbs; ~ unu fine white flour.

galeyan [. . .] 1. rage, agitation, excitement; 2. ebullition; -a gelmek to get worked up, to be agitated.

galiba [- . .] [x . -] 1. most probably, presumably; 2. I think so.

galibiyet, -ti [ā] victory, win.

galip, -bi [ā] 1. victorious; 2. victor, vanquisher; 3. overwhelming, superior; ~ çıkmak to emerge victorious (-den from); ~ gelmek (b-ne) to defeat s.o., to overcome s.o.; ~ ihtimale göre = ağlebi ihtimal.

galiz [î] 1. filthy, dirty; 2. obscene, indecent.

galon 1. gallon; 2. gas can.

galoş galosh.

galsame anat. gill (of a fish).

galvaniz galvanization.
galvanize galvanized; ~ etm. to galvanize.
galvanizlemek to galvanize.
galvanizli galvanized.
galyum ♔ gallium.
gam¹ ♪ scale.
gam² grief, anxiety, worry; ~ çekmek to grieve; ~ değil it does not matter; ~ yememek not to worry.
gamalı *hist.* comprising a gamma; ~ haç swastika, gammadion.
Gambiya *pr. n.* Gambia.
gambot, -tu 1. gunboat; 2. *ichth.* small mullet.
gamet, -ti *biol.* gamete.
gamlanmak to worry (-e about).
gamlı worried, sorrowful, grieved.
gamma gamma; ~ ışınları gamma rays.
gammaz [. -] sneak, informer, telltale.
gammazlamak to inform (against), to tell on, to tell tales (about), to denounce, to peach (against, on).
gammazlık tale-bearing, spying, informing.
gamsele [x . .] raincoat, oilskin, mackintosh.
gamsız carefree, lighthearted, happy-go-lucky.
gamsızlık lightheartedness, untroubledness.
gamze 1. dimple; 2. coquettish glance, twinkle.
Gana *pr. n.* Ghana.
gangster gangster, gunman.
gangsterlik gangsterism.
gani [ı] 1. abundant; 2. rich; ~ ~ abundantly; ~ gönüllü generous; -si olm. to have enough, not to be in need of.
ganimet, -ti [ı] 1. spoils, booty, loot; 2. windfall, godsend; 3. ♔ *wf.; ~* bilmek (or görmek) to look on as a godsend; to seize (an opportunity).
Ganj *pr. n.* Ganges.
gant, -tı *sports:* boxing glove.
ganyan the winner (horse); winning ticket.
gar large railway station; ~ şefi station-master.
garabet, -ti strangeness, oddity.
garaip, -bi [. - .] strange things.
garaipten odd, strange, queer.
garaj garage.
garam [. -] passionlove; eager desire.
garami lyric(al).
garanti 1. guaranty, guarantee; 2. F sure, certain; certainly, without doubt; ~ etm. to guarantee.

garantilemek 1. to guarantee; 2. to make certain, to make sure (-i of).
garantili 1. guaranteed; 2. *fig.* certain, sure.
garaz 1. grudge, ranco(u)r, malice, animosity; 2. aim, object, goal, purpose; ~ bağlamak (b-ne) to hold a grudge against s.o.; ~ beslemek (or tutmak) to nourish a spite; ~ olm. (b-ne) to bear a grudge against s.o., to bear s.o. malice.
garazkâr rancorous, spiteful.
garazkârlık spitefulness.
garazsız unbiased, unprejudiced, disinterested.
garben [x .] westwards.
garbi [ı] western.
gardenparti [x . . .] garden party.
gardenya ♔ gardenia.
çardıfren brakeman.
gardırop, -bu 1. wardrobe, armoire; 2. cloakroom.
gardiyan gaoler, warder, *Am.* jailer.
garez *s.* garaz.
gargar water jug with a filter.
gargara 1. gargle; 2. mouthwash; ~ yapmak to gargle; -ya getirmek *sl.* to deflect on purpose.
gariban pitiable, pathetic (person).
garibe strange thing, curiosity.
garip, -bi [ı] 1. strange, odd, peculiar, unusual; 2. destitute, needy; 3. stranger; garibine gitmek (b-nin) to strike as odd, to appear strange to s.o.
gariplik strangeness, oddity.
garipsemek 1. to find strange (or curious); 2. to feel lonely and homesick.
gark, -kı drowning; ~ etm. to overwhelm; ~ olm. to be overwhelmed (-e with), to be submerged.
garnitür 1. garnish, garniture, trimmings (of a dish); 2. trimmings (of a dress).
garnizon 1. garrison; 2. garrison town; ~ komutanı (or kumandanı) garrison commander.
garp, -bı 1. west; 2. Europe.
garpçı westernizer.
garplı Westerner, Occidental.
garplılık Occidentalism.
garson waiter.
garsoniye service charge.
garsoniyer bachelor's establishment.
gaseyan [. . .] 1. nausea; 2. vomiting; ~ etm. to vomit.
gasıp¹, -spı usurpation, seizure by violence.
gasıp² [â] usurper.
gasil, -sli washing of the dead.
gasletmek [x . .] to wash (the dead).
gaspetmek [x . .] to seize by force, to

usurp.

**gassal** washer of the dead.

**gastrit,** -ti gastritis.

**gastrula** *biol.* gastrula.

**gaşiy,** -şyi ecstasy, rapture.

**gaşyetmek** [x . .] to enrapture.

**gaşyolmak** [x . .] to be enraptured.

**gauss** *phys.* gauss.

**gâvur 1.** giaour, unbeliever, non-Moslem, infidel, Christian; **2.** *fig.* merciless, cruel; obstinate; ~ etm. F to squander, to blow *(money)*; ~ ınadı pigheadedness, obstinacy; ~ ölüsü gibi as heavy as lead.

**gâvurca 1.** in a European language; **2.** heartlessly, cruelly.

**gâvurcasına** mercilessly.

**gâvurluk 1.** unbelief; **2.** *fig.* cruelty; ~ etm. to act cruelly.

**gaybubet,** -ti [ü] absence; -inde in the absence of.

**gayda** [x .] ♪ bagpipe.

**gaydacı** ♪ bagpiper.

**gaye** [â] aim, object, end, goal; ~ edinmek *(bşi)* to aim at *s.th.*; -siyle for the purpose of; -ye ulaşmak to attain the aim, to succeed.

**gayet,** -ti [â] very, extremely, greatly.

**gaygay** with a shrill grating sound.

**gaygaylı** shrill.

**gayr** someone else; -e muhtaç olmamak not to be in need of anyone.

**gayret,** -ti **1.** zeal, energy, ardo(u)r, effort, perseverance; **2.** solicitude, protectiveness; ~ etm. to endeavo(u)r, to try hard; ~ vermek **1.** to encourage; **2.** to console; -e gelmek **1.** to get into working spirit; **2.** to become enthusiastic, to show zeal; -i elden bırakmamak to keep trying, to persist; -ten düşmek to become discouraged.

**gayretkeş 1.** zealous; **2.** zealot; **3.** partisan.

**gayretlenmek 1.** to get into working spirit; **2.** to display zeal.

**gayretli 1.** zealous; **2.** hard-working, persevering.

**gayretsiz** slack, without enthusiasm, lacking zeal.

**gayrı 1.** now, well then, at length, finally; **2.** *emph. of* ayrı; **3.** (not) any more, (no) longer.

**gayri 1.** other *(den* than), besides, apart from; **2.** *(before adjectives)* un-, non-; ihtiyari involuntarily; ~ kabil impossible; ~ menkul **1.** immovable, real *(property)*; **2.** real estate; ~ meşru illegitimate; unlawful; illicit *(gain)*; unjust *(war)*; ~ muntazam **1.** irregular(ly); **2.** disorderly;

~ müslim non-Moslem; ~ resmi unofficial; informal; ~ safi † gross; ~ tabii unnatural, abnormal, strange.

**gayya** a well in hell; ~ kuyusu place of confusion.

**gayzer** geyser, hot spring.

**gaz¹** gauze.

**gaz² 1.** kerosene; **2.** *phys.* gas; **3.** flatus; ~ bombası gas bomb; ~ hali gaseous state; ~ lambası kerosene lamp; ~ maskesi gas mask; ~ ocağı kerosene cookstove; ~ sobası kerosene heater; -a basmak **1.** *mot.* to step on the gas, to accelerate; **2.** *sl.* to go away, to scram; -ı kesmek *mot.* to throttle back *(gas).*

**gazal,** -li [. -] *zo.* gazelle; antelope.

**gazap,** -bı wrath, rage; -a gelmek to get in a rage.

**gazaplı** wrathful, infuriated.

**gazdan(lık)** oil-can, oiler.

**gazel¹ 1.** lyric poem of a certain pattern; **2.** extemporaneous vocal taksim.

**gazel²** autumn leaf.

**gazete** [. x .] newspaper; ~ çıkarmak to publish a newspaper.

**gazeteci 1.** journalist, newspaperman; **2.** newspaper seller, news-vendor, newsboy, paperboy; **3.** owner of a newspaper.

**gazetecilik** journalism.

**gazhane** [. - .] gasworks.

**gazışıl** *phys.* luminescent.

**gazi** [- -] **1.** ghazi; **2.** fighter for Islam. Gazi Atatürk.

**gazino** [. x .] casino, café.

**gazlamak 1.** to smear *(or* sprinkle) with kerosene; **2.** *mot.* to accelerate; **3.** *sl.* to run away.

**gazlanmak 1.** *pass. of* gazlamak; **2.** to be flatulent.

**gazlaştırmak** to gasify.

**gazlı 1.** gaseous; **2.** containing kerosene; ~ bez gauze.

**gazoil, gazoyl** diesel oil.

**gazojen** gas generator.

**gazolin** gasoline.

**gazoma** [. x .] seam around the edge of a stitched sole.

**gazometre** gasometer.

**gazoz** soda pop, fizzy lemonade.

**gazozcu** seller of gazoz.

**gazölçer** gas meter.

**gazyağı,** -nı kerosene.

**gebe** pregnant, expectant; ~ bırakmak *(or* etm.) to make pregnant; ~ kalmak to fall pregnant, to become pregnant *(-den* by); ~ olm. *(bşe or* bş için) *fig.* to be pregnant with *s.th.*

**gebelik** pregnancy; ~ önleyici contraceptive.

**geberik** *contp.* dead.

**gebermek** *contp.* to die, to croak, to kick the bucket, to perish.

**gebertmek** *contp.* to kill, to bump off.

**gebeş** 1. dumpy, squat; 2. *sl.* idiot, blockhead.

**gebre¹** haircloth glove *(for grooming horses).*

**gebre²** ✦ caper.

**gece** 1. night; 2. at night; last night; to-night; ~ gündüz night and day, continuously; ~ kasası night safe; ~ kuşu 1. bat; 2. *fig.* night owl, night bird, nighthawk; ~ lambası night-light; ~ vakti at night; ~ yarısı midnight; ~ yatısı overnight visit; -ler gebedir nights are pregnant with new events; -niz hayrolsun! good night!; -yi gündüze katmak to work night and day.

**gececi** worker on a night shift.

**geceki** nocturnal.

**gecekondu** shanty; ~ bölgesi shanty-town.

**gecelemek** to spend the night *(in a place).*

**geceleyin** [. x . .] by night.

**geceli:** ~ gündüzlü day and night, continuously.

**gecelik** 1. nightdress, nightgown, nightshirt; 2. pertaining to the night; lasting the night; 3. fee for the night.

**gecesefası,** -nı ✦ four-o'clock.

**gecikme** delay.

**gecikmek** to be late, to be delayed.

**geciktirmek** to delay, to retard.

**geç** late, delayed; ~ kalmak to be late; ~ vakit late in the evening.

**geçe** past *(time);* beşi on ~ 10 minutes past five.

**geçeğen** temporary, transitory.

**geçen** past, last; ~ gün the other day; ~ sefer last time; ~ yıl last year.

**geçende, geçenlerde** lately, recently.

**geçenek** *neol.* corridor.

**geçer** 1. current, in circulation; 2. desired, in demand.

**geçerli** valid.

**geçerlik** validity, currency.

**geçersiz** invalid, null; ~ saymak to annul; to cancel.

**geçersizlik** invalidity.

**geçici** 1. temporary, transitory, passing; 2. contagious; ~ hükümet caretaker government; ~ madde temporary article; ~ olarak temporarily; ~ tutku passing fad *(or whim).*

**geçilmek** *pass. of* geçmek 1. to pass, to traverse; 2. to be left aside; geçilmez! no passage!; geçilmemek *(bşden)* to have a

great abundance of *s.th.;* to have too much of *s.th.*

**geçim** 1. livelihood, living; 2. harmony, getting alone with one another; ~ derdi the struggle to make a living; ~ indeksi cost of living indekx; ~ masrafı cost of living; ~ seviyesi the standard of living; ~ yolu means of subsistence.

**geçimli** affable, easy to get along with.

**geçimlik** livelihood.

**geçimsiz** fractious, quarrelsome, shrewish, unsociable.

**geçimsizlik** fractiousness.

**geçindirmek** to support *(a person),* to maintain.

**geçinecek** 1. income; 2. livelihood, living.

**geçinge** budget.

**geçinim, geçinme** subsistence, getting by.

**geçinmek** 1. to live *(ile* on), to subsist *(ile* on); 2. to rub along *(ile* with), to get on well *(ile* with), to get along *(ile* with); 3. to pretend to be, to pass (for); 4. *(b-den)* to live on *s.o.,* to sponge on *s.o.;* 5. P to die.

**geçirgen** *phys.* permeable.

**geçirgenlik** *phys.* permeability.

**geçirimli** permeable.

**geçirimsiz** impermeable.

**geçirimsizlik** impermeability.

**geçirmek** *caus. of* geçmek *part.* 1. to infect *(s.o. with a disease);* 2. to fix, to fit, to insert *(glass into a frame);* 3. to slip on *(a cover on a book, etc.);* 4. to spend, to pass *(time);* 5. to enter, to register *(in an account);* 6. to undergo *(an operation);* 7. to copy out; 8. to get over *(a disease);* 9. to accompany s.o., to see s.o. out; 10. to see s.o. off; 11. to have *(an attack);* 12. to pass *(s.th. through s.th.);* 13. to transmit *(heat);* 14. *sl.* to fuck, to screw.

**geçiş** 1. passing, crossing; 2. change, transfer; 3. ♪ transition; ~ üstünlüğü right of way.

**geçişli** *gr.* transitive.

**geçişmek** to intermix, to be diffused.

**geçişsiz** *gr.* intransitive.

**geçiştirmek** 1. *caus. of* geçişmek; 2. to pass over lightly; 3. to get over *(an illness);* 4. to escape with little harm.

**geçit,** -di 1. mountain pass; 2. passageway, passage; 3. ford; 4. parade; 5. *ast.* transit; ~ resmi *(or* töreni) parade; ~ vermek to be fordable.

**geçkin** 1. elderly; 2. overripe *(fruit);* 3. overmatured *(wood);* otuzu ~ over thirty.

**geçkinlik** 1. elderliness; 2. overripeness *(fruit).*

**geçme 1.** *vn. of* geçmek; **2.** dovetailed; telescoped; **3.** tenon.

**geçmek, (-çer) 1.** to pass (-*den* over, along), to cross, to traverse; **2.** to undergo, to go through; **3.** to pass by; **4.** to give up on, to renounce; **5.** to move (-*e* to); **6.** to penetrate, to affect; to influence; **7.** to come into (*power*); **8.** (*b-den b-ne*) to spread from *s.o.* to *s.o.*; **9.** (*b-den b-ne*) to pass from *s.o.* to *s.o.* through heredity; **10.** to be recorded (*in a book*); **11.** (*ta-rihe*) to go down in history; **12.** to exceed, to pass; to cross, to go past; **13.** to omit, to skip, to leave out; **14.** to pass (*time*); **15.** to be mentioned; **16.** to be current, to be in force; **17.** to be popular, to be the fad; **18.** to pass, to come to an end, to end (*season, period, illness*); **19.** to pass one's class; to pass (*an exam*); **20.** to be overripe (*fruit*); to spoil, to go stale; **21.** to practise (*music*); **22.** (*k-den*) to faint; geç! (*or* geç efendim!) F leave it!, it is not worth talking about!; (gün) geç-tikçe as the day goes on, in the course of time.

**geçmelik** toll.

**geçmiş 1.** past; **2.** the past; **3.** overripe, spoiled; ~ ola (*or* olsun)! I wish you a speedy recovery!; ~ olsuna gitmek to visit *s.o.* who has been ill; ~ zaman *gr.* past tense; -i kandilli (*or* tenekeli) F damned (*for a person*); -i olm. (*b-le*) to have known *s.o.* in the past.

**gedik 1.** gap, breach; **2.** fault, defect; **3.** mountain pass; **4.** privilege; ~ açmak to make a breach (-*de* in); ~ kapamak to fill the gap.

**gedikli 1.** breached; gapped; notched; **2.** constant frequenter, patron; **3.** ✕ regular non-commissioned officer (NCO); ~ çavuş ✕ sergeant; warrant officer.

**geğirmek** to belch, to burp, to eructate.

**geğirti** belch, burp, eructation.

**geğrek** lower (*or* false) rib; ~ batması stitch in the side.

**gelberi** poker, rake; ~ etm. *sl.* to swipe, to nick, to pilfer.

**gele** *backgammon:* blank throw.

**gelecek 1.** future; **2.** next, coming; ~ se-fer next time; ~ zaman *gr.* future tense; ~ zaman ortacı *gr.* future participle.

**gelecekbilim** futurology.

**gelecekbilimci** futurologist.

**gelecekçi** futurist.

**gelecekçilik** futurism.

**geleğen** tributary (*river*).

**gelembe** sheepfold.

**gelen 1.** comer; **2.** *phys.* incident; ~ ge-çen(ler) passer(s)-by; ~ giden(ler) visitor(s), comer(s); ~ gidene rahmet oku-tur (*or* ~ gideni aratır) *fig.* the new is often worse than the old.

**gelenek** tradition.

**gelenekçi** traditionalist.

**gelenekçilik** traditionalism.

**gelenekli, geleneksel** traditional.

**geleneksellik** traditionalism.

**geleni** *zo.* meadow mouse.

**gelgeç** fickle, inconstant.

**gelgelelim** but, only.

**gelgit, -ti 1.** tide, flood-tide; **2.** useless coming and going.

**gelin 1.** bride; **2.** daughter-in-law; ~ alayı bridal procession; ~ güvey olm. (*kendi k-ne*) to build castles in Spain; ~ odası bridal chamber; ~ odası gibi attractive and very tidy (*room*); ~ olm. to get married (*girl*); ~ teli silver tinsel.

**gelinböceği, -ni** *zo.* ladybug.

**gelince [. x .]** -e as for, regarding.

**gelincik 1.** ✿ poppy; **2.** *zo.* weasel; **3.** (il-leti) P hectic fever; dropsy; sty.

**gelinfeneri, -ni** ✿ winter cherry.

**gelinhavası, -nı** fine weather.

**gelinkuşu, -nu** *zo.* pencilled lark.

**gelinlik 1.** wedding-dress; **2.** nubile, mar-riageable (*girl*).

**gelinsaçı, -nı** ✿ dodder.

**gelir** income, revenue; ~ dağılımı income distribution; ~ gider income and outgo; ~ vergisi income tax.

**geliş** coming.

**gelişigüzel** superficial(ly), by chance, at random; haphazard, desultory.

**gelişim** development, progress.

**gelişme 1.** development; **2.** growing, ma-turing.

**gelişmek 1.** to grow up; to mature; to grow healthy (*or* fat); **2.** to develop, to prosper, to thrive; gelişmekte olan ülke developing country.

**gelişmiş 1.** developed; **2.** grown-up (*person*).

**geliştirmek** to develop, to improve, to ad-vance.

**gelme** *vn. of* gelmek *part.* **1.** arrival; **2.** *optics:* incidence; **3.** originating (-*den* from); derived (-*den* from); yeni ~ new-comer.

**gelmek, (-ir) 1.** to come; **2.** -e to seem, to appear; **3.** -e to suit, to fit; **4.** to come up to; **5.** to cost; **6.** to be felt, to come to one; **7.** to affect; **8.** to come around (-*e* to); **9.** -*den* to pretend, to feign; gel gele-lim all the same, however, and yet; gele gele eventually, finally; gelip çatmak to come round at last, to be finally at hand (*a time*); gelip geçici transient, passing; gel zaman git zaman long afterwards; gelip gitmek to frequent, to come and go.

**gem bit** (*of a horse*); ~ almak to take the bit (*horse*); ~ almaz unbridled; ~ vurmak -e to curb; to bridle; -i azıya almak to take the bit between the teeth (*a. fig.*); -ini kısmak *fig.* to rein in.

**gemi** ship, boat, vessel; ~ aslanı F stuffed dummy; ~ ızgarası shipway, ways; ~ işletimi cabotage, coasting trade; ~ izi wake; ~ kafilesi convoy; ~ karaya oturmak to go (*or* run) aground; ~ kiralamak to charter a ship; ~ leşi shipwreck; ~ mürettebatı crew; ~ tezgâhı stocks, dockyard; ~ yatağı ship's berth, port of shelter; -de teslim † free on board, f.o.b.; -ye binmek to embark, to go on board.

**gemici** sailor, mariner; ~ feneri barn lantern.

**gemicilik 1.** seamanship; **2.** navigation; seafaring.

**gemilik** dockyard, shipyard.

**gemlemek** to bridle (*a. fig.*).

**gen**[1] *biol.* gene.

**gen**[2] broad, vast; untouched (*ground*).

**gencecik** [x . .] very young.

**genç, -ci** young, youthful; youngster; ~ yaşında in his youth; -ler the young, youth.

**gençleşmek** to become youthful, to be rejuvenated.

**gençleştirmek** to rejuvenate.

**gençlik 1.** youth, youthfulness; **2.** the young, youth.

**gençten** young.

**gene** [x .] **1.** again; **2.** still, nevertheless; ~ görüşelim! see you soon!, be seeing you!; -de but still; yet again.

**genel** general; ~ af amnesty; ~ merkez headquarters; ~ müdür general director; ~ olarak in general, generally; ~ prova dress rehearsal; ~ seçim general election; ~ seferberlik general mobilization; ~ sekreter secretary general.

**genelev** brothel.

**genelge** circular, notice.

**genelkurmay** ✕ general staff.

**genelkurul** general meeting.

**genelleme** generalization.

**genellemek** to generalize.

**genelleşme** generalization.

**genelleşmek** to become general.

**genelleştirme** generalization.

**genelleştirmek** to generalize.

**genellik** generality.

**genellikle** generally, in general, usually.

**general, -li** ✕ general.

**generallik** ✕ generalship.

**genetik** genetics.

**gengüdüm** ✕ strategy.

**geniş 1.** wide. broad; **2.** extensive, spacious. vast: **3.** carefree (*person*); ~ açı Ⱥ obtuse angle; ~ fikirli *fig.* broad-minded, ~ gönüllü (*or* yürekli) *fig.* easygoing, serene; ~ mezhepli very tolerant; ~ ölçüde on a large scale; ~ yapraklı ♦ broad-leaved; ~ zaman *gr.* simple present tense, aorist; ~ zaman ortacı *gr.* present participle.

**genişlemek 1.** to widen, to broaden; to expand; **2.** to ease up.

**genişletmek** to widen, to broaden; to expand, to enlarge.

**genişlik 1.** width, wideness; extensiveness; **2.** abundance, wealth, comfort.

**geniz, -nzi** nasal passages( *or* fossae); -den konuşmak to speak through the nose; -e kaçmak to go down the wrong way (*food*); genzi yakmak to stifle, to choke on.

**genleşme** dilatation.

**genleşmek** to dilate, to be dilated.

**genlik 1.** comfort; **2.** *phys.* amplitude.

**genom** genome.

**gensoru** *pol.* interpellation.

**genzel** nasal.

**geometri** geometry.

**geometrik** geometric(al); ~ dizi geometrical progression.

**gepegenç** very young.

**gerçek 1.** real, true, genuine; **2.** reality, truth; **3.** really, in truth; gerçeğe gözlerini yummak to blink the facts.

**gerçekçi 1.** realist; **2.** realistic.

**gerçekçilik** realism.

**gerçekdışı** unreal.

**gerçeklemek 1.** to confirm; **2.** to verify.

**gerçekleşme** realization, fulfillment.

**gerçekleşmek** to come true, to materialize, to turn out to be true.

**gerçekleştirmek** to realize; to certify, to verify.

**gerçekli** real, true.

**gerçeklik** reality, truth.

**gerçekten** really, truly.

**gerçeküstü** surrealistic.

**gerçi** [x .] although, though, it is true that.

**gerdan 1.** neck, throat; **2.** double chin; dewlap; ~ kırmak *fig.* to put on coquettish airs.

**gerdanlık** necklace, neckband.

**gerdek** bridal chamber; ~ gecesi wedding (*or* nuptial) night; gerdeğe girmek to enter the bridal chamber.

**gerdel** wooden (or leather) bucket.

**gerdirmek** to have s.o. make s.th. taut.

**gereç** requisite, material, necessaries.

**gereğince** in accordance with, following.

**gerek 1.** necessary, needed; **2.** requisite, need, necessity; ~ ... ~ whether ... or; both ... and; gereği gibi as is due, properly; gereği yok it is not necessary.

**gerekçe 1.** reason, justification; **2.** corollary.

**gerekçeli** justifiable, justified.

**gerekçesiz** unjustifiable, unjustified.

**gerekli** necessary, required, needed.

**gereklik** need, necessity; ~ kipi gr. necessitative mood.

**gereklilik** necessity, need.

**gerekmek,** (-ir) to be necessary, to be needed, to be required; gerekince when necessary; gerekirse if need be.

**gerekseme** necessity, need.

**gereksemek** to need, to consider necessary.

**gereksinim, gereksinme** necessity, need.

**gereksinmek** to need, to consider necessary.

**gereksiz** unnecessary, superfluous.

**gerektirmek 1.** to necessitate, to require; **2.** to imply, to entail.

**geren** clayey soil.

**gergedan** zo. rhinoceros.

**gergef** embroidery frame; ~ işlemek to embroider with a frame.

**gergi 1.** curtain; **2.** stretcher.

**gergin 1.** tight, stretched, taut; **2.** tense; strained (relations).

**gerginleşmek 1.** to get stretched; **2.** fig. to become tense.

**gerginleştirmek 1.** to tighten; **2.** fig. to strain, to make tense.

**gerginlik** tightness, tension.

**geri 1.** back, rear; **2.** the rest; **3.** backward, to the rear; **4.** fig. backward, reactionary; **5.** slow (clock); **6.** (go) back!; **7.** sl. fool; ~ almak **1.** to get (or take) back; **2.** to take back, to withdraw (word, order); **3.** to back up; **4.** to put back (clock); ~ basmak to back up, to move backwards; ~ bırakmak to postpone, to put off, to defer; ~ çekilmek to withdraw (-den from), to back away (-den from); ~ çevirmek to turn down, to turn away, to throw out, to toss out (a request); ~ dönmek to come (or go) back, to return, to turn back; ~ durmak to refrain, to abstain (-den from); ~ gitmek **1.** to go back, to return; **2.** to be slow, to lose time (clock); **3.** fig. to take a turn for the worse; ~ göndermek to send back; ~

~ hizmet ✕ supply service behind the front; ~ kafalı fig. reactionary, fogey, fogy; ~ kalmak **1.** to stay (or remain) behind; **2.** to be slow (clock); **3.** = geri durmak; ~ tepmek to recoil, to kick (gun); ~ vermek to give back, to return; ~ vites dişlisi mot. reverse (gear); -de bırakmak to leave behind, to pass; to surpass; -den bakmak fig. to look from a distance (-e at); to be an onlooker; -si aydın havası! fig. the rest is of no avail!

**gerici** reactionary.

**gericilik** reaction.

**geridon** round pedestal table.

**gerileme** vn. of gerilemek part. regression; retrogression.

**gerilemek 1.** to regress; to recede; to retreat; **2.** to be on the wane (sickness); **3.** to fall behind, to be left behind.

**gerili** stretched, taut, tight.

**gerilik** backwardness.

**gerilim 1.** phys. tension; **2.** ⚡ voltage; **3.** 🩸 blood pressure; **4.** tension (vocal cords).

**gerilimli** tense; under tension.

**gerilimsiz** slack; relaxed.

**gerilla** guerrilla.

**gerillacı** guerrilla.

**gerilme** tension.

**gerilmek 1.** to be tightened (or stretched); **2.** to be tensed.

**gerinmek** to stretch.

**gerisingeriye** backwards.

**geriz** sewer.

**germanyum** ⚗ germanium.

**germek,** (-er) **1.** to tighten, to stretch; **2.** to extend (muscle, limb).

**germen** biol. germen.

**getir, -tri** gaiter, spat.

**getirmek** to bring, to give, to yield.

**getirtmek 1.** to send for; **2.** to order, to import (-den from).

**gevelemek 1.** to chew, to mumble; **2.** fig. to hum and haw, to mumble.

**geveze** talkative, chattering, chatterbox, babbler; indiscreet.

**gevezelik 1.** chatter, chat, chitchat; **2.** chattering, prattling; ~ etm. **1.** to chatter, to chat, to babble, to prattle; **2.** to blab.

**geviş** rumination, cud; ~ getirmek to ruminate, to chew the cud.

**gevişgetirenler** zo. ruminants.

**gevmek** to mumble, to chew.

**gevrek 1.** crisp, brittle, crackly; **2.** crisp cake (or biscuit); ~ ~ gülmek to laugh in an easy and lively way.

**gevrekci** seller of gevrek.

**gevreklik** crispness.

**gevremek** 1. to become crisp, to be dry (*or* brittle); 2. P to starve.

**gevşek** 1. loose, slack, lax; 2. *fig.* soft, lax, lacking in backbone; ~ ağızlı indiscreet; ~ davranmak to be lax, to act in a lukewarm manner.

**gevşeklik** looseness, slack.

**gevşemek** 1. to loosen, to slacken; to become lax; 2. to relax, to become calm (*nerves*).

**gevşetici** relaxative.

**gevşetmek** 1. to loosen, to slacken; 2. to relax.

**geyik** 1. *zo.* deer, stag, hart; 2. *sl.* pander; ~ etine girmek to take on the physical appearance of a woman (*growing girl*); -ler kırkımında *co.* on the Greek calends.

**geyikdikeni**, -ni ♀ buckthorn.

**geyikotu**, -nu ♀ white dittany.

**gez¹** 1. notch (*in an arrow*); 2. rear sight (*of a gun*).

**gez²** rope with knots at intervals for measuring ground.

**gez³** plumbline.

**gez⁴** (*ağacı*) ♀ tamarisk tree.

**gezdirmek** *caus. of* gezmek *part.* 1. to show around, to take about, to take through, to lead about, to conduct; 2. to sprinkle (*as oil on salad*).

**gezegen** planet.

**gezelemek** 1. to pace up and down; 2. *fig.* to hesitate.

**gezente, gezenti** roving, peripatetic (*person*).

**gezer** mobile.

**gezge** patrol.

**gezgin** 1. wandering, roving; 2. travel-(l)er, tourist; ~ satıcı pedlar, hawker.

**gezginci** 1. roving, wanderig; 2. itinerant (*pedlar*).

**gezgincilik** travel(l)ing; roving; itinerancy.

**gezi¹** 1. excursion, outing; tour; 2. promenade; -ye çıkmak to go on a trip.

**gezi²** silk and cotton material.

**gezici** itinerant; ~ esnaf pedlar(s); ~ kütüphane bookmobile .

**gezicilik** peddling.

**gezim** tourism.

**gezimsel** touristic.

**gezinmek** 1. to stroll, to go about; 2. ♪ to pass slowly from one makam to another while improvising.

**gezinti** 1. stroll, walk, outing; tour; 2. corridor, floor; 3. ♪ slowly passing from one makam to another while improvising; ~ yeri promenade.

**gezlemek** 1. to measure a place; 2. to aim (*-i at*).

**gezlik** 1. sword edge; 2. pocketknife.

**gezme** 1. *vn. of* gezmek; 2. patrol; 3. watchman.

**gezmek**, (-er) 1. to stroll, to walk, to get about, to go about, to get round, to take about; 2. to go out; 3. to tour (*a place*); to walk around (*a place*); 4. to look round (*a place*); gezip tozmak to gallivant, to gad about (*or* around); gezmeğe gitmek to pay a visit.

**gezmen** tourist, travel(l)er.

**gıcık** 1. tickling sensation in the throat; 2. *sl.* pain (in the neck); ~ olm. to be irritated (*-e* by); ~ tutmak to have a tickle in the throat.

**gıcıklamak** 1. to tickle; 2. *fig.* to raise one's suspicion.

**gıcıklanmak** 1. to tickle; 2. *fig.* -den to suspect.

**gıcır** 1. gum of sarsaparilla used as chewing gum; 2. *sl.* new.

**gıcırdamak** to creak, to squeak, to rustle.

**gıcırdatmak** 1. to grind, to gnash (*one's teeth*); 2. to make creak.

**gıcır gıcır** 1. very clean; 2. brand-new; ~ ~ etm. to creak, to squeak.

**gıcırtı** creak, squeak.

**gıda** [â] food, nourishment; nutriment; ~ maddeleri foodstuffs.

**gıdaklamak** to cackle.

**gıdalı** nutritious, nourishing.

**gıdasız** undernourished; ~ kalmak to be undernourished.

**gıdgıd gıdak** cackle, cluck (*of a hen*).

**gıdık** 1. tickling; 2. under part of the chin.

**gıdıklamak** to tickle.

**gıdıklanmak** to tickle, to have a tickling sensation.

**gıgı** under part of the chin.

**gık:** ~ demek to be sick (*-den* of); ~ dedirtmemek to listen to no objections; ~ dememek not to say a word not to object.

**gıldır gıldır** with a roaring sound.

**gına** [â] 1. wealth; 2. sufficiency; ~ gelmek (*or* getirmek) to be sick (*-den* of). to be fed up (*-den* with), to be tired (*-den* of).

**gıpta** envy, longing; ~ etm. (*bşe*) to envy s.th.

**gır:** ~ atmak (*or* kaynatmak) *sl.* to chat; to gossip; ~ geçmek *sl.* to shoot the breeze, to chatter; ~ ~ geçmek *sl.* to make fun (*or* mock) (*ile* of); ~ -a almak *sl.* to hoax, to mock.

**gırgır** 1. tiresome noise; 2. carpet sweeper; 3. a clay jug for drinking water; 4.

large bag shaped fishing net; 5. raucously, annoyingly.

**gırgırlamak** to use a carpet sweeper (*-i* on).

**gırla [x .]** F amply, abundantly; incessantly, to the utmost; ~ gitmek F to be abundant.

**gırnata** ♪ clarinet.

**gırt,** -tı tearing sound; ~ ~ *or* ~ dıye with a tearing sound.

**gırtlak** throat, larynx; ~ gırtlağa gelmek to be at each other's throat, to be at daggers drawn; ~ kemiği *anat.* Adam's apple; gırtlağına basmak (*b-nin*) to get *s.o.* by the throat; gırtlağına düşkün greedy, gluttonous; gırtlağına kadar borcu olm. to be up to one's neck ın debt; gırtlağından kesmek to cut back on one's food expenses.

**gırtlaklamak** to strangle.

**gırtlaklaşmak** to be at each other's throats.

**gışa [. -]** membrane.

**gıyaben [ā] [. x .]** 1. in one's absence, in absentia; 2. by name (*or* repute); 3. ǧǒ by default; ~ tanımak (*b-ni*) to know *s.o.* by name.

**gıyabi [. - -]** 1. in absentia; 2. ǧǒ defaulting; ~ hüküm (*or* karar) ǧǒ judg(e)ment by default.

**gıyap,** -bı [ā] absence, default; gıyabında in one's absence.

**gıybet,** -ti slander, calumny, defamation; ~ etm. to slander, ot calumniate.

**gıybetçi** slanderer, backbiter.

**gibi** 1. like, similar; 2. nearly, almost, somewhat; -sine gelmek to seem, to appear; bunun ~ like this.

**gibice** somewhat like.

**gideğen** outlet (*of a lake*).

**gider** expenditure, expense, outgo, outlay.

**giderayak** just before leaving, at the last moment.

**giderek** gradually.

**giderici** remover.

**gidermek** to remove, to exterminate, to eradicate.

**gidi** 1. pander; 2. *in the exclamations:* senı ~ seni)! you little rascal!

**gidici** 1. on his way out, goer; 2. about to die.

**gidiş** 1. departure, going, leaving; 2. conduct, manner of living, way of life; ~ dönüş bileti return ticket, *Am.* round-trip ticket; ~ o ~ that was the last that was seen of him.

**gidişat,** -tı [ā] 1. conduct, goings-on, behavio(u)r; 2. the course of events.

**gidişgeliş** coming and going; traffic.

**gidişmek** to itch.

**gidon** handlebar (*of a bicycle*).

**Gine** *pr. n.* Guinea.

**girdap,** -bı [ā] whirlpool.

**girdi** input.

**girgin** sociable, gregarious.

**girginlik** sociability, gregariousness.

**girift,** -ti involved, intricate.

**giriftar** 1. captive (of); 2. victim (of), afflicted (with).

**girilir** entrance, way in.

**girilmek** enter; girilmez no entrance, no admittance.

**girim** entrance.

**girimlik** entrance ticket.

**girinti** indentation, recess.

**girintili** indented; ~ çıkıntılı wavy, toothed, zigzag.

**giriş** 1. entrance, entry; 2. going in; 3. introduction; ~ çıkış entrance and exit; going in and out; ~ serbesttir admission free; ~ sınavı entrance examination; ~ ücreti price of admission.

**girişik** intricate; complex; ~ tümce *gr.* complex sentence.

**girişim** 1. enterprise, iniative; 2. *phys.* interference.

**girişimci** entrepreneur.

**girişimölçer** interferometer.

**girişken** enterprising, pushing, pushy.

**girişkenlik** enterprise, initiative.

**girişli çıkışlı** movable, sliding.

**girişlik** introduction.

**girişmek** 1. to interfere, to meddle, to mix up (*-e* in); 2. to undertake, to attempt; to set about, to go about.

**Girit,** -ti *pr. n.* Crete.

**giritlalesi,** -ni ♣ ranunculus, crowfoot. buttercup.

**Giritli** Cretan.

**girive [. - .]** 1. rocky hill; 2. ravine; abyss; 3. *fig.* impasse.

**girizgâh [. - -]** introduction, prologue.

**girmek,** (-er) 1. -e to enter, to go in, to come in; 2. to join, to participate (*-e* in); 3. to fit (*-e* into); 4. to begin, to come (*season, time*); 5. to spread (*-e* into) (*contagion*); 6. to be enrolled; 7. to become, to turn; 8. to comprehend, to understand; gırdisi çıktısı the ins and outs (of); 2. intimacy; girip çıkmak 1. to pay a flying visit; 2. to frequent; girmiş çıkmış *fig.* with a screw loose.

**girmelik** entrance fee.

**gişe** ticket window, pay desk; cashier's desk; booking office; *thea.* box office.

**gitar** guitar.

**gitarcı, gitarist,** -ti guitarist.

**gitgide** [x . .] more and more, gradually.

**gitmek** (-der) **1.** to go (-e to); **2.** to lead, to go (road); **3.** to suit, to fit, to go well (-e with), to harmonize (-e with); **4.** to last, to be enough for, to suffice; **5.** (b-le) to accompany s.o.; **6.** to be spent, to be used up, to go; **7.** to travel, to go; **8.** to go away, to leave; **9.** to work (machine); **10.** to pass, to end; **11.** to turn to, to have recourse to; **12.** to disappear; to die; **13.** to get worn out; **git çişini et yat!** have a pee and go to bed!; **gitti gider** he's (or it's) gone forever.

**gittikçe** [. x .] gradually, little by little, by degrees, more and more.

**giydirici** dresser.

**giydirmek** caus. of giymek part. **1.** to dress, to clothe; **2.** fig. to dress down, to abuse.

**giyecek** clothes, clothing, dress.

**giyim** clothing, dress, attire; ~ **eşyası** clothing, clothes; ~ **kuşam** dress and finery, garments, attire; **-i kuşamı yerinde** carefully dressed, chic.

**giyimevi,** -ni clothing store.

**giyimli** dressed.

**giyinik** dressed.

**giyinmek 1.** to dress o.s.; **2.** to put on (hat, clothes, shoes); **3.** fig. to resent; **giyinip kuşanmak** to put on one's Sunday best, to dress o.s. up.

**giymek 1.** to put on, to wear; **2.** fig. to listen silently to (abuse).

**giyotin** guillotine.

**giysi** garment, dress; clothes, clothing; ~ **dolabı** wardrobe, armoire.

**giz** mystery.

**gizdüzen** conspiracy.

**gizem** mystery.

**gizemci** mystic.

**gizemcilik** mysticism.

**gizemli** mystical, mysterious.

**gizil** phys. potantial, latent.

**gizilgüç** phys. potential energy.

**gizlemek** to hide, to conceal, to secrete; to dissemble, to dissimulate (one's feelings).

**gizlenmek** pass. or refl. of gizlemek **1.** to hide o.s.; **2.** to be kept secret (-den from).

**gizli 1.** secret, confidential; **2.** concealed, hidden; **3.** occult; **4.** secretly; ~ **celse** (or oturum) secret session; ~ **kapaklı** clandestine, obscure; ~ **oy** secret vote, vote by ballot; ~ **pençe** half sole; ~ **sıtma 1.** dormant malaria; **2.** fig. insidious; ~ **tutmak** (bşi) to keep s.th. dark; **-den -ye** in the dark, in all secrecy.

**gizlice** in the dark, in secrecy, secretly.

**gizlilik** secrecy, stealth.

**gladyatör** gladiator.

**glase** patent leather.

**glayöl** ♀ gladiola.

**glikojen** ⚕ glycogen.

**glikol** glycol.

**glikoz** glucose.

**glikozit,** -ti glucoside.

**gliserin** glycerine, glycerol.

**glokoni** geol. glauconite.

**glüten** gluten.

**gnays** gol. gneiss.

**goblen** gobelin stitch.

**gocuk** sheepskin cloak.

**gocundurmak** to offend.

**gocunmak** to take offence (-den at).

**godoş** sl. pimp.

**gofre** puckered (material).

**gofret** a waffle-like chocolate cookie.

**gogo** sl. hashish.

**gol,** -lü football: goal; ~ **atmak** (or yapmak) to score (or kick) a goal; ~ **yemek** to let in a goal.

**golcü** football: scorer.

**golet,** -ti ⚓ schooner.

**golf** golf; ~ **pantolon** plus-fours, knickerbockers.

**golfstrim** Gulf Stream.

**gollük** football: good for making a goal.

**gomalak** schellac.

**gonca** bud.

**gondol,** -lü gondola.

**gondolcu** gondolier.

**gonk,** -gu gong.

**goril** zo. gorilla.

**gotik** Gothic; ~ **sanat** Gothic art; ~ **yazı** Gothic.

**Gotlar** pr. n. Goths.

**goygoycu** blind beggar.

**göbek 1.** navel; **2.** potbelly, paunch; **3.** the middle, heart, central part; **4.** generation; **5.** hub (of a bicycle wheel); ~ **adı** name given to a child when its umbilical cord is cut; ~ **atmak 1.** to belly dance; **2.** fig. to be wild with joy; ~ **bağı** infant's belly band; ~ **bağlamak** to develop a potbelly; ~ **havası** music for a belly dance; ~ **taşı** central massage slab; **çöbeği çatlamak** fig. to have a hard time; **göbeği sokakta kesilmiş** fig. **1.** gadabout; **2.** streetwalker, prostitute.

**göbeklenmek 1.** to get a potbelly, to become paunchy; **2.** to develop a heart (vegetables).

**göbekli 1.** paunchy, potbellied; **2.** naveled; with a central boss; ~ **salata** lettuce.

**göbel 1.** street urchin (or arab); **2.** bastard; **3.** mound (in a field used as a *marker).*

**göbelek** mushroom.

**göbelez** terrier.

**göç, -cü 1.** migration, emigration, immigration; **2.** transhumance; **3.** goods and chattels of migrating people; ~ etm. **1.** to migrate, to emigrate, to immigrate; **2.** to pass away.

**göçebe 1.** nomad; wanderer; **2.** nomadic; migrant, migratory.

**göçebelik** nomadic life; migration, emigration.

**göçelge** P migrant settlement.

**göçer** *s.* göçebe.

**göçeri, göçerkonar** nomadic, wandering.

**göçermek** to run over, to transfer.

**göçertmek** to demolish, to knock down.

**göçkün** dilapidated.

**göcmek, (-çer) 1.** to migrate, to move off, to move (-e to); to move out; **2.** to migrate seasonaly; **3.** to cave in, to fall down *(building)*; **4.** to pass away, to die.

**göçmen** immigrant, settler, refugee; ~ hücre *biol.* migratory cell; ~ kuşlar migratory birds.

**göcmenlik** migration.

**göçü 1.** migration; **2.** landslip, landslide.

**göçük** *geol.* subsidence.

**göçüm** *biol.* taxis.

**göçünmek** P to pass away, to die.

**göçürmek** *caus. of* göçmek *part.* **1.** to cause to move off (-e to), to make migrate; **2.** to make collapse *(roof, etc.)*; to make subside *(land)*; **3.** F to gobble up *(or* down).

**göçürtmek 1.** to cause to migrate; **2.** to make collapse.

**göçüş 1.** migration; **2.** collapse.

**göden** blind gut, caecum; rectum; large intestine.

**gödeş** *s.* ödeş.

**göğüs, -ğsü 1.** breast, chest; bosom; **2.** ↓ bow; ~ bağrı açık with one's shirt open; ~ cerrahisi thoracic surgery; ~ darlığı asthma; ~ geçirmek to sigh, to groan; ~ germek to face, to stand up (-e to, against); ~ göğüse gelmek to come face to face; ~ hastalıkları chest *(or* thoracic) diseases; ~ kafesi rib cage; ~ kemiği *anat.* breastbone, sternum; ~ tahtası **1.** = göğüs kemiği; **2.** ♪ soundboard, belly; göğsü kabarmak to swell with pride, to be proud.

**göğüslemek 1.** to breast; **2.** to block, to interpose o.s.

**göğüslü 1.** broad-chested; full-bosomed; **2.** ↓ having a flared bow.

**göğüslük 1.** bib, pinafore; apron; **2.** breastplate.

**gök, -ğü 1.** sky, heavens, firmament; **2.** azure, (sky) blue; aquamarine; ~ gözlü **1.** blue-eyed; **2.** *fig.* injurious, malevolent; gürlemesi *(or* gürültüsü) (a clap of) thunder; ~ gürlüyor it is thundering; ~ kandil *sl.* dead drunk, pissed; ~ kubbe the sky, the vault of heaven; göklere çıkarmak *fig.* to praise to the skies; göklere çıkmak *fig.* to rise to the sky; gökten zembille inmemiş ya! what's so special about him!

**gökada** *ast.* galaxy.

**gökbilim** *ast.* astronomy.

**gökbilimci** *ast.* astronomer.

**gökbilimsel** *ast.* astronomical.

**gökcismi, -ni** celestial *(or* heavenly) body.

**gökçe 1.** celestial, heavenly; **2.** sky-blue; aquamarine; **3.** pretty, beautiful *(person).*

**gökdelen** skyscraper.

**Gökhan** *ast.* Uranus.

**gökkır** blue-roan *(horse);* blue-gray *(hair).*

**gökkuşağı, -nı** rainbow.

**gökküresi, -ni** *ast.* celestial sphere.

**gökmen** P blue-eyed and blond.

**göksel** celestial, heavenly.

**göktaşı, -nı 1.** *ast.* meteor, meteorite, aerolite; bolide; **2.** turquoise.

**Göktürk** *pr. n.* Gök Turk.

**Göktürkçe** *pr. n.* the language of the Gök Turks.

**gökyolu, -nu** Milky Way.

**gökyüzü, -nü** sky, firmament.

**göl** lake; ~ ayağı outlet of a lake; ~ olm. to form a lake.

**gölalası** *zo.* lake trout.

**gölbaşı, -nı** inlet.

**gölcük** pond; small lake.

**gölcül** lacustrine.

**gölek** pond; puddle; small lake.

**gölermek** P to form a pond *(or* puddle).

**gölet** P **1.** pond; puddle; **2.** tank.

**gölge** shadow, shade; ~ düşürmek *fig.* to overshadow, to obscure; ~ etm. **1.** to shade, to cast a shadow (-e on); **2.** *fig.* to bother, to molest; ~ gibi shadowy; ~ oyunu *(or* tiyatrosu) shadow play; ~ vurmak to shade; -de bırakmak *fig.* to eclipse, to outshine, to overshadow; -sinden korkmak *fig.* to be afraid of one's (own) shadow.

**gölgebalığı, -nı** *zo.* grayling.

**gölgecil** ⚘ shade-loving.

**gölgelemek 1.** to overshadow *(a. fig.);* **2.** *art.* to shade in.

**gölgelendirmek** to shade, to overshadow

*(a. fig.).*
**gölgelenmek 1.** to be shaded, to grow shadowy; **2.** to sit *or* lie in the shade.
**gölgeli** shady, shaded, shadowy.
**gölgelik 1.** shady spot; **2.** arbo(u)r, bower; **3.** awning.
**gölgeolay** *phls.* epiphenomenon.
**göllenmek, göllemek** to form a. lake (*or* pond *or* puddle).
**gölük** pack animal.
**gömgök** [x .] **1.** dark blue, quite blue; **2.** *fig.* extremely.
**gömlek 1.** shirt; **2.** woman's slip; **3.** book jacket; **4.** smock; **5.** generation; **6.** gas mantle; **7.** level, degree; **8.** shade (*of a colour*); **9.** ⊕ sleeve; **10.** slough (*of a snake*); **11.** *biol.* coat, covering, tunic; **12.** *anat.* integument; ~ değiştirmek **1.** (*for a snake*) to cast off its skin, to slough off; **2.** *fig.* to change one's opinion, to be changeable; ~ eskitmek *fig.* to live a long life; gömleği kalın *fig.* well-to-do, well-off.
**gömlekçi** maker *or* seller of shirts.
**gömlekçilik** making *or* selling of shirts.
**gömlekli** wearing a shirt.
**gömleklik** shirting.
**gömme 1.** *vn. of* gömmek; **2.** built-in, set-in, sunken, recessed; buried; embedded, inlaid; ~ banyo sunken bathtub; ~ dolap built-in cupboard; ~ kilit inset lock.
**gömmek, (-er) 1.** to bury, to inter; **2.** to install, to build in, to set in.
**gömü** buried treasure.
**gömük** buried.
**gömülmek 1.** *pass. or refl. of* gömmek, *part.* to be buried; **2.** to sink deeply (*-e* into).
**gömülü 1.** buried, underground; **2.** sunk (*-e* into); grown (*-e* into).
**gömüt** tomb, grave.
**gömütlük** cemetery.
**gön** rawhide.
**gönder 1.** pole, staff; **2.** ox-goad.
**gönderen** sender.
**gönderi** sendoff.
**gönderilmek** *pass. of* göndermek, *part.* to be sent (*-e* to).
**göndermek, (-ir) 1.** to send, to dispatch, to forward; **2.** to see off; to send away.
**gönen 1.** moisture; humidity; **2.** moist (*soil*).
**gönence** comfort, ease.
**gönenceli** comfortable.
**gönenç** prosperity, comfort.
**gönençli** prosperous.
**gönenmek** to prosper.
**gönül, -nlü 1.** heart; mind; **2.** affection,

inclination, willingness, desire; **3.** ♀ *wf.*; ~ acısı pangs of love; ~ almak **1.** to please; **2.** to apologize and make up; ~ avcısı lady-killer; ~ bağı the ties of love; ~ bağlamak to set one's heart (*-e* on); ~ darlığı distress, foreboding; ~ eğlendirmek to amuse o.s.; ~ eri broad-minded; ~ ferahlığı contentment; ~ hoşluğu ile (*or* ~ rızasiyle) willingly; ~ işi love affair; ~ kırmak to break s.o.'s heart; ~ tokluğu contentment; ~ vermek (*or* bağlamak) to lose one's heart (*-e* to); (gönlü): ~ açık **1.** openhearted, frank; **2.** carefree; ~ alçak modest, unpretentious; ~ bulanmak **1.** to be nauseated, to have heartburn; **2.** *fig.* to suspect; ~ çekmek to desire; ~ olm. **1.** (*bşde*) to be in love with *s.th.*; **2.** (*bşe*) to agree to *s.th.*; ~ tez impatient; ~ tok satisfied, contented; ~ yufka soft-hearted, tender-hearted; ~ zengin generous; -nce to one's heart's content; -nden geçirmek to think (*-i* of); -ne doğmak to have a foreboding, to feel it in one's bones, to have a presentiment; -nü etm. (*or* yapmak) (*b-nin*) **1.** to please *s.o.*; **2.** to win *s.o.*'s assent, to persuade *s.o.*
**gönüldeş** sympathizer.
**gönüllü 1.** volunteer; **2.** (*bşin*) -sü keen on *s.th.*, eager for *s.th.*; **3.** lover; ~ kıtası ✕ volunteer corps.
**gönüllülük** willingness.
**gönülsüz 1.** = alçak gönüllü; **2.** unwilling, disinclined.
**gönülsüzce** unwillingly.
**gönülsüzlük** unwillingness, disinclination.
**gönye** [x .] triangle; -sinde olm. to be at right angles.
**göre** according (*-e* to), as (*-e* to), in respect (*-e* of), considering, regarding, respecting.
**görece** relative.
**göreceli** relative.
**göreli** relative.
**görelik** *phls.* relation.
**görenek** custom.
**göreneksel** customary, conventional.
**göresimek** to miss, to yearn (*-i* for).
**görev 1.** duty, obligation; **2.** function; **3.** office; -den alınmak **1.** to be removed from office; **2.** to be demoted; -den kaçmak to shirk, to goldbrick.
**görevlendirmek** to commission, to charge, to entrust (*ile* with).
**görevlenmek** to be assigned (*or* commissioned).
**görevli 1.** assigned, commissioned, charged; **2.** official, employee, jobhold-

**er; 3.** on duty.

**görevsel** functional.

**görevsiz** unemployed, out of work.

**görçü 1.** etiquette, good manners; **2.** experience; **3.** witnessing; ~ tanığı eyewitness.

**görgülü** polite, well-mannered.

**görgüsüz** impolite, rude, ill-mannered.

**görgüsüzlük** impoliteness, rudeness, lack of manners.

**görkem** splendo(u)r, magnificence, pomp.

**görkemli** splendid, magnificient, pompous.

**görme 1.** vn. of görmek; **2.** vision, sight.

**görmek,** (-ür) **1.** to see; **2.** to realize, to recognize, to see; **3.** to talk (-i with), to see; **4.** to spot; **5.** to regard, to consider, to see, to judge; **6.** to live through, to experience, to undergo, to see; **7.** to take (lessons); **8.** to perform (a duty); **9.** to pay (an expense); **10.** to receive, to get; **11.** to face; göreyim seni! **1.** just you try it! (threat); **2.** let's see if you can; görmüş geçirmiş worldly-wise, experienced.

**görmemiş 1.** upstart, parvenu; **2.** = görgüsüz.

**görmezlik, görmemezlik** pretending not to see; -ten gelmek (b-ni) to cut s.o. dead, to turn one's blind on to s.o.

**görmüşlük** having seen before; bu adamı görmüşlüğüm var I have seen this man before; ~ duygusu paramnesia.

**görsel** visual.

**görsel-işitsel** audio-visual.

**görücü** matchmaker, female go-between.

**görücülük** matchmaking.

**görüldüğünde** † at sight (draft, etc).

**görülmek** pass. of görmek to be seen.

**görülmemiş** never seen before.

**görüm 1.** vision; **2.** house call, hospital visit (of a physician).

**görümce** [. x .] sister of the husband, sister-in-law (of the wife).

**görümlük 1.** physician's fee for a house call or hospital visit; **2.** display window; **3.** = yüzgörümlüğü.

**görünmek 1.** to be seen, to be visible; to appear, to come in sight; **2.** to seem; **3.** (b-ne) fig. to scold s.o.; göründü Sıvas'ın bağları! iro. what we feared is starting to happen!

**görünmez** invisible; unforeseen, unexpected; ~ kaza unforeseen accident; ~ olm. to disappear.

**görüntü 1.** phantom, specter; **2.** image.

**görüntülemek** to project.

**görünüm 1.** appearance, view; **2.** gr. aspect.

**görünür(ler)de** in appearance (or sight); ~ yok not in sight.

**görünüş** appearance, sight, view, spectacle; aspect; -e aldanmamalı pro. all that glittters is not gold; -e göre (or bakılırsa) apparently, as far as can be seen.

**görünüşte** apparently, on the surface.

**görüş 1.** sight; **2.** opinion, point of view; ~ açısı point of view; ~ ayrılığı difference of opinion, conflict; ~ birliği agreement, consensus.

**görüşme 1.** vn. of görüşmek; **2.** interview; **3.** discussion, negotiation; **4.** meeting.

**görüşmeci** visitor.

**görüşmek 1.** to meet; to converse, to have an interview; **2.** to see (or visit) each other; **3.** to talk over, to discuss; görüşeni karışanı olmamak (b-nin) to be free from interference.

**görüştürmek** to arrange a meeting (for).

**gösterge 1.** phys. indicator; **2.** table, chart, index.

**gösteri 1.** show, display; **2.** showing (of a film), performance (of a play); **3.** demonstration; ~ yürüyüşü demonstration march.

**gösterici 1.** projector; **2.** demonstrator.

**gösterim** projection.

**gösteriş 1.** showing, demonstrating; **2.** showing off, ostentation; **3.** striking (or imposing) appearance; ~ yapmak to show off.

**gösterişçi** show-off, ostentatious; pretentious.

**gösterişçilik** showing off, ostentation.

**gösterişli** stately, imposing, showy.

**gösterişsiz** unimposing, poor-looking, inconspicuous.

**göstermek,** (-ir) **1.** to show; to indicate, to denote; **2.** to show, to manifest, to evidence, to evince, to demonstrate; **3.** to teach, to instruct, to show; **4.** to assign, to show; **5.** to expose (to light, etc.); **6.** (b-ne) to get even with s.o., to show s.o., to learn s.o.; **7.** to appear, to seem to be.

**göstermelik 1.** specimen, sample, showpiece; **2.** non-functional; **3.** scenery put up before the beginning of Karagöz.

**göt,** -tü sl. **1.** ass, arse; **2.** fig. courage, guts; **3.** silly arse; ~ üstü oturmak sl. to be in a jam; -üne kına yak! sl. kick him now that he's down!; -ünü yalamak (b-nin) sl. to lick s.o.'s arse; onu yapmaya ~ ister! sl. it takes guts to do it!

**götlek** sl. passive pederast.

**götün götün** sl. backwards.

**götürmek,** (-ür) **1.** to take (away), to carry, to convey; **2.** to remove, to destroy, to carry off; **3.** to accompany; **4.** to kill *(illness)*; **5.** to bear, to put up with, to stand for; **6.** to lead *(-e to)*; **7.** to take off to gaol.

**götürü** by the piece *(or* job), in a lump sum; ~ çalışmak to work by the job, to do piecework; ~ fiyat job lot *(or* contract) price; flat rate; ~ iş piecework, job work; ~ pazarlık &る contracting by the job.

**gövde 1.** body, trunk, stem; **2.** *gr.* stem, theme; **3.** whole carcass; ~ gösterisi public demonstration; -ye atmak *(or* indirmek) F to gulp down.

**gövdebilim** anatomy.

**gövdebilimci** anatomist.

**gövdelenmek 1.** to get husky; **2.** to develop a trunk *(tree)*.

**gövdeli** husky.

**gövdesel** corpor(e)al.

**gövermek** P **1.** to turn green; **2.** to turn blue.

**göynük 1.** burnt; **2.** rotten, decayed, putrid; **3.** overripe.

**göynümek** to be burned *(or* scorched).

**göz 1.** eye; **2.** sight; **3.** eye *(of a needle)*; **4.** division, drawer, compartment, cubbyhole; **5.** spring *(water)*; **6.** *fig.* the evil eye; **7.** love; esteem; friendship; **8.** bud; **9.** pan *(of a balance)*; ~ açıp kapayıncaya kadar in the twinkling of an eye; ~ açtırmamak to give no respite *(-e* to); ~ ağrısı **1.** eye-strain; **2.** ilk ~ ağrısı first love; ~ alabildiğine as far as the eye can see; ~ alıcı eye-catching, striking, dazzling; ~ almak to dazzle; ~ aşinalığı a slight acquaintance; ~ atmak to scan, to run an eye *(-e* over), to glance *(-e* at); ~ bankası eye bank; ~ boyamak to throw dust in s.o.'s eyes; ~ dikmek *(bşe)* to covet *s.th.*; ~ doktoru oculist; ~ etm. to wink *(-e* at); ~ gezdirmek to cast an eye *(-e* over), to run one's eye *(-e* over); ~ göre *(or* ~ göre göre) openly, publicly; knowingly; ~ görmeyince gönül katlanır *pro.* what the eye doesn't see, the heart doesn't grieve over; ~ hapsi surveillance; ~ kamaştırmak **1.** to dazzle; **2.** *fig.* to fascinate; ~ kararı by rule of thumb; visual estimation, judgement by the eye; ~ kırpmak to wink *(a. fig.)*, to blink; ~ kırpmamak not to sleep a wink, not to have a wink of sleep, not to bat an eyelid; ~ koymak to covet; ~ kulak olm. to keep an eye *(-e* on); ~ önünde in front of one's eyes; ~ önünde bulundurmak *(or* tutmak) to take into consideration *(or* account); ~ önüne getirmek to envisage, to envi-

sion; ~ yaşı tear; ~ yaşı dökmek to shed tears, to weep; ~ yummak *fig.* to close one's eyes *(-e* to), to turn a blind eye *(-e* to), to wink *(-e* at); ~ yuvası *anat.* eye socket; -den çıkarmak to sacrifice; -den düşmek to fall out of favo(u)r, to fall into disfavo(u)r; -den geçirmek to scrutinize, to look *(or* go) over; -den ırak olan gönülden de ırak olur *pro.* out of sight, out of mind; -den kaçmak to be overlooked; -den kaybolmak to vanish from sight; -e almak to risk, to venture; -e batmak **1.** to be very inappropriate; **2.** to attract attention; **3.** to be exasperating *(or* maddening); -e çarpmak to stand out, to strike one's eyes; -e girmek to curry favo(u)r; -e ~, dişe diş an eye for an eye a tooth for a tooth, tit for tat; -leri bağlı blindfolded; -leri fal taşı gibi açılmakı to be moon-eyed; -leri yollarda kalmak to wait a long time for s.o. to come; -lerine inanamamak cannot believe one's eyes; -lerinizden öperim kind regards; -ü açık wide awake, shrewd; sharp; -ü bağlı **1.** blindfolded; **2.** *fig.* unconscious; **3.** *fig.* bewitched; -ü dalmak to stare into space, to gaze vacantly; -ü dönmek to see red; -ü gibi sevmek *(b-ni)* to regard s.o. as the apple of one's eye; -ü görmeyen blind; -ü ısırmak *(b-ni)* not to be unfamiliar to s.o.; -ü kalmak *(bşde)* to long for s.th.; -ü keskin sharp-eyed, sharp-sighted; -ü kör olsun! damn it!, curse it!; -ü olm. *(bşde)* to have designs on s.th., to have one's eyes on s.th.; -ü pek brave, bold, daring; -ü tok contented; -ü tutmamak *(b-ni)* not to appeal to s.o.; -üm! *(or* -ümün nuru!) darling!, beloved!; -ünde tütmek to long for; -üne girmek *(b-nin)* to find favo(u)r in s.o.'s eyes, to curry favo(u)r; -ünü açmak **1.** to keep one's eye open, to keep one's eyes peeled *(or* skinned); **2.** *(b-nin)* to undeceive s.o.; -ünü dikmek to fasten *(or* fix) one's eyes *(-e* on); -ünü dört açmak to be all eyes; -ünü kan bürümek to see red; -ünü kapamak **1.** to pretend not to see; **2.** to die; -ünü korkutmak to daunt, to intimidate; -ünün bebeği gibi sevmek *(b-ni)* to love s.o. like the apple of one's eye; -ünün ucuyle bakmak to look out of the corner of one's eye; -ünün yaşına bakmamak *fig.* to have no pity *(-in* on).

**gözakı**, -nı the white of the eye.

**gözaltı**, -nı (house) arrest; ~ etm. *(or* -na almak) **1.** to put under house arrest; **2.** to take into custody.

**gözaşısı**, -nı ♀ bud graft.

**gözbağı,** -nı sleight of hand.

**gözbebeği,** -ni 1. *anat.* pupil; 2. *fig.* apple of the eye, honey, pet.

**gözcü** 1. watchman, sentry, observer, scout; 2. oculist.

**gözcülük** 1. observing, scouting; 2. medical treatment of the eyes; ～ etm. to watch.

**gözdağı,** -nı intimidation, threat; ～ vermek to intimidate, to threaten.

**gözde** favo(u)rite, pet.

**gözdemiri,** -ni ⚓ bower anchor.

**gözdikeği,** -ni object, aim, purpose.

**gözdişi,** -ni eyetooth, canine tooth.

**göze** 1. *anat.* cell; 2. spring, source.

**gözemek** 1. to patch, to mend; 2. to embroider with silk thread.

**gözenek** 1. stoma, pore; 2. window; 3. hemstitch; 4. *ast.* granulation; 5. beekeeper's mask.

**gözer** coarse sieve.

**gözerimi** 1. horizon; 2. (range of) sight.

**gözetici** guard, protector; observer.

**gözetim** supervision; care, watch.

**gözetleme** *vn. of* gözetlemek, *part.* X observation; ～ deliği 1. peephole, spyhole *(in a door)*; 2. X observation slit; ～ yeri X observation point, lookout.

**gözetlemek** to peep (-i at), to spy (-i on), to observe.

**gözetleyici** X observer; lookout.

**gözetmek,** (-ir) 1. to guard, to protect; to mind, to look after, to take care (-i of); 2. to consider, to respect; to regard, to observe *(law, rule).*

**gözevi,** -ni eye-socket.

**gözkapağı,** -nı eyelid.

**gözlem** observation.

**gözlemci** observer.

**gözlemcilik** observation.

**gözleme** 1. *vn. of* gözlemek, *part.* 1. X *or* *ast.* observation; 3. pancake.

**gözlemek** 1. to watch (-i for), to wait (-i for), to keep an eye (-i on); 2. to observe; 3. to prick with holes.

**gözlemen** observer.

**gözlemevi,** -ni observatory.

**gözlemlemek** to watch (-i for, over).

**gözleyici** observer.

**gözlü** 1. -eyed; 2. having drawers *or* pigeonholes.

**gözlük** (eye)glasses, spectacles; ～ camı spectacle lens; ～ çerçevesi frames *(or* rim) for glasses; ～ takmak *(or* kullanmak) to wear glasses.

**gözlükçü** optician.

**gözlüklü** wearing glasses.

**gözlüklüyılan** *zo.* hooded snake.

**gözpınarı,** -nı inner corner of the eye.

**gözsüz** 1. without pigeonholes *or* compartments; 2. blind.

**göztaşı,** -nı copper sulphate.

**gözükmek,** (-ür) 1: to appear, to be visible *(or* seen); 2. to show o.s., to turn up.

**grado** [x .] 1. proof (spirit);· 2. degree, grade.

**grafik** 1. graph, diagram; 2. graphic; ～ sanatlar graphics, graphic arts.

**grafit,** -ti *geol.* graphite.

**grafoloji** graphology.

**gram** gram(me).

**gramaj** weight in grams.

**gramer** grammar; ～ yönünden grammatically.

**gramerci** grammarian.

**gramkuvvet,** -ti gram force.

**gramofon** phonograph.

**grandi** [x .] ⚓ mainmast.

**grandük,** -kü grand duke.

**grandüşes** grand duchess.

**granit,** -ti granite.

**granül** *anat.* granule.

**granüle** granulated.

**granülit,** -ti *geol.* granulite.

**gravür** engraving.

**gravürcü** engraver.

**gravyer (peyniri)** Gruyère cheese.

**Grek** *pr. n.* Greek.

**Grekçe** *pr. n.* the ancient Greek language.

**grekoromen** greco-roman wrestling.

**grena** *geol.* garnet.

**grenadin** grenadine.

**gres (yağı)** ⊕ lubricating grease.

**grev** strike; ～ gözcüsü picket; ～ hakkı right of strike; ～ yapmak to strike, to go on strike; -i bozmak to break the strike.

**grevci** striker.

**greyder** bulldozer.

**greyfrut** ♣ grapefruit.

**gri** grey, *Am.* gray.

**grip,** -bi influenza, flu, grippe; ～ olm. to have influenza; gribe tutulmak to come down with flu.

**grizu** firedamp, pit gas, methane; ～ patlaması firedamp explosion.

**grogren** grosgrain.

**gros** gros; ～ ağırlık gross weight.

**grosa** † gross (= 12 dozen).

**grup,** -bu 1. group; 2. X section; ～ ～ in groups; ～ olm. to form a group.

**gruplandırmak** to group.

**gruplaşmak** 1. to separate into groups; 2. to gather into groups.

**guano** *geol.* guano.

**Guatemala** *pr. n.* Guatemala.

**guatr** ⚕ goitre, *Am.* goiter.

guatrlı ⚕ goitrous.

gudde *anat.* gland.

gudubet, -ti like the back (end) of a bus.

gufran [. -] God's mercy (*or* pardon).

guguk *zo.* cuckoo; ~ yapmak *fig.* to make mock (-*e* of).

guguklu having a cuckoo; ~ saat cuckoo clock.

gulfe foreskin, prepuce.

gulu(k) P turkey.

gulyabani [ū, ī] ogre, ogress.

gurbet, -ti 1. foreign land; 2. F absence from one's home; ~ çekmek to be homesick, to suffer absence from home; ~ eli (*or* diyarı) foreign land; -e (*or* ~ ellere) düşmek to be in a foreign land.

gurbetçi stranger.

gureba [ā] the poor and destitute; ~ hastanesi hospital for the poor.

gur gur rumling sound; ~ etm. to rumble.

gurk, -ku 1. broody (*hen*); 2. turkey cock; ~ ~ etm. to cluck (*broody hen*).

gurklamak to be broody (*hen*).

guruldamak to rumble, to growl.

gurul gurul rumbling sound; karnı ~ ötüyor his stomach is rumbling (*or* growling).

gurultu rumble.

gurup, -bu sunset, sundown.

gurur [. -] 1. pride; 2. conceit, vanity; ~ duymak to feel proud (-*den* of), to take pride (-*den* in); ~ gelmek (*b-ne*) *or* ~ getirmek (*b-i*) to be proud (of); to be conceited (about); -unu kırmak (*b-nin*) to hurt the pride of *s.o.*; -unu okşamak *fig.* to play on *s.o.*'s pride, to flatter *s.o.*'s pride.

gururlanmak to pride o.s. (*ile* on), to pique o.s. (*ile* on), to preen o.s. (*ile* on).

gururlu arrogant, vain, haughty, conceited.

gusletmek [x . .] to take a ritual bath.

gusto [x .] gusto, zest; taste.

gusül, -slü *isl.* total ablution of the body; ~ abdesti total ablution; ~ abdesti almak to perform a total ablution.

gusülhane [ā] bathroom for ritual washing.

guşa [x .] *s.* guatr.

gut ⚕ gout.

guvaş gouache.

gübre dung, manure, fertilizer, droppings; ~ şerbeti manure tea, liquid manure.

gübrelemek to manure, to fertilize, to dung.

gübreli manured, fertilized.

gübrelik dunghill.

gücendirmek to offend, to hurt.

gücenik offended, hurt, resentful.

gücenmek to resent, to take offence (-*e* at), to be offended (*or* hurt) (-*e* by).

gücü sley, weaver's reed.

gücün [x .] 1. just barely, hardly; 2. by force, forcibly.

güç[1], -cü 1. strength; 2. power; 3. force; 4. energy; ~ birliği cooperation; -ten düşmek to get weak; gücü yetmek to be strong enough; gücü yettiği kadar as well as he can, with all his might; gücünü yenmek to suppress one's anger.

güç[2], -cü 1. difficult, hard; 2. difficulty; ~ gelmek (*b-ne*) to seem difficult to *s.o.*; ~ halle (*or* gücü gücüne) with much effort, with great difficulty; ~ ile with difficulty, with great trouble; güce sarmak to get hard, to become difficult; gücüne gitmek to be offended, to be hurt, to take offence; gücüne koşmak to do s.th. the hard way.

güçbela with great difficulty, hardly.

güçlendirmek to strengthen.

güçlenmek to get strong, to strengthen.

güçleşmek to grow difficult.

güçleştirmek to render difficult, to complicate, to impede.

güçlü strong, powerful; ~ kuvvetli very strong and healthy.

güçlük difficulty, pain, trouble; ~ çekmek to experience difficulty; ~ çıkarmak (*or* göstermek) to make difficulties (-*e* for); güçlüğü yenmek to overcome difficulties.

güçlülük strength, power.

güçsüz weak, feeble, strengthless.

güçsüzlük weakness, feebleness, strengthlessness.

güderi 1. chamois (leather), chammy, shammy; 2. made of chamois; ~ eldiven chamois glove.

güdü motive, incentive; drive, push.

güdücü shepherd; cattle drover.

güdük 1. deficient, incomplete; 2. docked; tailless; 2. F thick-set, dumpy, squat; ~ kalmak F to be stunted; ~ tavuk 1. hen without tail feathers; 2. *fig.* nobody.

güdükleşmek to become stunted; to become truncated.

güdüleyici incentive.

güdüm guidance, direction, management.

güdümbilim cybernetics.

güdümlü controlled, directed; ~ mermi guided missile.

güfte words of a song, lyrics.

güğüm large jug.

gühercile ⚗ saltpetre, *Am.* saltpeter.

gül 1. ⚘ rose; 2. ♀ *wf.*; ~ ağacı rosewood; ~ gibi swimmingly; ~ gibi geçinmek to get along swimmingly; ~ goncası rose-bud; ~ reçeli rose jam; ~ rengi rose pink; ~ üstüne ~ koklamak to be disloyal to one's darling by loving another person; -ü seven dikenine katlanır *pro.* he that would have eggs must endure the cackling of hens, take the rough with the smooth.

**güldeste** anthology of poems.

**güldür güldür** with a crashing sound; ~ akmak to brawl *(river)*.

**güldürmek** *caus. of* gülmek to make laugh, to amuse.

**güldürü** *thea.* comedy, farce.

**güldürücü** comic, funny.

**güleç** smiling, joyful.

**gülhatmi** ✿ hollyhock.

**gülistan** [â] rose garden.

**gülizar** *poet.* rosy-cheeked.

**gülkurusu**, -nu violet-pink.

**güllabi(ci)** 1. warden *(in a lunatic asylum)*; 2. *fig.* flatterer, coaxer.

**güllaç**, -cı starch wafer.

**gülle** 1. cannon ball; shell; 2. *sports:* shot; weight; ~ atma *sports:* shot put; ~ atmak *sports:* to put the shot; ~ gibi as heavy as lead; ~ kaldırmak *sports:* to lift weights; ~ yağdırmak to shell, to bombard.

**gülleci** *sports:* shot-putter.

**güllük** rose garden *(or* bed*)*; ~ gülistanlık *fig.* a bed of roses.

**gülme** laughing, laughter; ~ almak to have a fit of laughter.

**gülmece** F funny story *or* novel.

**gülmek**, (-er) 1. to laugh; 2. *(b-ne)* to laugh at *s.o.*, to deride *s.o.*; 3. to be pleased; güle güle! good-bye!; 2. good luck!; güle güle gidin! have a good trip!; güle güle kullan! enjoy using it!; güle oynaya merrily, joyously; güleceği tuttu he had a fit of laughter; güler yüz cheerful, smiling face; güler yüz göstermek to behave cheerfully and hospitably *(-e* towards*)*; güler yüzlü cheerful, affable, merry; gülmekten çatlamak to split one's sides laughing; gülmekten kırılmak to be doubled up with laughter; gülüp oynamak *fig.* to have a good time.

**gülmez** sullen, sour-faced; unsmiling.

**gülsuyu**, -nu rose water.

**gülücük** smile.

**gülümseme** smile.

**gülümsemek** to smile.

**gülünç**, -cü ridiculous, ludicrous, laughable, funny.

**gülünçleştirmek** to caricature.

**gülünçlü** funny, comical.

**gülünçlük** funniness, comicality.

**gülünmek** 1. *pass. of* gülmek; 2. to laugh.

**gülüş** laughter.

**gülüşmek** to laugh together; to laugh at each other.

**gülyağı**, -nı attar of roses.

**güm** 1. bang!; 2. *sl.* fishy-story, tall-story; ~ atmak *sl.* to pull a fast one; ~ etm. to boom, to resound, to reverberate; ~ ~ atmak to throb *(heart)*; -e gitmek *sl. or* F 1. to go for nothing; 2. to die in vain, to peg out.

**gümbedek** [x . .] 1. with a booming sound; 2. out of the blue, all of a sudden.

**gümbürdemek** 1. to boom, to thunder, to reverberate; 2. *sl.* to peg out, to pop off.

**gümbür gümbür** with a booming noise.

**gümbürtü** boom, rumble, crash, thunder.

**gümeç**, -ci honeycomb; ~ balı honey in the comb.

**gümlemek** 1. to bang, to boom, to rumble; 2. *sl.* = güme gitmek.

**gümrah** [â] abundant, dense, copious.

**gümrük** 1. customs *(house)*; 2. duty; tariff; ~ almak to collect duty *(-den* on*)*; ~ kaçağı smuggled *(goods)*; ~ kaçakçısı smuggler; ~ komisyoncusu customs broker; ~ kontrolü customs inspection *(or* control*)*; ~ memuru customs officer; ~ resmî customs charges; ♀ ve Tekel Bakanlığı the Ministry of Customs and Monopolies; -ten muaf duty-free; gümrüğe tabi dutiable, subject to duty.

**gümrükçü** 1. customs officer; 2. customs agent.

**gümrüklenmek** to be cleared through customs.

**gümrüklü** 1. subject to customs duties; 2. with customs duties paid.

**gümrüksüz** duty-free.

**gümüş** silver; ~ kaplama silver-plated; silver plating; ~ madeni silver mine; ~ takımı silver (plate).

**gümüşbalığı**, -nı *zo.* sand-smelt, silversides, atherine.

**gümüşçü** silversmith.

**gümüşi** [î], **gümüşü** silvery, silver-grey, silver-colo(u)red.

**gümüşlemek** to silver-plate.

**gümüşlü** 1. containing silver; 2. ornamented with silver.

**gümüşservi** moonlight shining on water.

**gün** 1. day; daytime; 2. period; time; age; 3. happy *(or* better*)* days; 4. lady's at-home day; 5. sun; light; 6. date; 7. feast day; ~ ağarmak to break *(dawn)*; ~ ağarması daybreak; ~ batımı sunset, sundown; ~ bugün! now is the right time!;

~ doğmak **1.** to rise, to dawn *(sun)*; **2.** *(b-ne) fig.* to give *s.o.* an unexpected opportunity; ~ doğuşu sunrise, sun-up; ~ geçmek *(b-ne)* to get a sunstroke; ~ geçtikçe as the day goes on; ~ görmez sunless *(place)*; ~ görmüş **1.** who has seen better days; **2.** experienced; ~ tutulması eclipse of the sun; ~ yapmak to give an at-home; -den -e from day to day; -lerce for days; -lerden bir gün once upon a time; -leri sayılıdır his days are numbered; -ü -üne punctually; to the very day; -ün birinde one day, some day; -ünü ~ etm. to enjoy o.s. thoroughly.

günah [ā] **1.** sin; **2.** isn't it a crime!, shame!; ~ benden gitti it is no longer my responsibility; ~ çıkartmak to confess one's sins *(to a priest)*; ~ işlemek to sin, to commit a sin; ~ olm. to be a crime; -a girmek *s.* ~ işlemek; -a sokmak **1.** to tempt; **2.** to drive to blasphemy; -ı *(or* vebali) boynuna! the moral responsibility rests upon you *(or* him)!; -ını çekmek to suffer for one's sins; -ını vermez *fig.* he is very miser.

günahkâr **1.** sinner; culprit, wrongdoer; **2.** sinful, impious; culpable.

günahkârlık sinfulness.

günahlı = günahkâr 1 & 2.

günahsız sinless, innocent.

günahsızlık sinlessness, innocence.

günaşırı every other day.

günaydın good morning.

günbatısı, -nı west.

güncek P umbrella.

güncel current, up-to-date; ~ olaylar current events.

güncelleşmek to become current.

güncelleştirmek to make contemporary, to bring up-to-date.

güncellik currency.

günçiçeği, -ni ⚘ sunflower.

gündelik **1.** daily; **2.** daily wage *(or* fee); ~ gazete daily (paper); ~ ücret daily wage; -le çalışmak to work by the day.

gündelikçi day labo(u)rer, hired man; ~ kadın charwoman, *Am.* hired woman.

gündelikçilik day labo(u)r.

gündem agenda; -e almak to put on the agenda; -e geçmek to be put on the agenda.

gündeş happening on the same day.

gündoğ(r)usu, -nu **1.** ⬇ east; **2.** easterly wind.

gündönümü, -nü equinox, solstice.

gündüz **1.** daytime; **2.** by day *(or* daylight), in the daytime; ~ feneri *co.* Negro; ~ gözüyle by the light of day;

~ vakti in the daytime, during the day; -leri in the daytime, during the day.

gündüzcü **1.** on day duty; **2.** day student; **3.** day drinker.

gündüzlü **1.** day *(school)*; **2.** = gündüzcü 2.

gündüzsefası, -nı ⚘ bindweed.

gündüzün [x . .] by *(or* during the) day.

günebakan ⚘ sunflower.

güneş **1.** sun; **2.** sunshine; ~ açmak to become sunny; ~ almak *(or* görmek) to let in the sun; ~ banyosu sun bath(ing); ~ batması sunset, sundown; ~ çarpması sunstroke; ~ doğmak to rise *(sun)*; ~ gözlüğü sunglasses; ~ ışını sunbeam, sunray; ~ saati sundial; ~ sistemi solar system; ~ tutulması solar eclipse; ~ yanığı sunburn; ~ yılı solar year; -e göstermek to expose to the sun; -i balçıkla *(or* çamurla) sıvamak *fig.* to try to hide the truth; -in alnında *(or* altında) in full sun; -te yanmak to be sunburnt; to be tanned.

güneşle(n)mek to sunbathe.

güneşli sunny, sunlit.

güneşlik **1.** sunny place; **2.** sunshade, sunblind; **3.** sun hat; visor *(of a cap)*; **4.** sun-visor *(in a car)*; **5.** lens cover *(for a camera)*.

güneşsiz sunless.

güney **1.** south; **2.** southern; **1.** south wind; **4.** sunny side; ~ kutbu South Pole.

Güney Afrika Cumhuriyeti *pr. n.* Republic of South Africa.

güneybatı southwest.

güneydoğu southeast.

güneyli **1.** southerner; **2.** southern.

günlü dated.

günlük[1] **1.** daily; **2.** ... days old *(baby)*; **3.** sufficient for ... days; **4.** diary; **5.** everyday, usual; ~ emir ✗ order of the day; ~ gazete daily paper; ~ güneşlik sunny; ~ kur ✝ current rate of exchange; ~ rapor daily report, bulletin; ~ yumurta fresh egg.

günlük[2] incense, frankincense, myrrh.

günlükçü diarist.

günöte *ast.* apogee.

günübirlik, günübirliğine for the day.

güpegündüz [. x . .] in broad daylight.

gür **1.** abundant, dense, thick; rank; **2.** gushing.

gürbüz sturdy, robust, healthy.

gürbüzlük sturdiness, robustness.

Gürcistan *pr. n.* Georgia.

Gürcü Georgian.

güreş wrestling; ~ etm. *(or* tutmak) to wrestle.

güreşçi wrestler.

güreşçilik wrestling.

güreşmek to wrestle (ile with).

gürgen (ağacı) ♀ hornbeam, horn beech.

gürlemek 1. to thunder; to roar; 2. fig. to roar with rage; 3. sl. to peg out, to pop off.

gürleşmek to become abundant (or dense).

gürlük 1. abundance, luxuriance; 2. bountifulness.

güruh [ü] gang, group, lot, band, mob.

gürüldemek to thunder.

gürül gürül with a brawling sound; ~ ~ akmak to brawl (river).

gürültü 1. noise, uproar; 2. fig. brawl, row; ~ çıkarmak (or etm. or yapmak) to make a row; ~ koparmak to kick up (or make) a row; ~ patırtı noise, commotion; -ye boğmak to cause to be lost in the confusion; -ye gelmek to be lost in the confusion; -ye gitmek to be the victim of the confusion; (kuru) -ye pabuç bırakmamak not to be intimidated by mere threats.

gürültücü noisy, troublesome.

gürültülü noisy, tumultuous, clamorous.

gürültüsüz noiseless, quiet.

gürz hist. mace.

gütaperka [. . x .] guttapercha.

gütmek, (-der) 1. to herd, to drive (animal); 2. fig. to cherish, to nourish, to nurse (grudge, aim, ambition); 3. to impel.

güve zo. clothes moth; ~ yemiş moth--eaten; ~ yeniği moth hole.

güveç, -ci casserole; hotpot.

çüvelenmek to be moth-eaten.

güven 1. trust, confidence, reliance; 2. security, safety; -i olm. to have confidence (-e in); -i sarsılmak to lose confidence (in); -ini kazanmak (b-nin) to win s.o.'s confidence.

güvence guarantee.

çüvenç s. güven.

güvenışığı phot. safelight.

güvenilir trusty, trustworthy, dependable.

çüvenli dependable, trusty.

güvenlik 1. security, safety; 2. confidence; ♀ Konseyi Security Council.

güvenmek to trust (-e in), to rely (-e on); to confide (-e in); güvendiği dağlara kar

yağmak fig. to be let down.

güvenoyu, -nu vote of confidence; ~ almak to win a vote of confidence; ~ vermek to give a vote of confidence.

güvensiz distrustful.

güvensizlik distrustfulness, lack of confidence.

güvercin zo. pigeon; ~ postası pigeon post.

güvercinboynu, -nu multicolo(u)red, shot; dove colo(u)red.

güvercinlik dovecote, pigeon-loft.

güverte [. x .] ♪ deck.

güvey 1. bridegroom; 2. son-in-law; ~ olmadık, ama kapı dışında bekledik co. although we weren't there we know quite a lot about it.

güveyfeneri, -ni ♀ winter cherry.

güveyotu, -nu ♀ marjoram.

güvez purplish red.

güya 1. supposedly; 2. as if, as though.

güz autumn, Am. fall.

güzçiğdemi, -ni ♀ autumn crocus, meadow saffron.

güzel 1. beautiful, pretty, nice; 2. beauty, belle; 3. fine!, good!; 4. excellent, good; ~ ~ calmly, gently;~ hava fine weather; ~ sanatlar fine arts; ~ mi güzel! of breath-taking beauty, very beautiful; ♀ Sanatlar Akademisi pr. n. the Academy of Fine Arts; -im 1. darling, honey; 2. that beautiful (thing or person).

güzelavratotu, -nu ♀ belladonna, deadly nightshade.

güzelce 1. pretty, fair; 2. thoroughly.

güzelleme a kind of folk song of praise for a special person.

güzelleşmek to become beautiful.

güzelleştirmek to beautify.

güzellik 1. beauty, prettiness; 2. gentleness, kindness; ~ kraliçesi beauty queen; ~ salonu beauty-parlo(u)r, beauty-salon; ~ yarışması beauty contest.

güzellikle gently, with gentleness.

güzergâh route.

güzey geogr. shady side.

güzide [î] select, distinguished, outstanding; choice.

güzlük autumn..., Am. fall...; ~ ekim autumn (or fall) sowing.

güzün [x .] in the autumn, Am. in the fall.

# H

**ha 1.** what a...!, wow!; **2.** o yes!, I see!; **3.** come on now!; **4.** look here!; **5.** F eh?, huh?; **6.** P yes; **7.** either, or; **8.** on and on; ~ bire uninterruptedly; ~ deyince at a moment's notice.

**habaset,** -ti [. - .] villainy, wickedness.

**habazan** F starved, ravenous.

**habbe** grain, seed, kernel; -yi kubbe yapmak F to make a mountain out of a molehill.

**habe** [ā] sl. bread; ~ etm. (or kaymak or uçlanmak) sl. to get enough to eat.

**habeci** [ā] sl. fool, idiot, fucker.

**habeden** [ā] sl. for nothing, gratis.

**haber 1.** news, information, word, message; **2.** knowledge; **3.** gr. † predicate; ~ ajansı news agency; ~ alma X intelligence; ~ almak (bşi) to learn s.th., to get word of s.th., to hear s.th.; ~ göndermek to send a message (-e to); ~ kaynağı news source; ~ merkezi **1.** news bureau; **2.** information bureau; **3.** command post; ~ salmak F to send news (-e to); ~ sütunu news column; ~ toplamak to gather news; ~ uçurmak to send a message secretly or urgently (-e to); ~ vermek **1.** to let s.o. know; **2.** to inform, to announce; -i olm. (bşden) to be informed of s.th., to know about s.th.; -im var I know about it; -im yok I know nothing about it, I haven't heard it.

**haberci** herald, harbinger (a. fig.); forerunner, messenger; guguk kuşu baharın -sidir the cuckoo is a harbinger of spring.

**haberdar** [. . -] informed; ~ etm. (b-ni bşden) to inform s.o. of s.th.; ~ olm. to know (-den about); to find out (-den about), to possess information (-den about).

**haberleşme** communication.

**haberleşmek** to communicate (ile with), to correspond (ile with).

**haberli 1.** informed; **2.** having notified.

**habersiz 1.** uninformed, ignorant (-den of); **2.** without warning.

**habersizce** without warning, secretly.

**Habeş** pr. n. Abyssinian, Ethiopian; ~

maymunu zo. sacred baboon.

**Habeşi** s. Habeş.

**Habeşistan** pr. n. Abyssinia, Ethiopia.

**habis 1.** malicious, evil; **2.** malignant (tumour).

**hac,** -ccı pilgrimage to Mecca; -ca gitmek to go on the pilgrimage to Mecca.

**hacamat,** -tı **1.** bloodletting by cupping; **2.** sl. stabbing, knifing; ~ şişesi cupping glass.

**haccetmek** [x . .] to go on the pilgrimage to Mecca.

**hacet,** -ti [ā] **1.** need, necessity, requirement; **2.** feces; urine; ~ görmek **1.** to deem necessary; **2.** F to go to the toilet; ~ kalmamak to be no longer necessary; ~ kapısı (or penceresi) door (or window) of a saint's tomb; ~ yeri toilet; ~ yok it's not necessary.

**hacı** hadji; pilgrim; ~ ağa contp. parvenu, upstart, nouveau riche; ~ baba **1.** elderly hadji; **2.** F venerable old man; ~ bekler gibi beklemek to wait impatiently (-i for); ~ pintorosa kavuşmak sl. to get a good hiding; ~ sı hocası F everyone.

**hacılaryolu,** -nu the Milky Way.

**hacıyatmaz 1.** tumbler, roly-poly (toy); **2.** resilient person.

**hacim,** -cmi **1.** volume, capacity; bulk; **2.** ↓ tonnage.

**hacimli** voluminous, bulky.

**hacir,** -cri ⅋ putting under restraint.

**Hacivat,** -tı pr. n. one of the main characters of the Karagöz shadow play.

**haciz,** -czi seizure, sequestration, distraint; ~ altına almak to sequestrate; ~ kararı warrant of distraint; ~ koymak to sequestrate.

**hacizli** sequestered, sequestrated.

**haczetmek** to sequestrate, to seize.

**haç,** -çı the cross, crucifix; ~ çıkarmak to cross o.s.; -ı suya atma yortusu Epiphany.

**haçlamak** to crucify.

**Haçlılar** pr. n. hist. Crusaders.

**Haçlı seferleri** hist. the Crusades.

**had,** -ddi **1.** limit, boundary, degree, point; **2.** A, log. term; -di hesabı olmamak to be boundless (or bountiful); -di olmamak *(b-nin)* not to have the right to, not to be up to *s.o.*; -di zatında actually, essentially; -dinden fazla excessive, overmuch; -dini aşmak to go too far; -dini bildirmek *(b-ne)* to put *s.o.* in his place, to tell *s.o.* where to get off; -dini bilmek to know one's place.

**hâd,** -ddi **1.** sharp, pointed; **2. ⚡** acute; **3.** *fig.* critical, acute.

**hadde 1.** wire-drawer's plate; **2.** rolling machine; ~ fabrikası rolling mill; -den geçirmek *fig.* to examine minutely.

**haddehane** [. . - .] rolling mill.

**hademe** caretaker, *Am.* janitor.

**hadım** eunuch; ~ etm. to castrate.

**hadımağası,** -nı *hist.* chief eunuch in the sultan's palace.

**hadi** *s.* haydi.

**hadim 1.** manservant; **2.** serving.

**hadis 1.** hadith; **2.** the study of hadiths.

**hadise** event, incident, occurence, happening; ~ çıkarmak to make a scene, to stir up trouble.

**hadiseli** eventful.

**hadisene** F come on!

**hadisesiz** smoothly, eventless.

**hadsiz** unbounded, unlimited; ~ hesapsız countless, innumerable.

**haf** *sports:* half-back.

**hafakan** sudden exasperation; -lar boğmak (or basmak) to be bored stiff.

**hafazanallah** [. . . . -] may God protect us from such a misfortune!

**hafız** [â] **1.** hafiz; **2.** *sl.* fool, silly; **3.** *sl.* swot, grind, crammer.

**hafıza** memory.

**hafızıkütüp** librarian.

**hafızlamak** *sl.* to swot up, to mug up, to grind, to cram, to bone up on.

**hafızlık 1.** being a hafiz; **2.** *sl.* swotting; **3.** *sl.* stupidity.

**hafi** [ı] secret, hidden.

**hafif 1.** light; **2.** easy; **3.** frivolous, flighty; **4.** slight; **5.** slightly; **6.** insignificant, unimportant; ~ atlatmak to escape (or get off) lightly; ~ çay weak tea; ~ giyinmek to dress lightly; ~ ~ gently, slowly; ~ müzik light music; ~ sanayi light industry; ~ tertip **1.** small-scale: **2.** slightly, a little; -e almak to make light *(-i* of); -ten almak to trifle *(-i* with), to make light *(-i* of).

**hafifçe** lightly.

**hafiflemek 1.** to get lighter; **2.** to subside, to diminish; **3.** to be relieved.

**hafifleşmek 1.** to get light; **2.** *fig.* to become flighty (or light-héaded).

**hafifleştirmek, hafifletmek 1.** to lighten;

**2.** to abate, to diminish; **3.** to relieve.

**hafifletici 1.** extenuating; **2.** giving relief; ~ sebepler 🜚 extenuating circumstances.

**hafiflik 1.** lightness, slightness; **2.** relief, ease of mind; **3.** *fig.* flightiness.

**hafifmeşrep,** -bi loose, flighty, frivolous.

**hafifsemek** to make light *(-i* of), to trifle *(-i* with).

**hafifsiklet,** -ti welterweight.

**hafiften** lightly, gently.

**hafiye** detective, investigator, spy.

**hafriyat,** -tı [. . - ] excavation(s).

**hafriyatçı** [. . - .] excavator.

**hafta** week; ~ arasında (or içinde) during the week; ~ başı the first day of the week; ~ sonu (or tatili) weekend; -larca for weeks; -sına a week later; -sına kalmaz within a week; -ya in a week's time, next week; -ya bugün this day week.

**haftalık 1.** weekly; **2.** weekly wage; **3.** lasting ... weeks; ~ mecmua weekly; iki ~ bir çalışma a two-week work.

**haftalıkçı** wage earner *(paid by the week).*

**haftaym** [- .] [x .] *sports:* half time.

**hah** there!, now!, exactly!; ~ şöyle! there, that's good!

**haham** *eccl.* rabbi.

**hahambaşı,** -nı *eccl.* the chief rabbi.

**hahamhane** [. . - .] rabbinate.

**hahha** [. -], **hahhah** [x .] ha!, haha!

**hail** [â] barrier, screen, curtain.

**haile** [â] tragedy.

**hain** [â] **1.** traitor; **2.** treacherous. traitorous; **3.** malicious; ~ ~ maliciously.

**hainleşmek** to become (or act) treacherous, to become malicious.

**hainlik 1.** treachery, perfidy; **2.** malice; ~ etm. to act treacherously *(-e* towards).

**Haiti** *pr. n.* Haiti.

**haiz** [â] **1.** containing, having; **2.** provided *(-i* with); ~ olm. to possess, to obtain, to have.

**hak[1],** -kkı **1.** justice; **2.** right; due, share; **3.** fairness; **4.** true, right; **5.** remuneration, fee, pay; ~ etm. to deserve, to merit; ~ iddia etm. to claim; ~ kazanmak to deserve, to have a right *(-e* to); ~ sahibi holder of a right; ~ vermek *(b-ne)* to acknowledge *s.o.* to be right; ~ yemek to be unjust; ~ yemez rightful; ...hakkı için for the sake of...; hakkı olm. **1.** to have a right to; **2.** to be justified; hakkı var he is right; hakkından gelmek **1.** to get the better *(-in* of); **2.** *(b-nin)* to get even with *s.o.,* to pay *s.o.* back; hakkını almak to get one's due; to take one's share; hakkını vermek to give *s.o.* his due, to remunerate; hakkını yemek *(b-nin)* to do an injustice to *s.o.*

**hak²** -kkı **1.** engraving, incising; **2.** erasing by scraping.

**Hak,** -kkı *(a.* Cenabı Hak) God; Hakkın rahmetine kavuşanlar the dead, the deceased; Hakkın rahmetine kavuşmak to die, to go to meet one's Maker.

**hâk,** -ki † earth, soil; ~ ile yeksan etm. to raze to the ground, to bring down.

**hakan** [- .] khan, Turkish ruler; emperor.

**hakaret,** -ti [. - .] insult, contempt; ~ etm. to insult; ~ görmek *pass. of* ~ etm.

**hakça** [x .] **1.** truthfully, truly; **2.** justly.

**hakem 1.** arbitrator; **2.** *sports:* referee, umpire; ~ kararı ぬ arbitral award, arbitration; ~ kurulu arbitration committee.

**hakemlik** umpirage; arbitration; ~ etm. **1.** to arbitrate; **2.** *sports:* to umpire, to referee.

**hakeza** [- . -] [x . -] likewise.

**haki** [ā] khaki.

**hakikat,** -ti [ı] **1.** truth, reality; **2.** truly, really; ~ olm. to come true; -te in fact.

**hakikaten** [ı] [. x . .] truly, really.

**hakikatli** [. - . .] loyal, faithful.

**hakikatsiz** [. - . .] disloyal, unfaithful.

**hakiki 1.** true, real; **2.** genuine; **3.** sincere *(friend);* ~ mermi live cartridge; ~ şahıs ぬ natural person; ~ Türk tütünü genuine Turkish tobacco. '

**hakim 1.** sage; **2.** philosopher.

**hâkim 1.** dominating, ruling; **2.** dominant, supreme; **3.** ruler; **4.** ぬ judge; **5.** overlooking, dominating; ~ olm. **1.** to rule; **2.** to dominate; **3.** to overlook; ~ denize ~ bir ev a house overlooking the sea.

**hâkimiyet,** -ti sovereignty; rule, domination; hâkimiyeti milliye *(or mst* millî hâkimiyet *or* ulusal egemenlik) sovereignty of the nation.

**hâkimlik** judgeship.

**hakir** vile, worthless, mean; ~ görmek to despise.

**hakkâk,** -ki engraver; ~ kalemi scriber, engraver's chisel.

**hakkaniyet,** -ti [. - . .] justice, equity; ~ göstermek to do justice (-e to).

**hakketmek** [x . .] **1.** to engrave, to incise *(-e* on); **2.** to scrape away, to erase.

**hakkıhıyar** ぬ option.

**hakkıhuzur** daily allowance, *Am.* per diem.

**hakkında** about, regarding, concerning; dil ~ yazı an article about language.

**hakkısükût,** -tu hush money.

**hakkıyle 1.** thoroughly, properly; **2.** rightfully.

**haklamak 1.** to overcome, to beat, to suppress, to crush; **2.** F to eat up, to gulp down.

**haklaşmak** to settle mutual rights *or* claims, to be quits.

**haklı 1.** right, just; **2.** rightful; ~ çıkarmak to justify; ~ çıkmak to turn out to be right; ~ olm. to be in the right.

**haklılık** justice, rightfulness.

**haksever** just.

**hakseverlik** justness.

**haksız 1.** unjust, wrong; **2.** unjustifiable, in the wrong; ~ çıkmak to turn out to be in the wrong; ~ fiil ぬ wrong; ~ rekabet unfair competition; ~ yere unjustly, wrongfully.

**haksızlık** injustice, wrongfulness; ~ etm. **1.** to act unjustly; **2.** to do an injustice *(-e* to).

**hakşinas** [ .. -] just, fair, rightful.

**haktanır** just, righteous.

**hakuran** dove; ~ kafesi gibi F tumble-down *(place).*

**hal¹ 1.** condition, state; **2.** circumstances, state of affairs; **3.** attitude, behavio(u)r; **4.** *gr.* case; **5.** energy, strength; **6.** *fig.* trouble; **7.** the present time; ~ böyle iken and yet, nevertheless; ~ çaresi remedy; ~ hatır sormak to enquire *(or* inquire) after s.o., to ask after s.o.; ~ tercümesi **1.** biography; **2.** curriculum vitae; -den anlamak to sympathize; -e bak! how terrible!, how strange!; -e yola koymak to put in order; -i duman *(or* harap) olm. to fall into dire straits, to be in hot water; -i kalmamak to be exhausted; -i vakti yerinde *(b-nin)* well-off, wealthy; -im yok I am under the weather; -ine köpekler gülüyor F he is a laughingstock.

**hal²,** -li covered market-place.

**hal³,** -lli **1.** ぬ solution, resolution; **2.** melting, dissolving.

**hala** [x .] paternal aunt.

**hâlâ** [x -] still, yet.

**halas** salvation, deliverance; ~ etm. to save, to deliver; ~ olm. *(or* bulmak) to be saved; to escape *(-den* from).

**halaskâr** savio(u)r, deliverer.

**halat,** -tı rope, hawser; ~ çekme tug of war.

**halavet,** -ti sweetness, cuteness.

**halay** a folk dance performed by holding hands in a circle; ~ çekmek to dance the halay.

**halayık,** -kı concubine.

**halazade** [. . - .] cousin.

**halbuki** [x . .] *or* [. x .] whereas, however, but.

**haldeş** [ā] in the same boat *(another*

*person).*

**haldır haldır** speedily and noisily.

**hale** [ā] 1. halo; 2. *anat.* areola; 3. ♀ *wf.*

**halef** successor; ~ selef olm. to succeed.

**halel** harm, injury, damage; ~ gelmek 1. to be harmed; 2. to be blemished; ~ getirmek (*or* vermek) to harm, to injure, to spoil.

**haleldar** [. . -] injured, harmed; ~ etm. to injure, to harm.

**halelenmek** to form a halo.

**halen** [ā] [x .] at present, now, presently.

**Halep,** -bi *pr. n.* Aleppo; ~ çamı ♀ Aleppo (*or* Jerusalem) pine; ~ orada ise arşın burada! well, prove it!

**halet,** -ti [ā] condition, situation, aspect; haleti ruhiye mood, state of mind.

**haletmek** [x . .] to dethrone (*a sultan*).

**halfa(otu)** ♀ esparto (grass).

**halhal,** -li anklet, bangle.

**halı** carpet, rug; ~ döşemek to lay a carpet.

**halıcı** carpet maker *or* seller.

**halıcılık** the rug business.

**hali** [- -] 1. empty, vacant; 2. deserted, uninhabited.

**haliç,** -ci 1. inlet, bay, estuary; 2. ♀ *pr. n.* the Golden Horn.

**halife** [ı] *hist.* caliph.

**halifelik** *hist.* caliphate.

**halihazır** [ā, ā] the present (time); -da at present.

**halik,** -kı [ā] 1. creator; 2. creative; 3. the Creator, God.

**halim** mild, gentle; ~ selim docile, biddable.

**halis** [ā] pure, unmixed, genuine; ~ muhlis genuine, true.

**halisane** [- . - .] sincere(ly).

**halita** [ı] ⚛ alloy; ~ yapmak to alloy.

**haliyle** [- - .] 1. as it is, without change; 2. naturally, consequently.

**halk,** -kı 1. people, nation; 2. populace, people; 3. the common people; ~ ağzı vernacular; ~ dili colloquial language, vernacular; ~ edebiyatı folk literature; ~ müziği folk music; ~ oyunu folk dance; ~ şarkısı folk song, ballad; -a dönük popular.

**halka** 1. hoop; 2. circle; 3. link; 4. (finger) ring; earring; 5. ring-shaped biscuit; ~ ~ 1. in circles; 2. in rings; 3. in links; ~ olm. to form a circle; ~ oyunu 1. round dance; 2. quoits, hoop-la; -yı burnuna takmak to bring into submission.

**halkalamak** 1. to encircle; 2. to fasten with a ring.

**halkalı** ringed, linked.

**halkalıdamar** ♀ annular vessel.

**halkavcılığı** demagogy.

**halkavcısı** demagogue.

**halkbilgisi,** -ni folklore.

**halkbilimci** folklorist.

**halkçı** populist.

**halkçılık** populism.

**halkoylaması,** -nı referendum.

**halkoyu,** -nu public opinion.

**hallaç,** -cı wool *or* cotton fluffer; ~ pamuğu gibi atmak *fig.* to scatter about.

**hallenmek** [ā] 1. to acquire a new form *or* condition; 2. to feel faint; 3. *sl.* to desire, to want.

**halleşmek** [ā] to have a heart-to-heart talk.

**halletmek** [x . .] 1. to solve, to resolve; 2. to dissolve; 3. to finish up, to complete, to settle.

**hallice** somewhat better (-*den* than).

**hallihamur** olm. to conform, to accustom o.s. to circumstances.

**hallolunmak** 1. to be solved; 2. to be settled; 3. to be dissolved.

**halojen** ⚛ halogen; ~ lambası halogen reflector.

**halsiz** weak, exhausted, tired out; ~ düşmek to be exhausted (*or* tired out).

**halsizlik** weakness.

**halt,** -tı 1. mixup; 2. impertinence; ~ etm. to do s.th. rude; to say s.th. improper; ~ karıştırmak (*or* yemek) to do s.th. rude, to make a great blunder; ne ~ etmeye oraya gittin? what the dickens did you go there for?; ona ~ düşer he has no right at all to interfere.

**halter** *sports:* dumbbell, barbell.

**halterci** weight lifter.

**haluk,** -ku 1. good-natured; 2. ♀ [x .] *mf.*

**halvet,** -ti 1. solitude; 2. a very hot bathing cubicle in a public bath; ~ gibi like an oven; ~ o!m. to meet in private; -e dönmek to become like an oven (*room, etc.*).

**ham** 1. unripe, green; 2. crude, raw, unrefined; 3. *fig.* unrefined (*person*); 4. unrealistic (*aim, ambition, etc.*); 5. *sports:* out of shape (*or* condition); ~ çelik crude steel; ~ deri untanned leather; ~ fikir absurdity; ~ ipek raw silk; ~ meyve unripe fruit; ~ pamuk raw cotton; ~ petrol crude oil; ~ teklif unacceptable suggestion; ~ toprak uncultivated land; ~ ümit unrealizable hope.

**hamail** [. - .] 1. baldric; 2. amulet, charm.

**hamak** hammock.

**hamakat,** -ti [. - .] stupidity; ~ etm. (*or* göstermek) to act like a stupid.

**hamal** porter, carrier; stevedore; ~ camal F mob, rabble; ~ ücreti (*or* parası) porterage.

**hamaliye** [. - . .] porterage, porter's fee.

**hamallık 1.** porterage; **2.** porter's fee, porterage; **3.** *fig.* unnecessary burden; hamallığını etm. *(bir işin)* to do the dull and tiring part of *(a job)*.

**hamam 1.** Turkish *(or* public) bath; **2.** bathroom; **3.** *fig.* very hot room; ~ gibi like an oven *(room)*; ~ takımı set of supplies for the Turkish bath; ~ yapmak to have a bath.

**hamamanası**, -nı **1.** manageress in a public bath for women; **2.** *fig.* huge and shrewish woman.

**hamamböceği**, -ni *zo.* cockroach.

**hamamcı 1.** proprietor *or* keeper of a public bath; **2.** *eccl.* unclean and in need of a ritual bath; ~ kadın = hamamanası.

**hamamotu**, -nu depilatory agent.

**hamamtası**, -nı metal bowl.

**hamarat**, -tı hard-working, deft, industrious.

**hamaratlaşmak** to be industrious *(woman)*.

**hamaratlık** deftness, industriousness.

**hamaset**, -ti [. - .] heroism, valo(u)r.

**hamasi** [. - -] heroic. epic *(story, poem)*.

**Hamburg** *pr. n.* Hamburg.

**hamdolsun!** [x . .] God be praised!, thanks be to God!

**Hamel** *ast.* Aries.

**hamhalat**, -tı rough, boorish, loutish *(man)*.

**ham hum** F hemming and hawing; ~ etm. F to hem and haw; ~ şaralop *sl.* empty words, a lot of nonsense.

**hamız** 🔬 acid.

**hami** [- -] **1.** guardian, protector; **2.** sponsor, patron.

**hamil**, -mli **1.** 🕇 bearer; **2.** bearing, possessing; **3.** prop, support; ~ olm. to have, to possess; -ine 🕇 (pay) to bearer.

**hamile** pregnant *(woman)*; ~ bırakmak to impregnate, to make pregnant; ~ elbisesi maternity dress; ~ kalmak **1.** to get pregnant; **2.** *(b-den)* to be with child by *s.o.*; ~ olm. to be pregnant.

**hamilelik** pregnancy.

**haminne** [. x .] (< hanım nine) F grandma.

**haminto** [. x .] *sl.* swindle, ilicit gain.

**hamiş** postscript.

**hamiyet**, -ti patriotism.

**hamiyetli** patriotic.

**hamla** [x .] ⚓ stroke *(of the oars)*.

**hamlaç** 🔬 blowpipe.

**hamlamak, hamlaşmak** to get out of condition, to get rusty, to get out of practice.

**hamle 1.** attack, assault, onslaught; **2.**

dash, élan; **3.** *chess & draughts:* turn; ~ etm. *(or* yapmak) to make an attack; to dash.

**hamleci** enterprising, venturesome.

**hamletmet** [x . .] to attribute (-*e* to), to impute (-*e* to), to ascribe (-*e* to).

**hamlık 1.** unripeness, rawness, greenness; crudeness; **2.** being out of shape.

**hammadde** raw material.

**hampa** *s.* hempa.

**hamsi** *zo.* anchovy.

**hamt** giving praise to God; ~ olsun! praise be to God!, thank God!

**hamule** [ū] load, freight; ~ senedi waybill, bill of lading.

**hamur 1.** dough, paste, leaven; **2.** grade, quality *(of paper)*; **3.** half-cooked *(bread)*; **4.** paper pulp; **5.** clay *(for pottery)*; ~ açmak to roll out dough; ~ gibi **1.** overcooked, soggy, mushy; **2.** ~ gibi doughty, undercooked; **3.** F bushed, done up, worn out, exhausted; ~ işi pastry; ~ olm. to become doughty; ~ tahtası pastry board; ~ teknesi kneading trough.

**hamurlamak 1.** to cover with dough; **2.** to lute.

**hamurlaşmak** to get doughy *(or* soggy).

**hamursu** doughy.

**hamursuz** unleavened (bread); 2 Bayramı Passover.

**hamurumsu** *s.* hamursu.

**hamut**, -tu horse collar.

**han¹** [ā] khan, sovereign, ruler.

**han² [ā] 1.** inn; caravansary, caravanserai, khan; **2.** large commercial building; ~ gibi spacious, vast; ~ hamam sahibi a man nof property.

**hancı** innkeeper.

**hancılık** innkeeping.

**hançer** dagger. stab, khanjar.

**hançere** *anat.* larynx.

**hançerlemek** to stab, to knife.

**handikap** handicap.

**handiyse** [x . .] F **1.** all but, very nearly; **2.** any moment, soon.

**hane** [ā] **1.** house; **2.** household; **3.** square *(of a chessboard)*; **4.** section, division; **5.** blank *(in a printed form)*.

**hanedan** [- . -] **1.** dynasty; **2.** generous, hospitable.

**Hanefi** [. . -] *pr. n.* Hanafi, Hanafite.

**haneli** [ā] **1.** comprising ... houses; **2.** having ... places *(number)*.

**hanelik** of ... houses.

**hanende** [ā] singer.

**hangar** hangar.

**hangi** [x .] which; ~ biri? which one?; ~ dağda kurt öldü? fancy your doing it!; ~

rüzgâr attı? fancy seeing you here!, what on earth brought you here?; ~ taşı kaldırsan, altından çıkar he has a finger in every pie.

**hangisi** which of them, which one.

**hanım 1.** lady; **2.** *(after a first name)* Mrs.; Miss; **3.** wife; **4.** mistress *(of a household)*; **5.** ladylike; ~ abla sister; ~ evladı *sl.* **1.** mother's boy, milksop, mollycoddle; **2.** bastard; ~ hanımcık ladylike; ~ kızınız your daughter.

**hanımböceği,** -ni *zo.* ladybug.

**hanımefendi 1.** lady, gentlewoman; **2.** madam, ma'am.

**hanımefendilik** ladyship, being a lady.

**hanımeli,** -yi ♀ honeysuckle, woodbine.

**hanımgöbeği,** -ni ring-shaped syrupy pastry.

**hanımlık** ladyship, quality of a lady.

**hani¹** *(balığı)* *zo.* sea bass, cabrilla.

**hani² [x .] 1.** so where is...?; **2.** why ... not...?; **3.** you know!, you remember...?; **4.** let's suppose that...; **5.** in fact, besides; **6.** actually, to tell the truth; ~ yok mu? **1.** if only...; **2.** very nearly; -dir for ages, for a long time.

**hanlık 1.** khanate; **2.** sovereignty, rulership.

**hanos** *zo.* sea bass, cabrilla.

**hantal 1.** clumsy, coarse; **2.** huge, bulky.

**hantallaşmak** to become clumsy *(or* coarse).

**hantallık 1.** clumsiness, coarseness; **2.** bulkiness.

**hant hant ötmek** to crave.

**Hanya** Canea, Khania; -'yı Konya'yı göstermek *(b-ne)* to teach *s.o.* a lesson, to show *s.o.* what's what.

**hap,** -pı **1.** pill; **2.** *sl.* dope; -ı yutmak F to be in the soup, to be in hot waters.

**hapçı** *sl.* **1.** drug addict; **2.** opium addict, doper.

**hapır hapır, hapır hupur:** ~ ~ yemek to wolf down, to munch.

**hapis,** -psi **1.** imprisonment, confinement; **2.** prison, gaol, *Am.* jail; **3.** prisoner, gaoler, *Am.* jailer; **4.** imprisoned; ~ cezası prison sentence; ~ giymek *(or* yemek) to be sentenced to prison; ~ hakkı ♂ right of retention; ~ yatmak to be in prison; hapse tıkmak F to put s.o. in gaol, *Am.* to put s.o. in jail.

**hapishane [. - - .]** prison, gaol, *Am.* jail; ~ kaçkını **1.** criminal still at large; **2.** *fig.* scoundrel; -yi boylamak to end up *(or* land up) in gaol.

**hapislik** imprisonment.

**hapsetmek [x . .] 1.** to gaol, *Am.* to jail; to

imprison; **2.** to lock up *(-e* in); **3.** to confine; **4.** *fig.* to retain, to detain.

**hapşırmak** to sneeze.

**hapşu!** atishoo!, *Am.* achoo!

**hapt etm. [x . .]** F to silence.

**har:** ~ gür **1.** noisy squabble; **2.** tumultuously; ~ ~ violently, strongly; ~ ~ akmak to brawl; ~ hur chaos, confusion; ~ vurup harman savurmak F to play ducks and drakes (-i with), to squander; -ı başına vurmak to go wild; -ı geçmek **1.** to calm down, to cool down, to cool off, to simmer down; **2.** to lose one's enthusiasm.

**hara [x .]** stud (farm).

**harabat,** -tı **[. - -] 1.** ruins; **2.** *Ottoman lit.*: wineshops, taverns.

**harabati [. - - -]** unkempt, slovenly, untidy.

**harabe [. - .] 1.** ruins, remains; **2.** tumbledown house.

**haraç,** -cı **1.** tribute; **2.** protection money; **3.** † tax paid by non-Moslems; ~ mezat satmak to auction; ~ yemek *sl.* to sponge on another; haraca bağlamak to lay s.o. under tribute, to force s.o. to pay protection, money; haraca çıkarmak to put up to auction.

**haraççı 1.** extortioner who exacts protection money; **2.** † collector of tribute.

**harakiri** hara-kiri.

**haram [. -]** forbidden by religion, unlawful, wrong; ~ etm. *fig.* to take the pleasure out of s.th for s.o.; ~ mal ill gotten gains; ~ olm. *pass. of* ~ etm. to be spoiled; ~ olsun! may you get no benefit from it!; ~ yemek to get illegally *or* illegitimately; -a uçkur çözmek F to live in sin, to commit adultery.

**harami [. - -]** robber.

**haramzade [. - - .]** bastard.

**harap,** -bı **[. -] 1.** ruined, in ruins, devastated; **2.** bushed, done up, worn out, exhausted; ~ etm. to ruin, to destroy, to devastate, to vandalize; ~ olm. **1.** to be ruined *(or* destroyed *or* devastated), to fall into ruin; **2.** to be bushed, to be worn out *(or* exhausted).

**haraplaşmak** to fall into ruin.

**haraplık** ruin, desolation.

**harar** large haircloth sack.

**hararet,** -ti **[. - .] 1.** heat, warmth; **2.** temperature, fever; **3.** thirst; **4.** *fig.* vehemence, fervo(u)r, exaltation; ~ basmak to feel very thirsty; ~ kesmek *(or* söndürmek) to quench one's thirst; ~ vermek to make thirsty.

**hararetlendirmek** *fig.* to excite.

**hararetlenmek [. - . . .]** to get warm *(or* excited *or* heated).

**hararetli** [. - . .] vehement, excited, lively, heated.

**haraşo** [. x .] *sl.* Russian woman.

**haraza 1.** *sl.* quarrel, row; **2.** gallstone *(of a cow or ox).*

**harbe** short lance.

**harbi 1.** ramrod; **2.** *sl.* correct, straight; ~ konuşmak *sl.* to speak straightforwardly.

**harbiye 1.** military affairs; **2.** ♀ War Academy.

**harbiyeli** cadet.

**harcama 1.** *vn.* of harcamak; **2.** outgo, outlay, expenditure.

**harcamak 1.** to spend; **2.** to use (up); **3.** to sacrifice; **4.** *sl.* to kill, to finish off.

**harcı** cheap, affordable, inexpensive.

**hacıâlem 1.** ordinary, common; **2.** unoriginal cliché.

**harcırah** travel allowance, travelling expenses.

**harç[1]**, -cı **1.** mortar; **2.** plaster; **3.** ingredients; **4.** trimming *(of a garment)*; **5.** ✓ compost; harcı olm. *(b-nin)* to be within *one's* power.

**harç[2]**, -cı **1.** outgo, outlay, expenditure; **2.** customs duty; harcını vermek *sl.* to scold, to rebuke.

**harçlı 1.** containing mortar *or* plaster; **2.** trimmed *(garment)*; **3.** with the government fee paid; liable to duty.

**harçlık** pocket-money, allowance.

**hardal** mustard.

**hardaliye** [. - . .] grape juice flavo(u)red with mustard.

**hare** [- .] **1.** moiré, water *(of cloth)*; **2.** moiréd cloth.

**harekât**, -tı ✕ operation(s), campaign.

**hareket**, -ti **1.** movement, motion; **2.** act, deed; behavio(u)r, conduct; **3.** departure; **4.** activity, stir; **5.** tremor, earthquake; **6.** ♪ tempo; **7.** *sports:* exercise(s), exercising; **8.** 🚍 traffic; ~ cetveli 🚍 timetable; ~ dairesi dispatcher's office; ~ etm. **1.** to move, to act, to stir; **2.** to behave, to act; **3.** to set out *(or* off); to depart *(-den* from); **4.** to leave *(-e* for); ~ kolu starting handle; crank; ~ noktası starting point; -e geçmek to begin (to act), to start; -e getirmek **1.** to set in motion; **2.** to stir up.

**hareketlendirmek** to put into motion.

**hareketlenmek** to get into motion.

**hareketli 1.** active, moving; **2.** animated, vivacious.

**hareketlilik 1.** activity; **2.** vivacity, animation.

**hareketsiz** motionless, inactive.

**hareketsizlik** immobility.

**harelemek** to moiré, to water *(cloth)*.

**harelenmek** to have a sheen.

**hareli** [ā] moiréd, watered, wavy; ~ ipek watered silk, moiré.

**harem 1.** harem, women's apartments; **2.** wife; ~ ağası black eunuch in the sultan's palace.

**haremlik 1.** wifehood; **2.** harem; ~ selâmlık olm. *fig.* to sit in two groups, the women being separate from the men.

**harf**, -fi letter; ~ atmak to pester, to bother; -i -ine word for word, to the letter, literatim.

**harfiyen** word for word, to the letter, literatim.

**harharyas** *zo.* man-eater, a kind of shark.

**harıl harıl 1.** incessantly, continuously; **2.** with great effort; ~ çalışmak to work like mad; ~ yanmak to burn furiously.

**harıltı** roar *(of a fire)*; ~ gürültü din.

**harın 1.** intractable *(horse)*; **2.** *fig.* obstinate, pig-headed.

**haricen** externally, outwardly.

**harici** [ā] **1.** external, exterior; **2.** foreign.

**hariciye** [ā] **1.** foreign affairs; **2.** external diseases; ♀ Vekâleti † Ministry of Foreign Affairs; ♀ Vekili † Minister of Foreign Affairs.

**hariciyeci** [- . . . .] **1.** diplomat; **2.** 🖈 specialist in external diseases.

**hariç**, -ci [ā] **1.** outside, exterior; **2.** abroad; **3.** except (for), excluded, apart (from), besides; ~ olm. *(bşden)* to be excluded from *s th.*; -ten gazel okumak *(or* atmak) to butt in.

**harika** [- . .] **1.** wonder, miracle; **2.** *fig.* marvelous, extraordinary; ~ çocuk infant prodigy; -lar yaratmak to work miracles, to do wonders.

**harikulade** [- . . . .] **1.** wonderful, marvelous; **2.** unusual, extraordinary.

**haris** [i] greedy, avaricious, ambitious, acquisitive.

**harita** map.

**haritacı** cartographer.

**haritacılık** cartography.

**harlamak 1.** to burn furiously; **2.** *fig.* to flare up.

**harlatmak** to poke up *(fire)*.

**harlı** burning in flames.

**harman 1.** threshing (floor); **2.** harvest (time); **3.** stack of grain *(ready for threshing)*; **4.** blending; **5.** blend *(tea, tobacco)*; ~ corman mixed up; ~ dövmek to thresh grain; ~ etm. *(or* yapmak) **1.** to thresh; **2.** to blend *(tea, tabacco)*; ~ makinesi thresher; ~ savurmak to win-

**now** grain; ~ **sonu 1.** the end of the threshing season; **2.** gleanings; **3.** *fig.* remnants *(of a fortune or business).*

**harmancı 1.** thresher; **2.** blender *(of tea or tobacco).*

**harmancılık 1.** threshing; **2.** blending.

**harmandalı,** -nı a folk dance *(in Izmir and vicinity).*

**harmani** [. - -], **harmaniye** [. - . .] long cape.

**harmanlamak 1.** to blend; **2.** to go in circles; **3.** ↓ to go in a circle.

**harmoni** ♪ harmony.

**harmonik ,harmonili** ♪ harmonic.

**harmonisiz** ♪ inharmonious.

**harmonyum** ♪ harmonium.

**harnup** ⚘ carob (tree).

**harp¹,** -pı ♪ harp.

**harp²,** -bi war; battle, fight; ~ açmak to start a war; ~ esiri prisoner of war; ~ filosu war fleet; ~ gemisi warship; ~ malulü war casualty; ~ meydanı battlefield; ⓞ Okulu the Turkish Military Academy; ⓞ Şûrası Supreme War Council; ~ tazminatı war indemnity; ~ zengini war profiteer.

**harrangürra** [x . x .] in a disorderly and noisy manner.

**hars** † culture.

**hart:** ~ diye with a loud crunch.

**hartadak, hartadan** [x . .] with a loud crunch.

**hartası hurtası olmamak** to show disrespect.

**hart hart, hart hurt** with a crunching sound.

**hartuç,** -cu cartridge, shell.

**harup,** -bu *s.* harnup.

**has,** -ssı [ᵃ] **1.** peculiar (-e to); belonging (-e to); special (-e to); **2.** royal, belonging to the sultan; **3.** pure, unmixed, unadulterated; ~ boya fast dye; ~ işlemek *sl.* to gooble up another's food without permission.

**hasa** (bezi) heavy cambric.

**hasar** [. -] damage, loss; ~ görmek (*or* -a uğramak) to suffer damage; ~ yapmak to cause damage.

**hasat,** -dı harvest, reaping.

**hasatçı** reaper.

**hasatçılık** harvesting.

**hasbahçe** private garden of the sultan.

**hasbıhal,** -li [. . -] chitchat; ~ etm. to have a chitchat.

**hasbi** [ⁱ] **1** voluntary, volunteer; **2.** without reason; ~ geçmek *sl.* not to care at all.

**hasebiyle** [. - .] because of, by reason of.

**hasep** merits, personal qualities.

**haset,** -ti jealousy, envy; ~ **etm.** to envy.

**hasetçi** jealous, envious.

**hasetlenmek** to feel envy.

**hasetlik** envy.

**hasıl** grain still green in the field.

**hâsıl** resulting; produced; ~ etm. to produce; ~ olm. to result, to be produced, to be obtained (-den from).

**hâsıla** [- . .] result, outcome.

**hâsılat,** -tı [- . -] **1.** products; produce; **2.** returns, revenue; proceeds.

**hâsılı** [x . .] in brief (*or* short), in a word, to sum up; ~ kelam the long and the short of it.

**hasıllanmak 1.** to grow up; **2.** to mature (*crop).*

**hasım,** -smı **1.** opponent; **2.** enemy, adversary.

**hasımlık** enmity, antagonism.

**hasır 1.** rush mat; matting; canework; wickerwork; **2.** cane..., wicker...; ~ altı etm. to sweep s.th. under the carpet (*or* rug); ~ işi wickerwork; ~ koltuk wicker chair; ~ şapka boater, straw (*or* Panama) hat; -lara sarılmak (*or* yatmak) *sl.* to take a day off *(taxi driver).*

**hasırlamak** to cover with matting, to cane.

**hasırlı 1.** caned, covered with matting; **2.** large bottle covered with wickerwork.

**hasırotu,** -nu ⚘ rush.

**hasis** [ⁱ] **1.** miserly, stingy, niggardly; **2.** base, low, vile.

**hasislik** stinginess.

**hasiyet,** -ti [ᵃ] **1.** special virtue (*or* quality); **2.** wholesomeness.

**hasiyetli** wholesome *(food).*

**haslet,** -ti trait, virtue.

**haspa** F minx, baggage.

**hasret,** -ti longing, yearning; nostalgia, homesickness; ~ çekmek to long (-e for), to yearn (-e for); ~ gitmek to die longing (-e for); ~ kalmak to feel the absence (-e of), to miss; -ini çekmek to long to see again; to miss.

**hasretli 1.** longing, yearning; **2.** homesick.

**hasretlik 1.** longing, yearning; **2.** homesickness.

**hasretmek** [x . .] to devote (-e to), to consecrate (-e to), to appropriate (-e for).

**hassa** peculiarity; quality; ~ askeri bodyguard.

**hassas** [. -] **1.** sensitive, delicate, responsive; **2.** touchy, oversensitive; **3.** susceptible (-e to).

**hassasiyet,** -ti [. . . .] **1.** sensitivity, sensitiveness; **2.** touchiness, oversensitivity.

**hassaten** [- . .] [x . .] particularly, especially.

**hasse** s. hasa.

**hasta** 1. sick, ill; 2. patient; 3. addicted (to), fond (of); ~ düşmek to get sick, to fall (or be taken) ill; ~ etm. to make ill; ~ koğuşu X sickroom; ~ olm. to get sick, to become ill; ~ yatağı sickbed; -sı olm. (bşin) F to be a fan of s.th., to be nuts over s.th., to be wild about s.th.; -ya bakmak to nurse (or look after) a patient.

**hastabakıcı** nurse's aide.

**hastalanmak** to fall ill, to get sick.

**hastalık** 1. illness, sickness; 2. disease; 3. addiction; ~ almak (or kapmak) to catch a disease; ~ geçirmek to have an illness, to be sick; ~ hastası hypochondriac; ~ sigortası health insurance; hastalığa tutulmak to get sick; hastalığa yakalanmak to fall (or be taken) ill.

**hastalıklı** sickly, ailing.

**hastane** [. - .] hospital.

**hastanelik** requiring hospitalization; ~ etm. (b-ni) F to wallop s.o.

**hasut,** -du [ū] jealous.

**haşa** X saddlecloth.

**hâşa** [x -] God forbid!; ~ huzur(unuz)dan if you'll excuse my French.

**haşarat,** -tı [. . -] 1. vermin, insects; 2. fig. the mob, the rabble.

**haşarı** 1. impish, naughty, mischievous (child); 2. ungovernable (animal).

**haşarılaşmak** to become impish (or naughty).

**haşarılık** naughtiness, impishness.

**haşat** sl. 1. worn-out car; 2. worn-out; 3. in the soup, in hot waters.

**haşere** insect.

**haşhaş** ♀ opium poppy.

**haşıl** sizing (for cloth).

**haşırdamak** to rustle.

**haşır haşır, haşır huşur** with a scraping sound.

**haşin** [ı] rough, harsh, rude.

**haşinlik** harshness, rudeness.

**haşir,** -şri doomsday, Last Judg(e)ment; ~ neşir olm. (b-le) to be cheek by jowl with s.o.

**haşiş** hashish.

**haşiv,** -şvi redundancy, padding.

**haşiye** [ā] footnote, postscript; annotation.

**haşlama** 1. vn. of haşlamak; 2. boiled.

**haşlamak** 1. to boil; 2. to scald; 3. to sting all over (insect); 4. F to scold, to rebuke.

**haşlanmak** pass. of haşlamak to be boiled; to be scalded.

**haşmet,** -ti majesty, pomp, grandeur.

**haşmetli** 1. majestic, grand, splendid,

pompous; 2. His Majesty.

**haşmetmeap** [. . . .] His Majesty.

**haşyet,** -ti fear.

**hat,** -ttı 1. line; 2. contour (of a face); 3. handwriting; calligraphy; ~ çekmek to install a line; ~ işçisi lineman; trackman.

**hata** [. -] mistake, error, fault; ~ etm. (or işlemek) to make a mistake, to err; ~ yapmak to make a mistake; -ya düşmek to fall into error, to err.

**hatalı** [. - .] 1. faulty, defective, erroneous; 2. at fault, in the wrong.

**hatasız** [. - .] 1. flawless, faultless, errorless; 2. unerring; ~ kul olmaz nobody is perfect.

**hatıl** crossbeam, horizontal beam.

**hatır** [ā] 1. memory, mind; 2. sake; 3. feelings, sensitivities; 4. consideration, influence, weight; ~ almak to please, to delight; ~ gönül personal consideration; ~ senedi accommodation bill; ~ sormak to ask (or inquire) after s.o.; ~ yapmak to please, to delight; -a gelmemek not even to occur to one; -ı için for s.o.'s sake; -ı kalmak (b-nin) to feel hurt (or offended); -ı sayılır 1. considerable; 2. respected; -ına bir şey gelmesin as the actress said to the bishop; -ına gelmek to occur to one ,to come to mind; -ında kalmak to remember; -ında olm. to have in mind; -ında tutmak to keep in mind; -ından çıkmak to pass out of one's mind; -ından geçmemek not even to think (of); -ını kırmak to offend, to give offence; -ını saymak (b-nin) to show one's respect; -ını yapmak to please, to delight.

**hatıra** 1. memory, recollection, reminiscence; 2. keepsake, souvenir, memento, remembrance; ~ defteri diary; -larını yazmak to write one's memoirs; -sı olarak in memory of.

**hatıralık** s. hatıra 2.

**hatırat,** -tı memoirs.

**hatır hatır, hatır hutur** crunch crunch, with a crunching sound; hatır hutur yemek to munch, to crunch.

**hatırlamak** to remember, to recollect, to recall.

**hatırlatmak** (b-ne bşi) to remind s.o. of s.th.

**hatırlı** [ā] influential, esteemed.

**hatırşinas** [- . . .] considerate, obliging, courteous.

**hatim,** -tmi recitation of the Koran from beginning to end; ~ indirmek to finish repeating the whole Koran.

**hatime** epilogue.

**hatip,** -bı [ī] **1.** orator; **2.** *eccl.* preacher.

**hatmetmek** [x . .] **1.** to recite from beginning to end *(the Koran)*; **2.** *co.* to read from cover to cover.

**hatmi** ♀ marsh mallow.

**hatta** [x -] even, to the extent that; besides, moreover.

**hattat,** -tı [. -] calligrapher.

**hattatlık** calligraphy.

**hattıhareket,** -ti way of procedure, line of action.

**hatun** [ā] **1.** woman; **2.** lady *(after a given name)*; **3.** wife.

**hav** nap, pile *(of cloth)*.

**hava 1.** air, atmosphere; **2.** weather; **3.** climate; **4.** the sky; **5.** wind, breeze; **6.** desire, whim, fancy; **7.** ♪ pitch of a note; **8.** ♂♂ air rights; **9.** tune, melody, air; **10.** style; **11.** (social) environment; **12.** airs, affectation; **13.** F nothing; ~ acmak *(or* açılmak*)* to clear up; ~ akımı draught, *Am.* draft; ~ akını air raid *(or* attack*)*; ~ almak **1.** to breathe fresh air; **2.** to take in *(or* absorb*)* air; **3.** *sl.* to whistle for it; ~ atmak *sl.* **1.** to put on airs, to give o.s. airs; **2.** to speak claptrap; ~ basıncı atmospheric pressure; ~ basmak = ~ atmak; ~ boşluğu **1.** air pocket; **2.** air shaft *(in a building)*; ~ bozdu it turned stormy *or* rainy; ~ bulandı *(or* bulutlandı*)* it turned rainy; ~ cereyanı draught, *Am.* draft; ~ deliği **1.** ventilation hole; **2.** ventilation conduit *(in a building)*; ~ filosu air fleet; ~ fişeği rocket; ~ freni air *(or* pneumatic*)* brake; ~ geçirmez airtight; ~ hoş olm. *(b-ne)* to be all the same to *s.o.*; ~ kabarcığı bubble; ~ kaçırmak to lose air; ~ kapanmak to be overcast *(sky)*; ~ karardı it got dark; ~ kirliliği air pollution; ~ korsanı hijacker; ~ köprüsü airlift; ~ kuvvetleri air force; ~ meydanı airport, airfield; ~ oyunu speculative trading in futures; ~ parası lump cash payment *(demanded of a renter before he is given possession)*; ~ raporu weather report; ~ tahmini weather forecast; ~ üssü air base; ~ vermek **1.** to give air, to fill with air; **2.** to aerate *(s.o.'s lungs)*; -da kalmak **1.** to be up too high; **2.** to be left in suspense; -dan **1.** free, for nothing, as a windfall; **2.** empty, worthless; -dan sudan at random, randomly; -dan sudan konuşmak to have a chitchat; -sına uymak to adapt o.s. *(-in to)*, to fit in *(-in with)*; -sını bulmak to get into a good mood; -ya gitmek to go for nothing; -ya pala *(or* kılıç*)* sallamak to beat the air,

to plough the sand(s); -ya savurmak to make the money fly.

**havaalanı,** nı- airport, airfield.

**havaaltı,** nı- *geol.* subaerial.

**havacı** airman, pilot, aviator, flyer, flier.

**havacılık** aviation.

**havacıva 1.** ♀ alkanet; **2.** *sl.* trivial, nought; **3.** *sl.* nonsense, rubbish.

**havadar** airy, well-ventilated.

**havadis** news.

**havagazı,** -nı **1.** coal gas; **2.** *sl.* rubbish.

**havai** [. - -] **1.** aerial; **2.** fanciful, flighty: irresponsible, **3.** meaningless, nonsense; **4.** *(a.* ~ mavi*)* sky-blue; ~ fişek skyrocket; ~ hat overhead railway; funicular; ~ sözler idle talk.

**havailik** flightiness, inconstancy.

**havaküre** atmosphere.

**havalandırma** ventilation.

**havalandırmak 1.** to air, to ventilate; **2.** to take up into the air *(airplane)*; **3** to fly *(kite)*.

**havalanmak 1.** to be aired *(or* ventilated*)*; **2.** ✈ to take off; **3.** to become frivolous.

**havale** [. - .] **1.** assignment, referral; **2.** money order; bill of exchange; **3.** ♂ eclampsia; **4.** hoarding; ~ cekmek to fence off; ~ etm. **1.** to transfer, to assign; to endorse over *(-e to)*; **2.** to refer *(-e to)*; ~ gelmek ♂ to have an attack of eclampsia; ~ göndermek *(or* yollamak*)* to send a money order.

**havaleli** [. - . .] **1.** top-heavy; **2.** ♂ eclamptic; **3.** fenced, enclosed.

**havalename** [. - . - .] money order.

**havalı 1.** airy; well-ventilated; breezy; **2.** eye-catching, showy; swanky; **3.** restless; **4.** pneumatic; ~ korna *(or* klakson*)* air *(or* pneumatic*)* horn.

**havali** [. - -] vicinity, environs, neighbo(u)rhood.

**havalimanı,** -nı airport.

**havan** mortar; ~ dövücünün hınk deyicisi *iro.* flatterer who agrees with all that another says; ~ topu ✗ *(trench)* mortar, howitzer; -da dövmek to pestle; -da su dövmek *fig.* to beat the air.

**havaneli,** -ni pestle.

**havaölçer 1.** barometer; **2.** aerometer.

**havari** [. - -] **1.** apostle, disciple; **2.** assistant.

**havâs** the senses.

**havasız 1.** airless; **2.** stuffy.

**havasızlık 1.** airlessness; **2.** stuffiness.

**havas·zyaşar 1.** anaerobic; **2.** anaerobe.

**havayolu,** -nu airline; ~ ile by air.

**havayuvarı,** -nı atmosphere.

**havhav** bow-wow, doggie.

**havi** including, containing; ~ olm. to include, to contain.

**havil,** -vli fear; can havliyle fearing for one's life.

**havlamak** to bark, to bay.

**havlı** 1. downy, nappy, piled; 2. *s.* havlu.

**havlu** towel.

**havlucu** towel-dealer.

**havluluk** 1. toweling; 2. towel rack; 3. towel cupboard.

**havra** [x .] 1. synagogue; 2. *fig.* bedlam.

**havsala** 1. *anat.* pelvic cavity, pelvis; 2. *fig.* intelligence, comprehension; -sı almamak to be unable to comprehend; -sı geniş tolerant, accommodating; -sına sığmamak (b-nin) to be hard for s.o. to believe.

**havşa** ⊕ countersink.

**havuç,** -cu ♀ carrot.

**havut,** -tu camel's packsaddle.

**havuz** 1. pool; pond; 2. dry dock; ~ balığı *zo.* goldfish; -a çekmek ⚓ to dock (a ship).

**havuzcuk** *anat.* calyx.

**havuzlamak** ⚓ to dock (a ship).

**Havva** [. -] *pr. n.* Eve.

**havya** [x .] ⊕ soldering iron.

**havyar** caviar; ~ kesmek *sl.* to idle around, to moon away.

**havza** *geogr.* river basin, catchment area; sphere, domain.

**hay** what a...!, alas!; ~ Allah!! my God!; ~ anasını! F what a pity!; ~ ~! certainly!, by all means!; ~ lanet kör şeytan! damn it all!; -dan gelen huya gider *pro.* easy come easy go.

**haya** [ -.] testicle.

**hayâ** shame.

**hayal,** -li [. -] 1. image; 2. imagination, fancy; 3. *phys.* image; reflection; 4. daydream; 5. ghost, spectre, *Am.* specter, phantom; ~ âlemi the realm of the imagination; ~ etm. to imagine; ~ gibi 1. like a dream; 2. a bag of bones (person); ~ gücü imaginative power; ~ kırıklığı disappointment, let-down; ~ kırıklığına uğratmak to disappoint, to let s.o. down; kurmak to dream; ~ mahsulü imaginary, fancied; ~ meyal vaguely; ~ oyunu shadow play (or show); ~ peşinde koşmak to build castles in the air (or in Spain); -e dalmak to daydream; -e kapılmak to build high hopes, to be given to fancy; -inden geçirmek (bşi) to dream of s.th., to think of s.th.

**hayalci** [. - .] 1. unrealistic; 2. visionary, dreamer; 3. puppeteer in shadow plays.

**hayalet,** -ti [. - .] ghost, phantom, apparition, spectre, *Am.* specter.

**hayalhane** [. - - .] imagination, imaginative power.

**hayali** [. - -] 1. imaginary, fantastic, visionary, chimerical; 2. = hayalci 3.

**hayalifener** [. - . . .] *fig.* skinny (person).

**hayalperest,** -ti 1. fanciful; 2. visionary, daydreamer.

**hayalperestlik** fancifulness, daydreaming.

**hayâsız** shameless, impudent.

**hayat,** -tı [. - .] 1. life; 2. P courtyard (of a house); 3. P veranda, porch; ~ adamı man of the world; ~ arkadaşı life partner; ~ kadını prostitute, whore; ~ memat meselesi matter of life and death; ~ mücadelesi (or kavgası) life struggle; ~ pahalılığı high cost of living; ~ standardı standard of living; ~ sigortası life insurance; ~ sürmek to live a life; ~ vermek to enliven; -a atılmak to begin to work; -a gözlerini yummak (or kapamak) to depart this life, to die; -a küsmek to be weary of life; -ı kaymak *sl.* to go to the dogs; -ı zindan etm. (b-ne) *fig.* to make s.o.'s life a hell; -ım! my love!, my darling!; -ın baharı the prime of life; -ına mal olm. (b-nin) to cost s.o. his life; -ını kazanmak (or temin etm.) to earn one's living, to make a living; -ını yaşamak to lead a life of ease; -ta olm. to be living (or alive).

**hayatağacı,** -nı 1. *anat.* arborvitae; 2. family tree, genealogical chart.

**hayati** [. - -] 1. vital; 2. ♀ *mf.*

**hayatiyet,** -ti [. - . .] 1. vitality, vigo(u)r; 2. liveliness.

**haybeci** *sl.* sucker.

**haybeden** *sl.* free, gratis, for nothing.

**hayda** 1. giddap!; 2. what on earth!

**haydalamak** to urge (or drive) on (an animal).

**haydamak.** 1. = haydalamak; 2. *sl.* to sack. to fire.

**haydi** [x .], **hadi** 1. come on!; 2. let's say; 3. OK. all right; 4. come off it!, rubbish!; ~ bakalım come on then, hurry up; ~ canım sen de! F 1. that's bunk!, you're talking crap!; 2. who do you think you're fooling?; ~ gidelim come along, let's go; ~ git! off with you!; ~ ~ 1. cut it short!, there are no flies on us!; 2. easily, amply; 3. hurry up!; 4. at the very most; ~ oradan 1. clear out!, piss off!; 2. who do you think you're fooling?

**haydin** [x .] F come on all of you, hurry up!

**haydindi** F come along!, hurry up!

**haydisene** [. . x .] F come on!

**haydut**, -du brigand, bandit, robber; ~ yatağı brigands' den, robbers' roost, bandits' hide-out.

**haydutluk** brigandage.

**hayhay** by all means!, certainly!

**hayhuy 1.** tumult; confusion; **2.** *fig.* fruitless struggle.

**hayıf**, -yfı **1.** injustice; **2.** what a pity!

**hayıflanmak** to lament; to regret, to repent.

**hayır¹** [x .] no; ~ demek to say no.

**hayır²**, -yrı **1.** charity, philanthropy; **2.** fortune; **3.** use(fulness); ~ etm. to do good (-e to), to be of use; ~ gelmemek to be of no help; ~ görmemek (bşden) not to benefit from s.th.; ~ işlemek to do good, to be of use; ~ kalmamak to be of no more use; ~ kurumu charitable foundation, philanthropic institution; ~ ola (or hayrola)! what's up?, I hope nothing is wrong; ~ sahibi benefactor, philanthropist; ~ yok (b-den) he's of no use; hayra alamet good (or auspicious) sign; hayra alamet değil it bodes no good; hayra yormak to interpret favo(u)rably, to regard as auspicious (dream, omen); hayrı dokunmak to be of use (-e to), to be a help (-e to); hayrı yok it is good for nothing; -dır inşallah! **1.** I hope all is well!; **2.** I hope the dream is a good sign!; hayrını görün! may it bring you good luck!, enjoy using it!

**hayırdua** [. . . -] benediction, blessing.

**hayırhah** [. . -] benevolent, well-wishing.

**hayırlaşmak** to exchange good wishes after having concluded a bargain.

**hayırlı 1.** good, auspicious beneficial, advantageous, favo(u)rable; **2.** good, happy (journey); ~ haberler good news; ~ yolculuklar have a good trip; -sı (olsun)! let's hope for the best!

**hayırperver** benevolent.

**hayırsever** charitable.

**hayırsız 1.** good for nothing, useless; **2.** unfaithful, disloyal.

**hayız**, -yzı menstruation, period; ~ görmek to menstruate; -dan kesilme menopause.

**haykırı 1.** outcry, scream; **2.** *gr.* exclamation, interjection; ~ işareti exclamation mark.

**haykırış** shout, cry.

**haykırışmak** to scream (or shout) together.

**haykırmak 1.** to cry out, to bawl, to scream, to shout; **2.** to protest loudly.

**haylamak 1.** = haydalamak; **2.** to shove, to prod (a person); **3.** sl. to pay attention (to), to heed.

**haylaz 1.** idle, lazy; **2.** loafer, idler, lazybones.

**haylazlaşmak 1.** to get lazy, to loaf; **2.** to make mischief.

**haylazlık** idleness, laziness; ~ etm. **1.** to loaf; **2.** to make mischief.

**hayli** [x .] many, much; a good deal, very; fairly; bir ~ = ~.

**haylice** considerably, somewhat, much.

**haymana** prairie, pasture; ~ beygiri gibi dolaşmak to gad (or knock) about; ~ mandası (or öküzü or sığırı) *fig.* hulk, do-nothing, sluggard.

**haymatlos** stateless.

**hayran** [. -] **1.** admirer, lover, adorer, fan; **2.** astonished, perplexed; ~ bırakmak (or etm.) (b-ni) to charm s.o., to entrance s.o.; ~ kalmak (or olm.) (bşe) to be entranced by s.th., to admire s.th., to be astonished (or perplexed).

**hayranlık** [. - .] admiration, appreciation; adoration.

**hayrat**, -tı [. -] **1.** pious foundation; **2.** charities, pious deeds.

**hayret**, -tı **1.** astonishment, amazement, surprise; **2.** how surprising!; ~ etm. to be surprised (-e at), to be astonished (-e at); ~ verici amazing, astonishing, -e düşmek to be astounded; -te bırakmak to astound; -te kalmak to be lost in amazement.

**hayrola** s. hayır ola.

**haysiyet**, -tı self-respect, dignity, hono(u)r, amour-propre; ~ divanı (or kurulu) discipline committee; ~ sahibi self-respecting; -iyle because of.

**haysiyetli** self-respecting, dignified.

**haysiyetsiz** without dignity, lacking in self-respect.

**hayta** [x .] **1.** † mercenary cavalryman; **2.** *fig.* vagabond; **3.** F street urchin.

**haytalık** *fig.* vagabondage.

**hayvan 1.** animal; **2.** *fig.* beast, brute; ~ alım satımı livestock market; ~ gibi **1.** asinine, stupid; **2.** brutally, coarsely; ~ hırsızı rustler.

**hayvanat**, -tı [. . -] **1.** animals; **2.** † zoology; ~ bahçesi zoo. zoological garden.

**hayvanbilim** zoology.

**hayvanca(sına)** bestially, brutishly, brutally.

**hayvancık** animalcule.

**hayvancılık 1.** stockbreeding; **2.** cattle-dealing.

**hayvani** [. - -] **1.** brutal, brutish, animal-like, bestial; **2.** carnal, sensual; ~ kuvvet brute force.

**hayvankömürü**, -nü boneblack, animal charcoal.

**hayvanlaşmak** to become bestial (or brutal), to be brutalized.

**hayvanlık 1.** animalism; **2.** fig. bestiality, brutishness; ~ etm. to act like a turd.

**hayvansal** animal... (product).

**haz**, -zzı delight, pleasure, gusto, enjoyment; ~ duymak to be greatly gratified (-den by).

**hâzâ** [- -] F perfect, complete.

**hazakat**, -ti skill, ability.

**hazan** autumn, Am. fall.

**hazar** peace.

**Hazar** pr. n. Khazar; ~ Denizi Caspian Sea.

**hazcı** hedonist(ic).

**hazcılık** hedonism.

**hazfetmek** [x . .] to remove, to delete.

**hazık**, -kı [â] skillful, expert (doctor).

**hazım**, -zmı digestion; hazmı güc indigestible.

**hâzım** digestive.

**hazımlı** fig. tolerant, patient.

**hazımsız** fig. irritable, touchy.

**hazımsızlık** ₹ indigestion.

**hazır 1.** ready, prepared; **2.** ready-made (garment); **3.** present, in attendance; **4.** seeing that, now that, since; ~ bulunmak (or olm.) **1.** to be present (-de at); **2.** to be ready; ~ etm. to prepare, to get ready; ~ giyim ready-made clothing; ~ ol! X attention!; ~ para ready money, cash; ~ yiyici one who lives on his capital; -a konmak fig. to enjoy the fruits of others' labo(u)rs; -dan yemek to live on one's capital.

**hazırcevap**, -bı ready-witted, quick at repartee.

**hazırcı** seller of ready-made clothing, outfitter.

**hazırlamak 1.** to prepare, to make ready; **2.** ₼ to dispense.

**hazırlanmak 1.** pass. of hazırlamak; **2.** to get ready.

**hazırlık 1.** readiness; **2.** preparation; ~ görmek to get things ready, to make preparations; ~ okulu prep (or preparatory) school; ~ sınıfı preparatory year; ~ tahkikatı (or soruşturması) 🕮 preliminary investigations.

**hazırlıklı** (well) prepared; ~ olm. to be prepared.

**hazırlop**, -pu **1.** hard-boiled (egg); **2.** fig. effortless.

**hazin** [¹] sad, tragic, touching, pathetic, melancholic.

**hazine** [¹] **1.** treasure (a. fig.); **2.** treasury;

strongroom; **3.** national treasury; **4.** treasure-trove; **5.** depot; cistern; **6.** anat. uterus, womb.

**hazinedar** [. - . -] treasurer.

**haziran** [¹] June.

**hazmetmek** [x . .] **1.** to digest; **2.** fig. to stomach, to swallow.

**hazne** s. hazine.

**haznedar** [. . -] s. hazinedar.

**hazret**, -ti **1.** Excellency; **2.** co. old fellow; -leri (after a title) His Excellency.

**hazzetmek** [x . .] to like, to enjoy.

**he!** P yes!, yeah!; ~ demek (bşe) to accept s.th., to consent to s.th.; ~ mi? P is that all right?

**heba** [â] waste, loss; ~ etm. to waste, to spoil.

**hebenneka** idiot, fool.

**heccav** [â] ℞ satirist.

**hece** gr. syllable; ~ vezni syllabic meter.

**hecelemek** to spell.

**heceli** ...syllabled.

**hecin** [¹] (devesi) zo. dromedary.

**hedef 1.** target, mark; **2.** fig. aim, object, goal; ~ almak to aim (-i at); ~ olm. (bşe) to be the butt of s.th.; -e isabet etm. **1.** to hit the target; **2.** fig. to attain one's object.

**heder** loss, waste; ~ etm. to waste; ~ olm. to be wasted.

**hediye 1.** present, gift; **2.** price (of a sacred book); ~ etm. to give as a gift (-e to).

**hediyelik** fit for a present.

**hegemonya** hegemony.

**hekim** [¹] doctor, physician.

**hekimlik** [. - .] **1.** doctorship; **2.** medicine, medical science.

**hektar** hectare.

**hektogram** hectogram(me).

**hektolitre** hectolitre, Am. hectoliter.

**hektometre** hectometre, Am. hectometer.

**hela** toilet, loo, water closet, privy.

**helak**, -kı **1.** death; murder; **2.** destruction; **3.** fatigue, exhaustion; ~ etm. **1.** to kill, to finish off; **2.** fig. to tire out, to exhaust; ~ olm. **1.** to perish; **2.** fig. to be bushed.

**helal**, -li **1.** permissible, canonically lawful; **2.** fig. F lawful spouse; ~ etm. (bşi b-ne) to give up s.th. to s.o.; ~ olsun! take it with my blessings!, no need to thank!; ~ süt emmiş trustworthy; -ü hoş olsun! let it be yours to have and enjoy!; -inden lawfully .legitimately, honestly.

**helallaşmak** to forgive each other mutually.

**helalli** = helal 2.

**helallik** † **1.** = helal 2; **2.** waiving *(rights, etc.)*; ~ dilemek to ask forgiveness for an unlawful act.

**hele** [x .] **1.** especially, above all; **2.** you had better not; **3.** if (only); **4.** look here!; ~ bak! just look!; ~ bir **1.** you had better not...; **2.** let's wait until...; ~ ~ now tell me the truth; ~ şükür! thank goodness!, at last!

**helecan** palpitation.

**Helen** Greek, Grecian.

**helezon 1.** spiral, helix; helicoid; **2.** ₹ spiral.

**helezoni** [¹] spiral, helical; helicoidal; ~ merdiven spiral (or winding) staircase: ~ yay spiral spring.

**helezonlanmak** to form a spiral.

**helikoit** helicoid.

**helikon** helicon.

**helikopter** helicopter.

**helis** A helix.

**helke** pail, bucket.

**helme** thick liquid *(made by boiling starchy substances)*; ~ dökmek to become thick and soupy *(cooking water)*.

**helmelenmek** = helme dökmek.

**helmeli** thick and soupy.

**helva** halva(h); ~ demesini de biliriz, halva demesini de *fig.* I can speak politely, but at a pinch I can also speak rudely.

**helvacı** maker *or* seller of halva(h).

**helvacıkabağı**, -nı ❧ pumpkin.

**helvahane** [. . - .] shallow pan used for cooking halva(h).

**helyosta** [. x .] heliostat.

**helyum** ♁ helium.

**hem 1.** both ... and; **2.** and also, besides, too; **3.** even; (ve) ~ de and besides, moreover, and also, both ∴. and, as well as; ~ de nasıl! and how!; ~ nalına, ~ mıhına vurmak *fig.* to waver between two sides; ~ suçlu, ~ güçlü offensive though at fault; ~ ziyaret, ~ ticaret it's a combination of business and pleasure.

**hematit**, -ti hematite.

**hematoloji** hematology.

**hemayar** equal; of the same kind.

**hemcins** equal, fellow; of the same kind.

**hemdert**, -di fellow sufferer, confidant.

**hemen** [x .] **1.** right away; right now, immediately, at once; **2.** almost, nearly; about; ~ ~ **1.** almost, very nearly; **2.** pretty soon; ~ sonra **1.** immediately after, right after; **2.** immediately afterwards; ~ şimdi at once, right now.

**hemencecik** [. x . .] F at once.

**hemencek** [x . .] F = hemencecik.

**hemfikir** of the same opinion, like-minded.

**hemhal**, -li [ª] in the same boat.

**hemhudut**, -du contiguous.

**hemoglobin** *biol.* hemoglobin.

**hemoroit**, -di h(a)emorrhoids, piles.

**hempa** accomplice, confederate.

**hemşeri 1.** fellow townsman (or countryman), fellow citizen, compatriot; **2.** hey friend!

**hemşerilik** citizenship.

**hemşire** [¹] **1.** nurse; **2.** sister.

**hemşirelik 1.** nursing; **2.** sisterhood.

**hemşirezade** [. - . - .] nephew, niece *(of one's sister)*.

**hemze** *gr.* hamza.

**hendek** ditch, trench, dike, dyke, moat.

**hendese** geometry.

**hendesi** geometrical.

**hengâme** tumult, uproar.

**hentbol**, -lü handball.

**henüz** [x .] **1.** (only) just, a minute or so ago; **2.** *(in negative sentences)* yet.

**hep**, -pi **1.** all, the whole; **2.** always; ~ beraber all together; ~ bir ağızdan in unison, with one voice; ~ birlikte all together; -imiz all of us.

**hepçil** omnivorous.

**hepsi**, -ni [x .] all of it; all of them.

**hepten** F entirely.

**hepyek**, -ki *dice:* double one.

**her** every, each; ~ an at any moment; ~ bakımdan in every respect; ~ bir each, every single; ~ biri each one, every one (of); ~ daim always; ~ defa (or defasında) each time; ~ derde deva cure-all, panacea, nostrum; ~ durumda in any case; ~ gördüğün sakallıyı baban sanma *pro.* all that glistens (or glitters or glisters) is not gold; ~ gün every day; ~ günkü everyday; ~ günlük everyday clothes; ~ halde **1.** in any case; **2.** in all probability; for sure; ~ horoz kendi çöplüğünde öter *pro.* every cock crows on his own dunghill; ~ hususta in all respects in every way, from all points of view; ~ ihtimale karşı just in case; ~ inişin bir yokuşu, her yokuşun bir inişi vardır *pro.* every flow must have its ebb, and every ebb has its flow; ~ işe burnunu sokmak to poke one's nose into everything; ~ işte bir hayır vardır *pro.* every cloud has a silver lining; ~ kim whoever; ~ kim olursa olsun no matter who it is, whoever it may be; ~ nasılsa somehow or other; ~ ne whatever; ~ ne hal ise anyway, anyhow; ~ ne ise **1.** so anyhow; **2.** anyway; let's forget it; **3.** whatever the cost; ~ ne kadar although however much; ~ ne pahasına olursa olsun at any cost; ~ nerede wherever; ~ ne zaman whenever; ~ nedense somehow, I don't know why; ~ şey everything; ~ şeye burnunu sokmak = ~ işe burnunu sokmak; ~ tarafta (or yerde) everywhere, all around; ~ taraftan from everywhere; ~ tarakta bezi olm. to have a finger in every pie; ~ zaman always.

**hercai** [. - -] **1.** watered, shot (silk); **2.** fig. fickle, inconstant.

**hercailik** [. - - .] inconstancy.

**hercaimenekşe** [. - - ... .] ⚘ pansy.

**hercümerç,** -ci tumultuous, confused, disordered.

**herek,** -ki stake, pale.

**hereklemek** to stake (vine, plant).

**hergele 1.** unbroken horse; **2.** fig. scoundrel, rake, rascal.

**herhangi** whichever, whatever; (in negative sentences) whatsoever, any; ~ bir (just) any; ~ biri anyone, anybody.

**herif 1.** contp. fellow, rascal; **2.** P man, gent; **3.** P husband, hubby.

**herifçioğlu,** -nu sl. the fellow.

**herk,** -ki fallow field.

**herkes** [x .] everyone, everybody.

**Herkül** Hercules.

**herrü:** ya herrü ya merrü! we will have to take the consequences!

**Hersek** pr. n. Herzegovina.

**heryerdelik** omnipresence.

**herze** nonsense, rubbish; ~ yemek F to make a blunder.

**herzevekil** busyboody, nosy parker.

**hesabi** [. - -] economical, thrifty, closefisted.

**hesap,** -bı [â] **1.** arithmetic; **2.** account; **3.** calculation, computation; **4.** bill, Am. check; **5.** estimate; **6.** expectation, plan; ~ açmak to open an account; ~ bakiyesi balance; ~ arrears; ~ cetveli slide rule; ~ cüzdanı bankbook, passbook; ~ çıkarmak to make out the accounts; ~ etm. **1.** to calculate, to add up, to compute, to count; **2.** to estimate, to reckon, to project; **3.** to expect, to plan; ~ etmek kitap etm. to think twice; ~ görmek **1.** to pay (or foot) the bill; **2.** to settle accounts; ~ günü doomsday; ~ istemek to ask for the bill (or account); ~ kitap F **1.** after careful calculation; **2.** after full consideration; ~ makinesi calculator, calculating machine, adding machine; ~ müfettişi auditor; ~ sormak (b-den) to call s.o. to account; ~ tutmak **1.** to keep the books, to do the bookkeeping; **2.** to keep a record; ~ uzmanı trained accountant; ~ vermek (b-ne) to give s.o. an account;

(hesaba): ~ almak to take into account; ~ almamak to leave out of account; ~ çekmek (b-ni) to call s.o. to account; ~ geçirmek to enter in an account; ~ geçmek to debit s.o.'s account; ~ gelmez **1.** countless; **2.** unexpected, unforeseen; ~ katmak to take into account (or consideration); (hesabı): ~ kapa(t)mak to pay one's debt; ~ kesmek **1.** to stop doing business (ile with); **2.** fig. to cut all relations (ile with); ~ kitabı yok fig. it has no limits, it is uncontrolled; ~ kuvvetli good at figures; ~ yok innumerable; -na gelmek (b-nin) to fit one's views (or interest), to suit; -nı bilmek fig. to be economical; -nı görmek **1.** to pay the bill; **2.** to settle accounts; hesaptan düşmek **1.** to deduct; **2.** to write off (a person, etc.).

**hesapça** [. x .] according to calculation, supposedly.

**hesapçı 1.** thrifty; **2.** accountant.

**hesaplamak** = hesap etm.; ~ kitaplamak = hesap etmek kitap etm.

**hesaplaşmak 1.** to settle accounts mutually; **2.** fig. to settle (or square or balance) accounts (ile with), to get even (ile with).

**hesaplı 1.** economical, affordable; **2.** thrifty (person); **3.** well considered (or calculated); **4.** fig. moderate, rational, reasonable.

**hesapsız 1.** undocumented; **2.** innumerable, countless, incalculable; **3.** not properly considered; **4.** excessively; ~ kitapsız **1.** undocumented, unrecorded (expenses); **2.** fig. thoughtlessly, casually, at random.

**heterogen** ⚗ heterogeneous.

**hevenk,** -gi hanging bunch of fruit.

**heves 1.** desire, spirit, inclination, enthusiasm; **2.** fad, fancy, passing whim, crush; ~ etm. (bşe) to have a desire (or fancy or liking) for s.th.; -i kaçmak to lose interest; -ini almak ta satisfy one's desire; -ini kaçırmak to dishearten, to discourage.

**heveskâr** s. hevesli.

**heveslendirmek** to arouse s.o.'s interest.

**heveslenmek** to desire, to long (-e for).

**hevesli 1.** desirous (-e of), eager (-e for), enthusiastic (-e about, over); **2.** = amatör.

**hevessiz** uninterested, disinclined.

**hey!** hey (you)!, look here!; o...!

**heyamola** [. . x .] ⚓ heave, ho!; ~ ile F with great difficulty.

**heybe** saddlebag.

**heybet,** -ti grandeur, majesty, awe.
**heybetli** awesome, awe-inspiring, grand, majestic, imposing.
**heyecan** [ᵃ] **1.** excitement; **2.** enthusiasm; ~ **duymak 1.** to get excited; **2.** to be enthusiastic; -**a gelmek** (or **kapılmak**) to get excited.
**heyecanlandırmak** to excite, to thrill.
**heyecanlanmak** [. . - . .] **1.** to get excited, to be enthusiastic; **2.** to be upset.
**heyecanlı 1.** excited, thrilled; **2.** excitable; lively; **3.** exciting, thrilling.
**heyecansız 1.** unexcited, calm; **2.** unexciting, unemotional.
**heyelan** landslide.
**heyet,** -ti **1.** committee, commission; delegation; board; **2.** † astronomy; -**iyle** as it is, as a whole; **heyeti umumiye** the whole.
**heyhat,** -tı [. - ] alas!
**heyhey** nervous upset, jitters; -**ler geçirmek** (or -**leri tutmak**) to suffer from nervous fits; -**leri üstünde olm.** to have the jitters.
**heykel** statue; ~ **gibi** statuesque.
**heykelci** s. heykeltıraş.
**heykelcilik** s. heykeltıraşlık.
**heykeltıraş** sculptor.
**heykeltıraşlık** sculpture.
**heyula** [. - -] **1.** chaos; **2.** specter, bogy.
**hezaren** [ᵃ] 9 **1.** rattan palm; **2.** larkspur.
**hezel** parody, burlesque.
**hezeyan** [ᵃ] **1.** nonsensical talk; **2.** delirium, raving; ~ **e:m.** to drivel, to piffle.
**hezimet,** -ti [ⁱ] rout; -**e uğramak** to get clobbered; -**e uğratmak** to rout, to clobber.
**hı** F yes.
**hıçkıra hıçkıra** sobbingly.
**hıçkırık 1.** hiccup, hiccough; **2.** sob; ~ **tutmak** to have the hiccups (or hiccoughs); -**la ağlamak** to sob.
**hıçkırmak 1.** to hiccup, to hiccough; **2.** to sob.
**hıdrellez 1.** beginning of summer (May 6th); **2.** the half year from May 6th to November 8th.
**hıfız,** -fzı **1.** protection, preservation; **2.** memorization.
**hıfzetmek** [x . .] **1.** to protect, to preserve; **2.** to memorize.
**hıfzıssıhha** hygiene.
**hık** hiccup, hiccough; ~ **demiş anasının burnundan düşmüş** F he is the spit and image of his mother, he is the spitting image of his mother; ~ **mık etm.** F to hem and haw.
**hılt,** -tı biol. humo(u)r.

**hım** F hmm, I see.
**hımbıl** sluggish, indolent.
**hım hım** masally; ~ **konuşmak to na**salize.
**hımhım** one who nasalizes.
**hımış** ⊕ timber construction with brick filling.
**hıncahınç** [x . .] jammed, packed, chock-a-block.
**hınç,** -cı grudge, ranco(u)r, hatred; -**ını almak** to revenge; -**ını çıkarmak** to vent one's spleen (-**den** on), to take revenge (-**den** on).
**hındım** sl. orgy, carousal.
**hındımlamak** sl. to jump on, to attack.
**hınk deyici** F one who pretends to be helpful.
**hınt** sl. stupid, crazy.
**hınzır** F swine.
**hınzırlık 1.** nastiness; **2.** mischief; ~ **etm.** to behave nastily.
**hır** sl. row, quarrel; ~ **çıkarmak** sl. to kick up a row.
**hırbo** [x .] sl. oafish, loutish.
**hırçın 1.** ill-tempered, peevish, cross; **2.** fig. tempestuous (sea).
**hırçınlaşmak** to show a bad temper.
**hırçınlık** peevishness, irritability.
**hırdavat,** -tı **1.** hardware; **2.** junk.
**hırdavatçı 1.** hardware-seller; **2.** junkdealer, ironmonger.
**hırdavatçılık** ironmongery.
**hırgür** F squabble, row; ~ **çıkarmak** F to make a row (or scene).
**hırıldamak** to wheeze.
**hırıltı 1.** wheeze; **2.** snarl; **3.** fig. F squabble, row.
**hırıltıcı** fig. F quarrelsome.
**hırıltılı** wheezy.
**hırızma** [. x .] nose ring.
**Hıristiyan** pr. n. Christian.
**Hıristiyanlaşmak** to become a Christian.
**Hıristiyanlaştırmak** to Christianize.
**Hıristiyanlık** pr. n. **1.** Christianity; **2.** Christendom.
**Hıristo teyeli** cross-stitch.
**hırka** cardigan.
**hırlamak 1.** to snarl (at), to growl (at); **2.** to wheeze; **3.** F to rail (at).
**hırlanmak** to grumble, Am. to grouch.
**hırlaşmak 1.** to snarl at each other (dogs); **2.** F to rail at each other.
**hırlı:** ~ **mıdır, hırsız mıdır bilmiyorum** I don't know whether he is honest or not.
**hırpalamak 1.** to buffet; to ill-treat, to misuse; **2.** fig. to manhandle, to rough up.
**hırpani** [. - -] F ragged, in tatters, unkempt.
**hırs 1.** greed; **2.** anger, rage, fury; -**ını**

**alamamak** to be unable to control one's anger; **-ından çatlamak** to be ready to burst with anger; **-ını çıkarmak** *(b-den)* to vent one's spleen on *s.o.*

**hırsız** thief, burglar, robber; ~ **çetesi** gang of thieves; ~ **gibi** stealthily; ~ **yatağı** 1. den of thieves; 2. fence.

**hırsızlama** stealthily, surreptitiously.

**hırsızlık** theft, burglary, robbery; ♂♂ **larceny**; ~ **etm.** (*or* **yapmak**) to commit theft, to steal; ~ **malı** stolen goods.

**hırslandırmak** to infuriate, to anger.

**hırslanmak** to get angry, to become furious.

**hırslı** 1. angry, furious; 2. *fig.* greedy, avaricious.

**hırt, -tı** *sl.* conceited blockhead, pretentious fool.

**hırtapoz** *sl. s.* **hırt.**

**hırtı pırtı** F junk rubbish, lumber.

**hırtlamba** F shabby, dressed in rags; ~ **gibi** giyinmek to be dressed in several layers of shabby clothes; **-sı çıkmış** 1. in rags and tatters; 2. thin and bony.

**Hırvat, -tı** *pr. n.* 1. Croat; 2. Croatian.

**Hırvatça** *pr. n.* Croatian, the Croat language.

**Hırvatistan** *pr. n.* Croatia.

**hısım** 1. relative, kin; 2. in-law; ~ **akraba** kith and kin.

**hısımlık** kinship.

**hış hış** with a rustling sound; ~ **etm.** to rustle.

**hışıldamak** to rustle.

**hışıltı** rustle; froufrou.

**hışım, -şmı** rage, anger, fury; **hışmına uğramak** *(b-nin)* to be the object of *s.o.'s* rage.

**hışır** 1. unripe melon; 2. rind of a melon; 3. *sl.* uncouth; **-i çıkmak** F 1. to be worn out (*or* tattered); 2. to be bushed (*or* worn out).

**hışırdamak** to rustle, to grate.

**hışırdatmak** to rustle.

**hışır hışır** *s.* **hış hış.**

**hışırtı** rustle.

**hışlamak** *s.* **hışıldamak.**

**hıyanet, -ti** [ā] 1. treachery, perfidy, infidelity; 2. ♂♂ treason; 3. F disloyal, faithless (*person*).

**hıyar**[1] 1. ♀ cucumber; 2. *sl.* dolt, blockhead, swine.

**hıyar**[2] [ā] ♂♂ option.

**hıyarağa** *sl.* swine, dolt.

**hıyarcık, hıyarcıl** ♥ bubo, adenoma, glandular tumo(u)r.

**hıyarlaşmak** *sl.* to begin to act like a swine.

**hız** 1. speed; 2. momentum, impetus; 3. velocity; ~ **almak** to get up speed, to take a running start; ~ **vermek** 1. *(bşe)* to speed *s.th.* up; 2. to urge on; **-ını alamamak** 1. to be unable to slow down, to be out of control; 2. to be unable to get up to speed; **-ını almak** 1. to slow down; 2. to calm down, to subside.

**hızar** ⊕ large (*or* pit) saw.

**hızarcı** pit sawyer.

**Hızır** *isl. myth.*: ~ **gibi yetişmek** to come as a godsend, to be heaven-sent.

**hızlandırmak** to accelerate, to speed up.

**hızlanmak** to gain speed (*or* momentum), to be accelerated.

**hızlı** 1. speedy, rapid, quick, swift; 2. loud; 3. strong (*blow*); 4. forcefully, strongly; ~ **konuşmayınız, rica ederim!** be quiet, please!; ~ **yaşamak** F to live fast, to live it up.

**hızlılık** speed, velocity.

**hızölçer** ⊕ anemometer.

**hibe** donation, gift; ~ **etm.** to donate.

**hicap, -bı** shame, embarrassment; bashfulness; ~ **duymak** to feel ashamed, to be embarrassed.

**Hicaz** [ā] *pr. n.* the Hejaz.

**hicaz** [. -] ♪ a makam.

**hicazkâr** [. . -] ♪ a makam.

**hiciv, -cvi** satire; lampoon.

**hicivci** satirist; lampooner.

**hicran** [. -] 1. separation; 2. sadness.

**hicret, -ti** 1. emigration; 2. *eccl.* the Hegira; ~ **etm.** to migrate.

**hicri** of the Hegira; ~ **takvim** the Moslem calendar.

**hicvetmek** [x . .] to satirize; to lampoon.

**hicviye** satirical poem; lampoon.

**hiç, -çi** 1. never, not at all; 2. nothing (at all); 3. (*in negative sentences and questions*) ever; at all; 4. ♀ zero, nil; ~ **bir** not even one; ~ **biri** none of them; ~ **bir surette** in no way, by no means; ~ **bir şey** nothing (at all); ~ **bir yerde** nowhere; ~ **bir zaman** never; ~ **de** not at all; ~ **değil** no, not at all; ~ **değilse** at least; ~ **kimse** nobody, no one; ~ **kuşku yok** beyond a doubt, undoubtedly; ~ **mi** hiç really never; ~ **olmazsa** at least; ~ **öyle şey olur mu?** is it possible?. it won't do; ~ **yoktan** for no reason at all; ~ **yoktan iyi** better than nothing at all; ~ **yoktan kavga çıkarmak** to kick up a row for no reason; **-e saymak** to make light (*-i* of), to disregard.

**hicleşmek** to become insignificant.

**hiçlik** 1. nullity. nothingness; 2. poverty.

**hiçten** 1. worthless; 2. unnecessarily.

**hidayet,** -ti [ä] **1.** the way to Islam, the right way; **2.** ♀ *mf. or wf.*; **-e ermek to** become a Moslem.

**hiddet,** -ti anger, fury, rage.

**hiddetlendirmek** to anger.

**hiddetlenmek** to get angry (*or* furious).

**hiddetli** angry, furious.

**hidrasit** ♫ hydracid.

**hidrat,** -tı ♫ hydrate.

**hidrobiyoloji** hydrobiology.

**hidrodinamik** hydrodynamic(s).

**hidroelektrik** hydroelectric; **~ santralı** hydroelectric power plant.

**hidrofil 1.** hydrophilic; **2.** absorbent; **~ pamuk** absorbent cotton.

**hidrofobi** hydrophobia.

**hidrofor** pressure tank for a water supply.

**hidrojen** ♫ hydrogen; **~ bombası** hydrogen bomb, H-bomb.

**hidrokarbon** ♫ hydrocarbon.

**hidroklorik asit** ♫ hydrochloric acid.

**hidroksil** ♫ hydroxyl group.

**hidroksit,** -ti ♫ hydroxide.

**hidrolik** hydraulic(s); **~ fren** hydraulic brake.

**hidroliz** hydrolysis.

**hidroloji** hydrology.

**hidromekanik 1.** hydromechanics; **2.** hydromechanical.

**hidrometre** hydrometer.

**hidrosfer** hydrosphere.

**hidroskopi** water-divining, dowsing, rhabdomancy.

**hidrostatik** hydrostatic(s).

**hidroterapi** hydrotherapy.

**higrometre** hygrometer.

**higroskop,** -pu hygroscope.

**hikâye 1.** story, tale, narration; **2.** F tall story, whopper; **~ bileşik zamanı** *gr.* compound tense formed by adding the past tense; **~ etmek** to narrate, to tell, to relate.

**hikâyeci 1.** storyteller, narrator; **2.** short story writer.

**hikâyecilik 1.** the art of storytelling; **2.** short story writing.

**hikâyeleme** narration.

**hikmet,** -ti **1.** wisdom; **2.** philosophy; **3.** hidden (*or* inner) meaning; **4.** purpose, point; **5.** the unknowable intentions of God; **6.** † physics; **7.** ♀ *mf. or wf.*; **-inden sual olunmaz** Heaven only knows why.

**hilaf 1.** opposite, contrary; **2.** F lie; **~ olmasın!** F if I'm not mistaken!; **~ söylemek** to tell a lie; **-ına** contrary (*-in* to), in opposition (*or* contravention) (*-in* to).

**hilafet,** -ti Caliphate.

**hilafsız** for sure, surely, undoubtedly.

**hilal,** -li **1.** crescent moon; **2.** crescent; **3.** † pointer (*once used by children learning to read*); **~ gibi** narrow and arched (*eyebrow*).

**hile** [ï] **1.** trick, ruse, deceit, wile, fraud; **2.** adulteration; **~ hurda bilmez** (*or* **-si hurdası yok**) there is nothing tricky about him; **~ yapmak 1.** to cheat, to swindle, to trick; **2.** to adulterate.

**hilebaz, hilekâr** *s.* hileci.

**hileci** [- . .] **1.** deceitful, tricky, dishonest; **2.** swindler, trickster, fraud.

**hilecilik** trickery, fraud.

**hilekârlık** *s.* hilecilik.

**hileli** [- . .] **1.** tricky; ♂♀ fraudulent; **2.** adulterated, impure; **~ iflas** ♂♀ fraudulent bankruptcy.

**hilesiz 1.** honest, upright; **2.** aboveboard, free of fraud (*or* trickery); **3.** unadulterated, pure.

**hilkat,** -ti **1.** creation; **2.** natural disposition; nature; **~ garibesi** monstrosity, freak.

**himaye** [ä] **1.** protection, defence; **2.** support, patronage; **~ etm.** 'to protect; to patronize; **-sinde** (*b-nin*) under the protection of *s.o.*; **-sine almak** (*b-ni*) to take *s.o.* under one's protection, to take *s.o.* under one's wing.

**himayecilik** [ä] ♂♀ protectionism.

**himayeli** [ä] **1.** protected; **2.** ✗ escorted (*ship, etc.*).

**himayesiz** [ä] **1.** unprotected; **2.** ✗ unescorted (*ship, etc.*).

**himmet,** -ti **1.** auspices, help, favo(u)r; **2.** effort, labo(u)r, zeal; **~ etm.** to help, to exert *o.s.* (*-e* for); **-in var olsun!** all thanks for your help!; **-inizle** thanks to you, by your help.

**hındı** *zo.* turkey; **~ gibi kabarmak** *fig.* to be full of *o.s.*

**hindiba** [ä] ♀ chicory, succory.

**Hindistan** [ä] *pr. n.* India.

**hindistancevizi,** -ni ♀ **1.** coconut (palm); **2.** nutmeg (tree).

**Hindu** *pr. n.* Hindu.

**hınoğluhin** F **1.** devil; shyster; **2.** very sly (*or* tricky).

**Hint,** -di **1.** Indian; **2.** India; **~ Avrupa dilleri** Indo-European languages; **~ fakiri** fakir; **~ Okyanusu** Indian Ocean.

**hintarmudu,** -nu ♀ guave tree.

**hintbademi,** -ni ♀ cacao tree.

**hintbezelyesi,** -ni ♀ horse grain (*or* gram).

**hintdarısı,** -nı ♀ pearl millet.

**hinterlant,** -dı hinterland.

**hintfıstığı,** -nı ♀ physic nut.

**hintgüreşi,** -ni *sports:* Indian wrestling.

**hınthıyarı,** -nı ♀ cassia, drumstick tree.
**hınthurması,** -nı ♀ palmyra.
**hıntkamışı,** -nı ♀ rattan palm.
**hıntkeneviri,** -ni ♀ (Indian) hemp, bhang, cannabis.
**Hıntli** Indian.
**hıntyağı,** -nı castor oil.
**hiperbol,** -lü ⅄ hyperbola.
**hiperbolik** ⅄ hyperbolic.
**hiperboloit** ⅄ hyperboloid.
**hipermetrop,** -pu farsighted, hypermetropic.
**hipertansiyon** ⚕ hypertension, high blood pressure.
**hipnotizma** hypnosis, hypnotism.
**hipnoz** hypnosis.
**hipodrom** hippodrome.
**hipofiz** the pituitary gland.
**hipopotam** zo. hippopotamus.
**hipotansiyon** ⚕ low blood pressure.
**hipotenüs** ⅄ hypotenuse.
**hipotez** hypothesis.
**hippi** hippy. hippie.
**hippilik** hippiness.
**his,** -ssi 1. feeling, emotion, perception; 2. sensation, feeling, sentiment; 3. sense; -lerine kapılmak to be ruled by one's emotions; -sini vermek to give the impression that.
**hisar** [ā] 1. fort, fortress, castle; 2. ♪ B flat.
**hislenmek** to be touched (or affected or moved).
**hisli** sensitive, sentimental, emotional.
**hisse** 1. share, lot, part, allotted portion; 2. fig. lesson; ~ çıkarmak to take offence (-den at); ~ kapmak to draw a lesson (-den from); ~ sahibi shareholder; joint owner; ~ senedi † share.
**hissedar** [ā] = hisse sahibi.
**hisseişayia** [. . . . . .] ඊ co-ownership.
**hisseişayialı** [. . . . . .] ඊ jointly owned.
**hisseli** divided into shares; jointly owned.
**hisset,** -ti miserliness.
**hissetmek** [x .] to feel, to sense, to perceive; hissedilir perceptible, noticeable.
**hissettirmek** (b-ne bşi) 1. to cause s.o. to perceive s.th.; 2. to let s.o. know about s.th.
**hissi** emotional, sentimental; sensible, sensorial.
**hissiselim** [. . . -] common sense.
**hissiyat,** -tı [ā] feelings; emotions; -a kapılmak to be ruled by one's emotions.
**hissiz** 1. unfeeling, insensitive, callous; 2. numb, asleep.
**hissizlik** 1. insensitivity; 2. numbness.
**histeri** hysteria.

**histoloji** ⚕ histology.
**hişt, hişt,** -ti F hey!, look here!
**hitabe** [ā] address, speech.
**hitaben** [ā] addressing, speaking (-e to); addressed (-e to).
**hitabet,** -ti [ā] oratory, rhetoric, eloquence.
**hitam** [ā] end, conclusion, close; completion; ~ bulmak (or -a ermek) to come to a conclusion; ~ vermek to bring to an end.
**hitap,** -bı [ā] address, speech, discourse; ~ etm. to address.
**Hitit,** -ti pr. n. Hittite.
**Hititçe** pr. n. Hittite (language).
**hiyerarşi** hierarchy.
**hiyeroglif** hieroglyph.
**hiza** [ā] line, level; -sına kadar up to level (-in of); -ya gelmek 1. to line up, to form a line; 2. fig. F to get into line, to shape up; -ya getirmek 1. to line up (people); to straighten, to align; 2. fig. F (b-ni) to bring s.o. into line.
**hizalamak** to become aligned.
**hizip,** -zbi clique, faction (group).
**hizipçi** factionary.
**hizipçilik** cliquishness.
**hizipleşmek** to separate into factions.
**hizmet,** -ti 1. service; 2. duty; employment; 3. care, maintenance; ~ akdi ඊ contract of service; ~ eri ✗ orderly batman; ~ etm. to serve, to render service; ~ görmek to serve, to render service; -e girmek 1. to be put into service (or operation); 2. to begin working in the civil service; -inde bulunmak (b-nin) to be in the service of s.o.; -ine girmek (b-nin) to be in s.o.'s employment.
**hizmetçi** servant, maid, maidservant; ~ kadın charwoman; ~ kız maidservant; ~ tutmak to put in a maid.
**hizmetçilik** working as a maid.
**hizmetkâr** manservant.
**hizmetkârlık** working as a manservant.
**hizmetli** caretaker.
**hobi** hobby.
**hoca** [x .] 1. eccl. hodja; 2. teacher; -nın dediğini yap, yaptığını yapma pro. do as I say, not as I do.
**hocalık** 1. eccl. rank and duties of a hodja; 2. teaching.
**hodan** ♀ borage.
**hodbehot** [x . .] of one's own accord.
**hodbin** [¹] egoistic, selfish.
**hodkâm** = hodbin.
**hodpesent,** -ti conceited.
**hodri** [x .]: ~ meydan! come and try!, I dare you!
**hohlamak** to breathe (-e on), to blow one's breath (-e upon).

**hokey** *sports:* hockey.

**hokka 1.** inkwell, inkpot, inkstand; **2.** pot, cup; ~ **gibi oturmak** to fit like a glove (*clothes*).

**hokkabaz 1.** juggler, conjurer; **2.** *fig.* shyster, cheat.

**hokkabazlık 1.** juggling, sleight of hand; **2.** *fig.* put-up job; trickery.

**hol,** -lü entrance hall, vestibule.

**holding** ⊤ holding company.

**Hollanda** [. x .] *pr. n.* Holland, the Netherlands.

**Hollandalı** *pr. n.* Dutchman.

**holmiyum** ⌢ holmium.

**homo** F homo, homosexual.

**homogen, homojen** homogeneous.

**homoseksüel** homosexual.

**homurdanmak** to grumble (*-e* at), to mutter to o.s.

**homur homur** in a muttering way.

**homurtu 1.** mutter(ing); **2.** growl (*of a bear*).

**hop,** -pu **1.** all of a sudden; **2.** jump, skip; **3.** oops!; ~ ~! stop!, whoa!; ~ ~ sıçramak to jump for joy; ~ oturup ~ kalkmak to be like a cat on hot bricks.

**hoparlör** loudspeaker.

**hoplamak 1.** to jump; to skip along; **2.** to jump for joy.

**hoplatmak** *caus. of* hoplamak, *part.* to dandle; to bounce on one's knee (*a child*).

**hoppa** *flighty,* frivolous (*woman*).

**hoppala** [x . .] **1.** upsy-daisy!; **2.** how odd!, what an idea!; **3.** that's just it!; **4.** baby's play-chair hung by a spring; ~ bebek a childish person.

**hoppalık** levity, flightiness, frivolity.

**hopurdatmak** to slurp.

**hor** contemptible, despicable; ~ **bakmak** (*or* görmek) to look down on; ~ **kullanmak** to be hard (*-i* on), to misuse; ~ **tutmak** to mistreat; ~ a geçmek to be welcome.

**hora** [x .] a round dance; ~ **tepmek 1.** to dance a round dance; **2.** *fig.* to stamp noisily.

**horan** a folk dance of the Black sea region.

**horanta.** [. x .] P household, family.

**horda** horde.

**horgörü** contempt.

**horhor** water flowing noisily.

**herlamak 1.** to snore; **2.** *fig.* to insult, to treat with contempt, to ill-treat.

**hormon** *biol.* hormone.

**hornblent** *geol.* hornblende.

**horoz 1.** *zo.* cock, rooster; **2.** hammer (*of*

---

a gun), cock; **3.** bridge (*of a lock*); ~ **akıllı** (*or* kafalı) harebrained, brainless; ~ **döğüşü** cockfight; ~ **şekeri** lollipop in the shape of a rooster; **-dan kaçmak** to avoid the company of men (*woman*); **-lar öttü** morning has broken; **-u çok olan köyde sabah** ' **geç olur** *pro.* too many cooks spoil the broth.

**horozayağı,** -nı cartridge extractor.

**horozlanmak** to swagger, to bluster, to strut about.

**horezsıklet,** -ti *sports:* featherweight.

**hortlak** ghost, specter.

**hortlamak 1.** to rise from the grave and haunt people; **2.** *fig.* to rearrise (*trouble, etc.*).

**hortum 1.** *zo.* trunk, proboscis; **2.** ⊕ hose; **3.** *meteor.* whirlwind, waterspout; ~ **gibi long** (*nose*); ~ **sıkmak** to direct a fire hose (*-e* at).

**hortumlu 1.** having a trunk; **2.** *zo.* proboscidian; **3.** ⊕ with a hose attached.

**hortumlular** *zo.* proboscidea.

**horuldamak** *s.* horlamak 1.

**horul horul** snoring loudly.

**horultu** snore, snoring.

**hostes** stewardess; air hostess.

**hoş 1.** pleasant, nice, lovely; **2.** for that matter, as far as that's concerned; **3.** fine, but...; ~ **bulduk!** thank you! (*said in reply to a welcoming greeting*); ~ **geçinmek** (*b-le*) to get on well with s.o.; ~ **geldiniz!** welcome!; ~ **görmek** to tolerate, to overlook; ~ **tutmak** (*b-ni*) to treat s.o. warmly; **-a gitmek** to be pleasing; **-una gitmek** to please, to be agreeable (*-in* to).

**hoşaf** stewed fruit; ~ **gibi** bushed, worn-out; **-ın yağı kesilmek** (*b-de*) to be flabbergasted, to be at a loss for words; **-ına gitmek** F to please.

**hoşbeş** small talk; ~ **etm.** to have small talk, to chitchat.

**hoşça** [x .] pretty well, somewhat pleasant; ~ **kalın!** so long!, bye!, cheers!

**hoşgörü** tolerance.

**hoşgörülü** tolerant.

**hoşgörüsüz** intolerant.

**hoşgörüsüzlük** intolerance.

**hoşhoş** bow-wow, woof-woof, doggy, doggie.

**hoşlanmak** to like, to enjoy, to be pleased (*-den* with).

**hoşlaşmak 1.** to become pleasant and agreeable; **2.** to like each other.

**hoşluk 1.** pleasantness; **2.** strangeness.

**hoşnut,** -du [ü] pleased, satisfied, contented (*-den* with); ~ **etm.** (*b-ni*) to please

*s.o.*; ~ olm. to be pleased (*-den* with).
**hoşnutluk** contentment, satisfaction, pleasure.
**hoşnutsuz** displeased, discontented.
**hoşnutsuzluk** discontent, dissatisfaction.
**hoşor** *sl.* plump and pretty (*woman*).
**hoşsohbet**, -ti conversable, conversationalist.
**hoşt**, -tu shoo!, scram!
**hoşur** 1. worthless; 2. uncouth, crude.
**hotoz** 1. crest, tuft; 2. bun, topknot (*of hair*); 3. † headdress (*for women*).
**hovarda** 1. spendthrift, profligate; 2. womanizer, rake; 3. womanizing, rakish.
**hovardalaşmak** 1. to become a spendthrift; 2. to become a womanizer.
**hovardalık** 1. profligacy; 2. womanizing; ~ etm. 1. to womanize; 2. to spend money extravagantly.
**hoyrat**, -tı rough, coarse (*person*).
**hödük** boorish, uncouth.
**höpürdetmek** to slurp.
**höpürtü** slurp.
**hörgüç**, -cü *zo.* hump.
**hörgüçlü** humped.
**höst**, -tü 1. whoa!; 2. *sl.* hey you bastard!
**höt**, -tü boo!; ~ demek to bark (*-e* at), to speak sharply (*-e* to); ~ zöt browbeating.
**höyük** tumulus, artificial hill (*or* mound).
**hu** [- ] 1. hey there!; 2. He (*God*).
**hububat**, -tı [. - -] grain, cereals.
**Huda** [ᵃ] God.
**hud'a** trick.
**hudayinabit**, -ti [ᵃ, ᵃ] wild, self-sown, volunteer (*plant*).
**hudut**, -du [. -] 1. boundary, border, frontier; 2. end, limit; ~ dışı etm. (*b-ni*) to expel *s.o.* from the country.
**hudutlandırmak** to limit, to put a limit (to).
**hudutlu** limited.
**hudutsuz** unlimited, boundless.
**hukuk**, -ku [. -] 1. law, jurisprudence; 2. 🕮 rights; 3. friendship; 4. = Hukuk Fakültesi; ~ davası civil lawsuit; ~ doktoru doctor of law; ♀ Fakültesi law school; ~ mahkemesi civil court; ~ müşaviri legal adviser.
**hukukçu** jurist.
**hukuki** [. - -] legal, juridical; ~ muamele legal action.
**hukuklu** law student.
**hulasa** 1. summary, résumé; 2. in short (*or* brief), summing up; 3. 🕮 extract; ~ etm. to sum up, to summarize.
**hulliyat**, -tı [ᵃ] valuable jewelry.
**hulûl**, -lü 1. penetration; infiltration; 2. osmosis; 3. arrival, beginning (*of a season*).

**hulus** sincerity, purity of heart; ~ çakmak F (*b-ne*) to curry favo(u)r with *s.o.*
**huluskâr** 1. sincere, genuine; 2. flatterer.
**hulya** [ᵃ] daydream, fancy; -ya dalmak to daydream.
**hulyalı** [ᵃ] dreamy, romantic; fanciful.
**humar** [ᵃ] hangover (*from drink*); loginess (*from sleep*).
**humma** 🕮 fever.
**hummalı** 🕮 feverish (*a. fig.*)
**humus** humus.
**hunhar** [. -] bloodthirsty.
**hunharca** [. - .] 1. cruelly, brutally; 2. brutal, savage.
**hunharlık** bloodthirstiness.
**huni** funnel.
**hunnak**, -kı [ᵃ] 🕮 quinsy.
**hura** hurray!, hurrah!
**hurafe** [ᵃ] superstition.
**hurç**, -cu large leather saddlebag.
**hurda** 1. scrap iron (*or* metal), junk; 2. scrap (*metal*); 3. *fig.* worn-out; ~ demir scrap iron; ~ fiyatına very cheaply; -sı çıkmış worn-out.
**hurdacı** scrap iron dealer, junk dealer, secondhand metal dealer.
**hurdahaş** [ᵃ] bashed up, crushed; ~ etm. to smash to bits; ~ olm. 1. to be smashed to bits; 2. *fig.* to become bushed; araba kazadan sonra ~ oldu the car was a write-off after the accident.
**huri** [ᵘ] *isl. myth.* houri; ~ gibi as pretty as a picture (*girl*).
**hurma** ♀ date; ~ ağacı ♀ date palm; ~ tatlısı a date-shaped sweet.
**hurmalık** date grove.
**huruç** [. -] departure, exodus.
**hurufat**, -tı [. - -] *typ.* type(face); ~ dökmek to cast type; ~ kasası type case.
**husuf** [. -] eclipse (*of the moon*).
**husul**, -lü [. -] occurrence, appearance, coming into existence; ~ bulmak (*or* -e gelmek) to occur, to come into existence; -e getirmek to bring about, to accomplish.
**husumet**, -ti [. - .] hostility, enmity; ~ beslemek to nourish hostility (*-e* towards).
**husus** [. -] 1. subject, matter, question; case; 2. particularity, peculiarity; relation, respect; -unda regarding, with reference to, in connection with; bu -ta in this matter (*or* connection).
**hususi** [. - -] 1. particular, special, distinctive, characteristic; 2. personal, private; 3. reserved (*seat*); 4. F privately owned automobile.
**hususiyet**, -ti [. - . .] 1. characteristic, peculiarity, trait; 2. intimacy.
**hususuyla** [. - - .] [. - × .] particularly, es-

pecially.

**husye** ℥ testis, testicle.

**huş** ♦ birch.

**huşu,** -u [. -] **1.** modesty, humility; **2.** submission to God.

**huşunet,** -ti [. - .] severity, harshness.

**hutbe** *eccl.* khutbah *(sermon delivered at the noon prayer on Friday and on certain other occasions).*

**huy 1.** habit, temper, disposition, temperament; **2.** nature; ~ edinmek *(or* etm. *or* kapmak) to get into the habit (of), to take to; -u suyu *(b-nin)* one's nature and disposition; -una çekmek *(b-nin)* to take after *s.o.,* to resemble *s.o.;* -una suyuna gitmek to humo(u)r, to indulge.

**huylandırmak 1.** to upset, to molest; **2.** to frighten, to startle *(animal).*

**huylanmak 1.** to be irritated, to get nervous, to become uneasy; **2.** to get excited; **3.** to shy *(animal).*

**huylu 1.** ... tempered; **2.** bad-tempered, irritable, touchy, cross; **3.** suspicious.

**huysuz** bad-tempered, irascible; petulant, peevish.

**huysuzlanmak** to fuss, to fret *(child).*

**huysuzlaşmak** to become fretful *(child);* to become peevish.

**huysuzluk** fractiousness, bad temper, petulance; ~ etm. to show bad temper; huysuzluğu tutmak to have a fit of bad temper.

**huzme** *phys.* **1.** bundle, bunch; **2.** light beam.

**huzur** [. -] **1.** peace of mind, repose, comfort, quiet; **2.** presence, attendance; **3.** presence, access *(of an emperor);* ~ ve asayiş peace and security; ~ vermek *(b-ne)* **1.** to leave *s.o.* alone, not to bother *s.o.;* **2.** to bring *s.o.* comfort and joy, to soothe *s.o.;* -una çıkmak *(b-nin)* to have access to *s.o.;* -unda in the presence *(-in* of); -unu kaçırmak to trouble, to disturb.

**huzurevi,** -ni rest home.

**huzurlu 1.** peaceful, tranquil; **2.** happy, untroubled.

**huzursuz** troubled, uneasy.

**huzursuzluk** uneasiness, disquiet.

**hüccet,** -ti (legal) document; argument, proof.

**hücra** [. -] remote, solitary *(place).*

**hücre 1.** *biol.* cell; **2.** cell; chamber, room; **3.** niche, alcove.

**hücrelerarası,** -nı *biol. & anat.* intercellular.

**hücum** [ū] **1.** attack, assault; charge; **2.** sudden crowding, rush; **3.** lash of criticism, verbal attack; ~ etm. **1.** to attack,

to storm; **2.** *fig.* to mob, to rush to *(a place);* ~ kıtası *(or* kolu) ✕ storm troops; -a uğramak to be attacked *(or* assailed).

**hücumbot,** -tu ✕ assault boat.

**Hüda** [. -] God.

**hükmen** [x .] *sports:* by the decision of a referee; ~ galip *sports:* won by the decision of a referee.

**hükmetmek** [x . .] **1.** to rule, to govern, to dominate; **2.** to decide, to conclude.

**hükmi** [ı̄] **1.** legal; judicial; **2.** nominal; ~ şahıs *(or* şahsiyet) ₫ legal person.

**hüküm,** -kmü **1.** judg(e)ment, decision, decree, sentence; **2.** jurisdiction, sovereignty, sway, rule; **3.** opinion, thought, assumption; **4.** legality, validity, authority; **5.** influence, importance, effect; **6.** grip, force, hold; ~ giydirmek to pass sentence *(-e* on); ~ giymek to be condemned *(or* sentenced); ~ sürmek **1.** to reign, to rule; **2.** *fig.* to prevail; ~ vermek **1.** to bring in a verdict; **2.** to pass sentence, to condemn; hükmü geçmek **1.** to have authority *(-e* over), to carry weight *(-e* with); **2.** to expire *(validity),* to be over with; hükmü·Kalmadı *(or* yoktur) it is invalid; hükmünde olm. to be considered (as), to be of the same effect (as); hükmünü geçirmek to assert one's authority *(-e* over); hükümden düşmek to be invalid.

**hükümat,** -tı *sl.* prison warden.

**hükümdar** [ā] ruler, monarch, sovereign.

**hükümdarlık 1.** rulership, sovereignty; **2.** empire, kingdom.

**hükümet,** -ti **1.** government, administration, state; **2.** government building *(or* office); ~ darbesi coup d'état; ~ kapısı government office; ~ konağı government office; ~ merkezi capital, seat of government; ~ sürmek to rule, to reign, to govern; -i devirmek to overthrow the government; -i kurmak to form a government.

**hükümlü 1.** sentenced, condemned; **2.** convict.

**hükümran** [ā] sovereign.

**hükümranlık** [ā] sovereignty.

**hükümsüz** invalid, null; ~ kılmak to invalidate, to nullify, to annul.

**hükümsüzlük** nullity.

**hülle** † interim marriage necessary before a divorced couple could remarry.

**hümanist,** -ti humanist(ic).

**hümanizm** humanism.

**hümayun** [. - -] *hist.* royal, imperial.

**hüner** skill, talent, ability, dexterity; ~ göstermek to show skill *(or* proficiency)

(*-de* in).
**hünerli 1.** skillful, talented, dexterous, proficient; **2.** done with skill.
**hünersiz** unskilled.
**hüngürdemek** to sob violently, to wail loudly.
**hüngür hüngür** sobbingly; ~ ağlamak to sob, to blubber, to boohoo.
**hüngürtü** sob.
**hünkâr** *hist.* sovereign, sultan.
**hünnap,** -bı ♀ jujube.
**hünsa** [ā] *biol,* ♀, *zo.* **1.** hermaphrodite; **2.** hermaphroditic.
**hür** free; unconstrained, untrammeled; ~ düşünce free thought.
**hürmet,** -ti respect, regard, veneration; ~ etm. to respect, to hono(u)r, to venerate; -le respectfully; -lerimle respectfully yours, with my respects.
**hürmeten** [x . .] out of respect.
**hürmetkâr** respectful.
**hürmetli 1.** respectful, deferent; respected; **2.** *fig.* huge, large, considerable.
**hürmetsiz** disrespectful.
**hürmetsizlik** discrespect; ~ etm. to be disrespectful (-*e* to).
**hürriyet,** -ti freedom, liberty; -i seçmek to throw off the yoke.

**hürya** [x .] in a rush; ~ etm. to rush out (*or* in).
**hüsnühal,** -li [ā] good conduct; ~ kâğıdı certificate of good conduct, reference.
**hüsnükabul,** -lü [. . . -] warmly reception; ~ göstermek *(b-ne)* to receive *s.o.* warmly.
**hüsnükuruntu** *co.* wishful thinking.
**hüsnüniyet,** -ti good intention (*or* will *or* faith); ~ sahibi goodwilled.
**hüsnütelakki** favo(u)rably biased interpretation.
**hüsnüyusuf** ♀ sweet william.
**hüsran** [. -] **1.** disappointment, frustration, let-down; **2.** loss, damage; -a uğramak to be disappointed (*or* let down).
**hüsün,** -snü † beauty.
**hüthüt,** -tü *zo.* hoopoe, hoopoe.
**hüviyet,** -ti **1.** identity (card); **2.** *fig.* character, quality; ~ cüzdanı identity card, ID card.
**hüzün,** -znü sadness, sorrow, grief, melancholy.
**hüzünlendirmek** to sadden.
**hüzünlenmek** to feel sad, to sadden.
**hüzünlü** sad, sorrowful.
**Hz.** *abbr. of* Hazretleri.

# I

**ıcık:** ıcığını cıcığını çıkarmak F to go over with a fine-tooth comb.

**ığı!** P still water.

**ığıl ığıl** slowly; ~ akmak to flow slowly, to gurgle.

**ığrıp, -bı** trawl (net); ~ çevirmek *fig.* to make the best use of s.th.; ~ kayığı trawler.

**ıh!** *cry used to make a camel kneel.*

**ıhlamak** to groan, to moan.

**ıhlamur 1.** ♀ linden tree, lime-tree; **2.** linden-flower *(tea)*.

**ıhmak** to kneel down *(camel)*.

**ıkıl ıkıl** in gasps, gaspingly; ~ nefes almak to gasp for breath.

**ıkınmak 1.** to strain while defecating; **2.** to grunt, to moan; ıkınıp sıkınmak F **1.** to grunt and strain; **2.** to try hard.

**ıklamak 1.** to huff and puff, to breathe heavily; **2.** to sob; ıklaya sıklaya with the greatest effort.

**ıklım tıklım** up to the brim; brimful.

**ılgar 1.** gallop; **2.** cavalry raid; ~ etm. to raid.

**ılgarlamak** to raid, to foray.

**ılgım** mirage.

**ılgın** ♀ tamarisk.

**ılgıt ılgıt** gently, lighty.

**ılıca** hot spring, spa.

**ılıcak** tepid, warm, lukewarm.

**ılık** tepid, lukewarm; warmish, mild.

**ılıklaşmak** to become tepid (*or* lukewarm), to warm up slightly.

**ılıklaştırmak** to make lukewarm.

**ılıklık** tepidity, warmness.

**ılım** moderation.

**ılımak** *s.* ılıklaşmak.

**ılıman** temperate; ~ bölge Temperate Zone.

**ılımlı** moderate, middle-of-the-road.

**ılımlılık** moderateness.

**ılınmak** *s.* ılıklaşmak.

**ılıştırmak** to make lukewarm.

**ılıtmak** *s.* ılıklaştırmak.

**ımızganma 1.** dozing; **2.** wavering, indecision; **3.** smoldering; ~ halleri *psych.* hypnagogic images (*or* hallucinations).

**ımızganmak 1.** to doze, to be half asleep;

**2.** to waver *(between two opinions)*; **3.** to die down, to smolder *(fire)*.

**ıpıslak** completely wet, soaked.

**ıpıssız** very desolate, entirely uninhabited.

**ır** song; tune.

**ıra** characteristic, trait.

**ırabilim** characterology.

**ırak** far, distant, remote.

**Irak, -kı** *pr. n.* Iraq.

**ırakgörür** telescope.

**ıraklaşmak** to go (*or* move) away.

**Iraklı** *pr. n.* Iraqi.

**ıraklık** distance.

**ıraksak** ⅄ & *phys.* divergent.

**ıraksama 1.** *vn. of* ıraksamak; **2.** ⅄ & *phys.* divergence.

**ıraksamak** to consider improbable.

**ıralamak** to characterize.

**ıramak** to go (*or* move) away (-*den* from).

**ırgalamak 1.** to shake, to rock; **2.** *sl.* to interest, to concern.

**ırgamak** to shift, to move, to budge.

**ırgat, -tı 1.** day-labo(u)rer, workman; **2.** windlass, winch; ~ başı foreman, overseer; ~ gibi çalışmak *fig.* to sweat blood; ~ pazarı labo(u)r market.

**ırgatlık** day-labo(u)r.

**ırk, -kı 1.** race; **2.** lineage, blood; ~ ayrımı racial discrimination.

**ırkçı** racist.

**ırkçılık** racialism, racism.

**ırki** racial.

**ırkiyat, -tı** ethnology.

**ırktaş** of the same race.

**ırlamak** to sing.

**ırmak** river.

**ırz** chastity, purity ,hono(u)r; ~ düşmanı rapist; ~ ehli virtuous, chaste, honest; -a geçme (*or* tecavüz) ♂♀ rape; -ına geçmek (*or* tecavüz etm.) **1.** (*b-nin*) to rape *s.o.*, to violate *s.o.*; **2.** *fig.* to bastardize, to debase, to adulterate.

**ıs** (legal) owner.

**ısdar** [ā] loom.

**ısı 1.** heat, warm; **2.** temperature; ~ dam Turkish bath; ~ kuşak tropical zone.

**ısıalan** ⌕ endothermal, endothermic.

**ısıdenetir** thermostat.

**ısıldeğer** thermal value.

**ısın** *phys.* calorie.

**ısınma** warming; ~ koşusu *sports:* warm-up run.

**ısınmak** 1. to grow warm; 2. to warm o.s.: 3. *fig.* to warm *(-e* to), to get accustomed *(-e* to).

**ısıölçer** 1. thermometer; 2. calorimeter.

**ısırgan** 1. ♀ stinging nettle; 2. snappish, snappy *(animal).*

**ısırgın** heat rash, prickly heat.

**ısırıcı** 1. biting *(cold);* 2. snappish *(animal);* 3. scratchy *(cloth).*

**ısırık** 1. bite; 2. a bite *(or* mouthful).

**ısırmak** 1. to bite; 2. *fig.* to scratch, to irritate *(cloth);* ısıran it dişini göstermez *pro.* barking dogs seldom bite.

**ısıtıcı** heater.

**ısıtmak** to warm, to heat.

**ısıveren** ♁ exothermic, exothermal.

**ıska** *sl.* miss, muff; ~ geçmek *sl.* 1. to miss, to fail to hit; 2. *fig.* to overlook, to ignore.

**ıskaça** ⚓ step *(of a mast).*

**ıskala** [. x .] ♪ scale.

**ıskarça** [. x .] 1. ⚓ congestion *(in a harbour);* 2. packed, crowded.

**ıskarmoz** 1. ⚓ rib; 2. ⚓ oarlock, thole (pin); 3. *zo.* barracuda.

**ıskarta** [. x .] 1. *cards:* discard; 2. discarded; 3. † waste; ~ etm. *(or* -ya çıkarmak) to discard; ~ mal waste goods; -ya çıkmak to be discarded.

**ıskat,** -tı 1. dropping; 2. alms given on behalf of the dead as compensation for their neglected religious duties.

**ıskatçı** 1. person receiving alms from mourners; 2. beggar at the graveside.

**ıskonto** [. x .] 1. † discount; 2. price reduction; ~ etm. *(or* yapmak) 1. to reduce the price of; 2. † to discount.

**ıskota** [. x .] ⚓ sheet; clew line.

**ıskuna** [. x .] ⚓ schooner.

**ıslah** [ā] 1. improvement, correction, reform; 2. amendment, rectification; ~ etm. 1. to amend, to improve; 2. to discipline, to reform; ~ olmaz F incorrigible.

**ıslahat,** -tı [. - -] reform, improvement, amendment; ~ yapmak to make reforms.

**ıslahatçı** [. - - .] reformer, reformist.

**ıslahevi,** -ni [. - . .] reformatory, approved *(or* reform) school.

**ıslahhane** *s.* ıslahevi.

**ıslak** wet; damp.

**ıslaklık** wetness; dampness.

**ıslamak** *s.* ıslatmak 1.

**ıslanmak** to get wet, to be wetted.

**ıslatmak** 1. to wet ;to dampen; to moisten;

2. *sl.* to cudgel, to thrash; 3. F celebrate by a booze-up, to wet.

**ıslık** 1. whistle; 2. hiss; ~ çalmak 1. to whistle; 2. to hiss *(snake);* 3. to whistle *(-e* at, to).

**ıslıklamak** to boo, to give s.o. the bird, to hiss.

**ıslıklı** whistling, hissing *(sound);* ~ ünsüz *gr.* sibilant.

**ısmarlama** 1. *vn. of* ısmarlamak; 2. made-to-order, bespoke, custom made, made-to-measure; 3. slapdash, superficial; ~ elbise tailor-made *(or* custom-made) suit.

**ısmarlamak** 1. *(b-ne)* to order s.th. from s.o.; to have s.o. make s.th.; 2. *(b-ne)* to treat s.o. to *(drink, food);* 3. to entrust to s.o.; 4. *(b-ne)* to warn s.o. to behave *(in a certain manner).*

**ıspanak** 1. ♀ spinach; 2. *sl.* imbecile, idiot.

**ıspavli** ⚓ cord, twine.

**ıspazmoz** convulsion, spasm.

**ısrar** [ā] insistence, persistence; ~ etm. to insist *(-de* on), to persist *(-de* in).

**ısrarla** [. - .] insistently.

**ısrarlı** [. - .] insistent.

**ıssız** desolate, forlorn, solitary.

**ıssızlaşmak** to become desolate.

**ıssızlık** desolation, forlornness, solitariness.

**ıstakoz** *zo.* lobster.

**ıstampa** [. x .] 1. stamp; 2. ink *(or* stamp) pad.

**ıstavroz** cross, crucifix; ~ çıkarmak to cross o.s.

**ıstıfa,** -aı [ā] selection.

**ıstılah** [ā] technical term.

**ıstırap,** -bı [ā] 1. pain; anguish, misery; 2. bodily suffering; ~ çekmek to suffer; ~ vermek to make s.o. suffer, to afflict.

**ıstıraplı** [ā] suffering; miserable, anguished.

**ışığadoğrulum** ♀ phototropism.

**ışık** 1. light; 2. any source of light, *part.* lamp; ~ almak *phot.* to be fogged *(or* exposed); ~ oyunu play of light; ~ saçmak to shine, to give off light; ~ tutmak 1. to light the way *(-e* for); 2. to shine alight *(-e* on); 3. *fig.* to shed *(or* throw) light *(-e* on); ~ yılı light year; ışığı altında in the light of.

**ışıkçı** *thea.* electrician.

**ışıkgöçüm** ♀ phototaxy, phototaxis.

**ışıkkesen** *phot.* light trap.

**ışıkküre** photosphere.

**ışıklandırma** lighting, illumination.

**ışıklandırmak** to light up, to illuminate.

**ışıklı** illuminated, lighted up, floodlit;

reklam neon sign.
ışıklılık luminance.
ışıkölçer *phys.* photometer; light (*or* exposure) meter.
ışıkölçümü, -nü photometry.
ışıksız unlit, without light.
ışıkyuvarı, -nı *ast.* photosphere.
ışılamak *s.* ışıldamak.
ışıldak 1. bright, sparkling; 2. searchlight, spotlight, projector, floodlight.
ışıldamak to shine, to sparkle, to gleam, to twinkle.
ışıl ışıl sparklingly, glitteringly.
ışılküf ¶ actinomycete.
ışıltı flash, spark, glitter, twinkle.
ışıltılı sparkling, glittering, flashy.
ışıma 1. glowing; 2. *phys.* radiation.
ışımak 1. to glow, to radiate light; 2. to become light (*or* illuminated).
ışın A & *phys.* ray; ~ demeti pencil of rays.
ışınetki radioactivity.
ışınetkin radioactive.
ışınım radiation.
ışınımölçer *ast.* bolometer.
ışınlama radiation.

ışınlı 1. radiant; 2. radiolarian.
ışınölçer radiometer.
ışıtmak to illuminate.
ışkı drawknife, spokeshave.
ışkırlak cap worn by Karagöz.
ıştın clay lamp.
ıtır, -trı attar, essence, perfume; ~ çiçeği ¶ geranium.
ıtırlı fragrant, aromatic.
ıtnap, -bı [â] verbiage.
ıtri perfumed, fragrant.
ıtriyat, -tı [â] perfumes, essences, attars.
ıtriyatçı [â] perfumer, perfumier.
ıttıla, -aı [â] knowledge, information.
ıvır zıvır 1. bits and pieces, bobs and trinkets, baubles; 2. F nonsensical, rubbish; junky, trifling; 3. F nonsense, hooey.
ızbandut huge and terrifying man, hulk; ~ gibi burly, strapping (*man*).
ızgara [x . .] 1. grate, grating; 2. grill, grid, gridiron; 3. grilled (*fish, meat, etc.*); ~ köfte grilled meat balls; ~ yapmak to grill.
ızrar [â] † harming; ~ etm. to harm.

# I

**iade** [ā] 1. return(ing), giving back; 2. refusal, rejection; 3. restoration, restitution; ~ etm. 1. to return (-e to), to give back (-e to); 2. to refuse, to reject; 3. to restore; iadei ziyaret etm. (b-ni) to return s.o.'s call.

**iadeli** [ā] reply-paid (letter); ~ taahhütlü mektup registered and reply-paid letter.

**iane** [ā] subsidy, donation; 2. help, aid; ~ toplamak to collect contributions.

**iare** [ā] loan.

**iaşe** [ā] feeding, victualing; ~ etm. to feed, to sustain; ~ ve ibate room and board, board and lodging.

**ibadet,** -ti [ā] worship, prayer; ~ etm. to worship.

**ibadethane** [ā, ā] temple, sanctuary.

**ibadullah** [ā, ā] abundant.

**ibare** [ā] sentence; expression; paragraph.

**ibaret,** -ti [ā] composed (-den of), consisting (-den of); ~ olm. to consist (-den of), to be composed (-den of), to be made up (-den of).

**ibate** [ā] sheltering, giving lodging to; ~ etm. to house, to shelter.

**ibda,** -aı [ā] creating; ~ etm. to create.

**ibibik** zo. hoopoe.

**ibik** 1. zo. comb (of a fowl); 2. anat. crista; 3. red tassel (of a fez).

**ibikli** crested (bird).

**ibiş** name of the foolish servant in certain old Turkish plays; ~ gibi comically foolish.

**iblağ** 1. delivery; communication; 2. increase, augmentation; ~ etm. 1. to communicate, to transmit; to deliver; 2. to increase (-e to).

**iblis** [. -] 1. satan, the Devil; 2. fig. demon, devil, imp.

**ibne** sl. fag, gay, queen, queer.

**ibra** [ā] acquittance; ~ etm. to release (from debt); ~ kâğıdı quittance.

**ibraname** [ā, ā] quittance, release.

**ibrani** [. - -] pr. n. Hebrew.

**ibranice** [. - - .] [. - x .] pr. n. the Hebrew language.

**ibraz** [ā] presentation, showing; ~ etm. to present, to show (a document).

**ibre** ⊕ needle, pointer.

**ibret,** -ti [ā] warning, lesson, admonition; 2. P strange, queer; ~ almak (bşden) to take warning from s.th., to learn a lesson from s.th.; ~ olm. to be a warning (-e to); -in kudreti F strange and hideous.

**ibrik** ewer, pitcher.

**ibrişim** silk thread; ~ kurdu zo. silkworm.

**icabet,** -ti [ā] acceptance (of an invitation), attendance (at a gathering); ~ etm. 1. to accept (an invitation); 2. to accede (to a request).

**icap,** -bı [- -] 1. necessity, requirement, demand; 2. log. affirmation; ~ etm. to be necessary; -ına bakmak 1. to do what is necessary, to see to; 2. fig. F to take care of, to kill; -ında if nedeed, at a push (or pinch).

**icar** [- -] rent; -a vermek to lease, to let.

**icat,** -dı [- -] invention; ~ etm. 1. to invent; 2. to fabricate, to trump up.

**icaz** [- -] concision, succinctness.

**icazet,** -ti [ā] 1. permission; 2. † madrasa diploma.

**icazetname** [ā, ā] † madrasa diploma.

**icbar** [ā] compulsion, coercion; ~ etm. to force, to compel, to coerce.

**icik** F: iciğini ciciğini çıkarmak to go over (or through) s.th. with a fine-tooth comb.

**icmal,** -li [ā] summary; ~ etm. to summarize.

**icra** [ā] 1. execution, performance, carrying out; 2. (dairesi) court for claims; 3. ♪ performance; ~ etm. 1. to carry out, to execute; 2. ♪ to perform; to play; to sing; ~ heyeti 1. executive board (or committee); 2. ♪ performers; ~ kuvveti executive power; ~ memuru bailiff; ~ vekili minister, member of the cabinet; -ya vermek (b-ni) to take s.o. to court.

**icraat,** -tı [ā, ā] performances; operations, actions.

**iç,** -çi 1. inside, interior; 2. inner, internal; 3. in; among; 4. internal organs of the body; 5. domestic, home; 6. fig. mind, heart, will; ~ açı A interior angle; ~ açıcı heartwarming; ~ açmak to cheer up; 2 Anadolu Inner Anatolia; ~ bezelye shelled peas; ~ bulantısı nausea; ~ çamaşırı underwear; ~ çekmek **1.** to sigh; **2.** to sob; ~ deniz inland sea; ~ donu underpants; ~ etm. F to swipe, to pocket; ~ geçirmek to sigh; ~ gıcıklamak to arouse one's lust; ~ gömleği slip; ~ hat **1.** domestic line; **2.** domestic communications; ~ içe **1.** one inside the other, nested; **2.** one opening into another *(room)*; ~ lastik inner tube; ~ merkez focus *(of an earthquake)*; ~ organlar internal organs, viscera; ~ pazar domestic *(or home)* market; ~ pilav pilaf prepared with currants, pine nuts, spices and liver; ~ piyasa *s.* ~ pazar; ~ savaş civil war; ~ sıkıcı dull, boring, tedious; ~ sıkıntısı boredom; ~ sular inland rivers and lakes; ~ ticaret domestic *(or home)* trade; *(içi)*: ~ açılmak to feel relieved, to be cheered up; ~ almamak *(or* kabul etmemek*)* not to feel like eating; ~ bayılmak to feel faint with hunger, to be starving; ~ bulanmak **1.** to feel nauseated; **2.** *fig.* to get suspicious; ~ burkulmak to be very unhappy; ~ çekmek *(bşi)* to have a longing for *s.th.*, to desire *s.th.*; ~ çıfıt çarşısı *fig.* evil-minded; ~ dar *(or* tez*)* impatient, restless *(person)*; ~ daralmak to be depressed *(or distressed)*; ~ dışı bir unaffected, sincere; ~ dışına çıkmak to be nauseous; ~ erimek to be greatly grieved; ~ ezilmek to feel hungry, to have a sinking feeling; ~ geçmek **1.** to doze; **2.** F to be worn out; **3.** to become overripe *(fruit)*; ~ geniş *fig.* F easygoing, carefree; ~ gitmek **1.** to have diarrhea *(or* the squirts*)*; **2.** to starve *(-e* for*)*, to hunger *(-e* for*)*; ~ içine sığmamak to be up in the air; ~ içini yemek *(or* kemirmek*)* to eat one's heart out; ~ kalkmak to have a feeling of nausea; ~ kan ağlamak to be deeply grieved, to be in great sorrow; ~ kararmak to be dismayed; ~ kazınmak to feel very hungry, to starve; ~ paralanmak to be greatly upset; ~ rahat etm. to be relieved; ~ sıkılmak to feel bored; ~ sızlamak to be very unhappy *(-e* about*)*; ~ sürmek ? to have diarrhea; ~ yağ bağlamak to be filled with joy; ~ yanmak **1.** to be very thirsty; **2.** *fig.* to be very upset; *(içinde)*: ~ yüzmek to be rolling in *(money, etc.)*; *(içinden)*: ~ çıkmak to accomplish, to solve, to carry out; ~ geçirmek to think about, to consider; ~ geçmek *(b-nin)* to occur to *s.o.*, to cross *one's* mind; ~ gülmek *(b-ne)* to

laugh up one's sleeve at *s.o.*; ~ okumak **1.** to read to o.s.; **2.** *sl.* to swear under one's breath *(-e* at*)*; ~ pazarlıklı backstabbing, two-faced; *(içine)*: ~ almak to contain, to hold; to include, to encompass; ~ atmak **1.** to keep to o.s. *(problem)*; **2.** to brood over *(an insult)*; ~ çekmek to inhale; ~ doğmak to feel in one's bones, to have a presentiment *(or* hunch*)*; ~ etm. *(bşin) sl.* to make a hash *(or* mess*)* of *s.th.*; ~ işlemek **1.** to cut s.o. the quick; **2.** to chill s.o. to the bone *(cold)*; to soak s.o. to the skin *(rain)*; ~ kapanık introverted, withdrawn; ~ kurt düşmek to suspect; ~ sıçmak *s.* ~ etm.; ~ sokacağı gelmek *(b-ni)* to be nuts over *s.o.*, to be wild about *s.o.*; *(içini)*: ~ bayıltmak **1.** to make s.o. feel sick; **2.** to talk s.o.'s head off; ~ boşaltmak *s.* ~ dökmek; ~ çekmek to sigh; ~ dökmek to unburden o.s., to unbesom o.s., to make a clean breast of; *(içinin)*: ~ yağı erimek to pine away with anxiety; içler acısı heart-rendig, heart breaking; içten içe underhandedly, secretly.

**İçbükey** concave.

**İçderi** endoderm(is).

**İçebakış** *psych.* introspection.

**İçecek 1.** beverage, drink; **2.** potable, drinkable *(water)*; ~ su drinking water.

**İçedoğma** presentiment.

**İçedönük** introverted.

**İçek** *gr.* infix.

**İçekapanık 1.** schizoid; **2.** autistic.

**İçeri, içerisi, -nl 1.** inside, interior; **2.** inner; **3.** in; ~ atmak *(or* tıkmak*)* *fig.* F to put in clink; ~ buyurun! please come in!; ~ dalmak to barge in, to burst into; ~ düşmek *sl.* to go to clink; ~ girmek **1.** to go in, to enter; **2.** F to make a loss; **3.** F to go to clink; içerde **1.** losing; **2.** F in clink *(or* stir*)*; içerde olm. F **1.** to lose, to be out, to be to the bad *(money)*; **2.** to be in clink *(or* stir*)*.

**İçerik 1.** content(s); **2.** *log.* implicit.

**İçerlek 1.** sitting back *(building)*; **2.** indented *(line)*.

**İçerlemek** to resent.

**İçermek 1.** to contain, to include, to comprise; **2.** *log.* to imply.

**İçgeçit** tunnel.

**İçgözlem** introspection.

**İçgüdü** instinct.

**İçgüdüsel** instinctive.

**İçgüvey, içgüveyisi, -nl** man who lives with his wife's parents; *-den (or* -sinden*)* hallice *fig.* so so.

**İçici** drunkard, alcoholic.

**içim 1.** sip; **2.** taste, flavo(u)r.

**içimli 1.** having ... taste *(cigarette, etc.)*; **2.** pleasant to the taste *(cigarette, etc.)*.

**için 1.** for; **2.** because; **3.** so that, in order that; **4.** in order to, so as to, to; **5.** concerning, about; bunun ~ for this reason.

**içinde 1.** in, inside; **2.** within, in; **3.** under *(circumstances)*; **4.** having, full of, all; ~ olm. to be included.

**içindekiler** contents.

**için için 1.** internally; **2.** secretly; ~ ağlamak to weep inwardly.

**içirmek** *caus. of* içmek to make s.o. drink.

**içişleri,** -ni *pol.* internal *(or home)* affairs; ♀ Bakanı Minister of Internal Affairs; ♀ Bakanlığı Ministry of Internal Affairs.

**içken** tippler, boozer, alcoholic.

**içki 1.** drink, liquor, booze; **2.** drinking; ~ âlemi orgy, booze-up, spree; ~ içmek *(or* kullanmak*)* to drink, to tipple; ~ yasağı prohibition of alcoholic beverages; -ye düşkün addicted to drink.

**içkici 1.** liquor dealer; **2.** drunkard, tippler.

**içkili 1.** intoxicated; **2.** licensed to sell *(or* serve*)* alcoholic drinks.

**içkin 1.** immanent; **2.** intrinsic, inherent.

**içkulak** *anat.* inner ear.

**içlem** *log.* comprehension, connotation, intension.

**içlenmek** to be affected *(-den* by*)*, to take to heart.

**içli 1.** having an inside *(kernel, pulp, etc.)*; ⊾ oversensitive.

**içlidışlı** intimate, bosom, cheek by jowl; ~ olm. to be bosom friends, to be on intimate terms.

**içlik 1.** interior; **2.** undergarment.

**içme 1.** *vn. of* içmek; **2.** mineral spring; ~ suyu fresh *(or* drinking*)* water.

**içmek,** (-çer) **1.** to drink; **2.** to smoke; **3.** to drink, to tipple; **4.** to absorb, to imbibe *(fluid)*; içtikleri su ayrı gitmez *fig.* they are hail-fellow-well-met with each other.

**içmeler** mineral springs.

**içmimar** interior decorator.

**içplazma** *biol.* endoplasm.

**içsalgı** hormone.

**içsel 1.** internal, inner; **2.** spiritual.

**içten 1.** from within; **2.** sincere, from the heart; ~ gelen sincere; ~ yanmalı *mot.* internal-combustion.

**içtenlik** sincerity.

**içtepi** *psych.* compulsion.

**içtihat** [. . -] opinion, conviction.

**içtima,** -ı [⁸] **1.** meeting, gathering; assembly; **2.** ✕ muster; **3.** *ast.* conjunction; ~ etm. **1.** to meet, to assemble; **2.** ✕ to muster.

**içtimai** [. . - -] social.

**içtimaiyat,** -tı [⁸, ⁸] sociology.

**içtinap** [. .-] abstention, avoidance; ~ etm. to refrain *(-den* from*)*, to abstain *(-den* from*)*, to avoid.

**içtüzük** bylaws, internal regulations, standing rules.

**içyağı,** -nı suet.

**içyapı** internal structure.

**içyarıçap,** -pı Å apothem.

**içyüz** the inside story, the hidden side, the real truth, true colo(u)rs.

**içzar** ♀ intine.

**idadi** [- - -] *hist.* senior high school.

**idam** [- -] **1.** capital punishment; **2.** execution of a death sentence; ~ cezası death sentence; ~ etm. to execute, to put to death; ~ hükmü *(or* kararı*)* sentence of death; -a mahkûm etm. to condemn to death.

**idame** [⁸] continuation; ~ etm. to continue.

**idamlık 1.** capital *(crime)*; **2.** condemned to death.

**idare** [⁸] **1.** administration, management, direction; **2.** thriftiness, economy; ~ amiri chief, head administrator; ~ etm. **1.** to manage, to administer, to direct, to conduct, to lead; to govern; to control; **2.** to economize, to make ends meet; **3.** to be enough, to suffice; **4.** F *(b-ni)* to handle *s.o.* with kid gloves; **5.** F to hush up, to cover up; **6.** to drive, to use *(car)*; **7.** to stretch *(resources)*; ~ etmez it doesn't pay; ~ heyeti *(or* meclisi*)* administrative committee; board of directors; ~ hukuku administrative law.

**idareci** [⁸] **1.** manager, administrator, organizer; **2.** tactful.

**idarecilik** [⁸] **1.** administration; **2.** tact.

**idarehane** [⁸, ⁸] administrative office.

**idaremaslahat,** -tı [. - . . . . .] muddling through.

**idareli** [⁸] **1.** efficient, good at managing; **2.** thrifty; **3.** economical; ~ kullanmak to economize, to husband.

**idaresiz 1.** inefficient, incompetent; **2.** wasteful, uneconomical.

**idareten** on a day-to-day basis, temporarily.

**idari** [. - -] administrative, managerial.

**idbar** [⁸] adversity.

**iddia** [⁸] **1.** claim, assertion, thesis; **2.** insistence; **3.** pretension; **4.** bet, wager; ~ etm. **1.** to claim; to assert, to allege; **2.** to insist; **3.** to pretend; ~ makamı ♫ the public prosecutor; ~ olunan şey ♫ question at issue; -ya girişmek *(or* tutuşmak*)* to bet, to wager.

**iddiacı** obstinate, assertive.

**iddialı** 1. assertive, presumptuous; 2. disputed.

**iddianame** [â, â] *ðð* indictment.

**iddiasız** unassertive; unpretentious; simple, modest.

**ideal**, -li 1. ideal; 2. ideal, perfect.

**idealist**, -ti idealist(ic).

**idealizm** idealism.

**identik** *Å* identical.

**identiklik** *Å* identity.

**ideoloji** ideology.

**ideolojik** ideological.

**idi** 1. *(he, she, it)* was; 2. and so on *(or* forth)*; like, such as.

**idil** *lit.* idyl.

**idiş** 1. gelding; 2. gelded, castrated.

**idman** [â] 1. workout, training, exercise(s); 2. fitness; ~ yapmak to work out, to exercise, to train.

**idmancı** [â] 1. athlete in training; 2. gymnast, gym teacher.

**idmanlı** [â] 1. fit, in good shape; 2. *(bşe) fig.* experienced in *s.th.*

**idrak**, -ki [â] 1. perception, comprehension, understanding; 2. attainment, reaching; ~ etm. 1. to perceive, to apprehend, to comprehend; 2. to attain, to reach.

**idrakli** [â] perceptive, intelligent.

**idraksız** dull-witted, unintelligent.

**idrar** [â] urine; ~ torbası (urinary) bladder; ~ yolu urethra; ~ zorluğu dysuria.

**idrisağacı**, -nı ♀ St. Lucie's cherry, mahaleb (cherry).

**İETT** *(abbr. for* İstanbul Elektrik, Tünel, Tramvay İşletmesi) the Istanbul Electric Power, Funicular and Streetcar Board.

**ifa** [- -] fulfil(l)ment, performance; ~ etm. to fulfil(l), to execute, to carry out, to perform.

**ifade** [â] 1. expression, explanation; 2. statement; 3. *ðð* deposition; 4. *sl.* affair, business; ~ etm. 1. to be of value *(or* significance); 2. to explain, to express; ~ vermek *ðð* to give evidence, to testify; -sini almak 1. *ðð* to interrogate, to grill, to cross-examine; 2. *sl.* to beat up, to wallop.

**ifadelendirmek** [â] to make meaningful *(or* expressive).

**iffet**, -ti 1. chastity; 2. honesty, uprightness.

**iffetli** 1. chaste, virtuous; 2. honest, upright.

**iffetsiz** 1. unchaste; 2. dishonest.

**iflâh** restoration, recovery; ~ olm. to get well *(or* better); ~ olmaz 1. incorrigible *(person)*; 2. hopeless *(situation)*; -ı ke-

silmek F to be exhausted *(or* done for); -ını kesmek F to wear down.

**iflas** 1. bankruptcy, insolvency; 2. *fig.* failure; ~ dairesi bankruptcy office; ~ etm. 1. to go bankrupt; 2. *fig.* to fall flat *(idea, plan)*; ~ kararı decree of bankruptcy, adjudication of insolvency; ~ masası bankrupt's assets.

**ifrat**, -tı [â] 1. excess, overdoing; 2. exaggeration; -a kaçmak to overdo.

**ifraz** [â] 1. separation; 2. *ðð* allotment; 3. *biol.* secretion; ~ etm. 1. *ðð* to allot; 2. *biol.* to secrete.

**ifrazat**, -tı *biol.* secretions.

**ifrit**, -ti [ .-] malicious demon; ~ kesilmek *(or* olm.) to fly off the handle.

**ifsat**, -dı [â] 1. subversion; 2. corruption.

**ifşa** [â] disclosure, divulgence; ~ etm. to disclose, to divulge, to reveal, to expose.

**iftar** [â] *eccl.* 1. breaking one's fast; 2. the evening meal during Ramadan; ~ etm. to break one's fast; ~ topu *gun fired at sunset during Ramadan as a signal for breaking the fast.*

**iftarlık** [â] 1. snack eaten when breaking the fast; 2. suitable for eating when breaking the fast; 3. *fig.* very little.

**iftihar** [â] (laudable) pride; ~ etm. to take pride *(ile* in), to be proud *(ile* of); -a geçmek to get on the hono(u)r roll.

**iftira** [â] slander, calumny; ~ etm. *(or* atmak) to slander, to calumniate, to blacken.

**iftiracı** [â] slanderer.

**iğ** spindle.

**iğbirar** [â] resentment.

**iğde** ♀ oleaster, wild olive.

**iğdemir** ⊕ carpenter's chisel.

**iğdiş** 1. gelding; 2. castrated, gelded *(animal)*; ~ etm. to castrate, to geld.

**iğfal**, -li [â] rape; ~ etm. to rape.

**iğne** 1. needle; 2. pin; safety pin; 3. brooch, pin; 4. ⊕ pointer, needle; 5. *zo.* stinger; 6. ♀ style; 7. fishhook; 8. syringe; 9. ? injection, shot; 10. *fig.* pinprick; ~ atsan yere düşmez *fig.* it is packed-out; ~ deliği the eye of a needle; ~ deliğinden Hindistan'ı seyretmek *fig.* to read between the lines; ~ ile kuyu kazmak *fig.* 1. to do a hard job without proper means; 2. to work on a slow and difficult task; ~ ipliğe dönmek *fig.* to become skin and bones, to be worn away to a shadow; ~ vurmak *(or* yapmak) *(b-ne)* to give *s.o.* an injection; ~ yemiş köpeğe dönmek *fig.* to become a bag of bones; -den ipliğe kadar down to the smallest detail; -yi kendine batır, sonra çuvaldızı başkasına pro. do as you would be done by.

**iğneardı,** -nı backstitch.

**iğnedenlik** s. iğnelik.

**iğnelemek 1.** to pin (-e to); **2.** fig. to speak sarcastically.

**iğnelenmek 1.** pass. of iğnelemek; **2.** to have pins and needles.

**iğneleyici** biting, sarcastic; ~ söz biting word.

**iğneli 1.** having a needle (or pin or thorn or sting); **2.** pinned; **3.** fig. biting, sarcastic (words); ~ fıcı fig. hot water; ~ fıcıda olm. to be in hot water; ~ söz sarcastic remark.

**iğnelik** pincushion.

**iğneyapraklılar** ♀ Coniferales.

**iğrenç,** -ci detestable, repulsive, odious, loathsome, disgusting.

**iğrendirmek** to disgust.

**iğrengen** easily disgusted.

**iğrenme** s. iğrenti.

**iğrenmek** (bşden) to feel disgust at s.th., to be disgusted with s.th., to loathe.

**iğrenti** disgust, loathing.

**ihale** [â] tender, bid; ~ etm. to let a contract to.

**-i hali** gr. accusative case.

**ihanet,** -ti [â] **1.** treachery; **2.** unfaithfulness, infidelity; ~ etm. **1.** to betray; **2.** to be unfaithful (-e to).

**ihata** [. - .] surrounding, enclosing; **2.** comprehension; ~ etm. to surround.

**ihatalı 1.** vast; **2.** knowledgeable.

**ihbar** [â] denunciation, tip-off; ~ etm. **1.** to denounce, to tip off, to inform (-i against); **2.** to inform, to notify.

**ihbarcı** informer.

**ihbariye** [â] **1.** official notice, notification; **2.** reward for informing against s.o.

**ihbarlı** informed; ~ konuşma teleph. person-to-person call.

**ihbarname** [â, â] = ihbariye 1.

**ihdas** [â] creating, invention; ~ etm. to invent, to create, to introduce.

**ihlal,** -li infringement, violation; ~ etm. to infringe, to violate, to break (law, treaty, etc.).

**ihmal,** -li [â] negligence, omission; ~ etm. to neglect, to omit.

**ihmalci, ihmalkâr** [â] negligent, neglectful.

**ihmalkârlık** [â] neglectfulness.

**ihracat,** -tı [. - -] exportation, exporting; ~ malları exports; ~ yapmak to export.

**ihracatçı** [â] exporter.

**ihracatçılık** [â, â] exporting, the export business.

**ihraç,** -cı [â] **1.** expulsion; **2.** † exportation,

export; ~ bankası bank of issue; ~ etm. **1.** to expel; **2.** † to export.

**ihram** [â] **1.** garment worn by pilgrims in Mecca; **2.** Bedouin cloak; **3.** cover (for a sofa, etc.); ~a girmek to put on the pilgrim's garb.

**ihraz** [â] obtainment; ~ etm. to obtain, to attain.

**ihsan** [â] favo(u)r, kindness, benevolence; ~ etm. to grant, to bestow.

**ihsas** [â] **1.** hint, insinuation, indication; **2.** phys. perception; ~ etm. to insinuate, to indicate.

**ihtar** [â] warning; ~ cezası admonition; ~ etm. to warn, to remind; ~ vermek (or -da bulunmak) to warn, to remind.

**ihtarname** [â, â] **1.** official warning; **2.** ☼ = protesto.

**ihtifal,** -li commemorative ceremony.

**ihtikâr** profiteering.

**ihtilaç,** -cı convulsion.

**ihtilaf** conflict, difference, disagreement, dispute; ~a düşmek to conflict (ile with), to disagree (ile with).

**ihtilaflı** controversial.

**ihtilal,** -li **1.** revolution, rebellion, riot; **2.** disturbance, disorder; ~ yapmak to raise a rebellion.

**ihtilalci** rebel, revolutionary.

**ihtilam** [â] nocturnal emission.

**ihtilas** embezzlement; ~ etm. to embezzle.

**ihtilat,** -tı **1.** ☀ complication; **2.** social intercourse (or relations); ~ etm. ☀ to lead to complication.

**ihtimal,** -li [â] **1.** probability; **2.** probably; ~ vermek to consider likely, to regard as possible; -ki probably; her -e karşı just to be safe.

**ihtimali** [â] probable.

**ihtimam** [â] care, carefulness; ~ etm. (or göstermek) to take great pains (-e over, with).

**ihtimamlı** [â] painstaking, meticulous.

**ihtimamsız** [â] careless.

**ihtira,** -aı [â] invention; ~ beratı patent (right).

**ihtirak,** -kı [â] combustion.

**ihtiram** [â] veneration, reverence; ~ bölüğü guard of hono(u)r; ~ duruşu standing at attention.

**ihtiras** [â] ambition, greed, passion.

**ihtiraslı** [â] ambitious, greedy, passionate.

**ihtiraz** [â] avoidance; wariness, caution; ~ kaydı reservation.

**ihtisar** [â] abbreviation.

**ihtisas** [â] specialization, specialty; ~ yapmak to specialize (-de in), to major (-de in).

**ihtişam** [ā] splendo(u)r, magnificence, pomp, grandeur.

**ihtişamlı** [ā] splendid, magnificent, pompous.

**ihtiva** [ā] inclusion, containment; ~ etm. 1. to contain, to hold; 2. to include, to comprise.

**ihtiyaç,** -cı [ā] 1. need, necessity, want; 2. poverty; ~ duymak to feel the need (-e for); -ı karşılamak to serve (or meet) a need; -ı olm. (bşe) to need s.th., to be in need (or want) of s.th.

**ihtiyar**[1] [ā] 1. old, aged (person); 2. old person, Am. old-timer ~ meclisi (or heyeti) 𝕺 village council.

**ihtiyar**[2] [ā] selection, choice, option; ~ etm. 1. to choose, to select; 2. to endure, to put up with, to bear with.

**ihtiyari** [. . - -] optional.

**ihtiyarlamak** to grow (or get) old, to age.

**ihtiyarlatmak** to age.

**ihtiyarlık** old age, senility; ~ sigortası social security, old-age insurance.

**ihtiyat,** -tı [ā] 1. precaution, caution; 2. reserve; ~ akçesi reserve fund, nest egg; ~ kaydı ile with some doubt; ~ kuvvetleri reserve forces.

**ihtiyaten** [ā] 1. as a reserve; 2. as a precaution.

**ihtiyati** [. . - -] precautionary; ~ haciz 𝕺 provisional distraint; ~ tedbirler precautionary measures.

**ihtiyatkâr** [ā] cautious, prudent, foresighted.

**ihtiyatlı** s. ihtiyatkâr; ~ davranmak to act prudently.

**ihtiyatsız** imprudent, incautious, rash; improvident.

**ihtizaz** [ā] vibration; tremor.

**ihvan** [ā] 1. friends; 2. brethren, fellow members.

**ihya** [ā] 1. revitalization, resuscitation; 2. fig. revival; ~ etm. 1. to revitalize, to enliven; 2. fig. to revive, to revivify.

**ihzar** [ā] preparation.

**ihzari** [. - -] preparatory.

**ikame** [ā] 1. substitution; 2. establishment, appointment; 3. opening (a law case); ~ etm. 1. to substitute; 2. to establish, to appoint; 3. to open (a law case).

**ikamet,** -ti [ā] residence, dwelling; ~ etm. to live, to reside, to dwell; ~ tezkeresi 𝕺 residence permit.

**ikametgâh** [ā] (place of) residence, legal domicile; ~ kâğıdı (or ilmühaberi) residence paper.

**ikaz** [- -] warning; ~ etm. to warn.

**ikbal,** -li [ā] 1. prosperity, success; 2. †

wish, desire; ~ düşkünü person who has fallen from riches to poverty.

**iken** while, whilst.

**iki** two; ~ ahbap çavuşlar F inseparable friends; ~ arada kalmak to be at a loss as to whom to believe; ~ aslan bir posta sığmaz pro. two stars keep not their motion in one sphere; ~ ateş arasında kalmak to be caught between two fires; ~ ayağını bir pabuca sokmak F to put in a flurry; ~ büklüm olm. fig. to double up; ~ cami arasında kalmış beynamaz fig. fallen between two stools; ~ çift laf (or söz) a word or two; ~ dirhem bir çekirdek F dressed to kill, dressed (up) to the nines, dressed up like a dog's dinner; ~ eli kanda olsa fig. no matter how pressed he is; ~ elim yanıma gelsin! I swear I'm telling the truth; gözü ~ çeşme ağlamak to cry buckets; ~ günde in (or within) two days; ~ kat olm. to double up; ~ misli twofold; ~ nokta colon; ~ ucunu bir araya getirememek to be unable to make both ends meet; ~ yakası bir araya gelmemek to be unable to make both ends meet; ~ zamanlı motor ⊕ two-stroke engine; -de bir (or birde) frequently, all the time; -miz the two of us; -si aynı kapıya çıkar it is as broad as it is long; -ye ayırmak to halve.

**ikianlamlı** ambiguous, equivocal.

**ikicanlı** pregnant.

**ikicinsli, ikicinslikli** bisexual.

**ikideğerli** bivalent.

**ikidilli** bilingual.

**ikidüzlemli** ♀ dihedral.

**ikieşeyli** bisexual.

**ikikatlı** duplex apartment.

**ikilem** log. dilemma.

**ikilemek** 1. to make two (or a pair); 2. to plough twice (field).

**ikileşmek** to become two, to be doubled.

**ikili** 1. having two parts; 2. double, dual; 3. bilateral; 4. cards: two; 5. ♪ duet; 6. ♪ duo; ~ anlaşma bilateral treaty.

**ikilik** 1. discord, disagreement; 2. ♪ half note.

**ikinci** 1. second; 2. secondary; 3. vice-, sub-; ~ bir emre kadar until further notice; ~ hamur kâğıt lightly glazed paper; ~ mevki (or sınıf) 1. second-class; 2. the second-class section (in a boat, etc.).

**ikincil** secondary.

**ikindi** midafternoon; ~ ezanı the call to afternoon prayer; ~ kahvaltısı afternoon tea, snack; ~ namazı isl. the afternoon prayer.

**ikindiyin** [. . x .] F in the afternoon.

**ikişekilli** dimorphic, dimorphous.

**ikişer** two at a time; two each; ~ ~ two by two, in twos.

**ikiyanlı** bilateral.

**ikiyaşayışlı** *biol.* amphibian, amphibious.

**ikiyüzlü 1.** *fig.* two-faced, hypocritical; **2.** double-faced (*cloth*).

**ikiyüzlülük** hypocrisy.

**ikiz 1.** twins; **2.** a twin; **3.** twinned; ~ doğurmak **1.** to twin; **2.** *fig.* to have a devil of a hard time.

**ikizkenar** A isosceles; ~ üçgen isosceles triangle; ~ yamuk isosceles trapezoid.

**ikizler** *ast.* the Twins, Gemini.

**ikizli 1.** having twins; **2.** with two handles; **3.** of two kinds; **4.** *log.* ambiguous.

**iklim** climate.

**iklimleme aygıtı** air conditioner.

**iklimsel** climatic.

**ikmal, -li** [ā] **1.** completion; **2.** replenishment, supplying; **3.** X reinforcement; supply; **4.** (*imtihanı*) make-up examination; ~ etm. **1.** to finish, to complete; **2.** to replenish, to supply; -e kalmak to have to take a make-up examination.

**ikna, -aı** [ā] persuasion; ~ etm. to persuade, to convince; ~ olm. to be persuaded.

**ikon** icon.

**ikrah** [ā] disgust, detestation, abhorrence; ~ etm. to detest, to loathe, to abhor; ~ getirmek to begin to detest.

**ikrahlık** = ikrah.

**ikram** [ā] **1.** hono(u)ring; **2.** discount; **3.** s.th. offered a guest (*food, drink*); ~ etm. **1.** to offer, to serve, to help s.o. to (*food, drink*); **2.** to discount.

**ikramiye** [ā] **1.** bonus, gratuity; **2.** prize (*in a lottery*).

**ikramiyeli** [ā] **1.** with a premium; **2.** with a prize.

**ikrar** [ā] avowal, declaration, confession; ~ etm. to confess, to declare, to attest.

**ikraz** [ā] loan; ~ etm. to lend (*money*).

**iksir** [. -] elixir.

**iktibas** [ā] quotation; ~ etm. to quote.

**iktidar** [ā] **1.** power, capacity, ability; **2.** *pol.* the ruling party, government; **3.** potency, virility; ~ mevkii the position of being in power; ~ partisi the party in power; -da olm. *pol.* to be in power.

**iktidarlı** [ā] powerful, capable.

**iktidarsız 1.** weak; incompetent; **2.** impotent.

**iktidarsızlık 1.** wekaness; incapacity; **2.** impotence.

**iktifa** [ā] contentment; ~ etm. to be content (*ile* with).

**iktisadi** [. , - -] **1.** economic; **2.** economical; ~ devlet kuruluşu (*or* teşekkülü) corporation in which the government is the majority stock-holder; ~ ve ticari ilimler akademisi academy of economic and commercial sciences.

**iktisadiyat, -tı** [ā, ā] economy, economic state (*of a country*).

**iktisap, -bı** [ā] acquisition; ~ etm. to acquire.

**iktisat, -dı** [ā] **1.** economics, economy; **2.** economy, thrift, saving; ~ Fakültesi the School of Economics.

**iktisatçı** economist.

**iktiza** [ā] necessity, need; ~ etm. to be necessary.

**il 1.** province; **2.** country, nation; ~ genel meclisi provincial assembly; ~ özel idaresi the administration of a province.

**ila** [. -] from ... to..., between... and...; üç ~ beş kişi between three and five people.

**ilaç, -cı 1.** medicine, drug; **2.** chemical; **3.** cure, remedy; **4.** insecticide, pesticide; ~ içmek to take medicine.

**ilacbilim** pharmacology.

**ilaçlamak 1.** to apply medicine (to); **2.** to disinfect; **3.** to apply insecticide (to).

**ilaçlı 1.** medicated; **2.** treated (*with pesticide*).

**ilah** god, deity.

**ilahe** goddess.

**ilahi 1.** [. - -] hymn, psalm; **2.** [. x .] my God!

**ilahi** divine, heavenly.

**ilahileştirmek** to deify.

**ilahiyat, -tı** [ā, ā] theology, divinity; ~ Fakültesi the School of Theology.

**ilahiyatçı** theologian.

**ilam** [- -] writ.

**ilamaşallah 1.** until God knows when; **2.** bravo!

**ilan** [- -] **1.** notice; **2.** advertisement; **3.** proclamation, declaration; ~ etm. **1.** to declare, to announce; **2.** to advertise; **3.** to proclaim, to declare; ~ vermek to insert an advertisement (*in a newspaper*); -ı aşk declaration of love; -ı aşk etm. to declare one's love (-*e* to).

**ilancılık** advertising.

**ilarya** *zo.* a kind of mullet.

**ilave 1.** addition, increase; **2.** supplement; ~ etm. to add (-*e* to).

**ilaveten** in addition, additionally.

**ilbay** *s.* vali.

**ilçe** administrative district (*within an* il), borough.

**ilçebay** *s.* kaymakam.

**ile 1.** with, together with; **2.** and; **3.** by

means of, by.

**İlelebet** forever.

**İlenç** curse, malediction.

**İlenmek** to curse, to execrate.

**İlerde** s. İleride.

**İleri** 1. front part; 2. forward; 3. fore, front, forward; 4. *fig.* advanced, progressive; 5. fast *(clock)*; 6. forward!; ~ almak 1. to move forward; 2. to put forward *(clock)*; 3. to promote *(a person)*; ~ atılmak 1. to rush ahead, to spring forward; 2. *fig.* to act with courage; ~ gelenler notables; ~ gelmek to result *(-den* from), to be due *(-den* to); ~ gitmek 1. to go forward, to advance; 2. to be running fast *(clock)*; 3. *fig.* to go too far; ~ karakol X advance outpost, outlying picket; ~ kol X vanguard; ~ sürmek 1. to drive forwards; 2. to put forward *(idea)*; 3. to insist (on); -yi görmek *fig.* to take the long view, to be farsighted *(or* farseeing).

**İlerici** progressive.

**İlericilik** progressiveness.

**İleride** 1. in the future, later on; 2. ahead, further on; 3. in front.

**İlerlek** advanced, developed.

**İlerlemek** 1. to go forward, to move ahead, to advance; 2. to improve, to get better; 3. to progress, to develop; 4. to pass, to go by *(time)*.

**İleti** 1. message; 2. communiqué.

**İletim** transmission, transmittal.

**İletimli** transmitted; ~ yayın live broadcast.

**İletişim** communication.

**İletken** 1. *phys.* conductor; 2. *phys.* conductive.

**İletkenlik** *phys.* conductivity.

**İletki** ♣ protractor.

**İletmek** 1. to transmit, to convey; 2. *phys.* to conduct.

**İlga** [â] 1. annulment, nullification; 2. abolition; 3. repeal; ~ etmek 1. to annul; 2. to abolish; 3. to repeal.

**İlgeç** *gr.* postposition.

**İlgi** 1. relation, connection; 2. interest, concern; 3. *gr.* relational, relative; 4. ♠ affinity; ~ çekici interesting; ~ çekmek to draw attention, to arouse interest; ~ duymak to be interested *(-e* in); ~ göstermek to show an interest *(-e* in); ~ toplamak to arouse interest, to attract attention: ~ zamiri *gr.* relative pronoun.

**İlgilendirmek** 1. to interest; to concern; 2. to arouse s.o.'s interest *(ile* in).

**İlgilenmek** *(bşle)* to be interested in *s.th.*, to pay attention to *s.th.*, to show concern

for *s.th.*

**İlgili** 1. interested *(ile* in); 2. concerned *(ile* with), involving; 3. relevant, involved, concerned; ~ olm. to involve, to be concerned *(ile* with); to pertain *(ile* to); -ler those concerned.

**İlginç** interesting.

**İlgisiz** 1. indifferent; 2. irrelevant.

**İlgisizlik** 1. indifference; 2. irrelevance.

**İlhak,** -kı [â] annexation; ~ etm. to annex, to add *(-e* to).

**İlham** [â] inspiration; ~ almak to be inspired *(-den* by); ~ etm. to inspire; ~ perisi muse; ~ vermek to inspire.

**İlhan** 1. emperor; 2. ♀ *mf.*

**İlik,** -ği 1. *anat.* bone marrow; 2. buttonhole; button loop; ~ gibi 1. delicious; 2. *sl.* as pretty as a picture *(girl)*; ~ gibi pişmiş *(or* olmuş) done to a turn; iliğine işlemek *(or* geçmek) 1. to penetrate to one's marrow *(cold)*; 2. to drench to the skin; 3. to touch to the quick; iliğine kadar ıslanmak to be soaked to the skin, to get wet through; iliğini kemirmek *(b-nin)* to affect s.o. deeply; iliğini kurutmak *(b-nin)* *fig.* to wear s.o. out.

**İliklemek** to button up.

**İlikli** 1. containing marrow; 2. buttoned up.

**İlim,** -lmi science; ~ adamı scientist.

**İlimcilik** scientism.

**İlinti** 1. relevance, connection; 2. distress.

**İlintili** 1. related, connected; relevant; 2. distressed, upset.

**İlişik** 1. attached, enclosed; 2. related, connected; 3. connection, relation; ilişiği kalmamak to be through *(ile* with), to have no further connection *(ile* with); ilişiği olm. to be related *(ile* to), to be connected *(ile* with); ilişiğini kesmek 1. to sever one's connection *(ile* with); 2. to dismiss, to discharge *(ile* from).

**İlişikli** related, concerned, connected.

**İlişiksiz** unattached, free, independent.

**İlişki** 1. relation, connection; 2. communications; ~ kurmak to establish relations *(ile* with).

**İlişkili** related *(ile* to).

**İlişkin** concerning, regarding, relating *(-e* to).

**İlişkisiz** unrelated.

**İlişmek** 1. to graze, to touch; 2. to meddle *(-e* with), to touch; 3. to point out; 4. to bother, to disturb; 5. to perch, to sit on the edge.

**İliştirmek** to attach, to fasten *(-e* to).

**İlk,** -ki 1. (the) first; 2. initial; 3. primary; ~ adım first step; ~ ağızda the first time, at the first attempt; ~ defa for the first time; ~ fırsatta at the first opportunity; ~ görüşte at first sight; ~ göz ağrısı 1. first child; 2. F first love, old flame; ~ tahkikat *öö* preliminary inquiry; ~ yardım first aid; ~ yardım çantası first aid kit.

**Ilkah** [ā] fertilization, fecundation, insemination; ~ etm. to fecundate, to impregnate.

**Ilkbahar** spring.

**Ilkçağ** antiquity.

**Ilke** 1. principle, tenet; 2. element; 3. postulate, assumption; 4. fundamental, essential.

**Ilkel** 1. primitive; 2. primary.

**Ilkeleştirmek** to adopt as a principle.

**Ilkelleştirmek** to make primitive.

**Ilkellik** primitiveness.

**Ilkgirişim** initiative.

**Ilkin** [x .] 1. in the first place, first; 2. at first.

**Ilkkânun** † December.

**Ilkokul** primary school.

**Ilköğretim** primary education.

**Ilkönce** first (of all).

**Ilkteşrin** † October.

**Illa** [x -], **Illaki** 1. whatever happens, come what may; 2. or else; 3. especially, particularly; ~ ve lakin on the other hand, nevertheless.

**Illallah** [x . -] I'm fed up!; ~ demek to be fed up.

**Ille** [x .] s. Illa.

**Illet**, -ti 1. illness, disease; 2. defect, fault; 3. addiction; 4. *phls.* reason, cause.

**Illetli** 1. sickly, diseased; 2. faulty, defective.

**Illiyet**, -ti causality.

**Ilmek**[1] 1. to fasten (*or* tie) loosely; 2. to knot; 3. to graze.

**Ilmek**[2] s. Ilmik.

**Ilmen** scientifically speaking.

**Ilmi** scientific.

**Ilmihal**, -li [ā] catechism.

**Ilmik** 1. loop; 2. noose; ~ atmak to loop.

**Ilmiklemek** to loop.

**Ilmühaber** 1. certification, certificate of proof; 2. receipt.

**Iltibas** [ā] 1. confusion (*between two similar things*); 2. ambiguity; -a yol açmak to give rise to confusion.

**Iltica** [ā] taking (*or* seeking) refuge; ~ etm. to take refuge (-*e* with, in), to seek asylum (-*e* in); ~ hakkı right of asylum.

**Iltifat**, -tı [ā] 1. favo(u)r; 2. compliment; ~ etm. 1. to compliment; to flatter; 2. to enjoy, to like.

**Iltihak**, -kı [ā] adherence, joining; ~ etm. to join, to attach o.s. (-*e* to).

**Iltihap**, -bı [ā] *?* inflammation.

**Iltihaplanmak** [. - - .] *?* to get inflamed (*or* infected), to fester.

**Iltihaplı** *?* inflamed, infected.

**Iltimas** [ā] protection, patronage, favo(u)ritism, pull; ~ etm. to show favo(u)ritism (-*e* towards), to favo(u)r; -ı olm. to have s.o. at one's back, to have a pull.

**Iltimascı** [ā] backer, patron, protector.

**Iltimaslı** favo(u)red, privileged.

**Iltizam** [ā] 1. favo(u)ritism, partiality; 2. finding necessary; 3. tax farming; ~ etm. to favo(u)r.

**İlyada** the Iliad.

**Im** sign, signal; symbol.

**Ima** [- -] hint, allusion, innuendo; ~ etm. to hint (at), to imply, to allude (to).

**Imaj** image.

**Imal**, -li [ā] 1. manufacture, production; 2. product; ~ etm. to manufacture, to produce, to make.

**Imalat**, -tı [- - -] 1. products, manufactured goods; 2. production.

**Imalatçı** manufacturer.

**Imalathane** [- - - - .] workshop, factory, shop.

**Imalı** [- - .] allusive, implicit.

**Imam** 1. imam; 2. religious leader; 3. successor to the Prophet; ~ hatip okulu secondary school for the training of Islamic religious personnel; ~ kayığı *sl.* coffin; ~ nikâhı wedding performed by an imam; ~ suyu *sl.* raki.

**Imambayıldı** *a dish of eggplants with oil and onions.*

**Imame** [ā] junction bead in a string of prayer beads.

**Iman** [- -] 1. faith, belief; 2. religion; ~ getirmek to become a Muslim; ~ sahibi man of faith, believer; ~ tahtası F breastbone; -a getirmek (*b-ni*) 1. to convert s.o. to Islam; 2. *fig.* to persuade s.o. by force, to subdue s.o.; -ı gevremek (*or* ağlamak) F to wear o.s. out; -ı yok! 1. damn him!; 2. the callous swine!; -ım *sl.* hey, you!; -ına kadar up to the brim; -ına yandığım F damned; -ını gevretmek to wear out.

**Imanlı** [- - .] religious, faithful.

**Imansız** [- - .] 1. unbelieving, atheist; 2. unbeliever; 3. *fig.* cruel, unjust, wicked.

**Imar** [- -] public works, development; ~ etm. to improve, to render prosperous; ~ planı zoning and construction plan; ~ ve İskân Bakanlığı Ministry of Development and Housing.

**Imaret**, -ti [ā], **Imarethane** [ā] soup kitchen

*(for the poor).*

**imbat,** -tı daytime summer sea breeze.

**imbik** still, retort; -ten çekmek to distill.

**imdat,** -dı [â] **1.** help, assistance, aid; **2.** help!; ~ freni 🚗 emergency brake; ~ işareti SOS signal; ~ kapısı emergency exit; -ına yetişmek *(b-nin)* to come to *s.o.'s* rescue.

**imdi** [x .] **1.** therefore, so, thus; **2.** now.

**imece** cooperation for the community or one of its members.

**imge 1.** image; **2.** dream.

**imgelemek** to imagine.

**imgesel** imaginary.

**imha** [â] destruction, eradication; ~ etm. to destroy, to eradicate, to annihilate, to obliterate.

**imik** *anat.* throat.

**imkân 1.** possibility; **2.** opportunity, chance; ~ dahilinde as far as possible; ~ vermek to give an opportunity, to give a chance, to make possible; -ı yok! it's impossible *(or* out of question)!

**imkânsız** impossible.

**imla 1.** spelling, orthography; **2.** dictation; **3.** filling up; ~ etm. **1.** to dictate; **2.** to fill (up); ~ yanlışı spelling mistake; -sı bozuk **1.** bad at spelling; **2.** misspelled; -ya gelmemek *fig.* to go beyond all reason.

**imlemek 1.** to indicate; **2.** to hint (at), to imply.

**imparator** [.. x .] emperor.

**imparatoriçe** [... x . .] empress.

**imparatorluk 1.** empire; **2.** emperorship.

**imrendirmek** to arouse *s.o.'s* appetite *(or* desire) (-e for).

**imrenmek 1.** to long (-e for), to feel an appetite (-e for); **2.** to desire, to envy, to covet.

**imrenti** desire, envy.

**imsak,** -kı [â] **1.** fasting, abstinence; **2.** hour at which the daily Ramadan fast begins.

**imsel** symbolic.

**imtihan** [â] examination, test, trial; ~ etm. to test, to examine; ~ olm. to take *(or* sit for *or* go in for) an examination; vermek **1.** to pass an examination; **2.** *fig.* to get off scot-free; -da kalmak to fail *(or* flunk) in an examination.

**imtina,** -dı [â] avoidance; ~ etm. to avoid, to refrain (-den from).

**imtiyaz** [â] **1.** privilege; **2.** government concession, franchise; ~ sahibi **1.** concessionaire, concessioner; **2.** licensee; ~ vermek to give *s.o.* the privilege.

**imtiyazlı 1.** privileged; **2.** licensed.

**imtizaç** harmony, compatibility; ~ etm. **1.** to harmonize; **2.** to get on well together.

**imyazım** stenography.

**imza** [â] signature; ~ atmak *(or* etm.) to sign; ~ sahibi signatory; ~ toplamak to gather signatures.

**imzalamak** to sign.

**imzalı** signed.

**imzasız** unsigned.

**in**[1] **1.** den, lair; **2.** cave.

**in**[2]: ~ cin yok *(or* top oynuyor) there is nobody around, there isn't a soul around.

**inadına** [x - . .] out of obstinacy *(or* spite).

**inan 1.** belief; **2.** faith, confidence, trust; ~ olsun! take it from me!, take my word!

**inanç,** -cı **1.** belief; **2.** trust, confidence.

**inançlı** believing, faithful.

**inançsız** unbelieving.

**inandırıcı** convincing, plausible.

**inandırmak** to convince, to persuade.

**inanılır** believable, credible.

**inanılmaz** unbelievable, incredible.

**inanmak 1.** to believe, to trust; **2.** to have faith in *(God)*.

**inansız** faithless.

**inat,** -dı [â] **1.** obstinacy, stubbornness; **2.** F obstinate, stubborn, pigheaded; ~ etm. to be obstinate; -ı ~ F as stubborn as a mule; -ı tutmak to have a fit of obstinacy.

**inatçı** obstinate, stubborn, pigheaded.

**inatçılık** obstinacy, stubbornness.

**inatlaşmak** to behave stubbornly towards each other.

**inayet,** -ti [â] kindness, benevolence; ~ etm. to do a favo(u)r (-e to); ~ ola! may God help you!

**inayetli** [â] kind, gracious.

**ince 1.** slender, slim; **2.** thin, fine, small; **3.** refined, graceful, subtle; **4.** delicate, intricate; **5.** sensitive, delicate; **6.** dainty; **7.** high-pitched *(voice)*; **8.** front *(vowel)*; ~ elemek to sift fine; ~ eleyip sık dokumak *fig.* to split hairs; ~ görüşlü sharp-witted; ~ kesim small boned; ~ ses high *(or* treble) voice; -den -ye meticulously.

**inceağrı** twinge.

**incebağırsak** small intestine.

**incecik** very slender *(or* thin).

**inceleme** *vn.* of **incelemek**, *part.* examination, investigation.

**incelemek** to examine, to inspect, to scan, to scrutinize.

**incelik 1.** thinness, slenderness, slimness; **2.** delicacy, fineness; **3.** tact, finesse, delicacy; **4.** subtlety; **5.** detail.

**incelmek 1.** to become thin; **2.** to be thinned *(paint)*; **3.** to lose weight; **4.** F

to try to appear refined.
**inceltici** thinner.
**inceltmek 1.** to make thin; **2.** to thin *(paint)*.
**incesaz** ♪ *group of musicians who perform classical Turkish music.*
**inci** pearl; ~ avı pearl fishing; ~ avcısı pearl fisher *(or diver)*; ~ gibi pearly *(teeth)*.
**inciçiçeği,** -ni ♀ lily-of-the-valley.
**incik 1.** hurt, injured; **2.** *anat.* shin; **3.** P shinbone; **4.** P ankle.
**incik boncuk** cheap tawdry jewelry.
**İncil** *pr. n.* **1.** the New Testament; **2.** Gospel, Evangel.
**incili** pearly, pearled.
**incinmek 1.** to be hurt *(or injured)*; **2.** to be strained *(muscle)*; **3.** *fig.* to be offended *(-den* by).
**incir** ♀ fig (tree); ~ cekirdeğini doldurmaz *fig.* trifling, insignificant.
**incitici** painful, offensive.
**incitmebeni** P cancer.
**incitmek 1.** to hurt, to injure; to strain; **2.** *fig.* to offend.
**indeks** index.
**indi** subjective, personal.
**indifa,** -aı *eruption; ~ etm. to erupt.
**indirgeme** reduction.
**indirgemek** ♣, ♠ to reduce.
**indirim** discount, reduction.
**indirimli 1.** reduced, discount *(price)*; at a reduced price; ~ satış sale.
**indirmek** *caus. of* inmek, *part.* **1.** to lower, to bring down, to get down, to take down; **2.** to land, to deliver, to plant *(slap, blow)*; **3.** to reduce *(price, etc.)*; **4.** to destroy, to wreck.
**indiyum** ♠ indium.
**İndonezya** *pr. n.* İndonesia.
**indükleç** ≠ inductor.
**indükleme** *phys.* induction.
**indüklemek** *phys.* to induce.
**ineç,** -ci *geol.* syncline.
**inek 1.** *zo.* cow; **2.** *sl.* swot, *Am.* grind; **3.** *sl.* loose woman, tart.
**ineklemek** *sl.* to swot up, *Am.* to grind, to bone.
**ineklik 1.** cowshed; **2.** *sl.* imbecility.
**infaz** [â] execution, carrying out; ~ etm. to execute, to carry out.
**infial,** -li [â] indignation, resentment.
**infilak,** -kı explosion, ~ etm. to explode, to burst.
**İngiliz** [x . .] **1.** Englishman; Englishwoman; **2.** English; ~ anahtarı ⊕ monkey wrench, spanner; ~ lirası pound sterling; ♀ Uluslar Birliği the British Common-

wealth of Nations.
**İngilizce 1.** English, the English language; **2.** in English.
**İngiltere** [. . x .] *pr. n.* **1.** England; **2.** F Great Britain.
**ingin[1]** low.
**ingin[2]** (head) cold.
**inginlik 1.** lowness; **2.** *fig.* weakness.
**-in hali** *gr.* the genitive case.
**inhiraf** [â] deviation deflection; ~ etm. to deviate, to be deflected *(-den* from).
**inhisar** [â] **1.** restriction, limitation; **2.** monopoly; ~ etm. to be restricted *(or limited)* *(-e* to); -a almak to monopolize.
**inik 1.** pulled down, lowered *(curtain, etc.)*; flat *(tyre)*; **2.** *s.* encek; ~ deniz *geogr.* low tide.
**inikâs 1.** *phys.* reflection; **2.** echo; **3.** ↑ reaction; ~ etm. *phys.* to echo.
**inildemek** to groan, to moan, to whimper.
**inilti** groan, moan, whimper.
**inim inim:** ~ inlemek to whimper *(or moan or groan)* bitterly.
**inisiyatif** initiative.
**iniş 1.** *vn. of* inmek; **2.** downward slope; ~ aşağı downhill, downwards; ~ çıkış **1.** descent and ascent; **2.** ↑ rise and fall, fluctuation; ~ takımı ✈ undercarriage, undercart, landing gear.
**inişli** sloping downwards; ~ çıkışlı *(or yokuşlu)* hilly *(road)*.
**inkâr** denial; ~ etm. to deny.
**inkıbaz** [â] constipation.
**inkılap,** -bı revolution.
**inkılapçı** revolutionary.
**inkıraz** [â] collapse, end, extinction; ~ bulmak collapse, to end, to fall.
**inkıta,** -aı cessation; -a uğramak to cease.
**inkisar** [â] **1.** refraction; **2.** curse, malediction; ~ etm. to curse.
**inkişaf** [â] development *(a.* ♣*);* ~ etm. to develop.
**inlemek 1.** to groan, to whimper, to moan; **2.** to resound.
**inletmek 1.** *caus. of* inlemek; **2.** *fig.* to torture, to torment.
**inme 1.** *vn. of* inmek; **2.** ↑ stroke, apoplexy, paralysis; **3.** *geogr.* ebb tide; ~ inmek ↑ to have a stroke.
**inmek,** (-er) **1.** to descend, to come *(or go)* down; **2.** to get off *(a bus, plane, train, ship)*; to get out of *(a car)*; to dismount from *(a horse)*; **3.** to diminish, to decrease, to recede; to die down; **4.** to land *(-e* at) *(plane)*; **5.** to move down *(-e* to); **6.** to stay at *(a hotel)*; **7.** ♣ to be paralyzed; **8.** to collapse *(wall, etc.)*; **9.** to reduce *(price)*; **10.** to fall *(prices)*;

**11.** *sl.* to hit, to strike.

**İnmeli** *?* paralyzed, apoplectic.

**İnorganik** ⌐ inorganic.

**İnsaf** [â] **1.** justice, fairness; **2.** have a heart!; ~ etm. **1.** to take pity (*-e* on); **2.** to have a heart; -ına kalmış it's up to his discretion.

**İnsaflı** [â] equitable, just, fair.

**İnsafsız 1.** unmerciful, merciless; **2.** unjust, unfair.

**İnsan** [â] **1.** person, human being; **2.** person, man; **3.** moral, decent, good; **4.** *fig.* upright (*or* decent) person; ~ doğduğu yerde değil, doyduğu yerde *pro.* not where one is bred, but where he is fed; ~ hakları human rights; ~ müsveddesi inhuman person; ~ sarrafı a good judge of people; -ın adı çıkacağına canı çıksın *pro.* give a dog a bad name (and hang him).

**İnsanbilim** anthropology.

**İnsanca** [. - .] **1.** humanely, decently; **2.** humane (*act*).

**İnsancıl 1.** humanistic; **2.** domestic (*animal*).

**İnsani** [. - -] **1.** human; **2.** humane; **3.** humanely.

**İnsaniyet,** -ti [â] **1.** humanity, mankind; **2.** humaneness, kindness.

**İnsaniyetli** humane, kind, benevolent.

**İnsaniyetsiz** inhuman.

**İnsanlık** [â] *s.* insaniyet; ~ bilmez inhuman, cruel; -tan çıkmak **1.** to become a bag of bones; **2.** to become inhuman.

**İnsanoğlu,** -nu man, human being.

**İnsanüstü,** -nü [â] superhuman.

**İnsicam** [â] consistency, coherence.

**İnsicamlı** [â] consistent, coherent.

**İnsicamsız** [â] inconsistent, incoherent.

**İnsiyak,** -kı [â] instinct.

**İnsiyaki** [. - - -] instinctive.

**İnşa** [â] **1.** construction; **2.** writing, literary composition; ~ etm. to build, to construct.

**İnşaat,** -tı [â, â] (*pl. of* inşa) building, construction; ~ mühendisi civil engineer.

**İnşaatçı** [â, â] builder, contractor.

**İnşallah** [x . -] **1.** I hope that...; **2.** I hope so.

**İnşat,** -dı [â] recitation; declamation; ~ etm. to recite; to declaim.

**İntegral** Å integral.

**İntelek** intellect.

**İntelektüalizm** intellectualism.

**İnterpol,** -lü Interpol.

**İntiba,** -aı [â] impression; ~ bırakmak to make an impression (*-de* on).

**İntibak,** -kı [â] **1.** adaptation, adjustment, conformation, accommodation; **2.** suitability; ~ etm. to adjust o.s. (*-e* to), to

accustom o.s. (*-e* to); to conform (*-e* to).

**İntibaksız** maladjusted.

**İntifa,** -aı [â] benefit, advantage, gain; ~ etm. (*bşden*) to profit from *s.th.*; ~ hakkı usufruct; ~ senetleri preferred shares.

**İntihar** [â] suicide; ~ etm. to commit suicide.

**İntikal,** -li [â] **1.** transition, passage; **2.** comprehension, grasp; **3.** inference; **4.** transfer (*by inheritance or sale*); ~ devresi transition period; ~ etm. **1.** to pass to another place; **2.** to perceive, to grasp; **3.** to pass by inheritance, to be inherited (by).

**İntikam** [â] revenge, vengeance; ~ almak to take revenge (*-den* on), to revenge o.s. (*-den* on), to avenge o.s. (*-den* on).

**İntikamcı** [â] vengeful, vindictive.

**İntisap,** -bı [â] joining; affiliation; membership; ~ etm. to join, to become a member (*-e* of).

**İntişar** [â] **1.** diffusion; **2.** publication, dissemination; ~ etm. **1.** to spread, to radiate; **2.** to be published, to come out.

**İntizam** [â] order, orderliness, tidiness; -a sokmak to tidy up.

**İntizamlı** [â] tidy, orderly, regular.

**İntizamsız** [â] untidy, disorderly, irregular.

**İntizamsızlık** [â] untidiness, disorder.

**İntizar** [â] **1.** curse; **2.** expectation; ~ etm. to curse.

**İnzibat,** -tı [â] **1.** military police; **2.** discipline; ~ eri military policeman.

**İnziva** [â] seclusion; -ya çekilmek to seclude o.s.

**İp,** -pi **1.** rope, string, cord; **2.** P thread; ~ atlamak to jump rope, to skip; ~ cambazı ropedancer, tightrope walker; ~ kaçkını bad egg, tough; ~ merdiven rope ladder; ~ takmak to try to harm s.o. behind his back; -e çekmek to hang; -e gelesice! damned!; -e sapa gelmez inconsistent, nonsensical; -e un sermek *fig.* to make vain excuses; -i çürük *fig.* undependable; -i kırmak *sl.* to run away, to take to one's heels; -ini çekmek (*b-nin*) *fig.* to keep *s.o.* under control; -ini kırmak *sl.* to get out of hand; -iyle kuyuya inilmez you can't count on him; -le çekmek to look forward (to), to be counting the days until; -leri birinin elinde olm. to pull strings; -ten kazıktan kurtulmuş gallows bird.

**İpek 1.** silk; **2.** silken; ~ gibi silky.

**İpekböceği,** -ni *zo.* silkworm.

**İpekböcekçiliği,** -ni sericulture.

**İpekçilik** sericulture.

**İpekli 1.** of silk, silk; **2.** silk cloth.

**ipince** [x . .] very thin (or slender).

**iplemek** sl. to heed, to mind.

**iplememek** sl. not to give a damn (for), not to care 2 hoots, not to give a rap (for).

**iplik 1.** thread; yarn; **2.** fiber, filament; **3.** string (in a bean pod); ~ eğirmek to spin yarn; ~ ~ olm. to become threadbare; ipliği pazara çıkmak (b-nin) to come to light (one's faults).

**iplikhane** [ā] spinning mill.

**ipnotize** hypnotized; ~ etm. to hypnotize.

**ipnotizma** hypnotism.

**ipnotizmacı** hypnotizer.

**ipnoz** hypnosis.

**ipotek** mortgage.

**ipotekli** mortgaged.

**ipsiz 1.** ropeless; **2.** sl. vagabond; ~ sapsız **1.** senseless, meaningless (words); **2.** ne'er-do-well; vagabond; shiftless.

**iptal,** -li [ā] **1.** cancellation; **2.** δδ annulment; ~ etm. **1.** to cancel; **2.** δδ to annul.

**iptida** [ā] **1.** beginning, commencement, start; **2.** [x . .] at first, in the beginning.

**iptidal** [. . - -] **1.** primitive; **2.** primary, elementary.

**iptila** addiction.

**ipucu,** -nu **1.** clue; **2.** hint, indication; ~ vermek to give a clue.

**irade** [ā] **1.** desire, will; **2.** command, decree; **3.** psych. volition.

**iradedışı,** -nı psych. involuntary.

**iradeli** [ā] **1.** strong-willed, strong-minded, forceful, resolute; **2.** voluntary, volitional.

**iradesiz** [ā] **1.** irresolute, weak; **2.** involuntary.

**iradi** [. - -] voluntary, volitional.

**İran** [- .] pr. n. Iran.

**İranlı** [¹] [x . .] Iranian.

**irat,** -dı [- -] income, revenue; ~ getirmek to bring in revenue.

**irdeleme** investigation, examination.

**irdelemek** to consider at length, to examine, to scrutinize.

**irfan** [ā] **1.** comprehension, understanding, insight; **2.** knowledge; **3.** ♀ [x .] mf.

**iri 1.** large, huge, big; voluminous; **2.** coarse (-grained); ~ kum gravel; ~ taneli large-grained, large berried; coarse-grained.

**iribaş** zo. tadpole.

**irice 1.** fairly large, largish, siz(e)able; **2.** fairly coarse.

**iridyum** ⌐ iridium.

**irikıyım 1.** coarsely chopped; **2.** fig. huge, burly.

**irileşme 1.** vn. of irileşmek; **2.** biol. hypertrophy.

**irileşmek 1.** to grow large; **2.** biol. to hypertrophy.

**irili ufaklı** big and little.

**irilik** largeness, bigness.

**irin** pus; ~ toplamak to suppurate.

**irinlenmek** to suppurate, to fester.

**irinli** purulent.

**iris** [x .] anat. iris.

**iriyarı** burly, strapping, husky, portly.

**irkilmek 1.** to be startled; to start; **2.** ♂ to be inflamed, to tumefy.

**irkinti 1.** puddle; **2.** start.

**İrlanda** pr. n. Ireland, Eire.

**İrlandalı** pr. n. **1.** Irishman; Irishwoman; **2.** Irish.

**irmik** semolina; ~ helvası dessert made of semolina.

**irs** heredity, inheritance.

**irsal,** -li [ā] sending, forwarding.

**irsaliye** [. - . .] † waybill.

**irsen** [x .] through heredity, by inheritance.

**irsi** hereditary.

**irsiyet,** -ti heredity.

**irşat,** -dı [ā] guidance; ~ etm. to guide.

**irtibat,** -tı [ā] **1.** communications, contact; **2.** link, connection; ~ kurmak to get in touch (ile with); ~ subayı ✗ liasion officer.

**irtica,** -aı [ā] reaction.

**irticai** [. . - -] reactionary.

**irticalen** [ā] extempore, extemporaneously.

**irtifa,** -aı [ā] ast., geogr., ♣ altitude, elevation.

**irtifak** sharing, access; ~ hakkı easement, right of access.

**irtihal,** -li [ā] death, passing away; ~ etm. to die, to pass away.

**irtikâp** bribery, corruption.

**is** soot; lampblack; ~ kokmak to give off a scorched smell; -e tutmak to blacken with soot.

**İsa** [- -] pr. n. **1.** (a. Hazreti İsa) Jesus; **2.** mf.

**isabet,** -ti [ā] **1.** hitting (the mark); **2.** happy encounter; **3.** falling by chance to; **4.** thing done right; **5.** well done!; ~ almak to be hit (by a missile); ~ etm. **1.** to hit (the mark); **2.** to fall to (one's share); ~ kı luckily; ~ oldu it worked out well.

**isabetli** [ā] very fitting (or appropriate).

**isabetsiz** [ā] inappropriate, ineffective.

**ise 1.** if; **2.** as for; ~ de although; even if.

**İsevi** [- . -] Christian.

**İsevilik** [- . - .] Christianity.

**isfenks** sphinx.

**isfilt,** -ti ice field.

**ishakkuşu**, -nu *zo.* short-eared owl.
**ishal**, -li [â] diarrh(o)ea, the runs; ~ olm. to have diarrh(o)ea (*or* the runs).
**isilik** prickly heat, heat rash; ~ olm. to have heat rash.
**isim**, -smi 1. name; 2. title; 3. *gr.* noun; ~ cümlesi noun clause; ~ hali *gr.* case (*of a noun*); ~ koymak (*or* vermek) to name, to call; ~ takımı *gr.* genitive (*or* possessive) case; ~ takmak to nickname; ~ yapmak *fig.* to make a name for o.s.; ismi geçen aforementioned, above-mentioned; ismi var cismi yok titular; isminiz nedir? what is your name?
**isimfiil** *gr.* 1. gerund; 2. infinitive.
**iskambil** 1. playing card; 2. any card game; ~ kâğıdı 1. playing card; 2. deck of cards; ~ oynamak to play cards.
**iskân** settling, inhabiting; ~ etm. 1. to settle, to inhabit; 2. to house.
**iskandil** 1. ↓ sounding, plumb; 2. sounding line; 3. *fig.* investigating; ~ etm. 1. ↓ to sound, to fathom, to plumb; 2. to investigate; 3. *sl.* to put out feelers; 4. *sl.* to sound out.
**İskandinav** *pr. n.* Scandinavian.
**İskandinavya** *pr. n.* Scandinavia.
**iskarpela** [. . x .] carpenter's chisel.
**iskarpin** woman's shoe.
**iskele** 1. quay, wharf, pier, dock; 2. gangplank; 3. port (town); 4. scaffold(ing); 5. port side of a ship; ~ babası ↓ bollard; ~ vermek to lower the gangplank.
**iskelekuşu**, -nu *zo.* kingfisher, halcyon.
**iskelet**, -ti 1. skeleton; 2. framework; ~ gibi like a skeleton, a bag of bones; -i çıkmak to become skin and bone(s).
**iskemle** 1. chair; stool; 2. coffee (*or* end) table.
**İskender** *pr. n.* Alexander (the Great).
**İskenderiye** *pr. n.* Alexandria.
**İskenderun** [û] *pr. n.* Iskenderun.
**iskete** [. x .] *zo.* titmouse.
**İskoç**, -çu *pr. n.* 1. Scottish, Scots; Scotch; 2. Scot, Scotsman.
**İskoçya** [. x .] *pr. n.* Scotland.
**iskonto** discount; ~ yapmak to give a discount.
**iskorbüt**, -tü scurvy.
**iskorpit**, -ti *zo.* scorpion fish.
**İslam** *pr. n.* 1. Islam; 2. Islamic; 3. Muslim; -a gelmek to become a Muslim.
**İslamiyet**, -ti [. .-. .] *pr. n.* the Islamic religion.
**İslamlaşmak** to become a Muslim.
**İslav** *pr. n.* 1. Slav; 2. Slavic, Slavonic.
**İslavca** *pr. n.* Slavic.
**islemek** 1. to soot, to blacken with soot; 2.

to smoke (*fish, etc.*); 3. to burn slightly (*pudding, etc.*).
**isli** 1. sooty; 2. smoked.
**islim** steam; ~ arkadan gelsin *fig.* let's do it just any old way.
**ismen** [x .] by name.
**ismet**, -ti 1. chastity, purity; 2. 2 *mf. & wf.*
**isnat**, -dı 1. attribution, ascription; 2. imputation; ~ etm. 1. to attribute, to ascribe; 2. to impute.
**İspanya** [. x .] *pr. n.* Spain.
**İspanyol** *pr. n.* 1. Spanish; 2. Spaniard.
**İspanyolca** [. . x .] *pr. n.* 1. Spanish, the Spanish language; 2. in Spanish.
**ispanyolet**, -ti espagnolette.
**ispat**, -tı [â] 1. proof, evidence; 2. proving; ~ etm. to prove; ispatı vücut etm. to appear in person.
**ispati** [. x .] *cards:* clubs.
**ispatlamak** to prove.
**ispenç**, -ci *zo.* bantam; ~ horozu *fig.* hop-o'-my-thumb and cocky man.
**ispinoz** 1. *zo.* chaffinch; 2. *sl.* gabby, talkative.
**ispiralya** [. . x .] ↓ cabin skylight.
**ispirto** [. x .] grain (*or* ethyl) alcohol; ~ lambası spirit lamp; ~ ocağı spirit stove.
**ispirtolu** alcoholic, containing alcohol.
**ispiyonlamak** *sl.* (*b-ni*) to inform on *s.o.*, to squeal on *s.o.*, to peach on *s.o.*, to squeak.
**israf** [â] extravance, wastage, dissipation; ~ etm. to waste, to dissipate, to squander.
**İsrail** [. - -] *pr. n.* 1. Israel; 2. Israeli.
**İsraili** [. - . .] Israeli.
**İstanbul** *pr. n.* Istanbul; ~ Boğazı the Bosp(h)orus; ~ kazan ben kepçe *fig.* I left no stone unturned in Istanbul.
**İstanbullu** *pr. n.* native of Istanbul, Istanbulite.
**istasyon** (railway) station; ~ şefi stationmaster.
**istatistik** statistic(s).
**istatistikçi** statistician.
**istavrit**, -ti *zo.* horse mackerel, scad; ~ azmanı *zo.* bluefin.
**istavroz** cross, crucifix; ~ çıkarmak to cross o.s.
**istek** 1. wish, desire; 2. request; 3. appetite, inclination; ~ duymak to want, to desire, to long (*-e* for); ~ kipi *gr.* optative (mood).
**isteka** 1. *billiards:* cue; 2. *typ.* stick.
**isteklendirmek** to encourage, to motivate.
**istekli** desirous, willing.
**isteksiz** unwilling, reluctant, apathetic.
**istem** 1. request, demand; 2. volition, will.
**istemek** 1. to want, to wish, to desire; 2.

*(b-den bş)* to ask *s.o.* for *s.th.*; 3. to be necessary; to require; 4. *(kız)* to ask for a woman in marriage; ister istemez willy-nilly, perforce; ister... ister... whether... or...

**istemli** 1. optional; 2. voluntary.

**istemsiz** involuntary.

**isten(il)mek** 1. to be desired, to be in demand; 2. to be asked for.

**istep,** -pi steppe.

**istepne** *mot.* spare tyre.

**isteri** ? hysteria.

**isterik** ? hysterical.

**istiap,** -bı [ā] holding, containing; ~ haddi 1. load limit, capacity; 2. ↓ tonnage; 3. passenger capacity.

**istiare** [ā] *lit.* metaphor.

**istibdat,** -dı [ā] despotism.

**istida** [ā] petition.

**istidat,** -dı [. - -] aptitude, endowment.

**istidatlı** [. - -.] apt, capable, talented.

**istidatsız** [. - -.] inept, incompetent.

**istidlal,** -li deduction, inference.

**istif** stowage; ~ etm. to stow; -ini bozmamak *fig.* to keep up appearances.

**istifa** [. - -] resignation; ~ etm. to resign; -sını vermek to hand in one's resignation.

**istifade** [ā] profit, advantage, gain; ~ etm. to benefit (*-den* from), to profit (*-den* from).

**istifadeli** [ā] advantageous, profitable.

**istifçi** 1. stacker; stevedore; 2. *fig.* hoarder.

**istiflemek** = istif etm.

**istifrağ** [ā] vomit; ~ etm. to vomit, to bring up.

**istihale** [ā] 1. change of form; 2. *biol.* & *geol.* metamorphosis; ~ etm. 1. to change form; 2. *biol.* & *geol.* to undergo metamorphosis.

**istihbarat,** -tı [ā, ā] 1. news, information; 2. intelligence; ~ bürosu information bureau; ~ dairesi intelligence department; ~ servisi *newspaper:* news desk; ~ subayı intelligence officer; ~ şefi news editor.

**istihdam** [ā] employment; ~ etm. to employ.

**istihfaf** [ā] contempt; ~ etm. to despise.

**istihkak,** -kı [ā] merit, deserts; ration.

**istihkâm** 1. fortification, stronghold; 2. military engineering; ~ subayı engineer officer.

**istihlak,** -kı consumption; ~ etm. to consume, to use up.

**istihsal,** -li [ā] production; ~ etm. to produce.

**istihza** [ā] sarcasm, ridicule, irony; ~ etm.

*(b-le)* to ridicule *s.o.*

**istikamet,** -ti [ā] 1. direction; 2. straightness, integrity; ~ vermek to direct.

**istikbal,** -li [ā] the future.

**istiklal,** -li independence; ~ marşı the Turkish national anthem.

**istikrah** [ā] aversion; ~ etm. to loath.

**istikrar** [ā] stability, stabilization; ~ bulmak to become stabilized.

**istikrarlı** [ā] stable, stabilized; steady; settled.

**istikrarsız** [ā] unstable; inconsistent; unsettled; unsteady.

**istila** [. - -] 1. invasion, occupation; 2. infestation; ~ etm. 1. to invade; 2. to infest.

**istilacı** [. - -.] 1. invading, occupying *(army)*; 2. invader.

**istim** 1. steam; 2. *sl.* booze.

**istimator** customs evaluator.

**istimbot,** -tu steamboat.

**istimlak,** -ki expropriation, confiscation, condemnation; ~ etm. to expropriate, to confiscate, to condemn.

**istimna** masturbation.

**istinaden** [ā] based (*-e* on), supported (*-e* by).

**istinaf** [. - -] ♎ appeal; ~ mahkemesi court of appeals.

**istinat,** -dı [ā] 1. resting on, leaning against; 2. relying on, depending on; ~ duvarı retaining (*or* supporting) wall; ~ etm. 1. to rest (*-e* on), to lean (*-e* against); 2. to rely (*or* depend) (*-e* on).

**istinkâf** abstention; ~ etm. to abstain (*-den* from).

**istintaç,** -cı [ā] deduction, inference.

**istirahat,** -ti [. - -.] rest, repose; ~ etm. to rest, to relax, to repose.

**istirdat,** -dı [ā] restitution; ~ davası ♎ action for restitution; ~ etm. to retake.

**istirham** [ā] plea, petition; ~ etm. to plead, to petition.

**istiridye** [. x .] *zo.* oyster.

**istismar** [ā] exploitation; ~ etm. 1. to exploit; 2. to utilize.

**istismarcı** [ā] exploiter.

**istisna** [ā] exception; ~ etm. to except, to exclude; -lar kaideyi bozmaz the exception proves the rule.

**istisnai** [. - -] exceptional.

**istisnasız** [. - -.] without exception, unexceptionally.

**istişare** [ā] consultation; ~ etm. to consult; ~ kurulu advisory council.

**istişari** [. - -] consultative, advisory.

**istiva** [ā] levelness, evenness.

**istop** stoppage; ~ etm. 1. to stop; 2. *football:* to stop *(the ball)*.

**istor** 1. roller blind; 2. roller (or window) shade.

**İsveç,** -ci pr. n. Sweden.

**İsveççe** pr. n. 1. Swedish; 2. in Swedish.

**İsveçli** pr. n. Swede.

**İsviçre** [.x .] pr. n. Switzerland.

**İsviçreli** pr. n. Swiss.

**isyan** [â] rebellion, revolt; mutiny; ~ etm. rebel, to revolt, to mutiny.

**isyancı** [â] 1. rebel; 2. rebellious.

**isyankâr** rebellious.

**iş** 1. work, labo(u)r; 2. employment, job, work; 3. occupation, (line of) work; 4. duty, job; 5. trade, business, commerce; 6. affair, matter, business; 7. sl. trick, swindle; ~ arkadaşı colleague, co-worker, fellow-worker, collaborator; ~ başında 1. on the job; 2. during work time; ~ bilmek to be skilled; ~ bitirmek to complete a job successfully; ~ çıkarmak 1. to do a lot of work; 2. fig. to cause trouble; ~ eri skilled worker; ~ görmek 1. to work; 2. to be of use (or service); ~ güç occupation; ~ -ten geçti it is too late!; ~ sahibi employer; ~ yok fig. it is no use (or good); -e girmek to become employed, to get a job; -e yaramak to be of use, to come in handy; -i azıtmak fig. to go too far, to overstep the mark; -i başından aşkın olm. to be up to one's ears in work; -i ~ olm. to go very well; -i olm. 1. to have work to do; 2. to turn out well; -in başı the crux; -in içinde ~ var there are wheels within wheels, there is s.th. fishy in it; -inden olm. to lose one's job, -ine gelmek (b-nin) to suit one's interests; -ini bitirmek (b-nin) fig. to finish s.o. off, to bump s.o. off; -ini sağlama (or sağlam kazığa) bağlamak to make a matter safe; -ten atmak F to fire, to dismiss, to give the sack; -ten el çektirmek to remove from office.

**işadamı,** -nı businessman.

**işaret,** -ti [â] 1. sign; 2. mark; 3. signal, gesture; ~ etm. to point out, to indicate, to mark; ~ fişeği signal rocket; ~ sıfatı gr. demonstrative adjective; ~ vermek to signal, to give a signal; ~ zamiri gr. demonstrative pronoun.

**işaretçi** [â] signaler, flagger.

**işaretlemek** [â] 1. to mark; 2. to point out, to denote.

**işaretli** [â] marked, tagged.

**işaretparmağı,** -nı index finger, forefinger.

**işbaşı,** -nı hour at which work begins; ~ ~ yapmak to begin work.

**işbırakımcı** striker.

**işbırakımı,** -nı strike.

**işbıraktırımı,** -nı lockout.

**işbirliği,** -ni cooperation.

**işbirlikçi** 1. comprador; 2. collaborationist.

**işbirlikli** cooperative, collective.

**işbölümü,** -nü division of labo(u)r.

**işbu** [x .] this.

**işçi** 1. worker, workman, labo(u)rer; 2. sl. trickster, cardsharp; ~ sınıfı working class, proletariat; ~ sigortası worker's insurance; ~ ücreti wages.

**işçilik** 1. workmanship; 2. worker's pay.

**işemek** to urinate, to piss, to pee, to spend a penny.

**işgal,** -li [â] 1. occupation; 2. distraction; ~ altında under military occupation, occupied; ~ etm. 1. to occupy; 2. to take up, to occupy (space); 3. X to occupy, to take over; ~ kuvvetleri X occupation forces.

**işgalci** [â] 1. occupier; 2. occupying.

**işgücü,** -nü † 1. productive power; 2. work force (of a nation).

**işgüder** pol. chargé d'affaires.

**işgünü,** -nü weekday, workday.

**işgüzar** [â] officious, obtrusive.

**işitme** vn. of işitmek; ~ aleti hearing aid.

**işitmek** 1. to hear; 2. to learn (-i of).

**işitmemezlik** not hearing; -ten (or -liğe) gelmek to pretend not to hear, to feign deafness.

**işitsel** auditory.

**işittirmek** (b-ne) to cause s.o. to hear s.th.

**işkembe** 1. zo. rumen, paunch; 2. tripe (food); ~ çorbası tripe soup; -sini şişirmek F to make a pig of o.s.

**işkembeci** 1. tripe seller; 2. tripe restaurant.

**işkence** 1. torture, torment; 2. ⊕ carpenter's clamp; ~ etm. to torture, to torment.

**işkil** suspicion, doubt.

**işkolu,** -nu 1. the work force; 2. department.

**işlek** 1. busy; 2. flowing, cursive (handwriting).

**işlem** 1. A operation; 2. process; 3. transaction, procedure.

**işleme** 1. vn. of işlemek; 2. embroidery, handwork; 3. embroidered.

**işlemeci** embroiderer.

**işlemek** 1. to work up, to process, to treat; 2. to operate, to function, to perform; 3. to embroider; 4. to penetrate, to soak (-e into); 5. to cultivate (land); 6. to carry traffic (road); 7. to ply (ship, bus. etc.); 8. to discuss, to treat (subject); 9. to be enforced (or effective) (law); 10. to fester (boil); 11. sl. to steal, to swipe.

**işlemeli** embroidered.

işlenmemiş

işlenmemiş raw, untreated.
işletici operator.
işletme vn. of işletmek, part. business enterprise; ~ fakültesi school of business administration; ~ malzemesi rolling stock; ~ vergisi 1. excise tax; 2. sales tax.
işletmeci administrator, manager; business executive.
işletmecilik 1. business administration; 2. managership.
işletmek caus. of işlemek, part. 1. to run, to operate; 2. sl. hoodwink, to pull s.o.'s leg, to have s.o. on, to hoax, to kid.
işlev function.
işlevsel functional.
işlevsiz nonfunctional.
işleyim industry.
işli embroidered; ornamented; ~ güçlü 1. having business; 2. very busy.
işmar [ā] signal, gesture; wink; nod; ~ etm. to signal, to gesture; to wink.
işporta [. x .] 1. pedlar's pushcart; 2. basket, box (used by pedlars); ~ malı shoddy goods.
işportacı pedlar, peddler, pitchman.
işportacılık yapmak to peddle.
işret, -ti carousal; ~ etm. to carouse, to booze; ~ meclisi carousal, booze-up.
işsiz unemployed, out of work; ~ güçsüz idle.
işsizlik unemployment; joblessness; ~ sigortası unemployment insurance.
iştah 1. appetite; 2. desire, urge; ~ açıcı appetizing; ~ açmak to whet one's appetite; ~ kapamak (or kesmek or tıkamak) to spoil (or kill) one's appetite; -ı kapanmak (or kesilmek) to lose one's appetite; -ım yok I have no appetite; -la yemek to eat hungrily.
iştahlanmak 1. to get pleasantly hungry; 2. to get a craving (-e for).
iştahlı 1. having an appetite; 2. fig. desirous.
iştahsız without appetite.
iştahsızlık lack of appetite.
işte 1. here!, here it is!; 2. look!, see!, behold!; 3. as you see; ~ böyle such is the matter.
iştigal, -li [ā] occupation; ~ etm. (bşle) to occupy o.s. with s.th., to be busy with s.th.
iştirak, -ki [ā] 1. participation; 2. partnership; ~ etm. 1. to participate (-e in), to join in (-e on); 2. to share, to agree (-e with).
iştirakçi [ā] participant.
iştiyak, -kı [ā] longing, desire; ~ duymak

to long (-e for).
işve coquettishness, coquetry.
işveli coquettish, flirtatious.
işveren employer.
işyeri, -ni place of employment, practice.
it, -ti 1. zo. dog, cur; 2. fig. cur, swine, son of a bitch, bastard, punk; ~ canlı tough and strong; ~ gibi çalışmak to sweat blood; ~ oğlu ~ sl. cur, son of a bitch; ~ sürüsü fig. rabble.
ita [- -] 1. delivery; 2. payment; ~ etm. 1. to give; 2. to pay.
itaat, -ti [. - .] obedience; ~ etm. to obey.
itaatli obedient.
itaatsiz disobedient.
itaatsizlik disobedience.
italik typ. italic.
İtalya [. x .] pr. n. Italy.
İtalyan pr. n. Italian.
İtalyanca pr. n. 1. Italian; 2. in Italian.
itboğan ♀ autumn crocus, meadow saffron.
itburnu, -nu ♀ dog rose.
iteklemek F to manhandle, to shove.
itelemek 1. to shove, to nudge; 2. phys. to repel.
itenek ⊕ piston.
itfa [ā] 1. extinguishing, putting out; 2. † redemption, amortization; ~ akçesi (or bedeli) sinking fund; ~ etm. to pay off (debt), to redeem (bond).
itfaiye [ā] fire brigade, Am. fire department; ~ eri fireman.
itfaiyeci [ā] fireman.
ithaf [ā] dedication; ~ etm. to dedicate (-e to).
ithal, -li [ā] importation; ~ etm. to import; ~ malı imported goods.
ithalat, -tı [. - .] 1. importation; 2. imports.
ithalatçı [. - .] importer.
ithalatçılık importation.
itham [ā] accusation, imputation; ~ etm. to accuse.
ithamname [ā, ā] indictment.
ithıyarı, -nı s. acıhıyar.
itibar [- . -] 1. esteem, hono(u)r, consideration, regard; 2. † credit; ~ etm. to esteem, to show consideration; ~ görmek 1. to be respected; 2. to be in demand; -a almak to consider; -dan düşmek to fall from esteem; -ı olm. 1. to be held in esteem; 2. to have credit.
itibaren [- . - .] [- . x .] from ... on, beginning from, dating from.
itibarıyla [- . - - .] 1. concerning, considering; 2. as of...
itibari [- . - .] † 1. nominal; 2. conventional; ~ kıymet nominal value.

**itibarlı** [· . - .] 1. esteemed, valued; influential; 2. redeemable, acceptable *(bill)*.

**itibarsız** [· . - .] unesteemed.

**itici** propulsive.

**itidal,** -li [· . -] 1. moderation; 2. mildness, sobriety; ~ bulmak to calm down, to become moderate; ~ sahibi calm, composed, self-possessed.

**itidalli** [· . - .] calm; moderate.

**itikat,** -dı [· . -] belief, faith, creed; ~ etm. to believe (-e in).

**itilâf** [· . -] entente.

**itilim, itilme** *psych.* repression.

**itimat,** -dı [· . -] trust, confidence, reliance; ~ etm. to trust, to rely (-e on), to have confidence (-e in).

**itimatlı** [· . - .] trustworthy.

**itimatname** [- , - - .] letter of credence, credentials.

**itimatsızlık** [· . - . .] distrust, mistrust.

**itina** [· . -] care, attention; ~ etm. *(or* göstermek) to take great care (-e in), to take pains (-e to); ~ ile carefully.

**itinalı** [· . - .] careful, painstaking.

**itinasız** [· . - .] careless, inattantive, slipshod.

**itiraf** [· . -] confession, admission; ~ etm. to confess, to admit, to acknowledge.

**itiraz** [· . -] 1. objection, disapproval; 2. 𝔰̌ protest; ~ etm. to object (-e to); ~ götürmez incontestable.

**itirazcı** objector.

**itirazsız** [· . - .] without any objection.

**itişmek** 1. to push one another; 2. to scuffle, to tussle; itişip kakışmak to scuffle, to push and shove one another.

**itiyat,** -dı [· . -] habit; ~ edinmek to get into the habit (of), to make a habit.

**itizar** [· . -] apology; ~ etm. to apologize.

**itki** *psych.* motive, drive.

**itlaf** destruction; ~ etm. to destroy, to kill.

**itlik** *fig.* dirty trick, villainy.

**itmam** [ā] completion; ~ etm. to complete.

**itmek,** (-er) 1. to push, to shove; 2. to persuade, to compel; ite kaka pushing and shoving.

**itriyum** 𝔰̌ yttrium.

**ittırat,** -dı [ā] regularity.

**ittifak,** -kı [ā] 1. alliance, agreement; 2. accord, concord; ~ Devletleri *hist.* the Central Powers; ~ etm. to agree, to come to an agreement.

**ittifakla** [ā] unanimously.

**ittihat,** -dı [ā] union; ~ etm. to unite; 2 ve Terakki Cemiyeti *hist.* the Committee of Union and Progress.

**itüzümü,** -nü 𝔰̌ black nightshade.

**ivaz** 𝔰̌ consideration.

**ivdirmek** 1. to accelerate; to hasten; 2. to hurry, to urge on.

**ivedi** 1. haste; 2. hasty.

**ivedileşmek** to become urgent.

**ivedili** urgent.

**ivedilik** urgency; -le urgently.

**ivgi** hatchet.

**ivinti** speed, rapidity; ~ yeri *geogr.* rapids.

**ivme** 1. haste; 2. *phys.* acceleration.

**ivmek** to hurry.

**iye** possessor, owner.

**iyelik** possession, ownership; ~ eki' *gr.* possessive suffix; ~ zamiri *gr.* possessive pronoun.

**iyi** 1. good; 2. well, in good health; 3. abundant, plentiful; ~ etm. 1. to heal, to cure; 2. to do well; 3. *sl.* to rob; 4. *(b-ni) sl.* to give *s.o.* his comeuppance, to get even with *s.o.;* ~ gelmek 1. to help, to work *(medicine, etc.);* 2. to fit, to suit; ~ gitmek 1. to go well; 2. to suit; ~ gün dostu fair-weather friend; ~ hal kâğıdı certificate of good conduct; ~ hoş amma... that's all very well but...; ~ kalpli goodhearted, kind; ~ ki luckily, fortunately; ~ kötü mediocre, not bad; ~ olm. 1. to recover; 2. to go well; 3. to be good *(or* favo(u)rable); ~ saatte olsunlar the djinns; -den -ye completely, thoroughly; -si mi the best thing to do is...

**iyice** 1. [x . .] rather well, pretty good, fairly good; 2. [. x .] completely, thoroughly.

**iyicene** [. x . .] F thoroughly.

**iyicil** well-wishing, benevolent.

**iyileşmek** 1. to recover *(from illness);* 2. to improve, to get better.

**iyileştirmek** 1. to cure; 2. to repair, to improve.

**iyilik** 1. goodness; 2. favo(u)r, kindness; 3. advantage, benefit; ~ good health; ~ etm. to do a kindness *(or* favour); ~ güzellik *(or* sağlık) everything is all right; -le kindly, gently.

**iyilikbilir** grateful, thankful.

**iyilikçi, iyiliksever** kind, benevolent, good.

**iyimser** optimistic.

**iyimserlik** optimism.

**iyon** *phys.* ion.

**iyonlaşmak** *phys.* to ionize.

**iyot,** -du 𝔰̌ iodine.

**iz** 1. footprint, track; 2. *fig.* mark, trace, clue, evidence; 3. A trace; ~ düşürmek A, *phys.* to project; ~ sürmek to follow a trail; -i belirsiz olm. to leave no trace; -inden yürümek *(b-nin)* to follow in *s.o.'s* footsteps; -ine basmak *(b-nin)* to tail *s.o.*, to follow *s.o.*; -ine dönmek to change one's mind; -ine uymak *(b-nin) fig.* to tread in *s.o.'s* footsteps.

**izaç,** -cı [ā] vexation, worry; ~ etm. to vex, to harass.

**izafet,** -ti [ā] **1.** *gr.* nominal compound; **2.** *phls.* relativity.

**izafeten** [ā] after, in hono(u)r of.

**izafi** [. - -] **1.** relative; **2.** *phls.* nominal; **3.** *phys.* specific.

**izafiyet,** -ti [ā] relativity.

**izah** [- -] explanation; ~ etm. to explain.

**izahat,** -tı [- - -] explanations; ~ vermek to give an explanation.

**izale** [ā] removal; ~ etm. to remove, to wipe out.

**izam** [- -] exaggeration; ~ etm. to exaggerate.

**izan** [ā] understanding, intelligence; ~ etm. to be considerate.

**izbe 1.** hovel; **2.** out-of-the-way.

**izbiro** [. x .] rope sling *(used in lifting cargo).*

**izci 1.** scout; **2.** boy *(or girl)* scout.

**izcilik** scouting.

**izdiham** [ā] throng, crush, crowd.

**izdivaç,** -cı [ā] marriage, matrimony; ~ etm. to get married; ~ teklifi marriage proposal.

**izdüşüm** Å, *phys.* projection.

**izdüşümsel** Å, *phys.* projectional.

**izhar** [ā] display, manifestation; ~ etm. to display, to reveal, to show.

**izin,** -zni **1.** permission; **2.** leave (of absence); vacation; **3.** X discharge; ~ almak to get permission (*or* leave); ~ ko-

parmak F = ~ almak; ~ vermek **1.** to give permission; **2.** X to discharge; -e çıkmak to take a vacation, to go on vacation (*or* leave); iznini kullanmak to take one's vacation; to use one's leave.

**izinli** on vacation (*or* leave).

**izinsiz 1.** without permission; **2.** *school:* kept in; **3.** detention.

**İzlanda** *pr. n.* **1.** Iceland; **2.** Icelandic.

**İzlandalı** *pr. n.* Icelander.

**izlem** observation.

**izlemci** observer.

**izlemek 1.** to follow, to trace, to pursue; **2.** to watch, to view; to observe

**izlence** programme.

**izlendirmek** to make an impression (on).

**izlenim** impression.

**izlenmek 1.** *pass. of* izlemek; **2.** to get an impression.

**izleyici** spectator, onlooker; viewer.

**izmarit,** -ti **1.** cigarette butt (*or* end); **2.** *zo.* sea bream.

**izmihlâl,** -li destruction, annihilation.

**izobar** *geogr.* isobar.

**izohips** *geogr.* contour line.

**izolasyon** ⚡ insulation.

**izole** insulated; ~ bant electric (*or* friction) tape; ~ etm. ⚡, *phys.* to insulate, to isolate.

**izoterm** *geogr.* isotherm.

**izotop,** -pu *phys.* isotope.

**izzet,** -ti **1.** glory, might, hono(u)r, excellence; **2.** ♀ *mf.*

**izzetinefis,** -fsi self-respect, self-esteem amour propre.

# J

**jaguar** zo. jaguar.

**jaketatay** cutaway.

**jaluzi** Venetian blind.

**Jamayka** pr. n. 1. Jamaica; 2. Jamaican.

**Jamaykalı** pr. n. Jamaican.

**jambon** ham.

**jandarma** [. x .] 1. gendarme, police soldier; 2. gendarmerie, constabulary.

**jant**, -tı mot. rim (of a wheel); ~ kapağı hubcap.

**Japon** pr. n. Japanese.

**Japonca** [. x .] pr. n. Japanese.

**japongülü**, -nü ♣ camellia.

**Japonya** [. x .] pr. n. Japan.

**Japonyalı** pr. n. s. Japon.

**jarse** 1. jersey cloth; 2. jersey jacket.

**jartiyer** garter.

**jelatin** 1. gelatin(e); 2. a. ~ kâğıdı cellophane (paper).

**jelatinli** gelatinous.

**jeneratör** phys. 1. generator; 2. boiler.

**jeofizik** geophysics.

**jeofizikçi** geophysicist.

**jeolog** geologist.

**jeoloji** geology.

**jeolojik** geologic(al).

**jest**, -ti 1. gesture; 2. beau geste, gesture.

**jet**, -ti jet (airplane).

**jeton** token, slug; ~ düştü sl. the penny (has) dropped, Am. now it is registered; ~ geç düştü sl. it took a while for me to catch on.

**jigolo** gigolo.

**jile** jumper.

**jilet**, -ti razor blade, safety razor.

**jimnastik** 1. gymnastics; 2. gymnastic.

**jimnastikçi** gymnast.

**jinekolog**, -gu gynecologist.

**jorjet**, -ti georgette, Georgette crepe.

**jöle** jelly, Am. jello.

**jön** 1. handsome youngster; 2. actor playing the role of a young lover.

**jönprömiye** s. jön 2.

**Jöntürk** hist. Young Turk.

**judo** judo.

**judocu** judoka.

**jurnal** report of an informer; ~ etm. to denounce, to inform (on), to report.

**jurnalcı** informer, denouncer.

**jübile** jubilee.

**Jüpiter** Jupiter.

**jüpon** underskirt, slip, petticoat.

**jüri** jury; ~ üyesi juror.

**jüt**, -tü jute (fiber).

# K

**kaba 1.** puffed up, puffy; **2.** *fig.* boorish, coarse, rough, rude; unmannerly, uncouth; **3.** *fig.* vulgar, common; **4.** crudely made; **5.** coarse-grained; **6.** buttocks; ~ et(ler) buttocks; ~ iş rough (or unskilled) work; ~ saba **1.** rough and uneducated; **2.** credely made, rough-and-ready ~ sıva roughcast; ~ sofu bigoted; -sını almak **1.** to roughhew, to trim roughly; **2.** *fig.* to tidy up roughly, to clean up quickly.

**kababurun** *zo.* a kind of small fish.

**kabaca 1.** roughly, rather crudely, coarsely, in a rude way; **2.** biggish, somewhat grown up.

**kabadayı 1.** rough fellow, tough, bully, hooligan; **2.** intrepid, undaunted fellow; **3.** the best (of anything).

**kabadayılık** bravado, swagger; ~ etm. to swagger; ~ taslamak to act as if a tough, to play the tough.

**kabahat,** -ti [. - .] fault, defect; offence, guilt, sin, transgression, blame; ~ bende it is my fault; ~ bulmak to carp (or cavil) (-de at), to find fault (-de with); ~ işlemek (or etm.) to commit an offence, to offend, to do s.th. wrong.

**kabahatli** guilty, blameworthy, culpable, in the wrong.

**kabahatsiz** innocent, not guilty, inculpable.

**kabahatsizlik** innocence.

**kabak 1.** ♀ squash, pumpkin, gourd; **2.** hashish pipe; **3.** *fig.* inexperienced, rude, rough, boorish; **4.** unripe (melon); **5.** *fig.* bald, closeshaven, hairless; **6.** without hat; **7.** worn out (tyre); ~ bastısı stewed vegetable marrow; ~ başına patlamak (b-nin) *fig.* to carry the can; ~ çekirdeği pumpkinseed; ~ çıkmak to turn out to be unripe (melon); ~ çiçeği gibi açılmak *fig.* to display free and easy behavio(u)r; ~ dolması stuffed squash; ~ gibi bare, naked; ~ kafalı bald, hairless; *fig.* stupid; ~ tadı vermek to become boring gradually, to lose its appeal.

**kabakgiller** ♀ Cucurbitaceae.

**kabaklamak** to prune (a tree).

**kabaklaşmak** to go bald.

**kabaklık 1.** unripeness (melon); **2.** baldness; **3.** boorishness, rudeness.

**kabakulak** ☞ mumps, parotitis.

**kabala** cabala.

**kabalaşmak 1.** to become coarse (or vulgar); **2.** to act rudely.

**kabalık** rudeness, discourtesy, coarseness, vulgarity, impoliteness; sponginess.

**kaballama** propping (in mines).

**kaban** hooded (or casual) jacket.

**kabara** [. x .] **1.** hobnail; **2.** ornamental brass-headed stud.

**kabaralı** hobnailed.

**kabarcık 1.** ☞ bulla, bleb, blister; **2.** bubble; **3.** pimple, pustule.

**kabare** cabaret; ~ tiyatrosu revue.

**kabarık 1.** swollen, blistered, puffy; **2.** swelling; ~ deniz high tide.

**kabarma** *vn. of* kabarmak, *part.* high tide.

**kabarmak 1.** to swell up, to become fluffy; **2.** to rise (dough, paste), to bubble up (liquid); **3.** to increase considerably; **4.** to stand on end, to bristle (hair); **5.** *fig.* to be puffed up (with) (turkey); **6.** *fig.* to get furious (-e at); **7.** to increase, to swell (expences, figures); **8.** to become linty (or nappy) (cloth); **9.** to blister (paint); **10.** to boast, to be arrogant, to swell; **11.** to get rough (sea).

**kabartı** swelling, bulge; blister.

**kabartma 1.** *vn. of* kabartmak; **2.** embossed, (en)chased, stamping, in relief; **3.** relief..., embossed...

**kabartmak** *caus. of* kabarmak.

**kabasakal** bushy-bearded.

**kabataslak** roughly sketched out; in outline, without details.

**Kâbe** *pr. n.* the Kaaba at Mecca.

**kabız,** -bzı ☞ **1.** constipation; **2.** constipateq; ~ olm. to be constipated.

**kabızlık** ☞ constipation; ~ çekmek to suffer from constipation.

**kabil** [ᵃ] possible (-e for), practicable, cabaple (-e of), feasible; gayrikabil impossible.

**Kabil** [ᵃ] *pr. n.* Cain (Bible).

**kabil** kind, sort, type; bu ~ (or -den) such, of such a kind, this sort of.

**kabile¹** [ä] midwife.

**kabile²** 1. tribe; 2. ⚥ genus; ~ reisi tribal chieftain.

**kabiliyet,** -ti [ä] ability, capacity, aptitude, talent, capability, competence, possibility.

**kabiliyetli** [ä] capable (-e of), able (-e to), fit (-e for), qualified, talented, gifted, skil(l)ful (-e at, in), clever (-e at), adroit.

**kabiliyetsiz** [ä] unskil(l)ful, incapable, incompetent, untalented.

**kabiliyetsizlik** [ä] unskil(l)fulness, incapability, incapacity, incompetence.

**kabin** 1. cabin (of an airplane or ship or .spacecraft); 2. changing cubicle (at a beach).

**kabine** 1. cabinet (a. pol.), Cabinet Counsil; 2. surgery, consulting room (of a doctor); 3. small room; 4. toilet; 5. changing cubicle (at a beach, in a store); ~ çekilmek (for a government) to resign; ~ düşmek (for a government) to fall; ~ reisi prime minister; ~ toplantısı cabinet meeting.

**kabir,** -bri grave, burial-place, tomb; ~ azabı çekmek to suffer agonies; ~ suali F endless questioning.

**kablo** [x .] ✄ cable, cord, line; ~ döşemek to lay down a cable; ~ gemisi cable ship.

**kabotaj** ⏚ cabotage.

**kabristan** [. . -] churchyard, cemetery, graveyard.

**kabuk** -uğu 1. ⚥ bark; skin, shell, rind, peel, pod, husk, cod; 2. ⚘ crust, scab (wound); 3. outer covering; ~ bağlamak to form a crust (or scab) (wound); kabuğuna çekilmek to withdraw o.s. into solitude, to withdraw into one's shell; kabuğunu soymak to peel, to skin.

**kabuklanmak** 1. to form a crust (or scab) (wound); 2. to grow bark.

**kabuklu** 1. barky; 2. ... shelled; crustaceous.

**kabuklubit,** -ti zo. cochineal insect.

**kabuklular** zo. Crustacea.

**kabuksuz** shelled, peeled; without bark.

**kabul,** -lü [ū] 1. acceptance; 2. reception; 3. confession, consent, admission, avowal; 4. agreement, assent; 5. agreed!; ~ etm. 1. to accept; 2. to receive; 3. to put up with; 4. to admit, to confess, to avow; 5. to approve (of); 6. to agree, to consent to; ~ günü at-home; ~ havzası geogr. catchment basin; ~ resmi, resmî ~ official solemn reception; ~ salonu reception room; -ü olm. to accept willingly.

**kabullenmek** 1. to appropriate, to take away, to seize; 2. to accept unwillingly;

3. = kabul etm.

**kaburga** 1. rib; 2. anat. thorax, chest; 3. skeleton (or frame) (of a ship); -ları çıkmak (or sayılmak) to be only skin and bones.

**kâbus** [- -] nightmare; ~ çökmek (üzerine) or ~ geçirmek to have a nightmare.

**kâbuslu** [- - .] nightmarish.

**kabza** 1. grip, grasp, hold; heft, handle; 2. butt (end) (gun); 3. sl. a handful of hashish.

**kabzımal** fruit and vegetable wholesaler, middleman in fruit and vegetable.

**kaç,** -çı 1. how many?; how much?; ~ defa 1. how many times?, how often?; 2. many times, frequently, so often; ~ para eder? what's it good for?, what's the use?; ~ paralık (adam or şey) kıl F he (or it) is absolutely worthless!, he (or it) is good for nothing!; ~ parça olayım? F which of all these jobs can I cope with?; ~ yaşındasın? how old are you?; -a? what is the price?, how much is it?; -ın kur'ası fig. crafty, fox, wily fellow, old hand.

**kaçaburuk** shoemaker's awl.

**kaçak** 1. runaway, fugitive, truant (pupil), deserter; 2. contraband, smuggled (goods); 3. leakage, leak, escape (of gas); ~ içki F moonshine.

**kaçakçı** smuggler.

**kaçakçılık** smuggling; ~ yapmak to smuggle.

**kaçaklık** 1. desertion, fugitiveness; truancy; 2. tax or duty evasion.

**kaçamak** 1. neglect of duty, 2. evasion, flight, subterfuge, pretext, equivocation; 3. place of refuge, asylum, sheepfold; 4. F having a bit on the side; ~ yapmak 1. to shirk, to dodge, to goldbrick (a duty); 2. to prevaricate, to shuffle, to dodge; ~ yolu excuse, pretext, evasion.

**kaçamaklı** evasive, elusive.

**kaçar** how many at a time?, how many ... each?, how much per...?, how many to each?

**kaçarola,** kaçarula frying-pan, casserole.

**kaçık** 1. batty, mad (on), crazy (for, about), foolish, eccentric; 2. ladder, Am. run (in a stocking); 3. having a ladder (stocking); 4. crooked, warped.

**kaçıklık** craziness, battiness.

**kaçılmak** fig. to get out of the way.

**kaçımsamak** to goof off.

**kaçımsar** evasive.

**kaçıncı** which ... (in a series).

**kaçınık** reclusive.

**kaçınılmaz** inevitable, unavoidable, ineluctable.

**kaçınmak** to abstain (-*den* from), to avoid, to steer clear (-*den* of), to get out of the way, to stand aside, to shirk, to dodge, to shun, to evade.

**kaçıntı** leakage, leak.

**kaçırma** *vn. of* kaçırmak, ♫ abduction, kidnapping; hijacking.

**kaçırmak** *caus. of* kaçmak, *part.* 1. to make (*or* let) escape, to get away, to drive away; 2. to leak (*air, gas, etc.*); 3. *fig.* to rob (*or* deprive) s.o. of s.th.; 4. to conceal, to hide; 5. to cause s.o. to go away (*or* leave); 6. to miss (*a vehicle, school, chance*); 7. to kidnap, to abduct; to hijack; 8. to smuggle; 9. to withhold s.th. from s.o.; 10. to soil, to wet; 11. to go mad (*or* crazy); to lose one's mind; 12. to get overdrunk; 13. to overlook, to omit, to skip.

**kaçış** flight, escape, desertion.

**kaçışmak** to disperse, to flee in confusion, to run away in various directions.

**kaçkın** fugitive (*a. fig.*), deserter; truant.

**kaçlı** 1. from which number? (*card*); 2. from which annual set? (*of birth, graduation*).

**kaçlık** 1. at what price?; 2. contains how many?; of what size?; 3. how old?; bu adamı kaçlık tahmin edersiniz? How old do you think this man is?

**kaçmak**, (-ar) 1. to escape, to flee, to run away (-*den* from), to desert, 2. not to appear, not to show up, to shun; 3. to avoid, to shirk, to get out of the way, to stand aside, to steer clear; 4. to leak, to leak out; 5. to shift, to get out of place, to slip; 6. to ladder, *Am.* to run (*stocking*); 7. to withdraw without noticed; 8. to make haste, to hurry; 9. to disappear, to vanish, to come to nothing, to be frustrated; F to go to pot (*rest, joy, etc.*); 10. to turn out, to prove, to be (*good, bad, etc.*); 11. to draw near; 12. to slip into, to get into (*water, dust, etc.*); 13. to elope (*ile* with); kacacak delik aramak to look for a place to hide; kaçanın anası ağlamamış safety is in being cautious; -tan kovnlamaya vakit olmamak to have no time for lesser things because of important matters.

**kaçmaz** runnroof, non-laddering, *Am.* non--running (*stocking*).

**kadana** [. x .] 1. *name of a kind of horse* breed; 2. *sl.* huge woman; F dragon.

**kadar** 1. as much as, as far as, so long as, as big as; 2. to; up to; 3. about, say *Am.* around, like; 4. so much; bir ay öncesine ~ up to a month ago; istediğin ~ all take as much (*or* many) as you like; gözün görebildiği ~ as (*or* so) long as eye reaches.

**kadastro** [. x .] cadastration, land survey, land registry; -ya geçmek to be registered in a cadaster.

**kadavra** [. x .] cadaver, corpse, carcass.

**kadayıf** dry dough (*for various kinds of sweet pastry*).

**kadeh** glass, cup; wineglass, goblet; ~ arkadaşı drinking companion; ~ kaldırmak to raise one's glass in a toast; ~ tokuşturmak to clink glasses.

**kadem** 1. foot, pace; 2. good luck, good foreboding; 2. ♱, ✕ echelon, squadron; ~ in); ~ getirmek to bring good luck.

**kademe** 1. stage, level, grade, rank, degree; 2. ♱, ✕ echelon, squadron; ~ birliği ♱, ✕ squadron formation; ~ ~ 1. step by step, gradually, by degrees; 2. ✕ in echelons.

**kademelendirmek** ✕ to stagger.

**kademeli** 1. ✕ articulated, in echolons; 2. stepped, graded.

**kademhane** [. . - .] (water-)closet, lavatory, toilet.

**kademli** bringing luck, lucky, fortunate.

**kademsiz** unlucky, fatal, baneful, bringing bad luck.

**kademsizlik** inauspiciousness, ill omen.

**kader** destiny, fate, predestination; -in cilvesi the irony of fate; -in sillesi the buffet of fate.

**kadercilik** fatalism.

**kadı** Moslem judge, cadi, kadi.

**kadın** 1. woman; 2. matron; 3. *a title used after the names of older women*; 4. maid, charwoman; ~ berberi ladies' hairdresser; ~ doktoru gynecologist; ~ -a (*meeting, party, etc.*) with only women present; ~ -cık ideal housewoman; ~ milleti F womankind, women; ~ olm. 1. to lose her virginity; 2. to be a good housewife; ~ oyuncu actress; ~ sporcu sportswoman; ~ terzisi dressmaker; -lar hamamı gibi *fig.* like a bear garden.

**kadınbudu**, -nu *meat ball with eggs and rice.*

**kadıncık** poor woman.

**kadıncıl** woman-chaser, womanizer.

**kadıngöbeği**, -ni *sweet dish made with semolina and eggs.*

**kadınlık** 1. womanhood; 2. good housekeeping; 3. womankind, women; ~ gururu womanly pride; ~ hormonları woman hormones; ~ uzvu vagina.

**kadınsı** womanish. effeminate, sissy.

**kadıntuzluğu**, -nu ♀ barberry.

**kadırga** [. x .] † galley.

**kadırgabalığı,** -nı zo. whale, cachalot.

**kadife** [¹] velvet; corduroy; ~ gioı velvety.

**kadim** [ī] old, ancient *(times),* through eternal.

**kadir**¹, -dri 1. worth, value; 2. *ast.* magnitude; 2 gecesi the Night of Power *(the 27th of Ramadan, when the Koran was revealed);* ~ gecesi doğmuş 1. he is married to a very fine woman; 2. he is a very lucky person.

**kadir²** [ā] able *(-e* to), capable *(-e* of), fit *(-e* for), powerful, mighty *(God).*

**kadirbilir** appreciative *(of value or merit).*

**kadirbilirlik** appreciation.

**kadirşinas** [. . . -] appreciative *(of value or merit).*

**kadirşinaslık** appreciation.

**kadit,** -di [¹] 1. skeleton; 2. skin and bone, a mere skeleton; 3. jerked meat; -i çıkmak to turn into skin and bones.

**kadmiyum** ⚗ cadmium.

**kadran** 1. ⊕ dial (plate), face; 2. scale *(radio, etc.);* 3. quadrant.

**kadril** quadrille *(the dance and its music).*

**kadro** [x .] 1. personnel, staff; workers; teaching staff; roll; 2. ✕ cadre, establishment; 3. framework; 4. a permanent position; ~ dışı not on the permanent staff, temporary; not employed; ~ mevcudu ✕ authorized strength; -ya dahil on the permanent staff; -ya girmek to be put on the permanent staff.

**kadrolu** on the permanent staff.

**kadrosuz** not on the permanent staff; temporarily employed.

**kafa** 1. head, skull; 2. sight, view, opinion; 3. intelligence, understanding; 4. marble *(children's toy);* ~ değiştirmek to change one's mind, to change one's way of thinking; ~ dengi like-minded, intimate, kindred spirit; ~ göz yarmak *fig.* to be clumsy; ~ -ya vermek to put their heads together; ~ kalmamak not to be able think because of being worn out; ~ oyunu puzzle; ~ patlatmak to rack one's brain *(-e* over); ~ sallamak to be a yes-man, to approve everything; ~ şişirmek to talk s.o.'s head off, to talk the pants off one; ~ tutmak 1. to oppose, to resist, to struggle against, to contradict, to be rebellious, to be contrary; 2. *(b-ne)* to rebel, to revolt against *s.o.;* ~ ütülemek *sl.* to talk s.o.'s head off, to talk to s.o. to death; ~ yormak to rack one's brains *(-e* over), to ponder; -dan atmak to take a shot in the dark, to shoot off the belly; -dan gayrı müsellah *co.*

stupid, dull, nutty, obtuse; -dan kontak *sl.* having a screw loose, screwy, nutty; -sı almamak 1. not to be able to understand *(or* grasp); 2. not to be receptive any more; 3. not to be able to believe; -sı bozulmak to get angry; -sı bulanmak to get confused; -sı dönmek *fig.* to get perplexed, to fly into a broad passion; -sı dumanlı 1. tipsy, in one's cups; 2. confused and perplexed; -sı durmak to be too tired to think; -sı işlemek to be on the ball; -sı kazan olm. *s.* -sı şişmek; -sı kızmak to blow one's top, to get angry; -sı şişmek to be ringing *(from noise);* to feel fuddled; -sı taşa çarpmak *fig.* to suffer for one's mistake; -sı yerinde olmamak to woolgather; -sı yerine gelmek to regain self-control, to pull o.s. together; -sına dank etm. to dawn on one at last; -sına koymak to make up one's mind, to be determined to...; -sına sığmamak not to be able to conceive (of), to find unacceptable; -sına vur, ekmeğini elinden al he can't say boo to a goose; -sına vura vura by force; -sında şimşek çakmak to have a brainwave, to dawn on one suddenly; -sını kırmak *fig.* to knock s.o.'s block off; -sını kullanmak to use one's loaf; -sını kurcalamak to obsess; -sını taştan taşa çarpmak to regret bitterly; -sının dikine gitmek to behave stubbornly, to go one's own way; -yı bulmak *sl.* to be in one's cups; -yı çekmek *sl.* to be on the booze; -yı tütsülemek *sl.* to get tight; -yı (yere) vurmak to get laid up in bed; -yı vurup yatmak F to hit the sack.

**kafadanbacaklılar** zo. Cephalopoda.

**kafadar** like-minded; kindred spirit, buddy.

**kafaiçi,** -ni *anat.* brain, intercranial.

**kafakâğıdı,** -nı F identity card, ID card.

**kafalı** 1. ...headed; 2. *fig.* intelligent, brainy.

**kafasız** stupid, dull, obtuse.

**kafasızlık** stupidity.

**kafatascı** racist.

**kafatasçılık** racism.

**kafatası,** -nı *anat.* skull, cranium.

**kafein** caffeine.

**kafes** 1. cage; coop; 2. lattice, grating, latticework; 3. *sl.* clink; 4. framework *(wooden house);* 5. skeleton *(of a ship);* ~ gibi 1. a mere skeleton; 2. (entirely) perforated; ~ ~ full of holes, perforated; ~ tamiri a thoroughly overhauling of a building; -e girmek *sl.* to be duped *(or* tricked); -e koymak *sl.* to trick, to deceive, to make a dupe (of).

**kafesçi 1.** maker *or* seller of cages *or* latticework; **2.** *sl.* deceiver.

**kafeslemek** *sl.* to deceive, to trick, to con.

**kafesli** latticed.

**kafeterya** cafeteria.

**kâfi** [- -] sufficient, enough (-*e* for); ~ gelmek (*or* olm.) to be enough (*or* sufficient), to suffice.

**kafile** [ā] **1.** caravan, troop, band; **2.** X convoy, escort; **3.** sending, part.

**kâfir** [ā] **1.** unbeliever, infidel, misbeliever, non-Muslim; **2.** *fig.* chap, bloke, *Am.* guy; seni ~ seni! you mad chap!

**kâfirlik** infidelity, impiousness.

**kafiye** [ā] rhyme.

**kafiyeli** [ā] rhyming, rhymed.

**kafiyesiz** [ā] unrhymed.

**Kafkas (Dağları), Kafkasya** *pr. n.* Caucasus.

**Kafkasyalı** *pr. n.* Caucasian.

**kaftan** robe, caftan; ~ giymek to receive a robe of hono(u)r.

**kâfur** [- -] **kâfuru** [- . .] ⌐ camphor.

**kâgir** built of stone *or* brick; stone..., brick...

**kağan** khan, ruler.

**kağanlık** khanate.

**kâğıt, -dı 1.** paper; **2.** slip (of paper), note; **3.** letter; **4.** (playing) card; **5.** document, report; **6.** one lira; **7.** paper...; ~ açmak to turn up the trump card; ~ dağıtmak to deal cards; ~ fener Chinese lantern; ~ gibi olm. (*b-nin yüzü*) to turn pale in the face; ~ oynamak to play cards; ~ oyunu card game; ~ para paper money; ~ sepeti waste paper basket; ~ üzerinde kalmak to exist on paper only (*plan, etc.*); ~ üzerine koymak to commit to paper; kâğıda dökmek to write s.th. down; kâğıdı kim yaptı? who had the deal?

**kâğıtbalığı, -nı** *zo.* ribbonfish, dealfish.

**kâğıtçı** stationer.

**kâğıthelvası** disk-shaped wafers.

**kâğıtlamak** to paper.

**kâğıtlık 1.** paper case (*or* chest *or* stand); **2.** suitable for making paper.

**kağnı** two-wheeled ox-cart; ~ gibi (gitmek) (to go) at a snail's pace.

**kağşak** near to collapse; out of repair, dilapidated.

**kağşamak 1.** to become shaky, to become tottery: F to come apart (*furniture*); **2.** *fig.* to become old and feeble.

**kâh** sometimes, now and then, occasionally; ~ ... ~ sometimes ... sometimes.

**kahır, -hrı 1.** great sorrow, grief; **2.** unjust

treatment; ~ çekmek to bear difficulties for a long time, to endure, to put up with...; kahrı çekilir bearable; kahrı çekilmez unbearable; kahrından ölmek to die of grief; kahrını çekmek to lump (it), to endure.

**kahırlanmak** to be grieved (*or* distressed).

**kahırlı** extremely sad, deeply distressed, wretched.

**kâhin** soothsayer, seer.

**kâhinlik 1.** soothsaying; **2.** prophecy.

**kahir** [ā] overwhelming, irresistable, overpowering; ~ ekseriyet overwhelming majority.

**Kahire** [ā] *pr. n.* Cairo.

**kahkaha** peal of laughter, loud laughter; ~ atmak (*or* koparmak) to burst out laughing; ~ tufanı peals of laughter.

**kahkahaçiçeği, -ni** ♀ morning-glory.

**kahpe 1.** whore, prostitute; **2.** *sl.* fickle, inconstant, faithless, perfidious, base, mean; -nin dölü *sl.* son of a bitch.

**kahpelik 1.** prostitution, being a whore; **2.** villainy, knavish trick; ~ etm. **1.** to be a prostitute; **2.** to behave villainously.

**kahraman 1.** hero, gallant; heroine; **2.** *fig.* brave, heroic (*affair, etc.*).

**kahramanlık 1.** heroism, valo(u)r; **2.** heroic deed, exploit.

**kahretmek** [x . .] **1.** to crush (to death), to overcome, to overpower, to overwhelm, to ruin, to destroy, to wreck; **2.** *fig.* to be distressed, to torture; **3.** to grieve; **4.** to curse, to execrate.

**kahrolmak** [x . .] to grieve, to be depressed; Kahrolsun! damned!, to hell with him!

**kahvaltı 1.** (*a.* sabah kahvaltısı) breakfast; **2.** afternoon coffee; **3.** (*cold*) snack; ~ etm. **1.** to (have) breakfast; **2.** to have a snack.

**kahvaltılık 1.** ... for breakfast; **2.** food for breakfast.

**kahve 1.** ((*a.* kuru kahve) coffee, coffee-beans; **2.** coffee (*as drink*); **3.** Oriental coffee-house, café; ~ çekmek to grind coffee-beans; ~ değirmeni coffee-mill, coffee-grinder; ~ dolabı cylindrical coffee roaster; ~ fincanı coffee cup; ~ ocağı room where coffee, tea, etc. are made; ~ parası tip, gratuity.

**kahveci 1.** grower *or* seller of coffee; **2.** the owner *or* lessee of an Oriental coffee-house; **3.** coffee-boiler, coffee-maker.

**kahvehane** Oriental coffee-house, café.

**kahverengi, -yi, -ni** brown.

**kâhya 1.** (landowner's) steward, majordomo, bailiff, superintendent; **2.** warden of a trade guild; **3.** *fig. contp.* overseer;

**4.** *fig.* busybody; **5.** parking lot attendant; (Birinin başına) ~ kesilmek to meddle in affairs.

**kâhyalık 1.** stewardship; **2.** duty of a steward *or* a parking lot attendant; **3.** money paid to the parking lot attendant; **4.** *fig.* meddling in affairs; ~ etm. **1.** to work as a steward *or* a parking lot attendant; **2.** *fig.* to meddle in affairs.

**kaide** [â] **1.** basis, foundation; **2.** foot, base, pedestal; **3.** rule, principle *(a.* A*)*; **4.** norm, standard; **5.** *geom.* base-line; **6.** cardinal number; **7.** doctrine, teaching, theory; **8.** *sl.* buttocks, rump.

**kaidesiz** irregular.

**kail** [â] **1.** *(bşe)* convinced, positive; **2.** agreed! (with); **3.** speaker; ~ olm. to convince, to agree.

**kaim** [â] **1.** extant, lasting, existing, present; **2.** taking the place of; ~ olm. **1.** to exist, to be extant; **2.** to take the place of.

**kaime** [â] **1.** official list *(or* document*)*; **2.** † paper-money.

**kâin 1.** being, existent; **2.** situated.

**kâinat,** -tı [-. -] **1.** the universe, the cosmos; **2.** *fig.* everyone, everybody, the whole world.

**kak¹,** -kı **1.** dried fruit; **2.** *fig.* meagre, Am. meager, skinny.

**kak²,** -kı puddle, pool.

**kaka** *(child's language)* **1.** bad, ugly, bratty; **2.** dirt, filth, excrement; ~ yapmak to defecate, to go potty *(child)*.

**kakalamak 1.** to push *or* strike continuously; **2.** = kaka yapmak; **3.** *fig.* to put across *(or* one over on*)* *(in shopping)*.

**kakao** ⦷ cocoa; ~ yağı cocoa butter.

**kakavan 1.** stuck-up and stupid; **2.** *sl.* old and ugly.

**kakıç** gaff, a kind of harpoon.

**kakılmak** to be shoved and pushed; kakılıp kalmak to be stuck, to have to wait, to be rooted to (the spot).

**kakım** *zo.* ermine, stoat.

**kakımak** to blame, to reprove, to censure, to denounce, to criticize.

**kakınç** reproach; (başına) ~ etm. to rub it in.

**kakırdamak 1.** to rattle, to rustle, to crackle, to snap; **2.** *sl.* to die, to peg out.

**kakırtı** crackling sound, crackle, soft crack.

**kakışmak** to push and shove mutually, to keep nudging *(ile* with*)*.

**kakıştırmak** to cuff, to thump, to push, to nudge.

**kakma 1.** *vn. of* kakmak **2.** repousse work,

chased work, relief work.

**kakmacı** inlayer.

**kakmacılık** repoussage, ornamental inlaying.

**kakmak,** (-ar) **1.** to push, to shove, to drive in, to nail, to ram in; **2.** to encrust, to inlay; **3.** to chase.

**kakmalı** inlayed.

**kaknem** *sl.* **1.** meagre and misery; **2.** ugly, mean, bad-tempered.

**kaktüs** [â] ⦷ cactus.

**kakule** [â] ⦷ cardamom.

**kâkül** forelock, bangs, fringe.

**kâküllü** having forelock.

**kal¹ 1.** refining, purification *(from metal)*; **2.** ⦷ cupellation.

**kal²,** -li [â] word, talk, speech; -e almak to mention, to discuss, to take into consideration; -e almamak to consider insignificant *(or* negligible*)*, to take no notice *(-i* of*)*.

**kala** -e to *(for* time*)*; before *(a* time*)*; saat ona beş ~ at five to ten; köye iki kilometre ~ two kilometers from the village; on gün ~ ten days before.

**kalaazar** kala-azar, dumdum fever.

**kalaba** crowd, mass.

**kalabalık 1.** crowd, throng, press; **2.** crowded; **3.** numerous *(luggage)*; big *(family)*; **4.** overcrowded *(bus)*; overpopulated *(city)*; ~ etm. **1.** to crowd, to take up, to occupy *(a place)*, to be in the way *(object)*; **2.** F to stand about uselessly.

**kalabalıkça** a little crowded.

**kalabalıklaşmak 1.** to get crowded; **2.** to get cluttered.

**kalafat,** -tı **1.** ⦶ caulking; **2.** turban *(headdress worn by commander-in--chiefs and Janisseries)*; ~ yeri caulking wharf; -a çekmek to careen for caulking.

**kalafatçı** caulker.

**kalafatlamak 1.** to caulk, to careen; **2.** *fig.* to repair, to restore.

**kalafatsız** uncaulked, caulkless.

**kalak 1.** nostril *(of animals)*; **2.** winnings stones *(children's game)*.

**kalakalmak 1.** to be petrified, to be surprised, to be taken aback, to stand perplexed; **2.** to have a hard time.

**kalamar** *zo.* squid, cuttle-fish.

**kalan 1.** remaining; **2.** A remainder; **3.** the rest; **4.** staying.

**kalantor** well-heeled and ostentatious man.

**kalas** beam, plank, timber.

**kalastra** lifeboat chock on the deck of ships.

**kalay 1.** tin; **2.** *fig.* varnish; **3.** *sl.* swear, curse; -ı basmak *sl.* to swear a blue streak, to chew out.

**kalaycı** tinsmith, tinner; tinker.

**kalaylamak 1.** to tin; **2.** *sl.* to insult, to call s.o. names, to abuse; **3.** *fig.* to conceal by sham (*fault, etc.*).

**kalaylı 1.** tinned; **2.** containing tin; **3.** *fig.* sham.

**kalaysız 1.** untinned; **2.** containing no tin.

**kalben 1.** sincerely, wholeheartedly; **2.** ethical, spiritual, mental.

**kalbi** [. -] sincere, heartfelt, warm, cordial.

**kalbur** sieve, riddle; ~ gibi riddled, full of holes; ~ kemiği *anat.* ethmoid bone; -a cevirmek to fill with holes, to riddle; -a dönmek to be riddled, to be filled with holes; -dan geçirmek to sieve, to sift, to screen; -la su taşımak *fig.* to exert o.s. to purposeless work, to plough the sand(s).

**kalburcu 1.** maker *or* seller of sieves; **2.** sifter.

**kalburlamak** to sift, to sieve, to screen.

**kalburüstü**, -nü *fig.* select, elite, prominent; -ne gelmek (*or* kalmak) to become outstanding.

**kalcı** refiner of metals.

**kalça** [x .] *anat.* hip; ~ çevresi hip-measurement; ~ kemiği *anat.* hipbone.

**kalçalı 1.** hipped; **2.** with big hips, broad across the beam.

**kalçasız 1.** without hips; **2.** with narrow hips.

**kalçete** ⚓ gasket.

**kalçın** long felt hose.

**kaldıraç** lever, crowbar.

**kaldıran** *anat.* levator.

**kaldırıcı** jack.

**kaldırım** pavement, *Am.* sidewalk, causeway; ~ ciğnemek *fig.* to be experienced in the ways of the world, to be wordly wise; ~ döşemek to pave; ~ mühendisi *co.* loafer, idler; ~ süpürgesi (*or* yosması) streetwalker, prostitute; ~ taşı paving stone; -a düşmek **1.** to lose its value; **2.** to be sold cheap in the street.

**kaldırımcı 1.** paver; **2.** *sl.* swindler, crook, pickpocket.

**kaldırımsız** unpaved.

**kaldırımsı** *biol.* squamous (epithelium).

**kaldırma** *vn.* of kaldırmak; ~ cihazı forklift.

**kaldırmak** *caus.* of kalkmak **1.** to lift, to elevate, to raise; **2.** to move away, to remove, to clear away; **3.** to clear (*table*); **4.** to scare; **5.** to abolish, to do away with; **6.** to wake; **7.** to cause to

recover (from); **8.** to bear, to endure, to tolerate; **9.** to erect, to stand; **10.** F to steal, to pinch, to swipe; **11.** to start (*a motorcar*); **12.** to buy in bulky quantities; **13.** to kidnap; **14.** to carry the corpse to grave; **15.** to take the ill to hospital.

**kale 1.** fortress, castle, citadel; **2.** ✗ bunker, pillbox; **3.** *fig.* bullwark, bastion; **4.** *chess:* castle, rook; **5.** *sports:* goal; ~ gibi **1.** big, plain and solid (*building*); **2.** trustworthy and strong, portly (*person*); ~ sahası goal area.

**kalebent**, -di castle convict.

**kaleci** goalkeeper.

**kalem 1.** (lead) pencil, colo(u)red pencil, fountain-pen, writing reed; **2.** (government) office, chancellery; **3.** style, (im)personation, representation; **4.** chisel; **5.** carving knife; **6.** † item, entry, sum; **7.** ✓ graft; **8.** paintbrush; ~ açmak to sharpen a pencil; (üstüne) ~ çekmek to cross out, to cancel; ~ efendisi clerk in a government office; ~ işi **1.** hand-painting; **2.** hand-carved; ~ kaşlı having thin and long eyebrows; ~ kulaklı having small, upright ears (*horse, deer, etc.*); ~ oynatmak **1.** to write; **2.** to correct, to edit; **3.** to spoil by altering (*article, etc.*); ~ parmaklı having long, slim, tapering fingers; ~ sahibi author, writer, man of letters; -e almak to write, to draw up, to indite; -e gelir **1.** describable; **2.** reasonable; -e gelmemek to be indescribable; -e (*or* kâğıda) sarılmak to take pen in hand, to start to write promptly; (herhangi bir nitelikte) -i olm. to write well on any subject; -inden çıkmak to be written by s.o.; -inden kan damlamak *fig.* **1.** to write effectively; **2.** to write bitterly and harmfully; -iyle yaşamak (*or* geçinmek) to make a living by writing, to live by one's pen.

**kalemaşısı**, -nı graft, scion.

**kalembek 1.** aloes; **2.** a kind of maize.

**kalemis** civet (cat).

**kalemkâr** [. . -] **1.** decorator; **2.** engraver, chase-worker.

**kalemlik 1.** pencil box; **2.** penholder, pen rack.

**kalemşor** *co.* polemical writer.

**kalemtıraş** pencil sharpener.

**kalender 1.** wandering, mendicant friar; **2.** *fig.* unconventional, easy-going, easily satisfied.

**kalenderce 1.** unconventional and easy going, bohemian; **2.** philosophical.

**kalenderleşmek** to behave *or* live in an unconventional way.

**kalenderlik 1.** unconventionality; **2.** a bohemian existance.

**kalevi** alkaline.

**kaleydeskop** kaleidescope.

**kalfa [x .] 1.** assistant master; qualified workman; **2.** building contractor; **3.** chief palace maid-servant; **4.** † assistant (of a primary school teacher).

**kalgımak 1.** to leap up, to jump up, to rise, to scar up (dolphine); **2.** to rear, to rise, to prance (horse); **3.** to jump up angrily.

**kalhane [. - .]** ⊕ smelter(y).

**kalıcı** permanent, lasting.

**kalıcılık 1.** permanence; **2.** phys. retentivity.

**kalıç** sickle.

**kalık 1.** defective, incomplete; **2.** spinster.

**kalıklık** defectiveness, deficiency.

**kalım** survival, duration, life.

**kalımlı** everlasting, perpetual, permanent; immortal.

**kalımlılık 1.** permanence; **2.** immortality.

**kalımsız** transient, impermanent.

**kalın¹ 1.** thick, stout; **2.** viscous, stiff; **3.** sl. rich, wealthy, well-heeled; **4.** † coarse, uneducated; **5.** velar; ~ kafalı thickheaded, thickwitted, obtuse, stupid, dull; ~ kafalılık dullness; ~ ses deep voice; ~ ünlü back vowel (a, ı, o, u).

**kalın²** present given by the bridegroom to the bride.

**kalınbağırsak** anat. great gut, large intestine.

**kalınca** somewhat thick.

**kalınlaşmak** to become thick (or stout), to thicken.

**kalınlaştırmak** to thicken, to make s.th. thick.

**kalınlatmak** = kalınlaştırmak.

**kalınlık 1.** thickness (a. fig.); **2.** viscousness (gas, fluid); **3.** fig. coarseness; **4.** deepness (voice).

**kalınmak** to stay, to rest, to stop.

**kalıntı 1.** remnant, remainder, leftovers, leavings; **2.** ruin, ruins, debris, relic; **3.** mark, trace.

**kalınyağ** lubricating oil.

**kalıp, -bı 1.** mo(u)ld, press form; **2.** matrix, model; **3.** shoemaker last; **4.** block (hat); **5.** bar, bolt (cheese or scap); **6.** external apperance; model, pattern; ~ gibi still, without moving; ~ gibi oturmak to fit like a glove (suit, dress); ~ gibi serilmek (or yatmak) to lie stretched out like a log; ~ gibi uyumak to sleep like a log; ~ kesilmek to stand aghast, to be petrified; ~ kıyafet outer appearance; ~ sigarası machine-made cigarette; -a

dökmek to cast, to mo(u)ld; -a vurmak to put on a block (or last) (hat, etc.); -ı kıyafeti yerinde imposing and well dressed man; -ı değiştirmek (or dinlendirmek) sl. to die, to pop off; -ını basmak fig. to give (or provide) security, to stand surety; -ının adamı olmamak not to be the man as expected from his appearance; -tan -a girmek fig. to be fickle (or inconstant or valatile) for one's benefit.

**kalıpçı 1.** maker or seller of mo(u)lds; **2.** mo(u)lder, blocker.

**kalıplamak** to form, to block, to mo(u)ld.

**kalıplaşmak** to get fixed in one form (or type), to become stereotyped.

**kalıplaşmış 1.** stereotyped; **2.** clichéd; ~ iyelik gr. stereotyped possessed form.

**kalıplı** shaped by mo(u)lds.

**kalıpsız** out of shape.

**kalıt, -tı 1.** inheritance; **2.** inherited characteristic.

**kalıtçı** heir, inheritor.

**kalıtım 1.** biol. (genetic) heritage; **2.** inheritance, heritage.

**kalıtımbilim** genetics.

**kalıtımsal** hereditary.

**kalıtsal** hereditary.

**kalibre** caliber.

**kalifiye** qualified, skilled.

**kaliforniyum** californium.

**kalinos** ichth. a kind of sea bass.

**kalite** quality, class; ~ kontrolü quality control (or test).

**kaliteli 1.** high-quality, of good quality; **2.** of high value, high-class, high-grade.

**kalitesiz** poor-quality, shoddy.

**kalitesizlik** lack of quality, shooddiness.

**kalkan 1.** shield; **2.** zo. turbot; **3.** fig. defender.

**kalkanbezi, -ni** anat. thyroid gland.

**kalker** geol. limestone.

**kalkerleşmek** to calsify.

**kalkerli** calcareous.

**kalkık 1.** pointing upwards; **2.** upturned (brim, collar, etc.); **3.** peeled off (paint, polish, etc.); **4.** pulled up (curtain); **5.** high (eyebrow); **6.** standing on end (hair); **7.** retroussé (nose).

**kalkındırmak** to develop, to improve, to cause to recover, to lead towards progress.

**kalkınış** developing, improving.

**kalkınma 1.** development, progress improvement; **2.** recovery; **3.** ascent; ~ hızı rate of economic development; ~ planı development plan.

**kalkınmak** to develop, to make progress,

to advance.

**kalkış** 1. rising; 2. departure; -a geçmek ↑ to take off.

**kalkışmak** to attempt, to (dare to) undertake (-meğe to do s.th.), to try (-meğe to do s.th.).

**kalkmak,** (-ar) 1. to stand up, to rise to go up; 2. to get loose (polish); 3. to get up, to get out of bed; 4. to depart, to leave, to set out (or off), to start; 5. to rear (horse); 6. to be taken off (cloth, lid); 7. to recover (from an illness), 8. to be annulled, to be abolished, to be repealed; 9. to be cleared (or removed); 10. to set about, to undertake (to do s.th.), to venture; 11. to disappear, to vanish; 12. to rebel; 13. to be reaped (or gathered); 14. to move to; 15. to go out of circulation (money); Kalk borusu ✕ reveille; Kalkıp kalkıp oturmak to show one's anger by movements, to be hopping mad.

**kallavi** [. - -] 1. ceremonial turban (formerly worn by viziers); 2. F huge, very big.

**kalleş** F unreliable, treacherous, faithless, perfidious, backstabbing.

**kalleşçe** treacherously.

**kalleşlik** treachery, backstabbing, faithlessness, disloyalty, perfidiousness, perfidy; ~ etm. to play s.o. a dirty trick.

**kalma** 1. vn. of kalmak; 2. remaining, left; 3. handed down, inherited (-den from), descended (-den from).

**kalmak,** (-ır) 1. to remain, to be left; 2. to continue to exist, to survive; 3. to dwell, to stay; 4. not to make progress; 5. (sınıfta) not to get one's remove, to fail (a class); 6. to be detained, to be put off; 7. to be inherited (-den from); 8. to be postponed; 9. to be on s.o.'s duty, to be incumbent on s.o., to rest with s.o.; 10. to be kept from doing s.th.; 11. to be contented with; 12. to halt; 13. to cease; 14. to drop (wind); Kala kala there only remains, all that is left; kaldı ki besides, moreover; (şundan or bundan) Kalır yeri yok it is indistinguishable, it is perfectly the same; (Şuna or buna) Kalsa (or Kalırsa 1. if you ask (my, his, etc.) opinion; 2. if it were left up to (s.o.); kalsın! 1. leave it!, forget it!; 2. it is not important any more.

**kalmalı** locative; ~ tümleç gr. locative noun phrase with adverbial force.

**kaloma** [. x .] ↓ 1. slack of a hawser; 2. loose end of rope.

**kalomel** calomel.

**kalori** calorie.

**kalorifer** 1. central heating; 2. radiator;

~ dairesi furnace room; ~ kazanı boiler.

**kaloriferci** 1. furnaceman 2. stoker, fireman.

**kalorimetre** calorimeter.

**kaloş** overshoe, galosh.

**kalp¹** -bi 1. anat. heart; 2. heart desease; 3. fig. affection; 4. fig. feeling, sense; 5. centre, innermost part; ~ ağrısı lover's grief, heartache; ~ atışı heartbeat; ~ çarpıntısı beating (or palpitation) of the heart; ~ kazanmak (or fethetmek) to win the heart (of); ~ kırmak to hurt s.o.'s feelings, to break s.o.'s heart; ~ krizi heart attack from cardiac weakness; ~ olmamak (b-de) not to have sympathy, to be merciless; ~ sektesi heart attack; ~ yetersizliği (or kifayetsizliği) cardiac insufficiency; -den yaralı sad, grieved (at, about); -e doğmak to have a presentiment; ~ -e karşıdır feelings are mutual; -i çarpmak 1. to palpitate (or beat) fast; 2. to palpitate with excitement; -i fesat 1. envious, jealous; 2. suspicious; -i kırık broken-hearted; -ine doğmak s. -e doğmak; -ine girmek to win s.o.'s heart; -ine göre after one's own heart; -ini açmak to pour out one's troubles, to let one's hair down, to bare one's soul (-e to).

**kalp²** change, transformation.

**kalp³,** -pı 1. not genuine, spurious, false, forged; 2. fig. untrustworthy, liar.

**kalpak** fur cap.

**kalpazan** 1. counterfeiter, forger, faker; 2. fig. swindler, cheat, crook, liar.

**kalpazanlık** 1. counterfeiting; 2. swindling, cheating, trickery.

**kalplaşmak** to lose one's strength (or agility or diligence).

**kalplık** 1. falsity, spuriousness; 2. aversion to work.

**kalpli** having heart disease.

**kalpsiz** heartless, pitiless, merciless.

**kalpsizlik** heartlessness, pitilessness.

**kalseduan** chalcedony.

**kalsit,** -ti calcite.

**kalsiyum** calcium.

**kaltaban** 1. swindler, crook, tricky, unreliable; 2. † dishonest, without hono(u)r, pander.

**kaltabanlık** deceitfulness, dishonesty.

**kaltak** 1. saddle frame; 2. sl. whore, prostitute, slut, hussy.

**kaltaklık** 1. prostitution; 2. mean behavio(u)r (of a woman).

**kalubeladan beri** [- - . - x . ] from time immemorial.

**kalya** 1. potash; 2. squash or eggplant

*cooked with meat, onion and butter.*

**kalyon** galleon, galley.

**kalyoncu 1.** armed member of galley; **2.** seaman, sailor.

**kam** shaman.

**kâm** wish, desire; ~ almak (bşden) to get what one desires.

**kama** [x .] **1.** dagger, dirk; **2.** wedge; **3.** breechblock; ~ basmak to win a game.

**kamacı** artillary mechanic (or artificer).

**kamalamak 1.** to stab (with a dagger); **2.** ⊕ to fasten with wedges.

**kamanço etm.** sl. to burden s.o. with s.th., to exchange, to hand over.

**kamara** [x . .] **1.** ship's cabin; **2.** ♀ House (of Lords or Commons); **3.** joint edge (sole).

**kamarilla** [. . x .] camarilla, clique.

**kamarot**, -tu ship's steward.

**kamaşmak 1.** to be dazzled, to be blinded, to become dull; **2.** to be set on edge (teeth).

**kamaştırmak 1.** to dazzle; **2.** to set on edge (teeth).

**Kamber 1.** pr. n.; **2.** † faithful servant; -sız düğün olmaz he can't be left out.

**kambiyo** [x . .] † **1.** foreign exchange (dealing); **2.** foreign exchange or currency (office); ~ kuru foreign exchange rate.

**kambiyocu** foreign exchange dealer.

**kambiyoculuk** foreign exchange speculation.

**kambur 1.** humpback(ed), hunchback(ed); **2.** hump(back), hunch(back); **3.** bulge, curvature, projection; **4.** bulging, projecting; **5.** fig. trouble, grief; ~ felek adverse destiny, bad luck, misfortune; ~ üstüne (or ~ ~ üstüne) one trouble after another; ~ zambur (or ~ kumbur) crooked and hunchbacked, bumpy, over hedge and ditch; ~u çıkmak **1.** to become hunchbacked; **2.** fig. to be discredit; **3.** fig. to be having been worked very much (at work that requires bending, lifting); -unu çıkarmak to hunch one's back.

**kamburlaşmak 1.** to become hunchbacked; **2.** to become arched, to become warped, to become bulged.

**kamburlaştırmak** caus. of kamburlaşmak.

**kamburluk 1.** being hunchbacked; **2.** protuberance.

**kamçı 1.** whip; **2.** ↓ pendant, tail; **3.** biol. flagellum; ~ çalmak (or vurmak) to whip; ~ şaklatmak to crack a whip.

**kamçılamak 1.** to whip, to flog, to flagellate; **2.** fig. to stimulate, to whip up.

**kamelya** ♀ camellia.

**kamer** moon; ~ yılı lunar year.

**kamera 1.** camera; **2.** = kameraman.

**kameraman** cameraman.

**kameri** [. . -] lunar.

**kameriye** arbo(u)r, bower.

**kamet**, -ti [ā] **1.** height, stature; **2.** muezzin's call signalling the beginning of the namaz; ~ getirmek to recite the kamet.

**kamış 1.** ♀ reed; cattail, reed-mace; bamboo; **2.** reed...; **3.** fishing rod (or pole); **4.** penis, prick, dick; ~ kalem reed pen; -ı kırmak sl. to catch gonorrhea.

**kamışçık** jewel(l)er's blowpipe.

**kamışkulak** long-eared horse.

**kamışlı** reedy.

**kamışlık** reed bed.

**kâmil 1.** perfect, complete; **2.** mature; **3.** ♀ mf.

**kâmilen** [x . .] entirely, fully, completely.

**kamineto** [. . x .] single-burner.

**kamp**, -pı **1.** camp; **2.** camping; **3.** campground; ~ kurmak to pitch camp, to camp; ~ yeri campsite, campground; -a girmek sports: to go into camp.

**kampana** [. x .] bell.

**kampanacı** sl. quack, charlatan, mountebank.

**kampanya** [. x .] **1.** campaign, drive; **2.** cropping season; ~ açmak to start a campaign.

**kampçı** camper.

**kamping** campsite, campground.

**kamu** the public; ~ düzeni public order, the peace; ~ hizmeti public service; ~ kesimi (or sektörü) the public sector; ~ personeli civil servants; ~ yararı the public interest.

**kamuflaj** camouflage.

**kamufle** camouflaged; ~ etm. to camouflage.

**kamulaştırma** nationalization.

**kamulaştırmak** to nationalize.

**kamuoyu**, -nu public opinion; ~ yoklaması opinion poll.

**kamus** [- -] lexicon.

**kamusal** public.

**kamutanrıcılık** phls. pantheism.

**kamutay** joint session of the Turkish National Assembly.

**kamyon 1.** lorry, Am. truck; **2.** sl. prostitute, hooker.

**kamyoncu** truck driver.

**kamyonet** pickup (truck).

**kan 1.** blood; **2.** lineage, family; ~ ağlamak fig. to shed tears of blood; ~ akıtmak **1.** to sacrifice an animal; **2.** fig. to shed blood; ~ akrabalığı blood relationship, consanguinity; ~ alacak damarı bılmek to know which side one's bread is buttered; ~ almak to take blood (-den from), to bleed; ~ bağı blood tie; ~ bankası blood bank; ~ beynine sıçramak *fig.* to burst a blood vessel, to blow one's top, to see red; ~ çanağı gibi bloodshot *(eyes)*; ~ damarı blood vessel; ~ davası blood feud, vendetta; ~ dolaşımı circulation of the blood; ~ dökmek to shed blood; ~ emici blood-sucking; ~ gelmek to bleed; ~ gölü blood bath; ~ gövdeyi götürmek to be shed *(blood)*; ~ grubu blood group (or type); ~ istemek to want blood revenge; ~ kaybetmek to lose blood; ~ kaybı loss of blood; ~ kırmızı blood-red, crimson; ~ kusmak 1. to vomit blood; 2. *fig.* to be extremely grieved; ~ lekesi bloodstain; ~ merkezi blood transfusion centre; ~ muayenesi blood test; ~ nakli blood transfusion; ~ revan içinde blood-bespattered; ~ tahlili blood analysis; ~ vermek 1. to give a blood transfusion (-e to); 2. to donate blood; -a ~ istemek to want blood revenge; -a susamak to thirst for blood; -a susamış bloodthirsty; -ı donmak *fig.* s.o.'s blood runs cold; -ı kaynamak 1. to be hot--blooded; 2. *(b-ne)* to warm to s.o.; -ı kurumak to be exasperated; -ına dokunmak to make s.o.'s blood boil; -ına girmek 1. to have s.o.'s blood on one's hands; 2. to get a girl into trouble; -ına susamak *(kendi)* to court death.

**kana** ↓ load line.

**kanaat**, -ti [. - .] 1. opinion, conviction; 2. satisfaction, contentment; ~ etm. to be satisfied (or contented) (ile with); ~ getirmek to be of the opinion that; ~ notu mark based on the observation of the teacher; -ı olm. to have an opinion; -imce in my opinion.

**kanaatkâr, kanaatli** contented; satisfied with what he has.

**Kanada** pr. n. Canada.

**Kanadalı** pr. n. Canadian.

**kanağan** credulous, gullible.

**kanaktarım** blood transfusion.

**kanal** 1. canal; 2. *anat.* duct, canal; 3. ⊕ channel; ~ açmak to canalize.

**kanalizasyon** sewer system, sewerage, drains, sewers; ~ borusu sewer.

**kanama** bleeding, hemorrhage.

**kanamak** to bleed.

**kanara** [. x .] slaughterhouse.

**kanarya** [. x .] *zo.* canary; ~ sarısı canary yellow.

**kanat**, -tı [. -] 1. wing; 2. *ichth.* fin; 3. leaf *(of a door)*; 4. vane; 5. panel *(of a*

*curtain)*; ~ alıştırmak *fig.* to practise; ~ çırpmak to flutter; ~ germek *(b-nin üstüne) fig.* to take *s.o.* under one's protection; -ı altına almak *(b-ni) fig.* to take *s.o.* under one's wing.

**kanata** [. x .] mug, tumbler.

**kanatlanmak** to take wing, to fly away.

**kanatlı** 1. winged; 2. finned.

**kanatmak** to make bleed.

**kanatsız** wingless, apterous.

**kanava** [. x .], **kanevice** embroidery canvas.

**kanca** [x .] 1. hook; 2. grapnel; -yı takmak (or atmak) *fig.* to set one's cap (-e at), to get one's hooks (-e into).

**kancalamak** 1. to hook; 2. to grapple.

**kancalı** hooked; ~ iğne safety pin.

**kancık** 1. bitch; 2. *fig.* sneaky, low-down; 3. *sl.* woman.

**kancılar** *pol.* official in a consular or embassy secretariat.

**kandaş** cognate, consanguineous.

**kandırıcı** 1. deceptive, beguiling; 2. convincing; 3. thirst-quenching.

**kandırmaca** bluff; ~ yapmak to bluff.

**kandırmak** 1. to deceive, to fool, to cajole, to take in; 2. to convince, to persuade; 3. to quench *(thirst)*.

**kandil** 1. oil-lamp; 2. kerosene lamp; 3. *isl.* one of five Islamic holy nights when the minarets are illuminated; 4. *sl.* pissed, drunk; ~ gecesi *isl.* = ~ 3; ~ yağı poor quality olive oil; -in yağı tükenmek *fig.* to breathe one's last breath.

**kandilci** tender of oil lamps (in a mosque).

**kandilli** 1. illuminated by an oil lamp; 2. *sl.* pissed; ~ küfür resounding oath; ~ temenna (or selam) bowing and scraping.

**kanepe**[1] sofa, couch, settee.

**kanepe**[2] canapé.

**kangal** 1. coil; skein; 2. *anat.* loop, ansa.

**kangallamak** to coil up.

**kangren** ⚕ gangrene; ~ olm. to have gangrene.

**kanguru** *zo.* kangaroo.

**kanı** opinion, view.

**kanık** content, satisfied.

**kanıksamak, kanıksımak** 1. to become inured (-e to); 2. to become surfeited (-e with), to become sick (-e of).

**kanırtmak** to twist or bend loose.

**kanış** opinion.

**kanıt**, -tı evidence, proof.

**kanıtlamak** to prove.

**kanı**, -lı [â] convinced; ~ olm. to be convinced (-e of).

**kaniş** poodle.

**kankurutan** ⚕ mandrake.

**kanlamak** to blood.

**kanlanmak 1.** to become bloodstained; **2.** to become vigorous; **3.** to get bloodshot (*eyes*).

**kanlı 1.** bloody, bloodstained; **2.** bloodshot (*eyes*); **3.** sanguinary, bloody; **4.** blood-guilty; **5.** robust, vigorous; ~ basur dysentery; ~ bıçaklı olm. **1.** to get into a bloody fight; **2.** to be out for each other's blood; ~ canlı robust, vigorous; ~ katil bloodthirsty criminal.

**kanmak 1.** to be fooled (*or* taken in); **2.** to believe; **3.** to be contented (*or* satisfied) (*ile* with); **4.** to have had one's fill (*-e* of); kana kana içmek to drink thirstily, to quaff, to drink to one's heart's content.

**kano** canoe.

**kanon** ♪ canon.

**kansa** craw, maw, crop.

**kanser** cancer; ~ olm. to have cancer; to become cancerous.

**kanserli** cancerous.

**kansız 1.** bloodless; anemic; **2.** *fig.* spineless, cowardly.

**kansızlık** anemia.

**kantar 1.** scales, weighbridge; **2.** steelyard; **3.** kantar, cantar; ~ kavunu a large kind of muskmelon; ~ resmi (*or* parası) weighing fee; ~ topu ball of a steelyard; -a çekmek (*or* vurmak) to weigh (*a. fig.*); -a gelmek to be weighable; -ı belinde F alert, sly, cunning; -ın topunu kaçırmak *fig.* to overstep the limit, to go to extremes.

**kantariye** [. - . .] tax levied on weighable things.

**kantarlı 1.** heavy, severe; **2.** resounding oath; ~ küfür resounding oath; -yı atmak (*or* basmak *or* savurmak) *sl.* to cuss a blue streak.

**kantaron** ♀ centaury.

**kantaşı, -nı 1.** bloodstone, heliotrope; **2.** alum.

**kantin** canteen, snack bar.

**kanto** [x .] ♪ fin-de-siècle cabaret song.

**kantocu** fin-de-siècle cabaret chanteuse.

**kanton** canton.

**kanun** [- -] **1.** law, statute, act; **2.** ♪ zither-like instrument; ~ dışı illegal, outlaw; ~ gücü legal force (*or* power); ~ maddesi article of a law; ~ nazarında in the eyes of the law; ~ tasarısı bill, draft of a law; ~ teklifi bill; ~ yapmak to enact a law; ~ yolu ile by legal means; -a aykırı illegal, outlaw; -a uygun legal, licit, lawful; -ı esası ☪ constitution.

**kanunen** [- - .] legally, by law, according to law.

**kanuni** [- - -] **1.** legal, lawful, legitimate, statutory; **2.** kanun-player; ☾ Sultan Süleyman Suleiman the Magnificent; ~ yollara baş vurmak to take legal steps.

**kanuniyet, -ti** [- - . .] legality; ~ kesp etm. to become a law.

**kanunlaşmak** to become a law.

**kanunlaştırmak** to legalize.

**kanunname** [- - - .] statute book, code of laws.

**kanunsuz** illegal, unlawful.

**kanunsuzluk** illegality, unlawfulness, lawlessness.

**kânunuevvel** [- - . . .] † December.

**kânunusani** [- - . - .] † January.

**kanyak** cognac, brandy.

**kanyon** canyon.

**kaos** chaos.

**kap, -bı 1.** pot, vessel; **2.** cover; case; container, receptacle; **3.** dish, plate (*of food*); ~ kacak pots and pans.

**Kapadokya** *pr. n.* Cappadocia.

**kapak 1.** lid, cover; **2.** tap, stopper; **3.** cover (*of a book*); **4.** *anat.* valve; ~ kızı cover girl; kapağı atmak F to escape (*-e* to).

**kapakçık** *anat.* valvule, valvula.

**kapaklanmak 1.** to fall flat on one's face; **2.** to capsize, to overturn.

**kapaklı** covered.

**kapaksız** coverless; lidless.

**kapalı 1.** closed, shut; covered; **2.** roofed, covered; **3.** overcast (*sky*); **4.** blocked (*road*); **5.** oblique, indirect (*words*); **6.** secret (*meeting*); ~ celse closed (*or* executive) session; ~ duruşma closed hearing; ~ geçmek to pass over, to slide over, to slur over (*a point*); ~ gişe oynamak to play to a full house; ~ kutu *fig.* inscrutable person, pussyfooter; ~ oturum *s.* ~ celse; ~ sözler hints, innuendoes; ~ tribün covered grandstand; ~ zarf usulü ile by sealed tender.

**Kapalıçarşı** *pr. n.* the Grand Bazaar, the Covered Bazaar.

**kapama 1.** *vn. of* kapamak; **2.** lamb and onion stew; **3.** † complete suit of ready-made clothes.

**kapamak 1.** to close, to shut; **2.** to block (*road*); **3.** to stop up, to plug up; **4.** to shut down, to close down (*business*); to abolish, to suppress (*organization*); **5.** to hide, to cover, to conceal, to obscure; to veil; **6.** to turn off (*radio, faucet, electricity, etc.*); **7.** to lock up; **8.** to pay up, to settle (*account*); **9.** to drop (*matter*); **10.** to hoard, to stockpile; **11.** to draw (*curtain*).

**kapan 1.** trap; snare; **2.** *fig.* trap, trick; ~ kurmak to set a trap; -a düşmek to fall into a trap; -a düşürmek to entrap; -a kısılmak to be caught in a trap.

**kapanık 1.** closed, shut; **2.** *fig.* gloomy, oppressive *(place)*; **3.** confined, shut in; **4.** overcast *(weather)*; **5.** unsociable, shy.

**kapanış** closure; ~ saati closing time.

**kapanmak 1.** *pass. or refl. of* kapamak; **2.** *(bir yere)* to seclude o.s. in *(a place)*; **3.** to veil herself; **4.** to heal *(wound)*; **5.** to cease; **6.** to become cloudy *(or* overcast*) (sky)*; **7.** *(üstüne)* to hunch down *(over)*.

**kapari** [x . .] ♀ caper (plant).

**kaparo** [. x .] deposit, earnest money.

**kaparoz** *sl.* swag, pickings, spoils.

**kapasite** capacity.

**kapatma 1.** *vn. of* kapatmak; **2.** concubine, mistress; **3.** *basketball:* blocking.

**kapatmak 1.** *caus. of* kapamak; **2.** to close, to shut; **3.** to cover; **4.** to get very cheap; **4.** to keep *(mistress)*; **5.** to close down; to abolish, to suppress; **6.** to hang up *(telephone)*.

**kapcak** large hook with a long handle.

**kapçık 1.** small container; **2.** shell; **3.** ♀ capsule, pod.

**kapı 1.** door; **2.** gate; **3.** possibility; **4.** *backgammon:* point; ~ açmak to mention, to bring up; ~ almak *backgammon:* to block a point; ~ baca açık *fig.* unprotected *(place)*; ~ dışarı etm. *(b-ni)* to show *s.o.* the door, to throw *s.o.* out; ~ duvar no one answered the door; ~ gibi portly, full-bodied; ~ ~ dolaşmak to go from door to door; ~ kolu door handle; ~ komşu next-door neighbo(u)r; ~ kuzusu wicket; ~ mandalı door latch; ~ numarası street number *(of a house)*; ~ tokmağı (door) knocker; -sı herkese açık olm. to keep open house; -sını çalmak *(b-nin) fig.* to resort to *s.o.*; -ya dayanmak *fig.* to heave into sight; -yı kırıp odun etm. *fig.* to kill the goose that lays the golden egg(s); -yı *(or* -ya*)* vurmak to knock at *(or* on*)* the door.

**kapıcı** doorkeeper, doorman; caretaker, janitor.

**kapıkulu**, -nu † Janissary guard.

**kapılanmak** to find a job (-e with).

**kapılgan 1.** susceptible; **2.** easily deceived; **3.** quick to fall in love.

**kapılmak 1.** *pass. of* kapmak; **2.** to be carried *(or* washed*)* away *(-e* by*)*; **3.** to be entranced *(or* carried away*) (-e* by*)*.

**kapış** snatch; ~ ~ gitmek to be sold like hot cakes; ~ ~ yemek to gobble up, to

wolf down.

**kapışılmak** *s.* kapış kapış gitmek.

**kapışmak 1.** to snatch (at), to scramble (for); **2.** to rush to purchase; **3.** *(b-le)* to get to grips with *s.o.*; **4.** *sl.* to kiss each other, to bill and coo.

**kapik** kopeck, kopek.

**kapital**, -li capital.

**kapitalist**, -ti capitalist.

**kapitalizm** capitalism.

**kapitone** quilted *(cloth)*; tufted *(upholstery)*.

**kapitülasyon** capitulation.

**kapkaç** purse-snatching.

**kapkaççı** purse-snatcher; snatch-and-run thief.

**kapkara** [x . .] pitch-dark; pitch-black.

**kapkaranlık** completely dark.

**kaplam** *log.* extension, extent.

**kaplama 1.** *vn. of* kaplamak; **2.** coat; plate; **3.** coating; plating; **4.** crown; **5.** veneer; **6.** coated, plated, covered; ~ diş crowned tooth.

**kaplamacı 1.** metal plater; **2.** veneerer.

**kaplamak 1.** to cover; **2.** to coat, to plate; to veneer; **3.** to bind; to line; **4.** to spread over, to envelop; **5.** to encase, to cover.

**kaplan** *zo.* tiger.

**kaplı 1.** covered; plated; coated; **2.** bound *(book)*.

**kaplıca 1.** hot spring, thermal spring; hot spring resort, spa; **2.** ♀ einkorn wheat.

**kaplumbağa** [x . .] *zo.* turtle, tortoise.

**kapma 1.** *vn. of* kapmak; **2.** seized, snatched.

**kapmak**, (-ar) **1.** to snatch, to grasp, to seize, to catch, to snap up; **2.** to grab and devour; to catch *(disease)*; **4.** to catch and mangle *(machine)*; **5.** to pick up, to get the hang (of); **6.** to get, to develop, to acquire *(habit)*.

**kaporta 1.** *mot.* bonnet, *Am.* hood; **2.** ↓ hatch(way), companion, skylight.

**kapris** caprice, whim, fancy; ~ yapmak to behave capriciously.

**kaprisli** capricious.

**kapsam 1.** scope, radius, embrace, sphere; **2.** *log.* extent, extention.

**kapsamak** to contain, to comprise, to include.

**kapsamlı** extensive, comprehensive.

**kapsız** coverless.

**kapsol** percussion cap.

**kapsül** ♀, ⚗, ⌂, *anat.* capsule.

**kapşon** hood.

**kaptan** captain *(a. sports)*, skipper; ~ köşkü *(or* köprüsü*)* ↓ bridge; ~ pilot ✈ chief pilot.

                                                 **karakter**

**kaptanlık** captaincy, captainship; ~ etm. to captain.

**kaptıkaçtı 1.** minibus; **2.** purse-snatching; **3.** a card game.

**kaptırmak 1.** *caus. of* kapmak; **2.** to get *(a part of one's body)* caught in *(a machine).*

**kapuska** [. x .] cabbage stew.

**kaput, -tu 1.** military greatcoat; **2.** condom, contraceptive, sheath, rubber; **3.** bonnet, *Am.* hood; ~ gitmek to flunk all one's exams.

**kaputbezi, -ni** canvas, sail cloth.

**kar** snow; ~ fırtınası snowstorm; ~ gibi snowwhite; ~ topu snowball; ~ topu oynamak to have a snowball fight; ~ tutmak to stick *(snow)*; ~ yağmak to snow; -dan adam snowman.

**kâr 1.** profit; **2.** benefit; ~ bırakmak to yield a profit; ~ etm. to profit, to make a profit; ~ getirmek = ~ bırakmak; ~ haddi profit limit; ~ kalmak to remain as profit; ~ payı dividend; ~ ve zarar profit and loss; -ı olmamak *(b-nin)* not to be up *(or* equal) to; bu, benim kârım değil I am not equal to this; -ını tamam etm. *fig.* to kill, to polish off.

**kara¹ 1.** land, shore; **2.** terrestrial; ~ kuvvetleri X land forces, army; ~ vapuru F train; ~ yolculuğu overland journey; -da on land *(or* shore), ashore; -dan by land; -ya ayak basmak to go ashore, to disembark; -ya çıkmak to land, to go ashore, to disembark; -ya düşmek to run aground; -ya oturmak to run aground; -ya vurmak to run ashore.

**kara² 1.** black; **2.** swarthy; **3.** *phot.* negative; **4.** *fig.* unlucky; bad; ~ benizli swarthy, dark-complexioned; ~ cahil illiterate; ~ cümle *co.* the four arithmetical operations; ~ çalmak to slander, to calumniate; ~ et lean meat; ~ gün dostu true friend, a friend in need; ~ haber bad news; ~ haber tez duyulur *pro.* bad news travels fast; ~ ~ düşünmek to brood, to be in a brown study; ~ listeye almak to blacklist; ~ mizah black humo(u)r; ~ oğlan **1.** swarthy boy; **2.** gypsy; ~ sürmek *fig.* to slander, to blacken, to calumniate; ~ tahta blackboard; ~ talih bad luck, misfortune; ~ toprak black soil, chernozem; ~ yağız swarthy *(young man);* -lar bağlamak *(or* giymek) to put on *(or* wear) mourning, to be dressed in black.

**karaağaç, -cı** ♀ elm.

**karabasan 1.** nightmare; **2.** depression.

**karabaş 1.** monk; **2.** confirmed bachelor;

**3.** ♀ French lavender; **4.** P Anatolian sheep dog.

**karabatak** *zo.* cormorant.

**karabet, -ti** [ . - . ] **1.** affinity; **2.** relationship, kinship.

**karabiber 1.** ♀ black pepper; **2.** *fig.* cute brunette.

**karabina** [. . x .] carbine; blunderbuss.

**karaborsa** black market; -ya düşmek to go on the black market.

**karaborsacı** black marketeer.

**karaborsacılık** black-marketeering.

**karaboya** sulphuric acid.

**karabuğday** ♀ buckwheat.

**karabulut, -tu** black *(or* rain) cloud, nimbus.

**karaca¹** blackish; dark; ~ kemiği *anat.* humerus.

**karaca²** *zo.* roe (deer).

**karacı 1.** soldier; **2.** *fig.* slanderer; **3** gypsy.

**karaciğer** *anat.* liver.

**karaçalı** ♀ blackthorn.

**karaçam** ♀ black pine.

**karaçıban** ♀ carbuncle.

**Karadağ** *pr. n.* Montenegro.

**karadamga** smirch, stain, blot.

**Karadeniz** *pr. n.* the Black Sea; -de gemilerin mi battı? why are you in the dumps *(or* doldrums)?, why so worried?

**karadut** ♀ black mulberry.

**karaduygu** melancholia.

**karaelmas** coal.

**karafaki** [. . x .] small carafe *(or* decanter).

**karafatma** *zo.* cockroach, blackbeetle.

**karagöz 1.** *zo.* sargo; **2.** ♀ Turkish shadow play; **3.** Turkish Punch; ~ oyunu shadow play.

**karagül** karakul.

**karağı 1.** poker; **2.** blindness.

**karahumma** ♀ typhoid *(or* enteric) fever.

**karainçe** *zo.* red ant.

**karakaçan** black donkey.

**karakalem 1.** charcoal; **2.** charcoal drawing.

**karakehribar** black amber, jet.

**karakış** the dead of winter.

**karakol** police station; ~ gemisi coast-guard ship, patrol vessel; ~ gezmek to patrol his beat.

**karakolluk olm.** F to have to be taken to the police station.

**karakoncolos 1.** bugbear, black bogy, vampire, bugaboo; **2.** *fig.* person like the back (end) of a bus.

**karakter** character; ~ oyuncusu character actor; ~ rolü character part; ~ sahibi person of firm character.

**karakteristik** characteristic, distinctive.

**karakterli** of good character.

**karaktersiz** characterless.

**karakulak** *zo.* caracal.

**karakuş** 1. *zo.* black eagle; 2. farcy.

**karalama** 1. *vn. of* karalamak; 2. calligraphic exercise; 3. scribble, doodle; 4. (rough) draft; 5. slander; ~ defteri exercise book.

**karalamak** 1. to scribble, to doodle; 2. to cross out; 3. to draft, to sketch out; 4. *fig.* to slander, to blacken, to calumniate.

**karalaşmak** to blacken.

**karalı** spotted with black.

**karalık** blackness; darkness.

**karaltı** 1. indistinct figure; 2. silhouette; 3. smudge.

**karamak¹** to slander, to run down.

**karamak²** to look after, to take care of.

**karaman** fat-tailed sheep.

**karambol** 1. *billiards:* cannon, carom, billiard; 2. F collision, smashup.

**karamela** [. . x .] caramel.

**karamsar** pessimistic.

**karamsarlık** pessimism.

**karamsı** blackish.

**karamuk** 1. ♀ corncockle; 2. ☞ roseola infantum.

**karanfil** ♀ 1. carnation; 2. clove (tree).

**karanlık** 1. dark; 2. darkness, the dark; 3. bad, wicked; 4. obscure, unclarified; 5. dangerous; ~ basmadan before nightfall (*or* dark); ~ basmak to fall (*darkness*); ~ etm. to block the light, to stand in s.o.'s light; ~ oda *phot.* darkroom; ~ olm. to get dark; karanlığa kalmak to be benighted; -ta göz kırpmak *fig.* to wink in the dark.

**karantina** [. . x .] quarantine; ~ bayrağı quarantine flag; -ya almak to quarantine.

**karar** 1. decision, resolution, determination; 2. stability, predictability; 3. ☾ verdict; 4. estimate, approximation; ~ almak to make a decision; ~ kılmak (*bşde*) to decide on *s.th.*; ~ vermek 1. to decide (-*e* to); 2. to make a decision; -a bağlamak to make a decision about; -a varmak 1. to arrive at (*or* reach) a decision; 2. ☾ to bring in a verdict (of).

**karargâh** X headquarters.

**kararlama** 1. *vn. of* kararlamak; 2. estimated by guess, by rule of thumb.

**kararlamadan** at a guess.

**kararlamak** 1. to estimate by eye; 2. to make a rough estimate.

**kararlaşmak** to be decided (*or* agreed on).

**kararlaştırmak** to decide, to agree (on), to resolve (on); to determine, to fix (*date*).

**kararlı** decisive, determined, resolute.

**kararlılık** 1. decisiveness, determination, resolution; 2. stability.

**kararmak** 1. to get dark; to turn black, to darken; 2. to fade (*light*).

**kararname** [. . - .] decree.

**kararsız** 1. indecisive, undecided; 2. unstable, changeable; ~ olm. to be indecisive, to shilly-shally.

**kararsızlık** 1. indecision; 2. instability.

**karartı** 1. darkness; 2. smudge.

**karartma** blackout.

**karartmak** 1. to darken; 2. to black out.

**karasaban** primitive plough, *Am.* plow.

**karasal** terrestrial, territorial.

**karasevda** 1. passionate love; 2. melancholia; -ya düşmek (*or* tutulmak) to be passionately in love.

**karasevdalı** 1. passionately in love; 2. melancholic.

**karasığır** *zo.* water buffalo.

**karasinek** *zo.* housefly.

**karasu** ☞ glaucoma.

**karasuları**, -nı territorial waters.

**karatavuk** *zo.* blackbird.

**karate** karate.

**karateci** karateist.

**karavan** caravan, trailer.

**karavana** [. . x .] X 1. X cauldron, mess-tin; 2. X food, chow; mess; 3. miss; ~ borusu mess call; -dan yemek X to mess together.

**karavanacı** X mess carrier.

**karayazı** evil fate, ill luck.

**karayel** northwest wind.

**karayıkım** disaster.

**karayolu**, -nu highway, road; overland route.

**karbon** ⚗ carbon; ~ dioksit carbon dioxide; ~ kâğıdı carbon paper; ~ monoksit carbon monoxide.

**karbonat**, -tı ⚗ 1. carbonate; 2. sodium bicarbonate.

**karbonatlamak** ⚗ to carbonate.

**karbonhidrat**, -tı ⚗ carbohydrate.

**karbonik** ⚗ carbonic; ~ asit carbonic acid.

**karbonlaştırmak** ⚗ to carbonize, to char.

**karbonlu** ⚗ carbonaceous, carboniferous.

**karbüratör** ⊕ carburet(t)or; ~ ayarı carburet(t)or adjustment; ~ memesi carburet(t)or nozzle.

**kardan** Cardan (*or* universal) joint; ~ mili Cardan shaft.

**kardaş** *s.* kardeş.

**kardelen** ♀ snowdrop.

**kardeş** brother; sister; sibling; ~ payı yapmak to go halves.

**kardeşçe(sine)** 1. in a brotherly manner,

fraternally; in a sisterly manner; **2.** brotherly, fraternal; sisterly.

**kardeşlik** brotherhood; sisterhood.

**kardinal, -li** cardinal.

**kardinallik** cardinalate.

**kardiyografi** ₮ cardiography.

**kardiyogram** cardiogram.

**kare** square; -sini almak to square.

**karekök, -kü** square root; -ünü almak to extract the square root (-*in* of).

**kareli** chequered, *Am.* checkered, checked.

**karfiçe** [. x .] finishing nail.

**karga** *zo.* crow; ~ bok yemeden *sl.* bright and early, at (the) crack of dawn; -yı bülbül diye satmak F to swindle.

**kargaburnu, -nu** ⊕ roundnose pliers.

**kargaburun** hawknosed.

**kargabüken** ₴ nux vomica (tree).

**kargacık burgacık 1.** scrawly; **2.** in a scrawl; ~ ~ yazmak to write in a scrawl.

**kargaşa 1.** tumult, disorder; turmoil; anarchy; **2.** chaos, confusion, scramble; **3.** hullabaloo, commotion; ~ çıkarmak to kick up a row.

**kargaşalı** tumultuous.

**kargaşalık** = kargaşa.

**kargatulumba** carrying by arms and legs; ~ etm. to carry by arms and legs.

**kargı** pike; javelin; lance.

**kargılık** cartridge belt; bandoleer.

**kargımak** to curse.

**kargın** large carpenter's plane.

**kargo** [x .] cargo.

**karha** ₮ ulcer.

**karı 1.** wife, spouse; **2.** *sl.* broad, woman; ~ almak to marry; ~ kısmı womankind, weaker sex; ~ kızan P wife and children; ~ koca husband and wife, married couple; ~ koca hayatı married life; ~ kocalık matrimeny; ~ milleti = ~ kısmı; -sı ağızlı co. henpecked (*husband*).

**karık 1.** snow blindness; **2.** snow-blind; **3.** furrow.

**karılaşmak** to become effeminate.

**karılık** wifehood; wifeliness.

**karın, -rnı 1.** abdomen; **2.** stomach, belly; **3.** womb; **4.** *fig.* mind, head, loaf; **5.** *phys.* loop, antinode; ~ ağrısı **1.** stomach ache, colic; **2.** *fig.* a pain in the neck (*person*); **3.** F what-do-you-call-it, what-youmay jigger; ~ boşluğu abdeminal cavity; (**karnı**): ~ aç hungry; ~ ağrımak to have a stomach ache; ~ burnunda F in the (pudding) club, very much in the family way; ~ geniş easygoing, nonchalant; ~ -na geçmiş skeleton, a bag of bones; ~ tok full; ~ tok, sırtı pek well-

-off and contented with life; ~ zil (*or* dümbelek) çalmak to growl from hunger, to feel peckish; -ndan söylemek F to make up a yarn; -nı şişirmek (*b-nin*) F to put *s.o.* in the club.

**karınca 1.** *zo.* ant; **2.** ⩩ blowhole; ~ asidi ⚗ formic acid; ~ belli wasp-waisted; ~ duası gibi very illegible (*handwriting*); ~ kararınca (*or* kaderince) as much as one can; ~ yuvası ant nest, anthill; ~ yuvası gibi kaynamak *fig.* to teem (*or* be swarming) with people; -yı bile incitmez he will not say 'boo' to a goose.

**karıncalanmak 1.** to be crawling with ants; **2.** to have pins and needles; **3.** ⊕ to develop blowholes.

**karınlamak** ⬇ to pull up alongside.

**karınlı** potbellied.

**karınmak 1.** to be mixed (together); **2.** to mate (*fowls*).

**karınsa** molting (season) (*birds*).

**karıntı** whirlpool.

**karınzarı, -nı** *anat.* peritoneum; ~ yangısı peritonitis.

**karış** span, handspan; ~ ~ **1.** every inch (*of a place*); **2.** with a fine-tooth comb.

**karışık 1.** mixed; miscellaneous, assorted, heterogeneous; motley; **2.** adulterated; **3.** disorganized, jumbled, confused; **4.** complex; complicated.

**karışıklık 1.** confusion, disorder; **2.** tumult, civic turmoil; ~ çıkarmak to stir up trouble, to kick up a row.

**karışım 1.** ⚗ mix, mixture, blend; **2.** ₮ complication.

**karışlamak** to span.

**karışmak 1.** to mix (*ile* with); to be dispersed (*ile* in); **2.** to interfere (-*e* in), to meddle -*e* in); **3.** to get mixed up, to become confused (*or* jumbled); **4.** to join; **5.** to flow into (*another river*); **6.** to be in charge (-*e* of), to be responsible (-*e* for).

**karıştırıcı 1.** mixer; blender; **2.** *fig.* trouble-maker.

**karıştırmak** *caus. of* karışmak **1.** to mix, to stir; to blend; **2.** to confuse (*ile* with); **3.** to get confused (*in mind*); **4.** to rummage through; to thumb through; **5.** (*burnunu*) to pick one's nose.

**karides** [. x .] *zo.* shrimp; prawn.

**karikatür 1.** caricature; **2.** cartoon; comic strip; **3.** takeoff; -ünü yapmak to caricature.

**karikatürcü** caricaturist.

**karikatürist** = karikatürcü.

**karikatürize etm., karikatürleştirmek 1.** to caricature; **2.** to take off.

**karina** [. x .] ⬇ bottom (*of a ship*); ~ etm.

**karine** 220

(or -ya basmak) to careen (a vessel).
**karine 1.** evidence, trace; **2.** clue; ~ **ile**
anlamak to infer, to conjecture, to deduce
from the available information.
**kariyer** career; ~ yapmak to build a career.
**karkas** ⊕ concrete skeleton (of a building).
**karlamak** to snow.
**karlı** snowy; snow-clad; snow-capped.
**kârlı** profitable, advantageous; ~ çıkmak
to make a profit, to come out ahead; to
turn out profitable.
**karlık** snow-pit.
**karma 1.** vn. of karmak; **2.** mixed; **3.** coeducational; ~ eğitim coeducation; ~ ekono-
mi mixed economy; ~ okul coeducational
school.
**karmak 1.** to mix, to blend; **2.** cards: to
shuffle.
**karmakarış** [x . .], **karmakarışık** [x . . . .]
promiscuous, in utter confusion; ~ etm.
to mess up.
**karman çorman** s. karmakarışık.
**karmanyola** [. . x .] robbery; ~ etm. to rob,
to mug.
**karmanyolacı** robber, mugger.
**karmaşa 1.** complexity, confusion; **2.**
psych. complex.
**karmaşık** complicated, complex.
**karmaşıklık** complexity.
**karmuk** big hook.
**karnabahar, karnabit,** -ti ✿ cauliflower.
**karnaksı** s. karın ağrısı.
**karnaval** carnival.
**karne 1.** (student's) report card; **2.** card.
**karnıyarık** dish of aubergines stuffed with
mincemeat.
**karni** ✿ retort.
**karo** cards: diamond.
**karoser** mot. body.
**karpit** ✿ (calcium) carbide.
**karpuz 1.** ✿ watermelon; **2.** globe; ~ fener
chinese lantern.
**karpuzcu** watermelon-seller; watermelon-
-grower.
**karsak** zo. corsac.
**kârsız** unprofitable, profitless.
**karşı 1.** opposite; **2.** opposing; **3.** anti-,
counter-; **4.** in the direction (-e of), facing, towards; **5.** against, contrary (-e
to); **6.** in return (-e for); **7.** in response
(-e to); **8.** as a cure (-e for), as a counter-
measure (-e to), against; ~ çıkmak (b-ne)
**1.** to oppose s.o.; **2.** to object to s.o.; ~
durmak to resist, to oppose; ~ gelmek
(b-ne) to defy s.o., to go against s.o.;
~ görüşlü opponnent; ~ hücum counterattack; ~ hücuma geçmek to counterattack; ~ -ya face to face; ~ koymak to

resist, to oppose; ~ olm. to be against;
~ taarruz ✗ counteroffensive; ~ takım
opposing team; ~ taraf opposite side;
~ teklif counterproposal; counteroffer;
~ yaka opposite shore; -dan bakmak fig.
to watch idly; -dan -ya across; bu anı
kaza karşısında in face of this sudden
accident.
**karşıcasus** counterspy.
**karşıgelim** biol. antagonism.
**karşıki** (the) opposite, facing.
**karşılama** folk music played or sung when
meeting a bridal procession.
**karşılamak 1.** to go to meet, to welcome;
**2.** to pay, to cover; to be enough (for),
to suffice, to meet (a need); **3.** to defray
(expenses); **4.** to respond (or react) (to);
**5.** to prevent; to remedy.
**karşılaşma** vn. of karşılaşmak, part. **1.**
sports: game, match; **2.** ✿ reaction.
**karşılaşmak 1.** to meet; **2.** to run (ile into),
to meet; **3.** to face, to be up (ile against),
to be confronted (ile with); **4.** sports: to
play each other.
**karşılaştırılabilir** comparable.
**karşılaştırma 1.** comparison; **2.** confrontation.
**karşılaştırmak** caus. of karşılaşmak, part.
**1.** to compare (ile with); **2.** to confront
(ile with).
**karşılaştırmalı** comparative; ~ dilbilim
comparative linguistics.
**karşılık 1.** reply, retort, response, answer;
**2.** reaction, response; **3.** equivalent,
translation; **4.** appropriation; **5.** contrary,
opposite; **6.** in response (-e to); **7.** in
contrast (-e to); **8.** in payment (-e for);
~ olarak **1.** in return; **2.** in reply (-e to);
~ vermek to retort, to answer back, to
talk back.
**karşılıklı 1.** mutual, reciprocal; **2.** opposite; ~ olarak mutually; ~ sigorta mutual
insurance.
**karşılıksız 1.** complimentary, gratis; **2.**
dishono(u)red (cheque); **3.** unanswered
(love); **4.** unreturned, unrequited; ~ çıkmak to bounce (cheque).
**karşın** in spite (-e of).
**karşıt,** -ti **1.** opposite, contrary (-e to); **2.**
anti-, counter-; **3.** opposed, in disagreement; ~ anlamlı antonymous.
**karşıtdeğerli** ambivalent.
**karşıtduygu** antipathy.
**karşıtlı** gr. adversative.
**karşıtlık 1.** contrast; **2.** disagreement.
**kart[1],** -ti **1.** old; **2.** hard, tough; ~ kız old
maid, spinster.
**kart[2],** -ti **1.** card; **2.** visiting (or calling)

card; **3.** postcard.

**kartal** *zo.* eagle; ~ yavrusu eaglet.

**kartalağacı,** -nı ⚘ eaglewood.

**kartaloş, kartaloz** *sl.* over the hill, past it.

**kartel¹** cartel.

**kartel²** keg.

**kartlaşmak** to grow old, to get past it.

**kartlık 1.** oldness; **2.** staleness.

**kartograf** cartographer.

**kartografi** cartography.

**karton** pasteboard; cardboard; ~ kapak cover.

**kartonpiyer** papier-mâché.

**kartpostal** postcard.

**kartuk** large rake.

**kartuş** cartridge.

**kartvizit,** -ti visiting (*or* calling) card.

**Karun** [- -] **1.** *pr. n.* a rich man mentioned **in** the Koran; **2.** *fig.* Croesus.

**karyağdı** pepper-and-salt.

**karyola** bed, bedstead.

**kas** muscle; ~ kasılması muscular contraction; ~ teli muscular fibre; ~ tutukluğu muscle cramp.

**kasa** [x .] **1.** safe, strongbox; **2.** cash register, till; **3.** safe-deposit box; **4.** case, crate (for bottles); **5.** ⊕ body; **6.** games: the bank; **7.** gymnastics: horse; **8.** door frame; window frame; ~ açığı cash shortage, deficit; ~ dairesi strongroom; ~ defteri cashbook; ~ hesabı cash account; ~ hırsızı safecracker, safebreaker; ~ soymak to break (*or* crack) a safe.

**kasaba** small town.

**kasadar** cashier, teller.

**kasap,** -bı **1.** butcher (a. fig.); **2.** butcher shop, butcher's.

**kasaphane** [. . - .] slaughterhouse.

**kasaplık 1.** butchery; **2.** fit for slaughter (animal).

**kasara** [. x .] ⚓ castle; ~ altı steerage; ~ üstü poop deck.

**kasatura** [. . x .] sword bayonet.

**kasavet,** -ti [. - .] worry, sorrow.

**kasavetlenmek** [. - . . .] to become worried.

**kasbilim** myology.

**kasdoku** muscle tissue.

**kâse 1.** bowl; **2.** *sl.* rump.

**kasık 1.** *anat.* groin; **2.** inguinal; ~ kemiği *anat.* pubis; kasığı çatlamak (b-nin) to get a hernia.

**kasıkbağı,** -nı truss for a hernia.

**kasıkbiti,** -ni *zo.* crab louse.

**kasıksal** inguinal.

**kasıl** *anat.,* 𝔅 muscular.

**kasılduyumlar** *psych.* muscular sensations.

**kasılmak 1.** *pass. of* kasmak; **2.** to contract, to flex; **3.** to shorten; **4.** *fig.* to put on

airs, to swank, to show off, to swagger.

**kasım** November.

**kasımpatı,** -nı ⚘ chrysanthemum.

**kasınç** cramp, spasm.

**kasınmak 1.** to become cramped (*muscle*); **2.** *fig.* to give o.s. airs.

**kasıntı 1.** stitching used to shorten a garment; **2.** *fig.* swagger, swank.

**kasır,** -srı mansion, pleasure-house.

**kasırga** whirlwind, tornado; cyclone.

**kasıt,** -stı **1.** purpose, intention; **2.** evil intent; kastı olm. to harbo(u)r evil intentions (-e against).

**kasıtlı** deliberate, intentional; premeditated.

**kaside** qasida.

**kasis** open drainage ditch (cut across a road).

**kasiyer** cashier.

**kaskatı** [x . .] as hard as a stone, as hard as nails.

**kasket,** -ti cap.

**kasko** automobile insurance.

**kaslı** muscular, brawny.

**kasmak,** (-ar) **1.** to take in (garment); **2.** to reduce, to curtail (amount); **3.** to shorten (tie, etc.); **4.** to oppress; kasıp kavurmak **1.** to tyrannize, to terrorize; **2.** (ortalığı) to ruin, to destroy.

**kasnak 1.** rim, hoop; **2.** tambour; **3.** wrestling hold; ~ kayışı ⊕ belt.

**kasnaklamak 1.** to hoop; **2.** to hug.

**kaspanak** *sl.* by force, willy-nilly.

**kastanyola** [. . x .] ⚓ pawl, ratchet, detent.

**kastarlamak** to bleach.

**kasten** [x .] on purpose, intentionally, deliberately.

**kastetmek** [x . .] **1.** to mean; to intend, to purpose; **2.** to have designs (-e on, against).

**kasti** [ı] deliberate, intentional, premeditated.

**kastor** beaver (fur).

**kasvet,** -ti gloom, depression.

**kasvetli** gloomy.

**kaş 1.** eyebrow; **2.** projection, brow; **3.** pommel (of a saddle); ~ atmak (*or* etm.) to raise one's eyebrows (as a signal); ~ göz etm. to wink (-e at); ~ yapayım derken göz çıkarmak *fig.* to aggravate matters while trying to be helpful; -la göz arasında in the twinkling of an eye, in a trice; -larını çatmak to frown, to knit one's brows.

**kaşağı** currycomb.

**kaşağılamak** to curry, to groom.

**kaşalot 1.** *zo.* cachalot; **2.** *sl.* dunce, imbecile.

kaşamak s. kaşağılamak.
kaşan urinating, staling.
kâşane [- - .] mansion.
kaşanmak to stop and stale.
kaşar 1. (peyniri) sheep cheese; 2. kosher; 3. sl. clever, sly (gambler).
kaşarlanmak to become hackneyed.
kaşarlanmış hackneyed.
kaşe cachet.
kaşer s. kaşar.
kaşık 1. spoon; 2. spoonful; ~ atmak (or çalmak) eat heartily; ~ düşmanı co. one's wife, the missus; ~ ~ by spoonfuls; -la yedirip sapıyle (gözünü) çıkarmak to spoil a good deed with a bad one.
kaşıkçı elması the largest diamond in the Ottoman jewel collection.
kaşıkçıkuşu, -nu zo. pelican.
kaşıklamak to spoon out.
kaşımak to scratch.
kaşındırmak to make itch.
kaşınmak 1. to itch, to scratch o.s.; 2. fig. to be itching for a beating.
kaşıntı itch, pruritus.
kaşıntılı itchy, pruritic.
kâşif explorer; discoverer.
kaşkariko [. . x .] sl. trick, deceit.
kaşkaval 1. yellow cheese; 2. sl. dimwitted.
kaşkol scarf, neckerchief.
kaşkorse camisole.
kaşmer, kaşmerdikoz sl. clown; oddball.
kaşmir cashmere.
kat, -tı 1. storey; Am. story, floor; 2. layer, stratum; fold; 3. coat (of paint); 4. set (of clothes); 5. time(s); 6. presence; 7. multiple; ~ çıkmak to add a storey (to a building); ~ ~ 1. in layers; 2. many times more, much more; ~ mülkiyeti condominium; ~ yeri crease, fold.
katafalk, -kı catafalque.
katakofti [. . x .] sl. lie.
katakulli [. . x .] sl. trick, ruse; ~ yapmak sl. to swindle; to dupe; -ye gelmek sl. to be taken in.
kataliz catalysis.
katalizatör catalyst.
katalog catalogue.
katana artillery horse; ~ gibi F portly (woman).
katar 1. train (of wagons or animals); 2. caravan (of vehicles); 3. convoy (of military vehicles); ~ kılavuzu donkey at the head of a file of camels.
Katar pr. n. Qatar.
katarakt, -tı ∯ cataract.
katarlamak to form into a line (animals, vehicles).

katedral, -li cathedral.
kategori category.
katetmek [x . .] 1. to travel (over), to traverse, to cover; 2. to out (off), to terminate; 3. to intersect.
katgüt, tü catgut.
katı¹ 1. hard, rigid, stiff; 2. fig. tough, unbending; stern; insensitive; 3. ∯, phys. solid; ~ yumurta hard-boiled egg; ~ yürekli hardhearted.
katı² gizzard (of birds).
katık anything eaten with bread.
katılaşmak 1. to harden (a. fig.); to stiffen; 2. ∯, phys. to solidify.
katılaştırmak to harden.
katılgandoku anat. connective tissue.
katılık 1. hardness; stiffness, rigidity; 2. fig. hardheartedness; 3. ∯, phys. solidity.
katılmak¹ 1. pass. of katmak; 2. to join (a group); to enter (-e into), to participate (-e in); 3. (b-ne) to agree with s.o.
katılmak² to be out of breath (from laughing or weeping); katıla katıla ağlamak to choke with sobs; katıla katıla gülmek to split one's sides laughing, to choke with laughter, to be convulsed with laughter.
katım 1. adding, mixing; 2. s. koç katımı.
katıntı mixture.
katır 1. mule; hinny; 2. fig. mulish, obstinate; ~ gibi inatçı as stubborn as a mule.
katırcı muleteer.
katır kutur; ~ yemek to crunch, to munch.
katırtırnağı, -nı ⚘ broom, besome.
katışık mixed.
katışıksız unmixed, pure, unadulterated.
katışmak to join (a group).
katıştırmak to add (-e to).
katıyağ ∯ machine (or lubricating) grease.
kati definite, absolute, final; decisive; ~ karar unanppealable decision; ~ olarak definitely; ~ suretle absolutely; ~ teklif firm offer.
katil¹, -tli murder, homicide.
katil² [â] 1. murderer; 2. lethal, deadly; ~ kadın murderess.
katileşmek [î] to become definite.
kâtip, -bi clerk; secretary.
kâtiplik clerkship; ~ yapmak to clerk.
katiyen [î] [. x .] 1. never, by no means; 2. definitely, absolutely.
katiyet, -ti definiteness, finality, decisiveness.
katkı 1. help, assistance, aid; 2. contribution, addition, supplement; 3. additive; alloy; -da bulunmak to contribute (-e to).

**katkılı** alloyed.

**katkısız** unalloyed; pure.

**katlamak** to fold (up).

**katlanır** folding, collapsible.

**katlanmak 1.** pass. of katlamak; **2.** to endure, to bear, to put up (-e with); ... yapmak zahmetine ~ to take the trouble to do...

**katletmek** [x . .] to murder (a. fig.).

**katlı 1.** folded; **2.** ... storied (building).

**katliam** massacre.

**katma 1.** vn. of katmak; **2.** added; ~ bütçe supplementary budget; ~ değer vergisi value-added-tax.

**katmak,** (-ar) **1.** to add, to mix (-e in); **2.** to send with; **3.** to annex (-e to); **4.** (birbirine) to set a person against a person.

**katman** geol, geogr. layer; stratum; seam, bed.

**katmanbulut,** -tu meteor. stratus.

**katmanlaşmak** to stratify.

**katmer 1.** flaky pastry; **2.** layer; ~ ~ one on top of the other; one after the other.

**katmerleşmek** to become layered.

**katmerli 1.** in layers; **2.** double (flower); **3.** manifold, multiplied; ~ yalan whopping lie.

**Katolik** pr. n. Catholic.

**Katoliklik** pr. n. Catholicism.

**katra** [x .] drop.

**katran** tar; ~ gibi tarry.

**katranağacı,** -nı ♀ terebinth.

**katrançamı,** -nı ♀ Georgia pine.

**katranlamak** to tar.

**katranlı** tarry, tarred.

**katranruhu,** -nu ⚗ (wood) creosote.

**katrilyon** quadrillion.

**katsayı** ⚗ coefficient.

**kauçuk 1.** rubber; caoutchouc; **2.** ♀ rubber plant; ~ ağacı ♀ rubber tree.

**kav** tinder, punk.

**kavaf** cheap, ready-made shoes dealer; ~ işi shoddy; ~ malı shoddy goods.

**kavak** ♀ poplar.

**kavakincirl,** -nı purple fig.

**kaval** shepherd's pipe, flageolet; ~ kemiği anat. tibia; ~ tüfek smoothbored gun.

**kavalcı** piper.

**kavallanmak** sl. to pester.

**kavalye** escort, male partner (in a dance).

**kavalyelik** etm. to escort.

**kavanço** [. x .] **1.** ⚓ shifting (of a sail, etc.); **2.** sl. landing (s.o. with a job).

**kavanoz** jar, pot.

**kavara** [. x .] sl. outburst, noise.

**kavas** hist. kavass.

**kavata** [. x .] **1.** ♀ sour green tomato; **2.** large wooden bowl.

**kavela** [. x .] ⚓ treenail, trunnel.

**kavga 1.** fight, brawl; row, quarrel; **2.** struggle; ~ aramak to look for trouble; ~ çıkarmak to kick up (or make) a row, to pick a fight; ~ etm. to fight (ile with); to quarrel (ile with); ~ kaşağısı instigator, agitator; -ya girişmek (or tutuşmak) to take up a quarrel (ile with).

**kavgacı 1.** quarrelsome, pugnacious; **2.** puncher.

**kavgalı 1.** angry (ile with); **2.** disputed.

**kavgasız 1.** peaceable, peace-loving; **2.** peacefully, without a quarrel.

**kavi** [¹] strong; sound.

**kavil,** -vli **1.** † word; **2.** agreement.

**kavilleşmek** to agree, to reach an understanding.

**kavim,** -vmi people; tribe.

**kavis,** -vsi curve, arc.

**kavkı** zo. shell.

**kavlak 1.** barkless; **2.** peeled off (skin).

**kavlamak 1.** to scale off (bark); **2.** to peel, to desquamate (skin).

**kavlıç,** -cı **1.** hernia, rupture; **2.** ruptured.

**kavmantarı,** -nı ♀ punk, amadou.

**kavram¹** s. karınzarı.

**kavram²** log. concept.

**kavrama 1.** comprehension, grasp; **2.** mot. clutch (pedal); **3.** crosspiece, strut.

**kavramak 1.** to grasp, to clutch; **2.** fig. to comprehend, to grasp.

**kavramcılık** conceptualism.

**kavramsal** conceptual.

**kavrayış** psych. comprehension, grasp.

**kavrayışlı** quick-witted.

**kavrayışsız** slow-witted.

**kavruk 1.** scorched; **2.** fig. undersized, wizened, stunted.

**kavrulmak 1.** pass. of kavurmak; **2.** to be scorched.

**kavrulmuş** roasted; ~ kahve roasted coffee.

**kavşak** crossroads, junction, intersection.

**kavuk 1.** turban; **2.** bladder; ~ sallamak (b-ne) to fawn on s.o., to toady to s.o.

**kavuklu 1.** turbaned; **2.** ♀ a character in the ortaoyunu.

**kavun** ♀ muskmelon.

**kavuniçi,** -ni pale (or yellowish) orange.

**kavurga** roasted chickpeas, wheat or corn.

**kavurma 1.** vn. of kavurmak; **2.** roasted; **3.** fried meat.

**kavurmaç,** -cı roasted wheat.

**kavurmak 1.** to roast; **2.** to scorch, to parch (sun); **3.** to blight, to blast (wind, cold).

**kavurucu** parching, scorching (heat).

**kavuşma 1.** vn. of kavuşmak; **2.** ♀ isogamy.

**kavuşmak 1.** to be reunited (-e with); **2.** to reach, to arrive (-e at); **3.** to meet, to overlap; **4.** to join (roads); **5.** to flow (-e into) (rivers).

**kavuşum** conjunction.

**kay, -yyı** vomit.

**kaya 1.** rock; reef; **2.** palisade, rock cliff (or precipice); **3.** ♀ mf.; ~ gibi rocky; -lara bindirmek to run on the rocks.

**kayabalığı, -nı** zo. goby.

**kayağan** slippery, slick.

**kayağantaş** geol. slate.

**kayak 1.** ski; **2.** skiing; ~ yapmak to ski.

**kayakçı** skier.

**kayakçılık** skiing.

**kayalık 1.** rocky, reefy; **2.** rocky place; rock cliff.

**kayalifi, -ni** asbestos.

**kayan** mountain torrent.

**kayar 1.** path, goat trail; **2.** reusing an old horseshoe.

**kayasa** cinch, girth (of a saddle).

**kayatuzu, -nu** geol. rock salt, halite.

**kaybetmek** [x . .] to lose.

**kaybolmak** [x . .] to be lost; to vanish, to disappear.

**kaydetmek** [x . .] **1.** to register, to enroll; **2.** to enter, to write down, to record (a. with a tape recorder); **3.** sports: to score, to chalk up; **4.** to bear in mind.

**kaydıhayat, -tı: -la** (or ~ şartıyle) as long as one lives, for life.

**kaydırak 1.** slide; **2.** skid, stoneboat; **3.** hopscotch.

**kaydırmak** caus. of kaymak 2., to slide, to skid.

**kaydıye** registration fee.

**kaygan** slippery, slick.

**kaygana** omelet(te).

**kaygı** anxiety, worry.

**kaygılandırmak** to worry.

**kaygılanmak** to worry, to be anxious.

**kaygılı** worried, anxious, uneasy.

**kaygın** slippery, slick.

**kaygısız** carefree, untroubled.

**kaygısızlık** untroubledness.

**kayık 1.** boat, caique, skiff; **2.** slipped to one side; ~ salıncak boat-shaped swing; ~ tabak oval dish; ~ yarışı boat race; -la gezmek to go boating.

**kayıkçı** boatman.

**kayıkhane** [. . - .] boathouse.

**kayın¹** brother-in-law.

**kayın²** ♀ beech.

**kayınbaba** = kayınpeder.

**kayınbirader** brother-in-law.

**kayınpeder** father-in-law.

**kayınvalide** [. . - . .] mother-in-law.

**kayıp, -ybı 1.** loss; losses; **2.** ✕ casualties; **3.** lost, missing; ~ eşya bürosu lost

property office; ~ listesi casualty list; -lara karışmak co. to vanish into thin air, to disappear (or go off) into the blue.

**kayır** sandbank, sandbar.

**kayırıcı** patron, protector.

**kayırıcılık** favo(u)ritism.

**kayırmak 1.** to protect, to sponsor; **2.** to favo(u)r.

**kayısı** ♀ apricot.

**kayış¹** belt, strap, watch band; ~ gibi **1.** as tough as leather (meat); **2.** heavily sun-tanned (skin); -a çekmek to strop (a razor).

**kayış²** vn. of kaymak.

**kayışçı 1.** strap maker or seller; **2.** fig. trickster, con man.

**kayışdili, -ni** strong language.

**kayıt, -ydı 1.** registration, enrollment; **2.** entry; **3.** recording; **4.** restriction, limitation, restraint; **5.** giving importance (to); **6.** noting down; ~ altında restricted; ~ defteri register, record book; ~ ücreti registration fee; kayda değer noteworthy, remarkable; kayda geçirmek to register; kaydını silmek to delete; to expunge.

**kayıtlı 1.** registered, enrolled; **2.** entered, recorded; noted down; **3.** restricted.

**kayıtsız 1.** unregistered, unrecorded; **2.** unrestricted; **3.** fig. indifferent, carefree, unconcerned; ~ kalmak to be indifferent (-e to); ~ şartsız unconditionally; ~ şartsız teslim unconditional surrender.

**kayıtsızlık** indifference, uncorcern.

**kayma 1.** vn. of kaymak; **2.** landslide; **3.** cinema: misframe.

**kaymaç, -cı** slanting (eye).

**kaymak¹** cream; ~ altı skim milk; ~ bağlamak to form cream; ~ gibi **1.** snow-white; **2.** creamy and delicious.

**kaymak², (-ar)** to slip, to slide, to skid.

**kaymakam** kaimakam, head official (of a district).

**kaymaklanmak** = kaymak bağlamak.

**kaymaklı** creamy; ~ dondurma (creamy) ice cream.

**kaymaktaşı, -nı** alabaster, gypsum.

**kayme** P paper lira.

**kaynaç** geol. geyser.

**kaynak 1.** source, fountainhead; spring; **2.** origin source; **3.** ⊕ weld; **4.** patch (on rubber); ~ yapmak **1.** ⊕ to weld; **2.** to patch (rubber).

**kaynakça** bibliography.

**kaynakçı** welder.

**kaynakçılık** welding.

**kaynaklamak 1.** ⊕ to weld; **2.** to patch (rubber).

**kaynaklı 1.** ⊕ welded; **2.** patched (rubb-

*er)*.

**kaynama** *vn. of* kaynamak; ~ noktası boiling point.

**kaynamak 1.** to boil; **2.** to ferment; **3.** to teem, to swarm; **4.** to knit *(bone)*; **5.** to surge up, to seethe; **6.** ⊕ to become welded; **7.** to fidget; **8.** *sl.* to be wasted *(lesson)*.

**kaynana** mother-in-law.

**kaynanadili,** -ni ♀ cactus.

**kaynanazırıltısı,** -nı clacker, rattle.

**kaynar 1.** boiling *(water)*; **2.** *sl.* hashish.

**kaynarca** [. x .] **1.** hot spring, spa; **2.** fountainhead; spring.

**kaynaşma** *vn. of* kaynaşmak, *part.* uproar.

**kaynaşmak 1.** to fuse, to join *(ile* with); **2.** to go well *(ile* with), to blend *(ile* with); **3.** to teem, to swarm; **4.** ⚒ to combine; **5.** *fig.* to become bosom friends.

**kaynata** [x . .] father-in-law.

**kaynatmak 1.** *caus. of* kaynamak; **2.** to boil; **3.** ⊕ to weld; **4.** *sl.* to swipe, to nick, to pinch; **5.** *(dersi) sl.* to waste *(a lesson hour)* talking; **6.** *sl.* to gad about.

**kaypak 1.** slippery, slick; **2.** *fig.* slippery, shifty.

**kayrak 1.** ski area *(or* slope); **2.** slate.

**kayran** glade.

**kayser** [x .] *(Roman)* caesar; *(German)* kaiser.

**kayşa** landslide.

**kayşamak** to slide, to slip *(land)*.

**kayşat,** -tı *geol.* debris.

**kaytan** cotton *or* silk cord; ~ bıyıklı pointed mustachioed.

**kaytarıcı** shirker, goldbricker.

**kaytarmak 1.** to reject, to turn down; **2.** to shirk, to goldbrick *(work)*.

**kayyım 1.** caretaker of a mosque; **2.** ₺ट trustee, administrator.

**kaz 1.** *zo.* goose; **2.** *fig.* dumbbell, dolt; ~ gelen yerden tavuk esirgenmez *pro.* you must lose a fly to catch a trout, throw out a sprat to catch a mackerel; ~ kafalı F dumb. doltish; ~ kazla, daz dazla, kel tavuk topal horozla *pro.* birds of a feather flock together; ~ palazı gosling; -ı koz anlamak to get wrong, to misunderstand; -ın ayağı öyle değil it isn't like that at all.

**kaza** [. -] **1.** accident; misfortune; **2.** borough, county; district; **3.** *isl.* late performance of an act of worship; ~ geçirmek to have an accident; ~ ile by accident; ~ kurşunu stray bullet; ~ sigortası accident *(or* casualty) insurance; -ya uğramak to have *(or* meet with) an accident.

**kazaen** [. - .] **1.** by accident; **2.** by chance.

**Kazak**[1] Kazakh; Cossack.

**kazak**[2] pullover, sweater.

**kazak**[3] dominating, despotic *(husband)*.

**Kazakistan** *pr. n.* Kazakhstan.

**kazalı** [. - .] **1.** dangerous, unsafe; **2.** with ... boroughs.

**kazamat,** -tı ✕ casemate.

**kazan 1.** cauldron; **2.** boiler; furnace; ~ dairesi boiler room; İstanbul ~ ben kepçe I left no stone unturned in Istanbul.

**kazanç,** -cı **1.** gain, earnings; profit; **2.** benefit, advantage.

**kazançlı** profitable.

**kazançsal** economic.

**kazançsız** unprofitable, profitless.

**kazandırmak** *caus. of* kazanmak.

**kazandibi,** -ni *milk pudding slightly burnt on the bottom*.

**kazanmak 1.** to earn; **2.** to win; **3.** to acquire, to gain, to get.

**kazara** [. - .] [. x .] **1.** by accident; **2.** by chance.

**kazasker** *hist.* military judge.

**kazayağı,** -nı **1.** ♀ goosefoot, pigweed; **2.** ⚓ three-ended rope.

**kazazede** [. - - .] **1.** victim, casualty *(of an accident)*; **2.** shipwrecked; struck *(by an accident)*.

**kazboku,** -nu chartreuse.

**kazein** casein.

**kazı** excavation; ~ yapmak to excavate, to dig.

**kazıbilim** archeology.

**kazıbilimci** archeologist.

**kazıcı** excavator *(person)*.

**kazık 1.** stake, pale; pile, picket; **2.** *sl.* swindle, trick; **3.** *sl.* exorbitant *(price)*; ~ atmak F to overcharge, to fleece, to soak, to put it on, to rook; ~ gibi **1.** as stiff as a ramrod; **2.** as stiff as a board; ~ kadar grown-up; ~ marka too expensive; ~ yemek *sl.* to be rooked *(or* soaked); ~ yutmuş gibi as stiff as a ramrod; kazığa oturtmak *hist.* to impale.

**kazıkçı** swindler, trickster.

**kazıklamak 1.** to pile, to picket, to stake; **2.** *hist.* to impale; **3.** *sl.* to overcharge, to soak, to put it on, to fleece, to rook.

**kazıma 1.** *vn. of* kazımak; **2.** curettage.

**kazımak 1.** to scrape (off); **2.** to shave; **3.** to incise, to engrave; **4.** *sl.* to clean out, to pluck.

**kazınmak 1.** to scrape o.s.; **2.** to scratch o.s. hard; **3.** to give o.s. a very close shave

**kazıntı** scrapings.

**kazıyıcı** road grader.

**kaziye** *log.* proposition.

**kazma 1.** *vn. of* **kazmak; 2.** pick, pickax; mattock; **3.** excavated, dug; **4.** incised, engraved.

**kazmacı** ✕ sapper.

**kazmaç** excavator.

**kazmadiş** bucktoothed *(person)*.

**kazmak,** (-ar) to dig, to excavate, to trench.

**kazmir** cassimere, kerseymere.

**kazulet,** -ti *sl.* grotesque, portly.

**kebap,** -bı **1.** shish kebab; **2.** roasted; broiled; ~ şişi *sl.* dagger; ~ yapmak to roast; to broil.

**.kebe 1.** felt jacket; **2.** embroidered felt.

**kebir 1.** big; great; **2.** elderly, old.

**kebze** shoulder blade, scapula.

**keçe 1.** felt; **2.** mat.

**keçeleşmek 1.** to become matted *(hair, etc.);* **2.** *fig.* to become numb.

**keçeli** made of felt; ~ kalem felt-tip pen, felt-tipped pen.

**keçi 1.** *zo.* goat; **2.** nanny goat, she-goat; **3.** *fig.* stubborn, obstinate; ~ ağızlı *fig.* gluttonous; ~ çobanı goatherd; ~ derisi goatskin; ~ yavrusu kid; -leri kaçırmak F to go nuts.

**keçiboynuzu,** -nu ♀ carob, St. John's bread; ~ gibi insipid.

**keçileşmek** F to become mulish *(or* pigheaded).

**keçisakal** goatee.

**keçiyolu,** -nu path.

**keder** sorrow, grief; ~ vermek to grieve, to sadden.

**kederlenmek** to be grieved.

**kederli** sorrowful, grieved.

**kedersiz** free from grief.

**kedi** *zo.* cat; ~ ciğere bakar gibi bakmak to stare covetously; ~ yetişemediği ciğere pis dermiş *pro.* that's sour grapes; -yi sıkıştırırsan üstüne atılır *pro.* even a worm will turn.

**kedibalığı,** -nı *zo.* ray, stake.

**kedigözü,** -nü **1.** taillight; **2.** cat's-eye.

**kediotu,** -nu ♀ valerian.

**kefal 1.** *zo.* gray *(or* striped) mullet; **2.** *sl.* cigarette butt.

**kefalet,** -ti [â] bail; -le salıvermek to release on bail.

**kefaletname** bail bond, guaranty, surety bond.

**kefaret,** -ti [â] atonement, expiation; -ini ödemek to expiate, to atone (-*in* for).

**kefe**[1] *nan.* scale *(of a balance).*

**kefe**[2] haircloth bag *(used for grooming horses).*

**kefeki 1.** travertine, calsinter, scale; **2.** tartar, scale *(on teeth).*

**kefen** shroud, winding sheet; ~ soyucu grave robber; -i yırtmak *fig.* to turn the corner, to pass the danger point safely.

**kefenci 1.** shroud seller; shroud maker; **2.** *sl.* grave robber.

**kefenlemek** to shroud.

**kefere** non-Muslims; unbelievers.

**kefil** [í] guarantor, sponsor, surety; bondsman; ~ olm. to sponsor.

**kefillik** sponsorship, suretyship.

**kefir** kefir, kephir.

**kefiye** kaffiyeh.

**kehanet,** -ti [â] prediction; ~ etm. *(or* -te bulunmak) to predict, to foretell.

**kehkeşan** [â] *ast.* the Milky Way.

**kehle** *zo.* louse.

**kehlibar, kehribar** [â] amber; ~ balı clear yellow honey.

**kek,** -ki cake.

**kekâ, kekâh** [x-] F: oh ~! this is the life!

**keke** stammering, stuttering *(person).*

**kekelemek 1.** to stammer, to stutter; **2.** to hem and haw.

**kekeme** stammering, stuttering *(person).*

**kekemelik** stutter.

**kekik** ♀ thyme.

**keklik** *zo.* partridge, acrid.

**kekre** astringent.

**kekremsi 1.** somewhat acrid; **2.** *fig.* sour-faced.

**kel 1.** bald; **2.** ⚕ favus, ringworm; **3.** *fig.* bare, denuded; ~ başa şimşir tarak *fig.* out of place luxury; ~ kâhya *fig.* busybody; -i körü toplamak to assemble a band of incompetents.

**kelam 1.** remark, utterance; **2.** the Koran; **3.** Islamic theology.

**Kelamıkadim** [í] the Koran.

**kelebek 1.** *zo.* butterfly; moth; **2.** ⚕ distomatosis; **3.** ⊕ butterfly *(or* wing) nut; **4.** ⊕ butterfly valve; ~ cam butterfly window; ~ gözlük pince-nez; ~ kulacı butterfly stroke; ~ somun ⊕ butterfly *(or* wing) nut.

**kelek 1.** unripe melon; **2.** hairless; **3.** underdeveloped; **4.** *sl.* dunderhead; ~ herif *sl.* a bad hat *(or* egg).

**kelepçe** [. x .] **1.** handcuffs; **2.** ⊕ pipe clip; ~ vurmak *(or* takmak) *(b-ne)* to handcuff *s.o.*

**kelepçelemek** to handcuff.

**kelepçeli** handcuffed.

**kelepir 1.** bargain, steal; **2.** dirt-cheap.

**keler** *zo.* lizard.

**keleş** F **1.** beautiful; handsome; **2.** bald.

**kelime** *gr.* word; ~ hazinesi vocabulary; ~ word by word; ~ oyunu pun; kelimei şahadet *isl.* the confession of faith; -si

-sine word for word, literally.

**kelle 1.** *contp.* head, nut, crumpet, nob; **2.** boiled sheep's head; **3.** head *(of cabbage)*; **4.** ear, head *(of grain)*; ~ götürür gibi helter-skelter; -sini koltuğuna almak *fig.* to take one's life in one's hands; -sini uçurmak *(b-nin)* to behead *s.o.*, to decapitate *s.o.*; -yi vermek to sacrifice one's life; İngiltere kazanırsa kellemi keserim! F I'll eat my hat if England wins!

**kelli** since, seeing that.

**kellifelli** well-dressed and dignified *(person)*.

**kellik 1.** baldness; **2.** ringworm, favus.

**keloğlan** *name of a popular hero of Turkish folk tales.*

**Kelt** *pr. n.* Kelt, Celt.

**kem** evil, malicious.

**kemal,** -li [ª] **1.** perfection; **2.** maturity; ripeness; **3.** the highest price; **4.** ♀ [x .] *mf.*; -e ermek **1.** to reach perfection; **2.** to reach maturity.

**Kemalist** Kemalist.

**Kemalizm** Kemalism.

**keman** [ª] **1.** violin; **2.** *archery:* bow; ~ çalmak to play the violin; ~ yayı violin bow.

**kemancı** [ª] violinist.

**kemençe** [. x .] kemancha, kit.

**kement** -di lasso.

**kementlemek** *sl.* to swindle.

**kemer 1.** belt; **2.** arch; vault; **3.** waist *(of a garment)*; **4.** aqueduct; **5.** *anat.* arch; **6.** Roman *(nose)*; ~ altı vaulted bazaar; -ini *(or* -leri) sıkmak to tighten one's belt.

**kemerli 1.** girdled; **2.** arched; vaulted.

**kemerlik** leather belt *(used for holding tools, etc.)*.

**kemerpatlıcan** long, thin aubergine.

**kemgöz** evil eye.

**kemik 1.** bone; **2.** osseous; ~ atmak *(b-nin önüne) fig.* to throw *s.o.* a sop; ~ gibi **1.** as hard as a bone; **2.** bone-dry; ~ iltihabı osteitis; ~ yalayıcı *fig.* bootlicker, toady; -leri sayılmak to be a bag of bones.

**kemikbilim** osteology.

**kemikçik** ossicle.

**kemikdoku** bone tissue.

**kemikleşmek** to ossify.

**kemikli** bony.

**kemiksiz** boneless.

**kemircik** cartilage, gristle.

**kemirdek** tail bones.

**kemirgen** rodent.

**kemircenler** *zo.* Rodentia.

**kemirici 1.** rodent; **2.** corrosive.

**kemirmek 1.** to gnaw, to nibble; **2.** to

corrode.

**kemiyet,** -ti quantity.

**kem küm etm.** to hem and haw.

**kenar** [ª] **1.** edge; border; margin; hem; brink; **2.** isolated; **3.** suburb; ~ çekmek to edge, to hem, to border; ~ mahalle slums; -a çekilmek to get out of the way; -a çekmek to pull in, to pull over *(or off)* *(vehicle)*; -da kalmak *fig.* to remain aside; -da köşede in nooks and crannies.

**kenarlı** edged.

**kendi 1.** self, oneself; **2.** own; **3.** he; she; **4.** in person; ~ başına **1.** of one's own accord; **2.** by oneself, single-handedly; ~ bildiğini okumak *fig.* to get one's own way; ~ derdine düşmek to be preoccupied with one's own troubles; ~ düşen ağlamaz *pro.* you've made your bed and you must lie on it; ~ halinde innocuous, inoffensive *(person)*; ~ haline bırakmak *(b-ni)* to leave *s.o.* to his own devices; ~ -ne **1.** by oneself; **2.** to oneself; **3.** on one's own accord; ~ -ni yemek to eat one's heart out; ~ kuyusunu ~ kazmak *fig.* to dig one's own grave; ~ payıma as for me, for my part; ~ yağıyle kavrulmak *fig.* to get by on one's own means; -nden geçmek to faint; -ne gel! **1.** behave yourself!, come to your senses!; **2.** pull yourself together!; -ne gelmek **1.** to come to *(or* round)*; **2.** to behave o.s., to pull o.s. together; -ne yedirememek to be unable to stomach; -ni beğenmek to be full of o.s.; -ni bir şey sanmak to be too big for one's boots; -ni dev aynasında görmek to think no small beer of o.s.; -ni göstermek to prove one's worth; -ni gülmekten alamamak can't help laughing; -ni kaptırmak *fig.* to let o.s. get carried away (-e by); -ni kaybetmek **1.** to lose consciousness; **2.** to fly into a rage; -ni vermek *(bşe)* to put one's heart into *s.th.*; -sinden bahsettirmek to make a noise in the world.

**kendiliğinden 1.** by oneself; **2.** automatically; **3.** of one's own accord.

**kendilik** entity.

**kendince 1.** subjective, personal; **2.** in one's opinion.

**kendir** ♀ hemp.

**kene** *zo.* tick; ~ gibi yapışmak *fig.* to stick like a leech.

**kenef 1.** bog, toilet; **2.** filthy.

**kenegöz** small-eyed *(person)*.

**kenet,** -di ⊕ metal clamp, cramp iron.

**kenetlemek 1.** to clamp; **2.** to lock *(jaws)*.

**kenevir** *s.* kendir.

**kent,** -ti city, town.
**kental,** -li quintal.
**kentbilim** urbanology.
**kentilyon** quintillion.
**kentleşmek** to become urbanized.
**kentli** city-dweller.
**kentsel** urban.
**Kenya** pr. n. Kenya.
**kep,** -pi 1. cap; 2. mortarboard.
**kepaze** [ā] 1. ridiculous, vile, contemptible; 2. disgraceful, shameless; ~ etm. to disgrace; ~ olm. to become a laughing-stock.
**kepazelik** ignominy, degradation, vileness.
**kepbastı** double-netted fishing weir.
**kepçe** 1. ladle; 2. dip (or scoop) net; 3. butterfly net; 4. ↓ buttock; ~ gibi sticking out (ears).
**kepçekulak** having outstanding ears.
**kepçeli** having a ladle.
**kepek** 1. scurf, dandruff; 2. bran; ~ ekmeği whole-wheat bread; ~ unu whole-wheat flour.
**kepeklenmek** to become scurfy.
**kepekli** scurfy (hair).
**kepenek** 1. zo. flour (or wheat) moth; 2. shepherd's felt cloak.
**kepenk** rolling (or roll-down) shutter.
**kerahet,** -ti [ā] repugnance, nastiness; ~ vakti co. drinking-time.
**keramet,** -ti [ā] miracle, marvel; ~ buyurdunuz your words are wonderful; ~ göstermek to work miracles.
**kerametli** [ā] holy.
**kerata** 1. shoehorn; 2. F cuckold; 3. F son of a gun, dog.
**Kerbela** pr. n. Karbala; ~ gibi waterless (place).
**kere** time(s); iki ~ okudum I read it twice, üç ~ beş three times five.
**kerecik** diminutive of kere; bir ~ (only) just once.
**kerem** beneficence, kindness.
**kereste** [. x .] 1. timber, lumber; 2. sl. swine.
**keresteci** timber (or lumber) merchant.
**keresteli** [. x . .] P portly (man).
**kerevet,** -ti 1. plank-bed; 2. cinema: dolly.
**kerevides** [. . x .] zo. crayfish, crawfish.
**kereviz** 1. zo. celery, celeriac; 2. sl. dunce.
**kerez** sl. food or drink offered a guest.
**kerhane** [ā] brothel, cathouse.
**kerhaneci** [ā] 1. brothel keeper; 2. sl. son of a bitch, bastard.
**kerhen** [x .] 1. reluctantly, unwillingly; 2. disgustedly.
**kerih** [ī] disgusting, detestable.

**kerim** [ī] 1. gracious, kind, munificent; 2. ♀ [x .] mf.
**kerime** [ī] ♀ daughter.
**keriz** 1. s. geriz; 2. sl. sucker.
**kerkenez** zo. kestrel.
**kerki** large axe.
**kerliferli** s. kellifelli.
**kermes** 1. fete, kermis; 2. festival.
**kerpeten** pincers, pliers; forceps.
**kerpiç,** -ci 1. sundried (or mud) brick, adobe; 2. made of sundried bricks.
**kerrake** [ā] † a kind of light cloak; şimdi anlaşıldı Vehbi'nin kerrakesi! now all is clear!
**kerrat,** -tı † times; ~ cetveli times (or multiplication) table.
**kertan** sl. risky.
**kerte** 1. notch, score; 2. rhumb; 3. state, degree; -sine getirmek to bring to the very best time.
**kerteli** gradual.
**kertenkele** zo. lizard.
**kerteriz** ↓ bearing.
**kertik** notch, tally, score, gash.
**kertiklemek** to notch.
**kertikli** notched.
**kertmek,** (-er) 1. to notch; 2. to scrape.
**kervan** caravan; -a katılmak fig. to go with the crowd.
**kervanbaşı,** -nı leader of a caravan.
**kervancı** organizer or leader of a caravan.
**Kervankıran** pr. n. ast. Venus.
**kervansaray** caravanserai, caravansary.
**kes** sneaker.
**kesafet,** -ti [ā] density.
**kesat,** -dı [ā] 1. slack, stagnant, flat; 2. slackness.
**kesatlık** s. kesat 2.
**kesbetmek** [x . .] to acquire, to take on, to assume.
**kese[1]** 1. moneybag, purse; 2. zo. marsupium, pouch; 3. ♀ cyst, sac, bursa; 3. coarse glove-like cloth; 5. fig. wealth, purse; ~ sürmek to rub with a kese; -nin ağzını açmak to loosen the purse strings; -nin dibi görünmek to run out of money, to be short of money; -sine güvenmek to be able to afford, to be within one's purse; -sine hiç bir şey girmemek not to benefit at all.
**kese[2]** short cut; ~ yol short cut.
**kesecik** anat. saccule.
**kesedar** [ā] hist. treasurer, keeper of the purse.
**kesek** clod.
**kesekâğıdı,** -nı paper bag.
**keselemek** s. kese sürmek.

**keselenmek** to rub o.s. with a kese.
**keseli** zo. marsupial.
**keseliler** zo. Marsupialia.
**kesen** geom. secant.
**kesenek** deduction.
**kesenkes** P absolutely.
**keser** adze.
**kesici 1.** incisive, incisory, cutting; **2.** cutter; **3.** butcher.
**kesicidiş** incisor.
**kesif** [î] dense, thick.
**kesik 1.** cut; **2.** off (electricity, water, etc.); **3.** curdled; **4.** geom. truncated; **5.** clipping; **6.** interrupted, broken off; ~ ~ gaspingly.
**kesikli** discontinuous, intermittent.
**kesiksiz 1.** uninterrupted, continuous; **2.** continuously, on and on.
**kesilme** vn. of kesilmek, part. exhaustion.
**kesilmek 1.** pass. or refl. of kesmek; **2.** to be tired out (or bushed); **3.** to curdle, to sour; **4.** to be cut off (electricity, water, etc.); **5.** to stop, to die down, to let up (rain, etc.); **6.** to lose (appetite, strength); **7.** sl. to fall for.
**kesim 1.** slaughter; **2.** section (a. **%**), sector; **3.** period (of time).
**kesimevi**, -ni slaughterhouse.
**kesin** definite, certain.
**kesinleşmek** to become definite.
**kesinleştirmek** to make definite.
**kesinlik** certainty, certitude.
**kesinlikle** definitely, certainly.
**kesinti 1.** deduction; **2.** interruption; -ye almak (b-ni) F to make fun of s.o. behind his back.
**kesintisiz 1.** uninterrupted, continuous; **2.** without deductions.
**kesir**, -sri **1.** ⊕ fraction; **2.** **%** fracture.
**kesirli** ₳ fractional.
**kesişen** geom. intersecting.
**kesişmek 1.** to intersect, to cross; **2.** to come to an agreement; **3.** to exchange amorous glances.
**kesit**, -ti ₳ crosscut.
**keski 1.** billhook, coulter; **2.** chisel; **3.** hatchet.
**keskin 1.** sharp; **2.** acute, keen; **3.** pungent; **4.** severe; ~ gözlü eagle-eyed; ~ nişancı marksman, dead shot; ~ sirke küpüne (or kabına) zarar a bad temper harms its possessor most; ~ viraj sharp (or hairpin) curve.
**keskinleşmek** to get sharp.
**keskinleştirmek** to sharpen.
**keskinlik** sharpness, keenness.
**kesme 1.** vn. of kesmek; **2.** tin snips; **3.**

cut, faceted; **4.** sector; **5.** cinema: cut; **6.** cube-shaped; **7.** fixed (price); ~ almak F to pinch one's cheek; ~ işareti apostrophe.
**kesmece 1.** for a lump sum; **2.** at the same price.
**kesmek**, (-er) **1.** to cut (off); to cut down, to fell (tree); **2.** to slice, to cut up; **3.** to slaughter, to butcher; **4.** to stop, to interrupt; **5.** to turn off (electricity, water, gas); **6.** to determine, to fix; **7.** to deduct; **8.** to cut (cards); **9.** to coin, to issue (money); **10.** to block; to hinder, to impede; **11.** to take away, to kill (pain, etc.); **12.** sl. to shut up, to cut the cackle; **13.** sl. to shoot the bull; **14.** sl. to ogle at (a girl); kesip atmak to settle offhand, to settle once and for all; kesip biçmek to bluster; kestiği tırnak olamamak (b-nin) can't hold a candle to s.o.
**kesmelik** quarry.
**kesmeşeker** lump (or cube) sugar.
**kesmik 1.** chaff; **2.** curds.
**kesret**, -ti abundance.
**kestane** [â] **%** chestnut (tree); ~ kebabı roast chestnuts; ~ şekeri marron glacé, candied chestnuts.
**kestaneci** [â] chestnut man.
**kestanecik** [â] **%** prostate gland.
**kestanefişeği**, -ni firecracker.
**kestanelik** [â] chestnut grove.
**kestirme 1.** vn. of kestirmek; **2.** estimate; **3.** short cut; **4.** concise, direct (answer); ~ yol short cut; -den gitmek to take a short cut.
**kestirmek 1.** caus. of kesmek; **2.** to estimate, to guess, to predict; **3.** to take a nap, to nap, to doze off; **4.** to curdle.
**keş 1.** dry curd; skim-milk cheese; **2.** sl. idiotic; ~ etm. sl. to humiliate, to shame.
**keşfetmek** [x . .] **1.** to discover, to explore; **2.** to uncover, to find out (secret); **3.** ✕ to reconnoitre.
**keşide** [î] drawing; ~ etm. to draw.
**keşideci** [î] **%** drawer.
**keşif**, -şfi **1.** discovery, exploration; **2.** investigation; **3.** ✕ reconnaissance; ~ kolu reconnaissance patrol; ~ uçağı ✕ reconnaissance plane.
**keşiş** monk.
**keşişhane** [â] monastery.
**keşişleme 1.** southeast wind; **2.** ↓ southeast point (of the compass).
**keşke, keşki** [x .] I wish, if only, would that...!; ~ gelseydin if only you'd come!
**keşkül** milk pudding with coconut.
**keşlemek** sl. to take no notice (-e of).
**keşmekeş** disorder, rush.

**keşşaf** [ā] † X military scout.

**ket¹** = nişasta.

**ket²**, -ti obstacle; ~ vurmak to put back, to handicap, to hinder, to impede.

**ketçap** ketchup, catchup, catsup.

**keten 1.** linen; **2.** ⚥ flax; ~ bezi linen cloth.

**ketenhelvası**, -nı cotton candy.

**ketenkuşu**, -nu zo. linnet.

**ketentohumu**, -nu linseed, flaxseed; ~ yağı linseed oil.

**keton** ⚗ ketone.

**ketum** [ū] tightlipped, discreet.

**ketumiyet**, -ti [ū] reticence, discretion.

**kevgir 1.** skimmer; **2.** colander.

**Kevser** isl. myth. name of a river in Paradise; ~ gibi nectarous.

**keyfetmek** to enjoy o.s., to have fun.

**keyfi** arbitrary, discretionary.

**keyfiyet**, -ti **1.** situation; **2.** condition, nature; **3.** affair matter.

**keyif**, -yfi **1.** pleasure, delight, joy, enjoyment, merriment; **2.** humo(u)r, mood, spirits, disposition; **3.** high, kef; **4.** psych. euphoria; ~ çatmak to enjoy o.s., to have a good time; ~ halinde tipsy; ~ için for pleasure (or fun); ~ sürmek to live the good life; ~ vermek to make tipsy; keyfi bilmek to do as one pleases; keyfi bozuldu (or kaçtı) he is out of spirits; keyfi gelmek to get into a happy mood; keyfi olmamak to feel under the weather; keyfinden dört köşe olm. to be as happy as the day is long; keyfine bakmak to enjoy o.s.; keyfine gitmek (kendi) to do as one pleases; keyfini çıkarmak (bşin) to get a kick out of s.th.

**keyiflenmek 1.** to become merry; **2.** to get tipsy.

**keyifli 1.** merry, joyous ,in good spirits; **2.** tipsy.

**keyifsiz 1.** indisposed, under the weather; **2.** in bad humo(u)r.

**keyifsizlik** indisposition; depression.

**kez** time; bu ~ this time; dört ~ four times.

**keza** [x -], **kezalik** [. x .] [ā] **1.** the same, ditto; **2.** likewise; **3.** also, too.

**kezzap**, -bı [ā] aqua fortis, nitric acid.

**kıble 1.** kiblah, the direction of Mecca; **2.** south wind; ~ye dönmek to turn towards Mecca.

**Kıbrıs** pr. n. Cyprus.

**Kıbrıslı** pr. n. Cyprian, Cypriote.

**kıç**, -çı **1.** buttocks, butt, bottom, rump, behind; **2.** ↓ poop, stern; **3.** back, hind; ~ atmak **1.** to kick (animal); **2.** fig. to

long (-e for); ~ güverte quarter-deck; ~ üstü oturmak F to remain helpless; -ına kına yakmak F to gloat; -ına tekmeyi atmak sl. to give s.o. the boot, to boot out; -ını yırtmak sl. to rant and rave; -ının kılları ağarmış sl. old, past it.

**kıçın kıçın** backwards; astern.

**kıdem 1.** seniority, priority, precedence; **2.** length of service.

**kıdemli** senior (in service); ~ onbaşı X lance corporal.

**kıdemsiz** junior (in service).

**kığ**, kığı sheep, goat or camel droppings.

**kıh** dirty.

**kıkırdak 1.** anat. cartilage, gristle; **2.** greaves, crackling.

**kıkırdakdoku** anat. cartilaginous (or gristly) tissue.

**kıkırdaklı** cartilaginous, gristly.

**kıkırdamak 1.** to giggle, to chuckle; **2.** to be freezing; **3.** sl. to croak, to peg out, to pop off.

**kıkır kıkır** gigglingly.

**kıkırtı** giggle ,chuckle.

**kıl 1.** hair; bristle; **2.** goat hair; ~ çekmek sl. flatter, to soft-soap; ~ çuval haircloth sack; ~ gibi thin as a hair; ~ kaldı ödülü kazanacaktı he was within an ace (or inch) of winning the prize; ~ payı **1.** hairbreadth; **2.** by the skin of one's teeth; ~ payı kalmak to come within an inch (of); -ı şaşmadan painstakingly; ~ testere ⊕ fretsaw, scrollsaw; -ı kıpırdamamak not to turn a hair; -ı kırk yarmak to split hairs; -ını bile kıpırdatmamak = -ı kıpırdamamak.

**kılağı** burr.

**kılaptan** silvered cotton thread.

**kılavuz 1.** guide; **2.** ↓ pilot; **3.** matchmaker, go-between.

**kılavuzluk 1.** guidance; **2.** ↓ pilotage.

**kılburun** geogr. promontory.

**kılcal** biol. capillary; ~ damar anat. capillary.

**kılçık 1.** fishbone; **2.** string (of beans); kılçığını çıkarmak **1.** to bone (fish); **2.** to string (beans).

**kılçıklı 1.** bony (fish); **2.** string (beans).

**kılçıksız 1.** boneless (fish); **2.** stringless (bean).

**kılıbık** henpecked (husband).

**kılıbıklaşmak** to become henpecked.

**kılıcına** edgewise.

**kılıç**, -cı sword; saber; ~ çekmek to draw one's sword; ~ kabzası sword hilt; ~ kuşanmak to gird on a sword; ~ oynatmak to rule over; -tan geçirmek to put to the

sword.
**kılıçbacak** bowlegged, bandylegged.
**kılıçbalığı,** -nı zo. swordfish.
**kılıççı** sword maker or seller.
**kılıçlama** 1. = kılıcına; 2. crosswise.
**kılıf** 1. case, cover;  2. holster;  3. biol. sheath; 4. anat. zo. tunic.
**kılıflamak** to encase.
**kılık** 1. appearance, shape; 2. costume, dress; ~ kıyafet attire, dress; ~ kıyafet düşkünü dressed in shabby clothes.
**kılıklı** dressed like...; ~ kıyafetli well dressed.
**kılıksız** shabby.
**kılkıran** alopecia.
**kılkuyruk** F shabby and penniless.
**kıllanmak** to become hairy.
**kıllı** hairy; bristly; ~ bebek fig. big baby.
**kılmak,** (-ar) 1. to render, to make; 2. to perform.
**kılsız** hairless.
**kımılda(n)mak** to stir, to budge.
**kımıldatmak** caus. of kımıldamak to move, to shake.
**kımıltı** 1. movement, motion, agitation; 2. facial gesture.
**kımız** k(o)umiss.
**kın** 1. sheath, scabbard; 2. ♀ ocrea, stipule; -ına koymak to sheathe; -ından çıkarmak to unsheathe.
**kına** henna; ~ yakmak (or koymak or vurmak or sürmek) to henna; -lar yakmak (sevincinden) fig. to gloat, to rejoice.
**kınaçiçeği,** -ni ♀ garden balsam.
**kınagecesi,** -ni party during which a bride--to-be has her fingers hennaed.
**kınakına** [. . x .] ♀ cinchona.
**kınalamak** to henna.
**kınalı** 1. hennaed; 2. henna-colo(u)red.
**kınama** condemnation, censure.
**kınamak** to condemn, to censure.
**kınamsımak** to find fault with, to criticize.
**kınnap,** -bı twine, string, packthread.
**kıpık** half-closed (eyes).
**kıpırda(n)mak** to move, to stir, to quiver, to vibrate, to fidget.
**kıpırdaşmak** to stir, to fidget.
**kıpırdatmak** to stir, to budge.
**kıpır kıpır** fidgentingly.
**kıpırtı** stirring, quiver.
**kıpkırmızı** [x . . .] crimson, carmine.
**kıpkızıl** s. kıpkırmızı.
**kıpmak,** (-ar) to wink (an eye); to blink (one's eyes).
**kır¹** grey, Am. gray; ~ düşmek (saçına, sakalına) to turn grey.
**kır²** the country, countryside, rural area;

~ çiçeği wildflower; ~ gezisi country outing; ~ koşusu cross-country race.
**kıraat,** -ti [. - .] 1. reading; 2. reading-book, reader; ~ etm. to read.
**kıraathane** [. . . - .] café.
**kıraç** 1. arid (land); 2. sterile, unproductive, waste (land).
**kırağı** frost, hoarfrost; ~ çalmak to become frostbitten (plant); ~ düşmek (or yağmak) to frost.
**kırağılı** frosty.
**kıran** 1. edge; shore; bank; 2. murrain; pestilence.
**kıranta** [. x .] grayhead.
**kırat,** -tı 1. carat; 2. fig. value, character, quality.
**kırba** waterskin; ~ olm. to swell up.
**kırbaç,** -cı whip; ~ vurmak to whip, to flog; ~ yemek to be whipped (or flogged).
**kırbaçlamak** to whip, to flog.
**kırcın** murrain.
**kırçıl** graying (hair, beard).
**kırçıllaşmak** to gray.
**kırçoz** sl. = kıranta.
**kırgın** hurt, offended, resentful.
**kırgınlık** hurt, offence, resentment.
**Kırgız** pr. n. Kirghiz.
**Kırgızistan** pr. n. Kirghizia.
**kırıcı** hurtful, offensive (word, etc.).
**kırık** 1. broken; 2. ♥ fracture, break; 3. hybrid; mongrel; 4. (broken) piece; 5. failing grade; 6. fig. hurt, offended, resentful; ~ almak to get a failing grade; ~ dökük 1. broken, worn out; 2. odds and ends; ~ ışın refracted ray; ~ not failing grade; ~ tahtası ♥ splint.
**kırıkçı** bonesetter.
**kırıkkırak** breadstick.
**kırıklık** 1. brokenness; 2. fatigue; soreness.
**kırılgan** 1. brekable, fragile; 2. fig. touchy.
**kırılım** refraction.
**kırılmak** 1. pass. of kırmak; 2. (b-ne) to resent s.o., to be hurt (or offended) by s.o.; 3. phys. to be refracted; 4. to die, to perish; kırılıp dökülmek to speak in a flirtatious way.
**Kırım** pr. n. Crimea.
**kırım** 1. slaughter, massacre, genocide, carnage; 2. fold, pleat.
**kırım kırım** flirtatiously, coquettishly.
**kırınım** phys. diffraction.
**kırıntı** 1. fragment, piece; 2. crumb.
**kırışık** 1. wrinkly, wrinkled; 2. wrinkle, pucker.
**kırışmak** 1. to get wrinkled, to pucker, to crumple; 2. to bet with each other; 3. to

divide among *or* between themselves; 4.
F to flirt with each other.
**kırıştırmak 1.** to wrinkle, to crumple, to
pucker; **2.** to flirt (*ile* with), to carry on
(*ile* with).
**kırıtkan** coquettish, flirtatious, mincing.
**kırıtmak** to mince, to coquet.
**kırk, -kı** forty; ~ bir kere maşallah! touch
wood!; ~ (*or* bin) dereden su getirmek to
beat about the bush; ~ tarakta bezi olm.
to have too many irons in the fire; ~
yılda bir *fig.* once in a blue moon; ~ yılın
başında = ~ yılda bir.
**kırkambar 1.** general store; **2.** *fig.* omniscient person; **3.** ♨ mixed cargo.
**kırkar** forty at a time; forty to each.
**kırkayak** *zo.* **1.** centipede; **2.** millipede; **3.**
crab louse.
**kırkbayır** omasum, manyplies.
**kırkı** shearing.
**kırkım** shearing (season).
**kırkıncı** fortieth.
**kırklık 1.** fourty-year-old; **2.** layette; **3.** P
shears.
**kırkmak, (-ar) 1.** to shear, to clip (*animal*);
**2.** to trim.
**kırkmerak** nosy, inquisitive.
**kırkmerdiven** *fig.* very steep slope.
**kırlağan** pestilence, plague.
**kırlangıç, -cı 1.** *zo.* swallow; **2.** (house)
martin; **3.** *fig.* quack eye doctor; **4.** *hist.*
light galley; ~ kuyruğu dovetail.
**kırlangıçbalığı, -nı** *zo.* red gurnard.
**kırlangıçdönümü, -nü** early October.
**kırlaşmak** to turn grey.
**kırlık** open country.
**kırma 1.** *vn. of* kırmak; **2.** pleat, fold; **3.**
folding, collapsible; **4.** groats; **5.** *zo.*
hybrid, mongrel.
**kırmak, (-ar) 1.** to break; **2.** to split, to
chop (*wood*); **3.** to fold; **4.** to destroy, to
break (*resistance, pride, desire, etc.*); **5.**
to reduce (*price*); **6.** to offend, to hurt;
**7.** (*direksiyon*) to swerve; **8.** to mitigate,
to abate, to break; **9.** *sl.* to run away, to
clear out; kırıp geçirmek **1.** to wipe out,
to slay; **2.** (*gülmekten*) to have people
rolling in the aisles.
**kırmalı** pleated.
**kırmataş** gravel, ballast.
**kırmızı** red; crimson; carmine; ~ balık *zo.*
goldfish; ~ dut ♨ red mulberry; ~ oy
negative vote.
**kırmızıbiber** ♨ red (*or* cayenne) pepper.
**kırmızılaşmak** to redden, to turn red.
**kırmızılık** redness, ruddiness; flush.
**kırmızımsı, kırmızımtırak** reddish.

**kırmızıturp, -pu** ♨ radish.
**kırpık** clipped, shorn.
**kırpıntı 1.** clippings; **2.** bit, scrap.
**kırpıştırmak** to blink (*eyes*).
**kırpmak, (-ar) 1.** to shear, to clip; to trim;
**2.** to wink (*eye*).
**kırsal** rural, rustic, country; pastoral.
**kırtasiye [â]** stationery.
**kırtasiyeci [â] 1.** stationer; **2.** pettifogger,
bureaucrat.
**kırtasiyecilik [â] 1.** the stationery business;
**2.** red tape, bureaucracy.
**kırtıpil** *sl.* shabby, common, mean.
**kısa** short; ~ boylu squat, short; ~ dalga
*radio:* short wave; ~ devre *phys.* short
circuit; ~ geçmek to refer briefly; ~
kesmek to cut short (*talk*); ~ kollu short-
-sleeved; ~ ömürlü short-lived, ephemer-
al; ~ sürmek to take a short time; ~ vadeli short-term.
**kısaca 1.** squat; **2.** [. x .] in short, shortly,
briefly; -sı [. x .] in a word; in brief.
**kısacık** very short.
**kısalık** shortness.
**kısalmak 1.** to shorten; **2.** to shrink.
**kısaltma 1.** abbreviation; **2.** abridg(e)-
ment.
**kısaltmak 1.** to shorten; **2.** to abbreviate,
to abridge, to condense; **3.** to take up
(*garment*).
**kısaltmalı** shortened, abbreviated.
**kısas [â]** retaliation, reprisal; -a ~ an eye
for an eye, tit for tat.
**kısık 1.** hoarse (*voice*); **2.** turned down
(*radio, lamp*); **3.** slitted, narrowed
(*eyes*).
**kısıklık** hoarseness.
**kısılma 1.** *vn. of* kısılmak; **2.** reduction; **3.**
♥ heart contraction.
**kısılmak 1.** *pass. of* kısmak; **2.** to get hoarse
(*voice*); **3.** to be caught (*in a trap*); **4.**
to contract (*muscle*); **5.** to be slitted (*or*
narrowed) (*eyes*).
**kısım, -smı 1.** part, section, division, portion; **2.** kind; ~ ~ in parts (*or* sections);
kadın kısmı womankind.
**kısınmak** to refrain (-*den* from), to abstain
(-*den* from).
**kıs·ntı** reduction, cutback, restriction.
**kısır 1.** sterile, barren; **2.** unproductive; ~
döngü *log.* vicious circle.
**kısırganmak (bşi)** to grudge *s.th.*
**kısırlaşmak** to be sterilized, to become
barren (*or* unproductive).
**kısırlaştırmak** ♨ to sterilize.
**kısırlık** sterility, barrenness.
**kısıt, -tı** seizure, distraint.

**kısıtlamak** to restrict.

**kısıtlayıcı** restrictive.

**kısıtlı** restricted.

**kıskaç,** -cı 1. pincers, pliers; forceps; 2. claw, chela, pincer; 3. stepladder; ~ gözlük pince-nez.

**kıskanç,** -cı jealous.

**kıskançlık** jealousy.

**kıskandırmak** to arouse s.o.'s jealousy.

**kıskanmak** 1. to be jealous (-i of); 2. (b-den bşi) to grudge s.o. s.th., to envy s.o. s.th.

**kıs kıs gülmek** to laugh up one's sleeve, to snicker, to snigger.

**kıskıvrak** [x . .] very tightly; ~ bağlamak to bind tightly.

**kısmak,** (-ar) 1. to lessen,n to reduce; to shorten; 2. to lower (voice, sound); 3. to cut (expenses); 4. to turn down (lamp, light); 5. to narrow (eyes).

**kısmen** [x .] partly, partially.

**kısmet,** -ti 1. destiny, fate, fortune, luck, kismet; 2. change of marriage; 3. perhaps!, if fortune wills it!; ~ ise if fate so decrees; ~ olm. to be on the cards; -i çıkmak to receive a marriage proposal; -inde ne varsa kaşığında o çıkar pro. you can't avoid your destiny.

**kısmetli** lucky, fortunate.

**kısmetsiz** unlucky, unfortunate.

**kısmi** [î] partial; ~ seçim by-election.

**kısrak** zo. mare.

**kıssa** tale, story; anecdote; -dan hisse almak to draw a moral from a story.

**kıstak** geogr. isthmus.

**kıstas** [â] criterion.

**kıstelyevm** deduction from wages (for absence).

**kıstırmak** caus. of kısmak, part. to squeeze, to pinch; parmağımı kapıya kıstırdım I pinched my finger in the doorway.

**kış**[1] winter; ~ basmak to set in (winter); ~ günü wintery day; ~ kıyamet severe winter; ~ ortasında in the dead of winter; ~ uykusu zo. hibernation; ~ uykusuna yatmak zo. to hibernate; -ı geçirmek to winter.

**kış**[2] shoo!, scat!; ~ ~ etm. to shoo away.

**kışın** [x .] in (or during) the winter.

**kışır,** -şrı 1. bark; peel; rind; 2. geol. crust.

**kışkırtı** instigation, incitement, provocation, agitation.

**kışkırtıcı** 1. provocative; 2. instigator, fomenter, agitator.

**kışkırtmak** 1. to incite, to provoke, to stir, to agitate; 2. to shoo away (animals).

**kışla** [x .] X barracks; ~ hapsi detention in barracks; ~ hizmeti fatigue; -ya yer-

leştirmek to barrack.

**kışlak** winter quarters.

**kışlamak** 1. to set in (winter); 2. to winter.

**kışlık** 1. wintery; 2. winter residence.

**kıt,** -tı 1. scarce; 2. insufficient, inadequate; ~ kanaat geçinmek to live from hand to mouth, to make both ends meet; -ı -ına idare etm. to get by on a shoestring, to scrape by.

**kıta** 1. geogr. continent; 2. X detachment; 3. lit. quatrain, stanza; ~ ~ in sections; ~ sahanlığı continental shelf.

**kıtık** stuffing, tow.

**kıtıpiyos** sl. no-account, good-for-nothing.

**kıtır** 1. popcorn; 2. F lie, fib; ~ atmak (or yuvarlamak) F to fib.

**kıtırbom** sl. lie.

**kıtırdamak** to crackle.

**kıtır kıtır:** ~ doğramak (or kesmek) to kill in cold blood; ~ yemek to munch.

**kıtırtı** crackle.

**kıtlaşmak** to become scarce, to run short.

**kıtlık** 1. scarcity, shortage; 2. famine; kıtlığına kıran girmek to become as scarce as hen's teeth; -tan çıkmış gibi yemek to wade (or tuck) into the meal.

**kıvam** [â] 1. thickness, density, consistency; 2. the right moment (or stage); -ında 1. of the proper consistency; 2. at the most suitable time; 3. in top shape.

**kıvanç** 1. pride; 2. pleasure, joy; ~ duymak to take pride (-den in).

**kıvançlı** 1. proud; 2. pleased, glad.

**kıvılcım** spark; ~ saçmak to spark.

**kıvılcımlanmak** to spark.

**kıvırcık** curly; kinky; frizzy; ~ salata lettuce.

**kıvır kıvır** in curls; ~ yapmak to curl, to frizz.

**kıvırmak** 1. to curl, to twist, to coil; 2. to turn up (cuffs); 3. to fold back; 4. to crimp; 5. F to make up, to fabricate (lies); 6. F to pull off, to bring off.

**kıvır zıvır** 1. trifling, piddling; 2. kickshaw, odds and ends, bits and pieces.

**kıvıracık** [x . .] P orderly (place).

**kıvrak** 1. brisk, supple, agile; 2. fluent (speech, writing); 3. neat, elegant, spruce (clothing, etc.).

**kıvraklık** 1. briskness, agility; 2. fluency; 3. neatness.

**kıvramak** to kink.

**kıvranmak** to writhe (-den with), to double up (-den with).

**kıvrık** 1. curled, twisted; 2. curly (hair); 3. cuffed (trousers).

**kıvrılmak** 1. pass. of kıvırmak; 2. to curl, to

twist; 3. to curl up; to coil up.
**kıvrım** 1. curl, twist, undulation, convolution, fold *(a. geol.)*; 2. bend *(of a road)*; 3. ringlet *(of hair)*; 4. *anat.* plica, fold; ~ ~ 1. very curly *(hair)*; 2. twisty *(road)*; ~ ~ kıvranmak to be doubled up with pain.
**kıvrımlı** curled, twisted, folded.
**kıvrıntı** 1. = kıvrım; 2. turn, twist *(of a road)*.
**kıyafet**, -ti [ā] 1. dress, attire, clothes, costume; 2. appearance; ~ balosu fancy dress *(or* costume) ball; -ini değiştirmek to change one's clothes.
**kıyafetli** [ā] dressed in...
**kıyafetsiz** [ā] ill-dressed, untidy, shabby.
**kıyak** F great, super, swell.
**kıyam** [ā] 1. standing up; 2. endeavo(u)r, attempt; 3. rebellion, mutiny, revolt.
**kıyamet**, -ti [ā] 1. Doomsday, the Day of Judgement; 2. *fig.* ruction, tumult, uproar; ~ gibi *(or* kadar) heaps of, pots of; ~ günü Doomsday; ~ kopacak F there will be ructions, there will be hell to pay; ~ mi koptu? what the devil does it matter?; -e kadar till Doomsday, till kingdom come, till hell freezes over; -i *(or* -leri) koparmak to raise hell, to make a hell of a fuss.
**kıyas** [ā] 1. comparison; 2. ♋ analogy; 3. *log.* syllogism; ~ etm. to compare *(ile* with); ~ kabul etmez incomparable; -la in comparison (-e to, with).
**kıyasen** [ā] by comparison (-e to).
**kıyasıya** 1. cruelly, mercilessly; 2. murderous, savage.
**kıyasi** [. - -] 1. regular; 2. analogical; 3. syllogistical.
**kıyaslamak** to compare.
**kıyı** 1. shore, coast; bank; 2. edge, side; 3. outskirts; ~ balıkçılığı inshore fishing; ~ sıra inshore; -da bucakta *(or* köşede) in nooks and crannies; -ya çıkmak to go ashore, to land.
**kıyıcı** 1. beachcomber; 2. cutter; 3. *fig.* cruel.
**kıyılamak** to coast.
**kıyılmak** 1. *pass. of* kıymak; 2. *fig.* to ache.
**kıyım** massacre, genocide.
**kıyınmak** 1. to starve, to feel peckish; 2. to ache.
**kıyıntı** 1. languor; 2. scrap.
**kıyışmak** 1. to come to an agreement; 2. to compete *(ile* against).
**kıyma** 1. *vn. of* kıymak; 2. mince, mincemeat, minced meat; ~ makinesi mincer.
**kıymak**, (-ar) 1. to mince, to chop up; 2. to

part (-e with), to spare, to let go (-e of); 3. to slaughter, to massacre, to slay; 4. to perform *(marriage)*; paraya kıyıp kendime yeni bir elbise alacağım I'll treat myself to a new dress.
**kıymalı** with mincemeat.
**kıymet**, -ti value, worth; ~ biçmek to value, to evaluate; ~ koymak *(or* takdir etm.) to value, to appraise, to assess; ~ vermek to value, to esteem; -ini bilmek to appreciate, to value; -ten düş(ür)mek to depreciate.
**kıymetlendirmek** to raise the value (of), to utilize.
**kıymetlenmek** to appreciate.
**kıymetli** valuable, precious.
**kıymetsiz** worthless, valueless.
**kıymık** splinter, sliver.
**kıymıklanmak** to splinter.
**kız** 1. girl; 2. daughter; 3. virgin, maiden; 4. *cards:* queen; ~ alıp vermek to intermarry; ~ bozmak to deflower; ~ evlât daughter; ~ gibi 1. girlish, sissy; 2. brand-new; 3. shy; ~ kaçırmak 1. to kidnap a girl; 2. to elope with a girl; ~ kardeş sister; ~ kurusu old maid, spinster; ~ lisesi girls' high school; ~ oğlan ~ virgin, maiden; ~ tarafı the bride's family; ~ vermek to give a girl in marriage (-e to); -ını dövmeyen dizini döver *pro.* spare the rod and spoil the child.
**kızak** 1. sledge; sled; toboggan; sleigh; bobsled; 2. skid; 3. ↓ stocks, ways; ground *(or* sliding) ways; 4. ⊕ way; ~ koymak to slide, to sledge, to sled, to sleigh; ~ yapmak to skid *(vehicle)*; kızağa çekmek 1. ↓ to put on the stocks; 2. *fig.* to put on the shelf; to kick upstairs; -tan indirmek to launch *(ship)*.
**kızaklamak** to skid *(vehicle)*.
**kızamık** ♏ measles, rubeola; ~ çıkarmak to develop measles; ~ olm. to have measles.
**kızamıkçık** ♏ German measles.
**kızamıklı** ♏ measly.
**kızan** P 1. boy, lad; 2. hellraiser.
**kızarmak** 1. to redden, to turn red; 2. to blush, to flush; 3. to fry; to toast; to roast; 4. to glow *(coals)*; kızarıp bozarmak to blush as red as a rose; kızarmış ekmek toast.
**kızartı** red spot *(or* place).
**kızartma** 1. *vn. of* kızartmak; 2. fried *(food)*.
**kızartmak** *caus. of* kızarmak, *part.* to fry; to roast; to toast.

**kızböceği,** -ni zo. dragonfly.

**kızdırmak 1.** to anger, to irritate, infuriate, to exasperate; **2.** to heat.

**kızgın 1.** red-hot; **2.** angry; **3.** estral, in heat (or rut) (animal); ~ ~ angrily.

**kızgınlaşmak 1.** to get angry; **2.** to become red-hot.

**kızgınlık 1.** anger, rage, fury; **2.** rut; heat.

**kızıl 1.** red; **2.** fig. communist, red; **3.** ⚓ scarlet fever, scarlatina; ~ cahil as ignorant as they come; ~ kıyameti koparmak to raise a hell of a row; ~ saçlı redheaded.

**Kızılay** pr. n. the Red Crescent.

**kızılca** reddish; ~ kıyameti koparmak to raise a hell of a row.

**kızılcık** ⚓ cornelian cherry; ~ sopası fig. hiding, caning; ~ sopası yemek F to get caned.

**Kızıldeniz** pr. n. the Red Sea.

**Kızılderili** Red (or American) Indian.

**Kızılhaç,** -cı pr. n. the Red Cross.

**kızıllaşmak** to turn red, to redden.

**kızıllık 1.** redness; **2.** alpenglow.

**Kızılordu** the Red Army.

**kızılötesi,** -ni phys. infrared.

**kızıltı** reddish gleam (or glow).

**kızılyıldız** ast. Mars.

**kızışmak 1.** to become fierce; **2.** to become violent (or lively); **3.** to beat down (sun); **4.** to go into rut (animal).

**kızıştırmak 1.** to enliven, to liven up; **2.** to incite, to egg on; **3.** to make red-hot.

**kızkuşu,** -nu zo. lapwing, pewit.

**kızlık** girlhood, maidenhood, virginity; ~ adı maiden name; ~ zarı hymen, maidenhead.

**kızmak,** (-ar) **1.** to get angry; **2.** to get hot; **3.** to go into rut (or heat) (animal).

**kızmemesi,** -ni F grapefruit.

**ki 1.** who, which, that: bir çocuk ki çok yaramaz a child who is very naughty; **2.** so... that, such ... that: öyle pahalı ki alamıyorum it is so expensive that I cannot afford it; **3.** seeing (or considering) that; **4.** as, though; **5.** when: henüz televizyonu açmıştım ki telefon çaldı I'd just turned on the television when the telephone rang; **6.** ..., I wonder?: bilmem ki ne desem? what should I say, I wonder?; **7.** in; of: Türkiye'de'ki İngilizler the English in Turkey; bugünkü Türkiye Turkey of today.

**kibar** [â] polite, courteous, well-bred.

**kibarca** politely.

**kibarlaşmak** [â] to become polite (or courteous).

**kibarlık** [â] politeness, courtesy, refine-

ment.

**kibir,** -bri arrogance, haughtiness; pride; kibrine dokunmak to wound s.o.'s pride; kibrini kırmak to take s.o. down a peg or two, to humiliate.

**kibirlenmek** to become haughty (or arrogant).

**kibirli** arrogant, haughty; proud.

**kibrit,** -ti match; ~ çakmak to strike a match; ~ çöpü matchstick; ~ kutusu matchbox.

**kibritçi 1.** match seller; **2.** fig. miserly, niggardly.

**kifayet,** -ti [â] sufficiency; ~ etm. **1.** to be enough, to suffice; **2.** (bşle) to be satisfied (or contented) with s.th.

**kifayetli** [â] sufficient, adequate, enough.

**kifayetsiz** [â] insufficient, inadequate.

**kik,** -ki **1.** ⚓ gig; **2.** sl. nose, snout, conk.

**kikirik** F beanpole (person).

**kiklon** cyclone.

**kil** clay.

**kile** kileh.

**kiler** pantry, larder, storeroom.

**kilim** kilim; ~i kebeyi sermek F to settle down (in a place).

**kilise** [. x .] church.

**kilit,** -di **1.** lock; padlock; **2.** linchpin; **3.** clevis, shackle; ~ altında under lock and key; ~ noktası key position (or point); ~ vurmak to lock.

**kilitçi** locksmith.

**kilitlemek 1.** to lock (up); **2.** to dovetail; to interlock.

**kilitli 1.** locked; **2.** dovetailed; interlocked.

**kilitsiz** unlocked.

**kiliz** ⚓ reed, rush.

**killi** clayey, argillaceous.

**kilo** [x .] kilo(gram); ~ almak to put on weight; ~ vermek to lose weight.

**kilogram** kilogram(me).

**kilohertz** phys. kilocycle.

**kiloluk** weighing ... kilos.

**kilometre** [. . x .] kilometre, Am. kilometer; ~ doldurmak sl. to kill time; ~ kare square kilometre; ~ saati **1.** speedometer, odometer; **2.** taximeter; ~ taşı kilometre stone.

**kilosikl** phys. kilocycle.

**kilovat,** -tı kilowatt; ~ saati kilowatt-hour.

**kils** limestone.

**kim 1.** who; **2.** whoever; ~ bilir? who knows?; ~ -e, dum duma nobody knows anything about it; ~ o? who is it?; -i (or -isi) some (of them); o ~ kibarlık ~ he is wanting in courtesy.

**kimi,** -ni some; some people; some things; ~ kez sometimes; ~ köprü bulamaz geçmeye, ~ su bulamaz içmeye pro. water is a boon in the desert, but the drowning man curses it; ~ zaman sometimes; -miz some of us; -si some of them; some people.

**kimlik** identity (card); ~ cüzdanı identity (or ID) card.

**kimono** kimono.

**kimse 1.** somebody, someone; **2.** anyone, anybody; **3.** (with negative) nobody, no one.

**kimsecik** not a soul; -ler yok there's not a soul here.

**kimsesiz** without relations or friends; ~ çocuklar homeless children, waifs and strays.

**kimya** [ā] chemistry; ~ fakültesi department of chemistry; ~ mühendisi chemical engineer; ~ sanayii chemical industry.

**kimyacı** [ā] **1.** chemist; **2.** teacher of chemistry.

**kimyager** [ā] chemist.

**kimyasal** chemical; ~ madde chemical.

**kimyevi** [. . -] chemical.

**kimyon** ♀ cumin.

**kin** [ı] grudge, malice, ranco(u)r; ~ beslemek to nurse (or bear or nourish) a grudge (-e against).

**kinaye** [ā] allusion, hint; innuendo, insinuation.

**kinci** [-.], **kindar** [- -] vindictive, revengeful, rancorous.

**kinetik** kinetic(s).

**kinin** ♀ quinine.

**kinizm** Cynicism.

**kip,** -pi **1.** type; **2.** gr. mood; **3.** log., phls. mode.

**kir** dirt, filth; ~ götürmek (or kaldırmak) not to show dirt; ~ tutmak to show dirt easily.

**kira** [ā] rent, hire; ~ bedeli rent; ~ ile tutmak to rent; ~ kontratı lease; -da oturmak to live in a rented flat (or house); -ya vermek to let, to rent.

**kiracı** [ā] renter, lessee; tenant.

**kiralamak** [. - . .] **1.** (b-ne) to rent to s.o., to let to s.o., to lease to s.o.; **2.** (b-den) to rent from s.o., to lease from s.o.; to charter from s.o. (vehicle).

**kiralık** [ā] to let, for rent; ~ kasa safe-deposit box; ~ katil hired gun (or assassin), goon.

**kiraz** ♀ cherry; ~ dudaklı cherry-lipped.

**kirde** a kind of maize bread.

**kireç,** -ci lime; ~ gibi olm. to turn pale; ~ kuyusu lime pit; ~ ocağı limekiln.

**kireçkaymağı,** -nı bleaching powder.

**kireçlemek 1.** to lime; **2.** to whitewash.

**kireçlenme 1.** calcification; **2.** ♀ calcinosis.

**kireçlenmek 1.** to be limed; **2.** to calcify.

**kireçleşmek** to calcify.

**kireçli** limy, calcareous.

**kireçtaşı,** -nı limestone.

**kiremit** tile; ~ kaplamak to tile; ~ ocağı tile kiln; ~ rengi tile (or brick) red.

**kiremitçi** tiler.

**kiremitli** tiled.

**kiriş 1.** joist; rafter; beam; girder; **2.** geom. chord; **3.** ♪ string (of an instrument); **4.** bowstring (of a shooting bow); -i kırmak sl. to take to one's heels.

**kirişli 1.** joisted; **2.** tendinous.

**kirizma** [. x .] trenching (the soil); subsoiling.

**kirlenmek 1.** to (get) dirty, to foul; to become polluted; **2.** fig. to be defiled (or sullied) (honour); **3.** to menstruate, to have the curse; **4.** to be raped, to lose one's cherry.

**kirletmek 1.** to dirty ,to soil, to foul; to pollute; **2.** fig. to foul, to sully, to stain, to blot, to besmirch (honour); **3.** to rape.

**kirli 1.** dirty, filthy, soiled; polluted; **2.** fig. blemished, disreputable (honour); **3.** menstruating (woman); **4.** dirty laundry; ~ çamaşır dirty clothes, laundry; ~ çamaşırlarını ortaya dökmek fig. to wash one's dirty linen in public; ~ çıkı(n) fig. wealthy niggard; ~ sepeti laundry basket.

**kirlikan** venous blood.

**kirlilik** dirtiness, filthiness, foulness; pollution.

**kirpi** zo. hedgehog.

**kirpik 1.** eyelash; **2.** biol. cilium.

**kispet,** -ti leather pants (worn by a greased wrestler).

**kist,** -ti ♀ cyst.

**kisve** attire, apparel; dress, garb.

**kişi** person (a. gr.), human being; one.

**kişileştirmek** to personify.

**kişilik 1.** personality; **2.** individuality; **3.** for ... persons.

**kişiliksiz** characterless, styleless.

**kişioğlu,** -nu highborn person.

**kişisel** personal.

**kişizade** [ā] highborn.

**kişmiş** a kind of raisin grape.

**kişnemek** to neigh, to whinny.

**kişniş** ♀ coriander.

**KİT** (abbr. for Kamu İktisadi Teşekkülü) state-owned economic enterprise.

**kitabe** [ā] inscription, legend; epitaph.

**kitabet,** -ti [ā] **1.** rhetoric; **2.** secretaryship.

**kitabevi,** -ni bookstore, bookshop.

**kitabi 1.** bookish, book-learned; **2.** stilted.

**kitap,** -bı book; ~ delisi bibliomaniac; ~ ehli People of the Book; ~ kurdu book worm; kitaba el basmak to swear on the Koran.

**kitapçı 1.** bookseller; **2.** F bookstore.

**kitapçılık** bookselling.

**kitaplık 1.** bookcase; bookstand, bookrack; **2.** library.

**kitapsarayı,** -nı public library.

**kitapsız 1.** bookless; **2.** F heathen; pagan.

**kitara** [. x .] ♪ guitar.

**kitle** mass; ~ iletişimi mass media.

**kitlemek** s. kilitlemek.

**kitli** s. kilitli.

**kiyaset,** -ti [ā] cleverness.

**KKK** (*abbr. for* Kara Kuvvetleri Komutanlığı) Commandership of the Ground Forces.

**klakson** horn;· ~ çalmak to hoot.

**klan** clan.

**klapa** lapel.

**klarnet,** -ti clarinet.

**klarnetçi** clarinetist.

**klas** F first-rate, ace, A1.

**klasik 1.** classic; **2.** classic(al).

**klasman** *sports:* rating, classifying.

**klasör** file.

**klavye** keyboard; -si kuvvetli skillful (*typist, etc.*).

**kleptoman** kleptomaniac.

**kleptomani** kleptomania.

**klik** clique.

**klima (cihazı)** air conditioner.

**klinik 1.** clinic; **2.** clinical.

**klips** (spring) clip.

**klipsli** clip-on.

**kliring** ↑ clearing.

**klişe 1.** *typ.* cliché, plate; **2.** *fig.* trite, hackneyed.

**klişeleşmek** to become a cliché (*or* hackneyed).

**klor** chlorine.

**klorlamak** to chlorinate.

**klorlu** chlorinated.

**klorofil** ♀ chlorophyll.

**kloroform** ⚗ chloroform.

**kloş** bell-shaped (*skirt*).

**klüz** *geogr.* gap, col.

**koalisyon** coalition; ~ hükümeti coalition government.

**kobalt,** -tı ⚗ cobalt.

**kobay** *zo.* guinea pig, cavy.

**koca**[1] husband, hubby; ~ bulmak to find a hubby; -ya kaçmak to elope; -ya varmak to marry; -ya vermek to marry off (*a woman*).

**koca**[2] **1.** large, very big; **2.** grand, great; **3.** adult; aged, old; ~ herif olm. F to be fully grown; ~ oğlan *co.* bear.

**kocakarı** *sl.* hag, crone; ~ ilacı nostrum; ~ soğuğu cold spell in mid-March.

**kocamak** to age.

**kocaman** huge, enormous.

**kocasız** husbandless; widowed.

**kocatmak** to age, to put years on.

**koç,** -çu **1.** ram; **2.** *fig.* sturdy youngster; ~ burunlu hook-nosed.

**Koç,** -çu Aries, the Ram.

**koçan 1.** corncob; **2.** stump; **3.** heart (*or* stem) (*of a vegetable*).

**koçu 1.** a kind of horse-drawn carriage; **2.** granary (*built up on poles*).

**kod,** -du code.

**kodaman** *co.* **1.** big cheese (*or* shot *or* pot), bigwig; **2.** powerful, influential; -lar *co.* the big pots, the bigwigs.

**kodeks** codex.

**kodes** *sl.* clink, jug, cooler, stir, chokey; -e tıkmak *sl.* to throw in the clink.

**kodoş** *sl.* pimp, pander.

**kof 1.** hollow; **2.** weak; **3.** ignorant; ineffectual.

**kofana** [. x .] *zo.* large bluefish.

**koflaşmak 1.** to become hollow; **2.** to get weak.

**kofti** [x .] *sl.* lie.

**koğuş** dormitory; hospital ward.

**kok,** -ku (*a.* ~ kömürü) coke.

**kokain** cocaine.

**kokak** smelly, fetid, whiffy.

**kokarca** [. x .] *zo.* polecat, skunk.

**kokart,** -tı cockade.

**koket,** -ti coquettish.

**koklamak** to smell, to sniff.

**koklaşmak** *fig.* to neck, to pet.

**koklatmak** *caus. of* koklamak; koklatmamak *sl.* not even to give a very tiny bit of.

**kokmak,** (-ar) **1.** to smell; **2.** to stink, to putrefy, to whiff; **3.** *fig.* to reek (of).

**kokmuş 1.** smelly, whiffy, putrid; **2.** *fig.* bone-idle, bone-lazy.

**koko** coconut macaroon.

**kokoreç,** -ci roasted sheep's intestines.

**kokoroz 1.** ♀ corn; **2.** *sl.* person like the back (cnd) of a bus.

**kokorozlanmak** to become defiant.

**kokoz** *sl.* broke, penniless.

**kokteyl** cocktail (party).

**koku 1.** smell, scent, odo(u)r; **2.** perfume; **3.** *fig.* the tiniest bit of, a mote of; -su çıkmak to be divulged; -sunu almak (*bşin*) *fig.* to scent *s.th.*, to get wind of *s.th.*

**kokulu** sweet smelling, fragrant, odoriferous, odorous, perfumed.

**kokusuz** scentless, odo(u)rless.
**kokuşmak** to putrefy, to whiff.
**kokutmak** 1. to make smell; 2. to make stink; 3. to break wind.
**kol** 1. arm; 2. sleeve; 3. ⊕ handle, bar; lever; 4. limb *(of a tree)*; 5. crank; 6. ♪ neck *(of an instrument)*; 7. branch, division; 8. club *(in a school)*; 9. patrol; 10. ✕ column; 11. troupe; gang; 12. side; ~ askısı ⚓ sling; ~ demiri iron bar; ~ düğmesi cuff link; ~ gezmek 1. to patrol; 2. *fig.* to lurk, to prowl around; ~ kanat olm. *fig.* to take under one's wing; ~ kapağı shirt cuff; ~ -a arm in arm; ~ -a girmek to link arms; ~ nizamı ✕ column; ~ saati wristwatch; -larını sıvamak *fig.* to roll up one's sleeves; -u uzun *fig.* powerful, influential; -una girmek *(b-nin)* to take s.o.'s arm.
**kola** [x .] 1. (laundry) starch; 2. starch paste; ~ yapmak to starch.
**kolaçan etm.** to prowl, to have a look-see round.
**kolalamak** to starch.
**kolalı** starched, starchy.
**kolan** 1. stout band; 2. cinch, girth; 3. rope of a swing.
**kolay** 1. easy, simple; 2. easily; ~ gelsin! may it be easy!; ~ ~ easily; -da handy; -ına bakmak *(bir işin)* to look for the easiest way *(of doing s.th.)*; -ını bulmak *(bşin)* to find an easy way to do *s.th.*
**kolayca** [. x .] 1. easily; 2. fairly easy.
**kolaycacık** [. x . .] very easily.
**kolaylamak** to break the back of *(a job)*.
**kolaylaşmak** to get easy.
**kolaylaştırmak** to facilitate, to ease.
**kolaylık** 1. easiness; 2. facility, means; 3. convenience, labo(u)rsaving device; ~ göstermek to make things easier (-e for).
**kolcu** guard, watchman.
**kolçak** 1. mitten; 2. armlet, armband; 3. sleevelet; 4. chair arm.
**koldaş** colleague, co-worker.
**kolej** private high school.
**koleksiyon** collection; ~ yapmak to collect.
**koleksiyoncu** collector.
**koleksiyonculuk** collecting.
**kolektif** collective, joint; ~ ortaklık unlimited company.
**kolektör** ⚡ collector.
**kolera** cholera.
**kolesterol** ♥ cholesterol.
**koli** parcel, packet.
**kolibasil** coli *(or* colon*)* bacillus.
**kollamak** 1. to watch *(or* look out) for, to be on the alert for; 2. to look after, to protect; 3. to scan.

**kollu** 1. ... sleeved; 2. having ... arms; 3. ✕ of ... columns; 4. ⊕ handled; kısa ~ short-sleeved.
**kolluk** 1. cuff; 2. sleevelet; 3. armband, armlet.
**Kolombiya** *pr. n.* Colombia.
**kolon** 1. column; 2. riser, conduit; 3. *anat.* colon; 4. ⊕ (loud)speaker.
**koloni** colony.
**kolonya** cologne.
**kolordu** ✕ army corps.
**koltuk** 1. armchair, easy chair; 2. armpit; 3. *fig.* flattery; 4. out-of-the-way spot; 5. out-of-the-way shop; 6. *fig.* patronage, pull, favo(u)ritism; 7. *sl.* brothel; ~ altı armpit; ~ değneği crutch; ~ değneğiyle gezmek to go about on crutches; ~ vermek to flatter to his face; -ları kabarmak to swell with pride; -ta olm. *co.* to sponge on s.o.
**koltukçu** 1. maker *or* seller of armchairs; 2. *fig.* flatterer.
**koltuklamak** 1. to tuck under one's arm; 2. to take s.o.'s arm; 3. *fig.* to flatter.
**koltukluk** dress shield.
**kolye** necklace.
**kolyoz** [x .] *zo.* chub maçkerel.
**kolza** [x .] ♀ rape.
**koma** [- .] ⚕ coma; -dan çıkmak to come out of a coma; -ya girmek to go into a coma; -ya sokmak *sl.* to beat to a pulp.
**komak** *s.* koymak.
**komalık** *sl.* 1. enraged; 2. badly beaten up; ~ etm. *sl.* to beat the tar out of s.o.
**komandit,** -ti *(or* ~ şirket) limited *(or* special) partnership; commandite.
**komando** commando.
**komedi, komedya** comedy.
**komedyacı** [. x . .] faky, charlatanic.
**komedyen** comedian; comedienne.
**komi** busboy.
**komik** 1. comical, funny; 2. comedian, comic.
**komikleşmek** to become comical.
**komiklik** funniness, comicality.
**komiser** superintendent of police.
**komisyon** 1. commission, committee; 2. commission, percentage.
**komisyoncu** 1. commission agent, middleman, broker; 2. house agent. *Am.* realtor.
**komita** revolutionary committee.
**komitacı** comitadji.
**komitacılık** activities of an underground revolutionary.
**komite** committee.

komodin commode, bedstand.
komodor ⤋ commodore.
komot, -du dresser, chest of drawers.
kompartıman compartment.
kompas calipers, caliper compass.
kompetan expert, authority.
komple 1. full, filled up; 2. complete, full, entire.
kompleks *psych.* complex.
kompleksli *psych.* having a complex.
komplikasyon ⚕ complication.
komplike complicated.
kompliman compliment; ~ yapmak to compliment.
komplo plot, conspiracy; ~ kurmak to plot, to conspire.
komplocu conspirator, plotter.
komposto compote.
kompozisyon composition (a .*art.*, ♪).
kompozitör ♪ composer.
komprador comprador.
kompres ⚕ compress.
kompresör ⊕ compressor.
komprime tablet.
kompütür computer.
komşu 1. neighbo(u)r; 2. neighbo(u)ring, adjacent; ~ memleketler neighbo(u)ring countries; ~ olm. to become neighbo(u)rs; -nun tavuğu komşuya kaz görünür *pro.* the grass is greener on the other side of the hill (*or* fence).
komşuluk 1. neighbo(u)rhood; 2. neighbo(u)rliness.
komut, -tu ✕ order, command; ~ vermek to command.
komuta ✕ command; ~ etm. to command.
komutan ✕ commander.
komutanlık ✕ commandership.
komünist, -ti communist; ~ partisi communist party.
komünistlik, komünizm communism.
komütatör ⊕ commutator.
konak 1. mansion; 2. stopping place; ~ gibi stately (*house*).
konaklamak to pass (*or* spend) the night, to stay over night.
konca 1. flower bud; 2. *sl.* good-quality hashish.
konç, -cu leg (*of a boot or stocking*).
koncerto [. x .] ♪ concerto.
kondansatör ⊕ condenser.
kondisyon 1. physical fitness; 2. condition.
kondurmak 1. *caus.* of konmak; 2. to tack (-*e* on), to stick (-*e* on); 3. to label s.o. a..., put s.o. down as a...; 4. suddenly to land (-*e* on) (*blow*); suddenly to place (-*e* on) (*kiss*).

kondüktör conductor.
konfederasyon confederation.
konfederatif confederal, confederative.
konfedere confederated.
konfeksiyon ready-to-wear clothing.
konferans 1. lecture; 2. *pol.* conference; ~ salonu lecture theatre, assembly room, auditorium; ~ vermek to give a lecture.
konferansçı lecturer.
konfeti confetti.
konfor comforts, conveniences.
konforlu comfortable, comfy.
kongre [x .] congress.
koni *geom.* cone.
konik *geom.* conic(al).
konjonktür economic situation (*of a country*).
konkasör ⊕ rock crusher.
konkav concave.
konken cooncan, coon king.
konkordato [. . x .] 1. ↯ composition of debts; 2. concordat.
konkur competition, contest.
konkurhipik riding competition.
konmak 1. to stay for the night (-*e* at); 2. to camp (-*e* in); to bivouac (-*e* in); 3. to (a)light (-*e* on), to settle (-*e* on), to perch (-*e* on); 4. F to have s.th. fall in one's lap.
konsantrasyon concentration.
konsantre concentrated; ~ olm. to concentrate (-*e* on).
konsa gizzard.
konsept, -ti concept.
konser concert; ~ vermek to give a concert.
konservatuvar conservatory, conservatoire.
konserve tinned (*or* Am. canned) food.
konsey council.
konsol 1. chest (of drawers); 2. console, corbel, bracket; 3. console table; ~ saati bracket (*or* mantel) clock.
konsolidasyon ⊤ consolidation.
konsolide ⊤ consolidated.
konsolit, -ti consol, consolidated annuity.
konsolos consul.
konsolosluk consulate.
konsomasyon food *or* drink.
konsomatris B-girl.
konsorsiyum ⊤ consortium.
konsültasyon ⚕ consultation.
konşimento ⊤ bill of lading.
kont, -tu count; earl; ~ gibi yaşamak to live like a lord.
kontak 1. short (circuit); 2. *sl.* nutty, cracked; ~ anahtarı car (*or* engine) key; kontağı açmak to start the engine, to switch on the motor; kontağı kapamak

to shut off the engine.

**kontenjan** quota.

**kontes** countess.

**kontluk** countship, earldom.

**kontra** [x .] 1. counter, against; 2. plywood.

**kontrast,** -tı contrast.

**kontrat,** -tı contract.

**kontratak** sports: counterattack.

**kontrbas** ♪ contrabass.

**kontrol,** -lü 1. control; inspection; 2. inspector, controller; ~ etm. to control, to check, to inspect; ~ kalemi circuit- -tester; ~ kulesi ⚓ control tower.

**kontrolcu** controller, inspector.

**kontrplak** plywood.

**konu** topic, subject; matter, theme.

**konuk** guest.

**konukçu** host; hostess.

**konukevi,** -ni guest house.

**konuklamak** to host, to put up, to entertain (a guest).

**konu komşu** neighbo(u)rhood, the neigh- bo(u)rs.

**konuksever** hospitable.

**konukseverlik** hospitality.

**konum** location, site.

**konuşkan** talkative, loquacious, chatty.

**konuşkanlık** talkativeness, loquacity, chattiness.

**konuşma** 1. vn. of konuşmak; 2. speech, talk, lecture; 3. conversation; discus- sion; ~ dili colloquial language, everyday speech; ~ yapmak to make a speech.

**konuşmacı** 1. lecturer; 2. speaker, an- nouncer.

**konuşmak** 1. to speak (ile to), to talk (ile to); 2. to converse, to chat; 3. to com- municate; 4. to discuss, to talk (-i about); 5. to be on speaking (or friendly) terms (ile with) 6. F to look sharp, to be eye- -catching.

**konuşturmak** caus. of konuşmak, part. to make talk (a musical instrument).

**konuşucu** lecturer, speaker.

**konut,** -tu 1. house, dwelling, residence; 2. domicile.

**konveks** convex.

**konvektör** convector.

**konvoy** convoy.

**konyak** cognac, brandy.

**kooperatif** cooperative, co-op.

**kooperatifçi** 1. member of a co-op; 2. manager of a co-op.

**kooperatifçilik** economic cooperation, cooperative system.

**kooperatifleşmek** to become a cooperative.

**koordinasyon** coordination.

**koordinat,** -tı ∦ coordinate.

**kopanakı** bobbin (lace).

**koparmak** caus. of kopmak, part. 1. to break (or tear) off; 2. to pluck, to pick, to snap off; 3. to let out, to set up (noise); 4. (b-den bşi) F to get (or wangle) s.th. out of s.o.

**kopça** hook and eye.

**kopçalamak** to hook, to fasten.

**kopil** sl. street Arab, urchin, gamin.

**kopkolay** [x . .] as easy as pie.

**kopmak,** (-ar) 1. to break, to snap; 2. to break out (storm, war, etc.); 3. to ache violently.

**kopoy** hound.

**kopsi kefali** etm. sl. to behead.

**kopuk** 1. broken (or snapped) off; 2. F tramp, bum, punk; ~ alayı band of vagabonds.

**kopuz** lute-like instrument.

**kopya** 1. copy; 2. cheating; ~ çekmek to copy, to cheat; ~ defteri copybook; ~ etm. to copy; ~ kâğıdı carbon paper; ~ mürekkebi copying ink; -sını çıkarmak to copy.

**kopyacı** 1. copier; 2. cheater, cribber.

**kor**[1] ✕ corps.

**kor**[2] 1. ember; 2. fiery red; ~ dökmek to form a bed of glowing coals; ~ gibi red- -hot.

**koramiral,** -li vice admiral.

**kordele** ribbon.

**kordiplomatik** corps diplomatique, diplo- matic corps.

**kordon** 1. cord (a. ∮), cordon, braid; 2. cord, rope; pull; 3. cordon, stringcourse; 4. cordon (of police); ~ altına almak to cordon off, to isolate.

**Kore** pr. n. Korea.

**Koreli** pr. n. Korean.

**Korgeneral,** -li lieutenant general, corps commander.

**koridor** corridor.

**korkak** 1. cowardly, fearful, timid; 2. coward, poltroon.

**korkaklık** cowardice, fearfulness.

**korkmak,** (-ar) to be afraid (or scared) (-den of), to fear, to dread.

**korku** fear, dread, terror; phobia; fright; ~ filmi horror film; ~ saçmak to spread terror; ~ vermek to terrorize.

**korkulu** 1. scary, dreadful; 2. dangerous, perilous.

**korkuluk** 1. scarecrow; 2. balustrade, banister; parapet; 3. fig. figurehead, cipher.

**korkunç,** -cu 1. terrible, awful, dreadful; 2. tremendous, terrific, rightful; 3. terrifically, awfully.

**korkusuz 1.** fearless, intrepid; **2.** safe.

**korkutmak** *caus. of* korkmak, *part.* **1.** to scare, to frighten, to threaten; to intimidate; **2.** to scare off (*or* away).

**korna** [x .] horn; ~ çalmak to hoot, to honk.

**korner** *football:* corner (kick).

**kornet,** -ti ♪ cornet.

**korniş** cornice.

**korno** [x .] **1.** ♪ French horn; **2.** powder horn.

**koro** [x .] chorus, choir.

**koroydo** [. x .] *sl.* idiotic, foolish.

**korporasyon** corporation.

**korsa** corset; girdle.

**korsan** pirate, corsair; ~ gemisi pirate ship; ~ radyo pirate radio station.

**korsanlık** piracy.

**korse** = korsa.

**kort,** -tu court.

**korta, korte** courting; flirting; ~ etm. to court; to flirt (*ile* with).

**kortej** cortege.

**koru** grove, coppice, copse.

**korucu** forest watchman.

**korugan** *neol.* ✕ blockhouse.

**koruk** unripe grape; ~ lüferi small bluefish (*caught in August*).

**koruluk** grove, coppice, copse.

**koruma** *vn. of* korumak; ~ görevlisi bodyguard, bouncer; ~ polisi police bodyguard.

**korumak 1.** to protect, to guard, to watch over, to shield; to defend; **2.** to cover (*expense*).

**korunak** shelter.

**koruncak** *neol.* case, box.

**korunga** ✿ trefoil.

**korunmak** *pass. or refl. of* korumak, *part.* to safeguard (*or* protect) o.s. (*-den* against); to escape, to avoid.

**koruyucu 1.** protective; **2.** protector, defender.

**kosinüs** ▲ cosine.

**koskoca** [x . .] very big (*or* great).

**koskocaman** [x . . .] enormous, huge.

**kostüm 1.** suit; **2.** *thea.* costume.

**koşaltı** yoking *or* harnessing two animals together.

**koşmaca** tag.

**koşmak,** (-ar) **1.** to run; **2.** (*ardından, arkasından, peşinden*) to pursue, to run after, to chase; **3.** (*yardımına*) to run to s.o.'s assistance (*or* aid); **4.** (*şart*) to make it a condition, to stipulate; **5.** to harness, to hitch (-e to); **6.** to hitch up (*horse*); **7.** to put to work; koşar adımlarla at a run; koşar adım marş! run!

**koşturmak** *caus. of* koşmak, *part.* **1.** to send s.o. on (*an errand*); to hurry s.o.; **2.** to race (*horse*).

**koşu** race; ~ alanı hippodrome; ~ atı racehorse; ~ yolu racecourse, racetrack; bir ~ yardım getir run for help.

**koşucu** runner.

**koşuk** verse.

**koşul** condition, stipulation, provision.

**koşullandırmak** *psych.* to condition.

**koşullanmak** *psych.* to be conditioned.

**koşullu 1.** *psych.* conditioned; **2.** conditional.

**koşulsuz** unconditional.

**koşum** harness.

**koşuntu 1.** supporters, followers; **2.** accomplices.

**koşuşmak 1.** to run (*or* rush) together; **2.** to run hither and thither, to run about.

**koşuşturmak** to run hither and yon, to bustle about.

**koşut,** -tu parallel.

**kot,** -tu (blue) jeans, denius.

**kota** ↑ quota.

**kotarmak 1.** to dish up (*food*); **2.** *fig.* to finish, to complete.

**kotlamak** to spell out (*word*).

**kotlet,** -ti cutlet.

**kotletpane** breaded cutlet.

**kotonperle** pearl cotton.

**kotra** ↓ cutter.

**kova 1.** bucket, pail; **2.** ♌ *ast.* Aquarius.

**kovalamaca** tag.

**kovalamak** to chase, to pursue, to run after.

**kovan 1.** (bee)hive; **2.** cartridge case.

**kovboy** [x .] cowboy; ~ filmi western, cowboy film.

**kovcu 1.** backbiting; **2.** talebearing.

**kovlamak 1.** to run down, to disparage; **2.** to tell (*or* inform) (on).

**kovmak,** (-ar) **1.** to dismiss, to drive away, to repel; **2.** to expel, to get rid of.

**kovuk** hollow, cavity.

**kovuşturma** ⚖ prosecution, investigation; ~ yapmak to prosecute.

**kavuşturmak** ⚖ to prosecute, to investigate.

**koy** cove, small bay.

**koyncak** container.

**koyak** valley.

**koymak 1.** to put, to place (-e in); **2.** to let go; **3.** *fig.* to upset, to bother, to affect; to move; **4.** to set aside, to appropriate.

**koyu 1.** thick (*liquid*); **2.** dense (*fog*); **3.** deep, dark (*colour*); **4.** *fig.* fervid, extreme, rabid, dyed-in-the-wool; ~ kırmızı dark red; ~ yeşil dark green.

**koyulaşmak 1.** to thicken *(liquid);* **2.** to darken *(colour).*

**koyulaştırmak 1.** to thicken *(liquid);* **2.** to darken *(colour).*

**koyulmak** to set to *(or* about), to embark *(-e* upon).

**koyuluk 1.** thickness *(liquid);* **2.** deepness, darkness *(colour);* **3.** *fig.* extremeness, rabidity.

**koyun¹ 1.** *zo.* sheep; **2.** *F* simpleton; ~ bakışlı silly, simpleton *(in look);* ~ eti mutton; -un bulunmadığı yerde keçiye Abdurrahman Çelebi derler *pro.* in the country of the blind, the one-eyed man is king.

**koyun², -ynu 1.** bosom, breast; **2.** *fig.* arms, embrace; ~ koyuna in each other's arms; koynuna girmek *(b-nin)* to go to bed with *s.o.,* to sleep with *s.o.;* koynunda yılan beslemek *fig.* to nurse a viper in one's bosom, to have a snake in the grass.

**koyungözü, -nü ♀** feverfew.

**koy(u)vermek,** to set free, to let go.

**koz 1.** walnut; **2.** *cards;* trump *(a. fig.);* ~ kırmak **1.** to play a trump card; **2.** *F* to be up to no good; -u kaybetmek *fig.* to come out the loser; -unu oynamak *fig.* to play one's trump *(or* best) card; -unu paylaşmak *fig.* to settle *(or* square *or* balance) accounts *(ile* with).

**koza** [x .] **1.** cocoon; **2.** pod; boll.

**koza(la)k 1.** = koza; **2.** cone; **3.** unripe fruit.

**kozalaklı** coniferous.

**kozalaklılar ♀** Coniferae.

**kozalaksı** pineal; ~ bez pineal gland *(or* body).

**kozmetik** cosmetic.

**kozmik** cosmic.

**kozmonot, -tu** cosmonaut.

**kozmopolit, -ti** cosmopolitan.

**kozmos** *ast.* cosmos.

**köcek 1.** *zo.* foal *(of a camel);* **2.** boy dancer; **3.** *fig.* light-minded person.

**köfte** meatball; croquette.

**köfteci** maker and seller of meatball.

**köftehor** *co.* lucky dog.

**köfter** a kind of grape sweet.

**köftün** oil meal.

**köhne 1.** old, ramshackle, dilapidated; **2.** outmoded, autdated.

**kök, -kü 1.** root *(a. ♀);* **2.** origin; **3.** *♀* radical; ~ işareti *A* radical sign; ~ salmak to take root *(a. fig.);* ~ söktürmek *(b-ne)* to make things warm for *s.o.;* -ünden root and branch; -ünü kazımak to root out, to exterminate, to eradicate,

to extirpate.

**kökboyası, -nı 1. ♀** madder plant; **2.** madder (root); alizarin.

**kokçu** herbalist.

**köken 1.** origin, source; **2.** homeland, place of origin; **3.** *gr.* root (form).

**köklemek 1.** to uproot; **2.** to quilt, to tuft *(mattress);* **3.** to tune (saz).

**köklenmek, kökleşmek** to take root *(a. fig.).*

**köklü** rooted *(a. fig.)*

**köknar ♀** fir (tree).

**köksel** radicular.

**köksüz** rootless *(a. fig.)*

**kökten** radical, fundamental.

**köktencilik** radicalism.

**kökteş** cognate *(word).*

**köle** slave.

**kölelik** slavery, servitude, bondage.

**kölemen** *hist.* Mameluke.

**kömür 1.** coal; **2.** charcoal; **3.** coal-black; ~ gibi coal-black; ~ gözlü with coal-black eyes; ~ işçisi collier, coal miner; ~ ocağı coal mine.

**kömürcü 1.** coal dealer; **2.** stoker; ~ çırağına dönmek to get black all over.

**kömürleşmek** to coalify, to char.

**kömürlük 1.** coal cellar; coalbin; **2. ↓** bunker.

**köpek 1.** *zo.* dog; **2.** *sl.* cur; ~ gibi cringingly; köpeği öldürene sürütürler *pro.* it is the guilty one who suffers.

**köpekbalığı, -nı** *zo.* shark.

**köpekdişi, -ni** cuspid, canine tooth.

**köpeklemek 1.** to be dog-tired; **2.** *fig.* to be humiliated.

**köpeklenmek, köpekleşmek** to fawn, to cringe, to grovel.

**köpekmemesi, -ni** large bubo.

**köpoğlu, -nu** [x - .] *(a.* ~ köpek) *F* **1.** bastard; **2.** fox.

**köprü 1.** bridge; **2.** hasp *(of a lock);* ~ altı çocuğu guttersnipe; ~ başı **1.** *X* bridgehead; **2.** *fig.* foothold.

**köprücü 1.** bridge builder; **2.** *X* pontooning *(unit).*

**köprücük** *(a.* ~ kemiği) *anat.* collarbone, clavicle.

**köpük** foam, froth; suds.

**köpüklü** foamy, frothy; sudsy.

**köpürmek 1.** to foam, to froth, to spume; **2.** *fig.* to foam at the mouth.

**kör 1.** blind; **2.** dull, blunt *(knife. etc.);* **3.** dim *(light);* **4.** *fig.* evil; unlucky; ~ kütük *fig.* pissed, corked, as drunk as a lord; ~ olası! damn it!; ~ talih bad *(or* hard) luck, evil destiny; ~ topal *F* after a fashion; -le yatan şaşı kalkar *pro.* the rotten apple injures its neighbo(u)rs, who keeps company with the wolf will learn how to howl; -ü -une blindly, at random.

**körbağırsak** *anat.* cecum, blind gut.

**kördüğüm** *fig.* Gordian knot.

**körebe** blindman's buff.

**körelmek 1.** *biol.* to atrophy; **2.** to get dull *(or* blunt*) (knife, etc.);* **3.** to die down *(fire).*

**köreltmek** to dull, to blunt *(knife, etc.).*

**körfez** gulf; bay; inlet.

**körkandil** = kor kütük.

**körkuyu** dry well.

**körlemeden** blindly, at random.

**körlenmek, körleşmek 1.** to become dull *(or* blunt*) (knife, etc.);* **2.** to go dry *(well);* **3.** *fig.* to decline, to become blunt *(mental power).*

**körleştirmek, körletmek 1.** to dull, to blunt *(knife, etc.);* **2.** to cause to fail *(mental power);* **3.** to make go dry *(well).*

**körlük 1.** blindness; **2.** bluntness, dullness *(of a knife, etc.)*

**Köroğlu.** -nu **1.** *pr. n. name of a hero in Turkish folktales;* **2.** F wife, the missus.

**körpe** fresh, tender.

**körpecik** *emph. of* körpe very fresh *(or* tender*).*

**körpelik** freshness; tenderness.

**körük 1.** bellows; **2.** accordion coupling *(on a bus or train).*

**körüklemek 1.** to fan with bellows; **2.** *fig.* to incite.

**körükleyici** *fig.* instigative.

**kös** big drum; ~ dinlemiş *fig.* thick-skinned, hardened.

**köse** beardless; ~ sakal very sparse b ard.

**kösele** stout leather; ~ gibi leathery *(food);* ~ suratlı F shameless.

**köseletaşı,** -nı **1.** sandstone; **2.** lapstone; **3.** whetstone.

**kösemen** lead goat *(or* ram*);* bellwether.

**kös kös** looking neither right nor left.

**kösköturüm** [x . . .] completely paralyzed.

**kösnümek** to be in heat *(or* rut*).*

**köstebek 1.** zo. mole; **2.** ♀ scrofula.

**köstek 1.** hobble; **2.** watch *(or* key*)* chain; **3.** *fig.* obstacle, impediment; ~ olm to hinder. to impede; ~ vurmak to hobble *(horse);* kösteği kırmak *fig.* to beat it.

**kösteklemek 1.** to hobble. fo fetter *(horse);* **2.** *fig.* to hamper. to impede.

**köşe 1.** corner; **2.** *fig.* nook; ~ başı **1.** street corner; **2.** corner...; ~ bucak every

nook and cranny; ~ kadısı stay-at-home; ~ kapmaca puss in the corner; -sine çekilmek to retire into one's shell;'-yi dönmek F to strike it rich.

**köşebent** ⊕ **1.** angle iron; **2.** cornerpiece.

**köşegen** Å diagonal.

**köşeleme** diagonally.

**köşeli** cornered, angled; ~ ayraç *typ.* (square) bracket.

**köşk,** -kü villa, pleasure-house.

**kötek** beating; ~ atmak to cane; ~ yemek to get the cane.

**kötü 1.** bad; **2.** worthless; **3.** wicked, evil; **4.** F terribly; ~ beslenme malnutrition; ~ günler hard times; ~ huy bad habit; ~ kadın prostitute; ~ kişi olm. to be in s.o.'s bad books; ~ söylemek *(b-i için)* to speak ill of *s.o.;* ~ yola düşmek *(or* sapmak*)* to go on *(or* walk*)* the streets; -ye kullanmak to misuse, to abuse.

**kötücül** Malicious, evil, malevolent.

**kötülemek** to speak ill *(-i* of*),* to run down.

**kötüleşmek 1.** to become bad, to deteriorate; **2.** to be on the streets.

**kötülük 1.** badness, wickedness; **2.** harm, wrong; ~ etm. *(b-ne)* to do *s.o.* harm.

**kötülükçü** evil, wicked.

**kötümsemek** to belittle, to disparage, to think ill *(-i* of*).*

**kötümser** pessimistic.

**kötümserlik** pessimism.

**kötürüm** paralyzed, crippled.

**kötürümleşmek** to become paralyzed.

**köy** village; ♀ İşleri Bakanlığı Ministry of Village Affairs; ~ muhtarı village headman.

**köydeş** fellow villager.

**köylü** villager, peasant; fellow villager.

**köyodası,** -nı village social room.

**köz** ashes, embers.

**közlemek** to broil *(or* roast*)* over charcoal.

**kral 1.** king; **2.** *fig.* super, A1, top-notch.

**kraliçe** queen.

**kraliçelik** queenship, queenhood.

**kraliyet,** -ti **1.** kingdom; **2.** kingship; ailesi royal family.

**krallık 1.** kingdom; **2.** kingship.

**kramp,** -pı ♀ cramp; ~ girmek *(ayağına)* to be seized with cramp.

**krampon** screw-in stud.

**krank,** -kı ⊕ crankshaft.

**krater** crater.

**kravat,** -tı (neck)tie.

**kredi** credit; ~ kartı credit card; ~ mektubu letter of credit.

**krem** cream.

**krema** [x .] cream; icing.

kremkaramel crème caramel.
kremlemek to apply cream (-i to).
kremşantiyi creme chantilly.
krep, -pi crepe.
krepon crepon; ~ kâğıdı crepe paper.
kreş day nursery, crèche.
kriket, -ti *sports:* cricket.
kriko [x .] jack; -ya almak to jack up.
kriminoloji criminology.
kristal, -li crystal.
kriter criterion.
kritik 1. critique; 2. critical *(a. ₺)*, crucial.
kriz 1. crisis; 2. fit, attack; 3. fit of
hysterics; ~ geçirmek to have a fit of
hysterics.
krizalit, -ti *biol.* chrysalis.
kroke croquet.
kroki [x .] sketch; -sini . almak (or yapmak) to sketch, to outline.
krom chrome, chromium.
kromozom *biol.* chromosome.
kronik chronic.
kronoloji chronology.
kronometre [. . x .] chronometer, stop-
watch.
kros cross-country race.
kroscu cross-country runner.
kroşe *boring:* hook.
krupiye croupier.
kruvaze double-breasted *(garment)*.
kruvazör ⚓ cruiser.
kubbe dome, cupola.
kubbeli domed.
kubur 1. drain-hole; drainpipe; 2. quiver;
3. holster.
kuburluk 1. holster; 2. powder flask.
kucak 1. embrace; lap; 2. armful; ~ açmak *(b-ne)* to receive *s.o.* with open
arms; ~ çocuğu babe in arms; ~ dolusu
armful; ~ kucağa in each other's arms;
~ ~ by the armloads *(or armfuls)*; ku-
cağına düşmek to fall into the midst (-*in*
of).
kucaklamak 1. to embrace, to hug; 2. to
surround.
kucaklaşmak to embrace *(or hug)* each
other.
kuçukuçu doggy, bow-wow.
kudret, -ti 1. power, strength, might; 2.
omnipotence *(of God);* 3. capacity,
ability; 4. the wherewithal; ~ hamamı
Turkish bath; ~ helvası manna; -ten
natural.
kudretli powerful, mighty.
kudretsiz powerless, incapable.
kudurgan wild, uncontrollable *(person)*.
kudurmak 1. to become rabid, to go mad;

2. *fig.* to be foaming at the mouth, to be
beside o.s. with anger; 3. *fig.* to go wild,
to romp.
kuduruk 1. rabid, mad; 2. *fig.* wild *(person)*.
kuduz 1. rabies, hydrophobia; 2. rabid,
hydrophobic.
Kudüs *pr. n.* Jerusalem.
kuğu *zo.* swan.
kuğurmak to coo *(pigeon)*.
kuintet, -ti ♪ quintet.
kuka ball.
kukla [x .] 1. puppet; marionette; 2.
puppet show; 3. *fig.* puppet, tool; ~ hükümet puppet government.
kuklacı puppeteer.
kuku *zo.* cuckoo.
kukuleta [. . x .] hood; cowl.
kukuletalı hooded.
kukulya [. x .] silkworm cocoon; ~ fırtınası *storm occuring about the middle of
April.*
kukumav *zo.* owlet; ~ gibi all alone.
kul 1. slave; 2. mortal, man, human
being *(in relation to God);* ~ köle olm.
*fig.* to be at s.o.'s beck and call; ~ yapısı
manmade.
kula [x .] dun-colo(u)red *(horse)*.
kulaç 1. fathom; 2. *swimming:* stroke;
crawl; ~ atmak to crawl; to swim a
stroke.
kulaçlamak 1. to fathom; 2. to crawl.
kulağakaçan *zo.* earwig.
kulak 1. ear; 2. *zo.* gill *(of a fish);* 3. ♪
tuning peg; 4. lug, handle, handgrip; ~
asmak to lend one's ear(s); ~ asmamak
*fig.* to turn a deaf ear (-*e* to); ~ dolu un-
luğu knowledge picked up here and
there; ~ erimi earshot; ~ kabartmak to
prick up one's ears; ~ kepçesi *anat.*
earlap; ~ kesilmek to be all ears; ~ kiri
earwax; ~ misafiri olm. to overhear, to
eavesdrop; ~ tıkamak to stop one's ears
(-*e* to); ~ uğultusu ringing in the ears; ~
vermek to give *(or* lend an) ear (-*e* to); ~
yolu *anat.* auditory canal; kulağı ağır
işitmek to be hard of hearing; kulağı delik quick of hearing; kulağı okşamak to
be pleasant to the ear; kulağına çalınmak to come to one's ears; kulağına girmek *(b-nin)* to take note (of), to heed;
kulağına küpe olm. to be a lesson (-*in* to),
to serve as a warning (-*in* to); kulağını
çekmek *(b-nin)* to pull *s.o.'s* ear; kulağını doldurmak *(b-nin)* to put *s.o.* in the
know, to fill *s.o.* in; -ları cınlasın! I hope
his ears are burning!; -larına kadar kızarmak to blush to the top of one's ears;

-larını dikmek *fig.* to prick up its ears *(animal)*; -tan dolma picked up *(knowledge)*; -tan kulağa on the grapevine.

**kulakaltı**, -nı parotid; ~ bezi parotid gland.

**kulakçı** ear specialist.

**kulakçık** *anat.* atrium, auricle.

**kulakçın** ear(f)lap.

**kulaklı** eared.

**kulaklık 1.** earphone, headphone; earpiece; **2.** hearing aid; **3.** = kulakçın.

**kulakmemesi**, -ni earlobe.

**kulaksız** earless.

**kulakzarı**, -nı eardrum.

**kulampara** [. x . .] pederast.

**kule** tower; turret.

**kuleli** towered; turreted; ♀ Askeri Lisesi Kuleli Military High School.

**kulis 1.** *thea.* backstage, wings; **2.** † curb exchange; ~ yapmak to lobby, to work behind the scenes.

**kullanılmış** used, secondhand.

**kullanım 1.** use, using; **2.** *gr.* usage.

**kullanış** using; ~ tarzı usage, way of using.

**kullanışlı** useful, handy; serviceable.

**kullanışsız** useless, unhandy; unserviceable.

**kullanmak 1.** to use; **2.** to employ; **3.** to drive *(car)*; to fly *(plane)*; to steer *(ship)*; **4.** to take, to consume, to use.

**kullap**, -bı [ā] hasp.

**kulluk 1.** slavery, servitude; **2.** worship, adoration.

**kulp**, -pu **1.** handle; **2.** *fig.* pretext; ~ takmak to find a pretext; -unu bulmak *(bir işin)* to find a way out of *s.th.*

**kulplu** handled; ~ beygir *sports:* pommel horse.

**kuluçka** [. x .] **1.** broody; **2.** hen bird; ~ devri incubation period; ~ makinesi incubator; -ya oturmak *(or yatmak)* to brood, to incubate, to set.

**kulun** newborn foal.

**kulunç 1.** shoulder pain; **2.** colic; **3.** cramp.

**kulübe 1.** hut, shed, cottage; shanty, shack; **2.** ✕ sentry box; **3.** telephone box *(or booth)*; **4.** tollbooth.

**kulüp**, -bü **1.** club; **2.** clubhouse.

**kulvar** lane.

**kum 1.** sand; **2.** ⚕ gravel *(in the kidneys)*; ~ çölü sandy desert; ~ gibi loads of; ~ saati hourglass; ~ torbası sandbag; -da oynamak *fig.* to whistle for it.

**kuma** fellow wife.

**kumanda** [. x .] ✕ command; ~ etm. to command, to be in command *(-e of)*.

**kumandan** commander.

**kumandanlık** commandership.

**kumanya** [. x .] **1.** food *(to be eaten while traveling)*; **2.** ✕ soldier's *(or field)* rations.

**kumar** gambling *(a. fig.)*; ~ masası gaming table; ~ oynamak to gamble, to game.

**kumarbaz, kumarcı** gambler.

**kumarhane** [. . - .] gaming-house, gambling-house.

**kumaş** cloth, fabric, material.

**kumbara** [x . .] **1.** piggy bank, money-box; **2.** coin *(or token)* box *(of a pay telephone, etc.)*; **3.** † (bomb) shell.

**kumbaracı** † bombardier.

**kumkuma 1.** jug. vase; **2.** *fig.* instigator, spreader.

**kumlu** sandy.

**kumluk** sandy (place).

**kumpanya 1.** † company, firm; **2.** *thea.* troupe; **3.** *fig.* gang, band, bunch.

**kumpas** *s.* kompas.

**kumral 1.** brown *(hair)*; **2.** brown-haired *(person)*.

**kumru** *zo.* (turtle)dove; ~ göğsü iridescent. ·

**kumsal** sandy (beach).

**kumsallık** sandiness.

**kumtaşı**, -nı sandstone.

**kumul** (sand) dune.

**kunda** *zo.* a kind of poisonous spider.

**kundak 1.** swaddling clothes; **2.** gunstock; **3.** bundle of rags; ~ sokmak **1.** to set fire *(-e* to); **2.** to sabotage, to wreck; **3.** *(arasına) fig.* to set *persons* by the ears.

**kundakçı 1.** arsonist, incendiary, firebug; **2.** *fig.* mischief-maker.

**kundakçılık** arson, incendiarism.

**kundaklamak 1.** to swaddle; **2.** to set fire *(to);* **3.** *fig.* to sabotage, to wreck.

**kundaklı** swaddled.

**kundura** [x . .] shoe; ~ tamircisi shoe-repairer, cobbler.

**kunduracı 1.** shoemaker; **2.** shoe-repairer, cobbler; **3.** seller of shoes.

**kunduz** *zo.* beaver.

**kunt**, -tu stout, solid.

**kupa¹** [x .] **1.** cup; **2.** *cards:* heart; ~ finali cup final.

**kupa²** [x .] coupé.

**kupkuru** [x . .] *emph. of* kuru, bone-dry, as dry as a bone.

**kupon** coupon.

**kupür** clipping.

**kur¹ 1.** † rate of exchange; **2.** course *(of studies).*

**kur² courtship**, flirtation; ~ yapmak *(b-ne)* to court *s.o.,* to pay court to s.o.

**kura 1.** drawing of lots; **2.** lot; **3.** ✗ conscription; ~ çekmek to draw lots; -sı olm. *(bir yılın)* ✗ to be among those conscripted in *(a certain year)*.
**kurabiye** [ā] cooky, cookie.
**kurak** dry, rainless, arid.
**kuraklık** drought.
**kural** rule, regulation.
**kuraldışı** exceptional.
**kurallı** *gr.* regular.
**kuralsız** *gr.* irregular.
**kuram** theory.
**kuramcı** theorist, theoretician.
**kuramsal** theoretical.
**Kuran** *pr. n.* Koran, the Quran; ~ı Kerim the Holy Koran.
**kurander** draught, *Am.* draft.
**kurbağa** *zo.* frog; ~ adam frogman.
**kurbağacık 1.** froglet; **2.** small monkey wrench; **3.** handgrip.
**kurbağalama** *swimming:* breast stroke.
**kurban** [ā] **1.** sacrifice; **2.** victim *(of an accident)*; **3.** ♀ *(Bayramı) isl.* the Feast of the Sacrifice, the Greater Bairam; **4.** *fig.* martyr; **5.** P hey!, hello mate!; ~ etm. to sacrifice (-e to); ~ gitmek to fall victim *(or a prey)* (-e to); ~ kesmek to kill an animal as a sacrifice.
**kurbanlık** sacrificial *(animal)*.
**kurcalamak 1.** to monkey about *(or* tamper) (-i with); **2.** to rub, to irritate, to scratch; **3.** *fig.* to delve into, dwell on *(a matter)*.
**kurdele** ribbon.
**kurdeşen** (nettle) rash, urticaria.
**kurgu 1.** knob, winder; clock *(or* watch) key; **2.** ⊕ installation; **3.** *phls.* speculation; **4.** assembly and editing *(of a film)*.
**kurgubilim** science fiction.
**kurgusal** theoretical, speculative.
**kurlağan** ৠ whitlow, felon.
**kurmak,** (-ar) **1.** to set up, to assemble, to put together; **2.** to wind *(clock)*; **3.** to set, to lay *(table)*; **4.** to pitch *(tent)*; **5.** to set *(trap)*; **6.** to cock *(gun)*; **7.** to found, to establish; to form; **8.** to plan, to plot; **9.** to ponder, to dwell (on); **10.** to indulge in *(daydreams)*.
**kurmay** ✗ staff; ~ subay staff officer.
**kurna** [x.] marble basin.
**kurnaz** cunning, foxy, sly.
**kurnazca** cunningly, foxily.
**kurnazlık** cunning, foxiness.
**kuron** crown.
**kurs¹** course; ~ görmek to take a course.
**kurs²** disk *(a. ast.)*
**kursak 1.** crop, craw; **2.** F maw, stomach.

**kurşun 1.** ♊ lead; **2.** bullet; **3.** lead seal; ~ atmak to fire a gun; ~ dökmek to melt lead and pour it into cold water over the head of a sick person *(in order to break an evil spell)*; ~ gibi as heavy as lead; ~ işlemez bullet-proof; ~ yağdırmak to shower bullets (-e on); ~ yarası bullet wound; -a dizmek to execute by shooting.
**kurşuni** [. - -] leaden, gray.
**kurşunkalem** (lead) pencil.
**kurşunlamak 1.** to lead; **2.** to shoot.
**kurşunlu** leaden.
**kurt,** -du **1.** *zo.* wolf; **2.** worm, maggot; **3.** *fig.* fox; ~ dökmek to pass worms; ~ dumanlı havayı sever *pro.* a person who is up to no good loves a chaotic situation; ~ gibi *fig.* foxy, shrewd; ~ sürüsü a pack of wolves; ~ yemiş worm-eaten; -larını dökmek to have one's fling, to have the time of one's life; -unu kırmak to satisfy one's whims.
**kurtarıcı 1.** savio(u)r; **2.** *mot.* wrecker, breakdown lorry, tow truck.
**kurtarmak 1.** to save, to rescue; **2.** to extricate from *(trouble)*; **3.** to redeem *(s.th. pawned)*; **4.** to recover *(losses)*; **5.** to be enough to satisfy the seller; daha aşağısı kurtarmaz I can't sell it for less.
**kurtçuk** larva.
**kurtköpeği,** -ni Alsatian, German shepherd.
**kurtlanmak 1.** to get wormy; **2.** *fig.* to fidget; **3.** *fig.* to go stir crazy.
**kurtlu 1.** wormy; **2.** *fig.* fidgety; ~ peynir *fig.* fidgety child.
**kurtmasalı,** -nı cock-and-bull story.
**kurtulmak 1.** to escape; to be saved *(or* rescued); **2.** to get *(or* break) loose *(animal)*, **3.** to slip *(or* fall) out (of); **4.** to be completed *(or* finished); **5.** to get rid of *(s.th. or s.o. unpleasant)*; **6.** to give birth.
**kurtuluş 1.** liberation; **2.** salvation; **3.** escape; ♀ Savaşı the Turkish War of Independence.
**kuru 1.** dry; dried; **2.** bare, unfurnished, unadorned; **3.** empty, vain, hollow; **4.** dead *(plant)*; **5.** thin, emaciated; **6.** curt *(utterance)*; ~ fasulye kidney *(or* haricot) bean; ~ gürültü much ado about nothing; ~ hastalık P. tuberculosis; ~ hava dry air; ~ iftira sheer calumny; ~ incir dried fig; ~ kafes *fig.* skin and bones; ~ meyve dried fruit(s); ~ öksürük dry cough; ~ sıkı **1.** blank *(shot)*; *fig.* bluff; ~ soğuk dry cold; ~ temizle-

**me** dry cleaning; ~ temizleyici dry cleaner; ~ üzüm raisins; ~ yemiş nuts; -nun yanında yaş da yanar *pro.* the innocent suffers with the guilty.

**kurucu** founder; ~ meclis constitutional assembly (*or* convention).

**kurukafa 1.** skull; **2.** *fig.* dope.

**kurukahve** (roasted and ground) coffee.

**kurukahveci** seller of ground coffee.

**kurul** committee.

**kurulamak** to dry, to wipe dry.

**kurulanmak** *pass. or refl. of* kurulamak, *part.* to dry o.s.

**kurulmak 1.** *pass. of* kurmak; **2.** to nestle (*or* snuggle) down (-*e* in); **3.** to swagger, to show off.

**kurultay** general meeting (*or* assembly).

**kuruluk** dryness.

**kuruluş** organization, institution, establishment.

**kurum 1.** institution, foundation, association; **2.** soot; **3.** *fig.* swagger; ~ ~ kurulmak to be stuck-up; ~ satmak to put on airs.

**kurumak 1.** to dry, to get dry; **2.** to dry up (*stream*); **3.** to die (*plant*); **4.** to become skinny.

**kurumlanmak 1.** to put on airs; **2.** to get sooty.

**kurumlaştırmak** to institutionalize.

**kurumlu 1.** sooty; **2.** *fig.* conceited, stuck-up.

**kurumsal** institutional.

**kurunmak** to dry o.s.

**kuruntu** delusion, illusion, fancy.

**kuruntulu** neurotic, hypochondriac.

**kuruş** kurush, piastre, *Am.* piaster.

**kuruşlandırmak** to itemize.

**kurutma kâğıdı** blotting paper.

**kurutmak 1.** to dry; **2.** to wither (*plant*); **3.** to blot; **4.** to dehumidify; to desiccate.

**kurye** *pol.* courier.

**kuskun** crupper; -u düşük *fig.* in disgrace, out of favo(u)r.

**kuskus** couscous.

**kusmak,** (-ar) to vomit, to throw (*or* bring) up, to spew, to puke.

**kusmuk** vomit.

**kusturmak** to puke.

**kusturucu** emetic.

**kusur** [. -] fault, defect, flaw; shortcoming; drawback; ~ etm. to be at fault: -a bakmamak to overlook, to pardon, to let it pass; -a bakma! I beg your pardon!, excuse me!

**kusurlu 1.** faulty, defective; **2.** at fault, in the wrong.

**kusursuz** flawless, faultless, perfect.

**kuş 1.** *zo.* bird; **2.** *sl.* wet behind the ears; **3.** *sl.* penis, pecker, cock; ~ beyinli bird-brained, nit-witted, dizzy; ~ gibi as light as a feather (*or* air *or* thistledown); ~ kafesi gibi small and beautiful (*house*); ~ kanadıyle gitmek to go like a bird, to go off at a terrific bat; ~ uçmaz kervan geçmez bir yer desolate place; ~ uçurmamak *fig.* not to allow anyone *or* anything to escape; -a benzetmek to mess up, to spoil.

**kuşak 1.** sash; girdle, loin-cloth; cummerbund; **2.** generation; **3.** strap; **4.** brace; **5.** *geogr.* zone; **6.** *ast.* Saturn.

**kuşaklamak 1.** to band, to tie up; **2.** to brace.

**kuşam** *s.* giyim kuşam.

**kuşane** [ā] aviary.

**kuşanmak 1.** to gird (*or* put) on (*sword, etc.*); **2.** *s.* giyinip kuşanmak.

**kuşatma** *vn. of* kuşatmak, *part.* X siege.

**kuşatmak 1.** to gird (*ile* with); **2.** to surround; to besiege (*country*).

**kuşbakışı,** -nı bird's-eye view.

**kuşbaşı,** -nı **1.** in small chunks (*meat*); **2.** in big flakes (*snow*).

**kuşbilim** ornithology.

**kuşekâğıdı,** -nı glossy paper.

**kuşet,** -ti berth; couchette.

**kuşkonmaz** ♣ asparagus.

**kuşku** suspicion, doubt; -ya düşmek to feel suspicious.

**kuşkucu** suspicious, skeptical.

**kuşkulanmak** to get suspicious.

**kuşkulu 1.** suspicious, distrustful; **2.** unlikely, doubtful.

**kuşkusuz 1.** unsuspecting, trusting; **2.** certainly, for sure.

**kuşlamak** *sl.* to swot up, *Am.* to grind.

**kuşlokumu** small cookie.

**kuşluk** midmorning.

**kuşmar** bird trap.

**kuşpalazı,** -nı ☥ diphtheria.

**kuşsütü,** -nü any unobtainable thing; ~ ile beslemek to nourish with the choicest of food: -nden başka her şey var there's everything you can think of to eat.

**kuştüyü,** -nü down; ~ yatak feather bed.

**kuşüzümü,** -nü currant.

**kutlama 1.** congratulation; **2.** celebration; ~ töreni celebration.

**kutlamak 1.** to congratulate; **2.** to celebrate.

**kutlu** lucky; blessed; bayramınız ~ olsun! have a happy Bairam!

**kutlulamak** = kutlamak.

**kutsal** holy, sacred; ♀ kitap the (Holy) Bible.

kutsallık holiness, sacredness.
kutsamak to sanctify; to bless; to hallow; to consecrate.
kutsi [ī] = kutsal.
kutu box, case; ~ gibi small but cosy *(house)*.
kutup, -tbu 1. pole; 2. axle; 3. *fig.* authority, expert; ~ ayısı polar bear; ~ dairesi polar circle; ~ kuşağı *geogr.* polar *(or* frigid) zone.
kutuplaşmak to be polarized.
Kutupyıldızı, -nı *ast.* North Star, Polaris.
kutur, -tru Å 1. diameter; 2. diagonal.
kuvaför hairdresser, coiffeur.
kuvars quartz.
Kuvayı Milliye *hist.* the Nationalist Forces.
Kuveyt, -ti *pr. n.* Kuwait.
kuvöz incubator.
kuvve 1. potential; 2. X the effective forces and equipment *(of a unit);* -den fiile çıkarmak to put into action.
kuvvet, -ti strength, power *(a.* Å*);* force; vigo(u)r; ~ ilacı tonic; ~ macunu aphrodisiac with fruit and nuts; ~ vermek 1. to strengthen; 2. to hearten, to encourage; -le 1. by force; 2. emphatically; -ten düşmek to weaken.
kuvvetlendirmek to strengthen.
kuvvetlenmek to strengthen, to become strong.
kuvvetli strong, powerful; vigorous; forceful.
kuvvetsiz weak, feeble.
kuyruk 1. tail; 2. queue, *Am.* line; 3. *fig.* follower; suite, retinue; 4. ponytail; 5. train *(of a dress);* 6. corner *(of the eye);* ~ sallamak 1. to wag its tail; 2. *fig.* to fawn (-*e* over), to play up (-*e* to); kuyruğu kapana kısılmak F to have one's back against the wall; kuyruğu titretmek *sl.* to kick the bucket; kuyruğunu kısmak *fig.* to tuck one's tail.
kuyrukkakan *zo.* (stone)chat.
kuyruklu 1. tailed; 2. *zo.* scorpion; ~ kurbağa tadpole; ~ piyano grand piano; ~ yalan whopper, walloping lie.
kuyrukluyıldız *ast.* comet.
kuyruksallayan *zo.* yellow wagtail.
kuyruksokumu, -nu coccyx.
kuyruksuz tailless.
kuytu 1. snug, remote, secluded; 2. out-of-the-way.
kuyu 1. well; 2. pit; 3. X shaft; ~ açmak to dig a well *(or* pit); ~ bileziği wellcurb; -sunu kazmak *(b-nin) fig.* to set a trap for *s.o.*
kuyucu well digger *(or* driller).
kuyum † jewel(le)ry.

kuyumcu jewel(l)er.
kuyumculuk jewel(le)ry.
kuzen cousin.
kuzey 1. north; 2. northern.
kuzeybatı northwest.
kuzeydoğu northeast.
kuzeyli northerner.
kuzgun *zo.* raven; -a yavrusu şahin görünür *pro.* all his geese are swans.
kuzguncuk small iron grate.
kuzguni [. - -] as black as pitch *(or* ink).
kuzgunkılıcı, -nı ⚘ gladiolus.
kuzin cousin.
kuzu lamb; ~ derisi lambskin; ~ dolması stuffed and roasted lamb; ~ gibi *fig.* as meek as a lamb; -m! F dear!, honey!
kuzudişi, -ni milk *(or* baby) tooth.
kuzukestanesi, -ni small chestnut.
kuzukulağı, -nı ⚘ sorrel.
kuzulamak 1. to lamb; 2. to crawl on all fours *(baby).*
kuzulu pregnant *(ewe).*
kuzumantarı, -nı ⚘ a kind of mushroom.
Küba *pr. n.* Cuba.
kübik cubic(al).
küçücük [x . .] tiny, wee.
küçük 1. small, little; 2. young, little; 3. petty, small(-minded); 4. minor, petty; 5. petite, dainty; 6. small-scale, miniature; 7. hey little one!; ~ aptes urination, piss, pee; ~ dağları ben yarattım demek *fig.* to think no small beer of *o.s.;* ~ düşmek to lose face; ~ düşürmek to disgrace, to mortify, to humiliate; ~ görmek to belittle, to underrate, to underestimate, to undervalue; ~ harf minuscule; ~ köyün büyük ağası *iro.* he thinks he is something!; ~ parmak little finger *or* toe; ~ su dökmek to piss, to pee, to urinate; -ten beri ever since childhood.
Küçükayı *ast.* Ursa Minor, the Little Bear.
küçükbaş sheep, goat, *etc.;* ~ hayvanlar sheep, goats, *etc.*
küçükdil *anat.* uvula; -ini yutmak *fig.* to fall off one's chair.
küçükhindistancevizi, -ni ⚘ nutmeg (tree).
küçüklemek P to slight, to despise.
küçükleşmek 1. to grow smaller; 2. to humiliate o.s.
küçüklü büyüklü 1. big and small; 2. young and old.
küçüklük 1. littleness, smallness; 2. childhood; 3. *fig.* meanness, pettiness.
küçüksemek to despise, to belittle.
küçülmek 1. to shrink; 2. to be humiliated.
küçültme *vn. of* küçültmek, *part.* 1.

humiliation; **2.** deprecation; ~ **eki** *gr.* diminutive suffix.

**küçültmak** *caus. of* küçülmek **1.** to make smaller; to shrink, to reduce, to diminish; **2.** to deprecate; to underrate; **3.** to humiliate.

**küçültücü** derogatory, deprecatory.

**küçümen** tiny, peewee.

**küçümsemek** to despise, to lessen, to look down (-*i* on).

**küf** mo(u)ld; mildew; ~ **bağlamak** (*or* tutmak) to mo(u)ld, to get mo(u)ldy; ~ **kokmak** to smell musty; ~ **kokusu** musty smell.

**küfe 1.** pannier; **2.** *sl.* fanny, ass.

**küfelik 1.** basketful; **2.** *fig.* blotto, under the table, well-oiled, lit up.

**küflenmek 1.** to mo(u)ld, to get mo(u)ldy; to mildew; **2.** *fig.* to become fogyish (*or* fusty); **3.** *fig.* to rot, to get rusty.

**küflü 1.** mo(u)ldy; musty; mildewy; **2.** *fig.* fogyish, fusty, mo(u)ldy.

**küfran** [â] ingratitude.

**küfretmek** [x . .] to swear, to curse.

**küfür, -frü 1.** cuss, swearword, oath; **2.** blasphemy, impiety; ~ **etm.** (*or* savurmak *or* küfrü basmak) to swear, to cuss.

**küfürbaz** foulmouthed.

**küfürbazlık** swearing.

**küfür küfür:** ~ **esmek** to puff.

**küfüv, -ffü** peer, equal, match.

**küheylan** Arabian horse.

**kükremek 1.** to roar (*lion*); **2.** *fig.* to bellow, to roar.

**kükürt** ⚗ sulphur, *Am.* sulfur.

**kükürtçiçeği, -ni** flowers of sulphur.

**kükürtlemek** to dust with sulphur.

**kükürtlü** sulphurous, *Am.* sulfurous.

**kül¹, -lü** ash; ~ **etm.** *fig.* to ruin; ~ **gibi** ashen (*face*); ~ **tablası** ashtray; ~ **yutmak** *fig.* to get taken for a ride; -**ünü savurmak** *fig.* to play ducks and drakes with; **ben** ~ **yutmam** there are no flies on me.

**kül², -lli** all, the whole.

**külah 1.** conical hat; **2.** paper cone; **3.** *fig.* trick, deceit; ~ **kapmak** to get an important job by chicanery; -**ıma anlat!** tell that to the marines!; -**ını havaya atmak** *fig.* to throw one's hat in the air; **Ali'nin** -**ını Veli'ye, Veli'nin** -**ını Ali'ye giydirmek** to rob Peter to pay Paul.

**külbastı** grilled cutlet.

**külçe 1.** nugget, lump; **2.** ingot; ~ **gibi oturmak** *fig.* to flop (*or* plop) down, to plunk o.s. down.

**külek** tub.

**külfet, -ti** burden, onus, bother; ... **yapmak**

**külfetine katlanmak** to be at pains to do...

**külfetli** burdensome, troublesome.

**külfetsiz** untroublesome, easy.

**külhan** stokehole (*of a bath*).

**külhanbeyi, -ni** rowdy, toughie, hood(lum), hooligan.

**küllenmek 1.** to become ashy; **2.** *fig.* to cool (*or* die) down (*anger, etc.*).

**külli** [î] total, complete.

**külliyat, -tı** [â] complete works (*of an author*).

**külliye** complex of buildings (*adjacent to a mosque*).

**külliyen** entirely, totally.

**külliyet, -ti** completeness.

**külliyetli** a good many.

**küllü** ashy.

**küllük** ashtray.

**külot, -tu 1.** (*women's*) panties; (*men's*) underpants, briefs, undershorts; **2.** breeches; -**lu çorap** tights, *Am.* panty hose.

**külrengi, -ni** ashen; gray.

**külte 1.** = külçe; **2.** bunch; **3.** *geol.* rock formation.

**kültivatör** ↓ cultivator.

**kültür** culture; ~ **sahibi** cultured, cultivated.

**kültürel** cultural.

**kültür fizik** free exercise.

**kültürlü** cultured, cultivated.

**kültürsüz** uncultured.

**külünk** pick(ax).

**külüstür** ramshackle; junky-looking; araba crate, jalopy, rattletrap.

**küme 1.** pile, heap, mound; **2.** *sports:* league; **3.** group; ~ ~ in heaps (*or* groups).

**kümebulut, -tu** cumulus cloud.

**kümelemek** to heap (*or* pile) up.

**kümelenmek 1.** ✗ to group; **2.** to cluster (-*e* around).

**kümeleşmek** to group.

**kümes 1.** coop; **2.** *fig.* tiny house; ~ **hayvanları** poultry.

**künde 1.** hobble, fetter; **2.** *wrestling:* hold; -**den atmak** *fig.* to trip up.

**künk, -kü** pipe; tile.

**künye 1.** personal data; **2.** identification bracelet; identification (*or* dog) tag; ~ **defteri** personnel roster; -**si bozuk** with a blot on one's escutcheon.

**küp¹, -pü 1.** earthenware jar; **2.** *sl.* pissed, lit up; ~ **gibi** as fat as a pig; -**lere binmek** *fig.* to go up in the air, to blow one's top; -**ünü doldurmak** to feather one's nest.

küp[2] ⚥ **1.** cube; **2.** cubic.
küpe **1.** earring; **2.** *anat.* dewlap, wattle.
küpeçiçeği, -ni ⚥ fuchsia.
küpeli earringed.
küpeşte [.x.] **1.** ⚓ rail(ing); gunnel; **2.** banister, handrail.
kür health cure.
kürdan toothpick.
kürdanlık toothpick holder.
küre **1.** *geogr.* globe, sphere; **2.** ⚒ smelter; ~ kuşağı zone.
kürecik globule.
kürek **1.** shovel; **2.** oar; paddle; **3.** *(baker's)* peel; ~ çekmek to row; ~ kemiği *anat.* shoulder blade, scapula; ~ ~ by the shovelsful; ~ yarışı boatrace, rowing competition.
kürekçi **1.** oarsman, rower; **2.** stoker *(on a boat).*
küremek to shovel up.
küresel ⚥ spherical.
küret, -ti ⚕ curette.
kürevi [i] spherical.
kürk, -kü fur.
kürkçü furrier.
kürklü (be)furred.
kürsü **1.** lectern, rostrum, podium; pulpit; **2.** *(teacher's)* desk; **3.** *fig.* professorship, chair.
Kürt, -dü *pr. n.* **1.** Kurd; **2.** Kurdish.
kürtaj ⚕ curettage.
kürtün **1.** large packsaddle; **2.** snowdrift.
küs sullen.
küseğen **1.** touchy; **2.** ⚥ sensitive plant.
küskü crowbar.
küskün offended, disgruntled, peeved.
küs küs sullenly.

küsküt, -tü ⚥ dodder.
küskütük [x..] **1.** as stiff as a board; **2.** *jig.* blind, dead *(drunk).*
küsmek, (-er) to sulk, to pout, to be offended (-e by).
küspe bagasse; residue.
küstah insolent, impudent, cheeky, pert.
küstahlık insolence, impudence, cheek.
küstere **1.** *(carpenter's)* plane; **2.** grindstone.
küstümotu, -nu ⚥ mimosa.
küstürmek to offend.
küsur [ü] **1.** remainder; **2.** odd; beş yüz ~ five hundred odd.
küsurat, -tı remainder.
küsüşmek to get cross with each other.
küt, -tü **1.** stubby; **2.** blunt, dull; ~ diye kapatmak to slam *(door).*
küt küt: ~ atmak to pound, to thump, to throb *(heart).*
kütle mass.
kütleşmek to get blunt *(or dull).*
kütedek [x..] with a thud *(or clonk).*
kütük **1.** trunk; stub stump; **2.** log; **3.** ledger, register.
kütüphane **1.** library; **2.** bookcase; **3.** bookshop.
kütüphaneci librarian.
kütürdemek **1.** to crunch; **2.** to crack, to snap.
kütürdetmek **1.** to crunch; **2.** to crack, to snap.
kütür kütür **1.** crunchingly; **2.** crunchy *(fruit).*
kütürtü **1.** crunch; **2.** snap, crack.
küvet, -ti **1.** bath(tub); **2.** basin, sink; **3.** *phot.* developing tray; **4.** bedpan.

# L

**la** ♪ la; A.
**labada** ♀ patience.
**labirent**, -ti labyrinth.
**laborant**, -tı laboratory assistant.
**laboratuvar** laboratory.
**lacivert** dark (or navy) blue, ultramarine.
**laçka 1.** ⚓ untying a rope; **2.** *fig.* loose, lax; disorganized; indifferent, careless; ~ etm. to slacken, to cast off; ~ olm. *fig.* to get slack, to slacken off.
**laçkalaşmak** s. laçka olm.
**laden** ♀ cistus.
**lades** a bet with a wishbone; ~ kemiği *anat.* wishbone; ~ tutuşmak to pull a wishbone with one another.
**laf 1.** word, remark; **2.** empty words, hot air; **3.** talk, chat; **4.** that's bull!; ~ anlamaz thickheaded; obstinate; ~ aramızda between you, me and the gatepost, between you and me; ~ atmak **1.** to chat; **2.** to proposition; ~ etm. **1.** (b-le) to chat with s.o.; **2.** (bşi) to gossip about s.th.; ~ işitmek to be on the carpet; ~ -ı açar one topic leads to another; ~ olsun diye just for s.th. to say; ~ söyledi balkabağı! you're talking crap!; -a tutmak (b-ni) to engage s.o. in conversation; -ını (or -ınızı) balla kestim excuse me for interrupting you; -ını bilmek to weigh one's words; -ını etm. (bşin) to talk about s.th.; -la peynir gemisi yürümez actions speak louder than words.
**lafazan, lafçı** talkative, windy, chatty.
**lafebesi**, -ni talkative, garrulous.
**lafız**, -fzı utterance, word.
**lağap** s. lakap.
**lağar** skinny (animal).
**lağım 1.** sewer, drain; **2.** ✕ mine; underground tunnel; ~ açmak to dig a drain; ~ atmak to explode a mine; ~ çukuru cesspool, sinkhole; ~ kuyusu = ~ çukuru; ~ sıçanı zo. brown rat; ~ suları sewage; -ı atmak to blast.
**lağımcı** sewerman.
**lağv**, -ğvı abolition.
**lağvetmek** [x ..] to abolish, to do away

(-i with).
**lahana** [x ..] ♀ cabbage.
**lahavle** [- x .] my God!
**lahika 1.** appendix, addendum; **2.** *gr.* suffix.
**lahit**, -hdi **1.** sarcophagus; **2.** walled tomb.
**lahmacun** *a kind of meat pizza.*
**lahza** instant, moment, trice, second.
**lailaheillallah** there is no god but God.
**lak**, -kı s. laka.
**laka** [x .] lac; shellac; lacquer, varnish.
**lakap**, -bı nickname; ~ takmak to nickname.
**lakayt** indifferent, unconcerned; nonchalant; ~ kalmak (bşe or bşe karşı) to be indifferent towards s.th., to remain unmoved by s.th.
**lakaytlık** indifference, unconcern; nonchalance.
**lake** lacquered; shellacked.
**lakerda** salt bonito.
**lakırdı 1.** word(s), talk; **2.** conversation, chat; **3.** gossip; ~ altında kalmamak to give as good as one gets, to be quick to retort; ~ etm. **1.** to chat, to talk; **2.** to gossip; ~ taşımak to tell tales; -ya boğmak (bir konuyu) to drown a subject in a flood of words; -yı ağzına tıkamak (b-nin) to shut s.o. up.
**lakırdıcı** talkative, chatty.
**lakin** [x .] but, however.
**laklak** *fig.* chatter; clatter; ~ etm. to yak, to clatter, to natter, to prattle.
**lal**, -li **1.** ruby; garnet; **2.** red ink.
**lala** *hist.* manservant (who took care of a boy).
**lalanga** [. x .] a kind of pancake.
**lale 1.** ♀ tulip; **2.** forked stick; ≗ Devri *hist.* the Tulip Period (1718-1730); ~ soğanı tulip bulb.
**lalelik** vase.
**lalettayin 1.** at random, indiscriminately; **2.** any... whatsoever; unexceptional.
**lam**[1] (micro)slide.
**lam**[2]: -ı cimi yok I don't want any ifs and

buts.

**lama** 1. zo. llama; 2. lama.

**lamba¹** 1. lamp; 2. tube; ~ şişesi lamp chimney; ~yı açmak to run up the wick (of a lamp).

**lamba²** rabbet.

**lambalamak** to candle (eggs).

**lame** lamé.

**lamise** 1. the sense of touch; 2. zo. antenna.

**lan** 1. hey, you!; 2. say man!; 3. listen, buster!

**lanet**, -ti 1. curse, imprecation; 2. damnable, cursed, damned; ~ etm. (or okumak) to curse, to damn; ~ olsun! damn!

**lanetlemek** to curse, to damn.

**lanetli** = lanet 2.

**langır lungur** 1. rattling and banging; 2. brusquely; loutishly.

**langırt**, -tı 1. pinball; 2. fooseball.

**langust**, -tu zo. langouste.

**lanolin** lanolin(e).

**lanse** launced; ~ etm. to launch, to introduce.

**lantan** 🜞 lanthanum.

**lap**, -pı flop, plop; ~ diye with a flop; ~ ~ with a smacking sound.

**lapa** porridge; poultice, blister; ~ gibi soft, mushy; ~ ~ kar yağıyor it is snowing in large flakes; ~ koymak (or vurmak) to poultice; to blister.

**lapacı** 1. fond of lapa; 2. fig. flabby, languid.

**lappadak** with a plop.

**largetto** ♪ larghetto.

**largo** ♪ largo.

**larp**, -pı: ~ diye out of the blue.

**larpadak** s. larp diye.

**laser** laser.

**laskine** lansquenet.

**laso** lasso.

**lasta** [x .] ⚓ last.

**lasteks** Lastex.

**lastik** 1. rubber; 2. tyre, Am. tire; 3. galosh, rubber, overshoe; 4. rubber band; elastic band; 5. rubber, Am. eraser; ~ cizme waders, wellington (boot); ~ hortum rubber hose.

**lastikli** 1. made of rubber; 2. flexible, elastic; ~ konuşmak fig. to speak in double entendres.

**lata** [x .] lath.

**latarna, laterna** [. x .] hand (or barrel) organ.

**latif** [. -] nice, pleasant, lovely; amiable; dainty.

**latife** [. - .] joke, quip, leg-pull; ~ etm. to joke, to wisecrack; ~ latif gerek pro.

politeness should not be neglected even in a joke.

**latifeci** witty (person).

**latilokum** s. lokum.

**Latin** pr. n. 1. Latin; 2. Romance* (language); ~ Amerika Latin America; ~ harfleri Latin characters; ~ yelkeni lateen sail.

**Latince** [x . .] pr. n. Latin.

**latinçiçeği**, -ni 🜹 nasturtium.

**laubali** [- . - -] saucy, pert, free-and-easy.

**laubalileşmek** to become saucy.

**laubalilik** sauciness, pertness.

**lav** geogr. lava.

**lava** [x .] ⬇ pull! (on the oars).

**lavabo** washbasin, lavatory, Am. sink.

**lavaj** 1. ⚒ washing; sluicing; 2. ⚕ lavage.

**lavanta** [. x .] 1. 🜹 lavender; 2. lavender water.

**lavdanom** [x . .] pharm. laudanum.

**lavman** ⚕ 1. enema; 2. enemator.

**lavta¹** [x .] ♪ lute.

**lavta²** [x .] ⚕ 1. obstetrical forceps; 2. obstetrician.

**layık**, -ğı 1. worthy (-e of); fit to be; 2. suitable, proper, appropriate; ~ görmek (b-ni bşe) to deem s.th. worthy of s.o.; ~ olm. to deserve, to be worthy (-e of). to suit; layığını bulmak 1. to find a suitable mate; 2. to get one's deserts.

**layıkıyle** properly, adequately.

**layiha** 🜹 proposal, memorandum.

**layik**, -ki secular, nonclerical.

**layikleştirmek** to secularize, to laicize.

**layiklik** secularism, laicism.

**layter** ⬇ lighter.

**Laz** pr. n. Laz.

**laza** small trough (for honey).

**lazım** 1. necessary, needed; 2. gr. intransitive (verb); ~ olm. (or gelmek) to be necessary (or needed).

**lazımlık** potty, (chamber) pot.

**leb**: ~ demeden leblebiyi anlamak to be able to read s.o.'s **thoughts**.

**lebaleb** [x - .] brimful.

**lebiderya** 1. on the sea, seaside (building); 2. seashore.

**leblebi** 1. roasted chickpeas; 2. fig. bullet.

**ledün**, -nnü knowledge of the nature of God.

**leğen** 1. washtub; washbowl; 2. anat. pelvis.

**Leh** pr. n. 1. Pole; 2. Polish.

**leh** in favo(u)r of. for: -inde bulunmak to speak in favo(u)r (-in of); -inde olm. to be in favo(u)r (-in of); -te oy vermek to vote for; -te ve aleyhte pro and con,

for and against.
**Lehçe** *pr. n.* Polish.
**lehçe** dialect.
**lehim** solder.
**lehimci** solderer.
**lehimlemek** to solder.
**lehimli** soldered.
**Lehistan** *pr. n.* Poland.
**lehtar** [ā] ☾☾ beneficiary.
**leke 1.** stain *(a. fig.)*, blot *(a. fig.)*, spot; **2.** blemish, fleck, spot; birthmark; ~ etm. to stain; ~ getirmek *(b-ne)* *fig.* to blacken *s.o.*, to besmirch *s.o.;* ~ olm. to become stained; ~ sürmek *fig.* to blacken, to besmirch; ~ yapmak to stain, to leave *(or* make) a stain (on).
**lekelemek 1.** to stain; to soil; **2.** *fig.* to blacken, to besmirch, to sully.
**lekeli 1.** stained, spotted; **2.** *fig.* of bad repute, dishono(u)red.
**lekelihumma** typhus.
**lekesiz 1.** spotless; **2.** *fig.* of repute.
**leksikografi** lexicography.
**lenduha** [ū] hulking.
**lenf(a)** lymph.
**lenfatik** ⚗ lymphatic.
**lenger 1.** large deep dish; **2.** ⚓ anchor.
**lengüistik** linguistics.
**lento 1.** lintel; **2.** ♪ lento.
**leopar** *zo.* leopard.
**lepiska** [. x .] flaxen *(hair)*.
**lesepase** laissez-passer.
**leş** carcass; ~ gibi **1.** stinking to high heaven; **2.** bone-lazy; -ini çıkarmak *(b-nin)* to beat the tar out of *s.o.;* -ini sermek *(b-nin)* to do *s.o.* in, to bum *s.o.* off.
**leşkargası,** -nı *zo.* hooded crow.
**letafet,** -ti [ā] charm, grace, winsomeness; delicacy.
**Levanten** *pr. n.* Levantine.
**levazım** [ā] impedimenta, supplies, provisions.
**levha** sign(board); panel, slab.
**levye** rod, lever, crowbar.
**levrek** *zo.* sea bass.
**leydi** lady.
**leylak,** -kı ⚘ lilac.
**leylek** *zo.* stork.
**leyli** boarding; ~ mektep boarding school ~ talebe boarder.
**leziz** delicious, tasty, tasteful.
**lezzet,** -ti **1.** taste, flavo(u)r; **2.** pleasure; ~ almak *(or* duymak) *(bşden)* to enjoy *s.th.,* to find pleasure in *s.th.*
**lezzetlenmek** to become tasty.
**lezzetli** delicious, tasty, tasteful.
**lezzetsiz** tasteless.

**lığ** *geol.* alluvium.
**lığlı** *geol.* alluvial, alluvian.
**lıkırdamak** to glug, to gurgle.
**lıkır lıkır** with a gurgle.
**liberal,** -li liberal.
**liberalizm** liberalism.
**libre** [x .] **1.** pound; **2.** libra.
**libretto** ♪ libretto.
**Libya** *pr. n.* Libya.
**lider** [x .] **1.** leader; **2.** leading, first-rate.
**liderlik** leadership.
**lif** [i] **1.** fibre, *Am.* fiber; **2.** ⚘ luffa, loofah.
**lifli** fibrous.
**lig,** -gi *sports:* league.
**lika** [x .] lac(ca).
**liken** ⚘, ⚗ lichen.
**likidasyon** ⚡ liquidation.
**likide etm.** ⚡ to liquidate.
**likidite** ⚡ liquidity.
**likit** fluid, liquid.
**likorinoz** smoked fish.
**likör** liqueur.
**liman** harbo(u)r; (sea)port.
**limanlamak 1.** to come into harbo(u)r; **2.** to die down *(wind)*.
**limanlık 1.** suitable for a harbo(u)r; **2.** windless; **3.** calm *(sea)*.
**limba** [x .] ⚓ barge.
**limbo** [x .] *s.* limba.
**lime** [i]: ~ ~ in tatters *(or* rags).
**limit,** -ti limit.
**limitet,** -ti ⚡ limited; ~ şirket limited company.
**limon** ⚘ lemon; ~ gibi pale *(face)*; ~ sarısı lemon yellow; ~ sıkmak *fig.* to wet-blanket *(a conversation)*.
**limonata** [. . x .] lemonade; ~ gibi cool and pleasant *(weather)*.
**limonatacı** lemonade seller.
**limoni** [. - -] **1.** lemon *(or* pale) yellow; **2.** *fig.* bad, sour *(relations);* **3.** *fig.* snappish, fractious.
**limonküfü** bluish green.
**limonluk 1.** greenhouse; **2.** lemon squeezer; **3.** parapet.
**limontozu,** -nu, **limontuzu,** -nu citric acid.
**linç,** -ci lynching; ~ etm. to lynch.
**link,** -ki trot: ~ gitmek to trot.
**linolyum** linoleum.
**linotip,** -pi linotype.
**linyit,** -ti lignite.
**lir** ♪ lyre.
**lira** *(Turkish)* lira *(or* pound).
**liralık** worth... liras.
**liret,** -ti *(Italian)* lira.
**lirik** *lit.* lyrical.
**lisan** language, tongue; -a gelmek to

begin to speak *(for s.th. nonhuman).*

**lisans** 1. licence, *Am.* license; certificate; 2. bachelor's degree; 3. import *or* export licence; 4. licence to manufacture; ~ yapmak to study for a bachelor's degree.

**lisanslı** licenced; certified.

**lisansüstü** (post)graduate.

**lise** [x .] high school.

**liseli** high-school student.

**liste** [x .] list; -ye geçirmek to list.

**litografya, litografi** lithography.

**litre** [x .] litre, *Am.* liter.

**liva** † 1. ✕ brigade; 2. ✕ brigadier general; 3. banner, flag.

**livar** fishweir, fishgarth.

**liyakat,** -ti [. - .] merit, worthiness, suitability; competence; ~ göstermek to prove capable.

**liyakatli** [. - . .] worthy, deserving; competent.

**liynet,** -ti looseness *(of the bowels).*

**lizol,** -lü Lysol.

**lobi** lobby *(a pol.)*

**lobut,** -tu 1. *sports:* Indian club; 2. club, cudgel.

**loca** [x .] 1. *thea.* box; 2. Masonic lodge.

**lodos** 1. southwest wind; 2. south; ~ poyraz *fig.* he blows hot and cold.

**logaritma** ♫ logarithm.

**loğ** roller.

**loğlamak** to roll with a roller.

**loğusa** woman in childbed.

**loğusalık** childbed, confinement.

**lojistik** ✕ logistics.

**lojman** lodging *(for workers and employees).*

**lokal,** -li 1. local headquarters, clubroom; 2. local *(a. ♫)*; 3. rendezvous, haunt.

**lokanta** [. x .] restaurant.

**lokantacı** [. x . .] restaurateur.

**lokavt,** -tı lockout.

**lokma** 1. morsel, bite; 2. *anat.* condyle; 3. a kind of syrupy friedcake; 4. ⊕ wrench; -sını dökmek *(b-nin)* to make friedcake in memory of *s.o.* who has died.

**lokmanruhu,** -nu ♫ ether.

**lokomotif** 🚂 locomotive, engine.

**lokum** Turkish delight.

**lololo** *sl.* nonsense. bull.

**lombar** ⚓ gunport.

**lomboz** ⚓ porthole, scuttle.

**lonca** [x .] guild.

**Londra** [x .] *pr. n.* London.

**Londralı** *pr. n.* Londoner.

**long-play** long-playing record, LP.

**lop,** -pu 1. round and soft; 2. *anat.* lobe; ~ ~ yutmak to bolt down; ~ yumurta hard-boiled egg.

**loppadak** [x . .] with a plop.

**lopur** lopur yemek to bolt down.

**lort** 1. lord; 2. *F* nabob, moneybags; Lortlar Kamarası the House of Lords.

**lostra** [x .] shoe polish; ~ salonu shoeshine shop *(or* parlour).

**lostracı** [x . .] shoeshiner, shoeblack.

**lostromo** [. x .] ⚓ boatswain, bosun.

**losyon** lotion.

**loş** dim, murky, dark, gloomy.

**loşluk** dimness, murkiness, gloom.

**lotarya** [. x .] lottery.

**Lozan** *pr. n.* Lausanne.

**lök,** -kü 1. awkward, clumsy; 2. male camel.

**lökün** lute.

**lösemi** ♟ leukemia.

**lumbago** [x . .] ♟ lumbago.

**lunapark,** -kı fair, amusement park.

**lustur** *sl.* shoeshiner.

**lutr** *zo.* otter (fur).

**Lübnan** [ã] *pr. n.* Lebanon.

**Lübnanlı** [ã] *pr. n.* Lebanese.

**lüfer** *zo.* bluefish.

**lügat,** -tı 1. dictionary; 2. word; ~ paralamak to use a pompous language.

**lügatçe** glossary.

**lüks** 1. luxury; 2. luxurious; 3. lantern; ~ mevki luxury class; ~ vergisi luxury tax; şehrin en lüks otelleri the most luxurious hotels of the city.

**Lüksemburg** *pr. n.* Luxemb(o)urg.

**lüle** 1. curl, bob, fold, ringlet, lock *(of hair)*; 2. spout *(of a fountain)*; 3. clay bowl; ~ ~ in curls *(or* ringlets).

**lületaşı,** -nı *geol.* meerschaum.

**lüp,** -pü *sl.* 1. windfall; 2. kernel, essence, marrow; ~ diye yutmak to bolt down.

**lüpçü** *sl.* freeloader, parasite, hanger-on.

**lütfen** [x .] please.

**lütfetmek** [x . .] to condescend, to deign, to be so kind as to; to oblige.

**lütuf,** -tfu kindness, favo(u)r; lütfunda bulunmak to be so good as to, to be so kind as to.

**lütufkâr** gracious, kind.

**lüzum** necessity, need; ~ görmek to deem necessary; -unda at a pinch *(or* push), when it's necessary.

**lüzumlu** necessary, needed.

**lüzumsuz** unnecessary, unneeded.

# M

**maada** [.-.] **1.** except, apart from; **2.** besides, in addition to; -sı the rest; bundan ~ furthermore.

**maaile** with the whole family.

**maalesef** [.x..] unfortunately.

**maarif** [.-.] **1.** education, public instruction; **2.** ♀ the Ministry of Education; ~ müdürü superintendent of schools.

**maaş** salary, stipend, pay; pension; ~ bağlamak to salary, to put on a salary.

**maaşlı** salaried.

**maatteessüf** regrettably, I regret to say.

**maazallah** [.x.-] God forbid!

**mabat** [--] continuation, sequel.

**mabet** temple, place of worship.

**mablak** spatula; putty knife.

**mabut** [--] **1.** God; **2.** god, deity; idol.

**Macar**[1] pr. n. Hungarian; ~ salamı salami.

**macar**[2] sl. louse.

**Macarca** [.x.] pr. n. Hungarian.

**Macaristan** pr. n. Hungary.

**macera** [-.-] adventure; ~ filmi adventure film; ~ romanı adventure novel; ~ peşinde koşmak to seek adventure; -ya atılmak to get involved in a risky business.

**maceracı** adventuresome, adventurous.

**maceralı** adventurous.

**maceraperest**, -ti s. maceracı.

**macun** [â] **1.** putty; **2.** paste; **3.** ♀ paste; electuarv.

**macunlamak** [-...] to putty.

**maç**, -cı match; ~ yapmak to hold a match.

**maça** [x.] cards: spade; ~ beyi jack of spades; ~ beyi gibi kurulmak to sprawl; ~ kızı queen of spades.

**maçuna** [.x.] ⊕ crane.

**madalya** medal; -nın ters tarafı (or yüzü) the other side of the coin.

**madalyon** locket, medallion.

**madam** Madame.

**madama** Ma'am, Lady.

**madara** sl. **1.** worthless; **2.** vulgar, common; ~ olm. sl. to feel ashamed.

**madde** **1.** matter, substance; **2.** article, clause, paragraph; **3.** item, entry; **4.**
component, material; **5.** matter, topic, question; ~ ~ article by article, item by item.

**maddeci** materialist.

**maddecilik** materialism.

**maddesel** material.

**maddeten** [x..] materially.

**maddi** [î] material, physical.

**maddiyat**, -tı materiality.

**madem** [x.], **mademki** [.x.] [â] since, as, seeing that.

**maden** [â] **1.** ⚒ mine; **2.** ⚗ metal; **3.** mineral; ~ cevheri ore; ~ damarı lode, vein; ~ işçisi miner; ~ kuyusu mine shaft; ~ mühendisi mining engineer; ~ ocağı mine, pit; ~ ocağı işçisi pitman; ~ yatağı ore bed.

**madenci** [â] miner.

**madencilik** [â] mining.

**madeni** [â] **1.** metal(lic); **2.** mineral; ~ para coin, specie.

**madenkırmız** ⚗ kermesite.

**madenkömürü**, -nü hard coal, anthracite.

**madensel** s. madeni.

**madensuyu**, -nu mineral water.

**madik** **1.** marbles (game); **2.** sl. trick; ~ atmak to pull a fast one (-e on).

**madrabaz** cheat, swindler.

**maestro** ♪ maestro.

**Mafia** Maf(f)ia.

**mafiş** **1.** a kind of fritter; **2.** F nothing left, not to be found.

**mafsal** joint.

**mafsallı** articulate.

**magazin** magazine.

**magma** geol. magma.

**magnezyum** ⚗ magnesium.

**Magosa** [x..] pr. n. Famagusta.

**mağara** cave, cavern.

**mağaza** large store.

**mağdur** [û] wronged; ⚖ injured party.

**mağduriyet**, -ti [û] unjust treatment.

**mağfiret**, -ti forgiveness of God.

**mağfur** [û] whose sins have been forgiven by God.

**mağlubiyet**, -ti defeat, beating; -e uğramak to get a beating, to be defeated.

**mağlup**, -bu defeated, beaten, overcome;

~ etm. to defeat, to beat; ~ olm. to be defeated (or beaten).

mağrıp, -bi 1. the west; 2. ♀ pr. n. the Maghreb.

magrur [ü] 1. haughty, conceited; 2. proud.

mahal, -lli place, spot, locality, site; ~ kalmamak to be no longer necessary; -inde on the spot, in situ.

mahalle neighbo(u)rhood, quarter; district, ~ bekçisi night watchman; ~ çapkını timid womanizer; ~ çocuğu urchin, gamin; ~ karısı fishwife.

mahallebi s. muhallebi.

mahalli local; ~ idare local government.

maharet, -ti [.--] skill, proficiency.

maharetli skillful, proficient.

maharetsiz unskillful.

mahcubiyet, -ti [ü] shyness, bashfulness.

mahcup, -bu [ü] 1. shy, bashful; 2. ashamed; ~ etm. to shame, to put to the blush; ~ olm. to be ashamed.

mahcur [ü] ♂♂ under interdiction.

mahcuz [ü] ♂♂ seized, distrained.

mahdum [ü] ♀ son.

mahdut, -du [ü] 1. limited, restricted, definite; 2. bordered (or bounded) (ile by).

mahfaza case, box, cover.

mahfe howdah.

mahfil † 1. club, rendezvous; 2. maksoorah.

mahfuz [ü] 1. protected, sheltered; 2. guarded; ~ hisse ♂♂ legal (or compulsory) portion.

mahfuzen [ü] under guard.

mahıv, -hvı destruction.

mahir [ā] 1. skil(l)ful, expert; 2. ♀ mf.

mahiyet, -ti [ü] 1. reality; true nature, character; 2. the heart (of a matter).

mahkeme 1. law court; 2. trial, hearing; ~ celpnamesi summons, citation; ~ kadıya mülk değil. pro. place and power are not everlasting; ~ kararı judg(e)ment, verdict; -de dayısı olm. to have a friend at court, to have friends in high places; -ye düşmek to be taken to court; -ye vermek (b-ni) to go to law against s.o., to have the law on s.o., to bring s.o. to court.

mahkemelik matter for the courts; ~ olm. to go to court.

mahkûm 1. ♂♂ sentenced, condemned; 2. convict; 3. forced (or obliged) (-e to); 4. destined (or doomed) (-e to); ~ etm. to sentence (-e to), to condemn (-e to).

mahkûmiyet, -ti sentence, condemnation.

mahlas pen name, pseudonym.

mahlep, -bi ♀ mahaleb.

mahluk, -ku creature.

mahlukat, -tı [.--] creatures.

mahlul, -lü 1. ♂♂ escheated (property); 2. ♂ solution.

mahmude [ü] ♀ scammony (resin).

mahmur [ü] 1. logy, groggy (from sleep); 2. fuddled (from drink); 3. half-closed (eye); 4. heavy-eyed, sleepy-eyed; 5. lovesick, languishing (look).

mahmurluk 1. grogginess, loginess; 2. listlessness.

mahmuz [ü] 1. spur; 2. ↓ ram, rostrum.

mahmuzlamak to spur.

mahpus [ü] 1. prisoner; 2. imprisoned; captive.

mahpushane [ü] prison, gaol, Am. jail.

mahpusluk [ü] imprisonment.

mahreç, -ci 1. outlet; 2. source, origin; 3. Ӑ denominator.

mahrek, -ki ast. orbit.

mahrem 1. confidential, secret, intimate, private; 2. confidant(e).

mahremiyet, -ti confidentiality, intimacy, privacy.

mahrukat, -tı [.--] fuel; combustibles.

mahrum [ü] deprived (-den of), bereft (-den of), destitute (-den of); ~ etm. (or bırakmak) (b-ni bşden) to deprive s.o. of s.th., to bereave s.o. of s.th.; ~ kalmak (or olm.) (bşden) to be deprived (or bereft) of s.th.; bundan ~ kaldı he was deprived of this.

mahrumiyet, -ti [ü] deprivation, bereavement; ~ bölgesi hardship area.

mahsuben [ü] to the account (-e of), reckoning that...

mahsul, -lü [ü] 1. crop, yield, produce; product; 2. fig. product, result.

mahsup, -bu [ü] entered in an account; ~ etm. to enter in an account.

mahsur [ü] 1. stuck; 2. surrounded; 3. confined (-e to), limited (-e to); ~ kalmak to be stuck. (-de in).

mahsus 1. peculiar (-e to), unique (-e to), special (-e to); 2. reserved (-e for), set aside (-e for); 3. on purpose, intentionally, deliberately; 4. as a joke, jokingly; 5. particularly, especially.

mahşer 1. isl. myth. the place where people will gather on the Day of Judgment; 2. fig. throng, press; ~ günü Day of Judg(e)ment.

mahşeri tremendous, huge (crowd).

mahut [--] known.

mahvetmek [x..] to destroy, to ruin; to wipe out, to obliterate.

mahvolmak [x..] pass. of mahvetmek.

**mahya** *lights strung between minarets during Ramazan to form words or pictures.*
**mahzen** cellar, underground storeroom.
**mahzun** [ū] sad, depressed, dejected grieved.
**mahzunlaşmak** to become sad, to sadden.
**mahzunluk** sadness.
**mahzur** [ū] **1.** drawback, objection; **2.** obstacle, snag; ~ görmek to object (*-de* to).
**mahzurlu** objectionable; ill-advised, unwise.
**mail** [ā] **1.** slanting, leaning; **2.** with a bent (*-e* for); **3.** fond (*-e* of).
**maişet**, -ti [ī] livelihood, means of subsistence.
**maiyet**, -ti **1.** suite, entourage; **2.** employ, service; -inde (*b-nin*) in *s.o.'s* suite, at *s.o.'s* side.
**majeste** His (*or* Her) Majesty; -leri (His, Her, Your) Majesty.
**majör** ♪ major.
**majüskül** majuscule.
**makadam** macadam.
**makale** [. - .] article.
**makam** [. -] office, post, portfolio, position ~ arabası official car; ~ şoförü chauffeur.
**makamlı** [. - .] harmonious.
**makamsız** [. - .] inharmonious, discordant.
**makara** reel; bobbin; spool; pulley; drum, barrel; ~ gibi konuşmak to talk nonstop; -ları koyuvermek to burst into laughter; -ya almak to make fun (*-i* of); -yı takmak (*b-ne*) to pull *s.o.'s* leg.
**makarna** [. x .] macaroni; spaghetti.
**makas** **1.** scissors; shears; **2.** *mot.* spring; **3.** 🚂 switch, points; **4.** *sl.* pinch (*on one's cheek*); ~ almak (*b-den*) to pinch *s.o.'s* cheek; ~ ateşi ⚔ crossfire; ~ dili switch (*or* point) rail; ~ hakkı the remnants of cloth; ~ vurmak to put the scissors (*-e* to), to cut.
**makasçı** **1.** scissors man; **2.** 🚂 switchman, pointsman.
**makaslama** **1.** *vn. of* makaslamak; **2.** crosswise; **3.** *swimming:* scissors kick.
**makaslamak** **1.** to scissor; **2.** *sl.* to pinch (*s.o.'s cheek*).
**makastar** cutter.
**makat**, -tı anus; buttocks, rump.
**makber** grave.
**makbul**, -lü [ū] welcome, acceptable; satisfactory, liked; -e geçmek to be welcome, to touch the spot.
**makbuz** [ū] receipt; ~ kesmek to write a receipt, to receipt.
**Makedonya** [. . x .] *pr. n.* Macedonia.
**maket**, -ti maquette.
**maki** maquis, scrub.
**makine** [x . .] **1.** machine; **2.** motor, engine; mechanism; **3.** *P* car; **4.** *sl.* pistol; ~ dairesi ⚓ engine room; ~ gibi **1.** efficient; mechanical; **2.** mechanically; ~ gibi adam efficient man; ~ mühendisi mechanical engineer; ~ yağı machine (*or* lubricating) oil; -yi bozmak *co.* to get diarrhea (*or* the squirts).
**makineci** mechanic, machinist.
**makineleşmek** **1.** to become mechanized; **2.** to become machinelike.
**makineleştirmek** to mechanize.
**makineli** [x . . .] fitted with a machine; ~ tüfek machine-gun.
**makinist**, -ti **1.** engine-driver; **2.** machinist.
**makrama** **1.** tassel; **2.** head scarf.
**maksat**, -dı purpose, intention, aim, object, end; ~ gütmek to cherish a secret intention.
**maksatlı** purposeful.
**maksi** maxi; ~ etek maxi skirt.
**maksim** place containing a large reservoir.
**maksimum** maximum.
**maksure** [ū] maksoorah.
**maksut**, -du [ū] intention, purpose.
**maktu**, -uu [ū] **1.** fixed (*price*); **2.** for a lump sum; ~ fiyat fixed price.
**maktul**, -lü [ū] killed, murdered; ~ düşmek to be murdered (*or* killed).
**makul**, -lü [ū] sensible, reasonable; ~ konuşmak to talk sense.
**makyaj** make-up; ~ yapmak to make up, to put on make-up.
**mal** **1.** goods, merchandise; **2.** property, possession; **3.** wealth, riches; assets; **4.** cattle; **5.** *sl.* loose (*woman*); **6.** *sl.* heroin, skag; **7.** *sl.* bastard, scoundrel; ~ beyanı ⚖ declaration of property; ~ bulmuş Mağribi gibi as happy as a king; ~ canın yongasıdır *pro.* it is hard to part with anything one owns; ~ canlısı greedy, avaricious; ~ edinmek **1.** to acquire wealth; **2.** to appropriate; ~ etm. **1.** (*k-ne*) to appropriate for *o.s.*; **2.** to produce (*-e* at); ~ kaçırmak ⚖ to smuggle goods; ~ müdürü head of the finance office (*in a district*); ~ mülk property, goods; ~ olm. to cost; ~ sahibi landlord, landowner, proprietor; ~ sandığı financial office; -ın gözü **1.** tricky, sly, shifty; **2.** loose, promiscuous (*woman*).
**mala** [x .] trowel.

**malak** calf.

**malalamak** to trowel.

**malama** *sl.* gold lira.

**malarya** [ː x .] malaria.

**malca** [x .] as far as wealth is concerned, as to goods (*or* property).

**Malezya** *pr. n.* Malaysia.

**mali** financial; fiscal; ~ buhran financial crisis; ~ yıl fiscal year.

**malihulya** [â,â] 1. groundless fear; 2. † melancholy.

**malik**, -ki [â] 1. owner, possessor; 2. owning, possessing; ~ olm. to possess, to have, to own; kendine ~ değildir he is beside himself.

**malikâne** [â] stately home, country estate, mansion.

**maliye** 1. finance; 2. the Exchequer, the Ministry of Finance, the Treasury; 2 Bakanı Chancellor of the Exchequer, Minister of Finance; 2 Bakanlığı the Exchequer, Ministry of Finance.

**maliyeci** [â] financier; economist.

**maliyet**, -ti [â] cost; ~ fiyatı cost price, prime cost.

**malkıran** *vet.* cattle-plague.

**malt**, -tı malt.

**Malta** *pr. n.* Malta.

**Maltalı** *pr. n.* Maltese.

**maltaeriği**, -ni ♀ loquat.

**maltahumması**, -nı Malta fever.

**maltataşı**, -nı Malta stone.

**Maltız** = Maltalı.

**malul**, -lü 1. invalid, disabled; 2. victim (of war, disease); ~ gazi disabled veteran.

**maluliyet, malullük** disability, invalidity.

**malum** [- -] 1. known; 2. *gr.* active (voice); ~ olmak to feel in one's bones, to sense; ~ olduğu üzere as everybody knows; -unuz as you know.

**malumat**, -tı [- - -] information, knowledge; ~ almak (*or* edinmek) to get information; ~ sahibi knowledgeable person; ~ vermek to inform (hakkında of), to give information (-e to); -ı olm. (*bşden*) to know about s.th., to be in the know; -ım yok I know nothing about it.

**malumatfuruş** [- - . . . -] pedantic.

**malumatlı** [- - . .] well-informed, knowledgeable.

**malumatsız** [- - . .] uninformed.

**malzeme** material, necessaries, supplies; ingredients; equipment.

**mama¹** 1. baby food; 2. (baby talk) food; ~ bezi bib.

**mama²** *sl.* madam (of a brothel).

**mamafih** [- - .] nevertheless, however.

**mamaliga** [. . x .] dish made of corn flour.

**mamul**, -lü [- -] 1. product, manufacture; 2. made (-den of), manufactured (-den from).

**mamulat**, -tı [- - -] products, manufactures.

**mamur** [- -] prosperous, flourishing (place); well-cultivated (land).

**mamut**, -tu *zo.* mammoth.

**mana** 1. meaning; sense; significance; 2. expression (of the face, etc.); ~ çıkarmak to interpret amiss, to misunderstand; ~ vermek to interpret, to make sense (-e of); -sına gelmek to mean, to signify.

**manalı** 1. meaningful; 2. expressive, allusive, significant.

**manasız** 1. meaningless, senseless; pointless, 2. out of place, inappropriate.

**manastır** monastery.

**manav** 1. greengrocer, fruiterer; 2. greengrocer's, greengrocery.

**manca** [x .] pet food.

**mancana** [. x .] ↓ scuttle.

**mancınık** catapult; mangonel; ballista.

**manda¹** *zo.* water buffalo; ~ gibi hulk.

**manda²** *pol.* mandate.

**mandal** 1. clothes-peg, *Am.* clothespin; 2. latch; tumbler; catch; 3. ♪ tuning peg (of a violin, etc.); 4. ⊕ pawl.

**mandalina** [. . x .] ♀ tangerine, mandarin.

**mandallamak** 1. to peg up, *Am.* to pin up (laundry); 2. to latch (door).

**mandapost**, -tu postal money order.

**mandarin** = mandalina.

**mandater** ~ devlet mandatory, mandatary.

**mandepsi** *sl.* trick, deceit; -ye basmak *sl.* to be duped (*or* tricked).

**mandıra** [x .] dairy (farm), cheesery.

**mandıracı** dairyman; dairywoman.

**mandolin** ♪ mandolin.

**manej** manège.

**manen** [x .] spiritually; ~ ve maddeten in body and in spirit.

**manevi** [î] spiritual, moral; ~ destek olm. to give moral support; ~ evlat adopted child; ~ işkence 🕯 mental cruelty.

**maneviyat**, -tı [- - . .] morale, spirit; -ı bozulmak 1. to feel low; 2. to lose heart.

**manevra** [. x .] 1. manoeuvre, *Am.* maneuver (a. ✕, ↓, fig.); 2. 🚂 shunting; ~ fişeği ✕ blank (cartridge); ~ lokomotifi 🚂 shunting engine, shunter; ~ yapmak 1. ✕ to manoeuvre, *Am.* to maneuver; 2. 🚌 to shunt,

manga [x .] 1. ✕ squad; 2. ⬇ mess.

mangal brazier; ~ kömürü charcoal; -da kül bırakmamak *sl.* to talk big.

manganez, mangan ⚗ manganese.

mangır *sl.* money, dough, tin.

mangırsız *sl.* penniless, broke, without a bean.

mangiz *sl.* money, dough, tin; ~ tutmak *sl.* to be in funds.

mani[1] [ā] ballad.

mani[2] *psych.* mania.

mâni 1. obstacle, impediment, hindrance; 2. hindering, preventing; ~ olm. to prevent, to hinder.

mânia [-..] obstacle, hindrance, barrier.

mâniali [-...] rough, uneven *(country)*; ~ koşu hurdle race; steeplechase.

manidar [-.-] *s.* manalı.

manifatura [...x.] drapery, *Am.* dry goods.

manifaturacı draper.

manifesto [..x.] ⬇ manifest.

manikür manicure.

manikürcü manicurist.

maniple [. x ] *tel.* sending (*or* signalling) key.

manita [. x .] *sl.* 1. girlfriend, bird, *Am.* chick; 2. swindle.

manivela [..x.] lever, crank, crowbar, handspike; ~ kolu lever-arm.

mankafa [x .] blockheaded, thickheaded.

manken model; mannequin, manikin, dummy, lay figure.

manolya [. x .] ❦ magnolia.

manometre manometer.

mansiyon hono(u)rable mention.

Manş Denizi *pr. n.* the English Channel.

manşet, -ti 1. newspaper headline; 2. cuff.

manşon muff.

mantar 1. mushroom; fungus; toadstool; 2. (bottle) cork; 3. muzzle, snout; 4. cork *(for a popgun)*; 5. *sl.* lie; ~ atmak *sl.* to lie, to fib; ~ gibi yerden bitmek to mushroom; ~ tabancası popgun; -a basmak *sl.* to be duped *(or* taken in).

mantarlı corked *(bottle)*.

mantarmeşesi, -ni ❦ cork oak.

mantı[1] *a ravioli-like dish served with yogurt.*

mantı[2] ⬇ pulley *(for hoisting the topsail yard)*.

mantık logic.

mantıkçı logician.

mantıkdışı, -nı alogical.

mantıki [ī] logical.

mantıklı logical.

mantıksız illogical.

manto [x .] *(woman's)* coat.

manya ℞ mania.

manyak 1. ℞ maniac; 2. *F* crazy, nutty.

manyaklık *F* craziness, nuttiness.

manyetik magnetic; ~ alan magnetic field.

manyetizma magnetism.

manyeto magneto.

manyezit, -ti magnesium silicate.

manzara 1. scene, view; scenery, panorama; 2. appearance.

manzaralı scenic.

manzum *lit.* written in verse.

manzume [ū] 1. *lit.* poem, verses; 2. system.

maral *zo.* doe.

marangoz joiner, carpenter, cabinetmaker.

marangozbalığı, -nı *zo.* sawfish.

marangozluk joinery, carpentry.

maraton marathon.

maraz 1. ℞ disease, sickness; 2. *fig.* grouchy, bad-tempered.

maraza [-..] quarrel, row.

marazi [ī] pathological.

marda cullage, discarded goods.

mareşal, -li ✕ (field) marshal.

mareşallik ✕ marshalship.

margarin margarine.

margarit, -ti ❦ marguerite.

marifet, -ti [ā] 1. skill, talent, craft; 2. *iro.* piece of work, little masterpiece.

marifetli [ā] skilled, talented, skil(l)ful.

mariz[1] sick(ly), ill.

mariz[2] *sl.* beating; ~ atmak *(b-ne) sl.* to give *s.o.* a beating.

marizlemek *sl.* to beat up, to tan *s.o.*'s hide.

marj margin.

marjinal, -li † marginal.

mark, -kı mark.

marka [x .] 1. trademark; 2. brand, make; 3. *football:* blocking; 4. token; 5. sign, mark.

markalamak 1. to trademark; 2. to mark.

markalı 1. trademarked; 2. marked.

markasız unmarked.

marki marquis, marquess.

markiz marquise, marchioness.

markizet, -ti marquisette.

Marksist, -ti *pr. n.* Marxist.

Marksizm *pr. n.* Marxism.

Marmara Denizi, -ni *pr. n.* the Sea of Marmara.

marmelat, -tı marmalade.

**maroken** morocco (leather)

**marpuç,** -cu tube of a nargileh.

**mars** *etm. backgammon:* to skunk.

**Mars** *ast.* Mars.

**Marsilya** *pr. n.* Marseilles.

**marş 1.** ✕ forward, march!; **2.** *mot.* starter; **3.** ♪ march; ~ ~! **1.** ✕ run!; **2.** F get going!; -a basmak to press the starter.

**marşandiz** goods (*or* freight) train.

**marşpiye** *mot.* footboard.

**mart,** -tı March; ~ havası changeable (*or* unpredictable) weather; ~ kapıdan baktırır, kazma kürek yaktırır *pro.* cast not a clout ere May be out.

**martaval** *sl.* humbug, bull, hot air, guff, baloney; ~ atmak (*or* okumak) *sl.* to bullshit, to talk nonsense.

**martavalcı** *sl.* bullshitter, liar.

**martı** *zo.* (sea) gull.

**martini** martini.

**maruf** [- -] (well-)known, famous.

**marul** cos, romaine, lettuce.

**maruz** [- -] exposed (*or* subject) (-e to); ~ bırakmak to expose (-e to); ~ kalmak to be exposed (*or* subjected) (-e to); güneşe ~ kalmak to be exposed to the sun.

**maruzat,** -tı [- - - -] petitions, representations.

**marya** *zo.* **1.** ewe; **2.** female animal.

**mas,** -ssı *ast.*, *phys.* suction; soakage; absorption.

**masa** [x .] **1.** table; **2.** desk; ~ başında at table; ~ örtüsü tablecloth.

**masaj** massage; ~ yapmak to massage.

**masajcı** masseur; masseuse.

**masal 1.** story, tale; fable; **2.** *fig.* bull, cock-and-bull story; ~ okumak (*or* anlatmak) F to give a cock-and-bull story.

**masalcı** storyteller.

**masat** (*butcher's*) steel.

**masatenisi,** -ni table tennis, ping-pong.

**mask** (*actor's*) mask.

**maskara 1.** clown, buffoon, laughingstock; **2.** silly, ridiculous, ludicrous; **3.** droll person; cutup; **4.** mascara; ~ etm. (*b-ni*) to make *s.o.* a laughingstock, to pillory; ~ olm. to become a figure of fun: -ya çevirmek (*b-ni*, *bşi*) to make a fool of *s.o.*, *s.th.*

**maskaralanmak** to clown around, to play the buffoon.

**maskaralık 1.** clowning (around), buffoonery; **2.** disgrace; ~ etm. to play the buffoon, to clown around.

**maske** [x .] mask; -sini atmak *fig.* to let one's mask drop, to show one's true colo(u)rs; -sini kaldırmak (*b-nin*) *fig.* to

show *s.o.* up, to expose *s.o.*, to unmask *s.o.*

**maskelemek** to mask.

**maskeli** masked; ~ balo masked (*or* fancy dress) ball, masquerade.

**maskot,** -tu mascot.

**maslahat,** -tı business, affair.

**maslahatgüzar** [. . . . -] *pol.* chargé d'affaires.

**maslak 1.** pipe; **2.** stone trough.

**masmavi** [x - .] very (*or* deep) blue.

**mason** Freemason, Mason.

**masonluk** Freemasonry, Masonry.

**masör** masseur.

**masöz** masseuse.

**masraf 1.** expense(s), expenditure(s), outlay, cutgoings; ~ etm. to go to expense, to spend money; ~ görmek to shell out some money; ~ kapısı açmak to cause expenses; -a girmek to go to expense; -a sokmak to put to expense; -ı çekmek to bear the expenses; -ı kısmak to reduce (*or* cut) expenses; -tan kaçmak to avoid expense; -tan kaçmamak to spare no expense.

**masraflı** expensive, costly, dear.

**masrafsız** inexpensive, cheap.

**massetmek** [x . .] to suck (*or* soak) up, to absorb.

**mastar 1.** *gr.* infinitive; **2.** gage, template.

**mastika** [. x .] mastic.

**masturbasyon** masturbation; ~ yapmak to masturbate.

**masum** [- -] **1.** innocent, guiltless; **2.** little child.

**masumane** [- - - .] innocently.

**masumiyet,** -ti [- - . .] innocence.

**masun** [ū] **1.** guarded, protected (-den from); safe; **2.** ᪸ inviolable.

**masuniyet,** -ti [ū] **1.** safety, security; **2.** ᪸ immunity; inviolability.

**masura** [. x .] **1.** bobbin; **2.** spout.

**maşa 1.** (pair of) tongs; **2.** *fig.* cat's-paw, tool, dummy, front; ~ gibi dark and thin (*person*); ~ gibi kullanmak (*b-ni*) *fig.* to use *s.o.* as a cat's paw; ~ kadar teeny-weeny (*baby*); ~ varken elini yakmak *fig.* to burn one's fingers; -sı olm. (*b-nin*) *fig.* to be *s.o.'s* cat's paw (*or* tool).

**maşalamak** to crimp with a curling iron (*hair*).

**maşallah** [- . .] [x . .] **1.** may God preserve him from evil!; **2.** magnificent!, wonderful!; -ı var he is unusual today.

**maşatlık** non-Muslim cemetery.

**maşlah** long and open-fronted cloak.

**maşrapa** mug; dipper.

**mat¹**, -tı *chess:* (check)mate; ~ etm. **1.** to checkmate; **2.** *fig.* to silence; ~ olm. **1.** to be checkmated; **2.** *fig.* to be silenced.

**mat²**, -tı mat(t), *Am.* matte, dull, lusterless.

**matador** matador.

**matah** *contp.* prize package , great shakes.

**matara** [. x .] canteen, flask, water-bottle.

**matbaa** printing house, press.

**matbaacı** printer.

**matbaacılık** printing.

**matbu**, -uu [ū] printed *(matter)*.

**matbua** [ū] printed matter.

**matbuat**, -tı [. - -] the press; ~ hürriyeti freedom of the press.

**matem** [ā] mourning; ~ havası *(or* marşı) funeral march; ~ tutmak to mourn.

**matematik** mathematics.

**matematikçi 1.** mathematician; **2.** F mathematics teacher.

**matemli** [ā] **1.** in mourning; **2.** mournful.

**materyalist**, -ti materialist.

**materyalizm** materialism.

**materyel** material, supplies.

**matine** matinée.

**matiz¹** *sl.* dead drunk, pissed, soused.

**matiz²** ⚓ making a long splice.

**matkap**, -bı drill; auger; gimlet.

**matlaşmak** to become dull.

**matlaştırmak** to dull.

**matlup**, -bu [ū] † credit, receivable account.

**matmazel** Miss, Mademoiselle.

**matrah** category of taxed goods, standard.

**matrak** *sl.* funny, droll, amusing; ~ geçmek *sl.* to make fun *(or* mock) *(ile* of).

**matris** *typ.*, ⚓ matrix.

**matuf** [- -] aimed *(-e* at), directed *(-e* towards).

**maun** ⚘ mahogany.

**maval** *sl.* cock-and-bull story; ~ okumak *sl.* to give a cock-and-bull story.

**mavi** [- .] blue; ~ boncuk blue bead; ~ kâğıt almak to get fired; -ye çalmak to be bluish.

**mavileşmek** to turn blue.

**mavilik** blueness.

**mavimsi** [ā], **mavimtırak** [- . . .] bluish.

**maviş** blue-eyed.

**mavna** [x .] barge, lighter.

**mavzer** Mauser rifle.

**maya 1.** yeast, ferment; leaven; **2.** *fig.* origin, essence, marrow, blood; -sı bo-

zuk no-good, corrupt *(person).*

**mayalamak** to yeast, to leaven.

**mayalı** yeasted; leavened.

**mayasıl** eczema.

**mayasız** unleavened, unfermented.

**maydanoz** ⚘ parsley.

**mayhoş 1.** sourish, tart; **2.** *fig.* cool *(relations).*

**mayın** ✕ mine; ~ dökmek to mine, to lay mines *(-e* in); ~ tarama gemisi minesweeper; ~ tarlası minefield.

**mayınlamak** ✕ to mine.

**mayıs** May.

**mayısböceği**, -ni *zo.* cockchafer.

**mayışmak** *sl.* to get drowsy.

**mayi** [- -] liquid, fluid.

**maymun 1.** *zo.* monkey; ape; **2.** *fig.* droll *(person);* ~ gözünü açtı *fig.* he has learned his lesson; ~ iştahlı inconstant, fickle; ~ suratlı like the back (end) of a bus.

**maymuncuk** skeleton key, picklock.

**mayo** [x .] **1.** bathing suit, swimsuit; trunks; **2.** leotard.

**mayonez** mayonnaise.

**maytap**, -bı small fireworks, sparkler; -a almak *(b-ni)* to take the mickey out of *s.o.*

**mazbata** official report, protocol, minutes.

**mazbut**, -tu [. -] **1.** disciplined, orderly; **2.** well-built, solid *(building);* **3.** recorded.

**mazeret**, -ti [ā] excuse.

**mazeretli** [ā] excusable, justifiable.

**mazeretsiz** unjustifiable, unwarranted.

**mazgal** crenel, embrasure.

**mazhar 1.** the object of *(honours, favour, etc.);* **2.** ♀ *mf.;* ~ olm. *(bşe)* to be the object *(or* recipient) of *s.th.*

**mazı 1.** ⚘ arborvitae; **2.** gallnut, gall-apple.

**mazi** [- -] **1.** the past, bygones; **2.** *gr.* the simple past tense; -ye karışmak to belong to bygone days.

**mazlum** [ū] **1.** oppressed, wronged; **2.** *fig.* inoffensive, compliant; **3.** ♀ [x .] *mf.*

**mazmun** [ū] *lit.* witticism, pun.

**maznun** [ū] ♊ **1.** suspected, accused; **2.** suspect.

**mazot**, -tu diesel oil *(or* fuel).

**mazur** [- -] excused; excusable; ~ görmek to excuse, to pardon, to hold excused.

**meal**, -li [ā] meaning, purport.

**meblağ** amount, sum *(of money).*

**mebni** [ī] based *(-e* on), because *(-e* of).

**mebus** deputy, member of parliament.

**mebusluk** deputyship.

**mebzul**, -lü [ü] abundant, lavish.

**mecal**, -li [â] power, strength; ~ bırakmamak *fig.* to wear out.

**mecalsiz** [â] weak, exhausted, powerless.

**mecaz** [â] figure of speech, trope; metaphor.

**mecazen** [â] figuratively; metaphorically.

**mecazi** [. - -] figurative; metaphorical.

**mecbur** [ü] forced (-e to), compelled (-e to), obliged (-e to); ~ etm. to force, to oblige, to compel; ~ olm. (*or* kalmak) to be forced (*or* obliged *or* compelled) (-e to).

**mecburen** [ü] [. x .] compulsorily, out of necessity, perforce.

**mecburi** [. - -] compulsory, obligatory; ~ iniş ✈ forced landing, crash-landing; ~ istikamet one way.

**mecburiyet**, -ti [ü] compulsion, obligation; ~ halinde at a push (*or* pinch).

**meccanen** [â] free, gratis.

**meccani** [. - -] free, gratuitous.

**mecelle** 1. volume, book; 2. 📖 civil code.

**mecidiye**, **mecit** *hist.* silver coin.

**meclis** 1. assembly, council; 2. meeting; Meclisi Mebusan the Ottoman Parliament.

**mecmu**, -uu [ü] 1. whole, all; 2. A sum, total.

**mecmua** [ü] magazine, periodical.

**mecnun** [ü] 1. mad, insane, crackers; 2. love-crazed.

**mecra** [â] 1. watercourse, conduit; 2. *fig.* the course (*of events*).

**Mecusi** [. - -] *pr. n.* Zoroastrain, Mazdean.

**meczup**, -bu [ü] insane, crazy.

**meç** *fencing:* foil, rapier.

**meçhul**, -lü [ü] 1. unknown; 2. *gr.* passive.

**medar** [â] 1. *ast.* orbit; 2. *geogr.* tropic; 3. support, help; 4. means; reason, cause; ~ olm. to help, to aid.

**meddah** [â] 1. public storyteller; 2. eulogist.

**meddücezir**, -zri ebb and flow, tide.

**medeni** 1. civilized; 2. 📖 civil; ~ haklar civil rights; ~ hal marital status; ~ hukuk civil law; ~ kanun civil code; ~ nikâh civil marriage.

**medenileşmek** to become civilized.

**medenileştirmek** to civilize.

**medeniyet**, -ti civilization.

**medeniyetsiz** uncivilized.

**medet** help, aid; ~ Allah! help me, God!;

~ beklemek (*or* ummak) to hope for help (-den from).

**medih**, -dhi prise, eulogy.

**medikososyal** medico-social.

**Medine** *pr. n.* Medina.

**medrese** *hist.* medresseh, madrasa, madrasah.

**medreseli** student at a medresseh.

**medüz** *zo.* medusa, jellyfish.

**medyum** medium.

**medyun** [ü] indebted.

**mefhum** [ü] concept.

**mefkûre** ideal.

**mefkûrecilik** idealism.

**mefluç**, -cu paralyzed.

**mefruşat**, -tı [. - -] 1. furnishings; 2. fabrics.

**meftun** [ü] charmed, captivated; infatuated; ~ olm. to be charmed (*or* captivated) (-e by).

**megafon** megaphone.

**megaloman** megalomaniac.

**megavat**, -tı. *phys.* megawatt.

**meğer** [x .] it seems that..., apparently..., but, however.

**meğerki** [x . .] unless.

**mehil** respite, grace period, extension, delay.

**Mehmetçik** *pr. n.* the Turkish 'Tommy'.

**mehtap**, -bı [â] moonlight, moonglow.

**mehtaplı** [â] moonlit.

**mehter** member of a Janissary band; ~ takımı Janissary band.

**mekân** 1. place; 2. residence, abode; 3. *phls.* space.

**mekanik** 1. mechanics; 2. mechanical.

**mekanizm** *phls.* mechanism.

**mekanize** ✗ mechanized.

**mekanizma** [. . x .] mechanism.

**mekik** shuttle; ~ dokumak to shuttle.

**Mekke** *pr. n.* Mecca.

**mekruh** [ü] abominable.

**Meksika** *pr. n.* Mexico.

**Meksikalı** *pr. n.* Mexican.

**mektep**, -bi school; ~ arkadaşı schoolmate; ~ kaçağı truant; ~ medrese görmüş educated; mektebi asmak to play truant (*or* hooky), to cut school.

**mektepli** student, pupil, schoolkid.

**mektup**, -bu letter; ~ atmak to mail (*or* post *or* send) a letter; ~ üstü address on a letter.

**mektuplaşmak** to correspond (*ile* with).

**melaike** angels.

**melal**, -li boredom; tedium.

**melamin** melamine.

**melankoli** melancholy.

**melankolik** melancholic.

**melce** sanctuary, refuge, asylum.

**melek** 1. angel; 2. ♀ *wf.*

**meleke** 1. aptitude, knack, bent; 2. faculty; 3. skill.

**melemek** [- . .] to bleat.

**melez** 1. hybrid, crossbred; 2. of mixed race (or blood).

**melezlemek** to crossbreed, to hybridize.

**melezlik** hybridity, hybridism.

**melhem** s. merhem.

**melik, -ki** 1. sovereign, ruler, king; 2. ♀ *mf.*

**melike** 1. queen, ruler, sovereign; 2. ♀ *wf.*

**melodi** melody.

**melodik** melodic.

**melodram** melodrama.

**melon (şapka)** bowler, derby (hat).

**melun** damned, cursed.

**melûl, -lü** sad, blue, low-spirited.

**memba, -aı** spring; fountainhead, source (a. fig.).

**meme** 1. breast, boob, *anat.* mamma; 2. dug, udder; 3. ⊕ nozzle; ~ başı (or ucu) teat, nipple; ~ çocuğu suckling; ~ emmek to suck, to nurse; ~ vermek to suckle; -den kesmek (çocuğu) to wean (a child).

**memeli** zo. mammiferous; ~ hayvanlar mammals.

**memeliler** zo. mammals.

**memeş** slaver, slobber.

**memişhane** F loo, john.

**memleket, -ti** 1. country, land; 2. home town; 3. fatherland.

**memleketli** fellow countryman, compatriot.

**memnu, -uu** [û] forbidden, prohibited.

**memnun** [û] pleased, delighted, glad, contented, satisfied; ~ etm. to please, to satisfy; ~ olm. to be pleased (or satisfied), to be glad.

**memnuniyet, -ti** [û] pleasure, gladness, gratitude, delight, content, satisfaction; ~ verici satisfactory, pleasurable, delightful.

**memnuniyetle** [û] with pleasure, gladly.

**memorandum** [. . x .] memorandum.

**memul, -lü** [- -] hoped, expected; ~ etm. to hope, to expect.

**memur** civil servant, jobholder, official; employee; ~ etm. (b-ni bşe) to commission s.o. to do s.th., to charge s.o. with s.th.

**memure** female civil servant; female employee.

**memurluk, -tı** [- . . .] government job, civil service post.

**men, -ni** prohibition.

**menajer** manager.

**mendebur** 1. good-for-nothing (person); 2. F bastard.

**menderes** geogr. meander.

**mendil** handkerchief, hanky; ~ sallamak to wave one's handerchief.

**mendirek** breakwater, mole.

**menekşe** 1. ♀ violet; 2. sl. asshole.

**menenjit, -ti** ♀ meningitis.

**menetmek** [x : .] to prohibit, to forbid.

**meneviş** moire, water.

**menfaat, -ti** advantage, interest, benefit.

**menfaatçi** self-seeking.

**menfaatperest** s. menfaatçı.

**menfez** hole, vent.

**menfi** [î] negative; ~ cevap negative answer.

**menfur** [û] abhorrent, loathsome.

**mengel** P anklet.

**mengene** [x . .] 1. vice, Am. vise; 2. press; 3. clamp.

**menhus** [û] unluky, ill-omened.

**meni** biol. sperm, semen.

**menkıbe** legend, tale.

**menkul, -lü** [û] 1. movable, conveyable, transferable; 2. conveyed, transported; ~ kıymetler ⚅ stocks and bonds; ~ mallar ⚅ movable goods.

**menolunmak** [x . . .] pass. of menetmek.

**menopoz** ♀ menopause.

**mensucat, -tı** [. - -] textiles.

**mensup, -bu** [û] 1. belonging (-e to), connected (-e to), related (-e to); 2. member; ~ olm. to belong (-e to).

**mensur** [û] (in) prose.

**menşe, -ei** place of origin, source; ~ şahadetnamesi † certificate of origin.

**menteşe** hinge.

**mentol, -lü** menthol.

**mentollü** mentholated.

**menü** menu.

**menzil** 1. range; 2. stage, leg.

**mera** [â] pasture.

**merak, -kı** [â] 1. curiosity; 2. worry, anxiety; 3. passion, whim, interest, liking; ~ etme! don't worry!; ~ etm. (bşi) 1. to be curious about s.th.; 2. to be anxious about s.th.; ~ getirmek to suffer from melancholia; -ı kalkmak to become filled with curiosity; -tan çatlamak to be dying of curiosity, to be burning with curiosity.

**meraklanmak** 1. to worry (-e about), to be anxious (-e about); 2. to be aroused (s.o.'s curiosity).

**meraklı** 1. curious, inquisitive; 2. interested (-e in), fond (-e of); 3. scrupulous, particular.

meraksız 1. incurious, uninquisitive; 2. unworried, unanxious.

meram [ā] intention, purpose, goal, aim; ~ etm. to intend, to wish; -ın elinden bir şey kurtulmaz pro. where there is a will there is a way; -ını anlatmak to express o.s.

merasim [ā] 1. ceremony; 2. formalities; ~ kıtası X guard of hono(u)r, hono(u)r guard.

merbut, -tu [ū] 1. devoted (-e to); 2. attached (or connected) (-e to); 3. dependent (-e upon).

mercan [ā] zo. coral.

mercanada atoll.

mercanbalığı, -nı zo. red sea bream.

mercek lens.

merci, -ii reference, recourse; competent authority.

mercimek ¾ lentil; mercimeği fırına vermek co. to carry on with.

merdane [ā] 1. cylinder, roller; 2. mangle, wringer; 3. rolling pin.

merdiven 1. stairs, staircase; steps; 2. ladder; ~ basamağı step, stair; ~ dayamak fig. to push (a certain age); ~ sahanlığı landing.

meret, -ti damn.

merhaba [x . .] F hello!, hi!; -yı kesmek (b-le) to break off with s.o.

merhabalaşmak to greet one another.

merhale stage, phase; ~ ~ gradually, by stages.

merhamet, -ti mercy, pity, compassion; ~ etm. (or göstermek) to pity, to have mercy (-e on); -e gelmek to become merciful.

merhametli merciful, compassionate.

merhametsiz merciless, pitiless.

merhem ointment, salve.

merhum [ū] deceased, the late, the departed; ~ olm. to die, to pass away.

merhume [ū] deceased, the late, the departed (woman).

mer'i [i] † in force, valid.

meridyen meridian.

Merih [i] pr. n. ast. Mars.

merinos [. x .] (koyun) Merino sheep.

meriyet, -ti validity; -e girmek to come into force.

merkep donkey.

merkez 1. centre, Am. center; 2. headquarters; 3. police station.

merkezci centralist.

merkezci kuvvet phys. centripetal force.

merkezcilik centralism.

merkezi central.

merkezileşmek to centralize.

merkeziyet, -ti centralism.

merkezkaç kuvvet phys. centrifugal force.

mermer marble.

mermi missile, projectile.

merserize mercerized.

mersi! thanks!, cheers!

mersin 1. ¾ myrtle; 2. (balığı) zo. sturgeon.

mersiye elegy.

mert 1. brave, manly; 2. trustworthy.

mertebe 1. stage, step, degree; 2. rank, position.

mertek beam.

Meryem Ana pr. n. the Virgin Mary.

mesafe [ā] distance, interval, space.

mesaha [. - .] 1. surveying; 2. area; ~ memuru (land) surveyor.

mesai [. - -] efforts, work, pains; ~ arkadaşı colleague; ~ saatleri working hours; ~ yapmak (or -ye kalmak) to work overtime.

mesaj message.

mesame [ā] biol. pore.

mesane [ā] anat. bladder.

mescit masjid, small mosque.

mesel saying, proverb, parable.

mesela [x . -] for instance, for example.

mesele question, problem, matter; issue; ~ çıkarmak to make a fuss; ~ yapmak (bşi) to make a to-do about s.th.

meserret, -ti joy.

meshetmek [x . .] to wipe with the wet palm of one's hand.

Mesih [i] the Messiah, Christ.

mesire [i] promenade.

mesken dwelling, residence, house; ℔ domicile; ~ masuniyeti ℔ domiciliar inviolability.

meskûn inhabited; ~ kılmak to populate.

meslek 1. profession; 2. occupation, line of work; ~ okulu trade (or vocational) school; ~ sahibi professional (person).

mesleki 1. professional; 2. occupational, vocational.

mesleksiz having no profession, out of work.

meslektaş colleague, co-worker, associate.

mesnet, -di 1. support, prop; 2. position, office.

mest¹, -ti enchanted, captivated; ~ olm. to be in the seventh heaven.

mest², -ti light soleless boot.

mesul, -lü [ū] responsible (-den for); ~ tutmak (b-ni bşden) to hold s.o. responsible for s.th.

mesuliyet, -ti [ū] responsibility; ~ kabul etmemek to decline responsibility; ~ si-

gortası ⚹ liability insurance.
mesuliyetli [ū] responsible.
mesut [ū] 1. happy; 2. ♀ [x.] *mf.*
meşakkat, -ti trouble, hardship, fatigue; ~ çekmek to suffer hardship.
meşale cresset; torch.
meşe ⚹ oak; ~ odunu 1. oak wood; 2. *fig.* blockhead.
meşebüken *fig.* strong, brawny.
meşgale occupation, activity, pastime.
meşgul, -lü [ū] 1. busy (*ile* with), preoccupied (*ile* with), concerned (*ile* with), 2. *teleph.* busy, engaged (*line*); ~ etm. to busy, to occupy; to distract; ~ olm. to be busy, to busy o.s. (*ile* with).
meşguliyet, -ti [ū] occupation, activity, pastime, concern.
meşhur [ū] 1. famous, well-known; 2. celebrity; ~ olm. to become famous.
meşhut, -du [ū] witnessed.
meşin leather.
meşk, -ki 1. practice; 2. piece of calligraphy; ~ etm. to practise, *Am.* to practice.
meşrep, -bi temperament, disposition.
meşru, -uu [ū] legal, lawful, legitimate.
meşrubat, -tı [.--] beverages, drinks.
meşruten, -ti [.--] conditionally; ~ tahliye ⚹ release on probation.
meşruti [.--] *pol.* constitutional; ~ krallık constitutional monarchy.
meşrutiyet, -ti [ū] *pol.* constitutional monarchy.
meşum [ū] ill-starred, inauspicious.
meşveret, -ti consultation.
met, -ddi flood (*or* high) tide.
meta, -aı [â] goods, merchandise.
metabolizma *biol.* metabolism.
metafizik 1. metaphysics; 2. metaphysical.
metal, -li metal.
metalurji metallurgy.
metan ⚗ methane.
metanet, -ti [â] fortitude, backbone.
metanetsiz spineless; weak.
metazori [..x.] *sl.* by force.
metelik F bean, red cent; ~ vermemek (*bşe*) *fig.* not to give a damn about *s.th.*; meteliğe kurşun atmak F not to have a bean (*or* red cent), to be flat broke.
meteliksiz without a bean (*or* red cent), penniless, flat broke.
meteoroloji meteorology.
meteortaşı, -nı *ast.* meteorite.
metfen grave.
metfun [ū] buried.
methal, -li 1. entrance; 2. introduction; -i olm. (*b-nin bir işte*) to be involved in *s.th.*, to have a hand in *s.th.*

methaldar [..-] involved (-*e* in).
methetmek to praise, to extol, to laud.
methiye panegyric.
metin[1], -tni text.
metin[2] 1. firm, solid, strong; 2. ♀ [x.] *mf.*
metis *biol.* hybrid.
metodoloji methodology.
metot method.
metrdotel headwaiter.
metre [x.] 1. metre, *Am.* meter; 2. meterstick; ~ kare square metre; ~ küp cubic metre.
metres mistress.
metrik metric; ~ sistem metric system.
metris ✕ breastwork.
metro underground, tube, *Am.* subway.
metronom ♪ metronome.
metruk, -kü [ū] abandoned, deserted.
mevcudat, -tı [.--] assets.
mevcudiyet, -ti [ū] 1. existence; 2. presence.
mevcut, -du [ū] 1. existing; present, extant; 2. supply, stock; 3. ✕ the strength (*of a unit*); ~ olm. 1. to exist, to be; 2. to be present.
mevduat, -tı [.--] † deposits; ~ hesabı deposit account.
mevki, -ii 1. place, location; 2. position, portfolio, rank; 3. class; 4. situation, position.
mevkuf [ū] under arrest.
mevla † master, patron.
Mevla *pr. n.* God.
Mevlevi [î] *pr. n.* Mevlevi.
mevlit *the night of the birth of the Prophet Mohammed;* ~ kandili *the religious celebration held on the evening of the Prophet Mohammed's birth;* ~ okumak to chant the mevlit.
mevsim season.
mevsimlik seasonal.
mevsimsiz 1. untimely, ill-timed; 2. prematurely.
mevzi, -ii ✕ position; ~ almak ✕ to take up a position.
mevzii localized; scattered.
mevzilenmek ✕ to take up a position.
mevzu, -uu [ū] subject, topic; -a girmek to come to the point.
mevzuat, -tı [.--] 1. the laws; 2. containers.
mevzubahis, -hsi subject under discussion.
mevzun [ū] 1. shapely, well-proportioned; 2. *lit.* metrical (*verse*); rhythmical (*prose*).
mey wine.

meyan¹ [ā] = meyankökü.

meyan² [ā] 1. middle, centre, *Am.* center; 2. interval; bu -da while..., among them.

meyanbalı, -nı licorice extract.

meyancı [ā] go-between, mediator.

meyane [ā] 1. a kind of sauce; 2. correct degree of thickness *(for halvah);* -si gelmek to reach the right degree of thickness.

meyankökü, -nü [ā] ⚘ licorice.

meydan [ā] 1. open space; 2. public square; 3. field; 4. ring; arena; 5. opportunity, occasion; possibility; ~ almak to spread, to advance; ~ bulmak to find an opportunity; ~ dayağı public beating; ~ korkusu ⚘ agoraphobia; ~ okumak to challenge, to defy; ~ savaşı X pitched battle; ~ vermek to give a chance; -a atmak to bring up, to broach, to suggest; -a çıkarmak 1. to make public, to reveal, to disclose, to divulge; 2. to bring to light; to expose to view; -a çıkmak to come to light, to be revealed; -a gelmek to happen, to occur; to come into existence; -a getirmek to bring forth, to produce; -a vurmak to make public, to reveal; -da 1. in sight, around; 2. obvious, clear, evident; -ı boş bulmak to seize an opportunity to do s.th.

meydanlık open space, square.

meyhane [ā] pub, café, joint, dive.

meyhaneci [ā] publican, barkeep(er).

meyil, -yli 1. slope, slant, incline; 2. *phys.* inclination, tendency; 3. *fig.* penchant, predilection, fondness, liking.

meyletmek 1. to slant, to slope (-e towards); to lean (-e towards); 2. to be inclined (-e to); 3. *fig.* to have a liking (-e for).

meymenet, -ti fortune, auspiciousness.

meymenetsiz 1. unlucky, inauspicious; 2. disagreeable *(person).*

meyus [û] hopeless, desperate.

meyve fruit; ~ bahçesi orchard; ~ suyu fruit juice; ~ vermek to fruit.

meyveli 1. fruit-laden, fruited; 2. fruit...

meyvelik orchard, grove.

meyvesiz fruitless, unfruitful.

meyyal, -li [ā] inclined (-e to); fond (-e of).

mezalim [ā] cruelties, atrocities.

mezar [ā] grave, tomb; ~ kaçkını *fig.* person with one foot in the grave; ~ kitabesi epitaph.

mezarcı gravedigger.

mezarlık [ā] cemetery, graveyard.

mezat [ā] auction; ~ malı *fig.* bargain; -a çıkarmak to put up for auction.

mezatçı auctioneer.

mezbaha slaughterhouse, abattoir.

mezbele dump, pigsty, pigpen.

meze [x.] snack, appetizer, hors d'oeuvre.

mezgit, -ti *zo.* whiting.

mezhep, -bi denomination, creed, religion; -i geniş too tolerant.

meziyet, -ti virtue, merit, excellence.

meziyetli excellent, superior, virtuous.

mezkûr aforementioned.

mezmur [û] psalm.

Mezopotamya *pr. n.* Mesopotamia.

mezun [- -] 1. graduate; 2. graduated *(-den* from); 3. authorized *(-meğe* to *inf.);* ~ olm. to graduate (-den from).

mezuniyet, -ti [- -..] 1. graduation; 2. authorization, permission; ~ imtihanı leaving (or *Am.* final) examination.

mezura [.x.] tape measure.

mezzosoprano ♪ mezzo-soprano.

mıcır 1. fine gravel; 2. small bits of coal; 3. *sl.* bad egg *(person)*

mıh nail.

mıhladız *s.* mıknatıs.

mıhlamak 1. to nail; 2. to set, to place *(precious stone);* 3. *sl.* to skewer, to stab.

mıhsıçtı *sl.* very niggardly (or stingy).

mıknatıs magnet.

mıknatısi [î] magnetic.

mıknatısiyet, -ti magnetism.

mıknatıslamak to magnetize.

mıknatıslı 1. magnetic; 2. magnetized; ~ iğne magnetic needle.

mıncıklamak 1. to make squishy; 2. to pinch and squeeze.

mıncık mıncık squashed to a pulp; ~ etm. 1. to squash to a pulp; 2. to pinch *(a cheek).*

mıntıka zone, region, area, district.

mırılda(n)mak to mutter, to murmur, to mumble.

mırıl mırıl with a mutter, in low.

mırıltı mutter, mumble.

mırın kırın etm. F to hem and haw, to grumble.

mırlamak to purr.

mırıl mırıl with a mutter, in low.

mır mır with a mutter, in low.

mırnav! meow!

mısır ⚘ maize, corn; ~ buğdayı popcorn; ~ ekmeği corn bread (or pone); ~ koçan corncob.

Mısır *pr. n.* Egypt.

Mısırlı *pr. n.* Egyptian.

mısırözü yağı corn oil.

mısıryağı, -nı corn oil.

mıskal syrinx, panpipe.

**mısra,** -aı [ā] line *(of poetry).*

**mışıl mışıl** soundly; ~ uyumak to sleep soundly.

**mıymıntı** sluggish.

**mızıka** ♪ 1. harmonica, mouth-organ; 2. brass band.

**mızıkacı** ♪ harmonica player.

**mızıkçı** *F* spoilsport, killjoy, bad loser.

**mızıkçılık etm.** not to play the game.

**mızıklanmak** = mızıkçılık etm.

**mızmız** fussbudgety, persnickety, whiny.

**mızmızlanmak** to whine, to fuss.

**mızrak** spear, lance; ~ çuvala girmez (or sığmaz) *pro.* there are some things which cannot be kept secret.

**mızrap,** -bı plectrum, quill, pick.

**mi¹** (mı, mu, mü) *interrogative particle, sometimes adding emphasis;* cahil mi cahil! he is ignorant beyond words; geldi mi? has he come?; yapar mı yapar you can bet your bottom dollar he'll do it.

**mi²** ♪ mi; E.

**miat,** -dı 1. wear life *(of an object);* 2. fixed period; 3. deadline; due date; miadı dolmak to expire, to terminate.

**mibzer** ⊥ sower, seeder.

**miço** [x .] 1. young deckhand; 2. cabin boy.

**mide** [ī] stomach, belly; ~ borusu esophagus; ~ bozukluğu (or fesadı) indigestion; ~ bulantısı nausea; ~ iltihabı gastritis; ~ kanaması gastric bleeding; -si almamak (or kabul etmemek) to have no appetite (-i for); -si bozulmak to have indigestion; -si bulanmak 1. to feel nauseated; 2. *fig.* to smell a rat; -si ekşimek to have heartburn; -si kazınmak to feel peckish, to have a sinking feeling; -ye oturmak to lie heavy on the stomach.

**midesiz** [- . .] 1. eating anything; 2. *fig.* having bad taste.

**midevi** gastric, gastral.

**midi** midi; ~ etek midi skirt.

**midilli** [. x .] pony.

**midye** [x .] *zo.* mussel; ~ dolması stuffed mussel; ~ tavası fried mussel.

**migren** migraine.

**miğfer** helmet.

**mihenk** touchstone, test.

**mihmandar** [. - -] host; hostess.

**mihnet,** -ti trouble, hardship; ~ çekmek to suffer.

**mihrace** [. - .] maharaja(h).

**mihrak,** -kı [ā] *phys.* focus.

**mihrap,** -bı [ā] mihrab, altar.

**mihver** axis; axle, pivot.

**mika** [x .] *geol.* mica.

**mikado** mikado.

**mikâp,** -bı *s.* küp.

**miki (fare)** Mickey Mouse.

**mikrofilm** microfilm.

**mikrofon** microphone.

**mikrometre** micrometer.

**mikron** micron.

**mikroorganizma** microorganism.

**mikrop,** -bu 1. germ, microbe; 2. *fig.* viper, bad lot.

**mikroplu** germy, contaminated.

**mikropsuz** germless.

**mikropsuzlandırmak** to disinfect, to decontaminate.

**mikroskobik** microscopic.

**mikroskop,** -pu microscope.

**miktar** [ā] 1. amount, quantity; 2. portion, part.

**mikyas** [ā] scale, proportion.

**mil¹** ⊕ pivot, pin; axle; shaft; spindle.

**mil²** mile.

**mil³** *geol.* silt.

**mil⁴** † thousand, mille; ~ mersi! thank you very much!

**miladi** [- - -] of the Christian era; ~ takvim the Gregorian calendar.

**milat,** -dı [- -] birth of Christ; -tan önce B.C., before Christ; -tan sonra A.D., anno Domini.

**milföy** mille-feuille, napoleon.

**miligram** milligram(me).

**milim** millimetre, *Am.* millimeter.

**milimetre** millimetre, *Am.* millimeter.

**milis** militia; ~ kuvvetleri militia forces, militia.

**militan** militant.

**millet,** -ti nation, people; ♀ Meclisi the Turkish National Assembly.

**milletlerarası,** -nı international.

**milletvekili,** -ni deputy, M.P.

**milli** national; ~ bayram national holiday; ♀ Eğitim Bakanı the Minister of Education; ♀ Eğitim Bakanlığı the Ministry of Education; ♀ Güvenlik Kurulu the National Security Council; ♀ İstihbarat Teşkilatı the National Intelligence Organization; ~ marş national anthem; ~ takımı national team.

**millileştirmek** to nationalize.

**milliyet,** -ti nationality.

**milliyetçi** nationalist.

**milliyetçilik** nationalism.

**milyar** milliard, *Am.* billion, a thousand million.

**milyarder** billionaire.

**milyon** million.

**milyoner** millionaire.

**mimar** [- -] architect.

**mimari** [- - -] architectural.
**mimarlık** [- - -] architecture.
**mimber** pulpit, mimbar.
**mimik** facial expression.
**mimlemek** to mark down, to blacklist.
**mimli** marked, blacklisted.
**minare** [ā] minaret; ~ gibi as tall as a lamp-post; -yi çalan kılıfını hazırlar pro. if you venture to do s.th. illegal, you must plan it carefully in advance.
**minder** cushion; mattress, mat (a. sports); ~ çürütmek to sit idly, to be a bench warmer; ~ sermek to outstay one's welcome.
**mine** [x .] 1. enamel; 2. dial (of a clock); 3. ♀ wf.
**minelemek** to enamel.
**mineli** enameled.
**mineral,** -li mineral.
**mini** mini; ~ etek miniskirt.
**minibüs** minibus.
**minicik** [x ..] teeny, tiny, wee.
**minik** 1. tiny and cute; 2. tot, toddler.
**minimini** teen(s)y-ween(s)y, itty-bitty.
**minimum** minimum.
**minkale** protractor.
**minnacık** = minimini.
**minnet,** -ti gratitude, indebtedness, obligation; ~ altında kalmak to be obligated; ~ etm. to grovel, to plead.
**minnettar** [ā] grateful (-e to), indebted (-e to), obliged (-e to).
**minnettarlık** [ā] gratitude.
**minnoş** F little darling, honey.
**minör** ♪ minor.
**mintan** shirt.
**minüskül** minuscule.
**minval,** -li [ā] manner, way.
**minyatür** miniature.
**minyon** petite. mignon.
**mir** leader, chief; -im! governer!, my dear fellow!
**mira** surveyor's rod.
**miraç,** -cı [- -] the Prophet Mohammed's ascent to heaven.
**miralay** ✕ colonel.
**miras** [- -] inheritance, legacy; heritage; ~ yemek to inherit; -a konmak to inherit a fortune; -tan ıskat disinheritance; -tan mahrum etm. to disinherit.
**mirasçı** [- -] heir, inheritor, legatee.
**mirasyedi** 1. one who has inherited a fortune; 2. fig. extravagant.
**mis¹** musk; ~ gibi 1. fragrant; 2. super, first-rate.
**mis²** 1. miss; 2. Miss.
**misafir** [ā] 1. guest, visitor; 2. anat. nebula; ~ etm. to put up, to entertain, to have down; ~ gibi oturmak co. to sit in a constrained posture; ~ odası drawing-room, guest room; ~ sanatçı guest artist.
**misafirhane** [ā] 1. guesthouse; 2. hostelry, inn.
**misafirlik** visit; misafirliğe gitmek 1. to pay a visit (-e to); 2. to go on a visit.
**misafirperver** [ā] hospitable.
**misafirperverlik** [ā] hospitality.
**misak,** -kı [- -] pact, treaty.
**misal,** -li [ā] example, model, exemplar; precedent.
**misil,** -sli 1. equal, like, counterpart; 2. as much again; misli görülmemiş unique, matchless; misliyle mukabele ♂♂ retaliation, retortion.
**misilleme** retaliation, retortion.
**misina** fishline.
**misk** s. mis¹.
**miskal,** -li [ā] † miskal.
**misket,** -ti 1. marble; 2. (grape)shot; shrapnel ball.
**miskin** 1. indolent, supine, shiftless; 2. poor, wretched; 3. leprous, lazarous.
**miskinleşmek** to become indolent (or supine).
**miskinlik** supiness, shiftlessness.
**mister** Mister, Mr.
**mistik** mystic(al).
**misyon** mission.
**misyoner** missionary.
**-miş'li geçmiş zaman** gr. the inferential past tense.
**mit,** -ti myth.
**miting** meeting, demonstration; ~ yapmak to hold a meeting.
**mitingci** demonstrator.
**mitoloji** mythology.
**mitralyöz** machine-gun.
**miyar** [- -] 1. ♈ reagent; 2. standard.
**miyav!** meow!
**miyavlamak** to miaow, Am. to meow.
**miyop** nearsighted, shortsighted, myopic.
**miyopluk** nearsightedness, shortsightedness, myopia.
**mizaç,** -cı [ā] disposition, temperament. nature.
**mizah** [ā] humo(u)r; ~ dergisi humo(u)r magazine.
**mizahçı** [ā] humorist.
**mizahi** [. - -] humorous.
**mizan** [- -] 1. scales, balance; 2. ⚖ proof.
**mizana** [. x .] ⚓ mizzenmast.
**mizanpaj** typ. 1. layout; 2. paging up. make-up.
**mizanpli** set.
**mizansen** mise-en-scàne.
**mobilya** [. x .] furniture; ~ mağazası

furniture store.
**mobilyacı** maker *or* seller of furniture.
**mobilyalı** furnished.
**mobilyasız** unfurnished.
**moda** [x .] 1. fashion, vogue, style; 2. fashionable, stylish; ~ olm. to come into vogue, to be in; -sı geçmek to go out of fashion (*or* vogue), to be out, to become démodé; -ya uymak to keep up with fashions.
**modacı** stylist; couturier.
**model** 1. model; 2. pattern; 3. fashion magazine; 4. type, model, style; 5. *F* spitting image; ~ değiştirmek *sl.* to wreck one's car.
**modelci** patternmaker.
**modellik** being a model.
**modern** modern.
**modernize** modernized; ~ etm. to modernize.
**modernleştirmek** to modernize.
**modistra** [. x .] seamstress.
**modül** module.
**modülasyon** ♪ modulation.
**Moğol** *pr. n.* Mongol.
**Moğolistan** *pr. n.* Mongolia.
**moher** mohair.
**mokasen** moccasin.
**mola** [x .] 1. break, rest, pause, stopover; 2. ↓ ease it off!; ~ etm. ↓ to ease off (*rope*); ~ vermek to stop (*or* lay) over.
**molekül** molecule.
**molla** † mullah, mollah.
**molotofkokteyli** Molotov cocktail.
**moloz** 1. rubble, debris; 2. *sl.* swine.
**moment**, -ti *phys.* moment.
**monarşi** monarchy.
**monden** pleasure-loving.
**monogami** monogamy.
**monokl**, -lü monocle.
**monolog** monologue.
**monopol** monopoly.
**monoray** monorail.
**monoton** monotonous.
**monotonluk** monotony.
**monşer** mon cher.
**montaj** assembly, mounting.
**monte etm.** to assemble, to put together.
**mor** violet, purple; ~ etm. *sl.* to put to the blush; ~ olm. *sl.* to turn red in the face.
**moral**, -li morale; ~ vermek (*b-ne*) boost *s.o.*'s morale; -i bozuk low-spirited, down; -ini bozmak (*b-nin*) to get *s.o.* down, to destroy *s.o.*'s morale, to demoralize *s.o.*
**morarmak** 1. to turn purple; 2. to turn black-and-blue.

**morartı** bruise.
**moratoryum** [. . x .] moratorium.
**morfem** *gr.* morpheme.
**morfin** morphine.
**morfinoman** morphine addict.
**morfoloji** morphology.
**morg** morgue.
**morlaşmak** to turn purple.
**morötesi**, -ni ultraviolet.
**mors**[1] *zo.* walrus.
**mors**[2]: ~ alfabesi Morse code.
**mortlamak** *sl.* to kick the bucket, to peg out, to pop off.
**mortlatmak** *sl.* 1. to bump off, to do in, to kill; 2. to clean out, to pluck.
**morto** [x .] *sl.* corpse, stiff; -yu çekmek *sl.* = mortlamak.
**mortocu** 1. driver of a hearse; 2. pallbearer.
**mortu** *s.* morto.
**mortucu** *s.* mortocu.
**moruk** *sl.* old man, dotard.
**moruklaşmak** *sl.* to get old (*or* decrepit).
**morumsu, morumtırak** purplish.
**Moskof** *pr. n.* Russian.
**Moskova** [x . .] *pr. n.* Moscow.
**mosmor** [x .] 1. deep purple; 2. black and blue all over.
**mostra** [x .] sample, pattern, model; ~ olm. to be caught with one's pants down; -sını bozmak (*b-nin*) *sl.* to show *s.o.* up.
**mostralık** [x . .] 1. sample, model; 2. prize example (*or* package).
**motel** motel.
**motif** motif.
**motivasyon** motivation.
**motopomp**, -pu motor-driven pump.
**motor** 1. motor; engine; 2. = motorbot; 3. = motosiklet; 4. *sl.* loose (*woman*); 5. *sl.* dunce, fool; ~ açmak *mot.* to run in.
**motorbot**, -tu motorboat.
**motorcu** motorman.
**motorin** diesel fuel (*or* oil).
**motorize** X motorized; ~ etm. to motorize.
**motorlu** motorized (*a.* X), motor-driven.
**motorsuz** motorless.
**motosiklet**, -ti motorcycle.
**motör**, *s.* motor.
**motörcü** *s.* motorcu.
**motris** 🚋 motor car.
**mozaik** mosaic.
**mozole** mausoleum.
**M.Ö.** B.C.
**möble** furniture.
**möbleli** furnished.
**mönü** menu.
**mösyö** Monsieur.
**M.S.** A.D.

**muadelet**, -ti [â] equality.

**muadil** [â] equivalent.

**muaf** [â] 1. exempt (-den from), free (-den from); 2. ℱ immune; ~ tutmak to exempt (-den from).

**muafiyet**, -ti [â] 1. exemption; 2. ℱ immunity.

**muahede** [â] treaty, pact.

**muaheze** [â] criticism, censure; ~ etm. to criticize.

**muallak**, -kı 1. hung, suspended; 2. up in the air, undecided; -ta kalmak (or olm.) to be in the air, to hang in the balance.

**muallim** teacher, preceptor.

**muallime** schoolmistress.

**muamele** [â] 1. transaction, processing, procedure; 2. conduct, behavio(u)r, treatment; 3. trading, dealing; 4. ⸕ reaction; ~ etm. (b-ne) to treat s.o.

**muamma** [. x -] 1. enigma, mystery; 2. riddle.

**muammalı** enigmatic.

**muare** moiré.

**muarız** [â] opposed (-e to).

**muasır** [â] contemporary.

**muaşeret**, -ti [â] social intercourse; ~ adabı etiquette.

**muavenet**, -ti [â] help, assistance; ~ etm. to help, to assist.

**muavin** [â] assistant, helper.

**muayene** [â] inspection, examination (a. ℱ); ~ etm. to examine, to inspect.

**muayeneci** [â] 1. customs officer; 2. examiner.

**muayenehane** [â, â] surgery, consulting room.

**muayyen** fixed, determined, definite.

**muazzam** 1. huge, enormous; 2. F terrific, magnificent.

**mubah** [â] permissible, fair.

**mubayaa** [. - .] buying; ~ etm. to buy, to purchase.

**mubayaacı** [. - . .] stockbroker.

**mucibince** [- . x .] in accordance with, as required by.

**mucip**, -bi [û] cause, reason; ~ olm. to necessitate, to entail.

**mucit** [û] 1. inventor; 2. inventive, creative.

**mucize** [û] miracle; -ler yaratmak to work miracles.

**mucizevi** [- . . -] miracular, miraculous.

**mucur** 1. bits of coal; 2. fine gravel; 3. trash, debris, rubbish.

**muço** s. mıço.

**mudi**, -ii ⸕ depositor.

**mufassal** detailed.

**mufassalan** [. x .] in detail.

**muflon** zo. mouflon.

**mugayir** [â] contrary (-e to).

**muğlak**, -kı obscure, abstruse, recondite.

**muhabbet**, -ti 1. chat; 2. love, affection; ~ etm. to chat; ~ tellalı pimp, procurer.

**muhabbetçiçeği**, -ni ♀ mignonette.

**muhabbetkuşu**, -nu zo. lovebird, parakeet.

**muhabbetli** affectionate.

**muhaberat**, -tı [â, â] correspondence, communications.

**muhabere** [â] correspondence; communications; ~ etm. to correspond (ile with); to communicate (ile with); ~ sınıfı Signal Corps.

**muhabir** [â] correspondent, reporter.

**muhaceret**, -ti [â] immigration.

**muhacir** [â] immigrant, emigrant, refugee.

**muhafaza** [. - .] protection, care; maintenance, preservation; ~ altına almak to protect, to safeguard; ~ etm. to protect, to preserve, to guard.

**muhafazakâr** [. - . -] conservative.

**muhafazakârlık** conservatism.

**muhafız** [â] (body)guard, guardsman; ~ alayı ✕ troop of guardsmen.

**muhakeme** [â] 1. trial; adjudication; 2. judg(e)ment, discernment; ~ etm. 1. ⚖ to try; 2. to judge, to reason.

**muhakkak** 1. certain, sure; 2. certainly, without doubt, undoubtedly.

**muhalefet**, -ti [â] 1. opposition; 2. pol. the Opposition; ~ etm. to oppose; ~ partisi Opposition party.

**muhalif** [â] 1. contrary (-e to), against, adverse; 2. opposing; Opposition...

**muhallebi** pudding; ~ çocuğu milksop, namby-pamby, mollycoddle.

**muhammem** ⸕ estimated (value, etc.).

**Muhammet**, -di (a. Hazreti ~) Mohammed.

**muhammin** ⸕ appraiser.

**muharebe** [â] battle, war, combat; ~ etm. to fight, to battle; ~ meydanı battlefield.

**muharip**, -bi [â] ✕ 1. warrior, combatant; 2. belligerent; combat...

**muharrem** 1. Muharram; 2. ♀ mf., wf.

**muharrik**, -ki 1. moving, motive...; 2. fig. inciter, instigator.

**muharrir** writer, author.

**muhasara** [. - .] ✕ siege; ~ etm. to besiege, to beleaguer; -yı kaldırmak to raise a siege.

**muhasebe** [â] accountancy, bookkeeping; ~ memuru accountant, bookkeeper.

**muhasebeci** [â] accountant, bookkeeper.

**muhasebecilik** [â] accountancy, bookkeeping.

muhasım [ā] hostile, enemy; opponent.

muhasip, -bi [ā] accountant, bookkeeper.

muhatap, -bı [. - .] 1. collocutor; 2. ￢ drawee.

muhatara [. - . .] danger, risk.

muhataralı [. - . . .] dangerous.

muhavere [ā] conversation, talk; ~ etm. to converse.

muhavvile ✄ transformer.

muhayyel imaginary.

muhayyer 1. ￢ on trial (or approval); 2. ♪ a makam.

muhayyile imagination, fancy.

muhbir 1. informer; 2. reporter, correspondent.

muhit, -ti [ī] 1. surroundings, environment, milieu; 2. area, district, neighbo(u)rhood.

muhkem solid, tight, firm.

muhlis 1. sincere; 2. ♀ mf.

muhrip, -bi destroyer.

muhtaç, -cı [ā] needy, poor, destitute, indigent; ~ olm. to be in need (or want) (-e of), to need.

muhtar 1. [. -] autonomous, self-governing; 2. [. .] mukhtar, headman.

muhtariyet, -ti [ā] autonomy, self-government.

muhtarlık 1. being a mukhtar; 2. the mukhtar's office.

muhtasar short, brief, concise.

muhtasaran [. x . .] briefly, concisely.

muhtekir profiteer.

muhtelif various, diverse.

muhtelit, -ti 1. mixed; 2. ⚗ complex; ~ mahkeme ⚖ mixed court.

muhtemel likely, probable.

muhtemelen probably.

muhterem respected, hono(u)red, esteemed, venerable.

muhteris passionate.

muhteriz shy, timid.

muhteşem splendid, magnificent, imposing, grand.

muhteva [ā] content(s).

muhtevi [ī] containing.

muhteviyat, -tı [ā] contents.

muhtıra 1. pol. note, warning; 2. diary; 3. memorandum; ~ defteri notebook.

mukabele [ā] 1. retaliation, response, reciprocation; 2. comparison; ~ etm. to retaliate, to reciprocate.

mukabil [ā] 1. counter...; 2. counterpart; 3. in return (-e for); 4. in response (-e to); buna ~ in return for this; ~ dava ⚖ counterclaim; ~ taarruz ✗ counterattack; -inde by way of return.

mukaddeme preface, introduction.

mukadder predestined, fated, foreordained.

mukadderat, -tı [. . . .] destiny, fate.

mukaddes holy, sacred; blessed.

mukaddesat, -tı [ā] sacred things.

mukallit, -di imitator.

mukavele [ā] agreement, contract; ~ yapmak to make a contract.

mukaveleli [ā] bound by contract.

mukavelename [. - . . . .] contract, agreement; deed.

mukavemet, -ti [ā] 1. resistance; endurance; 2. phls. nolition; ~ etm. to resist; ~ yarışı long-distance race.

mukavemetçi [ā] pol. resistance fighter.

mukavemetli [ā] resistant.

mukavemetsiz [ā] irresisting.

mukavim [ā] resistant.

mukavva cardboard.

mukayese [ā] comparison; ~ etm. to compare.

mukayeseli [ā] comparative.

mukayyet, -di 1. recorded, registered; 2. bound (ile by), limited (ile by); ~ olm. to mind, to look after.

mukim [ī] who resides (or dwells) (-de in).

muktedir 1. capable, able; 2. potent, virile; ~ olm. to be able (-e to), to be capable (-e of).

mulaj 1. moulage (a. ✄); 2. impression, cast.

mum 1. candle; 2. wax; 3. ✄ candlepower; watt; ~ dibine ışık vermez pro. one who helps others sometimes is unable to help himself; ~ direk ramrod straight; ~ gibi 1. = ~ direk; 2. well-behaved; ~ ışığı candlelight; ~ olm. 1. to become obedient; 2. sl. to be willing to do s.th.; -a döndürmek (or çevirmek) to make obedient; -la aramak fig. to crave (or hanker) for.

mumcu candlemaker, chandler.

mumlamak to wax.

mumlu waxed; ~ kâğıt stencil.

mumya [x .] mummy.

mumyalamak to mummify, to embalm.

mumyalaşmak to be mummified.

munafık, -kı [ā] mischief-maker.

munis [ū] 1. sociable, friendly; 2. well-known, familiar; 3. tame.

munkabız constipated.

muntazam 1. regular, even, uniform; 2. regularly; 3. methodical; orderly.

muntazaman regularly, orderly.

munzam added; supplementary; additional.

murabaha [. - ..] ǒǒ usury.

murabba¹, -aı Ą square.

murabba² [. . -] preserved fruit.

murahhas delegate; ~ heyet delegation.

murakabe [. - ..] 1. inspection, supervision; 2. contemplation; ~ etm. to inspect.

murakıp, -bı [ā] 1. inspector; 2. Ṭ auditor.

murat, -dı [ā] 1. desire, wish; aim, intention, goal; 2. º mf.; muradına ermek to attain one's desire, to reach one's goal.

murdar dirty, filthy; ~ ilik spinal cord.

Musa [- -] pr. n. 1. Moses; 2. mf.

musahhih proofreader.

musahhihlik proofreading.

musakka moussaka.

musalla [. . -] 1. public place for prayer; 2. area within a mosque for performing a funeral service, ~ taşı stone on which the coffin is placed during the funeral service.

musallat, -tı worrying, annoying; ~ etm. (b-ni b-ne) to set s.o. to pester s.o., to cause s.o. to plauge s.o.; ~ olm. to pester, to bother, to pick on; to infest; to plague.

musandıra [. x ..] large cupboard.

musannif † 1. compiler (of a book); 2. classifier.

Musevi [. -.] 1. Jew; 2. Jewish.

Musevilik [- . -.] Judaism.

Mushaf the Koran.

musibet, -tı (i) 1. calamity, disaster; 2. F a pain in the neck, pest; 3. fig. ill-omened.

musikar [. . -] 1. panpipe; 2. a kind of mythical bird.

musiki [. . -] music.

musikişinas [- . -. - .] 1. musician; 2. lover of music.

muska amulet, charm.

muslin muslin.

musluk 1. tap, faucet, spigot; 2. F washbasin, lavatory; ~ taşı stone sink.

muslukçu 1. plumber; 2. sl. pickpocket.

muson meteor. monsoon.

mustarip, -bı suffering.

muşamba [. x .] 1. oilcloth; oilskin; 2. linoleum; 3. raincoat, slicker; ~ gibi very dirty (clothes).

muşmula [x . .] 1. Ұ medlar; 2. sl. antique, old person; ~ suratlı who has a wrinkled face.

muşta [x .] 1. blow with the fist; 2. brass knucks (or knuckles).

muştu good news.

mut, -tu happiness.

mutaassıp, -bı fanatical, bigoted, strict.

mutaassıplık fanaticism, bigotry.

mutabakat, -tı [. - ..] 1. agreement, conformity, correspondence, congruity; 2. Ą identity; -a varmak to come to an agreement.

mutabık, -kı [ā] 1. in agreement, agreeing, conformable; 2. appropriate (-e to), suited (-e to); ~ kalmak to come to an agreement (-de on).

mutaf [ū] weaver of goat's-hair articles.

mutarıza bracket, parenthesis.

mutasarrıf 1. ǒǒ owner, possessor; 2. hist. governer of a sancak.

mutasavvıf Sufi; mystic.

mutat customary, habitual.

mutavassıt, -tı go-between, intermediary.

muteber [ū] 1. valid, in force (or effect); 2. esteemed, eminent; 3. trustworthy; believable; ~ olm. to be valid, to be in force (or effect).

muteberan [- . . -] big shots, bigwigs.

mutedil [ū] 1. moderate, mild, temperate; 2. ♏ neutral.

mutekit, -dı [ū] religious, pious.

mutemet, -dı [ū] 1. paymaster, fiduciary 2. trustworthy.

mutena [- . -] 1. select, refined; 2. delicate; 3. carefully done.

mutfak 1. kitchen; 2. cuisine.

mutlak, -kı 1. absolute, unconditional; 2. absolutely, surely; by all means; ~ ekseriyet absolute majority.

mutlaka [x . -] absolutely, certainly, surely, definitely, undoubtedly; by all means.

mutlakiyet, -tı 1. absolutism; 2. autocracy.

mutlu 1. happy; 2. lucky, fortunate; ne mutlu Türküm diyene! he is a lucky person who can call himself a Turk!

mutluluk happiness.

mutsuz unhappy.

mutsuzluk unhappiness.

muttasıl 1. adjoining; 2. continuously.

muvacehe [ā] confrontation; -sinde in the face (-in of).

muvafakat, -tı [. - ..] consent; ~ etm. to consent (-e to).

muvaffak, -kı successful; ~ olm. to succeed (-de in), to be successful (-de in).

muvaffakiyet, -tı success.

muvaffakiyetli successful.

muvaffakiyetsiz unsuccessful.

muvaffakiyetsizlik unsuccess, failure.

muvafık, -kı [ā] suitable, appropriate, fit.

muvahhit monotheist.

muvakkat, -tı temporary, provisional; interim.

muvakkaten [. x ..] temporarily.

muvasala [. - ..] communication.

muvazaa [. - . .] ळ collusion.

muvazaalı [. - . . .] ळ collusive, collusory.

muvazene [ā] 1. balance, equilibrium; 2. ₹ sense of balance, equilibrium sense.

muvazeneli [ā] balanced, in equilibrium.

muvazenesiz [ā] unbalanced.

muvazi [. - -] parallel.

muvazzaf 1. X regular; 2. charged (ile with); ~ subay X regular (or active) officer.

muylu ⊕ hub.

muz ⚘ banana; ~ gibi olm. sl. to be rattled.

muzaffer 1. victorious, triumphant; 2. ♀ mf.

muzafferiyet, -ti victory, triumph.

muzır, -rrı 1. mischievous, naughty; 2. injurious, harmful.

muzırlık 1. mischievousness; 2. harmfulness.

muzip, -bi [ū] plaguing, tormenting; mischievous.

muziplik [ū] kidding, teasing; ~ etm. to kid, to tease.

mübadele [ā] exchange, barter, trade; ~ etm. to exchange, to trade, to swap.

mübadil [ā] exchangee.

mübalağa exaggeration; ~ etm. to exaggerate.

mübalağacı exaggerator.

mübalağalı exaggerated, blown-up.

mübarek, -ki [ā] 1. blessed; sacred, holy; 2. confounded, blasted; 3. F you son of a gun!; ~ olsun! may it be blessed!

mübaşir [ā] usher, crier.

mübayenet, -ti [ā] conflict.

mübrem inescapable.

mücadele [ā] struggle, fight, contention, fray, combat, strife; ~ etm. to struggle, to fight, to strive, to contend (ile with).

mücadeleci [ā] striver, fighter, contender.

mücahit, -di [ā] combatant, fighter, champion.

mücbir compelling; ~ sebepler ळ force majeure.

mücehhez 1. equipped (ile with) fitted out (ile with); 2. ready, prepared (ile with).

mücellit, -di bookbinder.

mücellithane [ā] bookbindery.

mücerret, -di 1. abstract; 2. unmarried; 3. gr. the nominative case; 4. [x . .] F only, solely.

mücessem 1. personified; 2. three-dimensional.

mücevher jewel.

mücevherat, -tı [ā] jewel(le)ry.

mücevherci jewel(l)er.

mücmel concise.

mücrim 1. guilty; 2. criminal, felon.

mücver croquette.

müdafaa [. - . .] defence, Am. defense; ~ etm. to defend; ~ hakkı ळ right of defence; ~ hattı X line of defence.

müdafaasız [. - . . .] defenceless, Am. defenseless, undefended.

müdafi, -ii [ā] 1. defender; 2. football: back.

müdahale [. - . .] interference, intervention; ~ etm. to interfere, to intervene, to step in.

müdana [. - -] gratitude, thankfulness.

müdavim [ā] frequenter, habitué.

müddei [ī] ळ plaintiff.

müddeiumumi [. . . - - .] ळ public prosecutor.

müddeiumumilik public prosecutorship.

müddet, -ti period, duration, space of time, interval, while; bir ~ for a while.

müderris 1. † professor; 2. hist. teacher in a medrese.

müdevver 1. circular, round, spherical; 2. transferred.

müdire [ī] 1. headmistress; 2. manageress, directress.

müdiriyet, -ti [. - . .] s. müdürlük.

müdrik, -ki perceiving, comprehending; ~ olm. to perceive, to comprehend.

müdür 1. director, head, chief; manager; 2. principal, headmaster.

müdürlük 1. directorate; 2. directorship.

müebbeden [. x . .] forever, eternally.

müebbet, -di 1. perpetual, eternal, endless; 2. life, lifelong; ~ hapis ळ life (sentence).

müellif writer, author.

müessese [. x . .] institution, foundation, establishment, organization.

müessif regrettable; sad.

müessir 1. touching, heart-moving; 2. influential, effective; 3. ⚕ active; ~ fiil ळ assault and battery.

müessis founder, establisher.

müeyyide ळ sanction.

müezzin isl. muezzin.

müfettiş inspector, supervisor.

müfettişlik inspectorship; inspectorate.

müflis bankrupt, insolvent.

müfredat, -tı [ā] items (of a list); ~ programı (bir okulun) curriculum.

müfreze X detachment, platoon.

müfrit, -di excessive.

müfsit, -di seditious.

müfteri [ī] slanderer, calumniator.

müftü isl. mufti.

müge 1. ⚘ lily of the valley; 2. ♀ wf.

mühendis engineer.

mühendislik engineering.

mühim, -mmi important.

mühimmat, -tı [ā] munitions.

mühimsemek to consider important, to regard as important.

mühlet, -ti period, respite, delay, extension.

mühre 1. stone used for polishing or grinding; 2. decoy.

mührelemek to grind with a mühre.

mühtedi [ī] convert to Islam.

mühür, -hrü 1. seal, signet; signet ring; 2. stamp; ~ basmak to seal; to stamp; ~ mumu sealing wax; mührünü basmak fig. to vouch (-e for); mührünü yalamak fig. to go back on one's word.

mühürcü engraver of seals.

mühürdar [ā] hist. private secretary of a high official.

mühürlemek 1. to seal; to stamp; 2. to seal up, to padlock (a place).

mühürlü sealed.

müjde good news; ~ vermek to give a piece of good news.

müjdeci harbinger, herald.

müjdelemek to give a piece of good news.

müjdelik present given to s.o. who brings good news.

mükâfat, -tı [. - -] reward; prize, recompense; ~ almak (or kazanmak) to win a prize; ~ vermek (b-ne) to give s.o. a prize (or reward).

mükâfatlandırmak [. - - . . .] to reward, to recompense.

mükâleme 1. conversation; 2. diplomatic conference, 3. X parley; ~ memuru (or subayı) X officer with the flag of truce.

mükellef 1. obliged (-mekle to inf.), charged (ile with); 2. elaborate, grand; 3. taxpayer.

mükellefiyet, -ti obligation, liability.

mükemmel excellent, perfect, superb, consummate.

mükemmeliyet, -ti mükemmellik perfection.

mükerrer repeated, reiterated; ~ ıskonto † rediscount; ~ sigorta † reinsurance.

müktesep, -bi acquired; ~ hak ٪٥ vested right.

mülahaza consideration; observation; ~ etm. to think twice; -sıyla in consideration of.

mülahazat, -tı [. . - .] observations; thoughts; ~ hanesi blank space; ~ hanesini açık bırakmak fig. to reserve comment.

mülakat, -tı [. - -] interview, audience;

~ yapmak to have an interview (ile with).

mülayemet, -ti 1. docility; 2. looseness in the bowels.

mülayim 1. docile, gentle, mild; 2. suitable, reasonable.

mülazım 1. † probationer; 2. X lieutenant.

mülhem inspired.

mülk, -kü property, real estate, possession; ~ almak to buy landed property; ~ sahibi property owner.

mülki [ī] civil(ian).

mülkiye 1. civil service; 2. ♀ (Mektebi) the School of Political Science.

mülkiyet, -ti ownership, proprietorship, possession; ~ hakkı ٪٥ property right.

mülteci [ī] refugee.

mültefit courteous, attentive.

mültezim hist. tax farmer.

mültimilyoner multimillionaire.

mümbit, -ti fertile.

mümessil 1. representative, agent; 2. prefect, monitor.

mümeyyiz 1. examiner; 2. distinctive.

mümin [- .] isl. believer, Muslim.

mümkün possible; ~ kılmak to render possible; ~ mertebe or ~ olduğu kadar as far as possible.

mümtaz [ā] 1. select, distinguished; 2. privileged, special; 3. ♀ mf.

münakale [. - . .] transport.

münakaşa [. - . .] argument, dispute, debate; wrangle, quarrel; ~ etm. to argue, to dispute; to quarrel.

münasebet, -ti [ā] 1. relation; 2. connection, tie-in; 3. opportunity; 4. reason; means; 5. fitness; ~ almaz it isn't fit; ~ kurmak to establish a relationship (ile with); -iyle on the occasion of, because of; -te bulunmak 1. to have relations (or dealings) (ile with); 2. to go to bed (ile with).

münasebetli [ā] 1. opportune, favo(u)rable; 2. appropriate; ~ münasebetsiz without considering whether it is suitable or not.

münasebetsiz [ā] 1. unfavo(u)rable, inopportune; 2. inappropriate; unseemly; 3. tactless, inconsiderate.

münasip 1. suitable, proper, fit; 2. opportune, reasonable, convenient; ~ görmek to see fit.

münavebe [ā] alternation, turn; ~ ile by turns.

münzaa [. - . .] quarrel, dispute.

münazara [. - . .] debate, discussion.

münderecat, -tı [ā] contents.

münebbih 1. stimulative; 2. (saat) †

alarm clock.
müneccim † astrologer.
münekkit, -di critic.
münevver 1. enlightened, intellectual, cultivated; 2. ♀ *wf.*
münfail offended.
münferit, -di separate, alone, isolated; ~ hücre solitary cell.
münfesih 1. dissolved, broken off; 2. abolished, annulled.
münhal, -li 1. vacant, vacated; 2. ♔ soluble; 3. ♔ dissolved.
münhasır limited (-e to), restricted (-e to).
Münih *pr. n.* Munich.
münkir 1. denier; 2. atheist.
müntahabat, -tı [. . . -] anthology.
müntahap, -bı select, choice.
münteha [ā] end, limit.
münteşir published.
münzevi [ī] reclusive, hermitic.
müphem vague, uncertain, indefinite.
müphemiyet, -ti vagueness.
müptela 1. addicted (-e to); 2. in love (-e with); 3. afflicted (-e with); ~ olm. to become addicted (-e to).
müptezel vulgar, common.
müracaat, -tı [. - . .] 1. application; 2. reference, recourse; 3. information desk (or office); ~ etm. 1. to apply (-e to); 2. to resort (-e to), to turn (-e to).
müracaatçı applicant.
mürai [. - -] two-faced, hypocritical.
mürdolmak [x . .] to die.
mürdümeriği, -ni ♀ damson (plum).
mürebbiye governess.
müreffeh well-off, well-heeled.
mürekkep¹, -bi ink; ~ hokkası inkwell; ~ lekesi inkstain; ~ yalamış *fig.* well educated.
mürekkep² composed (-den of), made up (-den of).
mürekkepbalığı, -nı *zo.* cuttlefish.
mürekkeplemek to ink.
mürekkepli inky; ink-stained.
mürekkeplik inkwell.
mürettebat, -tı [ā] crew.
mürettebatsız [ā] unmanned.
mürettip, -bi compositor, typesetter.
mürettiphane [ā] *typ.* composing room.
mürit, -di [ī] disciple.
mürşit, -di 1. guide; mentor; 2. sheikh.
mürteci, -ii reactionary.
mürtet, -ddi apostate Muslim.
mürur [ū] passage, transit.
müruriye 1. laissez-passer; 2. toll.
müruruzaman [. - . . -] ♔ prescription; limitation.

mürüvvet, -ti 1. joy *(felt by parents when they see their children reach certain stages in life)*; 2. generosity; -ini görmek to see one's children grow up and do well.
mürver ♀ elder(berry).
müsaade [. - . .] permission; leave; ~ etm. to permit, to let, to allow; -nizle! with your permission (or leave)!
müsabaka [. - . .] contest, competition.
müsabık, -kı [ā] competitor, contestant.
müsademe [ā] 1. collision, clash; 2. X skirmish.
müsadere [ā] ♔ confiscation, seizure; ~ etm. to seize, to confiscate.
müsait, -di [ā] suitable, favo(u)rable, convenient.
müsamaha [. - . .] tolerance, lenience, indulgence; ~ etm. (or göstermek) 1. (b-ne) to be lenient with *s.o.*, to tolerate *s.o.*; 2. (bşe) to overlook *s.th.*, to disregard *s.th.*
müsamahakâr müsamahalı tolerant, lenient, indulgent.
müsamere [ā] show.
müsavat, -tı [. - -] equality.
müsavi [. - -] equal.
müsebbip, -bi cause(r).
müseccel registered; ~ marka registered trademark.
müsekkin ♔ sedative, tranquilizer.
müselles ∆ 1. triangle; 2. triangular.
müshil ♔ laxative, aperient; purgative, cathartic.
müskirat, -tı alcoholic drinks, intoxicants.
Müslim Muslim.
Müslüman Muslim.
Müslümanlık 1. Islam; 2. the Moslem world.
müsmir fruitful, productive.
müspet, -ti 1. positive, affirmative; 2. proved, established; ~ cevap positive (or affirmative) answer.
müsrif wasteful, extravagant, spendthrift, prodigal.
müsriflik wastefulness, extravagance.
müstacel [ā] urgent.
müstaceliyet, -ti [ā] urgency.
müstahak, -kkı 1. condign; 2. worthy (-e of), deserving (-e of); -ını bulmak to get one's deserts.
müstahdem employee, servant, caretaker, *Am.* janitor.
müstahkem X fortified.
müstahsil producer.
müstahzar preparation.
müstahzarat, -tı [. . . -] preparations.
müstakbel (the) future.

müstakil, -lli 1. independent; autonomous; 2. detached, self-contained, separate; ~ ev detached house.

müstamel [ã] used; secondhand.

müstear [ã] 1. borrowed; 2. pseudo.

müstebit, -ddi despotic, tyrannical.

müstebitlik despotism.

müstecir [. - .] tenant, renter.

müstehcen obscene; pornographic, off colo(u)r.

müstehlik, -ki † comsumer.

müstehzi [î] mocking, sarcastic, ironical.

müstekreh loathsome.

müstemleke colony.

müstemlekeci colonialist.

müstemlekecilik colonialism.

müstenit, -di based (-e on), relying (-e on).

müsterih [î] at ease; ~ olm. to be set at ease.

müstesna [ã] 1. exceptional, extraordinary; 2. except for, with the exception for.

müsteşar [ã] 1. undersecretary; 2. counselor.

müsteşarlık [ã] 1. undersecretaryship; 2. counselorship.

müsteşrik, -kı orientalist.

müstevi [î] 1. ⅄ plane; 2. level, flat.

müsvedde 1. draft, rough copy; 2. manuscript; typescript; 3. fig. parody; ~ defteri notebook.

müşahede [ã] observation; ~ altında under medical observation; ~ etm. to observe, to see.

müşahhas concrete.

müşahit, -di observer.

müşavere [ã] consultation.

müşavir [ã] consultant, adviser.

müşerref 1. hono(u)red, exalted; 2. ♀ mf., wf.; ~ olm. to be (or feel) hono(u)red; ~ oldum I am hono(u)red to meet you.

müşfik kind, tender; compassionate.

müşir s. müşür.

müş'ir ⊕ gauge, indicator.

müşkül 1. difficult, hard; 2. difficulty, problem, trouble.

müşkülat, -tı difficulties, problems; ~ çıkarmak (or göstermek) (b-ne) to raise difficulties for s.o.

müşkülpesent, -di fastidious, fussy, hard to please, particular.

müşrik, -ki polytheist.

müstak[1], -kkı derived.

müstak[2], -kı longing (or pining) (-e for).

müsteki [î] complainant.

müstemilat, -tı outbuildings; additions, annexes.

müşterek, -ki common, joint; cooperative, combined; ~ bahis pari-mutuel; ~ duvar party wall; ~ mülkiyet co-ownership.

müştereken [. x ..] in common, jointly.

müşteri customer, buyer, purchaser, client; ~ avlamak to try to attract customers by artifice.

Müşteri ast. Jupiter.

müşür (field) marshal.

mütalaa [. - ..] 1. study; 2. observation, opinion; ~ etm. 1. to study, to peruse; 2. to ponder, to deliberate.

mütareke [ã] armistice, truce.

müteaddit numerous, many.

müteahhit builder, contractor.

müteakiben 1. afterwards, subsequently; 2. after, following.

mütebessim smiling.

mütecanis [ã] homogeneous.

mütecaviz [ã] 1. exceeding, over; 2. aggressive.

mütecessis inquisitive, nosy, curious.

mütedavil [ã] 1. current, in circulation; 2. working (capital); ~ sermaye working capital.

müteessif grieved, sorry, regretful; ~ olm. to be grieved, to regret.

müteessir 1. depressed, saddened; pained, hurt; 2. influenced; affected; ~ olm. (bşden) 1. to be saddened (or depressed) by s.th.; 2. to be influenced (or affected) by s.th.

mütefekkir thinker.

müteferrik, -kı scattered, dispersed; diverse, sundry.

müteferrika petty cash.

müteharrik, -ki 1. mobile, moving; 2 powered (or driven) (ile by).

mütehassıs specialist, expert.

mütehassis touched, moved; ~ etm. to touch, to move; ~ olm. to be touched (or moved).

mütehayyir amazed, taken aback.

mütekabil [ã] mutual, reciprocal; ~ dava ☪ cross action.

mütekabiliyet, -ti [ã] reciprocity.

mütekait, -di [ã] pensioner; retired.

mütekâmil mature.

mütekebbir haughty, arrogant.

mütemadi [. . - -] continuous.

mütemadiyen [ã] [.. x ..] continuously, continually.

mütenahi [. . - -] ⅄, phls. finite.

mütenasip, -bi [ã] 1. proportional; 2. well-proportioned, shapely.

mütenavip, -bi [ã] alternate.

mütenevvi, -ii various, diverse.

**müteradif** [ā] synonymous.

**müterakim** [ā] accumulated.

**mütercim** translator.

**mütereddit**, -di hesitant, undecided, indecisive.

**müteselsil** 1. continuous, successive; 2. ♒ joint; ~ alacaklılar ♒ joint creditors; ~ borçlular ♒ joint debtors; ~ mesuliyet ♒ joint liability; ~ suç ♒ crime involving another crime.

**müteşebbis** 1. enterprising *(person)*; 2. entrepreneur.

**müteşekkil** composed (-*den* of).

**müteşekkir** grateful, thankful.

**mütevazı**, -ıı modest, humble.

**müteveccih** 1. aimed *(-e* at), directed *(-e* towards); 2. sympathetic (-*e* to).

**müteveccihen** [..x..] in the direction (-*e* of), headed (-*e* towards), bound (-*e* for).

**müteveffa** [ā] the deceased.

**mütevekkil** who puts his trust in God.

**mütevelli** [ī] trustee *(of a* vakıf), mutawalli; ~ heyeti board of trustees *(of a* vakıf).

**mütevellit**, -di caused (-*den* by), resulting (-*den* from).

**müthiş** 1. terrible, awful, dreadful, terrific, frightful; 2. *fig.* amazing, astounding.

**müttefik**, -ki 1. ally; 2. allied; ~ devletler the allied powers, the allies.

**müttehit**, -di united.

**müvekkil** client.

**müverrih** historian.

**müvezzi**, -ii 1. distributor; 2. paperboy; postman.

**müzakere** [ā] 1. discussion, deliberation, negotiation; 2. oral test, recitation; ~ etm. to discuss, to debate, to talk over, to deliberate.

**müzakereci** [ā] tutor.

**müzayede** [ā] auction; ~ ile satış sale by auction; -ye koymak to put up for auction.

**müze** [x .] museum.

**müzeci** museum curator.

**müzecilik** museology.

**müzehhep**, -bi gilded, gilt.

**müzelik** [x ..] 1. museum...; 2. *fig. co.* ancient, antiquated.

**müziç**, -ci troublesome, vexatious.

**müzik** music.

**müzikal** musical.

**müzikçi** musician.

**müzikhol**, -lü music hall.

**müziksever** 1. music lover; 2. music-loving, fond of music.

**müzisyen** musician.

**müzmin** chronic *(disease);* ~ bekâr confirmed bachelor.

**müzminleşmek** to become chronic.

# N

**na!** *sl.* 1. take it!; 2. there it is; ~ kafa! what a fool I was!

**naaş,** -a'şı corpse, body.

**nabız,** -bzı pulse; ~ yoklamak *fig.* to put out feelers; nabzına göre şerbet vermek *fig.* to feel one's way with a person; nabzını tutmak to take s.o.'s pulse; nabzını yoklamak (b-nin) *fig.* to sound s.o. out.

**nacak** hatchet.

**naçar** [- -] 1. helpless; 2. hopeless.

**naçiz** [- -] 1. insignificant, worthless; 2. humble.

**naçizane** [- . - .] 1. humble *(opinion)*; 2. humbly; 3. = naçiz 1.

**nadan** [- -] unmannerly, rude, boorish.

**nadas** fallow; ~ etm. to fallow; -a bırakmak to leave the land fallow.

**nadide** [- - .] 1. rare, curious, precious; 2. ♀ [x . .] *wf.*

**nadim** regretful; ~ olm. to regret.

**nadir** [ā] 1. rare, scarce; 2. rarely; 3. ♀ *mf.*

**nadirat,** -tı [- . -] rarities; -tan olm. to be a rarity.

**nadiren** [ā] [x . .] rarely.

**nafaka** 1. ♫ alimony; 2. livelihood, living; ~ bağlamak to assign a subsistence.

**nafıa** [- . .] public works.

**nafile** [ā] 1. vain, useless, futile; 2. in vain, for nothing; ~ namaz *isl.* supererogatory prayer; ~ yere in vain.

**nafiz** [ā] 1. *fig.* influential; 2. ♀ *mf.*

**naftalin** ☊ naphthalene.

**naftalinlemek** to put naphthalene (-i among).

**nağme** 1. tune, melody, air; 2. tone; 3. song; 4. *fig.* sham protestation; -yi değiştirmek *fig.* to change one's tune.

**nah** *s.* na.

**nahak,** -kkı unjust; ~ yere unjustly, unjustifiably.

**nahif** [ī] gaunt, emaciated.

**nahiv,** -hvi *gr.* syntax.

**nahiye** [ā] 1. subdistrict; 2. region *(a. anat.)*: district; ~ müdürü governer of a subdistrict.

**nahoş** [ā] unpleasant, nasty, disagreea-

ble; ~ bir sürpriz an unpleasant surprise.

**nail** [ā] 1. who receives *(or gains)*; 2. ♀ *mf.;* ~ olm. to obtain, to attain, to acquire.

**naip,** -bi [ā] regent, viceroy.

**naiplik** [ā] regency, viceroyalty.

**nakarat,** -tı [. . -] 1. ♪ refrain, burden; 2. *fig.* the same old refrain.

**nakavt,** -tı *boxing:* knockout; ~ etm. to knock out.

**nakden** [x .] in cash *(or ready money)*.

**nakdi** monetary, pecuniary; ~ ceza fine; ~ teminat ☊ pecuniary warrant.

**nakıs** 1. minus, less; 2. Å negative *(number)*; 3. incomplete, deficient.

**nakış,** -kşı 1. embroidery, needlework; 2. miniature; 3. ♪ a kind of song; ~ işlemek to embroider.

**nakışlamak** = nakış işlemek.

**nakışlı** embroidered.

**nakız,** -kzı 1. violation, breach; 2. overthrowing *(of a court decision)*; 3. abrogation *(of a treaty)*.

**nakil,** -kli 1. transport, transfer; 2. transferring s.o. to a new post; 3. telling, recounting *(story)*; 4. moving to *(another residence)*; 5. ☙ transplanting; ~ vasıtası transport vehicle.

**nâkil** 1. transporter; 2. teller, narrator; 3. *phys.* conductor.

**nakit,** -kdi cash, ready money.

**nakkaş** [. - ] 1. muralist; frescoist; 2. miniaturist.

**naklen** [x .] live; ~ yayın live broadcast *(or telecast)*.

**nakletmek** [x . .] 1. to transport (-e to); to convey (-e to), to transfer (-e to); 2. to move (-e to); 3. to narrate, to recount, to tell.

**nakliyat,** -tı [. . -] transport, shipment, freighting, forwarding; ~ şirketi transport *(or shipping or forwarding)* company.

**nakliyatçı** freighter, shipper.

**nakliye** 1. freight(age); 2. transport, shipping; ~ gemisi troopship, transport; ~ senedi ✝ waybill; ~ uçağı troop carrier, transport plane; ~ ücreti freight(age).

carriage.

**nakliyeci** freighter, shipper; forwarding agent.

**nakşetmek** [x . .] to engrave (in one's memory).

**nakzen** [x .]: ~ görmek (davayı) to reexamine a case; ~ iade etm. (davayı) to send a case back.

**nakzetmek** [x . .] 1. to violate, to break; 2. to annul, to abrogate (treaty); 3. ठ to overthrow, to overturn (the decision of a lower court)

**nal** horseshoe; ~ çakmak to shoe (a horse); -ları dikmek sl. to kick the bucket, to peg out, to pop off.

**nalbant**, -dı blacksmith, farrier, horse-shoer.

**nalbur** iron-monger, hardwareman, hardware dealer; ~ dükkânı hardware store.

**nalburiye** hardware store.

**nalça** metal piece, iron tip (on a boot).

**naldöken** stony (road).

**nalet**, -ti F cursed, damned; ~ olsun! God damn him!

**nalın** bath clog.

**nallamak** 1. to shoe (a horse, etc.); 2. sl. to bump off, to kill.

**nam** [ā] 1. name; 2. reputation, fame, renown; ~ almak (or kazanmak or vermek) to make a name for o.s.; -ına 1. on behalf of; in s.o.'s name; 2. in the way of; -ında named, called; namı diğer alias.

**namağlup**, -bu undefeated.

**namahrem** canonically a stranger.

**namaz** prayer, namaz; ~ kılmak to perform the namaz, to pray; ~ seccadesi prayer rug; ~ vakti time of the namaz, prayer time; -ı kılındı he is dead.

**namazgâh** open-air prayer place.

**namazlık** prayer rug.

**namazsız** (woman) who is menstruating.

**namdar** [- -] famous, celebrated.

**name** [ā] 1. (love) letter; 2. document, certificate.

**namert**, -di 1. cowardly; 2. despicable, contemptible.

**namertlik** 1. cowardliness; 2. despicableness.

**namlı** famous, celebrated.

**namlu** 1. barrel (of a rifle, etc.); 2. blade (of a sword).

**namuhesabına** (b-nin) on s.o.'s behalf, on behalf of s.o.

**namus** [- -] 1. hono(u)r, integrity, probity; 2. chastity, virtue; ~ borcu debt of hono(u)r; ~ sözü word of hono(u)r; -una dokunmak (b-nin) to touch s.o.'s

hono(u)r; -uyla yaşamak to keep to the straight and narrow, to live honestly.

**namuslu** [ā] 1. hono(u)rable, upright; 2. virtuous, chaste.

**namussuz** [ā] 1. dishonest, dishonu(u)rable; 2. unvirtuous, unchaste; 3. rotten bastard, damned thing.

**namünasip** [- . - .] inappropriate; unsuitable; inconvenient.

**namütenahi** [- . . - -] endless, boundless.

**namzet** 1. candidate, prospect; nominee; 2. betrothed, fiancé(e); ~ göstermek to nominate, to put forward as a candidate.

**namzetlik** candidacy; namzetliğini koymak to put o.s. forward as a candidate (-e for); to stand (-e for), Am. to run (-e for).

**nanay** sl. there isn't...; bende para ~ I haven't a bean.

**nane** [ā] 1. ۴ (pepper)mint; 2. mint tea; ~ suyu peppermint water; ~ yemek F to make a blunder.

**naneli** [ā] (pepper)minty.

**nanemolla** [- . . .] weak Willy, cream puff.

**naneruhu**, -nu [- . - .] peppermint oil, essence of peppermint.

**nanesekeri**, -ni [- . . . .] peppermint drop.

**nanik**: ~ yapmak to cock a snook (-e at), to thumb one's nose (-e at).

**nankör** ungrateful, unthankful, thankless.

**nankörlük** ungratefulness, ingratitude; ~ etm. to act ungratefully.

**nar** ۴ pomegranate; ~ gibi well toasted (or roasted).

**nara** [- .] shout, cry, yell; ~ atmak to shout out, to yell; -yı basmak to let out a yell.

**narçiçeği**, -ni grenadine red.

**narenciye** [ā] ۴ citrus fruits.

**nargile** hookah, nargileh, water pipe, hubble-bubble.

**narh** officially fixed price; ~ koymak to put a fixed price (-e on).

**narin** [ā] delicate, slim, slender.

**narkotik** narcotic.

**narkoz** narcosis; ~ vermek to anesthetize.

**nasbetmek** [x . .] to appoint (-e to).

**nasıl** [x .] 1. how?; 2. how (much); 3. what sort of...?; 4. in the just same way; nasılsınız? how do you do?; ~ ki just as... so...; ~ olsa in any case, somehow or other.

**nasılsa** [x . .] = nasıl olsa.

**nasır** corn, clavus; callus, wart; ~ bağlamak to become calloused; -ına basmak (b-nin) F to tread on s.o.'s toes.

**nasırlanmak** = nasır bağlamak.

**nasırlı** calloused, warty; horny.

**nasihat,** -ti [İ] advice, counsel, admonition; ~ etm. (or vermek) to advise, to give advice, to counsel.

**nasip,** -bi [İ] portion, share, lot; ~ olm. to fall to one's lot; ~ olursa all being well; nasibini almak to enjoy.

**Nasrani** [. - -] Christian.

**naşi** [- -] owing (-den to), because (-den of).

**naşir** [ā] 1. publisher; 2. propagator.

**natamam** [- . -] incomplete, unfinished.

**natıka** [- . .] eloquence.

**natır** female bath attendant.

**natokafa** sl. numskull.

**natüralist,** -ti naturalist.

**natüralizm** naturalism.

**natürel** natural.

**natürmort,** -tu still life.

**navlun** freight(age).

**naylon** [x .] 1. naylon; 2. plastic.

**naz** coyness, reluctance; ~ etm. (or yapmak) to feign reluctance; -ını çekmek (b-nin) to put up with s.o.'s whims.

**nazar** 1. glance, look; 2. opinion; 3. the evil eye; ~ boncuğu blue bead, amulet; ~ değmek to cause misfortune by the evil eye, to hex; ~ değmesin! touch wood!; -ı dikkate almak to take into consideration; -ı dikkatini çekmek to attract s.o.'s attention; -ı itibara almak to take into consideration; -ıyla bakmak to regard as, to consider.

**nazaran** [x .] 1. in comparison (-e to); 2. according (-e to).

**nazari** [İ] theoretical, speculative.

**nazariye** theory.

**nazarlık** amulet, charm.

**nazenin** [- . -] 1. of delicate build; 2. hussy, minx; son of a gun; 3. coy.

**nazım,** -zmı verse; versification.

**nâzım** 1. regulatory; 2. phys. regulator; 3. writer of verse; 4. ♀ mf.

**nazır** [ā] 1. overlooking, facing, looking out on; 2. minister.

**Nazi** pr. n. Nazi.

**nazik,** -ki [ā] 1. polite, courteous; 2. delicate, fragile.

**nazikleşmek** [ā] 1. to become polite (or courteous); 2. to become delicate.

**naziklik** [ā] 1. politeness, courteousness, courtesy; 2. delicacy.

**nazır** [İ] 1. equal, counterpart; 2. ast. nadir.

**nazire** [İ] a poem written to resemble another poem in form and subject.

**nazlanmak** s. naz etm.

**nazlı** 1. reluctant; 2. coy, arch, coquet-

tish; 3. petted, coddled.

**ne** 1. what?; 2. whatever; 3. what a...!, how...!; ~ âlemdesiniz? how are you?, how are things with you?; ~ buyurdunuz? what did you say?; ~ çıkar? what does it matter?; ~ de olsa nevertheless, still; ~ .demek? what does it mean?; ~ dese beğenirsiniz? guess what he said to me!; ~ diye? why...?, for what purpose...?; ~ ekersen onu biçersin pro. as you sow, so shall you reap; ~ gibi? what, for example?, like what?; ~ görsem beğenirsiniz? guess what I saw!; ~ haber? what's the news?, how goes it?; ~ hacet? what need is there!; ~ hali varsa görsün let him stew in his own juice; ~ halt etmeye F why in the hell...?; ~ hıkmetse heaven knows why!; ~ ise in any case, at any rate, anyway; ~ kadar güzel! how beautiful!; ~ karın ağrısı! what a pain in the neck he is!; ~ malum? how do you know?; ~ mümkün! impossible!; ~ münasebet? of course not!; ~ oldu? 1. what happened?; 2. what is the matter with...?; ~ oldum delisi parvenu; ~ olur ~ olmaz just in case; ~ pahasına olursa olsun at any costs, at all costs; ~ sınır şey! what a pain in the neck it is!; ~ vakit (or zaman) when?, at what time?; ~ var? what's the matter?; ~ var ki only; but; however; ~ yalan söyleyeyim to tell you the truth...; ~ yapıp yapıp by hook or by crook, in some way or other; ~ yazık! what a pity!; -me lazım? what's it to me?

**nebat,** -tı [ā] plant.

**nebatat,** -tı [. - -] 1. plants; 2. botany; ~ bahçesi botanical garden.

**nebati** [. - -] botanical, vegetable; ~ yağ vegetable oil.

**nebi** [İ] prophet.

**nebülöz** ast. nebula.

**nebze** bit, particle.

**necat,** -tı [ā] salvation, safety.

**nece** [x .] what language...?

**neci** o, -dir? what's his job?, what does he do?; sen ~ oluyorsun? what's it to you?

**necip,** -bi [İ] 1. noble; 2. ♀ [x .] mf.

**nedamet,** -ti [ā] regret, remorse; ~ etm. (or getirmek) to regret.

**nedbe** ♀ scar.

**neden** 1. why?, what for?; 2. reason, cause; ~ olm. to cause; -iyle because of, owing to; because; bu -le for this reason, because of this.

**nedense** for some reason or other, I don't know why, but...

**nedensel** causal.

**nedensellik** causality.

**nedim** [i] 1. intimate friend; 2. ♀ [x .] *mf.*

**nedime** [i] 1. lady-in-waiting; 2. ♀ [x . .] *wf.*

**nefaset**, -ti [ā] excellence, exquisiteness.

**nefer** 1. individual, person; 2. ✕ private.

**nefes** 1. breath; 2. draw, puff, drag *(on a cigarette)*; 3. moment, instant; 4. *sl.* hash(ish); ~ aldırmamak *(b-ne)* to give *s.o.* no rest, not to give *s.o.* any respite; ~ almak 1. to breathe; to inhale; 2. *fig.* to catch one's breath, to take a short break, to rest; ~ borusu *anat.* trachea; ~ çekmek 1. to take a puff *(or draw or drag) (on a cigarette)*; 2. *sl.* to smoke some hash; ~ darlığı 1. shortness of breath; 2. asthma; ~ etm. *(b-ne)* to blow one's breath upon *s.o. (to cure him of an ailment)*; ~ -e out of breath; ~ -e kalmak to gasp for breath, to pant; ~ tüketmek to waste one's breath; ~ vermek to breathe out, to exhale; -i kesilmek to gasp for breath, to catch one's breath.

**nefeslemek** *s.* nefes etm.

**nefesli** 1. ♪ wind *(instrument)*; 2. long--winded *(person)*; ~ çalgı ♪ wind instrument.

**nefeslik** vent(hole), air hole.

**nefis**[1], -fsi 1. self; essence; 2. the body, the flesh; 3. soul, life; nefsine uymak to yield to the flesh, to sin; nefsine yedirememek to be unable to bring o.s. *(to do s.th.)*; nefsini körletmek *(or* öldürmek) 1. to take the edge off one's desire; 2. to stave off one's hunger; nefsini yenmek to master o.s.

**nefis**[2] excellent, choice, exquisite.

**nefiy,** -fyi 1. ⚖ banishment, exile; 2. denial; negation; ~ edatı *gr.* negative (particle).

**nefret,** -ti hate, hatred, detestation, abhorrence; aversion; ~ etm. to hate, to detest, to abhor, to loathe.

**nefrit,** -ti 🗲 nephritis.

**nefsani** [. - -] carnal, fleshly, bodily.

**nefsaniyet,** -ti [ā] enmity, malice.

**neft,** -ti *(yağı)* naphtha.

**nefyetmek** [x . .] 1. to exile; 2. *gr.* to negate.

**negatif** Å. *phot.*, 🗲 negative.

**neglije** negligee.

**nehari** [. - -] day *(student, school)*; ~ mektep day school; ~ talebe day student.

**nehir,** -hri river; ~ yatağı riverbed.

**nehiy,** -hyi 1. prohibition; 2. *psych.* inhibition.

**nehyetmek** [x . .] to prohibit, to forbid.

**nekahet,** -ti [ā] convalescence.

**nekes** stingy, mean.

**nekeslik** stinginess.

**nekre** witty.

**nektar** ⚕ nectar.

**neli** what... made of?

**nem** 1. damp(ness), moisture; 2. humidity; 3. dew.

**nema** [ā] 1. growth; 2. interest.

**nemelazımcı** indifferent.

**nemelazımcılık** indifference.

**nemlendirici** moisturizer; humidifier.

**nemlendirmek** to moisten; to humidify; to moisturize.

**nemlenmek** to become damp, to moisten.

**nemli** damp, humid, moist; dank.

**Nemrut,** -du [ū] 1. *pr. n.* Nimrod; 2. ♀ cruel, grim *(person)*.

**nenin** *s.* neyin.

**neogen** *geol.* the Neogene.

**neolitik** *(çağ)* Neolithic.

**neon** neon; ~ lambası neon lamp *(or* tube).

**Neptün** *ast.* Neptune.

**nere** [x .] where...?, what place...?; buranın ~ olduğunu biliyor musunuz? do you know what place this is?; burası neresi? what place is this?

**nerede** [x . .] where?; wherever...?

**nereden** [x . .] (from) where?, whence ...?; ~ geliyorsun? where are you coming from?; ~ nereye! what a coincidence!

**neredeyse** [x . . .] 1. almost, nearly, all but; 2. (pretty) soon, before long; ~ gelir he'll come pretty soon.

**nereli** [x . .] where... from?; siz nerelisiniz? where are you from?; benim nereli olduğumu biliyor musunuz? do you know where I am from?

**nereye** [x . .] where...?; wherever...?; ~ gidiyorsunuz? where are you going?

**nergis** ⚕ narcissus.

**nesep,** -bi ancestry, genealogy, lineage.

**nesiç,** -sci *(a.* ⚕, 🗲) tissue.

**nesil,** -sli 1. generation; 2. race, line; 3. offspring, progeny; nesli tükenmek to die out.

**nesir,** -sri prose.

**nesne** 1. thing; 2. *gr.* object.

**nesnel** objective.

**nesneleştirmek** to objectify.

**nesnelleşmek** to become objective.

**nesnellik** objectivity.

**neşe** merriment, gaiety, joy; -si yerinde he is in good spirits.

neşelendirmek to render merry, to put s.o. in good spirits.

neşelenmek to become merry.

neşeli merry, cheerful, joyful, joyous.

neşesiz low-spirited, out of sorts (or spirits), downcast.

neşet, -ti 1. origination; emergence; 2. ♀ mf.; ~ etm. 1. to originate (-den from), to arise (-den from); 2. to graduate (-den from).

neşetli who graduated in (a certain year).

neşir, -şri 1. publication; 2. dissemination, diffusion; 3. broadcasting.

neşren through the mass media; in print.

neşretmek [x . .] 1. to publish; 2. to diffuse, to spread; 3. to broadcast.

neşriyat, -tı [ā] publications.

neşter ₮ lancet.

neşvünema [ā] growth, development; ~ bulmak to grow.

net, -ti 1. clear, sharp; 2. net.

netameli [ā] 1. sinister; 2. accident-prone.

netice [i] result, consequence, outcome; end; -de in the end; -sinde as a result of...

neticelendirmek to bring to an end, to conclude.

neticelenmek to come to an end, to end; to result (ile in).

neticesiz inconclusive, useless, fruitless, futile.

neuzübillah! God help us!

nevale [ā] provisions, food, victuals; -yı düzmek to provide food.

nevazil [ā] (common) cold, catarrh.

nevi, -v'i kind, sort, variety; bu nevi(den) of this kind; nev'i beşer mankind; nev'i şahsına münhasır unique.

nevir, -vri the colo(u)r of s.o.'s face; nevri dönmek to fly off the handle.

nevralji ₮ neuralgia.

nevresim protective case (made of sheeting).

nevroloji neurology.

nevroz neurosis.

ney reed flute; ~ çalmak (or üflemek) to play the ney.

neye why?; ~ doğruyu söylemiyorsun? why aren't you telling the truth?

neyin gen. of ne.

neyle = ne ile.

neyse = ne ise.

neyzen ney player.

nezafet, -ti [ā] cleanliness.

nezaket, -ti [ā] courtesy, politeness; tact, delicacy; ~ kesp etm. to become delicate.

nezaketen [ā] [. x . .] as a matter of courtesy, out of politeness.

nezaketli [ā] courteous, polite; tactful.

nezaketsiz [ā] discourteous, impolite.

nezaret, -ti [ā] 1. superintendence, supervision; 2. surveillance; 3. direction, administration; 4. † ministry; ~ altında 1. under surveillance; 2. in police custody; ~ etm. to superintend, to oversee, to supervise; -e almak 1. to take into custody; 2. to put under surveillance.

nezarethane [. - . - .] lockup, jail.

nezih [i] 1. decent, clean; 2. ♀ [x .] mf.

nezir, -zri vow.

nezle (common) cold, catarrh; ~ olm. to catch cold, to get a cold.

nezretmek [x . .] to vow; to pledge (-e to).

nıkris [i] ₮ gout.

nısfiye short ney.

nısıf, -sfı half; ~ daire semicircle; ~ kutur radius; ~ küre hemisphere.

nışadır ₼ salamoniac; ammonia.

nışadırruhu, -nu ₼ ammonia.

nice [x .] how many...!, many a...!, so many...!; ~ ~ very many, a great many; ~ senelere! many happy returns of the day!

nicel quantitative.

nicelik quantity.

niçin [- .] [x .] why?, what for?

nida [ā] 1. cry, exclamation, shout; 2. gr. exclamation, interjection; ~ etm. to exclaim; ~ işareti exclamation mark (or point).

nifak, -kı [ā] discord, strife, dissension; ~ sokmak to sow the seeds of discord.

nihai [. - -] final, decisive; ~ karar ₰ final decision.

nihayet, -ti [ā] 1. end, conclusion; finish; 2. finally, at last; in the end; ~ bulmak to come to an end, to end, to finish; ~ vermek to conclude, to terminate, to bring to an end.

nihayetlendirmek [ā] to put an end to; to bring to an end.

nihayetlenmek [ā] to come to an end, to end.

nihayetsiz [ā] endless, unending; infinite, vast.

nikâh marriage (ceremony); ~ altına almak to marry; ~ dairesi marriage office; ~ düşmek (for a marriage) to be legally possible; ~ etm. (bir kadını) to marry a woman (-e to); to give a woman in marriage (-e to); ~ kıymak to perform a marriage ceremony; ~ şahidi witness at a marriage.

nikâhlamak 1. = nikâh etm.; 2. = nikâh kıymak.

nikâhlanmak to get married; to marry.

nikâhlı married, wedded.

nikâhsız unmarried, unwed.

nikbin [- -] optimistic.

nikbinlik [- -.] optimism.

nikel nickel.

nikelaj 1. nickeling; 2. nickel plate.

nikotin nicotine.

Nil pr. n. the Nile.

nilüfer [i] 1. ♀ water lily; 2. ♀ wf.

nim [i] half; semi-.

nimbus [x .] nimbus.

nimet, -ti [i] 1. blessing; 2. the staff of life, bread; 3. ♀ mf., wf.

nimresmi [- .-] semiofficial.

nine 1. grandmother, grandma, granny; 2. old woman.

ninni lullaby; ~ söylemek to sing a lullaby.

nisaiye gynecology.

nisan April.

nisanbalığı, -nı April fool.

nispet, -ti 1. proportion, ratio, rate; 2. relation(ship); 3. spite; ~ etm. 1. to compare; 2. to act spitefully; ~ vermek (or yapmak) to say or do s.th. out of spite.

nispetçi spiteful.

nispeten [x ..] 1. comparatively, relatively; 2 in comparison (-e to), compared (-e to).

nispi 1. proportional; 2. relative, comparative.

nişan [ä] 1. sign, indication, mark; 2. target; 3. engagement, betrothal; 4. engagement ceremony (or party); 5. pol. medal, decoration, order; ~ almak 1. to aim (-e at), to take aim (-e at); 2. pol. to receive a decoration; ~ koymak to make a mark; ~ merasimi (or töreni) engagement ceremony; ~ takmak 1. to put an engagement ring (-e on); 2. to pin a decoration (-e on); ~ vermek to bestow a decoration (-e on); ~ yapmak to have an engagement ceremony (or party): ~ yüzüğü engagement ring; -dan dönmek to break off an engagement.

nişancı [ä] sharpshooter, marksman.

nişane [ä] = nişan 1.

nişangâh [ä] 1. target; 2. rear sight (of a gun).

nişanlamak 1. to engage, to affiance, to betroth; 2. to take aim (-e at).

nişanlanma engagement, betrothal.

nişanlanmak 1. pass. of nişanlamak, to get engaged; 2. to be marked.

nişanlı engaged, betrothed, intended; fiancé(e).

nişanlılık engagement.

nişasta ♀ (corn)starch, amylum.

nite [x .] † how?

nitekim [x ..] just as; as a matter of fact; in just the same way.

nitel qualitative.

niteleme vn. of nitelemek, qualification; ~ sıfatı gr. descriptive adjective.

nitelemek 1. to describe, to characterize; 2. gr. to modify, to qualify.

nitelik quality, characteristic, attribute.

nitelikli 1. well-qualified; 2. of... quality.

niteliksiz of poor quality.

nitrat, -tı nitrate.

nitrikasit nitric acid.

nitrojen ♀ nitrogen.

niyabet, -ti [ä] regency; viceroyalty.

niyaz [ä] entreaty, supplication, plea; ~ etm. to plead, to entreat.

niye why?, what for?

niyet, -ti 1. intention, purpose, aim; 2. fortune (written on a slip of paper); ~ etm. to intend, to aim, to mean; ~ tutmak to think of the matter about which one is inquiring when consulting a fortuneteller; -i bozuk having evil intentions; -inde olm. (bşi yapmak) to be intent on doign s.th.

niyetçi person who lets his rabbit or bird draw a niyet 2.

niyetlenmek s. niyet etm.

niyetli 1. intent; 2. who intends to fast.

niza, -aı [ä] quarrel, dispute.

nizam [ä] 1. order, arrangement, system, method, organization; 2. regulation, rule; law; -a sokmak (or koymak) to put in order.

nizami [. - -] 1. regulative, regulatory; legal; 2. systematic, orderly, methodical.

nizamlı [ä] 1. orderly, organized, systematic; 2. lawful, legal.

nizamname [. - -.] regulations, statutes.

nizamsız [ä] 1. disorderly, disordered, unsystematic; 2. unlawful, illegal.

No. (abbr. for numara) No.

nobran harsh, rude, churlish.

Noel Christmas; ~ ağacı Christmas tree; ~ baba Father Christmas, Am. Santa Claus.

nohudi [. - -] buff-colo(u)red, manila.

nohut, -du ♀ chickpea; ~ oda, bakla sofa small house.

noksan [ä] 1. deficient, defective, missing; 2. deficiency, defect, shortcoming; 3. want, lack.

**noksanlık 1.** deficiency, defect(iveness), shortcoming, **2.** lack, want.

**noksansız 1.** complete; **2.** flawless, perfect.

**nokta 1.** point *(a. Ạ̇)*, dot; **2.** speck, spot; **3.** *gr.* full stop, *Am.* period; **4.** ✕ sentry, post; ~ koymak **1.** to put a full stop *(or period)*; **2.** to wind up, to finish; ~ olm. *sl.* **1.** to get lost, to beat it; **2.** *(for a dope-taker)* to be so high he cannot move a muscle; -sı -sına exactly, in every way; noktai nazar viewpoint, point of view.

**noktalama** punctuation; ~ işaretleri punctuation marks.

**noktalamak 1.** to punctuate; **2.** to dot, to mark.

**noktalı** dotted; speckled; ~ virgül semicolon.

**noktasız** undotted.

**nonoş** little darling, honey.

**norm** norm.

**normal,** -li normal *(a. Ạ̇)*.

**normalleşmek** to become normal.

**Norveç** *pr. n.* Norway.

**Norveçli** *pr. n.* Norwegian.

**nostalji** nostalgia, homesickness.

**not,** -tu **1.** note, memorandum; minute; **2.** *school:* mark, grade; ~ almak **1.** to take *(or make)* notes; **2.** to get a grade; ~ atmak to record a grade; ~ defteri notebook; ~ düşmek to write down a note; ~ etm to note down; ~ kırmak to give low grades; ~ tutmak to take notes; ~ vermek **1.** to give a grade *(-e* to); **2.** to pass judgment *(-e* on).

**nota** [x .] ♪ & *pol.* note.

**noter** notary public.

**noterlik 1.** notary public's office; **2.** notaryship.

**nöbet,** -ti **1.** turn *(of duty);* **2.** watch *(of a sentry);* **3.** shift; **4.** 🜍 onset, fit, attack; ~ beklemek **1.** to stand guard; to keep watch; to be on duty; **2.** to await one's turn; ~ değiştirmek to change guard; ~ gelmek *(b-ne)* to have a fit; ~ tutmak *s.* ~ beklemek **1.**

**nöbetçi 1.** sentry, watchman; **2.** on duty; ~ eczane pharmacy on night-duty; ~ kulübesi sentry box; ~ subayı ✕ duty officer.

**nöbetçilik** guard-duty.

**nöbetleşe** by turns.

**nöbetşekeri,** -ni sugar-candy.

**nöron** *biol.* neuron.

**nötr 1.** neutral; **2.** neuter.

**nötrlemek** to neutralize.

**nötrleşmek** to become neutral.

**nötron** neutron; ~ bombası neutron bomb.

**Nuh** [ū] *pr. n.* Noah; ~ der peygamber demez he is as stubborn as a mule; ~ Nebi'den kalma out of the ark; -un gemisi Noah's Ark.

**numara** [x ..] **1.** number; **2.** size, number *(shoe, etc.);* **3.** grade; **4.** *sl.* ruse, trick, stratagem; ~ koymak to number; ~ yapmak to fake, to pretend; -sı yapmak to pretend to be, to fake, to pose as; -sını vermek *(b-nin) fig.* to form a bad opinion of *s.o.*

**numaracı** *sl.* poseur, faker, phony.

**numaralamak** to number.

**numaralı** [x ...] numbered; yerler -dır the seats are numbered; iki numaralı ev the house number two.

**numarasız** numberless, unnumbered.

**numune** sample, model, pattern.

**numunelik** sample, specimen.

**nur** [ū] **1.** light, brilliance; radiance; **2.** ♀ *mf., wf.;* ~ içinde yatsın *(or* toprağı ~ olsun)! may he rest in peace; ~ ol! bravo!, well done!; ~ topu gibi very healthy and cute *(child);* ~ yüzlü benevolent looking *(old man).*

**nurani** [- - .], **nurlu** [- .] bright, radiant.

**nursuz** [- .]: ~ pirsiz *sl.* ugly and unlovely.

**nutuk,** -tku speech, oration, address; ~ atmak *(or* cekmek) to sermonize, to hold forth; ~ söylemek *(or* vermek) to make a speech; nutka gelmek to begin to speak; nutku tutulmak to be tongue-tied.

**nü** nude.

**nüans** nuance.

**nüfus** [ū] **1.** population, inhabitants; **2.** people, persons; ~ cüzdanı *(or* kâğıdı) identity card *(or* booklet); ~ dağılımı distribution of the population; ~ fazlalığı overpopulation; ~ kütüğü state register of persons; ~ memurluğu public registration office; ~ sayımı (population) census.

**nüfusça** as regards persons; ~ kayıp yoktur there is no loss of human life.

**nüfuslu 1.** having... inhabitants; **2.** made up of... persons *(family);* altı ~ bir aile a family of six persons; 500.000 ~ bir şehir a city of 500.000 people.

**nüfuz** [ū] **1.** influence, power, weight, pull; **2.** penetration; permeation; ~ etm. **1.** to penetrate; to permeate; **2.** to influence; ~ sahibi influential, powerful *(person).*

**nüfuzlu** [. - .] influential, powerful, dominant.

**nükleer** nuclear; ~ silah nuclear weapon.

**nüksetmek** [x ..] to relapse, to recur

*(disease).*

**nükte** witticism, wisecrack; ~ yapmak to wisecrack.

**nükteci, nüktedan** [â] **1.** witty; **2.** wit, wisecracker.

**nükteli** witty.

**nükûl,** -lü withdrawal, abstention; ~ etm. *(sözünden)* to withdraw, to go back on *(one's promise).*

**nümayiş** [â] **1.** demonstration; **2.** show, pomp.

**nümayişçi** [â] demonstrator,

**nüsha 1.** copy, specimen, transcript, duplicate; **2.** issue, number *(of a magazine, etc.);* iki ~ olarak in duplicate.

**nüve** nucleus.

**nüzul,** -lü [û] apoplexy, stroke.

# O

o¹ [-] ah!, oh!, o!, I say!

o² -nu 1. he, she, it; 2. that, those; 3. the former, previous; ~ anda at that moment; ~ bu whether this or that; everybody; ~ denli so much, that much; ~ duvar senin, bu duvar benim to walk along rolling *(drunk)*; ~ gün bu gün(dür) since then, from that day on; ~ halde in that case, therefore, hence, thus, so, consequently; ~ kadar so much, so... that; ~ kapı senin bu kapı benim dolaşmak to gallivant, to wander around; ~ saat 1. at that hour; 2. at once, immediately, directly, forthwith, straight, at that very moment, right away; ~ sırada at that straight moment; ~ taraflı olmamak not to pay attention to; ~ tarakta bezi olmamak not to have anything with..., not to be interested in...; ~ vakit *(or* zaman) 1. then, after that; 2. at that time; 3. in that case; ~ yolda in that way, like that; ~ yolun yolcusu 1. to live immorally; 2. he is in such a situation that he is going to end up with death; ~nun için that's why.

oba 1. large nomad tent; 2. nomad family; 3. temporary nomad camp.

obartı exaggeration.

obartıcı exaggerator.

obartılmak to be exaggerated.

obartma exaggeration, hyperbole.

obartmak to exaggerate.

obartmalı exaggerated.

obelisk, -ki obelisk.

obje object, thing.

objektif 1. objective; 2. *phot.* lens, objective.

objektivist objectivist.

objektivizm objectivism.

obligasyon † bond.

obruk 1. *phys.* concave; 2. funnel-shaped; 3. hollow ground.

observatuvar observatory.

obstrüksiyon 1. hindering, preventing, obstruction; 2. *sports:* blocking.

obua oboe.

obuacı oboist.

obur gluttonous, greedy, voracious.

oburca greedily.

oburlaşmak to become gluttonous *(or* greedy).

oburluk gluttony, voracity.

obüs 1. shell; 2. howitzer.

ocak¹ January; ~ ayı January.

ocak² 1. fireplace, hearth; 2. forge; 3. (gas)burner; 4. cooker, oven, range; 5. furnace; 6. distillary; 7. mine, kiln, pit; 8. quarry; 9. bed, plantation; 10. centre, focus, starting-point; 11. (local) club, local branch *(of a party, etc.);* 12. family, home; 13. dynasty; 14. military organization; ~ kaşı stone stand for saucepans *etc.* in front of the hearth; ocağı batmak to be exhausted, to be ruined; ocağı tütmek to keep continuing one's family; ocağına düşmek *(b-nin)* to take *s.o.'s* refuge, to plead with *s.o.* for help; ocağını söndürmek to destroy the family *(-in* of); to exhaust one's family, to ruin.

ocakçı 1. stoker; 2. chimney-sweep.

ocakçılık being a stoker *(or* chimney-sweep).

ocaklı 1. with a fireplace; 2. s.o. who belongs to a specific organization *(Janissary).*

ocaklık 1. family estate given by the sovereign; 2. fireplace; 3. (supporting) beam; 4. kitchen; 5. chimney.

od fire; ~ yok ocak yok *fig.* he is a poor devil *(or* wretch).

oda 1. room; 2. board, chamber, association, society; 3. † office; 4. room, space, hall; ~ müziği chamber music; ~ takımı suite of furniture.

odabaşı, -nı s.o. in charge of the rooms in an inn.

odacı servant *(at an office or public building).*

odak 1. *phys.* focus, focal point; 2. *fig.* starting-point.

odaklama focusing.

odaklamak to focus.

odaklaşma focalization.

odaklaşmak to focalize.

odaklaştırma focalization.

odaklaştırmak to focalize.

odaklayıcı assistant cameraman, lenser.

**odaksız** afocal.

**odalı** which has certain number of rooms.

**odalık** concubine, odalisque (up to 1908).

**oditoryum** [. . x .] auditorium.

**odun 1.** firewood, log; **2.** fig. (a. ~ aleyhisselam) foolish and rough fellow; **3.** a sound thrashing; ~ gibi blockhead, rude, rough; ~ kırmak to chop wood, to split firewood; ~ yarıcı woodchopper.

**oduncu 1.** wood-cutter; **2.** seller of firewood.

**odunkömürü,** -nü charcoal.

**odunlaşma** lignification.

**odunlaşmak 1.** to lignify; **2.** fig. to get rough, to become insensitive to others.

**odunluk 1.** woodshed; **2.** tree ready to be cut and used as firewood; **3.** fig. rudeness, insensitivity to others.

**odyometre** audiometer.

**odyovizüel** audio-visual.

**of! 1.** oof!; **2.** ow!, alas!, ah!, ouch!, oh!

**ofis** office, department, bureau.

**oflamak** to say 'ugh'; oflayıp puflamak to moan and groan, to huff and puff.

**oflaz** excellent, superb.

**ofris** twayblade.

**ofsayt,** -dı sports: offside.

**ofset,** -ti **1.** (baskısı) offset (printing); **2.** (makinesi) offset printing machine.

**oftalmoloji** ophthalmology.

**oftalmoskop** ophthalmoscope.

**oğalamak** s. ovalamak.

**Oğan** God.

**oğdurmak** s. ovdurmak.

**Oğlak 1.** ast. Capricorn; **2.** ♀ zo. kid.

**oğlan 1.** boy, lad; **2.** cards: knave; **3.** catamite.

**oğlancı** pederast.

**oğlancılık** pederasty.

**oğmaç** s. ovmaç.

**oğmak** s. ovmak.

**oğul,** -ğlu **1.** son; **2.** zo. swarm of bees; ~ balı virgin honey.

**oğulcuk 1.** dear little son; **2.** embryo.

**oğulluk 1.** sonship; **2.** stepson, adopted son.

**oğulotu,** -nu ♀ bee balm, lemon balm.

**oğunmak** s. ovunmak.

**oğuşturmak** s. ovuşturmak.

**Oğuz 1.** an Oghuz Turk; **2.** of the Oghuz Turks.

**oğuz 1.** young bull; **2.** honest, sincere; **3.** brave, valiant; **4.** severe, rigorous; **5.** provincial, peasant, villager; **6.** ♀ mf.

**Oğuzca** the Turkish spoken by the Oghuz Turks.

**oh** oh!, ah!, indeed!; ~ çekmek to be malicious (or gloating), to rejoice over

another's misfortune; ~ demek to (take a) rest, to have a breather; ~ olsun! it serves him right!

**oha** [x -] **1.** sl. whoa!, hey you!; **2.** whoa (said to stop cattle).

**oje** fingernail polish.

**ojit** augite.

**ok,** -ku **1.** arrow; **2.** pole, beam; **3.** plough -tail; **4.** A sine versus; **5.** prick, quill; ~ atmak to shoot an arrow; ~ gibi (yerinden) fırlamak to rush out of (a place); ~ meydanı archery ground; ~ meydanında buhurdan yakmak **1.** to try to heat a big place with an inadequate mean of heater; **2.** to try to use inadequate facilities to accomplish an important job; ~ yaydan çıktı fig. what's done is done, there's no turning back.

**okaliptüs** ♀ eucalyptus.

**okçu 1.** archer; **2.** maker or seller of arrows.

**okçuluk 1.** archery; **2.** making or selling of arrows.

**okka** † (Turkish weight measure) oke, oka (= 1283 gr. = 400 dirhem); ~ çekmek to weigh heavier than it looks; ~ dört yüz dirhem facts are facts; -nın altına gitmek to bear the brunt, to be the victim.

**okkalamak 1.** to estimate the weight of s.th. by weighing it in hand; **2.** fig. to flutter.

**okkalı 1.** heavy; **2.** important, profitable; **3.** big; **4.** significant; ~ kahve big cup of Turkish coffee.

**okkalık** which weighs ... okes.

**oklamak 1.** to shoot with an arrow; **2.** to dart like an arrow.

**oklanmak** to get shot with an arrow.

**oklava** rolling pin; ~ (or baston) yutmuş gibi standing as if a stick were swallowed.

**okluk** quiver.

**oklukirpi** zo. porcupine.

**okramak** (for a horse) to whinny (for water or food).

**oksalat** ⚗ oxalate.

**oksijen 1.** oxygen; **2.** hydrogen peroxide.

**oksijenlemek 1.** ⚗ to add oxygen into a compound, to oxygenize; **2.** to turn hair yellow with diluted oxygen.

**oksijensizlik** anoxia.

**oksilit** chemical substance containing peroxides of sodium and potassium.

**oksit** oxide.

**oksitlemek** to oxidize.

**oksitlenme** oxidation.

**oksitlenmek** to get oxidized.

**okşamak 1.** to stroke, to caress, to pat, to fondle; **2.** to touch lightly; **3.** to resemble; **4.** *sl.* to beat up, to trash; **5.** to please, to flatter.

**okşanmak** to be caressed.

**okşantı** caress.

**okşatmak** *caus. of* okşamak.

**okşayıcı** pleasing (*word, behave, etc.*).

**okşayış 1.** caressing, fondling; **2.** way of caressing; **3.** caress.

**oktan** octane.

**oktant, -tı** octant, mariner's quadrant.

**oktav** octave.

**oktruva** [x . .] octroi, excise, city customs.

**okul** school.

**okuldaş** schoolmate.

**okullu** student, pupil.

**okulöncesi, -ni 1.** preschool; **2.** preschool period.

**okulsonrası, -nı 1.** post-school; **2.** period relating to post-school.

**okuma** reading; ~ kitabı primer, reader; ~ yazma reading and writing; ~ yitimi word blindness, alexia.

**okumak 1.** to read; **2.** to learn, to study; **3.** to recite; **4.** to sing; **5.** to call, to invite; **6.** to review (*book*); **7.** *sl.* to curse, to swear; **8.** to ruin *s.o.*; **9.** to decipher; **10.** to exorcise.

**okumamış** illiterate.

**okume** okoume, Gaboon mahogany.

**okumuş** educated, learned.

**okumuşluk** being educated.

**okunaklı** legible, readable.

**okunaksız** difficult to read, illegible.

**okunmak 1.** to be read (*or* recited); **2.** to be sung.

**okuntu** invitation (card).

**okunuş** way of reading (*or* singing).

**okur** reader.

**okuryazar** literate.

**okuryazarlık** literacy.

**okutmak** *caus. of* okumak **1.** to have s.o. educate; **2.** to instruct s.o. in s.th.; **3.** to teach s.o. s.th.; **4.** *sl.* to sell, to dispose of.

**okutman** lecturer, reader.

**okuyucu 1.** reader; **2.** singer; **3.** exorcist; **4.** s.o. sent around to invite people to a wedding.

**oküler** *phys.* ocular, eyepiece.

**okyanus** *geogr.* ocean.

**Okyanusya** [. . x .] *pr. n.* Oceania.

**okyılanı, -nı** *zo.* water snake; viper.

**ol** † = $o^2$

**olabilir** possible.

**olabilirlik** possibility.

**olacak 1.** suitable, appropriate; **2.** which will happen; **3.** inevitable, unavoidable; **4.** so-called; ~ gibi değil impossible, it doesn't look s.th. will happen.

**olagelmek** to happen now and then (*or* often), to continue, to go on.

**olağan 1.** common, usual, ordinary, normal; **2.** frequent, commonly happening.

**olağandışı, -nı** unusual, exceptional, strange, out of the common, obnormal.

**olağanlaşmak** to become commonplace.

**olağanlık** normality.

**olağanüstü, -nü 1.** extraordinary; unusual, uncommon; **2.** unexpected, exceptional; **3.** excellent, stunning, wonderful.

**olağanüstülük** extraordinariness.

**olamaz** [. x .] impossible, impracticable.

**olanak** possibility; ~ sağlamak to provide (the) opportunity for (*or* to).

**olanaklı** possible.

**olanaksız** impossible.

**olanaksızlaşmak** to become impossible.

**olanaksızlaştırmak** to make s.th. impossible.

**olanaksızlık** impossibility.

**olanca** [. x .] utmost, all of...; ~ kuvvetiyle with all his might.

**olası** probable.

**olasıcılık** *phls.* probabilism.

**olasılı** based on probability.

**olasılık** probability.

**olay 1.** event, occurrence, indicent; **2.** *phys.* phenomenon; ~ çıkarmak to cause trouble, to provoke an incident.

**olayanlatım** narration.

**olaybilim** phenomenology.

**olaycılık** phenomenalism.

**olaylı** eventful; marked by unpleasant events.

**olaysız** uneventful.

**olçum 1.** quack doctor; **2.** quack; **3.** skilful.

**oldu** okey!, all right!, yes!

**oldubitti** fait accompli; -ye (*or* olupbitti-ye) getirmek to confront s.o. with a fait accompli.

**oldukça** [. x .] rather, pretty, to some extent.

**oldum olası** *s.* olmak.

**oldurgan** *gr.* causative (verb).

**oldurmak 1.** to cause to happen, to be; **2.** to ripen, to mature.

**olefin** olefin.

**oleik** oleic.

**olein** olein.

**olgu 1.** *phls.* fact; **2.** case.

**olgucu** positivist.

**olguculuk** positivism.

**olgun 1.** ripe *(fruit)*; mature *(human-being)*; **2.** experienced, mature.

**olgunlaşma** maturation.

**olgunlaşmak 1.** to become ripe; **2.** to become mature.

**olgunlaştırmak** to mature.

**olgunluk** ripeness; maturity; ~ çağı *(or* yaşı*)* age of maturity; ~ sınavı † university entrance examination.

**oligarşi** oligarchy.

**oligoklaz** oligoclase.

**oligosen** oligacene, the period between miocene and eocene.

**olijist** *geol.* hematite.

**olimpiyat** the Olympic games, the Olympics.

**olivin** *geol.* olivine.

**olmadık [x . .] 1.** unprecedented; **2.** incredible, unheard-of; **3.** out of place, inappropriate, insulting *(word)*; **4.** impossible.

**olmak,** (-ur) **1.** to be, to exist; **2.** to become, to happen, to occur, to take place, to come off; **3.** to be practicable, to be feasible, to be admissible; **4.** to ripen; to mature; **5.** to be prepared; **6.** to fade (away) *(time)*; **7.** to come on *(or* near) *(holiday)*; **8.** to have, to possess; **9.** to get, to catch *(disease)*; **10.** to fit s.o. s.th., to suit s.o.; **11.** *various verbal forms of it are used as helping verbs;* **12.** *(b-ne bş)* to happen to s.o.; **13.** *v/aux.* to have, to get; **14.** *pass. of* etmek; **15.** *sl.* to get drunk; **16.** to lose *(opportunity, etc.);* ola ki let's say...; olan biten *(or* olup biten) everything that took place; olan oldu it is too late now, there is nothing to do; oldu olacak kırıldı nacak it is too late to do anything about s.th.; oldu olanlar all the worst things happened to s.o.; oldum bittim *(or* oldum olası *or* oldum olasıya) as long as s.o. remembers, always; olsa olsa! *(or* olsun olsun) at (the) most; ... olsun, ... olsun both... and..., all.... olup olacağı that's all; olur olmaz **1.** ordinary, whatsoever; **2.** unnecessary, unimportant, inappropriate.

**olmamış 1.** unripe, immature; **2.** s.th. hasn't been worked out well; **3.** s.th. which didn't happen.

**olmayacak 1.** impossible; **2.** inappropriate, unsuitable.

**olmaz 1.** impossible!, that will not do!; **2.** incredible, unheard-of; ~ ~ nothing is impossible.

**olmazlı** *log.* absurd.

**olmazlık** *log.* absurdity.

**olmuş** ripe, mature; ~ *(or* pişmiş) armut

gibi eline düşmek to get s.th. without any effort.

**olta [x .]** fishing line; ~ balığı line-fish ~ iğnesi fish-hook; ~ yemi bait; -ya vurmak **1.** to bite *(fish)*; **2.** *fig.* to take the bait.

**oluk 1.** gutter-pipe, eaves; **2.** channel, chamfer; groove; **3.** transmittal; ~ gibi *(or* ~ ~) akmak to stream out, to flow in abundance *(water, money, etc.)*.

**olukçuk 1.** small groove; **2.** ⚕ sulculus.

**oluklu 1.** grooved; **2.** s.th. which has oluk attached to; ~ kalem gauge, engraver's tool; ~ sac corrugated iron sheet.

**olumlama** *log.* affirmation.

**olumlamak** *log.* to affirm.

**olumlu 1.** positive, affirmative; **2.** proved, useful; **3.** constructive, supportive; ~ eylem affirmative verb; ~ tümce affirmative sentence.

**olumluk** curriculum vitae.

**olumluluk 1.** positiveness; **2.** constructiveness.

**olumsal** *log.* possible.

**olumsallık** *log.* possibility, contingency.

**olumsuz 1.** negative; **2.** not constructive, negatory; ~ eylem negative verb; ~ tümce negative sentence.

**olumsuzluk** negativeness; ~ eki negative suffix.

**olunmak** *pass. of* olmak.

**olupbitti** *s.* oldubittl.

**olur 1.** possible, thinkable; **2.** all right!; ~ olmaz **1.** as soon as..., just after s.th. happens; **2.** anybody; **3.** any; ~ şey common, ordinary; ~ şey *(or* iş) değil! it is incredible!, it's impossible!; -una bakmak to try to see if s.th. is possible to (be) do(ne); (bir işi) -una bırakmak (or bağlamak) to let s.th. take its course; -uyla yetinmek to be contented with, to be satisfied with.

**olurluk** possibility.

**oluş 1.** way and nature of becoming; formation, genesis; **2.** event, happening.

**oluşma** formation, organization.

**oluşmak** to come into being, to be formed.

**oluşturma** formation, constitution.

**oluşturmak** to form, to constitute, to organize.

**oluşuk** *geol.* formation.

**oluşum 1.** formation, constitution; **2.** *geol.* & *ast.* formation period.

**om** *phys.* ohm.

**om, oma 1.** protuberance, tubercle; **2.** ⚕ coccyx.

**omaca 1.** = om; **2.** stump of a tree.

**ombra** umber.

**omça** 1. part of the hip-bone; 2. vinestock.

**omlet,** -ti omelette.

**omur** *anat.* vertebra.

**omurga** 1. *anat.* backbone, spine; 2. ↓ keel; 3. *fig.* vital part, base.

**omurgalılar** *zo.* Vertebrata.

**omurgasızlar** *zo.* Invertebrata.

**omurilik** *anat.* spinal marrow (*or* cord).

**omuz,** -mzu shoulder; ~ başı end of the shoulder; ~ çevirmek to cold-shoulder; ~ kaldırmak to pretend not to know; ~ -a 1. shoulder to shoulder; 2. *fig.* supportive, together; ~ öpüşmek to be almost equal; ~ silkmek to shrug the shoulders; ~ vermek 1. to press against s.th. with shoulder; 2. to support, to help; -da taşımak to hono(u)r, to hold in high esteem; -ları çökmek to get exhausted, to get ruined; -una binmek (*b-nin*) to be a burden to *s.o.*

**omuzdaş** *contp.* accomplice.

**omuzdaşlık** mutual support, cooperation, solidarity.

**omuzlamak** 1. to shoulder; 2. to press s.th. with shoulder; 3. *sl.* to steal, to walk off with; 4. *fig.* to support, to help.

**omuzluk** 1. shoulder strap, epaulet; 2. shoulder yoke; 3. ↓ quarter.

**on** ten; ~ kez (*or* defa *or* kere) ten times; ~ (*or* beş) para etmez worthless; ~ paralık etm. (*b-ni*) to insult *s.o.*, to put *s.o.* into a bad position; ~ parasız penniless, flat broke; ~ parmağında ~ hüner (*or* marifet) very skillful, capable, clever; ~ parmağında ~ kara slanderous.

**ona** to him; to her; to it; ~ buna dil uzatmak to speak tactlessly; ~ sebep P for that reason, therefore, that is why.

**onaltılık** ♪ sixteenth note.

**onama** approval; certification.

**onamak** 1. to approve; 2. = onaylamak.

**onanizm** masturbation.

**onanmak** to be appoved; to be certified.

**onar** ten each, ten apiece; ~ ~ ten at a time, in tens, by tens.

**onarılmak** to be repaired, to be mended, to be fixed, to be restored.

**onarım** 1. repair(s); 2. restoration.

**onarımcı** repairer, restorer.

**onarma** repair; restoration.

**onarmak** 1. to repair; 2. to restore; 3. *fig.* to make amendments, to make up for, to compensate.

**onat,** -tı 1. proper; 2. useful; 3. honest, straightforward.

**onay** 1. suitable, convenient; 2. approval; -ını almak (*b-nin*) to get *s.o.*'s approval (*or* consent).

**onayaklılar** Decapoda.

**onaylama** 1. approval; 2. ratification.

**onaylamak** 1. to approve; 2. to ratify; to certify.

**onaylı** approved; ratified; certified.

**onaysız** unapproved; unratified; uncertified.

**onbaşı,** -yı ✗ corporal.

**onbaşılık** 1. being a corporal; 2. corporalship.

**onca** [x .] 1. according to him (*or* her); 2. so many; so much.

**onculayın** 1. according to him (*or* her); 2. like him (*or* her).

**onda** tenth.

**ondalık** 1. a tenth; ten per cent compensation; 2. *hist.* a tax paid at the rate of ten per cent on crops; 3. ⅋ decimal; ~ kesir decimal fraction; ~ sayı decimal number.

**ondalıkçı** one who works on a ten per cent commission.

**ondurmak** 1. to improve; 2. to cure; to heal.

**ondüle** 1. curly, wavy (hair); 2. waterwave, permanent wave, F perm.

**ogun** 1. very productive; 2. developed, prosperous, flourishing; 3. happy; 4. lucky; 5. totem; 6. armorial bearings; ~ besisuyu ⅋ nourishment carried from the leaves to the rest of the plant.

**ongunculuk** totemism.

**ongunluk** 1. prosperity; 2. productivity; 3. happiness.

**onikiparmakbağırsağı,** -nı *anat.* duodenum.

**onikitelli** twelve-stringed guitar-shaped instrument.

**oniks** meerschaum.

**onlar** *pl. of* o, they.

**onlu** 1. *cards:* the ten; 2. having ten parts.

**onluk** 1. of ten parts; 2. ten kuruş piece, ten lira bill.

**onmak** 1. to improve, to get better; 2. to heal (up), to recover (from), to get well; 3. to find happiness.

**ons** ounce (28, 35. gramme).

**onsuz** without him (*or* her or it).

**ontoloji** ontology.

**onu** him, her, it.

**onulmak** *pass. of* onmak.

**onulmaz** incurable.

**onun** his, her, its.

**onuncu** tenth; in the tenth order.

**onur** 1. hono(u)r; 2. sense of hono(u)r, dignity, pride, self-respect; ~ kurulu discipline committee; ~ üyesi honorary member; -una dokunmak (*b-nin*) to hurt *s.o.'s* pride; -una yedirememek not to be able to stomach.

onurlandırmak-to hono(u)r, to do hono(u)r to, to hono(u)r s.o. with one's presence.

onurlanmak to acquire hono(u)r, to be hono(u)red; to feel proud.

onurlu self-respecting, dignified, proud.

onursal honorary; ~ başkan honorary president; ~ üye honorary member.

onursuz without dignity, lacking in self--respect.

onursuzluk lack of self-respect.

oosfer oosphere.

oosit, -ti oocyte.

opal, -li opal.

opera [x . .] ♪ 1. opera; 2. opera house.

operakomik comic opera.

operasyon 1. ¶ operation; 2. operation.

operatör 1. ¶ surgeon; 2. operator *(of a machine)*; 3. *typ.* type-setter; 4. cameraman.

operet, -ti operetta.

oportünist, -ti opportunist.

oportünizm opportunism.

optik 1. optics; 2. optical.

optimist, -ti optimist.

optimizm optimism.

optimum optimum; the most suitable *(or* favourable).

opus opus.

ora [x .] that place; ~ senin bura benim dolaşmak *(or* gezinmek) to go around from place to place; -da there; -da burada here and there; -dan from there; -larda there(abouts); -larda olmamak not to listen to; to pretend not to hear *(or* know); -ya there, thither.

oracıkta just over there.

orak 1. sickle; 2. *fig.* harvest time.

orakböceği, -ni *zo.* cicada.

orakçı reaper.

oralı [x . .] of that place; ~ olmamak *fig.* not to pay attention, not to take notice of; to feign indifference.

oramiral, -li vice-admiral.

oran 1. proportion *(a.* A); ratio; 2. indifferent proportion; 3. estimate; 4. measure, scale.

orangutan *zo.* orangutan.

oranla relatively, spitefully, in comparison with.

oranlamak 1. to calculate, to measure; 2. to estimate; 3. to compare *(ile* with).

oranlı 1. proportioned; 2. symmetrical; 3. appropriate.

oransız 1. badly proportioned; 2. unsymmetrical.

oransızlık lack of proportion.

orantı A proportion.

orantılı 1. balanced, well-proportioned; 2. A proportional.

orası, -nı 1. that place; 2. that aspect of the matter.

oratoryo [. . x .] oratorio.

ordinaryus [. . x .] senior professor holding a chair in a university, distinguished *(professor).*

ordinat, -tı A ordinate.

ordino [. x .] delivery order; † certificate of ownership; boarding slip.

ordonat, -tı X supply service.

ordövr hors d'oeuvres.

ordu 1. army; 2. army arrangement; 3. crowd.

ordubozan 1. P varicose veins; 2. public enemy; 3. spoilsport.

ordubozanlık being a spoilsport.

orduevi, -ni officers' club.

ordugâh X military camp; bivouac.

org, -gu ♪ organ.

organ 1. *anat.* & *pol.* organ; 2. publication, organ.

organaktarımı transplantation.

organik organic; ~ kimya organic chemistry; ~ kütle organik rock.

organizasyon organization.

organizatör organizer.

organizma [. . x .] organism.

organlaşmak *biol.* to develop organs, to become an organ.

organze organza.

orgazm climax.

orgeneral, -li X full general.

orijin source, origin.

orijinal, -li 1. original *(picture, etc.);* 2. *contp.* specific, peculiar; 3. original *(parts, etc.).*

orijinallik 1. originality; 2. *fig.* unusualness, differentness.

orkestra ♪ orchestra.

orkide [. x .] ¶ orchid.

orkinos [x . .] *zo.* tuna, tunny-fish.

orkit, -ti orchitis.

orman forest, wood; ~ gibi thick *(hair, eyebrow, etc.);* ~ kebabı stew *(made of mutton and vegetables);* ~ kibarı *iro.* rude fellow, boor, ruffian; ~ taşlamak *fig.* to sound s.o.

ormancı 1. forester; 2. forestry specialist.

ormancılık 1. forestry; 2. being a forester.

ormanhorozu, -nu blackcock.

ormanlaşmak to become forested.

ormanlık woodland; thickly wooded.

ormansıçanı, -nı *zo.* wood mouse.

ormansız forestless.

ornatmak to substitute.

**ornitolog** ornithologist.

**ornitoloji** ornithology.

**orojeni** *geol.* orogeny.

**orospu** prostitute, whore, harlot; ~ çocuğu *sl.* 1. bastard, son of a bitch; 2. cunning, crafty, wily.

**orospuluk** 1. prostitution; 2. dirty trick, treachery.

**orostopolluk** *sl.* trick, ruse.

**orsa** [x.] ↓ the weather side, luff; ~ alabanda down with the helm!; ~ etm. to luff up; ~ poca (*or* baca) 1. luffing and falling off; 2. *fig.* struggling along.

**orsalamak** ↓ to hug the wind, to luff.

**orta** 1. middle, centre; 2. *phys.* place, field; 3. ₳ proportion; 4. environment, culture, medium; 5. middle..., central..., intermediate...; 6. average, medium; ~ boy medium size, medium length; ~ boylu of medium height ~ dalga *phys.* medium wave; ~ dikme ₳ perpendicular bisector; ~ halli from middle-class; ~ hizmetçisi housemaid; ~ işi housework; ~ karar of middling quality, moderate, somewhat appropriate; ~ malı 1. common property; 2. common, usual; 3. prostitute, whore; ~ şekerli 1. having sugar neither too much nor too little (*coffee*); 2. moderate, so so (*situation*); ~ terim *log.* middle term; ~ yaşlı middle-aged; -da 1. in the middle; 2. seizable, visible, obvious; 3. in public, publicly; -da bırakmak to abandon, to desert, to leave in the lurch; -da fol yok yumurta yok F there is no apparent reason whatsoever; -da kalmak 1. to be left without home; 2. to be in a two-alternative situation; -da olm. to have to be considered; -dan kaldırmak 1. to hide; 2. to remove, to abolish, to do away with; 3. *fig.* to kill; -dan kalkmak 1. to disappear, to vanish; 2. to be removed, to be ruined; 3. to get killed; -dan kaybolmak to disappear, to vanish; -dan söylemek to speak in a group without mentioning anyone, to drop hints; -nın sağı *pol.* group which is to the right of centre; -nın solu *pol.* group which is to the left of centre; -ya almak 1. to circle, to surround; 2. *fig.* to press s.o. hard; -ya atılmak 1. to be proposed, to be suggested; 2. to volunteer; -ya atmak to bring up, to throw up, to suggest; -ya bir balgam atmak *b.s.* to throw up a malicious hint that upsets things; -ya çıkarmak to prove, to reveal, to bring to light; -ya çıkmak 1. to arise, to come into being; 2. to appear, to emerge; -ya dökmek 1.

to display, to disclose; 2. to explain, to tell; -ya düşmek to become a prostitute; -ya koymak 1. to put forward; 2. to expose, to present for consideration.

**ortaağırlık** 1. middleweight (*boxer, etc.*); 2. a class in boxing (*between 71-75 kg*); a class in wrestling, weightlifting and shot (*between 72-79 kg*).

**ortaç** *gr.* participle, verbal adjective.

**ortaçağ** the Middle Ages.

**ortadamar** ♦ the large vein in the middle of a leaf.

**ortaderi** mesoderm.

**ortadirek** *fig.* middle class.

**Ortadoğu** the Middle East.

**ortaelçi** minister plenipotentiary.

**ortak** 1. companion, ⊤ partner, associate, copartner; 2. *contp.* accomplice; 3. fellow wife; 4. common; ~ olm. to participate in, to share in; ~ ölçülmez sayılar ₳ incommensurable numbers; ~ tam bölen ₳ common divisor.

**ortakçı** s.o. who assists a farmer in return for a share of the crop; 2. *biol.* commensal.

**ortakkat**, -tı ₳ common multiple.

**ortaklaşa** 1. in common, jointly; 2. joint business; 3. common, joint, shared, collective.

**ortaklaşacı** collectivist.

**ortaklaşacılık** collectivism.

**ortaklaşmak** to enter into partnership with s.o., to become partners.

**ortaklık** 1. partnership; 2. ⊤ company, firm, corporation.

**ortakulak** *anat.* middle ear, tympanum.

**ortakyapım** joint production.

**ortakyaşama** *biol.* symbiosis.

**ortakyaşar** *biol.* symbiont.

**ortakyönetim** coalition.

**ortalama** 1. average, mean; 2. right through; 3. in the middle.

**ortalamak** 1. to reach the middle of; 2. to divide in the middle; 3. to put in the midst.

**ortalık** 1. surroundings, the area around; 2. *phys.* medium: 3. people, world, the public; ~ ağarmak (*for the dawn*) to break; ~ düzelmek to improve, to get better; ~ kararmak to get dark, (*for night*) to fall; ~ karışmak to be upside down, to be topsy-turvy; ~ yatışmak to calm down, to be restored; ortalığı birbirine katmak to cause tumult, to cause confusion and excitement, to make a mess; ortalığı... götürmek to cover the whole place; -ta in sight, around, within view.

ortam 1. environment, surroundings; 2. atmosphere.

ortanca¹ 1. second eldest *(for three brothers or sisters)*; 2. middle, middling.

ortanca² ⚘ hydrangea.

ortaokul secondary school, middle shool.

ortaoyunu, -nu a theatrical genre once popular in Turkey.

ortaöğretim secondary education.

ortaparmak middle finger.

ortayuvar mesosphere.

Ortodoks Orthodox.

Ortodoksluk Orthodoxy.

ortoklaz *geol.* orthoclase.

ortopedi orthopedics.

ortopedik orthopedic.

ortopedist orthopedist.

ortoz *s.* ortoklaz.

oruç, -cu *eccl.* fasting, fast, the Moslem daytime fast during the month of Ramazan; ~ açmak to break the fast *(at sunset)*; ~ bozmak to break the fast *(at an improper time, before sunset)*; ~ tutmak to fast; ~ yemek not to fast.

oruçlu fasting.

oruçsuz not fasting.

orun 1. private place; 2. place, abode, office.

orya [x .] *cards:* diamond.

oryantal Oriental.

oryantalist, -ti Orientalist.

Osmanlı 1. an Ottoman (Turk); 2. Ottoman; 3. *fig.* brave and noble.

Osmanlıca the Ottoman Turkish language.

Osmanlılık 1. being an Ottoman; 2. the period of Ottoman empire.

osmiyum ⚗ osmium.

osurgan *s.o.* who farts a lot.

osurganböceği, -ni *zo.* stag beetle.

osurmak to fart, to break wind.

osuruk *sl.* fart; osuruğu cinli *sl.* ill-humo(u)red, very touchy, easily effervesced.

oşinografi *geogr.* oceanography.

ot, -tu 1. herb, plant; 2. *(a.* yeşil ~) grass; 3. *(a.* kuru ~) hay; 4. weed; 5. poison; 6. medicine; 7. depilatory; 8. *sl.* hashish; 9. stuffed with grass *(pillow, cushion, etc.)*; 10. fodder; ~ tutunmak to rub a depilatory on one's body; ~ yiyenler *zo.* herbivorous; ~ yoldurmak *(b-ne)* to give *s.o.* a hard time, to put *s.o.* to trouble.

otağ, otak pavilion, large nomad tent.

otalamak 1. to poison; 2. to treat medically.

otamak to treat medically.

otantik authentic.

otarmak to pasture.

otarşi autarky.

otçul *zo.* herbivorous.

otel hotel.

otelci hotel-keeper, hotelier.

otelcilik hotel industry; hotel management.

otizm *psych.* autism.

otlak pasture, grassy area, pastureland.

otlakçı *sl.* sponger, parasite.

otlakçılık *sl.* being a sponger.

otlakıye [â] tax *(paid by those who pasture their animals on government land)*.

otlamak 1. to graze, to pasture; 2. *sl.* to sponge; 3. *sl.* to pitch, to steal.

otlanmak 1. to graze, to pasture; 2. to be grazed over.

otlatılmak *pass. of* otlatmak.

otlatmak to put out to graze.

otlubağa *zo.* toad.

otluk 1. pastureland, grassy area; 2. hayrick, haystack; 3. hay-barn.

oto¹ *prefix* with the meaning of «self».

oto² motor-car, car, auto, automobile.

otoban high-way, autobahn.

otobiyografi autobiography.

otobüs bus, motor coach, autobus.

otobüscü 1. *s.o.* who owns and runs a line of buses; 2. bus driver.

otodidakt, -tı self-taught person, autodidact.

otoerotizm autoerotism.

otogar bus station.

otokar large motor-car, bus.

otoklav autoclave.

otokrasi autocracy.

otokrat, -tı autocrat.

otokritik self-criticism, autocriticism.

otolit, -tı otolith, ear stone.

otoman 1. ottoman *(a kind of coach)*; 2. ottoman *(fabric)*.

otomasyon automation.

otomat, -tı 1. automaton, robot; 2. flash heater, geyser; 3. system in which electric lights are switched on manually and switched off automatically.

otomatik automatic.

otomatikman automatically.

otomatikleşmek to become automatic.

otomatizm automatism.

otomobil car, automobile.

otomotiv automotive industry.

otonom autonomous.

otonomi autonomy.

otopark, -kı car park; parking lot; parking building.

otoplasti ⚕ autoplasty.

otopsi autopsy, postmortem examination.

**otoray** autorail, rail-car.

**otorite 1.** authority, standing; **2.** authority (*scientifically*); **3.** ♔ supreme (*or executive*) power.

**otoriter** authoritarian.

**otosist,** -ti otocyst.

**otostop,** -pu hitchhiking; ~ yapmak to hitch-hike.

**otostopçu** hitchhiker.

**otoyol** super high-way, autobahn.

**otçu, otsul** ♔ herbaceous.

**oturacak** seat.

**oturak 1.** chamberpot; **2.** seat, foot, bottom; **3.** residence; **4.** oar-bench, thwart; ~ âlemi a drinking party with belly dancers.

**oturaklı 1.** solidly constructed, with solid foundation; **2.** *fig.* grave, sober, serious; **3.** striking, appropriate (*word*).

**oturaklılık** sedateness, dignity, sobriety.

**oturma 1.** sitting; **2.** residing; ~ belgesi residence permit; ~ grevi slow-down strike; ~ odası living room.

**oturmak 1.** to sit down on; **2.** to sit; **3.** to live; to dwell in, to reside; **4.** to fit; **5.** to loaf, to laze; **6.** to sink; **7.** ⚓ to run ashore; **8.** ♔ to precipitate; **9.** to settle; **10.** F to cost: **11.** to come to an agreement; **12.** to take up (*a post*); **13.** to take root, to be accepted; oturup kalkmak to act on.

**oturmuş** *fig.* rooted, settled.

**oturtma 1.** *vn. of* oturtmak; **2.** *a dish made with ground meat and vegetables.*

**oturtmak** *caus. of* oturmak **1.** to place, to put (*vase, etc.*); **2.** to seat, to sit s.o. down; **3.** to set, to mount, to emboss; **4.** ⚓ to run aground on.

**oturtmalık** △ basement, stereobate.

**oturulmak** *impersonal pass.* **1.** to sit; **2.** to live, to dwell in.

**oturum 1.** sitting, session; **2.** ♔ hearing.

**oturuş** way of sitting.

**oturuşmak** to calm down; to slow down.

**otuz** thirty; -bir a card game; -bir çekmek *sl.* to wank off, to jerk off, to masturbate, to beat one's meat.

**otuzar** A thirty at a time, thirty each.

**otuzuncu** thirtieth.

**ova** grassy plain, meadow.

**oval,** -li oval.

**ovalamak 1.** to grind, to rub, to powder, to pulverize, to crumble, to press with the hands; **2.** to massage, to knead.

**ovalı** s.o. who lives in a plain.

**ovalık** grassy land, plain, level and extensive (*area*).

**ovmak 1.** to massage, to knead, to rub; **2.** to rub, to scrub, to scour; **3.** to polish.

**ovogon** ♔ oogonium.

**ovolit,** -ti *geol.* oolite.

**ovulmak 1.** to be kneaded, to be massaged, to be rubbed; **2.** to be scoured, to be scrubbed.

**ovuşturmak** to massage, to rub, to knead, to wipe one's eyes.

**oy 1.** opinion, view, sight; **2.** vote; **3.** voting; ~ birliği **1.** unanimity; **2.** unanimous vote; ~ birliğiyle unanimously; ~ çokluğu majority; ~ hakkı the right of voting; ~ sandığı ballot box; ~ vermek to vote for; -a koymak (*bşi*) to put s.th. to the vote.

**oya** pinking, embroidery; ~ gibi fine and dainty.

**oyacı** maker *or* seller of embroidery.

**oyalamak 1.** to distract one's attention; **2.** to detain; **3.** to delay, to put off, to hold out, **4.** to keep busy, to amuse; **5.** to pink, to embroider.

**oyalanmak 1.** *pass of* oyalamak; **2.** to make o.s. merry; **2.** to kill time, to dawdle.

**oyalayıcı** amusing, keeping busy.

**oyalı** edged with embroidery.

**oydaş** of the same opinion, like-minded.

**oylama** voting, poll.

**oylamak** to vote on, to put s.th. to the vote.

**oylanmak** to be voted on.

**oyluk** thigh; ~ kemiği femur, thighbone.

**oylum 1.** volume, size; **2.** hollowed out, carved; **3.** depth, three dimensional effect (*painting*); ~ ~ curling (*smoke*), saw-toothed.

**oylumlama** modeling, giving s.th. three-dimensional shape (*fine arts*).

**oylumlu** bulk, voluminous; **2.** *fig.* large, great.

**oyma 1.** *vn. of* oymak; **2.** craving, engraving, wood-carving, fretwork, stamping, sculpture; **3.** carved, engraved, stamped, sculptured, hollowed out.

**oymabaskı** engraving (*printing process using the engraved plates*).

**oymacı** sculptor, engraver.

**oymacılık** the art of engraving (*or carving*).

**oymak[1] 1.** to scoop out, to dig out; **2.** to engrave, to carve.

**oymak[2] 1.** subdivision, tribe; **2.** troop of boy scouts; ~ beyi scoutmaster.

**oymalı** carved, engraved, chiselled; ~ yaprak ♔ lobate leaf.

**oynak 1.** frisky, restless (*horse*); **2.** playful; **3.** unstable; **4.** ⊕ loose, having much play; **5.** capricious, wayward; **6.** coquettish; **7.** *anat.* joint.

**oynaklık 1.** liveliness, being restless; **2.** capricious behavio(u)r.

**oynamak 1.** to play, to amuse o.s.; **2.** to frisk, to skip *(horse);* **3.** to be loose *(tooth, etc.);* **4.** † to fluctuate; **5.** to play *(cards, game, etc.);* **6.** to dance; **7.** to perform *(a play);* **8.** *(bşle)* to stake, to jeopardize; **9.** to trifle with, to risk; **10.** to be on *(film, play, etc.);* **11.** to flicker, to vibrate; **12.** to fool with, to tamper with; **13.** to show differences *(price);* **14.** to slip *(of the ground);* Oynama! *(negative)* **1.** do not dawdle! **2.** do not touch that!, do not play with it!; oynaya oynaya with great pleasure, joyfully.

**oynaş** lover, lovemate.

**oynaşmak 1.** to play with one another; **2.** to have a love affair.

**oynatmak 1.** *caus. of* oynamak; **2.** to cause to play; **2.** to keep amused *(child);* **3.** to cause to move, to stir; **4.** to make s.o. dance; **5.** to lose one's mind, to go off one's nut.

**oysa(ki)** [x . .] but, yet, however, whereas.

**oyuk 1.** hollowed out; **2.** cave, cavity, hole.

**oyulga** tacking, basting.

**oyulga(la)mak** to tack together, to bast together.

**oyulgan** ulcer.

**oyulmak** *pass. of* oymak.

**oyum 1.** hollowing; **2.** cutting, carving, engraving; **3.** cavity, cave hole.

**oyun 1.** game *(a. fig.);* **2.** *thea.* perform-

ance; **3.** (stage) play; **4.** dance; **5.** wrestling *(match);* **6.** wrestling technic; **7.** cheat, swindle; **8.** gambling; **9.** trick; ~ almak to win a game; ~ çıkarmak *sports:* to play a game; ~ etmek *(or* oynamak) to play a trick on, to fool, to dupe; ~ havası ♪ melody, tone, tune *(folk dances);* ~ kağıdı playing card; ~ vermek to lose a game; -a çıkmak *thea.* to appear on the stage; -a gelmek to be deceived, to be duped; -a getirmek to deceive, to swindle, to dupe; -u almak to win the game; Bizans -u trick, fraud, wile, intrigue.

**oyunbaz 1.** † playful, frollicsome; **2.** swindler; **3.** tricker.

**oyunbazlık** trickery, deceitfulness.

**oyunbozan** spoil-sport, kill-joy, intruder, troublemaker.

**oyunbozanlık** being a spoil-sport; ~ etm. to be a spoil-sport.

**oyuncak 1.** toy, plaything; **2.** *fig.* trifle, child's play, easy job; **3.** *fig.* sport, plaything.

**oyuncakçı** maker *or* seller of toys.

**oyuncakçılık** the toy business.

**oyuncu 1.** player; **2.** actor, player, actress; **3.** dancer; **4.** *s.* oyunbaz; **5.** gambler.

**oyunculuk 1.** being a player; **2.** acting, being an actor *(or* actress); **3.** trickery.

**oyunevi,** -ni theatre, *Am.* theater.

**oyuntu** hollow, hole, cavity.

**ozalit** Ozalid.

**ozan 1.** poet; **2.** wandering minstrel.

**ozanca** like a poet, in a poetic manner.

**ozanlık 1.** being a poet; **2.** poetic talent.

**ozansı** poetastrical.

**ozon** 🜍 ozone.

# Ö

**ö** [-] boo!, ugh!, phew!, oof!

**öbek** heap, pile, group, crowd; ~ ~ in groups, in heaps, in crowds.

**öbür** [x.] 1. the other (of two); 2. the former; ~ gün the day after tomorrow; ~ dünya the hereafter, the next world; ~ hafta the week after next.

**öbürkü** F s. öbürü.

**öbürü**, -nü the other one (person or thing).

**öcü** (child's language) bad man, evil, ogre, bogyman.

**öç**, -cü revenge, vengeance; ~ almak (or çıkarmak) (b-den) 1. to revenge o.s. (or be revenged) on s.o.; 2. to get revenge.

**öd**, -dü gall, bile; ~-ü kopmak (or patlamak) to be frightened to death, to be scared out of one's wits; ~-ünü koparmak (or patlatmak) to frighten to death, to scare s.o. out of his wits.

**ödağacı**, -nı ♀ agalloch tree.

**ödem** ⚕ edema.

**ödeme** payment, disbursement; ~ emri ⚖ default summons, writ of execution; ~ kabiliyeti solvency; -lerin tatili suspension of payment.

**ödemek** 1. to pay, to disburse; 2. to indemnify, to compensate; 3. ♸ to amortize, to redemp.

**ödemeli** 1. cash on delivery payment, Am. collect; 2. (to send s.th.) cash on delivery (c.o.d.); 3. teleph. reversed charge.

**ödenek** appropriations, allotments, allowance.

**ödenmek** pass. of ödemek.

**ödenti** 1. membership fee; 2. proceeds, receipts, income.

**ödeşmek** to settle (or square) accounts with each other.

**ödetmek** caus. of ödemek.

**ödev** 1. duty, obligation, liability, task, assignment, job; 2. homework.

**ödevbilim** deontology.

**ödkesesi**, -ni gall bladder.

**ödlek** 1. frightened, scared; 2. cowardly, timid.

**ödül** 1. prize; 2. reward, recompense, premium.

**ödüllendirmek** to award s.o. a prize, to give s.o. a prize.

**ödün** compensation, equalization, restitution, amends (for), indemnity; ~ vermek to compensate, to indemnify, to make a concession.

**ödünç**, -cü 1. lent, loaned; 2. borrowed, on loan; ~ almak to borrow; ~ para loan; ~ vermek to lend.

**ödünleme** compensation, concession.

**ödünlemek** to compensate, to make up (for).

**öf** phew!, ugh!, boo!, how nauseous!, how disgusting!, alas!, oh!, oof!

**öfke** anger, rage, wrath, fury; ~ baldan tatlıdır it is to shout at when you are angry; ~ topuklarına çıkmak (b-nin) to fill with great rage; -si burnunda hot--headed; -sini çıkarmak (or almak) (b-den) to vent one's anger on s.o.; -sini yenmek to control one's temper, to get hold of o.s.

**öfkelendirmek** to anger, to bring into a rage, to make angry, to infuriate.

**öfkelenmek** to get angry, to grow angry (-e at).

**öfkeli** choleric, hotheaded, angry, furious, Am. mad (with).

**öge** element, component.

**öğle** noon; ~ paydosu (or tatili or dinlencesi) lunch break; ~ üstü (or üzeri) about noon; ~ yemeği lunch; -(n)den önce (or evvel) in the morning, before noon; -(n)den sonra in the afternoon.

**öğlen** 1. F noon, midday; 2. ast. meridian.

**öğlende** at noon, about midday.

**öğleyin** s. öğlende.

**öğmek** s. övmek.

**öğrenci** student, pupil.

**öğrencilik** being a student.

**öğrenim** education, study, formation.

**öğrenme** learning.

**öğrenmek** 1. to learn; 2. to become familiar with; 3. to hear, to inquire.

**öğrenmelik** scholarship.

**öğreti**[1] doctrine, principles.

**öğretici** educational, didactic, instructive (film, etc.)

**öğretim** instruction, lessons; ~ bilgisi

didactics; ~ görevlisi lecturer; ~ izlencesi curriculum; ~ üyesi university teacher; ~ yardımcıları university teachers who are not lecturers and below in the rank than of associate professors; ~ yılı school year.

**öğretmek 1.** to teach, to impart, to instruct, to give lessons; **2.** to teach, to show (treat, menace).

**öğretmen** teacher.

**öğretmenlik** teaching, being a teacher.

**öğünmek** s. övünmek.

**öğür 1.** of the same age; **2.** familiar, intimate; **3.** used to, accustomed to; **4.** group, class, party; ~ olm. to get used to, to get very familiar with.

**öğürmek 1.** to retch; **2.** to bellow; öğüreceği gelmek fig. to feel very disgusted.

**öğürtmek** caus. of öğürmek.

**öğürtü 1.** retching; **2.** retching sound.

**öğüt, -dü** advice, counsel, admonition, lesson, warning; ~ vermek (or -te bulunmak) to advise, to counsel.

**öğütlemek** to advise, to counsel (s.o. to do s.th.).

**öğütmek 1.** to grind; **2.** fig. to digest.

**öğütücü 1.** grinder; **2.** digestive...

**öğütücüdiş** molar (tooth).

**öğütülmek** pass. of. öğütmek.

**öhö** coughing sound.

**ökçe 1.** heel; **2.** heel (of a boot); **3.** heel leather.

**ökçeli** heeled, high heeled (shoe).

**ökçesiz** heelless, flat-soled.

**öke** genius.

**ökse 1.** birdlime; **2.** fig. attractive woman; ~ çubuğu stick smeared with birdlime; -ye basmak to make a mistake or to lose carelessly.

**ökseotu, -nu** ♀ mistletoe.

**öksürmek** to cough, to clear one's throat, to have a cough; öksürmek tıksırmak to cough.

**öksürtmek** to cause to cough.

**öksürtücü** urgeing to cough, causing cough.

**öksürük** cough, clearing one's throat.

**öksüründü** s.o. who has a cough, coughing all the time, coughing slightly; ~ tıksırıklı F sickly.

**öksürükotu, -nu** ♀ coltsfoot.

**öksüz 1.** motherless, orphan; **2.** fig. alone (in the world), single, without friends; ~ babası fig. good benefactor; ~ kalmak **1.** to lose one's both father and mother; **2.** to be left alone; ~ sevindiren a common dawdry thing.

**öküz 1.** zo. ox; **2.** fig. fool, stupid, Am. sap(head), oaf; **3.** sl. loaded dice, die; ~ arabası ox-cart; ~ arabası gibi very slowly; ~ gibi stupid, fool; ~ gibi bakmak to stare like a fool; ~ trene bakar gibi bakmak to stare like a fool (or stupidly); -e boynuzu yük olmaz (or ağır gelmez) it is not a burden to help one's friends; -ün altında buzağı aramak to hunt for s.th. in the most unlikely place.

**öküzbalığı, -nı** zo. walrus.

**öküzburnu, -nu** zo. hornbill.

**öküzdili, -ni** ♀ bugloss.

**öküzgözü, -nü** arnica.

**öküzlük** fig. incredible stupidity.

**öl** moistness, wetness.

**ölçek 1.** measure, scale, standart; **2.** grain measure equal to four okka.

**ölçer** poker, fire-rake.

**ölçmek, (-er) 1.** to measure; **2.** fig. to weigh; ölçüp biçmek to consider carefully, to think s.th. over carefully.

**ölçü 1.** measure; **2.** unit of measurement; **3.** dimensions; **4.** fig. in reason; **5.** ♪ time, measure; **6.** poet. metre; **7.** fig. regard; ~ almak **1.** to measure; **2.** to compare; ~ vermek to give the measurements of (dress, shoe, etc.); -yü kaçırmak to behave excessively (or beyond reason).

**ölçülmek** to be measured.

**ölçülü 1.** measured; **2.** poet. metrical; **3.** fig. moderate, temperate; **4.** proportionally distributed; ~ biçili, elaborated; ~ balon ♏ gauge glass.

**ölçülülük** moderation.

**ölçüm 1.** measuring; **2.** measurement; **3.** appraisal.

**ölçümlemek 1.** to reason s.th. out, to consider s.th. carefully; **2.** to evaluate.

**ölçüsüz 1.** unmeasured; **2.** immeasurable, immense; **3.** excessive; **4.** immoderate, excessive, unbridled; **5.** without consideration.

**ölçüşmek (b-le)** to compete (or grapple) with s.o.

**ölçüt, -tü** criterion.

**öldüresiye** ruthlessly, murderously.

**öldürmek 1.** to kill, to murder, to slay (a. time); **2.** to remove the strong taste of (onion, etc.); **3.** to torture, to treat harshly; **4.** to exhaust, to wear out.

**öldürtmek** caus. of öldürmek.

**öldürücü 1.** mortal, fatal, deadly, lethal; **2.** suffocating.

**öldürülmek** to be killed.

**ölesiye** excessively, intensely.

**ölgün 1.** not fresh anymore, faded, withered; **2.** tired, exhausted, worn out; **3.** calm (sea).

**ölmek**, (-ür) **1.** to die; **2.** to fade, to wither; **3.** to suffer great grief (or anxiety); **4.** to perish; ~ var dönmek yok to come hell or high water; ölüp ölüp dirilmek to sweat blood; ölür müsün, öldürür müsün? to be between the rock and hard place.

**ölmez 1.** immortal, eternal; **2.** indestructible, tough.

**ölmezoğlu**, -nu indestructible, tough.

**ölmüş 1.** dead; **2.** dead (person).

**ölü 1.** dead; **2.** feeble, faint, weak, fatigued, motionless; **3.** dead (body); **4.** dead (person); **5.** out of fashion, not used any more; ~ açı ✕ dead angle; ~ dalga low wave, swell; ~ deniz swell; ~ fiyatına dirt cheap; ~ gözü gibi pale, weak (light); ~ nokta dead point (a. ✕); ~ salı wooden bench on which a corpse is washed; ~ veya sağ dead or alive; -sü kandilli (or kınalı) sl. the damned scoundrel, the wretch; -sü ortada kalmak not to be claimed by anybody (corpse); -yü güldürür very funny.

**ölük** weak, exhausted, feeble, faint.

**ölüm** death, decease, case of death; ~ Allah'ın emri death is the will of God; ~ döşeği deathbed; ~ kalım meselesi matter of life or death; ~ sessizliği deathly silence; ~ var dirim var death is an ever-present contingency; -e bağlı tasarruflar ☆ testimentary decrees (or orders); -le burun buruna gelmek to have a close brush with death; -ü göze almak to act in the face of death; -üne susamak to court death.

**ölümcül 1.** fatal, mortal; **2.** dying.

**ölümlü** mortal; ~ dünya (this) mortal world.

**ölümsü** deathlike, deathly.

**ölümsüz** immortal.

**ölümsüzlük** immortality.

**ömür**, -mrü **1.** life, existence; **2.** duration of life; **3.** happy life; **4.** fig. wonderful, marvel(l)ous; ~ adam **1.** a fine fellow; **2.** odd fellow; ~ boyunca all one's life; ~ çürütmek to spend one's time and energy in vain; ~ geçirmek to live, to spend one's life; ~ sürmek to lead a comfortable and happy life; ~ tehlikesi danger of life; ~ törpüsü a long and exhausting job; ömre bedel worth a life (beautiful, excellent); -ler olsun! may you live long!; ömrü billah **1.** up to now; **2.** never; ömrü vefa etmemek to die before attaining one's goal; ömründe never (in

one's life); ömrüne bereket! may you live long!

**ömürlü** long-lived, long-lasted.

**ömürsüz** short-lived.

**ön 1.** front; **2.** front (side), **3.** foremost; **4.** the future; ~ ayak olm. to be (the) pioneer, to be (the) first in doing s.th.; ~ plana geçmek to come to the fore; -de gelmek to be in (the) most important place; -e almak to give preference (to); -e düşmek to march in front, to lead the way; -e sürmek **1.** to propose, to suggest; **2.** to put forward (idea); -ü alınmak to be prevented; -ünde, -üne in front of; -üne bak! look out!, take care!, be careful!; -üne bakmak to hang one's head in shame; -üne geçmek to prevent, to avert; -üne gelen anybody; -ünü almak **1.** to prevent, to avert, to obviate; **2.** to dam up (a. fig.), to embank; -ünü ardını düşünmemek not to act circumspectly; -ünü kesmek to dam up, to embank.

**önad** gr. adjective.

**önavurt** anat. alveolar ridge.

**önce** [x .] **1.** before, previously; **2.** first, at first, first of all; **3.** the past, pre....

**önceden** [x ..] in the beginning, at first, beforehand, first of all.

**önceki** the preceding, the former, the previous.

**öncel** predecessor, ancestor; ~ düzen phls. the theory of preestablished harmony.

**önceleri** [x ...] previously, formerly.

**öncelik** priority.

**öncelikle** first of all, before all else.

**öncesiz** eternal, without beginning.

**öncesizlik** past eternity.

**öncü 1.** ✕ vanguard; **2.** advance courier; **3.** avant-garde; **4.** leader.

**öncül** phls. premise.

**öncülük** leadership.

**öndamak** anat. palate.

**öndelik** ✝ payment in advance.

**önder** leader, chief.

**önderlik** leadership.

**öndeyiş** prologue.

**önek** gr. prefix.

**önel** extension, delay, fixed period of time, due date; respite.

**önem** importance, consequence, significance; ~ vermek to consider important, to esteem, to appreciate.

**önemli** important, considerable.

**önemsemek** to consider important.

**önemsiz** unimportant, insignificant.

**önemsizlik** unimportance, insignificance.

**önerge** proposal, motion.

**öneri** offer, suggestion, proposal.

**önermek** to propose, to motion, to offer.

**önerti** *log.* antecedent.

**öngörmek** 1. to provide for, to foresee; 2. to consider, to bear in mind.

**öngörü** far-sightedness, prescience.

**öngörülü** foresighted, prescient.

**öngün** eve.

**önkol** *anat.* forearm.

**önlem** precaution, measure, action; ~ almak to take the necessary measurements.

**önlemek** 1. to prevent, to avert, to obviate, to guard against; 2. to stop, to forestall.

**önleyici** preventive.

**önlük** 1. apron; 2. pinafore; 3. smock.

**önseçim** primary election.

**önsel** a priori.

**önses** *gr.* first sound of a word; ~ düşmesi *gr.* ellision of the first sound of a word.

**önsezi** presentiment, foreboding.

**önsöz** preface, foreword.

**öntasar(ı)** preliminary draft.

**önyargı** prejudice.

**önyargılı** prejudiced.

**önyüz** front (*a.* ✕).

**önyüzbaşı**, -*yı* ✕ a senior captain, lieutenant commander.

**öpmek**, (-*er*) to kiss; ~ babanın elini! we are done for!; -üp te başına koymak to be thankful for small favo(u)rs, to accept s.th. with pleasure.

**öpücük** kiss; ~ göndermek (*or* yollamak) to blow kisses, to cast kisses to.

**öpülmek** to be kissed.

**öpüş** kissing.

**öpüşmek** to kiss one another.

**ördek** 1. *zo.* duck; 2. urinal (*for use in bed*); 3. *sl.* extra passenger picked up on the way; ~ yürüyüşü duckwaddle.

**ördekbaşı**, -*nı* greenish-blue.

**ördekgagası**, -*nı* reddish-yellow.

**ördürmek** to have s.th. knitted.

**öreke** distaff.

**ören** ruins.

**örf** custom, convention, common usage, sovereign right.

**örfi** [î] conventional, customary, consuetudinary; ~ idare ٌ state of siege, martial law.

**örge** motif.

**örgen** *biol.* organ.

**örgü** 1. plaited *or* knitted work, plait; 2. knitting; 3. knitted *or* plaited; 4. tress,

plait (of hair) 5. *anat.* plexus; 6. rush mat; ~ şişi knitting-needle.

**örgün** organic.

**örgüt**, -*tü* organization.

**örgütçü** organizer.

**örgütlemek** to organize.

**örgütlendirmek** to organize.

**örgütlenmek** to be organized.

**örgütleyici** organizer.

**örgütlü** organized.

**örgütsel** organizational.

**örgütsüz** unorganized.

**örme** 1. *vn. of* örmek 2. knitting, plaiting; 3. plaited, knitted; 4. braided (*hair*).

**örmek**, (-*er*) 1. to plait, to knit; 2. to tie, to knot, to crochet; 3. to darn, to mend (*linen, etc.*); 4. to build, to erect (*wall*); 5. to braid, to plait (*hair*); 6. *fig.* to make, to execute (*a. thea.*)

**örneğin** for example, for instance.

**örnek** 1. sample, design, pattern, specimen; 2. example, prototype; 3. equivalent (to), of the same value, like; 4. type, model; 5. typical..., model...; 6. form, blank (form); 7. copy, *typ.* proof; ~ almak (*b-den*) to take *s.o.* as one's model, to take a lesson from *s.o.*; ~ olmak to be a model; örneğini almak (*bşin*) to draw the design *or* model of *s.th.*; örneğini çıkarmak to make a copy of.

**örneklemek** to give an example of, to illustrate.

**örs** anvil.

**örselemek** 1. to use badly, to maul, to batter, to handle roughly, to damage, to spoil, to rumple; 2. to use *s.o.* ill, to play *s.o.* a nasty trick; 3. to exhaust, to weaken (*illness*).

**örselenmek** *caus. of* örselemek.

**örtbas etm.** to suppress, to hush up.

**örten** *anat.* mantle.

**örtmek**, (-*er*) 1. to cover (*a.* ✕, ⊤, *boxing*); to veil, to mask, to disguise (*a. fig.*); 3. to shut, to close; 4. to shovel, to cast; 5. to wrap; 6. to hush up.

**örttürmek** *caus. of* örtmek.

**örtü** 1. cover, wrap 2. blanket; 3. roof.

**örtük** covered, closed.

**örtülmek** 1. to be covered, to be wrapped up; 2. to be closed; 3. to be hushed up.

**örtülü** 1. covered, wrapped up; 2. roofed; 3. closed, shut; 4. hushed up, concealed; ~ ödenek discretionary fund in the government budget (*used to finance secret projects*).

**örtünmek** to cover o.s., to veil o.s.

**örtüsüz** uncovered, unveiled.

**örü** 1. plaited *or* knitted work; 2. building,

edifice, **3.** mending, repair; **4.** enclosed place.

**örücü 1.** knitter; **2.** darner, mender; **3.** stonemason, bricklayer.

**örülü 1.** knitted; **2.** darned, mended; **3.** braided.

**örümce** zo. a fig moth.

**örümcek 1.** zo. spider; **2.** (ağı) cobweb; ~ bağlamak **1.** to get covered with cobwebs; **2.** to be left without being used for a long time; ~ kafalı pej. reactioner, stone-conservative, old fashioned; (bir yeri) ~ sarmak to get covered with cobwebs.

**örümcekkuşu,** -nu zo. shrike.

**örümceklenmek 1.** to get covered with cobwebs; **2.** fig. to be left without being used; **3.** ℱ to become coated with dry mucous (around eyes, mouth, nostrils).

**örümcekler** zo. Araneida.

**örümcekli** covered with cobwebs; ~ kafa fig. old-fashioned, reactioner.

**östaki** anat. Eustachian; ~ borusu Eustachian tube.

**öşür,** -şrü **1.** ₳ tenth (part); **2.** tithe.

**öşürcü** tithe collector.

**öte 1.** the farther side; the other side; **2.** other, farther; **3.** the rest; ~ gün a few days ago, the other day, recently; -de beride here and there; -den beri from of old, at all times, -den beriden from here and there, from this and that; -si berisi **1.** one's goods and possessions; **2.** one's various places, various things; -si var mı? stick that in your pipe and smoke it!; -sinde berisinde here and there of...; -sini beri etm. (bşin) to leave no stone unturned (to); -ye beriye here and there.

**öteberi** this and that, various things.

**öteki,** -ni **1.** the other; **2.** the farther; **3.** the next but one; ~ beriki anybody and everybody.

**ötekisi,** -ni the other one.

**ötleğen** zo. warbler.

**ötleği** zo. lammergeier.

**ötmek** (-er) **1.** to sing (bird), to crow (cock); **2.** to sound, to echo; **3.** to ring, to tinkle, to sound; **4.** sl. to speak incessantly; **5.** sl. to vomit, to puke.

**öttürmek 1.** caus. of ötmek; **2.** to boast, to brag (of).

**ötücü** which sings habitually (bird).

**ötürü** because of, by reason of, on account of.

**ötüş** way of singing.

**ötüşmek** to sing at the same time (birds).

**öveç** two or three-year old ram.

**övendire** oxgoad.

**övgü** eulogy, panegyric.

**övgücü** flatterer.

**övme** praising, laudation.

**övmek,** (-er) to praise, to extol.

**övülmek** to be praised.

**övünç** pride; ~ çizelgesi hono(u)r roll.

**övüngen** boastful, boasting, braggard, boaster.

**övünmek 1.** to boast; **2.** to praise o.s., to boast, to brag, to bluster, to talk big, to show off; ~ gibi olmasın if I do say so myself..., I don't mean to boast but...

**öykü** story.

**öykücü 1.** story-teller; **2.** short-story writer.

**öykünme** imitating, imitation, mimicing.

**öykünmek** to imitate, to mimic.

**öyle 1.** such, such a, of such a kind; **2.** so, in such a way, like that; ~ ise if so, in that case; (b-ne) ~ gelmek it seems to..., to have the impression that...; ~ olsun all right, it is okay; ~ şey (or yağma) yok! (s.o. is) not going to get away with that, it's out of the question; ~ ya of course, certainly.

**öylece** [x . .], **öylelikle** [x . . .] in such a manner, thus, in this way, so that, so.

**öylesi** such..., like...

**öz 1.** (one's own) self; **2.** kernel, essence, heart substance; **3.** ♦ pith; **4.** core; **5.** own, proper; **6.** genuine, real; **7.** essential; **8.** cream; **9.** marrow; **10.** brook, stream; ~ hayat private life; ~ odun heartwood; ~ kardeş full brother (or sister); -ü sözü bir decent, sincere, honest, genuine, frank.

**özbağışıklık** ℱ autoimmunism.

**Özbek 1.** Uzbek; **2.** Uzbek, of the Uzbeks.

**Özbekçe** the Uzbek language.

**Özbekistan** Uzbekistan.

**özbeöz** real, genuine, true.

**özdek 1.** material; **2.** goods, merchandise; **3.** phls. matter.

**özdekçi** phls. materialist.

**özdekçilik** phls. materialism.

**özdeksel** phls. materialist.

**özden 1.** genuine, true, sincere; **2.** anat. thymus.

**özdeş** identical (a. phls. & ₳).

**özdeşlemek 1.** to equate; **2.** to identify.

**özdeşlik 1.** identity; **2.** identicalness.

**özdevim** automation.

**özdevinim** automatism.

**özdeyiş** epigram, aphorism.

**özdışı,** -nı phls. extrinsic.

**özdirenç** phys. resistivity.

**öze** phls. peculiar to, special.

özek center; ~ ağacı central pole of a four-wheeled cart.

özekdoku parenchyma.

özel s. hususi.

özeleştiri self-criticism.

özellik peculiarity, characteristic.

özellikle specially, especially, particularly.

özen care, carefulness, pains, trouble, attention; ~ göstermek to take great care (in), to take pains to.

özenç wishing, longing.

özendirmek caus. of özenmek.

özengen amateur.

özenli 1. with particular care, painstaking; 2. careful.

özenmek 1. to take pains about, to desire ardently; 2. to feel like; 3. to imitate, to ape; özene bezene carefully, willingly, painstakingly; özene özene with utmost care; özenip bezenmek to take great pains.

özensiz 1. superficial, casual; 2. careless, negligent.

özenti pretended, alleged, ostensible, pseudo-, swindle, fraut, cheat, false, counterfeit(ed), spurious, not genuine, fake(d), imitation.

özentili very careful, painstaking.

özentisiz 1. careless; 2. casual.

özerk pol. autonomous.

özerklik pol. autonomy.

özet, -ti 1. summary, résumé, synopsis; 2. subject; 3. extract.

özetlemek to sum up, to summarize, to recapitulate.

özge 1. other (than), apart from; 2. different, distinctive, unusual.

özgeci altruist.

özgecil altruistic, unselfish.

özgecilik altruism.

özgeçmiş biography.

özgü special, peculiar to, unique to.

özgül specific, special; ~ ağırlık specific gravity.

özgün 1. specific, peculiar; 2. original; creative; 3. authentic, genuine.

özgünlük originality.

özgür free, independant.

özgürce freely, independantly.

özgürleşmek to become free.

özgürleştirmek to free.

özgürlük freedom, liberty.

özgürlükçü partisan of freedom, which aims to promote freedom.

özgüven self-confidence.

özışın ❡ medullary rays.

özindükleme phys. self-induction.

özlem 1. longing, yearning; 2. inclination, aspiration, ardent desire.

özlemek to long for, to yearn for, to miss, to wish for.

özleşmek 1. to become purified; 2. to get ripen.

özletmek to make s.o. long for.

özleyiş longing, yearning.

özlü 1. marrowy, pithy; 2. pulpy, substential; 3. having kernel.

özlük 1. nature, character; 2. person, individual, employee; ~ işleri matters pertaining to personnel.

özne gr. & phls. subject.

öznel gr. & phls. subjective.

öznelci phls. subjectivist.

öznelcilik phls. subjectivism.

öznellik subjectivity.

özsaygı self-respect.

özsel essential.

özseverlik narcissism.

özsu 1. ❡ sap; 2. biol. juice.

özümleme biol. assimilation.

özümlemedokusu, -nu ❡ plant issue in which photosynthesis takes place.

özümlemek ❡ to assimilate.

özümlenmek ❡ to be assimilated.

özümseme s. özümleme.

özümsemek s. özümlemek.

özümsenmek s. özümlenmek.

özünerosluk autoeroticism.

özünlü intrinsic.

özür, -zrü 1. excuse, apology; 2. defect, shortcoming, infirmity; ~ dilemek 1. to apologize (to s.o.; for s.th.), to ask pardon; 2. to refuse, to decline; özrü kabahatinden büyük his excuse is worse than his fault.

özürlü 1. defective, flawed; 2. handicapped; 3. having an excuse.

özürsüz 1. flawless, perfect, nondefective; 2. lacking an excuse.

özveren self-sacrificing, self-denying.

özveri self-sacrifice, self-denial.

özverili self-sacrificing, self-denying.

özyaşamöyküsü, -nü autobiography.

# P

**pabuç,** -cu 1. shoe; 2. ⚓ base, pedestal; ~ bırakmamak *(bşe) fig.* not to be discouraged by *s.th.;* -tan aşağı despicable, low-down; -u dama atılmak *fig.* to lose favo(u)r, to fall into discredit; -unu eline vermek *(b-nin)* to give *s.o.* the boot *(or* the push).

**pabuççu** shoemaker, cobbler.

**paça** 1. lowest part of a trouser leg; 2. trotter; -sı düşük untidy, down-at-heels; -sından tutup atmak to give *s.o.* the chuck; -yı kurtarmak to elude, to evade.

**paçavra** [. x .] 1. rag; 2. *fig.* worn-out, worthless thing; ~ hastalığı *F* influenza, flu; -ya çevirmek *(or* döndürmek) to botch, to make a mess of.

**paçavracı** [. x .] ragman, ragpicker.

**paçoz** *sl.* prostitute.

**padavra** [. x .] shingle; -sı çıkmış *fig.* so thin that you can count his ribs.

**padişah** [- . -] padishah, sultan, ruler, sovereign.

**padişahlık** [- . . .] sovereignty, sultanate.

**pafta** [x .] 1. section of a map; 2. ⊕ diestock; 3. metal decoration *(on a horse's harness).*

**pagan** pagan.

**paha** [. -] price, value; ~ bicilmez priceless, invaluable; ~ biçmek to set a value (-*e* on), to price, to evaluate; -sına at the cost of; -ya çıkmak to rise in price, to become expensive.

**pahacı** who sells at a high price.

**pahalanmak** *s.* pahalılaşmak.

**pahalı** expensive, dear, costly; -ya oturmak to cost an arm and a leg.

**pahalılanmak** *s.* pahalılaşmak.

**pahalılaşmak** to become expensive, to increase in price.

**pahalılık** 1. expensiveness, costliness; 2. dearth.

**pak,** -ki [ā] 1. clean, pure; 2. *fig.* purehearted.

**paket,** -ti 1. pack(et); 2. package, parcel; 3. *sl.* ass. buttocks; ~ etm. to package; to wrap up; ~ postanesi parcel post office.

**paketlemek** to package, to wrap up.

**Pakistan** [- . -] *pr. n.* Pakistan.

**Pakistanlı** [- . - .] *pr. n.* Pakistani.

**paklamak** [- . .] 1. to clean, to purify; 2. *F* to deserve; 3. *F* to kill, to bump off.

**paklık** cleanness.

**pakt,** -tı pact, treaty.

**pala** 1. scimitar; 2. blade; ~ çalmak *(or* sallamak) to strive, to try hard.

**palabıyık** having a handlebar moustache.

**palamar** ⚓ hawser; ~ parası dockage, buoyage; -ı çözmek *(or* koparmak) *sl.* to show a clean pair of heels, to take to one's heels.

**palamut,** -tu 1. *zo.* bonito; 2. ♀ valonia oak.

**palan** a kind of saddle.

**palanga** [. x .] ⚓ pulley, tackle.

**palas** 1. sumptuous hotel; 2. palace.

**palaska** [. x .] ✕ bandolier, cartridge belt.

**palas pandıras** pell-mell, helter-skelter.

**palavra** [. x .] bunk, palaver, bullshit, baloney, humbug; ~ atmak *(or* savurmak *or* sıkmak) to talk bunk *(or* rot), to be full of bull.

**palavracı** braggart, bull-shooter.

**palaz** duckling, gosling, squab.

**palazla(n)mak** 1. to grow strong *(or* plump); 2. to grow up *(child);* 3. *sl.* to become lousy.

**paldır küldür** pell-mell, headlong.

**paleontoloji** paleontology.

**palet,** -ti 1. track, caterpillar tread; 2. flipper; 3. *(artist's)* palette.

**palikarya** [. . x .] Greek rowdy.

**palmiye** ♀ palm (tree).

**palto** [x .] (over)coat.

**palyaço** [. x .] clown, buffoon.

**palyoş** poniard, stiletto.

**pami** [x .] *sl.* let's get going!

**pamuk** ♀ cotton; ~ ağacı cotton tree; ~ atmak to fluff cotton *(with a bow and mallet);* ~ barutu guncotton; ~ gibi soft as cotton; ~ ipliği cotton thread; ♀ Prenses Snow White; ~ tarlası cotton field.

**pamukbalığı,** -nı *zo.* blue shark.

**pamuklu** 1. cotton...; 2. cotton (cloth).

**panayır** fair; ~ yeri fairground.

**pancar** ♦ beet; ~ kesilmek (or ~ gibi olm.) to turn as red as a beetroot, to go beet red; ~ şekeri beet sugar.

**pancur** s. panjur.

**panda** zo. panda.

**pandantif** pendant.

**pandispanya** [.. x .] sponge cake.

**pandomima** [.. x .] pantomime.

**pandûl** pendulum.

**panel** panel discussion.

**pangodoz** sl. drunkard (old man).

**panik** panic; ~ yaratmak to arouse (or create) panic; paniğe kapılmak to panic, to be seized with panic; paniğe kapılmış panic-stricken.

**panjur** shutter.

**pankart**, -tı placard, banner.

**pankreas¹** pancreas.

**pankreas²** a kind of wrestling.

**pano** 1. wall panel; 2. bulletin (or notice) board; panel.

**panorama** panorama.

**pansiyon** boarding house, pension, digs, lodgings.

**pansiyoner** boarder, lodger.

**pansuman** ♥ dressing; ~ yapmak to dress (a wound).

**panter** zo. panther, leopard.

**pantolon** trousers, pants.

**pantufla** [. x .] pantofle, felt slippers.

**panzehir** antidote.

**papa** the Pope.

**papağan** zo. parrot.

**papalık** the Papacy.

**papara** 1. dish made from pieces of dry bread and broth; 2. F scolding; ~ yemek F to get it in the neck, to cop it, to catch it.

**papatya** [. x .] ♥ daisy; camomile.

**papaz** 1. priest, minister; 2. cards: king; -a kızıp perhiz bozmak to cut off one's nose to spite one's face.

**papazlık** priesthood.

**papel** sl. one Turkish lira.

**papirüs** papyrus.

**papura** heavy plough (drawn by two yoke of oxen).

**papyebuvar** blotting paper.

**papyekuşe** glossy paper.

**papyon** bow tie.

**para** money; ~ babası moneybags; ~ bağlamak to lock up (-e in); ~ basmak to mint, to print (money); ~ bozmak to change money; ~ canlısı money-lover; ~ canlısı olm. to have an itching palm; ~ cezası fine; ~ cüzdanı wallet, billfold; ~ çantası money-bag, purse; ~ çekmek 1. to draw money (from a bank); 2. fig.

to squeeze money out of s.o.; ~ dökmek to pour money (-e into); ~ etm. to be worta s.th., to be valuable; ~ içinde yüzmek to be wallowing in money; ~ ile değil jig. it is dirt cheap; ~ kesmek 1. = ~ basmak; 2. fig. to rake it in; ~ -yı çeker pro. money breeds (or begets) money; ~ pul money and assets; ~ sızdırmak (b-den) to squeeze money out of s.o.; ~ tutmak 1. to save money; 2. to cost; ~ yardımı monetary aid, subsidy, donation; ~ yatırmak 1. to invest (-e in); 2. to deposit money (-e in); ~ yedirmek to bribe, to grease s.o.'s palm; ~ yemek 1. to play ducks and drakes with money; 2. to accept a bribe; ~ -dan çıkmak to have to spend money; ~ -nın üstü change; -yı veren düdüğü çalar pro. pay the piper and call the tune.

**parabellum** Parabellum.

**parabol**, -lü Å parabola.

**parafe** initialed; ~ etm. to initial (a document).

**parafin** paraffin (wax).

**paragöz** money-grubber.

**paragraf** paragraph.

**paraka** [. x .] groundline, setline.

**paralamak** 1. to tear to pieces; 2. to wear to pieces.

**paralanmak** 1. pass. of paralamak; 2. to wear (or lay) o.s. out; 3. to strain every nerve; 4. F to become lousy.

**paralel** 1. parallel; 2. sports: parallel bars.

**paralelkenar** parallelogram.

**paralı** 1. rich, well-heeled, moneyed; 2. requiring payment; ~ asker mercenary; ~ yol turnpike, toll road.

**parametre** Å parameter.

**paramparça** [. x ..] in tatters, ragged; smashed to bits; ~ etm. to smash to bits, to tatter, to tear to rags.

**parantez** parenthesis; ~ açmak fig. to digress.

**parapet**, -ti 1. ♣ bulwarks; 2. parapet.

**parasal** monetary.

**parasız** 1. penniless, poor, moneyless; 2. gratis, free (of charge); ~ yatılı öğrenci boarding student, boarder.

**parasızlık** pennilessness, poverty.

**paraşüt**, -tü parachute.

**paraşütçü** parachutist, parachuter, paratrooper.

**paratifo** ♥ paratyphoid.

**paratoner** lightning rod (or conductor).

**paravan(a)** (folding) screen.

**parazit**, -ti 1. biol. parasite (a. fig.); 2. ⊕ interference, static, atmospherics.

**parça 1.** piece, bit, fragment; **2.** *lit.*, ♪ passage; piece; **3.** item; **4.** *sl.* dope; **5.** *sl.* nice piece of goods, pretty woman; ~ başına ücret piece-wage; ~ mal piece goods; ~ ~ **1.** in bits and pieces, in smithereens; **2.** in rags, tattered; ~ ~ etm. to break (or tear) into pieces.

**parçacı I.** seller of piece goods; **2.** seller of spare parts.

**parçalamak** to tear (or smash or break) into pieces.

**parçalanmak 1.** *pass.* of parçalamak; **2.** *fig.* to lay (or wear) o.s. out.

**parçalı 1.** pieced, in parts; **2.** patchwork-(ed); ~ bulutlu cloudy in patches.

**pardesü, pardösü** (over)coat.

**pardon** pardon me, excuse me.

**pare** [ā] piece, fragment, bit.

**parfüm** perfume.

**parıldamak** to gleam, to glitter; to sparkle; to twinkle, to flash.

**parıl parıl** gleamingly, glitteringly.

**parıltı** gleam, glitter; sparkle; twinkle, flash.

**Paris** [ā] [x .] *pr. n.* Paris.

**parite** † parity.

**park, -kı 1.** park (a. ✕); **2.** car park, *Am.* parking lot; **3.** playpen; ~ etm. (or yapmak) to park; ~ sayacı parking meter; ~ yapılmaz no parking.

**parka** parka, windcheater.

**parke 1.** parquet(ry); **2.** cobblestone pavement; ~ döşeme parquet floor.

**parkur** (race)course.

**parlak 1.** bright, brilliant; luminous, radiant; **2.** *fig.* brilliant, great; successful; **3.** *sl.* sissy, sissified.

**parlaklık** brightness, brilliance (a. *fig.*).

**parlamak 1.** to shine, to glisten, to gleam; **2.** to flame up, to flare up (a. *fig.*).

**parlamenter 1.** member of parliament; **2.** parliamentary.

**parlamento** parliament.

**parlatmak 1.** *caus.* of parlamak, to polish, to rub up, to burnish; **2.** *sl.* to toss off, to knock back (booze).

**parmak 1.** finger; **2.** toe; **3.** spoke (of a wheel); **4.** inch; **5.** rail, bar; ~ basmak **1.** to draw attention (-e to); **2.** to put one's thumbprint (-e on); ~ emmek to suck one's finger; ~ hesabı **1.** counting on the fingers; **2.** *lit.* syllabic meter; ~ ısırmak to be taken aback, to be dumbfounded; ~ izi fingerprint; ~ kadar mere slip of (a child); ~ kadar çocuk hop-o'--my-thumb; ~ kaldırmak to raise one's hand; parmağı ağzında kalmak to be astounded, to fall off one's chair; par-

mağı olm. (b-nin bir işte) *fig.* to have a finger in s.th.; parmağında oynatmak (b-ni) *fig.* to twist s.o. round one's little finger.

**parmakçı** *fig.* agitator, inciter.

**parmaklamak 1.** to eat with one's fingers; **2.** to finger, to goose.

**parmaklık** railing, balustrade; grating, grate, grill.

**parodi** parody.

**parola** [. x .] password, watchword.

**pars** *zo.* leopard.

**parsa** [x .] money, collection; -yı başkası toplamak to reap the benefits of your work.

**parsal** *s.* partal.

**parsel** plot, lot, parcel.

**parsellemek** to divide into parcels, to subdivide.

**parşömen** parchment, vellum.

**partal** shabby, worn-out.

**parter** *thea.* parterre.

**parti 1.** party (a. *pol.*); **2.** † consignment (of goods); **3.** ♪ part; **4.** game, match; ~ vermek to give a party.

**partici** *pol.* party member.

**partisip, -pi** *gr.* participle.

**partisyon** ♪ full score.

**partizan** partisan.

**partizanlık** partisanship.

**parya** outcast, pariah.

**pas¹1.** rust, corrosion, tarnish; **2.** fur (on the tongue); ~ tutmak to rust, to corrode, to tarnish; ~ tutmaz rustproof.

**pas²** *sports, cards:* pass; ~ geçmek to disregard; ~ vermek *sl.* to give the glad eye (woman).

**pasaj 1.** arcade with shops; **2.** passage.

**pasak** dirt, filth.

**pasaklı** dirty, filthy; slovenly.

**pasaparola** [. . . x .] ✕ password.

**pasaport, -tu** passport; ~ çıkartmak to have a passport taken out; -unu eline vermek *fig.* to give s.o. the boot (or the bullet or the chop).

**pasavan** laissez-passer.

**pasif 1.** passive; **2.** † liabilities.

**paskal** funny, clownish.

**paskalya** [. x .] Easter.

**paslanmak 1.** to rust, to corrode, to tarnish; **2.** to fur (tongue); **3.** *fig.* to become rusty.

**paslanmaz** rustproof, tarnishproof, noncorrodible; ~ çelik stainless steel.

**paslaşmak 1.** *football:* to pass the ball to each other; **2.** *sl.* to give each other the glad eye.

**paslı** rusty.

**paso** [x .] pass.

**paspas** doormat.

**paspaslamak** to mop.

**pasta** [x .] 1. cake, pastry, tart; 2. fold, pleat.

**pastacı** maker *or* seller of pastry.

**pastane** [. - .] pastry shop, bakery.

**pastel** pastel.

**pastırma** pastrami-like beef; ~ yazı Indian Summer.

**pastil** pastille, troche, lozenge.

**pastoral** 1. pastoral; 2. ♪ pastorale.

**pastörize** pasteurized; ~ etm. to pasteurize.

**paşa** 1. pasha; 2. sedate, well-behaved *(child)*; ~ ~ sedately.

**pat¹**, -tı flat, snub *(nose)*.

**pat²** bam!, whop!, thud!; ~ diye with a thud; ~ ~ pit-a-pat.

**pat³**, -tı ⚘ aster.

**patagos** *sl.* five-kurush coin.

**patak** *F* beating, hiding.

**pataklamak** to beat, to thrash, to give a beating *(or* hiding).

**patates** [. x .] ⚘ potato.

**patavatsız** indiscreet, tactless.

**paten** 1. ice skate; 2. *(a.* tekerlekli ~) roller skate.

**patent**, -ti 1. patent; 2. ⚓ bill of health.

**patentli** patented.

**patırdamak** to patter, to clatter.

**patır patır** with a pattering sound.

**patırtı** 1. clatter, patter; noise; 2. tumult, row, disturbance; ~ çıkarmak to make a row, to raise a ruckus; -ya pabuç bırakmamak not to be scared off by empty threats; -ya vermek to put into confusion.

**patik** bootee.

**patika** [. x .] path, track, trail.

**patinaj** 1. ice skating; 2. *mot.* skidding, slipping; ~ yapmak 1. to skate; 2. *mot.* to skid, to slip, to spin; ~ zinciri anti--skid *(or* tyre) chain.

**patis** a fine kind of batiste.

**patiska** ! . x .] cambric, cotton batiste.

**patlak** 1. burst; cracked; 2. *mot.* puncture; ~ gözlü popeyed, bug-eyed; ~ vermek 1. to break out *(war. etc.)*; 2. to be discovered *(or* divulged) *(secret)*.

**patlama** *vn. of* patlamak, *part.* explosion.

**patlamak** 1. to explode, to burst, to blow up; 2. to break out *(war, etc.)*; 3. to burst *(or* split) open; 4. *fig.* to explode, to burst out *(with anger, etc.)*; 5. *F* to cost.

**patlamalı:** ~ motor ⊕ internal-combustion engine.

**patlangaç** popgun; peashooter.

**patlatmak** *caus. of* patlamak, *part.* 1. to blow up, to blast, to explode; 2. to infuriate; 3. to fire *(weapon)*; 4. to crack *(joke)*; 5. to land, to slap, to' plant *(blow)*.

**patlayıcı** explosive.

**patlıcan** ⚘ aubergine, *Am.* eggplant.

**patoloji** pathology.

**patrik** patriarch.

**patron** 1. boss, employer; 2. *(tailor's)* pattern.

**patrona** [. x .] *hist.* vice-admiral.

**pattadak, pattadan** suddenly, all of a sudden.

**pavurya** [. x .] *zo.* hermit crab.

**pavyon** 1. night club; 2. pavilion.

**pay** 1. share, portion, lot; 2. ₳ numerator; 3. *tailoring:* margin; 4. equal part; ~ biçmek 1. to take as an example; to compare; 2. to deduce, to judge (-*den* from); ~ etm. to share, to divide; ~ vermek to answer back, to sass; -ını almak 1. to get one's share; 2. to be scolded, to get told off.

**payanda** [. x .] prop, shore, support; ~ vurmak to prop up, to shore; -ları çözmek to run away, to beat it.

**payda** ₳ denominator.

**paydaş** shareholder.

**paydos** [x .] 1. break, rest; 2. it's break time!; ~ etm. to knock off, to quit work, to stop working.

**paye** rank, position; ~ vermek to show deference (-*e* to), to esteem.

**payidar** permanent, constant; ~ olm. to be permanent, to last.

**payitaht**, -tı † capital (city).

**paylamak** to scold, to tell off, to rebuke, to reprimand.

**paylaşmak** to share, to go shares.

**paytak** 1. knock-kneed; bowlegged, bandy--legged; 2. *chess:* pawn; ~ ~ yürümek to waddle.

**payton** phaeton.

**pazar** 1. market (place); bazaar; 2. Sunday; 3. trade; ~ bozmak to close an open-air market; ~ günü on Sunday; ~ kayığı gibi heavily loaded, top-heavy *(vehicle)*; ~ kurmak to set up an open market; ~ ola! good luck! *(said to sellers)*; ~ tatili Sunday rest; ~ yeri market place; -a çıkarmak to put up for sale, to put on sale.

**pazarbaşı**, -nı warden of a market.

**pazarcı** seller in a market.

**pazarlama** marketing.

**pazarlamacı** marketing expert, commercial traveller.

pazarlamak to market.
pazarlaşmak to bargain, to haggle.
pazarlık bargain, haggle; ~ etm. to bargain, to haggle.
pazartesi, -yi [. x . .] Monday.
pazen [â] flannel.
pazı¹ ⚘ chard.
pazı² anat. biceps; ~ kemiği anat. humerus.
pazıbent, -di armband, armlet.
pazval (shoemaker's) knee-strap.
pazvant, -tı night watchman.
peçe veil.
peçelemek fig. to camouflage.
peçeli veiled.
peçete napkin, serviette.
pedagog pedagogist.
pedagoji pedagogics.
pedal pedal, treadle.
peder father.
pederane fatherly.
pederşahi patriarchal.
pedikür pedicure.
pehlivan wrestler.
pehpeh! bravo!, well done!
pehriz ş. perhiz.
pejmürde shabby, worn-out, ragged.
pek, -ki 1. very, extremely; 2. a great deal, very much; 3. firm, hard; 4. sound, strong; 5. very fast; ~ çok 1. quite a few, a lot of, a great many; 2. very much, a great deal; ~ gözlü courageous, bold; ~ at the very most; ~ yürekli hardhearted; ~ yüzlü shameless, brazen.
pekâlâ [x - -] 1. all right, okay, very well; 2. very good, quite adequate; 3. most certainly.
peki [x .] 1. all right, okay; 2. if that's so, then...
pekin certain.
pekişmek 1. to harden; 2. to strengthen.
pekiştirmek 1. to strengthen, to consolidate, to reinforce, to intensify; 2. to harden, to stiffen.
peklik constipation; ~ çekmek to be constipated.
pekmez 1. grape molasses; 2. sl. blood.
peksimet, -ti hardtack, ship biscuit.
pelerin cape, cloak.
pelesenk, -gi balm, balsam.
pelesenkağacı, -nı ⚘ balm of Gilead.
pelikan zo. pelican.
pelin ⚘ wormwood.
pelit, -ti ⚘ valonia; camata.
pelte jelly, gelatine.
peltek lisping.
pelteklesmek to lisp.

pelteklik lisp.
peltelenmek, pelteleşmek to gel.
pelür onionskin.
pelüş plush.
pembe pink; ~ görmek fig. to see through rose-colo(u)red (or rosy) spectacles.
pembeleşmek to turn pink.
pembemsi pinkish.
penaltı, -yı sports: penalty.
pencere [x . .] window.
pencüdü a five and a two.
pencüse a five and a three.
pencüyek a five and a one.
pençe 1. paw, claw; 2. grip, clutches; 3. sole (of a shoe); ~ vurmak to sole (a shoe).
pençelemek 1. to paw, to claw, to maul; 2. to sole (a shoe).
pençeleşmek 1. to paw (or claw) at each other; 2. fig. to grapple (ile with), to wrestle (ile with), to battle (ile with), to struggle (ile against).
pençeli 1. having a paw (or claw); 2. resoled (shoe); 3. fig. aggressive; 4. fig. powerful.
pendifrank, -kı sl. clout, sock, punch.
penguen zo. penguin.
penisilin penicillin.
peniz etm. sl. to disclose (a secret).
pens¹ 1. pliers; 2. pincers; tweezers; nippers; 3. forceps; 4. pleat.
pens² pence.
pense [x .] pliers.
pentatlon sports: pentathlon.
pepe stammerer, stutterer.
pepelemek to stutter, to stammer.
pepelik stutter.
perakende [â] retail.
perakendeci [â] retailer.
perçem 1. bangs; 2. forelock (of a horse); 3. scalp lock.
perçin rivet, clinch bolt.
perçinlemek 1. to rivet, to clinch; 2. fig. to consolidate.
perçinli riveted, clinched.
perdah 1. polish, sheen, finish, glaze; 2. finishing shave; ~ vurmak to glaze, to polish, to finish, to burnish.
perdahlamak 1. to finish, to polish, to burnish; to glaze; 2. to buff; 2. to shave a second time (beard); 3. sl. to swear at; 4. sl. to fast-talk.
perdahlı burnished, polished, glazed.
perdahsız unburnished, unpolished, unglazed.
perde 1. curtain, drape; 2. thea. act; 3. (movie) screen; 4. ♪ fret; 5. pitch; 6. zo. web; 7. ⚕ cataract (on the eye);

~ arası intermission, interval; ~ arkası
*fig.* the hidden side *(of a matter)*; ~ arkasından *fig.* behind the scenes, backstage; ~ ayaklı *zo.* web-footed.

**perdelemek 1.** to curtain; **2.** *fig.* to conceal, to veil.

**perdeli 1.** curtained; **2.** *thea.* having... acts; **3.** ♪ fretted; **4.** *zo.* webbed.

**perende** [. x .] somersault, flip; ~ atmak to somersault, to turn a somersault; ~ atamamak *(b-nin yanında)* *fig.* can't hold a candle to *s.o.*

**perese 1.** plumbline; **2.** *fig.* state, condition, -sine getirmek to choose the right moment to do s.th.; -ye almak to take into consideration.

**perestiş** worship, adoration; ~ etm. to worship, to adore.

**performans** *sports:* performance.

**pergel** pair of compasses; -leri açmak F to shake a leg, to take long steps.

**pergellemek 1.** to measure with a pair of compasses; **2.** to pace off *(a distance)*; **3.** *fig.* to consider all the angles of *(a matter)*. z

**perhiz 1.** diet; **2.** Christian *or* Jewish fast; ~ etm. **1.** to diet; **2.** to fast; -i bozmak to violate one's diet.

**perhizli 1.** on a diet; **2.** fasting.

**peri** fairy; sprite, pixie; nymph; ~ gibi fairylike; ~ masalı fairy story *(or* tale).

**peribacası,** -nı **1.** fairy chimney; **2.** *geol.* earth pillar, demoiselle.

**perili** haunted; ~ köşk haunted house.

**periskop,** -pu periscope.

**perişan** [. - -] **1.** perturbed, upset, miserable, wretched, distraught; **2.** scattered; untidy, disordered; ~ etm. **1.** to upset, to perturb, to ruin; **2.** to scatter, to rout; ~ olm. **1.** to become miserable *(or* wretched); **2.** to be scattered *(or* routed).

**periton** *anat.* peritoneum; ~ kovuğu *anat.* peritoneal cavity.

**peritonit,** -ti ☞ peritonitis.

**perma, permanant,** -tı perm, permanent (wave).

**permanganat,** -tı ♔ permanganate.

**permeçe** ⚓ small hawser.

**permi 1.** ⸙ permit; **2.** 🚆 pass.

**peroksit** ♔ peroxide.

**peron** 🚆 platform.

**persenk,** -gi refrain.

**personel** personnel, staff.

**perspektif** perspective.

**perşembe** Thursday; -nin gelişi çarşambadan bellidir *pro.* coming events cast their shadows before.

**pertavsız** magnifying glass.

**Peru** *pr. n.* Peru.

**peruka** wig.

**perva** [ā] **1.** fear; **2.** attention, heed.

**pervane** [ā] **1.** propeller; **2.** screw; **3.** fanner; **4.** *zo.* moth; ~ olm. *(b-ne)* to be *s.o.'s* shadow.

**pervasız** [ā] fearless, unafraid, undauntable; unconcerned.

**pervaz** [ā] **1.** cornice, fringe, architrave; **2.** border, edging.

**peryodik 1.** periodic; **2.** periodical.

**pes[1] 1.** this is the last straw!; **2.** uncle!; ~ demek to submit, to give in, to say «uncle»; ~ etm. to yield, to submit, to give in.

**pes[2]** low, soft *(voice)*; ~ perdeden konuşmak *fig.* to speak softly.

**pesek** tartar *(on teeth)*.

**pesimist,** -ti pessimist.

**pespaye** [ā] vulgar, despicable.

**pespembe** rose-pink.

**pestenkerani** [ā] [... x .] nonsensical, idiotic.

**pestil** pressed and dried fruit pulp; ~ gibi olm. *fig.* to be too tired to move, to be bushed; -i çıkmak *fig.* to be worn to a frazzle, to be dog-tired; -ini çıkarmak *(b-nin)* *fig.* **1.** to beat *s.o.* to a pulp; **2.** to wear *s.o.* a frazzle; **3.** *(bşin)* to crush *s.th.* to a pulp.

**pesüs** oil lamp.

**peş** the back, the rear; ~ -e one after another; -i sıra right behind; -inde koşmak to run after; -inden gitmek *(b-nin)* *fig.* to follow in the footsteps of *s.o.;* -ine düşmek **1.** to follow s.o. around; **2.** to run after, to be after s.th.; -ine takılmak *(b-nin)* to tail after *s.o.,* to follow *s.o.* around; -ini bırakmak to stop following.

**peşin 1.** paid in advance, ready *(money)*; **2.** in advance, beforehand; earlier, in the first place; ~ almak to buy for cash; ~ cevap answer that anticipates a question; ~ hüküm *(or* yargı) prejudgement; ~ para cash, ready money, advance payment; ~ söylemek to tell in advance, to prognosticate.

**peşinat** [. - -] **1.** cash; downpayment; **2.** advance payment.

**peşinen** [î] *s.* peşin 2.

**peşkeş:** ~ çekmek *(b-ne bşi)* to make *s.o.* a present of *s.th.* that does not belong to one.

**peşkir 1.** (table) napkin, serviette; **2.** (hand) towel.

**peşrev 1.** ♪ overture, prelude; **2.** the entry

of wrestlers on to the wrestling field.

**peştamal** loincloth, waist cloth.

**peştamallık** † goodwill.

**petek** honeycomb; ~ balı honey in the comb.

**petekgöz** compound eye *(of insects)*.

**petrokimya** petrochemistry.

**petrol, -lü** petroleum, crude oil; ~ hattı oil pipeline; ~ kuyusu oil well; ~ şirketi oil *(or* petroleum) company.

**petrolcü** oilman.

**petunya** [ . x .] ♀ petunia.

**pey** deposit, earnest money; ~ sürmek *(or* vurmak) to make a bid.

**peyda** [ā] visible, manifest; ~ etm. 1. to beget, to give birth to; 2. to produce; ~ olm. to appear, to crop up, to spring up.

**peydahla(n)mak** 1. to give birth to, to sire; 2. to produce; 3. to acquire, to pick up.

**peyderpey** 1. bit by bit, step by step, little by little; 2. in succession.

**peygamber** prophet.

**peygamberlik** prophethood, prophecy.

**peyk, -ki** 1. *ast., pol.* satellite; 2. *fig.* adherent, follower.

**peyke** wooden bench.

**peyklik** being a satellite.

**peylemek** to reserve, to book, to engage.

**peynir** cheese.

**peynirhane** cheesery.

**peynirli** containing cheese; ~ sandviç cheese sandwich.

**peyzaj** landscape (picture).

**pezevenk, -gi** 1. procurer, pimp; 2. scoundrel, bastard, son of a bitch.

**pezevenklik** procuring, pimping; ~ etm. to procure, to pimp.

**pezo** 1. peso; 2. *sl.* procurer, pimp.

**pıhtı** clot, coagulate, coagulum.

**pıhtılanmak, pıhtılaşmak** to clot, to coagulate.

**pıhtılaştırmak** to clot, to coagulate.

**pılı pırtı** 1. junk, trash, traps; 2. belongings, bag and baggage.

**pınar** spring.

**pır** whir; ~ diye uctu it whirred away.

**pırasa** [ . x .] ♀ leek; ~ bıyıklı having a handlebar moustache.

**pırıldak** signal *(or* dark) lantern; heliograph.

**pırıldamak** to gleam, to glitter, to shine.

**pırıl pırıl** 1. gleaming, glittering; 2. spick-and-span.

**pırıltı** gleam, glitter, sparkle.

**pırlak** lure, decoy.

**pırlamak** 1. to whir away, to flutter; 2. *fiа.* to take to one's heels.

**pırlangıç, -cı** humming-top.

**pırlanta** [ . x .] brilliant; ~ gibi *F* top-notch, first-rate.

**pırnal** ♀ holly *(or* holm) oak.

**pırpır** tri-car, put-put.

**pırpırı** womanizer, skirt-chaser.

**pırpıt, -tı** 1. useless, worn-out; 2. a kind of coarse cloth.

**pırtı** 1. junk, traps; 2. bag and baggage, belongings.

**pırtık** torn, ragged.

**pısırık** fainthearted, pusillanimous, diffident.

**pıt, -tı** drip!; ~ yok you can hear a pin drop.

**pıtırdamak** to patter.

**pıtır pıtır** with a patter.

**pıtırtı** patter.

**pıt pıt** with a patter, pit-a-pat; ~ atmak to go pit-a-pat *(one's heart)*.

**pıtrak** ♀ burdock.

**piç** 1. bastard; 2. *fig.* brat, bratty child; ~ etm. to ball up, to make a balls-up of s.th.; ~ kurusu bratty child, brat; ~ olm. to be balled up *(or* spoiled).

**piçlik** bastardy.

**pide** [ x .] pizza-like bread; ~ gibi very flat.

**pijama** [ . x .] pyjamas, *Am.* pajamas.

**pik (demir)** ⊕ pig *(or* cast) iron.

**pikap¹** ♩ record player, gramophone, phonograph.

**pikap²** pickup (truck).

**pike¹** piqué.

**pike²** ⊥ nosedive; ~ yapmak 1. ⊥ to nosedive; 2. *billiards:* to make a massé shot.

**piknik** picnic; ~ yapmak to picnic, to have a picnic.

**piko** picot.

**pil** ≸ battery.

**pilaki** [ . x .] 1. *stew of beans or fish with oil and onions;* 2. *sl.* idiot.

**pilav** rice.

**piliç, -ci** 1. chick, pullet, fryer, broiler; 2. *sl.* chick, a bit of skirt, babe.

**pilot, -tu** pilot.

**pim** ⊕ pin, gudgeon.

**pineklemek** to doze, to slumber.

**pingpong** ping-pong, table tennis.

**pinti** stingy, niggardly, miserly, close-fisted.

**pintileşmek** to get stingy.

**pintilik** stinginess, tightness.

**pipet, -ti** ⚗ pipette.

**pipo** [ x .] pipe; ~ içmek to smoke a pipe; ~ tütünü pipe tobacco.

**pir** [ī] 1. master, patron saint; 2. thoroughly, completely.

**piramit**, -di pyramid.

**pire** zo. flea; ~ gibi very agile; ~ için yorgan yakmak to cut off one's nose to spite one's face; -yi deve yapmak to make a mountain out of a molehill; -yi nallamak fig. to attempt the impossible.

**pirelenmek 1.** to become flea-ridden; **2.** fig. to smell a rat.

**pirina** [.x.] oil cake.

**pirinç¹**, -ci brass.

**pirinç²**, -ci ♀ rice.

**pirit**, -ti geol. pyrite.

**pirüpak**, -ki [-.-] spotless, immaculate.

**pirzola** cutlet, chop.

**pis 1.** dirty, filthy, foul; **2.** nasty, vile, foul; **3.** obscene, foul, profane; ~ kokmak to stink; ~ koku stink; ~ ~ bakmak to leer (-e at); ~ ~ gülmek to grin, to chuckle; -i -ine for nothing, in vain.

**pisbıyık** sl. scraggly moustache.

**pisboğaz** greedy.

**pisi** pussycat, kitty; ~ ~ here kitty, kitty, kitty!

**pisibalığı**, -nı zo. plaice.

**pisin** swimming pool.

**pisipisi 1.** pussycat, kitty; **2.** here kitty, kitty, kitty!

**piskopos** bishop.

**pislemek 1.** to foul; **2.** to dirty, to soil.

**pislenmek** to get dirty.

**pisletmek 1.** to foul up, to make a balls-up of; **2.** to soil, to dirty.

**pislik 1.** dirt, filth; **2.** dirtiness, filthiness.

**pissu** sewage.

**pist¹**, -ti scat!

**pist²**, -ti **1.** running track; **2.** ✝ runway; **3.** dance floor.

**piston 1.** ⊕ piston; **2.** fig. friend at court; ~ kolu mot. connecting rod, piston-rod.

**pistonlu 1.** ⊕ having a piston; **2.** fig. having a friend at court.

**pisuar** urinal.

**pişik** heat rash, prickly heat.

**pişirmek 1.** to cook, to bake; **2.** to ripen, to mature; **3.** to fire (pottery); **4.** to heat-treat (metal); **5.** to learn well.

**pişkin 1.** well-cooked, well-done; **2.** fig. experienced, worldlywise; **3.** fig. brazen; **4.** used (-e to), accustomed (-e to).

**pişkinlik 1.** indifference to criticism; **2.** experience; maturity; pişkinliğe vurmak to brazen out.

**pişman** [â] regretful, remorseful, penitent; ~ olm. to regret, to repent.

**pişmaniye** candy made of sugar and oil with soapwort whipped into fibers.

**pişmanlık** [â] regret, repentance, remorse, penitence; ~ duymak to feel regret (or remorse).

**pişmek**, (-er) **1.** to be cooked; **2.** to mature, to ripen; **3.** to be fired (pottery); **4.** to become worldlywise; pişmiş aşa soğuk su katmak fig. to throw (or pour) cold water on; pişmiş kelle gibi sırıtmak to grin like a Cheshire cat, to simper.

**pişti** a card game.

**piştov** pistol.

**piton** zo. python.

**pitoresk**, -ki picturesque.

**piyade** [â] **1.** ✗ infantry; **2.** infantryman, foot soldier; **3.** chess: pawn.

**piyanço** [.x.] sl. louse.

**piyango** [.x.] lottery, raffle; ~ bileti lottery (or raffle) ticket; ~ çekmek to draw a lottery ticket.

**piyanist**, -ti pianist.

**piyano** [.x.] piano; ~ çalmak to play the piano; ~ resitali piano recital.

**piyasa** [.x.] **1.** market; **2.** the market, trading; **3.** the market price; **4.** promenading; ~ etm. to stroll about, to promenade; -ya çıkarmak to put on the market; -ya çıkmak **1.** to come on the market; **2.** to go out for a stroll; -ya düşmek **1.** to be on the market in abundance; **2.** fig. to go on the streets.

**piyata** [.x.] dinner plate.

**piyaz 1.** bean salad; **2.** chopped onions; **3.** sl. flattery.

**piyes** thea. play.

**piyiz** sl. raki.

**piyon** chess: pawn.

**piyoniye** fig. pioneer.

**pizza** pizza.

**plaçka** [x.] loot, plunder, booty.

**plaj** beach, plage.

**plak** record.

**plaka** [x.] **1.** mot. license plate, number plate; **2.** ⊕ plaque, tablet.

**plaket**, -ti plaquette.

**plan** plan, scheme, project; ~ kurmak to plan, to scheme.

**plançete** [.x.] surv. plane table.

**plankton** plankton.

**planlamak** to plan.

**planlı 1.** planned; **2.** premeditated (crime).

**planör** glider.

**planörcü** glider pilot.

**planörcülük** gliding.

**plantasyon** plantation.

**planya** [x.] carpenter's plane.

**planyalamak** to plane.

**plasman** ✝ investment.

**plaster** plaster, band-aid.

**plastik** plastic; ~ ameliyat plastic surgery; ~ sanatlar the plastic arts; ~ tutkal plastic glue.

**platform** platform *(a. geogr.)*, rostrum.

**plotin 1.** platinum; **2.** *mot.* points.

**plato** *geogr.* plateau.

**platonik** platonic.

**plazma** plasma.

**pli 1.** pleat; **2.** pleated.

**plise 1.** pleating; **2.** pleated; ~ yapmak to pleat.

**plonjon** *football: dive made by a goalkeeper to block a shoot.*

**poca** ↓ leeward.

**podüsüet**, -ti suede.

**podyum** podium, dais, platform.

**pof** sss!; ~ diye with a hiss.

**pofurdamak** to snort.

**pofur** pofur in great puffs.

**pofyos** *sl.* **1.** hollow, empty; **2.** no-count, worthless.

**poğaça** [.x.] flaky pastry.

**pohpoh** flattery, soft soap.

**pohpohçu** flatterer.

**pohpohlamak** to flatter, to pamper.

**poker** poker; ~ cevirmek *F* to play poker.

**pokerci** poker player.

**polarma** *phys.*, 🔊 polarization.

**polarmak** *phys.*, 🔊 to polarize.

**polemik** polemic; polemiğe girmek to joust.

**poliçe 1.** 🕇 draft, bill of exchange; **2.** insurance policy.

**poligami** polygamy.

**poligon 1.** polygon; **2.** 𝗫 gunnery *(or artillery)* range.

**poliklinik** polyclinic.

**polim** *sl.* lie; ~ atmak *sl.* to tell lies.

**polis 1.** the police; **2.** policeman.

**polisiye** detective...; ~ film detective movie; ~ roman detective novel, whodunit.

**polislik** policemanship.

**politik** political.

**politika 1.** politics; **2.** policy.

**politikacı 1.** politician; **2.** *fig.* politic *(person)*.

**poliüretan** polyurethane.

**poliyester** polyester.

**polo** polo.

**Polonya** [.x.] *pr. n.* Poland.

**Polonyalı** *pr. n.* **1.** Pole; **2.** Polish.

**pomat** 🕇 pomade.

**pompa** [x.] pump.

**pompalamak** to pump.

**pompuruk** *sl.* old, decrepit *(man.)*.

**ponpon 1.** pompon, pom-pom; **2.** powder puff.

**ponza** [x.] *(taşı)* pumice.

**poplin** poplin.

**pop (müzik)** pop (music).

**popo** bottom, buttocks, fanny.

**popüler** popular.

**pornografi** pornography.

**porselen** porcelain.

**porsiyon** helping, portion *(of food)*.

**porsuk** *zo.* badger.

**porsukağacı**, -nı 🌿 yew (tree).

**portakal** orange; ~ rengi orange.

**portatif** portable, movable, collapsible; ~ karyola camp bed, *Am.* cot.

**porte 1.** scope, range; **2.** ♪ stave, staff.

**Portekiz** *pr. n.* Portugal.

**portföy** wallet, billfold.

**portmanto** hallstand, hatstand.

**portör** 🕇 carrier.

**portre** portrait.

**posa** [x.] residue, pulp, bagasse.

**posbıyık** having a bushy moustache.

**post**, -tu **1.** skin, hide, pelt; **2.** *fig.* office, position, post; ~ elden gitmek to be killed *(or* bumped off); ~ kapmak to get an office; ~ kavgası struggle over official positions; ~u kurtarmak to save one's skin; -u sermek *fig.* to outstay one's welcome; -una oturmak *fig.* to put on airs.

**posta** [x.] **1.** post, mail; **2.** the post office, postal service; **3.** 𝗫 orderly; **4.** mail train; mail truck; mail steamer; **5.** crew, team; **6.** trip, run; ~ etm. to take to the police station; ~ güvercini carrier pigeon; ~ havalesi (postal) money order; ~ koymak to dupe, to con; ~ pulu postage stamp; ~ yapmak to ply; -ya vermek to post, *Am.* to mail; -yı kesmek *fig.* to cut relationships.

**postacı** [x..] postman; postwoman.

**postal 1.** 𝗫 combat *(or* half) boot; **2.** *F* hussy, trollop.

**postalamak** to post, *Am.* to mail.

**postane** [ā] post office.

**postrestant**, -tı poste restante, general delivery.

**poşet**, -ti pochette.

**pot¹**, -tu the pot, the pool.

**pot²**, -tu **1.** pucker, wrinkle; **2.** blunder, blooper, slip of the tongue; ~ gelmek (iş) to go wrong; ~ kırmak to put one's foot in it, to drop a brick, to blunder; ~ yeri *fig.* the sticky part *(of a matter)*.

**pot³** -tu raft, punt.

**pota** [x.] 🔊 crucible.

**potansiyel** potential.

**potas** 🔊 potash.

**potasyum** 🔊 potassium.

**potin** boot.

potpuri ♪ medley, potpourri.
potur 1. puckered, wrinkled; 2. Turkish breeches.
poyra [x .] ⊕ hub *(of a wheel)*.
poyraz boreas, northeast wind.
poz 1. pose; 2. *phot.* exposure; ~ vermek to pose.
pozitif positive.
pozometre [. . x .] *phot.* exposure *(or light)* meter.
pöf phew!, ugh!
pörsük flaccid, wizened, withered.
pörsümek to wizen, to shrivel up.
pösteki sheepskin, goatskin; ~ saymak *fig.* to be engaged in a tedious task; -si-ni çıkarmak (*or* sermek) *fig.* to beat to death; -yi sermek *fig.* to outstay one's welcome.
prafa [x .] a card game.
pranga [x .] fetters, irons, shackles; -ya vurmak to shackle, to fetter.
pratik 1. practical; handy; 2. practice, application; 3. applied; ~ yapmak to practise, *Am.* to practice.
pratikleşmek to become practical.
pratisyen hekim ♀ general practitioner.
prelüd ♪ prelude.
prens prince.
prenses princess.
prensip, -bi principle.
prenslik princedom, principate.
pres ⊕ press.
presbit, -ti presbyopic.
prese ⊕ (com)pressed.
prestij prestige.
prevantoryum [. . x .] ♀ preventorium.
prezantabl presentable.
prezante etm. to introduce.
prezervatif condom, rubber.
prifiks † fixed price.
prim 1. premium; 2. bonus.
priz ⚡ socket, wall plug, power-point, jack.
prizma prism.
problem problem *(a.* A*);* ~ çocuk problem child.
prodüktör producer.
profesör professor.
profesörlük professorship.
profesyonel professional.
profesyonellik professionalism.
profil profile.
program 1. program(me); 2. schedule.
programcı 1. programmer; 2. program(me) director.
programlamak to program.
programlı programmed.
proje project.

projeksiyon projection.
projectör projector, searchlight, spotlight.
proletarya proletariat.
prolog prologue.
propaganda propaganda; ~ yapmak to propagandize.
propagandacı propagandist.
prospektüs 1. instructions; 2. prospectus.
prostat, -tı ♀ prostate.
protein protein.
Protestan *pr. n.* Protestant.
Protestanlık *pr. n.* Protestantism.
protesto [. x .] protest, outcry; ~ etm. *(bşi)* to protest against. *s.th.*
protez 1. ♀ prosthesis; 2. denture, dental prosthesis.
protokol, -lü protocol.
protoplazma protoplasm.
prototip, -pi prototype.
prova [x .] 1. rehearsal; 2. *typ.* proof; 3. fitting; 4. *s.* pruva.
prömiyer premiere.
Prusya [x .] *pr. n.* Prussia.
pruva [x .] ⚓ bow, head.
psikanaliz psychoanalysis.
psikiyatri psychiatry.
psikiyatrist, -ti psychiatrist.
psikolog psychologist.
psikoloji psychology.
psikolojik psychological.
psikopat, -tı psychopath.
psikoterapi psychotherapy.
puan 1. point; 2. dot; ~ almak to score (points).
puanlamak to grade.
puantiye dotted *(cloth)*.
puding pudding.
pudra powder.
pudralamak to powder.
pudralık compact.
pudraşeker powdered sugar.
pudriyer compact.
puf hassock, pouf, ottoman.
pufla [x .] 1. *zo.* eider; 2. (eider)down; ~ gibi fluffy, downy.
puflamak to snort.
puhu (kuşu) *zo.* eagle owl.
pul 1. stamp; 2. *games:* piece, counter; 3. ⊕ washer; nut; 4. scale *(of a fish);* 5. sequin, spangle; ~ koleksiyonu collection of stamps.
pulcu 1. seller of stamps; 2. philatelist.
pullamak 1. to stamp; 2. to decorate with spangles.
pullu stamped.
pulluk plough. *Am.* plow.
pulsuz unstamped, stampless.
puluç impotent.

**puma** zo. puma.

**punç, çu** punch.

**punt, -du 1.** ↓ position; **2.** appropriate time; ~ tayini ↓ calculating a ship's position; -una getirmek (or -unu bulmak) to find a suitable opportunity.

**punto** [x .] typ. size.

**pupa** [x .] ↓ **1.** stern; **2.** astern; ~ gitmek **1.** to sail with the wind directly astern; **2.** fig. to go straight ahead; ~ yelken gitmek to go in full sail.

**puro** [x .] cigar.

**pus¹** inch.

**pus²** **1.** mist, haze; **2.** gum; **3.** bloom (on fruit); **4.** crust (on the nipple of a ewe).

**pusarık 1.** misty, hazy; **2.** mirage.

**pusat, -tı 1.** equipment, gear; **2.** armo(u)r, arms.

**puset, -ti** stroller.

**pusla** s. pusula.

**puslanmak** to get misty (or hazy).

**puslu** misty, hazy.

**pusmak** to crouch down.

**pusu** ambush; ~ kurmak to lay an ambush; ya düşürmek to ambush; -ya yatmak to lie in ambush, to lurk.

**pusula** [x . .] **1.** ↓ compass; **2.** memorandum, note; -yı şaşırmak fig. to be at a loss what to do, to be at sea.

**puşt, -tu** son of a bitch, bastard.

**put, -tu 1.** idol, effigy; **2.** the cross; ~ gibi as still as a statue; ~ kesilmek to become as still as a statue.

**putperest, -ti** idolater, pagan.

**putperestlik** idolatry, paganism.

**putrel** iron beam.

**puvan** s. puan.

**püf** puff, breath; ~ noktası (bir işin) the most delicate part (of a matter).

**püflemek** to blow on.

**püfür püfür** gently and coolingly; ~ esmek to blow gently, to puff.

**pünez** drawing pin, thumbtack.

**pürçek** lock, curl.

**püre** purée, mash.

**pürgatif** ℥ purgative.

**pürneşe** bright and merry.

**pürtük** knob.

**pürüz 1.** unevenness, roughness; **2.** fig. difficulty, snag, hitch.

**pürüzlenmek 1.** to get uneven (or rough); **2.** fig. to get snagged up, to go awry.

**pürüzlü 1.** uneven, rough; **2.** fig. difficult, marked by snags.

**pürüzsüz 1.** even, smooth; **2.** fig. free of snags (or hitches).

**püskül** tassel.

**püsküllü** tasseled; ~ bela F a peck of trouble, damnable nuisance.

**püskürgeç, -ci** atomizer; sprayer.

**püskürmek 1.** to spray from one's mouth; **2.** to erupt (volcano); **3.** to spew out, to spume forth (lava).

**püskürteç 1.** atomizer; spray gun, sprayer; **2.** aerosol (bomb).

**püskürtmek 1.** caus. of püskürmek, to spray; to dust; **2.** ✕ to repel, to drive back, to repulse.

**püskürtü** lava.

**püsür 1.** botherment, headache; **2.** petty; **3.** pain in the neck (person).

**pütürlenmek** to chap (skin).

**pütürlü** chapped, cracked.

**pütür pütür** chapped, cracked (skin).

# R

**Rab,** -bbı God, the Lord.
**Rabbena** [. . -]: ~ hakkı için by God.
**Rabbi(m)** my God!
**rabıt,** -ptı connection.
**rabıta** [- . .] 1. relation, connection, tie, bond; 2. conformity; 3. system, method, order.
**rabıtalı** [- . . . .] 1. orderly; well-conducted; 2. level-headed *(person);* 3. coherent, consistent.
**rabıtasız** [- . . . .] 1. disorderly, untidy; 2. incoherent, inconsistent.
**raca** raja(h).
**raci,** -ii [ā] returning; ~ olm. to concern, to touch.
**racon** *sl.* 1. custom, rule; 2. swagger; ~ kesmek to swagger, to show off.
**radar** [x .] radar.
**radarcı** 1. radar operator; 2. *sl.* talebearer, sneak.
**radde** degree, point;  -lerinde, -sinde a-round, about.
**radikal** radical.
**radyasyon** *phys.* radiation.
**radyatör** radiator.
**radyo** 1. radio, wireless; 2. radio (station); ~ dinlemek to listen to the radio.
**radyoaktif** radioactive.
**radyoculuk** radiobroadcasting.
**radyoevi,** -ni broadcasting station.
**radyofonik** radio...; ~ piyes radio play.
**radyofoto** radiophotograph.
**radyografi** radiography.
**radyogram** radiogram.
**radyotelefon** radiotelephone.
**radyotelgraf** radiotelegram.
**radyoterapi** radiotherapy.
**radyum** ⚛ radium.
**raf** shelf; -a koymak (*or* kaldırmak) to shelve *(a. fig.).*
**rafadan** 1. soft-boiled *(egg);* 2. *sl.* naive; ~ pişirmek to soft-boil *(egg).*
**rafine** refined; ~ etm. to refine.
**rafineri** refinery.
**rağbet,** -ti 1. demand, inclination, desire; 2. popularity; ~ etm. 1. to demand, to like; 2. to esteem; ~ görmek 1. to be in demand; 2. to be popular; -ten düşmek

1. to be no longer in demand; 2. to be out of favo(u)r.
**rağbetli** in demand.
**rağbetsiz** not in demand.
**rağmen** [x .] in spite (-*e* of).
**rahat,** -tı 1. comfort, ease; 2. peace; 3. comfortable; 4. easy, at ease, untroubled; 5. ✕ at ease!; 6. easygoing *(person);* ~ bırakmamak (*or* vermemek) to pester, to annoy, to devil; ~ durmak to behave o.s.; ~ etm. 1. to be at ease; 2. to rest, to take it easy; ~ ~ comfortably; easily; ~ yüzü görmemek to have no peace; -ına bakmak to mind one's own comfort, to see to one's pleasures; -ını kaçırmak to annoy, to pester, to molest.
**rahatça** 1. easily; 2. comfortably.
**rahatlamak** to feel relieved (*or* better): to feel at ease, to cheer up.
**rahatlık** 1. peace, quiet; 2. ease, comfort; 3. easygoingness.
**rahatsız** 1. uncomfortable; 2. uneasy, anxious; 3. unwell, under the weather, indisposed; ~ etm. 1. to annoy, to disturb, to trouble, to bother; 2. to pay a visit; ~ olm. 1. to feel uncomfortable; 2. to be under the weather, to feel indisposed.
**rahatsızlanmak** to feel ill (*or* unwell).
**rahatsızlık** 1. discomfort, uneasiness; 2. illness, sickness.
**rahibe** [ā] nun.
**rahibelik** [ā] nunhood.
**rahim,** -hmi womb, uterus.
**Rahim** the Merciful.
**rahip,** -bi [ā] 1. priest, minister, pastor; 2. monk.
**rahle** low reading-desk.
**Rahman** [. -] the Compassionate.
**rahmet,** -ti 1. God's mercy (*or* compassion); 2. *fig.* rain: ~ düşmek (*or* yağmak) to rain; ~ okumak 1. to pray for the soul (-*e* of); 2. to regret the loss (-*e* of); ~ okutmak to be a greater nuisance (-*e* than); -ine kavuşmak to pass away, to go to meet one's Maker.
**rahmetli(k)** the deceased, the late; ~ olm.

to pass away, to die.

**rahne** fissure, breach.

**rahvan** amble; ~ gitmek to amble *(horse)*

**rakam** 1. number, figure; 2. numeral, digit.

**raket,** -ti 1. racket, racquet; 2. snowshoe.

**rakı** raki, arrack.

**rakım** altitude, elevation.

**rakıs,** -ksı 1. dance; 2. *phys.* oscillation.

**rakip,** -bi rival.

**rakit,** -di [ā] still, stagnant *(water)*.

**rakkas** [. -] pendulum.

**rakkase** [. - .] belly dancer.

**rakor** ⊙ joint, union *(of pipes)*.

**raksetmek** [x . .] to dance.

**ralanti** *mot.* idling; -de çalışmak *mot.* to tick over, to idle; -ye almak *mot.* to idle.

**rali** rally.

**ram:** ~ etm. to master, to subjugate.

**ramak,** -kı: ~ kalmak to be within an ace *(or* inch) *(-e* of).

**Ramazan** 1. Ramazan; 2. *mf.;* ~ bayramı the Ramazan festival.

**rampa** [x .] 1. slope, incline, grade; 2. loading ramp; ~ etm. 1. to sidle up *(-e* to); 2. *sl.* to latch *(-e* onto).

**rampalamak** *s.* rampa etm.

**randevu** appointment, rendezvous, tryst, engagement, date; ~ almak to get an appointment *(-den* from); ~ vermek *(b·ne)* to make an appointment with *s.o.*

**randevuevi,** -ni unlicensed brothel.

**randıman** output, yield, production.

**randımanlı** productive.

**randımansız** unproductive.

**rant,** -tı ꝑ unearned income.

**rantabl** ꝑ profitable.

**ranza** [x .] 1. bunk bed; 2. ꝓ, 🚢 berth.

**rapido** drawing pen.

**rapor** report.

**raporcu** reporter.

**raporlu** on sick leave.

**raportör** reporter.

**rap rap** striking the ground smartly.

**rapsodi** ♪ rhapsody.

**raptetmek** [x . .] to attach, to fasten.

**raptiye** drawing pin. *Am.* thumbtack.

**raptiyelemek** to thumbtack.

**rasat,** -dı *ast.* observation.

**rasathane** [. . - .] observatory.

**rasgele** [x . .] haphazardly, at random; by chance.

**rasıt,** -dı *ast.* observer.

**raspa** [x .] 1. scraper; 2. *sl.* gluttony; ~ etm. to scrape.

**rast:** ~ gelmek 1. to chance *(-e* upon), to meet by chance; 2. to come *(-e* across),

to meet *(-e* with), to encounter; 3. to coincide *(-e* with), to fall *(-e* on); ~ getir-mek 1. to come across *(or* upon); 2. to approach, to collar s.o. *(at the right time);* 3. to hit the target; 4. to cause to succeed *(God);* ~ gitmek to go well, to turn out well.

**rastık** kohl.

**rastlamak** *s.* rast gelmek.

**rastlantı** coincidence, chance, accident.

**rastlaşmak** 1. to chance upon each other; 2. to coincide.

**rasyonalizm** rationalism.

**rasyonel** rational.

**raşitizm** ꝑ rickets, rachitis.

**raunt** *s.* ravnt.

**ravnt** *boxing:* round.

**ray** rail; track; -dan çıkmak 1. 🚂 to jump the rails, to go off the rails; 2. *fig.* to go awry *(or* haywire); -ına oturt-mak to set to rights.

**rayiç,** -ci ꝑ market *(or* current) value; ~ fiyat market *(or* current) price.

**rayiha** [- . .] fragrance.

**razakı** a kind of white grape.

**razı** [ā] willing, content; ~ etm. *(b·ni bşe)* to get *s.o.* to agree to *s.th.,* to get *s.o.* round to *s.th.;* ~ olm. to consent *(-e* to). to agree *(-e* to).

**re** ♪ re; D.

**reaksiyon** reaction.

**reaktör** reactor.

**realist,** -ti realist(ic).

**realite** reality.

**realizm** realism.

**Recep,** -bi 1. Rajab; 2. *mf.*

**reçel** jam.

**reçete** 1. prescription; 2. recipe.

**recine** [. x .] resin, rosin.

**recineli** resinous.

**redaksiyon** redaction.

**reddetmek** [x . .] 1. to refuse, to reject, to repudiate; 2. to disown, to cast off.

**redingot,** -tu frock coat.

**refah** [ā] welfare, prosperity, well-being; ~ içinde yaşamak to live in prosperity, to be at easy circumstances.

**refakat,** -ti [. - .] accompaniment *(a. ♪).* companionship; ~ etm. to accompany *(a. ♪);* to escort; -inde in the company *(-in* of).

**refakatçi** companion *(who stays with a patient while he is in hospital).*

**referandum** [. . x .] *pol.* referendum.

**referans** reference, letter of recommen-dation.

**refetmek** [x . .] to remove, to abolish.

**refik**, -kı [i] 1. friend, companion; 2. ♀ [x .] *mf.*

**refika** [i] 1. wife; 2. ♀ [x ..] *wf.*

**refleks** reflex.

**reflektör** reflector.

**reform** reform.

**reformcu** 1. reformer; 2. reformist(ic).

**refüj** *mot.* (traffic) island, refuge.

**refüze etm.** to refuse, to turn down.

**regaip**, -bi [ā]: ~ kandili *the 12 th of Recep. anniversary of the conception of Mohammad.*

**regülatör** ⊕ regulator.

**rehabilitasyon** ♀ rehabilitation.

**rehavet**, -ti [ā] languor, lassitude.

**rehber** 1. guide; 2. guidebook; 3. (telephone) directory.

**rehberlik** 1. guidance; 2. guiding; ~ etm. to guide.

**rehin** pawn, pledge, security, collateral; ~e koymak to pawn, to hock, to pop, to pledge.

**rehine** hostage.

**reis** [i] head, chief, leader; president; chairman; ~ vekili vice-president.

**reisicumhur** president.

**reislik** leadership, chieftaincy; presidency; chairmanship; ~ etm. to preside.

**reji** 1. the Regie; 2. *thea., cinema:* direction.

**rejim** 1. *pol.* regime; 2. ♥ diet; ~ yapmak to diet.

**rejisör** director.

**rekabet**, -ti [ā] rivalry, competition; ~ etm. *(b-le)* to rival *s.o.,* to compete against *s.o.,* to vie with *s.o.*

**rekâket**, -ti stammer, stutter.

**rekât**, -tı *isl. complete act of worship with the prescribed postures.*

**reklam** advertisement.

**reklamcılık** advertising.

**rekolte** [. x .] ⊤ harvest, crop.

**rekor** record; ~ kırmak to break a record; ~ sahibi record-holder.

**rekorcu, rekortmen** record-breaker.

**rektifiye etm.** ⊕ to rectify.

**rektör** *univ.* rector, president, chancellor.

**rektörlük** *univ.* rectorship, rectorate.

**remil**, -mli geomancy.

**remiz**, -mzi symbol, sign.

**remmal**, -li [ā] geomancer.

**rencide** [i] hurt, offended, wounded; ~ etm. to hurt *(s.o.'s feelings).*

**rençper** 1. farmer; 2. farmhand.

**rende** 1. *(carpenter's)* plane; 2. grater.

**rendelemek** 1. to plane; 2. to grate.

**rengârenk**, -gi colo(u)rful, multi-

**colo(u)red.**

**rengeyiği**, -ni *zo.* reindeer.

**renk**, -gi 1. colo(u)r, hue; 2. *fig.* character, colo(u)r; ~ ~ colo(u)rful, multicolo(u)red; ~ vermek *(or* katmak) to enliven, to liven up; ~ vermemek to keep up appearances; -i atmak *(or* uçmak) 1. to fade; 2. to go pale; -i çalık faded, discolo(u)red; -ten -e girmek *fig.* to go all shades of red.

**renkçideren** decolorant, bleach.

**renkkörlüğü**, -nü colo(u)r blindness.

**renkkörü**, -nü colo(u)r-blind.

**renklendirmek** 1. to make colo(u)rful, to give colo(u)r; 2. *fig.* to enliven, to liven up.

**renkli** 1. colo(u)red; 2. colo(u)rful, amusing, lively; ~ film colo(u)r film; ~ fotoğraf colo(u)r photograph; ~ işitme *psych.* colo(u)r hearing.

**renksecmezlik** colo(u)r blindness.

**renksemez** achromatic *(lens).*

**renksiz** 1. colo(u)rless, uncolo(u)red; 2. faded, pale; 3. *fig.* lackluster, non-descript.

**repertuvar** repertoire, repertory.

**replik** *thea.* rejoinder.

**re'sen** [x .] on one's own account, independently.

**resepsiyon** reception (desk).

**reseptör** ♀ receiver.

**resif** *geogr.* reef.

**resim**, -smi 1. picture; photograph; drawing; painting; illustration; 2. tax, duty, impost; 3. ceremony; ~ çekmek to take a photograph, to photograph; ~ dersi art lesson; ~ sergisi exhibition of pictures; ~ yapmak to paint; to draw; resmini çekmek to take a picture (-*in* of).

**resimci** 1. photographer; 2. illustrator; artist; 3. art teacher.

**resimlemek** to illustrate.

**resimli** illustrated, pictorial; ~ roman comic (strip).

**resimlik** 1. photograph album; 2. picture frame.

**resital**, -li ♪ recital.

**resmen** [x .] officially, formally.

**resmetmek** [x ..] 1. to picture, to draw; 2. to depict, to delineate, to describe, to represent.

**resmi** 1. official, government...; 2. authorized, official; 3. formal, ceremonious, official; ~ dil official language; ~ elbise uniform; ~ gazete official gazette; ~ nikâh civil marriage.

**resmiyet**, -ti 1. formality, ceremony; 2.

officialism, officiality; -e dökmek to officialize.

**ressam** painter, artist.

**rest**, -ti: ~ çekmek **1.** to stake all; **2.** *fig.* to have the last word.

**resto** *sl.* stop!, that's enough!

**restoran** restaurant.

**restorasyon** restoration.

**restore etm.** to restore.

**resul**, -lü [ā] prophet.

**resülmal**, -li [ - . - ] ϯ capital.

**reşit**, -di [ī] **1.** of age, adult; **2.** ♀ [x .] *mf.*; ~ olm. to come of age.

**ret**, -ddi **1.** refusal, rejection; **2.** repudiation, disownment.

**reva** [ā] suitable, worthy; ~ görmek to deem proper.

**revaç**, -cı **1.** salability, marketability; **2.** current (or market) price; ~ bulmak to be in demand; to be in vogue; ~ vermek to cause to be in demand.

**revani** [. - -] *a sweet made with semolina.*

**reverans** curts(e)y, bow; ~ yapmak to curtsy (-e to); to bow (-e to).

**revir** infirmary, sick bay.

**revizyon** ⊕ overhaul; -dan geçirmek ☉ to overhaul.

**revolver** revolver.

**revü** *thea.* revue, review.

**rey 1.** vote; **2.** view, opinion; -e koymak to put to the vote.

**reye** striped (cloth).

**reyon** department.

**rezalet**, -ti [ā] **1.** disgrace, outrage, scandal; **2.** disgraceful, scandalous; ~ çıkarmak to create a scandal.

**reze 1.** pintle hinge; **2.** hasp.

**rezene** ♀ fennel.

**rezerv(e)** reserve.

**rezervasyon** reservation; ~ yapmak to make a reservation.

**rezerve** reserved; ~ etm. to reserve, to book.

**rezervuar** reservoir.

**rezil** [ī] disgraceful, outrageous, scandalous; ~ etm. to disgrace, to pillory; ~ olm. to be disgraced.

**rezillik** [ī] disgrace, scandal, outrage.

**rezistans** ≠ resistance.

**rıhtım** quay, pier, wharf.

**rıza** [ā] **1.** consent, approval, assent; **2.** volition, choice; **3.** ♀ [x .] *mf.*; ~ göstermek to consent (-e to); -sını almak (b-nin) to get s.o.'s consent.

**rızk**, -kı one's daily bread, food; -ını çıkarmak to earn one's daily bread.

**riayet**, -ti [ā] **1.** obedience, compliance, observance; **2.** respect, esteem; regard;

**3.** hospitality; ~ etm. **1.** to comply (-e with), to obey; to observe; **2.** to respect; **3.** to show hospitality (-e to).

**riayetkâr** [ā] **1.** obedient; **2.** respectful.

**riayetsiz** [ā] **1.** disobedient; **2.** disrespectful.

**riayetsizlik** [ā] **1.** disobedience, noncompliance; **2.** disrespect.

**rica** [ā] request; ~ ederim! not at all!, please!; ~ etm. (b-den bşi) to request s.th. of s.o.

**rical**, -li [ā] men of importance; dignitaries.

**ricat**, -ti ≮ retreat; ~ etm. to retreat.

**rikkat**, -ti **1.** pity, compassion; mercy; **2.** gentleness, tenderness.

**rimel** mascara.

**rina** *zo.* stingray.

**ring**, -gi *sports:* ring.

**ringa** *zo.* herring.

**risale** [ā] **1.** treatise, pamphlet, booklet.

**risk**, -ki risk; -e girmek to take (or run) a risk.

**ritim**, -tmi rhythm.

**ritmik** rhythmic.

**rivayet**, -ti [ā] rumo(u)r, hearsay; ~ etm. to relate.

**riya** [ā] hypocrisy, two-facedness.

**riyakâr** [ā] hypocritical, two-faced.

**riyal**, -li ri(y)al.

**riyaset**, -ti [ā] headship, presidency; ~ etm. to preside (-e over).

**riyaseticumhur** presidency.

**riyazet**, -ti [ā] asceticism.

**riyaziye** [ā] ϯ mathematics.

**riyaziyeci** [ā] ϯ mathematician.

**riziko** [x .] risk.

**rizikolu** [x . . .] risky.

**roba 1.** dress; **2.** yoke (of a garment).

**robdöşambr** dressing gown.

**robot**, -tu robot.

**roka** ♀ (garden) rocket.

**roket**, -ti rocket.

**roketatar** bazooka.

**rokoko** rococo.

**rol**, -lü role, part; ~ almak to have a role (or part) (in a play); to perform; ~ kesmek F to put on an act, to playact; ~ oynamak (bşde) to play a part in s.th.; ~ yapmak = ~ kesmek.

**rom** rum.

**Roma** [x .] *pr. n.* Rome.

**Romalı** *pr. n.* Roman.

**roman** novel.

**romancı** novelist.

**romantik** romantic.

**romantizm** romance, romanticism.

**Romanya** [. x .] *pr. n.* Rumania.

Romanyalı *pr. n.* Rumanian.
romatizma [..x.] rheumatism.
romatizmalı rheumatic.
Romen: ~ harfleri *typ.* Roman letters; ~ rakamları Roman numerals.
rondela ⊕ washer.
rop, -bu dress, robe.
rosto [x.] roast.
rot, -tu *mot.* rod.
rota [x.] ⤓ course; -yı değiştirmek to change course *(a. fig.).*
roza [x.] rose (diamond).
rozbif roast beef.
rozet, -ti 1. rosette; 2. emblem, badge.
rölöve statistical survey.
rölyef relief.
römork, -ku trailer.
römorkör tug(boat).
rönar fox fur.
Rönesans the Renaissance.
röntgen 1. X-ray; 2. *sl.* peeping, voyeurism; -ini çekmek to X-ray.
röntgenci 1. X-ray specialist; 2. *sl.* Peeping Tom, voyeur.
röportaj report *(of a newspaperman).*
rötar delay.
rötarlı delayed *(train, bus, etc.).*
rötuş retouching; ~ yapmak to touch up.
rövanş *sports:* return match *(or game).*
ruam [â] 🐎glanders.
rubai [..-] quatrain.
ruble [x.] ruble.
rugan patent leather.
ruh 1. soul, spirit; 2. animation, life, spirit; 3. *psych.* psyche; 4. 🐎 essence, spirit; 5. heart, essence *(of a matter);* 6. spirit *(of a dead person);* ~ doktoru psychiatrist; ~ çağırma necromancy; ~ göçü metempsychosis; ~ haleti *(or* hali) mood, state of mind; ~ hastası mental patient; ~ hekimi psychiatrist; ~ hekimliği psychiatry; -unu teslim etm. to give up the ghost.
ruhani [- - -] spiritual.
ruhbilim psychology.
ruhbilimci psychologist.
ruhen [-.] spiritually, in spirit.
ruhi [- -] 1. psychological, mental; 2. ♀ [x.] *mf*
ruhiyat, -tı [-.-] psychology.
ruhlanmak to become animated, to revive.
ruhlu spirited, lively, energetic.
ruhsal psychological, mental.
ruhsat, -tı 1. permission, authorization; 2. license, permit; registration *(or* log) book.
ruhsatiye *s.* ruhsatname.

ruhsatlı 1. authorized, permitted; 2. licensed.
ruhsatname [...-.] permit, license; registration *(or* log) book.
ruhsatsız 1. unauthorized; 2. unlicensed.
ruhsuz spiritless, lifeless, inanimate.
ruj lipstick.
rulet, -ti roulette.
rulman ⊕ bearing.
rulo roll *(of paper).*
Rum Greek.
rumba r(h)umba.
Rumca [x.] Greek (language).
Rumen Romanian.
rumuz [.-] 1. symbol, sign; 2. pseudonym, alias.
Rus Russian.
Rusça [x.] the Russian language, Russian.
Rusya [x.] *pr. n.* Russia.
rutubet, -ti [.-.] humidity, damp(ness).
rutubetlenmek to become humid.
rutubetli [...] humid, damp.
ruva [.x] *cards:* king.
ruzname [- -.] 1. diary, journal; 2. agenda.
rücu, -uu [û] 1. recision; 2. withdrawal; ~ hakkı 🐎 right of recovery.
rüçhan [â] 1. preference, preemption; 2. ♀ *mf., wf.;* ~ hakkı 🐎 (right to) preference.
rükün, -knü mainstay, pillar, prop.
rüküş comically dressed.
rüsum [û] *pl.* of resim, duties, taxes.
rüsup, -bu [û] sediment.
rüşt, -tü 🐎 majority; -ünü ispat etm. *fig.* to evidence one's maturity.
rüştiye *hist.* junior high school.
rüşvet, -ti bribe, graft; bribery; ~ almak to take *(or* accept) a bribe, to graft; ~ vermek to give a bribe, to bribe; ~ yemek to take bribes, to graft.
rüşvetçi grafter, taker of bribes.
rüşvetçilik bribery.
rütbe ✗ rank.
rüya dream; ~ görmek to dream, to have a dream; -sında görmek to dream of, to see in one's dreams; -sını tabir etm. to interpret s.o.'s dream.
rüyet, -ti seeing, vision.
rüzgâr wind, breeze; ~ almak to be exposed to the wind; ~ ekip fırtına biçmek to sow the wind and reap the whirlwind; ~ ile gitmek to sail with the wind.
rüzgârgülü, -nü compass rose.
rüzgârlı windy, breezy.
rüzgârlık windbreaker, windcheater.

# S

**saadet**, -ti [. - .] **1.** happiness; **2.** ♀ *wf.;* -le! good luck!

**saat**, -ti **1.** hour; **2.** watch, clock; **3.** time; **4.** meter; taximeter; speedometer; ~ ayarı time signal; ~ başı on the hour; ~ kaç? what time is it?, what is the time?; ~ kulesi clock tower; ~ on birde **1.** at eleven o'clock; **2.** *fig.* very late in life; ~ tutmak to time; ~ vurmak to strike the hour *(clock);* -i kurmak to wind a watch *or* clock; -i -ine uymamak to chop and change.

**saatçi 1.** watchmaker; watch repairer; **2.** seller of watches *or* clocks.

**saatçilik** making, selling *or* repairing watches *or* clocks.

**saatli** fitted with a clock; ~ bomba time bomb.

**saatlik** lasting... hours.

**sabah 1.** morning; **2.** in the morning; ~ akşam all the time; ~ gazetesi morning paper; ~ kahvaltısı breakfast; ~ oldu it's morning, morning's come; ~ ~ early in the morning; ~ -a çıkmamak not to live through the night; -a doğru towards morning; -ın köründe at the crack of dawn; -lar hayrolsun! good morning!; -lardan bir ~ one morning.

**sabahçı 1.** person who works on a morning shift; **2.** pupil who goes to school in the mornings; **3.** person who sits up all night.

**sabahki** morning's.

**sabahlamak** to sit up *(or* work) all night; hasta çocuğunun başında sabahladı she kept vigil over her sick child.

**sabahleyin** [. x . .] in the morning.

**sabahlı akşamlı** mornings and evenings.

**sabahlık 1.** dressing gown, housecoat; **2.** enough for... mornings.

**saban** plough, *Am.* plow; ~ demiri ploughshare, *Am.* plowshare; ~ izi furrow; ~ sürmek to plough, *Am.* to plow

**sabık**, -kı [ā] previous, former, last, ex-; ~ kral ex-king.

**sabıka** [- . .] ♂ previous conviction, past offence.

**sabıkalı** [- . . .] ♂ previously convicted; recidivist.

**sabır**, -brı patience; forbearance; ~ taşı very patient person; sabrı taşmak (or tükenmek) *(for one's patience)* to come to an end; sabrın sonu selamettir patience is rewarded.

**sabırlı** patient; forbearing.

**sabırsız** impatient.

**sabırsızlanmak** to grow impatient.

**sabırsızlık** impatience.

**sabit**, -ti [ā] **1.** fixed, stationary; constant; stable; **2.** fast *(dye, colour);* **3.** fixed *(stare);* **4.** proved; ~ balon captive balloon; ~ fikir fixed idea, crank; ~ fiyat fixed price.

**sabitleşmek** to become fixed; to stabilize.

**sabo** clog.

**sabotaj** sabotage; ~ yapmak to sabotage.

**sabotajcı** saboteur.

**sabote etm.** to sabotage.

**sabretmek** [x . .] to show patience, to be patient; sabreden derviş muradına ermiş *pro.* everything comes to him who waits.

**sabuk** *s.* abuk sabuk.

**sabuklama** delirium.

**sabun** soap; ~ köpüğü lather.

**sabuncu** soap maker; soap seller.

**sabunlamak** to soap, to lather.

**sabunlanmak** to soap o.s.

**sabunlu** soapy.

**sabunluk** soap dish.

**sac** *s.* saç 2.

**sacayağı**, -nı, **sacayak** trivet.

**saç¹**, -çı hair; ~ bağı hair band; ~ boyası hair dye; ~ dibi hair bed; ~ filesi hair-net; ~ kurutma makinesi hair drier; ~ örgüsü plait; ~ örmek to braid the hair; ~ -a baş başa gelmek to come to blows; ~ sakal ağartmak to work on s.th. for a long time; -ına ak düşmek to turn grey; -ını başını yolmak to tear one's hair, to beat one's breast; -ını süpürge etm. to exert o.s. *(woman);* -ları diken diken oldu his hair stood on end; -ları iki türlü olm. to get old.

**saç²**, -cı, -çı ⊕ sheet iron.

**saçak 1.** eave(s) *(of a building);* **2.**

fringe.

**saçakbulul,** -tu cirrus (cloud).

**saçaklı 1.** eaved *(building)*; **2.** fringed.

**saçkıran** ☞ alopecia, loss of hair.

**saçlı** ... haired.

**saçma 1.** *vn.* of saçmak; **2.** (buck)shot; **3.** cast(ing) net; **4.** (*a.* ~ sapan) nonsensical, absurd; ~ sapan konuşmak to talk crap, to drivel, to talk nonsense.

**saçmak,** (-ar) to scatter, to strew; saçıp savurmak to play ducks and drakes with *(money)*, to squander.

**saçmalamak** to talk nonsense *(or* rot *or* crap), to drivel, to piffle, to ramble, to twaddle.

**saçmalık** piece of nonsense.

**sada** *s.* seda.

**sadak** quiver.

**sadaka** alms; ~ istemek to beg, to cadge; ~ vermek to give alms.

**sadakat,** -ti [. - .] loyalty, fidelity, devotion, allegiance; ~ borcu ☾☽ loyalty; ~ göstermek to show loyalty (-e to); ~ yemini oath of allegiance.

**sadakatli** [. - . .] loyal, faithful, devoted.

**sadakatsiz** [. - . .] disloyal, unfaithful.

**sadakatsizlik** disloyalty, unfaithfulness, infidelity.

**sadakor** raw silk.

**sadalı** *s.* sedalı.

**sadaret,** -ti [. - .] *hist.* grand vizierate *(or* viziership); ♀ Dairesi *hist.* the Sublime Porte.

**sadasız** *s.* sedasız.

**sade** [ā] **1.** plain, simple; **2.** black and unsweetened *(coffee)*; **3.** merely, only, solely, just; ~ suya çorba clear soup.

**sadece** [ā] *s.* sade 3.

**sadedil** [ā] simplehearted, guileless.

**sadeleşmek** [ā] to become simple *(or* plain).

**sadeleştirmek** [ā] to simplify, to purify.

**sadelik** [ā] simplicity, plainness.

**sadet,** -di main topic *(or* point); -e gelmek to come to the point; -ten ayrılmak to get off the subject.

**sadeyağ** clarified *(or* run) butter.

**sadık,** -kı [ā] **1.** loyal, faithful, devoted, fast; **2.** true, veracious; **3.** ♀ *mf.*; ~ kalmak to remain loyal (-e to).

**sadist,** -ti sadist(ic).

**sadistlik, sadizm** sadism.

**sadme** shock *(a. psych)*, jolt; collision.

**sadrazam** [. - .] *hist.* grand vizier.

**sadrazamlık** *hist.* grand viziership *(or* vizierate).

**saf¹,** -ffı **1.** row, line; **2.** ✗ rank, line; ~ bağlamak to form a line; ~ ~ in rows

*(or* ranks *or* lines).

**saf²** **1.** pure, unadulterated; **2.** credulous, naive, gullible.

**safa** [. -] **1.** ease, peace, untroubledness; **2.** delight, enjoyment, pleasure; **3.** entertainment, party; **4.** ♀ [x .] *mf.*; ~ bulduk! thank you! *(said in reply to the greeting ~* geldiniz!); ~ geldiniz! welcome!; ~ sürmek to enjoy o.s., to have a good time.

**safer** safar.

**saffet,** -ti **1.** purity; **2.** ♀ *mf., wf.*

**safha** phase, stage.

**safi** [- -] **1.** pure, unadulterated; **2.** net; **3.** only, merely, solely.

**safir** sapphire.

**safkan** [- .] purebred, thoroughbred *(horse)*.

**saflaştırmak** [- . . .] to purify; to refine.

**saflık** **1.** purity; **2.** credulousness, naiveté.

**safra¹** ⚓ ballast; ~ atmak to get rid of troublesome people *or* things.

**safra²** *anat.* bile, gall; ~ bastırmak to have a snack; ~ kesesi gall bladder; ~sı kabarmak *(or* bulanmak) to be seasick.

**safran** ⚘ saffron.

**safsata** sophistry, casuistry.

**safsatacı** sophist, casuist.

**sağ¹** **1.** right; **2.** *pol.* right-wing; ~ gözünü sol gözünden kıskanmak to be extremely jealous; -a bak! ✗ eyes right!; -a sola hither and thither; -dan gidiniz! keep to the right!; -dan soldan from the right and from the left; ~ı solu olmamak *fig.* to chop and change; -ını solunu şaşırmak not to know what to do.

**sağ²** **1.** alive, living; **2.** healthy, well; **3.** *s.* sağlam; ~ kalanlar the survivors; ~ kalmak to remain alive, to survive; ~ ol! thanks!, cheers!; ~ salim safe and sound, scot-free.

**sağaçık** *football:* outside right.

**sağanak** shower, downpour, cloudburst.

**sağbek,** -ki *football:* right back.

**sağcı** *pol.* rightist, right-winger.

**sağdıç** bridesmaid; groomsman.

**sağduyu** common sense.

**sağgörü** foresight.

**sağgörülü** foresighted.

**sağhaf** [. -] *football:* right halfback.

**sağılmak 1.** *pass.* of sağmak; **2.** to uncoil itself *(snake)*; **3.** to fray, to ravel *(cloth)*.

**sağın** exact, precise.

**sağır** **1.** deaf; **2.** blank, blind *(wall-etc.)*; **3.** muted, muffled *(sound)*; ~ sultan bile duydu everybody from here to China knows about it.

**sağırlaşmak** to grow deaf.

**sağırlık** deafness.

**sağiç**, -ci *football:* right centre *(or Am. center).*

**sağlam 1.** strong, sound; well-built, well--made; secure; **2.** healthy, strong; **3.** reliable, trustworthy, dependabie; ~ *(or sağ)* ayakkabı değildir he is unreliable; ~ kaba kotarmak *(bşi)* *fig.* to make *s.th.* profitable; ~ *(or sağ)* kazığa bağlamak *fig.* to make safe *(or sure).*

**sağlama 1.** *vn. of* sağlamak; **2.** *part.* ₳ proof, cross-check.

**sağlamak 1.** to provide, to get, to find, to obtain; **2.** to guarantee, to ensure; **3.** ₳ to prove, to cross-check; **4.** *mot.* to move to the right side *(of the road).*

**sağlamlamak** to strengthen, to fortify, to reinforce.

**sağlamlaşmak** to become strong.

**sağlamlaştırmak** to strengthen, to fortify, to reinforce, to consolidate.

**sağlamlık** strength, soundness.

**sağlı sollu 1.** on both sides of; **2.** using first one hand and then the other.

**sağlıcakla** [..x.] in good health, happily.

**sağlık¹** hcalth; ~ bilgisi hygiene; ~ ocağı village clinic; ~ olsun! never mind!; ~ raporu health report; ꭃ ve Sosyal Yardım Bakanlığı the Ministry of Health and Social Services; ~ sigortası health insurance; ~ yoklaması general medical checkup, physical examination; ~ yurdu convalescent home; sağlığında in his lifetime, while he is alive; sağlığınıza! cheers!, to your health!

**sağlık²** *s.* salık.

**sağlıklı 1.** healthy, in good health; **2.** *fig.* sound, reliable.

**sağlıksız** sickly.

**sağmak,** (-ar) **1.** to milk *(an animal)*; **2.** to extact from the hive *(honey)*; **3.** to unwind, to unravel *(threads)*; **4.** *sl.* to mulct, to milk.

**sağmal 1.** milch *(animal)*; **2.** *sl.* fit to be fleeced *(person)*; ~ inek milch cow *(a. fig.).*

**sağrı** rump *(of an animal)*; ~ kemiği *anat.* rump bone, sacrum.

**sah**, -hhı stet; ~ çekmek to stet.

**saha** [-.] field *(a. sports)*, area, zone, region.

**sahaf** [.-] dealer in secondhand books, bouquiniste.

**sahan** copper pan; -da yumurta fried egg.

**sahanlık 1.** landing *(on a staircase)*; **2.** platform.

**sahi** [î] really, truly.

**sahibe** [-..] proprietress; mistress.

**sahici** genuine, real.

**sahiden** really, truly.

**sahife** *s.* sayfa.

**sahil** [â] shore, coast; bank; ~ kordonu *geogr.* (sand)bar.

**sahip**, -bi [â] owner, possessor, proprietor, master; proprietress, mistress; ~ çıkmak **1.** *(bşe)* to claim *s.th.*; **2.** *(b-ne)* to look after *s.o.*, to see to *s.o.*; ~ olm. **1.** to own, to possess, to have; **2.** to get under control.

**sahipsiz** ownerless, unclaimed, unappropriated.

**sahne 1.** stage; **2.** *thea.* scene; ~ olm. to be the scene *(-e* of); -ye çıkmak to appear; -ye koymak to stage, to put on *(a play).*

**sahra** [.-] **1.** open plain; **2.** desert; **3.** X field...; ~ topu X field gun.

**sahre** *geol.* rock mass.

**sahte 1.** false, fake, counterfeit, spurious, phony; **2.** feigned, pretended.

**sahtekâr** forger, faker, falsifier.

**sahtekârlık** forgery, falsification; imposture.

**sahtiyan** morocco (leather).

**sahur** [û] *isl.* meal before dawn *(during Ramazan).*

**saik**, -kı [â] motive.

**saika¹** [-..] motive; incentive.

**saika²** [-..] † lightning.

**sair** [â] other.

**saka** water seller.

**sakakuşu**, -nu *zo.* (gold)finch.

**sakağı** ⅌ glanders.

**sakal** beard; whiskers; ~ bırakmak *(or* koyuvermek *or* salıvermek *or* uzatmak) to grow a beard; ~ı bitmek *(bir işin)* to be in the balance; ~ı ele vermek *fig.* to allow o.s. to be led by the nose; -ımı değirmende ağartmadım *fig.* I am not an old fool; -ına gülmek to laugh up one's sleeve.

**sakallı** bearded; whiskered.

**sakalsız** beardless.

**sakamonya** [..x.] ♀ scammony.

**sakandırık** chin strap.

**sakar 1.** blaze *(on an animal's forehead)*; **2.** butterfingered, clumsy, accident--prone.

**sakarin** saccharin.

**sakarlaşmak** to become butterfingered.

**sakarlık** clumsiness, awkwardness.

**sakat**, -tı **1.** disabled, invalid, handicapped; **2.** *fig.* unsound, crippled, defective.

**sakatat**, -tı [. . -] offal.

**sakatlamak** to disable, to mutilate, to maim, to cripple.

**sakatlanmak** to become disabled (*or* crippled).

**sakatlık 1.** disability, handicap, impairment; **2.** *fig.* flaw, defect.

**sakın** don't, beware!; ~ söylediklerimi unutmayın! don't forget what I said.

**sakınca** drawback, objection.

**sakıncalı** objectionable, inadvisable; unwise.

**sakıngan** cautious, prudent.

**sakınma** *vn. of* sakınmak; -sı olmamak to be heedless.

**sakınmak 1.** to avoid, to shun, to keep away (-*den* from), to steer clear (-*den* of); **2.** to watch out (-*den* for); to guard (-*den* against); **3.** to protect (-*den* from).

**sakırga** *zo.* tick.

**sakıt**, -tı **1.** falling; fallen; **2.** ⚥ stillborn; **3.** ♒ invalid.

**Sakıt**, -tı *ast.* Mars.

**sakız** (gum) mastic; ~ gibi **1.** sticky; **2.** very white and clean; ~ rakısı raki flavo(u)red with mastic.

**Sakız Adası**, -nı *pr. n.* Chios.

**sakızkabağı**, -nı vegetable marrow.

**saki** cupbearer.

**sakin** [ā] **1.** calm, tranquil, quiet, serene; **2.** resident, inhabitant, dweller.

**sakinleşmek** to become calm, to calm down.

**sakinleştirmek** to calm, to soothe, to tranquilize.

**sakinlik** calmness, tranquillity, serenity.

**sakit**, -ti silent.

**saklamak 1.** to hide, to conceal; **2.** to keep dark; **3.** to save (*or* keep) (-e for), to set aside (-e for); **4.** to store, to keep (-*de* in).

**saklambaç** hide-and-seek.

**saklanmak** *pass. or refl. of* saklamak, to hide (*or* conceal) o.s.

**saklı 1.** hidden, concealed; **2.** ♒ legally guaranteed (*right*).

**saksağan** *zo.* magpie.

**saksı** flowerpot.

**saksofon** ♪ saxophone.

**sal**, -lı raft.

**sala** *isl.* call to prayer *or* to a funeral.

**salacak** bench on which a corpse is washed.

**salah 1.** improvement; **2.** goodness, soundness; ~ bulmak to improve.

**salahiyet**, -ti authority, power, authorization; competence; ~ vermek to authorize.

**salahiyetli 1.** authoritative; competent

(-e for); **2.** authorized (-*meye* to *inf.*).

**salahiyetname** [. - - - .] credentials.

**salahiyettar** [. - - -] *s.* salahiyetli.

**salak** silly, doltish, dunderheaded, half-witted.

**salaklık** silliness, dunderheadedness.

**salam** salami.

**salamura** [. . x .] **1.** brine, pickle; **2.** pickled.

**salapurya** [. . x .] ⚓ small lighter.

**salaş** temporary wooden shed.

**salat**, -tı *isl.* ritual prayer.

**salata** [. x .] **1.** salad; **2.** lettuce.

**salatalık** cucumber.

**salavat**, -tı [. . -] *s.* salat.

**salbetmek** [x .] **1.** to hang; **2.** † to crucify.

**salça** [x .] tomato sauce (*or* paste).

**salçalı** gravied, covered with sauce.

**salçalık** sauceboat, gravy boat.

**saldırgan** aggressive, belligerent, truculent.

**saldırı** attack, assault; aggression.

**saldırmak 1.** to attack, to assault, to assail; to charge (at); to rush; **2.** ♒ to act (-e on); to dissolve.

**saldırmazlık** nonaggression; ~ antlaşması (*or* paktı) nonaggression treaty.

**salep**, -bi [ā] salep (*a.* ♥).

**salgı** *biol.* secretion.

**salgın 1.** epidemic (*disease*); **2.** epidemic, outbreak (*of a disease*); **3.** epidemic invasion (*of insects*); ~ hastalık epidemic disease.

**salhane** [. - .] slaughterhouse.

**salı** Tuesday.

**salık** advice; ~ vermek to advise, to recommend.

**salıncak 1.** swing; **2.** hammock.

**salıncaklı**: ~ koltuk rocking chair.

**salınım 1.** *phys.* oscillation; **2.** *ast.* libration of the moon.

**salınmak 1.** *pass. of* salmak; **2.** to sway; to oscillate; salına salına yürümek to walk along swaggeringly.

**salıntı 1.** swaying motion; **2.** swell, undulation (*of the sea*).

**salıvermek** to let go, to release, to set free.

**salih** [ā] **1.** suitable (*or* good) (-e for); **2.** authorized (-e to); **3.** ♀ *mf.*

**salim** [ā] **1.** healthy, sound; **2.** secure, safe.

**salip**, -bi [ī] cross.

**salkım 1.** bunch (*of grapes*); **2.** bunch, cluster; **3.** ♣ wisteria; ~ küpe ear pendant; ~ saçak hanging down in rags.

**salkımak** to hang down loosely.

salkımsı racemose.

salkımsöğüt ♀ weeping willow.

sallabaş afflicted with an involuntary shaking of the head.

sallamak 1. to swing, to shake, to rock; to wave, to wag; 2. to nod *(one's head)*; 3. to brandish *(sword)*; 4. *fig.* to put off, to postpone.

sallamamak *sl.* to pay no attention (-*i* to), not to care about.

sallandırmak 1. *caus.* of sallanmak; 2. F to hang, to make s.o. swing.

sallanmak 1. *pass. or refl.* of sallamak; 2. to sway, to swing; to wobble, to rock, to totter; 3. to be loose *(tooth)*; 4. *fig.* to fool around; 5. *fig.* to be about to get the sack.

sallantı swaying, swinging, rocking; -da bırakmak to leave up in the air.

sallasırt etm. to shoulder, to hoist onto one's shoulder(s).

salma 1. *vn.* of salmak; 2. a kind of stew with rice; 3. *hist.* policeman; 4. loft, cote; 5. running *(water)*.

salmak, (-ar) 1. to let go, to set free, to release; 2. to dispatch, to send; 3. to put forth *(or out)* *(roots)*; 4. to turn an animal out to graze; to direct, to channel (-*e* into); 5. to let attack, to turn loose (-*e* on); 6. to add (-*e* to); 7. to attack *(animal)*.

salmalık pasture.

salmastra [. x .] ⊕ gasket.

salon 1. hall; 2. drawing-room; ~ takımı drawing-room suite.

saloz *sl.* dunderheaded, stupid.

salpa loose, slack.

salt, -tı 1. mere, pure, simple; 2. simply, merely, solely; ~ çoğunluk absolute majority.

salta¹ [x .]: ~ durmak to stand on its hind legs *(dog)*.

salta² [x .] bolero.

saltanat, -tı 1. reign, sovereignty, rule, dominion; 2. sultanate; 3. *fig.* pomp, magnificence, splendo(u)r; ~ sürmek 1. to reign; 2. *fig.* to live in great splendo(u)r.

saltık absolute.

salvo [x .] salvo.

salya [x .] saliva; slaver, slobber, drool.

salyangoz zo. snail.

saman straw; chaff; ~ altından su yürütmek *fig.* to be as sly as a fox; ~ gibi insipid, tasteless; ~ nezlesi hay fever; ~ sarısı straw yellow.

samankâğıdı, -nı tracing paper.

samankapan amber.

samanlık hayloft, haymow.

samanrengi, -ni straw (yellow).

samanyolu, -nu *ast.* the Milky Way

samba samba.

Sami [ª] 1. Semite; 2. Semitic.

samia [- . .] ♀ hearing.

samimi [. - -] 1. intimate, close; 2. sincere, genuine; heartfelt.

samimiyet, -ti 1. intimacy, closeness, 2. sincerity.

samsa a kind of pastry.

samur *zo.* sable; ~ kaşlı having bushy eyebrows; ~ kürk sable fur.

samyeli, -ni samiel, simoom, sirocco.

san 1. repute, fame, reputation; 2. title, appellation.

sana to you; for you; ~ gelince as for you.

sanat, -tı 1. art; 2. trade, craft, skill; 3. craftsmanship, skill, craft; ~ eseri work of art; ~ filmi art film; ~ okulu trade *(or industrial)* school.

sanatçı, sanatkâr 1. artist; 2. craftsman, artisan.

sanatkârlık 1. artistry; 2. craftsmanship, artisanship.

sanatoryum sanatorium.

sanatsever art lover, lover of art.

sanayi, -ii [. . .] industry; ~ odası association of manufacturers.

sanayici industrialist.

sanayileşmek to become industrialized.

sanayileştirmek to industrialize.

sancak 1. flag, banner, standard; 2. ↓ starboard; 3. *hist.* sanjak, sub-province; ~ açmak to unfurl a flag.

sancakbeyi, -ni *hist.* governer of a sanjak.

sancaktar [. . -] standard-bearer.

sancı 1. pain, gripes, twinge, stitch; 2. labo(u)r pain, travail.

sancılanmak 1. to have a pain; 2. to have labo(u)r pains *(pregnant woman)*.

sancımak to ache, to twinge.

sandal¹ sandal.

sandal² sendal, brocade.

sandal³ sandalwood.

sandal⁴ rowboat.

sandalet, -ti sandal.

sandalye 1. chair; 2. *fig.* office, post; ~ kavgası struggle for a post; ~ sazı rush for caning chairs.

sandık 1. chest, trunk; 2. coffer, strongbox; 3. bank; credit union; 4. crate; ~ emini treasurer, cashier; ~ eşyası clothes, etc. *(kept in a bone chest)*; ~ lekesi stain made by mildew; ~ odası lumber room, storeroom; ~ sepet bag and baggage.

sandıklamak to box, to crate.

sanduka sarcophagus.

sandviç, -ci sandwich.

sanem idol.

sangı dazed, confused.

sanı supposition, surmise, imagination.

sanık ∴ suspect; accused.

sani [- -] second.

saniye [ā] second.

saniyelik [ā] taking a very short time.

sanki [x .] as if, as though; supposing that; sanki Fransızca'yı çok iyi bilirmiş gibi konuşuyor he speaks as if he knew French very well.

sanlı famous.

sanmak, (-ır) to suppose, to think, to imagine.

sanrı hallucination.

sanrılamak to hallucinate.

sansar zo. marten; ~ gibi sly.

sansasyon sensation.

sansasyonel sensational.

sansör censor.

sansür censorship; ~ etm. to censor.

sansürlemek to censor.

santigram centigram(me).

santigrat centigrade.

santilitre centilitre, Am. centiliter.

santim 1. centimetre, Am. centimeter; 2. centim ·.

santimetre [. . x .] centimetre, Am. centimeter.

santra sports: centre, Am. center.

santrafor s. santrfor.

santrahaf s. santrhaf.

santral, -li 1. switchboard, telephone exchange; 2. powerhouse; ~ memuru telephonist, (telephone) operator.

santrfor sports: centre forward, Am. center forward.

santrfüj 1 centrifuge; 2. centrifugal; ~ kuvvet phys. centrifugal force.

santrhaf sports: centre halfback, Am. center halfback.

santur ♪ dulcimer, santour.

santuri [. - -] ♪ dulcimer player.

sap, -pı 1. handle; 2. ♀ stem; stalk; 3. peduncle, pedicel; 4. sl. prick, cock, dick; -ına kadar to the backbone (or core).

sapa out-of-the-way (place); ~ düşmek to be off the beaten track.

sapak turning, turnoff.

sapaklık psych. abnormality.

sapan catapult. Am. slingshot.

sapanorya [. . x .] sl. very ugly.

saparta [. x .] ↓ broadside (a. fig.).

sapasağlam [x . . .] in the pink, very strong.

sapık 1. pervert; 2. perverted.

sapıklaşmak to become perverted.

sapıklık perversion.

sapır sapır: ~ dökülmek to rain down from every side; ~ titremek to shiver and shake.

sapıtmak 1. caus. of sapmak; 2. to go haywire (or nuts); 3. to talk crap, to drivel.

saplamak to stick (-e into), to thrust (-e into), to pierce (-e into).

saplanmak 1. pass. of saplamak; 2. to be fixed (or rooted) (-e to); 3. fig. to be obsessed (-e by), to be hipped (-e on).

saplantı fixed idea; obsession.

saplı 1. ...handled; 2. ♀ stemmed; stalked.

sapmak, (-ar) 1. to turn (-e to), to swerve (or veer) (-e to); 2. to deviate (or depart) (-den from); to digress (-den from); 3. to resort (-e to).

sapsağlam s. sapasağlam.

sapsarı [x . .] 1. bright yellow; 2. very pale (face).

saptamak 1. to fix, to determine, to establish; 2. to stabilize, to fix.

saptırmak 1. caus. of sapmak; 2. fig. to wrench, to distort (facts).

sara ♀ epilepsy; -sı tutmak to have an epileptic fit.

saraç, -cı saddler.

sarahat, -ti [. - .] clarity, clearness.

sarahaten [. - .] clearly.

sarak △ stringcourse.

saraka ridicule, mock; -ya almak to mock, to ridicule.

saralı epileptic.

sararmak 1. to turn yellow; 2. to pale, to grow (or turn) pale; sararıp solmak to pine away, to grow pale.

sarartmak to yellow.

saray 1. palace; 2. government house; ~ lokması a kind of sweet.

sardalye [. x .] zo. sardine, pilchard.

sardunya [. x .] ♀ geranium.

sarf 1. expenditure; 2. gr. morphology; ~ etm. 1. to spend (money); 2. to use up, to consume, to expend (time, effort); 3. to use (words).

sarfınazar apart from, regardless of; ~ etm. 1. to disregard, to overlook; 2. to relinquish, to give up.

sarfiyat, -tı [. - -] 1. expenditure, expenses, outgo; 2. consumption; wastage.

sargı bandage.

sargılı bandaged.

sarhoş 1. drunk, high, blotto, intoxicated;

2. *fig.* drunk *(with joy, etc.).*
**sarhoşluk** drunkenness, intoxication.
**sarı** 1. yellow; 2. blond; 3. yolk, yellow *(of an egg);* 4. ⊕ brass; 5. pale, wan, pallid *(face);* ~ çizmeli Mehmet Ağa *F* some Joe Doakes or other.
**sarıçalı** ✤ barberry.
**sarıçam** ✤ Scotch pine.
**sarığıburma** a sweet pastry.
**sarıhumma** ⚡ yellow fever.
**sarık** turban (cloth).
**sarıklı** turbaned.
**sarılgan** ✤ climbing, twining *(plant).*
**sarılı¹** 1. bandaged; 2. wrapped; 3. surrounded *(ile* by).
**sarılı²** mixed with yellow colo(u)r.
**sarılık** 1. yellowness; 2. ⚡ jaundice, icterus.
**sarılmak** 1. *pass. of* sarmak; 2. to embrace, to hug; 3. to coil *(or* twine) *(-e* around); 4. to cling *(-e* to), to hold fast *(-e* to); 5. to take up.
**sarımsak** s. sarmısak.
**sarımsı, sarımtırak** yellowish.
**sarınmak** to wrap o.s. up (-e in).
**sarısabır** 1. ✤ aloe; 2. aloes.
**sarışın** blond(e).
**sari** [- -] infectious, contagious *(disease).*
**sarih** [î] clear, explicit, evident.
**sarkaç** pendulum.
**sarkık** pendulous, flabby.
**sarkılmak** to hang down.
**sarkıntılık** molestation; ~ etm. to molest.
**sarkıt, -tı** *geol.,* △ stalactite.
**sarkıtmak** 1. *caus. of* sarkmak; 2. to dangle; to lower; 3. *sl.* to hang, to make s.o. swing.
**sarkmak** 1. to hang (down); to hang out; to lean out of *(a window);* to dangle; 2. to drop by; 3. to be left over.
**sarma** 1. *vn. of* sarmak; 2. *dish made of rice and meat wrapped up in grape leaves;* 3. *a wrestling maneuver.*
**sarmak,** (-ar) 1. to wrap up, to wind; to encircle; 2. to surround; 3. to bandage; 4. to wind *(or* coil) up; 5. to embrace; 6. to cover, to envelop; 7. to climb, to twine around *(vine);* 8. to infest *(insects);* 9. *F* to interest, to captivate; sarıp sarmalamak to wrap up.
**sarmal** spiral, helical.
**sarmalamak** to wrap up.
**sarmaş:** ~ dolaş olm. to be locked in a close embrace.
**sarmaşık** ✤ ivy.
**sarmaşmak** to embrace one another.
**sarmısak** ✤ garlic.

**sarnıç, -cı** 1. cistern; 2. tank; ~ gemisi tanker; ~ vagonu tank car.
**sarp, -pı** 1. steep, precipitous; 2. *fig.* difficult, hard; -a sarmak to become complicated.
**sarraf** moneychanger; moneylender.
**sarsak** shaky, quavery.
**sarsılmak** to be shaken *(or* jolted).
**sarsıntı** 1. shake, tremor, jolt; 2. *(brain)* concussion; 3. *psych.* shock.
**sarsmak,** (-ar) 1. to shake, to jolt, to jar; 2. to upset; to weaken *(one's health);* 3. to give a shock, to shock.
**sataşmak** to annoy, to tease, to provoke, to aggravate.
**saten** satin.
**sathi** [î] superficial, cursory; shallow.
**satı** sale; -ya çıkarmak to put up for sale.
**satıcı** seller; salesman; saleswoman; pedlar, *Am.* peddler.
**satıh, -thı** surface.
**satılık** for *(or* on) sale; satılığa çıkarmak to put up for sale.
**satım** sale.
**satın** almak to buy, to purchase.
**satır¹** line.
**satır²** chopper, cleaver; ~ atmak to slay.
**satırbaşı, -nı** paragraph indentation, head of a paragraph.
**satış** sale; ~ fiyatı selling price.
**satmak,** (-ar) 1. to sell; 2. to pretend, to put on a show of; 3. *sl. (b-ni)* to get rid of *s.o.;* satıp savmak to sell all one has.
**satranç, -cı** chess; ~ ~ checkered, checked; ~ tahtası chessboard; ~ taşı chessman; ~ turnuvası chess tournament.
**satrançlı** checkered, checked.
**Satürn** *ast.* Saturn.
**sauna** sauna.
**sav** 1. assertion, claim; 2. ⚖ indictment, allegation.
**savaş** 1. war, battle; 2. struggle, fight; ~ açmak to go to war *(-e* against), to start a war.
**savaşçı** warrior, combatant, fighter.
**savaşmak** to fight *(a. fig.),* to battle.
**savcı** public prosecutor; attorney general.
**savlet, -ti** assault, onslaught.
**savmak,** (-ar) 1. to get rid of, to dismiss, to drive away; 2. to get over *(an illness);* 3. to penetrate *(cold).*
**savruk** 1. inattentive, careless; 2. untidy, messy.
**savsak** 1. neglectful, negligent; 2. slipshod, careless.
**savsaklamak** 1. *(bsi)* to neglect *s.th.;* to put off *(doing s.th.);* 2. *(b-ni)* to put s.o.

off.

**savul!** gangway!, get out of the way!

**savulmak** to draw (or stand) aside, to get out of the way.

**savunma** defence, Am. defense.

**savunmak** to defend.

**sdvurgan** extravagant, wasteful, spendthrift, prodigal.

**savurganlık** extravange, prodigality.

**savurmak** 1. to throw, to fling, to hurl, to hurtle; 2. to winnow (grain); 3. to land (blow, kick); 4. to fling, to let fly (curse); 5. to brandish (sword); 6. to waste, to squander; 7. to bluster, to brag.

**savuşmak** 1. to slip away, to sneak off; 2. to pass (illness).

**savuşturmak** 1. to get rid of, to ward off; 2. to deflect, to parry (a blow).

**say** effort, work.

**saya** vamp.

**sayaç** meter, counter.

**saydam** transparent.

**saydamlık** transparency.

**saye** [ā] 1. shade, shadow; 2. protection, assistance, favo(u)r; -sinde thanks to; bu -de hereby, by this.

**sayfa** page; -yı çevirmek to turn over the leaf.

**sayfiye** summer resort (or house).

**saygı** respect, esteem; ~ göstermek to show respect, to pay tribute, to venerate, to revere; -larımla yours faithfully.

**saygıdeğer** estimable, venerable.

**saygılı** respectful.

**saygın** respected, esteemed.

**saygınlık** respect, esteem.

**saygısız** disrespectful.

**saygısızlık** disrespect(fulness).

**sayı** 1. number; 2. issue, number (of a magazine); 3. sports: point(s); 4. basketball: basket.

**sayıklamak** 1. to talk in one's sleep, to rave, to wander; 2. to dream (of s.th. longed for).

**sayılı** 1. numbered, counted; 2. limited; few and far between, 3. best, topnotch.

**sayım** enumeration, census, count.

**sayın** esteemed, hono(u)rable; dear (in a letter).

**sayısal** numerical.

**sayısız** countless, numberless, innumerable.

**Sayıştay** pr. n. the Government Accounting Bureau.

**saylav** s. mebus.

**saymak**, (-ar) 1. to count; 2. to respect, to value; 3. to consider, to take into

account; 4. to reckon, to deem, to regard, to look upon as; 5. to enumerate, to list.

**sayman** accountant.

**saz** 1. ♀ rush, reed; 2. ♪ musical instrument; 3. group of musicians; ~ benizli pale-faced; ~ şairi minstrel; ~ takımı group of musicians (who play traditional Turkish music).

**sazan** (balığı) zo. carp.

**sazlık** 1. rushy, reedy (place); 2. reedbed.

**se** dice: three.

**seans** 1. session, sitting; 2. performance (of a play); 3. treatment; 4. cards: game.

**sebat**, -tı [ā] perseverance, firmness, constancy; ~ etm. to persevere, to show resolution.

**sebatkâr** steady, constant, steadfast.

**sebebiyet**, -ti: ~ vermek to cause, to bring about.

**sebep**, -bi reason, cause; ~ olm. to bring about, to cause; -iyle because of, owing to.

**sebeplenmek** to get a share of the pie.

**sebepsiz** without any reason, causeless.

**sebil** [ī] 1. free distribution of water; 2. public fountain; ~ etm. 1. to distribute s.th. free; 2. fig. to ladle out.

**sebze** vegetable.

**sebzeci** vegetable seller.

**seccade** [ā] prayer rug.

**secde** prostrating o.s.; ~ etm. or -ye kapanmak or -ye varmak to prostrate o.s.

**seciye** character, disposition.

**seçenek** alternative.

**seçi** selection.

**seçici** selector; ~ kurul selection committee.

**seçim** pol. election; ~ bölgesi (or çevresi) election district; ~ sandığı ballot box.

**seçkin** select, choise, prominent.

**seçme** 1. vn. of seçmek; 2. select, choise, distinguished; -ler selections.

**seçmek**, (-er) 1. to choose, to select; 2. pol. to elect; 3. to perceive, to discern, to distinguish; 4. to be particular (or choosy) about.

**seçmeli** optional.

**seçmen** voter, elector; ~ kütüğü electoral roll.

**seda** 1. voice; 2. echo.

**sedalı** voiced, vocal.

**sedasız** voiceless, unvoiced.

**sedef** mother-of-pearl, nacre; ~ hastalığı ℟ psoriasis.

**sedefli** decorated with mother-of-pearl.

**sedir¹** divan.

**sedir²** ✻ cedar.
**sedrebeki** nonsense, rot.
**sedye** [x .] stretcher, litter.
**sefa** s. safa.
**sefahat,** -ti [ā] dissipation, debauch.
**sefalet,** -ti [ā] 1. poverty; 2. misery; ~ çekmek to suffer privation; -e düşmek to be reduced to poverty.
**sefaret,** -ti [ā] pol. 1. ambassadorship, envoyship; 2. embassy.
**sefarethane** [ā, ā] embassy, legation.
**sefer** 1. journey, voyage; 2. ✕ campaign, expedition; 3. time, occasion; bu ~ this time; on ~ ten times.
**seferber** mobilized (for war); ~ etm. to mobilize.
**seferberlik** mobilization.
**sefertası,** -nı travelling food box.
**sefih** [ī] dissolute, dissipated.
**sefil** [ī] 1. poor, miserable, destitute; 2. fig. mean, despicable.
**sefir** pol. ambassador; envoy.
**sefire** vol. ambassadress.
**seğirmek** to twitch.
**seher** 1. daybreak, dawn; 2. ♀ wf.
**sehpa** [ā] 1. coffee (or end) table; 2. tripod; 3. gallows; 4. easel; -ya çekmek to hang, to string up.
**sehven** [x .] by mistake.
**sek,** -ki dry, neat (wine).
**seki** 1. stone base; 2. doorsteps, stoop; 3. geol. terrace, bench.
**sekiz** eight.
**sekizer** eight apiece (or each); ~ ~ eight at a time.
**sekizgen** octagon.
**sekizinci** eighth.
**sekizli** 1. cards: the eight; 2. ♪ octet.
**sekizlik** ♪ eighth note.
**sekmek** 1. to hop; 2. to skip; 3. to ricochet.
**sekreter** secretary.
**sekreterlik** secretaryship.
**seks** sex; ~ filmi skin flick.
**seksek** hopscotch.
**seksen** eighty.
**sekseninci** eightieth.
**seksenlik** octogenarian.
**seksoloji** sexology.
**seksüel** sexual.
**sekte** stoppage, interruption, suspension, cessation; ~ vermek to cease, to come to a halt; ~ vurmak to put back, to interrupt, to impede.
**sektirmek** to cause to hop (or skip).
**sektör** sector.
**sel** flood, torrent, inundation.
**selam** 1. greeting, regards, salutation, hello; 2. ✕ salute; 3. ℉ hello!, hi!; ~ dur!

✕ present arms!; ~ etm. to send one's regards; ~ söylemek (or yollamak) to send (or give) one's regards (-e to), to say hello (-e to); ~ vermek to greet; -ı sabahı kesmek to break off relations (ile with).
**selamet,** -ti 1. security, safety; well-being; 2. healthiness, soundness; 3. salvation, deliverance; ~ bulmak to reach safety; -le 1. safe and sound; 2. God speed!
**selamlamak** 1. to greet; 2. ✕ to salute.
**selamlaşmak** to exchange greetings, to greet each other.
**selamlık** 1. the part of a Moslem house reserved for the men; 2. hist. public procession of the sultan to a mosque at noon on Fridays.
**selamünaleyküm** [. x .. x .] peace be with you; ~ demeden fig. without so much as by your leave.
**Selanik** pr. n. Salonika.
**selaset,** -ti fluency.
**Selçuk** Seljuk.
**sele** saddle, seat (of a bicycle).
**selef** predecessor.
**selektör** 1. selector; 2. mot. dimmer; ~ yapmak mot. to dim (or blink) the headlights.
**selfservis** self-service.
**selim** [ī] 1. sound, healthy; safe; 2. ✝ benign; 3. ♀ mf.
**selman** etm. sl. to beg.
**soleteyp** Scotch (or cellophane) tape.
**selp** etm. to destroy, to take away.
**selüloz** cellulose.
**selülozik** cellulosic.
**selvi** ✻ cypress.
**sema** [ā] 1. firmament, sky; 2. ♀ wf.
**semafor** semaphore.
**semahat,** -ti [. - .] 1. generosity; 2. ♀ wf.
**semai** [. - -] a poetic form.
**semantik** semantics.
**semaver** [ā] samovar, urn.
**semavi** [. - -] celestial, firmamental.
**sembol,** -lü symbol.
**sembolik** symbolic(al).
**sembolleştirmek** to symbolize.
**semen** corpulence, fatness.
**semer** 1. packsaddle; 2. stout, pad; 3. sl. buttocks; ~ vurmak to put a packsaddle (-e on).
**semere** fruit, outcome, consequence.
**semereli** fruitful.
**seminer** seminar.
**semirgin** fat and lazy.
**semirmek** to get (or grow) fat.
**semirtmek** to fatten.
**semiz** fat.

**semizlemek** s. semirmek.

**semizotu**, -nu ♃ purslane.

**sempati 1.** attraction, liking; **2.** psych. sympathy; ~ duymak to take to, to take kindly to; ~ sinirleri anat. sympathetic nerves.

**sempatik 1.** attractive, likable, simpatico; **2.** sympathetic.

**sempatizan** sympathizer.

**sempozyum** symposium.

**semt**, -ti **1.** neighbo(u)rhood, district, quarter; **2.** ast. azimuth; ~ ~ in every neighbo(u)rhood; -ine uğramamak to darken s.o.'s door(s).

**semtürreis**, -e'si ast. zenith.

**semum** [ü] simoom.

**sen** you; ~ de you too; -ce in your opinion; -den from you.

**sena** [â] praise; ~ etm. to praise.

**senarist**, -ti scenarist, script-writer.

**senaryo** [.x.] scenario, screenplay, script.

**senaryocu** s. senarist.

**senato** [.x.] senate.

**senatör** senator.

**senatörlük** senatorship.

**sendelemek 1.** to stagger, to totter, to lurch, to reel; **2.** fig. to be shocked, to be taken aback.

**sendik** ∮∿ receiver.

**sendika** trade (or labour) union.

**sendikacı** trade unionist.

**sendikacılık** trade unionism.

**sendikalaştırmak** to unionize.

**sene** year; 1961 -sinde in the year 1961.

**senelik 1.** lasting... years; **2.** yearly, annual; **3.** annual payment.

**senet** voucher; security; promissory note; ~ vermek fig. to guarantee.

**senetli** certified.

**senevi** [î] yearly, annual.

**senfoni** symphony.

**seni** acc. of sen, you; ~ it oğlu it! sl. you bastard!

**senin** gen. of sen, your; ~ için for you; -le with you.

**seninki** yours.

**senlibenli** familiar, intimate, free-and-easy; ~ olm. to be hail-fellow-well-met (ile with).

**sentaks** syntax.

**sentetik** synthetic.

**sentez** synthesis.

**sepet**, -ti **1.** basket; **2.** sidecar (of a motorcycle); ~ havası çalmak (b-ne) sl. to give s.o. the boot.

**sepetlemek 1.** to basket; **2.** sl. to send s.o. packing; to fire.

**sepettopu**, -nu basketball.

**sepilemek** to tan (a hide).

**sepmek** to sprinkle; to scatter.

**septik** skeptical.

**septisemi** ♀ septicemia.

**ser 1.** head; **2.** summit, top; ~ verip sır vermemek to die rather than disclose a secret.

**ser(a)** greenhouse, hothouse, conservatory.

**seramik 1.** ceramics; **2.** ceramic.

**seramikçi** ceramist, ceramicist.

**serap**, -bı [â] mirage.

**serasker** hist. Minister of War.

**serazat**, -dı [. - -] † unrestricted, free.

**serbest**, -ti **1.** free, independent, unrestricted; **2.** unconstrained; unconfined; **3.** open, unobstructed; ~ bırakmak to set free, to free, to release; ~ bölge free zone; ~ güreş catch-as-catch-can (wrestling); ~ meslek sahibi self-employed person.

**serbesti** [î] s. serbestlik.

**serbestlik 1.** freedom; independence; **2.** unconstrainedness.

**serçe** zo. sparrow.

**serçeparmak** little finger.

**serdar** [â] commander-in-chief.

**serdengeçti** who sacrifices his life.

**serdetmek** [x..] to put forward, to assert.

**serdümen** ⚓ **1.** helmsman; **2.** quartermaster.

**seremoni** ceremony.

**seren** ⚓ yard; boom.

**serenat** serenade.

**serencam** [â] **1.** conclusion, end; **2.** occurrence, adventure.

**sereserpe:** ~ yatmak to sprawl.

**sergi 1.** exhibition, show, display; **2.** mat, rug.

**sergilemek** to exhibit, to display, to put on display.

**sergin 1.** laid (or spread) out; **2.** bedridden, bedfast; ~ vermek to lie sick in bed.

**sergüzəşt**, -ti adventure.

**serhat**, -ddi frontier, border.

**seri¹** series; ~ bağlama ∮ series connection; ~ imalat mass production.

**seri²**, -li [î] swift, quick, speedy, rapid.

**serilmək 1.** pass. of sermek; **2.** to sprawl o.s. out.

**serin** cool; chill(y).

**serinkanlı** cool-headed, imperturbable.

**serinlemek 1.** to cool off, to get cool; **2.** fig. to feel relieved.

**serinleşmek** to cool off, to get cool (or

chilly).

**serinlik 1.** coolness; **2.** cool(ness), chill-(iness).

**serj** serge.

**serkeş** rebellious, unruly.

**serlevha** title, heading.

**sermaye** [ā] **1.** capital; **2.** cost price; production cost; **3.** *fig.* wealth; **4.** *sl.* prostitute; ~ koymak to invest capital (-e in).

**sermayedar** [ā] capitalist.

**sermek,** (-er) **1.** to spread, to lay; **2.** (işi) to neglect *(one's job)*; **3.** (yere) to beat down to the ground.

**sermest,** -ti drunk.

**serpantin** serpentine *(a. geol.)*

**serpelemek** to sprinkle down.

**serpilmek 1.** *pass.* of serpmek; **2.** *(for a child)* to grow.

**serpinti 1.** sprinkle, drizzle *(of rain);* **2.** spray; **3** vestiges.

**serpiştirmek 1.** *(yağmur)* to drizzle, to mizzle, to sprinkle down; **2.** *(kar)* to spit down; **3.** to scatter, to sprinkle.

**serpme** i. *vn.* of serpmek; **2.** scattered about; **3.** cast net.

**serpmek 1.** to sprinkle, to scatter; **2.** *s.* serpiştirmek 1, 2.

**serpuş** [ū] headgear.

**sersefil** very miserable.

**sersem 1.** stunned, dazed; **2.** scatterbrained, silly, muddleheaded; ~ etm. *(or* -e çevirmek)* to daze, to stupefy.

**sersemlemek 1.** to become dazed *(or* stupefied)*; **2.** to become muddleheaded.

**sersemletmek 1.** to daze, to stupefy, to stun; **2.** to confuse, to addle.

**serseri 1.** vagrant, vagabond, tramp, hobo; **2.** good-for-nothing, ne'er-do-well, loafer, bum, layabout; ~ kurşun stray bullet; ~ mayın floating mine.

**serserilik** vagrancy, vagabondage.

**sert,** -ti **1.** hard, tough; **2.** harsh, severe, rough; **3.** potent, strong; pungent; ~ konuşmak to speak harshly.

**sertabip,** -bi head doctor.

**sertifika** certificate.

**sertleşmek 1.** to harden, to toughen; to harshen; **2.** to turn bad *(weather)*.

**sertleştirmek** to harden, to toughen; to harshen.

**sertlik 1.** hardness, toughness; **2.** harshness, severeness.

**serum** ? serum.

**serüven** adventure.

**servet,** -ti **1.** wealth, riches, fortune; **2.** ♀ *mf., wf.;* -e konmak to come into a fortune.

**servetli** wealthy.

**servi** ş. selvi.

**servis 1.** service *(a. sports);* **2.** service charge; **3.** department, section; ~ atmak *sports:* to serve the ball; ~ yapmak **1.** to serve food (-e to); **2.** *sports:* to serve the ball.

**serzeniş** reproach.

**ses 1.** sound; **2.** voice; **3.** noise; ~ çıkarmak **1.** to voice one's opinion; **2.** to say s.th.; ~ çıkarmamak **1.** to raise no objection. to condone; **2.** to keep quiet; ~ düşmesi hyphaeresis; ~ etm. to shout (-e to), to call; ~ seda yok not a sound is heard; -i ayyuka çıkmak to shout to high heaven; -i çıkmaz taciturn; -ini kesmek **1.** *(kendi)* to shut *(or* clam) up; **2.** *(b-nin)* to shut s.o. up; -ini kısmak to turn down.

**sesbilgisi,** -ni phonetics.

**sesbilim** phonology.

**sescil** phonetic.

**seslemek** to give ear, to hearken.

**seslendirmek 1.** *caus.* of seslenmek; **2.** to dub.

**seslenmek 1.** to call out (-e to); **2.** to address, to speak (-e to).

**sesli 1.** voiced; **2.** *gr.* vowel; ~ film sound motion picture, talkie.

**sessiz 1.** silent, quiet; **2.** taciturn; **3.** *gr.* consonant; ~ film **1.** silent movie; **2.** F charades.

**sessizlik** silence, quietness.

**set¹,** -ti *sports:* set.

**set²,** -ddi dam, dyke, dike, levee; wall; ~ çekmek to dike.

**setir,** -tri hiding, concealing.

**setretmek** [x ..] to hide, to conceal; to cover.

**sevap,** -bı [ā] **1.** good deed; **2.** merit, reward, credit; ~ işlemek *(or* kazanmak)* to acquire merit; sevaba girmek to acquire merit in God's sight.

**sevda** [ā] love, passion; ~ çekmek to be passionately in love.

**sevdalanmak** [ā] to fall in love (-e with), to lose one's heart (-e to).

**sevdalı** [ā] lovesick.

**sevdiceğim** my darling.

**sevecen** compassionate, kind.

**sevgi** love, affection.

**sevgili 1.** darling, dear, beloved; **2.** sweetheart, beloved; **3.** dear *(in a letter)*.

**sevici** lesbian.

**sevicilik** lesbianism.

**sevimli** lovable, cute; likable.

**sevimsiz** unlovable; unlikable.

**sevinç**, -ci delight, joy, pleasure.
**sevinçli** joyful.
**sevindirmek** to please, to delight, to rejoice.
**sevinmek** to be pleased (-e with), to feel glad, to rejoice.
**sevişmek** 1. to make love; 2. to love each other.
**seviye** 1. level, plane; 2. standing, footing, level.
**sevk**, -kı 1. sending; 2. impulse; 3. dispatch; ~ etm. 1. to send; 2. to ship; to dispatch; ~ ve idare management, conduct.
**sevkıyat**, -tı [â] 1. dispatch (of troops); 2. consignment (of goods).
**sevkulceyş** ✕ strategy.
**sevmek**, (-er) 1. to love; to like; 2. to caress, to fondle; seve seve willingly.
**seyahat**, -ti [.-.] journey, travel, trip; voyage; ~ acentesi travel agency; ~ çeki traveler's cheque; ~ etm. to travel; -e çıkmak to go on a trip.
**seyahatname** [.-.-.] travel book.
**seyek** dice: three and one.
**seyelan** flow; ~ etm. to flow.
**seyir**, -yri 1. course, progress; movement; 2. show, spectacle; 3. onlooking, observation; ~ jurnalı ⚓ log(book); ~ yeri place of amusement; seyre çıkmak to go for a walk or ride.
**seyirci** spectator, onlooker, viewer; ~ kalmak to stand on the sidelines.
**seyis** stableman, groom, hostler.
**Seylan** pr. n. Ceylon.
**seylap**, -bı flood.
**seyran** [â] 1. outing; promenade; 2. observation, onlooking; ~ etm. to make an excursion.
**seyrek** 1. widely set; 2. sparse; 3. rare, uncommon, seldom.
**seyrekleşmek, seyrelmek** 1. to thin out (or down); to become sparse; 2. to become infrequent.
**seyretmek** [x..] 1. to watch, to look at, to see; 2. to progress, to proceed; 3. to develop (illness).
**seyrüsefer** traffic.
**seyyah** [â] travel(l)er, tourist.
**seyyal**, -li [â] fluid.
**seyyar** [â] 1. itinerant, peripatetic; 2. movable, portable; mobile; ~ satıcı pedlar, Am. peddler, hawker.
**seyyare** [â] ast. planet.
**seyyie** 1. wickedness; 2. sin.
**Sezar** pr. n. Caesar; -ın hakkını -a vermek to render to Caesar the things that are Caesar's.

**sezaryen** ⚕ cesarean.
**sezdirmek** to cause to sense, to imply.
**sezgi** intuition.
**sezi** s. sezgi.
**sezin(le)mek** to sense, to feel, to anticipate.
**sezmek**, (-er) to sense, to perceive, to discern, to feel, to anticipate.
**sezon** season.
**sfenks** sphinx.
**sıcacık** [x..] warm and cosy.
**sıcak** 1. hot, warm (a. fig.); 2. heat; ~ dalgası heat-wave; ~ tutmak to keep warm; sıcağı sıcağına while the iron is hot.
**sıcakkanlı** 1. warmblooded (animal); 2. fig. friendly, companionable, genial.
**sıcaklık** warmth, heat.
**sıçan** zo. rat; mouse.
**sıçandişi**, -ni hemstitch.
**sıçankırı**, -nı mouse-gray.
**sıçankuyruğu**, -nu rattail file.
**sıçanotu**, -nu arsenic.
**sıçanyolu**, -nu sewer.
**sıçmak** sl. to shit.
**sıçrama** 1. vn. of sıçramak; 2. jump; ~ tahtası springboard; diving board.
**sıçramak** 1. to jump, to leap, to spring; 2. to be startled, to start; 3. to splash; to spatter.
**sıçratmak** 1. to splash; to spatter, to splatter; 2. to startle.
**sıdık**, -dkı 1. truth; 2. sincerity; sıdkı sıyrılmak (b-den) to lose faith in s.o.
**sıfat**, -tı 1. capacity, position, role; 2. gr. adjective; 3. F appearance; face; 4. F title, honorific; -ıyle in the capacity of, as.
**sıfır** 1. zero; naught; nil; 2. fig. nothing; -dan başlamak to start from scratch (or square one).
**sığ** shallow.
**sığa** phys. capacity.
**sığamak** to roll up.
**sığdırmak** caus. of sığmak, part. to make s.th. fit (-e into).
**sığınak** shelter, bunker.
**sığınmak** to take shelter (-e in), to shelter.
**sığır** cattle; ~ eti beef.
**sığırcık** zo. starling.
**sığırtmaç** herdsman, herder, drover.
**sığışmak** to squeeze o.s. (-e into).
**sığıştırmak** to squeeze (-e into).
**sığlık** 1. shallowness; 2. shallow.
**sığmak**, (-ar) to fit (-e into).
**sıhhat**, -ti 1. health; 2. soundness, correctness; -inize! to your health!, cheers!; -ler olsun! good health to you!; -te bu-

lunmak to be in good health.
**sıhhatli** healthy.
**sıhhi** [i] 1. hygienic, sanitary; health...;
2. wholesome, salubrious, healthful.
**sıhhiye** sanitary matters.
**sıhhiyeci** 1. public health official; 2. X
medic.
**sıhriyet**, -ti affinity.
**sık** 1. dense, thick; 2. close; 3. frequent;
~ ~ frequently, often.
**sıkboğaz etm.** (b-ni) to keep on at s.o., to
push s.o., to importune s.o.
**sıkı** 1. tight; firm; 2. close (weave); 3.
tightly; 4. strict; 5. stingy, closefisted;
~ basmak to put one's foot down; ~ çalışmak to work hard; ~ fıkı 1. intimate;
2. on intimate terms, palsy-walsy; ~
tutmak 1. to hold tightly; 2. fig. to do
with care; ~ya koymak (b-ni) to urge
s.o., to push s.o.; -yı yemek to get it in
the neck.
**sıkıca** tightly.
**sıkıcı** boring, tiresome, irksome, tedious,
bothersome, wearisome.
**sıkılamak** 1. to wad; 2. fig. to put pressure on.
**sıkılgan** shy, timid, bashful.
**sıkılganlık** shyness, bashfulness.
**sıkılık** tightness.
**sıkılmak** 1. pass. of sıkmak; 2. to get
bored; 3. to feel embarrassed; 4. to be
pushed for money.
**sıkılmaz** shameless, brazen.
**sıkım** 1. squeeze; 2. fistful.
**sıkınmak** to restrain o.s.
**sıkıntı** 1. trouble, difficulty, distress;
worry, annoyance; 2. boredom; 3. financial straits; ~ çekmek 1. to have (or
experience) difficulty; 2. to experience
distress; ~ vermek to annoy, to bother;
to worry; -da olm. to be in straits, to be
on the rocks; ~ya gelememek to be unable to stand the gaff.
**sıkıntılı** 1. troubled; out of sorts; worried;
2. worrisome, difficult.
**sıkışık** 1. tight; jammed; congested; 2.
hard up (for money); 3. pushed (for
time).
**sıkışmak** 1. to be pressed together; to be
congested; 2. to be hard up (for money);
3. to be pinched (-e in), to get caught (-e
in); 4. to be taken short.
**sıkıştırmak** caus. of sıkışmak, part. 1. to
tighten, to compress; 2. to squeeze,
to crowd, to jam, to wedge; 3. to pinch,
to squeeze; 4. to catch, to pinch (one's
finger) (-e in); 5. to press, to pressure.
**sıkıt¹**, -tı abortus.

**sıkıt²**, -tı 👃 tablet.
**sıkıyönetim** martial law.
**sıklaşmak** to happen often, to become
frequent.
**sıklet**, -ti 1. weight; 2. fig. burden; ~ vermek to bore, to depress.
**sıklık** 1. frequency; 2. density.
**sıkmak**, (-ar) 1. to squeeze, to press; 2. to
tighten 3. to wring; 4. to bother, to annoy; 5. to fire, to shoot (bullet).
**sıla** reunion; -ya gitmek to go home.
**sımak**, (-ar) to break.
**sımsıkı** very tight.
**sınai** [. - -] industrial; ~ kuruluş industrial enterprise.
**sınamak** to test, to try out.
**sınav** examination, test; ~ vermek to pass
a test; -a girmek to take (or sit for or go
in for) an examination.
**sındı** scissors.
**sınıf** 1. class (a. zo., ♦), category; 2.
classroom; 3. X corps; ~ arkadaşı class-
mate; -ta kalmak (or çakmak) to fail, to
flunk.
**sınıflamak, sınıflandırmak** to classify.
**sınık** 1. broken; 2. defeated; 3. scattered.
**sınır** frontier, border.
**sınırdaş** bordering.
**sınırdışı etm.** to deport.
**sınırlamak, sınırlandırmak** to limit.
**sınırlı** limited, restricted.
**sınırsız** limitless, boundless, unlimited.
**sınmak** pass. of sımak 1. to get broken;
2. to be scattered; 3. to be defeated.
**sıpa** 1. colt, foal; 2. P = sehpa.
**sır¹** glaze.
**sır²**, -rrı secret; mystery; ~ küpü pussyfooter; ~ saklamak (or tutmak) to keep
a secret; -ra kadem basmak co. to vanish
into thin air.
**sıra** 1. row, line; queue; file; 2. turn; 3.
order, sequence; 4. desk; 5. bench; 6.
moment, time, point; ~ bızım! it's our
turn!; ~ evler row houses; ~ malı run-
-of-the-mill things; ~ ~ in rows; -dan
ordinary; -sı değil this isn't the right
time; -sı gelmişken by the way; -sıyla
respectively.
**sıraca** ⚕ scrofula.
**sıradağ(lar)** mountain range, chain of
mountains.
**sıralamak** 1. to arrange in rows, to line
up; 2. to enumerate, to tick off; 3. to file,
to arrange; 4. (for a child) to begin to
walk (by holding on to one thing after
another).
**Sırbistan** pr. n. Serbia.
**sırça** glass; ~ köşkte oturan başkasına

*(or* komşusuna) taş atmamalı *pro.* people who live in glass houses should not throw stones.

**sırdaş** confidant.

**sırf 1.** pure, utter; **2.** only.

**sırık** pole; stake; ~ gibi lanky; -la atlama *sports:* pole vaulting.

**sırılsıklam** [. x . .] *s.* sırsıklam.

**sırım** whipcord, thong, strap; ~ gibi wiry.

**sırıtkan** given to grinning.

**sırıtmak 1.** to grin; **2.** *fig.* to show up, to come out.

**sırlamak 1.** to glaze; **2.** to silver *(a mirror).*

**sırlı 1.** glazed; **2.** silvered *(mirror).*

**sırma 1.** silver thread; **2.** ✕ stripes; ~ saçlı golden-haired.

**sırnaşık** saucy, pert, pertinacious.

**sırnaşmak** to importune.

**Sırp** *pr. n.* Serb(ian).

**sırrolmak** [x . .] to vanish into thin air.

**sırsıklam** [x . .] soaking *(or* sopping *or* wringing) wet; ~ âşık madly in love; ~ olm. to get wet through, to be soaked to the skin.

**sırt, -**tı **1.** back; **2.** ridge *(of a hill, etc.);* **3.** the blunt side *(of a knife, etc.);* ~ çantası knapsack, rucksack; ~ çevirmek *(b-ne)* to turn one's back on *s.o.,* to give *s.o.* the cold shoulder; ~ omurları *anat.* dorsal vertebrae; ~ -a vermek **1.** to stand back to back; **2.** *fig.* to support each other; ~ üstü on one's back; -ı kaşınmak to ask for it, to itch for a beating; -ı pek warmly clad; -ı yere gelmek *fig.* to bite the dust; -ına almak **1.** to shoulder; **2.** to put on; -ından çıkarmak *(b-nin)* to saddle *s.o.* with the bill for; -ından geçinmek *(b-nin)* to sponge on *s.o.,* to live off *s.o.;* -ını dayamak *(b-ne) fig.* to have *s.o.* at one's back.

**sırtarmak 1.** to get one's dander *(or* hackles) up; **2.** to mass, to pile up *(clouds).*

**sırtlamak** to shoulder.

**sırtlan** *zo.* hyena.

**sıska** puny, thin and weak, scrawny.

**sıtma** ♂ malaria; ~ görmemiş ses rich and deep voice; ~ tutmak to get malaria.

**sıtmalı** malarious, malarial.

**sıva** plaster.

**sıvacı** plasterer.

**sıvalamak** to plaster.

**sıvalı 1.** plastered; **2.** rolled up *(sleeves, etc.).*

**sıvamak 1.** to plaster; **2.** to smear *(-e* on); **3.** to roll up *(sleeves, etc.).*

**sıvanmak 1.** *pass. of* sıvamak; **2.** *(bir işe)* to roll up one's sleeves and set to doing

*s.th.*

**sıvaşmak 1.** to get smeared *(-e* on); **2.** *fig.* to get sticky *(or* gooey).

**sıvazlamak** to stroke, to pet, to caress.

**sıvı** liquid, fluid.

**sıvık 1.** sticky; **2.** *sl.* importunate.

**sıvılaştırmak** to liquefy.

**sıvırya** [. x .] continually.

**sıvışık 1.** sticky, gooey; **2.** *fig.* troublesome.

**sıvışmak** to slip *(or* run) away, to sneak off, to take to one's heels.

**sıyanet, -ti** [â] protection; ~ etm. to protect.

**sıyga** *gr.* mood; -ya çekmek *F* to cross-examine.

**sıyırmak 1.** to graze, to scrape, to skin; **2.** to strip *(or* peel *or* take) off; **3.** to pick *(or* gnaw) clean *(bone);* **4.** to draw *(a sword);* **5.** *fig.* to get *s.o.* out of *(a predicament).*

**sıyrık 1.** graze, scrape; **2.** grazed, scraped; **3.** *fig.* brazen.

**sıyrılmak 1.** *pass. of* sıyırmak; **2.** *(bşden)* to get shut of *s.th.,* to squeak through *s.th.*

**sıyrıntı 1.** scrapings; **2.** strip of cloth.

**sızdırmak 1.** *caus. of* sızmak, *part.* to leak; **2.** *fig.* to squeeze *(or* wangle) money out of *s.o.,* to extort money from *s.o.*

**sızdırmaz** leakproof.

**sızı** ache, pain.

**sızıltı** complaint; discontent.

**sızım sızım:** ~ sızlamak to ache intensely.

**sızıntı** leakage, ooze; seepage; ~ yapmak to leak.

**sızlamak 1.** to hurt, to ache; **2.** *s.* sızlanmak.

**sızlanmak** to complain, to moan, to lament.

**sızmak,** (-ar) **1.** to leak, to ooze, to trickle, to exude; **2.** to leak out *(secret);* **3.** ✕ to infiltrate; **4.** to pass out *(after getting drunk).*

**si** ♪ ti.

**Sibirya** *pr. n.* Siberia.

**sicil 1.** register; **2.** dossier, employment record, file.

**sicilli 1.** registered; **2.** *fig.* previously convicted.

**Sicilya** *pr. n.* Sicily.

**sicim** string, twine, packthread.

**sidik** urine; ~ borusu ureter; ~ söktürücü diuretic; ~ torbası *anat.* bladder; ~ yarışı *iro.* futile rivalry.

**sidikli** enuretic.

**sidikyolu,** -nu urethra.

sidikzoru, -nu dysuria.

sif † C.I.F. *(cost, insurance and freight).*

sifon 1. siphon; 2. flush tank.

sifos *sl.* useless.

siftah 1. first sale of the day; handsel; 2. for the first time.

sigara cigarette; ~ içmek to smoke; ~ kâğıdı cigarette paper; ~ tablası ashtray; -yı bırakmak to give up smoking.

sigaralık 1. cigarette-holder; 2. cigarette box.

sigorta [. x .] 1. insurance; 2. ✄ fuse; ~ etm. to insure; ~ olm. to be insured; ~ poliçesi insurance policy; ~ şirketi insurance company.

sigortacı [. x . .] insurer, insurance agent, underwriter.

sigortalamak to insure.

sigortalı [. x . .] insured.

sigorya [. x .] *sl.* by all means.

sigil wart.

sihir, -hri magic, sorcery, witchcraft; charm.

sihirbaz magician, sorcerer.

sihirlemek to bewitch.

sihirli 1. bewitched, enchanted; 2. magical; 3. charming, bewitching.

sik *sl.* cock, dick, prick, penis.

sikişmek *sl.* to fuck, to screw.

sikke coin.

siklamen ✿ cyclamen.

siklememek *sl.* not to give a fuck *(or shit or damn).*

siklon cyclone.

sikmek, (-er) *sl.* to fuck, to screw.

siktir! *sl.* fuck off!

silah weapon, arm; ~ atmak to fire a weapon: ~ başına! ✗ to arms!; ~ çekmek to draw *(or pull out)* a weapon; ~ omuza! ✗ shoulder arms!; -a davranmak *(or* sarılmak) to go for a weapon.

silahendaz [. . . - .] ✗ marine.

silahhane [. . . - .] armo(u)ry, arsenal.

silahlamak, silahlandırmak to arm.

silahlı armed; ~ kuvvetler armed forces.

silahsız unarmed.

silahsızlandırmak to disarm.

silahsızlanma *pol.* disarmament.

silahşor man-at-arms, musketeer.

silecek 1. bath towel; 2. *mot.* windscreen *(or Am.* windshield) wiper.

silgi 1. eraser, duster; 2. rubber, eraser; 3. doormat; 4. mop; 5. *s.* silecek 2.

silgiç *neol. s.* silecek 2.

silik 1. indistinct; rubbed out, worn; 2. *fig.* colo(u)rless.

silikat, -tı silicate.

silikon silicone.

silindir 1. cylinder; 2. road roller; ~ şapka top hat.

silindiraj rolling.

silinmek 1. *pass. of* silmek; 2. to wipe o.s. dry, to rub o.s.

silinti wipings.

silis silica.

silkelemek 1. to shake (out); 2. *sl.* to drop off.

silkinmek 1. *(bşden)* to rid o.s. of *s.th.;* 2. to shake o.s.

silkinti start.

silkişmek to shake itself.

silkmek, (-er) 1. to shake (out); 2. to shrug *(one's shoulders).*

sille 1. slap, box, cuff; 2. *fig.* buffet; ~ atmak to slap, to cuff.

silme 1. *vn. of* silmek; 2. ⚒ mo(u)lding; 3. full to the brim.

silmek, (-er) 1. to wipe (up), 2. to dry; 3. to rub out, to erase; 4. to clean, to rub; silip süpürmek 1. to clean from stem to stern; 2. to polish off, to put away, to end *(or* finish) off.

silo [x .] silo.

silsile 1. chain, series; 2. ancestry, lineage; 3. (mountain) range.

silsilename [ᵃ] genealogical tree.

siluet, -ti silhouette.

sim silver.

sima [- -] 1. face; 2. figure, personage.

simetri symmetry.

simetrik symmetrical.

simge symbol, embodiment *(a. fig.).*

simgelemek to symbolize.

simgesel symbolical.

simit, -di 1. cracknel *(in the shape of a ring);* 2. ⬇ life buoy *(or* ring).

simitçi seller *or* maker of simits.

simsar [ᵃ] broker, middleman, commission agent.

simsariye [ᵃ] brokerage, commission.

simsiyah [x . .] jet-black, pitch-dark, pitch-black.

simya [ᵃ] alchemy.

simyager [ᵃ] alchemist.

sin¹ grave, tomb.

sin², -nni age.

sinagog synagogue.

sinameki [ᵃ] ✿ senna; ~ gibi tiresome and persnickety *(person).*

sinara [. x .] fishhook.

sinarit, -ti *zo.* dentex.

sincabi [. - -] dark gray.

sincap, -bı *zo.* squirrel.

sindirim digestion; ~ sistemi digestive system.

sindirmek *caus. of* sinmek, *part.* 1. to di

**gest**; 2. to cow, to intimidate.

**sine** breast, bosom; ~ye çekmek to take s.th. lying down.

**sinek** 1. (nouse)fly; 2. *cards:* club; ~ avlamak to potter about, to twiddle one's thumbs.

**sinekkaydı** very close *(shave)*.

**sineklik** flyswatter.

**sineksiklet**, -ti featherweight class.

**sinema** cinema, the pictures, the movies.

**sinemacı** 1. moviemaker; 2. movie distributor; 3. cinema actor *or* actress.

**sinemasever** movie fan *(or* buff).

**sinemaskop** cinemascope.

**sini** round metal tray.

**sinik¹** crouching.

**sinik²** cynical.

**sinir** 1. nerve; 2. sinew, tendon; 3. P quirk; 4. P equanimity; ~ argınlığı neurasthenia; ~ harbi war of nerves; -ine dokunmak *(b-nin)* to give *s.o.* the pip, to get on *one's* nerves.

**sinirlendirmek** to irritate, to make nervous.

**sinirlenmek** to get nervous, to become irritated, to get in a state.

**sinirli** 1. nervous, edgy; quick-tempered, angry; 2. tendinous, sinewy.

**sinirsel** neural.

**sinmek**, (-er) 1. to crouch down, to cower; 2. to penetrate, to pervade.

**sinonim** 1. synonym; 2. synonymous.

**sinsi** stealthy, insidious, sly.

**sinsice** slyly, stealthily, insidiously.

**sinüs** 1. Ⓐ sine; 2. *anat.* sinus.

**sinüzit**, -ti sinusitis.

**sinyal**, -li 1. signal; 2. *mot.* indicator light; ~ vermek to signal.

**sipahi** [. - -] *hist.* cavalry soldier.

**sipariş** [ā] order; ~ almak to receive an order; ~ etm. (*or* vermek) to order, to place an order.

**siper** 1. ✕ trench, foxhole; 2. shelter; shield; 3. visor, peak, bill *(of a cap)*; ~ almak to take shelter; ~ etm. to use as a shield; -e almak to take under one's protection.

**siperisaika** [. . . - . .] lightning rod.

**siperlenmek** ✕ to take shelter.

**siperlik** 1. canopy; awning; 2. visor, peak, bill *(of a cap)*.

**sipsi** 1. ♩ boatswain's whistle; 2. *sl.* cigarette, fag.

**sipsivri** [x . .] very sharp; ~ kalmak to be deserted by everyone.

**sirayet**, -ti [ā] propagation, contagion, infection; ~ etm. to spread.

**siren** siren, hooter.

**sirk**, -ki circus.

**sirkat**, -ti theft.

**sirke¹** vinegar.

**sirke²** nit.

**sirkülasyon** circulation.

**sirküler** circular.

**siroz** ⚕ cirrhosis.

**sirrus** [x .] *meteor.* cirrus.

**sirto** [x .] a dance.

**sis** fog, mist, haze; ~ basmak *(for the fog)* to come in; ~ bombası smoke bomb; ~ düdüğü foghorn; ~ lambası fog light *(or* lamp).

**Sisam** *pr. n.* Samos.

**sislenmek** 1. *pass. of* sislemek; 2. to get foggy.

**sisli** foggy, misty, hazy.

**sismograf** seismograph.

**sistem** system.

**sistematik** systematic.

**sistemleştirmek** to systematize.

**sistemli** 1. systematic; 2. systematically.

**sistemsiz** 1. unsystematic; 2. unsystematically.

**sistit**, -ti ⚕ cystitis.

**sitayiş** [ā] praise; ~ etm. to praise.

**sitayişkâr** [ā] laudatory, praiseful.

**site** 1. housing estate *(or* development), building, complex; 2. *hist.* city-state.

**sitem** reproach; ~ etm. to reproach.

**sitemkâr, sitemli** reproachful.

**sitil** large bucket.

**sittinsene** donkey's years.

**sivil** 1. civilian; 2. in civilian clothes, in mufti; 3. F stark naked, in the altogether; ~ polis plainclothes policeman.

**sivilce** pimple, pustule.

**sivilceli** pimply, pimpled.

**sivişmek** *s.* sıvışmak.

**sivri** sharp; ~ akıllı eccentric.

**sivribiber** ♦ hot pepper.

**sivrilmek** 1. to become pointed; 2. *fig.* to stand out.

**sivriltmek** to sharpen, to point.

**sivrisinek** *zo.* mosquito.

**siya** [x .] ↓ rowing backwards; ~ ~ gitmek *fig.* to backwater.

**siyah** 1. black; 2. dark; 3. Negro, Black; 4. *typ.* boldface *(letter)*; 5. *sl.* opium; ~ beyaz black-and-white.

**siyahımsı, siyahımtırak** blackish.

**siyahi** [. - -] Black, Negro.

**siyahlaşmak** to turn black.

**siyahlık** blackness.

**siyakusibak**, -kı [ā, ā] context.

**Siyam** *pr. n.* Siam; ~ kedisi Siamese cat.

**siyanür** cyanide.

**siyasa** *s.* siyaset.

**siyasal** political; ≗ Bilgiler Fakültesi *pr. n.* the School of Political Science.

**siyaset,** -ti [â] politics.

**siyasetçi** [â] politician.

**siyasi** [.--] 1. political; 2. politician.

**siyatik** ⚕ sciatica.

**siyek** *anat.* urethra.

**siymek** to urinate, to pee (*cat, dog*).

**Siyonist,** -ti *pr. n.* Zionist.

**Siyonizm** *pr. n.* Zionism.

**siz** you; ~ bilirsiniz 1. as you like; 2. the decision is up to you; ~ sağ olun! never mind!

**sizin** your; yours; ~ için for you.

**sizinki** yours.

**skandal** scandal.

**skeç,** -ci sketch, skit.

**ski** skiing; ~ yapmak to ski.

**Skoç,** -çu Scotch.

**skor** score.

**slayt** slide, transparency.

**slip,** -pi briefs.

**slogan** slogan; ~ atmak to shout slogans.

**smokin** [x.] tuxedo, dinner jacket.

**snop,** -bu snobby, snobbish.

**soba** [x.] stove; ~ borusu stovepipe.

**sobe** 1. home free!; 2. you're out!

**sobelemek** 1. to put a player out; 2. to reach base before s.o. else.

**soda** [x.] 1. sodium carbonate; 2. soda water.

**sodyum** sodium.

**sof** 1. woolen cloth; 2. silkaline.

**sofa** hall, anteroom.

**sofizm** sophism.

**sofra** table; ~ başına geçmek to sit down to a meal; ~ başında at the table; ~ kurmak to set the table; ~ örtüsü tablecloth; ~ takımı set of dinnerware; -sı açık hospitable; -yı kaldırmak (or toplamak) to clear the table.

**softa** 1. † Muslim theological student; 2. very pious; 3. *fig.* blind follower.

**sofu** religious, devout, puritanical.

**soğan** ⚘ onion.

**soğuk** 1. cold; 2. cold weather, the cold; 3. *fig.* cold, unfriendly, frosty; 4. ⚕ frigid; ~ algınlığı (common) cold; ~ almak to catch cold; ~ damga embossed stamp; ~ davranmak (b-ne) to give s.o. the cold shoulder; ~ harp cold war; ~ hava deposu cold store, cold-storage depot; ~ nevale cold fish.

**soğukkanlı** cool-headed, calm.

**soğukkanlılık** cool-headedness, calmness.

**soğuklamak** to catch cold.

**soğukluk** 1. cold(ness); 2. *fig.* chill; 3. ⚕ frigidity.

**soğumak** 1. to get cold, to cool; 2. *fig.* to lose one's love; to go off.

**soğurmak** ⚛ to absorb.

**soğutmak** 1. to cool, to chill; 2. *fig.* to put off.

**soğutucu** refrigerator, fridge.

**sohbet,** -ti chat, conversation, talk; ~ etm. to chat, to talk, to converse.

**sokak** street; ~ başı beginning of a street; ~ çocuğu guttersnipe, street Arab, urchin, gamin; ~ kadını streetwalker; ~ kapısı street door; ~ köpeği tyke, cur; sokağa atsan beş lira eder it's worth at least five liras; sokağa çıkma yasağı curfew; sokağa çıkmak to go out; sokağa düşmek to go on the streets.

**soket,** -ti sock.

**sokmak,** (-ar) 1. to insert (-e in), to put (-e in); to shove (-e in), to thrust (-e in), to stick (-e in); 2. to admit, to let in; 3. to bite, to sting (*insect*); 4. to smuggle (-e into).

**sokman** a high boot.

**sokra** ⬇ butt seam.

**sokulgan** sociable, friendly, companionable.

**sokulmak** 1. *pass. of* sokmak; 2. to insinuate o.s. (-e into), to slip (-e into), to work one's way (-e into); 3. to draw near (-e to).

**sokur** 1. mole; 2. sunken (*eye*); 3. blind.

**sokuşmak** to squeeze (-e into), to sneak (-e in).

**sokuşturmak** 1. to squeeze (-e into); 2. *fig.* to put it across, to put it over (-e on).

**sol¹,** -lu 1. left; 2. left side; 3. *pol.* the left; ~ tarafından kalkmak to get out of bed on the wrong side; ~ yapmak to steer to the left; -da sıfır unimportant, a mere nothing; -umda on my left.

**sol²,** -lü ♪ 1. sol; 2. G.

**solacık** *football:* left wing.

**solak** left-handed.

**solanahtarı,** -nı ♪ treble clef.

**solbek** *football:* left back, fullback.

**solcu** *pol.* leftist, lefty.

**solculuk** *pol.* leftism.

**solfej** ♪ solfège.

**solgun** 1. pale, faded; 2. wilted (*flowers*).

**solhaf** [â] *football:* left halfback.

**soliç,** -ci *football:* left inner.

**solist,** -ti soloist.

**sollamak** to pass a vehicle on its left side.

**solmak,** (-ar) 1. to fade, to get pale; 2. to wilt (*flowers*).

**solmaz** unfading, fast (*colour*); colo(u)r-fast (*cloth*).

**solo** solo.

**solucan** zo. 1. worm; 2. ascarid, round-worm; ~ gibi pale and thin.

**soluğan** 1. wheezy *(animal)*; 2. swell *(of the sea)*.

**soluk¹** s. solgun; ~ beniz paleface.

**soluk²** breath; ~ aldırmamak to give no respite; ~ almak 1. to breathe; 2. *fig.* to take a breather, to rest; ~ borusu *anat.* windpipe, trachea; ~ soluğa out of breath, panting for breath; soluğu kesilmek to get out of breath.

**soluklanmak** to rest, to take a breather.

**solumak** to pant, to snort.

**solungaç** *anat.* gill.

**solunmak** to breathe.

**solunum** respiration; ~ sistemi respiratory system.

**solüsyon** ♫ solution.

**som¹** 1. solid; 2. unalloyed, pure.

**som²** the part of a dock located above water.

**som³** *(balığı)* zo. salmon.

**somak** ♦ sumac.

**somaki** [. - -] porphyry.

**somata** [. x .] a kind of sweet.

**somun** 1. loaf *(of bread)*; 2. ⊕ nut.

**somurdanmak** to grumble to o.s.

**somurtkan** sulky, grouchy.

**somurtmak** to sulk, to grouch, to pout.

**somut, -tu** concrete.

**somutlamak** to concretize.

**somutlaşmak** to concretize.

**somutlaştırmak** to concretize.

**somya, somye** [x .] spring mattress.

**son** 1. end, termination, conclusion; 2. final; last; 3. afterbirth; ~ bulmak to come to an end, to end; ~ defa (for the) last time; ~ derece extremely; ~ gülen iyi güler *pro.* he laughs best who laughs last; ~ kozunu oynamak to play one's last card; ~ nefesini vermek to breathe one's last; ~ vermek to put an end (-e to), to abolish; to bring to an end; -a ermek to finish, to end; -a kalan dona kalır *pro.* first come, first served; -dan bir evvelki next to the last, penultimate; -una kadar to the last; -unda in the end, finally; -unu getirmek *(bşin)* to bring s.th. to a successful conclusion, to accomplish s.th.

**sonat, -tı** ♪ sonata.

**sonbahar** autumn, *Am.* fall.

**sonda** [x .] 1. ⚑ probe, sound; 2. ⊕ drill.

**sondaj** 1. ⊕ drilling; 2. ⚓ sounding; 3. *fig.* sounding out; ~ yapmak 1. ⊕ to drill, to bore; 2. ⚓ to sound, to fathom; 3. *fig.* to sound out.

**sondajcı** ⊕ driller.

**şondalamak** 1. ⚓ to sound, to fathom; 2. ⊕ to drill; 3. ⚑ to probe.

**sonek, -ki** *gr.* suffix.

**sonkânun** [ū] † January.

**sonra** [x .] 1. then, later, afterwards; 2. after; 3. the rest; 4. or else, otherwise; -ya atmak (or bırakmak) to postpone, to put off; ondan ~ after that.

**sonradan** [x .] later, subsequently; ~ görme parvenu, upstart, nouveau riche.

**sonraki** [x .] subsequent, following.

**sonraları** [x . . .] afterwards, later on.

**sonsuz** 1. endless, eternal; 2. infinite; -a dek eternally.

**sonsuzluk** 1. eternity; 2. infinity.

**sonteşrin** [i] † November.

**sonuç, -cu** result, conclusion, outcome; ~ olarak consequently; sonucuna katlanmak to take the consequences.

**sonuçlandırmak** to conclude, to bring to a conclusion.

**sonuçlanmak** to come to a conclusion; to result.

**sonuncu** last, final; latter.

**sopa** [x .] 1. stick, cudgel, club; 2. *fig.* beating; ~ atmak (or çekmek) *(b-ne)* to give s.o. a beating, to give s.o. the cane; ~ yemek to get a beating, to get the cane.

**soprano** ♪ soprano.

**sorgu** interrogation, cross-examination; -ya çekmek to interrogate, to cross-examine, to grill.

**sorguç, -cu** crest, tuft.

**sormak¹**, (-ar) 1. to ask; 2. to ask (or inquire) about; to ask after; sora sora Bağdat (or Kâbe) bulunur *pro.* you can find any place you want to go to by asking for directions; öyle bir sıcak oldu ki sormayın! you cannot imagine how hot it was!

**sormak²**, (-ur) to suck.

**sorti** ⚡ outlet.

**soru** question; ~ işareti question mark; ~ sormak to ask a question.

**sorum** responsibility.

**sorumak** s. sormak 2.

**sorumlu** responsible *(-den* for).

**sorumluluk** responsibility.

**sorumsuz** irresponsible.

**sorumsuzluk** irresponsibility.

**sorun** problem, matter, question; issue.

**soruşmak¹** P to dry up.

**soruşmak²** to question each other.

**soruşturma** 1. *vn.* of soruşturmak; 2. investigation; 3. questionnaire; ~ açmak to open an investigation.

**soruşturmak** to investigate, to inquire

about.

sos sauce.

sosis hot dog, frankfurter, wiener.

sosyal, -li social; ~ sigorta social insurance.

sosyalist, -ti socialist.

sosyalizm socialism.

sosyete society, the smart set.

sosyetik society...

sosyolog sociologist.

sosyoloji sociology.

sote sauté(ed).

Sovyet, -ti Soviet; ~ Sosyalist Cumhuriyetleri Birliği the Union of Soviet Socialist Republics.

soy 1. race; 2. line(age), family; 3. highbred; ~ sop family, relations; -a çekmek to take after one's family.

soya ♀ soybean.

soyaçekim heredity.

soyadı, -nı family name, surname.

soydaş of the same race.

soygun 1. robbery, holdup; stick-up; 2. = soyguncu; 3. ill-gotten gain.

soyguncu robber.

soykırım(ı) genocide.

soylu noble, highborn.

soymak 1. to peel (fruit, etc.); 2. to undress; 3. to skin (an animal); 4. to rob, to strip; soyup soğana çevirmek to clean out, to pluck, to take to the cleaners.

soysuz 1. of bad race; 2. base, good-for-nothing (person).

soysuzlaşmak to degenerate.

soytarı clown, buffoon.

soyunmak to undress o.s., to strip, to peel off, to take off one's clothes; soyunup dökünmek to change into casual clothes.

soyut, -tu abstract.

soyutlamak to abstract.

söbe oval.

söğüş cold meat; boiled meat.

söğüt ♀ willow.

sökmek, (-er) 1. to dismantle; to undo, to rip, to unstitch; to unravel; to undo, to pull up (or out); to rip out; 3. to decipher, to read (handwriting); 4. to learn to read (alphabet); 5. to appear, to come out; 6. to break through (obstacle); 7. to flow (mucus); 8. sl. to make a dent (-e on).

sökük 1. unstitched; unraveled; 2. dropped stitch.

sökülmek 1. pass. of sökmek; 2. sl. to shell (or fork) out (money).

sökün etm. to come one after the other.

söküntü rip.

sölpük flabby, lax.

sölpümek to hang flabbily.

sömestr semester.

sömikok (kömürü) semicoke.

sömürge colony.

sömürgeci colonialist(ic).

sömürgecilik colonialism.

sömürmek 1. to exploit (a. fig.); 2. to eat up, to gobble down; 3. to suck (a liquid).

sömürü exploitation.

söndürmek caus. of sönmek 1. to extinguish, to put out (fire); 2. to turn (or switch) off (light); 3. to deflate; 4. to reduce, to diminish (passion, fever).

söndürücü fire extinguisher.

sönmek, (-er) 1. to go out, to die down (fire); 2. to go out, to fade (light); 3. to go flat (tyre); 4. to die down (anger, etc.); 5. to go into a decline.

sönük 1. extinguished (fire, light); 2. flat (tyre); deflated (balloon); 3. dim, faint; 4. inactive, extinct (volcano); 5. dull, uninspired, lifeless (person).

sör [-] sister.

söve doorpost.

sövgü swearword, curse, cussword.

sövmek, (-er) to swear, to curse (-e at); sövüp saymak to swear a blue streak (-e at).

sövüşlemek sl. to swindle.

sövüşmek to swear at each other.

söylemek 1. to say, to utter; to tell; 2. to sing (a song); to recite (a poem); 3. to speak (-e to); söyleyecek kelime bulamıyorum I am at a loss for words.

söylenmek 1. pass. of söylemek; 2. to grumble, to mutter to o.s.

söylenti rumo(u)r, hearsay.

söyleşi chat.

söyleşmek to chat, to converse.

söylev speech, address; oration.

söz 1. remark, utterance; word; statement; 2. rumo(u)r; 3. promise; ~ anlamak to show understanding; ~ aramızda between you and me; ~ arasında in the course of the conversation; ~ bir, Allah bir! I am a man of my word!; ~ dinlemek to follow advice; ~ etm. 1. to talk about; 2. to gossip; ~ geçirmek to assert o.s.; ~ götürmez indisputable, beyond doubt; ~ işitmek to be told off; ~ kavafı F garrulous; ~ kesmek to agree to give in marriage; ~ konusu in question; ~ konusu etm. to discuss; ~ olm. to be the subject of gossip; ~ sahibi who has a say (in a matter); ~ vermek to promise; -ü ağzına tıkamak to squelch, to silence; -ü geçen aforementioned, said, aforesaid; -ü geçmek 1. to assert o.s.; **2.** to be mentioned; -ü uzatmak to be long-winded (*or* wordy); -üm meclisten dışarı (*or* yabana) present company excepted; -ün gelişi context; -ün kısası in short, the long and the short of it is that; -ünde durmak to keep one's word; -den dönmek to go back on one's word, to backpedal; -ünü esirgememek to call a spade a spade, not to mince words; -ünü kesmek to interrupt; -ünü tutmak **1.** (*b-nin*) to take the advice of *s.o.*; **2.** (*kendi*) to keep *one's* word; -ünün eri man of his word; sizin evde kimin sözü geçer? who wears the trousers in your house?

**sözbirliği,** -ni agreement.

**sözcü** spokesman.

**sözcük** word.

**sözde 1.** so-called, would-be; **2.** supposedly.

**sözdizimi,** -ni syntax.

**sözgelimi, sözgelişi** for instance, for example.

**sözleşme 1.** *vn.* of sözleşmek; **2.** agreement, contract.

**sözleşmek 1.** to promise each other; **2.** to make an appointment.

**sözleşmeli** contractual.

**söz'ü 1.** oral, verbal; **2.** engaged to be married; **3.** fiancé; fiancée; ~ sınav oral examination.

**sözlük** dictionary.

**sözlükbilgisi,** -ni lexicography.

**sözlükçü** lexicographer.

**sözlükçülük** lexicography.

**sözümona** *s.* sözde.

**spekülasyon** speculation.

**spekülatif** speculative.

**spekülatör** speculator.

**sperma** sperm.

**spesiyal,** -li special.

**spiker** announcer.

**spiral 1.** spiral; **2.** ₹ coil.

**spor 1.** sport; **2.** sport(s); ~ araba sports car.

**sporcu** sportsman.

**sporsever** sports fan.

**sportif** sports...

**sportmen 1.** sportsman; **2.** sportsmanlike.

**sportoto** the football pools, the pools.

**sprey 1.** spray; **2.** sprayer.

**stabilize** stabilized; ~ etm. to stabilize; ~ yol gravel (*or* macadam) road.

**stad, stadyum** stadium.

**staj** apprenticeship; internship; ~ yapmak to undergo training; to serve one's internship.

**stajyer** trainee; houseman, intern.

**standart** standard.

**statü** statutes.

**statüko** the status quo.

**steno 1.** shorthand, stenography; **2.** steno- (grapher).

**stenograf** stenographer.

**stenografi** shorthand, stenography.

**step,** -pi steppe.

**stepne** *mot.* spare tyre (*or Am.* tire).

**stereo** stereo.

**steril** sterile.

**sterilize etm.** to sterilize.

**sterlin** (pound) sterling.

**steyşin** estate car. *Am.* station wagon.

**stil** style.

**stilo** [x .] fountain pen.

**stok,** -ku stock; ~ etm. to stock.

**stokçu** stockpiler.

**stop,** -pu stop!; ~ etm. to stop.

**stopaj** stoppage at source.

**stoplazma** cytoplasm.

**strateji** strategy.

**stratejik** strategical.

**stratus** [x .] *meteor.* stratus.

**striptiz** striptease.

**striptizci** stripteaser, stripper.

**stüdyo** [x .] studio.

**su,** -yu **1.** water; **2.** river, stream; **3.** juice; **4.** sap; **5.** gravy; broth; **6.** temper (*of steel*); ~ akarken testiyi doldurmalı *pro.* strike while the iron is hot, make hay while the sun shines; ~ almak to leak, to make water (*boat*); ~ baskını flood; ~ basmak to flood, to inundate; ~ birikintisi puddle; ~ bölümü çizgisi *geogr.* watershed; ~ cenderesi hydraulic press; ~ çekmek to draw water; ~ dökmek to make water, to urinate; ~ gibi akmak to fly (*time*); ~ gibi bilmek to know perfectly; ~ gibi para harcamak to spend money like water; ~ götürmez indisputable; ~ içinde at least; ~ koyuvermek *fig.* to overstep the mark; ~ tabancası water pistol (*or* gun); ~ testisi su yolunda kırılır *pro.* the pitcher goes too often to the well; ~ vermek **1.** to water; **2.** ⊕ to temper, to quench (*steel*); ~ yüzüne çıkmak to come to light; -dan ucuz dirt cheap; -larında about, around; -ya düşmek *fig.* to fall to the ground, to go phut; -ya sabuna dokunmamak to avoid meddling; -ya salmak *fig.* to throw away (*money*); -yu görmeden paçaları sıvamak *fig.* to count one's chickens before they are hatched; -yunca gitmek *fig.* to comply with *s.o.'s* wishes; -yunu çekmek *fig.* to run out (*money*); -yunun suyu only a remote connection.

**sual**, -li [ā] question; inquiry; ~ açmak to interrogate; ~ etm. to question; ~ sormak to ask a question.

**sualtı**, -nı underwater.

**suare** evening performance *(of a play)*; evening showing *(of a movie)*.

**suaygırı**, -nı *zo.* hippopotamus.

**subaşı**, -nı *hist.* 1. police superintendent; 2. farm manager.

**subay** X officer.

**subilim** hydrology.

**subra** [x.] dress shield.

**subye** [x.] strap.

**sucu** water seller.

**sucuk** 1. sausage; 2. sweetmeat *(made of grape juice, nuts, etc.)*; ~ gibi olm. (or ıslanmak) to get wet through, to get drenched; sucuğunu çıkarmak *fig.* 1. to beat the tar out of; 2. to tire out.

**suç**, -çu 1. offence, *Am.* offense; guilt; fault; 2. crime; ~ atmak *(b-nin üstüne)* to put the blame on *s.o.;* ~ işlemek to commit an offence *or* crime; ~ ortağı accomplice, accessory; -unu bağışlamak *or* -undan geçmek to pardon, to forgive an offence.

**suçiçeği**, -ni chicken pox, varicella.

**suçlamak** *(b-ni bşle)* to accuse *s.o.* of *s.th.*

**suçlandırmak** to find guilty.

**suçlu** 1. guilty; 2. criminal, felon, offender; ~ çıkarmak to find guilty; -ların iadesi ⚖ extradition.

**suçsuz** not guilty, innocent.

**suçüstü**, -nü red-handed, in the act; ~ yakalamak to catch red-handed.

**sudak** *zo.* zander.

**sudan** trivial, weak.

**Sudan** [- -] *pr. n.* Sudan.

**sudolabı**, -nı waterwheel.

**sufi** [- -] Sufi.

**suflör** *thea.* prompter.

**sugeçirmez** waterproof.

**suiistimal**, -li [- . . . -] misuse, abuse; ~ etm. to misuse, to abuse.

**suikast**, -tı 1. conspiracy; 2. assasination; -ta bulunmak 1. to conspire; 2. to assassinate.

**suikastçı** 1. conspirator; 2. assassin.

**suiniyet**, -ti [ā] malice.

**suizan**, -nnı [ā] suspicion.

**sukabağı**, -nı 🌿 dipper gourd.

**sukemeri**, -ni aqueduct.

**sukut**, -tu [.-] fall; ~ etm. to fall; -u hayal disappointment; -u hayale uğramak to be disappointed; -u hayale uğratmak to disappoint, to let down.

**suküre** hydrosphere.

**sulak** 1. watery, well-watered; 2. marshy.

**sulama** *vn. of* sulamak, *part.* irrigation.

**sulamaç** *neol.* sprinkler.

**sulamak** 1. to water; to irrigate; 2. *sl.* to shell out *(money)*.

**sulandırmak** 1. *caus. of* sulanmak; 2. to water (down); 3. to dilute, to thin.

**sulanmak** 1. *pass. of* sulamak; 2. *(bşe) sl.* to hanker after *s.th.;* 3. *(b-ne) sl.* to make improper advances to *s.o.*

**sulfata, sulfato** [.x.] P quinine sulfate.

**sulh** peace; ~ hâkimi justice of the peace; ~ mahkemesi justice court; ~ olm. to settle their differences.

**sulhçu** 1. peace-loving; 2. pacifist.

**sulhname** [ā] peace treaty.

**sulhperver, sulhsever** *s.* sulhçu.

**sulp**, -bü 1. hard, tough; 2. loins; sulbünden gelmek to be the offspring (-*in* of).

**sulta** authority.

**sultan** 1. sultan; 2. sultana.

**sultanlık** sultanate; sultanship.

**sulu** 1. watery; dilute; 2. juicy; 3. *fig.* importunate, saucy, pert; ~ gözlü 1. tearful, lachrymose; 2. crybaby.

**suluboya** watercolo(u)r.

**suluk** 1. water cup; 2. 🍴 infantile seborrhea.

**sulusepken** sleet; ~ yağmak to sleet.

**sumak** 🌿 sumac.

**sumen** writing-pad, blotting-pad.

**suna** drake.

**sundurma** shed, lean-to.

**sungu** 1. gift; 2. sacrifice.

**sungur** *zo.* white falcon.

**suni** [ī] artificial, false; imitation.

**sunmak**, (-ar) 1. to present, to offer; to submit; 2. to perform; to play; to sing.

**sunta** fiberboard.

**sunturlu** awful, whopping.

**sunucu** compère, emcee.

**sup(anglez)** chocolate pudding.

**supap**, -bı ⊕ valve.

**suphanallah!** heavens above!, great Scott!

**suples** flexibility.

**sur[1]** rampart, city wall.

**sur[2]** *isl. myth.* good luck.

**surat**, -tı face; ~ asmak to pull (*or* make) a long face; ~ bir karış sour-faced; ~ düşkünü ugly; ~ etm. to pull a long face; -ı asık sour-faced, sulky; -ından düşen bin parça olur *fig.* very sour-faced; -ını ekşitmek to put on a sour face.

**suratlı** sour-faced, sulky.

**suratsız** 1. sour-faced; 2. ugly; 3. bad-tempered.

**surdin** ♪ mute.

sure [ü] sura (of the Koran).

suret, -ti [ü] 1. copy, transcript; 2. form, figure, shape; 3. way, manner, fashion; ~ almak (or çıkarmak) to make a copy of, to transcribe; -ine girmek to assume the form of; bu -le thus, so.

sureta [- . -] [x . -] 1. assumed, affected; 2. outwardly.

Suriye pr. n. Syria.

sus! be quiet!, silence!

susak 1. thirsty; 2. dipper.

susam ⚘ sesame.

susamak 1. to get thirsty; 2. fig. to thirst (-e for).

susamuru, -nu zo. otter.

susığırı, -nı zo. water buffalo.

suskun quiet, taciturn.

susmak, (-ar) to stop talking, to be quiet, to become silent, to hold one's tongue; sus payı hush money.

suspansuvar jock(strap).

suspus: ~ olm. to be silenced; to be as quiet as a mouse.

susta [x .] safety catch; ~ durmak 1. to stand on its hind legs (dog); 2. fig. to stand to heel.

sustalı switchblade.

susturmak to silence, to hush, to shut up.

susturucu 1. silencer (of a gun); 2. mot. silencer, muffler.

susuz waterless.

susuzluk 1. waterlessness; 2. thirst.

sut, -du soda.

sutopu, -nu water polo.

sutyen bra, brassiere.

Suudi Arabistan pr. n. Saudi Arabia.

suvare evening showing (of a movie); evening performance (of a play).

suvarmak to water (an animal).

suvat, -tı watering place.

suyolu, -nu 1. waterline; 2. watermark (in paper).

suyosunları, -nı ⚘ algae.

suyosunu, -nu seaweed, alga.

suyuk fluid.

suziş [ü] heartache, anguish.

suzişli [ü] full of anguish.

sübek urinal (for a baby).

sübjektif subjective.

sübut, -tu [ü] realization; ~ bulmak to become a reality.

sübyan children.

sübyancı F pedophiliac.

sübye [x .] 1. a kind of sweet; 2. 🧪 emulsion.

sücut [ü] prostration; ~ etm. to prostrate o.s. in worship.

südremek to get drunk.

süet, -ti suede.

süfli [ī] 1. contemptible, low-down; 2. shabby.

sühulet, -ti [ü] ease, facility.

sühunet, -ti [ü] meteor., phys. temperature.

süje subject (a. gr.).

süklüm püklüm cap in hand, in a hangdog manner.

sükna [ā] residence; ~ hakkı ⚖ right of residence.

sükse success, hit; ~ yapmak to be a hit (or success).

sükûn, sükûnet, -ti calm, quiet, rest, repose; ~ bulmak to quiet down.

sükût, -tu silence; ~ etm. to remain silent; ~ hakkı hush money; -la geçiştirmek to pass over in silence.

sükûti [ī] silent.

sülale family, line.

sülfat, -tı sulphate, Am. sulfate.

sülfit, -ti sulfite.

sülfür sulphide, Am. sulfide.

sülfürik sulphuric, Am. sulfuric.

sülük 1. zo. leech; 2. ⚘ tendril; ~ gibi yapışmak to stick like a leech.

sülün zo. pheasant; ~ gibi tall and graceful.

sümbül ⚘ hyacinth.

sümbüli [ī] overcast, cloudy (sky).

Sümer pr. n. Sumer.

sümkürmek to blow one's nose.

sümmettedarik [ā] last-minute.

sümsük shiftless, supine.

sümük mucus; snot; slime.

sümükdoku mucous membrane.

sümüklü snotty; snotty-nosed; slimy.

sümüklüböcek zo. slug.

sümüksü mucoid.

sünepe shiftless, supine.

sünger sponge; ~ avcılığı sponge fishing; ~ avcısı sponge fisherman; ~ geçirmek (bşin üzerinden) to pass the sponge over s.th.; ~ gibi spongy.

süngerci 1. sponge fisherman; 2. sponge seller.

süngerdoku ⚘ spongy parenchyma.

süngertaşı, -nı pumice.

süngü 1. bayonet; 2. poker (for a fire); -sü depreşmesin ama... I don't like to speak ill of the dead. but...; -sü düşük depressed, down in the dumps.

süngülemek to bayonet.

süngülü with fixed bayonets.

sünnet, -ti isl. 1. the Sunna; 2. circumcision; ~ düğünü circumcision feast; ~ etm. to circumcise; ~ olm. to be circumcised.

sünnetçi circumciser.

sünnetlemek *P* to eat up.

sünnetli circumcised.

sünnetsiz uncircumcised.

Sünni [î] Sunni.

Sünnilik [. - .] the Sunni branch of Islam.

süper super; ~ benzin high-octane gasoline.

süpermarket, -ti supermarket.

süpersonik supersonic.

süpozituvar ⚕ suppository.

süprüntü sweepings, rubbish, trash (a. fig.).

süprüntücü 1. dustman, street sweeper; 2. fig. junkman.

sünrüntülük dump, rubbish heap.

süpürge broom.

süpürgeci 1. maker or seller of brooms; 2. street sweeper.

süpürgelik baseboard, mopboard.

süpürgeotu, -nu ⚘ heath.

süpürmek 1. to sweep; 2. fig. to sweep away.

sürahi [. - .] decanter, jug, carafe.

sürat, -ti speed, velocity; ~ motoru speedboat; -ini artırmak to accelerate, to speed up; -le speedily, quickly.

süratlendirmek to accelerate, to speed up.

süratlenmek to speed up, to gain speed, to go faster.

süratli speedy, rapid, quick.

sürç, -cü; -ü lisan slip of the tongue.

sürçmek, (-er) 1. to stumble; 2. fig. to make a slip of the tongue.

sürdürmek 1. caus. of sürmek; 2. to carry on, to continue, to maintain.

süre period; extension.

süreç process, progression.

süredurum phys. inertia.

süregelmek to have gone on for a long time.

süreğen chronic.

sürek 1. duration, continuation; 2. drove (of cattle); ~ avı drive.

sürekli continuous, continual.

süreksiz transitory, transient.

süreksizlik transitoriness.

süreli periodic.

sürerlik continuousness.

Süreyya [â] pr. n. 1. ast. the Pleiades; 2. mf., wf.

sürfe larva.

sürgü 1. bolt; 2. bedpan; 3. harrow; 4. (plasterer's) trowel.

sürgülemek to bolt.

sürgülü bolted; ~ cetvel slide rule.

sürgün 1. ⚘ shoot, sucker; 2. exile, banishment; 3. ⚕ diarrhea; ~ avı drive; ~

etm. to exile, to banish; -e gitmek to go into exile; -e göndermek to send into exile.

sürme 1. vn. of sürmek; 2. drawer; 3. latch; 4. kohl; 5. sliding; ~ kapı sliding door.

sürmedan(lık) [â] container for kohl.

sürmek, (-er) 1. to drive (a vehicle, an animal) 2. to exile; 3. to plough, Am. to plow (a field); 4. to put into circulation (money); to put on the market (goods); 5. to rub, to smear; 6. to go on, to continue, to last; 7. to lead (a good life); 8. ⚘ to shoot out.

sürmelemek to bolt.

sürmelik s. sürmedan(lık).

sürmenaj nervous breakdown, neurasthenia.

sürpriz surprise; ~ yapmak (b-ne) to surprise s.o.

sürre the presents sent annually by the Sultan to Mecca and Medina; ~devesi gibi iro. overdressed woman.

sürrealist, -ti surrealist.

sürşarj surcharge (on a stamp).

sürtmek, (-er) 1. to rub (-e against); 2. to loiter, to wander about.

sürtük 1. gadabout (woman); 2. streetwalker.

sürtünme vn. of sürtünmek, part. phys. friction.

sürtünmek 1. to rub o.s. (-e against); 2. fig. to seek a quarrel.

sürtüşmek 1. to rub against each other; 2. to vex (or irritate) each other.

sürur [û] delight, joy.

sürü herd, drove, flock; ~ içgüdüsü psych. the herd instinct; ~ sepet F the whole kit and caboodle, the whole lot; -den ayrılmak fig. to go one's own way; -süne bereket a lot of, heaps of.

sürücü 1. drover; 2. driver, motorist.

sürüklemek 1. to drag; 2. to hold one's attention, to carry with one; 3. to drag (-e into).

sürüklenmek 1. pass. of sürüklemek; 2. to drag o.s.; 3. to drag on (or out).

sürükleyici fascinating, engrossing.

sürüm † demand, sale.

sürümek to drag.

sürümlü in demand.

sürüm sürüm: ~ sürünmek to suffer great misery.

sürünceme: -de bırakmak to procrastinate; -de kalmak to drag on, to be left hanging in the air.

süründürmek caus. of sürünmek, part. to drive from pillar to post.

sürüngen reptile.

sürünmek 1. to crawl, to creep, to grovel; 2. to rub (-e against); 3. *fig.* to live in misery.

sürüşmek to rub (*or* smear) on each other.

sürüştürmek to rub (*or* spread) slowly (-e on).

sürütme 1. *vn. of* sürütmek; 2. trawl(net).

sürütmek *caus. of* sürümek.

sürveyan supervisor.

süs 1. ornament, decoration; 2. ornamentation; ~ püs frippery, finery; -e düşkün dressy; ... süsü vermek (k-ne) to pass o.s. off as..., to set up as..., to pose as...

süsen ⚘ iris; ~ kökü orris(root).

süslemek 1. to adorn, to decorate, to embellish; 2. to doll up, to deck out; süsleyip püslemek to doll up fit to kill, to prank.

süslenmek *pass. or refl. of* süslemek, to deck o.s. out, to doll o.s. up; süslenip püslenmek to doll o.s. up fit to kill, to primp and preen, to prank o.s. up.

süslü 1. ornately, decorated, adorned; 2. fancy, ornate, dressy; ~ püslü dolled up fit to kill.

süsmek to butt, to gore.

süspansiyon ⊕ suspension.

süssüz undecorated, unadorned.

süt, -tü 1. milk; 2. latex; 3. *sl.* petrol, juice; ~ calmak (çocuğu) to make (a nursing baby) ill; ~ cocuğu 1. nursling; 2. *fig.* mollycoddle, babe in the woods; ~ dökmüş kedi gibi in a crestfallen manner; ~ gibi white and clean; ~ kesilmek to sour, to go off (*or* bad); ~ kuzusu 1. suckling lamb; 2. *fig.* baby; tot, toddler; ~ tozu milk powder; ~ vermek to suckle, to breast-feed, to nurse; -ten ağzı yanan yoğurdu üfleyerek yer *pro.* once bitten twice shy; -ten kesmek to wean; -ü bozuk *fig.* no-good, villain; -üne havale etm. (bir işi b-nin) to leave (a matter) to s.o.

sütana, sütanne wet nurse.

sütbaşı, -nı cream.

sütbeyaz milk white.

sütçü milkman.

sütçülük being a milkman.

sütdişi, -ni milk (*or* baby) tooth.

sütkardeş foster brother *or* sister.

sütkırı, -nı milk-white (horse).

sütkızı foster daughter.

sütlaç rice pudding.

sütleğen ⚘ spurge.

sütliman dead calm, as calm as a mill-pond, halcyon.

sütlü 1. milky, in milk; 2. made with milk (food); 3. full (ear of grain); ~ kahve white coffee, coffee with milk.

sütmavisi, -ni light sky-blue.

sütnine wet nurse.

sütoğul, -ğlu foster son.

sütre ✕ cover.

sütsüz milkless.

sütun [ū] column; post; pillar; ~ başlığı Δ capital of a column.

sütyen *s.* sutyen.

süvari [. - -] 1. cavalryman; 2. rider, horseman; 3. ⬇ captain; ~ alayı cavalry regiment.

süve *s.* söve.

süveter sweater.

Süveyş [. ✕] *pr. n.* Suez; ~ Kanalı Suez Canal.

süyek ☂ splint.

süzek strainer; filter.

süzeni a kind of embroidery.

süzgeç, -ci 1. strainer; filter; sieve; 2. *phot.* colo(u)r (*or* light) filter; ~ kâğıdı filter paper.

süzgün 1. languorous (look); 2. gaunt, thin.

süzme 1. *vn. of* süzmek; 2. filtered; strained; 3. *sl.* fox, rascal.

süzmek, (-er) 1. to filter; to strain; 2. to give the once-over; 3. to scan.

süzülmek 1. *pass. of* süzmek; 2. to glide; 3. to flow, to run; 4. to get thin; 5. to steal (*or* slip) in; 6. to be about to close (eyes).

süzüntü 1. filtrate; 2. residue, dregs.

# Ş

şa [ā]: ~ ~ ~ hip, hip, hurrah!
şaban[1] [- -] 1. *isl.* Sha'ban; 2. ♀ *mf.*
şaban[2] *sl.* dumb, nitwitted.
şablon pattern, template, former.
şad [ā] happy; joyful; ~ olm. to rejoice.
şadırdamak to plash (*water*).
şadırvan fountain.
şafak dawn, twilight; ~ atmak to dawn on s.o.; ~ sökmek (*for dawn*) to break.
şaft, -tı ⊕ shaft.
şah[1]: -a kalkmak to rear (*horse*).
şah[2] [ā] 1. shah; 2. *chess:* king; ~ iken şahbaz olm. *co.* to get even worse; ben şahımı bu kadar severim *fig.* I'll help my boss to this extent only.
şahadet, -ti [. - .] 1. witness, attestation; 2. martyrdom; ~ getirmek to repeat the Islamic testimony of faith; -te bulunmak to bear witness, to testify.
şahadetname [. - . - .] 1. diploma; 2. certificate.
şahadetparmağı, -nı index finger, forefinger.
şahane [- -.] 1. splendid, magnificent, superb; 2. imperial, royal.
şahap, -bı [. - ] 1. *ast.* shooting star; 2. ♀ *mf.*
şahbaz 1. *zo.* royal falcon; 2. courageous, brave.
şahdamarı, -nı *anat.* carotid artery, jugular vein.
şaheser masterpiece, masterwork.
şahıs, -hsı 1. person (*a. gr.*), individual; 2. *thea.* character; ~ zamiri *gr.* personal pronoun.
şâhis surveyor's rod.
şahika 1. summit; 2. ♀ *wf.*
şahin [ā] 1. *zo.* falcon; 2. ♀ *mf.*
şahit, -di [ā] (eye)witness; ~ olm. to witness.
şahitlik [ā] witnessing, testimony; ~ etm. to bear witness.
şahlanmak 1. to rear up (*horse*); 2. *fig.* to become angry and threatening.
şahlık shahdom.
şahmerdan ⊕ pile-driver; drop hammer.
şahniş(in) [- . - .] bay window.
şahrem şahrem in strips (*or* shreds).

şahsen [x .] 1. personally, in person; 2. for my part, personally; 3. by sight.
şahsi [ī] personal, private; ~ eşya personal effects, belongings.
şahsiyet, -ti 1. personality; 2. individuality; 3. personage.
şahsiyetli having personality.
şahsiyetsiz who lacks personality.
şaibe [ā] stain, blot.
şair [ā] poet.
şairane [- . - .] poetic(al).
şairlik poetship.
şak[1], -kı smack!
şak[2], -kkı split, fissure.
şaka joke, leg-pull, jest; gag; ~ bir tarafa (*or* yana) joking apart; ~ etm. to kid; ~ gibi gelmek to seem like a joke (-*e* to); ~ götürmez bir iş it is no joking matter; ~ iken kaka olm. to turn into a quarrel; to backfire; ~ kaldırmak to be able to take a joke; ~ maka (derken) imperceptibly; ~ söylemek to joke; -dan anlamak to take a joke; -sı yok it is no joke; -ya boğmak to turn into a joke; -ya gelmek to be able to take a joke; -ya vurmak to pretend to take as a joke.
şakacı joker.
şakacıktan 1. jokingly, as a joke; 2. inadvertently, unwittingly.
şakadan jokingly, as a joke.
şakak *anat.* temple.
şakalaşmak to joke with one another.
şakayık, -kı, -ğı ♀ peony.
şakımak to warble, to trill.
şakırdamak 1. to clatter, to rattle; 2. to snap (*fingers*); 3. to jingle; 4. to crack (*whip*); 5. to drum, to beat, to patter (*rain*).
şakırdatmak 1. to rattle, to clatter; 2. to jingle; 3. to crack (*a whip*); 4. to snap (*fingers*).
şakır şakır 1. with a patter; 2. with a rattle (*or* jingle).
şakır şukur clatteringly, with a rattle.
şakırtı 1. clatter, rattle; 2. patter, plash; 3. crack, snap; 4. jingle.
şaki robber, brigand.
şakirt, -di [ā] student.

şaklaban 1. jester, buffoon; 2. *fig.* sycophantic.

şaklamak to crack, to snap, to pop.

şaklatmak to crack, to snap.

şakrak mirthful, merry.

şakrakkuşu, -nu *zo.* bullfinch.

şakrämak *s.* şakımak.

şakşak 1. slapstick; 2. applause.

şakul, -lü [ä] plumb line.

şakuli [- . -] perpendicular.

şakullemek 1. to plumb, to plumb-line; 2. *fig.* to sound out.

şal shawl.

şalgam ❧ turnip.

şallak naked; ~ mallak stark naked.

şalter ⚡ switch; (circuit) breaker.

şalupa [. x .] ⚓ sloop.

şalvar baggy trousers, shalwar; ~ gibi very baggy.

Şam *pr. n.* Damascus.

şama [x .] wax taper.

şamama [. - .] muskmelon; ~ gibi small and cute-looking.

Şaman *pr. n.* shaman.

şamandıra [. x . .] 1. ⚓ buoy, float; 2. cork float.

şamar slap, box on the ear; ~ atmak to slap; to give a box on the ear; ~ oğlanı whipping boy, scapegoat; ~ yemek to get a slap on the face.

şamata whoopee, commotion, uproar, clamo(u)r; ~ yapmak to make whoopee, to make a commotion.

şamatacı noisy, boisterous.

şambriyel *mot.* inner tube (*of a tyre*).

şambrnuar *phot.* darkroom.

şamdan candlestick.

şamfıstığı, -nı pistachio (nut).

şamil [ä] 1. all-inclusive, comprehensive; 2. ≗ *mf.*; ~ olm. to include, to cover.

şamme [ä] *biol.* (sense of) smell.

şampanya [. x .] champagne.

şampiyon champion.

şampiyona championship.

şampiyonluk championship.

şampuan shampoo.

şan¹ [ä] glory, reputation, fame; ~ vermek to become famous; -ına düşmek (*or* yakışmak) to befit one's dignity; -ından olm. to befit.

şan² singing; ~ resitali recital given by a vocalist.

şangırdamak to crash.

şangır şungur with a crash.

şangırtı crash.

şanjan iridescence.

şanjman *mot.* gearbox, shift.

şanlı glorious, illustrious; ~ şöhretli illus-

trious and famous.

şano [x .] *thea.* stage.

şans luck; chance; ~ tanımak to give a chance; -ı yaver gitmek to have good luck, to be lucky enough.

şansız unrenowned.

şanslı lucky, fortunate.

şanssız unlucky.

şanssızlık unluckiness.

şantaj blackmail, extortion; ~ yapmak to blackmail.

şantajcı blackmailer.

şantiye 1. building (*or* construction) site; 2. shipyard.

şantör chanteur, male singer.

şantöz chanteuse, female singer.

şanzıman, şanzuman *s.* şanjman.

şap¹, -pı ⚗ alum; ≗ Denizi *pr. n.* the Red Sea; ~ hastalığı foot-and-mouth disease; -a oturmak *fig.* to get in a pickle (*or* quandary).

şap² smack.

şapırdamak to smack.

şapırdatmak to smack (*one's lips*).

şapır şapır *or* şapır şupur smacking one's lips loudly.

şapırtı smack.

şapka [x .] 1. hat; 2. truck (*of a mast*); 3. cowl, cap (*of a chimney*); -sını çıkarmak to take off one's hat; -sını giymek to put on one's hat.

şapkacı hatter.

şapkalık hatstand, hat rack.

şaplak whang.

şaplamak¹ to land with a smack.

şaplamak² ⚗ to treat with alum.

şappadak [x .] all of a sudden, out of the blue.

şaprak saddlecloth.

şapşal 1. slovenly, untidy, shabby; 2. stupid, lunkheaded.

şarabi [. - -] wine-red.

şarampol shoulder (*of a road*).

şarap, -bı wine.

şaraphane [. . - .] 1. winehouse; 2. winery.

şarapnel ✗ shrapnel.

şarbon ☤ charbon.

şarıldamak to splash.

şarıl şarıl splashingly.

şarıltı splash.

şarj 1. ⚡ charge; 2. *football:* rush; ~ etm. to charge.

şarjör (cartridge) clip, charger.

şark, -kı the east; the East, the Orient.

şarkadak [x . .] with a whop (*or* thump).

şarkı song; ~ okumak (*or* söylemek) to sing a song.

şarkıcı singer.

**şarki** [î] eastern.

**şarklı** easterner.

**şarküteri** delicatessen.

**şarlatan** charlatan.

**şarlatanlık** charlatanry.

**şarpi** ⚓ sharpie.

**şar şar** splashingly.

**şart**, -tı condition, stipulation, provision; ~ koşmak to make a condition (or stipulation), to stipulate; ~ şurt tanımaz F he refuses to be bound by any conditions.

**şartlandırmak** to condition.

**şartlanmak** to be conditioned.

**şartlaşmak** to agree to conditions.

**şartlı** conditional; stipulated.

**şartname** [. - .] list of conditions.

**şartsız** unconditional; unconditioned.

**şaryo** [x .] carriage (of a typewriter).

**şasi** chassis.

**şaşaa** splendo(u)r; glitter; brilliance.

**şaşaalı** splendid, pompous, grand, brilliant.

**şaşakalmak, şaşalamak** to be bewildered, to be taken aback.

**şaşı** cross-eyed, squint-eyed; ~ bakmak to squint.

**şaşılaşmak** to get cross-eyed.

**şaşılık** cross-eye, squint.

**şaşırmak** 1. to be confused (or puzzled), to be at a loss; 2. to lose (one's way).

**şaşırtma** vn. of şaşırtmak, part. transplanting (of seedlings).

**şaşırtmaca** tongue-twister, puzzle.

**şaşırtmak** caus. of şaşırmak, part. 1. to confuse, to bewilder, to mislead; to puzzle, to amaze; 2. to transplant (seedlings).

**şaşkaloz** sl. 1. cross-eyed; 2. confused.

**şaşkın** 1. confused, bewildered, at a loss; 2. silly, stupid; -a çevirmek to confuse, to bewilder; -a dönmek to be stupefied.

**şaşkınlık** confusion, bewilderment, daze; ~ içinde in a daze.

**şaşmak**, (-ar) 1. to be astonished (or amazed) (-e at); 2. to deviate (-den from), to depart (-den from); 3. (for a missile) to miss (its object); 4. to be mistaken; 5. to lose (one's way).

**şat**, -tı ⚓ lighter.

**şatafat**, -tı display, show, ostentation.

**şatafatlı** showy, ostentatious, splendiferous.

**şato** [x .] castle, château.

**şavalak** F stupid, thick, dense.

**şayan** [- -] worthy (-e of), deserving; -ı itimat trustworthy; -ı merhamet pitiful.

**şayet** [â] if (by chance), if perchance.

**şayi**, -ii [â] 1. widespread; 2. 𝔰 shared in common.

**şayia** [- . .] rumo(u)r.

**şaz** [â] irregular; exceptional.

**seamet**, -ti [â] bed luck.

**seametli** [â] unlucky, ill-omened.

**şebboy** ♀ 1. wallflower; 2. gillyflower, stock.

**şebek** 1. zo. baboon; 2. fig. ugly.

**şebeke** 1. network; 2. identity card (of a university student).

**şebnem** dew.

**şecaat**, -ti [. - .] courage.

**şecaatli** [. - . .] courageous.

**şecere** family tree, pedigree.

**şef** chief, leader; ~ garson head waiter.

**şefaat**, -ti [. - .] intercession; ~ etm. (b-ne) to intercede with s.o.

**şeffaf** [â] transparent.

**şeffaflık** [â] transparency.

**şefik**, -kı [î] 1. tender(hearted), kind, compassionate; 2. ♀ [x .] mf.

**şefkat**, -ti kindness, compassion, tenderness.

**şefkatli** kind, compassionate, tender(hearted).

**şeftali** [â] ♀ peach.

**şeftren** 🚩 guard, conductor.

**şehevi** [î] carnal.

**şehik**, -kı [î] biol. inhalation, inspiration.

**şehinşah** [â] the Shahinshah.

**şehir**, -hri city, town.

**şehirci** city planner.

**şehirlerarası**, -nı 1. intercity, interurban; 2. teleph. long-distance.

**şehirli** townsman, city dweller.

**şehit**, -di martyr; ~ düşmek to die a martyr.

**şehitlik** 1. martyrdom; 2. cemetery for Turkish soldiers.

**şehla** having a slight cast in the eye.

**şehremaneti**, -ni [â] municipality.

**şehremini**, -ni mayor.

**şehriye** vermicelli; ~ çorbası vermicelli soup.

**şehvani** [. - -] carnal, libidinal.

**şehvet**, -ti lust, concupiscence; ~ düşkünü lewd, prurient.

**şehvetli** lustful, concupiscent, libidinous.

**şehvetperest**, -ti lustful.

**şehzade** [â] prince, shahzadah.

**şek**, -kki suspicion, doubt.

**şekavet**, -ti [â] brigandage.

**şeker** 1. sugar; 2. candy; 3. ⚕ diabetes; 4. fig. darling, sweet; ♀ Bayramı the Lesser Bairam; ~ gibi darling, sweet; ~ hastası diabetic; ~ hastalığı diabetes; ~ kellesi sugarloaf; ~ pancarı sugar beet; -im F honey, sweetie, darling.

**şekerci** confectioner; candymaker; candyseller.

**şekercilik** confectionery.

**şekerkamışı,** -nı ♀ sugar cane.

**şekerleme 1.** *vn. of* şekerlemek; **2.** candied fruit; **3.** nap, doze; ~ yapmak to have (or take) a nap, to doze off.

**şekerlemek 1.** to sugar; **2.** to candy (fruit).

**şekerleşmek 1.** to turn into sugar, to sugar; **2.** *fig.* to become sweet.

**şekerli 1.** sugared; **2.** diabetic; ~ kahve well-sugared coffee.

**şekerlik 1.** sugar basin (or bowl); **2.** candy bowl (or dish).

**şekerrenk,** -gi cool, uncordial.

**şekersiz** unsugared, unsweetened.

**şekil,** -kli **1.** shape; **2.** figure, diagram; illustration; **3.** manner, way; **4.** sort, kind; şeklini değiştirmek to transform.

**şekilbilgisi,** -ni morphology.

**şekilci** formalist(ic).

**şekilcilik** formalism.

**şekillendirmek** to shape.

**şekillenmek** to take on a shape.

**şekilsiz** shapeless.

**şeklen** [x .] in shape (or appearance).

**şekva** [ā] complaint.

**şelale** waterfall.

**şema** [x .] diagram, scheme, plan; outline.

**şemacılık** [x ...] schematism.

**şematik** schematic.

**şempanze** zo. chimpanzee.

**şemse** sunburst (design).

**şemsiper** visor.

**şemsiye 1.** umbrella; parasol; **2.** umbel.

**şemsiyelik** umbrella stand.

**şen** happy, merry, cheerful, joyous.

**şenaat,** -ti [. - .] vileness, wickedness.

**şendere 1.** veneer; **2.** barrel stave; **3.** zo. red mullet.

**şeneltmek** to populate.

**şeni,** -ii vile, foul; wicked.

**şenia** [î] immoralty.

**şenlendirmek 1.** to cheer up, to enliven; **2.** to populate.

**şenlenmek 1.** to be cheered up; **2.** to be populated.

**şenlik 1.** gaiety, cheerfulness; **2.** merriment; festival, festivity; **3.** prosperity.

**şer,** -rri evil, wickedness.

**şerait,** -ti [ā] conditions, stipulations.

**şer'an** [x .] in accordance with canon law, canonically.

**şerare** [ā] *phys.* spark.

**şerbet,** -ti sherbet, sweet drink.

**şerbetçiotu,** -nu ♀ hop.

**şerbetli 1.** immune to snakebite; **2.** *fig.* incorrigible.

**şerç,** -ci *anat.* anus.

**şeref 1.** hono(u)r; **2.** ♀ *mf.;* ~ defteri honorarv-bock; ~ madalyası plume; ~ misafiri guest of hono(u)r; ~ sözü word of hono(u)r; ~ vermek to hono(u)r; -inize! cheers!, to your health!

**şerefe** balcony.

**şerefiye** betterment tax.

**şereflendirmek** to hono(u)r.

**şereflenmek** to be hono(u)red.

**şerefli** hono(u)red.

**şerefsiz** dishono(u)rable.

**şergil** naughty.

**şerh** explanation; ~ etm. to explain.

**şeriat,** -tı [î] Islamic (or canon) law.

**şerif[1]** [î] **1.** sacred; **2.** ♀ [x .] *mf.*

**şerif[2]** sheriff.

**şerik,** -ki [î] partner.

**şerir** [î] evil, wicked.

**şerit,** -di **1.** ribbon, tape; band; **2.** *mot.* lane; **3.** ✗ stripe; **4.** zo. tapeworm; ~ metre tape measure.

**şeş** six; -i beş görmek to be completely mistaken.

**şeşbeş** six and five.

**şeşcihar** six and four.

**şeşdüdü** six and two.

**şeşüse** six and three.

**şeşüyek** six and one.

**şetaret,** -ti [ā] gaiety, merriness.

**şetim,** -tmi execration, cursing.

**şetmetmek** [x .-] to curse, to execrate.

**şev 1.** slope, decline; **2.** slant; bevel.

**şevk,** -ki enthusiasm, eagerness, ardo(u)r, fervo(u)r; -e gelmek to become eager.

**şevket,** -ti **1.** majesty, grandeur; **2.** ♀ *mf.*

**şevval,** -li [ā] *isl.* Shawwal.

**şey 1.** thing; **2.** what-do-you-call-it; thingumbob, thingummy.

**şeyh** sheik(h).

**şeyhülislam** Sheikh ul-Islam.

**şeytan** [ā] **1.** Satan, the Devil; **2.** *fig.* fiend, demon, devil; ~ azapta gerek *fig.* it serves him right; ~ çekici little devil, clever urchin; ~ gibi as cunning as a fox; ~ kulağına kurşun! touch wood!; ~ tüyü *fig.* talisman supposed to give personal attraction; -a çarık giydirmek *fig.* to be clever enough to cheat the devil himself; -a uyma don't yield to temptation; -ın bacağını kırmak *fig.* to get the show on the road at last.

**şaytanarabası,** -nı cluster of feathery seeds floating in the air.

**şeytanca 1.** devilish; **2.** devilishly.

**şeytanet,** -ti [ā] *s.* şeytanlık.

**şeytani** [. - -] devilish.

**şeytanlık 1.** devilry; **2.** devilment, mischief.

**şezlong,** -gu chaise longue, deck chair.

**şık¹,** -kı smart, chic, neat, elegant, fashionable; ~ mı ~! she is dressed to kill.

**şık²,** -kkı choice, option; alternative.

**şıkırdamak** to clink, to rattle, to jingle.

**şıkırdatmak** to rattle, to jingle, to clink.

**şıkırdım** *sl.* lad, kid.

**şıkır şıkır 1.** with a clinking noise; **2.** jingling *(coins, etc.);* **3.** glittery, shiny.

**şıkırtı** clink, rattle, jingle.

**şıklık** smartness, chic, elegance.

**şıllık** loose woman, gaudily dressed woman.

**şımarık** spoiled.

**şımarmak** to get spoiled.

**ş:martmak** to spoil, to pamper.

**şıngırdamak** to clink, to rattle.

**şıngır şıngır** with a rattling sound.

**şıngırtı** rattle, clink.

**şıp,** -pı: ~ diye in a trice, all of a sudden; ~ ~ with a dripping sound.

**şıpıdık** scuff, slipper.

**şıpır şıpır** continuously, without letup.

**şıpırtı** splash.

**'şıppadak** [x . .] all of a sudden, out of the blue.

**şıpsevdi** susceptible.

**şıpşıp** *s.* şıpıdık.

**şıra** [x .] grape must.

**şırak** crack!, crash!, pop!

**şırakkadak** [. x . .] all of a sudden.

**şırfıntı** tramp, slut, floozy.

**şırıldamak** to plash, to purl, to ripple.

**şırıl şırıl** with a plash.

**şırıltı** plash, purl, ripple.

**şıringa** syringe; ~ yapmak to syringe.

**şırlağan 1.** sesame oil; **2.** flow.

**şırlamak** *s.* şırıldamak.

**şırlop** eggs served with yogurt.

**şırp:** ~ diye kesmek to cut off with a snip *(of scissors).*

**şırpadak** *s.* şıppadak.

**şırvan, şırvanı** loft, attic, garret.

**şıvgın 1.** shoot, twig; **2.** pine, fir.

**Sia** the Shi'a.

**şiar** [ā] **1.** mark, sign, token; **2.** password.

**şibih,** -bhi resemblance.

**şiddet,** -ti **1.** intensity; violence, severity; vehemence; **2.** harshness, stringency; ~ olayı act of terrorism; -e başvurmak to resort to brute force; -le **1.** violently, severely; **2.** passionately; vehemently.

**şiddetlendirmek** to intensify.

**şiddetlenmek** to become more intense, to

intensify.

**şiddetli** intense; violent, severe; passionate, vehement; ~ geçimsizlik *ʤ* extreme incompatibility.

**şifa** [ā] recovery, healing; ~ bulmak to recover one's health, to get well; -lar olsun! may it give you health!; -yı bulmak *(or* kapmak) to fall ill.

**şifahen** [ā] orally, verbally.

**şifahi** [. - -] oral, verbal; ~ imtihan oral examination.

**şifalı** [ā] restorative, healing, curative; ~ ot medicinal plant.

**şifon** chiffon.

**şifoniyer** chiffon(n)ier.

**şifre** [x .] cipher, code; ~ anahtarı key to a code; -yı açmak *(or* çözmek) to decode, to break a code, to decipher.

**şifrelemek** to encode, to encipher.

**şifreli** in cipher; ~ kilit combination lock.

**Şii** [- -] Shi'i.

**Şiilik** [- - .] *s.* Şia.

**şiir 1.** poem; **2.** poetry, verse.

**şiirsel** poetic(al).

**şikâyet,** -ti complaint; gripe, grouse; ~ etm. to complain; to gripe, to grouse; ~ hakkı *ʤ* right of petition.

**şikâyetçi** complainer, complainant; griper, grouser; ~ olm. to have a complaint to make *(-den* against).

**şikâyetname** [ā] written complaint.

**şike** chicane(ry); ~ yapmak to chicane.

**şikemperver** gluttonous.

**şilem** *bridge:* slam.

**şilep,** -bi freighter, cargo ship *(or* liner).

**Şili** *pr. n.* Chile.

**şilin** shilling.

**şilt,** -ti plaque.

**şilte** thin mattress.

**şimal,** -li [ā] north.

**şimalen** [ā] on the north.

**şimali** [ā] northern.

**şimdi** [x .] now; ~ bile still, yet; -ye kadar up to now.

**şimdicik** [x . .] just now.

**şimdiden** [x . .] already, right now; ~ sonra from now on, henceforth; ~ tezi yok right now, at once.

**şimdik** *s.* şimdicik.

**şimdiki** [x . .] of today, of the present time; ~ zaman *gr.* the present continuous tense.

**şimdilik** [x . .] for now, for the time being, for the present.

**şimendifer 1.** railway, railroad; **2.** train.

**şimik** chemical.

**şimşek** lightning; ~ çakmak *(for lightning)* to flash; ~ gibi like lightning, with lightning speed.

**şimşeklenmek** (for lightning) to flash.

**şimşir** ♦ boxwood, boxtree.

**şinanay** F 1. tra-la-la; 2. whoopee!, hur-rah!

**şipşak** sl. in an instant, in a flash.

**şipşakçı** street photographer.

**şipşirin** [. - -] very sweet.

**şirden** zo. abomasum.

**şirin** [- -] 1. sweet, charming, cute, cunning; 2. ♀ wf.

**şirk**, -ki polytheism; ~ koşmak to attribute a partner to God.

**şirket**, -ti company, firm; partnership; ~ kurmak to found (or establish) a company.

**şirpençe** [î] ♣ carbuncle.

**şirret**, -ti shrew, dragon, battle-ax, virago.

**şirürji** surgery.

**şiryan** [â] anat. artery.

**şist**, -ti geol. schist.

**şiş**[1] 1. spit, skewer; 2. knitting needle; ~ kebap shish kebab; -e geçirmek to skewer, to spit.

**şiş**[2] 1. swelling; 2. swollen.

**şişe** 1. bottle; flask; 2. cupping glass; 3. chimney (of a lamp); 4. lath; ~ çekmek to apply a cupping glass (-e to).

**şişeci** maker or seller of bottles.

**şişek** yearling (lamb).

**şişelemek** to bottle.

**şişirmek** caus. of şişmek 1. to inflate, to blow up; to distend; 2. to billow (sails, etc.); 3. F to exaggerate; 4. F to do hastily and carelessly; 5. sl. to stab.

**şişkin** swollen, puffed up, puffy.

**şişkinlik** 1. swelling; bulge, protuberance; 2. puffiness; 3. bloated feeling.

**şişko** [x .] co. fat(ty), paunchy.

**şişlemek** 1. to spit, to skewer; 2. sl. to stab.

**şişlik** s. şişkinlik 1 & 2.

**şişman** fat, obese, portly.

**şişmanlamak** to get (or grow) fat.

**şişmanlık** fatness, obesity.

**şişmek**, (-er) 1. to swell, to get swollen; 2. to billow (in the wind); 3. to feel too full (owing to overeating); 4. to get winded, to become out of breath; 5. to get fat; 6. sl. to feel sheepish, to be embarrassed; 7. F to give o.s. airs.

**şive** [î] 1. accent; 2. coquetry.

**şiveli** [- . .] coy, coquettish.

**şivesiz** [- . .] with a bad accent.

**şizofreni** ♣ schizophrenia.

**şofaj** heating system.

**şofben** geyser, flash heater.

**şoför** driver, chauffeur.

**şok**, -ku shock.

**şoke**: ~ etm. to shock; ~ olm. to be shocked.

**şom**: ~ ağızlı who always predicts misfortune.

**şorolo** sl. queen, homosexual.

**şorolop** P 1. in a gulp; 2. lie.

**şort**, -tu shorts.

**şose** [x .] paved road.

**şoset**, ti sock.

**şoson** galosh, overshoe.

**şov** show.

**şoven** chauvinist.

**şovenlik** chauvinism.

**şöhret**, -ti 1. fame, reputation, renown; 2. celebrity.

**şöhretli** famous, famed.

**şölen** feast, banquet.

**şömine** fireplace.

**şövale** easel.

**şövalye** knight, chevalier.

**şöyle** 1. thus(ly), in this way; like this; 2. such; this kind of; of that sort; ~ bir baktı he just glanced at it; ~ böyle 1. so-so; 2. approximately; ~ dursun let alone..., never mind about...; ~ ki such that.

**şöylece** [x . .] thus(ly), in this way; like that.

**şöylesi** this sort of...; such a... as that.

**şu**, -nu that, this; ~ günlerde in these days; ~ halde in that case; ~ var ki however, only; -na bak! just look at him!; -ndan bundan konuşmak to talk of this and that; -nu bunu bilmemek not to accept any excuses; -nun şurasında just, only.

**şua**, -aı [â] beam, ray.

**şubat**, -tı February.

**şube** [û] 1. branch (office); office; 2. division, section.

**şuf'a** ♣ preemption.

**şuh** [û] coquettish, pert.

**şule** [û] flame.

**şunca** [x .] this (or that) much.

**şura** [x .] this (or that) place.

**sûra** council.

**şuracık** [x . .] just there.

**şurada** over there.

**şuradan** from there; ~ buradan of this and that.

**şuralı** [x . .] inhabitant of that place.

**şurası** [x . .] that place; this fact; ~ muhakkak ki this much is certain.

**şuriş** disorder, tumult.

**şurup**, -bu syrup.

**şut**, -tu football: shoot; ~ çekmek to shoot.

şuur [. -] **1.** the conscious, consciousness.
şuuraltı, -nı (the) subconscious.
şuurlu conscious.
şuursuz unconscious.
şükran [ā] **1.** gratitude, thanks(giving);
**2.** ≟ *wf.; ~* borcu debt of gratitude.
şükretmek [x..] **1.** to thank God; **2.** to
give thanks (-*e* to).
şükür, -krü **1.** gratitude, thankfulness;
**2.** I thank God that..
şümul, -lü [ū] **1.** scope, sphere, inclu-
siveness; **2.** *log.* extension.
şümullendirmek [ū] to extend.
şümullu [ū] extensive, comprehensive.
şüphe **1.** suspicion, doubt; **2.** uncertainty;

*~* etm. to suspect, to doubt; *~* kurdu
gnawing doubt; *~* yok! there is no doubt
about it!; -ye düşmek to become suspicious.
şüpheci suspicious; sceptic.
şüphelenmek to suspect, to doubt, to be
in doubt (*den* about).
şüpheli **1.** suspicious, questionable; **2.**
doubtful; **3.** uncertain.
şüphesiz **1.** certain, sure; **2.** doubtless,
surely, certainly.
şüt, -tü ş. şut.
şüyu, -uu [ū] publicity; *~* bulmak to be
noised abroad.

# T

**1 cetveli**, -ni T square.

**ta** [ā] even until; even as far as; ~ eskiden beri from time immemorial; ~ kendisi his very self; ~ ki so that even.

**taabbüt**, -dü worship; ~ etm. to worship.

**taaccüp**, -bü astonishment; ~ etm. to be astonished.

**taahhüt**, -dü engagement, obligation, contract, commitment; ~ etm. to undertake, to commit o.s.; ~ senedi contract.

**taahhütlü** registered (letter).

**taahhütname** [ . . . - .] written contract.

**taalluk**, -ku relation, connection; ~ etm. to be related (-e to), to concern; -u olm. = ~ etm.

**taallukat**, -tı [ . . . - ] relatives, kin.

**taallül** evasion, subterfuge; ~ etm. to evade.

**taammüden** [ . x . . ] ﻋﺩ premeditatedly, deliberately.

**taammüm** generalization, spread; ~ etm. to spread.

**taarruz** attack, assault; ~ etm. to attack, to assault; -a geçmek to begin to attack.

**taarruzi** [ī] offensive.

**taassup**, -bu bigotry, fanaticism.

**taayyün 1.** manifestation, becoming clear; **2.** determination; ~ etm. **1.** to become manifest; **2.** to become determined.

**tab**, -b'ı s. tabı.

**taba** tobac.

**tabaat**, -tı [ . - .] printing.

**tababet**, -ti [ . - .] **1.** medical science; **2.** the medical profession.

**tabak¹** plate, dish; ~ yalamak fig. F to idle.

**tabak²** [ . - ] tanner.

**tabaka¹ 1.** layer, stratum; **2.** sheet (of paper); **3.** group, category, class (of people).

**tabaka²** tobacco box.

**tabakalaşma** geol. stratification.

**tabakhane** [ . . . - .] tannery.

**tabaklamak** to tan.

**tabaklık¹** tanning.

**tabaklık²** **1.** plate-rack; **2.** dish drainer.

**taban 1.** sole (of a shoe or foot); **2.** floor; **3.** flat top (of a hill, etc.); **4.** pedestal,

base (a. ⚓); **5.** bed (of a river); **6.** fine steel; **7.** P roller; **8.** T floor; ~ fiyat the minimum price; ~ tepmek (or patlatmak) to walk, to hoof it, to tramp, to trapes, to traipse; ~ a zıt diametrically opposite (-e to), antipodal (-e to); -a kuvvet by dint of hard walking; -ları kaldırmak iro. to run like anything; to make tracks; -ları yağlamak F to take to one's heels, to show a clean pair of heels.

**tab'an** [x .] naturally.

**tabanca** [ . x .] **1.** pistol, revolver; **2.** sprayer, spray gun; **3.** sl. bottle of raki or wine; ~ atmak to fire a pistol (-e at); ~ boyası spray paint; ~ çekmek to draw a pistol (-e on); ~ kılıfı pistol holster.

**tabanlı** soled.

**tabansız 1.** soleless; **2.** fig. cowardly, lily-livered.

**tabanvay** co.: -la gitmek to foot it, to hoof it, to go on foot.

**tabasbus** fawning, cringing; ~ etm. to fawn, to cringe, to grovel.

**tabela** [ . x .] **1.** sign; **2.** list of food (in schools, hospitals, etc.); **3.** card of treatment, chart.

**tabelacı** sign painter.

**tabetmek** [x . .] to print.

**tabı**, -b'ı **1.** print, edition, impression; **2.** character, nature.

**tabi¹**, -ii [ā] printer; publisher.

**tabi²**, -ii **1.** subject (-e to); bound (-e by); **2.** dependent (-e on), contingent (-e on); **3.** citizen; national; **4.** tributary (of a river, etc.); ~ kılmak to subject; ~ olm. (b-ne) to depend on s.o., to be dependent on s.o.; ~ tutmak (bşe) to subject to s.th., to make dependent on s.th.

**tabiat**, -tı [ . - .] **1.** nature; **2.** character, nature; **3.** taste, refinement; **4.** regularity (of the bowels); **5.** habit; ~ bilgisi nature study; ~ kanunu law of nature.

**tabiatıyla 1.** naturally; **2.** by his very nature.

**tabiatsız** ill-tempered.

**tabiatsızlık** ill-temperedness.

**tabiatüstü**, -nü supernatural.

**tabii** [ . - - ] **1.** natural; **2.** customary, habitual; **3.** unadulterated, pure; **4.** of course, naturally; ~ **afet** natural disaster; ~ **borçlar** $\frac{3}{6}$ natural obligations.

**tabiilik** naturalness.

**tabiiyat,** -tı [. - . -] the natural sciences.

**tabiiye** [. - . .] *phls.* naturalism.

**tabiiyet,** -ti nationality, citizenship.

**tabiiyetsiz** stateless *(person)*.

**tabip,** -bi [î] doctor, physician.

**tabir 1.** expression, term, phrase; idiom; **2.** interpretation *(of a dream);* ~ **caizse** if I may say so; ~ **etm. 1.** to express in words, to verbalize; **2.** to interpret *(a dream);* **tabiri diğerle** in other words.

**tabirname** [. - . .] book on the interpretation of dreams.

**tabiye** ✕ tactics.

**tabiyeci** ✕ tactician.

**tabla** [x .] **1.** circular tray; **2.** ashtray; **3.** disc; **4.** pan *(of a balance);* **5.** panel *(of a door);* **6.** metal pan or tray *(put under a stove).*

**tabldot,** -tu table d'hote.

**tablet,** -ti tablet.

**tablo** [x .] **1.** painting, picture; **2.** panorama, view, picture; **3.** table; **4.** tableau; **5.** *mot.* instrument board *(or panel).*

**tabu** taboo.

**tabur 1.** ✕ battalion; **2.** *fig.* row, line, file.

**taburcu 1.** discharged *(from a hospital);* **2.** *sl.* released from jail; ~ **etm.** to discharge, to dismiss; ~ **olm.** to be discharged.

**tabure 1.** stool; **2.** footstool; ottoman.

**tabut,** -tu **1.** coffin; **2.** egg crate.

**tabutlamak** to put into a coffin.

**tabutluk** place where empty coffins are stored.

**tabülatör** tabulator.

**tabya** [x .] ✕ bastion, redoubt.

**tacil** [- .] speeding up, hastening; ~ **etm.** to speed up, to hasten, to expedite.

**tacir** [â] merchant.

**taciz** [- -] annoyance, harassment; ~ **etm.** to annoy, to harass, to bother.

**tacizlik** harassment, bothering; ~ **getirmek 1.** to complain (-*den* about); **2.** to get fed up (-*den* with); ~ **vermek** to bother, to annoy, to harass.

**taç,** -cı **1.** crown; coronet; **2.** crest, crown *(of a bird);* **3.** $\frac{9}{6}$ corolla, petal; **4.** *ast.* corona; **5.** *football:* touchdown; ~ **giyme töreni** coronation; ~ **giymek** to be crowned.

**taçlı** crowned.

**taçsız** uncrowned.

**taçyapraklı** $\frac{9}{6}$ petaled, petalous.

**tadım** taste.

**tadımlık** just enough to taste.

**tadil** [- -] alteration, adjustment, modification; amendment; ~ **etm.** to change, to alter, to amend.

**tadilat,** -tı [- . -] *pl. of* **tadil,** changes, alterations; amendments.

**taflan** $\frac{9}{6}$ cherry laurel.

**tafra** pomposity, conceit; ~ **satmak** to talk big.

**tafracı** big talker.

**tafsil** [î] detailed explanation; ~ **etm.** to detail.

**tafsilat,** -tı details, particulars; ~ **vermek** to detail; **-a girmek** *(or* **girişmek)** to go into detail; **-iyle** in detail.

**tafsilatlı** detailed.

**tafta** taffeta.

**tagaddi** [î] nourishment; ~ **etm.** to feed; to be nurtured.

**tagallüp,** -bü **1.** tyranny; **2.** usurpation; ~ **etm.** to tyrannize (-*e* over).

**taganni** [î] singing; ~ **etm.** to sing.

**tagayyür** change, alteration; ~ **etm.** to change, to alter.

**tağdiye** feeding; ~ **etm.** to feed, to nourish.

**tağşiş** [î] adulteration; ~ **etm.** to adulterate.

**tağyir** [î] change, alteration; ~ **etm.** to change, to alter.

**tahaddüs** arising, coming into being; ~ **etm.** to arise, to come into being.

**tahaffuz** guarding o.s.; ~ **etm.** to guard o.s.

**tahaffuzhane** [. . . . - .] quarantine station.

**tahaffuzi** [î] precautionary.

**tahakkuk,** -ku **1.** realization; **2.** verification; **3.** accruement, accrual; ~ **etm. 1.** to be realized, to come true; **2.** to prove true; **3.** to fall due *(interest, tax);* ~ **memuru** tax assessor; ~ **tarihi** due date *(of a tax, interest).*

**tahakküm** tyranny; domination; ~ **etm.** *(b-ne)* to tyrannize over *s.o.;* ~ **dominate** over *s.o.*

**tahallül** $\frac{9}{6}$ dissolution; dissociation; ~ **etm.** to dissolve; to dissociate.

**tahammül 1.** patience, endurance, forbearance; **2.** durability *(of a thing);* ~ **etm.** to endure, to bear, to put up (-*e* with); ~ **olunamayacak derecede** unbearably.

**tahammülfersa** [. . . . -] $\frac{9}{6}$ unbearable, unendurable.

**tahammüllü** patient.

**tahammülsüz** impatient, intolerant.

**tahammür** fermentation; ~ **etm.** to ferment.

**taharet**, -ti [. - .] **1.** cleanliness, purity; **2.** canonical purification *(of the body);* ~ kâğıdı toilet paper.

**taharri** [ī] **1.** investigation, research; **2.** search; ~ etm. **1.** to investigate; **2.** to search; ~ memuru plainclothesman.

**taharrüş** ♀ itching; irritation; ~ etm. to itch; to be irritated.

**tahassul**, -lü resulting, emerging; ~ etm. to result, to emerge.

**tahassür** longing, yearning; ~ etm. to long *(-e* for), to yearn *(-e* for).

**tahassüs** sensation.

**tahaşşüt**, -dü concentration *(of troops);* ~ etm. to be concentrated *(or* amassed) *(troops).*

**tahavvül** change, conversion; ~ etm. to change.

**tahayyül 1.** imagination; fancy; **2.** daydreaming; ~ etm. **1.** to imagine; **2.** to fantasize; to daydream.

**tahdidat**, -tı [. - -] *pl. of* tahdit, limitations; restrictions.

**tahdit**, -di [ī] **1.** limitation; restriction; **2.** demarcation, delimitation; ~ etm. **1.** to limit; to restrict; **2.** to demarcate, to delimit.

**tahıl 1.** grain; **2.** cereal; ~ ambarı granary.

**tahin** [- .] sesame oil; ~ helvası hal(a)vah.

**tahini** [- . -] tan(-coloured).

**tahkik**, -ki [ī] investigation; ~ etm. to investigate.

**tahkikat**, -tı [. - -] *pl. of* tahkik, inquiry; probe, investigation; ~ yapmak to conduct an investigation.

**tahkim** [ī] **1.** fortification; **2.** strengthening; **3.** ₰ resolution of a dispute by arbitration; ~ etm. **1.** to fortify; **2.** to strengthen; **3.** ₰ to resolve by arbitration.

**tahkimat**, -tı [. - -] ✕ fortifications.

**tahkimli** [. - .] fortified.

**tahkir** [ī] insult, scorn; ~ etm. to insult, to despise, to scorn.

**tahlif** [ī] swearing *(a witness);* ~ etm. to swear *(a witness).*

**tahlil** [ī] analysis; ~ etm. to analyze.

**tahlili** [. - -] analytical.

**tahlisiye** [. - . .] lifeboat service; ~ sandalı lifeboat; ~ simidi life buoy; ~ yeleği life jacket.

**tahliye 1.** evacuation *(of people);* **2.** emptying; **3.** discharging, unloading *(cargo);* **4.** vacating *(a building);* **5.** releasing *(a prisoner);* ~ etm. **1.** to evacuate *(people, a place);* **2.** to empty; to unload, to discharge *(cargo);* **3.** to vacate *(a build-*

*ing);* **4.** to release, to set free *(a prisoner).*

**tahmil** [ī] **1.** loading; **2.** imposition *(of a task);* **3.** imputation, *(of blame, etc.)* ~ etm. **1.** to load; **2.** to impose *(a task)* (-e on); **3.** to lay *(the blame)* (-e on).

**tahmin** [ī] **1.** guess, conjecture, surmisal; **2.** estimation; prediction; ~ etm. **1.** to guess, to conjecture, to surmise; **2.** to estimate, to reckon, to judge; to predict, to forecast.

**tahminen** [ī] [. ✕ .] approximately; roughly.

**tahmini** [. - -] approximate; conjectural.

**tahminlemek** [ī] *s.* tahmin etm.

**tahnit**, -ti [ī] embalmment; ~ etm. **1.** to embalm *(a corpse);* **2.** to stuff *(a dead animal).*

**tahra** P pruning hook.

**Tahran** [. -] *pr. n.* Tehran.

**tahribat**, -tı [. - -] damage, destruction; ~ yapmak to damage, to destroy.

**tahrif** [ī] distortion, falsification; misrepresentation *(of facts);* ~ etm. to distort *(a meaning);* to misrepresent *(facts).*

**tahrifat**, -tı [. - -] distortions; misrepresentations.

**tahrik**, -ki [ī] incitement, instigation, provocation, fomentation; ~ etm. **1.** to incite, to instigate, to provoke, to foment; **2.** to stimulate, to excite, to arouse, to stir; **3.** to propel, to drive; to move.

**tahrikât**, -tı *pl. of* tahrik *pol.* incitements, provocations, instigations.

**tahrikçi** instigator, provocator, fomenter.

**tahril** stripe, line.

**tahrip**, -bi [ī] destruction, devastation, demolition; ~ etm. to destroy, to ruin, to devastate; to demolish.

**tahripçi** [. - .], **tahripkâr** [. - -] destructive.

**tahrir** [ī] **1.** composing, writing down; **2.** registration; **3.** essay, composition; ~ etm. to compose, to write down, to draft; -i nüfus population census.

**tahriri** [. - -] written.

**tahriş** ♀ irritation; ~ edici irritative; ~ etm. to irritate.

**tahsil** [ī] **1.** education, study; **2.** collection *(of money);* ~ etm. **1.** to study, to get an education; **2.** to collect *(money, taxes);* ~ görmek to get an education, to study.

**tahsilat**, -tı revenue, money received.

**tahsildar** [. - -] **1.** receiving teller *(in a bank);* **2.** tax collector.

tahsis [ⁱ] assignment, appropriation, allotment; ~ etm. to assign, to appropriate, to allot.

tahsisat, -tı [.--] pl. of tahsis. appropriation, allotment, allowance; ~ ayırmak to appropriate money (-e for).

tahşit, -di [î] concentration, amassing (of troops); ~ etm. to concentrate, to amass (troops).

taht, -tı throne; -a çıkarmak (or oturtmak) to enthrone; -a çıkmak (or geçmek or oturmak) to ascend the throne; -tan indirmek to dethrone.

tahta 1. board, plank; batten; 2. blackboard; 3. sheet (of metal); 4. wooden...; 5. bed (in a garden); ~ perde board fence, hoarding; -dan wooden; -sı eksik co. screwy, nutty, balmy.

tahtabiti, -ni s. tahtakurusu.

tahtaboş wooden balcony.

tahtakoz sl. policeman, fuzz, cop.

tahtakurusu, -nu zo. bedbug.

tahtalı 1. boarded; planked; 2. zo. ringdove; ~ köy sl. cemetery, boneyard; ~ köyü boylamak sl. to kick the bucket, to peg out, to go to one's long account.

tahtapuş s. tahtaboş.

tahtelhıfız, -fzı under guard; in custody.

tahterevalli [...x.] seesaw, teeterboard, teeter-totter.

tahteşşuur subconscious.

tahtezzemin [î] underground, subterranean.

tahtırevan [...-] 1. howdah; 2. palanquin.

tahvil [î] 1. transformation; transfer; conversion; 2. † bond, debenture; ~ etm. to transform; to transfer; to convert.

tahvilat, -tı † bonds, debentures, securities.

taife [-..] s. tayfa.

tak¹, -kı [â] arch.

tak² thump, knock; ~ ~ kapı vuruldu there was a knock on the door.

taka 1. small sailing boat; 2. sl. jalopy, rattletrap.

takaddüm 1. precedence; 2. antecedence; ~ etm. 1 to have precedence (-e over); 2. to antecede; 3. to act before s.o. else does.

takanak s. takıntı.

takarrüp, -bü approach; ~ etm. to approach, to near.

takarrür 1. establishment; 2. being decided; ~ etm. 1. to be established; 2. to be decided.

takas 1. barter, swap, exchange; 2. † clearing; ~ etm. 1. to barter, to swap,

to exchange; 2. † to clear; ~ tukas etm. to square accounts with each other.

takat, -ti [-.] strength (a. phys.); ~ getirmek to endure; -i kalmamak (or kesilmek or tükenmek) to be exhausted (or worn out).

takatlı strong.

takatsiz [-..] weak, debilitated.

takatuka [..x.] 1. noise, tumult, commotion; 2. spittoon; 3. typ. quoin.

takayyüt, -dü 1. attentiveness, attention, care; 2. vigilance; ~ etm. 1. to pay attention (-e to), to take care (-e of); 2. to be vigilant.

takaza [.--] taunt; ~ etm. to taunt, to rub it in.

takbih [î] disapproval; ~ etm. to disapprove.

takdim [î] 1. introduction; 2. presentation; ~ etm 1. to present, to tender, to offer; 2. (b-ni) to introduce s.o. to another; ~ tehir inversion.

takdimci compère, emcee.

takdir [î] 1. appreciation; 2. judg(e)ment, discretion; 3. commendation, approval, applause; 4. predestination, fate; ~ etm. 1. to appreciate; 2. to commend, to approve, to applaud; 3. to evaluate, to value; 4. (for God) to predestine, to foreordain; ~ hakkı ඇ judicial discretion; ~ toplamak to win general approval; -de in the event of..., if...; -e bağlı muamele ඇ discretionary act; -ine bırakmak (b-nin) to leave (a matter) to s.o.'s judg(e)ment; öldüğü -de in the event of his death.

takdirkâr [î] 1. appreciative; 2. appreciator.

takdirname [.--.] letter of commendation (or appreciation).

takdis [î] 1. sanctification, consecration; 2. veneration; ~ etm. 1. to bless, to sanctify, to consecrate, to hallow; 2. to venerate, to revere; 3. to glorify (God).

takı 1. wedding present; 2. gr. particle.

takılgan teaser.

takılı 1. gr. affixed; 2. attached (-e to); fastened (-e to).

takılmak 1. pass. of takmak; 2. to kid, to tease, to rally, to pull s.o.'s leg; 3. fig. (bş. üzerinde) to get stuck on s.th., to get snagged on s.th., to get hung up on s.th. 4. to get hung up in, to be delayed in (a place).

takım 1. team, group, band, gang, crew, troop; 2. set (of things); 3. ඇ. order; 4. ✕ platoon; 5. ⊕ train; ~ elbise suit; ~ mukavelesi ඇ collective agreement;

~ taklavat *F* the whole kit and caboodle, the whole push; ~ tutmak to support a team, to root for a team.

takımada archipelago.

takımyıldız *ast.* constellation.

takınmak 1. to assume *(an air)*; 2. to put on *(ornaments)*.

takıntı 1. ramification; 2. outstanding debt; 3. dealings, relationship; 4. *F* subject which a student has flunked; 5. piece of jewelry.

takırdamak to clatter, to rattle, to bang.

takırdatmak to rattle, to clatter.

takır takır 1. with a rattling noise; 2. very stale *(food)*; 3. hard and dry.

takırtı rattle, clatter; clop-clop.

takır tukur with a clattering noise.

takışmak 1. to tease each other; 2. to quarrel with each other.

takıştırmak to deck o.s. out in jewels.

takızafer [- . . . .] triumphal arch.

takibat, -tı [- - -] legal proceedings *(or* action); prosecution *(of a case).*

takip, -bi [- -] 1. following; pursuit; 2. ﻻ legal proceedings; prosecution *(of a case);* ~ etm. 1. to follow, to pursue, to trail; 2. to follow, to succeed; 3. to keep up with, to follow *(a fashion).*

takke skullcap.

takla somersault; cartwheel; ~ atmak *(or* kılmak) 1. to turn a somersault, to somersault; 2. *fig.* to jump for joy.

tak'ak *s.* takla.

taklidi [. - -] imitative.

taklit, -di [î] 1. imitation; 2. counterfeit, imitated, sham; 3. imitative; 4. mockery, impersonation; ~ etm. 1. to imitate, to copy, to duplicate, to reproduce; 2. to imitate, to ape; 3. to fake, to counterfeit; 4. to impersonate, to mimic, to mock.

taklitçi 1. imitator, copier; 2. impersonator; mimic.

takma 1. *vn.* of takmak; 2. artificial *(tooth, eye);* false *(beard);* 3. prefabricated; ~ ad 1. nickname; 2. pen name; ~ diş false teeth; ~ motor outboard motor; ~ saç wig.

takmak, (-ar) 1. to attach, to fasten, to put on, to affix, to fit; 2. to nickname; 3. to pick on; 4. *sl. school:* to fail, to flunk; 5. to put on; to wear; takıp takıştırmak to deck o.s. out in jewelry.

takmamak *sl.* to take no notice (-i of), to pay no heed (-i of).

takoz 1. wedge, chock; 2. shore, prop; 3. plug.

takozlamak 1. to shore up; 2. to put a

wedge under *or* behind s.th.

takriben [î] [. x .] approximately, about.

takribi [. - -] approximate.

takrir [î] 1. explaining, expounding; 2. report, memorandum; 3. proposal, motion; ~ etm. to present, to expound.

takriz [î] laudatory preface to a book.

taksa [x .] postage due; ~ pulu postage-due stamp.

taksi [x .] taxi, cab; ~ durağı taxi rank, cabstand.

taksim [î] 1. division; partition, distribution; 2. slash (mark), diagonal, virgule; 3. ♪ division sign; 4. ♪ instumental improvisation; ~ etm. 1. to divide up; to share out, to distribute; 2. ♪ to improvise; ~ geçmek = ~ etm. 2; ~ işareti slash (mark), diagonal, virgule.

taksimat, -tı [. - -] divisions, sections, parts.

taksimetre taximeter.

taksir [î] 1. cutting short; 2. failure in duty, remissness; ~ etm. 1. to cut short, to curtail; 2. to be remiss.

taksirat, -tı [. - -] 1. sins; 2. *F* fate, destiny.

taksit, -ti instal(l)ment; ~ ~ in instal(l)ments; -le in instal(l)ments.

tak tak *s.* tak².

taktik 1. tactic, manoeuvre, *Am.* maneuver; 2. ✕ tactics.

taktir [î] distillation; ~ etm. to distil(l).

tak tuk knock! knock!

takunya, takunye [. x .] clog, patten.

takvim [î] calendar; ~ yılı calendar year.

takviye reinforcement *(a.* ✕); ~ etm. to reinforce *(a.* ✕); to strengthen.

takyit, -di [î] restriction; ~ etm. to restrict, to limit.

talak, -kı *isl.* ﻻ divorce.

talan pillage, plunder, sack; ~ etm. to pillage, to plunder, to sack.

talaş 1. sawdust; wood shavings; 2. metal filings.

talaşlamak to sprinkle sawdust over *(a place).*

talaz 1. wave *(in the sea);* 2. ripple, undulation *(in a piece of silk).*

talebe student, pupil.

talebelik being a student *or* pupil.

talebetmek [. x .] to demand, to want, to require, to request.

talep, -bi demand, request; ~ etm. to demand, to want, to require, to request.

tali secondary; subordinate; ~ cümle *gr.* subordinate clause; ~ komisyon subcommittee

**talih** [ā] luck, good fortune; ~ kuşu good luck; -i olmamak to be unlucky; -i yaver gitmek to be lucky; -ine küsmek to curse one's luck.

**talihli** [ā] lucky, fortunate.

**talihsiz** [ā] unlucky.

**talihsizlik** [ā] bad luck, lucklessness, mischance.

**talik**, -kı [- -] 1. postponement; 2. depending on, hinging on; 3. calligraphic style; ~ etm. 1. to postpone, to put off; 2. to depend (-e on), to hinge (-e on).

**talika** [. x .] a small, horsedrawn vehicle.

**talim** [- -] 1. instruction, training; 2. practice, drill, exercise; 3. X drill; ~ etm. 1. to teach, to instruct; 2. to practice; 3. X to drill; ~ fişeği blank (cartridge); ~ meydanı X drill field; ~ ve terbiye training.

**talimat**, -tı [- - -] instructions, directions; ~ vermek to instruct, to give instructions.

**talimatname** [- . . . -] regulations book.

**talimgâh** [- . -] X training centre.

**talimhane** [- . - .] X drill field.

**talimli** [ā] trained; instructed; practiced.

**talimname** [- . - .] 1. X field manual; 2. technical manual.

**talip**, -bi 1. desirous, wishful; 2. suitor, wooer; 3. applicant; 4. customer; ~ çıkmak to become the suitor (-e of); ~ olm. 1. to desire, to want, to seek; 2. to seek the hand of a woman in marriage.

**talk**, -kı geol. talc(um); ~ pudrası talc, talcum powder.

**tallahi** [x . .] by God!

**taltif** [î] 1. favo(u)r, kindness; 2. recompense; ~ etm. 1. to gratify, to please, to win the heart of; 2. to reward.

**talveg** [x .] (hattı) geogr. thalweg.

**tam** 1. complete, perfect; full, whole; 2. fully, completely; 3. exactly; immediately; ~ acı A perigon; ~ adamını bulmak to choose the very man (for the job, etc.); ~ iki kilo a full two kilos; ~ pansiyon full pension; ~ -ına (or -ı -ına) completely; in full; ~ tertip thoroughly; ~ teşekküllü bir hastane a fully equipped hospital; ~ üstüne basmak to hit the nail right on the head; ~ vaktinde right on time; ~ yetki full authority; ~ yol at full (or top) speed.

**tamah** greed, avarice, cupidity.

**tamahkâr** 1. greedy, avaricious; 2. miserly, stingy, tight.

**tamam** 1. complete, finished; ready; 2. the whole of the.... all of the...; 3. correct; 4. O.K.!, all right!; 5. fully; for a whole; ~ etm. to finish, to complete, to termi-

nate; -ı -ına completely; in full.

**tamamen** [. - .] [. x .] completely, wholly, entirely, quite.

**tamamiyet**, -ti [. - . .] completeness, entirety.

**tamamıyla** s. tamamen.

**tamamlamak** to complete, to finish; to complement.

**tamamlayıcı** complementary, complemental; supplementary, supplemental.

**tambur** ♪ a kind of stringed instrument similar to the mandolin.

**tambura** [. x .] any stringed instrument.

**tamburi** [. - -] player of a tambur.

**tamim** [- -] 1. circular; 2. generalization; 3. circularization; ~ etm. 1. to circularize; 2. to generalize; 3. to diffuse.

**tamir** [- -] repair; restoration; ~ etm. to repair, to mend, to fix; ~ görmek to be repaired (or mended or fixed); -e vermek (bşi) to have s.th. repaired.

**tamirat**, -tı [- - -] repairs.

**tamirci** [ā] repairman, repairer.

**tamirhane** [- . - .] repair shop.

**tamlama** gr. 1. noun phrase; 2. prepositional phrase.

**tamlayan** gr. modifier.

**tampon** 1. mot. bumper; 2. 🚂 buffer; 3. ∯ tampon, plug, pack; 4. 🔬 buffer; 5. blotter; ~ devlet buffer state.

**tamsayı** A whole number.

**tamtakır** [x .] absolutely empty; ~ kuru bakır absolutely empty.

**tamtam** tom-tom.

**tan** dawn, daybreak; ~ ağarmak to dawn, (for day) to break.

**tanassur** conversion to Christianity; ~ etm. to become a Christian.

**Tanca** pr. n. Tangier(s).

**tandans** tendency.

**tandır** 1. oven (made in a hole in the earth); 2. heating arrangement; ~ kebabı dish of meat roasted in an oven.

**tandırname** [. . . .] old wives' tale.

**tane** [ā] 1. kernel, grain; 2. grain (of salt, sand, sugar, etc.); 3. item, piece, ~ -~ in separate pieces; ~ ~ konuşmak to speak distinctly; ~ tutmak (or -ye gelmek) to ear (up), to form ears.

**tanecik** [ā] 1. granule (of sand, salt, sugar, etc.); 2. tiny kernel; 3. particle.

**tanecikli** [ā] granular.

**tanecil** [ā] zo. granivorous (animal).

**tanelemek** [ā] 1. to granulate; 2. to shell.

**tanelenmek** [ā] 1. pass. of tanelemek; 2. to ear (up), to form ears (cereal plant).

**taneli** [ā] grainy.

**tanen** 🔬 tannin.

**tanga** very skimpy bikini, G-string.

**tangırdamak** to clatter, to clang.

**tangırdatmak** to clatter, to clang.

**tangır tangır** clatteringly.

**tangırtı** clatter, clang, racket.

**tangırtılı** clattery, clattering.

**tangır tungur** with a clatter.

**tango** [x .] **1.** ♪ tango; **2.** sl. loudly dressed woman.

**tanı** diagnosis.

**tanıdık** acquaintance; ~ çıkmak to have met before.

**tanık** (eye)witness; ~ olm. to witness.

**tanıklık** testimony, witness; ~ etm. to testify.

**tanılamak** to diagnose.

**tanım** definition.

**tanıma** vn. of tanımak, part. 🕸 recognition, acknowledgement.

**tanımak 1.** to recognize, to know; **2.** to be acquainted, to know; **3.** to be able to distinguish, to recognize, to know; **4.** to recognize, to acknowledge; **5.** to listen to, to pay attention to; to respect; **6.** to hold responsible.

**tanımlama** definition.

**tanımlamak** to define.

**tanımsal** definitional.

**tanınmak 1.** to be (well-)known; **2.** to be known for; **3.** to be acknowledged (or recognized); dürüstlüğüyle tanınır he is known for his honesty.

**tanınmış 1.** famous, well-known, famed, reputable; **2.** known for; doğru ~ bir hâkim a judge who's known for his honesty.

**tanış** F acquaintance; ~ çıkmak to have met before.

**tanışık:** ~ çıkmak to have met before.

**tanışıklık** acquaintance(ship).

**tanışmak** to get acquainted (ile with), to be acquainted (ile with), to make the acquaintance (ile of); to know one another.

**tanıştırmak** to introduce.

**tanıt, -tı** proof, evidence.

**tanıtıcı** introductory.

**tanıtım 1.** introduction, presentation; **2.** advertisement.

**tanıtlamak** to prove.

**tanıtmacı** 🕈 salesman, sales representative.

**tanıtmak 1.** to introduce, to present; **2.** to advertise, to publicize.

**tanjant, -tı** 📐 tangent.

**tank, -kı** tank.

**tankçı** ✕ tanker.

**tanker** tanker.

**tanksavar** ✕ **1.** antitank; **2.** antitank weapon.

**tanrı 1.** god, deity; **2.** ♀ God; ~ hakkı için for God's sake; ~ kayrası Providence; ~ misafiri unexpected guest; -nın günü every blessed (or doggone) day.

**Tanrıbilim** theology.

**Tanrıbilimci** theologian.

**Tanrıcılık** theism.

**tanrıça** goddess.

**tanrılaşmak** to become a god, to become divine.

**tanrılaştırmak** to deify.

**tanrılık** divinity, godhood.

**tanrısal** divine.

**tanrısız** godless, atheistic.

**Tanrıtanımazlık** atheism.

**tansiyon 1.** 🕈 blood pressure; **2.** tension; ~ aleti sphygmomanometer; ~ düşüklüğü 🕈 hypotension; ~ yüksekliği hypertension.

**tantana** pomp, display; grandiosity.

**tantanalı** pompous, grand; grandiose.

**tan tuna gitmek** sl. to be killed; to be done for.

**tanyeli, -ni** dawn breeze.

**tanyeri, -ni** dawn; ~ ağarmak (for dawn) to break.

**tanzifat, -tı** [. . -] street-cleaning.

**tanzim 1.** organizing, arranging; **2.** regulating; reorganizing; **3.** drafting, drawing up, preparing; ~ etm. **1.** to organize, to arrange, to determine; **2.** to regulate; to reorganize; to put in order; **3.** to draft, to draw up, to prepare; ~ satışı sale of foodstuffs by a municipality in order to regulate prices.

**Tanzimat, -tı** [. - -] pr. n. the political reforms made in the Ottoman state in 1839.

**tapa** [x .] **1.** stopper; cork; plug; bung; **2.** fuse (for a bomb).

**tapalamak** to stopper, to put a stopper (-ı on).

**tapalı** stoppered.

**tapı** god, deity.

**tapınak** temple, place of worship.

**tapınmak,** (-ır), **tapmak,** (-ar) **1.** to worship; **2.** to idolize, to adore.

**tapon** F shoddy, fourth-rate, crummy, sorry.

**taptaze** [x - .] very fresh.

**tapu 1.** (title) deed; **2.** (dairesi) deed (or land) office; ~ kütüğü register of title deeds; ~ senedi (title) deed.

**tapulamak 1.** to register with a title deed, to get title for (a piece of land); **2.** to issue a title deed for (a piece of land).

**tapyoka** [. x .] tapioca.

**taraça** [. x .] terrace.

**taraf** 1. side; part, portion; 2. region, area; direction; 3. party; litigant; 4. behalf; ~ tutmak to take sides; -a olm. *(b-den)* to side with *s.o.*, to be for *s.o.;* -ını tutmak *(b-nin)* to side with *s.o.*

**tarafeyn** the two parties; the prosecution and the defence.

**tarafgir** [i] partial, biased.

**taraflı** 1. -sided, -edged; 2. supporter, adherent; 3. person from a certain region; sen ne taraflısın? what part of the country are you from?

**tarafsız** 1. neutral; noncommittal; 2. impartial, unbiased.

**tarafsızlık** 1. neutrality; 2. impartiality.

**taraftar** [. . -] supporter, adherent, follower, advocate, partisan; ~ olm. to support, to be in favo(u)r (-e of).

**taraftarlık** 1. adherence, advocacy; 2. partiality, partisanship.

**tarak** 1. comb; 2. hackle, hatchel; 3. reed; 4. rake; harrow; 5. gill *(of a fish);* 6. *anat.* instep, metatarsus *(of the foot);* 7. *zo.* crest *(of a bird);* 8. *zo.* scallop; cockle; 9. dredge; 10. dragnet; ~ dubası dredger; ~ gemisi dredge; ~ vurmak to comb.

**tarakişi**, -ni serrated embroidery.

**taraklamak** 1. to comb; 2. to rake; 3. to dredge; 4. to hackle; to card, to comb *(wool).*

**tarakıl** 1. crested *(bird);* 2. serrated *(cloth);* 3. wide *(foot).*

**tarakotu**, -nu ♀ teasel.

**taralı** 1. combed; 2. raked; 3. dredged.

**tarama** 1. *vn.* of taramak; 2. hachure; 3. red caviar.

**taramak** 1 to comb; 2. to rake, to harrow; 3. to hackle; to card, to comb; 4. to dredge; 5. to search thoroughly, to comb; 6. to scan, to give the once-over; 7. to (cross)hatch; to hachure *(a map).*

**taranmak** 1. *pass.* of taramak; 2. to comb one's hair.

**tarantı** 1. combings; 2. rakings; 3. dredgings.

**tarassut**, -du *ast.*, X observation; surveillance; ~ etm. to observe; to keep under surveillance.

**tara'or** *sauce made with vinegar and walnuts.*

**taravet**, -ti [. - .] freshness; tenderness.

**taraz** ravels, ravelings, fuzz; ~ ~ olm. *s.* tarazlanmak.

**tarazlamak** to remove the ravelings from.

**tarazlanmak** 1. to ravel, to fuzz; 2. *(for hair)* to frizz.

**tarçın** cinnamon.

**tardetmek** [x . .] 1. to expel (-den from); to dismiss (-den from), to discharge (-den from); 2. X to repulse, to drive back.

**taret**, -ti X turret.

**tarh** 1. A subtraction; 2. imposition *(of a tax);* 3. *(a.* çiçek tarhı) flower bed.

**tarhana** [x . .] *preparation of yogurt and flour dried in the sun;* ~ çorbası *soup made with* tarhana.

**tarhetmek** [x . .] 1. to subtract; 2. to impose *(a tax).*

**tarhun** ♀ tarragon, estragon.

**tarım** agriculture, farming.

**tarımcı** agriculturist.

**tarımsal** agricultural.

**tarif** [- -] 1. description; 2. definition; 3. recipe; ~ edilemez indescribable; ~ etm. 1. to describe; 2. to define; -e uymak to match the description, to answer to the description.

**tarife** [â] 1. tariff; 2. timetable, schedule; 3. directions, instructions; 4. recipe.

**tarih** [â] 1. history; 2. date; 3. chronogram; ~ atmak *(or* koymak) to date; -e geçmek to go down in history as; -e karışmak to become a thing of the past.

**tarihçe** [â] short history.

**tarihçi** [â] 1. historian; 2. history teacher.

**tarihi** [- . -] historic(al).

**tarihli** [â] dated; 20 Nisan ~ bir mektup a letter dated 20 April.

**tarihöncesi**, -ni [â] 1. prehistory; 2. prehistoric(al).

**tarihsel** [â] historic(al).

**tarihsiz** [â] 1. undated; 2. historyless.

**tarik**, -kı 1. road; 2. way of life, path.

**tarikat**, -tı [i] 1. *isl.* tarekat, tariqa, dervish order; 2. tariqa(t). Sufi path.

**tarikatçı** [i] *isl.* member of a tariqa, dervish.

**tariz** [- -] allusion, hint, innuendo; ~ etm. to get in a dig (-e at), to allude (-e to).

**tarla** [x .] field; ~ açmak to clear a piece of land; ~ sürmek to plough, Am. to plow.

**tarlafaresi**, -ni *zo.* vole.

**tarlakuşu**, -nu *zo.* skylark.

**tarpan** tarpan.

**tarsin** [i] strengthening; ~ etm. to strengthen.

**tart**[1], -tı pie.

**tart**[2], -dı 1. expulsion; discharge, dismissal; 2. X repulse, repulsion.

**tartaklamak** to rough up, to manhandle.

**tartar** ʔ tartar.

**tartı 1.** weight, heaviness; **2.** balance, scales; **3.** ↓ line; **4.** *poetry:* meter; ~ aleti weighing device, scale; -ya gelmemek to be unweighable; -ya vurmak to weigh.

**tartıcı** weigher.

**tartıl** ʔ quantitative.

**tartılı 1.** weighed; **2.** well-considered; **3.** metrical *(poem)*.

**tartışma** *vn. of* tartışmak, *part.* debate, discussion; dispute, argument.

**tartışmacı** debater, discussant, disputant.

**tartışmak** to debate, to dispute, to argue, to discuss.

**tartışmalı** disputatious.

**tartmak,** (-ar) **1.** to weigh *(a. fig.);* **2.** to sound *(or* feel) out; **3.** to evaluate, to size up.

**tartura** [. x .] lathe wheel.

**tarumar** [- . -] confused, jumbled, topsy-turvy; ~ etm. to disarray, to make a mess of.

**tarz 1.** manner, way, sort, kind; **2.** style.

**tarziye** apology; ~ vermek to apologize (-e to).

**tas** cup, bowl; porringer; ~ gibi bald *(head);* ~ kebabı goulash *(a stew made of meat and vegetables);* -ı tarağı toplamak *fig.* to pack one's bags, to pack up one's belongings *(or* traps).

**tasa** worry, anxiety; ~ etm. *(or* çekmek) to worry, -mın on beşi! *F* I don't care!, what is it to me!; -sı sana mı düştü? what is it to you?, it's no concern of yours!

**tasaddi** attempt; ~ etm. to attempt, to try.

**tasalandırmak** to worry.

**tasalanmak** to worry.

**tasalı** worried, anxious, troubled.

**tasallut,** -tu **1.** molestation; **2.** attack; ~ etm. **1.** to molest; **2.** to attack.

**tasallüp,** -bü hardening; ~ etm. to harden.

**tasannu,** -uu simulation, pretense; artificiality.

**tasar** plan.

**tasarı 1.** plan, project, scheme; **2.** bill, draft law; proposal.

**tasarım 1.** conception, envisagement; **2.** concept, idea; **3.** *phls.* presentation.

**tasarımlamak** to imagine, to conceive, to envisage.

**tasarlamak 1.** to envisage, to envision, to plan, to project; **2.** to rough out, to

roughhew; tasarlayarak öldürmek ঠঠ to murder premeditatedly.

**tasarruf 1.** ঠঠ disposition, disposal; possession; management, administration! **2.** economy, thrift; saving *(money);* **3.** savings; ~ bankası savings bank; ~ bonosu a kind of savings bond; ~ etm. **1.** to save (up), to save money, to economize; **2.** to have the use of; ~ hesabı savings account; ~ mevduatı savings deposit; ~ sandığı savings bank.

**tasarruflu** thrifty, economical, frugal.

**tasasız** carefree, lighthearted.

**tasasızlık** carefreeness, lightheartedness.

**tasavvuf** *isl.* Sufism, Islamic mysticism.

**tasavvufi** *isl.* Sufistic, Sufic.

**tasavvur 1.** imagination, conception, envisagement; **2.** concept, idea; ~ etm. to imagine, to conceive, to envisage.

**tasdi,** -ii [i] discommoding, inconveniencing; ~ etm. to discommode, to inconvenience.

**tasdik,** -kı [i] **1.** confirmation; certification; **2.** ratification; ~ etm. to confirm, to certify, to ratify, to affirm.

**tasdikli** certified, ratified.

**tasdikname** [. . . -] **1.** certificate; letter of confirmation; **2.** certificate of attendance *(given to a student who leaves a school without graduating).*

**tasdiksiz** uncertified.

**tasfiye 1.** ✝ liquidation; **2.** purification; **3.** discharge, elimination *(of the employees);* ~ etm. **1.** to purify, to clarify, to refine; **2.** ✝ to liquidate; **3.** to discharge, to eliminate *(employees);* ~ memuru ঠঠ liquidator; -ye gitmek ✝ to go into liquidation.

**tasfiyeci** purist.

**tasfiyehane** [. . . - .] refinery.

**tashih** [i] correction; rectification, amendment; ~ etm. to correct; to rectify, to amend.

**tasımlamak 1.** to plan; **2.** to estimate, to reckon.

**taslak 1.** draft, sketch, outline; **2.** model, maquette; **3.** *contp.* would-be; şair taslağı would-be poet.

**taslamak 1.** to pretend, to make a show of, to feign, to fake, to simulate, to sham; **2.** to hew.

**tasma 1.** collar; **2.** strap *(of clogs);* **3.** *sl.* sucker, pushover; ~ takmak to put a collar (-e on).

**tasni,** -ii [i i] fabrication, invention; ~ etm. to fabricate, to make up, to concoct, to devise.

**tasnif** [i] classification; ~ etm. to classify.

**tasrif** [i] *gr.* inflection; conjugation; ~ etm. to inflect, to conjugate.

**tasrih** [i] clear expression; ~ etm. to explain clearly, to specify.

**tastamum** [x..] absolutely complete; altogether perfect.

**tasvip**, -bi [i] approval; sanction; ~ etm. to approve, to give one's approval; to sanction.

**tasvir** [i] 1. description, depiction; 2. *P* picture; ~ etm. to describe, to portray, to depict; ~ gibi as pretty as a picture.

**tasviri** [i] descriptive.

**taş** 1. stone; rock; 2. playing piece, counter; 3. stone, gem *(in a piece of jewelry)*; 4. ☏ calculus, stone; 5. *fig.* dig, allusion, innuendo; ~ arabası *sl.* blockhead, dodo; ~ atmak to get in a dig (*-e* at), to make an allusion (*-e* about); ~ bebek doll; ~ çatlasa by no means, whatever happens; ~ çıkartmak *(b-ne)* to be able to run rings around *s.o.*, to be far superior to *s.o.*; ~ devri *hist.* the Stone Age; ~ gibi 1. as hard as a rock; 2. stonyhearted, hardhearted; ~ kesilmek *fig.* to be dumbfounded; ~ ocağı stone quarry; ~ tahta slate; ~ ~ üstünde bırakmamak to leave no stone standing, to level with the ground; ~ tutmak *sl.* to have money; -a tutmak to stone, to stone to death; -ı gediğine koymak to hit the nail on the head; -ı sıksa suyunu çıkarır *fig.* he is very strong; -tan ekmeğini çıkarmak *fig.* to be able to make a living out of anything.

**taşak** testicle, testis, ball, nut.

**taşbaskı** lithography.

**taşbasması**, -nı lithograph.

**taşçı** 1. quarryman, quarrier; 2. stonecutter; 3. stonemason.

**taşeron** subcontractor.

**taşıl** fossil.

**taşıllaşmak** to fossilize.

**taşım**: ~ kaynamak *(for a liquid)* to come to the boil.

**taşıma** 1. *vn.* of taşımak; 2. transport.

**taşımacı** transporter, carrier; forwarder.

**taşımacılık** transportation, shipping.

**taşımak** 1. to carry, to transport; 2. to bear, to support, to sustain, to hold up *(a weight)*; 3. to carry, to bear, to possess *(a name, etc.)*.

**taşınır** movable, portable, transferable, conveyable.

**taşınmak** 1. *pass.* of taşımak; 2. to move (*-e* to), to remove (*-e* to); 3. to go too often (*-e* to).

**taşınmaz** immovable, real *(property)*.

**taşırmak** to overflow.

**taşıt**, -tı vehicle, conveyance, means of transportation; ~ giremez no entry; ~ kazası traffic accident.

**taşıyıcı** 1. porter, carrier; stevedore; 2. conveyor

**taşkın** 1. overflowing; 2. rowdy, boisterous, exuberant; 3. flood, inundation.

**taşkınlık** rowdiness, boisterousness, impetuosity.

**taşkömür(ü)** (pit)coal.

**taşlama** 1. *vn.* of taşlamak; 2. satirizing; 3. satire; lampoon.

**taşlamacı** 1. satirist; 2. honer.

**taşlamak** 1. to stone; 2. to stone to death; 3. *fig.* to satirize; to lampoon; 4. to hone; 5. to pave with stones; 6. *fig.* to get in a dig (*-i* at).

**taşlaşmak** to petrify, to turn to stone.

**taşlı** 1. stony; 2. set with stones.

**taşlık** 1. stony place; 2. gizzard *(of a bird)*.

**taşmak**, (*-ar*) 1. to overflow, to run over; 2. to boil over; 3. *fig.* to lose one's patience, to blow one's stack.

**taşra** [x.] the provinces, the sticks.

**taşralı** [x..] provincial.

**taşyürekli** stonyhearted, hardhearted.

**tat**, -dı 1. taste, flavo(u)r; 2. sweetness; 3. relish, pleasure, delight; ~ almak to relish, to get a kick (*-den* out of), to find pleasure (*-den* in); ~ vermek to flavo(u)r; -ı damağında kalmak to remember s.th. with relish; -ı tuzu kalmamak to lose its charm, to be no longer pleasurable; -ı tuzu yok it is insipid, it has no flavo(u)r at all; -ına bakmak to taste, to sample; -ına doyum olmamak to be very tasty; -ına varmak *fig.* to get the full flavo(u)r (*-in* of), to enjoy; -ında bırakmak *fig.* not to overdo, -ını çıkarmak *(bşin)* to make the most of *s.th.*, to enjoy *s.th.*; -ını kaçırmak to spoil; to cast a damper (*-in* on).

**tatar** 1. *hist.* mounted courier; postrider; 2. ♀ Ta(r)tar.

**tatarböreği**, -ni a kind of pastry.

**tatarcık** *zo.* sandfly; ~ humması ☏ sandfly fever.

**tatarımsı**, **tatarsı** half-cooked, underdone *(food)*.

**tatbik**, -ki [i] application; adaptation; ~ etm. 1. to apply; to put into effect *(or* practice); 2. to compare (*-e* with); ~ sahasına koymak to put into effect *(or* practice).

**tatbikat**, -tı [.--] 1. application; practice;

**2.** ✗ manoeuvres, *Am.* maneuvers, exercises; -ta in practice.

**tatbiki** [. - -] applied; ~ sanatlar applied arts.

**tatil** [- -] **1.** holiday, vacation; **2.** break *(for a meal);* **3.** suspension, temporary cessation; ~ etm. **1.** to close temporarily; **2.** to suspend; ~ günü **1.** holiday; **2.** off day, day off; ~ köyü holiday village; ~ olm. to be closed *(for a holiday);* ~ yapmak to take a holiday *(or vacation),* to holiday.

**tatlandırmak** to flavo(u)r.

**tatlanmak** to flavo(u)r, to sweeten.

**tatlı 1.** sweet; **2.** nice, pleasant, sweet; delicious; melodious, dulcet; **3.** sweet, dessert, ~ dil soft words; ~ dil yılanı deliğinden çıkarır *pro.* a soft answer turns away wrath; ~ dilli softspoken; ~ kaşığı dessert spoon; ~ su fresh water; -ya bağlamak to settle amicably.

**tatlıca** sweetish.

**tatlıcı 1.** maker *or* seller of sweets; **2.** fond of sweets, sweet-toothed.

**tatlılaşmak** to get sweet, to sweeten.

**tatlılaştırmak** to make sweet, to sweeten.

**tatlılık 1.** sweetness; **2.** *fig.* niceness, pleasantness, sweetness; deliciousness; -la with kindness; amicably.

**tatlımsı** sweetish.

**tatlısulevreği,** -ni *zo.* perch.

**tatmak,** (-ar) **1.** to taste; **2.** *fig.* to go through, to experience, to taste.

**tatmin** [i] satisfaction, gratification; ~ etm. to satisfy, to gratify, to content; ~ olm. to be satisfied *(or gratified or* contented).

**tatminkâr** satisfactory.

**tatsal** gustatory, gustatorial, gustative.

**tatsız 1.** tasteless, insipid, vapid; **2.** unsweet; **3.** *fig.* unpleasant, disagreeable; ~ tuzsuz insipid.

**tatula** [. x .] ♀ datura.

**taun** [- -] plague, pestilence.

**tav 1.** anneal *(of steel, etc.);* **2.** the exact state of heat *or* dampness; **3.** *fig.* opportune moment; **4.** *sl.* trick, deception; ~ olm. *sl.* to fall for s.o.'s trick; ~ vermek to dampen; -a düşürmek *sl.* to trick, to hoodwink; -ına getirmek to bring to the right condition.

**tava 1.** frying pan, skillet, frypan; **2.** fried *(food);* **3.** ladle *(for melting metal);* **4.** trough *(for slaking lime);* **5.** bed *(for young plants).*

**tavaf** [. -] circumambulation *(of the Kaaba);* ~ etm. **1.** to circumambulate *(the Kaaba);* **2.** *fig.* to wander around.

**tavan** ceiling; ~ arası attic, garret, loft; ~ fiyat ceiling price; ~ süpürgesi long-handled broom *(for cellings).*

**tavassut,** -tu mediation; interposition, intervention; ~ etm. to mediate, to interpose, to intervene.

**tavazzuh** becoming clear; ~ etm. to become clear.

**taverna** nightclub, tavern.

**tavır,** -vrı **1.** manner, attitude, air; **2.** airs, affectation, put-on; pose; ~ satmak to give o.s. airs.

**taviz** [- -] **1.** concession; **2.** compensation; ~ vermek to make a concession, to stretch a point.

**tavla¹** [x .] backgammon; ~ atmak *F* to play backgammon.

**tavla²** [x .] stable *(for horses).*

**tavlamak 1.** to dampen; **2.** to anneal *(steel, etc.);* **3.** *sl.* to trick, to hoodwink, to bamboozle; **4.** *sl.* to charm, to snow, to beguile.

**tavsamak** to abate, to moderate, to slacken.

**tavsif** [i] characterization; designation, qualification; ~ etm. to characterize; to designate, to qualify.

**tavsifi** [. - -] descriptive.

**tavsiye** recommendation, commendation; ~ etm. to recommend, to advise, to commend; ~ mektubu letter of recommendation; -ye şayan recommendable.

**tavsiyeli 1.** recommended; **2.** supported, backed.

**tavşan¹** *zo.* rabbit, hare; ~ kız Bunny (girl); ~ uykusu rabbit's sleep; ~ yavrusu young hare, leveret; ~ yürekli timid; -a kaç, tazıya tut demek ~ to run with the hare and hunt with the hounds; -ı araba ile avlamak *fig.* to do s.th. calmly and unhurriedly; -ın suyunun suyu *fig.* a very distant connection.

**tavşan²** cabinetmaker.

**tavşancıl** *zo.* vulture; eagle.

**tavşandudağı,** -nı harelip.

**tavşandudaklı** harelipped.

**tavşankanı,** -nı dark and strong *(tea).*

**tavşanlık** rabbit hutch.

**tavuk** *zo.* hen, chicken; ~ kümesi chicken coop; ~ suyu chicken broth.

**tavukçu 1.** poulterer; **2.** chicken farmer.

**tavukgöğsü,** -nü *a pudding made of rice flour and very finely shredded chicken.*

**tavukgötü,** -nü wart.

**tavukkarası,** -nı night blindness.

**tavus, tavuskuşu,** -nu *zo.* peacock, peafowl.

**tavzif** [i] appointing s.o. to a duty; ~ etm.

*(b-ni bşle)* to appoint *s.o.* to *s.th.*, to entrust *s.o.* with *s.th.*

**tavzih** [ī] explanation, elucidation; ~ etm. to explain, to elucidate.

**tay**[1] *zo.* colt, filly, foal.

**tay**[2] **1.** one of a pair, fellow, mate; **2.** peer, equal; ~ durmak *(for a baby)* to stand upright; ~ ~! up, up! *(said to a baby just learning to walk).*

**tay**[3], -yyı removal, deletion, expunction.

**taya** nursemaid, nanny.

**tayf 1.** apparition, specter; wraith; **2.** *phys.* spectrum.

**tayfa** [x .] **1.** crew; **2.** crewman, sailor; **3.** gang, bunch, band, troop.

**tayfun** typhoon.

**tayın** X ration.

**tayin** [- -] **1.** appointment; **2.** indication; **3.** designation; ~ etm. **1.** to appoint; **2.** to fix, to determine; -ı çıkmak to be appointed *(or* assigned).

**taylan** tall and well-set-up *(man).*

**Tayland** *pr. n.* Thailand.

**Taymis** *pr. n.* the Thames.

**tayyare** [. - .] airplane; ~ gemisi aircraft carrier; ~ meydanı airfield, aerodrome.

**tayyareci** [. - . .] **1.** pilot; **2.** airman.

**tayyarecilik** [. - . . .] pilotry; aviation.

**tayyetmek** [x . .] to remove, to delete, to expunge.

**tayyör** tailleur, *(woman's)* tailor-made suit.

**tazallüm** complaint, lamentation; ~ etm. to complain, to lament.

**tazammum 1.** including, comprising, embracing; **2.** *phls.* implication; ~ etm. **1.** to include, to comprise, to embrace; **2.** *phls.* to imply.

**tazarru,** -uu supplication; ~ etm. to supplicate.

**taze** [ā] **1.** fresh; **2.** new; young; **3.** newly, freshly; **4.** young girl; ~ biber green pepper; ~ ekmek fresh bread; ~ fasulye green beans.

**tazelemek** [ā] **1.** to freshen, to renew; **2.** to add water and reheat.

**tazeleşmek** [ā] to be rejuvenated.

**tazelik** [ā] freshness, newness, youth.

**tazı** greyhound; ~ gibi lean and agile *(person);* -ya dönmek **1.** to get very thin, to get as thin as a rail; **2.** to get soaked to the skin.

**tazim** [- -] hono(u)ring, respect; ~ etm. to hono(u)r, to revere.

**taziye** [ā] condolence; ~ etm. *(or* -de bulunmak) to offer one's condolences, to condole; ~ mektubu letter of condolence.

**taziz** [- -] **1.** cherishing; **2.** exaltation; **3.** Christianity: conferring sainthood upon; ~ etm. **1.** to cherish; **2.** to exalt; **3.** Christianity: to confer sainthood (-i upon).

**tazmin** [ī] indemnification; ~ etm. to indemnify; to make up for *(a mistake).*

**tazminat,** -tı [. - -] 𝟔𝟔 **1.** indemnity, damages, compensation, reparations; **2.** separation pay; ~ davası 𝟔𝟔 action for damages.

**tazyik,** -ki [ī] pressure; ~ etm. to press, to put pressure on, to pressure.

**tazyikli** [. - .] **1.** compressed *(air);* **2.** under compression.

**TBMM** *(abbr. for* Türkiye Büyük Millet Meclisi) the Turkish National Assembly.

**TC** *(abbr. for* Türkiye Cumhuriyeti) the Republic of Turkey.

**TCDD** *(abbr. for* Türkiye Cumhuriyeti Devlet Demiryolları) Turkish Rail.

**TDK** *(abbr. for* Türk Dil Kurumu) the Turkish Language Association.

**teadül** [ā] equivalence; ~ etm. to be equivalent *(-e* to).

**teakup,** -bu [ā] succession; ~ etm. to follow one another in succession.

**teali** [. - -] rise, ascent; ~ etm. to rise, to ascend.

**teamül** [ā] **1.** practice, custom; **2.** 🔥 reaction; ~ hukuku 𝟔𝟔 consuetudinary law.

**tearuz** [ā] conflict, contradiction.

**teati** [. - -] exchange; ~ etm. to exchange.

**teavün** [ā] cooperation; ~ etm. to cooperate.

**tebaa 1.** citizen; subject; **2.** citizens; subjects.

**tebadül** [ā] **1.** exchange; permutation; **2.** *biol.* mutation; ~ etm. to undergo permutation *or* mutation.

**tebahhur** vaporization, evaporation; ~ etm. to vaporize, to evaporate.

**tebarüz** [ā] becoming clear *(or* evident); ~ etm. to become clear *(or* evident); ~ ettirmek to make clear, to show clearly.

**tebcil** [ī] exaltation, glorification; ~ etm. to hono(u)r, to exalt, to glorify.

**tebdil** [ī] **1.** exchange, alteration; **2.** in disguise, incognito; ~ etm. to change, to alter, to exchange; ~ gezmek to go around in disguise, to travel incognito; -ı hava change of air; -i mekan etm. to move (house).

**tebeddül** [ā] alteration, exchange, replacement; ~ etm. to be changed *(or* altered).

**tebelleş** P pestiferous, importunate *(per-*

*son).*

**tebellür 1.** crystallization; **2.** *fig.* becoming clear; ~ etm. **1.** to crystallize; **2.** *fig.* to become clear.

**teber 1.** *hist.* battle-ax; **2.** knife *(for cutting leather).*

**teberru,** -uu donation, gift, contribution; ~ etm. to donate.

**tebessüm** smile; ~ etm. to smile.

**tebeşir** chalk.

**tebeyyün** becoming evident *(or* manifest); ~ etm. to become evident *(or* manifest).

**tebligat,** -tı [. - -] *pl. of* tebliğ **1.** notifications, communiqués; **2.** notification, communiqué.

**tebliğ** [i̇] **1.** communicating, notifying; **2.** communication, notification, communiqué; ~ etm. to communicate, to notify.

**tebrik,** -ki [i̇] **1.** congratulation; **2.** congratulatory card; ~ etm. to congratulate; ~ kartı greeting *(or* congratulatory) card.

**tebriye** ᴐ̃ acquittal, exoneration; ~ etm. to acquit, to exonerate.

**Tebriz** [i̇] *pr. n.* Tabriz.

**tebyiz** [i̇] **1.** making a fair copy of *(a document);* **2.** whitening; ~ etm. **1.** to make a fair copy of *(a document);* **2.** to whiten.

**tecahül** [â] feigning ignorance; ~ etm. to feign ignorance.

**tecanüs** [â] homogeneity.

**tecavüz** [â] **1.** aggression, attack; **2.** ᴐ̃ molestation; rape, assault; **3.** ᴐ̃ violation, infringement; encroachment; transgression; ~ etm. **1.** to attack; **2.** to molest, to assault, to rape; **3.** to violate, to infringe; to transgress; to encroach; to trespass *(-e* on); **4.** to surpass, to exceed.

**tecavüzi** [. - . -] aggressive, offensive.

**tecdit,** -di [i̇] renewal; restoration, renovation, refurbishment; ~ etm. to renew; to restore, to renovate, to refurbish.

**teceddüt,** -dü **1.** renewal; innovation; **2.** renaissance; ~ etm. to be renewed, to renew itself.

**tecelli** [i̇] **1.** manifestation; revelation; **2.** destiny, fate; ~ etm. to become manifest; to be revealed.

**tecemmu,** -uu **1.** assembling, gathering; **2.** ✕ concentration *(of troops);* ~ etm. **1.** to assemble, to gather; **2.** ✕ *(for troops)* to be concentrated.

**tecerrüt,** -dü **1.** isolation; **2.** abstraction; ~ etm. **1.** to isolate o.s. *(-den* from); **2.** to free o.s. *(-den* from), to set aside *(a prejudice, etc.);* **3.** to abstract.

**tecessüm 1.** embodiment; **2.** appearance; ~ etm. **1.** to become embodied *(or* tangible); **2.** to appear, to become apparent.

**tecessüs 1.** curiosity, inquisitiveness, nosiness, snoopiness; **2.** spying; ~ etm. **1.** to inquire pryingly; **2.** to spy *(-i* on).

**tecil** [- -] postponement; deferment; ~ etm. to postpone; to defer.

**tecim** commerce, trade.

**tecrit,** -di [i̇] isolation, separation, insulation; ~ etm. to isolate, to separate, to set apart, to insulate; to quarantine; ~ kampı *pol.* isolation camp; ~ siyaseti isolationism.

**tecrübe 1.** experience; **2.** ᴐ̃, *phys.* experiment, trial, test; ~ etm. **1.** to experience, to test, to experiment; **2.** to attempt, to try; ~ sahibi experienced; ~ tahtası *fig.* corpus vile, guinea pig.

**tecrübeli** experienced.

**tecrübesiz** inexperienced.

**tecrübesizlik** inexperience.

**tecrübi** [i̇] experimental.

**tecvit,** -di [i̇] recitation of the Koran with proper rhythm.

**teckiz** [i̇] permitting, allowing; ~ etm. to permit, to allow.

**tecziye** punishment; ~ etm. to punish.

**teçhiz** [i̇] equipment; ~ etm. to equip, to outfit.

**teçhizat,** -tı [. - -] equipment, gear, apparatus.

**tedafüi** [. - . -] defensive; ~ harp defensive war.

**tedahül** [â] **1.** interpenetration; permeation; **2.** delay in payment; **3.** *phys.* interference; -de kalmak *(or* -e binmek) *(for a payment)* to be overdue, to be in arrears.

**tedai** [. - -] *psych.* association.

**tedansan** tea dance, thé dansant.

**tedarik,** -ki [â] **1.** procurement, obtainment; **2.** preparation; **3.** accumulation; ~ etm. **1.** to procure, to obtain, to provide; **2.** to accumulate; -te bulunmak to make preparations *(-e* for), to get ready *(-e* for)

**tedarikli** [â] prepared, ready.

**tedariksiz** [â] unprepared, unready.

**tedavi** [. - -] 👁 treatment, cure; therapy; ~ etm. to treat, to cure; ~ görmek *(or* ~ olm.) to be treated.

**tedavül** [â] circulation; ~ bankası bank of circulation *(or* issue); ~ etm. to be in circulation; -den çekmek *(or* çıkarmak) to withdraw from circulation, to call in; -den kalkmak to go out of circulation;

-e çıkarmak to put into circulation, to issue.

**tedbir** [î] measure, step, precaution, action; ~ almak to take measures (or steps).

**tedbırli** provident, cautious, forethoughted, prudent.

**tedbirsiz** improvident, unforethoughtful, imprudent.

**tedbirsizlik** improvidence, imprudence.

**tedenni** [î] decline; ~ etm. to decline, to fall off.

**tedfin** [î] burial, interment; ~ etm. to bury, to inter.

**tedhiş** [î] terror, terrorization; ~ etm. to terrorize.

**tedhişçi** terrorist.

**tedhişçilik** terrorism.

**tedip**, -bi [- -] disciplining; chastisement; ~ etm. to discipline, to chastise.

**tedirgin** uncomfortable, uneasy, troubled, anxious, worried; ~ etm. to disquiet, to discompose.

**tedirginlik** disquiet, uneasiness, anxiety, worry.

**tediyat**, -tı [- . -] pl. of tediye payments.

**tediye** [- . .] payment, disbursement; ~ dengesi balance of payments; ~ etm. to pay, to disburse; ~ günü pay-day.

**tedricen** [î] [. x .] gradually, by degrees, by stages.

**tedrici** [. - -] gradual.

**tedris** [î] instruction, teaching; ~ etm. to teach.

**tedrisat**, -tı [. - - -] instruction, teaching.

**tedvin** [î] 1. ஃ codification (of laws); 2. compilation; ~ etm. 1. ஃ to codify (laws); 2. to compile.

**tedvir** [î] 1. rotation; 2. fig. administration, management; ~ etm. 1. to rotate, to turn, to revolve; 2. fig. to administer, to manage, to direct.

**teehhür** delay; ~ etm. to be delayed.

**teemmül** careful consideration, deliberation; ~ etm. to think carefully, to deliberate.

**teenni** [î] deliberation, caution; ~ etm. to exercise caution, to proceed slowly and carefully.

**teessüf** regret, sorrow, sadness; ~ etm. to feel sorry (-e about); to regret; ~ ederim it makes me very sad; I never expected you to do s.th. like this.

**teessür** 1. sorrow, sadness; 2. emotion.

**teessüs** 1. establishment; 2. foundation; ~ etm. 1. to become established (or rooted); 2. to be founded.

**teeyyüt**, -dü confirmation, substantiation;

~ etm. to be confirmed (or substantiated).

**tef** tambourine; ~ çalmak to play the tambourine; ~ çalsan oynayacak fig. it's all topsy-turvy, what a mess!; -e koymak (or -e koyup çalmak) (b-ni) fig. to make fun of s.o., to run s.o. down.

**tefcir** [î] drainage; ~ etm. to drain.

**tefeci** usurer.

**tefecilik** usury.

**tefehhüm** coming to understand; ~ etm. to come to understand.

**tefekkür** consideration, reflection, contemplation; thought; ~ etm. to think, to consider, to contemplate; -e dalmak to be lost in thought, to contemplate.

**teferruat**, -tı [â] details.

**teferruatlı** [â] detailed.

**teferrüç**, -cü walk, excursion, outing.

**teferrüt**, -dü being unique, standing alone; ~ etm. to be unique, to stand alone.

**tefessüh** rot, decay (a. ஃ); ~ etm. to rot, to decay.

**tefevvuk**, -ku superiority; ~ etm. (b-ne) to be superior to s.o.

**tefhim** [î] ஃ pronouncement (of a sentence); ~ etm. ஃ to pronounce (a sentence).

**tefrik**, -ki [î] distinction; ~ etm. to distinguish; to differentiate.

**tefrika** 1. serial; 2. disagreement, discord.

**tefriş** [î] 1. spreading over; 2. furnishing; ~ etm. 1. to spread; 2. to furnish; 3. to pave; to cover.

**tefrit**, -ti [î] remissness.

**tefsir** [î] 1. interpretation; 2. commentary on the Koran; ~ etm. 1. to interpret; to explain; to expound; 2. to comment (on a sura of the Koran).

**teftiş** [î] inspection; ~ etm. to inspect.

**teğelti** saddle blanket.

**teğet**, -ti Å tangent; ~ olm. to be tangent (-e to).

**teğmen** X lieutenant.

**teğmenlik** X lieutenancy.

**tehacüm** [â] 1. concerted attack; 2. rush; ~ etm. 1. to make a concerted attack; 2. to rush.

**tehdit**, -di [î] threat, menace; ~ etm. to threaten; to menace; ~ savurmak to bluster out threats.

**teheyyüç**, -cü emotional excitement; ~ etm. to get emotionally excited, to get worked up.

**tehir** [- -] 1. delay, postponement, deferment, deferral; 2. ஃ adjournment; ~ etm. 1. to delay, to postpone, to defer; 2. ஃ to adjourn.

tehirli delayed, late.

tehlike danger, hazard, peril, risk; ~ atlatmak to get through a dangerous situation successfully; -ye atmak to put in danger; -ye atılmak to court danger, to go into danger; -ye koymak (or sokmak) to endanger, to imperil, to put in danger.

tehlikeli dangerous, hazardous, perilous, risky.

tehlikesiz undangerous, dangerless, unhazardous, unperilous, riskless.

tehyiç, -ci [İ] excitation; ~ etm. to excite.

tehzil [İ] ridicule, making fun of; ~ etm. 'o ridicule, to make fun of.

tek, -ki 1. one, sole, single, solitary, only; 2. unique, unrivaled; 3. one of a pair, fellow, mate; 4. Ạ odd (number); 5. only, solely; ~ atmak F to knock back a drink; ~ başına alone, on one's own; ~ başına kalmak to be left alone; ~ meclisli hükümet sistemi ◊ unicameral system of government; ~ motorlu single--engined; ~ taraflı unilateral; ~ ~ one by one; ~ tük only a few; ~ yönlü one--way.

tekabül [ậ] correspondence, equivalence; ~ etm. to correspond.

tekâmül 1. evolution; 2. maturation; ~ etm. 1. to evolve; 2. to mature.

tekâsüf 1. condensation, inspissation; concentration; 2. opacification; ~ etm. 1. to condense, to inspissate, to thicken; 2. to opacify; 3. (for a crowd) to gather, to congregate.

tekaüt, -dü [ậ] 1. retirement; 2. F retired (person); 3. retired person, pensioner; ~ etm. (or -e sevk etm.) to retire, to pension off; ~ maaşı retirement pay, pension; ~ olm. to retire; ~ sandığı retirement fund.

tekaütlük [ậ] retirement.

tekbencilik phls. solipsism.

tekçe individual.

tekçilik phls. monism.

tekdeğerli ⚗ univalent.

tekdir [İ] reprimand, dressing down; ~ etm. to reprimand, to dress down, to upbraid.

tekdüze(n) monotonous.

tekdüzelik, tekdüzenlik monotony.

teke zo. 1. he-goat, billy goat; 2. shrimp; prawn.

tekeffül guaranteeing; ~ etm. to guarantee; to go bond (-e for).

tekel monopoly; -ine almak to monopolize.

Tekel pr. n. the Turkish State Liquor and Tobacco Monopoly.

tekelci monopolist.

tekelcilik monopolism.

tekellüf 1. empty show, false display; 2. formality, ceremoniousness.

tekellüflü ornate, sumptuous.

tekellüfsüz plain.

tekellüm speech; ~ etm. to speak.

tekemmül maturation; ~ etm. to reach maturity.

teker wheel; ~ meker yuvarlanmak to roll over and over.

tekerklik monarchy.

tekerlek 1. wheel; 2. sl. homosexual, fag, queer; ~ kırıldıktan sonra yol gösteren çok olur pro. it is easy to be wise after the event; ~ pabucu skidpan, dragshoe; ~ parmağı spoke of a wheel; tekerleğine çomak sokmak to put a spoke in one's wheel.

tekerlekli wheeled; ~ sandalye wheelchair.

tekerleme 1. vn. of tekerlemek; 2. rigmarole; 3. tongue-twister; 4. repartee.

tekerlemek to roll.

tekerlenmek 1. pass. of tekerlemek; 2. to roll.

tekerli wheeled.

tekerrür 1. repetition; 2. recurrence; ~ etm. 1. to be repeated; 2. to recur.

tekevlilik monogamy.

tekevvün coming into existence, origination; ~ etm. to come into existence.

tekfin [İ] (en)shrouding (a corpse); ~ etm. to (en)shroud (a corpse).

tekfir [İ] isl. accusing s.o. of being an infidel; ~ etm. to accuse s.o. of being an infidel.

tekfur hist. Christian princelet.

tekil gr. singular.

tekin 1. deserted, empty (place); 2. auspicious; 3. ⚖ mf.; ~ değil inauspicious, ill-omened, sinister.

tekinsiz 1. unlucky, of ill omen; 2. taboo.

tekir 1. tabby; 2. (balığı) surmullet, red mullet; ~ kedi tabby-cat.

tekke 1. dervish lodge, tekke; 2. sl. hashish den.

tekleme 1. vn. of teklemek; 2. ⊕ misfiring.

teklemek 1. to thin (seedlings); 2. ⊕ to miss, to misfire; 3. sl. to stammer, to stutter.

teklif [İ] 1. proposal, offer, motion; 2. formality, ceremony; ~ etm. to propose, to offer, to suggest; ~ kutusu suggestion box; ~ sahibi 1. mover (of a motion); 2. bidder; ~ tekellüf formality; ~ yok there's no need for ceremony.

teklifli formal, ceremonious.

teklifsiz informal, unceremonious.

**teklifsizce** unceremoniously, familiarly, casually.

**teklifsizlik** informality, casualness.

**teklik 1.** oneness; **2.** *sl.* lira.

**tekme** kick; ~ atmak to kick; ~ yemek to get kicked, to get a kick.

**tekmelemek** to kick.

**tekmil** [ï] **1.** completion; **2.** all, the whole; ~ etm. to complete, to finish; ~ haberi ✕ oral report; ~ vermek ✕ to give an oral report.

**tekne 1.** trough; vat; **2.** boat, vessel; **3.** hull *(of a ship)*; **4.** *typ.* galley; **5.** *geol.* basin; ~ kazıntısı *co.* the youngest child of the family, born when his or her parents are no longer young.

**teknik 1.** technique; **2.** technical; ~ resim drafting; ~ ressam draughtsman, *Am.* draftsman; ~ terim technical term.

**tekniker** technician.

**teknikokul** technical school.

**tekniköğretim** technical education.

**teknisyen** technician.

**teknoloji** technology.

**teknolojik** technological.

**tekrar** [x -] **1.** repetition, repeat, reiteration; **2.** recurrence; **3.** again, over again, once more; ~ etm. to repeat, to reiterate; ~ ~ repeatedly, again and again.

**tekrarlamak** to repeat, to reiterate.

**tekrarlanmak 1** *pass. of* tekrarlamak; **2.** to recur.

**teksif** [ï] **1.** concentration; condensation, inspissation; **2.** opacification; ~ etm. **1.** to concentrate, to densen, to thicken, to condense, to inspissate; **2.** to opacify.

**teksir** [ï] **1.** duplication; **2.** augmentation, increase, multiplication; ~ etm. **1.** to duplicate, to copy; **2.** to augment, to increase, to multiply; ~ kâğıdı paper used for making duplicates; ~ makinesi duplicating machine, duplicator, mimeograph.

**tekst**, -ti text.

**tekstil** textile; ~ sanayii textile industry.

**tektanrıcılık** monotheism.

**tekyazım** monograph.

**tekzip**, -bi [ï] denial, disclaimer; ~ etm. to deny, to disclaim, to declare false.

**tel 1.** wire; **2.** string *(of a musical instrument)*; **3.** thread; strand; fibre, *Am.* fiber; **4.** screen cloth, screening; window screen; door screen; **5.** *F* telegram, wire, cable; ~ çekmek **1,** to enclose with wire; **2.** *F* to telegraph, to send a wire, to cable, to wire; ~ çivi brad, wire-tack; ~ fırça wire brush; ~ kadayıf a kind of sweet pastry; ~ kafes wire cage; ~

kırmak **1.** to blunder; **2.** *sl.* to tread on s.o.'s toes; ~ örgü wire fence; ~ şehriye vermicelli; -ler takınmak *fig.* to rejoice greatly.

**tela** [x .] interfacing.

**telaffuz** pronunciation; ~ etm. to pronounce.

**telafi** [. - ] compensation; ~ etm. to compensate, to make up for; -si imkânsız irreparable, irremediable.

**telakki** [. . -] **1.** consideration, evaluation; **2.** view(point); ~ etm. to regard, to view.

**telaş 1.** flurry, flutter, commotion, hurry, bustle, to-do; **2.** agitation; ~ etm. to bustle, to behave agitatedly; ~ içinde in a bustle *(or hurry)*; -a düşmek to get agitated, to get in a swivet; -a vermek to get *(everybody in a place)* agitated, to alarm.

**telaşçı** nervous, restless *(person)*.

**telaşlandırmak** *(b-ni)* to get s.o. agitated.

**telaşlanmak** to get agitated.

**telaşlı** agitated.

**telaşsız** unagitated, unruffled, steady, calm.

**telatin** russia, Russia leather.

**telcik** fibril.

**teldolap** screen safe.

**telef 1.** waste; **2.** death; ~ etm. **1.** to waste, to throw away, to squander; **2.** to kill, to do away with; ~ olm. **1.** to be wasted *(or thrown away)*; **2.** to die.

**telefat**, -tı [â] losses, casualties; ~ verdirmek to inflict losses (-e on); ~ vermek to suffer losses.

**teleferik** telpher, teleferic.

**telefon 1.** telephone, phone; **2.** telephone *(or phone)* call; ~ etm. to telephone, to phone, to ring (up), to call (up); ~ kulübesi telephone box; ~ rehberi telephone directory *(or book)*; ~ santralı telephone exchange, switchboard; -la aramak *(b-ni)* to give s.o. a ring; -u kapamak to hang up.

**telefoncu 1.** telephone lineman; installer of telephones; **2.** telephonist, operator.

**telefonlaşmak** to talk on the telephone *(ile* with).

**telefoto, telefotografi 1.** telephotography; **2.** phototelegraphy.

**teleke** *zo.* remex.

**telekomünikasyon** telecommunication.

**teleks** telex; ~ çekmek to telex.

**telem** teletype(writer), teleprinter.

**telemetre** [. . x .] telemeter.

**teleobjektif** *phot.* teleobjective, telephoto *(lens)*, telelens.

**telepati** telepathy.

**telepatik** telepathic.

**teles** threadbare.

**telesimek 1.** to pant; **2.** to get thin; to pine away.

**telesinema** telephotography.

**teleskop,** -pu telescope.

**televizör** television set.

**televizyon 1.** television; **2.** television (set), TV, telly; ~ alıcısı television set (or receiver); ~ vericisi television transmitter; ~ yayını telecast; -la öğretim telecourse; -la yayınlamak to telecast, to televise.

**televizyoncu** maker, seller or repairer of television sets.

**televizyonculuk** making, selling or repairing television sets.

**telgraf 1.** telegraph; **2.** telegram, wire, cable; ~ çekmek to telegraph, to telegram, to wire, to cable.

**telgrafçı** telegrapher, telegraphist.

**telgrafçılık** telegraphy.

**telgrafhane** [. . - .] telegraph office.

**telif** [- -] **1.** reconciliation; **2.** compilation; ~ etm. **1.** to reconcile; **2.** to compile (a book); ~ hakkı copyright.

**tel'in** [î] damnation; ~ etm. to damn, to curse.

**telkâri** filigreed with gold or silver.

**telkin** [î] inspiration, inculcation, suggestion; ~ etm. to inspire, to inculcate, to instill.

**tellak** batlı attendant.

**tellal 1.** (town) crier; **2.** barker; hawker; crier; **3.** middleman, broker.

**tellemek 1.** to string wires on; **2.** to deck out; **3.** to embellish (a story); **4.** to send a telegram, to wire; telleyip pullamak **1.** to deck out, to prank, to fig out; **2.** fig. to praise to the skies.

**tellendirmek** to smoke, to enjoy a smoke.

**telli 1.** wired; **2.** adorned with gold or silver wires; ~ bebek fig. frivolous; ~ cam wire(d) glass; ~ çalgılar ♪ stringed instruments, strings; ~ pullu decked out; showy.

**telliturna** zo. demoiselle crane.

**telmih** [î] allusion, reference; ~ etm. to allude, to refer to.

**telsi** fibrous.

**telsiz 1.** wireless; **2.** radio, wireless; ~ telefon radiophone; ~ telgraf radio, wireless telegraph; -le bildirmek to radio.

**telsizci 1.** radiotelephonist; **2.** radiotelegraphist.

**telsizcilik 1.** radiotelephony; **2.** radiotelegraphy.

**teltik 1.** defect; **2.** deficiency; **3.** defi-

cient, insufficient, lacking, short.

**telve** coffee grounds; ~ falı fortune-telling by the appearance of coffee grounds.

**tema 1.** theme, topic, subject; **2.** ♪ theme, thema.

**temadi** [. - -] continuation; ~ etm. to continue.

**temaruz** [â] feigning illness; ~ etm. to feign illness, to pretend to be ill, to sham ill.

**temas** [â] **1.** contact, touch; **2.** contact, communication; ~ etm. **1.** to touch; **2.** to touch on (a subject); **3.** (b-le) to get in touch with s.o., to contact s.o.; ~ kurmak to establish contact (ile with); ~ noktası point of contact; -a geçmek to get in touch (ile with), to contact; -ta bulunmak (or olm.) (b-le) to be in touch with s.o.

**temaşa** [. - -] **1.** pleasure excursion, promenade; **2.** play, show, scene; the theatre; ~ etm. to view, to contemplate.

**temayül** [â] **1.** tendency, inclination, propensity; **2.** affection, liking, fondness; ~ etm. **1.** to have a tendency (-e to), to be inclined (-e to); **2.** to have a liking (-e for).

**temayüz** [â] becoming distinguished; ~ etm. to become distinguished, to stand out, to excel.

**tembel** lazy, indolent, supine, slothful.

**tembelhane** [â] den of idlers (or loafers).

**tembelleşmek** to get (or grow) lazy.

**tembellik** laziness, indolence, supinity, sloth.

**tembih** [î] **1.** warning, admonition, caution; **2.** psych. stimulation; ~ etm. **1.** to warn, to caution, to admonish; **2.** psych. to stimulate.

**tembihlemek** s. tembih etm. **1.**

**temcit,** -di [î] **1.** canticle intoned from minarets before dawn; **2.** meal eaten just before dawn during the month of Ramazan; ~ pilavı gibi ısıtıp ısıtıp öne sürmek fig. to keep bringing up the same topic time after time.

**temdit,** -di [î] extension, prolongation; ~ etm. to extend, to prolong.

**temel 1.** foundation; **2.** fig. basis; ground (work); **3.** fundamental, basic; **4.** main, principal, chief; ~ atmak to lay the foundation; ~ cümle gr. main clause; ~ direk main post (in a building); ~ kakmak (bir yere) to settle down in (a place) for good; ~ taşı foundation stone, cornerstone (a. fig.); ~ tutmak to become firmly fixed; -inden at bottom, fundamentally.

**temellenmek** to become firmly fixed (or

established).

**temelleşmek** s. temellenmek.

**temelli 1.** having a foundation; **2.** permanent; **3.** permanently, for good; **4.** completely, wholly; ~ bir iş a permanent job; ~ gitti he has gone for good.

**temellük**, -kü taking possession of; ~ etm. to take possession of.

**temelsiz** unfounded, groundless, baseless.

**temennᴂ(h)** [â] Oriental salute; ~ etm. to salute.

**temenni** [î] wish, desire; ~ etm. to wish, to desire.

**temerküz 1.** concentration; **2.** pol. coalition; ~ etm. to be concentrated (-de on), to centre, Am. to center (-de on); ~ kabinesi pol. coalition government; ~ kampı concentration camp.

**temerrüt**, -dü **1.** obstinacy, perverseness; **2.** ʃʃ default (in payment); ~ etm. to be obstinate (or perverse); ~ faizi ✝ moratory interest.

**temessül 1.** coming to resemble; **2.** biol. assimilation; ~ etm. **1.** to come to resemble; **2.** biol. to assimilate.

**temettü**, -üü **1.** profit; **2.** ✝ dividend; ~ etm. to profit; ~ hissesi ✝ dividend; ~ vergisi tax on profits.

**temevvüç** fluctuation; ~ etm. **1.** to fluctuate; **2.** to swell, to heave.

**temeyyüz** standing out, becoming distinguished; ~ etm. to stand out, to become distinguished.

**temhir** [î] sealing up; ~ etm. to seal up, to padlock (a place).

**temin** [- · ] **1.** assurance; **2.** procurement; ~ etm. **1.** to assure, to ensure; **2.** to secure, to achieve, to bring about; **3.** to obtain, to procure, to get.

**teminat**, -tı [- . · ] **1.** guarantee, guaranty; **2.** assurance.

**teminatlı** [- . · . ] guaranteed, secured.

**teminatsız** unsecured, insecure.

**temiz 1.** clean; **2.** fresh (air); **3.** fig. decent, clean-living; chaste, virtuous; **4.** net (amount of money); **5.** sl. poker; ~ çevirmek sl. to play poker; ~ hava almak to get some fresh air; ~ pak spotlessly clean; ~ raporu clean bill of health; ~ süt emmiş F decent, trustworthy; -e çekmek to make a fair copy (-i of); -e çıkarmak (b-ni) to put s.o. in the clear, to clear s.o., to exonerate s.o.; -e çıkmak to be in the clear, to be cleared (or exonerated); -e havale etm. sl. **1.** to finish in a jiffy; **2.** to kill, to bump off; **3.** to eat up, to polish off, to put away (food).

**temizkan 1.** arterial blood; **2.** purebred, pedigree (animal).

**temizlemek 1.** to clean, to purify; **2.** to clean, to gut, to dress (fish, etc.) **3.** F to finish; **4.** F to eat up, to put away, to polish off (food); **5.** sl. to clean out, to rob; **6.** sl. to kill, to bump off, to put away, to polish off.

**temizlenmek 1.** pass. of temizlemek; **2.** to clean o.s. (up).

**temizleyici 1.** cleanser, purificant; **2.** dry cleaner; **3.** cleaner.

**temizlik 1.** cleanliness; **2.** purity, pureness; **3** purification; ~ işleri street-cleaning, scavenging; ~ yapmak to do the cleaning, to clean.

**temizlikçi** charwoman, cleaning woman; cleaner.

**temkin** [î] **1.** self-possession, poise; **2.** deliberation, deliberateness.

**temkinli** [ . - . ] **1.** self-possessed, poised; **2.** deliberate.

**temlik**, -ki [î] ʃʃ alienation, transferral (of a property, right); ~ edilemeyen haklaı ʃʃ unassignable rights; ~ etm. to alienate, to transfer, to convey (property, etc.).

**temmuz** July.

**tempo** [x .] ♪ tempo, time; ~ tutmak to keep (or beat) time.

**temren** arrowhead; spearhead.

**temrin** [î] **1.** practice; **2.** exercise.

**temriye** ⚛, 🌿 lichen.

**temsil** [î] **1.** representation; **2.** thea. performance; **3.** analogy, comparison; **4.** biol. assimilation; **5.** P for example; ~ etm. **1.** to represent; **2.** thea. to perform, to put on; **3.** biol. to assimilate.

**temsilci** representative, agent.

**temsilcilik** representation.

**temsili** [ . - - ] **1.** representative; **2.** imaginative; **3.** composite; ~ hükümet pol. government by representation.

**temyiz** [î] **1.** discernment, distinguishing; **2.** ʃʃ appeal; ~ etm. **1.** to discern, to distinguish, to recognize; **2.** ʃʃ to appeal (a case); ~ kudreti ʃʃ power of discernment; ~ mahkemesi court of appeal.

**ten 1.** complexion; **2.** flesh, skin; **3.** body; ~ fanilası undershirt.

**tenafür** [â] cacophony.

**tenakus** [â] decrease, diminution; ~ etm. to decrease, to diminish.

**tenakuz** [â] log. contradiction.

**tenasüh** [â] transmigration of souls, metempsychosis.

**tenasül** [â] procreation, generation, reproduction; ~ aletleri genitals, genitalia.

tenasüp, -bü [ā] 1. proportion; 2. symmetry.

tencere [x . .] saucepot, saucepan, stewpot, stewpan; ~ dibin kara, seninki benden kara the pot calling the kettle black; ~ yuvarlanmış, kapağını bulmuş birds of a feather flock together.

tender [x .] 🚂 tender.

tendürüst, -tü robust (person).

teneffüs 1. respiration; 2. recess, break (in a school); ~ etm. to breathe, to respire.

teneke 1. tin, tinplate; 2. can, canister; ~ çalmak (arkasından) fig. to boo s.o., to jeer at s.o.; ~ kaplamak to tin; ~ mahallesi shantytown, favela; -sini eline vermek F to fire s.o., to give s.o. the boot.

tenekeci tinsmith, tinman, tinner.

tenekecilik tinsmithery.

teneşir wooden bench on which a corpse is washed; ~ horozu (or kargası) fig. bag of bones; -e gelmek fig. to kick the bucket, to die, to croak.

teneşirlik 1. place for washing corpses; 2. sl. about to die, at death's door.

tenevvü, -üü variety, diversity; ~ etm. to vary.

tenevvür enlightenment; ~ etm. to become lit (or enlightened).

tenezzüh excursion, outing, promenade; ~ gemisi cruise ship.

tenezzül condescension; ~ buyurmak to be so kind as to; ~ etm. 1. to condescend (-e to), to deign (-e to); 2. (for prices) to go down, to fall.

tenfiz [i] 🔅 execution, implementation (of a court order); enforcement (of a law); ~ etm. to carry out, to execute, to implement (a court order); to enforce (a law).

tenha [ā] lonely, solitary, unfrequented, uncrowded, isolated.

tenhalaşmak [ā] to become empty.

tenhalık [ā] 1. loneliness, solitude, isolation; 2. lonely (or solitary) place.

tenis [x .] tennis; ~ kortu tennis court; ~ raketi tennis racket; ~ topu tennis ball.

tenisçi tennis player.

tenkıye 1. enema, clyster; 2. enemator.

tenkil [i] getting rid of, doing away with; ~ etm. to get rid of, to do away with.

tenkit[1] 1. criticism; 2. (critical) review, critique; ~ etm. 1. to criticize; 2. to write a critical review (-i of), to review.

tenkit[2], -ti [i] punctuation; ~ etm. to punctuate.

tenkitçi 1. critic, reviewer; 2. critic, fault-finder; 3. critical, censorious (person).

tenor ♪ tenor.

tenperver fond of comfort.

tenrengi, -ni flesh-colo(u)red, flesh-pink.

tensel 1. fleshly, bodily; 2. material, corporeal.

tensik, -kı 1. putting in order; reorganization; 2. ✕ regroupment (of troops); ~ etm. 1. to put in order; to reorganize; 2. ✕ to regroup (troops).

tensip, -bi [i] seeing fit; ~ etm. to see fit.

tente [x .] awning.

tenteli [x . .] awninged.

tentene [x .] lace.

tentür tincture.

tentürdiyot tincture of iodine.

tenvir [i] 1. illumination; 2. fig. enlightenment; ~ etm. 1. to illuminate, to light; 2. fig. to enlighten, to inform.

tenvirat, -tı [. - -] illumination; ~ resmi municipal tax imposed on citizens living in areas illuminated at night by streetlights.

tenya [x .] zo. tapeworm, tenia.

tenzil [i] 1. lowering; 2. reduction, decrease; ~ etm. 1. to lower; 2. to reduce, to decrease.

tenzilat, -tı [. - -] reduction (of prices); ~ yapmak to make a reduction in price.

tenzilatlı reduced, discount (price); ~ satış sale.

teokrasi theocracy.

teoloji theology.

teorem Ȧ theorem.

teori theory.

teorik theoretic(al).

tepe 1. hill; 2. top; 3. crest, crown (of a bird); 4. Ȧ vertex; -den bakmak to look down (-e on), to look down one's nose (-e at), to despise; -den inme 1. unexpected, sudden; 2. from above, coming from one of the big guns; -den tırnağa kadar from head to toe (or foot), cap-a-pie; -si aşağı gitmek fig. to go downhill, to hit the skids, to fall flat on one's face; -si atmak to lose one's temper, to blow one's stack, to fly off the handle, to blow one's top; -sinden kaynar su dökülmek fig. to be left aghast, to be stunned; -sine binmek fig. to bedevil, to bug to death.

tepecamı, -nı skylight; bull's-eye.

tepecik hillock.

tepegöz 1. low-browed; 2. zo. cyclops.

tepeleme 1. vn. of tepelemek; 2. heaping portion of, heap of.

tepelemek 1. to give s.o. a severe beating, to wallop; 2. to clobber; 3. to kill.

tepeli crested *(bird)*.

tepetaklak 1. headlong, headfirst; 2. upside down.

tephir [i] vaporization, evaporation; ~ etm. to vaporize, to evaporate.

tephirhane [. - - .] fumigator; fumatorium.

tepinmek 1. to stamp; 2. to kick and stamp; 3. to jump for joy.

tepişmek 1. to kick at each other; 2. *fig.* to push and shove.

tepke reflex.

tepki 1. reaction; response; 2. recoil *(of a firearm)*; ~ göstermek to react.

tepkili reactive; ~ motor reaction engine *(or motor)*; ~ uçak jet (plane).

tepkime reaction *(a. ⚗)*.

tepkimek to react *(a. ⚗)*.

tepkisiz unreactive, inert.

tepme 1. *vn.* of tepmek; 2. kick.

tepmek, (-er) 1. to kick; 2. to turn down, to reject, to decline, to throw away *(an opportunity, etc.)*; 3. to recoil, to kick *(gun)*; 4. to tread on, to trample; 5. to crop up again, to recur; tepe tepe kullanmak to use as roughly as one pleases.

tepsi tray.

ter sweat, perspiration; ~ alıştırmak to cool off a little, to rest a bit; ~ basmak to break out in a sweat; ~ boşanmak to sweat like a pig; ~ dökmek to sweat *(a. fig.)*, to perspire; -e batmak to be covered with sweat; -e yatmak to make o.s. sweat; -ini soğutmak to cool off, to rest a bit.

terakki [i] progress, advance(ment); ~ etm. to progress, to advance.

terakkiperver [i] 1. progressive; 2. progressive-minded.

teraküm [ä] collection, accumulation; ~ etm. to collect, to accumulate, to gather.

terane [ä] 1. melody, air, tune; 2. *fig.* same old story, tired old refrain.

terapi therapy.

teras terrace; ~ katı penthouse.

teravi [. - -] *prayer special to the nights of Ramazan*.

terazi [ä] 1. balance, scales; 2. ♎ *ast.* Libra; ~ gözü pan *(or scale)* of a balance.

terbıyık youth whose moustache has just begun to sprout.

terbi, -ii [i] *ast.* quarter *(of the moon)*; ~ etm. ♪ to quadruple.

terbiye 1. (good) manners; 2. education, training *(of a person)*; 3. taming, training *(of an animal)*; 4. seasoning for food; sauce; 5. rein *(of a horse)*; ~ etm. 1.

to teach s.o. good manners; 2. to train, to educate; 3. to train, to tame *(an animal)*; ~ görmek to be trained *(or educated)*; -sini bozmak to forget one's manners, to be rude; -sini vermek *(b-nin)* to give s.o. a dressing down.

terbiyeci 1. educator, educationist; 2. trainer, tamer.

terbiyeli 1. well-mannered, polite, courteous, well-bred; 2. flavo(u)red *(with a sauce)*.

terbiyesiz ill-mannered, impolite, unmannerly, rude, discourteous, unmannered.

terbiyesizlik impoliteness, rudeness, unmannerliness; ~ etm. to behave rudely, to be impolite.

terbiyevi [. . . .] educational, educative; pedagogic(al).

tercih [i] preference; ~ etm. to prefer.

tercihen [i] by preference, preferably.

tercüman interpreter, translator.

tercümanlık interpretership; ~ yapmak to interpret; to be an interpreter.

tercüme translation; ~ etm. to translate.

tercümeihal, -li [ä] biography.

tere ♣ cress.

terebentin turpentine.

tereci seller of cress; -ye tere satmak to try to teach one's grandmother to suck eggs, to carry coals to Newcastle.

tereddi [i] degeneration, decline; ~ etm. to degenerate, to decline.

tereddüt, -dü hesitation, indecision; ~ etm. to hesitate; to falter, to waver.

tereddütlü hesitant; indecisive.

tereddütsüz unhesitant.

terek P shelf.

tereke estate.

terekküp, -bü 1. composition; 2. formation; ~ etm. to be composed (-den of).

terelelli [. . x .] F crazy, nutty.

terementi [. . x .] turpentine, resin; ~ ağacı ♣ turpentine tree.

teres 1. son of a bitch, bastard; 2. procurer, pimp, pander.

teressüp, -bü sedimentation; precipitation; ~ etm. to settle, to sediment; to precipitate.

terettüp, -bü being incumbent on, falling to; ~ etm. to be incumbent (-e on), to fall (-e to).

tereyağı, -nı 1. butter; 2. *sl.* stupid *(person)*; -ndan kıl çeker gibi as easy as taking candy from a baby, as easy as falling off a log.

terfi, -ii [i] promotion; ~ etm. to be promoted; ~ ettirmek to promote.

**terfian** [ī] by way of promotion.

**terfih** [ī] making prosperous; ~ etm. to make prosperous, to bring prosperity to.

**terfik**, -kı [ī] sending s.o. alongside another as an escort; ~ etm. to send s.o. alongside another as an escort.

**terhin** [ī] pawning, hocking; ~ etm. to pawn, to hock.

**terhis** [ī] X discharge, demobilization; ~ etm. to discharge, to demobilize; ~ olm. to be discharged (or demobilized), to get demobbed; ~ tezkeresi discharge (certificate).

**terilen** terrylene.

**terim** term (a. A̧, log.).

**terimsel** terminological.

**terk**, -ki abandonment, desertion; ~ etm. to abandon, to leave, to quit; to desert; to forsake; terki hayat etm. to die, to depart this life.

**terki 1.** the back part of a saddle; **2.** croup (of a horse); -sine almak to sit s.o. behind him.

**terkibi** [. - -] synthetic(al).

**terkip**, -bi [ī] **1.** combination; **2.** ♎, phls. synthesis; **3.** compound, union; **4.** ♎ compound; ~ etm. **1.** to compound, to put together; to combine; **2.** ♎, phls. to synthesize.

**terlemek 1.** to sweat, to perspire; **2.** (for a window) to fog (or steam) up; **3.** (for one's moustache) to sprout; **4.** fig. to work hard, to sweat.

**terli** sweaty, perspiry.

**terlik** slipper, scuff.

**termal**, -li thermal.

**termik** phys., ♎ thermic, thermal; ~ santral thermoelectric power plant.

**terminal**, -li terminal.

**terminoloji** terminology.

**terminüs** terminus.

**termoelektrik 1.** thermoelectricity; **2.** thermoelectric(al).

**termofor** hot-water bottle.

**termokimya** thermochemistry.

**termometre** thermometer.

**termonükleer** thermonuclear.

**termos** [x .] thermos (bottle), vacuum bottle.

**termosfer** thermosphere.

**termosifon 1.** hot-water heater; **2.** thermosiphon.

**termostat**, -tı thermostat.

**terör** terror.

**terörist**, -ti terrorist.

**terörizm** terrorism.

**ters 1.** back, reverse; converse; inverse, opposite; **2.** blunt edge (of a cutting implement); **3.** inverted, turned inside out; **4.** A̧ opposite (angle); **5.** P feces, excrement; **6.** wrong, opposite (road, direction); **7.** fig. bad-tempered, peevish, ornery, cantankerous, cross-grained; **8.** sharp, curt, brusque, cross (answer, word); **9.** backwards, in the opposite direction; **10.** sharply, curtly, brusquely; ~ anlamak to misunderstand, to misinterpret; ~ bakmak to leer (-e at); ~ düşmek to run counter (-e to), to go against; ~ gitmek to go wrong, to turn out badly; ~ tarafından kalkmak fig. to get out of bed on the wrong side; ~ ~ bakmak to look daggers (-e at); -i dönmek to lose one's bearings.

**tersane** [ā] shipyard.

**tersine** on the contrary.

**terslemek 1.** (b-ni) to snap at s.o., to bite s.o.'s head off; **2.** to dung.

**terslenmek 1.** pass. of terslemek; **2.** to growl (-e at), to be short (-e with), to talk sharply (-e to).

**terslik 1.** hitch, set-back; **2.** ill-temperedness, peevishness.

**tersyüz:** ~ etm. to turn inside out.

**tertemiz** [x . .] spotless, spotlessly clean.

**tertibat**, -tı [. - -] **1.** arrangement, setup; **2.** mechanism, apparatus; **3.** X disposition (of troops, etc.); ~ almak to take measures.

**tertip**, -bi [ī] **1.** arrangement, setup; contrivance; **2.** X disposition (of troops, etc.) **3.** typ. typesetting; **4.** ℞ recipe, prescription; **5.** A̧ ordinate; ~ etm. **1.** to arrange, to set up, to organize, to contrive; **2.** X to dispose (troops, etc.); **3.** typ to typeset.

**tertipçi 1.** arranger, planner; **2.** typ. typesetter.

**tertiplemek** to arrange, to set up, to organize, to contrive, to plan.

**tertipleyici** organizer, arranger, planner, contriver.

**tertipli** tidy, neat, orderly; organized.

**tertipsiz** untidy, messy; disorganized.

**tertipsizlik** untidiness, messiness; disorganization.

**terütaze** [ā] very fresh.

**tervic**, -ci [ī] supporting (an idea); ~ etm. to support, to advocate (an idea).

**terzi 1.** tailor, dressmaker; **2.** tailor's shop.

**terzihane** [ā] tailor's shop.

**terzil** [ī] disgracing; ~ etm. to disgrace.

**terzilik** tailorship, tailory.

**tesadüf** [ā] **1.** chance event, accident; happenstance; coincidence; **2.** chance, hazard; ~ etm. 1. to meet by chance, to chance upon, to come across, to come upon, to happen upon; 2. to coincide with.

tesadüfen [ā] [. x ..] by chance, by accident, by coincidence, coincidentally.

tesadüfi [. - .-] accidental, chance, casual, fortuitous, coincidental.

tesahup, -bu [ā] 1. claiming to be the owner of; 2. protection; ~ etm. 1. to claim to be the owner (-e of). 2. to protect.

tesanüt, -dü [ā] solidarity.

tesbit s. tespit.

tescil [i] registration; ~ etm. to register.

tescilli [i] registered; ~ marka registered trademark.

teselli [i] consolation, comfort, solace; ~ etm. (or vermek). to console, to comfort, to give consolation; ~ mükâfatı consolation prize.

tesellüm receiving; taking delivery; ~ etm. to receive; to receive a consignment of (goods); to take delivery on (a shipment).

teselsül concatenation; chain; ~ etm. to continue without interruption.

teshil [i] facilitation; ~ etm. to facilitate.

teshin [i] heating; warning; ~ etm. to heat; to warm.

teshir [i] bewitching, charming, enchanting; ~ etm. to bewitch, to charm, to enchant.

tesir [- -] effect, influence; impression; ~ etm. to affect, to act upon; to influence, to make an impression (-e on).

tesirli [- ..] effective, effectual, efficacious; impressive.

tesirsiz ineffective, ineffectual, inefficacious.

tesis [- -] 1. foundation, establishment; 2. institution, association, establishment, foundation; 3. facility; 4. installation, system; ~ etm. to found, to set up, to establish; to institute.

tesisat, -tı [- ..] 1. installation; 2. institutions, establishments, foundations; 3. facilities.

tesisatçı installer.

tesit, -di [i] celebration; ~ etm. to celebrate.

teskere [x ..] 1. † stretcher, litter; 2. handbarrow.

teskereci stretcher-bearer (a. X).

teskin [i] tranquilization; ~ etm. to tranquilize. to calm, to allay, to pacify.

teslih [i] armament; ~ etm. to arm.

teslihat, -tı [. - -] 1. armament; 2. armaments, arms, weaponry.

teslim [i] 1. delivery; 2. submission, surrender, capitulation; 3. concession; 4. surrender!, give up!; ~ almak 1. to take delivery of, to receive; 2. ✕ to possess, to seize control of (a place); ~ bayrağı çekmek F to strike one's flag, to throw in the sponge; ~ etm. 1. to deliver, to hand over; 2. to surrender; 3. to admit, to concede; ~ olm. to give in, to yield, to submit, to surrender; ~ ve tesellüm delivery and receipt.

teslimat, -tı [. - -] goods delivered, deliveries.

teslimiyet, -tı [. - ..] submission; ~ göstermek to submit (-e to).

tesmiye naming; ~ etm. to name.

tespih prayer beads, rosary; ~ çekmek to tell one's beads.

tespihböceği, -ni zo. wood louse, sow bug.

tespit, -ti determination, fixation; stabilization; ~ banyosu phot. fixing bath; ~ davası ⚖ declaratory action; ~ etm. 1. to fix; 2. to establish, to determine; 3. to fix, to set (prices).

tesri, -li [i] acceleration, speeding up; ~ etm. to accelerate, to speed up.

test, -ti test.

testere [x ..] saw.

testerebalığı, -nı zo. sawfish.

testi pitcher, jug.

tesviye 1. smoothing, flattening, leveling; 2. paying (a debt); 3. pass (given to travelling soldiers); ~ aleti level; ~ etm. 1. to smooth, to level, to flatten, to grade, to even; 2. to pay (a debt).

tesviyeci (pipe) fitter.

tesviyeruhu, -nu (spirit) level.

teşbih [i] 1. lit. simile; 2. comparison; ~ etm. to compare; -te hata olmaz (or olmasın)! pardon the crude expression!

teşdit, -di [i] 1. intensification; 2. harshening; ~ etm. 1. to intensify; 2. to harshen.

teşebbüs 1. enterprise, undertaking, attempt; 2. initiative, enterprise; ~ etm. to undertake, to set about. to enter upon, to attempt; -e gecmek to set about. to set to: -ü ele almak to take the initiative.

teşekkül 1. formation; 2. consisting of, being made up of: 3. organization. unit, body, group; ~ etm. 1. to be formed; to take shape: 2. to consist (-den of). to be made up (-den of).

teşekkür thanking; ~ ederim! thank you!; ~ etm. to thank.

**teşekkürname** [â] ·letter of thanks.

**teşerrüf** being hono(u)red; ~ etm. **1.** to be hono(u)red; **2.** to feel hono(u)red to meet s.o., to have the hono(u)r of meeting s.o.

**tesevvüş** confusion.

**teşhir** [î] **1.** display, exhibition; **2.** *fig.* pillorying; ~ etm. **1.** to display, to exhibit, to expose; **2.** *fig.* to pillory.

**teşhis** [î] **1.** ⚕ diagnosis; **2.** recognition, identification; **3.** *lit.* personification; ~ etm. **1.** ⚕ to diagnose; **2.** to recognize, to identify; ~ koymak ⚕ to diagnose.

**teşkil** [î] formation; ~ etm. to form; to constitute.

**teşkilat**, -tı organization; teşkilatı esasiye kanunu 𝒫𝒫 constitution.

**teşkilatçı** organizer.

**teşkilatçılık** organizing.

**teşkilatland:rmak** to organize.

**teşkilatlanmak** to be organized.

**teşkilatlı** organized.

**teşkilatsız** unorganized.

**teşne** thirsty (*a. fig.*); ~ olm. *(bşe) fig.* to thirst for *s.th.*

**teşrif** [î] **1.** visit; **2.** hono(u)ring; **3.** going to; ~ etm. (*or* buyurmak) **1.** to visit, to hono(u)r; **2.** to go (-*e* to); ~ nereye? where are you going?

**teşrifat**, -tı [. - .] **1.** protocol; **2.** formality, ceremonial.

**teşrifatçı 1.** master of ceremonies; **2.** protocolist.

**teşrih** [î] **1.** ⚕ dissection; **2.** anatomy; **3.** *P* skeleton; ~ etm. to dissect.

**teşrihhane** [. - .] dissecting room.

**teşrii** [. - .] legislative; ~ kuvvet legislative power; ~ masuniyet legislative immunity.

**teşrik**, -ki [î] making s.o. a partner; ~ etm. *(b-ni)* to make *s.o.* a partner (-*e* in).

**teşrikimesai** [. - . . - -] cooperation, collaboration; ~ etm. to cooperate (*ile* with), to collaborate (*ile* with).

**teşrinievvel** [. - . . .] † October.

**teşrinisani** [. - . . -] † November.

**teşvik**, -ki **1.** encouragement; **2.** incitement, provocation; ~ etm. **1.** to encourage, to spur on, to inspire; **2.** to incite, to provoke.

**teşviş** confusing; ~ etm. to confuse.

**teşyi** [î] seeing s.o. off; ~ etm. *(b-ni)* to see *s.o.* off.

**tetabuk**, -ku [â] agreement; coincidence; correspondence; ~ etm.· to be in harmony (*ile* with), to agree (*ile* with), to coincide (*ile* with).

**tetanos** [x . .] ⚕ tetanus, lockjaw.

**tetebbu**, -uu investigation, research; ~ etm. to investigate, to research.

**tetik 1.** trigger *(of a gun)*; **2.** alert, vigilant; **3.** delicate; ~ davranmak to act quickly; tetiğini bozmamak to keep one's cool, to keep a cool head; -te olm. to be on the alert, to be on the qui vive.

**tetkik**, -ki [î] investigation, examination; scrutiny; ~ etm. to investigate, to examine; to scrutinize.

**tetkikat**, -tı [. - -] investigations, examinations; scrutinies.

**tevafuk**, -ku [â] accordance; ~ etm. to accord (-*e* with), to agree (-*e* with).

**tevakkuf 1.** stopping; pausing; sojourning; **2.** depending on; ~ etm. **1.** to stop; to pause; to sojourn, to stay; **2.** to depend (-*e* on), to be subject (-*e* to).

**tevali** [. - -] **1.** succession, sequence; **2.** continuation; ~ etm. to continue without letup.

**tevarüs** [â] inheriting; ~ etm. to inherit.

**tevazu**, -uu [â] humility, humbleness; modesty; ~ göstermek to behave humbly.

**tevazün** [â] balance, equilibrium; ~ etm. to be balanced, to be in equilibrium.

**tevbih** [î] reprimand; ~ etm. to reprimand.

**tevcih** [î] **1.** turning towards; **2.** pointing, aiming, directing; **3.** bestowing, conferring; ~ etm. **1.** to turn (-*e* towards); **2.** to point (-*e* at), to aim (-*e* at), to direct (-*e* to); **3.** to bestow, to confer, to grant.

**tevdi**, -ii [î] entrusting, consigning; depositing; ~ etm. **1.** to entrust, to consign, to commit; to confide; **2.** to deposit (*money*).

**tevdiat**, -tı [. - -] deposits; -ta bulunmak to make a deposit, to deposit some money in (*a bank*).

**teveccüh 1.** kindness, consideration, favo(u)r; **2.** directing one's attention to; ~ etm. **1.** to be directed (-*e* toward); **2.** to betake o.s. (-*e* to); ~ göstermek to show kindness (-*e* to); -ünü kazanmak *(b-nin)* to win favo(u)r in *s.o.'s* eyes; -ünüz efendim! that's very kind of you!

**tevehhüm** imagining; ~ etm. to imagine.

**tevekkel** *P* happy-go-lucky.

**tevekkeli** *F* for no reason, for nothing; ~ değil it is not just a matter of chance that...

**tevekkül** resignation; ~ etm. **1.** to put o.s. in God's hands; **2.** to resign o.s. to one's fate.

**tevellüt**, -dü **1.** birth; **2.** date of birth.

**tevellütlü** born in...

**tevessü,** -üü expansion, enlargement; spreading; ~ etm. to widen, to expand, to enlarge; to spread.

**tevessül** 1. having recourse to; 2. undertaking, attempting; ~ etm. 1. to have recourse (-e to); 2. to undertake, to attempt.

**tevettür** tension.

**tevfik,** -ki [i] 1. divine guidance and assistance; 2. adaptation; 3. ♀ [- .] *mf.*

**tevfikan** [- . .] in accordance (-e with), in conformity (-e to).

**tevhit,** -di [i] 1. unification; combination; 2. monotheism; ~ etm. to unify, to unite; to combine.

**tevil** [- -] forced interpretation; ~ etm. to misinterpret intentionally.

**tevkif** [i] 1. arrest; custody, detention; 2. stopping, halting; ~ etm. 1. to arrest, to take into custody, to take under detention; 2. to stop, to halt; to detain; ~ müzekkeresi 🎲 warrant of arrest.

**tevkifhane** [. - - .] gaol, *Am.* jail, lockup.

**tevkil** [i] making s.o. one's proxy; ~ etm. (b-ni) to make s.o. one's proxy.

**tevlit,** -di [i] 1. giving birth to *(a child)*; 2. *fig.* producing, bringing about; ~ etm. 1. to give birth to *(a child)*; 2. *fig.* to produce, to bring about.

**tevliyet,** -ti trusteeship of a vakıf.

**Tevrat,** -tı [â] *pr. n.* 1. the Torah; 2. the Old Testament.

**tevsi,** -ii [i] extension, enlargement; ~ etm. to widen, to enlarge, to extend, to expand.

**tevsik,** -ki [i] documentation; ~ etm. to document.

**tevzi,** -ii [i] 1. distribution; 2. delivery *(of letters, etc.)*; ~ etm. 1. to distribute; 2. to deliver *(letters, etc.)*.

**tevziat,** -tı [. - -] 1. distributions; 2. deliveries.

**teyakkuz** vigilance; circumspection; ~ etm. to be vigilant.

**teyel** basting.

**teyellemek** to baste, to tack.

**teyelli** basted, tacked.

**teyit,** -di [- -] 1. strengthening; 2. confirmation, corroboration; ~ etm. 1. to strengthen; 2. to confirm, to corroborate.

**teyp** tape recorder; -e almak to tape, to tape-record.

**teyze** maternal aunt.

**tez**[1] 1. quick, speedy; 2. quickly, speedily; ~ beri P easily; ~ canlı impetuous, precipitate; ~ elden without delay, quickly;

~ olm. to hurry (up).

**tez**[2] thesis.

**tezahür** [â] 1. appearing; 2. sign, manifestation; ~ etm. to appear, to become visible.

**tezahürat,** -tı [. - -] 1. cheering; ovation; applause; 2. demonstration; 3. signs, manifestations; ~ yapmak to cheer *(-e* for), to root *(-e* for).

**tezat,** -dı [â] 1. contrast; oppositeness; 2. contradiction; -a düşmek to contradict o.s.

**tezayüt,** -dü [â] increase; ~ etm. to increase.

**tezebzüp,** -bü 1. disorder, confusion; 2. indecision, vacillation.

**tezek** dried dung.

**tezelzül** shaking; ~ etm. to shake, to quake.

**tezene** P plectrum, pick.

**tezgâh** 1. counter; 2. workbench; 3. loom; 4. stocks, ways, shipway; ~ başı yapmak F to stand at the bar and have a drink; -ından geçmek *sl. (for a woman)* to have sex with, to go to bed with.

**tezgâhlamak** to concoct, to cook up, to plan.

**tezgâhtar** shop assistant, *Am.* (sales) clerk, salesman, saleswoman, shopgirl, *Am.* salesgirl.

**tezgâhtarlık** clerking; ~ etm. to clerk.

**tezhip,** -bi [i] gilding; ~ etm. to gild.

**tezkere** [x . .] 1. message, note; 2. ✕ discharge papers; 3. permit; licence; -sini eline vermek *fig.* to fire, to give s.o. his walking papers.

**tezkereci** ✕ discharged soldier.

**tezkiye** 1. purification; 2. praise.

**tezlemek** P to speed up.

**tezlenmek** 1. *pass. of* tezlemek; 2. to hurry, to hasten.

**tezlik** 1. quickness, speed, haste; 2. impatience, impetuosity.

**tezvir** [i] 1. malicious misrepresentation; 2. trickery, deceit.

**tezyin** [i] ornamentation, embellishment, decoration; ~ etm. to adorn, to embellish, to ornament.

**tezyinat,** -tı [. - -] adornments, ornamentations, decorations.

**tezyini** [. - -] ornamental, decorative.

**THY** *(abbr. for* Türk Hava Yolları) Turkish Airlines.

**tıbben** medically, from a medical point of view.

**tıbbi** [i] medical.

**tıbbiye** medical school, school of medicine.

**tıbbiyeli** medical student.

**tıfıl,** -flı child.

**tığ 1.** crochet-hook; **2.** awl; **3.** plane iron; ~ gibi wiry.

**tığlamak 1.** to lance *(a wound)*; **2.** to pierce with a needle; **3.** to slaughter *(animal)*; **4.** *sl.* to stab, to knife, to bayonet.

**tığmak,** (-ar) *sl.* to make o.s. scarce, to split.

**tıka basa** as full as possible, crammed full; ~ yemek to make a pig of o.s.

**tıkaç,** -cı plug, stopper; gag.

**tıkalı** stopped (up); clogged, congested.

**tıkamak** to plug, to stop; to clog, to congest.

**tıkanık** stopped (up); clogged, congested.

**tıkanıklık** stoppage; cloggage, congestion.

**tıkanmak 1.** *pass.* of tıkamak; **2.** to gasp for breath; **3.** to lose one's appetite.

**tıkılmak 1.** *pass.* of tıkmak; **2.** to jump into *(a place)*.

**tıkınmak** F to cram it in, to pack it away, to tuck in.

**tıkır:** ~ ~ like clockwork; -ında gitmek to go like clockwork.

**tıkırdamak** to rattle, to clink.

**tıkırtı** rattle, click, clack, tap.

**tıkışık** crammed, squeezed.

**tıkışıklık** crowdedness.

**tıkışmak** *(for people)* to cram *(or* squeeze) themselves into *(a place)*.

**tıkıştırmak 1.** to cram, to squeeze, to jam; **2.** to bolt down *(food)*.

**tıkız 1.** hard, too tightly stuffed; **2.** underdone, undercooked *(bread)*.

**tıklım tıklım** very crowded, jammed, packed: ~ dolu jam-packed.

**tıkmak,** (-ar) to cram, to jam, to thrust, to stick (-e into).

**tıknaz** plump, dumpy.

**tıknefes 1.** short of breath, short-winded, pursy; **2.** shortness of breath.

**tıksırık** sneeze *(made with one's mouth shut)*.

**tıksırmak** to sneeze *(with one's mouth shut)*.

**tılsım** talisman, charm, amulet.

**tılsımlı** enchanted.

**tımar 1.** grooming *(a horse)*; **2.** dressing *(of wounds)*; **3.** pruning *(of trees)*; **4.** *hist.* fief; ~ etm. to groom, to curry.

**tımarhane** [. . -.] insane asylum, nut house, bughouse; ~ kaçkını *fig.* nut, kook.

**tımarlamak** to groom, to curry.

**tımarlı** groomed *(horse)*.

**tın tın** *sl.* dim-witted.

**tınaz** haystack.

**tıngadak** [x . .] with a metallic clang.

**tıngır 1.** clanging sound; **2.** *sl.* penniless, flat broke; **3.** *sl.* money, tin, dough.

**tıngırdamak 1.** to rattle, to clang; **2.** *sl.* to die, to croak, to peg out.

**tıngırdatmak** to thrum, to strum, to twang *(a stringed instrument)*.

**tıngır mıngır 1.** with a clanging sound; **2.** slowly.

**tıngırtı** clang, rattle.

**tıngır tıngır 1.** with a clanging sound; **2.** completely empty.

**tınlamak** to resound, to resonate, to ring, to clink.

**tınmak** to make a sound.

**tınmamak** *fig.* to take no notice (-e of).

**tınnet,** -ti tone, timbre.

**tıp,** -bbı medicine, medical science.

**tıpa** stopper, cork.

**tıpatıp** [x . .] perfectly, exactly.

**tıpırdamak 1.** to patter; **2.** to go pit-a-pat.

**tıpırtı** (pitter-)patter.

**tıpır tıpır 1.** with a pattering sound; **2.** pit-a-pat.

**tıpış tıpış:** ~ gitmek *(or* yürümek) to patter, to toddle.

**tıpkı** [x .] **1.** just like, in just the same way as; **2.** spitting image; ~ -sına exactly like.

**tıpkıbasım** facsimile.

**tıp tıp** pit-a-pat.

**tırabzan** stair rail(ing), banister; ~ başı **1.** newel; **2.** *fig.* ineffectual father.

**tırak** bang; ~ diye with a bang.

**tıraş 1.** shave, shaving; **2.** haircut; **3.** *sl.* pulling s.o.'s leg, having s.o. on; **4.** *sl.* boring talk, palaver; ~ bıçağı razorblade; ~ etm. **1.** to shave; **2.** to cut *(hair)*; **3.** *sl.* to pull s.o.'s leg, to have s.o. on; **4.** *sl.* to talk s.o.'s head off; ~ fırçası shaving brush; ~ kremi shaving cream; ~ losyonu after-shave (lotion); ~ makinesi **1.** (safety) razor; **2.** electric shaver; ~ olm. **1.** to shave; **2.** to get *(or* have) a shave; ~ sabunu shaving soap; ~ takımı shaving things; ~ı gelmek *(or* uzamak) to need a shave.

**tıraşlamak 1.** to plane, to prune; **2.** *sl.* to pull s.o.'s leg, to have s.o. on; **3.** *sl.* to talk s.o.'s head off.

**tıraşlı 1.** shaved, shaven; **2.** needing a shave.

**tıraşsız 1.** unshaved, unshaven; **2.** needing a shave.

**tırık** rattle; ~ diye with a rattle.

**tırıl** *sl.* **1.** naked; **2.** penniless, stone-broke.

**tırıs** trot; ~ gitmek to trot; -a kalkmak

to begin to trot.
**tırkaz** bolt, bar.
**tırmalamak 1.** to scratch, to claw; **2.** *fig.* to grate on, to irritate.
**tırmanma** *vn. of* tırmanmak; ~ şeridi *mot.* climbing lane.
**tırmanmak 1.** to climb; **2.** to increase, to escalate.
**tırmık 1.** scratch; **2.** rake.
**tırmıklamak 1.** to scratch, to claw; **2.** to rake.
**tırnak 1.** nail; fingernail; toenail; **2.** claw, hoof; **3.** quotation mark, quote, inverted comma; **4.** ⊕ ratchet, click, pawl; **5.** fluke, palm *(of an anchor);* ~ boyası *(or* cilası*)* nail varnish, *Am.* nail polish; ~ göstermek *fig.* to show one's claws; ~ işareti quotation mark, quote, inverted comma; ~ makası nail scissors; ~ törpüsü nail file; ~ yeri fingerhold; -larını yemek to bite one's nails.
**tırnakçı** *sl.* pickpocket.
**tırnaklamak** to claw, to scratch.
**tırpan** scythe; ~ atmak **1.** to kill off, to slay; **2.** to get rid (-e of), to weed out.
**tırpanlamak** to scythe.
**tırtık** nick; notch.
**tırtıklamak** *sl.* to steal, to nick, to swipe.
**tırtıklı 1.** nicked; notched; **2.** jaggy, jagged.
**tırtıl 1.** zo. caterpillar; **2.** caterpillar tread; **3.** serration *(on a knife blade);* **4.** perforation *(of a stamp);* **5.** rowel; jagging wheel; **6.** *sl.* sponger, freeloader.
**tırtıllı 1.** jagged; serrated; **2.** milled.
**tıs** hiss; ~ yok there is not a sound to be heard.
**tıslamak** to hiss.
**tıynet, -ti** nature, character, makeup *(of a person).*
**ti** [-] ✕ bugle call; ~ işareti bugle call; -ye almak *(b-ni)* *sl.* to make fun of *s.o.*, to poke fun at *s.o.*
**Tibet, -ti** *pr. n.* Tibet.
**ticaret, -ti** [ā] trade, commerce, traffic; ~ anlaşması trade agreement; ~ ataşesi commercial attaché; ♀ Bakanlığı Ministry of Commerce; ~ bankası commercial bank; ~ borsası exchange; stock exchange; ~ filosu merchant *(or* mercantile*)* mariné; ~ gemisi merchant ship, merchantman; ~ hukuku commercial law; ~ odası chamber of commerce; ~ unvanı trade name *(of a firm);* ~ yolu trade route.
**ticaretgâh** [ā] centre of commerce, trad-

ing centre.
**ticarethane** [. - . - .] trading establishment, firm, business.
**ticari** [. - -] commercial, trade.
**tifo** [x .] ✞ typhoid fever.
**tiftik** mohair, angora.
**tiftiklenmek** to fuzz, to become fuzzy *(cloth).*
**tifüs** [x .] ✞ typhus (fever).
**tik, -ki** tic.
**tiksindirici** repugnant, repellent, loathsome.
**tiksindirmek** to revolt, to fill with disgust.
**tiksinmek** to be disgusted (-den with), to loathe, to revolt, to abominate, to abhor.
**tiksinti** revulsion, repugnance, disgust, loathing, abomination.
**tilavet, -ti** chanting *(the Koran);* -le okumak to chant *(the Koran).*
**tilki 1.** zo. fox; **2.** *fig.* fox, cunning person, slyboots; ~ gibi foxy, sly, crafty; -nin dönüp dolaşıp geleceği yer kürkçü dükkânıdır *pro.* at length, the fox is brought to the furrier.
**tilkileşmek** to get foxy *(or* crafty*)*.
**tim** [i] *sports:* team.
**timbal, -li** ♪ kettledrum, timbal, tymbal.
**timsah** zo. crocodile; alligator.
**timsal, -li** [ā] symbol.
**tiner** thinner.
**tinsel** spiritual.
**tin tin** very quietly; on tiptoe.
**tip, -pi 1.** type, sort; **2.** unusual, odd; **3.** *fig.* geezer.
**tipi** snowstorm, blizzard.
**tipik** typical.
**tipsiz** *sl.* ugly, unattractive.
**tipografya** letterpress, typography.
**tirad** *s.* tirat.
**tiraj** circulation *(of a newspaper).*
**tiramola** ⬇ tacking; ~ etm. to tack.
**tirat** *thea.* tirade.
**tirbuşon** corkscrew.
**tirbuton** buttonhook.
**tire[1]** hyphen; dash.
**tire[2]** cotton thread.
**tirendaz** [. - -] **1.** archer; **2.** *fig.* skil(l)ful, adroit; **3.** *fig.* elegant.
**tirfil** ♣ trefoil, clover.
**tirfillenmek** to become threadbare.
**tirfon** large screw.
**tirhos** zo. sardine.
**tirildemek** to quiver, to shiver, to tremble.
**tiril tiril 1.** gauzy, filmy, gossamery *(cloth);* **2.** spotlessly clean.
**tirit** bread soaked in gravy; ~ gibi as old as the hills.

**tiriz** lath, batten.

**tirlin** ruling (or drawing) pen.

**tiroit,** -di anat. thyroid.

**tirpidin** small mattock.

**tirsi** (balığı) zo. shad.

**tirşe 1.** bluish green; **2.** vellum; parchment.

**tir tir titremek** to be all of a tremble, to shiver, to quiver, to tremble, to quake.

**tiryaki** [. - -] addict; -si olm. (bşin) to be addicted to s.th.

**tiryakilik** [. - ..] addiction.

**tişört,** -tü T-shirt, tee shirt.

**titiz 1.** fastidious, hard to please, finicky, picky, pernickety; **2.** particular, choosy; **3.** meticulous.

**titizlenmek 1.** to become hard to please, to get finicky; **2.** to become particular (or choosy); **3.** to become meticulous.

**titizlik 1.** fastidiousness, persnicketiness; **2.** particularity, choosiness; **3.** meticulousness.

**titrek** shaky, tremulous.

**titremek 1.** to shiver, to tremble, to shake, to quake, to quiver; **2.** to flicker (light); **3.** to be very afraid (-den of).

**titreşim 1.** phys. vibration; **2.** ♪ vibrato.

**titreşimli 1.** phys. vibratory, vibratile; **2.** voiced.

**titreşimsiz 1.** phys. vibrationless; **2.** unvoiced.

**titreşmek 1.** to tremble, to quake, to shake, to quiver; **2.** to vibrate.

**tiyatro** [.x.] theatre, Am. theater.

**tiyatrocu** [.x..] **1.** theatre owner; **2.** actor; actress.

**tiyatrolaştırmak** to dramatize for the stage.

**tiz** [i] **1.** shrill; **2.** ♪ high(-pitched); sharp.

**tizleşmek** [i] **1.** to become shrill; **2.** ♪ to sharp.

**TL** (abbr. for Türk Lirası) Turkish Lira.

**toğrul** zo. goshawk.

**tohum 1.** seed; **2.** sperm; **3.** fertilized egg; **4.** family, stock; ~ atmak to sow; ~ bağlamak to go to seed; ~ ekmek to sow seed, to seed; -a kaçmak to go to seed (a. fig.); -u dökülmek to reach the menopause.

**tohumlamak 1.** to inseminate artificially; **2.** to fertilize; **3.** to seed.

**tok,** -ku **1.** full; **2.** thick (cloth); **3.** deep (voice), ~ karnına on a full stomach; ~ sözlü blunt; plainspoken, outspoken.

**toka¹** [x.] **1.** buckle; **2.** barette (for the hair).

**toka²** [x.] **1.** shaking hands; **2.** clinking

glasses; ~ etm. **1.** to shake hands; **2.** to clink glasses (while toasting); **3.** ↓ to make taut, to draw tight; **4.** sl. to pay, to plank down.

**tokaç,** -cı clothes stick (used for beating washing).

**tokalaşmak** to shake hands.

**tokat¹,** -tı slap, cuff; ~ atmak (or aşketmek or yapıştırmak) to slap, to cuff; ~ yemek to be slapped.

**tokat²,** -tı sheepfold; pen.

**tokatlamak** to slap; to cuff.

**tokgözlü** contented.

**toklaşmak** (for a voice) to deepen.

**toklu** yearling sheep.

**tokluk 1.** fullness; **2.** deepness (of voice).

**tokmak 1.** mallet; tamper; beetle; gavel; **2.** knocker (for a door); **3.** wooden pestle.

**tokmakçı** sl. gigolo.

**tokmaklamak** to beat with a mallet; to tamp.

**toksik** toxic.

**toksin** toxin.

**toktağan** constant; ~ karlar perennial snow.

**tokurdamak** to bubble.

**tokurtu** bubble.

**tokuşmak 1.** (for animals) to butt each other; **2.** to collide.

**tokuşturmak 1.** caus. of tokuşmak; **2.** to clink (glasses).

**tokuz** s. tok 2.

**Tokyo** pr. n. Tokyo.

**tokyo** thong, flip-flop.

**tolerans** tolerance (a. ⊕).

**tolga** war helmet.

**tomak 1.** wooden mace; **2.** wooden ball; **3.** a kind of boot.

**tomar 1.** roll (of paper, etc.); **2.** a great deal of, a lot of, a wad of; **3.** rammer.

**tombala** tombola, lot(t)o; ~ çekmek to draw a number (while playing tombola).

**tombalacı** lotto man.

**tombalak** plump, chubby.

**tombaz 1.** flat-bottomed barge, lighter; **2.** pontoon, float (of a pontoon bridge); ~ köprü pontoon bridge.

**tombul** plump.

**tombullaşmak** to get plump.

**tombulluk** plumpness.

**tomruk 1.** log; **2.** bud (of a plant); **3.** ingot (of cast metal); **4.** † gaol, Am. jail.

**tomson** Thompson.

**tomurcuk** bud.

**tomurcuklanmak** to bud.

**ton¹** ton (= 1000 kg.); -la tons of.

**ton²** tone (a. ♪).

tonaj tonnage.

tonalite tonality.

tonbalığı, -nı zo. tunny.

tonga [x .] sl. trick, fast one; -ya basmak (or düşmek or oturmak) to be duped, to be taken in, to fall for; -ya bastırmak to dupe, to con, to trick.

tonik ₹ tonic.

tonilato [. . x .] ⚓ tonnage.

tonlama intonation.

tonoz ⌂ vault.

tonton darling, sweet, dear.

top, -pu 1. ball; 2. cannon; 3. roll, bolt (of cloth); 4. ream (of paper); 5. round-(ed); ~ gun carriage; ~ ateşi cannon fire; gunfire, artillery fire; ~ çehre round face; ~ gibi gitmek to go at once; ~ oynamak to play football; ~ sakal full, round beard; -a tutmak to bombard; -u atmak sl. 1. to go bankrupt, to go bust; 2. to flunk a grade, to fail a year; -u -u in all, all told, altogether; -un ağzında fig. at the lion's mouth, on the edge of the volcano.

topaç, -cı 1. (peg) top; teetotum; 2. rounded loom (of an oar); 3. round basket; ~ çevirmek to whip a top; ~ gibi plump and sturdy (child).

topak 1. ball, lump; 2. fetlock; 3. metall. pellet.

topaklamak metall. to pelletize.

topal lame, crippled; ~ ~ yürümek to limp.

topallamak to limp.

topallık lameness.

topaltı, -nı terreplein of a fort.

toparlak 1. round; 2. ✕ limber.

toparlamak 1. to collect, to gather together; 2. to summarize, to put in a nutshell; 3. to tidy o.s. up, to smarten o.s. up; 4. to tidy, to pick up; 5. to pull (or get) o.s. together.

toparlanmak 1. pass. of toparlamak; 2. to pull o.s. together; to shape up; 3. to recover, to get back on one's feet (after an illness).

topatan a kind of melon.

topçeker 1. gunboat; 2. artillery (animal, vehicle).

topçu 1. ✕ cannoneer; artilleryman; 2. ✕ the artillery; 3. sl. student who has flunked a grade; ~ sınıfı ✕ the artillery branch; ~ subayı ✕ artillery officer.

topçuluk gunnery.

tophane [ā] hist. 1. cannon foundry, arsenal; 2. artillery school.

toplaç ⚡ collector.

toplam ⅄ total; ~ olarak in all, all told.

toplama vn. of toplamak, part. ⅄ addition; ~ işareti ⅄ plus sign; ~ kampı concentration camp; ~ makinesi adding machine.

toplamak 1. to collect, to gather; 2. ⅄ to add (up), to total; 3. to pick, to harvest; 4. to accumulate, to amass; 5. to tidy (or pick) up, to straighten up; 6. to clear (the table); 7. to convene, to convoke; 8. to put on (or gain) weight.

toplanmak 1. pass. of toplamak; 2. to gather, to assemble, to congregate; 3. to shape up; 4. to put on (or gain) weight.

toplantı meeting, gathering; ~ salonu meeting room, assembly hall.

toplardamar anat. vein.

toplu 1. collected, gathered, assembled; 2. tidy, neat (place); 3. plump; 4. collective; 5. F pin; 6. cumulative; ~ konut housing estate; ~ mezar mass grave; ~ sigorta group insurance; ~ tabanca six--shooter; ~ taşıma mass transport(ation)

topluca 1. as a group; 2. plumpish.

topluiğne pin.

topluluk 1. group; 2. community; ~ adı gr. collective noun.

toplum society, community.

toplumbilim sociology.

toplumbilimci sociologist.

toplumcu socialist.

toplumdışı extrasocial.

toplumsal social, societal.

toplumsallaştırmak to socialize.

toplusözleşme collective agreement.

topografi topography.

toprak 1. earth, soil; dirt; 2. land; 3. ⚡ earth, ground; 4. earthen(ware); 5. unpaved, dirt (road); ~ aşınması geol. soil erosion; ~ doyursun gözünü! nothing on earth can satisfy you!; ~ kayması landslide, slump; ~ reformu land reform; ~ rengi earth-colo(u)red; ~ sahibi landowner; ~ yol dirt road; toprağa bakmak fig. to be at death's door, to have one foot in the grave; toprağa vermek to bury, to inter, to lay to rest; toprağı bol olsun may he rest in peace.

toprakaltı, -nı subsoil, underground.

toprakboya 1. oxide red; 2. earth colo(u)r.

topraklamak 1. to cover or fill with earth; 2. to dirty; 3. ⚡ to ground.

toptan 1. wholesale; 2. all at once, all at the same time.

toptancı wholesaler.

toptancılık wholesaling.

topuk 1. heel; 2. geogr. bar (of a river);

topuğuna basmak *(b-nin) fig.* to be at *s.o.'s* heels; -larına kadar up to the ankles.

**topuklamak** to heel.

**topuklu** high-heeled *(shoe).*

**topuksuz** flat-heeled, low-heeled *(shoe).*

**toput** *⚓* deposit.

**topuz 1.** mace; **2.** bun, knot *(of hair);* **3.** doorknob; **4.** head *(of a walking stick).*

**topyekûn 1.** in all, all told, altogether; **2.** total, all-out; ⁓ harp total war.

**tor 1.** fine-meshed net; **2.** *fig.* inexperienced, green *(youth).*

**toraman 1.** sturdy child; **2.** sturdy *(child).*

**torba 1.** bag, sack; **2.** *⚓* cyst; **3.** *anat.* scrotum; -ya koymak to acquire, to get.

**torbalamak** to bag.

**torbalanmak 1.** *pass. of* torbalamak; **2.** to bag, to become baggy.

**torik 1.** *zo.* large bonito; **2.** *sl.* acumen, brains; toriğini çalıştırmak *(or* işletmek*) sl.* to use one's loaf.

**torna** [x .] lathe; ⁓ etm. to lathe, to turn.

**tornacı** [x .] latheman, turner.

**tornacılık** turnery.

**tornavida** [. . x .] screwdriver.

**tornistan** [x . .] **1.** *⬇* stern-way; **2.** turning inside out *(a garment);* ⁓ etm. **1.** *⬇* to go astern; **2.** to turn *(a garment).*

**Toros Dağları** *pr. n.* the Taurus Mountains.

**torpido** [. x .] *⬇* torpedo boat; ⁓ gözü *mot.* glove compartment; ⁓ muhribi torpedo-boat destroyer.

**torpidobot,** -tu torpedo boat.

**torpil 1.** torpedo; **2.** *sl.* pull, influence; **3.** *sl.* big gun, a friend at court; ⁓ patlatmak *sl.* to pull, to pull strings *(or* wires).

**torpilbalığı,** -nı *zo.* torpedo fish.

**torpillemek 1.** to torpedo; **2.** *sl.* to flunk a grade.

**tortop,** -pu as round as a top *(or* ball).

**tortu** sediment, deposit, dregs, precipitate.

**tortul** sedimentary.

**tortullaşma** sedimentation.

**tortulu** turbid.

**tortusuz** free of sediment, clear.

**torun** grandchild; ⁓ torba *(or* tosun*)* sahibi olm. to have children and grandchildren.

**tos** butt; ⁓ vurmak to butt.

**tosbağa** *zo.* turtle, tortoise.

**toslamak 1.** to butt; **2.** to bump lightly *(-e* against); **3.** *sl.* to pay out to fork over *(money);* **4.** *sl.* to fail, to flunk.

**tost,** -tu toasted sandwich.

**tostoparlak** as round as a ball.

**tosun 1.** bullock; **2.** *fig.* lad.

**tosuncuk** big, healthy, newborn baby.

**totaliter** *pol.* totalitarian.

**totem** totem.

**toto** the pools, the football pools.

**toy¹** inexperienced, green.

**toy²** *zo.* bustard.

**toy³** feast, banquet.

**toydan** *zo.* great bustard.

**toyluk** inexperience, greenness.

**toynak** hoof.

**toynaklı** hoofed.

**toz 1.** dust; **2.** powder; **3.** *sl.* heroin, skag; ⁓ almak to dust; ⁓ bezi dustcloth, dustrag; ⁓ biber ground pepper; ⁓ etm. **1.** to crush, to pulverize, to annihilate; **2.** to raise dust; ⁓ kondurmamak not to allow anything to be said *(-e* against); ⁓ koparmak to raise dust; ⁓ olm. *sl.* to get lost, to beat it; -u dumana katmak **1.** to raise clouds of dust; **2.** *fig.* to kick up a dust, to raise a ruckus; -unu silkmek *(b-nin) fig.* to dust *s.o.'s* jacket.

**tozboya** powder paint.

**tozkoparan** very windy place.

**tozlanmak** to get dusty.

**tozlu** dusty.

**tozluk 1.** gaiter; spat; **2.** *sports:* sock.

**tozpembe** pale pink; ⁓ görmek to see the world through rose-colo(u)red glasses.

**tozşeker** granulated sugar.

**tozumak** to give off dust.

**tozutmak 1.** to raise dust; to make dusty; **2.** *sl.* to go nuts.

**töhmet,** -ti imputation; ⁓ altında bırakmak to implicate, to incriminate.

**tökezlemek** to stumble.

**tömbeki** Persian tobacco *(smoked in hookahs).*

**töre** custom(s), consuetudo.

**törebilim** ethics.

**törebilimci** ethician, ethicist.

**törebilimsel** ethical.

**töredışı** amoral, nonmoral.

**törel** ethical, moral.

**tören** ceremony, ritual; rite.

**törenli** ceremonial.

**törensel** ceremonial, ceremonious, ritual.

**töresel** customary, consuetudinary.

**töresiz** unethical, immoral.

**törpü** file, rasp.

**törpülemek** to file, to rasp.

**tövbe** repentance, penitence; forswearing; ⁓ etm. **1.** to forswear, to swear off; **2.** to repent, to vow not to do s.th. again; -ler -si! *(or* -ler olsun!) not on your life!, never again!

tövbekâr [. . -] penitent, repentant.
tövbeli repentant, penitent.
Trablus [x .] pr. n. Tripoli.
Trabzon pr. n. Trabzon.
trabzonhurması, -nı ♀ persimmon, kaki.
trafik traffic; ~ işareti traffic sign; ~ kazası traffic accident; ~ lambası traffic light; ~ polisi traffic policeman; ~ şeridi traffic lane; ~ tıkanması traffic jam, snarl-up.
trafo ⚡ transformer.
trahom ☞ trachoma.
trajedi tragedy.
trajik tragic.
traktör tractor.
Trakya [x .] pr. n. Thrace.
Trakyalı [x ..] Thracian.
trampa [x .] barter, swop; ~ etm. to barter, to swop.
trampet, -ti side (or snare) drum.
tramplen 1. diving board; springboard; 2. trampolin(e).
tramvay tram(car), streetcar, trolley.
transatlantik transatlantic (liner).
transfer transfer; ~ etm. to transfer; ~ olm. to be transferred.
transformasyon transformation.
transformatör ⚡ transformer.
transistor ⚡ transistor.
transistorlu ⚡ transistorized, transistor; ~ radyo transistor radio.
transit, -ti transit; ~ geçmek to go through in transit; ~ vizesi transit visa; ~ yolcu in-transit passenger; ~ yolu through highway.
transkripsiyon transcription.
transmisyon ⊕ transmission.
transplantasyon ☞ transplant(ation).
transport transport.
transportasyon transportation.
trapez trapeze.
trapezci trapezist.
traş s. tıraş.
trata [x .] small seine net.
travers ⚞ sleeper, crosstie.
travma ☞ trauma.
travmatoloji ☞ traumatology.
tren train; ~ istasyonu train (or railway) station; ~ tarifesi train timetable.
trençkot mackintosh, mack, trench coat, raincoat.
trete textbook.
treyler trailer.
tribün (grand)stand.
trigonometri trigonometry.
trigonometrik trigonometric.
triko [x .] machine-knit fabric, tricot.
trikotaj knitting; ~ sanayii knitting industry.
trilyon trillion, quintillion.
trinketa ⚓ foresail.
tripo [x .] sl. gambling den.
triportör 1. three-wheeler; 2. tricycle.
triyo ♪ trio.
triyör sorter; separator.
troleybüs trolley-bus.
trombon ♪ trombone.
trompet, -ti ♪ trumpet.
trompetçi ♪ trumpet player, trumpeter.
tropik(a) geogr. tropic.
tropikal, -li tropical; ~ kuşak tropical zone.
trotuvar pavement, Am. sidewalk.
tröst, -tü ⴕ trust.
TRT (abbr. for Türkiye Radyo Televizyon Kurumu) Turkish Radio and Television Company.
trup, -pu thea. troupe.
Truva pr. n. Troy; ~ atı Trojan horse.
tu [ü] ugh!, oof!
tuba ♪ tuba.
tufa sl. gravy.
tufacı sl. robber.
tufan [- -] 1. flood, deluge; 2. torrential rain, deluge; 3. ♀ the Flood.
tufeyli [î] 1. biol. parasite; 2. parasite; leech.
tugay brigade.
tuğ X horsetail.
tuğamiral, -li rear admiral.
tuğgeneral, -li brigadier (general).
tuğla [x .] brick.
tuğra hist. Sultan's signature.
tuğyan [â] rising up, springing up.
tuh oof!, ugh!
tuhaf 1. strange, odd, queer, curious; 2. funny; ridiculous; ~ına gitmek (b-nin) to seem strange to s.o.
tuhafiye sundries, notions, haberdashery.
tuhafiyeci haberdasher.
tuhaflaşmak to get odd, to become queer.
tuhaflık strangeness, oddity, queerness.
tul, -lü [û] 1. length; 2. longitude; ~ dairesi geogr. meridian.
tulu, -uu ast. rising (of the sun, etc.); ~ etm. ast. (for the sun, etc.) to rise.
tuluat, -tı [- - -] a kind of improvisatorial theatre; ~ yapmak to improvise, to ad-lib.
tulum 1. animal skin; 2. overalls; jump suit; 3. ♪ bagpipe; 4. tube (for toothpaste, etc.); ~ gibi 1. swollen all over; 2. as fat as a pig; ~ peyniri cheese encased in a skin.
tulumba [. x .] pump; ~ tatlısı a syrup-soaked pastry.

**tulumbacı 1.** maker *or* seller of pumps; **2.** *hist.* member of a fire brigade.

**tuman** long underpants, drawers.

**tumba** [x.] **1.** ↓ turning upside down; **2.** tumbling into bed; ~ etm. ↓ to upend *(a boat)*.

**tumturak** *lit.* bombast, fustian.

**tumturaklı** bombastic, pompous.

**Tuna** [x.] *pr. n.* **1.** the Danube; **2.** *mf.*

**tunç, -cu 1.** bronze; **2.** ♀ *mf.*

**tungsten** ♔ tungsten.

**Tunus** *pr. n.* Tunisia.

**Tunuslu** *pr. n.* Tunisian.

**tur 1.** tour; **2.** round *(of voting)*, ballot; **3.** round *(in a contest)*; **4.** spin; **5.** *sports:* lap; ~ atmak **1.** to take a stroll around, to have a walk round *(a place)*; **2.** to have *(or take)* a spin; ~ bindirmek to lap *(in a race)*.

**tura 1.** *s.* tuğra; **2.** skein, coil; **3.** knotted handkerchief used in a game.

**turaç** *zo.* francolin.

**turba** [x.] peat, turf.

**turbalık** [x..] peat bog.

**turfa 1.** not kosher; **2.** curiosity; ~ olm. *fig.* to fall into disgrace.

**turfanda 1.** early *(fruit, vegetables)*; **2.** out-of-season.

**turfandalık** garden for growing early fruit, *etc.*

**turgor** [x.] *biol.* turgor.

**turing,** -gl touring.

**turist,** -ti tourist.

**turistik** touristic(al).

**turizm** tourism.

**turkuaz** turquoise.

**turna** [x.] *zo.* crane; ~ katarı flock of people; ~ olm. *sl.* to lose *(while playing a card game)*; -yı gözünden vurmak *fig.* to hit the jackpot.

**turnabalığı,** -nı *zo.* pike.

**turne** *thea.* tour; -ye çıkmak to go on tour.

**turnike** turnstile.

**turnusol,** -lü ♔ turnsole.

**turnuva** tournament, tourney.

**turp,** -pu ♀ radish; ~ gibi hale and hearty, in the pink.

**turşu 1.** pickle; **2.** *sl.* pickled, blotto, soused; ~ gibi very tired, pooped, bushed; ~ kurmak to pickle; to make pickles; ~ olm. **1.** to go sour; **2.** *fig.* to be exhausted *(or pooped or bushed)*; ~ suratlı *fig.* sour-faced; -su çıkmak **1.** *(for fruit, etc.)* to be crushed to a pulp; **2.** *fig.* to get tired, to be pooped *(or bushed)*.

**turşucu** pickleman.

**turta** [x.] pie, tart.

**turuncu** orange.

**turunç, -cu** ♀ Seville orange, bitter orange.

**turunçgiller** citrus fruits.

**tuş 1.** key *(of a piano, typewriter, etc.)*; **2.** *wrestling:* fall; **3.** *paint.* touch; **4.** *fenc.* touch(é); -a getirmek to throw *(one's opponent)*.

**tutacak** potholder.

**tutaç 1.** potholder; **2.** tongs.

**tutak 1.** handle; **2.** potholder; **3.** hostage.

**tutam 1.** pinch; **2.** wisp; bir ~ saç a wisp of hair.

**tutamaç** handle.

**tutamak 1.** handle; **2.** evidence, proof.

**tutanak 1.** minutes, record; **2.** official report.

**tutar** total, sum; number.

**tutarak, tutarık 1.** fit, seizure; **2.** epilepsy.

**tutarlı** consistent; coherent.

**tutarlık, tutarlılık** consistency; coherence.

**tutarsız** inconsistent, incongruous; incoherent.

**tutarsızlık** inconsistency, incongruity; incoherence.

**tutkal** glue; size; ~ gibi importunate, obtrusive *(person)*.

**tutkallamak** to glue; to size.

**tutkallı** glued; sized.

**tutku** passion.

**tutkulu** passionate.

**tutkun 1.** in love (-e with); **2.** lover (-e of), admirer (-e of).

**tutma 1.** *vn.* of tutmak; **2.** farm hand.

**tutmak,** (-ar) **1.** to hold; to take hold of; to grip, to grab; **2.** to hunt *(birds)*; **3.** to restrain, to hold back; **4.** to arrest; to nab; **5.** to detain, to hold up; **6.** ✕ to capture, to occupy; **7.** to watch over, to look after; **8.** to take up *(space)*; **9.** to cover *(a place)*; **10.** to reserve *(a place)*; **11.** *(for cloth)* to show *(a stain, dust, etc.)*; **12.** to patrol; **13.** to support, to back; **14.** to keep *(one's promise, etc.)*; **15.** to approve, to like; **16.** to be accepted, to win general approval, to take on; **17.** to hire, to rent; **18.** to to hire, to employ, to take on; **19.** *(for s.o.'s curse)* to be realized, to come true, to come to pass; **20.** to grasp,, to understand; **21.** to reach, to arrive at, to come to *(a place)*; **22.** to accord with, to agree with, to jibe with; **23.** to take up, to embark on *(a job)*; **24.** P *(for a man)* to be married to; **25.** to be seized with *(the hiccups)*; **26.** to total, to come to, to amount to; **27.** *(for milk)* to form *(cream)*; **28.** to serve, to offer *(a guest)*;

29. (for a graft or vaccination) to take; 30. (for paint) to stick, to adhere; 31. to assume that..., to suppose that...; tutalım ki let's suppose that...; tuttu gitti he upped and left; tuttuğu dal elinde kalmak fig. to turn out to be a dud; tuttuğunu koparmak fig. to know how to get what one wants.

tutsak prisoner of war, captive.

tutsaklık captivity.

tutturmak 1. caus. of tutmak; 2. to fasten together; to sew together; 3. to maintain, to carry on, to keep s.th. going; 4. to get started (doing s.th.); 5. to hit (a mark, a target); 6. fig. to run his mind on.

tutturmalık fastener.

tutucu conservative.

tutuculuk conservatism.

tutuk 1. stuttering; tongue-tied; 2. shy, reserved; 3. stopped-up, blocked.

tutukevi, -ni gaol, Am. jail.

tutuklamak to arrest.

tutuklu prisoner; under arrest.

tutukluk 1. difficulty in talking; 2. shyness, timidity; 3. blockage.

tutukluluk arrest.

tutulan popular.

tutulma 1. vn. of tutulmak; 2. ast. eclipse.

tutulmak 1. pass. of tutmak; 2. to become popular, to catch on, to take on; 3. to become tongue-tied, to freeze up; 4. (for a part of one's body) to get stiff; 5. to fall in love (-e with), to fall for.

tutum 1. attitude, manner, conduct; 2. economy, thrift.

tutumlu thrifty, economical.

tutumluluk thriftiness.

tutumsuz thriftless, spendthrift, wasteful, extravagant.

tutumsuzluk thriftlessness, extravagance.

tutunmak 1. to grab hold of; 2. to hold on (-e to), to hang on (-e to); to cling (-e to); 3. to apply (leeches) to o.s.

tutuşkan (in)flammable; combustible.

tutuşma vn. of tutuşmak; ~ noktası ⌀ ignition point.

tutuşmak 1. to catch fire, to ignite, to kindle; 2. to start, to begin; 3. to hold (hands).

tutuşturmak 1. caus. of tutuşmak; 2. to set on fire, to ignite, to kindle; 3. to fasten together; 4. (eline) to thrust into (s.o.'s hands).

tutya ⌀ zinc.

tuval, -li paint. canvas.

tuvalet, -ti 1. toilet, water closet, lavatory; 2. toilet; 3. evening dress (or gown); 4. toilette, dress, outfit; ~ ispirtosu rubbing alcohol; ~ kâğıdı toilet paper; ~ masası dressing (or toilet) table, vanity.

tuz salt; ~ biber ekmek (bşe) fig. to make s.th. worse, to rub salt in une wound; ~ buz olm. to be smashed to smithereens; ~ ekmek to salt, to add salt (-e to); -la buz etm. to smash to smithereens; -u kuru well off, in easy circumstances; o, partinin tuzu biberiydi he was the life and soul of the party.

tuzak trap; snare; ~ kurmak (b-ne) to set (or lay) a trap for s.o.; tuzağa düşmek to fall into a trap; tuzağa düşürmek to trap.

tuzla [x.] saltpan.

tuzlama 1. vn. of tuzlamak; 2. a tripe soup; 3. salted, salt.

tuzlamak to salt; to brine; tuzlayayım da kokma! F what you're saying is nothing but a lot of tripe!

tuzlu 1. salty; 2. fig. expensive, pricy, high; ~ su salt water; -ya mal olm. (or oturmak) (b-ne) to cost s.o. a bundle, to cost s.o. an arm and a leg.

tuzluk saltshaker, saltcellar.

tuzluluk salinity.

tuzruhu, -nu ⌀ hydrochloric acid.

tuzsuz saltless; unsalted.

tü [-] s. tüh.

tüberküloz ⌀ tuberculosis.

tüccar [â] merchant; ~ gemisi trading vessel; ~ malı merchandise.

tüf geol. tufa.

tüfek rifle, gun; ~ atmak to fire a rifle; ~ çatmak to stack arms; ~ dipçiği butt of a rifle; ~ namlusu rifle barrel.

tüfekçi 1. gunsmith; 2. seller of guns.

tüfekhane armo(u)ry.

tüfeklik 1. armo(u)ry; gun-stand; 2. gun case.

tüh whew!, ouf!; ~ sana! shame on you!

tükenmek 1. to be used up (or exhausted), to give out, to run out; 2. to become exhausted, to give out.

tükenmez 1. inexhaustible; 2. ball-point (pen); ~ kalem ball-point pen.

tüketici ⌀ consumer.

tüketim ⌀ consumption.

tüketmek 1. to exhaust, to use up, to expend, to spend; 2. ⌀ to consume.

tükürmek to spit, to expectorate; tükürdüğünü yalamak fig. to eat humble pie, to eat one's words, to eat crow.

tükürük spit(tle); ~ bezi anat. salivary gland; ~ hokkası spittoon, cuspidor; tükürüğünü yutmak fig. (for s.o.'s *mouth)* to begin to water; to lick one's chops.

**tükürüklemek** to moisten with spittle.

**tül 1.** tulle; **2.** tulle curtain.

**tülbent**, -di muslin; gauze.

**tüm 1.** all (of); **2.** whole, entirety; **3.** completely; ~ **cahil** completely ignorant; -üyle completely.

**tümamiral**, -li vice admiral.

**tümbek 1.** small protuberance; **2.** small drum.

**tümce** *gr.* sentence.

**tümden** completely, totally, wholly.

**tümdengelim** *log.* deduction.

**tümel** *log., phls.* universal.

**tümen 1.** large heap *(or* pile); **2.** ten thousand; **3.** X division; ~ ~ thousands of...

**tümevarım** *log.* induction.

**tümgeneral**, -li major general.

**tümleç**, -ci *gr.* complement.

**tümlemek** to complete.

**tümler** Å complementary; ~ **açı** complementary angle.

**tümör** ₹ tumo(u)r.

**tümsayı** full number.

**tümsek 1.** small mound *(or* pile); **2.** protuberance; **3.** protuberant.

**tümsekli** convex.

**tümseklik** protuberance.

**tünaydın! 1.** good evening!; **2.** good night!

**tünek** perch, roost.

**tüneklemek** to perch, to roost.

**tünel** tunnel.

**tünemek** to perch, to roost.

**tünik** tunic.

**tüp**, -bü **1.** tube; **2.** (test) tube.

**tür 1.** kind, sort, type; **2.** *zo.,* ╬ species.

**türban** turban.

**türbe** tomb, turbe(h).

**türbin** *phys.* turbine.

**türe** justice.

**türedi** upstart parvenu.

**türel** judicial, juridical.

**türemek 1.** to spring up; to appear; **2.** to multiply, to increase, to mushroom; **3.** *gr.* to be derived (-den from).

**türeti** invention.

**türetici** inventor.

**türetmek 1.** to produce; to invent; **2.** *gr.* to derive.

**türev** *gr.* derivative.

**Türk**, -kü **1.** Turk; **2.** Turkish; ~ **ceza kanunu** Turkish penal code; ~ **dili** the Turkish language; ~ **Dil Kurumu** *pr. n.* The Turkish Language Association.

**Türkçe** [x .] **1.** Turkish. the Turkish language; **2.** (in) Turkish; ~ **öğretmeni**

teacher of Turkish; ~ **söylemek 1.** to speak in Turkish; **2.** *fig.* to say bluntly; ~ **sözlük** Turkish dictionary.

**Türkçeci** [x . .] **1.** supporter of the movement to purify Turkish of foreign words; **2.** teacher of Turkish.

**Türkçeleştirmek** to translate into Turkish.

**Türkçü** Turkist.

**Türkçülük** Turkism.

**Türkistan** [ā] *pr. n.* Turkistan.

**Türkiye** *pr. n.* Turkey; ~ **Büyük Millet Meclisi** *pr. n.* the Grand National Assembly of Turkey; ~ **Cumhuriyeti** *pr. n.* the Republic of Turkey, the Turkish Republic.

**Türkleştirmek** to Turkize, to Turkicize.

**Türklük 1.** Turkishness; **2.** the Turkish community.

**Türkmen** Turkoman, Turcoman.

**Türkmenistan** *pr. n.* Turkmenistan.

**Türkolog** Turcologist.

**Türkoloji** Turcology.

**türkuvaz** turquoise.

**türkü** folk song; ~ **çağırmak** *(or* söylemek) to sing a folk song; ~ **yakmak** to write a folk song; -sünü **çağırmak** *(b-nin) fig.* to sing the praises of *s.o.*

**türlü 1.** kind, sort, variety; **2.** various, diverse; **3.** meat and vegetable stew; ~ ~ all sorts of, various.

**türrühat**, -tı [ā] nonsense, rubbish.

**tüs** fuzz, down *(on a person's face).*

**tütmek**, (-er) **1.** to smoke, to fume; **2.** *(for smoke)* to rise.

**tütsü 1.** incense; **2.** smoke.

**tütsülemek 1.** to cense; **2.** to smoke *(fish, meat, etc.).*

**tütsülü 1.** censed; **2.** smoked *(fish, meat, etc.).*

**tütsülük** censer, incensory.

**tüttürmek 1.** *caus.* of tütmek; **2.** to smoke *(cigarette, pipe, etc.).*

**tütün** tobacco; ~ **içmek** *(or* kullanmak) to smoke *(tobacco).*

**tütüncü 1.** tobacconist; **2.** tobacco grower.

**tüvana** [. - -] vigorous.

**tüvit** tweed.

**tüy 1.** feather; down; quill; **2.** hair; **3.** fuzz, down; ~ **atmak** *(for a bird)* to mo(u)lt; ~ **dikmek** *(bşin üzerine)* to be the last straw. to be the straw that broke the camel's back; ~ **dökmek** *(for a bird)* to mo(u)lt; ~ **gibi** as light as a feather, featherlight; ~ **kalem** quill (pen); -ler **ürpertici** blood-curdling, spine-chilling, creepy; -leri **diken diken olm.** to get goose bumps, to get goose-

flesh, to stand on end *(hair);* -ü tüsü yok
he's still wet behind the ears; -ünü düzmek **1.** *(for a bird)* to preen; **2.** to start
to dress well.

**tüydöken** *sl.* razor, shiv.

**tüydürmek** *caus. of* tüymek, *sl.* **1.** to steal,
to pinch; **2.** to make s.o. leave.

**tüylenmek 1.** *(for a bird)* to grow feathers, to feather out, to fledge; **2.** *fig.* to
get rich, to get flush.

**tüylü 1.** feathered; feathery; downy; **2.**
fuzzy; shaggy; hairy.

**tüymek** *sl.* to slip away, to sneak off.

**tüyo** hint, tip; ~ vermek to drop *(or* give*)*
a hint.

**tüysıklet,** -ti *boxing:* featherweight.

**tüysüz 1.** unfeathered, unfledged; downless; **2.** fuzzless, downless *(plant, fruit);*
**3.** hairless *(animal);* **4.** beardless
*(youth).*

**tüysüzşeftali** ♀ nectarine.

**tüze 1.** jurisprudence, law; **2.** justice.

**tüzel 1.** jurisprudential, legal; **2.** judicial.

**tüzelkişi** ♫ juristic person.

**tüzük** regulations, statutes.

**TV** *(abbr. for* television*) TV,* television.

# U

**ubudiyet,** -ti [. x .] **1.** devotion to God; **2.** slavery, bondage.

**uca** coccyx, tailbone.

**ucube** [. - .] curiosity, monster, prodigy.

**ucuz 1.** cheap, inexpensive; **2.** *fig.* easy, easily acquired; ~ atlatmak *(or* kurtulmak) to get off lightly, to get away cheaply; ~ etin yahnisi yavan *(or* tatsız) olur *pro.* you can't make a silk purse out of a sow's ear; -a düşürmek to buy s.th. cheaply; -dur vardır illeti, pahalıdır vardır hikmeti *pro.* if s.th. is cheap, it is usually defective, if s.th. is expensive, there is a good reason.

**ucuzcu 1.** *F* the cheap real McCoy, s.o. who sells goods cheaply; **2.** s.o. who is always hunting for bargains, bargain hunter.

**ucuzlamak 1.** to become cheap, to go down in price *(goods);* **2.** *fig.* to become readily available, to become common, to become known by everybody.

**ucuzlatmak 1.** to reduce in price, to cheapen; **2.** to make readily available, to make s.th. easy.

**ucuzluk 1.** cheapness, inexpensiveness; **2.** sale.

**uç 1.** tip, point; **2.** (tree) top; **3.** end; **4.** † cause, reason; **5.** *hist.* border territory; **6.** *A* final point; **7.** extremity; **8.** frontier; ~ uca end to end; ~ uca gelmek to be just enough; ~ vermek **1.** to come to a head *(boil, etc.);* **2.** to appear, to turn out; **3.** to sprout, to come up *(plant);* -u bucağı olmamak *(or* görünmemek) to be endless; -u ortası belli olmamak not to know exactly, not to know how to start setting a job; -u dokunmak *(b-ne)* to be prejudicial to *s.o.,* to cause *s.o.* harm, to bring up a subject; -unda bir şey olm. to be some secret purpose behind s.th.; -unu kaçırmak *fig.* to lose the thread, to lose the control of.

**uçak** aeroplane, airplane, plane; ~ bileti air-travel ticket; ~ faciası air disaster; ~ gemisi aircraft carrier; ~ kaçırmak to hijack an airplane; -la **1.** by airplane, by air; **2.** by airmail, via airmail.

**uçaksavar** ✕ anti-aircraft gun.

**uçandaire** flying saucer.

**uçantop,** -pu volleyball.

**uçar 1.** flying; **2.** flying bird; **3.** volatile; -a atmak to shoot at a flying bird.

**uçarı 1.** philanderer, casanova; **2.** wild, uncontrollable.

**uçkun** spark.

**uçkur** belt, sash, band *(for holding up trousers);* ~ çözmek *F* to have sex with; -una gevşek olm. to sleep around, to have sex with, to be hot *or* horny; -una sağlam *fig.* chaste.

**uçlanmak** *sl.* to pay up, to fork out, to hand over, to shell out.

**uçlu** pointed, tipped.

**uçmak 1.** to fly; **2.** to evaporate *(perfume, etc.);* ~ to valatilize; **3.** to fade away *(colour);* **4.** to go downhill; **5.** *F* to disappear, to vanish; **6.** to get lost; **7.** to explode, to burst; **8.** to be wild with *(joy);* **9.** to go very fast; uçan kuşa borcu olm. to be in debt to everybody, to be up to the ears in debt; uçan kuştan medet ummak to try every mean in order to get out of trouble.

**uçman** aviator, airplane pilot.

**uçsuz** without a point; ~ bucaksız endless, vast, boundless.

**uçucu 1.** flying, able to fly; **2.** ~ volatile.

**uçucböceği,** -ni *zo.* ladybug.

**uçuk 1.** faded *(colour);* pale; **2.** ✂ cold sore, herpes (labialis); ~ benizli pale.

**uçuklamak** to develop cold sores; to get herpes.

**uçurmak** *caus. of* uçmak **1.** to fly *(kite);* **2.** to rise, to ascend *(plane);* **3.** to cut off, to separate *(head);* **4.** to blow up, to blast; **5.** *F* to kick out *(doors);* **6.** *sl.* to boast, to brag, to show off; **7.** *F* to lose, to steal, to purloin, to pilfer.

**uçurtma** kite.

**uçurtmak** *caus. of* uçurmak.

**uçurum 1.** abyss, chasm; precipice; **2.** *fig.* corruption, misfortune, disaster.

**uçuş** flight, flying; ~ hattı flight route.

**uçuşmak** to fly about; to fly together.

**udi** [. - .] lute player, lutist.

**uf** ouf!, oof!, ow!, oh my God!

**ufacık** very small, tiny, minute; ~ **tefecik** tiny, minute.

**ufak 1.** small; **2.** very young; **3.** insignificant; **4.** pedantic; **5.** crumb, small; ~ **çapta** small-scale; ~ **para** small change; ~ **tefek** small and thin, small, of no (or small) account; ~ ~ **1.** bit by bit; **2.** in small pieces.

**ufaklık 1.** smallness, littleness; **2.** small change (money); **3.** sl. vermin, esp. louse.

**ufalamak** to break up, to crumble, to powder, to pulverize.

**ufalanmak 1.** pass. of ufalamak; **2.** to crumble away.

**ufalmak** to diminish, to become smaller.

**ufarak** very small.

**ufki** horizontal, level.

**uflamak** to say 'oof'; **uflayıp puflamak** to keep saying 'oof'.

**ufuk, -fku 1.** horizon; **2.** skyline; **3.** fig. understanding, conception; **ufkunu genişletmek** fig. to broaden one's horizon.

**ufunet, -ti** [. - .] **1.** bad smell, stench; **2.** ♀ inflammation and suppuration.

**uğrak 1.** frequented place or region; **2.** haunt.

**uğramak 1.** to pass by, to call (on s.o., at a place); **2.** to (make a) halt, to stop, to touch at; **3.** to pass through; **4.** to get stricken (or afflicted) with; **5.** to rush out; **6.** to meet with, to suffer (a difficulty, etc.); **7.** to undergo; **8.** to encounter.

**uğraş, uğraşı 1.** occupation, work; pastime; **2.** struggle, striving, dispute.

**uğraşmak 1.** to exert o.s., to struggle, to strive; **2.** (başle) to busy (or occupy) o.s. with s.th.; to be engaged in s.th., to be busy; **3.** to create, to produce; **4.** fig. to struggle, to battle (ile with).

**uğraştırmak** caus. of uğraşmak; (b-ni) to give s.o. (a great deal of) trouble.

**uğratmak** caus. of uğramak; **1.** to expose s.o. to; **2.** to dismiss s.o. from.

**uğru** thief.

**uğrulamak** to steal.

**uğrun** secretly; ~ ~ secretly.

**uğuldamak 1.** to hum, to buzz, to growl, to grumble; **2.** to howl, to cry, to hoot. to wail.

**uğultu** hum, buzz, howl, roar.

**uğunmak 1.** to faint; **2.** to feel faint.

**uğur¹** -ğru purpose, aim, goal; **uğrunda** for the sake of, on account of.

**uğur²** good omen, good luck, lucky charm; ~ **getirmek** to bring good luck;

~ **ola** (or -lar olsun)! have a good trip!; **-u açık** lucky, fortunate.

**uğurböceği,** -ni zo. ladybug.

**uğurlamak** (b-ni) to accompany s.o., to see s.o. off.

**uğurlu** lucky, auspicious; ~ **kademli olsun!** may this bring you joy!

**uğursamak** to regard s.th. as a sign of good luck.

**uğursuz** inauspicious, ill-omened, ominous; unlucky, unfortunate, fatal.

**uğursuzluk** ill omen; bad luck, hoodoo.

**uhde** obligation, charge, responsibility, duty, engagement, undertaking; **-sinde ●km.** (b-nin) to be s.o.'s duty, to be incumbent on s.o.; **-sinden gelmek** to fulfil(l), to achieve, to manage, to deal with, to handle; **-sine almak** to carry over, to entrust.

**uhrevi** [. . -] pertaining to the other world.

**uhuvvet** brotherhood.

**ukala** [. . -] wiseacre, smart aleck; ~ **dümbeleği** smart aleck, smart ass, know-it-all.

**ukalalık** [. . . .] know-it-all behavio(u)r.

**ukde 1.** ♀, phys. knot; **2.** biol. ganglion; **3.** fig. pain, ache, torture.

**ukubet,** -ti [. - .] **1.** punishment; **2.** pain, torture; **3.** P coarse and ugly.

**ulaç** gr. gerund.

**Ulah** Wallachian, Vlach.

**ulak** courier, messenger.

**ulam 1.** group; **2.** category.

**ulama 1.** vn. of ulamak; **2.** adding, appendage; **3.** liaison.

**ulamak** to join, to attach, to add, to annex (-e to).

**ulan** sl. hi!, man alive!, hey you!, man!

**ulantı** addition, supplement.

**ulaşım** communication. transport(ation).

**ulaşmak 1.** to arrive (-e at), to get (-e to), to reach; **2.** to attain, to achieve; **3.** to reach, to hand, to pass; **4.** to get into contact with; **5.** to survive until.

**ulaştırma** transportation, communication; **♀ Bakanlığı** Ministry of Transport; ~ **sınıfı** X Transportation Corps.

**ulaştırmak** to cause to reach, to transport (-e to).

**ulema** [. . -] isl. doctors of Muslim theology, ulema.

**ulemalık** [. . - .] F scholarship.

**ulu** great. high. elevated. fig. exalted.

**ululamak** to extol, to exalt. to hono(u)r.

**ululuk** height, elevation, fig. loftiness, sublimity.

**ulumak** to howl.

**uluorta** rashly, recklessly, without reserve.

**ulus** nation, people.

**ulusal** national.

**ulusallaştırmak** to nationalize.

**ulusallık** nationality.

**ulusçu** nationalist.

**ulusçuluk** nationalism.

**uluslararası**, -nı international.

**ulussever** patriot.

**ulvi** [. -] high, sublime.

**umacı** bcgy man, ogre.

**umar** remedy, solution.

**umde** † principle.

**ummadık** [x . .] **1.** unexpected, unhoped-for; **2.** unforeseen.

**ummak**, (-ar) **1.** to hope; **2.** to expect, to await, to presume; *ummadığın taş baş yarar* it is the unexpected stone that wounds the head.

**umman** ocean.

**Umman** Oman.

**umran** *s.* ümran.

**umulmak** *pass. of* ummak.

**umum** [. -] **1.** all, general, universal; **2.** the public; ~ *müdür* general manager.

**umumhane** [. . - .] brothel.

**umumi** [ - - ] **1.** general, common, universal; **2.** public; ~ *efkâr* public opinion.

**umumiyet**, -ti [. - . .] generality.

**umumiyetle** in general, generally.

**umur** [. -] **1.** affairs, matters, concern; **2.** † things, belongings; ~ *görmek* **1.** to be experienced; **2.** to be in important positions *(person)*; ~ *görmüş* experienced; *-umda değil* I don't care; *-umun teki* what is that to me?, it is nothing to me.

**umursamak** to be concerned about, to consider important.

**umursamazlık** indifference, unconcern.

**umut**, -du hope, expectation, confidence; ~ *beslemek* to hope, to expect; ~ *etm.* to hope, to expect; ~ *kesmek* to lose hope; ~ *vermek* to give hope to; *-a düşmek* to be hopeful; *-unu kırmak* to dissappoint.

**umutlandırmak** to give hope to, to make s.o. hopeful.

**umutlanmak** to become hopeful.

**umutlu** hopeful.

**umutsuz** hopeless, desperate.

**umutsuzluk** hopelessness.

**un** flour; ~ *ufak etm.* to crumble s.th. finely; ~ *ufak olm.* to be broken into pieces; *-unu elemiş, eleğini asmış* **1.** he bas done all the useful work in his life; **2.** he is too old.

**unlamak** to flour, to sprinkle with flour.

**unluk 1.** suitable for making flour; **2.** flour bin *(in a mill)*.

**unsur** element, component.

**unutkan** forgetful.

**unutkanlık** forgetfulness.

**unutmabeni** ⚘ forget-me-not.

**unutmak 1.** to forget; to unlearn; **2.** to forgive.

**unvan** [. -] **1.** title; **2.** superscription.

**upuslu** very well-behaved.

**upuygun** [x . .] very suitable, perfectly appropriate.

**upuzun 1.** very long *or* tall; **2.** at full length.

**ur** tumo(u)r, outgrowth, swelling.

**urağan** *meteor.* hurricane.

**Uranus** *ast.* Uranus.

**uranyum** ⚛ uranium.

**urba** piece of clothing.

**Urduca** Urdu, the Urdu language.

**urgan** rope.

**uruk** clan.

**us** reason, state of mind, intelligence, intellect; ~ *pahası* warning, teaching.

**usanç** boredom, disgust; ~ *getirmek* to get bored, to get tired of; ~ *vermek* to bore, to disgust.

**usandırıcı** boring, disgusting.

**usandırmak** to bore, to disgust.

**usanmak** to become bored, to get tired of, to get disgusted.

**usare** [. - .] sap, juice.

**usavurmak** to reason, to think through.

**usçu** *phls.* **1.** rationalist; **2.** rationalistic.

**usçuluk** *phls.* rationalism.

**usdışı** irrational.

**uskumru** *zo.* mackerel.

**uskur** ⚓ screw, propeller.

**uskuru** ⊕ screw thread.

**uslamlamak** *s.* usavurmak.

**uslanmak 1.** to become sensible, to become well-behaved; **2.** to listen to reason.

**uslu 1.** well-behaved, sensible, good *(child)*; **2.** reasonable, sensible, rational; ~ *durmak (or* oturmak) to keep quiet, to sit still, to be good.

**ussal** mental, rational.

**usta 1.** skil(l)ful, clever (at), able; **2.** master craftsman, master workman; **3.** foreman, chief; ~ *elinden çıkmak* to be made by master; ~ *işi* work of a master.

**ustabaşı**, -nı foreman.

**ustaca** skil(l)fully.

**ustalaşmak** to become skilled.

**ustalık 1.** mastery, craftsman; **2.** proficiency, expertise.

ustalıkla skil(l)fully.

ustunç, -cu ☞ set of instruments.

ustura [x ..] 1. (straight) razor; 2. *sl.* strong *(drink)*; 3. *sl.* lie; ~ taşı whetstone; ~ tutunmak to get a shave.

usturlap astrolabe.

usturmaça ⚓ fender, padding.

usturpa [. x .] a kind of whip.

usturuplu F 1. properly, right; 2. masterly, striking, hitting the target.

usul, -lü 1. method, system, manner; 2. programme; 3. ♪ time, measure, rhythm; 4. ♫ procedure; ~ hukuku ♫ law of procedure; ~ tutmak ♪ to beat time; ~ ~ quietly, slowly and softly.

usulca 1. slowly; 2. quietly.

usulcacık slowly, gently, quietly.

usulsüz [. - .] 1. unmethodical; 2. contrary to regulations, irregular, incorrect.

usulsüzlük 1. lack of method *or* system; 2. irregularity.

uşak 1. boy, youth, lad; 2. servant, domestic, assistant; ~ olm. to undertake the duty of a servant.

uşakkapan *zo.* lammergeier.

uşaklık 1. being a manservant; 2. *fig.* degrading task; ~ etm. to be servitude.

ut¹ lute.

ut² shame, modesty; ~ yeri private parts, genitals.

utanç shame, modesty, shyness, embarrassment; -ından yere geçmek to feel very ashamed, to feel like 30 cents.

utandırmak to make s.o. ashamed, to cause s.o. to blush, to put s.o. to the blush.

utangaç, utangan bashful, shy, timid, embarrassed, confused, shamefaced.

utangaçlık bashfulness, shyness, shamefacedness.

utanmak 1. to be ashamed; 2. to feel embarrassed; 3. to be shy *or* bashful; 4. to be too timid to do, to recoil at.

utanmaz shameless, impudent, impertinent, insolent.

utanmazlık shamelessness, brazenness.

Utarit *ast.* Mercury.

utku victory, triumph.

utlu 1. chaste; 2. honest.

utmak 1. to defeat; 2. to win.

utopya utopia.

uvertür 1. ♪ uverture; 2. beginning *(poker game).*

uvunmak *s.* uğunmak.

uyak rhyme.

uyaklı rhymed.

uyaksız unrhymed.

uyandırmak *caus. of* uyanmak 1. to wake up, to awaken; 2. *fig.* to awaken, to arouse, to excite, to call forth; 3. to light, to kindle; 4. to revive, to stir.

uyanık 1. awake; 2. *fig.* bright, cunning; 3. watchful, vigilant, careful, mindful.

uyanıklık wakefulness, alertness, watchfulness.

uyanış awakening.

uyanmak 1. to wake (up); 2. *fig.* to awake; 3. to come up *(plant)*; 4. to appear again, to show up again *(pain, etc.)*; 5. to flame up *(fire)*; 5. to become aware of.

uyar conformable, fit, suitable.

uyaran stimulus, incentive, stimulant.

uyarı 1. warning; 2. stimulus.

uyarıcı 1. warning; 2. stimulative.

uyarım stimulation.

uyarınca in accordance with, following, according to.

uyarlaç adapter, adaptor.

uyarlamak 1. to accomodate, to adjust (-e to); 2. to fit, to adapt, to modify.

uyarlayıcı adapter, adaptor *(person).*

uyarlık conformity.

uyarmak 1. to warn, to remind; 2. to stimulate; 3. to awaken, to arouse.

uyartı 1. warning; 2. stimulation; 3. stimulus.

uydu satellite *(a. fig.)*

uydurma 1. *vn. of* uydurmak; 2. fictitious, improvised; 3. invented, false, made-up.

uydurmak *caus. of* uymak 1. to make fit, to adapt, to adjust; 2. to invent arbitrarily, to fabricate, to cook up; 3. to patch up; 4. F to pick up, to get; 5. F to manage, to engineer, to wangle; 6. ⊕ to fit in(to); 7. to seduce *(girl, woman).*

uydurmasyon *sl.* 1. invention, fable, bullshit; 2. made-up, invented.

uyduruk F fabricated, invented, made-up.

uydurukçu F bullshitter, fabricator.

uygar 1. civilized; 2. educated.

uygarlaşmak to become civilized.

uygarlık civilization.

uygulama *vn. of* uygulamak application, practice, carrying out *(plan, law, etc.).*

uygulamak 1. to apply, to carry through practice; 2. to superimpose s.th. on.

uygun 1. fit, suitable, corresponding, conformable, appropriate; 2. proper, qualified, apt; 3. in accord to, fitting; 4. reasonable *(price)*; 5. favo(u)rable, good; ~ bulmak *(or* görmek) to see fit, to agree to, to approve of; ~ düşmek to fit, to suit; ~ gelmek to suit; ~ katmanlaşma *geol.* concordant stratification.

uygunluk appropriateness, suitability.

uygunsuz unsuitable, inappropriate, unfitting, undue; ~ kadın prostitute, whore.

uygunsuzluk 1. inappropriate behavio(u)r; 2. unsuitableness, inappropriateness.

Uygur Uighur.

Uygurca the Uighur language, Uighur.

uyku 1. sleep; 2. *fig.* carelessness, sleepiness; ~ basmak *(or* bastırmak) to feel very sleepy; ~ durak (yok *or* ~ nedir bilmeden) (without a) chance to rest; ~ gözünden akmak to be very sleepy; ~ tulumu sleeping bag; ~ tutmamak not to be able to go to sleep; ~ vermek *(or* getirmek) to make s.o. feel sleepy; -su ağır heavy sleeper; -su bölünmek not to be able to go back to sleep; -su gelmek to feel sleepy; -su hafif light sleeper; -su kaçmak 1. to lose sleep over; 2. to be worried; -sunu almak to sleep well; -ya dalmak to fall asleep; -ya varmak 1. to sleep; 2. to calm down; -ya yatmak to lie down to sleep.

uykucu late riser, lie-abed, sleepyhead, fond of sleep.

uykulu sleepy.

uykusuz 1. sleepless; 2. blear-eyed, fatigued *(from lack of sleep).*

uykusuzluk lack of sleep, insomnia.

uyluk *anat.* thigh.

uylukkemiği, -ni thighbone.

uymak, (-ar) 1. to fit to, to conform; 2. to adapt o.s. to; to adjust to, to follow, to obey, to comply with, to observe, to submit to, to resign o.s. to, to listen to; 3. to harmonize with, to be homogeneous.

uyruk *pol.* citizen, subject.

uyruklu s.o. who is a citizen of *(a country).*

uyrukluk citizenship.

uysal conciliatory, easy-going, obedient, pliant, supple, compliant, docile, sociable, peaceable.

uysallaşmak to become docile *(or* compliant).

uysallık complaisance, docility.

uyuklamak to doze (off).

uyum 1. harmony, conformity; 2. ♪ accomodation *(of the eye);* 3. *gr.* harmony.

uyumak 1. to sleep, to go to sleep, to fall asleep; 2. *fig.* to be negligent; 3. to be unaware of what's going on.

uyumlu harmonious, in accord, well-proposed.

uyumsuz inharmonious.

uyuntu idle, lazy, indolent, sleepyhead.

uyur 1. sleeping; 2. still *(water).*

uyurgezer sleepwalker, somnambulist.

uyurgezerlik somnambulism, sleepwalking.

uyuşmak[1] 1. to become numb, to become insensible, to tingle *(hands from cold, etc.);* 2. to go to sleep; 3. to relax.

uyuşmak[2] 1. to come to an agreement *(ile* with), to come to terms *(price);* 2. to get on *(or* along) with.

uyuşmazlık disagreement, conflict.

uyuşturanbalığı *zo.* crampfish.

uyuşturmak[1] to anesthetize, to narcotize, to benumb, to deaden.

uyuşturmak[2] to cause to come to an agreement.

uyuşturucu narcotic, anesthetic.

uyuşuk numbed, insensible, asleep.

uyuşukluk 1. numbness; 2. laziness.

uyutmak *caus. of* uyumak 1. to lull to sleep, to send to sleep; 2. *fig.* to calm, to soothe, to ease, to alley, to hold out; 3. *fig.* to mitigate, to alleviate; 4. *fig.* to deceive, to fool; 5. to put off.

uyutucu 1. narcotic, soporific; 2. hypnotic.

uyuz 1. ♥ mange, itch; 2. itchy, scabious, mangy, scabby; 3. *fig.* miserable, wretched, sissy; ~ etm. to bug; ~ olm. 1. to get the itch; 2. *fig.* to be bugged.

uyuzböceği, -ni *zo.* itch mite.

uyuzotu, -nu ♥ scabious.

uyuzsineği, -ni *zo.* tiger beetle.

uz able, good, clever, skil(l)ful.

uzak 1. distant, far, out-of-the-way, remote; 2. unsuitable, unfit (for); 3. improbable, unlikely, inept, irrelevant; 4. distance, remoteness; 5. removal; ~ akraba distant relative; ~ durmak to stay at a distance, not to interfere; to keep *(or* stay) clear of; ~ düşmek *(birbirinden)* to be far from one another; -ı görmek to be able to see the future; -tan from far off; -tan bakmak to stay out of, to remain apart from; -tan uzağa 1. casually *(to know);* 2. from far away; -tan yakından it hasn't got the slightest connection.

Uzakdoğu the Far East.

uzaklaşmak 1. to go away, to remove, to retire; to be far away *(-den* from); 2. to become a stranger to.

uzaklaştırmak 1. to remove, to deport, to take away; 2. to turn off, to cause to lose interest.

uzaklık distance,, remoteness; interval.
uzam largeness, extent.
uzamak 1. to grow long, to extend; 2. to be prolonged, to drag out *(time)*; 3. to grow longer *(child)*.
uzanmak 1. to be down, to stretch o.s. out on; 2. to go on, to walk on; 3. to be extended to; 4. to stretch one's arm to.
uzantı 1. extension; 2. prolongation, lengthening.
uzatım prolongation, extension.
uzatma *vn. of* uzatmak lengthening, extension, stretch(ing), expansion; ~ işareti circumflex (accent).
uzatmak *caus. of* uzamak 1. to lengthen; 2. to extend, to stretch, to expand; 3. to let *(hair, etc.)* grow long; 4. to hand *(-e ...... -e* over), to pass *(-e* to); 5. to drag out, to prolong; uzatmayalım let's keep it short.
uzay *ast.*, Å, *phls.* space; ~ geometri solid geometry; ~ kapsülü space capsule; ~ uçuşu space flight.
uzayadamı astronaut. spaceman.
uzaygemisi spaceship, spacecraft.
uzgörür far-sighted.
uziletişim telecommunication.
uzlaşma *vn. of* uzlaşmak agreement, understanding, settlement, unification.
uzlaşmak to come to an agreement *(or*

understanding). to come to terms.
uzlaşmazlık unwillingness to come to an agreement.
uzlaştırıcı concillatory.
uzlaştırmak to reconcile, to compromise, to conciliate.
uzluk ability, cleverness, expertise, mastery.
uzman expert, specialist.
uzmanlaşmak to become an expert *(or* specialist), to specialize.
uzmanlık expertness, speciality.
uzun 1. long; 2. tall *(person);* 3. *contp.* diffuse, length, prolix; ~ araç long vehicle; ~ atlama long jump; ~ boylu 1. tall *(person);* 2. *fig.* diffuse, prolix; ~ etm. to draw out, to drag out; ~ hikaye long story; ~ lafın kısası in short, the long and the short of it; ~ oturmak to sprawl; ~ uzadıya detailed, full(length), long and broad.
uzunçalar long play, long-playing record. LP.
uzunlamasına lengthwise.
uzunluk 1. length *(a.* Å); 2. *contp.* diffuseness, prolixity.
uzuv, -zvu *anat.* member, organ; limb.
uzvi [. -] organic.
uzviyet, -ti 1. organism; 2. 卜 system.
uzyazım telex.

# Ü

**ücra** remote, out of the way, outermost.

**ücret,** -ti **1.** wage, pay(ment), compensation, stipend, salary; **2.** fee, charge; **3.** price, cost.

**ücretli 1.** paid, employed for pay; **2.** s.th. done for a fee.

**ücretsiz 1.** free, free of charge; **2.** gratis.

**üç,** -cü three; ~ aşağı beş yukarı approximately, roughly; ~ beş a few; ~ bucuk atmak to be very frightened; ~ günlük ömür short life.

**üçboyutlu** three-dimensional.

**üçer** three each, three apiece.

**üçgen** Å triangle; ~ piramit threelateral pyramid; ~ prizma triangular prism.

**üçkağıtçı** fig. swindler, crook.

**üçlemek 1.** to increase to three, to triple, to trebie; **2.** to lease the field in exchange for a third of the crop; **3.** to plough the field three times; **4.** to turn threefold (rope, etc.).

**üçlü 1.** three-figure number; **2.** ternary; **3.** (a) three (poker, dominoes, etc.) **4.** ♪ trio.

**üçüncü** third; ~ şahıs gr. the third person; ~ zaman geol. the Tertiary (period).

**üçüz** triplets, triplet.

**üçüzlü 1.** who has triplets (mother); **2.** threefold; **3.** (consisting of three parts.)

**üfleç,** -ci phys. nozzle, blower, blowpipe.

**üflemek 1.** to blow; **2.** to blow out; **3.** to blow (-e upon, at); **4.** to blow away (dust, etc.); **5.** to sound (flute, shawm, etc.).

**üfürmek 1.** to blow, to breathe on; **2.** to blow away; **3.** to cure by breathing on.

**üfürük** exhaled breath.

**üfürükçü** quack, sorcerer (who claims to cure by breathing on).

**üğrüm** ast. nutation.

**üleşmek** to share, to divide (ile with).

**üleştirmek** to distribute, to share out (-e to).

**ülfet,** -ti **1.** familiarity, acquaintance; **2.** intercourse, relation; **3.** friendship.

**ülger** fuzz, down.

**ülke 1.** country; **2.** ∷ territory.

**Ülker** ast. the Pleiades.

**ülkü** ideal.

**ülkücü** idealist.

**ülkücülük** idealism.

**ülser** ⚕ ulcer.

**ültimatom** pol. ultimatum.

**ültramodern** ultramodern.

**ültraviyole** ultraviolet.

**ümit,** -di **1.** hope, confidence; **2.** expectation, supposition, presumption; ~ bağlamak to set (or pin) one's hopes on; ~ dünyası one can always hope; ~ etm. to hope, to expect; ~ kapısı hope, anything that proves hope; ~ vermek to raise s.o.'s hopes (of), to hold out a prospect of, to promise; ümidi suya düşmek to lose hope; ümidini kesmek to give up hope.

**ümitlendirmek** to make hopeful.

**ümitlenmek** to become hopeful, to gather fresh hope.

**ümitli** hopeful, full of hope.

**ümitsiz 1.** hopeless (a. fig.); **2.** desperate.

**ümitsizlik** hopelessness, despair.

**ümmet,** -ti isl. religious community.

**ümmi** [. -] illeterate.

**ümmilik** illeteracy.

**ümük** P throat.

**ün 1.** F voice, sound; **2.** fame, reputation, esteem; ~ salmak (or kazanmak or yapmak) to become famous.

**üniforma** [. . x .] uniform.

**ünite 1.** unity; **2.** unit.

**üniversal** universal.

**üniversite** university.

**üniversiteli** university student.

**ünlem 1.** gr. interjection; **2.** exclamation, cry, shout; ~ işareti exclamation mark.

**ünlemek** P to call out (-e to).

**ünlü 1.** famous, well-known; **2.** gr. vowel.

**ünsiyet,** -ti **1.** familiarity; **2.** friendship.

**ünsüz 1.** unknown; **2.** gr. consonant; ~ uyumu consonant harmony.

**ürat** urate.

**Ürdünlü** Jordanian.

**üre** urea.

**ürem** † interest.

**üremek 1.** to reproduce; **2.** to multiply, to increase.

**üremi** ? uremia.

**üreteç** *phys.* generator.

**üretici 1.** producer; **2.** of production.

**üretim 1.** production, manufacture; **2.** product.

**üretken** productive.

**üretkenlik** productivity.

**üretmek** *caus. of* üremek **1.** to breed, to grow, to raise; **2.** to produce.

**ürik asit** ? uric acid.

**ürkek 1.** shy, timid; **2.** fearful, timorous; ~ ~ timidly, slowly and shyly.

**ürkeklik** timidity, shyness, bashfulness.

**ürkmek** (-er) **1.** to shy, to balk *(horse);* **2.** to start (at), to wince, to be terrified, to be shocked, to fear from, to be frightened of; **3.** to bear no fruit *(tree).*

**ürkünç** frightening, scary, terrifying.

**ürküntü** sudden fright, panic, scare.

**ürkütmek** *caus of* ürkmek **1.** to startle, to scare, to frighten; **2.** to lop *(tree).*

**ürolog** ? urologist.

**üroloji** ? urology.

**ürpermek 1.** to stand on end, to bristle up *(hair);* **2.** to shudder, to shiver (with, at); **3.** to rise, to start *(voice).*

**ürperti**[1] shudder, shiver.

**ürtiker** ? nettle-rash.

**ürümek** to howl, to bark, to bay; **ürüyen köpek ısırmaz** barking dogs never bite.

**ürün 1.** product, crop, harvest; **2.** dairy product; **3.** *fig.* result; **4.** work *(art).*

**üryan** naked, bare, nude.

**üs, -ssü 1.** base, basis, foundation; **2.** ₳ exponent; **3.** ✗ base.

**üsçavuş** ✗ sergeant.

**üslup,** -bu manner, form, style.

**üst, -tü 1.** upper side, top (side), upper surface; **2.** upper part; **3.** outside, surface; **4.** clothing, dress, clothes; **5.** ✗ superior; **6.** rest, remaining, residue; **7.** body; **8.** boss, superior; **9.** at *or* about *(time);* **10.** responsibility; ~ **bagaj** *mot.* roof rack; ~ **baş** clothes; ~ **çıkmak** *(or* gelmek) to win, to surpass, to exceed; ~ **perdeden konuşmak** to talk big, to bluster; ~ **-e 1.** one after *(or* upon) another, successively; **2.** one on top of the other; **3.** very crowded; **-e çıkmak** to be innocent seemingly; **-ten** superficially; **-ü başı dökülmek** to be in rags; **-ü kapalı** *(or* örtülü) in an indirect way, indirectly; **-üme iyilik sağlık** (-üne, -ünüze sağlık, -üne sağlık *or* -ünüze şifalar) may God preserve from such an ill luck; **-ünde durmak** to give a subject importance, to emphasize; **-ünde kalmak** to be left to the highest bidder *(auction);*

**-ünden atmak** not to take over the duty; to acquit o.s. of; **-ünden geçmek 1.** *(b-nin)* to violate, to rape; **2.** to pass over *(time);* **-üne almak 1.** to bind o.s. to do s.th., to lay o.s. under an obligation; **2.** to take offence *(-i* at); **-üne atmak** *(b-nin)* to put the blame for s.th. on *s.o.;* **-üne basmak** to hit the nail on the head; **-üne bir bardak** (soğuk) su **içmek** *(bşin)* to lose hope, to kiss s.th. goodbye; **-üne düşmek** to be persistent on; **-üne gitmek** to interfere; **-üne koymak** to add; **-üne olmamak** to be unique; **-üne oturmak** to appropriate illegally; **-üne titremek** to love tenderly, to dance attendance (on); **-üne kondurmamak** to overprotect; **-üne tuz biber ekmek** to rub salt in the wound; **-üne -üne gitmek** *(bşin)* to harp on *s.th.;* **-üne varmak 1.** to urge, to press s.o. hard, to give s.o. a hard time; **2.** to bid higher; **3.** to attack; **4.** to marry *s.o.* while he is already married; **-üne vazife olmamak** *(or* değil) to be none of one's business; **-üne yatmak** to arrogate; to appropriate s.th. for oneself, not to give s.th. back; **-üne yıkmak 1.** to dump on s.o. *(a hard job)* **2.** to cast the blame on, to impute; **-üne yok** superb, the best; **-üne yürümek** to pretend as if about attack; to march against; **-ünüze afiyet** *(or* sağlık) may you stay in good health.

**üstat** [. -] master, teacher, instructor.

**üstçene** *anat.* upper jaw.

**üstderi** *anat.* epidermis.

**üstdudak** *anat.* upper lip.

**üste** further, in addition; **-sinden gelmek** F to bring about, to manage, to realize, to achieve, to wangle.

**üsteğmen** ✗ first lieutenant.

**üstelemek 1.** to be added to; **2.** to renew incidence, to recur *(illness);* **3.** to insist on, to dominate, to urge; **4.** to renew *(request, etc.).*

**üstelik 1.** furthermore, besides, in addition; **2.** extra, addition.

**üstgeçit** overpass, overcrossing.

**üstinsan** superman.

**üstlük** overcoat.

**üstsubay** senior officer.

**üstübeç** ? white lead.

**üstün** superior *(-den* to), outstanding, excellent, exceeding, surpassing, victorious; ~ **gelmek** to surpass, to exceed; ~ **tutmak** to prefer s.th. *or* s.o. to another, to esteem *(or* appreciate) s.th. *or* s.o. more than another, to consider superior.

üstünkörü superficial(ly).

üstünlük superiority; supremacy; ~ derecesi gr. superlative (degree); ~ kompleksi superiority complex.

üstüpü tow, (cotton) waste.

üstyapı superstructure.

üşenç laziness, sloth.

üşengeç, üşengen lazy, slothful.

üşengeçlik laziness, sloth.

üşenmek to be slack, to be too lazy to do, to do with reluctance.

üşmek, (-er) to flock (-e to), to crowd.

üşniye ℈ algae.

üşümek 1. to feel cold; 2. to catch cold.

üşüntü flocking, crowding.

üşürmek caus. of üşmek.

üşüşmek to flock together, to crowd.

üşütmek 1. to cause to catch cold; 2. to catch cold; 3. sl. to go nuts.

üşütük sl. nutty.

ütmek¹, (-er) 1. to singe; 2. to hold to (or over) the fire; 3. to roast over the fire (corn, etc.).

ütmek², (-er) to win (in a game).

ütopik utopian, unrealizable, unattainable.

ütopist utopist, utopian.

ütopya, ütopi utopia.

ütopyacı utopist.

ütü 1. (flat-)iron; 2. crease; 3. ironing, pressing; ~ bezi press cloth; ~ tahtası ironing board; ~ yapmak to iron, to do the ironing.

ütücü ironer, presser.

ütülemek 1. to iron, to press; 2. to singe off.

ütülmek to get beaten (in a game).

ütülü 1. ironed, pressed; 2. singer.

ütüsüz 1. unironed, not ironed; 2. unsinged.

üvendire oxgoad.

üvey, -i, -si step-; ~ ana stepmother; ~ baba stepfather; ~ evlat stepchild; ~ evlat gibi tutmak (or bakmak) to treat s.o. unkindly (or unfairly).

üveyik zo. wood-pigeon.

üveymek to coo (dove, pigeon, etc.).

üvez¹ (ağacı) ℈ service tree.

üvez² zo. a kind of stinging fly.

üye 1. member (of a council, etc.); 2. anat. organ.

üyelik membership.

üzengi stirrup.

üzengikemiği, -ni anat. stapes.

üzengilemek to spur.

üzengitaşı, -nı △ impost.

üzere 1. (in order) to, just about to; 2. on condition that, provided that; 3. as; 4. of (or from) which; 5. at the point of (doing s.th.).

üzeri 1. top; 2. outer surface; 3. clothes; 4. body; 5. the rest, remainder; 6. at or about (time).

üzerinde 1. on, over, above, on top of; 2. with regard to, as to, corcerning, in respect of.

üzerlik harmal.

üzgü oppression, cruelty.

üzgün 1. sad (at), sorrowful, grieved (at, about); 2. weak, feeble, invalid.

üzmek, (-er) 1. to hurt the feelings of, to grieve, to sadden, to vex, to annoy; 2. to strain, to break.

üzücü distressing, annoying, tormenting, saddening.

üzülmek 1. pass. of üzmek; 2. to be sorry for, to regret, to be sad (at, about); 3. to be worn out.

üzüm ℈ grape; ~ şekeri glucose; ~ -e baka baka kararır a man is known by the company he keeps; -ün çöpü armudun sapı var demek to be hypercritical, to be fussy; -ünü ye de bağını sorma don't look a gift horse in the mouth.

üzüm üzüm (used in üzmek and üzülmek) very, terribly, dreadfully.

üzüntü 1. sorrow, anxiety, worry, trouble; 2. annoyance, vexation, chagrin; 3. grief, dejection.

üzüntülü 1. sad, worried, grieved unhappy; 2. tedious, troublesome; 3. annoying, vexatious; 4. anxious.

üzüntüsüz 1. carefree; 2. easy, simple, effortless.

# V

**vaat**, -dı promise; commitment, assurance: ~ etm. to promise; -te bulunmak to make a promise (-e to), to promise.

**vaaz** isl. sermon, homily; ~ etm. to give a sermon, to sermonize, to preach.

**vacip**, -bi 1. obligatory, incumbent; 2. isl. incumbent on a Muslim *(duty);* ~ olm. to be necessary.

**vade** 1. term, time; prompt; 2. due date; date of maturity; 3. one's hour of death; -si geçmiş overdue *(cheque, etc.);* -si gelmek 1. to fall due; 2. *fig.* to live one's last hour.

**vadeli** having a fixed term, time...; ~ hesap *(or* mevduat) time deposit; ~ satış time sale.

**vadesiz** having no fixed term, open...; ~ hesap *(or* mevduat) demand deposit.

**vadetmek** [ā] [x . .] to promise.

**vadi** [- -] 1. valley; 2. *fig.* topic, subject.

**vaftiz** baptism; ~ anası godmother; ~ babası godfather; ~ etm. to baptize.

**vagon** railway car; ~ restoran restaurant car, dining car, diner.

**vagonet**, -ti 🚋 car.

**vagonli** 🚋 wagon-lit, sleeping car, sleeper.

**vah** what a pity!, too bad!

**vaha** oasis.

**vahamet**, -ti [. . .] gravity, seriousness *(of a situation).*

**vahdaniyet**, -ti [. . . .] the unity of God.

**vahdet**, -ti 1. unity, oneness; 2. ♀ *mf.,* *wf.*

**vahi** [- -] futile; silly.

**vahim** serious, grave.

**vahimleşmek** to become serious.

**vahit**, -di 1. one, single, sole; 2. unique; 3. ♀ *mf.*

**vahiy**, -hyi *eccl.* inspiration, revelation.

**vahşet**, -ti 1. wildness, savageness; 2. brutality.

**vahşi** [ī] 1. wild, savage; barbarous; brutal; 3. untamed; 4. virgin *(forest).*

**vahşilik** *s.* vahşet.

**vaız**, -a'zı *isl.* sermon.

**vait**, -a'di *s.* vaat.

**vaiz** *isl.* preacher.

**vajina** *anat.* vagina.

**vajinal** *anat.* vaginal.

**vaka** event, happening, incident, occurrence *(a. 🏥);* ~ yeri scene.

**vakaa** [- . .] [x . -] although, though.

**vakanüvis** [. . . -] chronicler.

**vakar** [. -] gravity, dignity, sedateness.

**vakarlı** [. - .] sedate, dignified, grave.

**vakarsız** undignified.

**vaketa** [. x .] calfskin.

**vakfetmek** [x . .] 1. to make over to religious *or* charitable foundation *(property);* 2. to devote (-e to), to dedicate (-e to).

**vakfiye** *eccl.* deed of trust *(of a pious foundation).*

**vakıa** [- . .] 1. event, happening; 2. although, though.

**vakıf**, -kfı foundation, wakf; Vakıflar Genel Müdürlüğü *pr. n.* Directorate of Wakfs.

**vâkıf** aware, cognizant; ~ olm. to be aware *(or* cognizant) (-e of).

**vakıfname** [. . . -] deed of trust.

**vaki** [- -] happening, taking place; ~ olm. to happen, to occur, to take place.

**vakit**, -kti 1. time; 2. when; ~ almak to take time; ~ daralıyor time presses; ~ geçirmek to pass the time, to occupy o.s.; ~ kaybetmeden without losing any time, at once, promptly; ~ kazanmak to gain time; ~ nakittir *pro.* time is money; ~ öldürmek to kill time; ~ ~ from time to time, at times; -ler hayrolsun! good day!; vakti gelmek *(for s.o.'s hour of death)* to be at hand; vakti yerinde well-off, well-fixed; vaktini almak *(b-nin)* to take *s.o.'s* time; vaktiyle 1. at the proper time, in time; 2. in the past, once, once upon a time.

**vakitli** timely, opportune; ~ vakitsiz at all sorts of times.

**vakitsiz** untimely, inopportune, premature.

**vaktaki** [. - .] [. x .] † when.

**vokum** [x .] ⊕ vacuum.

**vakumlu** ⊕ vacuum-operated.

**vakur** [ū] sedate, dignified, grave.

**vak vak 1.** quack, quack!; **2.** guacking *(of a duck).*

**valans** ♯ valence.

**vale** *cards:* jack, knave.

**valf** valve.

**vali** [ā] governor *(of a province),* vali.

**valide** [ā] mother; ~ sultan *hist.* mother of the reigning sultan.

**valilik 1.** governorship; **2.** governor's office.

**valiz** valise, travel(l)ing bag.

**vallahi** [x - .] by God!, I swear it's true!; ~ billahi I swear to God it's true!

**vals** waltz; ~ yapmak to waltz.

**vamp,** -pı **1.** vamp; **2.** vampish.

**vampir 1.** vampire; **2.** *zo.* vampire bat.

**vana** valve.

**vandalizm** vandalism.

**vanilya** [. x .] ♀ vanilla.

**vantilasyon** ventilation.

**vantilatör** fan, ventilator; ~ kayışı fan *(or* ventilator) belt.

**vantrlok,** -ku ventriloquist.

**vantuz 1.** ♯ cupping glass; **2.** *zo.* sucker; ~ çekmek to cup.

**vaporizasyon** vaporization.

**vaporizatör** vaporizer.

**vapur 1.** steamer, steamship; **2.** *sl.* very drunk person; ~ seyahati voyage.

**vapurculuk** operating a steamship line.

**var 1.** existing, in existence; **2.** available, at hand; present, in attendance; **3.** there is; there are; **4.** one's all, everything one has; ~ etm. to create; ~ gücüyle *(or* kuvvetiyle)* with all his might; ~ ol! may you live long!; good for you!; ~ olm. to exist; -ı yoğu everything one owns.

**varagele** boat which is propelled by a guess-rope.

**varak 1.** sheet *(of paper, gold leaf);* **2.** leaf *(of a book).*

**varaka** printed form; certificate.

**varakçı 1.** gilder; **2.** silverer.

**varaklamak 1.** to gild; **2.** to silver.

**varaklı 1.** gilded; **2.** silvered.

**varda** [x .] ↓ keep clear!, make way!

**vardabandıra** ↓ signalman.

**vardakosta** [.. x .] **1.** ↓ coast guard cutter; **2.** *sl.* big and good-looking woman.

**vardiya** [x .. ] **1.** shift *(in a factory);* **2.** ↓ watch; ~ şefi shift boss.

**varılmak** *pass. of* varmak; oraya üç saatte varılır it takes three hours to get there.

**varış 1.** arrival; **2.** *fig.* comprehension, understanding; -ına gelişim, tarhana aşına bulgur aşım *pro.* as you treat others, so will they treat you.

**varışlı** clever, quick of comprehension.

**varidat,** -tı [- . -] income; revenue.

**varil** barrel, keg.

**varis** ♯ varix, varicosity.

**vâris** heir, inheritor.

**varisli** ♯ varicose.

**varit,** -di likely to happen; possible.

**variyet,** -ti [ā] P wealth, riches.

**varlık 1.** existence, being; **2.** presence; **3.** creature; **4.** wealth, riches; ~ göstermek to make one's presence felt; ~ içinde yaşamak to live in easy circumstances; ~ içinde yokluk scarcity despite wealth.

**varlıklı** wealthy, rich, well-to-do.

**varlıksal** existential.

**varma** *vn. of* varmak; ~ limanı port of discharge.

**varmak,** (-ır) **1.** to arrive (-e at, in), to reach; to get (-e to); **2.** *(for a woman)* to marry *(a man);* varsın gelmesin! it doesn't matter whether he comes or not.

**varoluş** existence.

**varoş** suburb.

**varsayılı** hypothetical.

**varsayım** hypothesis; supposition, assumption.

**varsaymak 1.** to suppose, to assume; **2.** to hypothesize.

**varta** great peril, dangerous situation, tight spot; -yı atlatmak to turn the corner.

**varyans** variance.

**varyant,** -tı **1.** variant; **2.** diversion, detour.

**varyasyon** ♪ variation.

**varyemez** miser, pinchpenny.

**varyete** variety show.

**varyos** sledge (hammer).

**vasat,** -tı **1.** average; mediocre; **2.** environment; **3.** centre, *Am.* center.

**vasati** [î] **1.** average, mean; **2.** central; ~ olarak on the average.

**vasıf,** -sfı **1.** quality, attribute; **2.** *gr.* adjective.

**vasıflandırmak** to characterize, to describe.

**vasıflı** qualified, skilled.

**vasıl olm.** to arrive (-e at, in), to reach.

**vasıta** [- . .] **1.** means; **2.** vehicle; **3.** intermediary; **4.** instrument, implement; -sıyla by means of, through.

**vasıtalı** [- . . .] **1.** indirect; **2.** indirectly, through an intermediary.

**vasıtasız** [- . . .] **1.** direct; **2.** directly.

**vasi** [. -] ♯ guardian; executor.

**vâsi,** -ii broad, wide.

**vasilik** ♯ guardianship, wardship.

**vasistas** transom (window).

**vasiyet, -ti 1.** will, testament; **2.** last request *(of a dying person);* ~ etm. to bequeath.

**vasiyetname [....].** will, testament.

**vasletmek [x ..]** *(bşi bşe)* to unite *s.th.* to *s.th.*

**vaşak** *zo.* lynx.

**vaşington** ⚓ navel orange.

**vat, -tı** ⚡ watt; ~ saat watt-hour.

**vatan** native country, motherland, fatherland, mother country; -a ihanet treason; -ı kurtarmak *sl.* to manage the situation.

**vatandaş** citizen, compatriot; national.

**vatandaşlık** citizenship; ~ hakları ⚖ civil rights.

**vatani [i]** patriotic; ~ görev *(or* vazife*)* military service.

**vatanperver, vatansever** patriotic.

**vatanperverlik, vatanseverlik** patriotism.

**vatansız** stateless.

**vatka** shoulder padding *(in a garment).*

**vatman** tram-driver, driver of a streetcar.

**vatoz** *(balığı)* *zo.* ray, skate.

**vaveyla [-.-]** shout; -yı koparmak to raise a shout.

**vay** oh!, woe!; ~ başıma! woe is me!

**vazelin** vaseline.

**vazetmek 1.** to impose *(a tax);* **2.** to make *(a law).*

**va'zetmek** to preach, to sermonize.

**vazgeçmek** to give up, to abandon, to quit; to renounce, to waive.

**vazıh [â]** manifest, clear.

**vazife [.-.] 1.** duty, responsibility; **2.** homework; **3.** employment, job; ~ aşkı love of one's job; senin ne üstüne ~? what's that to you?

**vazifelendirmek** to commission, to entrust, to charge.

**vazifeli [.-.]. 1.** charged with a duty; **2.** employed; **3.** on duty.

**vazifeşinas [.-..-]** dutiful; conscientious *(worker).*

**vaziyet, -ti 1.** situation, circumstances, plight; **2.** condition, state; **3.** position; ~ almak ⚔ to stand at attention; -e bağlı it all depends.

**vazo [x .]** vase.

**ve** and; ~ saire et cetera, etc., and so forth.

**veba [â]** ⚕ plague, pestilence.

**vebal, -li [â]** evil consequences *(of an evil action);* -i boynuna! on your head be it!, the responsibility is yours!; -ini çekmek to suffer the consequences *(of an evil action).*

**vebalı [â]** plague-stricken.

**veca, -aı [â]** pain, ache.

**vecibe [i]** duty, obligation.

**vecih, -chi 1.** face; **2.** way, manner; bu veçhile thus, in this way; hiç bir veçhile in no way.

**vecit, -cdi** ecstasy, rapture; vecde gelmek to become ecstatic.

**veciz [i]** pithy, meaty, laconic.

**vecize [i]** epigram, aphorism.

**veçhe 1.** direction, way, course; **2.** side, aspect.

**veda, -aı [â]** farewell, good-bye; ~ etm. to say farewell *(or* good-bye*)* *(-e* to); ~ partisi farewell party; ~ ziyareti farewell visit; -a gitmek *(b-ne)* to pay *s.o.* a farewell visit.

**vedalaşmak [....]** to say farewell *(ile* to), to say good-bye *(ile* to).

**vedia [i] 1.** deposit, trust; **2.** ♀ *wf.*

**vefa [â]** fidelity, loyalty, faithfulness; ~ etm. *(for one's life)* to last long enough, to suffice.

**vefakâr [.--], vefalı [.-.]** faithful, loyal.

**vefasız [â]** unfaithful, disloyal.

**vefasızlık [â]** unfaithfulness, disloyalty.

**vefat, tı [â]** death, decease; ~ etm. to die, to pass away.

**vehim, -hmi** groundless fear.

**vehmetmek [x ..]** to forebode, to fear.

**vejetalin** vegetable butter.

**vekâlet, -ti 1.** procuration, attorneyship; proxy; **2.** *pol.* ministry; ~ etm. to represent, to act for, to deputize; ~ vermek *(b-ne)* to give *s.o.* the right of representing.

**vekâleten [.x ..]** by proxy *(or* procuration*).*

**vekâletname [....].** proxy, procuration.

**vekil [i] 1.** agent, representative, attorney, deputy, proxy; **2.** *pol.* minister of state.

**vekilharç** majordomo, butler.

**vekillik 1.** proxy; attorneyship; **2.** *pol.* ministry.

**vektör** ⚓ vector.

**velayet, -ti 1.** ⚖ guardianship, wardship; **2.** sainthood.

**velense [. x .]** a kind of thick blanket.

**velespit, -tı** velocipede, bicycle.

**velet, -di** child, kid, brat.

**velev, velev ki** even if...

**velhasıl [x - .]** in short.

**veli [i] 1.** guardian, protector *(of a child);* **2.** saint, wali; **3.** ♀ *mf.*

**veliaht, -dı** heir apparent, crown prince, successor to the throne.

**veliahtlık** heir apparency.

velilik 1. guardianship, wardship; 2. sainthood.

velinimet, -ti [. - - .] benefactor, patron.

velur velure, velvet.

velvele clamo(u)r, outcry, hubbub; -ye vermek to kick up (or raise) a row, to cause a tumult.

velveleci clamorous, noisy.

Venedik [x . .] pr. n. Venice.

Venüs ast. Venus.

veranda veranda, porch.

veraset, -ti inheritance; heredity; ~ hakkı right of succession; ~ ve intikal vergisi death duties.

verecek debt, debit.

verecekli debtor.

verem ? tuberculosis; ~ olm. to get tuberculosis.

veremli tubercular, tuberculous.

veresiye 1. on credit; 2. fig. partially, halfway.

verev bias, diagonal.

vergi 1. tax; 2. gift, endowment; ~ beyannamesi tax statement (or return); ~ kaçakçılığı tax evasion; ~ mükellefi taxpayer; ~ tahsildarı tax-collector; -ye tabi taxable.

vergilemek to tax.

vergilendirmek to tax.

vergili 1. taxable, subject to taxation; 2. generous.

vergisiz tax-free.

veri datum.

verici transmitter; ~ istasyonu transmitting station.

verim output, production, yield.

verimli productive, fruitful.

verimlilik productivity, fruitfulness.

verimsiz unproductive, unfruitful.

verimsizlik unproductiveness, unfruitfulness.

veriştirmek 1. caus. of verişmek; 2. (b-ne) to give s.o. a dressing down.

verkaç, -cı football: passing and running.

vermek, (-ir) 1. to give; to hand; to deliver; 2. to leave, to bequeath; 3. to attribute (-e to); 4. to abandon o.s. (-e to), to give o.s. over (-e to); 5. to give in marriage (one's daughter); 6. to yield, to produce; 7. to hold (a party, etc.); to give (a concert); 8. to suffer (losses).

vermut, -tu vermouth.

vernik varnish.

verniklemek to varnish.

veryansın etm. to squander; to destroy without mercy.

vesait, -ti vehicles, means of transportation.

vesayet, -ti 𝔡𝔞 guardianship, wardship.

vesika 1. document, certificate; 2. ration card.

vesikalı licensed (prostitute).

vesikalık suitable for a document; ~ fotoğraf passport photograph.

vesile 1. means, cause; 2. opportunity; bu -yle thus, as a result of this.

vesselam [x . -] so that's that!

vestibül vestibule.

vestiyer cloakroom, checkroom, vestiary.

vestiyerci cloakroom attendant.

vesvese apprehension, misgiving.

vesveseli apprehensive.

veteriner veterinarian.

veterinerlik veterinary medicine.

vetire [İ] process.

veto [x .] veto; ~ etm. to veto.

veya, veyahut or.

veyöz night-light.

vezaret, -ti [â] hist. vizierate, viziership.

vezin, -zni poet. metre, Am. meter.

vezinli poet. metrical.

vezir [İ] 1. hist. vizier; 2. chess: queen.

veziriazam hist. grand vizier.

vezirlik hist. viziership, vizierate.

vezne cashier's desk (or window); teller's window; cashier's office.

vezneci s. veznedar 1.

veznedar [â] 1. cashier, teller; 2. treasurer (of a firm, etc.).

vıcık gooey, sticky; ~ ~ etm. to make gooey (or sticky).

vıdı vıdı etm. F to yak, to chatter.

vınlamak to whiz, to buzz, to whir.

vır vır etm. to nag, to grumble.

vırvırcı grumbler.

vız buzz; hum; ~ gelir tırıs gider F I don't give a damn (or tinker's cuss); ~ gelmek F to be a matter of indifference.

vızıldamak 1. to buzz; to hum; to ping; 2. to keep on complaining.

vızıltı 1. buzz; hum; 2. complaint.

vızır vızır constantly, continually.

vızlamak s. vızıldamak.

vibrato ♪ vibrato.

vibriyon vibrio.

vicdan conscience; ~ azabı pangs (or pricks) of conscience, remorse; ~ hürriyeti freedom of conscience; -ı sızlamak to suffer a pang of conscience.

vicdanen conscientiously.

vicdani of conscience, pertaining to conscience.

vicdanlı [â] conscientious, just, fair.

vicdansız [â] unjust, unfair; unscrupulous.

vida ⊕ screw.

**vidala** [.x.] calfskin.

**vidalamak** to screw.

**vidalı** [x..] screwed; ~ kapak screw cap.

**video** 1. video; 2. video player; video recorder.

**vikaye** [ā] protection; ~ etm. to protect.

**vikont,** -tu viscount.

**vikontes** viscountess.

**viladi** [.--] inborn, congenital.

**vilayet,** -ti province, vilayet.

**villa** villa.

**vinç,** -çi ⊕ crane; winch.

**viola** ♪ viola.

**vira** [x.] continuously; ~ etm. to lift; ~ söylemek to talk incessantly.

**viraj** curve, bend; ~ almak to go around (or take) a curve.

**viran** [--] ruined, in ruins.

**virane** [--.] ruin; -ye çevirmek to ruin, to destroy.

**virgül** comma.

**virtüöz** ♪ virtuoso.

**virüs** [x.] ⚕ virus.

**visamiral,** -li vice admiral.

**viski** whisky.

**viskonsül** vice-consul.

**viskoz** viscose.

**viskozite** viscosity.

**vişne** [x.] ⚘ morello, sour cherry, amarelle.

**vişneçürüğü,** -nü purple-brown, oxide-brown.

**vitamin** vitamin.

**vitaminli** vitamined, vitaminized.

**vitaminsizlik** ⚕ avitaminosis.

**vites** gear; ~ değiştirmek to shift gears; ~ kolu gear lever, gearshift; ~ kutusu gearbox, transmission; ~ küçültmek to change down, to downshift; -e takmak to put into gear.

**vitrin** 1. shopwindow; 2. china cabinet.

**viyadük** viaduct.

**viyaklamak** to cry, to wail.

**viyak viyak:** ~ ağlamak s. viyaklamak.

**Viyana** [.x.] pr. n. Vienna.

**viyola** [.x.] ♪ viola.

**viyolist,** -ti ♪ violist.

**viyolon** violon, violin.

**viyolonist,** -ti violinist.

**viyolonsel** (violon)cello.

**vize** visa.

**vizite** [x..] 1. visit, house call; 2. rounds (made by a doctor in a hospital); 3. doctor's fee.

**viziyer** visor, peak (of a cap).

**vizon** zo. mink.

**vizör** phot. view-finder.

**vokal,** -li vocal; ~ müzik vocal music.

**vokalist,** -ti vocalist.

**volan** 1. ⊕ flywheel; 2. volant, flounce (on a woman's dress).

**vole** [x.] football, tennis: volley.

**voleybol,** -lü volleyball.

**volfram** ⚗ wolfram, tungsten.

**volkan** volcano.

**volkanik** volcanic.

**volt,** -tu ⚡ volt.

**volta** 1. ⚓ fouling of a cable; 2. sl. pacing back and forth; pacing up and down; ~ atmak to pace back and forth; to pace up and down; -sını almak sl. to run away, to beat it.

**voltaj** ⚡ voltage.

**voltmetre** ⚡ voltmeter.

**vonoz** young mackerel or sardine.

**votka** vodka.

**voyvo** [x.] sl. hey!

**voyvoda** hist. voivode, vaivode.

**v.s.** (abbr. for ve saire) etc., et cetera.

**vual,** -li voile.

**vualet,** -ti veiling made of voile.

**vuku,** -uu [--] occurence; ~ bulmak (or -a gelmek) to occur, to happen, to take place; -u halinde in case (of).

**vukuat,** -tı [.--] 1. events, incidents; 2. police case, crime.

**vukuf** [.-] knowledge, knowing.

**vukuflu** well-informed.

**vukufsuz** uninformed, ignorant.

**vurdumduymaz** 1. thick-headed, stupid; 2. thick-skinned, insensitive, callous.

**vurgu** gr. stress, accent.

**vurgulamak** 1. to emphasize, to stress; 2. gr. to stress, to accent.

**vurgulu** gr. stressed, accented.

**vurgun** 1. in love with, sweet on, smitten with; 2. ill-gotten gain, gravy; 3. the bends, caisson disease, the chokes; 4. swindle; ~ vurmak F to pull a deal, to make a killing; ~ yemek to be crippled by the bends; to die from the bends.

**vurguncu** profiteer.

**vurgunculuk** profiteering.

**vurgusuz** gr. unstressed, unaccented.

**vurmak,** (-ur) 1. to hit, to strike; 2. to knock (-e on); to tap (-e on); 3. to hunt; 4. to shoot; to stab; 5. to kill; 6. to hit (a target); 7. (for a shadow, light) to hit, to strike, to fall on; 8. (for a clock) to strike (the hour); 9. to steal; 10. (for a shoe) to chafe, to pinch, to blister; 11. (for one's heart or pulse) to beat; 12. to strike out along, to head out along (a road); to head for; 13. to give (an injection); vur dedikse öldür demedik ya! fig. I didn't ask you to go that far!; vur patlasın çal oynasın enjoying o.s. by whooping it up *(or* by painting the town red).

**vurucu:** ~ güç striking power *(of an army);* ~ tim team of sharpshooters.

**vurulmak 1.** *pass. of* vurmak; **2.** *(b-ne)* to fall in love with *s.o.,* to be smitten with *s.o.*

**vuruntu yapmak** *mot.* to knock, to pink.

**vuruş 1.** blow, stroke; **2.** ♪ beat.

**vuruşkan** combative, belligerent.

**vuruşmak** to fight each other, to have a fight.

**vuslat,** -tı union *(with one's beloved).*

**vusul,** -lü [. -] arrival; ~ bulmak to arrive *(-e* at).

**vuzuh** [. -] clearness, clarity.

**vücut,** -du [ū] **1.** body; **2.** existence; ~ bulmak *(or* vücuda gelmek) to arise, to come into being; vücuda getirmek to create, to produce; -tan düşmek to grow thin.

**vücutlu** heavily built, hulking *(person).*

**vüsat,** -ti **1.** breadth; **2.** ♪ volume; **3.** spaciousness.

x ışınları, -nı X rays.

# Y

ya¹ [ã] o!, oh!; ~ Rabbi! o Lord!, oh my God!

ya² either... or...; ~ bu deveyi gütmeli, ya bu diyardan gitmeli when in Rome, do as the Romans do; ~ sen, ~ ben! it's either you or me!

yaba wooden pitchfork.

yabalamak to pitchfork.

yaban 1. wild, wilderness; 2. P stranger; -a atmak to disregard, to sneeze at, to sniff at, to brush aside; -a söylemek to talk nonsense (or rot).

yabanarısı, -nı zo. wasp; hornet.

yabancı 1. stranger; foreigner, alien; 2. foreign, alien; 3. unfamiliar, strange; ~ düşmanlığı xenophobia; -sı olm. (bsin) to be unfamiliar with s.th.; sesi ~ gelmedi ama ismini hatırlayamadım his voice struck a cord but I couldn't remember his name.

yabancılaşmak to become strangers to each other.

yabancılık 1. foreignnes; 2. unfamiliarity, strangeness.

yabandomuzu, -nu zo. wild boar.

yabangülü, -nü ♀ dog rose, dogberry.

yabani [ - -] 1. wild; 2. fig. shy, timid; 3. fig. boorish, crude.

yabanilik [ - . - .] 1. wildness; 2. fig. shyness; 3. fig. boorishness.

yabankedisi zo. wild cat.

yabanlaşmak to go wild.

yabanlık visiting clothes.

yabansı strange, odd.

yabansımak to find strange.

yad 1. strange, foreign; 2. enemy; 3. stranger, foreigner; ~ elde in a foreign land; away from home; ~ eller foreign lands.

yâd etm. to mention, to talk about, to remember.

yadımlama biol. catabolism, dissimilation.

yadımlamak biol. to catabolize, to dissimilate.

yadırgamak to find strange (or odd).

yadigâr [ - . -] keepsake, souvenir, remembrance.

yadsımak to deny; to reject.

yafa (portakalı) ♀ Jaffa (orange), Valencia (orange).

yafta [x .] label.

yağ 1. oil; fat; suet; tallow; 2. butter; margarine; 3. grease; lard; ~ bağlamak to get fat, to put on fat; ~ bal olsun! I hope you'll enjoy it (food); ~ çekmek to butter up, to flatter, to toady, to applepolish; ~ çubuğu mot. dipstick; ~ gibi gitmek (or kaymak) (for a vehicle) to go like a bird; ~ kutusu ⊕ crankcase; ~ süzgeci mot. oil filter; ~ tulumu fig. very fat person, tub of lard; -dan kıl çeker gibi as easy as taking candy from a baby, as easy as falling off a log.

yağbezi, -ni anat. sebaceous gland.

yağcı 1. seller of oil, butter, etc.; 2. lubricator; greaser; oiler; 3. fig. flatterer, toady.

yağcılık fig. flattery; ~ etm. to flatter, to butter up.

yağdanlık oilcan; lubricator.

yağdırmak 1. caus. of yağmak; 2. fig. to rain, to shower.

yağdoku anat. fatty tissue.

yağımsı oily, oleaginous; fatty.

yağır withers (of a horse).

yağış rain; precipitation.

yağışlı rainy, showery.

yağız dark, swarthy.

yağlama vn. of yağlamak lubrication.

yağlamak 1. to grease, to oil, to lubricate; 2. fig. to flatter, to butter up; yağlayıp ballamak to praise to the skies.

yağlanmak 1. pass. of yağlamak; 2. to get fat.

yağlayıcı 1. lubricant; 2. lubricator: grease gun; 3. lubricatory.

yağlı 1. oily, greasy; fatty; suety; tallowy; lardy; 2. fat, obese; plump; 3. fig. rich, well off, in the money; 4. fig. profitable; ~ ballı olm. to be on the sweetest of terms with each other; ~ carık sl. rich; ~ güreş greased wrestling; ~ kâğıt F oil paper; 2. tracing paper; ~ kapı F rich employer; ~ kuyruk fig. milch cow; ~ lokma fig. rich windfall;

~ müşteri profitable customer.

**yağlıboya 1.** oil paint; **2.** oil...; **3.** gangway!

**yağlık** napkin; handkerchief.

**yağma 1.** pillage, sack; **2.** loot, booty; ~ etm. to loot, to sack, to plunder, to pillage; ~ yok! nothing doing!, no way!

**yağmacı** [x . .] looter, sacker, plunderer, pillager.

**yağmacılık** [x . . .] pillage.

**yağmak,** (-ar) to rain, to shower.

**yağmalamak** to loot, to sack, to plunder, to pillage.

**yağmur** rain; ~ boşanmak to pour heavily, to come down in buckets; ~ duası ritual prayer for rain (said by villagers during a drought); ~ mevsimi rainy season; ~ yağarken küpünü doldurmak fig. to make hay while the sun shines; ~ yağıyor it is raining; ~ yemek to get wet through (in the rain); -dan kaçarken doluya tutulmak fig. to jump out of the frying pan into the fire.

**yağmurca** zo. chamois.

**yağmurkuşağı,** -nı rainbow.

**yağmurkuşu,** -nu zo. plover.

**yağmurlama sistemi** sprinkling system.

**yağmurlamak 1.** to turn into rain, to get rainy; **2.** to sprinkle.

**yağmurlu** rainy; ~ gün rainy day; ~ hava rainy weather.

**yağmurluk** raincoat, mackintosh; oilskin.

**yağsız 1.** oilless; greaseless; butterless; nonfat; **2.** lean, fatless (meat).

**yahey** [ā] hurrah!, yippee!

**yahni** fricassee, ragout.

**yahşi 1.** good, nice; **2.** pretty; beautiful; handsome.

**yahu** [ā] [x.] F see here!, look here!; ne yapıyorsun ~? what on earth are you doing?

**Yahudi 1.** Jew; **2.** Jewish; ~ pazarlığı fig. hard bargaining, haggle.

**Yahudice** Hebrew.

**Yahudilik 1.** Jewishness; **2.** Judaism.

**yahut** [ā] [x.] or.

**yaka 1.** collar; **2.** edge, bank, shore; ~ bir tarafta, paça bir tarafta fig. out at elbows, seedy, dishevel(l)ed; ~ paça by main force; ~ paça etm. to throw out by main force; ~ silkmek (b-den) to get fed up with s.o.; -dan atmak fig. to get rid (or shut) of; -dan geçirmek to adopt (a child); -sına yapışmak to badger, to hound, to bedevil; -sını bırakmamak fig. to badger, to bedevil; -yı ele vermek to get caught, to be collared; -yı

kurtarmak (or sıyırmak) to evade, to wriggle (-den out of).

**yakacak** fuel.

**yakalamak 1.** to catch, to collar, to nab; to grab, to seize, to get hold of; **2.** to notice, to see, to spot, to detect; **3.** to hold responsible.

**yakalanmak 1.** pass. of yakalamak; **2.** to catch (an illness); **3.** to be caught in (the rain, a storm).

**yakalı** collared.

**yakalık** collar.

**yakamoz** phosphorescence (in the sea).

**yakarış** prayer, entreaty.

**yakarmak** to beg, to implore, to entreat.

**yakı** plaster; blister; cautery; ~ vurmak (or yapıştırmak) to plaster; to blister; to cauterize.

**yakıcı 1.** burning; **2.** biting (to the taste); **3.** ⌐ caustic.

**yakın 1.** near (-e to), close (-e to), nearby; **2.** close (friend); **3.** very similar (-e to); **4.** nearby place, neighbo(u)rhood; **5.** relative, relation; ~ akraba close relative, near relation; ~ zamanda **1.** soon, in a short time; **2.** recently; -da **1.** nearby, close at hand; **2.** recently; **3.** in the near future, soon; -dan at close range; -dan bilmek to know well, to be closely acquainted with.

**yakınlaşmak 1.** to approach, to draw near; **2.** fig. to become close (-e to), to become a friend of s.o.

**yakınlık 1.** nearness, closeness proximity; **2.** fig. closeness, warmth, rapport, sympathy; ~ duymak to feel close (-e to); to feel a sympathy (-e for); ~ göstermek to show concern (-e for), to behave warmly (-e toward).

**yakınmak** to complain.

**yakınsak** Å, phys. convergent.

**yakışık almak** to be suitable (or proper); senin annenle böyle alay etmen yakışık almaz it is not fit that you should mock your mother so.

**yakışıklı** handsome, good-looking.

**yakışıksız** unsuitable, improper, unbecoming, unseemly.

**yakışmak 1.** to be suitable (or proper), to befit; **2.** to suit, to go well with.

**yakıştırmak 1.** caus. of yakışmak; **2.** (bşi b-ne) to regard s.th. as suitable for s.o.; to think that s.th. befits s.o.

**yakıt,** -tı fuel.

**yakinen** [. x .] for sure, for certain.

**yaklaşık** approximate.

**yaklaşım** approach.

**yaklaşmak** to approach, to draw near

(-e to); to come close (-e to).

**yaklaştırmak** 1. to bring near, to draw near; 2. to approximate.

**yakmak**, (-ar) 1. to light; to ignite; to set on fire, to set fire to; 2. to burn (up); 3. to scorch, to sear, to burn; 4. (for wool) to irritate; 5. to turn on, to light (electric lights); 6. fig. to ruin, to cook s.o.'s goose; 7. fig. to inflame with love; 8. to apply (henna); 9. to compose (a folk song); yakıp yıkmak to destroy utterly.

**yakşi** s. yahşi.

**yakut**, -tu [ā] ruby.

**yalak** 1. trough; 2. basin (of a fountain).

**yalama** 1. vn. of yalamak; 2. worn (by friction): ~ olm. to get worn.

**yalamacı** sl. toady, lickspittle.

**yalamak** 1. to lick; to lick up; to lap up; 2. to skim over; to graze.

**yalan** 1. lie, fib, falsehood. untruth; 2. false, untrue; ~ atmak to lie, to tell lies; ~ çıkmak to turn out untrue; ~ dolan pack of lies; ~ dünya this transitory life; ~ makinesi lie detector; ~ söylemek to lie, to tell lies; ~ yanlış false, erroneous; ~ yere yemin $\mathcal{J}\mathcal{J}$ perjury; ~ yere yemin etm. $\mathcal{J}\mathcal{J}$ to perjure o.s.; -a şerbetli prone to lying; -ını çıkarmak (b-nin) to give s.o. the lie; -ını tutmak (or yakalamak) (b-nin) to catch s.o. in a lie.

**yalancı** 1. liar; 2. imitation, false, artificial; ~ çıkarmak (b-ni) 1. to prove that s.o. is a liar; 2. to call s.o. a liar; ~ çıkmak to turn out to be a liar; ~ şahit $\mathcal{J}\mathcal{J}$ perjurer; -nın mumu yatsıya kadar yanar pro. It doesn't take long for a lie to come to light.

**yalancıakasya** ♦ black locust.

**yalancıktan** superficially; in pretence; ~ bayıldı he pretended to faint.

**yalancılık** lying.

**yalandan** superficially, only for appearance; ~ ağladı she pretended to cry.

**yalanlamak** to deny, to contradict.

**yalanmak** 1. pass. of yalamak; 2. to lick one's lips (or chops).

**yalapşap** superficially done.

**yalaz** flame.

**yalçın** 1. steep; 2. ♀ mf.

**yaldız** 1. gilding, silvering; 2. fig. veneer, gloss, glitter, gilt.

**yaldızcı** gilder, silverer.

**yaldızlamak** 1. to gild, to silver; 2. fig. to give a deceptive glitter; 3. F to cuckold.

**yaldızlı** 1. gilded, gilt, silvered; 2. fig. gilded, honeyed.

**yale (kilit)** Yale lock.

**yalelli** [- x .]: ~ gibi (or Arabın -si gibi) unending, monotonous.

**yalgın** P mirage.

**yalı** 1. shore; bank; beach; 2. waterside mansion; ~ boyu shore, beach; ~ kazığı big and tall.

**yalıçapkını**, -nı zo. kingfisher.

**yalın** 1. bare, naked; 2. gr. simple; ~ hal gr. nominative case.

**yalınayak** barefoot; ~ başı kabak 1. bareheaded and barefoot; 2. fig. clothed in rags.

**yalınkat**, -tı 1. one layer; 2. fig. superficial, shallow.

**yalıtım** insulation.

**yalıtkan** phys. nonconductive; insulative.

**yalıtmak** to insulate.

**yalıyar** geogr. cliff.

**yalız** anat. unstriated (muscle).

**yallah** [x .] go!, get going!

**yalnız** [x .] 1. alone, by o.s.; 2. lonely, lonesome; 3. solitary, isolated; lone; 4. just, only; 5. but, however; ~ başına alone, by o.s.; ~ bırakmak (b-ni) to leave s.o. alone, to leave s.o. on his own.

**yalnızca** alone, by o.s.

**yalnızcılık** pol. isolationism.

**yalnızlaşmak** to become isolated.

**yalnızlık** 1. loneliness, lonesomeness; 2. isolation, solitude, loneness.

**yalpa** [x .] ♪ rolling, lurching; ~ vurmak to roll, to lurch.

**yalpak** P friendly.

**yalpalamak** s. yalpa vurmak.

**yaltak(cı)** contp. fawning, cringing.

**yaltaklanmak** to toady (-e to), to fawn, to cringe, to lickspittle, to play up (-e to).

**yaltakçılık** toadying, fawning; ~ etm. to toady, to fawn, to lickspittle.

**yalvarmak** to beg, to entreat, to implore, to plead; yalvarıp yakarmak to beg earnestly.

**yama** 1. patch; 2. birhmark, nevus; ~ vurmak to put a patch (-e on), to patch.

**yamacı** cobbler, shoe repairman.

**yamaç**, -cı 1. side; 2. slope (of a hill); hillside; side (of a mountain).

**yamak** helper, apprentice.

**yamalak** s. yarım ~.

**yamalamak** to patch.

**yamalı** patched.

**yamamak** 1. to patch; 2. to foist (-e on), to palm off (-e on).

**yaman** 1. very clever and capable; 2. terrible, disastrous; 3. frightful, extreme; 4. violently, strongly.

yamanmak 1. *pass. of* yamamak; 2. *contp.* to be foisted (*or* palmed off) (-*e* on).

yampiri 1. lopsided; 2. crabwise; ~ gitmek to move crabwise, to crab.

yamrı yumru 1. misshapen; gnarled, uneven and lumpy; 2. very crooked.

yamuk 1. (a)skew, lopsided, crooked, bent; 2. Ӓ trapezoid.

yamuk yumuk very crooked; twisted out of shape.

yamulmak to become bent to one side; to lean to one side.

yamyam cannibal.

yamyamlık cannibalism.

yamyassı [x .] as flat as a pancake.

yamyaş [x .] very damp.

yan 1. side; 2. flank; 3. vicinity, neighbo(u)rhood; 4. direction; 5. part (*of one's body*); 6. aspect, side (*of a matter*); 7. secondary; ~ bakmak to look askance (-*e* at); to leer (-*e* at); ~ basmak *fig.* to be deceived (*or* taken in); ~ cümle *gr.* subordinate clause; ~ çizmek to avoid, to shirk, to evade, to dodge; ~ etki side effect; ~ gelmek (*or* ~ gelip yatmak) to take one's ease, to goof off; ~ gözle out of the corner of one's eye; ~ gözle bakmak 1. to look out of the corner of one's eye; 2. *fig.* to leer (-*e* at); ~ hakemi linesman; ~ sokak by-street; ~ tutmak to take sides; ~ ürün by-product; ~ ~ sideways; ~ ~ bakmak to look daggers (-*e* at), to leer (-*e* at); ~ -*a* side by side; ~ yatmak to lean to one side; -*a* 1. in favo(u)r of, for, pro; 2. concerning, as regards; -*dan* sideways. from one side; ın profile; -*dan* çarklı 1. paddle-wheel boat, paddle-steamer; 2. *F* tea served with the sugar brought in the saucer; -*ı* sıra right along with, together with; -*ına* bırakmamak (*or* koymamak) not to leave unpunished.

yanak cheek; yanağından kan damlamak to be rosy-cheeked and healthy; yanağından öpmek to kiss s.o. on the cheek.

yanal lateral; ~ yükseklik Ӓ apothem; ~ yüzey Ӓ lateral surface.

yanardağ volcano.

yanardöner shot (*silk*); chatoyant (*fabric, gem*).

yanaşık drawn up alongside; parked alongside; docked alongside.

yanaşma 1. *vn. of* yanaşmak; 2. farmhand.

yanaşmak 1. to approach, to draw near; to sidle up (-*e* to); 2. to draw up (*or* pull) alongside; 3. ♪ to dock; 4. to accede to (*a request*); to incline, to seem willing; to go along with (*a plan*); 5. (*b-ne*) to

cozy up to s.o.

yanaştırmak 1. *caus. of* yanaşmak; 2. to draw (*a vehicle*) up alongside (*a place*).

yandaş supporter, follower, advocate, adherent, partisan.

yandaşlık support, advocacy, adherence, partisanship.

yangaboz, yangabuç *F* hunchbacked, bent.

yangeçit bypass.

yangı ♀ inflammation, infection.

yangılanmak ♀ to become inflamed, to get infected.

yangılı ♀ 1. inflamed, infected; 2. inflammatory.

yangın 1. fire, conflagration; 2. *P* fever; 3. *F* madly in love, gone on; ~ bombası fire (*or* incendiary) bomb; ~ çıkarmak to start a fire; ~ kulesi fire tower; ~ sigortası fire insurance; ~ tulumbası hand fire pump; ~ var! fire!; -*a* körükle gitmek *fig.* to add fuel to the flames; -*dan* çıkmış gibi impoverished, destitute.

yanıbaşında right beside, right next to.

yanık 1. burn; scald; 2. burnt, burned; 3. (a)lit, alight, lighted; 4. love-sick; 5. doleful, touching, piteous; ~ kokusu burnt smell, smell of burning; ~ tenli sunburnt, sun-tanned.

yanıkara ♀ charbon, anthrax.

yanılgı mistake, error.

yanılmak 1. to be mistaken; 2. to make a mistake, to err.

yanılmaz infallible, unfailing.

yanılsama *psych.* illusion.

yanıltıcı misleading.

yanıltmaca sophism.

yanıltmaç tongue twister.

yanıltmak *caus. of* yanılmak to mislead.

yanıt, -*tı* answer, response, reply; ~ vermek to answer, to reply.

yanıtlamak to answer, to reply.

yani [ᵃ] [x .] that is (to say), I mean; namely.

yankesici pickpocket.

yankesicilik picking pockets.

yankı 1. echo; 2. repercussion; ~ uyandırmak 1. to echo; 2. to have repercussions.

yankıla(n)mak to echo.

Yanki Yankee.

yanlamak to get by (*or* around).

yanlı 1. ... sided; 2. supporter of, adherent of, advocate of, partisan of.

yanlış 1. mistake, error, blunder; mistep; 2. wrong, erroneous, incorrect; ~ çıkmak to turn out to be wrong; ~ doğru

cetveli list of errata; ~ düşmek *teleph.*
to get *(or* have) the wrong number; ~
kapı çalmak to bark up the wrong tree;
~ yere by mistake; -ını çıkarmak *(b-nin)*
to find *s.o.'s* mistake.

**yanlışlık** mistake, error, blunder.

**yanlışlıkla** by mistake.

**yanmak,** (-ar) 1. to burn, to be on fire; to
burn down *(or* up); 2. *(for electricity)*
to be on; 3. to be burned *(or* scorched
*or* singed); to get sunburned; 4. to get
tanned *(by the sun);* 5. to have fever,
to be feverish; 6. *fig.* to be done for, to
have had it, to be in the soup; 7. to expire; to become void; 8. to be out *(or*
eliminated); 9. to feel great sadness
(-e at); 10. *(for a place)* to be blazing
hot; 11. *fig.* to burn *(to do s.th.);* 12. to
be madly in love (-e with); to have the
hots (-e for); yanıp kül olm. to burn to
ashes; yanıp tutuşmak *(biri için)* to be
madly in love with *s.o.*

**yansı** 1. *biol.* reflex; 2. reflection.

**yansıma** reflection.

**yansımak** 1. *(for light)* to be reflected; 2.
*(for sound)* to echo.

**yansıtıcı** 1. reflector; 2. reflective.

**yansıtmak** 1. to reflect *(light);* 2. to echo
*(sound).*

**yansız** 1. impartial, unbiased; 2. *pol.*, ⌒,
⚡ neutral.

**yanşak** garrulous, talkative.

**yanşaklık** garrulity.

**yap yap** $P$ = yavaş yavaş.

**yapağı, yapak** spring wool.

**yapay** 1. artificial, imitation; 2. artificial,
affected.

**yapayalnız** [x . . -] all alone, completely
alone; all by himself; all by itself.

**yapaylık** artificiality.

**yapı** 1. building, edifice, construction,
structure; 2. physique; frame; construction; structure, build; 3. make,
origin; ~ iskelesi scaffolding; ~ ustası
master builder.

**yapıcı** 1. builder; constructor; maker;
2. constructive; creative; helpful.

**yapılı** 1. made of..., constructed of...; 2.
portly *(person).*

**yapım** 1. construction, building; 2. manufacture, production; 3. production *(of a
film, etc.).*

**yapımcı** 1. builder; 2. manufacturer,
maker; 3. producer *(of a film, etc.).*

**yapımevi** 1. factory, manufactory; mill;
plant; 2. *cinema:* production company.

**yapınmak** 1. to make s.th. for o.s.; 2. to
have s.th. made for o.s.; 3. to try to (-e

*inf.)*

**yapısal** structural.

**yapışık** 1. stuck (-e to, on); adhering (-e
to); 2. *fig.* boring, importunate *(person).*
~ kardeşler Siamese twins.

**yapışkan** 1. sticky, adhesive, viscid; 2.
*fig.* importunate, clingy *(person).*

**yapışmak** 1. to stick (-e to), to adhere (-e
to), to cling (-e to); 2. to set about (-e
*ger.);* 3. *fig.* to cling to s.o. like a leech,
to latch onto s.o. like a leech.

**yapıştırıcı** adhesive.

**yapıştırmak** *caus. of* yapışmak 1. to glue,
to paste, to stick, to tape; to adhere; 2.
to land, to deal, to plant *(a blow);* 3. to
say in quick reply.

**yapış yapış** very sticky.

**yapıt,** -tı work (of art), opus.

**yapıtaşı,** -nı building stone.

**yapkın** 1. rich, wealthy; 2. drunk.

**yapma** 1. *vn. of* yapmak; 2. artificial,
false, imitation; 3. affected, mock, feigned; ~ uydu artificial satellite.

**yapmacık** 1. artificiality, affectation,
pose, show; 2. artificial, affected, mock,
feigned.

**yapmak,** (-ar) 1. to make; to build, to
construct; to manufacture; to produce;
to prepare; to create; 2. to do; to carry
out, to perform, to execute; 3. to repair,
to fix; 4. to cause, to bring about *(an
illness);* 5. to make, to acquire *(money);*
6. *(for a vehicle)* to do *(speed);* 7. to defecate; to urinate, to wet; 8. to harm,
to do harm; 9. to do, to arrange; 10. to
have sexual intercourse with, to do it to
*(a woman);* Ahmet öğretmenlik yapıyor
Ahmet teaches, Ahmet's a teacher; geçen kış çok kar yaptı it snowed a lot last
year; gelmekle iyi yaptın you did well to
come; Orhan yapmadığını bırakmadı Orhan's committed every crime in the
book; yapma! stop it!, cut it out!

**yaprak** 1. leaf; 2. page, leaf *(of a book,
etc.);* 3. layer, sheet; 4. *geol.* folium;
~ aşısı bud graft; ~ dolması *(or* sarması) stuffed grape leaves; ~ dökümü
autumn. *Am.* fall; ~ kurmak to pickle
grape leaves; ~ oynamamak *(for the
air)* to be no wind at all; ~ sigarası
cigar; ~ tütün leaf tobacco; ~ ~ 1. mul-
tilayered; 2. in layers.

**yaprakbiti,** -ni *zo.* aphid, plant louse.

**yapraklanmak** to leaf, to come into leaf,
to leave (out).

**yapraklı** leafy; leafed.

**yapraksız** leafless.

**yaptırım** ⚡ sanction.

403

**yapyalnız** s. yapayalnız.

**yar** precipice, cliff, abyss; -dan atmak *fig.* to lead into deep trouble.

**yâr**, -ri 1. beloved, love; lover; 2. friend; 3. helper; ~ olm. to be a help, to help, to assist; -dan mı geçersin, serden mi? *fig.* I'm-faced with an impossible choice.

**yara** 1. wound; injury; 2. gash, rent, tear; 3. *fig.* pain, sorrow; ~ açmak to make a wound (-de in), to wound; ~ bağı bandage; ~ bere cuts and bruises; wounds and bruises; ~ işlemek to discharge (boil); ~ izi scar; ~ kabuğu scab, crust (over a wound); ~ kapanmak (for a wound) to heal; -sı olan gocunur! if the cap fits wear it!; -sını deşmek *fig.* to touch a sore spot, to open up an old wound; -ya tuz biber ekmek *fig.* to sprinkle salt on the wound.

**Yaradan** the Creator, the Maker, God; -a kurban olayım! oh Lord!, wow!; -a sığınıp mustering his strength.

**yaradılış** 1. nature, temperament, disposition; 2. creation; -tan by nature, naturally.

**yarak** sl. penis, cock, dick, prick, pecker, tool.

**yaralamak** 1. to wound, to injure; 2. to hurt.

**yaralanmak** pass. of yaralamak to be wounded (or injured).

**yaralı** wounded, injured; ~ kuşa kurşun sıkılmaz pro. don't hit (or kick) s.o. when he's down.

**yaramak** 1. to be of use (-e to), to be good (-e for), to come in handy; to serve, to avail; 2. to be good for s.o.'s health, to be good (-e for), to do s.o. good; 3. to befit.

**yaramaz** 1. useless, good-for-nothing; 2. naughty, mischievous.

**yaramazlık** naughtiness, mischievousness, misbehavio(u)r; ~ etm. to get into mischief, to play up, to cut up, to misbehave.

**yaranmak** to curry favo(u)r (-e with), to cozy up (-e to).

**yarar** 1. useful, serviceable; 2. benefit, profit; advantage; -ına for the benefit of.

**yararlanmak** to benefit (-den from), to profit (-den from), to make good use (-den of), to utilize.

**yararlı** useful; advantageous; worthwhile.

**yararlık** service, usefulness.

**yararlılık** usefulness.

**yararsız** useless, of no use.

**yararsızlık** uselessness.

**yarasa** zo. bat.

**yaraşık:** ~ olmak to be suitable (or fitting).

**yaraşıklı** suitable, becoming.

**yaraşıksız** unsuitable, unbecoming.

**yaraşmak** to suit, to become.

**yaratan** creator, maker.

**yaratıcı** creative.

**yaratıcılık** creativity, creativeness.

**yaratık** creature.

**yaratılış** creation, genesis.

**yaratmak** to create.

**yarbay** X lieutenant colonel.

**yarda** [x .] yard (= 91, 44 cm.).

**yardak** s. yardakçı.

**yardakçı** accomplice, henchman.

**yardakçılık** complicity; ~ etm. to aid, to be s.o.'s accomplice.

**yardım** help, assistance, aid; ~ elini uzatmak (b-ne) to give s.o. a hand; ~ etm. to help, to assist, to aid; -a muhtaç needy; -ına yetişmek (b-nin) to come to s.o.'s aid.

**yardımcı** 1. helper, assistant; aide; 2. vice-; 3. gr. auxiliary; 4. maid, cleaning woman; ~ fiil gr. auxiliary verb.

**yardımlaşmak** to help one another; to cooperate. to collaborate.

**yardımsamak** (b-den) to ask s.o. for help.

**yadımsever** philanthropic, helpful.

**yaren** [â] friend.

**yarenlik** [â] chit-chat; ~ etm. to chat.

**yarga** [x .] one-year-old hen.

**yargı** 1. idea, opinion; 2. 🕱 judg(e)ment; verdict (of a jury); decision (of a court); 3. adjudication; 4. phls., log. judg(e)ment; ~ yetkisi judicial power.

**yargıç**, -cı 🕱 judge.

**yargıçlık** 🕱 judgeship.

**yargılamak** to try; to judge, to adjudicate; to hear (a case).

**Yargıtay** pr. n. Supreme Court.

**yarı** 1. half; 2. half of, mid-; 3. sports: half time; 4. half(way), partially; ~ açık half open; ~ beline kadar to the waist; ~ fiyatına at half price; ~ resmi semiofficial; ~ -ya 1. half(way); 2. in half, fifty-fifty; ~ yolda bırakmak (b-ni) to leave s.o. in the lurch, to leave s.o. high and dry; ~ yolda kalmak to be left stranded in the middle of one's journey; -da bırakmak to discontinue, to interrupt; -da kalmak to be left half finished.

**yarıbuçuk** F 1. trivial, trifling, piddling; 2. poor, unsatisfactory.

**yarıcı** 1. chopper, splitter; 2. sharecropper.

yarıçap, -pı Å radius.

yarıfinal, -li *sports:* semifinal.

yarıgeçirgen semipermeable.

yarıiletken ⚡ semiconductor.

yarık 1. split, cleft, fissure; slit, chink; 2. split, cleft, cloven; slit.

yarıküre *geogr.* semisphere.

yarılamak 1. to be halfway through; to complete half of; 2. to be (or go) halfway down.

yarım 1. half; 2. half past noon, twelve-thirty; ~ ağızla *fig.* half-heartedly, with one's tongue in one's cheek; ~ daire Å half circle, semicircle; ~ doğru Å half line; ~ elmanın yarısı o, yarısı bu they're as like as two peas in a pod; ~ kalmak to be left half finished, to be left half done; ~ saat half an hour; ~ yamalak poor, sorry, crummy, two-bit.

yarımada peninsula.

yarımay half-moon.

yarımca ⚕ migraine.

yarımküre hemisphere.

yarımlamak 1. to halve; 2. to half-finish; 3. to be half through.

yarımşar a half each (or apiece).

yarın [x .] tomorrow; ~ değil öbür gün the day after tomorrow; ~ öbür gün soon; ~ sabah tomorrow morning.

yarınki tomorrow's; ~ gazete tomorrow's paper.

yarısaydam semitransparent, translucent.

yarış 1. race; 2. competition; ~ alanı racecourse, racetrack; ~ atı racehorse; ~ etm. to race; ~ pisti 1. speedway; 2. (race)track.

yarışçı contester, contender.

yarışma contest, competition.

yarışmacı competitor, contestant, contender.

yarışmak 1. to race; 2. to compete, to contest, to contend, to vie.

yarma 1. *vn.* of yarmak; 2. cut; 3. ✕ breakthrough; 4. coarsely ground (wheat, etc.); 5. split (wood); ~ gibi hugely built (person); ~ şeftali freestone peach.

yarmak, (-ar) to split, to cleave, to rend, to slit.

yarmalamak to split lengthwise.

yarpuz ✿ pennyroyal.

yas mourning; ~ tutmak to mourn, to be in mourning.

yasa 1. law; 2. law code, code of laws; ~ çıkarmak (or yapmak) to make laws; ~ koyucu lawmaker, legislator.

yasadışı illegal, unlawful.

yasak 1. prohibition; ban; 2. prohibited,

forbidden; ~ bölge off-limits area; ~ etm. to forbid, to prohibit; to ban; ~ savmak to do in a pinch, to serve in case of need, to be better than nothing.

yasakçı 1. prohibitor, prohibiter, forbidder; 2. *hist.* kavass.

yasaklamak to forbid, to prohibit; to ban.

yasaklayıcı prohibitive, prohibitory.

yasal legal, lawful, legitimate, licit.

yasalaşmak to become law.

yasalaştırmak to make law.

yasallaşmak to become lawful (or legal).

yasallaştırmak to legalize.

yasallık legality, lawfulness, legitimacy.

yasama legislation; ~ kurulu legislative body; ~ meclisi house, chamber; ~ yetkisi legislative power.

yasamak to legislate.

yasamalı legislative.

yasasız illegal, unlawful, illegitimate, illicit.

yasemin [- . -] 1. ✿ jasmine; 2. ♀ *wf.*

yaslamak to lean, to prop.

yaslanmak 1. to lean (-e against), to prop o.s. (-e against); 2. *fig.* to rely (-e on), to count (-e on).

yaslı in mourning.

yassı flat.

yassılaşmak to flatten (out).

yassılık flatness.

yastık 1. pillow; cushion; 2. seedbed (for plants); 3. ⊕ buffer, cushion; ~ kılıfı (or yüzü) pillowcase, tick.

yaş¹ age; ~ günü birthday; ~ haddi 1. age limit; 2. retirement age; -ı ne, başı ne? he's still wet behind the ears; -ı tutmamak to be under age; -ına başına bakmadan regardless of his age; -ında one year old; -ını (başını) almak to be old; kaç yaşındasınız? how old are you?; yirmi yaşındayım I am twenty years old.

yaş² 1. damp; moist; 2. fresh (fruit); 3. tears; 4. *sl.* bad, rough, tough; ~ akıtmak (or dökmek) to shed tears, to weep, to cry; ~ tahtaya basmak *fig.* to be duped (or taken in); -lara boğulmak to cry one's eyes out, to burst into tears, to cry buckets.

yaşa hurrah!, hurray!

yaşam life; ~ biçimi way of life.

yaşamak 1. to live; 2. to live, to inhabit; 3. to live well, to enjoy life; to live in clover; 4. to experience, to have, to enjoy.

yaşamöyküsü, -nü biography.

yaşamsal vital.

yaşantı life.

yaşarmak *(for one's eyes)* to fill with tears, to water.

yaşatmak *caus. of* yaşamak. *part.* to keep alive.

yaşayış way of living, life.

yaşıt, -tı of the same age; contemporary.

yaşlanmak to grow old, to age.

yaşlı[1] teary, tearful.

yaşlı[2] old, aged, elderly; ~ başlı elderly.

yaşlık damp(ness), moistness.

yaşlılık old age, senility.

yaşmak yas(h)mak, veil.

yaşmaklı veiled.

yat[1], -tı yacht; ~ kulübü yacht club; ~ limanı marina.

yat[2]: ~ borusu X taps, tattoo.

yatağan yataghan.

yatak 1. bed; 2. mattress; 3. bed *(of a river, lake)*; 4. den, lair, hide-out, hideaway *(of thieves)*; 5. bed, seam, vein *(of a mineral)*; 6. ⊕ bearing; 7. chamber *(of a gun)*; ~ çarşafı bed sheet; ~ liman big harbo(u)r; ~ odası bedroom; ~ örtüsü bedspread; ~ takımı bedding; ~ yüzü (bed)tick; yatağa düşmek to be bedfast, to be laid up, to take to one's bed *(because of illness)*; yatağa girmek to go to bed, to turn in; yatağını yapmak *(b-nin)* to make up s.o.'s bed; to prepare a bed for *s.o.;* ~-lar çekmek to feel like hitting the sack.

yatakhane [. . - .] dormitory.

yataklı 1. furnished with a bed *or* beds; 2. 🚃 sleeping car, sleeper; ~ vagon 🚃 sleeping car, sleeper.

yataklık etm. to receive and conceal *(stolen goods)*; to harbo(u)r *(a criminal)*.

yatalak bedridden, bedfast.

yatay horizontal.

yatı overnight stay; -ya gelmek to make an overnight visit, to come for an overnight stay.

yatık 1. leaning to one side; 2. low-lying; ~ yaka turndown collar.

yatılı 1. boarding *(school)*; 2. boarding student, boarder; ~ okul boarding school.

yatır place where a saint is buried.

yatırım ♀ investment; deposit.

yatırımcı ♀ investor; depositor.

yatırmak *caus. of* yatmak. *part.* 1. to put to bed; 2. to accommodate, to bed (down) *(an overnight guest)*; 3. to put s.o. in *(hospital)*; 4. to lay flat; 5. to invest, to deposit *(money)*.

yatısız day *(school, student)*.

yatışmak to die down, to subside; to calm down.

yatıştırıcı sedative, tranquilizing.

yatıştırmak to calm, to soothe, to tranquilize, to mollify, to appease, to allay.

yatkı wrinkle, crease.

yatkın susceptible (-e to); predisposed (-e to), inclined (-e to).

yatmak, (-ar) 1. to go to bed, to turn in; 2. to be lying down, to be in bed; 3. to keep to one's bed; to be bedridden; 4. to lie (flat); 5. to stay (-de in), to remain (-de in); 6. to enter, to go into *(hospital)*; 7. to lean to *(one side)*; 8. *(for a ship)* to list; 9. to be in prison; 10. to have sex, to sleep with; yatıp kalkmak 1. to sleep (-de in); 2. to have sex *(ile* with), to sleep *(ile* with).

yatsı time about two hours after sunset; ~ namazı isl. the ritual prayer performed two hours after sunset.

yavan 1. tasteless, insipid, flavo(u)rless *(food)*; 2. dry *(bread)*; 3. *fig.* vapid, dull, insipid.

yavanlaşmak to go flat, to lose its savo(u)r.

yavaş 1. slow; 2. soft, quiet; 3. gentle, mild; ~ gel! slow down!, take it easy!; ~ tütün mild tobacco; ~ ~ 1. slowly; 2. gradually, bit by bit.

yavaşça [. x .] 1. slowly; 2. quietly, softly.

yavaşçacık [. x . .] 1. rather slowly; 2. rather quietly.

yavaşlamak to slow down.

yavaşlatmak to slow (down); to slacken; to retard.

yavaşlık 1. slowness; 2. quietness, softness; 3 gentleness.

yave [ā] nonsense, rot, bunk.

yaver [ā] 1. helper, assistant; 2. X aide-de-camp; ~ gitmek to go well.

yavru 1. young animal; 2. child; 3. *sl.* chick, bird; ~ atmak *(for an animal)* to abort; -m! darling!, dear!, honey!

yavruağzı, -nı pinkish orange.

yavrucak poor little dear *(said of a child)*.

yavrucuk sweet little darling *(said of a child)*.

yavrukurt cub (scout).

yavrulamak to bring forth young.

yavşak nit.

yavuklamak P to give a token of betrothal.

yavuklanmak P to get engaged.

yavuklu P fiancé; fiancée.

yavuz 1. stern, tough; 2. gutsy, tough; 3. ♀ *mf.*

yay 1. bow; 2. ⊕ spring; 3. ⅄ arc, curve; 4. ♀ *ast* Sagittarius, the Archer.

yaya pedestrian; ~ bırakmak *(b-ni) fig.* to leave *s.o.* in the lurch; ~ geçidi **1.** pedestrian *(or* zebra) crossing, crosswalk; **2.** footbridge; ~ kaldırımı pavement, *Am.* sidewalk; ~ kalmak *fig.* to be left in the lurch.

yayan **1.** on foot; **2.** *fig.* uninformed; ~ gitmek to go on foot; ~ yapıldak bare-footed and travel(l)ing on foot.

yaygara howl, clamo(u)r; hullabaloo; ~yı basmak (*or* koparmak) to make a great to-do about nothing.

yaygaracı noisy person, brawler, crybaby, roisterer.

yaygı ground cloth.

yaygın widespread; prevalent.

yayginlaşmak to become widespread.

yayık[1] churn.

yayık[2] spread out; wide, broad; ~ ~ konuşmak to drawl.

yayılı spread (out).

yayılmak **1.** *pass. of* yaymak; **2.** to spread; **3.** to sprawl, to stretch out; **4.** to widen; **5.** to graze, to pasture.

yayım **1.** publication; **2.** broadcasting.

yayımcı publisher.

yayımcılık publishing.

yayımlamak **1.** to publish; **2.** to broadcast.

yayın **1.** publication; **2.** broadcast.

yayın(balığı) *zo.* sheatfish.

yayınevi, -ni publishing house.

yayla [x .] high plateau, wold.

yaylak mountain pasture.

yaylanmak **1.** to spring, to bounce; **2.** *sl.* to go away, to beat it.

yaylı **1.** having springs, sprung; **2.** ♪ played with a bow *(instrument);* **3.** spring-carriage.

yaylım **1.** *vn. of* yayılmak; **2.** *s.* yaylak; ~ ateşi X volley (fire), fussillade.

yayma **1.** *vn. of* yaymak; **2.** small trader's stall.

yaymak, (-ar) **1.** to spread; **2.** to scatter, to spread; **3.** to disseminate, to broadcast, to spread; **4.** to spread *(disease);* **5.** to take to pasture *(animals).*

yayvan broad and shallow; ~ ~ with a drawl *(speaking).*

yaz summer; ~ kış summer and winter, all the year round; ~ saati summer time, daylight saving time; ~ tarifesi summer time-table.

yazar writer; author.

yazarlık authorship.

yazgı destiny, fate, ordinance, predestination.

yazı[1] **1.** writing; **2.** article; **3.** handwriting; **4.** alphabet; **5.** *fig.* destiny, fate, ordi-

nance; ~ dili literary language; ~ makinesi typewriter; ~ masası writing table; ~ mı, tura mı? heads or tails?; ~ tahtası blackboard; ~ tura atmak to flip up, to toss up; ~ yazmak to write; -ya dokmek to indite; -yı çıkarmak (*or* sökmek) to be able to decipher s.o.'s handwriting.

yazı[2] plain.

yazıbilim graphology.

yazıcı **1.** scribe; copyist, transcriber; **2.** *cinema:* screenwriter, scriptwriter; **3.** ⊕ recorder.

yazıhane [. . - .] **1.** office; **2.** office desk.

yazık **1.** pity, shame; **2.** what a pity!, what a shame!; ~ etm. to spoil, to ruin; -lar olsun! shame!

yazıklanmak to pity; to be sorry (-*e* for).

yazıksız *P* innocent, sinless.

yazılı **1.** written; **2.** registered, enrolled; **3.** fated, destined to happen; **4.** written examination; ~ sınav written examination.

yazım spelling.

yazın[1] literature.

yazın[2] [x .] in summer, during the summer.

yazıncı literary man, man of letters, writer, author.

yazınsal literary.

yazışmak to correspond, to write to each other.

yazıt, -tı inscription; epitaph.

yazlık **1.** summer house *(or* place); **2.** summer..., estival; yazlığa gitmek to go to one's summer house.

yazma **1.** *vn. of* yazmak; **2.** handwritten manuscript; **3.** handwritten; **4.** hand-painted; hand-printed *(cloth);* **5.** hand-painted cloth; hand-printed cloth.

yazmak, (-ar) **1.** to write; **2.** to register, to enroll; yaz boz tahtası school slate.

yazman secretary.

yedek **1.** spare, reserve; standby; **2.** towrope; towline; ~ (*or* -te) çekmek to tow; ~ parça spare part; ~ subay reserve officer; yedeğe almak to tow, to take in tow.

yedi seven; ~ canlı invincible; ~ düvel **1.** the Great Powers; **2.** *fig.* everybody, all and sundry; ~ kat el *F* total stranger; ~ kubbeli hamam kurmak *fig.* to build castles in the air; ~ mahalle *fig.* everybody and his brother; -sinden yetmişine kadar everybody from nine to ninety.

yediemin [. . . -] ʤ̌ sequester, depositary, trustee.

yedigen **1.** heptagon; **2.** heptagonal.

**yedili** *cards:* the seven.
**yedinci** seventh.
**yedirmek** **1.** *caus. of* yemek; **2.** to feed; **3.** to let absorb.
**yedişer** seven each *(or* apiece); ~ ~ seven at a time.
**yediveren** ⚘ everblooming *(plant).*
**yedmek,** (-er) **1.** to tow; **2.** to lead *(an animal).*
**yegâne** sole, only, single.
**yeğ** preferable, better; ~ tutmak to prefer.
**yeğen** nephew; niece.
**yeğinlik** *phys.* intensity.
**yeğlemek** to prefer.
**yeis,** -e'si despair.
**yek,** -ki ⚒ one.
**yekdiğeri,** -ni each other, one another.
**yeknesak** monotonous.
**yeknesaklık** monotony.
**yekpare** in one piece; compact.
**yeksan** [ā] level *(ile* with); ~ etm. to level to the ground.
**yekta** [ā] **1.** unique, peerless, matchless; **2.** ♀ *mf., wf.*
**yekten** [x.] all at once; suddenly.
**yekûn** total, sum; ~ çekmek *F* to finish speaking.
**yel** **1.** wind; **2.** *P* flatus, wind, gas; **3.** *P* rheumatic pain; ~ yeperek yelken kürek *fig.* in a great hurry; -e vermek to throw away.
**yeldeğirmeni,** -ni windmill.
**yele** mane.
**yelek** **1.** waistcoat, vest; **2.** wing feather, pinion; **3.** feather *(of an arrow).*
**yeleli** maned.
**yelken** ⚓ sail; ~ açmak **1.** to hoist sail; **2.** to set sail; ~ bezi sailcloth; ~ gemisi sailing ship; -leri suya indirmek *fig.* to draw in one's horns.
**yelkenlemek** **1.** to set sail; **2.** *sl.* to vamoose, to make tracks.
**yelkenli** sailing ship; sailboat.
**yelkovan** **1.** minute-hand *(of a clock);* **2.** weather-cock.
**yellemek** to fan.
**yellenmek** **1.** *pass. of* yellemek; **2.** to break wind, to fart.
**yellim yelalim** *P* in great haste.
**yelloz** hussy, slut.
**yelmek,** (-er) to run in a fluster.
**yelpaze** [ā] fan.
**yelpazelemek** [ā] to fan.
**yelpazelenmek** [ā] **1.** *pass. of* yelpazelemek; **2.** to fan *o.s.*
**yelpik** *P* asthma.
**yeltek** fickle; inconstant.
**yeltenmek** to presume (-*e* to), to dare, to try.
**yem** **1.** feed; fodder; **2.** bait; **3.** primer *(for a gun);* ~ borusu **1.** ⚔ bugle call for horse fodder; **2.** *fig.* empty promise; ~ torbası nose *(or* feed) bag.
**yemek¹** **1.** food; meal; **2.** dish; **3.** dinner, supper; banquet; ~ borusu **1.** *anat.* esophagus; **2.** ⚔ mess call; ~ çıkarmak to serve food; ~ kitabı cookery-book, *Am.* cockbook; ~ masası dining table; ~ odası dining room; ~ pişirmek to cook; ~ seçmek to be choosy in eating; to be a picky eater; ~ yapmak to cook; ~ yemek to eat.
**yemek²** **1.** to eat; **2.** to spend *(money);* **3.** to bite; **4.** to corrode, to eat; **5.** to consume, to use up; **6.** *F* to kill, to do in; ye kürküm ye! fine feathers make fine birds; yeme de yanında yat! *sl.* it's finger-licking good!; yemeden içmeden *fig.* without losing any time; yemeden içmeden kesilmek to be off one's food, to have no appetite; yiyecek gibi bakmak to leer (-*e* at); yiyip bitirmek **1.** to eat up; **2.** to squander *(money).*
**yemekhane** [ā] dining hall.
**yemekli:** ~ vagon 🚃 dining car, diner.
**yemeni** **1.** hand-printed scarf *or* handkerchief; **2.** a kind of light shoe.
**yemin** [ī] oath; ~ billah etm. to swear to God; ~ etm. to swear; to take an oath; ~ ettirmek *(or* verdirmek) to administer an oath (-*e* to), to swear.
**yeminli** [. - .] under oath; sworn in; ~ tercüman certified *(or* official) interpreter.
**yemiş** **1.** dried fruit; **2.** nut; **3.** *P* fig; ~ vermek to bear fruit.
**yemişçi** fruiterer.
**yemlemek** **1.** to feed; **2.** to bait; **3.** to prime *(a gun).*
**yemlik** **1.** nose *(or* feed) bag; **2.** feedbox, manger; **3.** *fig.* bribe.
**yemyeşil** [x..] very green.
**yen** **1.** cuff; **2.** sleeve; **3.** ⚘ spathe; **4.** yen *(Japanese monetary unit).*
**yenge** [x.] **1.** affinal aunt, uncle's wife; **2.** sister-in-law, brother's wife.
**yengeç,** -ci **1.** *zo.* crab; **2.** ♀ *ast.* Cancer.
**yengi** victory.
**yeni** **1.** new; **2.** recent; **3.** newly; recently; ~ evliler newlyweds; ~ yetişen nesil the rising generation; -den *(or* ~ baştan) over again from the beginning.
**yeniay** *ast.* new moon.
**yenibahar** ⚘ allspice.
**yenice** fairly new.

**yeniçeri** *hist.* **1.** the Janissary corps; **2.** Janissary.

**yeniden** again; ~ doğmak to revive.

**yenidünya 1.** ♀ loquat; **2.** ♀ the New World.

**yenik 1.** defeated; **2.** moth-eaten hole; **3.** eroded; ~ düşmek to be defeated; kurt yeniği wormhole.

**yenilemek 1.** to renew, to renovate, to restore; to replenish; **2.** to renew (*a contract*); **3.** to repeat, to reiterate.

**yenilgi** defeat, beating; -ye uğramak to suffer defeat, to get a beating.

**yenilik 1.** newness; **2.** innovation; renewal; novelty; **3.** inexperience, greenness; ~ korkusu *psych.* neophobia; ~ yapmak to make a change.

**yenilikçi** innovator.

**yenilmek 1.** *pass. of* yemek²; **2.** *pass. of* yenmek²; yenilir yutulur gibi değil it is not to be stomached.

**yenişememek** to be unable to defeat each other.

**yeniyetme** adolescent.

**yeniyetmelik** adolescence.

**yenmek¹** *pass. of* yemek.

**yenmek²** to overcome, to conquer; to beat.

**yepyeni** [x . .] brand-new.

**yer 1.** place, spot; location; position; **2.** space, room; **3.** seat; **4.** place, position (*of employment*); **5.** *fig.* importance; **6.** the ground, the earth; **7.** floor; **8.** piece of land (*or* property); **9.** the earth; **10.** area, region, terrain; ~ açmak to make way (-e for); to make room; ~ almak **1.** to be situated (*or* located) (-de in); **2.** to take part (-de in), to be involved (-de in); ~ belirteci *gr.* adverb of place; ~ cücesi short but cunning; ~ etm. **1.** to leave a mark (-de on); **2.** to impress itself in; to be branded on (*s.o.'s mind*); ~ odası ground-floor room; ~ tutmak **1.** to take up space; **2.** to reserve a place; **3.** *fig.* to be of importance, to have an important place; ~ vermek **1.** to give s.o. a seat, to vacate one's seat; **2.** to include, to discuss (*in a book or speech*); ~ yarılıp içine girmek to vanish (*or* disappear *or* melt) into thin air; ~ yatağı bed spread on the floor; pallet; ~ ~ in places; here and there; ~ yurt place to live in, home; ~ zarfı *s.* ~ belirteci; -de instead of; -de kalmak *fig.* not to be appreciated; (**yerden**): ~ bitme squat, dumpy; ~ göğe kadar infinitely, greatly; ~ yapma squat, dumpy; ~ -e çalmak to throw (*or* hurl) to the ground; ~ -e vurmak (*b-ni*) *fig.* to chew *s.o.* out; (**yere**):

~ bakan yürek yakan butter wouldn't melt in his (*or* her) mouth, wolf in sheep's clothing; ~ bakmak *fig.* to have one foot in the grave; ~ göğe koyamamak *fig.* to hono(u)r greatly; ~ sermek (*b-ni*) to knock *s.o.* flying, to knock *s.o.* to the ground; (**yeri**): ~ olm. to be the right moment *or* time *or* place for s.th.; ~ öpmek *co.* to fall to the ground; ~ soğumadan *fig.* shortly after leaving one's place; ~ yurdu belirsiz homeless, vagrant; (**yerin**): ~ dibine geçmek to feel like 30 cents, to feel like sinking through the floor; ~ kulağı var walls have ears; (**yerinde**): ~ saymak *fig.* to mark time; ~ y-tler esmek to be gone with the wind, to have vanished; (**yerinden**): ~ ayrılmak to leave one's place; ~ oynamak **1.** to move from, to budge from, to stir from; **2.** to come (*or* get) loose; (**yerine**): ~ bakmak (*b-ni*) to stand in for *s.o.*; ~ geçmek to replace; ~ getirmek to carry out, to execute, to perform, to fulfil(l); ~ koymak to look on *s.o.* as, to regard *s.o.* as; (**yerini**): ~ bulmak to find one's place (*or* niche); ~ doldurmak (*b-nin*) *fig.* to fill *s.o.'s* shoes; ~ tutmak to be able to be used in place of another; (**yerle**): ~ beraber (*or* bir) leveled to the ground, razed; ~ bir etm. to level to the ground, to raze; ~ gök bir olsa no matter what happens, even if the sky should fall; yerlerde sürünmek to be down-and-out; yerlere kadar eğilmek *fig.* to bow and scrape; yerleri süpürmek to trail (*or* drag) on the ground (*long skirt, etc.*).

**yeraltı,** -nı underground; ~ geçidi underground passageway, subway; ~ örgütü underground; ~ sığınağı bunker; ~ suyu *geol.* subterranean water.

**yerbilim** geology.

**yerbilimci** geologist.

**yerçekimi,** -ni *phys.* gravity.

**Yerebatan Sarayı** *pr. n.* the underground cistern.

**yerel** local; ~ seçim *pol.* local election.

**yerelleştirmek** to localize.

**yerelması,** -nı ♀ Jerusalem artichoke.

**yerfıstığı,** -nı ♀ groundnut, peanut.

**yergi** satire.

**yergici** satirist.

**yerici 1.** critical, faultfinding; **2.** satirical.

**yerinde 1.** apt, appropriate; **2.** well-timed, timely; **3.** good, fine; **4.** old enough to be.

**yerine 1.** instead of, in place of; in lieu of; **2.** on behalf of, for, in the name of.

**yerinmek** to feel sad (*or* sorry) (*-e* about); to regret.

**yerkabuğu,** -nu *geol.* crust of the earth.

**yerküre 1.** the earth; **2.** globe.

**yerleşik 1.** settled, established; sedentary; **2.** endemic.

**yerleşim** settlement.

**yerleşmek 1.** to fit in; **2.** to get established in (*one's job*); **3.** to settle *o.s.* in (*a chair, etc.*); to get established in (*a new home*); **4.** to move into, to settle in (*a place*); **5.** to take root, to catch on.

**yerleştirmek 1.** *caus.* of yerleşmek; **2.** to place, to set, to put, to fit; **3.** to place, to put, to install *s.o.* in (*a job*); **4.** to deploy (*a missile*); **5.** to land, to plant (*a blow*).

**yerli 1.** local; native; indigenous; **2.** domestic; **3.** immovable, built-in (*piece of furniture*); ~ mal(ı) local product; ~ yerinde in apple-pie order.

**yermantarı,** -nı ♀ truffle.

**yermek,** (-er) **1.** to criticize, to run down, to speak ill of; **2.** to satirize; to deride; **3.** to condemn; to disapprove.

**yermeli** pejorative (*word*).

**yermerkezli** geocentric.

**yersarsıntısı,** -nı earthquake.

**yersiz 1.** homeless; **2.** irrelevant; **3.** unsuitable, inappropriate.

**yersolucanı,** -nı *zo.* earthworm.

**yeryuvarlağı,** -nı the earth.

**yeryüzü,** -nü the world, the face of the earth.

**yeşermek 1.** to leaf out; **2.** to green, to turn green; **3.** *fig.* to appear, to emerge.

**yeşil 1.** green; **2.** *sl.* one hundred lira note.

**Yeşilay** *pr. n.* the Green Crescent.

**yeşilaycı** F teetotaller.

**yeşilimsi, yeşilimtırak** greenish.

**yeşillenmek 1.** to green; **2.** to leaf out.

**yeşillik 1.** greenness; **2.** meadow; **3.** greens.

**yeşim** jade, jasper.

**yetenek** ability, talent, capability, competence, capacity; aptitude; ~ testi aptitude test.

**yetenekli** talented, capable, competent, able.

**yeteneksiz** untalented, incapable, incompetent; inept.

**yeteneksizlik** inability, incapability, incompetence.

**yeter 1.** enough, sufficient; **2.** that's enough!; -i kadar **1.** enough, sufficient, adequate; **2.** enough, sufficiently.

**yeterince 1.** enough, sufficient; **2.** enough, sufficiently.

**yeterli** enough, sufficient, adequate.

**yeterlik** adequacy, competence, qualification; sufficiency.

**yetersayı** quorum.

**yetersiz** insufficient, inadequate; ~ beslenme malnutrition, undernourishment.

**yetersizlik** insufficiency, inadequacy.

**yetim** [î] orphan.

**yetimhane** [. - - .] orphanage.

**yetinmek** (*bşle*) to be content with *s.th.*, to be satisfied with *s.th.*

**yetişkin** adult, grown-up.

**yetişmek 1.** to catch; **2.** to reach; to attain; to arrive; **3.** to catch up (*-e* with); **4.** to be enough, to suffice; **5.** (*for a plant*) to grow; **6.** (*for a person or animal*) to grow up; **7.** to be educated; yetiş(in)! help!

**yetişmiş 1.** mature, grown-up; **2.** trained; experienced.

**yetiştirici** producer, raiser, grower.

**yetiştirmek 1.** *caus.* of yetişmek; **2.** to raise, to bring up, to educate; **3.** to train; **4.** to convey (*news*).

**yetki** authority, authorization, warrant; askeri valiye tam ~ verildi the military governer has been invested with full authority.

**yetkili 1.** authorized; **2.** competent; **3.** authority; ~ merci ♂♂ competent authority.

**yetkin** perfect.

**yetkisiz 1.** unauthorized; **2.** incompetent.

**yetmek,** (-er) to be enough, to suffice, to do.

**yetmiş** seventy.

**yetmişer** seventy each (*or* apiece); ~ ~ seventy at a time.

**yetmişinci** seventieth.

**yetmişlik** septuagenarian.

**yevmiye** daily wage; ~ defteri † daybook.

**yezit** F scamp, devil, dickens.

**yığılı** heaped, piled, stacked.

**yığılışma** crowd, throng.

**yığılmak 1.** *pass.* of yığmak; **2.** to collapse in a heap; **3.** to crowd around.

**yığın 1.** heap, pile, stack; **2.** crowd, mass, throng, passel (*of people*); -la a heap of, a lot of.

**yığınak 1.** × concentration; **2.** ♀ colony.

**yığıntı** mass; heap, pile.

**yığışık** massed.

**yığışım** *geol.* conglomerate.

**yığışmak** to crowd together; to amass, to accumulate.

**yığmak,** (-ar) **1.** to heap (up), to pile (up), to stack (up); **2.** to amass, to accumulate, to concentrate.

**yıkamak 1.** to wash, to bath(e); to lave;

to launder; **2.** *phot.* to develop *(film).*

**yıkanmak 1.** *pass. of* yıkamak; **2.** to wash o.s., to take a bath, to bath(e).

**yıkayıcı 1.** washer; **2.** *phot.* developer.

**yıkıcı 1.** destructive; subversive; **2.** wrecker.

**yıkık 1.** ruined; **2.** demolished, destroyed.

**yıkılmak 1.** *pass. of* yıkmak; **2.** to collapse; **3.** to ccllapse in a heap, to fall to the ground; **4.** to wither *(hopes)*; **5.** *fig.* to clear out, to leave; yıkıl karşımdan! clear cut!, get lost!

**yıkım 1.** ruin, destruction; **2.** disaster; catastrophe.

**yıkımlık** damage.

**yıkıntı** ruin(s), debris.

**yıkkın** about to collapse, in ruins.

**yıkmacı** wrecker.

**yıkmak,** (-ar) **1.** to demolish, to wreck, to pull down, to destroy, to ruin; **2.** to overthrow; **3.** to topple; to lay s.o. flat; **4.** to tilt; **5.** to put *(the blame)* on s.o.

**yıl** year; -lar -ı for years.

**yılan 1.** *zo.* snake; serpent; viper; **2.** *fig.* snake in the grass, viper; ~ gibi malevolent and sneaky *(person)*; ~ gömleği slough; ~ sokması snakebite.

**yılanbalığı,** -nı *zo.* eel.

**yılancık 1.** small snake; **2.** ℣ erysipelas.

**yılankavi** [. . - -] serpentine, winding; ~ akmak to meander.

**yılbaşı,** -nı New Year's Day.

**yıldırım 1.** thunderbolt, lightning; **2.** ♀ *mf;* ~ gibi like lightning, with lightning speed; ~ savaşı blitzkrieg; ~ siperi lightning rod; ~ telgrafı urgent telegram; -la vurulmuşa dönmek to be thunderstruck.

**yıldırımkıran, yıldırımlık, yıldırımsavar** lightning rod.

**yıldırmak 1.** *caus. of* yılmak; **2.** to daunt; to cow; to intimidate; **3.** to terrorize.

**yıldız 1.** star; **2.** ⬇ north; ~ akmak *(or* kaymak *or* uçmak) *(for a shooting star)* to fall; ~ anasonu ♀ star aniseed, badian; ~ yılı *ast.* sidereal year; -ı dişi *fig.* popular; -ı parlak lucky; -ları barışmak to get along well with each other.

**yıldızbilim** astrology.

**yıldızböceği,** -ni *zo.* firefly.

**yıldızciçeği,** -ni ♀ dahlia.

**yıldızkarayel** ⬇ **1.** north-northwest wind; **2.** north-northwest.

**yıldızlı 1.** starry, starlit; **2.** starred.

**yıldızpoyraz** ⬇ **1.** north-northeast wind; **2.** north-northeast.

**yıldönümü,** -nü anniversary.

**yılgı** terror.

**yılgın 1.** daunted; intimidated; **2.** terror-

ized; terror-struck.

**yılışık** obtrusive, saucy, importunate, pert, smarmy; ~ ~ smarmily.

**yılışmak 1.** to grin *(or* smirk) smarmily; **2.** to smarm.

**yıllanmak 1.** to age, to grow old; **2.** to become a year old.

**yıllanmış 1.** aged, mellow *(wine)*; **2.** old *(thing)*.

**yıllık 1.** yearbook, annual; **2.** yearly salary; yearly fee; **3.** ... years old; **4.** yearly, annual; **5.** for one year.

**yılmak,** (-ar) to be daunted (-*den* by), to be intimidated (-*den* by).

**yılmaz 1.** undaunted; **2.** ♀ *mf.*

**yıpranmak 1.** to get worn-out, to wear out; **2.** to become burned-out *(or* worn-out).

**yıpratıcı** gruel(l)ing, exhausting, wearing.

**yıpratmak** to wear out, to burn out.

**yırılmak** P to split.

**yırmak,** (-ar) P to tear, to split.

**yırtıcı 1.** predatory, predacious; **2.** *fig.* blood-thirsty *(person)*; ~ hayvan beast of prey; ~ kuş bird of prey.

**yırtık 1.** torn, ripped, rent; **2.** tear, rip, rent; **3.** *fig.* shameless, brazen(faced); ~ pırtık in rags.

**yırtılmak 1.** *pass. of* yırtmak; **2.** to overcome one's shyness; **3.** *sl.* to fork over *(money).*

**yırtınmak 1.** to wear o.s. to a frazzle, to run o.s. ragged; **2.** to shout at the top of one's voice.

**yırtmaç,** -cı slit, vent *(in a garment).*

**yırtmaçlı** having a slit *(or* vent).

**yırtmak,** (-ar) **1.** to tear, to rip, to rend; **2.** to tear, to lacerate; **3.** to break in *(a colt).*

**yısa** [x .] hoist away!; ~ beraber! hoist together!; ~ etm. *(halatı)* to heave in *(a rope)*; ~ ~ at the very most.

**yiğit,** -di **1.** brave, bold, courageous; **2.** young man, young buck.

**yiğitlenmek** to pluck up courage.

**yiğitlik** bravery, courage; yiğitliğe leke sürmemek to save one's face.

**yine 1.** (once) again, once more; **2.** nevertheless, still.

**yinelemek** to repeat.

**yirmi** twenty; ~ yaş dişi *anat.* wisdom tooth.

**yirmilik 1.** twenty-lira note; **2.** twenty-year old.

**yirminci** twentieth.

**yirmişer** twenty each *(or* apiece); ~ ~ twenty at a time.

yisa *s.* yısa.

yitik lost, missing.

yitim loss.

yitirmek 1. *caus. of* yitmek; 2. to lose.

yitmek, (-er) to be lost (*or* missing); to disappear, to vanish.

ylv 1. groove, chamfer; 2. ⊕ thread; 3. flute (*on a column*).

yivli 1. grooved, chamfered; 2. ⊕ threaded; 3. fluted (*column*).

yiyecek food, edible, comestible.

yiyici 1. (*animal*) which feeds on (*a specified food*); 2. *fig.* taker of bribes, bribee.

yiyinti food.

yo [-] no.

yobaz 1. fanatic, bigot; 2. fogy, mossback.

yobazlaşmak to become fanatical.

yobazlık 1. fanaticism, bigotry; 2. fogyism.

yoga yoga.

yogi yogi.

yoğalmak to disappear.

yoğaltım consumption.

yoğaltmak to consume, to use up.

yoğun 1. dense, thick; 2. intensive, intense.

yoğunlaşmak 1. to densen, to thicken; 2. to intensify.

yoğunlaştırmak 1. to densen, to thicken; 2. to intensify.

yoğunluk 1. density, thickness; 2. intensity.

yoğurmak to knead.

yoğurt, -du yog(h)urt, yoghourt.

yoğurtçu maker *or* seller of yogurt.

yoğurtotu, -nu ♣ bedstraw.

yok, -ku *or* -ğu 1. non-existent; 2. absent; unavailable; 3. no (*negative reply*); 4. but if not...; ~ canım! F 1. you're kidding?, really?; 2. I wouldn't think of it!; 3. unbelievable!; ~ denecek kadar az next to nothing; ~ devenin başı! you're pulling my leg!; ~ etm. to do away with, to stamp out, to eradicate; ~ oğlu ~ F non-existent; ~ olm. to disappear, to vanish; to die out; ~ pahasına for nothing, for a song; ~ yere without reason; -tan from nothing; müdür yokken işin başında ben olurum in the absence of the manager I am in charge of the business.

yoklama 1. *vn. of* yoklamak; 2. roll call; 3. quiz; ~ yapmak to call the roll, to call over.

yoklamak 1. to search; to inspect; 2. to feel with the fingers, to finger; 3. to sound out; 4. to visit; 5. (*for an illness,*

*a pain*) to recur, to reappear.

yokluk 1. non-existence; 2. absence; 3. poverty.

yoksa [x .] 1. or; 2. otherwise, or else, if not; daha hızlı çalış, ~ patron seni kapı dışarı eder work faster or else the boss will give you the sack.

yoksul poor, destitute.

yoksullaşmak to become poor.

yoksullaştırmak to impoverish.

yoksulluk poverty, destitution, impoverishment.

yoksun deprived (-*den* of), bereft (-*den* of); ~ bırakmak to deprive (-*den* of), to bereave (-*den* of); ~ kalmak to be deprived (*or* bereft) (-*den* of).

yoksunluk deprivation.

yoksunmak to be deprived (*or* bereft) (-*den* of).

yokuş upward slope; hill; rise; ~ aşağı downhill; ~ yukarı uphill.

yol 1. road, way; path; course; route; passage; 2. manner, style; 3. method, system, 4. way, means; solution; 5. speed (*of a ship*); 6. stripe (*in cloth*); 7. time; ~ açmak 1. to open a road; 2. *fig.* to bring about, to give rise (-*e* to); ~ almak to proceed, to move forward; ~ aramak to look for a way (*to solve a problem*); ~ arkadaşı fellow-travel(l)er; ~ boyunca 1. along the road; 2. during the trip; ~ halısı hall rug, runner; ~ harcı travel allowance; ~ vermek 1. to make way (-*e* for); 2. (*b-ne*) *fig.* to fire s.o., to give s.o. the sack; ~ yakınken *fig.* before it's too late; ~ ~ striped (*cloth*); ~ yordam manners, behavio(u)r; ~ yürümek to walk; (yola): ~ çıkmak (*or* düzülmek *or* koyulmak) to set off (*or* out), to hit the road; ~ düşmek to set out for (*a place*); ~ germek (*or* yatmak) to come round; to see reason; ~ getirmek (*or* yatırmak) to bring round; to persuade; ~ gitmek to take a trip; ~ vurmak P to see off; yolda kalmak to be delayed on the road; yoldan çıkmak 1. to be derailed (*train*); to go off the road (*car*); 2. *fig.* to go astray; (yolu): ~ almak to reach the end of one's journey; ~ düşmek to happen to pass, to happen on, to chance on; yolun(uz) açık olsun! have a good trip!, bon voyage!; (yoluna): ~ bakmak (*b-nin*) to expect s.o., to await s.o.'s arrival; ~ çıkmak (*b-nin*) 1. to go to meet s.o.; 2. to meet s.o. by chance; ~ girmek to come all right; ~ koymak to put (*or* set) to rights; (yolunu): ~ beklemek (*b-nin*) to await *s.o.'s* arrival; ~ bulmak to find the way to do s.th.; ~ kaybetmek to lose one's way; ~ kesmek to stop, to waylay, to hold up; ~ sapıtmak *fig.* to go astray; ~ şaşırmak **1.** to take the wrong road, to lose one's way; **2.** *fig.* to go astray; -uyle **1.** by way of, via; **2.** by means of, through.

**yolcu 1.** travel(l)er; passenger; **2.** baby about to be born; **3.** sick person who is at death's door; ~ etm. to see off; ~ gemisi liner; ~ salonu passenger waiting room; ~ uçağı passenger aircraft.

**yolculuk** journey, trip; voyage; ~ etm. to travel; ~ ne zaman? when do you set out on your journey?

**yoldaş 1.** fellow travel(l)er; **2.** friend, companion; **3.** Communist, comrade.

**yolgeçen:** ~ hanı *used of a place which is much frequented.*

**yollamak** to send, to dispatch.

**yollanmak 1.** *pass. of* yollamak; **2.** to pick up speed.

**yollu 1.** having roads; **2.** striped *(cloth);* **3.** fast *(ship, etc.);* **4.** by way of; **5.** loose *(woman);* ~ yolsuz unlawful.

**yolluk 1.** food for a journey, victuals; **2.** hall rug, runner; **3.** travel allowance.

**yolmak,** (-ar) **1.** to pluck; **2.** to pull out, to tear out *(hair);* **3.** *fig.* to fleece, to milk, to bleed.

**yolsuz 1.** roadless; **2.** stripeless, unstriped *(cloth);* **3.** slow *(ship, etc.);* **4.** loose *(woman);* **5.** improper; unlawful, illegal; **6.** *sl.* flat broke, penniless.

**yolsuzluk 1.** lack of roads; **2.** irregularity, malpractice; graft; **3.** *sl.* pennilessness.

**yoluk** plucked *(chicken, etc.).*

**yolunmak 1.** *pass. of* yolmak; **2.** to tear one's hair with grief.

**yom** good luck; ~ tutmak to regard as lucky.

**yonca** ♣ clover, trefoil.

**yonda** down.

**yonga** chip, shaving *(of wood).*

**yont,** -tu unbroken mare.

**yontkuşu,** -nu *zo.* yellow wagtail.

**yontma 1.** *vn. of* yontmak; **2.** chiseled; hewn; ~ taş devri palaeolithic age.

**yontmak,** (-ar) **1.** to chisel; to hew, to whittle; to dress *(stone);* to sculpt; to chip; **2.** *fig.* to fleece.

**yontulmak 1.** *pass. of* yontmak; **2.** *fig.* to learn manners; yontulmamış *fig.* rough, uncouth.

**yordam 1.** agility; **2.** method, system; **3.** pomposity; swagger.

**yorga** jogtrot.

**yorgan** quilt, duvet, *Am.* comforter; ~ gitti, kavga bitti *iro.* the dispute is ended; ~ iğnesi quilting-needle.

**yorgancı** quilt-maker.

**yorgun** tired, weary, worn out; ~ argın dead tired, beat; ~ düşmek to be tired out; ~ ~ wearily.

**yorgunluk** tiredness, fatigue, weariness.

**yormak¹,** (-ar) to tire, to fatigue, to weary.

**yormak²,** (-ar) to interpret.

**yortmak** *P* to rove about.

**yortu** Christian feast.

**yorucu** tiring, tiresome, wearisome.

**yorulmak** to get tired, to tire.

**yorum** interpretation, commentary.

**yorumlamak** to interpret.

**yosma** loose woman.

**yosun** ♣ moss; alga.

**yosunlanmak** to moss, to get mossy.

**yosunlu** mossy.

**yoz 1.** uncultivated, virgin *(forest, land);* **2.** boorish, uncouth *(person);* **3.** degenerate; decadent.

**yozlaşmak** to degenerate.

**yozlaştırmak** to degenerate; to debase.

**yön 1.** direction; **2.** aspect, side; ~ vermek to give a direction (*-e* to); to direction; tarihî -den from the historical point of view.

**yönelim** inclination, tendency.

**yönelmek 1.** to head towards, to go towards; **2.** to incline towards.

**yöneltim** orientation.

**yöneltmek** to direct; to point (*-e* at).

**yönerge** directive; instructions.

**yönetici** manager; administrator.

**yöneticilik** management; administration.

**yönetim** management; administration; direction; government; ~ kurulu administrative committee, board of directors.

**yönetmek** to manage, to administer, to govern; to direct, to lead, to conduct; to control.

**yönetmelik** regulations, instructions, statutes.

**yönetmen** director *(a. thea., cinema);* manager.

**yönlendirmek** to direct, to orient, to steer.

**yöntem** method, system, procedure.

**yöntemli** methodical, systematic.

**yöntemsiz** unmethodical, unsystematic.

**yöre** vicinity, neighbo(u)rhood, region, environs.

**yöresel** local.

**yörünge** orbit; -sine oturmak to go into

orbit.

**yudum** sip, sup, gulp, swallow.

**yudumlamak** to sip.

**yuf** [ü] *int. expressing disgust; ~* borusu çalmak *(or ~* çekmek) to curse, to revile.

**yufka 1.** thin layer of dough; **2.** fragile, weak; ~ yürekli tender-hearted.

**Yugoslav** Yugoslav(ian).

**Yugoslavya** [..x.] *pr. n.* Yugoslavia.

**yuğmak** to wash.

**yuh(a)** boo!, ugh!, yuk!; ~ çekmek *(or* yuhaya tutmak) to boo, to jeer.

**yuhalamak** to boo, to jeer, to give s.o. the bird, to hoot.

**yukarı 1.** upper part; upstairs; **2.** upper; upstairs; **3.** up; -da above; upstairs; -da adı geçen above-mentioned, aforementioned; -dan **1.** from above, from upstairs; **2.** *fig.* from the boss; from the top (brass); -dan bakmak to look down (-e on); -dan aşağı süzmek *(b-ni)* to give s.o. the once-over.

**yulaf** 🌾 oat.

**yular** halter.

**yumak**[1] *s.* yıkamak.

**yumak**[2] ball *(of wool, etc.)*.

**yummak,** (-ar) to shut, to close *(eye)*; to clench, to double *(fist)*.

**yumru 1.** lump; knot; gnarl, knob; node; **2.** 🌾 tuber; ~ kök 🌾 tuber.

**yumruk 1.** fist; **2.** blow *(or* punch *or* sock) with the fist; **3.** *fig.* iron hand, fist; ~ atmak *(or* indirmek *or* vurmak) to hit *(or* punch *or* sock) with one's fist; ~ göstermek *fig.* to threaten; ~ hakkı s.th. gained by force; ~ kadar pea-sized, pint-sized; ~ yumruğa gelmek to come to blows; yumruğuna güvenmek to trust one's physical strength.

**yumruklamak** to hit with one's fist, to punch, to pummel, to sock.

**yumruklaşmak** to have a fist fight.

**yumrukoyunu,** -nu *sports:* boxing.

**yumrul(an)mak** to become knobby; to become nodular.

**yumuk** shut *(eye, mouth)*; clenched, doubled *(fist)*.

**yumulmak 1.** *pass. of* yummak; **2.** *(for* one's eyes) to shut, to close; to narrow; **3.** to hunch over, to hunker; **4.** to attack.

**yumurcak** brat, scamp, little dickens.

**yumurmak** to form a lump.

**yumurta 1.** egg; **2.** testicle, testis; ~ akı egg white, albumen; ~ kabuğu egg-shell; ~ kapıya dayanınca *fig.* when the chips are down; ~ sarısı yolk; -dan daha dün çıkmış *fig.* young and smart-alecky.

**yumurtacı** seller of eggs.

**yumurtacık** ovule.

**yumurtalık 1.** ovary; **2.** eggcup.

**yumurtlamak 1.** to lay (eggs); **2.** to ovulate; **3.** *fig.* to blurt out, to come out with *(a remark)*.

**yumuşacık** [x...] very soft, as soft as down.

**yumuşak** soft; tender; mild; gentle; ~ ağızlı that takes the bit easily *(horse)*; ~ başlı docile, mild; tractable; biddable; ~ iniş soft landing.

**yumuşaklık** softness; mildness.

**yumuşamak 1.** to soften; **2.** *fig.* to relent, to soften, to mellow, to unbend.

**yumuşatmak** to soften; to tenderize.

**Yunan** Greek, Grecian.

**Yunanca** [.x.] Greek.

**Yunanistan** *pr. n.* Greece.

**Yunanlı** Greek.

**yunus(balığı)** *zo.* dolphin.

**yurdu** eye of a needle.

**yurt,** -du **1.** native country, homeland; **2.** home; **3.** student dormitory, hostel; ~ bilgisi civics; ~ tutmak to settle in; yetiştirme yurdu orphanage.

**yurtlandırmak** to settle *(people)*.

**yurtlanmak 1.** to find a homeland; **2.** to settle in *(a place)*.

**yurtluk** country estate, domain.

**yurtsever 1.** patriotic; **2.** patriot.

**yurtseverlik** patriotism.

**yurttaş 1.** citizen; **2.** fellow countryman, compatriot.

**yurttaşlık** citizenship; ~ bilgisi civics.

**yusyumru** [x..] very round; very knobby.

**yusyuvarlak** [x...] as round as a ball *(or* top).

**yutak** *anat.* pharynx.

**yutkunmak** to swallow, to gulp.

**yutmak,** (-ar) **1.** to swallow, to gulp; **2.** *fig.* to swallow *(an insult)*; **3.** to believe, to fall for, to swallow; **4.** to beat, to skunk *(in a game)*; **5.** *fig.* to absorb *(knowledge)*.

**yutturmak 1.** *caus. of* yutmak; **2.** *(b-ne bşi)* to palm off *s.th.* on *s.o.*

**yuva 1.** nest; **2.** home; **3.** nursery school; **4.** den, nest *(of criminals)*; **5.** 🗲 socket; ~ kurmak to set up a home; -sını yapmak *(b-nin) fig.* to teach *s.o.* a lesson, to show *s.o.* a thing or two; -sını yıkmak *(b-nin) fig.* to break up *s.o.*'s marriage; -yı dişi kuş yapar *pro.* men make houses, women make homes.

**yuvak 1.** cylinder; **2.** stone roller.

**yuvalamak** to nest.

**yuvar** *biol.* corpuscle.

**yuvarlak** round, circular; globular, spherical; ~ hesap round figure; ~ sayı round number.

**yuvarlaklaşmak** to become round.

**yuvarlaklaştırmak** to round.

**yuvarlaklık** roundness; circularness.

**yuvarlamak 1.** to roll; **2.** to roll up; **3.** to round; **4.** to put away, to pack away, to polish off *(food)*; **5.** *F* to tell whoppers.

**yuvarlanmak 1.** *pass. of* yuvarlamak; **2.** to roll; to turn over and over; **3.** to fall (down); **4.** *fig.* to kick the bucket suddenly, to up and die; **5.** to get the sack *(or* push); yuvarlanan taş yosun tutmaz *pro.* a rolling stone gathers no moss; yuvarlanıp gitmek to rub along.

**yuvar yuvar** with a rolling motion.

**yuvgu** *s.* yuvak.

**yuvgulamak** to roll with a roller.

**yüce** exalted, high; lofty; eminent; sublime.

**yücelik** loftiness; eminence; sublimity.

**yücelmek** to become lofty *(or* exalted).

**yüceltmek** to exalt.

**yük, -kü 1.** load, burden; **2.** cargo; freight; lading; **3.** *fig.* burden; encumbrance; incubus; **4.** *phys.* charge; ~ asansörü goods lift, *Am.* freight elevator; ~ gemisi freighter; ~ hayvanı beast of burden; ~ olm. *(b-ne) fig.* to be a burden to *s.o.*; ~ treni goods train, *Am.* freight train; ~ vagonu goods wagon, *Am.* freight car; ~ vurmak to load *(an animal)*; -te hafif pahada ağır light in bulk, high in value; -ünü tutmak *fig.* to get rich, to make money.

**yükçü** porter.

**yüklem** *gr., log.* predicate.

**yüklemek 1.** to load, to freight; **2.** to lay *(a task)* on s.o., to burden s.o. with *(a task)*; **3.** *fig.* to lay *(or* put) *(the blame)* on s.o.

**yüklenmek 1.** *pass. of* yüklemek; **2.** to shoulder, to take on *(a burden, task, responsibility)*; **3.** to push, to press, to pressure.

**yükleyici** stevedore, longshoreman.

**yüklü 1.** loaded, freighted; **2.** overburdened with work; **3.** pregnant; **4.** *sl.* drunk, loaded; **5.** *sl.* rich, loaded.

**yüklük** large cupboard *(for bedding)*.

**yüksek 1.** high; lofty; **2.** high; great; big; **3.** noble, lofty; **4.** loud *(voice)*; **5.** high, superior; **6.** high place; height; ~ atlama *sports:* high jump; ~ basınç high pressure; ~ fiyat high price; ~ mühendis graduated engineer; ~ perdeden ko-

nuşmak *fig.* to talk big; 2 Seçim Kurulu Election Commission; ~ sesle aloud, loudly; ~ tansiyon high blood pressure; hypertension; -ten atınak to talk big; -ten bakmak *fig.* to look down one's nose *(-e* at); -ten uçmak *fig.* to chase after the impossible.

**yükseklik 1.** height; highness; **2.** altitude; elevation; **3.** loudness *(of a voice)*; **4.** high place, height.

**yüksekokul** college.

**yükseköğretim** higher education.

**yükselmek 1.** to rise, to ascend; **2.** to increase, to rise, to mount, to go up; **3.** to get louder *(voice)*; **4.** to advance, to rise; to come up in the world.

**yükselteç** *≶* amplifier.

**yükselti** altitude, elevation *(a. ast.)*.

**yükseltmek 1.** *caus. of* yükselmek; **2.** to raise, to elevate; to increase; **3.** *≶* to amplify; **4.** to promote.

**yüksük 1.** thimble; **2.** *♀* cupule.

**yüksükotu, -nu ♀** foxglove.

**yüksünmek** to regard as burdensome.

**yüküm** obligation, liability.

**yükümlü** obliged *(ile* to), obligated *(ile* to); bound *(ile* to).

**yükümlülük** obligation, liability.

**yün 1.** wool; **2.** wool, woolen.

**yünlü 1.** wool, woolen; **2.** woolen.

**yüpürmek** to run hither and thither.

**yürek 1.** heart; **2.** *fig.* courage, guts; **3.** *fig.* compassion, pity; ~ çarpıntısı **1.** palpitation of the heart, heartbeat; **2.** *fig.* anxiety; ~ vermek to give courage; to embolden; ~ yarası deep sorrow, heartbreak; **(yüreği):** ~ açık simple-hearted; sincere; ~ ağzına gelmek to have one's heart in one's mouth; ~ bayılmak to be starving *(or* caving in); ~ çarpmak *(for one's heart)* to palpitate; ~ dar impatient; ~ geniş carefree, happy-go-lucky; ~ kabarmak to feel nauseated; ~ kararmak to lose heart; ~ katılmak to gasp for breath; ~ parçalanmak *(for one's heart)* to be wrenched; ~ pek **1.** hardhearted; **2.** fearless; ~ sıkılmak to feel depressed *or* bored; **(yüreğine):** ~ dert olm. to take s.th. to heart; ~ inmek **1.** *(for a great sadness)* to kill, to deal a mortal blow; **2.** to die then and there; ~ işlemek to cut s.o. to the quick; **(yüreğini):** ~ pek tutmak to keep up one's courage; -ler acısı heartrending, heartbreaking, piteous; -ten from one's heart.

**yüreklendirmek** to give courage, to embolden.

yüreklenmek to take courage (or heart).
yürekli brave, courageous, stouthearted.
yüreksiz fainthearted, cowardly.
yürümek 1. to walk; 2. to march; 3. to hurry, to make haste; 4. to go on, to advance, to move forward; 5. to accumulate (interest); 6. to work, to function, to run (machine); 7. to die, to pass away; 8. to vanish; to be stolen; 9. to cross, to walk across; yürüyen merdiven moving staircase, Am. escalator.
yürürlük validity; operation; yürürlüğe girmek to come into force (or operation), to get into effect; -te olm. to be in operation (or force).
yürütmek 1. caus. of yürümek; 2. to perform, to carry out; 3. to get s.th. accepted; 4. to put forward (a thought, etc.); 5. to fire, to dismiss; 6. to put into force; 7. sl. to steal, to lift, to swipe, to nick, to pinch, to nip.
yürüyüş 1. walking; gait; 2. walk; 3. march; ~ yapmak 1. to go on a walk; 2. to hold a protest march; -e çıkmak to go out for a walk.
yüz¹ hundred; one hundred; -de ~ 1. one hundred percent; 2. sure, certain.
yüz² 1. face; 2. surface; 3. outer covering, case; 4. shame; 5. side; ~ bulmak to be emboldened; to get presumptuous; ~ bulunca astar ister s. ~ verince astar ister; ~ çevirmek fig. to turn one's back (-den on); ~ etm. 1. to hand over; 2. to face up (two things that are to be joined together); ~ göstermek to show up; ~ göz olm. (b-le) to make free with s.o.; ~ kızartıcı disgraceful, shameful; ~ tutmak to begin (-meğe to inf.); ~ verince astar ister give him an inch and he will take a yard (or mile); ~ vermek to indulge, to be indulgent (-e to); ~ vermemek (b-ne) to give s.o. the cold shoulder; ~ -e face to face; ~ -e gelmek to come face to face (ile with); (yüze): ~ çıkmak 1. to come to the surface; 2. fig. to get insolent; ~ gülmek to feign friendship; (yüzü): ~ ak alnı pak pure and honest; ~ asılmak to pull a long face; ~ gözü açılmak fig. to learn about the birds and the bees; ~ gülmek to be happy; ~ kızarmak to flush, to blush; ~ olmamak fig. not to have the face (or cheek) (-meğe to inf.); ~ pek brazenfaced, shameless; ~ sıcak attractive; ~ soğuk repulsive, repellent; ~ suyu hürmetine for the sake of; ~ tutmamak not to have the nerve (-meğe to inf.); ~ yazılı kalmak to remain untouched; ~ yerde

humble; ~ yere gelmek to feel ashamed on s.o.'s behalf; ~ yumuşak too kind to refuse; (yüzünden): ~ akmak to be evident from the look on s.o.'s face, to be written all over s.o.; ~ düşen bin parça olur sour-faced; ~ kan damlamak to be in the pink of health; ~ okumak to read in s.o.'s face; (yüzüne): ~ bakılmaz very ugly, like the back (end) of a bus; ~ gözüne bulaştırmak to make a mess (or balls or hash or bungle) of s.th.; ~ kan gelmek to recover one's health; ~ karşı to s.o.'s face; ~ vurmak to rub it in, to cast s.th. in s.o.'s teeth; (yüzünü): ~ ağartmak (b-nin) to do s.o. credit, to be a credit to s.o.; ~ buruşturmak (or ekşitmek) to make a face; ~ gören cennetlik you are a rare bird; you are a sight for sore eyes; ~ gözünü açmak (b-nin) to teach s.o. about the birds and the bees; ~ güldürmek (b-nin) to make s.o. happy; ~ şeytan görsün! the devil take him!; yüzünün akıyle çıkmak to succeed in doing s.th.
yüzakı, ·nı hono(u)r, good name.
yüzbaşı X captain.
yüzde 1. percent; percentage; 2. commission, percentage; ~ beş five percent.
yüzdelik commission, percentage.
yüzden superficial.
yüzdürmek 1. caus. of yüzmek; 2. to float (a ship); 3. sl. to fire, to give s.o. the sack.
yüzgelen prominent, important (people).
yüzer¹ a hundred each (or apiece); ~ ~ a hundred at a time.
yüzer² floating; ~ havuz floating dock.
yüzey 1. surface; 2. geom. plane.
yüzeysel superficial, surface; cursory; shallow.
yüzgeç, -ci 1. zo. fin (of a fish); 2. natatorial (animal).
yüzgörümlüğü, -nü, customary present given by a bridegroom to his bride on first seeing her unveiled face.
yüzkarası, -nı disgrace; black sheep.
yüzlemek to rub it in.
yüzleşmece face to face.
yüzleşmek to meet face to face; to be confronted with one another.
yüzleştirmek to confront.
yüzlü 1. ...faced; 2. impudent, insolent.
yüzlük 1. a hundred lira bill; 2. centenarian.
yüzme vn. of yüzmek; ~ havuzu swimming pool (or bath).
yüzmek¹, (-er) to skin, to flay.
yüzmek², (-er) 1. to swim; 2. to float; 3.

# Z

**zaaf** weakness; infirmity; debility.

**zabıt**, -ptı minutes; proceedings; court record: police report; ~ ceridesi printed proceedings; ~ kâtibi 1. keeper of the minutes; 2. 🜨 court reporter; ~ tutmak to take minutes; *(for a policeman)* to write down a report.

**zabıta** [- . .] police.

**zabıtname** [. . - .] minutes; proceedings; court record; police report.

**zabit**, -ti ✕ officer.

**zaç**, -cı vitriol.

**zaçyağı**, -nı oil of vitriol.

**zadegân** [- . -] elite; upper crust.

**zafer** 1. victory, triumph; 2. ♀ *mf.*; ~ alayı triumphal procession; ~ işareti V-sign; ~ kazanmak to gain the victory, to carry *(or* win) the day; ~ takı triumphal arch, arch of triumph.

**zafiyet**, -ti [â] weakness; infirmity; debility; inanition.

**zağ** burr.

**zağanos** *zo.* an eagle owl.

**zağar** terrier.

**zağara** fur collar *(of a coat)*.

**zahife** † reptile.

**zahir** 1. outer appearance; 2. clear, evident; 3. apparently; -de outwardly; to all appearances.

**zahire** [î] 1. provisions, stores; 2. stock of grain; ~ ambarı granary.

**zahiren** outwardly; to all appearances.

**zahiri** 1. external, outward; 2. feigned, artificial.

**zahit**, -di 1. ascetic; 2. ♀ *mf.*

**zahmet**, -ti trouble, difficulty, inconvenience; ~ çekmek to have trouble *(or* difficulty); ~ etm. to put o.s. out, to inconvenience o.s.; ~ etmeyin(iz)! don't trouble yourself!; ~ olmazsa if it doesn't put you to any trouble; ~ vermek to trouble, to inconvenience, to put out; -e değmek to be worth the trouble; -e girmek to put o.s. out, to inconvenience o.s.; -e sokmak *(b-ni)* to put s.o. to trouble, to put s.o. out, to trouble s.o., to inconvenience s.o.; bir ~ bana tuzu verir misiniz? may I trouble you for the salt?

**zahmetli** troublesome, hard, difficult, laborious, labo(u)red, onerous.

**zahmetsiz** easy.

**zaif** *s.* zaaf.

**zaika** [- . .] ♬ taste.

**zail** transitory, transient; evanescent; ~ olm. to disappear, to pass.

**zait**, -di [â] 1. unnecessary; 2. ♀ plus.

**zakkum** ♣ oleander, rosebay.

**zalim** [â] 1. tyrannical; unjust; cruel; 2. tyrant.

**zalimlik** [â] tyranny; injustice; cruelty.

**zam**, -mmı 1. rise, *Am.* raise; 2. additional charge, surcharge; ~ görmek 1. to get a rise *(or Am.* raise); 2. to be increased in price.

**zaman** [. -] 1. time; 2. age, epoch, era; 3. time, season; 4. free time; 5. *gr.* tense; 6. ♪ time; 7. when; ~ belirteci *gr.* adverb of time; ~ birimi unit of time; ~ geçtikçe as the time goes on; ~ kaybetmeden without delay, without loss of time; ~ kazanmak to gain time; ~ kollamak to bide one's time; ~ öldürmek to kill time; ~ ~ from time to time, every now and then, occasionally; ~ zarfı *s.* ~ belirteci; -ı geçmek 1. to be out of date *(or* outmoded); 2. to expire; -ında at the proper *(or* right) time; -la in the course of time; o -ın başkanı the then president.

**zamanaşımı**, -nı 🜨 prescription.

**zamane** [. - .] today, the present age; with it; ~ çocukları children of today, modern youth.

**zamanlamak** to time well.

**zamanlı** timely.

**zamansız** untimely.

**zamazingo** [. . x .] *sl.* mistress, paramour.

**zambak** ♣ lily.

**zamir** [î] 1. *gr.* pronoun; 2. inner self, heart.

**zamk**, -kı 1. gum; 2. glue; paste.

**zamkinos** [x . .] 1. thingumabob, what-do-you-call-it; 2. running away; ~ etm. *(or* -u çekmek) *sl.* to run away, to beat it.

**zamklamak** to glue, to paste.

**zamklı** 1. glued; pasted; 2. gummed.

**zammetmek** [x . .] to add, to annex.

**zampara** womanizer, woman (or skirt) chaser, lecher.

**zamparalık** skirt chasing, lechery; ~ etm. to chase after women, to womanize.

**zan**, -nnı 1. supposition, guess, surmise, conjecture; 2. suspicion, doubt; ~ altında bulunmak to be under suspicion; -ıma göre in my opinion; -ında olm. to be of the opinion that.

**zanaat**, -tı craft, trade.

**zanaatçı** craftsman.

**zangırdamak** 1. to rattle; 2. to tremble; 3. to chatter (teeth).

**zangırtı** rattle.

**zangır zangır** rattlingly; ~ titremek to be all of a tremble.

**zangoç** sexton, verger (of a church).

**zani** [- .] adulterer; fornicator.

**zanlı** accused; suspect.

**zannetmek** [x . .] to think, to suppose, to guess, to believe, to reckon; zannedersem I think that...

**zapt** 1. capturing; 2. seizure, confiscation; 3. taking down, recording; 4. keeping in mind; ~ etm. 1. to capture, to conquer; 2. to restrain; 3. to seize, to confiscate; 4. to take down, to record; 5. to keep in mind; 6. to grasp, to understand.

**zaptetmek** s. zapt etm.

**zaptiye**, hist. 1. zaptieh, gendarme; 2. zaptieh, gendarmerie.

**zapturapt**, -tı 1. discipline; 2. order.

**zar¹** 1. anat., ♥, zo. membrane, pellicle; 2. ♠ membrane.

**zar²** die; ~ atmak to throw dice; ~ tutmak to cheat in throwing dice.

**zarafet**, -tı [. - .] grace, elegance, refinement; delicacy.

**zarar** 1. damage, harm, injury, detriment; 2. ✝ loss; ~ etm. 1. to lose money; to make a loss; 2. to damage, to harm, to injure; ~ görmek to be damaged (or harmed or injured) (-den by); ~ ve ziyan damages; ~ vermek to damage, to harm, to injure; -ı yok! it doesn't matter!, never mind!, that's OK!; -ına satmak to sell at a loss (or sacrifice), to sacrifice.

**zararına** 1. at a loss (or sacrifice); 2. (b-nin) to s.o.'s disadvantage.

**zararlı** harmful, injurious, detrimental; ~ çıkmak to end up a loser; to come out of s.th. a loser.

**zararsız** harmless; innocuous; ~ hale getirmek to overpower.

**zarf** 1. envelope; 2. case, receptacle; 3. gr. adverb; üç saat -ında within three hours.

**zarflamak** to put into an envelope.

**zargana** [x . .] zo. needlefish, gar(fish).

**zarif** [î] 1. elegant, graceful; 2. elegant, gracious, refined (action, manner); 3. ♀ [x .] wf.

**zariflik** [î] elegance, grace; refinement.

**zari zari** [â, â] bitterly.

**zarp**, -bı 1. severity, violence; 2. blow; ~ etm. to hit, to strike; ~ musluğu main valve.

**zarta** [x .] fart, poop; -yı çekmek sl. to die, to kick the bucket.

**zartçı** sl. big talker, windbag.

**zart zurt** bluster; ~ etm. to bluster.

**zaruret**, -tı [û] 1. necessity, essentiality, vitalness; indispensability; unavoidability; 2. poverty, destitution.

**zaruri** [. - -] necessary, essential, requisite, vital; indispensable; unavoidable; inevitable.

**zar zor** 1. unwillingly, reluctantly; 2. by force, forcibly; 3. with difficulty.

**zat**, -tı [â] 1. person, individual; personality; 2. essence, core, heart; ~ işleri şubesi personnel department; -a mahsus private, personal; zatı âliniz your Worship.

**zaten**, **zati** [â] [x .] anyway, anyhow, in any case, at any rate.

**zati** [- -] personal, private; ~ eşya personal effects.

**zatülcenp**, -bi [â] [x . .] ♠ pleurisy.

**zatürree** [â] [x . . .] ♠ pneumonia.

**zavahir** s. zevahir.

**zavallı** [x . .] 1. poor, miserable, pitiful; 2. helpless; ~ adam! poor man!

**zaviye** [â] 1. corner; nook; 2. ♪ angle; 3. point of view, viewpoint.

**zayıf** 1. thin, meager; scrawny; 2. weak; faint; frail; 3. slim, small, slender (possibility); ~ almak to get a failing grade; ~ düşmek 1. to get thin; 2. to get weak.

**zayıflamak** 1. to get thin; 2. to lose weight, to slim down; 3. to get weak.

**zayıflık** 1. thinness, meagerness; 2. weakness; faintness, feebleness.

**zayi**, -ii [â] lost; ~ etm. to lose; ~ olm. to be lost.

**zayiat**, -tı [- . -] losses, casualties; ~ vermek to suffer losses (or casualties).

**zayiçe** [â] horoscope; -sine bakmak (b-nin) to cast s.o.'s horoscope.

**zeamet**, -tı [â] hist. fief, fee.

**zebani** [. - -] 1. demon of hell; 2. fig. hellhound.

**zebanzet**, -di commonly used (or popular) (word, etc.).

**zebella** [. . -] 1. ogre; 2. ogr(e)ish (person); ~ gibi ogr(e)ish (person).

**zebir** s. zebra.

**zebra** [x .] zo. zebra.

**zebun** [ü] weak, helpless.

**zebunküş** [ü] cruel.

**Zebur** [ü] pr. n. the Book of Psalms.

**zecir**, -cri force, compulsion; oppression.

**zecren** [x .] by force, by compulsion.

**zecri** forcible, coercive; ~ tedbirler coercive measures.

**zedelemek** 1. to bruise; 2. to harm, to damage, to injure.

**zefir¹** [i] ¥ exhalation, expiration.

**zefir²** zephyr.

**zehap**, -bı [â] supposition, surmise.

**zehir**, -hri poison, toxic; venom; ~ gibi 1. very hot (or peppery or pungent); 2. sharp, biting (cold); 3. very clever, crack, crackerjack.

**zehirlemek** 1. to poison; 2. fig. to poison, to contaminate.

**zehirli** poisonous, toxic; venomous.

**zehretmek** [x . .] fig. to make distasteful. to embitter, to take all the pleasure out of s.th. for s.o.

**zekâ** intelligence, intellect; ~ testi intelligence test; ~ yaşı mental age.

**zekât**, -tı isl. alms.

**zekâvet**, -ti acumen.

**zeker** anat. penis.

**zeki** [i] 1. intelligent; quick-witted. sharp, clever, acute; 2. ♀ [x .] mf.

**zeklenmek** P = zevklenmek.

**zelil** [i] despicable.

**zelzele** earthquake.

**zem**, -mmi disparagement.

**zemberek** spring (of a watch, etc.); zem bereği boşalmak fig. to have a fit of laughter.

**zembil** shopping bag.

**zemheri** the dead of winter; ~ zürafası person who wears light clothes in the dead of winter.

**zemin** [. -] 1. ground, earth; 2. floor; 3. ground floor; 4. basis, ground; 5. circumstances, conditions; ~ hazırlamak to lay the groundwork (-e for); ~ katı ground floor.

**zeminlik** ✕ underground shelter.

**zemmetmek** [x . .] to disparage, to speak ill of.

**zemzem** 1. Zamzam; 2. water from Zamzam; ~ kuyusuna işemek to do s.th. monstrous merely to acquire notoriety; -le yıkanmış olm. fig. to be an angel

compared to s.o. else.

**zencefil** ¥ ginger.

**zenci** Black, Negro.

**zengin** 1. rich, wealthy; 2. productive, fertile, rich; 3. rich person; 4. rich in, abounding in.

**zenginle(ş)mek** to get rich.

**zenginlik** 1. richness, wealthiness; 2. riches, wealth.

**zenne** 1. women's wear; 2. man taking a woman's part in the ortaoyunu.

**zenneci** seller of women's clothes.

**zeplin** [x .] zeppelin.

**zerdali** [â] ¥ wild apricot.

**zerdeva** zo. pine marten.

**Zerdüşt**, -tü pr. n. Zoroaster.

**zeretmek** [x . .] † to sow (seed).

**zeri**, -r'i sowing (seed).

**zerk**, -ki ¥ injection; ~ etm. to inject.

**zerre** 1. mote, atom; 2. 🔬 molecule; ~ kadar the least bit.

**zerrin** 1. gold(en) 2. ¥ jonquil.

**zerzevat**, -tı vegetables; produce.

**zerzevatçı** vegetable seller.

**zevahir** [. - .] appearances; -i kurtarmak to save face (or appearances).

**zeval**, -li [â] 1. disappearance; 2. decline, wane; ~ bulmak 1. to disappear; 2. to decline, to wane; ~ vakti noon; -e yüz tutmak fig. to begin to decline; -i olm. (b-ne) to be harmful to s.o.

**zevali** [. - -] reckoned from noon (time).

**zevalsiz** [â] permanent, everlasting.

**zevce** ✳ wife.

**zevc**, -ci † husband.

**zeveban** [â] melting, fusion; ~ etm. to melt, to fuse; ~ noktası phys. melting (or fusion) point.

**zevk**, -ki 1. pleasure, delight, enjoyment, fun; 2. taste, discrimination; 3. taste, liking, preference; 4. sense of taste, gustation; ~ almak (or duymak) (bşden) to find (or take) pleasure in s.th., to enjoy s.th.; ~ için for fun; ~ vermek to give pleasure; -ine düşkün addicted to pleasure; -ini çıkarmak (bşin) to enjoy s.th. to the full; -ler ve renkler tartışılmaz there is no accounting for tastes; -ten dört köşe olm. fig. to be as happy as a lark (or sandboy), to be as happy as the day is long, to be as happy as Larry.

**zevklenmek** 1. to take (or find) pleasure (ile in); 2. (b-le) to make fun of s.o.

**zevkli** 1. pleasurable, delightful, pleasant; 2. tasteful.

**zevksiz** 1. tasteless; 2. boring, dull, tiresome, insipid, tedious, unpleasant.

**zevzek** long-winded, talkative.

**zevzeklik** boring chatter; ~ etm. to rattle on.

**zeybek** *swashbuckling village lad of southwestern Anatolia.*

**zeyil,** -yli appendix, addendum.

**zeyrek** clever, quick-witted.

**zeytin** olive.

**zeytinlik** olive grove.

**zeytinyağı,** -nı olive oil; ~ gibi üste çıkmak *fig.* to come off best; to get the better of an argument.

**zeytuni** [. - -] olive-green.

**zıbarmak** *sl.* 1. to die, to croak, to peg out, to pop off; 2. to pass out *(after getting drunk);* 3. to fall asleep, to hit the sack.

**zıbın** quilted jacket for a baby.

**zıddiyet,** -ti opposition, contrariety; contrast.

**zıh** 1. edging; piping; 2. border; 3. mo(u)lding.

**zıkkım** poison; ~ olsun! may you choke on it!

**zıkkımlanmak** to eat, to cram food in one's gob, to stuff o.s. with food.

**zılgıt,** -tı *F* severe tongue-lashing; ~ yemek to get it in the neck, to cop it, to catch it

**zımba** [x .] punch, stapler.

**zımbalamak** 1. to punch, to staple; 2. *sl.* to stab, to knife; 3. *sl.* to fuck, to poke.

**zımbalı** [x . .] punched, stapled.

**zımbırdatmak** to strum, to thrum, to twang.

**zımbırtı** 1. discordant, twang; 2. what-do-·you-call-it, thingumabob.

**zımnen** [x .] 1. indirectly, by implication; 2. implicitly.

**zımni** [ī] indirect, implied, veiled; unspoken; implicit.

**zımpara** [x . .] emery; ~ kâğıdı sandpaper.

**zımparalamak** to sand(paper); to emery.

**zındık** *fig.* atheist, unbeliever.

**zıngadak** [x . .] suddenly and with a jolt.

**zıngıldamak** *s.* zangırdamak.

**zıngıl zıngıl** *s.* zangır zangır.

**zıngırdamak** *s.* zangırdamak.

**zıngır zıngır** *s.* zangır zangır.

**zınk:** ~ diye durmak to come to an abrupt stop.

**zıp:** ~ diye all of a sudden, suddenly.

**zıpçıktı** upstart, parvenu.

**zıpır** *F* screwy, cracked, loony, crack-pot.

**zıpkın** harpoon; (fish)gig.

**zıplamak** 1. to jump; 2. to bounce.

**zıppadak** [x . .] suddenly, all of a sudden.

**zıpzıp,** -pı marble.

**zıp zıp** 1. up and down; 2. with a bounce, bouncingly.

**zırdeli** [x . .] as mad as a hatter, stark staring mad.

**zırh** armo(u)r.

**zırhlanmak** to put on one's armo(u)r.

**zırhlı** 1. armo(u)red, armo(u)r-plated, armo(u)r-clad; 2. ↓ battleship, ironclad; ~ otomobil armo(u)red car; ~ tümen ✕ armo(u)red division.

**zırıldamak** 1. to yammer, to yak; 2. to cry, to blubber, to boohoo.

**zırıltı** 1. racket; 2. yammer; 3. squabble, row, quarrel; 4. *F* what-do-you-call-it, thingumabob.

**zırıl zırıl:** ~ ağlamak to cry buckets; ~ terlemek to sweat buckets.

**zırlak** 1. *zo.* cricket; 2. weepy.

**zırlamak** *s.* zırıldamak.

**zırnık** 1. arsenic, zarnich; 2. *fig.* the least little bit; ~ bile vermem! I won't leave him so much as a penny!

**zırtapoz** *sl.* crazy, screwy.

**zırt pırt** *F* at any time whatsoever.

**zırtullahıkermani** [. . - . . . -] *co.* nut, maniac, loon.

**zırt zırt** *s.* zırt pırt.

**zırva** [x .] 1. nonsense, rubbish, rot, bunk, hooey; 2. nonsensical, stupid; ~ tevil götürmez *pro.* it is no use trying to make sense out of foolish talk.

**zırvalamak** to talk nonsense (*or* rot), to drivel.

**zır zır:** ~ ağlamak to blubber, to boohoo.

**zırzop** *s.* zirzop.

**zıt,** -ddı opposite, contrary; ~ gitmek (b-le) to oppose *s.o.;* zıddı olm. (*bş b-nin*) to dislike *s.th.;* zıddına gitmek (*b-nin*) to rile *s.o.*

**zıtlaşmak** (*for people*) to become the opposite of each other.

**zıvana** [. x .] 1. liner; 2. tenon; 3. pin; 4. mortise; -dan çıkmak *fig.* to blow his stack, to fly off the handle.

**zıya,** -aı [ā] loss.

**zıykınefes, zıykısadır,** -drı ᵺ dyspnea.

**zibidi** 1. oddly dressed; 2. crazy, nutty, screwy.

**zifaf** [ā] entering the bridal chamber; ~ gecesi wedding night; ~ odası bridal chamber.

**zifir** deposit in a pipe stem.

**zifiri:** ~ karanlık 1. complete darkness; 2.

**pitch** black, inky (black), as black as pitch (*or* midnight *or* ink).

**zifos** [x .] 1. mud; 2. *F* nonsensical; ~ atmak (*b-ne*) to sling mud at *s.o.*

**zift**, -ti pitch; -in pekini yesin! let him starve for all I care!

**ziftlemek** to pitch.

**ziftlenmek** 1. *pass. of* ziftlemek; 2. *F* to make a pig of o.s.

**ziftli** coated with pitch.

**zihin**, -hni 1. mind, intellect; 2. memory, mind; 3. comprehension; ~ açmak to stimulate the mind; ~ bulanıklığı *mental confusion*; ~ yormak to think hard, to rack one's brains; (zihni): ~ açılmak to feel mentally alert; ~ bulanmak to get confused (*or* muddled up); ~ dağılmak (*for one's mind*) to wander; ~ durmak to be unable to think clearly, to be mentally fatigued; ~ saplanmak to get hipped on (*a mistaken idea*); -ni kurcalamak (*for s.th.*) to keep popping into one's mind, to recur to s.o. repeatedly.

**zihnen** mentally.

**zihni** mental, intellectual.

**zihniyet**, -ti mentality.

**zikir**, -kri 1. mention; 2. *isl.* zikr, dhikr (*repeating the word* Allah); zikri geçmek to be mentioned.

**zikretmek** [x . .] 1. to mention; 2. *isl.* to repeat the word Allah.

**zikzak** 1. zigzag; 2. zigzag(gy); ~ yapmak to zigzag.

**zikzaklı** zigzag(gy).

**zil** 1. bell; doorbell; buzzer; 2. cymbal; 3. finger cymbal; 4. jingle (*on a tambourine*); 5. *sl.* very hungry, peckish; ~ çalıyor the bell is ringing; ~ takıp oynamak *fig.* to jump for joy.

**zillet**, -ti abasement.

**zilli** 1. provided with a bell; 2. *sl.* shrewish (*woman*).

**zilyet** *öö* owner, possessor.

**zilyetlik** *öö* ownership, possession; ~ davası *öö* possessory action.

**zilzurna**: ~ sarhoş as drunk as a Lord, pissed as a newt, corked, blotto.

**zimamdar** [. - -] administrator, manager.

**zimmet**, -ti debit; -ine geçirmek 1. (*bir hesabı b-nin*) to debit (*an amount of money*) to s.o.'s account; 2. (*bir parayı kendi*) to embezzle, to peculate.

**zina** [ᵃ] *öö* adultery; fornication.

**zincifre** cinnabar.

**zincir** 1. chain; 2. necklace; 3. chain, series, succession; -e vurmak to chain, to put in chains, to fetter.

**zincirleme** 1. *vn. of* zincirlemek; 2. succes-

sive; ~ kaza pileup.

**zincirlemek** to chain.

**zincirli** chained.

**zindan** [ᵃ] prison; dungeon; ~ gibi pitch-dark.

**zindancı** [ᵃ] gaoler, jailer.

**zinde** energetic, alive, active; robust.

**zinhar** [ᵃ] never!, no way!

**zira** [- -] [x -] because.

**ziraat**, -ti [. - .] agriculture.

**ziraatçı** agriculturist.

**ziraatçılık** agriculture.

**zirai** [. - -] agricultural.

**zirman** *sl.* big, strapping (*man*).

**zirve** summit, peak, apex; ~ toplantısı summit meeting; mesleğinin zirvesinde at the top of the tree.

**zirzop**, -pu *F* crazy, screwy, loony, crackpot.

**ziya** [ᵃ] 1. light; 2. ♀ *mf.*

**ziyadar** [. - -] bright, luminous.

**ziyade** [ᵃ] 1. excess, surplus; 2. a lot of, much; many; 3. excessive; 4. courtyard (*of a mosque*); 5. rather (*-den than*), more (*-den than*); ~ olsun! thank you very much! (*said to s.o. after eating s.th. he has offered one*); -siyle 1. extremely, exceedingly; 2. excessively, too; burası evden ~ müzeye benziyor this place is more like a museum than a house.

**ziyafet**, -ti feast, banquet; ~ vermek (*or* çekmek) to give a banquet.

**ziyan** [ᵃ] loss; damage; harm; ~ etm. to waste; ~ olm. to go for nothing, to go to waste; ~ zebil olm. *P* to go to waste, to go for naught; -ı yok! never mind!

**ziyankâr** [ᵃ] destructive; wasteful.

**ziyankârlık** [ᵃ] destructiveness; wastefulness.

**ziyansız** [ᵃ] harmless.

**ziyaret**, -ti [ᵃ] 1. visit, call; 2. pilgrimage; ~ etm. to visit, to call on; -ine gitmek (*b-nin*) to go to visit s.o.

**ziyaretçi** [ᵃ] visitor, caller.

**ziyaretgâh** [. - -] place of pilgrimage.

**ziynet**, -ti 1. ornament, decoration; 2. jewel(le)ry; 3. ♀ *wf.*; ~ eşyası jewel(le)ry.

**zodyak** *ast.* zodiac.

**zoka** [x .] 1. fishhook; 2. *sl.* trap, trick; -yı yutmak *sl.* to take the bait, to fall for a trick.

**zom** *sl.* dead drunk, blotto, corked.

**zonklamak** to throb.

**zonk zonk**: ~ zonklamak to throb terribly.

**zoolog** zoologist.

**zooloji** zoology.

**zoolojik** zoological.

**zor 1.** difficult, hard; **2.** difficulty, trouble; **3.** obligation, necessity, compulsion; **4.** coercion, pressure; **5.** barely, just; ~ **bela 1.** with great difficulty; **2.** just barely; ~ **gelmek** (b-ne) to be difficult for s.o.; ~ **kullanmak** to use force; -a başvurmak to resort to force; -a gelememek to be unable to endure pressure; -a koşmak to make difficulties for s.o.; -la by force; -la güzellik olmaz it is no use forcing it; **-u** -una with great difficulty; -un ne? what's the matter with you?

**zoraki** [ā] forced; under compulsion.

**zorba** tyrant; bully; browbeater.

**zorbalık** tyranny.

**zorgulu** psych. compulsive.

**zorlama 1.** vn. of zorlamak; **2.** compulsion; coercion; **3.** strain; **4.** forced; ~ **yürüyüş** forced march.

**zorlamak 1.** to force, to compel, to coerce, to constrain; **2.** to strain; **3.** to put pressure on.

**zorlaşmak** to get difficult (or hard).

**zorlaştırmak** to make difficult.

**zorlayıcı** coercive, forcible; ~ **nedenler** ôô forces majeures.

**zorlu 1.** difficult, hard; **2.** powerful, violent; **3.** powerful, influential.

**zorluk** difficulty; ~ **çıkarmak** to make (or raise) difficulties, to make things difficult.

**zorunlu 1.** necessary, obligatory; indispensable; **2.** compulsory, imperative; **3.** unavoidable, inevitable.

**zorunluluk 1.** obligation; indispensability; **2.** imperativeness.

**zuhur** [.-] appearance; ~ **etm. 1.** to appear, to come into view; **2.** to take place suddenly, to come about suddenly.

**zuhurat,** -tı [. - -] unforeseen events, contingencies; -a bağlı contingent.

**zuhuri** [. - -] player in the ortaoyunu; ~ **kolu** troupe of ortaoyunu players.

**zula** sl. hiding place, cache; ~ **etm.** sl. **1.** to steal; **2.** to hide, to conceal.

**zulmet,** -ti darkness.

**zulmetmek** [x . .] to tyrannize.

**zulüm,** -lmü tyranny, cruelty; injustice; oppression.

**zurna** ♪ a kind of recorder; ~ **gibi** tightly fitting (trousers).

**zurnabalığı,** -nı zo. saury, skipper.

**zübde 1.** summary; **2.** the best part, the cream.

**zücaciye** [ā] glassware; china.

**züğürt,** -dü co. broke, penniless, skint; ~ **tesellisi** cold comfort.

**züğürtleşmek** co. to become penniless, to go broke.

**züğürtlük** co. pennilessness.

**Zühre** ast. Venus.

**zührevi** [i] ♂ venereal; ~ **hastalıklar** venereal diseases.

**zührevî** [i] ♂ venereal; ~ **hastalıklar** venereal diseases.

**z’uhd** asceticism. 

**zühul,** -lü [ū] inadvertance, slip; slip of the tongue.

**zülüf,** -lfü sidelock, earlock.

**zümre** class, group, set (of people).

**zümrüdi** [i] emerald.

**Zümrüdüanka** [. x . . -] a mythical bird; ~ **gibi** wonderful but imaginary.

**zümrüt,** -dü emerald; ~ **yeşili** emerald (-green).

**züppe** fop, coxcomb, snob, toff, la-di-da.

**züppelik** foppishness, coxcombry.

**zürafa** [. . .] **1.** zo. giraffe; **2.** sl. lesbian.

**zürra,** -aı [ā] † farmers.

**zürriyet,** -ti progeny, offspring.

# LANGENSCHEIDT'S
# STANDARD
# TURKISH DICTIONARY

*Second Part*

## English-Turkish

by
RESUHİ AKDİKMEN

Assistant Lexicographers
EKREM UZBAY
NECDET ÖZGÜVEN

# Contents

İçindekiler

# Foreword

Years of meticulous work have produced this new Standard English-Turkish/Turkish-English Dictionary. Containing 80,000 entries, it meets the needs of student, teacher, businessman and traveler alike – in short, it is an invaluable tool for anyone concerned with the Turkish language. The vocabulary reflects that used in modern, everyday Turkish. The dictionary furthermore contains the most important terminology from such specialist areas as trade and commerce, technology, and medicine.

The translations of the headwords are arranged according to frequency of use. Synonymous translations are separated by commas, and semantically distinct alternatives by semi-colons. For ease of reference, signs and abbreviations indicating parts of speech, stylistic register and subject areas have been used. Idioms, proverbs and colloquialisms have been given special consideration in this dictionary. Syllabification of English headwords is indicated by means of dots.

We trust that this up-to-date dictionary will prove to be indispensable to all those interested in the Turkish language.

# Önsöz

Uzun ve titiz bir çalışmanın ürünü olan bu yeni cep sözlüğü, 80.000'i aşkın kelime haznesiyle, öğrencilerin, öğretmenlerin, çevirmenlerin, kısacası İngilizce ile ilişkili herkesin gereksinimlerini büyük ölçüde karşılayacak biçimde hazırlanmıştır. Sözlüğün kapsamındaki sözcükler, günümüz modern İngilizcesinin konuşma dili, ticaret, teknik, tıp gibi dallarındaki en yaygın sözcükler arasından titizlikle seçilmiştir.

Bir sözcüğün anlamları, kullanımındaki önem sırasına göre dizilmiş, eşanlamlı olanlar virgülle, ayrı anlamlı olanlar ise noktalı virgülle ayrılmıştır. Bunun yanısıra, anlam karışıklığına meydan vermemek için kısaltmalardan başka özel işaretler de kullanılmıştır. Bu kısaltma ve işaretler sayesinde sözcüğün kullanım sahaları daha açık seçik olarak ortaya konmuştur.

Diğer pek çok sözlükte olduğu gibi İngilizce sözcüklerin okunuşlarının Türkçe olarak verilmesinden kesinlikle kaçınılmış, yerine uluslararası fonetik alfabesi tercih edilmiştir. Bunun yanısıra, okunuşlardaki vurgular da verilmiştir. Böylece sözlük sahibi, özellikle bilmediği sözcükleri doğru olarak söyleyebilecektir.

Sözcüklerin gerçek anlamlarının yanısıra, teknik, tıp, ticaret gibi pek çok alandaki kullanımları da kısaltma ve semboller yardımıyle verilmiştir. Ayrıca, deyimler, atasözleri ve argo sözcüklere de geniş yer ayrılmıştır.

İngilizcede en çok güçlük çekilen noktalardan biri olan sözcüklerin hecelenmesi de bu yeni sözlükte çözümlenmiştir. Harfler arasındaki noktalar bu hecelemeyi göstermektedir.

Tüm bu özelliklerinden dolayı bu yeni ve çağdaş sözlüğün büyük bir açığı kapatacağına ve İngilizce ile ilişkili herkes için vazgeçilmez bir yapıt olacağına inanıyoruz.

# Using the Dictionary

## Sözlüğün Kullanımı

**I. English Head-words.**

**1.** The alphabetical order of the head-words has been observed throughout, including the irregular forms.

**2.** Centred dots or stress marks within a head-word indicate syllabification,

*e.g.* **cul.ti.vat.ed ... cul.ti'va.tion**

**3.** In hyphenated compounds a hyphen coinciding with the end of a line is repeated at the beginning of the text.

**4.** The tilde (**~, ~**) represents the repetition of a head-word.

**a)** In compounds the tilde in bold type (**~**) replaces the catch-word,

*e.g.* **aft.er ... '~.birth** (= afterbirth)

**b)** The simple tilde (**~**) replaces the head-word immediately preceding (which itself may contain a tilde in bold type),

*e.g.* **dis.tance ...** at a **~** = at a distance **day ... '~.light ... ~-saving** time = daylight-saving time.

**5.** When the initial letter changes from small to capital or vice versa, the usual tilde is replaced by ♀ or ♀.

*e.g.* **foot...: ... ♀ Guards** = Foot Guards.

**II. Pronunciation.**

**1.** The pronunciation of English head-words is given in square brackets by means of the symbols of the International Phonetic Association.

**2.** To save space the tilde (**~**) has been made use of in many places within the phonetic transcription. It replaces any part of the preceding complete transcription which remains unchanged.

---

**I İngilizce Madde Başı Sözcükleri.**

**1.** Düzensiz şekilleri de dahil olmak üzere madde başı sözcüklerin alfabetik sırasına baştan sona dikkat edilmiştir.

**2.** Madde başı bir sözcükteki noktalar veya vurgu işaretleri hecelemeyi göstermektedirler,

*örnek:* **cul.ti.vat.ed ... cul.ti'va.tion**

**3.** Tire ile ayrılmış bileşik sözcüklerde satır sonuna gelen tire, diğer satırın başında tekrarlanmıştır.

**4.** Tekrar işareti (**~, ~**), madde başı sözcüğün tekrarını gösterir.

**a)** Bileşik sözcüklerdeki siyah tekrar işareti (**~**) asıl sözcüğün yerini alır.

*örnek:* **aft.er ... '~.birth** (= afterbirth).

**b)** Açık renkli tekrar işareti (**~**) kendisinden hemen önce gelen siyah harfli sözcüğün yerini alır,

*örnek:* **day ...** at a **~** = at a distance **day ... '~.light ... ~-saving** time daylight-saving time.

**5.** Bir sözcüğün ilk harfi küçük harften büyük harfe veya büyük harften küçük harfe dönüştüğünde ♀ veya ♀ tekrar işaretleri konulmuştur,

*örnek:* **foot...: ... ♀ Guards** = Foot Guards.

**II. Telaffuz.**

**1.** İngilizce madde başı sözcüklerin telaffuzları, Uluslararası Fonetik Kuruluşunun sembolleriyle köşeli ayraçlarda verilmiştir.

**2.** Yerden kazanmak için tekrar işareti (**~**) fonetik yazımda da pek çok yerlerde kullanılmıştır. Bu işaret, fonetik yazımın değişmeyen kısmının yerine geçmektedir.

X

e.g. **as.so.ci.a.ble** [ə'səuʃjəbl] ... **as<sup>t</sup>so.ci.
ate 1.** [~ʃieit] ... **2.** [~ʃiit] ... **as.so.ci.a.
tion** [~si<sup>t</sup>eiʃən]...

**III. Grammatical References.**

**1.** In the appendix you will find a list of
irregular verbs.

**2.** *(irr.)* following a verb refers to this
list, where you will find the principal
parts of this particular verb.

**3.** A reference such as *(irr. fall)* indicates that the compound verb is conju-
gated exactly like the primary verb as
given in the list of irregular verbs.

**4.** An adjective marked with □ takes
the regular adverbial form, *i.e.* by affixing ...ly to the adjective or by changing ...le into ...ly or ...y into ...ily.

**5.** (~ally) means that an adverb is formed by affixing ...ally to the adjective.

**6.** When there is only one adverb for
adjectives ending in both ...ic and ...ical,
this is indicated in the following way:

**his.tor.ic, his.tor.i.cal** □ *i.e.* historically
is the adverb of both adjectives.

**IV. Translations.**

**1.** Translations of a head-word have
been subdivided by Arabic numerals to
distinguish the various parts of speech.
Words of similar meanings have been
subdivided by commas, the various
senses by semicolons.

**2.** Explanatory additions have been
printed in italics,

*e.g.* **whip**... *v/t.* ... çalkamak, çırpmak
*(yumurta);* ... bastırmak *(kumaş);* döndürmek, çevirmek *(topaç)*...

**3.** Prepositions governing an English
catch-word (verb, adjective, noun) are
given in both languages,

*e.g.* **con.vers.a.ble** ... **con.verse** ... **3.**
[kən'vəːs] *vb.* konuşmak, görüşmek, soh-
bet etm. (with *ile)*...

*örnek:* **as.so.ci.a.ble** [ə'səuʃjəbl] ...
**as<sup>t</sup>so.ci.ate 1.** [~ʃieit] ... **2.** [~ʃiit] ...
**as.so.ci.a.tion** [~si<sup>t</sup>eiʃən]...

**III. Gramatik Başvurular.**

**1.** Sözlüğün ek kısmında düzensiz fiillerin bir listesini bulacaksınız.

**2.** Bir fiili izleyen *(irr.),* söz konusu
fiilin ikinci ve üçüncü şekillerinin olduğu bu listeye ilişkindir.

**3.** Örneğin *(irr. fall),* söz konusu bileşik fiilin düzensiz fiil listesinde verilen
esas fiil gibi çekildiğini göstermektedir.

**4.** □ işaretli bir sıfat, kendisine ...ly
eklenerek veya ...le ...ly'e veya ...y
...ily'e dönüştürülerek düzenli zarf şeklini alır.

**5.** (~ally), bir zarfın sıfata ...ally eklenerek yapıldığını göstermektedir.

**6.** Sonu ...ic veya ...ical ile biten sıfat-
lar için yalnızca bir zarf olduğunda, bu
şu şekilde gösterilmektedir:

**his.tor.ic, his.tor.i.cal** □, yani «historically» her iki sıfatın da zarfıdır.

**IV. Sözcüklerin Anlamları.**

**1.** Madde başı bir sözcüğün anlamları, sözcüklerin türlerine göre rakamlar-
la ayrılmıştır. Anlamdaş sözcükler virgüllerle, ayrı anlamlı sözcükler noktalı
virgüllerle ayrılmışlardır.

**2.** Açıklayıcı ek sözcükler italik olarak verilmiştir,

*örnek:* **whip**... *v/t.* ... çalkamak, çırpmak *(yumurta);* ... bastırmak *(kumaş);*
döndürmek, çevirmek *(topaç)*...

**3.** İngilizce bir sözcüğün (fiil, sıfat,
isim) aldığı edatlar her iki dilde de verilmiştir,

*örnek:* **con.vers.a.ble** ... **con.verse** ...
**3.** [kən'vəːs] *vb.* konuşmak, görüşmek,
sohbet etm. (with *ile)*...

# Symbols – Semboller

| | | |
|---|---|---|
| F | colloquial language | konuşma dili |
| P | provincialism | taşra dili |
| † | obsolete | eski |
| ⚕ | rare, little used | az kullanılan |
| ⚘ | botany | botanik, bitkibilim |
| ⊕ | mechanics | mekanik |
| ⚒ | mining | madencilik |
| ✕ | military term | askeri terim |
| ⚓ | nautical term | denizcilik terimi |
| ⟟ | commercial term | ticari terim |
| 🚋 | railway, railroad | demiryolu |
| ✈ | aviation | havacılık |
| ✆ | postal affairs | postacılık |
| ♪ | musical term | müzik terimi |
| ⌂ | architecture | mimarlık |
| ⚡ | electrical engineering | elektrik mühendisliği |
| ⚖ | jurisprudence | hukuk |
| A | mathematics | matematik |
| | agriculture | ziraat, tarım |
| ⚶ | chemistry | kimya |
| ⚕ | medicine | tıp |

# Abbreviations – Kısaltmalar

| | | |
|---|---|---|
| a. | also | keza |
| abbr. | abbreviation | kısaltma |
| acc. | accusative | -i hali |
| adj. | adjective | sıfat |
| adv. | adverb | zarf |
| Am. | Americanism | Amerikan dili |
| anat. | anatomy | anatomi, yapıbilim |
| ast. | astronomy | astronomi, gökbilim |
| attr. | attributively | niteleyici olarak |
| b-de | biri(si)nde | |
| b-den | biri(si)nden | |
| b-i | biri(si) | |
| biol. | biology | biyoloji, dirimbilim |
| b-le | biri(si)yle | |
| b-ne | biri(si)ne | |
| b-ni | biri(si)ni | |
| b-nin | biri(si)nin | |
| b.s. | bad sense | kötü anlamda |
| bş | bir şey | |
| bşde | bir şeyde | |
| bşden | bir şeyden | |
| bşe | bir şeye | |
| bşi | bir şeyi | |
| bşin | bir şeyin | |

| | | |
|---|---|---|
| bsle | bir şeyle | |
| cj. | conjunction | bağlaç |
| co. | comical | komik |
| coll. | collectively | topluluk ismi olarak |
| comb. | combining form | tamlama |
| comp. | comparative | üstünlük derecesi |
| contp. | contemptuously | aşağılayıcı olarak |
| dat. | dative | -e hali |
| eccl. | ecclesiastical | dini |
| etc. | et cetera | ve saire |
| etm. | etmek | |
| esp. | especially | özellikle |
| fenc. | fencing | eskrim |
| fig. | figuratively | mecazi olarak |
| gen. | genitive | -in hali |
| geogr. | geography | coğrafya |
| geol. | geology | jeoloji, yerbilim |
| ger. | gerund | isim-fiil |
| gr. | grammar | gramer, dilbilgisi |
| hist. | history | tarih |
| hunt. | hunting | avcılık |
| ichth. | ichthyology | balıklar bilimi |
| inf. | infinitive | mastar, eylemlik |
| int. | interjection | ünlem |
| Ir. | Irish | İrlanda dili |
| iro. | ironically | alaylı |
| irr. | irregular | düzensiz, kural dışı |
| k-de | kendi(si)nde | |
| k-den | kendi(si)nden | |
| k-le | kendi(si)yle | |
| k-ne | kendi(si)ne | |
| k-ni | kendi(si)ni | |
| k-nin | kendi(si)nin | |
| lit. | literary | edebi, yazınsal |
| metall. | metallurgy | metalurji, metalbilim |
| meteor. | meteorology | meteoroloji, havabilgisi |
| min. | mineralogy | mineraloji, mineralbilim |
| mot. | motoring | otomobilcilik |
| mount. | mountaineering | dağcılık |
| mst. | mostly | çoğunlukla |
| myth. | mythology | mitoloji, efsanebilim |
| n. | noun | isim |
| olm. | olmak | |
| opt. | optics | optik |
| orn. | ornithology | ornitoloji, kuşbilim |
| o.s. | oneself | kendi(si); kendi kendine |
| paint. | painting | ressamlık |
| parl. | parliamentary term | parlamento terimi |
| part. | particularly | özellikle |
| pharm. | pharmacy | eczacılık |
| phls. | philosophy | felsefe |
| phot. | photography | fotoğrafçılık |
| phys. | physics | fizik |
| physiol. | physiology | fizyoloji |
| pl. | plural | çoğul |
| poet. | poetry; poetic | şiir sanatı; şiirsel |
| pol. | politics | siyaset |
| p.p. | past participle | -mış yapılı ortaç |

| | | |
|---|---|---|
| *p.pr.* | *present participle* | *-en yapılı ortaç* |
| *pred.* | *predicatively* | *yüklem olarak* |
| *pret.* | *preterite* | *-di'li geçmiş zaman* |
| *pron.* | *pronoun* | *zamir* |
| *prp.* | *preposition* | *edat, ilgeç* |
| *psych.* | *psychology* | *psikoloji, ruhbilim* |
| *rhet.* | *rhetoric* | *sözbilim, konuşma sanatı* |
| *s.* | *see* | *bakınız* |
| *sg.* | *singular* | *tekil* |
| *sl.* | *slang* | *argo* |
| *s.o.* | *someone* | *biri(si)* |
| *s.th.* | *something* | *bir şey* |
| *sup.* | *superlative* | *enüstünlük derecesi* |
| *surv.* | *surveying* | *yeri ölçme bilimi* |
| *tel.* | *telegraphy* | *telgrafçılık* |
| *teleph.* | *telephony* | *telefonculuk* |
| *thea.* | *theatre* | *tiyatro* |
| *typ.* | *typography* | *basımcılık* |
| *univ.* | *university* | *üniversite* |
| *v/aux.* | *auxiliary verb* | *yardımcı fiil* |
| *v.b.* | *ve benzeri* | *fiil, eylem* |
| *vb.* | *verb* | |
| *vet.* | *veterinary medicine* | *veterinerlik* |
| *v/i.* | *verb intransitive* | *geçişsiz fiil* |
| *v/t.* | *verb transitive* | *geçişli fiil* |
| *zo.* | *zoology* | *zooloji, hayvanbilim* |

# Use of International Phonetic Alphabet

## Uluslararası Fonetik Alfabesinin Kullanımı

### A. Ünlüler ve Diftonglar

[ɑː] Türkçedeki (a) sesinin uzun şekli gibidir: *far* [fɑː], *father* [ˈfɑːðə].

[ʌ] Türkçedeki (a) sesinin kısa ve sert şeklidir: *butter* [ˈbʌtə], *come* [kʌm], *colour* [ˈkʌlə], *blood* [blʌd], *flourish* [ˈflʌriʃ], *twopence* [ˈtʌpəns].

[æ] Türkçedeki (a) sesi ile (e) sesi arasında bir sestir. Ağız, (a) diyecekmiş gibi açılır, daha sonra ses (e)'ye dönüştürülür: *fat* [fæt], *man* [mæn].

[ɛə] Türkçedeki (e) sesinin uzun ve yumuşak şeklidir: *bare* [bɛə], *pair* [pɛə], *there* [ðɛə].

[ai] Türkçedeki (ay) sesi gibidir: *I* [ai], *lie* [lai], *dry* [drai].

[au] Dudaklar önce (a) sesi çıkartmak için açılacak, daha sonra (u) sesi için uzatılacaktır: *house* [haus], *now* [nau].

[e] Türkçedeki (e) sesi gibidir: *bed* [bed], *less* [les].

[ei] Türkçedeki (ey) sesi gibidir: *date* [deit], *play* [plei], *obey* [əˈbei].

[ə] Türkçedeki (ı) sesi gibidir: *about* [əˈbaut], *butter* [ˈbʌtə], *connect* [kəˈnekt].

[əu] Dudaklar önce (o) sesi çıkartmak için yuvarlaklaştırılır, daha sonra (u) sesi için uzatılır: *note* [nəut], *boat* [bəut], *below* [biˈləu].

[iː] Türkçedeki (i) sesinin uzun şeklidir: *scene* [siːn], *sea* [siː], *feet* [fiːt], *ceiling* [ˈsiːliŋ].

[i] Türkçedeki (i) sesi gibidir: *big* [big], *city* [ˈsiti].

[iə] Dudaklar önce (i) sesi çıkartmak için açılacak, daha sonra ses (ı)'ya dönüştürülecektir: *here* [hiə], *hear* [hiə], *inferior* [inˈfiəriə].

[ɔː] Türkçedeki (o) sesinin uzun şeklidir: *fall* [fɔːl], *nought* [nɔːt], *or* [ɔː], *before* [biˈfɔː].

[ɔ] Türkçedeki (o) ile (a) sesleri arasında bir sestir. İngiliz İngilizcesinde (o) sesine, Amerikan Ingilizcesinde ise (a) sesine daha yakındır: *god* [gɔd], *not* [nɔt], *wash* [wɔʃ], *hobby* [ˈhɔbi].

[ɔi] Türkçedeki (oy) sesi gibidir: *voice* [vɔis], *boy* [bɔi], *annoy* [əˈnɔi].

[əː] Türkçedeki (ö) sesi gibidir: *word* [wəːd], *girl* [gəːl], *learn* [ləːn], *murmur* [ˈməːmə].

[uː] Türkçedeki (u) sesinin uzun şeklidir: *fool* [fuːl], *shoe* [ʃuː], *you* [juː], *rule* [ruːl], *canoe* [kəˈnuː].

[u] Türkçedeki (u) sesi gibidir: *put* [put], *look* [luk].

[uə] Dudaklar önce (u) sesi çıkartmak için uzatılır, daha sonra ses (ı) sesine dönüştürülür: *poor* [puə], *sure* [ʃuə], *allure* [əˈljuə].

# B. Ünsüzler

[r] Türkçedeki (r) sesi gibidir: *rose* [rəuz], *pride* [praid].

[ʒ] Türkçedeki (j) sesi gibidir: *azure* ['æʒə], *vision* ['viʒn].

[dʒ] Türkçedeki (c) sesi gibidir: *June* [dʒu:n], *jeep* [dʒi:p].

[tʃ] Türkçedeki (ç) sesi gibidir: *chair* [tʃɛə], *church* [tʃə:tʃ].

[ʃ] Türkçedeki (ş) sesi gibidir: *shake* [ʃeik], *washing* ['wɔʃiŋ], *she* [ʃi:].

[θ] Bu ses Türkçede yoktur. Dilin ucu üst kesicidişlere dokundurulup (t) sesi çıkarılır: *thank* [θæŋk], *thin* [θin], *path* [pɑ:θ], *method* ['meθəd].

[ð] Bu ses de Türkçede yoktur. Dilin ucu üst kesicidişlere dokundurulup (d) sesi çıkarılır: *there* [ðɛə], *father* ['fɑ:ðə], *breathe* [bri:ð].

[ŋ] Bu ses de Türkçede yoktur. Dil damağa dokundurularak genizden (n) sesi çıkarılır: *ring* [riŋ], *sing* [siŋ].

[s] Türkçedeki (s) sesi gibidir: *see* [si:], *hats* [hæts], *decide* [di'said].

[z] Türkçedeki (z) sesi gibidir: *rise* [raiz], *zeal* [zi:l], *horizon* [hə'raizn].

[w] Bu ses Türkçede yoktur. Dudaklar yuvarlaklaştırılıp (v) sesi çıkartılır: *will* [wil], *swear* [swɛə], *queen* [kwi:n].

[f] Türkçedeki (f) sesi gibidir: *fat* [fæt], *tough* [tʌf], *effort* ['efət].

[v] Türkçedeki (v) sesi gibidir: *vein* [vein].

[j] Türkçedeki (y) sesi gibidir: *yes* [jes], *onion* ['ʌnjən].

[p] Türkçedeki (p) sesi gibidir: *pen* [pen].

[b] Türkçedeki (b) sesi gibidir: *bad* [bæd].

[t] Türkçedeki (t) sesi gibidir: *tea* [ti:].

[d] Türkçedeki (d) sesi gibidir: *did* [did].

[k] Türkçedeki (k) sesi gibidir: *cat* [kæt].

[g] Türkçedeki (g) sesi gibidir: *got* [gɔt].

[h] Türkçedeki (h) sesi gibidir: *how* [hau].

[m] Türkçedeki (m) sesi gibidir: *man* [mæn].

[n] Türkçedeki (n) sesi gibidir: *no* [nəu].

[l] Türkçedeki (l) sesi gibidir: *leg* [leg].

# Suffixes in English

## İngilizcedeki Sonekler

İngilizcede en çok kullanılan sonekler, fonetik söylenişleriyle birlikte aşağıdaki listede gösterilmiştir.

-ability [-əbiliti]
-able [-əbl]
-age [-idʒ]
-al [-əl]
-ally [-əli]
-an [-ən]
-ance [-əns]
-ancy [-ənsi]
-ant [-ənt]
-ar [-ə]
-ary [-əri]
-ation [-eiʃən]
-cious [-ʃəs]
-cy [-si]
-dom [-dəm]
-ed [-d; -t; -id]
-edness [-dnis; -tnis; -idnis]
-ee [-i:]
-en [-n]
-ence [-əns]
-ent [-ənt]
-er [-ə]
-ery [-əri]
-ess [-is]
-fication [-fikeiʃən]
-ial [-əl]
-ible [-əbl]
-ian [-jən]
-ic(s) [-ik(s)]
-ical [-ikəl]

-ily [-ili]
-iness [-inis]
-ing [-iŋ]
-ish [-iʃ]
-ism [-izəm]
-ist [-ist]
-istic [-istik]
-ite [-ait]
-ity [-iti]
-ive [-iv]
-ization [-aizeiʃən]
-ize [-aiz]
-izing [-aiziŋ]
-less [-lis]
-ly [-li]
-ment(s) [-mənt(s)]
-ness [-nis]
-oid [-ɔid]
-or [-ə]
-ous [-əs]
-ry [-ri]
-ship [-ʃip]
-(s)sion [-ʃən]
-sive [-siv]
-ties [-tiz]
-tion [-ʃən]
-tious [-ʃəs]
-trous [-trəs]
-try [-tri]
-y [-i]

# English Alphabet

## İngiliz Alfabesi

a [ei], b [bi:], c [si:], d [di:], e [i:], f [ef], g [dʒi:], h [eitʃ], i [ai], j [dʒei], k [kei], l [el], m [em], n [en], o [əu], p [pi:], q [kju:], r [ɑ:], s [es], t [ti:] u [ju:], v [vi:], w [ˈdʌblju:], x [eks], y [wai], z [zed].

# Spelling of American English
## Amerikan İngilizcesinin Yazımı

İngiltere'de konuşulan İngilizcenin yazımından farklı olarak Amerikan İngilizcesinin yazımında başlıca şu özellikler vardır:

1. İki sözcüğü birleştiren çizgi çoğunlukla kaldırılır, örneğin: cooperate, breakdown, soapbox.

2. **-our** ekindeki **(u)** harfi Amerikan İngilizcesinde yazılmaz, örneğin: color, harbor, humor, favor.

3. **-re** ile biten birçok sözcük Amerikan İngilizcesinde **-er** olarak yazılır, örneğin: center, theater, fiber.

4. **(l)** ve **(p)** harfleri ile biten fiillerin türetmelerinde son ünsüz harf ikilenmez, örneğin: traveled, quarreled, worshiped.

5. **-ence** ile biten sözcükler Amerikan İngilizcesinde **-ense** ile yazılır, örneğin: defense, offense, license.

6. Fransızcadan gelen ekler çoğu kez kaldırılır veya kısaltılır, örneğin: dialog(ue), program(me), envelop(e), catalog(ue).

7. **ae** ve **oe** yerine çoğu kez yalnız **(e)** yazılır, örneğin: an(a)emia, man(o)euvers.

8. **-xion** yerine **-ction** kullanılır, örneğin: connection, reflection.

9. Söylenmeyen **(e)** harfi, judg(e)ment, abridg(e)ment, acknowledg(e)ment gibi sözcüklerde yazılmaz.

10. **en-** öneki yerine **in-** öneki daha çok kullanılır, örneğin: inclose.

11. Amerikan İngilizcesinde although yerine altho, all right yerine alright, through yerine thru biçimleri de kullanılabilir.

12. Tüm bunlardan başka, özel yazım biçimleri olan bazı sözcükler vardır, örneğin:

| English | American |
|---|---|
| cheque | check |
| cosy | cozy |
| grey | gray |
| moustache | mustache |
| plough | plow |
| sceptic | skeptic |
| tyre | tire |

# Pronunciation of American English
## Amerikan İngilizcesinin Söylenişi

Amerikan İngilizcesi (AE) ile İngiliz İngilizcesi (BE) arasında söyleniş bakımından bazı ayrılıklar vardır ki, en önemlileri şöyledir:

**1.** İngiliz İngilizcesinde (ɑ:) olarak söylenen ses, Amerikan İngilizcesinde (æ) veya (æ:) olarak söylenir: pass [BE pɑ:s = AE pæ(:)s], answer [BE'ɑ:nsə = AE'æ(:)nsər], dance [BE dɑ:ns = AE dæ(:)ns], half [BE hɑ:f = AE hæ(:)f], laugh [BE lɑ:f = AE læ(:)f].

**2.** İngiliz İngilizcesinde (o) olarak söylenen ses, Amerikan İngilizcesinde (a)'ya yakın olarak söylenir: dollar [BE 'dɔlə = AE 'dɑlər]. college [BE 'kɔlidʒ = AE 'kɑlidʒ], lot [BE lɔt, = AE lɑt], problem [BE 'prɔbləm = AE 'prɑbləm].

**3.** Sonda olup bir ünlüden sonra gelen veya bir ünlü ile bir ünsüz arasında bulunan (r), İngiliz İngilizcesinde söylenmez. Buna karşın Amerikan İngilizcesinde söylenir: car [BE kɑ: = AE kɑ:r], care [BE kɛə = AE kɛr], border [BE 'bɔ:də = AE 'bɔ:rdər].

**4.** Vurgulu hecedeki (u) sesi, İngiliz İngilizcesinde (ju:) olarak söylenir. Fakat bu ses Amerikan İngilizcesinde (u:) olarak söylenmektedir: Tuesday [BE 'tju:zdi = AE 'tu:zdi], student [BE 'stju:dənt = AE 'stu:dənt]. Fakat (music) ve (fuel) sözcükleri her iki söylenişte de aynıdır: [BE, AE = 'mju:zik] [BE, AE = 'fju:əl].

**5.** (p) ve (t) sesleri, Amerikan İngilizcesinde iki ünlü arasında olduklarında (b) ve (d) olarak söylenirler: property [BE 'prɔpəti = AE 'prɑbərti], united [BE ju:'naitid = AE ju'naidid].

**6.** İki veya daha fazla heceli sözcükler, Amerikan İngilizcesinde ana vurgudan sonra daha hafif ikinci bir vurgu alırlar: secretary [BE 'sekrətri = AE 'sekrəˌtɛri], dictionary [BE 'dikʃənri = AE 'dikʃənˌɛri].

**7.** Sözcük sonundaki (-ile) hecesi, İngiliz İngilizcesinde (-ail) olarak söylendiği halde, Amerikan İngilizcesinde (-əl) veya (-il) olarak söylenir: futile [BE 'fju:tail = AE 'fju:təl], textile [BE 'tekstail = AE 'tekstil].

**8.** Sözcük sonundaki (-ization) hecesi, İngiliz İngilizcesinde (-ai'zeiʃən) olarak söylendiği halde, Amerikan İngilizcesinde (-i'zeiʃən) olarak söylenir: civilization [BE sivəlai'zeiʃən = AE sivəli'zeiʃən].

**9.** (-able) ve (-ible) eklerinde bulunan (e) okunmamasına karşın, Amerikan İngilizcesinde (b) ile (l) arasında bir (ı) varmış gibi okunur: possible [BE 'pɔsəbl = AE 'pɑsəbəl], admirable [BE 'ædmərəbl = AE 'ædmərəbəl].

# Numerical Expressions
## Sayısal İfadeler

### Cardinal Numbers
### Asıl Sayılar

O nought, zero, cipher: *teleph.* O [əu] 41 forty-one *kırk bir*
   *sıfır*
1 one *bir*
2 two *iki*
3 three *üç*
4 four *dört*
5 five *beş*
6 six *altı*
7 seven *yedi*
8 eight *sekiz*
9 nine *dokuz*
10 ten *on*
11 eleven *on bir*
12 twelve *on iki*
13 thirteen *on üç*
14 fourteen *on dört*
15 fifteen *on beş*
16 sixteen *on altı*
17 seventeen *on yedi*
18 eighteen *on sekiz*
19 nineteen *on dokuz*
20 twenty *yirmi*
21 twenty-one *yirmi bir*
22 twenty-two *yirmi iki*
30 thirty *otuz*
31 thirty-one *otuz bir*
40 forty *kırk*

50 fifty *elli*
51 fifty-one *elli bir*
60 sixty *altmış*
61 sixty-one *altmış bir*
70 seventy *yetmiş*
71 seventy-one *yetmiş bir*
80 eighty *seksen*
81 eighty-one *seksen bir*
90 ninety *doksan*
91 ninety-one *doksan bir*
100 a *or* one hundred *yüz*
101 hundred and one *yüz bir*
200 two hundred *iki yüz*
300 three hundred *üç yüz*
572 five hundred and seventy-two *beş*
   *yüz yetmiş iki*
1000 a *or* one thousand *bin*
1066 ten sixty-six *bin altmış altı*
1971 nineteen (hundred and) seventy-one
   *bin dokuz yüz yetmiş bir*
2000 two thousand *iki bin*
1 000 000 a *or* one million *bir milyon*
2 000 000 two million *iki milyon*
1 000 000 000 a *or* one milliard. *Am.*
   billion *bir milyar*

### Ordinal Numbers
### Sıra Sayıları

1st first *birinci*
2nd second *ikinci*
3rd third *üçüncü*
4th fourth *dördüncü*
5th fifth *beşinci*
6th sixth *altıncı*
7th seventh *yedinci*
8th eighth *sekizinci*
9th ninth *dokuzuncu*
10th tenth *onuncu*
11th eleventh *on birinci*
12th twelfth *on ikinci*
13th thirteenth *on üçüncü*
14th fourteenth *on dördüncü*
15th fifteenth *on beşinci*
16th sixteenth *on altıncı*

17th seventeenth *on yedinci*
18th eighteenth *on sekizinci*
19th nineteenth *on dokuzuncu*
20th twentieth *yirminci*
21st twenty-first *yirmi birinci*
22nd twenty-second *yirmi ikinci*
23rd twenty-third *yirmi üçüncü*
30th thirtieth *otuzuncu*
31st thirty-first *otuz birinci*
40th fortieth *kırkıncı*
41st forty-first *kırk birinci*
50th fiftieth *ellinci*
51st fifty-first *elli birinci*
60th sixtieth *altmışıncı*
61st sixty-first *altmış birinci*
70th seventieth *yetmişinci*

**71st** seventy-first *yetmiş birinci*
**80th** eightieth *sekseninci*
**81st** eighty-first *seksen birinci*
**90th** ninetieth *doksanıncı*
**100th** a *or* one hundredth *yüzüncü*
**101st** hundred and first *yüz birinci*
**200th** two hundredth *iki yüzüncü*
**300th** three hundredth *üç yüzüncü*
**572nd** five hundred and   seventy-second

*beş yüz yetmiş ikinci*
**1000th** a *or* one thousandth *bininci*
**1950th** nineteen hundred and fiftieth *bin dokuz yüz ellinci*
**2000th** two thousandth *iki bininci*
**1 000 000th** a *or* one millionth   *bir milyonuncu*
**2 000 000th** two millionth *iki milyonuncu*

## Fractional and Other Numbers
### Kesirli ve Diğer Sayılar

1/2 one *or* a half *yarım*
1 ½ one and a half *bir buçuk*
2 ½ two and a half *iki buçuk*
1/3 one *or* a third *üçte bir*
2/3 two thirds *üçte iki*
1/4 one *or* a quarter, one fourth   *çeyrek, dörtte bir*
3/4 three quarters, three fourths *dörtte üç*
1/5 one *or* a fifth *beşte bir*
5/8 five eighths *sekizde beş*
2.5 two point five *iki onda beş*

once *bir kere*
twice *iki kere*
three times *üç kere*
$7 + 8 = 15$ seven and  eight are fifteen *yedi sekiz daha on beş eder*
$9 - 4 = 5$ nine less four are five *dokuzdan dört çıkarsa beş kalır*
$2 \times 3 = 6$ twice three are *or* make six *iki kere üç altı eder*
$20 : 5 = 4$ twenty  divided by five  make four *yirmide beş dört kere var*

# Weights and Measures
## Tartı ve Ölçü Birimleri

### Linear Measures
### Uzunluk Ölçüleri

**1 inch (in.)** = 2,54 cm
**1 foot (ft.)** = 12 inches = 30,48 cm
**1 yard (yd.)** = 3 feet = 91,44 cm

### Distance and Surveyors' Measures
### Uzaklık ve Yer Ölçüleri

**1 link (ll., İ.)** = 7.92 inches = 20,12 cm
**1 rod (rd.), pole** or **perch (p.)** = 25 links = 5,03 m
**1 chain (ch.)** = 4 rods = 20,12 m
**1 furlong (fur.)** = 10 chains = 201,17 m
**1 (statute) mile (mi.)** = 8 furlongs = 1609,34 m

### Nautical Measures
### Deniz Ölçüleri

**1 fathom (fm.)** = 6 feet = 1,83 m
**1 cable('s) length** = 100 fathoms = 183 m
**1 nautical mile (n. m.)** = 10 cable's length = 1852 m

### Square Measures
### Yüzey Ölçü Birimleri

**1 square inch (sq. in.)** = 6,45 qcm
**1 square foot (sq. ft.)**
 = 144 square inches
 = 929,03 qcm
**1 square yard (sq. yd.)**
 = 9 square feet
 = 0,836 qm
**1 square rod (sq. rd.)**
 = 30.25 square yards
 = 25, 29 qm
**1 rood (ro.)** = 40 square rods
 = 10, 12 a
**1 acre (a.)** = 4 roods = 40, 47 a
**1 square mile (sq. mi.)**
 = 640 acres = 2,59 qkm

### Cubic Measures
### Hacim Ölçüleri

**1. cubic inch (cu. in.)**
 = 16,387 ccm
**1 cubic foot (cu. ft.)**
 = 1728 cubic inches
 = 0,028 cbm
**1 cubic yard (cu. yd.)**
 = 27 cubic feet
 = 0,765 cbm
**1 register ton (reg. tn.)**
 = 100 cubic feet
 = 2,832 cbm

### British Measures of Capacity
### İngiliz Hacim Ölçüleri

Dry and Liquid Measures
Kuru ve Sıvı Ölçüler

**1 British** or **Imperial gill (gi., gl.)**
 = 0,142 l
**1 Brit.** or **Imp. bushel (bu., bsh.)**
 = 4 Imp. pecks = 36, 36 l
**1 Brit.** or **Imperial quarter (qr.)**
 = 8 Imp. bushels = 290, 94 l

Liquid Measure
Sıvı Ölçüsü

**1 Brit.** or **Imp. barrel (bbl., bl.)**
 = 36 Imp. gallons = 1,636 hl

### U.S. Measures of Capacity
### Amerikan Hacim Ölçüleri

Dry Measures
Kuru Ölçüler

**1 U.S. dry pint** = 0,550 l
**1 U.S. dry quart** = 2 dry pints
 = 1,1 l
**1 U.S. peck** = 8 dry quarts
 = 8,81 l
**1 U.S. bushel** = 4 pecks
 = 35,24 l

### Liquid Measures
### Sıvı Ölçüleri

**1 U.S. liquid gill** = 0,118 l
**1 U.S. liquid pint** = 4 gills
= 0,473 l
**1 U.S. liquid quart** = 2 liquid pints
= 0,946 l
**1 U.S. gallon** = 4 liquid quarts
= 3,785 l
**1 U.S. barrel** = 31 ½ gallons
= 119 l
**1 U.S. barrel petroleum**
= 42 gallons = 158, 97 l

### Apothecaries' Fluid Measures
### Eczacı Sıvı Ölçüleri

**1 minim (min., m.)** = 0,0006 dl
**1 fluid drachm, US dram (dr. fl.)**
= 60 minims = 0,0355 dl
**1 fluid ounce (oz. fl.)**
= 8 fluid dra(ch)ms = 0,284 dl
**1 pint (pt.)**
= 20 fluid ounces = 0,568 l
**US** 16 fluid ounces = 0,473 l

### Avoirdupois Weight
### Tartı Sistemi

**1 grain (gr.)** = 0,0648 g
**1 drachm, US dram (dr. av.)**
= 27.34 grains = 1,77 g

**1 ounce (oz. av.)** = 16 dra(ch)ms
= 28, 35 g
**1 pound (lb. av.)** = 16 ounces
= 0,453 kg
**1 stone (st.)** = 14 pounds
= 6,35 kg
**1 quarter (qr.)** = 28 pounds
= 12,7 kg
US 25 pounds = 11, 34 kg
**1 hundredweight (cwt).**
= 112 pounds = 50,8 kg
US 100 pounds = 45,36 kg
**1 ton (tn., t.)** = 2240 pounds
= 1016 kg
US 2000 pounds = 907,18 kg

### Troy and Apothecaries' Weight
### Kuyumcu ve Eczacı Tartısı

**1 grain (gr.)** = 0,0648 g
**1 scruple (s. ap.)** = 20 grains
= 1,296 g
**1 pennyweight (dwt.)**
= 24 grains = 1,555 g
**1 dra(ch)m (dr. t. or dr. ap.)**
= 3 scruples = 3,888 g
**1 ounce (oz. ap.)**
= 8 dra(ch)ms = 31,104 g
**1 pound (lb. t. or lb. ap.)**
= 12 ounces = 0,373 kg

# Irregular Verbs

| INFINITIVE | PAST | PAST PARTICIPLE |
| --- | --- | --- |
| abide | abode | abode |
| arise | arose | arisen |
| awake | awoke | awoke, awoken |
| be | was | been |
| bear | bore | borne, born |
| beat | beat | beaten |
| become | became | become |
| befall | befell | befallen |
| beget | begot | begotten |
| begin | began | begun |
| behold | beheld | beheld |
| bend | bent | bent, bended |
| bereave | bereft | bereft, bereaved |
| beseech | besought | besought |
| beset | beset | beset |
| bet | bet, betted | bet, betted |
| betake | betook | betaken |
| bethink | bethought | bethought |
| bid | bade, bid | bidden, bid |
| bide | bided | bided |
| bind | bound | bound |
| bite | bit | bitten, bit |
| bleed | bled | bled |
| blow | blew | blown |
| break | broke | broken |
| breed | bred | bred |
| bring | brought | brought |
| broadcast | broadcast | broadcast |
| build | built | built |
| burn | burnt, burned | burnt, burned |
| burst | burst | burst |
| buy | bought | bought |
| cast | cast | cast |
| catch | caught | caught |
| chide | chid | chidden, chid |
| choose | chose | chosen |
| cleave | clove, cleft | cloven, cleft |
| cling | clung | clung |
| clothe | clothed | clothed, clad |
| come | came | come |
| cost | cost | cost |
| creep | crept | crept |
| cut | cut | cut |
| deal | dealt | dealt |
| dig | dug | dug |
| do | did | done |
| draw | drew | drawn |
| dream | dreamt, dreamed | dreamt, dreamed |
| drink | drank | drunk, drunken |
| drive | drove | driven |

| INFINITIVE | PAST | PAST PARTICIPLE |
|---|---|---|
| dwell | dwelt | dwelt |
| eat | ate | eaten |
| fall | fell | fallen |
| feed | fed | fed |
| feel | felt | felt |
| fight | fought | fought |
| find | found | found |
| flee | fled | fled |
| fling | flung | flung |
| fly | flew | flown |
| forbear | forbore | forborne |
| forbid | forbade | forbidden |
| forecast | forecast | forecast |
| foreknow | foreknew | foreknown |
| foresee | foresaw | foreseen |
| foretell | foretold | foretold |
| forget | forgot | forgotten |
| forgive | forgave | forgiven |
| forsake | forsook | forsaken |
| forswear | forswore | forsworn |
| freeze | froze | frozen |
| gainsay | gainsaid | gainsaid |
| get | got | got |
| gild | gilded | gilded, gilt |
| gird | girded | girded, girt |
| give | gave | given |
| go | went | gone |
| grind | ground | ground |
| grow | grew | grown |
| hamstring | hamstrung | hamstrung |
| hang | hung | hung |
| have | had | had |
| hear | heard | heard |
| heave | heaved, hove | heaved |
| hew | hewed | hewn |
| hide | hid | hidden, hid |
| hit | hit | hit |
| hold | held | held |
| hurt | hurt | hurt |
| inlay | inlaid | inlaid |
| keep | kept | kept |
| kneel | knelt | knelt |
| knit | knitted, knit | knitted, knit |
| know | knew | known |
| lade | laded | laden |
| lay | laid | laid |
| lead | led | led |
| lean | leant, leaned | leant, leaned |
| leap | leapt, leaped | leapt, leaped |
| learn | learnt, learned | learnt, learned |
| leave | left | left |
| lend | lent | lent |
| let | let | let |
| lie | lay | lain |
| light | lighted, lit | lighted, lit |
| lose | lost | lost |

| INFINITIVE | PAST | PAST PARTICIPLE |
|---|---|---|
| make | made | made |
| mean | meant | meant |
| meet | met | met |
| melt | melted | melted, molten |
| miscast | miscast | miscast |
| misdeal | misdealt | misdealt |
| misgive | misgave | misgiven |
| mislay | mislaid | mislaid |
| mislead | misled | misled |
| misspell | misspelt | misspelt |
| misspend | misspent | misspent |
| mistake | mistook | mistaken |
| misunderstand | misunderstood | misunderstood |
| mow | mowed | mown |
| outbid | outbid | outbidden, outbid |
| outdo | outdid | outdone |
| outgo | outwent | outgone |
| outgrow | outgrew | outgrown |
| outride | outrode | outridden |
| outrun | outran | outrun |
| outshine | outshone | outshone |
| overbear | overbore | overborne |
| overcast | overcast | overcast |
| overcome | overcame | overcome |
| overdo | overdid | overdone |
| overhang | overhung | overhung |
| overhear | overheard | overheard |
| overlay | overlaid | overlaid |
| overleap | overleapt, overleaped | overleapt, overleaped |
| overlie | overlay | overlain |
| override | overrode | overridden |
| overrun | overran | overrun |
| oversee | oversaw | overseen |
| overset | overset | overset |
| overshoot | overshot | overshot |
| oversleep | overslept | overslept |
| overtake | overtook | overtaken |
| overthrow | overthrew | overthrown |
| partake | partook | partaken |
| pay | paid | paid |
| prove | proved | proved, proven |
| put | put | put |
| read | read | read |
| rebind | rebound | rebound |
| rebuild | rebuilt | rebuilt |
| recast | recast | recast |
| redo | redid | redone |
| relay | relaid | relaid |
| remake | remade | remade |
| rend | rent | rent |
| repay | repaid | repaid |
| rerun | reran | rerun |
| reset | reset | reset |
| retell | retold | retold |
| rewrite | rewrote | rewritten |
| rid | rid, ridded | rid, ridded |

## XXVIII

| INFINITIVE | PAST | PAST PARTICIPLE |
|---|---|---|
| ride | rode | ridden |
| ring | rang | rung |
| rise | rose | risen |
| rive | rived | riven, rived |
| run | ran | run |
| saw | sawed | sawn, sawed |
| say | said | said |
| see | saw | seen |
| seek | sought | sought |
| sell | sold | sold |
| send | sent | sent |
| set | set | set |
| sew | sewed | sewn, sewed |
| shake | shook | shaken |
| shave | shaved | shaved, shaven |
| shear | sheared/shore | shorn, sheared |
| shed | shed | shed |
| shine | shone | shone |
| shoe | shod | shod |
| shoot | shot | shot |
| show | showed | shown, showed |
| shrink | shrank | shrunk, shrunken |
| shrive | shrived | shriven |
| shut | shut | shut |
| sing | sang | sung |
| sink | sank | sunk, sunken |
| sit | sat | sat |
| slay | slew | slain |
| sleep | slept | slept |
| slide | slid | slid, slidden |
| sling | slung | slung |
| slink | slunk | slunk |
| slit | slit | slit |
| smell | smelt, smelled | smelt, smelled |
| smite | smote | smitten |
| sow | sowed | sown, sowed |
| speak | spoke | spoken |
| speed | sped | sped |
| spell | spelt, spelled | spelt, spelled |
| spend | spent | spent |
| spill | spilt, spilled | spilt, spilled |
| spin | spun, span | spun |
| spit | spat | spat |
| split | split | split |
| spoil | spoilt, spoiled | spoilt, spoiled |
| spread | spread | spread |
| spring | sprang | sprung |
| stand | stood | stood |
| stave | staved, stove | staved, stove |
| steal | stole | stolen |
| stick | stuck | stuck |
| sting | stung | stung |
| stink | stank | stunk |
| strew | strewed | strewn, strewed |
| stride | strode | stridden, strid |
| strike | struck | struck, stricken |

| INFINITIVE | PAST | PAST PARTICIPLE |
|---|---|---|
| string | strung | strung |
| strive | strove | striven |
| sunburn | sunburnt, sunburned | sunburnt, sunburned |
| swear | swore | sworn |
| sweep | swept | swept |
| swell | swelled | swollen, swelled |
| swim | swam | swum |
| swing | swung | swung |
| take | took | taken |
| teach | taught | taught |
| tear | tore | torn |
| tell | told | told |
| think | thought | thought |
| thrive | throve, thrived | thriven, thrived |
| throw | threw | thrown |
| thrust | thrust | thrust |
| tread | trod | trodden, trod |
| unbend | unbent | unbent |
| unbind | unbound | unbound |
| underbid | underbid | underbidden, underbid |
| undergo | underwent | undergone |
| understand | understood | understood |
| undertake | undertook | undertaken |
| undo | undid | undone |
| upset | upset | upset |
| wake | woke, waked | woken, waked |
| waylay | waylaid | waylaid |
| wear | wore | worn |
| weave | wove | woven, wove |
| wed | wedded | wedded, wed |
| weep | wept | wept |
| wet | wet, wetted | wet, wetted |
| win | won | won |
| wind | wound | wound |
| withdraw | withdrew | withdrawn |
| withhold | withheld | withheld |
| withstand | withstood | withstood |
| wring | wrung | wrung |
| write | wrote | written |

# A

**a** [ei, ə] *Sesli harfle başlayan sözcükten önce* **an** [æn;ən] *kullanılır. Ad belirteni, harfi tarif:* bir, herhangi bir; her bir, -de, -ne; twice *a* week haftada iki kere.

**A+F** [ˈeiˈwʌn] *adj.* birinci kalite.

**a.back** [əˈbæk] *adv.* geriye, geri tarafa; taken ~ şaşkın, afallamış.

**ab.a.cus** [ˈæbəkəs] *n, pl.* **ab.a.ci** [ˈ~sai] hesap tahtası; **⌀** abak, sütun gövdesi; direk bedeni.

**a.baft** ⌀ [əˈbɑːft] *adv.&prep.* geride, kıç tarafta.

**a.ban.don** [əˈbændən] *v/t.* terketmek, bırakmak, teslim etm., vazgeçmek; kendi haline bırakmak; *spor:* terketmek; ~ o.s. to hissiyatına kapılmak; bşe düşkün olm., bşin müptelâsı olm.; **a'ban.doned** *adj.* metruk, terkedilmiş; menfur, alçak; **a'ban.don.ment** *n.* terk, bırakma; sadakat, bağlılık.

**a.base** [əˈbeis] *v/t.* alçaltmak, gururunu kırmak; **a'base.ment** *n.* alçaltma, gururunu kırma, tezlil.

**a.bash** [əˈbæʃ] *v/t.* utandırmak, mahcup etm., yüzünü kızartmak; **a'bash.ment** *n.* mahcubiyet, hayâ, sıkılganlık.

**a.bate** [əˈbeit] *v/t.* azaltmak, kısaltmak, eksiltmek; kısmak: (*ağrı, sızı*) hafifletmek, teskin etm.; (*fiyat, vergi*) indirmek, azaltmak; ⌀ sona erdirmek; *v/i.* azalmak, çekilmek, hafiflemek; hükümsüz kalmak; (*fiyat*) düşmek; **a'bate.ment** *n.* azaltma, azaltılma; (*fiyat, vergi, resim*) indirim, tenzil, indirilmiş meblağ.

**ab.at.tis** ⋋ [əˈbætis] *n.* mâni, mania.

**ab.at.toir** [æbətwɑː] *n.* mezbaha, salhane.

**ab.bess** [ˈæbis] *n.* bir manastırın baş rahibesi, müdürü *veya* müdiresi; **ab.bey** [ˈæbi] *n.* manastır; manastır kilisesi; **ab.bot** [ˈæbət] *n.* bir manastırın baş papazı, müdürü.

**ab.bre.vi.ate** [əˈbriːvieit] *v.t.* kısaltmak,

özetlemek; **ab.bre.vi'a.tion** *n.* kısaltma, özetleme; özet.

**ABC** [ˈeibiːˈsiː] alfabe; alfabetik tarife *veya* rehber; ~ weapons nükleer, bakteriyolojik ve kimyasal silâhlar.

**ab.di.cate** [ˈæbdikeit] *v/i.* taç ve tahtını terketmek; *v/t.* (*görevden*) istifa etm., bşden vazgeçmek, feragat etm.; bşi bırakmak, terketmek; ~ the throne tahttan feragat etm., saltanattan çekilmek; **ab.di'ca.tion** *n.* vazgeçme, feragat; tahttan çekilme, terki saltanat.

**ab.do.men** [ˈæbdəmən; **⅋** æbˈdəumən] *n.* karnın alt kısmı, karın, batın; **ab.dom.i.nal** [æbˈdəminl] *adj.* karna ait.

**ab.duct** [æbˈdʌkt] *v/t.* zorla almak, gasbetmek; (*kadın veya çocuk*) kaçırmak; **ab'duc.tion** *n.* (*kadın veya çocuk*) kaçırma.

**a.be.ce.dar.i.an** [eibiːsiːˈdɛəriən] **1.** *adj.* çok basit; **2.** *n.* okumayı öğrenen öğrenci.

**a.bed** [əˈbed] *adv.* yatakta.

**ab.er.ra.tion** [æbəˈreiʃən] *n.* ayrılma, uzaklaşma, inhiraf; *fig.* delâlet, hata; *ast. & phys.* sapma.

**a.bet** [əˈbet] *v/t.* kışkırtmak, tahrik etm.; *mst.* aid and ~ bşe (*suç işlemesinde*) yardımcı olm.; **a'bet.tor** *n.* suç ortağı; tahrikçi, önayak.

**a.bey.ance** [əˈbeiəns] *n.* muallakta, askıda oluş; in ~ da karara bağlanmamış, muallakta, askıda; sahipsiz.

**ab.hor** [əbˈhɔː] *v/t.* bşden, b-den nefret, ikrah etm., tiksinmek; **ab.hor.rence** [əbˈhɔrəns] *n.* nefret, tiksinme; **ab'hor.rent** □ nefret verici, tiksindirici; aykırı, zıt, muhalif ⟨to -e⟩.

**a.bide** [əˈbaid] (*irr.*) *v/i.* kalmak; ~ by sebat etm.; kabullenmek; *v/t.* bşi beklemek; dayanmak, tahammül etm.; I cannot ~ him ona tahammül edemem; **a'bid.ing** □ daimi, devamlı.

**a.bil.i.ty** [əˈbiliti] *n.* iktidar, ehliyet, yetenek; to the best of one's ~ yapabildiği kadar; abilities *pl.* zihnî kabiliyetler, beceri.

**ab.ject** ☐ ['æbdʒekt] menfur, alçak, sefih; **ab'jec.tion, ab'ject.ness** *n.* alçaklık, adilik.

**ab.jure** [əb'ʒuə] *v/t.* tövbe etm., vazgeçmek; yeminle inkâr etm.

**a.blaze** [ə'bleiz] *adj. & adv.* alevli; *fig.* hararetli, şevkli.

**a.ble** ☐ ['eibl] güçlü, muktedir, yapabilen, be ~ to *bşe* gücü yetmek, bşi yapabilmek; ~ to pay ödeme güçlü; ~**-bodied** ['~'bɔdid] *adj.* vücudu sağlam, güçlü; ✕ askerliğe elverişli; ~ seaman ⬦ birinci sınıf tayfa.

**ab.lu.tion** [ə'blu:ʃən] *n.* yıkanma, aptes, gusül

**ab.ne.gate** ['æbnigeit] *v/t.* bşi inkâr etm., tanımamak, reddetmek; **ab.ne'ga.tion** *n. a.* self-~ feragat, yokluğa katlanma.

**ab.nor.mal** ☐ [æb'nɔːməl] anormal, doğal olmayan, usulsüz; **ab.nor'ma.li.ty** *n.* anormallik, usulsüzlük.

**a.board** [ə'bɔːd] *adv.* ⬦ gemide; gemiye; all ~! *Am.* 🚂, 🚆 etc. lûtfen yerlerinizi alınız!

**a.bode** [ə'baud] **1.** *pret & p.p. of* abide; **2.** *n.* oturulan yer, ikametgâh, mesken; kalma.

**a.bol.ish** [ə'bɔliʃ] *v/t.* kaldırmak, iptal etm., feshetmek; **a'bol.ish.ment, ab.o.li.tion** [æbəu'liʃən] *n.* kaldırılma, ilga; **ab.o'li.tion.ist** *n.* köleliğin kaldırılması taraftarı.

**A-bomb** ['eibɔm] = atomic bomb.

**a.bom.i.na.ble** ☐ [ə'bɔminəbl] iğrenç, nefret verici; **a'bom.i.nate** [~neit] *v/t. bşden, b-den* nefret, ikrah etm., tiksinmek; **a.bom.i'na.tion** *n.* nefret, iğrenme; çok iğrenç veya menfur şey veya hareket.

**ab.o.rig.i.nal** [æbə'ridʒənl] **1.** ☐ bir yerin en eski halkından olan; **2.** *n.* asıl yerli, ilk yerli; **ab.o'rig.i.nes** [~dʒiniːz] *n.pl.* asıl yerliler.

**a.bort** [ə'bɔːt] *vb.* 🟅 çocuk düşürmek; dumura uğramak; gelişememek; **a'bor.tion** *n.* 🟅 çocuk düşürme; düşük; *fig.* başarısızlık; **a'bor.tive** [~tiv] ☐ vaktinden evvel doğmuş; beyhude, boş; başarısız, gelişmeyen.

**a.bound** [ə'baund] *v/i.* bol olm.; ~ with (karınca gibi) kayna(ş)mak, bol olm.

**a.bout** [ə'baut] **1.** *prp.* hakkında, *bşe* dair; *bşin* etrafında, civarında, yakınında; her yerinde; talk ~ business işten konuşmak; send s.o. ~ his business *b-ne* yol vermek, *b-ni* defetmek; ~ the house evin herhangi bir yerinde; wander ~ the streets sokaklarda dolaşmak; what are

you ~ ? ne yapmak fikrindesiniz?; I had no money ~ me üstümde hiç para yoktu; be ~ to *bşi* yapmak üzere olm.; **2.** *adv.* aşağı yukarı, takriben, hemen hemen; her tarafta; etrafa, etrafına; şurada burada; it must be somewhere ~ bu civarda olmalı; a long way ~ uzun dolambaçlı yol; bring ~ husule getirmek, gerçekleştirmek; becermek, başarmak; come ~ husule gelmek, tahakkuk etm.; he is ~ my height aşağı yukarı benim boyumda; ~ ten o'clock saat 10 sularında; right ~! sağa dön!; ~-face *n.* geriye dönüş; fikir veya karar değişimi; ~ turn! ✕ geriye dön!

**a.bove** [ə'bʌv] **1.** *prp.* yukarıda; *bşin* üstünde; *bşden* yukarı, *bşden* fazla; *fig.* üstünde, fevkinde; ~ 300 300'den fazla; ~ all her şeyden önce, bunlardan başka; it is ~ me buna aklım ermez, beni aşıyor; **2.** *adv.* daha yukarıda olarak, önce olarak; over and ~ *bşe* ilave olarak, bundan başka; **3.** *adj.* yukarıdaki; yukarıda zikredilmiş; **a'bove-'board** *adj.* dürüst, hilesiz; **a'bove-'ground** *adj.* yeryüzünde, gömülmemiş.

**ab.ra.ca.dab.ra** [æbrəkə'dæbrə] *n.* sihirli kelime, muska; anlamsız söz.

**ab.rade** [ə'breid] *v/t.* aşındırmak, yemek *(esp. deri).*

**ab.ra.sion** [ə'breiʒən] *n.* aşınma, yenme; *(deri)* sıyrık, sıyrıntı; **ab'ra.sive** [~siv] **1.** *n.* ⊕ aşındırıcı veya törpüleyici madde; **2.** ☐ aşındırıcı, törpüleyici; rahatsız edici.

**a.breast** [ə'brest] *adv.* yan yana; aynı hizada; keep *veya* be ~ of the times devre uygun olm.

**a.bridge** [ə'bridʒ] *v/t.* kısaltmak, özetlemek; mahrum etm.; **a'bridg(e).ment** *n.* kısaltma, özet.

**a.broad** [ə'brɔːd] *adv.* yabancı ülkede, dışarıda; şurada burada, her tarafta; there is a report ~ rivayet ediliyor; the thing has got ~ *bş* duyuldu, şayi oldu; all ~ şaşırmış.

**ab.ro.gate** [æbrəugeit] *v/t.* ilga etm., iptal etm., feshetmek; **ab.ro'ga.tion** *n.* ilga, iptal, feshetme.

**ab.rupt** ☐ [ə'brʌpt] ani; sert; ters, haşin *(davranış);* çok dik *(yer);* **ab'rupt.ness** *n.* acele; sertlik, terslik.

**ab.scess** 🟅 ['æbsis] *n.* apse, çıban.

**ab.scond** [əb'skɔnd] *v/i.* kaçmak, firar etm., kanundan kaçmak.

**ab.sence** ['æbsəns] *n.* yokluk, bulunmayış; ~ of mind dalgınlık.

**ab.sent 1.** ☐ ['æbsənt] yok, bulunmayan;

**2.** [æb'sent] *vb.:* ~ o.s. gitmek, bulunmamak; **ab.sen.tee** [æbsən'tiː] *n.* (*görevinde vs.*) bulunmayan kimse; başka bir ülkede devamlı kalan; **ab.sen'tee.ism** *n.* iş veya görevde bulunmama alışkanlığı; devamsızlık; **'ab.sent-'mind.ed** □ dalgın; **'ab.sent-'mind.ed.ness** *n.* dalgınlık.

**ab.sinth(e)** ['æbsinθ] *n.* ♀ pelin otu, acı pelin.

**ab.so.lute** □ ['æbsəluːt] katî, kesin; sade, saf; sonsuz, sınırsız; kayıtsız şartsız; *gr.* soyut; ~ ceiling ✈ azami yükseliş haddi; ~ scale mutlak ölçü ve terazi; ~ temperature mutlak ısı derecesi; **'ab.so.lute.ness** *n.* mutlakiyet; **ab.so'lution** *n.* (*esp. Hıristiyanlık'da*) günahların affı; **'ab.so.lut.ism** *n.* istibdat, mutlakçılık.

**ab.solve** [əb'zɔlv] *v/t.* beraat ettirmek (from -*den*); (*günah veya cezayı*) affetmek.

**ab.sorb** [əb'sɔːb] *v/t.* emmek, içine çekmek; (*bilgi, fikir vs.*) anlamak; zaptetmek; ~ed (in) bşe dalmış; **ab'sorb.ent** *adj. & n.* içe çekici, emici (madde); ~ cotton wool hidrofil pamuk; **ab'sorb.ing** *adj.* çok ilgi çekici.

**ab.sorp.tion** [əb'sɔːpʃən] *n.* içe çekme, emme; dalgınlık.

**ab.stain** [əb'stein] *v/i.* çekinmek, kaçınmak (from -*den*); **ab'stain.er** *mst.* total ~ içkiye tövbeli.

**ab.ste.mi.ous** □ [æb'stiːmjəs] (*esp. yemek, içmek, zevk v.b. şeylerden*) azla kanaat eden, perhizkâr.

**ab.sten.tion** [æb'stenʃən] *n.* çekinme, kaçınma (from -*den*); *parl.* çekimser kalma.

**ab.sti.nence** ['æbstinəns] *n.* (*yiyecek, zevk v.b. şeyler*) perhiz, sakınma (from -*den*); total ~ (*esp.içki*) kullanmama; **'ab.sti.nent** *n.* perhizkâr.

**ab.stract 1.** □ ['æbstrækt] mücerret, soyut; nazarî ,kuramsal; **2.** *n.* özet; *a.* ~ noun *gr.* soyut isim; in the ~ kuramsal olarak; **3.** [æb'strækt] *v/t.* çıkarmak, ayırmak, tecrit etm.; çalmak, aşırmak; kimyasal usullerle ayırmak; özetlemek; **ab'stract.ed** □ dalgın; çıkarılmış; ayrılmış; **ab.strac.tion** [æb'strækʃən] *n.* soyutlama; çıkarma, ayırma; dalgınlık; çalma, aşırma.

**ab.struse** □ [æb'struːs] anlaşılması güç, çapraşık; **ab'struse.ness** *n.* çapraşıklık, muğlaklık.

**ab.surd** □ [əb'səːd] gülünç, anlamsız, saçma; imkânsız, olmayacak; **ab'surd.i-** ty *n.* gülünçlük, anlamsızlık, saçmalık: maskaralık.

**a.bun.dance** [ə'bʌndəns] *n.* bolluk, zenginlik, bereket; in ~ bol miktarda; **a'bun-dant** □ çok, bol; **a'bun.dant.ly** *adv.* bol bol.

**a.buse 1.** [ə'bjuːs] *n.* suiistimal, kötüye kullanma; küfür; **2.** [~z] *v/t.* suiistimal etm., kötüye kullanmak; † *b-ne* kötü muamele etm.; **a'bu.sive** □ [~siv] tahkir edici, aşağılayıcı; ağzı bozuk, küfürbaz.

**a.but** [ə'bʌt] *v/i.* dayanmak, bitişik olm. (on, upon, against -*e*); **a'but.ment** *n.* 🔺 mesnet, dayanak; köprü ayağı.

**a.bysm** [ə'bizəm] *poet.* = abyss.

**a.bys.mal** □ [ə'bizməl] dipsiz, derin; kesif, çok; **a.byss** [ə'bis] *n.* uçurum, boşluk; *fig.* derinlik.

**Ab.ys.sin.i.an** [æbi'sinjən] *adj. & n.* Habeş (istanlı).

**a.ca.cia** ♀ [ə'keiʃə] *n.* akasya.

**ac.a.dem.ic** [ækə'demik] *adj.* akademik, üniversiteye ait; pratiğe dayanmayan, soyut; **ac.a'dem.i.cal 1.** □ = academic; **2.** ~s *pl.* akademik kıyafet; **a.cad.e.mi-ci.an** [əkædə'miʃən] *n.* akademisyen, akademi üyesi.

**a.cad.e.my** [ə'kædəmi] *n.* akademi.

**a.can.thus** [ə'kænθəs] *n.* ♀ ayı pençesi; 🔺 Yunan mimarisinde ayı pençesi yaprağı süslemesi.

**ac.cede** [æk'siːd] *v/i.* ~ to bşe razı olm., bşi kabul etm.; iş başına geçmek, iktidara gelmek; tahta çıkmak.

**ac.cel.er.ate** [æk'seləreit] *v/t. & v/i.* hızlan(dır)mak, çabuklaş(tır)mak; *fig.* teşvik etm., canlandırmak; **ac.cel.er'a.tion** *n.* hızlandırma, süratin artması; **ac'cel-er.a.tor** *n. mot.* gaz pedalı.

**ac.cent 1.** ['æksənt] *n.* vurgu, aksan; şive, ağız; aksan işareti; **2.** [æk'sent] *v/t.* vurgu koymak; vurgulamak; *fig.* önemle belirtmek, üzerinde ısrarla durmak; **ac.cen.tu.ate** [æk'sentjueit] *v/t.* vurgulamak; önemle belirtmek; **ac.cen.tu'a.tion** *n.* aksan koyma, vurgulama.

**ac.cept** [ək'sept] *v/t.* bşi kabul etm., almak; † (*poliçe v.b.*) kabul etm.; bşi onaylamak; **ac.cept.a'bil.i.ty** *n.* kabul edilebilirlik; **ac'cept.a.ble** □ kabul edilebilir; kabule değer; **ac'cept.ance** *n.* kabul, bşe razı olma; bşi onaylama; † (*poliçe v.b.*) kabul; **ac.cep.ta.tion** [æk-sep'teiʃən] *n.* kabul; anlam; **ac.cept.ed** □ [ək'septid] kabul edilmiş; **ac'cept.er, ac'cept.or** *n.* kabul eden; † (*poliçe v.b.*) kabul eden taraf.

**ac.cess** ['ækses] *n.* giriş, yol, geçit; nöbet;

**♀ easy of** ~ kolay ulaşılabilir; ~ road giriş yolu; have ~ to girebilmek -*e*; **ac.ces.sa.ry** [əkˈsesəri] = accessory; **ac.ces.si.bil.i.ty** [~siˈbiliti] *n.* erişilebilme, yaklaşılabilme; **ac.ces.si.ble** □ [~-səbl] erişilebilir, tırmanılabilir; **acˈces.sion** *n.* ulaşma; artma, çoğalma; yeni gelen şey (to -*e*); ~ to the throne tahta çıkma: recent ~s *pl.* yeni tedarik edilen şeyler.

**ac.ces.so.ry** [əkˈsesəri] **1.** □ yardımcı olan; suç ortaklığı eden; **2.** *n.usu.pl.* aksesuar, yardımcı şey; ♉ ferî fail, ikinci derecede suç ortağı.

**ac.ci.dence** *gr.* [ˈæksidəns] *n.* sarf, morfoloji.

**ac.ci.dent** [ˈæksidənt] *n.* tesadüf; kaza, arıza; ~ insurance kaza sigortası; by ~ **tesadüfen**; **ac.ci.den.tal** [æksiˈdentl] **1.** □ tesadüfî, arızî; ~ death kazaî ölüm; **2.** *n.* ikinci derecede önemi olan şey; ♪ tesadüfî olarak gelen bemol veya diyez.

**ac.claim** [əˈkleim] *v/t.* alkışlamak; (*bağırarak*) ilân etm.

**ac.cla.ma.tion** [æklǝˈmeiʃən] *n. oft.* ~s *pl.* alkışlama, alkış; by ~ alkışlarla (*oylama yerine*).

**ac.cli.ma.ti.za.tion** [əklaimətaiˈzeiʃən] *n.* (*bir yerin hava koşullarına*) alış(tır)ma; **acˈcli.ma.tize** *v/t.* alıştırmak.

**ac.cli.ma.te** *part. Am.* [əˈklaimit] = acclimatize.

**ac.cliv.i.ty** [əˈkliviti] *n.* yokuş, bayır.

**ac.com.mo.date** [əˈkɔmədeit] *v/t.* uydurmak, intibak ettirmek (to -*e*); yerleştirmek, yer tedarik etm.; *b-ne* bşi sağlamak, temin etm.; **acˈcom.mo.dat.ing** □ uysal; yardıma istekli; **ac.com.moˈda.tion** *n.* uyma, intibak; uysallık; yerleşme; uzlaştırma; yatacak veya kalacak yer (*oda, ev, otel v.b.*); ~ bill ♉ hatır senedi, hatır bonosu; ~ ladder ♩ borda iskelesi; seating ~ oturacak yer; ~ train *Am.* birçok istasyonda duran yolcu treni.

**ac.com.pa.ni.ment** [əˈkʌmpənimənt] *n.* refakat eden şey; ♪ *b-ne veya bşe* eşlik eden parça; **acˈcom.pa.nist** *n.* ♪ refakat eden, beraber çalan kimse; **acˈcom.pa.ny** *v/t.* refakat etm. -*e*; ♪ eşlik etm. -*e*.

**ac.com.plice** [əˈkɔmplis] *n.* suç ortağı.

**ac.com.plish** [əˈkɔmpliʃ] *v/t.* bşi bitirmek, başarmak; tamamlamak; **acˈcom.plished** *adj.* hünerli, usta; başarılmış; **acˈcom.plish.ment** *n.* başarı, yapıp bitirme; başarılmış eser; *mst.* ~s *pl.* yetenekler.

**ac.cord** [əˈkɔːd] **1.** *n.* uyum, ahenk; uygunluk, anlaşma, uzlaşma; akort; ♉ mahkeme dışında uzlaşma; with one ~

hep birlikte; of one's own ~ kendiliğinden, kendi arzusu ile; **2.** *v/i.* birbirini tutmak, uymak (with -*e*); *v/t.* uzlaştırmak, uyum sağlamak, teslim etm.; **acˈcord.ance** *n.* uygunluk, ahenk; in ~ with -*e* göre, -*e* uygun olarak; **acˈcord.ant** □ (with, to) uygun gelen -*e*; **acˈcord.ing:** ~ to *e* göre, -*e* nazaran; ~ as göre, aynen; **acˈcord.ing.ly** *adv.* bundan dolayı.

**ac.cor.di.on** ♪ [əˈkɔːdjən] *n.* akordeon.

**ac.cost** [əˈkɔst] *v/t.* (*esp. bir yabancıya*) yaklaşıp konuşmak; sarkıntılık etm.

**ac.count** [əˈkaunt] **1.** *n.* hesap; rapor; hikâye, açıklama; sebep; önem, kıymet, değer; ♉ hesap; current ~ câri hesap; payment on ~ mahsuben ödeme; statement of ~ hesap hülâsası; of no ~ önemsiz, sayılmaz; on no ~ asla, katiyen; on ~ of sebebiyle, -den dolayı; place to s.o.'s ~ *b-nin* hesabına geçirmek; take into ~, take ~ of göz önünde tutmak, hesaba katmak -*i*; leave out of ~ bşe dikkat etmemek; bşi ihmal etm.; turn to ~ kullanmak, zayi etmemek; keep ~s hesap tutmak, bşin hesabını tutmak; call to ~ cevap istemek, hesap sormak; give *veya* render an ~ of anlatmak; bşin hesabını vermek; give an ~ of o.s. yaptıklarının hesabını vermek; make no ~ of saymamak, itibar etmemek; **2.** *v/i.* ~ for hesap vermek; bşden sorumlu olm.; *hunt.* avı vurmak; be much (little) ~ed of çok (az) sayılmak, itibar görmek; *v/t.* saymak, itibar etm.; ~ o.s. happy kendini mutlu saymak; **ac.count.aˈbil.i.ty** *n.* sorumluluk; **acˈcount.a.ble** □ sorumlu; anlatılabilir; **acˈcount.an.cy** *n.* muhasebecilik; **acˈcount.ant** *n.* muhasebeci, muhasip, hesap uzmanı; chartered ~, *Am.* certified public ~ yeminli hesap uzmanı; **acˈcount.ing** ~ muhasebe.

**ac.cou.tre.ments** ✕ [əˈkuːtəmənts] *n. pl.* teçhizat, malzeme (*elbise ve silâh dışında*).

**ac.cred.it** [əˈkredit] *v/t.* tasdik etm.; yetki vermek -*e*; inanmak, güvenmek; itimatname vererek atamak; ~ s.th. to s.o., ~ s.o. with s.th. *b-nin* hesabına geçirmek.

**ac.cre.tion** [æˈkriːʃən] *n.* ilâve, ek; gelişme.

**ac.crue** [əˈkruː] *v/i.* hâsıl olm., gelmek; ziyadeleşmek (from -*den*); hissesine düşmek.

**ac.cu.mu.late** [ə'kju:mjuleit] *v/t.* artır-mak, toplamak, yığmak; *v/i.* artmak, toplanmak, yığılmak; **ac.cu.mu'la.tion** *n.* toplama, yığın; **ac'cu.mu.la.tive** □ [~lə-tiv] toplayıcı; toplanmış; **ac'cu.mu.lator** ≠ [~leitə] *n.* akümülatör.

**ac.cu.ra.cy** [ˈækjurəsi] *n.* doğruluk, sıh-hat; tam vaktinde olma; **ac.cu.rate** □ [ˈ~rit] doğru, tam.

**ac.curs.ed** □ [ə'kə:sid], **ac.curst** [ə'kə:st] melûn, lânetlenmiş.

**ac.cu.sa.tion** [ækju:'zeiʃən] *n.* suçlama, itham; **ac.cu.sa.tive** [ə'kju:zətiv] *a.* ~ *case n.* & *adj. gr.* -*i* halinde; -*i* hali; **ac-cuse** [ə'kju:z] *v/t.* suçlamak, itham etm. (s.o. of s.t.h. *b-ni bşle*); the ~*d* sanık, maznun; **ac'cus.er** *n.* ♂♂ davacı, itham eden. **ac.cus.tom** [ə'kʌstəm] *v/t.* alıştırmak (to -*e*); **ac'cus.tomed** to alışık, alışkın -*e*.

**ace** [eis] *n.* (*iskambil*) birli, bey, as; *fig.* çok cesur savaş havacısı; ~ in the hole *Am.* F yedek koz; **he was within an** ~ **of** dying ölmesine ramak kaldı.

**a.cer.bi.ty** [ə'sə:biti] *n.* burukluk; (*söz*) acılık, sertlik, huysuzluk.

**ac.e.tate** ♂ [ˈæsitit] *n.* asetik asit tuzu; bir çeşit sentetik kumaş; **a.ce.tic** [ə'si:-tik] *adj.* sirke gibi, ekşi; ~ **acid** asetik asit, sirke asidi; **a.cet.i.fy** [ə'setifai] *v/t.* ekşitmek; *v/i.* ekşimek; **ac.e.tone** [ˈæsi-təun] *n.* aseton; **ac.e.tous** [ˈ~təs] *adj.* ekşi; **a.cet.y.lene** [ə'setili:n] *n.* asetilen.

**ache** [eik] 1. *n.* (*sürekli*) ağrı, sızı, acı; 2. *v/i.* ağrımak, sızlamak.

**a.chieve** [ə'tʃi:v] *v/t.* yapmak, icra etm., meydana çıkarmak, elde etm., başar-mak; **a'chieve.ment** *n.* başarı; başarıl-mış şey.

**ach.ing** [ˈeikiŋ] □ acıyan, ağrıyan, ıstı-raplı.

**ach.ro.mat.ic** [ækrəu'mætik] *adj.* renkleri doğal haliyle gösteren, renksiz

**ac.id** [ˈæsid] 1. *n.* asit; 2. *adj.* ekşi; **a.cid.i.fy** [ə'sidifai] *v/t.* asit yapmak, ek-şitmek; **a'cid.i.ty** *n.* ekşilik, ekşime; **ac.i.do.sis** [æsi'dəusis] *n.* kanın asitli hali; **'ac.id-proof** *adj.* aside dirençli; **a.cid.u.late** [ə'sidjuleit] *v/t.* ekşitmek; (*hamur*) mayalamak; *v/i.* ekşimek; **a.cid.u.lous** [ə'sidjuləs] *adj.* mayhoş, ek-şice.

**ac.knowl.edge** [ək'nɒlidʒ] *v/t.* kabul etm., tanımak; itiraf etm.; ♱ *bşin* alındığını bildirmek; *bşi* onaylamak; **ac'knowl-edg(e).ment** *n.* kabul, tasdik, itiraf; ♱ teslim makbuzu, alındı.

**ac.me** [ˈækmi] *n.* doruk, zirve; kriz.

**ac.ne** [ˈækni] *n.* akne, bir çeşit cilt has-talığı.

**ac.o.nite** ♣ [ˈækənait] *n.* kurtboğan.

**a.corn** ♣ [ˈeikɔ:n] *n.* meşe palamudu.

**a.cous.tic**, **a.cous.ti.cal** □ [ə'ku:stik(əl)] akustiğe ait; **a'cous.tics** *n. mst sg.* akus-tik.

**ac.quaint** [ə'kweint] *v/t.* bildirmek, tanıt-mak; (s.o. with *b-ne bşi*); be ~*ed* with *bşi* bilmek, -*den* haberdar olm.; **ac-'quaint.ance** *n.* tanışma; malûmat; ta-nıdık.

**ac.qui.esce** [ækwi'es] *v/i.* kabul etm., muvafakat etm., razı olm.; **ac.qui'es-cence** *n.* uysallık, razı olma, kabul et-me; **ac.qui'es.cent** □ itaatli, uysal, yu-muşak huylu.

**ac.quire** [ə'kwaiə] *v/t.* elde etm., kazan-mak; ~*d adj.* kazanılmış, müktesep; **ac'quire.ment** *n.* edinme; edinilen bilgi, hüner.

**ac.qui.si.tion** [ækwi'ziʃən] *n.* edinme, el-de edilen şey, kazanç; **ac.quis.i.tive** □ [ə'kwizitiv] haris, acgözlü; elde edilebi-len; **ac'quis.i.tive.ness** *n.* kazanç hırsı; tamahkârlık.

**ac.quit** [ə'kwit] *v/t.* ♱♱ beraat ettirmek (of -*den*); ~ o.s. of (*görev*) yerine ge-tirmek; ~ o.s. well (ill) görevini iyi (kötü) yapmak; **ac'quit.tal** *n.* beraat; (*görev*) yerine getirme; **ac'quit.tance** *n.* zimmet-ten kurtulma; ibraname.

**a.cre** [ˈeikə] *n.* İngiliz dönümü (*0,404 hek-tar*).

**ac.rid** [ˈækrid] *adj.* buruk, acı (a. *fig*).

**ac.ri.mo.ni.ous** □ [ækri'məunjəs] *fig.* acı, ters, sert; **ac.ri.mo.ny** [ˈækriməni] *n. fig.* acılık, terslik, sertlik.

**ac.ro.bat** [ˈækrəbæt] *n.* akrobat, cambaz; **ac.ro.bat.ic** [ækrəu'bætik] *adj.* (~*ally*) akrobatik; **ac.ro'bat.ics** *n. pl.* akrobasi; ♱ akrobasi (*uçuşu*)

**a.cross** [ə'krɒs] 1. *adv.* ortasından, için-den veya üstünden karşı yana geçerek; come ~ rast gelmek, tesadüf etm.; saw ~ testere ile ortasından ikiye böl-mek; a lake three miles ~ üç mil geniş-liğinde göl; with arms ~ çapraz kavuş-turulmuş (*kol*); 2. *prp.* karşıdan karşı-ya, öbür tarafa; çapraz; run ~ the road yolu koşarak geçmek; come ~, run ~ birdenbire *b-ne*, *bşe* rastlamak.

**act** [ækt] 1. *v/i.* hareket etm., harekete geçmek, davranmak (on, upon -*e göre*); *thea.* rol oynamak, temsil etm.; ~ (up) on s.o.'s advice *b-nin* önerisine göre ha-reket etm.; *v/t.* rol yapmak (*a.fig*), oy-namak; 2. *n.* fiil, hareket, iş, yapılan şey; ♂♂ kanun; *thea.* perde; ♀ of God mücbir sebep, meydana geleceği önceden kestirilemiyen olay; 2s of the Apostles havariyun tarihi; catch s.o. in the ~ b-ni suçüstü yakalamak; **'act.ing 1.** *n.* *thea.* temsil, oyun oynama; **2.** *adj.* yapan, işleyen; temsil eden; vekâlet eden. **ac.tion** ['ækʃən] *n.* fiil, hareket, iş, faaliyet, etki; 𝔰𝔰 dava; harekete geçme *(makine, at v.b.); thea.* oyundaki olaylar dizisi; *paint.* duruş, poz; ~ radius menzil, tesir, hareket sahası; bring an ~ against b-i aleyhine dava açmak; killed in ~ savaşta ölmek; take ~ harekete geçmek; **ac.tion.a.ble** ['~ʃnəbl] *adj.* dava edilebilir.

**ac.tive** □ ['æktiv] faal, enerjik, canlı, çevik, hareketli; etkin; faaliyette, iş başında, görevde; ✝ hareketli; aktif...; ✝ ~ demand fiili talep; ~ officer muvazzaf subay; ~ **voice** *gr.* etken çatı, aktif; **ac'tiv.i.ty** *n. (oft.pl.)* faaliyet; çeviklik; etki; faal oluş; *part.* ✝ hareketlilik, faaliyet; in full ~ tam faaliyette; *intense* ~ hummalı faaliyet.

**ac.tor** ['æktə] *n.* aktör, artist, rol oynayan; **ac.tress** ['æktrıs] *n.* aktris, kadın oyuncu.

**ac.tu.al** □ ['æktʃuəl] gerçek, hakiki, asıl; şimdiki, halihazırdaki; **ac.tu.al.i.ty** ['~æliti] *n.* gerçek, hakikat; **ac.tu.al.ly** ['æktʃuəli] *adv.* gerçekten, hakikatte; bilfiil.

**ac.tu.ar.y** ['æktjuəri] *n. (sigorta şirketi)* istatistikçi.

**ac.tu.ate** ['æktjueit] *v/t.* işletmek, harekete getirmek; *fig.* tahrik, teşvik etm.; **ac.tu'a.tion** *n.* teşvik, tahrik.

**a.cu.men** [ə'kju:men] *n.* feraset, basiret, zekâ keskinliği.

**a.cute** □ [ə'kju:t] şiddetli, keskin, ince; keskin akıllı; tiz, keskin *(ses);* 𝔰 akut; vahim, ağır, şiddetli; **a'cute.ness** *n.* zekâ, keskinlik.

**ad** F [æd] = advertisement.

**ad.age** ['ædidʒ] *n.* darbımesel, atasözü, vecize.

**ad.a.mant** ['ædəmənt] **1.** *n.* taş gibi katı, kaskatı şey; **2.** □ hoşgörüsüz, çok sert, insafsız; **ad.a.man.tine** ['~mæntain] *adj.* elmas gibi çok sert; *fig.* = adamant.

**a.dapt** [ə'dæpt] *v/t.* uydurmak, tatbik etm. (to, for -e); *lit.* adapte etm.; **a.dapt-a'bil.i.ty** *n.* uyma yeteneği, intibak kabiliyeti; **a'dapt.a.ble** *adj.* uyabilir; **ad.ap.ta.tion** [ædæp'teiʃən] *n.* uyma, intibak (to -e); *lit.* adaptasyon, uyarlama; **a.dap.ter** [ə'dæptə] *n. radyo:* adaptör; **a'dap.tive** *adj.* uyma yeteneğinde.

**add** [æd] *v/t.* katmak, eklemek, ilâve

etm.; zammetmek, toplamak; Ą toplamak; *v/i.* b-ne iltihak etm., katılmak; ~ up toplamak; neticelenmek; anlaşılmak; **'ad.ded** *adj.* ilâve edilen, munzam. **ad.den.dum** [ə'dendəm] *n., pl.* **ad'den.da** [~də] *(kitabın veya konuşmanın sonuna)* ek, ilâve.

**ad.der** ['ædə] *n. zo.* engerek yılanı.

**ad.dict 1.** [ə'dikt] *v/t.* ~ o.s.to bşe alışmak, kendini vermek, düşkün olm., bşin tiryakisi olm.; **2.** ['ædikt] *n.* (opium *etc.* ~) *(afyon vs. ye)* düşkün, müptelâ; **ad.dict-ed** [ə'diktid] **to** -e düşkün, -in tiryakisi.

**ad.di.tion** [ə'diʃən] *n.* ilâve, ek, zam; Ą toplama; in ~ to -den başka, -e ilâveten, ayrıca; **ad'di.tion.al** □ eklenilen, biraz daha.

**ad.dle** ['ædl] **1.** *adj.* çürük, cılk *(yumurta); fig.* boş, kof *(kafa, zekâ vs.);* **2.** *v/t.* bozmak, şaşırtmak; *v/i.* çürümek, cılk çıkmak.

**ad.dress** [ə'dres] **1.** *v/t.* hitap etm.; söylev vermek; -in üstüne adres yazmak; ~ o.s. to *(bir işe)* hazırlanmak; ele almak, girişmek; **2.** *n.* adres; hitabe, söylev; âdabımuaşeret; give an ~ hitap etm.; söylev vermek; pay one's ~es to b-ne kur yapmak; **ad.dress.ee** [ædre'si:] *n.* alacak olan.

**ad.duce** [ə'dju:s] *v/t. (delil vs.)* getirmek, göstermek.

**ad.e.noids** 𝔰 ['ædinɔidz] *n. pl.* bezeler.

**ad.ept** ['ædept] **1.** □ usta, mahir (in -de); **2.** *n.* uzman; be an ~ at usta olm. -de.

**ad.e.qua.cy** ['ædikwəsi] *n.* kifayet, yeterlilik, ehliyet; **ad.e.quate** □ ['~kwit] uygun, münasip, yeterli.

**ad.here** [əd'hiə] *v/i.* yapışmak, yapışık kalmak; iltihak etm.; bağlanmak (to -e); **ad'her.ence** *n.* (to) yapışma; vefa, bağlılık; **ad'her.ent 1.** *adj.* yapışık, merbut; **2.** *n.* taraftar.

**ad.he.sion** [əd'hi:ʒən] *s.* adherence; *fig.* rıza, muvafakat; *phys.* birbirine yapışma.

**ad.he.sive** [əd'hi:siv] **1.** □ yapışkan, yapışıcı; ~ plaster, ~ tape plaster, band; **2.** *n.* zamk, tutkal, çiriş.

**a.dieu** [ə'dju:] *int.* Allaha ısmarladık, elveda; **2.** *n.* veda; make one's ~(s) b-le vedalaşmak.

**ad.i.pose** ['ædipəus] *adj.* etin yağına ait; yağlı; *n.* etin yağlı tarafı; ~ tissue yağ dokusu.

**ad.it** ['ædit] *n.* giriş, methal; ✕ lâğım galerisi.

**ad.ja.cen.cy** [ə'dʒeisənsi] *n.* yakınlık, bitişik olma; adjacencies *pl.* civar, etraf.

çevre, dolay; **ad¹ja.cent** □ (to) bitişik, komşu -e.

**ad.jec.ti.val** □ [ædʒek¹taivəl] sıfat cinsinden; **ad.jec.tive** [¹ædʒiktiv] **1.** n. sıfat; **2.** adj. sıfat türünden.

**ad.join** [ə¹dʒɔin] v/t. bitişik olm. -e; **ad¹join.ing** adj. bitişik, yan yana.

**ad.journ** [ə¹dʒəːn] v/t. ertelemek, tehir etm.; v/i. oturuma son vermek, dağılmak; **ad¹journ.ment** n. erteleme; δδ ara.

**ad.judge** [ə¹dʒʌdʒ] v/t. b-ne bşi tanımak, vermek, hükmetmek; δδ karar vermek.

**ad.ju.di.cate** [ə¹dʒuːdikeit] s. adjudge; **ad¹ju.di¹ca.tion** n. hüküm verme, karar verme; mahkeme kararı; kararın tefhimi.

**ad.junct** [¹ædʒʌŋkt] n. ilâve, ek; iş arkadaşı, yardımcı; gr. tayini ilâve, başka kelimeleri tanımlamak için kullanılan kelime(ler).

**ad.ju.ra.tion** [ædʒuə¹reiʃən] n. ciddi dilek; yemin; **ad.jure** [ə¹dʒuə] v/t. istirham etm., yalvarıp yakarmak.

**ad.just** [ə¹dʒʌst] v/t. doğrultmak, düzeltmek; ayar etm., uydurmak (to -e); ~ o.s. to fig. intibak etm. -e; ~ing screw tanzim vidası; **ad¹just.a.ble** □ ayar edilebilir, uydurulabilir; **ad¹just.ment** n. uydurma, ayarlama, düzeltme; tasfiye.

**ad.ju.tan.cy** ✕ [¹ædʒutənsi] n. emir subaylığı; **¹ad.ju.tant** n. emir subayı.

**ad.lib** F [æd¹lib] v/t. (irticalen) söz söylemek; piyano çalmak.

**ad.man** F [¹ædmæn] n. reklâm uzmanı.

**ad.min.is.ter** [əd¹ministə] v/t. yönetmek, idare etm.; tatbik etm.; yerine getirmek; yemin ettirmek; ~ justice, ~ the law hâkimlik etm.; ~ punishment cezalandırmak, b-ni para cezasına çarpmak; v/i. hizmet etm. (to -e); **ad.min.is¹tra.tion** n. idare, yönetim; hükümet; esp. Am. başkanlık; ~ of justice kaza işleri, adliye; **ad¹min.is.tra.tive** [~trətiv] □ yönetimle ilgili, idarî; **ad¹min.is.tra.tor** [~treitə] n. idareci, müdür, yönetmen; δδ kayyım, vasi, tereke idare memuru.

**ad.mi.ra.ble** □ [¹ædmərəbl] takdire değer, çok güzel.

**ad.mi.ral** [ædmərəl] n. amiral; 2 of the Fleet donanma kumandanı; **¹ad.mi.ral.ty** n. amirallik; First Lord of the 2 (İngiltere'de) Bahriye Nazırı.

**ad.mi.ra.tion** [ædmə¹reiʃən] n. hayranlık, takdir; she was the ~ of all herkesin takdirini kazandı.

**ad.mire** [əd¹maiə] v/t. çok beğenmek, takdir etm.; zevkle seyretmek; **ad¹mir.er** n. hayran olan kimse; âşık.

**ad.mis.si.bil.i.ty** [ədmisə¹biliti] n. kabul

olunabilme; **ad¹mis.si.ble** □ kabul olunabilir; **ad¹mis.sion** n. itiraf, kabul (into, to -e); girme, giriş (into, to -e); giriş ücreti, duhuliye; ~ fee giriş ücreti, duhuliye.

**ad.mit** [əd¹mit] v/t. içeriye almak, kabul etm. (in, into, to), müsaade etm.; itiraf etm.; v/i. :~ of imkân vermek; it ~s of no excuse affedilemez, mazur görülemez; **ad¹mit.tance** n. kabul; giriş; no~! girilmez!; **ad¹mit.ted.ly** adv. itiraf edildiği gibi, gerçekten.

**ad.mix.ture** [əd¹mikstʃə] n. katma, ilâve; katıp karıştırılmış madde.

**ad.mon.ish** [əd¹mɔniʃ] v/t. ihtar etm., tenbih etm., azarlamak; **ad.mo.ni.tion** [ædmɔu¹niʃən] n. ihtar, tembih, öğüt; **ad.mon.i.to.ry** □ [əd¹mɔnitəri] ihtar mahiyetinde, nasihat şeklinde.

**a.do** [ə¹duː] n. telâş, gürültü, patırtı; without much ~ ses çıkarmadan, mesele yapmadan.

**a.do.be** [ə¹dəubi] n. kerpiç.

**ad.o.les.cence** [ædəu¹lesns] n. gençlik, büyüme çağı; **ad.o¹les.cent** adj. & n. delikanlı, genç; büyümekte olan (kimse); çocukça.

**a.dopt** [ə¹dɔpt] v/t. ¹benimsemek, kabul etm., edinmek; evlâtlığa kabul etm.; ~ed child evlât edinilmiş çocuk, evlâtlık; **a¹dop.tion** n. kabul; evlât edinme; **a¹dop.tive** adj. evlâtlığa kabul eden veya edilen.

**a.dor.a.ble** □ [ə¹dɔːrəbl] tapılacak, şayanı hürmet; **ad.o.ra.tion** [ædɔː¹reiʃən] n. tapma; aşk, aşırı sevgi; **a.dore** [ə¹dɔː] v/t. tapmak -e, aşırı derecede sevmek -i; v/i tapınmak; **a¹dor.er** adj. perestişkâr, tapan.

**a.dorn** [ə¹dɔːn] v/t. süslemek, donatmak; **a¹dorn.ment** n. süs, tezyinat, dekor.

**A.dri.at.ic** [eidri¹ætik] n. Adriya Denizi.

**a.drift** [ə¹drift] ⚓ adj. sularla sürüklenen; başıboş; turn s.o. ~ b-ni ortada bırakmak, kendi haline terketmek.

**a.droit** □ [ə¹drɔit] becerikli, usta; **a¹droit.ness** n. hüner, marifet.

**ad.u.late** [¹ædjuleit] v/t. dalkavukluk (veya müdahene, tabasbus) etm.; **ad.u¹la.tion** n. aşırı övgü, tabasbus, yaltaklanma; **ad¹u.la.tor** n. pohpohçu, komplimancı, yüze gülen, dalkavuk; **ad.u.la.to.ry** adj. fazla metheden, pohpohçu.

**a.dult** [¹ædʌlt] adj. & n. büyük, reşit, ergin, yetişkin; ~ education yetişkin eğitimi.

**a.dul.ter.ant** [ə¹dʌltərənt] n. karıştırılmış madde; **a¹dul.ter.ate 1.** [~reit] v/t. karıştırmak, bozmak; *fig. bşi yüzüne gözüne bulaştırmak, berbadetmek;* **2.** [~rit] *adj.* karışık; **a.dul.ter.a.tion** [ədʌltə'reiʃən] *n.* karıştırma; **a dul.ter.er** 𝒐̃ *n.* zâni, zina işleyen *(erkek);* **a'dul.ter.ess** *n.* zâniye, zina işleyen *(kadın);* **a'dul.ter.ous** □ zina eden; **a'dul.ter.y** *n.* zina.

**ad.um.brate** ['ædʌmbreit] *v/t.* ima etm., sezdirmek; taslağını çizmek; **ad.um'bration** *n.* ima, gösterme, işaret.

**ad.vance** [əd'vɑːns] **1.** *v/i.* ilerlemek, ileri gitmek, terfi etm.; yükselmek *(fiyat); v/t.* ilerletmek, ileri götürmek; terfi ettirmek; yükseltmek *(fiyat);* avans vermek; söylemek, teklif etm.; **2.** *n.* ilerleme, terakki; terfi; † avans, peşin; ✕ ileri yürüyüş; ileri harekât; yükselme *(fiyat);* in ~ *adv.* peşin olarak; be in ~ of s.o. yaşından daha olgun olm.; **ad'vanced** *adj.* ilerlemiş, ileri; ~ in years yaşı ilerlemiş, yaşlı; ~ English ileri düzeyde İngilizce; **ad'vance.ment** *n.* ilerleme; terfi.

**ad.van.tage** [əd'vɑːntidʒ] **1.** *n.* avantaj, yarar, fayda, kâr, kazanç; üstünlük; zaafından istifade; *(tenis)* düsten sonra gelen puan; avantaj; **2.** *vb.* kazan(dır)mak, ilerletmek; take ~ of faydalanmak *-den;* you have the ~ of me bilmediklerimi biliyorsun; benden daha kârlısın; **ad.van.ta.geous** □ [ædvən'teidʒəs] faydalı, yararlı, kârlı.

**ad.vent** ['ædvənt] *n.* gelme, baş gösterme; 2 *eccl.* Noel yortusundan önceki dört hafta; Hazreti Isa'nın dünyaya gelişi; **adven.ti.tious** □ [ædven'tiʃəs] arızî, dıştan gelen, tesadüfî.

**ad.ven.ture** [əd'ventʃə] **1.** *n.* macera, sergüzeşt; † rizikolu iş; **2.** *vb.* cesaret etm., göze almak; tehlikeye koymak; yapmağa kalkışmak, yeltenmek; **ad'ven.tur.er** *n.* avantüriye, maceracı; **ad'ven.tur.ess** *n.* dişi maceracı; **ad'ven.tur.ous** □ maceraya düşkün, cesaretli, tehlikeli.

**ad.verb** ['ædvəːb] *n. gr.* zarf; **ad.ver.bi.al** [əd'vəːbjəl] □ zarfa ait; ~ phrase zarf gibi kullanılan deyim.

**ad.ver.sar.y** ['ædvəsəri] *n.* düşman, muhalif; **ad.verse** □ ['~vəːs] zıt, ters, karşı gelen; ~ balance of trade bilânçoda açık; **ad.ver.si.ty** [əd'vəːsiti] *n.* zorluk; güçlük, sıkıntı, talihsizlik.

**ad.vert** [əd'vəːt] *vb.* zikretmek, ima etm., hissettirmek; bahsetmek (to *-den*).

**ad.ver.tise** [əd'vətaiz] *v/t.* ilân etm., bildirmek; reklâmını yapmak; **ad.ver.tisement** [əd'vəːtismənt] *n.* ilân, haber, reklâm; **ad.ver.tis.er** ['ædvətaizə] *n.* ilân

eden veya reklâm yapan kimse; ilân gazetesi; **'ad.ver.tis.ing** *n.* reklâm, ilân.

**ad.vice** [əd'vais] *n.* nasihat, öğüt; tavsiye; † haber, tebliğ, talimat; letter of ~ ihbar mektubu; take medical ~ doktora sormak.

**ad.vis.a.ble** □ [əd'vaizəbl] tavsiye edilebilir, makul, uygun; **ad'vise** *v/t.* nasihat etm., öğüt vermek; haber vermek; † haber vermek, teklifde bulunmak; ~ s.o. of s.th. *b-ni bş* hakkında uyarmak; *v/i.* danışmak, akıl sormak; **ad'vis.ed.ly** [~idli] *adv.* tedbirli olarak, akıllıca; **ad'vis.er** *n.* danışman, müşavir; **ad'vi.so.ry** [~əri] *adj.* istişari, tavsiye niteliğinde; 2 Board istişare kurulu.

**ad.vo.ca.cy** ['ædvəkəsi] *n.* avukatlık, müdafaa, savunma; **ad.vo.cate 1.** ['~kit] *n.* avukat; *fig.* müdafaasını yapan; **2.** ['~keit] *v/t.* müdafaa etm., savunmak, tavsiye etm..

**adze** *Am. a.* **adz** ⊕ [ædz] *n.* keser.

**Ae.ge.an Sea** [iː'dʒiːən'siː] Ege Denizi, Adalar Denizi.

**ae.gis** ['iːdʒis] *n.* kalkan, siper; koruma.

**ae.on, eon** ['iːən] *n.* çok uzun müddet; sonsuzluk.

**a.er.at.ed** ['eiəreitid] *adj.* karbonik, karbonatlı.

**a.e.ri.al** ['εəriəl] **1.** □ havaî, havaya ait; havada yapılan; ~ car hava hattı arabası; **2.** *n. (radyo, TV.)* anten.

**a.er.ie** ['εəri] *n.* kuş yuvası; *fig.* yuva.

**a.er.o...** ['εərəu] *comb.* hava...; **a.er.o.batics** [~'bætiks] *n. (uçakla, havada)* akrobasi; **a.er.o.drome** ['~drəum] *n.* hava alanı; **a.er.o.dy.nam'ic** [~dinæmik] □ hareket halinde olan hava veya gaza ait; **a.er.o.gram** ['~græm] *n.* telsiz telgraf.

**a.er.o.gramme** ['εərəugræem] *n.* zarfsız uçak mektubu; **a.er.o.lite** ['εərəulait] *n.* göktaşı; **a.er.o.naut** ['εərənɔːt] *n.* balon kullanan pilot; **a.er.o'nau.tic, a.er.o'nau.ti.cal** □ uçuculuğa ait; **a.er.o'nau.tics** *n. mst sg.* havacılık; **'a.er.o.plane** *n.* uçak, tayyare; **a.er.o.stat** ['εərəustæt] *n.* havada sabit durabilen balon; **a.er.o'stat.ics** *n.* hava kanunları ilmi.

**aes.thete** ['iːsθiːt] *n.* bediiyat ,estetik; **aesthet.ic, aes.thet.i.cal** □ [iːs'θetik(əl)] bedii, estetik; **aes'thet.ics** *n. pl.* estetik.

**a.far** [ə'fɑː] *adv. mst* ~ off uzak(ta); from ~ uzaktan.

**af.fa.bil.i.ty** [æfə'biliti] *n.* nezaket, hatırşınaslık.

**af.fa.ble** □ ['æfəbl] nazik, hatırşinas, sokulgan.

**af.fair** [ə'fεə] *n.* iş, mesele, olay; ilişki;

~ of honour şeref meselesi; love ~ aşk macerası.

**af.fect** [ə'fekt] *v/t.* tesir etm., dokunmak *-e*; etkilemek, değiştirmek, müteessir etm. *-i*; *bşi* yalancıktan yapmak, taslamak; gibi görünmek; *bşden* hoşlanmak; ~ ignorance tecahül etm., bilmez gibi görünmek; ~ sickness temaruz etm., hastalık taslamak; **af.fec.ta.tion** [æfek-'teiʃən] *n.* yapmacık, gösteriş, naz; **af.fect.ed** □ [ə'fektid] yapma, yapmacıklı; tutulmuş (with *-e*); meyyal, düşkün (towards s.o. *-e*); **af'fec.tion** *n.* sevgi, aşk (for, towards *-e*); düşkünlük; hastalık; **af'fec.tion.ate** □ [~kʃnit] şevkatli, sevgi gösteren; yours ~ly sevgilerle (*mektup sonunda*); **af'fec.tive** □ hissi, dokunaklı.

**af.fi.ance** [ə'faiəns] **1.** *n.* itimat, inanç, güven (in *-e*); nişan; **2.** *v/t.* nişanlamak (to *ile*).

**af.fi.da.vit** [æfi'deivit] *n.* (*yazılı*) yeminli ifade, beyan.

**cf.fil.i.ate** [ə'filieit] *vb.* üye olmak; kaynaştırmak, birleştirmek, yakın ilişki kurmak (with, to *ile, -e*); *b̃* babalığı tayin etm.; ~d company bağlı şirket; **af·fil.i'a.tion** *n.* yakın ilişki; il(ti)hak; evlâtlığa kabul.

**af.fin.i.ty** [ə'finiti] *n.* yakınlık, benzeşme (between, with arasında, ile); sıhrî hısımlık; güçlü cazibe (for, to, between *ile, -e, arasında*); ~ çekme.

**af.firm** [ə'fəːm] *v/t.* tasdik etm., onaylamak, yeminsiz olarak teyid etm.; **af.fir.ma.tion** [æfəː'meiʃən] *n.* tasdik, teyit, yeminsiz beyan; **af.fir.m.a.tive** □ [ə'fəːmətiv] **1.** müspet, olumlu, tasdik edilen; **2.** *n.:* answer in the ~ olumlu cevap vermek.

**af.fix 1.** [æfiks] *n.* ek. ilâve (*kelimenin başına veya sonuna*); **2.** [ə'fiks] (to) *v/t.* bağlamak, takmak, yapıştırmak; (*mühür*) basmak; (*yazı*) eklemek.

**af.flict** [ə'flikt] *v/t.* vermek *-e*, eziyet etm., müteessir etm., incitmek; ~ed tutulmuş (with *-e*); **af'flic.tion** *n.* dert, keder.

**af.flu.ence** ['æfluəns] *n.* bolluk, refah, servet; **'af.flu.ent 1.** □ bol (*akan*); bol; zengin; **2.** *n.* nehir kolu.

**af.flux** ['æflʌks] *n.* bir yere akış.

**cf.ford** [ə'fɔːd] *v/t.* meydana getirmek, vermek; bütçesi müsait olm. *-e*; I can ~ it onu alabilirim, param yeter.

**af.for.est** [æ'fɔrist] *v/t.* ağaçlandırmak, orman haline getirmek; **af.for.est'a.tion** *n.* ağaç dikme, ormanlaştırma.

**af.fran.chise** [ə'fræntʃaiz] *v/t.* azadetmek, muaf tutmak.

**af.fray** [ə'frei] *n.* kavga, arbede.

**af.front** ['əfrʌnt] **1.** *v/t.* (*alenen*) hakaret etm., tahkir etm.; **2.** *n.* hakaret, tahkir; put on ~ upon, offer an ~ to hakaret etm.

**a.field** [ə'fiːld] *adv.* (*evden*) uzak; kıra, kırda; far ~ çok uzakta.

**a.fire** [ə'faiə] *adj.* tutuşmuş, yanan.

**a.flame** [ə'fleim] *adj.* alevler içinde, tutuşmuş; *fig.* kızgın.

**a.float** [ə'fləut] *adj. & adv.* su üzerinde dolaşan; denizde; su basmış; keep ~ su üzerinde durmak; set ~ ↓ yüzdürmek; the rumour is ~ şayia dolaşıyor.

**a.foot** [ə'fut] *adv.* ayakta; hareket halinde, hazırlanmakta.

**a.fore** ↓ [ə'fɔː] *s.* before; **a'fore.men.tioned** [~menʃənd] *adj.*, **a'fore.named** [~neimd], **a'fore.said** evvelce belirtilen, mezkûr; **a'fore.thought** *n.* kasıt, taammüt.

**a.fraid** [ə'freid] *adj.* korkmuş, korkan; be ~ of korkmak *-den*; I am ~ korkarım, korkuyorum; maalesef, yazık ki.

**a.fresh** [ə'freʃ] *adv.* yeniden, tekrar.

**Af.ri.ca** ['æfrikə] *n.* Afrika; **Af.ri.can** ['æfrikən] **1.** *adj.* Afrika'ya ait; **2.** *n.* Afrikalı; *part.* Am. zenci.

**Af.ri.kaans** [æfri'kɑːns] *n.* Güney Afrika'da konuşulan lehçe (*Hollanda diline çok benzeyen*).

**aft** ↓ [ɑːft] *adj. & adv.* kıçda, kıça doğru.

**aft.er** ['ɑːftə] *adv., prp., cj., adj. -den* sonra; *-e* göre; *-e* rağmen; ardında; ardından; bunun üzerine; ertesi; *-e* nazaran; tarzında; ↓ sekiz kürekli skif; ~ all bununla birlikte, buna rağmen, yine de: in ~ days gelecekte, ileride; the day ~ tomorrow öbürgün; time ~ time tekrar tekrar; ~birth $\mathcal{P}$ *n.* meşime, etene, son; '~care *n.* (*hastalık vs.*) *-den* sonraki bakım: '~crop *n.* ikinci mahsül; '~din-ner *adj.* yemekten sonra gelen; '~ef.fect *n.* bşin bilvasıta neticeleri; '~glow *n.* akşam kızıllığı; '~hours *n. pl.* mesai saatleri dışında; ~math *n.* netice, akıbet, yan tesir; '~noon *n.* öğleden sonra, ikindi; '~pains *n. pl.* doğumdan sonraki ağrılar; '~sea.son *n.* mevsim sonu; '~taste *n.* ağızda kalan tat; '~thought *n.* sonradan akla gelen fikir; ~wards ['~wədz] *adv.* sonra, sonradan.

**a.gain** [ə'gen] *adv.* tekrar, gene, bir daha; bundan başka; ~ and ~; time and ~ bazen, arasıra; as much (many) ~ iki misli; now and ~ arasıra, bazen.

**a.gainst** [ə'genst] *prep. -e* karşı, *-e* rağmen: *-in* aleyhinde; ~ the wall duvara dayalı; ~ a background bir fon önünde (*veya üstünde*); over ~ karşı(sında); yüzyüze; karşılık olarak; run ~ s.o. *b-ne* rastgelmek.

**a.gape** [ə¹geip] *adv.* & *adj.* ağzı açık, şaşkın, şaşırmış.

**ag.ate** [¹ægət] *n.* akik taşı; bilye, zıpzıp; *Am. typ.* = ruby.

**a.ga.ve** ♦ [ə¹geivi] *n.* agave.

**age** [eidʒ] **1.** *n.* yaş; çağ, devir; (old) ~ yaşlılık; at the ~ of yaşında; in the ~ of Queen Anne Kraliçe Anne devrinde; of ~ reşit, ergin; over ~ yaşı geçkin; under ~ küçük, reşit olmayan; what is his ~? kaç yaşında?; come of ~, be of ~ reşit olm.; **2.** *v/i.* yaşlanmak; *v/t.* bşi eskitmek; **aged** [eidʒd] *adj.* yaşlı, ihtiyar; ~ twenty 20 yaşında; **a.ged** [¹-id] *adj.* yıllanmış, dinlendirilmiş *(içki)*; yaşındaki; **¹age.less** *adj.* eskimez, kocamaz, ihtiyarlamaz; **¹age-lim.it** yaş haddi.

**a.gen.cy** [¹eidʒənsi] *n.* faaliyet, işleme: tavassut, aracılık; † ajans, acentalık, vekillik, büro.

**a.gen.da** [ə¹dʒendə] *n.* gündem, ruzname.

**a.gent** [¹eidʒənt] *n.* acente, vekil; vasıta, âmil.

**age-old** [¹eidʒəuld] *adj.* çok eski, kadim.

**age-worn** [¹eidʒwɔːn] *adj.* eli ayağı tutmaz olmuş; takatten düşmüş.

**ag.glom.er.ate** [ə¹glɔməreit] **1.** *vb.* toplamak, bir araya getirmek, yığmak; **2.** *n.* toplama; volkanik parçaların eriyerek bir araya toplanması; **ag.glom.er¹a.tion** *n.* yığılma, toplanma, yığın.

**ag.glu.ti.nate** [ə¹gluːtineit] *vb.* bşi başka bş üzerine yapıştırmak; yapıştırarak örtmek: ♣, *gr.* bitiştirmek; **ag.glu.ti.na.tion** [~¹neiʃən] *n.* yapıştırma; *gr.* bitişme: ♣ aglütinasyon; **ag¹glu.ti.na.tive** [~nətiv] *adj.* yapıştırma işlemine ait; *gr.* bitişken.

**ag.gran.dize** [ə¹grændaiz] *v/t.* büyütmek *(boyut, güç veya rütbe)*; **ag¹gran.dize.ment** [~dizmənt] *n.* büyütme; *fig.* itibar veya değerinin yükseltme.

**ag.gra.vate** [¹ægrəveit] *v/t.* zorlaştırmak, fenalaştırmak; kızdırmak; abartmak; **ag.gra¹va.tion** *n.* zorlaştırma; hiddet.

**ag.gre.gate** **1.** [¹ægrigeit] *vb.* toplamak, yığmak, biriktirmek; yekûn tutmak; **2.** ☐ [¹-git] toplu, bütün; **3.** [¹-git] *n.* yığma, kümeleme; kütle: *(betonda)* çakıllı kum: in the ~ bir bütün olarak; **ag.gre.ga.tion** [~¹geiʃən] *n.* toplanma; hepsi, bütün.

**ag.gres.sion** [ə¹greʃən] *n.* saldırma, tecavüz: saldırganlık; **ag.gres.sive** ☐ [ə-

¹gresiv] saldırgan, mütecaviz; ~ war tecavüzî harp; **ag¹gres.sor** *n.* saldıran *(kimse veya ülke)*.

**ag.grieve** [ə¹griːv] *v/t.* incitmek, rencide etm., gücendirmek.

**a.ghast** [ə¹gaːst] *adj.* çok korkmuş, donakalmış; stand ~ donup kalmak.

**ag.ile** ☐ [¹ædʒail] çevik, faal, tetik.

**a.gil.i.ty** [ə¹dʒiliti] *n.* çeviklik, tetiklik.

**ag.i.o** † [¹ædʒəu] *n.* aciyo, paranın gerçek ve nominal değeri arasındaki fark; **ag.i.o.tage** [¹ædʒətidʒ] *n.* aciyotaj, borsa oyunu, sarraflık.

**ag.i.tate** [¹ædʒiteit] *v/t.* sallamak, oynatmak; rahatsız etm.; heyecan vermek; *v/i.* propagandasını yapmak (for bşin); **ag.i¹ta.tion** *n.* sallama, heyecana getirme; heyecan; tahrik; **¹ag.i.ta.tor** *n.* propagandacı; tahrikçi, kışkırtıcı; *(sallayıcı veya karıştırıcı)* makine.

**a.glow** [ə¹gləu] *adj.* (with *-den dolayı*) parlak, kor halinde; kızgın, kıpkırmızı; *fig.* şiddetli, hararetli.

**a.go** [ə¹gəu] *adv.* önce, evvel; a year ~ bir yıl önce; a little while ~ az önce; long ~ uzun zaman önce.

**a.gog** [ə¹gɔg] **1.** *adj.* bşe düşkün, haris, teşne, istekli; **2.** *adv.* heyecanla, can atarak (for *-a*).

**ag.o.nize** [¹ægənaiz] *v/t.* *b-ne* ıstırap vermek, işkence etm.; *v/i.* can çekişmek, ıstırap çekmek; **¹ag.o.niz.ing** ☐ eziyet verici, cefalı, işkenceli.

**ag.o.ny** [¹ægəni] *n.* ıstıraptan kıvranma, şiddetli acı; can çekişme; ~ of death, mortal ~ can çekişme; ~ column şahsi ilânlar sütunu *(gazete)*.

**a.grar.i.an** [ə¹grɛəriən] *adj.* zirai, tarımsal; tarlalara ait.

**a.gree** [ə¹griː] *v/i.* razı olm., aynı fikirde olm., muvafakat etm., uyuşmak (upon, ɔn); bşde anlaşmaya varmak, mutabık kalmak, uzlaşmak; ~ to razı olm. *-e*, kabul etm. *-i*; ~ with anlaşmak bir fikirde olm. *b-le*; ~ to differ münakaşayı kesmek; be ~d mukavafat etm., birlik olm.; ~d! kabul!, tamam!; **a.gree.a.ble** ☐ [ə¹griəbl] (to) uygun *-e*, münasip *-e*; hoş, nazik; **a¹gree.a.ble.ness** *n.* tatlılık, hoşluk; **a.gree.ment** [ə¹griːmənt] *n.* anlaşma, uyuşma, ittifak; sözleşme, mukavele, akit; come to an ~ bir karara varmak, uyuşmak; make an ~ anlaşma yapmak.

**ag.ri.cul.tur.al** [ægri¹kʌltʃərəl] *adj.* zirai, tarımsal; **ag.ri.cul.ture** [¹-tʃə] *n.* ziraat, tarım; **ag.ri¹cul.tur.ist** [~tʃərist] *n.* ziraatçı, çiftçi.

**a.ground** ↓ [ə'graund] *adj. & adv.* karaya oturmuş; run ~ karaya oturmak; run a ship ~ gemiyi karaya oturtmak.

**a.gue** ['eigju:] *n.* sıtma, malarya; **'a.gu-ish** *adj.* sıtmalı, sıtma getiren.

**ah** [ɑ:] *int.* ah!, ya!, vay!; bak!; hayret!

**a.ha** [ɑ:'hɑ:] *int.* şimdi anladım!; işte!, görüyorsun ya!

**a.head** [ə'hed] *adv.* önde, ileride; ileriye; straight ~ doğruca; go ~ ilerlemek; önden gitmek; *b-nin* önü sıra yürümek; devam etm.; go ~ ! yürüyünüz!, devam ediniz!; siz buyurunuz!

**a.hoi, a.hoy** ↓ [ə'hɔi] *int.* hey!, hu!, yahu!

**aid** [eid] **1.** *v/t.* yardım etm. -*e*; **2.** *n.* yardım, muavenet; by (with) the ~ of yardımıyle; *-den* bilistifade; in ~ of yararına; ~s and appliances vasıta, çare, medar.

**aide-de-camp** ✕ ['eiddə'kɑ:ŋ] *n.* yaver.

**ai.grette** ['eigret] *n.* sorguç, tuğ.

**ail** [eil] *v/i.* hastalıklı, dertli olm.; *v/t.* sıkıntı vermek, rahatsız etm.; what ~s him? nesi var?

**ai.ler.on** ['eilərən] *n.* uçak kanadının hareket eden arka kısmı.

**ail.ing** ['eiliŋ] *adj.* keyifsiz, hasta, rahatsız; **'ail.ment** *n.* rahatsızlık, hastalık.

**aim** [eim] **1.** *v/i.* nişan almak (at *bşi, b-ni*); ~ at *fig.* kastetmek *bşi, b-ni*; ~ to do *part. Am.* niyetinde bulunmak, kastetmek, maksat gütmek; *v/t.* (*top, tüfek, söz vs.*) doğrultmak, nişan almak (at -*ε*); **2.** *n.* emel, hedef, amaç; nişan alma; take ~ nişan almak; **'aim.less** □ gayesiz, hedefsiz.

**ain't** F [eint] = are not, am not, is not, have not, has not.

**air¹** [εə] **1.** *n.* hava; hava cereyanı, kuran; by ~ hava yoluyla; go by ~ uçmak, uçakla gitmek; in the open ~ açıkta, açık havada; castles in the ~ hayal, hülya; in the ~ havada; belli olmayan, sonuca bağlanmamış; on the ~ radyoda (dinlenebilir); go off the ~ yayını kesmek; ~ supply taze hava verme; take the ~ dışarıya çıkıp dolaşmak, temiz hava almak; ✝ havalanmak; **2.** *v/t.* havalandırmak; (*çamaşır*) kurutmak; açmak (*fikir, şikâyet vs.*); ~ one's views fikirlerini açmak.

**air²** [~] *n.* hal, tavır, eda; görünüş; give o.s. ~s kibarlık taslamak; with an ~ ~ vakarla, haşmetle; ~s and graces F numara yapma, hava atma.

**air³** ♩ [~] *n.* nağme, melodi; arya.

**air...:** '~.base *n.* ✕ hava üssü; '~.bath

*n.* açık hava banyosu; '~-bed *n.* deniz yatağı; '~.blad.der *n.* (*balık*) yüzme kesesi; '~-borne *adj.* havadan gelen (*toz, tohum vs.*); havadan nakledilen; uçmakta; ✕ hava indirme; we are ~ uçuyoruz; ~-brake *n.* hava freni; '~-cham.ber *n. biol.* hava hücresi; '~-con.di.tioned *adj.* otomatik ısıtma ve soğutma tesisatı olan; '~-con.di.tion.ing *n.* klimatizasyon tesisatı; '~-cooled *adj.* hava ile soğutulmuş; '~.craft *n.* uçak; uçaklar; ~ carrier uçak gemisi; '~-cush.ion *n.* şişirme yastık; '~-drop *n.* düşman gerisindeki personele havadan teçhizat ve malzeme yardımı; '~-field *n.* hava alanı; '~-force *n.* hava kuvvetleri; '~-gun *n.* hava tüfeği; ~ host.ess hostes.

**air.i.ness** ['εərinis] *n.* havadar olma; hafiflik, kolaylık, sühulet.

**air.ing** ['εəriŋ] *n.* (*elbise, çarşaf vs.*) havalandırma, kurutma; (*oda vs.*) havalandırma; gezinti, hava alma; açığa vurma.

**air...:** '~-jack.et *n.* yüzme yeleği; '~.less *adj.* havasız, ağır; '~-lift *n.* hava köprüsü; '~-line *n.* hava yolu; '~-lin.er *n.* yolcu uçağı; '~-mail *n.* uçak postası; '~.man *n.* havacı; '~-me'chan.ic *n.* uçak makinisti; '~-pas.sen.ger *n.* hava yolcusu; '~.pipe *n.* ⊕ hava borusu; '~.plane *n. part. Am.* uçak; '~.pock.et *n.* ✝ hava boşluğu; '~-port *n.* hava alanı; '~-proof *adj.* hava geçmez, hava geçirmez; '~-pump *n.* hava pompası; '~-raid *n.* ✕ hava hücumu; ~ precautions *pl.* hava hücumu önlemleri; ~ shelter sığınak; '~-route hava yolu; '~.ship *n.* hava gemisi, uçak; '~.sick *adj.* hava tutmuş; '~.strip *n.* ufak hava meydanı; '~-ter.mi.nal *n.* (*hava yollarının*) şehir bürosu; '~-tight *adj.* hava geçmez; '~-transport *n.* hava ulaşımı; '~-tube *n.* iç lâstik; ~ umbrel.la ✕ havaya karşı korunma şemsiyesi; '~.ways *n.* hava yolları; '~.wom.an *n.* kadın havacı; '~.worthy *adj.* ✝ uçabilir, uçuş güvenliğine sahip.

**air.y** □ ['εəri] havalı, havadar; hafif; havai, sudan.

**aisle** [ail] *n.* △ bir kilisenin yan kısmı; ara yol, geçit (*esp. kilise ve tiyatroda*); '~-sit.ter *n. Am.* F tiyatro eleştirmeni.

**aitch** [eitʃ] *n.* h harfinin İngilizce adı; drop one's aitches h harfini telaffuz etmemek.

**aitch.bone** ['eitʃbəun] *n.* sığır budu.

**a.jar** [ə'dʒɑ:] *adv.* yarı açık, aralık (*kapı*); *fig.* ahenksiz.

**a.kim.bo** [ə'kimbəu] *adv.:* with arms ~ el

leri kalçasına dayalı.
**a.kin** [ə'kin] *adj.* akraba, yakın, benzer (to -e).

**al.a.bas.ter** ['æləbɑːstə]*n.* su mermeri, kaymak taşı, albatr.

**a.lack** † [ə'læk] *int.* ah!, eyvah!; ~-a-day! *int.* yazık!, eyvah!

**a.lac.ri.ty** [ə'lækriti] *n.* çeviklik; istekli-lik, şevk.

**a.larm** [ə'lɑːm] 1. *n.* alarm, tehlike işare-ti; korku, telâş; ~ pistol patlangaç; give (raise, ring, sound) the ~ tehlikeyi haber vermek; 2. *v/t.* tehlikeyi bildirmek *-e*; korkutmak *-i*; a'larm-bell *n.* alarm çanı; a'larm-clock *n.* çalar saat; a'larm.ist *n.* etrafı telâşa veren kimse.

**a.las** [ə'læs] *int.* vay!, yazık!

**alb** [æib] *n.* katolik papazların kilisede giydikleri beyaz cübbe.

**Al.ba.ni.an** [æl'beinjən] *adj. & n.* Arnavutça; Arnavut.

**al.ba.tross** ['ælbətrɔs] *n.* bir cins deniz kuşu, albatros.

**al.be.it** [ɔːl'biːit] *cj.* her ne kadar, vakia, ise de.

**al.bi.no** *biol.* [æl'biːnəu] *n.* derisi, saçları ve kaşları doğuştan beyaz insan veya hayvan.

**al.bum** ['ælbəm] *n.* albüm.

**al.bu.men, al.bu.min** ⚗ ['ælbjumin] *n.* yumurta akı; albümin; **al.bu.mi.nous** [æl-'bjuːminəs] *adj.* albüminli.

**al.chem.ic, al.chem.i.cal** [æl'kemik(əl)] simya ilmine ait; al.che.mist [æl'kimist] *n.* simyager, alşimist; 'al.che.my *n.* simya, alşimi.

**al.co.hol** ['ælkəhɔl] *n.* alkol, ispirto; alkollü içki; al.co'hol.ic ⚗ & *n.* alkolik, ispirtolu: ayyaş; al.co.hol.ism *n.* alkolizm, içkiye düşkünlük, ayyaşlık; al.co.ho!.ize ['-laiz] *v/t.* alkol haline getirmek.

**al.cove** ['ælkouv] *n.* yatak köşesi, hücre-si; duvarda hücre; (bahçe) çardak, göl-gelik.

**al.der** ⚘ ['ɔːldə] *n.* kızılağaç.

**al.der.man** ['ɔːldəmən] *n.* kıdemli belediye meclisi üyesi; al.der.man.ship ['-mənʃip] *n.* belediye meclisi üyeliği.

**ale** [eil] *n.* bir çeşit bira.

**a.lee** ⬇ [ə'liː] *n.* rüzgâr altında.

**a.lem.bic** ⚗ [ə'lembik] *n.* imbik.

**a.lert** [ə'ləːt] 1. ☐ uyanık, dikkatli; 2. *n.* silâhbaşı hazırlığı; (hava) tehlike işare-ti; be on the ~ tetikte olm., hazır olm.; a'lert.ness *n.* tetiklik.

**al.fal.fa** ⚘ [æl'fælfə] *n.* kaba yonca.

**al.fres.co** [æl'freskəu] *adv. & adj.* açık havada; açık hava.

**al.ga** ⚘ ['ælgə] *n., pl.* **al.gae** ['ældʒiː] su yosunu.

**al.ge.bra** ⚗ ['ældʒibrə] *n.* cebir; al.gebra-ic [-'breiik] ☐ cebirsel.

**Al.ge.ri.a** [ældʒiːriə] *n.* Cezayir.

**a.li.as** ['eiliæs] 1. *adv.* namı diğer, diğer ismi; 2. *n.* namı müstear, takma isim.

**al.i.bi** ['ælibai] *n.* (suç işlendiği anda) başka yerde bulunduğu iddiası; Am., F özür, mazeret.

**al.ien** ['eiljən] 1. *adj.* yabancı uyruklu, ecnebi; *fig.* uymamış, intibak etmemiş (to *-e*); 2. *n.* yabancı, yabancı uyruklu kimse; 'al.ien.a.ble *adj.* satılabilir, devir ve ferağı kabil; al.ien.ate ['-eit] *v/t.* satmak, devir ve ferağ etm.; *fig.* soğut-mak, vazgeçirmek (from *-den*); al.ien'a-tion *n.* devir ve ferağ; ferağ yetkisi, tem-lik; *fig.* soğutma, vazgeçirme; ~ of mind cinnet; 'al.ien.ist *n.* akıl hastalıkları uz-manı, akliyeci.

**a.light¹** [ə'lait] *adj.* ateş içinde, yanmak-ta, tutuşmuş.

**a.light²** [~] *v/i.* çıkmak, inmek; ⚓ yere inmek, konmak.

**a.lign** [ə'lain] *v/t.* sıraya koymak, dizmek, hizaya sokmak: sıralamak; ~ o.s. with yanaşmak, bağlanmak *-e*; a'lign.ment *n.* dizilme, sıraya girme; hiza.

**a.like** [ə'laik] 1. *adj.* benzer, aynı; 2. *adv.* benzer, aynı şekilde, farksız olarak.

**al.i.ment** ['ælimənt] *n.* yiyecek, gıda; al.i-men.ta.ry [-'mentəri] *adj.* besleyici, yi-yeceğe dair; ~ canal hazım borusu; al.i-men'ta.tion *n.* beslenme, besleme.

**al.i.mo.ny** ⚖ ['æliməni] *n.* nafaka.

**a.line(.ment)** [ə'lain(mənt)] = align(ment).

**al.i.quot** ⚗ ['ælikwɔt] *adj.* bir sayıyı tam bölen.

**a.live** [ə'laiv] *adj.* canlı. yaşayan, sağ, di-ri. hayatta; pürhayat, faal; heyecanlı; haberdar, farkında; be ~ hayatta olm., yaşamak; ⚡ üzerinde cereyan olan: man ~ ! F be (mübarek) adam!; ulan!; keep ~ bşi yaşatmak, muhafaza etm.; look ~ ! F çabuk ol, sallanma!

**al.ka.li** ⚗ ['ælkəlai] *n.* alkali, kalevi; al-ka.line ['-lain] *adj.* alkali, kalevi.

**all** [ɔːl] 1. *adj.* bütün, hep; tam; her; ~ day (long) bütün gün; ~ kind(s) of books her çeşit kitap; *s.* above, after; for ~ that bununla beraber, buna rağmen; 2. *n.* herkes, herşey; my ~ herşeyim; ~ of them hepsi; not at ~ asla. hiç; for ~ (that) I know bana kalırsa; ~ hepsi, tama-mı; 3. *adv.* tamamen, tamamiyle, büs-bütün; ~ at once hep birden; ~ the better daha iyi ya: ~ but hemen hemen, aşağı yukarı, az daha; ~ right iyi!, pekâlâ, tamam; şöyle böyle.

**all-A.mer.i.can** [ɔːləˈmerikən] özbeöz Amerikalı.

**al.lay** [əˈlei] v/t. teskin etm., rahatlandırmak, hafifletmek, azaltmak, (harareti) gidermek.

**al.le.ga.tion** [æliˈgeiʃən] n. iddia, ileri sürme; **al.lege** [əˈledʒ] v/t. ileri sürmek, iddia etm., itham etm.; **al'leged** denen, iddia edilen; sözde, diye.

**al.le.giance** [əˈliːdʒəns] n. (vatan, hükümdar veya bir fikre) sadakat, bağlılık; (tebaa, vatandaş) sadakat, bağlılık (to -e); oath of ~ sadakat (veya bağlılık) yemini. '

**al.le.gor.ic(al)** [æliˈgɔrik(əl)] alegorik, kinaye yolu ile, remzî; **al.le.go.rize** [ˈæligəraiz] vb. (bir oyun, resim, hikâye vs.) alegorik yorumlamak; **'al.le.go.ry** n. alegori, remzî hikâye.

**al.le.lu.ia** [æliˈluːjə] n., int. sevinç veya teşekkür ifade eden bir kelime (veya şarkı vs.), elhamdülillâh.

**al.ler.gy** ⚡ [ˈælədʒi] n. alerji, aşırı duyu.

**al.le.vi.ate** [əˈliːvieit] v/t. azaltmak, hafifletmek; **al.le.vi'a.tion** n. hafifleme, azalma.

**al.ley** [ˈæli] n. dar sokak, aralık; iki tarafı ağaçlı yol; (bowling oyunu) dar yol; s. back ~; geçit; s. blind 1, skittle-~; it's up his ~ tam onun işi, biçilmiş kaftan; **'al.ley.way** n. Am. dar yol, geçit.

**All Fool's Day** [ˈɔːlˈfuːlzdei] 1 Nisan günü.

**al.li.ance** [əˈlaiəns] n. ittifak, birlik; sıhrî hısımlık; form an ~ ittifak yapmak (with ile).

**al.lied** [əlaid] adj. müttefik, dost; hısım, akraba; ↑ ~ company başka bir şirket tarafından idare edilen veya başka bir şirketi idare eden şirket.

**al.li.ga.tor** zo. [ˈæligeitə] n. Amerika timsahı.

**all-in** [ˈɔːlˈin] adj. her şey dahil.

**al.lit.er.ate** [əˈlitəreit] v/t. birbirine yakın iki veya daha çok kelimede aynı sesi tekrar etm.; **al.lit.er'a.tion** n. cümle içindeki kelimelerde aynı sesi tekrarlama; **al'lit.er.a.tive** [-rətiv] aynı sesin tekrar edildiği parçaya ait.

**al.lo.cate** [ˈæləukeit] v/t. tahsis etm., dağıtmak; **al.lo'ca.tion** n. tahsis etme, dağıtım, tahsisat.

**al.lo.cu.tion** [æləuˈkjuːʃən] n. söylev, nutuk, hitabe.

**al.lop.a.thist** ⚡ [əˈlɔpəθist] n. zıt tedavi

usulü uygulayan doktor; **al'lop.a.thy** ⚡ n. zıt tedavi usulü.

**al.lot** [əˈlɔt] v/t. ayırmak, tahsis etm., bölüştürmek, vermek; **al'lot.ment** n. hisselere ayırma, taksim etme; hisse, pay; (mahalli idarelerce kiraya verilen) küçük bostan.

**all-out** [ˈɔːlˈaut] adj. elinden gelen; bütün, toplam; ~ effort azamî güç.

**al.low** [əˈlau] v/t. bırakmak, müsaade etm., kabul etm., razı olm. -e; vermek -i; v/i. hesaba katmak (for -i); be ~ed to izni haiz olm., hakka sahip olm.; ~ for hesabetmek; it ~s of no excuse affedilemez, mazur görülemez; **al'low.a.ble** □ kabul edilebilir; caiz, meşru; **al'low.ance** 1. n. müsaade, göz yumma; tahsisat, harçlık, gelir (aylık, yıllık vs.); iskonto, indirim; itiraf, kabul; ⊕ tolerans, yedek pay; 2. v/t. nafakasını tayin etm.; (ekmek vs.) tayına bağlamak.

**al.loy** 1. [ˈæloi] n. alaşım, halita; fig. karışım; 2. [~] v/t. halita yapmak; fig. değerini veya kalitesini bozmak.

**all...:** **'~-'pur.pose** adj. her şeye yarayan; **'~-'round** adj. çok yeteneği olan; çok cepheli; ↑ götürü.

**All Saints' Day** [ˈɔːlˈseintsdei] rel. Azizler yortusu (1 Kasım).

**All Souls' Day** [ˈɔːlˈsəulzdei] rel. Ölüler günü (2 Kasım).

**al.lude** [əˈluːd] v/i. ima etm., kastetmek (to -i).

**al.lure** [əˈljuə] v/t. k-ne çekmek, cezbetmek; **al'lure.ment** n. çekicilik, cezbetme; **al'lur.ing** □ çekici, cazip.

**al.lu.sion** [əˈluːʒən] n. ima, kinaye (to -e); **al'lu.sive** □ ima yollu, cinaslı, mecazî.

**al.lu.vi.al** [əˈluːvjəl] suların bıraktığı toprak gibi, alüvyonlu; **al'lu.vi.on** [-vjən] n. suların bıraktığı toprak, alüvyon; **al'lu.vi.um** [-vjəm] n. suların bıraktığı toprak, lığ, alüvyon.

**al.ly** 1. [əˈlai] vb. birleşmek, ittifak e(tir)mek (to, with -le); akraba olm.; allied to fig. benzer, uygun, yakın; 2. [ˈælai] n. müttefik; dost, arkadaş; Allies pl. Müttefikler.

**al.ma.nac** [ˈɔːlmənæk] n. takvim, yıllık, almanak.

**al.might.i.ness** [ɔːlˈmaitinis] n. her şeye kadir olma; **al'might.y** 1. □ her şeye kadir, F kudretli, dehşetli, çok büyük; 2. ♀ Kadiri mutlak, Allah.

**al.mond** [ˈɑːmənd] n. badem; ~-eyed adj. badem gözlü.

**al.mon.er** [ˈɑːmənə] n. (hastanede hastaların ihtiyaçları ile ilgili) sosyal görevli.

**al.most** ['ɔːlmǝust] adv. hemen hemen, az kaldı; yaklaşık olarak.

**alms** [aːmz] n. sg. & pl. sadaka; **'~-bag** n. sadaka kesesi; **'~-house** n. fakirler yurdu, darülâceze.

**al.oe** ♀ & pharm. ['ælǝu] n. sarısabır.

**a.loft** [ǝ'lɔft] adv. yukarıda, yükseklerde; ⏚ yukarıda, gemi direğinde.

**a.lone** [ǝ'lǝun] adj. & adv. yalnız, tek başına, yalnız olarak; let veya leave s.o. ~ b-ni kendi haline bırakmak; let it ~! karışma!, dokunma!; let ~ ...... şöyle dursun, nerede kaldı ki.

**a.long** [ǝ'lɔŋ] adv. & prep. boyunca, müddetince, yanı sıra; all ~ öteden beri; her zaman; come ~! haydi gel!; get ~ with geçinmek, anlaşmak -le; get ~ with you! F haydi git!; amma yaptın ha!, sana inanmıyorum; a'long.shore adj. & adv. sahil boyunca; a'long'side 1. ⏚ adv. borda bordaya; yan yana; 2. prep. yanında, tarafında.

**a.loof** [ǝ'luːf] adj. & adv. uzak, uzakta; ⏚ alargada; sokulmaz, soğuk; keep ~ k-ni uzak(ta) tutmak; a'loof.ness n. uzaklık, çekingenlik, sokulmayış.

**a.loud** [ǝ'laud] adv. yüksek sesle.

**alp** [ælp] n. yüksek dağ; 2s pl. Alpler.

**al.pac.a** [æl'pækǝ] n. zo. (Peru'ya mahsus) koyuna benzer bir hayvan, alpaka; alpaka yünü; alpaka yününden kumaş.

**al.pen.stock** ['ælpinstok] n. (dağcılara mahsus) ucu demirli sopa.

**al.pha.bet** ['ælfǝbit] n. alfabe; **al.pha.bet.ic**, **al.pha.bet.i.cal** □ [~'betik(ǝl)] alfabe sırasına göre.

**Al.pine** ['ælpain] adj. Alp dağlarına ait; yüksek dağlara ait; **al.pin.ist** ['~pinist] n. dağcı, alpinist.

**al.read.y** [ɔːl'redi] adv. şimdiden; şimdiye kadar; zaten.

**Al.sa.tian** [æl'seiʃjǝn] 1. adj. Alsas'a ait; 2. n. Alsaslı; a. ~ dog (kurda benzer) iri bir çeşit köpek (Am. German Shepherd).

**al.so** ['ɔːlsǝu] adv. dahi, da (de, ta, te); bir de; ayrıca; ~-ran n. yarışçılık: dereceye giremiyen at; fig. başarısız sporcu veya politikacı.

**al.tar** ['ɔːltǝ] n. (üzerinde tanrıya sunulan şeylerin bulunduğu) Hıristiyan kiliselerindeki masa veya yüksek yer; **'~-piece** n. (mihrabın yakınındaki) resim veya tablo.

**al.ter** ['ɔːltǝ] v/t. değiştirmek; Am. F (hayvan) hadımlaştırmak, iğdiş etm.; v/i. değişmek; **'al.ter.a.ble** adj. değişir,

değiştirilebilir; **al.ter'a.tion** n. değişiklik (to -e).

**al.ter.cate** ['ɔːltǝkeit] v/i. kavga etm., çekişmek, dalaşmak; **al.ter'ca.tion** n. kavga, çekişme.

**al.ter.nate 1.** ['ɔːltǝneit] vb. nöbetleşe değiş(tir)mek. nöbetle yap(tır)mak; birbiri ardına gelmek; alternating current ⚡ dalgalı akım; 2. □ [ɔːl'tǝːnit] nöbetleşe değişen, münavebeli; on ~ days gün aşırı; 3. [ɔːl'tǝːnit] n. Am. mümessil, vekil; **al.ter.na.tion** [ɔːltǝ'neiʃǝn] n. değişiklik; münavebe; **al.ter.na.tive** [ɔːl'tǝː-nǝtiv] 1. □ ikisinden birini seçme imkânı olan, alternatifi olan, başka; ⊕ alternatif...; 2. n. iki şıktan biri, alternatif, tercih; imkân; I have no ~ başka çarem yok, yapacak başka birşey yok; **al.ter.na.tor** n. ⚡ alternatör.

**al.though** [ɔːl'ðǝu] cj. her ne kadar, -diği halde, bununla birlikte, gerçi.

**al.tim.e.ter** ['æltimiːtǝ] n. altimetre, yükseltiyi gösteren alet.

**al.ti.tude** ['æltitjuːd] n. yükseklik, irtifa; ~ recorder irtifa kayıtçısı.

**al.to** ♪ ['æltǝu] n. alto, kadın veya çocuk seslerinin en pesi.

**al.to.geth.er** [ɔːltǝ'geðǝ] adv. hep birlikte, tamamen, büsbütün; in the ~ F çıplak. anadan doğma.

**al.tru.ism** ['æltruizǝm] n. şahsî menfaatlerine bakmama, diğerkâmlık, fedakârlık; **'al.tru.ist** n. diğerkâm, başkalarını düşünen kimse; **al.tru'is.tic** adj. (~ally) başkalarını düşünen, diğerkâm.

**al.um** ♊ ['ælǝm] n. şap; **a.lu.mi.na** [ǝ'ljuːminǝ] n. alüminyum oksit; **al.u.min.i.um** [ælju'minjǝm], Am. **al.u.mi.num** [ǝ'luːminǝm] n. alüminyum; **al.u.mi.nous** [ǝ'ljuːminǝs] adj. şaplı.

**a.lum.na** [ǝ'lʌmnǝ] n., pl. **a'lum.nae** [~niː] Am. (bir okul veya üniversitenin) eski kız öğrenci; **a'lum.nus** [~nǝs] n., pl. **a'lum.ni** [~nai] Am. eski erkek öğrenci.

**al.ve.o.lar** [æl'viǝlǝ] 1. adj. anat. diş çukuruna ait; 2. n. gr. dilin üst damağa teması ile çıkarılan sessiz harf.

**al.ways** ['ɔːlweiz] adv. daima, her zaman.

**am** [æm; ǝm] vb. (irr. be) I ~ ben -im.

**a.mal.gam** [ǝ'mælgǝm] n. malgama, cıva ile başka bir maddenin karışımı; **a'mal.gam.ate** [~meit] v/t. cıva ile başka bir madeni karıştırmak; karıştırmak, birleştirmek; v/i. karışmak, birleşmek; **a.mal.gam'a.tion** n. karışma; alaşım; ℑ iki veya daha fazla şirketin birleşmesi, füzyon.

**a.man.u.en.sis** [ǝmænju'ensis] n., pl. a-

man.u'en.ses [~si:z] yazıcı, sekreter.
am.a.ranth ⚹ ['æmərænθ] n. tilki kuyruğu.
a.mass [ə'mæs] v/t. yığmak, toplamak.
am.a.teur ['æmətə:] n. amatör, meraklı,
hevesli kimse; am.a'teur.ish adj. acemice, yarımyamalak bilgili.
am.a.tive [æmətiv], am.a.to.ry ['~təri]
adj. aşkla ilgili, şehvani.
a.maze [ə'meiz] v/t. hayrette bırakmak,
şaşırtmak; a'mazed ☐ çok şaşırmış (at
-e); a'maze.ment n. şaşkınlık, hayret;
a'maz.ing ☐ şaşırtıcı, hayret verici, acayip.
Am.a.zon ['æməzən] n. Amazon Nehri; ♀
erkeksi kadın; savaşçı, yiğit kadın; Ama.zo.ni.an [~'zəunjən] adj. Amazon Nehrine ait; ♀ erkeksi (kadın).
am.bas.sa.dor [æm'bæsədə] n. büyükelçi,
sefir; am.bas.sa.do.ri.al [~'dɔ:riəl] adj.
büyükelçi ile ilgili, sefareti ilgilendiren;
am'bas.sa.dress [~dris] n. elçi karısı,
sefire, kadın elçi.
am.ber ['æmbə] n. kehribar;   kehribar
rengi; am.ber.gris ['~gri:s] n. amber.
am.bi.dex.trous ☐ ['æmbi'dekstrəs] iki
elini de aynı şekilde kullanabilen; fig.
iki yüzlü, riyakâr.
am.bi.ent ['æmbiənt] adj. dolaşan; kuşatan, çevreleyen.
am.bi.gu.i.ty [æmbi'gju:iti] n. iki manalılık, belirsizlik, müphemiyet; am'big.uous [~gjuəs] ☐ müphem, şüpheli, iki
anlamlı.
am.bit ['æmbit] n. mıntıka, bölge, çevre,
muhit.
am.bi.tion [æm'bifən] n. ihtiras, hırs; büyük istek; am'bi.tious ☐ hırslı, çok istekli (to -e).
am.bi.va.lent ['æmbi'veilənt] ☐ zıt hisler
veya fikirler taşıyan, kararsız (towards,
about -e karşı, için).
am.ble ['æmbl] 1. n. eşkin, rahvan; rahat
yürüyüş; 2. v/i. eşkin gitmek; fig. yavaş yavaş dolaşmak; 'am.bler n. eşkinli; rahvan yürüyen hayvan.
am.bro.si.a [æm'brəuzjə] n. (eski masallarda) tanrıların yemekleri; çok lezzetli veya nefis kokulu yiyecek veya içki;
am'bro.si.al ☐ nefis veya güzel kokulu;
fig. mükemmel, enfes.
am.bu.lance ['æmbjuləns] n. cankurtaran, ambulans; attr. sıhhi yardım...;
~ box ilk yardım kutusu; ~ station ilk
yardım istasyonu; 'am.bu.lant adj. seyyar, gezici.
am.bu.la.to.ry ['æmbjulətəri] 1. adj. seyyar, gezici; gezilebilir; 2. n. gezinti yeri, kemerli yol, kulvar.

am.bus.cade [æmbəs'keid], am.bush ['æmbuf] 1. n. pusu, tuzak; be veya lie in ~
for s.o. b-ne pusuya yatmak; 2. vb. pusuda beklemek, tuzak kurmak, pusuya
düşürmek.
a.mel.io.rate [ə'mi:ljəreit] vb. iyileş(tir)
mek, düzel(t)mek; a.mel.io'ra.tion n. iyileşme, düzelme.
a.men ['a:'men] int. âmin.
a.me.na.ble ☐ [ə'mi:nəbl] tâbi olan (to
-e), uysal; yükümlü, sorumlu.
a.mend [ə'mend] v/t. düzeltmek, ıslah
etm.; ☼ düzeltmek, tashih etm.; (kanun) değiştirmek, tadil etm.; v/i. iyileşmek, düzelmek; a'mend.ment n. düzeltme, tadil; ☼ bir kanunu değiştirme;
parl. tadilât, değişiklik; a'mends n. pl.
tazminat, zarar ödentisi; make ~ for
özür dilemek; kusurunu düzeltmek.
a.men.i.ty [ə'mi:niti] n. letafet, zerafet,
şirinlik; amenities pl. hayatın zevki, güzel tarafı.
A.mer.i.can [ə'merikən] 1. adj. Amerikalı, Amerikan; ~ cloth muşamba; 2. n.
Amerika kıtalarının yerlisi; Amerika Birleşik Devletleri tebaası; A'mer.i.can.ism
n. Amerikalılara mahsus kelime, deyim,
şive vs.; Am. Amerika Birleşik Devletleri inanç ve amaçlarına bağlılık; A.meri.can.i'za.tion n. Amerikalılaştırma; A
'mer.i.can.ize v/t. Amerikalılaştırmak.
am.e.thyst min. ['æmiθist] n. cebellokum,
ametist.
a.mi.a.bil.i.ty [eimjə'biliti] n. kanı sıcaklık, tatlılık, sevimlilik; 'a.mi.a.ble ☐ hoş,
sevimli, tatlı.
am.i.ca.ble ☐ ['æmikəbl] dostça, dostane,
sevimli, tatlı.
a.mid(st) [ə'mid(st)] prp. arasına, arasında, ortasında -in.
a.mid.ships ↓ [ə'midfips] adv. geminin
ortasında.
a.miss [ə'mis] adv. eksik, yanlış; kusurlu; take ~ gücenmek; fenaya almak,
yanlış anlamak -i; it would not be ~ (for
him) fena olmaz, zararı dokunmaz.
am.i.ty ['æmiti] n. dostluk, iyi ilişki, sevgi.
am.me.ter ⚡ ['æmitə] n. ampermetre.
am.mo.ni.a [ə'məunjə] n. amonyak; liquid ~ nişadır ruhu; am'mo.ni.ac [~niæk]
adj. amonyak ile ilgili; s. sal.
am.mo.nite ['æmənait] n. nesli tükenmis
bir deniz hayvanı kabuğunun fosili.
am.mu.ni.tion ✕ [æmju'nifən] n. cephane.
mühimmat.
am.ne.sia ⚕ [æm'ni:zjə] n. (kısmen veya
tamamen) hafıza kaybı, unutkanlık.
am.nes.ty ['æmnisti] 1. n. genel af; 2. v/t

genel af ilân etm., cezasını affetmek.
**a.m(o)e.ba** zo. [ə'mi:bə] n. amip.
**a.mok** [ə'mɔk] = amuck.
**a.mong(st)** [ə'mʌŋ(st)] prp. -in arasında, arasına; içinde; from ~ -in içinden, arasından.
**a.mor.al** [ei'mɔrəl] adj. ahlâk ile ilişiği olmayan.
**am.o.rous** □ ['æmərəs] âşık, tutkun (of -e); aşk...; **'am.o.rous.ness** n. âşıklık.
**a.mor.phous** □ [ə'mɔːfəs] min. şekilsiz, özelliği olmayan; fig. biçimsiz, çirkin.
**am.or.ti.za.tion** [əmɔːti'zeifən] n. itfa, herhangi bir borcu taksitle ödeme, amortisman; **am'or.tize** [~taiz] v/t. bir borcu taksitlerle ödemek, amortize etm..
**a.mount** [ə'maunt] **1.** v/i. ~ to -e varmak, baliğ olm.; **2.** n. miktar, meblağ, tutar, yekûn; to the ~ of -e baliğ olan.
**a.mour** [ə'muə] n. aşk, aşk macerası; ~-pro.pre ['æmuə'prɔpr] n. izzetinefis, onur.
**am.pere** ≠ ['æmpɛə] n. amper.
**am.phib.i.an** [æm'fibiən] **1.** n. iki yaşayışlı hayvan (kurbağa gibi); hem suya hem de karaya inip kalkabilen uçak; hem suda hem de karada gidebilen araç; **2.** = **am'phib.i.ous** □ hem havada hem de suda yaşayabilen.
**am.phi.the.a.tre,** Am. **am.phi.the.a.ter** ['æmfiθiətə] n. amfiteatr.
**am.ple** □ ['æmpl] geniş, bol; kâfi; etraflı.
**am.pli.fi.ca.tion** [æmplifi'keifən] n. genişletme, tevsi; rhet. geniş açıklama; phys. amplifikasyon; **am.pli.fi.er** ['~faiə] n. radyo: amplifikatör, büyültücü alet; **'am.pli.fy** vb. genişletmek, büyütmek; sesini kuvvetlendirmek; mübalâğa etm.; ~ing valve amplifikatör valfı; **am.pli.tude** ['~tjuːd] n. genişlik, bolluk; phys. genlik, amplitüd.
**am.poule** ≯ n. ['æmpuːl] ampul.
**am.pu.tate** ≯ ['æmpjuteit] v/t. (bir uzvu) kesmek; **am.pu'ta.tion** n. bir uzvun kesilmesi.
**a.muck** [ə'mʌk]: run ~ kudurmuş gibi etrafa saldırmak; run ~ at veya on veya against fig. üzerine atılmak.
**am.u.let** ['æmjulit] n. muska, tılsım.
**a.muse** [ə'mjuːz] v/t. eğlendirmek, güldürmek b-ni; **a'muse.ment** n. eğlence, zevk; ~ park, Am. funfair luna park; **a'mus.ing** □ eğlenceli, güldürücü, tuhaf; the ~ thing about it işin tuhafı.
**an** gr. [æn, ən] ad belirteni: s. a.
**a.nach.ro.nism** [ə'nækrɔnizəm] n. (bir olayı) ait olmadığı tarihte gösterme.

**an.a.con.da** zo. [ænə'kɔndə] n. boa yılanı.
**a.n(a)e.mi.a** ≯ [ə'niːmjə] n. kansızlık, anemi; **a'n(a)e.mic** adj. kansız, anemik.
**an.(a)es.the.si.a** ≯ [ænis'θiːzjə] n. anestezi, uyuşturma, narkoz; **an.(a)es.thet.ic** [~'θetik] **1.** adj. (~ally) uyuşturucu; **2.** n. uyuşturucu madde, narkotik.
**an.a.log.ic, an.a.log.i.cal** □ [ænə'lɔdʒik(əl)], **a.nal.o.gous** □ [ə'næləgəs] benzer, kıyas yoluyla olan; -vari; **a'nal.o.gy** [~dʒi] n. kıyas, karşılaştırma; benzerlik, benzeşme.
**an.a.lyse** ['ænəlaiz] v/t. tahlil etm., analiz etm.; çözümlemek, incelemek, tetkik etm., gr. çözümlemek, analiz etm.; **a.nal.y.sis** [ə'næləsis] n., pl. **a'nal.y.ses** [~siːz] analiz, çözümleme; **an.a.lyst** ['ænəlist] n. tahlilci, tahlil eden kimse; psikoanalist.
**an.a.lyt.ic, an.a.lyt.i.cal** □ [ænə'litik(əl)] çözümsel, tahlilî.
**an.ar.chic, an.ar.chi.cal** □ [æ'nɑːkik(əl)] anarşik; kanunsuz, nizamsız; **an.arch.ist** ['ænəkist] anarşist; **'an.arch.y** n. anarşi; kargaşalık.
**a.nath.e.ma** [ə'næθimə] n. afaroz; afaroz edilmiş veya lânetlenmiş kimse; nefret edilen şey (to... için); **a'nath.e.ma.tize** v/t. afaroz etm., lânetlemek.
**an.a.tom.i.cal** □ [ænə'tɔmikəl] anatomik, anatomi ile ilgili; **a.nat.o.mist** [ə'nætəmist] n. teşrihçi, anatom; **a'nat.o.mize** v/t. teşrih etm., dikkatle ayırmak; **a'nat.o.my** n. anatomi, (insan veya hayvan) vücut yapısı, teşrih; F iskelet.
**an.ces.tor** ['ænsistə] n. ata, cet, dede; **an.ces.tral** [~'sestrəl] adj. atadan kalma, atalara ait, geçmiş zamana ait; **'an.ces.try** n. ecdat, dedeler.
**an.chor** ⚓ & fig. ['æŋkə] **1.** n. çapa, gemi demiri; güven veren şey; at ~ demirli, demir atmış; **2.** vb. demirlemek, demir atmak; **'an.chor.age** n. geminin demir attığı yer; liman, koy.
**an.cho.ret, an.cho.rite** ['æŋkəret; '~rait] n. (Tanrıya ulaşmak için) bir köşeye çekilmiş olan kimse.
**an.cho.vy** ['æntʃəvi] n. hamsi balığı, ançüez.
**an.cient** ['einʃənt] **1.** adj. eski, kadim, eski zamandan kalma; **2.** n. the ~s pl. (eski zamandan kalma; **2.** n. the ~s pl. (eski Yunan ve Roma gibi) kadim milletler; **'an.cient.ly** eski zamanlarda, evvel zamanda.
**an.cil.lar.y** [æn'siləri] adj. tabi, bağlı, yardımcı (to -e); ~ road yan sokak.
**and** [ænd, ənd] cj. ve, ile; daha; thousands ~ thousands binlerce; ~ so on vesaire.

**and.i.ron** ['ændaiən] *n.* ocağın madeni ayaklığı.

**an.ec.do.tal** [ænek'dəutl], **an.ec.dot.i.cal** [‿'dɔtikəl] *adj.* fıkra tarzında; **an.ec.dote** ['ænikdəut] *n.* fıkra, hikâye.

**an.e.mom.e.ter** [æni'mɔmitə] *n.* rüzgârın şiddetini ölçen alet.

**a.nem.o.ne** ♣ [ə'neməni] *n.* Manisa lâlesi, anemon.

**an.er.oid** ['ænərɔid] *a.* ‿ barometer madeni barometre, aneroid.

**a.new** [ə'njuː] *adv.* yeniden, tekrar.

**an.gel** ['eindʒəl] *n.* melek; melek gibi kimse; **an.gel.ic, an.gel.i.cal** □ [æn'dʒelik-(əl)] melek gibi; meleklere mahsus.

**an.ge.lus** ['ændʒiləs] *n.* (Katoliklerce) günde üç defa okunan bir dua; bu duanın zamanını bildiren çan sesi.

**an.ger** ['æŋgə] 1. *n.* hiddet, öfke; 2. *v/t.* kızdırmak, öfkelendirmek.

**an.gi.na** ⚕ [æn'dʒainə] *n.* anjin, boğak; ‿ pectoris göğüs anjini.

**an.gle** ['æŋgl] 1. *n.* köşe açı; *fig.* görüş açısı; noktai nazar; ‿-dozer *n.* bir tip buldozer, yol düzenleme makinesi; ‿-iron köşebent demiri, korniyer; 2. *v/i.* (olta ile) balık tutmak; ‿ for F ima veya hile luyla bşi elde etmeğe çalışmak; **'an.gler** *n.* olta ile balık avlıyan kimse.

**An.gles** ['æŋglz] *n. pl.* Anglo'lar.

**An.gli.can** ['æŋglikən] 1. *n.* Anglikan, İngiliz kilisesine mensup kimse; 2. *adj.* İngiliz kilisesine ait.

**An.gli.cism** ['æŋglisizəm] *n.* (başka bir dilde çok kullanılan) İngilizce kelime veya deyim.

**an.gling** ['æŋgliŋ] *n.* olta ile balık avlama.

**An.glo-Sax.on** ['æŋgləu'sæksən] 1. *n.* Anglosakson; 2. *adj.* Anglosakson.

**an.gry** ['æŋgri] □ öfkeli, kızgın; darılmış (at, about ‿den dolayı); gücenmiş (with ‿e); ⚘ kızarmış, kabarmış.

**an.guish** ['æŋgwiʃ] *n.* ıstırap, keder, şiddetli acı.

**an.gu.lar** □ ['æŋgjulə] köşeli, açısal; sıska, bir deri bir kemik; *fig.* kaba, yontulmamış; **an.gu.lar.i.ty** [‿'læriti] *n.* açılı veya köşeli olma; *fig.* kabalık.

**an.i.line** ⚗ ['æniliːn] *n.* anilin.

**an.i.mad.ver.sion** ['ænimædvə:ʃən] *n.* tenkit, eleştiri, kınama; **an.i.mad.vert** [‿'vəːt] *v/i* tenkit etm., eleştirmek (on, upon ‿i).

**an.i.mal** ['æniməl] 1. *n.* hayvan; 2. *adj.* hayvanlara ait, hayvanî; ‿ spirits *pl.* canlılık, hayatiyet; **an.i.mal.cule** [‿'mælkjuː] *n.* kolayca görülemiyecek kadar

küçük hayvancık; **an.i.mal.ism** ['‿məlizəm] *n.* hayvan oluş, şehvaniyet.

**an.i.mate** 1. ['ænimeit] *v/t.* canlandırmak, diriltmek, hayat vermek; 2. ['‿mit] *mst* **an.i.mat.ed** ['‿meitid] *adj.* canlı; neşeli, hayat dolu; *fig.* canlı; ‿ cartoon canlı resimlerden ibaret film.

**an.i.ma.tion** [æni'meiʃən] *n.* canlılık, heyecan, şevk.

**an.i.mos.i.ty** [æni'mɔsiti] *a.* **an.i.mus** ['æniməs] *n.* düşmanlık, nefret, kin.

**an.ise** ⚘ ['ænis] *n.* anason.

**an.kle** ['æŋkl] *n.* ayak bileği, aşık kemiği.

**an.klet** ['æŋklit] *n.* ayak bileğine takılan bilezik; kısa çorap.

**an.nals** ['ænlz] *n. pl.* tarihî olaylar; vakayiname.

**an.neal** ⊕ [ə'niːl] *v/t.* (bir madeni) kızdırdıktan sonra yavaş yavaş soğutarak yumuşatmak, tavlamak; sertleştirmek (a.fig.).

**an.nex** 1. [ə'neks] *v/t.* ilhak etm., eklemek, katmak (to ‿e); 2. ['æneks] *n.* ek; müştemilât, ek bina; **an.nex'a.tion** *n.* ilhak (arazi); müsadere.

**an.ni.hi.late** [ə'naiəleit] *v/t.* imha etm., yok etm.; = annul; **an.ni.hi'la.tion** *n.* imha, yok etme; = annulment.

**an.ni.ver.sa.ry** [æni'vəːsəri] *n.* yıldönümü; yıldönümü merasimi.

**an.no.tate** ['ænəuteit] *v/t.* belirli kısımları açıklamak için bir kitaba kısa notlar ilâve etm., şerhetmek; şerhütefsir etm., bir metni açıklamak; **an.no'ta.tion** *n.* haşiye, not.

**an.nounce** [ə'nauns] *v/t.* bildirmek, ilân etm., haber vermek; tebliğ etm.; (radyo, TV vs. de haberleri) okumak veya (bir şahıs veya eylemi) sunmak; **an'nounce.ment** *n.* bildiri, ilân, tebliğ, anons; radyo: anons, mesaj; **an'nounc.er** *n.* radyo: sözcü; spiker.

**an.noy** [ə'nɔi] *v/t.* taciz etm., sıkmak, kızdırmak; **an'noy.ance** *n.* canını sıkma, üzüntü, rahatsızlık; **an'noyed** *adj.* dargın, kızgın (kimse); be ‿ kızmak; **an'noy.ing** □ can sıkıcı, nâhoş (şey).

**an.nu.al** ['ænjuəl] 1. □ senelik, yıllık; yıllık...; *part.* ⚘ bir yıl veya mevsimlik (bitki); 2. *n.* yıllık, almanak; bir yıl veya ya mevsimlik bitki.

**an.nu.i.tant** [ə'njuːitənt] *n.* kendisine ölünceye kadar veya belirli bir süre için gelir bağlanan (veya eşit miktarlarda para ödenen) kimse.

**an.nu.i.ty** [ə'njuːiti] *n.* (yıllık) taksit, tahsisat; ⚖ *a.* ‿ bond irat, gelir senedi; *s.* **life.**

**an.nul** [ə'nʌl] *v/t.* feshetmek, iptal etm., bozmak.

**an.nu.lar** ☐ ['ænjulə] halka şeklinde.

**an.nul.ment** [ə'nʌlmənt] *n.* iptal, fesih, kaldırma.

**an.nun.ci.a.tion** [ənʌnsi'eiʃən] *n.* bildirme, tebliğ etme, haber; ♀ İsa'ya hamile olduğunu Meryem'e bildiren haber (*Cebrail vasıtasıyla*); bu haberin kutlandığı yortu (*25 Mart*).

**an.ode** ⚡ ['ænəud] *n.* pozitif kutup, anod.

**an.o.dyne** ['ænəudain] *n. & adj.* uyuşturucu, yatıştırıcı, müsekkin (*ilâç*).

**a.noint** [ə'nɔint] *v/t. part. eccl.* yağlamak; takdis etm. (*a.fig.*).

**a.nom.a.lous** ☐ [ə'nomələs] anormal, kaideye uymayan, kural dışı; **a'nom.a.ly** *n.* anormallik, kural dışı oluş.

**a.non** [ə'nɔn] *adv.* hemen, biraz sonra; ever and ~ zaman zaman, arasıra.

**a.no.nym.i.ty** [ænə'nimiti] *n.* imzasızlık, anonimlik; **a.non.y.mous** ☐ [ə'nɔniməs] imzasız, anonim.

**a.noph.e.les** *zo.* [ə'nɔfiliːz] *n.* sıtma sivrisineği, anofel .

**an.oth.er** [ə'nʌðə] *adj.* başka, diğer, öbür, ayrı; in ~ ten years bundan on sene sonra; with one ~ birbirini.

**an.swer** ['ɑːnsə] **1.** *vb.* cevap vermek -*e*, yanıtlamak -*i*; sorumlu olm. (for -*den*); uymak (to -*e*); mukabele etm. (with -*ile*); ihtiyacı karşılamak; hesap görmek; ~ the bell *veya* door (*zili duyup*) kapıyı açmak; ~ for sorumluluğunu üzerine almak; garanti etm., bşi tekeffül etm.; **2.** *n.* cevap, yanıt (to -*e*); ♀ çözüm; ☒ cevap lâyihası; cevap; **'an.swer.a.ble** ☐ mesul, sorumlu; cevap verilebilir.

**ant** [ænt] *n.* karınca.

**an't** [ɑːnt] F = are not, am not; *sl. veya* P. = is not.

**an.tag.o.nism** [æn'tægənizəm] *n.* düşmanlık, zıddiyet (between-*arasında*); husumet (to -*e karşı*); **an'tag.o.nist** *n.* muhalif, düşman; **an.tag.o'nis.tic** ☐ (~ally) muhalif, düşman, zıt (to -*e*); **an'tag.o.nize** *v/t.* düşman etm.; zıtlık yaratmak, kışkırtmak.

**ant.arc.tic** [ænt'ɑːktik] **1.** *adj.* Güney Kutbuna ait; **2.** *n.* Güney Kutbu; the ♀ Antarktik; ♀ Circle Güney Kutup dairesi.

**an.te** *Am.* ['ænti] poker oyunu: **1.** *n.* (*oyunu açış için*) ortaya konulan para; **2.** *v/t.* mst ~ up para koymak, sürmek; *v/i. fig.* karınca kararınca yardım etm..

**an.te.ced.ence** [ænti'siːdəns] *n.* evvellik, öncelik, önce olan (*şey*); **an.te'ced.ent 1.** ☐ önce gelen, evvel, mukaddem; **2. n.**

b-*den*, bşden evvel gelen; *gr.* zamirin yerini aldığı isim veya tümleç; his ~s *pl.* geçmişi.

**an.te.cham.ber** ['æntitʃeimbə] *n.* bekleme odası. (*içinden daha büyük bir odaya geçilen*) küçük oda.

**an.te.date** ['ænti'deit] *v/t.* daha eski bir tarih koymak; bşden önce gitmek, önüne geçmek.

**an.te.di.lu.vi.an** ['æntidi'luːvjən] *adj.* Tufan öncesi.

**an.te.lope** *zo.* ['æntiləup] *n.* antilop; ceylan.

**an.te me.rid.i.em** ['æntimə'ridiəm] *adv.* öğleden evvel.

**an.ten.na** [æn'tenə] *n., pl.* **an'ten.nae** [~niː] *zo.* duyarga, böcek boynuzu; *radyo, televizyon:* anten.

**an.te.ri.or** [æn'tiəriə] *adj.* ön, önceki; önde bulunan.

**an.te-room** ['æntirum] *n.* bekleme odası.

**an.them** ['ænθəm] *n.* ilâhi, dinî şarkı; national ~ millî marş.

**an.ther** ♀ ['ænθə] *n.* başçık, haşefe.

**ant.hill** ['ænthil] *n.* karınca yuvası.

**an.thol.o.gy** [æn'θɔlədʒi] *n.* antoloji, (*çeşitli kitap ve yazarlardan derlenmiş*) şiir veya yazılar.

**an.thra.cite** *min.* ['ænθrəsait] *n.* antrasit; **an.thrax** *vet.* ['ænθræks] *n.* şarbon, ant-'raks'.

**an.thro.poid** ['ænθrəupɔid] **1.** *adj.* insana benzer; **2.** *n.* insanımsı maymun; **an.thro.pol.o.gist** [ænθrə'pɔlədʒist] *n.* antropoloji bilgini, antropolog; **an.thro'pol.o.gy** [~dʒi] *n.* antropoloji, insanbilim.

**an.ti...** ['ænti] *prefix* ...karşı, muhalif, zıt, ters.

**an.ti-air.craft** ['ænti'ɛəkrɑːft] *adj.* uçaksavar; ~ gun uçaksavar topu.

**an.ti.bi.ot.ic** ⚕ ['æntibai'ɔtik] *n.* antibiyotik.

**an.ti.bod.y** ⚕ ['æntibɔdi] *n.* vücutta yapılan ve hastalıklara karşı koyan madde, antikor.

**an.tic** ['æntik] *adj.* kaba komedi; ~s *pl.* maskaralık, tuhaflık, soytarılık.

**An.ti.christ** ['æntikraist] *n.* deccal.

**an.tic.i.pate** [æn'tisipeit] *v/t.* önceden görmek, tahmin etm., sezinlemek, beklemek, ummak; **an.tic.i'pa.tion** *n.* önceden görme, tahmin, bekleme, sezinleme; payment by ~ peşinen ödeme; avans; in ~ peşinen, önceden, evvelden; **an'tic.i.pa.to.ry** [~peitəri] *adj.* önceden yapılan, ilerisini düşünerek yapılan.

**an.ti.cli.max** *rhet. & fig.* ['ænti'klaimæks]

*n.* heyecan verici bir olayı takibeden tekdüzey şey; iniş.

**an.ti.cor.ro.sive    a.gent** [ˈæntikəˈrəusivˈeidʒənt] *n.* pasa mâni olan madde.

**an.ti.cy.clone** *meteor.* [ˈæntiˈsaikləun] *n.* yüksek basınç alanı.

**an.ti.dote** [ˈæntidəut] *n.* panzehir, çare (against, for, to -e karşı).

**an.ti-fas.cist** [ˈæntiˈfæʃist] *n. & adj.* antifaşist.

**an.ti-freeze** *mot.* [ˈæntifriːz] *n.* antifriz.

**an.ti-fric.tion** [ˈæntiˈfrikʃən] *adj.* sürtünmeye karşı; *attr.* kayma...

**an.ti-knock** *mot.* [ˈæntiˈnɔk] *n.* motorun vuruntusuz çalışması için benzine konan kimyevî madde.

**an.ti.mo.ny** *min.* [ˈæntiməni] *n.* rastık taşı, antimon.

**an.tip.a.thy** [ænˈtipəθi] *n.* antipati, sevişmezlik, hoşlanmama (against, to -e karşı).

**an.tip.o.dal** [ænˈtipədl] tam tersi, taban tabana zıddı; **an.ti.pode** [ˈ~pəud] *n., pl.* **an.tip.o.des** [~ˈpədiːz] birbirine zıt iki kimse veya şey; ≗ *pl.* Avustralya ve Yeni Zelanda.

**an.ti.quar.i.an** [æntiˈkwɛəriən] **1.** ☐ antikaya ait; **2.** *n.* antikacı, antika meraklısı; **an.ti.quar.y** [ˈ~kwəri] *n.* antikacı, antika meraklısı; **an.ti.quat.ed** [ˈ~kweitid] *adj.* eskimiş, modası geçmiş.

**an.tique** [ænˈtiːk] **1.** ☐ eski zamanlara **ait,** antika; **2.** *n.* antika; eski sanat **eseri;** **an.tiq.ui.ty** [~ˈtikwiti] *n.* eskilik, antikalık; eski zamana ait şey; eski zamanlar *pl.*; antiquities *pl.* âsarıatika.

**an.ti-rust** [ˈæntiˈrʌst] *n.* pasa mâni olan madde.

**an.ti-Sem.ite** [ˈæntiˈsiːmait] *n.* Yahudi düşmanı; **an.ti-Sem.i.tism** [ˈ~ˈsemitizəm] *n.* Yahudi düşmanlığı.

**an.ti.sep.tic** [æntiˈseptik] *n. & adj.* antiseptik.

**an.ti.so.cial** [æntiˈsəuʃəl] *adj.* topluma ve toplumsal yararlara karşı; bencil, uyumsuz.

**an.ti.tank** ✕ [æntiˈtæŋk] *adj.* tanksavar...

**an.tith.e.sis** [ænˈtiθisis] *n., pl.* **an·tith.e.ses** [~θisiːz] antitez, karşı tez; zıtlık; **an.ti.thet.ic, an.ti.thet.i.cal** ☐ [~ˈθetik(əl)] karşıt olan.

**ant.ler** [ˈæntlə] *n.* geyik boynuzu; ~s geyiğin boynuzları.

**an.to.nym** [ˈæntəunim] *n.* zıt anlama gelen kelime.

**A num.ber 1** [ˈəinʌmbəˈwʌn] *Am. F s.* A 1.

**a.nus** [ˈeinəs] *n.* anus, makat, şerç.

**an.vil** [ˈænvil] *n.* örs; örs kemiği.

**anx.i.e.ty** [æŋˈzaiəti] *n.* endişe, kuruntu, merak; şiddetli arzu; *fig.* endişe (for için); *fig.* istek (to -e); ≗ sıkıntı; nefes darlığı.

**anx.ious** ☐ [ˈæŋkʃəs] meraklı, endişeli, vesveseli, üzüntülü (about -den dolayı); müreddit; arzulu, istekli, hevesli (for, to, -e); be ~ to arzu etm. -i, can atmak -e.

**an.y** [ˈeni] *adj. & adv. & pron.* bir, herhangi, her bir; bazı, birkaç, biraz; hiç, hiçbir; not ~ hiç; ~ more artık; daha fazla; ˈ~.bod.y, ˈ~.one *pron.* herhangi bir kimse; not ~ hiçbiri, hiçkimse; ˈ~.how *adv.* her nasılsa; her halde; her ne olursa olsun; ˈ~.thing *pron.* her hangi bir şey; hiçbir şey; ~ but olmasın da ne olursa olsun; ˈ~.way = anyhow; zaten; esasen; ˈ~.where *adv.* her hangi bir yer(d)e; hiçbir yer(d)e.

**an.y.wise** [ˈeniwaiz] *adv.* her nasıl olursa.

**a.or.ta** ≗ [eiˈɔːtə] *n.* kanı yürekten vücuda taşıyan en büyük damar, aort.

**a.pace** [əˈpeis] *adv.* çabuk, süratle.

**a.part** [əˈpaːt] *adv. & adj.* ayrı, bir taraf(t)a; bağımsız olarak; başka (from -den); joking ~ şaka bertaraf, şaka bir tarafa; set ~ bir tarafa koymak, ayırmak, tahsis etm..

**a.part.heid** *pol.* [əˈpaːtheit] *n.* (Güney Afrika'da) ırk ayırımı.

**a.part.ment** [əˈpaːtmənt] *n.* büyük oda, salon; *Am.* apartman dairesi; ~s *pl.* apartman dairesi; ~ house apartman.

**ap.a.thet.ic** [æpəˈθetik] ☐ (~ally) hissiz, ilgisiz; uyuşuk; ˈap.a.thy *n.* duygusuzluk, ilgisizlik, soğukluk (to -e karşı).

**ape** [eip] **1.** *n.* maymun; **2.** *v/t.* taklit etm.

**a.peak** ⤵ [əˈpiːk] *adv. & adj.* amudî, şakuli, dikey.

**a.pe.ri.ent** [əˈpiəriənt] **1.** *n.* müshil, amel ilâcı; **2.** *adj.* müleyyin, yumuşatıcı, müshil.

**ap.er.ture** [ˈæpətjuə] *n.* aralık, delik, açık.

**a.pex** [ˈeipeks] *n., pl.* **ap.i.ces** [ˈeipisiːz] zirve, tepe, doruk; *mst fig.* en yüce yer, en üst derece.

**aph.o.rism** [ˈæfərizəm] *n.* vecize, darbımesel; **aph.o.ris.tic** ☐ (~ally) vecize kabilinden.

**a.pi.ar.y** [ˈeipjəri] *n.* arı kovanı; **a.pi.cul.ture** [ˈeipikʌltʃə] *n.* arıcılık.

**a.piece** [əˈpiːs] *adv.* her biri(ne), adam başına, beher.

**ap.ish** ☐ [ˈeipiʃ] maymun gibi, maymunca; taklitçi.

**A-plant** [ˈeiˈplaːnt] *n.* nükleer elektrik fabrikası.

**a.poc.a.lypse** [əˈpɔkəlips] *n.* vahiy.

**A.poc.ry.pha** [əˈpɔkrifə] *n. pl. İncil:* Mukaddes kitabın metnine dahil edilmeyen kitaplar; **aˈpoc.ry.phal** *adj.* bu kitaplara ait; sonradan uydurulmuş, doğruluğu kabul edilmeyen.

**ap.o.gee** [ˈæpəudʒi:] *n. ast. (bir uzay aracı, gök cismi, ay, güneş vs.nin)* yeryüzünden en uzak noktası; *(güç veya başarının)* en yüksek noktası, doruk.

**a.pol.o.get.ic** [əpɔləˈdʒetik] ☐ özür dileyen, af talep eden; savunan; ~ letter mazeret mektubu; **aˈpol.o.gist** *n.* bir inanç veya fikri savunan kimse; **aˈpol.o.gize** *v/i.* özür dilemek, itizar etm., af dilemek (for *-den*); **aˈpol.o.gy** *n.* özür dileme, tarziye; savunma; make an ~ özür dilemek.

**ap.o.plec.tic, ap.o.plec.ti.cal** ☐ [æpəuˈplektik(əl)] inme veya felce ait; inmeli, mefluc; **ap.o.plex.y** [ˈ~pleksi] *n.* inme, felç, nüzul.

**a.pos.ta.sy** [əˈpɔstəsi] *n.* irtidat, dininden dönme; parti değiştirme; inancından dönme; **aˈpos.tate** [~stit] **1.** *n.* dininden veya inancından dönmüş kimse; **2.** *adj.* din değiştiren; **aˈpos.ta.tize** [~stətaiz] *v/i.* ayrılmak (from *-den);* irtidat etm., dininden dönmek (from).

**a.pos.tle** [əˈpɔsl] *n.* havari; **ap.os.tol.ic, ap.os.tol.i.cal** ☐ [æpəsˈtɔlik(əl)] havariyuna veya papaya ait; yalnız İncil'e dayanan.

**a.pos.tro.phe** [əˈpɔstrəfi] *n. gr.* virgül, kesme işareti; *rhet.* hitabe, nutuk.

**a.poth.e.car.y** † [əˈpɔθikəri] *n.* eczacı.

**a.poth.e.o.sis** [əpɔθiˈəusis] *n.* ilâhlaştırma, tanrılaştırma, methüsena etme, ayyuka çıkarma.

**ap.pal** [əˈpɔ:l] *v/t.* korkutmak, ürkütmek; **ap.pall.ing** ☐ korkunç, müthiş.

**ap.pa.ra.tus** [æpəˈreitəs] *n.* cihaz, makine, takım, aletler; ~ work jimnastik aletleri.

**ap.par.el** [əˈpærəl] **1.** *n.* elbise, üst baş, kıyafet; **2.** *v/t.* giydirmek.

**ap.par.ent** ☐ [əˈpærənt] açık, belli; görünüşte olan; kolay anlaşılır; kolay görülür; *s. heir;* **ap.pa.ri.tion** [æpəˈriʃən] *n.* hayalet; görünüş; olay.

**ap.peal** [əˈpi:l] **1.** *vb.* ఴ daha yüksek mahkemeye müracaat etm., istinaf etm. (to *-e);* önemle rica etm., yalvarmak (to.s. o.for sth. *b-ne bş için*); başvurmak (to *-e);* beğenmek *-i; b-nin* hoşuna gitmek; *s.* country; **2.** *n.* baş vurma, müracaat (to *-e);* yalvarma, israrla isteme; temyiz; davet, çağrı (to *-e); fig.* ilân, beyanname; ~ for mercy af dilekçesi; **apˈpeal.er** *n.* başvuran; temyiz eden; **apˈpeal.ing** ☐ yalvaran; sevimli, cazip.

**ap.pear** [əˈpiə] *v/i.* görünmek, gözükmek, meydana çıkmak, belli olm.; mahkemeye çıkmak; var olm.; **apˈpear.ance** *n.* görünüş; gösteriş; dış görünüş; meydana çıkma, zuhur etme; olay; mahkemeye çıkma; keep up *veya* save ~s zevahiri kurtarmak, durumu idare etm.; make one's ~ ortaya *(veya* sahneye, meydana) çıkmak; alenen görünmek; put in an ~ ispatı vücut etm., görünüp gitmek; to *veya* by all ~s görünüşe göre.

**ap.pease** [əˈpi:z] *v/t.* yatıştırmak, teskin etm.; *(açlık vs.)* gidermek; *(dert)* azaltmak, hafifletmek; *(kavga, çarpışma vs.)* bastırmak; **apˈpease.ment** *n.* yatıştırma, teslim etme; *(politikada)* düşmana taviz vererek barışın sağlanabileceği düşüncesi.

**ap.pel.lant** [əˈpelənt] **1.** *adj.* istinaf yoluna giden, temyiz eden; **2.** *n.* istinaf yoluna giden taraf, temyiz eden kimse; **apˈpel.late** [~lit] *adj.* dâvaların yeniden görülmesine ait olan; temyizle ilgili; ~ court temyiz mahkemesi; **ap.pel.la.tive** *gr.* [əˈpelətiv] **1.** *n.a.* ~ name cins ismi; ünvan; **2.** *adj.* cins ismine ait; tanımlayıcı. *veya* istinaf yoluna başvurulan taraf.

**ap.pend** [əˈpend] *v/t.* eklemek, ilâve etm., katmak; **apˈpend.age** *n.* ilâve, katkı, ek; **ap.pen.dec.to.my** [~ˈdektəmi] *n.* apandis ameliyatı; **ap.pen.di.ci.tis** [~diˈsaitis] *n.* apandisit; **apˈpen.dix** [~diks] *n.pl.a.* **apˈpen.di.ces** [~disi:z] ek, zeyil; ♂ apandis.

**ap.per.tain** [æpəˈtein] *v/i.* ait olm.; bağlı olm. (to *-e); fig. b-ne* ait olm., *b-nin* olm.

**ap.pe.tence, ap.pe.ten.cy** [ˈæpitəns(i)] *n.* (for, after, of) iştiha, şiddetli arzu; insiyak; içgüdü.

**ap.pe.tite** [ˈæpitait] *n.* (for) iştah; arzu; istek; şehvet; *fig.* arzu.

**ap.pe.tiz.er** [ˈæpitaizə] *n.* iştah açan şey, çerez, aperatif; **ˈap.pe.tiz.ing** ☐ iştah açan.

**ap.plaud** [əˈplɔ:d] *vb.* alkışlamak; takdir etm.

**ap.plause** [əˈplɔ:z] *n.* alkış.

**ap.ple** [ˈæpl] *n.* elma; the ~ of s.o.'s eye *fig.* göz bebeği, favori, gözde; **ˈ~-cart** *n. (seyyar satıcının)* el arabası; upset s.o. 's ~ F bir işi bozmak, bir çuval inciri berbat etm.; **ˈ~.jack** *n. Am.* elma rakısı; **ˈ~-ˈpie** *n.* elma turtası; in ~ order çok düzenli; **ˈ~-pol.ish.er** *sl.* dalkavuk, yağcı; **ˈ~ˈsauce** *n.* elma püresi; *Am. sl.* zevzeklik, boş laf.

**ap.pli.ance** [əˈplaiəns] *n.* alet, cihaz.

**ap.pli.ca.bil.i.ty** [æplikə'biliti] *n.* uygulanabilme; **'ap.pli.ca.ble** *adj.* uygun, münasip, uygulanabilir (to -*e*); **'ap.pli.cant** *n.* istekli, başvuran kimse, aday (for -*e*, için); **ap.pli'ca.tion** *n.* uygulama, tatbik (of *bşin*); müracaat (to -*e*); dilekçe; ilâç, merhem; dikkat, özen; ~ form müracaat formu; make an ~ dilekçe vermek, başvurmak.

**ap.ply** [ə'plai] *v/t.* (to), yaklaştırmak; tatbik etm., uygulamak; üstüne koymak; atfetmek; tahsis etm., ayırmak -*e*; ~ o.s. to kendini bir işe vermek; *v/i.* müracaat etm., başvurmak (to, for -*e*, için); ~ for müracaat etm.; talep etm.; applied sciences *pl.* tatbikî tabii ilimler.

**ap.point** [ə'pɔint] *v/t.* tayin etm., atamak; görevlendirmek; kararlaştırmak, tayin etm.; donatmak; well ~ed iyi döşenmiş; **ap'point.ment** *n.* tayin, memuriyet, iş; randevu; ~s *pl.* donatım, teçhizat; by ~ sözleşme mucibince.

**ap.por.tion** [ə'pɔːʃən] *v/t.* paylaştırmak, taksim etm. (between, among, amongst ...*arasında*); **ap'por.tion.ment** *n.* pay; paylaştırma.

**ap.po.site** ☐ ['æpəuzit] uygun, münasip (to -*e*); **'ap.po.site.ness** *n.* uygunluk.

**ap.po.si.tion** [æpəu'ziʃən] *n.* gr. aynı şahıs veya şeyi açıklayan iki kelimenin bir cümlede yan yana konması.

**ap.prais.al** [ə'preizəl] *n.* değer biçme, tahmin; **ap'praise** *v/t.* değer biçmek, tahmin etm.; **ap'praise.ment** *n.* değer biçme, tahmin; **ap'prais.er** *n.* değer biçen kimse, muhammin.

**ap.pre.ci.a.ble** ☐ [ə'priːʃəbl] sezilebilir, tahmin edilebilir; değer biçilebilir; **ap'pre.ci.ate** [-ʃieit] *v/t.* kıymet takdir etm., paha biçmek; beğenmek, takdir ve teşekkür etm.; kıymetini anlamak -*in*; *v/i.* fiyatı yükselmek, değerlenmek; **ap.pre.ci'a.tion** *n.* değerlendirme, kıymet bilme; ✝ değer artışı; eleştiri; **ap.pre.ci.a.tive** ☐ [ə'priːʃiətiv], **ap'pre.ci.a.to.ry** takdir eden, kadirşinas; minnettar; be ~ of .....*den* anlamak ve zevk duymak.

**ap.pre.hend** [æpri'hend] *v/t.* yakalamak, tutuklamak; anlamak; korkmak -*den*; **ap.pre.hen.si.ble** ☐ [~'hensəbl] anlaşılabilir, farkolunabilir; **ap.pre'hen.sion** *n.* tutuklama; anlama, anlayış, kavrayış; korku, endişe; zihin; **ap.pre'hen.sive** ☐ çabuk kavrayan; endişe eden, korkan (of -*den*).

**ap.pren.tice** [ə'prentis] **1.** *n.* çırak; stajyer; **2.** *v/t.* çırak olarak vermek; **ap'pren.tice.ship** *n.* çıraklık.

**ap.prise** [ə'praiz] *v/t.* haber vermek, bilgi vermek (of -*den*).

**ap.pro** ✝ ['æprəu]: on ~ örnek olarak, muhayyer olarak.

**ap.proach** [ə'prəutʃ] **1.** *vb.* yaklaşmak, yanaşmak -*e*, yaklaştırmak, yakına getirmek; müracaat etm.; *fig.* yaklaşmak -*e*; **2.** *n.* yaklaşma, yanaşma; müracaat; giriş yolu; yaklaşım; make ~es to s.o. birine avans yapmak; **ap'proach.a.ble** *adj.* yaklaşılabilir, ulaşılabilir, varılması mümkün.

**ap.pro.ba.tion** [æprəu'beiʃən] *n.* beğenme; resmî müsaade, tasdik.

**ap.pro.pri.ate 1.** [ə'prəuprieit] *v/t.* tahsis etm., ayırmak; almak, kendine mal etm. (for için); **2.** ☐ [~priüt] uygun, münasip (for, to için, -*e*); **ap.pro.pri.a.tion** [~pri'eiʃən] *n.* ayırma, tahsis; ödenek, tahsisat; ♀ Committee *parl.* Bütçe Komisyonu.

**ap.prov.a.ble** [ə'pruːvəbl] *adj.* şayanı takdir, beğenilir; **ap'prov.al.** *n.* tasvip, uygun görme, onama, resmî izin; on ~ örnek olarak, muhayyer olarak; **ap'prove** *vb. a.* ~ of beğenmek, uygun görmek, onaylamak, kabul etm.; **ap'proved** ☐ tasdikli, izinli, onaylı; ~ school islah evi; **ap'prov.er** *n.* 🐍 başkalarını suç ortaklığı ile suçlayan sanık; suç ortağı.

**ap.prox.i.mate 1.** [ə'prɔksimeit] *vb.* yaklaşmak, yaklaştırmak; **2.** ☐ [~mit] yaklaşık olarak, takribi, yakın (to -*e*); **ap.prox.i.ma.tion** [~'meiʃən] *n.* yaklaşma, yakın olma; tahmin; **ap.prox.i.ma.tive** ☐ [~mətiv] takribî, tahminî.

**ap.pur.te.nance** [ə'pəːtinəns] *n.* *mst* ~s *pl.* teferruat, müştemilât; 🐍 irtifak hakları.

**a.pri.cot** 🌿 ['eiprikɔt] *n.* kayısı, zerdali.

**A.pril** ['eiprəl] *n.* Nisan; make an ~ fool of s.o. 1 Nisan'da birisine muziplik yapmak.

**a.pron** ['eiprən] *n.* önlük, prostela; peştamal; ✝ hangarın önündeki beton saha; *thea.* sahnenin seyirciye doğru olan çıkıntılı kısmı; '~-string *n.* önlük bağı; be tied to one's wife's (mother's) ~s aşırı derecede karısına (annesine) bağlı olm.

**ap.ro.pos** ['æprəpəu] *adj. & adv.* (of, to) yerinde olan, uygun, münasip; sırası gelmişken, bu münasebetle.

**apt** ☐ [æpt] uygun, elverişli, yerinde (*söz, fikir vs.*); zeki, anlayışlı (at -*de*); he is ~ to believe it ona inanmak eğiliminde; ~ to *bşe* mütemayil, taraflı; meyyal; **ap.ti.tude** ['~titjuːd], **'apt.ness**

**n.** eğilim, temayül (to -e); yetenek, kabiliyet (for, to için -e).

**aq.ua.lung** [ˈækwəlʌŋ] *n.* su altında kullanılan oksijen tüpü.

**aq.ua.ma.rine** *min.* [ækwəməˈriːn] *n.* akvamaren, cama benzer mavimsi yeşil bir ziynet taşı; mavimsi yeşil.

**aq.ua.plane** [ˈækwəplein] *n.* su kayağı.

**aq.ua.relle** [ækwəˈrel] *n.* sulu boya resim.

**a.quar.i.um** [əˈkwɛəriəm] *n.* akvaryum.

**a.quat.ic** [əˈkwætik] **1.** *adj.* suda yapılan, su...; ~ sports *pl.* su sporları; **2.** *n.* suda yetişen veya yaşayan, sucul bitki.

**aq.ue.duct** [ˈækwidʌkt] *n.* su kemeri; **a.que.ous** □ [ˈeikwiəs] sulu, su gibi, su ile yapılan.

**aq.ui.line** [ˈækwilain] *adj.* kartal gibi; kartal gagası gibi kıvrık; ~ nose gaga burunlu.

**Ar.ab** [ˈærəb] *n.* Arap, Arabistanlı; Arap atı; street ♀ sokak çocuğu; **ar.a.besque** [~ˈbesk] **1.** *n.* arabesk, çiçekli ve yapraklı süsleme; **2.** *adj.* arabesk tarzında olan; **A.ra.bi.an** [əˈreibjən] **1.** *adj.* Arabistan'a ait; The ~ Nights Binbir Gece Masalları; **2.** *n.* Arap, Arabistanlı; **Ar.a.bic** [ærəbik] **1.** *adj.* Araplara, Arabistan'a ait; **2.** *n.* Arapça.

**ar.a.ble** [ˈærəbl] **1.** *adj.* sürülebilir, ziraate elverişli; **2.** *n. a.* ~ land ekilebilir toprak.

**ar.bi.ter** [ˈɑːbitə] *n.* hakem; söz sahibi; **ar.bi.trage** † [ɑːbiˈtrɑːʒ] *n.* arbitraj; **ˈar.bi.tral** triˈbu.nal hakem mahkemesi; *spor:* hakem komitesi; **arˈbit.ra.ment** *n.* hakem kararı; *(hakem sıfatıyla)* karar verme; **ˈar.bi.trar.i.ness** *n.* keyfi hareket; **ˈar.bi.trar.y** □ keyfi, ihtiyari; **ar.bi.trate** [~ˈtreit] *vb. (hakem sıfatıyla)* karar vermek; *(hakemle)* halletmek; **ar.biˈtra.tion** *n.* hakem kararı; hakem kararıyla halletme, tahkim; ~ of exchange † döviz arbitraji; **ˈar.bi.tra.tor** *n.* ♂♀ hakem; **ˈar.bi.tress** *n.* kadın hakem; söz sahibi kadın.

**ar.bor** [ˈɑːbə] *n.* ⊕ mil, dingil; ♀ Day A.B.D.'de ağaç dikmeye ayrılan bir ilkbahar günü; **ar.bo.re.al** [ɑːˈbɔːriəl], **arˈbo.re.ous** *adj.* ağaç..., ağaçlı, ağaçlık; ağaç gibi; **arˈbo.res.cent** □ [ɑːbəˈresnt] ağaca benzeyen.

**ar.bour** [ˈɑːbə] *n.* çardak, gölgelik, kameriye.

**ar.bu.tus** ♦ [ɑːˈbjuːtəs] *n.* kocayemiş.

**arc** *ast.*, A *etc.* [ɑːk] *n.* ( ♪ ışık-) kavis; kemer, ark, yay; **ar.cade** [ɑːˈkeid] *n.* bir sıra kemer; kemer altı, pasaj.

**ar.ca.num** [ɑːˈkeinəm] *pl.* **ar'ca.na** [~nə] *n.* sır, muamma.

**arch¹** [ɑːtʃ] **1.** *n. part.* △ kemer, tak; ayak kemeri; ~ support düztabanlılara mahsus kundura tabanlığı; **2.** *vb.* kubbe, kemer gibi kabartmak; kabarmak, kubbelenmek.

**arch²** □ [~] *(kadın ve çocukların davranışları için)* şaklaban, soytarı; kurnaz, açıkgöz.

**arch³** □ [~] birinci, ilk, baş; baş... **ar.chae.ol.o.gist** [ɑːkiˈɔlədʒist] *n.* arkeolog; **ar.chae.ol.o.gy** *n.* arkeoloji.

**ar.cha.ic** [ɑːˈkeiik] *adj.* (~ally) eskiye ait, eski, kadim; artık kullanılmayan; **ˈar.cha.ism** *n.* artık kullanılmayan kelime veya deyim.

**arch.an.gel** [ˈɑːkeindʒəl] *n.* baş melek.

**arch.bish.op** [ɑːtʃˈbiʃəp] *n.* başpiskopos; **arch'bish.op.ric** [~rik] *n.* başpiskoposluk makamı veya bölgesi.

**arch.dea.con** [ɑːtʃˈdiːkən] *n.* başdiyakoz.

**arch.duch.ess** [ɑːtʃˈdʌtʃis] *n.* arşidüşes; **ˈarch'duch.y** *n.* arşidükün idaresi altındaki bölge; **ˈarch'duke** *n.* arşidük.

**arch.er** [ˈɑːtʃə] *n.* okçu; **ˈarch.er.y** *n.* okçuluk.

**ar.che.type** [ˈɑːkitaip] *n.* orijinal fikir veya örnek, ilk örnek.

**arch-fiend** [ɑːtʃˈfiːnd] *n.* baş şeytan, iblis.

**ar.chi.e.pis.co.pal** [ɑːkiiˈpiskəpəl] *adj.* başpiskosposluğa ait.

**ar.chi.pel.a.go** [ɑːkiˈpeligəu] *n.* takımadalar, arşipel; üzerinde çok sayıda küçük ada bulunan deniz.

**ar.chi.tect** [ˈɑːkitekt] *n.* mimar; yaratıcı, eser meydana getiren; **ar.chi.tec.ton.ic** [~ˈtɔnik] *adj.* (~ally) mimarlığa ait; **ar.chi.tec.tu.ral** [~tʃərəl] □ mimari, mimarlığa ait; **ˈar.chi.tec.ture** *n.* mimarlık; inşaat, yapı.

**ar.chives** [ɑːkaivz] *n. pl.* arşiv.

**arch.way** [ˈɑːtʃwei] *n.* kemeraltı yolu, kemerli geçit.

**arc-lamp** [ˈɑːklæmp] *n.*, **ˈarc-light** *n.* ♪ ark lâmbası.

**arc.tic** [ˈɑːktik] **1.** *adj.* arktik, Kuzey Kutbunda bulunan *(bölge)*; çok soğuk; the ♀ Kuzey Kutbu; ♀ Circle Kuzey Kutup dairesi; ♀ Ocean Kuzey Buz Denizi; **2.** *n. Am.* su geçirmez ve sıcak tutan pabuç, lastik, şoson.

**ar.den.cy** [ˈɑːdənsi] *n.* şevk; ateşlilik; içtenlik, samimiyet; **ˈar.dent** □ *mst fig.* ateşli, şevkli, heyecanlı; candan; ~ spirits *pl.* alkollü içkiler.

ar.do(u)r ['ɑːdə] n. fig. ateşlilik, gayret, şevk.

ar.du.ous ☐ ['ɑːdjuəs] zahmetli, güç.

are [ɑː] s. be.

a.re.a ['ɛəriə] n. saha, alan, bölge; yüzölçümü; (fikir, iş, çalışma) alan; danger ~ tehlikeli bölge; prohibited ~ yasak bölge.

a.re.na [ə'riːnə] n. arena, oyun meydanı, anfiteatrın ortasındaki meydan; mücadele alanı (a. fig.).

aren't F [ɑːnt] = are not.

a.rête mount. [æ'reit] n. sırt; hattıbalâ; tepeler hattı.

ar.gent ['ɑːdʒənt] adj. gümüş renginde; gümüş.

Ar.gen.tine ['ɑːdʒəntain] 1. adj. Arjantinli; 2. n. Arjantin; the ~ Arjantin.

ar.gil ['ɑːdʒil] n. kil, balçık; ar.gil.la.ceous [~'leiʃəs] adj. killi, balçıklı.

ar.gon ⚗ ['ɑːgɔn] n. argon.

ar.gu.a.ble ['ɑːgjuəbl] ☐ tartışılabilir; ar.gue ['ɑːgjuː] vb. münakaşa etm., tartışmak; ileri sürmek, ispat etm.; ~ s.o. into doing s.th. b-ni bşi yapmağa ikna etm.; ~ s.o. out of doing s. th. b-ni bşi yapmaktan caydırmak.

ar.gu.ment ['ɑːgjumənt] n. tartışma, münakaşa; delil, fikir; özet; ar.gu.men.ta.tion [~men'teiʃən] n. ispat; tartışma, münakaşa; ar.gu.men.ta.tive ☐ [~'mentətiv] tartışmacı, münakaşacı; delil nevinden.

a.ri.a ♪ ['ɑːriə] n. arya, şan solosu.

ar.id ['ærid] ☐ kurak, çorak; cansıkıcı (a. fig.); a'rid.i.ty n. kuraklık, çoraklık.

a.right [ə'rait] adv. doğru olarak.

a.rise [ə'raiz] irr. v/i. kalkmak, çıkmak, doğmak (from -den); a.ris.en [ə'rizn] p.p. of arise.

ar.is.toc.ra.cy [æris'tɔkrəsi] n. aristokrasi (a. fig); a.ris.to.crat [~'təkræt] n. aristokrat; a.ris.to'crat.ic, a.ris.to'crat.i.cal ☐ aristokrasiye ait; mümtaz, kibar.

a.rith.me.tic [ə'riθmətik] n. aritmetik, hesap; ar.ith.met.i.cal ☐ [æriθ'metikəl] aritmetiğe ilgili.

ark [ɑːk] n. tahta sandık; mavna; Kutsal Kitap: Noah's ~ Nuh'un gemisi; ⚥ of the Covenant On Emir'in yazılı olduğu taşları havi sandık.

arm[1] [ɑːm] n. kol; pazu; dal; şube; koy, küçük körfez; gü. otorite; within ~'s reach elin yetişeceği uzaklıkta, yakın; keep s.o. at ~'s length b-ni yanına yaklaştırmamak, yüz vermemek; infant in ~s meme çocuğu, bebek.

arm[2] [~] 1. n. mst ~s pl. silah; mst

~s sg. silahlı kuvvetlerin bir kolu; ~s pl. arma; s. coat; be (all) up in ~s ayaklanmak; öfkelenmek, ateş püskürmek, tepesi atmak; take up ~s silaha sarılmak; 2. vb. silahlandırmak, donatmak; silahlanmak, silaha sarılmak.

ar.ma.da [ɑːmɑːdə] n. donanma; the (Invincible) ⚥ İspanya tarafından 1588 de İngiltere'ye gönderilen ve İngilizere mağlûp olan donanma.

ar.ma.ment ['ɑːməmənt] n. teçhizat pl., silahlar; silahlandırma; mst pl. silahlı kuvvetler; naval ~ deniz kuvvetleri; ~ race silahlanma yarışı; ar.ma.ture ['~tjuə] n. zırh; ⚥, phys. armatur, mıknatısın iki kutbu arasına yerleştirilen demir parçası, endüvi.

arm.chair ['ɑːm'tʃɛə] n. koltuk.

armed [ɑːmd] adj. silahlı; ~ forces pl. silahlı kuvvetler.

...-armed [ɑːmd] adj. ...kollu.

Ar.me.ni.an [ɑː'miːnjən] adj. & n. Ermeni; Ermenice.

arm.ful ['ɑːmful] n. kucak dolusu.

ar.mi.stice ['ɑːmistis] n. mütareke, ateşkes (a. fig.).

arm.let ['ɑːmlit] n. pazıbent; haliç, koy.

ar.mo.ri.al [ɑː'mɔːriəl] adj. armaya ait.

ar.mo(u)r ['ɑːmə] 1. n. ✕ silah, (a. fig., zo.) zırh; dalgıç takımı; ✕ coll. zırhlı vasıta; 2. vb. zırh kaplamak, zırhlamak; ~ed car zırhlı otomobil; ~ed division zırhlı tümen; ~ed turret zırhlı taret; '~-clad, '~-plat.ed adj. zırhlı; zırhlı...; 'ar.mour.er n. zırhçı, silahçı; ✕, ⬇ tüfekçi ustası; 'ar.mo(u)r.y n. silah deposu (a. fig.); Am. silah fabrikası.

arm.pit ['ɑːmpit] n. koltuk altı; 'arm-rest n. kol dayanacak yer.

ar.my ['ɑːmi] n. kara ordusu; fig. ordu, kalabalık, sürü; ~ chaplain ordu papazı (veya imamı); s. service; '~-corps n. kolordu; '~-list n. ✕ ordu subay listesi.

a.ro.ma [ə'rəumə] n. güzel koku, rayiha, aroma; ar.o.mat.ic [ærəu'mætik] ☐ (~ally) güzel kokulu, rayihalı.

a.rose [ə'rəuz] pret. of arise.

a.round [ə'raund] 1. adv. -in etrafın(d)a, yakında, civarında; civarında, sularında; Am. ⬇ buralarda; 2. prp. etrafın(d)a; civarında; dört bir yanın(d)a; orada burada, oraya buraya.

a.rouse [ə'rauz] v/t. uyandırmak, canlandırmak; fig. b-ni harekete geçirmek; tahrik, teşvik etm.

ar.rack ['ærək] n. rakı.

ar.raign [ə'rein] v/t. suçlamák, itham etm., mahkemeye vermek; fig. azarla-

**mak,** paylamak; **ar'raign.ment** *n.* sanığın sorguya çekilmesi, iddianamenin tefhimi ve sorguya çekme muameleleri.

**ar.range** [ə'reɪndʒ] *v/t.* tanzim etm., düzenlemek; *part.* **J aranjman** yapmak: *(gün)* kararlaştırmak; *(anlaşmazlık)* arabuluculuk etm., bertaraf etm., bitirmek; hazırlamak; *v/i.* gerekli hazırlıkları yapmak (for *için*); **ar'range.ment** *n.* düzenleme, tanzim; düzen, sıra; hazırlık; anlaşma; düzenlenmiş şey; J aranjman; make one's ~s tertibatta bulunmak.

**ar.rant** [] ['ærənt] tamamen, son derece; çok kötü.

**ar.ray** [ə'reɪ] **1.** *n.* saf, sıra, düzen; ordu; teşhir; gösterişli kıyafet; **2.** *v/t.* sıraya koymak, düzenlemek; giydirmek, süslemek.

**ar.rear** [ə'rɪə] *n.* sürümcemede bırakılan *(iş vs.)*; ödenmemiş *(borç vs.)*; ~s of rent ödenmemiş kira borcu; be in ~s borcu vaktinde ödeyememek; **ar'rear.age** *n.* vaktinde ödenmemiş borcun bakiyesi.

**ar.rest** [ə'rest] **1.** *n.* tutuklama, tevkif; durdurma; under ~ tutuklu; **2.** *v/t.* tutuklamak, tevkif etm.; durdurmak; çekmek, celbetmek *(dikkat).*

**ar.riv.al** [ə'raɪvəl] *n.* geliş, varış; gelen kimse; a new ~ yeni gelen; **ar'rive** *v/i.* varmak, vâsıl olm. *(at* -e*),* yetişmek; başarmak.

**ar.ro.gance** ['ærəʊgəns] *n.* kibir, gurur; küstahlık, kendini bilmezlik; **'ar.ro.gant** [] kibirli, mağrur; küstah; **ar.ro.gate** ['-geɪt] *v/t. mst ~* to o.s. *(haksız yere)* benimsemek, kendine maletmek, iddia etm.; ~ s.th. to s.o. *bşi b-ne* maletmek.

**ar.row** ['ærəʊ] *n.* ok; '~-head *n.* ok başı, temren; '~.root *n.* ﬁ ararot.

**arse** *sl.* [ɑːs] *n.* göt, makat, kıç.

**ar.se.nal** ['ɑːsɪnl] *n.* silah ve mühimmat deposu, tophane; tersane.

**ar.se.nic** ['ɑːsnɪk] *n.* arsenik, sıçanotu; **ar.sen.i.cal** [ɑː'senɪkəl] *adj.* arseniğe ait, arsenikli.

**ar.son** ﬁ ['ɑːsn] *n.* kundakçılık, kasten yangın çıkarma.

**art¹** [ɑːt] *n.* sanat, hüner, marifet, maharet, ustalık; ilim dalı; ~s *pl.* ilimler; Master of ﬁs *(abbr.* **M.A.)** edebiyat fakültesi diploması ile doktora arasında bir derece; fine ~s *pl.* güzel sanatlar; Liberal ~s edebiyat ve beşeri ilimler; ~s and crafts el işleri; Faculty of ﬁs Edebiyat Fakültesi.

**art²** † [~] sen(sin).

**ar.te.ri.al** [ɑː'tɪərɪəl] *adj.* atardamara ait;

atardamara benzer; temiz kanla ilgili; ~ road anayol; **ar.te.ri.o.scle.ro.sis** ﬁ [ɑː'tɪərɪəʊskliə'rəʊsɪs] *n.* damar sertliği, arteriyoskleroz; **ar.ter.y** ['ɑːtərɪ] *n.* atardamar, arter; *fig.* büyük cadde, anayol.

**ar.te.sian well** [ɑː'tiːzjən'wel] *n.* artezyen kuyusu.

**art.ful** [] ['ɑːtful] kurnaz; ustalıklı, maharet isteyen.

**art gal.ler.y** ['ɑːt'gælərɪ] sanat galerisi.

**ar.thrit.ic** ﬁ [ɑː'θrɪtɪk] *adj.* mafsala ait, mafsal iltihabına ait; **ar.thri.tis** [ɑː'θraɪtɪs] *n.* mafsal iltihabı.

**ar.ti.choke** ﬁ ['ɑːtɪtʃəʊk] *n.* enginar.

**ar.ti.cle** ['ɑːtɪkl] **1.** *n.* makale; madde, fıkra, fasıl; nesne, madde; *gr.'* tanım edatı; ~s of apprenticeship usta ile çırak arasında anlaşma; ~s of association şirket mukavelenamesi, statüsü; **2.** *v/t. b-ni* mukavele ile başkasının yanına vermek *(tatbiki eğitim için)*; maddeler halinde düzenlemek; ~ed clerk staj gören kâtip.

**ar.tic.u.late 1.** [ɑː'tɪkjuleɪt] *vb.* eklem ile birleştirmek; eklem oluşturmak; ifade etm., açıkça söylemek, dikkatle telâffuz etm.; **2.** [] [-lɪt] açık, seçkin; düşünce ve hislerini rahatça anlatan; mafsallı, eklemli; **ar'tic.u.lat.ed** [~leɪtɪd] *adj.* mafsallı; **ar.tic.u'la.tion** *n.* ses teşkili; telâffuz; mafsal, eklem; bitiştirme.

**ar.ti.fact** ['ɑːtɪfækt] *n.* insan eliyle yapılan faydalı şey.

**ar.ti.fice** ['ɑːtɪfɪs] *n.* hile, oyun, kurnazlık; ustalık, marifet; **ar'tif.i.cer** *n.* usta işçi, sanatkâr; eser sahibi; askerî teknisyeni; **ar.ti.fi.cial** [] [~'fɪʃəl] *adj.* yapma, sunî; taklit; sahte, yapmacık; ~ silk sunî ipek; ~ insemination sunî ilkah; ~ person ﬁﬁ hükmî şahıs, tüzel kişi.

**ar.til.ler.y** [ɑː'tɪlərɪ] *n.* toplar, ağır silahlar; topçuluk; topçu *(sınıfı)*; **ar'til.ler.y-man** [~mən] *n.* topçu eri.

**ar.ti.san** [ɑːtɪ'zæn] *n.* zanaatçı, endüstri işçisi.

**art.ist** ['ɑːtɪst] *n.* sanatkâr, *part.* ressam; sahne sanatçısı; *sl.* düzenbaz, numaracı kimse; **ar.tiste** [ɑː'tiːst] *n. (profesyonel)* şarkıcı, oyuncu, dansöz; **ar.tis.tic, ar.tis.ti.cal** [] [ɑː'tɪstɪk(əl)] artistik, sanat yönü olan, sanatkârane, güzel sanatlara ait.

**art.less** [] ['ɑːtlɪs] sade, saf, hilesiz; işlenmemiş, doğal; kaba; **'art.less.ness** *n.* saflık, hilesiz oluş.

**art.y** ['ɑːtɪ] *adj.* sanatkârane, gösterişli.

**Ar.y.an** ['ɛərɪən] *adj.* Aryen, Hint-Avru-

**pa grubuna veya diline ait; 2. n.** Ari, Hint-Avrupalı.

**as** [æz, əz] *adv. & cj.* gibi, kadar; iken; -*diği* gibi; -*den* dolayı; -*mekle* beraber; çünkü, mademki, nitekim; ~ a rule genellikle; ~ if, ~ though sanki, güya; ~ for, ~ to -e gelince, -e sorarsanız, hakkında; so ~ to go gitmek için; ~ good ~ hemen hemen; gerçekten; be ~ good ~ one's word dediğini yapmak, sözünü tutmak; ~ long ~ mademki, ... olması şartıyle, ...dikçe, ...dıkça; olduğu sürece; I thought ~ much zaten bunu bekliyordum; ~ from -*den* başlıyarak, itibaren; ~ per -*e* göre, nazaran; ~ yet şimdiye kadar; ~ it were âdeta; sanki, güya; ~ well de, da, dahi, bile; ~ well ~ gibi, kadar, -*e* ilâveten.

**as.bes.tos** [æz'bestəs] *n.* amyant, asbest.

**as.cend** [ə'send] *vb.* çıkmak, yukarı çıkmak, yükselmek, tırmanmak -*e*; (*nehir*) akıntıya karşı gitmek; (*taht*) çıkmak -a; **as'cend.an.cy** *n.* (over) üstünlük; nüfuz; **as'cend.ant 1.** *adj.* yükselen; üstün, hâkim (over -*e*); **2. n.** = ascendancy; üstünlük; nüfuz, itibar; cet, dede; be in the ~ *fig.* itibarı artmak, yükselmek; **as'cend.en.cy, as'cend.ent** = ascendancy, ascendant.

**as.cen.sion** [ə'senʃən] *n.* yükselme, yukarı çıkış (*part. ast.*); ♀ (Day) Urucu İsa, İsa'nın göğe çıkışı (*günü*).

**as.cent** [ə'sent] *n.* çıkış, tırmanma; yokuş, bayır.

**as.cer.tain** [æsə'tein] *v/t.* soruşturmak, öğrenmek, gerçeği bulmak; **as.cer'tain.a-ble** ☐ soruşturulabilir, anlaşılabilir; **as-cer'tain.ment** *n.* soruşturma, anlama.

**as.cet.ic** [ə'setik] **1.** ☐ (~ally) zahit, münzevi, dünyevi zevklerden el çekmiş; **2.** *n.* din uğruna dünyevi zevklerden el çekmiş kimse, sofu kimse, derviş; **as'cet.i-cism** [~tisizəm] *n.* aşırı sofuluk, zahitlik; gösterişten uzak bir hayat sürme.

**as.cor.bic ac.id** [əs'kɔ:bik'æsid] *n.* C vitamini

**as.crib.a.ble** [əs'kraibəbl] *adj.* atfolunabilir, yüklenebilir (to -*e*); **as'cribe** *v/t.* (to) atfetmek, hamletmek, yüklemek -*e*.

**a.sep.tic** ♀ [æ'septik] *adj.* aseptik, mikropsuz.

**ash[1]** [æʃ] *n.* ♀ dişbudak ağacı; dişbudak kerestesi.

**ash[2]** [~] *mst* **ash.es** ['~ʃiz] *n. pl.* kül; **Ash Wednesday** Paskalyadan evvelki perhizin ilk Çarşambası.

**a.shamed** [ə'ʃeimd] ☐ mahcup, utanmış; be *veya* feel ~ of utanmak -*den*.

**ash-bin** ['æʃbin], *Am.* **ash-can** [ˈæʃkæn] *n.* çöp tenekesi.

**ash.en[1]** ['æʃn] *adj.* dişbudaktan yapılmış.

**ash.en[2]** [~] *adj.* kül gibi ;kül renginde, soluk renkli.

**a.shore** [ə'ʃɔ:] *adv.* karada, karaya, sahil(d)e; run ~, be driven ~ karaya oturmak.

**ash...:** '~-**pan** *n.* ocak küllüğü; '~-**tray** *n.* kül tablası.

**ash...:** '~-**tree** *n.* ♀ dişbudak ağacı; '~-**wood** *n.* dişbudak kerestesi.

**ash.y** ['æʃi] *adj.* küllü, külle kaplı; kül rengi.

**A.si.at.ic** [eiʃi'ætik] **1.** *adj.* Asya kıtasına veya halkına ait; **2. n.** Asyalı.

**a.side** [ə'said] *adv.* bir tarafa, yana, kendi kendine, başka (from -*den*); **2. n.** *thea.* bir oyuncunun sahnede seyirciye alçak sesle söylediği sözler.

**as.i.nine** ['æsinain] *adj.* eşekçe, eşeğe ait; aptal.

**ask** [ɑ:sk] *v/t. & v/i.* sormak -*e*; davet etm., teklif etm.; istemek; rica etm. -*den*; ~ for aramak, sormak -*i*; talep etm., istemek -*i*; ~ the price *b-şin* fiyatını sormak; ~ (s.o.) a question (*b-ne*) bir soru sormak; ~ (him) his name *b-ne* ismini sormak; ~ s.th. of s.o. birisinden *bş* talep etm.; you are ~ing too much çok şey istiyorsun; ~ s.o. for help (*b-den*) yardım istemek; ~ s.o. to come *b-ni* davet etm.; ~ s.o. to dinner *b-ni* yemeğe davet etm.; ~ s.o. in *b-ni* eve (*içeriye*) davet etm.; he ~ed for it *veya* for trouble çanak tuttu, kendi istedi; to be had for the ~ing istemeniz kâfidir, parasız verilir.

**a.skance** [əs'kæns], **a'skant**, **as.kew** [əs'kju:] *adv.* yan, yan tarafa, göz ucuyla; beğenmeyerek.

**a.slant** [ə'slɑ:nt] **1.** *adj. & adv.* bir yana doğru, eğri, meyilli; **2.** *prp.* üzerinden meyilli olarak.

**a.sleep** [ə'sli:p] **1.** *adj.* uykuda, uyumuş; uyuşmuş (*uzuv, organ*); **2.** *adv.* uyurken; be ~ uyumak, uykuda olm.; fall ~ uykuya dalmak; sound ~ derin uykuda.

**asp[1]** *zo.* [æsp] *n.* engerek yılanı.

**asp[2]** ♀ [~] *n.* telli (*a. titrek*) kavak.

**as.par.a.gus** ♀ [əs'pærəgəs] *n.* kuşkonmaz.

**as.pect** ['æspekt] *n.* görüş, bakış; görünüş; yüz, çehre; safha, durum, hal (*a. gr.*); the house has a southern ~ ev güneye bakıyor.

**as.pen** ['æspən] *n.* telli (*a. titrek*) kavak.

**as.per.gill, as.per.gil.lum** *eccl.* ['æspədʒil, ~'dʒiləm] *n.* Katoliklerin (*kilisede*) kutsal su serpmek için kullandıkları küçük fırça.

**as.per.i.ty** [æs'periti] *n.* kabalık, şiddet; pürüz, sertlik *(a. fig.)*; zorluk, güçlük.

**as.perse** [əs'pəːs] *v/t.* serpmek, atmak; *fig.* lekelemek, çamur atmak, iftira etm.; **as.per.sion** *n.* serpme; *fig.* iftira, leke.

**as.phalt** ['æsfælt] **1.** *n.* asfalt; **2.** *vb.* asfaltlamak.

**as.pho.del** ✤ ['æsfədel] *n.* çirişotu.

**as.phyx.i.a** [æs'fiksiə] *n.* asfeksi, boğulma *(havagası vs. ile)*; **as'phyx.i.ate** [~eit] *vb.* boğ(ul)mak; **as.phyx.i'a.tion** *n.* boğ(ul)ma.

**as.pic** ['æspik] *n.* dondurulmuş *(veya jelâtinli)* et.

**as.pi.dis.tra** ✤ [æspi'distrə] *n.* aspidistra, yaprakları yeşil benekli bir salon bitkisi.

**as.pir.ant** [əs'paiərənt] *n.* tâlip, namzet, istekli (to, after, for -*e*); ~ officer subay adayı; **as.pi.rate** ['æspərit] **1.** *gr. adj.* «h» sesiyle telâffuz edilen; **2.** *gr. n.* «h» sesi, «h» harfi; «h» gibi ses çıkarma; **3.** ['~reit] *vb. gr.* «h» sesiyle telâffuz etm.; ⊕, 🜚 emmek, içine çekmek; **as.pi'ra.tion** *n.* arzu, istek; önemli ve büyük bir işi gaye edinme; «h» harfinin telâffuzu; ⊕, 🜚 emme, içine çekme; **as'pire** [əs'paiə] *vb.* şiddetle arzu etm., elde etmeğe çalışmak (after *veya* to -*i*).

**as.pi.rin** *pharm.* ['æspərin] *n.* aspirin.

**as.pir.ing** □ [əs'paiəriŋ] gözü ileride olan, bir gayesi olan.

**ass** [æs] *n.* eşek; **make an ~ of** o.s. aptalca davranmak, aptallık etm.

**as.sail** [ə'seil] *v/t.* saldırmak, hücum etm. -*e* *(a. fig)*; *fig.* tecavüz etm., dil uzatmak (with *ile*); işe girişmek; **as'sail.a.ble** *adj.* tecavüz edilebilir; **as'sail.ant**, **as'sail.er** *n.* saldıran kimse, mütecaviz kimse.

**as.sas.sin** [ə'sæsin] *n.* katil; **as'sas.si.nate** [~neit] *v/t.* *(sinsice)* adam öldürmek; **as.sas.si'na.tion** *n.* suikast, adam öldürme.

**as.sault** [ə'sɔːlt] **1.** *n.* saldırı, taarruz, hücum, hamle *(a. fig.* on, upon -*e)*; ✕ hücum; 🜚 şahsa karşı fiili tecavüz, müessir fiil yapmağa teşebbüs; *s.* battery, indecent; **2.** *v/t.* saldırmak, hücum etm., tecavüz etm. -*e*; 🜚 müessir fiile teşebbüs etm.; ✕ hücum etm, saldırmak *(a. fig.).*

**as.say** [ə'sei] **1.** *n.* deneme, tecrübe; tahlil; ayar için alınan madde; **2.** *v/t.* tahlil etm., analiz yapmak; denemek; *v/i. Am.* kıymetli maden ihtiva etm..

**as.sem.blage** [ə'semblidʒ] *n.* toplantı; kalabalık; bir araya topla(n)ma; ⊕ montaj; **as'sem.ble** *vb.* topla(n)mak, birleş (tir)mek; bir araya gelmek *(veya* getirmek); ⊕ takmak, kurmak, monte etm.; **as'sem.bly** *n.* toplantı, kongre, meclis; ⊕ montaj; ~ shop montaj atelyesi; ~ hall konferans salonu; montaj atelyesi; ~ line sürekli iş bandı; ~ man *pol.* meclis üyesi.

**as.sent** [ə'sent] **1.** *n.* rıza, muvafakat, onay; **2.** *v/i.* razı olm., muvafakat etm. -*e*.

**as.sert** [ə'səːt] *v/t.* ileri sürmek, iddia etm.; ısrar etm.; ~ o.s. kendini göstermek, otoritesini kabul ettirmek; **as'ser.tion** *n.* öne sürme, iddia, teyit; **as'ser.tive** □ iddiacı; kendine fazla güvenir; **as'ser.tor** *n.* iddiacı kimse.

**as.sess** [ə'ses] *v/t. (vergi vs. için)* mülk değerini veya gelir miktarını hesaplamak, tayin *(takdir)* etm., tarh etm., bağlamak (at -*e*); **as'sess.a.ble** □ vergi tayini için değeri takdir olunabilen, takdiri kabil *(vergi)*; **as'sess.ment** *n.* vergi takdiri; vergi matrahı; tahakkuk; **as'ses.sor** *n.* vergi tahakkuk memuru; yalnız istişarı oya sahip olan mahkeme üyesi; muhammin.

**as.set** ['æset] *n.* 🜚 aktif; fayda temin eden şey; kâr; ~s *pl.* aktifler, mevcudat, değer; bir şahıs veya şirketin sahip olduğu menkul ve gayrimenkuller ile alacak haklarının tümü.

**as.sev.er.ate** [ə'sevəreit] *v/t.* tekrar tekrar beyan ve iddia etm.; **as.sev.er'a.tion** *n.* iddia, beyan.

**as.si.du.i.ty** [æsi'djuːiti] *n.* çalışkanlık, gayret, sebat; **as.sid.u.ous** □ [ə'sidjuəs] çalışkan, gayretli, sebatkâr.

**as.sign** [ə'sain] *v/t.* ayırmak, tahsis etm. (to -*e*); tayin etm., atamak (to -*e*); 🜚 alacağını temlik etm. veya devretmek; üstüne çevirmek, ferağ etm.; **as'sign.a.ble** □ tayini mümkün, tahsisi mümkün; devredilebilen, temlik edilebilen; **as.sig.na.tion** [æsig'neiʃən] *n.* randevu *(esp. gizli veya sevgili ile)*; *s.* assignment; **as.sign.ee** [æsiˈniː] *n.* devralan, temellük eden; 🜚 yedi adil, yediemin; ~ in bankruptcy müflisin mali üzerine hâkim tarafından tayin olunan vekil; **as.sign.ment** [ə'sainmənt] *n.* tayin, atama; *part. Am.* vazife, ödev, görev; 🜚 devir ve temlik; **as.sign.or** [æsi'nɔː] *n.* 🜚 bir menkul veya gayrimenkulü yahut bir hak veya menfaati başkasına devreden kimse.

**as.sim.i.late** [ə'simileit] *v/t.* (to, into, with) benzetmek, uydurmak -*e*; bağdaştırmak

-le; bşi özümsemek, hazmetmek, emmek; as.sim.iˈla.tion n. benzeyiş, benzeşme; özümseme, hazım, emme.
as.sist [əˈsist] v/t. yardım etm. -e, desteklemek; v/i. hazır bulunmak (at -de);
asˈsist.ance n. yardım, müzaheret, iane;
asˈsist.ant n. yardımcı, muavin, asistan.
as.size ⚖ [əˈsaiz] n. bir hakim ve jüri tarafından muhakeme; bu kurulda alınan
karar; ~s pl. geçici mahkeme (İngilte-
re'de).
as.so.ci.a.ble [əˈsəuʃjəbl] adj. birleş(tiril)
ebilir; uyum sağlıyabilir; bağlantısı olabilen (with ile); asˈso.ci.ate 1. [~ʃieit]
vb. birleştirmek, ortak etm., arkadaş
etm. -i; arkadaşlık etm., ortaklık kurmak (with ile); ortak olm. (with -e), katılmak -e; yakıştırmak, aralarında ilişki
kurmak; 2. [~ʃiit] n. arkadaş, dost; üye;
† ortak, şerik, hissedar; 3. [~ʃiit] adj.
tam yetki sahibi olmayan, yardımcı;
tam üyelik haklarından yararlanama-
yan; ortak olan; as.so.ci.a.tion [~siˈeiʃən]
n. kurul, kurum, cemiyet; birleşme, ortaklık; arkadaşlık, birlik; şirket; tedai,
çağrışım; ~ football futbol.
as.so.nance [ˈæsəunəns] n. ses benzeyişi;
yarım kafiye.
as.sort [əˈsɔːt] v/t. tasnif etm., sınıflandırmak; † mal çeşidi uydurmak; v/i.
(with) uymak, uygun olm., yakışmak -e;
~ed adj. çeşitli; asˈsort.ment n. tasnif,
sınıflandırma; † çeşit, mal çeşidi.
as.suage [əˈsweidʒ] v/t. yumuşatmak, yatıştırmak, hafifletmek, teskin etm.; (ağ-
lık vs.) gidermek.
as.sume [əˈsjuːm] v/t. (bir iş veya görevi) üzerine almak; gerçekmiş gibi kabul etm., farzetmek; (sahip olmadığı
bşi) var gibi göstermek; asˈsum.ing □
azametli, kibirli, küstah; as.sump.tion
[əˈsʌmpʃən] n. farz, zan; tavır, poz; üstüne alma; kibir, azamet, kendini satma; ♀ (Day) Urucu Meryem, Meryem'in
göğe kabulü yortusu; on the ~ that bean-
şart ki; asˈsump.tive □ farzolunan, zan-
nedilen; kibirli.
as.sur.ance [əˈʃuərəns] n. temin; güven,
itimat; söz, teminat; inanç; kendine gü-
venme; pişkinlik, yüzsüzlük; (part. hayat) sigorta; asˈsure v/t temin etm.;
söz vermek -e; sigorta etm. -i; ~ o.s.
bşden emin olm.; asˈsured 1. adj. (adv.
asˈsur.ed.ly [~ridli]) emin, şayanı itimat;
müemmen, sağlanmış; k-den emin olan;
b.s. sigortalı, küstah, 2. n. sigortalı kimse; asˈsur.er [~rə] n. sigortalı; a. = as-
ˈsur.or [~rə] n. sigorta eden, sigortacı.

As.syr.i.an [əˈsiriən] 1. adj. Asurca; 2. n.
Asurî.
as.ter ✸ [ˈæstə] n. yıldız çiçeği; as.ter.isk
typ. [ˈ~risk] n. yıldız işareti.
a.stern ⚓ [əˈstəːn] adv. geriye, arkaya,
arkada, kıç tarafında, kıçında; fall ~ (of)
bir geminin gerisinde kalmak.
as.ter.old ast. [ˈæstərɔid] n. küçük gezegen, asteroid.
asth.ma [ˈæsmə] n. nefes darlığı, astma;
asth.mat.ic [~ˈmætik] 1. a. asthˈmat.i.cal
□ astma ile ilgili, astmalı; 2. n. astmalı
kimse.
as.tig.mat.ic opt. [æstigˈmætik] adj. (~ally)
astigmatik; aˈstig.ma.tism [~mətizəm] n.
astigmatizm.
a.stir [əˈstəː] adj. harekette, faaliyette;
heyecanlı.
as.ton.ish [əsˈtɔniʃ] v/t. şaşırtmak, hayrete düşürmek; be ~ed şaşmak, hayret
etm. (at -e); asˈton.ish.ing □ şaşırtıcı,
hayret verici; asˈton.ish.ment n. şaşkınlık, hayret.
as.tound [əstaund] v/t. hayretten dondurmak; son derece şaşırtmak.
as.tra.khan [æstrəˈkæn] n. astragan, yeni
doğmuş kuzu postu.
a.stray [əsˈtrei] adj. & adv. yolunu şaşırmış, doğru yoldan çıkmış, sapıtmış (a.
fig.); go ~ yolunu şaşırmak; yanlış yola sapmak (a. fig).
a.stride [əsˈtraid] adv. bacakları ayrılmış, ata biner gibi.
as.trin.gent □ ⚕ [əsˈtrindʒənt] kanı durduran (ilaç); kabız, sıkıştırıcı, büzücü.
as.tro.dome ⚓ [ˈæstrədəum] n. uçağın üst
kısmında astronomik gözlem için kulla-
lanılan pencere.
as.trol.o.ger [əsˈtrɔlədʒə] n. müneccim,
astrolog; as.tro.log.i.cal □ [æstrə-
ˈlɔdʒikəl] astrolojiye ait; as.trol.o.gy
[əsˈtrɔlədʒi] n. müneccimlik, astroloji.
as.tro.naut [ˈæstrəunɔːt] n. astronot.
as.tro.nau.tics [ˈæstrəuˈnɔːtiks] n. uzay
araçları yapım ve işletme ilmi.
as.tron.o.mer [əsˈtrɔnəmə] n. astronom;
as.tro.nom.i.cal □ [æstrəˈnɔmikəl] 1. astronomi ile ilgili; 2. çok fazla, aşırı, astronomik; asˈtron.o.my [əsˈtrɔnəmi] n.
astronomi, yıldızlar ilmi; as.tro.phys.ics
[æstrəuˈfiziks] n. yıldızların ışığını inceleyen ve fizik yapılarını araştıran bilim
kolu, gökfiziği, astrofizik.
as.tute □ [əsˈtjuːt] keskin zekâlı, cin fikirli; as.tute.ness n. kurnazlık, cin fikirlilik.
a.sun.der [əˈsʌndə] adv. ayrı, ayrılmış,
parçalara ayrılmış.

**a.sy.lum** [əˈsailəm] *n.* melce, sığınacak (*veya* barınacak) yer; himaye, koruma; (lunatic) ~ tımarhane.

**a.sym.me.try** [æˈsimitri] *n.* oransızlık, simetrik olmama.

**at** [æt; ət] *prp.* -da, -de; -a, -e; -in üstün (d)e; yanın(d)a; halinde, üzere; ~ the door kapıda; ~ my expense masraflar bana ait olmak üzere, benim hesabıma; run ~ s.o. saldırmak -e; ~ daybreak şafakta; ~ table sofrada; ~ a low price düşük fiyatla; ~ peace sulhta, barışta; ~ the age of yaşında; ~ one blow bir vuruşta; ~ five o'clock saat beşte; ~ Christmas Noel'de.

**at.a.vism** *biol.* [ˈætəvizəm] *n.* atavizm, atacılık, atalara çekiş.

**a.tax.y.** 🏵 [əˈtæksi] *n.* beden faaliyetlerinde düzensizlik.

**ate** [et] *pret.* of eat 1.

**a.the.ism** [ˈeiθiizəm] *n.* ateizm, tanrıtanımazlık; **ˈa.the.ist** *n.* ateist, tanrıyı inkâr eden kimse; **a.theˈis.tic, a.theˈis.ti.cal** □ tanrıyı tanımayan, allahsız.

**A.the.ni.an** [əˈθiːnjən] 1. *adj.* Atina'ya ait, Atinalı; 2. *n.* Atinalı.

**a.thirst** [əˈθəːst] *adj.* istekli, susamış, teşne (for -e).

**ath.lete** [ˈæθliːt] *n.* atlet, sporcu; ~'s foot 🏵 mantar; **athˈlet.ic** [æθˈletik], **athˈlet.i.cal** □ atletik; kuvvetli; **athˈlet.ics** *n. pl.* atletizm.

**at-home** [ətˈhəum] *n.* küçük ve samimi ev toplantısı, kabul.

**a.thwart** [əˈθwɔːt] 1. *prp.* bir yandan karşı yana; karşı, zıt; 2. *adv.* aykırı, karşı; çapraz, ⬇ alabandadan alabandaya.

**a-tilt** [əˈtilt] *adj. & adv.* eğilmiş, çarpık, yana oturmuş.

**At.lan.tic** [ətˈlæntik] 1. *adj.* Atlas Okyanusu ile ilgili; 2. *n. a.* ~ Ocean Atlas Okyanusu.

**at.las** [ˈætləs] *n.* atlas (*kitap*).

**at.mos.phere** [ˈætməsfiə] *n.* havaküre, atmosfer; *fig.* hava, muhit, çevre; **at.mosˈpher.ic, at.mos.pher.i.cal** □ [~ˈferik(əl)]) havaya ait, atmosferik; **at.mosˈpher.ics** *n. pl.* (*radyoda*) parazit.

**at.oll** *geogr.* [ˈætɔl] *n.* atol, mercanada.

**at.om** 🔬, *phys.* [ˈætəm] *n.* atom, zerre (*a. fig.*); ~ bomb atom bombası; **a.tom.ic.** [əˈtɔmik] *adj.* atomla ilgili, atom...; ~ age atom çağı; ~ bomb atom bombası; ~ energy nükleer enerji; ~ nucleus atom çekirdeği; ~ number atomal sayı; ~ pile atom reaktörü; ~ power atom enerjisi; ~ research atom araştırması; ~ weight atomal ağırlık; **aˈtom.ic-powered** *adj.*

**atom** enerjisiyle işleyen; **at.om.ize** [ˈætəumaiz] *v/t.* atomlara ayırmak; (*sıvı*) püskürtmek; **ˈat.om.iz.er** *n.* pülverizatör, püskürgeç; **at.o.my** [ˈætəmi] *n. part. fig.* iskelet.

**a.tone** [əˈtəun] *v/i.:* ~ for bşi telâfi etm., bş için tarziye vermek, gönül onarımında bulunmak; **aˈtone.ment** *n.* tarziye, gönül onarımı.

**a.ton.ic** [æˈtɔnik] *adj.* 🏵 takatsız, zayıf; *gr.* vurgusuz; **at.o.ny** [ætəni] *n.* 🏵 takatsızlık, kuvvetsizlik.

**a.top** F [əˈtɔp] *adv. & prp.* üstte, üstünde, üzerinde (of -in).

**a.tro.cious** □ [əˈtrəuʃəs] vahşî, tüyler ürpertici, menfur; **a.troc.i.ty** [əˈtrɔsiti] *n.* gaddarlık, kötülük, canavarlık (*a. fig.*).

**at.ro.phy** 🏵 [ˈætrəfi] 1. *n.* (*kansızlıktan*) zafiyet; dumur, atrofi; 2. *vb.* dumura uğramak.

**at.tach** [əˈtætʃ] *v/t.* (to) bağlamak, yapıştırmak, bitiştirmek, takmak -e; (*imza*) basmak; 🛡 haczetmek, müsadere etm.; (*ad*) takmak; önem vermek; ~ o.s. to iltihak etm., takılmak -e; ~ value to bşe kıymet vermek, kıymet koymak; *v/i.* ~ to yapışmak -e, ittihat etm., birleşmek -le; **at.ta.ché** [əˈtæʃei] *n.* ateşe; ~ case evrak çantası; **at.tached** [əˈtætʃt]: ~ to bağlı, ait, müteallik -e; hissen bağlı, tutkun -e; **atˈtach.ment** *n.* bağlılık (to, for -e); sadakat, sevgi -e; ilâve, ek (to -e); ⊕ takılabilir bir parça; 🛡 tevkif, haciz; hapsen tazyik, icrai haciz.

**at.tack** [əˈtæk] 1. *vb.* hücum etm., saldırmak -e (*a. fig.*); başına gelmek (*hastalık*); (*işe*) girişmek; *b-nin* aleyhinde söylemek; 2. *n.* hücum, saldırma (*a. fig.*); 🏵 nöbet, kriz; *b-nin* aleyhinde söyleme; **atˈtack.er** *n.* mütecaviz, saldırgan.

**at.tain** [əˈtein] *v/t.* (*amaç*) ermek -e, elde etm. -i, kazanmak -i; *v/i.* ~ to varmak, yetişmek, ulaşmak -e; **atˈtain.a.ble** *adj.* varılması mümkün, ulaşılabilir; **atˈtain.der** 🛡 [~də] *n.* medenî ve siyasî haklardan iskat etme, eriş- me; hüner, marifet; ~s *pl.* hüner ve beceriler.

**at.tar** [ætə] *n.:* ~ of roses gülyağı.

**at.tem.per** [əˈtempə] *v/t.* yumuşatmak, sertliğini gidermek; uydurmak, intibak ettirmek (to -e).

**at.tempt** [əˈtempt] 1. *v/t.* teşebbüs etm. -e, kasdetmek -e; denemek -i; ~ the life of *b-nin* hayatına kasdetmek; 2. *n.* teşebbüs, gayret; suikast (on *veya* upon s.o.'s life -e).

**at.tend** [əˈtend] *v/t.* hazır bulunmak -de,

refakat etm. -e; (hasta) bakmak -e, hizmet etm. -e; (konferans vs.) takibetmek; v/i. dikkat etm. (to -e), dinlemek -i; ~ on (hasta) bakmak, hizmet etm.; ~ to hizmet etm. -e, meşgul olm. -le; at'tendance n. refakat; hizmet, bakım; devam, gitme (okul, kurs vs.) -e; hazır bulunanlar (at -de); hours of ~ mesai (veya iş) saatleri; be in ~ hizmete hazır, emre amade olm.; dance ~ on F b-nin etrafında dört dönmek; at'tend.ant 1. adj. b-nin refakatinde ve hizmetinde bulunan; refakat eden, eşlik eden; mevcut olan, devam eden; 2. n. hizmetçi; eşlik eden kimse; (mağaza, müze, tiyatro vs. de) görevli, memur.

at.ten.tion [ə'tenʃən] n. dikkat, ihtimam; iltifat, nezaket; ~! ✗ hazır ol!; s. call, give, pay; at'ten.tive ☐ dikkatli; nazik (to -e).

at.ten.u.ate [ə'tenjueit] v/t. inceltmek, seyrekleştirmek, hafifletmek, azaltmak; fig. hafifletmek, gevşetmek.

at.test [ə'test] vb. şahadet etm., tasdik etm. (a. fig.); açıkça söylemek, iddia etm.; ऊ tanıklık yapmak; part. ✗ b-ne yemin ettirmek, andiçirmek; at.tes.ta.tion [ætes'teiʃən] n. şahadet, tasdik; part. ✗ yemin; at.test.er, at.test.or [ə'testə] n. şahit, tanık.

At.tic¹ ['ætik] adj. Atinalı, Atina'ya ait; Atina lehçesi.

at.tic² [~] n. damaltı, tavan arası; ~s pl. tavan arası katı.

at.tire lit. [ə'taiə] 1. v/t. giydirmek; 2. n. elbise.

at.ti.tude ['ætitjuːd] n. davranış, tavır; vaziyet alma (to, towards -e); ✝ meyil; strike an ~ poz almak, yapmacık tavırlar takınmak; ~ of mind zihniyet, ideoloji; at.ti'tu.di.nize [~dinaiz] v/i. yapmacık tavır takınmak, vaziyet almak.

at.tor.ney [ə'təːni] n. vekil, mümessil, dâva vekili; Am. avukat; ~ at law avukat; power of ~ vekâletname; temsil yetkisi; ♀ General başsavcı; Am. adalet bakanı, başsavcı.

at.tract [ə'trækt] v/t. k-ne çekmek, cezbetmek (a. fig.); at'trac.tion [~kʃən] n. çekme gücü, çekim; fig. alımlılık; eğlence programı, atraksiyon; phys. çekim; at'trac.tive ☐ mst fig. çekici, alımlı, cazip.

at.trib.ut.a.ble [ə'tribjutəbl] adj. isnat olunabilir; atfolunabilir; at.trib.ute [ə'tribjuːt] v/t. yüklemek, isnat etm., atfetmek (to -e); at.tri.bute ['ætribjuːt] n. sıfat, nitelik; remiz, simge; gr. yüklem;

at.tri'bu.tion n. atfetme, hamletme, isnat; nitelik, sıfat; özellik; yetki; at.tribu.tive gr. [ə'tribjutiv] 1. ☐ niteleyici; 2. n. sıfat.

at.tri.tion [ə'triʃən] n. yıpranma, aşınma, sürtüşme; ⊕ aşınma, eskime; war of ~ yıpratma harbi.

at.tune [ə'tjuːn] v/t. ♪ akort etm.; ~ to fig. uydurmak, uyum sağlamak -e.

au.burn ['ɔːbən] adj. kestane rengi.

auc.tion ['ɔːkʃən] 1. n. artırma ile satış, mezat; sell by (Am. at) ~, put up for ~ açık artırma ile satma; 2. v/t. mst ~ off müzayedeye çıkarmak; ouc.tion.eer [~'niə] n. tellal, mezatçı.

au.da.cious ☐ [ɔː'deiʃəs] korkusuz, cüretkâr; b.s. küstah, arsız; au.dac.i.ty [ɔː'dæsiti] n. cüret; b.s. küstahlık.

au.di.bil.i.ty [ɔːdi'biliti] n. işitilebilme, duyulabilme; au.di.ble ☐ ['ɔːdəbl] işitilebilir, duyulabilir.

au.di.ence ['ɔːdjəns] n. dinleyiciler, seyirciler; huzura kabul, resmî görüşme; give ~ to huzura kabul etm.

au.di.o-fre.quen.cy ['ɔːdiəu'friːkwənsi] n. radyo: ses frekansı, alçak frekans.

au.di.o-vis.u.al ['ɔːdiəu'vizjuəl] 1. n. görsel-işitsel sistem; 2. adj. görsel-işitsel sistemle ilgili.

au.dit ['ɔːdit] 1. n. hesapların resmî kontrolu, murakabe; 2. v/t. hesapları kontrol etm.; au'di.tion n. işitme hassası, işitme kuvveti; thea. (bir şarkıcı, aktör vs.nin sesini sınamak için) dinleme; 'au.di.tor n. dinleyici; kontrolör, hesap uzmanı, murakıp, au.di.to.ri.um [~'tɔːriəm] n. konferans salonu; Am. festival salonu (konferans, konser, toplantı vs. için); au.di.to.ry ['~təri] 1. adj. işitme ile ilgili; 2. n. dinleyiciler pl.; = auditorium.

au.ger ⊕ ['ɔːgə] n. avger, burgu, matkap.

aught [ɔːt] n. & pron. bir şey, herhangi bir şey; hiçbir şey; hiçbir şekilde; for ~ I care umurumda değil!, bana ne!; for ~ I know bildiğim kadarıyla.

aug.ment [ɔːg'ment] v/t. büyütmek, artırmak, çoğaltmak; v/i. büyümek, artmak, çoğalmak; aug.men'ta.tion n. art(ır)ma, büyü(t)me, çoğal(t)ma.

au.gur ['ɔːgə] 1. n. (eski Roma'da) kâhin, falcı; 2. vb. kehanet etm., önceden haber vermek; ~ well (ill) hayra (kötüye) alâmet olm. (for için); au.gu.ry ['ɔːgjuri] n. kehanet; alâmet; falcılık.

Au.gust¹ ['ɔːgəst] n. Ağustos ayı; 2. ♀ ☐ [ɔː'gʌst] aziz, yüce; Augus.tan [ɔː'gʌstən] adj. Roma İmparatorluğu ve ya başka bir ülke edebiyatının en güzel çağına ait; klasik nitelikte.

**auk** *orn.* [ɔ:k] *n.* soğuk ülkelerde yaşayan bir cins deniz kuşu.

**aunt** [a:nt] *n.* teyze; hala; yenge *(dayı veya amca karısı)*; ♀ Sally oyuncuların eğlenmek için üzerine öteberi attıkları tahtadan yapılmış kadın; herkesin takıldığı kimse veya şey; **aunt.ie**, **aunt.y** F [¹~ti] *n.* sevgili teyze, teyzecik.

**au.ral** [¹ɔ:rəl] ☐ kulağa veya işitme duyusuna ait.

**au.re.ole** *eccl.*, *ast.* [¹ɔ:riəul] *n.* bale, nur.

**au.ri.cle** [¹ɔ:rikl] *n.* kulak kepçesi; *(kalp)* kulakçık; **au.ric.u.la** ♀ [ə¹rikjulə] *n.* ayı kulağı; **au.ric.u.lar** ☐ [ɔ:¹rikjulə] kulak veya işitme duyusu ile ilgili; ~ **witness** kulak misafiri.

**au.rif.er.ous** [ɔ:¹rifərəs] *adj.* içinde altın bulunan, altınlı...

**au.rist** [¹ɔ:rist] *n.* kulak mütehassısı.

**au.rochs** *zo.* [¹ɔ:rɔks] *n.* yaban sığırı, oroks.

**au.ro.ra** [ɔ:¹rɔ:rə] *n.* fecir, şafak; ♀ seher tanrıçası; ~ **borealis** kuzey fecri; **au¹ro.ral** *adj.* güneşin doğuşuna ait.

**aus.cul.ta.tion** ¥ [ɔ:skəl¹teiʃən] *n.* kulaklık ile dinleme.

**aus.pice** [¹ɔ:spis] *n.* kâhinlik, fal; ~**s** *pl.* himaye, koruma, nezaret; **under the** ~ **of** *b-nin* himayesinde; **aus.pi.cious** ☐ [~¹piʃəs] uğurlu, hayırlı.

**aus.tere** ☐ [ɔs¹tiə] sert, çetin; sade, şatafatsız; hoşgörüsüz; **aus.ter.i.ty** [~¹teriti] *n.* sertlik, haşinlik; sadelik, süssüzlük; kısıntılı yaşam şekli, imsâk.

**aus.tral** [¹ɔ:strəl] *adj.* güney.

**Aus.tra.lian** [ɔs¹treiljən] **1.** *adj.* Avustralya'ya ait; **2.** *n.* Avustralyalı.

**Aus.tri.an** [¹ɔstriən] **1.** *adj.* Avusturya'ya ait; **2.** *n.* Avusturyalı.

**au.tar.ky** [¹ɔ:ta:ki] *n.* otarşi, kendi kendine yeterlik.

**au.then.tic** [ɔ:¹θentik] *adj.* (~**əlly**) sahih, güvenilir, doğru; **au¹then.ti.cate** [~keit] *v/t.* bşin hakiki olduğunu göstermek, tevsik etm.; **au.then.ti¹ca.tion** *n.* bşin doğru olduğunu ispatlama, tevsik etme; **au.then¹ti.c.i.ty** [~siti] *n.* güvenilir olma, sıhhat.

**au.thor** [¹ɔ:θə] *n.* yazar, muharrir, yaratıcı, sebep olan; **¹au.thor.ess** *n.* kadın yazar; **au.thor.i.tar.i.an** [ɔ:θɔri¹teəriən] **1.** *adj.* otoriter; otorite taraftarı; **2.** *n.* otoriter veya otorite taraftarı kimse; **au¹thor.i.ta.tive** ☐ [~tətiv] otoriter; yetkili; **au¹thor.i.ty** *n.* otorite, salâhiyet; kudret, iktidar, yetki (for, to -*de)*; tesir, nü-

fuz (over, with -*de*, *üzerinde)*; bilirkişi, uzman; güvenilir, şayanı itimat; şahitlik, tanıklık; *mst* ~**s** *pl.* makam, idare, otorite; be an ~ on s.th. bir konuda uzman; olm.; have s.th. on good ~ bşi güvenilir kaynaktan öğrenmek; be under s.o.'s ~ *b-nin* emrinde olm.; **au.thor.i.za.tion** [ɔ:θərai¹zeiʃən] *n.* yetki verme, yetkilendirme; izin, ruhsat; **¹au.thor.ize** *v/t.* yetki vermek -*e*; müsaade etm. -*e*; izin vermek -*e*; bşi teyit etm., tasdik etm.; **¹au.thor.ship** *n.* yazarlık; asıl.

**au.to...** [¹ɔ:təu] *prefix* kendi kendine, kendiliğinden, oto...

**au.to.bi.og.ra.pher** [ɔ:təubai¹ɔgrəfə] *n.* otobiyograf; **au.to.bi.o.graph.ic**, **au.to.bi.o.graph.i.cal** ☐ [~əu¹græfik(əl)] kendi hayatından bahseden yazarın biyografisine ait; **au.to.bi.og.ra.phy** [~¹ɔgrəfi] *n.* otobiyografi, bir yazarın kendi hal tercümesi, hatırat.

**au.to.bus** [¹ɔ:təubʌs] *n.* otobüs.

**au.to.cade** *Am.* [¹ɔ:təukeid] = motorcade.

**au.toch.thon** [ɔ:¹tɔkθən] *n.* *(bir yerin)* esas yerlisi; **au¹toch.tho.nous** *adj.* yerli, kadim.

**au.toc.ra.cy** [ɔ:¹tɔkrəsi] *n.* otokrasi, istibdat; **au.to.crat** [¹ɔ:təukræt] *n.* otokrat, diktatör, müstebit kimse; **au.to¹crat.ic**, **au.to¹crat.i.cal** ☐ müstebit, zorba.

**au.tog.e.nous weld.ing** ⊕ [ɔ:¹tɔdʒənəs¹weldiŋ] otojen kaynağı.

**au.to.gi.ro** ✈ [¹ɔ:təu¹dʒaiərəu] *n.* otojir uçak, dikine yükselip alçalabilen uçak.

**au.to.graph** [¹ɔ:təgra:f] **1.** *n. b-nin* kendi el yazısı veya imzası; **2.** *v/t.* kendi eli ile yazmak, imzasını atmak; **au.to.graph.ic** [ɔ:təu¹græfik] *adj.* (~**əlly**) el yazısına ait; **au.tog.ra.phy** [ɔ:¹tɔgrəfi] *n.* insanların el yazısını bilme ilmi; el yazısı koleksiyonu.

**au.to.mat** [¹ɔ:təmæt] *n.* yemeğin otomatik makinelerden dağıtıldığı lokanta; **au.to¹mat.ic** [ɔ:tə¹mætik] **1.** *adj.* (~**əlly**) otomatik, mekanik, kendi *k-ne* hareket eden; gayrıiradi; gayriihtiyari; ~ **machine** otomatik satış makinesi; **2.** *n.* *Am.* otomatik tabanca; **au.to¹ma.tion** *n.* otomasyon, otomatik sistemle çalışma; **au.tom.a.ton** [ɔ:¹tɔmətən] *n. pl. mst* **au¹tom.a.ta** [~tə] kendi *k-ne* hareket eden şey veya kimse; robot *(a. fig.)*.

**au.to.mo.bile** *part.* *Am.* [¹ɔ:təməubi:l] *n.* oto(mobil); **au.to.mo.tive** [ɔ:tə¹məutiv] **1.** *adj.* otomobillerle ilgili; **2.** *n.* motorlu vasıta.

**au.ton.omous** [ɔ:¹tɔnəməs] ☐ özerk, muhtar; özerkliğe ait; **au¹ton.o.my** *n.* özerklik, muhtariyet, otonomi.

**au.top.sy** [ˈɔːtəpsi] *n.* otopsi.

**au.to.type** ⊕ [ˈɔːtəutaip] *n.* **suret, faksimile.**

**au.tumn** [ˈɔːtəm] *n.* sonbahar, güz; **autum.nal** ☐ [ɔːˈtʌmnəl] sonbahara ait, sonbahar...

**aux.il.ia.ry** [ɔːgˈziljəri] *n. & adj.* yardımcı, muavin; yedek; ~ *verb gr.* yardımcı fiil; auxiliaries *pl.* ✗ yardımcı kuvvet.

**a.vail** [əˈveil] **1.** *v/t.* faydalı olm., yaramak -*e*; ~ o.s. of *bşden* istifade etm., *bşi* kullanmak; **2.** *n.* yarar, fayda; of no ~ boşuna, beyhude; **a.vail.a¹bil.i.ty** *n.* hazır bulunma; geçerli olma; **a¹vail.a.ble** ☐ mevcut, elde edilebilir; geçer(li) (*bilet vs.*); kullanışlı; make ~ *b-nin* emrine vermek.

**av.a.lanche** [ˈævəlɑːnʃ] *n.* çığ; *fig.* yığın.

**av.a.rice** [ævəris] *n.* hırs, tamah; **av.a¹ri.cious** ☐ haris, tamahkâr.

**a.venge** [əˈvendʒ] *v/t.* -*in* intikamını almak, öç almak; ~ o.s., be ~ed intikam almak, öç almak (on. upon -*den*); **a¹veng.er** *n.* öç (*veya* intikam) alıcı.

**av.e.nue** [ˈævinjuː] *n.* cadde, iki tarafı ağaçlı yol; *fig.* bir sonuca ulaştıran yol.

**a.ver** [əˈvəː] *v/t.* kuvvetle söylemek, ispat etm., ᵴᵴ delil göstermek, iddia etm..

**av.er.age** [ˈævəridʒ] **1.** *n.* orta, ortalama, vasat; ⬩ avarya, denizde meydana gelen maddî zarar ve hasar; general (particular) ~ ⬩ umumî veya büyük (küçük veya hususî) avarya; on an ~ vasatî olarak, ortalama; **2.** ☐ ortalama, vasatî; **3.** *vb.* -*in* ortasını bulmak; -*in* ortalaması olm.

**a.ver.ment** [əˈvəːmənt] *n.* iddia, söz; ᵴᵴ delil, iddia; delil gösterme.

**a.verse** ☐ [əˈvəːs] muhalif, karşı (to, from -*e*); isteksiz; **a¹verse.ness, a¹ver.sion** *n.* antipati, isteksizlik, gönülsüzlük, nefret (to, from, for -*e karşı*); he is my ~ ondan nefret ediyorum.

**a.vert** [əˈvəːt] *v/t.* çevirmek, yön değiştirmek (*a. fig.*); önlemek.

**a.vi.ar.y** [ˈeivjəri] *n.* kuşhane.

**a.vi.ate** 🍂 [ˈeivieit] *v/i.* uçak kullanmak; **a.vi¹a.tion** *n.* havacılık; uçuş; ~ ground hava meydanı; ~ spirit uçak benzini; **¹a.vi.a.tor** *n.* havacı.

**av.id** ☐ [ˈævid] haris, hırslı, arzulu (for -*e*); **a.vid.i.ty** [əˈviditi] *n.* hırs, istek, arzu.

**av.o.ca.tion** [ævəuˈkeiʃən] *n.* meşguliyet, hobi.

**a.void** [əˈvɔid] *v/t.* sakınmak, çekinmek, uzak durmak, kaçınmak -*den*; ᵴᵴ feshet-

mek, iptal etm.; **a¹void.a.ble** *adj.* sakınılır, kaçınılır; fesholunur; **a¹void.ance** *n.* sakınma; ᵴᵴ fesih, iptal; ~ of taxation vergi kaçakçılığı.

**av.oir.du.pois** † [ævədəˈpɔiz] *n. a.* ~ weight İngiliz ağırlık ölçüsü sistemi.

**a.vouch** [əˈvautʃ] *v/t.* onaylamak, teyit ve tasdik etm., iddia etm.; = avow.

**a.vow** [əˈvau] *v/t.* itiraf etm., kabul etm., beyan etm., ikrar etm.; **a¹vow.al** *n.* itiraf, beyan, kabul, tasdik; **a¹vow.ed.ly** [-idli] *adv.* açıkça, alenen.

**a.wait** [əˈweit] *v/t.* *bşi* beklemek, *bşe* intizar etm. (*a. fig.*).

**a.wake** [əˈweik] **1.** *adj.* uyanık, tetikte; wide ~ tamamen uyanmış; *fig.* uyanık, açıkgöz; **2.** (*irr.*) *v/t.* mst **a¹wak.en** uyandırmak; uyarmak; kışkırtmak; ~ s.o. to s.th. *b-ne bşi* hissettirmek, *b-ni bş* hakkında uyarmak; *v/i.* uyanmak; harekete geçmek; farkına varmak (to s.th. -*in*).

**a.ward** [əˈwɔːd] **1.** *n.* hüküm, karar; ödül, mükâfat; **2.** *v/t.* (*mükâfat vs.*) vermek -*e*; hükmetmek, verilmesini istemek.

**a.ware** [əˈwɛə] *adj.* haberdar, farkında, bilir; be ~ bilmek (of -*i*), haberdar olm. (of -*den*); become ~ of öğrenmek -*i*; farkına varmak -*in*; **a¹ware.ness** *n.* farkında olma.

**a.wash** ⬇ [əˈwɔʃ] **1.** *adv.* su seviyesinde; **2.** *adj.* su üzerinde yüzen; dalgalarla yıkanan.

**a.way** [əˈwei] **1.** *adv.* uzakta; uzağa; bir yana; -*den,* -*dan;* **2.** *adj.* spor: değiştirmece. deplasman...; 2 miles ~ 2 mil uzakta; water has boiled ~ su kaynayıp buhar oldu; explain ~ tevil etm., sözü çevirmek; ~ back in the past çok uzak bir geçmişte, tâ geçmişte; right ~, straight ~ hemen, derhal; out and ~ fersah fersah.

**awe** [ɔː] **1.** *n.* saygıyla karışık korku, sakınma (of -*den*); **2.** *v/t.* korkutmak, dehşete düşürmek; **¹~-in.spir.ing** *adj.* korku veren, huşu telkin eden; **~.some** [ˈ~səm] *adj.* korku veren, huşu ifade eden; **¹~-struck** *adj.* huşu içinde, hayran olmuş.

**aw.ful** ☐ [ˈɔːful] korkunç, müthiş; berbat, çok kötü; F çok, muazzam; **aw.ful.ly** [ˈɔːfli] *adv.* F pek, çok, son derece; çok fena; I'm ~ sorry son derece üzgünüm.

**a.while** [əˈwail] *adv.* biraz, bir süre.

**awk.ward** ☐ [ˈɔːkwəd] beceriksiz, biçimsiz, sakar, hantal, münasebetsiz, kaba; sıkıntılı; **¹awk.ward.ness** *n.* beceriksizlik, sakarlık, acemilik.

**awl** [ɔːl] *n.* biz, kunduracı bizi.

awn ⁂ [ɔːn] *n*. başak bıyığı, kılçık.

awn.ing [ˈɔːnin] *n*. tente, güneşlik, güneş tentesi; ⬇ güneş tentesi.

a.woke [əˈwəuk] *pret. & p.p. of* awake 2.

a.wry [əˈrai] *adj. & adv.* eğri, yanlış, ters; *fig.* ters, aksi; go ~. turn ~ ters gitmek, bozulmak *(iş, olay)*.

ax(e) [æks] 1. *n.* balta; F give *(veya* get) the ~ aniden işten çıkar(ıl)mak; have an ~ to grind *(bir işte)* çıkarı olm.; 2. *v/t.* balta ile budamak; F aniden işten çıkarmak.

ax.i.om [ˈæksiəm] *n*. mütearife, belit, aksiyon, kabul edilmiş gerçek; ax.i.o.mat.ic [~siəuˈmætik] *adj.* (~ally) gerçek, kendiliğinden belli; aksiyonla ilgili olan.

ax.is [ˈæksis] *n.*, *pl.* ax.es [ˈ~siːz] mihver, eksen.

ax.le [ ⊕ [ˈæksl] *n*. aks, dingil, mil.

ay(e) [ai] 1. *adv.* daima, hep; evet, hay-hay; 2. *n. parl.* kabul oyu, olumlu oy, evet; the ~s have it kabul edilmiştir.

a.zal.ea ⁂ [əˈzeiljə] *n*. açalya, Amerikan hanımeli.

az.i.muth *ast.* [ˈæziməθ] *n*. semt, azimut, gök kürenin herhangi bir noktası ile güney arasındaki açı.

a.zo.ic *geol.* [əˈzəuik] 1. *n.* azoik çağ, hayat olmayan çağ; 2. *adj.* azoik, hayat olmayan çağa ait.

az.ure [ˈæʒə] *n. & adj.* açık mavi, gök mavisi.

# B

**baa** [bɑ:] **1.** *v/i.* melemek; **2.** *n.* koyun melemesi.

**bab.bitt** [ˈbæbit] *n.* teneke, bakır ve rastık taşı karışımı bir maden; ~ metal bebit metali, regül, yatak madeni.

**bab.ble** [ˈbæbl] **1.** *v/i.* saçmalamak; saçmalayarak ifade etm.; *(sır)* ağzından kaçırmak; *(bebek gibi)* anlamsız sesler çıkarmak; *(nehir vs.)* şarıldamak, çağlamak; **2.** *n.* saçma sapan konuşma; mırıltı; gevezelik; **ˈbab.bler** *n.* boşboğaz, geveze; mırıldayan kimse; çağlayan *(ırmak vs.).*

**babe** [beib] *n. poet.* küçük çocuk, bebek; *esp. Am. sl.* kız, bebek.

**Ba.bel** [ˈbeibəl] *n. Tevrat ve İncil:* Babil; ♀ *fig.* kargaşalık, gürültü patırtı.

**ba.boon** *zo.* [bəˈbuːn] *n.* Habeş maymunu.

**ba.by** [ˈbeibi] **1.** *n.* küçük çocuk, bebek; *bşin,* aile veya bir grubun en küçüğü; bebek gibi davranan kimse; *Am. sl.* kız, bebek; **2.** *adj.* bebek gibi; bebeğe ait; küçük; **3.** *v/t.* bebek muamelesi yapmak; şımartmak; **ˈ~-car.riage** *Am. s.* perambulator; **ˈ~-farm** *n. (ücretli)* çocuk bakımevi; ~ **grand** ♪ kısa kuyruklu piyano; **ba.by.hood** [ˈ~hud] *n.* çocukluk, bebeklik çağı; **ˈba.by.ish** ☐ çocukça, bebekçe, bebek gibi.

**Bab.y.lo.ni.an** [bæbiˈləunjən] **1.** *adj.* Babil'e ait; **2.** *n.* Babil'de oturan kimse; Babil dili.

**ba.by-sit.ter** [ˈbeibisitə] *(kısa süreli)* çocuk bakıcısı.

**bac.cha.nal** [ˈbækənl] = bacchant; **ˈbac.cha.nals** *pl.*, **bac.cha.na.li.a** [~ˈneiljə] *pl.* Baküs şenliği, sefih içki âlemi; **bac.cha.ˈna.li.an** *adj.* Baküs şenliğine ait; içki âlemine ait.

**bac.chant** [ˈbækənt] *n.* Baküs rahibi; ayyaş kimse; **bac.chante** [bəˈkænti] *n.* Baküs rahibesi; içkiye düşkün kadın.

**bac.cy** F [ˈbæki] *n.* tütün.

**bach.e.lor** [ˈbætʃələ] *n.* bekâr erkek; *univ.* fen veya edebiyat fakültesi mezunu;

~ **girl** bekâr kadın; **bach.e.lor.hood** [ˈ~hud] *n.* bekârlık.

**bac.il.la.ry** [bəˈsiləri] *adj.* basilli; **ba.cil.lus** [~ləs] *n., pl.* **ba.cil.li** [~lai] basil.

**back** [bæk] **1.** *n.* arka, sırt, geri; ters taraf, arka yüz; = full-back; behind s.o. 's ~ b-nin arkasından, gıyabında; put one's ~ into s.th. bir işe kendini tamamen vermek, olanca gücüyle çalışmak; put *veya* get *veya* set s.o.'s ~ up b-ni hiddetlendirmek, kızdırmak; break one's ~ belini kırmak; break the ~ of s.th. bşin çoğunu bitirmek, hakkından gelmek; be on one's ~ arka üstü yatmak; hasta yatmak; have one's ~ to the wall çıkmazda kalmak; at the ~ of içinde, arkasında, gerisinde; on the ~ of fazlasiyle; **2.** *adj.* arka, arkadaki; arkaya doğru olan, evvelki; eski; **3.** *adv.* arkada, arkaya; geri(ye); yeniden, tekrar; **4.** *v/t.* geri yürütmek; himaye etm.; desteklemek; para yatırımak, bahse girmek -e; ✝ ciro etm.; ~ the sails ↓ yelkenleri faça etm.; ~ water, ~ the oars ↓ siya etm.; ~ up bşi geri sürmek; desteklemek; *v/i.* geri gitmek; dönmek, caymak (out of -den); down F teslim olm., vazgeçmek (from -den); ~ **al.ley** *n. Am.* ka sokak *(esp. şehrin fakir bölgesinde);* **ˈ~-bend** jimnastik; köprü; **ˈ~.bite** *(irr. bite) v/t. b-ne* iftira etm., b-nin arkasından konuşmak; **ˈ~.bone** *n.* omurga, belkemiği *(a. fig.);* karakter kuvveti, metanet; to the ~ *fig.* tamamen, kapına kadar; **ˈ~-break.ing** *adj.* çok yorucu, yıpratıcı; **ˈ~-cloth** *n. thea.* arka perde; **ˈ~-ˈdoor.** *n.* arka kapı; *adj. fig.* el altından yapılan; **back.er** *n.* arka, taraftar, yardım eden kimse; yarışta bir ata para koyan kimse; ✝ ciranta ♪

**back...:** **ˈ~-ˈfire** *mot.* **1.** *n.* geri tepme *(vakitsiz ateşlemeden dolayı);* **2.** *vb.* geri tepmek *(a. fig.);* ~ **for.ma.tion** *gr.* bir kelimeden geriye gidilerek türetilen yeni kelime; **ˈ~gam.mon** *n.* tavla oyunu; **ˈ~.ground** *n.* arka plan; fon; mevcut şartlar; *fig.* muhit, görgü; ı~-ıhand 1. *n. tenis:* röver, bekhent; 2. *adj.* elin tersi öne doğru olarak yapılan ı~-hand.ed *adj.* elinin tersiyle; *fig.* samimi olmayan, sinsice; ı~hand.er *n.* elin tersiyle yapılan vuruş.

back.ing [ˈbækiŋ] *n.* yardım, destek; arkalık, arka.

back...: ı~.lash *n.* ani ve şiddetli geri itme; ⊕ diş boşluğu, ölü nokta, salgı; politik veya toplumsal gelişmeye karşı güçlü tepki; ı~.log *n.* sürüncemede bırakılan işler; yedek şeyler; ~ number 1. günü geçmiş gazete, dergi vs.; 2. modası geçmiş, itibardan düşmüş kimse veya şey; ~ pay ödenmesi gecikmiş maaş veya ücret; ı~-ped.al *v/t. (bisiklette)* ayak frenine basmak; sözünü geri almak, değiştirmek; ı~-room boy F işi önemli fakat gizli bilim adamı; ~ seat arka sırada oturacak yer, arka koltuk; ı~ˈside *n.* kıç, arka taraf; ı~.sight *n. gez;* ı~ˈslide *(irr.* slide) *v/i.* doğru yoldan tekrar kötüye dönmek; ı~ˈslid.er *n.* tekrar kötü yola dönen kimse; ı~ˈslid.ing *n.* tekrar hataya düşme; ı~ˈstairs 1. *n. pl.* arka merdiven *sg.*; 2. *adj.* gizlice yapılan, el altından olan; *b-ni* zemmeden; ı~.stitch 1. *n.* iğneardı; 2. *v/t.* iğneardı dikiş dikmek; ı~.stop *n. Am.* beysbol: topun kaçmasını önleyen engel; *poligon:* toprak siper; ı~.stroke *n.* sırtüstü yüzme; ~ talk küstahça konuşma; ~ to back arka arkaya, sırt sırta; ı~.track *vb. Am.* F *fig.* geriye dönüş yapmak, söylediğini değiştirmek.

back.ward [ˈbækwəd] 1. □ isteksiz, çekingen; geç kavrayan, gelişmemiş; gecikmiş; 2. *adv. a.* ˈback.wards geri; arkaya doğru; geri geri, tersine; back.wardˈa.tion ⊤ *n.* geriye hareket; depor, bir çeşit vadeli muamele; ˈback.ward.ness *n.* gerilik; geç kavrama.

back...: ı~.wa.ter *n.* bir nehrin akıntısı olmayan küçük kolu; dümen suyu; durgun su; ı~.woods *n. pl.* şehirlerden uzakta ve sık ağaçlardan arındırılmamış yerler; ı~.woods.man *n.* dağ adamı; kaba adam, hödük.

ba.con [ˈbeikən] *n.* tuzlanmış veya tütsülenmiş domuz eti, domuz pastırması; save one's ~ yakayı kurtarmak; bring home the ~ *sl.* başarılı olm. *(esp. evinin ihtiyaçlarını temin konusunda).*

bac.te.ri.al □ [bækˈtiəriəl] bakteriye ait; bac.te.ri.o.log.i.cal □ [~tiəriəˈlɔdʒikəl] bakteriyoloji ilmine ait; bac.te.ri.ol.o.gist [~tiəriˈɔlədʒist] *n.* bakteriyolog; bacˈte-

rı.um [~riəm] *n., pl.* bacˈte.ri.a [~riə] bakteri.

bad □ [bæd] fena, kötü, zararlı, kusurlu; yakışıksız *(söz vs.);* geçersiz *(para vs.);* yetersiz *(delil vs.);* bozuk, zararlı; keyifsiz, hasta; şiddetli, sert; çürük; not (too) ~, not so ~, not half ~ F hiç de fena değil, oldukça iyi; things are not so ~ mesele pek o kadar kötü değil; he is ~ly off mali durumu fenadır; ~ly wounded ağır yaralı; want ~ly bşi şiddetle arzu etm.

bade [bæd] *pret. of* bid 1.

badge [bædʒ] *n.* nişan, rozet.

badg.er [ˈbædʒə] 1. *n. zo.* porsuk; 2. *v/t.* tâciz etm.; kızdırmak.

bad.lands *Am.* [ˈbædləndz] *n. pl.* verimsiz, çorak arazi.

bad.min.ton [ˈbædmintən] *n.* tenise benzer bir çeşit oyun, badminton.

bad.ness [ˈbædnis] *n.* fenalık, kötülük.

bad-tem.pered [ˈbædˈtempəd] *adj.* aksi, huysuz.

baf.fle [ˈbæfl] *v/t.* şaşırtmak, bozmak; *(plan vs.)* akamete uğratmak; it ~s description tarifi imkânsız.

bag [bæg] 1. *n.* torba, çuval, kese; çanta; kese kâğıdı; ~s *pl. sl.* bol pantolon; it's in the ~ F garantili, çantada keklik; ~ and baggage tası tarağı toplayarak, her şeyi ile; ~s of *sl.* bol miktarda, çuvalla; 2. *vb.* torba veya çuvala koymak; F aşırmak, çalmak; *hunt.* yakalamak; şişirmek, germek.

bag.a.telle [bægəˈtel] *n.* ufak tefek şey; bir çeşit bilardo oyunu.

bag.gage [ˈbægidʒ] *n. Am.* bagaj; ✕ ordu ağırlığı; hafifmeşrep kadın; ~ car 🚃 *Am.* yük vagonu, furgon; ı~-check *n. Am.* bagaj kâğıdı, eşya makbuzu.

bag.ging [ˈbægiŋ] *n.* çuval bezi.

bag.gy [ˈbægi] *adj.* çok bol, torba gibi.

bag...: ~.man [ˈbægmən] *n.* F seyyar ticari mümessil; ı~.pipe *n.* gayda; ı~-snatch.er *n.* yankesici.

bah [baː] *int. b-ni* veya *bşi* aşağılayıcı ifade, Tu!

bail[1] [beil] 1. *n.* kefalet; kefil; teminat akçesi, kefalet; kefaletle salıverme; be ve ya go veya stand ~ for *b-ne* kefil olm, *b-i* için kefalet vermek; 2. *v/t. b-ne* kefalet etm.; ~ out kefaletle tahliye ettirmek.

bail[2] ↓ [~] *v/t. (suyu)* boşaltmak.

bail[3] [~] *n.* kriket; çubuk.

bail[4] [~] *n. (kova vs.)* sap, kulp.

bail.iff [ˈbeilif] *n.* çiftlik kâhyası; mübaşir; icra memuru; nezaretçi, idareci.

**bamboozle**

**bail.ment** 🔊 ['beilmənt] n. malları temi-nat olarak verme, kefalet.

**bail.or** 🔊 ['beilə] n. emaneten tevdi eden kimse, vedia veren.

**bairn** Scots [bɛən] n. çocuk.

**bait** [beit] 1. n. yem (a. fig.); çekici ve aldatıcı şey; mola; 2. vb. oltaya veya kapana yem koymak; hunt. köpekleri b-nin üzerine saldırtmak; fig. tâciz etm., rahatsızlandırmak; mola vermek.

**baize** [beiz] n. kaba yünlü kumaş (mst yeşil).

**bake** [beik] v/t. & v/i. (fırında) piş(ir)-mek; ateşte kurutmak; fig. sıcaktan piş-mek; '.~house n. fırın, ekmekçi dükkânı.

**ba.ke.lite** ⊕ ['beikəlait] n. bakalit.

**bak.er** ['beikə] n. ekmekçi, fırıncı; .~'s dozen on üç; 'bak.er.y n. fırın, ekmekçi dükkânı; 'bak.ing n. fırında pişirme; 'bak.ing-pow.der n. kabartıcı toz.

**bak.sheesh** ['bækʃiːʃ] n. bahşiş.

**bal.a.lai.ka** ♪ [bælə'laikə] n. balalayka, bir cins telli müzik aleti.

**bal.ance** ['bæləns] 1. n. terazi; denge; denklem; ✝ bilanço, bakiye, mizan; ka-lan; a. .~ wheel cep saati rakkası; be (hang) in the .~ muallâkta olm., nazik bir durumda bulunmak; keep (lose) one's .~ dengesini sağlamak (kaybetmek); throw s.o. off his .~ fig. b-nin dengesini kaybet-tirmek; turn the .~ kati etkili olm.; .~ of payments ödemeler dengesi; .~ of power pol. güçler dengesi; .~ of trade dış tica-ret bilançosu, dengesi; s. strike 2; 2. v/t. & v/i. tartmak, dengelemek; dengeli olm.; ✝ bilanço yapmak, denklemek; k-ni dengede tutmak; '.~-sheet n. ✝ bi-lanço.

**bal.co.ny** ['bælkəni] n. balkon (a. thea.).

**bald** [bɔːld] adj. saçları dökülmüş, daz-lak, kel; fig. çıplak, çorak.

**bal.da.chin** ['bɔːldəkin] n. gölgelik, çar-dak.

**bal.der.dash** ['bɔːldədæʃ] n. boş lâf, geve-zelik.

**bald...:** '.~-head, '.~-pate n. dazlak kimse, kel; go .~ into körüküne atılmak -e; 'bald.ness n. kellik.

**bale¹** ✝ [beil] n. denk, balya.

**bale²** ⬇ [.~] v/t. (suyunu) boşaltmak.

**bale.fire** ['beilfaiə] n. işaret ateşi.

**bale.ful** ☐ ['beilful] meşum, uğursuz.

**balk** [bɔːk] 1. n. kiriş, hatıl; engel; hata; tarlada sürülmemiş kısım; 2. v/t. (tar-lada) sürülmemiş yer bırakmak, dur-durmak, engel olm. -e; kaçırmak -ı; v/i. imtina etm., direnmek (at -de, için).

**Bal.kan** ['bɔːlkən] adj. Balkan, Balkan ül-keleri veya oturanlarına ait.

**ball¹** [bɔːl] 1. n. top; küre; yumak; bilye; top oyunu; spor: atış; Am. beysbol: ha-talı atılan top; ✗ gülle; keep the .~ roll-ing lâfı uzatmak, bşi devam ettirmek; start the .~ rolling bşi başlatmak, açmak; have the .~ at one's feet eline fırsat geç-mek, başarı yolu açılmak; the .~ is with you sıra sende; play .~ Am. F katılmak, beraber çalışmak; 2. vb. top, yumak yapmak; top olm.; .~ed up Am. sl. kar-makarışık, karman çorman.

**ball²** [.~] n. balo; open the .~ fig. dansı (veya baloyu) açmak.

**bal.lad** ['bæləd] n. balad, türkü.

**ball-and-sock.et** [bɔːlən'sɔkit] n.: .~ joint ⊕ bilyalı mesnet.

**bal.last** ['bæləst] 1. n. ⬇ denge ağırlığı, safra; 🚂 balast, kırma taş; mental .~ istikrar, metanet; 2. v/t. safra koymak; denge temin etm.; 🚂 çakıl döşemek.

**ball...:** '.~'bear.ing(s pl.) n. ⊕ bilye; bil-yeli yatak; '.~-boy tenis: top toplayan çocuk; '.~-car.tridge n. dolu fişek.

**bal.let** ['bælei] n. bale; bale trupu.

**bal.lis.tics** [bə'listiks] n. mst sg. balistik.

**bal.loon** [bə'luːn] 1. n. balon; 🎈 balon şi-şe; .~ barrage balon barajı; .~ tire mot. büyük lastik, balon lastik; 2. vb. balon gibi şişmek; balonla uçmak; **bal'loon.ist** n. balon kullanan kimse.

**bal.lot** ['bælət] 1. n. oy pusulası; gizli oy-la seçim; oy kullanma hakkı; 2. v/i. oy vermek; .~ for kura çekmek, oy vermek (... için); '.~-box n. oy sandığı.

**ball...:** .~-(point) pen tükenmez kalem; '.~-room n. balo salonu, dans salonu.

**bal.ly.hoo** F [bæli'huː] n. tamtam, gürül-tü, velvele; şamatalı propaganda.

**balm** [bɑːm] n. pelesenk, balsam; fig. merhem, teselli.

**balm.y** ☐ ['bɑːmi] yatıştırıcı, huzur veri-ci (a.fig.); yumuşak, ılık (hava, rüzgâr vs.); F kaçık.

**ba.lo.ney** Am. sl. [bə'ləuni] n. saçmasa-pan söz, zırva.

**bal.sam** ['bɔːlsəm] n. pelesenk; **bal.sam.ic** [.~'sæmik] adj. (.~ally) yatıştırıcı.

**Bal.tic** ['bɔːltik] adj. Baltık; .~ Sea Baltık Denizi.

**bal.us.ter** ['bæləstə] n. tırabzan kolonu.

**bal.us.trade** [bæləs'treid] n. tırabzon par-maklığı.

**bam.boo** [bæm'buː] 1. n. bambu; 2. adj. bambudan yapılmış.

**bam.boo.zle** F [bæm'buːzl] v/t. (into veya

out of) aldatmak, dolandırmak; şaşırtmak.

**ban** [ˈbæn] 1. *n.* yasak; *eccl.* afaroz; 2. *v/t.* bşi yasaklamak; afaroz etm.

**ba.nal** [bəˈnɑːl] *adj.* adî, bayağı.

**ba.nan.a** [bəˈnɑːnə] *n.* ☽ muz; ~ split *Am.* dondurmalı muz tatlısı.

**band** [bænd] 1. *n.* bağ, şerit, kayış; topluluk, gürüh; ♪ bando, orkestra, mızıka; ⊕ transmisyon kayışı; sargı; çizgi; 2. *v/t.* bağlamak; çizgilerle süslemek; *v/i.* toplanmak; ~ together birleşmek, bir araya gelmek.

**band.age** [ˈbændidʒ] 1. *n.* sargı, bağ; 2. *v/t.* sarmak, bağlamak.

**ban.dan.na** [bænˈdɑːnə] *n.* parlak renkli büyük mendil, şal.

**band.box** [ˈbændbɔks] *n.* mukavva şapka kutusu; as if one came out of a ~ iki dirhem bir çekirdek.

**ban.dit** [ˈbændit] *n.* haydut, eşkiya; **ban.dit.ry** *n.* haydutluk.

**band-mas.ter** ♪ [ˈbændmɑːstə] *n.* bando şefi.

**ban.do.leer** [bændəuˈliə] *n.* fişeklik.

**bands.man** [ˈbændzmən] *n.* mızıkacı, bando çalgıcısı; **band-stand** *n.* bandoya mahsus platform (*esp.* açık havada); **band wag.on** *Am.* bandoyu taşıyan araba.

**ban.dy** [ˈbændi] 1. *v/t.* (top *vs.*) öteye beriye vurmak; (sitem, söz *vs.*) teati etm.; 2. *adj.* eğri, çarpık; **~-leg.ged** *adj.* çarpık bacaklı.

**bane** [bein] *n.* afet, felâket; zehir; **bane.ful** □ zararlı; öldürücü, zehirli.

**bang** [bæŋ] 1. *n.* çat, pat, gürültü, patlama; şevk; (*usu. pl.*) kâkül, perçem; go over with a ~ *Am.* F çok başarılı olm.; 2. *v/t.* & *v/i.* gürültü ile kapa(n)mak, vur-(ul)mak; saç kesmek (*kâkül veya perçem*); *sl.* fiyatları indirmek; 3. *adv.* gürültülü bir şekilde, ansızın.

**ban.gle** [ˈbæŋgl] *n.* bilezik, halka, halhal.

**bang-up** *Am. sl.* [ˈbæŋʌp] *adj.* birinci sınıf, mükemmel.

**ban.ish** [ˈbæniʃ] *v/t.* sürgün etm.; uzaklaştırmak; **ban.ish.ment** *n.* sürgün.

**ban.is.ter** [ˈbænistə] *n.* tırabzan kolonu; **ban.is.ters** *pl.* tırabzan.

**ban.jo** ♪ [ˈbændʒəu] *n.* dört veya daha fazla telli bir müzik aleti.

**bank** [bæŋk] 1. *n.* (*nehir, göl*) kenar, kıyı; bayır; yığın, küme; sığ bölge; (*tekne*) kürekçi sırası; (*org veya piyano*) klavye; (*oyun*) banko; ╬ banka; ~ of deposit mevduat bankası; ~ of issue Merkez Bankası, ihraç bankası, emisyon bankası; 2. *v/t.* set, bent ile kapatmak;

╬ bankaya yatırmak; ╬ bir tarafa yatırmak; *v/i.* banka veya bankacılık gözevini yapmak; (bankada) para tutmak (with -de); ╬ bir tarafa yatmak; ~ on güvenmek, ümit bağlamak -e; ~ up yığmak, istif etm.; **bank.a.ble** *adj.* bankaca muteber; **bank(ing)-ac.count** *n.* banka hesabı; **bank-bill** *n.* banknot, kâğıt para; *Am. s.* bank-note; **bank.er** *n.* bankacı; (*şans oyunlarında*) bankocu; **bank-holiday** *n.* resmî tatil günü; **bank.ing** *n.* bankacılık; banka muamelesi; ╬ meyilli durum; **bank.ing-house** *n.* banka binası, banka; **bank-note** *n.* banknot, kâğıt para; **bank-rate** *n.* banka iskonto haddi, faiz oranı; **bank.rupt** [ˈ~rʌpt] 1. *n.* iflâs etmiş kimse, müflis; ~'s estate iflâs masası; müflisin malları; 2. *adj.* müflis, iflâs eden; go ~ iflâs etm.; 3. *v/t.* iflâs ettirmek, mahvetmek; **bank.rupt.cy** [ˈ~rəptsi] *n.* iflâs; declaration of ~ iflâs ilânı; ~ petition iflâs isteği.

**ban.ner** [ˈbænə] 1. *n.* bayrak, sancak; 2. *adj. Am.* çok iyi, mümtaz; ~ headline (*gazete*) manşet.

**banns** [bænz] *n. pl.* resmî ilân (*esp. evlenme*), askıya alma; put up the ~, publish the ~ resmen ilân etm., askıya almak.

**ban.quet** [ˈbæŋkwit] 1. *n.* şölen, ziyafet; 2. *vb.* ziyafet çekmek -e; ~ hall ziyafet salonu.

**ban.shee** *Scots, Ir.* [bænˈʃiː] *n.* ağlaması o evden ölü çıkacağına işaret sayılan ruh.

**ban.tam** [ˈbæntəm] *n.* küçük cins tavuk, ispenç; *fig.* ufak tefek kimse; ~ weight *spor:* horoz siklet.

**ban.ter** [ˈbæntə] 1. *n.* şaka, takılma, alay; 2. *vb.* şaka etm., takılmak, eğlenmek; **ban.ter.er** *n.* şaka eden kimse.

**bap.tism** [ˈbæptizəm] *n.* vaftiz, vaftiz ayini; ~ of fire bir askerin ilk girdiği düşman ateşi; bşin hoş olmayan ilk deneyimi; **bap.tis.mal** [~ˈtizməl] *adj.* vaftize ait.

**Bap.tist** [ˈbæptist] *n.* bir hıristiyan tarikatinin mensubu; **bap.tis.ter.y** *n.* (*kilise*) vaftiz bölümü; **bap.tize** [~ˈtaiz] *vb.* b-ni vaftiz etm.; ad koymak -e.

**bar** [bɑː] 1. *n.* çubuk, sırık, kol, kol demiri; engel, mania; (*çikolata, sabun v.b.*) kalıp, parça; nehir ağzında kum ve çakıl seti; *fig.* mâni; engel; ✕ toka, nişan şeridi; ♪ usul, ölçü, mezur; ♒ mahkemede dinleyici ve sanıkları diğerlerinden ayıran bölme; bar, içki satılan veya içilen yer, meyhane; ♒ men'i muhakeme; 🖰 sanık kürsüsü; 🖰 baro; horizontal ~ barfiks; parallel ~s *pl.* barparalel; be called to the ~ 🖰 baroya yazılmak; prisoner at the ~ muhakeme edilen kimse, sanık; behind the ~s hapiste; **2.** *v/t.* kapamak, sürgülemek; *bşi* önlemek, yasak etm.; geniş çizgi veya yollar yapmak; **3.** *prp.* maada, -den başka; ~ none istisnasız.

**barb** [bɑ:b] *n. (olta iğnesi, ok vs.)* keskin uç; kanca; kuş tüyünün bir kılı; *zo.* sakala benzer kısım; **barbed** *adj.* bir veya daha fazla keskin uçlu, kancalı, dikenli; *(söz)* alaylı ve kırıcı; ~ wire dikenli tel.

**bar.bar.i.an** [bɑ:'bɛəriən] **1.** *adj.* gaddar, zalim, barbar, medeni olmayan; **2.** *n.* barbar, vahşi kimse; yabancı; **bar.bar.ic** [~'bærik] *adj.* (~ally) barbarca, vahşice; uygar olmayan; **bar.ba.rism** [~'bɑri-zəm] *n.* barbarlık, kabalık; alışılmamış kelime veya deyim; **bar.bar.i.ty** [~'bæriti] *n.* barbarlık, vahşet, kabalık; **bar.ba.rize** [~'bɔraiz] *v/t.* vahşileştirmek; '**bar.ba.rous** ☐ barbarca, vahşi, uygar olmayan; yabancı.

**bar.be.cue** ['bɑ:bikju:] **1.** *n.* bütün bir hayvanı çeviren ızgara; hayvanın bütün olarak çevrildiği açık hava yemeği; bütün olarak çevrilmiş hayvan; baharlı ve salçalı bir çeşit et yemeği; **2.** *v/t.* bu çeşit ızgarada bütün hayvan çevirmek.

**bar.bel** *ichth.* ['bɑ:bəl] *n.* bir cins bıyıklı balık.

**bar.bell** ['bɑ:bel] *n. spor:* halter.

**bar.ber** ['bɑ:bə] *n.* berber; ~ shop berber dükkânı.

**bard** [bɑ:d] *n.* saz şairi, şair, ozan.

**bare** [bɛə] **1.** ☐ çıplak, açık; boş; sade; yoksul, mahrum (of *-den*); mübalâğasız, basit; **2.** *v/t.* açmak, örtüsünü kaldırmak; başını açmak, şapkasını çıkarmak; '~.back(ed) *adj.* eyersiz; '~.faced ☐ yüzsüz, utanmaz; '~.faced.ness *n.* yüzsüzlük; '~.foot *adj. & adv.* yalınayak; '~.foot.ed *adj.* yalınayak; '~.head.ed *adj.* başı açık, şapkasız; '**bare.ly** *adv.* sadece, ancak; '**bare.ness** *n.* çıplaklık.

**bar.gain** ['bɑ:gin] **1.** *n.* anlaşma, pazarlık; kelepir, elden düşme; ~ price ucuz fiyat, tenzilâtlı fiyat; a (dead) ~ yok pahasına, para ile değil; it's a ~! uyuştuk!, anlaştık!; into the ~ üstelik, caba; make *veya* strike a ~ uzlaşmak; **2.** *vb.* pazarlık etm. (about *için/hakkında*); anlaşmak, uyuşmak (for *için*); ~ for düşünmek, hesaplamak, tahmin etm.; '**bar.gain.er** *n.* pazarlık eden kimse.

**barge** [bɑ:dʒ] **1.** *n.* mavuna, salapurya; ↓ tahlisiye sandalı; işkampaviya; **2.** *vb.* F sendelemek, sersem sepet gitmek; **bar.'gee, barge.man** ['~mən] *n.* mavnacı.

**bar.i.ron** ['bɑ:aiən] *n.* çubuk halinde demir.

**bar.i.tone** ♪ ['bæritəun] *n.* tenor ile bas arasındaki erkek sesi, bariton.

**bar.i.um** 🧪 ['bɛəriəm] *n.* baryum.

**bark¹** [bɑ:k] **1.** *n.* ağaç kabuğu; **2.** *v/t.* kabuğunu soymak; tabaklamak.

**bark²** [~] **1.** *n.* havlama; F öksürük; **2.** *v/i.* havlamak; yüksek sesle konuşmak; *sl.* çığırtkanlık yapmak; F öksürmek.

**bark³** [~] *n.* ↓ = barque; *poet.* sandal, yelkenli gemi.

**bar-keep.er** ['bɑ:ki:pə] *n.* barmen.

**bark.er** ['bɑ:kə] *n.* havlayan; çığırtkan.

**bar.ley** ['bɑ:li] *n.* arpa.

**barm** [bɑ:m] *n.* bira köpüğü.

**bar.maid** ['bɑ:meid] *n.* içki tezgâhında çalışan kız.

**bar.man** ['bɑ:mən] *n. s.* bartender.

**barm.y** ['bɑ:mi] *adj.* köpüklü; havaî.

**barn** [bɑ:n] *n.* zahire ambarı; samanlık; *part. Am.* ahır, tavla.

**bar.na.cle** ['bɑ:nəkl] *n.* gemi diplerine, kayalara yapışan bir cins midye; *fig.* sırnaşık adam, çam sakızı.

**barn.storm** *Am. pol.* ['bɑ:nstɔ:m] *vb.* siyasî konuşmalar yapmak için dolaşmak; '**barn.yard** *n.* ahır ve ambarların çevrelediği avlu.

**ba.rom.e.ter** [bə'rɔmitə] *n.* barometre; **bar.o.met.ric, bar.o.met.ri.cal** ☐ [bærəu-'metrik(əl)] barometreye ait.

**bar.on** ['bærən] *n.* baron; *esp. Am.* önemli ve güçlü iş adamı; an oil ~ petrol kıralı; '**bar.on.ess** *n.* baronun karısı, kadın baron, barones; **bar.on.et** ['~nit] *n.* barondan bir derece aşağı asalet unvanı, baronet; **bar.on.et.cy** ['~nitsi] *n.* baronet payesi; **ba.ro.ni.al** [bə'rəunjəl] *adj.* barona ait; şaşaalı, debdebeli; **bar.o.ny** ['bærəni] *n.* baronun rütbesi.

**ba.roque** [bə'rɔk] **1.** *n.* barok; **2.** *adj.* barok üslûbuna ait, barok; çok süslü, şatafatlı.

**barque** ↓ [bɑ:k] *n.* barka.

**bar.rack** ['bærək] **1.** *n. mst* ~s *pl.* kışla; kışla gibi gösterişsiz bina; **2.** *vb. sl.* bağırarak tezahürat yapmak.

**bar.rage** ['bærɑ:ʒ] *n.* baraj, bent, set; ✕ baraj ateşi; ~ balloon savunmada kullanılan ve yerde bağlı balon.

**bar.rel** ['bærəl] **1.** *n.* fıçı, varil; *(top, tüfek)* namlu; ⊕ tambura, kasnak; silindir kovanı; 2. *v/t.* fıçıya koymak; **bar-rel-or.gan** *n.* ♪ laterna.

**bar.ren** ☐ [ˈbærən] kısır; kurak, çorak, verimsiz *(toprak)*; yavan; budala; faydasız; ✝ atıl, kullanılmayan *(sermaye)*; **bar.ren.ness** *n.* kısırlık.

**bar.ri.cade** [bæriˈkeid] 1. *n.* barikat, siper, engel; 2. *v/t.* siper yapmak; barikat kurmak.

**bar.ri.er** [ˈbæriə] *n.* mania, engel *(a. fig)*; çit, bariyer, parmaklık.

**bar.ring** [ˈbɑːriŋ] *prp.* hariç, -den maada, olmadığı takdirde.

**bar.ris.ter** [ˈbæristə] *n. a.* ~-at-law avukat, dava vekili.

**bar.row**[1] [ˈbærəu] *s.* hand-~, wheel-~; ~-man [ˈ~mən] *n.* seyyar satıcı.

**bar.row**[2] [~] *n.* mezar tümseği, tepe.

**bar.tend.er** [ˈbɑːtendə] *n.* meyhanede içki veren kimse, barmen.

**bar.ter** [ˈbɑːtə] 1. *n.* değişme, mübadele, trampa; 2. *vb.* takas yapmak; mübadele yolu ile alışveriş yapmak, trampa etm. (for, with *ile)*; *b.s.* yahudi pazarlığı etm., bezirgânlık etm.

**bar.y.tone** ♪ [ˈbæritəun] *n.* baso ile tenor arası ses, bariton.

**ba.salt** [ˈbæsɔːlt] *n.* bazalt, siyah mermer; **ba.sal.tic** [bəˈsɔːltik] *adj.* bazalta ait.

**base**[1] ☐ [beis] bayağı, alçak; değersiz; sahte, kalp *(para vs.)*.

**base**[2] [~] 1. *n.* temel, esas; taban, kaide; ✕ üs; ⚗ alkali; baz; 2. *v/t. fig.* kurmak, tesis etm.; istinat ettirmek, dayandırmak (on, upon -e, *üzerine)*; ~ o.s. on *bşe* dayanmak, istinadetmek *(a. fig.)*; be ~d (up)on *bşden* ileri gelmek, *bşe* bağlı olm.; *bşe* dayanmak.

**base...:** [ˈ~ball *n.* beysbol; [ˈ~born *adj.* soylu aileden gelmeyen; piç; alçak, zalim; [ˈ~less *adj.* asılsız, temelsiz; [ˈ~line *n.* esas alınan çizgi; *(tenis)* ana çizgi; [ˈbase.ment *n.* temel; bodrum katı, zemin katı.

**base.ness** [beisnis] *n.* alçaklık, aşağılık.

**bash.ful** ☐ [ˈbæʃful] utangaç, sıkılgan.

**bas.ic** [ˈbeisik] *adj.* (~ally) esas, temel, esas teşkil eden; ⚗ bazal; ♀ English *(İngilizce öğretiminde)* basit İngilizce; ~ slag fosfatlı bir cins gübre.

**basil** ♣ [ˈbæzl] *n.* fesleğen, reyhan.

**ba.sil.i.ca** ⚠ [bəˈzilikə] *(eski Roma'da)* dikdörtgen şeklinde ve iki tarafı sütunlu, nihayeti yarım daire şeklinde salondan ibaret kilise vs.; bu üslûpta yapılmış katolik kilisesi; bazilik, bazilika.

**bas.i.lisk** [ˈbæzilisk] *n. myth.* nefes *veya* bakışında öldürme gücü olduğuna inanılan yılana benzer yaratık; Güney Amerika kertenkelesi.

**ba.sin** [ˈbeisn] *n.* leğen, çanak, tas; havuz; havza.

**ba.sis** [ˈbeisis] *n., pl.* **ba.ses** [ˈ~siːz] esas, temel, dayanak; menşe, kaynak; ✕, ⚓ üs; take as ~ esas olarak kabul etm.; istinat ettirmek.

**bask** [bɑːsk] *v/i.* güneşlenmek, ısınmak için ateşe veya güneşe karşı oturmak veya uzanmak; tadını çıkarmak (in *bşin)*.

**bas.ket** [ˈbɑːskit] *n.* sepet, küfe, zembil; sepet dolusu; *spor:* sayı, basket; [ˈ~ball *n.* basketbol; basketbol topu; ~ dinner, ~ sup.per *n. Am.* piknik; [ˈbas.ket-work *n.* sepet örgüsü.

**bass**[1] ♪ [beis] *n.* basso, bas.

**bass**[2] *ichth.* [bæs] *n.* levrek.

**bas.si.net** [bæsiˈnet] *n.* sepet beşik; *(sepet beşiğe benzeyen)* çocuk arabası.

**bas.soon** ♪ [bəˈsuːn] *n.* fagot.

**bast** [bæst] *n.* lif, elyaf.

**bas.tard** [ˈbæstəd] 1. ☐ gayri meşru *(çocuk)*; sahte; alışılmışın dışında; 2. *n.* piç; *sl.* rezil herif; [ˈbas.tar.dy *n.* piçlik.

**baste**[1] [beist] *v/t.* -in üzerine erimiş yağ dökmek; F dayak atmak -e, pataklamak -i.

**baste**[2] [~] *v/t.* teyellemek -i, çatmak -i.

**bas.ti.na.do** [bæstiˈneidəu] 1. *n.* falaka; falaka sopası; 2. *v/t.* falaka çekmek -e; dayak atmak -e.

**bas.tion** ✕ [ˈbæstiən] *n.* kale burcu, tabya; müdafaada güçlü nokta.

**bat**[1] [bæt] *n.* yarasa; as blind as a ~ tamamen kör.

**bat**[2] [~] *spor:* 1. *n. (beysbol, kriket)* sopa, çomak; *(pingpong, tenis)* raket; sert sopa; vurucu *(oyuncu)*; off one's own ~ *fig.* kendiliğinden, yalnız başına; 2. *vb.* sopa ile vurmak; oynamak; ~ for s.o. *b-ne* sahip çıkmak, *b-nin* yardımına koşmak.

**batch** [bætʃ] *n.* bir ağız *(veya* fırın) ekmek; yığın *(mektup vs.)*.

**bate** [beit] *vb.* azaltmak -i, kısaltmak -i, eksiltmek -i; *(fiyat)* indirmek; *(nefes, soluk)* tutmak; with ~d breath nefesi kesilerek, soluk soluğa.

**bath** [bɑːθ] 1. *n. pl.* banyo, hamam; kaplıca; *(fotoğraf, film v.b.)* banyosu; 2. *v/t. (çocuk)* banyo etm., yıkamak; *v/i.* banyo yapmak.

**bathe** [beið] 1. *v/i. (nehir veya denizde)* yıkanmak; yüzmek; *v/t.* yıkamak -i,

banyo etm. -i; bşi ıslatmak, sulamak.
**bath.house** [ˈbɑːθhaus] n. hamam; soyunma kabini (plajda).
**bath.ing** [ˈbeiðiŋ] n. deniz banyosu, yüzme; ˈ~-cap n. lâstik başlık, bone; ˈ~-costume, ˈ~-dress n. mayo; ˈ~-hut n. soyunma kabini; ˈ~-maˈchine n. seyyar soyunma kabini; ˈ~-suit n. mayo.
**ba.thos** rhet. [ˈbeiθəs] n. çok güzel ve asil düşünce veya sözlerdeki ani değişme; beylik veya müptezel konuları işleme.
**bath**...: ˈ~.robe n. Am. bornoz; ˈ~room n. banyo dairesi; tuvalet; ˈ~-tow.el n. hamam havlusu; ˈ~.tub n. banyo küveti.
**ba.tik** [ˈbætik] n. batik, kumaşı boyama işi.
**ba.tiste** [bæˈtiːst] n. patiska.
**bat.man** [ˈbætmən] n. emir eri.
**ba.ton** [ˈbætən] n. asa; değnek, sopa, baston; ♪ orkestra şefinin değneği, baton; polis sopası.
**bats.man** [ˈbætsmən] n. kriket vs.: topa vurma sırası kendisinde olan oyuncu.
**bat.tal.ion** ✕ [bəˈtæljən] n. tabur, müfreze.
**bat.ten** [ˈbætn] 1. n. pervaz, tiriz, takoz; 2. vb. tiriz çekmek; semir(t)mek (on, upon -le); ~ down the hatches ↓ kaporta ağızlarını kapatmak.
**bat.ter** [ˈbætə] 1. n. kriket: topa vuran oyuncu; mutfak: sulu hamur; 2. v/t. şiddetle vurmak -e; dövmek; tahrip etm.; fig. durmadan hamle yapmak; ✕ bombardıman etm.; ˈbat.tered adj. hırpalanmış, eskimiş; çarpık; ˈbat.ter.ing ram (eski zamanlarda) kale duvarlarını veya kapılarını kırmak için kullanılan ucu demirli kalın kütük; ˈbat.ter.y n. ✕ batarya; ⚡ pil, akümülatör; beysbol: atıcı ve tutucu; ♛ dövme, müessir fiil; dizi, seri; assault and ~ müessir fiil.
**bat.tle** [ˈbætl] n. muharebe, savaş; dövüş; ~ royal korkunç savaş veya mücadele; 2. vb. mücadele etm., savaşmak (for için); muharebe etm., çarpışmak (against, with -e karşı, ile); ˈ~-axe n. cenk baltası; fig. hırçın kadın.
**bat.tle.dore** [ˈbætldɔː] n. tüylü mantarla oynanan bir oyun; bu oyuna ait raket.
**bat.tle-field** [ˈbætlfiːld], ˈbat.tle-ground n. savaş alanı (a. fig.).
**bat.tle.ment** [ˈbætlmənt] n. göğüs siperi; ~s pl. siper.
**bat.tle-ship** ✕ [ˈbætlʃip] n. zırhlı savaş gemisi.
**bat.tue** [bæˈtuː] n. sürgün avı.
**bat.ty** sl. [ˈbæti] adj. deli, kaçık.

**bau.ble** [ˈbɔːbl] n. gösterişli fakat değersiz şey, oyun, oyuncak.
**baulk** [bɔːk] = balk.
**baux.ite** min. [ˈbɔːksait] n. boksit.
**baw.bee** Scots [bɔːˈbiː] = halfpenny.
**bawd** [bɔːd] n. pezevenk, genelev patronu; ˈbawd.y ☐ açık saçık, müstehcen.
**bawl** [bɔːl] vb. bağırmak, haykırmak, feryat etm.; ~ out Am. sl. fena azarlamak, haşlamak.
**bay¹** [bei] 1. adj. doru (at), kızıl kahverengi; 2. n. doru rengi; doru at.
**bay²** [~] n. küçük körfez, koy; ~ salt kaba tuz.
**bay³** [~] n. ⚓ iki kiriş veya dikme arası; göz, çekme; çıkma, cumba; bölüm, kısım; sick-~ ↓ gemi hastanesi.
**bay⁴** ♈ [~] n. defne ağacı.
**bay⁵** [~] v/i. havlamak, ürümek (köpek); ~ at havlamak -e; stand at ~ ümitsizlik ve yeis içinde mücadeleye girişmek; bring to ~, keep veya hold at ~ sıkıştırmak, yanına kimseyi yaklaştırmamak (a. fig.).
**bay.o.net** ✕ [ˈbeiənit] 1. n. süngü, kasatura; 2. v/t. süngülemek; ˈ~-catch n. ⊕ süngü kilidi.
**bay.ou** Am. geogr. [ˈbaiuː] n. bir nehir veya gölün akıntısı az ve bataklıklı kolu.
**bay-win.dow** [ˈbeiˈwindəu] n. cumba; Am. sl. çıkıntı (göbek).
**ba.zaar** [bəˈzɑː] n. pazar, çarşı; kermes.
**be** [biː; bi] (irr.) vb. 1. olmak, bulunmak; mevcut olm., var olm.; hazır olm.; there is veya there are var, bulunur; here's to you(r health)! sıhhatinize!, şerefinize!; here you are buyur, al; ha geldin mi?; işte!; as it were gibi, sanki, güya; ~ about ... üzere olm.; ~ after s.o. b-nin peşinde olm., arkasına düşmek; ~ at bulunmak, olmak; ~ off ayrılmak, terketmek; yanılmak; (mal, bilet vs.) hepsi satılmış olm.; ~ off with you! defol!; 2. v/aux. p. pr. ile etken süreklilik kalıbını meydana getirir; ~ reading okumakta olm.; I am reading okuyorum; 3. v/aux. mastar ile zorunluluk, amaç, olabilirlik bildiren durumlarda: I am to inform you size bildirmem gerekir; it is (not) to be seen gözükme(me)li; if he were to die ölecek olursa; 4. v/aux. p.p. ile edilgen fiil yapmaya yarar: I am asked benden ....-mam isteniyor.
**beach** [biːtʃ] 1. n. kumsal, sahil, plâj; 2. vb. ↓ karaya çekmek; ˈ~.comb.er n. sahilde yaşayıp düzenli bir işi olmayan

kimse; okyanustan 'sahile vuran büyük dalga; *fig.* aylak; ↳~head *n.* ✕ köprübaşı.

**bea.con** [ˈbiːkən] **1.** *n.* fener; yüksek bir yerde yakılan işaret ateşi; işaret kulesi; ↓ nirengi feneri, şamandıra; yaya geçitlerdeki sarı ışık; *fig.* yol gösterici kimse veya şey; **2.** *vb.* yol göstermek; işaret koymak; *fig.* yol göstermek.

**bead** [biːd] **1.** *n.* boncuk, tesbih tanesi; damla, dane; ~s *pl.* tesbih; **2.** *v/t.* (*inci vs. ile*) süslemek; dizmek; *v/i.* (*ter vs.*) tane tane toplanmak; **'bead.ing** *n.* boncuklu işleme.

**bea.dle** [ˈbiːdl] *n.* bir kilise görevlisi.

**beads.man, beads.wom.an** [ˈbiːdzmən, ˈ~wumən] *n.* dua okuyucu.

**bead.y** [ˈbiːdi] *adj.* boncuk gibi; küçük, yuvarlak ve parlak (*göz*).

**bea.gle** [ˈbiːgl] *n.* tavşan avında kullanılan kısa bacaklı av köpeği.

**beak** [biːk] *n.* gaga, bir kabın ağzı; *sl.* kemerli burun; *sl.* hâkim; öğretmen; **beaked** *adj.* gagalı; sivri.

**beak.er** [ˈbiːkə] *n.* geniş ağızlı bardak.

**beam** [biːm] **1.** *n.* kiriş, direk, mertek, putrel; terazi kolu; ↓ kemere; şua, ışın (*radyo, güneş*); **2.** *v/t.* yaymak, neşretmek; *v/i.* parlamak; yayılmak; sevinç içinde gülümsemek; ˈ~-ˈends *pl.:* the ship is on her ~ gemi alabora olurcasına yan yatmış; on one's ~ *fig.* (*malî açıdan*) sıfırı tüketmiş.

**bean** [biːn] *n.* fasulye; tane (*kahve v.b.*); *Am. sl.* kafa; *sl.* metelik; full of ~s F kanlı canlı, hayat dolu; give s.o. ~s *sl.* dünyanın kaç bucak olduğunu göstermek, marizlemek; ˈ~-ˈfeast, **bean.o** *sl.* [biːnəu] *n.* şenlik.

**bear**[1] [bɛə] **1.** *n.* ayı, ayıya benzer hayvan; *fig.* hantal, hoyrat kimse; ⊤ *sl.* spekülatör; **2.** *v/t.* borsa fiyatlarını indirmeğe çalışmak; spekülâsyon yapmak.

**bear**[2] [~] *v/t.* taşımak, kaldırmak; tahammül etm., katlanmak -*e*; doğurmak -*i*; (*meyva*) vermek; üstüne almak -*i*; ~ away götürmek; meyletmek; ~ down bastırmak, yenmek -*i*; ~ out desteklemek, teyidetmek -*i*; ~ up (*güçlüklere rağmen*) cesareti elden bırakmamak; sabır ve tahammül etm.; *v/i* sabretmek, tahammül etm., dayanmak; ↓ (*adv. ile*) yönüne dönmek; ~ down upon ↓ ...yönüne seyretmek; ~ to the right saga meyletmek; ~ up dayanmak, mukavemet etm. (*against -e*); ~ up! cesaret!; ~ with

tahammül etm. -*e*, sabırlı olm. -*e karşı*; bring to ~ harekete getirmek; yönlendirmek (on, upon -*e*).

**beard** [biəd] **1.** *n.* sakal; ⚘ püskül, başak dikeni; **2.** *v/t.* b-ne meydan okumak, karşı gelmek; **'beard.ed** *adj.* sakallı; **'beardless** *adj.* sakalsız.

**bear.er** [ˈbɛərə] *n.* taşıyan kimse; *pasaport;* hâmil, taşıyan kimse; *çek:* hâmil; tabut taşıyan kimse; ⊕ destek.

**bear.ing** [ˈbɛəriŋ] *n.* tavır, davranma; ilgi (on -*ile*); etki (on -*e*); tahammül; doğurma, hâsıl etme; ↓ kerteriz; ~s *pl.* yol, yön; ⊕ yatak; ball ~s *pl.* ⊕ bilyeli yatak; beyond all ~ dayanılmaz; in full ~ iyi durumda, verimli (*ağaç*); lose one's ~s şaşırmak, nerede olduğunu bilmemek; take one's ~s bulunan yerin yönünü tayin etm..

**bear.ish** ☐ [ˈbɛəriʃ] ayı gibi kaba, hantal; ⊤ borsada fiyat indirmeye meyilli, fiyatların düşeceğinden ümitli.

**bear.skin** [ˈbɛəskin] *n.* ayı postu; İngiliz ordusunda törenlerde giyilen bir çeşit kalpak.

**beast** [biːst] *n.* hayvan (*esp.* dört ayaklı); vahşî hayvan, canavar (*a. fig*); ~ of burden yük hayvanı; ~ of prey yırtıcı hayvan; **beast.li.ness** [ˈ~linis] *n.* hayvan gibi davranış; **'beast.ly** *adj.* hayvan gibi; F çok fena; *adv.* çok, aşırı derecede.

**beat** [biːt] **1.** (*irr.*) *vb.* tekrar tekrar vurmak, çarpmak; dövmek; (*kalp*) atmak, çarpmak; (*davul vs.*) çalmak; yenmek, galip gelmek; (*yumurta vs.*) çalkamak; üstün olm.; *Am.* F bşin önünü almak; yol açmak; *hunt.* sürmek; önüne katmak; ~ it! *Am. sl.* defol!; ~ the band *Am.* F fevkalâde olarak; ~ one's brains zihnini karıştırmak; kafa yormak; parçalanmak; ~ a retreat geri çekilmek, ricat etm.; ~ time ♪ tempo tutmak; ~ one's way k-ne yol açmak; ~ down ezmek, çiğnemek; ⊤ pazarlıkta fiyat kırmak; ~ up (*yumurta vs.*) çırpmak; F dövmek, galip gelmek; ~ about bşi heyecanla ara(ştır)mak; ~ about the bush bin dereden su getirmek; **2.** *n.* vuruş, darbe; *fig.* kalp atışı; ♪ tempo; (*polis v.b.*) devriye; (*davul vs.*) çalma; *Am. gazete:* büyük yankı yaratan bir haberin yayınlanması; = beatnik; **3.** *adj.* F yorgun, yıpranmış; dead ~ bitkin; **'beat.en 1.** *p.p. of* beat **1**; **2.** *adj.* dövülmüş; yenik; çok kullanılmış; **'beat.er** *n.* çırpma makinesi (*aracı*); *hunt.* hayvanları yerinden çıkarıp sürten kimse.

**be.at.i.fi.ca.tion** *eccl.* [biːætifiˈkeiʃən] *n.*

ölünün ruhunu takdis etme; be'at.i.fy *v/t.* mutluluğa ulaştırmak; *eccl.* ölünün ruhunu takdis etm.

beat.ing ['bi:tiŋ] *n.* dövme, dayak; yenilgi; give s.o. a good ~ *b-ni* iyice dövmek.

be.at.i.tude [bi:'ætitju:d] *n.* büyük mutluluk, mutlak saadet.

beat.nik ['bi:tnik] *n. (1950'li yılların sonu 1960'lı yılların başı)* F bitnik, hipi.

beau [bəu] *n., pl.* beaux [~z] modaya uyan adam; sevgili, kavalye.

beau.teous *poet.* ['bju:tjəs] □ güzel, zarif.

beau.ti.ful □ ['bju:tǝful] güzel, hoş, zarif, latif.

beau.ti.fy ['bju:tifai] *v/t.* güzelleştirmek, süslemek.

beau.ty ['bju:ti] *n.* güzellik *(a. güzel kadın)*; F mükemmel, nefis şey; ~ parlo(u)r, ~ shop güzellik salonu, kuaför salonu; ~ sleep güzellik uykusu; ~ spot *(yüzdeki)* ben; güzel manzaralı yer.

bea.ver ['bi:vǝ] *n.* kunduz; kastor *(kürk)*; kastor şapka.

be.bop ♪ *Am.* ['bi:bɔp] *n.* bir tür caz müziği.

be.calm [bi'ka:m] *v/t.* teskin etm., yatıştırmak; rüzgârsızlıktan kımıldatamamak; be ~ed *(yelkenli)* rüzgârsızlıktan kımıldanamamak.

be.came [bi'keim]*pret. of* become.

be.cause [bi'kɔz] *cj.* çünkü, zira, diği için, -den dolayı, sebebiyle; ~ of -den dolayı, sebebiyle, yüzünden.

beck [bek] *n.* işaret; at one's ~ and call *b-nin* emrine amade.

beck.on ['bekǝn] *v/t.* işaret etm. -e.

be.cloud [bi'klaud] *v/t.* bulutlandırmak, karartmak.

be.come [bi'kʌm] *(irr.) v/i.* olmak; *v/t.* yakışmak, gitmek -e; what has ~ of him o ne oldu?, o şimdi ne halde?; be'coming □ uygun; yakışık.

bed [bed] **1.** *n.* yatak, yatacak yer, karyola; *(nehir vs.)* yatak; *(hayvan)* in; F sevişme; ✓ tarh, çiçeklik; *(arazi)* tabakat, kat; be brought to ~ of çocuk dünyaya getirmek; ~ and board yiyecek ve yatacak yer, iaşe ve ibate; take to one's ~ yatağa düşmek; as you make your ~ so you must lie on it kişi yaptıklarına katlanmalı; **2.** *v/t.* yatırmak, yerleştirmek; misafir etm.; *v/i.* yatmak; ✓ ~ (out) dikmek, ekmek.

be.daub [bi'dɔ:b] *v/t.* bulaştırmak, sürmek, karalamak.

be.dazzle [bi'dæzl] *v/t.* kamaştırmak -i.

bed...: '~.cham.ber *n.* yatak odası;

'~-clothes *n. pl.* yatak takımı *(örtü, battaniye v.b.)*.

bed.ding ['bediŋ] *n.* yatak takımı; hayvan yatağı.

be.deck [bi'dek] *v/t.* süslemek, donatmak (with *ile*).

be.dev.il [bi'devl] *v/t.* çıldırtmak, çileden çıkarmak; bozmak, berbadetmek; be-'dev.il.ment *n.* çileden çıkartma.

be.dew [bi'dju:] *v/t.* çiğ taneleri-ile ıslatmak; *poet.* ıslatmak, nemlendirmek.

bed.fel.low ['bedfelǝu] *n.* yatak arkadaşı; yakın arkadaş.

be.dight † [bi'dait] *v/t.* süslemek.

be.dim [bi'dim] *v/t.* karartmak, bulutlandırmak.

be.diz.en [bi'daizn] *v/t.* süsleyip püslemek, kabaca süslemek.

bed.lam ['bedlǝm] *n.* tımarhane; son derece gürültülü yer veya faaliyet, çıfıt çarşısı; bed.lam.ite ['~mait] *n.* akıl hastası, kaçık.

bed-lin.en ['bedlinin] *n.* yatak takımları.

Bed.ou.in ['beduin] *n. & adj.* bedevî.

bed-pan ['bedpæn] *n.* yatak lâzımlığı.

be.drag.gle [bi'drægl] *v/t. (elbise vs.)* kirletmek, bulaştırmak.

bed...: '~.rid(.den) *adj.* yatalak; '~-'rock *n. geol.* üstündeki toprağa destek olan asıl kaya; *fig.* temel, esas; '~.room *n.* yatak odası; '~.side *n.* yatak yanı, başucu; good ~ manner doktorun hastaya iyi davranması; ~ lamp gece lambası; ~ rug kaliçe, karyola halısı; ~ table komodin; '~'sit.ter F, '~'sit.ting-room *n.* hem oturma hem de yatma için kullanılan oda; '~.sore *n.* ? uzun zaman yatmaktan ileri gelen yatak yarası; '~.spread *n.* yatak örtüsü; '~-stead *n.* karyola, kerevet; '~.tick *n.* yatak yüzü; '~.time *n.* yatma zamanı.

bee [bi:] *n.* arı; *Am.* toplu çalışma toplantısı; arkadaşlar arasında yapılan yarışma: have a ~ in one's bonnet F kafasını *bşe* takmak, *bşle* bozmak.

beech ♀ [bi:tʃ] *n.* kayın ağacı; '~.nut *n.* kayın kozalağı.

beef [bi:f] **1.** *n.* sığır eti; F adele gücü; *sl. şikâyet;* **2.** *Am.* F *vb. şikâyet etm.:* '~.eat.er *n.* Londra Kalesi bekçisi; '~.steak ['bi:f'steik] *n.* biftek; '~-'tea *n.* sığır eti suyu; 'beef.y *adj.* etli butlu, iri yarı.

bee...: '~.hive *n.* arı kovanı; '~-keep.er *n.* arı yetiştiricisi; '~-keep.ing *n.* arıcılık; '~-line *n.* en kısa yol; make a ~ for *bşe* en kısa yoldan ulaşmak.

been [bi:n, bin] *p.p. of* be.

**beer** [biə] *n.* bira; small ~ hafif bira; F önemsiz şey; he thinks no small ~ of himself sanki küçük dağları o yarattı; **'beer.y** *adj.* F bira etkisiyle sarhoş olan.
**bees.wax** ['bi:zwæks] **1.** *n.* balmumu; **2.** *v/t.* balmumu ile cilâlamak.
**beet** ⚘ [bi:t] *n.* pancar; white ~ şeker pancarı.
**bee.tle¹** ['bi:tl] **1.** *n.* şahmerdan, kazık tokmağı; **2.** *v/t.* şahmerdan veya tokmakla kakmak, tokmaklamak.
**bee.tle²** [~] *n.* kınkanatlılardan herhangi bir böcek.
**bee.tle³** [~] **1.** *adj.* üstünden sarkan, taşan; **2.** *v/i.* *bşin* üstünden sarkmak, taşmak.
**beet.root** ['bi:tru:t] *n.* pancar.
**beet-sug.ar** ['bi:tʃugə] *n.* pancar şekeri.
**beeves** [bi:vz] *pl. of* beef.
**be.fall** [bi'fɔ:l] (*irr.* fall) *v/i.* zuhur etm., vuku bulmak; *v/t.* *-in* başına gelmek.
**be.fit** [bi'fit] *v/t.* uygun olm. *-e*, münasip olm. *-e*, yakışmak *-e*; **be'fit.ting** □ uygun, münasip.
**be.fog** [bi'fɔg] *v/t.* sisle kaplamak, dumanlandırmak.
**be.fool** [bi'fu:l] *v/t.* aldatmak, saptırmak.
**be.fore** [bi'fɔ:] **1.** *adv.* *yer:* önde, ileride, *-in* önünde, önüne; *zaman:* önce, evvel, daha önce; **2.** cj. *-den* önce; **3.** prp. *-in* huzurunda, huzuruna, yerine; be ~ one's time bir önceki çağda olm.; be ~ s.o. *fig.* gözü önünde bulunmak; ~ long çok geçmeden, az zamanda; ~ now şimdiye kadar; the day ~ yesterday evvelki gün; **be'fore.hand** *adv.* önce, önceden.
**be.foul** [bi'faul] *v/t.* kirletmek, pislemek.
**be.friend** [bi'frend]*v/t.* dostça hareket etm., yardım etm. *-e*.
**beg** [beg] *v/t.* dilemek, istemek, rica etm. (of *-den*); *v/i.* dilenmek (for s.th. of s.o. *-den bş*); *(köpek)* salta durmak; I ~ to inform you ☨ saygılarımla bildiririm; go ~ging *fig.* isteklisi, alıcısı olmamak.
**be.gan** [bi'gæn] *pret. of* begin.
**be.get** [bi'get] *(irr.)* *v/t.* *-in* babası olm., doğurmak; sebep olm.; **be'get.ter** *n.* meydana getiren kimse, baba.
**beg.gar** ['begə] **1.** *n.* dilenci; F adam, biri; çapkın; **2.** *v/t.* dilendirmek, sefalete düşürmek; *fig.* aşmak; it ~s all description tarif edilemez, kelimeler yetersiz kalır; **beg'gar.ly** *adj.* dilenci gibi; komik derecede az; **beg'gar.y** *n.* aşırı yoksulluk; reduce to ~ aşırı yoksulluğa düşmek.
**be.gin** [bi'gin] *(irr.)* *vb.* başlamak *-e*; meydana gelmek; başlatmak, önayak olm.; to ~ with ilk olarak, evvelâ; **be'ginner** *n.* yeni başlayan, başlayıcı; **be'ginning** *n.* başlangıç; menşe; baş, esas; from the ~ başlangıçtan.
**be.gird** [bi'gə:d] (*irr.* gird) *v/t.* kuşatmak, çevirmek.
**be.gone** [bi'gɔn] *int.* defol!, yıkıl!
**be.go.ni.a** ⚘ [bi'gəunjə] *n.* begonya.
**be.got ,be.got.ten** [bi'gɔt(n)] *pret.* & *p.p.* *of* beget.
**be.grime** [bi'graim] *v/t.* kirletmek, pisletmek.
**be.grudge** [bi'grʌdʒ] *v/t.* vermek istememek; çok görmek; *bşi* esirgemek *-den*.
**be.guile** [bi'gail] *v/t.* baştan çıkarmak, aldatmak (of, out of *-de*); hoşça vakit geçirmek (by, with); ~ s.o. into *b-ni bşle* kandırmak, aldatmak.
**be.gun** [bi'gʌn] *p.p. of* begin.
**be.half** [bi'ha:f]: on *veya* in ~ of adına, namına; lehinde.
**be.have** [bi'heiv] *v/t.* davranmak, hareket etm.; ~ o.s. terbiyesini takınmak, iyi hareket etm.; **be'hav.io(u)r** [~jə] *n.* davranış, tavır, muaşeret; be on one's good *veya* best ~ en iyi davranışı ortaya koymağa çalışmak; be of good ~ ⚖ iyi davranış göstermek; **be'hav.io(u)r.ism** *n.* *psych.* davranışçılık kuramı.
**be.head** [bi'hed] *v/t.* *-in* başını kesmek; **be'head.ing** *n.* *-in* başını kesme.
**be.hest** *poet.* [bi'hest] *n.* emir, buyruk.
**be.hind** [bi'haind] **1.** *adv.* geri, geride, geriye, arkada kalan; **2.** *prp.* arkada; *-in* arkasında, arkasına, *-in* gerisinde, geri; *s.* time; **be'hind.hand** *adv.* & *adj.* gecikmiş, geride.
**be.hold** [bi'həuld] **1.** (*irr.* hold) *v/t.* görmek; bakmak *-e*; **2.** *int.* işte!, bak!; **be'hold.en** *adj.* borçlu, medyun; **be'hold.er** *n.* seyirci.
**be.hoof** [bi'hu:f] *n:* to (for, on) (the) ~ of *-in* menfaatine, çıkarına.
**be.hoove** *Am.* [bi'hu:v] = behove.
**be.hove** [bi'həuv]: it ~s s.o. to *inf.* ...için gereklidir.
**beige** [beiʒ] **1.** *n.* bej *(kumaş)*; **2.** *adj.* bej *(renk)*.
**be.ing** ['bi:iŋ] *n.* oluş; varlık; mahlûk, yaratık; in ~ bilfiil mevcut; come into ~ meydana çıkmak, vücut bulmak.
**be.la.bo(u)r** [bi'leibə] *v/t.* dil uzatmak *-e*; adamakıllı dövmek *-i*.
**be.laid** [bi'leid] *pret.* & *p.p. of* belay.
**be.lat.ed** □ [bi'leitid] gecikmiş, geç kalmış.
**be.lay** [bi'lei] **1.** *(irr.)* *v/t.* ⚓ *(halat)* bağ-

lamak, volta etm.; *mount.* emniyete almak; **2.** *n. mount.* güvenlik çıkıntısı.

**belch** [beltʃ] **1.** *v/i.* geğirmek; *v/t.* püskürtmek, fırlatmak; **2.** *n.* geğirme; fırlatma, püskürtme.

**bel.dam** *contp.* ['beldəm] *n.* kocakarı; nine.

**be.lea.guer** [bi'li:gə] *v/t.* kuşatmak, muhasara etm..

**bel.fry** ['belfri] *n.* çan kulesi, çan kulesi sahanlığı.

**Bel.gian** ['beldʒən] **1.** *adj.* Belçika'ya ait; **2.** *n.* Belçikalı.

**be.lie** [bi'lai] *v/t.* yalancı çıkarmak, yalanlamak.

**be.lief** [bi'li:f] *n.* inanç, iman, itikat; güven (in *-e*); past all ~ inanılmaz; to the best of my ~ benim bildiğime göre.

**be.liev.a.ble** □ [bi'li:vəbl] inanılır.

**be.lieve** [bi'li:v] *v/t.* inanmak *-e*; zannetmek *-i*; *v/i.* itimat etm., güvenmek, inanmak (in *-e*); ~ in iman etm. *-e*, itimat etm. *-e*; **be'liev.er** *n.* inanan, inançlı, mümin.

**be.lit.tle** [bi'litl] *v/t. fig.* küçültmek, küçümsemek.

**bell**[1] [bel] **1.** *n.* zil, çıngırak, çan, kampana; çan şeklinde olan şey; **2.** *v/t.* ~ the cat başkalarının yanaşamadığı tehlikeli bir işi başarmak.

**bell**[2] [~] *v/i.* (geyik) bağırmak.

**bell.boy** *Am.* ['belbɔi] *n.* otellerde oda servisi yapan çocuk, otel oğlanı.

**belle** [bel] *n.* güzel ve çekici kadın, dilber.

**belles-let.tres** ['bel'letr] *n. pl.* edebiyat; edebiyatın seçme örnekleri.

**bell...:** '~.flow.er *n.* çançiçeği; '~.found.er *n.* çan dökümcüsü; '~.glass *n.* cam kılıf; fanus, karpuz; '~.hop *n. Am. sl.* otel oğlanı.

**bel.li.cose** ['belikəus] *adj.* kavgacı, döğüşken; savaşmayı seven.

**bel.lied.** ['belid] *adj.* göbekli.

**bel.lig.er.ent** [bi'lidʒərənt] **1.** *adj.* muharip; kavgacı, münakaşacı; harbe meyilli; **2.** *n.* harpte taraflardan biri.

**bel.low** ['beləu] **1.** *v/i.* böğürmek; bağırmak; **2.** *n.* böğürme, bağırma.

**bel.lows** ['beləuz] *n. pl.*: (a pair of) ~ körük; *phot.* körük.

**bell...:** '~.pull *n.* çan ipi; '~.push *n.* elektrikli zil düğmesi; '~.weth.er *n.* sürünün önünden giderek ona kılavuzluk eden koç ya da teke, kösemen.

**bel.ly** ['beli] **1.** *n.* karın; vücudun kısmı gibi yuvarlak veya şişkin olan şey; ~ landing ⚓ gövde üstüne iniş; **2.** *vb.*

**şiş(ir)mek; bel.ly.ful** F ['~ful] *n.* haddinden fazla.

**be.long** [bi'lɔn] *v/i.* ait olm., mensup olm. (to *-e*); **be'long.ings** *n. pl.* eşya; F pılı pırtı.

**be.lov.ed** [bi'lʌvd] **1.** *adj.* sevgili, aziz; **2.** [mst. ~vid] *n.* sevgili.

**be.low** [bi'ləu] **1.** *adj.* aşağıda, aşağı; *-in* altında; yeryüzünde; **2.** *prp. -den* aşağı.

**belt** [belt] **1.** *n.* kayış; kuşak, kemer, bel kayışı; ✗ kılıç kayışı; palaska; şerit; bölge; ⊕ transmisyon kayışı; *sl.* çok hızlı araba yolculuğu; hit below the ~ kahpece hareket etm.; **2.** *v/t.* kemer bağlamak; kayışla dövmek; ~ out *Am.* F yüksek sesle şarkı söylemek.

**be.moan** [bi'məun] *v/t.* bş için keder etm., üzüntüsünü belirtmek, *b-nin* yasını tutmak.

**bench** [bentʃ] *n.* sıra, bank; yargıç kürsüsü; mahkeme; yargıçlar heyeti; tezgâh; *s. treasury;* '**bench.er** *n.* baronun idare meclisi üyesi.

**bend** [bend] **1.** *n.* kavis, dönemeç, viraj; kıvırma, kıvrım; ⬇ bağ, düğüm; **2.** *(irr.)* *v/t.* bükmek, eğriltmek, kıvırmak; *b-ni* ikna etm., yola getirmek; ⬇ bağlamak; *v/i.* bükülmek, eğilmek, çevrilmek; teslim olm., râm olm.; *s.* bent[1].

**be.neath** [bi'ni:θ] = below.

**ben.e.dick** ['benidik] *n.* evlenen yaşı ilerlemiş bekâr; yeni evli adam.

**Ben.e.dic.tine** [beni'diktin] *n.* Sen Benuva tarikatından rahip; [~ti:n] bir cins likör.

**ben.e.dic.tion** *eccl.* [beni'dikʃən] *n.* takdis, takdis duası.

**ben.e.fac.tion** [beni'fækʃən] *n.* iyilik, ihsan, hayır; **ben.e.fac.tor** ['~tə] *n.* iyilik eden, velinimet; **ben.e.fac.tress** ['~tris] *n.* iyilik eden kadın.

**ben.e.fice** ['benifis] *n.* papazlık maaşı ve makamı; **be.nef.i.cence** [bi'nefisəns] *n.* iyilik, lütuf, hayır; **be'nef.i.cent** □ hayır sahibi, lütufkâr.

**ben.e.fi.cial** □ [beni'fiʃəl] hayırlı; yararlı (to *-e*); ~ interest ⚖ faydalanma hakkı; **ben.e'fi.ci.ar.y** *n.* lehtar, faydalanan kimse.

**ben.e.fit** ['benifit] **1.** *n.* yarar, fayda, menfaat, kâr; hayır için verilen konser *vs.*; yetki; for the ~ of lehine; yararına, menfaatine; **2.** *v/t.* yaramak, faydalı olm. *-e*; *v/i.* istifade etm., faydalanmak (by, from *-den*).

**be.nev.o.lence** [bi'nevələns] *n.* iyilikseverlik; yardım, sadaka; **be'nev.o.lent** □ iyi dilekli ,hayırhah; kâr gayesi gütmeyen.

**be.night.ed** □ [bi'naitid] gece karanlığında kalmış; *fig.* cahil, karanlıkta kalmış.

**be.nign** □ [bi'nain] yumuşak huylu, iyi kalpli, şefkatli, ₹ tehlikesiz, selim; **be.nig.nant** □ [bi'nignənt] iyi huylu, müşfik; **be'nig.ni.ty** *n.* yumuşaklık, iyi kalplilik.

**bent¹** [bent] **1.** *pret & p.p. of* bend 2; ~ on azmetmek *-e,* çok istemek *-i;* **2.** *n.* eğim; meyil, temayül; to the top of one's ~ canı istediği kadar.

**bent²** ¾ [~] *n.* birkaç tür sert çimen.

**be.numb** [bi'nʌm] *v/t.* uyuşturmak, hissini iptal etm..

**ben.zene** ⚗ ['benzi:n] *n.* benzol.

**ben.zine** ⚗ ['benzi:n] *n.* benzin.

**be.queath** [bi'kwi:ð] *v/t.* vasiyet etm., terketmek, vasiyetle bırakmak.

**be.quest** [bi'kwest] *n.* vasiyetname ile bırakılan şey, menkul vasiyeti.

**be.reave** [bi'ri:v] *(irr.) v/t.* mahrum etm. *-den,* elinden almak (of *-i);* be ~d of ölüm nedeniyle mahrum kalmak *-den;* ~d *adj.* geride kalan, ölen kişinin yakını; **be'reave.ment** *n.* elemli kayıp *(ölüm);* mahrumiyet *-den.*

**be.reft** [bi'reft] *pret. & p.p. of* bereave.

**be.ret** ['berei] *n.* bere.

**berg** [bə:g] = iceberg.

**ber.ry** ['beri] *n. (küçük meyva)* tane.

**berth** [bə:θ] **1.** *n. (vapur, tren, uçak)* ranza, yatak; ↓ geminin rıhtımdaki demir yeri; iş, görev; give s.o. a wide ~ *-den* uzak durmak, *-den* kaçınmak; **2.** *v/t.* gemiye yer vermek; rıhtıma yanaştırmak; yatacak yer vermek.

**ber.yl** *min.* ['beril] *n.* bir tür zümrüt.

**be.seech** [bi'si:tʃ] *(irr.) v/t.* istirham etm., yalvarmak *-e;* **be'seech.ing** □ yalvaran; **be'seech.ing.ly** *adv.* yalvararak.

**be.seem** [bi'si:m] *v/t.* yakışmak, yaraşmak, uymak; yakışık almak.

**be.set** [bi'set] *(irr.* set) *v/t.* kuşatmak, sarmak; *(savaş)* kuşatıp saldırıya hazır olm.; ~ting sin insanın yakasını bırakmayan hata veya günah.

**be.side** [bi'said] **1.** *adv. s.* besides; **2.** *prp.* *-in* yanın(d)a, *-in* tarafın(d)a *(a. fig.);* *-e* nazaran, üstelik; *-den* başka, *-in* dışında; ~ o.s. kendinden geçmiş, çılgın (with *-den, -den dolayı);* ~ the purpose amaca uymıyan; ~ the question konu ile ilgili olmıyan, sadet dışı; **be'sides** [~dz] **1.** *adv.* bundan başka, ayrıca; üstelik; **2.** *prp. -den* başka, *-den* gayrı, *-den* hariç.

**be.siege** [bi'si:dʒ] *v/t.* kuşatmak, muhasara etm.; *fig.* musallat olm., sıkıntı

vermek, baskı altında tutmak; **be'sieg.er** *n.* kuşatan kimse.

**be.slob.ber** [bi'slɔbə] *v/t.* salya bulaştırmak.

**be.smear** [bi'smiə] *v/t.* kirletmek, bulaştırmak.

**be.smirch** [bi'smə:tʃ] *v/t.* lekelemek, şerefine halel getirmek.

**be.som** ['bi:zəm] *n.* çalı süpürgesi.

**be.sot.ted** [bi'sɔtid] *adj.* sarhoş *(a. fig.).*

**be.sought** [bi'sɔ:t] *pret. & p.p. of* beseech.

**be.spat.ter** [bi'spætə] *v/t.* çamur sıçratmak, lekelemek; *fig.* iftira etm., çamur atmak.

**be.speak** [bi'spi:k] *(irr.) v/t.* göstermek, *bşe* delâlet etm.; tutmak, rezerve ettirmek.

**be.spoke** [bi'spəuk] *pret. of* bespeak; *adj.:* ~ tailor ısmarlama elbise yapan terzi; **be'spo.ken** *p.p. of* bespeak.

**be.sprin.kle** [bi'spriŋkl] *v/t.* serpmek, saçmak.

**best** [best] **1.** *adj.* en iyi, en çok, en uygun; ~ man sağdıç; the ~ part of çoğunluğu; *s.* seller; **2.** *adv.* en iyi şekilde; en çok; **3.** *n.* en iyisi; Sunday ~ pazarlık elbise, yabanlık; all for the ~ belki de daha iyi; to the ~ of son derece, haddinden fazla; *-i;* make the ~ of mümkün olduğu kadar yararlanmak *-den;* to the ~ of my knowledge bildiğime göre; at ~ olsa olsa, ancak; en çok; **4.** *v/t.* F yenmek, hakkından gelmek.

**be.ste(a)d** [bi'sted]: hard ~ müşkül durumda.

**bes.tial** □ ['bestjəl] hayvan gibi, hayvanca; çok kaba; vahşi; **bes.ti.al.i.ty** [~ti'æliti] *n.* hayvanlık; vahşilik.

**be.stir** [bi'stə:] *v/t.* harekete getirmek, kımıldatmak.

**be.stow** [bi'stəu] *v/t.* vermek, hediye etm.; bağışlamak (on, upon *-e);* yerleştirmek. koymak; **be'stow.al, be'stow.ment** *n.* verme, ihsan.

**be.strew** [bi'stru:] *(irr.* strew) *v/t.* saçmak; kaplamak (with *-le).*

**bet** [bet] **1.** *n.* bahis, iddia; **2.** *(irr.) vb.* bahse girmek, bahis tutuşmak; iddia etm.; you ~ F elbette, şüphesiz; I ~ you a shilling bir şilinine bahse girerim.

**be.take** [bi'teik] *(irr.* take) *v/t.:* ~ o.s. to gitmek, müracaat etm.

**be.think** [bi'θiŋk] *(irr.* think) *v/t.:* ~ o.s. düşünmek, hatırlamak (of *-i).*

**be.tide** [bi'taid] *vb.* başına gelmek, vuku bulmak, woe ~ him! Allah kahretsin!

**be.times** [bi'taimz] *adv.* erken, erkenden.

**be.to.ken** [bi'təukən] *v/t.* delâlet etm., göstermek.

**be.tray** [bi'trei] *v/t.* ihanet etm., ele vermek; ifşa etm., ağzından kaçırmak; göstermek, ortaya koymak; yanlış yola sevketmek; **be'tray.al** *n.* hıyanet, ele verme, ifşa; ~ of trust emniyeti suiistimal, inancı kötüye kullanma; **be'tray.er** *n.* hain, gammaz.

**be.troth** [bi'trəuð] *v/t.* nişanlamak (to *ile*); the ~ed nişanlı; **be'troth.al** *n.* nişan.

**bet.ter**[1] ['betə] 1. *adj.* daha iyi, daha güzel; daha çok; he is ~ daha iyi; get ~ iyileşmek; 2. *n.* daha iyisi; ~s *pl.* mafevk, kendinden üstün kimseler; get the ~ of yenmek -*i*, üstün olm. -*den;* 3. *adv.* daha iyi bir şekilde, daha çok; be ~ off daha iyi durumda olm.; so much the ~ daha iyi; isabet! you had ~ go gitsen iyi olacak; think ~ of it fikrini değiştirmek, vazgeçmek; 4. *v/t.* iyileştirmek, ıslah etm.; ~ o.s. (*ücret vs.*) daha iyi şekle sokmak; *v/i.* iyileşmek, ıslah olunmak.

**bet.ter**[2] [~] *n.* bahse giren kimse.

**bet.ter.ment** ['betəmənt] *n.* ıslah, iyileştirme.

**be.tween** [bi'twi:n], *poet & prov. a.* **betwixt** [bi'twikst] 1. *adv.* araya, arada, ortaya, ortada; betwixt and ~ ikisinin ortası, ne bu ne o; in ~ sallantıda; far ~ nadir, seyrek; 2. *prp.* -*in* arasına, arasında, aralarında, ortasına, ortasında; ~ ourselves aramızda; **be'tween-decks** *n.* ↓ ara güverte.

**bev.el** ['bevəl] 1. *adj.* mail, eğik, şevli; 2. *n.* ⊕ şev, açı, eğim; 3. *v/t.* şev vermek, eğik olarak kesmek; '~-wheel *n.* ⊕ konik dişli çark.

**bev.er.age** ['bevəridʒ] *n.* içecek, meşrubat.

**bev.y** ['bevi] *n.* kuş sürüsü; küme, zümre, takım; a ~ of beauties bir sürü güzel kadın.

**be.wail** [bi'weil] *v/t.* ağlamak -*e;* hayıflanmak -*e; v/i.* sızlanmak.

**be.ware** [bi'wɛə] *v/i.* dikkatli olm.; sakınmak, korunmak (of -*den*); *int.* dikkat!, sakın!

**be.wil.der** [bi'wildə] *v/t.* şaşırtmak, hayrette bırakmak; sersemletmek; **be'wil.der.ment** *n.* şaşkınlık, hayret.

**be.witch** F [bi'witʃ] *v/t.* büyülemek, teshir etm.; **be'witch.ment** *n.* büyü, cazibe.

**be.yond** [bi'jɔnd] 1. *adv.* öbür tarafta, öte, öteye, ötede, ileri; 2. *prp.* -*in* ötesine, ötesinde, karşısında; -*den* ötede; -*in* dışında, üstünde, haricin(d)e; ~ doubt şüphesiz; ~ endurance tahammülfersa, da-

yanılmaz; ~ measure hadsız, hesapsız, ifrat derecede; ~ dispute malûm, su götürmez, inkâr edilemez; ~ words ifade edilemez; it is ~ me anlamıyorum, buna aklım ermez.

**bi...** [bai] *prefix* iki kere, ikişer, iki...

**bi.as** ['baiəs] 1. *adj. & adv.* meyilli, çapraz; 2. *n.* meyil, temayül; peşin hüküm; terzilik: verev kesme; 3. *v/t.* meylettirmek; *(aleyhte)* tesir ve nüfuz altında bulundurmak; ~sed *adj.* taraf tutan, bitaraf olmıyan.

**bib** [bib] *n.* mama önlüğü; iş önlüğünün üst kısmı.

**Bi.ble** [baibl] *n.* Mukaddes Kitap, Tevrat, Zebur ve İncil.

**bib.li.cal** ☐ ['biblikəl] Kitabı Mukaddes'e ait.

**bib.li.og.ra.pher** [bibli'ɔgrəfə] *n.* bibliyografya bilgini *veya* uzmanı; **bib.li.o.graph.ic, bib.li.o.graph.i.cal** [~əu'græfik(əl)] *adj.* bibliyografyaya ait; **bib.li.og.ra.phy** [~'ɔgrəfi] *n.* bibliyografya; **bib.li.o.ma.ni.a** [~əu'meinjə] *n.* kitap merakı; **bib.li.o.ma.ni.ac** [~əu'meiniæk] *n. & adj.* kitap kolleksiyonu yapan; kitap delisi; **bib.li.o.phile** ['~əufail] *n.* kitap seven kimse.

**bib.u.lous** ☐ ['bibjuləs] ayyaş, içkiye düşkün, bekri; suyu çekici.

**bi.car.bon.ate** 🔬 [bai'ka:bənit] *n.* bikarbonat; ~ of soda bikarbonat de süt, soda.

**bi.ceps** ['baiseps] *n.* pazı; *fig.* güç, kuvvet.

**bick.er** ['bikə] *v/i.* kavga etm., çekişmek, dalaşmak; *(alev)* parıldamak; *(akarsu, yağmur)* şırıldamak; '**bick.er.ing(s** *pl.*) *n.* çirkin didişme, atışma.

**bi.cy.cle** ['baisikl] 1. *n.* bisiklet; ride a ~ = 2. *v/i.* bisiklete binmek, bisikletle dolaşmak.

**bid** [bid] 1. *(irr.) v/t.* emretmek, hükmetmek; demek, söylemek; davet etm.; *müzayede:* fiyat artırmak; *briç:* deklarasyon yapmak; teklif vermek; ~ fair to *int.* ihtimal dahilinde olm., vadetmek; ~ farewell vedalaşmak (to *ile*); ~ up fiyat artırmak; ~ welcome «Hoş geldin» demek; 2. *n.* teklif; girişim, teşebbüs (to *inf.* -*e*); *briç:* deklarasyon; davet; make a ~ for bşi elde etmeğe çalışmak, girişimde bulunmak; no ~ *iskambil:* pas; '**bid.den** *p.p. of* bid; '**bid.der** *n.* teklif veren kimse; *s.* high, low; '**bid.ding** *n.* artırma; emir; davet; *briç:* deklarasyon serisi.

**bide** [baid] *vb.:* ~ one's time uygun zamanı beklemek.

**bi.en.ni.al** [bai'eniəl] ☐ iki yılda bir olan.

**bier** [biə] *n.* cenaze teskeresi.

**bi.fur.cate** [ˈbaifəːkeit] *v/i. (yol, nehir vs.)* iki kola ayrılmak, çatallanmak; **bi.furˈca.tion** *n.* iki kola ayrılma.

**big** [big] *adj.* büyük, kocaman, iri; F önemli, etkili; gebe *(a. fig.* with *-e)*; ♀ Ben İngiliz parlamento binasındaki büyük saat kulesi; ~ business büyük sermayeli ticaret; ~ shot F kodaman; ~ stick *Am.* gözünü korkutma, gözdağı verme; ~ top sirk çadırı, sirk *(a. fig.)*; talk ~ F yüksekten atmak, atıp tutmak.

**big.a.mous** ☐ [ˈbigəməs] iki kadınla evli olan; iki karılılık suçunu işlemiş olan; **ˈbig.a.my** *n.* iki kadınla evlilik, iki karılılık.

**bight** ⬇ [bait] *n.* körfez, koy; halat bedeni.

**big.ness** [ˈbignis] *n.* büyüklük, irilik.

**big.ot** [ˈbigət] *n.* mutaassıp kimse; dar görüşlü kimse; **ˈbig.ot.ed** ☐ mutaassıp; dar görüşlü; **ˈbig.ot.ry** *n.* dar kafalılık.

**big.wig** F *co.* [ˈbigwig] *n.* kodaman, önemli kimse.

**bike** F [baik] *n.* bisiklet.

**bi.lat.er.al** ☐ [baiˈlætərəl] iki taraflı, iki cepheli.

**bil.ber.y** ⚘ [ˈbilbəri] *n.* yaban mersini.

**bile** [bail] *n.* safra; huysuzluk, terslik; ~-stone *n.* ♀ safra kesesi taşı.

**bilge** [bildʒ] *n.* ⬇ sintine, sintine suyu, karina; *sl.* saçmalık, herze.

**bi.lin.gual** [baiˈliŋgwəl] *n. & adj.* iki dili aynı derecede konuşan, iki dilli.

**bil.ious** ☐ [ˈbiljəs] safraya ait; safralı; *fig.* huysuz, aksi.

**bilk** [bilk] *v/t.* dolandırmak, aldatmak.

**bill¹** [bil] 1. *n.* gaga; sivri uc; 2. *v/i.* sevişip koklaşmak.

**bill²** [~] 1. *n.* hesap pusulası, fatura, kambiyo senedi, poliçe, bono, tahvil; *Am.* banknot, kâğıt para; kanun lâyihası, kanun tasarısı; dilekçe; afiş; basılı program; ~ of exchange kambiyo senedi, poliçe, tahvil; ~ of fare yemek listesi, mönü; ~ of health sağlık belgesi; ~ of lading konşimento, yükleme evrakı; ~ of sale satış bordrosu veya senedi; ~ of rights insan hakları beyannamesi; 2. *v/t.* faturasını yapmak; ilân etm.; programa almak; *Am.* kaydetmek, tescil etmek.

**bill.board** *Am.* [ˈbilbɔːd] *n.* ilân tahtası, afiş tahtası.

**bil.let** [ˈbilit] 1. *n.* ✗ konak yeri; konak tezkeresi; iş, görev; *(odun)* kütük; 2. *v/t.* ✗ konaklatmak (on *-de)*.

**bill.fold** *Am.* [ˈbilfəuld] *n.* cüzdan.

**bill.hook** ⬍ [ˈbilhuk] *n.* bağcı bıçağı.

**bil.liard** [ˈbiljəd] *comb.* bilardo..., ~-cue *n.* bilardo sopası; **ˈbil.liards** *n. pl. veya sg.* bilardo.

**bil.lion** [ˈbiljən] *n.* trilyon; *Am.* milyar.

**bil.low** [ˈbiləu] 1. *n.* büyük dalga; dalgalar halinde gelen şey *(alev, duman v.b.)*; 2. *v/i.* dalgalar halinde kabarmak, yükselmek; **ˈbil.low.y** *adj.* dalgalı.

**bill-stick.er** [ˈbilstikə] *n.* afiş yapıştıran kimse.

**bil.ly** *Am.* [ˈbili] *n.* kalın sopa, cop; ~-can *n.* teneke kap, tencere; **ˈ~.cock** *n.* F melon şapka; **ˈ~-goat** F erkek keçi, teke.

**bi.met.al.lism** ♱ [baiˈmetəlizəm] *n.* çift maden sistemi, altın ve gümüş gibi iki ayrı madeni birbirlerine olan oranlarına göre kullanma sistemi.

**bi-mo.tored** [ˈbaiməutəd] *adj.* iki motorlu.

**bin** [bin] *n.* kutu, sandık, teneke.

**bi.na.ry** [ˈbainəri] *adj.* iki kısımdan meydana gelen, çift.

**bind** [baind] *(irr.) v/t.* bağlamak, raptetmek; sarmak; ciltlemek; dondurmak; kenarını tutturmak; kabız vermek; mecbur etm.; *b-ne* vecibe yüklemek, bağlamak; ~ over ♣ teminata veya kefalete bağlamak; be bound up with *fig.* bağlı olm. *-e*; be bound up in *fig.* bağlı, düşkün; *s.* bound¹ 2; *v/i. (çimento vs.)* katılaşmak, donmak; *(makine vs.)* sıkışmak; **ˈbind.er** *n.* ciltçi; biçer bağlar makine; tutkal; cilt, kap; **ˈbind.ing** 1. *n.* ciltleme; cilt; kenar şeridi; 2. *adj.* bağlayıcı, tutucu; ♣ bağlayıcı, muteber, kesin; **ˈbind.weed** ⚘ *n.* boru çiçeği.

**binge** *sl.* [bindʒ] *n.* içki âlemi, cümbüş.

**bin.go** [ˈbiŋgəu] *n.* bingo oyunu.

**bin.na.cle** ⬇ [ˈbinəkl] *n.* pusula dolabı.

**bin.oc.u.lar** 1. [baiˈnɔkjulə] *adj.* iki gözle kullanılan; 2. [biˈnɔkjulə] *n.* mst ~s *pl.* dürbün.

**bi.o.chem.i.cal** [ˈbaiəuˈkemikəl] *adj.* biyoşimiye ait; **ˈbi.oˈchem.ist** *n.* biyoşimist; **ˈbi.oˈchem.is.try** *n.* biyoşimi, hayatî kimya.

**bi.og.ra.pher** [baiˈɔgrəfə] *n. b-nin* hayat hikâyesini yazan kimse, biyografi yazarı; **bi.o.graph.ic, bi.o.graph.i.cal** ☐ [~əuˈgræfik(əl)] hayat hikâyesine ait, biyografi ile ilgili; **bi.og.ra.phy** [~ˈɔgrəfi] *n.* biyografi, hayat hikâyesi, yaşam öyküsü.

**bi.o.log.ic, bi.o.log.i.cal** ☐ [baiəuˈlɔdʒik(əl)] biyoloji ilmine ait, biyolojik; **bi.ol.o.gist** [~ˈblədʒist] *n.* biyoloji bilgini, biyolog; **biˈol.o.gy** *n.* biyoloji, dirimbilim.

**bi.par.tite** [baiˈpɑːtait] *adj.* iki bölümlü; iki partinin paylaştığı.

**blackmailer**

**bi.ped** [ˈbaiped] **1.** *adj.* iki ayaklı; **2.** *n.* iki ayaklı yaratık.

**bi.plane** ✈ [ˈbaiplein] *n.* çift kanatlı uçak.

**birch** [bəːtʃ] **1.** *n.* ♀ huş ağacı; huş ağacı kerestesi; huş ağacından yapılmış değnek; **2.** *v/t.* huş dalı ile dövmek.

**bird** [bəːd] *n.* kuş; *sl.* herif; *sl.* kadın, bebek; kill two ~s with one stone F bir taşla iki kuş vurmak; give the ~ F ıslıklamak, yuha çekmek; '~.call *n.* kuş ıslığı; '~-fan.ci.er *n.* kuş meraklısı, kuşbaz; **bird.ie** [ˈbəːdi] *n.* F kuşcağız.

**bird...:** '~-lime *n.* ökse, tuzak; '~-seed *n.* kuş yemi; 'bird's-eye view kuş bakışı görünüş; 'bird's-nest **1.** *n.* kuş yuvası; **2.** *vb.* kuş yuvalarını aramak; kuş yumurtası çalmak.

**birth** [bəːθ] *n.* doğum, doğuş; soy; başlangıç, kaynak; meydana çıkma, zuhur; give ~ to doğurmak -*i*, meydana getirmek -*i*; *fig.* yaratmak; date of ~ doğum tarihi; '~-control *n.* doğum kontrolü; '~.day *n.* doğum günü; '~-mark *n.* doğuştan var olan vücut lekesi; '~-place *n.* doğum yeri; '~-rate *n.* doğum oranı; '~.right *n.* doğuştan kazanılan hak.

**bis.cuit** [ˈbiskit] *n.* bisküvi; fırınlanmış tabak çanak; açık kahverengi.

**bi.sect** ✂ [baiˈsekt] *v/t.* iki çeşit parçaya ayırmak; **bi'sec.tion** *n.* ikiye bölme.

**bish.op** [ˈbiʃəp] *n.* piskopos; *santraç oyunu*: fil; **bish.op.ric** [ˈ~rik] *n.* piskoposluk; piskoposluk bölgesi.

**bis.muth** ⚗ [ˈbizməθ] *n.* bizmut.

**bi.son** *zo.* [ˈbaisn] *n.* bizon.

**bis.sex.tile** [biˈsekstail] ~ year artık yıl.

**bit** [bit] **1.** *n.* küçük parça, lokmacık; gem; ⊕ matkap; anahtar dişi; ~ by ~ azar azar, yavaş yavaş; a ~ bir parça, biraz; a good ~ oldukça; not a ~ hiç de değil, asla; take the ~ between one's teeth gemi azıya almak (a. fig.) **2.** *v/t.* gemlemek; sınırlamak; **3.** *pret. of* bite 2.

**bitch** [bitʃ] **1.** *n.* dişi köpek; *sl.* kötü kadın; ~ fox dişi tilki; ~ wolf dişi kurt; **2.** *v/i.* şikâyet etm.

**bite** [bait] **1.** *n.* ısırım; ısırma; lokma; diş yarası, sokma *(arı, yılan v.b.)*; *(balık)* oltaya vurma; keskinlik *(içki, biber, soğuk)*; **2.** *(irr.) v/t.* ısırmak, dişlemek; sokmak *(arı, yılan v.b.)*; acıtmak, yakmak; aşındırmak *(soğuk, biber)*; ~ at ısırmağa çalışmak -*i*; ~ one's lips feciine hâkim olm.; 'bit.er *n.* ısırıcı; the ~ bit men dakka dukka.

**bit.ing** ☐ [ˈbaitiŋ] keskin; acı.

**bit.ten** [ˈbitn] *p.p. of* bite 2; be ~ with *fig.* çok arzu etm. -*i*, bş için yanıp tutuşmak.

**bit.ter** [ˈbitə] **1.** ☐ acı, keskin; sert; *fig.* kızgın, gazaplı; **2.** *n.* acı bira.

**bit.tern** *orn.* [ˈbitən] *n.* balaban kuşu.

**bit.ter.ness** [ˈbitənis] *n.* acılık; sertlik.

**bit.ters** [ˈbitəz] *pl.* bir tür içki, amer, bitter.

**bi.tu.men** [ˈbitjumin] *n.* zift, katran; **bi.tu.mi.nous** [biˈtjuːminəs] *adj.* ziftli, zift gibi.

**bi.valve** *zo.* [baiˈvælv] *n.* yumuşakçalardan çift kabuklu hayvanlar *(midye, istiridye gibi)*.

**biv.ou.ac** [ˈbivuæk] **1.** *n.* çadırsız ordugâh; **2.** *v/i.* çadırsız ordugâh kurmak; açıkta yatmak.

**biz** F [biz] *n.* iş.

**bi.zarre** [biˈzɑː] *adj.* tuhaf, garip, biçimsiz.

**blab** F [blæb] **1.** *n. a.* 'blab.ber geveze; boşboğaz; **2.** *v/i.* gevezelik etm.; boşboğazlık etm.

**black** [blæk] **1.** ☐ siyah, kara; karanlık; kirli; uğursuz; ~ cattle kasaplık sığır; ~ eye siyah göz; berelenmiş göz, morarmış göz; *s.* frost; ~ and white yazı; basılı şey; siyah beyaz resim veya görüntü; beat s.o. ~ and blue *b-ni* kıyasıya dövmek; be ~ in the face *(hiddet v.s. den)* morarmak; look ~ at s.o. *b-ne* surat asmak; **2.** *v/t.* siyahlatmak, siyaha boyamak; kara listeye almak; ~ out karartmak; örtmek; bayılmak, geçici olarak şuurunu kaybetmek; **3.** *n.* kara, siyah *(a. giysi)*; zenci.

**black...:** ~.a.moor [ˈ~əmuə] *n.* zenci *(esp. adam)*; '~.ball *v/t. (bir kulüpte üye seçiminde)* karşı oy vermek; '~.ber.ry *n.* ♀ böğürtlen; '~.bird *n.* karatavuk; '~.board *n.* yazı tahtası; '~.coat.ed: ~ worker kâtip, büroda çalışan kimse; '~.cock *n.* orn. siyah keklik *(erkek)*; '~-cur.rant *n.* siyah frenküzümü; 'black.en *v/t.* karartmak, karalamak; *fig.* lekelemek.

**black...:** '~.guard [ˈblæɡɑːd] **1.** *n.* alçak, ahlâksız kimse; **2.** *a.* '~.guard.ly ☐ alçak, rezil; **3.** *v/t.* küfretmek, sövüp saymak; ~.head ♀ [ˈblækhed] *n. (yüzde)* siyah benek; 'black.ing *n.* ayakkabı boyası, siyah boya; 'black.ish ☐ siyahımsı.

**black...:** '~.jack *n. part. Am.* cop; büyük içki bardağı *(siyah deri kaplı)*; ~.lead [ˈ~led] **1.** *n.* grafit, kurşun tozu; **2.** *v/t.* kurşun tozu ile boyamak; '~.leg *n.* greve katılmayan işçi; '~-let.ter *typ.* gotik harfler; ~.list **1.** *n.* kara liste; **2.** *v/t.* kara listeye koymak; '~.mail **1.** *n.* şantaj; **2.** *v/t.* şantaj yapmak -*e*; '~.mail.er *n.* şantajcı; ~ **mar.ket** karaborsa; ~ **market.eer** karaborsacı; **'black.ness** *n.* siyah oluş; karanlık olma; kötülük.

**black...**: **'~-out** *n.* karartma; *(elektrik kesilmesi dolayısiyle)* karanlıkta kalma; *thea.* ışıkların sönmesi; geçici olarak şuurunu kaybetme; *bşin* yayınını engelleme; ~ **pud.ding** hayvan kanı, yağ ve yulaftan yapılan siyah renkte bir tür sos; ~ **sheep** *fig.* saygıdeğer bir grup içinde değersiz kimse; **'~.smith** *n.* demirci, nalbant; **'~.thorn** *n.* ♀ alıç, yaban eriği.

**blad.der** ['blædə] *n.* anat. mesane, sidik torbası, kavuk; iç lastik *(top v.b.).*

**blade** [bleid] *n.* bıçak vs. ağzı; *(kürek, pervane v.b.)* *bşin* yassı ve geniş kısmı; *(arpa vs.)* ince uzun yaprak; **'~-bone** *n.* kürek kemiği.

**blae.ber.ry** ['bleibəri] *n.* ♀ yaban mersini.

**blah** F [blɑ:] *n.* zırva.

**blam.a.ble** □ ['bleiməbl] kötü, kabahatli; tevbihe müstahak.

**blame** [bleim] **1.** *n.* kabahat, kusur, ayıplama; sorumluluk; **2.** *v/t.* ayıplamak, suçlamak; sorumlu tutmak; be to ~ for *bşle* suçlu olm.; *bşin* sorumlusu olm.; lay the ~ on s.o. kabahati birine yüklemek.

**blame.ful** ['bleimful] □ kabahatli; **'blame.less** □ kabahatsiz, kusursuz; **'blame.less.ness** *n.* kusursuzluk; **'blame.wor.thy** *adj.* ayıplanmaya lâyık, sorumlu, kabahatli.

**blanch** [blɑ:ntʃ] *v/t.* beyazlatmak, ağartmak; ᵎkabuğunu soyarak beyazlatmak *(badem vs.);* haşlıyarak ağartmak *(et); v/i.* ağarmak; sararmak, rengi uçmak, benzi atmak.

**blanc.mange** [blə'mɔnʒ] *n.* mutfak: sütlü pelte. paluze.

**bland** □ [blænd] yumuşak, mülâyim; sert olmıyan; **'blan.dish** *v/t.* okşamak, tatlı dil kullanmak; **'blan.dish.ment** *n.* kompliman; çekici davranış.

**blank** [blæŋk] **1.** □ boş, açık, yazısız, beyaz; anlamsız; şaşkın; ~ **cartridge** ✗ manevra fişeği; **2.** *n.* boş ve açık yer; yazısız kâğıt; *(piyango)* boş kur'a; hedef; manevra fişeği.

**blan.ket** ['blæŋkit] **1.** *n.* battaniye; kalın örtü *(kar, karanlık v.b.);* wet ~ *fig.* keyif kaçıran; **2.** *adj.* geniş kapsamlı; **3.** *v/t.* battaniye ile örtmek; üstünü örtmek *-in; bşi* örtbas etm.. **blank.ness** ['blæŋknis] *n.* boşluk; anlamsızlık.

**blare** [blɛə] *v/i.* cayırdamak, boru gibi ses çıkarmak.

**blar.ney** ['blɑ:ni] **1.** *n.* dil dökme, *sl.* piyazlama, yağcılık; **2.** *vb.* dil dökmek, *sl.* yağcılık yapmak.

**bla.sé** ['blɑ:zei] *adj.* içi geçmiş, her şeyden bıkmış.

**blas.pheme** [blæs'fi:m] *vb. (din ve mukaddes şeylere)* küfretmek, sövüp saymak *(against -e);* **blas'phem.er** *n.* küfürbaz kimse; **blas.phe.mous** □ ['blæsfiməs] imansız, kâfir; **'blas.phe.my** *n.* küfür; mukaddes şeylere hürmetsizlik.

**blast** [blɑ:st] **1.** *n.* şiddetli ve ani rüzgâr esmesi, hava cereyanı; ⊕ patlama, infilâk; gürültülü boru veya düdük sesi; ♀ mildiyu; at full ~ tam süratle; in ~ işler halde; out of ~ hizmet dışı; **2.** *v/t.* berhava etm., yakmak, patlatmak; mahvetmek *(a. fig.)* ~ (it)! lânet olsun!; **'blast.ed** *adj. (yıldırımla)* yanmış; tahrip edilmiş, mahvolmuş *(a. fig.);* Allahın belâsı; **'blast-fur.nace** *n.* ⊕ izabe ocağı, yüksek fırın; **'blast.ing** *n.* berhava etme; patlama.

**bla.tant** □ ['bleitənt] gürültülü, gürültücü, şamatalı; *fig.* ayanbeyan, bâriz.

**blath.er** *Am.* ['blæðə] **1.** *n.* saçma lâf; **2.** *v/i.* saçma sapan konuşmak.

**blaze** [bleiz] **1.** *n.* büyük alev, ateş; parlaklık *(a. fig.);* yangın; alevlenme; atın alnındaki beyaz işaret, akıtma; ~s *pl.* cehennem; go to ~s! cehenneme git!, defol!; like ~s F çılgınca, alabildiğine; **2.** *v/i.* alevlenmek, parlamak, yanmak, ışık saçmak; ~ **away** durmadan ateş etm.; F durmadan çalışmak; *v/t.* alevlendirmek, neşretmek *(ışık vs.);* boru gibi çalmak; ilân etm.; *(ağaç)* gövdelerine işaret koymak; ~ **abroad** *(haber)* dört bir tarafa yaymak; ~ a trail yol çizmek, yol açmak; *fig.* çığır açmak; **'blaz.er** *n.* spor ceket.

**bla.zon** ['bleizn] **1.** *n.* arma; armacılık; **2.** *v/t.* arma çizmek, işaret koymak; *fig.* süslemek; ayyuka çıkarmak; bildirmek, ilân etm.; F yedi mahalleye davul zurna ile duyurmak; **'bla.zon.ry** *n.* arma çizimi.

**bleach** [bli:tʃ] *v/t.* ağartmak, beyazlatmak; *v/i.* ağarmak, beyazlanmak; **'bleach.er** *n.* çamaşır suyu; ~s *pl. Am. spor müsabakalarında:* açık tribün; **'bleach.ing** *n.* beyazlatma, beyazlanma; **'bleach.ing-pow.der** *n.* ağartma tozu.

**bleak** □ [bli:k] *(hava)* soğuk, tatsız; çıplak, rüzgârın etkisinde, açık; *fig.* ümitsiz, cesaret kırıcı; **ˈbleak.ness** *n.* rüzgâra açık oluş.

**blear** [bliə] **1.** ☐ çapaklı, kızarmış (göz); **2.** *v/t.* (göz) sulandırmak ve kızartmak; kamaştırmak, bulandırmak; ~-**eyed** [ˈbliəraid] *adj.* gözü akan; **ˈblear.y** ☐ uykulu (göz).

**bleat** [bliːt] **1.** *n.* meleme; **2.** *v/i.* melemek.

**bleb** [bleb] *n.* küçük kabarcık, sivilce.

**bled** [bled] *pret. & p.p. of* bleed.

**bleed** [bliːd] (irr.) *v/i.* kanamak, kanı akmak, kan kaybetmek; *fig.* kan ağlamak, çok kederli olm.; *v/t.* kan almak; *fig.* -*in* parasını sızdırmak; **ˈbleed.ing 1.** *n.* kanama; kan alma (verme); **2.** *adj. sl.* Allahın belâsı, uğursuz, gaddar.

**blem.ish** [ˈblemiʃ] **1.** *n.* kusur, hata; leke; **2.** *v/t.* güzellik ve kusursuzluğunu bozmak, lekelemek (a. fig.).

**blench** [blentʃ] *v/i.* ürkmek, çekinmek -*den*; benzi atmak; *v/t.* ağartmak.

**blend** [blend] **1.** *v/t.* (çay vs.) harman yapmak, karıştırmak (together, with ile); (şarap vs.) kupaj yapmak, hafifletmek; *v/i.* karışmak, harman olm.; *fig.* (ses, renk) uymak (well, with -e); bütünleşmek (into -e, ile); **2.** *n.* harman, karışım, kupaj; alaşım.

**blende** *min.* [blend] *n.* (çinko) sülfür.

**bless** [bles] *v/t.* kutsamak, takdis etm.; hayır dua etm. -e; Allahtan dilemek; mutlu kılmak (with ile); ~ me!, ~ my soul! aman ya Rabbi!, Allah Allah!; **bless.ed** [p.p. blest; *adj.* ˈblesid] mübarek, kutlu; F Allahın cezası; **bless.ed.ness** [ˈblesidnis] *n.* kutluluk; live in single ~ bekâr yaşamak; **ˈbless.ing** *n.* hayır dua, takdis, nimet; F onay, teşvik.

**blest** *poet.* [blest] *s.* blessed.

**bleth.er** [ˈbleðə] *s.* blather.

**blew** [bluː] *pret. of* blow[2] & blow[3] 1.

**blight** [blait] **1.** *n.* ♦ mildiyu, küf, mantar; samyeli; **2.** *v/t.* (güneş, rüzgâr v.b.) yakmak, kavurmak, soldurmak; **ˈblight.er** *n. sl.* herif, mübarek.

**Blight.y** ✕ *sl.* [ˈblaiti] *n.* memleket, ana vatan (part. İngiltere); a ~ one ana vatana dönmeyi gerektiren yasa.

**blind** [blaind] **1.** ☐ kör; gizli, saklı; *fig.* kısa görüşlü; gözü kararmış; anlaşılması güç; uzakta (yol); ~ alley çıkmaz sokak; *fig.* çıkmaz; ~ flying ✈ kör uçuş; ~ drunk *sl.* kör kütük sarhoş; turn one's ~ eye to s.th. göz yummak, bşi görmezlikten gelmek; **2.** *n.* perde, stor, kepenk; aldatmaca; pusu; **3.** *v/t.* kör etm.,

körleştirmek; gözünü kamaştırmak.

**blind.fold** [ˈblaindfəuld] **1.** *adj.* gözleri bağlı; körükörüne olan; **2.** *v/t.* gözlerini bağlamak; **3.** *n.* gözbağı; **ˈblind.ly** *adv. fig.* körükörüne; **ˈblind.manˈs-ˈbuff** *n.* körebe; **ˈblind.ness** *n.* körlük; **ˈblind.worm** *n. zo.* köryılan.

**blink** [bliŋk] **1.** *n.* göz kırpma; bakış; ⬇ pırıltı; **2.** *v/i.* göz kırpmak; gözleri yarı kapayarak bakmak; ışıldamak; ~ the facts gerçeğe gözlerini yummak; *v/t.* göz kırptırmak; **ˈblink.er** *n.* flaş lambası; *at:* meşin göz siperi; **ˈblink.ing** *adj.* F kötü, berbat.

**bliss** [blis] *n.* saadet, bahtiyarlık, mutluluk.

**bliss.ful** ☐ [ˈblisful] neşe dolu, mutlu; **ˈbliss.ful.ness** *n.* sonsuz haz, büyük mutluluk.

**blis.ter** [ˈblistə] **1.** *n.* kabarcık, su toplama; yakı; **2.** *vb.* kabar(t)mak, su toplamak; yakı koymak.

**blithe** ☐ [blaið], ~**.some** [ˈ~səm] *mst poet.* şen, neşeli; memnun.

**blith.er.ing** *sl.* [ˈbliðəriŋ] *adj.:* ~ idiot zırvalayan.

**blitz** [blits] **1.** *n.* ani hava saldırısı; *sl.* kampanya; **2.** *v/t.* bombardıman etm.

**bliz.zard** [ˈblizəd] *n.* tipi, kar fırtınası.

**bloat** [bləut] *v/t. & v/i.* şiş(ir)mek; kabar(t)mak; *balık:* tuzlamak ve tütsülemek; ~**.ed** *adj.* şişkin, kabarık; *fig.* şişirilmiş, abartılmış; **ˈbloat.er** *n.* tütsülenmiş ringa balığı.

**blob** [blɔb] *n.* damla, benek.

**block** [blɔk] **1.** *n.* kütük, kaya parçası; blok; klişe, kalıp; iki kavşak arasındaki mesafe; bitişik bir sıra bina; *Am.* sokak; ⊕ takoz, makara; engel; the ~ insanların başını kesmek için kullanılan ortası delik büyük tahta; **2.** *v/t.* tıkamak, kapamak, önünü kesmek, akamete uğratmak; döviz muamelesini kısıtlamak *veya* durdurmak; ~ in bşin krokisini yapmak, taslağını çizmek; *mst.* ~ up tıkamak; (liman vs.) kapatmak; bşe engel olm.; ~**.ed account** † bloke hesap.

**block.ade** [blɔˈkeid] **1.** *n.* abluka; run the ~ ablukayı yarmak; **2.** *v/t.* ablukaya almak; etrafını çevirmek; **blockˈade-runner** *n.* ablukayı yaran.

**block…:** ˈ~.bust.er *n. sl.* çok büyük ve güçlü uçak bombası; F çok etkili; ˈ~.head *n.* dangalak; ˈ~.house *n.* gözetleme kulesi, blokhavs; ~ let.ters *pl.* kitap yazısı.

**bloke** F [bləuk] *n.* herif.

**blond(e)** [blɔnd] *adj. & n.* açık renk, sarışın; ipek tül veya dantel.

**blood** [blʌd] *n.* kan; *fig.* kan, mizaç, huy; nesil, soy, ırk; kan bağı; in cold ~ soğukkanlı, tasarlayıp kurarak; *s.* run 1; '~-and-lthun.der *adj.* gürültülü patırtılı; '~-cur.dling *adj.* tüyler ürpertici; ~ do.nor kan veren.

**blood.ed** [ˈblʌdid] *adj.* cins, saf kan; ...kanlı.

**blood...**: '~-guilt.i.ness *n.* kanlı cinayet; adam öldürme; '~-heat *n.* kan ısısı; '~-horse *n.* safkan at; '~-hound *n.* bir cins av köpeği, zağar; *fig.* dedektif; 'blood.i.ness *n.* kana susamışlık, kanlı oluş; 'blood.less □ kansız, solgun; *fig.* renksiz; kan dökmeden olan; ruhsuz.

**blood...**: '~-let.ting *n.* kan alma; '~-poi.son.ing *n.* ⚡ kan zehirlenmesi; '~-pres.sure *n.* kan basıncı, tansiyon; '~-re'la.tion *n.* kan bağı; '~.shed *n.* kan dökme; '~.shot *adj.* kanlanmış, kızarmış; '~.stain *n.* kan lekesi; '~-suck.er *n.* sülük; *fig.* asalak kimse; '~.thirst.y *adj.* kana susamış, canavar ruhlu; '~-ves.sel *n.* kan damarı; 'blood.y □ kana bulanmış; kanlı; P kana susamış, gaddar.

**bloom** [bluːm] 1. *n.* çiçek, çiçek açma; *fig.* gençlik, tazelik; meyva üzerindeki buğu; *metall.* dökülmüş demir kütük; be in ~ çiçek açmak; 2. *v/i.* çiçek açmak; *fig.* gelişmek.

**bloom.er** [ˈbluːmə] *n. sl.* büyük hata, gaf; ~s *pl.* kadınların giydiği bir cins şalvar; (*şalvar şeklinde*) külot.

**bloom.ing** □ [ˈbluːmiŋ] çiçek açmış; bereketli, gelişen, serpilen; *sl.* Allahın belâsı, kör olası.

**blos.som** [ˈblɔsəm] 1. *n.* (*ağaç*) bahar çiçeği; 2. *v/i.* (*ağaç*) çiçek açmak; *fig.* gelişmek; ~ into büyümek, gelişip güzelleşmek.

**blot** [blɔt] 1. *n.* leke, mürekkep lekesi; *fig.* leke, kusur; 2. *v/t.* lekelemek (*a. fig.*), kirletmek, karartmak; kurutma kâğıdı ile kurutmak; *v/i.* lekelenmek, kirlenmek; (*kurutma kâğıdı*) emmek; *mst* ~ out örtmek, tanınmaz hale getirmek; yok etm., imha etm.

**blotch** [blɔtʃ] *n.* (*derideki*) leke veya büyük kırmızı kabartı; iri mürekkep lekesi.

**blot.ter** [ˈblɔtə] *n.* kurutma kâğıdı tamponu; *Am.* kayıt defteri (*esp. polis karakolunda*).

**blot.ting...**: '~-pad *n.* altlık, sumen; '~-pa.per *n.* kurutma kâğıdı.

**blot.to** *sl.* [ˈblɔtəu] *adj.* zil zurna sarhoş.

**blouse** [blauz] *n.* bluz.

**blow¹** [bləu] *n.* vuruş, darbe; şiddetli rüzgâr, sümkürme; saldırı; (*boru vs.*) çalma; at one ~ bir hamlede; come to ~s kavgaya tutuşmak.

**blow²** [~] (*irr.*) *v/i.* (*çiçek*) açmak, çiçeklenmek.

**blow³** [~] 1. (*irr.*) *v/i.* & *v/t.* (*rüzgâr*) esmek, üflemek; hohlamak; uç(ur)mak, atmak; (*toz vs.*) üfleyerek uzaklaştırmak; (*cama*) üfleyerek şekil vermek; (*boru vs.*) çal(ın)mak; solumak; (*elektrik sigortası*) atmak; (*ampul*) yanmak; *sl.* çarçur etm.; *sl.* ortadan kaybolmak, toz olm.; körüklemek; (*sinek*) yumurtlamak; (*sır vs.*) açıklamak; (*balina*) su fışkırtmak; ~ in ansızın gelmek; (*ocak vs.*) yakmak; ~ over (*fırtına*) dinmek; *fig.* bitmek, geçmek; ~ up havaya uç(ur)mak, patla(t)mak; (*fırtına*) patlak vermek; *phot.* büyütmek, agrantisman yapmak; *fig.* büyütmek; F aniden kızmak, tepesi atmak; ~ one's nose sümkürmek; ~ one's own horn övünmek, kendini methetmek; ~ one's brains out beynini patlatmak; I'll be ~ed if I...! *sl.* ...sam adam değilim!; 2. *n.* çiçek açma, çiçeklenme; 'blow.er *n.* üfleyici; esici; ⊕ kompresör, körük.

**blow...**: '~.fly *n.* et sineği, kurt sineği; '~-hole *n.* hava deliği; '~.lamp *n.* kaynak lâmbası, pirimüz lâmbası.

**blown** [bləun] *p.p. of* blow² & blow³ 1.

**blow...**: '~-lout *mot.* lâstik patlaması; '~.pipe *n.* üfleme borusu; ⊕ şalumo, hamlaç; '~.torch *n. s.* blowlamp; 'blow.y *adj.* rüzgârlı.

**blowz.y** [ˈblauzi] *adj.* pasaklı, kırmızı yüzlü (*kadın*).

**blub.ber** [ˈblʌbə] 1. *n.* balina yağı; ağlama; 2. *v/i.* bağıra bağıra ağlamak.

**bludg.eon** [ˈblʌdʒən] 1. *n.* sopa, kalın değnek, matrak; 2. *v/t.* matrak ile vurmak.

**blue** [bluː] 1. □ mavi; F kederli ve ümitsiz; 2. *n.* mavi renk; çivit; *pol.* muhafazakâr, tutucu; 3. *v/t.* maviye boyamak; çivitlemek.

**blue...**: '~.bell *n.* ⚘ çançiçeği; yabani sümbül; '~.ber.ry *n.* ⚘ yaban mersini; '~.bird *n. orn.* Kuzey Amerika'da yaşayan küçük mavi ve güzel sesli kuş türlerinden herhangi biri; '~-book *n. Am.* toplumun önemli kişilerinin adreslerinin yazılı olduğu defter; İngiliz hükümetinin yayınladığı resmî rapor; '~.bot.tle *n.* ⚘ peygamber çiçeği; *zo.* mavi sinek; '~.jack.et *n.* bahriyeli, gemici; '~-jay *orn.* mavi tüylü alakarga; ~ jeans *pl.* blucin; 'blue.laws *pl.* yutucu ve sert kanunlar; 'blue.ness *n.* mavilik; 'blue-lpen.cil *v/t.* sansür etm.; **'blue.print** *n.* mavi kopya; *fig.* tasarı; **blues** *pl. fig.* melankoli; ♪ bir tür caz müziği; **'blue.stock.ing** *n. fig.* okumuş kadın, entellektüel kadın.

**bluff** [blʌf] **1.** ☐ tok sözlü, açık; sarp, dik *(kıyı);* **2.** *n.* blöf; kayalık, uçurum; **3.** *v/t.* blöf yapmak *-e, b-ni* yanıltmak.

**blu.ish** ['bluːiʃ] *adj.* mavimsi.

**blun.der** ['blʌndə] **1.** *n.* gaf, büyük hata; **2.** *vb.* gaf yapmak, ahmakça hareket etm.; pot kırmak; ~ out F damdan düşercesine *bşi* ortaya atmak; **blun.der.buss** *hist.* ['blʌndəbʌs] *n.* geniş ağızlı eski zaman karabinası; **'blun.der.er, 'blun.der.head** *n.* ahmakça hareket eden kimse.

**blunt** [blʌnt] **1.** ☐ *(bıçak vs.)* kör, kesmez, *(kalem vs.)* küt; *fig.* körleşmiş; lafını sakınmayan, pervasızca konuşan; pervasız *(söz);* **2.** *v/t.* körleştirmek *-i,* körletmek *-i;* duyarlılığını gidermek *-in;* **'blunt.ness** *n.* pervasızlık; keskin olmayış.

**blur** [bləː] **1.** *n.* leke, bulanıklık *(a. fig.),* net olarak seçilemeyen şey; **2.** *v/t.* bulaştırmak, silmek; bulanıklaştırmak (with *-le);* ~red *adj. esp. phot.* bulanık.

**blurb** [bləːb] *n.* küçük kitap ilânı; yayıncının kitabın içeriği hakkında yazdığı abartmalı kısa yazı.

**blurt** [bləːt] ~ out *v/t.* ağzından kaçırmak *-i,* düşünmeden söylemek *-i.*

**blush** [blʌʃ] **1.** *n.* kızarma, utanma; pembelik; at the first ~ ilk bakışta; **2.** *v/i.* kızarmak, yüzü kızarmak (at, for, with *-den);* utanmak; (for *-den);* pembeleşmek; ~ to *bşden* dolayı utanmak, mahcup olm.; **'blush.ing** ☐ mahcup, utangaç.

**blus.ter** ['blʌstə] **1.** *n.* yüksekten atma, kabadayılık; sert rüzgâr ve dalga sesi; **2.** *v/i. (rüzgâr)* sert ve gürültüyle esmek; yaygara ile tehdit savurmak; patırtı etm.; *v/t. a.* ~ out *(küfür, tehdit v.b.)* savurmak; **'blus.ter.er** *n.* gürültücü kimse, övüngen, palavracı.

**bo.a** *zo.* ['bəuə] *n.* boğa yılanı.

**boar** [bɔː] *n.* erkek domuz; *hunt.* erkek yaban domuzu.

**board** [bɔːd] **1.** *n.* tahta, levha; mukavva; masa, sofra; yiyecek, içecek; kurul, idare heyeti; ↓ borda; *(satranç v.b.)* oyun tahtası; the ~s *pl. thea.* sahne; on ~ gemide; on ~ a train *Am.* trende; go by the ~ ↓ güverteden denize düşmek; *fig. (plan organizasyon vs.)* suya düşmek, bir kenara atılmak; above ~ dürüst, açıkça; sweep the ~ hemen hemen hepsini kazanmak; ~ of governers idare heyeti, yönetim kurulu; ♀ of Trade Ticaret Oda-

sı; Ticaret Bakanlığı; ~ and lodging yiyecek ve yatacak; **2.** *v/t. & v/i. (tahta)* döşemek, kaplamak; *(gemiye vs.)* binmek; ↓ *(gemiye)* saldırı sonucu girmek; para karşılığında yiyecek içecek ve kalacak yer temin etm.; pansiyoner olm.; ~ out pansiyona yerleştirmek; ~ up tahta ile kapatmak; ↓ borda etm.; **'board.er** *n.* pansiyoner; yatılı öğrenci.

**board.ing** ['bɔːdiŋ] *n.* tahta kaplama, tahta parmaklık; iaşe, erzak; **'~.house** *n.* pansiyon; **'~.school** *n.* yatılı okul.

**board...: '~.room** *n.* toplantı salonu; **'~.walk** *n. esp. Am.* plâj gezinti yeri *(tahta zeminli).*

**boast** [bəust] **1.** *n.* övünme; iftihar; **2.** *v/i.* yüksekten atmak, övünmek (of, about *-le);* iftihar etm. *-le;* **'boast.er** *n.* övünen kimse; **boast.ful** ☐ ['~ful] övüngen, palavracı.

**boat** [bəut] **1.** *n.* kayık, sandal, gemi; kayık tabak; burn one's ~s geri dönme şansını *k-ne* bırakmamak; take to the ~s filikayla gemiyi terketmek; be in the same ~ aynı durumda olm. *(esp. kötü);* s. sauce-~; **2.** *v/i.* kayıkla gezmek; **'boat-hook** *n.* kanca, çengelli sırık; **'boat-house** *n.* kayıkhane; **'boat.ing** *n.* sandal *vs.*'nin eğlence için kullanılması; **'boat-race** *n.* kayık yarışı; **boat.swain** ['bəusn] *n.* porsun, lostromo; **'boat-train** *n.* gemi yolcularını taşıyan tren.

**bob** [bɔb] **1.** *n.* püskül; pandül, sarkaç; *(saç)* kısa kesilmiş model; kâkül; âni hareket, birdenbire çekme veya sallama; *(at)* kısa kuyruk; küçük kızların reveransı; *sl.* bir şilin; **2.** *v/t. & v/i.* hafifçe hareket ettirmek; *(saç)* kısa kesmek; hafifçe vurmak; oynamak, kımıldamak; mantarlı olta ile balık avalmak; ~ up yükselmek, ortaya çıkmak.

**bob.bin** ['bɔbin] *n.* makara, bobin *(a. ♪);* ağaç bobin; **'~.lace** *n.* bir tentene türü, kopanaki.

**bob.ble** *Am.* F ['bɔbl] *n.* hata, yanılma, gaf.

**bob.by** *sl.* ['bɔbi] *n.* polis memuru; **'~.pin** *n.* saç tokası; **'~.socks** *n. pl.* kısa çorap, soket; **~.sox.er** *Am. sl.* ['~sɔksə] *n.* ondört ile onyedi yaş arasındaki genç kız.

**bob.cat** *zo.* ['bɔbkæt] *n.* vaşak.

**bob.o.link** *orn.* ['bɔbəliŋk] *n.* Kuzey Amerika'ya mahsus güzel sesli bir kuş.

**bob.sled** ['bɔbsled], **bob.sleigh** ['bɔbslei] *n.* bir tür kızak.

**bob.tail** ['bɔbteil] *n. (at veya köpek)* kısa kuyruklu; the rag-tag and ~ olur olmaz adamlar, sıradan adamlar.

bob.white *orn.* ['bɔb'wait] *n.* Kuzey Amerika bıldırcını.

bode [bəud] *v/t.* & *v/i.* işaret olm., delâlet etm.; ~ well (ill) hayra (uğursuzluğa) alâmet olm.

bod.ice ['bɔdis] *n.* korsaj, korse.

bod.i.ly ['bɔdili] 1. *adj.* bedenî, bedensel; maddî; ~ injury yaralama; cismanî zarar; 2. *adv.* bütün olarak, tamamen.

bod.kin ['bɔdkin] *n.* kalın ve uzun uçsuz iğne, biz.

bod.y ['bɔdi] 1. *n.* vücut, beden; ceset; gövde; *mot.* karoser; kurul, heyet, grup; bşin ana bölümü; F kişi; cisim; (içki) sertlik; X birlik; F büyük kısım; in a ~ birlikte, yekvücut olarak; 2. ~ forth *v/t.* şekil vermek; cisimlendirmek, şahıslandırmak; '~.guard *n.* hassa askeri.

Boer ['bəuə] 1. *n.* Hollanda asıllı Güney Afrikalı; 2. *adj.* Hollanda asıllı Güney Afrikalı ile ilgili.

bof.fin *sl.* ['bɔfin] *n.* araştırmacı, bilgin.

bog [bɔg] 1. *n.* batak, bataklık; bataklık çamuru; 2. *v/t.* & *v/i.* batağa bat(ır)mak; be *veya* get ~ged down bir yere saplanıp kalmak (*a. fig.*).

bog.gle ['bɔgl] *v/i.* çekinmek, ürkmek, korkmak (at *-den*).

bog.gy ['bɔgi] *adj.* bataklık.

bo.gie ['bəugi] *n.* 🚂 lokomotif veya vagonun alt kısmında bulunan çift dingilli kısım; *a.* = bogy.

bo.gus ['bəugəs] *adj.* sahte, yapma, yapmacık.

bo.gy ['bəugi] *n.* cin; umacı; the ~ (man) umacı, arap.

Bo.he.mi.an [bəu'hi:mjən] 1. *adj.* Bohemya'ya özgü; 2. *n.* Bohemyalı; Çek dili; Çingene; *fig.* Bohem, toplum kurallarını dikkate almadan yaşayan kimse, derbeder, kalender.

boil [bɔil] 1. *v/t.* & *v/i.* kayna(t)mak; haşla(n)mak; *fig.* öfkeden köpürmek; ~ over taşmak; ~ed egg rafadan yumurta; hard ~ed egg hazırlop yumurta; 2. *n.* çıban; kaynama; 'boil.er *n.* kazan; sıcak su deposu; 'boil.ing 1. *adj.* kaynar...; 2. *n.* kaynama; *sl.* the whole ~ takım taklavat.

bois.ter.ous □ ['bɔistərəs] (kişi *veya* davranışı) gürültülü, şiddetli; (hava) fırtınalı, sert; 'bois.ter.ous.ness *n.* gürültülü olma.

bold □ [bəuld] pervasız, cesur, yürekli, yiğit, atılgan; *b.s.* arsız, küstah; dik, sarp (*sahil, kıyı*); çarpıcı, göz alan; *typ.* siyah; make (so) ~ (as) to cesaret

etm., cüret etm. *-e*; 'bold.ness *n.* cesaret, yüreklilik; *b.s.* küstahlık.

bole [bəul] *n.* ağaç gövdesi.

bo.ler.o [bə'lɛərəu] *n.* bir tür İspanyol dansı; bu dansın müziği; cepken, bolero.

boll ⚕ [bəul] *n.* (*pamuk, keten*) tohum kabuğu veya zarfı.

bol.lard ['bɔləd] *n.* ⚓ iskele babası, duba.

bo.lo.ney *sl.* [bə'ləuni] *n.* saçma söz, zırva.

Bol.she.vism ['bɔlʃivizəm] *n.* Bolşeviklik; 'Bol.she.vist *adj.* & *n.* Bolşevik.

bol.ster ['bəulstə] 1. *n.* uzun yastık, minder; ⊕ yastık, plator; 2. *vb. mst* ~ up desteklemek *-i*, destek olm. *-e*.

bolt [bəult] 1. *n.* cıvata, bulon, sürme; kilit dili; kol demiri; (*kumaş*) top; (*kısa ve ağır*) ok; yıldırım; fırlama, kaçış; ~ upright dimdik; 2. *v/t.* & *v/i.* sürmelemek; cıvata ile bağlamak; fırlamak; ağzından kaçırmak; çiğnemeden yutmak; (*kumaş*) top veya rulo haline koymak; *Am. pol.* (*partisinden*) çekilmek; (*partisine*) destek olmaktan kaçınmak; gemi azıya almak (*a. fig.*); elemek, süzmek; dikkatle gözden geçirmek.

bolt.hole ['bəulthəul] *n.* sığınak, barınak.

bomb [bɔm] 1. *n. esp.* X bomba; 2. *v/t.* bombalamak, bombardıman etm.; ~ed out bombalanmış.

bom.bard [bɔm'bɑ:d] *v/t.* topa tutmak, bombardıman etm. (*a. fig.* & *phys.*); bom'bard.ment *n.* bombardıman, topa tutma.

bom.bast ['bɔmbæst] *n.* tumturaklı söz; bom'bas.tic, bom'bas.ti.cal □ tumturaklı.

bomb-bay ['bɔmbei] *n.* (*uçakta*) bombanın taşındığı bölüm.

bomb.er ✈ ['bɔmə] *n.* bombardıman uçağı.

bomb...: '~-proof 1. *adj.* bomba geçmez; 2. *n.* korugan, bunker; '~.shell *n. fig.* büyük sürpriz; '~-sight *n.* X bombardıman vizörü.

bo.nan.za *Am.* F [bəu'nænzə] *n.* zenginlik kaynağı; kârlı, kazançlı şey.

bon.bon ['bɔnbɔn] *n.* bonbon, şekerleme.

bond [bɔnd] 1. *n.* bağ, rabıta (*a. fig.*); ip, zincir; kişileri bir araya getiren ilişki; yapışıklık; yapıştırıcı madde; † bono, senet, tahvilât; sözleşme; kefalet; in ~ † antrepoda, ambarda; 2. *v/t.* malları antrepoya koymak; biraraya getirmek, yapıştırmak (together, to *-i*); ~ed warehouse gümrük antreposu; 'bond.age *n.* esirlik, serflik, kölelik (*a. fig.*); 'bond.hold.er *n.* tahvil (*senet*) hamili; 'bond(s)-

**man** *n*. erkek köle, serf; **¹bond(s).wom.an** *n*. cariye, halayık.

**bone** [bəun] **1.** *n*. kemik; kılçık; kemikten yapılmış şey; ~s *pl*. iskelet, vücut; zar; ~ of contention anlaşmazlık nedeni; feel in one's ~s derinden hissetmek; *bşden* çok emin olm.; have a ~ to pick with F paylaşacak kozu olm. -*le*, çözüm bekleyen işi olm. -*le*; make no ~s about F açıkça söylemek; **2.** *v/t*. & *v/i*. kemiklerini ayırmak, ayıklamak; *a*. ~ up F durmadan dinlenmeden çalışmak, ineklemek; *sl*. çalmak, araklamak; **boned** *adj*. kemikli; **¹bone-¹dry** *adj*. kupkuru; **¹bone-dust** *n*. kemik tozu; **¹bone-head** *n*. *sl*. aptal, mankafa kimse; **¹bon.er** *n*. *Am*. *sl*. hata, yanılma, gaf; **¹bone-set.ter** *n*. çıkıkçı, kırıkçı; **¹bone-shak.er** *n*. köhne otomobil veya bisiklet.

**bon.fire** [¹bɒnfaiə] *n*. şenlik ateşi; *(süprüntü yakmak için)* açık havada yakılan ateş.

**bon.net** [¹bɒnit] **1.** *n*. *(kadın ve çocukların giydiği)* başlık, bere; İskoç beresi; ⊕ motor kapağı, kaporta; **2.** *v/t*. başlık giydirmek.

**bon.ny** *part*. Scots [¹bɒni] □ güzel, zarif; sıhhatli, gürbüz.

**bo.nus** † [¹bəunəs] *n*. ikramiye, prim; hissedarlara verilen fevkalâde temettü.

**bon.y** [¹bəuni] *adj*. kemikleri görünen, zayıf; *(yiyecek)* kemikli, kılçıklı.

**boo** [bu:] **1.** *int*. yuha; **2.** *v/t*. yuhalamak, ıslık çalmak.

**boob** *Am*. *sl*. [bu:b] *n*. ahmak, herif, eşek kafalı; ~ tube F televizyon.

**boo.by** [bu:bi] *n*. hantal, beceriksiz, budala kimse; çeşitli deniz kuşu türlerinden biri; ~ prize sonuncuya verilen ödül, teselli mükâfatı; ¹~-trap *n*. iyi gizlenmiş ufak bomba; iyi gizlenmiş tuzak.

**boo.hoo** F [bu:¹hu:] *v/i*. çocuk gibi ağlamak; hüngür hüngür ağlamak.

**book** [buk] **1.** *n*. kitap; defter ♪ opera metni; cilt, bap; liste, cetvel; *(bilet, pul vs.)* blok: the ≗ Kutsal Kitap; be in s.o. ¹s good *(bad)* ~s *fig*. *b-nin* gözünde olm. (olmamak); bring s.o. to ~ *b-ni bşin* hesabını vermeğe zorlamak; *b-ni* sorumlu tutmak; **2.** *vb*. kaydetmek, deftere geçirmek; ismini kaydetmek; *(bilet, yer)* ayırtmak, rezervasyon yapmak; *(bagaj)* yollamak, sevkettirmek; ¹~.bind.er *n*. mücellit, ciltçi; ¹~.case *n*. kitap dolabı, kitaplık; ¹~-end *n*. kitap desteği; **book.le** [¹buki] *n*. F spor: yarış acentası; **¹book.ing.clerk** *n*. gişe memuru; **¹book.ing-of.fice** *n*. bilet gişesi; **¹book.ish** □ hayat tecrübesinden

fazla kitaplara bağlı olan; kitaplara bağlı, kitabî; **¹book-keep.er** *n*. muhasebeci, defter tutan; **book-keep.ing** *n*. defter tutma, muhasebecilik; **book.let** [¹~lit] *n*. broşür, küçük kitap. **book...**: ¹~-mak.er *n*. kitapçı; yarış acentası; ¹~-mark(.er) *n*. *(kitapta)* sayfayı belirlemek için kullanılan kâğıt; ¹~-plate *n*. kitabın kime ait olduğunu gösteren desenli kâğıt; ¹~.sell.er *n*. kitapçı, kitap satan kimse veya firma; ¹~.shop *n*. kitabevi; ¹~-stall *n*. kitap sergisi; ufak kitabevi; gazeteci köşesi; ¹~.worm *n*. kâğıt kurdu, kitap kurdu *(a. fig.)*.

**boom¹** ↓ [bu:m] *n*. seren, bumba; vinç kolu; kütüklerin akıntıyla gitmemesi ve gemilerin giriş çıkışına engel olunması için liman ağzına gerilmiş mania.

**boom²** [~] **1.** † fiyatların yükselmesi, piyasada canlılık; hamle; reklâmcılık; **2.** *vb*. *(iş vs.)* hızlı bir gelişme kaydetmek; ileri gitmek, ilerlemek; reklâm yapmak; överek tanıtmak.

**boom³** **1.** *vb*. *(top vs.)* gürlemek; *(rüzgâr)* uğultu yapmak; *(arı, böcek)* vızıldamak; **2.** *n*. gürleme, uğultu; vızıltı.

**boom.e.rang** [¹bu:məræŋ] *n*. Avustralya yerlilerinin silah olarak kullandığı ve fırlatıldıktan sonra geri gelen eğri değnek; *fig*. geri tepen kötü hareket *veya* plan.

**boon¹** [bu:n] *n*. lütuf, nimet, iyilik.

**boon²** [~] *adj*. şen, neşeli; ~ companion içki arkadaşı; çok yakın arkadaş.

**boor** *fig*. [buə] *n*. kaba adam.

**boor.ish** □ [¹buəriʃ] kaba, hoyrat; **¹boor-ish.ness** *n*. kabalık.

**boost** [bu:st] **1.** *n*. destek, yardım; artış; **2.** *v/t*. *b-ni* arkasından itmek; *(fiyat, vs.)* artırmak; destek olm. -e; lehinde konuşarak veya yazarak yardımcı olm. -e; *(radyo, elektrik, su v.b.)* gücü veya miktarını artırmak; reklâmını yapmak; **¹boost.er** *n*. destek veren kimse; ⊕, ≴ güç veya basıncı artıran alet; ≴ bir ilacın etkinliğini artıran madde.

**boot¹** [bu:t] *n*.: to ~ üstelik, ilâve olarak.

**boot²** [~] *n*. bot, potin, çizme; *(araba)* bagaj; tekme; the ~ is on the other leg durum değişti; give s.o. the ~ işinden çıkarmak -*i*; yol vermek -*e*; ¹~.black *Am*. = shoeblack; **¹boot.ed** *adj*. çizmeli; **boot-ee** [¹bu:ti:] *n*. kadın botu; patik.

**booth** [bu:ð] *n*. *(sergi, panayır, fuar)* satış pavyonu; kulübe, baraka; *Am*. telefon hücresi.

**boot...**: ¹~.jack *n*. çizme çekeceği; ¹~.lace *n*. ayakkabı bağı; ¹~.leg **1.** *vb*. *part*. *Am*.

içki kaçakçılığı yapmak; kaçak içki satmak veya üzerinde bulundurmak; **2.** *n.* kaçak içki; '~.leg.ger *n.* içki kaçakçısı; kaçakçı.

**boot.less** *poet.* ['buːtlis] *adj.* faydasız, beyhude, boş.

**boots** [buːts] *n.* (*otel*) ayakkabı temizleyen ve bavul taşıyan uşak.

**boot-tree** ['buːttriː] *n.* ayakkabı kalıbı.

**boo.ty** ['buːti] *n.* ganimet, yağma.

**booze** *sl.* [buːz] **1.** *v/i.* kafayı çekmek, içmek; **2.** *n.* alkollü içki; içki âlemi; 'booz.y □ sarhoş, kafası dumanlı.

**bop** [bɔp] = bebop.

**bo-peep** [bəu'piːp] *n.* bir yere saklanıp aniden ortaya çıkarak oynanan bir çocuk oyunu.

**bo.rax** ⚗ ['bɔːræks] *n.* boraks.

**bor.der** ['bɔːdə] **1.** *n.* kenar, pervaz; hu dut, sınır; (*resim, yazı*) çevreleyen süs; **2.** *v/t.* & *v/i.* sınırla(ndır)mak; sınırdaş olm., bitişik olm. (on, upon -*e*); 'bor.der.er *n.* sınırda oturan kimse; 'bor.der.land *n.* *mst* *fig.* sınır bölgesi; 'bor.der.line **1.** *n.* sınır; **2.** *adj.* şüpheli, güç ayırt edilebilen; belirli standardın altında olan.

**bore¹** [bɔː] **1.** *n.* çap, boru kutru; sonda, delgi; can sıkıcı kimse (*veya* olay); **2.** *v/t.* delik açmak, delmek, sondalamak; -*in* canını sıkmak, baş ağrıtmak.

**bore²** [~] *n.* şiddetli met hareketi.

**bore³** [~] *pret. of* bear².

**bo.re.al** ['bɔːriəl] *adj.* poyraza ait, kuzey rüzgârına ait; kuzey...

**bore.dom** ['bɔːdəm] *n.* can sıkıntısı, sıkıntı.

**bor.er** ['bɔːrə] *n.* burgu, matkap, delgi.

**bo.ric ac.id** ⚗ ['bɔːrik'æsid] *n.* asitborik.

**bor.ing** ['bɔːriŋ] **1.** *n.* sondaj, delme; **2.** *adj.* can sıkıcı.

**born** [bɔːn] *p.p. of* bear² doğmuş.

**borne** [bɔːn] *p.p. of* bear² taşınmış, götürülmüş.

**bo.ron** ⚗ ['bɔːrɔn] *n.* bor.

**bor.ough** ['bʌrə] *n.* belirli yasal haklara sahip kasaba veya şehir.

**bor.row** ['bɔrəu] *v/t.* ödünç almak, borç almak (from -*den*); (*fikir, kelime v.b.*) almak (from -*den*); 'bor.row.er *n.* borç alan, ödünç alan; 'bor.row.ing *n.* borç alma, istikraz; *gr.* başka bir dilden alınmış kelime veya deyim.

**Bor.stal** ['bɔːstl] *n.* suçlu çocuklara mahsus ıslâhhane.

**bos.cage** ['bɔskidʒ] *n.* ağaçlık, koru.

**bosh** F [bɔʃ] *n.* boş konuşma, zırva.

**bos.om** ['buzəm] *n.* göğüs, bağır, koyun;

*fig.* kucak, bağır; ~-friend *n.* candan arkadaş, samimi dost.

**Bos.pho.rus** ['bɔsfərəs] *n.* İstanbul Boğazı; the ~ and its shores Boğaziçi.

**boss¹** [bɔs] **1.** *n.* kambur, çıkıntı, şişkinlik; ⚙ kabartma, süs; **2.** *v/t.* kabartmalarla süslemek.

**boss²** [~] **1.** *n.* patron, şef, amir, ustabaşı; (*siyasi partide*) kodaman, nüfuzlu şahsiyet; **2.** *vb.* sevk ve idare etm. -*i*, kontrol etm. -*i*; *sl.* kumanda etm.

**boss.y** ['bɔsi] *adj.* kabartmalarla süslü; âmirane, sert, mütehakkim, despotça.

**bo.tan.ic, bo.tan.i.cal** □ [bə'tænik(əl)] botaniğe ait; bitkisel; **bot.a.nist** ['bɔtənist] *n.* botanist, bitkiler bilgini; **bot.a.nize** ['~naiz] *v/i.* inceleme için bitki örnekleri toplamak; bu iş için -*e* seyahat etm.; 'bot.a.ny *n.* botanik, bitki bilimi.

**botch** [bɔtʃ] **1.** *n.* kabaca yapılmış yama; kaba iş; **2.** *v/t.* bşi kötü ve kabaca yapmak; beceriksizce yamamak; 'botch.er *n.* yamacı, tamirci; *fig.* *contp.* eskici.

**both** [bəuθ] *pron., adj. & cj.* her iki(si), her ikisi de; ikisi de; ~ ... and hem ... hem de; ~ of them her ikisi.

**both.er** F ['bɔðə] **1.** *n.* canını sıkma, sıkıntı, üzüntülü iş; **2.** *v/t.* -*in* canını sıkmak. üzmek, rahatsız ıetm.; *v/i.* merak etm., endişelenmek (from -*den*); ~ it! Allah müstehakkını versin!; **both.er'a.tion** *n.* F can sıkıntısı, üzüntü; ~! Hay melûn şeytan!, Bırak şunu!; **both.er.some** ['~səm] *adj.* can sıkıcı, üzüntülü.

**bot.tle** ['bɔtl] **1.** *n.* şişe, biberon; **2.** *v/t.* şişeye koymak, şişelere dodurmak; ~ up sarmak, muhasara etm.; *fig.* (*öfke, hiddet vs.*) susturmak, zaptetmek; ~d beer şişe birası; '~-green *adj.* çok koyu yeşil; '~-neck *n.* şişe boğazı; *fig.* dar geçit; engel.

**bot.tom** ['bɔtəm] **1.** *n.* dip, alt; kıç; temel, esas; dere, vadi; kuvvet, can; ♱ karina, tekne; *at* ~ aslında, esasında; get to the ~ of a matter bir olayın aslını anlamak, içyüzünü öğrenmek; knock the ~ out of an argument bir yargıyı ret ve cerhetmek, çürütmek; **2.** *adj.* esaslı, alt, temel...; **3.** *vb.* (*iskemle vs.*) dip koymak; *fig.* bşe dayan(dır)mak (upon); dibine inmek, ulaşmak; 'bot.tom.less *adj.* dipsiz; çok derin; 'bot.tom.ry *n.* ♱ gemi rehni.

**bou.doir** ['buːdwaː] *n.* bir kadının yatak veya özel oturma odası.

**bough** [bau] *n.* ağaç; büyük dal.

**bought** [bɔːt] *pret. & p.p. of* buy.

**bouil.lon** ['buːjɔːŋ] *n.* et suyu, konserve.

**boul.der** ['bəuldə] *n.* çakıl; kaya parçası.

**bou.le.vard** ['bu:lvɑ:] *n.* bulvar; *Am.* geniş ana cadde.

**bounce** [bauns] 1. *n.* sıçrama, sıçrayış; F canlılık, hayatiyet; F övünme, yüksekten atma; 2. *v/t.* & *v/i.* sıçra(t)mak; fırla(t)mak; sek(tir)mek; F *(çek)* iade etm.; F işten atmak, yol vermek; ~ in (out) hızla girmek (çıkmak); ~ s.o. into doign stg. *b-ni* sıkboğaz ederek *bşi* yaptırmak; '**bounc.er** *n.* sıçrayan şey veya kimse; F iriyarı adam; *Am. sl. (bar, gece kulübü v.b.)* fedai; '**bounc.ing** *adj.* F gürbüz, neşeli *(çocuk).*

**bound¹** [baund] 1. *pret.* & *p.p. of* bind; 2. *adj.* bağlı, kayıtlı; ~ to *inf.* -meğe mecbur.

**bound²** [~] *adj.* yolda, gitmek üzere olan (for *-e).*

**bound³** [~] 1. *n.* hudut, sınır; keep within ~s sınırı aşmamak; ölçülü olm., haddini aşmamak; out of ~s yasak bölge; 2. *v/t.* & *v/i.* sınırla(ndır)mak, tahdit etm.; bitişik olm.

**bound⁴** [~] 1. *n.* sıçrayış, fırlayış, zıplama; 2. *v/t.* & *v/i.* sek(tir)mek, sıçra(t)mak, atlamak.

**bound.a.ry** ['baundəri] *n.* hudut, sınır; ~ line hudut hattı.

**boun.den** ['baundən] *adj.:* my ~ duty yapmakla zorunlu olduğum görevim, veci belerim.

**bound.less** ☐ ['baundlis] sınırsız, sonsuz, tükenmeyen.

**boun.te.ous** ['bauntiəs] cömert, eli açık; bol; **boun.tl.ful** ☐ ['~tiful] cömert; bol.

**boun.ty** ['baunti] *n.* cömertlik; cömertçe verilen şey; † ikramiye, prim.

**bou.quet** [bu:'kei] *n.* buket, demet; *(şarap)* koku.

**bour.geois** ['buəʒwɑ:] 1. *n.* burjuva, orta sınıf; 2. *adj.* orta sınıfa mensup.

**bour.geoi.sie** [buəʒwɑ:'zi:] *n.* burjuvazi, orta sınıf.

**bourn(e)** *poet.* [buən] *n.* hudut, sınır; hedef; ülke.

**bout** [baut] *n.* devre; maç, gösteri; *dans:* yarış, müsabaka; *hastalık:* nöbet.

**bou.tique** [bu:'ti:k] *n.* butik.

**bo.vine** ['bəuvain] *adj.* inek ve öküz gibi; ağır, durgun, sıkıcı.

**bov.ril** ['bɔvril] *n.* etsuyu hülâsası.

**bow¹** [bau] 1. *n.* baş eğerek selâmlama, reverans; 2. *v/t.* & *v/i.* reverans yapmak; eğmek; başını eğdirmek; başını eğerek yol göstermek; *fig.* boyun eğmek; ~ s.o. in (out) *b-ni* saygıyla içeri almak (yolcu etm.).

**bow²** ↓ [~] *n.* baş, pruva.

**bow³** [bəu] 1. *n.* yay, kavis; ilmek; fiyonk; 2. *vb.* ♪ yay ile çalmak.

**bowd.ler.ize** ['baudləraiz] *vb.* bir eserden müstehcen görülen kısımları çıkarmak.

**bow.els** ['bauəlz] *n. pl.* barsaklar; iç kısımlar.

**bow.er** ['bauə] *n.* çardak, kameriye; *poet.* bahçe köşkü; ↓ pruvada iki çapadan biri.

**bow.ie-knife** ['bəuinaif] *n.* av bıçağı.

**bow.ing** ♪ ['bəuiŋ] *n.* yay kullanma.

**bowl¹** [bəul] *n.* kâse, tas, çanak; pipo ağzı.

**bowl²** [~] 1. *n.* tahta top, yuvarlak; ~s *pl.* tahta toplarla oynanan bir tür oyun; 2. *v/t.* (top *vs.*) yuvarlamak, atmak; ~ out *kriket: b-ni* oyun harici yapmak; *fig. b-ni* kapı dışarı etm.; ~ over devirmek, düşürmek; *fig.* şaşkına çevirmek; *v/i.* yuvarlanmak; '**bowl.er** *n. kriket:* topu atan oyuncu; *a.* ~ hat melon şapka.

**bow.line** ↓ ['bəulin] *n.* borina; bir tür düğüm, izbarço bağı.

**bowl.ing** ['bəuliŋ] *n.* ağır topla oynanan bir tür oyun; ~ green bu oyunun oynandığı yeşil alan.

**bow...:** ~.man ['bəumən] *n.* okçu, ok atan kimse; '~.sprit *n.* ↓ civadra; '~.string *n.* ok kirişi.

**bow-wow!** [bau'wau] *int.* havhav!

**box¹** [bɔks] 1. *n.* kutu, sandık; arabacı yeri; kulübe; *thea.* loca; ⊕ yuva, mil yatağı; bir kutu dolusu; at tavlası; *mahkeme:* sanık veya tanık yeri; 2. *v/t.* kutuya veya sandığa koymak; *a.* ~ up ambalaj yapmak.

**box²** [~] 1. *v/i.* boks yapmak; ~ s.o.'s ear *b-ne* tokat atmak; 2. *n.* ~ on the ear tokat. şamar; '**box.er** *n.* boksör.

**Box.ing-Day** ['bɔksiŋdei] Noeli takip eden gün *(26 Aralık).*

**box...:** '~.keep.er *n. thea.* localara bakan kimse; '~.num.ber *n.* posta kutusu numarası; '~.of.fice *n. (sinema, tiyatro v.b.)* gişe.

**boy** [bɔi] *n.* erkek çocuk, oğlan; delikanlı; genç uşak; ~-friend *n.* erkek arkadaş; ~ scout erkek izci.

**boy.cott** ['bɔikət] 1. *v/t.* boykot etm.; 2. *n.* boykot.

**boy.hood** ['bɔihud] *n.* çocukluk çağı.

**boy.ish** ☐ ['bɔiiʃ] erkek çocuk gibi, oğlanlara yakışır.

**bra** F [brɑ:] = brassière.

**brace** [breis] 1. *n.* ⊕ matkap kolu, köşebent, payanda; kuşak; ₮ destek; *hunt.* çift; ↓ prasya; *(dişleri düzeltmeğe yarayan)* tel; *(satırları bağlıyan)* işaret;

pantolon askısı; **2.** *v/t.* sağlamlaştırmak, destek olm.; birbirine tutturmak; ↓ prasya etm..

**brace.let** ['breislit] *n.* bilezik.

**brac.ing** ['breisiŋ] *adj.* canlandırıcı, kuvvet verici *(hava vs.).*

**brack.en** ⚓ ['brækən] *n.* eğreltiotu.

**brack.et** ['brækit] **1.** *n.* ⚒ kol, destek, dirsek; raf; *typ.* ayraç, parantez; **2.** *v/t.* birleştirmek, birbirine bağlamak; parantez içine almak; *fig.* benzetmek, bir tutmak.

**brack.ish** ['brækiʃ] *adj.* tuzlumsu, acı.

**bract** ⚓ [brækt] *n.* çiçek yaprağı.

**brad** [bræd] *n.* tel çivi.

**brae** *Scots* [brei] *n.* bayır, yamaç.

**brag** [bræg] **1.** *n.* övünme, yüksekten atma; **2.** *v/i.* övünmek, yüksekten atmak, böbürlenmek (of, about *-le*).

**brag.gart** ['brægət] **1.** *n.* övüngen kimse, palavracı kimse, farfara; **2.** □ övüngen, palavracı.

**Brahm.an** ['brɑːmən], *mst* **Brah.min** ['-min] *n.* Brahma rahibi, Brehmen.

**braid** [breid] **1.** *n.* örgü, saç örgüsü; kurdele, örgülü şerit; **2.** *v/t.* örmek; kurdele takmak *-e.*

**brail** ↓ [breil] *n.* yelken ipi.

**braille** [breil] *n.* körlere mahsus kabartma yazı.

**brain** [brein] **1.** *n.* beyin, dimağ; *~s pl. fig.* kavrayış, zekâ, kafa; *have s.th.* on the *~* bşi aklından çıkarmamak; *pick veya* suck s.o.'s *~* F bilgisinden yararlanmak; *turn* s.o.'s *~ b-nin* başını döndürmek, ne oldum delisi etm.; **2.** *v/t.* kafasını yarmak, beynini patlatmak; *~ drain* beyin göçü; **brained** *comb.* ...beyinli.

**brain...:** *'~-fag n.* beyin yorgunluğu; *'~-fe.ver n.* beyin humması; *~.less adj.* akılsız; *fig.* kuş beyinli; *'~-pan n.* kafatası; *'~-storm n.* ani gelen cinnet; F müthiş ilham; **brain(s) trust** *Am.* bir grup danışman.

**brain...:** *'~-wash.ing n.* beyin yıkama; *'~-wave n.* F birdenbire akla gelen fikir; *'brain.y adj.* zeki, F kafalı.

**braise** [breiz] *v/t. mutfak:* kapalı kapta ve ağır ateşte pişirmek.

**brake¹** [breik] *n.* eğreltiotu; çalılık.

**brake²** [~] **1.** *n.* ⊕ fren *(a. fig.);* gezinti yapılan büyük yolcu arabası; *~ pedal* fren pedalı; **2.** *v/i.* fren yapmak; *v/t.* frenlemek; **brake(s).man** 🚂 ['~(s)mən] *n.* frenci.

**bram.ble** ⚓ ['bræmbl] *n.* böğürtlen çalısı.

**bran** [bræn] *n.* kepek.

**branch** [brɑːntʃ] **1.** *n.* dal; kol; şube. bö-

lüm; *local* ~ şube; chief of ~ şube âmiri; **2.** *v/i. a.* ~ out dallanmak, yayılmak, kollara ayrılmak; *a.* ~ off ikiye ayrılmak.

**brand** [brænd] **1.** *n.* marka, alâmet, alâmeti farika, cins; kızgın demir, dağ, damga; yanan odun; ⚓ buğdaypası; *poet.* kılıç; **2.** *v/t.* dağlamak; damgalamak; lekelemek.

**bran.dish** ['brændiʃ] *v/t.* sallamak, savurmak.

**bran(d).new** ['bræn(d)'njuː] *adj.* yepyeni.

**bran.dy** ['brændi] *n.* kanyak, brendi.

**brant** *orn.* [brænt] *n.* birkaç tür küçük kaz.

**brass** [brɑːs] *n.* pirinç; pirinçten yapılmış eşya; küstahlık, yüzsüzlük; the ~ ♪ pirinçten yapılmış müzik aletleri; bando; ~ band bando, mızıka; ~ hat ✕ *sl.* yüksek rütbeli subay; ~ knuckles *pl. Am.* pirinç muşta; ~ tacks *pl. sl.: get down to ~ tacks* asıl meseleye gelmek, sadede gelmek.

**bras.sard** ['bræsɑːd] *n.* kol askısı, pazıbent.

**bras.se.rie** ['bræsəriː] *n. (bira satılan)* lokanta.

**bras.sière** ['bræsiə] *n.* sütyen.

**bras.sy** ['brɑːsi] *adj.* pirinç kaplama- pirinç renginde; pirinçten yapılmış nefesli saz aleti gibi ses veren; *fig. (esp. kadın)* yüzsüz, arsız, cırtlak.

**brat** F [bræt] *n. contp.* arsız çocuk, yumurcak, piç kurusu.

**bra.va.do** [brə'vɑːdəu] *n. pl. ~(e)s* kabadayılık, kuru sıkı atma.

**brave** [breiv] **1.** □ cesur, yiğit; güzel. muhteşem; **2.** *v/t.* göğüs germek *-e*, karşı gelmek *-e*; **3.** *n.* Kızılderili savaşçı; *'brav.er.y n.* kahramanlık; ihtişam, tantana.

**bra.vo** ['brɑː'vəu] *int.* Aferin!, Bravo!

**brawl** [brɔːl] **1.** *n.* kavga, gürültü, ağız dalaşı; **2.** *v/i.* kavga etm., ağız dalaşı yapmak; *'brawl.er n.* kavgacı, yaygaracı.

**brawn** [brɔːn] *n. (insan)* kaba et, adale; *fig.* adale kuvveti; jelatinli domuz eti; *'brawn.i.ness n.* kuvvetlilik, adaleli oluş; *'brawn.y adj.* adaleli, kuvvetlili.

**bray¹** [brei] **1.** *n.* anırma, kulakları tırmalayan ses, çınlama; **2.** *v/i.* anırmak; gürültülü ses çıkarmak, çınlamak.

**bray²** [~] *v/t.* ezmek, rendelemek, dibekte dövmek.

**braze** ⊕ [breiz] *v/t.* pirinç ile lehimlemek, pirinç kaynağı yapmak.

**bra.zen** □ ['breizn] pirinçten, tunçtan; *fig. a.* ~-faced yüzsüz, arsız.

**bra.zier** [ˈbreizjə] *n*. mangal; pirinç işleri yapan kimse.

**Bra.zil.ian** [brəˈziljən] **1.** *adj*. Brezilya ile ilgili; **2.** *n*. Brezilyalı.

**Bra.zil-nut** [brəˈzilˈnʌt] *n*. Brezilya kestanesi.

**breach** [briːtʃ] **1.** *n*. delik, kırık; bozulma; ihlâl; riayetsizlik; ✕ gedik, rahne; ~ of contract sözleşmenin bozulması; akdin ihlâli; ~ of duty hizmet kusuru; ~ of peace asayişi ihlâl; **2.** *v/t*. kırmak, bozmak; gedik açmak.

**bread** [bred] *n*. ekmek, yiyecek; *fig*. geçim, maişet; ~ and butter tereyağlı ekmek; F geçim, maişet; take the ~ out of s.o.'s mouth rızkına engel olm., lokmasını ağzından çalmak; know which side one's ~ is buttered çıkarının nerede olduğunu bilmek; '~-bas.ket *n*. ekmek sepeti; *fig*. tahıl ambarı; *sl*. mide; '~-crumb *n*. ekmek kırıntısı; '~-fruit *n*. ♣ ekmek ağacı; '~-line *n*. ücretsiz yiyecek almak için fakirlerin oluşturduğu kuyruk.

**breadth** [bredθ] *n*. genişlik, en; *fig*. genişlik, şümul.

**bread-win.ner** [ˈbredwinə] *n*. evin geçimini sağlayan kimse.

**break** [breik] **1.** *n*. kırık; ara; açıklık, fasıla, dinlenme; âni değişiklik, arası kesilme; *typ*. fasıla; ✝ *Am*. *(fiyat)* düşüş; *(gün)* ağartı; kaçış; *bilardo*: sıra, dizi; F fırsat, şans; a bad ~ safdillik; şanssızlık; a lucky ~ şans, bahtiyarlık; **2.** *(irr.)* *v/t*. kırmak, koparmak, parçalamak; dağıtmak; açmak, yarmak; *(kanun)* ihlâl etm. -i, uymamak -e; *(söz)* tutmamak; *(rekor)* kırmak; mahvetmek; alıştırmak; ara vermek -e; sona erdirmek; ⚡ cereyanı kesmek; *(para)* bozdurmak; *(sır, şifre)* çözmek; iflâs ettirmek; ✔ nadas etm.; bozmak; ~ down yıkmak; ~ in *bşe* alıştırmak; kırıp girmek; ~ up parçalamak, kırmak; dağıtmak; sökmek, yıkmak; *v/i*. parçalanmak, kırılmak; kuvvetten düşmek; *(gün)* ağarmak; kesilmek; anî yön değiştirmek; fırlamak; ilgisi kesilmek; iflâs etm.; ~ away ayrılmak; dağılmak; kaçıp kurtulmak; kopmak; ~ down bozulmak, işlemez hale gelmek; başarısızlığa uğramak; morali bozulmak, kontrolunu kaybetmek; dönüşmek; kısımlara ayrılmak; 'break.a.ble *adj*. kırılır; kırılacak; 'break.age *n*. kır(ıl)ma; kırık yeri; 'break-down *n*. bozulma, yıkılma; *mot*. ârıza, bozukluk; nervous ~ asap bozulması. çökme; 'break.er *n*. kıran, parça-

layan *vs*. *(s*. break 2); ~s *pl*. sahile veya kayalara vurup kırılan dalga.

**break...:** ~.fast [ˈbrekfəst] **1.** *n*. kahvaltı; have ~ = **2.** *v/i*. kahvaltı etm.; ~.neck [ˈbreiknek] *adj*. çok süratli veya tehlikeli; '~-out *n*. kaçma, firar; ✕ çemberi yarma; '~-through *n*. ✕ yarma; *fig*. başarı: '~-ˈup *n*. bozulma, dağılma, parçalanma; *(hava)* değişme; '~.wa.ter *n*. dalgakıran.

**bream** *ichth*. [briːm] *n*. karagöz, mercan türü balık.

**breast** [brest] **1.** *n*. göğüs; meme; kalp, gönül; make a clean ~ of s.th. bütün gerçeği itiraf etm., içini boşaltmak; **2.** *v/t*. göğüs germek, karşı durmak; göğüslemek *(a. fig.)*; 'breast.ed *adj*. göğüslü.

**breast...:** '~-pin *n*. broş, kravat iğnesi; '~.plate *n*. göğüslük zırh; '~-stroke *n*. yüzme: kurbağalama; '~.work *n*. ✕ göğüs siperi.

**breath** [breθ] *n*. nefes, soluk; hafif rüzgâr; dem, an; buğu; under *veya* below one's ~ alçak sesle veya fısıldayarak; out of ~ soluğu kesilmiş, nefesi nefese; waste one's ~ boşuna nefes tüketmek; **breathe** [briːð] *v/t*. & *v/i*. nefes al(dır)mak, tenefüs etm.; hafifçe esmek; yaşamak; fısıldamak; belirtmek; hayat vermek; 'breath.er *n*. nefes alan kimse; ara, paydos, nefes alma.

**breath.ing** [ˈbriːðiŋ] *n*. nefes (alma); an; söyleme; püfürtü; '~-space, '~-time *n*. nefes alacak zaman, nefes alma fırsatı.

**breath.less** □ [ˈbreθlis] nefesi kesilmiş, nefes nefese; korkutucu; hareketsiz; 'breath.less.ness *n*. soluksuzluk.

**breath-tak.ing** □ [ˈbreθteikiŋ] nefes kesen, çok heyecanlı.

**bred** [bred] *pret*. & *p.p*. of breed 2.

**breech** ⊕ [briːtʃ] *n*. kıç, dip; top kuyruğu, kama; breech.es *pl*. pantolon, külot pantolon; 'breech.es-buoy *n*. ⬇ cankurtaran varagelesi; **breech-load.er** *n*. kuyruktan dolma top veya tüfek.

**breed** [briːd] **1.** *n*. soy, ırk, cins; çeşit; **2.** *(irr.)* *v/t*. & *v/i*. doğ(ur)mak, yavrulamak, üre(t)mek; yetiştirmek, beslemek; hâsıl etm., hasıl olm., türemek; 'breed.er *n*. yetiştirici; üretici, yavrulayan; *phys*. üretici reaktör; 'breed.ing *n*. üreme; yetiştirme; terbiye; ~ ground üreme yeri.

**breeze¹** [briːz] **1.** *n*. hafif rüzgâr, meltem, esinti; F münakaşa; **2.** *vb*. ~ in rahatlıkla gelmek.

**breeze²** ⊕ [~] *n*. kül ve sönmüş kömür

parçaları; ~ block *(bu madde ve çimento karışımı)* hafif yapı bloğu.

**breez.y** ['bri:zi] *adj.* hafif rüzgârlı, havadar; canlı, hareketli.

**Bren gun** X ['bren'gʌn] *n.* hafif makineli tüfek, mitralyöz.

**breth.ren** *eccl.* ['breðrin] *n. pl.* kardeşler.

**breve** [bri:v] *n.* sesli harflerin kısa okunması için üzerine konulan kavisli işaret.

**bre.vet** X ['brevit] *n.* üst rütbeye atama belgesi.

**bre.vi.ar.y** *eccl.* ['bri:vjəri] *n.* Katolik dua kitabı.

**brev.i.ty** ['breviti] *n.* kısalık.

**brew** [bru:] 1. *v/t.* yapmak *(bira v.b.),* hazırlamak, kaynatmak; *fig.* tertip etmek, hazırlamak *(esp.* kötü *bş);* 2. *n.* hazırlanmış içki; **'brew.age** *n. lit.* maya ile yapılmış içkiler; **'brew.er** *n.* bira yapan kimse, biracı; **'brew.er.y** *n.* bira fabrikası.

**bri.ar** ['braiə] = brier[1] & brier[2].

**bribe** [braib] 1. *n.* rüşvet; 2. *v/t.* rüşvet vermek *-e;* **'brib.er.y** *n.* rüşvet verme *veya* alma.

**brick** [brik] 1. *n.* tuğla; tuğla biçiminde şey; *sl.* mert adam; F a regular ~ yaman bir herif, çok iyi çocuk; drop a ~ F pot kırmak, çam devirmek; make ~s without straw parasız pulsuz iş çevirmek; 2. *v/t.* tuğla döşemek; **'~.bat** *n.* hırsla fırlatılan şey *(tuğla v.b.); fig.* eleştiri, taş; **'~.kiln** *n.* tuğla fırını; **'~.lay.er** *n.* duvarcı; **'~.work** *n.* tuğla işi; *pl.* tuğla ocağı.

**brid.al** ['braidl] 1. □ geline ait, düğüne ait; gelin...; ~ procession gelin alayı; 2. *n. mst poet.* düğün, nikâh, evlenme.

**bride** [braid] *n.* gelin, yeni evli kadın; **'~.groom** *n.* güvey, damat; **'brides.maid** *n.* düğünde geline refakat eden kız; **brides.man** ['~zmən] *n.* sağdıç; **bride.well** ['braidwəl] *n.* ıslahane.

**bridge**[1] [bridʒ] 1. *n.* köprü; ⫝̸ kaptan köprüsü; ♪ köprü; burnun kemikli üst kısmı; gözlüğün burna oturan kısmı; 2. *v/t.* köprü kurmak *-e; fig.* iki ucunu bir araya getirmek.

**bridge**[2] [~] *n. iskambil:* briç.

**bridge...: '~.head** *n.* köprübaşı; **'~.work** *n.* köprü inşaatı.

**bri.dle** ['braidl] 1. *n.* at başlığı; dizgin; 2. *v/t.* gem vurmak, dizgin takmak *-e;* hareketlerini kontrol altında tutmak; *v/i. a.* ~ up baş kaldırmak, terslenmek; **'~.path, '~.road** *n.* atlılara mahsus yol.

**brief** [bri:f] 1. □ kısa, özetli; 2. *n.* özet, yazılı belge; ⫝̸ dava özeti; *(papalık)* mühürlü mektubu; X, ⫝̸ görev ve yetki

talimatı; hold a ~ for b-ni mahkemede savunmak; 3. *v/t.* ⫝̸ *(avukat, a.* X) lüzumlu bilgi veya son talimatı vermek; avukat tutmak; **'~.bag, '~.case** *n.* evrak çantası; **'brief.ing** *n.* bilgi vermek için yapılan kısa toplantı, brifing; **'brief.ness** *n.* kısalık.

**bri.er**[1] ♣ ['braiə] *n.* funda, yabani gül.

**bri.er**[2] [~] *n. a.* ~ **pipe** funda kökünden yapılmış pipo.

**brig** ⚓ [brig] *n.* iki direkli yelkenli, brik; askeri hapishane.

**bri.gade** ['bri'geid] 1. *n.* X tugay; ekip; 2. *v/t.* birlikleri tugaylara göre düzenlemek; gruplar oluşturmak; **brig.a.dier** [brigə'diə] *n.* tuğbay.

**brig.and** ['brigənd] *n.* eşkıya, haydut; **'brig.and.age** *n.* eşkıyalık.

**bright** □ [brait] parlak, berrak, ışıldayan; neşeli, canlı; zeki; muhteşem; **'bright.en** *v/t. & v/i.* parla(t)mak, neşelen(dir)mek; *a.* ~ up aydınlatmak; aydınlanmak; **'bright.ness** *n.* parlaklık; uyanıklık.

**brill** *ichth.* [bril] *n.* çivisiz kalkan balığı.

**bril.liance, bril.lian.cy** ['briljəns(i)] *n.* parlaklık, pırıltı; *fig.* zekâ parlaklığı; **'bril.liant** 1. □ çok parlak; çok zeki; 2. *n.* pırlanta.

**brim** [brim] 1. *n. (bardak, kap v.b.)* ağız, *(şapka)* kenar; 2. *vb.* ağzına kadar dol(dur)mak; ~ over taşmak *(a. fig.);* **'~.ful, '~.full** *adj.* ağzına kadar dolu.

**brim.stone** ['brimstən] *n.* kükürt.

**brin.dle(d)** ['brindl(d)] *n. (esp. inek veya kedi)* benekli, lekeli hayvan.

**brine** [brain] 1. *n.* tuzlu su, salamura; *poet.* deniz suyu; 2. *v/t.* salamura etm., tuzlamak.

**bring** [briŋ] *(irr.) v/t.* getirmek; bşe vesile olm., sebebiyet vermek; şikâyet etm., dava açmak, ileri sürmek; ~ about. ~ to pass sebep olm.; beraberinde getirmek: ~ an action dava açmak; ~ along yanında getirmek; ~ down *(fiyat)* indirmek, azaltmak; ~ down the house *thea.* çok beğenilen gösteri yapmak, çılgınca alkışlanmak; ~ forth meydana çıkarmak; doğurmak; ~ forward ileri sürmek, ortaya atmak; öne almak; ⫝̸ *(hesap toplamı)* geçirmek, nakletmek; ~ home to gerçeği kabul ettirmek; ~ in kazandırmak; arzetmek, takdim etm.; içeri almak; ithal etm.; ~ in guilty suçlu olduğuna karar vermek; ~ off başarılı olm. *-de;* çıkarmak, kurtarmak *-den;* ~ on sebep olm. *-e;* geliştirmek *-i;* yardımcı olm. *-e;* ~ out meydana çıkarmak, üretmek,

59

neşretmek, yayımlamak; ~ round ayıltmak -i; iyileştirmek -i; *(gemi v.b.)* döndürmek; ~ s.o. to do *b-ne bşi* yaptırmak; ~ to ↓ orsa alabanda etm.; ~ s.o. to himself b-ni tekrar *k-ne* getirmek, ayıltmak; ~ under tâbi kılmak, boyunduruk altına almak; ~ up yetiştirmek, büyütmek; söz konusu etm.; yaklaştırmak.
**bring.er** ['briŋə] *n.* getiren, hâmil.
**brink** [briŋk] *n.* kenar, kıyı.
**brin.y** ['braini] *adj.* tuzlu.
**bri.quette** [bri'ket] *n.* briket.
**brisk** [brisk] **1.** ☐ faal, canlı, işlek; *(esp. rüzgâr, hava)* sert, kamçılayan; **2.** *v/t. & v/i. mst* ~ up canlan(dır)mak, diril(t)mek, hareketlen(dir)mek.
**bris.ket** [briskit] *n. (dört ayaklı hayvan)* göğüs eti, döş.
**brisk.ness** ['brisknis] *n.* canlılık, hareketlilik.
**bris.tle** ['brisl] **1.** *n.* sert kıl; **2.** *v/t. a.* ~ up tüyleri ürpermek, dimdik olm. (with *-den);* ~ with *fig.* bşle dolu taşmak; *b-ne,* bşe dik dik bakmak; **'bris.tled, 'bristly** *adj.* kıllı; anlaşması güç, öfkeli.
**Bri.tan.nic** [bri'tænik] *adj.* Britanya'ya ait.
**Brit.ish** ['britiʃ] *adj.* Britanya'ya ait; the ~ *pl.* Britanyalı, İngiliz; **'Brit.ish.er** *n. part. Am.* İngiliz.
**Brit.on** *hist., poet.* ['britn] *n.* Britanyalı.
**brit.tle** ['britl] *adj.* kolay kırılır, gevrek; *fig.* zayıf, hassas.
**broach** [brəutʃ] **1.** *n.* kebap şişi; ⊕ matkap, boşaltma tığı; **2.** *vb. (fıçı, varil)* delmek, delerek sıvıyı akıtmak, delik açmak *-e; (konu, fikir)* girişmek *-e,* bahis açmak, dermeyan etm.
**broad** ☐ [brɔːd] geniş, enli; hudutsuz, uçsuz bucaksız; sade, belli, açık *(öğüt, ikaz vs.);* güpe gündüz; genel; kaba *(espri);* erkinci, liberal; **'~axe** *n.* balta; **'~brimmed** *adj.* geniş kenarlı; **'~cast 1.** *adj.* ✔ saçılmış; yayınlanmış; yayına ait; **2.** *(irr. cast) vb. radyo:* yayınlamak, neşretmek; yayın yapmak; *fig.* etrafa yaymak *(haber, dedikodu);* ✔ saçarak tohum ekmek; **~ing station** yayın istasyonu; **3.** *n.* radyo yayını; **'~cast.er** *n.* spiker; **'~cloth** *n.* iyi cins yünden yapılmış kumaş; **'broad.en** *v/t. & v/i.* genişle(t)mek; **'broad'mind.ed** *adj.* açık fikirli; **'broad.ness** *n.* genişlik.
**broad...:** **'~sheet** *n.* el ilânı; **'~side** *n.* ↓ borda; borda ateşi; şiddetli hücum *(a. fig);* *a.* = broadsheet; **'~sword** *n.* pala.
**bro.cade** [brəu'keid] *n.* brokar; **bro'cad.ed** *adj.* kabartmalı, desenli dokunmuş.

**brother**

**broc.co.li** ['brɔkəli] *n.* karnabahara benzer bir bitki.
**bro.chure** [brəu'ʃjuə] *n.* broşür, risale.
**brogue** [brəug] *n.* bir tür kaba ve sağlam ayakkabı.
**broi.der** [brɔidə] = embroider.
**broil** [brɔil] **1.** *n.* gürültü, kavga; ızgara *(et);* **2.** *vb.* münakaşa etm.; ızgara yapmak; *fig.* güneşten yanmak; *fig.* pişmek; **~ing** *adj.* şiddetli sıcak; **'broil.er** *n.* ızgara yapan kimse veya alet; ızgaralık piliç.
**broke** [brəuk] **1.** *pret. of* break 2; **2.** *adj. sl.* meteliksiz.
**bro.ken** ['brəukən] *p.p. of* break 2; ~ health zayıf düşmüş, yıkılmış; ~ home yıkılmış yuva; ~ stones *pl.* balas, moloz; ~ English bozuk İngilizce; **'~heart.ed** *adj.* ümitsizliğe kapılmış, kalbi kırık; **'broken.ly** *adv.* ara vererek; kesik kesik hareket ederek; **'bro.ken-'wind.ed** *vet.* tıknefes, astmalı.
**bro.ker** ['brəukə] *n.* ✝ tellâl, simsar; borsa acentesi, komisyoncu; **'bro.ker.age** *n.* ✝ komisyonculuk, simsarlık; komisyon *(ücret).*
**bro.mide** ['brəumaid] *n.* ♔ bromür; *sl.* beylik söz veya fikir; **bro.mine** ['~miːn] *n.* ♔ brom.
**bron.chi.al** *anat.* ['brɔŋkjəl] *adj.* broşlara ait; **bron.chi.tis** *n.* ✝ bronşit.
**bron.co** ['brɔŋkəu] *n.* yabani veya yarı ehli at; **~-bust.er** ['~bʌstə] *n. sl.* at terbiyecisi.
**Bronx cheer** *Am.* ['brɔŋks'tʃiə] *n.* yuha, yuha çekme.
**bronze** [brɔnz] **1.** *n.* tunç, bronz; bronz rengi; tunçtan eşya; **2.** *adj.* tunçtan yapılmış, bronz...; **3.** *v/t.* bronzla kaplatmak; *fig.* güneşte yakmak, esmerleştirmek: ♀ Age Tunç Devri.
**brooch** [brəutʃ] *n.* broş, iğne.
**brood** [bruːd] **1.** *n.* yumurtadan çıkan hayvancıklar; sürü, gürüh; **2.** *v/i.* kuluçkaya yatmak; *fig.* kuruntularıyle *k-ni* yemek, derin düşüncelere dalmak; **'brood.er** *n.* kuluçka makinesi; düşünceye dalan kimse.
**brook[1]** [bruk] *n.* dere, çay, ırmak.
**brook[2]** *rhet.* [~] *v/t.* tahammül etm., çekmek; the matter ~s no delay meselenin beklemeye tahammülü yoktur.
**broom** ♀ [bruːm] *n.* katır tırnağı; süpürge; **~.stick** ['brumstik] *n.* süpürge sapı.
**broth** [brɔθ] *n.* etsuyu, etsuyuna çorba.
**broth.el** ['brɔθl] *n.* genelev.
**broth.er** ['brʌðə] *n.* erkek kardeş, bira

der; aynı cemiyette erkek üye; ~.hood ['~hud] n. kardeşlik, beraberlik, birlik; bir kuruluşun üyeleri; '~-in-law n. kayınbirader, bacanak, enişte; 'broth.er.ly adj. kardeşçe.

brougham ['bru:əm] n. kupa arabası.

brought [brɔ:t] pret. & p.p. of bring.

brow [brau] n. kaş, alın; poet. çehre, yüz; bayır sırtı; '~.beat (irr. beat) v/t. sert bakarak korkutmak.

brown [braun] 1. adj. kahverengi, kahve renkli, esmer; güneşten yanmış; ~ bread esmer ekmek; ~ paper koyu renkli ambalaj kâğıdı; be in a ~ study derin bir düşünce içinde olm.; 2. n. kahve rengi 3. v/t. & v/i. karar(t)mak; esmerletmek, esmerleşmek; be ~ed off sl. bıkmak; 'brown.ie ['~ni] n. masaldaki iyi huylu küçük peri; kız izci (8-11 yaşları arasında); 'brown.ish adj. esmerimsi; 'brown-stone n. kumtaşı; ön yüzü bu taştan yapılmış ev.

browse [brauz] 1. n. taze sürgün veya dal; 2. vb. otlamak, (yaprak, sürgün) yemek (on); fig. kitaplara göz gezdirmek.

bruise [bru:z] 1. n. bere, çürük; 2. v/t. berelemek, çürütmek; dövmek, ezmek; 'bruis.er n. sl. boksör, zorba.

brunch ['brʌntʃ] n. erken yenen öğle yemeği, geç yenen kahvaltı.

bru.nette [bru:net] 1. n. esmer kız veya kadın; 2. adj. esmer.

brunt [brʌnt] n. şiddetli darbe, yüklenme; bear the ~ sıkıntısını çekmek, asıl yüke katlanmak.

brush [brʌʃ] 1. n. fırça, fırçalama; tüylü kuyruk, tilki kuyruğu; ≠ fırça; kısa yumuşak temas; give a ~ fırçalayarak kaldırmak, çıkarmak; have a ~ with s.o. yumruk yumruğa gelmek -le, kavgaya tutuşmak -le; 2. vb. fırçalamak, süpürmek; hafifçe dokunmak -e; ~ aside, ~ away bertaraf etm., dikkate almamak, önemsememek; ~ down üstünü fırçalamak; ~ off tozunu almak; başından atmak, atlatmak, savmak; ~ up (bilgi) tazelemek; '~.wood n. çalılık, fundalık; çalı çırpı.

brusque ☐ [brusk] sert, haşin, kaba, ters. Brus.sels sprouts ❦ ['brʌsl'sprauts] n. frenk lahanası.

bru.tal ☐ ['bru:tl] hayvanca, vahşî; zalim, merhametsiz; çok sert, katlanması güç; kaba; bru.tal.i.ty [~'tæliti] n. vahşet, canavarlık; bru.tal.ize ['~təlaiz] vb. hayvanlaştırmak, kabalaştırmak; hayvanca davranmak; brute 1. adj. zalim,

hayvan gibi; düşüncesiz; 2. n. hayvan; hayvan gibi adam; canavar; 'brut.ish ☐ = brute 1; 'brut.ish.ness n. hayvanlık, kabalık.

bub.ble ['bʌbl] 1. n. hava kabarcığı; kaynayış, kaynama; fig. sabun köpüğü; 2. v/i. köpürmek, kaynamak, fıkırdamak; 'bub.bly 1. adj. kabarcıklı; coşkun, şakrak; 2. n. co. şampanya, köpüklü şarap.

buc.ca.neer ['bʌkə'niə] 1. n. korsan, deniz eşkiyası; 2. vb. korsanlık etm.

buck [bʌk] 1. n. zo. erkek hayvan (part. karaca, geyik); züppe, modaya düşkün adam; Am. sl. dolar; pass the ~ F sorumluluğu üzerinden atmak; 2. vb. sıçramak (esp. at); binicisini üzerinden atmak; Am. F muhalefet etm., karşı gelmek; ~ up F canlan(dır)mak, geliştirmeye çalışmak.

buck.et ['bʌkit] 1. n. kova, gerdel; a mere drop in the ~ fig. denizden katra, deve de kulak; 2. vb. (at) koşturarak yormak; delice bir süratle hareket et(tir)mek; (yağmur) bardaktan boşanırcasına yağmak; ~.ful ['~ful] n. bir kova dolusu; ~ seat mot. çanak biçiminde ve katlanır koltuk.

buck.le ['bʌkl] 1. n. toka, kopça; 2. v/t. & v/i. tokalamak, kopçalamak; ⊕ ısı veya basınç ile bük(ül)mek; ~ on tokalamak, takmak; ~ to girişmek -e, çok çalışmak; 'buck.ler n. kalkan, siper.

buck.ram ['bʌkrəm] n. çirişli pamuklu bez; fig. yapay davranış.

buck...: '~.skin n. güderi; '~.wheat n. ❦ kara buğday.

bud [bʌd] 1. n. tomurcuk, konca, sürgün; fig. gelişmemiş, olgunlaşmamış; nip in the ~ fig. bşin gelişmesine engel olm.; 2. v/t & v/i. tomurcuklan(dır)mak, konca vermek; (ağaç) aşılamak; ~ding tomurcuklanan; gelişmekte olan.

Bud.dhism ['budizəm] n. Budizm, Buda dini; 'Bud.dhist n. Budist.

bud.dy Am. F ['bʌdi] n. arkadaş, ahbap.

budge [bʌdʒ] v/t. & v/i. kımılda(t)mak. hareket et(tir)mek; fig. fikrini değiştir(t)mek.

budg.et ['bʌdʒit] 1. n. bütçe, devlet bütçesi; stok, miktar; ucuz, bütçeye uygun; 2. vb. bütçe yapmak; 'budg.et.ar.y adj. bütçeye ait, bütçe...

buff [bʌf] 1. n. (renk) deve tüyü; kalın bir tür deri; in (one's) ~ çırılçıplak; 2. v/t. boyamak, (metal) yumuşak bşle parlatmak.

buf.fa.lo zo. ['bʌfələu] pl. buf.fa.loes ['~z] n. manda.

**buff.er** [ˈbʌfə] *n*. 🚋 tampon; *fig. (saldı-rı, güçlük v.b.)* hafifletici; old ~ *sl*. beceriksiz moruk; ~ state tampon devlet.

**buf.fet¹** [ˈbʌfit] **1.** *n*. tokat, yumruk; **2.** *vb*. tokatlamak, yumruk atmak; mücadele etm.. savaşmak (with *ile*).

**buf.fet²** [ˈbufei] *n*. büfe; tezgâh; büfe şeklinde hazırlanan hafif yemek; ~ car 🚋 büfe, büvet.

**buf.foon** [bəˈfuːn] *n*. soytarı, maskara; **buf.foon.er.y** *n*. maskaralık.

**bug** [bʌg] *n*. tahtakurusu; *Am*. böcek; *Am. sl*. kusur, bozukluk, ârıza; gizli dinleme cihazı; *sl. -in* hastası; ~.a.boo [ ~əbuː], ˈ~.bear *n*. korku uyandıran hayali şey, umacı; ˈbug.gy **1.** *adj*. tahtakurusu üşüşmüş; **2.** *n*. tek atlı hafif araba; çocuk arabası.

**bu.gle¹** [ˈbjuːgl] *n*. borazan, boru.

**bu.gle²** [ ~ ] *n*. siyah boncuk.

**bu.gler** ✕ [ˈbjuːglə] *n*. boru çalan kimse.

**buhl** [buːl] *n*. kakma süslemeli eşya.

**build** [bild] **1.** *(irr.) vb*. inşa etm., kurmak, yapmak; *fig*. bina etm., dayanmak, güvenmek (on, upon *-e*); ~ in içine inşa etm.. sokmak, yerleştirmek; ~ up birik-(tir)mek; geliş(tir)mek; binalarla doldurmak, gelişmiş bir hale getirmek; *fig*. göklere çıkarmak; **2.** *n. (esp. insan vücudu)* yapı, bünye, biçim; ˈbuild.er *n*. inşaatçı; inşaat ustası; ˈbuild.ing *n*. bina, yapı, ev; inşa etme; ~ contractor inşaat müteahhidi; inşaatçı; ~ craftsman inşaat işçisi; ~ site şantiye, yapı yeri; ~ society inşaat şirketi, yapı kooperatifi; ˈbuild-up *n*. kurma, tanzim; kuruluş, organizasyon.

**built** [bilt] **1.** *pret. & p.p. of* build; **2.** *adj*. ... inşa edilmiş; ... şekillendirilmiş; ˈ~-ˈin *adj*. gömme; yerleşmiş; ˈ~-ˈup a-re.a meskûn bölge, yerleşme bölgesi.

**bulb** [bʌlb] *n*. ♀ *(kök)* soğan; *(termometre v.b.)* hazne; ⚡ ampul; ˈbulb.ous *n*. ♀ yumrulu, yumru köklü.

**Bul.gar** [ˈbʌlgaː] *n*. Bulgar; **Bul.gar.i.an** [ ~ ˈgɛərıən] **1.** *adj*. Bulgaristan'a ait; **2.** *n*. Bulgar; Bulgarca.

**bulge** [bʌldʒ] **1.** *n*. bel verme, şiş, çıkıntı; ani ve beklenmeyen yükselme; **2.** *v/i*. bel vermek, kamburlaşmak, çıkıntı yapmak.

**bulk** [bʌlk] *n*. hacım, kütle; en büyük kısım; hantal vücut; ↓ dökme yük, kargo; in ~ dökme, ambalajsız; toptan; ˈ~.head *n*. ↓ bölme; ˈbulk.i.ness *n*. irilik; ˈbulk.y *adj*. hacimli, büyük, cüsseli; ❀ havaleli.

**bull¹** [bul] **1.** *n*. boğa; *(iri)* erkek hayvan;

*sl. esp. Am*. polis memuru; boğa gibi, çok kuvvetli adam; 🗡 *sl*. spekülâtör, borsa hava oyuncusu; a ~ in a china shop sakar adam, patavatsız adam; take the ~ by the horns güçlükleri korkusuzca göğüslemek; ~ session *Am. sl*. erkeklerin bir araya gelerek yaptıkları toplantı; **2.** *v/t*. 🗡 *sl*. fiyatları yükselterek spekülasyon yapmak.

**bull²** [ ~ ] *n. (papalık)* ferman.

**bull³** [ ~ ] *n*. yanılma, gaf; Irish ~ boş lâkırdı, saçmasapan söz, zırva.

**bull.dog** [ˈbuldɔg] *n*. buldok köpeği; cesur ve kararlı adam; *univ*. laboratuvar yardımcısı.

**bull.doze** *Am*. F [ˈbuldəuz] *v/t*. üstünden buldozer geçirmek *-in*; tedhiş etm., zor kullanarak kabul ettirmek; ˈbull.doz.er *n*. buldozer.

**bul.let** [ˈbulit] *n*. kurşun, mermi.

**bul.le.tin** [ˈbulitin] *n*. günlük haber, tebliğ, bülten; dergi; ~ board *Am*. ilân tahtası.

**bull...:** ˈ~.fight *n*. boğa güreşi; ˈ~.finch *n*. *orn*. şakrakkuşu; çit, çalı; ˈ~.frog *n. zo*. bir tür iri kafalı kurbağa.

**bul.lion** [ˈbuljən] *n*. altın veya gümüş külçesi.

**bull.ock** [ˈbulək] *n*. iğdiş edilmiş boğa, öküz.

**bull.pen** *Am*. [ˈbulˈpen] *n*. F hapishane; *beysbol*: yedek oyuncuların bekledikleri yer.

**bull's-eye** [bulzai] *n*. hedefin ortası; tam vuruş; ↓ lomboz; nane şekeri.

**bul.ly¹** [ˈbuli] **1.** *n*. kabadayı, zorba, kendinden küçükleri ezen kimse *(esp. çocuk)*; **2.** *adj*. palavracı, farfara; *part. Am*. F şu, klâs. iyi, güzel *(a. int.)*; **3.** *v/t*. korkutmak, kabadayılık etm..

**bul.ly²** [ ~ ] *a*. ~ beef konserve sığır eti.

**bul.rush** ♀ [ˈbulrʌʃ] *n*. hasırotu, saz.

**bul.wark** [ˈbulwək] *n*. toprak tabya, siper *(mst fig.)*; ↓ küpeşte.

**bum¹** *sl*. [bʌm] *n*. kaba et, kıç.

**bum²** *Am*. F [ ~ ] **1.** *n*. serseri, başıboş kimse, sarhoş; be *veya* go on the ~ bozulmak. aşınmak; serseri hayatı yaşamak; **2.** *v/t*. başkalarının sırtından geçinmek, *sl*. otlamak; **3.** *adj*. fena, kötü, kıyafetsiz.

**bum.ble-bee** [ˈbʌmblbiː] *n. zo*. hezen arısı.

**bum.boat** [ˈbʌmbəut] *n*. erzak sandalı.

**bump** [bʌmp] **1.** *n*. çarpma, vuruş; şiş, yumru, tümsek; kabiliyet, Allah vergisi; **2.** *vb*. bindirmek, vurmak, çarpmak (against *-e*); çarpışmak (together), sarsı(l)mak; *sandal vs.* yarışı: geçmek, geride bırakmak -i; ~ **into** s.o. *b-ne* çarpmak, *b-ni* itmek; ~ **off** F öldürmek, mortlatmak.

**bump.er** [ˈbʌmpə] *n.* ağzına kadar dolu bardak; F çok dolu veya büyük şey; *mot.* tampon; ~ **crop** rekor teşkil eden hasat.

**bump.kin** [ˈbʌmpkin] *n.* hödük, ahmak.

**bump.tious** ☐ F [ˈbʌmpʃəs] kendini beğenmiş, küstah.

**bump.y** [ˈbʌmpi] *adj.* tümsekli, yamrı yumru; *fig.* inişli çıkışlı; ⸷ sallantılı.

**bun** [bʌn] *n.* kuru üzümlü çörek; *(saç)* topuz.

**bu.na** [ˈbuːnə] *n.* kauçuk.

**bunch** [bʌntʃ] **1.** *n.* demet, deste, salkım; grup, takım; kütle, yığın; ~ **of flowers** çiçek demeti, buket; ~ **of grapes** üzüm salkımı; **2.** *vb.* bir araya gelmek, demet yapmak.

**bun.combe** [ˈbʌŋkəm] *n.* boş laf, palavra.

**bun.dle** [ˈbʌndl] **1.** *n.* deste, demet, bohça, çıkın, paket, bağ; **2.** *v/t. a.* ~ **up** çıkınlamak, sarmalamak; ~ **away**, ~ **off** F kov(ala)mak, defetmek, sepetlemek.

**bung** [bʌŋ] **1.** *n.* fıçı tapası, tıkaç; **2.** *v/t.* tapa ile tıkamak; F fırlatmak; ~**ed up** tıkalı *(burun).*

**bun.ga.low** [ˈbʌŋgələu] *n.* tek katlı ev.

**bung-hole** [ˈbʌŋhəul] *n.* fıçı deliği.

**bun.gle** [ˈbʌŋgl] **1.** *n.* kötü iş, bozma, acemice iş; **2.** *vb.* bozmak, berbat etm., yüzüne gözüne bulaştırmak; **ˈbun.gler** *n.* üstünkörü iş gören adam; **ˈbun.gling 1.** ☐ beceriksiz, hantal; **2.** *n.* üstünkörü, kötü iş.

**bun.ion** ⸷ [ˈbʌnjən] *n.* ayak parmağı üzerinde oluşan şiş.

**bunk**[1] *sl.* [bʌŋk] *n.* boş lâf, gevezelik.

**bunk**[2] [~] *n.* yatak yeri, ranza.

**bunk.er** ⬇ [ˈbʌŋkə] **1.** *n.* kömürlük; **2.** *vb.* be ~**ed** *fig.* engele rastlamak.

**bun.kum** [ˈbʌŋkəm] = **buncombe.**

**bun.ny** [ˈbʌni] *n.* tavşan(cık).

**bun.sen** [ˈbʌnsn]: ~ **burner** Bunsen beki, Bunsen gaz lambası.

**bunt** *Am.* [bʌnt] *n. beysbol:* topa hafifçe vurma.

**bun.ting**[1] *orn.* [ˈbʌntiŋ] *n.* küçük kuş türlerinden biri.

**bun.ting**[2] [~] *n.* bayrak kumaşı, süs flamaları.

**buoy** ⬇ [bɔi] **1.** *n.* şamandıra; **2.** *v/t.* suyun gözüne tutmak, yüzdürmek; *mst* ~ **up** yüzdürmek, suyun üzerinde tutmak; *fig.* desteklemek, ümit vermek, cesaret vermek.

**buoy.an.cy** [ˈbɔiənsi] *n.* su yüzünde durabilme; *fig.* kudret, takat; ⸷ statik taşı-

ma gücü; *fig.* canlılık; neşe; **ˈbuoy.ant** ☐ yüzebilir, yüzen, batmaz; *fig.* neşeli; ⸷ fiyatların yükselme gücü.

**bur** ⬇ [bəː] *n.* dulavrat otu, pıtrak.

**Bur.ber.ry** [ˈbəːbəri] *n.* su geçirmez pardesü veya kumaş.

**bur.bot** *ichth.* [ˈbəːbət] *n.* morina cinsinden bir balık.

**bur.den**[1]- [ˈbəːdn] **1.** *n.* yük, ağırlık, ağır iş; sorumluluk; ♫ mükellefiyet, yükümlülük; ⬇ kargo; ⬇ tonilato, yük taşıma kapaistesi; **2.** *v/t.* yüklemek (s.o. with -e -i) *(a. fig.).*

**bur.den**[2] [~] *n.* ana fikir; nakarat.

**bur.den.some** [ˈbəːdnsəm] *adj.* külfetli, sıkıntı verici.

**bur.dock** ⬇ [ˈbəːdɔk] *n.* dulavrat otu.

**bu.reau** [ˈbjuərəu] *n., pl. a.* **bu.reaux** [~z] büro, yazıhane, daire, şube; *Am.* çekmeceli dolap; **bu.reau.ra.cy** [~ˈrɔkrəsi] *n.* bürokrasi, resmî formaliteler, kırtasiyecilik; **bu.reau.crat** [ˈbjuərəukræt] *n.* bürokrat, kırtasiyeci; **bu.reauˈcrat.ic** *adj.* (~ally) bürokratik.

**bu.rette** ⌕ [bjuəˈret] *n.* sıvı ölçmeye yarar cam tüp, büret.

**burg** *Am.* F [bəːg] *n.* kasaba, ufak şehir.

**bur.gee** ⬇ [ˈbəːdʒiː] *n.* üç köşeli flâma; flândra.

**bur.geon** *lit.* [ˈbəːdʒən] **1.** *n.* gonca, tomurcuk; rüşeym, embriyon; **2.** *vb.* tomurcuk ve filiz vermek, sürmek.

**bur.gess** [ˈbəːdʒis] *n.* oy verme hakkına sahip şehirli; *hist.* murahhas, delege, milletvekili.

**burgh** *Scots* [ˈbʌrə] *n.* kasaba; **bur.gher** *hist.* [ˈbəːgə] *n.* kasabada oturan kimse.

**bur.glar** [ˈbəːglə] *n. (ev soyan)* hırsız, gece hırsızı; **bur.glar.i.ous** ☐ hırsızlığa ait; **bur.gla.ry** [ˈ~gləri] *n.* ev soyma, hırsızlık; **ˈbur.gle** *vb.* ev soymak.

**bur.go.mas.ter** [ˈbəːgəumɑːstə] *n. (esp. Almanya ve Hollanda'da)* belediye başkanı.

**bur.gun.dy** [ˈbəːgəndi] *n.* Burgonya şarabı.

**bur.i.al** [ˈberiəl] *n.* gömme, defin; ~**-ground** *n.* mezarlık; ~ **serv.ice** cenaze töreni.

**bu.rin** ⊕ [ˈbjuərin] *n.* hakkâk kalemi.

**burke** [bəːk] *vb.* örtbas etm..

**burl** [bəːl] *n. (kumaş içinde)* düğüm.

**bur.lap** [ˈbəːlæp] *n.* çuval bezi.

**bur.lesque** [bəːˈlesk] **1.** *adj.* hicveden, gülünç, komik; **2.** *n.* hiciv, taşlama; **3.** *vb.* hicvetmek -i, taklidini yapmak -in, alaya almak -i.

**bur.ly** [ˈbəːli] *adj.* iriyarı, güçlü kuvvetli, sağlam yapılı.

63

**butt**

**Bur.mese** [bɔːˈmiːz] **1.** adj. Birmanyalı; **2.** n. Birmanya; Birmanya dili.

**burn** [bɔːn] **1.** n. yanık, yanık yarası; **2.** (irr.) v/t. & v/i. yakmak, yanmak, tutuş(tur)mak; parıldamak; ışık saçmak; **ˈburn.er** n. gaz ocağı memesi; yakıcı şey veya kimse; **ˈburn.ing** ☐ yanan, yanıcı; şiddetli, hararetli.

**bur.nish** [ˈbɔːniʃ] v/t. cilâlamak, perdahlamak, parlatmak (esp. maden); **ˈbur.nish.er** n. cilâcı; perdah taşı.

**burnt** [bɔːnt] pret. & p.p. of burn 2; ~ offering bir tanrıya sunmak için yakılan hayvan veya bitki.

**burp** Am. sl. [bɔːp] **1.** n. geğirme; **2.** v/t. & v/i. geğir(t)mek.

**burr** [bɔː] **1.** n. vızıltı; R harfinin boğazdan titrek şekilde söylenmesi; kozalak; ⊕ ince maden parçası, çapak, kalem pürüzü; **2.** v/i. R harfini boğazdan söylemek; **ˈ~-drill** n. ♀ matkap, delgi.

**bur.ro** F [ˈburəu] n. yük eşeği, merkep.

**bur.row** [ˈbʌrəu] **1.** n. oyuk, in, yuva; **2.** vb. oyuk açmak, tünel kazmak, yuva yapmak; kazdığı yerde saklanmak.

**bur.sar** [ˈbɔːsə] n. (esp. okullarda) muhasebeci, mutemet.

**bur.sa.ry** [ˈbɔːsəri] n. muhasebe; burs.

**burst** [bɔːst] **1.** n. patlama, fırlama, çatlama; ileri atılma; patlak, yarık; fig. coşkunluk, feveran; **2.** (irr.) v/t. & v/i. parla(t)mak (a. fig.); yar(ıl)mak, ayrılmak, ileri fırlamak; kırmak (a. fig.); ortaya dökülmek; görülür hale gelmek; ♦ birdenbire açmak; (çıban, apse v.b.) birdenbire çıkmak; (göz yaşı, kahkaha) boşanmak; ~ forth, ~ out birdenbire söylemek; fışkırmak; ~ into flame alevlenmek; ~ into tears ağlamaya başlamak, gözünden yaşlar boşanmak; ~ out laughing kahkaha koparmak; ~ upon s.o. b-ne birdenbire görünmek.

**bur.then** ↓ [ˈbɔːðən] = burden.

**bur.y** [ˈberi] v/t. gömmek, defnetmek; gizlemek, saklamak, örtmek; unutmak; **ˈbur.y.ing-ground** n. mezar(lık), kabir.

**bus** F [bʌs] **1.** n. otobüs; miss the ~ sl. fırsatı kaçırmak, geç kalmak; ~ boy Am. (lokantada) çırak; **2.** vb. otobüsle gitmek; otobüsle taşımak.

**bus.by** X [ˈbʌzbi] n. bir çeşit küçük kürklü şapka.

**bush** [buʃ] n. çalı, çalılık; ⊕ zıvana; burç; **bush.el** [ˈbuʃl] n. İngiliz kilesi (takriben 36.5 litre); hide one's light under a ~ yeteneğini gizlemek; **ˈbush.man** n. Güney Afrika yerlisi; **ˈbush-rang.er** n. fundalıklarda yaşıyan eşkiya.

**bush.y** [ˈbuʃi] adj. çalılık; (saç, sakal) fırça gibi.

**busi.ness** [ˈbiznis] n. iş, görev, meslek; ⊤ alışveriş, ticaret; iş yeri; mesele, problem; ~ of the day ruzname, gündem; on ~ iş için, iş hakkında; no admittance except on ~ işi olmıyan giremez; have no ~ to hakkı olmamak -e, ilgisi olmamak -le; mind one's own ~ kendi işine bakmak, karışmamak; send s.o. about his ~ b-ni defetmek, kovmak; ~ end F bşin tehlikeli tarafı; ~ hours pl. iş saatleri; **ˈ~-like** adj. ciddi, düzenli, sistemli; **ˈ~.man** n. iş adamı; ~ tour, ~ trip iş seyahati.

**bus.ker** [ˈbʌskə] n. sokak çalgıcısı.

**bus.kin** [ˈbʌskin] n. potin; trajedi.

**bus.man** [ˈbʌsmən] n. otobüs şoförü; ~'s holiday meslekle ilgili çalışmaları sürdürmek için yapılan tatil; **ˈbus-stop** n. otobüs durağı.

**bust¹** [bʌst] n. büst; göğüs.

**bust²** Am. F [~] n. mahvolma, iflâs, fiyasko.

**bus.tard** orn. [ˈbʌstəd] n. toy kuşu.

**bus.tle** [ˈbʌsl] **1.** n. faaliyet, telâş, koşuşma; eskiden kadın elbise eteklerine konulan kafes gibi yastık; **2.** v/i. telâşlanmak, telâşa vermek; acele et(tir)mek; kovalamak (a. fig.); **ˈbus.tler** n. faal, işgüzar adam; **ˈbus.tling** ☐ çalışkan, işgüzar.

**bust-up** F [ˈbʌstʌp] n. kavga, gümbürtü, yaygara.

**bus.y** [ˈbizi] **1.** ☐ faal, iş gören, meşgul (with -le); hareketli, canlı; teleph. meşgul; be ~ işi olm., meşgul olm.; **2.** vb. mst ~ o.s. meşgul olm., uğraşmak (with, in, at, about -le); **ˈ~.bod.y** n. her işe burnunu sokan kimse; işgüzar; **ˈbus.y.ness** n. gayret, faaliyet; işgüzarlık.

**but** [bʌt, bət] **1.** cj. ama, fakat, lâkin, ancak; halbuki; şu kadar ki; **2.** prp. -den başka, -den hariç; the next ~ one birinci değil ikinci; ~ for sayesinde, ...olmasaydı; **3.** adv. sadece, yalnız, sırf; ~ just demin, demincek; henüz; all ~ ...den gayrı, az kalsın; nothing ~ sırf, hepsi; ...den başka bir şey değil; I cannot ~ inf. ...memek mümkün değil, ...mek zorundayım; **4.** n. «fakat» kelimesi, itiraz.

**butch.er** [ˈbutʃə] **1.** n. kasap, celep; fig. katil, cani; **2.** v/t. (kasaplık) hayvan kesmek; fig. öldürmek, boğazlamak; **ˈbutch.er.y** n. kasaplık (a. fig.); mezbaha, salhane; ~ business kasaplık.

**but.ler** [ˈbʌtlə] n. kâhyâ; sofracı.

**butt¹** [bʌt] **1.** n. tos; a. ~ end bşin enli dibi *(ağaç vs.)*; izmarit; *silah*: dipçik; ⊕ manşet, birleştirme sathı; hedef levhası gerisindeki toprak siper; the ~s *pl.* atış alanı; *fig.* amaç, gaye; **2.** *vb.* tos vurmak; ~ in F karışmak *-e.*

**butt²** [~] *n.* büyük şarap fıçısı, damacana.

**but.ter** [ˈbʌtə] **1.** *n.* tereyağı; F kompliman, kur, yağcılık; as if ~ would not melt in his mouth çok nazik ve masum görünüyor *(öyle olmadığı halde)*; **2.** *v/t.* tereyağı sürmek *-e*; *fig.* kompliman yapmak, yağ çekmek; '~.cup *n.* ♣ düğünçiçeği; '~-fin.gers *n.* sakar kimse; '~.fly *n.* kelebek; *fig.* kelebek peşinde, havai kimse; '~.milk *n.* yayık ayranı; **but.ter.y 1.** *adj.* tereyağı gibi; tereyağlı...; **2.** *n.* kiler.

**but.tock** [ˈbʌtək] *n. mst* **but.tocks** *pl.* kalça, kıç, F popo.

**but.ton** [ˈbʌtn] **1.** *n.* düğme; ♣ konca, tomurcuk, sürgün; ~s *sg.* F otel oğlanı; **2.** *v/t. & v/i. oft.* ~ up düğmele(n)mek, ilikle(n)mek; '~.hole **1.** *n.* ilik; yakaya takılan çiçek; **2.** *v/t.* ilik açmak; yakalayıp zorla dinletmek; '~-hook *n.* düğme kancası; '~.wood *n.* ♣ çınar ağacı.

**but.tress** [ˈbʌtris] **1.** *n.* payanda, destek *(a. fig.)*; **2.** *v/t.* ~ up ayak koymak, payanda koymak; *fig.* desteklemek, takviye etm..

**bux.om** [ˈbʌksəm] *adj. (kadın)* dolgun, bıldırcın gibi, cazip, çekici, neşeli.

**buy** [bai] *(irr.) v/t.* almak, satın almak *(from -den)*; *fig.* bş karşılığında elde etm. (with *-le)*; 'buy.er *n.* alıcı, müşteri; satın alıcı, mübayaacı; 'buy.ing *comb.* satın alma...

**buzz** [bʌz] **1.** *n.* vızıltı, gürültü; F telefon konuşması; ~ saw *Am.* devvar testere; **2.** *vb.* vızıldamak, fısıldamak; *(kulak)* çınlamak; telefon etm.; ✈ alçaktan ve süratli uçmak.

**buz.zard** *orn.* [ˈbʌzəd] *n.* bir cins şahin.

**buzz.er** ⚡ [ˈbʌzə] *n.* vızıltılı sinyal veren elektrik zili; siren.

**by** [bai] **1.** *prp. -in* yanında, yakınında, nezdinde; ile, vasıtasiyle; tarafından, ...den; *-e* göre, *-e* nazaran; yakınından, yanından; *-e* kadar; hakkında; North ~ East kuzeydoğuya doğru; side ~ side yan yana; ~ day gündüz, gündüzün; ~ now şimdiye kadar; ~ the time (that) kadar, dek, değin; ~ the dozen düzine düzine; ~ far çok daha fazla, fersah fersah; 30 feet ~ 15 otuza onbeş ebadında; ~ o.s. yalnız, kendi kendine, bir köşede; ~ land karadan, yara yolu ile; ~ rail trenle; day ~ day her gün, günden güne; ~ twos ikişer ikişer; **2.** *adv.* bir yana, bir tarafa; yakın, yanında; ~ and ~ yavaş yavaş, çok. geçmeden, birazdan; ~ the ~ pek yakında, bu günlerde; yavaş yavaş, tedricen; close ~ yakında, civarda; go ~ geçip gitmek; ~ and large genellikle; **3.** *adj.* yan..., tali...

**bye** [bai] *n. spor:* yarışmacının tek kalması, otomatik olarak tur atlama.

**bye-bye** F [baiˈbai] *int.* Allaha ısmarladık!; Hoşça kalın!; Güle güle!

**by...:** '~-e.lec.tion *n.* ara seçim; '~.gone **1.** *adj.* geçmiş, eski; **2.** *n.* ~s *pl.* geçmiş olan şey; let ~s be ~s geçmişi unutmak, geçmişe sünger çekmek; '~-law *n.* nizamname, statü; '~-line *n. Am. (makalede)* yazar adının verildiği satır; '~-name *n.* lakap; '~-pass **1.** *n.* dolaştırma; kestirme yol, varyant; ⚡ kısa devre; **2.** *vb.* yanından geçmek, uğramamak; *(trafik)* başka yola vermek; bertaraf etm.; '~-path *n.* dolaylı yol, patika; '~-play *n. thea.* asıl oyunun yanısıra yapılan önemi az hareket; '~-prod.uct *n.* yan ürün.

**byre** [ˈbaiə] *n.* inek ahırı.

**by-road** [ˈbairəud] *n.* yan yol.

**by...:** '~.stand.er *n.* seyirci, olaya karışmadan seyreden kimse; '~-street *n.* yan sokak; '~-way *n.* gizli yol, dolaşık yol; '~-word *n.* darbımesel, atalarsözü; be a ~ for timsali olm. *-in.*

**By.zan.tine** [biˈzæntain] **1.** *adj.* Bizans'a ait; **2.** *n.* Bizanslı.

# C

cab [kæb] n. kira arabası, taksi; otobüs; lokomotifin kapalı kısmı, 🚂 makinist yeri, (otobüs) şoför yeri.

ca.bal [kə'bæl] 1. n. hile, entrika, fitne; 2. v/i. bşde hile, dalavere yapmak, entrika çevirmek, desise kurmak.

cab.a.ret [ˈkæbərei] n. çalgılı meyhane, kabare.

cab.bage [ˈkæbidʒ] n. bir baş lahana; ~ butterfly lahana yapraklarında yaşayan beyaz kelebek; ~ lettuce top salata.

cab.ba.lis.tic, cab.ba.lis.ti.cal □ [kæbə'listik(əl)] sırları açıklama ilmine ait.

cab.by [ˈkæbi] n. arabacı.

cab.in [ˈkæbin] 1. n. kulübe; hücre; ⚓ kamara; 2. vb. ağıllandırmak; bir yere sıkıştırmak, tıkmak; '~-boy n. ⚓ kamarot; subay hizmet eri; ~ class ikinci sınıf; ~ cruis.er ⚓ kamaralı büyük gemi.

cab.i.net [ˈkæbinit] n. kabine, küçük oda; çekmeceli, vitrinli dolap; kabine, bakanlar kurulu; ♀ Council vekiller meclisi; '~-mak.er n. doğramacı, marangoz.

ca.ble [keibl] 1. n. kablo; ⚓ palamar; telgraf; buried ~ yeraltı kablosu; 2. vb. telgraf çekmek; kablo ile bağlamak; '~-car n. kablo ile işlenen vagon, teleferik; ~.gram [ˈ~græm] n. telgraf.

cab.man [ˈkæbmən] n. arabacı, taksi şoförü.

ca.boo.dle sl. [kə'bu:dl]: the whole ~ bütün herkes, herşey.

ca.boose [kə'bu:s] n. ⚓ gemi mutfağı; Am. 🚂 yük treni işçilerine ait vagon.

cab.ri.o.let part. mot. [ˈkæbriə'lei] n. dört tekerlekli atlı araba; iki kapılı dört kişilik araba; bir vagonun arkasındaki ufak kompartman.

cab-stand [ˈkæbstænd] n. taksi, fayton durağı.

ca'can.ny ⊕ [ˈkɑːˈkæni] n. işçilerin işi yavaşlatma eylemi.

ca.ca.o [kə'kɑːəu] n. kakao ağacı, kakao.

cache [kæʃ] 1. n. bir şeyi saklamak için gizli yer, gizli yerde saklanan şey; 2. v/t. gizli bir yere bş saklamak.

cack.le [ˈkækl] 1 n. gevezelik; tavuk gıdaklaması; 2 v/i. gevezelik etm.; gıdaklamak; 'cack.ler n. gıdaklayan; fig. geveze.

ca.coph.o.ny [kæ'kɔfəni] n. kötü ses, ahenksizlik.

cac.tus ⚘ [ˈkæktəs] n. kaktüs.

cad F [kæd] n. kaba kimse; alçak adam.

ca.das.tre [kə'dæstə] n. tapu sicili, kadastro.

ca.dav.er.ous □ [kə'dævərəs] ölü gibi, sapsarı.

cad.die [ˈkædi] n. oyun sırasında golfçünün sopalarını taşıyan kişi.

cad.dis zo. [ˈkædis] n. kurtçuk, tırtıl.

cad.dish F □ [ˈkædiʃ] adj. kaba.

cad.dy [ˈkædi] n. çay kutusu; = caddie.

ca.dence [ˈkeidəns] n. ♪ ritim, ahenk; sesin derece derece inmesi.

ca.det [kə'det] n. askerî okul öğrencisi; ~ corps asker talimi gören yetişkinler taburu.

cadge [kædʒ] v/t. & v/i. yalvarıp yakarmak, dilenmek; seyyar satıcılık etm.; 'cadg.er n. bedavacı; dilenci; seyyar satıcı.

ca.di [ˈkɑːdi] n. (bazı İslâm ülkelerinde) kadı, yargıç.

cad.mi.um ⚗ [ˈkædmiəm] n. sembolü «Ca» olan beyaz, yumuşak bir maden, kadmiyum.

cad.re [ˈkɑːdə] n. çerçeve, plan; kadro; ✗ gerektiğinde kullanmak üzere iyi hazırlanmış birlik veya bu gruptan biri.

ca.du.cous ⚘ & zo. [kə'dju:kəs] adj. zamansız ve mevsimsiz dökülen.

cae.cum anat. [ˈsi:kəm] n. kör bağırsak, apandis.

Cae.sar [ˈsi:zə] n. Sezar; Cae.sar.i.an [si:'zɛəriən] adj. Sezar'a ait.

cae.su.ra [si:zjuərə] n. bir mısranın okunuşunda hafifçe duraklanacak yer.

ca.fé [ˈkæfei] n. kahvehane, küçük restoran, lokanta, pastahane.

caf.e.te.ri.a [kæfi'tiəriə] n. kafeterya, garsonsuz lokanta.

**caf.e.to.ri.um** *Am.* [kæfi'tɔːriəm] *n.* kantin ve dinlenme salonu.

**caf.fe.ine** ['kæfiːn] *n.* kahve ve çayda bulunan uyarıcı, kafein.

**cage** [keidʒ] **1.** *n.* kafes *(a. fig.); hapishane; ⚔ asansör; 2. v/t. kafese koymak; hapse atmak.

**cage.y** ☐ *part. Am.* ['keidʒi] kurnaz, hilekâr, pişkin.

**cairn** [kɛən] *n.* abide veya mezara benzer taş yığını.

**cais.son** [kə'suːn] *n.* ✕ cephane arabası; *hidrolik inşaat:* keson.

**ca.tiff** ['keitif] *adj. & n.* alçak, ahlâksız.

**ca.jole** [kə'dʒəul] *v/t. & v/i.* birisini tatlılıkla kandırmak veya aldatmak; **ca-jol.er** *n.* dalkavuk, pohpohçu, komplimancı; **ca'jol.er.y** *n.* kompliman, kur.

**cake** [keik] **1.** *n.* kek, pasta, kurabiye, çörek; parça, kısım, tane, kalıp *(sabun vs.); ~s and ale eğlence; a piece of ~ sl.* çocuk oyuncağı, çok kolay; like hot ~s kapış kapışa; **2.** *vb.* katılaş(tır)mak, kalıplaşmak.

**cal.a.bash** ['kæləbæʃ] *n.* sukabağı; sukabağından yapılmış su kabı.

**cal.a.mine** *min.* ['kæləmain] *n.* tutya taşı.

**ca.lam.i.tous** ☐ [kə'læmitəs] felâketli, belâlı; **ca'lam.i.ty** *n.* felâket, belâ, musibet, afet; **ca'lam.i.ty-howl.er** *n.* karamsar, kötümser; **ca'lam.i.ty-howl.ing** *n. Am.* karamsarlık.

**cal.car.e.ous** [kæl'kɛəriəs] *adj.* kalsiyumlu, kireçli.

**cal.ce.o.la.ri.a** ♀ [kælsiə'lɛəriə] *n.* çanta çiçeği.

**cal.ci.fi.ca.tion** [kælsifi'keiʃən] *n.* kireç tuzları ile sertleştirme, taş haline getirme işlemi; **cal.ci.fy** ['~fai] *vb.* kireçlenmek; kireç haline getirmek; **cal.ci.na.tion** ⚗ [kælsi'neiʃən] *n.* yakma, kavurma, damıtma; **cal.cine** ⚗ [kælsain] *vb.* yakarak toz haline getirmek veya gelmek; **'cal.cite** *n. min.* kalsiyum karbonat; **cal.ci.um** ⚗ ['~siəm] *n.* sembolü «Ca» olan eleman, Kalsiyum; **cal.ci.um car.bide** ⚗ karpit.

**cal.cu.la.ble** ['kælkjuləbl] *adj.* hesap edilebilir; güvenilir; **cal.cu.late** ['~leit] *v/t.* hesaplamak, hesap ederek bulmak, saymak; **~d** hesaplanmış; *v/i.* hesap etm., güvenmek (on, upon *-e*); F *Am.* tahmin etm.; calculating machine hesap makinesi; **cal.cu'la.tion** *n.* hesap, tahmin; **cal.cu.lus** ['~ləs] *n.* ⚕ entegral hesabı; ⚕ böbrek veya mesane taşı.

**cal.dron** ['kɔːldrən] *n.* kazan.

**cal.en.dar** ['kælində] **1.** *n.* takvim; liste;

**2.** *v/t.* zaman sırası ile kaydetmek.

**cal.en.der** ⊕ [~] **1.** *n.* perdah makinesi; **2.** *v/t.* perdahlamak, baskıya koymak.

**cal.ends** ['kælindz]: on the Greek ~ hiçbir zaman, asla, balık kavağa çıkınca.

**calf** [kaːf] *n., pl.* **calves** [kaːvz] dana, buzağı; *fig.* beceriksiz genç; *a.* ~-leather vidala; meşin cilt; kayış; *anat.* baldır; in ~, with ~ yüklü; gebe (buzağı); ~ love F. ilk aşk, ilk göz ağrısı; **'~-skin** *n.* dana postu.

**cal.i.brate** ⊕ ['kælibreit] *v/t.* çap ölçmek; ayar etm.; **cal.i.bre** ['~bə] *n.* çap; *fig. sanat:* kabiliyet, yetenek.

**cal.i.co** ⟝ ['kælikəu] *n.* pamuk bez, basma, empirme; hasse, kaliko.

**Cal.i.for.nian** [kæli'fɔːnjən] **1.** *adj.* Kaliforniya'ya ait; **2.** *n.* Kaliforniyalı.

**ca.liph** ['kælif] *n.* halife; **cal.iph.ate** ['~eit] *n.* hilâfet, halifelik.

**calk** [kɔːk] **1.** *n.* buzmıhı, kayar; **2.** *v/t.* ⚓ kalafat etm.; buzmıhı çakmak; **calk-in** ['kælkin] *s.* calk **1.**

**call** [kɔːl] **1.** *n.* seslenme, bağırma, içeri çağırma; *fig.* çağrı, davet (to *-e*); yoklama; *teleph.* arama; *thea.* sahneye çağırma; *hunt.* boru; kısa ziyaret; hak iddiası, talep; uğrama, görüşme; işaret; ~ money ⟝ vadesiz verilen borç para; port of ~ gemilerin kısa süreli uğradıkları liman, emir limanı; on ~ ⟝ vaki talep üzerine; **2.** *v/t.* çağırmak, *b-ne* gelsin diye bağırmak, seslenmek; uyandırmak; adlandırmak, demek; davet etm.; çağrıda bulunmak; telefon etm.; uğramak, ziyaret etm.; *iskambil:* istemek; bə ~ed bşe *(b-ne)* ...demek, bşi tasvif etm.; ~ s.o. names sövmek, sövüp saymak, hakaret etm.; ~ s.o. down *Am. sl. b-ni* azarlamak; ~ forth meydan vermek *-e*, yol açmak *-e*; gayrete getirmek; ~ in *(para)* geri çekmek, toplamak; celbetmek, davet etm., içeri çağırmak; ~ out bağırmak; *(işçi)* greve çağırmak; ~ up yukarı çağırmak; ✕ silah altına almak, celbetmek; hatırlamak; *teleph.* aramak; *v/i.* bağırmak, çağırmak; *b-ne* uğramak, *b-ni* ziyaret etm.; ~ at a port limana uğramak; ~ for *b-ni veya bşi* uğrayıp almak; *thea. b-ni* sahneye çağırmak; ~ to be (left till) ~ed for gelinip alınacak, postrestant; ~ on ziyaret etm. *-i*, uğramak *-e*; ~ to ...diye seslenmek *(veya* haykırmak) **'call.a.ble** *adj.* istenebilen *(para);* **'call-box** *n.* telefon kulübesi; **'call.er** *n.* ziyaretçi; *teleph.* telefon eden kişi; **'~-girl** *n.* fahişe, tele-kız.

cal.li.graph.ic [ˈkæliˈgræfik] adj. (~ally) güzel yazı, hattatlığa ait; cal.lig.ra.phy [kəˈligrəfi] n. güzel yazı, hattatlık.

call.ing [ˈkɔːliŋ] n. iş, meslek; ~ card Am. kartvizit, vizita kartı.

cal.li.pers [ˈkælipəz] n. pl. çap pergeli, kompas.

cal.lis.then.ics [kælisˈθeniks] adj. mst sg. özellikle bayanlar tarafından vücut güzelliği için aletsiz yapılan vücut hareketleri.

call-of.fice [ˈkɔːlɔfis] n. telefon dairesi, telefon kulübesi.

cal.los.i.ty [kælˈlɔsiti] n. nasır, nasırlanma; fig. nasırlaşmış olma, vurdumduymazlık; ˈcal.lous □ nasırlı, katı; fig. hissiz, duyguları körelmiş.

cal.low [ˈkæləu] adj. uçacak hale gelmemiş, tüysüz (kuş); fig. tecrübesiz, toy, acemi çaylak.

call-up [ˈkɔːlʌp] n. davet, çağrı.

calm [kɑːm] 1. □ sakin, durgun; ağırbaşlı (a. fig.); 2. n. sakinlik, hareketsizlik (a .fig.); ↓ rüzgârın kesilmesi; 3. (~ down) v/i.yatışmak; v/t. b-ni teskin etm., yatıştırmak; ˈcalm.ness n. sakinlik, durgunluk.

Cal.or gas [ˈkælɔˈgæs] n. bütan gazı.

ca.lor.ic phys. [kəˈlɔrik] n. ısı; ~-engine sıcak hava veren motor; cal.o.rie phys. [ˈkæləri] n. kalori, ısı birimi; cal.o.rif.ic [kæleˈrifik] adj. ısı meydana getiren, ısıtıcı.

cal.trop ↓ [ˈkæltrəp] n. boğa dikeni.

ca.lum.ni.ate [kəˈlʌmnieit] v/t. b-ne iftira etm.; ca.lum.ni.a.tion n. iftira; caˈlum.ni.a.tor n. iftiracı; caˈlum.ni.ous □ iftira türünden; cal.um.ny [ˈkæləmni] n. iftira.

Cal.va.ry [ˈkælvəri] n. Hazreti İsa'nın çarmıha gerildiği yer; İsa'nın haçlanmasının anlatımı; ♀ eza, cefa.

calve [kɑːv] v/i. buzağı doğurmak; calves [kɑːvz] n. pl. of calf.

Cal.vin.ism [ˈkælvinizəm] n. İsviçreli din bilimci Calvin'in doktrinleri, Kalvinizm.

ca.lyp.so [kəˈlipsəu] n. kalipso, Batı Hintlilerin isteklerini anlatmak için geliştirdikleri şarkı.

ca.lyx ♀ & zo. [ˈkeiliks] n., pl. cal.y.ces [ˈ~lisiːz] çiçek zarfı, çanak.

cam ⊕ [kæm] n. kam, mil dirseği; ~ gear eksantrik dişlisi.

cam.ber ⊕ [ˈkæmbə] 1. n. kubbe, kemer; hafif kavis; 2. v/t. kubbe, kemer gibi kabartmak.

cam.bric [ˈkeimbrik] n. ince pamuklu kumaş, patiska.

came [keim] pret. of come.

cam.el [ˈkæməl] n. zo. deve; ↓ tombaz, kayık biçiminde duba.

ca.mel.li.a ♀ [kəˈmiːljə] n. kamelya, çin gülü.

cam.e.o [ˈkæmiəu] n. işlemeli akik.

cam.er.a [ˈkæmərə] n. fotoğraf makinesi, kamera; in ~ ♕ yargıcın özel odasında gizli olarak, gizli celsede.

cami-knick.ers [ˈkæmiˈnikəz] n. pl. kadın kombinezonu.

cam.i.on [ˈkæmiən] n. kamyon.

cam.o.mile ♀ [ˈkæməumail] n. bir tür papatya; ~ tea papatya çayı.

cam.ou.flage ✕ [ˈkæmuflɑːʒ] 1. n. kamuflaj; 2. v/t. kamufle etm., gizlemek.

camp [kæmp] 1. n. kamp; ✕ ordugâh; ~ bed portatif karyola; ~ chair, ~ stool portatif iskemle; 2. v/i. ordugâh, kamp kurmak; ~ out kamp yapmak, çadırda yatmak.

cam.paign [kæmˈpein] 1. n. sefer, savaş; pol. & fig. meydan muharebesi, mücadele; kampanya; election ~ seçim kampanyası; 2. v/i. sefere çıkmak; mücadele etm.; kampanyaya katılmak; camˈpaign.er n. kampanyaya katılan kişi; old ~ F tecrübeli kişi.

camp.er [ˈkæmpə] n. kampçı, kamp yapan kişi; içinde yatılabilen özel döşenmiş kamp arabası.

cam.phor [ˈkæmfə] n. kâfur; cam.phor.at.ed [ˈ~reitid] adj. kâfurlu.

camp.ing [ˈkæmpiŋ] n. kamping, kamp yapma.

cam.pus Am. [ˈkæmpəs] n. üniversite veya okul arazisi, kampus.

cam.shaft ⊕ [ˈkæmʃɑːft] n. kamlı mil.

can¹ [kæn] (irr.) v/aux. -ebilmek.

can² [~] 1. n. kap, kutu; Am. konserve kutusu; 2. v/t. konserve yapmak, kutuya koymak.

Ca.na.di.an [kəˈneidjən] 1. n. Kanadalı; 2. adj. Kanada ile ilgili, Kanada...

ca.nal [kəˈnæl] n. kanal, mecra, suyolu; anat. vücuttaki sıvıların akıştığı yol; ~-boat mavuna, salapurya; ca.nal.i.za.tion [kænəlaiˈzeiʃən] n. kanal açma; kanalizasyon tesisatı; ca.nal.ize vb. kanalizasyon tesisatı yapmak, kanal açmak.

can.a.pé [ˈkænəpei] n. ekmek üzerine peynir vs. sürülerek yapılan ordövr, kanepe.

ca.nard [kæˈnɑːd] n. uydurma haber, asılsız havadis.

ca.nar.y [kəˈnɛəri] n. a. ~-bird kanarya.

can.cel [ˈkænsəl] v/t. silmek, çizmek; kaldırmak, iptal etm.; ~ out Ⓐ kısaltmak, götürmek; be ~led iptal edilmiş olm.;

can.cel'la.tion *n.* silme, bozma, iptal, iade; iptal damgası.

can.cer ['kænsə] *n.* ♊ kanser; ♀ *ast.* Yengeç Burcu; **'can.cer.ous** *adj.* kanserli, kanser gibi.

can.did □ ['kændid] samimi, candan; yalansız, dürüst.

can.di.da.cy ['kændidəsi] *n.* namzetlik, adaylık; **can.di.date** ['kændidit] *n.* talip, aday, namzet (for -e); **can.di.da.ture** ['ᵈᵗʃə] *n.* namzetlik, adaylık.

can.died ['kændid] *adj.* şekerle kaplanmış, şekerli; *fig.* göze hoş görünen, gönül okşayıcı; tatlı dilli.

can.dle ['kændl] *n.* mum, kandil; ~ power mum *(ışık kuvvet birimi);* hold a ~ to *fig.* eline su dökmek, tırnağı olm.; not worth the ~ zahmete değmez, astarı yüzünden pahalı; burn the ~ at both ends değişik işler yaparak kuvvetini tüketmek, gece gündüz eğlenmek; **'~.light** *n.* mum ışığı; **Can.dle.mas** *eccl.* ['ᵗməs] *n.* Şubat'ın ikisine rastlayan Hazreti Meryem yortusu; **'can.dle.stick** *n.* şamdan.

can.dour ['kændə] *n.* açık kalplilik, samimiyet; tarafsızlık, doğruluk.

can.dy ['kændi] **1.** *n.* şekerleme, şeker, bonbon; **2.** *v/i.* şekerlenmek; *v/t.* şekerleme yapmak; şekerleme haline getirmek.

cane [kein] **1.** *n.* ♣ kamış, bambu; baston, değnek; **2.** *v/t. b-ni* dövmek, *b-ne* dayak atmak; *(mobilya)* kamışla tamir etm.; ~ **sug.ar** şeker kamışından yapılmış şeker.

ca.nine **1.** ['keinain] *adj.* köpek gibi, kurt veya köpek ile ilgili; **2.** ['kænain] *n. a.* ~ tooth köpekdişi.

can.is.ter ['kænistə] *n. (kahve, çay v.b. konulan)* teneke kutu.

can.ker ['kæŋkə] **1.** *n.* ♊ ağız ve kulakta meydana gelen yara, pamukçuk; ♣ buğday pası; *fig.* çürütücü etki; **2.** *vb.* kemirmek; çürü(t)mek, mahvolmak; **'can.kered** *adj. fig.* kötü huylu; **'can.ker.ous** *adj.* yer yer çürümekte olan; yozlaştıran.

canned *Am* [kænd] *adj.* kutulanmış.

can.ner.y *Am.* ['kænəri] *n.* konserve imaâthanesi.

can.ni.bal ['kænibəl] **1.** *n.* yamyam; kendi cinsinin etini yiyen hayvan; **2.** *adj.* yamyamca, yamyamlıkla ilgili; **'can.ni.bal.ism** *n.* yamyamlık; **'can.ni.bal.ize** *v/t.* değişme için parçalara ayırmak *(araba vs.),* ⊕ çıkma parça takmak.

can.non ['kænən] **1.** *n.* ✕ top; *bilârdo:* karambol; **2.** *v/t.* karambol yapmak; topa

tutmak; çarpmak *(fig. against, with);* **can.non.ade** [~'neid] *n.* top ateşi, topla bombardıman; **'can.non-fod.der** *n.* harpte araç gibi düşünülüp harcanan askerler.

can.not ['kænɔt] *inf.* -ememek.

can.ny □ *Scots* ['kæni] dikkatli, itinalı, tedbirli, düşünceli; hareketsiz, sakin; açıkgöz, cin fikirli.

ca.noe [kə'nu:] **1.** *n.* hafif sandal, kano; **2.** *v/i.* botta kürek çekmek, kano ile geçmek, kano ile yük taşımak.

can.on ['kænən] *n.* kanun, kaide; kilise kanunu; dinî liste; katedralle bağlantı sağlayan rahip; ~ law kilise kanunu.

ca.ñon ['kænjən] = canyon.

can.on.ess ['kænənis] *n.* katedral veya büyük kiliselerin özel heyetlerinin kadın üyesi; **can.on.i.za.tion** [~nai'zeiʃən] *n.* bir azizi kilisenin resmen kabul edip tanıması; **'can.on.ize** *v/t. (ölmüş birini)* kilisece aziz diye resmen kabul edip tanımak; **'can.on.ry** *n.* katedral veya büyük kiliselerin özel heyetlerinde üyelik.

ca.noo.dle *sl.* [kə'nu:dl] *vb.* kucaklamak, okşamak.

can.o.py ['kænəpi] **1.** *n.* gölgelik, tente, çardak, sayvan; *fig.* saçak; ⚓ uçakların ön tarafındaki siper; **2.** *v/t.* üstünü örtmek.

cant¹ [kænt] **1.** *n.* meyil; eğilme; **2.** *v/t. & v/i.* eğ(il)mek; meylet(tir)mek, yan yat(ır)mak; ~ over devirmek, bir yanı üzerine çevirmek.

cant² [~] **1.** *n.* ikiyüzlülük, riyakârlık; argo; thieves' ~ hırsızların kullandığı dil, argo; **2.** *vb.* riyakârlıkla söylemek.

can't F [ka:nt] = cannot.

Can.tab F ['kæntæb] *n.* Cambridge ile ilgili (öğrenci).

can.ta.loup ♣ ['kæntəlu:p] *n.* bir tür kücük kavun.

can.tan.ker.ous F □ [kən'tæŋkərəs] ters, aksi, huysuz, kavgacı.

can.teen [kæn'ti:n] *n.* ✕ matara; kantin *(kışla, fabrika vs.'de);* ✕ yemek kabı; sofra takımı *(çatal, bıçak, kaşık).*

can.ter ['kæntə] **1.** *n.* atın eşkin gidişi; **2.** *v/i.* eşkin gitmek; *v/t. (atı)* eşkin yürütmek.

can.ter.bur.y ['kæntəbəri] *n.* nota sehpası; ♊ bell ♣ bir tür çan çiçeği.

can.thar.i.des ♊ ['kæn'θæridi:z] *n. pl., mst sg.* kunduz böceğinden yapılan bir müstahzar.

can.ti.cle ['kæntikl] *n.* temcit, methiye; ~s *pl.* İncil'den alınan kısa dini şarkı.

can.ti.le.ver ⌂ ['kæntili:və] *n.* dirsek, destek; ~ **bridge** destekler üzerine kurulmuş köprü.

**can.to** [ˈkæntəu] *n.* uzun şiirlerin bölümlerinden biri.

**can.ton 1.** [ˈkæntɔn] *n. (özellikle İsviçre'deki)* küçük eyalet, kanton; **2.** ✕ [kənˈtuːn] *v/t.* konaklatmak, konağa yerleştirmek; ˈ**can.ton.ment** *n.* ✕ konak, karargâh, ordugâh.

**can.vas** [ˈkænvəs] *n.* keten bezi, kanava, yelken bezi; çadır, tente; yelken; *paint.* yağlı boya resim, tablo, tuval.

**can.vass** [~] **1.** *n.* sipariş toplama, oy toplama, propaganda; seçim kampanyası; **2.** *vb.* müzakere etm., tartışmak, görüşmek; soruşturmak; dolaşarak oy veya sipariş toplamak; ˈ**can.vass.er** *n.* talip, müracaat eden; oy veya sipariş toplayan kişi.

**can.yon** [ˈkænjən] *n.* kanyon, derin ve uçurumlu dar boğaz, dere yatağı.

**caou.tchouc** [ˈkautʃuk] *n.* kauçuk, lastik.

**cap** [kæp] **1.** *n.* kasket, başlık; kapak; *univ.* kep, baret; ⊕, ⚔ *etc.* kapak, başlık, kapsül; ~ **and bells** çıngıraklı soytarı külahı; ~ **and gown** dört köşeli siyah başlık ve uzun siyah cüppeden oluşan üniversiteye ait kıyafet; ~ **in hand** *fig.* şapkası elinde, mütevazi tavırla; **set one's** ~ **at** s.o. *(bir erkeği)* cezbetmeye çalışmak; **2.** *vb.* başlık giydirmek -*e*; taçlandırmak -*i*; örtmek, kapamak.

**ca.pa.bil.i.ty** [keipəˈbiliti] *n.* kabiliyet, yetenek; ˈ**ca.pa.ble** ☐ muktedir, kabiliyetli, ehliyetli, yetenekli (**of** -*e*).

**ca.pa.cious** ☐ [kəˈpeiʃəs] geniş, büyük; **ca.pac.i.tate** [kəˈpæsiteit] *v/t.* olası kılmak; yetki vermek; **ca**ˈ**pac.i.ty 1.** *n.* istiap, sığdırma; yetenek, kabiliyet; kapasite; ⊕ verim; mevki, sıfat; **disposing** (or **legal**) ~ medeni hakları kullanma; **full to** ~ tamamen dolu.

**cap-à-pie** [kæpəˈpiː] *adv.* tepeden tırnağa kadar, her noktada.

**ca.par.i.son** *lit.* [kəˈpærisn] *n.* eyer örtüsü, çaprak, haşe; *fig.* süs, ziynet; moda kıyafet.

**cape¹** [keip] *n. geogr.* burun.

**cape²** [~] *n.* pelerin, kap, atkı.

**caper¹** ⚘ [ˈkeipə] *n.* kebere.

**ca.per²** [~] **1.** *n.* sıçrayıp oynama *(a. fig.)*, coşma, havada takla atma; **cut** ~**s** = **2.** *v/i.* **yaramazlık** etm., havada takla atmak, coşmak, sıçramak.

**ca.pi.as** ⅊ [ˈkeipiæs] *n.*: **writ of** ~ tutuklama emri.

**cap.il.lar.i.ty** *phys.* [kæpiˈlæriti] *n.* kapilarite, sıvıların kılcal borulara veya damarlara nüfuz etme özelliği; **cap.il.lar.y** [kəˈpiləri] **1.** *adj.* kılcal damarlara ait; **2.** *n. anat.* kılcal damar.

**cap.i.tal** [ˈkæpitl] **1.** ☐ **sermaye...**; sermayeye ait; baş, başlıca, asıl, ana; en büyük, mükemmel; ~ **crime** cezası idam olan suç; ~ **punishment** ölüm cezası; **2.** *n.* başkent, hükümet merkezi; sermaye, kapital; *a.* ~ **letter** *typ.* majüskül, büyük harf; ♠ direk başlığı; **cap.i.tal.ism** [ˈ~təlizəm] *n.* kapitalizm, anamalcılık; ˈ**cap.i.tal.ist** *n.* kapitalist, anamalcı; **cap.i.tal**ˈ**is.tic** *adj.* kapitalistliğe ait, anamalcılıkla ilgili; **cap.i.tal.i.za.tion** [kəpitəlaiˈzeiʃən] *n.* sermaye miktarı; sermayelendirme, sermayeye katma; **cap**ˈ**i.tal.ize** *v/t.* sermayeye çevirmek; sermaye olarak kullanmak; majüskül ile yazmak.

**cap.i.ta.tion** [kæpiˈteiʃən] *n. a.* ~ **tax** kişi başına vergi; baş vergisi.

**Cap.i.tol** [ˈkæpitl] *n.* Eski Roma'da Jupiter'in mabedi; Washington'da A.B.D. Kongresinin toplandığı bina, Amerika devletlerinden herhangi birinin eyalet meclisi binası.

**ca.pit.u.late** [kəˈpitjuleit] *v/i.* teslim olm.; silahları bırakmak, teslim şartlarını kararlaştırmak; **ca.pit.u**ˈ**la.tion** *n.* şartlı teslim; kapitülasyonlar, yabancılara özgü imtiyazlar.

**ca.pon** [ˈkeipən] *n.* semirmesi için kısırlaştırılmış horoz.

**ca.price** [kəˈpriːs] *n.* istek, geçici arzu, kapris; ♪ kapriçiyo; **ca.pri.cious** ☐ [kəˈpriʃəs] kaprisli, maymun iştahlı; **ca**ˈ**pri.cious.ness** *n.* maymun iştahlılık, havailik.

**Cap.ri.corn** *ast.* [ˈkæprikɔːn] *n.* Oğlak Burcu.

**cap.ri.ole** [ˈkæpriəul] *n.* keçi gibi sıçrama; havada takla atma.

**cap.size** ↓ [ˈkæpsaiz] *v/i.* alabora olm., devrilmek; *fig.* altüst olm., *v/t.* devirmek, alabora etm.

**cap.stan** ↓ [ˈkæpstən] *n.* ırgat, bocurgat.

**cap.su.lar** [ˈkæpsjulə] *adj.* kapsüle benzer; **cap.sule** ⚘ & ⚚ [ˈkæpsjuːl] *n.* kapsül; mahfaza.

**cap.tain** [ˈkæptin] *n.* kumandan, şef; *spor:* takım kaptanı; ↓ kaptan, süvari; deniz albayı; ✕ yüzbaşı; ~ **of industry** bir ülkenin endüstrisinde söz sahibi olan kişi; **cap.tain.cy, cap.tain.ship** [ˈ~si, ˈ~ʃip] *n.* kaptanlık; yüzbaşılık; liderlik.

**cap.tion** [ˈkæpʃən] **1.** *n.* başlık, serlevha; ünvan, resmî sıfat; *film:* yazılı tercüme; **2.** *v/t. Am.* isim, başlık vermek.

**cap.tious** ☐ [ˈkæpʃəs] tenkitçi, safsatalı, kılı kırk yaran.

**cap.ti.vate** *fig.* [ˈkæptiveit] *v/t.* cezbetmek; **cap.tiˈva.tion** *n.* büyüleme, cezbetme; **ˈcap.tive 1.** *adj.* esir düşmüş; baskı altında; ~ balloon sabit balon, yere iple bağlı balon; **2.** *n.* tutsak, esir *(a. fig.)*; **cap.tiv.i.ty** [~ˈtiviti] *n.* tutsaklık, esaret. **cap.tor** [ˈkæptə] *n.* esir eden, zapteden, tutan kişi; **cap.ture** [ˈ~tʃə] **1.** *n.* yakalama, esir alma; ↓ korsanlık etme; ganimet; **2.** *vb.* tutmak, yakalamak, zaptetmek; ↓ korsanlık etm., zaptetmek; *fig.* bşe el koymak.

**Cap.u.chin** *eccl.* [ˈkæpjuʃin] *n.* Fransiskan rahibi, Kapüsen rahibi.

**car** [kɑː] *n.* otomobil, araba; vagon; balon sepeti; *(asansör)* kabin.

**car.a.cole** [ˈkærəkəul] *binicilik:* **1.** *n.* yarım çark hareketi; **2.** *vb.* iki yana yarım çarklar yaparak at sürmek.

**ca.rafe** [kəˈræf] *n.* sürahi.

**car.a.mel** [ˈkærəmel] *n.* kavrulmuş şeker, karamel; karamela.

**car.a.pace** *zo.* [ˈkærəpeis] *n.* kaplumbağa gibi hayvanların üst kabuğu.

**car.at** [ˈkærət] *n.* kırat *(değerli taşların ağırlık ölçü birimi).*

**car.a.van** [ˈkærəvæn] *n.* kervan; arabaya bağlı küçük ev, treyler; **car.aˈvan.se.rai** [~sərai] *n.* kervansaray, büyük yolcu hanı.

**car.a.way** ¾ [ˈkærəwei] *n.* kimyon; çöreotu.

**car.bide** ⚗ [ˈkɑːbaid] *n.* karpit.

**car.bine** [ˈkɑːbain] *n.* kısa tüfek, süvari tüfeği, karabina.

**car.bo.hy.drate** ⚗ [ˈkɑːˈbəuˈhaidreit] *n.* karbonhidrat.

**car.bol.ic ac.id** ⚗ [kɑːˈbɔlikˈæsid] *n.* fenol. **car.bon** [ˈkɑːbən] *n.* ⚗ karbon; ✦ kömür; **a.** ~ paper karbon, kopya kâğıdı; ~ copy kopya, suret; ~ dioxide karbon dioksit; ~ monoxide karbon monoksit; **car.bo.na.ceous** [~bəuˈneiʃəs] *adj.* karbonlu; **car.bon.ate** [ˈ~bənit] *n.* karbonat; **car.bon.ic** [~ˈbɔnik] *adj.* karbonik; ~ acid karbonik asit; **car.bon.if.er.ous** *geol.* [~bəˈnifərəs] *adj.* kömürün oluştuğu jeolojik devre ait; kömürlü; karbonlu; **car.bon.i.za.tion** [~bənaiˈzeiʃən] *n.* karbonlaş(tır)ma; **ˈcar.bon.ize** *v/t.* & *v/i.* karbonlaş(tır)mak; kömürleş(tir)mek.

**car.bo.run.dum** [kɑːbəˈrʌndəm] *n.* karbon ve silikomdan oluşan ve maddeleri cilalamak ve keskinleştirmek için kullanılan madde.

**car.boy** [ˈkɑːbɔi] *n.* büyük sepetli şişe, damacana.

**car.bun.cle** [ˈkɑːbʌŋkl] *n. min.* kırmızı ziynet taşları; ✚ çıban, şirpençe.

**car.bu.ret** ⚗ [ˈkɑːbjuret] *v/t.* gaz haline getirmek; **ˈcar.bu.ret.ter,** *mst* **ˈcar.bu.ret.tor** *n. mot.* karbüratör.

**car.case,** *mst* **car.cass** [ˈkɑːkəs] *n. (hayvan)* ceste, kadavra, iskelet; *kasap dükkânı:* gövde, beden; *fig.* leş, *(gemi v.b.)* enkaz.

**card[1]** ⊕ [kɑːd] **1.** *n.* yün tarağı; kaşağı; **2.** *v/t. (yün)* taramak.

**card[2]** [~] *n.* kart, posta kartı; kartvizit; karton; oyun kâğıdı; house of ~s *(çocuk oyunu)* iskambilden ev; queer ~ F antika, tuhaf; have a ~ up one's sleeve gizli kozu olm.

**car.dan** ⊕ [ˈkɑːdən]: ~ joint kardan mafsalı, üniversal mafsal; ~ shaft kardan şaftı.

**card...:** **ˈ~.board** *n.* karton. mukavva. **car.di.ac** ✚ [ˈkɑːdiæk] **1.** *adj.* kalple ilgili, kalp...; **2.** *n.* kalp ilâcı.

**car.di.gan** [ˈkɑːdigən] *n.* örme yün ceket, hırka.

**car.di.nal** [ˈkɑːdinl] **1.** ☐ baş, esaslı, önemli, ana; koyu parlak kırmızı; ~ number asıl sayı; **2.** *n.* kardinal; *orn.* erkeği parlak kırmızı tüylü bir tür kuş *(Kuzey Amerika'da)*; **car.di.nal.ate** [ˈ~nəleit] *n.* kardinallik; kardinaller heyeti.

**card...:** **ˈ~.in.dex** *n.* klasör, fişler *pl.*; **ˈ~.sharp.er** *n.* iskambil oyununda hile yapan kimse.

**care** [kɛə] **1.** *n.* dikkat, bakım, koruma, ilgi; merak, üzüntü; *medical* ~ tıbbi bakım; ~ of the mouth ağız bakımı; ~ of the nails tırnak bakımı; ~ of *(abbr.* c/o*)* evinde, vasıtasiyle, eliyle; take ~ (of o.s.) *k-ne* bakmak, dikkat etm.; take ~ of muhafaza etm. *-i;* bakmak *-e,* dikkat etm. *-e;* with ~ dikkatle; **2.** *vb.* yapmak hevesinde olm. (to *-i);* ~ for ilgilenmek *-le;* bakmak *-e;* beğenmek *-i;* endişe etm. *-den;* I don't ~ (if I do)! F umurumda değil, bence aynı şey, Bana ne?; I don't ~ what he said ne söylerse söylesin (umurumda değil); well ~d-for iyi bakılmış, bakımlı.

**ca.reen** ↓ [kəˈriːn] *v/t. (gemiyi)* yan yatırmak; *v/i.* yan yatmak.

**ca.reer** [kəˈriə] **1.** *n.* meslek hayatı, kariyer; ~ diplomat meslekten yetişme diplomat; **2.** *v/i.* hızla gitmek, koşmak; **caˈreer.ist** *n.* mesleğinde herşeye rağmen ilerlemeye meraklı kimse, ikbalperest.

71

**cart**

**care.free** [ˈkɛəfriː] *adj.* kaygısız, kayıtsız, dertsiz.

**care.ful** ☐ [ˈkɛəful] dikkatli, ihtimamlı, itinalı, ihtiyatlı, ölçülü; be ~ to *inf.* dikkat etm. *-e;* **ˈcare.ful.ness** *n.* dikkat, dikkatli olma.

**care.less** ☐ [ˈkɛəlis] dikkatsiz, ihmalci, kayıtsız; düşüncesiz, pervasız (of); **ˈcare.less.ness** *n.* dikkatsizlik, ihmal; düşüncesizlik.

**ca.ress** [kəˈres] **1.** *n.* okşama, öpüş; **2.** *v/t.* sevmek, öpmek; *fig.* okşamak.

**care.tak.er** [ˈkɛəteikə] *n.* kapıcı; bina yöneticisi; ~ government geçici hükümet.

**care-worn** [ˈkɛəwɔːn] *adj.* kederden bitkin.

**car.fare** *Am.* [ˈkɑːfɛə] *n.* yolcu bilet parası.

**car.go** ⚓ [ˈkɑːgəu] *n.* yük, hamule; mixed *veya* general ~ karışık yük.

**car.i.bou** *zo.* [ˈkæribuː] *n.* Kuzey Amerika'ya ait ren geyiği.

**car.i.ca.ture** [kærikəˈtjuə] **1.** *n.* karikatür; kötü taklit; **2.** *v/t.* karikatürünü yapmak, karikatürleştirmek; **car.i.caˈtur.ist** *n.* karikatürist.

**car.i.es** ♥ [ˈkɛəriːz] *n.* diş ve kemik çürümesi.

**car.il.lon** [kæˈriljən] *n.* çeşitli tonlarda sesler veren çan takımı.

**car.i.ous** [ˈkɛəriəs] *adj.* (dişleri *veya* kemikleri) çürümüş.

**car.load** [ˈkɑːləud] *n.* araba veya vagon yükü; F araba dolusu şey.

**car.man** [ˈkɑːmən] *n.* arabacı.

**car.mine** [ˈkɑːmain] *n.* kızıl, kırmızı.

**car.nage** [ˈkɑːnidʒ] *n.* katliam, kan dökme, halkı kılıçtan geçirme; **ˈcar.nal** ☐ cinsî, şehvani; dünyevî; **car.nal.i.ty** [-ˈnæliti] *n.* maddiyat, cismaniyet; şehvet; **car.na.tion** [-ˈneiʃən] **1.** *n.* pembe veya açık kırmızı; ♥ karanfil; **2.** *adj.* açık kırmızı.

**car.ni.val** [ˈkɑːnivəl] *n.* karnaval, cümbüş, âlem.

**car.ni.vore** [ˈkɑːnivɔː] *n.* et yiyen hayvan, etobur; **car.niv.o.rous** [-ˈnivərəs] *adj.* et yiyen, et yiyen hayvanlara ait.

**car.ol** [ˈkærəl] **1.** *n.* neşeli şarkı, dini şarkı; **2.** *vb.* neşeyle şarkı söylemek; dini şarkı söylemek; şarkıyla methetmek.

**ca.rot.id** *anat.* [kəˈrɔtid] *n. a.* ~ artery karotis arteri, şahdamar.

**ca.rouse** [kəˈrauz] **1.** *n. a.* **caˈrous.al** ziyafet, içki âlemi; **2.** *v/i.* içmek, içki âlemi yapmak.

**carp**[1] [kɑːp] *n.* sazan balığı.

**carp**[2] [~] *v/i.* kusur bulmak, beğenmemek; ~ at tutturmak, tenkit etm., mızmızlanmak.

**car.pen.ter** [ˈkɑːpintə] **1.** *n.* marangoz, dülger, doğramacı; **2.** *vb.* marangozluk etm., yontmak, doğramak; **ˈcar.pen.try** *n.* doğramacılık, marangozluk, dülgerlik.

**car.pet** [ˈkɑːpit] **1.** *n.* kilim, halı (a. *fig.*); bring on the ~ bşin lafını etm., bşi dermeyan etm., müzakere mevkiine koymak; **2.** *v/i.* halı döşemek; F b-den hesap sormak, haşlamak; **ˈ~.bag** *n.* yol çantası, heybe; **ˈ~.bag.ger** *n.* Amerikan sivil savaşından sonra çıkarı için Güneye yerleşen Kuzeyli; prensipsiz politikacı; **ˈcar.pet.ing** *n.* döşemelik halı.

**car.pet...:** **ˈ~.knight** *n.* salon kahramanı; **ˈ~.sweep.er** *n.* halı süpürgesi.

**car.riage** [ˈkæridʒ] *n.* araba, vagon; taşıma, nakil; nakliye ücreti; davranış; ✗ kundak; ~ free, ~ paid nakliyesiz, navlun satıcıya ait; **ˈcar.riage.a.ble** *adj.* üzerinden araba geçebilir (yol).

**car.riage...:** **ˈ~.drive** *n.* park yolu; **ˈ~.way** *n.* araba yolu; dual ~ iki taraflı yol.

**car.ri.er** [ˈkæriə] *n.* nakliyeci; taşıyan; taşıyıcı (a. 🦠 = portör); **ˈ~.pi.geon** *n.* posta güvercini.

**car.ri.on** [ˈkæriən] **1.** *n.* leş; **2.** *adj.* leş gibi; leş yiyen.

**car.rot** [ˈkærət] *n.* havuç; **ˈcar.rot.y** *adj.* F havuç renginde (esp. saç).

**car.ry** [ˈkæri] **1.** *vb.* taşımak, götürmek, nakletmek; çekmek (yük); beslemek, desteklemek; üzerinde bulundurmak; k-ni idare etm.; (hastalık, mikrop) yayılmak; (silah) atıcı gücü olm.; satışa arzetmek; hamile olm. *-e;* 🅰 geçirmek; yayınlamak; (alkollü içki) dayanmak *-e,* tahammül etm. *-e;* kapsamak *-i;* desteğini kazanmak; (parlamentoda) kabul edilmek; ✗ (kale vs.) ele geçirmek, zaptetmek; (faiz) getirmek (ses) ...den işitilmek; ~ the day başarılı olm.; ~ away taşımak, alıp götürmek (a. *fig.*); ~ every thing before one her direnişi kırmak, tam bir zafer kazanmak; ~ forward *veya* over ⊤ yeni sayfaya nakletmek; yekûn nakletmek; ~ on devam et(tir)mek; ~ out, ~ through bitirmek; başarmak, yerine getirmek; ~ out 🅾🅾 (para cezasını vb.) icra etm., tenfiz etm.; **~ing capacity** taşıma kapasitesi; **2.** *n.* menzil, atış menzili; nakil, taşıma.

**cart** [kɑːt] **1.** *n.* iki tekerlekli yük arabası; el arabası; ~ grease araba dingil yağı; put the ~ before the horse *fig.* bir işi tersinden yapmak; in the ~ *sl.* hapı yutmuş, güç durumda; **2.** *v/t.* araba ile taşımak; **'cart.age** *n.* araba ile taşıma; nakliye ücreti.

**car.tel** [kɑː'tel] *n.* kartel, fabrikalar arasındaki anlaşma; ✕ mübadele, değişim, trampa.

**cart.er** ['kɑːtə] *n.* arabacı, yük arabasını kullanan kimse.

**car.ti.lage** ['kɑːtilidʒ] *n.* kıkırdak; **car.ti-lag.i.nous** [-'lædʒinəs] *adj.* kıkırdaklı; kıkırdağa benzer.

**cart-load** ['kɑːtlaud] *n.* araba dolusu yük.

**car.tog.ra.pher** [kɑː'tɒgrəfə] *n.* harita mütehassısı, haritacı; **car'tog.ra.phy** *n.* haritacılık.

**car.ton** ['kɑːtən] *n.* karton, mukavva kutu.

**car.toon** [kɑː'tuːn] **1.** *n. paint.* karikatür; ⊕ resim taslağı; **2.** *vb.* karikatürize etm., karikatürleştirmek; **car'toon.ist** *n.* karikatürcü, karikatürist.

**car.touche** ▲ [kɑː'tuːʃ] *n.* kralın ismini gösteren kabartma resim, şekil; fişeklik.

**car.tridge** ['kɑːtridʒ] *n.* hartuç, fişek; *phot.* kartuş, kaset; **'~-pa.per** *n.* kalın, kaba beyaz kâğıt.

**cart-wheel** ['kɑːtwiːl] *n.* araba tekerleği; *Am.* gümüş dolar; turn ~s elleri üzerinde takla atmak.

**cart.wright** ['kɑːtrait] *n.* araba imalâtçısı.

**carve** [kɑːv] *v/t.* oymak, hakketmek; *(esp. sofrada)* et kesmek; *(yolu)* düzleştirmek *(a. fig.);* **'carv.er** *n.* oymacı, hakkâk; **'carv.ing** *n.* oyulmuş sanat eseri; oymacılık; sofrada et kesme.

**cas.cade** [kæs'keid] *n.* çağlayan, şelale.

**case¹** [keis] **1.** *n.* kutu, kasa, göz, çekme, mahfaza, kılıf; *(fişek)* kovan; *typ.* hurufat kasası; **2.** *v/t.* kaplamak, örtmek; kutuya koymak.

**case²** [~] *n.* hal, husus, hâdise, olay *(a.* ₮, ⚘); ⚘ hasta; *Am.* F garip herif; ⚘ hukuki sebep, dava; *gr.* ismin hallerinden biri; make out one's ~ kuvvetli deliller ileri sürmek; as the ~ may be hal ve şartlara göre, gereğince, icabında; in ~ eğer, şayet; in any ~ her halde, mutlaka.

**case-hard.en** ⊕ ['keishɑːdn] *v/t.* dış yüzünü sertleştirmek, kalınlaştırmak; ~ed *adj. fig.* nasırlaşmış.

**case his.to.ry** ['keishistəri] *n.* evveliyat, hasta veya güçlük içinde bulunan kişinin geçmisi ile ilgili bilgiler.

**ca.se.in** ⚗ ['keisiːin] *n.* peynir özü, kazein.

**case.mate** ✕ ['keismeit] *n.* top yuvası, kazamat.

**case.ment** ['keismənt] *n.* pencere kanadı; ~ window kanatlı pencere.

**cash** [kæʃ] **1.** *n.* para, nakit; peşin para; ~ down, for ~ peşin para; in ~ peşin ola-

rak, nakit alarak; be in (out of) ~ üstünde parası ol(ma)mak; ~ and carry *adj.* peşin para ile alınan; ~ payment peşin ödeme; ~ on delivery ödemeli; ~ price peşin fiyat; ~ register otomatik kasa; **2.** *v/t.* paraya çevirmek, para bozmak; **'~-book** *n.* kasa defteri; **'~-cheque** *n.* çizgili olmayan çek; **cash.ier 1.** [kæ'ʃiə] *n.* veznedar, kasiyer; **2.** [kə'ʃiə] *v/t.* ✕ ordudan tard etm.; **cash.less** ['kæʃlis] *adj.* nakden olmayıp havale, çek vs. ile yapılan ödeme.

**cash.mere** [kæʃ'miə] *n.* kaşmir yünü; ince yün kumaş.

**cas.ing** ['keisiŋ] *n.* kaplama; çerçeve; ▲ zarf, sandık; ~ paper ambalaj kâğıdı.

**ca.si.no** [kə'siːnəu] *n.* gazino.

**cask** [kɑːsk] *n.* fıçı, varil; bir fıçı dolusu.

**cas.ket** ['kɑːskit] *n.* değerli eşya kutusu; *Am.* tabut.

**Cas.pi.an Sea** ['kæspiən'siː] *n.* Hazar Denizi.

**casque** ['kæsk] *n.* zırhlı başlık, miğfer.

**cas.sa.tion** [kæ'seiʃən] *n.* davayı temyiz; kararı bozma.

**cas.sa.va** ⚘ [kə'sɑːvə] *n.* manyok kökünden çıkartılan nişasta.

**cas.se.role** ['kæsərəul] *n.* saplı tencere, güveç; bu tencerede pişirilen yemek.

**cas.si.a** ⚘ ['kæsiə] *n.* Çin tarçını.

**cas.sock** ['kæsək] *n.* papaz cübbesi.

**cas.so.war.y** *orn.* ['kæsəwɛəri] *n.* devekuşu cinsinden büyük kuş; New Holland ~ Avustralya'ya mahsus iri devekuşu.

**cast** [kɑːst] **1.** *n.* atma, atış, fırlatma; döküm, dökme, kalıp; *(tiyatro oyunu veya filmde)* oynayanlar; rol dağıtımı; alçı; dış görünüş; renk tonu; tip, kalite; ↓ ağ atma, voli; **2.** *v/t.* atmak, saçmak; olta atmak, ağ sermek; *(diş, kıl vs.)* dökmek; *(oy)* vermek; *thea.* rol dağıtmak; rol vermek *-e; (dökům)* dökmek; *(hayvan)* doğurmak; *a.* ~ up sayıları toplamak; be ~ in a lawsuit ⚖ dava kaybetmek; ~ lots (for) *bş* için kura çekmek; ~ in one's lot with s.o. *b-i* ile herşeyi paylaşmak; ~ one's skin derisi soyulmak; ~ s.th. in s.o.'s teeth *b-ni bş* den dolayı muaheze etm., yüzüne vurmak; işe yaramaz diye atmak; be ~ away ↓ *(gemi)* kazaya uğramak; ~ down aşağı atmak, indirmek; ~ down yüreği karartmak, neşesiz ve kederli olm.; ~ up kusmak, kayyetmek; ~ up (accounts) ₮ *bşin* hesabını yapmak; *v/i.* eğrilmek; ⊕ kalıp lanmak; ~ about for çare aramak, düşünüp taşınmak; ~ off ↓ alarga etm.

**cas.ta.net** [kæstə'net] *n.* kastanyet, çengi zili.

**cast.a.way** ['kɑːstəwei] **1.** *n.* reddedilmiş kişi, şey; ⟟ kazazede; **2.** *adj.* reddedilmiş; kazazede.

**caste** [kɑːst] *n.* kast, birbirine karşı kapalı sınıf *(a. fig)*; ~ feeling zümre zihniyeti.

**cas.tel.lan** ['kæstələn] *n.* kale kumandanı, şato kâhyası; **cas.tel.lat.ed** ['kæsteleitid] *adj.* duvarları mazgallı, kuleli olan.

**cas.ter** ['kɑːstə] = castor[2]

**cas.ti.gate** ['kæstigeit] *v/t.* tenkit etm, cezalandırmak, kırbaçlamak; *fig.* teşhir etm.; **cas.ti'ga.tion** *n.* cezalandırma, paylama.

**cast.ing** ['kɑːstiŋ] **1.** *adj.* kati, kesin *(oy)*; **2.** *n.* atma, atış, fırlatma; döküm, dökme; hesap etme; rol dağıtımı; ~s *pl.* döküm kaplar.

**cast i.ron** ['kɑːstˌaiən] *n.* dökme demir; **'cast-'i.ron** *adj.* dökme demirden yapılmış; *fig.* sağlam, dayanıklı, demir gibi.

**cas.tle** ['kɑːsl] **1.** *n.* hisar, kale; şato; *satranç:* kale; ~s in the air, ~s in Spain hayal, hülya; **2.** *vb.* *satranç:* kaleyi şahın yanına koymak, rok yapmak.

**cast-off** ['kɑːst'ɔf] *n. (esp. giysi)* istenilmeyen veya atılmış şey.

**cas.tor[1]** *pharm.* ['kɑːstə] *n.:* ~ oil Hint yağı.

**cas.tor[2]** [~] *n.* koltuk vs. tekerleği; tuztuk, biberlik; ~ sugar pudra şekeri.

**cas.trate** [kæs'treit] *v/t.* hadımlaştırmak, iğdiş etm.; **cas'tra.tion** hadım etme, iğdiş etme.

**cast steel** ['kɑːst'stiːl] *n.* dökme çelik; **'cast-'steel** *adj.* dökme çelikten yapılmış.

**cas.u.al** □ ['kæʒjuəl] tesadüfî, rastgele; F gevşek, üşengeç. heyecansız, tembel, lâubali; sıradan, ciddi olmayan; gündelik *(elbise vs.)* ~ labourer geçici işçi; **'cas.u.al.ty** *n.* kaza; kayıp; casualties *pl.* ✕ zayiat.

**cas.u.ist** ['kæzjuist] *n.* ahlâk konularında doğru ile yanlışı isteği doğrultusunda yorumlayan kişi; safsatacı; **'cas.u.ist.ry** *n.* safsata, gerçeği aksettirmeyen fakat ustaca yapılmış yorum.

**cat** [kæt] **1.** *n.* kedi; *Am. sl.* caz meraklısı; wait for the ~ to jump, see which way the ~ jumps işlerin nasıl geliştiğini görmek, diğerlerinin tutumunu görünceye kadar işe karışmamak; not room to swing a ~ çok dar yer; ~ burglar duvardan tırmanarak içeri giren hırsız; **2.** *v/i.* P kusmak.

**cat.a.clysm** ['kætəklizəm] *n.* tufan, afet; felâket, musibet.

**cat.a.comb** ['kætəkuːm] *n.* yer altında dehliz gibi mezarlık.

**cat.a.logue,** *Am. a.* **cat.a.log** ['kætələg] **1.** *n.* katalog, liste; **2.** *v/t.* bşin kataloğunu yapmak.

**cat.a.pult** ['kætəpʌlt] *n.* mancınık; sapan; ✝ katapült.

**cat.a.ract** ['kætərækt] *n.* şelâle, büyük çağlayan; ✝ katarakt, perde.

**ca.tarrh** [kə'tɑː] *n.* akıntı, F nezle; **ca.tarrh.al** [kə'tɑːrəl] *adj.* nezleye ait.

**ca.tas.tro.phe** [kə'tæstrəfi] *n.* facia, felâket; **cat.a.stroph.ic** [kætə'strɔfik] *adj.* (~ally) dehşetli, korkunç, felâket getiren.

**ca.taw.ba** *Am.* ✦ [kə'tɔːbə] *n.* üzüm ve şarap.

**cat.bird** *zo.* ['kætbəːd] *n.* ardıç kuşu.

**cat.call** ['kætkɔːl] **1.** *n. thea. etc.* hoşnutsuzluk belirtmek için çıkarılan ıslık veya çıkarılan ses; **2.** *v/i.* ıslıklamak, yuhalamak.

**catch** [kætʃ] **1.** *n.* yakala(n)ma, tut(ul)ma; av, şikâr; tuzak, bityeniği; *fig.* kâr, kazanç, fayda; ⊕ kilit dili, çengel, kanca *(a. fig.)*; parola; slogan *s.* ~word; **2.** *(irr.) v/t. & v/i.* kapmak, tutmak, yakalamak, elde etm., ele geçirmek; cezbetmek, çekmek; *(tren vs.)* yetişmek *-e*; *(hastalık)* yakalanmak *-e*, duçar olm. *-e*; *(ateş)* tutuşmak, ateş almak; *(nefes, soluk)* tutmak; *(tokat, darbe)* aşketmek, indirmek; *fig.* anlamak, kavramak; ~ at tutmağa çalışmak *-i*; ~ it F azar işitmek; ~ in the act suçüstü yakalamak; ~ me! (doing such a thing) bunu yapmak mı? ne münasebet! ~ (a) cold soğuk almak, nezle olm., üşütmek; ~ on tutulmak, moda olm.; *Am.* kavramak, anlamak; ~ s.o.'s eye *b-nin* dikkatini çekmek; ~ the Speaker's eye *(İngiltere parlamentosunda)* söz almayı başarmak; ~ up yetişmek; kesmek, *bşe* ara vermek; ~ up with yetişmek *-e*; **'~-all** *n. Am.* yer; kap, mahfaza; **'~-as-'catch-'can** *n. spor:* serbest güreş; **'catch.er** *n.* tutan kimse; *beysbol:* topu yakalayan oyuncu; **'catch.ing** *adj.* çekici, cazibeli; ♪ giriş; ✝ sâri, bulaşıcı; **'catch-line** *n.* manşet; **'catch.ment ba.sin** su haznesi, toplama havuzu. **catch...:** '~.pen.ny *adj.* ✝ ucuz satmak için yapılan gösterişli fakat değersiz şey; **'~-phrase** *n.* slogan; **'~.pole** *n.* şerif vekili; **'~.word** *n.* parola; slogan; *thea.,* *typ.* replik; **'catch.y** *adj.* F *fig.* cazibeli; şüpheli.

**cat.e.chism** [ˈkætikizəm] *n.* soru cevaplı öğretme; **cat.e.chize** [ˈ‿kaiz] *v/t.* (dini konuları) soru cevap usulü ile öğretmek; **cat.e.chu.men** [‿ˈkjuːmen] *n.* Kateşizm öğrencisi.

**cat.e.gor.i.cal** □ [kætiˈgɔrikəl] kategorik, kesin, kati; **cat.e.go.ry** [ˈ‿gəri] *n.* kategori, sınıf, cins, zümre.

**ca.ter** [ˈkeitə]: *v/i.* ‿ for hazırlamak -i, temin etm. -i; *fig.* bşi bulmak, temin etm.; **ˈca.ter.er** *n.* yiyecek temin eden, vekilharç; **ˈca.ter.ing** *n.* yemek tedariki, ikram.

**cat.er.pil.lar** [ˈkætəpilə] *n.* tırtıl, kurt.

**cat.er.waul** [ˈkætəwɔːl] **1.** *n.* kedi sesi; **2.** *v/i.* kedi gibi miyavlamak.

**cat.fish** [ˈkætfiʃ] *n.* kedi balığı.

**cat.gut** [ˈkætgʌt] *n.* kiriş; ♀ katgüt.

**ca.thar.sis** [kəˈθɑːsis] *n.* ♀ ishal, amel; **caˈthar.tic** [‿tik] **1.** *n.* müshil ilâcı; **2.** *adj.* müshil, bağırsakları temizleyici.

**ca.the.dral** [kəˈθiːdrəl] *n.* katedral, piskoposluk kilisesi.

**Cath.er.ine-wheel** [ˈkæθərinwiːl] *n.* ☘ gül şeklinde yapılmış renkli pencere; rozas; döner hava fişeği, çarkıfelek.

**cath.ode** ⚡ [ˈkæθəud] *n.* katot, negatif elektrot; ‿ **ray** katot ışınları.

**cath.o.lic** [ˈkæθəlik] **1.** *adj.* (‿ally) Katolik kilisesine bağlı olan; **2.** *n.* Katolik; **ca.thol.i.cism** [kəˈθɔlisizəm] *n.* Katoliklik.

**cat.kin** ♀ [ˈkætkin] *n.* söğüt vs. gibi ağaçların çiçeği.

**cat.like** [ˈkætlaik] *adj.* kedi gibi; sessiz, sinsi; **ˈcat.nip** *n.* ♀ kedi nanesi.

**cat-o'-nine-tails** [ˈkætəˈnainteilz] *n.* dayak atmak için kullanılan uçları dokuz düğümlü ipten yapılmış kamçı.

**cat's-paw** *fig.* [ˈkætspɔː] *n.* başkası tarafından alet olarak kullanılan kişi, maşa.

**cat.tish** *fig.* [ˈkætiʃ] *adj.* kurnaz, şeytan, kinci, hain.

**cat.tle** [ˈkætl] *n.* sığır, davar; **ˈ‿-breed.ing** *n.* hayvan yetiştirme, sığırcılık; **‿.man** [ˈ‿mən] *n.* hayvan yetiştiricisi; hayvan güden kimse; **ˈ‿-plague** *n.* bulaşıcı sığır hastalığı; **ˈ‿-rus.tler** *n.* Am. davar veya at hırsızı; **ˈ‿-show** *n.* tarım sergisi; sığır sergisi.

**cat.ty** [ˈkæti] = cattish.

**Cau.ca.sian** [kɔːˈkeizjən] **1.** *adj.* Kafkasya'ya ait; Kafkas diliyle ilgili; **2.** *n.* Kafkasyalı; Kafkas dili.

**cau.cus** [ˈkɔːkəs] *n.* parti kurulu toplantısı; contp. klik; Am. pol. siyasi parti liderlerinin toplantısı.

**cau.dal** [ˈkɔːdl] *adj.* kuyruklu; kuyruğa ait; kuyruğa yakın; **cau.date** [ˈ‿deit]

*adj.* hem karada hem de denizde yaşayan ve kuyruklu olan.

**caught** [kɔːt] *pret. & p.p. of* catch 2.

**caul.dron** [ˈkɔːldrən] *n.* kazan.

**cau.li.flow.er** ♀ [ˈkɔliflauə] *n.* karnabahar.

**caulk** ⚓ [kɔːk] *v/t.* kalafatlamak; **ˈcaulk.er** *n.* kalafatçı.

**caus.al** □ [ˈkɔːzəl] sebep belirten; sebebe ait, nedensel; **cau.sal.i.ty** [‿ˈzæliti] *n.* sebebiyet, nedensellik; **ˈcaus.a.tive** *adj.* sebep olan (of -e); **cause 1.** *n.* sebep, neden; vesile; hedef, amaç; ☰ dava; büyük mesele; taraftarlık; **make common** ‿ **with** işbirliği yapmak -le; tarafını tutmak -in; **2.** *v/t.* bşe sebep olm.; sebebiyet vermek -e; meydan vermek -e; **ˈcause.less** □ sebepsiz, nedensiz, asılsız.

**cause.way** [ˈkɔːzweil], a. **cau.sey** [ˈ‿zeil] *n.* yayalar için yapılan geçici yol, geçit; şose.

**caus.tic** [ˈkɔːstik] **1.** *n.* yakıcı (veya aşındırıcı, dağlayıcı) madde; kostik, kezzap; **2.** *adj.* (‿ally) aşındırıcı; *fig.* dokunaklı, iğneli (söz), müstehzi.

**cau.ter.i.za.tion** ♀ [kɔːtəraiˈzeifən] *n.* dağlama; **ˈcau.ter.ize** *v/t.* yakmak, dağlamak; **ˈcau.ter.y** *n.* yakış, dağlayış; dağlama aleti.

**cau.tion** [ˈkɔːʃən] **1.** *n.* dikkat; ihtar, uyarma; sakınma; tedbir; ☰ kefalet, teminat ‿ **money** teminat akçesi, depozito, kefalet; **2.** *v/t.* b-ne bşi ihtar etm., uyarmak (against -e karşı); b-ne bş-den sakınmasını ihtar etm.; **cau.tion.ar.y** [ˈ‿ʃnəri] *adj.* ihtar cinsinden, uyarıcı.

**cau.tious** □ [ˈkɔːʃəs] ihtiyatlı, tedbirli, çekingen; **ˈcau.tious.ness** *n.* dikkat, ihtimam, itina, tedbirlilik.

**cav.al.cade** [kævəlˈkeid] *n.* süvari alayı; atlı ve arabalıların geçidi.

**cav.a.lier** [kævəˈliə] **1.** *n.* kavalye; centilmen; suvari, atlı; **2.** □ kibirli, gururlu.

**cav.al.ry** ✗ [ˈkævəlri] atlı asker, süvari sınıfı.

**cave** [keiv] **1.** *n.* mağara, in; **2.** ‿ **in** *v/i.* çökmek, yıkılmak; teslim olm., razı olm.; *v/t.* F oymak, (mağara) açmak.

**ca.ve.at** ☰ [ˈkeiviæt] *n.* işlemlerin durdurulması için yapılan başvurma, ihtar, ikaz.

**cave-dweller** [ˈkeivdwelə], **cave-man** [ˈ‿mæn] *n.* taş devri mağara adamı; F kaba adam.

**cav.en.dish** [ˈkævəndiʃ] *n.* kalıplanmış bir cins tütün.

**cav.ern** [ˈkævən] *n.* mağara, in; **ˈcav.ern-**

**ous** *adj.* mağaraları olan; *fig.* boş, kof, mağara gibi.

**cav.i.ar(e)** ['kæviɑ:] *n.* havyar.

**cav.il** ['kævil] **1.** *n.* anlamsız itiraz, bahane; **2.** *v/i.* bahane aramak, bahane bulmak, itiraz etm. (at, about -de, -e); **¹cav-il.ler** *n.* itirazcı kimse.

**cav.i.ty** ['kæviti] *n.* oyuk, çukur, boşluk.

**ca.vort** *Am.* F [kəvɔ:t] *v/i.* şahlanmak, coşmak, oynamak.

**caw** [kɔ:] **1.** *n.* karga sesi, gak; **2.** *v/i.* karga gibi gaklamak.

**cay.enne** [kei'en] *n. a.* ~ **pepper** ['keien] çok acı kırmızı biber.

**cay.man** *zo.* ['keimən] *n.* Güney Amerika'ya ait bir cins timsah.

**cease** [si:s] *v/i.* (from) bitmek ,sona ermek, durmak; *v/t.* bitirmek; (✕ *ateş*) kesmek; **¹.~¹fire** *n.* ✕ silahların geçici olarak bırakılması, ateşkes; **¹cease.less** ☐ durmadan, sürekli, fasılasız.

**ce.dar** ♀ ['si:də] *n.* sedir ağacı.

**cede** [si:d] *v/t.* bırakmak, terketmek.

**ce.dil.la** [si'dilə] *n.* Ç ve Ş harflerinin altındaki işaret, çengel.

**ceil** [si:l] *v/t.* tavan yapmak; **¹ceil.ing** *n.* tavan; tavan yapma; ⌀ uçağın azami yüksekliği; *fig.* azamî had; ~ **lighting** tavan aydınlatma düzeni; ~ **price** azamî fiyat, tavan fiyat.

**cel.an.dine** ♀ ['seləndain] *n.* kırlangıç otu.

**cel.a.nese** [selə'ni:z] *n.* bir çeşit suni ipek.

**cel.e.brate** ['selibreit] *vb.* kutlamak; şöhretini yaymak, övmek; *eccl.* ayin yapmak; **¹cel.e.brat.ed** *adj.* meşhur, ünlü (for *-le*); **cel.e¹bra.tion** *n.* kutlama; *eccl.* dini ayin yapma; **¹cel.e.bra.tor** *n.* kutlayan kimse.

**ce.leb.ri.ty** [si'lebriti] *n.* şöhret; ünlü kişi.

**ce.ler.i.ty** [si'leriti] *n.* sürat, çabukluk.

**cel.er.y** ♀ ['seləri] *n.* kereviz.

**ce.les.tial** ☐ [si'lestjəl] göğe ait, semavi; kutsal, ilâhi; göklerde oturan, melek.

**cel.i.ba.cy** ['selibəsi] *n.* bekârlık; **cel.i.bate** ['~bit] **1.** *adj.* bekâr, evlenmemiş *(esp. dinsel nedenlerle)*; **2.** *n.* bekâr.

**cell** [sel] *n.* hücre; ⚡ pil.

**cel.lar** ['selə] **1.** *n.* kiler, bodrum; şarap mahzeni; **2.** *v/t.* mahzene koymak; **¹cel.lar.age** *n.* mahzenlik yer; mahzen kirası; **cel.lar.et** [~'ret] *n.* içki dolabı. ...**celled** [seld] *comb.* ...hücreli.

**cel.list** ♪ ['tʃelist] *n.* viyolonsel çalan; **cel.lo** ['~ləu] *n.* viyolonsel.

**cel.lo.phane** ['seləufein] *n.* selofon, şeffaf kâğıt.

**cel.lu.lar** ['səljulə] *adj.* hücreye ait; hücreleri olan. hücreli, göz göz olan; **cel.lule**

**[¹.~ju:l]** *n.* küçük hücre, gözcük; **cel.lu-lose** ['.~juləus] *n.* selüloz.

**Celt** [kelt] *n.* Kelt, eski orta veya batı Avrupalı kişi; **¹Celt.ic** *n.* Keltlere ait; Keltçe.

**ce.ment** [si'ment] **1.** *n.* çimento; tutkal *(a. fig.)*; **2.** *v/t.* çimentolamak; yapıştırmak; **ce.men.ta.tion** [si:men'teiʃən] *n.* çimentolama.

**cem.e.ter.y** ['semitri] *n.* mezarlık.

**cen.o.taph** ['senəutɑ:f] *n. b-nin* hatırasını anmak için dikilen abide.

**cense** [sens] *v/t.* tütsülemek, buhur yakmak; **¹cen.ser** *n.* buhurdanlık.

**cen.sor** ['sensə] **1.** *n.* kontrol memuru, sansör; mümeyyiz; **2.** *v/t.* sansür etm.; yasak etm.; sansürcülük görevi yapmak; **cen.so.ri.ous** ☐ [sen'sɔ:riəs] kusur bulan, tenkit eden;\ **cen.sor.ship** ['.~səʃip] *n.* sansür, sansür idaresi.

**cen.sur.a.ble** ☐ ['senʃərəbl] kötü, cezayı haketmiş; **¹cen.sure 1.** *n.* azar(lama); tenkit, kınama; **2.** *v/t.* azarlamak, tenkit etm., kınamak.

**cen.sus** ['sensəs] *n.* sayım, nüfus sayımı; **¹.~pa.per** *n.* sayım formu.

**cent** [sent] *n. Am.* sent,·1/100 dolar; per ~ yüzde.

**cen.taur** ['sentɔ:] *n.* insan başlı at.

**cen.tau.ry** ♀ ['sentɔ:ri] *n.* kantaron.

**cen.te.nar.i.an** [senti'nɛəriən] **1.** *adj.* yüz yıllık, yüz yaşında; **2.** *n.* yüz yaşındaki kişi; **cen.te.nar.y** [sen'ti:nəri] *s.* centennial.

**cen.ten.ni.al** [sen'tenjəl] *adj.* & *n.* yüz yılı tamamlayan, yüz yıllık; yüzüncü yıl dönümü.

**cen.tes.i.mal** ☐ [sen'tesiməl] yüzüncü, yüzde bir, yüzde birine ait.

**cen.ti...** ['senti] '.~grade *adj.* santigrat, yüz dereceye bölünmüş; ~ **thermometer** yüz dereceli termometre, santigrat termometre; '.~gramme *n.* santigram, gramın yüzde biri; '.~me.tre *n.* santimetre, metrenin yüzde biri; ~.pede *zo.* ['.~pi:d] *n.* kırkayak.

**cen.tral** ['sentrəl] **1.** ☐ orta, merkezî; ana, en önemli; ~ **heating** merkezî ısıtma, kalorifer; ♀ **Powers** *pl. hist.* Merkezî Güçler *(Almanya ve Avusturya-Macaristan)*; ~ **office**, ⚡ **station** *n.* merkez, santral; **2.** *n. teleph.* telefon santralı; **cen.tral.i.za.tion** [~laizeiʃən] *n.* merkezileştirme; **¹cen.tral.ize** *v/t.* merkezileştirmek.

**cen.tre**, *Am.* **cen.ter** ['sentə] **1.** *n.* orta; *(a.* ✕, *pol.)* merkez; ~ forward *futbol:* santrfor: ~ half santrhaf; ~ of gravity ağırlık

merkezi; 2. *adj.* orta, merkezî; 3. *v/t.*
ortaya koymak, merkeze toplamak,
santralize etm.; '~-bit ⊕ *n.* matkap;
'~-board *n.* kontra omurga(lı tekne).

cen.tric, cen.tri.cal □ ['sentrik(əl)] merkezî, merkeze ait; cen.trif.u.gal □
[sen'trifjugəl] merkezden çıkan; santri-
fuj, merkezkaç; 'cen'trip.e.tal □ [~pitl]
merkeze doğru, merkezcil.

cen.tu.ple ['sentjupl] 1. □ yüz misli; 2.
*v/t.* yüzle çarpmak, yüz katına çıkarmak.

cen.tu.ri.on [sen'tjuəriən] *n.* eski Roma
yüzbaşısı.

cen.tu.ry ['sentʃəri] *n.* yüzyıl, asır.

ce.ram.ic [si'ræmik] *adj.* seramik; porselen, çini vb.'den yapılmış eşya ile ilgili;
ce'ram.ics *n. pl.* çinicilik; seramik; seramik eşya, çanak çömlek.

ce.re.al ['siəriəl] 1. *n.* tahıl, hububat, zahire; *mst* ~s *pl.* buğdaysı bitki; *part.Am.*
hububattan hazırlanmış kahvaltı yemeği; 2. *adj.* hububat türünden.

cer.e.bral *anat.* ['seribrəl] *adj.* beyne ait.

cere.cloth ['siəklɔθ] *n.* kefenlik olarak
kullanılan mumlu bez.

cer.e.mo.ni.al [seri'məunjəl] 1. □ *a.* cer-
e'mo.ni.ous □ törensel, resmî; 2. *n.* ayin,
tören; cer.e.mo.ny ['seriməni] *n.* tören;
ayin; *pol.* protokol, teşrifat; Master of
Ceremonies töreni yöneten kişi; stand
on ~ davranışlara dikkat etm.; resmî
davranmak; without ~ teklifsizce.

cert *sl.* [səːt] *n.* bşe kesin olmuş gözü ile
bakma.

cer.tain □ ['səːtn] muhakkak, kesin;
emin; belirli, kararlaşmış; güvenilir;
bazı; for ~ muhakkak, şüphesiz; make ~
bş hakkında emin olm.; 'cer.tain.ly *adv.*
elbette, tabii; 'cer.tain.ty *n.* kesinlik, katiyet.

cer.tes † ['səːtiz] *adv.* elbette, tabii.

cer.tif.i.cate 1. [sə'tifikit] *n.* tasdikname,
sertifika; diploma; ruhsat; belge; ilmühaber; ~ of birth nüfus (*veya* doğum) kâğıdı; ~ of death ölüm belgesi; ~ of marriage evlenme cüzdanı; ~ of employment
iş kâğıdı, çalışma belgesi; ~ of origin †
menşe şahadetnamesi; medical ~ sağlık
belgesi; 2. [sə'tifikeit] *v/t.* tasdik etm.,
onaylamak; belgelerle ispat etm., belgelemek, belge vermek; ~d *adj.* onaylı;
belgelenmiş, onaylanmış; cer.ti.fi.ca.tion
[səːtifi'keiʃən] *n.* belgeleme, onay, ruhsat; cer.ti.fy ['~fai] *v/t.* bşi onaylamak,
tasdik etm.; vesika vermek; doğrulamak; certified cheque karşılığı olduğu
onaylanan çek, vizeli çek; *s.* accountant;

cer.ti.tude ['~tjuːd] *n.* katiyet, kesinlik.

ce.ru.le.an [si'ruːljən] *adj.* gök mavisi.

cer.vi.cal [səː'vaikəl] *adj.* boyna ait, boyun...

ces.sa.tion [se'seiʃən] *n.* kesilme, durma,
ara.

ces.sion ['seʃən] *n.* vazgeçme, terk; devir.

cess.pit ['sespit], cess.pool ['sespuːl] *n.*
lağım çukuru.

ce.ta.cean [si'teiʃjən] 1. *n.* memeli deniz
hayvanı; 2. *adj. a.* ce'ta.ceous memeli
deniz hayvanları ile ilgili.

chafe [tʃeif] *v/t.* sürtmek, sürterek berelemek; yıpratmak; ovarak ısıtmak; *v/i.*
bşe sürtünmek; sinirlenmek, kızmak.

chaff [tʃɑːf] 1. *n.* saman tozu, çöp, atlara yem için kesilmiş ot, saman; F saçma söz; 2. *v/t.* ufak ufak kesmek; F alay
etm., *b-ne* takılmak; '~-cut.ter *n.* ot, saman kesme makinesi.

chaf.fer ['tʃæfə] *v/t.* & *v/i.* sıkı pazarlık
etm., çekişmek; alışverişte bulunmak.

chaf.finch zo. ['tʃæfintʃ] *n.* ispinoz.

chaf.ing-dish ['tʃeifiŋdiʃ] *n.* sofrada yemek ısıtmaya veya pişirmeye yarayan
kap.

cha.grin ['ʃægrin] 1. *n.* iç sıkıntısı, keder;
2. *v/t. b-nin* canını sıkmak, kederlendirmek.

chain [tʃein] 1. *n.* zincir, kelepçe; *(dağ)*
silsile; *fig. (olay, mağaza vs.)* zincir;
2. *v/t.* zincirle bağlamak, zincirlemek;
*fig.* kayıt altına almak, zincirlemek;
~ re.ac.tion *phys.* zincirleme reaksiyonu;
'~-smoker *n.* peş peşe sigara içen;
'~-store *n.* büyük bir mağazanın şubesi.

chair [tʃeə] 1. *n.* iskemle, sandalye; *Am.*
*a.* elektrikli sandalye; başkanlık makamı; kürsü; *a.* professorial ~ kürsü; be
in the ~, take the ~ başkanlık makamın-
da olm.; başkanlık etm.; 2. *v/t.* toplantıya başkanlık etm.; kürsüye oturtmak;
omuzlarında taşımak; '~-lift *n.* telesiyej;
~.man ['~mən] *n.* başkan, reis; '~.man-
ship *n.* başkanlık, riyaset; '~.wom.an *N.*
kadın başkan.

chaise [ʃeiz] *n.* hafif gezinti arabası.

chal.ice ['tʃælis] *n.* tas, ayinde kullanılan kadeh.

chalk [tʃɔːk] 1. *n.* tebeşir; red ~ kırmızı
tebeşir; by a long ~ F fersah fersah; 2.
*vb.* beyazlatmak, tebeşir katmak, tebeşirle yazmak, resim yapmak; *mst* ~ up
tebeşirle yazmak; hesabına katmak, sayı kaydetmek; ~ out tebeşirle taslak çizmek; *fig.* karalamak; 'chalk.y *adj.* kireçli; tebeşir gibi.

**chal.lenge** [ˈtʃælindʒ] **1.** *n.* meydan okuma, davet; X düelloya davet; *part.* ᴔ reddi hâkim; ~ prize *spor:* çalenç; **2.** *v/t.* çağırmak; meydan okumak; düelloya davet etm.; X parola veya kimlik sormak; ᴔ hâkim veya jüriyi reddetmek; *bşin* doğruluğundan şüphelenmek; ˈchal.leng.er *n.* meydan okuyan, mücadeleye davet eden kişi.

**cha.lyb.e.ate** [kəˈlibiit] *adj.* demirli, demir tadı olan.

**cham.ber** [ˈtʃeimbə] *n.* oda, yatak odası, özel oda; salon; ⊕ fişek yatağı; bölme, hücre; *parl.* meclis; ~s *pl.* yazıhane, büro, hâkimin özel odası; ⌷ of Commerce ticaret odası; **cham.ber.lain** [ˈ-lin] *n.* mabeyinci, teşrifatçı; kâhya; ˈcham.ber.maid *n.* oda hizmetçisi; ˈcham.ber-mu.sic *n.* oda müziği; ˈcham.ber-pot *n.* lâzımlık, oturak.

**cham.bray** *Am.* [ˈʃæmbrei] *n.* ince elbiselik kumaş.

**cha.me.le.on** *zo.* [kəˈmiːljən] *n.* bukalemun.

**cham.fer** ⚙ [ˈtʃæmfə] **1.** *n.* küçük oluk, şev (açmaya yarayan alet); **2.** *vb.* oluk açmak, şev yapmak.

**cham.ois** [ˈʃæmwɑː] **1.** *n. zo.* dağ keçisi; *a.* ~ leather keçi derisi, güderi; **2.** *adj.* açık sarı renkli.

**champ¹** [tʃæmp] *v/t. & v/i.* ısırmak, çiğnemek; *fig.* sinirden dişlerini sıkmak, sabırsızlanmak.

**champ²** F [~] *s.* champion 1.

**cham.pagne** [ʃæmˈpein] *n.* şampanya.

**cham.paign** [ˈtʃæmpein] *n.* ova, kır.

**cham.pi.on** [ˈtʃæmpjən] **1.** kahraman, savunucu kimse; *spor:* şampiyon; **2.** *v/t. b-ni* müdafaa etm., korumak; **3.** *adj.* galip; muhteşem, mükemmel; ˈcham.pi.on.ship *n.* şampiyonluk; şampiyona.

**chance** [tʃɑːns] **1.** *n.* şans, talih; tesadüf; fırsat; ihtimal; by ~ tesadüfen; take a ~, take one's ~ işi şansa bırakmak, şans denemek; **2.** *adj.* şans eseri olan, tesadüfi; **3.** *v/t. & v/i.* bir kere denemek; göze almak; tesadüfen olm.; tesadüfe bırakmak; I ~d to be there tesadüfen oradaydım; ~ upon rastlamak -*e*; şans eseri bulmak -*i*.

**chan.cel** ⚙ [ˈtʃɑːnsəl] *n.* kilisede mihrabın etrafında rahip ve koronun durduğu yer; ˈchan.cel.ler.y *n.* kançılarya, rektörlük *(makamı, bürosu)*; ˈchan.cel.lor *n.* rektör; yüksek rütbeli devlet memuru; saray kâtibi; *(Almanya'da)* başbakan, şansölye.

**chan.cer.y** [ˈtʃɑːnsəri] *n. (İngiltere'de)* en yüksek mahkeme; *(Amerika'da)* temyiz mahkemesi; in ~ temyiz mahkemesindeki dava; *fig.* müşkül durumda.

**chanc.y** F [ˈtʃɑːnsi] *adj.* tehlikeli, rizikolu.

**chan.de.lier** [ˈtʃændiˈliə] *n.* avize.

**chan.dler** [ˈtʃɑːndlə] *n.* mum yapan veya satan kişi; ˈchan.dler.y *n.* hırdavatçı dükkânı.

**change** [tʃeindʒ] **1.** *n.* değiş(tir)me, değişiklik; sapma; yenilik; paranın üstü; bozukluk; for a ~ değişiklik olsun diye; **2.** *v/t.* değiştirmek; boz(dur)mak; *tren:* aktarma yapmak; *(üstünü)* değiştirmek; ~ over *endüstri vs.:* yöntem değiştirmek; I've ~d my mind fikrimi değiştirdim; *v/i.* başkalaşmak, değişmek; ~ into second gear *mot.* ikinci vitese geçmek; *a.* ~ trains *(trende)* aktarma yapmak; change.aˈbil.i.ty *n.* değişebilirlik; ˈchange.a.ble değişebilir; kararsız, dönek; ˈchange-gear *n.* ⊕ sürat değiştirme düzeni; ˈchange.less □ değişmez, sabit; changeling [ˈ-liŋ] *n.* bebekken değiştirilmiş çocuk; cin veya perilerin lohusa yatağına koyduğu bozuk şekilli çocuk; ˈchange-lo.ver *n.* yöntem değiştirme.

**chan.nel** [ˈtʃænl] **1.** *n.* kanal, boğaz; nehir yatağı; yol *(a. fig.);* by the official ~s resmî yoldan; **2.** *v/t.* kanal açmak; oymak; kanala dökmek; *fig.* yönlendirmek.

**chant** [tʃɑːnt] **1.** *n.* şarkı, dinî şarkı; monoton bir melodi, monoton ses tonu; *fig.* can sıkıcı şarkı; **2.** *v/t.* şarkı söylemek, türkü çağırmak; teganni etm.; chan.ti.cleer *poet.* [tʃæntiˈkliə] *n.* evcil horoz; chan.try *eccl.* [ˈtʃɑːntri] *n. (kilise)* dua okunan bölüm; dua okutma parası; chan.ty [ˈ-ti] *n.* gemici şarkısı, heyamola.

**cha.os** [ˈkeiɔs] *n.* karışıklık; kaos; chaˈot.ic *adj.* (~ally) karmakarışık, altüst olmuş, düzensiz.

**chap¹** [tʃæp] **1.** *n.* yırtık, yarık, çatlak *(esp. deride);* **2.** *v/t. & v/i. (cildi)* çatla(t)mak; yar(ıl)mak; kızar(t)mak.

**chap²** [~] *n.* çenenin etli kısmı *(esp. hayvanlarda).*

**chap³** [~] *n.* oğlan, delikanlı, genç adam, arkadaş; ˈ~-book *n.* küçük, ucuz kitap.

**chap.el** [ˈtʃæpəl] *n.* küçük kilise, mabet; *(okul v.b. yerlerde)* ibadete ayrılmış bölüm; *typ.* matbaa bürosu, matbaacılar birliği.

**chap.er.on** [ˈʃæpərəun] **1.** *n.* bir genç kıza refakat eden yaşlıca kadın, yenge ka-

dın, şaperon; **2.** *v/t.* şaperon olarak refakat etm.

**chap-fall.en** [ˈtʃæpfɔːlən] *adj.* kederli,
mahzun.

**chap.lain** [ˈtʃæplin] *n.* papaz; **¹chap.lain.cy**
*n.* papazlık *(makam, bina veya bürosu)*.

**chap.let** [ˈtʃæplit] *n. (başa takılan)* çelenk; *eccl.* tesbih.

**chap.man** [ˈtʃæpmən] *n.* seyyar satıcı.

**chap.py** ☐ [ˈtʃæpi] çatlamış, yarılmış,
çatlak, yarık.

**chap.ter** [ˈtʃæptə] *n.* bölüm, kısım; bahis;
katedrale bağlı rahipler.

**char¹** *ichth.* [tʃaː] *n.* bir tür alabalık.

**char²** [~] *v/t.* & *v/i.* kömürleş(tir)mek;
karbonlaş(tır)mak.

**char³** [~] **1.** *v/i.* gündelikle ev, ofis temizlemek; **2.** = **charwoman**.

**char-à-banc** [ˈʃærəbæn] *n.* açık omnibüs,
gezinti otobüsü.

**char.ac.ter** [ˈkærəktə] *n.* karakter, seciye;
şöhret; vasıf, nitelik; özellik; işaret,
harf, yazı; *F* orijinal *b-i; thea., roman:*
canlandırılan kişi; sanatçının oynadığı
rol, karakter; **char.ac.ter¹is.tic 1.** *adj.*
(~ally) karakteristik, kendine özgü, tipik: **2.** *n.* karakter özelliği, vasıf; **char-
ac.ter.i.za.tion** [~raiˈzeiʃən] *n.* tasvir, tarif, tanımlama; **¹char.ac.ter.ize** *v/t.* tanımlamak; vasıflandırmak, karakterize
etm.

**cha.rade** [ʃəˈraːd] *n.* hece bilmecesi.

**char.coal** [ˈtʃaːkəul] *n.* mangal kömürü;
**¹~-burn.er** *n.* kömürcü.

**chard** ♣ [ˈtʃaːd] *n.* pazı.

**chare** [tʃɛə] **1.** *vb.* temizlemek, yıkamak;
**2.** *n. mst* ~s *pl.* ev işleri.

**charge** [tʃaːdʒ] **1.** *n.* yük, hamule; şarj; ✕
hamle, saldırı; sorumluluk; görev, memuriyet; masraf, fiyat; vergi, rüsum;
bedel, ücret; *♫, eccl.* suçlama, suç isna-
dı, itham; ✕ bir cihazdaki elektrik miktarı, yükleme, şarj; ~s *pl.* masraflar; **bə**
**in ~ of** *bş* ile görevli olm., *bşden* sorumlu olm.; **be in the ~ of** *s.o.* birisinden sorumlu olm.; **take ~ of** *bşi* yüklenmek, sorumluluğunu üstüne almak; **free of ~**
karşılıksız, ücretsiz; **2.** *v/t.* & *v/i.* yüklemek, doldurmak; suçlamak (**with** *ile*);
hesabına geçirmek (**on, upon** *-in*); hücum etm. *-e;* ♫ şarj etm.; istemek *(fiyat)*; hesabına kaydetmek, geçirmek;
görev vermek; önermek, emretmek;
**~** *s.o.* **with the duty of** *b-ni* *bş* ile görevlendirmek; **¹charge.a.ble** ☐ itham edilebilir, suçlanabilir (**with** *ile*); hesaba geçirilebilir; ödenebilir (**to** *-e*).

**char.gé d¹af.faires** *pol.* [ˈʃaːʒeidæˈfɛə] *n.*
maslahatgüzar, işgüder.

**charg.er** *poet.,* ✕ [ˈtʃaːdʒə] *n.* savaş atı.

**char.i.ot** *poet., hist.* [ˈtʃæriət] *n.* hafif iki
tekerlekli araba, savaş arabası; **char.i-
ot.eer** [~tiə] *n.* savaş arabasını süren
arabacı.

**char.i.ta.ble** ☐ [ˈtʃæritəbl] cömert, hayırsever, yardımsever, fukara babası;
**~ society** yardımsevenler derneği; **¹char-
i.ta.ble.ness** *n.* cömertlik, hayırseverlik;
merhamet, hoşgörülük.

**char.i.ty** [ˈtʃæriti] *n.* hayırseverlik; şefkat, merhamet; hayır, sadaka; **sister of
~** fakire yardım eden rahibe; **~ begins
at home** şefkat insanın ev halkına yardım etmesi ile başlar; **¹~-¹child** *n.* yetimler yurdunda yetişen çocuk; **¹~-¹school**
*n.* yetimler yurdu.

**cha.ri.va.ri** [ʃaːriˈvaːri] *n.* alay etm. için
tencereye vurularak yapılan gürültü.

**char.la.tan** [ˈʃaːlətən] *n.* şarlatan, yalandan beceri sahibi olduğunu iddia eden
kişi; **¹char.la.tan.ry** *n.* şarlatanlık.

**char.lock** ♣ [ˈtʃaːlɔk] *n.* çalgıcıotu, yabani hardal.

**char.lotte** [ˈʃaːlət] *n.* bir tür puding.

**charm** [tʃaːm] **1.** *n.* sihir, büyü, muska;
*fig.* cazibe, çekicilik; **2.** *v/t.* büyülemek,
sihirlemek; *fig.* teshir etm.; meftun etm.;
**~ away** *etc.* büyü ile etkileyerek *bşi* ortadan kaldırmak, yoketmek; **¹charm.er**
*n.* sihirbaz kadın, büyücü; *fig.* teshir
eden, etkileyen kadın veya erkek; **¹charm-
ing** ☐ çekici, cazip, cana yakın.

**char.nel-house** [ˈtʃaːnlhaus] *n.* ölü kemik-
lerinin toplandığı mahzen.

**chart** [tʃaːt] **1.** *n.* ↓ deniz haritası; plan,
çizelge, kroki; **2.** *v/t.* haritasını yapmak,
haritada göstermek; grafiğini çıkarmak.

**char.ter** [ˈtʃaːtə] **1.** *n.* berat, imtiyaz, patent; ↓ gemi kira kontratı; *mst* ~-**party**
gemi kira kontratı, navlun mukavelesi;
**2.** *v/t.* berat, imtiyaz veya patent vermek; *(uçak, gemi)* kiralamak; **s. accountant.**

**char.wom.an** [ˈtʃaːwumən] *n.* temizleyici,
gündelikçi *(kadın).*

**char.y** ☐ [ˈtʃɛəri] (of) dikkatli, itinalı;
düşünceli; tutumlu, pinti.

**chase¹** [tʃeis] **1.** *n.* av, takip, kovalama;
kovalanan şey veya kişi; **give ~ to** pe-
şinde(n) koşmak *-in;* **2.** *vb.* kovalamak,
takip etm.; avlamak; *fig.* acele etm.,
koşmak.

**chase²** [~] *v/t.* çizmek, oymak, hakketmek; kabartma işleri yapmak *(maden, tahta üzerine).*

**chase³** *typ.* [~] *n.* harfler için kullanılan demir çerçeve.

**chas.er** ['tʃeisə] *n.* avcı, kovalayan; sert içkinin üzerine alınan hafif içki veya su; ✝ avcı uçağı.

**chasm** ['kæzəm] *n.* yarık, uçurum *(a. fig.)*; kanyon, dar boğaz.

**chas.sis** *mot.* ['ʃæsi] *n. pl.* **chas.sis** ['ʃæsiz] *(top, uçak, otomobil)* alt iskelet, şasi.

**chaste** ☐ [tʃeist] temiz, iffetli, nezih; basit, sade, gösterişsiz, tantanasız *(üslup, stil).*

**chas.ten** ['tʃeisn] *v/t.* terbiyesini vermek -*in,* uslandırmak -*i,* yola getirmek -*i.*

**chas.tise** [tʃæs'taiz] *v/t.* dövmek, cezalandırmak; **chas.tise.ment** ['~tizmənt] *n.* dayak, kötek, ceza.

**chas.ti.ty** ['tʃæstiti] *n.* iffet, saffet, temizlik.

**chas.u.ble** *eccl.* ['tʃæzjubl] *n.* ayinde papazın giydiği kolsuz kıyafet.

**chat** [tʃæt] **1.** *n.* konuşma, çene çalma, sohbet; **2.** *v/i.* sohbet etm., konuşmak, çene çalmak.

**châ.teau** ['ʃætəu] *n.* şato, büyük köşk *(Fransa'da).*

**chat.tels** ['tʃætlz] *n. pl.* **mst goods and ~** her türlü taşınır mal.

**chat.ter** ['tʃætə] **1.** *n.* gevezelik, boş lâf; diş çatırdaması; **2.** *v/i.* çene çalmak; *(diş)* çatırdamak; '~.box *n.* F boşboğaz, geveze; '**chat.ter.er** *n.* geveze, farfaracı. **chat.ty** ['tʃæti] *adj.* sohbet meraklısı, geveze.

**chauf.feur** ['ʃəufə] *n.* şoför, araba sürücüsü; **chauf.feuse** [~'fəːz] *n.* kadın şoför.

**chau.vin.ism** ['ʃəuvinizəm] *n.* aşırı milliyetçilik, şovenlik, şovenizm; '**chau.vin.ist** *n.* şoven; **chau.vin'is.tic** *adj.* (~ally) şovenistliğe ait.

**chaw** *sl.* [tʃɔː] *v/t.* çiğnemek; ~ **up** *Am. sl.* **mst** *fig.* mahvetmek, imha etm., yok etm.; '~.ba.con *n.* budala, aptal.

**cheap** ☐ [tʃiːp] ucuz; değersiz *(a. fig.)*; bayağı, adi; feel ~ F keyifsiz olm.; mahcup olm.; hold ~ bşe önem vermemek; on the ~ F ucuza, ucuz olarak; make o.s. ~ k-ni küçük düşürmek; ♀ Jack seyyar satıcı; '**cheap.en** *v/t.* ucuzlatmak; *fig.* küçük düşürmek; *v/i.* ucuzlamak; '**cheap-skate** *n. Am. sl.* cimri, avantacı kişi.

**cheat** ['tʃiːt] **1.** *n.* hile, düzen; hileci, *sl.* üçkağıtçı; **2.** *v/t.* aldatmak, dolandırmak, bşi hile ile birinin elinden almak

*(out of s.th.);* '**cheat.ing** *n.* aldatma, dolandırma.

**check** [tʃek] **1.** *n.* engel, durdurma; kontrol, teftiş; fiş, marka; ✗ yenilgi, hezimet; *Am.* kontrol işareti; *Am.* eşya makbuzu; *Am.* ✝ = cheque; *satranç:* şah; *Am. (lokantada)* hesap pusulası; ~ pattern ekoseli kumaş; pass *veya* hand in one's ~s *Am.* F ölmek; keep s.o. in ~ b-ni kontrol etm., gözetmek; **2.** *v/t.* & *v/i.* önlemek, durdurmak; karşılaştırmak, kontrol etm.; *Am.* defterine işaret koymak; *satranç:* şah çekmek; ~ in *Am.* otel defterine kaydolmak; ~ one's baggage *Am. b-nin* bavullarını kontrol etm.; ~ out otelden parasını ödeyip ayrılmak; ~ up kontrol etm.; ~ up on soruşturmak, araştırmak; **checked** *adj.* kareli, ekose; '**check.er** *n.* gözcü, müfettiş; dama, kare, ekose desen; ~s *pl. Am.* dama oyunu; = chequer; '**check.ered** *adj.* kareli, damalı; '**check.ing** *n.* kontrol; '**check-mate 1.** *n.* satranç: mat; yenilgi; **2.** *v/t.* satranç: mat etm., yenmek *(a. fig)*; '**check-point** *n.* kontrol noktası; '**check-room** *n. Am.* vestiyer; '**check-up** *n. Am.* tıbbî kontrol.

**Ched.dar** ['tʃedə] *n.* bir çeşit krem peynir, çedar peyniri.

**cheek** [tʃiːk] **1.** *n.* yanak; F arsızlık, yüzsüzlük; ⊕ fren takozu; *s.* jowl; **2.** *v/t.* F küstahlık etmek -*e;* '**cheek-bone** *n.* elmacık kemiği; '**cheek.y** *adj.* F yüzsüz, küstah.

**cheep** [tʃiːp] *v/i.* cıvıldamak, kuş gibi cik cik etm.

**cheer** [tʃiə] **1.** *n.* alkış, ‹yaşa!› sesi; neşe; be of good ~ yüreğini ferah tutmak; three ~s! üç defa ‹yaşa!, yaşa!, yaşa!›; **2.** *v/t.* alkışlamak, neşelendirmek; *a.* ~ up *b-ni* teselli etm, avutmak; *a.* ~ on teşvik etm, alkışla cesaret vermek; *v/i.* sevinçle bağırmak, sevinç sesleri çıkarmak; *a.* ~ up cesaretlenmek; keyiflenmek; sevinmek; '**cheer.ful** ☐ neşeli, şen; '**cheer.ful.ness,** '**cheer.i.ness** *n.* neşelilik, neşe; '**cheer.ing** *n.* alkış, cesaret verme; '**cheer.i.o** ['~ri'əu] *int.* F Allaha ısmarladık!; merhaba!; '**cheer.less** ☐ neşesiz, kederli; kasvetli; '**cheer.y** ☐ neşeli, şen.

**cheese** ['tʃiːz] *n.* peynir; *sl.* mükemmel; ~.burg.er *n.* peynirli köfte; '~.cake *n.* peynirli kek; *sl.* duvara yapıştırılan güzel kadın posteri; '~.cloth *n.* tülbent; '~.mon.ger *n.* peynirci; '~.par.ing **1.** *adj.* cimri, pinti; hesabî; **2.** *n.* değersiz şey; hesabilik.

**chees.y** ['tʃiːzi:] *adj.* peynirli, peynir gibi.

**80**

**chee.tah** zo. [ˈtʃiːtə] n. avda kullanılan parsa benzer bir hayvan.

**chef** [ʃef] n. şef, ahçıbaşı.

**chem.i.cal** [ˈkemikəl] 1. ☐ kimyevî, kimyasal; 2. ¹**chem.i.cals** n. pl. kimyevî maddeler.

**che.mise** [ʃəˈmiːz] n. (kadın) iç gömleği.

**chem.ist** [ˈkemist] n. kimyager; eczacı; ~'s shop eczane; ¹**chem.is.try** n. kimya.

**chem.o.ther.a.py** ⚕ [keməuˈθerəpi] n. kemoterapi, kimyevî maddelerle tedavi.

**cheque** † [tʃek] n. çek; not negotiable ~, crossed ~ çizgili çek; ¹**~-book** n. çek defteri.

**chequer** [ˈtʃekə] 1. n. mst ~s pl. dama oyunu; 2. v/t. damalı yapmak, ekose desen ile kaplamak; ¹**cheq.uered** adj. kareli, satrançlı; fig. karışık, değişik.

**cher.ish** [ˈtʃeriʃ] v/t. beslemek; gütmek; b-ni aziz ve el üstünde tutmak.

**che.root** [ʃəˈruːt] n. bir çeşit yaprak sigara, puro.

**cher.ry** [ˈtʃeri] 1. n. kiraz; kiraz ağacı; 2. adj. parlak kırmızı.

**cher.ub** [ˈtʃerəb] n. melek; nur yüzlü kimse; nur topu gibi çocuk; **che.ru.bic** [~ˈruːbik] adj. melek gibi.

**cher.vil** ♀ [ˈtʃəːvil] n. frenk maydanozu.

**chess** [tʃes] n. satranç oyunu; ¹**~-board** n. satranç tahtası; ¹**~.man** n. satranç taşı.

**chest** [tʃest] n. sandık, kutu, kasa; anat. göğüs; ~ of drawers konsol, çekmeceli dolap; get s.th. off one's ~ b-ne içini dökmek; ¹**chest.ed** comb. ...göğüslü.

**ches.ter.field** [ˈtʃestəfiːld] n. uzun palto; kabarık kanepe.

**chest.nut** [ˈtʃesnʌt] 1. n. kestane; kestane ağacı; F bayat espri; 2. adj. kestane rengi, maron.

**che.val-glass** [ʃəˈvælglɑːs] n. boy aynası.

**chev.a.lier** [ʃevəˈliə] n. şövayle, silahşör; cesur ve mert kimse.

**chev.i.ot** [ˈtʃeviət] n. bir çeşit İskoç koyunu; bu koyunun yününden yapılan kumaş, şevyot.

**chev.ron** ✕ [ˈʃevrən] n. çavuş ve onbaşı rütbelerine ait kol şeridi.

**chev.y** F [ˈtʃevi] 1. n. av (narası); 2. v/t. & v/i. avla(n)mak.

**chew** [tʃuː] v/t. & v/i. çiğnemek; derin düşüncelere dalmak (on, upon, over); ~ the fat veya rag sl. çene çalmak, laklak etm.; ¹**chew.ing-gum** n. çiklet.

**chi.cane** [ʃiˈkein] 1. n. hile, şike; 2. v/t. & v/i. hile yapmak; **chi¹can.er.y** n. hilekârlık; fig. dalavere.

**chick** [tʃik] s. chicken.

**chick.a.dee** Am. orn. [ˈtʃikədiː] n. iskete kuşu.

**chick.a.ree** Am. zo. [ˈtʃikəriː] n. kırmızı Amerikan sincabı.

**chick.en** [ˈtʃikin] n. piliç, civciv; tavuk eti; sl. korkak; ¹**~-feed** n. Am. tavuk yemi; sl. bozuk para, az para; ¹**~-heart.ed** adj. korkak; ¹**~-pox** n. ⚕ suçiçeği; ¹**chick-pea** n. ♀ nohut; ¹**chick.weed** n. ♀ kuş otu.

**chic.o.ry** [ˈtʃikəri] n. hindiba.

**chid** [tʃid] pret. & p.p., ¹**chid.den** p.p. of chide.

**chide** lit. [tʃaid] (irr.) vb. b-ni azarlamak, ayıplamak; b-ne çıkışmak, söylenmek.

**chief** [tʃiːf] 1. ☐ büyük, en önemli, baş..., ana..., belli başlı; ~ clerk daire şefi, kalem amiri; 2. n. baş, reis, şef, âmir, **chieftain** [ˈ~tən] n. kabile reisi.

**chif.fon** [ˈʃifɔn] n. şifon; **chif.fo.nier** [ʃifəˈniə] n. aynalı, çekmeceli dolap, şifoniyer.

**chil.blain** [ˈtʃilblein] n. ⚕ soğuk şişliği.

**child** [tʃaild] n., pl. **chil.dren** [ˈtʃildrən] çocuk; be a good ~! uslu dur!, iyi çocuk ol!; from a ~ küçükten beri; with ~ hamile; ~'s play fig. çocuk oyuncağı, kolay, basit iş; ¹**~-bed** n. lohusa yatağı; ¹**~-birth** n. doğum; ¹**child.hood** n. çocukluk; second ~ bunaklık; ¹**child.ish** ☐ çocukça; b.s. aptal, budala; ¹**child.ish.ness** n. çocuksuluk, çocukçalık; b.s. dar düşüncelilik; ¹**child.less** n. çocuksuz; ¹**child-like** adj. fig. çocuk gibi, çocuk ruhlu; **chil.dren** [ˈtʃildrən] pl. of child.

**chil.i** Am. ♀ [ˈtʃili] n. kırmızı biber cinsi.

**chill** [tʃil] 1. adj. lit. buz gibi soğuk; 2. n. soğuk; titreme, üşüme; fig. soğuk davranış; soğuk algınlığı; take the ~ off a liquid sıvıyı hafifçe ısıtmak; 3. v/t. soğutmak; üşütmek; metall. soğutmak, su vermek; ~ed meat dondurulmuş et; v/i. soğumak; soğuktan titremek, donmak; ¹**chill.ness, ¹chill.i.ness** n. soğuk; soğuk davranış; ¹**chill.y** adj. soğuk, serin; hep üşüyen.

**chime** [tʃaim] 1. n. ahenkli çan sesi; fig. ahenk; 2. v/t. & v/i. çan çal(ın)mak; fig. hepbir ahenk olm.; ~ in uymak (with -e).

**chi.me.ra** [kaiˈmiərə] n. hayalî canavar, ejderha; korkunç hayal; **chi.mer.i.cal** ☐ [~ˈmerikəl] hayalî; imkânsız.

**chim.ney** [ˈtʃimni] n. baca; lamba şişesi; yanardağ ağzı (a. mount.); ¹**~-piece** n. şömine üstü, ocak rafı; ¹**~-pot** n. ocak külâhı; F fig. silindir şapka; ¹**~-stalk** n.

baca tepesi; fabrika bacası; **ı~-sweep-** (.er) *n.* baca temizleyicisi.

**chim.pan.zee** *zo.* [tʃimpən¹ziː] *n.* şempanze.

**chin¹** [tʃin] *n.* çene; keep one's ~ up F güçlüğe korkmadan göğüs germek; wag one's ~ konuşmak, çene çalmak.

**chin²** *sl.* [~] *v/i.* yarenlik etm., çene çalmak.

**chi.na** [¹tʃainə] *n.* porselen; ¹2.**man** *n.* Çinli.

**chine** [tʃain] *n.* belkemiği, sırt; sırttan çıkarılan et.

**Chi.nese** [¹tʃaiˈniːz] 1. *n.* Çince; Çinli; 2. *adj.* Çin'e ait, Çince'ye ve Çinlilere ait.

**chink¹** [tʃiŋk] *n.* yarık, çatlak.

**chink²** [~] 1. *n.* şıkırtı; çınlama; 2. *v/t.* & *v/i.* şıngırda(t)mak, tıngırda(t)mak.

**chintz** [tʃints] *n.* basma, perdelik pamuklu ve desenli kumaş.

**chip** [tʃip] 1. *n.* çentik; yonga; küçük parça; kırıntı; kuşun «çip» sesi; kızarmış patates; fiş, marka; have a ~ on one's shoulder meydan okumak, kavgaya hazır olm.; 2. *v/t.* yontmak, çentmek; *v/i.* *(kuş)* çip sesi çıkarmak; ~ in F bşe iştirak etm., para koymak; *Am.* F aniden konuşmaya girmek, sözünü kesmek; **chip.muck** [¹~mʌk], **chip.munk** [¹~mʌŋk] *n.* derisi çizgili ufak sincap; ¹**chip.py** *adj.* kurak, verimsiz, zayıf; F sarhoşluktan sonra olan mide bulantısı.

**chi.rop.o.dist** [kiˈrɔpədist] *n.* ayak rahatsızlıkları mütehassısı; **chiˈrop.o.dy** *n.* ayak hastalıkları tedavisi; **chi.ro.practor** ? [kairəuˈpræktə] *n.* oynak yerleri tedavi ederek hastalıkları iyileştiren kimse.

**chirp** [tʃəːp] 1. *n.* cıvıltı; 2. *v/t.* & *v/i.* cıvıldamak, cırcır ötmek; ¹**chirp.y** *adj.* F neşeli, şen.

**chirr** [tʃəː] *v/i.* *(çekirge v.b.)* sesi çıkarmak.

**chir.rup** [¹tʃirəp] 1. *v/i.* neşe ile cıvıldamak; 2. *n.* cıvıltı.

**chis.el** [¹tʃizl] 1. *n.* çelik kalem, kalem keski; 2. *v/t.* kalemle oymak, yontmak; F dolandırmak; ¹**chis.el.er** *n.* oymacı; F dolandırıcı, üçkâğıtçı.

**chit** [tʃit] *n.* çocuk, yavrucuk; a ~ of a girl delişmen kız.

**chit-chat** [¹tʃittʃæt] *n.* lâf, sohbet.

**chiv.al.rous** □ [¹ʃivəlrəs] mert, kibar, şövalye gibi; ¹**chiv.al.ry** *n.* şövalyelik, kahramanlık, cömertlik, mertlik; şövalyeler.

**chive** ❧ [tʃaiv] *n.* bir tür taze soğan.

F.6

**chiv.y** F [¹tʃivi] = chevy.

**chlo.ral** ⚗ [¹klɔːrəl] *n.* kloralhidrat; **chloride** [¹~aid] *n.* klorid; ~ of lime kalsiyum klorid; **chlo.rin.ate** [¹~ineit] *v/t.* *(suyu)* sterilize etm., klorlamak; **chlo.rine** [¹~iːn] *n.* klor; **chlo.ro.form** [¹klɔrəfɔːm] 1. *n.* kloroform; 2. *v/t.* kloroformla bayıltmak; **chlor.o.phyl(l)** [¹~əfil] *n.* bitkilere yeşillik veren madde, klorofil.

**choc-ice** [¹tʃɔkais] *n.* dışı çikolata ile kaplı dondurma.

**chock** ⊕ [tʃɔk] 1. *n.* odun parçası, takoz, kama; difizör; 2. *v/t.* tıkamak, takozlamak, destek koymak; **ı~-a-¹block** hıncahınç, tıkabasa (with *ile*); **ı~-¹full** *adj.* dopdolu.

**choc.o.late** [¹tʃɔkəlit] *n.* çikolata; ~ cream çikolatalı şekerleme; fondan.

**choice** [tʃɔis] 1. *n.* seçme, tercih; tercih hakkı; seçenek, seçilen şey; have one's ~ b-nin seçme hakkı olm.; make veya take one's ~ kendi tercihini yapmak, almak; multiple ~ çok seçenekli *(soru şekli)*; 2. □ seçkin, seçme, güzide, titiz; ~ fruit dikkatlice seçilmiş meyva.

**choir** [¹kwaiə] *n.* koro; *(kilisede)* koro yeri.

**choke** [tʃəuk] 1. *v/t.* & *v/i.* tıka(n)mak, boğ(ul)mak *(a. fig.)*; ⊕ boğmak; ∮ kısmak; *mst* ~ down zorla yutmak; ~ off F durdurmak; vazgeçirmek, menetmek (from -*den*); *mst* ~ up tıkanmak; 2. *n.* boğma, tıkama; ⊕ daraltma; *mot.* jigle; ~ coil ∮ kısma bobini; **ı~-bore** *n.* ⊕ namlu çapının yavaş yavaş azalması; **ı~--damp** *n.* ⚒ patlamadan sonra madendeki karbondioksit gazı, boğucu gaz; ¹**chok.er** *n.* co. boğan şey *veya* kimse; madeni gerdanlık; dik yaka; ¹**chok.y** 1. *adj.* boğazı tıkayan, boğucu; 2. *n.* *sl.* hapishane.

**chol.er.a** ? [¹kɔlərə] *n.* kolera; ¹**chol.er.ic** *adj.* canıtez; öfkesi burnunda.

**choose** [tʃuːz] *(irr.)* *v/t.* seçmek, tercih etm.; ~ to *inf.* bşi üstün tutmak, öne almak; ¹**choos.y** *adj.* titiz, zor beğenen.

**chop¹** [tʃɔp] 1. *n.* darbe, kesme; çırpıntı; parça; pirzola; ~s *pl.* çene, hayvan ağzı; ⊕ marangoz mengenesi; ~s and changes *pl.* devamlı değişmeler; 2. *v/t.* balta ile kesmek, yarmak; *usu.* ~ up bşi kıymak, doğramak; *v/i.* değişmek; ~ about *(rüzgâr)* değişmek, dönmek *(a. fig.)*; ~ and change ne yapacağını bilmemek, bir dakikası bir dakikasına uymamak.

**chop²** † [~] *n.* nişan, alamet, marka; first ~ birinci sınıf, en üstün kalite.

**chop-chop** *sl.* [ˈtʃɔpˈtʃɔp] *adv.* süratle, gecikmeksizin.

**chop-house** [ˈtʃɔphaus] *n.* kebapçı, lokanta; ˈ**chop.per** *n.* el baltası, kasap satırı; F helikopter; ˈ**chop.ping** *n.* kesiş, vuruş; ˈ**chop.py** *adj.* değişken, yön değiştiren *(rüzgâr)*; çırpıntılı *(deniz)*; = chappy; ˈ**chop.stick** *n.* Çinlilerin yemek yerken kullandıkları çubuk; **chop-su.ey** [~ˈsuːi] *n.* Çin lokantalarına ait et suyu veya balıkla pişirilen pirinçli yemek.

**cho.ral** □ [ˈkɔːrəl] koro ile ilgili; koro için yapılmış; **cho.ral(e)** ♪ [kɔˈraːl] *n.* kilise ilâhisi, koral.

**chord** [kɔːd] *n.* ♪, *poet.* kiriş, tel; *fig.* his, duygu; A veter, kiriş; ♪ akort.

**chore** *part.* *Am.* [tʃɔː] = chare 2.

**chor.ine** [ˈkɔːriːn] *s.* chorus-girl.

**chor.is.ter** [ˈkɔristə] *n.* koro üyesi, korodaki çocuk; *Am. a.* koro şefi.

**cho.rus** [ˈkɔːrəs] 1. *n.* koro, koro parçası; nakarat, şarkının koro kısmı; 2. *v/t.* koroda şarkı söylemek; ˈ**~-girl** revüde şarkı söyleyip dans eden kız.

**chose** [tʃouz] *pret.*, ˈ**cho.sen** *p.p. of* choose.

**chough** *orn.* [tʃʌf] *n.* küçük karga.

**chouse** F [tʃaus] 1. *n.* hile, oyun; 2. *v/t.* aldatmak, dolandırmak, hile yapmak.

**chow** *Am. sl.* [tʃau] *n.* yemek, yiyecek.

**chow.der** *Am.* [ˈtʃaudə] *n.* bir çeşit balık türlüsü.

**chrism** [ˈkrizəm] *n.* kutsal mesh yağı.

**Christ** [kraist] *n.* Hazreti İsa.

**chris.ten** [ˈkrisn] *v/t.* vaftiz etm., isimlendirmek; **Chris.ten.dom** [ˈ~dəm] *n.* Hıristiyan âlemi; ˈ**chris.ten.ing** *n.* vaftiz; vaftiz etme, isimlendirme.

**Chris.tian** [ˈkristjən] 1. □ Hiristiyan, İsa'ya inanan kişi; ~ name vaftizde verilen isim; ~ Science İsa'nın prensipleri ile kötülük ve fenalıkların yok olabileceğine inanan mezhep; 2. *n.* Hıristiyan; **Chris.ti.an.i.ty** [~tiˈæniti] *n.* Hıristiyanlık; **Chris.tian.ize** [ˈ~tjənaiz] *v/t.* Hıristiyanlaştırmak.

**Christ.mas** [ˈkrisməs] *n.* Noel, İsa'nın doğum yortusu; ~ Day Noel *(25 Aralık günü)*; ~ Eve Noel arifesi; ˈ**~-box** *n.* Noel hediyeleri ile dolu kutu; ˈ**~-tree** *n.* Noel ağacı.

**chro.mat.ic** *phys.*, ♪ [krəuˈmætik] *adj.* (~ally) renklere ait; seslerin yarımşar ton ara ile birbirini takip etmesine ait, kromatik; **chroˈmat.ics** *n. pl. & sg.* renkler ilmi.

**chrome** 🜍 [krəum] *n.* krom; krom boyası; **chro.mi.um** [ˈ~jəm] *n.* krom *(metal)*;

ˈ**chro.mi.um-**ˈ**plat.ed** krome, kromlu; **chro-mo.lith.o.graph** [ˈ~ouˈliθəugraːf] *n.* renkli taş basma.

**chron.ic** [ˈkrɔnik] *adj.* (~ally) sürekli, süreğen, müzmin, kronik *(mst ⚶)*; P tiksindirici; iğrenç, nefret uyandırıcı; **chron.i.cle** [ˈ~l] 1. *n.* tarih, vakayiname; 2. *v/t.* tarih sırası ile yazmak; ˈ**chron.i.cler** *n.* tarihçi, tarihe kaydeden kimse.

**chron.o.log.i.cal** □ [krɔnəˈlɔdʒikəl] kronolojik, tarih sırası ile düzenlenmiş; **~ly** *adv.* tarih sırasına göre; **chro.nol.o.gy** [krəˈnɔlədʒi] *n.* kronoloji; olayların tarih sırası ile hazırlanmış listesi .

**chro.nom.e.ter** [krəˈnɔmitə] *n.* vakti inceden inceye ölçen alet, kronometre.

**chrys.a.lis** [ˈkrisəlis] *n.* böceğin kelebek olmadan koza içindeki hali, krizalit.

**chrys.an.the.mum** ♣ [kriˈsænθəməm] *n.* kasımpatı, krizantem.

**chub** *ichth.* [tʃʌb] *n.* kefal, sazan balığı cinsinden tatlı su balığı; ˈ**chub-by** *adj.* F tombul, hantal *(a. fig.)*.

**chuck**[1] [tʃʌk] 1. *vb.* gurklamak; my ~! şekerim!, yavrum!, kuzum!; 2. *n.* gurklama; 3. ~! ~! bili! bili! *(tavuk çağırmak için)*.

**chuck**[2] F [~] 1. *v/t.* atmak, fırlatmak; ~ out atmak, çöpe atmak; kapı dışarı etm.; ~ under the chin çenesini okşamak; ~ it! *sl.* bırak!; durdur!; 2. *n.* atma, fırlatma.

**chuck**[3] ⊕ [~] *n.* torna bağlama aynası.

**chuck.le** [ˈtʃʌkl] *v/i.* kendi kendine gülmek, kıkır kıkır gülmek.

**chug** [tʃʌg] *n.* çalışırken çıkan ses *(motor vs.)*.

**chum** F [tʃʌm] 1. *n.* yakın arkadaş; be great ~s yakın arkadaş olm.; 2. *v/i.* arkadaşlık etm., beraber oturmak.

**chump** F [tʃʌmp] *n.* odun parçası, kütük, takoz; sersem ,budala, odun kafalı; off one's ~ ahmak.

**chunk** F [tʃʌŋk] *n.* kısa kalın parça; kısa boylu tıknaz adam; ˈ**chunk.y** *adj.* kısa ve kalın, tıknaz; topak topak.

**church** [tʃəːtʃ] 1. *n.* kilise, dini örgüt; din adamlığı; ♀ of England Anglikan kilisesi; ~ service ayini ruhani; 2. *vb.* be ~ed kilisede şükran duası etm. *(doğumdan sonra kadınlar)*; ˈ**~-go.er** *n.* devamlı kiliseye giden kişi; ˈ**church.ing** *n. (doğum yapan kadının)* kilisedeki şükran duası, ibadet; ˈ**church.man** *n.* papaz, kiliseye mensup kimse; ˈ**church**ˈ**ward.en** *n.* kilise mütevellisi; kilise işlerini idare eden fahri görevli; **'church'yard** *n.* kilise avlusu; mezarlık.

**churl** [tʃəːl] *n.* köylü, herif; kaba adam; pinti; **'churl.ish** □ vahşi, kaba; ters; paraya önem veren.

**churn** [tʃəːn] **1.** *n.* yayık; süt kabı; **2.** *v/t.* yayıkta çalkalamak, köpürtmek; *v/i.* yayık dövmek; çalkalanmak.

**chute** [ʃuːt] *n.* çağlayan, şelale, su oluğu; paraşüt.

**chut.ney** [ˈtʃʌtni] *n.* baharlı bir çeşit salça.

**chyle** [kail] *n.* barsaklarda bulunan beyaz bir sıvı, kilüs.

**chyme** [kaim] *n.* midede yarı hazmedilmiş gıda, kimus.

**ci.ca.da** *zo.* [siˈkɑːdə] *n.* ağustosböceği.

**cic.a.trice** [ˈsikətris] *n.* yara kapatan zar, yara izi; **cic.a.tri.za.tion** [~traiˈzeiʃən] *n.* *(yaranın)* zar *veya* deri bağlayarak iyileşmesi; **'cic.a.trize** *v/t. & v/i.* kapatmak; iyileşmek, kabuk bağlamak *(yara).*

**ci.ce.ro.ne** [tʃitʃəˈrəuni] *n.* turist gezdiren rehber, tercüman.

**Cic.e.ro.ni.an** [sisəˈrəunjən] *adj.* Çiçero gibi; belâgat sahibi.

**ci.der** [ˈsaidə] *n.* elma suyu, elma şarabı.

**ci.gar** [siˈgaː] *n.* yaprak sigarası, puro; **ci'gar-case** *n.* puro tabakası.

**cig.a.rette** [sigəˈret] *n.* sigara; **cig.a'rette--case** *n.* tabaka, sigaralık.

**ci.gar-hold.er** [siˈgəːhəuldə] *n.* ağızlık.

**cil.i.a** [ˈsiliə] *n. pl.* kirpikler; **cil.i.ar.y** [ˈsiliəri] *adj.* kirpiksi.

**cinch** *Am. sl.* [sintʃ] *n.* çok kolay şey, çantada keklik.

**cin.cho.na** ♣ [siŋˈkəunə] *n.* kınakına ağacı.

**cinc.ture** [ˈsiŋktʃə] *n.* kuşak, kemer.

**cin.der** [ˈsində] *n.* dışık, cüruf, maden artığı; köz, kor; ~s *pl.* kül; **Cin.der.el.la** [~ˈrelə] *n. (ünlü hikâyedeki gibi)* yeteneği ve güzelliği takdir edilmemiş kız, Sinderella; *fig.* ihmal edilmiş şey *veya* kimse; **'cin.der-track** *n.* spor: atletizm pisti.

**cin.e-cam.er.a** [ˈsinikæmərə] *n.* film çekme makinesi.

**cin.e.ma** [ˈsinəmə] *n.* sinema; sinema dünyası; **cin.e.mat.o.graph** [~ˈmætəgrɑːf] *n.* sinema makinesi, film çekme makinesi; **cin.e.mat.o.graph.ic** [~mætəˈgræfik] *adj.* (~ally) sinema makinesiyle ilgili.

**cin.er.ar.y** [ˈsinərəri] *adj.* kül ile ilgili.

**cin.na.bar** [ˈsinəbaː] *n.* zincifre.

**cin.na.mon** [ˈsinəmən] *n.* tarçın.

**cinque** [siŋk] *n.* iskambil: beşli; zar: beş *(penç)*; ~ foil ♣ beşparmak otu.

**ci.pher** [ˈsaifə] **1.** *n.* şifre; sıfır; *fig.* solda sıfır, hiç; in ~ şifreli; **2.** *vb.* şifre ile yazmak, şifrelemek; hesap yapmak.

**cir.ca** [ˈsəːkə] *adv.* takriben, yaklaşık olarak.

**cir.cle** [ˈsəːkl] **1.** *n.* daire, halka, çevre; grup; devir; ring; meydan; *thea.* balkon; **2.** *vb.* devretmek, dönmek; çevirmek, kuşatmak; **cir.clet** [ˈ~klit] *n.* halkacık, küçük daire.

**circs** F [səːks] = circumstances.

**cir.cuit** [ˈsəːkit] *n.* daire, dolaşım; ∮ devre; ⁂ *(İngiltere'de)* seyyar mahkeme; ✈ uçakla tur atma; short ~ ∮ kısa devre, kontak; ~ breaker ∮ devre kapatan anahtar; make a ~ of *bşin* etrafını dolaşmak; **cir.cu.i.tous** □ [səːˈkjuːitəs] dolaşık, dolmabaçlı; ~ route dolmabaçlı yol.

**cir.cu.lar** [ˈsəːkjulə] **1.** □ dairevi, dairesel; dolaylı, dolambaçlı; ~ letter sirküler; ~ note ✝ tamim, kredi mektubu; ~ saw daire testere; ~ skirt kloş etek; **2.** *n.* tamim, genelge, sirküler; **'cir.cu.lar.ize** *v/t.* sirküler yollamak.

**cir.cu.late** [ˈsəːkjuleit] *v/t. & v/i.* deveran etm.; dağıtmak; dolaş(tır)mak; dön(dür)mek; ✝ tedavül (et(tir)mek; yay(ıl)mak; **'cir.cu.lat.ing:** ~ decimal devirli ondalık kesir; ~ library dışarıya ödünç kitap veren kütüphane; ~ medium değişim aracı, para; **cir.cu'la.tion** *n.* dolaşma; deveran; dağıtım miktarı, tiraj; piyasadaki para miktarı.

**cir.cum...** [ˈsəːkəm] *prefix* takriben, ...kadar; **cir.cum.cise** ♣, eccl. [~ˈsaiz] *v/t.* sünnet etm.; **cir.cum.ci.sion** [~ˈsiʒən] *n.* sünnet etm.; **cir.cum.fer.ence** [səˈkʌmfərəns] *n.* daire çevresi, çember; **cir.cum.flex** [ˈsəːkəmfleks] *n. gr.* uzatma işareti; **cir.cum.ja.cent** [~ˈdʒəisənt] *adj.* dört taraftan bitişik, efraftaki; **cir.cum.lo.cu.tion** [~ləˈkjuːʃən] *n.* dolambaçlı söz; **cir.cum.loc.u.tory** [~ˈlɔkjutəri] *adj.* dolambaçlı, uzun uzadıya; **cir.cum'nav.i.gate** *v/t.* gemi ile etrafını dolaşmak; **cir.cum'nav.i.ga.tor** *n.* gemi ile dünyanın etrafını dolaşan kişi; **cir.cum.scribe** Ⓐ [ˈ~skraib] *v/t.* bir şeklin etrafına başka bir şekil çizmek, daire içine almak -i; sınırlamak -i *(a. fig.);* **cir.cum.scrip.tion** Ⓐ [~ˈskripʃən] *n.* etrafını çizme, kuşatma sınırlama; sınır çizgisi; **cir.cum.spect** □ [ˈ~spekt] dikkatli, ihtiyatlı; **cir.cum.spec.tion** [~ˈspekʃən] *n.* dikkat, özen, dikkatlilik; **cir.cum.stance** [ˈ~təns] *n.* hal, durum, keyfiyet; olay; ayrıntı; ~s *pl.* durum, ahval; mali durum; in *veya* under

the ~s bu şartlar altında; **'cir.cum-
stanced** *comb.* ...bir halde bulunan;
poorly ~ kötü, fakir durumda olan kişi;
**cir.cum.stan.tial** [~'stænʃəl] □ tafsilatlı,
ayrıntılı, uzun uzadıya; tâli, ikinci derecede önemi olan; ~ evidence ೋ emare,
ikinci derecede delil; **cir.cum.vent** [~
-'vent] *v/t.* aldatmak, hile ile galip gelmek.

**cir.cus** ['sɜːkəs] *n.* sirk; meydan.

**cir.rus** ['sirəs] *n.*, *pl.* **cir.ri** ['~rai] saçak
bulut, sirrus.

**cis.sy** ['sisi] = sissy.

**cis.tern** ['sistən] *n.* sarnıç, su deposu.

**cit.a.del** ['sitədl] *n.* hisar, kale.

**ci.ta.tion** /sai'teiʃən/ *n.* mahkemeye davet, celp; başka eserden alınan metin
parçası; *(iyi hal veya kahramanlığı belirten)* resmi bildiri; **cite** *v/t.* celbetmek,
mahkemeye davet etm.; beyan etm.; zikretmek, anmak; *(iyi hal veya kahramanlığı)* resmi bildiri ile açıklamak.

**cit.i.zen** ['sitizn] *n.* hemşeri; vatandaş; ✕
sivil; **cit.i.zen.ship** ['~ʃip] *n.* vatandaşlık,
tabiiyet.

**cit.ric ac.id** ['sitrik'æsid] *n.* sitrik asit; **citron.** ['~rən] *n.* ağaçkavunu; ağaçkavunu
kabuğu şekerlemesi; **cit.rus** ['~rəs] *adj.*
turunçgillere ait.

**cit.y** ['siti] **1.** *n.* şehir, kent; site; the ♀
Londra'nın iş merkezi; **2.** *adj.* şehir veya belediyeye ait; ~ editor *Am.* yöresel
haberler yazım sorumlusu; ~ hall *Am.*
belediye; belediye dairesi; ~ manager
*Am.* belediye başkanı; ~ state site kent,
şehir devleti.

**civ.ic** ['sivik] *adj.* şehre ait, belediye ile
ilgili; yurttaşlık ile ilgili; madenî; sivil; ~ rights *pl.* vatandaşlık hakları;
**'civ.ics** *n. sg.* yurttaşlık bilgisi.

**civ.il** □ ['sivl] vatandaşlarla ilgili; sivil;
nazik; uygar, medenî; iç, dahilî; ೋ medeni hukukla ilgili; ~ defence pasif korunma, sivil savunma; ~ war iç savaş;
♀ Servant devlet memuru; ♀ Service devlet hizmeti; **ci.vil.ian** ✕ [si'viljən] *n.* sivil şahıs; ~ population sivil halk, sivil-
ler; **ci'vil.i.ty** *n.* nezaket; **civ.i.li.za.tion**
[~lai'zeiʃən] *n.* medeniyet, uygarlık;
**'civ.i.lize** *v/t.* medenileştirmek, uygar dü-
zeye çıkarmak; ~d nation uygar, mede-
ni millet.

**civ.vies** *sl.* ['siviz] *n. pl.* sivil kıyafet; **'civ-
vy street** *sl.* başıbozuk hayat.

**clack** [klæk] **1.** *n.* tıkırtı, çıtırtı; *fig.* zevzeklik; ⊕ klape, subap; **2.** *v/i.* takırdamak; *fig.* laklak etm., boşboğazlık etm.

**clad** *lit.* [klæd] *pret, & p.p. of* clothe; hills

~ in verdure *poet.* yamaçlar yeşillendi.

**claim** [kleim] **1.** *n.* istek, talep; ೋ iddia;
✕ paylaştırılan arazi; lay ~ to sahip çıkmak -e; **2.** *vb.* iddia etm.; istemek; sahip çıkmak; ~ to be ... olduğunu iddia
etm.; **'claim.a.ble** *adj.* talep edilebilir;
**'claim.ant** *n.* iddialı; ೋ davacı, alacaklı,
hak talep eden.

**clair.voy.ance** [klɛə'vɔiəns] *n.* geleceği
görme yeteneği *(a. fig.)*; **clair'voy.ant(e)**
*n.* görünmez şeyleri gören, gaipten haber veren kişi.

**clam** *zo.* [klæm] *n.* bir tür istiridye, tarak.

**cla.mant** *lit.* ['klemənt] *adj.* gürültülü; ısrarlı.

**clam.ber** ['klæmbə] *v/i.* (güçlükle) tırmanmak.

**clam.mi.ness** ['klæminis] *n.* yapışkanlık;
**'clam.my** □ soğuk ve ıslak, nemli, yapışkan.

**clam.or.ous** □ ['klæmərəs] gürültülü, şamatalı; **clam.our** **1.** *n.* gürültü, patırtı;
**2.** *vb.* gürültü etm.; yaygara koparmak
*(for için)*.

**clamp¹** ⊕ [klæmp] **1.** *n.* kenet, köşebent;
**2.** *v/t.* bşi bağlamak, raptetmek, tesbit
etm.

**clamp²** [~] *n.* yeraltı stoğu *(patates vs.)*.

**clan** [klæn] *n.* kabile, klan; takım, zümre; *fig.* geniş aile.

**clan.des.tine** □ [klæn'destin] gizli, el altından.

**clang** [klæŋ] **1.** *n.* şakırtı, takırtı, çınlama; **2.** *v/t.* & *v/i.* yüksek sesle çal(dır)
mak; **clan.gor.ous** ['~gərəs] *adj.* gürültülü ses çıkaran; **'clang.o.(u)r** = clang.

**clank** [klæŋk] **1.** *n.* maden sesi, tınlama,
çınlama; **2.** *v/t.* & *v/i.* madenî ses çıkart-
(tır)mak.

**clan.nish** ['klæniʃ] *adj.* klana, kabileye
ait; *(bir grup insan)* yalnız birbirini destekleyen ve yabancıları sevmeyen.

**clap** [klæp] **1.** *n.* gürleme, patlama; tokat; vuruş, el çırpma; **2.** *vb.* tokat atmak, el çırpmak, alkışlamak; ~ eyes on
s.o. *b-ne* gözü ilişmek; **'~.board** *n.* ince
tahta, padavra; **'clap.per** *n.* çan tokmağı; alkışlayan kişi; **'clap.trap** *n.* palavra,
sahte iltifat, yaygara.

**clar.et** ['klærət] *n.* kırmızı şarap; *sl.* kan.

**clar.i.fi.ca.tion** [klærifi'keiʃən] *n.* aydınlatma, açıklama; **clar.i.fy** ['~fai] *v/t.* tasfiye etm.; *fig.* aydınlatmak; *v/i.* açılmak, berraklaşmak.

**clar.i.net** [klæri'net], **clar.i.o.net** [~ə'net]
*n.* klarnet.

**clar.i.on** ['klæriən] *n.* berrak ve tiz ses.

**clar.i.ty** [ˈklæriti] *n.* açıklık, berraklık.

**clash** [klæʃ] **1.** *n.* şakırtı, çarpışma (sesi); *fig.* çatışma; **2.** *vb.* şakırdamak, takırdamak; çarpışmak; uyuşmamak, çatışmak (with *ile*).

**clasp** [klɑːsp] **1.** *n.* toka, çengelli iğne, kopça; el sıkma, kucaklama; *fig. b-ne* sarılma; **2.** *v/t.* toka ile tutturmak, bağlamak; (*el*) sıkmak, kavramak, yakalamak; ~ s.o.'s hand elleri kavuşturmak; *v/i.* sıkı tutmak; '~-knife *n.* sustalı çakı.

**class** [klɑːs] **1.** *n.* sınıf, tabaka; kategori; *(tren. vapur v.b.)* mevki; *Am. univ.* aynı yıl okulu bitirenler; ders; *attr.* F kibarlık, üstünlük, şıklık; **2.** *v/t.* sınıflara ayırmak, tasnif etm.; F düşünmek, saymak; ~ with *bşle* kıyas etm.; benzetme yapmak; '~-Icon.scious *adj.* sınıf farkı gözeten; '~-fel.low *n.* sınıf arkadaşı.

**clas.sic** [ˈklæsik] **1.** *n.* klasik yazar; ~s *pl.* eski Yunan ve Latin edebiyatı eserleri; **2.** = 'clas.si.cal □ klasik; mükemmel, birinci derece.

**clas.si.fi.ca.tion** [klæsifiˈkeiʃən] *n.* tasnif, sınıflandırma; **clas.si.fy** [ˈ~fai] *v/t.* sınıflandırmak, tasnif etm.

**class...:** '~-mate *s.* class-fellow; '~-room *n.* sınıf, derslik; '~-war.fare *n.* sınıflar arası mücadele.

**clat.ter** [ˈklætə] **1.** *n.* takırtı; **2.** *v/t.* & *v/i.* takırda(t)mak.

**clause** [klɔːz] *n.* madde, şart; *(kanun, kontrat v.b.)* bent, fıkra; *gr.* cümlecik; subordinate ~ yan cümlecik.

**claus.tral** [ˈklɔːstrəl] *adj.* manastıra ait.

**clav.i.cle** [ˈklævikl] *n.* köprücük kemiği.

**claw** [klɔː] **1.** *n.* hayvan pençesi; pençe tırnağı; *(a.* ⊕*)* tırnak, kavrama, kurtağzı; **2.** *vb.* pençe atmak, yırtmak, tırmalamak; **clawed** *adj.* pençeli, tırnaklı.

**clay** [klei] *n.* balçık, kil; *fig.* toprak, yerküre; insan vücudu; ~ pigeon, ~ bird makine ile havaya atılan balçık hedef; **clay.ey** [ˈkleii] *adj.* balçıklı, killi.

**clean** [kliːn] **1.** *adj.* temiz, pak; açık; masum; *fig.* hatasız, kusursuz; **2.** *adv.* tamamen, iyice; temiz olarak; **3.** *v/t.* & *v/i.* temizle(n)mek, pak ve ayıklamak; be ~ed out F meteliksiz kalmak; ~ up iyice temizlemek; bitirmek; düzenlemek; **'clean.er** *n.* temizlikçi; silgi; temizleyici ilâç; *mst* ~s *pl.* kuru temizleyici; send to the ~s temizleyiciye göndermek; **'clean.ing** *n.* temizleme; ~ woman temizlikçi kadın; **clean.li.ness** *n.* temizlik; **cleanse** [klenz] *v/t.* temizlemek, arıtmak.

**clean-up** [ˈkliːnʌp] *n.* temizleme; *pol.* temizleme, tasfiye işlemi; *Am. sl.* avanta.

**clear** [kliə] **1.** □ açık, berrak, parlak; sarih, aşikâr; boş, serbest; kesin; *fig.* saf, lekesiz; ⊤ net; ~ of ...den uzak, ...den arınmış; as ~ as day gün gibi aşikâr; get ~ of *bşden* kurtulmak; **2.** in the ~ ⚠ içten içe ölçümde; **3.** *v/t. a.* ~ up halletmek; aydınlatmak; açmak, açık hale getirmek; *fig.* aydınlatmak, tenvir etm.; kurtarmak, temizlemek (of, from *-den*); temize çıkarmak (of *-den*); *(at vs.)* engeli aşmak; *a.* ~ away, ~ off toparlayıp kaldırmak, ortadan kaldırmak; *(hesap, fatura)* ödemek, yoluna koymak; ⊤ *s.* ~ off; ⊤ gümrükten çıkarmak; ⚹ *b-ni* herhangi bir taahhüdünden kurtarmak, muaf tutmak (from *-den*); ⊤ net kâr elde etm.; ~ off boşaltmak, tahliye etm., tasfiye etm.; ~ a port limanı boşaltmak; ~ a ship for action gemiyi savaş için hazırlamak; F bir iş için hazırlanmak; ~ one's throat öksürerek boğazını temizlemek; *v/i. a.* ~ up *(hava)* açılmak; anlaşılmak; *(dert, hastalık)* iyiye gitmek; *a.* ~ off *(bulut vs.)* dağılmak; sıvışmak; ~ out F ortadan kaybolmak, sıvışmak; ~ through geçip gitmek; **'clear.ance** *n.* temizleme; ⊤ kliringten çekleri geçirme; ⬇, ⊤ geminin gümrük işlemlerini bitirme; ⊕ makinenin iki kısmı arasındaki boşluk; ~ sale tasfiye satışı, likidasyon; **'clear-Icut** düzgün, biçimli; açık, vazıh; **'clear.ing** *n.* açma; temizleme *etc. s.* clear[3]; açıklık, meydan; ⊤ takas, kliring; ~ agreement kliring anlaşması; ~ bank ciro bankası; ~ house kliring odası, takas odası; ~-hospital seyyar hastane; **'clear.ness** *n.* berraklık, açıklık.

**cleat** [kliːt] *n.* ⬇ koç boynuzu; mesnet takozu.

**cleav.age** [ˈkliːvidʒ] *n.* yarılma, ayrılma, ayrılık *(a. fig.)*; *min.* parçalayarak elde edilen madlen.

**cleave[1]** [kliːv] *(irr.) v/t.* yarmak; be in a cleft stick çıkmaza girmek; cleft palate ⚕ yarık damak; show the cloven hoof şeytan ruhunu göstermek, ne mal olduğunu göstermek.

**cleave[2]** [~] *v/i.* çatlamak; yapışmak; *fig.* sevgi ile bağlanmak (to *-e*); ~ together bir arada tutulmak.

**cleav.er** [ˈkliːvə] *n.* balta, kasap satırı.

**cleek** [kliːk] *n.* demir topuzlu golf sopası.

**clef** ♪ [klef] *n.* nota anahtarı.

**cleft** [kleft] **1.** *n.* yarık, çatlak; **2.** *pret.* & *p.p. of* cleave[1].

**clem.a.tis** ⚶ [ˈklemətis] *n.* orman asması, filbahar, klemetis.

**clem.en.cy** [ˈklemənsi] *n.* şefkat, yumuşaklık; **ˈclem.ent** ☐ merhametli, şefkatli; *(esp. hava)* mülayim, yumuşak.

**clench** [klentʃ] *v/t. (diş, yumruk vs.)* sıkmak; kavramak; = clinch.

**clere.sto.ry** ⚠ [ˈkliəstəri] *n.* binanın pencereli üst kısmı.

**cler.gy** [ˈkləːdʒi] *n.* rahipler sınıfı; **ˈ~.man**, **cler.ic** [ˈklerik] *n.* papaz, rahip.

**cler.i.cal** [ˈklerikəl] **1.** ☐ kâtibe ait; daire işiyle ilgili; rahiplere ait; kilisenin siyasete karışmasını isteyen; ~ error yazı hatası, sürçü kalem; ~ work büro işi; **2.** *n.* rahip, papaz; *pol.* dinci, ümmetçi.

**clerk** [klɑːk] *n. (büroda)* kâtip, sekreter; † satıcı; *part. Am.* tezgâhtar; *eccl.* rahip.

**clev.er** ☐ [ˈklevə] akıllı, becerikli, marifetli; zarif; **ˈclev.er.ness** *n.* zekâ, akıllılık.

**clew** [kluː] *n.* yumak, topak; *s.* clue.

**cli.ché** [ˈkliːʃei] *n.* klişe, basmakalıp söz; *typ.* klişe.

**click** [klik] **1.** *n.* şıkırtı; çatırtı; *(dil)* şaklama; ⊕ kilit çengeli; **2.** *v/i.* şıkırdamak, «klik» sesi çıkarmak; *sl.* başarmak, şansı olm.; *sl.* uyuşmak, birbirinden hoşlanmak.

**cli.ent** [ˈklaiənt] *n.* müşteri; müvekkil; **cli.en.tèle** [kliːãːnˈteil] *n.* müşterilerin, müvekkillerin hepsi.

**cliff** [klif] *n.* kayalık, uçurum.

**cli.mate** [ˈklaimit] *n.* iklim; **cli.mat.ic** [~ˈmætik] *adj.* (~ally) iklime ait.

**cli.max** [ˈklaimæks] **1.** *n.* zirve, doruk; dönüm noktası; düğüm noktası; doyum; **2.** *v/i.* en yüksek dereceye gelmek; *v/t.* en yüksek dereceye getirmek.

**climb** [klaim] **1.** *n.* tırmanma; **2.** *v/t. & v/i.* tırmanmak -*e*; **ˈclimb.er** *n.* tırmanan, dağcı; *fig.* ikbalperest, yükselmek isteyen kimse; ⚶ sarmaşık; **ˈclimb.ing** *n.* tırmanma; **ˈclimb.ing-i.ron** *n.* tırmanma demiri, krampon.

**clinch** [klintʃ] **1.** *n.* ⊕ perçinleme; *fig.* kucaklama; *boks:* girift olma; **2.** *v/t.* bağlamak, perçinlemek ; hüküm vermek; *s.* clench; *v/i.* girift olm.; **ˈclinch.er** *n.* ⊕ kenet, perçinleme; F koz, düğüm noktası.

**cling** [kliŋ] *(irr.) v/i.* sıkı sarılmak, yapışmak (to -*e*); vazgeçmemek; **ˈcling.ing** *adj. (elbise)* sıkı, dar; *fig.* başkasına fazla bağımlı, yapışkan.

**clin.ic** [ˈklinik] *n.* klinik, muayenehane;

**ˈclin.i.cal** ☐ kliniğe ait; ~ thermometer doktor termometresi, derece.

**clink¹** *sl.* [kliŋk] *n.* hapishane, kodes.

**clink²** [~] **1.** *n.* şakırtı, şıngırtı; **2.** *v/i.* şakırdamak, şıngırdamak; *v/t.* şakırdatmak, şıngırdatmak, tokuşturmak; **ˈclink.er** *n.* maden kömürü cürufu; *sl.* fiyasko; **ˈclink.er-built** *adj.* ↓ üstüste bindirilmiş kaplama parçaları ile yapılmış *(gemi)*; **ˈclink.ing** *sl.* efsanevî; F yaman, fevkalâde, mümtaz.

**clip¹** [klip] **1.** *n.* kırpma, kırkım; at one ~ *Am.* F ansızın, hep birden; **2.** *v/t.* makasla kesmek, kırpmak, kırkmak; *(hece)* kısaltmak; yutmak; *(bilet)* zımbalamak; ~ s.o.'s wings *fig.* kısıtlamak, engel olm.

**clip²** [~] **1.** *n.* raptiye, mandal, klips, pens; **2.** *v/t.* kenetlemek; mandallamak.

**clip.per** [ˈklipə] *n.* kırpma makası; hızlı giden at; ↓ çok yollu bir tür yelkenli; süratli giden şey; *sl.* yaman şey; *(a.* pair of*)* ~s *pl.* saç kesme makinesi; **ˈclippings** *n. pl. Am.* gazete kupürü; *pl.* kırpıntı, talaş.

**clique** [kliːk] *n.* takım, komite, hizip, klik.

**cloak** [kləuk] **1.** *n.* manto, palto, pelerin; *fig.* perde, bahane; **2.** *v/t. fig.* örtbas etm., örtmek, gizlemek; **ˈ~-room** *n.* gardrop, vestiyer, helâ, tuvalet; 🚉 bagaj gişesi.

**clock** [klɔk] **1.** *n.* masa saati; duvar saati; *spor:* *sl.* kronometre; put the ~ back *fig.* eskiye dönmek; **2.** *v/t. spor:* *sl.* saat tutmak; *v/i.* ~ in (out) *(fabrikada işe gelme, işten çıkma saatlerinde)* kart basmak; **ˈ~-wise** *adj. & adv.* saat yelkovanlarının döndüğü yönde; like ~ saat gibi, muntazam.

**clod** [klɔd] *n.* toprak parçası, kesek; *a.* ~-hopper *n.* köylü, kaba adam, hödük.

**clog** [klɔg] **1.** *n.* kütük; *fig.* engel; **2.** *v/i.* tıkanmak, sıkılmak; *v/t. fig.* b-*ne* engel olm.; sıkıntı vermek; -*e*; **ˈclog.gy** *adj.* toptop olan şey, düğümlü.

**clois.ter** [ˈklɔistə] **1.** *n.* manastır; dehliz; **2.** *v/t.* manastıra kapamak.

**close 1.** [kləuz] *n.* son, sonuç, nihayet; avlu, kilise avlusu; **2.** [kləuz] *v/t.* kapamak. kapatmak; son vermek, bitirmek; ~ down *(işletme)* kapamak; ~ one's eyes to göz yummak, görmemezlikten gelmek; *v/i.* sona ermek, kapanmak (with *ile*); ~ in (on) *b*şin etrafını çevirmek; ~ up X safları sıklaştırmak; closing time *(ticarethane vs.)* kapatma saati; **3.** ☐ yakın, bitişik; dikkatli; sık, sıkı, dar; samimî, yakın; kapalı, havasız, ağır; ağzı sıkı; cimri; ~ by, ~ to yanıbaşında, yanında; ~ fight, ~ combat, ~ quarters *pl.* göğüs göğüse çarpışma; ~ prisoner sıkı göz altında olan mahkûm; ~ season, ~ time *hunt.* avlanmanın yasak olduğu mevsim; sail ~ to the wind ⬍ rüzgâra karşı yol almak, orsa gitmek; *fig.* kanun ve ahlâk kurallarına uymamak; a ~ shave *fig.* kazadan ucuz kurtulma; '~-'cropped, '~-'cut *adj.* kısa kesilmiş *(saç, çimen vs.).*

closed [kləuzd] *adj.* kapalı; ~ book *fig.* az bilinen konu; ~ circuit kapalı devre; ~circuit television kapalı devre televizyon; ~ shop yalnız sendika üyesi olanların çalıştığı fabrika vs.

close...: '~-'fist.ed *adj.* cimri; '~-'fit.ting *adj.* dar, iyi oturan *(elbise);* '~-'grained *adj.* çizgileri sık *(kereste, deri v.b.);* '~-'hauled *adj.* ⬍ orsa giden; 'close.ness *n.* kapalılık *vs. (s.* close 3).

clos.et ['klɔzit] 1. *n. part. Am.* küçük oda; dolap; tuvalet, helâ; *s.* water-~; 2. *vb.:* be ~ed with *b-le* odaya kapanmak.

clos.ing ['kləuziŋ]: ~ date kapanma tarihi.

close-up ['kləusʌp] *n. film:* çok yakından çekilen fotoğraf.

clo.sure ['kləuʒə] 1. *n.* kapa(n)ma; son verme; *parl.* mecliste müzakereyi bitirip oylamaya koyma; apply the ~ müzakerelerin yeterliliğine karar vermek; 2. *v/t. (tartışma vs.)* bitirip oylamaya koymak.

clot [klɔt] 1. *n.* pıhtı; 2. *v/t. & v/i.* pıhtılaş(tır)mak; kesilmek *(süt).*

cloth [klɔθ] *n.* kumaş, bez, masa örtüsü; the ~ F rahiplik; ~ lay the ~ sofrayı kurmak; ~ binding bez cilt.

clothe [kləuð] *(irr.) v/t.* giydirmek, örtmek.

clothes [kləuðz] *n. pl.* elbise(ler), giysi; üniforma; çamaşır; '~-bas.ket *n.* çamaşır sepeti; '~-line *n.* çamaşır ipi; '~-peg *n.* çamaşır mandalı; '~.pin *n. part. Am.* çamaşır mandalı; '~-press *n.* elbise dolabı.

cloth.ier ['kləuðiə] *n.* kumaş, elbise satıcısı.

cloth.ing ['kləuðiŋ] *n.* giyim, elbise.

cloud [klaud] 1. *n.* bulut; leke; *fig.* bulut gibi toplanmış kalabalık; be under a ~ şüphe altında olm.; in the ~s dalgın, hayal aleminde olma; 2. *v/t.* bulutla örtmek; lekelemek; bulandırmak *(a. fig.); v/i.* bulutlanmak; bulanmak; '~-burst *n.* ani sağanak yağışı; 'cloud.less ☐ bulut-

suz, açık; 'cloud.y ☐ bulutlu; bulanık; dumanlı; açık olmayan, müphem.

clough [klʌf] *n.* boğaz, dağ geçidi.

clout [klaut] 1. *v/t.* F tokat atmak -*e;* 2. *n.* tokat, darbe; bulaşık bezi; kumaş parçası, bez; yama; F etki, nüfuz.

clove[1] [kləuv] *n.* karanfil *(bahar).*

clove[2] [~] *n.* diş sarmısak.

clove[3] [~] *pret. of* cleave[1]; 'cloven 1. *p.p. of* cleave[1]; 2. *adj.* yarık, çatlak, ayrık.

clo.ver ⚘ ['kləuvə] *n.* yonca, tirfil; live *veya* be in ~ refah içinde yaşamak, hali vakti yerinde olm.; '~-leaf *n.* otoyol: yonca yaprağı.

clown [klaun] *n.* palyaço, soytarı; *lit.* kaba adam, hödük; 'clown.ish ☐ kaba saba, yontulmamış; budala.

cloy [klɔi] *v/t.* gına getirmek, kanıksatmak, içini bayıltmak.

club [klʌb] 1. *n.* çomak, tokmak; kulüp, cemiyet; ~s *pl. oyun kartı:* ispati, sinek, trefli; 2. *v/t.* sopa ile vurmak; ~ together *(para)* yatırmak; *v/i.* mst ~ together masrafa ortak olm.; 'club.a.ble *adj.* kulüp...; kulüp üyeliğine lâyık; girişken; 'club-'foot *n.* yumru ayak; 'club-'house *n.* spor kulübü binası; 'club-'law *n.* yumruk hakkı, zorbalık.

cluck [klʌk] *v/i.* gıdaklamak *(tavuk).*

clue *fig.* [klu:] *n.* işaret, delâlet, ipucu.

clump [klʌmp] 1. *n.* yığın, küme; mst ~ sole çifte taban; 2. *vb.* ağır adımlarla yürümek; yığmak, kümelemek.

clum.si.ness ['klʌmzinis] *n.* hantallık, becerisizlik; 'clum.sy ☐ hantal, beceriksiz, acemi.

clung [klʌŋ] *pret. & p.p. of* cling.

clus.ter ['klʌstə] 1. *n.* ⚘ salkım; demet; küme *(yıldız);* oğul *(arı);* grup; 2. *v/i.* toplanmak ,demet haline gelmek.

clutch[1] [klʌtʃ] 1. *n.* tutma; ⊕ kavrama, ambreyaj; in his ~es ...in pençesinde; ~ pedal *mot.* debriyaj; 2. *v/t.* yakalamak, tutmak, kavramak *(at -i).*

clutch[2] [~] *n.* kuluçka; kuluçkadan çıkan civciv ler.

clut.ter ['klʌtə] 1. *n.* karmakarışıklık, hercümerç, dağınıklık; 2. *v/t.* ~ up darmadağınık etm., altüst etm.; tıka basa doldurmak.

clys.ter ['klistə] *n.* tenkiye, lavman.

co... [kəu] *prefix* bazı sözcüklerin başına gelerek beraber, müşterek, ortak *an*lamını verir.

coach [kəutʃ] 1. *n.* araba; 🚌 vagon; gezinti arabası; *spor:* hoca, antrenör; 2. *v/t.* alıştırmak, hazırlamak (for -*e); v/i.* özel öğretim yapmak; '~.man *n.* arabacı.

**co.ad.ju.tor** *esp. eccl.* [kəu'ædʒutə] *n.* yardımcı (*piskopos*).

**co.ag.u.late** [kəu'ægjuleit] *v/t. & v/i.* koyulaş(tır)mak, pıhtılaş(tır)mak; **co.ag-u'la.tion** *n.* pıhtılaşma.

**coal** [kəul] 1. *n.* kömür, maden kömürü; *coll.* kor; carry ~ to Newcastle denize su taşımak, tereciye tere satmak; haul *ve-ya* call s.o. over the ~s *fig. b-ni* azarlamak, tehditle korkutmak, yıldırmak; 2. ⇓ *v/i.* kömür almak; *v/t.* kömür vermek; kömür haline gelinceye kadar yakmak; ~ing station kömür ikmal limanı veya iskelesi; **'~-'dust** *n.* kömür tozu.

**co.a.lesce** [kəuə'les] *v/i.* birleşmek, birlik oluşturmak, yekvücut olm.; **co.a-'les.cence** *n.* birlik, beraberlik, birleşme.

**coal...: '~-field** *n.* maden kömürü havzası; **'~-gas** *n.* havagazı.

**co.a.li.tion** [kəuə'liʃən] *n.* birleşme; *pol.* koalisyon.

**coal...: '~-mine,** **'~-pit** *n.* kömür ocağı; **'~-scut.tle** *n.* kömür kovası.

**coarse** □ [kɔːs] kaba, bayağı, adî; *fig.* yontulmamış, terbiyesiz, dangıl dungul; pişmemiş (*yiyecek*); pürüzlü (*yüzey*); **'coarse.ness** *n.* kabalık, terbiyesizlik.

**coast** [kəust] 1. *n.* kıyı, sahil; *esp. Am.* kızak kayma yolu (*yokuş*); yokuş aşağı güç harcamadan inme (*kızak, bisiklet, oto vs.*); 2. *v/i.* sahil boyunca gitmek; yokuş aşağı güç harcamadan inmek (*bisiklet, kızak, oto vs.*); **'coast.al** *adj.* sahile ait; kıyı... sahil...

**coast.er** ['kəustə] *n. Am.* el kızağı; ⇓ sahil boyunca işleyen ticaret gemisi; altlık (*bardak, şişe*); ~ brake *Am.* bisiklette fren pedalı.

**coast-guard** ['kəustgɑːd] *n.* sahil muhafızı; **'coast.ing** *n.* kıyı seyri, kabc'aj; kızakla kayma; ~ trade sahil ticareti, kabotaj; **'coast-line** *n.* sahil boyu, kıyı şeridi.

**coat** [kəut] 1. *n.* ceket, palto, manto; kat, tabaka; hayvan postu; ~ of mail *n.* zırh elbise; ~ of arms arma; cut the ~ according to the cloth ayağını yorganına göre uzat; turn one's ~ parti *vs.* değiştirmek, başka tarafa geçmek; 2. *v/t.* kaplamak, örtmek; **'~-hang.er** *n.* elbise askısı; **'coat-ing** *n.* kaplama; boya tabakası.

**coax** [kəuks] *v/t.* kandırmak, gönlünü yapmak (into, to); ~ s.o. out of s.th. tatlı sözlerle kandırarak *b-den* bşi elde etm.

**cob** [kɔb] *n.* mısır koçanı; erkek kuğu; kısa bacaklı bir tür binek atı; = ~-nut.

**co.balt** *min.* [kəu'bɔːlt] *n.* kobalt.

**cob.ble** ['kɔbl] 1. *n.* arnavut kaldırım ta-

şı; ~s *pl.* = cob coal; 2. *v/t.* kaldırım taşı döşemek; ayakkabı tamir etm., pençe vurmak; **'cob.bler** *n.* ayakkabı tamircisi; acemi çaylak, yaptığı işi yüzüne gözüne bulaştıran kimse; buzlu karışık bir tür içki; **'cob.ble-stone** *n.* parke taşı.

**cob...: '~-coal** *n.* parke taşı iriliğinde kömür parçası; **'~.loaf** *n.* yuvarlak sandviç ekmeği; **'~-nut** *n.* iri fındık.

**co.bra** *zo.* ['kəubrə] *n.* kobra yılanı.

**cob.web** ['kɔbweb] *n.* örümcek ağı.

**co.caine** *pharm.* [kə'kein] *n.* kokain.

**coch.i.neal** ['kɔtʃiniːl] *n.* kırmız.

**cock** [kɔk] 1. *n.* horoz; erkek kuş; ⊕ horoz (*silah*); valf, musluk; önder; kumandan; rüzgârgülü; *sl.* penis; 2. *usu.* ~ up *v/t. & v/i.* dik(il)mek; kulak kabartmak; (*silah horozunu*) ateşe hazır duruma getirmek; kurmak (*fotoğraf makinesi*); yana yatırmak (*baş, şapka*); ~ one's eye (at s.o. -e) göz kırpmak.

**cock.ade** [kɔ'keid] *n.* şapkaya takılan rozet *veya* şerit, kokart.

**cock-a-doo.dle-doo** ['kɔkədu:dl'du:] *n.* horoz ötmesi, kukuriku.

**cock-a-hoop** ['kɔkə'hu:p] *adj.* neşeli, memnun; *Am.* darmadağınık.

**Cock.aigne** [kɔ'kein] *n.* hayali bir tembellik ve lüks ülkesi.

**cock-and-bull story** ['kɔkənd'bulstɔːri] *n.* gerçekmiş gibi anlatılan aptalca, inanılması zor hikâye; yalan olduğu aşikâr mazeret.

**cock.a.too** [kɔkə'tu:] *n.* ibikli ve rengârenk tüylü birkaç tür papağan.

**cock-a.trice** ['kɔkətrais] *n.* horoz yumurtasından varolduğu varsayılan efsanevi bir yılan.

**cock.boat** ⇓ ['kɔkbəut] *n.* küçük sandal.

**cock.chaf.er** ['kɔktʃeifə] *n.* mayısböceği.

**cock-crow(.ing)** ['kɔkkrəu(iŋ)] *n.* tan, şafak.

**cocked hat** ['kɔkt'hæt] *n.* eskiden giyilen kenarları kıvrık üç köşeli bir tür şapka; knock into a ~ *sl.* eze eze yenmek.

**cock.er¹** ['kɔkə]: ~ up *v/t.* özenli yetiştirmek, yüz vermek, şımartmak.

**cock.er²** *hunt.* [~] *n.* bir tür spanyel köpeği.

**cock...: '~-eyed** *adj. sl.* aptal, budala, saçma; *Am.* sarhoş, küfelik; **'~-fight(.ing)** *n.* horoz dövüşü; **'~-'horse** *n.* tahta oyuncak at.

**cock.le¹** ⇝ ['kɔkl] *n.* buğdaygiller arasında yetişen zararlı bir ot.

**cock.le²** [~] 1. *n. zo.* midye türünden bir deniz hayvanı; kıvrım, kırışık, pli; warm *veya* delight the ~s of one's heart *b-ni* mutlu etm.; 2. *v/t.* & *v/i.* buruş(tur)-mak.

**cock.ney** [ˈkɔkni] *n.* Londralı adam, Londra aksanı ile konuşan kimse; ˈcock.ney.ism *n.* Londra aksanı veya özelliklerinden biri.

**cock.pit** [ˈkɔkpit] *n.* horoz dövüş alanı *(a. fig.)*; ↓ alçak güverte; ✈ pilot yeri, uçağın baş tarafı.

**cock.roach** *zo.* [ˈkɔkrəutʃ] *n.* hamamböceği.

**cocks.comb** [ˈkɔkskəum] *n.* horoz ibiği *(a. ♀)*; ˈcock-ˈsure F kendinden fazla emin; ˈcock.tail *n.* kokteyl; ˈcock.y ☐ F kendini beğenmiş, kibirli.

**co.co** [ˈkəukəu] *n.* hindistancevizi ağacı.

**co.coa** [ˈkəukəu] *n.* kakao.

**co.co.nut** [ˈkəukənʌt] *n.* hindistancevizi.

**co.coon** [kəˈkuːn] *n. (ipek böceği)* koza.

**cod** *ichth.* [kɔd] *n.* morina balığı; dried ~ kurutulmuş tuzsuz balık *(morina)*.

**cod.dle** [ˈkɔdl] *v/t.* şımartmak -*i*, yüz vermek -*e*; hafif ateşte kaynatmak *(yumurta vs.)*.

**code** [kəud] 1. *n.* kanun; düstur; şifre, şifre anahtarı; 2. *tel.* *v/t.* şifre ile yazmak.

**co.de.ine** ♫ [ˈkəudiːn] *n.* kodein.

**co.dex** [ˈkəudeks] *n.*, *pl.* **co.di.ces** [ˈ~disiːz] eski el yazısı veya el yazması kutsal kitap.

**cod.fish** [ˈkɔdfiʃ] = cod.

**codg.er** F [ˈkɔdʒə] *n.* yaşlı antika adam.

**co.di.ces** [ˈkəudisiːz] *pl. of* codex.

**cod.i.cil** [ˈkɔdisil] *n.* ek vasiyetname; **cod.i.fi'ca.tion** *n.* kanun halinde toplama; **cod.i.fy** [ˈ~fai] *v/t.* bir sisteme bağlamak, kanun halinde toplamak.

**cod.ling** [ˈkɔdliŋ] *n.* ♀ pişirmekte kullanılan bir tür ham elma; *ichth.* yavru morina balığı.

**cod-liv.er oil** [ˈkɔdlivərˈɔil] *n.* balıkyağı.

**co-ed** *Am.* F [ˈkəuˈed] *n.* karma yüksek okullarda kız öğrenci.

**co-ed.u.ca.tion** [ˈkəuedjuːˈkeiʃən] *n.* karma öğretim.

**co.ef.fi.cient** [kəuiˈfiʃənt] 1. *adj.* işbirliği yapan; 2. *n.* katsayı.

**co.erce** [kəuˈəːs] *v/t.* zorlamak, zorla yaptırmak, mecbur etm.; **co'er.ci.ble** *adj.* zorunlu, mecburi; **co'er.cion** [~ʃən] *n.* baskı, zorlama; under ~ baskı altında, zorunlu; **co'er.cive** [~siv] ☐ zorunlu, mecburi...

**co.e.val** ☐ [kəuˈiːvəl] yaşıt, akran, çağdaş.

**co.ex.ist** [ˈkəuigˈzist] *v/i.* bir arada var olm.; **ˈco.exˈist.ence** *n.* bir arada var

oluş; ˈco.exˈist.ent *adj.* bir arada var olan.

**cof.fee** [ˈkɔfi] *n.* kahve; ˈ~-bean *n.* kahve çekirdeği; ˈ~-grounds *n. pl.* kahve telvesi; ˈ~-house *n.* çayevi, kahvehane; ˈ~-pot *n.* kahve ibriği, cezve; ˈ~-room *n.* *(otel)* yemek salonu; ˈ~-set *n.* kahve servis takımı.

**cof.fer** [ˈkɔfə] *n.* sandık, kasa, kutu *(para, mücevher)*; 🏛 *n.* girintili ve tahta tavan panosu; ~s *n. pl.* hazine, sandıkta birikmiş para; *a.* ~-dam *n.* batardo, koferdam, batan gemileri kurtarmakta kullanılan duba.

**cof.fin** [ˈkɔfin] 1. *n.* tabut; 2. *v/t.* tabuta koymak.

**cog** ⊕ [kɔg] *n.* çark dişi.

**co.gen.cy** [ˈkəudʒənsi] *n.* inandırıcılık, ikna etme yeteneği; ˈco.gent ☐ inandırıcı, ikna edici.

**cogged** ⊕ [kɔgd] *comb.* dişli.

**cog.i.tate** [ˈkɔdʒiteit] *v/i.* düşünmek, tasarlamak (about, on, upon); *v/t.* icat etm., bulmak, planlamak; **cog.iˈta.tion** *n.* düşünme, tasarlama.

**co.gnac** [ˈkɔnjæk] *n.* kanyak.

**cog.nate** [ˈkɔgneit] 1. *adj.* aynı kökten gelen *(dil, sözcük)*; akraba, hısım; 2. *n.* kandaş, aynı soydan veya türden olan şey.

**cog.ni.tion** [kɔgˈniʃən] *n.* anlayış, idrak, kavrama.

**cog.ni.za.ble** [ˈkɔgnizəbl] *adj.* tanınabilir, idrak olunur; 🏛 mahkemenin yetki kapsamına giren; ˈcog.ni.zance *n.* bilgi, malûmat; idrak, anlayış; 🏛 karar, hüküm; (görev ve) yetki; işaret, alâmet; ˈcog.ni.zant *adj.* haberdar, farkında olan, bilen (of *-den, -in -i)*.

**cog.no.men** [kɔgˈnəumen] *n.* soyadı; lâkap.

**cog-wheel** ⊕ [ˈkɔgwiːl] *n.* dişli çark.

**co.hab.it** [kəuˈhæbit] *v/i.* karı koca gibi bir arada yaşamak *(gayrimeşru)*; **co.habˈi'ta.tion** *n.* nikâhsız bir arada yaşama.

**co.heir** [ˈkəuˈtɛə] *n.* ortak mirasçı; **co.heir.ess** [ˈkəuˈtɛəris] *n.* ortak mirasçı *(kadın)*.

**co.here** [kəuˈhiə] *v/i.* yapışmak, tutmak; tutarlı olm.; **co'her.ence, co'her.en.cy** *n.* tutarlık, uygunluk; yapışma; **co'her.ent** ☐ yapışık; uygun, birbirini tutan; **co'her.er** *n. radyo:* eski tip dalga almacı.

**co.he.sion** [kəuˈhiːʒən] *n.* yapışma, birleşme, kavuşma; **co'he.sive** [~siv] *adj.* yapışık, bağlı.

**co.hort** [ˈkəuhɔːt] *n. eski* Romalılarda bir lejyonun onda biri.

coif **90**

coif [kɔif] n. takke, bone, külâh; saç tuvaleti.

Ꞌcoif.feur [kwaːꞋfəː] n. kuaför, kadın berberi ;coif.fure [~Ꞌfjuə] 1. n. saç biçimi, saç tuvaleti; 2. v/t. b-nin saçını tarayıp düzeltmek.

coign of van.tage [kɔinəvꞋvɑːntidʒ] n. bir iş veya gözlem için uygun nokta, yer.

coil [kɔil] 1. part. ~ up v/t. sarkmak; v/i. kıvrılmak, burulmak; 2. n. kangal, roda, halka; ✗ bobin; ⊕ halka şeklinde kıvrılmış saç.

coin [kɔin] 1. n. madeni para, sikke; pay s.o. back in his own ~ b-ne aynı şekilde karşılık vermek; 2. v/t. madeni para bas(tır)mak; uydurmak (a. fig.); ~ing money para kırıyor olm.; Ꞌcoin.age n. para basma; para sistemi; yeni bir sözcük uydurma, icat etme; Ꞌcoin-box tel.e.phone n. kasalı telefon, ankesör.

co.in.cide [kəuinꞋsaid] v/i. tesadüf etm., uymak (with -e); fig. bir olm., birbirini tutmak; co.in.ci.dence [kəuꞋinsidəns] n. tesadüf, rastlantı; fig. bir olma, mutabakat; mere ~ tamamen rastlantı; coꞋin.ci.dent □ tesadüfî, rastlantı sonucu olan; uygun gelen.

coin.er [Ꞌkɔinə] n. para basan kimse, esp. kalp para basan, kalpazan.

coir [Ꞌkɔiə] n. hindistancevizi lifi.

coke [kəuk] 1. n. kok kömürü (a. sl. = kokain); Am. F Coca-Cola; 2. v/t. kok kömürü yapmak.

co.ker.nut [Ꞌkəukənʌt] = coco-nut.

col.an.der [Ꞌkʌləndə] n. mutfak: süzgeç; kevgir.

cold [kəuld] 1. □ soğuk (a. fig.); donuk (renk); throw ~ water on pişmiş aşa su katmak, b-nin hevesini kursağında bırakmak; give s.o. the ~ shoulder, = ~-shoulder; ~ feet F cesaretsizlik, korkaklık, cayma; 2. n. soğuk(luk); soğuk algınlığı; usu. ~ in the head nezle; be left in the ~ açıkta veya yarı yolda bırakılmak; Ꞌ~-Ꞌblood.ed adj. soğukkanlı, duygusuz (a. fig.); Ꞌ~Ꞌ-heart.ed adj. acımasız, duygusuz; Ꞌcold.ness n. soğukluk.

cold...: Ꞌ~-Ꞌshoul.der b-ne omuz çevirme, yüz vermeyiş; ~ steel kesici ve dürtücü silah; Ꞌ~Ꞌ-Ꞌstor.age n. soğuk havada depo etme; attr. soğuk hava (deposu)...; Ꞌ~-Ꞌstore vb. soğuk havada depolamak; ~ war soğuk harp.

cole ✿ [kəul] mst in compound word(s) n. lahana.

cole-seed ✿ [Ꞌkəulsiːd] n. turp lahanası, şalgam.

cole-slaw Am. [Ꞌkəulslɔː] n. lahana salatası.

col.ic ✿ [Ꞌkɔlik] n. sancı, kolik.

col.lab.o.rate [kəꞋlæbəreit] v/i. işbirliği yapmak, birlikte çalışmak (with, on ile, -le, -de); col.lab.oꞋra.tion n. işbirliği; in ~ with ortaklaşa, ...ile beraber; col.labꞋoꞋra.tion.ist n. pol. işgal edilmiş ülkenin düşman ile işbirliği yapan vatandaşı, işbirlikçi; colꞋlab.o.ra.tor n. beraber çalışan kimse, iş arkadaşı.

col.lapse [kəꞋlæps] 1. v/t. & v/i. çök(ert)mek, yık(ıl)mak; katlayıp bükmek, açılır kapanır olm. (masa v.b.); ✗ çökmek, yığılmak; ciğerlere hava gitmemek; düşmek; sönmek (balon); suya düşmek (plan vs.); 2. n. çökme, yıkılma, göçme, ani düşüş; colꞋlaps.i.ble adj. açılır kapanır, katlanır (masa, sandalye v.b.); ~ boat sökülüp takılabilen kayık.

col.lar [Ꞌkɔlə] 1. n. yaka; gerdanlık; tasma; ⊕ yatak ,mesnet, yüksük, burç, manşon; 2. v/t. yakalamak -i, yakasına yapışmak -in; sl. izinsiz almak, ele geçirmek; et: pişirmek için sarmak; Ꞌ~-bone n. anat. köprücük kemiği; Ꞌ~-stud n. yaka düğmesi.

col.late [kɔꞋleit] v/t. metin: karşılaştırmak, karşılaştırarak okumak; typ. (sayfaları) sıraya koymak, harman yapmak.

col.lat.er.al [kɔꞋlætərəl] 1. □ yan yana, paralel, aynı eğilimde olan; ikincil, tali; tamamlayıcı, vasıtalı; aynı soydan gelen; 2. n. maddî teminat; soydaş.

col.la.tion [kɔꞋleiʃən] n. metin: karşılaştırma; soğuk hafif yemek.

col.league [Ꞌkɔliːg] n. meslekdaş, mesai arkadaşı.

col.lect 1. [Ꞌkɔlekt] n. kilisede okunan kısa dua; 2. [kəꞋlekt] v/t. toplamak; bir araya getirmek (fikir); tahsil etm. (para); kafasını toplamak, kendine gelmek; koleksiyon yapmak, biriktirmek; b-ni veya bşi uğrayıp almak; ~ one's wits kendini toplamak; ~ing business para, vergi tahsil etme; v/i. birikmek, toplanmak; colꞋlect.ed □ fig. aklı başında, sakin; colꞋlect.ed.ness n. fig. sükûnet, itidal; colꞋlec.tion n. topla(n)ma; koleksiyon; toplanmış şeyler, yığın; kilisede toplanan para; forcible ~ cebrî icra, takip; colꞋlec.tive adj. toplu, müşterek, ortak, toplanan...; kolektif...; ~ bargaining (işveren ve işçi temsilcileri arasındaki) toplu görüşme ve pazarlık; colꞋlec.tive.ly adv. topyekûn, birlikte; colꞋlec.tiv.ism n. pol. kolektivizm, ortaklaşacılık; colꞋlec.tiv.ize vb. (sanayi, tarım vs.'yi) devletleştirmek, *(sanayi, tarım vs. de)* devletleşmek; col**lector** *n.* toplayan, koleksiyon sahibi; tahsildar; 🔲 biletçi; *≠* cereyan toplayıcı, kollektör.

**col.leen** *Ir.* [kɔˈliːn] *n.* kız.

**col.lege** [ˈkɔlidʒ] *n.* kolej; yüksek okul, üniversite, akademi; **col.le.gi.an** [kəˈliːdʒjən] *n.* üniversite öğrencisi veya mensubu; col**le.giate** [ˈdʒiit] *adj.* üniversiteye ait; üniversite öğrencilerine özgü.

**col.lide** [kəˈlaid] *v/i.* çarpmak (with -e); çarpışmak *(ile)*; *fig.* bşe karşı olm., muhalif olm.

**col.lie** [ˈkɔli] *n.* iskoç çoban köpeği.

**col.lier** [ˈkɔliə] *n.* maden işçisi; ⚓ kömür gemisi; **col.lier.y** [ˈkɔljəri] *n.* kömür ocağı.

**col.li.sion** [kəˈliʒən] *n.* çarp(ış)ma; *fig.* fikir ayrılığı.

**col.lo.ca.tion** [kɔləʊˈkeiʃən] *n.* sıraya koyma, düzenleme, sözdizimi.

**col.lo.di.on** [kəˈləʊdjən] *n.* kolodyum.

**col.logue** [kəˈləʊg] *v/i.* gizli konuşmak, entrika hazırlamak.

**col.lo.qui.al** 🔲 [kəˈləʊkwiəl] konuşma diline ait, teklifsiz konuşma ile ilgili; col**lo.qui.al.ism** *n.* konuşma dili üslubu; konuşma dilinde kullanılan deyim.

**col.lo.quy** [ˈkɔləkwi] *n.* karşılıklı konuşma, diyalog; sohbet.

**col.lude** [kəˈluːd] *v/i.* b-le gizlice anlaşmak; dolap çevirmek; col**lu.sion** [ˈʒən] *n.* gizli anlaşma, tuzak; ♋ sahte gizli anlaşma *(boşanma için)*.

**co.lon** [ˈkəʊlən] *n. typ.* iki nokta üst üste; *anat.* kolon, kalın bağırsak.

**colo.nel** ✕ [ˈkəːnl] *n.* albay; **colo.nel.cy** *n.* albaylık.

**co.lo.ni.al** 🔲 [kəˈləʊnjəl] *adj.* koloniye ait, sömürgelere ait; col**lo.ni.al.ism** *n. pol.* sömürgecilik; **co.lo.nist** [ˈkɔlənist] *n.* sömürgede yerleşen insan; **col.o.ni.za.tion** [kɔlənaiˈzeiʃən] *n.* sömürge kurma; bir yere ahali yerleştirme; **col.o.nize** *v/t.* & *v/i.* sömürge kurmak -de; yerleş(tir)mek -e.

**col.on.nade** [kɔləˈneid] *n.* sıra sütunlar, kemeraltı.

**col.o.ny** [ˈkɔləni] *n.* sömürge, koloni.

**Col.o.ra.do bee.tle** [kɔləˈraːdəʊˈbiːtl] *n.* Kolorado böceği.

**co.los.sal** 🔲 [kəˈlɔsl] muazzam, olağanüstü büyük; col**los.sus** [ˈsəs] *n.* dev heykel; dev gibi şey.

**col.our**, *Am.* **col.or** [ˈkʌlə] **1.** *n.* renk, boya; ten, cilt rengi; *fig.* sözü çevirme, tevil, tandans; görünüş; canlılık; *~s pl.* ✕ bayrak, bandıra; *local ~* yöresel özellikler; **2.** *v/t.* boyamak, renklerle süslemek; *fig.* olduğundan başka göstermek; *v/i.* renklenmek; rengi değişmek, kızarmak; **col.o.(u)r.a.ble** 🔲 aldatıcı, yanıltıcı, göz boyayıcı, su götürür; **col.o(u)r'a.tion** *n.* renk verme, renklendirme.

**col.o(u)r...:** **~bar** *n.* ırk ayırımı; **~blind** *adj.* renkkörü; **colo(u)red** *adj.* renkli; zenci, beyaz ırka mensup olmayan; *~ film* renkli film; *~ pencil* renkli kurşun kalemi; *~ wo(man)* zenci kadın (erkek); **col.o.(u)r.ful** *adj.* renkli, canlı; **col.o.(u)ring** *n.* renk; boya; bşe renk verme, boyama; renklendirme; nüans; *fig.* sahte görünüş; mazur gösterme; **col.o(u)r.ist** *n.* renkleri ustalıkla kullanan sanatçı; **col.o.(u)r.less** 🔲 renksiz *(a. fig.)*; **col.o(u)r scheme** renk düzenlemesi; **col.o(u)r wash** renkli badana.

**colt** [kəʊlt] *n. zo.* tay, sıpa; *fig.* acemi, tecrübesiz kimse; **colts.foot** *n.* ♣ öksürük otu.

**col.um.bine** ♣ [ˈkɔləmbain] *n.* haseki küpesi.

**col.umn** [ˈkɔləm] *n.* sütun, direk; *typ.* gazete sütunu; ✕ kol (nizamı), kafile; **co.lum.nar** [kəˈlʌmnə] *adj.* sütunlar halinde olan, sütun veya direk şeklinde; **col.um.nist** [ˈkɔləmnist] *n. Am.* fıkra yazarı, gazetede belirli bir köşesi olan yazar.

**col.za** ♣ [ˈkɔlzə] *n.* kolza, lahana türü sebzeler veya bunların tohumu.

**co.ma** [ˈkəʊmə] *n.* ✾ koma, derin baygınlık; ♣ püskül.

**comb** [kəʊm] **1.** *n.* tarak; horoz ibiği; dağ sırtı *(a. dalga)*; ⊕ kenevir tarağı; *s. curry-~*; *s. honey-~*; **2.** *v/t.* taramak *(a. fig.)*; taraklamak, taraktan geçirme *(keten)*; *~ out fig.* taramak, ayırmak, elemek; *v/i.* taranmak; tümselip kırılmak *(dalga)*.

**com.bat** [ˈkɔmbət] **1.** *n.* dövüş, savaş, çarpışma; *single ~* düello; **2.** *v/t.* & *v/i.* karşı durmak, dövüşmek, çarpışmak, boğuşmak; **com.bat.ant** *n.* savaşçı; **com.bat.ive** 🔲 cengâver, kavgacı.

**comb.er** [ˈkəʊmə] *n.* ⊕ yün, keten vs. tarayan kimse ya da makine; ⚓ *n.* uzun ve tümsekli dalga.

**com.bin.a.ble** [kəmˈbainəbl] *adj.* birleş(tiril)ebilir; **com.bi.na.tion** [kɔmbiˈneiʃən] *n.* birleş(tir)me, bağla(n)ma; bileşim, terkip *(esp. ♈)*; birlik; kilit şifresi *(rakam veya harf)*; *~s pl.* külot ve gömleği tek parça olan kadın iç çamaşırı; yan arabalı motosiklet; ~ lock şifreli kilit; **com.bine 1.** [kəmˈbain] *v/t.* & *v/i.* birleş(tir)mek, kombine etm., uyuş(tur)mak; **2.** [ˈkɔmbain] *n.* ✝ kartel, tröst, çıkar birliği; *a.* ~ harvester biçer-döğer makinesi.

**com.bus.ti.ble** [kəmˈbʌstəbl] **1.** *adj.* tutuşabilir, yanabilir; **2.** ~s *n. pl.* yakacak, yakıt; ʼ *mot.* akaryakıt; **com.bus.tion** [~ˈbʌstʃən] *n.* yanma; ~ engine yanmalı, ihtiraklı motor.

**come** [kʌm] *(irr.) vb.* gelmek, ulaşmak, vasıl olm. (to -*e*); F orgazma ulaşmak; to ~ önümüzdeki, gelecek, müstakbel; how ~? F nasıl oluyor da?; ~ about olmak, vaki olm., husule gelmek; ~ across rast gelmek -*e*, karşılaşmak -*le*; ~ along ilerlemek; acele etm.; birlikte gelmek; ~ at varmak -*e*; uğraşmak *ile*; saldırmak -*e*; ~ by yakınından geçmek, uğramak; elde etm., edinmek; ~ down inmek, düşmek *(a. fig.)*; intikal etm., geçmek; ~ down upon s.o. *b-ne* haddini bildirmek, terbiyesini vermek; ~ down upon s.o. for £ 10 10 £ borcunu istemek, talep etm. -*den*; ~ down with kesenin ağzını açmak, paraları sökülmek; *Am.* F hastalanmak; ~ for alıp götürmek -*i*; üstüne yürümek; ~ in girmek; katılmak; ⚓ limana girmek; yaygın olm.; moda olm.; iktidara gelmek; gelir olarak almak *(para)*; yükselmek *(deniz)*; çıkmak *(meyva)*; ~ in! giriniz!; ~ in for hak olarak almak, elde etm.; ~ off kaçıp kurtulmak, yakasını kurtarmak; olmak; kopmak *(düğme v.b.)*; dökülmek *(saç)*; başarıyla sonuçlanmak; ~ on yaklaşmak; gelişmek, ilerlemek; baş göstermek; sahneye çıkmak; ~ on! Haydi gel!, Çabuk ol!; Yok canım!; ~ out yerinden çıkmak; yayınlanmak, neşredilmek; açmak *(çiçek)*; meydana çıkmak; açıklığa kavuşmak; çıkmak *(fotoğraf[ta])*; sosyeteye takdim edilmek *(genç kız)*; çıkmak *(yıldız, kir)*; çalışmayı reddetmek; sonuçlanmak; ~ out right doğru çıkmak *(hesap)*; ~ round *b-ne* uğramak, *b-ni* ziyaret etm.; dönmek, yinelenmek; tekrar *k-ne* gelmek, ayılmak; *fig.* razı olm., başka perdeden konuşmak *(b-ni teskin etm. için)*; ~ to adv. = ~ to o.s.; ⚓ orsa etm., demirlemek; bulmak, erişmek, yekûn tutmak; iğilendirmek; ~ to o.s. *veya* to one's senses tekrar *k-ne* gelmek, ayılmak; ~ to anchor demir atmak; ~ to know *b-le* tanışmak; *bşi* öğrenmek; ~ up olmak; yükselmek; yaklaşmak; se-

çilmek; meydana çıkmak; yukarı gelmek; çimlenmek; ~ up against *fig.* karşılaşmak -*le*, çatmak -*e*; ~ up to uymak, tekabül etm.; eşit olm.; aynı başarıyı elde etm.; aynı ölçü, durum vs. ye erişmek; ~ up with yetişmek, ulaşmak; telafi etm.; öne sürmek, ortaya atmak; ~ upon rast gelmek -*e;* baskına uğratmak, gafil avlamak; ~ˈat-a.ble F *adj.* erişilebilir, varılması mümkün; ˈ~·back *n. thea.* sahneye dönüş; eski duruma dönüş; *Am. sl.* hazırcevap karşılık.

**co.me.di.an** [kəˈmiːdjən] *n.* komik aktör, komedyen; komedi yazarı.

**com.e.dy** [ˈkɔmidi] *n.* komedi, komedya, güldürücü piyes veya film.

**come.li.ness** [ˈkʌmlinis] *n.* zerafet, şirinlik; ˈcome.ly *adj.* lâtif, zarif, hoş, sevimli, güzel, yakışıklı, uygun, yakışan.

**com.er** [ˈkʌmə] *n.* gelen kimse; katılan kimse.

**co.mes.ti.ble** [kəˈmestibl] *mst* ~s *n. pl.* yiyecek şey, gıda maddesi.

**com.et** [ˈkɔmit] *n. astr.* kuyruklu yıldız.

**com.fort** [ˈkʌmfət] **1.** *n.* konfor, rahat(lık), refah; teselli, avuntu; *fig.* yardım, himaye; serinletici *(ferahlatıcı)* şey; **2.** *v/t.* teselli etm; rahat ettirmek; yatıştırmak; ˈcom.fort.a.ble □ rahat, konforlu, ferahlatıcı; teselli edici, avutucu; ˈcom.fort.er *n.* rahatlatıcı şey; teselli eden kimse; yün boyun atkısı; emzik; *Am.* yorgan; ˈcom.fort.less □ huzursuz, rahatsız, konforsuz; can sıkıcı, kasvetli; şekil verme; ˈcom.fort.sta.tion *Am.* umumî helâ.

**com.frey** ♀ [ˈkʌmfri] *n.* karakafes otu.

**com.fy** □ F [ˈkʌmfi] = comfortable.

**com.ic** [ˈkɔmik] *adj.* (~ally) komik, garip, tuhaf, orijinal; komedi...; *fig. mst* ˈcom.i.cal □ komik, neşeli; güldürücü, eğlendirici; gülünç, tuhaf; ~ journal, ~ paper gülmece dergisi; ˈcom.ics, comic strips *n. pl.* karikatür şeklinde hikâye serisi.

**com.ing** [ˈkɔmiŋ] **1.** *adj.* gelen; gelecek, yaklaşan; *fig.* gelecek vaat eden; ~, Sir! hemen geliyorum efendim!; **2.** *n.* geliş, yaklaşma, varış.

**com.i.ty** [ˈkɔmiti]: *n.* ~ of nations uluslararası dostluk.

**com.ma** [ˈkɔmə] *n. gr.* virgül.

**com.mand** [kəˈmaːnd] **1.** *n.* emir; otorite, yetki; hakimiyet; ✗ kumanda, komut; at *veya* by ~ of emri ile; have ~ of hakim olm., iyi bilmek, vâkıf olm.; be *(ha-ve)* at ~ *b-nin* emrine hazır olm., emrine amade olm.; be in ~ of ✗ *b-nin* komutası altında olm.; **2.** *v/t.* & *v/i.* emretmek, hâkim olm. -*e*; *kafile, gemi vs.*-

kumanda etm. -e, ✕ komuta etm. -e; bş üzerinde kullanım yetkisi olm.; ✕ ateş altına alıp taramak; bakmak, görmek -e, -i (manzara); **com.man.dant** ✕ [kɔmən-ˈdænt] n. kumandan, komutan; kaptan, süvari (gemi); **com.man.deer** [ˌ-ˈdiə] v/t. ✕ askeri hizmete zorunlu kılmak; zaptetmek, müsadere etm.; **com.mand.er** ✕ [kəˈmɑːndə] n. komutan, kumandan; ⚓ binbaşı; **comˈmand.er-in-ˈchief** n. başkumandan; **comˈmand.ing** adj. emreden, hükmeden; etkili; hâkim; fig. mükemmel, birinci kalitede; ~ point stratejik nokta; **comˈmand.ment** n. emir; rel. Allahın emri; **comˈman.do** ✕ [ˌ-dəu] n. komando (birliği); **comˈmand per.form.ance** thea. devlet başkanının emriyle yapılan tiyatro veya müzik gösterisi.

**com.mem.o.rate** [kəˈmeməreit] v/t. kutlamak -i, hatırasını anmak -in; **com.mem.oˈra.tion** n. kutlama, anma; **comˈmem.o.ra.tive** ☐ b-nin, bşin anısına (of), hatıra..., yadigâr...

**com.mence** [kəˈmens] v/t. başlamak -e; ♌ başlamak (dava); **comˈmence.ment** n. başlangıç; diploma töreni.

**com.mend** [kəˈmend] v/t. övmek, salık vermek; emanet etm. (to -e); ~ me to ... F... e saygılarımı ilet; **comˈmend.a.ble** ☐ övgüye değer, salık verilir; **com.men.da.tion** [kɔmenˈdeiʃən] n. övme; salık verme; **comˈmend.a.to.ry** [ˌ-dətəri] adj. öven; salık veren.

**com.men.su.ra.ble** ☐ [kəˈmenʃərəbl] aynı birim ile ölçülebilen, orantılı (with, to -le, -e); **comˈmen.su.rate** ☐ [ˌ-rit] (with, to' -le, -e) orantılı, aynı değerde, eşit, uygun.

**com.ment** [ˈkɔmənt] 1. n. tefsir, yorum; açıklama; düşünce, fikir (on); eleştiri, kritik; 2. v/i. (upon -i) tefsir etm., yorumlamak; detaylarıyla anlatmak; eleştirmek; **ˈcom.men.tar.y** n. tefsir, şerh, yorum, izah; **com.men.ta.tor** [ˈˌ-teitə] n. yorumcu, eleştirmeci, tefsirci; radyo: muhabir.

**com.merce** [ˈkɔmə:s] n. ticaret, alım satım; toplumsal ilişkiler; cinsel ilişki; Chamber of ⚷ ticaret odası; **com.mer.cial** ☐ [kəˈmə:ʃəl] 1. ticarî, ticaret...; meslekî; ~ traveller ticari ticarî mümessili; 2. P = ~ traveller; esp. Am. radyo, TV: reklâm, ilân, ticari yayın; **comˈmer.cial.ism** n. ticarî anlayış, tutum; ticarî deyim; **comˈmer.cial.ize** v/t. ticarileştirmek.

**com.mie** F [ˈkɔmi] n. komünist.

**com.min.gle** [kɔˈmiŋgl] vb. karış(tır)mak, kaynaş(tır)mak.

**com.mis.er.ate** [kəˈmizəreit] v/t. b-ne acımak, merhamet etm., kederini paylaşmak (with -in); **com.mis.er.a.tion** [ˌ-ˈreiʃən] n. acıma, teselli (for).

**com.mis.sar** pol. [kɔmiˈsɑː] n. komiser, eskiden Sovyetler Birliğinde herhangi bir idarî örgütün başı.

**com.mis.sar.i.at** [kɔmiˈsɛəriət] n. eskiden Sovyetler Birliğinde siyasî örgüt; ✕ levazım sınıfı; **com.mis.sar.y** [ˈˌ-səri] n. vekil, yardımcı delege; ✕ levazım subayı; levazımat mağazası ve kantin.

**com.mis.sion** [kəˈmiʃən] 1. n. görev, vazife, iş; eylem; işleme; komisyon, yüzde; salahiyetname, yetki belgesi; komisyon, kurul; emir, sipariş; ⚓ sefere hazır gemi; ~ sale komisyonlu satış, yüzde hesabı satış; on ~ yüzde ile, komisyon ile; 2. v/t. yetki vermek -e, tayin etm., atamak -e, görevlendirmek, vazifelendirmek, memur etm.; hizmete koymak -i; ✕ terfi ettirmek; ⚓ sefere hazırlamak (gemi); **com.mis.sion.aire** [ˌ-ˈnɛə] n. üniformalı uşak; **comˈmis.sion.er** n. komisyon üyesi, delege, vekil; görevli memur; komiser.

**com.mit** [kəˈmit] v/t. işlemek, yapmak; teslim etm., tevdi etm., emanet etm. (to -e); söz vermek, vaat etm. (to -e); ~ (o.s. k-ni) adamak, hasretmek -e; taahhüt altına girmek; ~ (to prison) hapsetmek; ~ for trial daha sonra yargılanmak üzere hapsetmek; **comˈmit.ment** n. taahhüt, vaat, söz; bağlılık; sorumluluk; (suç) işleme; teslim etme; **comˈmit.tal** = commitment; (suç) işleme; **comˈmit.tee** [ˌ-ti] n. komite, kurul, komisyon.

**com.mode** [kəˈmoud] n. konsol, komodin; lâzımlık, oturak; **comˈmo.di.ous** ☐ [ˌ-djəs] geniş, ferah, rahat, kullanışlı; **com.mod.i.ty** [kəˈmɔditi] n. mal, ticaret eşyası, emtia; ~ value hakiki kıymet.

**com.mo.dore** ⚓ [ˈkɔmədɔː] n. komodor; yat kulübü yöneticisi.

**com.mon** [ˈkɔmən] 1. ☐ ortak, müşterek; genel, yaygın, umumî; bayağı, adi, kaba; alışılmış, çoğu yerde bulunan, mutat; of ~ gender gr. hem eril hem dişil; ~ noun cins isim; ⚷ Council Belediye Meclisi; Book of ⚷ Prayer Anglikan kilisesi dua kitabı; ~ weal kamu yararı, toplum refahı; in ~ ortaklaşa, müşterek (with ile); in ~ with fig. -ile aynı, ...gibi; 2. n. umumî otlak, halkın malı olan yer; **com.mon.al.ty** [ˈˌ-nlti] n. halk tabakası, avam; **ˈcom.mon.er** n. halk tabakasından olan kimse, burjuva.

**com.mon...: ~ law** örf ve âdete dayanan

hukuk; ♀ **Mar.ket** Ortak Pazar; ~.place
**1. n.** alışılmış herhangi *bş,* basmakalıp
iş; beylik lâf, klişe; **2.** *adj.* adî, sıradan,
olağan; *fig.* beylik.
**com.mons** ['kɒmənz] *n. pl.* halk tabakası,
avam; herkesin paylaştığı erzak; short ~
yiyecek kıtlığı; *mst* House of ♀ Avam
Kamarası.
**com.mon...:** ~ **sense sağduyu;** '~.wealth
*n.* devlet, ulus; *part.* cumhuriyet; the
British ♀ İngiliz Milletler Topluluğu; the
♀ of Australia Avustralya Devletler Kon-
federasyonu.
**com.mo.tion** [kə'məuʃən] *n.* heyecan,
ayaklanma; karışıklık, gürültü velvele.
**com.mu.nal** □ ['kɒmjunl] toplumsal...,
halk...; umumî..., ortak..., müşterek...;
**com.mu.nal.ize** ['~nəlaiz] *v/t.* toplumsallaştırmak; yöresel idare altına sokmak.
**com.mune 1.** [kə'mjuːn] *v/i.* sohbet etm.,
söyleşmek, senli benli konuşmak; **2.**
['kɒmjuːn] *n.* komün; yöresel idare;
avam.
**com.mu.ni.ca.bil.i.ty** [kəmjuːnikə'biliti] *n.*
bulaşıcılık *(hastalık);* com'mu.ni.ca.ble
□ bulaşıcı, sâri *(hastalık);* söylenebilir, ifade edilebilir *(fikir);* com'mu.ni-
cant *n.* bilgi veren kimse, ele veren kimse; komünyon ayinine katılan kimse;
com'mu.ni.cate [~keit] *v/t.* bildirmek;
ifade etm., anlatmak; geçirmek, nakletmek; bulaştırmak; *v/i.* haberleşmek
(with *ile);* bitişik olm. (with *ile);* com-
mu.ni'ca.tion *n.* haberleşme; bulaşma;
tebliğ, haber; ulaşım; bağlantı, irtibat,
ulaştırma; be in ~ with *b-le* temasta olm.;
~ cord [imdat freni; com'mu.ni.ca-
tive □ [~kətiv] konuşkan, lakırdıcı, geveze; hislerini açıklamaktan hoşlanan;
com'mu.ni.ca.tor [~keitə] *n.* konuşkan
kimse; *tel.* sinyal veren alet; [imdat
freni.
**com.mun.ion** [kə'mjuːnjən] *n.* cemaat, birlik, mezhep; paylaşma; katılma; *eccl.*
şarap içme ve yemek yeme ayini.
**com.mu.ni.qué** [kə'mjuːnikei] *n.* resmi
tebliğ, bildiri.
**com.mu.nism** ['kɒmjunizəm] *n.* komünizm;
'com.mu.nist **1.** *n.* komünist; **2.** = com-
mu'nis.tic *adj.* (~ally) komünist...; komünizm...
**com.mu.ni.ty** [kə'mjuːniti] *n.* topluluk, cemiyet, cemaat; müşterek olma, paylaş-
ma; the ~ ahali, halk, toplum; ~ ownership ortak mülkiyet; ~ service kamu
hizmeti; ~ of interests çıkar grubu, tröst;
~ chest *Am.* fakirlere yardım fonu.
**com.mut.a.ble** [kə'mjuːtəbl] *adj.* değiştiri-

lebilir, dönüştürülebilir (into, for *-e);*
**com.mu.ta.tion** [kɒmjuː'teiʃən] *n.* değiştirme, değiş (into, for *-e);* cezanın hafif-
letilmesi; ~ ticket *Am.* abone bilet *veya*
kartı; **com.mu.ta.tive** [kə'mjuːtətiv] *adj.*
değiştirilebilen...; değişme ile ilgili;
**com.mu.ta.tor** ⚡ ['kɒmjuːteitə] *n.* çevirgeç, komütatör; **com.mute** [kə'mjuːt] *v/t.*
(for, into) değiştirmek, değiş tokuş etm.,
takas etm.; hafifletmek *(ceza); v/i.* telafi etm.; toptan ödemek; *Am.* her gün
iş ile ev arasında gidip gelmek; com-
'mut.er *n. Am.* her gün işi ile evi arasında gidip gelen kimse.
**com.pact 1.** ['kɒmpækt] *n.* sözleşme, mukavele, kontrat, anlaşma; pudralık; *Am.*
küçük otomobil; **2.** [kəm'pækt] *adj.* sıkı,
kesif, yoğun; kısa, öz; **3.** [~] *vb.* sıkılaş-
tırmak, yoğunlaştırmak, basınçla sıkıştırmak; anlaşma yapmak; com'pact.ness
*n.* yoğunluk, kesiflik, sıkılık; özet.
**com.pan.ion** [kəm'pænjən] *n.* arkadaş,
yoldaş, dost; eş; çift olan şeylerin teki
*(eldiven vs.);* refakatçı, bakıcı; el kitabı, rehber; † ortak; ⚓ kamara görevlisi; ~ in arms askerlik arkadaşı; com-
'pan.ion.a.ble □ arkadaş canlısı, samimi, girgin; com'pan.ion.ate [~nit]: ~
marriage anlaşmalı evlilik; com'pan.ion-
ship *n.* arkadaşlık, dostluk; eşlik, refakat; ortaklık.
**com.pa.ny** ['kʌmpəni] *n.* arkadaşlık, be-
raberiik, eşlik, refakat; misafirler, ziyaretçi grubu; arkadaşlar; † kumpanya, ortaklık, şirket; ✕ bölük; ⚓ mürettebat, tayfa; *thea.* grup, oyuncu topluluğu; be good (bad) ~ iyi (kötü) arkadaş olm.; bear s.o. ~ b-ne eşlik etm., refakat etm., arkadaş olm.; have ~ misafirleri olm.; keep ~ with *b-ne* eşlik etm.,
arkadaşlık etm., refakat etm.
**com.pa.ra.ble** □ ['kɒmpərəbl] karşılaştırılabilir, karşılaştırılması mümkün; com-
**par.a.tive** [kəm'pærətiv] **1.** □ orantılı,
mukayeseli, karşılaştırmalı; ~ degree =
**2.** *gr.* üstünlük derecesi; com'par.a.tive.ly
*adv.* orantılı olarak, karşılaştırmalı olarak; com.pare [~'pɛə] **1.** *n.* beyond ~,
without ~, past ~ fevkalâde, eşsiz, üstün,
tartışmasız; **2.** *v/t.* karşılaştırmak, mukayese etm. (with *ile);* benzetmek (to
*e-);* *gr.* üstünlük derecesini göstermek;
(as) ~d with *-e* nisbetle, *-e* oranla; *v/i.*
benzemek (to *-e),* karşılaştırılmak, mukayese kabul etm.; **com.par.i.son** [~
'pærisn] *n.* karşılaştırma, mukayese;
münasebet, ilişki, benzerlik; *gr.* sıfat
*veya* zarfın üstünlük *veya* enüstünlük de-

recesini gösteren çekim şekli; **in ~ with**
-e nispeten, -e oranla.

**com.part.ment** [kəm'pɑ:tmənt] *n.* bölüm,
şube, kısım; **⚠** bölme, göz; **⛁** kompartıman.

**com.pass** ['kʌmpəs] **1.** *n.* pusula; çevre;
sınır, hacim; saha, alan, menzil; **♪** genişlik, kapsam; (*usu.* pair of) **~es** *pl.*
pergel; **2.** *vb.* çevirmek, sarmak, kuşatmak; içine almak, kapsamak; etrafını
dolaşmak; başarmak; elde etm., almak;
kavramak, anlamak; gizli plan kurmak.

**com.pas.sion** [kəm'pæʃən] *n.* merhamet,
acıma, şefkat; **have ~ on** -e acımak;
**com¹pas.sion.ate** ☐ [~nit] şefkatli, merhametli, sevecen; **on ~ ground** acıdığın-
dan -e.

**com.pat.i.bil.i.ty** [kəmpætə'biliti] *n.* uygunluk, uyma, uygun düşme; **com¹pat.i.ble**
☐ uygun, münasip, tutarlı (with *ile*).

**com.pa.tri.ot** [kəm'pætriət] *n.* vatandaş,
yurttaş.

**com.peer** [kɔm'piə] *n.* akran, eş, arkadaş.

**com.pel** [kəm'pel] *v/t.* zorlamak, mecbur
etm. (*a. fig.*).

**com.pen.di.ous** ☐ [kəm'pendiəs] kısa, öz,
özet halinde; **com¹pen.di.ous.ness** *n.* kısalık, özlük.

**com.pen.di.um** [kəm'pendiəm] *n.* özet.

**com.pen.sate** ['kɔmpenseit] *v/t.* tazmin
etm., telâfi etm., karşılamak, bedelini
ödemek (for *için;* with *ile;* by *ile*); **⊕**
denkleştirmek, denklemek, eşitlemek;
*v/i.* **~ for** -*in* yerini tutmak; **com.pen¹sa-
tion** *n.* tazmin, telâfi; bedel, karşılık;
*Am.* maaş, ücret; **⊕** dengeleme; **com-
¹pen.sa.tive** [~sətiv], **com¹pen.sa.to.ry**
*adj.* telâfi edici.

**com.père** ['kɔmpɛə] **1.** *n.* eğlence programı sunucusu; **2.** *vb.* sunuculuk yapmak.

**com.pete** [kəm'pi:t] *vb.* boy ölçüşmek,
müsabakaya girmek, yarışmak (for *için*);
rekabet etm., mücadele etm. (with *ile*);
**~ with s.o.** b-*le* rekabet etm.; yarışmak,
aşık atmak.

**com.pe.tence, com.pe.ten.cy** ['kɔmpi-
təns(i)] *n.* yeterlik, kifayet; kabiliyet,
yetenek, güç; gelir, yetki, salâhiyet;
**¹com.pe.tent** ☐ yeterli, işinin ehli, kabiliyetli, kompetan; yetkili, salâhiyetli.

**com.pe.ti.tion** [kɔmpi'tiʃən] *n.* yarışma,
müsabaka; **†** müsabaka; **~** atıcılık
müsabakası; **com.pet.i.tive** ☐ [kəm-
¹petitiv] rekabet edilebilir; rakip olan;
rekabet ile ilgili; yarışma türünde; **com-
¹pet.i.tor** *n.* rakip, yarışmacı.

**com.pi.la.tion** [kɔmpi'leiʃən] *n.* derleme;

**derleme eser; com.pile** [kəm'pail] *v/t.*
derlemek, toplamak (from -*den*).

**com.pla.cence, com.pla.cen.cy** [kəm-
¹pleisns(i)] *n.* kendi halinden memnun
olma; memnuniyet, gönül rahatlığı;
**com¹pla.cent** ☐ kendini beğenmiş, ukalâ; halinden memnun, rahat.

**com.plain** [kəm'plein] *v/i.* şikâyet etm.,
yakınmak (about, of -*den;* that -*ki;* to
-*e*); suçlamak; **com¹plain.ant** *n.* davacı,
şikâyetçi; **com¹plain.er** *n.* şikâyetçi; **com-
¹plaint** *n.* şikâyet, yakınma, dert; **♥** hastalık, rahatsızlık.

**com.plai.sance** [kəm'pleizəns] *n.* hoşgörü,
müsamaha, göz yumma, tolerans; **com-
¹plai.sant** ☐ hoşgörülü, müsamahakâr.

**com.ple.ment** ['kɔmplimənt] **1.** *n.* tamamlayıcı herhangi bir şey, tümleç (*a. gr.*);
tüm, bütün; **⚠** bütünler açı; **com.ple-
¹men.tal, com.ple¹men.ta.ry** *adj.* tamamlayan, tamamlayıcı, tümleyici (to -*e*).

**com.plete** [kəm'pli:t] **1.** ☐ tam, tamam, bütün, eksiksiz; bitmiş, tamamlanmış; mükemmel, dört başı mamur; **2.** *v/t.* tamamlamak, bitirmek, bütünleştirmek;
**com¹plete.ness** *n.* bütünlük, tam olma hali; **com¹ple.tion** *n.* tamamlama, bitirme;
sona erme; yerine getirme.

**com.plex** ['kɔmpleks] **1.** ☐ karmaşık, çapraşık, anlaşılması güç; *fig.* karışık, bileşik; **~ sentence** *gr.* girişik cümle; **2.** *n.*
karmaşa; karışık *veya* bileşik herhangi
birşey; kompleks; **com.plex.ion** [kəm-
¹plekʃən] *n.* cilt, ten; genel görünüm,
yön, gidişat; **com¹plex.i.ty** *n.* güçlük, zorluk; karmaşa.

**com.pli.ance** [kəm'plaiəns] *n.* rıza; uyma, itaat, baş eğme, uysallık (with -*e*);
**in ~ with** -*e* uygun olarak; **com¹pli.ant** ☐
uysal, yumuşak başlı, itaatkâr.

**com.pli.cate** ['kɔmplikeit] *v/t.* karıştırmak, güçleştirmek, zorlaştırmak; **¹com-
pli.cat.ed** *adj.* karmaşık, çapraşık, anlaşılması güç; **com.pli¹ca.tion** *n.* karmaşıklık, güçlük, zorluk, engel; **♥** ihtilât,
hastalığın başka bir hastalıkla karışması.

**com.plic.i.ty** [kəm'plisiti] *n.* suç ortaklığı
(in -*de*).

**com.pli.ment 1.** ['kɔmplimənt] *n.* iltifat,
kompliman; **2.** ['~ment] *v/t.* (on) kompliman yapmak -*e*, övmek -*i*; iltifat etm.
-*e*; **com.pli¹men.ta.ry** *adj.* övücü...; parasız..., ücretsiz...; **~ dinner** ziyafet; **~ ticket** parasız bilet.

**com.ply** [kəm'plai] *vb.* razı olm., uymak,
itaat etm. (with -*e*); **~ with the rules** kurallara uymak.

**com.po.nent** [kəm'pəunənt] **1.** *n.* parça.

unsur, eleman; **2.** *adj.* tamamlayıcı, birleştirici; ~ part = ~ 1.

**com.port** [kəm'pɔ:t] *vb.* uymak, uygun olm. (with *-e*); ~ o.s. davranmak, hareket etm.

**com.pose** [kəm'pəuz] *v/t.* meydana getirmek, oluşturmak; bestelemek *(şarkı)*; yazmak *(şiir)*; *typ.* dizmek, tertip etm.; sakinleştirmek, kontrol altına almak; **com'posed** *adj.* kendi halinde, sakin; ibaret (of *-den*); **com'pos.ed.ly** [~zidli] *adv.* sakince, sakin sakin; **com'pos.er** *n.* bestekâr, besteci, kompozitör; **com'pos.ing 1.** *adj.* rahatlatıcı, yatıştırıcı, sakinleştirici; **2.** *n.* tertip, dizgi; besteleme; ~ **machine** dizgi makinesi; ~ **room** dizgi evi; **com.pos.ite** ['kɔmpəzit] **1.** *adj.* bileşik, karma, karışık; **2.** *n.* alaşım, bileşim; ♥ bileşikgillerden herhangi bir bitki; **com.po'si.tion** *n.* kompozisyon; ♪ beste, eser; ♣ bileşim, terkip; *paint.* kompozisyon; ↑ uzlaşma, anlaşma; derleme, biraraya getirme; nitelik, yapı; **com.pos.i.tor** [kəm'pɔzitə] *n.* *typ.* dizgici, dizici; **com.post** ['kɔmpɔst] **1.** *n.* çürümüş organik maddeli gübre; **2.** *vb.* gübrelemek; **com.po.sure** [kəm'pəuʒə] *n.* sakinlik, huzur, sükunet.

**com.pote** ['kɔmpɔt] *n.* komposto.

**com.pound¹** **1.** ['kɔmpaund] *adj.* bileşik; ~ **fracture** ⚕ açık kırık; ~ **interest** bileşik faiz; **2.** [~] *n.* bileşim, alaşım, terkip; *a.* ~ **word** *gr.* bileşik kelime; **3.** [kəm'paund] *v/t.* birleştirmek, terkip etm., bütün halinde getirmek; çoğaltmak, arttırmak, şiddetlendirmek; *v/i.* birleşmek; ↑ anlaşmak ,uzlaşmak (for *husunda*).

**com.pound²** ['kɔmpaund] *n.* içinde binalar bulunan etrafı çevrili arazi.

**com.pre.hend** [kɔmpri'hend] *v/t.* anlamak, kavramak, idrak etm.; içine almak, kapsamak.

**com.pre.hen.si.ble** □ [kɔmpri'hensəbl] anlaşılır, makul; **com.pre'hen.sion** *n.* anlayış, idrak; kapsam; **com.pre'hen.sive** □ geniş, etraflı, şumüllü; idrakli, anlama yeteneği olan; ~ **school** bir tür sanat okulu; **com.pre'hen.sive.ness** *n.* büyüklük, genişlik; anlayışlılık.

**com.press 1.** [kəm'pres] *v/t.* sık(ıştır)mak, bas(tır)mak, tazyik etm., basınç yapmak; özetlemek, kısaltmak; **2.** ['kɔmpres] *n.* ⚕ kompres; **com.pressed** [kəm'prest] *adj.* sıkıştırılmış, basınçlı; ~ **air** sıkıştırılmış hava, basınçlı hava; **com'press.i.ble** *adj.* sıkıştırılabilir; **com.pres.sion** [~'reʃən] *n.* özetleme, kısalt-

ma; *phys.* basınç, tazyik, sıkıştırma; ⊕ kompresyon; **com'pres.sor** [~sə] *n.* ⊕ kompresör.

**com.prise** [kəm'praiz] *v/t.* kapsamak, içine almak, ihtiva etm.

**com.pro.mise** ['kɔmprəmaiz] **1.** *n.* uzlaşma, uyuşma, anlaşma; **2.** *v/t.* uzlaştırmak, aralarını bulmak; *-in* şerefini tehlikeye atmak, *bşi* tehlikeye atmak; *v/i.* uzlaşmak, anlaşmak, uyuşmak (on *konusunda*).

**comp.trol.ler** [kən'trəulə] *n.* hesap kontrol memuru, kontrolör, denetçi.

**com.pul.sion** [kəm'pʌlʃən] *n.* zorla(n)ma, mecburiyet, yüküm; **com'pul.so.ry** [~səri] *adj.* mecburî, zorunlu; ~ **military service** mecburî askerlik; ~ **subject** zorunlu ders.

**com.punc.tion** [kəm'pʌŋkʃən] *n.* vicdan azabı; pişmanlık, esef.

**com.put.a.ble** [kəm'pju:təbl] *adj.* hesaplanabilir; **com.pu.ta.tion** [kɔmpju:'teiʃən] *n.* hesap, hesaplama; **com.pu'ta.tor** = computer; **com.pute** [kəm'pju:t] *v/t.* hesaplamak, hesap etm. (at *olarak*); **com'put.er** *n.* kompütür, bilgisayar.

**com.rade** ['kɔmrid] *n.* arkadaş, dost; yoldaş; **'com.rade.ship** *n.* arkadaşlık.

**con¹** [kɔn] *vb.* incelemek, tetkik etm., dikkatle okumak.

**con²** ↓ [~] *vb.* dümen kullanmak.

**con³** [~] *adv. abbr.* = contra aleyhte, karşı; pro and ~ lehte ve aleyhte; the pros and ~s lehte ve aleyhte olan tartışmalar.

**con⁴** *Am. sl.* [~] **1.** *s.* confidence man; **2.** *vb.* dolandırmak, kandırmak, aldatmak, yutturmak.

**con.cat.e.nate** [kɔn'kætineit] *vb. mst fig.* birbirine bağlamak; **con.cat.e'na.tion** *n.* birbirine bağlama *(a. fig.)*.

**con.cave** ['kɔn'keiv] içbükey..., konkav...; **con.cav.i.ty** [~'kæviti] *n.* içbükeylik; içbükey yüzey.

**con.ceal** [kən'si:l] *v/t.* gizlemek, saklamak, saklı tutmak, örtbas etm. (from *s.o. b-den*); **con'ceal.ment** *n.* gizle(n)me, sakla(n)ma; *a.* place of ~ gizlenme yeri.

**con.cede** [kən'si:d] *vb.* kabul etm., kabullenmek; vermek, bahşetmek. müsaade etm.; **con'ced.ed.ly** *adv.* kabullenerek.

**con.ceit** [kən'si:t] *n.* kendini beğenmişlik, ukalâlık, kibir, gurur; out of ~ with *-den* artık memnun olmayan; **con'ceit.ed** □ kibirli, gururlu, kendini beğenmiş, ukala; **con'ceit.ed.ness** *n.* kendini beğenmişlik, gurur, kibir.

**con.ceiv.a.ble** ☐ [kən'si:vəbl] akla uygun, düşünülebilir, inanılabilir; **con'ceive** v/i. hamile kalmak, gebe kalmak -den; anlamak, kavramak (of -i); v/t. ortaya atmak, yaratmak, çıkarmak; anlamak, anlam vermek; fikrinde olm.; hayal etm., zannetmek, tahmin etm.; ~d in ...fikrinde olan.

**con.cen.trate** ['kɔnsəntreit] 1. v/t. & v/i. bir yere topla(n)mak; fig. kendini vermek -e, zihnini bir noktaya toplamak; ⌂ koyulaştırmak; 2. n. koyu madde; **con'cen'tra.tion** n. topla(n)ma; kendini verme, dikkat; ⌂ koyulaş(tır)ma, konsantrasyon; ~ camp toplama kampı; **con'cen.tre, con'cen.ter** [~tə] vb. merkezileş(tir)mek, merkeze topla(n)mak; **con'cen.tric** adj. (~ally) ortak merkezli..., merkezleri aynı olan...

**con.cept** ['kɔnsept] n. kavram, görüş, fikir; **con.cep.tion** [kən'sepʃən] n. fikir, görüş, düşünce, kavram; biol. gebe olma, hamile kalma.

**con.cern** [kən'sə:n] 1. n. ilgi, alâka (in -de. for için); münasebet, irtibat, bağlantı (with ile); † ticarethane, kuruluş; pay, hisse; tasa, kaygı, merak; F şey, nesne; 2. v/t. ilgilendirmek, alâkadar etm.; ilişkisi olm., karışmak, bulaşmak; endişeye düşürmek, üzmek, canını sıkmak; ~ o.s. with karışmak, müdahale etm.; be ~ed endişeli olm., kaygı duymak; ilgi duymak, meşgul olm.; bşe bulaşmak, karışmış olm.; be ~ed that ... -den kaygı duymak; I am ~ed to inf. -mekle mecburum; be ~ed with ... ile meşgul olm., uğraşmak; **con'cerned** ☐ ilgili, alâkalı, meşgul (in ile); endişeli, kaygılı (at, about, for -de, hususunda); those ~ ilişkisi olanlar; **con'cern.ing** prp. hakkında, hususunda, -e dair,... ile ilgili olarak.

**con.cert** 1. ['kɔnsət] n. konser; ['~sə:t] n. uyum, ahenk; birleşme; 2. [kən'sə:t] vb. planlamak, beraberce karar vermek, anlaşmak; **con'cert.ed** adj. kararlaştırılmış, planlı, birlikte yapılmış...; ♪ bölüm bölüm düzenlenmiş; **con.cer.ti.na** ♪ [kɔnsə'ti:nə] n. akordeon, körüklü armonika; **con.cer.to** ♪ [kən'tʃə:təu] n. konçerto.

**con.ces.sion** [kən'seʃən] n. kabul, teslim, tasdik; bağış, ihsan, teberru; imtiyaz, ayrıcalık; hizmete karşılık devletçe verilen arazi; **con.ces.sion.aire** [~'nɛə] n. imtiyazlı kimse, ayrıcalık sahibi.

**con.ces.sive** ☐ [kən'sesiv] teslim veya kabul niteliğinde olan.

**conch** [kɔŋk] n. helezonî sedef kabuk.

**con.cil.i.ate** [kən'silieit] v/t. uzlaştırmak, barıştırmak, aralarını bulmak; sakinleştirmek, yatıştırmak; gönlünü almak; **con.cil.i'a.tion** n. uzlaştırma, barıştırma; yatıştırma, sakinleştirme; **con'cil.i.a.tor** n. uzlaştıran kimse, barıştıran kimse; **con'cil.i.a.to.ry** [~ətəri] adj. gönül alıcı, barıştırıcı, uzlaştırıcı; ~ proposal anlaşma önergesi.

**con.cin.ni.ty** [kən'siniti] n. ahenk, uyum, tutarlık.

**con.cise** ☐ [kən'sais] öz, kısa, özlü, muhtasar; **con'cise.ness** n. kısa ve öz olma.

**con.clave** ['kɔnkleiv] n. özel veya gizli toplantı.

**con.clude** [kən'klu:d] v/t. & v/i. bit(ir)mek, sona er(dir)mek, sonuçlan(dır)mak, neticelen(dir)mek; netice çıkarmak; karar vermek (to inf. -meğe); to be ~d in our next sonu gelecek sayıda; **con'clud.ing** adj. son..., bitiş...

**con.clu.sion** [kən'klu:ʒən] n. son, nihayet, netice, karar, sonuç; akdetme; netice çıkarma; in ~ son söz olarak, sözü bitirirken, son olarak; try ~s with s.o. b-le yarışmak, boy ölçüşmek; **con'clu.sive** [~siv] ☐ son, nihai; kati, kesin.

**con.coct** [kən'kɔkt] vb. birbirine karıştırarak hazırlamak, yapmak; fig. uydurmak; **con'coc.tion** n. karışım, tertip; karıştırma; fig. uydurma.

**con.com.i.tance, con.com.i.tan.cy** [kən'kɔmitəns(i)] n. eşlik eden şey, birlikte olan şey; **con'com.i.tant** 1. ☐ eşlik eden, beraberinde olan; 2. n. eşlik eden şey, birlikte olan şey.

**con.cord** ['kɔŋkɔ:d] n. uygunluk, bağdaşma, ahenk, uyum (a. gr.); barış, antlaşma; ♪ uyum, harmoni, armoni; **con.cord.ance** [kən'kɔ:dəns] n. uyum, ahenk, uygunluk, uyuşma; eccl. bir kitaptaki önemli kelimelerin alfabetik sırası; **con'cord.ant** ☐ uyumlu, uygun; ♪ ahenkli; **con'cor.dat** eccl. [~dæt] n. antlaşma, kilise ile devlet arasındaki anlaşma.

**con.course** ['kɔŋkɔ:s] n. toplanma, biraraya gelme; kalabalık, izdiham; Am. tren istasyonundaki geniş bina.

**con.crete** 1. ☐ ['kɔnkri:t] somut, maddî, belirli, kesin; betondan yapılmış, beton...; 2. [~] n. beton; phls., gr. somut varlık; in the ~ somut olarak; 3. [kən'kri:t] vb. katılaş(tır)mak; bütünleş(tir)mek; sertleş(tir)mek; somutlaş(tır)mak; ['kɔnkri:t] beton dökmek, betonla kaplamak (yol); ~ noun gr. somut isim;

**con.cre.tion** [kənˈkriːʃən] n. don(dur)ma, katılaş(tır)ma; donmuş madde.

**con.cu.bi.nage** [kɔnˈkjuːbinidʒ] n. gayri meşru olarak birarada yaşama, metres hayatı; **con.cu.bine** [ˈkɔŋkjubain] n. kapatma, cariye, odalık, metres.

**con.cu.pis.cence** [kənˈkjuːpisəns] n. şehvet, cinsel arzu; **conˈcu.pis.cent** adj. şehvetli.

**con.cur** [kənˈkəː] vb. uymak, razı olm., uyuşmak, aynı fikirde olm., mutabık olm. (with ile; in -de); beraber olm., aynı anda olm. (to -mek için); **con.cur.rence** [~ˈkʌrəns] n. uyum, anlaşma, fikir birliği, mutabakat; aynı anda olma; in ~ with müştereken, beraberce, birlikte; **conˈcur.rent** □ uygun, mutabık; aynı anda olan, beraber bulunan (s. concur); işbirliği yapan.

**con.cus.sion** [kənˈkʌʃən] n.: ~ of the brain beyin sarsıntısı.

**con.demn** [kənˈdem] v/t. kınamak, ayıplamak; suçlamak; çarptırmak, mahkûm etm. (a. fig.) (to -e); istimlâk etm., kamulaştırmak, elinden almak; ele vermek; his looks ~ him bakışları onun suçlu olduğunu gösteriyor; ~ed cell ölüm hücresi; **conˈdem.na.ble** [~nəbl] adj. mahkûm edilebilir; kınanmaya lâyık; istimlâk edilebilir; **con.dem.na.tion** [kɔndemˈneiʃən] n. kınama, ayıplama; suçlu çıkarma; mahkûmiyet; istimlâk; **con.dem.na.to.ry** □ [kənˈdemnətəri] kınayıcı.

**con.den.sa.ble** [kənˈdensəbl] adj. yoğunlaştırılabilir; kısaltılabilir, özetlenebilir; **con.den.sa.tion** [kɔndenˈseiʃən] n. kısaltma, özet; yoğunlaş(tır)ma, koyulaş(tır)ma; **con.dense** [kənˈdens] v/t. & v/i. koyulaş(tır)mak, yoğunlaş(tır)mak; ⊕ sıvılaştırmak; özetlemek, kısaltmak; **conˈdens.er** n. ⚡, ⊕ kondansatör.

**con.de.scend** [kɔndiˈsend] vb. tenezzülde bulunmak, lütfetmek; **con.deˈscend.ing** □ tenezzül eden; **con.deˈscen.sion** n. tenezzül, alçak gönüllülük gösterme.

**con.dign** □ [kənˈdain] lâyık, müstahak, hak etmiş (cezayı).

**con.di.ment** [ˈkɔndimənt] n. yemeğe çeşni veren şey.

**con.di.tion** [kənˈdiʃən] 1. n. koşul, şart, kayıt; durum, hal, vaziyet; medenî hal; sağlık; ~s pl. şartlar; on ~ that... şartı ile; out of ~ sağlık yönünden iyi durumda olmayan, bedenen uygun olmayan; 2. vb. ayarlamak, uygun bir hale getirmek, eğitmek; düzenlemek; şart koşmak, kayıt altına sokmak; havalandır-

mak; **conˈdi.tion.al** □ şartlı, şarta bağlı, şart...; bağlı (on, upon -e); ~ (mood) gr. şart kipi; **con.di.tion.al.i.ty** [~ˈnæliti] n. şarta bağlılık; **conˈdi.tion.al.ly** [~əli] adv. şartlı olarak; **conˈdi.tioned** adj. şarta bağlı; uygun durumda olan; **conˈdi.tioned re.flex** psych. şartlı refleks, şartlı davranış.

**con.dole** [kənˈdəul] vb. taziyede bulunmak, (üzüntüye) ortak olm., başsağlığı dilemek (with -e); **conˈdo.lence** n. taziye, başsağlığı.

**conˈdo.min.i.um** [ˈkɔndəˈminiəm] n. bir ülke üzerinde birkaç devletin ortak hâkimiyeti; Am. kat mülkiyeti.

**con.do.na.tion** [kɔndəuˈneiʃən] n. göz yumma, görmezden gelme; telâfi, yerini doldurma; **con.done** [kənˈdəun] v/t. göz yummak, affetmek, görmezden gelmek; karşılamak, telâfi etm.

**con.dor** orn. [ˈkɔndɔː] n. büyük akbaba.

**con.duce** [kənˈdjuːs] vb. yardım etm., katkıda bulunmak, sebep olm., vesile olm. (to -e); **conˈdu.cive** adj. yardım eden, sebep veya vesile olan (to -e).

**con.duct** 1. [ˈkɔndʌkt] n. davranış, tavır, hareket; idare, yönetim; 2. [kənˈdʌkt] vb. yol göstermek, önderlik etm., rehberlik etm.; idare etm., yürütmek, yönetmek; phys. nakletmek, geçirmek, iletmek; davranmak, hareket etm.; ♪ orkestra idare etm.; ~ o.s. davranmak, hareket etm.; para toplamak (yolcudan); **con.duct.i.bil.i.ty** [kɔndʌktiˈbiliti] n. phys. iletkenlik; **conˈduct.i.ble** [~təbl] adj. phys. ...iletebilen, ...geçirebilen; **conˈduct.ing** adj. iletken...; **conˈduc.tion** n. iletme, geçirme, nakletme; **conˈduc.tive** □ [~tiv] phys. iletken..., ...geçirici; **con.duc.tiv.i.ty** [kɔndʌkˈtiviti] n. phys. iletkenlik; **con.duc.tor** [kənˈdʌktə] n. biletçi, kondüktör; ♪ orkestra şefi; ⚡ iletken madde; rehber, kılavuz; **conˈduc.tress** n. kadın biletçi.

**con.duit** [ˈkɔndit] n. oluk, su yolu, kanal; [ˈ~djuit] ⚡ elektrik borusu.

**cone** [kəun] n. koni, mahrut; ⚜ kozalak.

**co.ney** [ˈkəuni] n. tavşan; tavşan kürkü.

**con.fab** F [ˈkɔnfæb] 1. = con.fab.u.late [kənˈfæbjuleit] v/i. sohbet etm., çene çalmak; 2. = con.fab.u.la.tion n. sohbet, hoşbeş.

**con.fec.tion** [kənˈfekʃən] n. şekerleme, bonbon; hazırlama, imalât; konfeksiyon, hazır giyim; **con.fec.tion.er** [~ˈfekʃnə] n. şekerci, pastacı; **conˈfec.tion.er.y** n. şekerlemeler; part. Am. şekerci dükkânı, pastane.

**con.fed.er.a.cy** [kən'fedərəsi] *n.* birlik, konfederasyon; the 2 *Am.* 1860-1861 yıllarında onbir Güney Eyaletin oluşturduğu konfederasyon; **con'fed.er.ate 1.** [~rit] *adj.* müttefik, birleşmiş; **2.** [~rit] *n.* müttefik kimse *veya* devlet; suç ortağı; **3.** [~reit] *v/t.* & *v/i.* birleş(tir)mek, ittifak et(tir)mek; **con.fed.er'a.tion** *n.* birlik, konfederasyon.

**con.fer** [kən'fə:] *v/t.* vermek, bahşetmek (on *-e*); *v/i.* danışmak, görüşmek (with *ile;* about, upon *hususunda);* **con.fer.ence** ['kɔnfərəns] *n.* müzakere, konferans, toplantı.

**con.fess** [kən'fes] *vb.* itiraf etm., ikrar etm.; doğrulamak; ~ to *eccl.* günah çıkar(t)mak; **con'fess.ed.ly** [~sidli] *adv.* itiraf edildiği gibi, kendi itirafı ile; **con'fes.sion** [~ʃən] *n.* itiraf, ikrar, doğrulama; *eccl.* günah çıkar(t)ma; **con'fes.sion.al** [~ʃən] **1.** *adj.* itiraf *veya* günah çıkar(t)ma ile ilgili, itiraf...; **2.** *n.* günah çıkar(t)ma hücresi; **con'fes.sor** [~sə] *n.* itiraf eden kimse; *eccl.* günah çıkartan papaz.

**con.fet.ti** [kən'feti:] *n. pl.* konfeti.

**con.fi.dant** [kɔnfi'dænt] *n.* sırdaş, dert ortağı; **con.fi'dante** [~] *n.* kadın dert ortağı.

**con.fide** [kən'faid] *v/t.* emanet etm., teslim etm., sır vermek, gizlice söylemek (to s.o. *b-ne);* güvenmek, itimat etm. (in *-e*).

**con.fi.dence** ['kɔnfidəns] *n.* güven, emniyet, itimat (in *-e*); gizlilik, mahremiyet; ~ **game** = confidence trick; ~ **man** dolandırıcı, üçkâğıtçı; ~ **trick** dolandırıcılık, üçkağıtçılık; **'con.fi.dent** □ emin, güvenli (of *-den);* **con.fi.den.tial** □ [~'denʃəl] gizli, mahrem; güvenilir; güvenen, inanan; ~ **clerk** özel kâtip.

**con.fig.u.ra.tion** [kənfigju'reiʃən] *n.* şekil, suret, görünüş; gruplaşma.

**con.fine 1.** ['kɔnfain] *n. mst* ~s *pl.* sınır, hudut; **2.** [kən'fain] *v/t.* sınırlamak, sınırlar içinde tutmak, toplamak, hasretmek (to *-e);* hapsetmek, evde *veya* yatakta tutmak; be ~d to bed yatakta yatmak: lohusa olm.; be ~d (of) doğurmak; **con'fine.ment** *n.* hapsedilme, kapalı tutulma; lohusalık.

**con.firm** [kən'fə:m] *v/t.* teyit etm., saptamak, sağlama bağlamak, kuvvetlendirmek, tasdik etm., onaylamak; **con.fir.ma.tion** [kɔnfə'meiʃən] *n.* tasdik, teyit, doğrulama, belgeleme; **con.firm.a.tive** □ [kən'fə:mətiv], **con'firm.a.to.ry** [~təri] teyit edici, doğrulayıcı, sağlamlaştırıcı;

**con'firmed** *adj.* kökleşmiş, yerleşmiş, müzmin *(part.* ♀); düşkün, müptela, tiryaki; ╥ teyitli, onaylı.

**con.fis.cate** ['kɔnfiskeit] *v/t.* müsadere etm., haczetmek, el koymak *-e;* istimlâk etm., kamulaştırmak; **con.fis'ca.tion** *n.* müsadere, haciz, el koyma; istimlâk, kamulaştırma; **con'fis.ca.to.ry** [~kətəri] *adj.* müsadereye ait, hacze ait.

**con.fla.gra.tion** [kɔnflə'greiʃən] *n.* büyük yangın.

**con.flict 1.** ['kɔnflikt] *n.* kavga, çekişme, mücadele, çarpışma, zıtlaşma, çatışma; *fig.* ayrılık, fikir ayrılığı, ihtilâf, anlaşmazlık; **2.** [kən'flikt] *v/i.* (with) zıtlaşmak *-le,* ihtilâfa düşmek *-le,* çekişmek *-le,* mücadele etm. *-le,* muhalif olm. *-e.*

**con.flu.ence** ['kɔnfluəns], **con.flux** ['~flʌks] *n.* iki akarsuyun birleştiği nokta, kavşak; birlikte akma; **con.flu.ent** ['~fluənt] **1.** *adj.* birlikte akarak birleşen; bir araya birikip karışmış; **2.** *n.* bir ırmağa karışan akarsu.

**con.form** [kən'fɔ:m] *v/t.* uydurmak *-e,* ayarlamak *-e,* alıştırmak *-e; v/i.* ~ to uymak *-e,* itaat etm. *-e,* boyun eğmek *-e;* ~ with uymak *-e,* uyum içinde olm. *ile;* **con'form.a.ble** □ (to) uygun *-e,* yerinde, uyumlu; itaatkâr, uysal, boyun eğen; **con.for.ma.tion** [kɔnfɔ:'meiʃən] *n.* şekil, yapı, çatı; oluşma; uyma, adaptasyon, uygunluk; **con.form.ist** [kən'fɔ:mist] *n.* toplum kurallarına uyan kimse; uyumlu kimse, uysal kimse; **con'form.i.ty** *n.* uygunluk, benzeyiş; in ~ with uyarak *-e,* uygun olarak *-e,* mucibince.

**con.found** [kən'faund] *v/t.* şaşırtmak, zihnini karıştırmak, kafasını allak bullak etm., karman çorman etm.; yenmek, mağlûp etm., yıkmak; ~ it! F Allahın cezası!; ~ you! F Allah belânı versin senin!; **con'found.ed** □ F Allahın cezası, baş belâsı; şaşırmış, zihni karışmış.

**con.fra.ter.ni.ty** [kɔnfrə'tə:niti] *n.* hayır kurumu, kardeşlik cemiyeti.

**con.front** [kən'frʌnt] *v/t.* karşılaştırmak, yüzleştirmek (with *ile);* karşı durmak, göğüs germek, karşısına çıkmak; karşısında olm. *-in,* bakmak *-e (evin cephesi);* find o.s. ~ed with *k-ni* bşle karşı karşıya bulmak; **con.fron.ta.tion** [kɔnfrʌn'teiʃən] *n.* yüzle(ştir)me; mücadele, kavga, ihtilâf *(pol.);* karşılaşma, mukayese.

**con.fuse** [kən'fju:z] *v/t.* karıştırmak, karmakarışık etm.; şaşırtmak; ayırt edememek; zihnini allak bullak etm.; **con'fused** □ kafası karışmış, zihni allak bullak, şaşkın; ayırt edilemez, seçile-

confusion

mez; karışık, karman çorman; **con'fu-sion** [~ʒən] *n.* karışıklık, düzensizlik; şaşkınlık.

**con.fut.a.ble** [kən'fjuːtəbl] *adj.* çürütüle-bilir *(iddia)*; **con.fu.ta.tion** [kɔnfjuː-'teiʃən] *n.* tekzip, çürütme *(iddia, fikir)*; **con.fute** [kən'fjuːt] *vb.* tekzip etm., çü-rütmek *(iddia, fikir)*, yalanlamak, aksi-ni ispat etm.

**congé** ['kɔːnʒei] *n.* ayrılma izni; yol ver-me, sepetleme, kovma; referans; give s.o. his ~ *b-nin* gitmesine izin vermek.

**con.geal** [kən'dʒiːl] *v/t.* & *v/i.* don(dur)-mak *(a. fig.)*; pıhtılaş(tır)mak; **con-'geal.a.ble** *adj.* donabilir, pıhtılaşabilir. **con.ge.la.tion** [kɔndʒiː'leiʃən] *n.* donma; pıhtılaşma.

**con.gen.ial** □ [kən'dʒiːnjəl] uygun, cana yakın (with *ile*); benzer (to *-e*); hoş; **con.ge.ni.al.i.ty** [~ni'æliti] *n.* uygunluk, benzerlik, yakınlık.

**con.gen.i.tal** [kən'dʒenitl] *adj.* doğuştan olan, fıtrî, Tanrı vergisi; **con'gen.i.tal.ly** [~təli] *adv.* doğuştan.

**con.ger** (eel) *ichth.* ['kɔŋgə(r'iːl)] *n.* bü-yük yılanbalığı.

**con.gest** [kən'dʒest] *v/t.* & *v/i.* topla(n)-mak; yığ(ıl)mak; tıka(n)mak *(damar, trafik)*; **con'ges.tion** *n.* kan birikmesi; tıkanıklık; izdiham, kalabalık; ~ of po-pulation fazla nüfus yoğunluğu; traffic ~ trafik tıkanıklığı.

**con.glom.er.ate** 1. [kən'glɔmərit] *adj.* kü-me halinde toplanmış, yığılmış; 2. [~] *n.* küme, yığın; ♱ holding; 3. [~reit] *vb.* bir araya toplamak, yığmak, kümele-mek; ♱ holdingleşmek; **con.glom.er'a-tion** *n.* yığın, küme; yığ(ıl)ma.

**con.grat.u.late** [kən'grætjuleit] *v/t.* tebrik etm., kutlamak (s.o. on *veya* upon s.th. *b-ni bşden dolayı)*; **con.grat.u'la.tion** *n.* tebrik, kutlama; **con'grat.u.la.tor** *n.* teb-rik eden, kutlayan; **con.grat.u.la.to.ry** *adj.* tebrik..., kutlama...

**con.gre.gate** ['kɔŋgrigeit] *vb.* topla(n)-mak, birleş(tir)mek, biraraya gelmek, biraraya getirmek; **con.gre'ga.tion** *n.* *eccl.* cemaat; toplantı, topla(n)ma; **con-gre'ga.tion.al** [~ʃənl] *adj.* cemaate ait.

**con.gress** ['kɔŋgres] *n.* kongre, toplantı; ♀ *Am. pol.* Millet Meclisi *(Senato ve Tem-silciler Meclisi)*; **con.gres.sion.al** [~-'greʃənl] *adj.* Meclise ait, Meclis...; **'Con-gress.man**, **'Con.gress.wom.an** *n. Am. pol.* Millet Meclisi üyesi, senatör.

**con.gru.ence**, **con.gru.en.cy** ['kɔŋgruəns-(i)] *n.* = congruity; ♀ benzeşim; **'con-gru.ent** *adj.* = congruous; ♀ benzer;

**con.gru.i.ty** [~'gruːiti] *n.* uygunluk, uyum; **con.gru.ous** □ ['~gruəs] uygun, müna-sip (to *-e*); uyumlu, ahenkli (to, *mst* with *ile)*.

**con.ic**, **con.i.cal** □ ['kɔnik(əl)] koni şek-linde, konik...; ~ section ♠ konik kesit eğrisi.

**co.ni.fer** ['kəunifə] *n.* kozalaklı ağaç; **co-'nif.er.ous** *adj.* kozalaklı, kozalak veren.

**con.jec.tur.al** □ [kən'dʒektʃərəl] tahmini, farazi, varsayılı; **con'jec.ture** 1. *n.* zan, sanı, tahmin, varsayı, farz; 2. *v/t.* tah-min etm., farzetmek, tasavvur etm., zan-netmek, sanmak.

**con.join** [kən'dʒɔin] *vb.* birleş(tir)mek, bi-tiş(tir)mek, bağlamak; **con.joint** ['kɔn-dʒɔint] *adj.* birleşmiş, ortak; **'con.joint-ly** *adv.* birleşmiş olarak.

**con.ju.gal** □ ['kɔndʒugəl] evlilikle ilgili, karıkocalığa ait, evlilik...; **con.ju.gate** 1. ['~geit] *v/t.* çekmek *(fiil)*; *v/i. biol.* bir-leşmek; 2. ['~git] *adj.* ♀ birleşmiş; **con-ju.ga.tion** [~'geiʃən] *n.* fiil çekimi; bir-leşme.

**con.junct** □ [kən'dʒʌŋkt] birleşmiş, biti-şik, ortak, müşterek; **con.junc.tion** *n.* bir-leşme; *ast.* konjonksiyon; *gr.* bağlaç; rastlantı, tesadüf, aynı zamanda olma *(olaylar)*; **con.junc.ti.va** *anat.* [kɔndʒʌŋk-'taivə] *n.* konjonktiv; **con.junc.tive** [kən-'dʒʌŋktiv] *adj.* birleştiren, bitiştiren; ~ mood şart kipi; **con'junc.tive.ly** *adv.* bir-leştirerek, bitiştirerek, bağlayarak; **con-junc.ti.vi.tis** ♀ [~'vaitis] *n.* konjonktivit; **con'junc.ture** [~tʃə] *n.* çeşitli olay *veya* durumların biraraya gelmesi, hal ve şartlar; ♱ konjonktür.

**con.ju.ra.tion** [kɔndʒuə'reiʃən] *n.* büyü, sihir; sihirbazlık; ruh çağırma; **con.jure** [kən'dʒuə] *v/t.* yalvarmak *-e*, rica etm. *-e*; ['kʌndʒə] *vb.* el çabukluğu ile yap-mak; ruh çağırmak; hokkabazlık yap-mak, el çabukluğu ile marifet yapmak; ~ up büyü yoluyla çağırmak; **'con.jur.er**, **'con.jur.or** *n.* hokkabaz, sihirbaz, büyü-cü; **'con.jur.ing-trick** *n.* hokkabazlık, el çabukluğu.

**conk** F [kɔŋk] *vb.* işlememek, çalışma-mak, durmak; grev yapmak; bayılmak;' ölmek, uyumak; başına vurmak.

**con.nate** ['kɔneit] *adj.* doğuştan olan, fıt-rî; akraba olan, benzer; ♀ & *anat.* biti-şik; **con.nat.u.ral** [kə'nætʃrəl] *adj.* do-ğuştan, fıtrî, tabii; aynı tabiatta olan.

**con.nect** [kə'nekt] *v/t.* & *v/i.* bağla(n)-mak, bitiş(tir)mek, birleş(tir)mek; ara-larında ilgi kurmak; ♂ cereyana bağla-mak, devreyi açmak; **con'nect.ed** □ bağlı, bitişik; anlamca ilgili; be ~ with irtibatta olm. -le; bağlı olm. -le; akraba olm. -le; be well ~ iyi bir çevreden gelmek, yüksek tabakadan olm.; con'necting adj. bağlayıcı, bağlantı..., bağlama..., irtibat...; ~ rod biyel, krank kolu, bağlama çubuğu; con'nec.tion s. connexion; con'nec.tive □ bağlayıcı, birleştirici; ~ tissue anat. katılgan doku.

con.nex.ion [kə'nekʃən] n. bağlantı, irtibat, ilgi, alâka, ilişki, münasebet; ≠ bağlama vasıtası, ekleme; süreklilik, devamlılık; akrabalık, hısımlık; ✝ müşteriler; ticarî ilişki; iş, görev; sınıf, mezhep, grup, parti.

conn.ing-tow.er ⬇ ['kɔniɳtauə] n. harp gemilerinde kumanda kulesi.

cón.niv.ance [kə'naivəns] n. göz yumma, suç ortaklığı (at, in, with -e); con'nive vb.: ~ at göz yummak -e, suç ortağı olm. -e, görmezlikten gelmek -i.

con.nois.seur [kɔnə'sə:] n. (of veya in wine etc. şarapta vs.) erbap, ehil, mütehassıs, uzman ,bir işten iyi anlayan kimse.

con.no.ta.tion [kɔnəu'teiʃən] n. çağrışım, diğer anlam, asıl anlamından başka kavram; con'note vb. akla getirmek, anlamına gelmek, demeye gelmek, ifade etm.

con.nu.bi.al □ [kə'nju:bjəl] evliliğe ait, evlilik..., karı koca...

con.quer ['kɔɳkə] v/t. fethetmek, zaptetmek, galip gelmek; fig. yenmek (korku); 'con.quer.or n. fatih, galip; F final maçı.

con.quest ['kɔɳkwest] n. fetih, zapt; zafer, başarı.

con.san.guin.e.ous [kɔnsæn'gwiniəs] adj. aynı soydan, aynı ırktan, akraba; con'san'quin.i.ty n. kan akrabalığı, aynı soydan gelme.

con.science ['kɔnʃəns] n. vicdan; in all ~ F doğrusu, vicdanen; mutlaka, elbette; have the ~ to do bşi yapmaya vicdanı elvermek; ~ money vicdanı rahatlatmak için verilen para; 'con.science.less adj. vicdansız.

con.sci.en.tious □ [kɔnʃi'enʃəs] vicdanının sesini dinleyen, vicdan sahibi; temiz iş yapan, dürüst, insaflı; ~ objector askerlik hizmetini reddeden kimse; con.sci'en.tious.ness n. vicdan, vicdanlılık; dürüstlük.

con.scious □ ['kɔnʃəs] bilinçli, şuurlu, farkında olan; ayık; be ~ of -in farkında olm., bilincinde olm.; 'con.scious.ness n. bilinç, şuur, idrak, anlayış, akıl, his.

con.script ✕ 1. [kən'skript] vb. askere çağırmak, askere almak; 2. ['kɔnskript]

adj. askere alınmış; 3. [~] n. askere alınmış nefer, kur'a neferi, acemi asker; con.scrip.tion ✕ [kən'skripʃən] n. askere çağırma; mecburi askerlik; savaş zamanında alınan mecburi vergi; industrial ~ bedenen çalışma yükümlülüğü.

con.se.crate ['kɔnsikreit] v/t. takdis etm.; Tanrıya adamak, tahsis etm., vakfetmek; con.se'cra.tion n. takdis merasimi; adama, vakfetme, takdis, ithaf; 'con.se.cra.tor n. kendini adamış kimse; bş bağışlayan kimse.

con.sec.u.tive [kən'sekjutiv] adj. arka arkaya, birbirini takibeden, art arta gelen; gr. ardıl; con'sec.u.tive.ly adv. birbirini takip ederek, art arta gelerek.

con.sen.sus [kən'sensəs] n. umumun fikri, fikir birliği, oy birliği, ittifak.

con.sent [kən'sent] 1. n. (to -e) müsaade, izin, rıza, muvafakat; oy birliği, ittifak; age of ~ erginlik yaşı; with one ~ oy birliği ile, tam ittifakla; 2. vb. razı olm., muvafakat etm., rıza göstermek (to, in -e); con.sen.tient [~'senʃənt] adj. razı, muvafık, kabul eden.

con.se.quence ['kɔnsikwəns] n. sonuç, netice, akıbet; eser, semere; ehemmiyet, önem; in ~ of neticesinde, sonucu olarak, sebebiyle; 'con.se.quent 1. adj. neticesi olan, sonucu olan, bağlı; 2. n. netice, sonuç; con.se.quen.tial [~'kwenʃəl] neticesi olan, bağlı olan (on, upon -e); con.se.quent.ly ['~kwəntli] adv. netice olarak, bu sebeple, sonuç olarak, binaenaleyh.

con.ser.va.tion [kɔnsə:'veiʃən] n. koruma, muhafaza, himaye; doğal kaynakları koruma; con.serv.a.tism [kən'sə: vətizəm] n muhafazakârlık, tutuculuk; con'serv.a.tive 1. □ ihtiyatlı, tedbirli, ılımlı, mutedil (of); pol. muhafazakâr, tutucu; 2. n. tutucu kimse, muhafazakâr kimse; tedbirli kimse; con'ser.va.toire [~twa:] n. ♪ konservatuvar; con'ser.va.tor n. koruyucu, himaye eden kimse, koruma görevlisi; con'ser.va.to.ry [~tri] n. limonluk, ser; ♪ konservatuvar; con'serve v/t. muhafaza etm., korumak; şeker ile muhafaza etm., konserve yapmak.

con.sid.er [kən'sidə] v/t. düşünmek, göz önünde tutmak; hesaba katmak, dikkate almak; addetmek, saymak, farzetmek, sanmak; hürmet etm.; incelemek, mütalâa etm.; v/i. tefekkür etm., durup düşünmek; all things ~ed enine boyuna düşünülürse, herşey göz önünde tutulursa; con'sid.er.a.ble □ hayli; çok, epey; büyük; önemli, hatırı sayılır; con'sid.er.a-

**bly** *adv.* epeyce, oldukça; **con¹sid.er.ate** [~rit] □ saygılı, nazik, düşünceli, hürmetkâr; **con.sid.er.a.tion** [~¹reiʃən] *n.* göz önüne alma; saygı, itibar, nezaket, hürmet; düşünce; faktör, husus; karşılık, bedel, ödül; önem, ehemmiyet; † pey akçesi; **be under ~** görüşülmekte olm., tetkik edilmekte olm., gözden geçirilmekte olm.; **take into ~** göz önüne almak, hesaba katmak; **money is no ~** para önemli değil; **on no ~** hiç bir surette, asla; **con¹sid.er.ing 1.** *prp.* **-e göre, -e** nazaran; **-i** göz önünde tutulursa; yine de, rağmen; **2.** *adv.* F şartlar göz önünde tutulursa.

**con.sign** [kən¹sain] *v/t.* göndermek, yollamak; teslim etm., vermek, tahsis etm., adamak; † mal göndermek; **con.sig.na.tion** [kɔnsai¹neiʃən], **con.sign.ment** [kən¹sainmənt] *n.* gönderme, sevk, teslim, sevkiyat; † gönderilen mallar; **con.sign.ee** [kɔnsai¹ni:] *n.* kendisine mal gönderilen kimse, alıcı; **con.sign.er, con.sign.or** [kən¹sainə] *n.* mal gönderen kimse.

**con.sist** [kən¹sist] *vb.* ibaret olm., mürekkep olm., meydana gelmek, oluşmak (of **-den**); dayanmak, bağlı olm. (in **-e**); uygun olm., uymak (with *ile*); **con¹sist.ence, con¹sist.en.cy** *n.* birbirini tutma, tutarlık, uyum, ahenk; yoğunluk, kesafet, kıvam, koyuluk; **con¹sist.ent** □ birbirini tutan, tutarlı; uygun, aralarında bağ olan (with *ile*); **~ly** her zaman, devamlı olarak, mütemadiyen; **con¹sis.to.ry** *n. eccl.* kilise idare heyeti, kilise yönetim kurulu.

**con.sol.a.ble** [kən¹səuləbl] *adj.* tesellisi mümkün, avutulabilir; **con.so.la.tion** [kɔnsə¹leiʃən] *n.* teselli, avunç.

**con.sole 1.** [kən¹səul] *v/t.* teselli etm., avutmak, avundurmak; **2.** [¹kɔnsəul] *n.* konsol, radyo *veya* televizyon kasası; org klavyesi; ⊿ dirsek; **~ table** konsol. **con.sol.er** [kən¹səulə] *n.* teselli eden kimse.

**con.sol.i.date** [kən¹sɔlideit] *v/t. & v/i.* sağlamlaş(tır)mak, pekiş(tir)mek; *fig.* birleş(tir)mek; konsolide etm., vadesini uzatmak; **~d annuities = consols**; **con.sol.i¹da.tion** *n.* birleş(tir)me, sağlamlaştırma, takviye; borçları birleştirme.

**con.sols** [kən¹sɔlz] *n. pl.* konsolide borçlar; Duyunu Umumiye'de kayıtlı uzun vadeli borç.

**con.so.nance** [¹kɔnsənəns] *n.* uygunluk, uyum, ahenk, ses uygunluğu; **¹con.so.nant 1.** □ ♪ ahenkli, aynı ses-lere sahip olan (with, to **-le**); **2.** *n. gr.* konsonant, sessiz harf.

**con.sort 1.** [¹kɔnsɔ:t] *n.* eş, karı, koca; ↓ yoldaş gemi; **2.** [kən¹sɔ:t] (with) *vb.* arkadaşlık etm. **-le**, vakit geçirmek **-le**; uymak **-e**, uygun olm. **-e**.

**con.spec.tus** [kən¹spektəs] *n.* taslak, genel plan, özet.

**con.spic.u.ous** □ [kən¹spikjuəs] göze çarpan, farkedilir, bariz, dikkati çeken, açık seçik; *fig.* çarpıcı, mükemmel, cazip; **be ~ by** one's absence yokluğunda aranmak, değeri yokluğunda belli olm.; **make o.s. ~** dikkat çekmek.

**con.spir.a.cy** [kən¹spirəsi] *n.* fesat dolu gizli anlaşma, suikast; **con¹spir.a.tor** [~tə] *n.* suikastçı; **con¹spir.a.tress** *n.* kadın suikastçı; **con.spire** [kən¹spaiə] *vb.* fesat maksadı ile anlaşmak, suikast hazırlamak, entrika çevirmek; elbirliği ile çalışmak.

**con.sta.ble** [¹kʌnstəbl] *n.* polis memuru; kraliyet ailesinin valisi *veya* muhafızı; **con.stab.u.lar.y** [kən¹stæbjuləri] *n.* polis teşkilâtı; jandarma.

**con.stan.cy** [¹kɔstənsi] *n.* değişmezlik, sabitlik; tahammül, dayanıklılık; sadakat, bağlılık; **¹con.stant 1.** □ devamlı, sürekli, daimî; sabit, değişmez; sadık, bağlı; **2.** *n.* A konstant, sabite.

**con.stel.la.tion** *ast.* [kɔnstə¹leiʃən] *n.* takımyıldız, burç.

**con.ster.na.tion** [kɔnstə:¹neiʃən] *n.* donup kalma, korku, dehşet, hayret, şaşkınlık.

**con.sti.pate** ⚕ [¹kɔnstipeit] *vb.* kabızlığa sebep olm., sıkmak; **con.sti¹pa.tion** *n.* ⚕ kabızlık, peklik.

**con.stit.u.en.cy** [kən¹stitjuənsi] *n.* seçim çevresi, seçim bölgesi; F seçmenler; **con¹stit.u.ent 1.** *adj.* anayasayı değiştirme yetkisi olan; seçme hakkı olan; bir bütünü oluşturan; **2.** *n.* seçmen; öğe, unsur.

**con.sti.tute** [kɔnstitju:t] *v/t.* teşkil etm., oluşturmak, meydana getirmek; tayin etm., atamak; kurmak, tesis etm., kanunî yetki vermek; **~ s.o.** judge *b-ni* hakim olarak atamak; **con.sti¹tu.tion** *n.* anayasa; bünye, beden yapısı; terkip, bileşim; **con.sti¹tu.tion.al** [~ʃənl] **1.** □ anayasal, anayasaya uygun; bünyesel, bünyevî, sıhhi, yapısal; **~ law** anayasa; **2.** *n.* F sağlık için yapılan kısa yürüyüş; **con¹sti.tu.tion.al.ist** [~ʃnəlist] *n.* meşrutiyetçi, anayasa taraftarı; **con.sti.tu.tive** □ [¹kɔnstitju:tiv] yapıcı, kurucu, teşkil eden; temelli, köklü, esaslı.

**con.strain** [kən¹strein] *v/t.* zorlamak, mecbur etm., zorla yaptırmak; **con.straint** [~'streint] *n.* zorlama, mecbur etme, sınırlama, tahdit; yapmacıklık, sunilik; &ŏ tehdit, hürriyetin sınırlanması, manevî zorlama.

**con.strict** [kən'strikt] *vb.* sık(ıştır)mak; büzmek; daraltmak; kısaltmak; **con- 'stric.tion** *n.* sıkma, büzme, kasılma, kısalma; **con'stric.tor** *n.* anat. büzgen, sıkıcı adale; *zo. a.* boa ~ boa yılanı.

**con.strin.gent** [kən'strindʒənt] *adj.* büzen, kısaltan.

**con.struct** [kən'strʌkt] *v/t.* inşa etme., yapmak, kurmak; *fig.* düzenlemek, tertip etm.; **con'struc.tion** *n.* yapı, bina, inşaat; yorum, mana; under ~ inşa halinde; **con'struc.tive** *adj.* yapıcı, olumlu, yapısal; **con'struc.tor** *n.* kurucu, yapıcı, inşaatçı.

**con.strue** [kən'struː] *vb. gr.* tercüme etm., mana vermek, yorumlamak; cümleyi tahlil etm.; gramatik olarak cümle kurmak.

**con.sue.tu.di.nar.y** [kɔnswi'tjuːdinəri] *adj.* alışılagelen, alışılmış...

**con.sul** ['kɔnsəl] *n.* konsolos; ~ general başkonsolos; **con.su.lar** ['kɔnsjulə] *adj.* konsolosa ait, konsolos..., konsolosluk...; **con.su.late** ['L~lit] *n.* konsolosluk, konsoloshane; ~ general başkonsolosluk; **con- sul.ship** ['kɔnsəlʃip] *n.* konsolosluk.

**con.sult** [kən'sʌlt] *v/t.* baş vurmak -*e*, müracaat etmek -*e*, danışmak -*e*, sormak -*e*; göz önünde bulundurmak, hesaba katmak, düşünmek; ~ing engineer danışman mühendis; ~ing physician danışman doktor; *v/i.* istişare etm., görüşme yapmak; danışmanlık yapmak; **con'sult- ant** *n.* müşavir, danışman; **con.sul.ta.tion** [kɔnsəl'teiʃən] *n.* başvurma, danışma, müzakere; konsültasyon; ~ hour muayene saati; **con.sult.a.tive** [kən'sʌltətiv] *adj.* danışmanlıkla ilgili, danışma...

**con.sum.a.ble** [kən'sjuːməbl] *adj.* tüketilir, sarfolunur, kullanılır; **con'sume** *v/t.* yiyip bitirmek, tüketmek, israf etm., ziyan etm., sarfetmek, yoğaltmak; yakıp kül etm.; *fig. k-ni* yemek; deliye dönmek; *v/i.* tükenmek, uçmak, ziyan edilmek, yok olm.; **con'sum.er** *n.* tüketici, yoğaltıcı; ~ goods *pl.* tüketim maddeleri.

**con.sum.mate** 1. □ [kən'sʌmit] tam, mükemmel, şahane; 2. ['kɔnsəmeit] *v/t.* tamamlamak; mükemmelleştirmek; **con- sum.ma.tion** [~'meiʃən] *n.* tamamlama, yerine getirme; *fig.* son, sonuç.

**con.sump.tion** [kən'sʌmpʃən] *n.* tüketim,

yoğaltım; **⅋** verem; **con.sump.tive** □ tüketilecek...; veremli.

**con.tact** 1. ['kɔntækt] *n.* temas, dokunma, değme, sürtünme; ilişki, münasebet; haberleşme; bulaşıcı hastalık geçirebilecek kimse; ⅋ bağlantı; make (break) ~ teması temin etm. (kesmek); elektrik devresini bağlamak (kesmek); 2. [kən'tækt] *v/t.* temasa geçmek -*le*, temas kurmak -*le*, konuşmak -*le*; ~ lens.es ['kɔntækt- 'lensiz] *n. pl.* kontakt lensler, mercekler.

**con.ta.gion** **⅋** [kən'teidʒən] *n.* bulaşma, geçme (*hastalık*); bulaşıcı hastalık; *fig.* kötü tesir; **con'ta.gious** □ bulaşıcı, sâri; yayılan.

**con.tain** [kən'tein] *v/t.* ihtiva etm., içine almak, kapsamak; eşit olm. -*e*; sınırlamak; kontrol altına almak; tam bölünmek (*sayı*); ✕ tutuklamak; *fig. k-ni* tutmak; ~ o.s. *k-ni* tutmak, geri durmak; **con'tain.er** *n.* kap; konteyner; **con'tain- ment** *n.* alıkoyma, kontrol etme; *pol.* bir devletin etki alanını genişletmesini önleme politikası.

**con.tam.i.nate** [kən'tæmineit] *v/t.* kirletmek, pisletmek, lekelemek; bulaştırmak, geçirmek (*hastalık, mikrop*); *fig.* bozmak (*ahlâkını*); **con.tam.i'na.tion** *n.* bulaştırma; kirletme, pisletme; pislik.

**con.temn** *lit.* [kən'tem] *vb.* hor görmek, küçük görmek, adam yerine koymamak.

**con.tem.plate** ['kɔntempleit] *vb. fig.* seyretmek; düşünmek, tasarlamak, niyetinde olm.; düşünceye dalmak; **con'tem- 'pla.tion** *n.* derin düşünce; niyet, maksat; umut, bekleme; düşünme, tasarlama; have in ~ niyetinde olm.; **'con.tem- pla.tive** □ düşünceli, dalgın.

**con.tem.po.ra.ne.ous** □ [kəntempə'rein- jəs] aynı zamanda olan; ~ performance &ŏ aynı anda olan icraat; **con'tem.po- rar.y** 1. *adj.* çağdaş, modern; aynı anda olan; aynı yaşta olan, 2. *n. b-le* akran olan kimse, aynı yaşta olan kimse.

**con.tempt** [kən'tempt] *n.* nefret, küçük görme, yukarıdan bakma; hürmetsizlik, saygısızlık; kurallara karşı gelme; ~ of court mahkemeye itaatsizlik; hold in ~ hor görmek, hakir görmek; in ~ of önemsemeyerek; karşı gelerek; **con'tempt.i.ble** □ alçak, rezil, aşağılık, adî; **con'temp- tu.ous** □ [~tjuəs] kibirli, küçük gören, hor gören (of *-i*).

**con.tend** [kən'tend] *v/i.* çarpışmak, mücadele etm., müsabakaya girmek, çekişmek (for *için*); *v/t.* iddia etm., ileri sürmek, tartışmak, münakaşa etm.

content

104

con.tent [kənˈtent] 1. adj. memnun, hoşnut, razı; not ~ memnun değil; 2. v/t. memnun etm., hoşnut etm.; ~ o.s. yetinmek, idare etm. (with ile); 3. n. rahatlık; to one's heart's ~ canı istediği kadar, doya doya; [ˈkɔntent] n. hacim, istiap, kapasite; öz, esas, içerik, muhteva, gerçek anlam; ~s pl. içindekiler; table of ~s fihrist, endeks; con.tent.ed ☐ [kənˈtentid] memnun, hoşnut, rahat, halinden memnun.

con.ten.tion [kənˈtenʃən] n. kavga, çekişme, mücadele, münakaşa, iddia; conˈten.tious ☐ kavgacı, münakaşacı; ihtilâflı.

con.tent.ment [kənˈtentmənt] n. memnuniyet, rahatlık, gönül huzuru.

con.test 1. [ˈkɔntest] n. yarışma, müsabaka; mücadele, çekişme; tartışma, münakaşa; iddia, bahis; 2. [kənˈtest] v/t. itiraz etm. -e, karşı koymak -e, muhalefet etm. -e; ~ s.o.'s right to do s.th. b-nin bş yapma hakkına itiraz etm.; v/i. müsabakaya girmek, mücadele etm., çekişmek; ~ a borough bir ilçede seçilmek için mücadele etm.; conˈtest.a.ble adj. itiraz kaldırır, tartışma götürür, münakaşa edilebilir; conˈtest.ant n. yarışmacı; bir karar veya ödüle itiraz eden kimse; conˈtest.ed adj. münakaşalı, ihtilâflı.

con.text [ˈkɔntekst] n. sözün gelişi, münasebet; şartlar ve çevre; con.tex.tu.al ☐ [kənˈtekstjuəl] sözün gelişine göre; conˈtex.ture [~tʃə] n. yapı, bünye; düzen, tertip; sözün gelişi.

con.ti.gu.i.ty [kɔntiˈgjuːiti] n. yakınlık, komşuluk, hemhudutluk; con.tig.u.ous ☐ [kənˈtigjuəs] yakın, komşu, bitişik, hemhudut, sınırdaş (to -e).

con.ti.nence [ˈkɔntinəns] n. kendini tutma, ölçülülük, kendine hâkim olma; ˈcon.ti.nent 1. ☐ kendine hâkim, ölçülü; 2. n. kıta, anakara; con.ti.nen.tal [~ˈnentl] 1. ☐ kıtaya ait, kıtasal, karasal (iklim); Avrupa kıtasına ait; 2. n. Avrupa kıtasında yaşayan kimse.

con.tin.gen.cy [kənˈtindʒənsi] n. ihtimal; beklenmedik olay; conˈtin.gen.cies n. pl. rastlantı sonucu olan olaylar, kazara olan olaylar; conˈtin.gent 1. ☐ kesin olmayan, şüpheli, olması başka şeye bağlı olan, kazara olan, rastlantı eseri olan, tesadüfî; ~ on bağlı -e, dayalı -e; 2. n. × asker grubu, grup.

con.tin.u.al ☐ [kənˈtinjuəl] devamlı, sürekli, daimî, ardı arkası kesilmez, mütemadî; sık sık; conˈtin.u.ance n. devam, süreklilik, sürdürme; süre, müddet; er-

teleme; arta kalan şey; con.tin.uˈa.tion n. devam (etme), sürme, sürüp gitme; uzantı; † uzatma, temdit, zeyil; ~ school (boş zamanları değerlendirmek için gidilen) akşam okulu; conˈtin.ue [~njuː] v/t. devam etm. -e; uzatmak, sürdürmek; görevde tutmak; ertelemek, tehir etm.; ~ reading okumaya devam etm.; to ~ devam etm.; conˈtin.u.ous ☐ [kənˈtinjuəs] devamlı, sürekli, fasılasız, aralıksız; ~ current ≠ devamlı cereyan, doğru akım.

con.tort [kənˈtɔːt] v/t. burmak, bükmek, eğmek, çarpıtmak; conˈtor.tion n. bur-(ul)ma, bük(ül)me, eğ(il)me; conˈtor-tion.ist [~ʃnist] n. vücudunu türlü şekillere sokan akrobat, vücudu lastik gibi olan akrobat.

con.tour [ˈkɔntuə] n. dış hatlar, çevre; şekil; düzey çizgisi; ~ line surv. eşyükselti çizgisi; ~ map düzey haritası.

con.tra [ˈkɔntrə] pref. karşı, zıt, aksi; per ~ † öbür taraftan.

con.tra.band [ˈkɔntrəbænd] 1. adj. kaçak...; 2. n. kaçak eşya, kaçak mal.

con.tra.cep.tion [kɔntrəˈsepʃən] n. gebelikten korunma; con.traˈcep.tive adj. & n. gebeliği önleyici (hap veya alet).

con.tract 1. [kənˈtrækt] v/t. daraltmak, kısaltmak; büzmek, kasmak; buruşturmak; hastalık: tutulmak; çatmak (kaş); anlaşma yaparak üstlenmek; girmek (borca); v/i. mukavele yapmak, anlaşma yapmak; kasılmak, daralmak, büzülmek, buruşmak; ~ for ...için mukavele yapmak; ~ing parties âkit taraflar, sözleşme aktedenler; 2. [ˈkɔntrækt] n. sözleşme, anlaşma, mukavele, akit kontrat; by ~ sözleşmeye dayanan, mukavele ile; under ~ mukaveleli, sözleşmeli; con.tract.ed ☐ [kənˈtræktid] kasılmış, büzülmüş, kısaltılmış; fig. az, kıt, mahdut; ~ form gr. kaynaştırılmış şekil; con.tract.iˈbil.i.ty n. kısaltılabilirlik; conˈtract.i.ble adj. kısaltılabilir; conˈtrac.tile [~tail] adj. toplanabilen, kısal(tıl)abilen; conˈtrac.tion n. büzülme, kasılma; gr. kaynaştırma; conˈtrac.tor n. müteahhit, akdi yapan taraf, mukaveleli kimse veya firma; anat. doğum anında gerilen rahim adeleleri, büzgen; conˈtrac-

**tu.al** [ˌtjuəl] *adj.* akitten doğan, mukaveleden doğan, mukavele...

**con.tra.dict** [kɒntrəˈdikt] *v/t.* yalanlamak, -*in* aksini söylemek, ...ile ters düşmek, ...ile tezat teşkil etm.; **con.tra'dic.tion** *n.* yalanlama; çelişme, aykırılık, tezat; **con.tra'dic.tious** □ aykırı, zıt, aksi, ters; **con.tra'dic.to.ry** [~təri] □ aykırı, zıt, aksi, ters.

**con.tra.dis.tinc.tion** [kɒntrədisˈtiŋkʃən] *n.* fark, zıt, aksi, tezat; **con.tra.dis'tin.guish** [~gwiʃ] *vb.* zıddı ile ayırmak, ayırt etm.

**con.trap.tion** *sl.* [kənˈtræpʃən] *n.* garip alet, cihaz.

**con.tra.ri.e.ty** [kɒntrəˈraiəti] *n.* zıtlık, tezat, terslik, aksilik; **con.tra.ri.ly** [ˈ~trəlili] *adv.* aksine, bilâkis; **'con.tra.ri.ness** *n.* terslik, zıtlık, aksilik, inatçılık; **con.tra.ri.wise** [ˈ~waiz] *adv.* aksine, bilâkis; ters yönde, aksi yönde; zıt giderek; **'con.tra.ry** 1. *adj.* ters, zıt, aksi, muhalif, karşı, aykırı; F [kənˈtrɛəri] dik kafalı, aksi, inatçı, asi; ~ *to prp.* -*e* aykırı, -*e* ters; 2. *n.* aksi, zıt, ters, karşıt; on the ~ aksine, bilakis, tersine; to the ~ aksi yönde, olumsuz yönde, ...rağmen.

**con.trast** 1. [ˈkɒntrɑːst] *n.* tezat, zıtlık, fark, ayrılık; *fotoğraf:* açık ve koyu kısımlar arasındaki fark; in ~ to -*e* zıt olarak, -*in* aksine, -*e* ters olarak; by ~ aksine; 2. [kənˈtrɑːst] *v/t.* karşılaştırmak, mukayese etm. (with *ile*); *v/i.* ters düşmek, tezat teşkil etm., zıt olm. (with *ile*).

**con.tra.vene** [kɒntrəˈviːn] *vb.* karşı gelmek -*e*, muhalefet etm. -*e*; itiraz etm. -*e*; ihtilâfa düşmek -*le*, zıtlaşmak -*le*, uyumsuz olm. -*le*; **con.tra.ven.tion** [~ˈvenʃən] *n.* karşı gelme, ihlâl (of -*e*, -*i*).

**con.trib.u.te** [kənˈtribjuːt] *v/t.* bağışlamak -*e*, katkıda bulunmak -*e*, iane vermek -*e*; *v/i.* yazı vermek (to -*e*); **con.tri.bu.tion** [kɒntriˈbjuːʃən] *n.* yardım, bağış, iane, teberru; makale, yazı; vergi; aidat, prim; ✕ işgal kuvvetlerinin elkoyması; **con.trib.u.tor** [kənˈtribjutə] *n.* yardım eden kimse, bağış yapan kimse; yazı yazan kimse (to a newspaper *bir gazeteye*); **con'trib.u.to.ry** *adj.* yardımcı, sebep olan (to -*e*).

**con.trite** □ [ˈkɒntrait] pişman, tövbekâr; **con.tri.tion** [kənˈtriʃən] *n.* pişmanlık.

**con.triv.ance** [kənˈtraivəns] *n.* buluş, icat; hüner; tertibat, cihaz; gizli plan, entrika; **con'trive** *v/t.* icat etm., bulmak; başarmak, becermek; *v/i.* plan yapmak (to *inf.* -*mek için*); **con'triv.er** *n.* çekip çevi-

ren kimse *(part. ev kadını)*; she is a good ~ iyi bir ev kadınıdır.

**con.trol** [kənˈtrəul] 1. *n.* kontrol, denetleme; idare, hâkimiyet, egemenlik; ☼ tasarruf; *attr.* kontrol...; ~ surfaces *pl.* ✈ kumanda sathı, uçak dümen tertibatı; remote *veya* distant ~ uzaktan kontrol; ~ board ⊕ kontrol paneli; ~ column ✈ kumanda kolonu, volanlı lövye; ~ knob ayar düğmesi, kontrol düğmesi; ~ valve *radyo:* ayar supapı; be in ~ yönetici durumda olm., kontrolü elinde bulundurmak, yönetmek (of -*i*); put s.o. in ~ *b-ni* yönetici yapmak, başa geçirmek; 2. *v/t.* kontrol etm., denetlemek, tetkik etm.; idare etm., hâkim olm.; düzenlemek; ⊕ ayar etm.; ✈ uçak kullanmak; **con'trol.la.ble** *adj.* idare edilebilir, yönetilebilir; **con'trol.ler** *n.* murakıp, denetleyici, muhasebeci, kontrolör; regulatör.

**con.tro.ver.sial** □ [kɒntrəˈvɜːʃəl] çekişmeli, ihtilâflı; **con.tro.ver.sy** [ˈ~vəːsi] *n.* çekişme, münakaşa, tartışma, ihtilâf, mücadele; **con.tro.vert** [ˈ~vəːt] *vb.* yalanlamak, inkâr etm.; itiraz etm.; **con.tro'vert.i.ble** □ itiraz edilebilir, inkâr edilebilir.

**con.tu.ma.cious** □ [kɒntjuˈmeiʃəs] inatçı, asi, dik başlı, isyankâr; ☼ itaatsiz; **con.tu.ma.cy** [ˈkɒntjuməsi] *n.* inat, inatçılık, asilik; ☼ itaatsizlik, mahkeme emrine uymama.

**con.tu.me.li.ous** □ [kɒntjuˈmiːljəs] terbiyesiz, arsız, küstah; utandırıcı, yüz kızartıcı; **con.tu.me.ly** [ˈkɒntjuːmli] *n.* küfür, hakaret, tahkir.

**con.tuse** ⚕ [kənˈtjuːz] *v/t.* berelemek, çürütmek, ezmek, yaralamak; **con'tu.sion** [~ʒən] *n.* bere, çürük, ezik.

**co.nun.drum** [kəˈnʌndrəm] *n.* şaşırtıcı soru, bilmece.

**con.ur.ba.tion** [kɒnəːˈbeiʃən] *n.* şehirlerin genişleyip birleşmesi.

**con.va.lesce** [kɒnvəˈles] *vb.* iyileşmek; **con.va'les.cence** *n.* iyileşme, nekahet; **con.va.les.cent** 1. □ nekahet devresi ile ilgili, iyileşme...; 2. *n.* iyileşen, şifa bulan kimse.

**con.vec.tion** *phys.* [kənˈvekʃən] *n.* ısı nakletme; **con'vec.tor** *n.* konvektör.

**con.vene** [kənˈviːn] *vb.* topla(n)mak, biraraya getirmek, toplantı yapmak, biraraya gelmek; ☼ dava açmak, mahkemeye celbetmek.

**con.ven.ience** [kənˈviːnjəns] *n.* uygunluk, rahatlık, kolaylık, elverişlilik; konfor; tuvalet, helâ; *at your earliest* ~ sizce mümkün olan en kısa zamanda; make a ~ of s.o. *b-nin* iyi niyetini suiistimal etm.; marriage of ~ maddiyat evliliği, menfaate dayanan evlilik; **con¹ven.ient** ☐ uygun, elverişli, münasip, rahat, müsait (to, for -*e*).

**con.vent** [ˈkɔnvənt] *n.* (*part. rahibelerin olduğu*) manastır; **con.ven.ti.cle** [kənˈventikl] *n.* gizli dinî toplantı, gizli dinî toplantının yapıldığı bina; **con¹ven.tion** *n.* toplantı, kongre; anlaşma, mukavele; âdet, gelenek; **con¹ven.tion.al** [~ʃənl] *adj.* göreneksel, geleneksel, âdetlere uygun; ~ weapons *pl.* nükleer silahlar dışındaki silahlar; **con¹ven.tion.al.ism** [~ʃnəlizəm] *n.* âdetlere bağlılık; **con.ven.tion.al.i.ty** [~ʃəˈnæliti] *n.* toplum geleneklerine bağlılık; **con¹ven.tu.al** [~tjuəl] ☐ manastır ile ilgili, manastır...

**con.verge** [kənˈvəːdʒ] *vb.* bir noktada birleşmek; ⅄ birbirine yaklaşmak (*doğrular*); **con¹ver.gence, con¹ver.gen.cy** *n.* birleşme; birbirine yaklaşma; **con¹vergent, con¹verg.ing** *adj.* birleşen; birbirine yaklaşan.

**con.vers.a.ble** [kənˈvəːsəbl] *adj.* hakkında konuşulabilir; sohbeti tatlı; **con¹ver.sant** (with) *adj.* iyi bilen, bilgisi olan, erbap; **con.ver.sa.tion** [~vəˈseiʃən] *n.* konuşma, sohbet; **con¹sa.tion.al** [~ʃənl] *adj.* konuşma..., konuşabilir..., konuşma diline ait; **con.verse 1.** ☐ [ˈkɔnvəːs] zıt, aksi, ters; **2.** [~] *n.* ters fikir, ters ifade; ⅄, *phls.* evirtim, akis; **3.** [kənˈvəːs] *vb.* konuşmak, görüşmek, sohbet etm. (with *ile*); **con¹ver.sion** *n.* değiş(tir)me; ⊕, ≠ çevirme; *phls.* evirme, evirtim; *eccl.* ihtida, din değiştirme; *pol.* başka bir görüşü benimseme; ✝ borçların tahvili, tahvil.

**con.vert 1.** [ˈkɔnvəːt] *n.* dönme, muhtedi, din değiştiren kimse; **2.** [ˈkɔnvəːt] *vb.* değiştirmek, tahvil etm., döndürmek, çevirmek; ⊕, ≠ şeklini değiştirmek; *eccl. b-nin* inançlarını değiştirmek (to -*e*); ✝ paraya çevirmek; **con¹vert.er** *n.* değiştiren şey; ⊕, ≠ konverter, çevirgeç; **con-vert.i.bil.i.ty** [~əˈbiliti] *n.* değiştirilebilme; ✝ konvertibilite, çevrilebilme; **con-¹vert.i.ble 1.** ☐ değiştirilebilir; ✝ tahvili mümkün, çevrilebilir; **2.** *n. mot.* üstü açılıp kapanabilen spor araba; değiştirilebilen şey.

**con.vex** ☐ [ˈkɔnˈveks] dışbükey, konveks; **con¹vex.i.ty** *n.* dışbükeylik.

**con.vey** [kənˈvei] *v/t.* taşımak, götürmek, nakletmek; ifade etm.; *phys.* nakletmek, iletmek; ♂ devretmek; **con¹vey.ance** *n.* taşıma, nakil, taşıt; ♂ feragatname,

terk, temlik, ferağ; ≠ geçirme, iletme, transmisyon; *public* ~ toplu taşıma aracı; **con¹vey.anc.er** *n.* ♂ temlik ve ferağ muamelelerini hazırlayan avukat; **con-vey.or** ⊕ *a.* ~ belt taşıma bandı.

**con.vict 1.** [ˈkɔnvikt] *n.* mahkûm, suçlu; **2.** [kənˈvikt] *v/t.* ikna etm., inandırmak (of -*e*); suçlandırmak, suçlamak, mahkûm etm. (of *ile*); **con¹vic.tion** *n.* ♂ suçlandırma, mahkûmiyet, hükümlülük; inanç, katiyet, kesinlik, kanaat (of -*e*); *previous* ~ sabıka.

**con.vince** [kənˈvins] *v/t.* inandırmak, ikna etm. (of -*e*); **con¹vinc.ing** *adj.* inandırıcı, ikna edici.

**con.viv.i.al** [kənˈviviəl] *adj.* neşeli..., şen...; eğlenceye düşkün...; **con.viv.i.al.i.ty** [~ˈæliti] *n.* neşe, eğlence, şamata.

**con.vo.ca.tion** [kɔnvəuˈkeiʃən] *n.* toplantı, meclis; kilise temsilcileri meclisi.

**con.voke** [kənˈvəuk] *v/t.* toplantıya çağırmak.

**con.vo.lu.tion** [kɔnvəˈluːʃən] *n.* büklüm, kıvrım; sarılma, dürülme.

**con.vol.vu.lus** ⚘ [kənˈvɔlvjuləs] *n.* kahkahaçiçeği.

**con.voy** [ˈkɔnvɔi] **1.** *n.* konvoy; koruma, himaye; **2.** *v/t.* rehberlik etm., korumak.

**con.vulse** *fig.* [kənˈvʌls] *vb.* sarsmak, sıkıntı vermek, rahatsız etm., kıvrandırmak; be ~d with laughter gülmekten katılmak; **con¹vul.sion** *n.* ihtilâç, kıvranma, çırpınma, katılma; ~s of laughter gülmekten katılma; **con¹vul.sive** ☐ ihtilâç gibi, çırpınma...

**co.ny** [ˈkəuni] *n.* tavşan; tavşan kürkü.

**coo** [kuː] *vb.* ötmek (*kumru*); kumru gibi ses çıkarmak; mırıldanmak.

**cook** [kuk] **1.** *n.* aşçı; **2.** *v/t. & v/i.* piş(ir)-mek; *fig.* uydurmak (*hikâye*); F üzerinde oynamak (*hesaplar*); ¹~.book *n.* Am. yemek kitabı; **¹cook.er** *n.* soba, ocak; F uydurukçu; **¹cook.er.y** *n.* aşçılık, mutfak işleri; ~ book yemek kitabı; **¹cook-house** *n.* dışarıda olan mutfak; ♪ gemi mutfağı; **cook.ie** Am. [¹~i] *n.* kurabiye, çörek, bisküvi; *Am. sl.* şahıs; *Am. sl.* güzel kadın; **¹cook.ing** *n.* pişirme (sanatı); **cook.y** [¹~i] = cookie.

**cool** [kuːl] **1.** ☐ serin, soğuk; *fig.* soğukkanlı, sakin, kayıtsız, kendine hâkim; *b.s.* yüzsüz, küstah; *sl.* hoş, güzel, iyi, mükemmel; ~ a thousand pounds F abartmasız bin pound; **2.** *n.* serinlik; serin hava *veya* yer; sükûnet, soğukkanlılık; **3.** *v/t. & v/i.* soğu(t)mak, serinle(t)mek; yatışmak, geçmek (*sinir*); let him ~ his heels bırak beklesin; **¹cool.er** *n.* soğutma cihazı, soğutucu; *sl.* hapishane, kodes; **ᴵcool-ᴵhead.ed** *adj.* soğukkanlı, serinkanlı.

**coo.lie** [ᴵkuːli] *n.* hamal.

**cool.ing** ⊕ [ᴵkuːliŋ] *n.* soğutma; *attr.* soğutucu...; **ᴵcool.ness** *n.* serinlik; *fig.* soğukkanlılık.

**coomb** [kuːm] *n.* derin vadi.

**coon** *Am.* F [kuːn] *n.* *zo.* ayıya benzer bir hayvan türü; zenci; ɑ gone ~ ümitsiz durumda olan kimse; ~ song zenci şarkısı.

**coop** [kuːp] 1. *n.* kümes; 2. *vb.* ~ up *veya* in kümese sokmak; tıkmak, sokmak.

**co-op** F [ᴵkəuɔp] *n.* = co-operative (store) kooperatif.

**coop.er** [ᴵkuːpə] *n.* fıçıcı; **ᴵcoop.er.age** *n.* fıçıcılık; fıçı imalathanesi.

**co-op.er.ate** [kəuᴵɔpəreit] *v/i.* işbirliği yapmak, beraber çalışmak; **co-op.erᴵa.tion** *n.* işbirliği; **co-ᴵop.er.a.tive** [~rətiv] 1. *adj.* işbirliği yapan, işbirliğine ait; ~ society tüketim kooperatifi; ~ store kooperatif; 2. = ~ store; **co-ᴵop.er.a.tor** [~reitə] *n.* iş arkadaşı.

**co-opt** [kəuᴵɔpt] *vb.* oy ile seçmek, atamak, tayin etm.; **co-opᴵta.tion** *n.* oy ile seçme, atama.

**co-or.di.nate** 1. □ [kəuᴵɔːdinit] eşit, aynı derecede; 2. [~neit] *v/t.* ayarlamak, ahenk kazandırmak, alıştırmak, düzeltmek; **co-or.diᴵna.tion** *n.* tanzim, ayarlama, düzenleme, tertip, koordinasyon.

**coot** [kuːt] *n.* su tavuğu, sakarmeki; F zararsız kimse, beceriksiz kimse; **coot-le** ✕ *sl.* [ᴵ~i] *n.* bit.

**cop** *sl.* [kɔp] 1. *vb.* yakalamak, kapmak; çalmak, aşırmak; ~ it cezalandırılmak, dövülmek; 2. *n.* polis memuru, aynasız.

**co.pal** [ᴵkəupəl] *n.* bir reçine türü, kopal.

**co.part.ner** [ᴵkəuᴵpɑːtnə] *n.* ortak; **ᴵco-ᴵpart.ner.ship** *n.* ortaklık.

**cope¹** [kəup] 1. *n.* papaz cüppesi; *fig.* örtü; 2. *vb.* örtmek.

**cope²** [~] *vb.*: ~ with başa çıkmak, uğraşmak.

**Co.per.ni.can** [kəuᴵpəːnikən] *adj.* Kopernik'e ait ,Kopernik...

**cope.stone** [ᴵkəupstəun] *n.* *mst* *fig.* taç, süsleme.

**co-pi.lot** [kəuᴵpailət] *n.* ikinci pilot.

**cop.ing** [ᴵkəupiŋ] *n.* duvar tepeliği *veya* üstlüğü **ᴵ~-stone** *n.* *fig.* taç, süsleme.

**co.pi.ous** □ [ᴵkəupjəs] bol, çok, mebzul, bereketli; **ᴵco.pi.ous.ness** *n.* bolluk, bereket.

**cop.per¹** [ᴵkɔpə] 1. *n.* bakır; bakır para;

kazan; 2. *adj.* bakıra benzer; bakır...; 3. *vb.* bakır kaplamak.

**cop.per²** *sl.* [~] *n.* polis memuru, aynasız.

**cop.per.as** ⌃ᵐ [ᴵkɔpərəs] *n.* demir sulfat, zaç.

**cop.per...**: ~ **beech** ⚘ kızıl kayın ağacı; **ᴵ~.plate** *n.* işlemeli bakır tabak; bir tür ince el yazısı; **ᴵ~-smith** *n.* bakırcı.

**cop.pice** [ᴵkɔpis], **copse** [kɔps] *n.* küçük koru, ağaçlık, çalılık.

**cop.u.late** *zo.* [ᴵkɔpjuleit] *vb.* çiftleşmek *(hayvanlar)*; **cop.uᴵla.tion** *n.* çiftleşme; **cop.u.la.tive** [ᴵ~lətiv] 1. *adj.* birleştiren, bağlayıcı; 2. *n.* *gr.* bağlaç.

**cop.y** [ᴵkɔpi] 1. *n.* kopya, nüsha, suret, numune, örnek; müsvedde; metin, yazı; fair *veya* clean ~ temiz kopya; rough *veya* foul ~ müsvedde, karalama, eskiz; 2. *v/t.* kopya etm., -in suretini çıkarmak; taklit etm.; kopya çekmek *(imtihanda)*; ~ fair temiz kopyasını çıkarmak; ~ing stand *phot.* kopya masası; **ᴵ~-book** *n.* defter; **ᴵ~-hold** *n.* zeamet, tımar; **ᴵcop.y.ing-ink** *n.* kopya çıkarma mürekkebi; **ᴵcop.y.ing-press** *n.* kopya presi; **ᴵcop.y.ist** *n.* kopya eden, taklitçi; **ᴵcop.y.right** *n.* telif hakkı; *attr.* telif hakkı sakıp olan.

**cor.a.cle** [ᴵkɔrəkl] *n.* bez *veya* deri kaplı bir çeşit kayık.

**cor.al** [ᴵkɔrəl] 1. *n.* mercan; 2. *adj.* *a.* **cor.al.line** [ᴵ~lain] mercana benzer, mercan...

**cor.bel** ⚐ [ᴵkɔːbəl] *n.* dirsek.

**cord** [kɔːd] 1. *n.* ip, sicim, kaytan, şerit, tel; *fig.* manevî bağ; *anat.* ribat, veter, kiriş; = corduroy; 2. *v/t.* iple bağlamak; iple süslemek; yığmak *(kütükleri)*; **ᴵcord.ed** *adj.* iple bağlı; gergin *(adale)*; kabarık çizgili; **ᴵcord.age** *n.* geminin halat takımı.

**cor.dial** [ᴵkɔːdjəl] 1. □ samimi, candan, yürekten, içten; 2. *n.* likör; **cor.dial.i.ty** [~diᴵæliti] *n.* samimiyet, içtenlik.

**cord-mak.er** [ᴵkɔːdmeikə] *n.* ipçi, urgancı, halatçı.

**cor.don** [ᴵkɔːdn] 1. *n.* ⚔ kordon; ✕ süslü bant, kordon; *(asker, polis araç vs.)* kordon; 2. *vb.* ~ off kordon oluşturarak uzak tutmak.

**cor.do.van** [ᴵkɔːdəvən] *n.* bir çeşit ince deri.

**cor.du.roy** [ᴵkɔːdərɔi] *n.* fitilli kadife; ~s

*pl.* kadife pantolon; ~ road bataklık üzerindeki kütüklerden yapılmış yol.

**core** [kɔː] 1. *n.* ✤ göbek, meyvaların çekirdek kısmı; *fig.* iç, öz, esas, nüve; 2. *vb.* içini çıkarmak *(meyvanın)*; ¹**cor.er** *n.* oyma bıçağı.

**co-re.li.gion.ist** [¹kəuri¹lidʒənist] *n.* dindaş, aynı dinden olan kimse.

**Co.rin.thi.an** [kə¹rinθiən] *adj.* Korint üslûbu.

**cork** [kɔːk] 1. *n.* mantar, tapa, tıpa; 2. *v/t.* mantarla kapamak, tıpalamak; *fig. a.* ~ up saklamak *(duygularını)*; ¹**cork.age** *n.* lokantada müşterilerin beraberinde getirdiği şarap için verilen açma ve servis ücreti; ¹**corked** *adj.* mantar kokusuyla bozulmuş *(şarap)*; *sl.* körkütük sarhoş; ¹**cork.er** *n. sl.* olağanüstü şey, muazzam şey; tıpalayan kimse *veya* şey; ¹**cork.ing** *adj. Am.* F fevkalâde, mükemmel, nefis.

**cork...**: ~**jack.et** *n.* can kurtaran yeleği; ¹**~.screw** 1. *n.* tirbuşon, tıpa burgusu; 2. *adj.* helezoni; 3. *vb.* vidalamak, dön(dür)mek; ¹**~.tree** *n.* ✤ mantar meşesi; ¹**cork.y** *adj.* mantara benzer, mantar gibi; F hayat dolu, canlı.

**cor.mo.rant** *orn.* [¹kɔːmərənt] *n.* karabatak kuşu.

**corn¹** [kɔːn] 1. *n.* hububat, buğday, tahıl; *a.* Indian ~ *Am.* mısır; *Am.* ~ bread mısır ekmeği; 2. *v/t.* tuzlayıp kurutmak; ~ed beef konserve sığır eti.

**corn²** ✤ [~] *n.* nasır.

**corn...**: ¹**~.chan.dler** *n.* mısırcı, tohumcu; ¹**~.cob** *n. Am.* mısır koçanı.

**cor.ne.a** *anat.* [¹kɔːniə] *n.* kornea, gözün dış tabakası.

**cor.nel** ✤ [¹kɔːnəl] *n.* karaniya.

**cor.nel.ian** *min.* [kɔː¹niːljən] *n.* akik taşı.

**cor.ne.ous** [¹kɔːniəs] *adj.* boynuzdan yapılmış, boynuz gibi.

**cor.ner** [¹kɔːnə] 1. *n.* köşe, köşebaşı; gizli yer; bölge, bucak; *fig.* sıkıntı, çıkmaz; ✝ piyasayı ele geçirme; ~ kick köşe vuruşu, korner atışı; 2. *v/t.* çıkmaza sokmak, köşeye sıkıştırmak *(a. fig.)*; ✝ ele geçirmek *(piyasayı)*; ¹**cor.nered** *comb.* ...köşeli.

**corner...**: ¹**~.house** *n.* köşebaşı evi; ¹**~.stone** *n.* temel taşı; *fig.* temel, esas.

**cor.net** [¹kɔːnit] *n.* ♪ kornet; kağıt külâh.

**corn...**: ¹**~.ex.change** *n.* tahıl borsası; ¹**~.field** *n.* buğday tarlası; *Am.* mısır tarlası; ~ flakes *n. pl.* mısır gevreği; ¹**~.flour** = corn-starch; ¹**~.flow.er** *n.* peygamberçiçeği.

**cor.nice** [¹kɔːnis] *n.* ⩜ korniş, geniş silme.

**Cor.nish** [¹kɔːniʃ] *adj.* Kelt diline ait.

**corn...**: ¹**~.juice** *n. Am. sl.* mısır viskisi; ~ pone *Am.* kızartılmış mısır ekmeği; ¹**~.pop.py** *n.* ✤ gelincik çiçeği; ¹**~.stalk** *n.* buğday sapı; *Am.* mısır sapı; ¹**~.starch** *n. Am.* mısır nişastası.

**cor.nu.co.pi.a** *poet.* [kɔːnju¹kəupjə] *n.* sanatçılar tarafından bolluk sembolü olarak kullanılan ve içinden meyva, çiçek ve tahıl taşan boynuz şeklinde süslü kap.

**corn.y** [¹kɔːni] *adj.* eskimiş, basmakalıp; *sl.* adi, bayağı; *part. Am.* ♪ çok duyulan *veya* tekrarlanan.

**co.rol.la** ✤ [kə¹rɔlə] *n.* taçyapraklar, korol; **cor¹ol.la.ry** *n.* sonuç, netice; *fig.* akıbet.

**co.ro.na** [kə¹rəunə] *n., pl.* **co¹ro.nae** [~niː] *ast.* hale, ağıl, ayla; ⚕ damlık, sıçan oluğu; **co¹ro.nal** *adj. anat.* kafatasının üst düzeyine ait; **cor.o.na.tion** [kɔrə¹neiʃən] *n.* taç giyme töreni; ¹**cor.o.ner** *n.* şüpheli ölüm vakalarını tahkik eden memur; **cor.o.net** [¹~nit] *n.* asillerin giydiği küçük taç.

**cor.po.ral** [¹kɔːpərəl] 1. ☐ bedenî, cismanî, gövdesel; 2. *n.* ✕ onbaşı; **cor.po.rate** [¹~rit] ☐ anonim şirkete ait, ortaklığa ait; birlik olmuş, toplu; ~ body birlik, özel hukuk tüzel kişisi; **cor.po.ra.tion** [~¹reiʃən] *n.* birlik; tüzel kişi; *Am.* anonim ortaklık; F şiş göbek; ~ tax kurumlar vergisi; **cor.po.ra.tive** [¹~rətiv] *adj.* anonim ortaklık...; korporatif...; **cor.po.re.al** ☐ [~¹pɔːriəl] bedenî, maddî, cismanî; **cor.po.re.i.ty** [~pə¹riːiti] *n.* bedenen var oluş, mevcudiyet.

**corps** [kɔː] *n., pl.* **corps** [kɔːz] kolordu, müfreze, kıta; topluluk, heyet; Diplomatic ⚥ kordiplomatik.

**corpse** [kɔːps] *n.* ceset, ölü.

**cor.pu.lence**, **cor.pu.len.cy** [¹kɔːpjuləns(i)] *n.* şişmanlık; ¹**cor.pu.lent** *adj.* şişman, etli butlu.

**cor.pus** [¹kɔːpəs] *n., pl.* **cor.po.ra** [¹~pərə] bir yazarın tüm eserlerini içeren yapıt, külliyat; esas; ana para, sermaye; ⚥ Christi [¹kristi] bir katolik yortusu; **cor.pus.cle** [¹kɔːpʌsl] *n.* hücre, yuvar, kan küreciği.

**cor.ral** *part. Am.* [kɔː¹rɑːl] 1. *n.* ağıl; 2. *vb.* ağıla kapamak; *fig.* yakalamak.

**cor.rect** [kə¹rekt] 1. ☐ doğru, sahih, yanlışsız, tam; dürüst; münasip, uygun; be ~ doğru, dürüst olm.; 2. *v/t.* düzeltmek, ayarlamak, doğrultmak; cezalandırmak; 🖉 yumuşatmak; **cor¹rec.tion** *n.* düzeltme, tashih, ıslah, ayarlama; cezalandırma; 🖉 yumuşatma; house of ~ ıslahha-

ne; hapishane; I speak under ~ yanlış-
larım olduğunu bilerek konuşuyorum;
cor'rect.i.tude [~tit.ju:d] n. doğruluk, dürüstlük; cor'rec.tive 1. adj. düzeltici, ıslah edici; *ʌ* yumuşatıcı; 2. n. ıslah eden
veya düzelten şey, çare; cor'rec.tor n.
düzletici, düzeltmen; *ʌ* yumuşatıcı.
cor.re.late ['kɔrileit] 1. vb. karşılıklı ilişkisi olm.; aralarında uygunluk sağlamak; aralarında ilişki kurmak; 2. n. aralarında ilişki olan şeylerden her biri;
cor.re'la.tion n. karşılıklı ilişki; bağlantı; cor.rel.a.tive □ [~'relətiv] karşılıklı;
bağlantılı, ilişkili.
cor.re.spond [kɔris'pɔnd] vb: (with, to ~e,
ile) uymak, uygun gelmek, benzemek,
aynı olm.; mektuplaşmak (with ile); cor-
re'spond.ence n. uygunluk, benzerlik;
mektuplaşma, yazışma, muhabere; cor-
re'spond.ent 1. □ karşılıklı, uygun; 2.
n. mektup arkadaşı; muhabir; my ~s
mektup arkadaşlarım; cor.re'spond.ing
adj. uyan, yerini tutan, aynısı; mektup-
laşan, muhabere eden.
cor.ri.dor ['kɔridɔ:] n. koridor, geçit, dehliz; ~ train bir vagondan diğerine geçi-
lebilen tren, koridorlu tren.
cor.ri.gi.ble □ ['kɔridʒəbl] düzeltilebilir;
ıslah edilebilir (kimse).
cor.rob.o.rant [kə'rɔbərənt] 1. adj. kuvvetlendirici, destekleyici; 2. n. kuvvetlendirici şey; cor'rob.o.rate [~reit] v/t.
doğrulamak, teyit etm., desteklemek (fikir); cor.rob.o'ra.tion n. doğrulama,
onaylama, destekleme; cor'rob.o.ra.tive
[~rətiv] adj. doğrulayan, destekleyen.
cor.rode [kə'rəud] v/t. & v/i. aşın(dır)-
mak, çürü(t)mek, paslan(dır)mak; cor-
'ro.dent 1. adj. aşındırıcı, çürütücü, pas-
landırıcı; 2. n. aşındırıcı madde, paslan-
dırıcı madde; cor'ro.sion [~ʒən] n. pas-
lanma, aşınma, çürüme; ⊕ asitlenme,
korozyon; cor'ro.sive [~siv] 1. □ çürütücü, aşındırıcı, kemirici; fig. yıpratıcı;
2. n. çürütücü madde; cor'ro.sive.ness
n. çürütücülük, aşındırıcılık.
cor.ru.gate ['kɔrugeit] vb. kırıştırmak,
buruşturmak; ⊕ yiv açmak, oluk açmak; ~d cardboard oluklu mukavva; ~d
iron oluklu demir levha.
cor.rupt [kə'rʌpt] 1. □ namussuz, fırsatçı, rüşvet almaya alışkın; kötü, pis; bozuk, çürük; ~ practices pl. pol. rüşvet
alma veya verme; 2. v/t. & v/i. boz(ul)-
mak, çürü(t)mek; ahlâkını bozmak,
ayartmak, baştan çıkartmak; rüşvet vermek; cor'rupt.er n. rüşvet yiyen kimse;
cor.rupt.i.bil.i.ty [~tə'biliti] n. rüşvet ye-

me; cor'rupt.i.ble □ rüşvet yiyen; cor-
'rup.tion n. çürü(t)me; rüşvet yeme; ahlâk bozukluğu, fesat; cor'rup.tive □ çürütücü.
cor.sage [kɔ:'sɑ:ʒ] n. kadın elbisesinin
üst kısmı, korsaj; Am. göğse takılan çiçek buketi.
cor.sair ['kɔ:sɛə] n. korsan; korsan gemisi.
corse [kɔ:s] poet. = corpse.
cors(e).let ['kɔ:slit] n. zırh (yalnız gövdeyi örten).
cor.set ['kɔ:sit] n. korse; 'cor.set.ed adj.
korseli.
cor.tège [kɔ:'tei3] n. kortej, merasim alayı; maiyet.
cor.tex *ʖ*, zo., anat. ['kɔ:teks] n., pl. cor-
ti.ces ['-tisi:z] kabuk, korteks, kışır.
cor.ti.cal ['kɔ:tikəl] adj. kabuk...; fig. harici, dış.
co.run.dum min. [kə'rʌndəm] n. korin-
don; zımpara.
cor.us.cate ['kɔrəskeit] vb. parıldamak,
ışıldamak (a. fig.).
cor.vette ↓ [kɔ:'vet] n. korvet, ufak torpido muhribi; kadırga.
cor.vine ['kɔ:vain] adj. karga gibi, karga...
cosh sl. [kɔʃ] 1. n. cop; 2. vb. cop ile vurmak; '~-boy n. sl. genç haydut.
cosh.er ['kɔʃə] vb. şımartmak, pohpohlamak.
co-sig.na.to.ry ['kəu'signətəri] 1. adj. birlikte imzalayan; 2. n. müşterek imza
atan kimse.
co.sine *ʖ* ['kəusain] n. kosinüs.
co.si.ness ['kəuzinis] n. rahatlık, konfor.
cos.met.ic [kɔz'metik] 1. adj. makyaja ait,
kozmetik..., güzelleştirici; 2. n. makyaj
malzemesi; cos.me.ti.cian [kɔzme'tiʃən]
n. güzellik uzmanı.
cos.mic, cos.mi.cal □ ['kɔzmik(əl)] evrensel, kâinata ait, kozmik; cosmic rays
pl. kozmik ışınlar.
cos.mo.naut ['kɔzmənɔ:t] n. kozmonot.
cos.mo.pol.i.tan [kɔzməu'pɔlitən], cos.mop-
o.lite [~'mɔpəlait] 1. adj. kozmopolit; 2.
n. kozmopolit kimse.
cos.mos ['kɔzmɔs] n. acun, evren, kâinat,
kozmos; düzen, sistem.
Cos.sack ['kɔsæk] n. Kazak.
cos.set ['kɔsit] 1. n. evde beslenen kuzu;
2. vb. şımartmak, çok iyi davranmak.
cost [kɔst] 1. n. fiyat, değer, paha, kıymet; zarar, ziyan; masraf, bedel; ~s pl.
mahkeme harcı, dava masrafları; first
veya prime ~ maliyet fiyatı; ~ of living
hayat pahalılığı, geçim masrafı; at all

~s ne pahasına olursa olsun; to my ~ benim zararıma; as I know to my ~ başıma geldiği için bilirim; 2. (irr.) vb. mal olm., para tutmak; çok tutmak (zaman); † -in fiyatı olm., mal olm.; hesap etm.; ~ dearly pahalıya mal olm.

**cos.ter** F ['kɔstə] n. = '~.mon.ger seyyar satıcı.

**cost.ing** ['kɔstiŋ] n. fiyat tesbiti.

**cos.tive** □ ['kɔstiv] kabız.

**cost.li.ness** ['kɔstlinis] n. değer, kıymet, paha; 'cost.ly adj. değerli, pahalı, kıymetli; fig. pahalıya malolan.

**cost-price** † ['kɔstprais] n. maliyet fiyatı. **cos.tume** ['kɔstjuːm] n. kostüm, elbise, kıyafet, giysi; cos'tum.i.er [~miə] n. kostümleri hazırlayan kimse.

**co.sy** ['kəuzi] 1. □ rahat, konforlu, sıcacık, keyifli; 2. = teɑ.cosy.

**cot** [kɔt] n. çocuk karyolası; ✓ gemi ranzası; portatif karyola.

**cote** [kəut] n. kulübe, sığınacak yer (hayvanlar için).

**co.te.rie** ['kəutəri] n. zümre, grup, heyet.

**cot.tage** ['kɔtidʒ] n. küçük ev, kulübe; yazlık ev, sayfiye evi; ~ cheese Am. süzme peynir; ~ piano küçük piyano; 'cot.tag.er n. rençper; Am. sayfiye evinde oturan kimse.

**cot.ter** ⊕ ['kɔtə] n. anahtar, kama.

**cot.ton** ['kɔtn] 1. n. pamuk, pamuk bezi, pamuk ipliği; 2. adj. pamuklu...; ~ wool ham pamuk, hidrofil pamuk; 3. vb. F yaltaklanmak, yağcılık yapmak (to s.o. b-ne); ~ to s.th bşi anlamak, çakmak; ~ up geçinmek, anlaşmak (with, to ile); '~-grass n. pamuk otu; '~-seed n. ✿ çiğit; '~-wood n. ✿ bir nevi kavak ağacı; 'cot.ton.y adj. pamuk gibi, pamuklu, pamuk...

**cot.y.le.don** ✿ [kɔti'liːdən] n. tohumdan çıkan ilk yaprak, katiledon.

**couch** [kautʃ] 1. n. yatak, divan, sedir, kanepe; 2. v/t. yatırmak; indirmek; ifade etm., arz etm.; v/i. yatmak; çömelmek; pusuya yatmak; '~-grass n. ✿ ayrıkotu.

**cou.gar** zo. ['kuːgə] n. puma.

**cough** [kɔf] 1. n. öksürük; 2. v/i. öksürmek; ~ down öksürerek duyulmasını önlemek; ~ up öksürerek çıkarmak; sl. nazlanarak söylemek, zorla vermek.

**could** [kud] pret. of can.

**couldn't** ['kudnt] = could not.

**coul.ter** ['kəultə] n. sapan demiri.

**coun.cil** ['kaunsl] n. meclis, divan, konsey, encümen, şura, danışma kurulu;

**coun.ci(l).lor** ['~silə] n. meclis üyesi, encümen üyesi.

**coun.sel** ['kaunsəl] 1. n. danışma, fikir, düşünce, öğüt, nasihat; † avukat, dava vekili; ~ for the defence savunma avukatı; ~ for the prosecution iddia makamı, dava avukatı; keep one's (own) ~ fikirlerini kendine saklamak; take ~ with -e başvurmak, danışmak; 2. v/t. öğüt vermek -e, akıl vermek -e; coun.se(l).lor ['~slə] n. müşavir, danışman, müsteşar; avukat, dava vekili; s. coun.ci(l).lor.

**count¹** [kaunt] 1. n. sayma, hesap; ✿ şikâyet fıkrası, madde; boks: birden ona kadar sayma; a. ~-out parl. yeterli üye olmadığından meclisi başka bir tarihe erteleme; lose ~ hesabı şaşırmak, sayısını unutmak (of -in); take no ~ of what s.o. says b-nin söylediklerine kulak asmamak; 2. v/t. saymak, hesap etm.; hesaba katmak, göz önünde tutmak; fig. addetmek, ... gözü ile bakmak; be ~ed out boks: nakavt olm.; v/i. sayılmak; güvenmek, itimat etm. (on, upon -e); değeri olm. (for little az).

**count²** [~] n. kont.

**count.a.ble** ['kauntəbl] adj. sayılabilen.

**count-down** ['kauntdaun] n. hazırlık devresi; geriye doğru sayma.

**coun.te.nance** ['kauntinəns] 1. n. yüz, çehre, sima, görünüş, ifade; destek, onay; put s.o. out of ~ b-ni utandırmak, mahcup etm.; 2. vb. desteklemek, tasvip etm.

**count.er¹** ['kauntə] n. tezgâh; sayaç; marka, fiş.

**coun.ter²** [~] 1. adv. (to -e) karşı, aykırı, zıt, ters; 2. n. karşıt şey; karşılık (to -e); 3. v/t. karşılamak, önlemek; karşı koymak; boks: bertaraf etm. (yumruk).

**coun.ter.act** [kauntə'rækt] v/t. karşılamak, önlemek, karşı koymak, tesirsiz hale getirmek; coun.ter'ac.tion n. karşı hareket.

**coun.ter-at.tack** ['kauntərətæk] n. karşı hücum, kontra atak.

**coun.ter.bal.ance** 1. ['kauntəbæləns] n. karşılık, eş ağırlık; 2. [~'bæləns] v/t. eşit kuvvetle karşı koymak; † denkleştirmek.

**coun.ter.blast** ['kauntəblɑːst] n. sert cevap.

**coun.ter.charge** ['kauntətʃɑːdʒ] n. karşı suçlama.

**coun.ter.check** ['kauntətʃek] n. engel, mani, zorluk.

**coun.ter-claim** ⚖ [ˈkauntəkleim] *n.* karşı dava.

**coun.ter-clock.wise** [ˈkauntəˈklɔkwaiz] *adv.* saat yelkovanının ters yönünde, sola doğru.

**coun.ter-cur.rent** [ˈkauntəˈkʌrənt] *n.* ana for, ters akıntı.

**coun.ter-es.pi.o.nage** [ˈkauntərespiəˈnɑːʒ] *n.* karşı casusluk.

**coun.ter.feit** [ˈkauntəfit] 1. ☐ sahte, kalp; 2. *n.* taklit; 3. *v/t.* taklit etm.; sahte para basmak; ˈcoun.ter.feit.er *n.* kalpazan.

**coun.ter.foil** [ˈkauntəfɔil] *n.* makbuz koçanı.

**coun.ter.fort** ⚏ [kauntəfɔːt] *n.* payanda.

**coun.ter-ir.ri.tant** ⚕ [kauntərˈiritənt] *n.* panzehir.

**coun.ter.mand** [kauntəˈmɑːnd] 1. *n.* iptal emri; 2. *vb.* yeni bir emir ile eski emri iptal etm.; siparişi iptal etm.

**coun.ter.march** [ˈkauntəmɑːtʃ] 1. *n.* geri yürüyüş; 2. *vb.* geri yürümek.

**coun.ter.mark** [ˈkauntəmɑːk] *n.* karşı marka.

**coun.ter.mine** 1. [ˈkauntəmain] *n.* savunma mayını; 2. [ˌmain] *vb.* savunma mayını ile durdurmak; savunma mayını dökmek; *fig.* karşı tedbir almak.

**coun.ter-move** [ˈkauntəmuːv] *n. fig.* karşı hareket; tedbir.

**coun.ter-or.der** [ˈkauntərɔːdə] *n.* karşı emir.

**coun.ter.pane** [ˈkauntəpein] *n.* yatak örtüsü.

**coun.ter.part** [ˈkauntəpɑːt] *n.* akran, emsal; karşılık; kopya, suret, ikinci suret.

**coun.ter.point** ♪ [ˈkauntəpɔint] *n.* kontrpuan, polifoni.

**coun.ter.poise** [ˈkauntəpɔiz] 1. *n.* mukabil ağırlık; denge; 2. *vb.* dengede tutmak, denkleştirmek (*a. fig.*).

**coun.ter-rev.o.lu.tion** [ˈkauntərevəluːʃən] *n.* karşı devrim.

**coun.ter.scarp** ✕ [ˈkauntəskɑːp] *n.* karşı siper.

**coun.ter.shaft** ⊕ [ˈkauntəʃɑːft] *n.* ara mili, transmisyon mili.

**coun.ter.sign** [ˈkauntəsain] 1. *n.* ikinci imza; ✕ parola; 2. *vb.* ikinci olarak imzalamak.

**coun.ter.sink** ⊕ [ˈkauntəsiŋk] *vb.* havşa açmak.

**coun.ter-stroke** [ˈkauntəstrəuk] *n.* karşı darbe.

**coun.ter-ten.or** ♪ [ˈkauntənə] *n.* kontrtenor.

**coun.ter.vail** [ˈkauntəveil] *vb.* eşit kuvvet-

le karşı koymak; karşılamak, denkleştirmek.

**coun.ter.weight** [ˈkauntəweit] *n.* eş ağırlık, karşılık (to *-e*).

**count.ess** [ˈkauntis] *n.* kontes.

**count.ing-house** [ˈkauntiŋhaus] *n.* muhasebe dairesi.

**count.less** [ˈkauntlis] *adj.* sayısız, hesapsız, pek çok.

**coun.tri.fied** [ˈkʌntrifaid] *adj.* kırsal, köye ait, köylümsü; basit, sade.

**coun.try** [ˈkʌntri] 1. *n.* memleket, yurt, vatan, milet, ulus; taşra, kır, sayfiye, şehir dışı; jüri; taşrada oturanlar; seçmenler; *appeal* veya *go to the* ~ seçime gitmek; 2. *adj.* taşra..., sayfiye...; ülke...; ~ **club** şehir dışındaki spor kulübü; ˈ~-**dance** *n.* eşlerin karşılıklı sıralandıkları İngiliz köy dansı; ~ **gen.tle.man** sayfiyede oturan zengin; ˈ~-ˈ**house** *n.* yazlık, sayfiye evi; ˈ~.**man** *n.* yurttaş, vatandaş; taşralı; ˈ~-**side** *n.* kır, kırlık, kırsal alan; sayfiye; ˈ~.**wom.an** *n.* vatandaş, yurttaş, taşralı kadın.

**coun.ty** [ˈkaunti] *n.* kontluk; vilayet, il; *Am.* ilçe, kaza; ~ **coun.cil** il komisyonu; ~ **seat** *Am.* = ~ **town** ilçe merkezi.

**coup** [kuː] *n.* askerî darbe, darbe, hükümet darbesi; ~ *d'état* hükümet darbesi.

**cou.pé** [ˈkuːpei] *n. mot.* iki kapılı dört kişilik otomobil, kupa arabası.

**cou.ple** [ˈkʌpl] 1. *n.* çift, eş, karı koca; *a* ~ *of* iki, *F* bir iki, bir kaç; 2. *v/t. & v/i.* birleş(tir)mek, bitiş(tir)mek, ekle mek, ilave etm.; çiftleş(tir)mek; cinsi münasebette bulunmak; ⊕ bağlamak; radyo: devreye sokmak; ˈ**cou.pler** *n.* radyo: bağlama kolu; devreye sokup çıkarma kolu; ˈ**cou.ple-skat.ing** *n. spor:* çiftli buz pateni; **cou.plet** [ˈkʌplit] *n.* beyit, çift mısra.

**cou.pling** ⊕ [ˈkʌpliŋ] *n.* kavrama; *radyo:* bağlama; *attr.* bağlama..., ekleme...

**cou.pon** [ˈkuːpɔn] *n.* kupon; faiz koçanı; müracaat kuponu.

**cour.age** [ˈkʌridʒ] *n.* cesaret, mertlik, yiğitlik, yüreklilik; *take* veya *muster up veya pluck up* ~ cesur olm., yiğit olm., cesaretini toplamak; **cou.ra.geous** ☐ [kəˈreidʒəs] cesur, yiğit, yürekli, mert.

**cour.i.er** [ˈkuriə] *n.* haberci, kurye; turist rehberi.

**course** [kɔːs] 1. *n.* yön, cihet, istikamet; ⬇ rota, yol, pist; saha, alan; rayiç; *univ.* ders, kurs; kap, tabak, servis; ♈ vade, zaman; *in due* ~ zamanı gelince, sırası gelince, vadesi gelince; *of* ~ tabii, elbette; *matter of* ~ tabiilik, doğal oluş;

~ of exchange kambiyo rayici; stay the ~ sonuna kadar devam etm., vaz geçmemek; 2. *v/t.* kovalamak *(av)*; *v/i.* hızla akmak *(kan, gözyaşı)*.

**cours.er** *poet.* [ˈkɔːsə] *n.* süvari atı.

**cours.ing** [ˈkɔːsiŋ] *n.* tazıyla tavşan kovalama.

**court** [kɔːt] 1. *n.* avlu, iç bahçe, saha, meydan, kort; mahkeme; hükümet sarayı, saray; kralın maiyeti; kur; at ~ mahkemede; pay (one's) ~ *b-ne* kur yapmak; 2. *v/t.* aramak, davet etm. *(hastalık)*; kur yapmak *-e*; flört etm. *ile*; yol açmak *-e (hastalığa, tehlikeye)*; **ˈ~-card** *n.* resimli iskambil kâğıdı *(kız, vale veya papaz)*; ~ **cir.cu.lar** saray genelgesi; **ˈ~-day** *n.* duruşma günü; **cour.te.ous** □ [ˈkəːtjəs] nazik, kibar, saygılı, ince; **cour.te.san,** *a.* **cour.te.zan** [kɔːtiˈzæn] *n.* zenginlerle düşüp kalkan fahişe, orospu; **cour.te.sy** [ˈkəːtisi] *n.* nezaket, saygı, kibarlık, incelik, hürmet; **court-guide** [ˈkɔːtgaid] *n.* liste, cetvel, katalog; **court-house** [ˈkɔːthaus] *n.* adliye sarayı, mahkeme salonu; *Am. a.* ilçe hükümet binası; **cour.ti.er** [ˈkɔːtjə] *n.* saraylı, padişahın nedimi; **ˈcourt.li.ness** *n.* nezaket, saygı, kibarlık; **ˈcourt.ly** *adj.* nazik, kibar.

**court...: ˈ~-ˈmar.tial** ⚔ 1. *n.* askerî mahkeme; 2. *vb.* askerî mahkemede yargılamak; **ˈ~-ˈplas.ter** *n.* yapışkan bant; **ˈ~.room** *n.* mahkeme salonu; **ˈ~.ship** *n.* kur yapma; **ˈ~.yard** *n.* avlu, iç bahçe.

**cous.in** [ˈkʌzn] *n.* kuzen, kuzin, amca *(veya* dayı, hala, teyze) çocuğu; first ~, ~ german amca *veya* teyze çocuğu; **cous.in.hood** [ˈ~hud], **ˈcous.in.ship** *n.* kuzenlik; **ˈcous.in.ly** *adj.* kuzene yakışır..., kuzen...

**cove¹** [kəuv] 1. *n.* koy, küçük körfez; *fig.* sığınak, barınak; ⌂ kemer; 2. *vb.* üstünü kubbe ile örtmek.

**cove²** P [~] *n.* herif, adam.

**cov.e.nant** [ˈkʌvənənt] 1. *n.* ⚖ sözleşme, anlaşma, mukavele, akit, ahit, söz; 2. *v/t.* vadetmek, söz vermek, ahdetmek; *v/i.* anlaşmak, uyuşmak, uzlaşmak (with s.o. for s. th. *b-le bş için*).

**Cov.en.try** [ˈkɔvəntri]: send s.o. to ~ *b-le* arkadaşlığı kesmek, *b-nin* yüzüne bakmamak.

**cov.er** [ˈkʌvə] 1. *n.* kap, kapak, örtü, kılıf; cilt; zarf; sığınak, barınak, siper; çalılık, ağaçlık; sofra takımı; † karşılık, kuvertür; sigorta; ~ charge *(lokantada)* giriş ücreti, duhuliye; under separate ~ ayrı bir zarfta *(veya* pakette); 2. *v/t.* kaplamak, kapamak, örtmek (with *ile*); korumak, müdafaa etm.; *(yol)* almak, katetmek; hâkim olm; silah ile tehdit etm.; † karşılamak, kâfi olm.; *fig.* kapsamak, içine almak; saklamak, gizlemek; yazmak; ~ed button kapalı düğme; ~ed court *tenis:* üstü kapalı kort; ~ed wire sarılı tel; **ˈcov.er.age** *n.* olayın takip edilip yazılması (of); **ˈcover girl** kapak kızı; **ˈcov.er.ing** *n.* kaplama, muhafaza, örtü, perde; kat, tabaka; floor ~ taban döşemesi, taban halısı; **cov.er.let** [ˈ~lit] *n.* yatak örtüsü.

**co.v.ert** 1. [ˈkʌvət] □ gizli, saklı, örtülü; ⚖ kocanın himayesi altında; 2. [ˈkʌvə] *n.* hayvan barınağı, sığınak; kuşların kanat örtü tüyleri.

**cov.et** [ˈkʌvit] *vb.* şiddetle arzu etm., gıpta etm., imrenmek, göz dikmek; **ˈcov.et.ous** □ hırslı, açgözlü (of); **ˈcov.et.ous.ness** *n.* açgözlülük.

**cov.ey** [ˈkʌvi] *n.* aynı kuluçkadan çıkan yavruların hepsi; keklik *veya* bıldırcın sürüsü.

**cov.ing** ⌂ [ˈkəuviŋ] *n.* sundurma.

**cow¹** [kau] *n.* inek; dişi manda, dişi fil, dişi balina.

**cow²** [~] *vb.* korkutmak, gözünü korkutmak, yıldırmak.

**cow.ard** [ˈkauəd] 1. □ korkak, yüreksiz, ödlek; 2. *n.* korkak kimse, ödlek kimse; **cow.ard.ice** [ˈ~dis], **ˈcow.ard.li.ness** *n.* korkaklık, alçaklık, namertlik; **ˈcow.ard.ly** *adj.* korkak, ödlek, yüreksiz; korkakça..., alçakça...

**cow.boy** [ˈkaubɔi] *n.* kovboy, sığırtmaç; **ˈcow-catch.er** *n.* 🚂 *Am.* lokomotif mahmuzu.

**cow.er** [ˈkauə] *v/i.* çömelmek, korkudan yere çökmek, korkup çekilmek, büzülüp saklanmak, sinmek (from *den*).

**cow.herd** [ˈkauhəːd] *n.* kovboy, çoban, sığırtmaç; **ˈcow.hide** 1. *n.* sığır derisi, inek derisi; 2. *vb.* kamçılamak, kamçı ile dövmek; **ˈcow-house** *n.* ahır.

**cowl** [kaul] *n.* başlıklı rahip cüppesi; kukuleta, başlık; baca şapkası.

**cow...: ˈ~.man** *n.* sığırtmaç; *Am.* hayvan yetiştiricisi, çiftlik sahibi; **ˈ~-pox** *n.* ineklerde çiçek hastalığı; **ˈ~-punch.er** *n. Am.* F kovboy, sığırtmaç.

**cow.rie** [ˈkauri] *n.* eskiden para yerine geçen küçük tropikal deniz hayvanı kabuğu.

**cow...: ˈ~-shed** *n.* ahır; **ˈ~.slip** *n.* ⚘ çuha-çiçeği.

**cox** F [kɔks] 1. = **coxswain**; 2. *vb.* dümen kullanmak.

**cox.comb** [ˈkɔkskəum] *n.* züppe adam, hoppa kimse; **cox¹comb.i.cal** □ züppe, hoppa.

**cox.swain** [ˈkɔkswein, ↓ ˈkɔksn] *n.* dümenci, filika *veya* kik serdümeni.

**coy** [kɔi] □ çekingen, ürkek, utangaç, mahcup; cilveli, nazlı; **¹coy.ness** *n.* mahcubiyet, çekingenlik; cilve, naz.

**coy.ote** *zo.* [ˈkɔiəut] *n.* kır kurdu.

**coy.pu** *zo.* [ˈkɔipuː] *n.* kürkü için beslenen bir çeşit kemirgen hayvan.

**coz.en** *lit.* [ˈkʌzn] *vb.* aldatmak, dolandırmak, kandırmak; **¹coz.en.age** *n.* dolandırıcılık, hilekârlık.

**co.zy** [ˈkəuzi] = cosy.

**crab¹** [kræb] *n.* yengeç, pavurya; *ast.* yengeç burcu; ⊕ vinç, palan, kriko; catch a ~ kürek çekerken sandalın dengesini bozmak.

**crab²** [~] **1.** *n.* ⚓ yaban elma ağacı; bu ağacın meyvası; F şikâyet, homurdanma, tenkit; **2.** *vb.* homurdanmak, şikâyet etm., tenkit etm.; bozmak, mahvetmek; yengeç avlamak; **¹crab.bed** □ ters, aksi, huysuz, sert; okunması *veya* anlaşılması güç (*yazı*).

**crab-louse** [ˈkræblaus] *n.* kasık biti.

**crack** [kræk] **1.** *n.* çatlak, yarık; çatırtı, şaklama, keskin ses; F kuvvetli darbe; *spor: sl.* top; kurnazca cevap; deneme, teşebbüs, girişim; have a ~ at *s.th.* zor olan *bşi* yapmayı denemek; **2.** *adj.* F birinci sınıf, en iyi kalite; usta; **3.** *int.* çatır!; **4.** *v/t.* & *v/i.* kır(ıl)mak, çatla(t)mak, yar(ıl)mak; şakla(t)mak, çatırda(t)mak; çatallaşmak (*ses*); açmak (*kasa*); ⚗ ayrıştırmak (*petrol*); ~ a bottle bir şişe içkiyi içip bitirmek; ~ a crib *sl.* zorla eve girmek (*hırsız*); ~ a joke şaka yapmak, takılmak; ~ down on *sl.* sıkı tedbirler almak; ~ up F elden ayaktan düşmek, bunamak; get ~ing ...ile meşgul olm.; **¹~-brained** *adj.* saçma, aptalca, acayip; kaçık; **¹~-down** *n. sl.* sıkı tedbir; **¹cracked** *adj.* çatlak, çatlamış; F kaçık, deli, **¹crack.er** *n.* patlangaç; fındık *veya* ceviz kıracağı; *Am.* gevrek bisküvit, kraker; **¹crack.er-bar.rel** *Am.* F *attr.* samimi...; **¹crack.er-jack** *adj. Am.* F mükemmel, kabiliyetli; **¹crack.ers** *adj.* F deli, çatlak; **¹crack-jaw** *n.* şaşırtmaca; **crack.le** [ˈkrækl] *v/i.* çatırdamak, hışırdamak; **¹crack.ling** *n.* çıtırtı, çatırdama, hışırtı; jambon rostosunun kızarmış kısmı; **crack.nel** [ˈ~nl] *n.* gevrek bisküvi; **¹cracks.man** *n. sl.* hırsız; **¹crack-up** *n.* sinir krizi, şok; ✈ feci uçak kazası; **¹crack.y** = cracked.

**cra.dle** [ˈkreidl] **1.** *n.* beşik (*a. fig.*); *teleph.* ahize yatağı; ↓ gemi kızağı; **2.** *v/t.* beşiğe yatırmak, ihtimamla tutmak; yerine koymak.

**craft** [kraːft] *n.* hüner, el sanatı, zanaat; tekne, gemi; *coll.* gemiler; esnaf; hile, şeytanlık, üçkâğıtçılık, kurnazlık; the gentle ~ olta ile balık avlama; **¹craft.i.ness** *n.* kurnazlık, şeytanlık; **¹crafts.man** *n.* sanat erbabı, sanatkâr, usta, zanaatçı; **¹crafts.man.ship** *n.* hünerli iş, ince iş; **¹craft.y** □ kurnaz, şeytan, hilekâr.

**crag** [kræg] *n.* sarp kayalık, uçurum; **¹crag.gy** *adj.* sarp; **¹crags.man** *n.* sarp kayalıklara tırmanmakta usta kimse.

**crake** *orn.* [kreik] *n.* su yelvesi.

**cram** [kræm] **1.** *v/t.* doldurmak, tıkmak; çiğnemeden yutmak, alelacele yemek; imtihana hazırlamak (*öğrenciyi*); *v/i.* tıkabasa yemek yemek, tıkınmak; imtihana çalışmak; **2.** *n.* kalabalık, izdiham; **¹~-full** *adj.* dopdolu, ağzına kadar dolu; **¹cram.mer** *n.* öğrencileri imtihana hazırlayan okul, öğretmen *veya* kitap; imtihana hazırlanan öğrenci.

**cramp** [kræmp] **1.** *n.* kramp, adale kasılması; şidetli karın ağrısı; ⊕ mengene, kenet ,krampon; *fig.* engel, mani; **2.** *v/t.* ⊕ kenetlemek; adale kasılmasına sebep vermek, krampa neden olm.; *fig.* engel olm., mani olm., kısıtlamak; **¹cramped** *adj.* okunması zor (*yazı*); kasılmış; **¹cramp-frame** *n.* ⊕ vida mengenesi, işkence; **¹cramp-i.ron** *n.* mengene, mandal, kopça.

**cram.pon** [ˈkræmpən] *n.* krampon, mengene, kanca, kenet, perşin çivisi.

**cran.ber.ry** ⚓ [ˈkrænbəri] *n.* kırmızı yaban mersini.

**crane** [krein] **1.** *n.* turna kuşu; ⊕ maçuna, vinç; **2.** *v/t.* uzatmak (*boynunu*); ⊕ vinç ile kaldırmak; ~ at tereddüt etm., bir türlü karar verememek; **¹crane.fly** *n. zo.* sivrisinek; **¹crane's-bill** *n.* ⚓ sardunya çiçeği, turna gagası.

**cra.ni.um** *anat.* [ˈkreinjəm] *n.* kafatası, kafa kemiği.

**crank** [kræŋk] **1.** *adj.* ⊕ gevşek, burkulmuş; ↓ kolayca yan yatabilen; neşeli, şen; kendini beğenmiş, kendine güvenen; **2.** *n.* manivela, krank, dirsek, kol; garip huylu *veya* sabit fikirli *b-i*; starting ~ *mot.* krank kolu; fresh air ~ temiz hava hastası *b-i*; **3.** *v/t.* ~ off krankla hareket ettirmek; ~ up *mot.* harekete getirmek, çalıştırmak; krankla hareket etm. (*a. v/i.*); **¹~-case** *n.* motor karteri, krank karteri; **¹crank.i.ness** *n.* gariplik,

tuhaflık; delilik, kaçıklık; **'crank-shaft**
*n.* ⊕ krank mili; **'crank.y** *adj.* garip,
acayip, tuhaf; budala, aptal, bön; güvenilmez *(makine)*; çok virajlı *(yol)*.
**cran.nied** ['krænid] *adj.* yarık..., çatlak...; **'cran.ny** *n.* yarık, çatlak.
**crape** [kreip] 1. *n.* krepon, krep; yas tu-
tarken giyilen siyah tül; 2. *vb.* siyah tül
ile örtmek.
**craps** *Am.* [kræps] *n. pl.* çift zarla oynanan bir oyun.
**crap.u.lence** ['kræpjuləns] *n.* sarhoşluk,
mide fesadı; içkiye aşırı düşkünlük; F
sarhoşluktan gelen mahmurluk, akşam-
dan kalmış olma.
**crash¹** [kræʃ] 1. *n.* çatırtı, gürültü, şangırtı, şiddetli ses; ✝ düşme *(hisse)*; iflâs, topu atma; ✝ kaza; 2. *v/t. & v/i.*
parçala(n)mak; kır(ıl)mak; çökmek, yıkılmak; çarpmak, bindirmek; ✝ düşüp
parçalanmak, kaza geçirmek; bir yere
davetsiz olarak girmek; geceyi bir yerde geçirmek; 3. *adj. Am.* F şimşek gibi,
çok süratli.
**crash²** [~] *n.* havlu yapımında kullanılan
kaba bez.
**crash...: '~-dive** ↓ 1. *n.* birden dalma, ani
dalış *(denizaltı)*; 2. *vb.* aniden dalmak;
**'~-hel.met** *n.* motosikletçi miğferi, kask;
**'~-land** *vb.* ✝ mecburi iniş yapmak;
**'~-land.ing** *n.* ✝ mecburi iniş.
**crass** *lit.* [kræs] *adj.* hissiz, duygusuz;
dangalak, bön, aptal; çok aşırı.
**crate** [kreit] *n.* kafesli sandık, küfe, kasa; *sl.* külüstür araba.
**cra.ter** ['kreitə] *n.* krater; huni şeklinde
çukur, bombanın açtığı çukur.
**cra.vat** [krə'væt] *n.* fular, kravat, boyunbağı.
**crave** [kreiv] *v/t.* yalvarmak, rica etm.,
çok ihtiyacı olm.; *v/i.* şiddetle arzu etm.
(for *-i*).
**cra.ven** ['kreivən] 1. *adj.* korkak, namert;
2. *n.* korkak kimse.
**crav.ing** ['kreiviŋ] *n.* şiddetli arzu, özlem.
**craw** [krɔ:] *n.* kursak, hayvan midesi.
**craw.fish** [krɔ:fiʃ] 1. *n.* kerevides, kara-
vide, istakoza benzer bir deniz hayvanı;
2. *vb. Am.* F geri çekilmek; tutmamak
*(sözünü)*, caymak.
**crawl** [krɔ:l] 1. *n.* sürünme, çok yavaş
ilerleme; 2. *vb.* sürünmek; çok yavaş
ilerlemek; emeklemek; kaynıyor olm.
(with *ile*) *(göl balık kaynıyordu)*; tüyleri ürpermek; krol yüzmek; it makes one's
flesh ~ insanın tüylerini ürpertiyor;

**'crawl.er** *n. fig.* dalkavuk, yağcı; ~s *pl.*
bebek tulumu.
**cray.fish** ['kreifiʃ] *n.* kerevides, istakoza
benzer bir deniz hayvanı.
**cray.on** ['kreiən] 1. *n.* renkli kalem, mum
boya, kreyon; blue ~, red ~ mavi, kırmızı boya kalemi; 2. *vb.* mum boya ile resim yapmak.
**craze** [kreiz] *n.* geçici moda, geçici heves; delilik, çılgınlık (for *-için*); be the ~
moda olm.; **'crazed** *adj.* çılgın, kaçık,
çıldırmış (with *-den*); **'cra.zi.ness** *n.* delilik, çılgınlık; **'cra.zy** □ çılgın, deli; deli olan, düşkün; âşık (for, about *-e*); çö-
kecek gibi, emniyetsiz *(yapı)*; gelişigüzel.
**creak** [kri:k] 1. *n.* gıcırtı; 2. *vb.* gıcırdamak; **'creak.y** □ gıcırtılı.
**cream** [kri:m] 1. *n.* krema, kaymak;
krem; *fig.* kalbur üstü, en iyisi; krem
rengi; cold ~ yağlı krem; ~ of tartar
krem tartar; 2. *vb. -in* kaymağını almak; kaymak bağlamak; krema haline
getirmek; *fig.* kaymağını yemek, en iyi
kısmını almak; **'cream.er.y** *n.* sütçü dükkânı; yağ ve peynir imalâthanesi;
**'cream.y** *adj.* kaymaklı, kaymak gibi.
**crease** [kri:s] 1. *n.* kırma, pli, kat; çizgi;
buruşuk; ütü çizgisi, kat yeri; *kriket:*
sahadaki beyaz çizgi; 2. *v/t. & v/i.* bu-
ruş(tur)mak, katla(n)mak.
**cre.ate** [kri:'eit] *v/t.* yaratmak, meydana getirmek; *thea.* yaratmak; bırakmak,
uyandırmak *(izlenim)*; atamak, tayin
etm., paye vermek; **cre'a.tion** *n.* yaradılış, yaratma; atama, tayin; evren, acun,
kozmos, âlem; **cre'a.tive** *adj.* yaratıcı;
**cre'a.tor** *n.* yaratıcı kimse, mucit, meydana getiren kimse; **cre'a.tress** *n.* kadın
mucit; **crea.ture** ['~tʃə] *n.* yaratık, varlık, mahlûk; insan; kul, köle, kukla;
~ comforts *pl.* yiyecek, içecek gibi maddî ihtiyaçlar.
**crèch.e** [kreiʃ] *n.* kreş, çocuk yuvası.
**cre.dence** ['kri:dəns] *n.* güven, itimat;
give ~ to inanmak, güvenmek *-e*; letter
of ~ tavsiyename, bonservis; **cre.den-
tials** [kri'denʃəlz] *n. pl.* itimatname.
**cred.i.bil.i.ty** [kredi'biliti] *n.* güvenirlik;
**cred.i.ble** □ ['kredəbl] inanılabilir, güvenilir, itimada şayan.
**cred.it** ['kredit] 1. *n.* güven, itimat; emniyet; itibar, şeref, ün; ✝ kredi; ✝ borç;
*Am. school:* ders kredisi; ~ note ✝ kredi
bildirim belgesi; do s.o. ~ ününü arttırmak, ününe ün katmak; get ~ for s.th.
*-den* dolayı şeref kazanmak; give s.o. ~
for s.th. *b-ni...* sanmak; letter of ~ ✝

akreditif; on ~ veresiye; put *veya* place *veya* pass to s.o.'s ~ *b-nin* matlubuna geçirmek, alacağına kaydetmek 2. *v/t.* inanmak *-e,* itimat etm. *-e;* † matluba geçirmek *-i;* ~ s.o. with s. th. *b-ni* ...sanmak; ¹cred.it.a.ble □ şerefli, beğenilen, takdir edilen, şeref kazandıran (to *-e);* ¹cred.i.tor *n.* alacaklı.

cred.it...: ~ squeeze † kredi darlığı; ~ titles *pl.* filmde oynayan ve yönetenlerin isimleri.

cre.du.li.ty [kri¹dju:liti] *n.* herşeye inanma, saflık; cred.u.lous □ [¹kredjuləs] herşeye inanan, saf.

creed [kri:d] *n.* iman, itikat, dinî inanç.

creek [kri:k] *n.* koy; *Am.* çay, dere.

creel [kri:l] *n.* balık sepeti.

creep [kri:p] 1. *(irr.)* *vb.* sürünmek, emeklemek, yavaşça hareket etm.; nüfuz etm., sokulmak, yavaş yavaş etkilemek; sarılmak, dal sürmek; ürpermek; it makes my flesh ~ tüylerimi ürpertiyor; 2. *n.* sevilmeyen, yaramaz adam; ~s *pl.* tüyleri diken diken olma, ürperme; it gave me the ~s tüylerimi diken diken yaptı; ¹creep.er *n.* sürüngen; ♀ sürüngen bitki; ¹creep.y *adj.* tüyler ürpertici.

creese [kri:s] *n.* kama, hançer, bıçak.

cre.mate [kri¹meit] *v/t.* *(ölüyü)* yakmak; cre¹ma.tion *n.* ölüyü yakma; crem.a.to.ri.um [kremə¹tɔːriəm], *part. Am.* cre.ma.to.ry [¹-təri] *n.* ölülerin yakıldığı yer, krematoryum.

cren.el.(l)at.ed [¹krenileitid] *adj.* mazgallı.

cre.ole [¹kri:əul] 1. *n.* Fransız asıllı kimse; 2. *adj.* bunların konuştuğu dile ait.

cre.o.sote ♏ [¹kriəsəut] *n.* kreozot, katran ruhu.

crêpe [kreip] *n.* krep; ~ pa.per krepon kâğıdı; ~ rub.ber krepsol, tırtıklı taban lâstiği.

crep.i.tate [¹krepiteit] *vb.* çatırdamak; crep.i¹ta.tion *n.* çatırdama.

crept [krept] *pret. and p.p. of* creep.

cre.pus.cu.lar [kri¹pʌskjulə] *adj.* alaca karanlığa ait, alaca karanlık...

cres.cen.do ♪ [kri¹ʃendəu] *n.* kreşendo; *fig.* zirveye doğru yükselme.

cres.cent [¹kresnt] 1. *adj.* hilâl şeklinde; büyüyen, gelişen; 2. *n.* hilâl, dilim ay, ayça; ♀ City *Am.* New Orleans kenti.

cress ♀ [kres] *n.* tere.

cres.set [¹kresit] *n.* demir kandil, meşale, fener.

crest [krest] *n.* ibik, taç; tepe; miğfer püskülü; tepe, zirve, doruk; family ~

aile arması; ¹crest.ed *adj.* armalı; tepeli, ibikli; ~ lark tepeli toygar; ~ note-paper armalı kağıt; ¹crest.fall.en *adj.* üzgün, yılgın, başı önünde.

cre.ta.ceous [kri¹teiʃəs] *adj.* tebeşirli.

cre.tin [¹kretin] *n.* kreten; ¹cre.tin.ous *adj.* kretenli.

cre.tonne [kre¹tɔn] *n.* üstü desenli pamuklu kumaş, kreton.

cre.vasse [kri¹væs] *n.* buzul yarığı; *Am.* su bendi.

crev.ice [¹krevis] *n.* çatlak, yarık.

crew¹ [kru:] *n.* takım, grup, kitle; ⚓, ✚ tayfa, mürettebat.

crew² [~] *pret. of* crow 2.

crew.el ✚ [¹kru:il] *n.* gevşek bükülmüş iplik.

crib [krib] 1. *n.* yemlik, ambar; kulübe, odacık; ahır; kopya malzemesi; anahtar kitap; F kopya; *part. Am.* çocuk karyolası; crack a ~ *sl.* zorla içeri girmek; 2. *vb.* kapamak, bir yere tıkmak; F kopya çekmek; F çalmak, aşırmak; ¹crib.bage *n.* bir tür iskambil oyunu; crib.ble [¹-bl] *n.* iri delikli kalbur.

crick [krik] 1. *n.* adale kasılması, boyun tutulması; ~ in the neck boyun tutulması; 2. *vb.* adalesi kasılmak, boynu tutulmak.

crick.et¹ zo. [¹krikit] *n.* cırcır böceği, küçük çekirge.

crick.et² [~] 1. *n.* kriket oyunu; not ~ F adil olmayan, sportmenliğe aykırı, oyun kurallarına aykırı; 2. *vb.* kriket oynamak; ¹crick.et.er *n.* kriket oyuncusu.

cri.er [¹kraiə] *n.* ağlayan kimse; tellâl; mübaşir.

crime [kraim] *n.* cinayet, suç, cürüm; günah, ayıp.

Cri.me.an War [krai¹miən¹wɔ:] *n.* Kırım savaşı.

crim.i.nal [¹kriminl] 1. *adj.* ağır cezalarla ilgili, kanuna karşı gelen..., cinayet...; 2. *n.* suçlu, cani; crim.i.nal.i.ty [~¹næliti] *n.* suç, kabahat; suçluluk; crim.i.nate *lit.* [¹-neit] *vb.* suçlamak, itham etm.; crim¹i¹na.tion *n.* *lit.* suçlama, itham.

crimp¹ ⚓, ✕ [krimp] 1. *n.* zorla *veya* kandırarak asker *veya* denizci toplayan kimse; 2. *vb.* zorla askere almak.

crimp² [~] 1. *vb.* kıvırmak, kıvırcık yapmak *(saçı);* 2. *n.* ~ cut dalgalı, kıvırcık saç.

crim.son [¹krimzn] 1. *adj.* koyu kırmızı, fes rengi; 2. *n.* koyu kırmızı renk; 3. *v/t.* & *v/i.* kırmızılaş(tır)mak, koyu kırmızıya boyamak; kıpkırmızı olm.

cringe [krindʒ] 1. *v/i.* korkuyla çömelmek, sinmek; *fig.* yaltaklanmak, köpeklenmek (to *-e*); **2.** *n.* çömelme, sinme; *fig.* yaltaklanma.

**crin.kle** ['kriŋkl] **1.** *n.* kırışık, buruşuk; **2.** *vb.* buruş(tur)mak, kırış(tır)mak.

**crin.o.line** ['krinəli:n] *n.* kaba bir kumaş; eskiden kadınların eteklerinin içine geçirdikleri çember.

**crip.ple** ['kripl] **1.** *n.* sakat, topal, kötürüm; **2.** *v/t.* sakatlamak; *fig.* hasar vermek, bozmak.

**cri.sis** ['kraisis] *n., pl.* **cri.ses** ['-si:z] buhran, kriz; dönüm noktası.

**crisp** [krisp] **1.** *adj.* gevrek; serin, kuru *(hava)*; kıvırcık *(saç)*; kesin, katı, kararlı; kırışık, buruşuk; temiz, bakımlı; **2.** *vb.* gevre(t)mek; kıvırcıklan(dır)mak; **3.** *n. a.* potato *-s pl.* cips, patates kızartması.

**criss.cross** ['kriskrɔs] **1.** *n.* birbirini kesen çapraz doğrular; **2.** *adj.* çapraz, çaprazvarî; **3.** *vb.* çapraz doğrular çizmek; çaprazvarî hareket et(tir)mek.

**cri.te.ri.on** [krai'tiəriən] *n., pl.* **cri.te.ri.a** [-ə] ölçüt, kriter, değer birimi, mikyas.

**crit.ic** ['kritik] *n.* eleştirmen; tenkitçi kimse, kusur bulan kimse; **'crit.i.cal** ☐ tehlikeli, kritik, vahim, nazik; tenkitçi, eleştiren; be *-* of *-i* eleştirmek, tenkit etm.; **crit.i.cism** ['-sizəm] *n.* tenkit, eleştiri; yerme, kınama (of *-i*); **crit.i.cize** ['-saiz] *v/t.* eleştirmek, tenkit etm.; yermek, kınamak, kusur bulmak *-de*; **cri.tique** [kri-'ti:k] *n.* eleştiri yazısı, tenkit yazısı.

**croak** [krouk] **1.** *vb.* vak vak diye bağırmak, kurbağa gibi bağırmak; F ölmek; nalları dikmek; **2.** *n.* boğuk ses; vaklama; **'croak.er** *n. fig.* herşeyden şikâyet eden kimse; **'croak.y** ☐ boğuk sesli.

**Cro.at** ['krouət] *n.* Hırvat.

**cro.chet** ['krouʃei] **1.** *n.* tığla işlenen dantel, kroşe; **2.** *vb.* tığ ile işlemek, kroşe yapmak.

**crock** [krɔk] **1.** *n.* çanak, çömlek, toprak tencere; F yaşlı at; F âciz *veya* beceriksiz kimse; F külüstür araç; **2.** *vb. mst* *-* up *sl.* kuvvetten düş(ür)mek; **'crock.er.y** *n.* çanak çömlek.

**croc.o.dile** ['krɔkədail] *n. zo.* timsah; F törende ikişer ikişer yürüyen öğrenciler; *-* tears *pl. fig.* yalancıktan ağlama, sahte gözyaşları.

**cro.cus** ♀ ['kroukəs] *n.* çiğdem.

**Croe.sus** *fig.* ['kri:səs] *n.* çok zengin adam, para babası kimse.

**croft** ['krɔft] *n.* etrafı çevrili küçük tarla, küçük çiftlik; **'croft.er** *n.* bir tarlayı

kiralayan ve işleten kimse, tarla sahibi.

**crom.lech** ['krɔmlek] *n.* dolmen.

**crone** F [kroun] *n.* kocakarı, ihtiyar kadın.

**cro.ny** F ['krouni] *n.* yakın arkadaş, samimi dost, kafadar.

**crook** [kruk] **1.** *n.* kanca; değnek, sopa, asa; dönemeç, dirsek, viraj; *sl.* dolandırıcı, hırsız, sahtekâr; on the *-* namussuzca, dolandırıcılıkla, üçkâğıtla; **2.** *vb.* bükmek, kıvırmak, eğmek; **crook.ed** [-kt] *adj.* eğri, çarpık; ['-kid] ☐ *fig.* namussuz, alçak, dolandırıcı, sahtekâr.

**croon** [kru:n] *vb.* mırıldanmak, alçak sesle şarkı söylemek; **'croon.er** *n.* duygulu şarkılar söyleyen popüler şarkıcı.

**crop** [krɔp] **1.** *n.* ekin, ürün, mahsul, rekolte; kursak; kırbaç sapı; çok kısa saç; *fig.* hasılat, kazanç, kâr; **2.** *v/t.* kesmek, biçmek, kırpmak, kırkmak, kesip kısaltmak *(saç)*; ekmek, dikmek; *v/i.* ürün vermek; *-* up meydana çıkmak, doğmak *(sorun)*; **'-dust.ing** *n.* uçakla ekini ilâçlama; **'-eared** *adj.* kesik kulaklı; çok kısa saçlı; **'crop.per** *n.* kırkma aleti *veya* makinesi; mahsul veren bitki; F bozgun, yıkım, sukut; *Am. sl.* kiracı olup ekine ortak olan tarımcı; come a *-* F bozguna uğramak, yıkılmak; *fig.* başarısızlığa uğramak.

**cro.quet** ['kroukei] **1.** *n.* tahta topla oynanan bir oyun, kroke; **2.** *vb.* kroke oynamak.

**cro.quette** [krɔ'ket] *n.* bir tür köfte, kroket.

**cro.sier** ['krouʒə] *n.* piskopos âsası.

**cross** [krɔs] **1.** *n.* çapraz işareti; çarmıh; ıstavroz; haç, salip, put; keder, gam, elem, cefa, dert; dörtyol ağzı, kavşak; melez; *sl.* alçak kimse, hilekâr kimse; **2.** ☐ karşıdan gelen *(rüzgâr)*; F huysuz, ters, aksi, öfkeli, kızgın (with, at *-e*); çapraz...; karşılıklı..., mütekabil...; melez...; namussuz..., alçak...; **3.** *v/t.* geçmek, aşmak; üstüne çizgi çekmek, iptal etm., çıkarmak; karıştırmak; üst üste atmak *(bacak)*; kavuşturmak *(kolların)*; *fig.* karşı durmak, engellemek, isini bozmak; *fig.* aldatmak; boydan boya geçmek; ulaşmak, varmak; çapraz koymak; melez olarak yetiştirmek; *-* o.s. ıstavroz çıkarmak; *-* out çizmek, silmek, çıkarmak; keep one's fingers *-ed* şans dilemek; *v/i.* karşıdan karşıya geçmek; birbirine çapraz olm.; karşılaşmak; melez elde etm.; karışmak; **'-bar** *n. futbol:* kalenin üst direği; **'-beam** *n.* kiriş; **'-bench** *n. parl.* Avam Kamarasında bağımsızlara ait koltuk; **'~.bones** n. pl. tehlike işareti olan *veya* korsan bayraklarında bulunan çapraz kemikler; **~-bow** ['krɔsbəu] n. tatar yayı, arbalet, yaylı tüfek; **'~-breed** n. melez; **'~-'country** adj. ülkeyi baştan başa geçen...; ülke çapında...; **~** runnig kır koşusu; **'~-cut saw** n. testere, ince dişli bıçkı; **'~-ex.ami'na.tion** n. sorgu; **'~-ex'amine** vb. sorguya çekmek; **'~-eyed** adj. şaşı; **~ fire** yaylım ateşi, çaprazlama ateş; *fig.* soru yağmuru; **'~-grained** adj. damarları ters olan *(tahta)*; *fig.* ters, huysuz, aksi; **'cross.ing** n. geçiş; geçit, geçiş yeri; **'cross-legged** adj. bacak bacak üstüne atarak; adj. bacak bacak üstüne atmış; **'cross.ness** n. hırçınlık, aksilik, terslik. **cross...: '~-patch** n. F ters ve huysuz kimse; **~ pur.pos.es** pl. birbirini yanlış anlama, ayrı gaye; be at **~** birbirini yanlış anlamak, amaçları ayrı olm.; **~** refer.ence kitapta bakılması gereken yeri gösteren not; **'~-road** n. yan yol, ara yol; **'~-roads** n. pl. *veya* sg. dörtyol ağzı, kavşak; *fig.* dönüm noktası; **'~-'sec.tion** n. enine kesit; **'~-stitch** n. kanaviçe işi; **'~.wise** adv. çapraz, birbirini keserek; **'~.word** puz.zle n. çapraz bilmece.

**crotch** [krɔtʃ] n. çatal, gövde ile dalın birleştiği yer; **crotch.et** ['~it] n. garip fikir, akıl almaz düşünce; ♪ dörtlük; **'crotch.et.y** adj. F garip fikirli; aksi, ters, huysuz.

**cro.ton** ♀ ['krəutən] n. kroton.

**crouch** [krautʃ] **1.** vb. çömelmek, yere çökmek, eğilmek, sinmek; **2.** n. çömelme vaziyeti.

**croup¹** [kru:p] n. hayvanın but kısmı.

**croup²** ♀ [~] n. krup hastalığı.

**crou.pi.er** ['kru:piə] n. krupiye, kumar masasını idare eden kimse.

**crow** [krəu] **1.** n. karga; horoz ötüşü; **eat ~** Am. F küçük düşürücü bş yapmak zorunda olm., yaltaklanmak; **have a ~ to pick with** b-le paylaşılacak kozu olm.; in a **~** line, as the **~** flies kuş uçuşu; **2.** *(irr.)* v/i. horoz gibi ötmek; *fig.* sevinmek, havalara uçmak (over -e; -den dolayı); **'~-bar** n. kaldıraç, manivela.

**crowd** [kraud] **1.** n. kalabalık, izdiham; kitle, yığın; halk; F arkadaş grubu; bir sürü şey, yığın; **2.** v/t. doldurmak (with ile), sıkıştırmak; v/i. toplanmak, birikmek; **~ out** b-ni bir yerden atmak, çıkarmak; **~ on sail** ♪ bütün yelkenleri açmak; **'crowd.ed** adj. kalabalık..., dolu..., tıkış tıkış...

**crow.foot** ♀ ['krəufut] n. düğünçiçeği, kazayağı.

**crown** [kraun] **1.** n. mst taç; hükümdarlık; hükümdar; başa takılan çiçek demeti; kuron; beş şilinlik eski İngiliz parası; baş, tepe; dişin görünen kısmı; taça benzer süs; **2.** v/t. taç giydirmek -e; ödüllendirmek; tepesinde olm.; süslemek, tamamlamak; *(dişe)* kron takmak; to **~** all: üstelik, bu da yetmiyormuş gibi; **'crown.ing** adj. *fig.* tamamlayıcı..., en son...; **'crown-'jew.els** n. pl. saray mücevherleri.

**crow's...** [krəuz]: **'~-feet** n. pl. göz kenarlarındaki kırışıklıklar; **'~-nest** n. ♪ direk üstündeki gözcü yeri.

**cru.cial** □ ['kru:ʃəl] kesin, önemli, kritik, can alıcı; **cru.ci.ble** ['kru:sibl] n. pota, maden eritme kabı; *fig.* zorlu deneme; **cru.ci.fix** ['~fiks] n. üzerinde İsa'nın resmi olan haç *veya* heykel; **cru.cifix.ion** ['~fikʃən] n. çarmıha ger(il)me; **'cru.ci.form** adj. haç şeklinde; **cru.ci.fy** ['~fai] v/t. çarmıha germek; *fig.* azap çektirmek.

**crude** □ [kru:d] ham, rafine edilmemiş *(petrol)*; kaba; yarım yamalak, tamamlanmamış; **'crude.ness, cru.di.ty** ['~diti] n. hamlık; F kabalık, terbiyesizlik.

**cru.el** □ ['kruəl] zalim, gaddar, insafsız, merhametsiz, acımasız; *fig.* dayanılmaz, çetin, müşkül; **'cru.el.ty** n. zulüm, gaddarlık.

**cru.et** ['kru:it] n. küçük şişe, küçük sirke *veya* yağ şişesi; **'~-stand** n. şişelik, şişelerin konulduğu kap.

**cruise** ♪ [kru:z] **1.** n. deniz gezintisi; **2.** v/i. gemi ile gezmek; seyrüsefer etm.; cruising speed normal sürat, ekonomik sürat; **'cruis.er** n. ♪ kruvazör; Am. telsizli devriye arabası; **~ weight** boks: yarı ağır siklet.

**crumb** [krʌm] **1.** n. ekmek kırıntısı, parça, zerre; *fig.* biraz, azıcık; ekmek içi; sl. değersiz kimse; **2.** vb. ufalamak; sofradan kırıntıları temizlemek; = **crum.ble** ['~bl] v/t. & v/i. ufala(n)mak, parçala(n)mak; *fig.* harap olmak, çökmek; suya düşmek *(ümit)*; **'crum.bling, 'crumbly** adj. kolayca ufalanan; **crumb.y** ['krʌmi] adj. ufalanabilen.

**crump** sl. [krʌmp] n. çatırtı, ses; X bomba, patlama sesi; mermi kovanı.

**crum.pet** ['krʌmpit] n. bir nevi pasta; sl. kafa, baş; sl. seksi kız *veya* kadın; **be off one's ~** aklı başında olmamak.

**crum.ple** ['krʌmpl] v/t. & v/i. buruş(tur)mak; *fig.* çökmek, düşmek.

**crunch** [krʌntʃ] *vb.* çiğnemek, çatır çutur yemek, ezmek; çatırdatmak.

**crup.per** [ˈkrʌpə] *n.* at sağrısı; kuskun, eyer kayışı.

**cru.ral** *anat.* [ˈkruərəl] *adj.* bacağa ait, bacak...

**cru.sade** [kruːˈseid] 1. *n.* Haçlı seferi; *fig.* kampanya, mücadele; 2. *vb.* mücadeleye katılmak; **cruˈsad.er** *n.* Haçlı; mücadeleye katılan kimse.

**crush** [krʌʃ] 1. *n.* kalabalık; izdiham; ezme, baskı; sıkma meyva suyu; F geçici aşk, tutku; have a ~ *sl.* tutulmak, aşık olm. (on -e); 2. *v/t.* & *v/i.* ez(il)-mek; tık(ıştır)mak; *fig.* yenmek, mahvetmek; kırışmak; kalabalığı yararak ilerlemek; sarılmak, kucaklamak; *Am. sl.* flört etm.; ~ out *fig.* suyunu çıkarmak, ezmek; ~ **bar.ri.er** izdihamı önlemek için kurulan barikat; **ˈcrush.er** *n.* sıkma makinesi; F darbe, vuruş; **ˈcrush room** *n. thea.* fuaye.

**crust** [krʌst] 1. *n.* ekmek kabuğu; kabuk, dış tabaka; şarap tortusu; *Am. sl.* yüzsüzlük, arsızlık; 2. *v/t.* & *v/i.* kabukla kapla(n)mak, kabuklanmak, kabuk bağlamak.

**crus.ta.cean** *zo.* [krʌsˈteiʃjən] *n.* kabuklular sınıfından bir hayvan.

**crust.ed** [ˈkrʌstid] *adj.* kabuklu; yaşlı, saygıdeğer, muhterem; sabit, içine işlemiş; ~ snow buz tutmuş kar; **ˈcrust.y** ☐ kabuklu; kabuk gibi; huysuz, aksi, ters.

**crutch** [krʌtʃ] *n.* koltuk değneği; manevi destek; çatal; **crutched** *adj.* koltuk değnekli...

**crux** [krʌks] *n. fig.* çözülmesi zor mesele, pürüzlü nokta, zor kısım; püf noktası; çetin ceviz.

**cry** [krai] 1. *n.* ağlama; bağırma, feryat; ses, nida; nara, avaz; rica, yalvarma; parola; genel düşünce, istek; uzaklık, mesafe; kovalama, takip; a far ~ from... to ...den çok uzak; *fig.* ...den çok farklı; within ~ (of) duyulabilecek uzaklıkta; 2. *v/i.* ağlamak; feryat etm.; bağırmak; *v/t.* yalvarmak, rica etm.; reklamını yapmak, bağırarak bildirmek; ~ for istemek, arzu etm. -i; ~ off vazgeçmek, caymak; ~ out haykırmak, bağırmak (against -e); ~ up göklere çıkarmak, çok övmek; **ˈ~-ba.by** *n.* mızmız çocuk; **ˈcry.ing** *adj. fig.* dikkat gerektiren; acele, ivedi, mübrem; iğrenç.

**crypt** [kript] *n.* yeraltı kemeri *veya* türbesi; **ˈcryp.tic** *adj.* gizli, örtülü, kapalı; gizli anlamlı; **cryp.to-** [ˈ~təu] *prefix* gizli-, saklı-, kapalı-.

**crys.tal** [ˈkristl] 1. *n.* kristal, billûr; *part. Am.* kol saati camı; 2. *adj.* billûr, şeffaf, berrak, kristale benzer; **ˈ~-gaz.ing** *n.* billûr küre ile fal bakma; **crys.tal.line** [ˈ~təlain] *adj.* kristal gibi, parlak, temiz, şeffaf; kristal...; **crys.tal.li.za.tion** *n.* billûrlaşma; **ˈcrys.tal.lize** *v/t.* & *v/i.* billûrlaş(tır)mak; kesinleş(tir)mek *(fikir)*; şekerle kaplamak; ~d şekerlenmiş, şekerli *(meyve)*.

**cub** [kʌb] 1. *n.* hayvan yavrusu; genç kimse; tecrübesiz kimse, çırak; 2. *vb.* yavrulamak; **ˈcub.bing** *n.* av.

**cu.bage** [ˈkjuːbidʒ] *n.* kübik hacim.

**cub.by-hole** [ˈkʌbihəul] *n.* kapalı ufak yer; rahat yer; masa gözü.

**cube** Δ [kjuːb] 1. *n.* küp; 2. *vb.* küp çıkarmak; sayıyı kendiyle iki kere çarpmak; ~ root küp kök; **ˈcub.ic**, **ˈcub.i.cal** ☐ küp şeklinde, kübik.

**cu.bi.cle** [ˈkjuːbikl] *n.* odacık, kabin.

**cu.bit** [ˈkjuːbit] *n.* 45-56 cm. arası eski bir uzunluk ölçüsü.

**cub.hood** [ˈkʌbhud] *n. pl.* büyüme çağı.

**cuck.old** [ˈkʌkəuld] 1. *n.* boynuzlanan erkek, karısı tarafından aldatılan adam; 2. *vb.* kocayı aldatmak, boynuz taktırmak.

**cuck.oo** [ˈkukuː] 1. *n.* guguk kuşu; guguk kuşunun ötüşü; 2. *adj. sl.* kafadan çatlak, kaçık.

**cu.cum.ber** [ˈkjuːkʌmbə] *n.* hıyar, salatalık; as cool as a ~ *fig.* kendine hâkim, soğukkanlı.

**cu.cur.bit** [kjuˈkəːbit] *n.* kabakgillerden bir bitki.

**cud** [kʌd] *n.* geviş; chew the ~ geviş getirmek; *fig.* derin derin düşünmek.

**cud.dle** [ˈkʌdl] 1. *n.* F kucaklama, sarılma; 2. *v/t.* kucaklamak, bağrına basmak, sarılmak; *v/i.* sarılıp yatmak.

**cudg.el** [ˈkʌdʒəl] 1. *n.* sopa, değnek, çomak; take up the ~s ...in tarafını tutmak, savunmak, müdafaa etm.; 2. *v/t.* sopa ile dövmek, dayak atmak; ~ one's brains kafa patlatmak, hatırlamaya çalışmak (about -e; for -i).

**cue** [kjuː] *n.* isteka, bilardo sopası; *part. thea.* aktörün sözü arkadaşına bırakmadan önceki son sözü; işaret, üstü kapalı söz, ima; take the ~ from s.o. b-ni k-ne örnek almak.

**cuff¹** [kʌf] 1. *n.* sille, tokat, yumruk; 2. *vb.* tokat atmak.

**cuff²** [~] *n.* kolluk, yen, kol ağzı, manşet; **ˈ~-links** *n. pl.* kol düğmesi.

**cui.rass** [kwiˈræs] *n.* göğüs zırhı.

**cui.sine** [kwiːˈziːn] *n.* yemek pişirme usulü, mutfak.

**cul-de-sac** [ˈkuldəˈsæk] *n.* çıkmaz sokak.

**cu.li.nar.y** [ˈkʌlinəri] *adj.* yemek pişirme ile ilgili, mutfağa uygun.

**cull** *lit.* [kʌl] *vb.* koparmak, devşirmek *(çiçek)*; seçmek, ayırmak.

**cul.len.der** [ˈkʌlində] = colander.

**culm** [kʌlm] *n.* kömür tozu.

**cul.mi.nate** [ˈkʌlmineit] *vb. ast.* neticelenmek, sonuçlanmak ,sona ermek, bitmek; *fig.* zirvesine ermek, doruğuna yükselmek; **cul.mi!na.tion** *n. ast.* netice, son, bitme; *fig.* zirve, doruk.

**cul.pa.bil.i.ty** [kʌlpəˈbiliti] *n.* suç, kabahat, kusur; **ˈcul.pa.ble** □ kusurlu, kabahatli.

**cul.prit** [ˈkʌlprit] *n.* suçlu, sanık, mücrim.

**cult** [kʌlt] *n.* ibadet, tapınma, inanç; mezhep, çığır.

**cul.ti.va.ble** [ˈkʌltivəbl] *adj.* ekilebilir; ✓ ziraate elverişli.

**cul.ti.vate** [ˈkʌltiveit] *v/t.* işlemek, sürüp ekmek ,yetiştirmek; *fig.* terbiye etm.; *b-ni* kendine bağlamaya çalışmak; **ˈcul.ti.vat.ed** *adj.* ekili; *fig.* görgülü, terbiyeli, kültürlü, münevver; **cul.ti.va.tion** *n.* tarım; toprağı işleme; yetiştirme; **ˈcul.ti.va.tor** *n.* çiftçi, ekici, yetiştirici; tırmık makinesi.

**cul.tur.al** □ [ˈkʌltʃərəl] kültürel...; uygarlığa ait.

**cul.ture** [ˈkʌltʃə] *n.* kültür; terbiye, irfan; medeniyet, uygarlık; yetiştiricilik; ✹ kültür; **ˈcul.tured** *adj.* kültürlü, görgülü, kibar, münevver; **ˈcul.ture-me.di.um** *n. biol.* kültür maddesi; **ˈcul.ture-pearl** *n.* üretilmiş inci, kültüve inci.

**cul.vert** [ˈkʌlvət] *n.* yeraltı kanalizasyonu, su yolu, ark; *(yolun altında elektrik kablolarının geçtiği)* tünel.

**cum.ber** [ˈkʌmbə] *vb.* engel olm., mâni olm.; yükle(n)mek, yük olm., ağırlık vermek; **ˌsome** [ˈ-səm], **cum.brous** □ [ˈ-brəs] hantal, ağır; külfetli, sıkıntı verici; ✺ havaleli.

**cum.in** ✤ [ˈkʌmin] *n.* kimyon.

**cu.mu.la.tive** □ [ˈkjuːmjulətiv] birikten..., birikmiş..., birikerek çoğalan...; **cu.mu.lus** [ˈ-ləs] *n.*, *pl.* **cu.mu.li** [ˈ-lai] yığın, bulut yığını; höyük.

**cu.ne.i.form** [ˈkjuːniifɔːm] *adj.* çivi şeklinde..., kama şeklinde..., çivi yazısı...

**cun.ning** [ˈkʌnin] **1.** □ kurnaz, açıkgöz, şeytan, hilekâr; *Am.* sevimli, şirin, cazibeli; **2.** *n.* kurnazlık; şeytanlık; marifet, hüner.

**cup** [kʌp] **1.** *n.* fincan, kâse, bardak, kadeh; *spor:* kupa; deneyim, tecrübe; ✤ çanak; **2.** *vb.* fincan şekline sokmak; şişe çekmek, vantuz çekmek; **ˌboard** [ˈkʌbəd] *n.* dolap, yüklük; ~ love *fig.* bir çıkar uğruna gösterilen sevgi; **ˌful** [ˈ-ful] *n.* fincan dolusu ölçek.

**Cu.pid** [ˈkjuːpid] *n.* eski Roma'da aşk tanrısı.

**cu.pid.i.ty** [kjuːˈpiditi] *n.* açgözlülük, hırs.

**cu.po.la** [ˈkjuːpələ] *n.* küçük kubbe; kubbe tavanı; ✕, ✥ zırhlı kule.

**cup.ping-glass** ✹ [ˈkʌpinglɑːs] *n.* şişe, vantuz.

**cu.pre.ous** *min.* [ˈkjuːpriəs] *adj.* bakırlı, bakır gibi; **cu.pric** [ˈ-prik] *adj.* içinde bakır bulunan, bakır...

**cur** [kəː] *n.* sokak köpeği, azgın köpek; alçak adam, it.

**cur.a.bil.i.ty** [kjuərəˈbiliti] *n.* tedavi edilebilme, iyileştirilebilme; **ˈcur.a.ble** *adj.* tedavisi mümkün.

**cur.a.cao** [kjuərəˈsəu] *n.* portakal likörü.

**cu.ra.cy** [ˈkjuərəsi] *n.* papazlık; **cu.rate** [ˈ-rit] *n.* papaz; **cu.ra.tor** [ˌ-ˈreitə] *n.* müze *veya* kütüphane müdürü.

**curb** [kəːb] **1.** *n.* atın suluk zinciri; *fig.* engel, mâni, fren; kaldırım taşı *(a.* ˌstone)*; **2.** *vb.* atı kontrol altına almak; *fig.* hâkim olm., yenmek, tutmak, durdurmak; **ˌˈmar.ket** *n. Am. borsa:* tahvil borsası; **ˌroof** *n.* tavanarası çatısı.

**curd** [kəːd] **1.** *n.* kesilmiş süt, lor peyniri; **2.** *mst* **cur.dle** [ˈ-dl] *v/t. & v/i.* kes(il)mek *(süt);* pıhtılaş(tır)mak.

**cure** [kjuə] **1.** *n.* tedavi, çare, derman, şifa, ilaç, kür; ~ of souls papazlık, imamlık; **2.** *vb.* tedavi etm., iyi etm., çare bulmak, şifa vermek; tuzlamak; tütsülemek.

**cur.few** [ˈkəːfjuː] *n.* eskiden gece ışıkları mecburî söndürme zamanı; *pol.* sokağa çıkma yasağı.

**cu.ri.o** [ˈkjuəriəu] *n.* nadir ve pahalı sanat eseri; **cu.ri.os.i.ty** [ˌ-ˈɔsiti] *n.* merak; tecessüs; az bulunan *veya* tuhaf şey; **ˈcu.ri.ous** □ meraklı, mütecessis; garip, tuhaf, acayip; dikkati çeken.

**curl** [kəːl] **1.** *n.* büklüm, bukle, kıvrım, saç lülesi, kıvırcık saç; **2.** *v/t.* kıvırmak, bukle yapmak, lüle lüle yapmak, bükmek; *v/i.* kıvrılmak, büklümek.

**cur.lew** *orn.* [ˈkəːljuː] *n.* çulluk.

**curl.ing** [ˈkəːliŋ] *n. spor:* buz üzerinde ağır taşlarla oynanan bir İskoç kış oyunu; **ˌˈi.ron, ˌtongs** *n. pl.* saç maşası; **ˈcurl.y** *adj.* kıvırcık..., kıvrımlı...

**cur.mudg.eon** [kəːˈmʌdʒən] *n.* huysuz

adam, aksi kimse; tamahkâr kimse.
**cur.rant** [ˈkʌrənt] *n.* frenk üzümü; *a.* dried ~ kuşüzümü.

**cur.ren.cy** [ˈkʌrənsi] *n.* revaç, geçerlik; ✝ nakit para; *fig.* değer, önem; **¹cur.rent 1.** ☐ bugünkü, geçerli, hali hazırdaki; ✝ tedavülde olan, cari; ~ events *pl.* günlük olaylar, aktüalite; ~ account ✝ cari hesap; **2.** *n.* akım, cereyan *(a. ⚡)*; akıntı; *fig.* gidişat *(olayların)*; ~ impulse ⚡ akımın ani artışı; ~ junction elektrik bağlantısı.

**cur.ric.u.lum** [kəˈrikjuləm] *n., pl.* **cur.ric.u.la** [~lə] müfredat programı; ~ **vi.tae** [ˈvaitiː] *n.* hal tercümesi, özgeçmiş.

**cur.ri.er** [ˈkʌriə] *n.* deriyi işleyen kimse, sepici.

**cur.rish** ☐ [ˈkəːriʃ] *fig.* it gibi, serseri.

**cur.ry¹** [ˈkʌri] **1.** *n.* baharatlı yemek türü; ~-powder *n.* Hint mutfağında kullanılan baharat; **2.** *vb.* baharatlı yemek yapmak.

**cur.ry²** [~] *vb.* tabaklamak, sepilemek, işlemek *(deri)*; tımar etm., kaşağılamak *(at)*; dövmek, dayak atmak, pataklamak; ~ favour with *b-ne* yaltaklanmak, *b-nin* gözüne girmeye çalışmak; **¹~-comb** *n.* kaşağı.

**curse** [kəːs] **1.** *n.* lânet, beddua, küfür; belâ, felâket; **2.** *vb.* lânetlemek, beddua etm., sövmek, küfretmek; belâ getirmek, cezalandırmak *(with ile)*; **curs.ed** ☐ [ˈkəːsid] lânetli, Allahın cezası, başbelâsı.

**cur.sive** [ˈkəːsiv] *adj.* el yazısı...

**cur.so.ry** ☐ [ˈkəːsəri] gelişigüzel, aceleyle yapılan, itinasız, üstünkörü, yarımyamalak.

**curt** ☐ [kəːt] kısa, sert *(söz veya davranış)*.

**cur.tail** [kəːˈteil] *v/t.* kısaltmak, azaltmak, kısmak *(a. fig.)*; *fig.* kısıtlamak, sınırlamak *(of -i)*; **cur¹tail.ment** *n.* kısal(t)ma, azal(t)ma.

**cur.tain** [ˈkəːtn] **1.** *n.* perde; tiyatro perdesi; *fig.* maske, örtü; ✕ siper, koruma; draw a ~ over s.th. *fig.* konuyu bırakmak, artık konuşmamak; **2.** *vb.* perde takmak, perdelemek; ~ off perdeyle ayırmak; **¹~-call** *n. thea.* alkışlayarak sanatçıyı tekrar sahneye çağırma; **¹~-fire** *n.* ✕ baraj ateşi; **¹~-lec.ture** *n.* F yalnızken kadının kocasını haşlaması; **¹~-rais.er** *n. thea. & fig.* asıl piyesten önce oynanan kısa oyun.

**curt.s(e)y** [ˈkəːtsi] **1.** *n.* reverans, diz bükerek selâmlama; drop a ~ reverans yapmak; **2.** *vb.* reverans yapmak (to -e).

**cur.va.ture** [ˈkəːvətʃə] *n.* eğilme, bükülme, kavislenme, eğrilik; ~ of the spine ✝ belkemiği kayması.

**curve** [kəːv] **1.** *n.* kavis, eğri, kıvrım; viraj, dönemeç; *Am. beysbol:* topun vurulduktan sonra havada eğri çizmesi; **2.** *v/t. & v/i.* eğ(il)mek, bük(ül)mek, kavis oluşturmak.

**cush.ion** [ˈkuʃən] **1.** *n.* yastık, minder; bilardo masasının lastikli iç kenarı; **2.** *v/t.* kıtıkla doldurmak, minderlemek, minderle hızını kesmek; *fig.* korumak, etkisini azaltmak; ⊕ beslemek, doldurmak.

**cush.y** *sl.* [ˈkuʃi] *adj.* rahat, kolay, hafif *(iş)*.

**cusp** [kʌsp] *n.* sivri uç; uç nokta; zirve; dilim.

**cus.pi.dor** *Am.* [ˈkʌspidɔː] *n.* tükürük hokkası.

**cuss** *Am.* F [kʌs] **1.** *n.* küfür; lânet; *co.* herif; **2.** *vb.* küfretmek, sövmek, lânetlemek; **cuss.ed** [ˈkʌsid] *adj.* inatçı, dik kafalı, ters.

**cus.tard** [ˈkʌstəd] *n.* süt ve yumurtadan yapılan bir çeşit tatlı; **¹~-pow.der** *n.* muhallebi tozu.

**cus.to.di.an** [kʌsˈtoudjən] *n.* muhafız, koruyucu, nezaret eden kimse; kapıcı; **cus.to.dy** [~tədi] *n.* muhafaza, koruma, himaye, nezaret, hapis.

**cus.tom** [ˈkʌstəm] *n.* âdet, örf, görenek, gelenek, anane; alışkanlık; ✝ alışveriş, müşterisi olma; ⊗ gelenek hukuku; ~s *pl.* gümrük; **¹cus.tom.ar.y** ☐ alışılmış, âdet olan, geleneksel; **¹cus.tom.er** *n.* müşteri; **¹cus.tom-house** *n.* gümrük dairesi; ~ officer gümrük memuru; **¹cus.tom-¹made** *adj. Am.* ısmarlama yapılmış, ısmarlama...; **¹cus.toms clear.ance** gümrük muayene belgesi.

**cut** [kʌt] **1.** *n.* kesim, kesme, kesiş; kesit; tenzilât, iskonto, kesinti; kesik kısım; parça, dilim, bölüm; ⚡ elektrik kesintisi; sert vuruş; biçki; *fig.* incitici söz, taş; *iro.* küçük parça, parçacık; *typ.* klişe; oyulmuş geçit; *oyun kağıdı:* kesme; short-cut kestirme yol; cold ~s *pl.* soğuk et yemekleri; give s.o. the ~ (direct) F *b-ni* görmezden gelmek; **2.** *(irr.) v/t.* kesmek, biçmek, kısaltmak; selam vermemek; dilimlemek; sansür etm. *(film)*; azaltmak, kesintiye uğratmak; acmak *(yol, kanal)*; F asmak *(okul, ders)*; kesmek *(doğru, çizgi)*; kenarına vurmak *(topun)*; durdurmak *(film çekimini)*; ~ one's finger parmağını kesmek; ~ teeth diş çıkarmak *(çocuk)*; ~ a figure F şekil vermek; ~ and come again bol bol, çokça almak; ~ it fine F ucu ucu-na yetişmek; ~ short kısa kesmek; lafı-nı yarıda kesmek; to ~ a long story short uzun lafın kısası; ~ and run F sıvışmak, tüymek; ~ back budamak; azaltmak; ~ down kesmek (ağaç); öldürmek, yara-lamak; azaltmak; fiyatını indirmek; kı-saltmak (elbise); ~ off kesmek, kesip koparmak; teleph. kesilmek (hat); mah-rum etm. (from -den); Am. ayırmak, ayıklamak; ∲ tecrit etm.; radyo: kapa-mak; ~ out kesip çıkarmak; fig. yer aç-mak -e; F bırakmak (içki, sigara v.b.); kesmek (konuşma vs.); sürüden ayır-mak: be ~ out for istenilen nitelikte olm.; have one's work ~ out (for one) F yapıla-cak dünya kadar işi olm.; ~ it out! sl. bırakın kavgayı!, kesin artık!; ~ up doğ-ramak; tahrip etm.; çok etkilemek, sars-mak; fig. şiddetle eleştirmek, taş atmak; v/i. ~ in arabanın önüne dalmak; dahil etm.: lafını kesmek; 3. adj. kesik, kesil-miş, biçilmiş; sl. sarhoş; ~ flowers pl. kesilmiş çiçekler; ~ glass billûr, kristal; ~ and dry veya dried sabit, yerleşmiş (fikir vs.); önceden hazırlanmış.

cu.ta.ne.ous [kju:'teinjəs] adj. deriye ait, deri..., cilt...

cut-a.way ['kʌtəwei] a. ~ coat n. frak, bonjur.

cut-back ['kʌtbæk] n. film: tekrar oynat-ma.

cute □ F [kju:t] zeki, kurnaz, açıkgöz; Am. F zarif, hoş, sevimli, şirin.

cu.ti.cle anat., ∲ ['kju:tikl] n. epiderma, üst deri, tırnakları çevreleyen ölü deri; ~ scissors pl. tırnak makası, et makası.

cut-in ['kʌtin] n. film: kesilen parça.

cut.lass ['kʌtləs] n. ↓ bahriye kılıcı; ke-sici alet, pala.

cut.ler ['kʌtlə] n. bıçakçı; 'cut.ler.y n. sof-ra takımı, çatal bıçak takımı; bıçakçı-lık.

cut.let ['kʌtlit] n. pirzola, kotlet.

cut...: '~-off n. Am. kestirme yol; kesici alet; kesilen herhangi birşey; bşin sona erme tarihi; '~-out n. mot. arıza; ∲ dev-re kesici; Am. mahrumiyet, yoksunluk; '~-purse n. yankesici; 'cut.ter n. kesici; ↓ tek direkli gemi; filika; kotra; film: montajcı; ⚔ çukur açan alet; ⊕ kesici alet, bıçak, freze; Am. hafif kızak; 'cut-throat 1. n. katil, cani; 2. adj. zalim, acımasız; amansız; kıyasıya (mücade-le); 'cut.ting 1. □ iğneleyici, acı (söz); ⊕ delici..., keskin...; dondurucu (so-ğuk): bıçak gibi, müthiş (ağrı); ~ edge keskin kenar; ~ nippers pl. kesici kıs-

kaç, kerpeten; 2. n. kesme; gazete kü-pürü; ⚡ daldırma, çelik; kesim, kayıt; 🚂 yol, pasaj; ⊕ kesme.

cut.tle ichth. ['kʌtl] = ~-fish; '~-bone n. mürekkep balığının cilacılıkta kullanı-lan kabuğu; '~-fish n. mürekkep balığı.

cy.a.nide ⚗ ['saiənaid] n. siyanür; ~ of potassium potasyum siyanür.

cy.ber.net.ics [saibə:'netiks] n. sg. ayarla-ma-yönleme bilgisi, sibernetik.

cyc.la.men ⚘ ['sikləmən] n. siklamen, tav-şankulağı, buhurumeryem çiçeği.

cy.cle ['saikl] 1. n. devre, dönem; ⊕ de-vir, dönme, dönüş; bisiklet, motosiklet; ↑ dalgalanma, konjonktür; four-~ engine mot. dört zamanlı motor; 2. v/i. bisik-letle gitmek, bisiklete binmek; 'cy.clic, 'cy.cli.cal □ devirli; ↑ devresel...; cy-cling ['saikliŋ] 1. n. bisiklete binme; 2. adj. devreden..., dönen...; 'cy.clist n. bi-sikletçi.

cy.clone ['saikləun] n. siklon, kiklon; ka-sırga; cy.clon.ic [~'klɔnik] adj. siklon..., kiklon...

cy.clo.pae.di.a [saiklɔu'pi:djə] n. ansiklo-pedi.

Cy.clo.pean [sai'kləupjən] adj. dev gibi, muazzam, büyük. heybetli; eski Yunan mitolojilerindeki deve ait.

cy.clo.style ['saiklɔustail] n. teksir maki-nesi; cy.clo.tron phys. ['saiklətrɔn] n. siklotron.

cyg.net ['signit] n. kuğu yavrusu.

cyl.in.der ['silində] n. silindir; cy'lin.dric, cy'lin.dri.cal □ [~drik(əl)] silindir şek-linde.

cym.bal ♪ ['simbl] n. büyük zil.

cyn.ic ['sinik] 1. a. 'cyn.i.cal □ toplum tö-relerini hor gören, kötü gözle gören, ki-nik, sinik; alaycı; 2. n. toplum töreleri-ni hor gören kimse; alaycı kimse; cyn.i-cism ['~sizəm] n. toplum törelerini hor görme, kinizm.

cy.no.sure fig. ['sinəzjuə] n. dikkati çe-ken şey veya kimse.

cy.press ⚘ ['saipris] n. servi.

Cyp.rian ['sipriən], Cyp.ri.ot ['sipriət] 1. n. Kıbrıslı kimse; 2. adj. Kıbrıs'a ait, Kıbrıslı..., Kıbrıs...

cyst [sist] n. ⚕ kist; 'cyst.ic adj. kiste ait, kist...; cys.ti.tis ⚕ [sis'taitis] n. si-dik torbası iltihabı, sistit.

Czar [zɑ:] n. Rus çarı, çar.

Czech [tʃek] 1. n. Çek; 2. adj. Çek'lere ait; Çek diline ait.

Czecho.-Slo.vak ['tʃəkəu'sləuvæk] 1. adj. Çekoslavakyalı; 2. n. Çek; Çek dili.

# D

**dab** [dæb] **1.** *n.* hafif vuruş, *bşe* temas, *bşe* değme; *ichth.* bir tür yassı balık; **be a ~** (hand) at s. th. *bşin* ustası olm.; **2.** *v/t.* hafifçe vurmak *-e*, dokunmak *-e*; *(boya)* hafifçe sürmek.

**dab.ble** [ˈdæbl] *v/t.* & *v/i.* hafifçe ıslatmak, su serpmek; *(amatörce)* meşgul olm., uğraşmak (*in, at ile*); **ˈdab.bler** *n.* amatör, üstünkörü iş gören adam; şarlatan.

**dace** *ichth.* [deis] *n.* bir tür tatlısu balığı.

**dac.tyl** *poet.* [ˈdæktil] *n.* bir açık ve iki kapalı heceden oluşan mısra.

**dad** F [dæd], **dad.dy** F [ˈ~di] *n.* baba, babacık.

**dad.dy-long.legs** F *zo.* [ˈdædiˈlɔŋlegz] *n.* tipula sineği.

**daf.fo.dil** ❖ [ˈdæfədil] *n.* nergis, zerrin, fulya.

**daft** ☐ F [dɑːft] kaçık, ahmak, saçmasapan.

**dag.ger** [ˈdægə] *n.* hançer, kama; **be at ~s drawn** kanlı bıçaklı olm. (*with ile*).

**dag.gle** [ˈdægl] *v/t.* & *v/i.* çamura sür(ün)mek, çamurlamak.

**da.go** *Am. sl.* [ˈdeigəu] *n.* *contp.* İspanyol *veya* İtalyan asıllı kimse.

**dahl.ia** ❖ [ˈdeiljə] *n.* dalya, yıldızçiçeği.

**Dail Eir.eann** [dailˈɛərən] *n.* İrlanda millet meclisi.

**dai.ly** [ˈdeili] **1.** *adj.* gündelik, günlük; **2.** *adv.* her gün; **3.** *n.* gündelik gazete; gündelikçi *(hizmetçi).*

**dain.ti.ness** [ˈdeintinis] *n.* zarafet, incelik; titizlik; **ˈdain.ty 1.** ☐ narin, zarif, ince, sevimli; titiz; **2.** *n. (yemek)* nefis şey, leziz şey.

**dair.y** [ˈdɛəri] *n.* süthane, mandıra; sütçü dükkânı; **~ cat.tle** süt veren hayvan; **ˈ~farm** *n.* süt üretilen çiftlik, mandıra; **ˈ~maid** *n.* sütçü kız; **ˈ~man** *n.* sütçü.

**da.is** [ˈdeiis] *n.* kürsü, salonun baş tarafında yükseltilmiş zemin.

**dai.sy** [ˈdeizi] **1.** *n.* papatya; **2.** F *adj.* hoş, sevimli.

**dale** [deil] *n.* vadi, dere.

**dal.li.ance** [ˈdæliəns] *n.* tembellik, üşeniklik; oynaşma, cilveleşme; **ˈdal.ly** [ˈ~li] *vb.* cilveleşmek, oynaşmak (*with ile*); boşuna vakit geçirmek, oyalanmak (*about, over ile*).

**dam¹** [dæm] *n.* ana hayvan.

**dam²** [~] **1.** *n.* set, baraj, su bendi; **2.** *v/t.* set yapmak, bentle durdurmak; *fig.* durdurmak, engellemek, kapatmak, geri tutmak (*in, up bşi*).

**dam.age** [ˈdæmidʒ] **1.** *n.* zarar, hasar; **~s** *pl.* 💰 tazminat; **2.** *v/t.* zarar vermek *-e*, bozmak *-i*; **dam.age.a.ble** *adj.* bozulabilir, hasara uğrayabilir.

**dam.a.scene** [ˈdæməsiːn] **1.** *adj.* damasko ile ilgili, kakma işi ile ilgili; **2.** *v/t.* *bşi* kakma işi ile süslemek; **dam.ask** [ˈdæməsk] **1.** *n. (kumaş)* damasko; Şam çeliği; koyu pembe renk; **2.** *adj.* Şam işi; damasko; gül rengi, pembe; **3.** *v/t.* *(çelik)* kakma ile süslemek; *(kumaş)* damasko ile döşemek; gül rengi vermek.

**dame** [deim] *n.* hanım, bayan (*a. un van*); *sl.* kadın.

**damn** [dæm] **1.** *v/t.* lânetlemek, beddua etm.; mahkûm etm.; *thea.* reddetmek; kınamak; **~ it!** kahrolası!; Allah belâsını versin!; **2.** *n.* lânet, beddua; *fig.* değersiz şey; **I don't care a ~!** umurumda değil!; **dam.na.ble** ☐ [ˈdæmnəbl] melûn, lânetlenmeyi hak eden; **damˈna.tion** *n.* lânet, kargıma, belâ, mahkûm etme; **dam.na.to.ry** ☐ [ˈ~nətəri] lânete (*veya* bedduaya) neden olan; **damned** [dæmd] *adj.* *veya* *adv.* lânetli, melûn (*a. = ziyade, çok fazla)*; **damn.ing** [ˈdæmiŋ] *adj.* şiddetle karşı olan.

**Dam.o.cles** [ˈdæməkliːz] *n.*: **sword of ~** Demoklesin kılıcı, insanı her an bekleyen tehlike.

**damp** [dæmp] **1.** ☐ rutubetli, nemli; **2.** *n.* rutubet, nem; *fig.* cesaretini kırma, ak satma; ⚒ madenlerde oluşan tehlikeli bir gaz; **3.** *a.* **ˈdamp.en** *v/t.* & *v/i.* ıslatmak, ıslanmak, nemlen(dir)mek; *(ateş,* *şevk)* bastırmak, azaltmak; *fig.* neşesini kaçırmak; **'damp.er** *n.* ♪ yastık; pedal; soba borusu kapağı; *fig.* sevinci, heyecanı vs. yi azaltma; *mot.* ses titreşimini azaltan araç, damper; **'damp.ish** *adj.* rutubetli, nemli; **'damp-proof** *n.* nem geçirmeyen şey.

**dam.sel** † [ˈdæmzəl] *n.* genç kız, küçük hanım.

**dam.son** ♀ [ˈdæmzən] *n.* mürdümeriği; ~ **cheese** erik reçeli.

**dance** [dɑːns] **1.** *n.* dans; balo; **lead s.o.** a ~ *b-ni* üzmek, *b-ne* ezivet etm.; **2.** *v/t.* & *v/i.* dans et(tir)mek, oyna(t)mak; **'~-band** *n.* dans orkestrası; **'~-hall** *n.* dans salonu; **'~-hos.tess** *n.* beraber dansetmek için ücretle tutulan kız; **'danc.er** *n.* danseden; dansöz;

**danc.ing** [ˈdɑːnsiŋ] *n.* dans etme; dans; **~-girl** *n.* danseden, dansöz; **'~-les.son** *n.* dans dersi; **'~-room** *n.* dans salonu.

**dan.de.li.on** ♀ [ˈdændilaiən] *n.* kara hindiba.

**dan.der** *sl.* [ˈdændə] *n.* öfke, hiddet; **get s.o.'s** ~ **up** *b-ni* kızdırmak, öfkelendirmek.

**dan.dle** [ˈdændl] *v/t. (çocuk)* kolda veya dizde hoplatmak.

**dan.druff** [ˈdændrʌf] *n. pl. (saçta)* kepek, konak.

**dan.dy** [ˈdændi] **1.** *n.* züppe, bobstil; F şık; **2.** *part. adj.* F klâs, şık, en iyi nitelikte; **dan.dy.ish** [ˈ~diiʃ] *adj.* züppece; **'dan.dy.ism** *n.* züppelik.

**Dane** [dein] *n.* Danimarkalı.

**dan.ger** [ˈdeindʒə] *n.* tehlike; **'~-list:** **be on the** ~ F ölüm tehlikesi içinde olm.; ~ **mon.ey** tehlikeli iş için ödenen ek para; **'dan.ger.ous** □ tehlikeli; **'dan.ger--sig.nal** 🚦 *n.* tehlike işareti.

**dan.gle** [ˈdæŋgl] *v/t.* & *v/i.* ası(lı)p salla(n)mak; *fig.* sallanmak, sendelemek; ~ **about, after, round s.o.** *b-nin, bşin* peşinden koşmak; **'dan.gler** *n.* çapkın, hovarda.

**Dan.ish** [ˈdeiniʃ] **1.** *n.* Danimarka dili; **2.** *adj.* Danimarkalı.

**dank** [ˈdæŋk] *adj.* nemli, ıslak.

**Da.nu.bi.an** [dæˈnjuːbjən] *adj.* Tuna nehri'ne ait.

**daph.ne** [ˈdæfni] *n.* ♀ defne ağacı.

**dap.per** □ F [ˈdæpə] minyon, zarif; atik, çevik.

**dap.ple** [ˈdæpl] *v/t.* & *v/i.* benekle(n)mek; **'dap.pled** *adj.* benekli, lekeli; **'dap.ple--grey** *adj.* & *n.* bakla kırı rengi (at).

**dare** [dɛə] *v/i.* cesaret etm.; kalkışmak *-e;* **I** ~ **say** diyebilirim ki, sanırım her-

halde; *v/t.* cesaretli olm.; meydan okumak *b-ne;* **'~-dev.il** *n.* & *adj.* gözüpek, yiğit, atılgan; **'dar.ing** □ **1.** cüretkâr, pervasız; cesur; **2.** *n.* cesaret, yiğitlik.

**dark** [dɑːk] **1.** □ *mst* karanlık, koyu; esmer; anlaşılması güç olan; esrarlı; üzüntülü; **2.** *n.* karanlık; **before (after)** ~ güneş batmadan önce (sonra); **leap in the** ~ körü körüne veya bilmeden bir işe atılma, cüretli iş; ♀ **A.ges** *pl.* ortaçağın ilk yarısı; **'dark.en** *v/t.* & *v/i.* karar(t)mak; *fig.* karanlıklaş(tır)mak; karıştırmak; **never** ~ **s.o.'s door** *b-nin* eşiğine bir daha ayak basmamak; **dark horse** *n.* favori olmayan yarış atı; *fig.* süpriz aday; **'dark.ish** *adj.* siyahımsı; **dark.ling** [ˈ~liŋ] *adj.* karanlık; **'dark.ness** *n.* karanlık; koyuluk; **'~.room** *n.* karanlık oda; **dark.some** [ˈ~səm] *poet.* = dark 1; **'dark-** y *n.* F zenci.

**dar.ling** [ˈdɑːliŋ] **1.** *n.* sevgili, şirin; **2.** *adj.* sevgili, gözde; sevilen.

**darn**[1] *sl.* [dɑːn] = damn.

**darn**[2] [~] **1.** *n.* gizli yama örgüsü; **2.** *v/t.* & *v/i.* örerek tamir etm., yamamak; **'darn.er** *n.* örgü yumurtası.

**darn.ing** [ˈdɑːniŋ] *n.* örülmesi gereken şeyler; **'~-cot.ton** *n.* örme ipliği; **'~-nee-dle** *n.* örme iğnesi.

**dart** [dɑːt] **1.** *n.* kargı, cirit, kısa mızrak; sıçrayış, hamle, fırlayış; ~**s** *pl.* küçük okları numaralı, daire şeklinde bir hedefe atarak oynanan bir oyun; **2.** *v/t.* fırlatmak; atmak; *v/i. fig.* fırlamak, atılmak; hızla atılmak (at, on *-e).*

**Dar.win.ism** [ˈdɑːwinizəm] *n.* Darwin kuramı, Darvincilik.

**dash** [dæʃ] **1.** *n.* kısa mesafe koşusu; canlılık, enerji; gösteriş; darbe, vuruş; *fig.* hamle, atılış, saldırma, hızla atılma (for *-e,* için); *fig.* az miktar; bir tutam (tuz vs.); bir yudum (içki vs.); çizgi, tire, hat (a. ♪, tel.); *typ.* uzun çizgi; cut a ~ çaka yapmak; çalım satmak; at a ~ çabuk, seri; **2.** *v/t.* fırlatmak, atmak, savurmak; *mst* ~ **to pieces** parampaça etm.; kırmak (ümit); üstüne su vs. sıçratmak; karıştırmak; dolaştırmak; ~ **down,** ~ **off** karalamak, çiziktirmek (mektup vs.); ~ **it!** *sl.* Allah belâsını versin!; *v/i.* çarpmak; atılmak, fırlamak (at *-e);* seğirtmek; küplere binmek, çılgınlık etm.; ~ **off** süratle uzaklaşmak, fırlamak, acele gitmek; çiziktirmek; **through** yarmak, delmek, (su vs.) içinden yürümek; ~ **up** acele gelmek; **'~-board** *n. mot.* kontrol paneli; tekerlek çamurluğu (at arabasında); **'dash.er** *n*

F şık, modaya uygun giyimli; **'dash.ing** □ cesur, atılgan; F atik; şık.

**das.tard** ['dæstəd] *n.* korkak, zorba, kötü niyetli kimse; **'das.tard.ly** *adj.* korkak, hain, alçak.

**da.ta** ['deitə] *n. pl., Am. a. sg.* bilgi, haber; veriler; ayrıntılar; *personal* ~ kişiye ait bilgi; ~ **pro.cess.ing** *komputer:* bilgi toplayıp aktarma işlemi.

**date¹** [deit] *n.* hurma.

**date²** [~] **1.** *n.* tarih; zaman; randevu; flört edilen kimse; δό, ✝ vade, önel, mühlet, mehil; *esp. Am.* F randevulaşma, sözleşme; *make a* ~ randevu tayin etm., sözleşmek; *out of* ~ modası geçmiş, eski; *to* ~ şimdiye kadar; *up to* ~ modern, modaya uygun; **2.** *v/t.* tarih koymak *-e*; *esp. Am.* F randevulaşmak (*with ile*); ~ *back to,* ~ *from bşden* ileri gelmek, sebebi ... olm.; *that is* ~*d* modası geçmiş; **'~-block** *n.* yapraklı takvim; **'~.less** *adj.* tarihsiz; **'~-line** *n.* gün değişim meridyeni (*Greenwich'in 180° karşısındaki*); **'~-stamp** *n.* postalanma tarihi, posta damga tarihi.

**da.tive** ['deitiv] *adj. & n. a.* ~ *case gr.* *-e* hali, datif.

**da.tum** ['deitəm] *n.* haber; ayrıntı; veri, bilinen.

**daub** [dɔ:b] **1.** *n.* harç, çamur; acemice yapılmış resim, karalama; üstünkörü görülen iş; **2.** *v/t.* bulaştırmak, kirletmek; *paint,* karalamak; **daub.(st)er** ['~(st)ə] *n.* boyacı; acemi ressam.

**daugh.ter** ['dɔ:tə] *n.* kız evlât; ~**-in-law** ['dɔ:tərinlɔ:] *n.* gelin; **'daugh.ter.ly** *adj.* kız evlâda yakışır.

**daunt** [dɔ:nt] *v/t.* cesaretini kırmak, yıldırmak; *nothing* ~*ed adj.* korkmamış, pervasız; **'~.less** □ cesur, korkusuz, yürekli.

**dau.phin** ['dɔ:fin] *n.* eski Fransa krallığında veliaht.

**dav.en.port** ['dævnpɔ:t] *n.* dolaplı yazı masası; sedir, divan.

**dav.it** ⌁ ['dævit] *n.* matafora.

**da.vy¹** ⚒ ['deivi] *a.* ~*-lamp n.* bir tür emniyetli madenci feneri.

**da.vy²** *sl.* [~] *n.* yemin, ant; *take one's* ~ yemin etm., andiçmek.

**daw** *orn.* [dɔ:] *n.* küçük karga.

**daw.dle** F ['dɔ:dl] *v/i.* tembellikle vaktini harcamak; dolaşmak, oyalanmak; **'daw.dler** *n.* F haylaz, avare; *fig.* uykucu, üsengeç, miskin, tembel.

**dawn** [dɔ:n] **1.** *n.* şafak, gün ağarması, tan; *fig.* başlangıç, uyanma; **2.** *v/i.* şa-

fak sökmek, gün ağarmak; *it* ~*ed upon* (*on*) *him* nihayet anladı ki.

**day** [dei] *n.* gün; gündüz; zaman, devir; *usu.* ~*s pl.* (*esp. yaşam*) zaman, süre; ~ *off* boş gün; *carry veya* win *the* ~ *b-ne* galebe çalmak, kazanmak; *the other* ~ geçenlerde; *this* ~ *week* gelecek hafta bugün; *bundan bir hafta evvel*; *let's call it a* ~ bu günlük bu kadar iş yeter; *pass the time of* ~ *with s.o. b-le* günaydınlaşmak; **'~.book** *n.* ✝ yevmiye defteri; **'~.boy** *n.* yatısız (*veya* gündüzcü) öğrenci; **'~.break** *n.* şafak, tan; **'~.dream 1.** *n.* hülya, hayal; **2.** *v/i.* hayal kurmak, dalmak; **'~.fly** *n.* günü birliğine uçakla yolculuk; **'~.la.bo(u)r.er** *n.* gündelikçi; **'~.light** *n.* gün ışığı, aydınlık; ~*-saving time n.* yazın saatleri ileri alarak kazanılan zaman, yaz saati; **'~.long** *adj. & adv.* gün boyu; **'~.nur.se.ry** *n.* ana okulu; **'~.star** *n.* sabah yıldızı; **'~.time** *n.* gündüz; **'~.to-'day** her günkü, sürekli.

**daze** [deiz] *v/t.* kamaştırmak; sersemletmek; **dazed** *adj.* uyuşuk ,sersem, şaşkın

**daz.zle** ['dæzl] *v/t. -in* gözünü kamaştırmak (*a. fig.*); ⚓ gizlemek, kamuflaj yapmak.

**D-Day** ['di:dei] *n.* İkinci Dünya Savaşı sırasında İngiliz ve Amerikan askerlerinin kuzey Fransa'ya çıktıkları gün (*6 Haziran 1944*).

**dea.con** ['di:kən] *n.* diyakoz, hasta ve fakirleri gözeten papaz; **'dea.con.ess** *n.* hastabakıcı hemşire; **'dea.con.ry** *n.* diyakozluk.

**dead** [ded] **1.** *adj.* ölü, ölmüş; duygusuz (*to -e*); ıssız; sakin, durgun (*su,* ✝); mat, soluk (*renk*); sönük (*ateş vs.*); tatsız, tuzsuz (*içecek*); derin (*uyku*); işlemeyen, ölü (*para, kapital vs.*); ✄ tamamiyle, büsbütün; ani; ~ *bargain* çok ucuz mal, eşya; *at a* ~ *bargain* çok ucuz fiyata; ~ *calm fig.* ölüm sessizliği, ıssızlık; ~ *centre,* ~ *point* ölü nokta; ~ *heat* birden fazla kişinin aynı anda bitirdiği yarış; ~ *letter fig.* uygulamaya konmamış yasa; sahibi bulunamayıp postanede kalan mektup; ~ *load* boş, kendi ağırlığı; ~ *loss* tam kayıp, zarar; ~ *march* cenaze marşı; ~ *set* kararlı; karşıt olma, ters davranma (*against -e*); *a* ~ *shot* keskin nişancı; ~ *wall* ses geçirmez duvar; ~ *water* durgun su; dümen suyu; ~ *weight* net ağırlık; *fig.* külfet, ağır gelen yük; ~ *wood* çalı çırpı; *Am.* eski püskü şey, pılı pırtı; **2.** *adv.* büsbütün; tamamen; harfi harfine; kati; ~ *against* tamamen karşısında; ~ asleep derin uykuda; ~ drunk körkütük sarhoş; ~ sure hiç kuşkusuz; ~ tired bitkin, yorgun argın; **3.** the ~ ölüler; ıssızlık, sessizlik; in the ~ of winter karakışta; in the ~ of night gecenin ortasında; **'~-a'live** adj. ölü gibi, yarı ölü; can sıkıcı, monoton; **'~-'beat 1.** adj. bitkin, perişan; **2.** n. Am. sl. avantacı, otlakçı, bedavacı (beleşçi) kimse; **'dead.en** v/t. körletmek, azaltmak, hafifletmek; fig. öldürmek; zayıflatmak, bşe gem vurmak; ⊕ parlaklığını gidermek. **dead...:** ~ end çıkmaz sokak; fig. çıkmaz; **'~-end** n. çıkmaz yol; fig. umutsuz; ~ kids pl. sokak çocuğu; ~ street çıkmaz yol; **'~-head** n. kaçak yolcu; serbest giriş kartı sahibi; **'~-line** n. Am. yasak bölge sınırı (hapishane); son teslim tarihi; **'~-lock** n. durgunluk; tıkanıklık, çıkmaz; fig. olduğu yerde sayma; **'dead.ly** adj. öldürücü; ölüm derecesinde; ölüm gibi; ~ pale sapsarı; ~ enemy can düşmanı; ~ sin büyük günah; **'deadness** n. uyuşukluk; duyarsızlık (duygusuzluk); durgunluk; bitkinlik; ⬇ rüzgârın kesilmesi.

**dead...:** **'~'net.tle** ⚘ n. ballıbaba; **'~-'çan** Am. sl. adj. & n. sönük, cansız (yüz, çehre).

**deaf** □ [def] sağır; ~ and dumb sağır-dilsiz; turn a ~ ear işitmemezlikten gelmek (to -i); **'deaf.en** v/t. sağır etm., sağırlaştırmak; **'deaf-'mute** n. sağır-dilsiz; **'deaf.ness** n. sağırlık.

**deal¹** [di:l] n. çam tahtası; laden ağacı.

**deal²** [~] **1.** n. parça, kısım; miktar; oyun kağıdını dağıtma; F alış veriş; iş, meşguliyet; Am. mst uzlaşma, anlaşma; a good ~ çok; a great ~ bir hayli, oldukça çok; give a square ~ to b-ne dürüst davranmak; **2.** (irr.) v/t. paylaşmak; oyun kağıdını dağıtmak; dayak atmak, tokat aşketmek (at s.o. b-ne); v/i. alış veriş etm., ticaret yapmak; davranmak; ~ with uğraşmak, meşgul olm. ile, iştigal etm. ile; muamele etm. -e; have ~t with s.o. b-le artık hiç bir alâkası kalmamak; **'deal.er** n. satıcı, tüccar; oyun kağıdını dağıtan; plain ~ samimi, doğru; sharp ~ kurnaz, hilekâr, çıkarcı; **'deal.ing** n. mst deal.ings pl. ilişkiler, muamele, usul; (esp. ticaret) alış veriş.

**dealt** [delt] pret. & p.p. of deal² 2.

**dean** [di:n] n. dekan; **'dean.er.y** n. dekanlık.

**dear** [diə] **1.** □ pahalı; aziz, sevgili, kıymetli; **2.** n. sevgili; gözde; sevimli, hoş; **3.** F o(h) ~!, ~ me! aman tanrım!; süp-

hanallah!; vah vah, yazık!; **'dear.ness** n. pahalılık, kıymet; sevgi, muhabbet; **dearth** [də:θ] n. pahalılık; yokluk, kıtlık; **dear.y** F ['diəri] n. sevgili, favori; sevgilim, nonoşum, kuzum.

**death** [deθ] n. ölüm, vefat; ~s pl. ölüm hali, vefat; ~ penalty ölüm cezası; tired to ~ yorgun argın, bitkin; **'~-bed** n. ölüm döşeği; **'~-blow** n. öldürücü darbe; **'~-du.ty** n. veraset vergisi; **'~.less** □ ölümsüz; **'~.like** adj. ölüm gibi; öldürücü; **'death.ly** adj. öldürücü; **'death-rate** n. ölüm oranı; **'death-roll** ✗ n. şehit düşenler listesi; **'death's-head** n. kuru kafa; **'death-trap** n. ölüm tuzağı (a. fig.); **'death-war.rant** n. idam kararı; fig. ölüm fermanı.

**dé.bâ.cle** [dei'ba:kl] n. felâket, musibet; yıkım, çökme, mağlûbiyet.

**de.bar** [di'ba:] v/t. yoksun bırakmak, mahrum etm. (from -den); men etm. (from -den).

**de.bar.ka.tion** [di:ba:'keiʃən] n. gemiden karaya çık(ar)ma.

**de.base** [di'beis] v/t. itibarına halel getirmek, alçaltmak, indirmek; bşin içine başka bir şey katarak değerini, kalitesini düşürmek; **de'base.ment** n. değerini düşürme, kötüleştirme.

**de.bat.a.ble** □ [di'beitəbl] tartışma götürür; ihtilâflı; **de'bate 1.** n. tartışma, müzakere; **2.** v/t. tartışmak; danışmak; bsi düşünüp taşınmak (on s.th., with s.o. ile); **de'bat.er** n. tartışmacı; becerikli, eli çabuk.

**de.bauch** [di'bɔ:tʃ] **1.** n. sefahat, ayyaşlık, ahlâksızlık; **2.** v/t. ahlâkını bozmak; ayartmak, baştan çıkarmak; **deb.au.chee** [debɔ:'tʃi:] n. zevk ve eğlenceye düşkün, ahlâksız, ayyaş; **de.bauch.er.y** [di'bɔ:tʃəri] n. sefahat, ayyaşlık.

**de.ben.ture** [di'bentʃə] n. tahvil, borç senedi.

**de.bil.i.tate** [di'biliteit] v/t. b-ni kuvvetten düşürmek, zayıflatmak; **de.bil.i.tation** n. zayıflatma; **de'bil.i.ty** n. zayıflık, kuvvetsizlik.

**debt** [det] ['debit] **1.** n. borç, zimmet, açık; to one's ~ b-nin hesabına; **2.** v/t. -in zimmetine geçirmek; b-nin borç hanesine yazmak (against veya to s.o.).

**deb.o.nair** [debə'nɛə] adj. neşeli, güler yüzlü, nazik.

**de.bouch** [di'bautʃ] v/t. & v/i. dar bir yerden açığa çık(ar)mak; dökülmek; akmak, üzerine yayılmak.

**de.bris** ['deibri:] n. yıkıntı, enkaz, moloz, süprüntü.

**debt** [det] *n.* borç; active ~ ödenmemis alacak; owe s.o. a ~ of gratitute şükran borcu olm. -e; pay the ~ of nature, pay one's ~ to nature ölmek; **'debt.or** *n.* borçlu.

**de.bunk** F ['di:'bʌŋk] *v/t. fig. (yüceltilmiş)* bir kişi, düşünce *veya* kuruluş hakkındaki yanlış kanıları, inanışları kaldırmak, gerçeği göstermek.

**de.bus** [di:'bʌs] *v/t.* yük boşaltmak *(kamyon vs.'den); v/i.* inmek *(kamyon vs.'-den).*

**dé.but** ['deibu:] *n.* ilk ortaya çıkış, görünüş *(esp. bir genç kızın ilk olarak parti vs.'de görünmesi; sanatçıların ilk sahneye çıkışları);* **dé.butan.te** ['debju:ta:nt] *n.* sosyeteye ilk kez takdim olunan genç kız.

**dec.ade** ['dekeid] *n.* onluk; on yıl.

**de.ca.dence** ['dekədəns] *n.* düşkünlük, çöküş, gerileme; **'de.ca.dent** *adj.* düşkün, çökmüş, yozlaşmış.

**Dec.a.log(ue)** ['dekələg] *n.* Musa peygambere bildirilen *(veya* inen) on emir, evamiri aşere.

**də.camp** [di'kæmp] *v/i.* kampı bozup çekilmek; kaçmak, sıvışmak; **de'campment** *n.* yola koyulma, hareket.

**de.çant** [di'kænt] *v/t.* kaptan kaba boşaltmak *(şarap);* **de'cant.er** *n.* sürahi.

**de.cap** [di:'kæp] *v/t. (bomba vs.)* etkisiz hale getirmek.

**de.cap.i.tate** [di'kæpiteit] *v/t.* -in başını kesmek, boynunu vurmak; *Am.* işten çıkarmak, azletmek; **de.cap.i'ta.tion** *n.* başını kesme, boynunu vurma.

**de.car.bon.ize** *mot.* [di:'ka:bənaiz] *v/t.* karbonu temizlemek.

**de.car.tel.i.za.tion** [di:ka:təlai'zaiʃən] *n.* kartelleşmeyi önleme.

**de.cath.lon** [di'kæθlən] *n. spor.* dekatlon.

**de.cay** [di'kei] **1.** *n.* çökme, gerileme, çürüme, bozulma, zeval bulma; **2.** *v/i.* çürümek, bozulmak, zeval bulmak; *fig.* azalmak, eksilmek, zayıflamak; ~ed with age eli ayağı tutmaz olmuş, takatten düşmüş.

**de.cease** *esp.* ☆ [di'si:s] **1.** *n.* ölüm, vefat; **2.** *v/i.* ölmek, vefat etm.; the ~ed *adj.* ölmüş, merhum.

**de.ceit** [di'si:t] *n.* hile, yalan; aldatma, hilekârlık; **de'ceit.ful** ☐ hilekâr; yalancı, aldatıcı; **de'ceitful.ness** *n.* hilekârlık, yalancılık.

**de.ceiv.a.ble** [di'si:vəbl] *adj.* kolay aldanan, saf, kanan; **de'ceive** *v/t.* aldatmak; yalan söylemek -e; be ~ed aldanmak;

yanılmak; **de'ceiv.er** *n.* hilekâr, dubaracı.

**de.cel.er.ate** [di:'seləreit] *v/t. & v/i.* yavaşla(t)mak.

**De.cem.ber** [di'sembə] *n.* aralık ayı.

**de.cen.cy** ['di:snsi] *n.* terbiye, iffet; **'decen.cies** *pl.* âdabı muaşeret, davranış töresi.

**de.cen.ni.al** [di'senjəl] *adj.* on yıllık, on yılda bir olan; **de'cen.ni.um** [~jəm] *n.* on yıllık süre.

**de.cent** ☐ ['di:snt] edepli, terbiyeli, kibar; F makûl, kabul edilebilir.

**de.cen.tral.i.za.tion** [di:sentrəlai'zeiʃən] *n.* bir merkezden idare edilmeyiş, ademi merkeziyet sistemi; **de'cen.tral.ize** *v/t.* bir merkezden idare etmemek, ademi merkeziyetleştirmek.

**de.cep.tion** [di'sepʃən] *n.* aldatma, hile; aldanış; **de'cep.ti.ve** ☐ aldatıcı.

**dec.i.bel** *phys.* ['desibel] *n.* desibel, ses yüksekliğini ölçme birimi.

**de.cide** [di'said] *v/t.* kararlaştırmak (in favour of, on, upon); karar vermek *(hakkında);* bitirmek, bşe son vermek; karar almak; **de'cid.ed** ☐ kesin, kararlaştırılmış; tereddütsüz; kesin fikirli, inatçı; **de'cid.er** *n. spor.* final, son maç.

**de.cid.u.o.us** ♀, *zo.* ☐ [di'sidjuəs] *(her sene)* dökülen, düşen; ~ tree yapraklı ağaç.

**dec.i.mal** ['desiməl] *n. &* ☐ ondalık, ondalık...; ~ point ondalık nokta *(ondalık kesirde);* ~ system ondalık sistem; go ~ ondalık sisteme girmek; **dec.i.mate** ['~meit] *v/t.* onda birini *veya* daha büyük bir kısmını öldürmek *veya* ortadan kaldırmak; *fig.* tırpan atmak; **dec.i'ma.tion** *n.* öldürme, yok etme, imha.

**de.ci.pher** [di'saifə] *v/t.* -in şifresini çözmek; **de'ci.pher.a.ble** [~rəbl] *adj.* deşifre edilebilir; **de'ci.pher.ment** *n.* deşifre etme.

**de.ci.sion** [di'siʒən] *n.* karar, hüküm; ☆ ilâm, emir; sebat; take a ~ bşi karara bağlamak; bir karar vermek; **de.ci.sive** ☐ [di'saisiv] kati, kesin; azimkâr.

**deck** [dek] **1.** *n.* ↓ güverte; *esp. Am.* bir deste oyun kâğıdı; on ~ güvertede; *Am.* F hazır, âmade; tetikte, müteyakkız; **2.** *lit. v/t.* süslemek, güzelleştirmek; ↓ güverte kaplamak; **'~-chair** *n.* şezlong; **'~-hand** ↓ *n.* tayfa, deniz eri.

**deck.le-edged** ['dekl'edʒd] *adj.* kenarları kesilip düzlenmemiş *(kâğıt).*

**de.claim** [di'kleim] *v/t. & v/i.* bir koşuk veya edebi parçayı yüksek sesle ve etkileyici üslupla okumak; sövüp saymak *(against ~e).*

dec.la.ma.tion [deklə'meiʃən] n. söz söyleme sanatı; resmi nutuk; **de.clam.a.to.ry** [di'klæmətəri] adj. coşturucu, şatafatlı; hitabete ait.

de.clar.a.ble ['di'klɛərəbl] adj. gümrük vergisine tabi; **dec.la.ra.tion** [deklə'reiʃən] n. beyanname; bildiri: make a ~ demeç vermek; **de.clar.a.to.ry** [di'klɛərətəri] adj. açıklayıcı; sarih, kati; **de'clare** v/t. bildirmek, ilân etm.; (gümrükte) beyan etm., deklare etm.; ~ o.s. iddia etm., savunmak; ~ off geri almak; feshetmek; bozmak; v/i. bş hakkında fikir beyan etm.; b-nin lehinde söz söylemek; bşi önermek; well, I ~! F (şaşkınlık ifadesi) yapma yahu!; ey!; **de'clared** □ kati, belirgin.

de.class.i.fy ['di:'klæsifai] v/t. (artık gizliliği kalmayan askeri veya politik bir sırrı) açıklamak, ilân etm.

de.clen.sion [di'klenʃən] n. meyil ,iniş; çöküş; gr. isim çekimi.

de.clin.a.ble [di'kainəbl] adj. çekilebilir; **dec.li.na.tion** [dekli'neiʃən] n. meyil, eğim: ast., phys. açılım, sapma; **de.cline** [di'klain] 1. n. azalma; fig. çöküş, gerileme; ≇ zayıflama, kuvvetten düşme; 2. v/t. eğmek, eğriltmek; gr. çekmek; reddetmek, kabul etmemek; v/i. eğilmek; çökmek, gerilemek; azalmak, kuvvetten düşmek.

de.cliv.i.ty [di'kliviti] n. iniş, meyil; **de'cliv.i.tous** adj. meyilli, inişli.

de.clutch mot. ['di:klʌtʃ] v/i. debriyaj yapmak.

de.coct [di'kɔkt] v/t. kaynatmak; **de'coction** n. kaynatma; esp. pharm. kaynatarak hazırlanan öz.

de.code tel. ['di:'kəud] v/t. bşin şifresini çözmek.

dé.colle.té(e) [dei'kɔltei] adj. dekolte.

de.col.o(u)r.ize [di:'kʌləraiz] v/t. rengini gidermek, ağartmak.

de.com.pose [di:kəm'pəuz] v/t. parçalara ayırmak; ayrıştırmak; v/i. çürümek, bozulmak; **de.com.po.si.tion** [di:kɔmpə'ziʃən] n. ayrışma; çürüme.

de.con.tam.i.nate ['di:kən'tæmineit] v/t. bşi veya bir yeri zararlı maddelerden arıtmak, dezenfekte etm.

de.con.trol ['di:kənt'trəul] 1. v/t. alış verişte kontrolu kaldırmak, ticareti serbest bırakmak; 2. n. kontrolu kaldırma.

dé.cor thea. ['deikɔː] n. sahne dekoru, mizansen.

dec.o.rate ['dekəreit] v/t. süslemek, donatmak; nişan vermek; **dec.o'ra.tion** n. süs; nişan, madalya; ♀ **Day** Am. Birle-

şik Amerika'da harpte ölenlerin anıldığı gün (30 Mayıs); **dec.o.ra.tive** ['dəkərətiv] n. süsleyici, süs, ziynet; **dec.o.ra.tor** ['~reitə] n. süsleyen, dekoratör.

dec.o.rous □ [dekərəs] terbiyeli; uygun. **de.cor.ti.cate** [di'kɔːtikeit] v/t. kabuğunu soymak.

de.co.rum [di'kɔːrəm] n. edebe uygun olma; uygun davranış.

de.coy [di'kɔi] 1. n. tuzak, yem; a. ~ bird, ~ duck çığırtkan, pırlak, avcı kuş, tuzakçı (a. fig.); 2. v/t. tuzağa düşürmek, hile ile cezbetmek.

de.crease 1. ['di:kri:s] n. azalma, eksilme; on the ~ azalmakta olan; 2. [di:'kri:s] v/t. & v/i. azal(t)mak.

de.cree [di'kriː] 1. n. kararname; emir; tâmim; ∅∅ hüküm, karar; takdiri ilâhi; 2. v/t. karara bağlamak; emretmek; ~ ni.si ∅∅ [~'naisai] n. belirli bir süre geçtikten sonra kesin hüküm haline gelen geçici boşanma hükmü.

dec.re.ment ['dekrimənt] n. eksilme, azalma; kayıp.

de.crep.it [di'krepit] adj. dermansız, zayıf; **de'crep.i.tude** [~tjuːd] n. dermansızlık, çökmüşlük.

de.cres.cent ['di:kresnt] adj. küçülen; azalan.

de.cry [di'krai] v/t. b-ni rezil rüsva etm.; b-ni haşlamak; yermek.

dec.u.ple ['dekjupl] 1. adj. on misli; on kat; 2. n. on kez tekrarlanan rakam; 3. v/t. on misli yapmak, onla çarpmak.

ded.i.cate ['dedikeit] v/t. vakfetmek, adamak, ithaf etm. (to -e); **ded.i'ca.tion** n. tahsis, ithaf; feda etme; açılış töreni; **'ded.i.ca.tor** n. vakfeden, adayan, tahsis eden; **ded.i.ca.to.ry** ['~kətəri] adj. ithaf kabilinden.

de.duct [di'dʌkt] v/t. hesaptan çıkarmak; sonuç çıkarmak; **de'duc.tion** n. çıkarılan miktar; sonuç; † iskonto; çıkarma; **de'duc.tive** adj. tümdengelimli, istidlâli.

deed [diːd] 1. n. iş, eylem; kahramanlık; hareket; belge; senet; 2. v/t. Am. senetle devretmek (to -e).

deem [diːm] vb. zannetmek; saymak; düşünmek; fikrinde olm.; hüküm vermek (of ...hakkında).

deep [diːp] 1. □ derin; detaylı; kurnaz; zeki; samimi; dalgın; tok (ses); koyu (a. fig.); gizli; ~ in bkz: favullü vuruş; in ~ water(s) fig. zor durumda; 2. n. derinlik; poet. deniz; '~-'breathing

128

nefes egzersizi; **deep.en** v/t. & v/i. derinleş(tir)mek; koyulaş(tır)mak; art(ır)mak.

**deep...:** '~-'**freeze** 1. v/t. (yiyecek) dondurmak; 2. n. dipfriz, dondurucu; '~-'**laid** adj. özenle ve gizlice plânlanmış; **deep.ness** n. derinlik; tokluk (ses).

**deep...:** '~-'**root.ed** adj. köklü; '~-sea n. açık deniz; '~-'**seat.ed** adj. kök salmış, yerleşmiş; '~-set adj. çukur (göz).

**deer** [diə] n. geyik, karaca; '~-**lick** n. geyiğin su içtiği tuzlu su kaynağı; '~-**shot** n. saçma, dum dum kurşunu; '~-**skin** n. güderi; '~-**stalk.er** n. geyik avcısı; '~--**stalk.ing** n. geyik avcılığı.

**de.face** ['di'feis] v/t. şeklini bozmak, silmek, çirkinleştirmek; **de'face.ment** n. bozma; silme; silinti, kazıntı.

**de.fac.to** [di:'fæktəu] adj. & adv. bilfiil, gerçekte, fiilen.

**de.fal.ca.tion** [di:fæl'keiʃən] n. zimmete geçirme; para aşırma, suiistimal.

**def.a.ma.tion** [defə'meiʃən] n. iftira; lekeleme; **de.fam.a.to.ry** [di'fæmətəri] adj. iftira kabilinden; iftiralı; **de.fame** [di-'feim] v/t. iftira etm. -e; b-nin şeref ve haysiyetine leke sürmek; b-nin adını kötüye çıkarmak; **de'fam.er** n. iftiracı.

**de.fault** [di'fɔ:lt] 1. n. bulunmama (duruşmada); ihmal; gecikme; gıyab; judgement by ~ ∿ gıyabî hüküm; in ~ of which hazır bulunmadığı için; aksi halde; 2. v/t. görevini, sözünü yerine getirmemek; ihmal etm.; ∿ gıyabında hüküm vermek; **de'fault.er** n. ihmalkâr; töhmetli; ✕ suçlu er; borçlarını ödemeyen kimse; ∿ gaip, hazır bulunmayan.

**de.fea.sance** [di'fi:zəns] n. iptal, fesih, lağvetme.

**de.feat** [di'fi:t] 1. n. yenilgi, bozgun, hüsran; 2. v/t. ✕ yenmek, yok etm., başarısızlığa uğratmak; parl. düşürmek; **de-'feat.ist** n. bozguncu.

**de.fect** [di'fekt] n. kusur, eksiklik, hata; **de'fec.tion** n. ayrılma (from -den); ihanet; **de'fec.tive** ☐ kusurlu, eksik; gr. bazı eckim sekileri kullanılmayan.

**de.fence**, Am. **de.fense** [di'fens] n. müdafaa, savunma: witness for the ~ savunma sahidi; **de'fence.less** adj. himayeden yoksun, desteksiz; ✕ savunmasız.

**de.fend** [di'fend] v/t. müdafaa etm.; savunmak (against -e karşı); korumak (from -den); **de'fen.dant** ☼ n. davalı; **de'fend.er** n. savunucu; koruyucu.

**de.fen.si.ble** [di'fensəbl] adj. savunulabilir; **de'fen.sive** 1. ☐ korumada olan, savunan; 2. n. savunma; be on the ~ sa-

vunmada olm.; act veya stand on the ~ savunmada kalmak.

**de.fer** [di'fə:] v/t. ertelemek; Am. ✕ tecil etm.; payment on ~ red terms taksitle ödeme.

**de.fer** [~] (to) v/i. itaat etm., hürmet etm. -e; **def.er.ence** ['defərəns] n. uyma, itaat; hürmet; in ~ to, out of ~ to hürmeten -e, uyarak -e; **def.er.en.tial** ☐ [~-'renʃəl] saygılı, hürmetkâr.

**de.fer.ment** [di'fə:mənt] n. önel, vade, erteleme; Am. ✕ tecil etme.

**de.fi.ance** [di'faiəns] n. meydan okuma; karşı koyma; bid ~ to b-ne karşı durmak; meydan okumak; in ~ of b-ne nispet için, göze alarak; **de'fi.ant** ☐ meydan okuyan, karşı gelen, serkeş.

**de.fi.cien.cy** [di'fiʃənsi] n. eksiklik, noksan; açık; **de'fi.cient** ☐ eksik, noksan; be ~ in bşde eksik olm.

**def.i.cit** ['defisit] n. (bütçe, hesap) açık; noksan; dezavantaj.

**de.fi.er** [di'faiə] n. meydan okuyan; hakir gören.

**de.file** 1. ['di:'fail] n. geçit, boğaz; 2. [di-'fail] v/i. birerli kolda yürümek; resmi geçit yapmak.

**de.file** [di'fail] v/t. kirletmek, pisletmek; ırzına geçmek; bir yerin kutsallığını bozmak; **de'file.ment** n. kirletme; pislik.

**de.fin.a.ble** [di'fainəbl] adj. tanımlanabilir; **de'fine** v/t. tanımlamak; açıklamak; sınırlamak; **def.i.nite** ['definit] ☐ kesin; açık; belirli; sınırlı; **def.i'ni.tion** n. tanım; açıklama; opt. netlik; **de.fin.i.tive** ☐ [di'finitiv] kesin; son; sınırlandıran.

**de.flate** [di'fleit] v/t. havasını boşaltmak -in; enflasyonu ortadan kaldırmak; gururunu kırmak; **de'fla.tion** n. boşaltma; deflasyon; fiyatların düşmesi; **de'fla.tion.a.ry** adj. deflasyonal, deflasyon doğurucu.

**de.flect** [di'flekt] v/t. saptırmak, çevirmek; **de.flec.tion**, mst **de.flex.ion** n. sapma. dönme.

**de.flow.er** [di:'flauə] v/t. çiçeklerini koparmak; bekâretini bozmak; fig. ırzına geçmek.

**de.form** [di'fɔ:m] v/t. şeklini bozmak, çirkinleştirmek; deforme etm.; ~ed adj. çirkin, biçimsiz, şekli bozulmuş; sakat; **de.for.ma.tion** [di:fɔ:'meiʃən] n. çirkinleştirme, şeklini bozma; sakatlık; **de-form.i.ty** [di'fɔ:miti] n. biçimsizlik, sakatlık; fazlalık (a. fig. vücutta ur vs.); hilkat garibesi.

**de.fraud** [di'frɔ:d] v/t. b-ni dolandırmak (of); aldatmak.

**de.fray** [di'frei] *v/t.* masrafı *b-ne* ait olm.; karşılamak, ödemek.

**de.freez.er** *mot.* [di:'fri:zə] *n.* anti-friz perde.

**de.frost** ['di:'frɔst] *v/t.* buzlarını çözmek *-in*; **de.frost.er** *mot.* ['di:'frɔstə] *n.* (*otomobil camı, buzdolabı vs. de*) buzları eritme düzeni.

**deft** ☐ [deft] çevik, eli çabuk, becerikli.

**de.funct** [di'fʌŋkt] 1. *adj.* ölmüş, merhum; *fig.* eskimiş, modası geçmiş; 2. *n.* ölü.

**de.fy** [di'fai] *v/t. b-ne* meydan okumak, kafa tutmak, karşı koymak; *bşi* hiçe saymak; aldırış etmemek *-e*; alnını karışlamak *-in*; dayanmak *-e*.

**de.gen.er.a.cy** [di'dʒenərəsi] *n.* soysuzluk, ahlâk bozukluğu; yozlaşma, dejenere olma; **de.gen.er.ate** 1. [~reit] *v/t.* yozlaşmak; soysuzlaşmak; 2. ☐ [~rit] yozlaşmış, soysuzlaşmış, dejenere; **de.gen.er.a.tion** [~'reiʃən] *n.* yozlaşma, soysuzlaşma, bozulma; **de.gen.er.a.tive** [~rətiv] *adj.* yozlaş(tır)an; soysuzlaş(tır)an.

**deg.ra.da.tion** [degrə'deiʃən] *n.* indirme; alçal(t)ma; azletme; **de.grade** [di'greid] *v/t.* alçaltmak; *-in* rütbesini indirmek; aşağılamak; *fig.* azaltmak, kısaltmak; *v/t.* gerilemek; düşmek, derecede alçalmak; bozulmak.

**de.gree** [di'gri:] *n.* derece (*a. geogr., gr., A, phys., univ.*); akrabalık derecesi; *fig.* basamak, adım (to *-e*); rütbe; seviye; by ~s gittikçe, aşama aşama; in no ~ katiyen; to a ~ bir dereceye kadar; take one's ~ bir üniversiteden mezun olm.

**de.hu.man.ize** [di:'hju:mənaiz] *v/t.* insanlıktan çıkarmak, canavarlaştırmak.

**de.hy.drat.ed** [di:'haidreitid] *n.* susuz, kurumuş şey; ~ eggs *pl.* yumurta tozu; ~ potatoes *pl.* kurutulmuş patates; ~ vegetables kurutulmuş sebze.

**de.ice** 🌡 ['di:'ais] *v/t.* buzlanmayı önlemek, buzu eritmek; **de.ic.er** *n.* buzlanmayı önleyen *veya* buzu eriten aygıt *veya* madde.

**de.i.fi.ca.tion** [di:ifi'keiʃən] *n.* tanrılaş(tır)ma; **de.i.fy** ['di:ifai] *v/t.* tanrılaştırmak; tapmak.

**deign** [dein] *vb.* tenezzül etm. (to *-e*); alçak gönüllü olm.

**de.ism** ['di:izəm] *n.* yaradancılık, bir dine bağlı olmadan tanrıya inanma; **de.ist** *n.* yaradancı, tanrıya inanan; **de.is.tic, de.is.ti.cal** ☐ bu inanışa ait.

**de.i.ty** ['di:iti] *n.* tanrı(ça);tanrılık.

**de.ject** [di'dʒekt] *v/t.* cesaretini kırmak, keyfini kaçırmak, karamsar kılmak; **de-**

'**ject.ed** ☐ kederli, karamsar; **de'ject.ed.ness**, **de'jec.tion** *n.* keder, umutsuzluk, neşesizlik.

**de jure** [di:'dʒuəri] *adj. & adv.* haklı olarak; yasal...

**de.lay** [di'lei] 1. *n.* gecikme, tehir, erteleme; 2. *v/t.* geciktirmek, ertelemek; *b-ni* oyalamak; *v/i.* gecikmek; tereddüt etm; zaman kaybetmek.

**de.le** *typ.* ['di:li:] 1. *n.* silme işareti; 2. *v/t.* silmek.

**de.lec.ta.ble** *usu. iro.* ☐ [di'lektəbl] hoş, nefis, leziz; **de.lec.ta.tion** [di:lek'teiʃən] *n.* zevk, eğlence, haz.

**del.e.ga.cy** ['deligəsi] *n.* delegasyon; üyelik; **del.e.gate** 1. ['~geit] *v/t.* üye atamak *veya* göndermek; yetki vermek, devretmek (to s.o. *-e*); 2. ['~git] *n.* temsilci, mümessil, elçi, delege, raportör; **del.e.gation** [~'geiʃən] *n.* delegasyon; *Am. parl.* kongre üyesi; atama.

**de.lete** [di'li:t] *v/t.* çizmek, silmek, kazımak; **del.e.te.ri.ous** ☐ [deli'tiəriəs] zararlı, bozucu, sıhhate dokunur; **de.le.tion** [di'li:ʃən] *n.* silip çıkarma; kazıma, bozma.

**delf(t)** [delf(t)] *n.* Hollanda porseleni.

**de.lib.er.ate** 1. [di'libəreit] *v/t.* düşünmek, tartmak; *v/i.* düşünüp taşınmak; danışmak, istişare etm. (on); 2. ☐ [~rit] tedbirli, dikkatli; iyi düşünülmüş; kasti, kasıtlı; **de'lib.er.ate.ness** *n.* dikkatlilik, tedbirli olma; **de.lib.er.a.tion** *n.* düşünüp taşınma; tartışma, görüşme; tedbirli olma; **de'lib.er.a.tive** ☐ [~rətiv] düşünceli, ihtiyatlı; üzerinde düşünülmüş.

**del.i.ca.cy** ['delikəsi] *n.* lezzetli şey; nefaset; zarafet, hassasiyet, kibarlık, incelik, nezaket; **del.i.cate** ☐ ['~kit] nazik, narin, ince (*a. fig.*); hassas, nefis, titiz; **del.i.ca.tes.sen** [delikə'tesn] *n.* mezeci dükkânı; meze, hazır yemekler.

**de.li.cious** ☐ [di'liʃəs] nefis, hoş, leziz, lezzetli.

**de.light** [di'lait] 1. *n.* zevk, sevinç, haz; take ~ in *-den* zevk almak; eğlenmek; 2. *v/t.* sevindirmek, zevk vermek *-e*; *v/i.* sevinmek, zevk almak (in); ~ to *bşden* hoşlanmak; **de'light.ful** ☐ [~ful] hoş, zevkli.

**de.lim.it** [di'limit], **de.lim.i.tate** [di'limiteit] *v/t.* sınırlandırmak; tahdit etm.; **de.lim.i'ta.tion** *n.* sınırlandırma.

**de.lin.e.ate** [di'linieit] *v/t.* taslak çizmek; tarif etm., tasvir etm., betimlemek; **de.lin.e'a.tion** *n.* resim, kroki, tasarı; tarif, betim.

**de.lin.quen.cy** [di'liŋkwənsi] *n.* kusur, kabahat, hata; suçluluk; **de'lin.quent** **1.** *adj.* kabahatli, suçlu, savsakçı; **2.** *n.* kabahatli kimse, suçlu kimse.

**del.i.quesce** [deli'kwes] *v/i.* *(havadan rutubet kapıp)* sıvı hale gelmek, erimek.

**de.lir.i.ous** □ [di'liriəs] sayıklayan; şaşkın, cinnet getirmiş, çılgına dönmüş (with *-den, ile*); **de'lir.i.ous.ness** *n.* cinnet, çılgınlık, delilik; **de'lir.i.um** [~əm] *n.* sayıklama, hezeyan; çılgınlık, taşkınlık; ~ tremens [~əm'tri:menz] içki alışkanlığından ileri gelen hezeyan.

**de.liv.er** [di'livə] *v/t.* kurtarmak (from *-den*); *a.* ~ up teslim etm., haber iletmek; bildirmek; konferans vermek; ⚕ doğurtmak (of a child *-i*); teslim etm. *(eşya vs.)*; ✉ vermek, dağıtmıak; tokat atmak; fırlatmak *(top vs.)*; **de'liv.er.a.ble** *adj.* dağıtılabilir, teslim edilebilir; **de'liv.er.ance** *n.* kurtarış; kurtuluş; ileri sürme; **de'liv.er.er** *n.* kurtaran; dağıtan; **de'liv.er.y** ⚕ doğurma; teslim; ✉ dağıtım; konferans; fırlatma *(top vs.)*; special ~ ekspres, özel postacı ile; on ~ of tesliminde; **de'liv.er.y-note** *n.* teslim kâğıdı; **de'liv.er.y-truck, de'liv.er.y-van** *n.* dağıtım arabası.

**dell** [del] *n.* küçük vadi, dere.

**de.louse** ['di:'laus] *v/t.* *b-ni* bitlemek, bitten temizlemek; **de'lous.ing cen.tre** bitleri temizlemeye mahsus **buğuevi.**

**del.ta** ['deltə] *n.* Yunan **alfabesinin dör**düncü harfi; delta.

**de.lude** [di'lu:d] *v/t.* **aldatmak**; **ayart**mak (into).

**del.uge** ['delju:dʒ] **1.** *n.* tufan, sel, su baskını; **2.** *v/t.* (with) su basmak, tufana boğmak *(a. fig.)*.

**de.lu.sion** [di'luʒən] *n.* aldatma, aldanma; vehim; **de'lu.sive** [~siv] □, **de'lu.so.ry** [~səri] aldatıcı, hayalî.

**delve** [delv] *vb.* kazmak; araştırmak.

**dem.a.gog.ic, dem.a.gog.i.cal** [demə'gɔgik(əl)] *adj.* demagojiye dayanan; **dem.a.gogue** ['~gɔg] *n.* demagog, halk avcısı; **'dem.a.gog.y** *n.* demagogluk, demagoji.

**de.mand** [di'ma:nd] **1.** *n.* talep, istem, istek (on); gereksinim (for); ✝ talep, rağbet; ⚖ talep, dava, hak iddiası (on); in ~ çok aranılan, rağbet gören; on ~ talep vukuunda; **2.** *v/t.* istemek, talep etm. (of); gerektirmek; ⚖ hak talep etm.; *b-den (veya b-ne) bşi* sormak; ~ **note** ödeme talebi.

**de.mar.ca.tion** [di:ma:'keiʃən] *n.* sınır saptama, ayırma; *mst* line of ~ sınır çizgisi.

**dé.marche** *pol.* ['deima:ʃ] *n.* diplomatik girişim.

**de.mean¹** [di'mi:n] *v/t.* *mst* ~ o.s. kendini alçaltmak, küçültmek.

**de.mean²** [~] *v/t.*: ~ o.s. davranmak, hareket etm.; **de'mean.o(u)r** *n.* davranış, tavır.

**de.ment.ed** [di'mentid] □ deli, çılgın.

**de.mer.it** [di:'merit] *n.* kusur, hata; sakınca.

**de.mesne** [di'mein] *n.* mülk; arazi, toprak; malikâne.

**demi...** ['demi] *prefix* yarım, buçuk, yarı...

**dem.i.god** ['demigɔd] *n.* yarı tanrı yarı insan; **'dem.i.john** *n.* damacana, hasırlı büyük şişe.

**de.mil.i.ta.ri.za.tion** ['di:militərai'zeiʃən] *n.* askerden arındırma; **'de'mil.i.ta.rize** *v/t.* askerden arındırmak.

**dem.i.mon.daine** ['demimɔn'dein] *n.* yüksek sosyeteye zengin birini bularak girmeye çalışan kadın; **dem.i.monde** ['~'mɔ:nd] *n.* dömimond.

**de.mise** [di'maiz] **1.** *n.* ölüm; devir; ferağ; kiralama; kira haddi; **2.** *v/t.* geçirmek, *bşi* vasiyetle devretmek, icar etm.

**de.mist** *mot.* [di:'mist] *v/t.* buğulanmayı önlemek; **de'mist.er** *n.* buğulanmayı önleyen aygıt.

**demo** F ['deməu] *n.* ispat; göster(il)me; gösteri.

**de.mob** *sl.* [di:'mɔb] = demobilize; **de.mo.bi.li.za.tion** ['di:məublai'zeiʃən] *n.* seferberliğin sona ermesi, terhis; **de'mo.bi.lize** ⚔ v/t. terhis etm.

**de.moc.ra.cy** [di'mɔkrəsi] *n.* demokrasi; **dem.o.crat** ['deməkræt] *n.* demokrat, demokrasi yanlısı; **dem.o'crat.ic, dem.o'crat.i.cal** □ demokratik, halkçı; **de.moc.ra.tize** [di'mɔkretaiz] *vb.* demokratlaş(tır)mak.

**dé.mo.dé** [dei'məudei] *adj.* modası geçmiş, demode.

**de.mog.ra.phy** [di:'mɔgrəfi] *n.* demografi, sayısal nüfus bilgisi *(doğum, ölüm vs. oranı)*.

**de.mol.ish** [di'mɔliʃ] *v/t.* yıkmak; *fig.* yok etm.; çekip indirmek; F silip süpürmek *(yemek)*; **dem.o.li.tion** [demə'liʃən] *n.* tahrip, yık(ıl)ma; yok olma.

**de.mon** ['di:mən] *n.* şeytan, iblis, cin; he is a ~ for work F kendini işe kaptırır, deli gibi çalışır; **de.mo.ni.ac** [di'məuniæk] **1.** *a.* **de.mo.ni.a.cal** □ [di:məu'naiəkəl] şeytanî, çılgın; **2.** *n.* çılgın kimse, cinli kimse; **de.mon.ic** [di:'mɔnik]

*adj.* doğaüstü; cin *veya* şeytanlara ait.
**de.mon.stra.ble** ☐ [ˈdemənstrəbl] gösterilebilir, kanıtlanabilir; **dem.on.strate** [ˈ~streit] *v/t.* kanıtlamak, göstermek; *v/i.* gösteri yapmak; **dem.on'stra.tion** *n.* kanıt, ispat, göster(il)me; nümayiş, gösteri; *pol.* gösteri, tezahürat; ✗ manevra, tatbikat; **de.mon.stra.tive** [diˈmɒnstrətiv] **1.** ☐ açıkça gösteren, bşi işaret eden (of); inandırıcı; gösteri şeklinde; *gr.* bir noktaya işaret eden; anlamlı; göze çarpan; coşkun; **2.** *n. gr.* işaret zamiri; **dem.on.stra.tor** [ˈdemənstreitə] *n.* ispat eden, anlatan; *anat.* laboratuvar asistanı; *pol.* gösteri yapan, nümayişçi.
**de.mor.al.i.za.tion** [dimɔrəlaiˈzeiʃən] *n.* karamsarlık; ahlâk bozulması; **deˈmor.al.ize** *v/t.* ahlâkını bozmak *-in*; karamsar kılmak.
**de.mote** *Am.* [diːˈməut] *v/t.* rütbesini indirmek; *okul:* bir aşağı sınıfa indirmek; **deˈmo.tion** *n.* indirme vs.
**de.mur** [diˈməː] **1.** *n.* itiraz; **2.** *v/i.* karşı koymak, itiraz etm. (to, at *-e*).
**de.mure** ☐ [diˈmjuə] ciddi, temkinli; hassas; uslu, ağır başlı; **deˈmure.ness** *n.* ciddiyet; duyarlılık, alçak gönüllülük.
**de.mur.rage** ⚓, 🚂 [diˈmʌridʒ] *n.* süristarya, istarya müddeti, yükleme süresini geçirme ve bu süre için ödenen para; **deˈmur.rer** *n.* ♣♣ itiraz.
**den** [den] *n.* in, mağara; *sl.* küçük özel oda.
**de.na.tion.al.ize** [diːˈnæʃnəlaiz] *v/t.* devlet tekelinden çıkarmak, serbest bırakmak; ulusal haklarından yoksun kılmak *-i*.
**de.na.ture** ⚗ [diːˈneitʃə] *v/t.* özelliklerini değiştirmek, doğal halinden çıkarmak.
**de.ni.a.ble** [diˈnaiəbl] *adj.* yadsınabilir, inkâr olunabilir; **deˈni.al** *n.* inkâr, yadsıma, yalanlama; ret.
**de.ni.er**[1] [diˈnaiə] *n.* yadsıyan, yalanlayan; reddeden.
**de.nier**[2] [ˈdeniəi] *n.* ipek, naylon vs. ipliğinin kalitesini ölçmekte kullanılan eski bir Fransız ölçü birimi.
**den.i.grate** [ˈdənigreit] *v/t.* iftira etm. *-e*; kara çalmak.
**den.im** [ˈdenim] *n.* kaba pamuklu kumaş.
**den.i.zen** [ˈdenizn] *n.* sakin, oturan, ora ahalisinden, yerleşmiş.
**de.nom.i.nate** [diˈnɒmineit] *v/t.* ad vermek (to *-e*); tefrik etm., ayırmak, belirtmek; **de.nom.i.na.tion.al** [~ˈneiʃənl] *adj.* bir mezhebe bağlı; ~ school mezhep okulu; **deˈnom.i.na.tive** [~nətiv] *adj.* ad veren, ad gibi

kullanılan; **deˈnom.i.na.tor** ♣ [~neitə] *n.* payda; common ~ ortak payda.
**de.no.ta.tion** [diːˈnəuˈteiʃən] *n.* işaret; anlam; **de.no.ta.tive** [diˈnəutətiv] *adj.* karakteristik, ayırt eden; önemli (of); **deˈnote** *v/i.* göstermek, delâlet etm., nitelendirmek.
**de.nounce** [diˈnauns] *v/t.* bildirmek, ihbar etm.; suçlamak; *(anlaşmanın)* sona erdiğini bildirmek; **deˈnounce.ment** *n.* açıklama, ihbar.
**dense** ☐ [dens] sık, yoğun, kalabalık; anlayışı kıt; **ˈdense.ness** *n.* sıklık, yoğunluk, kalınlık, yakınlık; *fig.* darlık, sıkışıklık; **ˈden.si.ty** *n.* yoğunluk, sıklık, koyuluk; *phys.* yoğunluk, sıklık.
**dent** [dent] **1.** *n.* çentik, basınç *veya* darbe sonucu olan çökük; **2.** *v/t.* çentmek, göçürmek.
**den.tal** [ˈdentl] **1.** *adj.* diş ya da dişçiliğe ait; ~ surgeon diş doktoru; **2.** *n.* dişsel ünsüz; **den.tate** [ˈ~teit] *adj.* 🌿 kenarı dişli, tarak şeklinde; **den.ti.frice** [ˈ~tifris] *n.* diş temizleme tozu *veya* macunu; **ˈden.tist** *n.* diş doktoru, dişçi; **ˈden.tist.ry** *n.* dişçilik; **denˈti.tion** [~ˈtʃə] *n.* diş çıkarma; diş yapısı; **den.ture** *n.* takma dişler.
**den.u.da.tion** [diːnjuːˈdeiʃən] *n.* soyulma, açma, çıplak etme; *geol.* aşındırma, erözyon; **de.nude** [diˈnjuːd] *v/t.* (of) açmak, çıplak hale koymak; *fig.* soymak.
**de.nun.ci.a.tion** [dinʌnsiˈeiʃən] *n.* ihbar, ifşa, itham, uyarma; feshetme; **deˈnun.ci.a.tor** muhbir, ithamcı; **deˈnun.ci.a.to.ry** [~ətəri] *adj.* suçlayıcı, itham edici; gammazlayıcı; küçük düşürücü.
**de.ny** [diˈnai] *v/t.* yadsımak, inkâr etm.; reddetmek; esirgemek; yalanlamak, tanımamak; ~ o.s. s.th. *k-ni bşden* yoksun bırakmak; ~ o.s. (to a visitor) evde iken yok dedirtmek.
**de.o.dor.ant** [diˈəudərənt] *n.* hoş olmayan kokuları gideren madde, deodoran; **deˈo.dor.ize** *v/t.* kokusunu gidermek; **deˈo.dor.iz.er** *n.* koku giderici şey.
**de.part** [diˈpɑːt] *vb.* ayrılmak, gitmek; hareket etm. (for *-e*); F ayırmak (from); uzakta durmak, uzaklaşmak, sapmak, ayrılmak (from *-den*); vefat etm.; the ~ed merhum, vefat edenler; ~ this life bu dünyadan göçmek; **deˈpart.ment** *n.* kısım, bölüm, şube, daire; † branş, şube; *Am.* bakanlık; State ♔ Dış İşleri Bakanlığı; ~ store büyük mağaza; **deˈpart.men.tal** [diːpɑːtˈmentl] *adj.* bir şube *veya* daireye ilişkin; **de.par.ture** [diˈpɑːtʃə] *n.* gidiş, 🚂, ⚓ hareket, kalkış

(from -den); a new ~ yeni bir akım, yenilik; ~ platform hareket peronu.

**de.pend** [di'pend] *v/i.* bağlı olm., tabi
olm.; *b-nin* elinde olm. (on, upon); *b-ne,*
*bşe* güvenmek (on, upon); ♋ karar bağlanmamış olm.; it ~s F belli olmaz, duruma göre; **de'pend.a.ble** *adj.* güvenilir,
emin; **de'pend.ant** *n.* bağlı (on, upon -e);
hizmetçi, uşak; taraftar; aile bireylerin-
den olan; **de'pend.ence** *n.* bağlılık (upon
-e); sınırlı olma (on); güven, inanç (on);
**de'pend.en.cy** *n.* bağımlılık; sömürge,
müstemleke; ek bina; **de'pend.ent 1.** □
bağımlı (on); muhtaç; güvenen; **2.** *s.*
dependant.

**de.pict** [di'pikt] *v/t.* göstermek, betimlemek, anlatmak; resmetmek, çizmek.

**de.pil.a.to.ry** [de'pilətəri] **1.** *adj.* kıl dökücü; **2.** *n.* kıl döken ilaç.

**de.plane** [di:'plein] *v/i.* uçaktan inmek.

**de.plete** [di'pli:t] *v/t.* azaltmak, boşaltmak, dökmek; *fig.* tüketmek; **de'ple.tion**
*n.* tüketme, azaltma, boşalt(ıl)ma; **de-
'ple.tive** *adj.* boşaltıcı.

**de.plor.a.ble** □ [di'pɔ:rəbl] acınacak, acıklı, perişan; **de'plore** *v/t.* acımak -*e;* beğenmemek.

**de.ploy** ✕ [di'plɔi] *vb.* açmak, yaymak,
yanaşık düzenden dağınık düzene geçmek; **de'ploy.ment** *n.* açılma, yayılma.

**de.po.nent** [di'pəunənt] *n.* ♋ yazılı ifade
veren şahit, tanık; *gr.* kipi pasif, anlamı aktif olan fiil.

**de.pop.u.late** [di:'pɔpjuleit] *v/t.* nüfusunu
azaltmak; **de.pop.u'la.tion** *n.* nüfusunu
azaltma.

**de.port** [di'pɔ:t] *v/t.* yurt dışı etm., sürgün etm.; ~ o.s. davranmak, hareket
etm.; **de.por.ta.tion** [di:pɔ:'teiʃən] *n.* yurt
dışı etme; **de.port'ee** *n.* sürgün, hudut
harici edilen kimse; **de.port.ment** [di-
'pɔ:tmənt] *n.* davranış, hareket.

**de.pos.a.ble** [di'pəuzəbl] *adj.* azledilebi-
lir; **de'pose** *v/t.* azletmek; ♋ yeminle
yazılı ifade vermek (to s.th., that).

**de.pos.it** [di'pɔzit] **1.** *n. geol.* çöküntü (*a.*
♀ ); maden yatağı; ♒ tortu; ♈ depo,
ambar; mevduat, teminat akçesi; rehin;
♈ pey, avans; *attr.* depozito; **2.** *v/t.* yatırmak, tevdi etm.; depo etm.; çökeltmek; **de'pos.i.ta.ry** *n.* depo, emanetçi;
**dep.o.si.tion** [depə'ziʃən] *n.* çöküntü; şa-
hidin ifadesi, delil; azil (from -den); **de-
pos.i.tor** [di'pɔzitə] *n.* mudi, para yatı-
ran; emanet eden; **de'pos.i.to.ry** *n.* depo;
*fig.* zengin kaynak, depo.

**de.pot** ['depəu] *n.* depo, ambar, antrepo;
toplanma yeri; *Am.* tren istasyonu.

**dep.ra.va.tion** [deprə'veiʃən] = depravity;
**de.prave** [di'preiv] *v/t.* ayartmak, ahlâkını bozmak; **de'praved** *adj.* ahlâkı bozuk; **de.prav.i.ty** [di'præviti] *n.* ahlâk bozukluğu; fesat.

**dep.re.cate** ['diprikeit] *v/t.* onaylamamak, hoş görmemek, reddetmek; **dep-
re'ca.tion** *n.* ayıplama, hoşnutsuzluk, beğenmeyiş, ret; **dep.re.ca.to.ry** ['~kətəri]
*adj.* küçümseyen, beğenmeyen; olumsuz.

**de.pre.ci.ate** [di'pri:ʃieit] *v/t.* değerini düşürmek, azaltmak, fiyatını kırmak, ucuzlatmak; *fig. b-ne, bşe* hor bakmak; *v/i.*
değer kaybetmek; **de.pre.ci'a.tion** *n.* alçaltma, kötüleme; indirim; ♈ değerin
azalması; aşınma payı, amortisman;
**de'pre.ci.a.to.ry** [~ʃjətəri] *adj.* değerini
düşürücü, küçümseyici.

**dep.re.da.tion** [depri'deiʃən] *n.* yağmala-
ma; tahribat; ~s *pl.* yıkıp bozma; **'dep-
re.da.tor** *n.* yağmacı, çapulcu; **dep.re.da-
.to.ry** *adj.* yağmacılık türünden; F müthiş, korkunç, feci.

**de.press** [di'pres] *v/t.* indirmek, alçaltmak (*fiyat, ses*); basmak -*e*; *fig.* sıkıştırmak, eziyet vermek; **de'pressed** *fig.*
*adj.* kederli, karamsar; **de.pres.sion** [di-
'preʃən] *n.* çökme, depresyon; keder;
indir(il)me; ♈ durgunluk, ekonomik
kriz; ♈ yorgunluk, kuvvetten düşme; ⊕,
*phys., ast.* düşme, alçalma; *geogr.* arazi çöküntüsü, çukur; *meteor.* alçak basınç bölgesi.

**dep.ri.va.tion** [depri'veiʃən] *n.* yoksunluk,
mahrumiyet; kayıp; **dep.ri.ve** [di'praiv]
*v/t.* yoksun bırakmak (of -*den*); ~ s.o. of
s.th. elinden bşi almak; *b-ni bşden* yoksun bırakmak; *bşe* katılmamak.

**depth** [depθ] *n.* derinlik (*a. fig.*); derin
yer; ~ bomb, ~ charge su altı bombası;
~ of focus *phot.* odak derinliği; go beyond one's ~ (*suda*) ayağı yerden kesilmek; be out of one's ~ *fig.* bilginin ötesinde.

**dep.u.ta.tion** [depju'teiʃən] *n.* murahhas
hevet, delegasyon; delegelik; **de.pute**
[di'pju:t] *v/t.* atamak (*temsilci*), göndermek (*delege*); çıkarmak (*milletvekili*);
**dep.u.tize** ['depjutaiz] *v/t.* delege tayin
etm.; ~ for *v/i. b-ne* vekalet etm.; **'dep-
u.ty** *n.* vekil; milletvekili; delege; ♋
temsilci; yardımcı, muavin.

**de.rac.i.nate** [di'ræsineit] *v/t.* kökünden
çıkarmak, ayırmak (*a. fig.*).

**de.rail** ⚒ ['direil] *v/t. & v/i.* raydan
çık(ar)mak; **de'rail.ment** *n.* raydan çıkma.

**de.range** [di'reindʒ] *v/t.* karıştırmak, bşi

bozmak; (mentally) ~d aklı bozuk; **de-lrange.ment** *n.* düzensizlik; geçimsizlik; çılgınlık, akli dengesizlik.
**de.rate** [di:ˈreit] *v/t.* (*yerel vergileri*) hafifletmek.
**Der.by** [ˈdɑːbi] *spor.* İngiltere'de geleneksel at yarışı; ˈ**der.by** *Am.* melon şapka.
**der.e.lict** [ˈderilikt] **1.** *adj.* terkedilmiş, sahipsiz; *esp. Am.* savsak, kayıtsız; **2.** *n.* sahipsiz mal; gemi enkazı; **der.e.lic-tion** *n* terketme; savsaklama; ~ of duty kayıtsız kalma, görevin ihmali.
**de.ride** [diˈraid] *v/t.* b-le, bşle alay etm.; **deˈrid.er** *n.* alaycı.
**de ri.gueur** [dəriˈɡəː] *adj.* mutlaka gerekli.
**de.ri.sion** [diˈriʒən] *n.* alay, hor görme; **de.ri.sive** [diˈraisiv], **deˈri.so.ry** [~səri] alaylı, istihza kabilinden; gülünç; önemsiz.
**de.riv.a.ble** [diˈraivəbl] çıkarılabilir, türetilebilir; **der.i.va.tion** [deriˈveiʃən] *n.* türetme; başka tarafa çevirme; kaynak, asıl; **de.riv.a.tive** [diˈrivətiv] **1.** türetilmiş; **2.** *n.* türetme (*sözcük vs.*); incicil, tali; **de.rive** [diˈraiv] *v/t.* çıkarmak, türetmek (from -*den*); ~ from, be ~d from *b-nin* neslinden olm., gelmek.
**der.ma.tol.o.gist** [dəːməˈtɔlədʒist] *n.* cilt doktoru, dermatolog; **derˈma.tol.o.gy** *n.* cildiye, dermatoloji, cilt hastalıkları ilmi.
**der.o.gate** [ˈderəugeit] *v/i.* zarar vermek, saygınlığını bozmak (from); küçültmek; değerinden düşürmek (from); **der.oˈga-tion** *n.* küçültme (from); ket vurma; **de-rog.a.to.ry** [diˈrɔɡətəri] zararlı (to -e); ket vurucu.
**der.rick** [ˈderik] *n.* ⊕ döner vinç; ↓ vinç kolu; ⚔ petrol sondaj kulesi.
**der.ring-do** [ˈderiŋˈduː] *n.* atılganlık, cüret, gözüpeklik.
**derv** [dəːv] *n.* dizel motor yakıtı.
**der.vish** [ˈdəːviʃ] *n.* derviş.
**de.scale** [diˈskeil] *v/t.* (*kaplarda oluşan kireç taşını*) çıkarmak.
**des.cant** [disˈkænt] *v/t.* bir konu üzerinde uzunca bir söylev vermek (upon); daha yüksek sesle çalmak *veya* söylemek.
**de.scend** [diˈsend] *v/i.* inmek, alçalmak; k-ni küçültmek, düşmek; ⚔ maden ocağına inmek; ☂ yere inmek; ~ (up)on üzerine atılmak, sökün etm., çullanmak; ~ to miras kalmak; bşe yanaşmak; ~ from, be ~d from *b-nin* soyundan gelmek, nesebi olm.; **deˈscend.ant** *n.* torun, oğul.
**de.scent** [diˈsent] *n.* iniş; yokuş; soy, nesil; baskın, istilâ; ⚔ iniş, geçit; alçal-

ma, düşme; meyilli yüzey; karaya çıkma; ⚔ miras kalması, tevarüs.
**de.scrib.a.ble** [disˈkraibəbl] *adj.* tanımlanabilir; **deˈscribe** *v/t.* tanımlamak, nitelendirmek; anlatmak.
**de.scrip.tion** [diˈskripʃən] *n.* tanımlama, tarif; F cins, çeşit; **deˈscrip.tive** ☐ tanımlayıcı, açıklayıcı.
**de.scry** [disˈkrai] *v/t.* görmek, seçmek, keşfetmek.
**des.e.crate** [ˈdesikreit] *v/t.* bir yerin kutsallığını bozmak; **des.eˈcra.tion** *n.* kutsallığa saygısızlık, kirletme.
**de.seg.re.gate** *Am.* [diːˈsegrigeit] *v/t.* & *v/i.* ırk ayırımını kaldırmak; ˈ**de.seg-reˈga.tion** *n.* ırk ayırımına son vermek.
**des.ert¹** [ˈdezət] **1.** *adj.* ıssız, boş; **2.** *n.* çöl.
**de.sert²** [diˈzəːt] *v/t.* bırakmak, terketmek; *v/i.* askerlikten kaçmak; sıvışmak.
**de.sert³** [diˈzəːt] *mst* ~s *n. pl.* eder, ücret; hakedilen ceza.
**de.sert.er** [diˈzəːtə] *n.* firari, asker kaçağı; **deˈser.tion** *n.* terketme; firar; ⚔ terk; askerden kaçma; ıssızlık.
**de.serve** [diˈzəːv] *v/t.* hakkı olm.; bşe lâyık olm. (of); **deˈser.ved.ly** [~vidli] *adv.* haklı olarak; **deˈserv.ing** *adj.* lâyık (of), değerli.
**des.ha.bille** [ˈdezæbiːl] = dishabille.
**des.ic.cate** [ˈdesikeit] *vb.* kuru(t)mak; **des.icˈca.tion** *n.* kuru(t)ma; kuruluk; ˈ**des.ic.ca.tor** *n.* kurutucu aygıt.
**de.sid.er.ate** [diˈzidəreit] *v/t.* arzu etm., istemek; eksikliğini duymak; **de.sid.er-a.tum** [~ˈreitəm] *n.* gereksinim, koşul.
**de.sign** [diˈzain] **1.** *n.* plan, resim, proje, taslak, model; tasarım, niyet; *b.s.* entrika; maksat, kasıt; ⊕ resmini yapma; desen, şekil; by ~ kasıtlı olarak; with the ~ of amacıyla; protection of ~s, copyright in ~s alâmeti farikaların korunması; **2.** *vb.* keşfetmek; taslak çizmek; tasarlamak, hazırlamak; çizmek; amaçlamak; kastetmek.
**des.ig.nate** **1.** [ˈdezigneit] *v/t.* belirtmek, işaretlemek (as); seçmek, atamak (for); **2.** [ˈ~nit] *adj.* geçici olarak atanmış; **des ig.na.tion** [~ˈneiʃən] *n.* atama, tayin; tahsis; isim, ünvan, sıfat.
**de.sign.ed.ly** [diˈzainidli] *adv.* kasıtlı olarak; **deˈsign.er** *n.* düzenleyen kimse; modelist, teknik ressam; *fig.* dalavereci; **deˈsign.ing** *adj.* düzenci, entrikacı.
**de sir.a.bil.i.ty** [dizaiərəˈbiliti] *n.* arzu edilir olma, hoşa gitme; **deˈsir.a.ble** ☐ istenilir; makbul; hoş; sempatik; beğenilir; **de.sire** [diˈzaiə] **1.** *n.* arzu, istek (for, to

*için, -e)*, emel; at s.o.'s. ~ *b-nin* arzusu üzerine; **2.** *vb.* arzulamak; arzu etm., istemek; what do you ~ me to do? ne yapmamı arzu edersiniz?; **de.sir.ous** □ [di'zaiərəs] istekli (of, to do).

**de.sist** [di'zist] *v/i.* vazgeçmek, çekilmek (from *-den*).

**desk** [desk] *n.* kürsü, yazı masası; okul sırası.

**des.o.late 1.** ['desəleit] *v/t.* boş bırakmak; perişan etm., tahrip etm., harabeye döndürmek; **2.** □ ['~lit] tenha, ıssız; harap, perişan; **des.o.la.tion** [~'leiʃən] *n.* harap etme; ıssızlık; viranlık, perişanlık.

**de.spair** [dis'peə] **1.** *n.* ümitsizlik, üzüntü, keder; **2.** *v/i.* ümidi kesmek (of *-den*); **de'spair.ing** □ ümitsiz, çaresiz.

**des.patch** [dis'pætʃ] = dispatch.

**des.per.a.do** [despə'ra:dəu] *n.* gözü dönmüş haydut.

**des.per.ate** □ ['despərit] *adj. & adv.* ümitsiz, deliye dönmüş; F çok; müthiş; aşırı; **des.per.a.tion** [~'reiʃən] *n.* ümitsizlik, çaresizlik; her şeyi göze alma.

**des.pi.ca.ble** □ ['despikəbl] alçak, aşağılık; küçümsenen.

**de.spise** [dis'paiz] *v/t.* hor görmek, küçümsemek, yukarıdan bakmak; nefret etm.

**de.spite** [dis'pait] **1.** *n.* kin, kötülük, nefret; in ~ of *-e* rağmen; ile beraber; **2.** *prp. a.* ~ of *-e* rağmen; **de'spite.ful** □ *poet.* [~ful] gafazkâr, kinci, fena, kötü.

**de.spoil** [dis'pɔil] *v/t.* soymak, yağmalamak (of); **de'spoil.ment** *n.* soygun, çapulculuk.

**de.spond** [dis'pɔnd] *v/i.* ümitsizliğe kapılmak, cesaretini kaybetmek; *bşden* ümidini kesmek (of); **de'spond.en.cy** *n.* ümitsizlik; **de'spond.ent** □, **de'spond.ing** □ ümitsiz, cesaretsiz.

**des.pot** ['despɔt] *n.* despot, zorba hükümdar; **des'pot.ic** *adj.* (~ally) despotlukla, zorbalıkla; **des.pot.ism** *n.* despotluk, zorbalık, istibdat.

**des.qua.ma.tion** [deskwə'meiʃən] *n.* derinin pul pul dökülmesi, soyulması.

**des.sert** [di'zə:t] *n.* yemek sonunda yenen tatlı, yemiş vs.; *Am.* tatlı; ~ *powder* tatlı kabartma tozu; **des'sert-spoon** *n.* tatlı kaşığı.

**des.ti.na.tion** [desti'neiʃən] *n.* amaç, hedef; gidilecek yer; **des.tine** ['~tin] *v/t.* ayırmak, tahsis etm. (to, for *-e*); be ~d to do alın yazısı olm.; **'des.ti.ny** *n.* kader, yazgı; şans, talih.

**des.ti.tute** □ ['destitjuːt] yoksul, mah-

rum; *bşden* yoksun (of); **des'ti.tu.tion** *n.* yoksulluk.

**de.stroy** [dis'trɔi] *v/t.* yıkmak, ortadan kaldırmak; öldürmek; **de'stroy.er** *n.* yok edici; ⚓ destroyer, muhrip.

**de.struct.i.bil.i.ty** [distrʌktiˈbiliti] *n.* bozulma niteliği; **de'struct.i.ble** [~təbl] *adj.* yok edilebilir; **de'struc.tion** *n.* yıkım, imha, tahrip; âfet; **de'struc.tive** □ yıkıcı, tahrip edici (of, to); zararlı, öldürücü; **de'struc.tive.ness** *n.* yıkıcılık; **de'structor** *n.* yakma fırını; yok eden.

**des.ue.tude** [di'sjuːitjuːd] *n.* kullanılmama durumu; fall into ~ yürürlükten kalkmak, kullanılamamak.

**des.ul.to.ri.ness** ['desəltərinis] *n.* düzensiz olma, tutarsızlık; maymun iştahlılık; **'des.ul.to.ry** □ düzensiz, daldan dala atlayan.

**de.tach** [di'tætʃ] *v/t.* ayırmak, çıkarmak, çözmek, sökmek; ✗ bir göreve atamak; **de'tach.a.ble** *adj.* yerinden sökülebilir, ayrılabilir; **de'tached** *adj.* ayrı, bağımsız, tarafsız; **de'tach.ment** *n.* ayırma; ✗ müfreze, kol; tarafsızlık, bağımsız olma.

**de.tail** [di'teil] **1.** *n.* teferruat, ayrıntı, ayrıntılı plan; ✗ müfreze, komando birliği; ~s *pl.* ayrıntılar; in ~ ayrıntılı; go into ~s ayrıntılara girmek; **2.** *v/t.* ayrıntılarıyle anlatmak; ✗ bir göreve atanmak; **'de.tailed** *adj.* mufassal, ayrıntılı.

**de.tain** [di'tein] *v/t.* alıkoymak; geciktirmek; ♕ *b-ni bşden* yoksun bırakmak; hapsetmek, gözaltına almak; **de.tain'ee** *n.* gözaltına alınmış, hapsedilmiş; **de'tain.er** *n.* alıkoyma; ♕ tutukluluk süresini uzatma emri.

**de.tect** [di'tekt] *v/t.* ortaya çıkarmak, keşfetmek; bulmak; **de'tect.a.ble** *adj.* ortaya çıkarılabilir; **de'tec.tion** *n.* keşif, bulma, ortaya çıkarma; **de'tec.tive** *n.* gizli polis, hafiye, sivil polis, dedektif; ~ *force* cinayet masası görevlileri; ~ *story*, ~ *novel* polis romanı; **de'tec.tor** *n.* ortaya çıkaran; *radyo:* dedektör.

**de.tent** ⊕ [di'tent] *n.* çalar saat vs.'de tutma mandalı.

**dé.tente** *pol.* [dei'tä:t] *n.* yumuşama.

**de.ten.tion** [di'tenʃən] *n.* alıkoyma; tutuklama; *(okulda)* izinsizlik, cezaya kalma.

**de.ter** [di'tə:] *v/t.* caydırmak, vazgeçirmek (from *-den*).

**de.ter.gent** [di'tə:dʒənt] **1.** *adj.* temizleyici; **2.** *n.* temizleme maddesi, deterjan.

**de.te.ri.o.rate** [di'tiəriəreit] *v/t. & v/i.* fenalaş(tır)mak; kötüleş(tir)mek; **de.te.ri-**

o'ra.tion n. fenalaşma, bozulma; soysuzlaşma.

de.ter.ment [di'tə:mənt] n. korkutma vasıtası.

de.ter.mi.na.ble ☐ [di'tə:minəbl] saptanabilir; de'ter.mi.nant 1. adj. belirleyici; 2. n. belirleyici etken; de'ter.mi.nate ☐ [-nit] sınırlı, belirli, kesin; de.ter.mi.na.tion [-'neiʃən] n. saptama; tesbit, sınırlama; azim; hüküm, yargı, karar; de'ter.mi.na.tive [-nətiv] adj. & n. niteleyici, sınırlayıcı; de'ter.mine [-min] vb. sınırlamak, belirtmek; azmetmek; saptamak; özendirmek (to -e); esp. 🐂 karara bağlamak; ᴅᴇ -d kararlı olm.; kararlaştırmak; tasarlamak (on, to); de'ter.mined adj. azimli, kararlı; kesin.

de.ter.rent [di'terənt] 1. adj. caydırıcı; 2. n. caydıran, vazgeçiren; nuclear ~ pol. nükleer caydırıcı.

de.test [di'test] v/t. nefret etm., iğrenmek -den; de'test.a.ble ☐ iğrenç, berbat; de.tes.ta.tion [di:tes'teiʃən] n. nefret, tiksinme (of -den).

de.throne [di'θrəun] v/t. tahttan indirmek (a. fig.); de'throne.ment n. düşürülme, tahttan indirilme.

det.o.nate ['detəuneit] vb. patla(t)mak; infilâk et(tir)mek; 'det.o.nat.ing n. patlama, ateş alma; ~ cap kapsol; det.o'na.tion n. patlama, infilâk; 'det.o.na.tor n. 🎖 sis işareti; ✕ kav, kapsol, fitil, funya.

de.tour ['di:tuə], dé.tour ['deituə] n. dolambaçlı yol, sapak; make a ~ dolambaçlı yoldan gitmek.

de.tract [di'trækt] vb. ~ from s.th. azaltmak, eksiltmek; yermek; de'trac.tion n. eksiltme; yerme; de'trac.tive adj. yerici; iftiralı; de'trac.tor n. yeren, kara çalan.

de.train [di:'trein] vb. trene bin(dir)mek ya da in(dir)mek.

de trib.al.i.za.tion [di:traibəlai'zeiʃən] n. critme; dağıtım; arıtma; de'trib.al.ize v/t. aşiret üyesi olarak saymamak.

det.ri.ment ['detrimənt] n. zarar, ziyan, hasar (to); det.ri.men.tal ☐ [-'mentl] zarar veren, zararlı (to -e).

de.tri.tus geol. [di'traitəs] n. hayşat, döküntü taş, kum vs.

de.tune [di'tju:n] v/t. radyo: yayın metresini bozmak.

deuce [dju:s] n. ikili (kart, zar vs.); tenis: düs, berabere; F kör talih; the ~! şeytan!; Allah belâsını versin!; deu.ced F [dju:st] ☐ berbat, Allahın belâsı.

de.val.u.a.tion [di:vælju'eiʃən] n. devalüasyon, para değerinin düşürülmesi; de.val.ue [di:'vælju:] v/t. -in değerini düşürmek.

dev.as.tate ['devəsteit] v/t. harap etm., mahvetmek; dev.as'ta.tion n. yakıp yıkma.

de.vel.op [di'veləp] vb. geliş(tir)mek; genişle(t)mek; phot. develope etm., banyo etm.; işlenecek hale getirmek; Am. görünmek, meydana çıkmak; meşhur olm.; de'vel.op.er n. phot. revelâtör, develope eden ilaç; de'vel.op.ing n. phot. develope etme; de'vel.op.ment n. gelişme; genişletme; meydana çıkma; phot. developman.

de.vi.ate ['di:vieit] v/i. sapmak, yoldan çıkmak (a. fig.) (from -den); de.vi'a.tion n. sapma; ⬇ pusulanın sapması; de.vi'a.tion.ism n. pol. partiden ayrılma; de.vi'a.tion.ist n. pol. partiden ayrılan, politik düşüncelerinde sapma olan kimse.

de.vice [di'vais] n. buluş; alet, aygıt; hile, oyun; arma, nişan; slogan; leave s.o. to his own ~s b-nin işine karışmamak; kendi haline bırakmak.

dev.il ['devl] 1. n. şeytan, iblis (a. fig.); şeytan herif; 🐂 avukat yardımcısı; fig. yamak; ⊕ lehimci ocağı; the ~! Allah belâsını versin!; between the ~ and the deep sea aşağı tükürsen sakal, yukarı tükürsen bıyık; 2. v/t. bol baharatla kızartmak; ⊕ bez, kâğıt vs.'yi paçavra etm.; rahatsız etm., canını sıkmak; v/i. yamak olarak çalışmak; 'dev.il.ish ☐ şeytanca; F müthiş; kahrolası; 'dev.il--may-'care adj. pervasız, kayıtsız; 'dev.il.ment n. şeytanlık, muziplik; 'dev.il(t)-ry n. şeytanlık; kötülük; yaramazlık.

de.vi.ous ☐ ['di:vjəs] dolaşık, sapa, eğri büğrü; hatalı (a. fig.); dürüst olmıyan; ~ step yanlış adım.

de.vis.a.ble [di'vaizəbl] adj. tasavvur edilebilir; vasiyet olunabilir; de'vise 1. 🐂 n. bşi vasiyetle bırakma, vasiyet; 2. v/t. tasarlamak; icat etm.; 🐂 vasiyet etm.; dev.i.see 🐂 [devi'zi:] n. mirasçı, varis; de.vis.er [di'vaizə] n. mucit; de.vi.sor 🐂 [devi'zɔ:] n. vasiyet eden.

de.vi.tal.ize [di:'vaitəlaiz] v/t. cansızlaştırmak, şevkini kırmak.

de.void [di'vɔid] ( dj. (of) boş, hali; ...siz: ...sız, -den yoksu n.

dev.o.lu.tion [di:v ʲ'lu:ʃən] n. 🐂 miras kalması; havale; ⊕ görevi devretme; biol. gerileme; de.volve [di'vɔlv] (upon, to) v/t. b-ne devretmek; yuvarlamak;

*v/i.* b-ne, bşe geçmek, hissesine düşmek, kalmak.

**de.vote** [di'vəut] *v/t.* vakfetmek, adamak (to *-e*); **de'vot.ed** □ sadık, bağlı (to *-e*); **dev.o.tee** [devəu'ti:] *n.* düşkün, hayran; sofu; **de.vo.tion** [di'vəuʃən] *n.* derinden bağlılık (to s.o. *-e*), fedakârlık, özveri; adayış, tapma; **~s** *pl.* ibadet, dua; **de-'vo.tion.al** □ [~ʃənl] ibadete ilişkin, dindar.

**de.vour** [di'vauə] *v/t.* tıkınmak, yutmak (*a. fig.*); yok etm., bitirmek; **~ed** with hırs ve istekli; **de'vour.ing** □ yiyip bitiren, son derece üzücü, içini kemiren.

**de.vout** □ [di'vaut] dindar; sadık; samimi; **de'vout.ness** *n.* dindarlık.

**dew** [dju:] **1.** *n.* çiy, şebnem; **2.** *v/t.* çiyle ıslatmak, nemlendirmek; **~-drop** *n.* çiy damlası; **'~-lap** *n.* (*öküz vs.*) boynun altında sarkan deri; **'dew-pond** *n.* çiyden oluşmuş ufak ve sığ göl; **'dew.y** *adj.* çiyle kaplı.

**dex.ter** ['dekstə] *adj.* sağ, sağa ilişkin, sağda olma.

**dex.ter.i.ty** [deks'teriti] *n.* beceri, ustalık; **dex.ter.ous** □ ['~tərəs] becerikli, usta.

**di.a.be.tes** [daiə'bi:ti:z] *n.* şeker hastalığı, diyabet.

**di.a.bol.ic, di.a.bol.i.cal** □ [daiə'bɔlik(el)] şeytanca.

**di.a.dem** ['daiədem] *n.* taç; (*çiçek veya yapraklardan*) başlık.

**di.ag.nose** ['daiəgnəuz] *v/t.* teşhis etm.; **di.ag'no.sis** [~-sis] *n. pl.*, **di.ag'ni.ses** [~-si:z] *n.* teşhis, tanılama.

**di.ag.o.nal** [dai'ægənl] **1.** □ çapraz, diyagonal; **2.** *n.* köşegen, çapraz örgü.

**di.a.gram** ['daiəgræm] *n.* diyagram. değişimi gösteren grafik; şema, plân; **di-a.gram.mat.ic** [daiəgrə'mætik] *adj.* (~ally) şematik, grafiksel.

**di.al** ['daiəl] **1.** *n.* kadran; güneş saati; taksimatlı daire: *teleph.* diks, kurs; radyo: dereceli disk: ~ light kurs lâmbası; **2.** *v/t. teleph.* numaraları çevirmek.

**di.a.lect** ['daiəlekt] *n.* lehçe, sive, ağız; **di.a'lec.tic, di.a'lec.ti.cal** □ lehçeye ait; mantık ve münazaraya ait; **di.a'lec.tic-(s)** *sg n.* diyalektik, eytişim; mantıksal konusmaları yürütme sanatı.

**di.a.logue** *Am. a.* **di.a.log** ['daiəlɔg] *n.* diyalog, biriyle konuşma; ~ track *film:* ses şeridi.

**di.al...: '~-sys.tem** *teleph. n.* otomatik telefon sistemi; **'~-tone** *teleph.* çevir sesi.

**di.am.e.ter** [dai'æmitə] *n.* çap.

**di.a.met.ri.cal** □ [daiə'metrikəl] çapla ilgili.

**di.a.mond** ['daiəmənd] **1.** *n.* elmas; eşkenar dörtgen şekil; *Am .beysbol:* oyun sahası; oyun kartı; karo; ~ cut ~ dinsizin hakkından imansız gelir; he is a rough ~ kaba fakat iyi kalpli kimsedir; **2.** *adj.* kareli, baklava şeklinde; **'~-'cut-ter** *n.* elmastraş; **~ wed.ding** evliliğin altmışıncı yıldönümü.

**di.a.pa.son** ♪ [daiə'peisn] *n.* uyum, armoni; ölçü; orgun ana sesleri, sekizinciden itibaren boruları; diyapazon.

**di.a.per** ['daiəpə] **1.** *n.* baklava desenli keten bezi, *Am.* kundak bezi; **2.** *v/t.* baklava şeklinde desenlemek; *Am.* bebeğin bezini değiştirmek.

**di.aph.a.nous** [dai'æfənəs] *adj.* şeffaf.

**di.a.phragm** ['daiəfræm] *n. anat.* diyafram; ⊕ bölme, ara duvarı; *opt.* mercek perdesi; *teleph.* diyafram.

**di.a.rist** ['daiərist] *n.* günlük tutan; **'di.a-rize** *vb.* günlük tutmak.

**di.ar.rhoe.a** 💊 [daiə'riə] *n.* ishal, amel.

**di.a.ry** ['daiəri] *n.* hatıra defteri, günlük, takvimli defter (*ajanda*).

**Di.as.po.ra** [dai'æspərə] *n.* Yahudilerin sürgünden sonra dünyanın her yanına dağılmaları.

**di.a.ther.my** ♨ ['daiəθə:mi] *n.* elektrikle vücuda ısı vererek tedavi.

**di.a.tribe** ['daiətraib] *n.* hiciv, hakaret.

**dib.ble** ['dibl] **1.** *n.* fide kazığı; **2.** *v/t.* fide dikmek; fide kazığı ile çukur açmak.

**dibs** *sl.* [dibz] *n. pl.* mangır, mangiz.

**dice** [dais] **1.** *n. pl.* oyun zarları; **2.** *vb.* zar oynamak, zar atmak (for *için*); zar şeklinde parçalara kesip ayırmak; **'~-box** *n.* zar atmaya yarar meşin kap; **'dic.er** *n.* zar oyuncusu.

**dick¹** *Am. sl.* [dik] *n.* dedektif, hafiye, sivil polis.

**dick²** *sl.* [~] *n.* açıklama; take one's ~ yemin etm.

**dick.ens** F ['dikinz] *n.* şeytan.

**dick.er** *Am.* ['dikə] *v/i.* pazarlık etm. (with, for *b le., için*).

**dick.(e)y** ['diki] **1.** *sl. adj.* kötü, adi, çürük, zavıf; **2.** *n.* F araba arkasında uşak yeri; takma gömlek yakası; *a.* ~-bird *n.* (*çocuk dilinde*) kuş.

**dic.ta.phone** ['diktəfoun] *n.* diktafon.

**dic.tate 1.** ['dikteit] *n.* dikte; emir; **2.** [dik'teit] *vb.* yazdırmak; dikte etm.; *fig.* zorla kabul ettirmek; emretmek; **dic'ta-tion** *n.* emir; dikte; dikte etme; **dic'ta-tor** *n.* diktatör; **dic.ta.to.ri.al** □ [diktə'tɔ:riəl] diktatörce, zorbaca, otokratik; **dic.ta.tor.ship** [dik'teitəʃip] *n.* diktatörlük, zorbalık.

**dic.tion** ['dikʃən] *n.* anlatım şekli, diksiyon; **dic.tion.ar.y** ['~ri] *n.* sözlük, lügat. **dict.um** ['diktəm], *pl.* **dic.ta** ['~tə] *n.* yetkili söz; özdeyiş; ẞ́ẞ mütalâa.

**did** [did] *pret. of* do.

**di.dac.tic** [di'dæktik] *adj.* (~ally) öğretici, didaktik, öğretsel.

**did.dle** *sl.* ['didl] *v/t.* aldatmak, dolandırmak, kandırmak.

**didn't** ['didnt] = did not; *s.* do.

**die¹** [dai] *v/i.* ölmek, vefat etm. (of, from *-den*); mahvolmak; yavaş yavaş ölmek; ⌐ özlemini duymak, şiddetle arzu etm. (for s.th., to *inf. -i*); ~ away yavaş yavaş ölmek, kesilmek *(rüzgâr)*; yavaş yavaş sönmek *(ses)*; yavaş yavaş uçmak *(renk)*; sönmek *(ışık, ateş)*; ~ down kaybolmak, küçülmek, sönmek; ~ off yavaş yavaş ölmek, kurumak; ~ out nesli tükenmek, ortadan kalkmak; ~ hard direnmek, *(eski inanç, âdet vs.)* ortadan kalkması çok zaman almak; never say ~! umudunu yitirme!; cesaretini kaybetme!

**die²** [~], *n. pl.* **dice** [dais] zar; *pl.* **dies** [daiz] ⊕ kalıp; mühür; lower ~ matris, harf kalıbı; upper ~ zımba; as straigh as a ~'dimdik; the ~ is cast ok yaydan çıktı.

**die...**: '~'way *adj.* azalıp kaybolan, zayıf, süzgün; uzaklaşan *(ses vs.)*; '~'casting *n.* ⊕ basınçlı döküm; '~'hard *n.* inatçı, gerici, eski kafalı, tutucu kimse.

**di.e.lec.tric** [daii'lektrik] *adj.* elektrik geçirmez, izolatör, yalıtkan.

**Die.sel en.gine** ['di:zl'endʒin] *n.* dizel motoru.

**die-sink.er** ['daisiŋkə] *n.* pafta kalıpçısı.

**die-stock** ⊕ ['daistɔk] *n.* el paftası.

**di.et** ['daiət] 1. *n.* perhiz, rejim; gıda, yiyecek; ulusal meclis, diyet; 2. *v/t. & v/i.* perhiz et(tir)mek; rejim yap(tır)mak; 'di.e.tar.y 1. *n.* beslenme rejimi; perhiz kuralları; 2. *adj.* perhize ait; **di.e.tet.ics** [daii'tetiks] *n.* diyet bilimi; **di.e.ti.cian, di.e.ti.tian** [~'tifən] *n.* diyet uzmanı.

**dif.fer** ['difə] *v/i.* farklı olm., ayrılmak (with, from *-den*); uygun bulmamak, anlaşamamak (about, on, over *-de*); they agreed to ~ anlaşamadıklarını kabul ettiler; **dif.fer.ence** ['difrəns] *n.* ayrılık, fark; ihtilâf, anlaşmazlık; ⅄ & ⊤ fark; split the ~ farkı paylaşmak; 'dif.fer.ent □ farklı (from, to *-den*), ayrı, başka; çeşitli; değişik; **dif.fer.en.ti.a** [difə'renʃiə] *n.* alâmeti farika. karakteristik; **dif.fer-'en.tial** [~əl] 1. *adj.* farklı, farklılık gösteren; ~ calculus diferensiyel hesap; 2.

**mot.** *n.* diferansiyel dişlisi; **dif.fer'en.ti.ate** [~ʃieit] *vb.* ayırt etm.; değişiklik göstermek; farklılaşmak; **dif.fer.en.ti'a.tion** *n.* ayırma, ayırt etme, fark.

**dif.fi.cult** □ ['difikəlt] zor, güç; titiz; inatçı; 'dif.fi.cul.ty *n.* zorluk, güçlük; be in difficulties parasız kalmak, sıkıntıda olm.

**dif.fi.dence** ['difidəns] *n.* çekingenlik, utangaçlık; 'dif.fi.dent □ çekingen, utangaç.

**dif.frac.tion** *phys.* [di'frækʃən] *n.* elektromanyetik dalgaların *ya da* ışınların kırılarak ışık tayfını *(gökkuşağını)* oluşturması.

**dif.fuse** 1. [di'fju:z] *fig. v/t. & v/i.* yay(ıl)mak, dağıtmak; dağılmak; ⁊̃ bşe nüfuz etm.; 2. □ [~s] ayrıntılı; yayılmış, yaygın, dağılmış, geniş; **dif'fused** [~zd] *adj.* yayılmış *(ışık)*; **dif'fu.sion** [~ʒən] *n.* yayılma; ⁊̃ dağılma; **dif'fu.sive** □ [~siv] yayılmış, fazla açıklamalı, uzun uzadıya.

**dig** [dig] 1. *vb.* kazmak; kazı yapmak; kafa yormak; bşi deşelemek (in); ⌐ itip kakmak; dürtmek; ~ for eşeleyerek aramak; ~ in gömmek; ✕ siper kazmak; ~ into kazıp delmek; yemeğe girişmek, ~ up kazıp çıkarmak; ortaya çıkarmak; 2. *n.* kazı, hafriyat; ⌐ dürtme, kinaye; ~s *pl.* F oda, pansiyon.

**di.gest** 1. [di'dʒəst] *v/t. & v/i.* düzenlemek; hazmetmek, sindir(il)mek *(a. fig.)*; 2. ['daidʒest] *n.* özet, derleme, seçme; ẞ́ẞ yasalar toplamı; **di.gest.i.bil.i.ty** [didʒestə'biliti] *n.* sindirebilme; **di'gest.i.ble** *adj.* hazmı kolay, sindirilebilir; **di'ges.tion** *n.* hazım, sindirim; **di'gestive** 1. *n.* sindirici ilâç; 2. *adj.* hazmettirici, midevi.

**dig.ger** ['digə] *(esp. altın) n.* kazıcı, arayıcı; toprak kazan kimse; *sl.* Birinci Dünya Savaşı'nda Avustralyalı ya da Yeni Zelandalı asker; **dig.gings** F ['~giŋz] *pl.* pansiyon; *Am.* altın madeni.

**dig.it** ['didʒit] *n.* parmak; ⅄ rakam; bir parmak genişliği; 'dig.it.al *adj.* parmağa ait.

**dig.ni.fied** ['dignifaid] *adj.* ağırbaşlı, vakur; **dig.ni.fy** ['~fai] *v/t.* değer vermek, yükseltmek, şeref vermek; *fig.* asilleştirmek.

**dig.ni.tar.y** *esp. eccl* ['dignitəri] *n.* yüksek rütbeli kimse, ruhani; 'dig.ni.ty *n.* ağırbaşlılık, vakar, değer; stand (up)on one's ~ kendisine saygılı davranılmasında ısrar etm.

**di.graph** *gr.* ['daigrɑ:f] *n.* tek sesi temsil

eden iki harf (örneğin «heat» sözcüğündeki «ea»).

**di.gress** [dai'gres] v/i. konunun dışına çıkmak, ayrılmak (from -den); **di'gression** n. konudan ayrılma, sapma; **di'gressive** □ yersiz, gereksiz, konu dışı.

**dike** [daik] 1. n. set, bent; hendek; 2. vb. bentle kapatmak; hendek açmak, kazmak.

**di.lap.i.date** [di'læpideit] v/t. harap etm.; v/i. harap olm.; **di'lap.i.dat.ed** adj. harap, yıkılmaya yüz tutan; **di.lap.i'da.tion** n. harap olma; viranlık.

**di.lat.a.bil.i.ty** phys. [daileitə'biliti] n. genleşme yeteneği; **di'lat.a.ble** adj. genişliyebilir, uzayabilir; **dil.a'ta.tion** n. genleşme, genişleme, yayılma; **di'late** v/t. & v/i. genişle(t)mek; ~ upon ayrıntılara girmek; **di'la.tion** = dilatation; **dil.a.to.ri.ness** ['dilətərinis] n. tembellik, işini sonraya bırakma; **'dil.a.to.ry** □ tembel, ağırdan alan, yavaş, b-ni oyalayıcı.

**di.lem.ma** [di'lemə] n. dilem, ikilem; fig. kötü durum, sıkıntı.

**dil.et.tan.te** [dili'tænti], pl. **dil.et.tan.ti** [dili'tænti:] n. güzel sanatlara meraklı; amatör; adj. yüzeysel merakı olan.

**dil.i.gence** ['dilidʒəns] n. gayret, çalışkanlık; **'dil.i.gent** □ gayretli, çalışkan.

**dill** ♦ [dil] n. dereotu.

**dil.ly-dal.ly** F ['dilidæli] v/i. boş vakit geçirmek, oyalanmak, bşi yapmağa üşenmek.

**dil.u.ent** ['diljuənt] 1. n. sulandırıcı madde; 2. adj. sulandırıcı, çözücü; **di.lute** [dai'lju:t] 1. v/t. sulandırmak; fig. ruhsuzlaştırmak; 2. adj. sulandırılmış; fig. ruhsuz; **di'lu.tion** n. sulandırma, çözme; fig. ruhsuzlaşma, heyecanını yitirme.

**di.lu.vi.al** [dai'lu:vjəl], **di'lu.vi.an** adj. geol. sel sonucu oluşmuş.

**dim** [dim] 1. □ bulanık, donuk; loş; F an!ayışsız; 2. v/t. & v/i. bulan(dır)mak; karar(t)mak (ışık); mot., film: donuklaş(tır)mak.

**dime** Am. [daim] n. on sentlik para: ~ novel ucuz roman; ~ store tek fiyatla ucuz satış yapan mağaza.

**di.men.sion** [di'menʃən] n. boyut, ebat; ~s pl. buut; uzaklık.

**di.min.ish** [di'miniʃ] v/t. & v/i. azal(t)mak; küçül(t)mek; eksil(t)mek; **dim.i.nu.tion** [dimi'nju:ʃən] n. azal(t)ma; eksil(t)me; ⚔ küçül(t)me; **di'min.u.tive** [~njutiv] 1. □ gr. küçültme eki; ufak; 2. n. küçültme eki almış sözcük.

**dim.ness** ['dimnis] n. donukluk, matlık.

**dim.ple** ['dimpl] 1. n. çene veya yanak çukuru, gamze; 2. v/t. & v/i. çukur oluş(tur)mak; **'dim.pled** adj. gamzeli.

**din** [din] 1. n. gürültü, patırdı, şamata; 2. v/t. & v/i. gürültü ile sersemletmek; gürültü etm.; ~ s.th. into s.o.('s ears) tekrar tekrar söyleyerek bşi b-nin kafasına sokmak, hatırlatmak.

**dine** [dain] v/i. akşam yemeğini yemek; v/t. ağırlamak, yedirip içirmek, ziyafet vermek -e; ~ out akşam yemeğini dışarda yemek; **'din.er** n. akşam yemeği yiyen; akşam yemeğine gelen misafir; esp. Am. vagon restoran, vagon restoran şeklinde düzenlenmiş lokanta; **'din.er-'out** n. dışarıda akşam yemeğine çok davet edilen kimse; **di.nette** [dai'net] n. mutfağa açılan küçük yemek odası.

**ding** [diŋ] v/i. tınlamak, çınlamak; **~-dong** ['~'dɔŋ] 1. n. çan, zil vs. sesi, dan dan; 2. adj. çekişmeli bir oyun veya mücadelede önce bir tarafın sonra öteki tarafın üstün gelmesi şeklinde.

**din.gey, din.ghy** ['diŋgi] n. küçük sandal, bot; rubber ~ lastik sandal.

**din.gle** ['diŋgl] n. ağaçlık küçük vadi.

**din.gus** Am. sl. ['diŋgəs] n. şey.

**din.gy** □ ['dindʒi] bulanık, rengi solmuş, kirli görünen.

**din.ing...** ['dainiŋ]: **'~-'al.cove** n. duvar da yemek koymak için girinti; **'~-car** n. ∰ vagon restoran; **'~-room** n. yemek odası.

**dink.ey** Am. ['diŋki] n. küçük manevra lokomotifi.

**dink.y** F ['diŋki] adj. küçük ve zarif, sevimli, cici bici.

**din.ner** ['dinə] n. (öğleyin veya akşam yenen) esas yemek; akşam yemeği; ziyafet; **'~-jack.et** n. smokin; **'~-pail** n. Am. sefertası; **'~-par.ty** n. yemek daveti eri; **'~-serv.ice, '~-set** n. sofra takımı.

**di.no.saur** zo. ['dainəuso:] n. çok büyük ve nesli tükenmiş sürüngen, dinazor.

**dint** [dint] 1. n. çizgi, iz, ufak oyuk; bere; by ~ of vasıtasiyle, -den ötürü, kuvvetiyle; 2. v/t. berelemek, yamrı yumru etm.

**di.o.ce.san** eccl. [dai'ɔsisən] 1. adj. piskoposluğa ait; 2. n. piskopos; **di.o.cese** ['daiəsis] n. piskoposluk ruhanî dairesi.

**di.op.tric** opt. [dai'ɔptrik] 1. adj. ışınları kırıcı; 2. n. ışık kırılması ile ilgili bilim dalı.

**di.ox.ide** ♠ [dai'ɔksaid] n. molekülde bir diğer elemente bağlanan iki oksijen atomlu oksit, dioksit.

**dip** [dip] 1. v/t. daldırmak, batırmak; ↓ selâm amacıyla sancağı yarıya indirmek; (kumaş) boyamak; su çekmek (out of, from *-den*); *mot.* farları kısmak; *(bir hayvanı)* antiseptik suya batırmak; *v/i.* dalmak, batmak; eğilmek; *geol.* meyletmek; çökmek; *~* into göz gezdirmek; **2.** *n.* dal(dır)ma; bat(ır)ma; dezenfektan banyo *(hayvanlar için)*; F deniz banyosu; yokuş, iniş; bayrak gibi bir şeyi indirip kaldırma.

**diph.the.ri.a** [dif'θiəriə] *n.* difteri.

**diph.thong** ['difθɔŋ] *n.* iki ünlünün bir hece oluşturması, diftong.

**di.plo.ma** [di'pləumə] *n.* diploma; **di'plo.ma.cy** *n.* diplomasi, diplomatlık; görüşmelerde ustalık, incelik; **dip.lo.mat** ['dipləmæt] *n.* diplomat, Dışişleri Bakanlığı memuru; görüşmelerde incelik gösteren kimse; **dip.lo'mat.ic, dip.lo'mat.i.cal** □ diplomatik, uluslararası siyasete ait; ilişkilerinde usta, siyasi; **dip.lo'mat.ics** *n. sg.* eski resmî belgeleri çözme ve gerçekliğini saptama ilmi; **di.plo.ma.tist** *n.* diplomat, siyaset adamı.

**dip.per** ['dipə] *n.* kepçe, maşrapa; *Am.* Big ♀ *ast.* Büyükayı; **'dip.py** *sl. adj.* deli.

**dip.so.ma.ni.a** [dipsəu'meinjə] *n.* içki tutkunluğu, ayyaşlık; **dip.so'ma.ni.ac** [*~*niæk] *n.* alkolik, ayyaş.

**dip-stick** ['dipstik] *n. (esp. mot)* daldırma çubuk ölçek.

**dire** ['daiə] *adj.* korkunç, müthiş, dehşetli; uğursuz.

**di.rect** [di'rekt] **1.** □ doğru, vasıtasız; açık, belirgin; içten, samimi, dürüst; tam; *~* current doğru akım; *~* hit tam isabet; *~* speech konuşmacının gerçek sözleri, dolaysız söz; *~* tax vasıtasız vergi; *~* train aktarmasız tren; **2.** *adv.* doğrudan doğruya; hemen, derhal; açıkça; *=* *~*ly **1**; **3.** *v/t.* doğrultmak, yöneltmek (to, towards, at *-e*); yol göstermek, idare etm.; düzenlemek; emretmek (to *-i*); zarfa adres yazmak; *~* to ulaştırmak; **di'rec.tion** *n.* yön, cihet, taraf; emir; düzenleme; idare, nezaret; **di'rec.tion.al** [*~*ʃənl] *adj. radyo:* yön saptamaya ait; **di'rec.tion-find.er** *n. radyo:* yön bulucu alet; sinyal alıcı alet; **di'rec.tion-find.ing** *n. radyo:* yön, sinyal bulma; *~* set yön bulma aleti; **di'rec.tion in.di.ca.tor** *mot.* yol, yön göstergesi; ⚓ rota göstergesi; **directions** *n. pl.* tarifname, kullanış tarzı; **di'rec.tive** *adj.* idare edici, yönlendirici; **di'rect.ly 1.** *adv.* doğrudan doğruya; **2.** *cj.* yapar yapmaz; **di'rect.ness** *n.* doğru gidiş; *fig.* doğruluk, dürüstlük.

**di.rec.tor** [di'rektə] *n.* direktör, müdür; *film:* rejisör; idare kurulu üyesi; *board of ~s* idare kurulu; **di'rec.to.rate** [*~*rit]

*n.* idare kurulu; müdürlük; *a.* **di'rec.tor.ship** müdürlük, direktörlük; **di'rec.to.ry** *n.* adres defteri; telephone *~* telefon rehberi.

**di.rec.tress** [di'rektris] *n.* müdire, kadın direktör.

**dire.ful** □ ['daiəful] korkunç, dehşet veren.

**dirge** [dəːdʒ] *n.* ağıt, mersiye.

**dir.i.gi.ble** ['diridʒəbl] **1.** *adj.* yönlendirilebilir; **2.** *n.* güdümlü balon *veya* hava gemisi.

**dirk** [dəːk] **1.** *n.* bir çeşit kama; **2.** *v/t.* hançerlemek.

**dirt** [dəːt] *n.* kir, pislik, çamur *(a. fig)*; treat s.o. like *~* *b-ni* hiçe saymak, hor görmek; fling *veya* throw *~* at s.o. *b-ni* çamura bulamak, iftira atmak; **'~-'cheap** F *adj.* sudan ucuz, bedava; **'~-track** *n. spor:* yarış yapılan toprak yol; **'dirt.y 1.** □ kirli *(a. fig.)* pis, bulanık; iğrenç, alçak; **2.** *v/t.* kirletmek, pisletmek, lekelemek.

**dis.a.bil.i.ty** [disə'biliti] *n.* kuvvetsizlik, yetersizlik; sakatlık; yetkisizlik.

**dis.a.ble** [dis'eibl] *v/t. (esp. savaşta)* sakatlamak, kuvvetten düşürmek, kullanılmaz hale getirmek; **dis'a.bled** *adj.* sakat, malul; **dis'able.ment** *n.* sakatlık; yetkisizlik.

**dis.a.buse** [disə'bjuːz] *v/t.* yanlış düşünceyi düzeltmek, *b-nin* gözünü açmak, aklını başına getirmek (of).

**dis.ac.cord** [disə'kɔːd] *v/i.* anlaşmazlık halinde olm. (with *ile*); *n.* anlaşmazlık, ihtilâf.

**dis.ac.cus.tom** ['disə'kʌstəm]: *~* s.o. to s. th. *v/t.* bir alışkanlıktan vazgeçirmek.

**dis.ad.van.tage** [disəd'vɑːntidʒ] *n.* mahzur, sakınca, aleyhte oluş; sell to *~* zararına satış; **dis.ad.van.ta.geous** □ [disædvɑːn'teidʒəs] sakıncalı, mahzurlu, zararlı; elverişsiz.

**dis.af.fect.ed** □ [disə'fektid] (to, towards *-e*) muhalif, aykırı, hoşnutsuz; **dis.af'fec.tion** *n.* antipati, isteksizlik, hoşnutsuzluk.

**dis.af.firm** 🕸 [disə'fəːm] *v/t.* reddetmek, bozmak.

**dis.af.for.est** [disə'fɔrist] *v/t.* ormanları tahrip etm. ormansız bırakmak.

**dis.a.gree** [disə'griː] *v/i.* uyuşamamak, anlaşamamak (with *ile*); araları açık olm. (on); uygun gelmemek (with *-e*); *(yiyecek)* dokunmak; **dis.a.gree.a.ble** □ [*~*'griəbl] nahoş, cansıkıcı, hoş olmayan *(a. fig.)*; **dis.a.gree.ment** *n.* anlaşmazlık, uyuşmazlık. çekişme.

dis.al.low ['disə¹lau] v/t. müsaade etmemek, engel olm.; reddetmek.

dis.ap.pear [disə¹piə] v/i. gözden kaybolmak; yok olmak; dis.ap.pear.ance [~¹piərəns] n. gözden kaybolma; yok olma.

dis.ap.point [disə¹point] v/t. hayal kırıklığına uğratmak; ümidini boşa çıkarmak, yarı yolda bırakmak; dis.ap¹point.ment n. hayal kırıklığı, hüsran; ~ in love karşılık görmeyen aşk.

dis.ap.pro.ba.tion [disæprəu¹beiʃən] n. beğenmeyiş, uygun görmeyiş, onaylamama.

dis.ap.prov.al [disə¹pruːvl] n. beğenmeyiş, ayıplama, onaylamama; dis.ap¹prove v/t. beğenmemek, uygun görmemek (of -i).

dis.arm [dis¹aːm] v/t. silahsızlandırmak; zararsız hale getirmek (a. fig.); v/i. silahları bırakmak, azaltmak; dis¹ar.ma.ment n. silahsızlanma, silahların sınırlandırılması, silahları bırakma.

dis.ar.range ['disə¹reindʒ] v/t. karıştırmak, -in düzenini bozmak; disar¹range.ment n. karışıklık, düzensizlik.

dis.ar.ray ['disə¹rei] 1. n. karışıklık; düzensiz kıyafet; 2. v/t. karıştırmak.

dis.as.sem.bly ⊕ [disə¹sembli] n. sökme, parçalara ayırma; dağılma.

dis.as.ter [di¹zaːstə] n. felâket, belâ, facia; dis¹as.trous ☐ felâket getiren, uğursuz, talihsiz, feci, dehşetli, korkunç.

dis.a.vow ['disə¹vau] v/t. inkâr etm., onaylamamak, tanımamak, tekzip etm., yalanlamak; dis.a¹vow.al n. inkâr, tanımama, onaylamama, tekzip.

dis.band [dis¹bænd] v/t. terhis etm., dağıtmak; v/i. dağılmak; dis¹band.ment n. dağılma; terhis.

dis.bar [dis¹baː] v/t. barodan ihraç etm.

dis.be.lief ['disbi¹liːf] n. imansızlık; güvensizlik; şüphe (in); dis.be.lieve [¹disbi¹liːv] v/t. inanmamak -e; şüphe etm.; dis.be¹liev.er n. inanmayan kimse, şüpheci.

dis.bud [dis¹bʌd] v/t. meyve ağaçlarının tomurcuklarını seyreltmek.

dis.bur.den [dis¹bəːdn] v/t. b-nin yükünü hafifletmek; kurtarmak (of); kalp ferahlatmak (a. fig.).

dis.burse [dis¹bəːs] v/t. ödemek; b-nin hesabına para vermek; dis¹burse.ment n. ödeme; harcama; ödenen para.

disc [disk] = disk.

dis.card 1. [dis¹kaːd] v/t. atmak, ihraç etm., azletmek; ıskartaya çıkarmak; kâğıt oyunu: boş kâğıt atmak; 2. ['dis.kaːd] n. oyun kâğıdı: ıskarta, boş kâğıt; esp. Am. çöp.

dis.cern [di¹səːn] v/t. ayırt etm., bşin far-

kına varmak, anlamak, kavramak; dis¹cern.i.ble ☐ farkedilebilir, görülebilir; dis¹cern.ing 1. ☐ anlayışlı, zeki; 2. n. anlama, kavrama; dis¹cern.ment n. idrak, kavrama, muhakeme; görüş, seziş.

dis.charge [dis¹tʃaːdʒ] 1. v/t. boşaltmak, tahliye etm.; terhis etm.; ↓ yük boşaltmak; ⚡ cereyanı boşaltmak; bşden affetmek; ateş etm.; ödemek (borç); yerine getirmek (görev); işten çıkarmak; öfkesini b-den çıkarmak; v/i. boşalmak, dökülmek; akmak (in); 2. n. boşaltma (a. ⚡ ); ↓ yük indirme; salıverme; terhis; işten çıkarılma; ateş etme; ödeme, ifa; makbuz; görev; cerahat; dis¹charg.er n. boşaltma işini yapan kişi ya da alet.

dis.ci.ple [di¹saipl] n. öğrenci, mürit; İsa paygamberin öğütlerini yaymakla görevlendirdiği oniki çömezi, havari; dis¹ci.ple.ship n. öğrencilik; havarilik.

dis.ci.pli.nar.i.an [disipli¹nɛəriən] n. sert amir, disiplini sağlayan kimse; he is a poor ~ disiplini sağlayamayan kimsedir; ¹dis.ci.pli.nar.y adj. disipline ait, eğitimsel; ¹dis.ci.pline 1. n. disiplin, terbiye; eğitim; cezalandırma; bilim dalı; 2. v/t. disiplin altına almak, terbiye etm.; cezalandırmak.

dis.claim [dis¹kleim] v/t. inkâr etm.; vazgeçmek -den; dis¹claim.er n. vazgeçme, feragat; tekzip, yalanlama.

dis.close [dis¹kləuz] v/t. ifşa etm., açmak; açığa çıkarmak; dis¹clo.sure [~ʒə] n. ifşa, açma.

dis.col.o(u)r [dis¹kʌlə] v/t. -in rengini bozmak, soldurmak, rengini değiştirmek; dis.col.o(u)r¹a.tion n. rengini bozma, soldurma, solma.

dis.com.fit [dis¹kʌmfit] v/t. yenmek, mağlûp etm.; sinirlendirmek; bozmak; dis¹com.fi.ture [~tʃə] n. yenilgi; şaşkınlık; bozgun.

dis.com.fort [dis¹kʌmfət] 1. n. rahatsızlık, sıkıntı, huzursuzluk; 2. v/t. rahatsız etm., sıkıntı vermek, üzmek.

dis.com.pose [diskəm¹pəuz] v/t. şaşırtmak, rahatını bozmak, düzenini bozmak; dis.com¹po.sure [~ʒə] n. rahatsızlık, kaygı, telaş.

dis.con.cert [diskən¹səːt] v/t. şaşırtmak; karıştırmak, telaşlandırmak.

dis.con.nect [¹diskə¹nekt] v/t. ayırmak, bağlantısını kesmek (from, with -den. -le); ⊕ durdurmak; birbirinden ayırmak; ⚡ fişi çözmek; ¹dis.con¹nect.ed ☐ bağlantısız; ¹dis.con¹nec.tion n. ayrılma; ⊕ bağlantının kesilmesi.

**dis.con.so.late** □ [diskɔnsəlit] teselli kabul etmez, çok kederli.

**dis.con.tent** [ˈdiskənˈtent] **1.** ✤ = ~ed; **2.** n. hoşnutsuzluk; ˈdis.conˈtent.ed □ hoşnutsuz.

**dis.con.tin.u.ance** [diskənˈtinjuəns] n. ara, duraklama, kesilme; vazgeçme; ˈdis.conˈtin.ue [~njuː] v/t. kesmek, devam etmemek -e; vazgeçmek -den; gazete: aboneyi kesmek; ˈdis.conˈtin.u.ous □ [~njuəs] düzensiz, fasılalı, aralıklı, ayrılmış.

**dis.cord** [ˈdiskɔːd], **disˈcord.ance** n. anlaşmazlık, uyuşmazlık; ♪ ahenksizlik; **disˈcord.ant** □ uyumsuz; farklı (to, from, with); aralarında anlaşmazlık bulunan; ♪ ahenksiz.

**dis.count** [ˈdiskaunt] **1.** n. † iskonto, tenzilât; at a ~ iskonto ile, değerinden ucuza; **2.** v/t. iskonto etm., hesaptan indirmek; çıkarmak (a. fig.); kır(dır)mak (senet, bono); **disˈcount.a.ble** adj. iskonto edilebilir; **disˈcoun.te.nance** [~tinəns] v/t. utandırmak; onaylamamak; cesaretini kırmak.

**dis.cour.age** [disˈkʌridʒ] v/t. -in cesaretini kırmak, gözdağı vermek, yıldırmak, vazgeçirmek (from -den); **disˈcour.age.ment** n. cesaretsizlik, hevesin kırılması; güçlük, zorluk.

**dis.course** [disˈkɔːs] **1.** n. söylev, nutuk; karşılıklı konuşma; bilimsel araştırma; **2.** v/t. (on, upon, about) bş. hakkında konuşmak, söylev vermek, konferans vermek; bşle ilgili görüşmek.

**dis.cour.te.ous** □ [disˈkeːtjəs] saygısız, kaba; **disˈcour.te.sy** [~tisi] n. saygısızlık, kabalık.

**dis.cov.er** [disˈkʌvə] v/t. keşfetmek, bulmak, ortaya çıkarmak; **disˈcov.er.a.ble** □ keşfedilebilir, ortaya çıkarılabilir; **disˈcov.er.er** n. bulucu, kâşif, ortaya çıkaran; **disˈcov.er.y** n. keşif, buluş, ortaya çıkarma; keşfedilen şey, bulgu.

**dis.cred.it** [disˈkredit] **1.** n. güvensizlik; şüphe; saygısızlık, itibarsızlık; **2.** v/t. kötülemek, itibardan düşürmek, güvenini sarsmak ,şüpheye düşürmek; **disˈcred.it.a.ble** □ ayıplanacak, onur kırıcı, küçük düşürücü.

**dis.creet** □ [disˈkriːt] ketum, ağzı sıkı, sır saklayan; tedbirli, akıllı, denli.

**dis.crep.an.cy** [disˈkrepənsi] n. ayrılık, anlaşmazlık ,zıtlık.

**dis.crete** □ [disˈkriːt] ayrı, farklı, ayrılmış.

**dis.cre.tion** [disˈkreʃən] n. ağzı sıkılık, ketumluk; akıllılık; naziklik; yetki;

banker's ~ bankanın hesabı gizli tutması; at one's ~ isteği doğrultusunda, istediği kadar, isteğe bağlı; age veya years of ~ cezaî ehliyet, aklın hakim olduğu yaşlar; surrender at ~ koşulsuz teslim; **disˈcre.tion.ar.y** [~ʃnəri] adj. isteğe bağlı, ihtiyari.

**dis.crim.i.nate** [disˈkrimineit] vb. ayırmak, ayırt etm.; ayırım yapmak, ayrı tutmak, fark gözetmek; ~ against farklı davranmak -e, daha kötü davranmak -e; **disˈcrim.i.nat.ing** □ ayırt eden; zevk sahibi olan, en iyiyi seçen, görüş sahibi olan; temyiz hakkı olan; **dis.crim.iˈna.tion** n. aleyhte davranma, ayırım, fark gözetme, temyiz; **disˈcrim.i.na.tive** [~nətiv] □ ayırt edici, fark gözeten; **disˈcrim.i.na.to.ry law** olağanüstü hal yasası.

**dis.cur.sive** □ [disˈkəːsiv] konudan konuya geçen, tutarsız; F daldan dala konan; phls. içeren, sonuca varan.

**dis.cus** [ˈdiskəs] n. spor: disk; disk atma oyunu.

**dis.cuss** [disˈkʌs] v/t. görüşmek, müzakere etm., tartışmak; F (yemek veya içki) tadına bakmak; **disˈcuss.i.ble** adj. tartışılabilir, müzakere edilebilir; **disˈcus.sion** n. görüşme, müzakere, tartışma.

**dis.dain** [disˈdein] **1.** n. hakaret, küçük görme; **2.** v/t. aşağısamak, hafifsemek, hor görmek; **disˈdain.ful** □ [~ful] hafifseyen, hor gören (of), küçümseyen, mağrur.

**dis.ease** [diˈziːz] n. hastalık, rahatsızlık, illet, maraz; **disˈeased** adj. hasta.

**dis.em.bark** [ˈdisimˈbaːk] v/t. & v/i. gemiden karaya çık(ar)mak; **dis.em.bar.ka.tion** [disəmbaːˈkeiʃən] n. karaya çık(ar)ma.

**dis.em.bar.rass** [ˈdisimˈbærəs] v/t. rahatlatmak; mahcubiyetten kurtarmak (of).

**dis.em.bod.y** [disimˈbɔdi] v/t. bedenden ayırmak; ✗ terhis etm.

**dis.em.bogue** [disimˈbəug] v/t. & v/i. (nehir) denize dök(ül)mek; ak(ıt)mak.

**dis.em.bow.el** [disimˈbauəl] v/t. bağırsaklarını çıkarmak.

**dis.em.broil** [disimˈbrɔil] v/t. karışık ve zor durumdan kurtarmak.

**dis.en.chant** [ˈdisinˈtʃaːnt] v/t. büyüden kurtarmak; ayıltmak, aklını başına getirmek.

**dis.en.cum.ber** [ˈdisinˈkʌmbə] v/t. b-ni yük veya sıkıntıdan kurtarmak (of, from).

**dis.en.gage** [ˈdisinˈgeidʒ] v/t. ayırmak; çözmek; ⊕ kavramayı gevşetmek; mot. debriyaj yapmak; **dis.enˈgaged** adj. serbest, boş; **¹dis.en¹gage.ment** *n.* ilgiyi kesme; salıverme, serbest bırakma.

**dis.en.tan.gle** [ˈdisinˈtæŋgl] *v/t. & v/i.* çıkarmak, çöz(ül)mek, kurtulmak (from *-den*); *fig.* serbest bırakmak (from *-den*); **¹dis.en¹tan.gle.ment** *n.* çözülme, serbest kalma.

**dis.en.tomb** [disinˈtuːm] *v/t.* kazmak, hafriyat yapmak, mezardan kazıp çıkarmak.

**dis.e.qui.lib.ri.um** [ˈdisekwiˈlibriəm] *n.* dengesizlik, denksizlik.

**dis.es.tab.lish** [ˈdisisˈtæbliʃ] *v/t. (kilise)* devletten ayırmak, ilişkisini kesmek; **dis.es¹tab.lish.ment** *n.* devletle olan ilişkisini kesme.

**dis.fa.vo(u)r** [ˈdisˈfeivə] **1.** *n.* gözden düşme; *b-nin* hoşuna gitmeme; isteksizlik; **2.** *v/t.* gözden düşürmek, istememek; hoşlanmamak; onaylamamak.

**dis.fig.ure** [disˈfigə] *v/t.* çirkinleştirmek, şeklini bozmak; **dis¹fig.ure.ment** *n.* çirkinleştirme, şekilsizlik.

**dis.fran.chise** [ˈdisˈfræntʃaiz] *v/t.* oy verme *veya* vatandaşlık hakkından yoksun bırakmak; **dis.fran.chise.ment** [disˈfræntʃizmənt] *n.* vatandaşlık haklarından yoksun etme, oy verme hakkını elinden alma.

**dis.frock** [disˈfrɔk] *v/t.* papazlık hakkını elinden almak.

**dis.gorge** [disˈgɔːdʒ] *v/t.* kusmak; boşaltmak; çalınan *bşi* geri vermek.

**dis.grace** [disˈgreis] **1.** *n.* gözden düşme; yüz karası, utanç; **2.** *v/t* gözden düşürmek; rezil etm.; be ~d rezil olm.; **dis¹grace.ful** □ [~ful] ayıp, yüz kızartıcı, rezil.

**dis.grun.tled** [disˈgrʌntld] *adj.* üzgün, canı sıkılmış.

**dis.guise** [disˈgaiz] **1.** *v/t. & v/i.* kıyafet değiştirmek; ses vs. tanınmaz hale getirmek; gizle(n)mek, sakla(n)mak; **2.** *n.* kıyafet değiştirme, gizlenme; blessing in ~ gizli ama gerçek.

**dis.gust** [disˈgʌst] **1.** *n.* nefret, tiksinme, iğrenme (at, for *-den*); **2.** *v/t.* tiksindirmek, bıktırmak; be ~ed with nefret etm., kızmak, bıkmak *-den*; **dis¹gust.ing** □ iğrenç, tiksindirici, nefret uyandırıcı.

**dish** [diʃ] **1.** *n.* tabak, çanak; yemek; *sl.* güzel kız; the ~es *pl.* sofra takımı (*tabak, çatal, kaşık vs.*); standing ~ *fig.* hep güncel olan konu, temcid pilavı; **2.** *v/t.* tabağa koymak; *mst* ~ up sofraya koymak; sunmak için hazırlamak (*a. fig.*); *sl.* aldatmak; berbat etm.

**dis.ha.bille** [disæˈbiːl] *n.* sabahlık, ev elbisesi; yarı giyinik olma.

**dish-cloth** [ˈdiʃklɔθ] *n.* tabak yıkama *veya* durulama bezi.

**dis.heart.en** [disˈhɑːtn] *v/t.* cesaretini kırmak, ümidini kırmak.

**di.shev.el(l)ed** [diˈʃevəld] *adj. (saç, giyim)* darmadağınık, düzensiz; *fig.* pasaklı.

**dis.hon.est** □ [disˈɔnist] namussuz, haysiyetsiz, şerefsiz; **dis¹hon.est.y** *n.* namussuzluk, sahtekârlık.

**dis.hon.o(u)r** [disˈɔnə] **1.** *n.* namussuzluk, yüzkarası, leke, ayıp, alçaklık; **2.** *v/t.* -*in* namusuna leke sürmek; *-in* ırzına geçmek; *poliçe:* kabul etmemek, ödememek; **dis¹hon.o(u)r.a.ble** □ namussuz, haysiyetsiz.

**dish...:** **¹~.pan** *n. Am.* bulaşık kabı; **¹~.rag** *Am.* = dish-cloth; **¹~.wash.er** bulaşıkçı, bulaşık yıkama makinesi; **¹~.wa.ter** *n.* bulaşık suyu.

**dis.il.lu.sion** [disiˈluːʒən] **1.** *n.* hayal kırıklığı, gözünü açma; **2.** *v/t.* hayal kırıklığına uğratmak, gerçekleri göstermek; *fig.* aklını başına getirmek; **dis.il¹lu.sion.ment** = disillusion 1.

**dis.in.cen.tive** [disinˈsentiv] *n.* yıldırma, gözünü korkutma.

**dis.in.cli.na.tion** [disinkliˈneiʃən] *n.* isteksizlik, gönülsüzlük (for, to *-e*); **dis.in.cline** [ˈ~ˈklain] *v/t.* *bşden*, *b-den* soğutmak, caydırmak; **¹dis.in¹clined** *adj.* isteksiz (for, to *-e*).

**dis.in.fect** [disinˈfekt] *v/t.* dezenfekte etm.; **dis.in¹fect.ant** *n.* antiseptik ilaç, dezenfektan; **dis.in¹fec.tion** *n.* dezenfekte etme.

**dis.in.fla.tion** [disinˈfleiʃən] *n.* enflasyondan fiyat ve ücretlerin çok değişmediği duruma geçme, paranın satın alma gücünün yükseltilmesi.

**dis.in.gen.u.ous** □ [disinˈdʒenjuəs] samimi olmayan, iki yüzlü.

**dis.in.her.it** [ˈdisinˈherit] *v/t.* mirastan yoksun bırakmak, reddetmek; **dis.in¹her.it.ance** *n.* mirastan yoksunluk.

**dis.in.te.grate** [disˈintigreit] *v/t.* parçalara ayırmak, ayrıştırmak; *v/i.* parçalanmak, ayrışmak; **dis.in.te¹gra.tion** *n.* ayrılıp dağılma.

**dis.in.ter** [ˈdisinˈtəː] *v/t.* kazıp çıkarmak, eşmek.

**dis.in.ter.est.ed** □ [disˈintristid] tarafsız, önyargısız, çıkar gözetmeyen.

**dis.join** [disˈdʒɔin] *v/t.* ayırmak; **dis.joint** [ˈ~ˈdʒɔint] *v/t.* düzenini bozmak; ayırmak; sökmek; **dis.joint.ed** *adj.* ayrılmış; düzensiz, tutarsız (*söz*).

**dis.junc.tion** [disˈdʒʌŋkʃən] *n.* ayrılma;

**dis·junc·tive** ☐ [~tiv] ayıran; *gr.* bağlaç.

**disk** [disk] *n.* yuvarlak levha, disk, kurs; plâk; ~ **brake** *mot.* fren diski; ~ **clutch** *mot.* kavrama diski, debriyaj diski; ~**·har·row** *n.* keskin çarklarla işleyen tırmık; ~ **jock·ey** plâk sunucusu, disk-cokey.

**dis·like** [dis'laik] 1. *n.* beğenmeyiş, antipati (for, of, to *-e*); 2. *v/t.* beğenmemek, sevmemek; *b̦den, b-den* hoşlanmamak; ~d *adj.* sevilmeyen.

**dis·lo·cate** ['dislʌukeit] *v/t.* yerinden çıkarmak, yerinden oynatmak; *fig.* altüst etm., şaşırtmak; **dis·lo·ca·tion** *n.* ⚓ çıkık; yer değiştirme (*esp.* ✕); *geol.* yeryüzü tabakasını delip açma; *fig.* şaşırtma.

**dis·lodge** [dis'lɔdʒ] *v/t.* yerinden çıkarmak; defetmek; siperden çıkarmak; evden taşınmak.

**dis·loy·al** ☐ ['dis'lɔiəl] sadık olmayan, vefasız; **dis·loy·al·ty** *n.* sadakatsizlik, vefasızlık, hıyanet.

**dis·mal** ['dizməl] 1. ☐ *fig.* kederli, sıkıntılı, kasvetli, sönük; 2. **the** ~**s** *pl.* F melankoli, kuruntu.

**dis·man·tle** [dis'mæntl] *v/t.* sökmek; (*kale*) yerle bir etm.; ⚓ armasını soymak; (*ev*) eşyasını boşaltmak; ⊕ parçalara ayırmak; ⊕ makinaları sökmek; **dis·'man·tling** *n.* sökme; boşaltma; parçalara ayırma.

**dis·mast** ⚓ [dis'mɑːst] *v/t.* gemi direğini çıkarmak.

**dis·may** [dis'mei] 1. *n.* korku, dehşet, şaşkınlık, endişe; 2. *v/t.* korkutmak, ürkütmek, yıldırmak.

**dis·mem·ber** [dis'membə] *v/t.* parçalamak; uzuvları gövdeden ayırmak; **dis·'mem·ber·ment** *n.* parçala(n)ma.

**dis·miss** [dis'mis] *v/t.* işten çıkarmak, yol vermek *-e*; reddetmek; gitmesine izin vermek; (*konu, fikir*) vazgeçmek; ♂♂ davayı reddetmek; be ~ed the service işten atılmak; *v/t.* ✕ saftan çıkmak; **dis·'miss·al** *n.* yol verme, azledilme; izin; ♂♂ davanın reddi.

**dis·mount** ['dis'maunt] *v/t.* (*bisiklet veya attan*) indirmek; ⊕ parçalara ayırmak; sökmek; *v/i.* attan inmek.

**dis·o·be·di·ence** [disə'biːdjəns] *n.* itaatsizlik; **dis·o·be·di·ent** ☐ itaatsiz (to *-e*); **dis·o·'bey** *v/t.* itaat etmemek *-e*; söz dinlememek.

**dis·o·blige** ['disə'blaidʒ] *v/t.* hatırını kırmak, ricasını kabul etmemek, gücendirmek; **dis·o·'blig·ing** ☐ nezaketsiz, hatır kıran, aksi; **dis·o·'blig·ing·ness** *n.* nezaketsizlik, kabalık.

**dis·or·der** [dis'ɔːdə] 1. *n.* karışıklık; rahatsızlık; ⚡ hastalık; mental ~ aklî dengesizlik; 2. *v/t.* düzenini bozmak, rahatsız etm.; **dis·or·dered** ☐ düzensiz, karışık; bozuk (*mide*); **dis·or·der·ly** *adj.* düzensiz; itaatsiz; çapaçul; rahatsız.

**dis·or·gan·i·za·tion** [disɔːgənai'zeiʃən] *n.* düzensizlik, karışıklık; **dis·or·gan·ize** *v/t.* düzenini bozmak *-in*; karıştırmak *-i*.

**dis·o·ri·en·tate** [dis'ɔːrienteit] *v/t. b-nin* yolunu şaşırtmak, zihnini karıştırmak; he was ~d yönünü şaşırdı.

**dis·own** [dis'əun] *v/t.* inkâr etm., yadsımak, tanımamak, reddetmek.

**dis·par·age** [dis'pæridʒ] *v/t.* kötülemek *-i*, hor görmek *-i*, *b-nin* şeref ve onuruna leke sürmek, küçük düşürmek *-i*; **dis·'par·age·ment** *n.* kötüleme, aşağılama; **dis·'par·ag·ing** ☐ aşağılayıcı, hor gören.

**dis·pa·rate** ['dispərit] 1. ☐ eşit olmayan, farklı; 2. ~**s** *n. pl.* kıyaslanamayacak ölçüde farklı şeyler; **dis·par·i·ty** [dis'pæriti] *n.* eşitsizlik, farklılık.

**dis·part** [dis'pɑːt] *v/t.* ikiye ayırmak; *v/i.* ikiye ayrılmak; ⊕ çapını ayar etm.

**dis·pas·sion·ate** ☐ [dis'pæʃnit] tarafsız, soğukkanlı, sakin.

**dis·patch** [dis'pætʃ] 1. *n.* acele; göndermek; rapor, haber; telgraf; öldürme, idam etme; mentioned in ~es savaştaki kahramanlığı raporda belirtilmiş; happy ~ harakiri; 2. *v/t.* süratle tamamlamak (*a.* = öldürmek); göndermek; **dis·'patch-box** *n.* resmî evrak çantası; **dis·'patch-goods** *n. pl.* ekspresle gönderilen eşya; **dis·'patch-rider** *n.* ✕ haberci.

**dis·pel** [dis'pel] *v/t.* defetmek, uzaklaştırmak, dağıtmak (*a. fig.*).

**dis·pen·sa·ble** [dis'pensəbl] *adj.* vazgeçilebilir, zorunlu olmayan; **dis·'pen·sa·ry** *n.* dispanser; eczane; **dis·pen·sa·tion** [dispen'seiʃən] *n.* dağıtma, bölme; takdiri ilahi; dağıtma bırakma.

**dis·pense** [dis'pens] *v/t.* dağıtmak; hazırlamak (*ilâç reçetesi*); üstesinden gelmek; ~ from muaf tutmak, *b̦den* affetmek; *b-ne* işten el çektirmek; *v/i.* ~ with vazgeçmek *-den*; *b̦şe* muhtaç olmamak; **dis·'pens·er** *n.* ilâç hazırlayan kimse; dağıtıcı.

**dis·per·sal** [dis'pəːsəl] = dispersion; **dis·'perse** *v/t.* dağıtmak, yaymak; *v/i.* ayrılmak, dağılmak; **dis·'per·sion** *n.* dağıtma (*a. opt.*), dağılma, dağıtım, yayılma.

**dis·pir·it** [di'spirit] *v/t.* cesaretini kırmak, keyfini kaçırmak; **dis·'pir·it·ed** ☐ cesaretsiz ,yüreksiz, keyifsiz.

**dis·place** [dis'pleis] *v/t.* yerinden çıkarmak, götürmek; yerine başka b$i (b-ni) geçirmek; b-ni azletmek; ~d person ülkesini terketmeye zorlanan kimse; dis-'place.ment n. yerinden çıkar(ıl)ma; bir geminin boşalttığı suyun ağırlığı; yer değişme.

dis.play [dis'plei] 1. n. gösteriş, nümayiş, teşhir; 2. v/t. göstermek, teşhir etm., göz önüne sermek, vurgulamak.

dis.please [dis'pli:z] v/t. b-nin hoşuna gitmemek; fig. gücendirmek; dis'pleased ☐ dargın, kızgın (at, with -e); dis'pleasing ☐ can sıkıcı, hoş olmayan; dis.pleas-ure [~'pleʒə] n. gücenme, hoşnutsuzluk, can sıkıntısı (at, over).

dis.port [dis'pɔːt] vb.: ~ o.s. neşe içinde koşuşturmak; eğlenmek, oyna(ş)mak.

dis.pos.a.ble [dis'pəuzəbl] adj. elde hazır bulunan; gerektiğinde kullanılabilen; bir kez kullanılıp atılan; dis'pos.al n. tertip, düzen; bertaraf etme, tasarruf hakkı (of); satma, satış, başkasına verme, elden çıkarma; at one's ~ b-nin emrine âmade, hizmetinde; dis'pose vb. düzenlemek; dağıtmak; idare etm.; b$e sebep olm. (for, to); ~ of -in tasarrufunda olm.; kullanmak -i; bertaraf etm. -i; satmak; k-ni yiyip bitirmek; dis'posed ☐ hazır (to, for -e); well (ill) ~ towards s.o. b-ne arkadaşça (düşmanca) davranış, yaklaşım; dis.po.si.tion [~pə'ziʃən] n. düzen; eğilim; tabiat, huy; tasarruf hakkı (of).

dis.pos.sess [dispə'zes] (of) v/t. malına mülküne el koymak, yoksun bırakmak; evden çıkarmak; fig. bir alışkanlıktan vazgeçmek; dis.pos.ses.sion [~'seʃən] n. mal ve mülke el konulması; evden çıkar(ıl)ma.

dis.praise [dis'preiz] 1. n. kötüleme, azarlama, ayıplama; 2. v/t. kötülemek, azarlamak; b-ne, b$e hor bakmak.

dis.proof ['dis'pruːf] n. aksini kanıtlama; ret.

dis.pro.por.tion [disprə'pɔːʃən] n. oransızlık; dis.pro'por.tion.ate ☐ [~ʃnit] oransız, gereğinden fazla, aşırı; dis.pro'por-tion.ate.ness n. oransızlık; 'dis.pro'por-tioned [~ʃənd] = disproportionate.

dis.prove [dis'pruːv] v/t. yanlış olduğunu göstermek, aksini kanıtlamak.

dis.pu.ta.ble [dis'pjuːtəbl] adj. yadsınabilir, inkâr edilebilir, tartışılır; dis'pu.tant n. tartışmacı; dis.pu'ta.tion n. tartışma, münakaşa; dis.pu'ta.tious ☐ münakaşacı, kavgacı; dis'pute 1. n. münakaşa, kavga, tartışma; in ~ münakaşalı, ihtilâflı; beyond (all) ~, past ~ tartışma götürmez, apaçık; 2. v/t. tartışmak, kabul etme-

mek; v/i. münakaşa etm., kavga etm. (about).

dis.qual.i.fi.ca.tion [diskwɔlifi'keiʃən] n. yetkisizlik, ehliyetsizlik; spor: oyundan çıkarma cezası; engel; dis'qual.i.fy [~fai] v/t. yetkisiz kılmak (for); spor: oyundan atmak, diskalifiye etm.

dis.qui.et [dis'kwaiət] 1. n. merak, endişe; 2. v/t. huzurunu kaçırmak, endişe vermek, üzmek; dis.qui.e.tude [~'kwaiit-juːd] n. rahatsızlık, üzüntü.

dis.qui.si.tion [diskwi'ziʃən] n. araştırma, tetkik; nutuk, söylev (on).

dis.re.gard ['disri'gɑːd] 1. n. ihmal, kayıtsızlık, saymayış; 2. v/t. ihmal etm., saymamak, aldırmamak, önemsememek.

dis.rel.ish [dis'reliʃ] 1. n. tiksinme, beğenmeyiş, nefret (for); 2. v/t. hoşlanmamak, tiksinmek.

dis.re.pair ['disri'pɛə] n. tamire muhtaç olma, viranlık, bakımsızlık; fall into ~ bakıma muhtaç hale gelmek.

dis.rep.u.ta.ble [dis'repjutəbl] rezil; itibarsız; dis.re.pute [~ri'pjuːt] n. kötü şöhret, itibarsızlık.

dis.re.spect ['disris'pekt] n. saygısızlık, kabalık; dis.re'spect.ful [~ful] ☐ saygısız, kaba, hürmetsiz.

dis.robe [dis'rəub] v/t. & v/i. soy(un)-mak; elbisesini çıkarmak.

dis.root [dis'ruːt] v/t. kökünden sökmek.

dis.rupt [dis'rʌpt] v/t. yarmak, ayırmak; dis'rup.tion n. parçalama, kırılma, ayrılma, engel olma.

dis.sat.is.fac.tion ['dissætis'fækʃən] n. hoşnutsuzluk, tatminsizlik; dis.sat.is.fac.to-ry [~'fæktəri] adj. uygun olmayan, hoşnutsuz kılan, tatmin etmeyen; 'dis'sat.is-fied [~faid] adj. hoşnutsuz, memnun olmayan; 'dis'sat.is.fy [~fai] v/t. memnun etmemek, tatmin etmemek, b-nin hoşuna gitmemek.

dis.sect [di'sekt] vb. parçalara ayırmak; anat. kadavrada çalışmak; fig. bir konuyu en ince ayrıntılarıyle anlatmak, açımlamak; dis'sec.tion n. parçalama; anat. otopsi; fig. analiz, tahlil.

dis.sem.ble [di'sembl] v/t. gizlemek, saklamak; görmezlikten gelmek; v/i. b-ne karşı sahte tavır takınmak, iki yüzlülük etm.

dis.sem.i.nate [di'semineit] v/t. saçmak, yaymak; dis.sem.i'na.tion n. saç(ıl)ma; yay(ıl)ma.

dis.sen.sion [di'senʃən] n. ihtilâf, çekişme.

dis.sent [di'sent] 1. n. ihtilâf, ayrılık, reddetme; 2. v/i. bir konuda ayrılmak (from -den); aynı görüşte olmamak (with -le);

Anglikan kilisesinden ayrılmak; **dis'sent-er** *n.* muhalif; kiliseden ayrılan; **dis'sen-tient** [~ʃiənt] 1. *adj.* muhalif olan; 2. *n.* muhalif.

**dis.ser.ta.tion** [disə:'teiʃən] *n.* bilimsel araştırma; nutuk, söylev (on).

**dis.serv.ice** ['dis'sə:vis] *n.* (to) kötülük, zarar.

**dis.sev.er** [dis'sevə] *v/t.* tamamen ayırmak, kesip ayırmak; **dis'sev.er.ance, dis-'sev.er.ment** *n.* ayrılık, ayrılma.

**dis.si.dence** ['disidəns] *n.* fikir ayrılığı, karşı koyma, muhalefet; **'dis.si.dent** 1. *adj.* muhalif, karşı koyan; 2. *n.* muhalif, karşı gelen kimse.

**dis.sim.i.lar** □ ['di'similə] farklı (to, from *-den*); **dis.sim.i.lar.i.ty** [~'læriti] *n.* başkalık, farklılık, benzemeyiş (to).

**dis.sim.u.late** [di'simjuleit] = dissemble; **dis.sim.u'lation** *n.* iki yüzlülük, sahte tavır.

**dis.si.pate** ['disipeit] *v/t.* dağıtmak; israf etm., har vurup harman savurmak; *v/i.* dağılmak; müsrif olm.; harcanmak; **'dis.si.pat.ed** *adj.* müsrif; sefih; hovarda; **dis.si'pa.tion** *n.* zevk ve eğlenceye düşkünlük, sefahat.

**dis.so.ci.ate** [di'səuʃieit] *v/t.* ayırmak; ~ o.s. *bşden* ilgisini kesmek, ayrı tutmak ayrılmak (from *-den*); **dis.so.ci.a-tion** [~si'eiʃən] *n.* ayırma, ayrılma; *psych.* düşüncelerin duygulardan ayrıldığı ana ortaya çıkan müdafaa mekanizması, şahsiyetin çözülmesi.

**dis.sol.u.bil.i.ty** [disɔlju'biliti] *n.* çözülebilirlik, ayrılabilirlik; **dis'sol.u.ble** [~jubl] *adj.* erir, eritilebilir; çözülebilir; feshedilebilir.

**dis.so.lute** [di'zɔlu:t] ahlâksız, sefih, çapkın; **dis.so'lu.tion** *n.* eri(t)me; sona erme; ölüm.

**dis.solv.a.ble** [di'zɔlvəbl] *adj.* erir, eritilebilir; çözülebilir; feshedilebilir; **dis-'solve** 1. *v/t.* eritmek; feshetmek; çözmek, halletmek *(a. fig.)*; *v/i.* erimek; *fig.* eriyip gitmek; 2. *n. Am. film:* resmi yeni bir resim ile yavaş yavaş ortadan kaldırma; **dis'solv.ent** 1. *adj.* eritici, çözücü; 2. *n.* eritici madde.

**dis.so.nance** ['disənəns] *n.* ♪ ahenksizlik, uyumsuzluk; akortsuzluk; **'dis.so.nant** *adj.* ♪ ahenksiz; akortsuz; *fig.* farklı olan (from *-den*).

**dis.suade** [di'sweid] *v/t.* vazgeçirmek, caydırmak (from *-den*); **dis'sua.sion** [~ʒən] *n.* vazgeçirme; **dis'sua.sive** [~siv] □ caydırıcı.

**dis.taff** ['distɑ:f] *n.* öreke, yün eğirmekte kullanılan bir ucu çatal değnek; *fig.* kadın işi; ~ side ailenin kadın tarafı.

**dis.tance** ['distəns] 1. *n.* mesafe; uzaklık; ara; menzil; at a ~ uzakta; belirli bir mesafede; in the ~ uzakta; a great ~ away oldukça uzak; striking ~ vurulabilecek uzaklık; tesir sahası; keep one's ~ mesafe bırakmak, sokulmamak; keep s.o. at a ~ fazla samimi olmamak; 2. *v/t.* geride bırakmak *(a. fig.)*; **'dis.tant** □ uzak, ırak; soğuk, mesafeli; ~ control uzaktan kontrol.

**dis.taste** ['dis'teist] *n.* tiksinme, nefret (for); hoşlanmayış; *fig.* antipati (for); **dis'taste.ful** □ iğrenç, nahoş, antipatik.

**dis.tem.per¹** [dis'tempə] 1. *n.* su ile inceltilebilen bir tür boya; 2. *v/t.* bu boya ile boyamak.

**dis.tem.per²** [~] *n.* bir tür köpek hastalığı; *pol.* rahatsızlık; **dis'tem.pered** *adj.* çılgın, hasta, deli.

**dis.tend** [dis'tend] *v/t. & v/i.* şiş(ir)mek; yay(ıl)mak; ger(il)mek; **dis'ten.sion** *n.* şişme, yayılma, gerilme.

**dis.tich** ['distik] *n.* beyit, iki mısra.

**dis.til(l)** ['dis'til] *vb.* imbikten çek(il)mek; ⌃ damıtmak; *fig.* sızdırmak; damla damla ak(ıt)mak; *(kitap, fikir, konu)* özünü çıkarmak *veya* almak; **dis.til.late** ['~lit] *n.* damıtılmış sıvı, öz; **dis.til.la-tion** [~'leiʃən] *n.* damıtma, öz; **dis'till.er** *n.* viski, rakı gibi alkollü içki imal eden kimse; **dis'till.er.y** *n.* içki imal edilen yer.

**dis.tinct** □ [dis'tiŋkt] ayrı, farklı; belli, açık; **dis'tinc.tion** *n.* ayırma, ayırt etme, temayüz, üstünlük; nişan; draw a ~ be tween arasında farklılık yaratmak; have the ~ of üstünlük veya farklılığa sahip olm.; **dis'tinc.tive** □ ayıran, özellik belirten, orijinal, karakteristik (of); **dis-'tinct.ness** *n.* fark, çeşitlilik; açıklık.

**dis.tin.guish** [dis'tiŋwiʃ] *v/t.* ayırmak, ayırt etm.; anlamak; sivrilmek, temayüz etm.; **dis'tin.guish.a.ble** *adj.* ayırt edilebilir, farkedilebilir; **dis'tin.guished** *adj.* seçkin, mümtaz, kibar, meşhur.

**dis.tort** [dis'tɔ:t] *v/t.* bükmek, burkmak; *fig.* yanlış anlam vermek, saptırmak; bozmak, tahrif etm.; ~ing mirror eğlence aynası, dev aynası; **dis'tor.tion** *(söz)* ters anlam verme; çarpıklık, bozukluk.

**dis.tract** [dis'trækt] *v/t.* *(kişi veya aklını)* başka yöne çekmek; rahatsız etm.; şaşırtmak; **dis'tract.ed** □ şaşırmış, deli, çılgın; *k-den* geçmiş (with *ile)*; **dis'tract.ing** □ deli eden, çıldırtan; **dis'trac.tion** *n.* karışıklık; eğlence; çılgınlık; dikkati başka yöne çekme.

**dis.train** [dis'trein] *v/i.* haczetmek (on, upon); **dis'train.a.ble** *adj.* haczolunabilir; **dis.traint** [~'treint] *n.* haciz, el koyma.

**dis.traught** [dis'trɔːt] *adj.* aklı başından gitmiş, çılgın.

**dis.tress** [dis'tres] **1.** *n.* sıkıntı, zaruret, dert, ıstırap; tehlike; = distraint; ~ rocket ⚓ tehlike işareti; **2.** *v/t.* sıkıntıya sokmak, rahatsız etm., canını sıkmak, ıstırap çektirmek; **dis'tressed** *adj.* endişeli; sıkıntı çeken (for için); ~ area işsizliğin yoğun olduğu bölge; **dis'tress.ful** □ [~ful] *lit.* ıstıraplı, keder verici, acıklı; **dis'tress.ing** □ eziyetli; acıklı.

**dis.trib.ut.a.ble** [dis'tribjutəbl] *adj.* dağıtılabilir, yayılabilir; **dis'trib.ute** [~juːt] *v/t.* dağıtmak, yaymak (among, to); bölüştürmek, taksim etm. (mal); *typ.* yazı harflerini yerlerine dağıtmak; **dis.tri'bu.tion** *n.* dağıtım; yayılma; taksim etme; **dis-'trib.u.tive** *adj.* dağıtan, yayan; *gr.* «her», «her bir» gibi sıfatların anlamını ifade eden **dis'trib.u.tor** *n.* dağıtan; ⊕ distribütör; † satıcı, dağıtım yeri.

**dis.trict** ['distrikt] *n.* bölge; ilçe, kaza, mahalle.

**dis.trust** [dis'trʌst] **1.** *n.* güvensizlik, şüphe (of); **2.** *v/t.* inanmamak, güvenmemek -e); **dis'trust.ful** □ [~ful] şüpheci, kuşkulu; ~ (of o.s.) çekingen, utangaç.

**dis.turb** [dis'təːb] *v/t.* karıştırmak, düzenini bozmak; rahatsız etm.; **dis'turb.ance** *n.* karışıklık; rahatsızlık; ~ of the peace ☏ b·nin hak ve hukukuna saldırı, güvenliğin bozulması; **dis'turb.er** *n.* huzuru bozan.

**dis.un.ion** ['dis'juːnjən] *n.* ayrılma; anlaşmazlık, ara bozukluğu; **dis.u.nite** ['~'nait] *vb.* ayrılmak; aralarını bozmak, ayırmak.

**dis.use 1.** ['dis'juːs] *n.* kullanılmayış; fall into ~ kullanılmaz olm.; **2.** ['dis'juːz] *v/t.* bşi artık kullanmamak; **dis.used** *adj.* eski, vaktini doldurmuş.

**di.syl.lab.ic** ['disi'læbik] *adj.* (~ally) iki heceli; **di.syl.la.ble** [di'siləbl] *n.* iki heceli sözcük.

**ditch** [ditʃ] **1.** *n.* hendek; die in the last ~ sonuna kadar dayanmak; **2.** *v/t.* hendeğe yuvarlamak; *v/i.* hendek açmak; hendekle çevirmek; *Am. sl.* kurtulmak, kaçmak -den; **'ditch.er** *n.* hendek açan kimse ya da makine.

**dith.er** ['diðə] *v/i.* titremek; şaşırıp kalmak.

**dith.y.ramb** ['diθiræmb] *n.* coşkulu ve duygulu bir deyişle yazılmış yazı, şiir.

**dit.to** ['ditəu] *adj.* yukarıdaki gibi; aynen; *adv.* keza, aynı veçhile, gibi; (suit of) ~s aynı tip elbise, üniforma.

**dit.ty** ['diti] *n.* şarkı sözü.

**di.ur.nal** □ [dai'əːnl] günlük; gündüze ait, gündüz olan.

**di.va.ga.tion** [daivə'geiʃən] *n.* sapma, ayrılma, konu dışına çıkma.

**di.van** [di'væn] *n.* sedir, divan; ~-bed ['daivænbed] *n.* divan, yatak.

**di.var.i.cate** [dai'værikeit] *v/i.* çatallaşmak; *biol.* kollara, şubelere ayrılmak.

**dive** [daiv] **1.** *v/i.* dalmak (into -e); 🕇 pike yapmak; F başını eğmek, sinmek; ~ into elini daldırmak; **2.** *n.* yüzme: dalış, balıklama dalma (a. fig.); batakhane; pike uçuşu, baş aşağı dalış; *Am.* F *boks:* rakibin kasıtlı olarak yenmesini sağlama; '~-bomb *v/t.* dalış yaparak bombalamak; **'div.er** *n.* dalgıç.

**di.verge** [dai'vəːdʒ] *v/i.* birbirinden ayrılmak, farklı olm.; **di'ver.gence, di'vergen.cy** *n.* ayrılma, uzaklaşma; **di'vergent** □ birbirine karşı, muhalif, farklı.

**di.vers** ['daivəːz] *adj.* muhtelif, çeşitli.

**di.verse** □ [dai'vəːs] çeşitli, değişik; **di.ver.si.fi.ca.tion** [~fiˈkeiʃən] *n.* çeşitlilik, değişiklik; **di'ver.si.fy** [~fai] *v/t.* çeşitli ve değişik şekle sokmak; **di.ver.sion** [dai'vəːʃən] *n.* başka tarafa çevirme, saptırma; eğlence; **di'ver.sion.a.ry** *n.* ✗ şaşırtma hareketi, taktikler; **di'ver.si.ty** [~siti] *n.* fark, başkalık, çeşit, tür.

**di.vert** [dai'vəːt] *v/t.* saptırmak; (trafik) başka yöne çevirmek; eğlendirmek.

**di.vest** [dai'vest] *v/t.* soymak, çıkarmak; mahrum etm.; ~ o.s. of bşden özveride bulunmak, k-ni yoksun bırakmak; **di'vest.ment** *n.* soy(ul)ma; yoksun ol(un)-ma.

**di.vide** [di'vaid] **1.** *v/t. usu.* ~ up bölmek, ayırmak, taksim etm. (among); dağıtmak; aralarını açmak; ⚖ bölmek (by); ayrılmak, bölünmek (into); *parl.* oy vermek; **2.** *n.* su bölümü çizgisi; **div.i.dend** ['dividend] *n.* † kâr hissesi; temettü; ⚖ bölünen; **'div.i.dend-war.rant** † kupon (esham ve tahvilat); **di.vi.ders** [di'vaidəz] *n. pl.* pergel; **di'vid.ing** bölen...; ~ ridge su bölüm çizgisi; çatı sırtı.

**div.i.na.tion** [divi'neiʃən] *n.* fal açma, kehanette bulunma; **di.vine** [di'vain] **1.** □ ilahi (a. fig.), kutsal; ~ service ibadet; **2.** *n.* imam, papaz; **3.** *vb.* sezmek, hissetmek; fala bakarak kehanette bulunmak;

**di'vin.er** *n.* falcı, önceden haber veren kimse; değnekle su *veya* maden damarı arayan kimse.

**div.ing** ['daiviŋ] *n. yüzme:* tramplenden atlama; *attr.* dalgıç...; '**~-bell** *n.* dalgıç fanusu, haznesi; '**~-board** *n.* tramplen; **'~dress, '~-suit** *n.* dalgıç elbisesi.

**di.vin.ing-rod** [di'vainiɳrɔd] *n.* yeraltında su *ya da* maden damarı aramakta kullanılan çatal şeklinde çubuk; **di.vin.i.ty** [di-'vinitiĵ] *n.* tanrılık niteliği; ilâhiyat.

**di.vis.i.bil.i.ty** [divizi'biliti] *n.* bölünebilme; **di'vis.i.ble** ☐ [~zəbl] bölünebilir; **di'vi-sion** [~ʒən] *n.* böl(ün)me, taksim; ayırma; bölüm; ayrılma; kısım, daire; bölge: kaza, nahiye; ✕ tümen; ♬ bölme; *parl.* oylamada ikiye ayrılma; ~ of labo(u)r işbölümü; **di'vi.sion.al** [~zənl] *adj.* bölme *veya* bölünme ile ilgili; ✕ kıta...; birlik...; **di.vi.sive** [di'vaisiv] *adj.* bölen; anlaşmazlık çıkaran; **di'vi.sor** ♬ [~zə] *n.* bölen.

**di.vorce** [di'vɔːs] **1.** *n.* boşanma; *fig.* ayrılış, ayrılma; **2.** *v/t. & v/i.* boşa(n)mak; ayrılmak; ilgisini kesmek; **di'vor.cee** [diːvɔ'siː] *n.* boşanmış kadın; **di.vorc.er** [diːvɔːsə] *n.* boşanmaya neden olan.

**di.vulge** [dai'vʌldʒ] *v/t.* ifşa etm., açığa vurmak, söylemek, yaymak.

**dix.ie** ✕ *sl.* ['diksi] *n.* karavana; ♀ *Am. pl.* Amerika Birleşik Devletleri'nin güney eyaletleri; ♂crat *Am. pol.* bu eyaletlerdeki muhalefet; demokrat partililer.

**diz.zi.ness** ['diziniz] *n.* baş dönmesi, sersemlik; **'diz.zy 1.** ☐ *(kişi)* baş döndürücü; *(nesne)* baş döndüren; **2.** *v/t.* baş döndürmek, sersemletmek.

**do** [duː] *(irr.) (s. a. done)* **1.** *v/t.* yapmak; etmek; hazırlanmak; bitirmek; mesafe katetmek; pişirmek; *(rol)* oynamak; F dolandırmak, kafese koymak; uygun gelmek, yakışmak; ~ London F Londra'yı gezmek; ~ s.o. F *b-ne* bakmak. beslemek; what is to be done? yapılacak ne var?; ~ the polite *etc.* nezaket taslamak; have done reading okumayı bitirmiş olm.; ~ a room odayı toplamak; ~ (over) again bir kere daha yapmak; ~ down üstesinden gelmek, alt etm.; ~ in F öldürmek; ~ into tercüme etm.; ~ out süpürmek .temizlemek; ~ over *(boya vs.)* üzerine sürmek; ~ up tamir etm., yenileştirmek; ambalaj yapmak; bağlamak. iliklemek; güzelleştirmek *-i;* F benzetmek. sakatlamak; **2.** *v/i.* davranmak; bulunmak. olmak; kâfi gelmek, yetmek; elverişli olm.. uymak; that will ~ yeter, yetişir; that won't ~ yetmez; how ~ you

~? nasılsınız?; ~ well işi iyi gitmek, iyi para kazanmak; ~ badly işini becereememek; have done! yetişir!, sus!; ~ away with feshetmek, kaldırmak; öldürmek; ~ for *b-ne* bakmak; ~ with *bşde* rolü olm.; ...le ilgili olm.; ihtiyacı olm. *-e;* I could ~ with... ...olsa fena olmaz; have done with bitirmek, son vermek; ~ without muhtaç olmamak *-e;* **3.** *v/aux. soru:* ~ you know him? onu tanıyormusunuz?; *olumsuz:* I ~ not know him onu tanımıyorum; *vurgulama:* I ~ feel better kendimi gerçekten iyi hissediyorum; ~ come and see me ne olur gel ve beni gör; ~ be quick acele etsene; *bir önceki fiilin yerine:* ~ you like London? — I do. Londra'yı severmisiniz? — Evet; you write better than I ~ benden daha iyi yazıyorsunuz; I take a bath every day. — So ~ I her gün banyo yaparım. — Ben de; **4.** F *n.* dalavere; büyük olay; şenlik; ziyafet, parti.

**doc** F [dɔk] = doctor.

**doc.ile** ['dəusail] *adj.* uslu, uysal, yumuşak başlı; **do.cil.i.ty** [~'siliti] *n.* usluluk, uysallık, yumuşak başlılık.

**dock¹** [dɔk] *v/t. (kuyruk vs.)* kısaltmak, kırpmak; *(ücret)* azaltmak (off).

**dock²** ♀ [~] *n.* kuzukulağı otu.

**dock³** [~] **1.** *n.* ♻ havuz, dok; *esp. Am.* rıhtım; ☸ sanık yeri; dry ~. graving ~ kuru havuz; floating ~ yüzer havuz; wet ~ su bentli havuz; **2.** *vb.* ♻ havuza çekmek; rıhtıma yanaşmak; '**~-dues** *n. pl.* havuz *veya* rıhtım ücreti; '**dock.er** *n.* liman işçisi.

**dock.et** ['dɔkit] **1.** *n.* yafta, yapılacak işler listesi, gündem; sipariş listesi; etiket; adres etiketi; ☸ bekleyen davalar listesi; **2.** *v/t.* listeye kaydetmek, özetlemek; etiketlemek.

**dock.yard** ['dɔkjɑːd] *n.* tersane.

**doc.tor** ['dɔktə] **1.** *n.* doktor, hekim; **2.** *vb.* F *b-ni* tedavi etm.; tamir etm.; tahrif etm.. üzerinde değişiklik yapmak, hile karıştırmak; **doc.tor.ate** ['~rit] *n.* doktora.

**doc.tri.naire** [dɔkri'nɛə] **1.** *n.* kuramcı, nazariyeci, doktriner; **2.** *adj.* kuramsal, nazari; **doc.tri.nal** ☐ [~'trainl] *n.* kuram *veya* doktrine ait; **doc.trine** ['~trin] *n.* doktrin, öğreti.

**doc.u.ment 1.** ['dɔkjumənt] *n.* belge, vesika, senet, delil; **2.** ['~ment] *v/t.* belgelerle kanıtlamak, belgelemek; **doc.u'men.ta.ry 1.** ☐ dökümanter, belgelere dayanan, yazılı, belgesel; ~ film = **2.** *n.* belgesel film; **doc.u'men.ta.tion** *n.* belgeleme, belgelerle kanıtlama.

**dod.der** ['dɔdə] **1.** *n.* ❖ küsküt; **2.** *v/i.* yaşlılık nedeniyle titremek, sallanmak, sendelemek.

**dodge** [dɔdʒ] **1.** *n.* oyun, kurnazlık; kurtulma, yana kaçış; **2.** *v/t.* atlatmak; bertaraf etm.; *v/i.* kaçamak bulmak, kenara sıçramak; kaçınmak *-den*; *fig.* dolambaçlı yoldan gitmek, ağız yapmak; *bşden* sıyrılmak; **dod.gem** F ['dɔdʒəm] *n.* (*esp. pl.*) çarpışan otomobil; **¹dodg.er** *n.* hilekâr kimse, madrabaz, vurguncu; *Am.* küçük el ilânı; *Am.* mısır unundan yapılan bir tür kek.

**do-do** *orn.* ['dəudəu] *n.* nesli tükenmiş ve güvercin cinsinden uçmayan bir tür kuş.

**doe** [dəu] *n. zo.* dişi geyik *veya* tavşan.

**do.er** ['du:ə] *n.* yapan, eden kimse, fail.

**does** [dʌz] (he, she, it) yapmak (*s.* do).

**doe.skin** ['dəuskin] *n.* dişi geyik *veya* karaca derisi.

**doesn't** F ['dʌznt] = does not (*s.* do).

**dog** [dɔg] **1.** *n.* köpek, it; kurt; ⊕ mandal; sac ayağı; maşa, raptiye; kanca; ✗ kömür vagonu; F herif; *Am.* F fazla naz, tafra; go to the ~s sefalete düşmek, mahvolmak; **2.** *v/t. b-nin* peşine takılmak, izini araştırmak; **'~-bis.cuit** *n.* köpek bisküviti; **'~-cart** *n.* arka arkaya iki kişilik oturacak yeri olan tek atlı araba, büyük bir köpek tarafından çekilen hafif araba; **'~-cheap** *adj.* sudan ucuz; **'~-days** *n. pl.* yılın en sıcak günleri.

**doge** [dəudʒ] *n.* eski Venedik ve Cenova Dükası.

**dog...:** **'~-eared** = dog's-eared; **'~-fight** *n.* F hava savaşı; **'~-fish** *n. zo.* bir kaç tür küçük köpek-balığı.

**dog.ged** □ ['dɔgid] inatçı, bildiğinden şaşmaz.

**dog.ger.el** ['dɔgərəl] *n. a.* ~ rhymes *pl.* edebî değeri olmayan şiir.

**dog.gish** ['dɔgiʃ] *adj.* köpek gibi; homurdanan; huysuz, ters; **dog.go** *sl.* ['dɔgəu] *adv.:* lie ~ sessizce ve hareket etmeden saklandığı yerde durmak; **'dog.gy 1.** *n.* (*çocuk dilinde*) köpek; **2.** *adj.* köpeksever, köpeğe düşkün; köpeğe ait; **'dog--'Lat.in** *n.* kötü ve yanlış Latince; **'~-like** *adj.* köpek gibi sadık.

**do.gie** *Am.* ['dəugi] *n.* annesiz buzağı.

**dog.ma** ['dɔgmə] *n.* dogma, inak, doktrin; akide: **dog.mat.ic, dog.mat.i.cal** □ [~'mætik(əl)] dogmatik, kesin; iman ve itikada ait; öğretici; kestirip atan, başına buyruk; **dog'mat.ics** *n. sg.* dini dogmaların sistematik olarak incelenmesi; **dog.ma.tism** ['~mətizəm] *n.* dogmatizm,

inakçılık; fikir açıklamada kesinlik; **'dog.ma.tist** *n.* dogmatik kimse, kesin fikir beyan eden kimse; **dog.ma.tize** ['~mətaiz] *v/i.* kesin olarak fikrini söylemek, kestirip atmak.

**dog's-bod.y** *sl.* ['dɔgzbɔdi] *n.* köle gibi çalışan; rençber, hamal; **'dog's-ear** *n.* (*kitap*) sayfanın kıvrılan köşesi; **'dog's--eared** *adj.* köşesi kıvrık (*sayfa*).

**dog...:** **'~-tired** *adj.* çok yorgun, bitkin; **'~.tooth** *n.* (*kumaş*) kareli desen (*ekose*), ▲ taş oymacılığında küçük piramit şeklinde süsleme; **'~.trot** *n.* yavaş koşma; **'~-watch** ⚓ akşam üzeri 4-6 *ya da* 6-8 nöbeti; **'~.wood** ❖ *n.* kızılcığa benzer bir tür ağaç.

**doi.ly** ['dɔili] *n.* tabak *ya da* süs eşyası altına konan dantel *veya* işlemeli küçük örtü.

**do.ing** ['du:iŋ] **1.** *p. pr. of* do **1.** *vb.* nothing ~ ağzınla kuş tutsan bile nafile; ↑ iş güç yok; **2.** *n.* eylem, hareket, iş; **~s** *pl.* yapılan işler, olan şeyler; davranış.

**doit** [dɔit] *n.* metelik, mangır; eski Avusturya kronunun yüzde biri.

**dol.drums** ['dɔldrəmz] *n. pl.* ümitsizlik, kasvet, durgunluk, canı sıkkın olma; ⚓ okyanusun rüzgârsız olan ekvatora yakın kısımları.

**dole** [dəul] **1.** *n.* teberru, sadaka, muhtaç kimselere yiyecek, giyecek vs. dağıtımı; F işsizlere verilen haftalık hükümet yardımı; be *veya* go on the ~ hükümetten işsizlik parası almak; **2.** *v/t. mst* ~ out azar azar dağıtmak (to *-e*).

**dole.ful** □ ['dəulful] üzüntülü, mahzun, melânkolik; **'dole.ful.ness** *n.* hüzün, üzüntü, keder, gam.

**doll** [dɔl] **1.** *n.* bebek, kukla (*a. fig.*); **2.** *vb.* ~ up F süsle(n)mek, şık giyinmek, giydirmek.

**dol.lar** ['dɔlə] *n.* dolar, 100 sent karşılığı olan Amerikan para birimi.

**dol.lop** F ['dɔləp] *n.* topak, toparlak parça, bir miktar.

**doll.y** ['dɔli] *n.* (*çocuk dilinde*) bebek; iki tekerlekli yük taşıyıcısı; film *veya* televizyon kamerasını taşıyan tekerlekli araç.

**dol.o.mite** *min.* ['dɔləmait] *n.* kalsiyum, magnezyum ve karbonattan ibaret bir tür beyaz mermer, dolomi.

**dol.o(u)r** *mst poet., co.* ['dəulə] *n.* keder, elem, dert, azap., **dol.o.rous** ['dɔlərəs] *adj.* kederli, elemli, üzüntülü.

**dol.phin** *ichth.* ['dɔlfin] *n.* yunusbalığı.

**dolt** [dəult] *n.* ahmak, budala, kalın kafalı kimse; **¹dolt.ish** ☐ kafasız, budala, ahmak.

**do.main** [dəu¹mein] *n.* mülk, arazi, alan; *fig.* nüfuz sahası, çevre, muhit.

**dome** [dəum] *n.* kubbe; ⊕ kapak, dosya gömleği, kitap kabı; **domed** *adj.* kubbeli, kemerli.

**Domes.day Book** [¹du:mzdei¹buk] *n.* 1086'-da İngiltere'de Kral I. William'ın emri ile hazırlanan tapu sicili.

**do.mes.tic** [dəu¹mestik] **1.** *adj.* (~ally) eve ait, ehli, evcil; yerli; ~ animal evcil hayvan; ~ coal ev için kullanılan kömür; ~ science ev idaresi bilimi; **2.** *n. a.* ~ servant hizmetçi kız; ~s *pl.* evde kullanılan eşyalar; **do¹mes.ti.cate** [~keit] *v/t.* evcilleştirmek, ehlileştirmek, alıştırmak; **do.mes.ti¹ca.tion** *n.* alıştırma, evcilleş-(tir)me; **do.mes.tic.i.ty** [~¹tisiti] *n.* aile hayatı; evcimenlik.

**dom i.cile** [¹dɔmisail] **1.** *n.* *esp.* ฿ daimi ikametgah yeri, mesken, oturma yeri, konut; **2.** *vb.* ϯ *(kambiyo)* tediye etm., ödemek; oturmak, ikamet etm., yerleş-(tir)mek; **¹dom.i.ciled** *adj.* yerleşmiş, mukim, sakin; **dom.i.cil.i.ar.y** [~¹siljəri] *adj.* eve ait; ~ visit arama, ev araştırması; ϯ hasta ziyareti, vizita.

**dom.i.nance** [¹dɔminəns] *n.* hâkimiyet, selâhiyet, tahakküm, üstünlük; **¹dom.i.nant 1.** *adj.* hâkim ,üstün; **2.** *n.* ♪ dominant, sol notasına ait; **dom.i.nate** [~¹neit] *v/t.* & *v/i.* idaresi altına almak, hakim olm. *-e;* üstün olm.; **dom.i¹na.tion** *n.* egemenlik, hükmetme; **¹dom.i.na.tor** *n.* hükümdar; **dom.i.neer** [dɔmi¹niə] *v/t.* tahakküm altında tutmak; zorbalık etm.; ~ over *b-ne* zulmetmek, gaddarlık etm.; **dom.i¹neer.ing** ☐ otoriter, despotça davranan, zalim.

**do.min.i.cal** [də¹minikəl] *adj.* pazar *(veya* Rab [İsa]) gününe ait; ~ prayer Hıristiyanların fatihaya benzetilebilen duası. **Do.min.i.can** [də¹minikən] *n.* Sen Dominik papazı.

**do.min.ion** [də¹minjən] *n.* hüküm, hakimiyet, dominyon; *usu.* ~s *pl.* arazi, ülke; nüfuz sahası *(a. fig.);* ♀ *pol.* dominyon, müstemleke *(İngiliz milletler topluluğu içinde).*

**dom.i.no** [¹dɔminəu] *n.* domino taşı; maskeli kostüm; **dom.i.noes** [¹~z] *n. pl.* domino oyunu.

**don¹** *univ.* [dɔn] *n.* öğretim görevlisi. **don²** [~] *v/t.* giydirmek.

**do.nate** *Am.* [dəu¹neit] *v/t.* bağışlamak *-e,* hediye etm. *-e,* iane vermek *-e;* **do¹na-**

**tion, don.a.tive** [¹~nətiv] *n.* bağış, iane, hibe.

**done** [dʌn] **1.** *p.p. of* do; be ~ *usu.* yapılmak; bitkin olm.; **2.** *adj.* tamamlanmış, bitmiş; *a.* ~ up bitkin; hazır; well ~ *(yemek)* iyi pişmiş; he is ~ for mahvolmuş, bitkin; **3.** *int.* tamam!, kabul!. **do.nee** ฿ [dəu¹ni:] *n.* bağışta bulunan kimse *veya* kurum.

**don.jon** [¹dɔndʒən] *n.* eski zaman şatolarındaki muazzam kule, burç.

**don.key** [¹dɔŋki] *n.* eşek; eşek adam, inatçı kimse; *attr.* yardımcı...; **¹~en.gine** *n.* yardımcı motor, palamar çekmek için kullanılan küçük yardımcı makine.

**don.na** [¹dɔnə] *n.* hanım.

**do.nor** [¹dəunə] *n.* veren; *(kan, böbrek vs.)* verici.

**do-noth.ing** F [¹du:nʌθiŋ] **1.** *n.* tembel, haylaz kimse; **2.** *adj.* tembel.

**don't** [dəunt] **1.** = do not; ~! Yapma!; **2.** *n.* yasak, memnuiyet.

**doom** [du:m] **1.** *n. mst b.s.* kötü kader, kötü talih; kıyamet; **2.** *v/t.* mahkûm etm. (to *-e);* hüküm giydirmek; **dooms.day** [¹du:mzdei] *rel. n.* kıyamet günü.

**door** [dɔ:] *n.* kapı; next ~ (to) kapı komşu; *fig.* yakın, iki adımlık yer; two ~s off iki ev ötede; (with) in ~s içerde, evde; out of ~s dışarda, açık havada; show s.o. the ~ *b-ni* kovmak, kapıyı göstermek; turn out of the ~ *b-ni* kapı dışarı etm.; lay s.th. to *veya* at s.o.'s ~ *b-ne* kabahat yüklemek; **¹~bell** *n.* kapı zili; **¹~case, ¹~frame** *n.* kapı çerçevesi; **¹~han.dle** *n.* kapı mandalı; **¹~keep.er, ¹~man** *n.* kapıcı; **¹~mat** *n.* paspas; **¹~nail** *n.* eskiden kullanılan iri başlı kapı çivisi; dead as a ~ ölmüş gitmiş; **¹~plate** *n.* isim yazılı kapı tabelâsı; **¹~post** *n.* kapı pervazı; **¹~step** *n.* eşik; **¹~.way** *n.* kapı yeri, giriş; **¹~.yard** *n. Am.* ev avlusu.

**dope** [dəup] **1.** *n.* yağlı ve yapışkan madde; *esp.* ϯ vernik, cilâ; sinir uyarıcı, uyuşturucu madde, esrar, afyon; *Am. sl.* haber, malumat; budala; baş dönmesi; **2.** *v/t.* cilâlamak, verniklemek; ilaçla sersemletmek; *spor:* doping yapmak, uyarıcı ilaç vermek; *Am. sl.* halletmek; **¹dope.y** *adj. Am. sl.* budala, uyuşuk.

**Dor.ic** [¹dɔrik] *adj.* Dorlara ait; ~ order en eski ve basit Yunan mimari tarzı. **dorm** F [dɔ:m] = dormitory.

**dor.mant** [¹dɔ:mənt] *adj. mst fig.* uyuyan, uyuşuk, cansız, uykuda gibi hareketsiz; ~ partner özel ortak, komanditer.

**dor.mer(-win.dow)** [¹dɔ:mə(¹windəu] *n.* çatı penceresi.

**dor.mi.to.ry** [ˈdɔːmitri] *n.* yatakhane, koğuş; *esp. Am.* öğrenci yurdu.

**dor.mouse** [ˈdɔːmaus] *n., pl.* **dormice** [ˈdɔːmais] sincaba benzer bir tür küçük orman faresi.

**dor.sal** ☐ [ˈdɔːsəl] sırta ait; arkada, arka tarafa ait.

**do.ry** ↓ [ˈdɔːri] *n.* bir tür yassı kayık; bir tür büyük deniz balığı.

**dose** [dəus] **1.** *n.* doz; **2.** *v/t. a.* ~ **with** belirli miktarda ilaç vermek; *(şarap vs.)* su katmak *-e.*

**doss-house** *sl.* [ˈdɔshaus] *n.* ucuz kalacak yer *(han).*

**dos.si.er** [ˈdɔsiei] *n.* evrak dosyası.

**dost** † [dʌst, dəst] you do *(s.* **do**).

**dot** [dɔt] **1.** *n.* nokta, benek, ufak leke; on the ~ tam vaktinde; **2.** *v/t.* noktalamak, benek benek yapmak; *a.* ~ about *fig.* dağıtmak, oraya buraya saçmak; ~ted *adj.* noktalı, benekli.

**dot.age** [ˈdəutidʒ] *n.* bunaklık, ikinci çocukluk; aşırı düşkünlük, iptilâ; **do.tard** [ˈdɔtəd] *n.* bunak kimse; **dote** [dəut] *v/t. & v/i.* bunamak; düşkün olm., aşırı sevmek, çılgınca sevdalanmak (on, upon *-e).*

**doth** † [dʌθ, dəθ] = **does** *(s.* **do**).

**dot.ing** [ˈdəutiŋ] ☐ çılgınca seven (on *-i).*

**dot.ty** *sl.* [ˈdɔti] *n.* sarsak, aptal, budala.

**dou.ble** [ˈdʌbl] **1.** ☐ çift, iki misli, iki kat; bükülmüş, katlı; iki kişilik. **2.** *n.* iki kat, çift; aynı, eş; dublör, tam benzeri; hile, oyun, ✕ koşar adım; **3.** *v/t.* ikilemek, iki kat etm., duble etm.; *a.* ~ up eğmek, kıvırmak, iki büklüm etm., *(bilek)* bükmek; ~d up *adj.* eğilmiş, iki büklüm olmuş; be ~d up with eğilmek, iki büklüm olm.; *v/i.* iki misli olm.; *a.* ~ back aynı yoldan geri dönmek; ✕ koşar adım ilerlemek; *kâğıt oyunu:* duble etm., kontr etm.; ~ up bükülmek, ikiye katlanmak; ˈ~-bar.relled *adj.* çift namlulu; *fig.* iki anlamlı, şüpheli *(söz);* ~ name iki addan oluşan soyadı; ˈ~-ˈbass ♪ *n.* kontrbas; ˈ~-bed.ded *n.* çift yataklı; ˈ~-ˈbreast.ed *adj.* çift düğmeli, kruvaze *(ceket);* ˈ~-ˈcroos *sl. v/t.* (ortak) kazık atmak, al datmak; ˈ~-ˈdeal.er *n.* iki yüzlü kimse, dolandırıcı; ˈ~-ˈdeal.ing *n.* iki yüzlülük, dolandırıcılık; ˈ~-ˈdeck.er *n.* iki katlı *(yatak, tekne, otobüs, sandviç);* ˈ~-ˈdyed *adj. fig.* ıslah olmaz, kaşarlanmış *(hırsız, yalancı);* ˈ~-ˈledged *adj.* iki taraflı *(a. fig.);* ˈ~-ˈen.try ↓ *n.* muzaaf kayıt, muhasebede çift defter tutma usulü; ˈ~-faced *adj.* iki yüzlü, iki taraflı; ˈ~-ˈfea.ture *n. Am.* iki film birden *(sinema);* ˈ~-ˈhead.er *n. Am. beysbol:* iki ta-

kım arasında üst üste yapılan iki karşılaşma; ˈ~-ˈline 🚧 *n.* çift ray; ˈdou.ble.ness *n.* çift olma durumu; *fig.* iki anlamlılık; ˈdou.ble- park *vb.* kaldırıma paralel park etmiş bir arabanın yanına park etm.; ˈdou.ble-ˈquick ✕ *n.* hızlı yürüyüş.

**dou.blet** [ˈdʌblit] *n.* eş, çift, aynısı; *hist.* ceket; ~s *pl.* çift gelen zarlar.

**dou.ble...**: ˈ~-talk *n.* lastikli söz; ˈ~-time *sl. v/t.* dolandırmak, kafese koymak; ˈ~-ˈtrack *n.* çift hat.

**doub.ling** [ˈdʌbliŋ] *n.* ikileme, duble etme; katlama; geminin burnu dolaşması; ˈdoub.ly *adv.* çifte, iki kat.

**doubt** [daut] **1.** *v/i.* kuşkulanmak, şüphelenmek *(about -den); v/t.* şüphe etm.; tereddüt etm.; **2.** *n.* şüphe, tereddüt, endişe; güvensizlik; no ~ hiç şüphesiz, elbette; ˈdoubt.er *n.* şüpheci, septik; **doubt.ful** ☐ [ˈ~ful] şüpheli, kararsız, karanlık, muğlak, belirsiz; be ~ kestirememek, bir türlü bilememek; ˈdoubt.ful.ness *n.* şüpheli durum, tereddüt; ˈdoubt.less *adv.* şüphesiz, muhakkak.

**douche** [duːʃ] **1.** *n.* duş; 🌡 şırınga; **2.** *vb.* duş yapmak, sudan geçirmek; şırınga etm.

**dough** [dəu] *n.* hamur; *sl.* para; ˈ~.boy *n. Am.* F piyade; ˈ~.nut *n.* çörek.

**dough.ty** *co.* [ˈdauti] *adj.* yiğit, cesaretli.

**dough.y** [ˈdəui] *adj.* hamurumsu, iyice pişmemiş.

**dour** *Scots.* [ˈduə] *adj.* asık suratlı, ters, aksi, haşin.

**douse** [daus] *s.* dowse.

**dove** [dʌv] *n.* güvercin, kumru; *fig.* barış taraftarı kimse, masum ve iyi huylu kimse; ˈ~-col.o(u)red *adj.* pembemsi kurşuni; ~.cot(e) [ˈ~kɔt] *n.* güvercinlik; ˈ~.tail **1.** *n.* ⊕ lambalı erkek tahta; **2.** *v/t.* bu tahta ile birleştirmek; *v/i. fig.* iki şeyi uydurmak, telif etm.

**dow.a.ger** [ˈdauədʒə] *n.* ölen kocasından *k-ne* ünvan ve mal mülk kalan dul kadın.

**dow.dy** F [ˈdaudi] **1.** *adj.* derbeder, üstü başı dökülen, kılıksız; **2.** *n.* pasaklı kadın.

**dow.el** ⊕ [ˈdauəl] *n.* ağaç çivi, takoz, kama.

**dow.er** [ˈdauə] **1.** *n.* kadının ölen kocasının terekesi üzerindeki kanuni hissesi; *fig.* drahoma; **2.** *v/t.* çeyiz *veya* ağırlık vermek.

**down[1]** [daun] *n.* ince kuş tüyü, pufla; ayva tüyü, hav.

**dow[2]** [~] = dune; ~s ağaçsız tepeler, dağ sırtları, eksibe, kumul.

**down³** [~] **1.** *adv.* aşağı(ya); aşağıda; ~ and out *fig.* bitkin, argın, hayatta yenilgiye uğramış; be ~ *(fiyat)* düşmek, azalmak; be ~ upon F *b-ne* acımasız davranmak; ~ in the country şehir dışında, köyde, taşrada; ~ under F Avustralya *veya* Yeni Zelanda'da; **2.** *prp.* aşağı(ya); ~ the river ırmağın aşağısına doğru; ~ (the) wind rüzgâr yönünde; **3.** *int.* alçak!; **4.** *adj.* ~ train Londra'dan kalkan tren; **5.** F *v/t.* indirmek; yenmek -*i*; ~ tools grev yapmak; **6.** *s.* up 4; **'~.cast** *adj.* üzgün; **'~-'draft, '~-'draught** *n.* aşağı doğru giden hava akımı; **~--'East.er** *n. Am.* New England'dan olan *(esp. Maine'den)*; **'~.fall** *n.* düşüş, yıkılış, gerileme; düşüşün nedeni olan şey *veya* kişi; *(yağmur)* boşanma; **'~.grade** *v/t.* alçaltmak, derecesini indirmek; **'~-'heart.ed** *adj.* cesareti kırılmış, kederli; **'~-'hill 1.** *adv.* yokuş aşağı; **2.** *adj.* inişli, meyilli; **'~.pour** *n.* şiddetli yağmur, sağanak; **'~-'right 1.** *adv.* tamamiyle, büsbütün, kesin olarak; **2.** *adj.* tamam; kesin, kati; çok; **'~.right.ness** *n.* açıklık, samimiyet, doğruluk, dürüstlük; **'~.stairs 1.** *adv.* aşağıda, aşağıya; **2.** *adj.* aşağıda olan, aşağı, alt; **'~.'stream** *adv.* akıntı yönünde; **'~-stroke** *n.* alt çizgi; ⊕ pistonun inişi; **'~-'town** *n. esp. Am.* şehrin merkezi; **'~.trod.den** *adj.* haksızlığa uğramış, ezilmiş; **~.ward** ['~wəd] **1.** *adj.* aşağı doğru olan; *fig.* kötüye doğru olan; **2.** *adv. a.* ~s aşağı(ya) doğru; **'~.wash** *n.* **✝** hava akımının aşağı sapması.

**down.y** ['dauni] *adj.* ince tüylü, havlı; *fig.* kurnaz, şeytana külahını ters giydiren; pişkin.

**dow.ry** ['dauəri] *n.* çeyiz, drahoma; *fig.* Allah vergisi, yetenek.

**dowse** ['dauz] **1.** *v/t.* sulamak; söndürmek; **2.** *v/i.* değnekle yeraltında su *veya* maden damarı aramak; **'dows.er** *n.* değnekle su *veya* maden damarı araştıran; **'dows.ing-rod** *n.* yeraltında su aramak için kullanılan ucu çatal şeklinde değnek.

**doze** ['dəuz] **1.** *v/i.* uyuklamak, (~ away) dalmak; **2.** *n.* hafif uyku, şekerleme.

**doz.en** ['dʌzn] *n.* düzine; talk nineteen to the ~ hiç durmadan konuşmak, çene çalmak.

**drab** [dræb] **1.** *adj.* sarımtrak kurşuni; *fig.* monoton, usandırıcı; **2.** *n.* bu renk kumaş; fahişe, orospu; *fig.* monotonluk.

**drachm** [dræm] *n.* dirhem; = **drach.ma** ['drækmə] *n.* Yunan drahmisi.

**draff** [dræf] *n.* tortu, posa.

**draft** [dra:ft] **1.** *n.* tasarı, taslak, müsvedde, kroki; **✝** poliçe, çek; **✗** mecburi askerliğe alma; = draught; ~ agreement mukavele taslağı; **2.** *v/t.* tasarlamak, çizmek; **✗** ifraz etm., bir işe ayırmak; *Am.* askere almak, silah altına çağırmak; **draft.ee** *n.* **✗** *Am.* askere çağrılan; **'drafts.man** *n.* teknik ressam.

**drag** [dræg] **1.** *n.* sürükleme; sürüklenen şey; tırmık; takoz, engel *(a. fig.)*; tomruk vagonu; hava direnci; *sl.* sıkıcı şey *veya* kimse; **2.** *v/t.* sürüklemek, çekmek; ✓ tırmıklamak; *(tekerlek)* durdurmak; = dredge 2; ~ along sürüklemek; ~ out *bşi* uzatmak; bir yere sürüklemek; ~ one's feet kasıtlı olarak yavaş hareket etm. *veya* çalışmak; ~ up a child gelişi güzel yetiştirmek, terbiye etmemek; *v/i.* sürüklenmek, sürünmek; ağla suyun dibini taramak (for); **✝** durgun gitmek.

**drag.gle** ['drægl] *v/t. & v/i.* çamur içinde sürükleyerek ıslatıp kirletmek *veya* kirlenmek; bulaş(tır)mak; **'~-tail** *n.* pasaklı kadın.

**drag.o.man** ['drægəumən] *n.* Orta Doğu'da tercüman, rehber.

**drag.on** ['drægən] *n.* ejderha; **'~-fly** *n. zo.* yusufçuk.

**dra.goon** [drə'gu:n] **1.** *n.* ağır süvari; *fig.* vahşi, hayvani; **2.** *v/t.* zorlamak, mecbur etm. (into -e).

**drain** [drein] **1.** *n.* lağım, su yolu, kanalizasyon, kanal; F yudum, damla; alıp götürme (on); ~s *pl.* kanalizasyon şebekesi; **2.** *v/t.* akıtmak, kurutmak, akaçlamak, drenaj yapmak; *(şişe)* boşaltmak; *a.* ~ off içip bitirmek, tüketmek; süzmek; *v/i.* süzülmek, suyu süzülmek; **'drain.age** *n.* akaçlama, drenaj; kanalizasyon; çekilen su; **'drain.ing** *n.* boşaltma, süzme, drenaj; ~s *pl.* kanalizasyon şebekesi; **'drain.ing-board** *n.* yıkanmış bulaşıkların süzüldüğü oluklu kab; **'drain-pipe** *n.* suyu ve artıkları dışarı akıtan boru, oluk.

**drake** [dreik] *n.* erkek ördek.

**dram** [dræm] *n.* dirhem; yudum; sert içki.

**dra.ma** ['drɑ:mə] *n.* dram, tiyatro eseri, oyun; tiyatro edebiyatı; **dra.mat.ic** [drə'mætik] *adj.* (~ally) dramatik; heyecanlı; tiyatro ile ilgili; **dra'mat.ics** *n. mst sg.* tiyatro, sahne faaliyeti; **dram.a.tist** ['dræmətist] *n.* oyun yazarı, piyes yazarı; **dram.a.tis per.so.nae** ['dra:mətispə-'səunai] *n. pl.* oyundaki karakterler, oyuncu listesi; **dram.a.tise** ['dræmətaiz] *v/t. & v/i.* dram şekline sokmak, tiyatro oyunu şeklinde ifade etm.; **dram.a-tur.gy** ['~tə:dʒi] *n.* tiyatro eseri yazma sanatı.

**drank** [dræŋk] *pret. of* drink 2.

**drape** [dreip] *v/t.* kumaşla kaplamak; -in kıvrımlarını düzeltmek; asarak süslemek *veya* donatmak; **'drap.er** *n.* kumaşçı; **'dra.per.y** *n.* çuhacılık, kumaşçılık; perdelik kumaş, manifatura; kıvrımların düzeltilmesi.

**dras.tic** ['dræstik] *adj.* (~ally) şiddetli; açık, kesin.

**draught** [drɑːft] *Am.* draft *n.* çekme, içme, yudum; hava cereyanı; ↓ su çekimi; büyük kabtan verilen (*bira vb.*); ~s *pl.* dama oyunu; *s.* draft; ~ beer fıçı birası; at a ~ bir yudumda; **'~-board** *n.* dama tahtası; **'~-horse** *n.* koşum atı; **'draughts.man** *n.* teknik ressam; = draftsman; **'draught.y** *adj.* cereyanlı.

**draw** [drɔː] **1.** (*irr.*) *v/t.* çekmek; uzatmak; çekip çıkarmak; sürüklemek, celbetmek, cezbetmek; (*silah*) çekmek; (*para*) bankadan çekmek; (*eşya vs.*) taşımak; (*kümes hayvanı*) içini temizlemek; (*faiz*) getirmek; çizmek, taslağını çizmek -*in*; (*belge, evrak*) ele geçirmek; berabere kalmak; su çekmek; (*hava, sıvı*) emmek, çekmek; germek; (*perde*) kapamak; ~ away *v/t. & v/i.* çekilmek, kendini çekmek (from -*den*); ~ down *v/t.* indirmek; ~ forth *v/t.* çekip çıkarmak, ~ near *v/i.* sokulmak, yaklaşmak; ~ on *v/t.* bşe sebep olm.; ~ out *v/t.* uzatmak; taslağını çizmek; ~ up *v/t.* tasarlamak, hazırlamak; dimdik durmak; *v/i.* yaklaşıp durmak; yerini almak; ~ (up)on † (*senet, plan*) düzenlemek, çekmek, keşide etm.; *fig.* talebetmek, istemek; **2.** *n.* çekme; (*kur'a, piyango*) çekiliş; *spor:* berabere biten oyun; F cazibe, çok rağbetli şey; F para sızdırma; **'~.back** *n.* engel, sakınca; bilinmeyen tarafı -*in*; † reddi rüsum; vergi iadesi, ihraç primi; *Am.* tazminat; **'~.bridge** *n.* iner kalkar köprü; **draw'lee** *n.* † poliçe keşidesinde ödeyecek olan, muhatap kişi; **'draw.er** *n.* ressam; [mst drɔː] çekmece, göz; † keşideci, çeken kimse; (pair of) ~s *pl.* don, külot; *mst* chest of ~s konsol, şifonyer.

**draw.ing** ['drɔːiŋ] *n.* resim; çizim; kroki, plan; piyango, çekiliş; † keşide; out of ~ kötü çizilmiş; ~ instruments *pl.* çizim takımı, pergel takımı; **'~-ac'count** *n.* açık hesap, vadesiz hesap ve mevduat; **'~-board** *n.* resim tahtası; plançete; **'~-pen** *n.* cetvel kalemi; **'~-pin** *n.* rapti-

ye, pünez; **'~-room** *n.* misafir odası, salon, kabul resmi salonu..

**drawl** [drɔːl] **1.** *vb. a.* ~ out ağır ağır söylemek, konuşmak; **2.** *n.* ağır ağır konuşma.

**drawn** [drɔːn] **1.** *p.p. of* draw 1; **2.** *adj.* berabere; karara bağlanmamış; (*çehre*) süzük, gergin.

**draw-well** ['drɔːwel] *n.* kuyu.

**dray** [drei] *n. a.* ~-cart yük arabası, kızak; **'~.man** *n.* arabacı.

**dread** [dred] **1.** *n.* korku, dehşet; çekinme; **2.** *v/t.* korkmak -*den*, endişe duymak -*den*; **dread.ful** □ ['~ful] **1.** korkunç, dehşetli, tüyler ürpertici; **2.** penny ~ ucuz korku romanı; **dread.nought** ['~nɔːt] *n.* kalın yünlü palto; ↓ eskiden kullanılan bir tür zırhlı.

**dream** [driːm] **1.** *n.* rüya; hülya; rüya görme; hedef, amaç; F mükemmel (*rüya gibi*) şey *veya* kişi; **2.** (*irr.*) *vb.* rüya görmek (of), bşi rüyasında görmek; ~ away vaktini hayal kurarak geçirmek; **'dream.er** *n.* rüya gören kimse; hayalperest kimse; **'dream-land** *n.* rüyalar ülkesi; **'dream-like** *adj.* rüya gibi; **'dream-read.er** *n.* rüya yorumcusu; **dreamt** [dremt] *pret. & p.p. of* dream 2.; **'dream-y** □ dalgın; hayalperest; rüya gibi; belirsiz, müphem; yatıştırıcı.

**drear** *poet.* [driə] = dreary.

**drear.i.ness** ['driərinis] *n.* hüzün, üzüntü, keder, melânkoli; **'drear.y** □ mahzun, üzüntülü, melânkolik; can sıkıcı, ıssız.

**dredge[1]** [dredʒ] **1.** *n.* tarak makinesi; ağlı kepçe, ekskavatör; **2.** *v/t. a.* ~ up, ~ out deniz dibini taramak, tarakla temizlemek (*liman, nehir*).

**dredge[2]** [~] *v/t.* üzerine serpmek (*un, kum, şeker vs.*) (over); bulamak (with -*e*).

**dredg.er[1]** ['dredʒə] *n.* tarak dubası; tarak makinesi.

**dredg.er[2]** [~] *n.* (*un, şeker, tuz, biber, kum vs.*) serpmeğe yarayan kap, tuzluk, şekerlik vs.

**dregs** [dregz] *n. pl.* tortu, telve, posa, cüruf; drink *veya* drain to the ~ son damlasına kadar içmek.

**drench** [drentʃ] **1.** *n.* sağanak; hayvanlara zorla içirilen ilaç, posyon; **2.** *v/t.* ıslatmak, sırılsıklam etm.; hayvana ilaç içirmek; *fig.* iliklerine kadar ıslatmak; **'drench.er** *n.* F fena ıslatan sağanak; hayvanlara ilaç içirilen alet.

**dress** [dres] **1.** *n.* kadın elbisesi, giysi, kıyafet, *fig.* üstbaş; full ~ frak, tören elbisesi; **2.** *vb.* giydirmek, giyinmek; ✕ hizaya getirmek, sıralamak; hazırlamak;

düzenlemek; süslemek, donatmak, tezyin etm.; *(yara)·* sarmak; *(kütük)* biçmek, yontmak; *b-nin* saçını tarayıp düzeltmek; ✓ ekip biçmek ,gübrelemek; ~ s.o. down *b-ni* paylamak, sövüp saymak, pataklamak; ~ it *thea.* kostümlü prova yapmak; ~ up giyinip süslenmek; *(çocuklar)* büyüklerin kıyafetini giymek; '~-'cir.cle *n. thea.*   protokol yeri; '~-coat *n.* frak; 'dress.er *n.* giydiren kimse, *b-nin* giyinmesine yardım eden kimse; dekoratör; asistan doktor; pansumancı; dresuvar; *Am.* tuvalet masası; mutfak dolabı.

dress.ing ['dresiŋ] *n.* giy(in)me; giydirme; pansuman, sargı; apre; mutfak harcı *(esp. salata ve hindi dolması için sirke, salça, mayonez vs.);* ✓ gübre; temiz bir dayak; ~s *pl.* sargı malzemesi; ~ down şiddetli azarlama; '~-case *n.* makyaj çantası; ilk yardım çantası; '~-cub.ic.le *n.* soyunma kabinesi; '~-glass *n.* tuvalet aynası; '~-gown *n.* sabahlık; '~-jack.et *n.* ropdöşambr, sabahlık; ~ room giyinme odası, gardırop; '~-ta.ble *n.* tuvalet masası.

dress...: '~.mak.er *n.* kadın terzisi; '~-pa.rade *n.* defile; ✗ üniformalı geçit töreni; ~ re.hears.al *thea.* kostümlü prova; '~-shield *n.* subra, koltukluk; '~-'shirt *n.* frak gömleği; '~-'suit *n.* frak takım; 'dress.y *adj.* F giyimine özen gösteren, şık, gösterişli giyinen.

drew [dru:] *pret. of* draw 1.

drib.ble ['dribl] *vb.* damla damla ak(ıt)mak, damla(t)mak; salyası akmak; *futbol:* topu zıplatarak ileri götürmek.

drib.let ['driblit] *n.* ufak tefek şey; nebze; damla(cık).

dried [draid] *adj.* kurutulmuş...; kuru...; ~ fruit kuru meyve.

dri.er ['draiə] *n.* kurutan kimse; kurutucu makine; çabuk kuruması için boyaya katılan madde.

drift [drift] **1.** *n.* sürüklenme, kar; kum vs. yığıntısı; hedef; ↓ geminin akıntı ve rüzgâr ile sürüklenmesi; *fig.* eğilim, tandans; *geol.* birikinti, moren; ✗ kanal, geçit; **2.** *v/t. & v/i.* sürükle(n)mek; yığ-(ı)lmak, birik(tir)mek; '~-ice *n.* yüzer buz kütleleri, aysberk; '~-net *n.* balık tutmada kullanılan büyük ağ; '~-wood *n.* su üstünde sürüklenen odun parçaları.

drill¹ [dril] **1.** *n.* delgi, matkap; sapan izi; tohum dizisi; ✓ tohum ekme makinesi; ✗ talim *(a. fig.);* alıştırma; ~ ground talim alanı; **2.** *v/t. & v/i.* delmek;

✗ talim et(tir)mek *(a. fig.);* alıştırma yap(tır)mak; ✓ tohum ekmek.

drill², drill.ing [dril, '~-iŋ] *n.* çuval bezi.

drink [driŋk] **1.** *n.* içki, içecek; içme; *sl.* deniz; in ~ sarhoş; **2.** *(irr.) vb.* içmek; ~ s.o.'s health *b-nin* sıhhatine içmek; ~ away varını yoğunu içkide bitirmek; ~ in zevk duyarak doya doya seyretmek *veya* dinlemek; ~ to *b-nin* şerefine kadehini kaldırıp içmek; ~ off *veya* out *veya* up içip bitirmek; 'drink.a.ble *adj.* içilebilir; 'drink.er *n.* içki içen kimse; sarhoş, ayyaş, bekri.

drink.ing ['driŋkiŋ] *n.* içme; içki içme alışkanlığı; '~-bout *n.* içki alemi; '~-foun.tain *n.* su içilen fıskiye; '~-song *n.* içki âlemlerinde söylenen şarkı; '~-wa.ter *n.* içecek su.

drip [drip] **1.** *n.* damlama, su sızma; **2.** *v/t. & v/i.* damla(t)mak, damla damla akmak; ~ping wet sırsıklam; '~-'dry shirt *n.* buruşmaz, ütü gerektirmeyen gömlek; 'drip.ping *n.* kızartılan etten damlayan yağ, erimiş yağ; ~s *pl.* damlayan şey; ~ pan damlayan su *veya* yağı toplamaya yarayan kap.

drive [draiv] **1.** *n.* gezinti, araba gezintiti; araba yolu; *tenis vs.:* topa vuruş; *mot.* işletme mekanizması; *fig.* canlılık, neşe ;işleme; teşebbüs, gayret; hamle; dürtü; *(hayvan)* gütme; sürgün avı; **2.** *(irr.) v/t.* sürmek; kullanmak; götürmek; sevketmek; zorlamak (to, into -e); *usu.* ~ away sürüp götürmek; kovmak; *v/i.* sürülmek *(a. ↓ & hunt.);* araba ile gitmek, araba kullanmak; acele etm.; ~ at s.th. amaçlamak, demek istemek; ~ on gitmeğe devam etm.; ~ out kovmak, çıkarmak; ~ up arabasiyle *b-nin* kapısı önüne gelmek.

drive-in *Am.* ['draivin] **1.** *adj. mst attr.* müşterilerine araba içinde servis yapan...; ~ cinema bu tür sinema; **2.** *n.* seyircilerin arabada oturarak film seyrettikleri açık hava sineması; müşterilere araba içinde servis yapılan lokanta.

driv.el ['drivl] **1.** *v/t. & v/i.* ağzından salya ak(ıt)mak; saçmasapan söylemek, saçmalamak; **2.** *n.* salya; saçmasapan söz.

driv.en ['drivn] *p.p. of* drive 2.

driv.er ['draivə] *n.* şoför, sürücü, ~~~~ makinist; † arabacı; ⊕ işletme *(hareket)* kasnağı, çarkı; 'drive.way *n. Am.* bahçe kapısından eve kadar olan özel oto yolu.

driv.ing ['draiviŋ] **1.** *n.* sürme, kullanma; araba gezintisi; **2.** *adj.* hareket ettiren; çeviren; enerjik, canlı, şiddetli; '~-belt

*n.* çark kayışı; transmisyon kayışı; '~-
-gear *n.* makine tertibatı; ~ li.cence şoförlük ehliyetnamesi; ~ mir.ror dikiz aynası; ~ school şoförlük okulu; '~-wheel
*n.* işletme dişlisi, ana çark.

driz.zle ['drizl] 1. *n.* çiseleme; 2. *v/i.* çiselemek, ince ince yağmak, serpiştirmek
*(yağmur);* 'drizz.ly *adj.* çiseleyen.

droll [drəul] *adj. (adv.* drooly) tuhaf, gülünç; 'droll.er.y *n.* mizah; tuhaf kimse,
maskara, soytarı.

drom.e.dar.y *zo.* ['drʌmədəri] *n.* hecin devesi, tek hörgüçlü binek devesi.

drone¹ [drəun] 1. *n. zo.* erkek arı; *fig.*
tembel, asalak kimse; uzaktan kuman-
dalı uçak *veya* gemi; 2. *vb.* tembellik,
haylazlık etm.

drone² [~] 1. *n.* vızıltı, çınlama; ♪ telli ve
nefesli çalgıların pes tonu; 2. *vb.* vızıldamak; monoton, pes bir ses tonuyla konuşmak.

drool [dru:l] 1. *v/i.* ağzı sulanmak, ağzının suyu akmak; 2. *n. Am.* F boş laf.

droop [dru:p] *v/t. & v/i.* indirmek; sark-
(ıt)mak; bükülmek; halsiz olm., süngü-
sü düşük olm., cesareti kırılmak; solmak, tazeliğini kaybetmek; 'droop.ing □
sarkık; yorgun, bitkin; soluk; ümitsiz.

drop [drɔp] 1. *n.* damla; düşme, sukut;
bonbon şekeri, draje; tavanda *veya* yerde bulunan kapak şeklinde kapı; *thea.*
perde; düşüş uzaklığı; paraşütle atılan
şey; *(mektup vs.)* bırakıldığı yer; get
*veya* have the ~ on *Am.* atik davranarak birinden önce silah çekmek; ~ light
asma lamba; in ~s, ~ by ~ damla damla
*(a. fig.);* 2. *v/t.* düşürmek, atmak; damlatmak; *(mektup)* posta kutusuna atmak; *(bomba)* atmak; *(gözyaşı)* akıtmak; *(söz, mevzu)* sarfetmek; *(yolcu)*
indirmek; *(ses)* alçaltmak; *(surat)* asmak; *(reverans)* yapmak; ~ s.o. a few
lines *b-ne* birkaç satır mektup yazmak;
~ it! F yapma!, bırak bunu!; *v/i.* damlamak, sızmak *(fıçı);* düşmek; inmek;
azalmak; düşüp ölmek; ~ behind geri
kalmak; ~ in uğramak (at, on, upon -e);
~ off yavaş yavaş azalmak; uykuya dalmak; düşmek; ~ out ayrılmak *(üyelik-
ten);* okulu bitirmeden ayrılmak; çıkmak; 'drop.ping *n.* damlama; düşme; ~s
*pl.* gübre, hayvan tersi; 'drop.scene *n.*
*thea.* son perde.

drop.si.cal □ ['drɔpsikəl] su toplanması
ile ilgili; 'drop.sy *n.* deri altında *veya* or-
ganlarda çeşitli hastalıklar yüzünden su
toplanması, hidropizi.

dross [drɔs] *n.* cüruf, tortu, maden po-
sası.

drought [draut], drouth [drauθ] *n.* kuraklık, susuzluk; kıtlık; 'drought.y,
'drouth.y *adj.* kurak, susuz; kıt.

drove [drəuv] 1. *n.* sürü, sığır sürüsü,
*fig.* kalabalık; 2. *pret. of* drive 2; 'drover *n.* davar sürücüsü, çoban, celep.

drown [draun] *v/t.* suda boğmak; bir yeri su basmak; *fig.* susturmak, sesiyle
bastırmak, boğmak; be ~ed boğulmak;
*v/i.* suda boğulmak.

drowse [drauz] *v/i.* uyuklamak, pineklemek; 'drow.si.ness *n.* uykulu olma, uyuşukluk; 'drow.sy *adj.* uykusu basmış, uyku gözünden akan; uyuşuk; uyutucu.

drub [drʌb] *v/t. b-ne* sopa çekmek, dayak
atmak; adamakıllı yenmek *-i; v/i.* par-
makların ucuyla tıkırdatmak *(masayı);*
'drub.bing *n.* dayak, kötek.

drudge [drʌdʒ] 1. *n. fig.* esir, köle, yük
eşeği, hamal, ağır ve kötü işlerde çalışan kimse; 2. *v/i.* ağır işler yapmak;
'drug.er.y *n.* ağır ve sıkıcı iş.

drug [drʌg] 1. *n.* ilaç, tıbbî ecza; uyuşturucu madde; esrar; ~ on the market sa-
tılmayan mal; 2. *v/t.* ilaçla uyutmak;
ilaç vermek, uyuşturucu vermek; *v/i.*
uyuşturucu almak; 'drug.gist *n.* eczacı;
bakkal; 'drug.store *n. Am.* bakkaliye;
eczane.

dru.id *hist.* ['dru:id] *n.* Hıristiyanlıktan
önce İngiltere, İrlanda ve Fransa'da
Kelt rahibi.

drum [drʌm] 1. *n.* davul, trampete, darbuka; ⊕ tambura, kasnak; *anat.* kulak
zarı; 2. *vb.* davul çalmak; davul sesi çıkarmak; davul çalarak biraraya toplamak, çağırmak; '~.fire *n.* ✗ aralıksız
şiddetli ateş; '~.head *n.* davul derisi;
~ court-martial ✗ harp divanı; '~-lma.jor
*n.* ✗ bando şefi; 'drum.mer *n.* davulcu,
trampeteci, baterist; *esp. Am.* F gezgin
satıcı; 'drum.stick *n.* davul tokmağı,
trampet sopası, baget; *(kümes hayvanı)* budun alt kemiği.

drunk [drʌŋk] 1. *p.p. of* drink 2.; 2. *adj.*
sarhoş; get ~ sarhoş olm.; drunk.ard
['~əd] *n.* ayyaş, sarhoş; drunk.en *adj.*
*attr.* sarhoş, ayyaş; 'drunk.en.ness *n.*
sarhoşluk; içki tutkunluğu.

drupe ⚘ [dru:p] *n.* tek çekirdekli ve etli
meyve.

dry [drai] 1. □ kuru, kurak; susuz; yavan, can sıkıcı; ince ve düşündürücü
*(mizah);* sek *(içki);* süt vermez *(inek);*
F susamış; F içki yasağı uygulanan; ~
cell kuru pil; ~ goods *pl.* F *Am.* tuhafi-

ye, manifatura; **2.** *n. Am.* F içki yasağı yanlısı; **3.** *v/t.* kurutmak, kurulamak; *v/i.* kurumak; ~ **up** tamamen kuru(t)-mak; ~ **up** F kes sesini!

**dry.ad** ['draiəd] *n. myth.* orman perisi.

**dry...:** ~ **bat.ter.y** kuru pil; ~ **bulb** ther-mom.e.ter atmosferdeki nemi ölçmekte kullanılan farklı kuru biri ıslak biri kuru olan iki termometreden biri; **'~-'clean** *v/t. (elbi-se vs.'yi)* su yerine benzen, trikloretilen vs. kullanarak temizlemek; **'~-'clean.ing** *n.* kuru temizleme.

**dry.er** ['draiə] = drier.

**dry...:** **'~-'nurse 1.** *n.* çocuğu emzirmeyen dadı; **2.** *v/i.* b-ne dadılık etm., candan bakmak; **'~-'rot** *n.* kerestenin içindeki «ev süngeri» denilen toz gibi çürüklük; *fig.* yozlaşma; **'~-'shod** *adv.* ayaklarını ıslatmadan; **'~-'wall.ing** *n.* harçsız duvar örme.

**du.al** □ ['dju:əl] iki kat, iki misli, çifte; çift...; **'du.al.ism** *n.* ikilik, dualizm.

**dub** [dʌb] *v/t.* b-nin omuzuna kılıçla do-kunarak şövalye yapmak; b-ne yeni bir isim *veya* unvan vermek; dublaj yap-mak; *(kösele)* yağlayıp yumuşatmak; **'dub.bing** *n.* vidala yağı.

**du.bi.e.ty** [dju:'baiəti] *n.* şüpheli olma; şüpheli şey *veya* durum.

**du.bi.ous** □ ['dju:bjəs] şüpheli, belirsiz, müphem; be ~ kestirememek, şüphe etm., bir türlü bilememek (of, about, over -i, -den, -i); **'du.bi.ous.ness** *n.* şüphe, belir-sizlik.

**du.cal** ['dju:kəl] *adj.* düke ait.

**duc.at** ['dʌkət] *n.* Avrupa'da eskiden bazı ülkelerde kullanılan değişik değerlerde altın para.

**duch.ess** ['dʌtʃis] *n.* düşes.

**duch.y** ['dʌtʃi] *n.* dükalık.

**duck¹** [dʌk] *n.* ördek; ördek eti; *Am. sl.* herifin biri, adam.

**duck²** [~] **1.** *n.* başını eğme, eğilme; sin-me; dalış; **2.** *v/t. & v/i.* dal(dır)mak; başını eğmek, sinmek *(a. fig.)*; b-den, bşden sakınmak için yana çekilmek, giz-lenmek; *Am.* b-le karşılaşmamağa çalış-mak; F sıvışmak.

**duck³** F [~] *n.* sevgili, yavru.

**duck⁴** [~] *n. (yelken)* keten bezi.

**duck...:** **'~-'bill** *n. zo.* Avustralya'ya mah-sus perde ayaklı, gagalı, vücudu kundu-za benzeyen bir hayvan; **'~-'boards** *n. pl.* lata, ızgara.

**duck.ling** ['dʌkliŋ] *n.* yavru ördek.

**duck.weed** ♀ ['dʌkwi:d] *n.* su mercimeği.

**duck.y** F ['dʌki] **1.** = duck³; **2.** *adj.* sevgi-li, güzel, zarif.

**duct** [dʌkt] *n.* guddelerden sıvı maddele-ri, salgıları akıtan kanal, boru, tüp, da-mar *(bitki).*

**duc.tile** □ ['dʌktail] *(metal)* genişleyebi-lir, uzayabilir; *(çamur)* şekil verilebilir; *fig.* uysal, yumuşak; **duc.til.i.ty** [~'tiliti] *n.* uzayıp genişleyebilme özelliği; uysal-lık.

**dud** *sl.* [dʌd] **1.** *n.* patlamayan mermi *ve-ya* bomba; *fig.* kendisinden bekleneni ya-pamayan, başarıya ulaşamayan kimse *veya* şey; ~**s** *pl.* kişisel eşya; **2.** *adj.* sah-te, kalp; yararsız.

**dude** *Am.* [dju:d] *n.* züppe, giyimine aşı-rı düşkün erkek; ~ **ranch** tatil köyü ola-rak düzenlenmiş çiftlik.

**dudg.eon** ['dʌdʒən] *n.* öfke, hiddet; in high ~ çok öfkeli, çok gücenmiş.

**due** [dju:] **1.** *adj.* gerekli; ödenmesi ge-rekli; uygun; süresi dolan; bşe layık; in ~ time tam vaktinde, zamanı gelince; the train is ~ at... trenin saat ...te gel-mesi bekleniyor; in ~ course zamanı ge-lince; zamanında; be ~ to yüzünden, -den dolayı; be ~ to *inf.* zorunda olm.; yapması istenilmek; *Am.* ...mak üzere olm.; fall ~ ♦ vadesi gelmek; ~ date ödeme günü, vade bitimi; **2.** *adj.* ♦ doğ-ru; ~ east tam doğuya doğru; **3.** *n.* hak; alacak, istihkak; mst ~**s** *pl.* vergi, re-sim; üye aidatı.

**du.el** ['dju:əl] **1.** *n.* düello; **2.** *v/i.* düello etm.; **'du.el.list** *n.* düellocu.

**du.et(.to)** [dju:'et(əu)] *n.* ♪ düet, iki kişi tarafından söylenen şarkı.

**duf.fel** ['dʌfəl] *n.* kalın havlı ve kaba bir tür yünlü kumaş; ~ coat bir tür kapşon-lu *(başlıklı)* kaban.

**duff.er** F ['dʌfə] *n.* ahmak herif, eşek ka-falı.

**dug** [dʌg] **1.** *pret. & p.p. of* dig; **2.** *n.* inek memesi, emcik; **'~-'out** *n.* ✕ sığınak; *sl.* göreve çağırılan emekli subay; *Am. beysbol:* üzerinde oyuncuların oturduğu üstü kapalı sıra *veya* yer.

**duke** [dju:k] *n.* dük, düka; **duke.dom** *n.* dükalık.

**dul.cet** ['dʌlsit] *adj.* tatlı, hoş, lâtif, ahenk-li; **'dul.ci.mer** ♪ [~'simə] *n.* simbalom, santur.

**dull** [dʌl] **1.** □ aptal, budala, kalın kafa-lı; ağır, hantal; *(göz, renk)* donuk, sö-nük; *(ses)* cansız; can sıkıcı; hissiz, alâ-kasız; kör, kesmez; *(ağrı, sızı)* belirsiz, pek hissedilmeyen; *(hava)* kapalı, kas-vetli; *(ticaret)* durgun, kesat; ♦ sakin, sütliman; **2.** *v/t. & v/i.* körleş(tir)mek, *fig.* duygusuzlaş(tır)mak, hayvanlaş-

(tır)mak; donuklaş(tır)mak; sersem-
le(t)mek; **dull.ard** [ˈ~əd] *n.* ahmak kimse; **ˈdull.ness** *n.* ahmaklık, hantallık; donukluk, matlık; sıkıcılık; monotonluk;
ilgisizlik, lâkaytlık; dert, keder, sıkıntı;
durgunluk.

**du.ly** [ˈdjuːli] *adv. s.* due; uygun olarak,
gereğince; tam zamanında.

**dumb** ☐ [dʌm] dilsiz; dili tutulmuş, sessiz, konuşmayan; *Am.* F aptal, budala,
deaf and ~ sağır ve dilsiz; *s.* show 2;
strike ~ hayretten dondurmak, şaşırt-
mak; **ˈ~bell** *n.* jimnastik güllesi; *Am. sl.*
aptal adam; **~ˈfound** *v/t.* F susturmak,
serseme çevirmek; **~ˈfounded** *adj.* hayretler içinde; **ˈdumb.ness** *n.* dilsizlik; dili tutulma; **ˈdumb-ˈwait.er** *n.* seyyar masa; *Am.* mutfak asansörü.

**dum.my** [ˈdʌmi] *n.* aldatmaca; *fig.* kulis;
*fig.* kukla adam, figüran; manken *(elbise)*; emzik; *attr.* taklit...; uydurma...;
~ whist üç kişi ve hayali bir dördüncü
ile oynanan bir iskambil oyunu.

**dump** [dʌmp] **1.** *vb.* boşaltmak, atmak
*(moloz. süprüntü)*; bşden kurtulmak *(a.
fig.)*; *(mal)* ucuza ihraç etm., damping
yapmak, fiyatları düşürmek, düşmek; **2.**
*n.* çöp, moloz vs. yığını; çöplük, mezbele; X cephanelik; = ~ing; **ˈdump.ing** †
*n.* ucuza ihraç etme, damping, ucuzluk,
fiyat indirme; **ˈdump.ing-ground** *n.* çöplük, mezbele; **ˈdump.ling** bir tür meyvalı hamur tatlısı; F kısa boylu ve tombul
kimse; **ˈdumps** *n.* F *pl.:* (down) in the ~
keyifsiz, ümitsiz; **ˈdump.y** *adj.* tıknaz,
bodur.

**dun¹** [dʌn] **1.** *adj.* boz, kurşunî; **2.** *n.* boz
at.

**dun²** [~] **1.** *n.* sıkıştıran alacaklı; **2.** *v/t.*
borçluyu sıkıştırmak; ~ning letter *n.* ihbarname.

**dunce** [dʌns], **dun.der.head** [ˈdʌndəhed]
*n.* aptal kimse.

**dune** [djuːn] *n.* kumul, eksibe.

**dung** [dʌŋ] **1.** *n.* hayvan tersi, gübre; **2.**
*v/t.* gübrelemek.

**dun.ga.ress** [dʌŋgəˈriːz] *n. pl.* kaba pamuklu kumaştan dikilmiş tulum.

**dun.geon** [ˈdʌndʒən] *n.* zindan.

**dung.hill** [ˈdʌŋhil] *n.* gübre yığını.

**dunk** [ˈdʌŋk] *vb.* suya dal(dır)mak; *(çay,
çorba vs.'ye)* batırmak, banmak.

**du.o** [ˈdjuːəu] *n.* düet; çift, eş.

**du.o.dec.i.mal** [djuːəuˈdesiməl] *adj.* on iki
veya on ikinciye ait; on ikişer on ikişer;
*n.* on ikide bir kısım; **du.oˈdec.i.mo**
[~məu] *n. typ.* bir kitap boyu, oniki yapraklı forma; *fig.* bücür, bacaksız.

**du.o.de.nal** *anat.* [djuːəuˈdiːnl] *adj.* onikiparmak bağırsağı...; **du.oˈde.num** [~nəm]
*n.* onikiparmak bağırsağı.

**dupe** [djuːp] **1.** *n.* kolayca aldatılabilen,
ahmak kimse; **2.** *v/t.* aldatmak, dolandırmak; **ˈdup.er.y** *n.* aldatma, hile, işletme.

**du.plex** [ˈdjuːpleks] **1.** *adj.* çift..., dubleks...; *tel.* karşılıklı aynı anda iki gönderme sistemi olan; **2.** *n. Am.* iki katlı
apartman dairesi.

**du.pli.cate 1.** [ˈdjuːplikit] *adj.* çift, eş, aynı, kopya; **2.** [ˈ~kit] *n.* eş, kopya, ikinci
nüsha, suret; in ~ iki nüsha olarak; **3.**
[ˈ~keit] *v/t. -in* suretini çıkarmak, ikilemek; iki misline çıkarmak; **du.pliˈca-
tion** *n.* teksir etme, teksir suret; **du.pli-
ca.tor** *n.* teksir makinesi; **du.plic.i.ty**
[djuːˈplisiti] *n.* iki yüzlülük, düzenbazlık, hile.

**du.ra.bil.i.ty** [djuərəˈbiliti] *n.* dayanıklılık,
sağlamlık; sürekli oluş; **ˈdu.ra.ble** ☐ dayanıklı, sağlam, devamlı; **ˈdur.ance** *n.* †
tutukluluk, mahpusluk; **du.ra.tion** [~
ˈreiʃən] *n.* devam, süre, süreklilik.

**du.ress** ☼☼ [ˈdjuəˈres] *n.* cebir, ikrah, tehdit, şantaj; zorlama, baskı.

**du.ring** [ˈdjuəriŋ] *prp.* esnasında, müddetince, zarfında.

**durst** [dəːst] *pret. of* dare.

**dusk** [dʌsk] *n.* akşam karanlığı, alacaka-
ranlık; **ˈdusk.y** ☐ oldukça karanlık *(a.
fig.)*; koyu esmer, siyahımsı.

**dust** [dʌst] **1.** *n.* toz; çiçek tozu; toprak;
çöp; küçültücü durum; **2.** *v/t. -in* tozunu silkmek, tozunu almak; *v/i.* toz serpmek, tozlanmak; **ˈ~bin** *n.* çöp tenekesi;
**ˈ~bowl** *n. Am.* A.B.D.'nin batısında kum
fırtınaları etkisinde olan bölge; **ˈ~cart**
*n.* çöp kamyonu; **ˈ~cloak**, **ˈ~coat** *n.* el-
biseyi tozdan korumak için giydirilen örtü, kaşpusiyer; **ˈdust.er** *n.* toz bezi, toz
alan şey, kuş tüyü; *Am.* kaşpusiyer;
**ˈdust.i.ness** *n.* tozluluk, toz; **ˈdust.ing** *n.*
*sl.* bir iki dayak; **ˈdust-ˈjack.et** *n.* kitap
cildini tozdan koruyan kitap kabı; **ˈ~.man**
*n.* çöpçü; **ˈ~.pan** *n.* faraş; **ˈdust-ˈup** *n.*
patırtı, şamata; **ˈdust.y** ☐ tozlu, toz gibi.

**Dutch** [dʌtʃ] **1.** *adj.* Hollandalı, Felemenkli; *hist. & Am. sl.* Almanyalı; ~ treat
*Am.* F yemekte hesabı paylaşma, eşit
ödeme *(Alman usulü)*; **2.** *n.* Felemenkçe,
Hollanda dili; the ~ *pl.* Hollanda halkı;
double ~ çetrefil lisan; ~ auc.tion *(mezat)* fiyat indirimi; ~ courage çakır ke-
yifliliğin verdiği cesaret; **ˈ~.man** *n.* Hollandalı; *hist. & Am. sl.* Alman, **ˈ~.wom-
an** *n.* Hollandalı kadın.

du.te.ous ['dju:tjəs] = dutiful; du.ti.a.ble ['~tjəbl] adj. gümrüğe tabi, du.ti.ful □ ['~tiful] görevini bilen, vazifeşinas; itaatli, saygılı.

du.ty ['dju:ti] n. ödev, görev, hizmet, sorumluluk, vazife (to); gümrük resmi, vergi; on ~ hizmette, vazife başında; off ~ izinli, serbest; ~ call resmî ziyaret, nezaket ziyareti; in ~ bound vazifesine uygun olarak; do ~ for bşin, b-nin yerini almak, işlevini görmek; fig. b-nin yanında çalışmak, hizmetçilik etm.; '~-'free adj. gümrüksüz, gümrük resmi ödemeden.

dwarf [dwɔ:f] 1. n. cüce, bodur (insan, ağaç, hayvan) 2. v/t. büyümesini önlemek, cüceleştirmek; kıyaslayarak küçük göstermek, gölgede bırakmak; ~ed adj. dumura uğramış, körelmiş; 'dwarf-ish □ cüceyi andıran, bodurca; 'dwarf-ish.ness n. cücelik.

dwell [dwel] (irr.) v/i. oturmak, durmak (on, upon üzerinde); ~ up(on) bir konu üzerinde durmak, ısrar etm.; 'dwell.er n. oturan, mukim, sakin, ora ahalisinden; 'dwell.ing n. ev, mesken, oturma yeri; 'dwell.ing-house n. ev, mesken, konut; 'dwell.ing-place n. ikametgâh, konut.

dwelt [dwelt] pret. & p.p. of dwell.

dwin.dle ['dwindl] v/i. yavaş yavaş azalmak veya küçülmek veya ufalmak; 'dwin.dling n. azalma, ufalma, küçülme.

dye [dai] 1. n. boya; of deepest ~ fig. en kötü şekilde; 2. v/t. & v/i. boya(n)mak; 'dy.er n. boyacı; 'dye-stuff n. boya ilacı; 'dye-works n. pl. boyahane.

dy.ing □ ['daiiŋ] (s. die¹) 1. adj. ölmekte olan; ölen...; lie ~ can çekişmek; 2. n. ölüm, ölme.

dyke [daik] = dike.

dy.nam.ic [dai'næmik] 1. a. dy'nam.i.cal □ dinamik, kuvvetli, faal, enerjik; 2. n. devitken güç, muharrik kuvvet; dy'nam-ics mst sg. dinamik birimi; dy.na.mite ['dainəmait] 1. n. dinamit; 2. v/t. dinamitle havaya uçurmak; 'dy.na.mit.er n. dinamitle uçuran kimse; dy.na.mo ['~məu] n. dinamo.

dy.nas.tic [di'næstik] adj. (~ally) hanedana ait; dy.nas.ty ['dinəsti] n. hanedan, soy.

dyne phys. [dain] n. din (güç birimi).

dys.en.ter.y ⚕ ['disntri] n. dizanteri, kanlı basur.

dys.pep.sia ⚕ [dis'pepsiə] n. hazımsızlık, dipepsi; dys'pep.tic [~tik] 1. adj. (~ally) hazımsızlığa ait; 2. n. hazımsızlık çeken kimse.

# E

**each** [iːtʃ] adj. her, beher, her bir; adv. her biri, tanesi; ~ other birbiri(ni); they cost a shilling ~ tanesi bir şilin.

**ea.ger** □ [ˈiːgə] hevesli; istekli (about, after, for), sabırsız; fig. gayretli; şevkli, hararetli; **ˈeager.ness** n. istek, gayret, şevk.

**ea.gle** [ˈiːgl] n. kartal, karakuş; on dolarlık madeni para; **ˈ~-ˈeyed** adj. keskin gözlü; **ea.glet** [ˈ~lit] n. kartal yavrusu.

**ea.gre** [ˈeigə] n. şiddetli met hareketi.

**ear¹** [iə] n. başak.

**ear²** [~] n. kulak; işitim; müziğin inceliklerini sezebilme yeteneği; kulp, sap; kulak verme, dikkat; be all ~s kulak kesilmek, can kulağı ile dinlemek; keep an ~ to the ground esp. Am. yeni haberleri almak veya gelişmeleri bildirmek; up to the ~s fig. fazla meşgul (çalışma); set by the ~s birbirine karşı kışkırtmak; **~-ache** [ˈiəreik] n. kulak ağrısı; **~-deaf.en.ing** [ˈ~defniŋ] adj. kulakları sağır edecek kadar gürültülü; **ˈ~-drum** n. kulak zarı.

**earl** [əːl] n. (İngiliz) kont; ♀ Marshal n. protokol başkanı; **ˈearl.dom** n. kontluk. **earl.li.ness** [ˈəːlinis] n. erken olma.

**ear.ly** [ˈəːli] adj. & adv. erken(den), erken...; başlangıçta...; eski; ilk; yakında; ~ life gençlik (zamanı); as ~ as ...kadar erken; earlier on evvelce, eskiden.

**ear-mark** [ˈiəmɑːk] 1. n. hayvanların kulağına takılan marka, işaret; fig. alâmet, karakteristik; 2. v/t. kulağa işaret koymak; fig. karakterize etm.; belirli bir amaç için kenara koymak (para vs.).

**earn** [əːn] v/t. kazanmak, hak etm.; ~ed income hak edilmiş, çalışarak kazanılmış gelir.

**ear.nest¹** [ˈəːnist] a. ~money n. pey akçesi, kaparo, pey, avans; temiant; fig. tadımlık, ilk tat; delil.

**ear.nest²** [~] 1. □ ciddi, ağırbaşlı; istekli, samimi; gerçek, hakiki; 2. n. ciddiyet; be in ~ ciddi olarak, samimiyetle; **ˈear.nest.ness** n. ciddiyet; istekli olma.

**earn.ings** [ˈəːniŋz] n. pl. kazanç, kâr, gelir.

**ear...:** **ˈ~-phones** n. pl. radyo, teyp vs.: kulaklık; **ˈ~.piece** n. teleph. işitme cihazı; **ˈ~-pierc.ing** adj. kulakları sağır edici (ses); **ˈ~-ring** n. küpe; **ˈ~.shot** n. kulak erimi, kulak menzili; **ˈ~-split.ting** adj. kulakları sağır edici.

**earth** [əːθ] 1. n. dünya; toprak; kara; yeryüzü; (tilki vs.) in; a. ~-connection n. radyo: toprak bağlantı; 2. v/t. ⚡ toprağa bağlamak; ~ up toprak ile örtmek; **ˈearth.en** adj. topraktan yapılmış; **ˈearth-en.ware** 1. n. çanak çömlek; 2. adj. toprak işi; **ˈearth.ing** n. ⚡ toprak bağlantı; **earth.li.ness** n. dünyevî oluş, maddilik; **ˈearth.ly** adj. dünyaya ait, dünyevî; F düşünülebilir, olası; no ~ ... hiç bir ...yoktu; **ˈearth.quake** n. deprem; **ˈearth.worm** n. zo. yer solucanı; fig. yaltakçı b-i; **ˈearth.y** adj. dünyevî, madde ile ilgili; topraklı, toprağa benzer; fig. zevk düşkünü. ruhsuz, kaba.

**ear...:** **ˈ~-trum.pet** n. eskiden ağır işiten kimselerin kullandığı kulak borusu; **ˈ~-wax** n. kulak kiri; **ˈ~.wig** n. zo. kulağakaçan.

**ease** [iːz] 1. n. rahat, konfor, huzur, refah; kolaylık; at ~ rahat, hoş; teklifsiz; be veya feel at ~ içi rahat olm.; ill at ~ huzursuz, endişeli; stand at ~! ✕ yerinde rahat!, rahat!; take one's ~ rahat etm., dinlenmek, yangelmek; with ~ kolaylıkla: live at ~ rahat koşullarda yaşamak: 2. v/t. hafifletmek; (ağrı) yatıştırmak; b-nin rahat ve huzurunu sağlamak; (halat vs.) gevşetmek; kurtarmak (of -den); gerginliğini kaybetmek (koşullar); ~ nature hacet görmek, tuvalete gitmek; hafiflemek; **ease.ful** □ [ˈ~ful] rahat, hoş; sakin.

**ea.sel** [ˈiːzl] n. ressam sehpası, şövale.

**eas.i.ly** [ˈiːzili] adv. kolaylıkla, kolayca; rahat rahat; şüphesiz; **ˈeas.i.ness** n. kolaylık, rahatlık, doğal davranma, tabiilik; ~ of belief safdillik, kolay aldatılma.

**east** [i:st] **1.** *n.* doğu, şark; the 2 *Am.*
A.B.D.'de doğu eyaletleri; **2.** *adj.* doğu..., doğu ile ilgili; **3.** *adv.* doğuya doğru.
**East.er** [ˈiːstə] *n. rel.* Paskalya yortusu;
~ egg paskalya yumurtası.
**east.er.ly** [ˈiːstəli] *adj. & adv.* doğuda;
doğu...; doğuya doğru, doğudan; **eastern** [ˈ-tən] = easterly; doğu(da); doğu-
lulara ait, oryantal; **ˈeast.ern.er** *n.* doğulu *b-i;* 2 *Am.* A.B.D.'de doğu eyaletlerinden olan *b-i;* **east.ern.most** [ˈ-məust]
*adj.* en uzak doğu.
**east.ing** ↓ [ˈiːstiŋ] *n.* doğu yönünde hareket; doğuya doğru giderek katedilen mesafe.
**east.ward(s)** [ˈiːstwəd(z)] *adj. & adv.* doğuya doğru (olan).
**eas.y** [ˈiːzi] **1.** ☐ kolay, rahat, sıkıntısız;
sakin; uysal; doğal davranışları olan;
rahat *(elbise);* ⊤ durgun; in ~ circumstances hali vakti yerinde, varlıklı; on ~
street iyi koşullarda; on ~ terms ⊤ uygun
koşullarda, uygun taksitlerle; make o.s.
~ rahatına bakmak; take it ~ *k-ni* fazla
yormamak, yangelmek; take it ~! acele
etmeyiniz!, telaşlanmayınız!, darılma-
yınız!; **2.** *n.* kısa mola; **ˈ~-ˈchair** *n.* koltuk; **ˈ~-go.ing** *adj. fig.* kayıtsız, kaygısız.
**eat** [iːt] *(irr.) v/t.* yemek; aşındırmak
*(away -i);* ~ up hepsini yemek, silip süpürmek, yiyip bitirmek *(a. fig.); v/i.* yemek yemek; lezzetli olm.; aşındırmak
*(into, through);* biriktirileni yemeğe başlamak; **2.** ~s *n. pl. Am. sl.* yemek, yiye-
cek(ler); **ˈeat.a.ble** *adj.* yenilebilir; **ˈeat-
a.bles** *n. pl.* yiyecek, gıda; **ˈeat.en** *p.p.
of* eat 1; **ˈeat.er** *n.* yiyen *b-i;* be a great
(poor) ~ çok (az) yiyen *b-i* olm.; **ˈeat.ing**
*n.* yemek yeme; **ˈeat.ing-house** *n.* aşevi,
lokanta.
**eau-de-Co.logne** [ˈəudəkəˈləun] *n.* kolonya.
**eaves** [iːvz] *n. pl.* çıkıntı, saçak; **ˈ~-drop**
*v/i.* kulak kabartmak, gizlice dinlemek;
**ˈ~-drop.per** *n.* kulak misafiri, gizlice dinleyen *b-i.*
**ebb** [eb] **1.** *n.* cezir, deniz sularının çekilmesi; *fig.* bozulma, düşüş, başarısızlık;
at a low ~ harap, perişan, zor durum-
da; **2.** *v/i.* çekilmek *(deniz); fig.* bozulmak; azalmak; zor durumda olm.;
**ˈ~-ˈtide** *n.* cezir, inik deniz; *fig.* suyunu
çekme.
**eb.on** *poet.* [ˈebən] *adj.* abanozdan yapılmış; abanoz gibi siyah; **eb.on.ite** [ˈ-nait]
*n.* ebonit, bir tür siyah sert kauçuk; **ˈeb-
on.y** *n.* abanoz (ağacı).
**e.bri.e.ty** [iːˈbraiəti] *n.* sarhoşluk.

**e.bul.li.ent** [iˈbʌljənt] *n.* taşkın, coşkun, içi
içine sığmayan; *fig.* fıkır fıkır (with);
**eb.ul.li.tion** [ebəˈliʃən] *n.* taşkınlık, coşkunluk; kaynama.
**ec.cen.tric** [ikˈsentrik] **1.** *a.* **ecˈcen.tri.cal**
☐ eksantrik; *fig.* garip, tuhaf; deliş-
men, kaçık; **2.** *n.* ⊕ dışmerkezli, eksantrik; kendi bildiğini okuyan kimse; **ec-
cen.tric.i.ty** [eksenˈtrisiti] *n.* tuhaflık;
dışmerkezlilik; *fig.* delişmenlik, eksantrik olma.
**ec.cle.si.as.tic** [ikliːziˈæstik] *n.* papaz, rahip; **ec.cle.si.as.ti.cal** ☐ kiliseye at, dinî.
**ech.e.ion** ✗ [ˈeʃələn] **1.** *n.* kademe, mevzi; **2.** *v/t. & v/i.* kademelen(dir)mek.
**e.chi.nus** *zo.* [eˈkainəs] *n.* deniz kestanesi.
**ech.o** [ˈekəu] **1.** *n.* yankı, aksiseda; **2.** *v/t.
& v/i.* yansı(t)mak; *(ses)* akset(tir)mek;
*fig.* taklit etm., tekrarlamak; **ˈ~-sound.er**
*n.* ↓ sesli iskandil.
**e.clat** [ˈeiklɑ:] *n.* büyük başarı, herkesin
övgüsünü kazanan mükemmel sonuç.
**ec.lec.tic** [ekˈlektik] **1.** *adj.* (insan, yöntem, fikir) bir sistem *ya da* düşünceye
bağlanmayan fakat hepsinden yararla-
nan; seçme şeylerden oluşmuş, derlenmiş; **2.** *n.* felsefe ve sanatta belirli bir
düşünceye değil fakat çeşitli düşünce ve
yöntemlerden *k-ne* uygun olanı seçen
kimse; **ecˈlec.ti.cism** [~sizəm] *n.* seçip
toplama eğilimi.
**e.clipse** [iˈklips] **1.** *n.* ay tutulması, güneş
tutulması; *fig.* şöhretini kaybetme; **2.**
*v/t.* karartmak; gölgede bırakmak *(a.
fig.); b-nin* yıldızını söndürmek; **eˈclip-
tic** *ast.* [~tik] *n.* ekliptik, güneşin sabit
yıldızlara göre bir yılda takip ettiği dairesel yol.
**ec.logue** [ˈeklɔg] *n.* karşılıklı konuşma
şeklinde pestoral şiir.
**e.col.o.gy** [iːˈkɔlədʒi] *n.* çevrebilim, canlıların çevreleriyle olan ilişkilerini inceleyen biyoloji dalı.
**e.co.nom.ic** [iːkəˈnɔmik], **e.coˈnom.i.cal** ☐
iktisadî, ekonomik; idareli, tutumlu; iktisat...; **e.coˈnom.ics** *n. sg.* iktisat bilimi; **e.con.o.mist** [iˈkɔnəmist] *n.* iktisatçı, ekonomist; **eˈcon.o.mize** *vb.* idareli
kullanmak (in, on, with *-i), bşden* tasarruf etm.; **eˈcon.o.my** *n.* iktisat, ekonomi;
tutum, idare; ekonomik sistem; econo-
mies *pl.* tasarruf, tutum; ekonomik önlem; political ~ ekonomi politik, iktisat
bilimi.
**ec.sta.size** [ˈekstəsaiz] *v/t. & v/i.* coş-
(tur)mak, kendinden geç(ir)mek; hayran bırakmak, hayran olm.; **ˈec.sta.sy** *n.*
coşkunluk, kendinden geçme, vecit, esri-

me; go into ~ coşkuyla övmek; **ec.stat.ic** [eks'tætik] *adj.* (~ally) coş(tur)an, vecde düşmüş; ~ fit coşkunluk hali, ulu bş karşısında heyecan duyma.

**ec.ze.ma** 🐝 ['eksimə] *n.* egzama, mayasıl.

**e.da.cious** [i'deifəs] *adj.* obur, açgözlü, pisboğaz.

**ed.dy** ['edi] **1.** *n.* girdap, anafor; **2.** *v/t.* & *v/i.* şiddetle dön(dür)mek; *fig.* velveleye getirmek.

**e.den.tate** *zo.* [i'denteit] *adj.* dişsiz; dişsiz memeli hayvanlara ait.

**edge** [edʒ] **1.** *n.* kenar, sırt; uç; bıçak ağzı; kıyı, sınır; *(kitap)* kenar; *(dağ)* sırt; şiddet, sertlik; bə on ~ sinirli olm.; have the ~ on s.o. *sl.* b-den üstün olm.; put an ~ on bilemek, keskinleştirmek, zağlamak; lay on ~ yanlamasına koymak *(alanı geniş, ince şeyler için: madeni para vs. gibi)*; set s.o.'s teeth on ~ b-ni sinirlendirmek; dişbilemek; **2.** *vb.* bilemek, keskinleştirmek; kenar geçirmek, teyellemek, kenarını süslemek *(with ile)*; yan yan ve yavaşça ilerle(t)mek, sokulmak, sürmek, çekmek. **edged** *adj.* keskin; ~ kenarlı.

**edge**...: '~.less *adj.* kör, keskin olmayan; *fig.* yavan; '~-tool *n.* kesici alet; '~.ways, ~.wise ['~waiz] *adv.* yandan, kenardan; dolaylı olarak; yana doğru; get a word in ~ fırsat bulup konuşabilmek.

**edg.ing** ['edʒiŋ] *n.* kenarlık, şerit, dantelâ; bordür; '~-shears *n. pl.* çim biçme makası.

**edg.y** ['edʒi] *adj.* keskin kenarlı; F sinirli.

**ed.i.ble** ['edibl] *adj.* yenir, yenilebilir; 'ed.i.bles *n. pl.* yiyecek(ler).

**e.dict** ['i:dikt] *n.* emir, ferman, buyrultu, kararname.

**ed.i.fi.ca.tion** *fig.* [edifi'keifən] *n.* yüksek duygulara ulaşma, karakter ve düşünce gelişimi; **ed.i.fice** ['~fis] *n.* büyük bina, yapı; bünye, yapılış *(a. fig.)*; **ed.i.fy** *fig.* ['~fai] *v/t.* yüksek duygular ilham etm.; öğretmek; doğru yolu göstermek; duyguca yüceltmek; 'ed.i.fy.ing ☐ yüksek duygulara ulaştıran; iyi bir örnek olan.

**ed.it** ['edit] *v/t. (metin, konu)* yayımlamak, baskısının yazdığı bir yazıyı basılmak için hazırlamak, telif etm.; *(gazete)* idare etm.; **e.di.tion** [i'difən] *n.* baskı, *(kitap)* yayım; **ed.i.tor** ['editə] *n.* yayımlayan; yazı işleri müdürü; **ed.i.to.ri.al** [~'tɔ:riəl] **1.** *adj.* yazı işleri müdürlüğüne ait; **2.** *n.* başyazı; **ed.i.tor.ship** ['~təfip] *n.* yazı işleri müdürlüğü, editörlük; redaksiyon.

**ed.u.cate** ['edju:keit] *v/t.* eğitmek, yetiştirmek, bşi öğretmek; ~ed *adj.* okumuş, aydın; **ed.u'ca.tion** *n.* eğitim, öğretim, maarif; Ministry of ☿ Milli Eğitim Bakanlığı; **ed.u.ca.tion.al** ☐ ['~keifənl], **ed.u.ca.tive** ['~kətiv] *adj.* eğitimsel, pedagojik; eğitim...; eğitici; educational film öğretici film; **ed.u.ca.tion(.al)-ist** [~'keifn(ə)list] *n.* pedagog, eğitimci; 'ed.u.ca.tor *n.* eğitmen, öğretmen.

**e.duce** [i:'dju:s] *v/t.* sonuca varmak, tümevarım; *fig.* hedefinden çevirmek; ☿ bir karışımdan bir elemanı ayırmak. **e.duc.tion** [i'dʌkʃən] *n. (anlam, sonuç)* çıkarma, çıkan şey; ⊕ egzos; istim sahverme; **e'duc.tion-pipe** *n.* istim borusu, egzos borusu.

**eel** [i:l] *n.* yılanbalığı.

**e'en** [i:n] = even.

**e'er** [cə] = ever.

**ee.rie, ee.ry** ['iəri] *adj.* tekin olmayan, endişe verici, korkutucu, tüyler ürpertici.

**ef.face** [i'feis] *v/t.* silmek, bozmak *(yüzey)*, üstünden sünger geçirmek; *fig.* yok etm., imha etm.; *fig.* unutturmak; ~ o.s. bir köşeye çekilmek; **ef'face.a.ble** *adj.* silinebilir; **ef'face.ment** *n.* silme, yok etme; sinme.

**ef.fect** [i'fekt] **1.** *n.* etki, sonuç; gösteriş; ☿ meriyet, yürürlük; ⊕ randıman, verim; ~s *pl.* menkul kıymetler, taşınır mallar, eşya; † alacak, matlup; bring to ~, carry into ~ gerçekleştirmek, realize etm.; tahakkuk ettirmek; take ~, be of ~ yürürlüğe girmek; işlemek; of no ~ etkisiz, faydasız, tesirsiz; in ~ hakikaten, gerçekten, aslında; halen yürürlükte; to the ~ genel olarak, anlamında; to this ~ bu anlamda; **2.** *v/t.* etkilemek; başarmak; be ~ed etkili olm.; **ef'fec.tive 1.** ☐ etkili, tesirli; ☿ yürürlükte, geçerli; ✕, ⬍ muharebeye elverişli, hizmete hazır; ⊕ verimli, randımanlı; ~ capacity ⊕ verimli kapasite; ~ date geçerli tarih, yürürlüğe girdiği tarih; ~ range etkili top menzili; ~ use kullan(ıl)ma; **2.** *n.* ✕ mst ~s *pl.* hazır güç; † efektif, nakit para; **ef'fec.tive.ness** *n.* etki, geçerlilik, itibar; **ef'fec.tu.al** [~'tfuəl] *adj. (davranış)* etkili, sonuç veren, geçerli; **ef'fec.tu.ate** [~tjueit] *v/t.* yapmak, yerine getirmek, sonuçlandırmak, becermek, basarmak.

**ef.fem.i.na.cy** [i'feminəsi] *n.* kadınca davranış, erkekçe olmayan durum; **ef'fem.i.nate** [~nit] ☐ kadınımsı, kadın tavırlı, yumuşak.

**ef.fer.vesce** [efə'ves] *v/i.* *(sıvı)* köpürmek, kabarmak; *fig.* coşmak, taşmak, neşelenmek; **ef.fer'ves.cence** *n.* köpürme, kabarma; coşma; **ef.fer'ves.cent** *adj.* köpüren, kabaran; coşkun; ~ powder kabartma tozu.

**ef.fete** [e'fi:t] *adj.* bitkin, yıpranmış, güçsüz; kısır, verimsiz.

**ef.fi.ca.cious** ☐ [efi'keiʃəs] etkili, tesirli *(esp. ilaç, tedavi)*; **ef.fi.ca.cy** ['~kəsi] *n.* etki, yarar, fayda.

**ef.fi.cien.cy** [i'fiʃənsi] *n.* kifayet, yeterlik, uzluk, etki; ⊕ verim, randıman; ~ expert rasyonalizasyon uzmanı; **ef'fi.cient** ☐ etkili, yeterli, uz, ehliyetli; verimli.

**ef.fi.gy** ['efidʒi] *n.* resim, tasvir, şekil, portre; burn s.o. in ~ *(halkın nefret ifadesi olarak b-nin)* resim *veya* modelini yakmak .

**ef.flo.resce** [eflɔ:'res] *v/i.* ❦ çiçek açmak; *fig.* çiçek gibi açılmak; ⚗ su kaybederek toz haline gelmek; **ef.flo'res.cent** *adj.* çiçeklenen; hava ile temas edince tozlanan.

**ef.flu.ence** ['efluəns] *n.* *(sıvı, gaz, ışık)* dışarı akma, dökülme; **'ef.flu.ent 1.** *adj.* dışarı akan, akıp giden; **2.** *n.* akıntı, dökülme; fabrika vs.'den dökülen artık sıvı *vs.*

**ef.flux** ['eflʌks] *n.* dışarı akış, akıntı.

**ef.fort** ['efət] *n.* gayret, çaba, uğraş (at); F elde edilen başarı; **'ef.fort.less** ☐ zahmetsiz, çaba sarfetmeyen; kolay.

**ef.fron.ter.y** [i'frʌntəri] *n.* küstahlık, yüzsüzlük, hayasızlık.

**ef.ful.gence** [e'fʌldʒəns] *n.* parlaklık, parıltı; debdebe, görkem, şaşaa, ihtişam; **ef'ful.gent** ☐ parlak, ışıyan; şaşaalı, görkemli.

**ef.fuse** [e'fju:z] *v/t.* dışarı akıtmak, dökmek. sızdırmak; **ef.fu.sion** [i'fju:ʒən] *n.* dökme, içini boşaltma *(a. fig.)*; akma; dökülen, akan *veya* sızan sıvı *veya* gaz; **ef'fu.sive** ☐ [~siv] taşkın, taşan, bol, coşkun; **ef'fu.sive.ness** *n.* taşkınlık, coşkunluk. bolluk.

**eft** *zo.* [eft] *n.* ufak semender *veya* kertenkele.

**egg¹** [eg] *mst* ~ on *v/t. b-ni* bşi yapması için sıkıştırmak, tahrik etm., gayrete getirmek.

**egg²** [~] *n.* yumurta, tohum; in the ~ ilk aşamada, başlangıç devresinde; bad ~ F ciğeri beş para etmez adam; put all one's ~ in one basket varını yoğunu tek bir şeye bağlayarak tehlikeye atmak; tüm sermayesini bir işe yatırmak; as

sure as ~s is ~s F hiç şüphesiz, kaçınılması olanaksız; **'~cup** *n.* yumurta kabı; **'~flip** *n.* yumurtalı içki; **'~head** *n.* Am. *sl.* entellektüel, aydın *b-i;* **'~nog** = egg-**flip**; **'~plant** *n.* ❦ patlıcan; **'~shell** *n.* yumurta kabuğu; **'~whisk** *n.* yumurta çırpma teli.

**eg.lan.tine** ❦ ['eglantain] *n.* bir tür kokulu gül, yaban gülü.

**e.go** ['egəu] *n.* benlik, mevcudiyet, varlık, varoluş, ben, ego; **'e.go.ism** *n.* bencilik, egoizm, yalnız kendi öz varlığını düşünme ve sevme, hodbinlik; **'e.goist** *n.* egoist, bencil, hodbin, yalnız kendi çıkarını düşünen *b-i;* **e.go'is.tic,** **e.go'is.ti.cal** ☐ egoist, bencil, kendi çıkarını düşünen, hodkâm, menfaatperest; **e.go.tism** ['~tizəm] *n.* kendini beğenme, hodpesentlik; **'ego.tist** *n.* kendinden çok bahseden kimse, benbenci; *k-ni* beğenmiş *b-i;* **e.go'tis.tic,** **e.go'tis.ti.cal** ☐ *k-ni* beğenmiş, *k-ni* dev aynasında gören.

**e.gre.gious** *iro.* ☐ [i'gri:dʒəs] fevkalâde kötü, çok kötü, işitilmemiş.

**e.gress** ['i:gres] *n.* çıkış, çıkılacak yer; *fig.* çıkar yol, çare.

**e.gret** ['i:gret] *n. orn.* bir tür küçük beyaz balıkçıl; sorguç, kuş tepeliği.

**E.gyp.tian** [i'dʒipʃən] **1.** *adj.* Mısır'a ait; **2.** *n.* Mısırlı.

**eh** [ei] *int.* nasıl?; ya?; Vay!; Ey!

**ei.der** ['aidə] *n. a.* ~-duck *orn.* pufla, kuzey kutbuna yakın yerlerde yaşayan bir tür ördek; ~ down pufla tüyünden yapılan yastık, yorgan vs.

**eight** [eit] **1.** *adj.* sekiz; **2.** *n.* sekiz rakamı; ⚓ sekiz kişilik skif; behind the ~ ball *Am.* sıkıntıda, zor durumda; **eight.een** ['ei'ti:n] *n. & adj.* onsekiz; **'eight.**teenth** [~θ] *n. & adj.* onsekizinci; **eight.fold** *adj. & adv.* sekiz misli; **eighth** [eitθ] **1.** *adj.* sekizinci; **2.** *n.* sekizde bir; **'eighth.ly** *adv.* sekizinci olarak; **eight-'hour day** sekiz saatlik çalışma günü; **eight.i.eth** ['~iiθ] *adj.* sekseninci; **'eight.some** [~səm] *n. (8 dansçı ile yapılan)* bir İskoç dansı; **'eight.y** *n. & adj.* seksen.

**eis.tedd.fod** [ais'teðvəd] *n.* Gal ülkesinde müzisyenler, edebiyatçılar ve saz şairlerinin yıllık yarışması.

**ei.ther** ['aiðə] **1.** *adj. & pron.* ikisinden biri, ya o ya bu, her iki; **2.** *cj.* ~ ... or ...ya ...yahut...

**e.jac.u.late** [i'dʒækjuleit] *vb.* birdenbire söyleyivermek; atmak, fışkırtmak; **e.jac.u'la.tion** *n.* ünlem, nida; dışarı atma, fışkırtma.

e.ject [i:dʒekt] v/t. dışarı atmak, kovmak (from -den), çıkarmak, fışkırtmak; (görev) azletmek; e'jec.tion n. çıkarma, kovma, azil; fışkıran şey; e'ject.ment n. öö boşaltma, tahliye, çıkarma; e'jec.tor n. ⊕ tırnak, tüfekten boş kovanları atan mekanizma; ~-seat n. ✈ fırlatma koltuğu.

eke [i:k]: ~ out v/t. tamamlamak, ikmal etm. (with, by ile), (maaş) katkı sağlamak, idareli kullanmak, idare etmek; ~ out a miserable existence kıt kanaat geçinmek.

el Am. F [el] = elevated railroad.

e.lab.o.rate 1. □ [i'læbərit] dikkatle işlenmiş, özenilmiş, kusursuz; komplike, detaylı; 2. [~reit] vb. incelikle işlemek, ayrıntılı olarak hazırlamak; e'lab.o.rate-ness [~ritnis], e.lab.o.ra.tion [~'reiʃən] n. özenli işleme; detay.

e.lapse [i'læps] v/i. (zaman) geçmek, akmak.

e.las.tic [i'læstik] 1. adj. (~ally) elâstiki, esnek (a. fig.), eski şeklini alan; hoşgörü sahibi, kendini çabuk toparlayan; 2. n. lastik bant; e.las.tic.i.ty [elæs'tisiti] n. elastikiyet, esneklik; fig. takat, kudret.

e.late [i'leit] v/t. sevindirmek, mutlu etm., gurur vermek; e'lated adj. sevinçli, mutlu, gururlu (at, with); e'la.tion n. sevinç, kıvanç, gurur.

el.bow ['elbəu] 1. n. dirsek; kavis, dönemeç, viraj; ⊕ dirsek, açı; at one's ~ elinin altında yardıma hazır; out at ~s kılıksız, pejmürde; fig. sefil, perişan; 2. v/t. dirsekle dürtmek; ~ one's way through ite kaka k-ne yol açmak; ~ out b-ni bir yerden atmak, defetmek; '~-chair n. koltuk; '~-grease n. F (parlatma, temizleme) el emeği; '~-room n. hareket serbestliği olan yer.

eld.er¹ ['eldə] 1. adj. daha yaşlı, büyük; 2. n. ihtiyar; kilise mütevelli heyeti üyesi; my ~s ailedeki büyüklerim.

el.der² ⌗ [~] n. mürver ağacı.

eld.er.ly ['eldəli] adj. yaşlı(ca), geçkin.

eld.est ['eldist] adj. en yaşlı, en büyük; the ~ born ilk doğan çocuk.

e.lect [i'lekt] 1. adj. seçilmiş, seçimi kazanmış; eccl. cennete gidecek; bride ~ nişanlı; 2. vb. seçilmek; karar vermek (to do); 3. n. pl. eccl. the ~s cennete gidecek olanlar; e'lec.tion n. seçim; e.lec.tion.eer [~ʃə'niə] v/i. seçim propagandası yapmak; e.lec.tion'eer.ing n. seçim propagandası; e'lec.tive 1. □ seçimle getirilen; seçme yetkisi olan; seçim...; Am.

isteğe bağlı, ihtiyarî; 2. n. Am. seçmeli ders; e'lec.tive.ly adv. seçimle, seçim yoluyla; e'lec.tor n. seçmen, seçme yetkisi olan b-i; hist. kutsal Roma imparatorunu seçen altı seçiciden b-i; e'lec.tor.al adj. seçim...; seçmen...; seçimle ilgili; ~ address seçim nutku; ~ college Am. seçmenler kurulu; ~ roll seçmen listesi; e'lec.tor.ate [~tərit] n. seçmenler; e'lec-trees n. hist. kutsal Roma imparatorunu seçen altı seçiciden kadın olanı; kadın seçmen.

e.lec.tric [i'lektrik], e'lec.tri.cal □ elektrik(li); elektro...; fig. elektriklen(dir)-ilmiş; e'lec.tri.cal en.gi.neer elektrik mühendisi.

e.lec.tric...; ~ blue çelik mavisi; ~ chair elektrikli sandalye.

e.lec.tri.cian [ilek'triʃən] n. elektrik teknisyeni, elektrikçi; e.lec'tric.i.ty [~siti] n. elektrik; elektrik akımı; e.lec.tri.fi'ca-tion n. elektrikle(n)me; e'lec.tri.fy [~fai], n. elektrik...; e'lec.trize v/t. elektrikle(ndir)mek (a. fig.); elektrikleştirmek; heyecana getirmek, coşturmak.

e.lec.tro [i'lektrəu] prefix elektrikle işleyen, elektro...; e'lec.tro.cute [~trəkju:t] v/t. elektrikli sandalyede idam etm., elektrik akımı vererek öldürmek; e.lec-tro'cu.tion n. elektrikle idam veya ölüm; e'lec.trode [~trəud] n. elektrot; e'lec.tro--dy'nam.ics n. mst sg. elektrodinamik; e.lec.tro.lier [~'liə] n. elektrikli avize; e'lec.tro.lyse [~laiz] v/t. elektrikle ayrıştırmak; e.lec.trol.y.sis [ilek'trolisis] n. elektroliz; e.lec.tro.lyte [i'lektrəulait] n. elektrolit; e.lec.tro.lyt.ic [~'litik] adj. elektrolitik; e'lec.tro'mag.net n. elektrikli mıknatıs; e'lec.tro'met.al.lur.gy n. madenleri alaşımlarından ayırmada kullanılan elektrikli yöntem bilimi; e'lec.tro-'mo.tive adj. elektrik akımının geçmesini sağlayan; e'lec.tro'mo.tor n. elektromotor.

e.lec.tron [i'lektrɔn] n. elektron; attr. elektron...; e.lec'tron.ic adj. elektronik...; e.lec'tron.ics n. sg. elektronik bilimi.

e.lec.tro.plate [i'lektrəupleit] 1. v/t. elektroliz usulü ile kaplamak; 2. n. bu şekilde kaplanmış eşya; e'lec.tro type n. galvanize klişe, elektrikle yapılmış klişe.

e.lee.mos.y.nar.y [elii:'mɔsinəri] adj. sadaka olarak verilmiş.

el.e.gance ['eligəns] n. zarafet, şıklık. incelik; 'el.e.gant □ zarif, şık, ince, kibar, nazik, Am. birinci sınıf.

**el.e.gi.ac** [eli'dʒaiək] **1.** *adj.* hüzünlü, elemli, hazin, mersiye tarzında; **2.** *n.* mersiye tarzında yazılmış şiir.

**el.e.gy** ['elidʒi] *n.* ağıt, mersiye, eleji.

**el.e.ment** ['elimənt] *n.* öğe, unsur, eleman; cüz, esas *(hava, ateş, toprak, su gibi)* dört ana unsurdan her biri; *≠* pil; *⚗* element; *∼s pl.* esaslar, elementer bilgiler; kötü hava şartları; **el.e.men.tal** [∼ment] ☐ temel, ilkel, basit, elemanter, esas(lı); doğaya ait; **el.e'men.ta.ry** ☐ basit, öz, başlangıç; ilk...; *∼* school ilkokul; elementaries *pl.* esaslar, unsurlar.

**el.e.phant** ['elifənt] *n. zo.* fil; white *∼* değerli fakat işe yaramayan mal, mülk; **el.e.phan.tine** [∼'fæntain] *adj.* fil gibi..., hantal, kaba.

**el.e.vate** ['eliveit] *v/t.* yükseltmek; *fig.* sesini yükseltmek, yaygara koparmak; **'el.e.vat.ed 1.** *adj.* yüksek, yüce, ulu; F çakırkeyf; *∼* railroad = **2.** *n. Am.* F şehir içinde yapılmış sütunlar üzerinden geçen demiryolu; **el.e'va.tion** *n.* yükseltme, yüceltme; yükseklik, yücelik, irtifa, rakım, altitüt; yüksek yer, tepe; *ast.* yıldızların yüksekliği; ⊕ dikey kesit; **'el.e.va.tor** *n.* ⊕ kaldırma mekanizması; *Am.* asansör; ⊥ irtifa dümeni; (grain) *∼ Am.* tahıl ambarı; bucket *∼* ⊕ tahılı üst katlara nakleden makine.

**e.lev.en** [i'levn] **1.** *adj.* onbir; **2.** *n.* onbir rakkamı; *∼-'plus ex.am.i.na.tion n.* İngiltere'de 11 yaşına gelen çocuğun girdiği ortaokul giriş sınavı; **e'lev.enth** [∼θ] *adj.* onbirinci; *at the* *∼* hour son dakika, son anda.

**elf** [elf] *n., pl.* **elves** [elvs] peri, cin; cüce; **elf.in** ['∼in] *adj.* cin gibi, ele avuca sığmaz; **'elf.ish** *adj.* yaramaz, şirret.

**e.lic.it** [i'lisit] *v/t. (bilgi vs.)* sağlamak; *(gerçek)* aydınlığa kavuşturmak.

**e.lide** *gr.* [i'laid] *v/t.* hızlı konuşurken atlamak. telaffuz etmemek *(harf, hece).*

**el.i.gi.bil.i.ty** [elidʒə'biliti] *n.* uygunluk, tercih; **'el.i.gi.ble** ☐ seçilebilir, uygun, elverişli; evlilik için uygun *(koca).*

**e.lim.i.nate** [i'limineit] *v/t.* ayırmak, bertaraf etm.; ortadan kaldırmak, çıkarmak *(esp. ⚗, ♈, ♓);* **e.lim.i'na.tion** *n.* çıkarma, ayırma.

**e.li.sion** *gr.* [i'liʒən] *n.* çıkarma, şiirde özellikle sözcük sonundaki harf *ya da* hecenin okunmaması.

**é.lite** [ei'liːt] *n.* seçkin kimseler, elit tabaka.

**e.lix.ir** [i'liksə] *n.* iksir.

**E.liz.a.be.than** [ilizə'biːθən] **1.** *adj.* İngil-

tere'de kraliçe I. Elizabeth devrine ait; **2.** *n.* o devirde yaşamış kimse.

**elk** *zo.* [elk] *n.* iri boynuzlu bir geyik türü.

**ell** *hist.* [el] *n.* endaze, arşın.

**el.lipse** A [i'lips] *n.* elips; **el'lip.sis** [∼sis] *n., pl.* **el'lip.ses** *gr.* [∼siːz] bir tümcenin anlamı bozulmaksızın öğelerinden birinin atılması; **el'lip.tic,** **el'lip.ti.cal** ☐ [∼tik(əl)] oval, eliptik, beyzi; anlatılmak isteneni tam açıklamayan, dolambaçlı *(söz).*

**elm** ♣ [elm] *n.* karaağaç.

**el.o.cu.tion** [elə'kjuːʃən] *n.* söz söyleme sanatı, hitabet; **el.o'cu.tion.ar.y** [∼ʃnəri] *adj.* hitabete ait; **el.o'cu.tion.ist** *n.* hatip, belagat sahibi *b-i.*

**e.lon.gate** ['iːlɔŋgeit] *v/t.* gerip uzatmak; **e.lon'ga.tion** *n.* uza(t)ma ,uza(n)mış kısım; *ast.* bir gezegenin güneş *ya da* uydusu arasındaki açı farkı.

**e.lope** [i'ləup] *v/i.* aşığı ile kaçmak, evlenmek için evden kaçmak; **e'lope.ment** *n. b-le* kaçma.

**el.o.quence** ['eləukwəns] *n.* belâgat, güzel söz söyleme sanatı; **'el.o.quent** ☐ beliğ, dokunaklı, belâgatli.

**else** [els] *adj. & adv.* yoksa; başka, daha; başka yer, başka zaman, başka şekilde; *all* *∼* başka herşey; *anyone* *∼* başka herhangi *b-i; what* *∼*? bundan başka ne var?; *or* *∼* yoksa, aksi halde; **else-'where** başka yer(de).

**e.lu.ci.date** [i'luːsideit] *v/t.* açıklamak, izah etm., *(güçlük).* sır) aydınlatmak; **e.lu.ci'da.tion** *n.* açıklama, izah; **el'lu.ci.da.to.ry** *adj.* aydınlatıcı, açıklayıcı.

**e.lude** [i'luːd] *v/t.* sakınmak, sıyrılmak, paçayı kurtarmak *-den.*

**e.lu.sion** [i'luːʒən] *n.* kaçıp kurtulma, sıyrılma, sakınma; kaçamaklı söz; **e'lu.sive** [∼siv] *adj.* tutulmaz, ele geçmez; **e'lu.sive.ness** *n.* ♣yakalanmayış, sakınma. kaçamak; **e'lu.so.ry** *adj.* aldatıcı, yanıltıcı.

**elves** [elvz] *pl.* of **elf.**

**E.lys.i.an** [i'liziən] *adj.* cennete ait. cennet gibi; semavi. ilahi; **E'lys.i.um** [∼iəm] *n.* cennet, mutluluk bahçesi.

**em** [em] *n. typ.* katrat. harfler arasına konan yazısız maden parçası.

**e.ma.ci.ate** [i'meifieit] *v/t.* çok zayıflatmak. bir deri bir kemik bırakmak; **e.ma.ci.a.tion** [imeisi'eifən] *n.* çok zayıflatma.

**em.a.nate** ['eməneit] *vb.* çıkmak. yayılmak (from *-den);* **em.a'na.tion** *n.* çıkma, yayılma.

**e man ci.pate** [i'mænsipeit] *v/t.* serbest bırakmak. özgür kılmak: **e.man.ci'pa.tion** *n.* serbest bırakma. eşit hakları verme; e'man.ci.pa.tor *n.* serbest bırakan, azat eden *b-i.*

e.mas.cu.late 1. [i'mæskjuleit] *v/t.* hadım etm., iğdiş etm.; kuvvetten düşürmek; *(metin)* sansür ederek hafifletmek; 2. [~lit] *adj.* kuvvetten düşmüş; efemine, kadın tavırlı; e.mas.cu.la.tion [~'leiʃən] *n.* hadım etme *veya* edilme; kuvvetten düş(ür)me; *(metin)* sansür etme.

em.balm [im'baːm] *v/t.* mumyalamak, tahnit etm.; anmak, anısını yaşatmak; be ~ed unutulmamak; em'balm.ment *n.* ınumyalama, tahnit.

em.bank [im'bæŋk] *vb. (toprak, taş vs. ile)* etrafına set yapmak; em'bank.ment *n.* set, bent; rıhtım; set yapma.

em.bar.go [em'baːgəu] 1. *n.* ambargo, ticareti sınırlama, yasaklama; 2. *vb.* ambargo koymak, müsadere etm.

em.bark [im'baːk] *v/t. & v/i.* gemiye bin-(dir)mek (for); *(para)* yatırmak; *bşe* girişmek, yanaşmak (in, on, upon); em.bar.ka.tion [embaː'keiʃən] *n.* gemiye bin-(dir)me; girişim.

em.bar.rass [im'bærəs] *v/t.* şaşırtmak; utandırmak, mahcup etm., sıkmak; engellemek, mani olm.; ~ed *adj.* mahcup, sıkılgan, çekingen, şaşkın; *(para)* sıkıntıda; em'bar.rass.ing □ utandırıcı; nahoş, sıkıntılı; em'bar.rass.ment *n. (para)* sıkıntı; sıkılganlık, utanma, şaşkınlık.

em.bas.sy ['embəsi] *n.* büyük *veya* orta elçilik; sefarethane.

em.bat.tle [im'bætl] *vb.* meydan savaşına hazırlamak; harp düzeninde mevzilemek; mazgal yapmak.

em.bed [im'bed] *v/t.* gömmek, yerleştirmek.

em.bel.lish [im'beliʃ] *v/t.* süslemek, güzelleştirmek; *(hikâye)* gerçek olmayan ayrıntılar ekleyerek ilginç hale sokmak; em'bel.lish.ment *n.* süsleme, güzelleştirme, süs.

em.ber-days ['embədeiz] *n .pl.* bazı hıristiyan kiliselerinde dua ederek ve oruç tutarak *(et yemeyerek)* geçirilen üçer günlük dört mevsim perhizi.

em.bers ['embəz] *n. pl.* sönmekte olan ateş, kor, köz; *fig.* kıvılcım.

em.bez.zle [im'bezl] *vb.* zimmetine geçirmek; em'bez.zle.ment *n.* zimmetine geçirme; em'bez.zler *n.* zimmetine para geçiren *b-i.*

em.bla.zon [im'bleizən] *vb.* aileye ait armalarla süslemek; *fig.* ayyuka çıkar-

mak; em'bla.zon.ry *n.* arma ressamlığı; süsleme.

em.blem ['embləm] *n.* sembol, simge, amblem, işaret; em.blem.at.ic, em.blem-at.i.cal □ [embli'mætik(əl)] sembolik.

em.bod.i.ment [im'bɔdimənt] *n.* cisimlenme, şekil alma; düzenleme; em.bod.y *v/t.* cisimlendirmek, temsil etm., ifade etm., belirtmek; içermek; düzenlemek; *(ülke)* ilhak etm.

em.bold.en [im'bəuldən] *vb.* cesaret vermek, teşvik etm.

em.bo.lism [embəlizəm] *n.* amboli, damar tıkanması.

em.bos.om [im'buzəm] *v/t.* kucaklamak, bağrına basmak; ~ed with etrafı ... ile çevrili.

em.boss [im'bɔs] *vb.* kabartma işleri yapmak, kakmak, çekiçle dövmek; em-'bossed *adj.* kabartmalı; ~ note-paper kabartma simgeli kağıt.

em.bow.el [im'bauəl] *v/t. (ölen hayvanın)* bağırsaklarını çıkarmak.

em.brace [im'breis] 1. *v/t. & v/i.* kucakla(ş)mak, kolları arasına almak; *(meslek)* seçmek, tutmak; kabul etm., benimsemek; 2. *n.* kucakla(ş)ma, sarılma.

em.bra.sure [im'breiʒə] *n.* bir kapı *veya* pencerenin meyilli pervazı, mazgal eğimi.

em.bro.cate ['embrəukeit] *v/t.* ovmak, friksiyon yapmak; em.bro'ca.tion *n.* ovuşturma, friksiyon.

em.broi.der [im'brɔidə] *v/t.* -in üzerine nakış işlemek; *fig.* abartmak, ballandırmak; em'broi.der.y *n.* nakış işleme; *fig.* abartı, mübalâğa.

em.broil [im'brɔil] *vb.* ara bozmak, karmakarışık etm., dallandırıp budaklandırmak, karıştırmak; em'broil.ment *n.* karışıklık, anlaşmazlık.

em.bry.o ['embriəu] *n.* cenin, dölüt; in ~ gelişmemiş halde, tasarı halinde; em.bry.on.ic [~'ɔnik] *adj.* cenine ait; gelişmemiş, ilkel *(a. fig.).*

em.bus [im'bʌs] *vb.* (motorlu araca) bin-(dir)mek.

e.mend [iːmend] *v/t.* (metin) düzeltmek, tashih etm.; e.men'da.tion *n.* tashih, düzeltme; 'e.men.da.tor *n. (metin)* tashihçi, düzelten; e'mend.a.to.ry [~dətəri] *adj.* düzeltme kabilinden, tashihî.

em.er.ald ['emərəld] 1. *n.* zümrüt; 2. *adj.* zümrüt yeşili rengi.

e.merge [iˈməːdʒ] *v/i.* ortaya çıkmak (from, out of -den); *fig.* sökün etm.; görünmek, doğmak, gözükmek; hasıl olm.; e'mer.gence *n.* çıkma, zuhur.

e.mer.gen.cy [i'məːdʒənsi] *n.* olağanüstü durum, tehlike; ~ **brake** imdat freni; ~ **call** istimdat, imdat isteme; ~ **decree** geçici yasa, kararname; ~ **ex.it** ihtiyat, imdat kapısı; ~ **land.ing** ⚓ zorunlu iniş; ~ **man** *spor:* yedek oyuncu.

e.mer.gent [i'məːdʒənt] *adj.* çıkan, zuhur eden; ~ **countries** *pl.* fakir ve bağımlı durumdan zengin ve bağımsız duruma geçen devletler.

e.mer.sion [i'məːʃən] *n.* yeniden görünme; *ast.* bir gök cisminin tam *veya* yarım tutulmadan sonra yeniden görünmesi.

em.er.y ['eməri] *n.* zımpara; '~-cloth *n.* zımpara bezi; '~-pa.per *n.* zımpara kağıdı.

e.met.ic [i'metik] 1. *adj.* kusturucu; 2. *n.* kusturucu ilaç.

em.i.grant ['emigrənt] 1. *adj.* göç eden; 2. *n.* göçmen; em.i.grate ['~greit] *v/i.* göçmek, göç etm.; em.i'gra.tion *n.* göç, hicret; em.i.gra.to.ry ['~greitəri] *adj.* göçmen...

em.i.nence ['eminəns] *n.* yükseklik; yüksek yer, tepe; yüksek rütbe, itibar; 'em.i.nent □ *fig.* seçkin, yüksek, mümtaz, güzide (in, for); 'em.i.nent.ly *adv.* pek, gayet, fevkalade.

e.mir [e'miə] *n.* emir; e.mir.ate [e'miərit] *n.* emirlik.

em.is.sar.y *n.* kurye, özel bir görevle gönderilen memur, gizli ajan; e.mis.sion [i'miʃən] *n.* yayma, çıkarma, neşretme; çıkarılan şey; *phys.* yayılma; *fig.* sonuç, tesir; ↑ tahvil çıkarma.

e.mit [i'mit] *v/t.* çıkarmak, neşretmek, dışarı vermek, fışkırtmak, yaymak; ↑ tedavüle çıkarmak; *fig.* söylemek.

e.mol.u.ment [i'mɔljumənt] *n.* ücret, bir hizmet karşılığı alınan şey; ~s *pl.* gelir, irat, varidat.

e.mo.tion [i'məuʃən] *n.* heyecan, duygu, his; e'mo.tion.al [~ʃənl] □ duygulu, heyecanlı, hassas, duygusal, dokunaklı, hislerine kolay kapılan; e.mo.tion.al.i.ty [~ʃə'næliti] *n.* duygunluk, hassasiyet, duyarlık; e'mo.tion.less *adj.* hissiz, duyarsız, soğuk neva; e'mo.tive *adj.* duygusal, hissi.

em.pan.el [im'pænl] *vb. (jüri heyeti)* adını listeye yazmak.

em.pa.thy *psych.* ['empəθi] *n.* duyarlık, *b-nin* duygularını seziş inceliği.

em.per.or ['empərə] *n.* imparator.

em.pha.sis ['emfəsis] *n., pl.* em.pha.ses ['~siːz] şiddet, vurgu, kuvvet; önem; em.pha.size ['~saiz] *v/t.* önem vermek

-e; vurgulamak -i; em.phat.ic [im'fætik] *adj.* (~ally) etkili; vurgulu, önemli; be ~ that kesinlikle ...ki .

em.pire ['empaiə] *n.* imparatorluk; the British ♀ Büyük Britanya İmparatorluğu.

em.pir.ic [em'pirik] 1. *n.* bilginin kitaplardan değil, deneyle edinileceğine inanan *b-i;* şarlatan; em'pi.ri.cal □ edinilen deneyimlere göre, deneysel, ampirik; em'pir.i.cism [~sizəm] *n.* bilginin esasının deneye dayandığını ileri süren felsefi görüş, görgücülük; şarlatanlık; em'pir.i.cist *n.* bu görüşe inanan *b-i;* şarlatan.

em.place.ment × [im'pleismənt] *n.* top mevzii, tabya.

em.plane [im'plein] *v/t. & v/i.* uçağa bin(dir)mek.

em.ploy [im'plɔi] 1 *v/t.* kullanmak, istihdam etm., çalıştırmak -i, iş vermek -e; *(vakit, enerji)* sarfetmek, vermek; 2. *n.* görev, hizmet; in the ~ of hizmetinde; em.ploy.é, em.ploy.ée [ɔm'plɔiei], em.ploy.ee [emplɔi'iː] *n.* işçi, müstahdem, işalan; em.ploy.er [im'plɔiə] *n.* işveren, patron; em'ploy.ment *n.,* iş verme, memuriyet, istihdam; ~ **agency** iş ve işçi bulma kurumu; **place** of ~ işyeri; ♀ **Exchange** iş ve işçi bulma bürosu.

em.po.ri.um [em'pɔːriəm] *n.* alışveriş merkezi, dükkân, bonmarşe, ticaret merkezi.

em.pow.er [im'pauə] *v/t.* yetki vermek e, ehil kılmak -i.

em.press ['empris] *n.* imparatoriçe.

emp.ti.ness ['emptinis] *n.* boşluk; 'emp.ty 1. □ boş; anlamsız; *fig.* kof; F aç; 2. *vb.* boşal(t)mak, dökmek, akıtmak, tahliye etm.; 3. *n.* içi boş şey; empties *pl.* ↑ bos *(sandıklar, şişeler vs.).*

em.pur.ple [im'pəːpl] *v/t.* mor renge boyamak, morartmak.

e.mu *orn.* ['iːmjuː] *n.* Avustralya'da yaşayan devekuşuna benzer bir tür kuş.

em.u.late ['emjuleit] *v/t.* rekabet halinde bulunmak, yarışmak, *b-ni k-ne* örnek almak, aynı başarıları elde etm.; em.u'la.tion *n.* rekabet, yarışma gayreti; em.u.la.tive ['~lətiv] *adj.* rekabet edici (of); em.u.la.tor ['~leitə] *n. b-ni k-ne* örnek alan *b-i;* 'em.u.lous □ (of) *b-ne* benzemeye çalışan, gıpta eden, *b-ni* kıskanan.

e.mul.sion ⚗ [i'mʌlʃən] *n.* emulsiyon, sübye, mustahlep.

en.a.ble [i'neibl] *v/t.* muktedir kılmak, kuvvet vermek -e, yetki vermek, imkân vermek -e; izin vermek.

en.act [i'nækt] *v/i.* kararlaştırmak, hükmetmek; *(yasa)* çıkarmak; *thea.* temsil etm., oynamak; be ~ed oynana oynana aşınmak; en**'act.ment** *n.* yasalaştırma; yasa, kararname.

en.am.el [i'næməl] **1.** *n.* emay, (diş) mine, sır; **2.** *vb.* mine ile kaplamak, sırlamak; *poet.* süslemek.

en.am.o(u)r [i'næmə] *v/t.* aşık etm.; be ~ed of aşık, tutkun -e.

en.cage [in'keid3] *v/t.* kafese koymak, kafese kapamak.

en.camp X [in'kæmp] *v/i.* ordugâh kurmak, kamp kurmak; en**'camp.ment** *n.* ordugâh, karargâh, kamp.

en.case [in'keis] *v/t.* kılıflamak, örtmek; en**'case.ment** *n.* kılıf, mahfaza, örtü.

en.cash.ment † [in'kæʃmənt] *n.* tahsil etme, paraya çevirme, ahzu kabz.

en.caus.tic [en'kɔːstik] **1.** *adj.* renkli mumlar ısıtılarak boyanmış (kiremit, çini vs.); **2.** *n.* renkli mumları bir yüzeye sürüp ısı ile sabitleştirerek yapılan bir boyama metodu.

en.ceph.a.li.tis ⚕ [enkefə'laitis] *n.* beyin iltihabı, ansefalit.

en.chain [in'tʃəin] *v/t.* zincirlemek, zincire vurmak (in, with, by); k-ne bağlamak, celbetmek.

en.chant [in'tʃaːnt] *v/t.* büyülemek, k-ne bağlamak; *fig.* aklını başından almak, çıldırtmak; en**'chant.er** *n.* büyüleyen kimse, büyücü; en**'chant.ment** *n.* büyü, sihir, cazibe; en**'chant.ress** *n.* büyücü kadın; büyüleyen kadın, dilber.

en.chase [in'tʃeis] *vb.* kalemle kazımak (çizmek, oymak); (kıymetli taş) yerleştirmek, oturtmak; *fig.* süslemek.

en.cir.cle [in'səːkl] *v/t.* (by, with, in) kuşatmak, etrafını çevirmek, sarmak; en**'cir.cle.ment** *n.* kuşatma, ihata; *pol.* kuşatma politikası.

en.close [in'klouz] *v/t.* (by, in) çitle etrafını çevirmek, kuşatmak, katmak, ilâve etm.; ilişikte göndermek; en**'clo.sure** [~3ə] *n.* çit; çit veya duvarla çevrili arazi; ilişik kağıt, ilisikte gönderilen şey.

en.co.mi.ast [en'koumiæst] *n.* methiye yazan kimse, kaside yazarı; en**'co.mi.um** [~mjəm] *n.* methiye, övücü nutuk.

en.com.pass [in'kʌmpəs] *v/t.* -in etrafını çevirmek, kuşatmak.

en.core [ɔŋ'kɔː] **1.** *int.* bir daha!, tekrar!; **2.** *v/i.* gelsin diye bağırmak; *v/t.* bir şarkı vs.'nin tekrarlanmasını istemek; **3.** *n.* tekrar etme; program dışı parçası, bis.

en.coun.ter [in'kauntə] **1.** *n.* karşılaşma, rastlantı. tesadüf, karşı karşıya gelme; çarpışma; **2.** *v/t.* karşılamak; b-ne, bşe birdenbire rastlamak, karşı karşıya gelmek; çarpışmak.

en.cour.age [in'kʌrid3] *v/t.* teşvik etm., cesaret vermek -e; en**'cour.age.ment** *n.* teşvik, cesaret verme; en**'cour.ag.er** *n.* teşvik eden, cesaret veren b-i.

en.croach [in'kroutʃ] *v/i.* tecavüz etm., el uzatmak (on, upon -e); sokulmak, nüfuz etm.; halel getirmek -e; ~ upon s.o.'s kindness b-nin iyiliğini suistimal etm.; en**'croach.ment** *n.* tecavüz, müdahale, karışma (on, upon, in -e).

en.crust [in'krʌst] *vb.* kabuk bağlamak, sert bir tabaka oluşturmak (with ile); ⊕ üstüne katıca bir kabuk çekmek.

en.cum.ber [in'kʌmbə] *v/t.* yüklemek; tıkabasa doldurmak; mani olm., engel olm. -e; tıkamak (yol); en**'cum.brance** *n.* yük; *fig.* engel, mani; ipotek, borçlar yükü; without ~ çocuksuz; ipoteksiz.

en.cyc.li.cal *eccl.* [en'siklikəl] *n.* Papanın Katolik piskoposlara gönderdiği mektup, tamim.

end [end] **1.** *n.* son; amaç, gaye; sonuç, âkıbet; be at an ~ bitmiş tükenmiş olm.; no ~ of sonsuz, pek çok, sayısız; have s.th. at one's finger's ~s hükmetmek; in the ~ sonunda; on ~ dik, ayakta; aralıksız, arka arkaya, biteviye; stand on ~ (tüyleri) ürpermek; dikine koymak; to the ~ that ...amacı ile, böylece, bu suretle; to no ~ nafile, boşuna; to this ~ bu amaçla; come to an ~ son bulmak, bitmek; go off the deep ~ *fig.* kontrolnu kaybetmek ,öfkelenmek; make an ~ of, put an ~ to son vermek, bitirmek; make both ~s meet (para) geçinebilmek, iki yakasını bir araya getirmek; **2.** *v/t.* & *v/i.* bit(ir)mek, son vermek, son bulmak.

en.dan.ger [in'deind3ə] *v/t.* tehlikeye düşürmek.

en.dear [in'diə] *v/t.* sevdirmek (to -e); en**'dear.ing** *adj.* cazip, çekici, alımlı, edalı; şefkatli, müşfik; en**'dear.ment** *n.* okşama; sevgi dolu söz ya da davranış.

en.deav.o(u)r [in'devə] **1.** *n.* emek, çaba, gayret; **2.** *vb.* çalışmak, çabalamak, gayret etm., bşi elde etmeğe çalışmak (after).

en.dem.ic ⚕ [en'demik] **1.** *a.* en**'dem.i.cal** ☐ bir bölge veya zümreye ait, yöresel; **2.** *n.* yöresel hastalık.

end.ing ['endiŋ] *n.* son, nihayet; *gr.* sonek.

en.dive ♣ ['endiv] *n.* hindiba, andılya.

**end.less** □ ['endlis] sonsuz, ebedî; ⊕ (kayış, zincir vs.) uçları birleştirilmiş, dairevi.

**en.dorse** [in'dɔːs] v/t. † ciro etm.; kloz koymak; onaylamak; endorsing ink ıstampa mürekkebi; **en.dor.see** [endɔːsiː] n. k-ne ciro edilen kimse; lehdar; **endorse.ment** [in'dɔːsmənt] n. onay; † ciro; **en¹dors.er** n. ciro eden kimse, ciranta.

**en.do.sperm** ⬥ ['endəuspəːm] n. besidoku, endosperm, tohumun içindeki besleyici doku.

**en.dow** [in'dau] v/t. donatmak; bahşetmek, (bir hayır kurumu vs.'ye) bağış yapmak; **en¹dow.ment** n. bağış, teberru; vakıf, tahsisat; yetenek; Allah vergisi.

**en.due** mst fig. [in'djuː] v/t. giy(dir)mek; b-ni bşle donatmak, teçhiz etm. (with); bahş ve ihsan etm., nasip etm.

**en.dur.a.ble** [in¹djuərəbl] adj. dayanılabilir, tahammül edilebilir; **en¹dur.ance** n. tahammül, sabır, metanet; past ~ tahammül edilmez, çekilemez; ~ flight havada kalış süresi; ~ run mukavemet koşusu; **en¹dure** v/t. tahammül etm., dayanmak -e; **en¹dur.ing** adj. sürekli; sabırlı; dayanıklı.

**end.way(s)** ['endwei(z)], **end.wise** ['~waiz] adv. dik, dikine; uzunluğuna.

**en.e.ma** ⚕ ['enimə] n. lavman, tenkiye, şırınga.

**en.e.my** ['enimi] 1. n. düşman, hasım; the ⚲ şeytan, iblis; 2. adj. düşmanca, hasmane.

**en.er.get.ic** [enə'dʒetik] adj. (~ally) enerjik, faal; etkili; **en.er.gize** vb. ⚡ enerji, güç vermek; harekete geçmek; **en.er.gy** n. enerji, güç, erke, kuvvet (a. phys.), gayret, azim; faaliyet, hareket.

**en.er.vate** ['enəveit] v/t. kuvvetten düşürmek, zayıflatmak; **en.er¹va.tion** n. kuvvetten düşürme, zayıflatma.

**en.fee.ble** [in'fiːbl] v/t. kuvvetten düşürmek; **en¹fee.ble.ment** n. kuvvetten düşürme; zayıflatma.

**en.feoff** [in'fef] vb. tımar veya zeamet şeklinde vermek; **en¹feoff.ment** n. tımar veya zeamet fermanı.

**en.fi.lade** ✕ [enfi'leid] 1. n. yan ateşi; 2. vb/ yan ateşi ile taramak.

**en.fold** [in'fəuld] v/t. sarmak, katlamak; bağrına basmak, kucaklamak.

**en.force** [in'fɔːs] vb. zorlamak, zorla yaptırmak; zorla kabul ettirmek (upon s.o. -e), sözünü geçirmek (upon s.o. -e); ısrar etm.; yasaları uygulamak, icra etm., yü

rütmek; **en¹force.a.ble** adj. uygulanabilir; **en¹force.ment** n. uygulama, tatbik.

**en.fran.chise** [in'fræntʃaiz] vb. pol. seçim hakkı vermek -e; (köle) özgür kılmak, azat etm.; **en¹fran.chise.ment** [~ʃizmənt] n. oy verme hakkı, vatandaşlık haklarının tanınması; özgür kılma, azat etme.

**en.gage** [in'geidʒ] v/t. hizmete almak, tutmak, işe koymak, angaje etm.; işgal etm.; ilgi çekmek; ✕ saldırmak, taarruz etm.; be ~ed nişanlı olm. (to ile); meşgul olm. (in ile); dolu olm.; ~ the clutch tutturmak, kavramak; v/i. meşgul olm. (to ile); söz vermek, garanti etm.; meşgul olm. (in ile); ✕ çarpışmak; ⊕ birbirine geçmek; **en¹gage.ment** n. söz, vaat; angajman, hizmete alma; nişanlanma; randevu; ✕ çarpışma; ⊕ (dişli, çark vs.) birbirine geçme; **en.gage.ment ring** nişan yüzüğü.

**en.gag.ing** fig. □ [in'geidʒiŋ] cazip, alımlı, sempatik.

**en.gen.der** fig. [in'dʒendə] v/t. meydana getirmek, oluşturmak, yaratmak, sebep olm.

**en.gine** ['endʒin] n. makine, motor; 🚂 lokomotif; yangın tulumbası; fig. vasıta, çıkar yol; alet edevat; ...¹en.gined ...motorlu; **¹en.gine-driv.er** n. makinist.

**en.gi.neer** [endʒi'niə] 1. n. mühendis; makinist; makineci; ✕ istihkamcı; ⚓ çarkçı; Am. makinist; 2. vb. mühendislik yapmak, inşa etm.; F becermek, başarmak; idare etm.; **en.gi¹neer.ing** n. mühendislik, makinistlik; F hünerle kullanma; attr. teknik.

en.gine...: '~-fit.ter n. tesviyeci; '~.man n. makinist.

**en.gird** [in'gəːd] (irr. gird) v/t. kemer gibi sarmak; fig. kuşatmak.

**Eng.lish** ['iŋgliʃ] 1. adj. İngiliz, İngilizce; 2. n. İngilizce; the ~ pl. İngilizler, İngiltere halkı; İngilizce tercüme; in plain ~ fig. sözünü esirgemeden, dobra dobra; the Queen's (King's) ~ temiz İngilizce; '~.man n. İngiliz erkeği; '~.wom.an n. İngiliz kadını.

**en.gorge** [in'gɔːdʒ] vb. oburca yemek, tıka basa doldurmak.

**en.graft** [in'grɑːft] v/t. aşılamak (into, on, onto -e); fig. b-nin hafızasına iyice yerleştirmek (in); dikmek (on -e).

**en.grain** [in'grein] v/b. boyayı iyice emdirmek; fig. (alışkanlık, zevk) aşılamak; **en¹grained** adj. ıslah olmaz, akıllanmaz; kök salmış, iyice yerleşmiş.

**en.grave** [in'greiv] v/t. hakketmek, oymak; fig. b-nin kafasına iyice yerleştir

engraver 168

mek; **en'grav.er** *n.* hakkâk, oymacı; ~ on copper bakır hakkâkı; **en'grav.ing** *n.* hakkâk işi, ksilografi.

**en.gross** [in'grəus] *v/t.* zaptetmek, meşgul etm., işgal etm.; *(yazı)* temize çekmek; ~ed in dalmış -e, dalgın; meşgul; ~ing *adj.* ilginç, cezbedici *(kitap vs.)*; ~ing hand büro yazısı; **en'gross.ment** *n.* yığma, stok *(mal)*; bşle meşgul olma (of, with); temize çekilmiş yazı.

**en.gulf** [in'gʌlf] *fig. vb.* yutmak, içinde kaybolmak; girdap içine çekip yutmak.

**en.hance** [in'ha:ns] *v/t.* artırmak, yükseltmek, ziyadeleştirmek, çoğaltmak *(değer, güç, güzellik)*; **en'hance.ment** *n.* artma, çoğalma; artırma.

**e.nig.ma** ['inigmə] *n.* bilmece, muamma; **en.nig.mat.ic**, **e.nig.mat.i.cal** ☐ [enig-'mætik(əl)] akıl ermez, muammalı, anlaşılmaz.

**en.join** [in'dʒɔin] *v/t.* emretmek, tembih etm. (on, upon s.o. -e); yasaklamak, menetmek (from, -den).

**en.joy** [in'dʒɔi] *v/t.* sevmek, hoşlanmak -den, bşden dolayı sevinmek, bşden zevk, lezzet almak; did you ~ it? hoşunuza gitti mi?; ~ o.s. zevk almak, hoşça vakit geçirmek; **en'joy.a.ble** *adj.* zevkli, enfes, eğlenceli, hoş, tatlı; **en'joy.ment** *n.* eğlence, zevk, haz.

**en.kin.dle** [in'kindl] *v/t.* tutuşturmak, alevlendirmek; uyandırmak, tahrik etm. *(a. fig.)*.

**en.lace** [in'leis] *v/t.* sarmak, dolamak.

**en.large** [in'la:dʒ] *v/t. & v/i.* büyü(lt)mek, genişle(t)mek *(a. phot.)*; *fig.* yayılmak (on, upon); **en'large.ment** *n.* büyü(lt)me; agrandisman; **en.larg.er** *n. phot.* agrandisör.

**en.light.en** [in'laitn] *v/t. fig.* aydınlatmak, bilgi vermek; ~ed *adj.* aydın; **en'lighten.ment** *n.* aydınlatma, aydınlanma; açıklama.

**en.list** [in'list] *v/t.* askere almak, kaydetmek; bir yardım sağlamak (in); ~ed man ✕ asker; *v/i.* asker olm., gönüllü olm.; ~ in b-ne sahip çıkmak, kayırmak; **en'list.ment** *n.* ✕ kaydetme, kaydedilme; *fig.* kazanma.

**en.liv.en** [in'laivn] *v/t.* canlandırmak, gayrete getirmek, teşvik etm.

**en.mesh** [in'meʃ] *v/t.* ağa düşürmek, b-ni kendi tuzağına düşürmek.

**en.mi.ty** ['enmiti] *n.* düşmanlık.

**en.no.ble** [i'nəubl] *v/t.* asilleştirmek *(a. fig.)*, yükseltmek, kıymetlendirmek.

**e.nor.mi.ty** [i'nɔ:miti] *n.* alçaklık, büyük

kötülük; büyüklük, **e'nor.mous** ☐ kocaman, iri, muazzam.

**e.nough** [i'nʌf] **1.** *adj.* yetişir, elverir; **2.** *int.* yeter!, kâfi!; **3.** *n.* yeterince, gerekli miktar; **4.** *adv.* kâfi derecede; sure ~ elbette!, şüphesiz!; well ~ fena değil, oldukça iyi; be kind ~ to *inf.* ...mek lûtfunda bulunmak.

**en.plane** [in'plein] = emplane.

**en.quire** [in'kwaiə] = inquire.

**en.rage** [in'reidʒ] *v/t.* kızdırmak -i, öfkelendirmek -i; **en'raged** *adj..*kızgın, öfkeli (at, by).

**en.rap.ture** [in'ræptʃə] *v/t.* kendinden geçirmek, sonsuz hazlara boğmak -i.

**en.rich** [in'ritʃ] *v/t.* zenginleştirmek, zengin etm.; süslemek (by, with *ile*); **en'rich.ment** *n.* zenginleş(tir)me; süs, dekor.

**en.rol(l)** [in'rəul] *vb. b-ni veya k-ni* kaydetmek *(liste)*; ✕ askere almak, yazmak; asker olm.; üyeliğe kaydetmek *(dernek)*; sicile kaydetmek; ~ (o.s.) yazılmak, kaydedilmek; askere yazılmak; **en'rol(l).ment** *n.* kaydolma; kaydedilenlerin sayısı.

**en.san.guined** [in'sæŋgwind] *adj.* kana bulanmış, kan lekeli.

**en.sconce** [in'skɔns] *v/t.* yerleştirmek; yataklık etm.; *mst* ~ o.s. F rahat bir şekilde oturmak, koltuğa gömülmek.

**en.sem.ble** [ã:n'sã:mbl] *n.* genel tesir, izlenim, parçaların tümünün bir arada algılanması; *thea.* topluluk; ♪ küçük topluluk; küçük orkestra için yazılmış eser; koro *(opera)*; piyesteki oyuncuların tümü; bir müzik topluluğunun birlik, denge ve başarı derecesi; takım *(elbise)*, döpiyes, iki *veya* daha fazla parçadan ibaret kadın kostümü.

**en.shrine** [in'ʃrain] *v/t.* mabede koymak; kutsal olarak kabul etm.

**en.shroud** [in'ʃraud] *v/t.* kefenlemek; örtmek, gizlemek.

**en.sign** ['ensain] *n.* bayrak, sancak, bandıra, alem; alâmet, nişan; ⬇ *Am.* ['ensn] teğmen.

**en.si.lage** ['ensilidʒ] **1.** *n.* siloya doldurma *(yem)*; **2.** = **en.sile** [in'sail] *v/t.* siloya depolamak *(yem)*.

**en.slave** [in'sleiv] *v/t.* köle yapmak, esir etm. (to -e), *k-ne* kul etm.; **en'slave.ment** *n.* köleleş(tir)me, esaret, kölelik; **en'slaver** *n. k-ne* köle eden, boyunduruk altına alan *b-i*.

**en.snare** [in'snɛə] *v/t.* (by, in, into) tuzağa düşürmek; *fig.* baştan çıkarmak, ayartmak -i.

**en.sue** [in'sju:] *v/i.* ardından gelmek; hasıl olm., gelmek, meydana çıkmak (from, on -den).

en.sure [in'fuə] v/t. sağlamak, temin etm., sağlama almak, garanti etm., korumak (against, from -den).

en.tab.la.ture ⊕ [en'tæblətʃə] n. saçaklık, direk üstü tabanı, sütun pervazı.

en.tail [in'teil] 1. v/t. bşe neden olm., gerektirmek; b-ne bir mülkü başkasına devredilmemek üzere miras bırakmak; 2. n. devredilemez mülk.

en.tan.gle [in'tæŋgl] v/t. dolaştırmak, karıştırmak; fig. b-ni bir işe karıştırmak, b-nin başını derde sokmak; en'tan.gle.ment n. karışıklık, dolaşıklık; ✕ engel, mania (dikenli tel).

en.tente [ãːn'tãːnt] n. anlaşma, ittifak, uyuşma, itilâf.

en.ter ['entə] v/t. girmek; dahil olm., yazılmak, katılmak; ayak basmak; bşe girişmek (iş); sokulmak, zorla girmek; söze karışmak; yazmak, kaydetmek; ✝ deftere geçirmek; (itiraz) koymak; b-ne bşi bildirmek; hayvan, motor: alıştırmak, hazırlamak (koşum, yarış); it ~ed his head kafasına girdi, anladı; ~ s.o. at school b-ni okula kaydettirmek; ~ up ✝ hesap defterine geçirmek; v/i. girmek (into -e); girişmek -e; ismini yazmak; spor: müsabakaya girmek, yazılmak (for); işe koyulmak; ~ Macbeth thea. Makbet sahneye girer; ~ into unsuru olm. -in; söze karışmak; fig. incelemek (teklif); fig. taahhüt altına girmek (anlaşma); eşelemek (konu); ~ (up)on bşe başlamak, girişmek (konu, iş); ♋ mirasa konmak.

en.ter.ic ♏ [en'terik] adj. bağırsaklarla ilgili, bağırsak...; en.ter.i.tis [~tə'raitis] bağırsak iltihabı, anterit.

en.ter.prise ['entəpraiz] n. girişim, teşebbüs, iş, yatırım; girişkenlik; 'en.ter.pris.ing □ müteşebbis, girişken, uyanık, açıkgöz; pervasız, cesur.

en.ter.tain [entə'tein] vb. eğlendirmek, ağırlamak, misafirliğe kabul etm.; göz önünde bulundurmak; hatırda tutmak; they ~ a great deal misafirleri eksik olmaz (sık sık parti verirler); ~ s.o. to supper b-ni akşam yemeğine davet etm.; cn.ter'tain.er n. prezantatör, eğlendiren aktör (veya aktris); davet veren kimse; en.ter'tain.ing □ eğlenceli, hoşsohbet, eğlendiren; en.ter'tain.ment n. eğlence; ağırlama, davet; ~ tax eğlence vergisi.

en.thral(l) [in'θrɔːl] v/t. fig. büyülemek, cezbetmek, hayran bırakmak.

en.throne [in'θrəun] v/t. tahta çıkarmak;

b-ni gönlünde yüceltmek, yüksek yer vermek; en'throne.ment, en.thron.i.za.tion [enθrəunai'zeiʃən] n. tahta oturtma; tahta çıkma, cülûs (hükümdar).

en.thuse F [in'θjuːz] vb.: ~ over bşe bayılmak, b-ne hayran kalmak, coşmak.

en.thu.si.asm [in'θjuːziæzəm] n. coşkunluk; can atma, heves, istek; en'thu.si.ast [~æst] n. bşin hayranı, aşırı taraftar (for, of); şevkli kimse; en.thu.si'as.tic adj. (~ally) heyecanlı, coşkun, hislerine kapılan, şevkli, hevesli (at, about).

en.tice [in'tais] v/t. ayartmak, vaatlerle baştan çıkarmak -i; en'tice.ment n. ayartma, kandırma, baştan çıkarma; cazibe, alımlılık; en'tic.er n. ayartan, baştan çıkaran, iğfal eden b-i; en'tic.ing □ ayartıcı, kandırıcı, cazip, çekici; işveli, fettan.

en.tire □ [in'taiə] tam, bütün, tamam, eksiksiz, bölünmemiş; iğdiş edilmemiş (hayvan); en'tire.ly adv. büsbütün, tamamen; en'tire.ness n. bütünlük, tamamlık, yekparelik; en'tire.ty n. bütünlük, mükemmellik, tamamiyet.

en.ti.tle [in'taitl] v/t. yetki vermek -e, hak kazandırmak (to -e); ad vermek; be ~d to hakkı, yetkisi olm.

en.ti.ty ['entiti] n. varlık, mevcudiyet; legal ~ tüzelkişi, hukuki varlık.

en.tomb [in'tuːm] v/t. gömmek, defnetmek; mezar olm.; en'tomb.ment n. defin töreni, mezara koyma.

en.to.mol.o.gy zo. [entə'mɔlədʒi] n. entomoloji, böcek ilmi.

entr'acte thea. ['ɔntrækt] n. perde arası, antrakt.

en.trails ['entreilz] n. pl. bağırsaklar, iç uzuvlar (hayvan).

en.trance¹ ['entrəns] n. giriş, duhul, girme; giriş yeri, antre, giriş kapısı; vazifeye giriş (into veya upon office); thea. sahneye çıkış, sahneye giriş; (liman) boğaz, ağız.

en.trance² [in'trɑːns] v/t. kendinden geçirmek -i, coşturmak -i, büyülemek -i, hayran bırakmak -i.

en.trance... ['entrəns] ~ ex.am.i.na.tion giriş sınavı; ~ fee, ~ mon.ey girmelik, duhuliye, giriş ücreti.

en.trant ['entrənt] n. giren, başlayan b-i; spor: müsabık, yarışmacı.

en.trap [in'træp] v/t. tuzağa düşürmek, avlamak, yakalamak; ayartmak (into, to -e).

en.treat [in'triːt] v/t. ısrarla rica etm. -den, yalvarmak, dilemek (of); en'treat.y n. yalvarma, rica, dilek, niyaz.

en.trée [ˈɔntrei] *n.* giriş, giriş izni, giriş hakkı; ziyafetlerde balık ile asıl yemek arasında verilen yemek.

en.trench [inˈtrentʃ] *vb.* ✗ hendek *veya* siper kazmak, istihkâma yerleştirmek; *fig.* kök salmak; *fig.* bşin arkasına gizlenmek; en·trench.ment *n.* istihkâma yerleşme; istihkâm, siper.

en.tre.pre.neur [ɔntrəprəˈnəɪ] *n.* müteahhit, müteşebbis; müzikaller hazırlayan kimse, emprezaryo.

en.trust·[inˈtrʌst] *v/t.* emniyet etm., emanet etm. (s.th. to s.o. *b-ne bşi*).

en.try [ˈentri] *n.* girme, giriş, girilecek yer, antre, methal; ☆ mülke giriş (on, upon *-e*); kayıt, not; gümrüğe giriş kaydı yaptırma; *(para)* tahsil, alınma; *spor:* iştirak için kaydolunma, müsabakaya katılma; ~ permit giriş müsaadesi; make an ~ of s.th. hesap defterine geçirmek, giriş yapmak *(tahsilat)*; book-keeping by double (single) ~ çifte (tek taraflı) defter tutma yöntemi.

en.twine [inˈtwain], en.twist [inˈtwist] *v/t.* etrafını *bşle* çevirmek, sarmak, birbirine geçirmek, bükmek, dolaştırmak.

e.nu.mer.ate [iˈnjuːməreit] *v/t.* birer birer sayma, sıralamak; e.nu.mer'a.tion *n.* sayma, sayım, tadat.

e.nun.ci.ate [iˈnʌnsieit] *vb.* bildirmek, ilan etm.; *(dogma, dava)* ileri sürmek, iddia etm.; *(akıcı ve kesin)* telâffuz etm.; e.nunci'a.tion *n.* telaffuz; bildirme; ileri sürme, ifade ve beyan tarzı.

en.vel.op [inˈveləp] *v/t.* bşi bşe sarmak, örtmek; ✗ kuşatmak; en.ve.lope [ˈenvəloup]. *Am. a.* en.vel.op [inˈveləp] *n.* zarf; ☥ örtü; kılıf *(balon)*; en.vel.op.ment [inˈveləpmənt] *n.* örtü; sarma, kuşatma.

en.ven.om [inˈvenəm] *v/t.* zehirlemek, zehir katmak *-e*; *fig. a.* şiddetlendirmek, kin aşılamak.

en.vi.a.ble □ [ˈenviəbl] gıpta edilir, mesut, talihli, başarılı, fevkalâde iyi; ˈen.vi.er *n.* gıpta eden *b-i,* kıskanan *b-i;* ˈen.vi.ous □ kıskanç, hasut, gıpta eden (of *-c*).

en.vi.ron [inˈvaiərən] *vb.* etrafını çevirmek, kuşatmak, içine almak; en·vi.ron.ment *n.* muhit, çevre, etraf; ~al *adj.* çevresel, etrafındaki çevre...; ~al pollution çevre kirlenmesi; en.vi.rons [ˈenvirənz] *n. pl.* civar, havali, etraf, dolay.

en.vis.age [inˈvizidʒ] *v/t.* hiçe saymak, göze almak *(tehlike)*; planlamak *(amaç)*; tasavvur etm., düşünmek, ...gibi telâkki etm.

en.voy¹ [ˈenvɔi] *n.* (orta) elçi, delege, murahhas.

en.voy² [~] *n.* düzyazı *veya* şiirde yazar *veya* şairin özellikle ithaf şeklindeki ve parçanın ana fikrini açıklayan son sözü.

en.vy [ˈenvi] 1. *n.* kıskançlık, haset, gıpta, imrenme (of s.o. *b-ne;* of *veya* at s.th. *bşe*); his car is the ~ of his friends arabası arkadaşlarını kıskandırıyor,: 2. *v/t.* kıskanmak, gıpta etm.; imrenmek *-e,* haset etm., çekememek (s.o. s.th. *b-ni, bşi*).

en.wrap [inˈræp] *v/t.* sarmak, örtmek.

en.zyme *biol.* [ˈenzaim] *n.* enzim, ferment, organizmada kimyasal reaksiyonları hızlandıran madde.

e.on [ˈliːɔn] = aeon.

ep.au.let(te) [ˈepəulet] *n.* apolet.

e.pergne [ˈipəːn] *n.* yemek masası ortasına çiçek, meyve vs. koymak için konan süs tabak *veya* kâse.

e.phem.er.a *zo.* [iˈfemərə] *n.,* eˈphem.er.on [~rɔn] *pl. a.* eˈphem.er.a [~rə] kısa ömürlü böcekler sınıfı; eˈphem.er.al *adj.* kısa ömürlü, bir gün yaşayan, geçici, süresiz.

ep.ic [ˈepik] 1. □ destan tarzında, destan gibi; 2. *n.* destan, epope.

ep.i.cure [ˈepikjuə] *n.* düşkün, zevk, lezzet alan *b-i (yemek, içki);* ep.i.cu.re.an [~ˈriːən] 1. *adj.* zevk ve sefaya düşkün; 2. = epicure.

ep.i.dem.ic [epiˈdemik] 1. *adj.* (~ally) salgın, yaygın, genel; ~ disease =2. *n.* salgın *(hastalık),* epidemi.

ep.i.der.mis *anat.* [epiˈdəːmis] *n.* üst deri, dış zar.

ep.i.gram [ˈepigræm] *n.* nükteli kısa şiir, hicivli söz, nükte; ep.i.gram.mat.ic, ep.i.gram.mat.i.cal □ [~grəˈmætik(əl)] nükteli, hicivli, vecizeli.

ep.i.lep.sy ☥ [ˈepilepsi] *n.* sara, tutarak, yilbik, peri hastalığı; ep.i.ˈlep.tic ☥ 1. *adj.* sara ile ilgili; 2. *n.* saralı *b-i.*

ep.i.logue [ˈepilɔg] *n.* sonsöz, hatime.

E.piph.a.ny [iˈpifəni] *n.* Mecusilerin Hazreti İsa'yı görmek için Bethlehem'e gelmelerini kutlayan yortu *(6 Ocak).*

e.pis.co.pa.cy [iˈpiskəpəsi] *n.* kiliseyi piskoposlar vasıtasıyla idare yöntemi; piskoposluk; eˈpis.co.pal *adj. rel.* piskoposa ait: piskoposlarca idare edilen; e.pis.co.pa.li.an [~kəuˈpəiljən] 1. *n.* piskoposlarca yönetilen kilise hükümeti taraftarı *b-i;* 2. *adj.* piskoposlarca yönetilen kilise hükümeti ile ilgili; eˈpis.co.pate [~kəupit] *n.* piskoposluk; piskoposlar sınıfı.

ep.i.sode [ˈepisəud] *n.* olay, hadise, vaka; fıkra, bölüm, parça *(roman, hikâye vs.):* ep.i.sod.ic, ep.i.sod.i.cal □ [~ˈsɔdik(əl)]|

hadise kabilinden; bölümler halinde olan.
**e.pis.tle** *n.* çok uzun ve önemli mektup, name, risale; sirküler, tamim; **e'pis.to-lar.y** [~-tɔlǝri] *adj.* mektup (yazma) ile ilgili; mekuplaşma ile yürütülen; mektup türünde.

**ep.i.taph** [ˈepitɑːf] *n.* mezar kitabesi.

**ep.i.thet** [ˈepiθet] *n.* sıfat, lâkap, vasıf; hakaret *veya* hoşnutsuzluk belirten söz.

**e.pit.o.me** [iˈpitǝmi] *n.* özet, öz, hülâsa; örnek, tüm özellikleri gösteren *b-i veya bş;* **e'pit.o.mize** *v/t.* özetlemek, hülâsa etm.; örnek teşkil etm.

**ep.och** [ˈiːpɔk] *n.* devir, çağ, çığır; '~-mak-ing *adj.* çok önemli, çığır açan.

**Ep som salts** [ˈepsǝmˈsɔːlts] *n. pl.* müshil olarak kullanılan magnezyum sülfat, İngiliz tuzu.

**eq.ua bil.i.ty** [ekwǝˈbiliti] *n.* ılımlılık, yeknesaklık, soğukkanlılık, yumuşaklık; **'eq-ua.ble** □ yeknesak, düzenli, ılımlı, sakin; *fig.* istifini bozmayan, soğukkanlılığını yitirmeyen.

**e.qual** [ˈiːkwǝl] **1.** □ eşit, denk, aynı; esdeğerli; dengeli, düzenli, düzgün; aynı haklara sahip olan; yeterli; ~ to emsal -c; yeterli *-e; b-nin, bşin* üstesinden gelmek, yeterli olm.; **2.** *n.* eş, emsal; my ~s *pl.* yaşıtlarım; **3.** *v/t.* eşit olm. *-e,* eşdeğerde olm.; not to be ~!ed eşi emsali *(ve-ya* misli menendi) olmamak; **e.qual.i.ty** [iːˈkwɔliti] *n.* eşitlik, aynılık; akranlık; o **qual.i.za.tion** [iːkwǝlaiˈzeiʃǝn] *n.* eşit-le(n)me, aynı olma, uyuşma; **'e.qual.ize** *v/t.* eşitlemek (to, with *-e, ile); v/i.* spor: beraberliği sağlamak.

**e.qua.nim i.ty** [ekwǝˈnimiti] *n.* ılım, vakar, soğukkanlılık.

**e.quate** [iˈkweit] *v/t.* eşitlemek; eşit saymak, kıyaslamak (to, with *-e, ile);* **e'qua-tion** *n.* eşitleme; A denklem; **e'qua.tor** *n. gco.* ekvator; **e.qua.to.ri al** □ [ekwǝˈtɔːriǝl] ckvator ile ilgili, ekvatoral.

**eq.uer.ry** [iˈkwǝri] *n.* imrahor, ahır bakıcısı; İngiliz Kraliyet ailesinden birinin özel hizmet'inde bulunan kimse.

**e.ques.tri.an** [iˈkwestriǝn] **1.** *adj.* biniciliğe ait; atlı; **2.** *n.* süvari, atlı; at cambazı.

**e.qui.dis.tant** [iːkwiˈdistǝnt] *adj.* eşit uzaklıkta olan.

**e.qui.lat cr.al** □ [ˈiːkwiˈlætǝrǝl] eşkenar (üçgen).

**e.qui.li.brate** [iːkwiˈlaibreit] *v/t.* denge sağlamak, denk kılmak *(ağırlık, güç vs.); v/i.* dengede olm., denk olm.; **e-quil-i.brist** [iːˈkwilibrist] *n.* akrobat, ip cambazı; **e.qui'lib.ri.um** [~ǝm] *n.* denge, muvazene.

**e.quine** *zo.* [ˈiːkwain] *adj.* at ile ilgili, ata benzer; at gibi...

**e.qui.noc.tial** [iːkwiˈnɔkʃǝl] *adj.* gece ile gündüzün eşit olduğu zamanla ilgili; **e-qui.nox** [ˈ~nɔks] *n.* gündönümü, gün-tün eşitliği.

**e.quip** [iˈkwip] *v/t.* donatmak, teçhiz etm.; silahlandırmak; **eq.ui.page** [ˈekwipidʒ] *n.* harp levazımatı; konak arabası *(at-lı);* **e.quip.ment** [iˈkwipmǝnt] *n.* teçhizat, donatım, levazım; *fig.* bir amaca ulaşmak için gerekli olan araçlar.

**c.qui.poise** [ˈekwipɔiz] **1.** *n.* muvazene, denge; karşıt ağırlık; **2.** *vb.* muvazene sağlamak, dengeyi korumak.

**eq.ui.ta.ble** □ [ˈekwitǝbl] âdil, insaflı, tarafsız; **'eq.ui.ty** *n.* insaf, adalet; ↯↯ *(esp. İngiliz dilinin konuşulduğu ülkelerde)* örf ve âdet hukukundan ayrı olarak gelişen ve farklı prensiplere dayanan haktanıyct hukuku; equities *pl.* hisse senedi.

**o.quiv.a lence** [ˈikwivǝlǝns] *n.* eşitlik, eşdeğerlik, denk olma; **e'quiv.a.lent 1.** *adj.* muadil, eşit (to *-e);* **2.** *n.* bedel, karşılık, eşit miktar.

**e.quiv.o.cal** □ [iˈkwivǝkǝl] iki anlamlı, iki an'ama gelebilen *(sözcük);* şüpheli, belirsiz, müphem *(davranış, olay);* **e'quiv-o.cal ness** *n.* şüpheli olma, belirsizlik, iki anlamlılık; **e'quiv.o.cate** [~keit] *v/i.* kaçamaklı dil kullanmak, iki anlama gelecek söz söylemek; **e.quiv.o'ca.tion** *n.* kaçamak, iki anlamlı sözle aldatma, müphem davranma.

**c.qui.voque, eq.ui.voke** [ˈekwivǝuk] *n.* kelime oyunu; belirsizlik, çift anlam, kaçamak.

**e.ra** [ˈiǝrǝ] *n.* devir, çağ; tarih.

**e.rad i.cate** [iˈrædikeit] *v/t.* yok etm., kökünü kurutmak *(hastalık, suç, kötü alışkanlık vs.);* **e.rad.i'ca.tion** *n.* yok etme, imha.

**e.rase** [iˈreiz] *v/t.* silmek, çizmek, kazımak; *fig.* yok etm., öldürmek; **e'ras.er** *n.* lastik, silgi, yazı kazımağa mahsus gakı; **e'ra sure** [~ʒǝ] *n.* silme, bozma; silinen yerde kalan iz, silinti.

**ore** *poet.* [ǝǝ] *cj. & prp.* evvel, önce, -den önce; ~ this evvelce, bundan önce; ~ long yakında, neredeyse, birazdan; ~ now bundan önce, vaktiyle.

**o.rect** [iˈrekt] **1.** □ dik, doğru, dik duran, dikili, dikilmiş *(saç);* **2.** *v/t.* kaldırmak, inşa etm., dikmek *(anıt vs.);* **e'rec.tion** *n.* dikme, kurma; yapı, bina; kalkma, dikilme, penis dokusunun kan dolması ile sertleşmesi, ereksiyon; **e'rec.ness** *n.* doğruluk, dik duruş; **e'rec.tor** *n.* kaldıran, diken *veya* inşa eden *b-i veya bş.*

**er.e.mite** ['erimait] *n.* inzivaya çekilmiş kimse, keşiş; **er.e.mit.ic** (*~'mitik) *adj.* bir köşeye çekilmiş, insandan kaçan, inziva kabilinden.

**erg** *phys.* [ə:g] *n.* erg, enerji birimi.

**er.got** ⚓ ['ə:gət] *n.* çavdar mahmuzu *(çavdar başağı üzerinde türeyen bir tür askıı mantar).*

**er.mine** ['ə:min] *n. zo.* kakım, as; kakım kürkü; *fig.* hakim edasıyla.

**e.rode** [i'rəud] *v/t. & v/i.* azar azar yiyerek kemir(il)mek, aşın(dır)mak.

**e.ro.sion** [i'rəuʒən] *n.* aşın(dırma); *geol.* erozyon; **e'ro.sive** (*~siv) *adj.* aşındırıcı, kemirici.

**e.rot.ic** [i'rɔtik] 1. *adj.* aşka ait, şehvanî; cinsel arzu uyandıran, erotik, şehvetli; 2. *n.* âşıkane şiir, erotik şiir; şehevî *b-i;* **e'rot.i.cism** (*~sizəm) *n.* şehvet, erosallık, şehvetperestlik.

**err** [ə:] *v/i.* yanılmak, yanlış yapmak; günah işlemek.

**er.rand** ['erənd] *n.* iş, sipariş; habercilik; fool's *~* yararsız çaba, boşuna gayret; go (on) *~s* bir haber götürmek *veya* bir iş için bir yere gitmek; '*~-boy n.* ayak işlerine koşulan çocuk, çırak.

**er.rant** ☐ ['erənt] maceraperest, doğru yoldan sapan, serseri, delâlete düşen; *s.* knight-*~;* **'er.rant.ry** *n.* serserilik, avarelik, maceraperestlik *(şövalye).*

**er.rat.ic** [i'rætik] *adj.* (*~ally) seyyar, dolaşan; düzensiz; sebatsız, ne yapacağı belirsiz, *sl.* osuruğu cinli; *~* fever belirli aralıklarla gelen ateş; **er.ra.tum** [e'ra:təm] *n., pl.* **er'ra.ta** [*~tə] dizgi hatası, sehiv.

**er.ro.ne.ous** ☐ [i'rəunjəs] hatalı, yanlış.

**er.ror** ['erə] *n.* hata, yanlışlık; *~* of judgement muhakemede usul hatası; *~s* excepted *(hesap)* olası yanlışlar müstesna, hatalar kabul edilir.

**Erse** [ə:s] 1. *adj.* İrlanda diline ait; 2. *n.* İrlanda dili.

**erst.while** ['ə:stwail] *adj.* eski, sabık, evvelce olan.

**e.ruc.ta.tion** [i:rʌk'teifən] *n.* geğirme.

**er.u.dite** ['eru:dait] çok bilgili, âlim, bilgin; **er.u.di.tion** (*~'difən) *n.* âlimlik, bilginlik.

**e.rupt** [i'rʌpt] *v/i.* indifa etm. *(volkan),* fışkırmak, püskürmek; çıkmak *(diş);* **e'rup.tion** *n.* indifa *(volkan),* fışkırma, püskürme, patlama *(a. fig.);* ⚓ isilik, kızartı; diş çıkması; **e'rup.tive** *adj.* patlayan, indifa eden, püsküren, fışkıran; kızartı ile ilgili.

**er.y.sip.e.las** ⚓ [eri'sipiləs] *n.* yılancık.

**es.ca.la.tion** *pol.* [eskə'leifən] *n.* kızışma, gerginlik, artış, yükseliş; **es.ca.la.tor** ['eskəleitə] *n.* yürüyen merdiven.

**es.ca.pade** [eskə'peid] *n.* haylazlık, yaramazlık, gençlik çılgınlığı; *fig.* hoppalık, yoldan çıkma; **es.cape** [is'keip] 1. *v/t.* -den çıkmak *(ses, sözcük);* gözünden kaçmak, hatırından çıkmak *(olay vs.);* -den kaçmak, kurtulmak, *bşden* sakınmak; *v/i.* kaçmak, kurtulmak (from, out of -*den);* *(gaz)* sızmak (from -*den);* 2. *n.* kaçma, kurtuluş; akma, sızma, sızıntı; have a narrow *~* güçbelâ kurtulmak; **es.ca.pee** [eskei'pi:] *n.* firari, kaçak; **es.cape.ment** ⊕ [is'keipmənt] *n.* saat çarklarının çalışmasını sağlayan maşa; **es'cap.ism** *n.* hoş olmayan hayatın gerçeklerinden kaçma; hayal kurma; **es'cap.ist** 1. *adj.* gerçeklerden kaçan, hayal kuran; 2. *n.* gerçeklerden kaçan kimse.

**es.carp** [is'ka:p] 1. *a.* **es'carp.ment** *n.* az meyilli yüzey, şev, bayır; 2. *v/t.* meyillendirmek, şev şeklini vermek.

**es.cheat** ⚓ [is'tfi:t] 1. *n.* mirasçısız ölen kimsenin mülkünün devlete geçişi; 2. *v/i.* devlete kalmak *(mülk);* *v/t.* müsadere etm., zoralımına çarptırmak.

**es.chew** [is'tfu:] *v/t. bşden* kaçınmak, vazgeçmek, sakınmak.

**es.cort** 1. ['eskɔ:t] *n.* muhafız; maiyet; kavalye; refakatçı; 2. [is'kɔ:t] *v/t.* refakat etm. *-e.*

**es.cri.toire** [eskri:twa:] *n.* yazı masası, yazıhane.

**es.cu.lent** ['eskjulənt] 1. *adj.* yenilebilir; 2. *n.* gıda maddeleri, yiyecekler.

**es.cutch.eon** [is'kʌtfən] *n.* arma, armalı levha, ad tablası; anahtar deliği çevresindeki süslü madenî çerçeve.

**Es.ki.mo** ['eskiməu] *n.* Eskimo; Eskimo dili.

**e.soph.a.gus** [i:'sɔfəgəs] = oesophagus.

**es.o.ter.ic** [esəu'terik] *adj.* gizli, anlaşılması güç; belirli bir grup tarafından anlaşılan.

**es.pal.ier** ✓ [is'pæljə] *n.* meyve ağacı dallarının bir duvar vs. boyunca gelişmesini sağlayan çerçeve; böyle yetişmiş ağaçlar sırası.

**es.pe.cial** [is'pefəl] *adj.* özel, mahsus, husüsî; fevkalâde; seçkin; **es'pe.cial.ly** *adv.* özellikle, bilhassa

**Es.per.an.to** [espə'ræntəu] *n.* Esperanto dili.

**es.pi.al** [is'paiəl] *n.* gözetleme, keşfetme.

es.pi.o.nage [espiə'nɑ:ʒ] *n.* casusluk.

es.pla.nade [esplə'neid] *n.* gezinti yeri, deniz kenarında piyasa yapılan yer, kordonboyu.

es.pous.al [is'pauzəl] *n.* benimseme, bir düşünceyi destekleme (of), kabullenme; evlenme *veya* evlenme sözü, nişan; es-'pouse *v/t. b-le* evlenmek; *bşi* benimsemek, desteklemek.

es.pres.so [es'presəu] *n.* İtalyan usulü kahve, espreso kahve; ~ bar, ~ ca.fé bu tür kahve içilen yer.

es.py [is'pai] *v/t.* uzaktan görmek, gözüne ilişmek.

es.quire [is'kwaiə] *n.* mülk sahibi; *(mektup)* kısaltılmış şekilde ad ve soyadından sonra yazılan ve beyefendi, bay anlamına gelen unvan: John Smith, Esq. Bay John Smith.

es.say 1. [e'sei] *v/t.* denemek, tecrübe etm., prova etm.; 2. ['esei] *n.* makale, yazı; deneme, tecrübe (at); 'es.say.ist *n.* deneme yazarı.

es.sence ['esns] *n.* öz, esas, cevher, asıl, öz varlık, nitelik; ⚛ esans; es.sen.tial [i'senʃəl] 1. □ (to) esaslı, karakteristik, önemli; elzem, gerekli; ~ likeness özü, esası bir olma; ~ oil uçucu yağ; 2. *n.* esas özellik; esas mesele; gerekli olan şey, esas; es'sen.tial.ly *adv.* esasen, esas itibariyle, aslında.

es.tab.lish [is'tæbliʃ] *v/t.* kurmak, tesis etm.; saptamak; atamak *(memur vs.)*; *b-ne* iş bulmak, *b-ni* işe yerleştirmek; tanıtmak; ~ o.s. yerleşmek; ♗ed Church resmi *(veya* ulusal) kilise; es'tab.lish.ment *n.* kurma, kurum, tesis, müessese, teşkilat; egemen çevreler, ileri gelenler, kodamanlar; ✕, ⚓ erler, mürettebat; military ~ sürekli ordu.

es.tate [is'teit] *n.* mal, mülk, arsa, gayrımenkul; çiftlik, yalı; miras, tereke; durum, hal; tabaka, sınıf, mevki; itibar, yüksek mertebe; personal ~ taşınabilir, menkul mallar; real ~ taşınamaz, gayrımenkul mallar; housing ~ iskân bölgesi, bahçeli evler; industrial ~ endüstri bölgesi; ~ a.gen.cy emlâk bürosu; ~ a-gent emlâk simsarı, emlâk komisyoncusu; ~ car pikap; ~ du.ty intikal vergisi, veraset vergisi.

es.teem [is'ti:m] 1. *n.* saygı, takdir, itibar (with); 2. *v/t.* takdir etm. *-i;* hürmet etm. *-e;* zannetmek, telâkki etm., sanmak.

es.ter ⚛ ['estə] *n.* ester, asitlerin alkollere etkisiyle elde edilen organik bileşik.

es.thet.ic [i:s'θetik] = aesthetic.

Es.tho.ni.an [es'təunjən] 1. *n.* Estonyalı;

Estonya dili; 2. *adj.* Estonya'ya özgü.

es.ti.ma.ble ['estiməbl] *adj.* saygıdeğer, itibarlı, değerli, hürmete lâyık, takdire değer.

es.ti.mate 1. ['estimeit] *vb.* takdir etm., tahmin etm., değer biçmek (at); 2. *n.* hesap; tahmin, takdir, değer biçme the ⚖ pl. parl. bütçe; es.ti.ma.tion [~'meiʃən] *n.* hesap etme; itibar, hürmet; fikir, tahmin, görüş, rey; 'es.ti.ma.tor *n.* değer biçen, maliyet hesabını yapan *b-i.*

es.trange [is'treindʒ] *v/t.* soğutmak, uzaklaştırmak (from s.o. *-den*), yabancılaştırmak; es'trange.ment *n.* yabancılaş-(tır)ma, soğu(t)ma, bozuşma.

es.tu.ar.y ['estjuəri] *n. geol.* nehir ağzı, haliç.

et.cet.er.as [it'setrəz] *n. pl.* ufak tefek çeşitli şeyler.

etch [etʃ] *vb.* kezzapla hakkatmek, madeni bir levhayı asitle yakarak resim kalıbı çıkarmak.

e.ter.nal □ [i:tə:nl] ebedî, sonsuz; ezelî, öncesiz; e'ter.nal.ize [~nəlaiz] *v/t.* ebedileştirmek; e'ter.ni.ty *n.* ebediyet, sonsuzluk, ezeliyet; ölümsüzlük; e'ter.nize [~naiz] *v/t.* ebedileştirmek, ölümsüzleştirmek.

e.ther ['i:θə] *n.* esir, evreni ve atomlar arasındaki boşluğu dolduran ve ağırlığı olmayan bir töz, değişmeden kalan varlık; ⚛ eter, lokman ruhu; e.the.re.al □ [i:'θiəriəl] dünyevi olmayan aydınlık ve hassasiyet; ruh gibi, peri gibi; 'e.ther.ize *v/t.* eterle bayıltmak, sersemletmek, uyuşturmak.

eth.i.cal □ ['eθikəl] ahlâki, manevi, törel; 'eth.ics *n. mst sg.* ahlâk (ilmî).

E.thi.o.pi.an [i:θi'əupjən] 1. *adj.* Habeşistan'a ait, Habeş...; 2. *n.* Habeşistanlı, Habeş.

eth.nic ['eθnik] *adj.* etnik, ırka ait, ırksal. eth.nog.ra.phy [eθ'nɔɡrəfi] *n.* etnografya, budunbetim, kavimler ilmi; eth'nol.o.gy [~lədʒi] *n.* etnoloji, (kıyaslamalı) budunbilim.

eth.yl ['eθil] ⚛ 'i:θail] *n.* etil; *(arabada motor sesini azaltmak için)* benzine konulan kurşunlu bir bileşim; eth.yl.ene ['eθili:n] *n.* etilen (gazı), hidrokarbon.

e.ti.o.late ['i:tiəuleit] *v/t.* ışıksızlıktan soldurmak *(bitki); fig.* zayıflatmak, kuvvetten düşürmek.

e.ti.ol.o.gy [i:ti'ɔlədʒi] *n.* hastalıkların nedenlerini araştırma ilmi.

et.i.quette ['etiket] *n.* görgü kuralları, adabımuaşeret, topluluk töresi, protokol.

E.ton crop ['i:tn'krɔp] *n.* alagarson saç,

erkek saçı gibi kısa kesilmiş saç *(kadın)*.
**E.trus.can** [i'trʌskən] **1.** *adj.* eski İtalya'-
da Etrurya'ya ait; **2.** *n.* Etrurya'lı; Etrurya dili.
**et.y.mo.log.i.cal** ☐ [etimə'lɔdʒikl] etimo-
lojik, iştikaka ait, türeme ile ilgili; **et.y-
mol.o.gy** [~'mɔlədʒi] *n.* etimoloji, işti-
kak, sözcük türetme; sözcük kökü bilgisi.
**eu.ca.lyp.tus** ♀ [juːkə'liptəs] *n.* okaliptüs,
sıtma ağacı.
**Eu.cha.rist** ['juːkərist] *n.* Hıristiyan kilisesine ait Aşai Rabbanî *(şarap ve ekmek yeme)* ayini; bu ayin için kutsanan
şaarp ve ekmek.
**Eu.clid** ♀ ['juːklid] *n.* Öklit geometri.
**eu.gen.ic** [juːdʒenik] *adj.* (~ally) insan ırkının soyaçekim yoluyla mükemmelleş-
tirilmesine ait; gelecek nesillerin ıslahına ait; **eu'gen.ics** *n. pl.* insan ırkının soyaçekim yoluyla ıslahına çalışan bilim
dalı.
**eu.lo.gist** ['juːlədʒist] *n.* methiye yazan ve
söyleyen kimse, kaside yazarı; **eu.lo.gıze**
['~dʒaiz] *v/t.* övmek, methetmek, sita-
yişle bahsetmek; **eu.lo.gy** ['~dʒi] *n.* methiye, kaside, senakâr nutuk.
**eu.nuch** ['juːnək] *n.* hadım, harem ağası.
**eu.phe.mism** ['juːfimizəm] *n.* kaba sayılan
sözcükler kullanmayıp kavramı üstü örtülü olarak anlatan başka sözcükler kullanma; **eu.phe'mis.tic, eu.phe'mis.ti.cal** ☐
bu tür sözcükler içeren, bu tür sözcüklerle ilgili.
**eu.phon.ic, eu.phon.i.cal** ☐ [juː'fɔnik(əl)]
ahenkli, armonik, öfonik, kulağa hoş gelen; **eu.pho.ny** ['juːfəni] *n.* ahenk, armoni, öfoni.
**eu.phor.ia** [juː'fɔːriə] *n.* öfori, *k-ni* aşırı
derecede mutlu ve zinde hissetme hali.
**eu.phu.ism** ['juːfjuːizəm] *n.* yapmacık, zor
ve tumturaklı edebî dil *(16 yy.'da İngil-
tere'de)*.
**Eur.a.sian** [juə'reiʒən] **1.** *n.* bir Avrupalı
ile bir Asyalı'nın evlenmesinden doğan
çocuk; **2.** *adj.* Avrupa ile Asya'ya ait.
**eu.re.ka** [juə'riːkə] *int.* buldum!
**Eu.ro.pe.an** [juərə'piːən] **1.** *adj.* Avrupa
ile ilgili; **2.** *n.* Avrupalı.
**eu.tha.na.si.a** [juːθə'neiʒə] *n.* acısız ölüm;
ümitsiz durumda *veya* çok yaşlı olan hastaların acılarını dindirmek için hayatla-
rına son verme.
**e.vac.u.ate** [i'vækjueit] *v/t.* boşaltmak,
dökmek, tahliye etm., terketmek *(toprak)*; ⚕ ishal, amel vermek, vücuttan çıkarmak; **e.vac.u'a.tion** *n.* boşaltma, tahliye; **e.vac.u'ee** *n.* tehlike yerinden uzak-
laştırılan *b-i.*

**e.vade** [i'veid] *v/t.* sakınmak *-den,* kaçınmak *-den, bşden* çekinmek, kaçamaklı
yol aramak.
**e.val.u.ate** *esp.* A [i'væljueit] *v/t.* değerini *veya* derecesini hesap etm. *-in,* değerlendirmek *-i,* sayısını tahmin etm. *-in;*
**e.val.u'a.tion** *n.* değerlendirme, paha biçme.
**ev.a.nesce** [iːvə'nes] *v/i.* ortadan kaybolmak, yok olm., yavaş yavaş gözden kaybolmak, unutulmak; **ev.a'nes.cence** *n.*
yok olma, gözden kaybolma; **ev.a'nes-
cent** ☐ yok olan, gözden kaybolan, unutulan.
**e.van.gel.ic, e.van.gel.i.cal** ☐ [iːvæn-
'dʒelik(əl)] protestan; dört İncil'de ya-
zılanlara göre İsa'yı tanıtma ve öğretme
ile ilgili; **e.van.ge.list** [i'vændʒilist] *n.* gezici vaiz; dört İncili yazanlardan biri;
**e'van.ge.lize** *v/t. & v/i.* İncil'i va'zetmek,
Hıristiyanlığa sevketmek.
**e.vap.o.rate** [i'væpəreit] *v/t. & v/i.* buhar-
laş(tır)mak, uç(ur)mak; *fig.* uçup gitmek, yok olm.; *~ed* milk kondanse süt.
kısmen suyu alınmış süt; **e.vap.o'ra.tion**
*n.* buharlaş(tır)ma, buğulan(dır)ma.
**e.va.sion** [i'veiʒən] *n.* kaçınma, sakınma;
kaçamak, bahane; **e'va.sive** ☐ [~siv] kaçamaklı (of), baştan savma; **be ~** *fig.*
yan çizmek.
**eve** [iːv] *n.* arife; arife gecesi; *poet.* gece; on the ~ of arifesinde *-in.*
**e.ven¹** ['iːvən] **1.** *adj.* ☐ düz, pürüzsüz,
müstevi, düzlem; eşit, müsavi; düzgün,
muntazam, düzenli; çift, tam *(sayı)*; paralel, denk, aynı seviyede; tarafsız; **make**
~ with the ground yerle bir etm., yıkıp
yok etm.; **be ~** with s.o. *b-le* alacağı ver-
receği kalmamak, ödeşmek; **get ~ with**
s.o. *b-le* hesaplaşmak, *b-den bşin* acısını
çıkarmak, intikam almak; **odd or ~** tek
mi çift mi; **of ~ date** † aynı tarihte;
**break ~** F kârsız *veya* zararsız kapamak
*(hesap)*, ancak masrafını karşılamak;
**2.** *adv.* hatta, bile, dahi; tamamiyle, tıpkı; not ~ hatta ...bile değil; ~ though,
~ if her ne kadar... ise de. olsa bile, (olmasına) rağmen; **3.** *v/t.* düzlemek, düzeltmek, tesviye etm.; kıyas etm. (to,
*-e),* benzetmek.
**even²** *poet.* [~] *n.* akşam.
**eve-hand.ed** ['iːvən'hændid] *adj.* tarafsız, bitaraf.
**eve.ning** ['iːvnin] *n.* akşam; suvare; ~
dress gece elbisesi, tuvalet, smokin *veya* frak.
**e.ven.ness** ['iːvənnis] *n.* doğruluk, dürüst-

lük, tarafsızlık; eşitlik; düz oluş; kalp huzuru; sükûnet.

**e.ven.song** [ˈiːvənsɔn] *n.* akşam duası.

**e.vent** [iˈvent] *n.* olay, hadise, vaka; hal; *fig.* sonuç, âkıbet; müsabaka, maç, turnuva *(sportif)*; numara *(program)*; athletic ~s *pl.* atletizm yarışmaları; table of ~s festival *(şenlik, ziyafet)* programı; at all ~s mutlaka, behemehal, her halde, ne olursa olsun; in any ~ zaten, esasen, haddizatında; in the ~ of şayet, ...olduğu takdirde.

**e.ven-tem.pered** [ˈiːvəntempəd] *adj.* sakin, soğukkanlı.

**e.vent.ful** [iˈventful] *adj.* olaylarla dolu.

**e.ven.tide** *poet.* [ˈiːvəntaid] *n.* akşam, akşam vakti.

**e.ven.tu.al** [iˈventʃuəl] muhtemel, olası; nihaî, sonuncu, sonraki; ~ly sonunda, nihayet, ilerde **e.ven.tu.al.i.ty** [~tʃuˈæliti] *n.* ihtimal, olasılık; **e.ven.tu.ate** [~tʃueit] *v/t.* sonuçlanmak; çıkmak, oluşmak.

**ev.er** [ˈevə] *adv.* herhangi bir zamanda; hiç, asla; daima, her zaman, tekrar tekrar; ~ so pek, çok; as soon as ~ I can elimden geldiğince çabuk; ~ after, ~ since -den beri; ~ and anon arada sırada; for ~, for ~ and ~, for ~ and a day ilelebet, daima, ebediyete kadar; liberty for ~ sonsuza dek özgürlük; ~ so much pek çok; I wonder who ~ kim olabilir, kim olduğunu merak ediyorum; the best ~ F en iyisi; yours ~ daima senin... *(mektup sonunda)*; ~.glade *n.* Am. bataklık alan; ~.green 1. *adj.* yaprağını dökmeyen; 2. *n.* yaprağını dökmeyen ağaç; ~.last.ing 1. ☐ sonsuz; devamlı; ölümsüz; 2. *n.* ebediyet, sonsuzluk; ✤ kuruduğu zaman rengini ve şeklini koruyan bir tür çiçek; ~.more *adv.* daima, ebediyen, sürekli.

**ev.er.y** [ˈevri] *adj.* her, her bir, her biri; ~ bit as much tam onun kadar; ~ now and then arasıra; ~ one of them istisnasız hepsi; ~ other day iki günde bir, gün aşırı; ~ twenty years her yirmi yılda bir; her ~ movement her hareketi; ~.bod.y *pron.* herkes; ~.day *adj.* her günkü, günlük, olağan; ~.one *pron.* herkes; ~.thing *pron.* herşey; ~.way *adv.* her bakımdan; ~.where *adv.* her yer(d)e.

**e.vict** [iˈvikt] *v/t.* kapı dışarı etm., tahliye et(tir)mek; **e.vic.tion** *n.* tahliye etme *veya* edilme, geri al(ın)ma.

**ev.i.dence** [ˈevidəns] 1. *n.* delil, ispat, tanıt, tutanak; ☼ şahitlik, şahadet, tanıklık; şahit, tanık; be in ~ göze çarpmak,

kendini göstermek; furnish ~ of, be ~ of kanıtlamak, ispat etm., göstermek, belirtmek, açığa vurmak; give ~, bear ~ tanıklık etm., şahadet etm. (of, for. against -e); 2. *v/t.* kanıtlamak, göstermek, belirtmek, -e delâ;et etm.; **ev.i.dent** ☐ aşikâr, belli, açık, sarih; **ev.i.den.tial** ☐ [~ˈdenʃəl] delile dayanan, kanıt *veya* tanık türünden.

**e.vil** [ˈiːvl] 1. ☐ fena, kötü, kem; the ~ eye kem göz, nazar değme; the ⵛ One Şeytan, İblis; 2. *n.* fenalık, kötülük, bela, dert; ~-ˈdo.er *n.* muzır, şerir, kötülük eden b-i; ~-ˈmind.ed *adj.* kötü niyetli, suniyet sahibi, kötü yürekli, kötücül.

**e.vince** [iˈvins] *v/t.* ortaya koymak, göstermek, izhar etm., açığa vurmak, kanıtlamak.

**e.vis.cer.ate** [iˈvisəreit] *v/t. (vurulan hayvanın)* karnını yarıp temizlemek, bağırsaklarını çıkarmak.

**ev.o.ca.tion** [evoˈkeiʃən] *n.* aklına getirme -i, zihinde canlandırma i-; **e.voc.a.tive** [iˈvɔkətiv] *adj.* hatırlatan, andıran, uyandıran.

**e.voke** [iˈvəuk] *v/t.* uyandırmak, mucip olm., davet etm., hissettirmek, neden olm., doğurmak.

**ev.o.lu.tion** [iːvəˈluːʃən] *n.* gelişme, inkişaf, evrim; Ａ kök alma; ✕ manevra, tatbikat; **ev.oˈlu.tion.a.ry** [~ʃnəri] *adj.* evrimsel, gelişme ile ilgili.

**e.volve** [iˈvɔlv] *v/t. & v/i.* aç(ıl)mak, yay(ıl)mak, geliş(tir)mek, evrim geçirmek.

**ewe** [juː] *n. zo.* dişi koyun.

**ew.er** [ˈjuːə] *n.* ibrik.

**ex** [eks] *prefix* † -de teslim; -den dışarı *(fabrika, liman vs.); (borsa)* -siz, olmadan; sabık, eski, önceki; ex-minister *n.* sabık bakan.

**ex.ac.er.bate** [eksˈsæsəːbeit] *v/t.* kötüleştirmek, vahimleştirmek, şiddetlendirmek, kızdırmak, öfkelendirmek.

**ex.act** [igˈzækt] 1. ☐ tam, doğru; kati, kesin; fiilî, hakikî; tamamen; aynen; dakikası dakikasına; 2. *v/t.* tahsil etm., talep etm., ödeme zorunda bırakmak; icbar etm.; **exˈact.ing** *adj.* titiz, müşkülpesent, kibirli; hoşgörüsüz; fazla dikkat ve güç gerektiren; **exˈac.tion** *n.* zorla alma. haraç kesme; zorla yaptırılan iş *veya* alınan para; **exˈact.i.tude** [~titjuːd] *n.* sıhhat, doğruluk, hatasızlık, tam ve doğru olma; **exˈact.ly** *adv. (cevap)* tamamen, aynen; not ~ tam olarak değil, tamamen öyle değil; **exˈact.ness** = exactitude.

**ex.ag.ger.ate** [igˈzædʒəreit] *vb.* mübalağa

etm., abartmak; **ex.ag.ger¹a.tion** *n.* mübalağa, abartma, aşırılık.

**ex.alt** [ıg¹zɔːlt] *v/t.* yükseltmek, yüceltmek; övmek, göklere çıkarmak; **ex.al.ta.tion** [egzɔːl¹teiʃən] *n.* heyecan, aşka gelme, coşkunluk, esrime; yüksel(t)me; yükseklik, ululuk; **ex.alt.ed** [ıg¹zɔːltid] *adj.* yüce, ulu, yüksek, ulvî; coşkun.

**ex.am** *okul: sl.* [ıg¹zæm] *n.* sınav, imtihan.

**ex.am.i.na.tion** [ıgzæmi¹neiʃən] *n.* sınav, imtihan; muayene, yoklama, teftiş, tetkik; **ex¹am.ine** *v/t.* sınava tabi tutmak, imtihan etm.; yoklamak, muayene etm., teftiş etm., tetkik etm. *(a. ~* into s.th.); sorguya çekmek; **ex¹am.i¹nee** *n.* sınava giren *b-i;* **ex¹am.in.er** *n.* sınav yapan *b-i,* ayırtman; muayene eden *b-i;* sorgu hâkimi; müfettiş.

**ex.am.ple** [ıg¹zaːmpl] *n.* örnek, misal, numune; beyond ~ emsalsiz, eşsiz; for ~ örneğin, meselâ; make an ~ of başkalarına ders olsun diye *b-ni* cezalandırmak; set an ~ örnek olm.

**ex.as.per.ate** [ıg¹zaːspəreit] *v/t.* kızdırmak, sinirlendirmek, çileden çıkarmak, şiddetlendirmek; **ex.as.per¹a.tion** *n.* öfke, hiddet, sinirlenme, dargınlık (of).

**ex.ca.vate** [¹ekskəveit] *v/t.* kazmak, hafriyat yapmak; kazıp açmak; **ex.ca¹va.tion** *n.* kazı, hafriyat, çukur; **¹ex.ca.va.tor** *n.* ekskavator, kazma makinesi; toprak işçisi.

**ex.ceed** [ik¹siːd] *vb.* aşmak, geçmek; *b-ne* üstün gelmek (in); aşırıya kaçmak, ileri gitmek; **ex¹ceed.ing** *adj.* aşırı, müfrit, ölçüsüz; **ex¹ceed.ing.ly** *adv.* son derece, fazlasıyla, gayet fevkalâde.

**ex.cel** [ik¹sel] *vb.* geçmek, üstün olm. *-den; k-ni* göstermek, temayüz etm., sivrilmek (in, at); **ex.cel.lence** [¹eksələns] *n.* üstünlük, seçkin oluş, mükemmel oluş, fazilet; **¹Ex.cel.len.cy** *n.* ekselans *(ünvan);* **¹ex.cel.lent** □ mükemmel, çok iyi, kusursuz, mümtaz, üstün.

**ex.cept** [ik¹sept] **1.** *vb.* hariç tutmak, müstesna kılmak, ayrı tutmak; itiraz etm., karşı çıkmak; present company ~ed sizden iyi olmasın; hatırınız kalmasın; **2.** *cj.* haricinde; meğer ki, olmadıkça; **3.** *prp.* -den başka, -den maada; ~ for bir yana, hariç; olmasaydı; **ex¹cept.ing** *prp.* -den başka, in dışında, müstesna, hariç (olmak üzere); **ex¹cep.tion** *n.* istisna; itiraz (to *-e*); take ~ to *bşi* sakıncalı bulmak, hoş görmemek, itiraz etm.; **ex¹cep.tion.a.ble** [~ʃnəbl] *adj.* itiraz olunabilir, yakışıksız, ahlâka aykırı; **ex-**

**¹cep.tion.al** *adj.* müstesna; olağan üstü, fevkalâde, harikulâde; **ex¹cep.tion.al.ly** *adv.* müstena olarak, fevkalâde olarak bir defaya mahsus olmak üzere.

**ex.cerpt 1.** [ek¹sɔːpt] *vb.* aktarmak, iktibas etm., almak (from *-den) (yazı, kitap vs.);* **2.** [¹eksəːpt] *n.* seçme parça, pasaj, alıntı (from *-den).*

**ex.cess** [ik¹ses] *n.* ifrat, aşırılık, fazlalık, taşkınlık, ölçüsüzlük; *attr.* fazla...; in ~ of *-den* daha çok, -i geçen; carry to ~ ifrat dereceye vardırmak; ~ fare bilet ücretine yapılan zam, ücret farkı; ~ luggage fazla bagaj; ~ postage taksa, pulsuz gönderilen mektup için alıcının ödediği posta ücreti; ~ profit fazla kazanç; **ex¹ces.sive** □ aşırı, fazla müfrit.

**ex.change** [iks¹tʃeindʒ] **1.** *vb.* değiştirmek, mübadele etm., trampa etm. (for), bozmak *(para);* **2.** *n.* değişme, trampa; kambiyo; *a.* bill of ~ ticaret senedi, poliçe; *a.* ♀ borsa; telefon santralı; *a.* foreign ~s *pl.* döviz; in ~ for *-e* bedel olarak; ~ control döviz kontrolu, kambiyo denetimi; ~ list kur cetveli; par of ~ kambiyo paritesi, borsa değeri; (rate of) ~ döviz kuru, kambiyo rayici; **ex¹change.a.ble** *adj.* değiştirilebilir, mübadele edilebilir (for); ~ value mübadele değeri.

**ex.cheq.uer** [iks¹tʃəkə] *n. pol.* devlet hazinesi; bir kimsenin kişisel gelirinin tümü; Chancellor of the ♀ *(İngiltere)* Maliye Bakanı; ~ bond hazine bonosu.

**ex.cise¹** [ek¹saiz] **1.** *n.* vasıtalı vergi, ülkede üretilip kullanılan mallardan alınan vergi; **2.** *vb.* vergi koymak.

**ex.cise²** [~] *v/t.* kesip almak, kesip çıkarmak; oymak, temizlemek *(ur);* budamak; **ex.ci.sion** [ek¹siʒən] *n.* kesip alma, kesip çıkarma; kesip alınan, çıkarılan şey.

**ex.cit.a.bil.i.ty** [iksaitə¹biliti] *n.* kolay heyecanlanma, telaşlanma; **ex¹cit.a.ble** *adj.* kolay heyecanlanır, aşırı derecede hassas, çabuk kızan; **ex.cit.ant** [¹eksitənt] *adj.* uyarıcı, uyandırıcı; **ex.ci.ta.tion** [~¹teiʃən] *n.* heyecanlandırma, tahrik, uyarma; **ex.cite** [ik¹sait] *v/t. b-ni* bşe kışkırtmak, tahrik etm.; heyecanlandırmak; uyandırmak, uyarmak; **~d** *adj.* heyecanlı; get **~d** heyecanlanmak, sinirlenmek; **ex¹cite.ment** *n.* heyecan; telaş; tahrik, uyarı; **ex¹cit.er** *n.* ♀ uyarıcı, münebbih; ⚡ dinamonun sabit sarmalarına akım veren yardımcı dinamo; **ex¹cit.ing** *adj.* heyecanlı, meraklı, ilginç, enteresan.

**ex.claim** [iks¹kleim] *vb.* bağırmak, hayret ifade etm., haykırmak, çağırmak; sövüp saymak (against -e).

**ex.cla.ma.tion** [eksklə'meiʃən] n. ünlem, nida, ani olarak söylenen söz; bağırış, çığlık; ~s pl. yaygara, şamata, bağrışma; note of ~, point of ~, ~ mark gr. ünlem işareti; **ex.clam.a.to.ry** □ [~'klæmətəri] sevinç, hayret veya keder belirten.

**ex.clude** [iks'kluːd] v/t. hariç tutmak (from -den), dahil etmemek, engel olm.; kabul etmemek; yoksun bırakmak.

**ex.clu.sion** [iks'kluːʒən] n. hariç tutma; spor: diskalifikasyon veya boykot; ret, ihraç. tart; to the ~ of -i hariç tutarak, dışında bırakarak; **ex'clu.sive** □ [~siv] has, özgü; tek, yalnız, hariç tutan; özel, sırf; ~ of -siz, -den hariç, müstesna.

**ex.cog.i.tate** [eks'kɔdʒiteit] v/t. düşünüp bulmak, tasar(ım)lamak, icat etm. (plan, fikir, vs.); **ex.cog.i'ta.tion** n. düşünme, tasarım, icat, buluş.

**ex.com.mu.ni.cate** [ekskə'mjuːnikeit] v/t. kiliseden aforoz etm.; **ex.com.mu.ni'ca-tion** n. aforoz.

**ex.co.ri.ate** [eks'kɔːrieit] v/t. sıyırmak, yüzmek (deri); fig. şiddetle eleştirmek, suçlamak.

**ex.cre.ment** ['ekskrimənt] n. dışkı, pislik, ters.

**ex.cres.cence** [iks'kresns] n. ur, şiş, yumru gibi cisim, fazlalık (bitki, hayvan vs.' de); **ex'cres.cent** adj. normalden fazla büyüyen, gereğinden fazla, gereksiz.

**ex.crete** [eks'kriːt] vb. ifraz etm., salgılamak, çıkarmak (vücuttan); **ex'cre.tion** n. ifrazat, salgı; ifraz etme, boşaltım; **ex'cre.tive**, **ex'cre.to.ry** [~təri] adj. ifraz eden, salgı çıkaran, salgı...

**ex.cru.ci.ate** [iks'kruːʃieit] v/t. azap vermek, eziyet etm., ıstırap vermek, işkence etm., cefa çektirmek; **ex'cru.ci.at.ing** □ ıstıraplı, eziyetli, cefalı, işkenceli, dayanılmaz.

**ex.cul.pate** ['eksʌlpeit] v/t. mazur göstermek, haklı çıkarmak, aklamak, beraatine karar vermek (from); **ex'cul'pa.tion** n. beraat, aklanma, af.

**ex.cur.sion** [iks'kəːʃən] n. gezinti, kısa süreli seyahat; ~ train özel indirimli tren; **ex'cur.sion.ist** [~ʃnist] n. gezinti yapan b-i.

**ex.cur.sive** □ [eks'kəːsiv] belirli bir çizgi izlemeyen, dolaşan, kararsız.

**ex.cus.a.ble** □ [iks'kjuːzəbl] affedilebilir, affolunacak, mazur; **ex'cuse 1.** v/t. affetmek, mazur görmek; ~ s.o. s.th. b-ni bşden affetmek, muaf tutmak; be ~d from s.th. bşden muaf tutulmak, affedil-

mek; ~ me affedersiniz, kusuruma bakmayın; **2.** [iks'kjuːs] n. özür, mazeret; bahane.

**ex.e.at** ['eksiæt] n. okul vs.: izin.

**ex.e.cra.ble** □ ['eksikrəbl] iğrenç, menfur, tiksindirici, berbat, kötü, lânet, melun; **ex.e.crate** ['~kreit] v/t. lânet etm., tel'in etm., beddua etm., belâ okumak; bşden, b-den nefret, ikrah etm.; **ex.e'cra-tion** n. nefret, istikrah, tiksinme, lânet, beddua.

**ex.e.cu.tant** ♪ [ig'zekjutənt] n. icra eden b-i; resital veren b-i; **ex.e.cute** ['eksikjuːt] v/t. icra etm., tatbik etm., yerine getirmek, yapmak; idam etm.; ♪ resital vermek; ♬ hükmü infaz etm.; yürürlüğe koymak, geçerli kılmak; (vasiyet) icra, tenfiz etm.; **ex.e'cu.tion** n. icra, ifa, tatbik, yapma; infaz, idam; (belge) verme, tevdi; (vasiyet) cebrî icra, zorlayışlı yerine getirme; ♪ resital; teknik, yapış tarzı; a man of ~ azimkâr kimse; take out an ~ against. b-nin malına haciz koymak, malını haczetmek; do ~ tesir etm.; put veya carry a plan into ~ bir planı gerçekleştirmek; **ex.e.cu.tion.er** [~'kjuːʃnə] n. cellat, idam hükmünü yerine getiren kimse; **ex.ec.u.tive** [ig'zekjutiv] **1.** □ icra eden, idare eden; yetki sahibi; ~ committee idare heyeti; ~ editor başyazar; **2.** n. yetkili kimse, idareci; icra gücü; yürütme organı; Am. devlet başkanı; ✝ sevk ve idare eden kimse, müdür; **ex'ec.u.tor** n. vasiyeti tenfiz memuru, yerine getiren kimse; **ex.ec.u.to.ry** adj. icraî; idarî...; ♬ bir süre sonra veya beklenmedik bir olayda geçerli olması planlanan; müeccel, ertelenen **ex'ec.u.trix** [~triks] n. vasiyet hükümlerini yerine getiren kadın.

**ex.e.ge.sis** [eksi'dʒiːsis] n. yorum, tefsir, şerh (esp. kutsal kitap).

**ex.em.plar** [ig'zemplə] n. örnek, numune, model; **ex'em.pla.ri.ness** n. örnek olma, kusursuzluk; **ex'em.pla.ry** adj. örnek verici, numune olarak; ibret verici.

**ex.em.pli.fi.ca.tion** [igzemplifi'keiʃən] n. örnek, misal; örnekleme, açıklama; izah; ♬ onaylı kopya, resmî suret; **ex'em.pli.fy** [~fai] v/t. örnek olarak vermek; izah etm., anlatmak; canlandırmak; ♬ onaylı kopyasını çıkarmak.

**ex.empt** [ig'zempt] **1.** adj. muaf, bağışık, ayrı tutulan (from -den); imtiyazlı; **2.** v/t. muaf tutmak, hariç tutmak, müstesna kılmak (from -den); **ex'emp.tion** n. muafiyet, bağışıklık (from -den).

**ex.e.quies** [ˈeksikwiz] *n. pl.* cenaze alayı, merasimi.

**ex.er.cise** [ˈeksəsaiz] **1.** *n.* uygulama, tatbik, yerine getirme, kullanma; talim, idman, jimnastik, beden eğitimi; egzersiz, alıştırma; take ~ talim, spor yapmak; ~s *pl. Am.* merasim, tören; ✗ manevra; **2.** *v/t. (beden)* talim ve terbiye etm.; *(güç vs.)* kullanmak; antrene etm.; talim yaptırmak; sinirlendirmek, rahatsız etm. *-i*; *v/i.* idman yapmak, talim, spor yapmak.

**ex.ert** [igˈzɔːt] *v/t.* sarfetmek, kullanmak *(güç, hak, nüfuz vs.)*; ~ o.s. çabalamak, uğraşmak; zahmete girmek, yorulmak; **exˈer.tion** *n.* kullanma, sarfetme; çaba, gayret, zahmet, çabalama, uğraşma.

**ex.e.unt** *thea.* [ˈeksiʌnt] *vb.* sahneden çıkarlar.

**ex.fo.li.ate** [eksˈfəulieit] *v/t.* yaprakları yolmak, koparmak; *v/i.* yaprak dökmek.

**ex.ha.la.tion** [ekshəˈleiʃən] *n.* koku *(buhar, ter vs.)* çıkarma, nefes verme; çıkış; çıkan buhar, koku vs.; **ex.hale** [~ˈheil] *v/t. & v/i.* koku vs. çık(ar)mak, nefes vermek; can vermek; ölmek; *(duygu)* açığa vurmak.

**ex.haust** [igˈzɔːst] **1.** *v/t.* tüketmek, bitirmek *(a. fig.)*; bitap düşürmek, yormak; boşaltmak, dökmek (of); *(hava)* tulumba ile çekmek, boşaltmak; **2.** *n.* ⊕ çürük gaz, çürük istim; egzoz, egzoz borusu; ~ box sustúrucu; ~ pipe egzoz borusu; **exˈhaust.ed** *adj.* bitkin, yorgun; tükenmiş *(a. fig.)*; satılıp bitmiş *(kitap vs.)*; **exˈhaust.i.ble** *adj.* tükenir, biter; **exˈhaust.ing** ☐ yorucu, zahmetli; ⊕ boşaltıcı...; **exˈhaus.tion** [~tʃən] *n.* bitkinlik; **exˈhaus.tive** ☐ = exhausting; ayrıntılı, detaylı, etraflı.

**ex.hib.it** [igˈzibit] **1.** *vb.* teşhir etm., sermek, göstermek; ✗ ibraz etm., arzetmek; **2.** *n.* ✗ delil olarak ibraz edilen şey; sergilenen şey; **ex.hi.bi.tion** [eksiˈbiʃən] *n.* sergi; gösterme, teşhir; burs; make an ~ of o.s. elâleme gülünç olm.; on ~ sergilenmekte; **ex.hiˈbi.tion.er** [~ʃnə] *n.* burslu öğrenci; **ex.hiˈbi.tion.ism** *n. psych. k-ni* teşhir merakı, teşhir hastalığı; **ex.hiˈbi.tion.ist** *n. k-ni* teşhir eden kimse, teşhir meraklısı.

**ex.hil.a.rate** [igˈziləreit] *v/t. b-ni* neşelendirmek, keyiflendirmek, canlandırmak; **ex.hil.aˈra.tion** *n.* neşe, canlılık; keyiflenme.

**ex.hort** [igˈzɔːt] *v/t. bşe* teşvik etm.; *b-ni bşi* yapması için uyarmak, ihtar etm.;

**ex.hor.ta.tion** [egzɔːˈteiʃən] *n.* teşvik, nasihat, öğüt; uyarı.

**ex.hu.ma.tion** [ekshjuːˈmeiʃən] *n.* mezardan çıkarma; **exˈhume** *v/t.* mezardan çıkarmak *(ceset)*.

**ex.i.gence, ex.i.gen.cy** [ˈeksidʒəns(i)] *n.* ivedi gereksinim, ihtiyaç; ivedi önlem almayı gerektiren endişe verici durum; koşul, zaruret; lüzum; **ex.i.gent** *adj.* ivedi, acele, gecikme kabul etmez; zorunlu, elzem; zorlayıcı; be ~ of gerektirmek, icabetmek, istemek.

**ex.ile** [ˈeksail] **1.** *n.* sürgün, sürülme; **2.** *v/t.* sürmek, sürgüne göndermek.

**ex.ist** [igˈzist] *v/i.* var olm., mevcut olm.; bulunmak, olmak; yaşamak, geçinmek; **exˈist.ence** *n.* varlık, mevcudiyet; vücut, oluş, hayat; be in ~ var olm.; in ~ = **exˈist.ent** *adj.* mevcut, bulunan, var olan; **ex.is.ten.tial.ism** *phls.* [egzisˈtenʃəlizəm] *n.* varoluşluk, egzistansializm.

**ex.it** [ˈeksit] **1.** *n.* çıkış; çıkış yeri, çıkış kapısı; sahneden çıkış; ölüm; make one's ~ sahneden çıkmak; ~ permit çıkış izni; ~ visa çıkış vizesi; **2.** *thea.* sahneden çıkar.

**ex.o.dus** [ˈeksədəs] *n.* çıkış, özellikle Musa peygamber zamanında Musevilerin Mısır'dan çıkışları; *fig.* toplu çıkış, panik; ♀ Eski Ahit'te ikinci İncil'in adı.

**ex of.fi.ci.o** [eksəˈfiʃiəu] *adj. & adv.* resmî, resmen; memuriyeti nedeniyle.

**ex.on.er.ate** [igˈzɔnəreit] *v/t. fig. b-nin* yükünü hafifletmek, *b-ne* yardım etm.; *bşden* affetmek, muaf tutmak *(from -den)*; suçsuzluğunu kanıtlamak, temize çıkarmak; **ex.on.erˈa.tion** *n.* beraat, temize çıkarma; muafiyet, azadoluş.

**ex.or.bi.tance, ex.or.bi.tan.cy** [igˈzɔːbitəns(i)] *n.* aşırılık, fazlalık; **exˈor.bi.tant** ☐ aşırı, müfrit, ölçüsüz, fahiş *(fiyat)*.

**ex.or.cism** [ˈeksɔːsizəm] *n.* dualarla cin, şeytan, kötü ruh vs.'yi defetme; **ex.or.cist** *n.* cinci hoca, böyle dua okuyan kimse; **ex.or.cize** [ˈ~sáiz] *v/t.* efsunla ruhları defetmek, cinleri defetmek *(from -den)*; kurtulmak (of).

**ex.ot.ic** [igˈzɔtik] *adj.* dışardan gelen, yabancı; yabancı iklimden gelen, egzotik; garip, alışılmamış.

**ex.pand** [iksˈpænd] *v/t. & v/i.* genişle(t)mek, yay(ıl)mak, aç(ıl)mak (into -e); büyü(t)mek; kısaltmadan tam olarak yazmak; (samimi, konuşkan) güleryüzlü olm.; **exˈpand.er** *n.* yayılan, genişleyen şey; **ex.panse** [iksˈpæns] *n.* genişlet(il)me, yay(ıl)ma; genişlik, en, enginlik; geniş yüzey; **ex.pan.si.bil.i.ty** [~sə-

**ᴵbiliti]** *n.* genişleyebilirlik, yayılabilirlik; **exᴵpan.si.ble** *adj.* yayılabilir, genişleyebilir, uzatılabilir; **exᴵpan.sion** *n.* yayılma, genişleme, genleşme, uzama; genişlik, uzam; *pol.* yayılma, genişleme; **exᴵpan.sive** ☐ geniş, engin; yay(ıl)ıp genişle(t)meye uygun; *fig.* duygu ve düşüncelerini belli etmekten hoşlanan, konuşkan; **exᴵpan.sive.ness** *n.* yayılma, genişleme; konuşkanlık; coşma.

**ex.pa.ti.ate** [eksᴵpeiʃieit] *v/t.* detaylı olarak anlatmak *veya* yazmak (on); **ex.patiᴵa.tion** *n.* detaylı olarak görüşme, anlatma; boş lâkırdı, gevezelik.

**ex.pa.tri.ate** [eksᴵpætrieit] *v/t.* vatandaşlıktan çıkarmak, memleket dışına sürmek; ~ o.s. göç etm., göçmek; 2. *n.* ülkesini terkedip başka ülkeye yerleşen *b-i*; **ex.pa.triᴵa.tion** *n.* vatandaşlıktan çıkarılma; başka ülkeye yerleşme.

**ex.pect** [iksᴵpekt] *v/t.* beklemek (of, from); F sanmak, farzetmek, düşünmek; ummak, ümit etm.; **exᴵpect.an.cy** *n.* bekleyiş, ümit; adaylık; %o beklenen haklar; **exᴵpect.ant** 1. *adj.* bekleyen, sabırsızlanan, uman; be ~ bebek bekliyor olmak; ~ mother hamile ~ kadın; 2. *n.* aday, namzet, bekleyen *b-i*; **ex.pec.ta.tion** [ekspekᴵteiʃən] *n.* bekleme, umma, ümit, olasılık, şans; contrary to ~ umulanın aksine; beyond ~ umulanın ötesinde; on *veya* in ~ of olasılığına karşı; ~ of life yaşanılacağı ümit edilen süre; **exᴵpect.ing** = expectant.

**ex.pec.to.rate** [eksᴵpektəreit] *vb.* öksürerek balgam, tükürük vs.'yi çıkarmak, atmak; **ex.pec.toᴵra.tion** *n.* tükürme; balgam, tükürük.

**ex.pe.di.ence, ex.pe.di.en.cy** [iksᴵpiːdjəns (i)] *n.* amaca uygunluk, yararlılık; kişisel çıkar; **exᴵpe.di.ent** 1. ☐ yararlı, uygun; her davranışında kendi çıkarlarını düşünen; 2. *n.* çare, tedbir, önlem, vasıta; **ex.peᴵdite** [ᴵekspidait] *v/t.* çabuklaştırmak, hızlandırmak, kolaylaştırmak; **ex.pe.di.tion** [~ᴵdiʃən] *n.* acele, çabukluk, sürat; X sefer (keşif); gezi; sevkiyat; sefer, hareket; **ex.peᴵdi.tion.ar.y** [~ʃnəri] *adj.* sürat *veya* gezi vs. ile ilgili, gönderilen, sevkedilen; **ex.peᴵditious** ☐ süratli, çabuk, seri, eli çabuk, işbilir; acelesi olan.

**ex.pel** [iksᴵpel] *v/t.* kovmak, çıkarmak, defetmek (from -den); ~ from school *b-ni* okuldan tardetmek, kovmak.

**ex.pend** [iksᴵpend] *v/t.* sarfetmek (para), harcamak (on, in -e) (zaman, emek); **exᴵpend.a.ble** *adj.* harcanabilen, sarfedi-

lebilir...; **exᴵpend.i.ture** [~ditʃə] *n.* harcama, masraf, sarfiyat (of); masraflar; **ex.pense** [iksᴵpens] *n.* masraf, gider, harcamalar; harcanan şey (para, zaman, emek vs.); ~s *pl.* masraflar; at my ~ kendi hesabıma; at the ~ of -in zararına, pahasına; at great ~ çok masraflı; go to the ~ of masrafa girmek, para sarfetmek; put s.o. to great ~ *b-ni* masrafa sokmak; **exᴵpense ac.count** masraf (veya gider) hesabı; **exᴵpen.sive** ☐ masraflı, pahalı.

**ex.pe.ri.ence** [iksᴵpiəriəns] 1. *n.* tecrübe, deneme, görgü; 2. *v/t.* bşi görmek, geçirmek, tatmak; bşe maruz kalmak, uğramak, tecrübe etm., denemek; (kayıp, zayiat v.b.) vermek; **exᴵpe.ri.enced** *adj.* tecrübeli, deneyimli, görgülü, görmüş geçirmiş.

**ex.per.i.ment** 1. [iksᴵperimənt] *n.* tecrübe, deney, deneme; 2. [~ment] *vb.* tecrübe etm., denemek; deney yapmak (on, with); **ex.pe.ri.men.tal** ☐ deneysel..., tecrübeye dayanan, ampirik, görgül; **ex.per.i.menᴵta.tion** *n.* deney yapma; deneme, deneyim, tecrübe; **ex.perᴵi.ment.er** [iksᴵperimentə] *n.* deney yapan, deneyen, tecrübe eden *b-i*.

**ex.pert** [ᴵekspəːt] 1. ☐ [*pred.* eksᴵpəːt] usta, mahir, becerikli (at, in -de); uzman, ihtisas..., bilirkişi...; ~ opinion (report) ekspertiz; 2. *n.* uzman, eksper, mütehassıs (at, in), bilirkişi; **ex.per.tise** [~ᴵtiːz] *n.* bilirkişi raporu, ekspertiz; ihtisas, ehliyet, eksperlik; **ex.pert.ness** *n.* ustalık, mahir olma, uzmanlık.

**ex.pi.a.ble** [ᴵekspiəbl] *adj.* kefaret edilebilir, cezası çekilebilir; **ex.pi.ate** [~pieit] *v/t.* kefaret etm., cezasını çekmek, gönül onarımında bulunmak; **ex.piᴵa.tion** *n.* kefaret, tarziye, gönül onarımı; **ex.pi.ato.ry** [~piətəri] *adj.* kefaret olarak.

**ex.pi.ra.tion** [ekspaiəᴵreiʃən] *n.* nefes verme; son, hitam, nihayet; at the time of ~ ᵀ vade bitiminde; **ex.pir.a.to.ry** [iksᴵpaiərətəri] *adj.* nefes vermekle ilgili; **exᴵpire** *v/i.* nefes vermek, ölmek; son bulmak (zaman, mukavele vs.); ᵀ vadesi gelmek; sönmek, bitmek (ateş, dava vs.); **exᴵpi.ry** *n.* vade bitimi, sona erme; ölüm.

**ex.plain** [iksᴵplein] *v/t.* & *v/i.* açıklamak -i, anlatmak -i, izah etm. -i; beyan etm., belirtmek; ~ away örtbas etm., tevil etm., sözü çevirmek; **exᴵplain.a.ble** *adj.* açıklanabilir, izah edilebilir.

**ex.pla.na.tion** [ekspləᴵneiʃən] *n.* izah, açıklama, beyanat; **ex.plan.a.to.ry** ☐ [iks-

**ǀplænətəri]** izahlı, açıklayıcı, izahat olarak.

**ex.ple.tive** [eksǀpliːtiv] **1.** ☐ dolduran, tamamlayıcı, yazımla ilgili; **2.** *n.* tamamlayıcı, anlamı kuvvetlendirici söz; heyecan ifade eden söz, küfür.

**ex.pli.ca.ble** [ǀeksplikəbl] *adj.* anlatılabilir; anlaşılabilir; **ex.pli.cate** [ǀ‿keit] *v/t.*
yorumlamak, detaylı olarak açıklamak;
*(fikir)* açıklamak.

**ex.plic.it** ☐ [iksǀplisit] açık, kesin, kat'î,
sarih; *fig.* aleni.

**ex.plode** [iksǀpləud] *v/t. & v/i.* patla(t)-
mak, infilâk et(tir)mek; patlamak (in,
with) *(kızgınlık, gözyaşı, kahkaha vs.)*;
*(kuram)* çürütmek, yanlışlığını kanıtlamak; devirmek, altüst etm.; açığa vurmak, ortaya çıkarmak; **exǀplod.ed view**
⊕ parçaları ayrı ayrı fakat birbiriyle
ilişkisini anlatan grafik *veya* model.

**ex.ploit 1.** [iksǀplɔit] *v/t.* sömürmek, istismar etm., kullanmak, işletmek, *k-den*
yana yontmak; **2.** [ǀeksplɔit] *n.* kahramanlık, yiğitlik; macera; **ex.ploiǀta.tion**
*n.* sömürü, istismar, kendi çıkarına kullanma; işletme, kullanım.

**ex.plo.ra.tion** [eksplɔːreiʃən] *n.* araştırma, keşif, inceleme; **exǀplor.a.to.ry**
[‿rətəri] *adj.* araştırma ile ilgili, araştırma...; **ex.plore** [iksǀplɔː] *v/t.* araştırmak, keşfetmek, incelemek, tetkik etm.,
yoklamak; **exǀplor.er** *n.* kâşif, bulucu;
araştırmacı kimse.

**ex.plo.sion** [iksǀpləuʒən] *n.* patlama, infilâk; galeyan, feveran, parlama, hid-
detlenme; **exǀplo.sive** [‿siv] **1.** ☐ patlayıcı...; **2.** *n.* patlayıcı madde; *gr.* patlama sesi.

**ex.po.nent** [eksǀpəunənt] *n.* Å üs; açıklayan, destekleyen kimse; temsil eden
kimse; örnek, misal.

**ex.port 1.** [eksǀpɔːt] *vb.* ihraç etm., yurt
dışına mal satmak, ihracat yapmak; **2.**
[ǀekspɔːt] *n.* † ihraç malı; ihracat, dışsatım ‿s *pl.* ihraç edilen mallar; **exǀport-
a.ble** *adj.* ihraç edilebilir; **ex.porǀta.tion**
*n.* ihraç, ihracat, dışsatım; **ex.port.er** *n.*
ihracatçı, yurt dışına mal satan kimse.

**ex.po.sé** [eksǀpəuzei] *n.* suçu ortaya koyma, gizli bir şeyi açığa vurma; *(esp.
utanç verici gerçekleri açıklayan)* makale *veya* kitapçık.

**ex.pose** [iksǀpəuz] *vb.* açığa vurmak, ifşa
etm.; meydana koymak, teşhir etm.;
*phot.* film üzerine çıkarmak, almak;
poz vermek; maruz bırakmak, karşı karşıya getirmek; terk etm., bırakmak *(çocuk)*; *fig.* maskesini düşürmek, foyası-

nı ortaya çıkarmak; **ex.po.si.tion**
[ekspəuǀziʃən] *n.* sergi, fuar; açıklama,
ortaya koyma *(fikir)*; **exǀpos.i.tor** *n.* yorumlayan, açıklayan *b-i.*

**ex.pos.tu.late** [iksǀpɔstjuleit] *v/i.* bşi protesto etm., bşe itiraz etm. (with, about,
on); ‿ with s.o. *b-ne* sitem etm., *b-ne* serzeniş ve ihtarda bulunmak; **ex.pos.tu-
ǀla.tion** *n.* sitem, ihtar, ikaz, uyarma;
**exǀpos.tu.la.to.ry** [‿lətəri] *adj.* tenkit, ihtar olarak.

**ex.po.sure** [iksǀpəuʒə] *n.* maruz olma, açık
olma; açığa vurma; keşfetme, açma;
teşhir; *phot.* poz; cephe *(ev)*; ‿ meter
*phot.* ışıkölçer, pozometre; *death from* ‿
soğuktan ölme.

**ex.pound** [iksǀpaund] *v/t.* açıklamak, izah
etm., yorumlamak.

**ex.press** [iksǀpres] **1.** ☐ açık, sarih, belli, kesin; özel, mahsus; süratli, hızlı,
ekspres...; ‿ company *Am.* nakliye şirketi; ‿ highway ekspres yol; **2.** *n.* ekspres,
res; sürat postası; *a.* ‿ train ekspres,
sürat postası; by ‿ = **3.** *adv.* ekspresle,
sürat postası ile; **4.** *v/t. (fikir vs.)* ifade etm., beyan etm., anlatmak, söyle-
mek, göstermek; sıkarak çıkarmak *(suyunu vs.)*; be ‿ed ifade edilmek; **ex-
ǀpress.i.ble** *adj.* ifade edilebilir; **ex.pres-
sion** [‿ǀpreʃən] *n.* ifade, deyim *(lisan,
yüz, ♪, boya, Å)*; **exǀpres.sion.ism** *n. sanat:* ekspresyonizm, dışavurumculuk;
**exǀpres.sion.less** *adj.* sönük, cansız;
ifadesiz, anlamsız; **exǀpres.sive** ☐ açık,
sarih; anlamlı (of); etkileyici; canlı;
**exǀpress.ly** *adv.* açık açık, kesinlikle;
özellikle; **exǀpress.way** *n. Am.* otoyol.

**ex.pro.pri.ate** [eksǀprəuprieit] *v/t.* kamulaştırmak, istimlâk etm., elinden almak
(s.th. *bşi*; s.o. *b-nin*; s.o. from s.th. *bşi
b-nin*) **ex.pro.priǀa.tion** *n.* kamulaştırma,
istimlâk.

**ex.pul.sion** [iksǀpʌlʃən] *n.* kov(ul)ma, çı-
kar(ıl)ma, ihraç; **exǀpul.sive** *adj.* ihraç
edici, defedici.

**ex.punge** [eksǀpʌndʒ] *v/t.* çıkarmak, silmek (from ‿den); *fig.* üstünden sünger
geçirmek.

**ex.pur.gate** [ǀekspəːgeit] *vb. (kitap vs.)*
sansürden geçirmek, silip çıkarmak; temizlemek, arıtmak; **ex.purǀga.tion** *n.* temizleme, arıtma, tasfiye, ıslah; **exǀpur-
ga.to.ry** [‿gətəri] *adj.* ıslah edici, ıslah
kabilinden.

**ex.qui.site** ☐ [ǀekskwizit] ince, seçkin,
zarif, enfes, mükemmel; şiddetli, sert,
keskin *(soğuk, acı vs.)*; **ǀex.qui.site.ness**

**n.** mükemmellik, zariflik, incelik, kibarlık, duyarlılık; sertlik, keskinlik.

**ex-serv.ice.man** ✕ [ˈeksˈsəːvismən] **n.** terhis edilmiş asker.

**ex.tant** [eksˈtænt] *adj.* hâlâ mevcut, günümüze dek gelen.

**ex.tem.po.ra.ne.ous** □ [ekstempəˈreinjəs], **ex.tem.po.ra.ry** [iksˈtempərəri], **ex.tem po.re** [eksˈtempəri] düşünülmeden, hazırlıksız, irticalen, doğaçtan, ani olarak yapılan *veya* söylenen; **ex.tem.po.rize** [iksˈtempəraiz] *v/i.* düşünmeden, hazırlıksız söy söylemek, irticalen söylemek; **exˈtem.po.riz.er** *n.* hazırlıksız söyleyen, çalan, yazan *veya* bşi yapan kimse.

**ex.tend** [iksˈtend] *v/t.* yaymak, büyütmek, uzatmak *(el vs.)*; genişletmek *(arazi vs.)*; uzatmak, temdit etm. *(süre)*; çekmek *(çizgi, tel vs.)*; bşe devam etm.; *steno:* detaylı yazmak; göstermek *(lütuf)*; *(yardım)* el uzatmak; sunmak *(yardım, dostluk vs.)*; ✕ avcı hattına yayılmak; *spor:* tüm gücünü kullanmak; ⁓ed order avcı hattı, açılma düzeni; *v/i.* uzanmak, genişlemek, büyümek, sürmek (to -e); **exˈtend.ed** *adj.* uzatılan, uzayan, genişletilmiş, büyütülmüş.

**ex.ten.si.bil.i.ty** [ikstensəˈbiliti] *n.* uza(tıl)ma kabiliyeti; **exˈten.si.ble** *adj.* uzatılabilir; **exˈten.sion** *n.* uzatma; uzanma; yay(ıl)ma, genişle(t)me *(a. gr.)*; büyütme, yetiştirme; *teleph.* tâli hat, munzam telefon, dahili numara; † vadenin uzatılması; ⁓ cord ⚡ uzatma kordonu; University ≙ üniversite derslerinin devam edemeyenlere verilmesi, öğretilmesi; **exˈten.sive** □ geniş, yaygın; şümullü; uzatılmış; **exˈten.sive.ness** *n.* genişlik; şümul.

**ex.tent** [iksˈtent] *n.* derece, had, ölçü, nisbet; büyüklük, saha; mesafe, uzunluk, boy; kapsam, şümul; to the ⁓ of derecede; to a certain ⁓ bir dereceye kadar; to a great ⁓ büyük ölçüde; to some ⁓ kısmen, oldukça, bir ölçüde; to that ⁓ o derecede; grant ⁓ for süre vermek -e.

**ex.ten.u.ate** [eksˈtenjueit] *v/t.* hafifletmek, gevşetmek, yumuşatmak, mâzur göstermek, ayıbını örtmek; hafiften almak; **ex.ten.uˈa.tion** *n.* hafifletme, azaltma; hafiften alma.

**ex.te.ri.or** [eksˈtiəriə] **1.** □ dış, harici, zahiri; dışardan bakan, yabancı; **2.** *n.* dış taraf, dış, hariç; görünüş; *film:* açık havada çekilen resim.

**ex.ter.mi.nate** [iksˈtəmineit] *v/t.* imha etm., yok etm., kökünü kurutmak; **ex-**

**ter.mi.na.tion** *n.* imha, izale; **exˈter.mi.na tor** *n.* imha eden ilâç *veya* kimse.

**ex.ter.nal** [eksˈtəːnl] **1.** □ dış, zahiri, harcî; gözle görülen; dıştan gelen, haricî; yabancı ülkelerle ilgili, dış...; haricen kullanılan *(ilâç)*; **2.** *n.* ⁓s *pl.* dış görünüş, dışta kalan olaylar, durumlar; *fig.* formalite(ler).

**ex.ter.ri.to.ri.al** [ˈeksteriˈtɔːriəl] *adj.* bulunduğu ülkenin yasalarına bağlı olmayan.

**ex.tinct** [iksˈtiŋkt] *adj.* sönmüş, sönük; nesli tükenmiş, yok olmuş *(a. fig.)*; **exˈtinc.tion** *n.* sön(dür)me *(a. fig.)*; bir neslin tükenmesi.

**ex.tin.guish** [iksˈtiŋgwiʃ] *v/t.* söndürmek *(a .fig.)*, bastırmak, yok etm., imha etm., kökünü kurutmak; *(görev, iş)* lağvetmek, feshetmek; *(kusur)* silmek; *(düşman)* susturmak, bertaraf etm.; **exˈtin.guish.er** = fire-⁓.

**ex.tir.pate** [ˈekstəːpeit] *v/t.* imha etm., yok etm., kökünü kurutmak; ⚕ kesip almak; **ex.tirˈpa.tion** *n.* imha, yok etme; ⚕ kesip alma.

**ex.tol** [iksˈtəul] *v/t.* övmek, yüceltmek; ⁓ s.o. to the skies *fig.* b-ni överek göklere çıkarmak.

**ex.tort** [iksˈtɔːt] *v/t.* zorla almak, şantajla almak (from -*den*), gaspetmek; **exˈtor.tion** *n.* zorla alma, gasp; **exˈtor.tion.ate** [⁓ʃnit] *adj.* fahiş; zorbalığa ait; şantaj; **exˈtor.tion.er** *n.* zorba b-i, görevini kötüye kullanan b-i.

**ex.tra** [ˈekstrə] **1.** *adj.* fazla, gereksiz, ziyade, zait; ekstra, alâ, fevkalâde..., seçkin, ayrı...; ⁓ pay ücret zammı, fazla ödeme; **2.** *adv.* -den başka, ilâveten, ek olarak, ayrıca, bir de; **3.** *n.* ilâve, ek, zam, katma; fevkalâde nüsha, ikinci, üçüncü vs. baskı *(gazete)*; *thea., film:* figüran *(kız veya kadın)*.

**ex.tract 1.** [ˈekstrækt] *n.* özet, hülâsa *(a. 🜍 )*; ruh, esans; kupür *(gazete)*; † ekstre, hesap hülâsası; **2.** [iksˈtrækt] *v/t.* çıkarmak, çekip çıkarmak; *(metin, 🜍)* özetini *veya* özünü çıkarmak; ⚕ *(kök)* almak, çıkarmak; itiraf ettirmek; seçmek; koparmak; **exˈtrac.tion** *n.* çıkarma, çekme *(diş vs.)*; nesil, soy, sülâle; öz, hülâsa, özet.

**ex.tra.dit.a.ble** [ˈekstrədaitəbl] *adj.* iade edilebilir *(suçlu)*; **ˈex.tra.dite** *v/t. (suçlu)* iade et(tir)mek; **ex.tra.di.tion** [⁓ˈdiʃən] *n.* suçluları iade.

**ex.tra...:** ⁓ˈjuˈdi.cal *adj.* mahkeme dışı, yasaların dışında; ⁓ˈmu.ral *adj.* şehir *veya* okul duvarları dışında, okullarası *(karşılaşma)*; ~ student misafir öğ-renci.

**ex.tra.ne.ous** [eks'treinjəs] *adj*. ikincil, ta-lî (to *-e)*; konu dışı; dıştan gelen, ya-bancı.

**ex.traor.di.nar.y** [iks'trɔːdnri] *adj*. olağan-üstü, fevkalâde, müstesna, garip, seç-kin; envoy ~ yetkili temsilci, murahhas. **ex.tra.sen.so.ry per.cep.tion** *psych*. ['ekstrə'sensəri pə'sepʃən] altıncı his.

**ex.tra.ter.ri.to.ri.al** ['ekstrəteri'tɔːriəl] = exterritorial.

**ex.trav.a.gance** [iks'trævigəns] *n*. israf; aşırılık, ifrat, taşkınlık, delibozukluk; **ex'trav.a.gant** ☐ tutumsuz, müsrif; deli-bozuk; aşırı, müfrit, bol bol; **ex.trav.a-gan.za** *thea*. [ekstrævə'gænzə] *n*. zengin dekorlu piyes, büyük mizansenli piyes, fantezi.

**ex.treme** [iks'triːm] **1.** ☐ son derece, fev-kalâde; aşırı, müfrit; en uçta *veya* en kenarda olan; son; ~ unction *eccl*. Ka-tolik kilisesi geleneğine göre ölüm halin-deki kişiye mukaddes yağ sürülmesi; **2.** *n*. sınır, uç; ifrat; go to ~s aşırıya kaç-mak; in the ~ aşırı derecede; **ex'trem.ist** *n*. aşırı giden *b-i*; **ex.trem.i.ty** [~'tremiti] *n*. uç; sınır, had; son; aşırı tehlike; son çare; ıstırap; **ex'trem.i.ties** [~z] *n. pl. anat*. eller ve ayaklar.

**ex.tri.cate** ['ekstrikeit] *v/t*. kurtarmak, çıkarmak; açmak, ayırmak; ᵐ ayrıştır-mak; **ex.tri'ca.tion** *n*. kurtarma, kurtul-ma, çıkarma, ayırma.

**ex.trin.sic** [eks'trinsik] *adj*. (~əlly) haricî, dıştan gelen (to *-e)*.

**ex.tro.vert** ['ekstrəuvəːt] *n*. dışa dönük karakter, kendi düşünce ve duygularıy-la ilgilenmek yerine vaktini başkaları ile geçiren kimse.

**ex.trude** [eks'truːd] *v/t*. çıkarmak, ihraç etm., dışarı çıkarmak, sıkıp çıkarmak; *b-ni* bir yerden atmak.

**ex.u.ber.ance** [ig'zjuːbərəns] *n*. coşkun-luk, taşkınlık; bolluk; **ex'u.ber.ant** *adj*. coşkun, heyecanlı, taşkın; aşırı; bol, be-reketli.

**ex.u.da.tion** [eksjuː'deiʃən] *n*. sızıntı, sı-zan şey, ifrazat, ter; **ex.ude** [ig'zjuːd] *vb*. sızıntı yapmak, sızdırmak, ifraz etm. **ex.ult** [ig'zʌlt] *vb*. çok sevinmek (at *veya* in s.th *bşe*), *(bir zafer sonucu)* coşmak, övünmek, hakkından gelip sevinmek (over s.o. *b-nin*); **ex'ult.ant** *adj*. sevinçli, coşkun, neşeli; **ex.ul.ta.tion** [egzʌl-'teiʃən] *n*. sevinç, coşku; övünme.

**eye** [ai] **1.** *n*. göz *(a. fig. &* ♀*)*; bakış, nazar; delik ,iğne deliği *(veya* gözü, kula-ğı), ilik, dişi kopça; budak; have an ~ for *bşin* iyisini seçebilmek, *bşden* iyi anla-mak; my ~s! *sl*. vay iki gözüm benim!, yok canım!; it's all my ~! *sl*. zırva, boş lâkırdı; make ~s at s.o. *b-ne* aşıkâne bak-mak, *b-ne* sevgiyle bakmak, F *b-ne* kaş göz etm.; up to the ~s in work başını ka-şıyacak vakti yok, işi başından aşkın, çok meşgul; mind your ~! dikkatli ol!, gözünü aç; with an ~ to göz önünde tuta-rak, hesaba katarak; **2.** *v/t*. göz atmak *-e*, gözden geçirmek *(şaşkınlıkla)*, ince-lemek, bakmak; '~.**ball** *n*. göz küresi; '~.**brow** *n*. kaş; '~.**catch.er** *n*. göz alan, dikkati çeken şey; **eyed** [aid] *comb*. ...gözlü.

**eye...:** '~.**glass** *n*. tek gözlük, oküler; (pair of) ~es *pl*. gözlük; '~.**hole** *n*. gözçukuru; gözetleme deliği; '~.**lash** *n*. kirpik; **eye-let** [~'lit] *n*. küçük delik, göz deliği; tek-nelere açılan küçük delik, matafyon; kopça iliği.

**eye...:** '~.**lid** *n*. gözkapağı; '~.**o.pen.er** *n*. aydınlatan *veya* şaşırtan haber *veya* olay; sürpriz olay; insanın gözünü açan şey; sabahları mahmurluk gideren ilk içki; '~.**piece** *n. opt*. dürbün *vs*.'nin göz camı, oküler; '~.**shot** *n*. görüş mesafesi; '~.**sight** *n*. görme kuvveti, görüm; '~.**sore** *n*. göze çirkin görünen şey; '~.**tooth** *n*. köpekdişi, gözdişi; '~.**wash** *n. sl*. göz bo-yama, aldatma; '~.**wit.ness** *n*. ♂♀ görgü tanığı, şahit.

**ey.rie, ey.ry** ['aiəri] = aerie.

# F

**Fa.bian** ['feibjən] **1.** *adj.* ihtiyatlı, tedbirli, işi ağırdan alan, sürüncemede bırakan, ağır *(kimse);* ~ policy işi ağırdan alma politikası, sürüncemede bırakma politikası; **2.** *n. (İngiltere'de)* ılımlı sosyalist bir derneğe mensup kişi.

**fa.ble** ['feibl] *n.* masal, özellikle hayvanları anlatan hikâye, fabl, efsane, mit; yalan, sahte.

**fab.ric** ['fæbrik] *n.* kumaş, bez, dokuma; bünye, yapı; **fab.ri.cate** ['~keit] *v/t.* imal etm., yapmak, biraraya getirmek; *fig.* yalan söylemek, uydurmak, sahtesini yapmak; **fab.ri'ca.tion** *n.* imal etme, yapma, biraraya getirme; *fig.* yalan, uydurma, sahte; **'fab.ri.ca.tor** *n.* imalatçı; uydurukçu.

**fab.u.list** ['fæbjulist] *n.* hayal ürünü hikâyeler yazan kimse; yalancı, uydurukçu; **'fab.u.lous** □ hayal mahsulü, uydurma, efsanevî; inanılmaz, olması imkânsız, abartılmış; F harika, şahane, müthiş, mükemmel, fevkalâde.

**fa.çade** ⚠ [fə'saːd] *n.* binanın ön yüzü, cephe; *fig.* dış görünüş, sahte görünüş.

**face** [feis] **1.** *n.* yüz, çehre, surat, sima; görünüş, ifade; yüzey, satıh, *(binanın)* cephesi; yüzsüzlük; in (the) ~ of karşısında, rağmen; ~ to ~ with yüz yüze *ile*; save one's ~ onurunu kurtarmak, kabahatini örtbas etm.; lose ~ itibarını kaybetmek, saygınlığını yitirmek; on the ~ of it görünüşe bakılırsa, görünüş itibariyle; set one's ~ against karşı çıkmak -e, engel olm. -e; **2.** *v/t. & v/i.* yüzüne bakmak, bakmak, yönelmek, cesaretle karşılamak; -*in* karşısında olm.; -*in* kenarını çevirmek; kaplamak, astarlamak; be ~d with karşısında olm.; karşı çıkmak -*e*; ~ about ters yöne dönmek; left ~! ✕ sola dön!; about ~! geriye dön!; ~ card *iskambil:* resimli iskambil kağıdı *(papaz, kız veya vale);* '~-cloth ~. yüz havlusu; **faced** *comb.* ... yüzlü, yüzü olan; **'face-lift.ing** *n.* ⚕ yüzü ameliyatla gerdirme, yüz estetik ameliyatı; **'fac.er**

*n.* aniden karşılaşılan ciddi zorluk, beklenmedik engel.

**fac.et** ⊕ ['fæsit] *n.* kıymetli taşın bir yüzeyi, faseta; *fig.* yön, görünüş; **'fac.et.ed** *adj.* yüzlü, fasetalı.

**fa.ce.tious** □ [fə'siːʃəs] uygunsuz şaka yapan, alaycı, nükteli, esprili, şakacı.

**face val.ue** ['feis'væljuː] *n.* ✝ itibarî kıymet, üzerindeki değer, nominal değer; *fig.* dış görünüşündeki değer *veya* önem; take s.th. at its ~ bşi dış görünüşüne göre değerlendirmek.

**fa.ci.a** ['feiʃə] = fascia.

**fa.cial** ['feiʃəl] **1.** □ yüz ile ilgili, yüze ait; **2.** *n.* yüz masajı.

**fac.ile** ['fæsail] □ kolay, basit; herşeyi kolayca yapan *(kimse),* becerikli; kolay yapılan; uysal; **fa.cil.i.tate** [fə'siliteit] *v/t.* kolaylaştırmak; **fa.cil.i'ta.tion** *n.* kolaylaştırma; **fa'cil.i.ty** *n.* kolaylık, rahatlık; *pl.* vasıta, imkânlar, bina, tesis.

**fac.ing** ['feisiŋ] *n.* ⊕ kaplama, astar; ✕ dönüş; ~s *pl.* volan, süs.

**fac.sim.i.le** [fæk'simili] *n.* faksimile, kopya, suret, aynısı, tıpkısı; resim *veya* yazının radyo *veya* telgrafla gönderilmesi.

**fact** [fækt] *n.* gerçek, hakikat; durum; ~s *pl.* (of the case) olayın unsurları; after the ~ suç işlendikten sonra; before the ~ suç işlenmeden önce; in (point of) ~, as a matter of ~ gerçekten, hakikatte, işin doğrusu; know for a ~ kesinlikle bilmek, adı gibi bilmek; '~-find.ing *n.* gerçekleri ortaya çıkarma.

**fac.tion** ['fækʃən] *n.* grup, bölünme, çekişme, hizip, ihtilâf, ayrılık; **'fac.tion.ist** *n.* ihtilafçı, partizan, arabozucu, bölücü, fitneci.

**fac.tious** □ ['fækʃəs] ihtilafçı, partizan, arabozucu, fitneci; **'fac.tious.ness** *n.* fitnecilik, ihtilafçılık, hizipçilik.

**fac.ti.tious** □ [fæk'tiʃəs] yapmacık, suni, tabii olmayan.

**fac.tor** ['fæktə] *n.* ⚠ çarpılanlardan biri; âmil, sebeplerden biri, faktör; ✝ komisyonla satış yapan kimse; **¹fac.to.ry** *n.* fabrika, atölye, imalathane.

**fac.to.tum** [fæk¹təutəm] *n.* kâhya, uşak, hizmetçi.

**fac.tu.al** [¹fæktʃuəl] *adj.* gerçeklere dayalı, olaylarla ilgili.

**fac.ul.ty** [¹fækəlti] *n.* yetenek, kabiliyet; güç, iktidar; ⌂ öncelik hakkı, ayrıcalık, imtiyaz; *univ.* fakülte, üniversite dalı, branş.

**fad** F [fæd] *n.* geçici merak, heves, ilgi; **¹fad.dish, ¹fad.dy** *adj.* geçici heves kabilinden; **¹fad.dist** *n.* geçici hevesleri olan kimse.

**fade** [feid] *vb.* rengini soldurmak, solmak, sararıp solmak, canlılığını kaybetmek; gözden kaybolmak, hafızadan silinmek; *radyo:* şiddetini artırmak *veya* azaltmak, şiddeti artmak *veya* azalmak; ~ away, ~ out gözden kaybolmak, duyulmamak; ~ in sesi yavaş yavaş yükseltmek; ~ out sesi yavaş yavaş azaltmak; **¹fade.less** *adj.* solmaz; **¹fad.ing** ☐ geçici, süreksiz, fani; *radyo:* zayıflama, kaybolma, feding.

**fae.ces** *physiol.* [¹fi:si:z] *n. pl.* tortu, posa, pislik, dışkı.

**faer.ie, faer.y** [¹feiəri] *n.* † periler ülkesi; *attr.* hayali.

**fag** F [fæg] **1.** *n.* yorucu iş; *(İngiltere'de)* üst sınıftaki öğrenciye hizmet eden öğrenci; *sl.* sigara; homoseksüel erkek. **2.** *v/t. & v/i.* didinmek, çalışıp yor(ul)-mak, uşak gibi çalış(tır)mak; ~-¹end *n.* işe yaramaz kısım, artık; izmarit.

**fag.ot, fag.got** [¹fægət] *n.* ince odun demeti, çubuk demeti; ⊕ demir çubuk demeti; *Am.* F homoseksüel erkek.

**Fahr.en.heit** [¹færənhait] *n.* fahrenhayt; ~ thermometer fahrenhayt termometresi.

**fail** [feil] **1.** *v/t. & v/i.* başaramamak *(in -i)*, başarısız olm., kalmak *(sınavda)*, boşa çıkmak; bırakmak *(sınavda)*; yetersiz olm., bitmek, zayıflamak; ihmal etm., iflâs etm.; yoksun olm. *(in -den)*; he ~ed to do *veya* in doing ...yapmayı başaramadı; he cannot ~ to *inf.* ...yapmadan bırakmaz; his heart ~ed him cesareti kırıldı, cesaret edemedi; **2.** *n.* without ~ elbette, mutlaka, şüphesiz; **¹fail.ing 1.** *n.* kusur, zayıflık, zaaf; **2.** *prp.* yokluğunda, olmadığı takdirde; ~ which olmadığı takdirde; **fail.ure** [¹~jə] *n.* başarısızlık; başarısız kimse; başarısızlıkla sonuçlanan şey *veya* teşebbüs; bitme, tükenme; iflâs; ihmal, yetersizlik.

**fain** *poet.* [fein] *adv.* seve seve, isteyerek, memnuniyetle.

**faint** [feint] **1.** ☐ zayıf, cılız *(ses)*, silik, belirsiz, başı dönmüş, baygın; **2.** *v/i.* bayılmak; solmak; gevşemek, zayıflamak; **3.** *n.* baygınlık, bayılma; ~-¹heart.ed ☐ yüreksiz, korkak; çekingen, mahcup; ~-¹heart.ed.ness *n.* korkaklık, çekingenlik; **¹faint.ness** *n.* baygınlık, halsizlik, zayıflık.

**fair¹** [fɛə] **1.** *adj.* dürüst, adil, doğru, haklı; orta, vasat, iyi; açık *(hava)*; elverişli *(rüzgâr)*; tatminkâr, bol, çok; sarışın, kumral; hoş, güzel; iyi seçilmiş *(kelime)*; temiz, açık, lekesiz; ~ copy temiz kopya; ~ name iyi nam, şöhret; ~ play temiz oyun, tarafsızlık; the ~ sex kadınlar, cinsi lâtif; **2.** *adv.* dürüstce, adilane, tam, temiz olarak; write s.th out ~ hatasız yazmak.

**fair²** [~] *n.* pazar, panayır, fuar, sergi.

**fair-haired** [¹fɛəˈhɛəd] *adj.* sarışın.

**fair.ly** [¹fɛəli] *adv.* dürüstçe, adilane; tamamen; âdeta; oldukça; **¹fair.ness** *n.* doğruluk, dürüstlük, güzellik; **¹fair-¹spoken** *adj.* nazik, tatlı dilli; **¹fair.way** *n.* ↓ serbest geçit, gemilerin seyredebildiği geçit; **¹fair-weath.er friend** iyi gün dostu.

**fair.y** [¹fɛəri] **1.** *n.* peri; *sl.* homoseksüel erkek; **2.** *adj.* peri gibi, perilere ait; **¹Fair.y.land** *n.* periler ülkesi, büyülü yer, güzel yer; **¹fair.y.like** *adj.* peri gibi; **¹fair.y--tale** *n.* peri masalı; yalan, uydurma hikâye.

**faith** [feiθ] *n.* inanç, itikat, iman; itimat, güven; din; söz, vaat; sadakat, vefa; have ~ in s.th. itimadı, güveni, inancı olm. -e; in good ~ iyi niyetle, samimiyetle, dürüstlükle; ~-¹cure = faith-healing; **faith.ful** ☐ [¹~ful] iman sahibi; sadık, vefakâr, güvenilir, doğru; the ~ *pl.* müminler, inananlar; yours ~ly saygılarımla, saygılarımızla; **¹faith.ful.ness** *n.* sadakat, iman; **¹faith-heal.ing** *n.* itikatla iyileşme, şifa bulma; **¹faith.less** ☐ güvenilmez, sadakatsiz, hain; imansız, dinsiz; **¹faith.less.ness** *n.* güvensizlik; imansızlık.

**fake** *sl.* [feik] **1.** *n.* sahte, yapma; uydurma; sahtekâr, şarlatan; *Am. a.* **¹fak.er** *n.* sahtekâr, dolandırıcı; **2.** *a.* ~ up *v/t.* sahtesini yapmak, uydurmak.

**fal.con** [¹fɔ:lkən] *n.* şahin, doğan; **¹fal.con.er** *n.* şahin *veya* doğanla avlanan avcı, şahinci, doğancı; **¹fal.con.ry** *n.* doğancılık, kuşçuluk.

**fall** [fɔ:l] **1.** *n.* düşme, düşüş, çöküş, çökme; yağış; şelale, çağlayan; *Am.* sonbahar, güz; yıkılma; düşüş mesafesi; ucuzlama; dökülme; *(güreşte)* düşüş;

elbise fırfırı; the ♀ (of Man) Hz. Adem ve Havva'nın işlediği günah ve sonuçları; have a ~ düşmek; 2. v/i. düşmek, yağmak, dökülmek; doğmak *(hayvan)*; inmek; uzanmak; azalmak, kesilmek *(rüzgâr)*; vaki olm.; çökmek, düşmek *(kale)*; meyletmek *(toprak)*; rastlamak *(tarih)*; his countenance fell suratı asıldı; ~ asleep uykuya dalmak; ~ away terketmek, çekilmek, ortadan kaybolmak; ~ back geri çekilmek; ~ back (up)-on yeniden müracaat etm., başvurmak *(güvenilen bşe)*; ~ behind geri kalmak, yetişememek; ~ between two stools iki cami arasında beynamaz olm., iki seçenek arasında tereddütten dolayı bir fırsatı kaçırmak; ~ down düşmek; çökmek, yıkılmak; ~ due vadesi dolmak; ~ for F çok beğenmek, bayılmak, kesilmek; aldatılmak, tongaya basmak; ~ from düşmek *-den*; ~ ill *veya* sick hastalanmak; ~ in çökmek, yıkılmak; X sıraya girmek, dizilmek; ~ in with uymak, kabul etm.; rast gelmek; ~ in love with aşık olm. *-e*; ~ into başlamak; bölünmek, ayrılmak; ~ into line with diğerlerinin yaptığına uymak; ~ off eksilmek, azalmak; düşmek *(a .fig.)* (from *-den)*, düşüş göstermek; ~ on saldırmak, hücum etm.; gelmek düşmek; ~ out X sıradan çıkmak; vaki olm., meydana gelmek; kavga etm., bozuşmak, bırakmak; ~ short kısa düşmek, ulaşamamak (of *-e)*; ~ short of umduğu gibi çıkmamak, yetersiz olm.; ~ to başlamak, girişmek; ~ under altına düşmek, altında toplanmak, altında sınıflandırmak.

**fal.la.cious** ☐ [fɔ'leiʃəs] yanıltıcı, aldatıcı, yanlış, hatalı, boş.

**fal.la.cy** [ˈfæləsi] n. yanlış fikir, aldatıcı kavram; aldatma, hile, yanlışlık.

**fall.en** [ˈfɔːlən] p.p. of fall 2.

**fall guy** Am. sl. [ˈfɔːlˈgai] n. kolayca aldatılan kimse, keriz, başkalarının cezasını ve sorumluluğunu yüklenen kimse.

**fal.li.bil.i.ty** [fæliˈbiliti] n. yanılma payı.

**fal.li.ble** ☐ [ˈfæləbl] yanılabilir, hataya düşebilir, yanlış olabilir.

**fall.ing** [ˈfɔːliŋ] n. düşüş, çöküş; ~ off azalma, eksilme; ~ sick.ness sara, epilepsi; ~ star göktaşı.

**fal.low** [ˈfæləu] 1. adj. açık sarı, deve tüyü; ✓ ekilmemiş, nadasa bırakılan; 2. n. nadasa bırakılan arazi, nadas; nadas etme; '~-deer n. zo. geyik; **'fal.low.ness** n. nadasa bırakma.

**false** ☐ [fɔːls] sahte, yanlış, yapma, taklit, hatalı, yalan, takma *(saç, diş)*, sözde; ~ imprisonment haksız yere hapis,

sözde mahkûmiyet; ~ key maymuncuk; play s.o. ~ ihanet etm., aldatmak; **false-hood** [ˈhud] n. yalan; **'false.ness** n. yalan, sahtelik.

**fal.set.to** ♪ [fɔːlˈsetəu] n. çok ince ses *(erkekte)*; bu sesle şarkı söyleyen kimse, kontrtenor.

**fal.si.fi.ca.tion** [ˌfɔːlsifiˈkeiʃən] n. tahrif, taklit, sahtesini yapma, uydurma; **fal.si.fi.er** [ˈ~faiə] n. yalancı, düzenbaz, tahrifçi, kalpazan; **fal.si.fy** [ˈ~fai] v/t. tahrif etm., bozmak; taklit etm.; yalan olduğunu söylemek; **fal.si.ty** [ˈ~ti] n. yalan; yanlışlık, hata; hainlik.

**al.ter** [ˈfɔːltə] v/t. & v/i. sendelemek, yalpalamak; kekelemek, tutuk konuşmak, titremek *(ses)*, duraklamak, teredüt içinde söylemek, kısık sesle söylemek.

**fame** [feim] n. şöhret, ün, şan, nam; **famed** adj. ünlü, meşhur.

**fa.mil.iar** [fəˈmiljə] 1. ☐ bilen *-i*, malûmatı olan, haberdar olan, bilinen, her zaman görülen *veya* duyulan, alışılmış; lâubali, senli benli; alışkın (with *-e)*; be ~ with bilmek, tanımak; samimi, yakın, teklifsiz olm.; 2. n. samimi arkadaş; **fa.mil.i.ar.i.ty** [~li'æriti] n. iyi bilme, aşinalık, teklifsizlik, alışkanlık; pl. lâubalilik, serbestlik, teklifsizlik; **fa.mil.iar.i.za.tion** [~ljərai'zeiʃən] n. tanıtma, alıştırma, tanıma; **fa'mil.iar.ize** v/t. tanıtmak, alıştırmak; ilişki kurmak.

**fam.i.ly** [ˈfæmili] n. aile, çoluk çocuk, ecdat, akraba; soy, cins; ✻ familya; in the ~ way F hamile, gebe; ~ allowance çocuk zammı; ~ doctor aile doktoru; ~ man aile babası; ~ planning aile planlaması; ~ tree soy ağacı, şecere.

**fam.ine** [ˈfæmin] n. kıtlık, açlık.

**fam.ish** [ˈfæmiʃ] v/t. & v/i. çok acıkmak, açlıktan öl(dür)mek, aç bırakmak, aç kalmak.

**fa.mous** ☐ [ˈfeiməs] ünlü, meşhur, tanınmış; F mükemmel, çok iyi, tatmınkâr.

**fan[1]** [fæn] 1. n. yelpaze, ventilatör, yelpaze kanadına benzeyen şey; ↓ pervane; 2. v/t. yelpazelemek, hava vermek, körüklemek serinletmek; ~ out X yelpaze gibi açılmak, yayılmak.

**fan[2]** [~] n. spor, etc.: bşin hayranı, meraklısı, delisi, hastası, tiryakisi.

**fa.nat.ic** [fəˈnætik] 1. a. **fa'nat.i.cal** ☐ mutaassıp, fanatik, aşırı meraklı, çok düşkün, aşırı fikirli; **fa'nat.i.cism** [~sizəm] n. tutuculuk, aşırılık, taassup.

**fan.ci.er** [ˈfænsiə] n. meraklısı, düşkünü, seven b-i.

**fan.ci.ful** □ ['fænsiful] hayalperest, gerçeklerden uzak, kaprisli; **'fan.ci.ful.ness** *n.* hayali olma.

**fan.cy** -['fænsi] **1.** *n.* hayal, düş, kapris, geçici arzu, beğeni, düşkünlük, merak, kuruntu; take a ~ to beğenmek, hoşlanmak, sevmek; **2.** □ süslü, parlak renkli; aşırı; iyi kalite *(mal)*; hayale dayalı; ~ apron aşırı bağ; ~ dress karnaval kıyafeti, maskeli balo kıyafeti; ~-dress ball maskeli balo; ~ fair yardım pazarı; ~ goods fantezi eşya, iyi kalite mallar; ~ man sevgili; *sl.* pezevenk; ~ price fahiş fiyat; **3.** *v/t.* hayal etm., tasavvur etm., zannetmek, sanmak; istemek, arzu etm., beğenmek, sevmek; just ~! hayret doğrusu!; **'~-work** *n.* ince el işi.

**fane** *poet.* [fein] *n.* mabet, kilise.

**fan.fare** ['fænfɛə] *n.* ♪ merasim borusu, nefesli çalgıların çaldığı parça, fanfar; **fan.fa.ron.ade** [~færə'naːd] *n.* yüksekten atma. palavra, martaval, övünme.

**fang** [fæŋ] *n.* azı dişi *(köpek veya kurtların)*; yılanın zehirli dişi; ⊕ pençe, tırnak.

**fan.ner** ⊕ ['fænə] *n.* vantilatör, havalandırma tertibatı, üfleç, hamlaç.

**fan.tail** *zo.* ['fænteil] *n.* bir çeşit evcil güvercin; yelpaze şeklinde kuyruk.

**fan.ta.sia** ♪ [fæn'teizjə] *n.* fantezi; **fan.tas.tic** [~'tæstik] *adj.* hayali; garip, acayip, tuhaf, saçma; F harika, şahane, fevkalâde; **fan.ta.sy** ['~təsi] *n.* hayal, garip fikir; ♪ fantezi.

**far** [faː] *adj.* uzak, uzun; daha uzak; ilerlemiş; *adv.* uzağa, uzakta, daha, oldukça, epeyce, çok; ~ better çok daha iyi; ~ the best en iyisi; as ~ as -e kadar, -e kalırsa; by ~ hatırı sayılır derecede, büyük farkla; ~ from hiç, hiç mi hiç,... bir yana; in so ~ as bir dereceye kadar, -den dolayı, olduğuna göre; ~ and near, ~ and wide her yerde; ~-a.way ['faːrə-wei] *adj.* uzak, uzakta; dalgın *(bakış).*

**farce** *thea.* [faːs] *n.* komik tiyatro oyunu, fars; yapmacık, yararsız şey; **far.ci.cal** □ ['~sikəl] tuhaf, komik, gülünç.

**fare** [fɛə] **1.** *n.* yol parası, bilet ücreti; yolcu; yiyecek; **2.** *v/i.* olmak, yaşamak; başından geçmek, gitmek, gelişme göstermek; how did you ~? nasıl gitti?; ~ well! güle güle!; ~ stage kıta, iki durak arası; **'~'well 1.** *int.* uğurlar olsun, güle güle!; **2.** *n.* ayrılma, gitme, veda, uğurlama; **3.** *adj.* veda, son; ~ party veda partisi.

**far...** [faː]: **'~-'fetched** *adj. fig.* zoraki, **'~-'flung** *adj.* çok yaygın; *fig.* uzak; ~

**gone** F çok ilerlemiş *(hastalık, delilik, sarhoşluk, borç v.b.).*

**far.i.na.ceous** [færi'neiʃəs] *adj.* nişastalı, un gibi.

**farm** [faːm] *n.* çiftlik; chicken ~ tavuk çiftliği; **2.** *vb.* ekip biçmek, çiftçilik yapmak; işletmek; *a.* ~ out kiraya vermek, ekip biçmek; çocuğun bakımı için anlaşmak; **'farm.er** *n.* çiftçi; çiftlik sahibi; **'farm.hand** *n.* Am. rençber; **'farm-house** *n.* çiftlik evi; **'farm.ing** *n.* çiftçilik; **farmstead** ['~sted] *n.* çiftlik ve içindeki binalar; **'farm.yard** *n.* çiftlik avlusu.

**far.o** ['fɛərəu] *n.* kağıdı dağıtana karşı oynanan kumar oyunu.

**far-off** ['faːr'ɔːf] *adj.* uzak.

**far.ra.go** [fə'raːgəu]*n.* karışım, karmakarışık şey.

**far-reach.ing** ['faː'riːtʃiŋ] *adj.* geniş kapsamlı.

**far.ri.er** ['færiə] *n.* nalbant.

**far.row** ['færəu] **1.** *n.* bir batında doğan domuz yavruları; **2.** *v/i.* yavrulamak *(domuz).*

**far-see.ing** ['faː'siːiŋ], **'far-'sight.ed** *adj. fig.* uzağı gören, basiretli.

**far.ther** ['faːðə], **far.thest** ['~ðist] *comp. & sup. of* far.

**far.thing** ['faːðiŋ] *n.* çeyrek peni; not worth a ~ beş para etmez.

**fas.ci.a** *mot.* ['feiʃə] *n.* arabada kontrol paneli; uzun tabelâ.

**fas.ci.nate** ['fæsineit] *v/t.* büyülemek, cezbetmek, teshir etm., hayran bırakmak; **fas.ci'na.tion** *n.* cazibe, çekicilik, büyüleme, teshir.

**fas.cine** [fæ'siːn] *n.* çalı demeti.

**Fas.cism** *pol.* ['fæʃizəm] *n.* faşizm; **'fascist** *n.* faşist; **fa'scis.tic** *adj.* [~əlly] faşistliğe ait.

**fash.ion** ['fæʃən] **1.** *n.* moda, şekil, tarz, usül; rank and ~ yüksek zümre; in (out of) ~ moda ol(may)an; set the ~ modada öncülük etm.; **2.** *v/t.* yapmak; şekil vermek; **'fash.ion.a.ble** □ ['fæʃnəbl] modaya uygun, şık; zenginler arasında tutulan; **'fash.ion.a.ble.ness** *n.* modaya uygunluk. sıklık; **'fash.ion-pa'rade** *n.* defile; **'fash.ion-plate** *n.* elbise modeli; son modayı izleyen.

**fast¹** [faːst] **1.** *adj.* çabuk, tez, hızlı, süratli; seri; ileri *(saat);* sıkı, sabit; solmaz *(renk);* sadık, vefalı *(arkadaş);* zevke düşkün; ahlâksız *(kadın);* to light ışığa dayanıklı; ~ train süratli tren, ekspres; my watch is ~ saatim ileri gitmiş; **2.** *adv.* çabuk, süratle; sıkıca; derin bir şekilde; ~ asleep derin uykuda.

**fast²** [~] 1. *v/i.* oruç tutmak, perhiz etm.; 2. *n.* oruç; '~-day *n.* oruç günü, perhiz günü.

**fas.ten** ['fɑːsn] *v/t.* & *v/i.* bağlamak, tut(tur)mak, sürmelemek; dikmek, ayırmamak; birleştirmek; ~ (up)on dikmek, ayırmamak *(gözünü)*; ~ upon kavramak, iyice anlamak; 'fas.ten.er *n.* tutacak, bağ, bağlayan şey, toka kıskacı, çıtçıt; 'fas.ten.ing *n.* sürgü, toka.

**fas.tid.i.ous** □ [fəs'tidiəs] titiz, müşkülpesent, memnun edilmesi güç; fas'tid.i.ous.ness *n.* titizlik.

**fast.ness** ['fɑːstnis] *n.* sağlamlık; sürat; solmazlık, solmama *(renk)*; X kale, istihkâm.

**fat** [fæt] 1. □ şişman, semiz, yağlı, kalın, dolu; bereketli, verimli *(toprak)*; 2. *n.* yağ; live on the ~ of the land herşeyin iyisiyle geçinmek; the ~ is in the fire kıyamet kopacak, iş patlak verecek; 3. *v/t.* semirtmek, beslemek.

**fa.tal** □ ['feitl] öldürücü, mahvedici, yok edici; mukadder, alında yazılı; ~ accident öldürücü kaza; fa.tal.ism ['~təlizm] *n.* herşeyi kadere bağlama inancı, kadercilik, fatalizm; 'fa.tal.ist *n.* herşeyi kadere bağlayan kimse, fatalist; fa.tal.i.ty [fə'tæliti] *n.* felâket, talihsizlik, akıbet, belâ, afet.

**fate** [feit] *n.* kader, kısmet, talih; ecel; akıbet; the 2s *pl.* üç Yunan kader tanrıçası; 'fat.ed *adj.* kadere bağlı; 'fate.ful □ ['~ful] kaderi tayin eden, önemli; tarihi önem taşıyan *(karar)*; mukadder.

**fa.ther** ['fɑːðə] 1. *n.* baba; *pl.* ata, soy; kurucu; tanrı; papaz; 2. *v/t.* icat etm., yaratıcısı olm., babası olm.; to ~ an article on s.o. bir yazıyı birine atfetmek; fa.ther.hood ['~hud] *n.* babalık; 'fa.ther- -in-law *n.* kayınpeder; 'fa.ther.land *n.* anavatan; 'fa.ther.less *adj.* babasız, yetim; 'fa.ther.ly *adj.* baba gibi, babacan, babaya ait.

**fath.om** ['fæðəm] 1. *n.* anlama, kavrama; ↓ kulaç; 2. *v/t.* ↓ iskandil etm., derinliğini bulmak; derinliğine inmek; *fig.* *-in* içyüzünü anlamak, kavramak; 'fath.om.less *adj.* çok derin, dibine erişilemeyen; anlaşılmaz.

**fa.tigue** [fə'tiːg] 1. *n.* yorgunluk, bitkinlik; X kışla hizmeti; ~s *pl.* X kışla hizmeti sırasında askerlerin giydiği üniforma; 2. *v/t.* yormak, yorgunluk vermek; fa'tigue-par.ty *n.* X kışla hizmeti verilen askerler.

**fat.ling** ['fætliŋ] *n.* kesim için beslenen genç hayvan; 'fat.ness *n.* şişmanlık, se-

mizlik; 'fat.ten *v/t.* & *v/i.* şişmanla(t)-mak, semir(t)mek; gübrelemek; 'fat.ty 1. *adj.* yağlı, şişman, semiz; gübreli; ~ degeneration yağ dejenerasyonu, aşırı şişmanlık; 2. *n.* F şişko, dobiş.

**fa.tu.i.ty** [fə'tjuːiti]*n.* anlamsızlık, ahmaklık, budalalık; fat.u.ous □ ['fætjuəs] aptal, budala, salak, ahmak.

**fau.cet** *part.* Am. ['fɔːsit] *n.* musluk.

**faugh** [fɔː] *int.* püf!, pöf!, ne kötü!

**fault** [fɔːlt] *n.* faul, hata *(a. tennis)*; ⚡ hata, yanlış, kusur; ⊕ hata, bozukluk; *geol.* fay, çatlak; find ~ with kusur bulmak *-de*; be at ~ yanılmış olm., şaşmış olm.; kabahatli olm.; to a ~ *fig.* aşırı derecede; '~-find.er *n.* tenkitçi, kusur bulan kimse; '~.find.ing *n.* tenkit, eleştiri; 'fault.i.ness *n.* kusurlu olma, bozukluk; 'fault.less □ kusursuz, mükemmel; 'faults.man *n.* teleph. tamirci; 'fault.y □ hatalı, kusurlu, bozuk.

**faun** [fɔːn] *n.* myth. yarısı keçi yarısı insan olan ilâh.

**faun.a** ['fɔːnə] *n.* fauna, direy, bir bölgeye *veya* çağa ait tüm hayvanlar.

**fa.vo(u)r** ['feivə] 1. *n.* dostça bakış, teveccüh, güleryüz; yardım, destek, kayırma, iltimas, iyilik, rica, lütuf, nişan; in ~ of *-in* lehinde, *-in* taraftarı; † lehine, emrine *(çek)*; I am (not) in ~ of it onun lehindeyim (değilim); under ~ of night gecenin karanlığından yararlanarak; do s.o. a ~ *b-ne* bir iyilikte bulunmak; 2. *v/t.* kayırmak *-i*; iltimas geçmek *-e*, tercih etm. *-i*, destek olm. *-e*, lütuf göstermek *-e*, *-in* tarafını tutmak; müsaade etm. *(hava)*; fa.vo(u)r.a.b!e □ ['~vərəbl] taraf tutan, öven; olumlu, memnuniyet verici, uygun, elverişli, müsait, münasip; 'fa.vo(u)r.a.ble.ness *n.* taraf tutma, övme, elverişli olma; fa.vo-(u)red ['~vəd] *adj.* avantajlı, belli bir özelliği olan, iltimas geçilen; most-~ nation clause † bir ülkenin en düşük ithalat vergisini ödeyeceğini belirten özel hüküm; fa.vo(u)r.ite ['~vərit] 1. *adj.* daha çok sevilen, gözde; 2. *n.* kayırılan kimse; *spor:* favori, kazanması beklenen; 'fa.vo(u)r.it.ism *n.* taraf tutma, adam kayırma.

**fawn¹** [fɔːn] 1. *n.* zo. geyik *veya* karaca yavrusu; açık kahverengi; 2. *vb.* doğurmak, yavrulamak *(geyik)*.

**fawn²** [~] *v/i.* kuyruk sallamak *(köpek)*: *fig.* yaltaklanmak, dalkavukluk etm. (upon *-e*); 'fawn.er *n.* yağcı, yaltakçı, dalkavuk; 'fawn.ing *n.* dalkavukluk, yağcılık, yaltaklanma.

**fay** *poet.* [fei] *n.* peri.

**faze** *part. Am.* F [feiz] *v/t.* telaşa düşürmek, sıkıntı vermek, iki ayağını bir pabuca sokmak.

**fe.al.ty** [ˈfiːəlti] *n.* sadakat.

**fear** [fiə] **1.** *n.* korku, dehşet; endişe, kuruntu; through *veya* from ~ of korkusuyla, korkusundan; for ~ of doing yapma korkusuyla, korkusundan, endişesiyle; in ~ of one's life hayatından endişe ederek, ölüm tehlikesiyle; **2.** *vb.* korkmak *-den*, çekinmek *-den*, endişe etm. *-den*, korkuyla bakmak *-e*; **fear.ful** □ [ˈ~ful] korkunç, dehşetli; berbat, can sıkıcı; korkan, endişeli; be ~ that korkmak, endişelenmek *-den*; **ˈfear.ful.ness** *n.* korkaklık; **ˈfear.less** □ korkusuz, gözü pek; **ˈfear.less.ness** *n.* korkusuzluk.

**fea.si.bil.i.ty** [fiːzəˈbiliti] *n.* tatbik edilebilme, uygulanabilme, mümkün olma; **ˈfea.si.ble** *adj.* yapılabilir, mümkün, tatbik edilebilir, makûl, münasip.

**feast** [fiːst] **1.** *n.* bayram, festival, yıldönümü, yortu; ziyafet; **2.** *v/t. & v/i.* (on, upon) ziyafete katılmak; ziyafet vermek, ziyafette vakit geçirmek; yiyip içmek; hissi zevk vermek; ~ one's eyes on doya doya bakmak *-e*.

**feat** [fiːt] *n.* yapılması beceri, güç *veya* cesaret isteyen şey; başarı.

**feath.er** [ˈfeðə] **1.** *n.* tüy; *a.* ~s *pl.* kuşun tüyleri; show the white ~ F korkaklık göstermek; that is a ~ in his cap gurur duyabileceği bir başarıdır; in high ~ neşesi yerinde; **2.** *vb.* tüy takmak *-e*; tüylenmek, tüyleri bitmek; ↓ pala çevirmek *(kürek)*; ~ one's nest küpünü doldurmak, zenginleşmek, *k-ne* emanet edilen seyden pay çıkarmak; ˈ~bed **1.** *n.* kuştüyü yatak; **2.** *v/t. (bir gurup insana)* cömertçe avantaj sağlamak; ˈ~brained, ˈ~head.ed *adj.* kuş beyinli, aptal; **ˈfeath.ered** *adj.* tüylü; **ˈfeath.er-edge** *n.* ⊕ kolayca kırılan *veya* bükülen çok ince uç; **ˈfeath.er.ing** *n.* tüy; **ˈfeath.er.stitch** *n.* terzilik: zikzak, civankaşı dikiş; **ˈfeath.er--weight** *n. boks:* tüysiklet; **ˈfeath.er.y** *adj.* tüylü; tüy gibi hafif ve yumuşak.

**fea.ture** [ˈfiːtʃə] **1.** *n.* yüz organlarından biri: *pl.* yüz, surat, çehre; özellik, hususiyet; makale; asıl film; **2.** *vb.* özelliği olm.; önem vermek; baş rolde oynamak; a film N.N.'nin başrolde oynadığı film; ~ film asıl film; **ˈfea.ture.less** *adj.* hiç bir özelliği olmayan, çekici olmayan.

**feb.ri.fuge** [ˈfebrifjuːdʒ] *n.* 🌡 ateş düşürücü ilaç.

---

**fe.brile** [ˈfiːbrail] *adj.* ateşli, hummalı.

**Feb.ru.ar.y** [ˈfebruəri] *n.* şubat.

**feck.less** [ˈfeklis] *adj.* bir işe yaramayan, yetersiz, beceriksiz, zayıf, sorumsuz.

**fe.cun.date** [ˈfiːkəndeit] *v/t.* gebe bırakmak, döllemek; bereketlendirmek; **fe.cun.da.tion** *n.* dölleme; bereketlendirme; **fe.cun.di.ty** [fiˈkʌnditi] *n.* verimlilik; doğurganlık, üreyebilme.

**fed** [fed] *pret. & p.p. of* feed 2.

**fed.er.al** [ˈfedərəl] *adj.* federal, federasyona ait, federe; **ˈfed.er.al.ism** *n.* federalizm; **ˈfed.er.al.ist** *n.* federalist, federal sistem taraftarı; **ˈfed.er.al.ize** *v/t.* devletleri birleştirmek, federal sistem altında toplamak; **fed.er.ate 1.** [ˈ~reit] *v/t. & v/i.* federasyon halinde birleş(tir)mek; **2.** [ˈ~rit] *adj.* birleşik, müttefik; **fed.er.a.tion** [ˈ~ˈreifən] *n.* federasyon, birlik; **fed.er.a.tive** [ˈ~rətiv] *adj.* federasyon esasına dayalı, federatif.

**fee** [fiː] **1.** *n.* ücret; giriş ücreti; vizite; 🏛 mülk; ~ simple mülk, şartsız veraset; **2.** *v/t.* ücretini ödemek, ücretle tutmak.

**fee.ble** □ [fiːbl] zayıf, kuvvetsiz, dermansız, takatsiz, cılız; ˈ~ˈmind.ed *adj.* geri zekâlı, aptal, iradesiz, kararsız; **ˈfee.ble.ness** *n.* zayıflık, kuvvetsizlik.

**feed** [fiːd] **1.** *n.* yemek, yiyecek, gıda, yem; ⊕ malzemeyi makineye veren boru; ⊕ makineye verilen malzeme; × yük; **2.** *v/t. & v/i.* beslemek (on, with *-le*), yemlemek, yiyeceğini vermek; ihtiyacını temin etm.; desteklemek; otlamak, yemlenmek; yemek yemek; ~ o.s. yemek yemek; ~ off *veya* down besini bir yerden almak; ~ up fazla yiyecek vermek. besleyici yiyecek vermek, semirtmek; be fed up with *sl.* bıkmak, usanmak, bezmek *-den*; well fed iyi beslenmiş; ˈ~ˈback *n. radyo:* geri itilim; eleştiri; **ˈfeed.er** *n.* besleyici; beslenen; biberon; mama önlüğü; ana yola bağlı hat; ⊕ elektrik taşıyan hat; radyo vericisinden antene giden hat; **ˈfeed.er line** 🚃 ana demiryoluna bağlı hat; **ˈfeed.er road** besleme hattı; **ˈfeed.ing** *n.* besleme, yiyecek verme, yemleme; ⊕ besleme; high ~ lüks hayat, zevk ve sefa hayatı; **ˈfee.ding-bottle** *n.* biberon; **ˈfeed-ing-stuff** *n.* yem, yiyecek maddesi.

**feel** [fiːl] **1.** *(irr.)* *v/t & v/i.* hissetmek, duymak, dokunmak, elle yoklamak; anlamak, kavramak; fikrinde olm.; × keşif yapmak, araştırma yapmak; ~ bad about s.th. acımak *-e*; ~ cold üşümek; ~ like doing canı yapmak istemek; ~ for acımak *-e*; *-in* üzüntüsünü paylaşmak;

**2.** *n.* his, duygu; temas, dokunarak anlama; **¹feel.er** *n.* dokunan şey; hisseden kimse; *zo.* anten *(a. fig.)*; dokunaç; ✕ gözleyici, casus; **¹feel.ing** *n.* his, duygu, duyu, dokunma; dokunma hissi; his dünyası; merhamet, hassasiyet; good ~ nezaket, iltifat, teveccüh.

**feet** [fiːt] *pl. of* foot.

**feign** [fein] *v/t.* yapar gibi görünmek, taklit etm., uydurmak; ~ illness hasta numarası yapmak; ~ to do yapar gibi görünmek; ~ o.s. mad deli numarası yapmak; **feigned** *adj.* sahte, yapmacık; **feign.ed.ly** [ˈ~idli] *adv.* sahte olarak, yapmacıklı.

**feint** [feint] *n.* sahte, yapmacık; bahane, hileli söz; gösteriş, caka, fiyaka; ✕ savaş hilesi; **2.** *v/i.* sahte taarruzda bulunmak, yanıltıcı harekette bulunmak.

**feld.spar** *min.* [ˈfeldspɑː] *n.* feldispat.

**fe.lic.i.tate** [fiˈlisiteit] *v/t.* bşi kutlamak, tebrik etm. (on); **fe.lic.iˈta.tion** *n.* kutlama, tebrik; **feˈlic.i.tous** ☐ mutlu; münasip, iyi seçilmiş, yerinde *(kelime)*; **feˈlic.i.ty** *n.* mutluluk, saadet; etkileyici yazı *veya* konuşma; iyi seçilmiş deyim.

**fe.line** [ˈfiːlain] *adj.* kedi gibi, kedilere ait.

**fell¹** [fel] **1.** *pret. of* fall 2; **2.** *v/t.* yere düşürmek, devirmek, kesmek *(ağaç).*

**fell²** *poet.* [~] *adj.* vahşî, korkunç, zalim; öldürücü.

**fell³** [~] *n.* hayvan derisi *veya* postu.

**fel.loe** [ˈfeləu] *n.* ispit, jant.

**fel.low** [ˈfeləu] *n.* adam, kişi, herif; arkadaş, dost, hemcins, akran; *univ.* hoca; akademi üyesi; dernek üyesi; bir çift şeyin teki *(ayakkabı vs.)*; old ~ F eski dost; the ~ of a glove eldivenin teki; be ~s arkadaş olm.; he has not his ~ akranı, arkadaşı yok; **¹~ˈbe.ings** *pl.* aynı türden insanlar; **¹~ˈcit.i.zen,** **¹~ˈcoun.try.man** *n.* vatandaş, yurttaş; **¹~ˈcrea.ture** *n.* hemcins, aynı türden yaratık; **¹~ˈfeel.ing** *n.* ortak duygu, halden anlama; **¹~ˈpas.sen.ger** *n.* yol arkadaşı; **¹~.ship** *n.* arkadaşlık, dostluk; cemiyet, dernek; üyelik; ~ sol.dier askerlik arkadaşı; **¹~ˈstu.dent** *n.* okul arkadaşı; **¹~-¹trav.el.ler** *n.* yol arkadaşı, yoldaş; *pol.* Komünist parti sempatizanı.

**fel.ly** [ˈfeli] *n.* ispit, jant.

**fel.on** [ˈfelən] *n.* 𝔰𝔱 mücrim, suçlu; 𝔗 tırnak etrafında oluşan yara; **fe.lo.ni.ous** ☐ 𝔰𝔱 [fiˈləunjəs] caniyane, suç unsuru olan; **fel.o.ny** 𝔰𝔱 [ˈfeləni] *n.* cinayet, silahlı soygun, kundakçılık gibi ağır suç.

**fel.spar** [ˈfelspɑː] = feldspar.

**felt¹** [felt] *pret. & p.p. of* feel 2.

**felt²** [~] **1.** *n.* keçe; fötr; **2.** *vb.* keçeyle kaplamak; keçe yapmak; keçelenmek.

**fe.male** [ˈfiːmeil] **1.** *adj.* dişi, dişil, kadın cinsine ait; ~ child kız çocuk; ~ screw dişi vida; **2.** *n.* kadın; dişi hayvan *veya* bitki.

**fem.i.nine** ☐ [ˈfeminin] kadın gibi, kadınımsı, kadına ait; *gr.* dişil; **fem.iˈnin.i.ty** *n.* kadınlık; **¹fem.i.nism** *n.* kadın haklarını tanıtma mücadelesi, feminizm; **¹fem.i.nist** *n.* kadın hakları savunucusu, feminist; **fem.i.nize** [ˈ~naiz] *v/t. & v/i.* kadınlaş(tır)mak, kadın gibi olm.

**fe.mur** *anat.* [ˈfiːmə] *n.* kalça kemiği, uyluk kemiği.

**fen** [fen] *n.* bataklık.

**fence** [fens] **1.** *n.* parmaklık, çit, tahta perde; *sl.* çalıntı malların satıldığı yer; çalıntı mal alıp satan kimse; sit on the ~ kararsız olm., tarafsız olm.; **2.** *v/t. a.* ~ in *-in* etrafını çitle çevirmek; korumak (from *-den*); *v/i.* eskrim yapmak; *fig.* kaçamaklı konuşmak, direk cevap vermekten kaçınmak; *sl.* çalıntı mal almak; **¹fence.less** *adj.* kararsız; korunmasız.

**fenc.ing** [ˈfensiŋ] *n.* eskrim; çit *veya* parmaklık malzemesi; çit, parmaklık; **¹~-foil** *n.* eskrim kılıcı; **¹~-mas.ter** *n.* eskrim antrenörü.

**fend** [fend] *vb.*: ~ off kendini korumak *-den*; uzak tutmak, defetmek; ~ for geçindirmek *-i*; **¹fend.er** *n.* şömine önündeki paravana; araba çamurluğu; koruyucu herhangi bir şey; lokomotif mahmuzu; ♣ çarpışmanın şiddetini azaltan iki gemi arasındaki lastik, usturmaça.

**Fe.ni.an** [ˈfiːnjən] *n.* M.S. 2. ve 3. yüzyıllarda İrlanda'yı savunan savaşçılar; İrlanda'daki İngiliz yönetiminin yıkılmasına kendilerini adamış 19. yüzyıl İrlanda ve İrlanda-Amerikan gizli örgüt üyesi.

**fen.nel** ♣ [ˈfenl] *n.* rezene.

**fen.ny** [ˈfeni] *adj.* bataklıklı; bataklık gibi.

**feoff** [fef] *n.* tımar, fief; feodal emlâk; **feoff.ee** [feˈfiː] *n.* tımar sahibi, zaim; **¹feoff.ment** *n.* arazi bağışlama; **feof.for** [feˈfɔː] *n.* arazi bağışlayan kimse.

**fer.ment 1.** [ˈfəːmənt] *n.* maya; mayalanma: *fig.* telaş, galeyan, heyecan; **2.** [fəːˈment] *v/t. & v/i.* mayalan(dır)mak; *fig.* heyecanlan(dır)mak, galeyana getirmek; **ferˈment.a.ble** *adj.* mayalanabilir ,maya tutabilen; **fer.menˈta.tion** *n.* mayalanma, fermantasyon; *fig.* heyecan, galeyan; **ferˈment.a.tive** [~tətiv] *adj.* mayalanan; mayalayan.

**fern** ♣ [fəːn] *n.* eğreltiotu.

fe.ro.cious ☐ [fə'rəuʃəs] vahşi, yırtıcı, zalim, yabani, canavar ruhlu; fe.roc.i.ty [fə'rɔsiti] n. vahşilik, vahşet, saldırganlık, zalimlik, canilik.

fer.ret ['ferit] 1. n. zo. tavşan ve sıçan tutmakta kullanılan kır sansarı, mustela; fig. araştırmacı; 2. v/i. bu hayvanlarla avlanmak; ~ out araştırıp bulmak, araştırmak.

fer.ric ⚗ ['ferik] adj. demirli, içinde demir olan, demire ait; fer.rif.er.ous [fe-'rifərəs] adj. demirli; fer.ru.gi.nous [fe'ru:dʒinəs] adj. demirli, pas renginde; fer.ro-con.crete ⊕ ['ferəu'kɔŋkri:t] n. betonarme; fer.rous ⚗ ['ferəs] adj. demirli.

fer.rule ['feru:l] n. demir halka, yüzük.

fer.ry ['feri] 1. n. feribot; 2. vb. vapurla karşı tarafa geçirmek; fig. götürüp getirmek; '~-boat n. feribot; 'fer.ry.man n. feribot kullanan kimse.

fer.tile ☐ ['fə:tail] verimli, bereketli; fig. yaratıcı (kimse veya zekâ); fer.til.i.ty [fə:tiliti] n. verimlilik, bereket; fig. yaratıcılık; fer.ti.li.za.tion [~lai'zeiʃən] n. gübreleme, verimini artırma; 'fer.ti.lize v/t. gübrelemek; biol. döllemek, tohumlamak; verimini artırmak; 'fer.ti.liz.er n. (kimyevi) gübre.

fer.ule ['feru:l] n. öğrencinin eline vurmaya yarayan sopa.

fer.ven.cy ['fə:vənsi] n. mst fig. tutku, aşk, aşırı heves, şevk; 'fer.vent ☐ sıcak, hararetli; fig. deli gibi seven, kara sevdalı, şiddetli, ateşli.

fer.vid ☐ ['fə:vid] = fervent.

fer.vo(u)r ['fə:və] n. şiddetli arzu, şevk, gayret, istek.

fes.tal ☐ ['festl] bayrama ait, festivalle ilgili; şen, eğlenceli.

fes.ter ['festə] 1. v/i. iltihaplanmak, azmak; fig. kuruntu etm.; 2. n. iltihap.

fes.ti.val ['festəvəl] n. bayram, yortu, festival, şenlik, eğlence; fes.tive ☐ ['~tiv] festivale ait, bayramla ilgili; neşeli; fes-'tiv.i.ty n. şenlik, eğlence; pl. bayram, yortu, festival.

fes.toon [fes'tu:n] 1. n. çiçek, yaprak veya kurdeladan yapılmış kordon; 2. v/t. çiçek veya kurdelayla süslemek.

fetch [fetʃ] v/t. & v/i. gidip getirmek, alıp getirmek; çıkarmak (inilti); çekmek (iç); F para getirmek, para kazandırmak; F vurmak (tokat, yumruk); ~ and carry for s.o. b-ne hizmet etm., onun için koşuşturmak; ~ up dur(dur)mak; varmak; kusturmak; 'fetch.ing F ☐ çekici, alımlı, cazibeli.

fête [feit] 1. n. açık hava eğlencesi; ~-day bir azizin yortusu; 2. v/t. ziyafet vermek -e, ağırlamak -i, saygı göstermek -e.

fet.id ☐ ['fetid] pis kokan, kokmuş, kuşmuş.

fe.tish ['fi:tiʃ] n. tılsım, putperestlerin taptığı şey, fetiş (a. fig.).

fet.lock ['fetlɔk] n. atın topuk kılları; topuk mafsalı.

fet.ter ['fetə] 1. n. pranga, zincir, köstek, bukağı; pl. fig. engel, mani, ayak bağı; 2. v/t. ayağını zincire vurmak; fig. engel olm., mani olm., ayak bağı olm.

fet.tle ['fetl] n. durum, şart, şekil; in fine ~ iyi durumda, neşesi yerinde.

feud [fju:d] n. kavga, kan davası, çekişme; feu.dal ☐ ['~dl] derebeyliğe ait; feodal; feu.dal.ism ['~dəlizəm] n. derebeylik; feu.dal.i.ty [~'dæliti] n. derebeylik; feu.da.to.ry ['~dətəri] 1. adj. hizmet borcu olan; 2. n. hizmetli, köle, vasal.

fe.ver ['fi:və] n. ateş, humma, hararet, sıcaklık; fig. heyecan, sinirlilik; 'fe.vered adj. part. fig. ateşli, heyecanlı; 'fe.ver.ish ☐ ateşli, hummalı, hararetli; fig. heyecanlı, telaşlı.

few [fju:] adj. az; a ~ birkaç; quite a ~, a good ~ birçok, pek çok; the ~ azınlık.

fez [fez] n. fes.

fi.an.cé(e) [fi'ã:nsei] n. nişanlı.

fi.as.co [fi'æskəu] n. başarısızlık, hezimet, bozgun, fiyasko.

fi.at ['faiæt] n. emir, karar; ~ money Am. hükümetin kararına dayanarak çıkarılan kağıt para, karşılıksız para.

fib [fib] 1. n. yalan, palavra; 2. v/i. yalan söylemek, uydurmak, atmak; 'fib.ber n. yalancı, palavracı.

fi.bre ['faibə] n. lif, tel; iplik; yapı; karakter; '~.board n. liften yapılmış tahta; '~.glass n. cam elyafı, fiberglas; fi.brin ['~brin] n. fibrin; 'fi.brous ☐ lifli, telli; ~ material dokuma maddesi.

fib.u.la anat. ['fibjulə] n. kamış kemik, fibula.

fick.le ['fikl] adj. değişken, dönek, kararsız; 'fick.le.ness n. döneklik, kararsızlık.

fic.tion ['fikʃən] n. roman; roman ve hikâye edebiyatı; hayal; uydurma; yalan; ♙ varsayım; fic.tion.al ☐ ['~ʃənl] roman edebiyatına ait; hayalî.

fic.ti.tious ☐ [fik'tiʃəs] hayalî, uydurma; 'fic.tive adj. hayalî, uydurma, sahte.

fid.dle ['fidl] 1. n. keman; 2. v/i. keman çalmak; v/t. sl. dalavere yapmak, tevil etm.; ~ away israf etm., boşa harcamak; fid.dle.de.dee ['~di'di:] int. saçma!, zırva!; **fid.dle.fad.dle** F [ˈ~fædl] n. saçma söz; ~! saçma!; 2. vb. tembellikle vaktini israf etm.; **ˈfid.dler** n. kemancı; sl. vergi kaçakçısı; **ˈfid.dle.stick** n. keman yayı; ~s! saçma!; **ˈfid.dling** adj. önemsiz ,değersiz.

**fi.del.i.ty** [fiˈdeliti] n. vefa, sadakat (to -e); doğruluk.

**fidg.et** F [ˈfidʒit] 1. n. oft. ~s pl. huzursuzluk, rahatsızlık, sinirlilik; yerinde duramayan kimse; have the ~s yerinde duramamak; 2. v/t. rahat oturamamak, yerinde duramamak; **ˈfidg.et.y** adj. yerinde duramayan, kıpır kıpır.

**fi.du.ci.ar.y** [fiˈdjuːʃjəri] adj. güvene dayanan, itimat kabilinden; † itibarî; 2. n. emin, kendisine güvenilen kimse, mutemet.

**fie** [fai] int. ayıp!, yuh!

**fief** [fiːf] n. zeamet, tımar.

**field** [fiːld] 1. n. çayır, kır, otlak, mera, tarla; meydan, alan; spor: saha; pl. bir yarışmaya katılanlar; hold the ~ yerini muhafaza etm.; take the ~ sefere çıkmak; 2. vb. kriket: topu yakalamak veya durdurmak; **ˈ~-day** n. X askeri harekât ve manevraların yapıldığı gün; fig. önemli gün; Am. spor bayramı; Am. beklenmedik başarı; **ˈfield.er** n. kriket: dış meydan oyuncusu.

**field...:** ~ e.vents pl. atlama ve atma yarışları; **ˈ~.fare** n. ardıçkuşu; **ˈ~-glass.es** n. pl. çifte dürbün; **ˈ~-gun** n. X hafif top; **ˈ~-ˈhos.pi.tal** n. X sahra hastanesi; **ˈ~-ˈmar.shal** n. mareşal; **ˈ~-of.fi.cer** n. binbaşı veya albay; **ˈ~-sports** n. pl. açık hava sporları.

**fiend** [fiːnd] n. iblis, şeytan, canavar, zalim; fig. tiryaki; **ˈfiend.ish** □ şeytanî, vahşi, zalim, gaddar.

**fierce** □ [fiəs] vahşi, azgın, şiddetli, sert; öfkeli, hiddetli, hararetli; **ˈfierce.ness** n. şiddet, sertlik, vahşet.

**fi.er.i.ness** [ˈfaiərinis] n. hararet, şiddetli sıcaklık; hiddet; **ˈfi.er.y** □ hararetli; ateşli, alevli, kızgın.

**fife** [faif] 1. n. fifre, küçük flavta; 2. vb. düdük çalmak; **ˈfif.er** n. düdük çalan kimse.

**fif.teen** [ˈfifˈtiːn] n. & adj. on beş; **ˈfif.teenth** [~θ] n. & adj. on beşinci; **fifth** [fifθ] 1. adj. beşinci; 2. n. beşte bir; **fifth col.umn** pol. beşinci kol; **ˈfifth.ly** adv. beşinci olarak, beşinci sırada; **fif.ti.eth** [ˈ~tiiθ] 1. adj. ellinci; 2. n. ellide bir; **fif.ty** n. elli; **ˈfif.ty-ˈfif.ty** F yarı yarıya; go ~ yarı yarıya bölüşmek.

**fig¹** [fig] n. incir; a ~ for...! ... Allah belâsını versin!; I don't care a ~ for him Allah onun belâsını versin, o hiç umurumda bile değil.

**fig²** [~] 1. n. F donanım; hal; in full ~ giyimli, tam teçhizatlı; 2. vb. ~ out F telleyip pullamak.

**fight** [fait] 1. n. dövüş, kavga, savaş, mücadele; make a ~ for ...için mücadele etm.; put up a good ~ cesaret ve azimle mücadele etm.; show ~ mücadeleye hazır olm.; 2. v/t. & v/i. mücadele etm., dövüşmek, kavga etm.; defetmek, yapmak, uğraşmak; X savaşmak; ~ off püskürtmek, defetmek, mücadele etm.; ~ one's way mücadele ederek ilerlemek; ~ against s.th. bşle mücadele etm.; ~ back püskürtmek; ~ shy of kaçınmak -den, uzak durmak -den, karışmamak -e; **ˈfight.er** n. savaşçı; X avcı uçağı; ~ pilot avcı uçağı pilotu; **ˈfight.ing** n. kavga, mücadele, savaş; ~ chance büyük çabalar sonucunda kazanılabilecek başarı şansı.

**fig.ment** [ˈfigmənt] n. icat, hayal, uydurma.

**fig-tree** [ˈfigtriː] n. incir ağacı.

**fig.u.rant(e)** [ˈfigjurənt; (~ˈrɑːnt)] n. balede figüran; figüran.

**fig.u.ra.tion** [figjuˈreiʃən] n. şekil verme, şekle sokma; şekil, tasvir; **fig.ur.a.tive** □ [ˈ~rətiv] mecazî, sembolik, simgesel; süslü.

**fig.ure** [ˈfigə] 1. n. rakam, şekil (a. A); endam, boy bos, vücut yapısı; şahsiyet, şahıs; mecaz; dans: figür; fiyat; ~ of speech mecaz, istiare, kinaye; what's the ~? kaç para?; at a high ~ pahalı, yüksek fiyata; be good at ~s matematiği kuvvetli olm.; 2. v/t. & v/i. temsil etm.; desenlerle süslemek; tasavvur etm., hayal etm., resmetmek, zihinde canlandırmak; a. ~ to o.s. hayal etm.; ~ on güvenmek -e, hesaba katmak -i; ~ up veya out hesaplamak; anlamak; ~ out at ...miktarına erişmek; **ˈ~-head** n. ♩ gemi pruvasındaki şekil; fig. gerçek yetkisi olmayan kimse, mostralık, kukla; **ˈ~-skat.ing** n. figür yaparak paten kayma.

**fig.u.rine** [ˈfigjuriːn] n. heykelcik.

**fil.a.ment** [ˈfiləmənt] n. tel, lif; ♀ ercik sapı; ✗ lamba teli.

**fil.a.ture** [ˈfilətʃə] n. iplik fabrikası.

**fil.bert** ♀ [ˈfilbəːt] n. fındık.

**filch** [filtʃ] v/t. çalmak, aşırmak, yürütmek (from -den).

**file¹** [fail] 1. n. dosya dolabı; dosya, klasör; X dizi, küme; on ~ dosyalanmış; 2. v/t. & v/i. dosyalamak, dosyaya koymak, tasnif etm.; vermek *(dilekçe vs.)*; X sırayla yürümek; ~ in (out) sırayla, arka arkaya yürümek.

**file²** [~] 1. *n.* eğe, törpü; 2. *v/t.* eğelemek, törpülemek.

**fil.i.al** □ [¹filjəl] evlâda ait, evlâda yakışır; **fil.i.a.tion** [fili¹eiʃən] *n.* birinin evlâdı olma, aynı soydan gelme, menşe, nesep.

**fil.i.bus.ter** [¹filibʌstə] 1. *n. Am.* uzun uzun konuşarak bir kanunun kabulünü engelleme; engelleyici konuşma; isyana teşvik eden kimse; 2. *vb. Am.* engellemek.

**fil.i.gree** [¹filigri:] *n.* telkâri iş; filigran.

**fil.ings** [¹failiŋz] *n. pl.* eğe talaşı.

**fill** [fil] 1. *v/t. & v/i.* dol(dur)mak; doyurmak; kabarmak; işgal etm.; şişirmek; tatmin etm.; *Am.* yapmak, icra etm., tamamlamak; ~ in doldurmak *(eksiklik, form, çek vs.)*; ~ out büyü(t)mek; şiş(ir)mek; doldurmak *(fiş vs.)*; ~ up tamamen dol(dur)mak; 2. *n.* doyumluk, dolumluk, dolduracak miktar; eat (drink) one's ~ doyana kadar yemek (içmek), doymak (of -e), gına gelmek (of -*den*).

**fill.er** [¹filə] *n.* astar verniği; huni; dolgu maddesi.

**fill.let** [¹filit] 1. *n.* fileto, dilim; saça takılan bant; pervaz, silme, tiriz *(part.* △); kitap kapağına basılan süs çizgisi; 2. *v/t.* dilimlemek, (fileto) çıkarmak.

**fill.ing** [¹filiŋ] *n.* doldurma, dolgu; ~ **station** *Am.* benzin istasyonu.

**fil.lip** [filip] 1. *n.* fiske; 2. *v/t.* fiske vurmak; teşvik etm.

**fil.ly** [¹fili] *n.* kısrak; *fig.* genç kız.

**film** [film] 1. *n.* zar, ince tabaka; film; take *veya* shoot a ~ film çekmek, çevirmek; 2. *v/t. & v/i.* film çevirmek, filme geçirmek; ince örtüyle kaplanmak, zarla kaplamak; **¹film.y** □ zarlı, ince tabaka ile kaplı; puslu, dumanlı, bulanık.

**fil.ter** [¹filtə] 1. *n.* filtre, süzgeç; 2. *v/t. & v/i.* süzgeçten geç(ir)mek, süz(ül)mek; sızmak, duyulmak; ~ in *mot.* trafik kırmızı ışıkta durduğunda sola dönmek; **¹fil.ter.ing** *n.* süzme; **¹fil.ter tip** sigara filtresi; filtreli sigara.

**filth** [filθ] *n.* kir, pislik *(part. fig.)* **¹filth.y** □ pis, kirli; iğrenç, çirkin.

**fil.trate** [¹filtreit] *v/t. & v/i.* süz(ül)mek; **fil¹tra.tion** *n.* süzme.

**fin** [fin] *n. zo.* yüzgeç, yüzgece benzeyen şey; ✈ kanatçık; *mot.* kanatçık, kulak, pancur.

**fi.nal** [¹fainl] 1. □ son, nihaî; kesin, ka- 2. *n* ⁚ ~s *pl.* sömestr sonu sınavı; *spor:*

**fi.nal** [¹fainl] 1. □ son, nihaî; kesin, katî; final, son yarış; *gazete:* son baskı; **fi.na.le** [fi¹na:li] *n.* ♪ final, bitiş; **fi.nal.ist** [¹fainəlist] *n. spor:* finale kalan yarışmacı, finalist; **fi.nal.i.ty** [~¹nӕliti] *n.* kelinlik, katiyet; son olma.

**fi.nance** [fai¹nӕns] 1. *n.* maliye; ~s *pl.* malî durum, gelir; 2. *v/t. & v/i. -in* masraflarını karşılamak, finanse etm. -i; malî işleri idare etm.; **fi¹nan.cial** □ [~ʃəl] malî; **fin¹an.cier** [~siə] *n.* maliyeci; sermayedar.

**finch** *orn.* [fintʃ] *n.* ispinoz.

**find** [faind] 1. *(irr.) v/t.* bulmak, keşfetmek; ulaşmak; rastlamak -e; öğrenmek; tedarik etm., sağlamak; ∞ karar vermek, hüküm vermek, hükmüne varmak; ~ o.s. kabiliyetlerini keşfetmek, kendini bulmak; kendine gelmek; all found ücretsiz yemek ve kalacak yer; ~ out öğrenmek; keşfetmek, ortaya çıkarmak; I cannot ~ it in my heart gönlüm elvermiyor, bu kadar zalim olamam; 2. *n.* bulunmuş şey; keşif, buluş; bulgu; **¹find.er** *n.* bulucu, bulan; *opt.* vizör; **¹find.ing.** *n.* bulgu, bulunan şey; *a.* ~s *pl.* sonuç, netice; ∞ karar.

**fine¹** [fain] 1. □ ince; güzel, zarif; hoş, nazik; açık *(hava);* hassas; halis, saf; şatafatlı *(konuşma veya yazı);* sağlıklı; you are a ~ fellow! *iro.* sen yaramaz adamsın!; ~ arts *pl.* güzel sanatlar; 2. *adv.* çok iyi, güzel, hoş; cut ~ ucu ucuna hesabetmek *(para, zaman);* 3. *n. meteor.* güzel hava; 4. *vb.* berraklaş(tır)mak; ~ away, ~ down, ~ off incel(t)mek, saflaş(tır)mak; azalmak.

**fine²** [~] 1. *n.* para cezası; in ~ kısaca, özetle; 2. *v/t.* para cezasına çarptırmak; ~ s.o. 5 sh. ceza olarak 5 şilin almak.

**fine-draw** [fain¹drɔ:] *v/t.* inceltmek.

**fine.ness** [¹fainnis] *n.* incelik, zarafet, güzellik; saflık.

**fin.er.y** [¹fainəri] *n.* gösteriş, süslü giyim, şıklık; şık elbiseler.

**fi.nesse** [fi¹nes] *n.* incelik, ustalık; *iskambil:* fines; kurnazlık, hile.

**fin.ger** [¹fiŋgə] *n.* parmak; have a ~ in the pie işe karışmak, bir işte parmağı olm.; *s.* end 1; 2. *v/t.* parmakla dokunmak; belirtmek, teşhis etm.; göstermek; ♪ parmakla çalmak; **¹~-al.pha.bet** *n.* işaretlerle anlaşma; **¹~-board** *n.* ♪ çalgı aletinin sapı; **¹~-bowl** *n.* eltası; **¹fin.gerea** *comb.* ...parmaklı; **¹fin.ger.ing** *n.* parmakla dokunma; ♪ parmakları kullanma usulü.

**fin.ger...:** **¹~-lan.guage** *n.* işaret dili; **¹~-**

-mark *n.* parmak izi; '~-nail *n.* tırnak; '~-plate *n.* kilit aynası, parmak izini önlemek için kapıya takılan plaka; '~-post *n.* işaret direği, yön gösteren levha; '~-print 1. *n.* parmak izi; 2. *v/t.* -in parmak izini almak; '~-stall *n.* sargı.

fin.i.cal □ ['finikəl], fin.ick.ing ['~iŋ], fin.i.kin ['~kin] titiz, müşkülpesent, kılı kırk yaran.

fin.ish ['finiʃ] 1. *v/t.* & *v/i.* bit(ir)mek, tamamlamak; sona er(dir)mek; cilâlamak; *a.* ~ off, ~ up bitirmek; ⊕ apre yapmak; ~ed goods *pl.* fabrika ürünü, mamûl eşya; ~ing touch son cilâ, rötuş; have ~ed bitmiş olm.; 2. *n.* son; son iş; cilâ, rötuş; ⊕ apre; 'fin.ish.er *n.* bitiren, tamamlayan; ⊕ apre yapan.

fi.nite □ ['fainait] sınırlı, mahdut; ölümlü; ~ verb *gr.* çekimli fiil; 'fi.nite.ness *n.* fanilik.

fink *Am. sl.* [fiŋk] *n.* ihbar eden işçi, grevi bozan işçi; sevilmeyen kimse.

Finn [fin] *n.* Finlandiyalı, Finli.

Finn.ish ['finiʃ] 1. *adj.* Finlandiya'ya ait; 2. *n.* Fin dili.

fin.ny ['fini] *adj.* yüzgeçleri olan, yüzgeçli; yüzgeçlerle ilgili.

fiord [fjɔːd] *n.* fiyord.

fir [fəː] *n.* çam ağacı, köknar; Scotch ~ sarı çam; '~-cone *n.* köknar kozalağı.

fire ['faiə] 1. *n.* ateş; yangın; soba, ocak; şevk, ihtiras; cehennem, cehennem azabı; on ~ tutuşmuş ,yanan, alevler içinde; lay a ~ ateş yakmak; set ~ to ateşe vermek, tutuşturmak; 2. *v/t.* & *v/i.* tutuş(tur)mak, yakmak, ateşe vermek; patlatmak, ateş etm.; pişirmek, fırınlamak; *fig.* tahrik *veya* teşvik etm.; *a.* ~ off ateşlemek, ateş etm.; F işinden çıkarmak, koymak; ~ up sinirlenmek, parlamak; ateş etm. (at, upon -e); ~ away! F haydi başla!; '~-a.larm *n.* yangın işareti (*veya* alarmı); '~-arms *n. pl.* ateşli silahlar; '~-ball *n.* atom bombasının merkezi; akanyıldız; '~-bomb *n.* yangın bombası; '~-box *n.* ⊕ lokomotifin yakıt bölümü; '~-brand *n.* alevli odun parçası; *fig.* tahrikçi, fesatçı; '~-break *n.* ağaçsız orman yolu, yangın duvarı; '~-brick *n.* ateş tuğlası; '~-bri.gade *n.* itfaiye; '~-bug *n. Am.* F kundakçı; '~-clay *n.* ateş tuğlası yapımında kullanılan kil, çamur; '~-con.trol *n.* ✕ top ateşini idare sistemi; '~-crack.er *n.* kağıt fişeği; '~-damp *n.* ✕ grizu; '~-de.part.ment *n. Am.* itfaiye; '~-dog *n.* ocağın demir ayaklığı; '~-eat.er *n.* ateş yutan hokkabaz; çabuk sinirlenen kimse, kavgacı kimse; '~-en.gine *n.* ⊕ yan-

gın tulumbası, itfaiye arabası; '~-es.cape *n.* yangın merdiveni; '~-ex.tin.guish.er *n.* yangın söndürme aleti; '~-fly *n.* ateşböceği; '~-guard *n.* şömine pervazı; '~-in.sur.ance *n.* yangın sigortası; '~-i-rons *n. pl.* şömine takımı; '~-light.er *n.* ateş yakmak için çalı çırpı; '~-man *n.* itfaiyeci; ateşçi; '~-of.fice *n.* yangın sigortası bürosu; '~-place *n.* ocak, şömine; '~-pow.er *n.* ✕ ateş gücü; '~-plug *n.* yangın musluğu; '~-proof *adj.* ateşe dayanır, yanmaz; '~-screen *n.* ateş siperi; '~-side *n.* ocak başı; ev (hayatı); yurt; '~-sta.tion *n.* yangın istasyonu, itfaiye merkezi; '~-wood *n.* odun; '~-works *n. pl.* donanma fişekleri; *fig.* çıngar.

fir.ing ['faiəriŋ] *n.* yakma, ateşleme; ✕ ateş etme; '~-line *n.* ✕ ateş hattı; '~-par.ty, ~ squad *n.* ✕ idam mangası; cenazede saygı gösterisi olarak ateş eden bölük.

fir.kin ['fəːkin] *n.* ufak fıçı.

firm [fəːm] 1. □ sabit, metin, bükülmez, katı, sıkı, sert; kararlı; 2. *n.* firma.

fir.ma.ment ['fəːməmənt] *n.* sema, gökkubbe, asuman.

firm.ness ['fəːmnis] *n.* sağlamlık, metanet.

first [fəːst] 1. *adj.* birinci, ilk; temel; at ~ hand doğrudan doğruya, aracısız; at ~ sight ilk görüşte, ilk bakışta; 2. *adv.* önce, başta, evvelâ, ilk kez, öncelikle; tercihen; at ~ ilk önce, evvelâ; ~ of all herşeyden önce; ~ and last genelde; 3. *n.* başlangıç; birinci; birincilik; ~ of exchange ⬍ ilk poliçe; from the ~ baştan itibaren; go ~ önce gitmek, önde gitmek; için birinci mevkiyle seyahat etm.: '~-'aid post *n.* ilk yardım istasyonu; '~-born 1. *adj.* ilk doğan; 2. *n.* ilk çocuk; ~ class birinci mevki; '~-'class *adj.* birinci sınıfa ait, mükemmel; '~-fruits *n. pl.* ilk sonuç, ilk hasılat; '~-'hand *adj.* & *adv.* dolaysız, vasıtasız, direk olarak, doğrudan doğruya; 'first.ly *adv.* evvelâ, ilkin, ilk olarak, en başta.

first...: ~ name isim, ad; ~ pa.pers *pl. Am.* vatandaşlığa kabul için yapılan ilk müracaat; '~-'rate *adj.* birinci sınıf, en iyi cinsten; = first-class.

firth [fəːθ] *n.* haliç, dar körfez.

fis.cal ['fiskəl] *adj.* mali.

fish [fiʃ] 1. *n.* balık; balık eti; ✂✂ sağlamlaştırma tahtası; F adam, herif; odd ~ garip herif; have other ~ to fry daha önemli bir işi olm.; a pretty kettle of ~ karmaşık durum; 2. *v/t.* & *v/i.* balık tutmak, balık avlamak; ağız aramak (for);

**❧** sağlamlaştırmak; ~ out çekip çıkartmak; ~ in troubled waters *fig.* bulanık suda balık avlamak, karışık bir durumdan çıkar sağlamaya çalışmak; **'~-bone** *n.* kılçık.

**fish.er** [ˈfiʃə], **fish.er.man** [ˈ~mən] *n.* balıkçı; **'fish.er.y** *n.* balıkçılık; balık tarlası.

**fish-hatch.er.y** [ˈfiʃhætʃəri] *n.* balık yetiştirme (*veya* üretme).

**fish-hook** [ˈfiʃhuk] *n.* olta.

**fish.ing** [ˈfiʃiŋ] *n.* balık avı, balıkçılık; **'~-boat** *n.* balıkçı kayığı *veya* gemisi; **'~-line** *n.* olta (ipi); **'~-rod** *n.* olta kamışı; **'~-tack.le** *n.* balıkçı takımı.

**fish...**: **'~-liv.er oil** *n.* balıkyağı; **'~.monger** *n.* balıkçı, balık satan kimse; **'~-wife** *n.* balıkçı kadın; küfürbaz kadın; **'fish.y** *adj.* balık gibi; F şüpheli, inanılmaz.

**fis.sion** [ˈfiʃən] *n.* ortadan ikiye bölünme; *s.* atomic; **fis.sure** [ˈfiʃə] 1. *n.* yarık, çatlak; 2. *v/t.* & *v/i.* çatla(t)mak, yarmak, ayrılmak.

**fist** [fist] *n.* yumruk; F el yazısı; **fist.i.cuffs** [ˈ~ikʌfs] *n. pl.* yumruk yumruğa kavga.

**fis.tu.la** ♀ [ˈfistjulə] *n.* fistül.

**fit¹** [fit] 1. ☐ uygun, yaraşır, münasip; lâyık; hazır; doğru; zinde, sıhhatli; it is not ~ yakışık almaz, uygun değildir; ~ as a fiddle çok iyi, zinde, sağlıklı, turp gibi; 2. *v/t.* & *v/i.* uymak, yakışmak; yerleştirmek; donatmak; üstüne olm. (*elbise*); takmak; prova etm.; uygun hale getirmek (for, to -e); ⊕ ~ in takmak; ~ on prova etm.; takmak, uydurmak, uymak (with -e); ~ out donatmak; ~ up kurmak, hazırlamak; 3. *n.* biçim, vücuda uyma; it is a bad ~ iyi oturmuyor (*elbise*).

**fit²** [~] *n.* tutarak, hastalık nöbeti, sara; hal, ruh durumu; by ~s and starts arasıra, düzensiz olarak, kısa aralıklarla; give s.o. a ~ b-ni şaşırtmak, kızdırmak.

**fitch.ew** *zo.* [ˈfitʃuː] *n.* kokarca.

**fit.ful** ☐ [ˈfitful] düzensiz, kesik kesik; *fig.* kararsız, daldan dala konan; **'fit.ment** *n.* mobilya parçası; ~s *pl.* takım (*mobilya*); **'fit.ness** *n.* uygunluk, sağlık; **'fit-out** *n.* teçhizat; mobilya; **'fit.ter** *n.* boru işlerine bakan kimse, tesisatçı, montajcı; **'fit.ting** 1. ☐ uygun, münasip, yerinde; 2. *n.* prova; takma, montaj; ~s *pl.* tertibat; bağlantı parçaları; eşya, mobilya; **'fit-up** *n.* F geçici, kısa süreli tiyatro; *a.* ~ company seyyar tiyatro.

**five** [faiv] 1. *adj.* beş; 2. *n.* beş sayısı; ~s *sg.* bir çeşit top oyunu; **'five.fold** *adj.*

beş misli, beş kat; **fiv.er** F [ˈ~və] *n.* beş dolar *veya* pound.

**fix** [fiks] 1. *v/t.* & *v/i.* takmak; yerleş-(tir)mek; otur(t)mak; sabitleştirmek; kararlaştırmak; hazırlamak; tamir etm.; çekmek (*dikkat*); hile *veya* rüşvete başvurarak satın almak; hakkından gelmek; *part. Am.* F düzene sokmak, tamir etm.; hazırlamak; *phot.* tesbit banyosu yapmak; gözlerini dikmek (on -*e*); ~ o.s. *k-ni* bir yere yerleştirmek; ~ up kurmak, düzeltmek, ayarlamak; tedarik etm.; ~ on seçmek, karar vermek 2. *n.* F güç durum, çıkmaz; yön bulma; **fix'a-tion** *n.* tesbit; sabit fikir, gelişmemiş ve anormal bağlılık; **fix.a.tive** [ˈ~ətiv], **fix.a-ture** [ˈ~ətʃə] *n.* koruma maddesi, tesbit maddesi; **fixed** *adj.* sabit, bağlı (*a.* ♠); **fixed i.de.a** *psych.* sabit fikir; **fix.ed.ly** [ˈfiksidli] *adv.* değişmeden; gözlerini dikerek; **'fix.ed.ness** *n.* sabitlik, hareketsizlik (*a. fig.*); **fixed star** durağan yıldız; **'fix.er** *n. phot.* fiksatif, tesbit maddesi; **'fix.ing** *n.* bağlama, sağlamlaştırma, tesbit; ~s *pl. Am.* tertibat, teçhizat; garnitür; **'fix.i.ty** *n.* sabitlik, karar, sebat; **fix.ture** [ˈ~tʃə] *n.* sabit bş., demirbaş (*a. fig. person*); *spor:* fikstür; ~s *pl.* teçhizat; lighting ~ elektrik teçhizatı.

**fizz** [fiz] 1. *v/i.* fışırdamak, fıslamak; 2. *n.* fışırtı, tıslama, vızıltı; F köpüklü içki; **fiz.zle** [ˈfizl] 1. *v/i.* vızlamak, cızırdamak; *mst* ~ out vızlayıp sönmek; başarısızlığa uğramak; 2. *n.* vızıltı; fışırtı; başarısızlık, fiyasko.

**flab.ber.gast** F [ˈflæbəɡɑːst] *v/t.* şaşırtmak; be ~ed şaşırmak, hayrete düşmek.

**flab.by** ☐ [ˈflæbi] gevşek, yumuşak, sarkık; zayıf, iradesiz.

**flac.cid** ☐ [ˈflæksid] gevşek, yumuşamış, sarkmış.

**flag¹** [flæɡ] 1. *n.* bayrak, sancak, bandıra, flama; black ~ korsan bayrağı; 2. *v/t.* bayraklarla donatmak; bayrakla işaret vermek.

**flag²** [~] 1. *n.* kaldırım taşı; 2. *v/t.* bu taşlarla döşemek.

**flag³** ♀ [~] *n.* zambak, süsen.

**flag⁴** [~] *v/i.* sarkmak, bükülmek, eğilmek; kuvvetten düşmek, canlılığını kaybetmek.

**flag-cap.tain** ⚓ [ˈflæɡˈkæptin] *n.* amiral gemisi süvarisi.

**flag-day** [ˈflæɡdei] *n.* yardım toplama günü; *Am.* Flag Day Amerikan bayrağının 1777'de resmen kabulünün yıldönümü (14 Haziran).

**flag.el.lant** [ˈflædʒilənt] *n. k-ni* kırbaçlayan kimse; **flag.el.late** [ˈ~dʒəleit] v/t. kırbaçlamak; **flag.elˈla.tion** n. kırbaçlama; dövünme.

**flag.eo.let** ♪ [flædʒəuˈlet] n. küçük flüt.

**fla.gi.tious** □ [fləˈdʒiʃəs] alçakça, kötü, iğrenç; cinaî.

**flag.on** [ˈflægən] n. büyük şişe, bir çeşit sürahi.

**flag.post** [ˈflægpəust] n. bayrak direği, gönder.

**fla.grant** □ [ˈfleigrənt] iğrenç, çirkin, rezalet kabilinden; bariz, göze batan.

**flag...**; **ˈ~.ship** n. amiral gemisi; **ˈ~.staff** n. bayrak direği, gönder; **ˈ~.stone** n. kaldırım taşı.

**flail** ↙ [fleil] n. harman döveni.

**flair** [flɛə] n. yetenek, kabiliyet, Allah vergisi; seziş, anlayış.

**flake** [fleik] 1. n. kuşbaşı, lapa; ince tabaka; 2. v/i. tabaka tabaka ayrılmak; lapa lapa yağmak; **ˈflak.y** adj. lapa lapa, kat kat.

**flam** F [flæm] n. yalan, hile, saçma, martaval.

**flam.beau** [flæmbəu] n. fener.

**flame** [fleim] 1. n. alev, ateş, yalaz; fig. hiddet, hırs; aşk ateşi; 2. v/i. alevlenmek, alev alev yanmak; parlamak (a. fig.); ~ out, ~ up alevlenmek, tutuşmak; **ˈflam.ing** adj. yanmakta, tutuşmuş, alevler içinde; çok sıcak, ateşli (a. fig.).

**fla.min.go** orn. [fləˈmiŋgəu] n. flamingo.

**flan** [flæn] n. meyvalı pasta, kek.

**flange** ⊕ [flændʒ] n. yanak, halka, kenar, yaka, kulak, flanş.

**flank** [flæŋk] 1. n. böğür; yan, yan taraf, kanat; 2. v/t. bitişik olm. -e, yan tarafında olm.; kanadı geçmek; kanada hücum etm.; yandan kuşatmak.

**flan.nel** [ˈflænl] n. fanila, pazen; sabunlama bezi, mutfak bezi; **flan.nel.ette** [~ˈet] n. fanilaya benzer pamuklu kumaş, pazen; **ˈflan.nels** n. pl. fanila, fanila pantolon, fanila ceket.

**flap** [flæp] 1. n. sarkık parça, kapak; kanat; vuruş; aşırı heyecan; 2. v/t. & v/i. hafifçe vurmak -e, çarp(tır)mak, çırpmak; **ˈflap.jack** n. bir tür börek, gözleme; **ˈflap.per** n. sineklik, balığın geniş yüzgeci; sl. (1920'lerde) son moda giyinen genç kız.

**flare** [flɛə] 1. v/t. & v/i. alevlen(dir)mek; ~ up birden alevlenmek, parlamak; fig. öfkelenmek, parlamak; 2. n. ışık, parlaklık; işaret fişeği; **ˈ~ˈup** n. alevlenme, parlama; fig. ani öfke, parlama, hiddet.

**flash** [flæʃ] 1. adj. gösterişli fakat sahte, göz boyayan; 2. n. ışıltı, parıltı; fig. an; ani alev; gösteriş, fiyaka, hava; part. Am. bülten; in a ~ hemen, derhal, kısa sürede; ~ of wit aniden akla esen fikir: ~ in the pan kısa sürede neticesiz kalan teşebbüs; 3. vb. parlamak; birden gelmek; birden parıldamak; radyo veya TV ile haber yayınlamak; it ~ed on me birden aklıma geldi; **ˈ~.back** n. film: geri dönme; **ˈ~.light** n. phot. flaş; el feneri, fener; **ˈ~.point** n. yanma ısısı; **ˈflash.y** □ parıltılı, alevli; gösterişli, frapan, göze çarpan.

**flask** [flɑːsk] n. küçük şişe; matara; termos; ♔ boynuzlu imbik.

**flat** [flæt] 1. □ düz, yassı; tatsız, yavan; inik veya patlak; sıkıcı, monoton; kesin; mat; zayıflamış (akü); yüzüstü, sırtüstü; † durgun, kesat; ♪ bemol; ~ price tek fiyat; fall ~ başarısızlığa uğramak, sonuç vermemek; sing ~ ♪ bemolden okumak; 2. n. apartman dairesi; yüzey; ↓ sığlık kumsal; ♪ bemol; F basit; mot. patlak lastik; **ˈ~-boat** n. ↓ altı düz gemi; **ˈ~-foot** n. düztaban; Am. sl. polis; denizci; **ˈ~-ˈfoot.ed** adj. düztaban; Am. F açık açık, dobra dobra, kesin; **ˈ~.i.ron** n. ütü; **ˈflat.ness** n. düzlük, yassılık: tatsızlık, yavanlık; † durgunluk, kesatlık; **ˈflat.ten** v/t. & v/i. yassılatmak, yassılaşmak, düzleş(tir)mek; ~ out düzleş(tir)mek, açmak yassılaş(tır)mak; dalıştan sonra uçağı yerle paralel duruma getirmek.

**flat.ter** [ˈflætə] v/t. pohpohlamak, göklere çıkarmak, yağ çekmek; **ˈflat.ter.er** n. dalkavuk, yağcı; **ˈflat.ter.ing** n. pohpohlama, yağ çekme; **ˈflat.ter.y** n. dalkavukluk, yağcılık, övgü.

**flat.u.lence, flat.u.len.cy** [ˈflætjuləns(i)] n. gaz, şişkinlik; **ˈflat.u.lent** □ midede gaz yapan; gaza ait; şişkin.

**flaunt** [flɔːnt] vb. gösteriş yapmak, hava atmak, kibirle göstermek; dalgalanmak (bayrak).

**fla.vo(u)r** [ˈfleivə] 1. n. tat, lezzet, çeşni, koku; 2. v/t. tat veya lezzet vermek -e; **ˈfla.vo(u)red** comb. ...lezzetinde; **ˈfla.vo(u)r.ing** n. baharat, tat veren bş; **ˈfla.vo(u)r.less** adj. tatsız, lezzetsiz.

**flaw** [flɔː] 1. n. çatlak, yarık; noksan, kusur (♉, ⊕), defo; ↓ kısa süreli şiddetli rüzgâr; 2. v/t. & v/i. çatla(t)mak; defolu olm.; kusurlu olm.; fig. hasara uğratmak; zarara sokmak; **ˈˈflaw.less** □ kusursuz.

**flax** ♀ [flæks] *n.* keten; **'flax.en**, **'flax.y** *adj.* keten; ketene benzer; soluk sarı.

**flay** [flei] *v/t.* derisini yüzmek; *fig.* azarlamak, haşlamak; **'flay.er** *n.* hayvan derisi yüzen.

**flea** [fli:] *n.* pire; **'~.bane** *n.* ♀ pireotu; **'~-bite** *n.* pire ısırması; *fig.* hafif rahatsızlık.

**fleck** [flek] **1.** *n.* nokta, benek, leke, zerre; **2.** *v/t.* beneklemek; lekelemek.

**flec.tion** [ˈflekʃən] *s.* flexion.

**fled** [fled] *pret. and p.p. of* flee.

**fledge** [fledʒ] *v/t. & v/i.* tüylenmek; tüy takmak; tüyleninceye kadar beslemek; **fledg(e).ling** [ˈ~liŋ] *n.* yeni tüylenmiş yavru kuş; *fig.* acemi çaylak.

**flee** [fli:] *(irr.) v/t. & v/i.* kaçmak, tüymek, firar etm. (from *-den*); *a.* ~ from sakınmak, kaçınmak *-den*.

**fleece** [fli:s] **1.** *n.* yapak, yünlü, koyun postu; **2.** *v/t.* kırkmak *(koyun)*; *b-ni* soymak, çok parasını almak, kazıklamak, yolmak; **'fleec.y** *adj.* yün gibi.

**fleer** [fliə] **1.** *n.* alay, eğlenme, dalga geçme; **2.** *v/i.* alay etm., dalga geçmek (at).

**fleet** [fli:t] **1.** ☐ *poet.* çevik, süratli, hızlı, çabuk, atik; **2.** *n.* donanma, filo; ♀ Street basın, Londra basını; **3.** *v/t. & v/i.* çabuk geçmek; yok olm.; hızla uçmak; hareket etm.; yerini değiştirmek; **'fleet.ing** ☐ çabuk geçen, kısa süren, ömürsüz.

**Flem.ing** [ˈflemiŋ] *n.* Flaman; **'Flem.ish 1.** *adj.* Flamanlar bölgesine ait; **2.** *n.* Flaman dili.

**flesh** [fleʃ] **1.** *n.* et; vücut, ten; meyvenin etli kısmı; beden; *fig.* şehvet duygusu; make s.o.'s ~ creep tüylerini ürpertmek, tüylerini diken diken yapmak; **2.** *v/t. & v/i.* kan dökmek *(a. fig.)*; eti sıyırmak; etle beslemek; etle kaplamak; şişmanlamak; **'~-brush** *n.* masaj fırçası; **'flesh.ings** *n. pl.* ten renginde külotlu çorap; **'flesh.ly** *adj.* etli, şişman; vücuda ait, bedene ait; **'flesh.y** *adj.* şişman, etli butlu; ete ait.

**flew** [flu:] *pret. of* fly¹ 2.

**flex** ∮ [fleks] *n.* esnek kablo; **flex.i.bil.i.ty** [~ə'biliti] *n.* esneklik, elastikiyet; *fig.* uysallık, yumuşak başlılık; **'flex.i.ble** ☐ bükülebilir, esnek; uysal; **flex.ion** [ˈflekʃən] *n.* bükülme, esneme; *gr.* çekim; dirsek; **flex.or** [ˈ~ksə] *n.* fleksör kas; **flex.ure** [ˈflekʃə] *n.* bükülme, katlanma; dirsek.

**flib.ber.ti.gib.bet** [ˈflibəti'dʒibit] *n.* dedikocu kimse.

**flick** [flik] **1.** *v/t.* hafifçe vurmak, fiske

vurmak (at *-e*); **2.** *n.* hafif vuruş, fiske; **~s** *n. pl. sl.* sinema.

**flick.er** [ˈflikə] **1.** *v/i.* titremek, oynamak, titrek yanmak; ileri geri oynamak; **2.** *n.* titrek ışık; *Am.* ağaçkakan.

**flick-knife** [ˈfliknaif] *n.* sustalı bıçak.

**fli.er** [ˈflaiə] *s.* flyer.

**flight** [flait] *n.* uçuş, uçma; uçak yolculuğu; çabuk geçme; yükselme; sıra; *a.* ~ of stairs bir kat merdiven; ⚓, ✕ hava filosu; firar, kaçış; put to ~ kaçırtmak; take (to) ~ kaçmak, *sl.* tüymek; **'~-com'mand.er** *n.* uçuş pilotu; **'~-deck** *n.* ⚓ *(uçak gemisi)* uçuş güvertesi; pilot mahalli; **'~-lieu'ten.ant** *n.* pilot yüzbaşı; **'flight.y** ☐ dönek, kararsız; hafifmeşrep, havaî; sorumsuz; budala.

**flim.sy** [ˈflimzi] **1.** *adj.* ince, gevşek, seyrek; sudan *(bahane)*; kolayca yırtılabilen; **2.** *n.* pelür, kopya kâğıdı; *sl.* kâğıt para; telgraf.

**flinch** [flintʃ] *v/i.* sakınmak, kaçınmak, ürkmek, çekinmek (from *-den*).

**fling** [fliŋ] **1.** *n.* fırlatma, atma, atış; fırlayış; *fig.* taş, iğneli söz; hareketli dans; have one's ~ dilediğince eğlenmek, kurtlarını dökmek; have a ~ at teşebbüs etm., denemek; **2.** *(irr.) v/t. & v/i.* at(ıl)mak, fırlatmak, savurmak *(küfür)*; sallamak; hışımla çıkmak; *a.* ~ out dış. kıyameti koparmak, gürültü yapmak; ~ o.s. hızla atılmak; ~ away kaldırıp atmak; ~ forth atmak, savurmak; ~ open hızla açmak.

**flint** [flint] *n.* çakmaktaşı; **'flint.y** *adj.* çok sert; *fig.* katı yürekli, haşin.

**flip** [flip] **1.** *n.* fiske, hafif vuruş; ✈ *sl.* uçakla zevk için yapılan kısa gezinti; takla; bir içki çeşidi; **2.** *vb.* fiske vurmak; parmakla havaya fırlatmak; öbür yüzünü çevirmek *(plak vs.)*; sinirlenmek.

**flip-flap** [ˈflipflæp] *n.* takla, perende.

**flip.pan.cy** [ˈflipənsi] *n.* küstahlık, düşüncesizlik; **'flip.pant** ☐ küstah, kendini bilmez.

**flip.per** [ˈflipə] *n.* balık kanadı; palet.

**flirt** [flə:t] **1.** *n.* flört eden; işvebaz *b-i*; ani hareket; **2.** *v/i.* flört etm.; fırlamak; **flir'ta.tion** *n.* flört; **flir'ta.tious** *adj.* flörtçü, işvebaz, F fındıkçı.

**flit** [flit] *v/i.* geçmek; çırpınmak; oradan oraya dolaşmak.

**flitch** [flitʃ] *n.* domuz döşü.

**flit.ter** [ˈflitə] *v/i.* kanat çırpmak, çırpınmak.

**fliv.ver** *Am.* F [ˈflivə] **1.** *n.* külüstür otomobil; **2.** *vb.* başarısızlığa uğramak.

**float** [fləut] **1.** *n.* olta mantarı; şamandıra, duba; ⊕ flotör; ⬦ pervane tahtası; *thea.* ön sahne ışıkları; geçit resminde kullanılan araba; meyvalı gazoz; **2.** *v/t. & v/i.* yüz(dür)mek; suyun yüzünde durmak; hava akımına kapılıp sürüklenmek; *fig.* başlatmak, harekete geçirmek; kurmak; ⊤ satışa arzetmek *(hisse senedi, tahvil)*; yaymak; **ıfloat.a.ble** *adj.* yüzebilen, su üstünde durabilen; **ıfloat.age** *n.* yüzen şey; **floatˈa.tion** *s.* flotation; **ıfloat.ing** *adj.* yüzen, değişen, seyyar; ~ bridge tombaz köprü, dubalı köprü; ~ capital döner sermaye; ~ ice suda yüzen buz kütlesi; ~ kidney yer değiştiren böbrek; ~ light fener dubası, fenerli şamandıra; **ıfloat-plane** *n.* deniz uçağı.

**flock¹** [flɔk] **1.** *n.* sürü; küme; kalabalık, yığın; cemaat; **2.** *v/i.* toplanmak, başına üşüşmek.

**flock²** [~] *n.* *(part. yün)* yumak, saç yumağı; yün artığı.

**floe** [fləu] *n.* buz kitlesi.

**flog** [flɔg] *v/t.* kamçılamak, dövmek; ~ a dead horse boşuna çaba sarfetmek; **ıflog.ging** *n.* dayak, kamçılama.

**flood** [flʌd] **1.** *n. a.* ~-tide sel, seylap, taşkın; tufan; met ,kabarma; the 2 Nuh tufanı; **2.** *v/t. & v/i.* coşmak, taşmak, su basmak, sel basmak; istilâ etm.; **ˈ~-dis-as.ter** *n.* sel felâketi; **ˈ~-gate** *n.* set, bent kapağı; **ˈ~.light 1.** *n.* projektör; **2.** *v/t.* projektörle aydınlatmak.

**floor** [flɔː] **1.** *n.* döşeme, zemin; kat; dip; asgari ücret; ✓ harman yeri; *parl.* meclis salonunun üyelere ayrılmış kısmı; mecliste konuşma hakkı; *sl.* borsa binası; ~ leader *Am. (yasama meclisi)* grup başkanı; ~ price asgari ücret, taban ücret; ~ show eğlence programı; hold the ~ *parl.* mecliste konuşma yapmak; be kept on the ~ ortaya atılmak, ileri sürülmek; take the ~ mecliste söz almak; **2.** *v/t.* tahta *veya* parke döşemek *-e*; yere yıkmak *-i*; şaşırtmak *-i*; yenmek *-i*; **ˈ~-cloth** *n.* tahta bezi; **ıfloor.er** *n.* döşemeci; **ıfloor.ing** *n.* döşemelik; **ıfloor-lamp** *n.* ayaklı abajur; **ıfloor-walk.er** *n. Am.* mağazada müşterilere yardım eden görevli; **ıfloor-wax** *n.* döşeme cilası.

**flop** F [flɔp] **1.** *v/t. & v/i.* çırpınmak; çöküvermek; düşürmek; devrilmek; *sl.* başarısızlığa uğramak, tutmamak *(kitap, piyes)*; **2.** *n.* çarpma; çarpma sesi; başarısız teşebbüs; başarısızlık; çökme; ~ house *Am. sl.* ucuz otel; **ıflop.py** *adj.* yumuşak; gevşek; başarısız.

**flo.ra** [ˈflɔːrə] *n.* flora, bitey, bir bölgede yetişen bitkilerin tümü; **ıflo.ral** *adj.* çiçeklere ait; ~ design çiçek deseni.

**flo.res.cence** [flɔːˈresns] *n.* çiçek açma, çiçeklenme devresi.

**flor.id** □ [ˈflɔrid] çok süslü; kırmızı *(yüz)*; yüzüne ateş basmış; **ıflor.id.ness** *n.* süslülük; kırmızılık; canlılık.

**flor.in** [ˈflɔrin] *n.* iki şilin kıymetinde İngiliz parası; Hollanda florini.

**flo.rist** [ˈflɔrist] *n.* çiçekçi.

**floss** [flɔs] *n.* bükülmemiş ham ipek, floş; kısa ipek telleri; ~ silk ham ibrişim; **ıfloss.y** *adj.* ince tüylü; ipeğe ait; süslü.

**flo.ta.tion** [fləuˈteiʃən] *n.* yüzme; su üzerinde durma; ⊤ sermaye temini, mali destek temini.

**flo.til.la** ⬦ [fləuˈtilə] *n.* küçük filo, flotilla.

**flot.sam** ⚓ [ˈflɔtsəm] *n.* gemi enkazı.

**flounce¹** [flauns] **1.** *n.* fırfır, volan; **2.** *v/t.* fırfırla süslemek, volan koymak.

**flounce²** [~] *v/i.* yerinden fırlayıp yürümek; fırlamak; sabırsızlıkla hareket etm.

**floun.der¹** *ichth.* [ˈflaundə] *n.* pisibalığı.

**floun.der²** [~] *v/i.* boşuna çabalamak; zorluk çekmek; bata çıka yürümek.

**flour** [ˈflauə] **1.** *n.* un; **2.** *v/t.* una bulamak, un serpmek.

**flour.ish** [ˈflʌriʃ] **1.** *n.* gösterişli hareket; paraf. gösteriş, süs; sallama, savurma; ♪ coşkulu parça, fanfar; **2.** *v/t. & v/i.* sallamak, savurmak; gelişmek; bayındır olm.; sağlıklı olm.; gözde olm.; ortaya çıkmak.

**flout** [flaut] *v/t. & v/i.* karşı koymak, itaat etmemek; alay etm., eğlenmek; küçümsemek.

**flow** [fləu] **1.** *n.* cereyan, akıntı; met, kabarma; ~ of spirits neşe; neşe dolu; **2.** *v/i.* akmak; dalgalanmak; sallanmak; sarkmak; kabarmak; ~ from *-in* sebebi olm., *-den* gelmek.

**flow.er** [ˈflauə] **1.** *n.* çiçek; *fig.* seçkin ve güzide *bş*; olgunlaşmış *bş*; en iyi kısım; say it with ~s süslü bir şekilde söylemek; **2.** *v/i.* çiçeklenmek, çiçek açmak; **flow.er.et** [ˈ~rit] *n.* küçük çiçek; **ıflow.er.i.ness** *n.* gösteriş *(a. fig.);* **ıflow.er-pot** *n.* saksı; **ıflow.er.y** *adj.* çiçekli; süslü, gösterişli.

**flown** [fləun] *p.p. of* fly¹ 2.

**flu** F [fluː] = influenza.

**flub.dub** *Am. sl.* [ˈflʌbdʌb] *n.* boş laf; palavra. saçmalık, saftasa.

**fluc.tu.ate** [ˈflʌktjueit] *v/i.* değişmek, düzensiz olm., dalgalanmak; **fluc.tuˈa.tion** *n.* değişme, dalgalanma.

**flue** [fluː] *n.* baca, boru.

**flu.en.cy** ['flu:ǝnsi] *n.* akıcılık, ifade düzgünlüğü; **'flu.ent** □ akıcı *(söz)*, düzgün, pürüzsüz.

**fluff** [flʌf] **1.** *n.* tüy, hav; kuştüyü; kırpıntı; yumuşak kürk; *fig.* acemice yapılan atılım; **2.** *v/t.* silkinip tüylerini kabartmak; sallamak, kabartmak *veya* yaymak; söyleyeceği sözü unutmak *veya* yanlış söylemek; **'fluff.y** *adj.* tüy gibi yumuşak, yumuşacık; kabarık.

**flu.id** ['flu:id] **1.** *adj.* akıcı, sıvı, akışan; *fig.* sabit olmayan *(fikir)*; **2.** *n.* sıvı madde; **flu'id.i.ty** *n.* akıcılık.

**fluke** [flu:k] *n.* gemi demirinin tırnağı; F şans, rastlantı, tesadüf.

**flume** [flu:m] *n.* suni kanal.

**flum.mer.y** ['flʌmǝri] *n.* bir çeşit yemek; bir tatlı çeşidi; boş laf.

**flum.mox** F ['flʌmǝks] *v/t.* şaşırtmak.

**flung** [flʌŋ] *pret. & p.p. of* fling 2.

**flunk** *Am.* F [flʌŋk] *v/t. & v/i.* başaramamak, çakmak, kalmak *(sınavda)*; sınavda bırakmak.

**flunk.(e)y** ['flʌŋki] *n.* üniformalı uşak, hizmetçi; dalkavuk, yağcı; **'flunk.ey.ism** *n.* uşaklık.

**flu.o.res.cence** *phys.* [fluǝ'resns] *n.* fluoresans, flüorışı; **flu.or'es.cent** *adj.* fluoresans, flüorışıl; ~ lamp fluoresan lambası.

**flur.ry** ['flʌri] **1.** *n.* ani rüzgâr; sağanak; telaş; heyecan; acele; **2.** *v/t.* telaşlandırmak, telaşa sokmak, sinirlendirmek.

**flush** [flʌʃ] **1.** *adj.* ⊕ bir seviyede, düz; bol parası olan; *fig.* bol, dopdolu, çok; **2.** *n.* kızarma; taşkınlık; galeyan; akıtma; *iskambil:* floş; **3.** *v/t. & v/i.* birden akmak; yüzü kızar(t)mak; cesaretlendirmek; bol suyla yıkamak; taşmak; kanatlanıp uçmak; ürkütüp kaçırmak; düzlemek, bir seviyeye getirmek.

**flus.ter** ['flʌstǝ] **1.** *n.* telaş, şaşkınlık; **2.** *v/t.* telaşa düşürmek, şaşırtmak; *v/i.* şaşırmak, telaş etm.

**flute** [flu:t] **1.** *n.* ♪ flavta, flüt; ⚠ yiv, oluk; **2.** *v/t. & v/i.* flüt çalmak; *fig.* ötmek; oluk *veya* yiv açmak; **'flut.ist** *n.* flütçü.

**flut.ter** ['flʌtǝ] **1.** *n.* çırpınma; telaş, heyecan; kanat sarsıntısı; F bahis; have a ~ bahse girmek; **2.** *v/t. & v/i.* çırpınmak; kanat çırpmak; telaşa düşürmek; telaşlanmak; düzensiz hareket etm.

**flux** [flʌks] *n. fig.* akış; akıntı; değişme; eritici madde; ⚇ akıntı; ~ and reflux gelgit, meddücezir.

**fly¹** [flai] **1.** *n.* sinek; uçuş; fermuar; pantolonun düğmeli ön kısmı; çadırdaki bez kapı; bayrak ucu; *Am. beysbol:* havaya atılan top; *flies pl. thea.* sahne yukarısındaki dekor değiştirme teçhizatı; **2.** *(irr.) v/t. & v/i.* uçmak; uçakla gitmek; uçakla taşımak; çabuk gitmek; fırlamak; atılmak; uçurmak; dalgalandırmak; *-den* kaçmak; ~ high hırslı olm.; ~ at üstüne saldırmak; ~ in the face of açıkça karşı gelmek; ~ into a passion *veya* rage öfkelenmek, sinirlenmek; ~ off uçup gitmek; ~ blind *veya* on instruments köruçuş yapmak, sadece aletler yardımıyla uçmak; ~ out at karşı çıkmak; ~ open hızla açılmak; send s.o. ~ing vurup düşürmek, kaçırtmak.

**fly²** *sl.* [~] *adj.* uyanık, kurnaz, haberdar, aldatması güç.

**fly...:** '~-blow **1.** *n.* sinek yumurtası; sinek kurdu istilası; **2.** *v/t. -e* yumurta bırakmak; *fig.* kirletmek; bozmak; '~-blown *adj.* bozulmuş, kurtlanmış; *fig.* kötü durumda; '~-catch.er *n.* sinekcil; sinek kapanı.

**fly.er** ['flaiǝ] *n.* hızlı giden bş, *(part. ✈)*, pilot, havacı; take a ~ *Am.* F riskli bir işe girmek; ~s *pl.* ⚠ dış merdiven.

**fly-flap** ['flaiflæp] *n.* sinek raketi.

**fly.ing** ['flaiiŋ] **1.** *n.* uçma, havacılık, uçuş; **2.** *adj.* uçan; havacılıkla ilgili; ~ boat deniz uçağı; ~ buttress ⚠ duvar dirseği; ~ deck uçuş güvertesi; ~ field havaalanı; ~ jump koşarak atlama; ~ machine uçak, tayyare; ~ school uçuş okulu; ~ squad hızlı polis ekibi; ~ start hızlı başlangıç; ~ visit kısa ziyaret, kapıdan uğrama; '~-of.fi.cer *n.* üsteğmen.

**fly...:** '~-leaf *n. typ.* bir kitabın başında ve sonundaki boş sayfa; '~-o.ver *n.* üstgeçit; ✈ = '~-past *n.* hava geçit resmi; '~-weight *n. boks:* sineksiklet; '~-wheel *n.* volan, düzenteker.

**foal** [fǝul] **1.** *n.* tay, sıpa; in ~, with ~ gebe *(kısrak)*; **2.** *v/i.* tay doğurmak.

**foam** [fǝum] **1.** *n.* köpük; **2.** *v/i.* köpürmek *(a. fig.)*; '~-rub.ber *n.* sünger; '**foam.y** *adj.* köpüklü.

**fob¹** [fɔb] *n.* saat cebi; saat kösteği.

**fob²** [~] *vb.:* ~ off *fig.* hile yapmak, kazık atmak, aldatmak.

**fo.cal** ['fǝukǝl] *adj.* odaksal; ~ length, ~ distance *phot.* odak uzaklığı; ~-plane shutter *phot.* yarıklı diyafram.

**fo'c's.le** ['fǝuksl] = forecastle.

**fo.cus** ['fǝukǝs] **1.** *n. pl. a.* **fo.ci** ['fǝusai] odak, mihrak; *fig. a.* merkez; **2.** *v/t. & v/i.* bir noktaya getirmek; biraraya gelmek; ayar etm.; dikkatini toplamak;

konsantre olm.; ¹fo.cus.(s)ing screen phot. buzlu cam.

fod.der ['fɔdə] 1. n. yem; 2. v/t. yemlemek, beslemek.

foe poet. [fəu] n. düşman; ¹.-man n. † düşman.

foe.tus ⅋ ['fi:təs] n. cenin, dölüt.

fog [fɔg] 1. n. sis; fig. bunaklık, zihin karışıklığı; phot. donukluk; 2. vb. mst fig. şaşırtmak; phot. bulanıklaşmak, donuklaşmak; ¹.-bank n. kalın sis tabakası; ¹.-bound adj. ⅃ sise yakalanmış; sis yüzünden hareket edemeyen.

fo.gey F ['fəugi] n.: old ~ geri kafalı kimse.

fog.gy □ ['fɔgi] sisli; fig. bulanık, belirsiz; ¹fog-horn n. sis düdüğü; ¹fog-sig.nal n. sis işareti.

fo.gy Am. ['fəugi] = fogey.

foi.ble fig. ['fɔibl] n. kusur, zaaf.

foil¹ [fɔil] n. ince yaprak, foya, yaldız kâğıdı; ayna sırı; fig. engel.

foil² [~] 1. v/t. engellemek, işini bozmak, boşa çıkarmak; 2. n. fenc. kılıç.

foist [fɔist] vb.: ~ s.th. (off) on s.o. hile ile kabul ettirmek, yutturmak.

fold¹ [fəuld] 1. n. ağıl; sürü; fig. cemaat; 2. v/t. ağıla kapamak.

fold² [~] 1. n. kat, kıvrım, büklüm; 2. v/t. & v/i. bükmek; katla(n)mak; karıştırmak; (elleri) kavuşturmak; a. ~ up sarmak; ~ down bükmek, katlamak, kıvırmak; ~ in one's arms kollarını kavuşturmak, ~ up F çökmek, sona ermek; ¹fold.er n. dosya, klasör; broşür; kutu, kap.

fold.ing ['fəuldiŋ] adj. katlama; katlanabilir; kırma; ¹.-bed n. katlanır karyola; ¹.-boat n. sökülüp takılabilen kayık; ¹.-door(s pl.) katlanır kapı; ¹.-screen n. katlanır paravana; ¹.-seat n. katlanır sandalye.

fo.li.age ['fəuliidʒ] n. ağaç yaprakları.

fo.li.o ['fəuliəu] n. kitap yaprağı; sayfa numarası; hesap defterindeki karşılıklı iki sayfa; iki yapraklık kâğıt tabakası; büyük boy kitap, cilt.

folk [fəuk] n. pl. halk, insanlar, ahali; ~s pl. F ev halkı; aile; akrabalar; ¹.-dance n. halk oyunu; ~.lore ['~lɔ:] n. folklor; ¹.-song n. halk şarkısı, türkü.

fol.low ['fɔləu] v/t. & v/i. takip etm., izlemek; anlamak; mesleğinde çalışmak; riayet etm., uymak; örnek almak; sonucu çıkmak; to ~ arkadan, geriden; it ~s that ...sonucu çıkıyor, ...demektir; ~ out sonuna kadar götürmek; ~ the sea denizci olm.; ~ up kovalamak; ¹fol.low.er

n. taraftar, F hayran; ¹fol.low.ing 1. n. taraftarlar, tabi olanlar; the ~ şunlar, aşağıdakiler; 2. adj. izleyen; ertesi, müteakip; ~ wind arkadan esen rüzgâr.

fol.ly ['fɔli] n. aptallık, ahmaklık; aptalca şey.

fo.ment [fəu'ment] v/t. ⅋ pansuman yapmak; fig. kışkırtmak; fo.men¹ta.tion n. pansuman; pansuman için kullanılan şey; tahrik, kışkırtma; fo¹ment.er n. fig. kışkırtıcı, tahrikçi.

fond [fɔnd] seven (of -i); düşkün -e; be ~ of düşkün olm. -e, hoşlanmak -den; be ~ of dancing dansa düşkün olm.

fon.dant ['fɔndənt] n. bir çeşit tatlı, fondan.

fon.dle ['fɔndl] v/t. okşamak, sevmek.

fond.ness ['fɔndnis] n. sevgi, düşkünlük.

font eccl. [fɔnt] n. vaftiz kurnası.

food [fu:d] n. yiyecek, besin, yemek, gıda; yem; ¹.-stuff n. gıda maddesi.

fool¹ [fu:l] 1. n. budala, enayi, aptal, ahmak, alık kimse; make a ~ of s.o. enayi yerine koymak, küçük düşürmek; make a ~ of o.s. rezil olm., kepaze olm.; ~ 's paradise geçici mutluluk, aylaklık; 2. adj. Am. F sersem, şaşkın; 3. v/t. & v/i. aldatmak; boşuna vakit geçirmek; aptalca davranmak; ~ about aptalca davranıp durmak; ~ (a)round part. Am. aylak aylak dolaşmak, boşuna vakit geçirmek; ~ away F tembellikle vakit geçirmek, israf etm.

fool² [~] n. kremalı meyve.

fool.er.y ['fu:ləri] n. aptalca hareket, budalalık, ahmaklık; ¹fool.hard.y □ delice cesur; ¹fool.ish □ aptal, akılsız, budalaca; ¹fool.ish.ness n. enayilik, akılsızlık; ¹fool-proof adj. ⊕ emniyetli, sağlam; kusursuz; fool.scap ['fu:lskæp] n. kâğıt ölçüsü.

foot [fut] 1. n. pl. feet [fi:t] ayak; kadem (30.48 cm); adım; dip, (dağ) etek; en alçak kısım; temel, esas; ✕ piyade; poet. vezin tef'ilesi; on ~ yaya, yürüyerek; be on one's feet ayakta olm.; fig. hastalıktan sonra ayağa kalkmak, iyileşmek; put one's ~ down ayak diremek, kararlı olm., karşı çıkmak; I have put my ~ into it F pot kırdım, çam devirdim; set on ~ başlatmak, yürütmek; set ~ on ayak basmak; 2. v/t. & v/i. ayak kısmını örmek; dansetmek; yaya gitmek; seyretmek (gemi); ödemek; yekûnunu çıkarmak, mst ~ up toplamak, yekûn çıkarmak; ~ it yaya gitmek; ~ the bill hesabı ödemek; ¹foot.age n. uzunluk.

foot...: ¹.-and-¹mouth dis.ease bir sığır

200

hastalığı; **'~.ball** *n.* futbol; **'~.board** *n.*
ayakları dayayacak tahta; **'~.boy** *n.* bel-
boy, *(otelde)* uşak; **'~-brake** *n.* ayak freni; **'~-bridge** *n.* yaya köprüsü, köprü geçit.
**foot.ed** ['futid] *comb.* ...ayaklı; **'foot.er** *n.*
F futbol.
**foot**...: **'~.fall** *n.* ayak sesi; **'~-gear** *n.* ayak
giyecekleri; **♀ Guards** *pl.* ✗ piyade mu-
hafız alayı; **'~-hills** *n. pl.* dağ eteklerin-
deki tepeler; **'~.hold** *n.* ayak basacak
yer; *fig.* sağlam yer.
**foot.ing** ['futiŋ] *n.* ayak basacak yer;
mevki; ilişki; ✗ hal, durum, vaziyet; **be
on a friendly ~ with s.o.** ...ile arası iyi
olm.; **upon the same ~ as** ... ile aynı durumda; **get a ~** yer edinmek; **lose one's
~** ayağı kaymak, tökezlemek.
**foo.tle** F ['fuːtl] *vb.* boşuna vakit geçirmek, maskaralık etm., aptalca konuş-
mak *veya* hareket etm.; **2.** *n.* ahmaklık,
budalalık.
**foot.lights** *thea.* ['futlaits] *n. pl.* sahne
önündeki bir sıra ışık; sahne hayatı.
**foot.ling** ['fuːtliŋ] *adj.* önemsiz, değersiz,
ufak tefek.
**foot**...: **'~.man** *n.* üniformalı uşak; **'~-mark**
*n.* ayak izi; **'~-note 1.** *n.* dipnot; **2.** *vb.*
dipnot koymak; **'~.pad** *n.* eşkiya, haydut; **'~-pas.sen.ger** *n.* yaya; **'~-path** *n.*
keçi yolu, patika; **'~-print** *n.* ayak izi;
**'~-race** *n.* koşu; **'~-rule** *n. (tahta veya
madeni)* metre; **'~-slog** *v/i. sl.* bata çıka yürümek, zorlukla yürümek; **'~-sore**
*adj.* yürümekten ayakları şişmiş;
**'~.stalk** *n.* ♣ çiçek sapı, yaprak sapı;
**'~.step** *n.* adım; ayak sesi; ayak izi;
**'~.stool** *n.* ayak taburesi; **'~.wear** = foot-
-gear; **'~.work** *n. spor.* ayak hakimiyeti.
**fop** [fɔp] *n.* züppe; **'fop.per.y** *n.* züppelik; **'fop.pish** ☐ züppece.
**for** [fɔː; fə; f] **1.** *prp. mst* için; hususunda; amacıyla; *-e* karşı; *-e* göre; yerine;
adına; lehinde, taraftarı, *-den* dolayı;
sebebiyle; sonucu olarak; *-e* rağmen;
zarfında, *-den* beri; **come ~** dinner yemeğe gelmek; **the train ~** London Londra'ya
gidecek tren; **it is ~** you to decide karar
vermek size kalmış; **were it not ~** that o
olmasaydı; **he is a fool ~** doign that onu
yaptığı için aptaldır; **~** three days üç
gündür, üç günden beri; **I walked ~** a
mile bir mil yürüdüm; **I ~** one kendi hesabıma; **ben de;** **~** sure! şüphesiz!, elbette!; **it is good ~** us to be here burada
olmamız iyi olur; **the snow was too deep
~** them to go on kar devam edemeyecek-

leri kadar kalındı; **2.** *cj. -den* dolayı,
*-diği* için, çünkü, zira.
**for.age** ['fɔridʒ] **1.** *n.* ot, saman, hayvan
yemi, arpa; **2.** *v/i.* yiyecek peşinde koşmak, yiyecek aramak.
**for.as.much** [fərəz'mʌtʃ] *cj.:* **~ as** madem
ki, *-den* dolayı, sebebiyle.
**for.ay** ['fɔrei] **1.** *n.* çapul, akın, yağma;
**2.** *v/i.* yağma etm.
**for.bade** [fə'bæd] *pret. of* forbid.
**for.bear¹** ['fɔːbɛə] *n.* ata, cet.
**for.bear²** [fɔː'bɛə] *(irr.) v/t. & v/i.* kaçınmak, sakınmak, çekinmek (from *-den*);
sabretmek; **for'bear.ance** *n.* sabır, tahammül; sakınma, kaçınma.
**for.bid** [fə'bid] *(irr.) v/t.* yasak etm., yasaklamak, menetmek; **God ~!** Allah esirgesin!; **for'bid.den** *p.p. of* forbid; **~ fruit**
yasak meyve, ahlak dışı zevk; **for'bidding** ☐ sert, haşin, ürkütücü, nahoş.
**for.bore, for.borne** [fɔː'bɔː(n)] *pret. & p.p.
of* forbear².
**force** [fɔːs] **1.** *n. mst* güç, kuvvet, kudret;
şiddet, zor, baskı, tazyik; otorite, nü-
fuz; **the ~** polis; **armed ~s** *pl.* silahlı kuvvetler; **by ~** zorla; **come (put) in ~** yürürlüğe girmek (koymak); **2.** *v/t.* zorlamak,
mecbur etm.; sıkıştırmak; zorla almak;
kırıp açmak; turfanda sebze ve meyve
yetiştirmek; zorla yapmak; **~ back** geri
sürmek, püskürtmek; **~ down** ✈ inişe
zorlamak; **~ s.o.'s hand** *b-ne* istemiye-
rek *bş* yaptırmak, bir işi yapmaya zorlamak; **~ on** harekete geçirmek; kışkırtmak; **~ open** kırıp açmak; **forced** *(adv.*
**forc.ed.ly** ['~idli]) mecburî; **~ loan** mecburî borçlanma; **~ landing** mecburî iniş;
**~ march** mecburî yürüyüş; **~ sale** mecburî satış; **force.ful** ☐ ['~ful] güçlü, etkili, tesirli, kuvvetli; **'force.meat** *n.* baharatlı kıyma.
**for.ceps** ♀ ['fɔːseps] *n. sg. & pl.* pens, kıskaç, forseps.
**force-pump** ['fɔːspʌmp] *n.* tazyik pompası.
**forc.er** ⊕ ['fɔːsə] *n.* piston.
**for.ci.ble** ☐ ['fɔːsəbl] zora dayanan, mecburî; etkili; ikna edici.
**forc.ing-house** ['fɔːsiŋhaus] *n.* limonluk,
ser.
**ford** [fɔːd] **1.** *n.* nehir geçidi, sığ geçit;
**2.** *v/t. (nehir vs.)* sığ yerden geçmek;
**'ford.a.ble** *adj.* yürüyerek geçilebilir.
**fore** [fɔː] **1.** *adv.* ön tarafta, baş tarafta,
önde; **~ and aft** ⬇ baştan kıça
kadar; **2.** *n.* ön; baş taraf, pruva; **to the
~** elde mevcut, hazır bulunan; önemli;
**come (bring) to the ~** başa geç(ir)mek,

öne geç(ir)mek; 3. *adj.* ön taraftaki, öndeki; ilk; '~.**arm**¹ *n.* önkol; ~'**arm**² *v/t.* önceden silahlandırmak; ~'**bode** *v/t.* işareti olm.; önceden haber vermek; önceden hissetmek; ~'**bod.ing** *n.* önsezi; '~.**cast** 1. *n.* hava tahmini, tahmin; 2. (*irr. cast*) *v/t.* önceden söylemek; önceden tahmin etm.; '~.**cas.tle** ↓ ['**fɑuksl**] *n.* baş kasarası; ~.**close** [fɔ:'klǝuz] *v/t.* & *v/i.* engel olm.; ipotekli malı sahibinin elinden almak; ~'**clo.sure** [~ʒǝ] *n.* ipotekli malı sahibinin elinden alma; '~.**court** *n.* ön avlu, ön bahçe; ~'**date** *v/t.* önceden tarih koymak; ~'**doom** *v/t.* önceden hüküm vermek; önceden belli etm.; '~.**fa.ther** *n.* ata, cet; '~.**fin.ger** *n.* işaret parmağı; '~.**foot** *n.* önayak; '~.**front** *n.* en ileri taraf; en ileri yer; ~'**go** (*irr.* go) *v/t.* & *v/i.* önce gitmek; ~**ing** daha önce belirtilen; ~'**gone** *adj.* geçmiş, bitmiş, önceki; ~ **conclusion** kaçınılmaz sonuç; '~.**ground** *n.* ön plan; '~.**hand** 1. *n. tenis:* sağ vuruş; 2. *adj.* evvelki, önceden yapılan; ~.**head** ['fɔrid] *n.* alın.

**for.eign** ['fɔrǝn] *adj.* yabancı, ecnebi; dış; ilgisi olmayan; ~ **body** yabancı cisim; ~-**born** yabancı ülkede doğmuş; '**for.eign.er** *n.* yabancı, ecnebi; '**for.eign.ness** yabancılık, ecnebilik.

**for.eign...:** ≙ **Of.fice** Dışişleri Bakanlığı; ~ **pol.i.cy** dış politika; ~ **trade** dış ticaret.

**fore...:** ~'**judge** *v/t.* önceden hüküm vermek; ~'**know** (*irr.* know) *v/t.* önceden bilmek; '~.**knowl.edge** *n.* önceden bilme; ~.**land** [fɔ:lǝnd] *n.* burun, çıkıntı; '~.**leg** *n.* ön ayak; '~.**lock** *n.* kâkül, perçem; take time by the ~ fırsatı kaçırmamak, fırsatı hemen kullanmak; '~.**man** *n.* ᴆ̌ jüri başkanı; ✗ ustabaşı; '~.**mast** *n.* ↓ baş direği, pruva direği; '~.**most** 1. *adj.* başta gelen; ana, en tanınmış; 2. *adv.* başta, ilkönce; '~.**name** *n.* birinci isim; '~.**noon** *n.* öğleden önceki zaman, sabah.

**fo.ren.sic** [fǝ'rensik] *adj.* mahkemeye ait, adlî, kazai.

**fore...:** '~.**or'dain** *v/t.* önceden takdir etm.; önceden tayin etm.; '~.**paw** *n.* ön aygın pençesi; '~.**run.ner** *n.* haberci, müjdeci; öncü; ~.**sail** ['~seil; ↓ '~sl] *n.* trinketa yelkeni; ~'**see** (*irr.* see) *v/t.* önceden görmek, ileriyi görmek, önceden bilmek; ~'**see.a.ble** *adj.* önceden bilinebilen; ~'**shad.ow** *v/t.* önceden belirtmek, önceden haber vermek; '~.**shore** *n.* deniz kıyısı, sahil; '~.**short.en** *v/t.* orantılı olarak küçültmek; '~.**sight** *n.* basiret, ön-

ceden görme; '~.**skin** *n.* sünnet derisi.

**for.est** ['fɔrist] 1. *n.* orman (*a. fig.*); 2. *v/t.* ağaçlandırmak.

**fore.stall** [fɔ:stɔ:l] *v/t.* önüne geçmek; önce davranıp önlemek; önce davranmak.

**for.est.er** ['fɔristǝ] *n.* ormancı; '**for.est.ry** *n.* ormancılık; orman.

**fore...:** '~.**taste** *n.* önceden tadına varma; önceden alınan tat; ~'**tell** (*irr.* tell) *v/t.* önceden haber vermek, kehanette bulunmak; '~.**thought** *n.* basiret; önceden düşünme.

**for.ev.er** [fǝ'revǝ] *adv.* devamlı olarak, edebiyen, daima; durmadan.

**fore...:** ~'**warn** *v/t.* önceden uyarmak; '~.**wom.an** *n.* kadın ustabaşı; '~.**word** *n.* önsöz.

**for.feit** ['fɔ:fit] 1. *adj.* ceza olarak kaybedilen; 2. *n.* ceza, bşin ceza olarak kaybedilmesi; † & *spor:* cayma, vazgeçme; ~**s** *pl.* bir oyun çeşidi; '**for.feit.a.ble** *adj.* kaybedilebilir; **for.fei.ture** ['~tʃǝ] *n.* kaybetme, hakkın kaybedilmesi.

**for.gath.er** [fɔ:'gæðǝ] *v/i.* toplanmak, biraraya gelmek, içtima etm.; rastlamak.

**for.gave** [fǝ'geiv] *pret. of* forgive.

**forge**¹ [fɔ:dʒ] 1. *n.* demirhane, demirci ocağı; 2. *v/t.* demiri kızdırıp işlemek, dövmek; *fig.* kurmak; sahtesini yapmak, uydurmak.

**forge**² [~] *mst* ~ **ahead** *v/i.* ilerlemek, öne geçmek.

**forg.er** ['fɔ:dʒǝ] *n.* sahtekâr; demirci; '**for.ger.y** *n.* sahte bş; kalpazanlık; sahtekârlık, sahte imza atma.

**for.get** [fǝ'get] (*irr.*) *vb.* unutmak; ihmal etm.; I ~ F unuttum; **for'get.ful** ☐ [~ful] unutkan, ihmalci; **for'get.ful.ness** *n.* unutkanlık, ihmal; **for'get-me-not** *n.* ᴥ unutmabeni.

**for.give** [fǝ'giv] (*irr.*) *v/t.* affetmek, bağışlamak; **for'giv.en** *p.p. of* forgive; **for'give.ness** *n.* af, bağışla(n)ma; **for'giv.ing** ☐ affeden, bağışlayan, merhametli.

**for.go** [fɔ:gǝu] (*irr.* go) *v/t.* vazgeçmek.

**for.got** [fǝ'gɔt], **for'got.ten** [~tn] *pret. & p.p. of* forget.

**fork** [fɔ:k] 1. *n.* çatal; bel; 2. *vb.* çatallaş(tır)mak; ayrılmak; çatalla kaldırmak; bellemek; **forked** *adj.* çatallı; '**fork-lift** *n.* çatallı kaldırıcı.

**for.lorn** [fǝ'lɔ:n] *adj.* kimsesiz, terkedilmiş, sahipsiz; ümitsiz; ~ **hope** boş ümit; ümitsiz bir girişim; ✗ fedailer takımı.

**form** [fɔ:m] 1. *n.* şekil, biçim, suret; hal; üslup, tarz; *typ.* forma; formül, kâğıt, okul: sınıf; in (good) ~ *spor:* formda;

good (bad) ~ iyi (kötü) durum, davranış; 2. *v/t.* teşkil etm., kurmak; şekil vermek -*e*; geliştirmek; düzenlemek; ✕ tertiplemek; *v/i.* şekil almak, oluşmak.

**for.mal** ☐ [ˈfɔːməl] resmî, usule uygun; biçimsel, şekli; ˈ**for.mal.ism** *n.* şekilcilik, biçimselcilik; dış görünüşüne önem verme; ˈ**for.mal.ist** *n.* biçimci kimse; resmiyet taraftarı; **for.mal.i.ty** [ˈfɔːmæliti] *n.* usül, formalite; resmiyet; **for.mal.ize** [ˈfɔːməlaiz] *v/t.* şekillendirmek; resmileştirmek.

**for.mat** [ˈfɔːmæt] *n.* kitabın genel düzeni, kitabın şekli ve boyutları; düzenleme, tertip.

**for.ma.tion** [fɔːˈmeiʃən] *n.* teşkil, kurma; şekillendirme; oluşum, formasyon; *esp.* ✕ & *geol.* düzen, tertip, oluşum; ~ flying ✈ filo uçuşu; **form.a.tive** [ˈfɔːmətiv] *adj.* şekil vere(bile)n; geliştirici, öğretici; ~ years *pl.* gelişme yılları.

**form.er¹** ⊕ [ˈfɔːmə] kalıp; şablon; bobin şablonu; *fig.* biçimlendirici şey *veya* kimse.

**for.mer²** [~] *adj.* önceki, eski, sabık; ilk bahsedilen; ˈ**for.mer.ly** *adv.* eskiden.

**for.mic** [ˈfɔːmik] *adj.*: ~ acid karınca asidi, formik asid.

**for.mi.da.ble** ☐ [ˈfɔːmidəbl] heybetli, korkulur; müthiş, çok zor; çok büyük.

**form.less** ☐ [ˈfɔːmlis] şekilsiz, biçimsiz.

**For.mo.san** [fɔːˈmousən] *n.* Formaza'lı kimse.

**for.mu.la** [ˈfɔːmjulə] *n. pl. mst* **for.mu.lae** [ˈ~liː] formül; usül, kaide; ℞ reçete, tertip; **for.mu.lar.y** [ˈ~ləri] *n.* formüler; kodeks; **for.mu.late** [ˈ~leit] *v/t.* hazırlamak *(plan, öneri vs.)*; açıkça belirtmek; **for.mu¹la.tion** *n.* formülleştirme; kesin ve açık ifade.

**for.ni.ca.tion** [fɔːniˈkeiʃən] *n.* evlilik dışı cinsel ilişki.

**for.rad.er** F [ˈfɔrədə] *adv.* daha ileriye.

**for.sake** [fəˈseik] *(irr.) v/t.* terketmek, bırakmak; vazgeçmek -*den*; **forˈsak.en** *p.p. of* forsake; **for.sook** [~ˈsuk] *pret. of* forsake.

**for.sooth** *iro.* [fəˈsuːθ] *adv.* gerçekten, hakikaten.

**for.swear** [fɔːˈswɛə] *(irr.* swear) *v/t.* yeminle bırakmak, vazgeçmek -*den*; ~ o.s. yalan yere yemin etm.; **forˈsworn** *adj.* yalan yere yemin etmiş.

**fort** ✕ [fɔːt] *n.* kale, hisar; istihkâm.

**forte** *fig.* [fɔːt] *n.* özel yetenek, bir kimsenin asıl hüneri.

**forth** [fɔːθ] *adv.* ileri, dışarı, açığa; sonra; from this day ~ bugünden itibaren;

~ˈcom.ing *adj.* gelecek, çıkacak; hazır, mevcut; F kolaylık gösteren, yardımsever; be ~ kolaylık göstermek; güleryüz göstermek; ˈ~.right *adj.* açık, doğru sözlü, içten; ˈ~ˈwith *adv.* derhal, hemen, vakit kaybetmeden.

**for.ti.eth** [ˈfɔːtiiθ] 1. *adj.* kırkıncı; 2. *n.* kırkta bir.

**for.ti.fi.ca.tion** [fɔːtifiˈkeiʃən] *n.* tahkim, kuvvetlendirme; ✕ istihkâm; **for.ti.fy** [ˈ~fai] *v/t.* ✕ takviye etm., kuvvetlendirmek; *fig.* canlandırmak, zindelik vermek; **for.ti.tude** [ˈ~tjuːd] *n.* metanet, sabır, tahammül.

**fort.night** [ˈfɔːtnait] *n.* iki hafta; this day ~ iki hafta sonra bugün; this ~ bu iki hafta; ˈ**fort.night.ly** *adj. & adv.* iki haftada bir.

**for.tress** [ˈfɔːtris] *n.* kale, hisar, istihkâm.

**for.tu.i.tous** ☐ [fɔːˈtjuːitəs] rastlantı sonucu olan, tesadüfî; **forˈtu.i.tous.ness**, **forˈtu.i.ty** *n.* tesadüf, rastlantı.

**for.tu.nate** [ˈfɔːtʃnit] *adj.* talihli, şanslı; ˈ**for.tu.nate.ly** *adv.* iyi ki, çok şükür, Allahtan, bereket versin, hamdolsun.

**for.tune** [ˈfɔːtʃən] *n.* baht, talih, şans; kader, kısmet; servet; uğur; good ~ iyi şans; bad ~, ill ~ kötü talih; marry a ~ zengin bir kadınla evlenmek; tell ~s fal bakmak; ˈ~-hunt.er *n.* servet avcısı; ˈ~-tel.ler *n.* falcı.

**for.ty** [ˈfɔːti] 1. *adj.* kırk; ~-niner *Am.* F 1849'da Kaliforniya'ya altın aramaya giden kimse; ~ winks *pl.* kısa uyku, şekerleme, kestirme; 2. *n.* kırk; the forties 40 ile 49 yılları arası.

**fo.rum** [ˈfɔːrəm] *n.* Eski Roma'da meydan, forum.

**for.ward** [ˈfɔːwəd] 1. *adj.* öndeki, ilerdeki, önde olan; gelişmiş; küstah; aşırı; ℣ ilerideki...; ~ planning ilerisi için planlama; 2. *adv.* ileri, ileri doğru; from this time ~ bundan böyle; 3. *n. futbol:* forvet; 4. *v/t.* sevketmek, göndermek (to -*e*); yeni adrese göndermek; ilerlemesine yardımcı olm.; please ~ ☞ lütfen yeni adrese gönderin; ˈ**for.ward.er** *n.* nakliyeci, sevkiyatçı.

**for.ward.ing** [ˈfɔːwədiŋ] *n.* gönderme, sevkiyat, nakliye; ~ a.gent sevkiyat acentesi.

**for.ward.ness** [ˈfɔːwədnis] *n.* ilerleme; düşüncesizlik, küstahlık, cüret; **for.wards** [ˈfɔːwədz] *adv.* ileriye doğru, ileri; itibaren.

**fosse** [fɔs] *n.* ✕ hendek; *anat.* çukur.

**fos.sil** [ˈfɔsl] 1. *adj.* fosilleşmiş, taşlaşmış; *fig.* eski kafalı, zamana uymayan; **2.** *n.* fosil, taşıl; eski kafalı kimse.

**fos.ter** [ˈfɔstə] *v/t. fig.* beslemek, bakıp büyütmek, bakmak; teşvik etm.; ~ up büyütmek, yetiştirmek; **2.** *adj.* süt..., evlatlık...; ˈ**fos.ter.age** *n.* evlatlık büyütme; bakım, besleme, teşvik; ˈ**fos.ter-child** *n.* evlâtlık, evlât gibi büyütülmüş çocuk; **fos.ter.ling** [ˈ~liŋ] *n.* evlâtlık, manevi evlât.

**fought** [fɔːt] *pret. & p.p. of* fight 2.

**foul** [faul] **1.** ☐ pis, kirli; bozuk; iğrenç; *fig.* çirkin, ayıp, bayağı, kaba, kötü, fırtınalı *(hava)*; müstehcen, açık saçık; dolaşmış, karışmış; tıkalı, tıkanık; ↓ bozuk, arızalı, çaparız; ~tongue kötü lisan, küfürlü konuşma; fall ~ of başı derde girmek; ↓ çarpmak, çarpışmak; **2.** *n.* çarpışma, bindirme *(gemi); spor:* faul; through fair and ~ iyi veya kötü zamanlarda; **3.** *v/t. & v/i.* kirletmek, kirlenmek, pisletmek; rezil etm.; dolaş(tır)mak, karışmak; faul yapmak; ~-mouthed [ˈ~mauðd], ˈ~-spo.ken *adj.* ağzı bozuk, küfürbaz.

**found¹** [faund] *pret. & p.p. of* find 1.

**found²** [~] *v/t.* kurmak, temelini atmak, tesis etm. *(a. fig.)*.

**found³** [~] *v/t.* kalıba dökmek, eritmek.

**foun.da.tion** [faunˈdeiʃən] *n.* kurma, tesis; vakıf, kuruluş; temel, esas, dayanak *(a. fig.)*; ~ cream makyaj kremi; ~ gar.ment korse; ~-s.tone *n.* temel taşı.

**found.er¹** [ˈfaundə] *n.* kurucu.

**found.er²** ⊕ [~] *n.* dökmeci.

**found.er³** [~] *v/i.* ↓ su dolup batmak; *fig.* batmak, iflas etm.; sakatlanmak; tökezlenmek; çökmek; olmamak, suya düşmek; *v/t.* suyla doldurup batırmak; yıkmak.

**found.ling** [ˈfaundliŋ] *n.* sokakta bulunmuş çocuk, buluntu; ~ hos.pi.tal kimsesiz çocuklar yurdu.

**found.ress** [ˈfaundris] *n.* kadın kurucu.

**found.ry** ⊕ [ˈfaundri] *n.* dökümhane.

**fount** [faunt] *n. poet.* pınar, kaynak, memba; *typ.* [a. fɔnt] baskı harfleri takımı, hurufat takımı.

**foun.tain** [ˈfauntin] *n.* çeşme, pınar, kaynak, memba; fıskiye; ⊕ döküm kanalı; ˈ~-ˈhead *n.* kaynak *(a. fig.)*; ˈ~-ˈpen *n.* dolmakalem.

**four** [fɔː] **1.** *adj.* dört; **2.** *n.* dört rakamı; *spor:* dört kişilik takım; ˈ~-ˈflush.er *n. Am. sl.* blöfçü, blöf yapan kimse; ˈ~-ˈfold *adj. & adv.* dört kat, dört kez; ˈ~-in-ˈhand *n.* dört katlı araba; kravat; ˈ~-part *adj.* ♩ dört sesli; ˈ~.pence *n.* dört penilik ma

deni para; ˈ~-ply *adj.* dört katlı, dörtkat; ˈ~-ˈpost.er *n.* dört direkli karyola; ˈ~ˈscore *adj. & n.* seksen; ~.some [ˈfɔːsəm] *n. golf:* dörtlü grup oyunu; ˈ~-ˈsquare *adj.* dört köşe, kare; *fig.* metin, sağlam; ˈ~-ˈstroke *adj. mot.* dört zamanlı...

**four.teen** [ˈfɔːˈtiːn] *adj. & n.* on dört; ˈ**four**ˈ**teenth** [~θ] **1.** *adj.* on dördüncü; **2.** *n.* on dörtte bir; **fourth** [fɔːθ] **1.** *adj.* dördüncü; **2.** *n.* dörtte bir; ˈ**fourth.ly** *adv.* dördüncü olarak; ˈ**four**-ˈ**wheel.er** *n.* dört tekerlekli atlı araba.

**fowl** [faul] **1.** *n.* kuş, tavuk; kümes hayvanı; bu hayvanların eti; **2.** *vb.* yabanî kuş avlamak; ˈ**fowl.er** *n.* yabani kuş avcısı.

**fowl.ing** [ˈfauliŋ] *n.* yabanî kuş avı; ~-piece *n.* av tüfeği.

**fowl-run** [ˈfaulrʌn] *n.* kümes.

**fox** [fɔks] **1.** *n.* tilki; tilki kürkü; kurnaz adam; **2.** *vb.* aldatmak, şaşırtmak, zihnini karıştırmak; ˈ~-brush *n.* tilki kuyruğu; ˈ~-earth *n.* tilki ini; **foxed** *adj.* lekeli, sararmış.

**fox...**: ˈ~.glove *n.* ♣ yüksükotu; ˈ~-hole *n.* ✕ askerin sığınacağı çukur; ˈ~.hound *n.* tilki avında kullanılan köpek; ˈ~-hunt *n.* tilki avı; ˈ~-ˈter.ri.er *n. zo.* tilki teriyeri; ˈ~.trot *n.* fokstrot, bir dans müziği; ˈ**fox.y** *adj.* kurnaz, şeytani görünüşlü; cazibeli, çekici; tilki renginde.

**foy.er** *thea.* [ˈfɔiei] *n.* fuaye, giriş salonu.

**fra.cas** [ˈfrækɑː] *n., pl.* ~ [ˈ~z] gürültü, kavga, velvele.

**frac.tion** [ˈfrækʃən] *n.* ♣ kesir; parça; kır(ıl)ma; oran; ~ line kesir çizgisi; **frac.tion.al** [ˈ~ʃənl] ☐ kesri, cüzi, az, azıcık.

**frac.tious** [ˈfrækʃəs] *adj.* ters, aksi, huysuz, kavgacı.

**frac.ture** [ˈfræktʃə] **1.** *n. (esp. kemik)* kırık; kır(ıl)ma; **2.** *v/t. & v/i.* kır(ıl)mak; çatla(t)mak.

**frag.ile** [ˈfrædʒail] *adj.* kolay kırılır, kolay bozulur; kolay yok olan; *fig.* zayıf, nazik; **fra.gil.i.ty** [ˈ~dʒiliti] *n.* kolay kırılma, narinlik.

**frag.ment** [ˈfrægmənt] *n.* kırılmış parça, kısım, eksik parça; ˈ**frag.men.tar.y** ☐ eksik kalmış, parça parça, kısım kısım, tamamlanmamış.

**fra.grance** [ˈfreigrəns] *n.* güzel koku; ˈ**fra.grant** ☐ güzel kokulu, mis kokulu.

**frail¹** [freil] *n.* küfe, sepet.

**frail²** ☐ [~] zayıf, narin, kolay kırılır, kolay bozulan; *(esp. ahlakı)* zayıf; ˈ**frail.ty** *n. fig.* zayıflık, manevi zaaf; hata.

**frag.ment** [ˈfrægmənt] *n*. kırılış parça, kırıntı.

**frame** [freim] **1.** *n*. çerçeve, gergef; beden, vücut; yapı; kafes; düzen; ⬇, ⬆ kaburga, gövde; *phot*. poz; ✓ limonluk, sera; ～ of mind mizaç, hal, ruhsal durum; **2.** *vb*. şekil vermek -*e*, uydurmak -*i*; çerçevelemek -*i*; düzenlemek, tertip etm.; *a*. ～ up *sl*. yalan yere suçlamak; ～ **aer.i.al** çerçeve anten; ～ **house** ahşap ev; **ˈfram.er** *n*. çerçeveleme sistemi; **ˈframe-up** *n. esp. Am*. F hileli düzen, iftira, yalan yere suçlama; **ˈframe.work** *n*. ⊕ şasi; ⚃ çatı, iskelet; *fig*. yapı, bünye.

**franc** [fræŋk] *n*. (*Fransa, Belçika, İsviçre*) frank.

**fran.chise** ȡ [ˈfræntʃaiz] *n*. oy verme hakkı; *esp. Am*. imtiyaz, özel hak.

**Fran.cis.can** *eccl*. [frænˈsiskən] *n*. Fransiskan mezhebine mensup rahip.

**Fran.co-** [ˈfræŋkəu] *prefix* Fransız.

**fran.gi.ble** [ˈfrændʒibl] *adj*. kırılabilir.

**Frank¹** [fræŋk] *n*. Ortaçağda German kavimlerinden birine mensup kimse; Frenk.

**frank²** [～] **1.** ☐ açık sözlü, samimi, içi dışı bir, dobra; **2.** *v/t*. posta ücretinin ödendiğini göstermek için mektuba damga vurmak.

**frank.furt.er** [ˈfræŋkfəːtə] *n*. bir tür baharatlı sosis.

**frank.in.cense** [ˈfræŋkinsens] *n*. günlük, buhur, tütsü.

**frank.ing-ma.chine** [ˈfræŋkiŋməʃiːn] *n*. pul yapıştırma makinesi, damgalama makinesi.

**frank.ness** [ˈfræŋknis] *n*, açık sözlülük, samimiyet.

**fran.tic** [ˈfræntik] *adj*. (～ally) çılgınca heyecanlanmış, çılgın, çileden çıkmış.

**fra.ter.nal** [frəˈtəːnl] kardeşçe; **fraˈter.ni.ty** *n*. kardeşlik; kardeşlik cemiyeti; *univ. Am*. erkek öğrenci birliği; **frat.er.ni.za.tion** [frætənaiˈzeiʃən] *n*. arkadaşlık; **ˈfrat.er.nize** *v/i*. arkadaş olm., kardeş gibi olm.

**frat.ri.cide** [ˈfreitrisaid] *n*. kardeş katili; kendi kardeşini öldürme.

**fraud** [frɔːd] *n*. hile; F dolandırıcılık, sahtekârlık; F hilekâr, sahtekâr, dolandırıcı kimse; **fraud.u.lence** [ˈ～juləns] *n*. hilekârlık; **ˈfraud.u.lent** ☐ hilekâr, sahtekâr, dolandırıcı; hile ile kazanılan.

**fraught** *poet*. [frɔːt] *adj*. dolu, yüklü (with *ile*).

**fray¹** [frei] *v/t*. yıpratmak; *v/i*. yıpranmak (*kumaş vs*.).

**fray²** [～] *n*. kavga, karışıklık, mücadele, çekişme.

**fraz.zle** *esp. Am*. F [ˈfræzl] **1.** *n*. tamamen yıpranma; yorulma; beat to a ～ bitkin, çok yıpranmış; **2.** *v/t*. yıpratmak, eskitmek; *v/i*. yıpranmak, eskimek.

**freak** [friːk] *n*. acayiplik, kapris; hilkat garibesi, eksantrik kimse; ～ of nature şeklen anormal olan insan, hayvan *veya* bitki; **ˈfreak.ish** ☐ acayip, garip, anormal, kaprisli.

**freck.le** [ˈfrekl] **1.** *n*. çil; leke, benek; *fig*. kusur; **2.** *v/i*. çillenmek, çil basmak; **freck.led** [ˈ～ld] *adj*. çilli.

**free** [friː] **1.** ☐ *com*. serbest; özgür, hür, azat, kurtulmuş (from, of -*den*); bağımsız; açık; bedava, parasız; ⚄ terkipsiz; muaf; ...sız, ...meyerek; *bşin* dışında; boş; eli açık, cömert; teklifsiz, rahat; ～ of debt borçtan kurtulmuş; he is ～ to *inf*. ...mekte serbesttir; ～ and easy teklifsiz, laubali, gayrı resmi; have a ～ hand hareketlerinde bağımsız olm.; give *veya* allow s.o. a ～ hand istediğini yapmakta serbest bırakmak; have one's hands ～ *fig*. serbest olm., istediğini yapmak; make ～ with laubali olm., yüzgöz olm.; kendi malı gibi kullanmak; make ～ of ayrıcalığa ortak olmak hakkını vermek; make s.o. ～ of the city fahri hemşeri sıfatını vermek; set ～ serbest bırakmak, azat etm. **2.** *v/t*. serbest bırakmak, kurtarmak (from, of -*den*); tahliye etm.; **～.boot.er** [ˈ～buːtə] *n*. korsan, haydut; **ˈfree.dom** *n*. özgürlük, hürriyet, serbestlik (from -*den*); açık sözlülük; aşırı samimiyet, laubalilik; ～ of the city şehrin fahri hemşerilik sıfatı; ～ of movement davranış özgürlüğü; ～ of speech konuşma özgürlüğü; **free...**; ～ **en.ter.prise** serbest teşebbüs; ～ **fight** serbest dövüş; **ˈ～-for-all** *n*. herkese açık yarış, tartışma *veya* kavga; ＝ free fight; **ˈ～-ˈhand.ed** *adj*. cömert, eli açık; **ˈ～.hold** *n*. ȡ mülkiyet, mülk, sahiplik hakkı; **ˈ～.hold.er** *n*. mülk sahibi; ～ **kick** *spor*: serbest vuruş, frikik; **ˈla.bo(u)r** sendikaya bağlı olmayan işçiler; **ˈ～-ˈlance** **1.** *n*. serbest çalışan yazar, gazeteci *vs*.; **2.** *v/i*. serbest çalışmak; **ˈ～-ˈlist** *n*. gümrüksüz giren eşya listesi; bir yere parasız girenlerin listesi; ～ **liver** her şeyden bol bol yiyip içen kimse, boğazına düşkün, zevkperest; **ˈ～.man** *n*. hür kimse, fahri hemşeri; **ˈ～.ma.son** *n*. mason; **ˈ～.ma.son.ry** *n*. masonluk; ～ **port** serbest liman; ～ **speech** serbest konuşma hakkı; **ˈ～-ˈspo.ken** *adj*. açık sözlü.

düşündüğünü söyleyen, sözünü esirgemeyen; ~ **state** bağımsız devlet; **¹~-stone** n. kolay yontulan taş, kumtaşı, kireçtaşı; **¹~-think.er** n. serbest düşünür; **¹~¹think-ing,** **¹~-thought** **1.** n. serbest düşünce; **2.** adj. serbest düşünceli; ~ **trade** serbest ticaret; **¹~-¹trad.er** n. serbest ticaret taraftarı; **¹~-¹wheel** **1.** n. pedal çevirmeden gitme; **2.** v/i. pedal çevirmeden gitmek.

**freeze** [fri:z] **1.** (irr.) v/i. donmak, buz kesmek, buz tutmak; çok üşümek; ~ **to** death donarak ölmek; soğuktan ölmek; v/t. dondurmak; fiyatları dondurmak; ~ **out** sl. işten veya toplumdan uzaklaştırmak, iş veya toplumun dışına itmek; **2.** n. donma, don; **wage-**~ ücretleri dondurma; **¹freez.er** n. dondurucu; dondurma makinesi; 🍴 soğuk hava vagonu; **¹freez.ing** ☐ dondurucu, donmakta; çok soğuk; ~ **mixture** phys. soğutucu karışım, dondurucu karışım; ~ **point** donma noktası.

**freight** [freit] **1.** n. navlun, nakliye ücreti; hamule, yük; attr. Am. yük...; ~ **out** (home) dönüş yükü (veya hamulesi); **2.** v/t. yüklemek; nakletmek, göndermek, taşımak; **¹freight.age** = freight 1.; **¹fre-ight-car** n. 🚂 Am. yük vagonu; **freight.** er n. ⚓ şilep, yük vapuru; ✈ nakliye uçağı; **freight train** Am. yük treni, marşandiz.

**French** [frentʃ] **1.** adj. Fransa'ya veya Fransızlara ait; ~ **beans** pl. taze fasulye; ~ **fried potatoes** pl. yağda kızarmış patates; **take** ~ **leave** izinsiz sıvışmak, izin almadan çekip gitmek; ~ **window** balkona vs. giden camlı kapı; **2.** n. Fransızca; **the** ~ pl. Fransızlar, Fransız halkı; ~ **horn** ♪ Fransız kornosu; **¹~.man** n. Fransız (erkek); **¹~.wom.an** n. Fransız (kadın).

**fren.zied** [¹frenzid] adj. çılgın; **¹fren.zy** n. çılgınlık, taşkınlık.

**fre.quen.cy** [¹fri¹kwənsi] n. sık sık olma, çok meydana gelme; ≠ frekans; ~ **mod-u.la.tion** ≠ frekans modülasyonu; **fre-quent 1.** ☐ [¹~kwənt] sık sık olan, alışılmış, daimi; **2.** [fri¹kwent] v/t. sık sık gitmek -e, çok uğramak -e; **fre.quen.ta-tion** n. bir yere sık gitme; **fre.quent.er** [fri¹kwentə] n. devamlı müşteri, müdavim.

**fres.co** [¹freskəu] n., pl. **fres.co(e)s** [¹~z] fresk, yaş sıva üzerine yapılan duvar resmi.

**fresh** [freʃ] **1.** ☐ com. taze, yeni; dinç; acemi; yeni toplanmış (çiçek); yeni gelmiş; yeni büyümüş; yeni ayrılmış; tatlı (su); temiz, serin (hava); parlak, canlı (renk); Am. sl. küstah, yüzsüz; **break** ~ **ground** fig. bir şeye yeni başlamak; yeni gerçekler bulmak; yepyeni bşe başlamak; ~ **water** tatlı su; **2.** n. serinlik; taşma, kabarma; **¹fresh.en** v/t. & v/i. canlan(dır)mak; tazelemek (içki); sertleşmek (rüzgâr); serinle(t)mek; **fresh.et** [¹~it] n. fig. kabarma, taşma, seyelân; **¹fresh.man** n. univ. birinci sınıf öğrencisi; **¹fresh.ness** n. tazelik; acemilik; **¹fresh-wa.ter** adj. tatlı suya ait, tatlı su...; ~ **college** Am. sl. ufak kolej.

**fret¹** [fret] **1.** n. üzüntü, sıkıntı, öfke; **2.** v/t. & v/i. üz(ül)mek; sık(ıl)mak; aşın-(dır)mak; ye(n)mek; sinirlen(dir)mek; rahatsız etm.; kız(dır)mak; ~ **away,** ~ **out** yıpratmak, aşındırmak, yenmek.

**fret²** [~] **1.** n. ⚗ kabartma, oyma; **2.** v/t. kabartma yapmak, oymak.

**fret³** [~] n. ♪ telli sazlarda perde.

**fret.ful** ☐ [¹fretful] sinirli, huysuz, aksi, ters.

**fret-saw** [¹fretsɔ:] n. kıl testere.

**fret.work** [¹fretwə:k] n. oyma işi.

**fri.a.bil.i.ty** [fraiə¹biliti] n. gevreklik, çabuk ufalanma; **¹fri.a.ble** adj. kolay ufalanabilir, gevrek.

**fri.ar** [fraiə] n. bazı katolik örgütlerinde rahip, keşiş; **¹fri.ar.y** n. manastır.

**frib.ble** [¹fribl] **1.** vb. eğlenmek, oynamak; tembel davranmak; boşa harcamak; **2.** n. uçarı, hoppa, hafifmeşrep.

**fric.as.see** [frikə¹si.] **1.** n. yahni; **2.** v/t. -in yahnisini yapmak.

**fric.tion** [¹frikʃən] n. sürtme, sürtünme, friksiyon; sürtüşme (a. fig.); attr. = **fric.tion.al** [¹~ʃənl] adj. sürtünme...

**fridge** F [fridʒ] n. buzdolabı.

**Fri.day** [¹fraidi] n. cuma.

**friend** [frend] n. dost, arkadaş, ahbap; yardımcı; ♀ Kuveyker mezhebine mensup kimse; **make** ~**s with** b-le arkadaş olm.; b-le tanışmak; **¹friend.less** adj. dostu olmayan; **¹friend.li.ness** n. dostça duygu ve hareket; **¹friend.ly** adj. dostça, samimi, arkadaşça, dostane; ♀ **Society** yardımlaşma cemiyeti; **¹friend.ship** n. dostluk, arkadaşlık.

**frieze** [fri:z] n. duvar süsü (kumaş veya ⚗).

**frig.ate** ⚓ [¹frigit] n. savaş gemisi, firkateyn.

**frig(e)** F [fridʒ] = fridge.

**fright** [frait] n. dehşet, korku; fig. çirkin kılıklı kimse veya şey; **¹fright.en** v/t. korkutmak, ürkütmek, korkutup kaçırmak, dehşete düşürmek; be ~ed of F *bşden* korkmak, ürkmek; **fright.ful** □ [ˈ~ful] korkunç, müthiş, berbat; ˈ**fright.ful.ness** *n.* korkunçluk, dehşet.

**frig.id** □ [ˈfridʒid] soğuk; buz gibi *(a. fig.)*; *psych.* cinsel bakımdan soğuk *(kadın)*; **friˈgid.i.ty** *n.* soğukluk *(a. psych.)*; duygusuzluk.

**frill** [fril] **1.** *n.* fırfır, volan; farbala; put on ~s F *fig.* aşırı süslemek; **2.** *vb.* farbala yapmak, kıvırmak.

**fringe** [frindʒ] **1.** *n.* saçak; kenar; kâkül; *a.* ~s *pl.* yele, püskül; **2.** *v/t.* saçak *veya* kenar takmak; çevrelemek, sınır oluşturmak.

**frip.per.y** [ˈfripəri] **1.** *n.* elbisede gereksiz süs, cicili bicili şeyler, değersiz süs; **2.** *adj.* kıymetsiz, değersiz...

**frisk** [frisk] **1.** *n.* sıçrama; oyun, neşe; üstünü arama, silah arama; **2.** *v/t. & v/i.* sıçramak, oynamak; üstünü aramak, üstünde silah aramak; ˈ**frisk-i.ness** *n.* neşe, canlılık; ˈ**frisk.y** □ neşeli, oynak.

**frith** [friθ] = firth.

**frit.ter** [ˈfritə] **1.** *n.* gözlemeye benzer börek; **2.** *vb.* ~ away boşuna sarfetmek, ziyan etm., israf etm.

**fri.vol** [ˈfrivəl] *vb.* sarfetmek, vakit öldürmek, israf etm.; **fri.vol.i.ty** [~ˈvɔliti] *n.* hoppalık, hafifmeşreplik; saçmalık, manasızlık; **friv.o.lous** □ [ˈ~vələs] önemsiz, ehemmiyetsiz, anlamsız; uçarı, zevk düşkünü.

**frizz** [friz] *v/t.* kıvırmak, bukle yapmak; **friz.zle** [ˈ~l] *a.* ~ up *v/t. & v/i.* kıvırmak, kıvrılmak, kıvrım kıvrım olm., bukle yapmak; ˈ**friz.z(l)y** *adj.* kıvır kıvır, kıvırcık, bukle bukle.

**fro** [frou] *adv.*: to and ~ öteye beriye, ileri geri.

**frock** [frɔk] *n.* kadın elbisesi, rop; rahip cüppesi; cüppe; iş elbisesi; ˈ~ˈ**coat** *n.* redingot.

**frog** [frɔg] *n.* kurbağa; 🎖 makas göbeği; ✕ kılıç kayışı; ˈ~**.man** *n.* kurbağa adam, balıkadam; ˈ~**-march** *v/t.* el ve ayaklarını tutarak (mahkûmu) yüzükoyun taşımak.

**frol.ic** [ˈfrɔlik] **1.** *n.* neşe, eğlence, coşma; **2.** *v/t.* oynamak, gülüp eğlenmek; **frol.ic.some** □ [ˈ~səm] eğlenceyi seven, şen, neşeli.

**from** [frɔm, frəm] *prep.* -den, -dan; -den itibaren; -den dolayı; defend ~ -den korumak; draw ~ nature doğaya bakarak çizmek; hide ~ -den saklamak; ~ above yukarıdan, tepeden; ~ amidst arasından; ~ before -den evvel.

**frond** ❦ [frɔnd] *n.* eğreltiotu yaprağı; hurma ağacı yaprağı.

**front** [frʌnt] **1.** *n.* ön, yüz; ön taraf; ön saf; ✕ cephe; yol kenarı; birleşik hareket, cephe; paravan kişi *veya* kurum; *poet.* alın, yüz; in ~ önde; in ~ of -*in* önünde; come to the ~ *fig.* göze çarpmak, tanınmak, meşhur olm.; **2.** *adj.* öndeki...; **3.** *vb. a.* ~ on, ~ towards -*e* bakmak; ˈ**front.age** *n.* 🏠 bina cephesi, cephe; ˈ**fron.tal 1.** *adj.* alna ait; ön...; **2.** *n.* 🏠 cephe; front door sokak kapısı, ön kapı; **fron.tier** [ˈ~tiə] *n.* sınır, hudut; yerleşilmemiş bölge, boş bölge; ˈ**fron.tiers.man** *n.* sınırda oturan adam; *fig.* öncü; **fron.tis.piece** [ˈ~tispiːs] *n.* 🏠 binanın yüzü; *typ.* kitabın başındaki resimli sayfa; **front.let** [ˈfrʌntlit] *n.* alın bağı; **front.man** *fig.* gizli maksatları örtmek için kullanılan kimse; ˈ**front-page** *n.* baş sayfa; ˈ**front-ˈwheel drive** *mot.* önden çekişli.

**frost** [frɔst] **1.** *n.* don, ayaz, *a.* hoar ~, white ~ kırağı; F başarısızlık; black ~ don; **2.** *v/t. & v/i.* don(dur)mak; kırağı tutmak; buz tutmak; şekerle kaplamak; ~ed glass buzlucam; ˈ~**-bite** *n.* soğuk ısırması, soğuğun yakması; ˈ**frost.bit.ten** *adj.* donmuş; ˈ**frost-bound** *adj.* buz tutmuş, donmuş; ˈ**frost.i.ness** *n.* soğuk, don; ˈ**frost.ing** *n.* pastaya sürülen şekerli karışımı; ˈ**frost.y** □ ayazlı; buz tutmuş; soğuk *(a. fig.)*.

**froth** [frɔθ] **1.** *n.* köpük; *fig.* boş laf, saçmalık; **2.** *v/i.* köpürmek; ˈ**froth.i.ness** *n.* köpük; *fig.* boş laf, saçmalık; ˈ**froth.y** □ köpüklü; *fig.* yavan, tatsız.

**fro.ward** † [ˈfrouəd] *adj.* ters, aksi, inatçı, asi, serkeş.

**frown** [fraun] **1.** *n.* kaş çatma, hiddetli bakış; **2.** *vb.* kaşlarını çatmak; hiddetle bakmak; ~ at, ~ (up)on uygun görmemek, tasvip etmemek, hoş görmemek.

**frowst** F [fraust] *n.* küf kokusu, küflülük, havasızlık; ˈ**frowst.y** □, **frowz.y** [ˈfrauzi] küf kokulu, havasız; dağınık, pasaklı, şapşal.

**froze** [frouz] *pret. of* freeze 1; ˈ**fro.zen 1.** *p.p. of* freeze 1; **2.** *adj.* donmuş, buz kesilmiş; buz gibi, soğuk davranışlı; † donmuş *(kıymetler)*; ~ meat dondurulmuş et.

**fruc.ti.fi.ca.tion** [frʌktifiˈkeiʃən] *n.* verimlilik, bereket; **fruc.ti.fy** [ˈ~fai] *v/t.* meyve verir hale getirmek, verimli hale getirmek; *v/i.* meyve vermek, verimli olm., bereketli olm. *(a. fig.)*.

**fru.gal** □ [ˈfruːgəl] tutumlu, idareli, ekonomik; ucuz; **fru.gal.i.ty** [~'gæliti] *n*. tutumluluk, idareli olma.

**fruit** [fru:t] **1.** *n*. meyve, yemiş; *fig.* verim, sonuç; semere; **2.** *v/i.* meyve vermek; **¹fruit.age** *n*. meyve verme; meyve; sonuç, netice; **frui.ta.ri.an** [fru:-¹teəriən] *n*. meyve ile beslenen kimse; **¹fruit-cake** *n*. meyveli pasta, kek; **¹fruit.er** *n*. meyve veren ağaç; meyve taşıyan gemi; **¹fruit.er.er** *n*. manav, yemişçi; **fruit ful** □ [¹~ful] meyve veren, yemiş veren, verimli *(a. fig.)*; **¹fruit.ful.ness** *n*. verim, bereket *(a. fig.)*; **fru.i.tion** [fru:¹iʃən] *n*. gerçekleşme, muradına erme, istediğini elde etme; **fruit knife** meyve bıçağı; **fruit less** □ meyvesiz; *fig.* verimsiz; faydasız, nafile; **¹fruit-ma.chine** *n*. F kumar makinesi; **fruit sal.ad** meyve salatası; **¹fruit y** *adj.* meyve lezzetinde; meyveli; F çatlak; dolgun, yumuşak *(ses)*; süslü.

**frump** [frʌmp] *n*. *fig.* derbeder kılıklı kimse, üstü başı dökülen kimse; **¹frump.ish**, **¹frump.y** *adj.* derbeder kılıklı, üstü başı dökük, demode, rüküş.

**frus.trate** [frʌs¹treit] *v/t.* önlemek, engel olm., işini bozmak; hüsrana uğratmak, hayal kırıklığına uğratmak; **frus¹tra.tion** *n*. önleme, engel olma; *psych.* hüsran, hayal kırıklığı.

**fry** [frai] **1.** *n*. kızartma; yeni doğmuş balık; small ~ F çocuklar; çoluk çocuk; önemsiz kimse; **2.** *v/t.* & *v/i.* kızar(t)mak; fried potatoes *pl.* kızarmış patates; **¹fry.ing-pan** *n*. tava; get out of the ~ into the fire yağmurdan kaçıp doluya tutulmak.

**fuch.sia** ⚲ [¹fju:ʃə] *n*. küpeçiçeği.

**fud.dle** [¹fʌdl] **1.** *v/t.* şaşırtmak, sersemletmek, sarhoş etm; **2.** *n*. sersemlik, şaşkınlık, sarhoşluk.

**fudge** F [fʌdʒ] **1.** *vb.* ileri gitmek; umulduğu gibi başaramamak; tahrif etm., uydurmak; abartmak, yalan söylemek, aldatmak; **2.** *n*. yumuşak bir şekerleme; saçma, boş laf; ~! saçma!.

**fu.el** [¹fjuəl] **1.** *n*. yakacak, yakıt, akaryakıt; *mot.* benzin; ~ oil mazot, akaryakıt; **2.** *vb.* yakıt sağlamak, yakıt yüklemek; desteklemek, teşvik etm.; *mot.* benzin almak.

**fug** [fʌg] **1.** *n*. havasızlık; **2.** *v/i.* havasız bir yerde dolaşmak; *v/t.* havasını kirletmek.

**fu.ga.cious** [fju:¹geiʃəs] *adj.* çabuk uçan, uçucu; kısa süreli, geçici.

**fu.gi.tive** [¹fju:dʒitiv] **1.** *adj.* geçici, muvakkat, kısa süreli, fani *(a. fig)*; **2.** *n*. kaçak ,firarî; mülteci.

**fu.gle.man** [¹fju:glmæn] *n*. talimli asker; şef.

**fugue** ♪ [fju:g] *n*. füg, çok sesli müzikte beste.

**ful.crum** [¹fʌlkrəm] *n*. ⊕ dayanak noktası, dayanma noktası, manivela dayanağı.

**ful.fil(l)** [ful¹fil] *v/t.* yerine getirmek, yapmak, icra etm.; tamamlamak, bitirmek; **ful¹fill.er** *n*. yerine getiren, yapan, icra eden, görevini tamamlayan *b-i*; **ful¹fil(l)-ment** *n*. icra, yapma, yerine getirme, tamamlama.

**ful.gent** *poet.* [¹fʌldʒənt] *adj.* göz kamaştıracak derecede parlak.

**full¹** [ful] **1.** □ *com.* dolu; dolgun, tombul; bol ,geniş; meşgul; tam; bütün; tok; olgun; at ~ length etraflıca, tafsilatıyla, uzun uzadıya; tam boy *(resim)*; of ~ age reşit, ergin; ~ stop *gr.* nokta; ~ up tamamen dolu, dopdolu; ~ house *thea.* her yerin dolu olması; **2.** *adv.* tam, tamamen; fazlasıyla, pek çok; doğru; **3.** *n*. son had, aşırı derece doluluk; in ~ tam olarak, eksiksiz; pay in ~ tamamen ödemek; to the ~ tamamiyle, son haddine kadar.

**full²** ⊕ [~] *v/t.* büzüp kalınlaştırmak; bollaştırmak, genişletmek.

**full...:** **¹~-¹back** *n.* *futbol:* bek, defans oyuncusu; **¹~-¹blood.ed** *adj.* safkan; kuvvetli, dinç; **¹~-¹blown** *adj.* tamamen açmış *(çiçek)*; **¹~-¹bod.ied** *adj.* cüsseli, kapı gibi; önemli; kuvvetli derecede *(içki)*; ~ **dress** resmi elbise, merasim elbisesi; **¹~-dress** *adj.* ayrıntılı; ~ **debate** geniş kapsamlı müzakere, tartışma; ~ **rehearsal** *thea.* kostümlerle yapılan prova, genel prova.

**full.er** [¹fulə] *n*. çırpıcı; demirci çekici.

**full...:** **¹~-¹fledged** *adj.* *orn.* kanatları olan, uçabilen; **¹~-¹grown** *adj.* olgun, kemale ermiş, reşit, ergin.

**full-ing-mill** ⊕ [¹fuliŋmil] *n*. çırpıcı dibeği.

**full-length** [¹ful¹leŋθ] *adj.* tam boy *(portre)*; standart uzunlukta.

**ful(l).ness** [¹fulnis] *n*. dolgunluk; bolluk, çokluk; şişmanlık; olgunluk, kemal; bütünlük.

**full...:** **¹~-¹page** *adj.* tam sayfa; **¹~-¹scale** *adj.* orijinal boyutta; tam; eldeki bütün kaynakları kullanarak yapılan; **¹~-¹time** *adj.* bütün günlük.

**ful.ly** [¹fuli] *adv.* tamamen, bütünüyle; en azından, hiç olmazsa; ~ **two hours** en azından iki saat; **¹~-¹fash.ioned** *adj.* vücuda tam uyacak şekilde yapılmış *(kadın çorabı vs.)*.

**ful.mar** *orn.* [ˈfulmə] *n.* martıya benzer bir tür deniz kuşu.

**ful.mi.nate** *fig.* [ˈfʌlmineit] *v/i.* ateş püskürmek, karşı çıkmak; patlamak, gürlemek (against -*e*); **ful.miˈna.tion** *n.* patlama, ateş püskürme, lânet okuma.

**ful.some** ☐ [ˈfulsəm] aşırı, fazla; samimiyetsiz, yalancı, dalkavukça.

**fum.ble** [ˈfʌmbl] *v/i.* el yordamıyla aramak (for -*i*), elleri beceriksizce kullanmak; *v/t.* tutamamak; becerememek; (oyunda topu) düşürmek; **ˈfum.bler** *n.* beceriksiz kimse.

**fume** [fjuːm] **1.** *n.* duman, buhar, pis kokulu duman; öfke, hiddet; in a ~ hiddetle, öfkeyle; **2.** *v/t.* tütsülemek; *v/i.* kızmak, öfkelenmek; duman çıkarmak.

**fu.mi.gate** [ˈfjuːmigeit] *v/t.* buharla dezenfekte etm.; **fu.miˈga.tion** *n.* buharla dezenfekte etme.

**fum.ing** ☐ [ˈfjuːmiŋ] hiddetli, kızgın; duman çıkaran.

**fun** [fʌn] *n.* eğlence; şaka, lâtife, alay; make ~ of *ile* alay etm., eğlenmek.

**func.tion** [ˈfʌŋkʃən] **1.** *n.* görev, vazife, iş; tören, merasim; *physiol, A* fonksiyon; **2.** *v/i.* iş görmek, işlemek, çalışmak, görevini yapmak; **func.tion.al** ☐ [ˈ~ʃənl] görevsel, vazifeye ait, işlevsel; vücut organlarının görevine ait; *A* fonksiyonel; pratik; **func.tion.ar.y** [ˈ~ʃnəri] *n.* görevli memur.

**fund** [fʌnd] **1.** *n.* stok; sermaye, kapital; fon; ~s *pl.* para, sermaye, fon; in ~s eldeki para; **2.** *vb.* sermaye bulmak, para temin etm.; kısa vadeli bir borcu uzun vadeli borca çevirmek.

**fun.da.men.tal** [fʌndəˈmentl] **1.** ☐ esaslı, önemli, mühim, temele ait, temel...; **2.** *n.* ~s *pl.* kurallar, prensipler.

**fu.ner.al** [ˈfjuːnərəl] **1.** *n.* cenaze töreni, cenaze alayı, gömme merasimi, defnetme; **2.** *adj.* cenaze törenine ait, cenaze...; ~ pile üzerinde cesetlerin yakıldığı odun yığını; **fu.ne.re.al** ☐ [~ˈniəriəl] cenaze...; kasvetli, sıkıcı, hazin.

**fun.fair** [ˈfʌnfɛə] *n.* lunapark.

**fun.gous** [ˈfʌŋgəs] *adj.* mantara benzer, mantara ait, mantardan oluşan; **fun.gus** [ˈ~gəs] *n.*, *pl.* *mst* **fun.gi** [ˈ~gai] ⚘ mantar; ⚕ yara etrafındaki mantar, ur.

**fu.nic.u.lar** [fjuːˈnikjulə] **1.** *adj.* kablolu...; **2.** *n.* *a.* ~ railway kablolu demiryolu, füniküler.

**funk** F [fʌŋk] **1.** *n.* korku, dehşet; korkak kimse; **2.** *v/t.* & *v/i.* çok korkmak; korkup kaçmak; **ˈfunk.y** *adj.* F duygulu ve ritmik (*müzik*); korkak.

**fun.nel** [ˈfʌnl] *n.* huni; boru; ⚓, 🚂 baca.

**fun.nies** *Am.* [ˈfʌniz] *pl.* = comics.

**fun.ny** ☐ [ˈfʌni] eğlenceli, komik, gülünç; garip, acayip, tuhaf; ˈ~-bone *n.* dirsekteki çok duyarlı bir sinirin geçtiği yer.

**fur** [fəː] **1.** *n.* kürk, post; kürk manto; pas, kir; ~s *pl.* kürklü giyecekler; make the ~ fly ortalığı birbirine katmak, olay çıkarmak; **2.** *v/t.* kürkle kaplamak, kürkle süslemek; *v/i.* paslanmak, kirlenmek; ~red paslı (*dil*).

**fur.be.low** [ˈfəːbiləu] *n.* elbisede gereksiz süs, fırfır, farbala.

**fur.bish** [ˈfəːbiʃ] *v/t.* parlatmak, yeni gibi yapmak; tazelemek.

**fur.ca.tion** [fəːˈkeiʃən] *n.* çatallanma, dallanma.

**fu.ri.ous** ☐ [ˈfjuəriəs] öfkeli, kızgın, küplere binmiş, tepesi atmış; şiddetli, sert, hiddetli.

**furl** [fəːl] *v/t.* & *v/i.* sar(ıl)mak, katla(n)mak.

**fur.long** [ˈfəːlɔŋ] *n.* bir milin sekizde biri, 201 metrelik mesafe.

**fur.lough** [ˈfəːləu] **1.** *n.* sıla (izni); **2.** *v/t.* sıla izni vermek (*part.* ✕).

**fur.nace** [ˈfəːnis] *n.* ocak, kalorifer ocağı.

**fur.nish** [ˈfəːniʃ] *v/t.* döşemek; tedarik etm., sağlamak, teçhiz etm., vermek (with *ile*); **ˈfur.nish.er** *n.* mobilyacı; **ˈfur.nish.ings** *n.* *pl.* mobilya, eşya, takım, teçhizat.

**fur.ni.ture** [ˈfəːnitʃə] *n.* mobilya, eşya, malzeme; ⊕ matbaa yazılarının arasını doldurmak için kullanılan parçalar.

**fu.ro.re** [fjuəˈrɔːri] *n.* taşkınlık, heyecan, kızgınlık, velvele.

**fur.ri.er** [ˈfʌrə] **1.** *n.* kürkçü; **ˈfur.ri.er.y** *n.* kürkçülük.

**fur.row** [ˈfʌrəu] **1.** *n.* saban izi, tekerlek izi; yüz ve alındaki kırışıklık; **2.** *vb.* saban izi yapmak; yüzde kırışıklık oluşturmak.

**fur.ry** [ˈfəːri] *adj.* kürk kaplı, kürke benzer; kürk...

**fur.ther** [ˈfəːðə] **1.** *adj.* & *adv.* daha fazla, daha öteye, daha ileriye; ayrıca, bundan başka; daha çok; **2.** *v/t.* ilerletmek, ilerlemesine yardımcı olm.; **ˈfur.ther.ance** *n.* ilerleme; yardım; **ˈfur.ther.er** *n.* ilerleten; yardım eden; **ˈfur.therˈmore** *adv.* ayrıca, bundan başka, ilaveten; **ˈfur.thermost** *adj.* en ilerideki.

**fur.thest** [ˈfəːðist] *s.* furthermost; at (the) ~ en fazla; en ileride; en son.

**fur.tive** ☐ [ˈfəːtiv] gizli, sinsi.

**fu.ry** [ˈfjuəri] *n.* kızgınlık, öfke, hiddet; şiddet; sinirli kadın *veya* kız, şirret kadın.

**furze** ₄ [fəːz] *n.* katırtırnağına benzer bir bitki.

**fuse** [fjuːz] **1.** *v/t.* & *v/i.* eri(t)mek; eriyip kaynaşmak; eritip kaynatmak; sigorta atmak; sigorta takmak; birleştirmek; ✕ tapa koymak; **2.** *n.* ✗ sigorta; ✕ tapa; patlama cihazı; time-~ saniyeli tapa.

**fu.se.lage** [ˈfjuːzilɑːʒ] *n.* uçak gövdesi, gövde.

**fu.si.bil.i.ty** [fjuːzəˈbiliti] *n.* erime kabiliyeti; **fu.si.ble** [ˈfjuːzəbl] *adj.* eritilebilir.

**fu.sil.ier** ✕ [fjuːziˈliə] *n. (Bazı İngiliz alaylarında)* eski tip tüfekli asker.

**fu.sil.lade** [fjuːziˈleid] *n.* yaylım ateşi.

**fu.sion** [ˈfjuːʒən] *n.* eri(t)me; birleş(tir)me; ~ **bomb** ✕ hidrojen bombası.

**fuss** F [fʌs] **1.** *n.* telaş, yaygara, karışıklık; itiraz, şikâyet; tartışma; aşırı övgü; make a ~ about mesele yapmak; make a ~ of s.o. *b-ne* aşırı itina göstermek; **2.** *v/t.* & *v/i.* titiz davranmak, aşırı itina göstermek; ufak ayrıntılarla uğraşmak; yakınmak; sinirlen(dir)mek; telaşa vermek; **ˈfuss.y** □ F titiz, kılı kırk

yaran, telaşçı; sinirli, huysuz; çok süslü, cicili bicili.

**fus.tian** ⊤ [ˈfʌstiən] *n.* kalın ve kaba yünlü kumaş, dimi; *fig.* laf bolluğu, saçma konuşma.

**fust.i.ness** [ˈfʌstinis] *n.* küflülük, kokmuşluk, çürük kokma; demodelik, geri kafalılık; **ˈfust.y** □ küflü, kokmuş; *fig.* modası geçmiş, demode, eski kafalı.

**fu.tile** □ [ˈfjuːtail] beyhude, boş, sonuçsuz, nafile; değersiz; **fu.til.i.ty** [-ˈtiliti] *n.* yararsızlık, faydasızlık, sonuç vermeyiş, abes oluş.

**fu.ture** [ˈfjuːtʃə] **1.** *adj.* gelecekteki, istikbalde olan, müstakbel; ~ **tense** *gr.* gelecek zaman; **2.** *n.* gelecek, istikbal; ~**s** *pl.* ⊤ vadeli alım satım; **ˈfu.tur.ism** *n. paint.* fütürizm; **fu.tu.ri.ty** [fjuːˈtjuəriti] *n.* istikbal, gelecek; ileride olacak olay.

**fuzz** [fʌz] **1.** *n.* tüy, hav; kabarık *veya* kıvırcık saç; **2.** *v/i.* tüylenmek; *v/t.* tüylerle kaplamak; bulanıklaştırmak; **ˈfuzz.y** □ tüy gibi; bulanık, donuk, belirsiz; kabarık *(saç)*.

# G

**gab** F [gæb] *n.* gevezelik, boş laf, konuşma; the gift of the ~ konuşkanlık, konuşma yeteneği, çenebazlık.

**gab.ar.dine** [ˈgæbədiːn] *n.* gabardin.

**gab.ble** [ˈgæbl] **1.** *n.* gevezelik, boş laf, anlamsız söz, anlaşılmaz konuşma; **2.** *vb.* çok hızlı konuşmak; gevezelik etm.; anlamsız şeyler söylemek; **ˈgab.bler** *n.* geveze, boşboğaz, lakırdıcı; **ˈgab.by** *adj.* F konuşkan, geveze, boşboğaz, çenebaz.

**gab.er.dine** [ˈgæbədiːn] *n.* palto, aba; iş elbisesi; Ortaçağda Musevilerce giyilen kaba ve bol cüppe; = gabardine.

**ga.ble** [ˈgeibl] *n.* çatı altındaki üç köşeli duvar; **ˈga.bled** *adj.* böyle duvarı olan.

**ga.by** [ˈgeibi] *n.* ahmak *veya* budala kimse.

**gad** F [gæd]: ~ about *v/i.* başıboş dolaşmak, aylak aylak gezmek; ♀ üremek, türemek; **ˈgad.a.bout** *n.* F avare kimse, başıboş kimse.

**gad.fly** *zo.* [ˈgædflai] *n.* atsineği.

**gadg.et** *sl.* [ˈgædʒit] *n.* küçük alet, hünerli alet, cihaz.

**Gael.ic** [ˈgeilik] *n.* İskoçya Keltlerinin dili; Gal dili.

**gaff** [gæf] *n.* balıkçı zıpkını; döğüş horozunun ayağına geçirilen madenî mahmuz; ⚓ randa yelkeninin üst sereni; *sl.* hile, oyun, dolap; blow the ~ *sl.* sırrı söylemek, gizli planı açıklamak.

**gaffe** F [gæf] *n.* gaf (yapma), pot kırma, çam devirme.

**gaf.fer** F [ˈgæfə] *n.* yaşlı adam, ihtiyar, taşralı yaşlı kimse; ustabaşı.

**gag** [gæg] **1.** *n.* ağız tıkacı (*a. fig.*); *parl.* mecliste serbest konuşmayı engelleme; *thea.* sahnede oyuncu tarafından eklenen söz *veya* hareketler; şaka, latife; **2.** *vb.* ağzını tıkamak, susturmak; *thea.* oyuna söz *veya* hareketler eklemek; *fig.* serbest konuşmasını önlemek, b-nin ağzını tıkamak.

**ga.ga** *sl.* [ˈgaːgaː] *adj.* bunak, deli, **ka**çık.

**gage**[1] [geidʒ] **1.** *n.* rehin; pey; düelloya davet için yere atılan eldiven; **2.** *vb.* **b**şi rehin vermek, pey vermek.

**gage**[2] [~] = gauge.

**gag.gle** [ˈgægl] *n.* kaz sürüsü; *fig.* **çene**baz kadınlar grubu.

**gai.e.ty** [ˈgeiəti] *n.* neşe, şenlik, eğlence; parlak görünüş, gösteriş.

**gai.ly** [ˈgeili] *adv.* of gay.

**gain** [gein] **1.** *n.* kâr, kazanç, gelir; yarar; artma, artış (*part.* ♰ ~s *pl.*); **2.** *vb.* kazanmak, elde etm., arttırmak, eklemek, kâr etm.; ileri gitmek (*saat*); varmak -e; ~ in kilo almak, şişmanlamak; ~ on yaklaşmak, aradaki mesafeyi kapatmak; **ˈgain.er** *n.* kazanan kimse *veya* şey; **gain.ful** □ [ˈ~ful] kazançlı, kârlı; ~ employment para karşılığı yapılan iş, kazançlı iş; ~ly occupied para ile tutulmuş b-i, meslek sahibi; **ˈgain.ings** *n. pl.* kazanç, kâr, gelir.

**gain.say** *lit.* [geinˈsei] (*irr.* say) *v/t.* inkâr etm., reddetmek.

**gainst** *poet.* [geinst] = against.

**gait** [ˈgeit] *n.* yürüyüş, gidiş, yürüme *veya* koşma şekli.

**gai.ter** [ˈgeitə] *n.* tozluk, getir.

**gal** *Am. sl.* [gæl] *n.* kız.

**ga.la** [ˈgaːlə] *n.* gala, bayram, şenlik.

**ga.lac.tic** *ast.* [gəˈlæktik] *adj.* gökadaya ait, gökada...

**gal.an.tine** [ˈgæləntiːn] *n.* galantin, haşlanmış söğüş et.

**gal.ax.y** [ˈgæləksi] *n. ast.* gökada; samanyolu; *fig.* seçkin kimseler topluluğu.

**gale** [geil] *n.* bora, fırtına; *fig.* kahkaha tufanı.

**ga.le.na** *min.* [gəˈliːnə] *n.* kükürt kurşunu, galen.

**gall**[1] [gɔːl] *n.* safra, öd; *fig.* acı duygu; *part. Am. sl.* yüzsüzlük, arsızlık, terbiyesizlik.

**gall**[2] ♀ [~] *n.* mazı, ağaç uru.

**gall**[3] [~] **1.** *n.* yara, acı veren şişkinlik, sürtünmekten açılmış yer; *fig.* duygularını incitme, utandırma; **2.** *v/t.* sürterek yara etm.; üzmek, incitmek.

**gal.lant** [ˈgælənt] **1.** □ cesur; gösterişli; nazik, kibar; **2.** *n.* çapkın adam; kadınlara karşı hep nazik olan delikanlı; centilmen delikanlı; moda budalası kimse; **3.** *vb.* kadınlara kur yapmak; kadınlara nezaket göstermek; modaya uygun giyinmek; **ˈgal.lant.ry** *n.* cesaret, kahramanlık, yiğitlik; kadınlara karşı nezaket; âşıkane söz *veya* davranış.
**gal.leon** ⚓ [ˈgæliən] *n.* kalyon.
**gal.ler.y** [ˈgæləri] *n.* galeri; tiyatroda en ucuz yerlere oturan kimseler; üstü kapalı balkon; dehliz, koridor, tünel; ⚒ galeri; play to the ~ halkın sempatisini kazanmaya çalışmak.
**gal.ley** [ˈgæli] *n.* ⚓ kadırga; ⚓ gemi mutfağı; *typ.* dizilmiş harflerin konulduğu tekne, gale; ~ **proof** ilk düzeltme; **ˈ~-slave** *n.* kürek mahkûmu, forsa.
**Gal.lic** [ˈgælik] *adj.* Galya ile ilgili; *co.* Fransa'ya ait; **Gal.li.can** [ˈ~kən] *adj.* Galya *veya* Fransa'ya ait; **gal.li.cism** [ˈ~sizəm] *n.* Fransızca'dan alınmış terim.
**gal.li.vant** [gæliˈvænt] *v/i.* başıboş dolaşmak, aylak aylak gezmek, gezip tozmak, zevk peşinde koşmak, gününü gün etmeye bakmak.
**gall-nut** [ˈgɔːlnʌt] *n.* mazı, yumru.
**gal.lon** [ˈgælən] *n.* galon *(4,54 litre, Am. 3,78 litre).*
**gal.lop** [ˈgæləp] **1.** *n.* dörtnala gidiş; **2.** *vb.* dörtnala gitmek; koşuşturmak; acele etm.; hızla gelişmek.
**gal.lows** [ˈgæləuz] *n. sg.* darağacı; **ˈ~-bird** *n.* asılmaya layık herif, ip kaçkını.
**Gal.lup poll** [ˈgæləpˌpəul] *n.* kamuoyu yoklaması.
**ga.lore** [gəˈlɔː] *adv.* bol bol, bol miktarda.
**ga.losh** [gəˈlɔʃ] *n.* kaloş, şoson, yağmurlu havada giyilen lastik.
**ga.lumph** [gəˈlʌmf] *v/i.* çalım atarak yürümek, fiyakalı biçimde yürümek.
**gal.van.ic** [gælˈvænik] *adj.* (~ally) galvanik, galvanizme ait; **gal.va.nism** [ˈgælvənizəm] *n.* galvanizm, kimyasal güçle üretilen elektrik; **ˈgal.va.nize** *v/t.* galvanizlemek, galvanizle kaplamak; harekete geçirmek (into -e); **gal.va.no.plas.tic** [~nəuˈplæstik] *adj.* galvanoplastik.
**gam.bit** [ˈgæmbit] *n.* *satranç:* gambit, daha iyi bir mevki kazanmak için taş feda etme; *fig.* ilk hareket, başlangıç, ilk söz, açış.
**gam.ble** [ˈgæmbl] **1.** *v/i.* kumar oynamak *(a .fig.)*; **2.** *n.* F kumar, riskli iş *(mst fig.)*; **ˈgam.bler** *n.* kumarbaz; **ˌgam.bling-den, ˈgam.bling-house** *n.* kumarhane.
**gam.boge** [gæmˈbuːʒ] *n.* sanatçıların kullandığı turuncu madde, Hint zamkı, gomagota.
**gam.bol** [ˈgæmbəl] **1.** *n.* sıçrama, zıplama, hoplama; **2.** *v/i.* sıçrayıp oynamak, hoplayıp zıplamak.
**game¹** [geim] **1.** *n.* oyun, eğlence; oyun aleti; spor; atletizm yarışmaları; oyun partisi; plan, tertip, hile; av; av eti; parti; beat s.o. at his own ~ *b-ni* kendi oyunuyle yenmek; play the ~ usule uygun oynamak, kurallara uymak; *fig.* açık sözlü ve dürüst olm.; be off one's ~ formda olmamak, oynayacak durumda olmamak; make ~ of s.o. *b-le* alay etm.; *b-ni* küçük düşürmek; **2.** *adj.* F cesur, yiğit, gözüpek; die ~ ölesiye dayanmak, sebat etm.; **3.** *vb.* kumar oynamak.
**game²** [~] *adj.* topal, sakat, kötürüm.
**game...:** **ˈ~-cock** *n.* dövüş horozu; **ˈ~.keeper** *n.* avlak bekçisi; **ˈ~-laws** *n. pl.* av hukuku, avlanma kuralları; **ˈ~-li.cence** *n.* avcı tezkeresi; **ˈgames-mas.ter** *n.* beden eğitimi öğretmeni; **game.ster** [ˈ~stə] *n.* kumarbaz; **ˈgam.ing-house** *n.* kumarhane.
**gam.ma rays** *phys.* [ˈgæməˈreiz] *n. pl.* gamma ışınları.
**gam.mon** [ˈgæmən] *n.* tütsülenmiş jambon; F zırva, saçma, boş laf.
**gamp** *co.* [gæmp] *n.* büyük şemsiye.
**gam.ut** [ˈgæmət] *n.* ♪ gam; *fig.* *bşin* tümü.
**gam.y** [ˈgeimi] *adj.* cesur, yiğit, gözüpek; av eti kokulu.
**gan.der** [ˈgændə] *n.* erkek kaz.
**gang** [gæŋ] **1.** *n.* takım, ekip, güruh; *b.s.* çete; **2.** *vb.* ~ up karşı gelmek, saldırmak (against, on -e); **ˈ~-board** *n.* ⚓ iskele tahtası; **gang.er** [ˈgæŋə] *n.* işçi ekibinin başı.
**gan.gli.on** [ˈgæŋliən] *n.* *anat.* sinir düğümü, ganglion, lenfa bezi; *fig.* kavuşma noktası, ilgi merkezi.
**gang-plank** ⚓ [ˈgæŋplæŋk] *n.* iskele tahtası.
**gan.grene** ⚕ [ˈgæŋgriːn] *n.* kangren.
**gang.ster** *Am.* [ˈgæŋstə] *n.* gangster.
**gang.way** [ˈgæŋwei] *n.* geçit, yol, pasaj; ⚓ borda iskelesi; ⚓ iskele tahtası.
**gan.net** *orn.* [ˈgænit] *n.* bir tür deniz kuşu.
**gan.try** [ˈgæntri] *n.* 🚂 sinyal köprüsü; ⚓ yükleme iskelesi.
**gaol** [dʒeil], **ˈ~-bird, ˈgaol.er** *s.* jail *etc.*
**gap** [gæp] *n.* yarık, çatlak, boşluk, aralık, açıklık; eksiklik; geçit; *fig.* ayrılık *(fikir).*
**gape** [geip] **1.** *v/i.* açık olm., açılmak, yarılmak; ~ at esnemek; ağzını açmak; hayretten ağzı açık kalmak; ağzı açık

bir şekilde bakakalmak; **2.** *n.* the ~s *pl.*
kümes hayvanlarının ölünceye kadar ga-
galarının açık kaldığı bir hastalık; esneme nöbeti.

**ga.rage** [ˈgærɑːʒ] **1.** *n.* garaj; *Am.* benzin istasyonu; **2.** *v/t.* *(oto)* garaja koymak, garaja sokmak.

**garb** [gɑːb] **1.** *n.* kıyafet, kılık, üst baş;
**2.** *v/t.* giydirmek.

**gar.bage** [ˈgɑːbidʒ] *n.* çöp, süprüntü; ~
can *Am.*, ~ pail çöp kutusu.

**gar.ble** [ˈgɑːbl] *v/t.* tahrif etm., bozmak,
bazı parçaları seçip kötü bir maksada
alet etm.

**gar.den** [ˈgɑːdn] **1.** *n.* bahçe; ~s *pl.* park;
bostan; lead s.o. up the ~ path *b-ni* kötü
yola sevketmek; **2.** *v/i.* bahçıvanlık etm.,
bahçe işiyle uğraşmak; ˈgar.den.er *n.*
bahçıvan.

**gar.de.nia** ⚕ [gɑːˈdiːnjə] *n.* gardenya.

**gar.den.ing** [ˈgɑːdniŋ] *n.* bahçıvanlık;
ˈgar.den-par.ty *n.* garden parti, bahçede
verilen parti.

**gar.gle** [ˈgɑːgl] **1.** *v/t.* gargara etm.; **2.** *n.*
gargara.

**gar.goyle** ⚘ [ˈgɑːgɔil] *n.* çirkin insan ve-
*ya* hayvan şeklindeki oluk ağzı.

**gar.ish** □ [ˈgɛəriʃ] aşırı parlak, çok süslü, nazarı çekecek, cafcaflı, gösterişli.

**gar.land** [ˈgɑːlənd] **1.** *n.* çelenk; **2.** *v/t.* çe-
lenkle süslemek.

**gar.lic** ⚘ [ˈgɑːlik] *n.* sarmısak.

**gar.ment** [ˈgɑːmənt] *n.* elbise, giysi.

**gar.ner** [ˈgɑːnə] **1.** *n.* tahıl ambarı; *fig.*
biriktirilen şey; **2.** *v/t.* toplamak, biriktirmek.

**gar.net** *min.* [ˈgɑːnit] *n.* lâl taşı, grena,
kıymetli bir kırmızı taş.

**gar.nish** [ˈgɑːniʃ] *vb.* süslemek, donatmak; yemeği süslemek; garnitür katmak; **gar.nish.ing** *n.* süsleme, garnitür.

**gar.ret** [ˈgærit] *n.* çatı arası, tavan arasındaki oda.

**gar.ri.son** ✕ [ˈgærisn] **1.** *n.* garnizon; **2.**
*vb.* garnizon kurmak; bir yere asker yerleştirmek.

**gar.ru.li.ty** [gæˈruːliti] *n.* gevezelik, boşboğazlık; **gar.ru.lous** □ [ˈgæruləs] geveze, boşboğaz.

**gar.ter** [ˈgɑːtə] *n.* çorap bağı; *Am.* jartiyer; Order of the ♀ dizbağı nişanı.

**gas** [gæs] **1.** *n.* gaz, havagazı; F boş laf,
anlamsız konuşma, övünme; *Am.* =
gasoline; step on the ~ gaza basmak,
süratlendirmek; **2.** *vb.* gazla zehirlemek;
F saçmalamak, boş boş konuşmak;
ˈ~-bag *n.* ⚓ gaz zarfı, uçakta gaz tut-
maya yarayan torba; F laf ebesi, geve-

ze; ˈ~-brack.et *n.* gaz kolu; ˈ~-burn.er *n.*
bek, havagazı memesi; ˈ~-cham.ber *n.*
gaz odası; ˈ~-en.gine *n.* gaz motoru, gazla işleyen makine; **gas.e.ous** [ˈgeizjəs]
*adj.* gazlı, gaz gibi, gaz...

**gas...**: ˈ~-fire *n.* gaz ocağı; ˈ~-fit.ter *n.* havagazı tesisatçısı; ˈ~-fit.tings *n. pl.* havagazı aletleri.

**gash** [gæʃ] **1.** *n.* uzun ve derin yara, kesik; **2.** *vb.* yaralamak, derin yara açmak.

**gas.ket** [ˈgæskit] *n.* ⚓ kalçeta, sarılı yelkeni serene bağlamaya yarayan küçük
ipler, salmastra; ⊕ conta.

**gas...**: ˈ~-light *n.* gaz ışığı; ˈ~-mask *n.* gaz
maskesi; ˈ~-me.ter *n.* gaz saati, gaz sayacı; **gas.o.lene, gas.o.line** *Am. mot.*
[ˈgæsəuliːn] *n.* benzin; **gas.om.e.ter**
[gæˈsɔmitə] *n.* gazometre; ˈgas-oven *n.*
havagazı fırını.

**gasp** [gɑːsp] **1.** *n.* soluma, nefes; **2.** *v/i.*
solumak; soluyarak konuşmak; *a.* ~ for
breath nefes nefese kalmak, nefesi kesilmek.

**gas-pok.er** [ˈgæsˈpəukə] *n.* ocak demiri;
ˈgas-ˈproof *adj.* gaz geçirmez; ˈgas-range
*n.* havagazı ocağı; ˈgas-ring *n.* bek;
**gassed** *adj.* gazlanmış, gazlı; gazdan ze-
hirlenmiş; ˈgas-stove *n.* gaz ocağı, fırın;
ˈgas.sy *adj.* gaz..., gaz gibi, gazla dolu;
ˈgas-tar *n.* kömür katranı.

**gas.tric** ⚕ [ˈgæstrik] *adj.* mideye ait, midevi, mide...; **gas.tri.tis** [gæsˈtraitis] *n.*
mide iltihabı, gastrit.

**gas.tron.o.my** [gæsˈtrɔnəmi] *n.* iyi yemek
seçme, pişirme ve yeme sanatı.

**gas-works** [ˈgæswəːks] *n.* *mst* *sg.* havagazı üretilen yer, gazhane.

**gat** *Am. sl* [gæt] *n.* tabanca.

**gate** [geit] *n.* kapı, giriş, kanal kapağı,
su yolu kapağı; dağ geçidi, patika;
*spor:* seyirci sayısı; = ~-money;
ˈ~-crash.er *n. sl.* parasız *veya* davetiye-
siz giren kimse; ˈ~-house *n.* kapıcı odası, bekçi kulübesi; ˈ~-leg(ged) ta.ble açılır kapanır ayaklı kanatları olan masa;
ˈ~.man 🚉 geçit bekçisi; ˈ~-mon.ey
*n. spor:* hâsılat; ˈ~-post *n.* kapı direği;
between you and me and the ~ laf aramızda, aramızda kalsın; ˈ~.way *n.* giriş
yeri, kapı, geçit; *fig.* geçiş.

**gath.er** [ˈgæðə] **1.** *v/t.* toplamak, biraraya getirmek; devşirmek, seçmek; yavaş
yavaş kazanmak; anlamak, kavramak,
sonuç çıkarmak (from -*den*); büzmek; ~
speed hızlanmak; *v/i.* toplanmak, çoğalmak, biraraya gelmek; cerahat toplamak; *a.* ~ to a head 🕇 iltihaplanıp şiş-

mek; **2.** *n.* ~s *pl.* kıvrım, büzük; **'gath-er.ing** *n.* toplantı, toplanma; ⚶ cerahat, apse, iltihap.

**gauche** [gəʊʃ] *adj.* beceriksiz, acemi; kaba; patavatsız; savruk; **gau.che.rie** [¹~əriˑ] *n.* beceriksizlik; kabalık, münasebetsizlik.

**gaud.y** [¹gɔːdi] **1.** ☐ zevksizce süslenmiş, aşırı süslü, cicili bicili; **2.** *n. univ.* yıllık ziyafet.

**gauge** [geidʒ] **1.** *n.* ölçü, mikyas, ayar, miktar; kalibre; geyç, ölçme aleti; 🚂 raylar arasındaki açıklık; ⊕ enine kesit, çap; ✝ dokunmuş kumaşın inceliği; **2.** *v/t.* ayar etm., ölçüsünü bulmak, ölçmek; *fig.* tahmin etm.; **'gaug.er** *n.* ölçü aleti, ayar aleti.

**Gaul** [gɔːl] *n.* Gal; Galya; Gal'li; *co.* Fransız.

**gaunt** ☐ [gɔːnt] zayıf, irˑce, kuru, cılız, gıdasızlıktan kurumuş, bir deri bir kemik; tenha, ıssız, korkunç, kasvetli.

**gaunt.let¹** [gɔːntlit] *n.* zırh eldiveni; uzun eldiven, kolçak; *fig.* meydan okuma; throw down (pick up, take up) the ~ meydan okumak (düelloyu kabul etm., meydan okumayı kabul etm.).

**gaunt.let²** [~] : run the ~ sıra dayağı yemek; *fig.* şiddetli eleştirilere maruz kalmak.

**gauze** [gɔːz] *n.* tül, gazlı bez; tül kafes; pus, duman; sılk ~ ipek tül; **'gauz.y** *adj.* tül gibi, hafif, şeffaf.

**gave** [geiv] *pret. of* give 1 & 2.

**gav.el** *Am.* [¹gævl] *n.* açık arttırmacı veya hakimlerce kullanılan çekiç, tokmak.

**gawk** F [gɔːk] *n.* beceriksiz *veya* utangaç kimse; ahmak kimse, budala kimse, hantal kimse; **'gawk.y** *adj.* beceriksiz; utangaç, ahmak; hantal.

**gay** ☐ [gei] neşeli, şen, keyifli, neşe dolu, mutlu, neşe saçan; zevk düşkünü; parlak, canlı *(renk)*; *Am. sl.* homoseksüel; **gay.e.ty** [¹geiəti] = gaiety.

**gaze** [geiz] **1.** *n.* dik bakış; **2.** *v/i.* dik dik bakmak, gözlünü dikip bakmak (at *-e*); **'gaz.er** *n.* dik dik bakan kimse.

**ga.zelle** *zo.* [gə¹zel] *n.* ceylan, ahu, gazal.

**ga.zette** [gə¹zet] **1.** *n.* (resmi) gazete; **2.** *v/t.* resmi gazetede ilan etm.; **gaz.et.teer** [gæziˈtiə] *n.* coğrafi isimler indeksi.

**gear** [giə] **1.** *n.* ⊕ dişli (takımı); *mot.* şanjman, vites; donanım, tertibat, teçhizat; elbise, eşya, giyim; in ~ viteste; out of ~ boşta; landing-~ ✈ iniş takımı; steering-~ 🔧 dümen makinesi; *mot.* direksiyon dişli mekanizması; hunting-~ av malzemesi; **2.** *vb.* vitese takmak;

⊕ birbirine geçmek; *fig.* uydurmak (to *-e*); ~ up (down) vites büyültmek (küçültmek); **'~-box** *n.* dişli kutusu, vites kutusu; **'gear.ing** *n.* şanjman, mekanizma, dişli takımı; **'gear-le.ver** *n.*, *part.* *Am.* **'gear-shift** vites kolu.

**gee** [dʒiː] **1.** *n.* g harfi; **2.** *int.* deh!; *Am.* vay canına!, Allah Allah!, ya!, öyle mi?

**geese** [giːs] *pl. of* goose.

**Gei.ger** [¹gaigə]: ~ counter radyoaktivite ölçme aracı, geyger sayacı.

**gei.sha** [¹geiʃə] *n.* geyşa.

**gel.a.tin(e)** [dʒelə¹tiˑn] *n.* jelatin; **ge.lat.i-nize** [dʒi¹lætinaiz] *vb.* jelatin yapmak, jelatinle kaplamak; **ge¹lat.i.nous** *adj.* jelatinli, jelatin gibi.

**geld** [geld] *(irr.)* *v/t.* hadım etm., kısırlaştırmak, iğdiş etm.; **'geld.ing** *n.* kısırlaştırılmış hayvan *(mst at)*.

**gel.ig.nite** [¹dʒelignait] *n.* gelignit, jelatinli dinamit.

**gelt** [gelt] *pret.* & *p.p. of* geld.

**gem** [dʒem] **1.** *n.* kıymetli taş, cevher, mücevher; *fig.* kıymetli şey, pahalı şey; **2.** *v/t.* kıymetli taşlarla süslemek, donatmak.

**Gem.i.ni** [dʒenimai] *n.* İkizler burcu.

**gen.darme** [¹ʒãːndɑːm] *n.* jandarma.

**gen.der** *gr.* [¹dʒendə] *n.* cins, ismin cinsi.

**gene** *biol.* [dʒiːn] *n.* gen.

**gen.e.a.log.i.cal** ☐ [dʒiːnjə¹lɔdʒikəl] soy *veya* şecereye ait, soy...; ~ tree şecere, soy ağacı; **gen.e.al.o.gy** [dʒiːni¹ælədʒi] *n.* nesep, şecere, soy, silsile.

**gen.er.a** [¹dʒenərə] *pl. of* genus.

**gen.er.al** [¹dʒenərəl] **1.** ☐ genel, umumi, genel...; şef, amir, reis; ~ election genel seçim; as a ~ rule, in ~ genellikle, ekseriya; ~ knowledge genel bilgi; **2.** *n.* X general; F *a.* ~ servant hizmetçi kız; **gen.er.al.i.ty** [~¹ræliti] *n.* genel kural, genellik, umumiyet; şüpheli söz; **gen.er.al-i.za.tion** [~rəlai¹zeiʃən] *n.* genelleştirme, umumileştirme, genellik, umumilik; genel bir sonuç çıkarma; **'gen.er.al.ize** *vb.* genelleştirmek, umumileştirmek, genel bir sonuç çıkarmak, genel olarak ifade etm.; **'gen.er.al.ly** *adv.* genellikle, ekseriya, geniş ölçüde; detaylara inmeden, genel olarak; **'gen.er.al.ship** *n.* generallik; liderlik, başkanlık, önderlik, müdürlük. şeflik.

**gen.er.ate** [¹dʒenəreit] *v/t.* husule getirmek, doğurmak, üretmek, meydana getirmek, oluşturmak *(a. fig.)*; **'gen.er.at-ing sta.tion** elektrik santralı; **gen.er¹a-tion** *n.* meydana getirme, üretme; nesil, döl, soy; ortalama olarak insan nesli sa-

yılan otuz yıl; batın; **gen.er.a.tive**
[ˈ~rətiv] *adj.* üretken; doğuşa ait; üreme kabiliyeti olan; **gen.er.a.tor** [ˈ~reitə]
*n.* üreten kimse, doğuran kimse, meydana getiren kimse; ⊕ jeneratör; *part.*
*Am. mot.* dinamo.

**ge.ner.ic** [dʒiˈnerik] *adj.* cinse ait; genel, umumi; geniş kapsamlı.

**gen.er.os.i.ty** [dʒenəˈrɔsiti] *n.* cömertlik, eli açıklık; gönlü yücelik; **ˈgen.er.ous** □ cömert, eliaçık; yüce gönüllü, asil; bol, bereketli, verimli.

**gen.e.sis** [ˈdʒenisis] *n.* başlangıç, başlama noktası, menşe, yaradılış; ♀ *İncil ve Tevrat:* İlk kitap; **ge.net.ic** [dʒiˈnetik] *adj.* (~ally) bir şeyin aslına ait; genetiğe ait, genetik...; **geˈnet.ics** *n. pl.* genetik, soyaçekim olaylarını inceleyen biyoloji dalı.

**gen.ial** □ [ˈdʒiːnjəl] güler yüzlü, hoş, sempatik, arkadaş canlısı; elverişli, müsait, uygun *(iklim);* **ge.ni.al.i.ty** [~niˈæliti] *n.* sempatiklik, sevimlilik, nezaket, güler yüzlülük.

**ge.nie** [ˈdʒiːni] *n.* cin, peri *(Arap hikâyelerinde).*

**ge.ni.i** [ˈdʒiːniai] *pl. of* genius.

**gen.i.tals** [ˈdʒenitlz] *n. pl.* tenasül *(veya* üreme) organları.

**gen.i.tive** *gr.* [ˈdʒenitiv] *n. a.* ~ case -in hali.

**gen.ius** [ˈdʒiːnjəs] *n., pl.* **ge.ni.i** [ˈ~niai] deha; üstün kabiliyet, istidat, yetenek; dâhi; cin, ruh, iblis, peri, doğaüstü yaratık; **gen.ius.es** [ˈ~njəsiz] *n.* deha, dâhilik.

**gen.o.cide** [ˈdʒenəsaid] *n.* soykırım, katliam.

**Gen.o.ese** [dʒenəuˈiːz] **1.** *n.* Cenovalı kimse; **2.** *adj.* Cenovalı, Cenevizli.

**genre** [ʒãːŋr] *n.* tarz, tür, nevi; ~-painting günlük hayatı anlatan üslup.

**gent** F [dʒent] *n.* kibar adam, beyefendi, centilmen.

**gen.teel** □ *sl. veya iro.* [dʒenˈtiːl] soylu, kibar, nazik, terbiyeli; yüksek tabakaya mensup.

**gen.tian** ♀ [ˈdʒenʃiən] *n.* yılanotu.

**gen.tile** [ˈdʒentail] **1.** *adj.* Musevî olmayan; **2.** *n.* Musevi olmayan kimse.

**gen.til.i.ty** *mst iro.* [dʒenˈtiliti] *n.* kibarlık, asalet, soyluluk.

**gen.tle** □ [ˈdʒentl] nazik, kibar; yumusak; tatlı; ılımlı, mutedil; dikkatli; soylu. asil; **ˈ~.folk(s** *pl.)* soylu kişiler, yüksek tabaka; **ˈ~.man** *n.* centilmen, kibar adam. beyefendi; gentlemen! baylar! efendiler!; **ˈ~.man.like,** **ˈ~.man.ly** *adj.*

centilmence, beyefendiye yakışır şekilde; **ˈ~.man.ı.s a.gree.ment** centilmen anlaşması, söz anlaşması, kontratsız anlaşma; **ˈgen.tle.ness** *n.* kibarlık, nezaket; **ˈgen.tle.wom.an** *n.* hanımefendi, kibar kadın.

**gen.try** [ˈdʒentri] *n.* küçültücü soyluluk; *contp.* orta sınıf.

**gen.u.flec.tion, gen.u.flex.ion** [dʒenjuːˈflekʃən] *n.* diz çökme *(ibadet ederken).*

**gen.u.ine** □ [ˈdʒenjuin] hakiki, gerçek, taklit olmayan; içten, samimi.

**ge.nus** [ˈdʒiːnəs] *n., pl.* **gen.er.a** [ˈdʒenərə] cins, nevi, çeşit, tür, sınıf.

**ge.o.cen.tric** [dʒiːəuˈsentrik] *adj.* yeryüzünün merkezine ait.

**ge.od.e.sy** [dʒiˈɔdisi] *n.* yeryüzü düzlemini ölçme bilgisi, jeodezi.

**ge.og.ra.pher** [dʒiˈɔgrəfə] *n.* coğrafyacı, coğrafya uzmanı; **ge.o.graph.ic, ge.o.graph.i.cal** □ [~əˈgræfik(əl)] coğrafi, coğrafyaya ait; **ge.og.ra.phy** [~ˈɔgrəfi] *n.* coğrafya; coğrafya konusunda bilimsel inceleme.

**ge.o.log.ic, ge.o.log.i.cal** □ [dʒiəˈlɔdʒik-(əl)] jeolojiye ait, jeolojik; **ge.ol.o.gist** [~ˈɔlədʒist] *n.* jeolog; **geˈol.o.gy** *n.* jeoloji, yerbilim.

**ge.om.e.ter** [dʒiˈɔmitə] *n.* geometri uzmanı; bir tür tırtıl; **ge.o.met.ric, ge.o.met.ri.cal** □ [dʒiəˈmetrik(əl)] geometrik; geometrical progression geometrik artma *veya* eksilme; **ge.om.e.try** [~ˈɔmitri] *n.* geometri.

**ge.o.phys.ics** [dʒiːəuˈfiziks] *n. sg.* jeofizik.

**ge.o.pol.i.tics** [dʒiːəuˈpɔlitiks] *n. sg.* jeopolitik; siyasi ve iktisadi coğrafya.

**geor.gette** [dʒɔːˈdʒet] *n.* ince ipekli kumaş, jorjet.

**ge.ra.ni.um** ♀ [dʒiˈreinjəm] *n.* ıtır, sardunya çiçeği.

**ger.i.at.rics** ♀ [dʒeriˈætriks] *n. pl.* yaşlıların tıbbi bakımı, yaşlılarla ilgili tıp ihtisası.

**germ** [dʒəːm] **1.** *n.* mikrop; tohum; başlangıç, başlama noktası *(bir fikrin);* **2.** *vb.* çimlenmek, topraktan fışkırmak, filiz vermek *(a. fig.).*

**Ger.man¹** [ˈdʒəːmən] **1.** *adj.* Almanya *veya* Almanlara ait; **2.** *n.* Alman(ca).

**ger.man²** [~]: brother *etc.* ~ öz kardeş *vs.;* **ger.mane** [dʒəːˈmein] *adj.* (to) *b-le* ilgili, alâkalı, ilişkili.

**Ger.man.ic** [dʒəːˈmænik] *adj.* Almanya, Almanca *veya* Almanlarla ilgili; German dil ailesine ait; **Ger.man.ism** [ˈdʒəːmənizəm] *n.* Alman dili (özelliği);

Almanya *veya* Alman geleneklerine karşı özel sevgi.

**germ-car.ri.er** ['dʒəːmkæriə] *n.* portör, mikrop taşıyıcı b-i.

**ger.mi.cide** ['dʒəːmisaid] *n.* mikrop öldürücü madde, antiseptik dezenfektan.

**ger.mi.nal** ['dʒəːminl] *adj.* oluşum safhasında; mikrop...; **ger.mi.nate** ['-neit] *v/t.* & *v/i.* filizlen(dir)mek; **ger.mi'na.tion** *n.* filizlenme, sürme, filiz verme.

**germ...:** '-**proof** *adj.* mikrop geçirmez; ~ **war.fare** ✕ savaşta mikrop kullanılması.

**ger.on.tol.o.gy** ⚡ [dʒerɔn'tɔlədʒi] *n.* yaşlılıkla ilgili bilim dalı.

**ger.ry.man.der** *pol.* ['dʒerimændə] *n.* seçim bölgesini bir siyasî partinin çıkarına göre ayarlama.

**ger.und** *gr.* ['dʒerənd] *n.* fiilimsi, eylemsi, ulaç, isim-fiil.

**ges.ta.tion** [dʒes'teiʃən] *n.* gebelik (süresi), hamilelik (süresi).

**ges.tic.u.late** [dʒes'tikjuleit] *v/i.* konuşurken el hareketleri yapmak; el hareketleri yaparak konuşmak, jestler yapmak; **ges.tic.u'la.tion** *n.* konuşurken el hareketleri yapma; konuşurken yapılan el hareketi.

**ges.ture** ['dʒestʃə] *n.* hareket, jest.

**get** [get] *(irr.)* **1.** *v/t.* almak, elde etm., ele geçirmek; olmak; sağlamak, hazırlamak, tedarik etm.; başlamak; yaptırmak; ikna etm.; sebep olm.; kazanmak; yakalanmak *(hastalığa);* ceza yemek, hapse mahkûm edilmek; anlamak, kavramak; şaşırtmak; *b-ni* sıkıştırmak; başarmak; *-mek* fırsatı bulmak, *-mek* fırsatına erişmek; have got sahip olm., ...si olm.; you have got to obey F itaat etmeye mecbursun, itaat etmelisin, itaat etmen gerekir, itaat etmek zorundasın; one's hair cut saçını kestirmek; ~ me the book! kitabı bana getir!; ~ by heart ezberlemek; ~ with child hamile bırakmak, gebe bırakmak; ~ away kaçmak, kurtulmak; ~ down masadan kalkmak; canını sıkmak, moralini bozmak; yutmak; yazmak, not etm.; aşağı inmek; ~ in varmak; içeri girmek; seçilmek; toplamak; tedarik etm.; kaldırmak *(ürün);* ~ s.o. in *b-ni* eve çağırmak; ~ off inmek *(araçtan);* başlamak; göndermek; cezadan kurtarmak; çıkarmak; ~ on binmek *(araca);* uyuşmak, anlaşmak, geçinmek; ~ out dışarı çıkmak; açığa çıkmak, ortaya çıkmak *(sır);* güçlükle söylemek; yayınlamak; dağıtmak; kaç(ın)mak; yavaş yavaş bırakmak *(kötü alışkanlık);* çı-

karmak; ~ over unutmak; üzerinden atmak *(öfke, şok);* yenmek anlaşılmasını sağlamak; ~ through geçmek *(imtihanı);* bitirmek; anlamasını sağlamak; geçirmek *(imtihanda öğrenciyi, tasarıyı, kanunu);* ~ up binmek; yataktan kaldırmak; düzenlemek; ~ up steam kuvvetini toplamak; heyecanlanmak *veya* öfkelenmek; hızlanmak, istim kaldırmak; **2.** *v/i.* gelmek; varmak; ulaşmak; ~ ready hazırla(n)mak; ~ about dolaşmak, ayağa kalkmak *(hastalıktan sonra);* yayılmak *(söylenti);* ~ abroad yurt dışına çıkmak; ~ ahead geçmek, geride bırakmak, üstün olm.; ilerlemek; ~ along geçinmek; idare etm.; başarmak, ilerleme kaydetmek; ~ along with *b-le* geçinmek, anlaşmak, uyuşmak, araları iyi olm.; ~ around to s.th. *bşi* geç yapmak, *bşe* eli geç değmek; ~ at ulaşmak, yanına varmak; rüşvet vermek; azarlamak; açığa çıkarmak, ortaya çıkarmak *(gerçekleri);* ~ away kurtulmak, kaçmak; ~ away with alıp kaçmak, yakayı ele vermemek, şüphe uyandırmadan atlatmak; ~ by geçmek; geçinmek; yaşamak; ~ down to uğraşmak, kendini vermek; F .işe koyulmak; ~ in içeri girmek; varmak; seçilmek; binmek; ~ into giymek; girmek; edinmek, sahip olm.; ~ off yakayı kurtarmak, paçayı kurtarmak, kaçmak, sıvışmak; ⚓ yola çıkmak; ~ off with s.o. *b-le* tanışmak; hissi *veya* cinsel ilişkiye girmek; ~ on ilerlemek, gelişme kaydetmek; geçmek *(zaman);* ~ over atlatmak *(hastalık);* ~ through temas kurmak; çıkarmak *(telefonda);* ~ to hear *veya* know *veya* learn duymak *veya* bilmek, tanımak *veya* öğrenmek; ~ up yataktan kalkmak; ayağa kalkmak; yükselmek, yukarı çıkmak; sertleşmek *(hava);* **get-at--a.ble** [get'ætəbl] *adj.* yanına girilebilir, ulaşılabilir; **get-a.way** ['getəwei] *n. spor:* start; kaçış, kaçıp kurtulma; kaçan şey; make one's ~ kaçmak; '**get.ter** *n.* alan, kazanan, elde eden *b-i;* gaz giderici şey; '**get.ting** *n.* elde etme, kazanma, geçim, kazanç; '**get-up** *n.* tertip, düzen; *Am.* F garip kıyafet.

**gew.gaw** ['gjuːgɔː] *n.* süslü değersiz şey, biblo, kıymetsiz şey, oyuncak; ~**s** *pl.* süs müs, cici bici, değersiz şeyler.

**gey.ser** ['gaizə] *n. geogr.* gayzer, aralıklarla sıcak su fışkırtan kaynak; ['giːzə] şofben.

**ghast.li.ness** ['gaːstlinis] *n.* ölü gibi olma, soluk olma; korku, dehşet; '**ghast.ly** *adj.* ölü gibi, sapsarı, solgun, beti benzi atmış; korkunç, dehşetli.

**gher.kin** [ˈgəːkin] *n.* turşuluk salatalık, ufak hıyar.

**ghet.to** [ˈgetəu] *n.* eskiden bazı ülkelerdeki Musevi mahallesi; azınlık mahallesi.

**ghost** [gəust] *n.* hayalet, hortlak; cin; iz, gölge; ruh; = ~ writer; **ˈghost.like** *adj.* hortlak gibi; **ˈghost.ly** *adj.* hayalet gibi; manevî; **ghost writ.er** başkasının adına çalışan yazar.

**ghoul** [guːl] *n.* gulyabani; mezar hırsızı; *fig.* korkunç zevk ve alışkanlıkları olan kimse, canavar ruhlu kimse.

**gi.ant** [ˈdʒaiənt] 1. *adj.* dev gibi, iri, kocaman, muazzam; 2. *n.* dev; anormal ölçüde insan, hayvan *veya* bitki; olağanüstü yetenekli kimse; **ˈgi.ant.ess** *n.* dişi dev, dev gibi kadın.

**gib.ber** [ˈdʒibə] *v/i.* çok hızlı ve anlaşılmaz biçimde konuşmak; **gib.ber.ish** [ˈ~riʃ] *n.* anlaşılmaz söz, karışık söz.

**gib.bet** [dʒibit] 1. *n.* darağacı; ⊕ maçuna kolu; 2. *v/t.* asmak, idam etm., darağacına asmak; *fig.* rezil etm., teşhir etm.

**gib.bon** *zo.* [ˈgibən] *n.* uzun kollu bir maymun cinsi.

**gib.bos.i.ty** [giˈbɔsiti] *n.* dışbükeylik; kamburluk; **gib.bous** *adj.* dışbükey; kambur.

**gibe** [dʒaib] 1. *v/i.* alay etm., eğlenmek, dalga geçmek (*a.* at s.o. *b-le*); 2. *n.* alay, pis şaka, eşek şakası.

**gib.lets** [ˈdʒiblits] *n. pl.* tavuğun yenebilen iç kısımları, tavuk sakatatı.

**gid.di.ness** [ˈgidinis] *n.* baş dönmesi, sersemleme; *fig.* hoppalık, uçarılık, havailik; **ˈgid.dy** ☐ baş döndürücü, sersemletici; başı dönen, başı dönmüş; *fig.* hoppa, uçarı, havaî.

**gift** [gift] 1. *n.* hediye, armağan; Allah vergisi, doğuştan kabiliyet, hüner; verme hakkı, hibe; ~ shop hediyelik eşya satan dükkân; *s.* horse; 2 *.vb.* hediye vermek, hibe etm.; **ˈgift.ed** *adj.* hünerli, kabiliyetli.

**gig** [gig] *n.* iki tekerlekli tek katlı hafif araba; ⚓ kik, hafif filika.

**gi.gan.tic** [dʒaiˈgæntik] *adj.* (~ally) kocaman, dev gibi, aşırı ölçüde.

**gig.gle** [ˈgigl] 1. *vb.* kıkır kıkır gülmek; kıkırdayarak belirtmek; 2. *n.* kıkırdama, kıkır kıkır gülme.

**gig.o.lo** [ˈʒigələu] *n.* jigolo, tokmakçı.

**gild** [gild] (*irr.*) *v/t.* yaldızlamak, altın rengine boyamak, süslemek, parlak gösttermek, altın kaplamak; ~ the pill *fig.* göz boyamak; ~ed youth zengin ve moda düşkünü gençlik; **ˈgild.er** *n.* yaldızcı; **ˈgild.ing** *n.* yaldız, altın kaplama.

**gill¹** [dʒil] *n.* litrenin sekizde biri kadar bir sıvı ölçü birimi.

**gill²** [gil] *n. ichth.* solungaç; *fig.* insanlarda çene altındaki kısım; ❀ ince yaprak.

**gill³** [dʒil] *n.* kız, sevgili.

**gil.lie** [ˈgili] *n.* avcı *veya* balıkçı yardımcısı.

**gilt** [gilt] 1. *pret. & p.p. of* gild; 2. *n.* yaldız; **ˈ~-edged** *adj.* kenarı yaldızlı; ⸸ emin, sağlam, çok güvenilir; ⸸ *sl.* en iyi kalite, birinci sınıf, mükemmel.

**gim.bal** [ˈdʒimbəl] *n. mst* ~s *pl.* pusula yalpalıkları, yalpa çemberleri.

**gim.crack** [ˈdʒimkræk] 1. *n.* işe yaramaz süs, değersiz süs, süslü adi şey; 2. *adj.* değersiz, adi, kıymeti olmayan, kötü yapılmış.

**gim.let** ⊕ [ˈgimlit] *n.* burgu, delgi, matkap.

**gim.mick** *Am. sl.* [ˈgimik] *n.* hile, tertip, dalavere; hileli alet; bit yeniği.

**gin¹** [dʒin] *n.* cin, ardıç rakısı.

**gin²** [~] 1. *n.* tuzak, kapan; ⊕ çiğidi pamuktan ayıran makine, çırçır; 2. *vb.* tuzağa düşürüp yakalamak; ⊕ pamuk çekirdeklerini çıkarmak.

**gin.ger** [ˈdʒindʒə] 1. *n.* zencefil (kökü); canlılık, enerji; 2. *vb.* ~ up canlandırmak, hareketlendirmek; 3. *adj.* koyu kahverengi, kızılımsı; ~ ale, ~ beer zencefilli alkolsüz içki, gazoz; **ˈ~.bread** *n.* zencefilli çörek *veya* bisküvi; **ˈgin.ger.ly** *adj. & adv.* ihtiyatlı, tedbirli; yavaşça, ihtiyatla, dikkatle; **ˈgin.ger-nut** *n.* zencefilli bisküvi.

**ging.ham** [ˈgiŋəm] *n.* çizgili *veya* kareli pamuklu kumaş.

**gip.sy** [ˈdʒipsi] *n.* çingene.

**gi.raffe** *zo.* [dʒiˈrɑːf] *n.* zürafa.

**gird¹** [gəːd] *n.* iğneli söz, alaycı söz; 2. *v/t.* alay etm.; küçümsemek (at *-i*).

**gird²** [~] (*irr.*) *vb.* kayışla bağlamak; kuşak sarmak; bağlamak; sarmak, kuşatmak, çevrelemek; hazırlanmak; giydirmek, teçhiz etm.

**gird.er** ⊕ [ˈgəːdə] *n.* kiriş, direk.

**gir.dle** [ˈgəːdl] 1. *n.* kemer, kuşak; korsa; kuşak gibi saran herhangi birşey; 2. *vb.* çevrelemek, sarmak, kuşatmak; kabuğunu soyarak ağacı kurutmak.

**girl** [gəːl] *n.* kız; kız evlât; genç kadın; sevgili; hizmetçi kız; ~-friend kız arkadaş ,sevgili; ♀ Guide kız izci; **girl.hood** [ˈ~hud] *n.* kızlık (çağı); **girl.ie** [ˈ~i] *n.* açık saçık kızları gösteren; **ˈgirl.ish** ☐ kızlara ait, kız gibi, kıza yakışır; **ˈgirl-**

**ish.ness** n. genç kızlık hali; **'girl.y** adj. Am. F açık saçık kızları gösteren (dergi, program).

**girt** [gə:t] **1.** pret. & p.p. of gird²; **2.** n. ⊕ çevre, daire çevresi; genişlik.

**girth** [gə:θ] n. kolan, çevre; kuşak.

**gist** [dʒist] n. ana fikir, meselenin esası, özet, öz, sadet.

**git** sl. [git] = get.

**give** [giv] **1.** (irr.) v/t. vermek; emanet etm., teslim etm.; hak vermek; sağlamak, temin etm.; kaynağı olm.; geçirmek, bulaştırmak (hastalık); bağışlamak. hibe etm. ,adamak; ~ attention to dikkat etm.; ~ battle savaş vermek, savaşmak; ~ birth to doğurmak; ~ chase to kovalamak; ~ credit to kredi açmak; ~ ear to kulak vermek, dinlemek; ~ one's mind to dikkatini vermek; ~ it to s.o. b-ni cezalandırmak, azarlamak, haşlamak; ~ away feda etm.; hediye etm.; vermek; dağıtmak; F ele vermek, belli etm., sırrını açığa vurmak; ~ away the bride düğünde gelini damada teslim etm.; ~ back geri vermek, geri göndermek; geri çekilmek; ~ forth dışarı vermek, çıkartmak, yaymak, salmak (koku, duman); ~ in vermek, teslim etm.; ~ out dağıtmak, göndermek; ~ over vazgeçmek, kesmek, bırakmak; teslim etm.; ayrılmak; ~ up vazgeçmek; pes etm.; ümidi kesmek; terketmek, bırakmak; ~ o.s. up teslim olm.; **2.** v/i. mst ~ in vazgeçmek, teslim olm., boyun eğmek, kabul etm.; ~ into, ~ (up)on bakmak -e; bşi küçümsemek, hor görmek; ~ out bitmek, tükenmek; kuvveti kesilmek; ~ over durmak, vazgeçmek, kesmek; **3.** n. elastikiyet, esneklik; kabullenme; ~ and take ['givən'teik] n. karşılıklı fedakârlık; uzlaşma, uyuşma; elbirliği; ~-a.way ['~əwei] n. hediye, armağan; açığa vurma, belli etme, istemeyerek ağzından kaçırma; ~ show, ~ program radyo, TV: hediyeli, ödüllü yarışma, program; **'given** p.p. of give 1 & 2; ~ to bşe düşkün, müptelâ, meyilli; **'giv.er** n. veren, hediye eden kimse; saçan kimse (neşe); ~ of a bill keşideci.

**giz.zard** orn. ['gizəd] n. taşlık, boğaz, kursak; it sticks in my ~ çok gücüme gidiyor, hazmedemiyorum, bana ağır geliyor.

**gla.ci.al** □ ['gleisjəl] buza ait, buzlu; buz devrine ait; buz gibi; buz..; ~ era buzul devri; **gla.ci.a.tion** geol. [glei'eiʃən] n. buzul ile kaplanma; **gla.cier** ['glæsjə] n. buzul; **gla.cis** ['glæsis] n. hafif meyilli;

kaleden inen bayır; tampon devlet, tampon bölge.

**glad** □ [glæd] memnun, mutlu, sevinçli (of, at -den); mutluluk veren; güzel...; give s.o. the ~ eye F b-ne âşıkane bakmak, göz etm.; ~ rags pl. sl. bayramlık giysi, en süslü elbise; **glad.den** ['~dn] v/t. memnun etm., sevindirmek.

**glade** [gleid] n. ormanda açıklık yer; Am. bataklık bölgesi.

**glad.i.a.tor** ['glædieitə] n. gladyatör.

**glad.i.o.lus** ♀ [glædi'əuləs] n. kılıççiçeği, glayol, kuzgunkılıcı, kuzgunotu, keklik çiğdemi.

**glad.ly** ['glædli] adv. memnuniyetle, seve seve; **'glad.ness** n. memnunluk, sevinç; **glad.some** ['~səm] adj. memnun, sevinçli, neşeli, şen.

**Glad.stone** ['glædstən] n. a. ~ bag bir çeşit seyahat çantası, bavul, valiz.

**glair** [glɛə] **1.** n. yumurta akı; yumurta akına benzer yapışkan madde; **2.** vb. böyle bir madde sürmek.

**glam.or.ous** ['glæmərəs] adj. göz alıcı, cazibeli, çekici, cazip, büyüleyici; **glam.our** ['~mə] **1.** n. parlaklık, cazibe, çekicilik, göz alıcılık; ~ girl cazibeli kız, çekici kız, seksi kız; **2.** vb. büyülemek, cezbetmek.

**glance** [gla:ns] **1.** n. bakış; göz atma; parıltı; **2.** vb. göz gezdirmek (over -e); ~ at göz atmak -e, bakmak -e; parlamak; mst ~ off sıyırmak, sıyırıp geçmek; ~ over göz gezdirmek -e.

**gland** anat., ♀ [glænd] n. bez, gudde, salgı hücresi, salgı bezi; **glan.dered** vet. ['~dəd] adj. ruamlı, sakağı hastalığına tutulmuş; **glan.ders** vet. ['~dəz] n. sg. bir çeşit at hastalığı, sakağı, ruam; **glan.du.lar** ['~djulə] adj. gudde gibi, guddeye ait, gudde..

**glare** [glɛə] **1.** n. göz kamaştırıcı ışık, parıltı; dargın bakış, öfkeli bakış, sabit bakış; **2.** v/i. parıldamak, göz kamaştıracak şekilde parlamak; ters ters bakmak, yiyecekmiş gibi bakmak (at -e); **glar.ing** □ ['~riŋ] göz kamaştırıcı, çok parlak; hemen göze çarpan, apaçık, bariz; aşırı parlak (renk); fig. kızgın, hiddetli, öfkeli.

**glass** [gla:s] **1.** n. cam; bardak; camdan yapılmış herhangi bş; bir bardak dolusu; ayna; teleskop; barometre; pl. dürbün; (cam eşya); ~es pl. gözlük; mercek; cam eşya; **2.** adj. camdan yapılmış cam...; **3.** v/t. camla kaplamak; cam takmak; cam kaba koymak; cam gibi yapmak; v/i. cam gibi olm.; **'~-blow.er** n. üfleyerek cam ve şişe yapan kimse;

'~-case *n.* küçük vitrin, cam dolap; '~-cut.ter *n.* cam kesen kimse; camcı elması; **glass.ful** ['~ful] *n.* bir bardak (dolusu); '**glass-house** *n.* limonluk, ser; ✕ *sl.* askeri hapishane; '**glass.i.ness** *n.* cam gibi olma; çarşaf gibi olma *(deniz)*; donukluk, anlamsızlık; '**glass.ware** *n.* züccaciye; '**glass.y** *adj.* cam gibi; dümdüz, çarşaf gibi *(deniz)*; donuk, anlamsız, dalgın *(bakış)*.

**glau.co.ma** ❦ [glɔːˈkəumə] *n.* bir göz hastalığı, gözde karasu hastalığı, glokom; '**glau.cous** *adj.* mat grimsi yeşil *veya* mavi; üstü toza benzer beyaz bir maddeyle kaplı *(yaprak, üzüm)*.

**glaze** [gleiz] **1.** *n.* cam gibi sır, cila, perdah; **2.** *v/t.* cilalamak; cam geçirmek -e, cam takmak; sırlamak; cam gibi bir tabakayla kaplamak; ~d paper parlak kâğıt, cilalı kâğıt; ~d(-in) veranda camlı taraça; *v/i.* donuklaşmak, anlamsızlaşmak, dalmak; **gla.zier** ['~jə] *n.* camcı; '**glaz.ing** *n.* cam takma; camcılık; sır, mine, cila, emaye; '**glaz.y** *adj.* cam gibi, cama benzer; donuk, dalgın.

**gleam** [gliːm] **1.** *n.* parıltı; ışın, şua, hafif ve geçici ışık; **2.** *v/i.* parıldamak, ışın saçmak.

**glean** [gliːn] *v/t.* hasattan sonra toplamak; azar azar toplamak *(bilgi)*; ortaya çıkarmak; *v/i.* hasattan sonra ekin toplamak; azar azar bilgi toplamak; '**glean.er** *n.* ekinci; *fig.* bilgi toplayan kimse; '**glean.ings** *n. pl.* çeşitli kaynaklardan toplanmış bilgi.

**glebe** [gliːb] *n.* vakıf arazisi, papazlığa ait arazi; *poet.* yer, toprak.

**glee** [gliː] *n.* neşe; birkaç sesle söylenen şarkı; ~ club koro kulübü, koro birliği; **glee.ful** □ ['~ful] şen, neşeli, sevinçli.

**glen** [glen] *n.* küçük vadi, dere.

**glib** □ [glib] *fig.* süratli konuşan; içten olmasa da kolayca söylenen; kayıtsız; çevik; üstün körü, yarım yamalak; '**glib.ness** *n.* çabuk konuşma, akıcılık; kayıtsızlık, hareketlerde serbestlik.

**glide** [glaid] **1.** *n.* kayma; ✈ havada süzülme; *gr.* sesin yavaş değişmesi; **2.** *v/i.* kaymak, kayıp gitmek, akmak, süzülmek; motoru işletmeden inmek; '**glid.er** *n.* planör; ~ pilot planörcü; '**glid.ing** *n.* planörcülük; kayma, süzülme, akış.

**glim.mer** ['glimə] **1.** *n.* parıltı, hafif ışık, cılız ışık, donuk ışık; benze, zerre, azıcık olan şey; *min.* mika; **2.** *v/i.* parıldamak, hafif ışık vermek, sönük sönük parıldamak.

**glimpse** [glimps] **1.** *n.* kısa bakış, bir an

için görme, gözüne ilişme; **2.** *v/t.* bir an için görmek, gözüne ilişmek; *v/i.* parlayıp sönmek; ~ at bir an için bakmak. **glint** [glint] **1.** *v/i.* parlamak, parıldamak; **2.** *n.* parıltı, parlaklık.

**glis.sade** *mount.* [gliˈsɑːd] **1.** *v/i.* kaymak; buzlu dağ eteğinde kaymak; **2.** *n.* kayma.

**glis.ten** ['glisn], **glis.ter** † ['glistə], **glitter** ['glitə] *v/i.* parlamak, parıldamak, pırıldamak; '**glit.ter.ing** *adj.* parlak, cezbedici, göz alıcı, şaşaalı; ~ personality mükemmel kişilik.

**gloam.ing** ['gləumiŋ] *n.* akşam karanlığı, alaca karanlık.

**gloat** [gləut]: ~ (up)on, ~ over *v/i.* şeytanca bir zevk duymak, şeytani bir zevkle seyretmek; başkalarının başarısızlığını zevkle seyretmek.

**glob.al** ['gləubəl] *adj.* tüm dünyayı kapsayan; küresel; dünya çapında; **globe** *n.* küre, top, yuvarlak; dünya; dünya küresi modeli; lamba karpuzu; '**globe-fish** *n. ichth.* kirpibalığı; '**globe-trot.ter** *n.* durmadan dünyayı dolaşan kimse; **globose** ['~bəus], **glob.u.lar** □ ['gləbjulə] küre şeklinde, küresel; küreciklerden meydana gelen; **glo.bos.i.ty** [gləuˈbɔsiti] *n.* küresellik, yuvarlak olma; **glob.ule** ['glɔbjuːl] *n.* kürecik, küçük yuvarlak; küçük damla.

**gloom** [gluːm] **1.** *n.* (yarı) karanlık; belirsizlik, çapraşıklık; üzgünlük, hüzün, kasvet; ümitsizlik; **2.** *v/i.* ümitsiz *veya* hüzünlü bakmak *veya* davranmak; surat asmak; kararmak; uzakta hayal gibi gözükmek; *v/t.* canını sıkmak; kasvetlendirmek; karartmak; '**gloom.i.ness** *n.* karanlık, kasvet; sıkıcılık; ümitsizlik; mahzunluk, hüzün; '**gloom.y** □ karanlık, kapanık; kederli, endişeli; üzüntülü; kasvetli, sıkıcı; ümitsiz.

**glo.ri.fi.ca.tion** [glɔːrifiˈkeiʃən] *n.* övme, ululama, yüceltme; tapma; fazlasıyla büyültme; **glo.ri.fy** ['~fai] *v/t.* yüceltmek, methetmek, göklere çıkarmak, büyültmek, yükseltmek; tapmak; ululamak, şereflendirmek; F güzelleştirmek, olduğundan daha muhteşem göstermek; '**glo.ri.ous** □ şanlı, şerefli, parlak, muhteşem, mükemmel, fevkalâde; eğlenceli. **glo.ry** ['glɔːri] **1.** *n.* şan, şeref, ihtişam; övgü, medih; tapınma; şaşaa; **2.** *v/i.* iftihar etm., övünmek, şeref duymak, gururlanmak (in *ile)*.

**gloss**[1] [glɔs] **1.** *n.* açıklama *(dipnot veya kitap sonudaki)*, yorum; **2.** *v/t.* açıklamak; açıklayıcı yazı eklemek; yorumlamak; açımlamak.

**gloss²** [~] **1.** *n.* cilâ, perdah; parlaklık; parlak ve düzgün yüzey; aldatıcı görünüş, dış güzellik; **2.** *v/t.* parlatmak, cilâlamak; ~ over sahte bir biçimde gizlemek, kusurlarını örtmek, hatalarını örtbas etm.

**glos.sa.ry** [ˈglɔsəri] *n.* ek sözlük, özel kelimelerin açıklamaları.

**gloss.i.ness** [ˈglɔsinis] *n.* parlaklık; **'gloss.y** □ parlak, cilâlı; ~ periodical iyi kalite parlak kâğıda basılmış mecmua, *part.* moda mecmuası.

**glot.tis** *anat.* [ˈglɔtis] *n.* nefes borusunun ağzı, glotis.

**glove** [glʌv] *n.* eldiven; *s.* hand 1; **'glov.er** *n.* eldivenci.

**glow** [gləu] **1.** *n.* kızıllık, kızartı, parlaklık; hararet, ısı; şevk ve gayret; **2.** *v/i.* parıldamak; ısı vermek; kızarmak; yanakları al al olm.; kor haline gelmek, kızıllaşmak; yüzü kızarmak; coşmak, şevklenmek.

**glow.er** [ˈglauə] *v/i.* dik dik bakmak, öfkeyle bakmak, yiyecekmiş gibi bakmak.

**glow-worm** [ˈgləuwəːm] *n.* ateşböceği.

**gloze** [gləuz]: ~ over *v/t.* örtbas etm.

**glu.cose** [gluːkəus] *n.* glikoz.

**glue** [gluː] **1.** *n.* tutkal, yapışkan; **2.** *v/t.* tutkallamak, yapıştırmak; *fig.* iyice yaklaştırmak, gözünü dikmek (to *-e*); **'glue.y** *adj.* tutkal gibi, yapışkan, yapış yapış.

**glum** □ [glʌm] asık suratlı, somurtkan; hüzünlü, üzgün; kasvetli.

**glut** [glʌt] **1.** *n.* bolluk, tokluk; **2.** *v/t.* piyasaya fazla sürmek (*mal*); tıka basa doyurmak; ağzına kadar doldurmak; tam manasıyla memnun etm.

**glu.ten** [ˈgluːtən] *n.* glüten, nişasta çıkarıldıktan sonra geri kalan albuminli madde; **glu.ti.nous** □ [ˈ-tinəs] yapışkan, yapış yapış; yapışkan gibi, tutkal cinsinden.

**glut.ton** [ˈglʌtn] *n.* obur, boğazına düşkün kimse, pisboğaz, açgözlü kimse (of, for, at); *zo.* kutup porsuğu; **'glut.ton.ous** □ obur, açgözlü, pisboğaz; **'glut.ton.y** *n.* oburluk, pisboğazlık, açgözlülük.

**glyc.er.in** [ˈglisərin], **glyc.er.ine** [~ˈriːn] *n.* gliserin.

**G-man** *Am.* F [ˈdʒiːmæn] *n.* Federal soruşturma Bürosu (FBI) memuru.

**gnarl** [naːl] *n.* budak, yumru, boğum; **gnarled**, *a.* **'gnarl.y** *adj.* budaklı, boğumlu, boğum boğum; yıpranmış, şekli bozuk (*el, parmak*).

**gnash** [næʃ] *v/t.* gıcırdatmak (*diş*).

**gnat** [næt] *n.* tatarcık, sivrisinek.

**gnaw** [nɔː] *vb.* kemirmek; azap çektirmek, eziyet vermek; aşındırmak; **'gnaw.er** *n.* kemirgen hayvan, kemiren hayvan *veya* insan.

**gnome** [nəum] *n.* yeraltındaki hazinelerin bekçileri farzolunan yaşlı cüce; [ˈnəumiː] vecize, atasözü; **gnom.ish** [ˈnəumiʃ] *adj.* cüce gibi.

**go** [gəu] **1.** (*irr.*) *vb. com.* gitmek (*s.a.* going, gone); ayrılmak; hareket etm., kalkmak; yeri olm.; sığmak; ulaşmak, uzanmak, erişmek; olmak; işlemek, çalışmak; ilerlemek, gelişmek; mevcut olm.; satılmak; harcanmak; elden gitmek, kaybolmak; devam etm.; çökmek, düşmek, kırılmak; iflas etm.; ölmek; sonuçlanmak; uymak; ses çıkarmak; bahse girmek; başlamak; çıkmak; gezmek; ~ bad kötüye gitmek; bozulmak, çürümek; *s.* mad; *s.* sick; the dog must ~ köpeğin gitmesi lâzım, köpeği satmalıyız; the story ~es deniliyor ki..., söylendiğine göre; here ~es! *sl.* hadi! yürü! başla!; ~ it *sl.* bir işe koyulmak; ~ it! *sl.* atıl! durma yürü!; as men, *etc.* ~ diğer kişilere göre, diğerleri gözönüne alınırsa; let ~ bırakmak, salmak; ~ shares bölüşmek, paylaşmak; ~ to see, ~ and see görmeye gitmek, gidip görmek; just ~ and try! bir denesenize!, bir deneyiverin!; ~ about gezmek; dolaşmak (*söylenti*); tiramola etm.; ~ abroad yurt dışına çıkmak; ~ ahead ilerlemek, gelişmek, ileri gitmek; başlamak; ~ at saldırmak; üzerinde çalışmak, bşi ele almak; ~ back geri dönmek; eskiye uzanmak; ~ back from, F on vazgeçmek, caymak (*sözünden*); ~ behind aslını araştırmak; ~ between araya girmek, aralarını bulmak; ~ by geçmek; -e göre davranmak; ~ by the name of ... ...ismiyle tanınmak, ...ismini kullanmak; ~ down batmak; yutulmak; üniversiteden mezun olm.; sakinleşmek, durulmak, kesilmek (*deniz, rüzgâr*); ucuzlamak, azalmak, düşmek (*fiyat*); yenilmek (before *tarafından*); geçmek (*tarihe*); yazılı, kayıtlı olm.; kabul edilmek, beğenilmek, benimsenmek (with *tarafından*); ~ for almaya gitmek, gidip getirmek; saldırmak; sayılmak, geçerli olm.; beğenmek; kabul etm.; ~ for a walk yürüyüşe çıkmak; ~ in girmek, sığmak; bulutlarca engellenmek (*güneş*); *kriket:* vuruş yapmak; katılmak (*yarışmaya*); ~ in for girmek, katılmak (*imtihana, yarışmaya*); meraklısı olm., ilgi duymak; ~ in for an examination imtihana girmek; ~ into girmek; araştırmak, soruşturmak, incelemek; tutulmak *(hastalık)*; ~ off patlamak. ateş almak; bozulmak, kalitesi düşmek; ekşimek; uyumak; fenalaşmak, bayılmak; satılmak; elden çıkmak; iyi gitmek; çıkmak *(sahneden)*; ~ on geçmek *(zaman)*; devam etm; olmak; sahneye çıkmak; *kriket:* topu savurmak; ~ on! devam et!; sana inanacağımı sanma!; ~ out dışarı çıkmak; gezip tozmak, sosyal faaliyetlere katılmak; sönmek; modası geçmek; görevden ayrılmak; iktidardan çekilmek *(hükümet)*; grev yapmak; bitmek, sona ermek *(yıl)*; ~ over başarı kazanmak, tutmak *(oyun)*; etkilemek; tetkik etm., incelemek; prova etm., gözden geçirmek; karşı tarafa geçmek, partisini değiştirmek; ~ through kabul edilmek *(tasarı)*; neticelenmek, sonuca bağlanmak; gözden geçirmek, incelemek; aramak, araştırmak, yoklamak; yapmak; atlatmak *(zorluk)*; geçirmek *(hastalık, tecrübe)*; satılmak; harcamak, sarfatmek, yiyip bitirmek; ~ through with bşi sonuca bağlamak, bitirmek, tamamlamak, yarım bırakmamak; ~ to katkıda bulunmak; ~ up yükselmek, çıkmak, artmak; havaya uçmak, patlamak, infilâk etm.; üniversiteye girmek; şehre inmek; tırmanmak; ~ with eşlik etm., beraber gitmek; aynı görüşte olm.; uymak, yakışmak; flört etm.; ~ without -siz olm., mahrum kalmak, yoksun olm.; **2.** *n.* F gitme, gidiş, hareket; moda; olay, vaka; gayret, enerji; başarı; sefer, sıra; hamle, teşebbüs; izin, müsaade, başlama işareti; 🎵 nöbet, tutulma; little ~ *univ. sl.* ilk imtihan; great ~ ana imtihan; on the ~ meşgul, aktif, faal, hareket halinde; it is no ~ olacak iş değil, hayret edilecek şey; faydasız; in one ~ bir seferde; have a ~ at s.th. bşe teşebbüs etm., bşi denemek.

**goad** [gəud] **1.** *n.* üvendire, davarı dürtmeye yarayan değnek; *fig. b-ni* harekete geçiren şey; **2.** *v/t. fig.* dürtmek, harekete geçirmek, kışkırtmak, isteklendirmek, teşvik etm.

**go-a.head** F [ˈgəuəhed] **1.** *adj.* ilerleyen, gelişen, gelişmekte olan; gelişme ümidi gösteren; başlama...; **2.** *n. part. Am.* F enerji, canlılık; izin, müsaade; izni olan kimse; başlama işareti.

**goal** [gəul] *n.* hedef, amaç, gaye; *futbol:* gol; kale; '~-keep.er *n. futbol:* kaleci.

**goat** [gəut] *n. zo.* keçi, teke; Oğlak burcu; zampara adam, çapkın kimse; başkalarının günah ve sorumluluğunu yük-

lenen kimse; get s.o.'s ~ *sl. b-ni* kızdırmak, sinirlendirmek, *b-nin* sinirine dokunmak; seperate the sheep from the ~s *fig.* iyileri kötülerden ayırmak; play the giddy ~ kaba ve budalaca davranmak, aptal aptal hareket etm.; **goat'ee** *n.* keçi sakalı, sivri sakal; **'goat.ish** *adj.* keçi gibi; kaba, pis; **'goat.skin** *n.* keçi derisi, keçi postu.

**gob** [gɔb] *n. sl.* büyük miktar, çok; parça, küme; ağız; *Am.* F denizci, deniz eri; **gob.bet** [ˈgɔbit] *n.* parça, külçe, küme.

**gob.ble** [ˈgɔbl] *v/i.* hindi gibi ses çıkarmak, glu glu etm.; *v/t.* çabuk çabuk yemek, oburca yutmak; kapmak; hızlı hızlı okumak; **gob.ble.dy.gook** *Am. sl.* [ˈgɔbldiguk] *n.* karışık ve anlamsız söz; **'gob.bler** *n.* baba hindi, erkek hindi.

**go-be.tween** [ˈgəubitwiːn] *n.* aracı, arabulucu; simsar, tellal.

**gob.let** [ˈgɔblit] *n.* kadeh.

**gob.lin** [ˈgɔblin] *n.* gulyabani, cin.

**go-by** [ˈgəubai] *n.:* give s.o. the ~ *b-ni* görmezden gelmek, tanımazlıktan gelmek, *b-ne* yüz vermemek.

**go-cart** [ˈgəukaːt] *n.* hafif el arabası; çocuğu yürümeye alıştırmakta kullanılan tekerlekli sandalye; portatif bebek arabası; hafif araba, motorlu küçük yarış arabası.

**god**, *eccl.* 2 [gɔd] *n.* Tanrı, Allah, Cenabı Hak; ilâh; put, sanem; *fig.* çok sevilen kimse, herkesin hayran olduğu kimse; çok nüfuzlu kimse; çok önem verilen şey; the gods *pl. thea.* balkonda oturan seyirciler; **'god.child** *n.* vaftiz evlâdı; **'god.dess** *n.* tanrıça, ilâhe; çok cazip kadın; **'god.fa.ther** *n.* vaftiz babası, manevi baba; **'god.fear.ing** *adj.* dindar; **'god-head** *n.* Allah, Tanrı, mabut; **'god.less** *adj.* Allahı tanımayan, Allahsız, dinsiz; günahkâr; **'god.like** *adj.* Allah gibi, tanrısal; **'god.li.ness** *n.* dindarlık; **'god.ly** *adj.* dindar, Allaha saygı duyan; **'god-moth.er** *n.* vaftiz anası; **'god.send** *n.* beklenmedik anda gelen ve ihtiyaç duyulan şey, Hızır gibi gelen yardım; **'god'speed:** bid *veya* wish s.o. ~ *b-ne* iyi yolculuklar dilemek, 'yolun açık olsun' demek, 'Tanrıya emanet ol' demek, 'uğurlar olsun' demek.

**go.er** [ˈgəuə] *n.* giden kimse.

**gof.fer** [ˈgɔufə] *v/t.* kırma yapmak, kırmak, kıvırmak.

**go-get.ter** *Am.* F [ˈgəuˈgetə] *n.* girişken kimse, uyanık kimse, açıkgöz kimse, çok faal kimse.

**gog.gle** [ˈgɔgl] **1.** *v/i.* şaşı bakmak, gözlerini devirmek; gözlerini faltaşı gibi açarak bakmak; **2.** *n.* ~s *pl.* gözlük *(pilot, motosiklet yarışçısı, balıkadam)*; ˈ~-eyed *adj.* patlak gözlü.

**go.ing** [ˈgəuiŋ] **1.** *adj.* işleyen, hareket eden; yaşayan, hayattaki; şu anki; be ~ to *inf.* -*mek* üzere olm., ... yapacak olm; keep ~ devam etm., durmadan yürümek; set ~ kurmak *(saat)*; a ~ concern başarılı iş; ~, ~, gone! satıyorum, satıyorum, sattım! *(açık arttırmada)*; **2.** *n.* gidiş, ayrılış; yol durumu; gidişat; gidiş hızı, sürat; ˈgo.ings-ˈon *n. pl.* F olup bitenler; gidişat; hal ve hareket.

**goi.tre** ⚕ [ˈgɔitə] *n.* guatr; **goi.trous** [ˈgɔitrəs] *adj.* guatrı olan; guatra ait, guatr...

**go-kart** *mot.* [ˈgəukɑːt] *n.* motorlu küçük yarış arabası.

**gold** [gəuld] **1.** *n.* altın; servet, zenginlik; altın rengi, sarı renk; değerli herhangi bş; **2.** *adj.* altın, sırmalı, yaldızlı; altından yapılmış; ˈ~-bear.ing *adj.* altınlı, altın madeni ihtiva eden; ˈ~.brick **1.** *n. fig.* kıymetli görünen değersiz şey; görevden kaçınan kimse; **2.** *v/t.* aldatmak; *v/i.* görevden kaçmak, işten kaçınmak; ˈ~.dig.ger *n. Am.* altın arayıcısı; *sl.* erkeklerden para sızdırmaya çalışan kadın, fındıkçı; ˈgold.en *adj. mst fig.* altın gibi; altından yapılmış; altın renkli; çok kıymetli; şahane, fevkalade; önemli; ˈgold.en.rod *n.* 🌿 uzun saplı sarı bir çiçek.

**gold...:** ˈ~.finch *n. orn.* saka kuşu; ˈ~.fish *n. ichth.* havuz balığı, kırmızı balık; ˈ~.mine *n.* altın madeni; *fig.* servet kaynağı; ~ plate altın kaplama eşya; ˈ~.rush *n.* altına hücum; ˈ~.smith *n.* kuyumcu.

**golf** [gɔlf] **1.** *n.* golf oyunu; **2.** *vb.* golf oynamak; ˈ~.course = golf-links; ˈgolf.er *n.* golf oyuncusu; ˈgolf-links *n. pl.* golf alanı.

**gol.li.wog(g)** [ˈgɔliwɔg] *n.* siyah yüzlü acayip oyuncak bebek, zenci oyuncak bebek; *fig.* garip kimse, umacı.

**go.losh** [gəˈlɔʃ] *n.* kaloş, şoson, yağmurlu havada giyilen lastik.

**gon.do.la** [ˈgɔndələ] *n.* ⚓ gondol; altı düz mavna; üstü açık yük vagonu; ✈ uçağın alt kısmına takılan ek kısım; **gon.do.lier** [~ˈliə] *n.* gondolcu.

**gone** [gɔn] **1.** *p.p. of* go; **2.** *adj.* geçmiş; ilerlemiş *(hastalık)*; âşık olmuş, sevdalanmış; hamile; ölmüş; F mahvolmuş; kaybolmuş; F ümitsiz; büyük, çok iyi, fevkalade; be ~!, get you ~! kaybol gözümden!, gözüm görmesin seni!; ~ on

s.o. *sl. b-ne* abayı yakmış, aşık olmuş; ˈgon.er *n. sl.* hayatından ümit kesilmiş kimse, yolcu, mahvolmuş kimse, bedbaht kimse.

**gong** [gɔŋ] *n.* gong; *sl.* madalya.

**good** [gud] **1.** *adj. com.* iyi, güzel, âla, hoş; uygun, münasip, yerinde; faydalı, sağlığa yararlı; yetenekli, kompetan; memnuniyet verici; nazik, kibar, hayır sahibi; kuvvetli, sağlıklı, sağlam; eğlenceli, komik; taze, bozulmamış; güvenilir, sağlam, emin; † ödeme kabiliyeti olan, ticari yönden sağlam; uslu, edepli, iyi huylu; faziletli, kerim; çok, hayli, fazla; tam; the ~ Samaritan merhametli kimse, hayır sahibi, yardıma muhtaçlara yardım eden kimse; ~ at bşde becerikli, başarılı; in ~ earnest çok ciddi olarak, gayet samimiyetle; **2.** *n.* iyilik; fayda, yarar; doğruluk; iyi ve hayırlı şey; kâr; ~s *pl.* eşya, mallar, emtia; *pl. (the ile kullanıldığında)* iyi insanlar; *pl.* suçun kanıtları; that's no ~ yararı yok, faydalı değildir; it is no ~ talking konuşmanın yararı yok; for ~ temelli olarak, daimi olarak; piece of ~s F kadın, parça; ~s in process işleme konulmuş mallar, yarı mamûl; ~-bye, *Am. a.* ~-by **1.** [ˈgudˈbai] 🌿 veda; **2.** [ˈgudˈbai] *int.* Allahaısmarladık!, hoşça kal!, güle güle!, selâmetle!; ˈ~-for-ˈnoth.ing **1.** *adj.* bir işe yaramaz; **2.** *n.* hiç bir işe yaramayan kimse, serseri; ♀ Fri.day Paskalyadan önceki Cuma; ˈ~.hu.mo(u)red *adj.* şakacı, şen, hoş, sevimli; ˈgood.li.ness *n.* iyilik, iyi huyluluk; ˈgood-look.ing *adj.* yakışıklı, güzel; ˈgood.ly *adj.* güzel, hoş görünüşlü; *fig.* büyük, çok; ˈgood-ˈna.tured *adj.* iyi huylu, yumuşak huylu, halim, nazik, kibar; ˈgood.ness **1.** *n.* iyilik, erdem, fazilet; faydalı kısım; **2.** *int.* Allah!, Tanrım!, Yarabbim!; *s.* gracious; **goods train** yük treni, marşandiz; ˈgood.wife *n.* ev kadını, karı, eş; ˈgoodˈwill *n.* iyi niyet, hüsnüniyet, hayırhahlık, dostça duygu *(towards -e karşı)*; † prestij; † firma itibarı ve değeri.

**good.y¹** [ˈgudi] *n.* şekerleme, bonbon.

**good.y²** [~], *a.* ˈgood.y-ˈgood.y **1.** *adj.* aşırı iyi, melek gibi, yapmacık iyilik gösteren; **2.** *n.* aşırı iyi görünen kimse, yapmacık iyilik yapan kimse.

**goof.y** *sl.* [ˈguːfi] *adj.* aptal, ahmak, budala, akılsız.

**goon** *Am. sl.* [guːn] *n.* ahmak kimse, budala kimse, beecriksiz kimse; *part. grev:* işverenin grevcilere karşı şiddet kullanan adamı.

**goose** [guːs] *n.*, *pl.* **geese** [giːs] kaz *(a. fig.)*; cook s.o.'s ~ *b-nin* işini bozmak; *pl.* **'goos.er** *n.* terzi ütüsü; *sl.* parmaklama, parmak atma.

**goose.ber.ry** ['guzbəri] *n.* bektaşi üzümü; play ~ F iki sevgiliye eşlik etm.

**goose…:** '~**-flesh** *n.* tüyleri ürpermiş deri; '~**.herd** *n.* kaz çobanı; ~**ıplm.ples** *pl. Am.* = goose-flesh; '~**-step** *n.* kaz adımı, dizleri kırmadan atılan adım; **'goos.ey**, **'goos.ie** *n.* F kaz kafalı kimse.

**go.pher** *part. Am.* ['gəufə] *n.* Kuzey Amerika'da yaşayan sıçana benzer bir hayvan.

**Gor.di.an** ['gɔːdjən]: ~ knot kördüğüm; zor iş.

**gore**¹ [gɔː] *n.* pıhtılaşmış kan.

**gore**² [~] **1.** *n.* peş, apışlık; **2.** *vb.* kumaşı üç köşeli kesmek, apışlık koymak.

**gorge** [gɔːdʒ] **1.** *n.* boğaz, dar geçit, koyak, vadi; gırtlak; mide içindeki şeyler; tiksinti; my ~ rises midem bulanıyor, tiksiniyorum; **2.** *vb.* oburcasına yemek yemek; tıka basa doldurmak, yutmak, tıka basa yemek; ağzına kadar doldurmak.

**gor.geous** ['gɔːdʒəs] parlak, tantanalı, muhteşem, harikulâde, debdebeli, göz kamaştırıcı; zevk veren, güzel; **'gorgeous.ness** *n.* ihtişam, parlaklık.

**go.rilla** *zo.* [gəˈrilə] *n.* goril.

**gor.mand.ize** ['gɔːməndaiz] *vb.* oburca yemek, çok yemek, yiyip yutmak, mideye indirmek.

**gorse** ['gɔːs] *n.* katırtırnağına benzer bir bitki.

**gor.y** ['gɔːri] kanlı; kan dondurucu, korkunç, ürpertici.

**gosh** P [gɔʃ] *int.* aman Yarabbi!, hay Allah!

**gos.hawk** *orn.* ['gɔshɔːk] *n.* atmaca.

**gos.ling** ['gɔzliŋ] *n.* kaz yavrusu, kaz palazı.

**gos.pel** ['gɔspəl] *n.* İncil; *fig.* doğru söz, hakikat; **'gos.pel.(l)er** *n.* İncil okuyan kimse.

**gos.sa.mer** ['gɔsəmə] *n.* havada uçan ince örümcek ağı; yumuşak, hafif, ince kumaş.

**gos.sip** ['gɔsip] **1.** *n.* dedikodu; gevezelik, çene çalma, boş laf; dedikoducu kimse; **2.** *v/i.* dedikodu etm.; gevezelik etm., çene çalmak.

**got** [gɔt] *pret. & p.p. of* get.

**Goth** [gɔθ] *n. hist.* Got, Got kavminden biri; *fig.* kaba adam, barbar kimse; **'Goth.ic** *adj.* Got'lara ait, Gotik; Gotik tarzına ait; Gotik diline ait; Gotik yazıya ait; *fig.* barbarlık, yıkıcılık.

**got.ten** *Am.* ['gɔtn] *p.p. of* get.

**gouge** [gaudʒ] **1.** *n.* ⊕ oluklu keski, marangoz kalemi, heykeltıraş kalemi; **2.** *vb.* *mst* ~ out kalemle işlemek, kesmek, şekil vermek; gözünü oymak; *Am.* F kazıklamak, fazla para almak.

**gou.lash** ['guːlæʃ] *n.* taş kebabı, biberli haşlanmış et ve sebze.

**gourd** ⚘ [guəd] *n.* sukabağı, kabak.

**gour.mand** ['guəmənd] **1.** *adj.* obur, pisboğaz, boğazına düşkün; **2.** *n.* obur kimse, boğazına düşkün kimse.

**gout** ⚕ [gaut] *n.* gut, nıkris; **'gout.y** ☐ gut hastalığına tutulmuş.

**gov.ern** ['gʌvən] *v/t.* yönetmek, idare etm.; hâkim olm. *-e (a. fig.)*; kontrol etm.; kontrol altında tutmak; almak, *ile* kullanılmak; *v/i.* hükümet sürmek; hüküm sürmek; ~**ing body** idare, yönetim, hükümet; **'gov.ern.ess** *n.* mürebbiye; **'gov.ern.ment** *n.* hükümet; idare, yönetim, hüküm; yönetme, hükümet sürme; **gov.ern.men.tal** [~'mentl] *adj.* devlet…, devletle ilgili; **'gov.er.nor** *n.* vali, eyalet reisi; yönetim kurulu üyesi; F patron, şef, baba; ⊕ düzengeç, regülatör; **gov.er.nor** *gen.er.al* genel vali; **'gov.er.nor.ship** *n.* valilik; idarecilik, yöneticilik.

**gown** [gaun] **1.** *n.* rop; cüppe; kadın elbisesi, kadın geceliği; resmi elbise; **2.** *v/t.* elbise giydirmek; **'gowns.man** *n.* cüppe giyme hakkı olan kimse; üniversiteli; ✕ sivil.

**grab** F [græb] **1.** *v/t.* kapmak, ele geçirmek, zorla almak, gaspetmek, çabucak yakalamak; **2.** *n.* kapma, kapış, gasp, el koyma; ⊕ eşya kaldırmaya mahsus kıskaçlı alet; ~**-bag** *Am.* eşya piyangosu torbası; **'grab.ber** *n.* herşeyi kapmak isteyen kimse, aç gözlü kimse, hayatta tek amacı servet yapmak olan kimse.

**grace** [greis] **1.** *n.* zarafet; lütuf; fazilet, erdem, iyi niyet; sofrada şükran duası; rahmet, kerem, merhamet; borç ertelemesi, mühlet, vade; ♪ asıl notalara eklenen ufak nota; ~**s** *pl.* cazibe; **2s** *pl. myth.* çeşitli güzellikleri temsil eden üç ilahe; act of ~ genel af; with (a) good (bad) ~ isteyerek (istemeyerek, nazlanarak); Your 2 Yüce Başpiskoposum; Yüce Düküm *veya* Düşesim; good ~s *pl.* iltimas, teveccüh; tasvip, beğeni; period of ~ bekleme müddeti, borcun vadesinden sonra tanınan süre; *s.* say 1; **2.** *v/t.* süslemek; lütuf göstermek; şeref vermek; **grace.ful** ☐ ['~ful] zarif, lâtif, nazik; **'grace.ful.ness** *n.* zarafet, incelik, nezaket; **'grace.less** ☐ kötü, nahoş, hoşa gitmeyen, ahlâksız.

**gra.cious** ☐ ['greiʃəs] cana yakın, şirin; merhametli; nazik, kibar, ince; cömert; good ~!, goodness ~!, ~ me! Allah Allah!, olacak iş değil!, yok canım!; **'gracious.ness** *n.* zarafet; sıcakkanlılık, cana yakınlık; merhamet.

**grack.le** *orn.* ['grækl] *n.* sığırcık *veya* ona benzer kuş.

**gra.da.tion** [grə'deiʃən] *n.* derece, basamak, sıralama; bir durumdan diğerine yavaş yavaş geçiş; yavaş değişim; *gr.* sesli harfi yavaş yavaş değiştirme.

**grade** [greid] **1.** *n.* derece; rütbe; mertebe; sınıf; basamak; cins; *part. Am.* = gradient; *Am. okul:* sınıf, dönem; not; make the ~ *Am.* F başarmak, muvaffak olm.; ~ crossing *Am.* hemzemin geçit; ~(d) school *Am.* ilkokul; **2.** *v/t.* sınıflandırmak, tasnif etm.; derecelere ayırmak; tesviye etm., aynı seviyeye getirmek *(yol);* neslini ıslah etm. *(at, davar);* 🐑 *etc.* düzleştirmek, aynı seviyeye getirmek.

**gra.di.ent** ['greidjənt] *n.* 🐑 *etc.* yokuş, meyil, irtifa.

**grad.u.al** ☐ ['grædʒuəl] derece derece, tedricî, kademeli, yavaş yavaş olan; **'grad.u.al.ly** *adv.* derece derece, tedricen, yavaş yavaş; **grad.u.ate 1.** ['~djueit] *v/i.* mezun olm., diploma almak; derecelere ayrılmak; *v/t.* derecelere ayırmak -*i;* sınıflarına göre ayırmak -*i;* mezun etm., diploma vermek -*e;* **2.** ['~dʒuit ] *n.* mezun, diplomalı *(üniversiteden etc.);* **grad.u.a.tion** [~dju'eiʃən] *n.* mezuniyet, mezun olma, diploma alma; diploma töreni; ölçü bardağındaki derece işareti.

**graft¹** [gra:ft] **1.** *n.* ✔ ağaç aşısı; **2.** *v/t.* & *v/i.* aşıla(n)mak (in, upon); ⚕ ameliyatla doku yerleştirmek, transplante etm.

**graft²** *Am.* [~] **1.** *n.* rüşvet; para yeme; yolsuzluk, suiistimal; **2.** *v/i.* F rüşvet almak, para yemek; **'graft.er** *n.* F *part. pol.* menfaatçi kimse, rüşvetçi.

**gra.ham** ['greiəm]: ~ bread buğday ekmeği.

**Grail** [greil] *n.* son akşam yemeğinde Hz. İsa'nın kullandığı farzolunan sahan *veya* kâse.

**grain** [grein] *n.* tane, habbe, tohum, zerre; damar, doku; hububat; 0,065 gram; *fig.* huy, mizaç; in ~ esaslı, inceden inceye, natürel; dyed in the ~ iyice boyanmış; against the ~ *fig.* tabiatına zıt, ho-

şuna gitmeyen; **grained** *adj.* taneli, damarlı.

**gram** [græm] = gramme.

**gra.mer.cy** † [grə'mə:si] *int.* çok teşekkür!, sağolun!, minnettarım!; Allah Allah!, nasıl olur!

**gram.i.na.ceous** [greimi'neiʃəs], **gra.min.e.ous** [grei'miniəs] *adj.* ota benzer, ot gibi, ot...

**gram.ma.logue** ['græmələg] *n.* stenografi: kısaltma, özet.

**gram.mar** ['græmə] *n.* gramer, dilbilgisi; gramer kitabı; gramatik kurallara göre hazırlanmış konuşma *veya* yazı; **gram.mar.i.an** [grə'mɛəriən] *n.* gramer uzmanı, dilbilgisi kitabı yazarı, gramerci; **'gram.mar-school** *n.* İngiltere'de üniversiteye hazırlık okulu; *Am. a.* ilk ve orta okul; **gram.mat.i.cal** ☐ [grə'mætikəl] gramatik, gramere ait, dilbilgisi kurallarına uygun.

**gramme** [græm] *n.* gram.

**gram.o.phone** ['græməfəun] *n.* gramofon; ~ record gramofon plağı.

**gran.a.ry** ['grænəri] *n.* tahıl ambarı; çok tahıl yetiştiren bölge.

**grand** [grænd] **1.** ☐ *fig.* muhteşem, fevkalade, enfes, mükemmel, depdebeli, saltanatlı; heybetli, muazzam; büyük, ulu, baş; tam; ♀ Duchess grandüşes; ♀ Duke grandük; ♀ Old Party *Am.* Cumhuriyetçi parti; ~ stand tribün; **2.** *n. a.* ~ piano ♪ kuyruklu piyano; *Am. sl.* bin dolar; miniature ~ kısa kuyruklu piyano; **grandad** F ['grændæd] *n.* büyükbaba, dede; **gran.dam(e)** ['~dæm] *n.* nüfuzlu yaşlı kadın; **'grand.child** *n.* torun; **'grand.daughter** *n.* kız torun; **gran.dee** [græn'di:] *n.* ekâbir, itibarlı kimse; İspanyol *veya* Portekiz soylusu; **gran.deur** ['grændʒə] *n.* büyüklük, azamet, ihtişam, güzellik; **'grand.fa.ther** *n.* büyükbaba, dede; ~ clock sarkaçlı büyük dolap saati.

**gran.dil.o.quence** [græn'diləkwəns] *n.* tantanalı, süslü kelimeler kullanma; tumturak; **gran'dil.o.quent** ☐ süslü, tantanalı, tumturaklı.

**gran.di.ose** ☐ ['grændiəus] heybetli, muhteşem, göz alıcı, tantanalı, gösterişli.

**grand.moth.er** ['grænmʌðə], F **grand.ma** ['grænma:] *n.* anneanne, babaanne, nine; **'grand.ness** = grandeur.

**grand...:** '~.pa ['grænpa:] = grandfather; '~.par.ents *n. pl.* büyükanne ve büyükbaba, dede ve nine ~.sire ['~saiə] *n.* † büyükbaba, dede; yaşlı adam; '~.son *n.* erkek torun.

**grange** [greindʒ] *n.* binalarıyla birlikte

çiftlik; *Am.* çiftçi birliği; **'grang.er** *n.* çiftçi; çiftçi birliği üyesi.

**gran.ite** ['grænit] *n.* granit; **gra.nit.ic** [~'nitik] *adj.* granit cinsinden, granit...

**gran.ny** F ['græni] *n.* babaanne, anneanne, nine; titiz kadın; ebe.

**grant** [gra:nt] 1. *n.* bağış, teberru; tahsisat; bahşedilen arazi *veya* para; öö ferağ, terk, hibe; 2. *v/t.* vermek, ihsan etm., bahşetmek; kabul etm., onaylamak, tasdik etm., farzetmek; öö devretmek, ferağ etm., hibe etm.; take for ~ed doğru olarak kabul etm., muhakkak olacak gözüyle bakmak, olmuş gibi kabul etm.; ~ing this (to) be so bunun böyle olduğunu farzederek; God ~ ...! inşallah...!; **gran'tee** *n.* öö kendisine birşey hibe edilen kimse; **grant-in-aid** ['gra:ntin'eid] *n.* para yardımı, iane, tahsisat; **grant.or** öö [~'tɔ:] *n.* devreden, temlik eden, hibe eden kimse.

**gran.u.lar** ['grænjulə] *adj.* taneli, tane tane olan, granüle; **gran.u.late** ['~leit] *v/t. & v/i.* tanele(n)mek; **'gran.u.lat.ed** *adj.* taneli; ~ sugar tozşeker; **gran.u'la.tion** *n.* taneleme; **gran.ule** ['~ju:l] *n.* tanecik, zerre, habbe; **gran.u.lous** ['~juləs] *adj.* üstü taneli, granüle.

**grape** [greip] *n.* üzüm; asma; **'~.fruit** *n.* ♀ greyfrut; **'~-shot** *n.* ✕ top mermisi; **'~-sug.ar** *n.* glikoz, desktroz, levüloz, üzüm şekeri; **'~-vine** *n.* asma; dedikodu yoluyla haber alma; *a.* ~ telegraph ağızdan duyma, dedikodu yoluyla duyma.

**graph** [græf] *n.* grafik; **'graph.ic, 'graph.i-cal** □ resim *veya* yazıya ait, şeklî, çizgili; tam tasvir edilmiş, canlı; graphic arts *pl.* grafik sanatlar; **graph.ite** *min.* ['~fait] *n.* grafit; **graph.ol.o.gy** [~'fɔlədʒi] *n.* grafoloji; **graph pa.per** çizgili kâğıt.

**grap.nel** ⚓ ['græpnəl] *n.* filika demiri; dört tırnaklı demir; borda kancası.

**grap.ple** ['græpl] 1. *n.* ⚓ borda kancası, filika demiri; yakalama, sıkıca sarılma; göğüs göğüse savaşma; ⊕ kanca, tırnaklı demir; 2. *vb.* yakalamak, kavramak, sıkıca tutmak; göğüs göğüse mücadele etm.; kanca ile tutmak; uğraşmak; ~ with sıkıca tutmak, kavramak, yakalamak.

**grasp** [gra:sp] 1. *n.* tutma, yakalama, yakalayış, kavrama, kavrayış; anlama, idrak; 2. *vb.* tutmak, kavramak, yakalamak; kavramak, idrak etm.; yakalamayı denemek, istekle kabul etm. (at ~i); **'grasp.ing** □ haris, açgözlü, cimri, pinti.

**grass** [gra:s] 1. *n.* ot, çimen, çim, yeşillik; çayır, otlak; *sl.* haşiş; at ~ otlamakta *(hayvan); fig.* izinli; emekliye ayrılmış; send to ~ = 2. *v/t. & v/i.* otla(t)-mak; otla kaplamak; *sl.* ispiyon etm. on ~i); **'~.hop.per** *n.* çekirge; **'~-'plot** *n.* çimenlik; ~ roots *pl. Am.* taşra halkı *veya* seçmenleri; yüzeye yakın toprak; **'~-wid.ow(.er)** *n.* eşinden bir süre ayrı kalmış kadın *(veya* erkek); **'grass.y** *adj.* otlu, çimenli, yeşillikli.

**grate**[1] [greit] *n.* demir parmaklık, ızgara; *fig.* hapishane, kodes.

**grate**[2] [~] *v/t.* rendelemek; gıcırdatmak, sürterek ses çıkarmak; *v/i.* sürtünerek ses çıkarmak; ~ (up)on *fig.* sinirine dokunmak, sinirlendirmek; gıcırdamak.

**grate.ful** □ ['greitful] minnettar, müteşekkir; hoş, güzel, rahatlatıcı.

**grat.er** ['greitə] *n.* rende.

**grat.i.fi.ca.tion** [grætifi'keiʃən] *n.* memnuniyet, haz, zevk; **grat.i.fy** ['~fai] *v/t.* memnun etm., hoşnut etm.; tatmin etm.; **'grat.i.fy.ing** *adj.* memnuniyet verici, hoş, güzel; tatminkâr.

**grat.ing** ['greitiŋ] 1. □ tiz, cırlak, kulakları tırmalayan; 2. *n.* demir parmaklık, pencere kafesi; ızgara.

**gra.tis** ['greitis] *adv. & adj.* bedava, parasız, ücretsiz.

**grat.i.tude** ['grætitju:d] *n.* minnettarlık, şükran.

**gra.tu.i.tous** □ [grə'tju:itəs] bedava, parasız, ücretsiz; sebepsiz; **gra'tu.i.ty** *n.* hediye, teberru; bahşiş.

**gra.va.men** öö [grə'veimen] *n.* suçun esasını oluşturan şey, suçlamanın ağırlık merkezi.

**grave**[1] □ [greiv] ciddi, ağır, vahim, önemli; ~ accent *gr.* sesli harf üzerindeki aksan işareti.

**grave**[2] [~] 1. *n.* mezar, kabir; 2. *(irr.) v/t. mst fig.* oymak, hakketmek, işlemek *(hafızaya);* **'~-dig.ger** *n.* mezarcı.

**grav.el** ['grævəl] 1. *n.* çakıl; ⚕ kum, idrar taşı; 2. *v/t.* çakıl döşemek; F şaşırtmak, aklını karıştırmak; **grav.el.ly** ['grævəli] *adj.* çakıllı; kalın ve kaba ses.

**grav.en** ['greivən] *p.p. of* grave[2] 2.

**grav.er** ⊕ ['greivə] *n.* hakkâk, oymacı (kalemi).

**grave...:** '~.side: at his ~ bir ayağı çukurda; '~.stone *n.* mezar taşı; '~.yard *n.* mezarlık, kabristan.

**grav.ing dock** ⚓ ['greiviŋ'dɔk] *n.* kalafat havuzu, kuru havuz.

**grav.i.tate** ['græviteit] *vb.* çekilmek, yer çekimi ile hareket etm.; cezbedilmek, meyletmek (towards -e doğru); **grav.l'ta-tion** n. yerçekimi; fig. cazibe; **grav.l'ta-tion.al** pull [~ʃənl'pul] yerçekimi kuvveti.

**grav.i.ty** ['græviti] n. yerçekimi; ağırlık; önem, ciddiyet, ehemmiyet; centre of ~ ağırlık merkezi; specific ~ özgül ağırlık.

**gra.vy** ['greivi] n. etsuyu, sos, salça; kolay kazanılan para; '~-boat n. sosluk.

**gray** part. Am. [grei] adj. gri, kurşuni, boz, kır (saç); gri giysili; F neşesiz, kasvetli; **gray.ish** part. Am. ['~iʃ] adj. grimsi, grimtrak.

**graze** [greiz] 1. v/t. & v/i. otla(t)mak; sıyırmak, sıyırıp geçmek; 2. n. sıyrık, bere.

**gra.zier** ['greizjə] n. çoban.

**grease** 1. [griːz] v/t. yağlamak, yağ sürmek; ~ s.o.'s palm fig. b-ne rüşvet vermek; 2. [griːs] n. yağ, et yağı, kuyruk yağı; makine yağı; '~-cup n. ⊕ gres kabı, yağlama kutusu, yağdanlık; '~-gun n. mot. gres pompası; '~-proof adj. yağ geçirmez; **greas.er** ['griːzə] n. Am. sl. Meksikalı; gemide makine yağcısı.

**greas.y** ⊡ ['griːzi] yağlı, yağlanmış.

**great** ⊡ [greit] 1. adj. com. büyük, kocaman, iri, heybetli, cüsseli, azametli; fig. kabiliyetli, yetenekli, usta, mahir; F mükemmel,l şahane, harikulâde, fevkalâde; önemli; meşhur; yüksek; çok iyi; s. deal² 1. many; 2. n. the ~ pl. kodamanlar, büyükler; ~s pl. gözde kimseler, önemli kişiler; '~.coat n. palto; '~-'grand.child n. evlâdının torunu; '~-'grand.fa.ther n. büyük dede; **lgreat.ly** adv. çokça, pek çok; **lgreat.ness** n. büyüklük; şöhret; önem.

**Gre.cian** ['griːʃən] adj. Yunan...

**greed** [griːd], **lgreed.i.ness** n. açgözlülük, oburluk, hırs; **lgreed.y** ⊡ obur, açgözlü; hırslı, haris; hevesli, arzulu.

**Greek** [griːk] 1. adj. Yunanistan, Yunanlı veya Yunanca'ya ait; 2. n. Yunanlı, Grek, Rum; Yunanca; that is ~ to me hiç birşey anlayamıyorum, anlıyorsam arap olayım.

**green** [griːn] 1. ⊡ yeşil; ham, olmamış; yaş, taze; F tecrübesiz, toy, acemi, cahil; 2. n. yeşil renk; ~s pl. yeşil yapraklı sebzeler; yeşillik, çimen, çayır; ortak arazi; mera; golf oyununda hedef deliğinin etrafındaki çimen; '~.back n. Am. arkası yeşil banknot; **green.er.y** ['~nəri] n. yeşillik, çimen, botanik.

**green...:** ~ **fin.gers** pl. bahçıvanlıktan anlama; '~.gage n. ♣ frenkeriği, bardakeriği; '~.gro.cer n. manav, yemişçi; '~.gro.cer.y n. manavlık; '~.horn n. acemi

veya toy kimse; '~.house n. limonluk, ser; **lgreen.ish** adj. yeşilimsi, yeşilimtrak.

**Green.land.er** ['griːnləndə] n. Grönland Adası'nda yaşayan kimse.

**green light** ['griːn'lait] n. yeşil ışık (F fig. = izin, salâhiyet, yetki); **lgreen.ness** n. yeşillik.

**green...:** '~-room n. thea. oyuncuların dinlenme odası; '~.sick.ness n. ❢ kloroz, genç kızlarda demir eksikliğinden oluşan hastalık; ~.sward ['~swoːd] n. çimen.

**Green.wich** ['grinidʒ] : ~ time Greenwich saat ayarı.

**green.wood** ['griːnwud] n. yemyeşil orman.

**greet** [griːt] v/t. selâmlamak, selâm vermek; karşılamak; **lgreet.ing** n. selâm.

**gre.gar.i.ous** [gri'gɛəriəs] adj. toplu halde yaşayan, topluluğu seven.

**gre.nade** ✕ [gri'neid] n. el bombası; **gren.a.dier** [grenə'diə] n. eskiden el bombası atan asker; İngiliz piyade alayında er.

**grew** [gruː] pret. of grow.

**grey** [grei] 1. ⊡ gri, kurşuni, kül rengi, kır, boz, ağarmış (saç); ❩ Friar Fransiskan mezhebine ait rahip; 2. n. gri renk, kurşuni renk; 3. v/t. & v/i. ağar(t)mak; '~.beard n. yaşlı adam, ak sakallı adam; **grey.cing** ['~sin] n. tazı yarışı.

**grey...:** '~-'head.ed adj. fig. eski; yaşlı; '~.hound n. tazı; **lgrey.ish** adj. grimsi, grimtrak; **grey mat.ter** anat. gri madde; fig. beyin, akıl.

**grid** [grid] n. part. radyo: valfta kontrol voltajı taşıyan ızgara; şebeke; haritada kesişen dikey ve yatay hatlar sistemi; ray şebekesi; Am. futbol: saha.

**grid.dle** ['gridl] n. (alçak kenarlı) tava.

**grid.i.ron** ['gridaiən] n. ızgara; Am. futbol: saha.

**grief** [griːf] n. keder, acı, ıstırap, dert, elem; felâket, belâ.

**griev.ance** ['griːvəns] n. keder verici şey, dert; **grieve** v/t. & v/i. kederlen(dir)mek, üz(ül)mek, eseflen(dir)mek; **lgriev.ous** ⊡ kederli, acıklı, üzücü, keder verici, elem verici; şiddetli; **lgriev.ous.ness** n. acıklı durum, dert, keder; şiddet, tehlike.

**grif.fin** ['grifin] n. yarısı aslan yarısı kartal farzolunan garip yaratık.

**grig** [grig] n. hayat dolu kimse, neşeli kimse, şen şakrak kimse.

**grill** [gril] 1. v/t. & v/i. ızgarada pişir(il)mek, çok ısıtmak, çok sıcağa maruz bırakmak; sl. soru yağmuruna tutmak, sorguya çekmek; **2.** *n.* ızgara, tava; ızgarada pişmiş et; *a.* ~-room otel *veya* lokantada ızgaraların pişirildiği yer.

**grim** ☐ [grim] haşin, vahşi, gaddar, zalim, merhametsiz, korkunç, çetin; ~ facts *pl.* acı gerçekler; ~ humour uğursuz, meşum neşe.

**gri.mace** [gri'meis] **1.** *n.* yüz buruşturma, surat ekşitme; **2.** *v/i.* yüz buruşturmak, surat ekşitmek.

**grime** [graim] **1.** *n.* kir, pislik, pasak; **2.** *v/t.* kirletmek, pisletmek; **'grim.y** ☐ kirli, pis.

**grin** [grin] **1.** *n.* sırıtma, sırıtış; **2.** *v/i.* sırıtmak, dişlerini göstererek gülmek; *v/t.* sırıtarak belirtmek.

**grind** [graind] **1.** *(irr.)* *v/t.* öğütmek, ufalamak; bilemek; ezmek; sürterek parlatmak; gıcırdatmak *(diş)*; *fig.* eziyet vermek; *sl.* ineklemek, hafızlamak *(ders)*; döndürerek çalıştırmak; ~ out durmadan üretmek *(esp. yazı veya müzik)*; *v/i.* öğütülmek; sürtünmeden dolayı parlamak; gıcırdamak; *sl.* dersini ineklemek, hafızlamak; seksi biçimde kalçalarını kıvırmak *(striptizci)*; **2.** *n.* bitip tükenmek bilmeyen iş, uzun ve monoton iş, sıkıcı iş; öğütme, ezme; *sl.* inek, hafız *(öğrenci)*; kalça kıvırma; **'grind.er** *n.* öğütücü, bileyici; ~s *pl.* dişler; büyük sandviç; *sl.* inek, hafız; **'grind.ing** *n.* öğütme, çekme *(kahve)*; bileme; parlatma, cilalama; **'grind.stone** *n.* bileği taşı; keep s.o.'s nose to the ~ *b-ni* durmadan çalıştırmak, köle gibi çalıştırmak.

**grip** [grip] **1.** *v/t.* sıkı tutmak, sarılmak, kavramak *(a. fig.)*, yakalamak; etkilemek, -*in* dikkatini çekmek, tesir etm.; **2.** *n.* sıkı tutma, kavrama; kabza, sap; ⊕ kıskaç, kenet; *Am.* = gripsack; get to ~s with *bşle* uğraşmak.

**gripe** [graip] **1.** *n.* tutma, yakalama; kontrol, yönetme; şikâyet, sızlanma; sap, kabza; tutan alet *(fren)*; ~s *pl.* F sancı, karın ağrısı; *part. Am.* sıkıntı, dert; **2.** *v/t.* tutmak, yakalamak; keder vermek, ıstırap çektirmek, sıkıntı vermek; kızdırmak, sinirlendirmek; sancı vermek *(karın)*; *v/i. part. Am.* F mızmızlanmak, sızlanmak.

**grip.sack** *Am.* ['gripsæk] *n.* yolcu çantası.

**gris.ly** ['grizli] *adj.* korkunç, dehşetli, tüyler ürpertici.

**grist** [grist] *n.* öğütülecek zahire, hububat; bring ~ to the mill *fig.* ele geçen her şeyden yararlanmak: all is ~ that comes to his mill eline geçen her şeyden istifade eder.

**gris.tle** ['grisl] *n. anat.* kıkırdak; **gris.tly** *adj.* kıkırdaklı, kıkırdaktan ibaret.

**grit** [grit] **1.** *n.* çakıl, iri taneli kum; *fig.* metanet, cesaret, yiğitlik; **2.** *v/t.* çakıl döşemek, kum döşemek; gıcırdatmak *(diş)*; cesaret göstermek; **'grit.ty** *adj.* kumlu; cesur, yiğit.

**griz.zle** F ['grizl] *v/i.* sızlanmak, homurdanmak, halinden şikâyet etm.; **'grizzled** = grizzly 1; **'griz.zly 1.** *adj.* gri, kurşuni, boz; ~ bear = **2.** *n.* boz ayı.

**groan** [grəun] **1.** *n.* inilti, figan; **2.** *v/i.* inlemek, ah etm., figan etm.; *v/t.* *bşi* inleyerek belirtmek, inleyerek söylemek, üzülerek anlatmak.

**groat** [grəut]: not worth a ~ beş para etmez.

**groats** [grəuts] *n. pl. (part. yulaf)* dövülmüş hububat.

**gro.cer** ['grəusə] *n.* bakkal; **gro.cer.ies** ['~riz] *n. pl.* bakkaliye, bakkalın sattığı şeyler; **'gro.cer.y** *n.* bakkal dükkânı.

**grog** [grɔg] *n.* su katışmış içki; **'grog.gy** *adj.* sallanan, düşecek gibi, sersemlemiş.

**groin** [grɔin] **1.** *n. anat.* kasık; ⚕ iki kemerin birleştiği kenar; **2.** *v/t.* böyle kenarlarla donatmak.

**groom** [grum] **1.** *n.* seyis; güvey; = bridegroom; **2.** *v/t.* tımar etm.; çekidüzen vermek; bir işe hazırlamak; *Am. pol.* aday göstermek; well ~ed iyi giyimli, şık; **grooms.man** ['~zmən] *n.* sağdıç.

**groove** [gru:v] **1.** *n.* oluk, yiv, saban izi; *fig.* alışkanlık, âdet; in the ~ *fig.* keyfi yerinde, neşeli; **2.** *v/t.* oluk açmak; F *bşe* kendini vermek; **'groov.y** *adj. Am.* son modaya uygun, şık, mükemmel.

**grope** [grəup] *v/t.* & *v/i.* el yordamıyla aramak; körü körüne araştırmak; one's way el yormadıyla yürümek, yolunu bulmak.

**gross** [grəus] **1.** ☐ kaba, çirkin, kötü; iğrenç, tiksindirici, adi; hantal, şişko; göze batan, bariz; bereketli; bol; toptan; † brüt...; **2.** *n.* on iki düzine; in the ~ toptan, bütünüyle; genel olarak; **'gross.ness** *n.* kabalık; toptancılık; hantallık, iri yarılık.

**gro.tesque** ☐ [grəu'tesk] acayip, tuhaf, garip; kaba.

**grot.to** ['grɔtəu] *n., pl.* **'grot.to(e)s** mağara; yapay yeraltı odası.

**grouch** *Am.* F [grautʃ] **1.** *v/i.* şikâyet etm., homurdanmak, söylenmek, mırıldanmak; **2.** *n.* suratsızlık, homurdanma; söylenme, şikâyet; suratı asık kimse, memnun olmamış kimse, şikâyetçi kimse; **'grouch.y** *adj.* suratsız, asık suratlı, somurtkan.

**ground¹** [graund] *pret. & p.p. of* grind 1; ~ glass kristal cam; *phot.* buzlucam.

**ground²** [~] 1. *n.* mst yer, zemin; toprak, arsa; yeryüzü; meydan, saha, alan; ≠ toprak; *paint.* astar boya, üstüne desen çizilen düz satıh; ~s *pl.* bahçe; dip, denizin dibi; kahve telvesi, dibe çöken kısım, tortu; neden, sebep; on the ~(s) of sebebiyle, -*den* dolayı, ...yüzünden; fall to the ~ düş(ür)mek; *fig.* suya düşmek *(plan)*; give ~ geri çekilmek; avantajını koruyamamak; stand *veya* hold *veya* keep one's ~ ayak diremek, boyun eğmemek, davasından vazgeçmemek; 2. *v/t.* yere oturtmak, kurmak; esaslı olarak öğretmek; bir esasa dayandırmak; ≠ toprağa bağlamak; ✈ kalkışa izin vermemek; ⚓ karaya oturtmak; ⊕ zemin boyası sürmek; *v/i.* temeli olm.; karaya oturmak; topa vurmak; well ~ed temeli iyi; sağlam temeller üzerine kurulmuş; **'ground.age** *n.* ✝ demirleme için ödenen ücret, liman resmi.

**ground...:** **'~-con.nex.ion** *n.* ≠ toprak hattı; ~ **crew** = ground-staff; ~ **floor** zemin katı; **'~-'hog** *n.* zo. *part. Am.* dağsıçanı; **'~.less** ☐ temelsiz, yersiz, sebepsiz, asılsız; **ground.ling** ['~liŋ] *n. thea.* ayakta duran seyirci; basit zevkleri olan kimse; toprağa yakın çalışan *veya* yaşıyan bitki *veya* hayvan.

**ground...:** **'~-nut** *n.* yerfıstığı; **'~-'plan** *n.* binanın zemin planı; **'~-rent** *n.* arsa kirası.

**ground.sel** 🌿 ['graunsl] *n.* kanaryaotu.

**ground...;** ~ **speed** ✈ yer sürati; **'~-staff** *n.* ✈ hava meydanı ekibi, yer mürettebatı; ~ **swell** soluğan, uzakta esen rüzgârdan oluşan ölü dalga; **'~-wire** *n.* ≠ toprak teli; **'~.work** *n.* temel, esas.

**group** [gru:p] 1. *n.* grup, küme, öbek; heyet, topluluk; 2. *v/i.* gruplaşmak, grup halinde toplanmak; bir gruba ait olm.; *v/t.* toplamak; gruplara ayırmak.

**grouse¹** *orn.* [graus] *n.* ormantavuğu.

**grouse²** F [~] *v/i.* homurdanmak, söylenmek, sızlanmak, şikâyet etm.

**grove** [grəuv] *n.* koru, ormancık, ağaçlık.

**grov.el** ['grɔvl] *v/i.* mst *fig.* yerde sürünmek; ayaklarına kapanmak; kendini alçaltmak; yaltaklanmak; **'grov.el.(l)er** *n.* alçalmış kimse, hor görülen kimse; dalkavuk; **'grov.el.(l)ing** 1. *adj.* dalkavuk, alçalmış, rezil; 2. *n.* dalkavukluk, kendini küçük düşürme.

**grow** [grəu] *(irr.) v/i.* büyümek, geliş-

mek; olmak; serpilmek; çoğalmak, artmak, genişlemek; kökleşmek, yerleşmek *(alışkanlık)*; çekici olm.; ~ out of çok büyük gelmek; içine sığmamak *(elbise)*; bırakmak *(kötü alışkanlık)*; ~ (up)on s.o. b-*nin* içine yerleşmiş olm.; ~ up büyümek, olgunlaşmak; gelişmek; *v/t.* büyütmek, yetiştirmek; üretmek; geliştirmek; **'grow.er** *n.* yetiştirici, üretici; belirli şartlarla büyüyen bitki.

**growl** [graul] 1. *n.* homurtu, homurdanma, hırlama; 2. *v/i.* hırlamak, homurdanmak; guruldamak *(mide)*; gümbürdemek *(şimşek)*; *v/i.* homurdanarak söylemek; **'growl.er** *n. fig.* homurdanan kimse; *Am. sl.* bira kabı; küçük buzul.

**grown** [grəun] 1. *p.p. of* grow; 2. *adj.* büyümüş, yetişkin, olgun; **'~-up** 1. *adj.* yetişkin, olgun, büyümüş; 2. *n.* yetişkin kimse, olgun kimse; **growth** [grəuθ] *n.* büyüme, gelişme; artma, yükselme, çoğalma; mahsul, ürün; hastalıklı durum; of one's own ~ kendi eliyle yetiştirmiş.

**groyne** [grɔin] *n.* set, erozyonu önlemek için yapılmış duvar.

**grub** [grʌb] 1. *n.* tırtıl, kurtçuk; *sl.* yiyecek; *contp.* meşe odunu; köle gibi çalışan kimse; 2. *v/t.* kazmak, eşelemek, kökünden sökmek, kökünden sökerek temizlemek; *sl.* yedirmek *(yemek)*; ~ up kökünden sökmek; mst ~ out yuvasından çıkarmak; *v/i.* toprağı kazmak (for için); didinmek, çalışıp yorulmak (for için); **'grub.by** *adj.* pis, kirli, yıkanmamış; kurtlu.

**grudge** [grʌdʒ] 1. *n.* kin, garez, diş bileme; 2. *v/t.* isteksizce vermek, çok görmek, kıskanmak, gözü kalmak, vermek istememek; diş bilemek; ~ no pains özen göstermek, itina etm., hiçbir zahmetten kaçınmamak; **'grudg.er** *n.* kıskanç, bşde gözü kalan kimse; **'grudg.ing.ly** *adv.* istemeye istemeye, istemeyerek, isteksizce.

**gru.el** ['gruəl] *n.* pişirilmiş yulaf ezmesi; get *veya* have one's ~ *sl.* cezasını bulmak, hak ettiğini bulmak; **'gru.el.(l)ing** *adj.* çok yorucu, bitap düşürücü; şiddetli.

**grue.some** ☐ ['gru:səm] korkunç, dehşetli, ürkütücü; iğrenç.

**gruff** [grʌf] *adj.* kaba, ters, aksi; sert; boğuk *(ses)*; boğuk sesli.

**grum.ble** [grʌmbl] *v/i.* mırıldanmak; şikâyet etm. (at -*den*); homurdanmak; guruldamak; gürlemek; *v/t.* mırıldanarak söylemek, homurdanarak söylemek; **'grum.bler** *n. fig.* homurdanan kimse, halinden şikâyetçi kimse.

**grump.y** □ F ['grʌmpi] aksi, ters, kaba, kötü huylu.

**Grun.dy.ism** ['grʌndiizəm] n. iffet taslama, dar görüşlülük.

**grunt** [grʌnt] 1. n. homurtu, hırıltı; 2. vb. domuz gibi hırıldamak; homurdanmak; homurdanarak söylemek; **'grunt.er** n. domuz.

**guar.an.tee** [gærən'tiː] 1. n. garanti, kefalet, teminat; kefil; = guaranty; 2. v/t. garanti etm.; kefil olm.; **guar.an.tor** [~tɔː] n. kefil; **'guar.an.ty** n. garanti, kefalet.

**guard** [gɑːd] 1. n. koruma, muhafaza, himaye, müdafaa; gardiyan; koruyucu alet; X nöbet; nöbetçi; muhafız; 🚂 tren memuru, frenci; ♎ s pl. X muhafız alayı; be on (off) ones ~ hazırlıklı (hazırlıksız) olm., dikkatli olm., (gafil avlanmak); mount ~ X nöbet tutmak; relieve ~ X nöbet değiştirmek, nöbeti devralmak; 2. v/t. korumak, muhafza etm., himaye etm. (from -den; against -e karşı); beklemek; göz altına almak; v/i. uyanık bulunmak; nöbet tutmak; korunmak (against -e karşı); **'~-boat** n. ↓ karakol gemisi; **'guard.ed** □ uyanık, tetikte; korunan, muhafazalı; tedbirli; **'guard.house** n. askeri karakol; **'guard.i.an** n. koruyucu, muhafız, gardiyan; ♙ vasi, veli; ~ angel koruyucu melek; ~ of the poor fakirlerin koruyucusu, fakir babası; **'guard.i.an.ship** n. muhafızlık; vasilik, velilik; **guards.man** X ['gɑːdzmən] n. muhafız askeri.

**gudg.eon** ['gʌdʒən] n. ichth. yem için kullanılan ufak tatlı su balığı; fig. saf kimse, bön kimse; ⊕ mil, pin, menteşe kovanı, çengel, kanca.

**guer.don** lit. ['gəːdən] 1. n. ödül, mükâfat; 2. v/t. ödüllendirmek, mükâfat vermek.

**guer(r).ril.la** [gə'rilə] n. gerilla, çeteci; ~ war çete harbi, gerilla savaşı.

**guess** [ges] 1 .n. tahmin, zan; at a ~ tahminen; 2. v/t. tahmin etm., sanmak, zannetmek, farzetmek; inanmak; v/i. tahminde bulunmak (at -e hakkında); part. Am. zannetmek, farzetmek, sanmak; **'guess.work** n. tahmin, varsayı.

**guest** [gest] n. misafir, davetli, konuk, otel veya pansiyon müşterisi; paying ~ pansiyoner; **'~-house** n. pansiyon; **'~-room** n. misafir yatak odası.

**guf.faw** [gʌ'fɔː] 1. n. kaba gülüş, kahkaha 2. v/i. kabaca kahkaha atmak.

**guid.a.ble** ['gaidəbl] adj. yönetilebilir, idare edilebilir; **guid.ance** ['~dəns] n.

rehberlik, yol gösterme, liderlik; yönetme; eğitim sırasında çocuğa verilen öğüt.

**guide** [gaid] 1. n. rehber, kılavuz; yönetmelik; s. ~-book; ⊕ yatak, kızak, ray; 2. v/t. yol göstermek -e; sevketmek, idare etm. -i; ~d missile X güdümlü roket; **'~-book** n. seyahat rehberi; ~ dog körlere yol gösteren köpek; **'~-post** n. yol işareti; **'~-rope** n. 🕆 kılavuz ipi.

**gui.don** X ['gaidən] n. tabur sancağı, flama; sancak taşıyan er.

**guild** [gild] n. esnaf birliği,'lonca, hayır kurumu; **'guild.er** n. Hollanda para birimi; **'Guild'hall** n. esnaf birliği merkez binası; Londra belediye dairesi.

**guile** [gail] n. aldatma, hile, kurnazlık, şeytanlık; **guile.ful** □ ['~ful] hilebaz, düzenbaz, şeytan gibi, kurnaz; **'guile.less** □ saf, bön, samimi, temiz kalpli; **'guile.less.ness** n. samimiyet, saflık.

**guil.lo.tine** [gilə'tiːn] 1. n. giyotin; ⊕ kağıt bıçağı; pol. tartışma sınırlaması; 2. v/t. giyotinle idam etm.

**guilt** [gilt] n. suç, kabahat; **'guilt.i.ness** n. suçluluk; **'guilt.less** □ masum, suçsuz (of -den); **'guilt.y** □ suçlu, kabahatli; plead ~ suçu kabul etm.

**guin.ea** ['gini] n. 21 şilin değerindeki eski İngiliz parası; **'~-fowl** n. Afrika tavuğu, beç tavuğu; **'~-pig** n. kobay; fig. üzerinde deney yapılan insan.

**guise** [gaiz] n. elbise; aldatıcı görünüş, maske, kisve.

**gui.tar** ♪ [gi'tɑː] n. gitar.

**gulch** Am. [gʌlʃ] n. küçük ve derin dere.

**gulf** [gʌlf]n. körfez; uçurum, derin yarık; fig. ayrılık (fikir).

**gull**[1] orn. [gʌl] n. martı.

**gull**[2] [~] 1. n. hile, oyun, aldatma; kolay aldatılan kimse, saf kimse; 2. v/t. aldatmak, dolandırmak, hile yoluyla almak.

**gul.let** ['gʌlit] n. boğaz, gırtlak.

**gul.li.bil.i.ty** [gʌli'biliti] n. kolay aldanma, saflık, bönlük; **gul.li.ble** □ ['~ləbl] kolay aldanır, saf, ahmak, bön.

**gul.ly** ['gʌli] n. sel ve yağmur suyunun oluşturduğu dere; su kanalı.

**gulp** [gʌlp] 1. n. yudum, yutma; 2. v/t. yutmak, yutuvermek.

**gum**[1] [gʌm] n. a. ~s pl. dişeti.

**gum**[2] [~] 1. n. zamk; sakız, çiklet; jelatinli şekerleme; sakız ağacı; ~s pl. Am. lastik ayakkabı; 2. v/t. zamklamak, yapıştırmak.

**gum.boil** 🕆 ['gʌmbɔil] n. dişeti iltihabı.

**gum.my** ['gʌmi] adj. yapışkan, sakız gibi, yapış yapış.

**gump.tion** F [ˈgʌmpʃən] *n.* girişkenlik, cesaret, beceriklilik.

**gun** [gʌn] 1. *n.* top, tüfek, silâh; *part. Am.* tabanca, revolver; **big** *veya* **great** ~ F kodaman, nüfuzlu kimse; **stick to one's** ~ ayak diremek, davasından vazgeçmemek; 2. *vb. Am.* tüfekle ateş etm.; tüfekle avlanmak; '~.**boat** *n.* ↓ gambot; '~-**car.riage** *n.* ✕ top arabası; '~-**cot.ton** *n.* pamuk barutu; '~-**li.cence** *n.* silah taşıma ruhsatı; '~.**man** *n. part. Am.* silahlı kimse, silahlı gangster, silahlı soyguncu; '~-**met.al** *n.* top dökümü, kızıl döküm; '**gun.ner** *n.* ✕, ↓ topçu (subayı); '**gun**ner.**y** *n.* ✕ topçuluk (tekniği).

**gun.ny** [ˈgʌni] *n.* çuval bezi, çul.

**gun...**; '~.**pow.der** *n.* barut; ♀ Plot *hist.* 5 Kasım 1605'te Parlamento binasını havaya uçurmayı amaçlayan suikast; '~-**room** *n.* ↓ subaylara ait oda; '~-**run**ning *n.* silah kaçakçılığı; '~.**shot** *n.* silah atışı; top menzili; '~-**shy** *adj.* silah sesinden ürken (*esp. köpek, at*); '~.**smith** *n.* silahçı, tüfekçi; '~-**tur.ret** *n.* taret, zırhlı kule.

**gun.wale** ↓ [ˈgʌnl] *n.* filika küpeştesi, borda tirizi.

**gur.gle** [ˈgəːgl] 1. *n.* çağıltı, gurultu, fokurtu; 2. *v/i.* çağıldamak, guruldamak, fokurdamak; çağıltı gibi ses çıkarmak.

**gush** [gʌʃ] 1. *n.* fışkırma, taşma; *fig.* coşku, hayranlık; 2. *v/i.* fışkırmak (from *-den*); *fig. b-ne* hayran kalmak, bayılmak; '**gush.er** *n. fig.* hayran olmuş kimse; petrol kuyusu; '**gush.ing** □ coşkun, taşkın, heyecanlı.

**gus.set** [gʌsit] *n.* elbiseleri bollaştırmak için yanlarına eklenen kumaş parçası, üç köşeli peş.

**gust** [gʌst] *n.* ani rüzgâr, bora; coşku.

**gus.ta.to.ry** [ˈgʌstətəri] *adj.* tatma duyusuyla ilgili, tatma...

**gus.to** [ˈgʌstəu] *n.* zevk alma, haz, kişisel arzu, istek (for *-e*).

**gus.ty** □ [ˈgʌsti] rüzgârlı, fırtınalı.

**gut** [gʌt] 1. *n.* bağırsak; ♩ bağırsaktan yapılan çalgı teli; ~s *pl.* bağırsaklar; *sl.* cesaret, azim, kararlılık; 2. *v/t.* bağırsaklarını dışarı çıkarmak (*ölü hayvanın*); içini tamamen tahrip etm., yağma etm.

**gut.ta-per.cha** [ˈgʌtəˈpəːtʃə] *n.* gutaperka, Malezya'da bazı ağaçlardan elde edilen kauçuğa benzer bir madde.

**gut.ter** [ˈgʌtə] 1. *n.* oluk, suyolu, hendek; *fig.* bayağılık, sefalet; 2. *v/t.* hendek açmak, oluk açmak, su yolu kazmak; *v/i.* oluk gibi akmak; eriyip akmak (*mum*); ~ **press** müstehcen hikâyelere veya skandallara daha çok yer veren gazeteler; '~-**snipe** *n.* sokak çocuğu, köprüaltı çocuğu, kenar mahalle çocuğu.

**gut.tur.al** [ˈgʌtərəl] 1. □ gırtlağa ait, gırtlak...; 2. *n. gr.* gırtlaktan çıkarılan ses.

**guy¹** [gai] 1. *n.* F acayip kılıklı herif; *part. Am.* F herif, adam; 2. *v/t.* alay etm., dalga geçmek.

**guy²** [~] *n.* bşi yerinde tutan halat *veya* zincir; ↓ gemi direklerini yerinde tutan halat.

**guz.zle** [ˈgʌzl] *vb.* obur gibi yemek, çok ve hızlı içmek.

**gym** F [dʒim] = gymnasium, gymnastics.

**gym.kha.na** [dʒimˈkɑːnə] *n.* atletizm yarışması; araba yarışı.

**gym.na.si.um** [dʒimˈneizjəm] *n.* spor salonu; **gym.nast** [ˈ~næst] *n.* beden eğitimi öğretmeni *veya* uzmanı; **gym'nas.tic** 1. *adj.* (~ally) beden eğitimine ait, atletizm...; ~ **competition** jimnastik müsabakası; 2. ~**s** *n. pl.* jimnastik, idman, beden eğitimi; '**gym-shoes** *n. pl.* F beden ayakkabısı, jimnastik ayakkabısı.

**gyn.ae.col.o.gist** [gainiˈkɔlədʒist] *n.* jinekolog, kadın-doğum hastalıkları mütehassısı; **gyn.ae'col.o.gy** *n.* jinekoloji, kadın-doğum hastalıkları bilgisi.

**gyp** [dʒip] *n.* (*Cambridge Üniversitesi'nde*) öğrencilere hizmet eden erkek hizmetçi; hilebaz, dolandırıcı; **give** s.o. ~ *b-ni* acımasızca azarlamak *veya* cezalandırmak, dövmek.

**gyp.se.ous** [ˈdʒipsiəs] *adj.* alçı gibi; alçılı.

**gyp.sum** *min.* [ˈdʒipsəm] *n.* alçıtaşı.

**gyp.sy** *part. Am.* [ˈdʒipsi] = gipsy.

**gy.rate** [dʒaiəˈreit] *v/i.* dönmek, deveran etm., devretmek; **gy'ra.tion** *n.* dönüş, dönme, deveran; **gy.ra.to.ry** [ˈ~rətəri] *adj.* dönen..., devreden...

**gy.ro-com.pass** *phys.* [ˈdʒaiərəuˈkʌmpəs] *n.* giroskoplu pusula, topaç pusulası; **gy-ro.scope** [ˈdʒaiərəskəup] *n.* giroskop, topaç; **gy.ro.scop.ic** **sta.bi.liz.er** [gaiərəsˈkɔpikˈsteibilaizə], **gy.ro'sta.bi.liz.er** *n.* giroskopik stabilizatör.

**gyve** *poet.* [dʒaiv] 1. *n.* ~**s** *pl.* ayak zinciri, pranga; 2. *v/t.* prangaya vurmak.

# H

**h** [eitʃ]: drop one's h's h harfini söyle-
memek.

**ha** [hɑː] *int.* ha!, vay!, ya!, oh!

**ha.be.as cor.pus** ȫ [ˈheibjəsˈkɔːpəs] *n. a.*
writ of ~ bir suçluyu hakim huzuruna çıkarma emri, ihzar emri.

**hab.er.dash.er** [ˈhæbədæʃə] *n.* tuhafiyeci;
*Am.* erkek giyimi satan mağaza; **ˈhab-
er.dash.er.y** *n.* tuhafiye dükkânı; tuhafiye (eşyası); *Am.* erkek giyim eşyası.

**ha.bil.i.ments** [həˈbilimənts] *n. pl.* elbise,
kıyafet, kılık; teçhizat, tertibat.

**hab.it** [ˈhæbit] **1.** *n.* âdet, alışkanlık, huy,
tabiat; iptilâ, düşkünlük; zihni yapı; yaradılış; din adamlarının giydiği özel kıyafet; fall *veya* get into bad ~s kötü huy-
lar edinmek; get out of a ~ bir alışkanlıktan kurtulmak, bir alışkanlığı bırakmak;
get into the ~ of smoking sigara içmeye
alışmak, sigara içmeyi alışkanlık haline
getirmek; be in the ~ of ...alışkanlığın-
da olm., alışmak -e; **2.** *vb.* giydirmek;
**ˈhab.it.a.ble** *adj.* oturmaya elverişli, oturulabilir; **hab.i.tat** ȣ, *zo.* [ˈ~tæt] *n.* bir
hayvan *veya* bitkinin büyüdüğü yer;
**hab.iˈta.tion** *n.* ikamet, oturma; ikametgâh, mesken, ev.

**ha.bit.u.al** ☐ [həˈbitjuəl] âdet olmuş, alışılmış; daimi...; **haˈbit.u.ate** [~eit] *vb.*
alıştırmak (to -e); **hab.i.tude** [ˈhæbitjuːd]
*n.* âdet, alışkanlık; eğilim, istidat; **ha-
bit.u.é** [həˈbitjuei] *n.* müdavim, daimi ziyaretçi, gedikli müşteri.

**hack¹** [hæk] **1.** *n.* vuruş, darbe; madenci
kazması; kesici alet, çentik aleti; çentik,
kertik, diş; kuru öksürük; *futbol:* tekme yarası; **2.** *v/t.* çentmek, yarmak, yontmak; kıymak, doğramak; keserek temizlemek; becermek; *futbol:* tekme atmak;
~ing cough kuru öksürük.

**hack²** [~] **1.** *n.* kira beygiri; yaşlı at; kiralık at arabası; taksi; taksi şoförü; *a.*
~ writer değersiz yazılar yazan kalitesiz
yazar **2.** *adj.* kiralık...; *fig.* âdi, bayağı,
basmakalıp; bayatlamış; **3.** *vb.* yıpratmak, eskitmek, âdileştirmek; rahvan yü-

rüyüşle ata binmek; araba kullanmak;
taksi şoförlüğü yapmak.

**hack.le** [ˈhækl] **1.** *n.* ⊕ kendir *veya* keten
tarağı; *orn.* horozun boynundaki uzun
tüyler; get s.o.'s ~ up *fig. b-ni* kızdırmak, öfkelendirmek; **2.** *vb.* keten tarağı ile taramak; olta ucuna suni sinek yemi takmak; yarmak, yontmak, çentmek,
parçalamak.

**hack.ney** [ˈhækni] *n.* binek *veya* koşum
atı; ~ car.riage, ~ coach kiralık at arabası; **ˈhack.neyed** *adj. fig.* adi, bayağı;
eskimiş, yıpranmış; basmakalıp; kaşarlanmış.

**hack-saw** ⊕ [ˈhæksɔː] *n.* demir testeresi.

**had** [hæd, həd] *pret. & p.p. of* have.

**had.dock** *ichth.* [ˈhædək] *n.* mez(g)it balığı.

**Ha.des** [ˈheidiːz] *n.* ölülerin ruhlarının bulunduğu yer, ölüler diyarı.

**h(a)e.mal** [ˈhiːməl] *adj.* kanla *veya* da-
marlarla ilgili, kan...

**h(a)e.ma.tite** *min.* [ˈhemətait] *n.* hematit.

**h(a)e.mo...** [ˈhiːməu] *prefix* kan...

**h(a)e.mo.glo.bin** ȣ [hiːməuˈgləubin] *n.* hemoglobin; **h(a)e.mo.phil.i.a** [~ˈfiliə] *n.* he-
mofili, kanın pıhtılaşmaması.

**h(a)em.or.rhage** [ˈheməridʒ] *n.* kanama;
**h(a)em.or.rhoids** [ˈ~rɔidz] *n. pl.* basur,
emeroit.

**haft** [hɑːft] *n.* balta *veya* bıçak sapı, kılıç kabzası.

**hag** [hæg] *n. mst fig.* acuze, cadı, çirkin
kadın, kocakarı, büyücü kadın.

**hag.gard** ☐ [ˈhægəd] bitkin görünüşlü,
çökmüş, çelimsiz, bir deri bir kemik.

**hag.gle** [ˈhægl] *vb.* sıkı pazarlık etm.; çekişmek, münakaşa etm.; doğramak, parçalamak.

**hag.i.ol.o.gy** [hægiˈɔlədʒi] *n.* azizlerin hayatı ile ilgili edebiyat.

**hag.rid.den** [ˈhægridn] *adj.* bitkin, yorgun,
usanmış.

**hah** [hɑː] *int.* ha!, vay!, ya!, oh!

**ha-ha** [hɑːˈhɑː] *n.* alçak çit.

**hail¹** [heil] **1.** *n.* dolu; dolu gibi yağan

şey; **2.** *vb.* dolu yağmak; yağdırmak ·*(küfür);* hızlı ve şiddetli gelmek *(yumruk).*

**hail²** [~] **1.** *vb.* çağırmak; demek; alkışlarla karşılamak, selâmlamak; ~ from ...limanından kalkmak; ...li olm.; **2.** *n.* selâmlama, seslenme; ~! selâm!; within ~ duyulacak mesafede, yakın; be ~-fellow -well-met with *b-le* samimi dost olm., yakın arkadaş olm. canciğer olm. **hail.stone** [ˈheilstəun] *n.* dolu tanesi; **ˈhailstorm** *n.* dolu fırtınası; *fig.* yağmur *(soru, küfür, mermi).*

**hair** [hɛə] *n.* saç, kıl, tüy; kıl payı mesafe; keep your ~ on! *sl.* sakin ol!; not turn a ~ kılını kıpırdatmamak; ~'s breadth = ˈ~-breadth *n.* kıl payı mesafe, ucuz kurtulma; by *veya* within ~ az kaldı, ramak kaldı; ˈ~-cut *n.* saç kesme, saç traşı; saç kesilme biçimi; ˈ~-do *n.* *Am.* saç tuvaleti; ˈ~.dress.er *n.* *(part. kadın)* ku(v)aför, berber; ˈ~-dri.er *n.* saç kurutma makinesi; **haired** *comb.* ...saçlı; **ˈhairi.ness** *n.* tüylülük, kıllılık; tehlike, risk. **hair...**; ˈ~.less *adj.* saçsız, kel, saçlara dökülmüş; ˈ~.pin *n.* firkete, saç tokası; ~ bend keskin viraj; ˈ~-rais.ing *adj.* tüyler ürpertici, korkunç; ˈ~-shirt *n.* sert hayvan kılından yapılmış gömlek; ˈ~-split.ting *n.* kılı kırk yarma; ˈ~-spring *n.* ⊕ saat içindeki kıl yay; **ˈhair.y** *adj.* kıllı, tüylü; kıldan yapılmış; kıl gibi; *sl.* tehlikeli, riskli.

**ha.la.tion** *phot.* [həˈleiʃən] *n.* resmin sürekspoze kısmı.

**hal.berd** × [ˈhælbəːd] *n.* Ortaçağda kullanılan baltalı kargı.

**hal.cy.on** [ˈhælsiən] **1.** *n.* yalıçapkını, iskelekuşu, emircik; **2.** *adj.* durgun, sakin, dingin.

**hale** [heil] *adj.* sağlam, dinç, zinde; ~ and hearty dinç ve canlı.

**half** [hɑːf] **1.** *adj.* yarımbuçuk; ~ a crown iki buçuk şilin değerindeki eski İngiliz parası; a pound and a ~ bir buçuk pound; not ~ *sl.* hem de nasıl; çok fazla; adamakıllı; **2.** *n. pl.* **halves** [hɑːvz] yarı; eş; yarım saat; *okul:* sömestr, dönem; yarım dolar; *s.* ~-back; too clever by ~ gereğinden fazla akıllı; by halves yarımyamalak, tamamlanmamış; go halves yarı yarıya bölüşmek *-i;* ˈ~-ˈback *n. futbol:* hafbek; ˈ~-ˈbaked *adj. fig.* acemi, deneyimsiz, toy; aptalca, iyi düşünülmemiş; iyi pişmemiş; ˈ~-bind.ing *n.* arkası ve köşeleri daha iyi kalite bezle kaplı cilt; ˈ~-ˈblood *n.* melez, yarım kan; ˈ~-ˈbound *adj.* arkası ve köşeleri daha

iyi kalite bez kaplı; ˈ~-ˈbred *adj.* melez...; ˈ~-breed *n.* melez; ˈ~-ˈcalf *n.* kitabın arkasını ve köşelerini kaplama derisi; ˈ~-caste *n.* melez; ˈ~-ˈcrown *n.* iki buçuk şilin değerindeki eski İngiliz parası; ˈ~-ˈheart.ed □ isteksiz, gayretsiz; ˈ~-ˈhol.i.day *n.* yarım günlük tatil; ˈ~-ˈhour **1.** *n.* yarım saat; **2.** *adj.* yarım saatlik; ˈ~-ˈhour.ly *adj. & adv.* yarım saatte bir; ˈ~-ˈlength *n.* vücudun yukarı kısmını gösteren resim; ˈ~-ˈlife (pe.ri.od) *n. phys.* yarıla(n)ma süresi; ˈ~-ˈmast: (at) ~ yarıya indirilmiş *(bayrak);* ˈ~-ˈmoon *n.* yarımay; ˈ~-ˈmourn.ing *n.* yarı matem elbisesi; ˈ~-ˈpay *n.* yarım maaş; açıkta bekleme maaşı; ~.pen.ny [ˈheipni] *n.* yarım peni; ~-seas-o.ver F [ˈhɑːfsiːzˈəuvə] *adj.* çakırkeyf; ˈ~-ˈtime *n. spor:* haftaym, yarı devre; ˈ~-ˈtone proc.ess ⊕ resmi hafif noktalarla gösterme işlemi; ˈ~-ˈtrack *n.* yarısı paletli askeri araç; ˈ~-ˈway *adj.* yarı yolda; yetersiz; ~ house yarı yolda bulunan otel *veya* han; *fig.* akıl hastası *veya* uyuşturucu madde kullananları toplum hayatına alıştıran yer; ˈ~-ˈwit *n.* aptal *(veya* ahmak, budala) kimse; ˈ~-ˈwit.ted *adj.* aptal, ahmak, budala.

**hal.i.but** *ichth.* [ˈhælibət] *n.* kalkana benzer yassı bir balık.

**hall** [hɔːl] *n.* salon; resmi bina; hol; koridor; *univ.* yemek salonu; ~ of residence yurt, lojman.

**hal.le.lu.jah** [hæliˈluːjə] *n.* Tanrıya şükretme.

**hall...**; ˈ~-mark **1.** *n.* altın *veya* gümüşte ayar damgası; *fig.* kalite işareti; **2.** *vb.* ayar damgası basmak; ˈ~-ˈstand *n.* portmanto.

**hal.lo(a)** [həˈləu] *int.* alo!, hey!, yok ya!, bana bak!.

**hal.loo** [həˈluː] **1.** *int.* hadi yavrum! *(köpeklere);* **2.** *n.* avda köpekleri saldırtma ünlemi; **3.** *v/i.* 'saldır' diye bağırmak; *v/t.* saldırtmak, tahrik etm.

**hal.low** [ˈhæləu] *vb.* kutsallaştırmak; kutsamak, takdis etm.; **Hal.low.mas** [ˈ~mæs] *n.* Azizler yortusu.

**hal.lu.ci.na.tion** [həluːsiˈneiʃən] *n.* varsanı, sanrı, kuruntu, vehim.

**hall.way** [ˈhɔːlwei] *n.* koridor; hol.

**ha.lo** [ˈheiləu] *n. ast.* ağıl, hale, ışık halkası.

**halt** [hɔːlt] **1.** *n.* duruş; durma, duraklama; mola; 🚂 ara istasyon; **2.** *v/t. & v/i.* dur(dur)mak; *mst fig.* tereddüt etm., duraksamak; **3.** *adj.* topal, aksak.

**hal.ter** [ˈhɔːltə] *n.* yular; idam ipi.

**halve** [haːv] *v/t.* yarıya bölmek; yarıya indirmek; **halves** [~z] *pl. of* half 2.

**hal.yard** ⚓ [ˈhæljəd] *n.* bayrak *veya* seren ipi, kandilisa, abli.

**ham** [hæm] *n.* jambon, domuz budu; *sl.* amatör radyocu; amatör; *a.* ~ actor *sl.* amatör oyuncu.

**ham.burg.er** *Am.* [ˈhæmbəːgə] *n.* hamburger, köfteli sandviç; sığır kıyması; köfte.

**ham-hand.ed** [ˈhæmhændid] *adj.* eli ağır, beceriksiz.

**ham.let** [ˈhæmlit] *n.* küçük köy.

**ham.mer** [ˈhæmə] **1.** *n.* çekiç, tokmak; çekiç kemiği; tüfek horozu; ~ and tongs F büyük gürültü ve gayretle; **2.** *v/t.* çekiçle işlemek, çekiçle vurmak, çekiçle çakmak, çekiçlemek; yumruklamak; ~ at didinmek, uğraşıp durmak, durmadan çalışmak; ~ out düzeltmek, şekil vermek, plan yapmak.

**ham.mock** [ˈhæmək] *n.* hamak; ~ chair şezlong.

**ham.per** [ˈhæmpə] **1.** *n.* büyük sepet, sandık, çamaşır sepeti; **2.** *v/t.* engel olm. -e, mâni olm. -e.

**ham.ster** *zo.* [ˈhæmstə] *n.* sıçan türünde bir hayvan.

**ham.string** [ˈhæmstriŋ] **1.** *n. anat.* diz arkasındaki iki büyük kirişten biri; **2.** (*irr.* string) *vb.* bu kirişleri kesmek, kötürümleştirmek, sakatlamak; *fig.* gücünü kesmek, etkinliğini azaltmak, kolunu kanadını kırmak.

**hand** [hænd] **1.** *n.* el; kuvvet, etki; elleri kullanmadaki hüner; *zo.* ön ayak; işçi, amele; gemi tayfası; işe karışma, parmak; akrep, ibre; F adam, herif, biri; el yazısı; imza; *iskambil:* el, oyun; *pl.* sorumluluk, yetki, salahiyet; sahip olma; alkış; at ~ yakında, yakın, yanında; be at ~ yakın olm., yakında olm.; at first ~ doğrudan doğruya, ilk elden; at s.o.'s ~s ...den; a good (poor) ~ aı ...de becerikli (beceriksiz); ~ and glove el ele, yardımlaşarak; bear a ~ yardım etm. -e; by ~ el ile; elden *(mektup)*; change ~s el değiştirmek; sahip değiştirmek; have a ~ in ...de parmağı olm.; in ~ elde, mevcut, hazırda; bitirilmek üzere; † nakit para; lay ~s on el atmak -e; şiddet kullanmak -e; bulmak -i; kutsamak, takdis etm. -i; lend a ~ yardım etm. -e; off ~ derhal, hemen, doğrudan doğruya; ~s off! elini sürme!, dokunma!; on ~ elde; † mevcut, stokta; *part. Am.* hazır, rezerve edilmiş; on one's ~s ...nin elinde; on all ~s her tarafta, her

yerde; on the one ~ bir taraftan; on the other ~ diğer taraftan; out of ~ derhal, hemen, gecikmeksizin; bitirilmiş; kontrolden çıkmış, çığrından çıkmış, elden çıkmış; ~ over fist süratle ve başarıyla; take a ~ at *(oyun v.b.)* katılmak -e; to (one's) ~ ...nin eline, ...nin elinde, eline geçmiş; ~ to ~ göğüs göğüse, yumruk yumruğa; come to ~ varmak, ele geçmek; you can feed him out of your ~ *fig.* onu kendine kul köle yapabilirsin; ona kendi fikirlerini kabul ettirebilirsin; get the upper ~ of ...in kontrolünü ele geçirmek, üstünlük sağlamak; put one's ~ to el koymak -e; he can turn his ~ to anything on parmağında on marifet var; ~s up! eller yukarı!; *s.* high 1; **2.** *v/t.* el ile vermek, uzatmak; yardım etm.; teslim etm.; ~ down nesilden nesile devretmek; ~ in teslim etm.; ~ out dağıtmak; sadaka olarak vermek; ~ over vermek, teslim etm., devretmek (to -e); **'~-bag** *n.* kadınların el çantası; para cüzdanı; **'~-bar.row** *n.* el arabası; **'~.bill** *n.* el ilanı; **'~.book** *n.* el kitabı, rehber; **'~-brake** *n.* ⊕ el freni; **'~.cart** *n.* el arabası, çekçek; **'~.clap** *n.* alkış; **'~.cuff 1.** *n.* kelepçe; **2.** *v/t.* kelepçe vurmak; **'hand.ed** *comb.* ...elli; **hand.ful** [~ful] *n.* avuç dolusu; F avuç kadar miktar, çok az miktar; F ele avuca sığmayan kimse; **'hand-glass** *n.* saplı küçük ayna.

**hand.i.cap** [ˈhændikæp] **1.** *n.* engel, mâni, sekte, ket *(a. fig.)*; handikap, elverişsiz durum; engelli koşu; **2.** *v/t.* sakatlamak engel olm. -e, mâni olm. -e; *fig. a.* ket vurmak -e, sekte vurmak -e.

**hand.i.craft** [ˈhændikrɑːft] *n.* el sanatı, el hüneri; **'hand.i.crafts.man** *n.* zanaatçı, küçük sanat; **'hand.i.ness** *n.* beceri, maharet, ustalık; **'hand.i.work** *n.* iş, elişi.

**hand.ker.chief** [ˈhæŋkətʃif] *n.* mendil.

**han.dle** [ˈhændl] **1.** *n.* sap, kulp, tokmak, kabza, tutamaç, tutamak; *fig.* vasıta, imkân, bahane; F ünvan, paye, rütbe; fly off the ~ F tepesi atmak, küplere binmek; **2.** *v/t.* ellemek, ele almak, el sürmek, dokunmak, kullanmak; idare etm., muamele etm., davranmak; alıp satmak; **'~-bar** *n.* gidon *(bisiklette)*.

**hand...:** **'~.loom** *n.* el dokuma tezgâhı; **'~-lug.gage** *n.* elde taşınabilir bagaj; **'~-'made** *adj.* elişi, el yapımı; **'~-maid-(.en)** *n. fig.* hizmetçi kız, besleme, kız evlâtlık; **'~-me-downs** *n. Am.* F *pl.* kullanılmış herhangi bş *(part. elbise)*; **'~-or.gan** *n.* latarna, kollu çalgı aleti; **'~-out** *n.* F sadaka; bildiri; **'~-rail** *n.* trabzan, merdiven parmaklığı; '~.saw n. el testeresi; **hand.sel** [ˈhænsəl] n. uğur getirsin diye verilen hediye; siftah; pey; ilk taksit; **hand.shake** [ˈhændʃeik] n. el sıkma; **hand.some** □ [ˈhænsəm] yakışıklı, güzel; cömert; iyi; bol.

**hand**...: '~.work n. elişi, el yapımı; '~.writing n el yazısı; '**hand.y** □ yakın, el altında; eli işe yatkın, becerikli, usta, mahir; kullanışlı, elverişli, faydalı; ~ man elinden her iş gelen kimse.

**hang** [hæŋ] 1. (irr.) v/t. asmak; asarak idam etm. (pret. & p.p. mst ~ed); takmak; yapıştırmak; sarkıtmak; eğmek (baş); galeride sergilemek (resim); I'll be ~ed if ... F ...irsem kahrolayım; ~ it! F lânet olsun!; ~ fire zamanında ateş almamak; yavaşlamak, gecikmek; ~ out asmak (çamaşır); sarkıtmak; sl. yaşamak, oturmak; ~ up kapamak (telefonu); asmak; fig. ertelemek, tehir etm., geri bırakmak; v/i. asılı olm. (on -de); asılmak, sallanmak; üstünde dolaşmak; sallantıda olm., muallakta olm.; sarkmak; ~ about aylak aylak dolaşmak, başıboş gezerek beklemek, avare dolaşmak; ~ back tereddüt etm., çekinmek; ~ on sıkı tutmak, yapışmak; fig. peşini bırakmamak, azimle devam etm., bağlı olm. -e; ~ by a hair, ~ by a single thread fig. pamuk ipliğine bağlı olm.; let things go ~ F olayları gidişatına bırakmak, hiç aldırış etmemek; 2. n. duruş (elbise, perde); F anlam, mana, kullanış şekli; get the ~ of s.th. F bşin nasıl çalıştığını öğrenmek, anlamını kavramak; I don't care a ~ sl. vız gelir tırıs gider, hiç umurumda değil, iplemem.

**hang.ar** [ˈhæŋə] n. hangar.

**hang.dog** [ˈhæŋdɔg] 1. n. sinsi adam, alçak adam; 2. adj. sinsi, kurnaz, alçak, adi...

**hang.er** [ˈhæŋə] n. askı, kanca, çengel; '~-ˈon n. contp. fig. beleşçi, çanak yalayıcı, asalak.

**hang.ing** [ˈhæŋiŋ] adj. asılı..., sarkan...; idama layık; ~ committee paint. asılacak tablo seçimi yapan jüri; '**hang.ings** n. pl. oda duvarlarına asılan kumaş.

**hang.man** [ˈhæŋmən] n. cellat.

**hang.nail** 💯 [ˈhæŋneil] n. şeytantırnağı.

**hang.out** F [ˈhænˈaut] n. ev, mesken, sık gidilen yer.

**hang.over** [ˈhæŋəuvə] n. sl. içkiden gelen baş ağrısı, içkinin verdiği mahmurluk; Am. eski zamandan kalmış şey, kalıntı.

**hank** [hæŋk] n. çile; kangal.

**han.ker** [ˈhæŋkə] vb. arzulamak, özlemek,

istemek (after, for -i); '**han.ker.ing** n. özlem, istek, arzu.

**han.kie, han.ky** F [ˈhæŋki] n. mendil.

**han.ky-pan.ky** F [ˈhæŋkiˈpæŋki] n. hilekârlık, üçkâğıtçılık, dümen, dolap.

**Han.sard** [ˈhænsɑːd] n. parlamento tutanağı (İngiltere'de).

**Hanse** [hæns]: the ~ hist. tüccar loncası.

**han.sel** [ˈhænsəl] = handsel.

**han.som** [ˈhænsəm] n. a. ~-cab iki tekerlekli ve tek atlı araba.

**hap** 🏚 [hæp] n. şans, talih; **hapˈhaz.ard 1.** n. şans, rastlantı; at ~ rasgele, şansa, gelişigüzel; 2. adj. rasgele, gelişigüzel; 'hap.less □ şanssız, talihsiz, bahtsız; 'hap.ly adv. † şansa, belki, muhtemelen.

**haˈpˈorth** F [ˈheipəθ] = halfpennyworth.

**hap.pen** [ˈhæpən] vb. olmak, vuku bulmak, meydana gelmek, vaki olm.; he ~ed to be at home bereket versin ki evdeydi, Allahtan evdeydi; ~ on, ~ upon rast gelmek -e, şans eseri bulmak -i; ~ in Am. F pat diye çıkıp gelmek; ~ to inf. rasgele olm.; 'hap.pen.ing n. olay, vaka, hadise.

**hap.pi.ly** [ˈhæpili] adv. mutlulukla, sevinçle.

**hap.pi.ness** [ˈhæpinis] n. mutluluk, saadet, bahtiyarlık.

**hap.py** □ [ˈhæpi] com. mutlu, mesut, bahtiyar, memnun, sevinçli, neşeli; şanslı, talihli; yerinde, uygun, münasip; '~-go-ˈluck.y adj. F kaygısız, gamsız, bir şeye aldırmaz, vurdumduymaz.

**ha.rangue** [həˈræŋ] 1. n. uzun konuşma, tirad, nutuk; 2. v/t. nutuk çekmek -e; v/i. uzun uzun konuşmak, tirad söylemek.

**har.ass** [ˈhærəs] v/t. taciz etm. -i, tedirgin etm. -i, üzmek -i, rahat vermemek e, canını sıkmak; aralıksız saldırmak -e.

**har.bin.ger** [ˈhɑːbindʒə] 1. n. haberci, müjdeci; 2. vb. olacağını önceden söylemek, haber vermek, müjdelemek.

**har.bo(u)r** [ˈhɑːbə] 1. n. liman; sığınak, barınak; 2. v/t. & v/i. barın(dır)mak, korumak, saklamak, gizlemek; beslemek; akılda tutmak; sığınmak; yaşamak, oturmak; 'har.bo(u)r.age n. barınak, sığınak; har.bo(u)r dues ⚓ pl. liman ücreti.

**hard** [hɑːd] 1. adj. com. sert, katı; zor, güç, ağır, müşkül; çetin; kötü, acı; merhametsiz, acımasız, gaddar, kalpsiz; kuvvetli ve adaleli; gr. kalın sesli (harf); part. Am. sert (içki), alkol derecesi yüksek; the ~ facts pl. kesin deliller; ~ of hearing kulağı ağır işiten; ~ to deal with uğraşması zor; be ~ (up)on s.o. b-ne haşin davranmak, acımasızca muamele etm.; 2. adv. sıkıca, zorla, kuvvetle, kuvvetlice, hızla; güçlükle, zorlukla, acıyla, mücadeleyle; katı, sıkı; ~ by pek· yakın, yanıbaşında; ~ up parasız, eli dar, muhtaç (for -e); be ~ put to it büyük güçlükle karşılaşmak, zor durumda olm.; ride ~ atı çatlatırcasına sürmek; 3. n. F çalışma yükümlülüğü; ~ and fast değişmez, kati (kanun); '~-back n. ciltli kitap; '~-'bit.ten adj. inatçı, bildiğini okuyan; '~-'boiled adj. lop, katı (yumurta); part. Am. sert, katı; eski kurt, pişkin; ~ cash madeni para; nakit para; '~-cov.er = hard-back; ~ curren.cy sağlam döviz, sağlam para; 'harden v/t. & v/i. katılaş(tır)mak, sertleş-(tir)mek, pekiş(tir)mek, kuvvetlen(dir)-mek, don(dur)mak; fig. hissizleştirmek; † yükselmek (fiyat).

hard...: '~-'fea.tured adj. sert ifadeli; '~-'fist.ed adj. eli sıkı, cimri, pinti; bileği kuvvetli; '~-'head.ed adj. makûl düşünen, gerçekçi; inatçı, dik kafalı; '~-'heart.ed □ taş yürekli, kalpsiz, vicdansız, acımasız.

hard.di.hood ['hɑːdihud] n. yiğitlik, cesaret; cüret; arsızlık, küstahlık; 'hard.di.ness n. dayanıklılık, mukavemet, tahammül; ~ cesaret, yiğitlik.

hard.ly ['hɑːdli] adv. hemen hiç; ancak; güçlükle, güçbelâ; az bir ihtimalle; 'hard-'mouthed adj. inatçı, dik kafalı; azimkâr, azimli; 'hard.ness güçlük, zorluk; sertlik (a. fig.); terslik, aksilik.

hard...: '~.pan n. Am. sert toprak, killi toprak; fig. sağlam temeller, temel ilkeler; '~-'set adj. donmuş (çimento vs.); sert, katı, sabit; acıkmış; '~.shell adj. sert kabuklu; fig. sabit fikirli; 'hard.ship n. sıkıntı, güçlük, zorluk, meşakkat, cefa; 'hard.ware n. madeni eşya, hırdavat; silah; kompütür: mekanik aksam; 'hard.wood n. sert tahtalı ağaç (kerestesi); 'hard-working adj. çok çalışkan.

har.dy □ ['hɑːdi] dayanıklı, tahammüllü, mukavim; cesur, yiğit, gözüpek; küstah, arsız, yüzsüz; soğuğa dayanıklı (bitki).

hare [heə] n. tavşan; ~ and hounds yola kâğıt parçaları saçarak oynanan tavşantazı oyunu; '~.bell n. çançiçeği, yaban sümbülü; '~-'brained adj. aptal, kuş beyinli, kafasız; '~.lip n. ⊗ tavşandudağı, yarık dudak.

ha.rem ['hɛərəm] n. harem (dairesi).

har.i.cot ['hærikəu] n. fasulye; a. ~ bean kuru fasulye.

hark [hɑːk] v/i. dinlemek (to -i); ~! dinle!, kulağını aç!; ~ back hunt. geri çağırmak (tazı); fig. sadede gelmek, aynı konuya değinmek·(to); 'hark.en = hearken.

har.lot ['hɑːlət] n. fahişe, orospu; 'har.lot.ry n. fahişelik, orospuluk.

harm [hɑːm] 1. n. zarar, ziyan, hasar; kötülük; felâket; out of ~'s way emin yerde, emniyette, kötülükten uzak; 2. v/t. zarar vermek -e, kötülük etm. -e; 'harm.ful □ ['~ful] zararlı, kötü, fena; 'harm.less □ zararsız, masum, suçsuz.

har.mon.ic [hɑːˈmɔnik] adj. (~ally) uyumlu, ahenkli, harmonik, kulağa hoş gelen; har'mon.i.ca ♪ [~kə] n. armonika, ağız mızıkası; har.mo.ni.ous □ [hɑːˈməunjəs] ahenkli, uyumlu (a. fig.); düzenli, muntazam; iyi geçinen; tatlı sesli, hoş sesli; har.mo.nize ['hɑːmənaiz] v/t. akord etm., harmonisini yapmak, düzen vermek; v/i. ahenkli çalmak veya şarkı söylemek; uymak -e, uyum sağlamak -e; 'har.mo.ny n. uyum, ahenk; harmoni, ses uyumu.

har.ness ['hɑːnis] 1. n. koşum; iş donanımı; işbaşı; zırh; die in ~ iş başında ölmek, çalışırken ölmek; 2. v/t. koşmak (atı), koşum takımını vurmak; boyunduruk vurmak; kullanmak, yararlanmak; istifade etm.

harp ♪ [hɑːp] 1. n. harp; 2. vb. harp çalmak; ~ (up)on bşin üzerinde çok durmak, bşi defalarca anlatmak; be always ~ing on the same string hep aynı telden çalmak; 'harp.er, 'harp.ist n. harpçı.

har.poon [hɑːˈpuːn] 1. n. zıpkın; 2. v/t. zıpkınlamak, zıpkınla öldürmek.

harp.si.chord ♪ ['hɑːpsikɔːd] n. eski tip piyano, harpsikord.

har.py ['hɑːpi] n. myth. yüzü kadına, kanatları kuşa benzeyen vahşi yaratık; fig. zalim kadın, merhametsiz kadın.

har.ri.dan ['hæridən] n. huysuz kocakarı.

har.ri.er ['hæriə] n. hunt. tavşan tazısı; kros koşucusu.

har.row ✔ ['hærəu] 1. n. sürgü, tapan, tırmık; 2. vb. sürgü geçirmek -e, tırmık çekmek -e, kesek kırmak; fig. sinirlendirmek -i, keder vermek -e; ~ing üzücü.

har.ry ['hæri] vb. yağma etm., talan etm., soymak; saldırmak; üzmek, canını sıkmak, rahat vermemek.

harsh □ [hɑːʃ] sert, haşin, merhametsiz, gaddar, ters, huysuz; kalın, kaba, kulağı tırmalayan (ses); 'harsh.ness n.

kabalık, haşinlik, terslik, gaddarlık.

**hart** zo. [haːt] n. erkek karaca; **harts-horn** ↗ ['haːtshɔːn] n. amonyum karbonatı, nişadır kaymağı.

**har.um-scar.um** F ['hɛərəm'skɛərəm] **1.** adj. patavatsız, pervasız, kayıtsız, dünyayı umursamayan; **2.** n. düşüncesizce hareket eden kimse, delidolu kimse.

**har.vest** ['haːvist] **1.** n. hasat (mevsimi); ürün, mahsül, rekolte; fig. semere, sonuç, netice; ~ festival, ~ thanksgiving hasattan sonra yapılan şenlik; **2.** v/t. toplamak (ürün); biçmek -i, hasat etm. -i; **'har.vest.er** n. orakçı, hasatçı; orak makinesi, biçerdöver; **'har.vest-'home** n. harman sonunda verilen ziyafet.

**has** [hæz, həz] s. have; **'~-been** n. F eski özelliği kalmamış şey veya kimse, modası geçmiş şey veya kimse.

**hash** [hæʃ] **1.** n. kıymalı yemek; Am. F haşiş; fig. karmakarışık şey, karman çorman şey; make a ~ of F bşi karman çorman etm., yüzüne gözüne bulaştırmak; settle s.o.'s ~ F b-nin defterini dürmek; **2.** v/t. doğramak -i, kıymak -i.

**hasp** [haːsp] **1.** n. asma kilit köprüsü, kenet; **2.** vb. kenetlemek, kopçalamak.

**has.sock** ['hæsək] n. diz dayayacak minder; eccl. kilisede üstünde diz çökülüp dua edilen minder.

**hast** † [hæst] 2nd sg. of have.

**haste** [heist] n. acele, hız, sürat, telaş, ivedilik; make ~ acele etm.; çabuk davranmak; more ~ less speed, make ~ slowly acele işe şeytan karışır; **has.ten** ['heisn] v/t. & v/i. acele et(tir)mek, hızlan(dır)mak, sıkış(tır)mak; **hast.i.ness** ['heistinis] n. acelecilik, telaş; **'hast.y** □ acele, çabuk, ivedi, süratli, tez; üstünkörü.

**hat** [hæt] n. şapka; my ~! sl. hayret doğrusu!, vay canına!; hang up one's ~ F devam etmemek, noktalamak; talk through one's ~ aptal aptal konuşmak, palavra atmak.

**hatch¹** [hætʃ] **1.** n. kuluçka, civcivler; yumurtadan çıkan hayvancıklar; ↓, ☂ ambar ağzı, ambar kapağı, kaporta; üstü açık kapı; under ~es güverte altında; **2.** v/t. & v/i. yumurtadan çık(ar)mak; fig. kurmak (plan), tasarlamak (entrika).

**hatch²** [~] vb. ince çizgilerle süslemek -i, paralel çizgiler çekmek -e.

**hatch.er.y** ['hætʃəri] n. üretme çiftliği (esp. balık).

**hatch.et** ['hætʃit] n. küçük balta; bury

the ~ barışmak, dost olm.; **'~-face** n. ince yüz.

**hatch.way** ↓ ['hætʃwei] n. lombar ağzı, ambar ağzı.

**hate** [heit] **1.** n. poet. nefret, kin, garez, düşmanlık (to, towards -e karşı); **2.** v/t. nefret etm. -den; kin beslemek -e karşı; F üzülmek -e, pişman olm. -e; **hate.ful** □ ['~ful] nefret verici, iğrenç, kötü; **'hat.er** n. kinci kimse.

**ha.tred** ['heitrid] n. kin, nefret, düşmanlık (of -e karşı).

**hat.ter** ['hætə] n. şapkacı; as mad as a ~ zırdeli.

**haugh.ti.ness** ['hɔːtinis] n. gurur, kurum, kibir, kendini beğenmişlik; **'haugh.ty** □ kibirli, mağrur, kendini beğenmiş.

**haul** [hɔːl] **1.** n. çekme, çekiş; bir ağda çıkarılan balık miktarı, foroz; Am. taşıma mesafesi; çalınmış mal; çekici alet; yük; **2.** vb. çekmek (at -i); ↓ geminin yönünü değiştirmek; ☇ çıkarmak, taşımak; ↓ çekerek taşımak; ~ down one's flag bayrağını indirmek; fig. teslim olm.; **'haul.age** n. taşıma, nakliye; nakliye ücreti; ☇ çıkarma, çekme; **haul.ier** ['~jə] n. nakliye şirketi; nakliyeci.

**haulm** [hɔːm] n. ekin sapı, saman; bitki sapı.

**haunch** [hɔːntʃ] n. kalça, but; sağrı.

**haunt** [hɔːnt] **1.** n. uğrak, sık sık gidilen yer; **2.** v/t. sık sık uğramak -e; sık sık görünmek -de, sık sık ziyaret etm. -i (hortlak olarak); akıldan çıkmamak, devamlı aklına gelmek; the house is ~ed house perili (veya tekin olmayan) ev; **'haunt.er** n. devamlı müşteri, müdavim.

**hau.boy** ♪ ['ʼəubɔi] n. obua.

**hau.teur** ['əuˈtəː] n. kibir, gurur, azamet.

**Ha.van.a** [həˈvænə] n. a. ~ cigar Havana purosu.

**have** [hæv, həv] **1.** (irr.) v/t. malik olm., sahip olm. -e; olmak; fikir taşımak, fikri olm.; izin vermek -e; ettirmek; almak, elinde tutmak; yemek; çekmek, katlanmak -e, geçirmek; aldatmak, üç kağıda getirmek; yenmek, alt etm., mat etm. -i; yaptırmak -i; ~ to inf. -meğe mecbur olm.; I ~ my hair cut saçımı kestiririm; he had his leg broken ayağı kırıldı. düşüp bacağını kırdı; I would ~ you know bilmeni isterim ki, şunu bilesin ki; he will ~ it that... ...diğini iddia ediyor, iddia ediyor ki; I had better (best) go git-sem iyi olur (en iyisi ben gideyim); I had rather go gitmeyi tercih ederim; let s.o. ~ it b-ni cezalandırmak, dövmek; ~

about one üzerinde bulundurmak *(para vs.)*; ~ at him! saldır ona!; ~ on taşımak, üzerinde giyiyor olm.; *fig.* kastetmek, niyetinde olm.; kandırmak, oyun oynamak; ~ it out with *b-le bşi* tartışarak *veya* kavga ederek çözümlemek; ~ s.o. up F *b-ni* misafir olarak ağırlamak; mahkemeye çıkarmak (for *için*); 2. *v/aux.* *(yardımcı fiil olarak bileşik fiil şekillerine katılır)* I ~ come geldim; 3. *n.* F dolandırıcılık, dalavere, yalan dolan, düzen, hile.

ha.ven ['heivn] *n.* liman; sığınak, barınak *(a. fig.)*.

have-not ['hævnɔt] *n.* fakir kimse, yoksul kimse.

haven't ['hævnt] = have not.

hav.er.sack ['hævəsæk] *n.* ✗ asker çantası, kumanya torbası.

hav.ing ['hæviŋ] *n.* ~s *pl.* mal, mülk, servet, zenginlik.

hav.oc ['hævək] *n.* zarar, ziyan, hasar, tahribat; make ~ of, play ~ with *veya* among harabeye çevirmek *-i*, çok zarar vermek *-e*, tahrip etm. *-i*, yerle bir etm. *-i*.

haw¹ ♀ [hɔː] *n.* alıç.

haw² [~] 1. *vb.* 'hım' demek, kaçamaklı konuşmak; kekelemek; hafifçe öksürmek; 2. *n.* kekeleme, kaçamaklı konuşma, hafifçe öksürme.

Ha.wai.ian [haː'waiiən] 1. *adj.* Hawaii'ye ait, Hawaii...; 2. *n.* Hawaii'li kimse.

haw.finch *orn.* ['hɔːfintʃ] *n.* flurcun.

haw-haw ['hɔː'hɔː] *vb.* şiddetli kahkaha atmak.

hawk¹ [hɔːk] 1. *n. orn.* şahin, doğan, atmaca; 2. *vb.* doğan şahin *veya* atmacayla avlamak (at *-i*).

hawk² [~] *vb.* 'öhö öhö' diye öksürmek; balgam çıkarmak.

hawk³ [~] *vb.* seyyar satıcılık yapmak, işportacılık yapmak, sokak sokak dolaşıp öteberi satmak; hawk.er *n.* seyyar satıcı, işportacı.

hawk-eyed ['hɔːkaid] *adj.* keskin bakışlı; 'hawk.ing *n.* doğancılık, doğanla avlanma.

hawse ♀ [hɔːz] *n. a.* ~-hole loça deliği.

haw.ser ♀ ['hɔːzə] *n.* palamar, yoma, kablo.

haw.thorn ♀ ['hɔːθɔːn] *n.* yabani akdiken, alıç.

hay [hei] 1. *n.* kuru ot, saman; make ~ of karmakarışık etm. *-i*; 2. *vb.* kuru ot biçmek; samanla beslemek *-i*, saman yedirmek *-e*; '~-box *n. a.* ~ cooker yemek pişirme kutusu; '~.cock *n.* ot yığını; tı-

naz; '~.fe.ver *n.* ♀ saman nezlesi; '~.loft *n.* otluk, samanlık; '~.mak.er *n. sl.* kuvvetli darbe, oturaklı yumruk; '~.rick = haycock; '~.seed *n. part. Am.* F hödük kimse, budala kimse, ahmak kimse; '~.stack = haycock; '~.wire: go ~ sapıtmak, kafayı üşütmek.

haz.ard ['hæzəd] 1. *n.* riziko, tehlike; talih, baht, şans; run a ~ tehlikeye atılmak, riske girmek; 2. *v/t.* talihe bırakmak *-i*, şansa bırakmak *-i*; tehlikeye atmak *-i*; 'haz.ard.ous ☐ tehlikeli, rizikolu; şansa bağlı.

haze¹ [heiz] *n.* hafif sis, pus; *fig.* belirsizlik, çapraşıklık, şüphe.

haze² ⬇ & *Am.* [~] *vb.* zulmetmek *-e*, fazla çalıştırarak yormak *-i*; eşek şakaşı yaparak üzmek *-i*.

ha.zel ['heizl] 1. *n.* ♀ fındık (ağacı); 2. *adj.* elâ *(göz)*; '~-nut *n.* fındık.

ha.zy ☐ ['heizi] sisli, dumanlı, puslu; *fig.* belirsiz, sişpheli, bulanık, kararsız; be ~ kararsız olm., şüpheli olm.

H-bomb ✗ ['eitʃbɔm] *n.* hidrojen bombası.

he [hiː; hi] 1. *pron.* o, kendisi, kimse *(erkek)*; ~ who o ki; 2. *prefix* erkek...

head [hed] 1. *n. com.* baş, kafa, kelle; *fig.* akıl, zihin, zekâ; tura, madeni paranın resimli yüzü; kişi, adam başı; üst kısım ;baş taraf, ön taraf; zirve, doruk; ekin başı, başak; *(pl. değişmez)* baş, adet, tane *(= elli baş sığır)*; başkan, şef, amir, reis, yönetici; *geogr.* burun; suyun düşme yüksekliği; birikmiş basınç; başlık, manşet, konu; bira köpüğü; ~ and shoulders above the rest diğerlerinden üstün; bring to a ~ sonuçlandırmak, karar noktasına getirmek; come to a ~ bitmek, sona ermek, doruğa ulaşmak; baş vermek *(sivilce, çıban)*; gather ~ yayılmak, çoğalmak; get it into one's ~ that... ...kafasına koymak, ...sanmak; keep one's ~ soğukkanlılığını korumak, kendine hâkim olm.; ~(s) or tail(s)? yazı mı tura mı?; ~ over heels havada perende atma; adamakıllı, tamamen; over ~ and ears aklının almadığı *veya* duymadığı; I can't make ~ or tail of it hiçbir şey anlayamıyorum, anlıyorsam Arap olayım; take the ~ idareyi eline almak, yönetmek, başa geçmek; 2. *adj.* başa ait; başta olan; baş...; şef...; 3. *v/t.* başında olm. *-in*, önünde olm. *-in*, birinci sırasında gelmek *-in*; başını kesmek *-in*, budamak *-i*; baş takmak *-e*; baş olm. *-e*; başına geçmek *-in*, lider olm. *-e*; önüne geçmek *-in (yarışta)*; başa koymak *-i (listede)*; başını çevirmek *(ge-*

*mínin*); *futbol:* kafa vurmak *(topa)*; be ~ed gidiyor olm. *-e;* ~ off yolunu kesmek *-in;* *v/i.* baş vermek *(lahana, turp)*; ↓ başı bir yöne doğru olm., gitmek, yönelmek (for *-e doğru*); meydana çıkmak, olmak; *Am. futbol:* topa kafa atmak; **Ihead.ache** *n.* baş ağrısı; *fig.* dert, sorun; **Ihead.ach.y** *adj.* başı ağrıyan; **Iheadband** *n.* saç bantı; **Ihead-boy** *n.* okul temsilcisi erkek; **Ihead-dress** *n.* başlık; saçın taranış şekli; **Ihead.ed** *comb.* ...başlı, ...kafalı; **Ihead.er** *n.* ⚘ bağlantı taşı; F balıklama (suya dalış); *futbol:* kafa vuruşu; **Ihead-gear** *n.* başlık, şapka, baş örtüsü; dizgin, yular; **Ihead-girl** *n.* okul temsilcisi kız; **Ihead-hunt.er** *n.* kelle avcısı; F teknik eleman avcısı; **Ihead.i.ness** *n.* sabırsızlık, acelecilik, düşüncesizlik; haşinlik, sertlik, zorbalık, dikkafalılık; baş döndürücülük, çarpıcılık *(içki)*; **Ihead.ing** *n.* serlevha, başlık; *spor:* kafa atma; **Ihead.land** *n.* burun, çıkıntı; **Ihead.less** *adj.* kafasız *(a. fig.)*; başkansız, amirsiz.

**head...:** **I~.light** *n. mot.* ön ışık, far; **I~.line** *n.* başlık, serlevha; ~s *pl. radyo:* haberlerden özetler; he hits the ~s F afişte ismi baştadır; **I~.long 1.** *adj.* düşüncesiz, kayıtsız, aceleci; **2.** *adv.* düşüncesizce, aceleyle, paldır küldür, önünü ardını düşünmeden; başı önde olarak; **I~Iman** *n.* kabile reisi; muhtar; cellat; idareci, ustabaşı; **I~Imas.ter** *n.* okul müdürü; **I~Imis.tress** *n.* okul müdiresi; **I~.most** *adj.* en ilerideki, en baştaki; **I~-Ion** *adj.* baştan, önden, kafadan; ~ collision kafadan çarpışma; **I~-phone** *n. radyo:* kulaklık; **I~-piece** *n.* baş zırhı, miğfer; F akıl, kafa, zekâ; *typ.* bölüm başlarına konan süs; **I~Iquar.ters** *n. pl.* ✕ karargâh; merkez büro; **I~-room** *n.* araç üzerinde bırakılan güvenlik boşluğu, boş yer; **I~-set** *n. radyo:* kulaklık; **Ihead.ship** *n.* müdürlük, başkanlık, reislik, amirlik; **Iheads.man** *n.* cellat.

**head...:** **I~.stone** *n.* mezar taşı; **I~.strong** *adj.* dikkafalı, inatçı, kafasının dikine giden, bildiğini okuyan; **I~.wa.ters** *n. pl.* ırmağı besleyen kaynak; **I~.way** *n.* gelişme, ilerleme; make ~ gelişmek, ilerlemek; **I~.wind** *n.* karşıdan esen rüzgâr; **I~.word** *n.* *(sözlükte)* madde başı sözcük; **I~.work** *n.* kafa işi; **Ihead.y** ☐ inatçı, dik başlı; sert, çarpıcı *(içki)*.

**heal** [hiːl] *v/t.* & *v/i.* iyileş(tir)mek, kapanmak *(yara)*; tedavi etm. (of *-i*), şifa vermek *-e;* bitirmek, sonuçlandırmak, sona erdirmek; ~ up kapanmak *(yara)*;

**I~-all** *n.* her derde deva; **Iheal.er** *n.* iyileştiren kimse *veya* şey, doktor; time is a great ~ zaman en iyi tedavi yoludur; **Iheal.ing 1.** ☐ iyileştirici..., tedavi edici, faydalı; **2.** *n.* iyileşme, şifa.

**health** [helθ] *n.* sağlık, sıhhat; Ministry of 2 Sağlık ve Sosyal Yardım Bakanlığı; **health.ful** ☐ [I~ful] sıhhat için faydalı, sıhhî, sağlıklı; **Ihealth.i.ness** *n.* sıhhat, sağlık; **Ihealth-re.sort** *n.* ılıca; **Ihealth.y** ☐ sağlıklı, sıhhatli, sağlam; sıhhî, sıhhate yarar.

**heap** [hiːp] **1.** *n.* yığın, küme, öbek; F çok miktar, kalabalık, izdiham; all of a ~ darmadağınık; struck *veya* knocked all of a ~ şaşırmış, sersemlemiş; **2.** *v/t.* *a.* ~ up yığmak *-i*, kümelemek *-i*.

**hear** [hiə] *(irr.) v/t.* işitmek, duymak, dinlemek, kulak vermek; mektup almak (from *-den*); haber almak (of *-den*); öğrenmek (about *-i*); ~ s.o. out *b-ni* sonuna kadar dinlemek; **heard** [həːd] *pret.* & *p.p. of* hear; **hear.er** [Ihiərə] *n.* dinleyici; **Ihear.ing** *n.* işitme (duyusu), işitim, dinleme; ☆ celse, duruşma, oturum, sorgu; ses erimi; **heark.en** [Ihɑːkən] *vb.* dinlemek (to *-i*); **hear.say** [Ihiəsei] *n.* söylenti, dedikodu.

**hearse** [həːs] *n.* cenaze arabası.

**heart** [hɑːt] *n. com.* kalp, yürek, gönül, sevgi, can; göğüs; vicdan; merkez, can damarı, orta yer; verimlilik; *iskambil:* kupa; cesaret; sevilen kimse; *a.* dear ~ sevgili; ~ and soul tamamen, canı gönülden, seve seve; at ~ içten; hakikatte, aslında, içyüzünde; I have a matter at ~ çok ilgilendiğim bir konu var; by ~ ezbere, ezberden; for one's ~ kendi canı için; in good ~ iyi durumda; in his ~ (of ~s) kalbinin derinliklerinde; out of ~ kötü durumda, verimsiz; speak from one's ~ samimi olarak konuşmak; cut to the ~ yüreğine inmek; with all my ~ tüm kalbimle; lose ~ cesaretini yitirmek, cesareti kırılmak; take ~ cesaretlenmek; take *veya* lay to ~ içine işlemek, çok etkilenmek; **I~.ache** *n.* ıstırap, keder, kalp ağrısı; **I~-beat** *n.* kalp atışı; **I~-break** *n.* keder, büyük acı, kalp kırıklığı; **I~-break.ing** ☐ son derecede keder verici; **I~-bro.ken** *adj.* kalbi kırık, acılı, kederli; **I~-burn** *n.* mide ekşimesi; **I~-burn.ing** *n.* kıskançlık, imrenme, kin; **I~-com.plaint,** **I~-dis.ease** *n.* kalp hastalığı; **Iheart.ed** *comb.* ...kalpli; **Iheart.en** *v/t.* yüreklendirmek, cesaretlendirmek, canlandırmak, memnun etm., neşelendirmek; **Iheart-fail.ure** *n.* kalp yetmezliği;

**¹heart.felt** *adj.* samimi, içten, yürekten, candan.

**heart** [hɑːθ] *n.* ocak *(a. fig.)*, şömine; aile ocağı, yurt; **¹.~-rug** *n.* ocağın önüne yayılan halı; **¹.~-stone** *n.* ocak taşı; ocak, yuva, yurt.

**heart.i.ness** [¹hɑːtinis] *n.* içtenlik, samimiyet; dinçlik, sıhhatlilik *(s.* hearty); **¹heart.less** ☐ kalpsiz, merhametsiz, acımasız, zalim, vicdansız; **¹heart.rend.ing** *adj.* yürekler acısı, yürek parçalayıcı, çok acıklı.

**heart...:** **¹.~'s.ease** *n.* ♀ viola; **¹.~-sick** *adj.* *fig.* kederli, üzgün, acı dolu; **¹.~-strings** *n. pl. fig.* kalbin en kuvvetleri hisleri; **~ trans.plant** kalp nakli; **¹.~-whole** *adj.* âşık olmayan, kalbi boş; samimi, içten; **¹heart.y** **1.** ☐ içten, samimi, yürekten, candan; sağlam, sıhhatli, dinç; bol, çok; **~** eater obur, çok yemek yiyen kimse, iştahı açık kimse; **2.** *n.* ⚓ denizci; *univ.* sporcu.

**heat** [hiːt] **1.** *n. com.* hararet, sıcaklık, ısı, vücut ısısı; sıcak yer; tav, ısıtma; cinsi heyecan *(dişi hayvanlarda)*; yarışın tek ayağı; eleme yarışı, final koşusu; *sl.* baskının artması; *sl.* polis; baskı; dead **~** iki *veya* daha çok atletin aynı anda ipi göğüslediği yarış; **2.** *v/t.* ısıtmak *-i*; kızdırmak *-i*; *fig.* heyecanlandırmak *-i*; *v/i.* ısınmak, kızmak; **¹heat.ed** ☐ heyecanlı, hararetli, öfkeli, kan beynine sıçramış; **¹heat.er** *n.* ⊕ ısıtıcı, soba, ocak, radyatör; **¹heat-flash** *n.* radyasyon.

**heath** [hiːθ] *n.* çalılık, fundalık; ♀ funda, süpürgeotu.

**hea.then** [¹hiːðən] **1.** *n.* dinsiz kimse, kâfir kimse, putperest kimse; **2.** *adj.* dinsiz, kâfir, putperest; **¹hea.then.dom** *n.* putperestler ülkesi; **¹hea.then.ish** ☐ *mst fig.* barbar; **¹hea.then.ism** *n.* putperestlik, dinsizlik.

**health.er** ♀ [¹heðə] *n.* süpürgeotuna benzer bir çalı; **¹.~-bell** *n.* kara süpürgeotu.

**heat.ing** [¹hiːtiŋ] *n.* ısıtma; *attr.* ısıtıcı...; **~** battery ısıtma batarya; **~** pad elektrik yastığı.

**heat...:** **~** **light.ning** *Am.* gök gürlemesi olmadan çakan şimşek; **¹.~-stroke** *n.* güneş çarpması, sıcak çarpması; **¹.~-val.ue** *n.* ısı değeri; **¹.~-weve** *n.* sıcak dalgası.

**heave** [hiːv] **1.** *n.* kaldırma; fırlatma, kaldırıp atma; **2.** *(irr.)* *v/t.* kaldırmak, çekmek; atmak, fırlatmak; güçlükle çıkarmak *(inilti)*; yükseltmek, kabartmak, şişirmek; **~** the anchor demir almak; **~** down ⚓ karina etm.; **~** out atmak, fır-

latmak; *v/i.* yükselmek, kabarıp inmek, şişmek; solumak; öğürmek; vira etm.; **~** for breath nefes nefese kalmak; **~** in sight ⚓ aniden görünmek; **~** to ⚓ dur(dur)mak *(gemi)*.

**heav.en** [¹hevn] *n.* cennet; gök, sema; ☯ Tanrı, Cenabı Hak; mutluluk, saadet; **~s** *pl.* gök kubbe, asuman; move **~** and earth elinden geleni yapmak, mümkün olan herşeyi yapmak; **¹heav.en.ly** *adj.* göksel..., tanrısal...; *fig.* çok güzel, nefis; **heav.en.ward(s)** [¹.~wəd(z)] *adj.* & *adv.* cennete doğru (giden).

**heav.er** [¹hiːvə] *n.* manivela, kaldıraç.

**heav.i.ness** [¹hevinis] *n.* ağırlık, siklet; *fig.* yavaşlık; sıkıcılık.

**heav.y** ☐ [¹hevi] *com.* ağır; güç, zor *(iş)*; şiddetli, kuvvetli *(yağmur)*; kederli, üzgün; sert *(toprak)*; berbat *(yol)*; bulutlu, kapalı *(hava)*; dalgalı *(deniz)*; hazmı güç *(yemek)*; ciddi, önemli; uyuşuk, tembel, mıymıntı; kasvetli, sıkıcı; uyku basmış, ağırlaşmış *(göz)*; sıkışık *(trafik)*; kalın, kaba *(kumaş, elbise)*; ağır *(koku)*; dik, sarp; vurgulu; ✕ tepeden tırnağa silahlı; **~** **cur.rent** ✒ kuvvetli akım; **¹.~-hand.ed** *adj.* eli ağır, beceriksiz, sakar; **¹.~-¹heart.ed** *adj.* kederli, üzgün; **¹.~-¹lad.en** *adj.* ağır yüklü; *fig.* kalbi kırık, kederli; **¹.~-weight** *n. boks:* ağır siklet.

**heb.dom.a.dal** ☐ [heb¹dɔmədl] haftalık, haftada bir olan.

**He.bra.ic** [hiˈbreiik] *adj.* (.~ally) İbrani...; İbranice...

**He.brew** [¹hiːbruː] **1.** *adj.* İbranilere ait, İbrani...; İbraniceye ait, İbranice...; Musevi...; **2.** *n.* İbrani; Yahudi; İbranice.

**hec.a.tomb** [¹hekɑtuːm] *n.* katliam; 100 öküzlük kurban.

**heck.le** [¹hekl] *vb.* sözünü kesip soru sormak, soru yağmuruna tutmak, sıkıştırmak; **¹heck.ler** *n.* konuşmacının sözünü kesip soru soran kimse.

**hec.tic** ⚕ [¹hektik] **1.** *adj.* veremli, hummalı; *sl.* heyecanlı, telaşlı; **2.** *n.* verem kızartısı; *mst* **~** fever humma.

**hec.tor** [¹hektə] *v/t.* gözünü korkutmak, yıldırmak, sindirmek; *v/i.* kabadayılık etm., zorbalık etm.

**hedge** [hedʒ] **1.** *n.* çit, çalı; *fig.* mânia, engel; tedbir; **2.** *v/t.* çit ile çevirmek, kuşatmak, sarmak; engel olm., önlemek; **~** off etrafını çit ile çevirmek; **~** up önlemek, engel olm.; **~** a bet iki taraf için bahse girişmek; *v/i.* etrafına çalı dikmek; dolaylı konuşmak; önlem almak, tedbir almak; **¹.~.hog** *n. zo.* kirpi; *Am.*

oklu kirpi; '~-hop *v/i. sl.* ♈ alçaktan uçmak; '~.row *n.* çit; '~-spar.row *n. orn.* çit serçesi.

heed [hiːd] 1. *n.* dikkat, özen, ihtimam; take ~ of, give *veya* pay ~ to -e dikkat etm., kulak asmak, önemsemek; 2. *v/t.* dikkat etm., kulak vermek -e, önemsemek -i; heed.ful □ ['~-ful] dikkatli, önem veren (of -e); 'heed.less □ dikkatsiz, düşüncesiz, önem vermeyen (of -e).

hee-haw ['hiːˈhɔː] 1. *n.* eşek anırması; *fig.* kaba kahkaha; 2. *v/i.* anırmak; *fig.* kabaca gülmek.

heel¹ ⚓ [hiːl] *v/t. & v/i.* bir yana yat⟨ır⟩mak *(gemi).*

heel² [~] 1. *n.* topuk, ökçe; *part. Am. sl.* alçak herif, namussuz kimse, aşağılık adam; *at veya* on *veya* upon s.o.'s ~**s** hemen ardında, peşi sıra; down at ~ topukları çok eskimiş; *fig.* perişan kılıklı, hırpani, pejmürde; take to one's ~s, show a clean pair of ~s kaçmak, tüymek, sıvışmak, tabanları yağlamak; lay s.o. by the ~s *b-ni* hapsetmek, kodese tıkmak; come to ~ çağrılınca gelmek *(köpek);* uslanmak; 2. *vb.* ökçe takmak; dizinin dibinden ayrılmamak *(köpek); a.* ~ out *futbol:* topukla geri pası vermek; heeled *adj. Am.* F ensesi kalın, para babası; 'heel.er *n. Am. sl. pol.* bir politikacının adamı.

heel-tap ['hiːltæp] *n.* içki artığı; no ~! artık bırakmak yok! *(içki).*

heft [heft] 1. *n.* ağırlık, siklet; *Am.* F önem, etki, tesir; 2. *v/t.* kaldırmak; kaldırarak ağırlığını bulmak; 'heft.y *adj.* F güçlü, kuvvetli, tesirli.

he.gem.o.ny *pol.* [hiːˈgeməni] *n.* üstünlük, egemenlik, hakimiyet, hegemonya.

he.goat ['hiːgəut] teke, erkeç.

helf.er ['hefə] *n.* düve, doğurmamış genç inek.

heigh [hei] *int.* hey!, bana bak!; ~-ho ['~-həu] *int.* a!, ya!, yazık!, tüh be!

height [hait] *n.* yükseklik, irtifa, yükselti; tepe, dağ; doruk, zirve, en yüksek nokta; what is your ~? boyunuz kaç?; 'height.en *v/t. & v/i.* yüksel(t)mek, art-(tır)mak, çoğal(t)mak.

hei.nous □ ['heinəs] iğrenç, kötü, berbat, çirkin, tiksindirici; 'hei.nous.ness *n.* iğrençlik, tiksindiricilik.

heir [εə] *n.* vâris, mirasçı; be ~ to -e vâris olm.; ~ apparent, ~ at law kanuni vâris; ~ presumptive muhtemel vâris; 'heir.dom *n.* vârislik, mirasçılık; 'heir.ess *n.* kadın vâris; 'heir.less *adj.* vârissiz, mirasçısı olmayan; heir.loom

[''~luːm] *n.* evlâdiyelik, nesilden nesile intikal eden değerli şey.

held [held] *pret. & p.p. of* hold 2.

hel.i.bus *Am.* F ['helibʌs] *n.* helikopter.

hel.i.cal ['helikəl] *adj.* helezoni, spiral, sarmal.

hel.i.cop.ter ['helikɔptə] *n.* helikopter.

hel.li.o... ['hiːliəu] *prefix* güneş...; he.li-o.graph ['~əugraːf] *n.* güneş ışığı yansıtılarak sinyal gönderen alet, helyosta, pırıldak; he.li.o.trope ['heljətrəup] *n.* ♥ güneş çiçeği.

he.li.um ☊ ['hiːljəm] *n.* helyum.

he.lix ['hiːliks] *n., pl. mst* hel.i.ces ['helisiːz] helis; *zo.* sümüklüböcek, salyangoz; ⚘ sarmal eğri; *anat.* dışkulak kıvrımı.

hell [hel] *n.* cehennem; *attr.* cehennem...; like ~ çok, son derecede, müthiş; hiç; oh ~! Allah kahretsin!; go to ~! canın cehenneme!; what the ~...? F Allahaşkına ne...?; a ~ of a noise çok fazla gürültü; raise ~ kıyameti koparmak; ride ~ for leather mümkün olduğu kadar hızlı at sürmek, dolu dizgin gitmek; '~-'bent *adj. Am. sl.* istekli, şevkli, azimli; '~-cat *n. fig.* öfkeli kimse; cadı; şirret kadın.

hel.le.bore ♥ ['helibɔː] *n.* çöpleme.

Hel.lene ['heliːn] *n.* Helen, Yunanlı; Hel'len.ic [he'liːnik] *adj.* Helen, Yunanlı; Yunan...

hell.ish □ ['helifʃ] korkunç, dehşetli, şeytani; cehennemi.

hel.lo [he'ləu] *int.* merhaba!, selâm!, günaydın!; alo!

helm ⚓ [helm] *n.* dümen; *fig.* idare.

hel.met ['helmit] *n.* miğfer, tolga; kask; 'hel.met.ed *adj.* miğferli; kasklı.

helms.man ⚓ ['helmzmən] *n.* dümenci.

hel.ot *hist.* ['helət] *n.* esir, köle; *fig.* kul, köle.

help [help] 1. *n. com.* yardım, imdat; çare, çözüm; yardımcı, hizmetçi, uşak; by the ~ of -in yardımı ile; 2. *v/t.* yardım etm. -e; rahatlatmak, ferahlaştırmak; kurtarmak, imdadına yetişmek, çare bulmak; faydası olm. -e, yararı dokunmak e-; kendini tutmak, kendini almak -den; önlemek, önüne geçmek; ikram etm. *(yemek);* ~ o.s. kendi kendine servis yapmak, yemeğe buyurmak; ~ o.s. to s.th *bşden* almak, *bşe* buyurmak *(yemek);* I could not ~ loughing gülmemek elimde değildi, gülmekten kendimi alamadım: that cannot be ~ed ne yapalım, elden bir şey gelmez; *v/i. bşe* faydası dokunmak, işe yaramak; 'help.er *n.* yardımcı, muavin, çırak; hizmetçi, uşak;

**help.ful** □ [ˈ~ful] yardımsever; yardımcı, faydalı, yararlı, işe yarar; **ˈhelp.ing** *n.* porsiyon *(yemek)*; **ˈhelp.less** □ âciz, çaresiz, kendini idare edemeyen, beceriksiz, kabiliyetsiz, gücü yetmez; **ˈhelp.less.ness** *n.* âcizlik, beceriksizlik, güçsüzlük; **ˈhelp.mate, help.meet** [ˈ~miːt] *n.* arkadaş, eş, yardımcı; karı *veya* koca.

**helter-skel.ter** [ˈheltəˈskeltə] *adv.* aceyle, telâşla, alelacele, apar topar.

**helve** [helv] *n.* sap, tutamak.

**Hel.ve.tian** [helˈviːʃjən] **1.** *adj.* İsviçreli...; İsviçre...; **2.** *n.* İsviçreli *(kimse)*.

**hem¹** [hem] **1.** *n.* kenar *(elbise)*, baskı; **2.** *v/t.* -*in* kenarını kıvırıp dikmek, bastırmak; ~ *in* kuşatmak, etrafını ıçevirmek, içine almak.

**hem²** [~] **1.** *v/i.* hafifçe öksürmek; 'hım' demek; tereddütlü konuşmak; **2.** *int.* hım!

**he-man** *sl.* [ˈhiːmæn] *n.* erkek adam, yiğit adam, güçlü kuvvetli erkek.

**hem.i.sphere** [ˈhemisfiə] *n.* yarımküre.

**hem-line** [ˈhemlain] *n.* etek ucu *(elbise)*; lower (raise) the ~ elbisenin boyunu uzatmak (kısaltmak).

**hem.lock** ♀ [ˈhemlɔk] *n.* köknara benzer bir çam ağacı.

**he.mo...** [ˈhiːməu] *s.* haemo...

**hemp** [hemp] *n.* kenevir, kendir; **ˈhemp.en** *adj.* kendir gibi, kendirden yapılmış, kendir...

**hem.stitch** [ˈhemstitʃ] **1.** *n.* ajur, antika, gözenek; **2.** *vb.* kenarına ajur yapmak.

**hen** [hen] *n.* tavuk; dişi kuş; ~'s egg tavuk yumurtası.

**hen.bane** ♀ [ˈhenbein] *n.* banotu.

**hence** [hens] *adv. usu.* from ~ buradan, bundan, bu zamandan itibaren; bu sebeple, bundan dolayı; ~! defol!, yıkıl karşımdan!; *a year* ~ bundan bir yıl sonra; ˈ~ˈforth, ˈ~ˈfor.ward *adv.* bundan böyle, şu andan itibaren ,gelecekte.

**hench.man** *pol.* [ˈhentʃmən] *n.* kendi çıkarı için taraf tutan kimse; bir kimsenin sağ kolu, hizmetkâr.

**hen...**: ˈ~-coop *n.* tavuk kümesi; ˈ~ˈpar.ty *n.* F kadınlar toplantısı; ˈ~pecked *adj.* kılıbık *(koca)*; ˈ~-roost *n.* tavuk tüneği.

**hep** *Am. sl.* [hep]: be ~ to -*in* farkında olm., -*den* haberi olm.

**he.pat.ic** *anat.* [hiˈpætik] *adj.* karaciğere ait, karaciğer...

**hep.cat** *Am. sl.* [ˈhepkæt] *n.* caz hastası *(veya* delisi*).*

**hep.ta...** [ˈheptə] *adj.* yedi...; **hep.ta.gon** [ˈ~gən] *n.* yedigen, yedi kenarlı çokgen.

**her** [həː, hə] *adv. & adj. (dişil)* onun; ona, onu.

**her.ald** [ˈherəld] **1.** *n.* haberci, müjdeci; **2.** *v/t.* ilân etm., haber vermek, müjdelemek; selâmlamak; ~ *in* tanıtmak, takdim etm.; **he.ral.dic** [heˈrældik] *adj.* (~ally) hanedan armacılığına ait; **her.ald.ry** [ˈherəldri] *n.* hanedan armacılığı.

**herb** [həːb] *n.* ot, bitki; **her.ba.ceous** [~ˈbeiʃəs] *adj.* ot cinsinden; **ˈherb.age** *n.* yeşillik, ot; ⅛⅜ başkasının merasında hayvan otlatma hakkı; **ˈherb.al** **1.** *adj.* otlara ait, ot..., bitkisel...; **2.** *n.* şifalı bitkiler kitabı; **ˈherb.al.ist** *n.* şifalı bitki satan kimse; **her.bar.i.um** [~ˈbɛəriəm] *n.* kurutulmuş bitki koleksiyonu; kurutulmuş bitki koleksiyonu saklanan yer; **her.biv.o.rous** [~ˈbivərəs] *adj.* otçul *(hayvan)*; **her.bo.rize** [ˈ~bəraiz] *vb.* bitki yetiştirmek.

**Her.cu.le.an** [həːkjuˈliːən] *adj.* Herkül'e ait, Herkül...; çok güçlü, çok zor...

**herd** [həːd] **1.** *n.* sürü, davar sürüsü; *fig.* avam, ayak takımı; **2.** *v/t. & v/i.* sürü gibi biraraya topla(n)mak; sürüyü gütmek; sürüye kat(ıl)mak; ~ *together* biraraya topla(n)mak; **ˈherd.er, ˈherds.man** *n.* çoban, sığırtmaç.

**here** [hiə] **1.** *adv.* buraya; burada; şu anda, şimdi; bu noktada; bu dünyada, bu hayatta; **2.** *int.* ~! bana bak! baksana!, dur!; ~'s to...! ... -*in* şerefine!

**here.a.bout(s)** [ˈhiərəˈbaut(s)] *adv.* buralarda, bu yakınlarda, bu civarda; **here.aft.er** [hiərˈɑːftə] **1.** *adv.* ileride, gelecekte, bundan sonra; **2.** *n.* gelecek; öbür dünya, ahiret; **ˈhereˈby** *adv.* bu vesile ile, bundan dolayı.

**he.red.i.ta.ble** [hiˈreditəbl] *adj.* kalıtsal, irsî; **her.e.dit.a.ment** ⅛⅜ [heriˈditəmənt] *n.* miras yoluyla kalan mal; **he.red.i.tar.y** [hiˈreditəri] *adj.* kalıtsal, irsî, miras yoluyla kalan...; **heˈred.i.ty** *n.* kalıtım, irsiyet, soyaçekim.

**here.in** [ˈhiərˈin] *adv.* bunda, bunun içinde; **here.of** [hiərˈɔv] *adv.* bununla ilgili olarak.

**her.e.sy** [ˈherəsi] *n.* bir akideye aykırı mezhep.

**her.e.tic** [ˈherətik] **1.** *n.* kabul olunmuş doktrinlere karşı olan kimse; **2.** = **he.ret.i.cal** □ [hiˈretikəl] kabul olunmuş doktrinlere karşı olan.

**here.to.fore** [ˈhiətuˈfɔː] *adv.* şimdiye dek, bundan önce; **here.up.on** [ˈhiərəˈpɔn] *adv.* bunun üzerine; **ˈhereˈwith** *adv.* bununla, ilişikte, beraberce.

**her.it.a.ble** [ˈheritəbl] *adj.* miras yoluyla

intikali mümkün; **ı her.it.age** *n.* miras, tereke.

**her.maph.ro.dite** [həˈmæfrədait] *n.* çift
cinsiyetli bitki *veya* hayvan.

**her.met.ic, her.met.i.cal** □ [həˈmetik(əl)]
hava geçirmez, sımsıkı kapalı.

**her.mit** [ˈhəːmit] *n.* yalnız kalmayı seven
kimse, münzevi; **ı her.mit.age** *n.* yalnız
kalmayı seven kişi *veya* kişilerin hücresi, inziva yeri.

**her.ni.a** ⚵ [ˈhəːnjə] *n.* fıtık, kasık yarığı,
kavlıç; **ı her.ni.al** *adj.* fıtıklı, fıtık...

**he.ro** [ˈhiərəu] *n.*, *pl.* **he.roes** [ˈ~rəuz]
kahraman, yiğit; baş karakter; **he.ro.ic**
[hiˈrəuik], **heˈro.i.cal** *adj.* kahramanca,
cesur; gerçek boyutundan büyük *(heykel)*; kahramanlıklar anlatan, destansı,
epik *(şiir)*; abartmalı sözlere ait.

**her.o.in** *pharm.* [ˈherəuin] *n.* eroin.

**her.o.ine** [ˈherəuin] *n.* kadın kahraman;
**ı her.o.ism** *n.* kahramanlık, cesaret.

**her.on** *orn.* [ˈherən] *n.* balıkçıl; **ı her.on.ry**
*n.* balıkçılların yumurtladığı yer.

**her.ring** *ichth.* [ˈheriŋ] *n.* ringa; **ı her.ring-
-bone** *n.* ringa kemiğine benzer dikiş,
çapraz dikiş.

**hers** [həːz] *pron.* onun(ki) *(dişil).*

**her.self** [həːˈself] *pron.* kendisi *(dişil).*

**Hertz.i.an** ⚡ [ˈhəːtsiən] *n.*: ~ waves elektromanyetik dalgalar, radyo dalgaları.

**he's** [ˈhiːz] = he is; he has.

**hes.i.tance, hes.i.tan.cy** [ˈhezitəns(i)] *n.* tereddüt, duraksama; **hes.i.tate** [ˈ~teit]
*v/i.* tereddüt etm., duraksamak (about,
over *-de*); kem küm etm., kekelemek (to
*inf. -mekte*); **hes.iˈta.tion** *n.* tereddüt, duraksama, şüphe; kekeleme.

**Hes.sian** [ˈhesiən] **1.** *adj.* Almanya'nın
Hesse eyaletine ait; Hesse'li; **2.** *n.* Hesse'li kimse; ⚵ çuval bezi.

**het.er.o.dox** [ˈhetərəudɒks] *adj.* kabul edilmiş dini esaslara aykırı olan; **ı het.er.o-
dox.y** *n.* kabul edilmiş doktrinlere karşı
çıkma; **het.er.o.dyne** [ˈ~dain] *adj. radyo:*
gelen sinyali devamlı bir frekansa karıştıran...; **het.er.o.ge.ne.i.ty** [~dʒiˈniːiti]
*n.* farklı oluş; **het.er.o.ge.ne.ous** □
[ˈ~rəuˈdʒiːnjəs] heterojen, ayrı cinsten.

**hew** [hjuː] *(irr.)* *vb.* yontmak, yarmak,
kesmek, çentmek; ⊕ yontarak şekil vermek; **ı hew.er** *n.* baltacı, oduncu; ⚒ kömür madencisi; **hewn** [hjuːn] *p.p. of*
hew.

**hex.a...** [ˈheksə] *prefix* altı...; **hex.a.gon**
[ˈ~gən] *n.* altıgen; **hex.ag.o.nal** □ [hek-
ˈsægənl] altıgen, altı kenarlı; **hex.am.e-
ter** [hekˈsæmitə] *n.* altı ayaklı mısra.

**hey** [hei] *int.* hey!, haydi!, a!

**hey.day** [ˈheidei] **1.** *int.* yaşasın!, yok ya!;
**2.** *n. fig.* en enerjik çağ, altın çağ.

**hi** [hai] *int.* hey!; selam!, merhaba!

**hi.a.tus** [haiˈeitəs] *n.* aralık, açıklık, boşluk; *gr.* hemze.

**hi.ber.nate** [ˈhaibəneit] *v/i.* kış uykusuna
yatmak; **hi.berˈna.tion** *n.* kış uykusu.

**hi.bis.cus** ⚵ [hiˈbiskəs] *n.* amberçiçeği.

**hic.cup, a. hic.cough** [ˈhikʌp] **1.** *n.* hıçkırık; **2.** *v/i.* hıçkırmak, hıçkırık tutmak.

**hick** F [hik] *n.* taşralı, kaba köylü; *attr.*
taşralı...

**hick.o.ry** [ˈhikəri] *n.* Kuzey Amerika'da
bulunan bir tür ceviz ağacı.

**hid** [hid] *pret. of* hide²; **hid.den** [ˈhidn]
*p.p. of* hide².

**hide¹** [haid] **1.** *n.* hayvan derisi, post; F
insan derisi, cilt; **2.** *v/t.* F pataklamak,
dayak atmak.

**hide²** [~] *(irr.)* *v/t. & v/i.* sakla(n)mak,
gizle(n)mek (from s.o. *b-den*); örtbas
etm.; **ı hide-and-ı seek** *n.* saklambaç oyunu; **play (at)** ~ saklambaç oynamak.

**hide.bound** *fig.* [ˈhaidbaund] *adj.* dar görüşlü, geri kafalı.

**hid.e.ous** □ [ˈhidiəs] çirkin, iğrenç, korkunç; **ı hid.e.ous.ness** *n.* iğrençlik, çirkinlik, korkunçluk.

**hid.ing¹** F [ˈhaidiŋ] *n.* dayak, kötek.

**hid.ing²** [~] *n.* sakla(n)ma, gizle(n)me;
in ~ saklı, gizli; **ı ~-place** *n.* gizlenecek
*(veya* saklanacak) yer.

**hie** *poet.* [hai] *vb. (p. pr.* hying) çabucak
gidivermek.

**hi.er.arch.y** [ˈhaiərɑːki] *n.* hiyerarşi.

**hi.er.o.glyph** [ˈhaiərəuglif] *n.* hiyeroglif, resimlerden oluşan yazı; **hi.er.oˈglyph.ic,** *a.*
**hi.er.oˈglyph.i.cal** □ hiyerogliflere ait, hiyeroglif...; **hi.er.oˈglyph.ics** *n. pl.* hiyeroglif.

**hi-fi** *Am.* [ˈhaiˈfai] = high fidelity.

**hig.gle.dy-pig.gle.dy** [ˈhigldiˈpigldi] *adj. &
adv.* karmakarışık, karman çorman, altüst.

**high** [hai] **1.** *adj.* □ *(s. a. ~ly) com.* yüksek, yukarı; önemli *(mevki)*, yüce, baş;
tiz, cırlak *(ses)*; aşırı, şiddetli; fahiş
*(fiyat)*; kibirli, kendini beğenmiş; kızgın, öfkeli; coşkun, taşkın *(neşe)*; lüks;
asil, soylu; kokmuş *(et, yemek)*; sarhoş,
kafayı bulmuş; esrarın etkisinde; dolgun; ~ and dry karaya oturmuş *(gemi)*;
suyun dışında; çaresiz, terkedilmiş; be
on one's ~ horse, ride the ~ horse kendini beğenmiş olm., kibirli olm., yukarıdan bakmak; with a ~ hand kibirle, küstahça; in ~ spirits neşeli, keyfi yerinde; a
~ Tory aşırı tutucu kimse; ~ colo(ur),

~ complexion koyu kırmızı renk; ~ life sosyete hayatı; ~ words pl. ağır sözler; öfkeli sözler; ~ time tam vakit; 2. n. meteor. yüksek basınç bölgesi; Am. F = high school; ~ and low toplumun her kesimi, zengin fakir; her yerde; on ~ yüksekte, gökte; hızla, süratle ;3. adv. yüksekçe, yüksekte; pahalı olarak; lüks içinde; I~.ball n. Am. sodalı viski; I~-born ajd. soylu olarak doğmuş; I~-bred adj. asil, soylu; I~-brow F 1. n. entelektüel kimse, fikir adamı; 2. adj. entelektüel; I~-class adj. birinci sınıf, kaliteli, I~-!col-o(u)red adj. parlak renkli..., kırmızı...; 2 Com.mis.sion.er büyükelçi ayarındaki temsilci; I~-ex'plo.sive n. kuvvetli patlayıcı madde; ~fa.lu.tin(g) [I~fə'lu:tin, I~fə'lu:tiŋ] 1. n. şatafat, gereksiz süs; 2. adj. şatafatlı, aşırı süslü; I~-fi'del.i.ty adj. sesi çok tabii şekilde veren... Hi-Fi; I~.fli-er = highflyer; I~-flown adj. şatafatlı, çok süslü (söz, yazı); I~.fly.er n. hırslı kimse, ihtiraslı kimse; I~-grade adj. üstün kaliteli; I~-!hand.ed adj. amirlik taslayan, küstah; I~-!hat sl. 1. n. züppe kimse; 2. adj. züppe; I~-!heeled adj. yüksek ökçeli; I~.land.er n. dağlı kimse; I~.lands n. pl. dağlık bölge; I~-!lev.el adj. yüksek seviyeli (konferans); I~.light v/t. dikkati çekmek -e; önem vermek -e; I~-lights n. pl. fig. ilgi çekici olay; ~ liv.ing lüks hayat; Ihigh.ly adv. yüksek derecede, çok, fazlasıyla; speak ~ of s.o. b-den övgüyle bahsetmek; ~ descended asil, soylu; Ihigh-!mind.ed adj. âlicenap, yüce gönüllü; Ihigh-!necked adj. balıkçı yakalı, dik yakalı; Ihigh.ness n. yükseklik; fig. yücelik; His veya Your 2 Ekselansları. high...; I~-!pitched adj. çok tiz (ses); dik (çatı); I~-!pow.er: ~ station yüksek güçlü santral; ~ radio station güçlü radyo istasyonu; I~-!pow.ered adj. güçlü, dinamik, enerjik (kimse); I~-!priced adj. pahalı; ~ road anayol; ~ school lise; I~-!spir.it.ed adj. neşeli, şen; oynak, yerinde duramayan (at); I~-!strung adj. çok sinirli, sinir küpü. hight poet. veya co. [hait] adj. isminde, adında, denilen. high...; ~ tea ikindi kahvaltısı; I~-!toned adj. kaliteli, sosyetik; ~ wa.ter taşkın, kabarma; I~.way n. anayol, karayolu; fig. en kolay ve kısa yol; ~ code karayolları nizamnamesi; I~.way.man n. eşkiya, soyguncu.
hi.jack [Ihaidʒæk] v/t. kuvvet zoru ile çalmak, kaçırmak; Ihi.jack.er n. uçak korsanı; yol kesici.

hike F [haik] 1. v/i. yürümek, yürüyüşe çıkmak; 2. n. uzun yürüyüş; part. Am. F artış, yükselme; Ihik.er n. uzun yürüyüşe çıkan kimse.
hi.lar.i.ous □ [hi'lɛəriəs] çok şamatalı, neşeli ve gürültülü.
hi.lar.i.ty [hi'læriti] n. neşe, kahkaha.
Hil.a.ry [Ihiləri]: ~ term ᴺᴬ, univ. ocak ayında başlayan devre.
hill [hil] n. tepe; bayır, yokuş; küme, yığın; ~.bil.ly Am. F [I~-bili] n. çiftçi, orman köylüsü; ~ climb mot. tırmanma yarışı; hill.ock [Ihilək] n. tepecik, tümsek; Ihill.side n. yamaç, dağ eteği; Ihill-top n. tepe doruğu; Ihill.y adj. tepelik.
hilt [hilt] n. kabza; up to the ~ fig. tamamiyle, tamamen.
him [him] pron. onu, ona (eril).
him.self [him'self] pron. kendi(si), bizzat (eril); of ~ kendinden; by ~ yalnız başına; kendisi, kimsenin yardımı olmaksızın.
hind¹ [haind] n. dişi geyik.
hind² [~] adj. arkadaki, geride olan, arka...; ~ leg arka bacak; ~ wheels pl. arka tekerlekler.
hind.er¹ [Ihaində] adj. arkadaki, gerideki, arka..;
hin.der² [Ihində] v/t. engellemek, mâni olm. -e, alıkoymak (from -den).
hind.most [Ihaindməust] adj. en arkadaki, en gerideki.
hin.drance [Ihindrəns] n. engel, mâni (to -e).
Hin.du, a. Hin.doo [Ihin'du:] n. Hintli, Hindu.
Hin.du.sta.ni [hindu'sta:ni] adj. Hindistan'a ait, Hindistan...; Hintli...
hinge [hindʒ] 1. n. menteşe, reze; fig. dayanak noktası, esas; off the ~s fig. dayanağı olmayan; 2. vb. ~ upon fig. dayanmak, bağlı olm.
hin.ny [Ihini] n. (at ile dişi eşekten hasıl olan) katır.
hint [hint] 1. n. ima, üstü kapalı söz, çıtlatma; 2. v/i. ima etm., çıtlatmak, dokundurmak (at -i).
hin.ter.land [Ihintəlænd] n. iç bölge, arka bölge, hinterland.
hip¹ [hip] n. kalça, kaba et; attr. kalça...
hip² ⚜ [~] n. kuşburnu.
hip³ [~] int.: ~.~, hurra(h)! şa! şa! şa!
hip...; I~-bath n. yarım banyo (küvet); I~-flask n. cebe konan küçük yassı şişe.
hip.po F [Ihipəu] = hippopotamus.
hip-pock.et [Ihippɔkit] n. arka cep.
hip.po.pot.a.mus [hipə'pɔtəməs] n., pl. a. hip.po'pot.a.mi [~mai] suaygırı.

hip.py ['hipi] *n. a.* hippie hipi.

hip-roof ♠ ['hipruːf] *n.* ortası kabarık çatı.

hip-shot ['hipʃɔt] *adj.* çıkık kalçalı.

hire ['haiə] 1. *n.* kira, ücret; kiralama; on ~ kiralık; 2. *vb.* kiralamak, ücretle tutmak; ücretle çalışmak; ~ out kiraya vermek; hire.ling *contp.* ['-lin] 1. *n.* ücretli adam, uşak; 2. *adj.* kiralık; 'hire--'pur.chase *n.* taksit; by ~ taksitle.

hir.sute ['həːsjuːt] *adj.* kıllı, tüylü, saçlı.

his [hiz] *adj. & pron.* onun(ki) *(eril).*

hiss [his] 1. *n.* tıslama, yılan sesi; ıslıklama; 2. *vb.* tıslamak; ıslık çalmak; *a.* ~ off ıslık çalarak yuhalamak, ıslıklamak.

hist [sːt] *int.* hişt!, dur!, sus!

his.to.ri.an [his'tɔːriən] *n.* tarihçi, tarih bilgini; his.tor.ic, his.tor.i.cal ☐ [~'tɔrik-(əl)] tarihî, tarihsel; önemli, mühim; his.to.ri.og.ra.pher [~tɔːri'ɔgrəfə] *n.* tarihçi, tarih yazarı; his.to.ry ['-təri] *n.* tarih, tarihî olaylar; make ~ tarihe geçmek.

his.tri.on.ic [histri'ɔnik] *adj.* sahneye ait, oyuna ait, sahne..., tiyatro..., oyunculuk...; dramatik..., yapmacık, suni, sahte.

hit [hit] 1. *n.* vuruş, vurma, darbe; başarı; şans, talih; isabet; *fig.* iğneli söz, taş; *thea.,* ♪ başarı kazanmış eser; 2. *(irr.) vb.* vurmak, çarpmak -*e*; isabet et(tir)mek -*e*; tesir etm. -*e*; *Am.* F ulaşmak, varmak, erişmek -*e*; gitmek -*e*; bulmak -*i*; uymak -*e*; çok içmek *(içki)*; yumruk atmak; olmak, vuku bulmak; uygun olm.; ~ s.o. a blow *b-ne* yumruk atmak; ~ at vurmak; ~ or miss rasgele, şansa, tesadüfî; gayesiz, amaçsız; ~ off F kısaca tarif etm.; süratle yapmak; ~ it off with F *ile* uyuşmak, anlaşmak, geçinmek; ~ out yumruklamak, saldırmak; ~ (up)on rastgele bulmak -*i*; he ~ his head against a tree başını bir ağaca çarptı; '~-and--'run driv.er *mot.* çarpıp kaçan şoför.

hitch [hitʃ] 1. *n.* ani çekme *veya* itme, çekiş; ⚓ adi düğüm; *fig.* engel, arıza, mâni, pürüz; 2. *v/t. & v/i.* çek(iştir)mek; bağla(n)mak, iliştir(il)mek, tak(ıl)mak (on -*e*); topallamak, aksamak; evlen(dir)mek; otostop yapmak; ~ up yukarı çekmek *(pantolon);* '~-hike *v/i.* F otostop yapmak.

hith.er *lit.* ['hiðə] *adv.* buraya, buraya doğru; hith.er.to ['-'tuː] *adv.* şimdiye kadar, bu zamana kadar; hith.er.ward(s) ['-wəd(z)] = hither.

hive [haiv] 1. *n.* kovan; kovandaki arı kümesi; *fig.* çok hareketli yer, arı kovanı gibi kaynaşan yer; ~s *pl.* ❦ kurdeşen,

ürtiker; 2. *v/t.* kovana doldurmak, kovanda biriktirmek, toplamak; ~ up toplamak, biriktirmek; *v/i.* kovana girmek; birarada oturmak.

ho [həu] *int.* ya!, yok ya!, hadi canım!

hoar [hɔː] *adj.* kır, ak, ağarmış *(saç);* kır saçlı.

hoard [hɔːd] 1. *n.* saklanan stok, biriktirilmiş şey; 2. *v/t. a.* ~ up saklamak, biriktirmek, istif etm.; 'hoard.er *n.* istifçi, biriktirip saklayan kimse.

hoard.ing ['hɔːdin] *n.* geçici tahta perde; ilan tahtası.

hoar.frost ['hɔː'frɔst] *n.* kırağı.

hoar.i.ness ['hɔːrinis] *n.* ak saç, kırlık.

hoarse [hɔːs] *adj.* boğuk, kısık *(ses);* boğuk sesli; 'hoarse.ness *n.* boğukluk, boğuk seslilik.

hoar.y ['hɔːri] *adj.* kır, ak, ağarmış, ak düşmüş; eski.

hoax [həuks] 1. *n.* şaka, muziplik; hile, oyun; 2. *v/t.* aldatmak, oyun etm., işletmek, gırgır geçmek.

hob¹ [hɔb] *n.* şömine pervazı.

hob² [~] = hobgoblin; raise ~ *part. Am.* F yaramazlık yapmak.

hob.ble ['hɔbl] 1. *n.* topallama, aksama; F engel, mâni, köstek; 2. *v/i.* topallamak, aksamak *(a. fig.); v/t.* kösteklemek; topal etm.; bukağı vurmak *(ata);* engel olm., mâni olm.

hob.ble.de.hoy ['hɔbldi'hɔi] *n.* beceriksiz delikanlı.

hob.by *fig.* ['hɔbi] *n.* merak, özel zevk, hobi; '~-horse *n.* sallanan oyuncak at; atlıkarınca atı; çocuğun at diye bindiği değnek; bir kimsenin hoşlandığı konu.

hob.gob.lin ['hɔbgɔblin] *n.* gulyabani, ifrit.

hob.nail ['hɔbneil] *n.* iri başlı kısa çivi, ayakkabıların altına vurulan çivi, kabara.

hob.nob ['hɔbnɔb] *v/i.* arkadaşlık etm., sıkıfıkı olm., araları iyi olm.

ho.bo *Am. sl.* ['həubəu] *n.* serseri, aylak, boş gezenin boş kalfası.

Hob.son's choice *fig.* ['hɔbsnz'tʃɔis] *n.* tek çözüm yolu, yapılacak tek şey.

hock¹ ['hɔk] 1. *n. zo.* hayvanların içdizi; 2. *v/t.* topal etm. *(at).*

hock² [~] *n.* Ren şarabı, beyaz Alman şarabı.

hock³ [~] 1. *n.* rehin; 2. *v/t.* rehine koymak; '~-shop *n.* rehinci dükkânı.

hock.ey ['hɔki] *n. spor:* hokey oyunu.

ho.cus ['həukəs] *v/t.* aldatmak, kandırmak; uyuşturucu vererek sersemletmek; ~-po.cus ['-'pəukəs] *n.* hokus pokus.

**hokkabazlık**, hile; sihirbazın sözleri; aldatıcı hareketler.

**hod** [hɔd] *n.* harç *veya* tuğla teknesi.

**hodge-podge** [ˈhɔdʒpɔdʒ] = hotchpotch.

**hod.man** [ˈhɔdmən] *n.* yamak, el ulağı.

**hoe** ✓ [həu] 1. *n.* çapa; 2. *vb.* çapalamak, çapa kullanmak.

**hog** [hɔg] 1. *n.* domuz; *fig.* obur ve pis kimse; go the whole ~ *sl.* bir işi tam yapmak; 2. *v/t.* açgözlülükle kapmak; hakkından fazlasını almak; *v/i. mot.* yolun ortasında gitmek; **hogged** *adj.* açgözlü; ˈhog.gish ☐ açgözlü ve bencil; ˈhog.gishness *n.* açgözlülük, bencillik.

**hog.ma.nay** *Scots* [ˈhɔgmənei] *n.* yılbaşı arifesi.

**hogs.head** [ˈhɔgzhed] *n.* büyük fıçı; 240 litrelik sıvı ölçü birimi; ˈhog.skin *n.* domuz derisi; ˈhog.wash *n.* çerçöp, artık şey; F saçma şey, atmasyon.

**hoi(c)k** [hɔik] *v/t.* birden çekmek, aniden yukarıya doğru döndürmek *(uçak).*

**hoi pol.loi** [hɔiˈpɔlɔi] *n. pl.* halk yığını, ayak takımı, avam.

**hoist** [hɔist] 1. *n.* kaldıraç; yük asansörü; itme *veya* çekme; 2. *v/t.* yükseltmek, kaldırmak; çekmek *(bayrak).*

**hoi.ty-toi.ty** F [ˈhɔitiˈtɔiti] 1. *adj.* kibirli, kendini beğenmiş; 2. *int.* yok yahu!, deme!

**ho.kum** *Am. sl.* [ˈhəukəm] *n.* boş laf, palavra; seyircinin ilgisini çekmek için başvurulan oyunlar.

**hold** [həuld] 1. *n.* tutma, tutuş; nüfuz, hüküm, otorite; dayanak, destek; tutunacak yer; kale, istihkam; hapis; hapishane, kodes; kavrama, anlama, idrak; ♪ uzatma işareti; ⬇ gemi ambarı; catch, get, lay, take, seize ~ of yakalamak, tutmak, kavramak; have a ~ of *veya* on ...üzerinde etkisi olm., otoritesi olm.; keep ~ of -i kontrol altına almak; 2. *(irr.) v/t. com.* tutmak; kavramak; dayanmak e; malik olm. -e, sahip olm. -e, elinde tutmak -i; zapt etm., işgal etm., ele geçirmek -i; kontrol atına almak, hükmetmek -e; alıkoymak, salıvermemek, durdurmak -i; kanunen bağlamak, mecbur etm.; germek *(kas);* çekmek, tartmak, tasımak *(ağırlık);* hapsetmek, gözaltına almak -i; içine almak, kapsamak -i; stok etm. -i; desteklemek *(teori);* düzenlemek *(toplantı);* çevirmek, yöneltmek, doğrultmak *(silah);* 🜚 hüküm vermek, karara bağlamak; ~ a job down F bir işi yürütmek; ~ one's ground, ~ one's own ayak diremek, yerini korumak, dayanmak, durumunu muhafaza etm.; ~ the

line *teleph.* telefonu açık tutmak, telefonda beklemek, kapatmamak; ~ water su kaldırmak; *fig.* makul olm., mantıklı olm., geçerli olm.; ~ off uzak tutmak, uzaklaştırmak; ✝ rotasında gitmek; ~ on devam etm., dayanmak; beklemek; yerinde tutmak; ~ out dayanmak, karşı koymak; yetmek; tutmak; ileri sürmek; ~ over ertelemek, tehir etm.; -i silah olarak kullanmak; ~ up geciktirmek, durdurmak, engel olm., tutmak; 3. *(irr.) v/i.* durumunu korumak, dayanmak, karşı koymak; sürmek, devam etm.; bağlı olm.; geçerli olm.; doğru gitmek, ilerlemek; durmak, ara vermek; uyuşturucu maddesi olm.; ~ forth nutuk atmak, gururla konuşmak; ileri sürmek, teklif etm.; ~ good *veya* true geçerli olm.; ~ hard! F sıkı tut!; ~ in tutmak, zapt etm., kontrol altına almak; ~ off uzakta kalmak, uzak durmak; ~ on devam etm.; *teleph.* durmak, beklemek; ~ on! F dur!, bekle!; ~ to devam etm.; sadık kalmak, tutmak; yönelmek; ~ up yolunu kesip soymak; ˈhold-all *n.* valiz, çanta, bavul; ˈhold.er *n.* ✝ sahip, hamil; kulp, tutacak, tutamak, sap; ~ of shares hisse senedi sahibi; ˈhold.fast *n.* kenet, mandal, çengel, kanca; ˈhold.ing *n.* holding; mülk, mal; arazi; tutma; small ~ ekilip biçilen küçük arazi; ~ company holding; ˈhold.o.ver *n. Am.* artık, posa; bakiye, geriye kalan kısım; ˈhold-up *n.* gecikme; yol kesme, soygun.

**hole** [həul] 1. *n.* delik, çukur, boşluk, oyuk, gedik; F *fig.* güç durum, çıkmaz; hayvan ini, barınağı, yuvası; pis yer; golf çukuru; pick ~s in kusur bulmak, ince eleyip sık dokumak; 2. *vb.* delik açmak; *golf:* topu deliğe sokmak; ˈhole-and- -ˈcor.ner *adj.* gizli, el altından.

**hol.i.day** [ˈhɔlədi] *n.* tatil günü; bayram günü; ~s *pl.* tatil; ˈ~-mak.er *n.* tatile çıkmış kişi.

**ho.li.ness** [ˈhəulinis] *n.* kutsallık, kutsiyet.

**hol.la** [ˈhɔlə] 1. *int.* haydi! *(köpeklere);* 2. *vb.* bağırmak, seslenmek *(köpeğe).*

**hol.land** [ˈhɔlənd] *n. a.* brown ~ ağartılmamış keten bezi; 2s *sg.* ardıç suyu, cin.

**hol.ler** *Am.* F [ˈhɔlə] 1. *vb.* bağırmak, haykırmak; 2. *n.* bağırış, haykırış.

**hol.lo(a)** [ˈhɔləu] = holla.

**hol.low** [ˈhɔləu] 1. ☐ içi boş, oyuk; derin; boşluktan gelen *(ses);* yalan, sahte, aldatıcı; çökük, çukurlaşmış; 2. F *adv. a.* all ~ tamamen, büsbütün; sahte, aldatıcı; çökük; çukurlaşmış; 3. *n.* çukur, boşluk; küçük dere; ⊕ oyuk, yiv; 4. *vb.* oy(ul)mak, çukurlatmak, içini oymak; **¹hol.low.ness** *n.* boşluk, oyukluk; *fig.* sahtelik, aldatıcılık.

**hol.ly** ⚓ [ˈhɔli] *n.* çobanpüskülü.

**hol.ly.hock** ⚓ [ˈhɔlihɔk] *n.* gülhatmi.

**holm** [həum] *n. a.* **¹⌣-¹oak** ⚓ pırnal.

**hol.o.caust** [ˈhɔləkɔːst] *n.* tahribat, büyük yıkım. yangın felâketi.

**hol.ster** [ˈhəulstə] *n.* deri tabanca kılıfı.

**ho.ly** [ˈhəuli] 1. *adj.* kutsal, mukaddes, kutsi. mübarek; ♀ Week paskalyadan önceki hafta; 2. *n.* ~ of holies İncil: en kutsal yer; Musevi tapınağının en iç kısmı; **¹⌣.stone** *n.* ⚓ maltataşı.

**hom.age** [ˈhɔmidʒ] *n.* hürmet, saygı; biat, *b-nin* egemenliğini tanıma; do *veya* pay *veya* render ~ saygı göstermek, hürmet etm. (to *-e*).

**home** [həum] 1. *n.* ev, yuva, aile ocağı, mesken; vatan, yurt, memleket; bazı oyunlarda hedef; at ~ evde; memleketinde; *spor:* kendi sahasında; make o.s. at ~ rahatına bakmak, kendi evindeymiş gibi davranmak; be at ~ evde bulunmak; *b-ni* evinde kabul etm.; 2. *adj.* eve ait; memleketine ait; yerli; ♀ Office İçişleri Bakanlığı; ♀ Rule muhtariyet, özerklik; ♀ Secretary İçişleri Bakanı; ~ trade iç ticaret; 3. *adv.* evde, eve; kendi ülkesine, ülkesinde; tam yerine; be ~ evde olm.; bring *veya* drive s.th. ~ to s.o. *bşi b-nin* kafasına sokmak, *bşi* iyice anlamasını sağlamak; come ~ eve gelmek; come ~ to s.o. *fig.* tamamiyle farkına varmak; *b-ni* çok etkilemek; that comes ~ to you onu iyice anlıyorsunuz; hit *veya* strike ~ *fig.* tam yerine vurmak; 4. *v/i.* eve gitmek *veya* dönmek; yuvasına dönmek *(hayvan)*; dikkatini bir yöne çevirmek; evi olm.; **¹⌣-¹brewed** *adj.* evde yapılma *(içki)*; **¹⌣-com.ing** *n.* eve *veya* yurda dönüş; mezunlar günü; ♀ Coun.ties *pl.* kontluklar; ~ e.co¹nom.ics *mst sg. Am.* ev idaresi bilgisi, ev ekonomisi; **¹⌣-felt** *adj.* kendini evindeymiş gibi hisseden; **¹⌣-¹grown** *adj.* ülkede yetişen; **¹home.less** *adj.* evsiz barksız, yurtsuz; **¹home.like** *adj.* ev gibi, rahat; **¹home.li.ness** *n.* basitlik, sadelik, gösterişsizlik; *Am.* cazibesizlik, çirkinlik; **¹home.ly** ☐ *fig.* basit, sade, gösterişsiz, süssüz; ev gibi, evi andıran; *Am.* cazibesiz, çirkin. **home...:** **¹⌣-¹made** *adj.* evde yapılmış; **¹⌣.mak.er** *n.* ev kadını; **¹⌣.sick:** be ~ yurt hasreti çekmek, sıla hasreti çekmek; **¹⌣.sick.ness** *n.* sıla hasreti; **¹⌣.spun**

1. *adj.* evde dokunmuş; temiz, saf; 2. *n.* evde dokunmuş kumaş; **¹⌣.stead** *n.* ev ve eklentileri; çiftlik evi; ~ *team spor:* ev sahibi takım; **⌣.ward(s)** [ˈ⌣wəd(z)] *adj. & adv.* eve doğru (giden); **¹⌣.work** *n.* ev ödevi.

**hom.i.cide** [ˈhɔmisaid] *n.* adam öldürme; adam öldüren kimse, katil.

**hom.i.ly** [ˈhɔmili] *n.* vaız, uzun ve sıkıcı konuşma.

**hom.ing** [ˈhəumiŋ] *adj.* salıverildiğinde tekrar yuvaya dönebilen *(güvercin);* ~ instinct tekrar yuvayı bulabilme içgüdüsü; ~ pigeon posta güvercini.

**hom.i.ny** [ˈhɔmini] *n.* mısır lapası.

**ho.m(o)e.o.path** [ˈhɔumjəupæθ] *n.* hastalığı benzeri ile tedavi eden doktor; **ho-m(o)e.o¹path.ic** *adj.* (⌣ally) benzeri ile tedavi olunan hastalığa ait; **ho.m(o)e.op.a-thist** [⌣miˈɔpəθist] *n.* hastalığı benzeri ile tedavi eden doktor; **ho.m(o)e¹op.a.thy** *n.* hastalığı benzeri ile tedavi etme usulü. **ho.mo.ge.ne.i.ty** [hɔmɔudʒeˈniːiti] *n.* aynı cinsten olma, cinsdeşlik, türdeşlik; **ho-mo.ge.ne.ous** ☐ [⌣ˈdʒiːnjəs] aynı cinsten olan, cinsdeş, türdeş, homojen; **hom.o-graph** [ˈhɔməugrɑːf] *n.* yazılışı aynı fakat anlam *veya* telaffuzu farklı olan kelime; **ho.mol.o.gous** [hɔːˈmɔləgəs] *adj.* birbirine benzer *veya* eşit; **ho¹mol.o.gy** [⌣dʒi] *n.* benzeşim, benzeyiş; eşitlik; **hom.o.nym** [ˈhɔmənim] *n.* eşsesli, anlamları farklı fakat telaffuzu aynı olan kelime; **hom.o.phone** [ˈ⌣fəun] = homonym; **ho.mo.sex.u.al** [ˈhɔuməuˈseksjuəl] *adj.* homoseksüel, eşcinsel. **hom.y** F [ˈhɔumi] = homelike.

**hone** ⊕ [həun] 1. *n.* bileğitaşı; 2. *v/t.* bilemek.

**hon.est** ☐ [ˈɔnist] doğru, dürüst, namuslu, güvenilir, doğru sözlü, açık kalpli; **¹hon.es.ty** *n.* namusluluk, dürüstlük, doğruluk. iffet.

**hon.ey** [ˈhʌni] *n.* bal; F tatlılık; sevgili; canım; **¹hon.ey-bee** *n.* bal arısı; **¹hon.ey-comb** 1. *n.* bal peteği; 2. *v/t.* delikler açmak; **hon.eyed** [ˈhʌnid] *adj.* tatlı *(söz);* **¹hon.ey.moon** 1. *n.* balayı; 2. *vb.* balayı geçirmek; **¹hon.ey.suck.le** *n.* ⚓ hanımeli.

**honk** *mot.* [hɔŋk] 1. *n.* klakson sesi; 2. *v/i.* klakson çalmak.

**honk.y-tonk** *Am. sl.* [ˈhɔŋkitɔŋk] *n.* ucuz gece kulübü .batakhane.

**hon.o.rar.i.um** [ɔnəˈreəriəm] *n.* ücret; **hon-or.ar.y** [ˈɔnərəri] *adj.* onursal, fahrî; ücretsiz.

**hon.o(u)r** [ˈɔnə] 1. *n.* şeref, onur, namus, itibar, saygıdeğerlik; şöhret, nam; ün;

şeref kaynağı, yüz akı; yargıçlara verilen ünvan; ayrıcalık; imtiyaz; iskambilde en yüksek kart; ~s *pl.* üstün başarılı ünversite öğrencilerine verilen şeref payesi; Your ♀ Sayın Yargıç; in ~ of s.o. *b-nin* şerefine; do the ~s of the house ev sahipliği yapmak, misafir ağırlamak; 2. *v/t.* şereflendirmek, şeref vermek, saygı göstermek; ♀ *-in* karşılığını ödemek.

**hon.o(u)r.a.ble** ☐ ['ɔnərəbl] şerefli, namuslu, itibarlı; muhterem, sayın; Right ♀ pek muhterem, çok saygıdeğer *(markizin altındaki kişilere söylenir)*; **¹hono(u)r.a.ble.ness** *n.* şeref, itibar, namus.

**hooch** *sl.* [huːtʃ] *n.* içki.

**hood** [hud] *n.* kukuleta, başlık, kapşon; kukuletaya benzer herhangi bir şey; *mot.* arabanın üst kısmı; *Am.* motor kapağı; ⊕ kapak; *univ.* rütbe göstermek için cüppelere takılan başlık şeklindeki parça; gangster, azılı katil, serseri; **¹hooded** *adj.* başlıklı, kukuletalı, kapşonlu.

**hood.lum** *Am.* F [ʲhuːdləm] *n.* serseri, kabadayı, gangster, azılı katil.

**hoo.doo** *part. Am.* [ʲhuːduː] 1. *n.* uğursuz kimse *veya* şey; 2. *v/t.* uğursuzluk getirmek.

**hood.wink** [ʲhudwiŋk] *v/t.* aldatmak, hile yapmak, oyuna getirmek.

**hoo.ey** *Am. sl.* [ʲhuːi] *n.* saçma şey, zırva, saçmalık; martaval, dümen.

**hoof** [huːf] *n., pl.* hoofs *veya* hooves [huːvz] *at. vs.* tırnağı, toynak; **¹~-beat** *n.* toynak sesi; **¹hoofed** [huːft] *adj.* toynaklı.

**hook** [huk] 1. *n.* çengel, kanca, kopça; orak; *boks:* kroşe; ~s and eyes erkek ve dişi kopçalar; by ~ or by crook şu veya bu şekilde; ~, line, and sinker F tamamen tümüyle; 2. *v/t.* kıvırmak, bükmek, eğmek; kancayla yakalamak, tutmak, çekmek, bağlamak; *sl.* çalmak, araklamak, aşırmak; ~ it *sl.* kaçmak, tüymek; ~ up birleştirmek, bağlamak; *v/i. a.* ~ on kanca şeklini almak; takılmak, asılmak.

**hook.a(h)** [ʲhukə] *n.* nargile.

**hooked** [hukt] *adj.* çengelli; çengel şeklinde; tığ ile örülmüş; müptelâ, düşkün; **¹hook.er** *n.* ↓ tek direkli balıkçı gemisi; eski ve hantal gemi; fahişe, orospu; **¹hook.ey** = hooky; **¹hook-up** *n.* birleşme, bağlantı; birkaç elektrik devresinin birbirine bağlanması; *radyo:* birkaç radyo istasyonunu birleştirme; **¹hook.y** *n.* okul kaçağı; play ~ *Am. sl.* okula asmak, okulu kırmak.

**hoo.li.gan** [ʲhuːligən] *n.* serseri, külhanbeyi, kabadayı.

**hoop** [huːp] 1. *n.* kasnak, çember; ka-

dınların eteklerinin içine geçirilen çember; ⊕ tasma kelepçe; 2. *v/t.* çemberlemek, çemberle bağlamak; **¹hoop.er** *n.* fıçıcı, varilci.

**hoop.ing-cough** [ʲhuːpiŋkɔf] *n.* boğmaca.

**hoo.poe** *orn.* [ʲhuːpuː] *n.* çavuşkuşu, ibibik, hüthüt.

**hoot** [huːt] 1. *n.* baykuş sesi; klakson sesi; vapur düdüğü; bağırma, azarlama; yuhalama; 2. *v/i.* yuhalamak, yuha çekmek; bağırmak ,azarlamak; baykuş gibi ötmek; ötmek *(baykuş)*; *mot.* klakson çalmak; *v/t. a.* ~ at, ~ out, ~ away ıslıklamak, yuhalamak; **¹hoot.er** *n.* fabrika düdüğü, siren; *mot.* klakson.

**Hoov.er** [ʲhuːvə] 1. *n.* elektrik süpürgesi; 2. *v/t.* elektrik süpürgesiyle temizlemek.

**hop¹** [hɔp] 1. *n.* ♀ şerbetçiotu; ~s *pl.* şerbetçiotu *(biraya katılan ve ona lezzet veren)*; **¹~-picker** şerbetçiotu toplayan kimse *veya* makine; 2. *v/t.* yetiştirmek *(şerbetçiotu)*; *v/i.* şerbetçiotu toplamak.

**hop²** [~] 1. *n.* sekme, sıçrama, zıplama; ♀ uçak seferi; F dans partisi; 2. *vb.* sıçramak, sekmek, zıplamak, seke seke yürümek; uçakla seyahat etm.; ~ it *sl.* yaylanmak, gidivermek; ~ off ♀ havalanmak, kalkmak.

**hope** [həup] 1. *n.* umut, ümit (of *-den*); umut kaynağı; of great ~s umut veren; 2. *vb.* ummak, ümit etm., beklemek (for *-i*); ümitle aramak; umutla beklemek; ~ in güvenmek, itimat etm. *-e*; ~ against ~ ümidini kesmeyerek beklemek; **hope.ful** ☐ [ʲ~ful] ümitli, ümit verici; be ~ that *b-şden* ümitli olm.; **¹hope.less** ☐ ümitsiz.

**hop-o'-my-thumb** [ʲhɔpəmiʲθʌm] *n.* cüce.

**hop.per** [ʲhɔpə] *n.* ⊕ besleme hunisi; tahıl ambarı; büyük kova; sıçrayan herhangi bir böcek.

**horde** [hɔːd] *n.* göçebe aşiret; kalabalık, izdiham; çokluk, fazlalık.

**ho.ri.zon** [həʲraizn] *n.* ufak, çevren; **hor.i.zon.tal** ☐ [hɔriʲzɔntl] yatay, ufki, ufka paralel.

**hor.mone** [ʲhɔːməun] *n.* hormon.

**horn** [hɔːn] *n.* ♪ boru; *zo.* boynuz; *mot.* korna, klakson; boynuz şeklindeki herhangi bş; draw in one's ~s *fig.* korkup geri çekilmek, yelkenleri suya indirmek; (stag's) ~s *pl.* geyik boynuzları; ~ of plenty bolluk (sembolü); **¹~.beam** *n.* ♀ gürgen; **~.blende** [ʲ~blend] *n. min.* hornblent; **¹horned** [ʲ~id] *adj.* boynuzlu.

**hor.net** *zo.* [ʲhɔːnit] *n.* eşekarısı, büyük sarı arı.

**horn.less** [ʲhɔːnlis] *adj.* boynuzsuz, boy-

nuzları olmayan; **¹horn.pipe** *n. a.* sailor's
~ gemici dansı; bu dansın müziği; **¹horn-
rimmed:** ~ spectacles *pl.* bağa gözlük,
boynuzdan yapılma gözlük; **horn.swog-
gle** *Am. sl.* [¹~swɔgl] *v/t.* faka bastırmak, aldatmak, dolandırmak, işletmek;
**¹horn.y** □ boynuzlu; boynuzdan yapılmış; sert, nasırlaşmış, nasır tutmuş *(el);*
şehvetli, tahrik olmuş.

**ho.rol.o.gy** [hɔ¹rɔlədʒi] *n.* vakit ölçme ilmi; saatçilik; **hor.o.scope** [¹hɔrəskəup]
*n.* zayiçe, yıldız falı; cast a ~ yıldız falına bakmak.

**hor.ri.ble** □ [¹hɔrəbl] dehşetli, korkunç,
müthiş, iğrenç; kötü, berbat; **hor.rid** □
[¹hɔrid] korkunç, dehşetli, iğrenç; kötü;
berbat; **hor.rif.ic** [hɔ¹rifik] *adj.* dehşetli,
korkunç; **hor.ri.fy** [¹~fai] *v/t.* korkutmak,
dehşete düşürmek; **hor.ror** [¹hɔrə] *n.* dehşet, korku, yılgı; nefret, tiksinme *(of
-den);* chamber of ~s mumyalar müzesi; ~ fiction (film) korku romanı (filmi);
**¹hor.ror-strick.en** *adj.* korkudan donakalmış.

**horse** [hɔ:s] **1.** *n.* at, beygir; aygır; *coll.*
süvari birliği; ⊕ sehpa, kasa; look a gift
~ in the mouth *fig.* bahşiş atın dişine bakmak, bir armağanı beğenmeyip kusur
bulmak; a ~ of another colo(u)r tamamiyle farklı bir konu, apayrı bir mesele;
(straight) from the ~'s mouth asıl kaynağından öğrenilmiş *veya* alınmış; **2.** *vb.*
ata bin(dir)mek, at koşmak; hayvan gücüyle hareket ettirmek; *sl.* eşek şakası
yapmak; **¹~.back:** on ~ ata binmiş, at üstünde; atla; go on ~ atla gitmek; **¹~-bean**
*n.* ♀ bakla; **¹~-box** *n.* at taşımak için kullanılan kapalı araç; **¹~-break.er** *n.* at terbiyecisi; ~ chest.nut *n.* ♀ atkestanesi;
**¹~-col.lar** *n.* hamut; **¹~-deal.er** *n.* at satıcısı; **¹~-flesh** *n.* at eti; *coll.* atlar, at sınıfı; **¹~-fly** *n. zo.* atsineği; ⚥ Guards *n.*
*pl.* atlı muhafız bölüğü; **¹~.hair** *n.* at kılı; **¹~.laugh** *n.* F kaba kahkaha; **¹~.man**
*n.* binici, süvari; **¹~.man.ship** *n.* binicilik; ~ op.er.a *Am.* kovboy filmi; **¹~-play**
*n.* eşek şakası; **¹~-pond** *n.* at sulama *veya* yıkama havuzu; **¹~.pow.er** *n.* beygir
gücü; **¹~.rad.ish** *n.* ♀ yabanturbu, acırga; **¹~-sense** *n.* sağduyu; **¹~.shoe** *n.* at
nalı; **¹~.whip** *n.* kamçı, kırbaç; **¹~.wom.an**
*n.* kadın binici.

**hors.y** [¹hɔ:si] *adj.* ata ait, at...; at yarışları...; ata benzeyen...; binici...

**hor.ta.tive** □ [¹hɔ:tətiv], **hor.ta.to.ry**
[¹~təri] teşvik edici, gayret verici, yü-
reklendirici; nasihat verici, öğütleyici.

**hor.ti.cul.tur.al** [hɔ:ti¹kʌltfərəl] *adj.* bah-

çıvanlığa ait, bahçıvanlık...; **¹hor.ti.cul-
ture** *n.* bahçıvanlık, bahçecilik, çiçekçilik; **hor.ti¹cul.tur.ist** *n.* bahçıvan, bahçecilik uzmanı.

**ho.san.na** [həu¹zænə] *n.* şükretme *(Tanrıya)*

**hose** [¹həuz] **1.** *n.* hortum; *coll.* çorap; **2.**
*v/t.* hortumla sulamak *veya* yıkamak.
**ho.sier** [¹həuziə] *n.* çorapçı ve iç çamaşırcı; **¹ho.sier.y** *n.* çorap ve iç çamaşırı,
mensucat.

**hos.pice** [¹hɔspis] *n.* misafirhane; darülaceze, düşkünler evi.

**hos.pi.ta.ble** □ [¹hɔspitəbl] misafirperver;
açık *(to -e).*

**hos.pi.tal** [¹hɔspitl] *n.* hastane; ✕ askeri
hastane; **hos.pi.tal.i.ty** [~¹tæliti] *n.* konukseverlik, misafirperverlik; **hos.pi.tal.ize**
[¹~təlaiz] *v/t.* hastaneye yatırmak; **¹hos-
pi.tal-train** *n.* ✕ askeri hastane treni.

**host¹** [həust] *n.* ev sahibi *(erkek),* mihmandar; otelci, hancı; *zo.,* ♀ bir asa-
lağı besleyen organizma; reckon without
one's ~ güçlükleri düşünmeden plan yapmak; ilgili kişilere danışmadan hesap
yapmak.

**host²** [~] *n. fig.* kalabalık, çokluk; ordu;
Lord of ~s *İncil:* ordulara zafer veren
Allah; he is a ~ in himself bir çok ada-
ma bedeldir.

**Host³** *eccl.* [~] *n.* okunmuş ekmek, takdis edilen fodla.

**hos.tage** [¹hɔstidʒ] *n.* rehine, tutak.

**hos.tel** [¹hɔstəl] *n.* han; *univ.* talebe yurdu; **¹hos.tel.(l)er** *n.* handa kalan kimse;
**¹hos.tel.ry** [¹~ri] *n.* han, otel.

**host.ess** [¹həustis] *n.* ev sahibesi; hancı
kadın; konsomatris; hostes.

**hos.tile** [¹hɔstail] *adj.* düşmanca; saldırgan; düşmana ait, düşman...; **hos.til.i.ty**
[~¹tiliti] *n.* düşmanlık *(to -e);* ~s *pl.* savaş, çarpışmalar.

**hos.tler** [¹ɔslə] *n.* seyis.

**hot** [hɔt] **1.** □ sıcak, kızgın; acı, yakıcı,
biberli; hiddetli, öfkeli; yeni, taze *(iz,
haber);* ritmik, hareketli *(müzik);* *Am.*
*sl.* elden çıkarması güç *(çalıntı mal);*
şiddetli, sert, hararetli; şehvetli; istekli; şevkli; inanılmaz, imkânsız; yüksek
gerilim taşıyan *(tel);* radyoaktif; çalıntı *(mal);* polisçe aranan; hızlı, süratli
*(araç);* ~ air F boş laf, atmasyon, martaval; go like ~ cakes kapışa kapışa satın alınmak, çok hızlı gitmek; ~ stuff *sl.*
birinci sınıf şey; değerli kimse; get into
~ water başını belâya sokmak; **2.** *v/t. &
v/i. mst.* ~ up F ısıtmak; heyecanlan-
(dır)mak; ısınmak; **¹hot.bed** *n.* camlık,

ısıtılmış gübreli toprak; *fig.* huzursuzluk (*veya* kötülük) kaynağı, yuvası, yatağı; **¹hot-¹b.ood.ed** *adj.* hiddetli, kan beynine sıçramak üzere olan.

**hotch.potch** F [¹hɔtʃpɔtʃ] *n.* karmakarışık şey, karman çorman şey; düzensizlik, intizamsızlık; türlü (*yemek*).

**hot dog** F [¹hɔt¹dɔg] *n.* sosis, sıcak sosisli sandviç.

**ho.tel** [həu¹tel] *n.* otel.

**hot...**: **¹~.foot 1.** *adv.* aceleyle, telaşla; **2.** *vb.* aceleyle gitmek; **¹~.head** *n.* öfkeli (*veya* çabuk kızan, ateşli) kimse; **¹~.house** *n.* limonluk, ser, camlık; **¹hot-ness** *n.* sıcaklık, hararet; heyecan; hiddet, öfke; acılık, yakıcılık.

**hot...**: **¹~-plate** *n.* küçük elektrik ocağı; **¹~-pot** *n.* güveç; **¹~-press** *vb.* sıcak saç ütüsüyle ütülemek (*kağıt, kumaş*); **~ rod** *mot. Am. sl.* takviyeli külüstür araba; **¹~.spur** *n.* çabuk öfkelenen adam; **~-water bot.tle** sıcak su torbası.

**hough** [hɔk] = hock¹.

**hound** [haund] **1.** *n.* av köpeği, tazı; *fig.* it herif, adi adam, aşağılık herif; **2.** *v/t.* tazı ile avlamak (*veya* kovalamak); peşini bırakmamak, izlemek, takip etm.

**hour** [¹auə] *n.* saat (*60 dakika*); vakit, zaman; **~s** *pl.* belirli süre; mesai (*veya* iş) saatleri; *eccl.* dua vakti; *s.* eleventh; **¹~-glass** *n.* kum saati; **¹~-hand** *n.* akrep (*saatteki*); **¹hour.ly 1.** *adv.* saatte bir, saat başı; herhangi bir saatte; **2.** *adj.* her saat başı olan; devamlı, sürekli.

**house 1.** [haus] *n., pl.* **hous.es** [¹hauziz] *com.* ev, mesken, hane; *parl.* hükümet meclis binası; † ticarethane, müessese; *parl.* meclis; ev halkı, aile; soy; hanedan; tiyatro; *thea.* seyirciler; the 2 borsa; Avam Kamarası, Lordlar Kamarası; **~ and home** ev bark; keep **~** ev idare etm., ev işlerini görmek; on the **~** masrafı patrona *veya* şirkete ait; **2.** [hauz] *v/t.* barındırmak, evinde misafir etm.; yerleştirmek, yığmak; eve koymak; korumak, muhafaza etm.; *v/i.* evde oturmak, barınmak; **~-a.gent** [¹hauseidʒənt] *n.* ev komisyoncusu; **~ ar.rest** evde göz hapsi; **¹~-boat** *n.* yüzen ev; **¹~.break.er** *n.* ev hırsızı; **¹~-flag** *n.* ↓ gemi bayrağı; **¹~-fly** *n.* karasinek; **¹~.hold** *n.* ev halkı, aile; *attr.* eve ait, ev...; King's **~** Kral'ın saray hayatı; **~** troops *pl.* hassa askeri; **~ word** hergün kullanılan kelime; **¹~.hold.er** *n.* ev sahibi; aile reisi; **¹~.keep.er** *n.* kâhya kadın; evi idare eden kadın; **¹~.keep.ing 1.** *n.* ev idaresi; **2.** *adj.* ev..., aile...; **¹~.less** *adj.* evsiz barksız, evi ol-

mayan; **¹~.maid** *n.* orta hizmetçisi; **¹~.mas.ter** *n.* yatılı okulda bir binayı idare eden öğretmen; **~ of cards** çocuğun iskambil kağıtlarından yaptığı ev; *fig.* sallantılı iş; 2 of God tapınak, kilise; **~ of ill fame** genelev; **¹~-paint.er** *n.* badanacı, boyacı; **¹~-phy.si.cian** *n.* revir doktoru; **¹~-room** *n.* bir evde barınacak yer, bir evdeki boş yer; give s.o. **~** *b-ni* evine kabul etm., *b-ne* evinde oda vermek; **¹~-to-¹house** *adj.* kapı kapı; **~ collection** kapı kapı dolaşarak toplama; **¹~-top** *n.* dam; proclaim from the **~s** herkese ilan etm., *fig.* davul çalmak, sağır sultana bile duyurmak; **¹~-train.ed** *adj.* evcil, ehli, uysal (*hayvan*); **¹~-warm.ing** *n.* yeni eve taşınanların verdikleri ziyafet; **~.wife** [¹~waif] *n.* ev kadını; [¹hʌzif] *n.* dikiş kutusu; **~.wife.ly** [¹hauswaifli] *adj.* ev kadınına ait, ev kadınının...; **~.wif.er.y** [¹~wifəri] *n.* ev kadınlığı; **¹~.work** *n.* ev işi; **¹~-wreck.er** *n. Am.* ev yıkıcısı.

**hous.ing¹** [¹hauziŋ] *n.* iskân; evler; barınacak yer; **~ conditions** *pl.* yaşam şartları; **~ shortage** evsizlik sorunu.

**hous.ing²** [**~**] *n.* eyer bellemesi, süslü koşum takımı.

**hove** [həuv] *pret. & p.p. of* heave 2.

**hov.el** [¹hɔvəl] *n.* açık ağıl; harap kulübe.

**hov.er** [¹hɔvə] *v/i.* havada durmak (*helikopter*); etrafında dolaşıp durmak (*kuş*); dolaşmak, sallanmak; *fig.* tereddüt etm., arada kalmak; **~ing** accent şüpheli konuşma; **¹~.craft** *n.* basınçlı hava üzerinde gidebilen taşıt, hoverkraft.

**how** [hau] *adv.* nasıl, ne, kadar; ne derecede, ne durumda; **~** do you do? nasılsınız?; **~** large a room! ne geniş bir oda!; **~** about... ?... ne dersin?; **~.be.it** † F [¹~¹bi:it] *cj.* bununla beraber, yine de; **~-d¹ye-do** *sl.* [¹~djə¹du:] *n.* sıkıntılı, durum; **~.¹ev.er,** *a.* howe'er [~¹εə] *adv. & cj.* ne kadar... olursa olsun; F nasıl oldu da...?; mamafih, bununla beraber.

**how.itz.er** × [¹hauitsə] *n.* havan topu, obüs.

**howl** [haul] **1.** *v/i.* ulumak; inlemek, feryat etm.; kahkaha atmak; uğuldamak (*rüzgâr*); *v/t.* bağırmak -*e*, yuhalayarak susturmak; **2.** *n.* uluma; inleme, inilti, feryat, bağırma; uğultu; *radyo:* vınlama; **¹howl.er** *n.* uluyan hayvan; bağıran kimse; *sl.* gülünç hata, budalaca yanlışlık; **¹howl.ing 1.** *adj.* uluyan; uğuldayan; ıssız, tenha, vahşi (*yer*); F çok büyük, göz kamaştırıcı; **2.** *n.* uluma; feryat, inleme.

**how.so.ev.er** [ˈhausəuˈevə] *adv.* her nasıl olursa olsun, her ne kadar olursa olsun, her ne derecede olursa olsun.

**hoy** [hɔi] **1.** *int.* hey! *(dikkat çekmek için)*; ho! *(hayvanları uzaklaştırmak için)*; **2.** *n.* ⤶ direksiz *veya* tek direkli mavna *veya* duba.

**hoy.den** [ˈhɔidn] *n.* kaba ve arsız kız, erkek Fatma.

**hub** [hʌb] *n.* tekerlek poyrası, tekerlek göbeği; *fig.* merkezi yer.

**hub.ble-bub.ble** [ˈhʌblbʌbl] *n.* nargile.

**hub.bub** [ˈhʌbʌb] *n.* gürültü, velvele.

**hub(.by)** F [ˈhʌb(i)] *n.* koca.

**hub.ris** [ˈhjuːbris] *n.* kibir, gururlanma, kasılma.

**huck.a.back** [ˈhʌkəbæk] *n.* havluluk bir çeşit kumaş.

**huck.le** [ˈhʌkl] *n.* kalça, but; ʰ~.ber.ry *n.* ⤶ Kuzey Amerika'da yetişen bir cins ufak ve siyah meyve; ʰ~-bone *n.* kalça kemiği.

**huck.ster** [ˈhʌkstə] **1.** *n.* seyyar satıcı, işportacı; reklamcı; **2.** *vb.* sıkı pazarlık etm.; *bşi* dolaşa dolaşa satmak.

**hud.dle** [ˈhʌdl] **1.** *v/t. & v/i. a.* ~ together sıkı halde topla(n)mak, biraraya sıkış-(tır)mak, karmakarışık tık(ıştır)mak; ~ (o.s.) up *b-ne* sokulup sarılmak; **2.** *n.* karışıklık, düzensizlik, yığın; go into a ~ F baş başa verip konuşmak.

**hue**[1] [hjuː] *n.* renk (tonu).

**hue**[2] [~] *n.*: ~ and cry çığlık, bağrışma; protesto, karşı çıkma.

**huff** [hʌf] **1.** *n.* huysuzluk, surat asma, dargınlık, içerleme; **2.** *vb.* şişirmek; kabadayılık etm.; zulmetmek; öfkelendirmek, kızdırmak; solumak; püfür püfür esmek; tehdit etm., göz dağı vermek; kızmak, öfkelenmek; ʰhuff.ish □ çabuk kızan; öfkeli, darılmış, gücenmiş, içerlemiş; ʰhuff.i.ness, ʰhuff.ish.ness *n.* öfke, kızgınlık, dargınlık; ʰhuff.y □ çabuk kızan ,parlamaya hazır; öfkeli, sinirli, dargın, gücenmiş, içerlemiş.

**hug** [hʌg] **1.** *n.* kucaklama, sarılma; **2.** *v/t.* kucaklamak, sarılmak -*e*; bağrına basmak -*i*; *fig.* benimsemek -*i*, bağlı olm. -*e*; ~o.s. *k-ni* kutlamak, tebrik etm., kendi halinden memnun olm. (on -*den dolayı*).

**huge** □ [hjuːdʒ] pek büyük, kocaman, cüsseli, heybetli, muazzam; ʰhuge.ness *n.* irilik, kocamanlık, büyüklük, muazzamlık.

**hug.ger-mug.ger** F [ˈhʌgəmʌgə] **1.** *adj.* gizli; karışık, düzensiz; **2.** *t/t.* gizli tutmak, örtbas etm., sır olarak saklamak; *v/i.*

gizlice, sinsice, çaktırmadan hareket etm. *veya* görüşmek; **3.** *n.* gizlilik; düzensizlik, karışıklık; ağzı sıkılık.

**Hu.gue.not** *hist.* [ˈhjuːgənɔt] *n.* *(16 ve 17. yüzyıllarda)* Fransız Protestan.

**hu.la** [ˈhuːlə] *n.* Hawaii dansı.

**hulk** ⤶ [hʌlk] *n.* kullanılmaz hale gelmiş gemi teknesi, hurda gemi, eskiden hapishane olarak kullanılan gemi; *fig.* büyük ve kaba gemi; iri ve hantal kimse *veya* şey; ʰhulk.ing *adj.* hantal, eli ağır, beceriksiz, sakar.

**hull** [hʌl] **1.** *n.* ✿ kabuk; çanak; ⤶ tekne, gövde; ~ down yalnız direk, yelken ve bacası görünecek kadar uzakta; **2.** *v/t. -in* kabuğunu soymak; ⤶ geminin teknesine gülle isabet ettirmek.

**hul.la.ba.loo** [hʌləbəˈluː] *n.* gürültü, velvele, yaygara.

**hul.lo** [ˈhʌˈlʌu] *int.* merhaba!, selam!; hey!; hadi canım!; alo!

**hum** [hʌm] **1.** *n.* vızıltı; mırıltı; uğultu; **2.** *int.* hım!, ya!, öyle mi?; **3.** *vb.* mırıldanmak; vınlamak, vızıldamak; faaliyette olm., harıl harıl çalışmak; *sl.* kötü kokmak, kokuşmak; mırıldanarak söylemek *(şarkı)*; mırıldanarak belirtmek *veya* etkilemek; ~ and haw kem küm etm., mırın kırın etm.; make things ~ F faaliyete geçirmek, harıl harıl çalıştırmak.

**hu.man** [ˈhjuːmən] **1.** □ insana ait, insanî, beşerî; ~ly insanca, insanın yapabileceği kadar, insanın yeteneği dahilinde; ~ly possible insanın elinden geldiği kadar; ~ly speaking beşerî bakımdan; **2.** *n.* F insan; **hu.mane** □ [hjuˈmein] insancıl, merhametli, şefkatli, müşfik; uygarlaştırıcı; ~ killer hayvanları acı vermeden öldürmeye yarayan alet; ~ learning beşeriyet kültürü; **hu.man.ism** [ˈhjuːmənizəm] *n.* insanlık çıkarlarına bağlılık, hümanizm; edebi kültür; ʰhu.man.ist *n.* insan tabiatı *veya* toplumsal olay dalında okuyan öğrenci; Hümanizm görüş ve felsefesini tutan kimse *(veya* düşünce, davranış*)*, hümanist kimse; **hu.man.i.ta·r.i.an** [hjuːmænɪˈtɛəriən] **1.** *n.* yardımsever kimse; **2.** *adj.* hayırsever, yardımsever, insancıl, insaniyetperver; **hu-**ʰman.i.ty *n.* beşeriyet, insanlık; insan, beşer; merhamet, şefkat; the humanities *pl.* klasik Yunan ve Latin edebiyatı üzerine çalışma; konusu insan olan bilimler, hümaniter bilimler; **hu.man.i.za.tion** [hjuːmənaiˈzeiʃən] *n.* insanlaştırma; insanileştirme; ʰhu.man.ize *v/t. & v/i.* insanlaş(tır)mak; insanileş(tir)mek; **hu.man-**

**kind** [ˈhjuːmənˈkaind] *n.* insanoğlu, beşeriyet.

**hum.ble** [ˈhʌmbl] **1.** □ alçak gönüllü, mütevazi; önemsiz; fakir, yoksul; vasat, orta; saygılı, hürmetkâr; my ~ self bendeniz, kulunuz; your ~ servant âciz kulunuz; eat ~ pie kibri kırılmak, burnu sürtülmek, kabahatini kabul edip özür dilemek, tükürdüğünü yalamak; **2.** *v/t.* kibrini kırmak, burnunu sürtmek, aşağılamak, boyun eğdirmek.

**hum.ble-bee** [ˈhʌmblbiː] *n.* bir çeşit iri gövdeli arı.

**hum.ble.ness** [ˈhʌmblnis] *n.* alçak gönüllülük, tevazu.

**hum.bug** [ˈhʌmbʌg] **1.** *n.* şarlatanlık, yalan, hile, dolap, dümen, martaval; yalancı kimse; üçkağıtçı kimse; **2.** *v/t.* aldatmak, kazıklamak, hile yapmak.

**hum.ding.er** *Am. sl.* [hʌmˈdiŋə] *n.* olağanüstü şey *veya* kimse.

**hum.drum** [ˈhʌmdrʌm] **1.** *adj.* can sıkıcı, tekdüzen, monoton, yavan; âdi, bayağı, değersiz, sıradan; **2.** *n.* can sıkıcı şey *veya* kimse; monoton şey; boş ve sıkıcı söz.

**hu.mer.al** *anat.* [ˈhjuːmərəl] *adj.* kol kemiği *veya* omuza ait, kol kemiği..., pazı kemiği...

**hu.mid** [ˈhjuːmid] *adj.* rutubetli, nemli, yaş; **hu¹mid.i.ty** *n.* rutubet, nem.

**hu.mil.i.ate** [hjuːˈmilieit] *v/t.* küçültmek, -in kibrini kırmak, aşağılamak, utandırmak, rezil etm.; **hu.mil.i¹a.tion** *n.* küçültme, kibrini kırma, aşağılama, rezil etme, utandırma.

**hu.mil.i.ty** [hjuːˈmiliti] *n.* alçak gönüllülük, tevazu; boyun eğme.

**hum.mer** [ˈhʌmə] *n.* cızırtı yapan alet (*part. teleph.*); *sl.* harıl harıl çalışan kimse.

**hum.ming** F [ˈhʌmiŋ] *adj.* vızıldayan, uğuldayan, mırıldanan; ¹~-bird *n. orn.* sinekkuşu; ¹~-top *n.* Alman topacı.

**hum.mock** [ˈhʌmək] *n.* yuvarlak tepe, tümsek yer, tepecik.

**hu.mor.ist** [ˈhjuːmərist] *n.* şakacı kimse, nüktedan kimse; mizahçı, güldürü yazarı.

**hu.mor.ous** □ [ˈhjuːmərəs] komik, gülünç, mizahî; ¹hu.mor.ous.ness *n.* komiklik, gülünçlük; şakacılık.

**hu.mo(u)r** [ˈhjuːmə] **1.** *n.* güldürü, mizah, komiklik, nükte; huy, mizaç, tabiat; out of ~ canı sıkkın, keyifsiz; **2.** *v/t.* memnun etm., hoşnut etm., kaprisine boyun eğmek; ¹hu.mo(u)r.less *adj.* keyifsiz, canı sıkkın; hu.mo(u)r.some □ [ˈ~səm] somurtkan, huysuz, ters, kaprisli.

**hump** [hʌmp] **1.** *n.* hörgüç; kambur; tümsek, tepe; *sl.* huzursuzluk, iç sıkıntısı; give s.o. the ~ *b-nin* canını sıkmak, içini karartmak; **2.** *vb.* kamburlaştırmak; ~ o.s. *Am. sl.* gayret sarfetmek, çabalamak, uğraşmak; ¹hump.back, ¹hump-backed *s.* hunchback.

**humph** [mm; hʌmf] *int.* hım! (*şüphe veya tereddüt belirtmek için dudakları hareket ettirmeden çıkarılan ses*).

**hump.ty-dump.ty** F [ˈhʌmptiˈdʌmpti] *n.* düşüp kırılınca tamir edilemeyen şey.

**hump.y** [ˈhʌmpi] *adj.* kambur, girintili çıkıntılı.

**hu.mus** [ˈhjuːməs] *n.* humus.

**hunch** [hʌntʃ] **1.** *s.* hump; iri parça; *Am.* F önsezi; **2.** *v/t. a.* ~ out, ~ up kamburlaştırmak; eğmek, bükmek; omuzlamak, itmek, dürtmek; ¹hunch.back *n.* kambur kimse; ¹hunch.backed *adj.* kambur.

**hun.dred** [ˈhʌndrəd] **1.** *adj.* yüz; **2.** *n.* yüz sayısı, yüz rakamı; hun.dred.fold [ˈ~fəuld] *adv.* yüz misli, yüz kat; hun.dredth [ˈ~θ] **1.** *adj.* yüzüncü; **2.** *n.* yüzde bir; ¹hun.dred.weight *n.* 50.8 kilo, *Am.* 45.4 kilo.

**hung** [hʌŋ] **1.** *pret. & p.p. of* hang **1.**; **2.** *adj.* asılmış, asılı.

**Hun.gar.i.an** [hʌŋˈgɛəriən] **1.** *adj.* Macar, Macaristan halkından; **2.** *n.* Macar; Macar dili, Macarca.

**hun.ger** [ˈhʌŋgə] **1.** *n.* açlık; *fig.* arzu, özlem, kuvvetli istek (for -e); **2.** *v/i.* acıkmak; şiddetle arzulamak (for, after -i); *v/t.* aç bırakmak.

**hun.gry** □ [ˈhʌŋgri] aç, karnı acıkmış; pek istekli, arzulu (for -e); kıraç, verimsiz (*toprak*); ~ work zahmetli iş, acıktıran iş.

**hunk** F [hʌŋk] *n.* iri parça; ¹hun.kers *n. pl.* kalça, popo.

**hunks** F [hʌŋks] *n.* cimri (*veya* pinti) kimse.

**hunt** [hʌnt] **1.** *n.* av, avlanma, avcılık, avcı grubu; avlanma bölgesi; *fig.* arama; **2.** *v/t.* avlamak; kovalamak; peşine düşmek, aramak; ~ out *veya* up aramak, arayıp bulmak; *v/i.* avlanmak; bulmaya çalışmak (for, after -i); ¹hunt.er *n.* avcı; av atı; ¹hunt.ing **1.** *n.* avcılık; **2.** *adj.* avcı...; ¹hunt.ing-box *n.* avcı kulübesi; ¹hunt.ing-ground *n.* avlanma bölgesi; ¹hunt.ress *n.* kadın avcı; ¹hunts.man *n.* avcı; av köpekleri bakıcısı.

**hur.dle** [ˈhəːdl] *n.* çit, engel (*a. fig.*); ¹hur.dler *n.* çit yapan kimse; engelli yarış koşucusu; **'hur.dle-race** *n.* engelli koşu.

**hur.dy-gur.dy** ['hə:ldigə:di] *n.* latarna, kolu çevrilerek çalınan müzik sandığı.

**hurl** [hə:l] **1.** *n.* fırlatma, savurma; **2.** *v/t.* hızla atmak, fırlatmak, savurmak.

**hurl.y-burl.y** ['hə:libə:li] *n.* gürültü, karışıklık, velvele.

**hur.ra(h)** [hu'ra:], **hur.ray** [~'rei] *int.* yaşa!, hura!

**hur.ri.cane** ['hʌrikən] *n.* kasırga, bora; ~ **lamp** gemici feneri, rüzgâr feneri.

**hur.ried** ☐ ['hʌrid] aceleyle gelen, acele ile yapılmış, telaşlı.

**hur.ry** ['hʌri] **1.** *n.* acele, telaş; in a ~ acele ile, telaşla; isteyerek; kolayca, kolay kolay; be in a ~ acelesi olm; is there any ~? aceleye gerek var mı?, telaşa lüzum var mı?; **2.** *v/t.* aceleleştirmek, çabuklaştırmak, hızlandırmak; acele ile göndermek; dürtmek, tahrik etm., sıkıştırmak; ~ on, ~ up acele ettirmek; *v/i.* acele etm., acele ile gitmek; *a.* ~ up acele etm., çabuk olm.; ~ over s.th. b-şi acele ile yapmak; **'~-'scur.ry 1.** *n.* karışıklık, koşuşturma, telaş; **2.** *adv.* telaşla, acele ile.

**hurt** [hə:t] **1.** *n.* yara, bere; zarar, hasar; acı, sızı, ağrı; **2.** (*irr.*) *v/t.* (*a. fig.*) yaralamak, incitmek, acıtmak; zarar vermek, hasara uğratmak; engel olm.; *v/i.* ağrımak, acımak; F incinmek; **hurt.ful** ☐ ['~ful] zararlı (to *-e*).

**hur.tle** ['hə:tl] *v/i.* fırlamak, uçup gitmek; *v/t.* savurmak, fırlatıp atmak.

**hus.band** ['hʌzbənd] **1.** *n.* koca, eş; **2.** *v/t.* idareli kullanmak; **'hus.band.man** *n.* çiftçi; **'hus.band.ry** *n.* ziraat, tarım, çiftçilik; idarecilik; good *etc.* ~ iyi *vs.* ev idaresi.

**hush** [hʌʃ] **1.** *adj.* durgun, sessiz; **2.** *n.* susma, sessizlik, sukût; **3.** *v/t.* & *v/i.* sus(tur)mak; yatış(tır)mak, sakinleş(tir)mek; ~ up örtbas etm., gizli tutmak; **'~-'hush** *adj.* gizli, örtülü, gizli kapaklı; **'~-mon.ey** *n.* sus payı.

**husk** [hʌsk] **1.** *n.* ❦ kabuk; kılıf; *fig.* işe yaramayan dış kısım; **2.** *v/t. -in* kabuğunu soymak; **'husk.i.ness** *n.* boğukluk, kısıklık (*ses*).

**husk.y¹** ['hʌski] **1.** ☐ kabuklu; kabuk gibi (*kuru*); boğuk, kısık (*ses*); F dinç, gürbüz, sağlıklı, kuvvetli, dayanıklı; **2.** *n.* F dinç (*veya* gürbüz) kimse.

**hus.ky²** [~] *n.* Eskimo köpeği; Eskimo.

**hus.sar** ✕ [hu'za:] *n.* süvari eri.

**hus.sy** ['hʌsi] *n.* adı çıkmış kadın; şirret kız.

**hus.tings** ['hʌstiɳz] *n. pl.* seçim hazırlığı.

**hus.tle** ['hʌsl] **1.** *v/t.* itip kakmak; acele ettirmek; hile ile satmak *veya* almak; *v/i.* itişip kakışmak, itişmek; acele etm.; fahişelik yapmak; **2.** *n.* itişip kakışma, acele, telaş; ~ and bustle telaş, koşuşma; **'hus.tler** *n.* eline çabuk kimse, çok faal kimse; fahişe.

**hut** [hʌt] **1.** *n.* kulübe, baraka; ✕ asker barakası; **2.** *v/t.* barakaya yerleştirmek *veya* koymak.

**hutch** [hʌtʃ] *n.* tavşan kafesi; dolap; kümes; kulübe, baraka.

**hut.ment** ✕ ['hʌtmənt] *n. a.* ~ camp kargâh, ordugâh.

**huz.za** [hu'za:] *int.* yaşa!, varol!

**huz.zy** ['hʌzi] = hussy.

**hy.a.cinth** ♀ ['haiəsinθ] *n.* sümbül.

**hy.ae.na** zo. [hai'i:nə] *n.* sırtlan.

**hy.brid** ['haibrid] **1.** *n.* melez hayvan *veya* bitki; iki ayrı dilden alınmış kelimelerden oluşan bileşik kelime; **2.** *adj.* melez...; karışık...; **'hy.brid.ism** *n.* melezlik; **hy'brid.i.ty** *n.* melezlik; **'hy.brid.ize** *v/t.* & *v/i.* melez olarak yetiş(tir)mek.

**hy.dra** ['haidrə] *n.* Herkül tarafından öldürülen çok başlı yılan.

**hy.dran.gea** ♀ [hai'dreindʒə] *n.* ortanca.

**hy.drant** ['haidrənt] *n.* yangın musluğu.

**hy.drate** ⚗ ['haidreit] **1.** *n.* hidrat; **2.** *vb.* su ile karıştırmak; su ile karıştırarak bileşik meydana getirmek.

**hy.drau.lic** [hai'drɔ:lik] **1.** *adj.* (~ally) hidrolik, su kuvvetiyle işleyen; su altında sertleşen; **2.** *n.* ~s *sg.* hidrolik bilimi.

**hy.dro** ['haidrəu] *n.* ılıca, kaplıca.

**hy.dro...** ['haidrəu] *prefix* su.... hidro-; **'~.car.bon** *n.* hidrokarbon; **'~.chlo.ric ac.id** hidroklorik asit, tuzruhu; **'~.dy.nam.ics** *n. sg.* hidrodinamik; **'~-e!lec.tric** *adj.* hidroelektrik; ~ generating station hidroelektrik santrali; **hy.dro.gen** ⚗ ['haidridʒən] *n.* hidrojen; **hy.dro.gen.at.ed** [hai'drɔdʒineitid] *adj.* hidrojenle birleştirilmiş; **'hy.dro.gen bomb** hidrojen bombası; **hy.drog.e.nous** [hai'drɔdʒinəs] *adj.* hidrojenli; **hy'drog.ra.phy** [~'grəfi] *n.* hidrografi; **hy.dro.path.ic** ['haidrəu-'pæθik] **1.** *adj.* hidropatik, su kürü ile yapılan; **2.** *n. a.* ~ establisment hidroterapi müessesesi; **hy.drop.a.thy** [hai'drɔpəθi] *n.* hidropati, su kürü.

**hy.dro...**: **~.pho.bi.a** ['haidrəu'fəubjə] *n.* kuduz; sudan korkma hastalığı; **'~.plane** *n.* deniz uçağı, suya inebilen uçak; **~.po.nics** *n. sg.* ilaçlı suda bitki yetiştirme bilimi; **~'stat.ic 1.** *adj.* hidrostatik...; ~

press hidrostatik basınç; 2. *n.* ~s *sg.* hidrostatik.

**hy.e.na** *zo.* [hai'i:nə] *n.* sırtlan.

**hy.giene** ['haidʒi:n] *n.* sağlık bilgisi, hıfzısıhha; **hy'gien.ic** *adj.* (~ally) sağlıkla ilgili; ~s *sg.* = hygiene.

**hy.grom.e.ter** [hai'grɔmitə] *n.* higrometre.

**Hy.men** ['haimen] *n.* evlilik tanrısı; kızlık zarı; **hy.me.ne.al** [~'ni:əl] *adj.* evlenme (*veya* düğün) ile ilgili, evlilik..., düğün...

**hymn** [him] 1. *n.* ilahi; 2. *v/t.* ilahi okuyarak kutlamak *veya* ifade etm.; **hym.nal** [ı~nəl] 1. *adj.* ilahi ile ilgili; 2. *n. a.* **ʰhymn-book** ilahi kitabı.

**hy.per.bo.la** ⅄ [hai'pə:bələ] *n.* hiperbol; **hy'per.bo.le** *rhet.* [~bəli] *n.* abartma, büyütme, mübalağa; **hy.per.bol.ic** ⅄ [~ 'bɔlik] *adj.* hiperbolik; **hy.per'bol.i.cal** □ *rhet.* çok abartılmış; **hy.per.crit.i.cal** □ ['~'kritikəl] aşırı eleştiri niteliğinde; **'hyper'mar.ket** *n.* büyük süpermarket; **hy-'per.tro.phy** [~trəufi] *n.* bir organın anormal irileşmesi.

**hy.phen** ['haifən] 1. *n.* tire, çizgi; 2. *v/t.* tire ile birleştirmek; **hy.phen.at.ed** ['~eitid] *adj.* tire ile birleştirilmiş; ~ Americans *pl.* yarı Amerikalılar.

**hyp.no.sis** [hip'nəusis] *n.*, *pl.* **hyp'no.ses** [~si:z] ipnoz, suni uyutma.

**hyp.not.ic** [hip'nɔtik] 1. *adj.* (~ally) uyutucu; 2. *n.* uyuşturucu madde; **hyp.no.tism** ['~nətizəm] *n.* hipnotizma, suni uyutma; **ʰhyp.no.tist** *n.* hipnotizmacı; **hyp.no.tize** ['~taiz] *v/t.* hipnotize etm., uyutmak.

**hy.po** *phot.* ['haipəu] *n.* fotoğrafçılıkta kullanılan sabitleştirici ilaç.

**hy.po.chon.dri.a** [haipəu'kɔndriə] *n.* hastalık kuruntusu; **hy.po'chon.dri.ac** [~driæk] 1. *adj.* kuruntulu...; 2. *n.* kuruntulu kimse; **hy.poc.ri.sy** [hi'pɔkrəsi] *n.* ikiyüzlülük. riyakârlık; **hyp.o.crite** ['hipəkrit] *n.* ikiyüzlü kimse; **hyp.o.crit.i.cal** □ [hipəu-'kritikəl] ikiyüzlü; **hy.po.der.mic** ⅊ [haipəu'də:mik] 1. *adj.* deri altına ait; ~ injection = 2. *n.* şırınga, iğne; **hy.pot.e.nuse** ⅄ [hai'pɔtinju:z] *n.* hipotenüs; **hy'poth.e.cate** [~θikeit] *v/t.* ipotek etm.; rehin olarak vermek; **hy'poth.e.sis** [~θisis] *n.*, *pl.* **hy'poth.e.ses** [~θisi:z] varsayım, hipotez, kuram, faraziye; **hy.po.thet.ic, hy.po.thet.i.cal** □ [haipəu'θetik-(əl)] kuramsal, nazari.

**hys.sop** ⅊ ['hisəp] *n.* zufa otu, çördük.

**hys.te.ri.a** ⅊ [his'tiəriə] *n.* isteri, peri hastalığı; **hys.ter.ic, mst hys.ter.i.cal** □ [his-'terik(əl)] isterik, isteriye ait; **hys'ter.ics** *n. pl.* isteri nöbeti; go into ~ isterikleşmek, sinir buhranına girmek.

# I

**I** [ai] *pron.* ben.

**i.am.bic** [ai'æmbik] **1.** *adj.* bir kısa bir uzun vezinle yazılmış...; **2.** *n. a.* **i'am.bus** [~bəs] bir kısa bir uzun vezin.

**i.bex** *zo.* ['aibeks] *n.* kıvrık boynuzlu dağ keçisi.

**i.bi.dem** [i'baidem] *adv.* evvelce bahsedilen yerde, aynı kitapta.

**ice** [ais] **1.** *n.* buz; meyveli dondurma; dondurma; buza benzeyen şey; pırlanta, mücevher; cut no ~ F önemi *veya* etkisi olmamak; **2.** *v/t.* buz ile kaplamak, soğutmak, dondurmak, buz gibi yapmak; krema ile kaplamak *(pasta); v/i.* buzlanmak; *a.* ~ up buzla kaplanmak, buz tutmak; buz gibi soğumak; **'~-age** *n.* buzul devri; **'~-axe** *n.* dağcıların kullandıkları buz baltası; ~ **bag** ⁊ buz torbası; **ice-berg** ['~bəːg] *n.* aysberk, buz adası, buzdağı *(a. fig.).*

**ice...:** **'~-boat** *n.* yelkenli kızak; **'~-bound** *adj.* her tarafı donmuş *(liman);* etrafı buzla çevrilmiş *(gemi);* **'~-box** *n.* buzluk; *Am. a.* buzdolabı; **'~-break.er** *n.* ↓ buzkıran; **'~-cap** *n.* buzul; **'~-'cream** *n.* dondurma; **'~-fall** *n.* donmuş şelâle; **'~-field** *n.* büyük buz kitlesi, buzul; **'~-floe** *n.* buzul, denizde yüzen geniş buz kitlesi; **'~-free** *adj.* buzsuz; **'~-hock.ey** *n.* buz hokeyi; **'~-house** *n.* buz deposu, buzhane.

**ice.land.er** ['aisləndə] *n.* İzlandalı; **Ice-lan.dic** [~'lændik] *n.* İzlanda dili.

**ich.thy.ol.o.gy** [ikθi'ɔlədʒi] *n.* zoolojinin balıklar bölümü; balıklar üzerine tez.

**i.ci.cle** ['aisikl] *n.* buz parçası, buz saçağı, buz salkımı.

**i.ci.ness** ['aisinis] *n.* soğukluk, buz gibi olma, çok soğuk olma.

**ic.ing** ['aisin] *n.* şekerli krema.

**i.con** ['aikɔn] *n.* Ortodoks kiliselerinde azizlerin resmi, ikon.

**i.con.o.clast** [ai'kɔnəuklæst] *n.* yerleşmiş gelenekleri hiçe sayan kimse; putkıran, azizlerin resimlerini parçalayan kimse.

**I.cy** □ ['aisi] buz gibi soğuk *(a. fig.);* buzlu, buz kaplı.

**I'd** [aid] = I had; I would.

**i.de.a** [ai'diə] *n.* fikir, düşünce; sanı, tahmin; plan, tasarı; kavram, idrak, anlayış; düşünme şekli, kafa, akıl; form an ~ of -*in* hakkında kafada bir fikir oluşturmak; **i'de.al 1.** □ ideal; ülküsel; istenilen...; hayali...; mükemmel; şahane...; **2.** *n.* ülkü, ideal; örnek alınacak kimse; amaç, gaye, erek; **i'de.al.ism** *n.* idealizm, ülkücülük; **i'de.al.ist** *n.* idealist, ülkücü; **i.de.al'is.tic** *adj.* (~ally) ülkücü..., idealizme ait; kamu yararına çalışan...; **i'de.al.ize** [~laiz] *vb.* idealleştirmek, mükemmel olarak görmek.

**i.den.ti.cal** □ [ai'dentikəl] aynı, bir, tıpkı, özdeş; **i'den.ti.cal.ness** = identity; **i.den-ti.fi'ca.tion** *n.* hüviyet, kimlik tesbiti; ~ card = identity card; ~ mark *mot.* marka, alâmeti farika; **i'den.ti.fy** [~fai] *vb.* -*in* hüviyetini göstermek, teşhis etm., ispatlamak *(hüviyetini);* bir tutmak, fark gözetmemek (with *ile);* desteklemek; **i'den-ti.ty** *n.* aynılık, özdeşlik; hüviyet, kimlik; ~ card kimlik cüzdanı, hüviyet kartı; ~ disk X üzerinde askerlerin kimliği yazılı olan madalyon.

**Id.e.o.gram** ['idiəugræm], **'id.e.o.graph** ['~grɑːf] *n. gr.* ideogram, bir fikri ifade etmek için harf yerine kullanılan şekil.

**id.e.o.log.i.cal** □ [aidiə'lɔdʒikl] ideolojik; **id.e.ol.o.gy** [~'ɔlədʒi] *n.* ideoloji.

**ides** [aidz] *n. pl.* eski Roma takviminde mart, mayıs, temmuz, ekim'in 15'i *veya* diğer ayların 13'ü.

**id.i.o.cy** ['idiəsi] *n.* ahmaklık, bönlük, aptallık; aptalca hareket.

**id.i.om** ['idiəm] *n.* şive, lehçe; deyim, tabir; **id.i.o.mat.ic** ['mætik] *adj.* (~ally) deyimsel; dilin anlatım özelliklerini belirten.

**id.i.o.syn.cra.sy** [idiə'sinkrəsi] *n.* kişisel özellik, hususiyet; mizaç, huy.

**id.i.ot** ['idiət] *n.* anadan doğma deli, geri zekâlı kimse; aptal, salak, bön kimse; **id.i.ot.ic** [idi'ɔtik] *adj.* (~ally) ahmak, bön, aptal, salak.

**I.dle** ['aidl] **1.** □ aylak, işsiz güçsüz, başıboş; tembel; işlemeyen; boş; aslı esası olmayan, değersiz, işe yaramaz; faydasız, yararsız, nafile; ~ hours *pl.* boşa geçen zaman; **2.** *v/t.* mst ~ away boşa harcamak *(zaman)*; sarfetmek; *v/i.* oyalanmak, boş şeylerle meşgul olm.; boş gezmek; boşa zaman harcamak; ⊕ boşta çalışmak; **'i.dle.ness** *n.* tembellik, işsizlik, aylaklık; **'i.dler** *n.* boş gezen kimse, başıboş kimse, tembel kimse, aylak kimse.

**I.dol** ['aidl] *n.* put, sanem, mabut; *fig.* tapılan kimse, çok sevilen kimse *veya* şey; **i.dol.a.ter** [ai'dɔlətə] *n.* putperest kimse; taparcasına seven kimse, hayran; **I'dol.a.trous** *n.* putperest kadın; **I'dol.a.try** *n.* putperestlik; çılgınca sevgi; hayranlık; **i.dol.ize** ['aidəlaiz] *v/t.* tapınmak -e, aşırı derecede sevmek -i; putlaştırmak -i.

**I.dyll** ['idil] *n.* idil, pastoral şiir *veya* düzyazı; **i.dyl.lic** [ai'dilik] *adj.* (~ally) pastoral; saf ve sevimli.

**if** [if] **1.** *cj.* eğer, şayet, ise, rağmen; **2.** *n.* şart, madde; **'if.fy** *adj. Am.* F şüpheli.

**ig.loo** ['iglu:] *n.* Eskimo evi.

**ig.ne.ous** ['igniəs] *adj.* volkanik; ateş gibi, kızgın; ateş...

**ig.nit.a.ble** [ig'naitəbl] *adj.* kolay tutuşan; **ig'nite** *v/t.* & *v/i.* tutuş(tur)mak, ateşlemek, yakmak; ateş almak, yanmak; ⌐ ısıtmak; **ig.ni.tion** [ig'niʃən] *n.* ateşleme, tutuş(tur)ma, ateş alma, yakma; *mot.* marş; ⌐ ısıtma.

**ig.no.ble** □ [ig'nəubl] alçak, âdi, şerefsiz, haysiyetsiz; utanç verici, çirkin, yüzkarası.

**ig.no.min.i.ous** □ [ignəu'miniəs] alçakça, namussuzca, şerefsizce, haysiyetsizce; **ig.no.min.y** ['ignəmini] *n.* rezalet, kepazelik; alçaklık, şerefsizlik; namussuzca davranış.

**ig.no.ra.mus** F [ignə'reiməs] *n.* cahil kimse; **'ig.no.rance** *n.* cahillik, cehalet; **'ig.no.rant** *adj.* cahil, bilgisiz, bilmez; habersiz (of *-den*); **ig.nore** [ig'nɔ:] *vb.* önem vermemek *-e*, bilmezlikten gelmek, anlamazlıktan gelmek; ∅∅ reddetmek, kabul etmemek, tanımamak.

**I.gua.na** *zo.* [i'gwɑ:nə] *n.* büyük kertenkele.

**i.kon** ['aikɔn] = **icon.**

**i.lex** ⚕ ['aileks] *n.* çobanpüskülü.

**II.I.ad** ['iliəd] *n.* Homer'in 'İlyada' adlı destanı.

**ill** [il] **1.** *adj.* hasta, rahatsız, keyifsiz; fena, kötü; uğursuz; ahlâka aykırı, ahlâksız, edepsiz; zor, güç; düşmanca; haşin, sert, zalim, gaddar; **2.** *adv.* düşmanca; keyifsizce; haşince; sertçe; aleyhinde; güç belâ, zar zor; uğursuzca; fall ~, be taken ~ hastalanmak, yatağa düşmek; *s. ease;* **3.** *n.* fenalık, kötülük, zarar; uğursuzluk; acı, belâ, dert, sıkıntı; hastalık, rahatsızlık.

**I'll** [ail] = I will *veya* I shall.

**ill...:** '~-ad'vised *adj.* tedbirsiz, ihtiyatsız; '~-af'fect.ed *adj.* kötü niyetli (to *-e, -e* karşı); '~-'bred *adj.* terbiyesiz, kaba; ~ breed.ing kötü davranışlar; '~.con'ditioned *adj.* kötü durumda; '~-dis'posed *adj.* kötü niyetli; karşı (to *-e*).

**il.le.gal** □ [i'li:gəl] kanuna aykırı, kanunsuz, yolsuz; **il.le.gal.i.ty** [ili:'gæliti] *n.* kanunsuzluk, kanuna aykırılık, yolsuzluk.

**il.leg.i.ble** □ [i'ledʒəbl] okunmaz, okunaksız *(yazı).*

**il.le.git.i.ma.cy** [ili'dʒitiməsi] *n.* gayrı meşruluk. yolsuzluk; kanuna aykırılık; piçlik; mantıksızlık; **il.le'git.i.mate** □ [~mit] kanuna aykırı; gayrı meşru, evlilik dışı doğan; mantıki olmayan, saçma.

**ill...:** '~-'fat.ed *adj.* talihsiz, bahtsız; uğursuz, nahoş; '~-'fa.vo(u)red *adj.* çirkin; '~-'got.ten *adj.* kötülükle *veya* kanunsuzlukla elde edilmiş; '~-'hu.mo(u)red *adj.* aksi, huysuz, fena huylu, sinirli, alıngan.

**il.lib.er.al** □ [i'libərəl] cimri, pinti, eli sıkı, hasis; dar görüşlü; hoşgörüsüz; kültürsüz, bilgisiz; **il.lib.er.al.i.ty** [~'ræliti] *n.* cimrilik; dar görüşlülük; hoş görmeme; bilgisizlik.

**il.lic.it** □ [i'lisit] kanuna aykırı, caiz olmayan, yasaklanmış; ~ trade karaborsa, kanunsuz ticaret.

**il.lim.it.a.ble** □ [i'limitəbl] hudutsuz, sınırsız, limitsiz, sınır tanımayan, sonsuz.

**il.lit.er.a.cy** [i'litərəsi] *n.* cehalet, okumamışlık, cahillik, okuma yazma bilmeme, kara cahillik; **il'lit.er.ate** [~rit] **1.** *adj.* okumamış, kara cahil, okuma yazma bilmeyen; **2.** *n.* kara cahil kimse, okumamış kimse.

**ill...:** '~-'judged *adj.* tedbirsiz, düşüncesiz; '~-'man.nered *adj.* terbiyesiz, kaba; '~-'na.tured □ huysuz, ters, serkeş.

**ill.ness** ['ilnis] *n.* hastalık, rahatsızlık, keyifsizlik.

**il.log.i.cal** □ [i'lɔdʒikəl] mantıksız, mantığa aykırı.

ill...: ~-o.mened [ˈilʲʲumend] adj. uğursuz; ~-ˈstarred adj. bahtı kara, talihsiz, şanssız; ~-ˈtem.pered adj. huysuz; ~-ˈtimed adj. vakitsiz, zamansız; ~-ˈtreat v/t. kötü davranmak, kötü muamele etm. -e.

il.lume poet. [iˈljuːm] v/t. aydınlatmak (a. fig.).

il.lu.mi.nant [iˈljuːminənt] 1. adj. parlak; 2. n. aydınlatıcı alet veya madde, lamba; il.lu.mi.nate [~neit] v/t. aydınlatmak (a. fig.); ışıklarla donatmak, süslemek; renkli resim ve harflerle süslemek; anlatmak, açıklamak, izah etm.; ~d advertising ışıklı reklam; il.lu.mi.nat.ing adj. aydınlatıcı; fig. açıklayıcı; il.lumi.na.tion n. aydınlatma, tenvir; kitaptaki süslemeler; il.lu.mi.na.tive [~nətiv] adj. aydınlatıcı; il.lu.mi.na.tor n. aydınlatıcı kimse veya şey; kitap yaldızcısı; il.lu.mine = illuminate.

ill-use [ˈilʲjuːz] v/t. kötü muamele etm., kötü davranmak -e.

il.lu.sion [iˈljuːʒən] n. hayal, kuruntu, aldanma, hülya; yanlış görüş, hata; il.lusive ☐ [~siv], il.lu.so.ry ☐ [~səri] aldatıcı, yanıltıcı, asılsız.

il.lus.trate [ˈiləstreit] v/t. tasvir etm., anlatmak, tanımlamak, izah etm., açıklamak, tarif etm.; resimlerle süslemek, resimlemek; il.lus.tra.tion n. resim, şema, diyagram, çizelge; izah, açıklama; örnek, misal; il.lus.tra.tive ☐ tarif eden, tanımlayan, tasvir edici; be ~ of izah etm., açıklamak -i; il.lus.tra.tor n. tasvir eden kimse veya şey; kitap veya dergilere resim çizen kimse.

il.lus.tri.ous ☐ [iˈlʌstriəs] ünlü, meşhur, şöhretli; şanlı, şerefli.

ill will [ˈilˈwil] n. kötü niyet, düşmanlık, garez, kin.

I'm [aim] = I am.

im.age [ˈimidʒ] 1. n. şekil, suret, tasvir, heykel; fikir, hayal; teşbih, mecaz; yansıma, akis; 2. vb. tasvirini yapmak, tanımlamak, tarif etm.; yansıtmak, aksettirmek; hayal etm., zihinde canlandırmak; im.age.ry n. betim, betimleme, tasvir, tanımlama; düş, imge, hayal.

im.ag.i.na.ble ☐ [iˈmædʒinəbl] hayal edilebilir, göz önüne getirilebilir; im'ag.inar.y adj. hayali, hayal mahsulü; im.agi.na.tion [~neiʃən] n. hayal gücü, yaratıcılık, yaratma kabiliyeti; hayal, kuruntu; im'ag.i.na.tive ☐ [~nətiv] yaratıcı, hayal gücü kuvvetli...; im'ag.ine v/t. hayal etm., tasavvur etm., tasarımlamak; düşünmek, sanmak, farzetmek.

im.bal.ance [imˈbæləns] n. dengesizlik; oransızlık.

im.be.cile [ˈimbisiːl] 1. ☐ ahmak, budala, bön, aptal; 2. n. ahmak kimse, aptal kimse; im.be.cil.i.ty [~ˈsiliti] n. ahmaklık, aptallık, budalalık.

im.bed [imˈbed] = embed.

im.bibe [imˈbaib] v/t. içmek, içine çekmek; emmek; fig. öğrenmek, kapmak.

im.bro.glio [imˈbrəuliəu] n. karmakarışık küme; karışık durum, dolambaçlı mesele; ciddi anlaşmazlık.

im.brue [imˈbruː] vb. ıslatmak, sırılsıklam etm., batırmak (sıvıya) (in, with ile).

im.bue [imˈbjuː] vb. boyamak, iyice ıslatmak, emdirmek; fig. doldurmak (his, fikir vs. ile).

im.i.ta.ble [ˈimitəbl] adj. taklit edilebilir; im.i.tate [ˈ~teit] v/t. taklit etm., benzetmek, taklidini yapmak; b-ni örnek almak ⊕ taklidini yapmak, kopya etm.; im.i.tation n. taklit, sahte şey; taklit etme, benzetme; ⊕ yapma; attr. taklit..., suni..., yapma...; ~ leather suni deri; im.i.ta.tive ☐ [ˈ~tətiv] taklit eden, örnek alan (of -i); ~ word sesi taklit eden sözcük; im.ita.tor [ˈ~teitə] n. taklitçi.

im.mac.u.late ☐ [iˈmækjulit] saf, tertemiz, lekesiz, pak; kusursuz.

im.ma.nent [ˈimənənt] adj. her yerde mevcut, hazır ve nazır; içinde olan, tabiatında olan.

im.ma.te.ri.al ☐ [iməˈtiəriəl] önemsiz, ehemmiyetsiz (to için); maddî olmayan, manevi, cisimsiz, tinsel.

im.ma.ture [iməˈtjuə] adj. olgunlaşmamış, ham, olmamış; kemale ermemiş, toy, gelişmemiş, pişmemiş; im.ma'tu.ri.ty n. hamlık; toyluk.

im.meas.ur.a.ble ☐ [iˈmeʒərəbl] ölçülemez; sınırsız, hudutsuz, çok geniş.

im.me.di.ate ☐ [iˈmiːdjət] doğrudan doğruya, vasıtasız, en yakın; şimdiki, hazır, derhal olan, elde mevcut; im'me.di.ate.ly 1. adv. derhal, hemen, doğrudan doğruya; 2. cj. ...ir ...irmez.

im.me.mo.ri.al ☐ [imiˈmɔːriəl] hatırlanamayacak kadar çok eski; from time ~ çok eskiden beri, ezelden beri.

im.mense ☐ [iˈmens] çok büyük, engin, geniş, hudutsuz; sl. harika, şahane, fevkalade; im'men.si.ty n. genişlik, enginlik, uçsuz bucaksız olma; çok büyük şey.

im.merse [iˈməːs] v/t. daldırmak, sokmak, suya batırmak; ~ o.s. in fig. dalmak -e; ~d in -e dalmış; im'mer.sion n. daldırma; bat(ırıl)ma; bütün vücudu suya daldırarak vaftiz etme; fig. dalma;

~ heater elektrikli su ısıtıcısı, daldırma ısıtıcı.

im.mi.grant ['imigrənt] *n.* göçmen, muhacir; im.mi.grate ['~greit] *v/i.* göç etm., hicret etm.; *v/t.* göçmen olarak yerleştirmek (into -*e*); im.mi'gra.tion *n.* göç, hicret; göçmenlik.

im.mi.nence ['iminəns] *n.* yakında olabilecek durum, tehdit eden şey; 'im.mi.nent □ yakında olan, hemen olacak olan, yakın.

im.mit.i.ga.ble □ [i'mitigəbl] hafifletilemez, yatıştırılamaz, bastırılamaz.

im.mo.bile [i'məubail] *adj.* hareketsiz; kımılda(tıla)maz; im.mo.bil.i.ty [~'biliti] *n.* hareketsizlik, yerinden kımıldamama; im'mo.bi.lize [~bilaiz] *v/t.* hareketsizleştirmek, yerinde tutmak, tesbit etm., kımıldamaz hale getirmek; askeri kuvvetleri savaşamaz hale getirmek; piyasadaki parayı tedavülden çekmek.

im.mod.er.ate □ [i'mədərit] ölçüsüz, ifrata kaçan, aşırı, çok fazla; im'mod.er.ate.ness *n.* aşırılık, ölçüsüzlük, ifrat.

im.mod.est □ [i'mədist] açık saçık, utanmaz, arsız, yüzsüz; haddini bilmez, terbiyesiz, küstah; im'mod.es.ty *n.* küstahlık, haddini bilmezlik; utanmazlık, arsızlık.

im.mo.late ['iməleit] *v/t.* kurban etm., kurban olarak kesmek; im.mo'la.tion *n.* kurban etme, kesme.

im.mor.al □ [i'mərəl] ahlâkı bozuk, ahlâksız, terbiyesiz, edepsiz; im.mo.ral.i.ty [imə'ræliti] *n.* ahlâksızlık, edepsizlik.

im.mor.tal [i'mɔːtl] **1.** □ ölümsüz, ölmez, ebedî, sonsuz, baki; **2.** *n.* ölümsüz varlık, ebedî varlık, unutulmayan şey; im.mor.tal.i.ty [~'tæliti] *n.* ölmezlik, ölümsüzlük, ebedîlik; im'mor.tal.ize [~tə'laiz] *v/t.* ebedîleştirmek, ölümsüzleştirmek.

im.mov.a.ble [i'muːvəbl] **1.** □ kımıldamaz, yerinden oynamaz, sabit; değişmez, dönmez; **2.** *n.* ~s *pl.* gayrımenkul, taşınmaz mallar.

im.mune [i'mjuːn] *adj.* ⚕ & *fig.* bağışık; muaf (from -*den*); im'mu.ni.ty *n.* muafiyet (from -*den*); bağışıklık (from -*e karşı*); dokunulmazlık; im.mu.nize ['~naiz] *v/t.* muaf kılmak; bağışık kılmak.

im.mure [i'mjuə] *v/t.* hapsetmek; kendini vermek; duvara gömmek.

im.mu.ta.bil.i.ty [imjuːtə'biliti] *n.* değişmezlik; im'mu.ta.ble □ değişmez, sabit.

imp [imp] *n.* küçük şeytan; şeytanın çocuğu; afacan (*veya* haşarı, yaramaz) çocuk.

im.pact ['impækt] *n.* vuruş, vur(uş)ma, çarpışma; etki, tesir.

im.pair [im'pɛə] *v/t.* bozmak, zayıflatmak; eksiltmek, azaltmak.

im.pale [im'peil] *v/t.* kazığa sokarak öldürmek.

im.pal.pa.ble □ [im'pælpəbl] dokunulunca hissedilemeyen; *fig.* kolayca kavranılmayan.

im.pan.el [im'pænl] = empanel.

im.part [im'paːt] *v/t.* vermek; bildirmek, söylemek.

im.par.tial □ [im'paːʃəl] tarafsız, bitaraf; im.par.ti.al.i.ty [~ʃi'æliti] *n.* tarafsızlık.

im.pass.a.ble □ [im'paːsəbl] geçil(e)mez, aşılamaz, geçit vermez.

im.passe [æm'paːs] *n.* çıkmaz (*a. fig.*); *fig.* içinden çıkılmaz durum, kördüğüm.

im.pas.si.ble □ [im'pæsibl] hissiz, duygusuz (to -*e karşı*); ağrı duymaz, acı çekmeyen.

im.pas.sion [im'pæʃən] *v/t.* hırslandırmak, kızdırmak, çileden çıkarmak; heyecanlandırmak; im'pas.sioned *adj.* ateşli, hararetli, heyecanlı.

im.pas.sive [im'pæsiv] duygusuz, hissiz, vurdumduymaz, kayıtsız, soğuk; im'pas.sive.ness *n.* vurdumduymazlık, kayıtsızlık.

im.pa.tience [im'peiʃəns] *n.* sabırsızlık, tahammülsüzlük; im'pa.tient □ hoşgörüsüz, müsamaha etmeyen (at, of -*e*); be ~ of s.th. bşe anlayış göstermemek, müsamaha etmemek; ~ for çok arzu eden -*i*; sabırsız, tahammülsüz.

im.peach [im'piːtʃ] *v/t.* suçlamak (of, with *ile*); şüphe etm. -*den*; mahkemeye sevketmek (*devlet memurunu*); im'peach.a.ble *adj.* suçlanabilir; im'peach.ment *n.* suçlama; devlet memuruna karşı dava açma.

im.pec.ca.bil.i.ty [impekə'biliti] *n.* hatasızlık, kusursuzluk; im'pec.ca.ble □ hatasız, kusursuz; günahsız.

im.pe.cu.ni.ous [impi'kjuːnjəs] *adj.* parasız, züğürt, fakir.

im.pede [im'piːd] *v/t.* engellemek, mâni olm.

im.ped.i.ment [im'pedimənt] *n.* mania, engel (to -*e*); ~ in one's speech pelteklik; im.ped.i.men.ta X [~'mentə] *n. pl.* levazım.

im.pel [im'pel] *v/t.* sevketmek, tahrik etm., harekete geçirmek, zorlamak, sürmek, mecbur etm.; im'pel.lent **1.** *adj.* sevkeden, harekete geçiren; **2.** *n.* tahrik edici unsur.

**im.pend** [im'pend] *v/i.* asılı olm., dolaşmak (over *üzerinde*); olmasına az kalmak, meydana gelmesi yakın olm.; tehdit etm.; **im'pend.ence** *n.* asılı olma; vukuu yakın olma; **im'pend.ent, im'pend.ing** *adj.* olması yakın.

**im.pen.e.tra.bil.i.ty** [impenitrǝ'biliti] *n.* içine girilememe, nüfuz edilememe; *fig.* anlaşılamama; **im'pen.e.tra.ble** ☐ nüfuz edilemez, delinmez, içine girilemez, geçilemez (to, by -*e*); *fig.* anlaşılmaz, kestirilemez; idrak edilemez; *fig.* kabul edilemez, uygun düşmez (to -*e*).

**im.pen.i.tence** [im'penitǝns] *n.* pişmanlık duymama, pişman olmama; **im'pen.i.tent** ☐ pişman olmayan, pişmanlık duymayan.

**im.per.a.tive** [im'perǝtiv] **1.** ☐ mecburi, zorunlu, zarurî; gerekli, lüzumlu, âcil; emredici, buyurucu; *gr.* emir belirten; ~ **mood** = **2.** *n. gr.* emir kipi.

**im.per.cep.ti.ble** ☐ [impǝ'septǝbl] hissolunamaz, görülemez, seçilemez, farkedilemez, algılanamaz.

**im.per.fect** [im'pǝ:fikt] **1.** ☐ eksik, kusurlu, tamam olmayan, noksan, bitmemiş; ~ **tense** = **2.** *n. gr.* bitmemiş bir eylemi gösteren zaman; **im.per.fec.tion** [~pǝ'fekʃǝn] *n.* kusur, eksiklik, noksan, hata.

**im.pe.ri.al** [im'piǝriǝl] **1.** ☐ imparator(luğ)a ait; şahane, görkemli, haşmetli, muhteşem; İngiliz ölçü standartlarına uygun; **2.** *n.* keçi sakalı; çok büyük şey; görkemli şey; imparator; **im'pe.ri.al.ism** *n.* emperyalizm, sömürgecilik; imparatorluk sistemi; **im'pe.ri.al.ist** *n.* emperyalist, sömürgecilik taraftarı; imparator(luk) taraftarı; **im.pe.ri.al'is.tic** *adj.* emperyalizme ait, sömürgeci.

**im.per.il** [im'peril] *v/t.* tehlikeye düşürmek, tehlikeye atmak.

**im.pe.ri.ous** ☐ [im'piǝriǝs] zorba, zalim, hükmeden; kibirli, küstah; zaruri, mecburi; âcil.

**im.per.ish.a.ble** ☐ [im'periʃǝbl] ölümsüz, yok olmaz; bozulmaz, çürümez.

**im.per.ma.nent** [im'pǝ:mǝnǝnt] *adj.* sürekli olmayan, devam etmeyen.

**im.per.me.a.ble** ☐ [im'pǝ:mjǝbl] *(su veya hava)* geçirmez; nüfuz edilemez.

**im.per.son.al** ☐ [im'pǝ:snl] kişisel olmayan, şahsi olmayan; *gr.* yalnız üçüncül tekil şahsı kullanılan *(fiil)*; **im.per.sonal.i.ty** [~sǝ'næliti] *n.* kişisel olmama, şahsi olmama.

**im.per.son.ate** [im'pǝ:sǝneit] *v/t.* kişilik kazandırmak; *thea.* temsil etm.; taklit

etm.; **im.per.son'a.tion** *n.* şahıslandırma, kişilik kazandırma; *thea.* temsil etme, oynama; taklit etme.

**im.per.ti.nence** [im'pǝ:tinǝns] *n.* küstahlık, arsızlık, saygısızlık, münasebetsizlik, laubalilik, sululuk; **im'per.ti.nent** ☐ terbiyesiz, arsız, saygısız, küstah, münasebetsiz, laubali, sulu, sırnaşık; *b̆* konuyla ilgisi olmayan, tali, ikincil.

**im.per.turb.a.bil.i.ty** ['impǝ:tǝ:bǝ'liti] *n.* ağırbaşlılık, soğukkanlılık, sakinlik; **imper'turb.a.ble** ☐ ağırbaşlı, soğukkanlı, sakin, nefsine hakim.

**im.per.vi.ous** ☐ [im'pǝ:vjǝs] *(su veya hava)* geçirmez, dayanıklı (to -*e*) *(a. fig.)*; nüfuz edilemeyen, kapalı.

**im.pe.ti.go** ⁊ [impi'taigǝu] *n.* impetigo, bir çeşit deri hastalığı.

**im.pet.u.os.i.ty** [impetju'ositi] *n.* tez canlılık, atılganlık, acelecilik, coşkunluk; **im'pet.u.ous** ☐ coşkun, atılgan, aceleci, düşünmeden hareket eden; zorlu, sert, şiddetli; **im.pe.tus** ['impitǝs] *n.* hız, güç, zor, şiddet; güdü, hızlandırıcı güç, dürtü.

**im.pi.e.ty** [im'paiǝti] *n.* saygısızlık, hürmetsizlik *(esp. dinsel)*; saygısız söz *veya* davranış.

**im.pinge** [im'pindʒ] *v/i.* çarpmak (on, upon, against -*e*); ~ **on** tecavüz etm. *(b-nin hakkına)*; **im'pinge.ment** *n.* çarpma (on, upon -*e*); *fig.* tecavüz etme *(b-nin hakkına)*.

**im.pi.ous** ☐ ['impiǝs] kâfir, Allahın varlığını tanımayan, dine karşı hürmetsiz.

**imp.ish** ☐ ['impiʃ] cin gibi, şeytan gibi, afacan, yaramaz.

**im.pla.ca.bil.i.ty** [implækǝ'biliti] *n.* amansızlık, affetmezlik; **im'pla.ca.ble** ☐ yatıştırılamaz, bastırılamaz, teskin edilemez, amansız, affetmez.

**im.plant** [im'pla:nt] *v/t. mst fig.* aşılamak (in -*e*), aklına sokmak; dikmek, ekmek.

**im.plau.si.ble** [im'plɔ:zǝbl] *adj.* inanılmaz, inanılması güç, makul olmayan.

**im.ple.ment 1.** ['implimǝnt] *n.* alet, araç; **2.** [~ment] *v/t.* yerine getirmek, tamamlamak, yürütmek; **im.ple.men'ta.tion** [~men'teiʃǝn] *n.* yürütme, yerine getirme.

**im.pli.cate** ['implikeit] *v/t.* sokmak, karıştırmak, bulaştırmak (in -*e*); dokundurmak, ima etm.; **im.pli'ca.tion** *n.* bulaştırma, karıştırma *(suç)*; ima, üstü kapalı söyleme; what are the ~s ? anlatılmak istenilen nedir?

**im.plic.it** [im'plisit] ima edilen, zımnî, altık; aslında olan; tam, kesin, katî; **im'plic.it.ly** *adv.* zımnen, dolayısıyla, üs

tü kapalı olarak; tamamiyle, kesinlikle.
**im.plied** □ [im'plaid] ima edilen, demek istenen, kastedilen.
**im.plore** [im'plɔː] *v/t.* yalvarmak, istirham etm., dilemek, rica etm. -*e*; **im'plor.ing** □ [~riŋ] yalvaran, yakaran, rica eden.
**im.ply** [im'plai] *v/t.* ima etm., demek, belirtmek, ifade etm.; içine almak, kapsamak; do you ~ that...? ...mi demek istiyorsunuz?
**im.po.lite** □ [impə'lait] nezaketsiz, terbiyesiz, kaba.
**im.pol.i.tic** □ [im'pɔlitik] siyasete aykırı, politik olmayan; uygun olmayan, uygunsuz, isabetsiz, münasip olmayan.
**im.pon.der.a.ble** [im'pɔndərəbl] **1.** *adj.* tartılamayan...; ölçülemeyen...; **2.** *n.* ~s *pl.* önceden etkisi ölçülemeyen şeyler.
**im.port 1.** ['impɔːt] *n.* anlam, mana; önem, ehemmiyet; † ithal, ithalat, dışsatım; ~s *pl.* ithal malları; **2.** [im'pɔːt] *vb.* ithal etm.; belirtmek, ifade etm., ima etm., demek istemek; önemi olm., hükmü olm.; **im'por.tance** *n.* önem, ehemmiyet; etki, tesir, nüfuz, itibar; **im'por.tant** □ önemli, ehemmiyetli, mühim; etkili, nüfuzlu, itibarlı; **im.por.ta.tion** [~'teiʃən] *n.* ithal (malı), ithalat, dışsatım; **im'port.er** *n.* ithalatçı.
**im.por.tu.nate** □ [im'pɔːtjunit] ısrarla isteyen, defalarca talep eden; acil; **im'por.tune** [~tju:n] *vb.* sıkıştırmak, ısrarla istemek, tekrar tekrar istemek; **im.por'tu.ni.ty** *n.* usandırıcı ısrar, tekrar tekrar isteme, sıkıştırma.
**im.pose** [im'pəuz] *v/t.* koymak, yüklemek (*vergi*) (on -*e*); zorla kabul ettirmek (on, upon -*e*); dizilmiş sayfaları sıraya koymak, düzenlemek; hile ile kabul ettirmek; *v/i.* ~ upon -*den* yararlanmak, istifade etm.; aldatmak -*i*, kazıklamak -*i*; **im'pos.ing** □ heybetli, muhteşem, görkemli; **im.po.si.tion** [impə'ziʃən] *n.* üzerine koyma, yükleme; vergi; yük; ceza; istenmeyen misafir; hile, aldatma.
**im.pos.si.bil.i.ty** [impɔsə'biliti] *n.* olanaksızlık, imkânsızlık; **im'pos.si.ble** □ imkânsız, olanaksız; çekilmez, dayanılmaz.
**im.post** ['impəust] *n.* vergi, gümrük resmi; **im.pos.tor** [im'pɔstə] *n.* sahtekâr (*veya* hilekâr) kimse, dolandırıcı; **im'pos.ture** [~tʃə] *n.* hile, sahtekârlık, dolandırıcılık.
**im.po.tence** ['impətəns] *n.* güçsüzlük, etkisizlik, tesirsizlik; *physiol.* iktidarsız-

lık; **im.po.tent** *adj.* kudretsiz, âciz, zayıf, etkisiz; iktidarsız.
**im.pound** [im'paund] *v/t.* haczetmek, kanunen el koymak; ağıla kapamak.
**im.pov.er.ish** [im'pɔvəriʃ] *v/t.* fakirleştirmek, yoksullaştırmak; kuvvetini kesmek, tüketmek, bitirmek.
**im.prac.ti.ca.bil.i.ty** [impræktikə'biliti] *n.* elverişsizlik, pratik olmama, kullanışsızlık; **im'prac.ti.ca.ble** □ yapılamaz, uygulanamaz; kullanışsız, elverişsiz, pratik olmayan; geçilmez, geçit vermez (*yol*).
**im.prac.ti.cal** [im'præktikəl] *adj.* elverişsiz, kullanışsız, pratik olmayan.
**im.pre.cate** ['imprikeit] *v/t.* lânet okumak, beddua etm. (upon -*e*); **im.pre'ca.tion** *n.* lânet, beddua; **im.pre.ca.to.ry** ['~keitəri] *adj.* lânet..., beddua...; lânet kabilinden.
**im.preg.na.bil.i.ty** [impregnə'biliti] *n.* zaptedilememe, ele geçirilememe; **im'preg.na.ble** □ zaptedilemez, ele geçirilemez, dayanıklı; **im.preg.nate 1.** ['~neit] *v/t.* hamile bırakmak, gebe bırakmak; ♀ döllemek; ⚗ emdirmek, doyurmak (*a. fig.*); *fig.* zihnini doldurmak; ⊕ emprenye etm.; **2.** [im'pregnit] *adj.* gebe, hamile; dolu; doymuş; **im.preg.na.tion** [~'neiʃən] *n.* dölleme, hamile bırakma; doyurma, emdirme; emprenye etme.
**im.pre.sa.ri.o** [impre'sɑːriəu] *n.* tiyatro temsillerini düzenleyip yöneten kimse, impresario.
**im.pre.scrip.ti.ble** [impris'kriptəbl] *adj.* hükmü geçmez; sürekli, daimi.
**im.press 1.** ['impres] *n.* damga, basma, nişan, iz, eser, işaret; *fig.* etkileme; **2.** [im'pres] *v/t.* basmak (on s.th. *veya* s.th. with -*e*); etkilemek, aklına sokmak (on, upon -*i*); izlenim bırakmak, yer etm. (on -*de*); ~ s.o. with s.th. *b-ni bşle* etkilemek; ⚓ çalışmaya zorlamak; sıkıştırmak; **im'press.i.ble** *adj.* etkilenebilir, hassas; **im'pres.sion** [~ʃən] *n.* basma; baskı; tabetme; damga; *fig.* izlenim, intiba, tesir, etki; *typ.* kopya, nüsha; be under the ~ that ...izleniminde olm., ...zannetmek, ...gibi gelmek; **im'pres.sion.a.ble** [~ʃnəbl] *adj.* aşırı duygulu, çok hassas; kolay etkilenen; kolay kalıplanır; **im'pres.sion.ism** *n.* empresyonizm, izlenimcilik; **im'pres.sion.ist** *n.* empresyonist, izlenimci; **im'pres.sion.is.tic** *adj.* empresyonistik, izlenimciliğe ait; **im'pres.sive** □ [~siv] etkili, tesirli, müessir; **im'press.ment** *n.* ⚓ sıkıştırma.
**im.print 1.** [im'print] *v/t.* basmak (*damga, mühür*) (on -*e*); *fig.* etkilemek, tesir etm., zihnine sokmak (on, in); **2.**

['imprint] *n.* damga; baskı; *typ.* bir kitaptaki yayınevi ve basımevinin adları; *fig.* etki, tesir, izlenim, intiba.

**im.pris.on** [im'prizn] *v/t.* hapsetmek, zından a kapamak, içeri atmak; **im'pris.on.ment** *n.* hapis, tutukluluk, mahpusluk.

**im.prob.a.bil.i.ty** [improbə'biliti] *n.* ihtimal dahilinde olmama, olasılığı olmama; ihtimal dahilinde olmayan şey; **im'prob.a.ble** ☐ ihtimal dahilinde olmayan.

**im.pro.bi.ty** [im'prəubiti] *n.* şerefsizlik, iffetsizlik, haysiyetsizlik.

**im.promp.tu** [im'prɔmptjuː] 1. *n.* ♪ empromptü, küçük parça; 2. *adj.* hazırlıksız; 3. *adv.* hazırlıksız olarak.

**im.prop.er** ☐ [im'prɔpə] yersiz, yakışıksız, uygunsuz, münasebetsiz, yakışık almaz, çirkin; yanlış, hatalı; ~ fraction ℞ payı paydasından büyük olan kesir; **impro.pri.e.ty** [imprə'praiəti] *n.* uygunsuzluk, yersizlik, münasebetsizlik; yanlışlık; uygunsuz söz *veya* hareket.

**im.prov.a.ble** ☐ [im'pruːvəbl] düzeltilmesi mümkün, ıslah edilebilir, yoluna girebilir; tarıma elverişli *(toprak)*.

**im.prove** [im'pruːv] *v/t.* & *v/i.* düzel(t)mek; geliş(tir)mek; değerlen(dir)mek, kıymeti(ni) art(tır)mak; yoluna koymak; ıslah etm.; yola girmek; ıslah olm.; ~ *upon* mükemmelleştirmek; **im'prove.ment** düzelme, ıslah; gelişme, ilerleme (on, upon -de); **im'prov.er** *n.* ıslahatçı, reformcu.

**im.prov.i.dence** [im'prɔvidəns] *n.* tedbirsizlik, ihtiyatsızlık; israf, ziyankârlık; **im'prov.i.dent** ☐ tedbirsiz, ihtiyatsız; savurgan, müsrif.

**im.pro.vi.sa.tion** [imprəvai'zeiʃən] *n.* önceden düşünmeden şiir söyleme *veya* şarkı besteleme; o anda uydurma; **im.provise** ['ˌ-vaiz] *vb.* doğaçtan söylemek *veya* yapmak, önceden düşünmeden söylemek *veya* bestelemek; o anda uydurmak; **'im.pro.vised** *adj.* uydurma, eğreti.

**im.pru.dence** [im'pruːdəns] *n.* tedbirsizlik, ihtiyatsızlık, düşüncesizlik; **im'pru.dent** ☐ tedbirsiz, ihtiyatsız, düşüncesiz, sağgörüsüz.

**im.pu.dence** ['impjudəns] *n.* yüzsüzlük, arsızlık, küstahlık, terbiyesizlik; **'im.pu.dent** ☐ arsız, edepsiz, saygısız, terbiyesiz, yüzsüz, küstah.

**im.pugn** [im'pjuːn] *v/t.* dil uzatmak, aksini iddia etm., aleyhinde olm., yalanlamak. yalancı çıkarmak; **im'pugn.a.ble** *adj.* inkâr edilebilir, yalanlanabilir.

**im.pulse** ['impʌls], **im'pul.sion** *n.* dürtme, itme, dürtü, itici kuvvet, sevk, tahrik;

*fig.* içtepi, güdü; **im'pul.sive** ☐ tahrik edici. itici; *fig.* atılgan, düşüncesizce hareket eden; **im'pul.sive.ness** *n.* düşünmeden hareket etme.

**im.pu.ni.ty** [im'pjuːniti] *n.* cezadan muaf olma; with ~ cezasız.

**im.pure** ☐ [im'pjuə] pis, kirli *(a. fig.)*; karışık, katışık; **im'pu.ri.ty** [~riti] *n.* pislik, kirlilik; pis *(veya* kirli) şey.

**im.put.a.ble** [im'pjuːtəbl] *adj.* başkasının üstüne atılabilir; başkasına yüklenebilir; **im.pu.ta.tion** [~'teiʃən] *n.* suçlama; başkasına yükleme, başkasının üstüne atma; **im'pute** *v/t.* itham etm., suçlamak (to *ile)*, üstüne yıkmak, yüklemek.

**in** [in] 1. *prp.* içinde, içine, dahilinde, -de, -e, -(y)e; esnasında, sürecinde, zarfında; giy(in)miş, kılığında, bürünmüş; düzenlenmiş; vasıtasıyla; olarak; bakımından, yönünden; ile meşgul; -den yapılmış; halinde, durumunda, vaktinde, mevsiminde; ~ 1983 1983'de; there is nothing ~ it temelsiz, asılsız, boş; F önemsiz; it is not ~ her içinde yok; he hasn't it ~ him o yaradılışta değil; ~ that... ...den dolayı, ...yüzünden, ...için; 2. *adv.* içeriye, içerde, içine; evde; varmakta; hasat edilmekte; mevsimi gelmiş; moda; iktidarda, seçilmiş; yanmakta; be ~ evde olm.; varmak; hasat edilmek, toplanmak *(ürün)*; mevsimi olm. *(yiyecek)*; moda olm.; iktidarda olm.; görevde olm.; yanıyor olm.; be ~ for başına gelecek olm.; *bşle* karşı karşıya olm.; -*e* katılmayı kabul etmiş olm.; be well ~ with F *b-le* araları iyi olm., arkadaş olm.; 3. *adj.* dahili, iç; görevdeki; iktidardaki; yürürlükteki; içeri doğru gelen; yanmakta olan; son derece moda olan...; 4. *n. su.*: the ~s *pl. parl.* iktidardaki parti; the ~s and outs *pl.* bir işin bütün ayrıntıları, girdisi çıktısı.

**in.a.bil.i.ty** [inə'biliti] *n.* yetersizlik, kifayetsizlik, iktidarsızlık, beceriksizlik, âcizlik.

**in.ac.ces.si.bil.i.ty** ['inæksesə'biliti] *n.* erişilmezlik, yanına varılamama; **in.ac'cessi.ble** ☐ erişilmez, yanına varılamaz.

**in.ac.cu.ra.cy** [in'ækjurəsi] *n.* yanlışlık, hatalı olma; kusur, hata, yanlış; **in'accu.rate** ☐ [~rit] yanlış, kusurlu, hatalı.

**in.ac.tion** [in'ækʃən] *n.* hareketsizlik, faaliyetsizlik; tembellik, avarelik.

**in.ac.tive** ☐ [in'æktiv] hareketsiz; tembel, üşengeç; † durgun, atıl, kesat; ℞ tesirsiz, etkisiz; **in.ac'tiv.i.ty** *n.* hareketsizlik; tembellik; durgunluk; tesirsizlik.

**in.ad.e.qua.cy** [in'ædikwəsi] *n.* yetersizlik,

kif.ayetsizlik, yetmezlik, eksiklik, noksanlık; **in¹ad.e.quate** ☐ [~kwit] yetersiz, kifayetsiz, eksik, noksan.

**in.ad.mis.si.bil.i.ty** [¹inədmisə¹biliti] *n.* kabul olunmama, uygun görülmeme; **inad¹mis.si.ble** ☐ kabul olunmaz, uygun görülmez.

**in.ad.vert.ence, in.ad.vert.en.cy** [inəd¹vəːtəns(i)] *n.* dikkatsizlik; kasıtsızlık; **in.ad¹vert.ent** ☐ dikkatsiz; kasıtsız; ~ly istemeyerek, kasıtsız olarak.

**in.ad.vis.a.ble** ☐ [inəd¹vaizəbl] tavsiye edilmez; akla yakın olmayan, makul olmayan.

**in.al.ien.a.ble** ☐ [in¹eiljənəbl] geri verilemez, devrolunamaz, satılamaz.

**in.al.ter.a.ble** ☐ [in¹ɔːltərəbl] değiş(tirile)mez.

**in.am.o.ra.ta** [inæməˡrɑːtə] *n.* sevgili, sevilen kadın, âşık olunan kadın; **in.amoˡra.to** [~təu] *n.* âşık kadın.

**in.ane** ☐ [i¹nein] *mst fig.* boş, anlamsız, aptalca; budala, ahmak.

**in.an.i.mate** ☐ [in¹ænimit] cansız, ruhsuz, ölü; *fig.* donuk, sönük, sıkıcı.

**in.a.ni.tion** ⚇ [inəˡniʃən] *n.* zafiyet; boşluk.

**in.an.i.ty** [i¹næniti] *n.* anlamsızlık; boş laf, anlamsız söz (s. inane).

**in.ap.pli.ca.bil.i.ty** [¹inæplikəˡbiliti] *n.* uygun olmama, tatbik edilememe; **in¹ap.plica.ble** *adj.* uymaz, tatbik edilemez (to -e); ilgisiz, alâkasız.

**in.ap.po.site** ☐ [in¹æpəzit] uygunsuz, münasebetsiz.

**in.ap.pre.ci.a.ble** ☐ [inəˡpriːʃəbl] takdir edilemez; azıcık, cüzî.

**in.ap.pre.hen.si.ble** ☐ [inæpri¹hensəbl] anlaşılmaz, idrak edilemez.

**in.ap.proach.a.ble** [inəˡprəutʃəbl] *adj.* yaklaşılamaz, erişilemez.

**in.ap.pro.pri.ate** ☐ [inəˡprəupriit] münasebetsiz, uygunsuz, yakışmaz.

**in.apt** ☐ [in¹æpt] beceriksiz, yeteneksiz, hünersiz; uygunsuz, yakışıksız; **in¹apt.itude** [~titjuːd], **in¹apt.ness** *n.* yeteneksizlik, kabiliyetsizlik; uygunsuzluk.

**in.ar.tic.u.late** ☐ [inɑː¹tikjulit] anlaşılmaz, açık seçik olmayan, belirsiz; iyi birleşmemiş; derdini anlatmaktan âciz; mafsalsız. oynak yeri olmayan; açıkça konuşmayan; **in.ar¹tic.u.late.ness** *n.* derdini anlatamama; anlaşılmazlık, belirsizlik.

**in.as.much** [inəz¹mʌtʃ]: ~ as madem ki, çünkü, -i göz önünde bulundurarak.

**in.at.ten.tion** [inə¹tenʃən] *n.* dikkatsizlik, ihmal; **in.at¹ten.tive** ☐ [~tiv] dikkatsiz, ihmalkâr, dikkat etmeyen (to -e).

**in.au.di.ble** ☐ [in¹ɔːdəbl] işitilemez, duyulamaz.

**in.au.gu.ral** [i¹nɔːgjurəl] **1.** *adj.* açılışa ait, açılış...; ~ lecture açılış konuşması; **2.** *n.* açılış konuşması; açılış töreni; **in¹augu.rate** [~reit] *v/t.* açmak; törenle göreve getirmek; törenle başlamak -e; başlatmak; **in.au.gu¹ra.tion** *n.* resmen göreve başlama; açılış (töreni); ♀ Day *Am.* Amerika Cumhurbaşkanı'nın resmen göreve başladığı gün. .

**in.aus.pi.cious** ☐ [inɔːs¹piʃəs] uğursuz.

**in.board** ⚓ [¹inbɔːd] **1.** *adj.* geminin içindeki; **2.** *adv.* geminin içinde, bordalarında.

**in.born** [¹in¹bɔːn] *adj.* doğuştan, fıtrî, tabii, yaradılıştan.

**in.bred** [¹in¹bred] *adj.* tabii, yaradılıştan, fıtrî, doğuştan, tanrı vergisi; aynı soydan gelen hayvanların dölünden elde edilmiş.

**in.breed.ing** [¹in¹briːdiŋ] *n.* aynı soy ve cinsten hayvan ve bitkilerin çiftleştirilmesi.

**in.cal.cul.a.ble** ☐ [in¹kælkjuləbl] hesap edilemez, hesaplanamaz, hesap edilemeyecek kadar; belirsiz, kararsız, dönek, değişken.

**in.can.des.cence** [¹inkæn¹desns] *n.* akkorluk; **¹in.can¹des.cent** *adj.* akkor; ~ light akkor ışık; ~ mantle akkor gaz fitili.

**in.can.ta.tion** [inkæn¹teiʃən] *n.* büyü, sihir; sihirli söz.

**in.ca.pa.bil.i.ty** [inkeipə¹biliti] *n.* güçsüzlük, yetersizlik, âcizlik, ehliyetsizlik; kabiliyetsizlik, iktidarsızlık; **in¹ca.pa.ble** ☐ güçsüz, yeteneksiz, kabiliyetsiz, kudretsiz, iktidarsız, ehliyetsiz, âciz (of -den); **in.ca.pac.i.tate** [inkə¹pæsiteit] *v/t.* kudretsizleştirmek, kuvvetten düşürmek, zayıflatmak (for, from -de); **in.ca¹pac.i.ty** *n.* kabiliyetsizlik, güçsüzlük, yetkisizlik, ehliyetsizlik, salahiyetsizlik (for için, -de).

**in.car.cer.ate** [in¹kɑːsəreit] *v/t.* hapsetmek, kapatmak; **in.car.cer¹a.tion** *n.* hapsetme, hapsedilme.

**in.car.nate** **1.** [in¹kɑːnit] *adj.* vücudu olan, vücutlu, vücut bulmuş, insan şekline girmiş; *fig.* şahıslanmış, cisimlenmiş; **2.** [¹inkɑːneit] *v/t.* vücut kazandırmak, canlandırmak; *fig.* cisimlendirmek; **in.car¹na.tion** *n.* belirme, canlanma, vücut bulma; *fig.* cisimlenme.

**in.case** [in¹keis] = encase.

**in.cau.tious** ☐ [in¹kɔːʃəs] düşüncesiz, tedbirsiz, dikkatsiz, ihtiyatsız; **in¹cau.tiousness** *n.* düşüncesizlik, tedbirsizlik, dikkatsizlik.

**in.cen.di.ar.y** [in'sendjəri] **1.** *adj.* yangın çıkarıcı, kasten yangın çıkaran; çok ısı meydana getirebilen; *fig.* tahrik edici, ortalığı karıştırıcı; ~ (bomb) yangın bombası; **2.** *n.* kundakçı; ortalığı karıştıran kimse.

**in.cense**[1] ['insens] **1.** *n.* tütsü, buhur, günlük; **2.** *v/t.* tütsülemek; günlük yakmak.

**in.cense**[2] [in'sens] *v/t.* öfkelendirmek, kızdırmak, darıltmak (with *hususunda*).

**in.cen.tive** [in'sentiv] **1.** *adj.* teşvik edici; harekete geçirici; **2.** *n.* dürtü, saik, güdü.

**in.cep.tion** [in'sepʃən] *n.* başlama, başlangıç; **in'cep.tive** [~tiv] *adj.* başlayan..., başlayıcı...; *gr.* bir hareketin başladığını gösteren (*fiil*).

**in.cer.ti.tude** [in'səːtitjuːd] *n.* belirsizlik, kararsızlık; şüphe, tereddüt.

**in.ces.sant** ☐ [in'sesnt] sürekli, devamlı, daimî, ardı arkası kesilmeyen.

**in.cest** ['insest] *n.* akraba arasında cinsi temas, akraba ile zina; **in.ces.tu.ous** ☐ [in'sestjuəs] akrabası ile cinsi temasta buiunmuş; akraba ile zina kabilinden.

**inch** [intʃ] *n.* pus (*2,54 cm*), inç; *fig.* az miktar; ~es *pl.* boy; by ~es yavaş yavaş, ağır ağır, azar azar, kıl payı; every ~ tepeden tırnağa, tamamiyle, tam manasıyla; **inched** *comb.* ...inçlik.

**in.cho.a.tive** ['inkəueitiv] *adj.* başlayan, başlayıcı; *gr.* bir hareketin başladığını gösteren (*zaman, kip*).

**in.ci.dence** ['insidəns] *n.* isabet, tesadüf etme; tekrar oranı; oluş derecesi; **angle** of ~ geliş açısı; **'in.ci.dent 1.** *adj.* bağlı, tabi (to ~e); **2.** *n.* olay, vaka, hadise; önemsiz olay; *thea.* perde; **in.ci.den.tal** ☐ [~'dentl] tesadüfi..., rastlantıya bağlı...; küçük ve önemsiz; doğal olarak takip eden...; be ~ to ~e bağlı olm., ait olm.; ~ly tesadüfen, şans eseri, şansa; aklıma gelmişken.

**in.cin.er.ate** [in'sinəreit] *v/t.* yakıp kül etm.; **in.cin.er'a.tion** *n.* yakıp kül etme; **in'cin.er.a.tor** *n.* (işe yaramaz *maddelerin yakıldığı*) fırın, ocak.

**in.cip.i.en.cy** [in'sipiənsi] *n.* başlangıç; **in'cip.i.ent** *adj.* başlangıç halinde, yeni başlayan...

**in.cise** [in'saiz] *v/t.* oymak, hakketmek; **in.ci.sion** [~'siʒən] *n.* yarma, deşme, kesme; ♀ ensizyon, yarık; **in.ci.sive** ☐ [~'saisiv] sivri, keskin; zeki, açıkgöz; açık seçik; **in.ci.sor** [~'saizə] *n.* ön diş, kesici diş.

**in.ci.ta.tion** [insai'teiʃən] = **incitement**; **in'cite** *v/t.* teşvik etm., tahrik etm., kış-

kırtmak; **in'cite.ment** *n.* teşvik, tahrik, kışkırtma.

**in.ci.vil.i.ty** [insi'viliti] *n.* kabalık, nezaketsizlik; kaba davranış *veya* söz.

**in.clem.en.cy** [in'klemənsi] *n.* fırtınalı, (*veya* sert, şiddetli, soğuk) hava; **in'clem.ent** *adj.* sert, fırtınalı, şiddetli, soğuk (*hava*).

**in.cli.na.tion** [inkli'neiʃən] *n.* meyil, eğilim, yatma; bayır, yokuş, eğiklik; *fig.* istek, rağbet, heves; **in.cline** [~'klain] **1.** *v/t.* & *v/i.* eğ(il)mek, meylet(tir)mek, yat(ır)mak; ~d plane eğri yüzey; ~ to *fig.* ~e meyletmek, eğilim göstermek; **2.** *n.* eğri yüzey; yokuş, meyil, eğilme.

**in.close** [in'kləuz], **in'clos.ure** [~ʒə] = enclose, enclosure.

**in.clude** [in'kluːd] *v/t.* içine almak, dahil etm., kapsamak, ihtiva etm., hesaba katmak.

**in.clu.sion** [in'kluːʒən] *n.* dahil olma, dahil etme, kapsama, hesaba kat(ıl)ma; **in'clu.sive** [~siv] *adj.* kapsayan, dahil, ihtiva eden, içine alan; be ~ of dahil olm., katılmış olm.; ~ terms *pl.* herşey dahil olan fiyatlar.

**in.cog** F [in'kɔg], **in'cog.ni.to** [~'niːtəu] **1.** *adv.* takma adla; kıyafet değiştirerek; **2.** *n.* takma ad.

**in.co.her.ence**, **in.co.her.en.cy** [inkəu-'hiərəns(i)] *n.* anlaşılmazlık, manasızlık, tutarsızlık; **in.co'her.ent** ☐ anlaşılmaz, manasız, tutarsız, abuk sabuk.

**in.com.bus.ti.ble** ☐ [inkəm'bʌstəbl] yanmaz, ateş almaz, tutuşmaz.

**in.come** ['inkʌm] *n.* gelir, irat, kazanç; **'in.com.er** *n.* yeni gelen; muhacir; ⚄ yerine geçen, halef, ardıl; **in.come-tax** ['inkəmtæks] *n.* gelir vergisi.

**in.com.ing** ['inkʌmiŋ] **1.** *n.* girme, geliş, varış; ~s *pl.* gelir, kazanç; **2.** *adj.* gelen, varan; yeni gelen; göreve yeni başlayan.

**in.com.men.su.ra.bil.i.ty** ['inkəmenʃərə'biliti] *n.* nisbetsizlik, kıyas kabul etmezlik, ölçülemezlik, karşılaştırılamaz olma; **in.com'men.su.ra.ble** ☐ oransız, nisbetsiz, kıyaslanamaz, ölçülemez, orantı kabul etmez; **in.com'men.su.rate** [~rit] *adj.* orantısız, nisbetsiz, kıyaslanamaz (with, to *ile*); = incommensurable.

**in.com.mode** [inkə'məud] *v/t.* rahatsız etm., zahmet vermek, tedirgin etm.; **in.com'mo.di.ous** ☐ [~djəs] rahatsız, kullanışsız; zahmetli, işe yaramaz.

**in.com.mu.ni.ca.ble** ☐ [inkə'mjuːnikəbl] ☐ ifade edilemez, söylenilemez; nakledilemez; **in.com.mu.ni.ca.do** *part.* Am. [~ ˈkɑːdəu] *adj.* kimseyle görüştürülmeyen *(hapiste)*; **in.comˈmu.ni.ca.tive** ☐ [~kətiv] fikrini başkasına açıklamayan, ağzı sıkı, ağzı pek.

**in.com.mut.a.ble** ☐ [inkəˈmjuːtəbl] değiş(tirile)mez.

**in.com.pa.ra.ble** ☐ [inˈkɔmpərəbl] emsalsiz, eşsiz; kıyas kabul etmez, karşılaştırılamaz.

**in.com.pat.i.bil.i.ty** [ˈinkəmpætəˈbiliti] *n.* uygunsuzluk, birbirine uymama, tutarsızlık; **in.comˈpat.i.ble** ☐ birbirine uymayan, birbirine zıt, tutarsız, bir diğerine uymayan.

**in.com.pe.tence,    in.com.pe.ten.cy** [inˈkɔmpitəns(i)] *n.* ehliyetsizlik, yetersizlik, işinin ehli olmama; **inˈcom.pe.tent** ☐ ehliyetsiz, yetersiz, kifayetsiz, işinin ehli olmayan.

**in.com.plete** ☐ [inkəmˈpliːt] tam olmayan, eksik, noksan, bitmemiş, kusurlu.

**in.com.pre.hen.si.bil.i.ty** [inkəmprihensəˈbiliti] *n.* anlaşılmazlık; **in.com.preˈhensible** ☐ anlaşılamaz, kavranmaz, akıl ermez; **in.com.preˈhen.sion** *n.* anlayışsızlık, akıl erdirememe, kavrayamama.

**in.com.press.i.ble** [inkəmˈpresəbl] *adj.* sıkıştırılamaz; sert ve dayanıklı.

**in.con.ceiv.a.ble** ☐ [inkənˈsiːvəbl] tasavvur olunamaz, anlaşılamaz, inanılmaz; idrak edilemez, kavranamaz.

**in.con.clu.sive** ☐ [inkənˈkluːsiv] sonuçsuz, neticesiz, bir sonuca varmayan, ikna edici olmayan, kifayetsiz, yetersiz; **in.conˈclu.sive.ness** *n.* sonuçsuzluk, neticesizlik, bir sonuca varmama.

**in.con.gru.i.ty** [inkɔŋˈgruːiti] *n.* uyuşmazlık, uyumsuzluk;   uyuşmayan şey; **inˈcon.gru.ous** ☐ [~gruəs] uymayan, uyuşmaz, bağdaşmaz, uyumsuz, aykırı (with *ile*); uygunsuz, yersiz, münasebetsiz.

**in.con.se.quence** [inˈkɔnsikwəns] *n.* mantıksızlık; irtibatsızlık,  birbirini tutmama; **inˈcon.se.quent** ☐ mantıksız, birbirini tutmaz, irtibatsız; **in.con.se.quen.tial** [~ˈkwenʃəl] *adj.* önemsiz; = inconsequent.

**in.con.sid.er.a.ble** ☐ [inkənˈsidərəbl] önemsiz, ehemmiyetsiz, düşünmeye değmez; ufak, küçük, az; **in.conˈsid.er.ate** ☐ [~rit] düşüncesiz, saygısız, terbiyesiz (towards *-e karşı*); tedbirsiz, ihtiyatsız; **in.conˈsid.er.ate.ness** *n.* düşüncesizlik, saygısızlık, tedbirsizlik.

**in.con.sist.en.cy** [inkənˈsistənsi] *n.* tutarsızlık, uyuşmazlık, uyumsuzluk; zıtlık, tezatlık; **in.conˈsist.ent** ☐ kararsız, se

batsız; uyuşmaz, uyumsuz, aykırı, tutarsız.

**in.con.sol.a.ble** ☐ [inkənˈsəuləbl] teselli edilemez, avutulamaz.

**in.con.spic.u.ous** ☐ [inkənˈspikjuəs] önemsiz, ehemmiyetsiz; göze çarpmayan, farkedilemeyen.

**in.con.stan.cy** [inˈkɔnstənsi] *n.* kararsızlık, değişkenlik, döneklik; vefasızlık; **inˈconstant** ☐ kararsız, dönek, değişken; vefasız.

**in.con.test.a.ble** ☐ [inkənˈtestəbl] malûm, bilinen, su götürmez, inkâr edilemez, muhakkak, itiraz kaldırmaz.

**in.con.ti.nence** [inˈkɔntinəns] *n.* kendini tutamama, nefsine hâkim olamama; ~ of urine ⚡ idrarını tutamama; **inˈcon.ti.nent** ☐ kendini tutamayan, nefsine hâkim olamayan; iradesiz; idrarını tutamayan; ~ly kendini tutamayarak; hemen, derhal.

**in.con.tro.vert.i.ble** ☐ [ˈinkɔntrəˈvəːtəbl] itiraz kabul etmez, tartışma götürmez, su götürmez, muhakkak.

**in.con.ven.ience** [inkənˈviːnjəns] **1.** *n.* zahmet, rahatsızlık, güçlük, zorluk; uygunsuzluk, münasebetsizlik; **2.** *v/t.* zahmet vermek, rahatsız etm.; **inˈcon.ven.ient** ☐ zahmetli, müşkül, güç, zor, çetin; uygunsuz, elverişsiz, münasebetsiz (to *için, -e*).

**in.con.vert.i.bil.i.ty** [ˈinkənvəːtəˈbiliti] *n.* değiştirilemezlik; ✝ altına çevrilemez olma; **in.conˈvert.i.ble** ☐ değiştirilemez; ✝ altına çevrilemez (para).

**in.con.vin.ci.ble** ☐ [inkənˈvinsəbl] inandırılamaz, kandırılamaz, ikna edilemez.

**in.cor.po.rate** **1.** [inˈkɔːpəreit] *v/t. & v/i.* birleş(tir)mek (into *-e*); 🏛 anonim şirket haline getirmek; biraraya getirmek; biraraya gelmek; **2.** [inˈkɔːpərit] *adj.* anonim...; birleşik, birleşmiş...; **inˈcorpo.rat.ed** [~reitid] *adj.* anonim; **in.corpoˈra.tion** *n.* birleş(tir)me; şirket, tüzel kişi.

**in.cor.po.re.al** ☐ [inkɔːˈpɔːriəl] tinsel, manevî, ruhanî, cisimsiz.

**in.cor.rect** ☐ [inkəˈrekt] yanlış, hatalı, kusurlu; uygunsuz, yakışıksız, yakışmaz, münasebetsiz; **in.corˈrect.ness** *n.* hata, kusur, yanlış.

**in.cor.ri.gi.bil.i.ty** [inkɔridʒəˈbiliti] *n.* yola getirilemez olma, ıslah edilememe, düzeltilememe; **inˈcor.ri.gi.ble** ☐ düzelmez, ıslah edilemez, değiştirilemez, yerleşmiş.

**in.cor.rupt.i.bil.i.ty** [ˈinkərʌptəˈbiliti] *n.* dürüstlük, rüşvet yememe; bozulmazlık, çürümezlik; **in.corˈrupt.i.ble** ☐ dürüst, rüşvet yemeyen; bozulmaz, çürümez, kokuşmaz.

**In.crease 1.** [in'kri:s] *v/t.* & *v/i.* art(tır)-mak, çoğal(t)mak, büyü(t)mek, geliş-(tir)mek, verimlen(dir)mek; **2.** ['inkri:s] *n.* çoğalma, artma, büyüme; üreme, yav-rulama, döl; in'creas.ing.ly *adv.* gittikçe artarak; ~ difficult gittikçe zorlaşan.

**in.cred.i.bil.i.ty** [inkredi'biliti] *n.* inanıl-mazlık, inanılmaz hal; in'cred.i.ble □ [~dəbl] inanılmaz.

**in.cre.du.li.ty** [inkri'dju:liti] *n.* inanılmaz-lık, kuşku, şüphecilik; in.cred.u.lous □ [in'kredjuləs] inanmaz; güvenmez, kuş-kulu, kuşkusu olan.

**in.cre.ment** ['inkrimənt] *n.* artma, çoğal-ma, kâr, fazlalık.

**in.crim.i.nate** [in'krimineit] *v/t.* suçlamak, suç yüklemek *-e*; in'crim.i.na.to.ry [~nətəri] *adj.* suçlayıcı.

**in.crust** [in'krʌst] = encrust; in.crus'ta-tion *n.* üstü kabuk bağlama, kabuk tut-ma, kabuklanma; ⊕ kaplama.

**in.cu.bate** ['inkjubeit] *v/t.* üstüne otura-rak *veya* sıcak ısı ile çıkarmak *(civciv)*; uygun şartlarda geliştirmek *(bakteri)*; *v/i.* kuluçkaya yatmak; in.cu'ba.tion *n.* kuluçkaya yatma; *biol.*, ⚕ bir hastalığın vücuda girmesiyle ilk belirtilerinin or-taya çıkması arasındaki zamanda mik-ropların gelişmesi; 'in.cu.ba.tor *n.* kuluç-ka makinesi; kuvöz; in.cu.bus ['inkjubəs] *n.* kâbus, karabasan, ağırlık basması; kâbus gibi şey.

**in.cul.cate** ['inkʌlkeit] *v/t.* iyice kafasına sokmak, telkin etm., aşılamak (upon); in.cul'ca.tion *n.* telkin.

**in.cul.pate** ['inkʌlpeit] *v/t.* suçlamak, suç yüklemek; in.cul'pa.tion *n.* suçlama, it-ham; in'cul.pa.to.ry [~pətəri] *adj.* suçla-yıcı.

**in.cum.ben.cy** [in'kʌmbənsi] *n.* görev, va-zife, ödev; görev süresi; in'cum.bent 1. *adj.* zorunlu, mecburi, yükümlü, görev-li; be ~ on s.o. *b-ne* düşmek, *b-nin* vazi-fesi olm.; 2. *n. eccl.* görevli kimse, me-mur.

**in.cu.nab.u.la** [inkju:'næbjulə] *n. pl.* 1501 yılından önce basılmış kitaplar; eskiden kalma sanat eserleri.

**in.cur** [in'kə:] *v/t.* uğramak *-e*, girmek *-e*, yakalanmak *-e*, tutulmak *-e*, maruz kalmak *-e*.

**in.cur.a.bil.i.ty** [inkjuərə'biliti] *n.* tedavi edilemezlik, çaresizlik, şifa bulmazlık; in'cur.a.ble 1. □ şifa bulmaz, devasız, tedavi edilemez, iyileşmez; 2. *n.* şifasız hasta, tedavi edilemeyen hasta.

**in.cu.ri.ous** □ [in'kjuəriəs] meraksız, me-

raklı olmayan; kayıtsız, lâkayt, ilgisiz, dikkatsiz.

**in.cur.sion** [in'kə:ʃən] *n.* akın, hücum, bas-kın, saldırı; *fig.* tecavüz, el atma.

**in.cur.va.tion** [inkə:'veiʃən] *n.* eğme, bük-me; 'in'curve *v/t.* eğmek; bükmek.

**in.debt.ed** [in'detid] *adj.* borçlu (to *-e*); *fig.* minnettar, müteşekkir (to *-e*); in'debt.ed.ness *n.* borçluluk; borç miktarı.

**in.de.cen.cy** [in'di:snsi] *n.* ahlâksızlık; in'de.cent □ utanmaz, yüzsüz; edepsiz, ahlâksız, çirkin, kaba; 🕸 toplum töresi-ne aykırı.

**in.de.ci.pher.a.ble** [indi'saifərəbl] *adj.* okunmaz, çözülmez, sökülmez, anlaşıl-maz, karışık.

**in.de.ci.sion** [indi'siʒən] *n.* kararsızlık; te-reddüt, duraksama; in.de.ci.sive □ [~'saisiv] kararsız; kesin olmayan.

**in.de.clin.a.ble** [indi'klainəbl] *adj.* çe-kilmez, kipsiz.

**in.dec.o.rous** □ [in'dekərəs] edebe aykı-rı, ayıp, yakışmaz, çirkin, utandırıcı, uy-gunsuz, yakışık almaz; in'dec.o.rous-ness = in.de.co.rum [indi'ko:rəm] *n.* ede-be aykırı hareket, uygunsuz davranış, terbiyesizlik.

**in.deed** [in'di:d] **1.** *adv.* gerçekten, haki katen, doğrusu; **2.** *int.* öyle mi?

**in.de.fat.i.ga.ble** □ [indi'fætigəbl] yorul-maz, yorulmaz bilmez.

**in.de.fea.si.ble** □ [indi'fi:zəbl] feshedile-mez, iptal edilemez *(hak)*.

**in.de.fect.i.ble** □ [indi'fektəbl] çürümez, bozulmaz; hatasız, kusursuz.

**in.de.fen.si.ble** □ [indi'fensəbl] savunu-lamaz, savunmasız, müdafaasız; affedi-lemez, mazur görülemez.

**in.de.fin.a.ble** □ [indi'fainəbl] tarif edile-mez, tanımlanamaz, anlatılamaz.

**in.def.i.nite** □ [in'definit] belirsiz, bellisiz, şüpheli, bulanık; *gr.* belgisiz.

**in.del.i.ble** □ [in'delibl] silinmez, çıkmaz; ~ ink silinmez mürekkep; ~ pencil kopya kalemi.

**in.del.i.ca.cy** [in'delikəsi] *n.* kabalık, uy-gunsuzluk; kaba davranış *veya* söz; in'del.i.cate □ [~kit] kaba, nezaketsiz, ter-biyesiz.

**in.dem.ni.fi.ca.tion** [indemnifi'keiʃən] *n.* tazminat; in'dem.ni.fy [~fai] *v/t. -in* za-rarını ödemek (from, against *-e karşı*); geri ödemek, tazmin etm.; in'dem.ni.ty *n.* tazminat; kefalet, teminat, güvence.

**in.dent 1.** [in'dent] *v/t. -in* kenarını oy-mak, diş diş oymak; çentmek, kertmek; içerden başlamak, içerlek yazmak *(sa-tır)*; 🕸 senede bağlamak; † ısmarlamak, sipariş etm. (upon s.o. for s.th. *b-ne bş*); ~ed coastline girintili çıkıntılı sahil; *v/i.* anlaşma yapmak; çentik açmak; **2.** [ˈindent] *n.* çentik, kertik, bere; †́ yabancı ülkeden alınan sipariş; ✗ resmi emir; içerlek yazma; = indenture; **in-denˈta.tion** *n.* çentik, kertik, diş; çentme, kertme; içerlek yazma; girinti, oyuntu; **inˈden.tion** *n. typ.* içerlek yazma; **inˈden-ture** [~tʃə] **1.** *n.* sözleşme, senet, mukavele, iki taraflı kontrat; **2.** *v/t.* sözleşmeye bağlamak.

**in.de.pend.ence, in.de.pend.en.cy** [indiˈpendəns(i)] *n.* bağımsızlık, hürriyet, istiklâl; Independence Day *Am.* Birleşik Amerika'da Bağımsızlık Günü *(4 Temmuz);* **in.deˈpend.ent 1.** ☐ bağımsız, hür, özgür (of *-den);* başlı başına, ayrı, serbest; ~ means özel imkânlar; **2.** *n. pol.* bağımsız *(veya* parti üyesi olmayan) kimse.

**in.de.scrib.a.ble** ☐ [indisˈkraibəbl] tanımlanamaz, anlatılmaz, nitelendirilemez.

**in.de.struct.i.ble** ☐ [indisˈtrʌktəbl] yıkılmaz, tahrip edilemez, yok edilemez, bozulmaz, çok dayanıklı.

**in.de.ter.mi.na.ble** ☐ [indiˈtəːminəbl] çözümlenemez, halledilemez, karara bağlanamayan, kararlaştırılamaz; **in.deˈter-mi.nate** ☐ [~nit] belirsiz, bellisiz, bilinmeyen, şüpheli, belli olmayan; **in.deˈter-mi.nate.ness, in.de.ter.mi.na.tion** [ˈ~ˈneiʃən] *n.* belirsizlik, bilinmezlik.

**in.dex** [ˈindeks] **1.** *n., pl. a.* **in.di.ces** [ˈindisiːz] indeks, fihrist; gösterge, işaret, ibre; işaret parmağı; *eccl.* okunması yasak kitaplar listesi; *a.* ~ üs; *a.* ~ number indeks sayı; **2.** *v/t. -in* indeksini yapmak, indeks içine koymak.

**in.di.a.man** [ˈindjəmən] *n.* ↓ eskiden Hindistan ile yapılan ticarette kullanılan gemi.

**in.di.an** [ˈindjən] **1.** *adj.* Hindistan'a ait, Hindistan...; Amerika kızılderilisine ait; **2.** *n.* Hintli, Hint; Amerikan kızılderilisi; *a.* Red ~ kızılderili; ~ club lobut; ~ corn mısır; ~ file: in ~ tek sıra *(yürüyüş);* ~ ink çini mürekkebi; ~ pud.ding *Am.* mısır muhallebisi; ~ sum.mer pastırma yazı.

**India**...: ~ paper ince Çin kağıdı, pelür kağıdı; ˈȷrub.ber kauçuk, lastik.

**in.di.cate** [ˈindikeit] *v/t.* göstermek, işaret etm., belirtmek; **in.diˈca.tion** *n.* belirti, delil, kanıt; bildirme, belirtme, gösterme. işaret etme; **in.dic.a.tive** ☐ [inˈdikətiv] belirten, gösteren, bildiren (of *-i);* ~ mood *gr.* bildirme kipi; **in.di.ca.tor**

[ˈ~keitə] *n.* gösteren şey *veya* kimse, işaret eden şey, delil, belirti; ⊕ müşir, ibre, gösterge; *tel.* kayıt ibresi; **inˈdi.ca-to.ry** [~kətəri] *adj.* gösteren (of *-i);* belirtici..., işaret edici.

**in.di.ces** [ˈindisiːz] *pl. of.* index.

**in.dict** [inˈdait] *v/t.* suçlamak (for, on charge of *-den);* **inˈdict.a.ble** *adj.* suçlanabilir; **inˈdict.er** *n.* şikâyetçi, davacı; **inˈdict.ment** *n.* suçlama; iddianame.

**in.dif.fer.ence** [inˈdifrəns] *n.* aldırmazlık, kayıtsızlık, tasasızlık; hissizlik, duygusuzluk (to, towards *-e, -e karşı);* **inˈdif-fer.ent** ☐ kayıtsız, tasasız, aldırmaz, lakayt, umursamaz (to *-e);* şöyle böyle, orta derecede, vasat.

**in.di.gence** [ˈindidʒəns] *n.* fakirlik, yoksulluk, züğürtlük.

**in.di.gene** [ˈindidʒiːn] *n.* yerli insan, hayvan *veya* bitki; **inˈdig.e.nous** [~dʒinəs] *adj.* yerli; doğuştan ait (to *-e).*

**in.di.gent** ☐ [ˈindidʒənt] yoksul, fakir, züğürt.

**in.di.gest.ed** [indiˈdʒestid] *adj.* iyice düşünülmemiş; düzensiz, biçimsiz, intizamsız; sindirilmemiş, hazmolunmamış; **diˈgest.i.ble** ☐ sindirilemeyen, hazmı güç, hazmolunmaz; **in.diˈges.tion** *n.* hazımsızlık, mide fesadı.

**in.dig.nant** ☐ [inˈdignənt] dargın, öfkeli, kızgın, hiddetlenmiş (at *-e);* **in.digˈna-tion** *n.* dargınlık, öfke, kızgınlık, hiddet (with *hususunda);* ~ meeting bir haksızlığı protesto için yapılan toplantı; **inˈdig-ni.ty** [~niti] *n.* hürmetsizlik, saygısızlık, hakaret; kaba muamele *veya* söz.

**in.di.go** [ˈindigəu] *n.* çivit; ~ blue çivit mavisi.

**in.di.rect** ☐ [indiˈrekt] dolaşık, dolambaçlı, dolaylı, dolayısıyla olan; *gr. a.* dolaylı.

**in.dis.cern.i.ble** [indiˈsəːnəbl] *adj.* ayırt edilemez, seçilemez, farkına varılamaz.

**in.dis.ci.pline** [inˈdisiplin] *n.* disiplinsizlik, itaatsizlik.

**in.dis.creet** ☐ [indisˈkriːt] boşboğaz, patavatsız, geveze, ağzı gevşek, düşüncesiz, sağgörüsüz; **in.dis.cre.tion** [~ˈkreʃən] *n.* boşboğazlık, patavatsızlık, düşüncesizlik; düşüncesiz söz *veya* davranış.

**in.dis.crim.i.nate** ☐ [indisˈkriminit] gelişigüzel, rastgele, tesadüfi; karışık, karmaşık, karman çorman; = **in.disˈcrim.i-nat.ing** [~neitiŋ], **in.disˈcrim.i.na.tive** [~nətiv] farkı göremeyen, ayırt edemeyen, ayıramayan; *fig.* kör; **in.dis.crim.i-na.tion** [ˈ~ˈneiʃən] *n.* ayırt edememe, farkı görememe, birbirinden ayıramama.

**in.dis.pen.sa.ble** □ ₜindis'pensəbl] zaruri, zorunlu, elzem, mecburi, kaçınılmaz.

**in.dis.pose** [indis'pəuz] v/t. soğutmak, caydırmak, hevesini kırmak (towards, from -e karşı, -den); elverişsizleştirmek (for s.th, to inf. bş için, -mek için); **in.dis'posed** adj. rahatsız, keyifsiz; isteksiz (to -e karşı); **in.dis.po.si.tion** [indispə-'ziʃən] n. rahatsızlık, keyifsizlik; isteksizlik, gönülsüzlük (to -e karşı).

**in.dis.pu.ta.ble** □ ['indis'pju:təbl] söz götürmez, su götürmez, tartışma götürmez, şüphe götürmez, muhakkak.

**in.dis.so.lu.bil.i.ty** ['indisəlju'biliti] n. erimezlik, çözülmezlik; fig. bozulmazlık, ayrılmazlık, daimilik, süreklilik; **in.dis.so-lu.ble** □ [~'sɔljubl] erimez, çözülmez; fig. bozulmaz, ayrılmaz, sabit, sürekli, daimi.

**in.dis.tinct** □ [indis'tiŋkt] iyice görülmez, seçilmez, ayırt edilmez, bulanık, belirsiz, sönük; **in.dis'tinct.ness** n. belirsizlik, bulanıklık.

**in.dis.tin.guish.a.ble** □ [indis'tiŋgwiʃəbl] ayırt edilemez, seçilemez, fark edilemez.

**in.dite** [in'dait] v/t. kaleme almak, yazıya dökmek, yazmak; bestelemek.

**in.di.vid.u.al** [indi'vidjuəl] 1. □ bireysel, ferdî; tek, yalnız; ayrı, başlı başına, kendine özgü; 2. n. birey, fert, kimse, şahıs; **in.di'vid.u.al.ism** n. ferdiyetçilik, bireycilik; bencillik, kendini beğenmişlik, egoizm; **in.di'vid.u.al.ist** n. bireyci, ferdiyetçi, erkinci, liberal; **in.di.vid.u.al-i.ty** [~'æliti] n. ferdiyet, hususiyet, kendine özgülük; erkinlik; **in.di'vid.u.al.ize** [~əlaiz] v/t. bireyleştirmek, ferdileştirmek; tek tek ele almak.

**in.di.vis.i.bil.i.ty** ['indivizi'biliti] n. bölünmezlik; **in.di'vis.i.ble** □ bölünmez, taksim olunmaz.

**in.do...** ['indəu] prefix Hintli, Hint...

**in.doc.ile** [in'dəusail] adj. yola gelmez, adam olmaz, inatçı, serkeş; **in.do.cil.i.ty** [~'siliti] n. kolay yola getirilememe, adam edilememe.

**in.doc.tri.nate** [in'dɔktrineit] v/t. aşılamak (fikir), telkin etm., kafasını doldurmak (with ile).

**' in.do-Eu.ro.pe.an** ['indəujuərə'pi:ən] n. Hint-Avrupa dillerinden birini konuşan kimse.

**in.do.lence** ['indələns] n. tembellik, üşengeçlik; **'in.do.lent** □ tembel, üşengeç; ❡ ağrısız, acısız.

**in.dom.i.ta.ble** □ [in'dɔmitəbl] boyun eğmez, itaat etmez, direngen, inatçı, ayak direyici.

**in.door** ['indɔ:] adj. ev içinde olan, ev içinde yapılan; spor: ev içinde oynanan...; ~ aerial oda anteni; ~ game ev içinde oynanan oyun; ~ swimming-bath ev içindeki yüzme havuzu; **'in'doors** adv. ev içinde, evde; ev içine, eve.

**in.dorse** [in'dɔ:s], **in'dorse.ment**, etc = endorse, etc.

**in.du.bi.ta.ble** □ [in'dju:bitəbl] şüphe edilmez, kuşku duyulmaz, kati, kesin.

**in.duce** [in'dju:s] vb. teşvik etm., kandırıp yaptırmak, ikna etm.; sebep olm. -e, meydana getirmek, oluşturmak; ❢ indüklemek; ~d current ❢ indüksiyon cereyanı; **in'duce.ment** n. neden, sebep, vesile, dürtü, güdü; ikna, teşvik, tahrik.

**in.duct** [in'dʌkt] v/t. eccl. resmen göreve getirmek; üye olarak kabul etm.; askere almak; **in'duct.ance** n. ❢ indüktans; ~ coil indüktans bobini; **in'duc.tion** n. göreve getirme; başlama; askere alma; phls. tümevarım; phys. indüksiyon; **in-'duc.tive** □ phls. tümevarımsal, tümevarımlı...; phys. indüksiyon yapan, indüksiyon...

**in.due** [in'dju:] = endue.

**in.dulge** [in'dʌldʒ] v/t. müsamaha etm. -e, anlayış göstermek -e, hoşnut etm.; boyun eğmek -e (istek, kapris); şefkatle muamele etm. -e; v/i. düşkün olm., müptelâ olm., kapılmak (in -e); ~ with bşle sevindirmek, memnun etm.; ~ (o.s.) in s.th. -e kapılmak, -in müptelâsı olm.; **in'dul.gence** n. müsamaha, hoşgörü, göz yumma; düşkünlük, iptilâ (of, in -e); eccl. kilise tarafından cezanın affedilmesi; **in'dul.gent** □ müsamahakâr, hoşgörülü.

**in.du.rate** ['indjuəreit] v/t. & v/i. katılaş-(tır)mak, sertleş(tir)mek; sağlamlaş-(tır)mak; **in.du'ra.tion** n. katılaş(tır)ma, sertleş(tir)me; sağlamlaş(tır)ma.

**in.dus.tri.al** [in'dʌstriəl] 1. □ sınai, endüstriyel, endüstri ile ilgili...; ~ area endüstri alanı, sanayi sahası; ~ estate endüstri bölgesi; ~ school teknik okul; çocuk suçlular için sanayi okulu; 2. = in-'dus.tri.al.ist n. sanayici, fabrikatör; in-'dus.tri.al.ize [~laiz] v/t. & v/i. sanayileş(tir)mek; **in'dus.tri.ous** □ çalışkan, gayretli.

**in.dus.try** ['indəstri] n. sanayi, endüstri; çalışkanlık, gayret; heavy industries pl. ağır sanayi.

**in.dwell** ['in'dwel] (irr. dwell) vb. oturmak, ikamet etm.; fig. içinde olm.

**in.e.bri.ate 1.** [i'ni:brieit] v/t. sarhoş etm., mest etm., kafayı buldurmak; **2.** [~briit] adj. sarhoş, mest; 3. [~briit] n. sarhoş kimse; in.e.bri'a.tion, in.e.bri.e.ty [~'braiəti] n. sarhoşluk, ayyaşlık.

in.ed.i.ble [in'edibl] adj. yenmez.

in.ed.it.ed [in'editid] adj. yayınlanmamış.

in.ef.fa.ble [] [in'efəbl] tarif olunamaz, anlatılamaz; söylenemez, ağıza alınmaz.

in.ef.face.a.ble [] [ini'feisəbl] silinemez.

in.ef.fec.tive [ini'fektiv], in.ef'fec.tu.al [] [~tʃuəl] etkisiz, tesirsiz; başarısız; (part. X) kabiliyetsiz, beceriksiz, âciz.

in.ef.fi.ca.cious [] [inefi'keiʃəs] etkisiz, tesirsiz, yetersiz; in'ef.fi.ca.cy [~kəsi] n. tesirsizlik, etkisizlik, yetersizlik.

in.ef.fi.cien.cy [ini'fiʃənsi] n. etkisizlik, tesirsizlik, verimsizlik, randımansızlık; in-ef'fi.cient [] etkisiz, tesirsiz, verimsiz, randımansız.

in.el.e.gance [in'eligəns] n. zarafetsizlik, çirkinlik, incelikten yoksunluk; in'el.e-gant [] zarafetsiz, çirkin, incelikten yoksun.

in.el.i.gi.bil.i.ty [inelidʒə'biliti] n. uygun olmama, münasip olmama, yeterli niteliği olmama; in'el.i.gi.ble [] uygun olmayan, yeterli niteliği olmayan; part. X hizmete yaramaz, çürük.

in.e.luc.ta.ble [ini'lʌktəbl] adj. kaçınılamaz.

in.ept [] [i'nept] yersiz, uygunsuz, aptalca; hünersiz, beceriksiz, toy; in'ept.i.tude [~titju:d], in'ept.ness n. beceriksizlik; yersizlik; yersiz söz veya davranış.

in.e.qual.i.ty [ini:'kwɔliti] n. eşitsizlik, farklılık; düzensizlik, intizamsızlık.

in.eq.ui.ta.ble [] [in'ekwitəbl] insafsız, haksız, adaletsiz; in'eq.ui.ty n. insafsızlık, haksızlık, adaletsizlik.

in.e.rad.i.ca.ble [] [ini'rædikəbl] sökülemez, kökünden çıkarılamaz, giderilmesi olanaksız.

in.ert [i'nə:t] [] hareketsiz, süreduran; tembel, uyuşuk, ağır; tesirsiz; in.er.tia [i'nə:ʃiə], in'ert.ness n. atalet, süredurum; tembellik, uyuşukluk.

in.es.cap.a.ble [inis'keipəbl] adj. kaçınılamaz.

in.es.sen.tial [ini'senʃəl] adj. gereksiz, lüzumsuz (to -e).

in.es.ti.ma.ble [] [in'estiməbl] hesaplanamaz, hesaba sığmaz; çok kıymetli, paha biçilmez.

in.ev.i.ta.ble [] [in'evitəbl] kaçınılamaz, sakınılamaz, çaresiz; in'ev.i.ta.ble.ness n. kaçınılmazlık; in'ev.i.ta.bly adv. kaçınılmaz surette.

in.ex.act [] [inig'zækt] doğru olmayan, yanlış, hatalı; in.ex'act.i.tude [~titju:d],

in.ex'act.ness n. tam doğru olmama, yanlışlık, hata.

in.ex.cus.a.ble [] [iniks'kju:zəbl] affedilemez, bağışlanamaz, mazur görülemez.

in.ex.haust.i.bil.i.ty [i'inigzɔ:stə'biliti] n. yorulmazlık; bitmeme, tükenmeme; in.ex-'haust.i.ble [] tükenmez, bitmez; yorulmaz.

in.ex.o.ra.bil.i.ty [ineksərə'biliti] n. merhametsizlik, amansızlık, insafsızlık; boyun eğmezlik, direngenlik; in'ex.o.ra.ble [] merhametsiz, insafsız; boyun eğmez, direngen.

in.ex.pe.di.en.cy [iniks'pi:djənsi] n. uygunsuzluk, münasebetsizlik; in.ex'pe.di.ent [] uygunsuz, münasebetsiz.

in.ex.pen.sive [] [iniks'pensiv] ucuz, masrafı az.

in.ex.pe.ri.ence [ineks'piəriəns] n. tecrübesizlik, deneyimsizlik, acemilik; in.ex-'pe.ri.enced adj. tecrübesiz, deneyimsiz, acemi.

in.ex.pert [] [in'ekspə:t] acemi, tecrübesiz, deneyimsiz.

in.ex.pi.a.ble [] [in'ekspiəbl] kefaretle ödenemez (suç); yatıştırılamaz, bastırılamaz (öfke).

in.ex.pli.ca.ble [] [in'eksplikəbl] izah edilemez, açıklanamaz.

in.ex.press.i.ble [] [iniks'presəbl] ifade edilemez, anlatılamaz, tarif edilemez.

in.ex.pres.sive [] [iniks'presiv] anlatımsız, ifade etmeyen; in.ex'pres.sive.ness n. anlatımsızlık.

in.ex.tin.guish.able [] [iniks'tingwiʃəbl] söndürülemez; bastırılamaz, yatıştırılamaz (öfke).

in.ex.tri.ca.ble [] [in'ekstrikəbl] sökülemez, içinden çıkılmaz, çözümlenemez; kaçınılmaz; karmaşık, karman çorman.

in.fal.li.bil.i.ty [infælə'biliti] n. yanılmazlık; şaşmazlık; in'fal.li.ble [] yanılmaz, şaşmaz.

in.fa.mous [] ['infəməs] ahlâkı bozuk, rezil, kepaze, adı çıkmış; utanç verici, ayıp; 'in.fa.my n. rezalet, kepazelik; utanç verici davranış.

in.fan.cy ['infənsi] n. çocukluk, bebeklik, küçüklük; ȫȫ ergin olmama, reşit olmama; başlangıç; in its ~ başlangıcında; in.fant ['infənt] 1. n. küçük çocuk, bebek; ȫȫ ergin (veya reşit) olmayan kimse; ~ school anaokulu, çocuk yuvası; 2. adj. çocuksu, çocuk...; başlangıç safhasında olan.

in.fan.ta [in'fæntə] n. Portekiz veya İspanya prensesi; in'fan.te [~ti] Portekiz *veya* İspanya prensi.

**In.fan.ti.cide** [in'fæntisaid] *n.* çocuk öldürme; istenmeyen yeni çocukları öldürme; çocuk katili; **In.fan.tile** ['infəntail] *adj.* çocuğa ait, çocukça, çocuk...; ~ paralysis çocuk felci; **In.fan.tine** ['-tain] = infantile.

**In.fan.try** X ['infəntri] *n.* piyade, yaya asker; 'In.fan.try.man *n.* piyade, yaya er.

**In.fat.u.ate** [in'fætjueit] *v/t.* çıldırtmak, aklını çelmek, kara sevdaya düşürmek; ~d meftun, deli gibi âşık (with -e); **In.fat.u'a.tion** *n.* delicesine sevdalanma, kara sevdaya düşme (for *için*).

**In.fect** [in'fekt] *v/t.* bulaştırmak, geçirmek (*a. fig.*); become ~ed yakalanmak (*hastalık*); **In'fec.tion** *n.* bulaş(tır)ma, geç(ir)me; **In'fec.tious** □, **In'fec.tive** [~tiv] bulaşıcı, bulaşık...; başkalarına hemen geçen (*gülme, neşe*).

**In.fe.lic.i.tous** [infi'lisitəs] *adj.* açıklaması zor, anlaşılması güç, beceriksizce yapılmış, münasebetsiz; **In.fe'lic.i.ty** *n.* uygunsuz söz *veya* davranış, talihsizlik, hoşnutsuzluk.

**In.fer** [in'fə:] *v/t.* anlamak, çıkarmak, sonuca varmak (from -*den*); **In'fer.a.ble** *adj.* anlaşılır; **In.fer.ence** ['infərəns] *n.* sonuç çıkarma; netice, sonuç; **In.fer.en.tial** [~'renʃəl] sonuç olarak çıkarılabilir; **In.fer'en.tial.ly** *adv.* dolayısıyle anlayarak, sonuca vararak.

**In.fe.ri.or** [in'fiəriə] 1. *adj.* aşağı, alt; ikinci derecede, adi, bayağı; ast; önemi az; 2. *n.* aşağı derecede olan kimse *veya* şey; **In.fe.ri.or.i.ty** [~ri'ɔriti] *n.* aşağılık, adilik, bayağılık; ~ complex aşağılık duygusu.

**In.fer.nal** □ [in'fə:nl] cehenneme ait, cehennemi...; şeytanca..., şeytani...; F iğrenç, berbat; ~ machine suikast bombası; **In'fer.no** [~nəu] *n.* cehennem; cehennem gibi yer.

**In.fer.tile** [in'fə:tail] *adj.* verimsiz, kısır, kıraç, çorak; **In.fer.til.i.ty** [~'tiliti] *n.* verimsizlik; kıraçlık.

**In.fest** [in'fest] *v/t.* zarar vermek -*e*; *fig.* sarmak, istilâ etm. (*bit, kurt, fare*); **In.fes'ta.tion** *n.* istilâ (*bit, kurt, fare*).

**In.fi.del** [infidəl] 1. *adj.* kâfir, imansız; 2. *n.* kâfir kimse; **In.fi.del.i.ty** [~'deliti] *n.* sadakatsizlik, hıyanet (to -*e*); zina; imansızlık, kâfirlik.

**In.field** ['infi:ld] *n.* kriket, beysbol: dört esas çizgi dahilindeki saha; bu saha oyuncuları.

**In.fight.ing** ['infaitiŋ] *n.* boks: yakın dövüş.

**In.fil.trate** ['infiltreit] *v/t.* & *v/i.* süz(ül)-mek; girmek; içeri süzülmek, nüfuz etm.; **In.fil'tra.tion** *n.* süz(ül)me.

**In.fi.nite** □ ['infinit] sonsuz, nihayetsiz, hudutsuz, bitmez, tükenmez, pek çok, sayısız; **In.fin.i.tes.i.mal** [~'tesiməl] *adj.* bölünemeyecek kadar küçük, parçalara ayrılamayan; **In'fin.i.tive** *n.* gr. *a.* ~ mood mastar; **In'fin.i.tude** [~tju:d], **In'fin.i.ty** *n.* sonsuzluk, nihayetsizlik.

**In.firm** □ [in'fə:m] zayıf, kuvvetsiz, halsiz; hastalıklı; ~ of purpose amaçsız; kararsız; **In'fir.ma.ry** *n.* hastane; revir; **In'fir.mi.ty** *n.* zayıflık, hastalık, sakatlık; *fig.* kusur, hata, zaaf.

**In.fix** [in'fiks] *v/t.* tutturmak, bağlamak (in -*e*); kelimenin ortasına yerleştirmek; *fig.* telkin etm., aşılamak.

**In.flame** [in'fleim] *v/t.* & *v/i.* tutuş(tur)-mak, alevlen(dir)mek; *fig.* kızdırmak, öfkelen(dir)mek; ♈ iltihaplan(dır)mak.

**In.flam.ma.bil.i.ty** [inflæmə'biliti] *n.* tutuşabilme; **In'flam.ma.ble** 1. □ tutuşur, yanar, alev alır; parlar, çabuk kızar; 2. *n.* ~s *pl.* yanabilen maddeler; **In.flam.ma.tion** [inflə'meiʃən] *n.* iltihap(lanma), yangı, kızarıklık; alevlenme, tutuşma; **In.flam.ma.to.ry** [in'flæmətəri] *adj.* tahrik edici; iltihaplı...

**In.flate** [in'fleit] *v/t.* şişirmek; piyasaya çok sürmek (*para*); suni olarak yükseltmek (*fiyat*); *fig.* gururlandırmak; **In'flat.ed** *adj.* şiş(iril)miş; abartmalı, süslü; **In'fla.tion** *n.* şişkinlik; şiş(iril)me; ♈ enflasyon; *fig.* kendini beğenmişlik; **In'fla.tion.ar.y** ♈ [~ʃnəri] *adj.* enflasyon..., enflasyona neden olan; ~ spiral enflasyon sonucu ücretlerin artması.

**In.flect** [in'flekt] *v/t.* değiştirmek (*ses tonu*); kıvırmak, eğmek; *gr.* çekmek; **In'flec.tion** = inflexion.

**In.flex.i.bil.i.ty** [infleksə'biliti] *n.* eğilmezlik; *fig.* azim, kararlılık; **In'flex.i.ble** □ eğilmez, bükülmez; sarsılmaz; *fig.* azimli, kararlı; **In'flex.ion** [~ʃən] *n.* bükülme, eğilme, eğrilik; *gr.* çekim.

**In.flict** [in'flikt] *v/t.* getirmek, uğratmak, vermek (*ağrı, ceza*), atmak (*yumruk*) (on, upon s.o. *b-ne*); *fig.* yüklemek, yamamak (on -*e*); **In'flic.tion** *n.* ceza; sıkıntı, eziyet.

**In.flo.res.cence** ♈ [inflɔ:'resns] *n.* çiçeklenme; çiçeklerin sapları üzerindeki duruşu.

**In.flow** [infləu] = influx.

**In.flu.ence** ['influəns] 1. *n.* nüfuz, etki, tesir (with, on, upon -*e*); baskı, hüküm (on, upon -*e*); 2. *v/t.* etkilemek, tesir etm, sö-

zünü geçirmek; **in.flu.en.tial** □ [~'enʃəl]
sözü geçer, nüfuzlu.

**in.flu.en.za** ⁊ [influ'enzə] *n.* grip, enflü-
anza.

**in.flux** ['inflʌks] *n.* içeriye akma; *fig.* akın
*(turist vs.).*

**in.fold** [in'fəuld] = enfold.

**in.form** [in'fɔːm] *v/t.* haber vermek *-e*, bilgi vermek *-e* (of, about hakkında); bildirmek *-i*, söylemek *-i*; haberdar etm.
(s.o. of s.th. *b-ni bşden*); şekil vermek
*-e*, şekillendirmek *-i*; canlandırmak *-i*;
well ~ed bilgili; herşeyden haberi olan;
keep s.o. ~ed *b-ni* haberdar etm., *b-ne*
bilgi vermek; *v/i.* ihbar etm., şikayet
etm. (against s.o. *b-ni*); **in'for.mal** □ resmi olmayan, gayri resmi, teklifsiz, me-
rasimsiz, formalitesiz; **in.for.mal.i.ty**
[~'mæliti] *n.* teklifsizlik, resmiyetsizlik;
**in'form.ant** [~mənt] *n.* bilgi veren kimse,
ihbarcı; = **informer**; **in.for.ma.tion** [infə-
'meiʃən] *n.* bilgi, haber, malûmat; danışma; ȡ̃ iddia; gather ~ bilgi toplamak
(about *hakkında*); **in.form.a.tive** [in'fɔː-
mətiv] *adj.* aydınlatıcı, bilgi verici, eğitici; **in'form.er** *a.* common ~ muhbir, jurnalcı, ele veren kimse.

**in.fra** ['infrə] *adv.* aşağıda, altta; see ~
aşağıya bakınız *(kitap).*

**in.frac.tion** [in'frækʃən] *n.* suç, kurall bozma, kanuna karşı gelme.

**in.fra...:** ~ **dig** F ['infrə'dig] *adj.* şanına yakışmaz; **'~-'red** *adj. phys.* kızılötesi.

**in.fre.quen.cy** [in'friːkwənsi] *n.* seyreklik;
**in'fre.quent** [~] seyrek, nadir, az bulunur.

**in.fringe** [in'frindʒ] *vb. a.* ~ upon tecavüz
etm. *(hak)*; bozmak, ihlâl etm., çiğnemek *(kanun, kural, yemin)*; **in'fringe.
ment** *n.* tecavüz *(hak)*; bozma, ihlâl, çiğneme *(kanun, kural, yemin).*

**in.fu.ri.ate** [in'fjuərieit] *v/t.* çıldırtmak, çileden çıkartmak, küplere bindirtmek.

**in.fuse** [in'fjuːz] *v/t.* aşılamak, telkin etm.
(into *-e*); ⁀, *pharm.* suya batırmak;
demlendirmek *(çay)*; **in'fu.sion** [~ʒən] *n.*
suya batır(ıl)ma; demlendirme; demlen-
miş *veya* kaynamış sıvı *(çay, ilâç)*; karıştırma, katma; *fig.* telkin, aşılama; **in-
fu.so.ri.a** *zo.* [~ızɔ:riə] *n. pl.* haşlamlılar;
**in.fu'so.ri.al** *adj.* haşlamlı...

**in.gath.er.ing** ['ingæðəriŋ] *n.* hasat *(veya*
ürün) toplama.

**in.gen.ious** □ [in'dʒiːnjəs] hünerli, marifetli, becerikli; usta; zeki; yaratıcı; ustaca yapılmış; **in.ge.nu.i.ty** [indʒi'njuːiti]
*n.* hüner, marifet, maharet, yaratıcılık;
**in.gen.u.ous** □ [in'dʒenjuəs] açık, samimi, candan; masum, saf; doğal, tabii.

**in.gle** ['ingl] *n.* alev, ateş; şömine; köşe;
**'~-nook** *n.* baca kenarı, ocak başı.

**in.glo.ri.ous** □ [in'glɔːriəs] utanç verici,
yüz kızartıcı; alçakça, şerefsiz; tanınmamış, belirsiz.

**in.go.ing** ['ingəuiŋ] **1.** *n.* içeri girme; başlama; **2.** *adj.* içeri giren; başlayan.

**in.got** ['ingət] *n.* külçe; **'~-steel** *n.* akma
çelik.

**in.grain** [in'grein] *adj.* kökleşmiş; ham
iken boyanmış; *fig. a.* ~ed kökleşmiş,
yerleşmiş, tam.

**in.gra.ti.ate** [in'greiʃieit]: ~ o.s. *v/t.* çıkarı için yaltaklanmak, yağcılık yaparca-
sına sokulmak (with *-e*); **in.grat.i.tude**
[in'grætitjuːd] *n.* nankörlük.

**in.gre.di.ent** [in'griːdjənt] *n.* cüz, parça,
harç; *fig.* unsur.

**in.gress** ['ingres] *n.* giriş, girme; girme
yetkisi.

**in.grow.ing** ['ingrəuiŋ] *adj.* içe doğru büyüyen.

**in.gui.nal** *anat.* ['iŋgwinl] *adj.* kasığa ait;
kasık...

**in.gur.gi.tate** [in'gəːdʒiteit] *v/t.* oburcasına yutmak.

**in.hab.it** [in'hæbit] *v/t.* oturmak, ikamet
etm., sakin olm. *-de*; **in'hab.it.a.ble** *adj.*
oturulabilir, oturmaya elverişli; **in'hab-
it.an.cy** *n.* oturma, ikamet, sakin olma;
**in'hab.it.ant** *n.* oturan, sakin, ikamet
eden kimse.

**in.ha.la.tion** [inhə'leiʃən] *n.* nefes alma,
solukla içeri çekme, teneffüs, enhalâsyon; ⁊ solukla içeri çekilen ilâç; **in.hale**
[in'heil] *v/t.* ⁊ içine çekmek; *v/i.* nefes
almak, teneffüs etm., solumak; **in'hal.er**
*n.* ⁊ enhalâsyon aleti.

**in.har.mo.ni.ous** □ [inhɑː'məunjəs] uyumsuz, ahenksiz.

**in.here** [in'hiə] *v/i.* içinde. olm., tabiatında olm. (in *-in*); **in'her.ence, in'her.en.cy**
[~rəns(i)] *n.* içinde olma, tabiatında olma; **in'her.ent** □ içinde olan, tabiatında
olan (in *-in*).

**in.her.it** [in'herit] *v/t.* miras almak, kalıt
almak; vâris olm. *-e*; **in'her.it.a.ble** □
miras kalması mümkün olan; irsî, kalıtsal; **in'her.it.ance** *n.* miras, kalıt; veraset; *biol.* kalıtım, irsiyet, soyaçekim; **in-
'her.i.tor** *n.* vâris, mirasçı; **in'her.i.tress,
in'her.i.trix** [~triks] *n.* kadın vâris.

**in.hib.it** [in'hibit] *v/t.* engel olm. *-e*, mâni
olm. *-e*; bırakmamak, geri tutmak, alıkoymak (s.o. from s.th. *b-ni bşden*); **in.hi-
bi.tion** [~'biʃən] *n.* yasak; alıkoyma, engelleme durdurma; **in'hib.i.to.ry** [~təri]
*adj.* yasaklayıcı; engelleyici...

**in.hos.pi.ta.ble** ☐ [in'hɔspitəbl] misafir sevmez; barınılmaz *(yer)*; **in.hos.pi.tal.i.ty** ['ᵕ‿'tæliti] *n.* misafir sevmezlik, soğuk muamele.

**in.hu.man** ☐ [in'hjuːmən] gaddar, kıyıcı, zalim, şefkatsiz, merhametsiz, insanlık dışı; **in.hu.man.i.ty** [ᵕ‿'mæniti] *n.* insaniyetsizlik; zalim davranış.

**in.hu.ma.tion** [inhjuː'meiʃən] *n.* ölüyü gömme, defin.

**in.hume** [in'hjuːm] *v/t.* gömmek, defnetmek.

**in.im.i.cal** ☐ [i'nimikəl] düşman, zarar verici; zıt, karşı, ters, aksi.

**in.im.i.ta.ble** ☐ [i'nimitəbl] emsalsiz, eşsiz; taklit edilemez, aynı yapılamaz.

**in.iq.ui.tous** ☐ [i'nikwitəs] günahkâr; kötü; haksız, kanunsuz, adaletsiz; **in.iq.ui.ty** *n.* günah; kötülük; haksızlık, adaletsizlik.

**in.i.tial** [i'niʃəl] **1.** ☐ ilk baştaki, birinci; evvelki; **2.** *n.* ilk harf; büyük harf; **3.** *v/t.* adının baş harfleriyle imzalamak, parafe etm.; **in.i.ti.ate 1.** [i'niʃiit] *n.* yeni üye (in *-de*); **2.** [ᵕ‿ʃieit] *v/t.* başlatmak *-i*; başlamak *-e*; *pol.* sunmak, teklif etm.; kabul etm. (into *-e*); göstermek, bilgi vermek, alıştırmak; **in.i.ti.a.tion** *n.* başla(t)ma; üyeliğe kabul (töreni); *part. Am.* ᵕ fee kayıt ücreti; **in.i.ti.a.tive** [ᵕ‿ətiv] **1.** *adj.* başlatan, ilk, ön; **2.** *n.* öncelik, inisiyatif; ilk adım, ilk hareket; girişim, kişisel teşebbüs; on one's own ᵕ kendi kararıyla, kimseden emir almadan; take the ᵕ ilk adımı atmak; **in.i.ti.a.tor** [ᵕ‿eitə] *n.* önayak olan kimse; **in.i.ti.a.to.ry** [ᵕ‿ətəri] *adj.* tanıtıcı, başlatan, başlangıç türünden.

**in.ject** [in'dʒekt] *v/t.* şırınga etm., enjeksiyon yapmak, iğne yapmak (into *-e*); iğne ile içine sokmak, zerk etmek (with *-e*); **in.jec.tion** *n.* içeri atma; içeri atılan şey; ₷ enjeksiyon, iğne yapma, zerk.

**in.ju.di.cious** ☐ [indʒuː'diʃəs] akılsız, tedbirsiz, düşüncesiz, basiretsiz.

**in.junc.tion** [in'dʒʌŋkʃən] *n.* uyarı, ihtar, nasihat, öğüt; yasaklama; mahkeme emri.

**in.jure** ['indʒə] *v/t.* incitmek *-i*, zarar vermek *-e*, dokunmak *-e*; bozmak *-i*, ihlâl etm. *-i*; rencide etm. *-i*, haksızlık etm. *-e*; **in.ju.ri.ous** ☐ [in'dʒuəriəs] zararlı, zarar verici, dokunur; yerici, aşağılayıcı, onur kırıcı *(söz)*; rencide edici, haksız; **in.ju.ry** ['indʒəri] *n.* zarar ziyan, hasar; haksızlık, adaletsizlik; yara, bere.

**in.jus.tice** [in'dʒʌstis] *n.* haksızlık, adaletsizlik; haksız davranış.

**ink** [iŋk] **1.** *n.* mürekkep; mürekkep balığının çıkardığı sıvı; *mst* printer's ᵕ matba mürekkebi; *attr.* mürekkep...; **2.** *v/t.* mürekkep bulaştırmak, üzerinden mürekkeple geçmek; ᵕ in *veya* over *-i* mürekkeplemek.

**ink.ling** ['iŋkliŋ] *n.* ima, işaret, iz, ipucu; seziş, kuşku.

**ink...:** 'ᵕ‿pad *n.* ıstampa; 'ᵕ‿pen.cil *n.* mürekkepli kalem; 'ᵕ‿pot *n.* mürekkep hokkası; 'ᵕ‿stand *n.* yazı takımı; 'ink.y *adj.* mürekkepli, mürekkep gibi, simsiyah, zifiri *(karanlık)*.

**in.laid** ['inleid] *adj.* kakma, işlemeli...; ᵕ floor parke döşeme.

**in.land 1.** ['inlənd] *adj.* iç, dahili, ülkenin iç kısmında olan; ₷ Revenue vergilerden elde edilen devlet geliri; **2.** [ᵕ‿] *n.* ülke içi, dahil; **3.** [in'lænd] *adv.* içeriye doğru, içerilerde, denizden uzakta; **in.land.er** ['inləndə] *n.* ülkenin iç kısmında oturan kimse.

**in.lay 1.** ['inlei] *(irr.* lay) *v/t.* kakma ile süslemek, kakma işlemek, içini kakmak; **2.** ['inlei] *n.* kakmacılık; kakmacılık malzemesi; kakma deseni; dolgu *(diş)*.

**in.let** ['inlet] *n.* giriş yolu; koy; ⊕ giriş, giriş deliği.

**in.mate** ['inmeit] *n.* oturan, sakin; başkası ile aynı yerde oturan kimse *(esp. hastane, hapishane)*.

**in.most** ['inməust] *adj.* en içerideki, dahili; çok özel *veya* gizli.

**inn** [in] *n.* otel, han; ₷s *pl.* of Court Londra Barosu.

**in.nards** F ['inədz] *n. pl.* iç organlar; mide ve bağırsaklar; iç kısımlar *(makine)*.

**in.nate** ☐ ['i'neit] fıtrî, doğuştan olan, Tanrı vergisi; tabii, yaradılıştan olan.

**in.ner** ['inə] *adj.* iç, içerideki, dahilî; manevî, ruhanî; ᵕ tube iç lastik; the ᵕ man insan ruhu *veya* aklı; *co.* mide, iştah; **in.ner.most** ['ᵕ‿məust] *adj.* en içerideki, en içteki.

**in.nings** ['iniŋz] *n. sg. spor:* bir oyuncu *veya* takımın atış yaptığı zaman; iktidar devresi; have one's ᵕ atış yapmak; *fig.* uzun ve mutlu yaşamak; uzun süre iktidarda kalmak.

**inn.keep.er** ['inkiːpə] *n.* otelci, hancı.

**in.no.cence** ['inəsns] *n.* suçsuzluk, masumiyet; saflık; **in.no.cent** ['ᵕ‿snt] **1.** ☐ suçsuz, masum, günahsız (of *-den*); zararsız; saf, aklı ermez; ᵕ of F -sız, -siz,

-sızın; **2.** *n.* masum kimse *veya* çocuk; saf kimse, aptal kimse.

**in.noc.u.ous** ☐ [i'nɔkjuəs] zararsız *(esp. hareket, söz vs.).*

**in.nom.i.nate** [i'nɔminit] *adj.* adsız, isimsiz.

**in.no.vate** ['inəuveit] *v/t.* yenilik yapmak, değişiklik yapmak; **in.no'va.tion** *n.* yenilik, icat, buluş; **'in.no.va.tor** [~tə] *n.* yenilikçi.

**in.nox.ious** ☐ [i'nɔkʃəs] zararsız.

**in.nu.en.do** [inju:'endəu] *n.* ima, kinaye; imleme, dolayısıyla söyleme.

**in.nu.mer.a.ble** ☐ [i'nju:mərəbl] sayısız, pek çok, bir sürü.

**in.nu.tri.tious** [inju:'triʃəs] *adj.* gıdasız, yeterli beslenmeyen.

**in.ob.serv.ance** [inəb'zə:vəns] *n.* (of) dikkatsizlik; yerine getirememe.

**in.oc.cu.pa.tion** ['inɔkju'peiʃən] *n.* işsizlik.

**in.oc.u.late** [i'nɔkjuleit] *v/t.* ⚕ & *fig.* aşılamak (with *ile,* for *-e karşı*); ✓ aşı yapmak *(ağaç)*; **in.oc.u'la.tion** *n.* aşı(lama).

**in.o.dor.ous** [in'əudərəs] *adj.* kokusuz.

**in.of.fen.sive** ☐ [inə'fensiv] zararsız, incitmez, dokunmaz; **in.of'fen.sive.ness** *n.* zararsızlık.

**in.of.fi.cial** [inə'fiʃəl] *adj.* resmi olmayan, gayri resmi.

**in.op.er.a.ble** [in'ɔpərəbl] *adj.* ⚕ ameliyat edilemez *(ur)*; işlemez, çalışmaz.

**in.op.er.a.tive** [in'ɔpərətiv] *adj.* tesirsiz, etkisiz; işlemeyen; boş, hükümsüz, geçersiz.

**in.op.por.tune** ☐ [in'ɔpətju:n] vakitsiz, zamansız, uygunsuz, sırasız, münasebetsiz; mevsimsiz.

**in.or.di.nate** ☐ [i'nɔ:dinit] aşırı, haddinden fazla; düzensiz, intizamsız.

**in.or.gan.ic** [inɔ:'gænik] *adj.* cansız, inorganik.

**in.pa.tient** ['inpeiʃənt] *n.* hastanede yatan hasta.

**in.put** ['input] *n.* ⊕ *part.* ⚡ giriş, besleme; emiş gücü; elektronik beyne verilen bilgi; ⚡ girdi.

**in.quest** ☐ ['inkwest] *n.* resmi soruşturma (on *hakkında*); coroner's ~ nedeni bilinmeyen ölümlerle ilgili resmi soruşturma.

**in.qui.e.tude** [in'kwaiitju:d] *n.* endişe, kaygı, tasa.

**in.quire** [in'kwaiə] *v/t.* & *v/i.* ara(ştır)mak, tahkikat yapmak, sor(uştur)mak *(about, after, for -i; of -e)*; ~ into araştırmak, soruşturmak *-i;* **in'quir.er** *n.* soruşturan kimse, araştıran kimse; **in'quir.ing** ☐ soruşturan, araştıran, meraklı;

**in'quir.y** *n.* sorgu, soruşturma, araştırma; make inquiries soruşturma yapmak (of *-i hakkında*); on, about *hakkında*): **in'quir.y-'of.fice** *n.* soruşturma bürosu.

**in.qui.si.tion** [inkwi'ziʃən] *n.* soruşturma, araştırma, tahkikat; sorgu, sorguya çekme *(a. ⚖)*; ⚖ *hist.* Engizisyon mahkemesi; **in'quis.i.tive** ☐ [~tiv] çok sual soran; meraklı; **in'quis.i.tive.ness** *n.* meraklılık; **in'quis.i.tor** *n.* soruşturmacı, tahkikat yapan kimse; *hist.* Engizisyon mahkemesi üyesi; **in.quis.i.to.ri.al** ☐ [~'tɔ:riəl] soruşturma..., araştırma...; Engizisyona ait, Engizisyon...

**in.road** ['inrəud] *n.* akın, baskın, saldırı (in, on *-e).*

**in.rush** ['inrʌʃ] *n.* içeriye hücum, akın, baskın.

**in.sa.lu.bri.ous** [insə'lu:briəs] *adj.* sağlığa zararlı, sıhhate dokunur.

**in.sane** ☐ [in'sein] deli, çıldırmış; delice, manasız, anlamsız; ~ asylum tımarhane, akıl hastanesi; **in.san.i.tar.y** ☐ [in'sæni-təri] sağlığa zararlı, pis; **in'san.i.ty** *n.* akıl hastalığı, delilik, cinnet.

**in.sa.ti.a.bil.i.ty** [inseifjə'biliti] *n.* doymazlık, açgözlülük; **in'sa.ti.a.ble** ☐, **in'sa.ti-ate** [~ʃiit] çok obur, doymak bilmez, hiç kanmaz (of *-e).*

**in.scribe** [in'skraib] *v/t.* kaydetmek, yazmak (with *-i*); hakketmek; ↑ tescil etm.; ∱ içine çizmek; *fig.* iz bırakmak (in, on *-de*); ithaf etm. (to *-e*); ~d stock *pl.* müseccel hisse senedi.

**in.scrip.tion** [in'skripʃən] *n.* kayıt; yazıt, kitabe, yazı; ithaf; ↑ tescil.

**in.scru.ta.bil.i.ty** [inskru:tə'biliti] *n.* anlaşılmazlık; esrarengizlik; **in'scru.ta.ble** ☐ anlaşılmaz, esrarengiz *(insan veya davranışlar).*

**in.sect** ['insekt] *n.* böcek, haşere; **in'sec-ti.cide** [~'tisaid] *n.* haşarat ilâcı; **in.sec-tiv.o.rous** [~'tivərəs] *adj.* böcek yiyen, böcekçil.

**in.se.cure** ☐ [insi'kjuə] emniyetsiz, sağlam olmayan, garantisiz, güvenilmez; endişeli; korumasız; **in.se'cu.ri.ty** [~riti] *n.* emniyetsizlik, güvenilmezlik.

**in.sem.i.nate** *biol.* [in'semineit] *v/t.* tohum ekmek, tohumlamak; döllemek; *fig.* aşılamak *(fikir)*; **in.sem.i'na.tion** *n.* dölleme.

**in.sen.sate** [in'senseit] *adj.* hissiz, duygusuz; insafsız, merhametsiz; cansız; **in-sen.si.bil.i.ty** [~sə'biliti] *n.* duygusuzluk, hissizlik; aldırmazlık, ilgisizlik (of, to *-e karşı*); **in'sen.si.ble** ☐ hissiz, duygusuz (of, to *-e karşı*); baygın, şuursuz, kendinden geçmiş; farkına varılamaz, hissedilemez; aldırış etmeyen, ilgisiz, lâkayt, kayıtsız; farkında olmayan; yavaş, az; anlamsız; ~ of *veya* to s.th. bşin farkında olmayan; **in'sen.si.tive** [~sitiv] *adj.* duygusuz, hissiz (to *-e karşı*).

**in.sen.ti.ent** [in'senʃənt] *adj.* cansız; duygusuz, hissiz; farkında olmayan.

**in.sep.a.ra.bil.i.ty** [insepərə'biliti] *n.* ayrılmazlık; **in'sep.a.ra.ble** ☐ ayrılmaz.

**in.sert 1.** [in'səːt] *v/t.* sokmak, sıkıştırmak, arasına koymak; vermek *(ilân);* **2.** ['insəːt] *n.* ortaya eklenen şey; kitap ortasına eklene sayfalar; **in'ser.tion** *n.* ekleme; eklenen şey; ilân.

**in.set** ['inset] *n.* ilâve, ek; kitabın ortasına konan ilâve sayfalar.

**in.shore** ⚓ ['in'ʃɔː] *adj.* kıyıya yakın, kıyı..., sahil...

**in.side** ['in'said] **1.** *n.* iç, iç taraf, dahil, iç yüz; F mide, karın; turn ~ out ters yüz etm., içini dışına çevirmek; altüst etm.; **2.** *adj.* iç..., içteki, dahili; ~ information içeriden sızan haberler; ~ left *futbol:* solaçık; ~ right sağaçık; **3.** *adv.* içerde, içeriye; ~ of F icinde, süresinde, zarfında; **4.** *prp. -in* içerisinde, içerisine; **'in'sid.er** *n.* bilgi elde edebilecek durumda olan kimse, içerideki kimse.

**in.sid.i.ous** ☐ [in'sidiəs] sinsi, gizlice zarar veren, görünmez; hain, hilekâr.

**in.sight** ['insait] *n.* bilgi, iyice anlama, öğrenme; ~ into idrak, anlayış, kavrama *-i*.

**in.sig.ni.a** [in'signiə] *n. pl.* nişanlar; rütbe işaretleri.

**in.sig.nif.i.cance,** *a.* **in.sig.nif.i.can.cy** [insig-'nifikəns(i)] *n.* önemsizlik; anlamsızlık, manasızlık; **in.sig'nif.i.cant** *adj.* önemsiz, ehemmiyetsiz; anlamsız, manasız; değersiz, değmez; cüzî, pek az.

**in.sin.cere** ☐ [insin'siə] ikiyüzlü, riyakâr, samimiyetsiz, vefasız, sadakatsiz; **in.sin.cer.i.ty** [~'seriti] *n.* samimiyetsizlik, vefasızlık, ikiyüzlülük.

**in.sin.u.ate** [in'sinjueit] *v/t.* ima etm., üstü kapalı söylemek, çıtlatmak; yavaş yavaş girmek; ~ o.s. into sokulmak, yavaş yavaş girmek *-e*; **in'sin.u.at.ing** ☐ üstü kapalı, imalı; **in.sin.u'a.tion** *n.* ima, üstü kapalı itham, çıtlatma; göze girmeye yöneltilmiş söz *veya* hareket.

**in.sip.id** ☐ [in'sipid] yavan, lezzetsiz, tatsız; sönük, cansız; **in.si'pid.i.ty** *n.* yavanlık, tatsızlık; sönüklük, cansızlık.

**in.sist** [in'sist]: ~ on, ~ upon *v/i.* üzerinde ısrar etm., diretmek, direnmek; ~ that ...konusunda ısrar etm.; **in'sist.ence** *n.* ısrar (on, upon *üzerinde*); at his ~ ısrarı üzerine; **in'sist.ent** ☐ ısrarlı, inatçı, di-

rengen (on, upon *-de*); zorlayıcı, âcil.

**in.so.bri.e.ty** [insəu'braiəti] *n.* sarhoşluk, içkiye düşkünlük, ayyaşlık.

**in.so.la.tion** [insəu'leiʃən] *n.* güneşe bırakma, güneşlendirme; güneş çarpması.

**in.sole** ['insəul] *n.* ayakkabının iç tabanı; taban astarı, keçe.

**in.so.lence** ['insələns] *n.* küstahlık, terbiyesizlik, arsızlık; **'in.so.lent** ☐ küstah, terbiyesiz, arsız.

**in.sol.u.bil.i.ty** [insɔlju'biliti] *n.* erimezlik *(sıvı);* çözülemezlik *(problem);* **in'sol.u.ble** ☐ [~jubl] erimez *(sıvı);* çözülemez, halledilemez, açıklanamaz *(problem, sorun).*

**in.sol.ven.cy** [in'sɔlvənsi] *n.* iflâs; **in'sol.vent 1.** *adj.* iflâs etmiş, borcunu ödeyemez; **2.** *n.* müflis.

**in.som.ni.a** [in'sɔmniə] *n.* uykusuzluk, uyumama.

**in.so.much** [insəu'mʌtʃ] *adv.:* ~ that o kadar ki.

**in.spect** [in'spekt] *v/t.* teftiş etm., denetlemek; muayene etm., yoklamak, bakmak; **in'spec.tion** *n.* teftiş, denetleme, yoklama, muayene; for ~ ⚔ örnek olarak, denenmek üzere; **in'spec.tor** *n.* müfettiş, tetkik memuru, enspektör; kontrol memuru; **in'spec.tor.ate** [~tərit] *n.* müfettişlik.

**in.spi.ra.tion** [inspə'reiʃən] *n.* ilham, esin; ilham kaynağı; parlak fikir; vahiy; nefes alma; **in.spire** [in'spaiə] *v/t.* ilham etm., esinlemek; içine çekmek *(nefes);* sevketmek; etkilemek; sebep olm., vesile olm.; yaymak *(dedikodu); fig.* telkin etm., aklına sokmak (s.th. in s.o., s.o. with s.th. bşi *b-ne, b-nin*); *v/i.* nefes almak; **in.spir.it** [in'spirit] *v/t.* canlandırmak, şevklendirmek, neşelendirmek.

**in.spis.ate** [in'spiseit] *v/t.* kalınlaştırmak, koyulaştırmak, yoğunlaştırmak.

**in.sta.bil.i.ty** [instə'biliti] *n.* dayanıksızlık; *part. fig.* kararsızlık, sebatsızlık.

**in.stall** [in'stɔːl] *v/t.* yerleştirmek (in *-e);* makamına getirmek; ⊕ kurmak, tesis etm., takmak; **in.stal.la.tion** [instə-'leiʃən] *n.* yerleştirme; ⊕ tesisat, tertibat, donanım; ⚔ kurma, montaj; askeri üs.

**in.stal(l).ment** [in'stɔːlmənt] *n.* taksit; kısım, bölüm; by ~s taksitle, taksit taksit; payment by ~s taksitle ödeme; ~ plan taksit usulü.

**in.stance** ['instəns] **1.** *n.* misal, örnek; rica, istek; defa, kere, sefer; ⚖️ dava; aşama, basamak, durum; for ~ örneğin, meselâ; in the first ~ ilk olarak, öncelikle; at the ~ of -in isteği üzerine; **2.** *v/t.* örnek olarak göstermek; örnek ile belirtmek.

**in.stant** ['instənt] **1.** ☐ hemen olan, derhal olan; âcil; şimdiki, şu anki; cari, içinde bulunulan ayda olan; çabuk ve kolay hazırlanabilen (*yiyecek, içecek*); ~ coffee sıcak su *veya* süt katılarak yapılan toz kahve; on the 10th ~ bu ayın onunda; **2.** *n.* an, dakika; the ~ you call sen telefon eder etmez; **in.stan.ta.ne.ous** ☐ [~'teinjəs] ani, bir anlık, bir anda olan...; **in.stant.ly** *adv.* hemen, derhal.

**in.state** [in'steit] *v/t.* yerleştirmek, koymak (in *-e*); yatırmak, vermek (*para*); bağışlamak, hediye etm.

**in.stead** [in'sted] *adv.* yerine, karşılık olarak, yerinde ~ of -*in* yerine; ~ of going gitmek yerine.

**in.step** ['instep] *n.* ayağın üst kısmı; ayakkabı *veya* çorabın üst kısmı; be high in the ~ F burnu havada olm.

**in.sti.gate** ['instigeit] *v/t.* kışkırtmak, tahrik etm., teşvik etm., ayartmak; **in.sti-'ga.tion** *n.* kışkırtma, tahrik, teşvik, ayartma; at the ~ of -*in* teşvikiyle; 'in-sti.ga.tor *n.* kışkırtıcı.

**in.stil(l)** [in'stil] *v/t.* damla damla akıtmak (*ilâç*); *fig.* aşılamak (*fikir*) (into *-e*); **in.stil'la.tion, in'stil(l).ment** *n.* damla damla akıtma; fikir aşılama.

**in.stinct 1.** ['instiŋkt] *n.* içgüdü, insiyak; sezgi, içe doğma; **2.** [in'stiŋkt] *adj.* dolu; ~ with life hayat dolu; **in'stinc.tive** ☐ içgüdülü, içgüdüsel.

**in.sti.tute** ['institjuːt] **1.** *n.* enstitü, okul; kuruluş, müessese; kurum, cemiyet; **2.** *v/t.* kurmak, tesis etm.; atamak, tayin etm. (to into *-e*); **in.sti'tu.tion** *n.* kuruluş, müessese, kurum, tesis; yerleşmiş gelenek *veya* kanun; kurma, yerleştirme; atama, tayin etme; **in.sti'tu.tion.al** [~ʃənl] *adj.* kuruluş..., kurum...; geleneksel...; care ~ huzurevi, yetimhane, ıslahane *vs.* bakımı; **in.sti'tu.tion.al.ize** [~ʃnəlaiz] *v/t.* müesseseleştirmek, kurum haline getirmek; gelenekselleştirmek, âdet haline getirmek; F düşkünler evine yatırmak.

**in.struct** [in'strʌkt] *v/t.* eğitmek, öğretmek, okutmak, ders vermek; talimat vermek *-e*, emir vermek *-e*, direktif vermek *-e*; bilgi vermek *-e*; **in'struc.tion** *n.* eğitim, talim, öğrenim, öğretim; bilgi verme; ~s *pl.* emir, talimat, direktif; **in-'struc.tion.al** [~ʃənl] *adj.* eğitici..., öğretici...; ~ film eğitici film; **in'struc.tive** ☐ öğretici, eğitici; **in'struc.tor** *n.* eğitmen, okutman, öğretmen; *Am. univ.* doçent;

**in'struc.tress** *n.* kadın okutman, öğretmen.

**in.stru.ment** ['instrumənt] *n.* alet; ♪ enstruman, saz, çalgı; *fig.* maşa, alet; ⚙ belge; ~ board *mot.*, ⚓ dağıtım (*veya* kontrol) tablosu; fly on ~s ⚓ aletler yardımıyla uçmak, kör uçuş yapmak; **in.stru.men.tal** ☐ [instru'mentl] yardımcı, aracı olan; ♪ enstrumental; faydalı, yararlı, tesirli, etkili; be ~ to *-e* yardımcı olm.; be ~ in *-de* aracı olm.; **in.stru'men.tal.ist** ♪ [~təlist] *n.* çalgıcı; **in.stru.men.tal.i.ty** [~'tæliti] *n.* vasıta, araç.

**in.sub.or.di.nate** [insə'bɔːdnit] *adj.* itaatsiz, asi, baş kaldıran, kafa tutan, isyankâr; **in.sub.or.di.na.tion** ['~di'neiʃən] *n.* itaatsizlik, baş kaldırma, asilik.

**in.sub.stan.tial** [insəb'stænʃəl] *adj.* gerçek olmayan, hayalî; zayıf, temelsiz, esassız, asılsız.

**in.suf.fer.a.ble** ☐ [in'sʌfərəbl] tahammül olunamaz, çekilmez, katlanılmaz; çok gururlu, fazla kibirli.

**in.suf.fi.cien.cy** [insə'fiʃənsi] *n.* yetersizlik, yetmezlik, eksiklik, kifayetsizlik; **in-suf'fi.cient** ☐ eksik, yetersiz, kifayetsiz.

**in.su.lar** ☐ ['insjulə] adaya özgü, ada...; adada yaşayan; *fig.* dar görüşlü; **in.su.lar.i.ty** [~'læriti] *n.* adalı olma; *fig.* dar görüşlülük; **in.su.late** ['~leit] *v/t.* ayırmak, izole etm., yalıtmak, tecrit etm. (*a.* ⚡); 'in.su.lat.ing *adj.* izole eden, izole...; ~ tape izole bant; **in.su'la.tion** *n.* tecrit, izolasyon, yalıtım (*a. phys.*); 'in.su.la.tor *n.* ⚡ izolatör, fincan.

**in.su.lin** ⚕ ['insjulin] *n.* insülin.

**in.sult 1.** ['insʌlt] *n.* hakaret, onur kırma, aşağılama, hor görme; **2.** [in'sʌlt] *v/t.* hakaret etm., hor görmek, aşağılamak; şerefini kırmak.

**in.su.per.a.bil.i.ty** [insjuːpərə'biliti] *n.* başa çıkılmazlık, yenilemezlik; geçilemezlik, aşılmazlık; **in'su.per.a.ble** ☐ başa çıkılmaz, yenilemez; geçilemez, aşılamaz.

**in.sup.port.a.ble** ☐ [insə'pɔːtəbl] çekilmez, dayanılmaz, tahammül edilemez; haksız, yersiz.

**in.sup.press.i.ble** [insə'presəbl] *adj.* bastırılamaz, söndürülemez, önlenemez.

**in.sur.ance** [in'ʃuərəns] *n.* sigorta, sigorta etme; sigorta parası; sigorta taksidi; sigorta poliçesi; *attr.* sigorta...; ~ pol.i.cy sigorta poliçesi; ~ sigorta primi ödeyen kimse; **in'sure** *v/t.* sigorta etm.; temin etm., sağlamak; *v/i.* sigorta olm.; **in'sured** *n.* sigortalı kimse; **in'sur.er** *n.* sigorta şirketi; sigortacı.

**in.sur.gent** [in'səːdʒənt] **1.** *adj.* asi, baş

kaldıran, kafa tutan; **2.** *n.* ihtilâlci, asi kimse.

**in.sur.mount.a.ble** ☐ [insəːˈmauntəbl] yenilemez, başa çıkılmaz, üstesinden gelinemez, seçilemez.

**in.sur.rec.tion** [insəˈrekʃən] *n.* isyan, ayaklanma, ihtilâl; **in.surˈrec.tion.al** [~ʃənl] *adj.* isyan kabilinden; **in.surˈrec.tion.ist** [~ʃnist] *n.* asi kimse, isyan taraftarı, ihtilâlci.

**in.sus.cep.ti.ble** [insəˈseptəbl] *adj.* duygusuz, hissiz, vurdumduymaz (of, to -e *karşı*).

**in.tact** [inˈtækt] *adj.* bozulmamış, dokunulmamış, el sürülmemiş, tam, eksiksiz.

**in.take** [ˈinteik] *n.* giriş, ağız; içeri giren miktar, alınan miktar; tarıma uygun hale getirilen arazi.

**in.tan.gi.bil.i.ty** [intændʒəˈbiliti] *n.* tutulamazlık, dokunulamazlık; kavranamazlık; **inˈtan.gi.ble** ☐ tutulamaz, dokunulamaz; *fig.* kavranamaz, idrak edilemez; manevî (*değer*).

**in.te.ger** [ˈintidʒə] *n.* A tam sayı; bütünlük, tam mevcudiyet; **in.te.gral** [ˈ~grəl] **1.** ☐ gerekli, lüzumlu; tam, bütün, yekpare; A tam sayılardan oluşan, tam sayı...; **2.** *n.* A integral; **in.te.grant** [ˈ~grənt] *adj.* bir bütünü oluşturan, bütünleyici; **in.te.grate** [ˈ~greit] *v/t.* tamamlamak, bütünlemek; katmak, ilâve etm., eklemek (into, in -e); kaldırmak (*ırk ayırımını*); **in.teˈgra.tion** *n.* *mst pol.* ırk ayırımını kaldırma; bütünleme, tamamlama; **in.teg.ri.ty** [inˈtegriti] *n.* bütünlük; dürüstlük, doğruluk.

**in.teg.u.ment** [inˈtegjumənt] *n.* deri, zar, kabuk, gömlek (*a.* ♥, *anat.*).

**in.tel.lect** [ˈintilekt] *n.* akıl, zihin, idrak; anlık; **in.telˈlec.tu.al** [~tjuəl] **1.** ☐ akla ait, aklî, zihnî; bilgili, akıllı, zekâ sahibi, okumuş, âlim, münevver; **2.** *n.* entelektüel (*veya* münevver) kimse; **in.telˈlec.tu.al.i.ty** [ˈ~tjuˈæliti] *n.* münevverlik, zihnî kabiliyet.

**in.tel.li.gence** [inˈtelidʒəns] *n.* akıl, zekâ, anlayış; haber, bilgi, malûmat; ~ department istihbarat bölümü; **inˈtel.li.genc.er** *n.* casus, gizli ajan; muhbir, muhabir.

**in.tel.li.gent** ☐ [inˈtelidʒənt] akıllı, zeki, anlayışlı; becerikli, maharetli, kabiliyetli, usta; **in.tel.li.gent.si.a** [~ˈdʒentsiə] *n.* aydınlar sınıfı, münevver sınıf; **in.tel.li.gi.bil.i.ty** [~dʒəˈbiliti] *n.* anlaşılabilme, açıklık; **inˈtel.li.gi.ble** ☐ anlaşılır, açık (to *için*).

**in.tem.per.ance** [inˈtempərəns] *n.* aşırılık, taşkınlık; düşkünlük, ayyaşlık; **inˈtem-**

**per.ate** ☐ [~rit] taşkın, aşırı; şiddetli, sert, bozuk, fırtınalı (*hava*); ayyaş.

**in.tend** [inˈtend] *v/t.* niyet etm., niyetlenmek, tasarlamak, zihninde kurmak; kastetmek, demek istemek (by *ile*); ~ for -e, için niyet etm.; **inˈtend.ant** *n.* idare memuru; **inˈtend.ed 1.** *adj.* tasarlanmış, amaçlı; müstakbel; ~ husband müstakbel koca; **2.** *n.* F nişanlı kimse.

**in.tense** ☐ [inˈtens] şiddetli, kuvvetli, hararetli, ateşli, gergin; **inˈtense.ness** *n.* şiddet, kuvvet, hararet, gerginlik.

**in.ten.si.fi.ca.tion** [intensifiˈkeiʃən] *n.* kuvvetlendirme, koyulaştırma (*a. phot.*); **inˈten.si.fy** [~fai] *v/t.* & *v/i.* şiddetlen-(dir)mek; -in şiddetini arttırmak, koyulaştırmak.

**in.ten.sion** [inˈtenʃən] *n.* keskinlik, şiddet; koyuluk, yoğunluk; **inˈten.si.ty** = intenseness; **inˈten.sive** ☐ = intense; şiddetli, kuvvetli.

**in.tent** [inˈtent] **1.** ☐ gayretli, şevkli, istekli, arzulu (on -e); meşgul, niyetli, dalmış, kendini vermiş (on *ile*, -e); **2.** *n.* niyet, maksat, amaç, gaye, kasıt, meram; to all ~s and purposes esas itibariyle, her bakımdan, tamamiyle; with ~ to kill öldürmek amacıyla; **inˈten.tion** *n.* niyet, maksat, amaç; meram, kasıt; evlenme niyeti; önem, ehemmiyet; yaranın kapanması; **inˈten.tion.al** ☐ [~ʃənl] kasıtlı, maksatlı, mahsus; **inˈten.tioned** *comb.* ...niyetli; well-~ iyi niyetli; **inˈtent.ness** *n.* büyük dikkat, gayret, şevk, istek, arzu.

**in.ter** [inˈtəː] *v/t.* gömmek, defnetmek, toprağa vermek.

**in.ter...** [ˈintə] *prefix* arasında; ortasında; karşılıklı, birbiriyle.

**in.ter.act 1.** [ˈintərækt] *n. thea.* perde arası, antrakt; **2.** [~ˈækt] *v/i.* birbirini etkilemek; **in.terˈac.tion** *n.* birbirini etkileme.

**in.ter.breed** [ˈintəbriːd] (*irr. breed*) *v/i.* melez elde etm.; *v/t.* melezleştirmek.

**in.ter.ca.lar.y** [inˈtəːkələri] *adj.* takvime eklenen (*ay, gün*); ilâve edilmiş *ay veya* günü olan (*yıl*); **inˈter.ca.late** [~leit] *v/t.* araya eklemek (*gün*); ortasına ilâve etm.; **in.terˈca.la.tion** *n.* araya ekleme; ortaya ilâve etme.

**in.ter.cede** [intəˈsiːd] *v/i.* aracılık etm., arasına girmek (with *ile*); **in.terˈced.er** *n.* aracı.

**in.ter.cept** [intəˈsept] *v/t.* durdurmak, engellemek; -in yolunu kesmek, yolda iken yakalamak; **in.terˈcep.tion** *n.* durdurma, yolunu kesme, engelleme; **in.terˈcep.tor** *n.* yol kesen kimse *veya* şey; ✕ süratli avcı uçağı.

in.ter.ces.sion ['intəˈseʃən] *n.* iltimas, şefaat; başkaları için yalvarma, rica; in.ter.ces.sor [.ˈsesə] *n.* iltimasçı kimse, başkaları için yalvaran kimse; in.terˈces.so.ry *adj.* başkaları için yardım isteyen.

in.ter.change-1. [intəˈtʃeindʒ] *v/t. & v/i.* değiş(tir)mek, mübadele etm., değiş tokuş etm.; 2. [ˈ~ˈtʃeindʒ] *n.* mübadele, değiştirme, değiş tokuş etme; in.terˈchange.a.ble *adj.* birbiriyle değiştirilebilir.

in.ter.com.mu.ni.cate [intəkəˈmjuːnikeit] telefon sistemi.

in.ter.com.mu.ni.cate [intəkəˈmjuːnikeit] *v/i.* birbiriyle haberleşmek; ˈin.ter.com.mu.niˈca.tion *n.* birbiriyle haberleşme; ~ system = intercom; in.terˈcomˈmun.ion [.~njən] *n.* karşılıklı münasebet.

in.ter.con.nect [ˈintəˈkəˈnekt] *v/t.* birbiriyle birleştirmek.

in.ter.con.ti.nen.tal [ˈintəkɔntiˈnentl] *adj.* kıtalararası.

in.ter.course [ˈintəkɔːs] *n.* münasebet, ilişki; ticaret, iş, alışveriş; cinsî münasebet.

in.ter.de.pend.ence [intədiˈpendəns] *n.* karşılıklı dayanışma; in.ter.deˈpend.ent *adj.* birbirine bağlı olan, birbirine muhtaç.

in.ter.dict 1. [intəˈdikt] *v/t.* yasak etm., yasaklamak, menetmek (s.th. to s.o. *bşi b-ne*; s.o. from doing *b-ni bş yapmaktan*); kilise ayinlerinden menetmek; 2. [ˈintədikt], in.terˈdic.tion *n.* yasak(lama).

in.ter.est [ˈintrist] 1. *n.* ilgi, merak; alâka, hobi, özel zevk; hisse, pay; † faiz; ~s *pl.* kâr, kazanç; menfaat, çıkar; ~s *pl.* iktisadî hayatta hâkim grup; in the ~ of *-in* menfaatine, çıkarı için; be of ~ to *-in* çıkarına olm.; take an ~ in *-e* ilgi duymak, merak duymak; return a blow with ~ daha kuvvetli bir yumrukla karşılık vermek; banking ~s *pl.* banka faizleri; 2. *v/t. com.* ilgilendirmek, alâkadar etm.; merakını uyandırmak (for s.o. *b-nin*); be ~ed in *ile* ilgilenmek, ilgili olm.; *-e* merak duymak, meraklı olm.; ~ o.s. in *ile* ilgilenmek; ˈin.ter.est.ed □ ilgili, alâkalı (in *ile*); meraklı *-e*; ˈin.ter.est.ing □ ilgi çekici, ilginç, enteresan.

in.ter.face [ˈintəfeis] *n.* ortak yüzey.

in.ter.fere [intəˈfiə] *vb.* karıştırmak, kurcalamak (with *-i*); karışmak, müdahale etm., burnunu sokmak (in *-e*); mâni olm., engel olm. (with *-e*); in.terˈfer.ence *n.* karışma. müdahale; parazit; *phys.* girişim, karışım; engel, mâni; *spor:* obstrüksiyon.

in.ter.flow [intəˈfləu] (*irr.* flow) *vb.* içine akmak.

in.ter.fuse [intəˈfjuːz] *v/t.* karıştırmak, katmak; kaplamak, istilâ etm., nüfuz etm.

in.ter.im [ˈintərim] 1. *n.* aralık, fasıla; in the ~ arada, aradaki zamanda; 2. *adj.* geçici, muvakkat...; ~ report geçici rapor.

in.te.ri.or [inˈtiəriə] 1. □ içerdeki, içe ait, dahilî; kıyıdan *veya* sınırdan uzak; manevî; ~ decorator iç dekoratör; 2. *n.* iç, dahil; iç kısımlar; *pol.* içişleri; Department of the ♀ *Am.* İçişleri Bakanlığı.

in.ter.ja.cent [intəˈdʒeisənt] *adj.* ortasında bulunan.

in.ter.ject [intəˈdʒekt] *vb.* arasına katmak (*söz*); in.terˈjec.tion *n.* ünlem, nida; söz arasına koyma; in.terˈjec.tion.al □ [.~ʃənl] araya konulan (*söz*); ünlem şeklinde.

in.ter.lace [intəˈleis] *v/t. & v/i.* birbiriyle ör(ül)mek, beraber doku(n)mak, karış(tır)mak.

in.ter.lard [intəˈlaːd] *v/t. fig.* doldurmak (*süslü sözlerle*); içine karıştırmak (*yabancı kelime*).

in.ter.leave [intəˈliːv] *v/t.* kitabın yaprakları arasına eklemek (*boş sayfa*).

in.ter.line [intəˈlain] *v/t.* orta astarı koymak (*elbiseye*); *typ.* yazının satırları arasına koymak (*başka yazı*); in.ter.lin.e.ar [.~ˈliniə] *adj.* satır aralarına yazılmış; in.ter.lin.e.a.tion [ˈ~liniˈeiʃən] *n.* satır aralarına yazılan yazı.

in.ter.link [intəˈliŋk] *v/t. & v/i.* birleş(tir)mek. birbirine bağla(n)mak.

in.ter.lock [intəˈlɔk] *v/t. & v/i.* birbirine bağla(n)mak, kenetle(n)mek.

in.ter.lo.cu.tion [intələuˈkjuːʃən] *n.* konuşma; in.ter.loc.u.tor [.~ˈlɔkjutə] *n.* konuşan kimse, konuşmacı (*tartışmada*); in.terˈloc.u.to.ry *adj.* konuşmaya ait, konuşma...; ♰ geçici...

in.ter.lope [intəˈləup] *v/i.* başkasının işine burnunu sokmak; † başkalarının hakkına tecavüz etm.; ˈin.ter.lop.er *n.* başkasının işine burnunu sokan kimse; † başkasının hakkına tecavüz eden kimse.

in.ter.lude [ˈintəluːd] *n.* ara faslı; perde arası, antrakt; ara, fasıla; ~s of bright weather geçici güzel hava.

in.ter.mar.riage [intəˈmæridʒ] *n.* değişik aile, kabile, millet *vs.* arasında evlenme; ˈin.terˈmar.ry *v/i.* değişik aileden, kabileden, milletten *vs.* birisi ile evlenmek.

in.ter.med.dle [intəˈmedl] *v/i.* karışmak, müdahale etm. (with, in *-e*); in.terˈmed.dler *n.* herşeye burnunu sokan kimse.

**in.ter.me.di.ar.y** [intə'mi:djəri] **1.** *adj.* aracılık eden, vasıta olan, arada bulunan; **2.** *n.* vasıta; ortada olan şey; ⚓ aracı; **in.ter.me.di.ate** ☐ [~'mi:djət] ortadaki, aradaki; orta..., ara...; ~ **landing** ⚓ ara iniş; ~**range ballistic missile** orta menzilli roket; ~ **school** *Am.* ortaokul; ~ **stage** orta kademe, ara safha; ~ **trade** komisyonculuk.

**in.ter.ment** [in'tə:mənt] *n.* ölüyü gömme, defnetme; defin.

**in.ter.mez.zo** [intə'metsəu] *n.* küçük fasıl, aranağme.

**in.ter.mi.na.ble** ☐ [in'tə:minəbl] sonsuz, nihayetsiz, bitmez, tükenmez, sonu gelmez.

**in.ter.min.gle** [intə'mingl] *v/t.* & *v/i.* birbirine karış(tır)mak.

**in.ter.mis.sion** [intə'miʃən] *n.* aralık, fasıla, ara; antrakt; mola.

**in.ter.mit** [intə'mit] *v/t.* & *v/i.* dur(dur)mak; ara vermek, tatil etm.; tatil olm.; **in.ter'mit.tent 1.** ☐ arada kesilen, aralıklı, kesik kesik; ~ **fever** = **2.** *n.* ⚕ sıtma; **in.ter'mit.tent.ly** *adv.* ara ara, kesik kesik, zaman zaman durarak, aralıklı.

**in.ter.mix** [intə'miks] *v/t.* & *v/i.* birbirine karış(tır)mak; **in.ter'mix.ture** [~tʃə] *n.* birbirine karış(tır)ma; karışım, karışmış şey; alaşım.

**in.tern**[1] [in'tə:n] *v/t.* enterne etm., gözaltına almak, hapsetmek, alıkoymak.

**in.tern**[2] ['intə:n] *n.* stajyer doktor, stajını yapan tıp öğrencisi.

**in.ter.nal** ☐ [in'tə:nl] iç, içe ait, dahili, içinde bulunan; içilir *(ilâç)*; bir ülkenin içişlerine ait; ~**-com'bus.tion en.gine** içten yanmalı motor.

**in.ter.na.tion.al** [intə'næʃənl] **1.** ☐ uluslararası, milletlerarası, beynelmilel, enternasyonal; ~ **law** milletlerarası hukuk; **2.** *n. pol.* ② uluslararası ④ sol kanat kurumundan herhangi biri; **in.ter.na.tion.al.i.ty** [~'næliti] *n.* beynelmilellik, enternasyonellik; **in.ter'na.tion.al.ize** [~nəlaiz] *v/t.* beynelmilel kılmak, milletlerarası kontrole sokmak, enternasyonelleştirmek.

**in.terne** ['intə:n] = **intern**[2].

**in.ter.ne.cine war** [intə'ni:sain'wɔ:] *n.* iki tarafa da büyük kayıplar verdiren savaş.

**in.tern.ee** [intə:'ni:] *n.* gözaltındaki *(veya* enterne edilmiş) kimse; tutuklu; **in'tern.ment** *n.* enterne edilme, gözaltına alınma, hapsedilme; ~ **camp** toplama kampı.

**in.ter.pel.late** [in'tə:pəleit] *v/t.* gensoru açmak; **in.ter.pel'la.tion** *n.* gensoru.

**in.ter.phone** ['intəfəun] *n.* ⚓ *Am.* dahili telefon.

**in.ter.plan.e.ta.ry** [intə'plænitri] *adj.* gezegenlerarası.

**in.ter.play** ['intə'plei] *n.* karşılıklı etkileme.

**in.ter.po.late** [intə:pəleit] *v/t.* katmak, ilâve etm., eklemek *(metne)*; **in.ter.po'la.tion** *n.* ekleme, ilâve etme, metni değiştirme.

**in.ter.pose** [intə'pəuz] *v/t.* arasına koymak, araya sokmak; ortaya atmak; *v/i.* araya girmek, karışmak, müdahale etm.; arabuluculuk yapmak; **in.ter.po.si.tion** [intəpə'ziʃən] *n.* araya girme, karışma, müdahale.

**in.ter.pret** [in'tə:prit] *v/t.* -*in* anlamını açıklamak, izah etm.; yorumlamak; tercüme etm.; *v/i.* tercümanlık yapmak; **in.ter.pre'ta.tion** *n.* yorum, tefsir, izah, açıklama, mana; **in'ter.pre.ta.tive** [~tətiv] *adj.* açıklayıcı, yorumlayıcı (of -*i*); **in'ter.pret.er** *n.* tercüman, çevirmen.

**in.ter.ra.cial** [intə'reiʃjəl] *adj.* ırklararası.

**in.ter.reg.num** [intə'regnəm] *n.* hükümetin kanunen çalışmadığı devre; ara, fasıla.

**in.ter.re.la.tion** ['intəri'leiʃən] *n.* karşılıklı münasebet.

**in.ter.ro.gate** [in'terəgeit] *v/t.* sorguya çekmek; **in.ter.ro'ga.tion** *n.* sorgu, sorguya çekme; **note** *veya* **mark** *veya* **point of** ~ soru işareti; **in.ter.rog.a.tive** [intə'rogətiv] **1.** ☐ sorulu..., soru sorar gibi, soru ifade eden..., soru...; **2.** *n. gr.* soru kelimesi; **in.ter'rog.a.to.ry** [~təri] **1.** *adj.* soru belirten, soru türünden; **2.** *n.* yazılı olarak bildirilen resmi soru.

**in.ter.rupt** [intə'rʌpt] *vb.* kesmek, ara vermek -*e,* durdurmak, engellemek; *b-nin* sözünü kesmek; **in.ter'rupt.ed.ly** *adv.* aralıkarla; **in.ter'rupt.er** *n.* ⚡ devre kesici, şalter; **in.ter'rup.tion** *n.* ara, fasıla, kesilme, kesiklik.

**in.ter.sect** [intə'sekt] *v/t.* & *v/i.* kes(iş)mek, ikiye bölmek; **in.ter'sec.tion** *n.* kes-(iş)me, kavşak; ⬛ kesişme hattı.

**in.ter.space** ['intə'speis] *n.* ara, aralık, fasıla.

**in.ter.sperse** [intə'spə:s] *v/t.* arasına serpmek, serpiştirmek; değişik hale sokmak (with *ile*).

**in.ter.state** *Am.* ['intə'steit] *adj.* eyaletlerarası.

**in.ter.stice** [in'tə:stis] *n.* yarık, çatlak, küçük aralık; **in.ter.sti.tial** ☐ [~'stiʃəl] çatlağa ait, çatlak..., yarık...

**in.ter.tri.bal** [intə'traibəl] *adj.* kabilelerarası.

in.ter.twine [intə'twain], in.ter.twist [.-'twist] v/t. & v/i. birbiriyle ör(ül)mek, birbirine sar(ıl)mak.

in.ter.ur.ban [intər'əːbən] adj. şehirlerarası.

in.ter.val ['intəvəl] n. ara, fasıla, aralık; müddet, zaman; ♪ es, enterval, aralık.

in.ter.vene [intə'viːn] v/i. araya girmek, karışmak, müdahale etm.; arada bulunmak; diğer olaylar arasında olm.; in.terven.tion [.-'venʃən] n. araya girme, müdahale, karışma; aracılık.

in.ter.view ['intəvjuː] 1. n. görüşme, mülâkat; röportaj; 2. v/t. görüşmek, röportaj yapmak 'in.ter.view.er n. röportajcı, mülâkat yapan kimse.

in.ter.weave [intə'wiːv] (irr. weave) v/t. beraber dokumak, birbirine dokumak, birbirine karıştırmak (a. fig.).

in.tes.ta.cy [in'testəsi] n. vasiyetsiz ölme; in'tes.tate [.- [.-tit] 1. adj. vasiyetname bırakmadan ölmüş; 2. n. vasiyetname bırakmadan ölmüş kimse.

in.tes.ti.nal anat. [in'testinl] adj. bağırsaklara ait, bağırsak...; in'tes.tine 1. adj. iç..., içe ait; 2. n. bağırsak; .-s pl. bağırsaklar.

in.ti.ma.cy ['intiməsi] n. samimiyet, yakın dostluk, sıkı dostluk, içlidışlı olma, teklifsizlik; in.ti.mate 1. ['.-meit] v/t. ima etm., üstü kapalı anlatmak, dolayısiyle anlatmak; açıklamak, ilan etm., bildirmek; 2. □ ['.-mit] sıkı fıkı, içten, candan, samimi, içlidışlı; gizli, mahrem; 3. ['.-mit] n. yakın dost, samimi arkadaş; in.ti.ma.tion [.-'meiʃən] n. ima, dolayısiyle anlatma; bildirme, haber verme; teklif, öneri.

in.tim.i.date [in'timideit] v/t. korkutmak, sindirmek, yıldırmak, gözdağı vermek; in.tim.i'da.tion n. gözdağı verme, yıldırma, korkutma.

in.to ['intu] prp. -e, -ye, içeri, -in içerisine.

in.tol.er.a.ble □ [in'tɔlərəbl] tahammül olunmaz, çekilmez, dayanılmaz; in'tol.er.ance n. hoş görmeme, taassup; in'tol.er.ant □ hoşgörüsüz, müsamahasız; tahammülsüz.

in.to.na.tion [intə'neiʃən] n. düz bir sesle okuma; ♪ doğru ses perdesi, seslem, tonötüm; gr. ses tonunun yükselip alçalma şekli, tonlama; in.to.nate ['.-neit], in'tone vb. monoton bir makamla okumak; monoton bir sesle konuşmak.

in.tox.i.cant [in'tɔksikənt] 1. adj. sarhoş edici; 2. n. sarhoş edici içki; in'tox.i.cate [.-keit] vb. sarhoş etm., mest etm. (a.

fig.); in.tox.i'ca.tion n. sarhoşluk, mest olma (a. fig.).

in.trac.ta.bil.i.ty [intræktə'biliti] n. kolayca yola getirilememe, kolay kontrol edilememe; in'trac.ta.ble □ kolay yola getirilemeyen, kolay kontrol edilemeyen, ele avuca sığmaz.

in.tra.mu.ral ['intrə'mjuərəl] adj. bir bina içinde olan veya yapılan; okul içinde olan veya yapılan.

in.tran.si.gent [in'trænsidʒənt]˙ adj. uzlaşmaz, uzlaşması olanaksız.

in.tran.si.tive [in'trænsitiv] □ gr. geçişsiz, nesnesiz (fiil).

in.tra.state Am. [intrə'steit] adj. eyaletlerarası.

in.trench [in'trentʃ], in'trench.ment = entrench etc.

in.tre.pid □ [in'trepid] yılmaz, korkusuz, cesur, yiğit, gözüpek; in.tre.pid.i.ty n. yiğitlik, korkusuzluk, cesurluk, gözüpeklik.

in.tri.ca.cy ['intrikəsi] n. karışıklık, anlaşılmazlık; şaşırtıcılık; in.tri.cate ['.-kit] karışık, anlaşılması zor, çaprašık; şaşırtıcı.

in.trigue [in'triːg] 1. n. entrika, hile, dolap, desise, dalavere; gizli aşk macerası; 2. v/i. entrika çevirmek, dalavere yapmak, dolap çevirmek; v/t. merakını uyandırmak, ilgisini çekmek; in'tri.guer n. hilekâr (veya dalavereci, entrikacı, düzenbaz) kimse.

in.trin.sic, in.trin.si.cal □ [in'trinsik(əl)] aslında olan, esası, asıl, hakiki; yaradılıştan.

in.tro.duce [intrə'djuːs] v/t. teklif etm., sunmak, öne sürmek, tanıştırmak, tanıtmak, takdim etm. (to -e); ortaya çıkarmak, ortaya koymak, getirmek (yeni fikir); öğretmek; sokmak, arasına koymak; in.tro.duc.tion [.-'dʌkʃən] n. takdim, tanıştırma; önsöz; başlangıç, giriş; letter of .- tavsiye mektubu; in.tro'duc.to.ry [.-təri] adj. tanıtıcı, tanıtma maksadiyle yapılan.

in.tro.spect [intrə'spekt] vb. kendi düşünce ve hislerini tahlil etm.; in.tro'spec.tion n. kendi düşünce ve hislerini tahlil etme; iç gözlem; in.tro'spec.tive □ [.-tiv] kendi kendini tetkik kabilinden.

in.tro.vert 1. [intrə'vəːt] v/t. içeri doğru çevirmek, kendi üzerine çevirmek (düşünce); 2. ['intrəvəːt] n. içine kapanık (veya içedönük) kimse.

in.trude [in'truːd] v/t. & v/i. zorla sok(ul)mak (into -e); davetsiz olarak girmek, izinsiz dalmak; kendini zorla kabul ettirmek (upon s.o. b-ne); ihlâl etm., boz-

mak (upon -i); **in'trud.er** n. davetsiz misafir; zorla sokulan kimse *veya* şey; a. ~ aircraft düşman uçağı.
**in.tru.sion** [in'truːʒən] n. içeri sokulma, zorla içeri girme; davetsiz olarak girme.
**in.tru.sive** ☐ [in'truːsiv] zorla içeri giren, izinsiz içeri giren; davetsiz olarak giren.
**in.trust** [in'trʌst] = entrust.
**in.tu.i.tion** [intjuː'iʃən] n. sezgi, içine doğma, sezi; **in'tu.i.tive** ☐ [~tiv] sezgi yolu ile öğrenilen; sezgili.
**in.un.date** ['inʌndeit] v/t. sel basmak, su ile kaplamak; garketmek, boğmak; **in.un'da.tion** n. sel, tufan; garketme, boğma.
**in.ure** [i'njuə] v/t. alıştırmak (to -e); **in'ure.ment** n. alıştırma.
**in.u.til.i.ty** [injuː'tiliti] n. faydasızlık, lüzumsuzluk, yararsızlık.
**in.vade** [in'veid] vb. saldırmak, hücum etm. -e, istilâ etm. -i; *fig.* tecavüz etm. *(hak);* ihlâl etm. -i; **in'vad.er** n. saldırgan; istilâcı.
**in.val.id¹** ['invəliːd] 1. *adj.* hasta, sakat, yatalak, zayıf; 2. n. hasta kimse; ✕, ✠ sakat *(veya* malûl) kimse; 3. v/t. ✕, ✠ çürüğe çıkarmak, hastaneye göndermek; hasta diye memleketine göndermek.
**in.val.id²** [in'vælid] *adj.* hükümsüz, geçersiz; **in.val.i.date** v/t. zayıflatmak, kuvvetten düşürmek; ∅₿ hükümsüz kılmak, geçersiz saymak; **in.val.i'da.tion** n. hükümsüz kılma, geçersiz sayma; **in.va.lid.i.ty** [invə'liditi] n. hükümsüzlük, geçersizlik.
**in.val.u.a.ble** ☐ [in'væljuəbl] paha biçilmez, çok kıymetli.
**in.var.i.a.ble** ☐ [in'vɛəriəbl] değişmez, sabit, daimi, sürekli, devamlı; **in'var.i.a.bly** *adv.* değişmeyerek, aynı şekilde, mütemadiyen, devamlı, her zaman.
**in.va.sion** [in'veiʒən] n. akın, saldırı, hücum, istilâ; ∅₿ ihlâl, tecavüz (of -i, -e); 🏴 nöbet, kriz; **in'va.sive** [~siv] *adj.* saldıran...; ihlâl eden, bozan (of -i); yayılan.
**in.vec.tive** [in'vektiv] n. küfür, sövüp sayma, hakaret, aşağılama.
**in.veigh** [in'vei] vb. çatmak, çıkışmak, sözle saldırmak *(against -e).*
**in.vei.gle** [in'viːgl] vb. kandırmak, ayartmak, baştan çıkarmak, aldatmak, cezbetmek, çekmek (into *-mesi için, -e);* **in'vei.gle.ment** n. aldatma, kandırma, baştan çıkarma.
**in.vent** [in'vent] v/t. icat etm., bulmak, keşfetmek; uydurmak, düzmek, atmak; **in'ven.tion** n. icat, buluş, keşif; uydur-

ma, atma, yalan; **in'ven.tive** ☐ [~tiv] yaratıcı; **in'ven.tive.ness** n. yaratıcılık; **in'ven.tor** n. mucit, türeten kimse, yaratıcı kimse; **in.ven.to.ry** ['invəntri] 1. n. envanter, mal stoku, mevcut; mal sayımını gösteren defter *veya* liste, envanter defteri; 2. v/t. envanterini çıkarmak.
**in.verse** ☐ ['in'vəːs] ters, ters çevrilmiş, tersyüz edilmiş; **in'ver.sion** n. ters dönme, altüst olma; ters çevirme; tersine dönmüş şey; değişim, değişme; homoseksüellik; *gr.* cümledeki kelime sırasının değişmesi.
**in.vert** 1. [in'vəːt] v/t. tersine çevirmek, tersyüz etm.; sırasını değiştirmek; ~ed. commas *pl.* tırnak işareti; ~ed flight ✈ sırtüstü *(veya* ters) uçuş; 2. ['invəːt] n. homoseksüel, sevici.
**in.ver.te.brate** [in'vəːtibrit] 1. *adj.* omurgasız, vertebrasız; *fig.* zayıf iradeli, dayanıksız, kuvvetsiz; 2. n. omurgasız hayvan; *fig.* kuvvetsiz kimse.
**in.vest** [in'vest] v/t. yatırmak *(para)* (in -e); sarfetmek *(para, güç, zaman);* giydirmek; süslemek, donatmak (with *ile);* vermek *(yetki);* kaplamak, sarmak (with *ile);* ✕ kuşatmak -i, çevirmek -i; v/i. ~ in F satın almak -i.
**in.ves.ti.gate** [in'vestigeit] vb. araştırmak, incelemek, tetkik etm., gözden geçirmek, teftiş etm., tahkik etm.; **in.ves.ti'ga.tion** n. araştırma, tetkik, inceleme, tahkik, teftiş; **in'ves.ti.ga.tor** [~geitə] n. araştırmacı.
**in.ves.ti.ture** [in'vestitʃə] n. resmen görevine getirme, tayin; **in'vest.ment** n. yatırma, para koyma, yatırım; resmen göreve getirme; yatırılan sermaye; ✕ kuşatma, muhasara, çevirme; **in'vest.or** n. sermayedar, yatırım yapan kimse.
**in.vet.er.a.cy** [in'vetərəsi] n. yerleşme, kökleşme *(alışkanlık, duygu);* tiryakilik; **in'vet.er.ate** ☐ [~rit] kökleşmiş, yerleşmiş *(alışkanlık, duygu);* tiryaki, düşkün, müptelâ.
**in.vid.i.ous** ☐ [in'vidiəs] kıskandırıcı; kıskanç; iğrenç, tiksindirici, çirkin.
**in.vig.i.late** [in'vidʒileit] vb. gözcülük etm., nezaret etm.; **in'vig.i.la.tor** n. gözcü, nezaretçi.
**in.vig.or.ate** [in'vigəreit] v/t. kuvvet vermek, kuvvetlendirmek, cesaret vermek, cesaretlendirmek, canlandırmak, zindelik vermek; **in.vig.or'a.tion** n. kuvvetlendirme, canlandırma.
**in.vin.ci.bil.i.ty** [invinsi'biliti] n. yenilmez-

lik, yılmazlık; **in'vin.ci.ble** ☐ yenilmez, yılmaz.
**in.vi.o.la.bil.i.ty** [invaiələ'biliti] *n*. dokunulmazlık; bozulmazlık; **in'vi.o.la.ble** ☐ dokunulmaz; bozulamaz, ihlâl edilemez; **in'vi.o.late** [~lit] *adj*. şeref ve haysiyetine dokunulmamış; bozulmamış, ihlâl edilmemiş; kutsal sayılmış.
**in.vis.i.bil.i.ty** [inviza'biliti] *n*. görülmezlik; **in'vis.i.ble** ☐ görülmez, görünmez; ~ mending dokuma kumaşları gözle farkedilemeyecek kadar iyi onarma.
**in.vi.ta.tion** [invi'teifən] *n*. davet, çağrı, çağırma; davetiye; **in.vite** [in'vait] *v/t*. davet etm., çağırmak; istemek; cezbetmek, celbetmek; **in'vit.ing** *adj*. çekici, davetkâr, cezbedici.
**in.vo.ca.tion** [invə'keifən] *n*. dua, niyaz, Tanrı'ya yakarış; **in.voc.a.to.ry** [in-'vɔkətəri] *adj*. dua kabilinden.
**in.voice** † ['invɔis] 1. *n*. fatura; gönderilen mal; 2. *v/t*. faturasını çıkarmak, fatura etm.
**in.voke** [in'vəuk] *v/t*. yalvarmak -*e*, yakarmak -*e*, dua etm. -*e*; çağırmak -*i*, davet etm. -*i*; istemek -*i*, rica etm. -*i*; yerine getirmek -*i*, yürütmek -*i*; sebep olm. -*e*.
**in.vol.un.tar.y** ☐ [in'vɔləntəri] tasarlanmamış, istenilmeden yapılan; bilinçsizce yapılan.
**in.vo.lute** ['invəlu:t] *adj*. dolaşık, karışık, karmaşık, çapraşık, girift, girişik; girintili çıkıntılı (*dişli*); helezonî kıvrılmış; **in.vo'lu.tion** *n*. kıvırma, sarma; kıvrılmış şey; karışıklık, dolaşıklık, karmaşıklık; karışık herhangi bir şey; eski haline dönme.
**in.volve** [in'vɔlv] *v/t*. sarmak, kuşatmak; içine almak, ihtiva etm., kapsamak; sokmak, karıştırmak, bulaştırmak (in -*e*); gerektirmek, icap ettirmek; etkilemek, tesir etm.; **in'volved** *adj*. karmaşık, karışık, çapraşık, anlaşılması güç; **in'volve-ment** *n*. ilgi, alâka, bağlılık; sarılma; karıştırılma, bulaştırılma.
**in.vul.ner.a.bil.i.ty** [invʌlnərə'biliti] *n*. yaralanamazlık, incitilemezlik; zaptedilemezlik; **in'vul.ner.a.ble** ☐ yaralanamaz, incitilemez; zaptedilemez, fethedilemez; *fig*. sağlam (*mevki*).
**in.ward** ['inwəd] 1. *adj* içerde olan, iç, dahilî (*a. fig.*); manevi, ruhsal; içe kıvrık; 2. *adv*. = inwards; 3. *n. fig*. maneviyat; ~s *pl*. iç organlar; **'in.ward.ly** *adv*. içte, içeride; akıl yoluyla, manen (*a. fig.*); **'in.ward.ness** *n*. içyüz, gerçek du-

rum; maneviyat; **in.wards** ['~z] *adv*. içe doğru; ruhun derinliğine doğru.
**i.od.ic** ⌢ [ai'ɔdik] *adj*. iyot..., iyotlu...; **i.o.dide** ['aiədait] *n*. iyodür; **i.o.dine** ['~di:n] *n*. iyot.
**i.o.do.form** ⌢ [ai'ɔdəfɔ:m] *n*. iyodoform.
**i.on** *phys*. ['aiən] *n*. iyon.
**I.o.ni.an** [ai'əunjən] 1. *adj*. İyonya *veya* İyonyalılara ait; 2. *n*. İyonyalı.
**I.on.ic¹** [ai'ɔnik] *adj*. İyonik; İyonya'ya ait.
**i.oni.c²** *phys*. [~] *adj*. iyon...; **i.on.ize** *phys*. ['aiənaiz] *v/t*. & *v/i*. iyonlaş(tır)mak.
**i.o.ta** [ai'əutə] *n*. Yunan alfabesinin dokuzuncu harfi, yota; çok küçük herhangi bir şey.
**I O U** ['aiəu'ju:] (= I owe you) size olan borcum; borç senedi.
**ip.so fac.to** ['ipsəu'fæktəu] *adv*. yalnız bu sebeple.
**I.ra.ni.an** [i'reiniən] 1. *adj*. İran'a ait; 2. *n*. İranlı.
**I.ras.ci.bil.i.ty** [iræsi'biliti] *n*. kızgınlık, huysuzluk, çabuk parlama; **i'ras.ci.ble** ☐ [~sibl] çabuk öfkelenir, sinirli, huysuz, çabuk parlar.
**i.rate** [ai'reit] *adj*. öfkeli, kızgın, hiddetli.
**ire** *poet*. ['aiə] *n*. öfke, hiddet, kızgınlık.
**ire.ful** ☐ ['aiəful] öfkeli, kızgın, tepesi atmış.
**ir.i.des.cence** [iri'desns] *n*. yanardönerlik; **ir.i'des.cent** *adj*. yanardöner, oynadıkça renk değiştiren, gökkuşağı gibi renkleri olan.
**i.rid.i.um** [i'ridiəm] *n*. iridyum.
**i.ris** ['aiəris] *n*. *anat*. iris tabakası; ♀ iris; ~ diaphragm *phot*. iris diyaframı, ayarlı diyafram.
**I.rish** ['aiərif] 1. *adj*. İrlanda'ya ait; İrlanda diline ait; 2. *n*. İrlandalılar; İrlanda dili, İrlanda şivesiyle konuşulan İngilizce; the ~ *pl*. İrlanda halkı, İrlandalılar; **'I.rish.ism** *n*. İrlandalılara özgü deyim, deyim *veya* ifade; **'I.rish.man** *n*. İrlandalı erkek; **'I.rish.wom.an** *n*. İrlandalı kadın.
**irk** [ə:k] *v/t*. bıktırmak, usandırmak, canını sıkmak, bezdirmek.
**irk.some** ☐ ['ə:ksəm] bıktırıcı, usandırıcı, sıkıcı, bezdirici.
**i.ron** ['aiən] 1. *n*. demir; *fig*. kuvvet, dayanıklılık; *a*. flat~ ütü; ~s *pl*. pranga, zincir; strike while the ~ is hot *fig*. demir tavında dövülür; 2. *adj*. demirden yapılmış; demir gibi; *fig*. sağlıklı, dinç, sapasağlam; değişmez, sabit; merhametsiz, zalim, katı yürekli, taş kalpli; 3. *v/t*. & *v/i*. ütüle(n)mek; demir kaplamak; zincirle bağlamak, prangaya vurmak;

**ı.~-bound** *adj.* engebeli, girintili çıkıntılı *(kıyı)*; katı *(gelenek)*; sert, haşin, şiddetli, kuvvetli; sabit; demirle takviye edilmiş; **ı.~.clad 1.** *adj.* demir kaplı, zırhlı; kuvvetli, bozulmaz *(yemin, söz)*; katı *(kural)*; **2.** *n.* zırhlı gemi; **~** cur.tain *pol.* demirperde **ı.ron.er** *n.* ütücü; **ı.ron--found.ry** *n.* dökümhane, demirhane; **ı.ron-ıheart.ed** *adj. fig.* taş kalpli, zalim, insafsız.

**ı.ron.ic, ı.ron.i.cal** ☐ [aiˈrɔnik(əl)] alay eden, alaylı, cinaslı.

**ı.ron.ing** [ˈaiəniŋ] **1.** *n.* ütüleme, ütü işi; ütülenen *veya* ütülenecek elbiseler; **2.** *adj.* ütü...; **~**-board ütü tahtası.

**ı.ron...: ~ lung 🟊** suni akciğer; **ı.~.mas.ter** *n.* demirci ustası; **ı.~.mon.ger** *n.* demirci, hırdavatçı, nalbur; **ı.~.mon.ger.y** *n.* demircilik, hırdavatçılık, nalburluk; demir eşya; **ı.~.mould** *n.* pas lekesi; **ı2.sides** *n. pl.* Cromwell'in süvari askerleri; **ı.~.work** *n.* demir eşya; **ı.~.works** *n.* ⊕ *mst sg.* demirhane, dökümhane.

**ı.ro.ny¹** [ˈaiəni] *adj.* demirden yapılmış, demire benzer.

**ı.ro.ny²** [ˈaiərəni] *n.* alay, istihza; kötü tesadüf, cilve *(kaderin)*.

**ir.ra.di.ance, ir.ra.di.an.cy** [iˈreidjəns(i)] *n.* parlaklık, aydınlık; *fig.* şaşaa; **ir.ra.di.ant** *adj.* ışık saçan, ışıldayan, parlayan (with *ile*).

**ir.ra.di.ate** [iˈreidieit] *v/t.* 🟊 röntgen ışınlarına tutmak; aydınlatmak, parlatmak (with *ile*); *fig.* aydınlığa kavuşturmak *(bir konu)*; **ir.ra.diˈa.tion** *n.* aydınlatma, parlaklık; *phys.* röntgen ışınlarına tutma; *fig.* aydınlığa kavuşturma.

**ir.ra.tion.al** ☐ [iˈræʃənl] akla uymaz, akılsız, mantıksız; yersiz, sebepsiz, münasebetsiz, saçma; Ⱥ yadrasyonel; **ir.ra-tion.al.i.ty** [~ˈnæliti] *n.* mantıksızlık, saçmalık, yersizlik.

**ir.re.claim.a.ble** ☐ [iriˈkleiməbl] ıslah olmaz, akıllanmaz, yola gelmez.

**ir.rec.og.niz.a.ble** ☐ [iˈrekəgnaizəbl] tanınamaz.

**ir.rec.on.cil.a.ble** ☐ [iˈrekənsailəbl] uzlaştırılamaz, barıştırılamaz; uyuşmaz *(fikir, tutum)*.

**ir.re.cov.er.a.ble** ☐ [iriˈkʌvərəbl] geri alınamaz, telâfi edilemez; düzeltilemez; tahsili mümkün olmayan, tahsil edilemeyen.

**ir.re.deem.a.ble** ☐ [iriˈdi:məbl] ıslah olunamaz, çaresiz, düzeltilemez; nakde tahvil olunamaz; bedeli ödenerek kurtarılamaz.

**ir.re.duc.i.ble** [iriˈdju:səbl] *adj.* azaltıla-

maz, küçültülemez, ufaltılamaz (into, to *-e*).

**ir.ref.ra.ga.bil.i.ty** [irefrəgəˈbiliti] *n.* aksi iddia edilemezlik, inkâr edilemezlik; değişmezlik, sabitlik; kırılmazlık; **ir.ref.ra-ga.ble** ☐ aksi iddia edilemez, inkâr edilemez, itiraz kabul etmez; değişmez, sabit *(kural)*; kırılmaz, sert.

**ir.ref.u.ta.ble** ☐ [iˈrefjutəbl] inkâr edilemez, reddedilemez, itiraz kaldırmaz, su götürmez.

**ir.reg.u.lar** [iˈregjulə] **1.** ☐ düzensiz, kuralsız, nizamsız, intizamsız; usule aykırı, yolsuz, usulsüz; *gr.* kural dışı; çarpık, düz olmayan, eğri; başıbozuk *(asker)*; **2.** *n.* **~s** *pl.* başıbozuk asker, çeteci; **ir.reg.u.lar.i.ty** [~ˈlæriti] *n.* düzensizlik, intizamsızlık, karışıklık, yolsuzluk, aykırılık.

**ir.rel.a.tive** [iˈrelətiv] *adj.* ilgisi olmayan, ilgisiz, alâkasız, konu dışı (to *ile*).

**ir.rel.e.vance, ir.rel.e.van.cy** [iˈrelivəns(i)] *n.* konu dışı olma; konu dışı olan şey; **ir.ˈrel.e.vant** ☐ konu dışı, ilgisiz, alâkasız (to *ile*).

**ir.re.li.gion** [iriˈlidʒən] *n.* dinsizlik; din aleyhtarlığı; **ir.reˈli.gious** ☐ dinsiz, dine karşı olan.

**ir.re.me.di.a.ble** ☐ [iriˈmi:djəbl] çaresiz, telâfi olunamaz, düzeltilemez; tedavisi mümkün olmayan.

**ir.re.mis.si.ble** ☐ [iriˈmisəbl] affolunamaz, bağışlanamaz; zorunlu, mecburi, kaçınılmaz.

**ir.re.mov.a.ble** ☐ [iriˈmu:vəbl] sabit, oynamaz; yerinden atılamaz, azlonulamaz.

**ir.rep.a.ra.ble** ☐ [iˈrepərəbl] tamir olunamaz, çaresiz, düzeltilemez; telâfisi imkânsız.

**ir.re.place.a.ble** [iriˈpleisəbl] *adj.* yeri doldurulamaz; yenisi teḋarik edilemez.

**ir.re.press.i.ble** ☐ [iriˈpresəbl] söndürülemez, bastırılamaz; baskıya gelmez; önüne geçilemez; kontrol edilemez, ele avuca sığmaz, zaptolunamaz.

**ir.re.proach.a.ble** ☐ [iriˈprəutʃəbl] hatasız, kusursuz; **ir.reˈproach.a.ble.ness** *n.* kusursuzluk, hatasızlık.

**ir.re.sist.i.bil.i.ty** [irizistəˈbiliti] *n.* karşı konulamazlık; **ir.reˈsist.i.ble** ☐ karşı konulamaz, dayanılamaz, çok çekici, pek cazip.

**ir.res.o.lute** [iˈrezəlu:t] *adj.* kararsız, mütereddit, zayıf; **irˈres.o.lute.ness, ir.res-oˈlu.tion** *n.* kararsızlık, tereddüt, zayıflık.

**ir.re.solv.a.ble** [iriˈzɔlvəbl] *adj.* çözümlenemez, tahlil edilemez, analiz edilemez.

**ir.re.spec.tive** ☐ [iriˈspektiv] (of) *-e* bakmaksızın; -i düşünmeden, -i hesaba katmayan, -i göz önünde bulundurmadan.

**ir.re.spon.si.bil.i.ty** ['irispɔnsɔ'biliti] *n.* sorumsuzluk, güvenilmezlik; **ir.re'spon.si.ble** ☐ sorumsuz, mesuliyetsiz, güvenilmez.

**ir.re.triev.a.ble** ☐ [iri'tri:vəbl] telâfi edilemez, bir daha ele geçmez, yeri doldurulamaz, karşılanamaz.

**ir.rev.er.ence** [i'revərəns] *n.* saygısızlık, hürmetsizlik; **ir'rev.er.ent** ☐ saygısız, hürmetsiz.

**ir.re.vers.i.ble** ☐ [iri'və:səbl] ters çevrilemez; değiştirilemez, geri döndürülemez, geri alınamaz, kesin, kati *(karar)*.

**ir.rev.o.ca.bil.i.ty** [irevəkə'biliti] *n.* geri alınamazlık, değiştirilemezlik, feshedilemezlik; **ir'rev.o.ca.ble** ☐ değiş(tirile)-mez, geri alınamaz, feshedilemez, gayri kabili rücu.

**ir.ri.gate** ['irigeit] *v/t.* sulamak; tazelendirmek; ‡ antiseptik su ile yıkamak *(yara)*; **ir.ri'ga.tion** *n.* sulama.

**ir.ri.ta.bil.i.ty** [iritə'biliti] *n.* alınganlık, titizlik, havadan nem kapma, çabuk öfkelenme; **ir.ri.ta.ble** ☐ çabuk kızan, alıngan, titiz, sinirli; **ir.ri.tant 1.** *adj.* sinirlendirici, öfkelendirici; tahrik edici; tahriş edici; **2.** *n.* tahriş edici madde; sinirlendirici herhangi bir şey; **ir.ri.tate** ['-teit] *v/t.* gücendirmek, kızdırmak, sinirlendirmek; tahrik etm.; tahriş etm.; **ir.ri.tat.ing** sinirlendirici, sinir bozucu, kızdırıcı; tahrik edici; tahriş edici; **ir.ri'ta.tion** *n.* sinirlilik, dargınlık, öfke, hiddet.

**ir.rup.tion** [i'rʌpʃən] *n.* içeriye baskın, hücum, akın, istilâ; **ir'rup.tive** [~tiv] *adj.* baskın kabilinden.

**is** [iz] -dir, -dır, -tir, -tur *(s. be)*.

**i.sin.glass** ['aizinglɑ:s] *n.* balık tutkalı; mika.

**Is.lam** ['izlɑ:m] *n.* İslâm; İslâm âlemi; İslâmiyet, Müslümanlık.

**is.land** ['ailənd] *n.* ada, ada gibi yer; refüj; **'is.land.er** *n.* adalı *(veya* adada oturan) kimse.

**isle** [ail] *n. poet.* ada; **Is.let** ['ailit] *n.* adacık.

**ism** *mst contp.* ['izəm] *n.* özel bir doktrin *veya* meslek.

**isn't** ['iznt] = is not.

**I.so...** ['aisəu] *prefix* aynı..., eşit...

**i.so.bar** *meteor.* ['aisəbɑ:] *n.* izobar, eşbası.

**i.so.late** ['aisəleit] *v/t.* ayırmak, tecrit etm., yalıtmak, izole etm.; karantinaya almak; **'i.so.lat.ed** *adj.* tek, ayrı, ayrıl-

mış, kendi başına olan, tecrit edilmiş, ücra, yalıtılmış; **i.so'la.tion** *n.* ayırma, tecrit, yalıtma, izole etme; karantinaya alma; ~ ward karantina odası; **i.so'la.tion.ist** *Am. pol.* [~ʃnist] *n.* tecrit politikası taraftarı, kendi memleketinin diğerlerinden ayrı hareket etmesi taraftarı.

**i.sos.ce.les** Å [ai'sɔsili:z] *adj.* ikizkenar...

**i.so.therm** *meteor.* ['aisəθə:m] *n.* eşsıcak, izoterm, eşsıcağı gösteren çizgi.

**i.so.tope** ⚛ ['aisətəup] *n.* izotop.

**i.so.type** ['aisəutaip] *n.* diyagram, grafik.

**Is.ra.el.ite** ['izriəlait] *n.* İsrail kavminden bir kimse; **'Is.ra.el.it.ish** *adj.* İsrail kavmine ait.

**is.sue** ['iʃu:] **1.** *n.* boşalma, çıkış, gidiş; çıkış kapısı, boşalma yeri, yol, ağız, delik; ♂ füru, çocuklar, torunlar, nesil, soy, döl; *fig.* sonuç, netice, son, nihayet, akıbet; ♂ dava konusu olan ihtilâf, münakaşalı mesele, tartışma konusu, sorun; boşalma, akıntı, akış, cerahat; ‡ ihraç, emisyon, tedavüle çıkarma *(papa)*; yayınlama, yayın, basım; sayı *(dergi)*; dağıtım, tevzi, donatma; ~ of fact asıl sorun; ~ of law kanun konusu, hukuk meselesi; force an ~ zorla karar ver(dir)mek; join (the) ~ tartışmak, münakaşa etm. (on *konusunda)*; join ~ with s.o. *b-le* tartışmak, münakaşa etm.; be at ~ tartışma konusu olm., üzerinde konuşulmak; point at ~ tartışma konusu, bahis konusu; **2.** *v/i.* çıkmak, dışarı akmak (from *-den)*; meydana gelmek, ortaya çıkmak, doğmak, hâsıl olm.; basılıp yayınlanmak; hak olarak hissesine düşmek; sonuç vermek, sonuçlanmak, neticeye varmak, bitmek (in *içinde)*; *v/t.* çıkarmak, dağıtmak; yayınlamak; vermek, ihraç etm.; ‡ tedavüle çıkarmak *(para)*; dağıtmak, tevzi etm. (with *-i)*; **'is.sue.less** *adj.* çocuksuz, torunsuz.

**isth.mus** ['isməs] *n.* kıstak, berzah.

**it** [it] **1.** *pron.* o, onu, ona *(cinssiz)*; *edat tan sonra:* onun... (= by it onun ile; for it onun için); how is ~ with...? ...nasıl?, ...den ne haber?; *s.* lord 2, foot 2; go ~ F cesaret etm., yapmağa kalkmak, yeltenmek; go ~! hadi!, yürü!, atıl!; we had a very good time of ~ doya doya tadını çıkardık; **2.** *n. oyun:* ebe; *sl.* önemli nokta.

**I.tal.ian** [i'tæljən] **1.** *adj.* İtalya, İtalyanlar ve İtalyanca ile ilgili; **2.** *n.* İtalyan; İtalyanca.

**I.tal.ics** *typ.* [i'tæliks] *n. pl.* italik; **i'tal.i.cize** [~saiz] *vb.* italik harflerle basmak.

**itch** [itʃ] **1.** *n.* ℰ kaşıntı, kaşınma; uyuz hastalığı; şiddetli arzu, özlem (for *için*, -e; to *inf. -meye*); **2.** *vb.* kaşınmak; *fig.* şiddetle arzu etm., özlem duymak, can atmak; be ~ing to *inf. -meye* can atmak; have an ~ing palm paraya düşkün olm., para canlısı olm.; **itch.ing** *n.* kaşıntı, kaşınma; *fig.* şiddetli arzu, özlem; **itch.y** *adj.* kaşıntılı, kaşınan.

**i.tem** [ˈaitəm] **1.** *adv.* keza, dahi; **2.** *n.* parça, kalem, adet; bent, madde, fıkra; **3.** *vb.* not etm., kaydetmek; **i.tem.ize** [ˈ~maiz] *vb.* ayrıntıları ile yazmak.

**it.er.ate** [ˈitəreit] *vb.* tekrarlamak, tekrar tekrar söylemek; **it.er.a.tion** *n.* tekrarla(n)ma, tekerrür; **it.er.a.tive** □ [ˈitərə-tiv] mükerrer, tekrarlanmış, yinelemeli.

**i.tin.er.ant** □ [iˈtinərənt] dolaşan, gezgin, seyyar...; **i.tin.er.ar.y** [aiˈtinərəri] **1.** *n.*

yol; yolcu rehberi; seyahat kitabı, seyahatname; seyahat programı; **2.** *adj.* yola (*veya* seyahate) ait, yol..., seyahat...; **i.tin.er.ate** [iˈtinəreit] *vb.* yolculuk etm., seyahat etm.; gezici vaizlik etm.

**its** [its] *adv.* onun(ki) (*cinssiz*).

**it's** F [its] = it is, it has.

**it.self** [itˈself] *adv.* bizzat, kendi(si); of ~ kendi kendine, kendiliğinden; in ~ haddi zatında, aslında, başlı başına; by ~ kendi kendine, otomatikman; yalnız başına, tek başına.

**I've** F [aiv] = I have.

**i.vied** [ˈaivid] *adj.* sarmaşık kaplı, sarmaşıklarla örtülü.

**i.vo.ry** [ˈaivəri] **1.** *n.* fildişi; fildişi rengi; fildişinden yapılmış eşya; **2.** *adj.* fildişi...; fildişi renginde...

**i.vy** ⚘ [ˈaivi] *n.* sarmaşık.

# J

**jab** F [dʒæb] 1. *v/t.* dürtmek, itmek; ucu keskin bir şeyle dürtmek; 2. *n.* dürtme, itme; *boks:* direk; F şırınga, iğne, enjeksiyon.

**jab.ber** [ˈdʒæbə] 1. *vb.* hızlı konuşmak, çabuk çabuk konuşmak; anlaşılmaz şekilde söylemek; 2. *n.* hızlı konuşma; anlamsız söz.

**jab.ot** [ˈʒæbəu] *n.* kadın elbisesinin önüne takılan süslü fırfır.

**Jack¹** [dʒæk] *n.* 'John' ismi; ~ Frost Ayaz Paşa, şiddetli ayaz; before one could say ~ Robinson çok hızlı *veya* ani, apansız.

**jack²** [~] 1. *n.* kriko; adam, herif; denizci, gemici; hizmetçi, uşak, işçi; bocurgat, kaldıraç; erkek hayvan *(eşek);* ↓ cıyadra sancağı; beş taş oyunu; *iskambil:* vale, bacak; pot, ortada biriken para; *sl.* para, mangır; *sl.* polis memuru, aynasız; priz; elma rakısı; çakı; 2. *v/t.* a. ~ up bocurgat ile kaldırmak, kriko ile kaldırmak.

**jack.al** [ˈdʒækɔːl] *n. zo.* çakal; *fig.* başkasının hesabına karanlık işler gören kimse.

**jack.a.napes** [ˈdʒækəneips] *n.* kendini beğenmiş kimse; yaramaz çocuk; **¹jack.ass** *n.* erkek eşek; *fig.* eşek herif, ahmak adam; **¹jack.boots** *n. pl.* eskiden süvarilerin giydiği dizi aşan çizme; **¹jack.daw** *n. orn.* küçük karga.

**jack.et** [ˈdʒækit] *n.* ceket; ⊕ kaplama, kılıf, gömlek, silindir ceketi; kitap zarfı, ciltli kitabın üstüne geçirilen kağıt kap; dust s.o.'s ~ F b-ni dövmek, pataklamak; potatoes in their ~s kabuğu soyulmamış patates.

**jack...: ¹~-in-of.fice** *n.* kılı kırk yaran ukalâ memur; **¹~-in-the-box** *n.* kutu açılınca içinden fırlayan yaylı kukla; ⊈ **Ketch** cellât; **¹~-knife** *n.* büyük çakı; **¹~-of-¹all--trades** *n.* elinden her iş gelen kimse, becerikli kimse, on parmağında on marifet olan kimse; **~-o'-¹lan.tern** [ˈdʒækəulæntən] *n.* bataklık yakamozu; içi oyulmuş ve bir tarafına insan çehresi şekli ve-

rilmiş kabaktan oyuncak fener; **¹~-plane** *n.* kaba planya, marangoz rendesi; **¹~.pot** *n. poker:* pot, ortada biriken para; hit the ~ *Am.* F turnayı gözünden vurmak, büyük başarı kazanmak; ~ **pud-ding** maskara, soytarı, palyaço; ~ **tar** gemici, denizci; **¹~-tow.el** *n.* el havlusu.

**Jac.o.bin** *hist.* [ˈdʒækəubin] *n.* Fransız ihtilâli sırasında örgütlenen ihtilâlci grupların üyesi; **Jac.o.bite** *hist.* [ˈ~-bait] *n.* 1685-1688 yılları arasında hüküm süren II. James yanlısı kimse.

**jade¹** [dʒeid] 1. *n.* yaşlı ve işe yaramaz beygir; *contp.* adı kötüye çıkmış kadın, cilveli kız; 2. *v/t. & v/i.* çok yor(ul)mak, bitkin düş(ür)mek, ağır işler vererek yormak.

**jade²** *min.* [~] *n.* yeşim, yeşil renkte değerli bir taş.

**jag** [dʒæg] 1. *n.* diş, sivri uç, ok ucu, kanca; *sl.* sarhoşluk, ayyaşlık; içki âlemi; 2. *vb.* diş diş etm., çentmek; **¹jag.ged** □, **¹jag.gy** dişli, çentikli, kertikli; *part. Am. sl.* jagged sarhoş, ayyaş.

**jag.uar** *zo.* [ˈdʒægjuə] *n.* jaguar.

**jail** [dʒeil] 1. *n.* cezaevi, tutuevi, hapishane, kodes; 2. *v/t.* hapsetmek, tutuklamak, hapse atmak; **¹~-bird** *n.* hapishane gediklisi, mahkûm; ip kaçkını; pranga kaçağı.

**jail.er** [ˈdʒeilə] *n.* gardiyan.

**ja.lop.(p)y** *part. Am.* F *mot.,* ⊰ [dʒəˈlɔpi] *n.* külüstür otomobil *veya* uçak.

**jam¹** [dʒæm] *n.* reçel, marmelat.

**jam²** [~] 1. *n.* sıkış(tırıl)ma; ⊕ kasılma, tekleme, kilitlenme; *radyo:* yayına karışan parazit; kalabalık, izdiham, sıkışıklık; zor durum, çıkmaz; *trafik* ~ trafik sıkışıklığı; be in a ~ *sl.* zor durumda olm., hapı yutmak, ayvayı yemek; ~ session caz müzisyenlerinin toplanarak müzik yapmaları; 2. *v/t. & v/i.* sıkış(tır)mak; tık(ıştır)mak; *radyo:* parazit yapmak; ⊕ kasılmak, sıkışıp durmak, kenetlenmek, bloke etm.; ~ the brakes frenleri kenetlemek, kasmak, kilitlemek.

**Ja.mai.ca** [dʒə'meikə] *n. a.* ~ rum Jamaika romu.

**Jamb** [dʒæm] *n.* kapı *veya* pencere pervazı.

**jam.bo.ree** [dʒæmbə'riː] *n. (part. izcilerin yaptığı)* toplantı; *sl.* eğlenti, cümbüş, âlem, şamata, gırgır.

**jam-jar** ['dʒæmdʒaː] *n.* reçel kavanozu.

**jan.gle** ['dʒæŋgl] **1.** *vb.* kavga etm., çekişmek, ağız münakaşası etm.; ahenksiz ses çıkarmak; ahenksiz bir şekilde söylemek; **2.** *n.* gürültü; ahenksiz ses; **'jan-gling** *adj.* tiz, cırlak, kulakları tırmalayan *(ses)*.

**jan.i.tor** ['dʒænitə] *n.* kapıcı, odacı; *Am.* hademe.

**Jan.'u.ar.y** ['dʒænjuəri] *n.* ocak (ayı).

**Jap** F [dʒæp] *n.* Japon.

**ja.pan** [dʒə'pæn] **1.** *n.* laka, parlak ve sert cila, Japon verniği; **2.** *v/t.* Japon lakası ile cilalamak.

**Jap.a.nese** [dʒæpə'niːz] **1.** *adj.* Japonya'ya ait; **2.** *n.* Japon(yalı); Japonca; the ~ *pl.* Japon halkı.

**ja.pan.ner** [dʒə'pænə] *n.* cilacı, vernikçi, lakacı.

**jar¹** [dʒaː] *n.* kavanoz.

**jar²** [~] **1.** *n.* sarsıntı, titreşim; şok; çatlak ses, bozuk ses; **2.** *v/t. & v/i.* sars(ıl)-mak, titre(t)mek, salla(n)mak; çatlak ses çıkarmak, ahenksiz ses vermek; sinirlendirmek (upon *-i*); dokunmak *(sinirine)*; tırmalamak *(kulak)*; ~ with *ile* uyuşmamak, *-e* uymamak.

**jar.gon** ['dʒaːgən] *n.* anlaşılmaz dil *veya* söz; teknik lisan.

**jas.min(e)** ♀ ['dʒæsmin] *n.* yasemin.

**jas.per** *min.* ['dʒæspə] *n.* yeşime benzer bir taş.

**jaun.dice** ['dʒɔːndis] *n.* ♥ sarılık hastalığı; *fig.* sağduyuyu bozan hissi durum, kıskançlık, haset, gıpta; **'jaun.diced** *adj.* sarılık olmuş; *fig.* kıskanç.

**jaunt** [dʒɔːnt] **1.** *n.* gezinti; **2.** *v/i.* gezmek; **'jaun.ti.ness** *n.* neşe; kibarlık; şıklık; **'jaunt.ing-car** *n.* iki tekerlekli hafif at arabası; **'jaun.ty** ☐ soylu, kibar; şık, gösterişli, fiyakalı; neşeli, canlı.

**Jav.a.nese** [dʒaːvə'niːz] **1.** *adj.* Cava'ya *veya* Cava diline özgü; **2.** *n.* Cava halkı *veya* dili; the ~ *pl.* Cava halkı, Cavalılar.

**jave.lin** ['dʒævlin] *n.* kargı, mızrak; *spor:* cirit; throwing the ~ cirit atma.

**jaw** [dʒɔː] **1.** *n.* çene; ~s *pl.* ağız; dar geçit, boğaz; ⊕ sap, çene; F konuşkanlık, gevezelik; sıkıcı konuşma; **2.** *v/i.* çene çalmak, gevezelik etm., laklak etm.; *v/t.*

P veríp veriştirmek, çıkışmak, dırlanmak; '~-bone *n.* çene kemiği; '~-break-er *n.* F telaffuzu zor kelime.

**jay** [dʒəi] *n. orn.* alakarga, kestane kargası; F geveze kimse, lakırdıcı; '~.walk-er *n.* bir caddeyi trafik kurallarını çiğneyerek geçen kimse.

**jazz** [dʒæz] **1.** *n.* caz; *caz* müziği parçası; yalan, martaval, dümen; şey, zımbırtı, falan filan; **2.** *adj.* F göz kamaştırıcı, fiyakalı; **3.** *v/t.* caz türünde çalmak *veya* düzenlemek *(şarkı)*; ~ up canlandırmak, hareketlendirmek; '~-band *n.* cazbant, caz orkestrası; **'jaz.zy** = jazz 2.

**jeal.ous** ☐ ['dʒeləs] kıskanç, kıskanan (of *-i*); aşırı titiz, dikkatli; şüpheci; **'jeal-ous.y** *n.* kıskançlık, haset.

**jean** [dʒiːn] *n.* bir çeşit kaba pamuklu bez; ~s *pl.* blucin pantolon.

**jeep** [dʒiːp] *n.* cip.

**jeer** [dʒiə] **1.** *n.* alay, alaylı söz, taş, yuha; **2.** *v/i.* alay etm., eğlenmek, dalga geçmek *(at ile)*; *v/t.* alaya almak, küçümsemek; **'jeer.er** *n.* alaycı kimse; **'jeer-ing** ☐ alaylı, iğneli, taşlı.

**je.june** ☐ [dʒi'dʒuːn] yavan, anlamsız, manasız, kuru, sıkıcı, *esp. Am.* çocukça.

**jell** F [dʒel] *v/t. & v/i.* pelteleş(tir)mek, pelte gibi donmak; *fig.* şekillenmek, şekil almak.

**jel.ly** ['dʒeli] **1.** *n.* pelte, meyve özünden yapılmış jelatinli marmelat; jelatin; **2.** *v/t. & v/i.* pelteleş(tir)mek, pelte gibi donmak; '~-fish *n. zo.* denizanası, medüz.

**jem.my** ['dʒemi] *n.* kısa demir çubuk, levye.

**jen.ny** ⊕ ['dʒeni] *n.* pamuk eğirme makinesi, çıkrık; = spinning-~.

**jeop.ard.ize** ['dʒepədaiz] *v/t.* tehlikeye atmak, tehlikeye koymak; **'jeop.ard.y** *n.* tehlike.

**jer.bo.a** *zo.* [dʒəː'bəuə] *n.* Asya ve Kuzey Afrika'da yaşayan tarla faresi.

**jer.e.mi.ad** [dʒeri'maiəd] *n.* yakınma, figan, feryat, dert yanma, can sıkıcı şikâyet.

**jerk** [dʒəːk] **1.** *n.* ani çekiş, itme, başlama, duruş, bükme, kaldırma *veya* fırlatma; silk(in)me; büzülme, burkulma, gerilme; *sl.* aptal, ayı; by ~s hamle ile; *physical* ~s *pl.* F jimnastik hareketleri, idman, beden eğitimi; **2.** *vb.* atmak, fırlatmak; kesik kesik söylemek; uzun parçalar halinde kesip güneşte kurutmak *(et)*; birdenbire çekmek.

**jer.kin** ['dʒəːkin] *n.* dar deri yelek.

**jerk.wa.ter** *Am.* ['dʒəːkwɔːtə] **1.** *n.* banliyö

treni; **2.** *adj.* F taşra...; küçük, önemsiz; **'jerk.y 1.** ☐ sarsıntılı; *sl.* aptal, salak, ahmak; **2.** *n. Am.* güneşte kurutulmuş sığır eti.

**jer.ry** *sl.* ['dʒeri] *n.* ✕ ♀ Alman askeri; lâzımlık, oturak; **'~-build.er** *n.* kötü malzeme kullanan inşaatçı; **'~-build.ing** *n.* kötü malzeme kullanarak inşa etme; **'~-built** *adj.* kötü malzeme kullanılarak yapılmış; ~ house kötü malzeme ile yapılmış (*veya* derme çatma) ev; **'~.can** *n.* benzin *veya* yağ bidonu.

**jer.sey** ['dʒəːzi] *n.* jarse; yün kazak; ♀ *n. zo.* Jersey adasında bulunan sütü çok yağlı bir cins inek.

**jes.sa.mine** ♀ ['dʒesəmin] *n.* yasemin.

**jest** [dʒest] **1.** *n.* şaka, lâtife, alay; **2.** *vb.* şakaya almak; hafife almak, yabana atmak; alaya almak; şaka söylemek; şaka etm.; alaylı konuşmak; **'jest.er** *n.* şakacı, dalkavuk, soytarı.

**Jes.u.it** ['dʒezjuit] *n.* Cizvit; **Jes.u'it.ic, Jes.u'it.i.cal** ☐ Cizvit gibi.

**jet¹** *min.* [dʒet] *n.* siyah kehribar, kara amber, Erzurum taşı; simsiyah renk.

**jet²** [~] **1.** *n.* fışkırma, püskürme; tepki; jet uçağı; jet motoru; ⊕ meme; ~ propulsion jetle tepki, jetle çalıştırma; ~ set jet sosyete; **2.** *v/t. & v/i.* fışkır(t)-mak, püskür(t)mek; jet uçağı ile seyahat etm.

**jet-black** ['dʒet'blæk] *adj.* simsiyah, kapkara.

**jet...:** ~ en.gine jet motoru; **'~-plane** *n.* jet uçağı, tepkili uçak; **'~-pow.ered** *adj.* tepki ile çalışan, tepkili.

**jet.sam** ['dʒetsəm] *n.* tehlike anında gemiyi hafifletmek için denize atılan mal; bu şekilde atıldıktan sonra karaya vuran eşya; flotsam and ~ denizin attığı enkaz; *fig.* serseriler, ayaktakımı.

**jet.ti.son** ['dʒetisn] **1.** *n.* tehlike anında gemiyi hafifletmek için eşyayı denize atma; bu suretle denize atılan mal; **2.** *v/t.* tehlike anında gemiyi hafifletmek için denize atmak (*eşya*); *fig.* feda etm.; **'jet.ti.son.a.ble** *adj.* atılabilir türden, atılabilir...

**jet.ty** ↓ ['dʒeti] *n.* dalgakıran, set, mendirek; iskele, rıhtım.

**Jew** [dʒuː] *n.* Yahudi; *attr.* Yahudi...

**jew.el** ['dʒuːəl] **1.** *n.* kıymetli taş, mücevher, cevher (*a. fig.*); **2.** *v/t.* kıymetli taşlarla süslemek; **'jew.el(l)er** *n.* kuyumcu; **'jew.el.ry, 'jew.el.ler.y** *n.* kuyumculuk; *pl.* mücevherat.

**Jew.ess** ['dʒuːis] *n.* Yahudi kadın; **'Jew.ish** *adj.* Musevi..., Yahudi...; **Jew.ry**

['dʒuəri] *n.* Musevi halkı; Yahudilik.

**jib** [dʒib] **1.** *n.* ↓ flok yelkeni; ⊕ vinç kolu; the cut of his ~ dış görünüşü; **2.** *v/i.* aniden durmak (*at*); inat edip ileri gitmemek (*at*); *fig.* ayak diremek, dayatmak; ~ at -e isteksizlik göstermek, -i istememek, beğenmemek; **'jib.ber** *n.* inat edip ileri gitmeyen at; **'jib'boom** *n.* ↓ bumba, gemi bastonu.

**jibe** [dʒaib] *vb. Am.* F uy(uş)mak; = gibe.

**jif.fy** F ['dʒifi] *n.* an; in a ~ hemen, derhal, göz açıp kapayıncaya kadar.

**jig** [dʒig] **1.** *n.* oynak ve hızlı bir dans, cig dansı; bu dansın müziği; ⊕ delme cihazı, cig; **2.** *v/t. & v/i.* cig dansı yap-(tır)mak; iki yana salla(n)mak; bir aşağı bir yukarı zıpla(t)mak.

**jig.ger** ['dʒigə] *n.* pire; kene, sakırga; *Am.* kokteyller için ölçü olarak kullanılan ufak cam bardak.

**jig.gered** F ['dʒigəd] *adj.*: I'm ~ if ......irse hayret doğrusu.

**jig.gle** [dʒigl] *v/t. & v/i.* salla(n)mak.

**jig-saw** ['dʒigsɔː] *n.* makineli oyma testeresi; ~ puz.zle oyma testeresi ile kesilmiş tahta parçalarından ibaret bilmece.

**jill** [dʒil] = gill³.

**jilt** [dʒilt] **1.** *n.* sevgilisini reddeden kız; **2.** *v/t.* reddetmek, yüzüstü bırakmak (*sevgili*).

**Jim** *Am. sl.* [dʒim] *n.:* ~ Crow zenci.

**jim-jams** *sl.* ['dʒimdʒæmz] *n. pl.* aşırı sinirlilik.

**jim.my** ['dʒimi] *n.* hırsızların kullandıkları demir çubuk.

**jin.gle** ['dʒiŋgl] **1.** *n.* çıngırtı, şıngırtı; tekerleme gibi kelimeler; **2.** *v/t. & v/i.* çıngırda(t)mak, şıngırda(t)mak; alliterasyon ve kafiyelerle dolu olm. (*mısra*).

**jin.go** ['dʒiŋgəu] *n.* şoven, savaş taraftarı; by ~! *sl.* ya!, öyle mi!, vallahi!; **'jin-go.ism** *n.* aşırı milliyetçilik.

**jinks** [dʒiŋks] *n. pl.:* mst high ~ eğlence, şamata, gırgır, cümbüş, tantana.

**jinn** [dʒin] = genie.

**jinx** *sl.* [dʒiŋks] *n.* uğursuz şey *veya* kimse.

**jit.ney** *Am. sl.* ['dʒitni] *n.* beş sentlik para; minibüs, dolmuş.

**jit.ter** F ['dʒitə] **1.** *v/i.* sinirli olm.; sinirli davranmak; **2.** *n.* ~s *pl. sl.* aşırı sinirlilik; have the ~s heyheyleri üstünde olm.; **'~.bug** **1.** *n. fig.* heyheyleri üstünde (*veya* şaşalamış, şaşkın) kimse; 1940'lı yılların hareketli ve popüler bir dansı; caz müziğe delisi; **2.** *v/i.* deli gibi caz dansı yapmak; **'jit.ter.y** *adj. sl.* çok

sinirli, heyheyleri üstünde; korkmuş.
**jiu-jit.su** [dʒuːˈdʒitsuː] *n.* silahsız dövüş
sanatı.
**jive** *Am. sl.* [dʒaiv] *n.* caz müziği; caz
müziği argosu; yanıltıcı *veya* aptalca
konuşma, gevezelik.
**Job¹** [dʒəub] *n.*: ~'s comforter sözde teselli etmeye çalışarak bir kimsenin sıkıntısını arttıran kimse.
**job²** [dʒɔb] **1.** *n.* iş, görev, vazife, memuriyet; hizmet; soygun; dalavere, hileli
iş; † parti malı; by the ~ götürü usulü;
make a good ~ of it bşi başarmak, üstesinden gelmek; a bad ~ ümitsiz (*veya* kötü) şey *veya* durum; ~ lot satın alınan çeşitli eşya; ~ printer küçük matbaacı; ~
work götürü iş; **2.** *v/t.* götürü usulü çalıştırmak; kira ile tutmak; aldatmak, dolandırmak; † kâr amacıyla alıp satmak;
kötüye kullanmak, suiistimal etm.; *v/i.*
götürü iş yapmak; kişisel çıkarı için resmi işe girmek; komisyonculuk yapmak.
**job.ber** [ˈdʒɔbə] *n.* komisyoncu, simsar,
tellâl; götürü usulü çalışan kimse; resmi
görevini suiistimal eden kimse; toptancı; **¹job.ber.y** *n.* resmi işlerde dalaverecilik; **¹job.bing** *n.* komisyonculuk; götürü usulü çalışma; *s.* jobbery.
**jock.ey** [ˈdʒɔki] **1.** *n.* cokey; **2.** *vb.* aldatmak, dolandırmak; cokey sıfatıyla bin-
mek *(at)*; işletmek, çalıştırmak; yerini
değiştirmek.
**jo.cose** □ [dʒəuˈkəus] şakacı, latifeci;
komik, gülünç; şen, neşeli; **joˈcose.ness**
*n.* şakacılık, latifecilik; komiklik.
**joc.u.lar** [ˈdʒɔkjulə] *adj.* şaka yollu, şaka
türünden, şakalı; **joc.u.lar.i.ty** [~ˈlæriti]
*n.* şakacılık.
**joc.und** □ [ˈdʒɔkənd] neşeli, şen, hoş, keyifli, canlı.
**Jodh.purs** [ˈdʒɔdpuəz] *n. pl.* ata binerken
giyilen pantolon, potur.
**Joe** [dʒəu]: ~ Miller bayat espri.
**jog** [dʒɔg] **1.** *n.* sarsma, hafifçe itme, dürtme; tırıs yürüyüş; girinti *veya* çıkıntı;
keskin viraj; **2.** *v/t.* sarsmak, itmek,
dürtmek; canlandırmak *(hafıza)*; tırıs
yürütmek *(at)*; *v/i.* mst ~ along, ~ on
yavaş yavaş gezinmek, bir tempoda ilerlemek; yavaş yavaş koşmak; **jog.ging** *n.*
yavaş yavaş koşma, ağır ağır ilerleme.
**jog.gle** [ˈdʒɔgl] **1.** *v/t. & v/i.* hafifçe sars-
(ıl)mak, yavaşça salla(n)mak, ⊕ dişle-
mek, çentik açmak; **2.** *n.* sarsma, sallama; ⊕ geçme, dişli yiv.
**jog-trot** [ˈdʒɔgˈtrɔt] *n.* tırıs yürüyüş, yavaş yürüyüş; *fig.* lakaytlık, işi oluruna
bırakma.

**John** [dʒɔːn]: ~ Bull İngiliz milleti; tipik
İngiliz; ~ Hancock *Am.* bir kimsenin kendi el yazısı ile imzası.
**join** [dʒɔin] **1.** *v/t. & v/i.* birleş(tir)mek,
bağlan()mak, bitiş(tir)mek, kavuş(tur)-
mak (to *-e*); ⊕ raptetmek; katılmak *-e*
*(kulüp, parti, ordu)*; evlendirmek ~ battle
savaşa girmek; ~ company gruba katılmak (with); ~ hands el ele tutuşmak; *fig.*
birlik olm.; ~ in katılmak *-e*; ~ up askere yazılmak, orduya katılmak; üye kaydolunmak; I ~ with you ben senden tara-
fayım, sana katılıyorum; **2.** *n.* bitişim
noktası; birleşme, bitişme.
**join.er** [ˈdʒɔinə] *n.* doğramacı, marangoz;
**¹join.er.y** *n.* doğramacılık, marangozluk.
**joint** [dʒɔint] **1.** *n.* ek; ek yeri; et parçası; batakhane; *anat.* eklem, mafsal; ♣
nod, düğüm, boğum; *Am. sl.* esrarlı sigara; put out of ~ yerinden oynatmak,
burkmak, çıkarmak *(kol, bacak)*; out of
~ çıkık; *fig.* çığrından çıkmış; **2.** □ birleşik, ortaklaşa, müşterek...; ~ heir müşterek vâris; **3.** *v/t.* bitiştirmek, birleştirmek, eklemek; ⊕ raptetmek; **¹joint.ed**
*adj.* birleştirilmiş, bitiştirilmiş; mafsallı; ~ doll parçalardan yapılmış oyuncak
bebek; **joint stock** ana sermaye; **¹joint-
-stock com.pa.ny** anonim şirket; **join.ture**
ʤ [ˈ~tʃə] *n.* bir kadına kocasının ölümünden sonra kalmak şartıyla bağlanan
gelir.
**joist** [dʒɔist] *n.* kiriş.
**joke** [dʒəuk] **1.** *n.* şaka, latife, nükte; şaka konusu; practical ~ eşek şakası; **2.**
*v/i.* şaka yapmak, latife etm.; *v/t.* takılmak, şakadan aldatmak, alaya almak,
eğlenmek *(about -e, -i, ile)*; **¹jok.er** *n.*
iskambil: koz, joker; şakacı kimse:
*Am.* bir kanun tasarısına gizlice eklenen
ve anlamını değiştiren madde; herif,
adam; **¹jok.y** □ komik, gülünç, eğlendirici.
**jol.li.fi.ca.tion** F [dʒɔlifiˈkeiʃən] *n.* eğlence,
gırgır, şamata, cümbüş, âlem; **¹jol.li.ness,
¹jol.li.ty** *n.* neşe, zevk.
**jol.ly** [ˈdʒɔli] **1.** □ şen, neşeli, keyifli, neşe dolu, sevinçli, memnun, mutlu; F hoş,
güzel, sevimli, zarif, cazip; çakırkeyf;
**2.** *adv.* F çok, pek çok, fazlasıyla; **3.** *vb.*
F *b-nin* gönlünü yapmak, *b-ni* tatlı sözle kandırmak; eğlenmek, alay etm., takılmak.
**jol.ly-boat** ⚓ [ˈdʒɔliˈbəut] *n.* küçük filika.
**jolt** [dʒəult] **1.** *v/t. & v/i.* sars(ıl)mak; **2.**
*n.* sarsıntı, sarsma; sürpriz, şok; **¹jolt.y**
*adj.* sarsıntılı.

**Jonathan**

**Jon.a.than** [ˈdʒɔnəθən]: Brother ~ Amerikalı.

**jon.quil** ⚜ [ˈdʒɔŋkwil] *n.* fulya, zerrin.

**jo.rum** [ˈdʒɔːrəm] *n.* büyük içki kabı; bu kabın içindeki içki *(esp. punç).*

**josh** *Am. sl.* [dʒɔʃ] **1.** *n.* şaka, takılma; **2.** *v/t.* alay etm., takılmak; *v/i.* şaka yapmak.

**joss** [dʒɔs] *n.* Çin tanrısı; '~-house *n.* Çin mabedi, Çin tapınağı.

**jos.tle** [ˈdʒɔsl] **1.** *vb.* itip kakmak, it(tir)-mek, dürtüklemek; **2.** *n.* itip kakma, iteleme.

**jot** [dʒɔt] **1.** *n.* zerre, pek az şey, az miktar; **2.** *v/t.* ~ down yazıvermek, not almak; 'jot.ter *n.* not defteri; 'jot.tings *n. pl.* alınan notlar.

**jour.nal** [ˈdʒəːnl] *n.* gazete, dergi; † yevmiye defteri; ↓ seyir defteri; günlük, muhtıra; meclis zabıt defteri; ⊕ mil ucu, mihver mili; **jour.nal.ese** F [ˈ~nəˈliːz] *n.* gazeteci üslubu, gazeteci ağzı; 'jour.nal.ism *n.* gazetecilik; 'jour.nal.ist *n.* gazeteci; **jour.nal'is.tic** *adj.* (~ally) gazeteciliğe ait, gazetecilik...; 'jour.nal.ize *vb.* † yevmiye defterine geçirmek; † yevmiye defteri tutmak; günlük tutmak; gazetecilik yapmak.

**jour.ney** [ˈdʒəːni] **1.** *n.* yolculuk, seyahat, gezi, sefer, yol; **2.** *v/i.* yolculuk etm.; '~.man *n.* usta, kalfa; '~-work *n.* usta işi.

**joust** [dʒaust] **1.** *n.* at üstünde yapılan mızrak dövüşü; **2.** *v/i.* at üstünde mızrak dövüşü yapmak; polemiğe girmek.

**Jove** [dʒəuv] *n.* Jupiter, baş tanrı; by ~! Allah Allah!, yok ya!

**jo.vi.al** □ [ˈdʒəuvjəl] şen, neşeli, keyifli; **jo.vi.al.i.ty** [~viˈæliti] *n.* şenlik, neşe, keyif.

**jowl** [dʒaul] *n.* çene; gıdık; gerdan; cheek by ~ sıkı fıkı; yana yana.

**joy** [dʒɔi] *n.* sevinç, neşe, keyif, haz, memnuniyet; **joy.ful** □ [ˈ~ful] neşeli, sevinçli, keyifli, neşe dolu, memnun; 'joy.ful.ness *n.* neşelilik, sevinçlilik, keyiflilik; 'joy.less □ neşesiz, keyifsiz, kederli, üzgün, tasalı; 'joy.ous □ sevinçli, keyifli, neşeli; 'joy-ride *n. sl.* çalıntı araba ile zevk için yapılan gezinti; 'joy-stick *n.* ✈ *sl.* manevra kolu, kumanda levyesi.

**ju.bi.lant** [ˈdʒuːbilənt] *adj.* büyük neşe içinde, çok memnun, sevinçli, coşkulu; zafer sarhoşu; **ju.bi.late** [ˈ~leit] *v/i.* coşmak, çok sevinmek; **ju.bi'la.tion** *n.* çok sevinme, coşma; **ju.bi.lee** [ˈ~liː] *n.* yıldönümü şenliği; ellinci yıldönümü; neşeli kutlama, jübile.

**Ju.da.ism** [ˈdʒuːdeiizəm] *n.* Yahudilik.

**Ju.das** [ˈdʒuːdəs] *n. fig.* hain, asi; *a.* 2-hole gözetleme deliği.

**judge** [dʒʌdʒ] **1.** *n.* hâkim, yargıç; hakem; bilirkişi; Yahudilerde krallardan önce geçici hükümdarlık yetkisi verilen hâkim; **2.** *vb.* bş hakkında fikir edinmek; bir davayı çözmek; hâkimlik yapmak; bir hükme varmak (from, by -*den*; of *hakkında*); yargılamak, muhakeme etm.; hüküm vermek (by -*den*); eleştirmek, tenkit etm.; karar vermek *(hakkında).*

**judg(e).ment** [ˈdʒʌdʒmənt] *n.* hüküm, yargı, karar; mahkeme kararı, bildiri, tebligat; muhakeme, yargılama; fikir, düşünce; Allah tarafından verilen ceza; in my ~ bence, bana kalırsa, kanımca; pronounce ~ kararı bildirmek; sit in ~ duruşma yapmak; come to ~ karara varmak; Day of 2, 2-Day kıyamet günü, hüküm günü.

**judge.ship** [ˈdʒʌdʒʃip] *n.* hâkimlik, yargıçlık.

**ju.di.ca.ture** [ˈdʒuːdikətʃə] *n.* yargılama; hâkimler kurulu; mahkeme; yargılama işlemi.

**ju.di.cial** □ [dʒuːˈdiʃəl] mahkemeye ait, adli, hukuki; hâkime ait; şer'i; ~ murder mahkeme kararı ile fakat haksız yere ölüm cezası; ~ system hukuk sistemi.

**ju.di.ci.a.ry** [dʒuːˈdiʃiəri] *adj.* adli, hukukî.

**ju.di.cious** □ [dʒuːˈdiʃəs] akıllı, tedbirli; sağgörülü; **ju'di.cious.ness** *n.* sağgörülülük, basiretlilik.

**ju.do** [ˈdʒuːdəu] *n. spor:* judo.

**jug** [dʒʌg] **1.** *n.* testi, çömlek; *sl.* hapishane, kodes; **2.** *v/t.* çömlekte haşlamak; *sl.* kodese tıkmak; ~ged hare haşlanmış tavşan.

**Jug.ger.naut** *fig.* [ˈdʒʌgənɔːt] *n.* put, sanem; insanın kendisini körü körüne feda etmesini gerektiren inanç.

**jug.gins** F [ˈdʒʌginz] *n.* pısırık *(veya* sünepe, sümsük) kimse.

**jug.gle** [ˈdʒʌgl] **1.** *n.* hokkabazlık; hile, aldatmaca; **2.** *vb.* hokkabazlık yapmak; hile yapmak; aldatmak; *fig.* çarpıtmak, olduğundan değişik göstermek; mahrum etm. (out of -*den*); 'jug.gler *n.* hokkabaz, jonglör; hilekâr kimse, dolandırıcı; 'jug.gler.y *n.* hokkabazlık; hile.

**Ju.go.slav** [ˈjuːgəuˈslaːv] **1.** *n.* Yugoslav(yalı); **2.** *adj.* Yugoslav...

**jug.u.lar** *anat.* [ˈdʒʌgjulə] *n.* boyna ait, boyun...; ~ vein şahdamarı; **ju.gu.late** *fig.* [ˈ~leit] *v/t.* durdurmak, önüne geçmek, önlemek.

**juice** [dʒuːs] *n.* özsu, usare; sebze, meyve *veya* et suyu; insan vücudunun sıvı kısımları; *mot. sl.* benzin; ✗ *sl.* elektrik, cereyan; kuvvet, güç; **¹juic.i.ness** *n.* özlülük, sululuk; **¹juic.y** □ özlü, sulu; F ilginç, enteresan, merak uyandırıcı.

**ju.jube** [ˈdʒuːdʒuːb] *n.* ✿ hünnap; *pharm.* hünnap şekerlemesi.

**ju-jut.su** [dʒuːˈdʒutsuː] *n.* silahsız dövüş sanatı.

**juke-box** *Am.* F [ˈdʒuːkbɔks] *n.* para ile çalışan müzik dolabı, otomatik pikap.

**ju.lep** [ˈdʒuːlep] *n.* ilâca karıştırılan tatlı bir sıvı; *part. Am.* buzlu ve naneli içki.

**Ju.ly** [dʒuːˈlai] *n.*, temmuz.

**jum.ble** [ˈdʒʌmbl] **1.** *n.* karmaşa, karışıklık, karmakarışık iş; **2.** *vb. a.* ~ up karmakarışık etm.; karmakarışık olm.; **¹~-sale** *n.* eski *veya* elden düşme malların birarada satışı *(yardım için).*

**jump** [dʒʌmp] **1.** *n.* atlama, sıçrama, zıplama; irkilme; fırlama, yükselme, artış *(fiyat);* ~s *pl.* sinirlilik; **high (long)** ~ yüksek (uzun) atlama; **get (have) the** ~ **on** *Am.* F *-den* önce davranmak; **give a** ~ korkutmak, ürkütmek; **2.** *v/t. & v/i.* atla(t)mak, sıçra(t)mak, zıpla(t)mak, fırla(t)mak, üzerinden atla(t)mak; içine atlamak, binmek *(tren, taksi);* geçivermek *(konudan konuya);* küt küt atmak *(kalp); fig.* aniden fırlamak *(fiyat);* ~ **at** hemen kabul etm., *-e* dünden razı olm.; ~ **to conclusions** acele hüküm vermek; hemen karara varmak; ~ **on,** ~ **upon** saldırmak; azarlamak, çatmak, paylamak; ~ **the queue** bşi haksız yere elde etm., başkasının sırasını kapmak; **¹jump.er** *n.* atlayıcı, sıçrayan kimse, hayvan *veya* böcek; kazak; çocuk önlüğü, göğüslük; **¹jump.ing-¹off** *n.* başlangıç; **¹jump.y** *adj.* sinirli, diken üstünde.

**junc.tion** [ˈdʒʌŋkʃən] *n.* birleşme, bitişme; birleşme yeri, kavşak; ▨ makas, iki demiryolunun birleştiği yer; ~ **box** ✗ bağlantı kutusu, buat; **junc.ture** [ˈ~tʃə] *n.* birleşme yeri; bitişme, bağlantı; nazik zaman, önemli an; **at this** ~ bu kritik durumda.

**June** [dʒuːn] *n.* haziran.

**jun.gle** [ˈdʒʌŋgl] *n.* orman, cengel.

**jun.ior** [ˈdʒuːnjə] **1.** *adj.* yaşça küçük; ast; küçük *(babasıyla aynı ismi taşıyanın ismine eklenir); Am. univ.* üçüncü sınıfa ait; ~ **high school** *Am.* ortaokul *(7.8. ve 9. sınıfları kapsayan);* ~ **partner** ikinci derecede ortak; **2.** *n.* yaş, mevki *veya* kıdemce küçük kimse; *Am.* lise *veya* üniversitede üçüncü sınıf öğrencisi; erkek evlât, oğul; F küçük boy *(elbise vs.);* **he is my** ~ **by four years,** he is four years

my ~ benden dört yaş küçüktür; **jun.ior.i.ty** [dʒuːniˈɔritiǀ] *n.* yaşça küçüklük; astlık.

**ju.ni.per** ✿ [ˈdʒuːnipə] *n.* ardıç.

**junk¹** ⚓ [dʒʌŋk] *n.* altı düz ve yelkenli Çin gemisi.

**junk²** [~] *n.* pılı pırtı, çöp; hurda.

**jun.ket** [ˈdʒʌŋkit] **1.** *n.* kesilmiş sütten yapılmış bir çeşit kaymak; *Am.* ziyafet; piknik; **2.** *vb.* ziyafet vermek; ziyafete katılmak.

**jun.ta** [ˈdʒʌntə] *n.* cunta; **jun.to** [ˈ~təu] *n.* amaçları ortak olan grup, klik.

**ju.rid.i.cal** □ [dʒuəˈridikəl] adlî, hukukî, kanunî...

**ju.ris.dic.tion** [dʒuərisˈdikʃən] *n.* yargılama hakkı; yetki, salâhiyet; nüfuz dairesi, kaza dairesi; **ju.ris.pru.dence** [ˈ~pruːdəns] *n.* hukuk ilmi; **¹ju.ris.pru.dent** *n.* hukuk uzmanı, hukukçu.

**ju.rist** [ˈdʒuərist] *n.* hukuk uzmanı, hukukçu.

**ju.ror** ⚖ [ˈdʒuərə] *n.* jüri üyesi.

**ju.ry** ⚖ [ˈdʒuəri] *n.* jüri; **¹ju.ry-box** *n.* mahkemede jürinin oturduğu yer; **¹ju.ry.man** *n.* jüri üyesi.

**ju.ry-mast** ⚓ [ˈdʒuərimɑːst] *n.* yedek *(veya* geçici) direk.

**just** [dʒʌst] **1.** *adj.* □ âdil, haklı, insaflı, haktanır, doğru; akla yakın, makûl, mantıkî; **2.** *adv.* sadece, yalnız; tam, tam tamına, kesin olarak; hemen; şimdi, biraz önce, az evvel; neredeyse; güçbelâ, darı darına; çok, epey; ~ **now** hemen şimdi; az evvel, biraz önce; ~ **over** (below) hemen yukarıda (aşağıda); ~ **let me see!** bir bakayım!; it's ~ **splendid!** harika!

**jus.tice** [ˈdʒʌstis] *n.* adalet, hak, insaf; hâkim, yargıç; doğruluk, dürüstlük; **Ⓙ of the Peace** sulh hâkimi; **court of** ~ sulh mahkemesi; **do** ~ **to** s.o. *b-nin* hakkını gözetmek, *b-ne* âdil davranmak; **do** o.s. ~ elinden geleni yapmak; **¹jus.tice.ship** *n.* hâkimlik.

**jus.ti.fi.a.bil.i.ty** [dʒʌstifaiəˈbiliti] *n.* haklı olma; **¹jus.ti.fi.a.ble** □ doğruluğu ispatlanabilir, haklı çıkarılabilir, savunulabilir.

**jus.ti.fi.ca.tion** [dʒʌstifiˈkeiʃən] *n.* haklı çık(ar)ma; mazur gösterme; mazeret, sebep; **jus.ti.fi.ca.to.ry** [ˈ~təri] *adj.* haklı çıkaran, mazur gösteren.

**jus.ti.fi.er** *typ.* [ˈdʒʌstifaiə] *n.* satır düzenleyici; **¹jus.ti.fy** *v/t.* haklı çıkarmak, doğrulamak; temize çıkarmak; *typ.* düz olarak ayarlamak *(yazının sağ kenarını).*

**jus.tly** [ˈdʒʌstli] *adv.* haklı olarak.

# K

**Ka(f).fir** ['kæfə] *n.* Afganistan'da Kâfiristan halkından biri; Güney Afrika'da Bantu kabilesinden olan kimse; ~s *pl.* † *sl.* Güney Afrika'ya ait altın madeni hisseleri.

**kale** [keil] *n.* bir çeşit kıvırcık yapraklı lahana; *Am. sl.* para, mangır.

**ka.lei.do.scope** *opt.* [kə'leidəskəup] *n.* çiçek dürbünü, kaleydoskop.

**kal.ends** ['kælendz] = calends.

**kan.ga.roo** *zo.* [kæŋgə'ru:] *n.* kanguru.

**ka.o.lin** *min.* ['keiəlin] *n.* arıkil, kaolin.

**ka.pok** ['keipɔk] *n.* sıcak memleketlere özgü yumuşak pamuksu lif.

**ka.put** *sl.* [kæ'puːt] *adj.* mahvolmuş; harap olmuş.

**ka.yak** ['kaiæk] *n.* Eskimo balıkçı kayığı; küçük kano.

**keck** [kek] *vb.* öğürmek; iğrenmek, tiksinmek (at *-den*).

**kedge** ⚓ [kedʒ] **1.** *n.* tonoz çapası; **2.** *vb.* tonoz çapasına bağlı yoma ile yürütmek *(gemi)*.

**ked.ge.ree** [kedʒə'riː] *n.* balık, yumurta *vs.* ile pişirilen pilav.

**keel** ⚓ [kiːl] **1.** *n.* gemi omurgası; on an even ~ dengede *(gemi);* *fig.* muntazam, düzenli; **2.** *v/i.* ~ over alabora olm.; *v/t.* devirmek, yana yatırmak *(gemi);* **'keel-age** *n.* ⚓ liman resmi; **keel-haul** ⚓ ['~hɔːl] *v/t. b-ni* ceza olarak geminin altından geçirmek; şiddetle azarlamak; haşlamak; **keel.son** ⚓ ['kelsn] *n.* geminin iç omurgası.

**keen¹** ☐ [kiːn] keskin, sivri; şiddetli, sert; zeki, akıllı; kuvvetli, canlı, yoğun; hassas; şahane; ~ on F düşkün, meraklı, hevesli *-e;* be ~ on hunting avcılığa meraklı olm.

**keen²** *Ir.* [~] *n.* ağıt.

**keen-edged** ['kiːnedʒd] *adj.* keskin kenarlı; **'keen.ness** *n.* keskinlik; düşkünlük; akıllılık.

**keep** [kiːp] **1.** *n.* geçim; *hist.* kale, hisar; zindan, hapishane; himaye; for ~s F temelli olarak, her zaman için, ebediyen; **2.** *(irr.) v/t. com.* tutmak, korumak, himaye etm., saklamak, muhafaza etm.; yerine getirmek; sürdürmek, devam ettirmek; yönetmek, işletmek; beslemek, bakmak, geçindirmek; ücretle tutmak; geri tutmak, alıkoymak; biriktirmek, bir *b.o.* company *b-ne* refakat etm.; ~ company with *ile* arkadaşlık etm.; ~ silence susmak; ~ one's temper *k-ne* hâkim olm.; ~ time doğru işlemek, doğru gitmek *(saat);* ♩ tempo tutmak; ✕ aynı adımlarla yürümek; ~ *s.o.* waiting *b-ni* bekletmek; ~ away uzak tutmak; ~ down baskı yapmak; kontrol altına almak; kısıtlamak, sınırlamak; ~ *s.o.* from *b-ni -den* alıkoymak; ~ *s.th.* from *s.o. bşi b-den* saklamak; ~ in yanmaya devam etm. *(ateş);* içeride tutmak, alıkoymak, saklamak; ~ in money parayı idare etm.; ~ in view gözönünde bulundurmak; ~ off uzak tutmak (from *-den);* ~ on çıkarmamak *(elbise);* söndürmemek; devam etm.; ~ out yaklaştırmamak, uzak tutmak, çıkarmak; ~ up korumak; devam ettirmek, sürdürmek; *b-ni* ayakta tutmak; toplamak *(cesaret);* ~ it up dayanmak; **3.** *(irr.) v/i.* F oturmak, yaşamak; devam etm., sürüp gitmek; kalmak, durmak; açık olm. *(okul);* geri durmak, *k-ni* alıkoymak; ~ doing yapmaya devam etm.; ~ away uzak durmak; ~ clear of *-den* uzak durmak, kaçınmak, sakınmak; ~ from *-den* uzak durmak; ~ in with *ile* iyi geçinmek, dost kalmak; ~ off uzak kalmak; ~ on devam etm.; ~ on talking konuşmaya devam etm., konuşmayı sürdürmek; ~ on at *s.o. b-ni* sıkboğaz etm.; ~ to *-e* sadık olm., *-e* bağlı kalmak; ~ up ayakta durmak; ~ up with *-de* geri kalmamak, *-e* ayak uydurmak; ~ up with the Joneses komşularıyla rekabet etm.; toplumsal değişmelere ayak uydurmak.

**keep.er** ['kiːpə] *n.* bakıcı; bekçi; gardiyan; **'keep.ing** *n.* koruma, tutma, muhafaza etme, bakım; geçim; be in (out of) ~ with -e uygun ol(ma)mak; **keepsake** [¹~seik] n. hatıra, andaç, yadigâr.

**keg** [keg] n. küçük fıçı, varil.

**kelp** ♥ [kelp] n. büyük deniz yosunu, varek.

**kel.son** ⚓ [¹kelsn] = keelson.

**ken** [ken] n. bilgi alanı, görüş açısı, görüş sahası.

**ken.nel¹** [¹kenl] n. su kanalı, oluk.

**ken.nel²** [~] n. köpek kulübesi; köpek yetiştirilen yer; köpek sürüsü.

**kept** [kept] pret. and. p.p. of keep 2.

**kerb** [kə:b], ¹~.stone = curb etc.

**ker.chief** [¹kə:tʃif] n. başörtüsü, eşarp; boyun atkısı, fular; mendil; ¹**ker.chiefed** adj. başörtülü, eşarplı.

**kerf** [kə:f] n. çentik; yarık; kesilmiş parça.

**ker.nel** [¹kə:nl] n. tahıl tanesi; iç; çekirdek; fig. öz, cevher, esas, ruh.

**ker.o.sene** [¹kerəsi:n] n. gazyağı, gaz.

**kes.trel** orn. [¹kestrəl] n. kerkenez.

**ketch** ⚓ [ketʃ] n. iki direkli bir çeşit yat, kotra.

**ketch.up** [¹ketʃəp] n. keçap, domates sosu.

**ket.tle** [¹ketl] n. çaydanlık; kazan; güğüm; tencere; ¹~.drum n. ♪ tembal, bir çeşit davul, dümbelek.

**key** [ki:] 1. n. anahtar; fig. çözüm yolu; ⊕ kama, dil; cevap cetveli, şifre cetveli; tercüme, çeviri; ♪ düğme, buton; ♪ tuş, anahtar (işareti), ses perdesi; fig. ton, tel; telgraf maniplesi; 2. v/t. ~ up ♪ perdesini yükseltmek; fig. heyecanlandırmak, coşturmak; ¹~.board n. klavye; ¹~-bu.gle n. ♪ boru, korno; ¹~.hole n. anahtar deliği; ~ In.dus.try temel endüstri; ¹~-man n. kilit adam; ¹~.mon.ey n. hava (veya anahtar) parası; ¹~.note n. esas perde, ana nota; fig. temel, ilke, anafikir; ¹~.stone n. anahtar taşı, kilit taşı; fig. temel, ilke, esas madde.

**khak.i** [¹ka:ki] 1. adj. hâki; toprak rengi; 2. n. bu renk kumaş; bu kumaştan üniforma.

**khan¹** [ka:n] n. han, emir, kağan.

**khan²** [~] n. kervansaray, han.

**kibe** [kaib] n. el ve ayakta soğuktan oluşan çatlak, yarık.

**kib.itz.er** Am. F [¹kibitsə] n. iskambil oynayanların arkasında durup ellerini gören seyirci; istenmeyen öğüt veren kimse.

**ki.bosh** sl. [¹kaibɔʃ] n. zırva, saçma; put the ~ on son vermek -e, altüst etm. -i.

**kick** [kik] 1. n. tekme, tepme; F heyecan,

zevk, haz; fig. kuvvet, enerji, canlılık; silahın geri tepmesi; karşı gelme, yakınma, şikâyet; kuvvet, sertlik (içki); merak, heves; topa vurma; more ~s than halfpence takdirden çok eleştiri; get a ~ out of F bşin tadını çıkarmak, -den zevk duymak; 2. v/t. tekmelemek, çiftelemek; sl. -den yakasını kurtarmak, bırakmak (uyuşturucu madde); F baştan savmak, atlatmak; futbol: atmak (gol); ~ the bucket sl. nalları dikmek, ölmek, gebermek; ~ one's heels F çok beklemek, ağaç olm.; ~ out F kovmak, defetmek; ~ up a row veya fuss veya dust F kavga çıkarmak, ortalığı birbirine katmak; v/i. tekme atmak, çifte atmak; topa vurmak; geri tepmek (silah); karşı durmak (against, at -e); ~ in with Am. sl. para yardımında bulunmak; ~ off futbol: oyuna başlamak; ¹**kick.back** n. part. Am. F kârdan hisse, komisyon; ¹**kick.er** n. vuran şey veya kimse; vurucu; futbolcu; ¹**kick-¹off** n. futbol: başlama (vuruşu); ¹**kick.shaw** n. çerez türünden yiyecek, abur cubur; değersiz şey, ıvır zıvır; ¹**kick-start.er** n. ayakla basılan marş; ¹**kick-¹up** n. sl. kavga, gürültü, patırtı.

**kid** [kid] 1. n. oğlak, keçi yavrusu; oğlak eti; oğlak derisi; sl. çocuk; 2. vb. sl. takılmak -e, gırgır geçmek ile, işletmek -i; şaka yapmak; oğlak doğurmak; ¹**kid.dy** n. sl. çocukcağız, yavrucak; **kid glove** oğlak derisinden eldiven; fig. yumuşaklık; ¹**kid-glove** adj. yumuşak, nazik.

**kid.nap** [¹kidnæp] v/t. zorla kaçırmak (part. çocuk); ¹**kid.nap.(p)er** n. zorla insan kaçıran kimse.

**kid.ney** [¹kidni] n. anat. böbrek; F soy, tip, huy ,karakter; ~ bean ♥ fasulye.

**kike** Am. sl. contp. [kaik] n. Yahudi.

**kill** [kil] 1. v/t. öldürmek, katletmek; fig. yok etm., mahvetmek; bitirmek, sona erdirmek; parl. veto etm., reddetmek; fig. yenmek, mağlûp etm., durdurmak; geçirmek, boşa harcamak, öldürmek (zaman); çok yormak; hepsini bitirmek (içki); tesirini yok etm.; çok etkilemek; ~ off hepsini öldürmek, kırıp geçirmek; ~ time vakit öldürmek; 2. n. öldürme; avda öldürülen hayvan, av; ¹**kill.er** n. adam öldüren kimse, katil, cani; ¹**kill.ing 1.** □ öldürücü; çok yorucu; F komik, gülünç; 2. n. Am. F vurgun, büyük kazanç; ¹**kill-joy** n. neşe bozan kimse.

**kiln** [kiln, ⊕ kil] n. tuğla veya kireç ocağı, fırın; ¹~-dry v/t. ocakta kurutmak, fırınlamak.

**kil.o.cy.cle** *phys.* [ˈkiləusaikl] *n.* kilosikl, kilo elektron volt; **kil.o.gram, kil.o.gramme** [ˈ~græm] *n.* kilo(gram); **kil.o.me.ter, kil.o.me.tre** [ˈkiləumiːtə] *n.* kilometre; **kil.lo.watt** ⚡ [ˈkiləuwɔt] *n.* kilovat.

**kilt** [kilt] **1.** *n.* İskoç erkeklerinin giydiği eteklik; **2.** *v/t.* pli yapmak; etek giydirmek; *v/i.* çevik davranmak.

**kl.mo.no** [kiˈməunəu] *n.* uzun Japon entarisi, kimono.

**kin** [kin] **1.** *n.* akraba, hısım; soy, nesep; akrabalık; the next of ~ yakın akraba; **2.** *adj.* akraba olan (to *-e*).

**kind** [kaind] **1.** ☐ müşfik, iyi kalpli, nazik, iyi, iyi huylu, sevimli; insancı(l); uysal, yumuşak başlı (to *-e, -e karşı*); **2.** *n.* cins, çeşit, tür, nevi; huy, karakter, mizaç, tabiat; people of all ~s her türden insan; different in ~ başka çeşitten; pay in ~ eşya ile borç ödemek, aynıyla ödemek; *fig.* aynen karşılık vermek; I ~ of expected it F biraz da bunu bekliyordum.

**kin.der.gar.ten** [ˈkindəgaːtn] *n.* anaokulu.

**kind.heart.ed** [ˈkaindˈhaːtid] *adj.* iyi kalpli.

**kin.dle** [ˈkindl] *v/t. & v/i.* tutuş(tur)mak, alevlen(dir)mek; aydınlatmak, yakmak; yanmak; *fig.* parlamak, uyan(dır)mak, çekmek (*ilgi*).

**kind.li.ness** [ˈkaindlinis] *n.* şefkat, insancıllık, sevecenlik, yumuşaklık.

**kin.dling** [ˈkindliŋ] *n. a.* ~s *pl.* çalı çırpı.

**kind.ly** [ˈkaindli] **1.** *adj.* müşfik, şefkatli, dostça; **2.** *adv.* doğal olarak; içten, gönülden; şefkatle; nazikçe, kibarca.

**kind.ness** [ˈkaindnis] *n.* şefkat, yumuşaklık.

**kin.dred** [ˈkindrid] **1.** *adj.* akraba olan; birbirine benzer; **2.** *n.* akraba, hısım; akrabalık; soy, sülâle.

**kine** † [kain] *pl. of* cow¹.

**ki.ne.ma** [ˈkinimə] = cinema.

**kin.e.mat.o.graph** [kainiˈmætəugraːf] = cinematograph.

**ki.net.ic** [kiˈnetik] *adj.* devimsel, kinetik; ki²net.ics *n. sg.* kinetik bilimi.

**king** [kiŋ] *n.* kral *(a. fig.)*; satranç: şah; başta olan kimse; *iskambil:* papaz; dama olan taş; ~'s evil ⚕ sıraca hastalığı; turn ~'s evidence suç ortağı aleyhinde ifade vermek; **¹king.bird** *n. orn.* kral kuşu; **¹king.craft** *n.* krallık hüneri; **¹king.cup** *n.* ⚘ düğünçiçeği; altıntabak; **¹king.dom** *n.* krallık, kraliyet, hükümdarlık; hükümet; saltanat; *part.* ⚘, *zo.* âlem; ~ come F öteki dünya, ahret; **¹king.fish.er** *n.* yalıçapkını, iskelekuşu, emircik; **king.let** [ˈ~lit] *n.* küçük kral; **¹king.like** *adj.* kral

gibi, krala yaraşır; haşmetli, muhteşem, mükellef; **¹king.li.ness** *n.* haşmet; **¹king.ly** *adj.* krala ait; krala yaraşır; haşmetli, muhteşem, şahane; **¹king.pin** *n.* dingil başı pimi, göbek mili; *fig.* çok gerekli kimse *veya* şey, baş ,elebaşı; **¹king.post** *n.* ⚙ baba, çatının orta direği; **¹king.ship** *n.* krallık, hükümdarlık; **¹king-size** *adj.* F normalden büyük, büyük boy.

**kink** [kiŋk] **1.** *n.* halat, tel *veya* ipin dolaşması; *fig.* kaçıklık, üşütüklük; acayiplik, tuhaflık; *Am.* kapris, garip fikir; have a ~ F tahtası eksik olm.; **2.** *v/t. & v/i.* halat gibi dolaş(tır)mak.

**kins.folk** [ˈkinzfɔuk] *n. pl.* akraba, hısım; **¹kin.ship** *n.* akrabalık, hısımlık; benzerlik; **¹kins.man** *n.* erkek akraba; **¹kins-wom.an** *n.* kadın akraba.

**ki.osk** [ˈkiːɔsk] *n.* küçük kulübe; telefon kulübesi; köşk, sayfiye.

**kip.per** [ˈkipə] **1.** *n.* tuzlanmış isli ringa balığı, çiroz; *sl.* delikanlı, adam; **2.** *v/t.* tuzlayıp tütsülemek *veya* kurutmak *(balık).*

**kirk** [kəːk] *n.* kilise.

**kir.tle** † [ˈkəːtl] *n.* kadın fistanı; erkek ceketi *veya* paltosu.

**kiss** [kis] **1.** *n.* öpüş, öpücük, buse; *fig.* hafif temas; **2.** *vb.* öpmek; hafifçe dokunmak; ~ the book kutsal kitabı öperek ant içmek, kitaba el basmak; ~ the dust boyun eğmek, mağlûp olm.; vurulup ölmek, öldürülmek; **¹~-proof** *adj.* silinmez.

**kit** [kit] *n.* avadanlık, alet takımı; takım, malzeme *(a.* ✕ *& spor)*; takım çantası; do-it-yourself ~ monte edilmemiş takım; **¹~-bag** *n.* ✕ asker hurcu, sırt çantası; ⚓ denizci çantası.

**kitch.en** [ˈkitʃin] *n.* mutfak; **¹kitch.en.er** *n.* mutfak ocağı; **kitch.en.ette** [~ˈnet] *n.* ufak mutfak.

**kitch.en...:** [ˈ~-ˈgar.den] *n.* sebze bahçesi; **¹~-maid** *n.* aşçı yamağı kız; **¹~-range** *n.* ocak, fırın.

**kite** [kait] *n. orn.* çaylak; uçurtma; *fig.* balon; † *sl.* sahte bono; ~ balloon ✕ yere bağlı sabit balon; fly a ~ uçurtma uçurmak; *fig.* balon uçurmak, nabız yoklamak.

**kith** [kiθ] *n.:* ~ and kin dostlar ve akrabalar, hısım akraba.

**kit.ten** [ˈkitn] **1.** *n.* yavru kedi; **2.** *v/i.* yavrulamak *(kedi)*; **kit.ten.ish** [ˈkitniʃ] *adj.* kedi yavrusu gibi; oynamayı seven.

**kit.tle** *fig.* [ˈkitl] *adj.* nazik, tehlikeli, korkulur.

**kit.ty¹** [ˈkiti] *n.* yavru kedi, kedicik.

**kit.ty²** [~] *n. iskambil:* kasa.

**ki.wi** *orn.* [¹kiːwiː] *n.* Yeni Zeland'a ait bir kuş, kivi.

**Klan** *Am.* [klæn] *n. Birleşik Amerika'da iç savaştan sonra güney eyaletlerinde zencilerin siyasi hakları olması aleyhinde kurulan gizli bir cemiyet;* **Klansman** [¹klænzmən] *n.* bu cemiyetin üyesi.

**klax.on** *mot.* [¹klæksn] *n.* otomobil kornası, klakson.

**klep.to.ma.ni.a** [kleptəu¹meinjə] *n.* hırsızlık hastalığı, kleptomani; **klep.to¹ma.ni.ac** [~niæk] *n.* hırsızlık hastası, kleptoman.

**knack** [næk] *n.* ustalık, marifet, hüner.

**knack.er** [¹nækə] *n.* sakat at alıp kesen ve hayvan maması olarak satan kimse; malzemesi için eski ev *veya* gemi alan kimse; **¹knack.er.y** *n.* sakat atları kesip satma; malzemesi için eski ev *veya* gemi alma.

**knag** [næg] *n.* budak.

**knap.sack** [¹næpsæk] *n.* sırt çantası.

**knar** [naː] *n.* budak.

**knave** [neiv] *n.* herif, düzenbaz kimse, üçkağıtçı; *iskambil:* bacak; **¹knav.er.y** *n.* hilekârlık, düzenbazlık; **¹knav.ish** □ hilekâr, dolandırıcı.

**knead** [niːd] *v/t.* yoğurmak; masaj yapmak.

**knee** [niː] **1.** *n.* diz; diz yeri; dize benzer şey; ⊕ dirsek, mafsal; bring s.o. to his ~s *b-ni* yola getirmek, dize getirmek; on the ~s of the gods Allaha kalmış, henüz belli olmayan; **2.** *v/t.* diz ile vurmak; **¹~-breech.es** *n. pl.* kısa pantolon; **¹~-cap** *n.* dizkapağı; **¹~¹deep** *adj.* diz boyu derinliğinde; **¹~-joint** *n.* diz mafsalı; **kneel** [niːl] *(irr.) v/i.* diz çökmek (to *-in önünde*); diz üstü oturmak; **¹kneel.er** *n.* diz çökmüş kimse; **¹knee-pan** *n.* dizkapağı.

**knell** [nel] *n.* matem çanı sesi; salâ; ölüm haberi, kara haber.

**knelt** [nelt] *pret. & p.p. of* kneel.

**knew** [njuː] *pret. of* know 1.

**knick.er.bock ers** [¹nikəbɔkəz] *n. pl.* diz altından büzgülü bol pantolon, golf pantolonu; **¹knick.ers** *n. pl.* F dizde büzülen kadın donu; = knickerbockers.

**knick.knack** [¹niknæk] *n.* ufak süs eşyası, biblo; ~s *pl.* süs müs, cici bici.

**knife** [naif] **1.** *n., pl.* **knives** [naivz] bıçak, çakı; makine bıçağı; get one's ~ into s.o. *fig. b-ne* karşı kötü niyetler beslemek, diş bilemek; **2.** *v/t.* bıçaklamak; bıçakla kesmek; arkadan vurmak; **¹~-grind.er** *n.* bıçak bileyici.

**knight** [nait] **1.** *n.* silahşör, şövalye; asılzade, soylu kimse; *satranç:* at; *k-ni* bşe adayan kimse; **2.** *v/t. b-ne* şövalyelik payesi vermek; **knight-er.rant** [¹~¹erənt] *n.* kahramanlık göstermek için dolaşan seyyar silahşör; **knight.hood** [¹~hud] *n.* silahşörlük payesi, şövalyelik; şövalyeler; **¹knight.li.ness** *n.* şövalyeye yakışırlık; **¹knight.ly** *adj.* şövalyeye ait; şövalyeye yakışır; şövalye gibi.

**knit** [nit] *(irr.) vb.* örmek; birleştirmek; kavuşturmak; kaynatmak *(kemik)*; çatmak *(kaş)*; birbirine yapışmak; kayna(ş)mak *(kemik)*; ~ the·brows kaşlarını çatmak; **¹knit.ter** *n.* örgü ören kimse; = knitting-machine; **¹knit.ting 1.** *n.* örme; örgü; **2.** *adj.* örgü...; **¹knit.ting-ma.chine** *n.* örgü makinesi; **¹knit.ting-nee.dle** *n.* örgü şişi; **¹knit.wear** *n.* trikotaj eşyası, örme.

**knives** [naivz] *pl. of* knife.

**knob** [nɔb] *n.* top, yumru; topuz, tokmak; pürtük; tepecik, yuvarlak tepe; **¹knobbed**, **¹knob.by** *adj.* yumrulu; tokmak gibi; **¹knob-stick** *n.* topuzlu sopa; grev bozan *(veya* kırıcı) kimse.

**knock** [nɔk] **1.** *n.* vuruş, vurma, darbe, çalma, kapı çalınması; *mot.* vuruntu; **2.** *v/i.* vurmak, çalmak (at *-e, -i)*; çarpışmak; koşuşmak; gezip tozmak; vuruntu yapmak *(motor)*; tenkitçilik yapmak; ~ off *sl.* yüzüstü bırakıp gitmek; ~ under meydana çıkmak; *v/t.* vurmak; çarpmak *e-*; çarpıştırmak; *Am. sl.* kusur bulmak, tenkit etm.; ~ about tekrar tekrar vurmak, şiddetle sarsmak; ~ down vurup yere devirmek, yere sermek, yıkmak; açık arttırma: son fiyatı verenin üstüne bırakmak; kazanmak, kırmak *(para)*; ⊕ sökmek, parçalara ayırmak; ~ off aceleyle yapmak; tatil etm., işi bırakmak; indirmek *(fiyat)*; öldürmek; soymak; ~ out *boks:* nakavt etm.; ~ up kapıya vurup uyandırmak; yormak; hamile bırakmak; ~.a.bout [¹~əbaut] **1.** *adj.* kaba ve dayanıklı *(eşya)*; gürültülü; *thea.* güldürücü, komik; **2.** *n.* komedi oyuncusu; kaba ve dayanıklı şey; **¹~-¹down** *adj.* yıkıcı, yere serici, mat edici; portatif, sökülür takılır; düşük, indirimli *(fiyat)*; **¹knock.er** *n.* kapı tokmağı; çalan *veya* vuran şey *veya* kimse; *Am. sl.* tenkitçi; **knock-¹kneed** *adj.* çarpık bacaklı; *fig.* topal, aksak; **¹~-out** *n. boks:* nakavt; oyun dışı etme; *sl.* çekici kimse *veya* şey.

**knoll¹** [nəul] *n.* tepecik.

**knoll²** [~] *vb.* matem çanı ile ilân *veya* davet etm.; ağır ağır çalmak *(çan)*.

**knot** [nɔt] **1.** *n.* düğüm, bağ; güç durum,

zorluk; ⚓ deniz mili; halat cevizi; ⚓
nod; küme; **2.** *v/t.* & *v/i.* düğümle(n)-
mek, bağla(n)mak *(a. fig.)*; düğüm olm.;
**'knot.hole** *n.* budak deliği; **'knot.ti.ness**
*n.* karışıklık, zorluk; **'knot.ty** *adj.* düğümlü; budaklı; *fig.* karışık, güç, zor;
**'knot.work** *n.* düğüm işi.

**knout** [naut] **1.** *n.* kamçı; **2.** *v/t.* kamçılamak.

**know** [nəu] **1.** *(irr.)* *vb.* bilmek; tanımak;
seçmek, ayırmak, farketmek; tecrübey-
le bilmek; haberdar olm., farkında olm.;
~ French Fransızca bilmek; come to ~
öğrenmek, haber almak; get to ~ bilmek, tanımak; ~ one's business, ~ the
ropes, ~ a thing or two, ~ what's what
usulünü bilmek, çaresini bilmek, işini
bilmek, dünyadan haberi olm.; do you ~
how to play chess? satranç oynamayı biliyor musunuz?; you ought to ~ better
than to do that o işi yapmayacak kadar
akıllı olmalısınız; I don't ~ one from the
other birini diğerinden ayıramıyorum;
you ~ biliyorsunuz ki; **2.** *n.* be in the ~
F haberdar olm. (of *-den)*; **'know.a.ble**
*adj.* bilinmesi mümkün, bilinir; **'know-
-all 1.** *adj.* herşeyi bilen; **2.** *n.* herşeyi
bilen *veya* bildiğini iddia eden kimse;
**'know-how** *n.* yaratıcılık; teknik ustalık,
maharet, hüner, kabiliyet; **'know.ing 1.**
□ bilgisi olan; akıllı, zeki, kurnaz; fikir
sahibi, düşünceli; F şeytan, kurnaz, açıkgöz; **2.** *n.* bilgi, malumat; **'know.ing.ly**
*adv.* bilerek, bile bile, kasten; **knowledge** ['nɔlidʒ] *n.* bilgi, malumat; anla-

yış; to my ~ bildiğime göre, bildiğim kadarıyla; **'knowl.edge.a.ble** *adj.* F bilgili,
zeki; **known** [nəun] *p.p. of* know **1;** come
to be ~ tanınmak, meşhur olm.; make ~
b-ni b-le tanıştırmak; make o.s. ~ k-ni tanıtmak.

**knuck.le** ['nʌkl] **1.** *n. a.* '~-bone **parmak**
orta eklemi, aşık kemiği; **2.** *v/i.* ~ **down.**
~ under boyun eğmek, pes demek, tes-
lim olm.; işe koyulmak; '~-dust.er *n.*
muşta.

**ko.a.la** *zo.* [kəu'ɑːlə] *n.* keseli ayı.

**ko.dak** *phot.* ['kəudæk] *n.* küçük fotoğraf
makinesi.

**Ko.ran** [kɔ'rɑːn] *n.* Kur'an.

**Ko.re.an** [kə'riən] **1.** *n.* Koreli; Korece;
**2.** *adj.* Kore'ye ait.

**kosh.er** ['kəuʃə] *n.* Musevi şeriatına göre temiz sayılan et, kaşer.

**ko.tow** ['kəu'tau] **1.** *n.* Çinlilerde diz çö-
küp alnı yere vurarak yapılan ibadet
*veya* hürmet; **2.** *vb.* bu şekilde ibadet
*veya* hürmet etm.; *fig.* yaltaklanmak
(to *-e)*.

**Krem.lin** ['kremlin] *n.* Kremlin, Moskova'da yüksek duvarlı kale.

**ku.dos** *co.* ['kjuːdɔs] *n.* şöhret, şan, şeref,
itibar.

**Ku-Klux-Klan** *Am.* ['kjuː'klʌks'klæn] *n. Bir
leşik Amerika'da iç savaştan sonra Güney eyaletlerinde zencilerin siyasi haklara sahip olması aleyhinde kurulan gizli cemiyet.

**Kurd** [kəːd] *n.* Kürt.

**Kurdish** [kəːdiʃ] *adj.* & *n.* Kürt(çe).

# L

**la** ♪ [lɑː] *n.* la notası.

**lab** F [læb] = laboratory.

**la.bel** [ˈleibl] **1.** *n.* etiket, yafta; *fig.* sıfat, ünvan; ☼ sınıf; ⚓ saçak, pervaz; **2.** *v/t.* etiketlemek; † üzerine fiyatını yazmak; *fig.* ...damgasını vurmak (as).

**la.bi.al** [ˈleibjəl] **1.** *adj.* dudaklarla ilgili; dudaksıl...; **2.** *n.* dudak ünsüzü, dudaksıl ses.

**lab.o.ra.to.ry** [ləˈbɔrətri] *n.* laboratuvar; ~ assistant laborant, deneme hazırlayıcısı.

**la.bo.ri.ous** ☐ [ləˈbɔːriəs] çalışkan, işgüzar; yorucu, zahmetli.

**la.bo(u)r** [ˈleibə] **1.** *n.* iş, çalışma; emek; işçi sınıfı; ☈ doğum ağrıları; zahmet, sıkıntı, zorluk; Ministry of ♀ Çalışma Bakanlığı; hard ~ çalışma yükümlülüğü, ağır iş cezası; **2.** *adj.* iş..., çalışma...; **3.** *v/i.* çalışmak, uğraşmak, çabalamak; emek vermek, sıkıntı çekmek; zorlukla ilerlemek; ~ under sıkıntı çekmek, zorluk altında olm., -*in* kurbanı olm.; *v/t.* emekle meydana getirmek; işlemek (*toprak*); sıkıntı vermek, yüklenmek; detayına girmek; ~ **camp** çalışma kampı; **ˈla.bo(u)red** *adj.* zorlu, zahmetli; şaşaalı, şatafatlı; **ˈla.bo(u)r.er** *n.* işçi, emekçi, rençber; **La.bo(u)r Ex.change** İş ve İşçi Bulma Kurumu; **ˈla.bo(u)r.ing** *adj.* zorlu; yorucu...; ~ breath tıknefes; **la.bo(u)r.ite** [ˈ~rait] *n.* İşçi Partisi üyesi *veya* yandaşı; **La.bour Par.ty** *pol.* İşçi Partisi; **ˈla.bo(u)r-sav.ing** *adj.* işi kolaylaştıran; **la.bor un.ion** *Am.* işçi sendikası.

**Lab.ra.dor** [ˈlæbrədɔː] *n.:* ~ dog *zo.* Labrador cinsi köpek.

**la.bur.num** ♣ [ləˈbəːnəm] *n.* sarısalkım.

**lab.y.rinth** [ˈlæbərinθ] *n.* labirent, dolambaçlı ve çok karışık yer *veya* iş; **lab.yˈrin.thi.an** [~θiən], *rıst* **lab.yˈrin.thine** [~θain] *adj.* çapraşık, karmaşık.

**lac** [læk] *n.* reçineli sıvı, laka; a ~ of rupees yüz bin rupi.

**lace** [leis] **1.** *n.* bağ (*ayakkabı*), şerit; dantel(a); kaytan; kordon; **2.** *v/t. & v/i.*

bağla(n)mak (*ayakkabı bağı vs.*); dantel ile süslemek; karıştırmak (with *ile*); ~ (into) s.o. *b-ni* pataklamak, paylamak.

**lac.er.ate** [ˈlæsəreit] *v/t.* yırtmak, yaralamak; *fig.* kırmak (*kalp*), incitmek (*his*); **2.** [ˈ~rit] *adj.* yaralı, yırtık, parçalanmış, ezilmiş; **lac.er.a.tion** [~ˈreiʃən] *n.* yırtma, yaralama, incitme.

**lach.es** ☼ [ˈleitʃiz] *n.* hakkını aramakta ihmal.

**lach.ry.mal** [ˈlækriməl] *adj.* gözyaşına ait, gözyaşı...; **lach.ry.mose** [ˈ~məus] *adj.* sulu gözlü; göz yaşartıcı.

**lack** [læk] **1.** *n.* noksan, eksiklik, kusur; ihtiyaç, gereksinme; yoksunluk; **2.** *v/t.* muhtaç olm. -*e*; ihtiyacı olm. -*e*; yoksun olm. -*den*; he ~s money paraya ihtiyacı var, para sıkıntısı çekiyor; *v/i.* eksik olm., yetmemek; be ~ing eksikliği olm., mevcut olmamak, bulunmamak; he is ~ing in courage yeteri kadar cesur değil, o kim cesur olmak kim.

**lack.a.dai.si.cal** ☐ [lækəˈdeizikəl] canından bezmiş gibi; ilgisiz, uyuşuk.

**lack.ey** [ˈlæki] **1.** *n.* uşak, erkek hizmetçi; *fig.* dalkavuk; **2.** *vb.* uşaklık etm.

**lack.ing** [ˈlækiŋ] *s.* lack 1.

**lack.land** [ˈlæklænd] *adj.* topraksız, arazisiz; **lack.lus.tre**, *Am.* **lack.lus.ter** [ˈ~lʌstə] *adj.* cansız, donuk, sönük.

**la.con.ic** [ləˈkɔnik] *adj.* (~ally) az ve öz, özlü, veciz; az konuşur.

**lac.quer** [ˈlækə] **1.** *n.* vernik; **2.** *v/t.* vernik ile kaplamak, verniklemek; ~ed vernikli...

**lac.quey** [ˈlæki] = lackey.

**la.crosse** [ləˈkrɔs] *n.* spor: raketle oynanan bir top oyunu.

**lac.ta.tion** [lækˈteiʃən] *n.* süt salgılama; emzirme.

**lac.tic** [ˈlæktik] *adj.* süte ait, süt...; ~ acid süt asidi, laktik asit.

**la.cu.na** [ləˈkjuːnə] *n.* boşluk, aralık, eksiklik.

**lac.y** [ˈleisi] *adj.* dantel gibi; dantelli...

**lad** [læd] *n.* genç erkek, delikanlı.

**lad.der** ['lædə] **1.** *n.* el merdiveni; *fig.* basamak; çorap kaçığı; ↓ ip merdiven; **2.** *v/i.* kaçmak *(çorap);* '**~-proof** *adj.* kaçmaz *(çorap).*

**lad.die** ['lædi] *n.* genç erkek, delikanlı.

**lade** [leid] *(irr.)* = load; '**lad.en 1.** *p.p. of* lade; **2.** *adj.* yüklü.

**la-di-da** ['lɑːdiˈdɑː] **1.** *n.* gösterişçi kimse; **2.** *adj.* gösterişçi.

**la.ding** ['leidiŋ] *n.* hamule, yük, kargo; yükleme.

**la.dle** ['leidl] **1.** *n.* kepçe; ⊕ büyük kepçe, pota; **2.** *v/t.* ~ out kepçe ile servis yapmak; *fig.* bahşetmek, bol keseden vermek.

**la.dy** ['leidi] *n.* bayan, hanım(efendi); asilzade kadın, leydi; Ladies *sg.* kadınlar tuvaleti; Ladies and Gentlemen! bayanlar baylar!; ♀ Day 25 Martta kutlanan bir kilise yortusu; ~ doctor kadın doktor; ~'s maid bir hanımın oda hizmetçisi; ~'s *veya* ladies' man kadınlara karşı nazik ve onların hoşlandığı adam, kadın düşkünü, kadıncıl; '**~-bird** *n.* gelinböceği; '**~-in-ˈwait.ing** *n.* kraliçe nedimesi; '**~-kill.er** *n.* kadın avcısı, çapkın; '**~.like** *adj.* hanıma yakışır, hanım hanımcık; *contp.* kadınsı *(erkek);* '**~-love** *n.* sevgili, metres; ~ of the bed-**cham.ber** kraliçe nedimesi; '**~.ship** *n.* hanımefendilik; her *veya* your ~ hanımefendi.

**lag**[1] [læg] **1.** *v/i.* oyalanmak; *a.* ~ behind geri kalmak; **2.** *n.* geri kalma, gecikme.

**lag**[2] *sl.* [~] **1.** *n.* suçlu, mahkûm; **2.** *v/t.* tutuklamak; hapse atmak.

**lag**[3] [~] *v/t.* kaplamak *(su boruları, kazan vs.);* tecrit *(veya* izole) etm.

**la.ger (beer)** ['lɑːgə(ˈbiə)] *n.* Alman birası.

**lag.gard** ['lægəd] *n.* uyuşuk kimse; geri kalan şey *veya* kimse.

**la.goon** [ləˈguːn] *n.* denizkulağı.

**la.ic** ['leiik] **1.** *a.* 'la.i.cal □ layik; **2.** *n.* layik kimse; **la.i.cize** ['~saiz] *v/t.* layikleştirmek.

**laid** [leid] *pret. & p.p. of* lay[4] 2; ~ up biriktirilmiş; yatağa düşmüş (with *-den).*

**lain** [lein] *p.p. of* lie[2] 2.

**lair** [leə] *n.* in, yatak *(a. fig.).*

**laird** *Scots* [leəd] *n.* mülk sahibi.

**la.i.ty** ['leiiti] *n.* ruhbandan olmayanlar; meslekten olmayanlar.

**lake**[1] [leik] *n.* göl.

**lake**[2] [~] *n.* morumsu kırmızı boya.

**lake-dwel.lings** ['leikdweliŋz] *n. pl.* göl kıyısındaki kazık temelli evler.

**lam** *sl.* [læm] *v/t.* dövmek, sopa çekmek,

pataklamak; *v/i.* tüymek, sıvışmak; ~ into *s.o.* b-ni adamakıllı dövmek, b-ne çıkışmak.

**la.ma** ['lɑːmə] *n.* Lama, Tibet'li Buda rahibi; 'la.ma.se.ry ['~səri] *n.* lama manastırı.

**lamb** [læm] **1.** *n.* kuzu (eti); *fig.* kuzu gibi kimse; like a ~ *fig.* kuzu gibi; **2.** *v/i.* kuzulamak.

**lam.baste** *sl.* [læmˈbeist] *v/t.* dövmek, pataklamak; haşlamak, paylamak.

**lam.bent** ['læmbənt] *adj.* yalayarak yayılan *(alev);* hafifçe parlayan *(göz, gök).*

**lamb.kin** ['læmkin] *n.* kuzucuk; 'lamb.like *adj.* kuzu gibi; 'lamb.skin *n.* kuzu derisi.

**lame** [leim] **1.** □ topal, ayağı sakat, aksak *(a. fig.); fig.* eksik, kusurlu, sudan *(sebep);* Am. *sl.* dünyadan habersiz; **2.** *v/t.* topal etm.; *v/i.* topallamak; 'lame-**ness** *n.* topallık.

**la.ment** [ləˈment] **1.** *n.* inilti, feryat, figan, keder; **2.** *v/t. & v/i.* inlemek; ağlamak, figan etm., matem tutmak (for için); **lam.en.ta.ble** □ ['læməntəbl] acınacak, içler acısı; matemli, kederli; **lam.en'ta.tion** *n.* ağlayış, inleme, feryat, figan.

**lam.i.na** ['læminə] *n., pl.* lam.i.nae ['~niː] ince levha; ♀ varak, tabaka; 'lam.i-**nar** *adj.* levha şeklinde; lam.i.nate ['~neit] *v/t.* ince tabakalara ayırmak; ~d glass katmerli cam.

**lamp** [læmp] *n.* lamba, ışık *(a. fig.);* '**~.black** *n.* kandil isi; '**~-chim.ney** *n.* lamba şişesi; '**~.light** *n.* lamba ışığı; '**~.light-er** *n.* fenerleri yakan adam, fenerci; '**~-oil** *n.* gazyağı.

**lam.poon** [læmˈpuːn] **1.** *n.* taşlama, yergi, hicviye; **2.** *v/t.* yermek, taşlamak, hicvetmek.

**lamp-post** ['læmppəust] *n.* sokak feneri direği, elektrik direği.

**lam.prey** *ichth.* ['læmpri] *n.* yılanbalığına benzer su hayvanı.

**lamp.shade** ['læmpʃeid] *n.* abajur.

**lance** [lɑːns] **1.** *n.* mızrak; *a.* **3'**; '**~-ˈcor.po.ral** *n.* ✗ geçici onbaşı; **lan.ce.o.late** ♀ ['lænsiəlit] *adj.* mızraksı, lanseolat; **lanc.er** ✗ ['lɑːnsə] *n.* mızraklı süvari; ~s *pl.* dörtlü kadril dansı.

**lan.cet** ['lɑːnsit] *n.* neşter; ~ arch ⌂ sivri kavisli dar kemer; ~ win.dow sivri kavisli pencere.

**land** [lænd] **1.** *n.* toprak, kara; ülke, memleket; arsa, yer; by ~ karadan, kara yolu ile; ~s *pl.* emlâk, arazi; see how the ~ lies nabzını yoklamak, gidişata bakmak; 2. *v/t.* & *v/i.* karaya çık(ar)mak, yere in(dir)mek; elde etm., kazanmak; vurmak, indirmek *(yumruk vs.);* ↓ boşaltmak; yakalamak *(balık);* ~ on one's feet dört dört ayak üstüne düşmek; ~ up in prison hapsi boylamak; '~-a.gent *n.* emlâkçi, emlâk komisyoncusu.

**lan.dau** ['lændɔ:] *n.* landon, dört tekerlekli ve çift körüklü binek arabası.

**land.ed** ['lændid] *adj.* arazi sahibi; gayrimenkul...

**land...:** '~.fall *n.* ↓ karanın ilk görünmesi; '~-forc.es *n. pl.* kara kuvvetleri; '~-grab.ber *n.* hile ile başkasının arazisine tecavüz eden kimse; '~.hold.er *n.* mülk sahibi.

**land.ing** ['lændiŋ] *n.* iniş; karaya çık(ar)ma; iskele; sahanlık; '~-craft *n.* ↓, ✕ çıkartma gemisi; '~-field *n.* ✝ havaalanı; '~-gear *n.* ✝ iniş takımı; '~-net *n.* ağ kepçe; '~-par.ty *n.* ✕ çıkartma birliği; '~-stage *n.* ↓ iskele; '~-strip = landing-field.

**land.la.dy** ['lændleidi] *n.* pansiyoncu kadın; ev sahibesi.

**land.less** ['lændlis] *adj.* arazisiz.

**land...:** '~.locked *adj.* kara ile çevrilmiş; '~.lop.er *n.* serseri, derbeder; ~.lord ['lændlɔ:d] *n.* mal sahibi; hancı, otelci, pansiyoncu; ~-lub.ber ↓ *contp.* ['lændlʌbə] *n.* deniz ve gemiden anlayan kimse; '~.mark *n. part.* ↓ uzaktan görülebilen işaret; sınır taşı; *fig.* dönüm noktası; '~-own.er *n.* arazi sahibi; ~.scape ['lændskeip] *n.* manzara, peyzaj; ~.slide ['lændslaid] *n.* toprak kayması, kayşa, heyelân; *pol.* büyük çoğunluğun kazanılması; a Democratic ~ Demokratik partinin zaferi; '~-slip *n.* kayşa, heyelân, toprak kayması; ~.s.man ↓ ['~zmən] *n.* denizci olmayan kimse; '~-sur.vey.or *n.* mesahacı, yüzölçümü memuru; ~.tax *n.* arazi vergisi; ~.ward ['~wəd] *adj.* karaya doğru uzanan.

**lane** [lein] *n.* dar sokak, dar yol, dar geçit; kulvar; *mot.* şerit.

**lang syne** *Scots* ['læŋ'sain] *n.* & *adv.* eski zaman(da), geçmiş(te).

**lan.guage** ['læŋgwidʒ] *n.* dil, lisan; konuşma yeteneği; bad ~ küfür; strong ~ sert dil, ağır söz.

**lan.guid** ☐ ['læŋgwid] gevşek, cansız, sönük, yavaş, ağır; isteksiz, gayretsiz; ✝ durgun, kesat; '**lan.guid.ness** *n.* cansızlık, yavaşlık; durgunluk.

**lan.guish** ['læŋgwiʃ] *v/i.* gevşemek, zayıf düşmek, kuvveti kesilmek; isteği kalmamak (for *-e* karşı); ✝ kesat gitmek;

'**lan.guish.ing** ☐ kuvvetsiz, zayıf; ✝ kesat, durgun.

**lan.guor** ['læŋgə] *n.* gevşeklik, cansızlık, ağırlık, bitkinlik, isteksizlik, halsizlik; '**lan.guor.ous** ☐ bitkinlik veren, halsiz düşüren.

**lank** ☐ [læŋk] uzun ve zayıf, boylu, ince; düz *(saç);* '**lank.y** ☐ uzun boylu ve zayıf, sırık gibi.

**lan.o.lin** ['lænəuli:n] *n.* lanolin.

**lan.tern** ['læntən] *n.* fener *(a.* ♠*); dark ~ hırsız feneri; '~-jawed *adj.* uzun çeneli; '~-slide *n.* hayalci feneri, diyapozitif; ~ lecture projeksiyonlu konferans.

**lan.yard** ↓ ['lænjəd] *n.* kordon, ince ip, savla.

**lap¹** [læp] 1. *n.* kucak; diz üstü; etek; ⊕ örtü, kat, bindirme dikişi; *spor:* tur; 2. *v/t.* & *v/i.* üst üste bin(dir)mek, katla(n)mak, sar(ıl)mak; kuşatmak, çevirmek, örtmek; *spor:* tur bindirmek.

**lap²** [~] 1. *n.* yalayarak içme; dalga sesi; 2. *v/t.* yalayarak içmek; can kulağı ile dinlemek; *v/i.* hafif hafif çarpmak *(dalga).*

**lap-dog** ['læpdɔg] *n.* küçük ev köpeği.

**la.pel** [lə'pel] *n.* klapa.

**lap.i.dar.y** ['læpidəri] 1. *adj.* yazıta elverişli...; taşlara ait, taş...; *fig.* özlü; 2. *n.* oymacı, hakkâk, kıymetli taş kesicisi.

**lap.is laz.u.li** [læpis'læzjulai] *n.* lacivert taş; bu taşın rengi.

**lapse** [læps] 1. *n.* kusur, yanlış, hata; kayma; ara; geçme, mürur, geçiş, düşme (into *-e);* ᵘᵘ sukut; 2. *v/i.* geçmek; başkasına intikal etm.; gömülmek, sapmak, düşmek, dalmak (into *-e);* ᵘᵘ hükmü kalmamak; yanılmak, hata etm.

**lap.wing** *orn.* ['læpwiŋ] *n.* kızkuşu.

**lar.ce.ny** ᵘᵘ ['lɑ:səni] *n.* hırsızlık.

**larch** ♣ [lɑ:tʃ] *n.* karaçam.

**lard** [lɑ:d] 1. *n.* domuz yağı; 2. *v/t.* domuz yağı ile yağlamak; *fig.* süslemek *(yazı veya söz);* '**lard.er** *n.* kiler; '**lard.ing-nee-dle**, '**lard.ing-pin** *n.* yağlama şişi.

**large** ☐ [lɑ:dʒ] büyük, geniş, iri; bol, çok; serbest; cömert; sınırsız *(yetki);* kaba *(dil);* elverişli *(rüzgâr);* abartmalı, övüngen; at ~ kontroldan çıkmış, serbest; ayrıntılı olarak, detaylı; genellikle; rasgele; talk at ~ ayrıntılı olarak konuşmak; in ~ büyük ölçüde; '**large.ly** *adv.* büyük ölçüde; başlıca; cömertçe, bol bol, çok; '**large.ness** *n.* büyüklük *(a. fig),* genişlik; '**large-'mind.ed** *adj.* geniş fikirli, serbest düşünüşlü; '**large-'scale** *adj.* büyük çapta; '**large-'sized** *adj.* büyük boy.

**lar.gess(e)** † [lɑːˈdʒes] *n.* cömertlik; bağış.

**lar.go** ♪ [ˈlɑːgəu] **1.** *n.* yavaş çalınan parça; **2.** *adv.* largo.

**lar.i.at** *Am.* [ˈlæriət] *n.* kement.

**lark¹** *orn.* [lɑːk] *n.* tarlakuşu.

**lark²** [~] **1.** *n.* şaka, eğlence, cümbüş, şamata; **2.** *v/i.* cümbüş yapmak, şamata yapmak, eğlenmek; **lark.some** [ˈ~səm] = larky.

**lark.spur** ♦ [ˈlɑːkspəː] *n.* hezaren çiçeği.

**lark.y** F [ˈlɑːki] *adj.* şamatacı, gırgır.

**lar.va** *zo.* [ˈlɑːvə] *n.*, *pl.* **lar.vae** [ˈ~viː] tırtıl, kurtçuk, sürfe; **lar.val** [ˈ~vəl] *adj.* tırtıla ait, tırtıl...; tırtıl şeklinde.

**lar.yn.gi.tis** ⚕ [lærinˈdʒaitis] *n.* larenjit; **lar.ynx** [ˈlærinks] *n.* gırtlak, boğaz, hançere.

**las.civ.i.ous** ☐ [ləˈsiviəs] şehvetli.

**lash** [læʃ] **1.** *n.* kamçı (darbesi); vuruş, vurma; kirpik; acı hiciv, zem; **the ~** kamçılama, dövme; **2.** *vb.* kamçılamak, dövmek, çarpmak, vurmak; *fig.* yermek, eleştirmek; sıkıca bağlamak; kışkırtmak, galeyana getirmek; **~ out** saldırmak; çifte atmak; *fig.* çatmak, çıkışmak; **lash.ing** *n.* ip, halat; kamçılama, dövme; azarlama; **~s** *pl.* çok miktar, bolluk.

**lass** [læs] *n.* kız; sevgili, kız arkadaş; **las.sie** [ˈlæsi] *n.* kızcağız.

**las.si.tude** [ˈlæsitjuːd] *n.* yorgunluk, bitkinlik; ilgisizlik.

**las.so** [ˈlæsəu] **1.** *n.* kement; **2.** *v/t.* kementle yakalamak.

**last¹** [lɑːst] **1.** *adj.* son(uncu), en sonraki, en gerideki; geçen, evvelki; eski, sabık; son derece, gayet; **~ but one** sondan bir evvelki; **~ night** dün gece; **2.** *n.* son, nihayet; **my ~** sonuncu (*çocuğum, mektubum vs.*); **at ~** sonunda, nihayet; **at long ~** en sonunda; **breathe one's ~** son nefesini vermek, ölmek; **3.** *adv.* en sonra, son olarak, nihayet; **~, but not least** özellikle, son fakat önemli.

**last²** [~] *v/i.* devam etm., sürmek; dayanmak, bitmemek, tükenmemek, yetmek.

**last³** [~] *n.* kundura kalıbı; **stick to one's ~** üstesinden gelemediği şeyi yapmaya kalkışmamak, çizmeden yukarı çıkmamak.

**last.ing** [ˈlɑːstiŋ] **1.** ☐ sürekli, devamlı, uzun süreli, dayanıklı; **2.** *n.* dayanma, sürme.

**last.ly** [ˈlɑːstli] *adv.* son olarak, nihayet.

**latch** [lætʃ] **1.** *n.* mandal, sürgü; kilit dili; **on the ~** sürgülü ,mandallanmış; **2.**

*v/t.* & *v/i.* mandalla(n)mak; **ˈ~-key** *n.* kapı anahtarı.

**late** [leit] *adj.* geç; gecikmiş, geri kalmış; sabık, geçmiş; ölü, rahmetli, merhum; yakında olmuş, yeni; **at (the) ~st** en geç; **as ~** as yesterday ancak dün; **of ~ son** zamanlarda, yakınlarda; **of ~ years** son yıllarda; **~r on** daha sonra; **be ~** geç kalmak, gecikmek; ⚙ rötar yapmak; **keep ~ hours** gece geç saatlere kadar yatmamak; **eve** geç gelmek; **ˈ~-com.er** *n.* geç gelen *veya* kalan kimse.

**la.teen** ⚓ [ləˈtiːn] *adj.*: **~ sail** latin yelkeni.

**late.ly** [ˈleitli] *adv.* geçenlerde, yakınlarda, bu günlerde.

**la.ten.cy** [ˈleitənsi] *n.* gelişmemişlik, gözükmezlik, gizli olarak varolma.

**late.ness** [ˈleitnis] *n.* gecikme, geçlik.

**la.tent** ☐ [ˈleitənt] gelişmemiş, gözükmez; gizli kalmış.

**lat.er.al** ☐ [ˈlætərəl] yana ait, yan...; yanal, yandan gelen; yana doğru olan.

**la.tex** ♦ [ˈleiteks] *n.* lateks; kauçuk hammaddesi.

**lath** [lɑːθ] **1.** *n.* lata, tiriz; **2.** *v/t.* lata ile kaplamak.

**lathe** [leið] *n.* torna tezgâhı; çömlekçi çarkı.

**lath.er** [ˈlɑːðə, ˈlæðə] **1.** *n.* sabun köpüğü; atın köpüklü teri; **2.** *v/t.* & *v/i.* köpür(t)-mek; sabunlamak; pataklamak, sopa çekmek.

**Lat.in** [ˈlætin] **1.** *adj.* Latin(ce)...; **2.** *n.* Latince; **~ A.mer.i.ca** Latin Amerika; **ˈLat.in.ism** *n.* Latin dili özelliği; **ˈLat.in.ize** *v/t.* Latinceye çevirmek.

**lat.i.tude** [ˈlætitjuːd] *n.* enlem, arz; *fig.* serbestlik, hoşgörü; genişlik; **~s** *pl.* bölge, mıntıka; **lat.iˈtu.di.nal** [~dinl] *adj.* enine...; **lat.i.tu.di.nar.i.an** [ˈ~diˈnɛəriən] **1.** *adj.* serbest fikirli, hoşgörülü; **2.** *n.* serbest fikirli kimse.

**la.trine** [ləˈtriːn] *n.* helâ çukuru.

**lat.ter** [ˈlætə] *adj.* son(raki)..., *poet.* daha sonraki...; **~ end** son; ölüm; **ˈ~-day** *adj.* çağa uygun, modern..., çağdaş...; **ˈlat.ter.ly** *adv.* bu yakınlarda, son zamanlarda.

**lat.tice** [ˈlætis] **1.** *n. a.* **~-work** kafes; **2.** *v/t.* kafesle çevirmek.

**Lat.vi.an** [ˈlætviən] **1.** *adj.* Letonya...; **2.** *n.* Letonyalı; Letonya dili.

**laud** [lɔːd] *v/t.* övmek, methetmek, yüceltmek; **ˈlaud.a.ble** ☐ övgüye değer; **lauˈda.tion** *n.* övme; **laud.a.to.ry** ☐ [ˈ~dətəri] övücü, öven (of *-i*).

**laugh** [lɑːf] **1.** *n.* gülme, gülüş, hande; **have a ~** gülmek; **raise a ~** güldürmek;

2. *vb.* gülmek (at *-e*); ~ at s.o. *b-le* alay etm.; ~ off gülerek geçiştirmek, gülüp geçmek; ~ out of gülerek meseleyi kapatmak; you will ~ on the wrong side *veya* on the other side of your mouth *veya* face bu kadar gülme pişman olursun; he ~s best who ~s last son gülen iyi güler; *s.* sleeve; **'laugh.a.ble** ☐ gülünç, komik; **'laugh.er** *n.* gülen kimse; **'laugh.ing 1.** *n.* gülme, gülüş; **2.** ☐ gül(dür)en; it is no ~ matter işin şaka götürür yanı yok; **'laugh.ing-gas** *n.* güldürücü gaz; **'laugh.ing-stock** *n.* alay konusu kimse *veya* şey; **laugh.ter** [ˈ~tə] *n.* gülüş, gülme, kahkaha.

**launch** [lɔːntʃ] **1.** *n.* ↓ kızaktan suya indirme; işkampaviye; roketi fezaya fırlatma; **2.** *v/t.* kızaktan suya indirmek *(gemi)*; fırlatmak *(roket)*; atmak, fırlatmak, savurmak *(a. fig.)*; *fig.* başlatmak; *v/i.* ~ out başlamak, girişmek; ~ (out) into *-e* girişmek, *-e* başlamak; **'launch.ing-pad** *n.* fırlatma *(veya* atış) rampası.

**laun.der** [ˈlɔːndə] *v/t. & v/i.* yıka(n)mak, yıkayıp ütül(en)mek *(veya* çamaşır); **laun.der.ette** [lɔːndəˈret] *n.* çamaşırhane.

**laun.dress** [ˈlɔːndris] *n.* çamaşırcı kadın; **'laun.dry** *n.* çamaşır(hane); çamaşırcılık; **'laun.dry-man** *n.* çamaşırcı.

**lau.re.ate** [ˈlɔːriit] **1.** *adj.* defne dallarından çelenk giymiş; **2.** *n.* the ♀, the Poet ♀ saray şairi.

**lau.rel** ↓ [ˈlɔrəl] *n.* defne ağacı; win ~s *fig.* şöhret kazanmak; **'lau.relled** *adj.* defne dallarından çelenk giymiş; şan, şeref kazanmış.

**lav** F [læv] *n.* helâ, kenef.

**la.va** [ˈlɑːvə] *n.* lav.

**lav.a.to.ry** [ˈlævətri] *n.* helâ, tuvalet; lavabo; yıkanma yeri; public ~ umumî helâ.

**lave** *mst poet.* [leiv] *v/t. & v/i.* yıka(n)mak; banyo yapmak; yanısıra akıvermek *(nehir)*.

**lav.en.der** ↓ [ˈlævində] *n.* lavanta.

**lav.ish** [ˈlæviʃ] **1.** ☐ savurgan, müsrif, tutumsuz; çok, bol, aşırı; **2.** *v/t.* bol bol harcamak, çarçur etm.; aşırı... göstermek; **'lav.ish.ness** *n.* savurganlık.

**law** [lɔː] *n.* kanun, yasa; kaide, kural; nizam; ᎏᎏ kanunlar; tabiat kanunu; usül, töre; at ~ kanunî, meşru; be a ~ unto o.s. bildiğini okumak; go to ~ mahkemeye başvurmak; dava etm.; have the ~ of s.o. *b-ni* dava etm.; ...-in-law kayın...; necessity knows no ~ ihtiyaç kanun tanımaz; lay down the ~ dediği dedik olm.;

practise ~ avukatlık *(veya* hukukçuluk) etm.; **'~-a.bid.ing** *adj.* ᎏᎏ kanuna uyan; **'~-break.er** *n.* kanunu çiğneyen kimse; **'~.court** *n.* mahkeme; **law.ful** ☐ [ˈ~ful] kanuna uygun, meşru, kanunî; **'law-giv.er** *n.* kanun yapan kimse; **'law.less** ☐ kanuna aykırı, kanun tanımaz; kanunsuz; vahşi, azılı; **'law.mak.er** *n.* kanun koyucu; meclis üyesi.

**lawn¹** [lɔːn] *n.* patiska.

**lawn²** [~] *n.* çimen(lik), çayır; **'~-mow.er** *n.* çim biçme makinesi; **'~-sprin.kler** *n.* çim sulama aleti; **'~-ten.nis** *n.* çim tenisi. **law.suit** [ˈlɔːsjuːt] *n.* dava; **law.yer** [ˈ~jə] *n.* avukat, dava vekili.

**lax** ☐ [læks] gevşek *(a. fig.)*; ihmalci, kayıtsız, savsak, lâkayt; **lax.a.tive** [ˈ~ətiv] **1.** *adj.* ishal edici *(ilâç)*; **2.** *n.* sürgün ilâcı, müshil; **'lax.i.ty, lax.ness** *n.* gevşeklik; kayıtsızlık.

**lay¹** [lei] *pret. of* lie² 2.

**lay²** [~] *n.* türkü, balad; poet. şiir, gazel.

**lay³** [~] *adj.* layık; işin ehli olmayan...

**lay⁴** [~] **1.** *n.* durum, duruş, yatış, mevki; *sl.* iş güç, meşgale; **2.** *(irr.)* *v/t.* koymak, yatırmak, yaymak, sermek; kurmak *(masa)*; gömmek; yumurtlamak; yatıştırmak; koymak *(vergi)*; yüklemek *(suç)*; hazırlamak *(plan vs.)*; dayamak, yaslamak; *sl. ile* cinsi münasebette bulunmak; ~ aside bir tarafa koymak; biriktirmek *(para)*; terketmek, bırakmak, vazgeçmek; ~ bare açmak; ortaya çıkarmak *(sır vs.)*; ~ before s.o. *b-ne* sunmak, takdim etm., *b-ne* göstermek; ~ by yığmak, biriktirmek *(para)*; ~ down bırakmak; feda etm.; planlamak; yapmak, inşa etm.; yatırmak; saklamak, depo etm.; emretmek; ~ s.o. (fast) by the heels *b-ni* yakalamak, tutuklayıp hapsetmek; ~ in biriktirmek, stoklamak; ~ low yere sermek; yatağa düşürmek; ~ off geçici olarak işten çıkarmak; *Am. sl.* bırakmak, vazgeçmek, kesmek; ~ on sağlamak, temin etm.; saldırmak, yüklenmek; ~ it on (thick) *fig.* abartmak; pohpohlamak, göklere çıkarmak; ~ open ortaya çıkarmak; kesmek, yarmak; ~ (o.s.) open to s.th *k-ni* ...ile karşı karşıya bırakmak; ~ out yaymak, sermek; sergilemek; tasarlamak; düzenlemek; tertiplemek; gömülmeye hazırlamak, kefenlemek *(ölü)*; harcamak, sarfetmek *(para)*; yere sermek *b-ni*; ~ o.s. out *k-ni* paralamak, paralanmak (for *için)*; ~ s.o. under an obligation *veya* a necessity *b-ni* mecbur bırakmak; ~ up biriktirmek, saklamak; ↓ kızağa çekmek; be laid up yatağa düş-

mek; ~ with ... ile yatmak; *v/i.* yumurtlamak; *a.* ~ a wager bahse girmek; ~
about saldırmak, sağına soluna vurmak;
çıkışmak; ~ into s.o. *sl. b-ne* girişmek,
*b-ni* pataklamak; *b-ne* verip veriştirmek;
~ (it) on F saldırmak, yüklenmek, veriştirmek.

**lay.a.bout** *sl.* [ˈleiəbaut] *n.* aylak *(veya*
serseri) kimse; **ˈlay-by** *n.* yol kenarındaki park yeri.

**lay.er 1.** [ˈleiə] *n.* kat, tabaka; tavuk;
daldırma; **2.** ✓ [ˈlɛə] *v/t.* daldırmak.

**lay.ette** [leiˈet] *n.* yeni doğmuş bebeğin çamaşır ve elbise takımı.

**lay-fig.ure** [ˈleiˈfigə] *n.* manken.

**lay.man** [ˈleimən] *n.* meslek sahibi olmayan kimse.

**lay...:** **ˈ~-off** *n.* işçilerin geçici olarak işten çıkartılması; **ˈ~-out** *n.* düzen, tertip;
mizanpaj.

**laz.a.ret,** *mst* **laz.a.ret.to** [læzəˈret(əu)] *n.*
karantina merkezi; ↓ erzak ambarı.

**laze** F [leiz] *v/i.* ense yapmak; *v/t.* aylak
aylak geçirmek *(zaman);* **ˈlaz.i.ness** *n.*
tembellik, uyuşukluk, aylaklık; **ˈla.zy** *adj.*
tembel, miskin, uyuşuk, aylak, hantal,
ağır; **ˈla.zy-bones** *n.* tembel kimse.

**lea** *poet.* [li:] *n.* çimenlik, çayırlık, mera.

**leach** [li:tʃ] *vb.* damıtmak, süzmek.

**lead¹** [led] **1.** *n.* kurşun; ↓ iskandil; *typ.*
anterlin; grafit; ~s *pl.* kurşun levha; ~
pencil kurşunkalem; swing the ~ *sl.* temaruz etm., hasta numarası yaparak işten kaçmak; **2.** *v/t.* kurşunlamak; *typ.*
anterlin ile açmak *(satır araları).*

**lead²** [li:d] **1.** *n.* kılavuzluk, öncülük, rehberlik; tasma kayışı; *thea.* başrol (oyuncusu); ✓ ana tel; başa geçme; *iskambil:* ilk oynama hakkı; ilk oynayacak
kimse; it's my ~ *iskambil:* sıra bende;
take the ~ başa geçmek; örnek olm.; **2.**
*(irr.) v/t.* yol göstermek -*e,* rehberlik
etm. -*e,* götürmek -*i;* kumanda etm. -*i;*
idare etm. -*i,* yönetmek -*i;* elinden tutarak götürmek -*i;* sürmek *(hayat);* önde
götürmek *(yarış vs.);* etkilemek -*i;* ikna
etm. -*i;* sebep olm. (to -*e); iskambil:*
...ile oyun açmak; ~ on ayartmak, kandırıp yaptırmak; *v/i.* gitmek, çıkmak
*(yol);* başta olm.; ~ off başlamak; *spor:*
oyuna başlamak; ~ up to -*e* getirmek,
-*e* sebep olm.

**lead.en** [ˈledn] *adj.* kurşun(dan); kurşun
renginde, kurşuni; *fig.* ağır, kasvetli, sıkıcı; hüzünlü.

**lead.er** [ˈli:də] *n.* önder, lider, kumandan,
baş, önayak; kılavuz, rehber; solo kemancı; orkestra şefi; ☼ *(çok avukatlı*

*davada)* kıdemli avukat; *gazete:* başmakale; ✤ filiz, sürgün; *anat.* kiriş, veter; **lead.er.ette** [~ˈret] *n. (baş makale-
den sonra gelen)* kısa makale; **ˈlead.er-
ship** *n.* önderlik, liderlik, öncülük.

**lead-in** ✤ [ˈli:din] *n.* anten iniş teli.

**lead.ing** [ˈli:diŋ] **1.** *adj.* önde olan, baş-
(lıca), ana, en önemli; yol gösteren; yöneten; ~ article başmakale; ✝ çok tutulan mal; ~ case ☼ emsal karar; ~ man
*thea.* baş aktör; ~ lady baş aktris; ~
question istenilen cevaba götüren soru;
**2.** *n.* yol gösterme, rehberlik, öncülük;
**ˈ~-strings** *n. pl.* çocuk yürütme kayışla-
rı; keep in ~ *b-nin* başına kâhya kesilmek.

**lead...** [led]: ~ **poi.son.ing** kurşun zehirlenmesi; **ˈ~-works** *n. mst sg.* kurşun dö-
kümhanesi.

**leaf** [li:f] *n., pl.* **leaves** [li:vz] yaprak; kanat *(kapı, masa);* in ~ yapraklanmış,
yeşermiş; come into ~ yapraklanmak;
**ˈleaf.age** *n.* yapraklar; **ˈleaf-bud** *n.* yaprak tomurcuğu; **ˈleaf.less** *adj.* yapraksız;
**leaf.let** [ˈ~lit] *n.* yaprakçık; ufak risale, broşür; **ˈleaf.y** *adj.* yapraklı.

**league¹** [li:g] **1.** *n.* birleşme, ittifak; birlik, cemiyet; *spor:* lig; ♀ of Nations Milletler Cemiyeti; **2.** *v/t. & v/i.* birleş(tir)-
mek.

**league²** *mst poet.* [~] *n.* fersah *(4,8 km.).*

**leak** [li:k] **1.** *n.* delik, akıntı, sızıntı *(a.
fig.);* **2.** *v/t. & v/i.* sız(dır)mak; ~ out
*fig.* sız(dır)mak *(haber);* **ˈleak.age** *n.* sızıntı, sızma *(a. fig.);* ✝ fire; **ˈleak.y** *adj.*
sızıntılı, delik.

**lean¹** [li:n] **1.** *adj.* zayıf, cılız; yağsız *(yemek);* verimsiz, kıraç; **2.** *n.* yağsız et.

**lean²** [~] *(irr.) v/t. & v/i.* daya(n)mak
yasla(n)mak *(against -e);* güvenmek (on,
upon -*e);* yana yat(ır)mak, eğilmek;
meyletmek (to, towards -*e);* **2.** *n. (fig. a.*
**ˈlean.ing)** eğilim, meyil.

**lean.ness** [ˈli:nnis] *n.* zayıflık; yağsızlık.

**leant** [lent] *pret. & p.p. of* lean² 1.

**lean-to** [ˈli:ntu:] *n.* sundurma.

**leap** [li:p] **1.** *n.* atlama, sıçrayış; atlanı-
lan mesafe; ani artış; by ~s (and bounds)
büyük hızla, çok hızlı; **2.** *(irr.) v/t. &
v/i.* atla(t)mak, sıçra(t)mak, fırla(t)-
mak; he ~t at the opportunity fırsatı ka-
çırmadı, fırsatı ganimet bildi; **ˈ~-frog 1.**
*n.* birdirbir oyunu; **2.** *v/i.* birdirbir oynamak; **leapt** [lept] *pret. & p.p. of* leap
2; **ˈleap-year** *n.* artıkyıl.

**learn** [lən] *(irr.) vb.* öğrenmek; işitmek,
haber almak; ezberlemek; *sl.* sormak;
göstermek; ~ from -*den* haber almak;

**learn.ed** □ ['~nid] âlim, bilgili; üstünde çok çalışılmış; **'learn.er** n. bşi öğrenen kimse, yeni başlayan; **'learn.ing** n. bilgi, öğrenme, ilim; **learnt** [lə:nt] pret. & p.p. of learn.

**lease** [li:s] 1. n. kira(lama); kira kontratı; let (out) 'on ~ kiraya vermek; a new ~ of life yeniden doğma; 2. v/t. kiralamak; kiraya vermek; **'~.hold** 1. n. kiralanmış mal; 2. adj. kiralanmış...; **'~.hold.er** n. kiracı.

**leash** [li:ʃ] 1. n. tasma sırımı (veya kayışı); hold in ~ fig. yuları elden bırakmamak; strain at the ~ fig. serbest kalmağa can atmak; 2. v/t. iple bağlamak.

**least** [li:st] 1. adj. en az, en ufak, en küçük, asgari; 2. adv. a. ~ of all hiç, zerre kadar; at (the) ~ hiç olmazsa, en azından, bari; at the very ~ en az, en aşağı; not in the ~ hiç; to say the ~ en azından, hiç olmazsa.

**leath.er** ['leðə] 1. n. deri, kösele, meşin; F meşin top; ~s pl. deri ürünleri; 2. adj. deriden mamul, deri...; 3. v/t. deri ile kaplamak; kayışla dövmek; **leath.er.ette** [~'ret] n. suni deri; **leath.ern** ['leðən] adj. deriden yapılmış; **'leath.er.neck** n. X Am. sl. bahriyeli; **'leath.er.y** adj. kösele gibi (a. fig.).

**leave** [li:v] 1. n. müsaade; a. ~ of absence izin; veda, ayrılma; izin süresi; by your ~ izninizle, müsaadenizle; take one's ~ veda etm., ayrılmak; take ~ of ile vedalaşmak; -den ayrılmak; take ~ of one's senses kafayı üşütmek, aklını kaçırmak; 2. (irr.) v/t. bırakmak, terketmek; ayrılmak -den; geçmek -i; ardında bırakmak; miras olarak bırakmak; vazgeçmek; be left (arta) kalmak; ~ it at that burada bırakmak, burada kesmek, üstelememek; s. call; ~ behind geride bırakmak; unutmak; ~ off bırakmak, vazgeçmek; giymemek; takmamak; ~ s.o. to himself veya to his own devices b-ni kendi haline bırakmak; ~ s.o. veya s.th. alone b-ne veya bşe karışmamak, dokunmamak; be (nicely) left F üçkağıda getirilmek, şapa oturtulmak; çıkmazda olm.; v/i. gitmek, yola çıkmak (for -e).

**leav.en** ['levn] 1. n. maya (a. fig.); 2. v/t. mayalamak; fig. bozmak, değiştirmek; etkilemek; **'leav.en.ing** n. mayalama; bozma.

**leaves** [li:vz] pl. of leaf.

**leav.ings** ['li:viŋz] n. pl. artık.

**lech.er** ['letʃə] n. zampara, çapkın erkek, şehvet düşkünü adam; **'lech.er.ous** adj.

şehvet düşkünü, çapkın; **'lech.er.y** n. şehvet (düşkünlüğü), çapkınlık.

**lec.tern** eccl. ['lektən] n. kürsü.

**lec.ture** ['lektʃə] 1. n. konferans; umumî ders; azarlama, paylama; s. curtain; read s.o. a ~ b-ni azarlamak, paylamak; ~ room konferans salonu; 2. v/i. konferans vermek, ders vermek (on üzerine, hakkında); v/t. azarlamak, paylamak; **'lec.tur.er** n. konferansçı; univ. doçent; eccl. vaiz; **'lec.ture.ship** n. doçentlik.

**led** [led] pret. & p.p. of lead[2] 2.

**ledge** [ledʒ] n. düz çıkıntı; kaya tabakası.

**ledg.er** ['ledʒə] n. ✝ defteri kebir; ⊕ travers; a. ~ line ♪ yardımcı çizgi.

**lee** ⌷ [li:] n. rüzgâr altı, boca.

**leech** [li:tʃ] n. zo. sülük (a. fig.); stick like a ~ fig. sülük gibi yapışmak.

**leek** ♣ [li:k] n. pırasa.

**leer** [liə] 1. n. yan gözle bakma; 2. v/i. kötü niyetle bakmak, yan gözle bakmak (at -e); **'leer.y** □ sl. kuşkulu (of -den).

**lees** [li:z] n. pl. tortu, posa.

**lee.ward** ⌷ ['li:wəd] adj. & adv. boca(ya doğru).

**lee.way** ⌷ ['li:wei] n. rüzgâr altına düşme; make ~ bocalamak; fig. geri kalmak; make up ~ fig. kaybolan zamanı telâfi etm., açığı kapatmak.

**left[1]** [left] pret. & p.p. of leave 2.

**left[2]** [~] 1. adj. sola ait, sol(daki)...; 2. adv. sola doğru; 3. n. sol taraf; sol kanat; **'~.hand** adj. sol soldaki...; sol elle yapılan; **'~.hand.ed** □ solak; solaklar için yapılmış; fig. sakar, beceriksiz, salak; içten olmayan (iltifat); ⊕ sağdan sola.

**left...:** **'~.llug.gage of.fice** eşya dairesi, emanet; **'~.o.vers** n. pl. artık yemek.

**left-wing** ['left'wiŋ] adj. pol. sol kanat.

**leg** [leg] n. bacak; mobilya ayağı; but; pantolon bacağı; A pergel ayağı; give s.o. a ~ up binmesine veya tırmanmasına yardım etm.; fig. b-ne kara gününde yardım etm.; be on one's last ~s F ayaklarına kara su inmek; ölüm döşeğinde olm.; pull s.o.'s ~ b-ne takılmak; not have a ~ to stand on fig. fikrini savunamamak, tutunacak dalı kalmamak.

**leg.a.cy** ['legəsi] n. miras, kalıt; **'~.hunt.er** n. miras avcısı.

**le.gal** □ ['li:gəl] kanunî, meşru, kanuna uygun; hukukî; ~ capacity medenî hakları kullanma ehliyeti; ~ entity tüzel kişi, hükmî şahıs; ~ remedy kanunî çözüm; ~ status hukukî durum; s. tender; **le.gal.i.ty** [li:'gæliti] n. kanunilik, kanuna uygunluk; **le.gal.i.za.tion** [li:gəlai'zeiʃən] n.

tasdik, onaylama, kanunlaştırma; **'le-gal.ize** v/t. kanunlaştırmak, meşru kılmak.

**leg.ate** ['legit] n. Papa elçisi; elçi, sefir.

**leg.a.tee** ☼ [legə'tiː] n. vâris, mirasçı, kalıtçı.

**le.ga.tion** [li'geiʃən] n. orta elçilik (dairesi).

**leg-ball** ['leg'beil] n.: give ~ tabanları yağlamak, sıvışmak.

**leg.end** ['ledʒənd] n. masal, hikâye, efsane; yazı; **'leg.end.ar.y** adj. efsanevî.

**leg.er.de.main** ['ledʒədə'mein] n. el çabukluğu, hokkabazlık.

**legged** [legd] adj. ...bacaklı; **'leg.gings** n. pl. tozluk; **'leg.gy** adj. uzun bacaklı.

**leg.horn** [le'gɔːn] n. legorn, bir çeşit tavuk.

**leg.i.bil.i.ty** [ledʒi'biliti] n. okunaklılık; **leg.i.ble** ['ledʒəbl] □ okunaklı (yazı).

**le.gion** ['liːdʒən] n. eski Roma alayı; fig. kalabalık; birçok; **'le.gion.ar.y** 1. adj. alaya ait, alay...; 2. n. alay eri.

**leg.is.late** ['ledʒisleit] v/i. kanun yapmak; **leg.is'la.tion** n. yasama; yasa, kanunlar; **leg.is.la.tive** ['~lətiv] yasamalı; **leg.is.la.tor** ['~leitə] n. kanun yapan kimse; **leg.is.la.ture** ['~leitʃə] n. yasama kurulu.

**le.git.i.ma.cy** [li'dʒitiməsi] n. kanuna uygunluk, kanunî olma, yasallık; **le'git.i.mate** 1. □ [~mit] kanuna uygun, kanunî, meşru; mantıklı, akla yatkın, makûl; meşru doğmuş; 2. [~meit] v/t. kanuna uygun kılmak; onaylamak; **le.git.i'ma.tion** n. kanunî kılma; **le'git.i.ma.tize** [~mətaiz], **le'git.i.mize** = legitimate 2.

**leg.ume** ['legjuːm] n. baklagillerden herhangi bir bitki; **le'gu.mi.nous** [~minəs] adj. baklagillere ait, baklagiller...

**lei.sure** ['leʒə] 1. n. boş vakit; serbestlik; be at ~ serbest olm., boş vakti olm.; acelesi olmamak; at your ~ boş vaktinizde, vaktiniz olduğunda; 2. adj. boş..., serbest...; **'lei.sured** adj. boş vakti olan; the ~ classes aristokrat sınıfı; **'lei.sure.ly** 1. adj. acelesiz iş yapan; acelesiz yapılan; 2. adv. rahatça, acelesiz, yavaş yavaş.

**lem.on** ['lemən] n. limon (ağacı); limon sarısı renk; **lem.on.ade** [~'neid] n. limonata; **'lem.on-'squash** n. limon suyu; **'lem.on-squeez.er** n. limonluk.

**lend** [lend] (irr.) v/t. ödünç vermek, borç vermek; vermek; ~ a hand yardım elini uzatmak; ~ o.s. to -e yanaşmak; -e elverişli olm.; ~ing library ödünç kitap veren kütüphane; **'lend.er** n. ödünç veren kimse; **'Lend-'Lease Act** ödünç verme veya

kiralama sistemi kanunu (Am. 1941).

**length** [leŋθ] n. uzunluk; boy; süre, müddet; mesafe; at ~ nihayet, sonunda; baştan sona kadar; at (great) ~ ayrıntılarıyle, uzun uzadıya; go all ~s sonuna kadar gitmek, her çareye başvurmak; go (to) great ~s ...için çok uğraşmak; her çareye başvurmak; he goes the ~ of saying ...diyecek kadar ileri gider; **'length.en** v/t. & v/i. uza(t)mak; **'length.ways, 'length.wise** adv. uzunluğuna, uzunlamasına; **'length.y** □ upuzun.

**le.ni.ence, le.ni.en.cy** ['liːnjəns(i)] = lenity; **'le.ni.ent** □ yumuşak huylu, merhametli; kibar; **'len.i.tive** ⚕, 1. adj. yatıştırıcı; 2. n. yatıştırıcı ilâç; **len.i.ty** ['leniti] n. yumuşaklık; merhamet; kibarlık.

**lens** [lenz] n. mercek, adese, pertavsız; phot. objektif; ~ system phot. mercek sistemi.

**lent¹** [lent] pret. & p.p. of lend.

**Lent²** [~] n. büyük perhiz.

**Lent.en** ['lentən] adj. büyük perhize ait, büyük perhiz...

**len.tic.u.lar** □ [len'tikjulə] merceğe ait, mercek...; mercekli...

**len.til** ⚕ ['lentil] n. mercimek.

**leop.ard** ['lepəd] n. pars, panter.

**lep.er** ['lepə] n. cüzamlı kimse.

**lep.re.chaun** Ir. ['leprəkɔːn] n. cin.

**lep.ro.sy** ☙ ['leprəsi] n. cüzam, miskin hastalığı; **'lep.rous** adj. cüzamlı; cüzama ait, cüzam...

**les.bian** ['lezbiən] n. sevici (kadın); **'les.bian.ism** n. sevicilik.

**lese-maj.es.ty** ☼ ['liːz'mædʒisti] n. hıyanet, hainlik.

**le.sion** ['liːʒən] n. yara, bere.

**less** [les] 1. adj. & adv. daha az, daha küçük; 2. prp. ♉ eksi; † indirimli, çıkarılmak üzere; no ~ than en azından; no ~ a person than ... kadar önemli; none the ~ yine de, bununla birlikte, hal böyle iken.

**...less** [lis] suffix ...sız, ...siz.

**les.see** [le'siː] n. kiracı.

**less.en** ['lesn] v/t. & v/i. küçül(t)mek, azal(t)mak, eksil(t)mek; fig. küçümsemek.

**less.er** ['lesə] adj. daha az, daha küçük.

**les.son** ['lesn] n. ders; ibret (a. eccl.); ~s pl. dersler, öğretim; teach s.o. a ~ b-ne ders vermek; b-ne ders olm.

**les.sor** [le'sɔː] n. kiraya veren kimse.

**lest** [lest] cj. olmasın diye, ...mesin diye; korkusu ile, belki, olmaya ki.

**let¹** [let] (irr.) v/t. müsaade etm. -mesine, izin vermek -mesine; bırakmak; kiraya vermek; ~ alone el sürmemek, dokunmamak; *adv.* ...saymazsak, ...bırak, ...şöyle dursun; ~ be dokunmamak, kendi haline bırakmak; ~ down indirmek; kısaltmak; düşürmek; hayal kırıklığına uğratmak, boşa çıkarmak; ~ s.o. down gently *b-ni* hafifçe cezalandırmak, *b-ni* alıştıra alıştıra hayal kırıklığına uğratmak; ~ drive at s.o. *b-ne* girişmek; ~ fly savurmak, fırlatmak, atmak; *fig.* bağırıp çağırmak; ~ go elinden bırakmak, koyvermek, salıvermek; ~ it go at that konuyu burada kesmek; ~ into *-e* ortak etm., *-e* sırdaş etm.; *-e* açmak (*pencere vs.*); ~ loose salıvermek, serbest bırakmak; ~ off cezasını affetmek, cezasını hafifletmek; patlatmak, ateşlemek; *s.* steam; ~ out boşaltmak; genişletmek, bollaştırmak (*elbise*); ağzından kaçırmak (*sır*); salıvermek; kiraya vermek; ~ the cat out of the bag ağzından kaçırmak; *v/i.* kiralanmak (at, for *-e*); ~ on F ağzından kaçırmak; ~ out at *-e* saldırmak, *-e* çifte atmak; *fig. -e* çıkışmak; ~ up durmak, dinmek (*yağmur*).

**let²** [~] *n. a.* ~ ball *tenis*: net; without ~ or hindrance hiç bir engelle karşılaşmadan.

**le.thal** □ [ˈliːθəl] öldürücü.

**le.thar.gic, le.thar.gi.cal** □ [leˈθɑːdʒik(əl)] uyuşuk (*a. fig.*); **leth.ar.gy** [ˈleθədʒi] *n.* bitkinlik; *fig.* uyuşukluk.

**Le.the** [ˈliːθiː] *n. myth.* suyundan içenlere geçmişi unutturan nehir.

**let.ter** [ˈletə] **1.** *n.* mektup; harf; ~s *pl.* edebiyat, ilim; by ~ mektupla; man of ~s edebiyatçı, ilim adamı; to the ~ harfi harfine, harfiyen; **2.** *v/t.* kitap harfiyle yazmak; '~.bal.ance *n.* mektup terazisi; '~-box *n.* mektup kutusu; '~-card *n.* katlanınca zarf olan mektup kağıdı; '~-car.ri.er *n. Am.* postacı; '~-case *n.* mektup mahfazası, portföy; '~-cov.er *n.* mektup zarfı; 'let.tered *adj.* okumuş, bilgili, tahsilli; 'let.ter-file *n.* mektup dosyası; 'let-ter-found.er *n.* harf dökümcüsü; 'let.ter-gram [~græm] *n.* indirimli telgraf; 'let-ter.head *n.* mektup başlığı; başlıklı kağıt; 'let.ter.ing *n.* harflerle yazma, harf sıralama; harfler.

**let.ter...**: '~.less *adj.* kültürsüz; '~-o.pen.er *n.* mektup açacağı; '~-'per.fect *adj. thea.* rolünü harfi harfine ezberlemiş; '~.press *n. typ.* kitabın yazılı kısmı; ~ printing tipo baskısı; '~-press *n.* linotip; '~-weight *n.* kağıdın uçmasını önlemek için üstüne konulan ağırlık, prespapye.

**let.tuce** ✿ [ˈletis] *n.* salata, marul.

**leu.co...** [ˈljuːkəu] *prefix* renksiz, beyaz: **leu.co.cyte** [ˈ~sait] *n.* akyuvar, lökosit; **leu.k(a)e.mi.a** ✿ [ljuːˈkiːmiə] *n.* lösemi, kan kanseri.

**le.vant¹** [liˈvænt] *v/i.* kaçmak (*esp.* alacaklılardan).

**le.vant²** [~] *n.* Akdeniz'in doğusu ve buradaki ülkeler; **le.vant.ine** [ˈlevəntain] **1.** *n.* Yakın Doğulu kimse, Levanten; **2.** *adj.* Yakın Doğu'da ticaret yapan; Yakın Doğu'ya ait.

**lev.ee¹** *hist.* [ˈlevi] *n.* kabul merasimi.

**lev.ee²** *Am.* [~] *n.* set; rıhtım.

**lev.el** [ˈlevl] **1.** *adj.* düz, düzlem; ufkî, yatay, bir hizada; dengeli, ölçülü; my ~ best elimden ne gelirse; ~ crossing 🚇 hemzemin geçit; ~ stress *gr.* serbest vurgu; **2.** *n.* seviye, hiza, derece; düzlük, düz yer, yüzey; tesviye aleti; *fig.* sosyal norm; ~ of the sea deniz seviyesi; on a ~ with *ile* aynı seviyede (*a. fig.*): dead ~ dümdüz yüzey; *fig.* tekdüzelik, monotonluk; on the ~ F dürüst, doğru sözlü; **3.** *v/t.* düzlemek, tesviye etm.; *surv.* tesviye aletleriyle ölçmek; *fig.* alıştırmak, uydurmak; doğrultmak (*silah*) (at *-e*); ~ with the ground yerle bir seviyeye getirmek; ~ down alçaltarak eşitlemek; ~ up yükselterek eşitlemek; *v/i.* ~ at, ~ against *-i* suçlamak; *-e* suç yüklemek; ~ off 🛫 havalandıktan sonra yatay olarak uçmak; '~-'head.ed *adj.* sağgörülü, mantıklı; 'lev.el.(l)er *n. surv.* düzlemci; *fig.* sınıf farklarını yok etmek isteyen kimse; 'lev.el.(l)ing *adj.* tesviye etme... düzeltme...

**le.ver** [ˈliːvə] **1.** *n.* manivela (kolu); **2.** *v/t.* manivela ile kaldırmak; 'le.ver.age *n.* manivela gücü; *sl.* piston.

**lev.er.et** [ˈlevərit] *n.* tavşan yavrusu.

**le.vi.a.than** [liˈvaiəθən] *n.* büyük su hayvanı.

**le.vis** [ˈliːvaiz] *n. pl.* blucin.

**lev.i.tate** [ˈleviteit] *v/t.* havaya kaldırmak; *v/i.* havaya kalkmak.

**Le.vite** [ˈliːvait] *n. İncil*: Levi kabilesinden biri.

**lev.i.ty** [ˈleviti] *n.* hoppalık; ciddiyetsizlik; hafife alma.

**lev.y** [ˈlevi] **1.** *n.* toplama, tarh; ✕ zorla asker toplama; toplanan asker; capital ~ varlık (*veya* sermaye) vergisi; **2.** *v/t.* tarh etm.. koymak (*vergi vs.*); zorla toplamak; haczetmek, el koymak; açmak (*savaş*) (on, against *-e* karşı).

**lewd** □ [luːd] şehvet düşkünü; müstehcen, açık saçık; 'lewd.ness *n.* şehvet düşkünlüğü; müstehcenlik.

**lex.i.cal** □ ['leksikəl] sözlüğe ait, kelimelere ait, kelime...

**lex.i.cog.ra.pher** [leksi'kɔgrəfə] *n.* sözlük düzenleyen kimse, sözlükçü; **lex.i.cograph.i.cal** □ [~kəu'græfikəl] sözlüğe ait, sözlük...; **lex.i.cog.ra.phy** [~ɪ'kɔgrəfi] *n.* sözlük düzenleme, sözlükçülük; **lex.i.con** ['~kən] *n.* sözlük.

**li.a.bil.i.ty** [laiə'biliti] *n.* sorumluluk, mesuliyet; ♂♂ mükellefiyet; *fig.* engel, ayak bağı; **liabilities** *pl.* borç; † pasif.

**li.a.ble** □ ['laiəbl] sorumlu (for *-den*); ♂♂ mükellef; maruz (to *-e*); ıstırap çeken (to *-den*); meyilli (to *inf. -meğe*); **be ~** to *-e* maruz olm.; **~** to duty gümrüğe tabi; **~** to punishment cezalandırılabilir, cezaya tabi.

**li.ai.son** [li'eizn] *n.* bağlantı, birleş(tir)me; gizli ilişki *(cinsel)*; ✗ irtibat; **~ officer** irtibat subayı.

**li.ar** ['laiə] *n.* yalancı.

**li.ba.tion** [lai'beiʃən] *n.* ſanrı'nın şerefine içilen içkinin yere dökülmesi; içki, işret.

**li.bel** ['laibəl] 1. *n.* hakaret (on *-e*); ♂♂ iftira; dava dilekçesi; 2. *v/t. -e* iftira etm., *-e* leke sürmek; ♂♂ dilekçe **vererek dava etm.; **li.bel.(l)ous** □ iftira **kabilinden;** iftiracı, lekeleyici...

**lib.er.al** ['libərəl] 1. □ serbest düşünceli, açık fikirli; *pol.* liberal; cömert, eli açık; bol, pek çok; yüksek *(tahsil)*; serbest; 2. *n.* liberal; **lib.er.al.ism** *n.* liberalizm, serbest fikirlilik; **lib.er.al.i.ty** [~'ræliti] *n.* cömertlik; serbest fikirlilik, liberallik.

**lib.er.ate** ['libəreit] *v/t.* kurtarmak, özgür kılmak (from *-den*); salıvermek, azat etm., serbest bırakmak; **lib.er'a.tion** *n.* kurtuluş; serbest bırakma, kurtarma; **lib.er.a.tor** *n.* kurtarıcı.

**lib.er.tine** ['libəti:n] 1. *n.* şehvet düşkünü kimse, ahlâksız adam; 2. *adj.* şehvet düşkünü, ahlâksız, hovarda, çapkın; **lib.er.tin.ism** ['libətinizəm] *n.* çapkınlık, hovardalık.

**lib.er.ty** ['libəti] *n.* hürriyet, serbestlik, özgürlük; ayrıcalık, hak; **take liberties** küstahlık etm., terbiyesizlik etm.; **be at ~** serbest olm., özgür olm.; **be at ~ to do** bş yapmaya hakkı olm.; **~ of conscience** vicdan hürriyeti; **~ of speech** konuşma özgürlüğü; **~ of the press** basın özgürlüğü.

**li.bid.i.nous** □ [li'bidinəs] şehvet düşkünü.

**li.brar.i.an** [lai'bɛəriən] *n.* kütüphane memuru, kütüphaneci; **li.brar.y** ['laibrəri] *n.* kütüphane, kitaplık; kitaplar serisi.

**li.bret.to** ♪ [li'bretəu] *n.* opera güftesi, opera kitabı.

**lice** [lais] *pl. of* louce.

**li.cence** ['laisəns] *n.* ruhsat(name), izin (tezkeresi), müsaade, lisans; çapkınlık, serbestlik, riayetsizlik; driving ~ ehliyet.

**li.cense** [~] 1. = licence; 2. *v/t.* ruhsat *veya* yetki vermek *-e*; izin vermek *-e*; **licensing hours** *pl.* meyhanelerde içki içilebilen saatler; **li.cen.see** [~'si:] *n.* ruhsat sahibi.

**li.cen.ti.ate** *univ.* [lai'senʃiit] *n.* resmen izinli kimse.

**li.cen.tious** □ [lai'senʃəs] şehvet düşkünü, **ahlâksız.**

**li.chen** ♀ & ♀ ['laikən] *n.* liken.

**lich.gate** ['litʃgeit] = lychgate.

**lick** [lik] 1. *n.* yalama, yalayış; *Am.* hayvanların tuz yalama yeri; *sl.* darbe, tokat, sille; F sürat, hız, tempo; 2. *v/t.* yalamak; F dayak atmak *-e*, pataklamak; yenmek, üstesinden gelmek; *v/i.* hızla gitmek; **~** the dust yenilmek; öldürülmek; yeri öpmek; **~** into shape hazırlamak; adam etm.; **lick.er.ish** *adj.* ahlâksız, hovarda; pisboğaz, obur, açgözlü; **lick.ing** *n.* yalama, yalayış; F dayak, kötek; F yenilgi; **lick.spit.tle** *n.* dalkavuk, yaltakçı kimse, çanak yalayıcı.

**lic.o.rice** ♀ ['likəris] *n.* meyan(kökü).

**lid** [lid] *n.* kapak; göz kapağı; *sl.* şapka; put the ~ on it F üzerine tüy dikmek, bardağı taşıran son damla olm.; sonu olm.

**li.do** ['li:dəu] *n.* havuz; plaj.

**lie¹** [lai] 1. *n.* yalan, palavra; give s.o. the ~ *b-ni* yalancılıkla suçlamak; tell a ~ yalan söylemek; white ~ zararsız yalan; 2. *v/i.* yalan söylemek.

**lie²** [~] 1. *n.* yatış; yer, mevki; the ~ of the land bir arazinin doğal özellikleri; durum, gidişat; 2. *(irr.) v/i.* yatmak, uzanmak; durmak, kalmak, olmak; ♂♂ kanunen uygun olm.; **~** by istifade edilmemek; istirahat etm., sakin olm.; **~** down yatmak, uzanmak; take it lying down alttan almak, sineye çekmek, ister istemez katlanmak; as far as in me ~s elimden geldiğince; **~** in geç saatlere kadar yatmak; loğusa olm.; **~** in wait for pusuya yatmak; **~** over † sonraya bırakılmak, ertelenmek; **~** to ♪ rüzgâra karşı giderken (neredeyse) durmak; **~** under *-e* bağlı olm.; **~** up çok yatmak; gizlenmek, saklanmak; it ~s with you o sizin işiniz. o size kalmış; let sleeping dogs ~ *fig.* uyuyan yılanın kuyruğuna basma.

**lie-a.bed** ['laiəbed] *n.* uykucu kimse; **lie-'down** *n.* kestirme, şekerleme.

**lief** *lit.* [li:f] *adv.* seve seve, memnuni-

yetle; **llef.er** *adv.* daha çok, tercihan.
**liege** *hist.* [liːdʒ] 1. *adj.* işini kullarına gördüren; 2. *n. a.* ~man derebeyi kölesi; *a.* ~ lord derebeylik lordu.
**lie-in** [laiˈin] *n.:* have a ~ sabahleyin geç vakţe kadar yatmak.
**li.en** ŏɔ̌ [ˈliən] *n.* ipotek.
**lieu** [ljuː] *n.:* in ~ of -*in* yerine.
**lieu.ten.an.cy** [lefˈtenənsi, ⬇ leˈtenənsi] *n.* teğmenlik; ⬇ yüzbaşılık.
**lieu.ten.aht** [lefˈtenənt, ⬇ leˈtenənt] *n.* teğmen; ⬇ yüzbaşı; vekil, yardımcı; '~-'colo.nel *n.* yarbay; '~-com'mand.er *n.* kıdemli yüzbaşı; '~-'gen.er.al *n.* korgeneral; '~-'gov.er.nor *n.* vali muavini.
**life** [laif] *n., pl.* **lives** [laivz] hayat, yaşam, ömür; can(lılık); biyografi, yaşam öyküsü; yaşam tarzı; ~ and limb hayat; for ~ hayat boyu; for one's ~, for dear ~ bütün gücü ile, canla başla; to the ~ tıpatıp, aynen; ~ sentence müebbet (*veya* ömür boyu) hapis cezası; have the time of one's ~ dilediğince eğlenmek, kurtlarını dökmek; '~-'an.nu.i.ty *n.* ömür boyu gelir; '~-'as.sur.ance *n.* hayat sigortası; '~-belt *n.* cankurtaran kemeri; '~-blood *n.* yaşam için gerekli olan kan (*a. fig.*); '~-boat *n.* cankurtaran sandalı, filika; '~-buoy *n.* cankurtaran simidi; '~-giv.ing *adj.* canlandırıcı, hayat verici; '~-guard *n.* cankurtaran yüzücüsü; '~-'in.ter.est *n.* kaydı hayat şartıyla intifa, yaşadığı sürece mülk hakkı (in -*de*); '~-jack.et *n.* ⬇ cankurtaran yeleği; '~-less □ cansız (*a. fig.*); ölü (gibi); '~-less.ness *n.* cansızlık; '~-like *adj.* canlı gibi görünen; '~-line *n.* cankurtaran halatı; '~-long *adj.* ömür boyu süren; '~-pre.serv.er *n. Am.* cankurtaran yeleği; topuzlu baston, lobut.
**lif.er** *sl.* [ˈlaifə] *n.* ömür boyu hapse mahkûm kimse.
**life**...: '~-sav.er *n.* cankurtaran kimse *veya* şey; '~-'size(d) *adj.* doğal büyüklükte (*resim, heykel vs.*); '~-strings *n. pl.* hayat bağları; '~-time *n.* hayat süresi, ömür; '~-'work *n.* tüm hayatın verildiği (*veya* ömür boyu) iş.
**lift** [lift] 1. *n.* kaldırma, kaldırış, yüksel(t)me; ⊕ sia; *phys.*, ⬆ kaldırma gücü: asansör; *fig.* neşe, canlılık; give s.o. a ~ b-ni arabasına almak; 2. *v/t. & v/i.* kaldırmak (*a. fig.*), yüksel(t)mek; *oft.* ~ up kaldırmak (*masa vs.*); yükseltmek (*ses*); dikmek (*kulaklarını*); kökünden sökmek (*bitki*); *sl.* aşırmak, yürütmek, araklamak; '~-at.tend.ant, '~-boy *n.* asansör görevlisi; '**lift.er** *n.* vinç,

kaldırıcı; hırsız, yankesici; '**lift.ing** *adj.* ⊕ kaldırıcı, kaldırma...; ~ power ⬆ kaldırma kuvveti; '**lift-off** *n.* kalkış, yükselme (*roket vs.*).
**lig.a.ment** *anat.* [ˈligəmənt] *n.* bağ.
**lig.a.ture** [ˈligətʃə] 1. *n.* bağ(lama); ⅌ kanı durduran bağ; ♪, *typ.* bağ; 2. *v/t.* tel ile bağlamak.
**light¹** [lait] 1. *n.* ışık (*a. fig.*), aydınlık; ateş; bilgi kaynağı; *fig.* parlaklık, canlılık; gün ışığı, gündüz; görüş; ~s *pl.* yetenekler, cevher; örnek alınacak kimse; pencere, aydınlık; *paint.* resmin aydınlık kısmı; in the ~ of -*in* ışığında, -*e* göre; come (bring) to ~ açığa çık(ar)mak, ortaya çık(ar)mak; will you give me a ~ ateşinizi rica edebilir miyim?, sigaramı yakar mısınız?; put a ~ to yakmak -*i*, tutuşturmak -*i*; see the ~ doğmak, dünyaya gelmek; ortaya çıkmak, meydana gelmek; *fig.* sonunda anlamak; 2. *adj.* aydınlık; soluk, solgun; açık (*renk*); 3. (*irr.*) *v/t. & v/i. oft.* ~ up yakmak, tutuş(tur)mak; aydınlatmak; neşelen(dir)mek, gül(dür)mek; canlan(dır)mak; yanmak, alev almak; parıldamak; ~ out *Am. sl.* yola koyulmak (*veya* düzülmek).
**light²** [~] 1. □ hafif; eksik; hazmı kolay (*yemek*); vurgusuz (*hece*); önemsiz; hafifmeşrep, mal (*kadın*); neşeli; endişesiz; başı dönmüş, sersemlemiş; çevik; az, küçük; ~ current ϟ zayıf akım; make ~ of hafife almak -*i*, önemsememek -*i*; 2. *n. su.* = lights; 3. *vb.* ~on, ~ upon rastlamak, tesadüfen bulmak.
**light-col.o(u)red** [ˈlaitkʌləd] *adj.* açık renk (*elbise vs.*).
**light.en¹** [ˈlaitn] *v/t.* aydınlatmak (*a. fig.*); *v/i.* aydınlanmak; şimşek çakmak.
**light.en²** [~] *v/t. & v/i.* hafifle(t)mek, yükü(nü) azal(t)mak; neşelen(dir)mek.
**light.er¹** [ˈlaitə] *n.* yakıcı alet; çakmak.
**light.er²** ⬇ [~] *n.* mavna, salapurya.
**light**...: '~-fin.gered *adj.* hırsızlığa yatkın, eli uzun; eli yatkın; '~-hand.ed *adj.* eli hafif; *fig.* becerikli; '~-hand.ed.ness *n.* beceriklilik, eli hafiflik; '~-'head.ed *adj.* başı dönen, sersemlemiş; düşüncesiz; kuş beyinli; '~-'heart.ed □ neşeli, şen şakrak, mutlu; '~-house *n.* fener kulesi.
**light.ing** [ˈlaitiŋ] *n.* aydınlatma; yakma; ışıklandırma sistemi; ~ up ışıklandırma.
**light.ly** [ˈlaitli] *adv.* hafifçe, az; kolayca: iyice düşünmeden; çevikçe; canlılıkla, neşeyle; '**light'mind.ed** *adj.* hafif, ciddiyetten yoksun, düşüncesiz; '**light.ness** *n.* hafiflik.
**light.ning** [ˈlaitniŋ] *n.* şimşek, yıldırım:

limpidne**ss**

like ~, with ~ speed şimşek *(veya* yıldırım) gibi, çok çabuk; '~-ar'rest.er *n.* elektrik aletleri̇ni yıldırımdan koruyan aygıt; ~ bug *Am.* ateşböceği; '~-con.duc.tor, '~-rod *n.* paratoner, yıldırımsavar, yıldırımkıran.

lights [laits] *n. pl.* hayvan akciğeri.

light.ship ['lait∫ip] *n.* fener gemisi *(veya* dubası).

light.some ['laitsəm] *adj.* neşeli, şen şakrak; kaygısız, endişesiz; parlak, ışıklı.

light-weight ['laitweit] 1. *n. spor:* tüysıklet; 2. *adj.* hafif; önemsiz; karaktersiz.

lig.ne.ous ['ligniəs] *adj.* odunsu..., oduna benzer; lig.nite ['lignait] *n.* linyit.

lik.a.ble ['laikəbl] *adj.* sevimli, hoş; çekici.

like [laik] 1. *adj. & prp.* gibi, benzer -e; eşit -e; ~ a man akışır(casına), adam gibi; such ~ böylesi, benzeri, gibi; feel ~ F hoşlanmak, canı istemek, arzulamak -i; *s.* look; something ~ ... ...gibi bir şey, takriben; ~ that öyle, böyle, onun gibi; what is he ~? neye benziyor, nasıl biridir?; that's more ~ it bu daha iyi, kulağa daha hoş geliyor; 2. *n.* benzeri, eşit; ~s *pl.* sevilen şeyler, tercihler; his ~ emsali, eşi, benzeri; the ~ gibi, aynı; the ~(s) of F ...gibi, -in benzeri; 3. *v/t.* sevmek -i, beğenmek, hoşlanmak -den; istemek, arzu etm. -i; ~ best en çok sevmek; how do you ~ London? Londra'yı nasıl buluyorsunuz?; I should ~ to know bilmek istiyorum.

like.a.ble ['laikəbl] = likable.

like.li.hood ['laiklihud] *n.* ihtimal, olasılık; 'like.ly 1. *adj.* muhtemel, olası; ...cek gibi; uygun, yerinde; sevimli, çekici; inanılır, güvenilir; 2. *adv.* muhtemelen, belki de, galiba; as ~ as not olabilir ki, büyük bir olasılıkla; he is ~ to die galiba ölecek.

like-mind.ed ['laik'maindid] *adj.* hemfikir, aynı görüşte; 'like.en *v/t.* benzetmek (to -e); 'like.ness *n.* benzerlik; görünüş; resim, tasvir; have one's ~ taken fotoğrafını çektirmek, resmini yaptırmak; 'like-wise *adv.* aynı şekilde, aynen, aynısı, dahi, keza; ayrıca, bundan başka.

lik.ing ['laikiŋ] *n.* (for) beğenme, meyil, beğeni, düşkünlük, sevme; to s.o.'s ~ b-nin istediği gibi, zevkine göre.

li.lac ['lailək] 1. *adj.* açık mor; 2. *n.* leylâk (rengi); açık mor.

Lil.li.pu.tian ['lili'pju:∫ən] 1. *n.* 'Guliver'in Seyahatleri' adlı kitaptaki adada yaşayan kimse; 2. *adj.* küçücük, minnacık.

lilt [lilt] 1. *v/i.* kıvrak şarkı söylemek; 2. *n.* kıvrak şarkı.

lil.y ✣ ['lili] *n.* zambak; ~ of the valley inciçiçeği; '~-'liv.ered *adj.* ödlek, yüreksiz; '~-white *adj.* bembeyaz.

limb¹ [lim] *n.* uzuv, örgen; ✣ dal; F haylaz çocuk; out on a ~ F desteksiz.

limb² *ast.*, ✣ [~] *n.* kenar.

limbed [limd] *suffix* ...uzuvlu.

lim.ber¹ ['limbə] 1. *n.* ✕ toparlak; 2. *vb.* ~st ~ up top arabasına koşum parçasını bağlamak.

lim.ber² [~] 1. *adj.* gevşek, oynak, bükülebilir, esnek; 2. *v/t. & v/i.* ~ up esne(t)-mek, ger(il)mek, ısın(dır)mak *(adale).*

lim.bo ['limbəu] *n.* vaftiz edilmeden ölenlerle İsa'dan önce yaşayanların ruhlarının olduğu yer; *sl.* kodes; *fig.* şüphe, tereddüt.

lime¹ [laim] 1. *n.* kireç; 2. *v/t.* kireçle-mek.

lime² ✣ [~] *n.* ıhlamur.

lime³ ✣ [~] *n.* misket limonu; '~-'juice **y** misket limonu suvu.

lime...: '~-kiln *n.* kireç ocağı; '~.light *n.* kireç lambası; in the ~ *fig.* göz önünde, halkın dilinde.

lim.er.ick ['limərik] *n.* beş ırısralı nükteli şiir.

lime...: '~.stone *n.* kireçtaşı; '~-tree *n.* ✣ ıhlamur ağacı; '~.twig *n.* ökse çubuğu.

lim.it ['limit] 1. *n.* had, sınır, uç, son, hudut; limit; in (off) ~s serbest *(yasak)* bölge (to *için*); that is the ~! F bu kadarı da fazla!, yetti be!; go the ~ *Am.* F sınıra dayanmak; her şeyi göze almak; 2. *v/t.* sınırlamak, kısıtlamak; hasretmek, vermek, ayırmak (to *e);* lim.i'ta-tion *n.* sınırlama, tahdit, kısıtlama *(a. fig.);* ✿ sınırlandırma, hudutlandırma, kayıtlama; 'lim.it.ed 1. *adj.* mahdut sayılı, sınırlı, az, kısıtlı (to -e); 'ı sınırlı sorumlu, limited; ~ (liability) company sınırlı sorumlu *(veya* limited) şirket; ~ in time zamanı kısıtlı; 2. *n.* ekspres; 'lim-it.less ☐ sınırsız, sayısız, sonsuz, uçsuz bucaksız.

limn † [lim] *v/t.* resmetmek; tasvir etm

lim.ou.sine ['limə:zi:n] *n. (bölmeli şoför mahalli olan)* lüks otomobil.

limp¹ [limp] 1. *v/i.* topallamak, aksamak; 2. *n.* topallama.

limp² [~] *adj.* gevşek, yumuşak; zayıf, kuvvetsiz.

lim.pet ['limpit] *n. zo.* denizminaresi; *fig.* sülük gibi kimse.

lim.pid ☐ ['limpid] berrak, şeffaf; 'lim-pid.ness *n.* berraklık, şeffaflık.

**lim.y** [ˈlaimi] *adj.* kireçli; kireç gibi.

**lin.age** [ˈlainidʒ] *n.* satır sayısı.

**linch.pin** [ˈlintʃpin] *n.* dingil çivisi.

**lin.den** ᛩ [ˈlindən] *n.* ıhlamur ağacı.

**line¹** [lain] **1.** *n.* sıra, dizi, seri; çizgi, yol, hat; ip, olta, sicim; *teleph.* hat; *fig.* yol, metod; satır, mısra; plan, desen; ⵜ mal; ✕ saf, sıra; pusula, not; hiza; ~s *pl.* çevre, şekil, anahat; *thea.* rol; silsile, sıra; soy; çığır, devir; meslek, iş; sınır, hudut; kuyruk; demiryolu hattı; ekvator çizgisi; ~ of battle savaş hattı; ~ of business meslek, branş; ~ of conduct hayat (*veya* hareket) tarzı; ship of the ~ savaş gemisi; hard ~s şanssızlık, kötü talih; all down the ~ tamamen, her yönden; in ~ with uygun -e; aynı hizada *ile*; that is not in my ~ bu benim işim değil; stand in ~ sıraya girmek, kuyrukta beklemek; fall into ~ with s.o. *b-ne* uymak, *b-le* hemfikir olm., *b-ne* katılmak; draw the ~ *fig.* reddetmek, geri çevirmek; party ~ *pol.* parti siyaseti; party ~, shared ~ *teleph.* birkaç abonenin birden bağlandığı telefon sistemi; toe the ~ *pol.* kanun *veya* kurala uymak; denileni yapmak; hold the ~ *teleph.* telefonu kapatmamak; **2.** *v/t.* dizmek, sıralamak; çizgilerle göstermek; *fig.* kırıştırmak (*yüz vs.*); ~ the streets caddelere dizilmek; ~ out taslağını çizmek; ~ through çizmek, karalamak; ~ up sıraya dizmek; *v/i.* ~ up sıraya girmek.

**line²** [~] *v/t.* astarlamak; kaplamak; doldurmak.

**lin.e.age** [ˈliniidʒ] *n.* soy, nesil; **lin.e.al** [ˈ~əl] babadan oğula geçen; **lin.e.a.ment** [ˈ~əmənt] *n.* yüz hattı; **lin.e.ar** [ˈ~ə] *adj.* doğrusal, çizgisel.

**line.man** [ˈlainmən] *n.* demiryolu *veya* telgraf hat memuru, monoton; *Am.* = linesman.

**lin.en** [ˈlinin] **1.** *n.* keten bezi; iç çamaşır; masa örtüleri ve yatak çarşafları; wash one's dirty ~ in public *fig. b-nin* kirli çamaşırlarını ortaya dökmek; **2.** *adj.* keten...; '~clos.et, '~cup.board *n.* çamaşır dolabı; '~drap.er *n.* bez satıcısı.

**lin.er** [ˈlainə] *n.* transatlantik; yolcu uçağı; makyaj kalemi; astar; **lines.man** [ˈlainzmən] *n. spor:* yan hakem; 'line- -up *n.* sıraya girme; sıra; program; *spor:* oyuncuların yerini alması, diziliş.

**ling¹** *ichth.* [liŋ] *n.* morinaya benzer bir balık.

**ling²** ᛩ [~] *n.* süpürgeotu.

**lin.ger** [ˈliŋə] *v/i.* gecikmek, ayrılamamak, oyalanmak (over, upon *başında*); ölüm döşeğinde yatmak; kolayca geçmemek (*ağrı vs.*); ~ at, ~ about oyalanarak gitmek.

**lin.ge.rie** [ˈlænʒəriː] *n.* kadın iç çamaşırı.

**lin.ger.ing** ▢ [ˈliŋgəriŋ] uzun süre geçmeyen.

**lin.go** [ˈliŋgəu] *n.* (yabancı) dil, lisan; anlaşılması güç deyimlerle dolu konuşma.

**lin.gua.fran.ca** [ˈliŋgwəˈfræŋkə] *n.* ortak dil.

**lin.gual** [ˈliŋgwəl] *adj.* dile ait, dil...

**lin.guist** [ˈliŋgwist] *n.* dil uzmanı, dilci; çok dil bilen kimse; **lin'guis.tic** *adj.* (~ally) dile at, dil...; dilbilime ait, dilbilim...; **lin'guis.tics** *n. sg.* dilbilim, lengüistik.

**lin.i.ment** ᛩ [ˈlinimənt] *n.* liniment, merhem.

**lin.ing** [ˈlainiŋ] *n.* astar(lama); every cloud has a silver ~ her işte bir hayır vardır.

**link¹** [liŋk] **1.** *n.* zincir halkası; *fig.* bağ(lantı), ilişki; ~s *pl.* kol düğmesi; **2.** *v/t. & v/i.* bağla(n)mak, birleş(tir)mek; zincirlemek.

**link²** *hist.* [~] *n.* meşale, fener.

**link.man** [ˈliŋkmən] *n.* fenerci.

**links** [liŋks] *n. pl.* kumullar; *a.* golf-~ golf oyunu alanı.

**lin.net** *orn.* [ˈlinit] *n.* ketenkuşuna benzer bir kuş.

**li.no** [ˈlainəu] = linoleum; '~cut *n.* linolyum gravürü.

**li.no.leum** [liˈnəuljəm] *n.* linolyum, mantarlı taban muşambası.

**li.no.type** *typ.* [ˈlainəutaip] *n.* linotip.

**lin.seed** [ˈlinsiːd] *n.* ketentohumu; ~ oil beziryağı, ketentohumu yağı.

**lin.sey-wool.sey** [ˈlinziˈwulzi] *n.* yarı keten kumaş.

**lint** ᛩ [lint] *n.* keten tiftiği.

**lin.tel** ⚠ [ˈlintl] *n.* üst eşik, lento.

**li.on** [ˈlaiən] *n.* aslan (*a. ast. & fig.*); *fig.* tanınmış şahsiyet, şöhretli kimse; place *veya* put one's head in the ~'s mouth tehlikeye atılmak, kellesini koltuğuna almak; the ~'s share aslan payı; 'li.on.ess *n.* dişi aslan; 'lion-heart.ed *adj.* aslan yürekli; '~.hunt.er *n. fig.* ünlü kişi avcısı; 'li.on.ize *v/t. b-ni* el üstünde tutmak.

**lip** [lip] *n.* dudak (*a.* ᛩ); kenar, uç; *sl.* küstahlık, yüzsüzlük; curl one's ~ dudak bükmek; none of your ~! yüzsüzlüğün lüzumu yok!, gevezelik istemez!; '~serv.ice *n.* sözde bağlılık; '~stick *n.* ruj.

**liq.ue.fac.tion** [likwiˈfækʃən] *n.* sıvılaş-(tır)ma, eri(t)me; **ˈliq.ue.fi.a.ble** [ˈ~faiəbl] *adj.* eritilebilir; **ˈliq.ue.fy** *v/t.* & *v/i.* sıvılaş(tır)mak, eri(t)mek; **ˈliq.ues.cent** [liˈkwesnt] *adj.* eriyebilir, eriyen.

**li.queur** [liˈkjuə] *n.* likör; alkollü içki.

**liq.uid** [ˈlikwid] **1.** □ sıvı..., akıcı..., akış-kan...; sulu, ıslak; berrak, şeffaf; net, tatlı *(ses);* † likit, kolayca paraya çev-rilebilen; **2.** *n.* sıvı, mayi; *gr.* yarım ses-li harf.

**liq.ui.date** [ˈlikwideit] *v/t.* † tasfiye etm., likide etm.; ortadan kaldırmak; gebert-mek, temizlemek; **liq.uiˈda.tion** *n.* tasfi-ye, likidasyon; **ˈliq.ui.da.tor** *n.* tasfiye me-muru.

**liq.uor** [ˈlikə] **1.** *n.* alkollü içki, sert içki; sıvı madde; et suyu; in *~,* the worse for ~ çakırkeyf, sarhoş; **2.** *v/t.* & *v/i. a.* ~ up *sl.* içki iç(ir)mek, kafayı çekmek.

**liq.uo.rice** ♧ [ˈlikəris] *n.* meyan(kökü).

**li.ra** [ˈliərə] *n., pl.* **li.re** [ˈ~ri] lira; liret.

**lisp** [lisp] **1.** *n.* peltek konuşma; **2.** *v/i.* peltek konuşmak.

**lis.som(e)** [ˈlisəm] *adj.* kıvrak, çevik, atik.

**list¹** [list] **1.** *n.* liste, cetvel, dizin, fihrist; **2.** *v/t.* listeye yazmak, kaydetmek; *-in* listesini yapmak; *v/i.* askere yazılmak.

**list²** ♩ [~] **1.** *n.* yan yatma; **2.** *v/i.* yan yatmak.

**lis.ten** [ˈlisn] (to) dinlemek *-i,* kulak ver-mek *-e;* ~ in *teleph., radyo:* gizlice din-lemek; ~ in to *radyo:* dinlemek *-i;* **ˈlis-ten.er** *n.* dinleyici.

**lis.ten.ing** [ˈlisniŋ] *adj.* dinleme...; ~ ap-paratus dinleme aleti; **ˈ~-post** *n.* dinle-me noktası.

**list.less** □ [ˈlistlis] halsiz, bitkin; kayıt-sız, kaygısız; **ˈlist.less.ness** *n.* halsizlik; kayıtsızlık.

**lists** [lists] *n. pl.* dövüş meydanı; enter the ~ *fig.* mücadeleye girişmek, yarışa katılmak.

**lit** [lit] **1.** *pret.* & *p.p. of* light¹ 3; **2.** *adj.* ~ up *sl.* küfelik, sarhoş.

**lit.a.ny** *eccl.* [ˈlitəni] *n.* münacaat; tekrar, nakarat.

**lit.er.a.cy** [ˈlitərəsi] *n.* okuryazarlık; **ˈlit.er-al 1.** □ harfi harfine, kelimesi kelimesi-ne; kelime ile ilgili, kelime...; kesin, doğ-ru, gerçek; *fig.* alelade, bayağı; kuru fi-kirli; **2.** *n. a.* ~ error basım hatası; **ˈlit-er.al.ism,** **ˈlit.er.al.ness** *n.* harfiyen uyma; gerçekçilik.

**lit.er.ar.y** □ [ˈlitərəri] edebiyatla (*veya* ya-zınla) ilgili, edebi...; ~ man edip, yazıncı, edebiyatçı; edebiyat meraklısı; **lit.er.ate**

**[ˈ~rit] 1.** *adj.* okuryazar; kültürlü, çok okumuş; **2.** *n.* okuryazar kimse; **lit.e.ra.ti** [litəˈraːtiː] *n. pl.* edebiyatçılar, yazıncı-lar; **lit.e¹ra.tim** [~tim] *adv.* kelimesi ke-limesine; **lit.er.a.ture** [ˈlitəritʃə] *n.* edebi-yat, yazın; edebi eserler; broşür.

**lithe(.some)** [ˈlaið(səm)] *adj.* elâstikî, es-nek, kıvrak.

**lith.o.graph** [ˈliθəugraːf] **1.** *n.* taşbasması resim, litograf; **2.** *v/t.* & *v/i.* taşbasma-sı ile (resim) yapmak; **li.thog.ra.pher** [liˈθɔgrəfə] *n.* litografyacı; **lith.o.graph-ic** [liθəuˈgræfik] *adj.* (~ally) litografiye ait, litografi...; **li.thog.ra.phy** [liˈθɔgrəfi] *n.* taşbasması, litografi, litografya.

**Lith.u.a.ni.an** [liθjuːˈeinjən] **1.** *adj.* Lituan-ya diline ve halkına ait; **2.** *n.* Lituanya-lı; Lituanya dili.

**lit.i.gant** ♫ [ˈlitigənt] **1.** *adj.* davacı...; **2.** *n.* davacı; **lit.i.gate** [ˈ~geit] *v/i.* mahke-meye başvurmak; dava açmak; *v/t.* mahkemeye sunmak; **lit.iˈga.tion** *n.* da-va (etme); **li.ti.gious** □ [liˈtidʒəs] dava seven; ♫ davaya ait, dava...; çekişme-li, kavgacı.

**lit.mus** ♫ [ˈlitməs] *n.* turnusol; **ˈ~-pa.per** *n.* turnusol kâğıdı.

**li.to.tes** *rhet.* [ˈlaitəutiːz] *n.* bir fikri olum-suz şekilde ifade etme.

**li.tre** [ˈliːtə] *n.* litre.

**lit.ter** [ˈlitə] **1.** *n.* çöp, süprüntü, çerçöp; düzensizlik, karışıklık; tahtırevan; sed-ye, teskere; *zo.* bir batında doğan yav-rular; hayvanlar için yataklık saman; **2.** *v/t.* karman çorman etm., karmaka-rışık etm., saçmak, dağıtmak; doğur-mak; ~ down altına yataklık saman ser-mek; ~ up altüst etm., karmakarışık etm.; **ˈ~-bas.ket,** **ˈ~-bin** *n.* çöp kutusu.

**lit.tle** [ˈlitl] **1.** *adj.* küçük, ufak; önemsiz, değersiz; kısa, az, biraz; a ~ one ufak-lık, çocuk; a ~ house küçük bir ev; my ~ Mary F midem; his ~ ways onun garip usulları, şeytanlıkları; ~ people periler; **2.** *adv.* az miktarda, birazcık, hemen hiç, nadiren, seyrek olarak; a ~ red hafif kır-mızı; **3.** *n.* ufak miktar; az zaman; ~ by ~, by ~ and ~ azar azar, yavaş yavaş; for a ~ kısa bir süre; not a ~ çok; **ˈ~-go** *n. F univ.* ön imtihan; **ˈlit.tle.ness** *n.* kü-çüklük.

**lit.to.ral** [ˈlitərəl] **1.** *adj.* sahile yakın...; **2.** *n.* sahil boyu.

**lit.ur.gy** *eccl.* [ˈlitədʒi] *n.* dua usulü.

**liv.a.ble** [ˈlivəbl] *adj.* F içinde yaşanabi-lir; yaşamaya değer; çekilir, tahammül edilir; *mst ~-*with F geçimli (*kimse*).

**live 1.** [liv] *v/t.* & *v/i. com.* yaşamak;

oturmak, ikamet etm.; geçirmek, sürmek *(hayat)*; geçinmek (on *ile*); ~ to see *bşi* görecek kadar yaşamak; ~ s.th. down· *bşi* unutturmak; üstesinden gelmek; ~ in (out) çalıştığı yerde (çalıştığı yer dışında) yatıp kalkmak; ~ through güçlüklere rağmen yaşamaya devam etm., geçirmek; ~ up to ulaşmak -*e*, *bşi* doğrulayacak şekilde yaşamak; ~ and learn yaşadıkça öğrenmek; ~ and let ~ hoşgörülü olm.; **2.** [laiv] *adj.* diri, canlı, zinde; hayat dolu; gerçek; yanan *(kömür)*; sönmemiş *(kor)*; direkt, doğrudan; .X patlamamış *(bomba)*; ≠ akımlı, cereyanlı *(tel)*; *radyo:* canlı *(yayın)*; ~ wire *fig.* enerjik kimse; ~ broadcast canlı yayın; **live.a.ble** [ˈlivəbl] *s.* livable; **lived** *comb.* ...ömürlü; **live.li.hood** [ˈlaivlihud] *n.* geçim, geçinme; rızk; **live.li.ness** *n.* canlılık, zindelik; parlaklık; **live.long** [ˈlivlɔŋ] *adj.:* the ~ day *poet.* bütün gün; **live.ly** [ˈlaivli] *adj.* canlı, neşeli, şen, keyifli; hayat dolu; parlak *(renk)*; zıplayan *(top)*; gerçekmiş gibi; make things ~ for s.o. *b-nin* başına iş açmak, başını derde sokmak.
**liv.en** [ˈlaivn] *v/t.* & *v/i. mst* ~ up F canlan(dır)mak, neşelen(dir)mek.
**liv.er¹** [ˈlivə] *n.* yaşayan kimse; fast ~ hızlı yaşayan, hovarda; good ~ zevkperest, iyi yaşamayı seven.
**liv.er²** [~] *n.* karaciğer; **ˈliv.er.ish** *adj.* F karaciğerinden rahatsız, hasta.
**liv.er.y¹** [ˈlivəri] = liverish.
**liv.er.y²** [~] *n.* hizmetçi üniforması; özel üniforma; *fig.* kılık, kıyafet; = ~-stable; ~ com.pa.ny Londra'da bulunan özel üniformalı loncalardan biri; ˈ~.man *n.* Londra'da lonca üyesi; ˈ~-sta.ble *n.* kiralık at ahırı.
**lives** [laivz] *pl. of* life; **ˈlive-stock** *n.* çiftlik hayvanları; **ˈlive-weight** *n.* ücrete tabi yük *(uçak vs.'de)*.
**liv.id** [ˈlivid] *adj.* mavimsi, morumsu; solgun, soluk; kanı beynine sıçramış, tepesi atmış; **liˈvid.i.ty** *n.* kurşun rengi; solgunluk.
**liv.ing** [ˈliviŋ] **1.** ☐ hayatta, canlı, yaşayan, diri, sağ; tıpkı; zinde, kuvvetli; the ~ image of *-in* tıpkısı, hık demiş burnundan düşmüş; the ~ theatre tiyatro; the ~ *pl.* yaşayanlar; in ~ memory yaşayanların hafızalarında; **2.** *n.* yaşayış; yaşama, geçim, geçinme; gelir; meslek; *eccl.* maaşlı papazlık makamı; ˈ~-room *n.* oturma odası; ˈ~-space *n.* hayat sahası.
**liz.ard** [ˈlizəd] *n. zo.* kertenkele.

**Liz.zie** *Am. co.* [ˈlizi] *n.* T model Ford otomobil.
**lla.ma** [ˈlɑːmə] *n.* lama.
**Lloyd's** [lɔidz] *n.* Lloyd sigorta şirketi.
**lo** † [ləu] *int.* bak!, işte!
**loach** *ichth.* [ləutʃ] *n.* çoprabalığı.
**load** [ləud] **1.** *n.* yük *(a. fig.)*, hamule; ≠ şarj; endişe, üzüntü; ağırlık; ⊕ mukavemet; ~s of F dünya kadar, kucak dolusu; **2.** *v/t.* & *v/i.* yükle(n)mek, yükletmek; doldurmak *(silah)*; yığmak; makineye koymak *(film)*; tıka basa doldurmak *(mide)*; *fig.* gark etm., boğmak (with -*e*); ~ test dayanıklılık deneyi, ~ed yüklü, dolu; *sl.* küfelik, sarhoş; şaşırtıcı *(soru)*; F ensesi kalın; ~ed dice *pl.* hileli zar; the ~ dice against s.o. *fig. b-nin* şansını azaltmak; *b-nin* aleyhine *bş* yapmak; **ˈload.er** *n.* .yükleyici; **ˈload.ing 1.** *adj.* yükleme...; yük...; **2.** *n.* yükleme; yük; **ˈload-line** *n.* ⊥ geminin yükleme sınırını gösteren çizgi; **ˈload.stone** *n.* mıknatıs taşı.
**loaf¹** [ləuf] *n., pl.* **loaves** [ləuvz] bütün bir ekmek, somun; *sl.* kafa, kelle; use your ~ kafanı çalıştır.
**loaf²** [~] *v/i.* vaktini boş geçirmek, aylak aylak vakit geçirmek; **ˈloaf.er** *n.* haylaz *(veya* aylak) kimse.
**loaf-sug.ar** [ˈləufʃugə] *n.* kesmeşeker.
**loam** [ləum] *n.* balçık, lüleci çamuru; verimli toprak; **ˈloam.y** *adj.* balçık gibi; balçığa ait, balçık...
**loan** [ləun] **1.** *n.* ödünç verme; ödünç alma, borçlanma; ödünç verilen şey; on ~ ödünç olarak; ask for the ~ of s.th. *bşi* ödünç istemek; put out to ~ ödünç vermek; **2.** *v/t. part. Am.* ödünç vermek.
**loath** [ləuθ] *adj.* isteksiz; be ~ for s.o. to do s.th. *b-nin bş* yapmasına karşı isteksiz olm.; nothing ~ isteyerek, seve seve.
**loathe** [ləuð] *v/t.* iğrenmek, nefret etm., tiksinmek -*den;* **ˈloath.ing** *n.* nefret; **loath.some** ☐ [ˈ~səm] iğrenç, nefret verici, tiksindirici; **ˈloath.some.ness** *n.* iğrençlik.
**loaves** [ləuvz] *pl. of* loaf¹.
**lob** [lɔb] *tenis:* **1.** *n.* havaya vurulan top; **2.** *v/t.* havaya vurmak *(top)*.
**lob.by** [ˈlɔbi] **1.** *n.* koridor; antre; *parl.* kulis faaliyeti; *thea.* fuaye; *parl.* kulis yapanlar; bekleme salonu, lobi; **2.** *v/i. parl.* meclis üyelerini etkilemek; kulis yapmak; *v/t.* kulis yaparak geçirtmek *veya* reddettirmek *(tasarı)*; **ˈlob.by.ist** *n. parl.* kulis yapan kimse.
**lobe** *anat.*, ♀ [ləub] *n.* kulak memesi; lop; ~ of the ear kulak memesi.

**lob.ster** ['lɔbstə] *n.* ıstakoz.

**lo.cal** ['ləukəl] **1.** □ mahalli, yöresel, yerel, bölgesel, lokal; kısmi; *s.* branch; ~ call *teleph.* şehiriçi telefon konuşması; ~ colour yöresel özellikler; ~ government mahalli idare; **2.** *n. gazete:* yerel haber; *a.* ~ train 🚂 banliyö treni; F semt meyhanesi; ~s *pl.* semt sakinleri; **lo.cale** [ləu'ka:l] *n.* mahal, yer, yöre, olayın geçtiği yer; **lo.cal.ism** ['~kəlizəm] *n.* belirli bir yere duyulan ilgi; yöresel şive *veya* töre; **lo.cal.i.ty** [~'kæliti] *n.* yer, yöre, mevki; semt, mahalle; **lo.cal.ize** ['~kəlaiz] *v/t.* sınırlamak; yerini bulmak.

**lo.cate** [ləu'keit] *v/t.* yerleştirmek; bulmak; *Am.* yerini tayin etm., be ~d bulunmak, yerleştirilmek; *v/i.* oturmak; **lo'ca.tion** *n.* yerleş(tir)me; yer, mahal; 🗽 kiraya verme; *film:* stüdyo dışındaki çekim yeri; on ~ stüdyo dışında film çekme.

**loch** *Scots* [lɔk] *n.* göl, haliç, körfez.

**lock**[1] [lɔk] **1.** *n.* kilit; yükseltme havuzu; ⊕ kilitlenme; tekerlek turu; silah çakmağı; ~. stock and barrel tamamen, ne var ne yok hepsi; **2.** *v/t. & v/i.* kilitle(n)mek, kapa(n)mak, kenetle(n)mek; ⊕ bloke etm.; ~ s.th. away *bşi* kitleyip kaldırmak; ~ s.o. in *b-nin* üzerine kapıyı kilitlemek; ~ s.o. out *b-ni* dışarda bırakmak; lokavt yapmak; ~ up kilitleyip kaldırmak, kilit altında saklamak; kapıları kilitlemek; hapsetmek; yatırmak, bağlamak *(para)*.

**lock**[2] [~] *n.* bukle, lüle; ~s *pl. co.* saç.

**lock.age** ['lɔkidʒ] *n.* gemiyi kanal havuzundan geçirme; havuzdan geçme parası; **'lock.er** *n.* dolap; go to Davy Jones's ~ denizin dibini boylamak, boğulmak; **lock.et** ['lɔkit] *n.* madalyon.

**lock...**: '~.gates *n. pl.* kanal kapıları; '~-jaw *n.* tetanos; '~.keep.er *n.* kanal görevlisi; '~-nut *n.* ⊕ kilit somunu; '~-out *n.* lokavt; '~.smith *n.* çilingir; '~-stitch *n.* mekik dikişi; '~-up **1.** *n.* tutukevi; † sermayenin dondurulması; **2.** *adj.* kilitlenebilen.

**lo.co** *Am. sl.* ['ləukəu] *adj.* deli, kaçık.

**lo.co.mo.tion** [ləukə'məuʃən] *n.* hareket; **lo.co.mo.tive** ['~tiv] **1.** *adj.* harekete ait, hareket...; hareket edebilen; **2.** *n. a.* ~ engine lokomotif.

**lo.cust** ['ləukəst] *n.* çekirge; *a.* ~-tree 💮 salkım (*veya* akasya) ağacı.

**lo.cu.tion** [ləu'kju:ʃən] *n.* konuşma şekli, tabir, terim.

**lode** 💥 [ləud] *n.* maden damarı; '~.star

*n.* Çobanyıldızı, Kutupyıldızı; *fig.* yol gösterici ilke; '~.stone *n.* mıknatıs taşı.

**lodge** [lɔdʒ] **1.** *n.* kulübe; in; masonlar *veya* toplanma yeri, loca; küçük ev; kapıcı odası; **2.** *v/t. & v/i.* yerleş(tir)mek, barın(dır)mak; misafir etm.; emaneten vermek; sunmak; arzetmek; kirada oturmak; misafir olm.; '**lodge.ment** *s.* lodgment; '**lodg.er** *n.* misafir, kiracı; '**lodg.ing** *n.* kiralık oda; geçici konut; ~s *pl.* pansiyon; '**lodg.ing-house** *n.* pansiyon; '**lodg.ment** *n.* 🗽 arzetme, sunma, emaneten verme; sığınak, barınak; ikamet etme, yerleşme.

**lo.ess** ['ləuis] *n.* lös, verimli sarımtırak toprak.

**loft** [lɔft] *n.* çatı arası (odası), tavan arası; samanlık; kilise balkonu; '**loft.i.ness** *n.* yükseklik; *fig.* yücelik; kibirlilik; '**loft.y** □ yüksek; yüce, asil; üstün, mükemmel; gururlu, kibirli, çalımlı.

**log** [lɔg] *n.* kütük; ⚓ parakete, geminin süratini ölçme aleti; = log-book; sleep like a ~ külçe gibi uyumak.

**lo.gan.ber.ry** ♧ ['ləugənbəri] *n.* yarı böğürtlen yarı ağaççileği türünden bir çeşit meyve.

**log.a.rithm** ⋏ ['lɔgəriθm] *n.* logaritma.

**log...**: '~-book *n.* ⚓ rota (*veya* seyir) defteri; gemi jurnalı; *mot.* ruhsatname; 🏕 rota defteri; ~ cab.in kütüklerden yapılmış kulübe; **logged** *adj.* ağırlaşmış (*su ile)*; **log.ger.head** ['lɔgəhed] *n.:* be at ~s kavgalı olm. (with *ile).*

**log.gia** ['lɔdʒə] *n.* kemeraltı, sundurma, kenarı açık sıra kemerler.

**log.ging** ['lɔgiŋ] *n.* kerestecilik; **log house,** **log hut** kütüklerden yapılmış kulübe.

**log.ic** ['lɔdʒik] *n.* mantık, eseme; '**log.i.cal** □ mantıklı, makûl, uygun, mantıklı, esemeli; **lo.gi.cian** [ləu'dʒiʃən] *n.* mantıkçı, mantık ilmi uzmanı.

**lo.gis.tics** ⋋ [ləu'dʒistiks] *n. oft. sg.* lojistik.

**log.roll** *part. pol.* ['lɔgrəul] *v/i* karşılıklı birbirini desteklemek.

**log.wood** ['lɔgwud] *n.* bakkam ağacı.

**loin** [lɔin] *n.* bel; fileto; gird up one's ~s harekete geçmeye hazırlanmak; '~-cloth *n.* peştamal, kuşak.

**loi.ter** ['lɔitə] *v/i.* gezmek, yolda sık sık durarak gitmek, aylak aylak dolaşmak; ~ away *v/t.* boşa geçirmek *(zaman)*; '**loi.ter.er** *n.* aylak (*veya* avare) kimse.

**loll** [lɔl] *v/i.* sallanmak; aylaklık etm.; ~ about avare dolaşmak; ~ out dışarı sark(ıt)mak *(dil).*

**lol.li.pop** F ['lɔlipɔp] *n.* lolipop, şekerleme.

**lol.lop** F [ˈlɔləp] *v/i.* ayağını sürüyerek yürümek.

**Lom.bard** [ˈlɔmbəd] *n.:* ~ Street Londra para piyasası.

**Lon.don.er** [ˈlʌndənə] *n.* Londralı.

**lone** [ləun] *adj.* yalnız, kimsesiz; ıssız, tenha; **lone.li.ness** [ˈ~linis] *n.* yalnızlık, kimsesizlik; **lone.ly**, **lone.some** □ [ˈ~səm] yalnız, kimsesiz; ıssız, tenha; sıkıcı, kasvetli.

**long¹** [lɔŋ] **1.** *n.* uzun zaman; uzun hece; before ~ çok geçmeden, yakında; for ~ uzun süre; take ~ uzun sürmek; the ~ and the short of it uzun lâfın kısası, doğrusu; **2.** *adj.* uzun; yorucu; uzak *(tarih)*; at ~ date † uzun vadeli; in the ~ run eninde sonunda; zamanla, uzun vadede; be ~ uzun sürmek; take the ~ view ileriyi görmek; **3.** *adv.* çok, pek; süresince, boyunca; çoktan; geç; as ~ ago as 1960 1960'dan beri; so ~! Allaha ısmarladık!, hoşça kal!; ~er daha uzun; daha çok; no ~er ago than ...den çok önce değil.

**long²** [~] *v/i.* can atmak (for -*e*), özlemek (for -*i*), özlemini çekmek (for -*in*), çok istemek (to *inf. -meği*).

**long...:** ˈ~.boat *n.* ⚓ yelkenli geminin en büyük sandalı; ~-bow [ˈ~bəu] *n.* *hist.* uzun yay; draw the ~ *fig.* atıp tutmak, tıraş etm., palavra atmak; ˈ~-ˈdated *adj.* uzun vadeli *(veya* süreli); ˈ~-ˈdis.tance *adj.* şehirlerarası; uzun mesafe...; ~ flight uzun mesafe uçuşu; ~ race uzun mesafe yarışı; ˈ~-drawn-ˈout, *a.*ˈ~-ˈdrawn *adj.* uzun süren; [lon.gev.i.ty [lɔnˈdʒeviti] *n.* uzun ömür(lülük); **long** firm dolandırıcılar, dolandırıcı takımı; ˈlong.hair *n.* F profesör tipli kimse; hippi; klasik müzik düşkünü; ˈlong.haired *adj.* F münevver, bilgili, entelektüel; hippi; uzun saçlı; ˈlong.hand *n.* el yazısı; ˈlong-ˈhead.ed *adj. fig.* ileriyi gören; zeki, akıllı.

**long.ing** [ˈlɔŋiŋ] **1.** □ özlem dolu, arzulu; **2.** *n.* özlem, hasret, iştiyak.

**long.ish** [ˈlɔŋiʃ] *adj.* uzunca, upuzun.

**lon.gi.tude** *geogr.* [ˈlɔndʒitjuːd] *n.* boylam, tul; **lon.gi.tu.di.nal** □ [~dinl] uzunlamasına...; boylama ait.

**long...:** ˈ~-ˈlived *adj.* uzun ömürlü; ˈ~-ˈrange *adj.* uzun vadeli; ✕ uzun menzilli...; † büyük hareket sahası olan...; ˈ~-shore-man *n.* dok işçisi; ˈ~-shot *n. film:* telefotografi; ˈ~-ˈsight.ed *adj.* presbit, uzağı iyi gören; *fig.* ileriyi görebilen, basiretli, sağgörülü; ˈ~-ˈstand.ing *adj.* eskisi gibi, uzun süren; ˈ~-ˈsuf.fer.ing **1.** *adj.* cefakâr, cefakeş, sabırlı; **2.** *n.* cefa, sabır, tahammül; ˈ~-ˈterm *adj.*

uzun vadeli; ~ **waves** *pl.* ⚡ uzun dalga; ˈ~.ways *adv.* uzunlamasına; ˈ~-ˈwind.ed □ sözü bitmez, kafa ütüleyen.

**loo¹** [luː] *n.* bir çeşit iskambil oyunu, lû.

**loo²** F [~] *n.* tuvalet.

**loo.fah** ⚘ [ˈluːfɑː] *n.* lif kabağı.

**look** [luk] **1.** *n.* bakış, nazar, bakma; *oft.* ~s *pl.* görünüş, güzellik, yüz ifadesi; new ~ yeni çehre *(veya* moda); have a ~ at *s.th.* bşi gözden geçirmek, bşe göz atmak; I don't like the ~ of it onu beğenmiyorum, onu gözüm tutmadı; **2.** *v/i.* bakmak (at, on -*e*), görmek; görünmek, gözükmek, benzemek; it ~s like rain yağmur yağacağa benziyor; he ~s like winning kazanacağa benziyor; ~ about bakınmak, araştırmak, kollamak, aramak (for -*i*); ~ after bakmak -*e*, gözetmek -*i*; ~ at seyretmek -*i*, bakmak -*e*; göz önüne almak -*i*, düşünmek -*i*; kontrol etm. -*i*; not much to ~ at yüzüne bakılmaz, görünüşü kötü; ~ down on tepeden bakmak -*e*, küçük görmek -*i*; ~ for aramak -*i*; beklemek -*i*; ~ forward to beklemek, ummak -*i*, iple çekmek -*i*, dört gözle beklemek -*i*; ~ in uğramak (on -*e*); ~ into araştırmak -*i*, soruşturmak -*i*, incelemek -*i*; içine bakmak -*in*; ~ on seyretmek, bakıp durmak; bakmak -*e* (as *gözüyle*); ~ on to bakmak -*e*; my bedroom ~s to the garden yatak odam bahçeye bakıyor; ~ out dikkat etm., sakınmak; seçmek, çıkarmak; ~ out for aranmak, bakınmak -*e*; ~ over *s.th.* bşi gözden geçirmek, incelemek, yoklamak, bşe göz gezdirmek; ~ round iyi düşünmek, enine boyuna düşünmek; kafasını çevirip bakmak; gezmek, dolaşmak; ~ through gözden geçirmek -*i*, incelemek -*i*; ~ to dikkat etm. -*e*, önem vermek -*e*, bakmak -*e*; ~ to *s.o.* to *inf. b-nin* ...ceğine güvenmek; ~ up yukarıya bakmak, başını kaldırıp bakmak; gelişmek ,düzelmek, iyileşmek; bulup ziyaret etm.; ~ up to *s.o. b-ne* saygı göstermek, *b-ni* saymak; ~ (up)on *fig.* bakmak -*e* (as *gözüyle*); *v/t.* ~ *s.o.* in the face (sıkılmadan) *b-nin* gözünün içine bakmak; ~ one's age yaşını göstermek; ~ disdain tepeden bakmak, hor görmek; ~ over gözden geçirmek -*i*, incelemek -*i*, yoklamak -*i*; ~ up sözlükte aramak; ziyaret etm. -*i*, uğramak -*e*, arayıp sormak -*i*.

**look.er-on** [ˈlukərˈɔn] *n.* seyirci.

**look-in** [ˈlukˈin] *n.* kısa bakış; kısa ziyaret, uğrama; F kazanma şansı.

**look.ing-glass** [ˈlukiŋglɑːs] *n.* ayna.

**look-out** [ˈlukˈaut] *n.* gözetleme (yeri); olasılık, ümit; gözleyici; be on the ~ gözetlemek, araştırmak, tetikte olm.; that is my ~ o benim bileceğim iş; **look-o.ver** n. gözden geçirme, tetkik; give s.th. a ~ bşi gözden geçirmek.

**loom**[1] [luːm] n. dokuma tezgâhı.

**loom**[2] [~] v/i. karaltı gibi görünmek, uzakta hayal gibi görünmek, belirmek; ~ large fig. kafasını kurcalamak, gözünde büyümek.

**loon**[1] Scots [luːn] n. işe yaramaz (veya serseri) kimse.

**loon**[2] orn. [~] n. gerdanlı dalgıç.

**loop** [luːp] 1. n. ilmik, düğüm, ilmek; kıvrık sap; doğum kontrolü için kullanılan cihaz, spiral; ~ aerial radyo: çerçeve anten; 2. v/t. ilmiklemek, düğümlemek; ~ up iğne ile tutturmak (elbise); firkete ile toplamak (saç); ~ the ~ ⟟ takla atmak; v/i. ilmik yapmak; ilmik olm., ilmikle tutulmak; **~-hole** n. gözetleme deliği; fig. kaçamak, açık (kapı); ✕ mazgal; **~-line** n. 🚂 & tel. ana hattan ayrılıp tekrar birleşen hat, şube hattı.

**loose** [luːs] 1. ☐ com. çözük, gevşek; sallantılı; boş, serbest; hafifmeşrep, başıboş; bol, dökümlü (elbise); şüpheli; seyrek, dağınık; dikkatsiz; ~ connection ⚡ gevşek bağlantı; at a ~ end yapacak işi olmayan, boşta; play fast and ~ with aldatmak, kandırmak; 2. v/t. gevşetmek, çözmek, açmak; a. ~ off salıvermek, serbest bırakmak (esir); atmak, fırlatmak (ok); ateşlemek (silah); ~ one's hold on s.th. bşi serbest bırakmak, bş üzerindeki baskıyı kaldırmak, gevşek bırakmak; v/i. ateş etm.; atış yapmak; 3. n. give (a) ~ to gevşetmek, salıvermek; **~-leaf** adj. sayfaları çıkarılıp yeniden takılabilen; ~ book, ~ ledger sayfaları çıkarılıp takılabilen defter; **loos.en** [ˈluːsn] v/t. & v/i. gevşe(t)mek, çöz(ül)mek; **loose.ness** n. gevşeklik; düzensizlik; kararsızlık; ☒ ishal.

**loot** [luːt] 1. v/i. yağma etm.; 2. n. yağma, ganimet, çapul.

**lop**[1] [lɔp] v/t. budamak, kesmek (ağaç); mst ~ away, ~ off budamak; kaldırmak, durdurmak.

**lop**[2] [~] v/i. sarkmak.

**lope** [ləup] 1. v/i. seke seke koşmak; 2. n. sekme, koşuş.

**lop**...: **~-ears** n. pl. sarkık kulaklar; **~-sid.ed** adj. bir tarafa yatkın; dengesiz, orantısız.

**lo.qua.cious** [ləʊˈkweiʃəs] adj. konuşkan, çenebaz, dilli, geveze; **lo.quac.i.ty** [ləʊˈkwæsiti] n. konuşkanlık, çenebazlık.

**lo.ran** ⟟, ⬇ [ˈlɔːrən] n. radyo sinyalleri ile uçağın veya geminin yerini tesbit eden sistem.

**lord** [lɔːd] 1. n. sahip, efendi; mal sahibi; lord; hükümdar; co. koca; nüfuzlu kimse; the 2 Allah, Tanrı; Hazreti İsa; my ~ efendim, lord hazretleri; the 2's Prayer İsa'nın öğrettiği dua; the 2's Supper Aşai Rabbani ayini, kudas, liturya; as drunk as a ~ kör kütük sarhoş; live like a ~ krallar gibi yaşamak; 2. vb. ~ it amirlik taslamak (over s.o. -e); **lord.li.ness** n. haşmet, heybet, görkem; b.s. gurur, kibir; **lord.ling** n. değersiz lord, küçük lord; **lord.ly** adj. lorda yaraşır; görkemli, haşmetli; gururlu, kibirli; **lord.ship** n. lordluk; üstünlük, egemenlik.

**lore** [lɔː] n. bilgi, ilim, bilim.

**lor.gnette** [lɔːˈnjet] n. saplı gözlük.

**lor.ry** [ˈlɔri] n. üstü açık yük arabası; kamyon; 🚂 furgon, dekovil vagonu.

**lose** [luːz] (irr.) v/t. & v/i. kaybet(tir)mek, yitirmek, kaçırmak; geri kalmak (saat); şaşırmak; kaybolmak; yenilmek; ~ o.s. kendini kaybetmek, kendinden geçmek; yolunu kaybetmek; dalmak, kendini vermek (in -e); ~ sight of gözden kaybetmek -i; dikkate almamak -i, unutmak -i; **los.er** n. kaybeden (veya yenik) kimse; come off a ~ yenik düşmek; **los.ing** 1. adj. kazançlı olmayan, zarar gören...; yenilen; 2. n. ~s pl. kayıplar, zaiyat.

**loss** [lɔs] n. kayıp; zarar, ziyan, hasar; at a ~ şaşırmış, afallamış; zararına (satış); be at a ~ for words söyleyecek kelime bulamamak; be at a ~ what to say ne diyeceğini bilememek; **~-lead.er** n. ⟟ müşteri çekmek için zararına satılan mal.

**lost** [lɔst] pret. & p.p. of lose; be ~ kaybolmak; fig. kendini kaptırmak, dalmak (in -e); this won't be ~ on me o beni etkilemez, o bana vız gelir; be ~ upon s.o. b-nin gözünde bir hiç olm; **~-prop.er.ty of.fice** kayıp eşya bürosu.

**lot** [lɔt] 1. n. kur'a, adçekme; hisse, pay; arazi parçası, yer; fig. şans, talih, kısmet, kader; ⟟ parti (mal), kısım, parça; nevi, tip, cins; F çok miktar, çokluk; Am. film: film stüdyosu; a ~ of people F pek çok (veya pek sürü) kimse; draw ~s kur'a çekmek, adçekmek (for için); fall to s.o.'s ~ b-nin payına düşmek; throw in one's ~ with -ile şansını denemek, ile alın yazısı birleştirmek; he is feeling a ~ better F kendini çok daha iyi

hissediyor; **2.** *v/t.* bölüştürmek, taksim etm., paylaştırmak.
**loth** [ləuθ] = loath.
**lo.tion** [ˈləuʃən] *n.* losyon.
**lot.ter.y** [ˈlɔtəri] *n.* piyango, lotarya; talih, kader.
**lo.tus** ♀ [ˈləutəs] *n.* nilüfer çiçeği; '~-eater *n.* hayal âleminde yaşayan kimse.
**loud** [laud] **1.** ☐ yüksek (*ses*); gürültülü, patırtılı; çiğ *(renk)*; kaba; **2.** *adv.* yüksek sesle, gürültü ile; '~-'hail.er *n.* ↓ megafon; '**loud.ness** *n.* gürültü; *radyo:* ses şiddeti; '**loud-'speak.er** *n.* hoparlör.
**lough** *Ir.* [lɔk] *n.* göl, haliç.
**lounge** [laundʒ] **1.** *v/i.* tembelce uzanmak, yayılıp oturmak; avare dolaşmak; **2.** *n.* dinlenme salonu, hol; bekleme salonu: şezlong; avarelik; *thea.* fuaye; '~-'chair *n.* şezlong; '~-liz.ard *n.* *sl.* jigolo, salon züppesi; '**loung.er** *n.* avare (*veya* aylak) kimse; '**lounge-'suit** *n.* günlük (takım) elbise.
**lour** [ˈlauə] *v/i.* surat asmak, kaşlarını çatmak, kötü kötü bakmak; kararmak *(hava)*; **lour.ing** ☐ [ˈ~rɪŋ] somurtkan; kapalı *(hava)*.
**louse 1.** [laus] *n.*, *pl.* **lice** [lais] bit, kehle; *sl.* ciğeri beş para etmez adam; **2.** [lauz] *v/t.* -*in* bitlerini ayıklamak; **lous-y** [ˈlauzi] *adj.* bitli; alçak; berbat, rezalet; **he is ~ with money** *sl.* denizde kum onda para.
**lout** [laut] *n.* kaba adam, *sl.* eşek; **lout.ish** *adj.* kaba..., maskara...
**lov.a.ble** ☐ [ˈlʌvəbl] sevimli, cana yakın, hoş, çekici.
**love** [lʌv] **1.** *n.* sevgi (*of*, *a.* **for**, to, towards -*e karşı*); aşk; sevgili; F sevimli kimse *veya* şey, şeker kimse *veya* şey; ♀ aşk tanrısı, Küpid; *spor:* sıfır; *attr.* aşk...; **for the ~ of God** Allah aşkı için; **play for ~** zevk için oynamak; **four (to) ~** sıfıra karşı dört; **give** *veya* **send one's ~ to** s.o. *b-ne* selâm yollamak (*veya* söylemek); **in ~ with** -*e* âşık; **fall in ~ with** âşık olm. -*e*, vurulmak -*e*; **make ~** sevişmek; **make ~ to** kur yapmak -*e*; **neither for ~ nor money** hiç bir surette; **2.** *vb.* sevmek, âşık olm. -*e*; tapmak -*e*; düşkün olm. -*e*; **~ to do** yapmayı sevmek; '~-af.fair *n.* aşk macerası; '~-bird *n.* muhabbetkuşu; '~-child *n.* aşk meyvesi, piç; '**love.less** *adj.* sevgisiz, aşksız, sevgiden yoksun; sevilmeyen; '**love-let.ter** *n.* aşk mektubu; '**love-ll.ness** *n.* güzellik, sevimlilik; '**love.lock** *n.* kâkül, zülüf, lüle; **love.lorn** [ˈ~lɔːn] *adj.* aşk acısı çeken, sevgilisi dönmemiş; '**love.ly** *adj.* sevimli, güzel, hoş, çekici;

eğlenceli; '**love-mak.ing** *n.* sevişme; aşk dolu kelimeler; '**love-match** *n.* aşk evliliği; '**love-phil.tre,** '**love-po.tion** *n.* aşk iksiri; '**lov.er** *n.* sevgili, dost, metres, yâr, âşık *(a. fig.);* **a ~ of art** sanat âşığı; **~s** *pl.* sevgililer; pair of **~s** sevişen çift; '**love.set** *n.* *spor:* sıfıra karşı alınan set; '**love.sick** *adj.* sevdalı; '**love-to.ken** *n.* aşk hatırası.
**lov.ing** ☐ [ˈlʌvɪŋ] seven, sevgi gösteren, sevgi dolu; '~-'kind.ness *n.* şefkat, merhamet, iyilik.
**low¹** [ləu] **1.** *(☐ ⚓)* aşağı, alçak; bayağı, adi, ucuz; düşük *(♥ nabız vs.);* yavaş, zayıf *(ses)*; kuvvetsiz, halsiz; neşesiz, üzgün; *fig.* karamsar; gelişmemiş; basit; alçak gönüllü; ufka yakın; kısa, bodur; **~est bid** en düşük teklif; **be brought ~** burnu sürtülmek; mahvolmak; **lay ~** yıkmak, mahvetmek; burnunu sürtmek; **lie ~** saklanmak; susup beklemek; **2.** *n.* *meteor.* düşük basınç bölgesi; *part. Am.* düşük şey *(fiyat, seviye vs.)*.
**low²** [~] **1.** *v/i.* böğürmek; **2.** *n.* böğürme.
**low...:** '~-'born *adj.* aşağı tabakadan; '~-'bred *adj.* soysuz, kaba, terbiyesiz; '~-brow **1.** *adj.* kültürsüz, basit; **2.** *n.* kültürsüz (*veya* basit) kimse; ~ **co.me.di.an** *mst fig.* maskara, soytarı; ~ **com.e.dy** konusu hafif güldürü; fars; ~ **coun.try** ova, düz arazi; '~-'down **1.** *adj.* F alçak(-ca), âdi(ce); **2.** *n.* *sl.* gerçek, bşin içyüzü.
**low.er¹** [ˈləuə] **1.** *adj.* daha aşağı, daha alçak (s. low¹); ~ **case** *typ.* küçük harf, minüskül; **2.** *v/t.* & *v/i.* in(dir)mek, alçal(t)mak, düş(ür)mek, azal(t)mak, eksil(t)mek; küçük düşürmek, rezil etm.; zayıflatmak; ~ **one's voice** sesini alçaltmak.
**low.er²** [ˈləuə] *s.* lour.
**low.er.most** [ˈləuəməust] *adj.* en düşük, en alçak, en aşağı; '**low.land** *n.* ova, düz arazi; '**low.land.er** *n.* ovalı kimse; '**low.li.ness** *n.* alçak gönüllülük; '**low.ly** *adj.* & *adv.* ikinci derecede, aşağı; alçak gönüllü; '**low-'necked** *adj.* dekolte *(elbise);* '**low.ness** *n.* düşüklük, alçaklık; ♪ peslik; ~ **of spirits** üzgünlük, ümitsizlik, neşesizlik; '**low-'pres.sure** *adj.* alçak basınçlı; '**low-'spir.it.ed** *adj.* kederli, üzgün, neşesiz, mutsuz; **low wa.ter** cezir, inik deniz; **in ~** *fig.* züğürt, cebi delik.
**loy.al** ☐ [ˈlɔiəl] sadık, vefalı; '**loy.al.ist** *n.* krala sadık kalan kimse; '**loy.al.ty** *n.* sadakat, bağlılık, vefa.
**loz.enge** [ˈlɔzindʒ] *n.* eşkenar dörtgen; *pharm.* pastil.

**£.s.d** F ['eles'di:] *n.* para.
**lub.ber** ['lʌbə] *n.* acemi kimse; **ᴵlub.ber.ly** *adj.* acemi, bön.
**lu.bri.cant** ['lu:brikənt] *n.* yağ(layıcı madde); **lu.bri.cate** ['ᴵ-keit] *v/t.* yağlamak; **lu.bri'ca.tion** *n.* ⊕ yağlama; **ᴵlu.bri.ca.tor** **ℝ.** ⊕ yağdanlık; yağcı; **luᴵbric.i.ty** [~siti] *n.* ⊕ kayganlık, yağlılık; *fig.* kaypaklık; zamparalık, şehvete düşkünlük.
**lu.cerne** ⚘ [lu:ᴵsəːn] *n.* kabayonca.
**lu.cid** □ ['lu:sid] *mst poet.* açık, kolay anlaşılır, berrak, vazıh, şeffaf, parlak; ~ **interval** .❡ hastanın aklı başına geldiği ara; **luᴵcid.i.ty**, **ᴵlu.cid.ness** *n.* açıklık, berraklık, şeffaflık, sağduyu.
**Lu.ci.fer** □ ['lu:sifə] *n.* şeytan, İblis; Venüs, sabah yıldızı.
**luck** [lʌk] *n.* şans, talih, baht, uğur; good ~ iyi şans; bad ~, hard ~, ill ~ aksilik, talihsizlik, fena talih, kötü şans; be down on one's ~ F şansı yaver gitmemek; worse ~ maalesef, ne yazık ki; **ᴵluck.i.ly** *adv.* Allahtan, bereket versin ki, iyi ki; **ᴵluck-l.ness** *n.* şanslılık; **ᴵluck.less** *adj.* şanssız, talihsiz, bahtsᴵz; **ᴵluck.y** □ şanslı, talihli, uğurlu; be ~ şanslı olm.; **ᴵluck.y-bag**, **ᴵluck.y-dip** *n.* piyango torbası.
**lu.cra.tive** □ ['lu:krətiv] kazançlı, kârlı; **lu.cre** ['lu:kə] *n.* para, servet, kazanç.
**lu.cu.bra.tion** [lu:kju:ᴵbreiʃən] *n.* emekle ortaya çıkarılmış eser; *mst* ~s *pl.* emek isteyen işler.
**lu.di.crous** □ ['lu:dikrəs] gülünç, komik; saçma, aptalca.
**luff** ⬇ [lʌf] **1.** *n.* orsa seyiri; **2.** *v/i. a.* ~ up orsa etm.
**lug.¹** [lʌg] **1.** *v/t.* çekmek, sürüklemek; ~ in *fig. b-ni* saçlarından sürüklemek; **2.** *n.* kulp, sap; kulak (memesi).
**lug²** [~] = lugsail.
**luge** [lu:ʒ] **1.** *n.* kızak; **2.** *v/i.* kızakla kaymak.
**lug.gage** ['lʌgidʒ] *n.* bagaj; **ᴵ~-car.ri.er** *n.* portbagaj; **ᴵ~-of.fice** *n.* 🚂 eşya bürosu; **ᴵ~-rack** *n.* bagaj filesi; üst bagaj; **ᴵ~-tick-et** *n.* bagaj bileti; **ᴵ~-van** *n.* 🚂 furgon, eşya vagonu.
**lug.ger** ⬇ ['lʌgə] *n.* bir *veya* daha çok aşırmalı yelkenli küçük gemi.
**ᴵug.sail** ⬇ ['lʌgseil, 'lʌgsl] *n.* aşırmalı (*veya* hasır) yelken.
**lu.gu.bri.ous** □ [lu:ᴵgu:briəs] dokunaklı, hazin, acıklı, kederli.
**luke.warm** ['lu:kwɔːm] *adj.* ılık; *fig.* kayıtsız, ilgisiz; **ᴵluke.warm.ness** *n.* ılıklık; kayıtsızlık.
**lull** [lʌl] **1.** *v/t. & v/i.* uyuş(tur)mak, sakinleş(tir)mek, yatış(tır)mak; uyutmak

(*bebek*); **2.** *n.* ara, fasıla; geçici sükû net, dinginlik.
**lull.a.by** ['lʌləbai] *n.* ninni.
**lum.ba.go** ❡ [lʌmᴵbeigəu] *n.* lumbago, bel ağrısı.
**lum.ber** ['lʌmbə] **1.** *n.* lüzumsuz eşya, ıvır zıvır; kereste; **2.** *v/t. a.* ~ **üp** lüzumsuz eşya ile (*veya* ıvır zıvırla) doldurmak; *v/i.* kereste kesmek; hantal hantal yürümek, ağır ağır ilerlemek; **ᴵlum.ber.er**, **ᴵlum.ber.man** *n.* keresteci, bıçkıcı; **ᴵlumber.ing** *adj.* hantal; gürültülü; **ᴵlum.ber-jack** *n.* ormanda ağaç kesen kimse, keresteci; **ᴵlum.ber-mill** *n.* hızarhane, bıçkıhane; **ᴵlum.ber-room** *n.* sandık odası; **ᴵlum.ber-yard** *n.* kereste deposu.
**lu.mi.nar.y** ['lu:minəri] *n.* ışık veren cisim (*yıldız, ay veya güneş*); *fig.* aydın kimse; **lu.mi.nos.i.ty** [~'nɒsiti] *n.* parlaklık; açıklık; **ᴵlu.mi.nous** □ parlak, aydınlık; *fig.* açık, anlaşılır, berrak; ~ **dial** ışıklı kadran; ~ **paint** fosforlu boya.
**lump** [lʌmp] **1.** *n.* toprak, yumru, küme; öbek; şiş(kinlik); *fig.* ahmak kimse; **in the** ~ toptan, hep birden; ~ **sugar** kesmeşeker; ~ **sum** toptan ödenen para, götürü; **have a** ~ **in the throat** *fig.* boğazı düğümlenmek; **2.** *v/t.* yığmak (into, in -e); bir araya toplamak; *fig.* tahammül etm., katlanmak; **if you don't like it you can** ~ **it** istesen de istemesen de; ~ **together** bir araya getirmek; *v/i.* yığılmak; hantal hantal dolaşmak; **ᴵlump.ish** *adj.* sakar; aptal, kalın kafalı; mıymıntı, tembel; **ᴵlump.y** □ yumru yumru, topak topak; şapşal; çırpıntılı (*su*).
**lu.na.cy** ['lu:nəsi] *n.* delilik, cinnet, kaçıklık; **lunacies** *pl.* deli deli hareketler.
**lu.nar** ['lu:nə] *adj.* aya ait, ay...; ~ **caustic** ⚕ cehennemtaşı, gümüş nitrat; ~ **module** ay modülü.
**lu.na.tic** ['lu:nətik] **1.** *adj.* deli..., akıl hastası...; saçma sapan; delice...; **2.** *n.* deli kimse, akıl hastası; ~ **a.sy.lum** tımarhane, akıl hastanesi; ~ **fringe** garip fikirli taşkın kimseler topluluğu.
**lunch** [lʌntʃ] **1.** *n.* öğle yemeği; **2.** *v/t. & v/i.* öğle yemeği ye(dir)mek; **lunch.eon** ['ᴵ-tʃən] = lunch 1; **ᴵlunch-hour** *n.* öğle tatili.
**lu.nettes** [lu:ᴵnets] *n. pl.* dalgıç (*veya* sualtı) gözlüğü.
**lung** [lʌŋ] *n.* akciğerlerin her biri; **the** ~**s** *pl.* akciğer.
**lunge** [lʌndʒ] **1.** *n. fenc.* hamle, saldırış; **2.** *v/i.* ileri atılmak, hamle etm., saldırmak (at -e); *v/t.* itmek, kakmak.
**lung.er** *sl.* ['lʌŋə] *n.* ciğerlerinden rahat-

sız kimse, veremli; **lung-pow.er** *n.* ses gücü.

**lu.pin(e)** ⚤ [ˈluːpin] *n.* acı bakla.

**lurch**[1] [ləːtʃ] 1. *n.* ⚓ birden sallanma *veya* silkinme; *fig.* sendeleme; 2. *v/i.* ⚓ sallanmak, silkinmek; *fig.* sendelemek, sendeleyerek yürümek.

**lurch**[2] [~] *n.: leave in the ~* yüzüstü bırakmak.

**lurch.er** [ˈləːtʃə] *n.* zağar, kopoy, bir cins melez av köpeği.

**lure** [ljuə] 1. *n.* yem; *fig.* cazibe, tuzak; 2. *v/t.* cezbetmek, çekmek.

**lu.rid** [ˈljuərid] *adj.* parlak, pırıl pırıl; dehşetli, korkunç, tüyler ürpertici.

**lurk** [ləːk] *v/i.* gizlenmek, saklanmak, gizli gizli dolaşmak, kol gezmek *(tehlike)*; **lurk.ing-place** *n.* pusu yeri.

**lus.cious** ☐ [ˈlʌʃəs] pek tatlı, nefis, bal gibi; çekici, güzel; olgun *(meyva)*; süslü; *b.s.* yapmacık; **lus.cious.ness** *n.* lezzetlilik, pek tatlılık.

**lush** [lʌʃ] 1. *adj.* bereketli, verimli, bol; lezzetli, leziz; çok sulu; şatafatlı, konforlu; 2. *n. Am. sl.* ayyaş kimse.

**lust** *lit.* [lʌst] 1. *n.* şehvet; *fig.* hırs, arzu; 2. *v/t.* şehvetle arzu etm. *(after, for -i)*; **lust.ful** ☐ [ˈ~ful] şehvetli.

**lust.i.ness** [ˈlʌstinis] *n.* dinçlik, kuvvet, canlılık.

**lus.tre** [ˈlʌstə] *n.* parlaklık, parıltı; perdah, cilâ; görkem, ihtişam; avize; şöhret, ün; **lus.tre.less** *adj.* donuk, mat; parıltısız.

**lus.trous** ☐ [ˈlʌstrəs] pırıl pırıl, parlak.

**lust.y** ☐ [ˈlʌsti] dinç, kuvvetli, gürbüz; *fig.* canlı; şehvetli.

**lu.ta.nist** [ˈluːtənist] *n.* udî, kopuzcu.

**lute**[1] ♪ [luːt] *n.* ut, lavta, kopuz.

**lute**[2] [~] 1. *n.* macun; 2. *v/t.* macunlamak, sıvamak.

**Lu.ther.an** [ˈluːθərən] 1. *adj.* Martin Luther'e ait; 2. *n.* Lüteriyen, Martin Luther taraftarı; **Lu.ther.an.ism** *n.* Martin Luther taraftarlığı, Luther doktrini.

**lut.ist** [ˈluːtist] = lutanist.

**lux.ate** [ˈlʌkseit] *v/t.* ⚕ mafsaldan çıkarmak, burkmak.

**lux.u.ri.ance** [lʌgˈzjuəriəns] *n.* bolluk; **lux.u.ri.ant** ☐ bol, bereketli; şatafatlı; **lux.u.ri.ate** [~rieit] *v/t.* büyük bir zevk almak (in *-den*), tadını çıkarmak *-in*; *v/i.* lüks içinde yaşamak; **lux.u.ri.ous** ☐ lüks, konforlu; pahalı; zevk verici; F süslü, tantanalı; **lux.u.ri.ous.ness** *n.* rahatlık, konfor; **lux.u.ry** [ˈlʌkʃəri] *n.* lüks, konfor; süs.

**ly.ce.um** [laiˈsiəm] *n. part. Am.* konferans salonu; lise.

**lych.gate** [ˈlitʃgeit] *n.* üstü damlı kilise kapısı.

**lye** [lai] *n.* kül *(veya* boğada) suyu.

**ly.ing** [ˈlaiiŋ] 1. *p.pr. of* lie[1] 2 & lie[2] 2; 2. *adj.* yalancı...; yanıltıcı...; **ˈ~-ˈin** *n.* loğusalık; ~ hospital doğumevi.

**lymph** [limf] *n.* ⚕ lenfa, akkan; *poet.* pınar, kaynak; **lym.phat.ic** [~ˈfætik] 1. *adj* (~ally) lenfatik...; lenfe ait, lenf...; *fig* mıymıntı, tembel; 2. *n.* lenf damarı.

**lynch** [lintʃ] *v/t.* linç etm.; **ˈ~-law** *n.* linç kanunu.

**lynx** *zo.* [liŋks] *n.* vaşak, karakulak; **ˈ~-eyed** *adj. fig.* keskin gözlü.

**lyre** [laiə] *n.* çenk, harp; **ˈ~-bird** *n. orn.* kuyruğu çenk şeklinde bir cins kuş.

**lyr.ic** [ˈlirik] 1. *adj.* lirik; 2. *n.* lirik şiir; ~s *pl.* güfte; **lyr.i.cal** ☐ liriğe ait, lirik...; heyecanlı, hevesli, gayretli.

**ly.sol** *pharm.* [ˈlaisɔl] *n.* lizol.

# M

ma F [mɑ:] *n.* anne.

ma'am [mæm] *n.* majeste; [məm] F *s.* madam.

mac F [mæk] = mackintosh.

ma.ca.bre [mə'kɑ:br] *adj.* ölümü hatırlatan, dehşetli, meş'um; danse ~ ölüm dansı.

mac.ad.am [mə'kædəm] *n.* şose, makadam; kırma taş, balast; mac'ad.am.ize *vb.* yol yüzeyini makadam ile kaplamak; şose yapmak.

mac.a.ro.ni [mækə'rouni] *n.* (düdüklü) makarna.

mac.a.roon [mækə'ru:n] *n.* bademli kurabiye.

mace¹ [meis] *n. hist.* gürz, topuz; süslü tören asası.

mace² [~] *n.* kurutulmuş küçük hindistancevizi kabuğundan yapılan baharat.

Mac.e.do.ni.an [mæsi'dəunjən] 1. *n.* Makedonyalı; Makedonya dili; 2. *adj.* Makedonya ile ilgili.

mac.er.ate ['mæsəreit] *vb.* katı maddeyi sıvıda yatırarak yumuşatmak; zayıfla(t)mak; mac.er'a.tion *n.* yumuşama; zayıflama.

Mach *phys.* [mæk] *n.:* ~ number Mah sayısı; ~ two ses hızının iki katı.

ma.che.te [mə'tʃeiti] *n.* Latin Amerika'da kullanılan bir çeşit mala.

Mach.i.a.vel.li.an [mækiə'veliən] *adj.* Makyavelce.

mach.i.na.tion [mæki'neiʃən] *n.* entrika, kumpas kurma; ~s *pl.* düzen, dolap; mach.i.na.tor ['~tə] *n.* düzenbaz kimse; ma.chine [mə'ʃi:n] 1. *n.* makine; alet; bisiklet; motorlu araç, araba; parti kontrol organizasyonu; mekanizma (*a. fig.*); 2. *vb.* şekil vermek *veya* makine ile imal etm.; ma'chine-gun *n.* X makineli tüfek, mitralyöz; ma'chine-made *adj.* makine yapımı; ma'chin.er.y *n.* mekanizma (*a. fig.*); makinenin işleyen bölümleri; makineler; ma'chine-shop *n.* torna, makine atölyesi; ma'chine-tool *n.* torna, plan-

ya makinesi; imalat aleti; ma'chin.ist *n.* makinist; makine yapımcısı.

mack F [mæk] = mackintosh.

mack.er.el ichth. ['mækrəl] *n.* uskumru.

mack.i.naw *Am.* ['mækinɔ:] *n.* yünlü kısa kruvaze palto, kaban.

mac(k).in.tosh ['mækintɔʃ] *n.* yağmurluk.

mac.ro... ['mækrəu] *prefix* büyük..., uzun...; ~.cosm ['~kɔzəm] *n.* kâinat, evren.

mad ☐ [mæd] deli, çılgın, çıldırmış; kuduz; öfkeli, çok kızmış, kudurmuş (with, at *-den,* *-den dolayı*); deli, çok düşkün (about, for *-e*); go ~ çılgına dönmek; drive ~ *b-ni* çileden çıkar(t)mak, çıldırtmak.

mad.am ['mædəm] *n.* madam, bayan, hanımefendi.

mad.cap ['mædkæp] 1. *adj.* vahşi, tehlikeli, zıpır; 2. *n.* delişmen (*veya* kudurgan) kimse; mad.den ['mædn] *vb. b-ni* çıldırtmak, sinirlendirmek.

mad.der ♀, ⊕ ['mædə] *n.* boya kökü; parlak kırmızı boya; kökboyası.

made [meid] *pret. & p.p.* of make 1.

made-up ['meid'ʌp] *adj.* uydurma; makyajlı, yüzü boyalı; tamamlanmış; zararı ödenmiş; ~ clothes *pl.* konfeksiyon; ~ of *-den* teşekkül etmiş, *-den* yapılmış.

mad.house ['mædhaus] *n.* akıl hastanesi; 'mad.man *n.* deli (*veya* mecnun) kimse; 'mad.ness *n.* delilik, çılgınlık; *vet.* kuduz hastalığı; *Am.* kızgınlık (at *-e*).

Ma.don.na [mə'dɔnə] *n.* Meryem Ana, Hazreti Meryem; Meryem Ana resmi *veya* heykeli; ~ li.ly ♀ beyaz zambak.

mad.ri.gal ♪ ['mædrigəl] *n.* çalgı eşliği olmadan söylenen çok sesli yarı şarkı.

mad.wom.an ['mædwumən] *n.* deli, çılgın, mecnun (*kadın*).

mael.strom ['meilstrəum] *n.* girdap.

ma.es.tro ['maistrəu] *n.* usta, üstat (*esp. virtüöz, mayestro, orkestra şefi*).

maf.fick ['mæfik] *v/i.* çılgınca eğlenmek.

mag.a.zine [mægə'zi:n] *n.* dergi, mecmua;

ambar, depo, kiler; ✕ cephanelik; şarjör.

**mag.da.len** ['mægdəlin] *n.* tövbekâr kimse.

**ma.gen.ta** ⚕ [mə'dʒentə] *n.* parlak koyu kırmızı boya.

**mag.got** ['mægət] *n.* kurt, sürfe; *fig.* kuruntu; **'mag.got.y** *adj.* kurtlu; kaprisli, şımarık.

**Ma.gi** ['meidʒai] *n. pl.* gördükleri yıldız aracılığı ile Hazreti İsa'yı ziyaret eden ve ona hediye sunan üç müneccim.

**mag.ic** ['mædʒik] 1. *a.* **'mag.i.cal** □ sihirli, büyülü..., cazip; 2. *n.* sihirbazlık, büyücülük; *fig.* sihir, büyü; **ma.gi.cian** [mə'dʒiʃən] *n.* sihirbaz, büyücü; **mag.ic lan.tern** projektör.

**mag.is.te.ri.al** □ [mædʒis'triəriəl] hükümeti ilgilendiren; devletçe, hükümetçe, resmî; yetkili, otoriter; *b.s.* âmirane, sert; **mag.is.tra.cy** ['ˌtrəsi] *n.* hâkimlik, yargıçlık; yargıçlar; **mag.is.trate** ['ˌtreit] *n.* sulh yargıcı.

**mag.na.nim.i.ty** [mægnə'nimiti] *n.* yüce gönüllülük; **mag.nan.i.mous** □ [ˌ'næniməs] yüce gönüllü, âlicenap.

**mag.nate** ['mægneit] *n.* patron, sermayedar, kodaman.

**mag.ne.sia** ⚕ [mæg'niːʃə] *n.* magnezyum oksit, manyezi; **mag'ne.si.um** ⚕ [ˌ'zjəm] *n.* magnezyum.

**mag.net** ['mægnit] *n.* mıknatıs; **mag.net.ic** [ˌ'netik] *adj.* (ˌ'ally) manyetik, mıknatısla çekilen; ˌ tape teyp bandı; **mag.net.ism** [ˌ'nitizəm] *n.* manyetizma; **mag.net.i.za.tion** [ˌnitai'zeiʃən] *n.* mıknatıslama; **'mag.net.ize** *v/t.* manyetize etm., mıknatıslamak; *fig.* cezbetmek, çekmek; **'mag.net.iz.er** *n.* manyetizmacı; **mag.ne.to** [mæg'niːtəu] *n. mot.* manyeto.

**mag.nif.i.cat** *eccl.* [mæg'nifikæt] *n.* Meryem Ana'nın Tanrı'ya övgü sunma ilâhisi; *fig.* methiye, övgü.

**mag.nif.i.cence** [mæg'nifisns] *n.* azamet, ihtişam, görkem; **mag'nif.i.cent** *adj.* muhteşem, görkemli; fevkalâde, harika; **mag.ni.fi.er** ['ˌfaiə] *n.* büyük gösteren şey, büyüteç; **'mag.ni.fy** *v/t.* büyütmek (*a. fig.*); ˌing glass büyüteç, pertavsız; **mag.nil.o.quence** [mæg'niləukwəns] *n.* tantanalı söz söyleme; **mag'nil.o.quent** *adj.* şatafatlı, abartmalı (*söz*); **mag.ni.tude** ['ˌtjuːd] *n.* büyüklük; önem, ehemmiyet; star of the first ˌ birinci kadirden olan yıldız.

**mag.no.lia** ⚘ [mæg'nəuljə] *n.* manolya.

**mag.pie** *orn.* ['mægpai] *n.* saksağan; *fig.* geveze kimse.

**Magyar** ['mægjɑː] *n. & adj.* Macar; Macarca.

**mahl.stick** *paint.* ['mɔːlstik] *n.* ressamın çalışırken fırçayı tutan elini dayadığı değnek.

**ma.hog.a.ny** [mə'hɔgəni] *n.* mahun, maun; kırmızımsı kahverengi.

**maid** [meid] *n. lit.* kız; † kız oğlan kız, bakire; kadın hizmetçi; old ˌ gençliği geçmiş kız, kız kurusu; ˌ of hono(u)r kraliçe *veya* prenses nedimesi; bir tür küçük kek.

**maid.en** ['meidn] 1. *prov. veya co.* = maid; 2. *adj.* evlenmemiş; el değmemiş, bakir; *fig.* ilk...; ˌ name kızlık adı, evli kadının bekârlık soyadı; ˌ speech (*milletvekili tarafından parlamentoda yapılan*) ilk konuşma; 'ˌhair *n.* ⚘ baldırıkara; 'ˌhead *n.* bikir; 'ˌhood *n.* kızlık, bakirelik, erdenlik; 'ˌlike, 'maid.en.ly *adj.* genç kız gibi; mahçup, iffetli.

**maid-of-all-work** ['meidəvˌɔːlwɔːk] *n.* her işe bakan hizmetçi.kız; **'maid.serv.ant** *n.* kız hizmetçi.

**mail¹** *hist.* [meil] *n.* zırh.

**mail²** [ˌ] 1. *n.* posta arabası; posta; 2. *v/t. part. Am.* postaya vermek, posta ile göndermek; **'mail.a.ble** *adj. Am.* posta ile gönderilebilir.

**mail...:** 'ˌbag *n.* posta torbası; 'ˌbox *n. part. Am.* mektup kutusu; ˌ car.ri.er *Am.* postacı; 'ˌman *n. part. Am.* postacı; 'ˌor.der firm, *part. Am.* 'ˌor.der house posta ile sipariş alan mağaza; 'ˌtrain *n.* posta treni.

**maim** [meim] *v/t.* sakatlamak, sakat etm. ˌi.

**main** [mein] 1. *adj.* asıl, esas, başlıca..., ana...; ˌ chance kişisel çıkar; ˌ station *teleph.* esas irtibat hattı, santral; by ˌ force var gücüyle, kuvvetle; ˌ plane unit ✈ ana uçak ünitesi, uçak kanadı; 2. *n.* güç, kuvvet; ana su boru hattı; *poet.* derya, açık deniz; ˌs *pl.* ≠ şebeke; ˌs aerial ışık ağlı anten; in the ˌ çoğu, ekseriyetle; *s.* might 1; 'ˌland *n.* (ana)kara; 'main.ly *adv.* başlıca, esasen.

**main...:** 'ˌmast ['ˌmɑːst, ↓ 'ˌməst] *n.* ana gemi direği; 'ˌsail ['ˌseil, ↓ 'ˌsl] *n.* mayıstra yelkeni; 'ˌspring *n.* ana yay, büyük zemberek; *fig.* asıl neden; 'ˌstay *n.* ↓ grandi çanaklarını pruva direğinin altına bağlayan payanda; *fig.* direk, başlıca dayanak; ≗ Street *Am.* kasabanın çarşısındaki cadde; taşra gelenekleri.

**main.tain** [mein'tein] *v/t.* sürdürmek; korumak, muhafaza etm.; bakmak, beslemek, geçindirmek; iddia etm.; ~ that öyle olduğunu iddia etm. ; **main¹tain.a.ble** *adj.* tutulabilir; müdafaası mümkün; **main¹tain.er** *n.* gözeten (*veya* koruyan, destekleyen) kimse.

**main.te.nance** [¹meintənəns] *n.* bakım; müdafaa; muhafaza; iddia; nafaka.

**main.top** ↓ [¹meintɔp] *n.* grandi çanaklığı.

**mai.son.(n)ette** [meizə¹net] *n.* küçük daire *veya* ev; dublex daire.

**maize** ⚜ [meiz] *n.* mısır, darı.

**ma.jes.tic** [mə¹dʒestik] *adj.* (~ally) muhteşem, heybetli, şahane; **maj.es.ty** [¹mædʒisti] *n.* heybet, haşmet, azamet.

**ma.jor** [¹meidʒə] 1. *adj.* daha büyük, daha önemli; iri; başlıca, asıl; ♩ majör; A ~ Do majör; ~ third tiyers majör; ~ key majör perdesi; ~ league *Am. beysbol:* en büyük iki ligden biri; 2. *n.* binbaşı; reşit olan kimse; *phls.* büyük terim, önerme; *Am. univ.* ana ders; 3. *v/i. Am.* üniversite öğrenimini belirli bir konuda yoğunlaştırmak, belirli bir konuyu izlemek; ¹~-¹gen.er.al *n.* tümgeneral; **ma.jor.i.ty** [mə¹dʒɔriti] *n.* çoğunluk, ekseriyet; erginlik, reşitlik; join the ~ çoğunluğa katılmak; ¹**ma.jor road** anayol.

**make** [meik] 1. (*irr.*) *v/t. com.* yapmak, yaratmak, meydana getirmek; teşkil etm.; sağlamak; kazanmak, elde etm.; yazmak (*şiir*); inşa etm.; hazırlamak, düzeltmek; karıştırmak (*oyun kâğıdı*); etmek, çıkarmak; atamak; yerine getirmek; koymak (*fiyat*); kapatmak (*devre*); zorlamak, yaptırmak; ulaşmak, varmak; olmak; girmek (*takıma*); dahil etm., içine almak; yakalamak, yetişmek; anlamak, kavramak; göstermek; katetmek, almak (*yol*); ~ believe that gibi görünmek, taklit etm.; ~ the best of it *bşden* en iyi biçimde yararlanmak; ~ capital out of *bşden* istifade etm., *bşi* istismar etm., kendi çıkarına kullanmak, kötüye kullanmak; ~ do with yetinmek *ile*, idare etm. *ile*; ~ good başarılı olm.; telâfi etm, karşılamak; refaha erişmek; ~ it F başarmak, kazanmak; zamanında varmak; ~ (the) land ↓ karayı görmek; ~ or mar s.o. *b-ni* ya yüceltmek ya da batırmak; do you ~ one of us? bize katılır mısınız?; ~ port ↓ limana uğramak; ~ shift idare etm., yetinmek (with *ile*); ~ way ilerlemek; ~ way for yol vermek *-e*.; ~ into dönüştürmek *-e*, çevirmek *-e*; ~ out yazmak; doldurmak; anlamak, çözmek, sökmek; görebilmek; iddia etm.; ~ over çevirmek, dönüştürmek, de-

ğiştirmek; devretmek; ~ up uydurmak; teşkil etm., hazırlamak; telâfi etm., tamamlamak (for *-i*); ⚜ ödemek (*borç*); kapatmak, örtmek; dikmek (*elbise vs.*); toplamak, bir araya getirmek; düzenlemek; hazırlamak, meydana getirmek, oluşturmak; yapmak (*yatak vs.*); ~ up one's mind karar vermek (to *inf. -meğe*); 2. (*irr.*) *v/i.* davranmak, hareket etm.; yola koyulmak; yükselmek, kabarmak (*met*); ~ as if yapar gibi görünmek, ...miş gibi davranmak; ~ after peşinden gitmek *-in,* kovalamak *-i*; ~ against zarar vermek *-e*, zararı dokunmak *-e*; ~ at üstüne yürümek *-in,* atılmak; ~ away F tüymek, sıvışmak; ~ away with F öldürmek; yok etm.; çalmak, yürütmek; ~ for gitmek *-e,* yolunu tutmak *-in;* koşmak *-e,* üşüşmek *-e,* saldırmak *-e;* sağlamak *-i,* katkıda bulunmak *-e;* ~ off sıvışmak, tüymek; ~ up barışmak; makyaj yapmak; ~ up to s.o. *b-nin* gözüne girmeye çalışmak; 3. *n.* şekil; yapı, biçim; marka; verim, randıman; ♪ devrenin kapanması; of poor ~ düşük kaliteli; on the ~ *sl.* kendi çıkarı peşinde; cinsi münasebet peşinde; ¹~-be.lieve 1. *n.* yalandan yapma, taklit; hile, bahane; 2. *adj.* sahte, samimiyetsiz; ¹**mak.er** *n.* yapan, fabrikatör; ♀ Allah, Tanrı.

**make...:** ¹~.shift 1. *n.* eğreti tedbir, geçici çare; 2. *adj.* eğreti, geçici...; ¹~-up *n.* mizanpaj, tertip; makyaj; fig. mizaç, tabiat; ¹~.weight *n.* tartı tam gelsin diye eklenen ağırlık; *fig.* bir açığı dolduran önemsiz kimse *veya* şey.

**mak.ing** [¹meikin] *n.* başarı nedeni; yapma, etme; ~s *pl.* F nitelikler; in the ~ yapılırken; yapılmakta; that was the ~ of him başarılı olmasının nedeni o oldu; have the ~s of ...olmak için gerekli niteliklere sahip olm.

**mal.a.chite** *min.* [¹mæləkait] *n.* bakırtaşı, malakit.

**mal.ad.just.ed** *psych.* [¹mælə¹dʒʌstid] *adj.* k-ni çevreye, topluma uyduramayan, uyumsuz; ¹**mal.ad¹just.ment** *n.* uyumsuzluk.

**mal.ad.min.is.tra.tion** [¹mælədminis¹treiʃən] *n.* kötü yönetim, idare.

**mal.a.droit** [¹mælə¹drɔit] *adj.* beceriksiz, sakar.

**mal.a.dy** [¹mælədi] *n.* hastalık, dert.

**ma.laise** [mæ¹leiz] *n.* huzursuzluk, rahatsızlık.

**mal.a.prop.ism** [¹mæləprɔpizəm] *n.* sözcükleri yanlış yerde kullanma; **mal.a.pro.pos** [¹~¹æprəpəu] 1. *adj.* uygunsuz, münasebetsiz; **2.** *adv.* uygunsuzca, münasebetsizce; **3.** *n.* münasebetsizlik, yakışıksızlık, yersizlik, vakitsizlik.

**ma.lar.i.a** 🌡 [mə'lɛəriə] *n.* sıtma; **ma'lar.i-al** *adj.* sıtmalı, malarya...

**Ma.lay** [mə'lei] **1.** *n.* Malaya dili; Malayalı; **2.** *adj.* Malaya'ya *veya* halkına ait.

**mal.con.tent** ['mælkəntent] **1.** *adj.* memnun olmayan, hoşnutsuz; **2.** *n.* tatmin olmayan kimse.

**male** [meil] **1.** *adj.* erkek, erkekçe; ~ child erkek çocuk; ~ screw vida; **2.** *n.* erkek.

**mal.e.dic.tion** [mæli'dikʃən] *n.* lânet, kargış, beddua; iftira.

**mal.e.fac.tor** ['mælifæktə] *n.* suçlu (*veya* kötülük eden) kimse.

**ma.lef.i.cence** [mə'lefisns] *n.* kötülük; **ma'lef.i.cent** *adj.* kötü, başkalarına zarar veren.

**ma.lev.o.lence** [mə'levələns] *n.* kötü niyet; **ma'lev.o.lent** ☐ kötü niyetli, hain.

**mal.for.ma.tion** ['mælfɔ:'meiʃən] *n.* sakatlık, kusurlu oluşum.

**mal.ice** ['mælis] *n.* garaz, kötü niyet; muziplik; ⚖ suiniyet, suç işleme kastı.

**ma.li.cious** ☐ [mə'liʃəs] kötü niyetli, garazkâr; muzip; ⚖ kasten, taammüden; **ma'li.cious.ness** *n.* kötü niyetlilik, kötülük.

**ma.lign** [mə'lain] **1.** ☐ zararlı; 🌡 habis, kötü, ağır; **2.** *v/t.* iftira etm.; **ma.lig.nan-cy** [mə'lignənsi] *n.* habislik; 🌡 habis tümör; **ma'lig.nant 1.** ☐ kötü yürekli, garazkâr, kötücül; 🌡 habis (*tümör*); **2.** *n.* kötü niyet; **ma'lig.ni.ty** *n.* kötülükçülük; şiddetli nefret; *part.* 🌡 habaset, kötülük.

**ma.lin.ger** [mə'lingə] *v/i.* hasta pozu yapmak, *k-ni* hasta gibi göstermek; **ma'lin-ger.er** *n.* hasta pozu yaparak görevden kaçan kimse.

**mall** [mɔ:l] *n.* gezinti yolu.

**mal.lard** *orn.* ['mæləd] *n.* bir tür yaban ördeği.

**mal.le.a.ble** ['mæliəbl] *adj.* dövülür (*metal*); *fig.* uysal, yumuşak huylu.

**mal.let** ['mælit] *n.* lastik *veya* tahta başlı çekiç; *spor:* (*kriket, polo*) sopa.

**mal.low** 🌿 ['mæləu] *n.* ebegümeci.

**malm.sey** ['mɑ:mzi] *n.* tatlı şarap.

**mal.nu.tri.tion** [mælnju:'triʃən] *n.* gıdasızlık, yetersiz *veya* kötü beslenme.

**mal.o.dor.ous** ☐ [mæ'ləudərəs] kötü kokulu.

**mal.prac.tice** ['mæl'præktis] *n.* yolsuzluk, 🌡 yanlış tedavi; ⚖ görevi kötüye kullanma, görevde ihmal *veya* suiistimal.

**malt** [mɔ:lt] **1.** *n.* bira yapılan çimlendirilmiş arpa, malt; ~ liquor malttan ma-

yalanma ile yapılan içki, *part.* bira; **2.** *vb.* arpa *veya* başka tahıldan malt yapmak.

**Mal.tese** ['mɔ:l'ti:z] **1.** *adj.* Maltız; Malta dili; **2.** *n.* Maltalı, Maltız.

**mal.treat** [mæl'tri:t] *v/t.* kötü davranmak -*e*, eziyet etm. -*e*; **mal'treat.ment** *n.* kötü davranma.

**malt.ster** ['mɔ:ltstə] *n.* malt imalâtçısı.

**mal.ver.sa.tion** [mælvə'seiʃən] *n.* rüşvet yeme, suiistimal, zimmete para geçirme.

**ma.ma, mam.ma** [mə'mɑ:] *n.* anne.

**mam.mal** ['mæməl] *n.* memeli hayvan; **mam.ma.li.an** [mə'meiljən] *adj.* memeli hayvanla ilgili, memeli hayvan...

**mam.mon** ['mæmən] *n.* hırs ve ihtirasın esiri olan servet.

**mam.moth** ['mæməθ] **1.** *n. zo.* mamut; **2.** *adj.* dev gibi, iri.

**mam.my** F ['mæmi] *n.* anne; *Am.* zenci sütnine, Arap dadı.

**man** [mæn, mən] **1.** *n., pl.* **men** [men] erkek, adam; er, asker; insan; uşak; erkek işçi; koca; satranç *veya* dama taşı; şahıs, kişi; to a ~, to the last ~ son kişiye kadar, hepsi birden; ~ on leave ✗ izinli er; be one's own ~ dilediğince hareket edebilmek, özgür olm.; **2.** *vb.* ✗, ⚓ (*kadro, kuvvet, tayfa*) koymak -*e*; ~ o.s. cesaretlenmek.

**man.a.cle** ['mænəkl] **1.** *n.* kelepçe; **2.** *v/t.* kelepçelemek, kelepçe takmak.

**man.age** ['mænidʒ] *v/t.* kullanmak; becermek; yönetmek, idare etm., çekip çevirmek (*ticarethane vs.*); terbiye etm. (*hayvan*); -*in* yolunu bulmak; ~ to *inf.* -*meği* başarmak; *v/i.* müdür olm.; *bşle* geçinmek, yet(iş)mek; işini uydurmak, işin içinden sıyrılmak; **'man.age.a.ble** ☐ idare edilebilir; kullanışlı; **'man.age.ment** *n.* idare, yönetim; müdürlük; yönetim kurulu; **'man.ag.er** *n.* müdür, direktör, yönetmen, idareci, yönetici; good (bad) ~ iyi (kötü) yönetici, idareci; **'man.ag.er-ess** *n.* müdire, kadın direktör, kadın yönetici; **man.a.ge.ri.al** ☐ [~ə'dʒiəriəl] yönetimsel, idari...

**man.ag.ing** ['mænidʒin] *adj.* idareci, yöneten; sevk..., idari...; ~ clerk büro şefi.

**man-at-arms** ['mænət'ɑ:mz] *n.* † asker, zırhlı süvari neferi.

**Man.ches.ter** ['mæntʃistə] *n.:* ~ goods *pl.* pamuklu mensucat.

**Man.chu** [mæn'tʃu:], **Man.chu.ri.an** [~'tʃuəriən] **1.** *adj.* Mançulara *veya* dillerine ait; **2.** *n.* Mançuryalı, Mançu; Mançurya dili.

**man.da.mus** ⚖ [mænˈdeiməs] *n.* daha yüksek bir mahkemeden alt mahkemeye verilen yazılı emir.
**man.da.rin** [ˈmændərin] *n.* mandalina likörü; mandalina rengi; F tutucu ve eyyamcı politikacı; *a.* **ˈman.da.rine** *n.* ⚘ mandalina.
**man.da.tar.y** ⚖ [ˈmændətəri] *n.* vekil, temsilci; **man.date** [ˈ~deit] **1.** *n.* manda, bir ulusun diğer bir ulus üzerindeki egemenliği; ferman, emir; vekillik; **2.** *v/t.* egemenlik altına almak *-i*; **manˈda.tor** *n.* müvekkil; **man.da.to.ry** [ˈ~dətəri] **1.** *adj.* emredici; *Am.* zorunlu, gerekli; **2.** *n.* vekil; mandater.
**man.di.ble** *anat.* [ˈmændibl] *n.* çene kemiği, alt çene.
**man.do.lin** ♪ [ˈmændəlin] *n.* mandolin.
**man.drag.o.ra** [mænˈdrægərə], **man.drake** ⚘ [ˈ~dreik] *n.* muhabbetotu, kankurutan, adamotu.
**man.drel** ⊕ [ˈmændril] *n.* toka dili, mil, mandrel.
**man.drill** *zo.* [~] *n.* bir tür iri ve yırtıcı maymun.
**mane** [mein] *n.* yele; **maned** *adj.* yeleli.
**man-eat.er** [ˈmæniːtə] *n.* yamyam; insan eti yiyen hayvan.
**ma.nes** [ˈmɑːneiz] *n. pl.* ölmüş kişilerin ruhları.
**ma.neu.ver** [məˈnuːvə] = manoeuvre.
**man.ful** □ [ˈmænful] erkekçe, mert; **ˈman.ful.ness** *n.* mertlik, yiğitlik.
**man.ga.nese** ⚗ [mæŋgəˈniːz] *n.* manganez; **man.gan.ic** [~ˈgænik] *adj.* manganez...; manganez türünden.
**mange** *vet.* [meindʒ] *n.* uyuz hastalığı.
**man.ger** [ˈmeindʒə] *n.* yemlik; dog in the ~ F *k-ne* yararı olmayan *bşden* başkasının yararlanmasını istemeyen kimse.
**man.gle**[1] [ˈmæŋgl] **1.** *n.* sıkma makinesi; ütü cenderesi; **2.** *v/t.* cendereden geçirmek, silindirli makine ile ütülemek.
**man.gle**[2] [~] *v/t.* vurarak ezmek, parçalamak, yırtmak; *fig.* sakatlamak; **ˈman.gler** *n.* iki silindirli ütü makinesi.
**man.go** ⚘ [ˈmæŋgəu] *n.* Hint kirazı, mango.
**man.grove** ⚘ [ˈmæŋgrəuv] *n.* tropikal bölgelerde yetişen bir bitki türü.
**man.gy** [ˈmeindʒi] *adj.* uyuz; yırtık pırtık; âdi, bayağı.
**man...:** **ˈ~-han.dle** *v/t. bşi* insan gücüyle hareket ettirmek; kabaca itmek; *sl.* itip kakmak; **ˈ~-hat.er** *n.* insanlardan kaçan kimse; **ˈ~.hole** *n.* ⊕ baca, yeraltında boru, kablo yapmak için caddelerdeki üstü kapaklı delik; **ˈ~.hood** *n.* erkeklik; mertlik; insanlık; **ˈ~-ˈhour** *n.* bir saatlik çalışma.
**ma.ni.a** [ˈmeinjə] *n.* tutku, mani, manya; delilik, cinnet, çılgınlık; **ma.ni.ac** [ˈ~niæk] **1.** *n.* manyak, çılgın; **2.** *a.* **ma.ni.a.cal** □ [məˈnaiəkəl] çılgın, deli.
**man.i.cure** [ˈmænikjuə] **1.** *n.* el ve tırnak tuvaleti, manikür; **2.** *v/t.* manikür yapmak; **ˈ~-case** *n.* manikür kutusu; **man.i.cur.ist** [ˈ~rist] *n.* manikürcü.
**man.i.fest** [ˈmænifest] **1.** □ belli, açık, anlaşılır; **2.** *n.* ⚓ manifesto, gümrük beyannamesi; **3.** *v/t.* açıkça göstermek, belirtmek, ortaya koymak; işaret etm.; eliyle *b-ni, bşi* göstermek; beyan etm., bildirmek; *v/i. k-ni* göstermek, belli etm.; **man.i.fesˈta.tion** *n.* gösteri, izhar; **man.iˈfes.to** [~təu] *n.* bildiri, beyanname.
**mani.fold** [ˈmænifəuld] **1.** □ türlü türlü, çok; **2.** *v/t.* teksir etm., çoğaltmak; **3.** *n.* ⊕ birçok giriş ve çıkışı olan ana boru, kollektör; intake ~ *mot.* ana emme borusu; ~ **writ.er** teksir makinesi.
**man.i.kin** [ˈmænikin] *n.* ufak adam, cüce; manken, insan şekli.
**Ma.nil.(l)a** [məˈnilə] *n. a.* ~ cheroot Manila purosu; *a.* ~ hemp kenevir muzu; Manila keneviri; ~ paper Manila kenevirinden yapılan bir cins ambalaj kağıdı.
**ma.nip.u.late** [məˈnipjuleit] *v/t.* becermek; beceriyle kullanmak, idare etm.; hünerle kullanmak; el ile idare etm., işletmek; *bşe* hile karıştırmak; *b-ni, k-nin* çıkarı için kullanmak, dalavere yapmak; **ma.nip.uˈla.tion** *n.* el ile işletme, beceriyle kullanma; suiistimal, hile, dalavere; **maˈnip.u.la.tive** [~lətiv] *adj.* el ile işletilebilir; dalavereci; **maˈnip.u.la.tor** [~leitə] *n.* yöneten kimse; *phys.* manipülatör; maniple.
**man.kind** [mænˈkaind] *n.* insanlık, beşeriyet; [ˈ~] erkekler; **ˈman.like** = manly; mannish; **ˈman.li.ness** *n.* mertlik, yiğitlik; **ˈman.ly** *adj.* mert, yiğit, erkekçe.
**man.na** [ˈmænə] *n.* kudret helvası.
**manned** [mænd] *adj.* içinde insan bulunan, insanlı...
**man.ne.quin** [ˈmænikin] *n.* manken; ~ parade defile.
**man.ner** [ˈmænə] *n.* tavır, yol, usül (*a. lit.*): *paint.* çeşit, stil; ~s *pl.* terbiye, görgü; üslûp; no ~ of doubt hiç şüphe yok; in a ~ belli bir düzeyde, bir bakıma, bir anlamda; in such a ~ that o derece ki, şöyle ki; **ˈman.nered** *adj.* yapma tavırlı, ... tavırlı; **ˈman.ner.ism** *n.* yapmacık; *(sanatçıya ait)* özellik; **ˈman.ner.li.ness** *n.*

görgülülük, nezaket; **'man.ner.ly 1.** *adj.* terbiyeli; **2.** *adv.* nazikçe.

**man.nish** ['mæniʃ] *adj.* erkeksi, erkek gibi *(esp.·kadın)*; erkeğe yakışır.

**ma.noeu.vra.ble,** *Am. a.* **ma.neu.ver.a.ble** [məˈnuːvrəbl] *adj.* manevralı, manevra yeteneği olan; **ma'noeu.vre,** *Am. a.* **ma-'neu.ver** [~vɔ]**1.** *n.* manevra *(a. fig.)*; **~s** *pl.* F *fig.* bahane, kaçamaklı söz, ağız yapma, hile, dolap; **2.** *vb.* manevra yapmak; sokmak (into **-e**); tedbir almak; dolap çevirmek.

**man-of-war** ['mænɔvˈwɔː] *n.* savaş gemisi.

**ma.nom.e.ter** *phys.,* ⊕ [məˈnɔmitə] *n.* manometre, basıölçer.

**man.or** ['mænə] *n.* tımar; malikâne; lord of the **~** derebeyi; malikâne sahibi; **'~-house** *n.* şato; **ma.no.ri.al** [məˈnɔːriəl] *adj.* malikâneye ait, malikâne...

**man.pow.er** ['mænpauə] *n.* el emeği, insan gücü; işçi sayısı, personel; işgücü.

**manse** *Scots* [mæns] *n.* papaz konutu.

**man.serv.ant** ['mænsɔːvənt] *n.* erkek hizmetçi, uşak.

**man.sion** ['mænʃən] *n.* konak, büyük ve güzel ev; **~s** *pl.* evler bloku.

**man.slaugh.ter** ['mænslɔːtə] *n.* tasarlamadan adam öldürme, kasıtsız adam öldürme.

**man.tel.piece** ['mæntlpiːs], **'man.tel.shelf** *n.* şömine rafı.

**man.til.la** [mæn'tilə] *n.* şal.

**man.tle** ['mæntl] **1.** *n.* kolsuz üstlük, harmani, pelerin; örtü *(a.* 4, *anat., zo.)*; *fig.* perde, örtü; *a.* incandescent **~** *(lamba)* lüks gömleği; **2.** *v/t.* üstünü örtmek; *fig.* örtbas etm., gizlemek; **~** on üstüne bşi örtmek, yaymak; *v/i.* kızarmak *(yüz)*; **~** with bşle kapla(n)mak.

**man.trap** ['mæntræp] *n.* tuzak.

**man.u.al** ['mænjuəl] **1.** □ ele ait, el ile yapılan...; **~** exercises *pl.* X tüfek talimi; **~** training elişi eğitimi; **2.** *n.* elkitabı, talimname; *(org)* klavye, tuş düzeni.

**man.u.fac.to.ry** [mænjuˈfæktəri] *n.* fabrika, yapımevi.

**man.u.fac.ture** [mænjuˈfæktʃə] **1.** *n.* imal, yapım; yapılmış şeyler, mamulât; **2.** *v/t.* imal etm., yapmak; *fig.* uydurmak; **~d** goods *pl.* fabrika mamulâtı; **man.u'fac.tur.er** *n.* fabrikatör; **man.u'fac.tur.ing** *n.* imalât; *attr.* imalât...

**ma.nure** [məˈnjuə] **1.** *n.* gübre; **2.** *v/t.* gübrelemek.

**man.u.script** ['mænjuskript] **1.** *n.* el yazması; müsvedde; yazma; **2.** *adj.* elle yazılı.

**Manx** [mæŋks] **1.** *adj.* Man adasına mensup; **2.** *n.* Man adası halkı.

**man.y** ['meni] **1.** *adj.* çok, birçok; **~** a sayıca çok; **~** a one birçoğu; as **~** as ...kadar çok; one too **~** gereğinden bir fazla; lüzumundan fazla, fuzuli; be one too **~** for s.o. *b-den* daha kurnazca davranmak; *b-ni* yenecek kadar akıllı olm.; **2.** *n.* bir çoğu; a great **~,** a good **~** hayli, pek çok, büyük sayıda; **'~-'sid.ed** *adj.* çok taraflı, çok cepheli.

**map** [mæp] **1.** *n.* harita; off the **~** F ortadan kaybolmuş; on the **~** F önemli; **2.** *v/t.* *bşin* haritasını yapmak; not etm., kaydetmek, geçirmek; **~** out ayrıntılarıyle planlamak, düzenlemek.

**ma.ple** ♀ ['meipl] *n.* akçaağaç.

**map.per** ['mæpə] *n.* harita ve plan yapan *veya* çizen kimse, haritacı.

**ma.quis** ['mækiː] *n. II.* Dünya savaşında Nazilere direnen Fransız örgütü.

**mar** [maː] *v/t.* zarar vermek, halel getirmek, bozmak, ihlâl etm.

**mar.a.bou** *orn.* ['mærəbuː] *n.* büyük Güney Afrika leyleği.

**mar.a.schi.no** [mærəˈskiːnəu] *n.* siyah kirazdan yapılan tatlı likör.

**mar.a.thon** ['mærəθən] *n. a.* **~** race uzun yol koşusu, maraton.

**ma.raud** [məˈrɔːd] *vb.* çapulculuk etm.; **ma'raud.er** *n.* yağmacı, çapulcu.

**mar.ble** ['maːbl] **1.** *n.* mermer; mermerden yapılmış eser; bilya, zıpzıp; **2.** *adj.* mermerden yapılı; *fig.* katı yürekli, hissiz, merhametsiz; **3.** *v/t.* ebrulamak, harelemek.

**mar.cel** [maːˈsel] **1.** *n. a.* **~** wave perma *(saç)*; **2.** *v/t.* perma yapmak *(saç)*.

**March**[1] [maːtʃ] *n.* mart.

**march**[2] [~] **1.** *n.* yürüyüş; marş; ilerleme, terakki; ♪ marş; **~** past X geçit töreni; steal a **~** on s.o. daha çabuk davranarak *b-ne* karşı üstünlük kazanmak; **2.** *vb.* yürümek, yürüyüş yapmak; zorla yürütmek; *fig.* ilerlemek; **~** off X götürmek, posta etm.; **~** past önünden yürüyüp geçmek.

**march**[3] [~] **1.** *n. mst* **~es** *pl. hist.* hudut, sınır, hudut bölgesi; **2.** *vb.* hemhudut *(veya* sınırdaş) olm. (with **ile**).

**march.ing** ['maːtʃiŋ] **~** order askeri araçların dizilişi; **~** orders *pl.* askere verilen yürüyüşe başlama emri, yürüyüş emri; in heavy **~** order seferi.

**mar.chion.ess** ['maːʃənis] *n.* markiz.

**march.pane** ['maːtʃpein] *n.* acıbadem kurabiyesi.

**mare** [mɛə] *n.* kısrak; **~'s nest** *fig.* uydurma haber, değersiz *veya* uydurma buluş.

**mar.ga.rine** [maːdʒəˈriːn] *n.*, F *a.* **marge** [maːdʒ] margarin.

**mar.gin** [ˈmaːdʒin] *n.* kenar, ara, marj, sınır, hudut; hareket serbestliği; *a.* ~ of profit kâr marjı; ~ of safety güvenlik payı; **ˈmar.gin.al** □ kenarda olan; kenarda bulunan..., marjinal; ~ note çıkma, derkenar, haşiye.

**mar.grave** [ˈmaːgreiv] *n.* Roma İmparatorluğunda prenslere verilen bir ünvan; **mar.gra.vine** [ˈ~grəviːn] *n.* Roma İmparatorluğunda prens eşi.

**mar.gue.rite** ♀ [maːgəˈriːt] *n.* çayır papatyası, margrit.

**Ma.ri.a** [məˈraiə] *n:* Black ~ F cezaevi arabası.

**mar.i.gold** ♀ [ˈmærigəuld] *n.* kadife çiçeği.

**mar.i.jua.na** [mæriˈhwaːnə] *n.* haşiş.

**ma.ri.nade** [mæriˈneid] **1.** *n.* şarap, sirke, yağ ve baharat karışımı salamura; salamuraya yatırılmış et *veya* balık; **2.** = **ma.ri.nate** [ˈ~neit] *v/t.* salamuraya yatırmak.

**ma.rine** [məˈriːn] **1.** *adj.* denize ait, deniz..., okyanus...; deniz kuvvetlerine ait, bahriye...; gemi...; **2.** *n.* silahendaz; deniz kuvvetleri; denizcilik, bahriye; *paint.* deniz tablosu; tell that to the ~s! külahıma anlat!; **mar.i.ner** *poet.* *veya* ☾ [ˈmærinə] *n.* gemici, denizci, bahriyeli.

**mar.i.o.nette** [mæriəˈnet] *n.* kukla.

**mar.i.tal** □ [ˈmæritl] evliliğe ait; ~ status medeni hal.

**mar.i.time** [ˈmæritaim] *adj.* deniz(ciliğ)e ait; denize yakın; deniz..., sahil...; gemicilik...; ~ power donanması olan devlet.

**mar.jo.ram** ♀ [ˈmaːdʒərəm] *n.* mercanköşk.

**mark¹** [maːk] *n.* Alman parası, mark.

**mark²** [~] **1.** *n.* nişan, alâmet, marka, işaret; † etiketleme, damga; yara izi; yer, nokta, benek; şöhret; iz, eser, delil, emare; numune, örnek, norm, standart; *okul:* not, derece, numara; *spor:* başlama çizgisi; nişan, hedef; *vet.* damga; a man of ~ meşhur (*veya* önemli) adam; up to the ~ *fig.* istenilen düzeyde, derecede; hit the ~ hedefi bulmak, nişanı vurmak; miss the ~ hedefe isabet ettirememek; *fig.* konu dışı olm.; beside the ~, wide of the ~ doğru olmayan, yanlış; **2.** *v/t.* işaretlemek, markalamak, etiketlemek, nişan koymak, damgalamak; etiketlere işaret koymak *(fiyat)*; not vermek -*e*; beyan etm.; nazarı dikkate almak -*i*, hesaba katmak

-*i*, dikkat etm. -*e*; bşi zihinde tutmak; ~ down fiyat indirmek, azaltmak; bşi not etm., kaydetmek, yazmak; ~ off ayırmak, tecrit etm., hudutlarını çizmek *ile*; ~ out işaretlemek, -*in* sınırlarını çizmek; seçip ayırmak; ~ time X yerinde saymak *(a. fig.)*; **3.** *v/i.* bşe dikkat etm.; ~! dikkat!; **marked** *adj.* işaretlenmiş; göze çarpan; hissolunabilecek; belli, aşikâr, meydanda; **mark.ed.ly** [ˈmaːkidli] *adv.* belirgin bir şekilde; **ˈmark.er** *n.* bilardo: *esp.* sayıları işaret eden *b*-*i*; işaretleyen *veya* belli eden *bş.*

**mar.ket** [ˈmaːkit] **1.** *n.* pazar (yeri), çarşı (meydanı); alışveriş, ticaret; piyasa; sürüm, revaç; in the ~ piyasada; satın almaya hazır; come into the ~ piyasada satışa çıkmak; play the ~ *Am. sl.* borsada alışveriş yaparak para kazanmak; **2.** *v/t.* satışa çıkarmak, çarşıda *veya* piyasada satmak; *v/i.* alışveriş etm., satın almak; **ˈmar.ket.a.ble** □ † satılabilir, revaçlı, sürümlü; satılık; **mar.ket.eer** [~ˈtiə] *n.*: black ~ karaborsacı, karapazarcı; **ˈmar.ket-gar.den** *n.* bahçe, bostan; **ˈmar.ket.ing** *n.* pazarlama; alışveriş etme; **ˈmar.ket-place** *n.* çarşı (meydanı); **ˈmar.ket-town** *n.* pazarı olan kasaba; **ˈmar.ket-va!ue** *n.* piyasa rayici (*veya* değeri).

**mark.ing** [ˈmaːkiŋ] *n.* işaret, marka, etiket; nişan; **ˈ~-ink** *n.* (*çamaşırlarda markayı belirtmeye yarayan*) mürekkep.

**marks.man** [ˈmaːksmən] *n.* nişancı, atıcı; **ˈmarks.man.ship** *n.* atıcılık, nişancılık.

**marl** [maːl] **1.** *n. min.* marn, pekmez toprağı, kireçli toprak; **2.** *v/t.* ✔ kireçli toprakla gübrelemek.

**mar.ma.lade** [ˈmaːməleid] *n.* portakal marmelatı, reçel.

**mar.mo.re.al** □ *poet. & rhet.* [maːˈmoːriəl] mermer gibi beyaz, soğuk ve cilalı; mermerden yapılmış.

**mar.mot** *zo.* [ˈmaːmət] *n.* marmot, dağ sıçanı.

**ma.roon¹** [məˈruːn] *adj.* kestane renginde.

**ma.roon²** [~] *v/t.* terketmek, *b-ni* ıssız bir kıyıya çıkarıp bırakmak.

**ma.roon³** [~] *n.* uyarı sinyali niteliğinde kullanılan patlayıcı fişek.

**mar.plot** [ˈmaːplɔt] *n.* meclisbozan.

**mar.quee** [maːˈkiː] *n.* büyük çadır, otağ.

**mar.quess** *mst* **mar.quis** [ˈmaːkwis] *n.* marki.

**mar.que.try** [ˈmaːkitri] *n.* mobilyacılıkta kakma işi, marketri.

**mar.riage** [ˈmæridʒ] *n.* evlenme, izdivaç, nikâh, evlilik; evlilik hali; civil ~ mede-

marriageable

nî nikâh; by ~ evlenme suretiyle elde edilmiş; related by ~ sıhrî hısım; take in ~ evlenmek, almak; **¹mar.riage.a.ble** *adj.* evlenmeye ehil, gelinlik, evlenecek çağda.

**mar.riage...:** ~ **ar.ti.cles** *n. pl.* evlenme sözleşmesi; ~ **lines** *pl.* evlenme kâğıdı (*veya* cüzdanı); ~ **por.tion** drahoma, çeyiz.

**mar.ried** [¹mærid] *adj.* evliliğe ait; evli. evlilik...; ~ **couple** karıkoca.

**mar.row** [¹mærəu] *n.* ilik; *fig.* öz, esas, asıl; vegetable ~ ♀ sakızkabağı; **¹~.bone** *n.* ilikli kemik; **~s** *pl.co.* çapraz iki kemik; **¹mar.row.y** *adj.* ilik gibi, ilik dolu; özlü, kuvvetli.

**mar.ry** [¹mæri] *v/t. & v/i.* evlenmek (*a. fig.*) (s.o. *ile*); evlendirmek (s.o. to *-i ile*), nikâh kıymak; birleş(tir)mek; get married evlenmek.

**marsh** [mɑːʃ] *n.* batak(lık); *attr.* bataklık...; ~ **fever** bataklık humması, sıtma, malarya; ~ **gas** bataklıkta oluşan metan gazı.

**mar.shal** [¹mɑːʃəl] **1.** *n.* mareşal, müşür; *hist.* saray nazırı; protokol sorumlusu, şenlik görevlisi; *Am.* polis müdürü; **2.** *v/t.* sıralamak, tertip etm., tanzim etm., dizmek; sevketmek, yerleştirmek; **mar.shal.ling-yard** [¹~ʃliŋjɑːd] *n.* 🚂 manevra istasyonu.

**marsh mal.low** [¹mɑːʃmæləu] *n.* ♣ hatmi; hafif yuvarlak şekerleme; **marsh mar.i.gold** sarı çuhaçiçeği; **¹marsh.y** *adj.* bataklığa ait, bataklık gibi.

**mar.su.pi.al** *zo.* [mɑːˈsjuːpjəl] **1.** *adj.* keseli...; **2.** *n.* keseli hayvan.

**mart** [mɑːt] *n.* pazar(yeri); çarşı; ticaret merkezi.

**mar.ten** *zo.* [¹mɑːtin] *n.* zerdeva.

**mar.tial** □ [¹mɑːʃəl] harbe ait, savaşa özgü; askerî; savaşkan, savaşçı; ~ **law** örfi idare, sıkıyönetim; state of ~ law sıkıyönetim hali; ~ **music** askeri mızıka.

**Mar.tian** [¹mɑːtin] **1.** *n.* Merihli; **2.** *adj.* Mars..., Merih...

**mar.tin¹** [¹mɑːtin] *n.* kırlangıç.

**Mar.tin²** [~] *n.:* St. ~'s summer pastırma yazı.

**mar.ti.net** [mɑːtiˈnet] *n.* eziyetçi; katı (*veya* sert) kimse.

**mar.ti.ni** [mɑːˈtiːni] *n.* martini, cin ve vermut karışımı bir içki.

**Mar.tin.mas** [¹mɑːtinməs] *n.* 11 Kasım'da yapılan St. Martin günü.

**mar.tyr** [¹mɑːtə] **1.** *n.* şehit, bir amaç uğrunda ölen kimse; **2.** *v/t.* şehit etm.; işkence etm.; **¹mar.tyr.dom** *n.* şehitlik; **¹mar-**

**tyr.ize** *vb.* eziyet *veya* işkence etm.; şehit etm.; şehit olm.

**mar.vel** [¹mɑːvəl] **1.** *n.* mucize, harika; şaşkınlık; **2.** *vb.* hayret etm., şaşmak (at *-e*).

**mar.vel.(l)ous** □ [¹mɑːvələs] hayret verici; şaşılacak nitelikte; fevkalâde; **¹mar.vel.(l)ous.ness** *n.* acayiplik, gariplik.

**Marx.ian** [¹mɑːksjən] **1.** *n.* Marksizm taraftarı; **2.** *adj.* Marks'ın kuramına ait; **¹Marx.ism** *n.* Marksizm; **¹Marx.ist** = Marxian.

**mar.zi.pan** [mɑːziˈpæn] *n.* acıbadem kurabiyesi.

**mas.ca.ra** [mæsˈkɑːrə] *n.* kirpikleri koyulaştırmak için kullanılan madde, rimel, maskara.

**mas.cot** [¹mæskət] *n.* tılsım, muska, maskot, uğur bebeği.

**mas.cu.line** [¹mæskjulin] **1.** □ erkeğe ait; erkeksi; **2.** *n. gr.* eril, müzekker.

**mash** [mæʃ] **1.** *n.* lapa, karışım; biracılıkta kullanılan arpa ezgil ile su karışımı; ✓ ezme; **2.** *v/t.* ezmek; püre yapmak; ezilmiş arpayı su ile karıştırmak; *sl.* baştan çıkarmak, teshir etm.; **~ed** potatoes *pl.* patates ezmesi, patates püresi; be **~ed** on *sl. b-ne* asılmak; **¹mash.er** *n.* ezen *b-i veya* bş; *sl.* çapkın erkek; sahte âşık.

**mask** [mɑːsk] **1.** *n.* maske; yüz kalıbı; *s.* masque; **2.** *vb.* maske ile örtmek, maskelemek (*a. fig.*), gizlemek; maske takınmak, kılık değiştirmek; **masked** *adj.* gizli, belli olmayan; maskeli...; ~ **ball** maskeli balo; **¹mask.er** *n.* maske takan kimse.

**ma.so.chism** *psych.* [¹mæzəukizəm] *n.* mazoşizm.

**ma.son** [¹meisn] *n.* taşçı, duvarcı; ♀ (far)mason; **ma.son.ic** [məˈsɔnik] *adj.* mason *veya* farmasonluğa özgü; **ma.son.ry** [¹meisnri] *n.* duvarcılık; duvarcı işi; masonluk.

**masque** [mɑːsk] *n.* 16 ve 17. yüzyıllarda İngiltere'de maske giyilerek oynanan konuşmasız dram türünde yapıt; **mas.quer.ade** [mæskəˈreid] **1.** *n.* maskeli balo; maskeli balo giysisi; **2.** *v/i. fig.* maskelenmek, olduğundan değişik görünmek.

**mass¹** *eccl.* [mæs] *n.* kuddas âyini; High ♀ (Katoliklerde) kuddas; Low ♀ kuddas âyininin basit düzeni.

**mass²** [~] **1.** *n.* kütle, küme, yığın; çokluk; the **~es** *pl.* halk kütlesi, avam takımı; in the ~ bütün olarak; **2.** *vb.* yığın olarak topla(n)mak.

**mas.sa.cre** [¹mæsəkə] **1.** *n.* katliam, kırım; **2.** *v/t.* katletmek, kırıp geçirmek.

**mas.sage** ['mæsɑːʒ] **1.** *n.* masaj, ovma; **2.** *v/t.* masaj yapmak, ovmak.

**mass com.mu.ni.ca.tions** ['mæskəmjuːni-ıkeiʃənz] *n. pl.* = mass media.

**mas.seur** [mæˈsəː] *n.* masajcı, masör; **mas.seuse** [mæˈsəːz] *n.* kadın masajcı.

**mas.sif** ['mæsiːf] *n.* dağ kitlesi.

**mas.sive** □ ['mæsiv] som, masif, kütle halinde; ağır; esaslı, derin; kuvvetli, kudretli; ı**mas.sive.ness** *n.* irilik, ağırlık.

**mass...: ~** me.di.a *pl.* kitle iletişim; **~ meet-ing** halka açık toplantı; **ı~-pro.duce** *vb.* seri halde üretmek; **~ pro.duc.tion** seri üretim.

**mas.sy** ['mæsi] *adj.* cüsseli, iri yapılı; ağır; sağlam, dayanıklı.

**mast¹** ⤵ [mɑːst] **1.** *n.* gemi direği; **2.** *v/t.* direk dikmek.

**mast²** [~] *n.* (*domuzlar için*) palamut, kayın kozalağı, kestane gibi ağaç yemişi.

**mas.ter** ['mɑːstə] **1.** *n.* üstat, usta (*a. fig.*); efendi (*a. fig.*); sahip, patron, âmir; erkek öğretmen; kaptan, süvari; dinî lider; *univ.* rektör; 2 of Arts üniversite mezuniyeti ile doktora arasında bir derece; 2 of Ceremonies teşrifatçı, protokol görevlisi; be one's own ~ başına buyruk olm.; **2.** *adj. fig.* mümtaz, ileri gelen; baş, esas, temel, asıl; **3.** *v/t.* yenmek, hakkından gelmek; hükmetmek, idare etm.

**mas.ter-at-arms** ⤵ ['mɑːstərət'ɑːmz] *n.* güvenlik görevlisi; **mas.ter build.er** kalfa; mimar; **mas.ter.ful** □ ['ı~ful] zorba, gaddar; üstatça; ı**mas.ter-key** *n.* ana anahtar; ı**mas.ter.less** *adj.* sahipsiz; yönetimsiz; ı**mas.ter.ly** *adj.* ustaca, hünerli.

**mas.ter...: ~.piece** *n.* şaheser; harika; 'ı~.ship *n.* ustalık, üstatlık; şampiyonluk; yöneticilik, yönetim; *okul:* müdürlük; 'ı~-stroke *n.* maharetli iş, çok ustalıklı iş; ı**mas.ter.y** *n.* hüküm, hakimiyet, hükümdarlık, saltanat, otorite; üstünlük; üstün gelme; ustalık, üstatlık, şampiyonluk; maharet, hüner.

**mast-head** ['mɑːsthed] *n.* çanaklık, direk ucu.

**mas.tic** ['mæstik] *n.* macun; sakız rakısı, mastika.

**mas.ti.cate** ['mæstikeit] *vb.* çiğnemek; **mas.ti'ca.tion** *n.* çiğneme.

**mas.tiff** ['mæstif] *n.* avcılıkta ve gözetlemede kullanılan köpek, mastı.

**mas.to.don** *zo.* ['mæstədɔn] *n.* mamuta benzer fil.

**mas.toid** ♈ ['mæstɔid] *n.* kulak arkası kemiği.

**mat¹** [mæt] **1.** *n.* hasır; minder; paspas;

altlık; **2.** *vb.* hasır ile örtmek; keçeleş-(tir)mek; birbirine dolaşmak.

**mat²** ⊕ [~] *adj.* donuk, mat.

**match¹** [mætʃ] *n.* kibrit.

**match²** [~] **1.** *n.* oyun, maç, müsabaka, turnuva; evlenme, izdivaç; eş, benzer, denk *bş*; be a ~ for ...e denk olm., eş olm., ayak uydurabilmek; meet one's ~ rakibi ile karşılaşmak, üstesinden gelebileceği *b-ni* bulmak; **2.** *v/t.* uydurmak, intibak ettirmek; mukayese etm., kıyaslamak, karşılaştırmak (with *ile*); uymak, benzemek, denk olm. *-e*; well ~ed uygun, münasip, yerinde; *v/i.* uymak; ~ with birbirine yakışmak, birbirini tutmak.

**match-box** ['mætʃbɔks] *n.* kibrit kutusu.

**match.et** ['mætʃet] = machete.

**match.less** □ ['mætʃlis] eşsiz, emsalsiz, rakipsiz; ı**match.mak.er** *n.* çöpçatan.

**match.wood** ['mætʃwud] *n.* kibritlik odun, kıymık.

**mate¹** [meit] *vb.* satranç: mat etm.

**mate²** [~] **1.** *n.* arkadaş, dost; koca, eş, karı, zevce; çiftin erkek *veya* dişisi (*hayvan*); yardımcı, muavin; ⤵ ikinci kaptan; **2.** *v/t. & v/i.* evlen(dir)mek, çiftleş(tir)mek; eşlemek; ı**mate.less** *adj.* yalnız, tek.

**ma.ter** *sl.* ['meitə] *n.* anne.

**ma.te.ri.al** [məˈtiəriəl] **1.** □ maddi, cismani; bedeni, bedensel; esaslı, mühim, önemli, etkili (to *için*); **2.** *n.* malzeme, levazım, harç, materyel, madde, cevher, unsur; dokuma, kumaş; *coll. veya* ~s *pl.* levazım, malzeme; bileşik unsur; working ~ iptidai madde; writing ~s *pl.* yazı malzemesi; **ma'te.ri.al.ism** *n.* materyalizm, maddecilik; **ma'te.ri.al.ist** *n.* materyalist, maddeci; **ma.te.ri.al'is.tic** *adj.* (~ally) materyalist, maddeci; **ma.te.ri.al.i.za.tion** [~riəlaiˈzeiʃən] *n.* maddileş(tir)me, cisimlenme; **ma'te.ri.al.ize** *v/t. & v/i.* maddileş(tir)mek, gerçekleşmek; realize etm.

**ma.ter.nal** □ [məˈtəːnl] anaya mahsus, anneye yakışır; ana..., anne..., valide...; ana tarafından; **ma'ter.ni.ty** [~niti] *n.* analık, annelik; *mst* ~ hospital doğumevi; ~ dress hamile elbisesi.

**mat.ey** ['meiti] *adj.* teklifsiz, samimi, senli benli ,arkadaşça.

**math.e.mat.i.cal** □ [mæθiˈmætikəl] matematiksel; **math.e.ma.ti.cian** [~məˈtiʃən] *n.* matematikçi; **math.e.mat.ics** [~ˈmætiks] *n. mst sg.* matematik.

**maths** F [mæθs] = mathematics.

**mat.ie** ['meiti] *n.* ringa balığının küçüğü.

**mat.in** ['mætin] **1.** *adj. poet.* sabah..., sabahleyin; **2.** *n.* ~s *pl. eccl.* sabaha karşı yapılan ibadet; *poet. (kuşların)* sabah şarkısı.

**mat.i.née** ['mætinei] *n.* matine.

**ma.tri.arch** ['meitriɑːk] *n.* aile *(veya* kabile) reisi *(kadın);* **¹ma.tri.ar.chy** *n.* anaerki; **ma.tri.cide** ['-said] *n.* anasını öldürme; anasını öldüren kimse, ana katili. **ma.tric.u.late** [məˈtrikjuleit] *v/t. & v/i.* üniversiteye öğrenci olarak kaydedilmek; kaydetmek; **ma.tric.uˈla.tion** *n.* öğrenci kaydı.

**mat.ri.mo.ni.al** [mætriˈməunjəl] evliliğe ait, evlilik...; **mat.ri.mo.ny** ['-məni] *n.* evlilik hali, evlilik.

**ma.trix** ['meitriks] *n. fig.* bşe şekil veren *veya* onu geliştiren canlı kısım; *geol.* fosilin bulunduğu kaya parçası; ⊕ *a.* ['mætriks] matris, hurufat kalıbı.

**ma.tron** ['meitrən] *n.* ağırbaşlı orta yaşlı evli kadın; ana kadın; amir kadın, başhemşire; **¹ma.tron.ize** *v/t. b-ne* analık etm; **¹ma.tron.ly** *adj.* ana gibi; toplu, etine dolgun; *fig.* temkinli, ağırbaşlı, ciddi *(kadın).*

**mat.ter** ['mætə] **1.** *n.* madde, cevher, unsur; ⚕ cerahat, irin; şey; konu; içindekiler, muhteviyat; illet, neden; iş, mesele, meşguliyet; *typ.* dizilecek metin, müsvedde; *~s pl.* hal, ahval, şartlar, vaziyet, durum; *postal ~* posta ile gönderilen her şey; *printed ~* basma, matbua; *in the ~ of ...* bakımından, ...in hususunda, *-e* gelince; *what's the ~?* ne var?; *what's the ~ with you?* neyiniz var?; *no ~* mühim değil, zararı yok; *no ~ who* her kim olursa olsun; *~ of course* kendiliğinden anlaşılan bş, doğal bş., işin tabii gidişi; *as a ~ of course* doğal olarak; *for that ~,* for the *~ of that* ona gelince, hatta; *~ of fact* hakikat, realite, gerçek; *as a ~ of fact* işin doğrusu, gerçekte, zaten; *~ in hand* söz konusu mevzu; *that is a hanging ~* cezasını kellen ile ödeyebilirsin, hayatına malolur; *no laughing ~* şakaya gelmez; **2.** *v/i.* ehemmiyeti olm., önemi olm. (*to için);* cerahatlenmek; *it does not ~* önemi yok, farketmez; **¹-ˈ-of-¹course** *adj.* doğal; **¹-ˈ-of-¹fact** *adj.* fiilî, hakiki, gerçek; soğukkanlı, sakin, heyecansız.

**mat.ting** ['mætiŋ] *n.* hasır (örme).

**mat.tock** ['mætək] *n.* kazma.

**mat.tress** ['mætris] *n.* döşek, şilte.

**ma.ture** [məˈtjuə] **1.** ⬜ olgun, ergin; reşit; dıkkatli, ölçüp biçen; *~* vadesi gelmiş; **2.** *v/t. & v/i.* olgunlaş(tır)mak, kemale er(dir)mek; erginleşmek; *~* vade-

si gelmek; **ma¹tu.ri.ty** *n.* olgunluk, erginlik; *~* vade.

**ma.tu.ti.nal** ⬜ [mætjuːˈtainl] sabaha ait, sabah...; erken.

**maud.lin** ⬜ ['mɔːdlin] aşırı duygusal, aşırı duygulanan.

**maul** [mɔːl] *v/t.* dövmek, berelemek, ezmek, hırpalamak; *fig. b-ni* fena halde hırpalamak.

**maul.stick** *paint.* ['mɔːlstik] *n.* resim çizerken dayanılan değnek.

**maun.der** ['mɔːndə] *v/i.* anlaşılmaz şekilde konuşmak, mırıldanarak söylenmek; düzensiz hareket etm.

**Maun.dy Thurs.day** ['mɔːndiˈθɔːzdi] *n.* Paskalya öncesi Perşembe günü.

**mau.so.le.um** [mɔːsəˈliəm] *n.* türbe, mozole.

**mauve** [məuv] *n. & adj.* leylâk rengi.

**mav.er.ick** *Am.* ['mævərik] *n.* damgalanmamış dana; *pol. & fig.* disipline uymayan, tek başına hareket eden kimse.

**maw** [mɔː] *n. (hayvanlarda)* kursak, mide; ağız.

**mawk.ish** ⬜ ['mɔːkiʃ] tiksindirici; **¹mawk-ish.ness** *n.* tiksindiricilik.

**maw.worm** ['mɔːwəːm] *n.* bağırsak kurdu.

**max.il.lar.y** [mækˈsiləri] *adj.* çene kemiğine ait, çene kemiği...

**max.im** ['mæksim] *n.* vecize, ata(lar) sözü; kural; **max.i.mum** ['-məm] **1.** *n.* en yüksek derece, maksimum; **2.** *adj.* azami..., en çok...; *~ wages pl.* en yüksek ücret, tavan ücreti.

**May¹** [mei] *n.* mayıs (ayı); ♀ ♣ yabani akdiken.

**may²** [~] *v/aux. (irr.)* -edebilmek, muhtemel olm., -meğe izinli olm.

**may.be** ['meibiː] *adv.* belki, olabilir.

**may-bee.tle** *zo.* ['meibiːtl] *n.,* **¹may-bug** mayısböceği.

**May Day** ['meidei] *n.* bahar bayramı ve işçi bayramı olarak kutlanan gün.

**may.fly** *zo.* ['meiflai] *n.* mayıssineği.

**may.hap †** ['meihæp] *adv.* belki, ihtimal ki.

**may.on.naise** [meiəˈneiz] *n.* mayonez.

**may.or** [mɛə] *n.* belediye reisi *(veya* başkanı); **¹may.or.al** *adj.* belediye başkan(lığ)ına ait; **¹may.or.al.ty** *n.* belediye başkanlığı; **¹may.or.ess** *n.* belediye başkanının eşi; kadın belediye başkanı.

**may.pole** ['meipəul] *n.* bahar bayramında etrafında dansedilen çiçeklerle süslü direk.

**maze** [meiz] *n.* labirent; *fig. a.* karışıklık; *be ~d,* be in a *~* şaşkına dönmek, şaşkınlık içinde olm.; **¹ma.zy** ⬜ dolaşık,

darmadağın, karmakarışık, muğlak.
**Mc.Coy** *Am. sl* [mə'kɔi] *n.*: the real ~ gerçeği.
**me** [miː, mi] *pron.* beni; bana; F ben.
**mead¹** [miːd] *n.* mayalı bal ve sudan yapılan bir içki.
**mead²** *poet.* [~] = meadow.
**mead.ow** ['medəu] *n.* çayır, çimen; **'~-'saf.fron** *n.* ✣ güzçiğdemi; **'mead.ow.y** *adj.* çimenli.
**mea.ger, mea.gre** □ ['miːgə] zayıf, yavan, cılız, çelimsiz, sıska, kuru *(a. fig.)*; noksan, eksik, az, kıt, kifayetsiz; **'mea.ger.ness, 'mea.gre.ness** *n.* zayıflık, cılızlık, sıskalık, çelimsizlik; kuruluk; noksanlık, eksiklik, azlık, kıtlık, kifayetsizlik.
**meal¹** [miːl] *n.* yemek, öğün.
**meal²** [~] *n.* un; **meal.ies** ['~iz] *n. pl. Güney Afrika:* mısır (buğdayı).
**meal.time** ['miːltaim] *n.* yemek vakti.
**meal.y** ['miːli] *adj.* un gibi, unlu; **'~-mouthed** *adj.* sinsi, samimiyetsiz.
**mean¹** [miːn] bayağı, alçak, pis, kaba, adi, aşağı; acınacak, zavallı; çirkin; lime lime olmuş, yırtık pırtık; cimri, pinti, hasis; dar kafalı.
**mean²** [~] **1.** *adj.* orta, alelade; ortalama, vasati; in the ~ time = ~time; **2.** *n.* orta, vasat; aleladelik; ılımlılık; ℞ ortalama, nicelik; ~s *pl.* para, sermaye, gelir, servet, mali vaziyet, mali durum; imkân, olanak; vasıta, araç; by all ~s kuşkusuz, şüphesiz; by no ~s hiçbir suretle, asla, katiyen; by this ~s bunun üzerine, sonradan; by ~s of vasıtasiyle, yardımıyla; by some ~s or other herhangi bir suretle, herhangi bir usulde, herhangi bir tarzda, ne yapıp yapıp.
**mean³** [~] *(irr.) v/t.* söylemek, demek istemek; yapmak niyetinde olm.; ifade etm., mana vermek, kastetmek, amaç gütmek, tasarlamak; uygun olm. *(for -e)*; arzuladığını söylemek, istediğini söylemek, niyetinde olduğunu söylemek *(by ile)*; ...manasına gelmek, demek; ~ well (ill) niyeti iyi (kötü) olm. *(by, a.* to *ile)*.
**me.an.der** [mi'ændə] **1.** *n.* dolambaç, dirsek; ~s *pl.* kıvrım, menderes; **2.** *v/i.* kıvrılmak, yılankavi akmak *(nehir, dere)*; avare dolaşmak *veya* konuşmak.
**mean.ing** ['miːniŋ] **1.** □ bşe delâlet eden, anlamlı; well ~ hüsnüniyet sahibi, iyi kalpli; **2.** *n.* mana, anlam; ✣ niyet, maksat, hedef, fikir, kasıt; **'mean.ing.less** *adj.* ehemmiyetsiz, önemsiz; anlamsız; sönük, cansız.

**mean.ness** ['miːnnis] *n.* alçaklık, adilik, aşağılık, kabalık.
**meant** [ment] *pret. & p.p. of* mean³.
**mean.time** ['miːn'taim], **mean.while** ['miːn'wail] *adv.* bu aralık, bu sırada, aynı zamanda.
**mea.sles** ['miːzlz] *n. pl.* ✤ kızamık; *vet.* uyuz; German ~ kızamıkçık; **'mea.sly** *adj.* kızamıklı; benekli; *sl.* acınacak, adi, değersiz, zavallı.
**meas.ur.a.ble** □ ['meʒərəbl] ölçülebilir.
**meas.ure** ['meʒə] **1.** *n.* ölçü; ♪ usül, ölçü, mezür; tedbir, önlem; ölçüm, ölçme; ~ of capacity istiap ölçüsü; beyond ~ son derece, haddinden fazla; in some ~ bir dereceye kadar, kısmen; in a great ~ ekserisi, en büyük kısmı; made to ~ ısmarlama yapılmış; for good ~ fazladan, ek olarak; set ~s to sınırla(ndır)mak; take s.o.'s ~ *b-nin* karakter ve yeteneklerini sınamak; take ~s önlem almak, hazırlıklı bulunmak; **2.** *vb.* ölçmek, kıymet biçmek, tartmak *(a. fig.)*; ölçüsü ...kadar olm.; ~ up *Am.* yeterli nitelikte olduğunu göstermek *(to -e)*; **'meas.ure.less** □ ölçüsüz, sınırsız; **'meas.ure.ment** *n.* ölçü, ölçme, tartı, ölçüm; ⚓ tonaj.
**meat** [miːt] *n. (yenecek)* et; † *veya prov.* yiyecek *(şey)*; *fig.* büyük zevk; butcher's ~ kasaplık et; fresh ~ taze et; preserved ~ konserve et; roast ~ kızartma et, rosto; '~-fly *n. zo.* etsineği, kurtsineği; ~pie kıymalı börek; '~-safe *n.* yemek dolabı; **'meat.y** *adj.* etli; *fig.* özlü, değerli fikirlerle dolu.
**mec.ca.no** [mi'kaːnəu] *n.* bir çeşit oyuncak.
**me.chan.ic** [mi'kænik] *n.* makinist, makine ustası; *mot.* tamirci; **me'chan.i.cal** □ makineye ait, mekanik, makine...; ~ engineering makine mühendisliği; **mech.a.ni.cian** [mekə'niʃən] *n.* makinist, mekanisyen; **me.chan.ics** [mi'kæniks] *n. mst sg.* mekanik, makine ilmi.
**mech.a.nism** ['mekənizəm] *n.* mekanizma; **'mech.a.nize** *v/t.* makineleştirmek; ✕ motörleştirmek, mekanize hale getirmek.
**med.al** ['medl] *n.* nişan, (hatıra) madalya(sı); **'med.al.(l)ed** *adj.* madalyalı; **me.dal.lion** [mi'dæljən] *n.* madalyon; süslü şekil; **med.al.(l)ist** ['medəlist] *n.* madalya kazanan *veya* yapan kimse.
**med.dle** ['medl] *v/i.* karışmak, müdahale etm., burnunu sokmak (in, with *-e*); **'med.dler** *n.* başkalarının işine burnunu sokan kimse; **med.dle.some** ['~səm] □ sırnaşık, usandıran, sıkıcı; herşeye burnunu sokan.

**me.di.a** [ˈmiːdjə] *n. pl. of* medium.

**me.di.ae.val** [mediˈiːvəl] = medieval.

**me.di.al** □ [ˈmiːdjəl], **ˈme.di.an** orta(lama), vasat(i), avaraj.

**me.di.ate 1.** □ [ˈmiːdiit] bilvasıta, vasıtalı, endirek(t), dolayısıyla olan; **2.** [ˈmiːdieit] *vb.* aracılık etm., vasıta olm.; aralarını bulmak; **me.di.a.tion** *n.* tavassut, aracılık; **ˈme.di.a.tor** *n.* aracı; *eccl.* arabulucu, şefaatçi; **me.di.a.to.ri.al** □ [ˌ-əˈtɔːriəl], **me.di.a.to.ry** [ˈ-ətəri] uzlaştırma ile ilgili, uzlaştırıcı; arabulucu...; **me.di.a.trix** [ˈ-eitriks] *n.* aracı kadın.

**med.i.cal** □ [ˈmedikəl] tedaviye ait, tıbbî; iyileştirici; ~ board sağlık kurulu, sağlık heyeti; ~ certificate doktor raporu; ~ evidence tıbbî delil; ~ jurisprudence adlî tıp; ~ man doktor, hekim, tabip; ~ officer devlet kademesinde tıp sorumluluğu olan kimse; ~ specialist uzman doktor; ~ student tıp öğrencisi; ♀ Superintendent baştabip, başhekim; **meˈdic.a.ment** *n.* ilâç.

**med.i.cate** [ˈmedikeit] *v/t.* ilâç ile tedavi etm.; bşin içine ilâç katmak; **med.iˈca.tion** *n.* ilâçla tedavi; bşin içine ilâç katma; ilâç *(esp. yatıştırıcı)*; **med.i.ca.tive** [ˈ-kətiv] *adj.* ilâçla tedavi kabilinden.

**me.dic.i.nal** □ [meˈdisinl] tıbbî, iyileştirici, tedavi *(veya* teskin) edici, şifalı.

**med.i.cine** [ˈmedsin] *n.* tıp, hekimlik; ilâç, deva; **ˈ~-ball** *n. spor:* ağır top, sağlık topu; **ˈ~-chest** *n.* ev ecza dolabı; **ˈ~-man** *n.* sihirbaz hekim.

**med.i.co** F *co.* [ˈmedikəu] *n.* doktor.

**me.di.e.val** □ [mediˈiːvəl] ortaçağa ait.

**me.di.o.cre** [miːdiˈəukə] *adj.* orta derecede, olağan; **me.di.oc.ri.ty** [ˌ-ˈɔkriti] *n.* orta, vasat olma; ne iyi ne kötü zekâsı olan *(veya* alelade) kimse.

**med.i.tate** [ˈmediteit] *v/t. & v/i.* düşünüp taşınmak, düşünceye dalmak *(on üzerinde);* bşi düşünmek, ölçüp biçmek; tasarlamak, planlamak, proje yapmak; **med.iˈta.tion** *n.* düşünüp taşınma, düşünceye dalma; dalgınlık; **med.i.ta.tive** □ [ˈ-tətiv] derin düşüncelere dalmış, düşünceli.

**Med.i.ter.ra.ne.an** [meditəˈreinjən] *n.* Akdeniz.

**me.di.um** [ˈmiːdjəm] *n., pl. a.* **me.di.a** [ˈ-djə] orta; çevre, ortam; araç, vasıta; *phys. & ispritizma:* medyum; *biol.* mikrop üretilebilir madde; **2.** *adj.* orta(lama), vasat(i); **ˈ~-ˈsized** *adj.* orta boylu.

**med.lar** ♀ [ˈmedlə] *n.* muşmula, beşbıyık, döngel (ağacı).

**med.ley** [ˈmedli] *n.* karmakarışıklık; *contp.* karışık insanlar *veya* şeyler; ♪ potpuri.

**me.dul.la** [meˈdʌlə] *n.* ilik; **medˈul.lar.y** *adj.* ilikli, ilik...; özlü, kuvvetli.

**me.du.sa** *zo.* [miˈdjuːzə] *n.* denizanası, medüz.

**meed** *poet.* [miːd] *n.* mükâfat, ödül.

**meek** □ [miːk] uysal, yumuşak huylu; mütevazı, alçakgönüllü; **ˈmeek.ness** *n.* alçakgönüllülük; uysallık.

**meer.schaum** [ˈmiəʃəm] *n.* eskişehirtaşı, lületaşı.

**meet¹** [miːt] *adj.* uygun, münasip, yerinde, yakışık alır.

**meet²** [~] **1.** *(irr.) v/t.* rast gelmek, rastlamak -e; karşılamak -i; tanışmak, görüşmek (s.o. *ile);* tediye etm., ödemek -i; bitişmek, kavuşmak; tatmin etm., cevap vermek *(ihtiyaca);* ~ one's death kaza sonucu ölmek; ~ the ear kulağa gelmek; ~ the eye göze ilişmek; ~ s.o.'s eye b-ne gözlerini dikmek; *v/i.* rastlamak -e; görüşmek, buluşmak; kavuşmak, bitişmek; toplanmak; uğramak (with -e); birdenbire b-ne, bşe rastlamak, karşılaşmak -le; toplantı yapmak -le; ~ with an accident kazaya uğramak; make both ends ~ geçinebilmek, ipin iki ucunu biraraya getirebilmek; **2.** *n. spor:* karşılaşma, yarışma.

**meet.ing** [ˈmiːtiŋ] *n.* toplantı, miting; heyet, meclis, cemaat; birleşme; **ˈ~-house** *n.* toplantı evi; kilise; **ˈ~-place** *n.* toplanma yeri.

**meg.a.cy.cle** ⚡ [ˈmegəsaikl] *n.* megasikl, bir milyon sikl; **meg.a.lith** [ˈ-liθ] *n.* megalit, büyük taş anıt; **meg.a.lo.ma.ni.a** [ˌ-ləuˈmeinjə] *n.* megalomani; **meg.a.phone** [ˈ-fəun] *n.* megafon, ses nakil borusu; **meg.a.ton** [ˈ-tʌn] *n.* büyükton, megaton.

**me.grim** [ˈmiːgːim] *n.* yarım baş ağrısı, migren, yarımca; **~s** *pl.* melankoli, karasevda, bunalım.

**mel.an.chol.ic** [melənˈkɔlik] *adj* hüzünlü, karasevdalı, melankolik; **mel.an.chol.y** [ˈ-kəli] **1.** *n.* karasevda, melankoli; **2.** *adj.* melankolik, karasevdalı; hüzünlü, mahzun.

**mé.lange** [meiˈlɑ̃ːŋ] *n.* karışık şey.

**mê.lée** [ˈmelei] *n.* saç saça baş başa dövüşme; kalabalık, izdiham.

**mel.io.rate** [ˈmiːljəreit] *v/t. & v/i.* iyileş(tir)mek, düzel(t)mek.

**mel.lif.lu.ent** [meˈlifl:uənt], *mst* **melˈlif.lu.ous** *adj.* bal gibi (tatlı).

**mel.low** [ˈmeləu] **1.** □ olgun, olmuş, ke-

male ermiş; *fig.* görmüş geçirmiş; yıllanmış (*şarap*); tatlı (*ses, renk*); yumuşak; *fig.* nazik, ince; *sl.* çakırkeyf; **2.**
*vb.* olgunlaş(tır)mak; yumuşa(t)mak;
**¹mel.low.ness** *n.* olgunluk, kemal; yumu-ı
şaklık; incelik, zayıflık.

**me.lo.di.ous** ☐ [mi¹ləudjəs] melodik,
ahenkli, armonik, hoş sesli; **me¹lo.di.ous-
ness** *n.* ahenk(lilik), armoni **mel.o.dist**
[¹melədist] *n.* kompozitör, şarkıcı; **¹mel.o-
dize** *vb.* ahenk vermek; bestelemek, kom-
poze etm.; **mel.o.dra.ma** [¹meləudrɑːmə]
*n.* melodram, heyecanlı dram; **me.lo.dra-
¹mat.ic** *adj.* melodrama uygun; aşırı duygusal; **mel.o.dy** [¹melədi] *n.* nağme, hava,
ezgi, melodi.

**mel.on** ⬥ [¹melən] *n.* kavun.

**melt** [melt] *v/t.* & *v/i.* eri(t)mek; *fig.* erimek; yumuşa(t)mak (*a. fig.*); ~ away
eriyip kaybolmak (*a. fig.*); ~ down (*hammadde olarak kullanılmak üzere*) eritmek; ~ into tears göz yaşlarına boğulmak.

**melt.ing** ☐ [¹meltiŋ] (*esp. ses*) yumuşak,
hoş; **¹~point** *n.* erime noktası; **¹~pot** *n.*
pota (*a. fig.*).

**mem.ber** [¹membə] *n.* aza, üye; *parl.* mebus, milletvekili; organ, uzuv; **¹mem.ber-
ship** *n.* azalık, üyelik; üye sayısı, üyeler;
~ fee üye aidatı.

**mem.brane** [¹membrein] *n.* (ince) zar, gışa; **mem¹bra.nous, mem¹bra.ne.ous** [~jəs]
*adj.* zarımsı, zardan ibaret.

**me.men.to** [mi¹mentəu] *n.* hatıra, yadigâr.

**mem.o** [¹meməu] = memorandum.

**mem.oir** [¹memwaː] *n.* biyografi; inceleme yazısı; ~s *pl.* hatırat, anılar; tuta-
naklar.

**mem.o.ra.ble** ☐ [¹memərəbl] anmağa değer.

**mem.o.ran.dum** [memə¹rændəm] *n.* not,
muhtıra, memorandum; *pol.* nota.

**me.mo.ri.al** [mi¹mɔːriəl] **1.** *adj.* hatırlatı-
cı; **2.** *n.* abide, anıt; muhtıra, dilekçe,
önerge; **me¹mo.ri.al.ist** *n.* dilekçe sahibi;
**me¹mo.ri.al.ize** *v/t.* anmak -i, hatırasını
yad etm. -*in.*

**mem.o.rize** [¹meməraiz] *v/t.* ezberlemek.

**mem.o.ry** [¹meməri] *n.* hatıra, andaç; hafıza, zihin, hatır; commit to ~ ezberlemek; within living ~ olayları hatırlanan
zaman içinde; in ~ of hatırasına, anısına -*in.*

**men** [men] *n. pl. of* man.

**men.ace** [¹menəs] **1.** *v/t.* tehdit etm., gözünü korkutmak, yıldırmak; **2.** *n.* tehlike; tehdit.

**me.nag.er.ie** [mi¹nædʒəri] *n.* gösteri için
kafeslerde tutulan vahşi hayvan koleksiyonu; bu hayvanların sergilendiği yer,
hayvanat bahçesi.

**mend** [mend] **1.** *v/t.* ıslah etm.; onarmak,
tamir etm., yamamak; daha iyi yapmak;
~ the fire ateşe daha fazla yakıt atmak;
~ one's ways davranışlarına dikkat etm.;
*v/i.* iyileşmek, ıslah olunmak, düzelmek,
şifa bulmak; **2.** *n.* tamir, onarım; tamir
olunmuş yer, yama; on the ~ iyileşmekte, gelişen, düzelen.

**men.da.cious** ☐ [men¹deiʃəs] yalan; yalancı, yalana şerbetli; **men.dac.i.ty**
[~¹dæsiti] *n.* yalancılık; yanlışlık; yalan.

**mend.er** [¹mendə] *n.* tamirci.

**men.di.can.cy** [¹mendikənsi] *n.* dilencilik;
**¹men.di.cant 1.** *adj.* dilenen, dilencilik
eden; **2.** *n.* dilenci; **men¹dic.i.ty** [~siti] *n.*
dilencilik.

**men.folk** F [¹menfəuk] *n.* erkekler, erkek
kısmı (*veya* milleti).

**men.hir** [¹menhiə] *n.* abide, büyük taş anıt.

**me.ni.al** *contp.* [¹miːnjəl] **1.** ☐ hizmetçi-
ye ait; süflî, bayağı; **2.** *n.* uşak, hizmetçi.

**men.in.gi.tis** ♆ [menin¹dʒaitis] *n.* beyin zarı iltihabı, menenjit.

**men.ses** [¹mensiːz] *n. pl.* âdet, aybaşı (*s.*
menstruation); **men.stru.al** [¹~struəl] *adj.*
âdetle ilgili; âdet (görme)..., aybaşı...;
**men.stru¹a.tion** *n.* âdet (görme), aybaşı.

**men.su.ra.ble** [¹menʃurəbl] *adj.* ölçülebilir; **men.su.ra.tion** [~sjuə¹reiʃən] *n.* ölçme.

**men.tal** ☐ [¹mentl] akılla ilgili, zihne ait,
zihnî...; ~ arithmetic akıldan yapılmış hesap; ~ institution tımarhane, asabiye hastanesi, akıl hastanesi; ~ly ill akıl hastası; **men.tal.i.ty** [~¹tæliti] *n.* zihniyet, düşünme tarzı.

**men.thol** *pharm.* [¹menθɔl] *n.* mantol, nane ruhu.

**men.tion** [¹menʃən] **1.** *n.* anma, ima, ifade, zikir; **2.** *v/t.* anmak, zikretmek, ima
etm.; don't ~ it! estağfurullah!, birşey değil efendim!; not to ~ ..., without ~ing ...
...den başka, üstelik; **men.tion.a.ble**
[¹~ʃnəbl] *adj.* kayda değer, anılabilir,
söylenebilir.

**men.tor** [¹mentɔː] *n.* akıllı ve güvenilir
danışman, akıl hocası.

**men.u** [¹menjuː] *n.* yemek listesi, mönü.

**Meph.is.to.phe.le.an** [mefistə¹fiːljən] *adj.*
şeytanca, haince.

**mer.can.tile** [¹məːkəntail] *adj.* ticarete ait,
ticari, ticaret...; ~ marine ticaret filosu.

**mer.ce.nar.y** [¹məːsinəri] **1.** ☐ ücretli; yal-

nız çıkar gözeten, kazanç düşkünü, para
canlısı; 2. n. X ücretli asker.
**mer.cer** [ˈməːsə] n. kumaş satıcısı, kumaşçı; ˈmer.cer.y n. kumaş, dokuma,
manifatura.
**mer.cer.ize** [ˈməːsəraiz] v/t. ipeğe benze-
yecek şekilde işlemek (pamuklu kumaş).
**mer.chan.dise** [ˈməːtʃəndaiz] n. ticaret eşyası, emtia, mal.
**mer.chant** [ˈməːtʃənt] 1. n. tacir, tüccar;
Am. perakendeci, satıcı; 2. adj. ticarete ait, ticari...; law ˏ ticaret kanunu;
ˈmer.chant.a.ble adj. satılabilir, satışı kolay; sürümlü; ˈmer.chant.man, mer.chant
ship n. ticaret gemisi.
**mer.ci.ful** □ [ˈməːsiful] merhametli, sevecen, şefkatli; ˈmer.ci.ful.ness n. rahmet,
merhametlilik.
**mer.ci.less** □ [ˈməːsilis] acımasız, merhametsiz, amansız; ˈmer.ci.less.ness n.
merhametsizlik.
**mer.cu.ri.al** [məːˈkjuəriəl] adj. cıvalı...;
ˏ cıva...; fig. bir türlü yerinde durmaz,
cıva gibi; değişken.
**Mer.cu.ry** [ˈməːkjuri] n. Merkür, Utarit;
fig. haberci, mesajcı, kurye; ♀ ˏ civa.
**mer.cy** [ˈməːsi] n. merhamet, şefkat; af,
rahmet, bereket; be at s.o.'s ˏ b-nin in-
safına kalmış olm., b-nin elinde olm.; at
the ˏ of the waves dalgalara karşı güçsüz, dalgaların· keyfine bağlı; have ˏ
upon b-ne acımak, merhamet etm.; it is
a ˏ that... iyi ki...; ˏ killing ıstırapsız (veya rahat) ölüm.
**mere¹** [miə] n. küçük göl.
**mere²** [ˏ] adj. halis, saf, sade, hakiki,
karışıksız, katıksız; önemsiz; ˏ(st)
nonsense son derece saçma; ˏ words pl.
sırf laf, boş söz; ˈmere.ly adv. sadece,
ancak, yalnız.
**mer.e.tri.cious** □ [meriˈtriʃəs] cicili bicili; fig. sırnaşık, usandırıcı, cıvık, lâubali, küstah.
**merge** [məːdʒ] v/t. & v/i. (in) kaynaş-
(tır)mak, birleş(tir)mek; içinde kaybolmak; ˈmerg.er n. ♀ birleşme, füzyon.
**me.rid.i.an** [məˈridiən] 1. adj. öğleye ait,
öğle...; fig. en yüksek; 2. n. geogr. meridyen, boylam dairesi; öğle vakti; fig. tepe, zirve, doruk; meˈrid.i.o.nal □ boylam
dairesine ait; güneye ait; güneyde olan.
**me.ringue** [məˈræŋ] n. yumurta akından
yapılan bir tür krema; bir tür kremalı
pasta, beze.
**me.ri.no** [məˈriːnou] n. merinos koyunu;
merinos yünü; merinos yününden yapılmış kumaş.
**mer.it** [ˈmerit] 1. n. liyakat; değer; fazi-

let; ˏs pl. part. ♂♂ esas, gerçek değer,
kıymet; on the ˏs of the case davanın
esasına göre; on its (own) ˏs değerine
göre; make a ˏ of övgüye değer davra-
nışta bulunmak; 2. v/t. fig. hak etm. -i,
lâyık olm. -e; mer.i.to.ri.ous □ [ˏˈtɔːriəs]
değerli, methedilmeye değer, hürmete
lâyık.
**mer.maid** [ˈməːmeid] n. denizkızı; **mer-**
**man** [ˈˏmæn] n. belinden aşağısı balık
şeklinde olan deniz adamı.
**mer.ri.ment** [ˈmerimənt] n. keyif, neşe,
şenlik, cümbüş.
**mer.ry** □ [ˈmeri] keyifli, neşeli, şen, sevinçli; neşe verici, eğlenceli, güldürücü,
eğlendirici; çakırkeyf; make ˏ cümbüş
(veya âlem) yapmak; ˏ-an.drew
[ˈˏˈændruː] n. maskara, soytarı, paskal,
palyaço; ˈˏ-go-round n. atlıkarınca;
ˈˏ-mak.ing n. eğlence, şenlik, bayram,
cümbüş; ˈˏthought n. lades kemiği.
**me.sa** geogr. [ˈmeisə] n. küçük plato.
**mé.sal.li.ance** [meˈzæliəns] n. daha düşük
seviyeden b-i ile olan evlilik.
**me.seems** † [miˈsiːmz] vb. bana öyle görünüyor.
**mes.en.ter.y** anat. [ˈmesəntəri] n. bağırsakları karın duvarına bağlayan zar.
**mesh** [meʃ] 1. n. ağ gözü, file ilmiği; fig.
oft. ˏs pl. tuzak; be in ˏ ⊕ birbirine
geçmek; 2. vb. ağla yakalamak; uygun
düşmek (nitelik, fikir vs.); ⊕ birbirine geçmek; **meshed** adj. ...gözlü, ...il-
mikli; ˈmesh-work n. ağ örgüsü.
**mes.mer.ism** [ˈmezmərizəm] n. ipnoz;
ˈmes.mer.ize v/t. ipnotize etm.; hayrette
bırakmak.
**mess¹** [mes] 1. n. karmakarışıklık, düzensizlik; kaos, karışık durum; kirlilik, pislik; sofra arkadaşları; sofra arkadaşla-
rıyla yenen yemek; F sıkıntı, darlık;
make a ˏ of bozmak, berbat etm. -i; 2.
v/t. a. ˏ up yüzüne gözüne bulaştırmak,
bozmak, karıştırmak, berbat etm.; v/i. ˏ
about düzensiz, plansız iş yapmak; tembellik etm.
**mess²** [ˏ] 1. n. porsiyon, tabak; X subaylara mahsus yemek ve dinlenme salonu; 2. vb. birlikte yemek yemek.
**mes.sage** [ˈmesidʒ] n. haber, mesaj.
**mes.sen.ger** [ˈmesindʒə] n. haberci, ulak;
kurye; ˏ boy özel haber vs. götüren çocuk.
**Mes.sieurs**, mst **Messrs.** [ˈmesəz] n. baylar, efendiler (özellikle firmalar için kullanılır).
**mess...:** ˈˏ-jacket n. X kısa üniforma ceket; ˈˏ-mate n. X, ⚓ sofra arkadaşı;

**ˈ~-room** *n.* orduevi; **ˈ~-tin** *n.* aş kabı.

**mes.suage** *ǒǒ* [ˈmeswidȝ] *n.* mesken, müştemilâtlı ev.

**met** [met] *pret. & p.p. of* meet² 1.

**met.a.bol.ic** [metəˈbɔlik] *adj.* metabolik; **me.tab.o.lism** *physiol.* [meˈtæbəlizəm] *n.* metabolizma.

**met.age** [ˈmiːtidȝ] *n.* ölçme ücreti.

**met.al** [ˈmetl] 1. *n.* maden, metal; çakıl, kırma taş; camın soğumadan önceki sıvı hali; ~s *pl.* F ray, yol; 2. *v/t.* çakılla kaplamak; **me.tal.lic** [miˈtælik] *adj.* (~ally) madenî, maden..., metal...; **met.al.lif.er.ous** [metəˈlifərəs] *adj.* madenli; **met.al.line** [ˈ~lain] *adj.* madenî; **ˈmet.al.lize** *v/t.* madene dönüştürmek, maden özelliği vermek; **met.al.log.ra.phy** [~ˈlɔɡrəfi] *n.* metalografi; **met.al.loid** [ˈ~lɔid] 1. *adj.* madene benzer; 2. *n.* metal olmayan cisim; **met.al.lur.gic, met.al.lur.gi.cal** [~ˈlɔːdȝik(əl)] metalurjiye ait; **met.al.lur.gy** [miˈtælədȝi] *n.* metalurji.

**met.a.mor.phose** [metəˈmɔːfəuz] *v/t. & v/i.* başkalaş(tır)mak; **met.aˈmor.pho.sis** [~fəsis] *n., pl.* **met.aˈmor.pho.ses** [~fəsiːz] metamorfoz, istihale, şekil değişimi, başkalaşım.

**met.a.phor** [ˈmetəfə] *n.* mecaz; **met.a.phor.ic,** *mst* **met.a.phor.i.cal** [~ˈfɔrik(əl)] mecazî.

**met.a.phys.ic** [metəˈfizik] 1. *mst* **met.aˈphys.i.cal** ☐ metafiziğe (*veya* fizikötesine) ait; 2. **met.aˈphys.ics** *n. oft. sg.* metafizik, fizikötesi.

**mete** [miːt] *v/t.* ölçmek; *mst* ~out hissesini ölçmek; paylaştırmak.

**me.te.or** [ˈmiːtjə] *n.* akanyıldız, meteor(taşı); **me.te.or.ic** [miːtiˈɔrik] *adj.* meteorortaşına benzer, meteortaşı...; *fig.* parlak, göz kamaştırıcı; **me.te.or.ite** [ˈmiːtjərait] *n.* yere düşen meteortaşı; **me.te.or.o.log.i.cal** ☐ [miːtjərəˈlɔdȝikəl] meteorolojik; **me.te.or.ol.o.gist** [~ˈrɔlədȝist] *n.* meteorolog, meteoroloji bilgini; **me.te.orˈol.o.gy** *n.* meteoroloji.

**me.ter** [ˈmiːtə] *n.* saat, sayaç, ölçü aleti.

**me.thinks** † [miˈθiŋks] *vb. (pret.* methought) sanırım, galiba.

**meth.od** [ˈmeθəd] *n.* usul, metod, yöntem; düzen; sistem; **me.thod.ic,** *mst* **me.thod.i.cal** ☐ [miˈθɔdik(əl)] yöntemli, düzenli, metodik, metotlu; **Meth.od.ism** *eccl.* [ˈmeθədizəm] *n.* Hıristiyanlıkta ibadet öğretimi ve düzeni; **ˈMeth.od.ist** *n. eccl.* metodist, Protestan mezhebi üyesi; **ˈmeth.od.ize** *v/t.* düzene sokmak, usule uydurmak.

**me.thought** † [miˈθɔːt] *pret. of* methinks.

**meth.yl** ⁿ̃ [ˈmeθil] *n.* metil; **meth.yl.at.ed spir.it** [ˈmeθileitidˈspirit].*n.* ısıtma ve ışıklandırma için kullanılan alkol; **meth.yl.ene** [ˈmeθiliːn] *n.* metilen.

**me.tic.u.lous** ☐ [miˈtikjuləs] titiz, çok dikkatli.

**me.tre** [ˈmiːtə] *n.* metre; vezin.

**met.ric** [ˈmetrik] *adj.* (~ally) metre sistemini kullanan, metrik; ~ **system** metre sistemi; **ˈmet.ri.cal** ☐ metrik; şiir veznine ait, ölçülü.

**met.ro** F [ˈmetrəu] *n.* metro, şehir çevresinde işleyen demiryolu, tünel; **ˈ~.land** *n.* F banliyö, dış mahalle.

**me.trop.o.lis** [miˈtrɔpəlis] *n.* başkent, başşehir; büyük şehir; **met.ro.pol.i.tan** [metrəˈpɔlitən] 1. *adj.* başşehre ait; ♀ Railway şehir çevresinde işleyen demiryolu; 2. *n.* başpiskopos, metropolit; başkentte oturan kimse.

**met.tle** [ˈmetl] *n.* cesaret, yiğitlik, yüreklilik, hararetli gayret; be on one's ~ elinden gelenin en iyisini yapmaya hazır olm.; put s.o. on his ~ en iyisini yapmaya teşvik etm.; **ˈmet.tled,** **met.tle.some** [ˈ~səm] *adj.* canlı, ateşli.

**mew¹** *orn.* [mjuː] *n.* martı.

**mew²** [~] 1. *n.* miyavlama; 2. *vb.* miyavlamak.

**mew³** [~] *v/t. mst* ~ up kilitlemek, kapa(t)mak.

**mewl** [mjuːl] *vb.* inlemek, sızla(n)mak.

**mews** [mjuːz] *n. hist.* dar sokak.

**Mex.i.can** [ˈmeksikən] 1. *adj.* Meksikalıya ait, Meksikalı...; 2. *n.* Meksikalı.

**mez.za.nine** [ˈmetsəniːn] *n.* asma kat; *Am. thea.* birinci balkon.

**mi.aow** [miˈau] 1. *n.* miyavlama; 2. *v/i.* miyavlamak.

**mi.as.ma** [miˈæzmə] *n., pl. a.* **mi.as.ma.ta** [~tə] pis ve zehirli sis; **miˈas.mal** ☐ zehirli, tehlikeli, mikroplu.

**miaul** [miˈɔːl] *v/i.* miyavlamak.

**mi.ca** *min.* [ˈmaikə] *n.* mika; **mi.ca.ce.ous** [~ˈkeifəs] *adj.* mıkalı; mıkaya ait; mikamsı.

**mice** [mais] *n. pl. of* mouse.

**Mich.ael.mas** [ˈmiklməs] *n.* 29 Eylül'de kutlanan St. Mişel festivali.

**mi.cro...** [ˈmaikrəu] *prefix* küçük..., ufak..., mikro...

**mi.crobe** [ˈmaikrəub] *n.* mikrop, bakteri; **ˈmi.cro.bi.al** [~bjəl] *adj.* mikrobik.

**mi.cro.cosm** [ˈmaikrəukɔzəm] *n.* küçük dünya; insan *(evreni temsil eden);* **mi.cro.film** [ˈ~film] 1. *n.* mikrofilm; 2. *v/t.* mikrofilm üzerine film çekmek.

**mil.age** [ˈmailidʒ] = mileage.
**mi.crom.e.ter** [maiˈkrɔmitə] *n.* mikrometre; **mi.cro.phone** [ˈmaikrɔfəun] *n.* mikrofon; **mi.cro.scope** [ˈ~skəup] *n.* mikroskop; **mi.cro.scop.ic, mi.cro.scop.i.cal** □
[~sˈkɔpik(əl)] mikroskobik; pek ufak;
**mi.cro.wave** ≠ [ˈmaikrɔuweiv] *n.* bir çeşit elektromanyetik dalga.
**mid** [mid] *s.* middle 2; *poet.* = amid arasında, ortasında; in ~ air havada; in ~
winter kış ortasında; **ˈ~.day** 1. *n.* öğle
vakti; 2. *adj.* öğle.
**mid.den** [ˈmidn] *n.* gübre (*veya* çöp) yığını.
**mid.dle** [ˈmidl] 1. *n.* merkez, orta (yer);
bel; ~s *pl.* ✝ orta kalite; 2. *adj.* orta,
vasat; aradaki, ortadaki; ♀ Ages *pl.* Ortaçağ; ~ class(es *pl.*) ortahalliler sınıfı,
orta sınıf, burjuva; ˈ~-ˈaged *adj.* orta
yaşlı; ˈ~-ˈclass *adj.* orta sınıfa ait, orta...; ~ dis.tance *paint.* arka ve ön görüntü arasındaki kısım; ~ King.dom *lit.*
Çin; ˈ~.man *n.* arabulucu; ✝ mutavassıt tüccar, komisyoncu; ˈ~.most *adj.* en
ortadaki; ~ name göbek adı; ˈ~-of-the-
-ˈroad *adj. pol.* ılımlı; ˈ~-ˈsized *adj.* orta
boy; ˈ~-weight *n. boks:* orta sıklet.
**mid.dling** [ˈmidliŋ] 1. *adj.* orta, alelade;
oldukça iyi; şöyle böyle; 2. *adv. a.* ~ly
orta halde, şöyle böyle; 3. *n.* ~s *pl.* ✝
orta kalite mahsül.
**mid.dy** F [ˈmidi] = midshipman.
**midge** [midʒ] *n.* tatarcık; **midg.et** [ˈmidʒ-
it] *n.* cüce.
**mid.land** [ˈmidlənd] 1. *adj.* ülkenin iç böl-
gelerinde bulunan; 2. *n.* the ♀s *pl.* İngil-
tere'nin iç bölgeleri; **ˈmid-ˈmorn.ing break**
öğleden evvelki büyük ara; **ˈmid.most**
*adj.* tam ortadaki; **ˈmid.night** 1. *n.* gece-
yarısı; 2. *adj.* gece yarısı olan, geceya-
rısı...; **mid.riff** [ˈ~rif] *n. anat.* diyafram;
**ˈmid.ship.man** *n.* deniz okulu öğrencisi;
deniz yarsubayı; *Am.* (*denizci*) asteğmen; **ˈmid.ships** *adv.* ♪ geminin orta-
sın(d)a; **midst** [midst] 1. *n.* orta, merkez; in the ~ of ~in ortasında; in our ~
aramızda, bizim ile; 2. *prp. poet. s.*
amidst arasında, ortasında; **ˈmid.stream**
1. *n.* nehrin orta yeri; 2. *adv.* nehrin orta yerinde; **ˈmid.sum.mer** *n.* yaz ortası;
yaz dönümü; ♀ Day 24 Haziran; **ˈmid-**
**ˈway** 1. *n.* yarı yol; *Am.* eğlence yeri, lunapark; 2. *adj.* yarı yolda olan; 3. *adv.*
yarı yolda; **ˈmid.wife** *n.* ebe; **mid.wife.ry**
[ˈ~wifəri] *n.* ebelik; **ˈmid-ˈwin.ter** *n.* karakış, kış ortası.
**mien** *lit.* [miːn] *n.* çehre, surat; eda, hal,
tavır.

**miff** F [mif] *n.* dargınlık, bozuşma.
**might** [mait] 1. *n.* kuvvet, kudret, güç, iktidar, takat; with ~ and main var kuvveti ile, elden geldiğince; 2. *pret. of* may;
**might.i.ness** [ˈ~tinis] *n.* güçlülük; **ˈmight-**
**y** 1. *adj.* güçlü, kuvvetli; F muazzam,
pek büyük; 2. F *adv.* pek çok, fazla, ziyade, son derecede.
**mi.gnon.ette** ♀ [minjəˈnet] *n.* muhabbetçiçeği.
**mi.graine** [ˈmiːgrein] *n.* migren, yarım
başağrısı.
**mi.grant** [ˈmaigrənt] 1. = migratory; 2. *n.*
*a.* ~ bird göçmen kuş.
**mi.grate** [maiˈgreit] *v/i.* göç etm., hicret
etm.; **miˈgra.tion** *n.* göç; **mi.gra.to.ry**
[ˈ~grətəri] *adj.* göçebe; göçle ilgili; göçmen.
**mike** *sl.* [maik] *n.* mikrofon.
**mil** [mil] *n.* bin; 1/1000 pus.
**mil.age** [ˈmailidʒ] = mileage.
**Mil.an.ese** [miləˈniːz] 1. *adj.* Milano'ya
ait; 2. *n.* Milanolu.
**milch** [miltʃ] *adj.* süt veren, sağmal; ~
cow süt ineği, sağmal inek.
**mild** □ [maild] yumuşak, zarif; hafif;
ılımlı; nazik; to put it ~ly en azından, en
hafif deyimiyle.
**mil.dew** [ˈmildjuː] 1. *n.* mildiyu; küf; 2.
*v/t. & v/i.* küflen(dir)mek.
**mild.ness** [ˈmaildnis] *n.* yumuşaklık; hafiflik; nezaket; ılımlılık.
**mile** [mail] *n.* mil (*1609,33 metre*).
**mile.age** [ˈmailidʒ] *n.* mil hesabıyla uzaklık; mil başına ödenen ücret.
**mil.er** [ˈmailə] *n. spor:* bir millik koşuya
katılan koşucu *veya* yarış atı.
**mile.stone** [ˈmailstəun] *n.* kilometre taşı;
*fig.* dönüm noktası.
**mil.foil** ♀ [ˈmilfɔil] *n.* civanperçemi.
**mi.lieu** [ˈmiːljə] *n.* çevre, muhit.
**mil.i.tan.cy** [ˈmilitənsi] *n.* saldırganlık;
**ˈmil.i.tant** □ militan, saldırgan; faal;
kavgacı; **mil.i.ta.rism** [ˈ~tərizəm] *n.* militarizm, savaşçı politika; askerlik ruhu;
**ˈmil.i.ta.rist** *n.* militarizm yandaşı; **ˈmil.i-**
**tar.y** 1. □ askerî; askerliğe *veya* savaşa ait; harp...; ~ college harp okulu,
harbiye (mektebi); ♀ Government askeri hükümet; ~ map kurmay haritası; 2.
*n.* asker, ordu; **mil.i.tate** [ˈ~teit] *v/t.:*
~ in favour of (against) lehine (aleyhine)
etkilemek; **mi.li.tia** [miˈliʃə] *n.* milis; yedek askerler; **miˈli.tia.man** *n.* yedek er.
**milk** [milk] 1. *n.* süt; the ~ of human
kindness insanın yapısında olan şefkati;
it's no use crying over spilt ~ olan oldu.
iş işten geçti, üzülmek için ~ çok geç; 2.

*vb.* süt sağmak; süt vermek *(inek, koyun vs.)*; almak, çekmek *-den; fig.* sağmak *-i;* faydalanmak *-den,* kötüye kullanmak *-i;* ¹**milk-and-¹wa.ter** *adj.* yavan, değersiz, tatsız *(bş veya b-i);* ¹**milk-bar** *n.* süt barı *(süt ve sütlü maddelerin satılıp içildiği ve yendiği dükkân);* ¹**milk-churn** *n.* süt kabı *(veya* güğümü); ¹**milk.er** *n.* süt sağan kimse; sağmal inek; ¹**milk.ing-ma-¹chine** *n.* süt sağma makinesi.

**milk...:** ¹**~.maid** *n.* süt sağıcı kız; ¹**~.man** *n.* sütçü; ¹**~.pow.der** *n.* süttozu; ¹**~-¹shake** *n.* dondurma ile karıştırılan süt; ¹**~.sop** *n.* çıtkırıldım, dandini bebek, muhallebi çocuğu; ¹**~.weed** *n.* ⚥ sütleğenotu; ¹**~-white** *adj.* süt gibi beyaz; ¹**milk.y** *adj.* süt gibi; sütlü; süt...; *fig.* yumuşak, nazik, uysal, ince; ♀ Way samanyolu.

**mill¹** [mil] 1. *n.* değirmen; fabrika, imalâthane; iplikhane; öğütme makinesi; *sl.* dövüşme; go through the ~ *fig. (zorluklar sonucu)* deneyim kazanmak; 2. *vb.* öğütmek, çekmek; ⊕ frezelemek; kenarını diş diş yapmak *(para);* çalkalamak.

**mill²** *Am.* [~] *n.* doların binde biri *(= 1/10 cent).*

**mill.board** [¹milbɔ:d] *n.* kalın karton; ¹**mill.dam** *n.* değirmen barajı.

**mil.le.nar.i.an** [mili¹nɛəriən], **mil.len.ni.al** [mi¹leniəl] *adj.* bininci; bin yıllık devreye ait; **mil.le.nar.y** [ᵃ~¹nəri] 1. *adj.* bin yıla ait; bin yıllık devreye ait; 2. *n.* bin yıllık devre; bu devre inanan kimse; **mil¹len.ni.um** [~niəm] *n.* bin yıllık devre; herkes için mutluluk içinde geçeceği düşünülen bin yıllık devre; mutluluk devresi.

**mil.le.pede** *zo.* [¹milipi:d] *n.* kırkayak.

**mill.er** [¹milə] *n.* değirmenci; ⊕ freze tezgâhı.

**mil.les.i.mal** [mi¹lesiməl] *n.* binde bir.

**mil.let** ⚥ [¹milit] *n.* darı.

**mill...:** ¹**~-girl** *n. part.* iplikçi *(kız);* ¹**~-hand** *n.* fabrika işçisi.

**mil.li.ard** [¹miljɑ:d] *n.* milyar, **mil.li.gram** [¹miligræm] *n.* miligram.

**mil.li.me.tre** [¹milimi:tə] *n.* milimetre.

**mil.li.ner** [¹milinə] *n.* kadın şapkacısı; ¹**mil.li.ner.y** *n.* kadın şapkacılığı; kadın şapkaları.

**mill.ing** [¹miliŋ] *n.* değirmencilik; ~ cutter ⊕ freze çakısı; ~ machine freze makinesi.

**mil.lion** [¹miljən] *n.* milyon; **mil.lion.aire** [~¹nɛə] *n.* milyoner; **mil.lionth** [¹miljənθ] 1. *adj.* milyonuncu; 2. *n.* milyonda bir.

**mill...:** ¹**~-pond** *n.* değirmen havuzu;

¹**~-race** *n.* değirmen deresi; ¹**~.stone** *n.* değirmentaşı; *fig.* engel, yük; see through a ~ F ukalâ dümbeleği olm.; ¹**~-wheel** *n.* değirmen dolabı, değirmen çarkı; ¹**~.wright** *n.* değirmenci, değirmen yapan ve tamir eden adam.

**mi.lord** [mi¹lɔ:d] *n.* lord; zengin, asılzade.

**milt¹** [milt] *n.* balık menisi.

**milt²** ⚥ [~] *n.* dalak.

**milt.er** *ichth.* [¹miltə] *n.* erkek ringa balığı.

**mime** [maim] 1. *n.* pandomima; pandomimci; 2. *vb.* taklidini yapmak; mimiklerle rol oynamak.

**mim.e.o.graph** [¹mimiəgrɑ:f] 1. *n.* teksir makinesi; 2. *v/t.* teksir etm.

**mi.met.ic** [mi¹metik] *adj.* taklide ait.

**mim.ic** [¹mimik] 1. *adj.* taklit eden; yanıltıcı; 2. *n.* taklitçi; taklit; 3. *v/t.* taklit etm., kopya etm; taklidini yapmak; ¹**mim.ic.ry** *n.* taklitçilik; *zo.* benzetme, tatbik.

**mi.mo.sa** ⚥ [mi¹məuzə] *n.* mimoza, küstümotu.

**min.a.ret** [¹minəret] *n.* minare.

**min.a.to.ry** [¹minətəri] *adj.* tehdit edici, korkutucu.

**mince** [mins] 1. *vb.* kıymak; ufaltmak; aşırı nezaketle konuşmak; kırıtarak yürümek; he does not ~ matters dobra dobra konuşur; ~ one's words açıkça söylemek; 2. *n. a.* ~d meat kıyma; ¹**~.meat** *n.* tatlı ve etli börek dolgusu; make ~ of hezimete uğratmak *-i,* parça parça etm. *-i;* ¹**~-¹pie** *n.* (mincemeat *dolgusu ile)* börek, poğaça; ¹**minc.er** *n.* et kıyma makinesi.

**minc.ing** □ [¹minsiŋ] işveli, nazlı; yapmacık, sahte tavırlı; ¹**~-ma.chine** = mincer.

**mind** [maind] 1. *n.* his, duygu; zihin, akıl, beyin; zekâ; düşünce, fikir, kanaat; niyet, maksat, hedef, kasıt; arzu, istek, heves; hafıza; dikkat, itina; to my ~ benim düşünceme göre; ~'s eye düş, hayal; out of one's ~, not in one's right ~ deli, kaçık; since time out of ~ ezelden beri, oldum olası; change one's ~ fikrini değiştirmek, caymak; bear s.th. in ~ bşi .hatırda tutmak, unutmamak; have (half) a ~ to bş yapmaya eğilim göstermek, niyet etm.; have s.th. on one's ~ zihnini işgal eden bşi olmak; have in ~ tasavvur etm., düşünmek; (not) know one's own ~ ne istediğini bil(me)mek; make up one's ~ karar vermek; make up one's ~ to s.th. kabullenmek *-i,* sonucuna razı olm. -*in*; put s.o. in ~ of *b-ne bşi* hatırlatmak; speak one's ~ düşündüğünü açıkça söylemek; 2. *vb.* bakmak, dikkat etm. -*e*; endişe etm., kaygı duymak; saymak; dikkatli olm.; önem vermek -*e*; karşı çıkmak -*e*; ~! dikkat!; never ~! önemi yok!, zararı yok!; ~ the step! önüne bak!, düşme!; I don't ~ (it) aldırmam; zararı yok; do you ~ if I smoke? sigara içmemde sakınca var mı?; would you ~ taking off your hat? lütfen şapkanızı çıkarır mısınız?; ~ your own business! kendi işine bak!, başkasının işine karışma!; **ımind.ed** *adj.* niyetli; gönlü yatmış; **ımind.er** *n. bşe* bakmakla görevli kimse; **mind.ful** ['~ful] *adj.* unutmaz, dikkatli (of -*e*); **ımind.ful.ness** *n.* dikkat, itina; **ımind.less** □ akılsızca yapılan, aptalca; aldırışsız, lâkayt, pervasız (of -*e*).

**mine¹** [main] *pron.* benim(ki); benimkiler.

**mine²** [~] 1. *n.* maden ocağı; lağım; *fig.* zengin kaynak, hazine; ✗ mayın; 2. *vb.* lağımlamak; kazmak; ✗ kazıp çıkarmak; ✗ mayın dökmek; ✗ tünel kazmak; '~.field *n.* ✗ mayın tarlası; ✗ maden alanı; '~.lay.er *n.* ⚓, ✗ mayın döken gemi; **ımin.er** *n.* madenci, maden işçisi; *part.* ✗ tünel kazan *veya* mayın döken kimse; ⚓ mayın dökme gemisi.

**min.er.al** ['minərəl] 1. *n.* mineral, maden; madensel madde; ~*s pl.*, ~ water madensuyu; 2. *adj.* mineral; madensel; **ımin.er.al.ize** *v/t.* mineralleştirmek; taşlaştırmak; **min.er.al.o.gist** [~'rælədʒist] *n.* madenler ilmi uzmanı; **min.er.al.o.gy** *n.* madenler ilmi, mineroloji.

**mine.sweep.er** ⚓ ['mainswi:pə] *n.* mayın temizleme *veya* tarama) gemisi.

**min.gle** ['miŋgl] *v/t. & v/i.* karış(tır)mak (in -*e*); kat(ıl)mak (with -*e*).

**min.gy** F ['mindʒi] *adj.* cimri.

**min.i.a.ture** ['minjətʃə] 1. *n.* minyatür; 2. *adj.* küçük, çok ufak...; çok ufak yapılmış; ~ camera 35 mm'lik *veya* daha dar film kullanılan fotoğraf makinesi.

**min.i.kin** ['minikin] 1. *adj.* pek ufak, cüzi; yapmacık, yapay, sahte tavırlı; 2. *n.* bücür, cüce, bodur, bacaksız.

**min.im** ['minim] *n.* ♩ yarım nota; damla; **ımin.i.mize** *v/t.* en aza indirgemek; *fig.* önemsememek; **min.i.mum** ['~məm] 1. *n.* en az miktar; 2. *adj.* minimum, asgari, en az..., en küçük...

**min.ing** ['maining] *n.* maden kazma; † madencilik, maden işletmeciliği; ✗, ⚓ mayın dökme.

**min.ion** ['minjən] *n.* efendisinin dedikle-

rini körü körüne yapan hizmetçi; *fig.* köle, peyk; *typ.* yedi puntoluk matbaa harfi; ~*s* of the law polis, zabıta memurları, gardiyan *vs.*

**min.is.ter** ['ministə] 1. *n.* papaz; *fig.* alet ve edevat; *pol.* bakan; devlet vekili; ortaelçi; 2. *vb.* bakmak, yardım etm., hizmet sunmak (to -*e*); **min.is.te.ri.al** □ [~.'tiəriəl] *pol.* bakanlığa ait; elçiliğe ait; *eccl.* ruhani.

**min.is.trant** ['ministrənt] 1. *adj.* hizmet eden; 2. *n. eccl.* destekleyen *veya* yardım eden kimse; **min.is'tra.tion** *n.* hizmet; yardım, servis (*part. eccl.*); **ımin.is.try** *n.* dinsel hizmet, papazlık; *pol.* bakanlık, vekâlet; yardım.

**min.i.ver** ['minivə] *n.* (*süs*) beyaz kürk.

**mink** zo. [miŋk] *n.* vizon.

**min.now** *ichth.* ['minəu] *n.* golyan balığı.

**mi.nor** ['mainə] 1. *adj.* daha küçük, önemi az, ikinci derecede olan; rüştünü ispat etmemiş; ♪ minör...; A ~ minör; ~ key minör anahtarı; 2. *n.* rüştünü kanıtlamamış kimse; *phls.* küçük önerme; *Am. univ.* ikinci branş; *spor: Am.* ikinci lig; **mi.nor.i.ty** [mai'nɔriti] *n.* azınlık; reşit olmama.

**min.ster** ['minstə] *n.* büyük kilise, katedral.

**min.strel** ['minstrəl] *n.* † saz şairi; ~*s pl.* yüzü siyaha boyanmış şarkıcı; **min.strel.sy** ['~si] *n.* saz şairliği; lirik şiir ve baladlar.

**mint¹** ♣ [mint] *n.* nane; ~ sauce naneli sos.

**mint²** [~] 1. *n.* darphane; *fig.* zengin kaynak; a ~ of money büyük miktar para; 2. *adj.* yeni, kirlenmemiş, iyi durumda (*madalya, kitap pul v.b.*); 3. *v/t.* basmak (*madeni para*); yaratmak, uydurmak (*kelime, deyim vs.*); **ımint.age** *n.* para basma ücreti; basılan para; paraya basılan damga.

**min.u.et** ♪ ['minjuʹet] *n.* menuetto, mönüe, gruplar halindeki çiftlerin yaptığı yavaş dans.

**mi.nus** ['mainəs] 1. *prp.* eksi; F -sız, -siz; 2. *adj.* eksi; sıfır, hiç; 3. *n.* eksi işareti; sıfırdan eksik miktar.

**mi.nute¹** [mai'nju:t] □ çok ufak; dikkatli, titiz.

**min.ute²** ['minit] 1. *n.* dakika; *fig.* an; ~*s pl.* tutanak; in a ~ uzun zamanda, şimdi; to the ~ tam zamanında; dakikası dakikasına; the ~ (that) olur olmaz, yapar yapmaz; 2. *v/t.* not tutmak; tutanak hazırlamak; **ımin.ute-hand** *n.* saat yelkovanı.

**min.ute.ly¹** ['minitli] *adv.* dikkatle, inceden inceye.

**mi.nute.ly²** [maiˈnjuːtli] *adj.* sürekli; **mi-ˈnute.ness** *n.* küçük olma.

**mi.nu.ti.a** [maiˈnjuːʃiə] *n., pl.* **miˈnu.ti.ae** [~ʃiː] önemsiz ayrıntılar.

**minx** [miŋks] *n.* lâubali kız, haspa.

**mir.a.cle** [ˈmirəkl] *n.* mucize, harika; to a ~ son derece güzel, enfes; ~ play Hazreti İsa ve havarilerini konu alan dinsel piyes; **mi.rac.u.lous** □ [miˈrækjuləs] mucize gibi, hayret verici, harikulâde; doğa yasalarına aykırı, doğaüstü; **miˈrac.u.lous.ness** *n.* mucize kabilinden oluş.

**mi.rage** [ˈmiraːʒ] *n.* ılgım, serap (*a. fig.*).

**mire** [ˈmaiə] 1. *n.* çamur, batak; pislik; be in the ~ güçlük içinde olm.; drag s.o. through the ~ b-ni rezil etm., ipliğini pazara çıkarmak; 2. *v/t. & v/i.* çamur ile kirletmek; çamura bat(ır)mak (*a. fig.*); his car was ~d arabası çamurlanmıştı.

**mir.ror** [ˈmirə] 1. *n.* ayna (*a. fig.*); 2. *v/t.* yansıtmak (*a. fig.*).

**mirth** [məːθ] *n.* neşe, şenlik, cümbüş; **mirth.ful** □ [ˈ~ful] neşeli, şen; **ˈmirth.less** □ neşesiz.

**mir.y** [ˈmaiəri] *adj.* çamurlu, pis.

**mis...** [mis] *prefix* yanlış, kötü, hatalı.

**mis.ad.ven.ture** [ˈmisədˈventʃə] *n.* talihsizlik, felâket, kaza.

**mis.al.li.ance** [ˈmisəˈlaiəns] *n.* yanlış evlilik.

**mis.an.thrope** [ˈmizənθrəup] *n.* insanlardan nefret eden kimse; **mis.an.throp.ic, mis.an.throp.i.cal** □ [~ˈθrɔpik(əl)] insanlardan nefret eden; **mis.an.thro.pist** [miˈzænθrəpist] *n.* merdümgiriz kimse, mizantrop; **misˈan.thro.py** *n.* insanlardan nefret etme *veya* kaçma.

**mis.ap.pli.ca.tion** [ˈmisæpliˈkeiʃən] *n.* yanlış uygulama; **mis.ap.ply** [ˈ~əˈplai] *v/t.* yerinde kullanmamak, yanlış uygulamak.

**mis.ap.pre.hend** [ˈmisæpriˈhend] *v/t.* yanlış anlamak; **ˈmis.ap.preˈhen.sion** *n.* yanlış anlama.

**mis.ap.pro.pri.ate** [ˈmisəˈprəuprieit] *v/t.* haksız kullanmak, emanete hıyanet etm.; **ˈmis.ap.pro.priˈa.tion** *n.* emanete hıyanet.

**mis.be.come** [ˈmisbiˈkʌm] *vb.* uygun olmamak, uymamak; **ˈmis.beˈcom.ing** *adj.* uygunsuz.

**mis.be.got(.ten)** [ˈmisbigɔt(n)] *adj.* gayet çirkin, iğrenç; piç.

**mis.be.have** [ˈmisbiˈheiv] *vb.* kötü davranmak; **ˈmis.beˈhav.io(u)r** [~jə] *n.* kötü davranış, yaramazlık.

**mis.be.lief** [ˈmisbiˈliːf] *n.* imansızlık, inançsızlık; **mis.be.lieve** [ˈ~ˈliːv] *vb.*

inanmamak; **ˈmis.beˈliev.er** *n.* imansız (*veya* inançsız) kimse, kâfir.

**mis.cal.cu.late** [ˈmisˈkælkjuleit] *vb.* yanlış hesap etm.; **ˈmis.calˈcuˈla.tion** *n.* yanlış hesap(lama).

**mis.call** [ˈmisˈkɔːl] *v/t.* yanlış isim vermek.

**mis.car.riage** [misˈkæridʒ] *n.* başarısızlık; yanlış sevkiyat; çocuk düşürme; ~ of justice adlî hata; **misˈcar.ry** *v/i.* başaramamak; doğru adrese ulaşamamak (*mektup v.b.*); çocuk düşürmek.

**mis.cast** *thea.* [misˈkɑːst] (*irr.* cast) *v/t.* yanlış rol vermek.

**mis.ce.ge.na.tion** [misidʒiˈneiʃən] *n.* ırk karışımı, değişik ırklardan kişilerin evlenmesi.

**mis.cel.la.ne.ous** □ [misiˈleinjəs] türlü türlü, çeşitli, muhtelif; **mis.celˈla.ne.ous.ness** *n.* çeşitlilik.

**mis.cel.la.ny** [miˈseləni] *n.* derleme; **misˈcel.la.nies** *n. pl.* edebî derlemeler.

**mis.chance** [misˈtʃɑːns] talihsizlik, şanssızlık, kaza.

**mis.chief** [ˈmistʃif] *n.* zarar, ziyan, hasar, telef; yaramazlık, haylazlık; fesat; F şeytan, haylaz kimse; make ~ between aralarını bozmak -in; get into ~ yaramazlık etm.; ˈ~-mak.er *n.* kavga çıkaran *veya* fitnecilik eden kimse.

**mis.chie.vous** □ [ˈmistʃivəs] zararlı; arabozucu; yaramaz; **ˈmis.chie.vous.ness** *n.* arabozuculuk; yaramazlık.

**mis.con.ceive** [ˈmiskənˈsiːv] *vb.* yanlış anlamak; **mis.con.cep.tion** [ˈ~ˈsepʃən] *n.* yanlış anlama, hata.

**mis.con.duct** 1. [misˈkɔndʌkt] *n.* kötü davranış; kötü yönetim; zina; suiistimal; 2. [ˈ~kənˈdʌkt] *v/i.* kötü yönetmek; ~ o.s. kötü (*veya* ahlâksızca) davranmak.

**mis.con.struc.tion** [ˈmiskənˈstrʌkʃən] *n.* yanlış yorumlama *veya* anlama; **mis.con.strue** [ˈ~ˈstruː] *v/t.* yanlış yorumlamak, yanlış anlamak.

**mis.count** [ˈmisˈkaunt] 1. *vb.* yanlış saymak, yanlış hesap etm.; 2. *n.* yanlış sayma.

**mis.cre.ant** [ˈmiskriənt] 1. *n.* alçak (*veya* kötülükçü) kimse; 2. *adj.* zalim, gaddar, merhametsiz.

**mis.cre.a.ted** [ˈmiskriˈeitid] *adj.* biçimsiz, çirkin.

**mis.date** [misˈdeit] 1. *n.* yanlış tarih koyma; 2. *v/t.* yanlış tarih koymak.

**mis.deal** [ˈmisˈdiːl] (*irr.* deal) *vb.* iskambil: yanlış dağıtmak.

**mis.deed** [ˈmisˈdiːd] *n.* kötülük, ahlâksızca hareket.

**mis.de.mean.ant** ☆ [misdi'mi:nənt] *n.* kabahat türünden bir suçtan dolayı suçlanan kimse; **mis.de'mean.o(u)r** ☆ [~nə] *n.* hafif suç, cürüm, kabahat.

**mis.di.rect** ['misdi'rekt] *v/t.* yanlış yere göndermek; yanıltmak; **'mis.di'rec.tion** *n.* yanlış yere gönderme; yanıltma.

**mis.do.ing** ['mis'du:iŋ] *n.* *mst* ~s *pl.* kötü davranma.

**mise-en-scène** *thea.* ['mi:zɑ:n'sein] *n.* mizansen.

**mi.ser** ['maizə] *n.* hasis (*veya* cimri, pinti) kimse.

**mis.er.a.ble** □ ['mizərəbl] mutsuz, dertli; sefil; hasta; pek kötü; utanmaz; **'mis.er.a.ble.ness** *n.* yoksulluk, sefalet.

**mi.ser.ly** ['maizəli] *adj.* hasis, pinti, cimri.

**mis.er.y** ['mizəri] *n.* yoksulluk, sefalet; bedbahtlık; F yoksulluk çeken *veya* yakınan kimse.

**mis.fea.sance** ☆ [mis'fi:zəns] *n.* yolsuzluk, kanunsuzluk.

**mis.fire** ['mis'faiə] **1.** *n.* ateş almama (*tabanca*); *mot.* ateşlememe, iştial bozukluğu; **2.** *v/i.* ateş almamak; *fig.* anlaşılmamak (*espri*); hedefine ulaşamamak (*plan*).

**mis.fit** ['misfit] *n.* iyi uymayan şey, oturmayan elbise; *fig.* pozisyonuna *veya* çevresine uymayan (*veya* uyumsuz) kimse.

**mis.for.tune** [mis'fɔ:tʃən] *n.* talihsizlik; şanssız kaza *veya* olay.

**mis.give** [mis'giv] (*irr.* give) *v/t.* şüpheye düşürmek; my heart misgave me şüpheye düştüm; **mis'giv.ing** *n.* şüphe, kuşku, endişe, güvensizlik.

**mis.gov.ern** ['mis'gʌvən] *v/t.* kötü yönetmek; **mis'gov.ern.ment** *n.* kötü yönetim.

**mis.guide** ['mis'gaid] *v/t.* yanlış bilgi *veya* yön vermek; **'mis'guid.ed** *adj.* yanlış yola yönlendirilmiş; yanlış değerlendirilmiş.

**mis.han.dle** ['mis'hændl] *v/t.* kötü kullanmak; kötü yönetmek.

**mis.hap** ['mishæp] *n.* talihsizlik, kaza, aksilik.

**mish.mash** ['miʃmæʃ] *n.* karmakarışıklık.

**mis.in.form** ['misin'fɔ:m] *v/t.* yanlış bilgi vermek -*e*; **'mis.in.for'ma.tion** *n.* yanlış bilgi.

**mis.in.ter.pret** ['misin'tə:prit] *v/t.* yanlış yorumlamak, yanlış anlamak -*i*; **'mis.in.ter.pre'ta.tion** *n.* yanlış yorum.

**mis.judge** ['mis'dʒʌdʒ] *vb.* yanlış hüküm vermek; yanlış kanaat oluşturmak; **'mis'judg(e).ment** *n.* yanlış yargı.

**mis.lay** [mis'lei] (*irr.* lay) *v/t.* bşi yanlış bir yere koymak, kaybetmek.

**mis.lead** [mis'li:d] (*irr.* lead) *v/t.* yanlış yönlendirmek; yanlış yapmaya neden olm.; aldatmak, yanlış fikir vermek; **mis'lead.ing** *adj.* yanlış etki *veya* izlenim veren, yanıltıcı.

**mis.man.age** ['mis'mænidʒ] *v/t.* kötü *veya* yanlış yönetmek; **'mis'man.age.ment** *n.* kötü (*veya* yanlış) yönetim.

**mis.name** ['mis'neim] *v/t.* yanlış isim ile çağırmak.

**mis.no.mer** ['mis'nəumə] *n.* isim *veya* sözcüğün yanlış kullanımı.

**mi.sog.a.mist** [mi'sɔgəmist] *n.* evlilikten nefret eden kimse.

**mi.sog.y.nist** [mai'sɔdʒinist] *n.* kadın düşmanı, kadınlardan nefret eden kimse; **mi'sog.y.ny** *n.* kadınlardan nefret etme.

**mis.place** ['mis'pleis] *v/t.* yanlış yere koymak; istismar etm.

**mis.print 1.** [mis'print] *v/t.* yanlış basmak; **2.** ['mis'print] *n.* baskı hatası.

**mis.pro.nounce** ['misprə'nauns] *v/t.* yanlış telaffuz etm.; **mis.pro.nun.ci.a.tion** ['~prənʌnsi'eiʃən] *n.* yanlış telaffuz.

**mis.quo.ta.tion** ['miskwəu'teiʃən] yanlış aktarma; **'mis'quote** *v/t.* yanlış aktarmak.

**mis.read** ['mis'ri:d] (*irr.* read) *v/t.* yanlış okumak; yanlış yorumlamak.

**mis.rep.re.sent** ['misrepri'zent] *v/t.* kötü temsil etm.; yanlış anlatmak; **'mis.rep.re.sen'ta.tion** *n.* kötü temsil etme; yalan.

**mis.rule** ['mis'ru:l] **1.** *n.* kötü yönetim; karışıklık; kanunsuzluk; **2.** *v/t.* kötü yönetmek.

**miss¹** [mis] *n.* *mst* ♀ bekâr bayan, genç kız; Bayan.

**miss²** [~] **1.** *n.* başarısızlık; isabet ettirememe, boşa gitme; **2.** *vb.* vuramamak, isabet et(tire)memek; bulamamak, kaçırmak, yetişememek; göreceği gelmek; özlemek, hasret çekmek; eksik olm.; ~ fire ateş almamak; ~ one's footing (ayağı) kaymak, sürçmek; ~ out atlamak, gözden kaçırmak; kaçırmak, bulunmamak (*şans*).

**mis.sal** *eccl.* ['misəl] *n.* Aşaî Rabbani ayini kitabı.

**mis.shap.en** ['mis'ʃeipən] *adj.* deforme olmuş, biçimsiz.

**mis.sile** ['misail] *n.* mermi; ok; atılan madde; füze.

**miss.ing** ['misiŋ] *adj.* hazır bulunmayan, eksik, nâmevcut; *part.* ✕ kayıp, âkıbeti meçhul kalan; be ~ yokluğu çok hissedilmek, onsuz yapılamamak.

**mis.sion** ['miʃən] *n.* görev, misyon, hizmet; görevle bir yere gönderilen kimseler; *eccl.* dinî propaganda; misyon; *pol.* delegasyon; sefarethane, elçilik; hedef, amaç; **mis.sion.ar.y** ['miʃənri] **1.** *n.* misyoner; **2.** *adj.* dinsel görev ile ilgili.

**mis.sis** F ['misiz] *n.* eş, hanım.

**mis.sive** ['misiv] *n.* uzun mektup.

**mis.spell** ['mis'spel] (*irr.* spell) *v/t.* yanlış hecelemek (*veya* yazmak).

**mis.spend** ['mis'spend] (*irr.* spend) *v/t.* israf etm., heba etm., saçıp savurmak, boş yere sarfetmek.

**mis.state** ['mis'steit] *v/t.* yanlış ifade etm.; **'mis'state.ment** *n.* yanlış ifade.

**mis.sus** F ['misəz] *n.* eş, hanım.

**miss.y** F ['misi] *n.* genç kız.

**mist** [mist] **1.** *n.* sis, duman; *fig.* karartı, bulanıklık; **in a ~** yolunu şaşırmış, şaşkın; **2.** *vb.* sis ile kapla(n)mak.

**mis.tak.a.ble** [mis'teikəbl] *adj.* yanlış anlaşılabilir; **mis'take 1.** (*irr.* take) *v/t.* tanımamak, teşhis etmemek; benzetmek (**for** -*e*); kazı koz anlamak, yanlış anlamak, karıştırmak (**with**); **be ~n** yanılmak; *v/i.* ⚓ yanılmak, hata etm.; **2.** *n.* yanlış(lık), hata, yanılma; **by ~** yanlışlıkla; **and no ~** F kesinlikle; **mis'tak.en** ☐ hatalı, yanlış.

**mis.ter** ['mistə] *n.* (*abbr.* Mr.) Bay, Efendi.

**mis.time** ['mis'taim] *v/t.* zamansız söylemek, zamansız yapmak, vaktini yanlış hesaplamak; **'mis'timed** *adj.* vakitsiz, zamansız, yersiz.

**mist.i.ness** ['mistinis] *n.* sis, pus, duman; *fig.* karanlık.

**mis.tle.toe** ⚘ ['misltəu] *n.* ökseotu.

**mis.trans.late** ['mistræns'leit] *v/t.* yanlış tercüme etm., yanlış çevirmek; **'mis.trans'la.tion** *n.* yanlış tercüme (*veya* çeviri).

**mis.tress** ['mistris] *n.* evin hanımı; (*kadın*) öğretmen; bilgili kadın; metres, dost.

**mis.tri.al** ⚖ ['mis'traiəl] *n.* geçersiz duruşma.

**mis.trust** ['mis'trʌst] **1.** *v/t.* güvenmemek, itimat etmemek -*e*; **2.** *n.* güvensizlik, itimatsızlık; **'mis'trust.ful** ☐ [~ful] kuşkulu, güvensiz, şüpheli.

**mist.y** ☐ ['misti] sisli, puslu, dumanlı; *fig.* bulanık, müphem, karanlık.

**mis.un.der.stand** ['misʌndə'stænd] (*irr.* stand) *vb.* yanlış anlamak, ters anlamak, kazı koz anlamak; **'mis.un.der'stand.ing** *n.* yanlış anlama.

**mis.us.age** [mis'ju:zidʒ] *n.* yanlış kullanılış; kötü davranma.

**mis.use 1.** ['mis'ju:z] *v/t.* yanlış kullanmak, suiistimal etm.; kötü davranmak;

**2.** ['~'ju:s] *n.* yanlış kullanma, suiistimal.

**mite¹** *zo.* [mait] *n.* kene, peynir kurdu, uyuz böceği.

**mite²** [~] *n.* çok ufak bş; a ~ (of a child) yavrucak.

**mit.i.gate** ['mitigeit] *v/t.* teskin etm., yatıştırmak (*a. fig.*); azaltmak, hafifletmek; **mit.i'ga.tion** *n.* yatıştırma; azaltma.

**mi.tre, mi.ter** ['maitə] **1.** *n.* piskoposluk tacı; ⊕ gönye; **2.** *vb.* piskoposluk tacı giymek; ⊕ gönye ile ölçmek; **'mi.tre-wheel** *n.* ⊕ konik dişli çark.

**mitt** [mit] *n.* beysbol, boks: eldiven; = mitten.

**mit.ten** ['mitn] *n.* kolçak, parmaksız eldiven; **get the ~** F ret cevabı almak, kovulmak.

**mix** [miks] **1.** *v/t.* & *v/i.* karış(tır)mak; karmak; katmak; birleşmek; kaynaşmak, uyuşmak, bağdaşmak; ~ **in society** toplum hayatına katılmak; ~ed karışık, karmaşık (*a. fig.*); karma; ~ed marriage değişik din ve ırklardan kimselerin evlenmesi; ~ed pickles *pl.* karışık turşu; ~ **up** (zihnini) karıştırmak; **be ~ed up with** karışmak -*e*, bulaşmak -*e*, atılmak -*e*; ~ **with** uyum sağlamak *ile*, geçinmek *ile*; **2.** *n.* karış(tır)ma; karışım; **'mix.er** *n.* karıştırıcı kimse *veya* şey; mikser (*a. radyo*); good (bad) ~ girişken (olmayan) kimse; **mix.ture** ['~tʃə] *n.* karışım; karış(tır)ma; kaynaşma (*a. fig.*); **'mix-up** *n.* karışıklık, anlaşmazlık.

**miz.en, miz.zen** ⚓ ['mizn] *n.* mizana direği (*veya* yelkeni); *attr.* mizana...

**miz.zle** F ['mizl] *v/i.* serpiştirmek, çiselemek (*yağmur*).

**mne.mon.ic** [ni:'mɔnik] **1.** *adj.* (~ally) hafızaya yardımcı olan; **2.** *n.*, **mne'mon.ics** *pl.* hafızayı kuvvetlendirme sanatı.

**mo co.** *veya* *sl.* [məu] = moment.

**moan** [məun] **1.** *n.* inilti, figan; uğultu (*rüzgâr*); şikâyet; **2.** *v/i.* inlemek, figan etm.; uğuldamak (*rüzgâr*); şikâyet etm., sızlanmak.

**moat** [məut] *n.* kale hendeği; **'moat.ed** *adj.* hendekli.

**mob** [mɔb] **1.** *n.* ayaktakımı, avam; izdiham, kalabalık; gangster çetesi; **2.** *v/t.* etrafını sarmak; saldırmak, hücum etm.; doluşmak; **'mob.bish** *adj.* kaba, âmiyane.

**mob-cap** ['mɔbkæp] *n.* kadın başlığı.

**mo.bile** ['məubail] **1.** *adj.* oynak, yer değiştirebilen, devingen, hareketli, değişken; ✕ seyyar (*ordu*); **2.** *n.* ince tellere bağlı parçaları hava akımı ile hareket eden bir tür süs eşyası *veya* sanat eseri; **mo.bil.i.ty** [~'biliti] *n.* hareketlilik; değişkenlik; **mo.bi.li.za.tion** ✕ [~bilai-'zeiʃən] *n.* seferberlik; **'mo.bi.lize** *v/t.* ✕ seferber etm., silah altına almak.

**mob-law** ['mɔblɔː] *n.* linç kanunu.

**mob.oc.ra.cy** [mɔ'bɔkrəsi] *n.* avamtakımı yönetimi; **mob.ster** ['mɔbstə] *n.* gangster.

**moc.ca.sin** ['mɔkəsin] *n.* mokasen.

**mo.cha** ['mɔkə] *n.* Yemen kahvesi.

**mock** [mɔk] **1.** *n.* alay, dalga geçme; **2.** *adj.* sahte, taklit, yapmacık...; ~ **fight** yalandan kavga; **3.** *v/t. & v/i.* taklit etm., taklidini yapmak; karşı koymak -*e*; alay etm., dalga geçmek, eğlenmek (at *ile*); **'mock.er** *n.* alaycı (*veya* dalgacı) kimse; **'mock.er.y** *n.* alay, dalga geçme; taklit; alaya alınan şey; **'mock-he'ro.ic** *adj.* destansı taşlama türünden; **'mock.ing 1.** *n.* alay etme, dalga geçme; **2.** ☐ alaycı..., dalgacı...; **'mock.ing-bird** *n.* alaycı kuş. **mock...**: **'~-king** *n.* kral müsveddesi, sözde kral; **'~-'tur.tle soup** kaplumbağa çorbası tadında et çorbası; **'~-up** *n.* model, kalıp.

**mod.al** ☐ ['mɔudl] *part. gr.* kipe ait, kip... **mo.dal.i.ty** [~'dæliti] *n.* usül, şekil, tarz.

**mode** [mɔud] *n.* tarz, usül, üslup, şekil, moda; *gr.* kip.

**mod.el** ['mɔdl] **1.** *n.* örnek, numune, model; şekil, kalıp; plan, resim; manken; *fig.* örnek alınacak kimse; *attr.* örnek...; model...; act as a ~ modellik yapmak (to -*e*); ~ aircraft model uçak; **2.** *v/i. -in* modelini yapmak; örneğine göre yapmak; *v/i.* mankenlik (*veya* modellik) yapmak; *fig.* kendine örnek almak (after, on, upon -*i*); **mod.el.(l)er** ['mɔdlə] *n.* modelci.

**mod.er.ate 1.** ☐ ['mɔdərit] ılımlı; orta; makûl; **2.** ['~reit] *v/t. & v/i.* hafifle(t)mek, azal(t)mak, yatış(tır)mak, yumuşa(t)mak; başkanlık etm.; **mod.er.ate.ness** ['mɔdəritnis] *n.* ılımlılık; **mod.er.a.tion** ['~reiʃən] *n.* itidal, ölçülülük, ılımlılık; in ~ ölçülü olarak, aşırıya kaçmadan, kararında; ²s *pl. univ.* Oxford Üniversitesinde edebiyat fakültesi diploması için ilk genel imtihan; **'mod.er.a.tor** *n.* toplantı başkanı; *univ.* imtihan gözcüsü; *phys.* yavaşlatıcı madde.

**mod.ern** ['mɔdən] **1.** *adj.* yeni, modern, çağdaş, çağcıl; ~ **languages** *pl.* çağdaş diller; **2.** *n.* the ~s *pl.* çağdaş kimseler; modern görüşlü kimseler; **'mod.ern.ism** *n.* çağdaşlık, modernlik; yenilik; **'mod.ern.ist** *n.* yenilikçi kimse; **mod.ern'is.tic**

*adj.* yenilikçi; **mo.der.ni.ty** [mɔ'dəːniti] *n.* yenilik, çağdaşlık; **mod.ern.ize** ['mɔdə-naiz] *v/t. & v/i.* modernleş(tir)mek, yenileş(tir)mek.

**mod.est** ☐ ['mɔdist] alçak gönüllü, mütevazı; gösterişsiz; tutarlı, ılımlı; **'mod.es.ty** *n.* tevazu, alçak gönüllülük; tutarlılık.

**mod.i.cum** ['mɔdikəm] *n.* azıcık miktar, nebze.

**mod.i.fi.a.ble** ['mɔdifaiəbl] *adj.* değiştirilebilir; **mod.i.fi.ca.tion** [~fi'keiʃən] *n.* değişiklik; değiştirme; **mod.i.fy** [~'fai] *v/t.* değiştirmek; azaltmak, hafifletmek; *gr.* nitelemek; tamlamak.

**mod.ish** ['mɔudiʃ] *adj.* modaya uygun, son model.

**mo.diste** [mɔu'diːst] *n.* kadın şapkacısı *veya* terzisi.

**mod.u.late** ['mɔdjuleit] *v/t.* ayarlamak; tatlılaştırmak, yumuşatmak, hafifleştirmek (*ses*); *radyo:* modüle etm.; **mod-u'la.tion** *n.* hafifle(t)me; modülasyon, geçiş; **'mod.u.la.tor** *n.* modülatör; ~ of tonality *film:* ses modülatörü; **mod.ule** ['~djuːl] *n.* sabit değer; çap, mikyas (*a.* ♚); *s.* lunar ~; **mod.u.lus** *phys.* ['~djuləs] *n.* modül.

**Mo.gul** [mɔu'gʌl]: the Great *veya* Grand ~ Timur hanedanından Hindistan imparatoru.

**mo.hair** ['mɔuhɛə] *n.* moher, tiftik yünü; moherden yapılan kumaş.

**Mo.ham.med.an** [mɔu'hæmidən] **1.** *n.* Müslüman etm.; **2.** *adj.* Müslüman.

**moi.e.ty** ['mɔiəti] *n.* yarı(m); kısım, pay.

**moil** [mɔil] *v/i.* çok çalışmak, didinmek.

**moi.ré** ['mwaːrei] *n.* hareli (ipek) kumaş.

**moist** [mɔist] *adj.* nemli, rutubetli; ıslak; yaşlı (*göz*); **mois.ten** ['mɔisn] *v/t.* ıslatmak; *v/i.* ıslanmak, nemlenmek, yaşarmak (*göz*); **moist.ness** ['mɔistnis], **mois.ture** ['~tʃə] *n.* nem, rutubet, ıslaklık.

**moke** *sl.* [mɔuk] *n.* eşek.

**mo.lar** ['mɔulə] *n. a.* ~ tooth azıdişi.

**mo.las.ses** [mɔu'læsiz] *n.* melas.

**mold** [mɔuld], **'mold.board** etc. *s.* mould etc.

**mole¹** *zo.* [mɔul] *n.* köstebek.

**mole²** [~] *n.* ben, leke.

**mole³** [~] *n.* dalgakıran, mendirek.

**mo.lec.u.lar** [mɔu'lekjulə] *adj.* moleküle ait, moleküllü; **mol.e.cule** *phys.* ['mɔlikjuːl] *n.* molekül, zerre, tozan.

**mole.hill** ['mɔulhil] *n.* köstebek tepesi; make a mountain out of a ~ pireyi deve yapmak; **'mole-skin** *n.* köstebek derisi; köstebek derisine benzer kumaş.

**mo.lest** [mɔu'lest] *v/t.* rahatsız etm.; tecavüz. etm., sarkıntılık etm.; **mo.les.ta-tion** [~'teiʃən] *n.* rahatsız etme; tecavüz, sarkıntılık.

**moll** F [mɔl] *n.* gangsterin sevgilisi; fahişe, orospu.

**mol.li.fy** ['mɔlifai] *v/t.* yumuşatmak, yatıştırmak, sakinleştirmek.

**mol.lusc** *zo.* ['mɔləsk] *n.* yumuşakçalar sınıfından bir hayvan; **'mol.lusk** = **mollusc.**

**mol.ly.cod.dle** ['mɔlikɔdl] **1.** *n.* muhallebi çocuğu, hanım evlâdı; **2.** *v/t.* üstüne titremek.

**mo.loch** ['mɔulɔk] *n.* üstü dikenli Avustralya kertenkelesi.

**mol.ten** ['mɔultən] *adj.* erimiş; dökme.

**mo.lyb.den.um** 🜍 [mɔ'libdinəm] *n.* molibden.

**mo.ment** ['mɔumənt] *n.* an; önem; kuvvet; unsur; = ~um; at *veya* for the ~ şimdi, şu anda; to the ~ dakikası dakikasına; **'mo.men.tar.y** ◻ anî, bir anlık...; geçici; **'mo.ment.ly** *adv.* her an; bir anlık; **mo.men.tous** ◻ [mɔu'mentəs] önemli, mühim, ciddî; **mo'mentum** *phys.* [~təm] *n.* moment; *fig.* hız, sürat.

**mon.a.chism** ['mɔnəkizəm] *n.* manastır hayatı.

**mon.ad** *phls.* ['mɔnæd] *n.* monad.

**mon.arch** ['mɔnək] *n.* kral, hükümdar; **mo.nar.chic, mo.nar.chi.cal** ◻ [mɔ'nɑːkik-(əl)] monarşiye ait, monarşik; **'mon.arch.ism** ['mɔnəkizəm] *n.* kraliyetçilik; **'mon.arch.ist** *n.* kraliyetçi; **'mon.arc.y** *n.* krallık, monarşi, tekerklik.

**mon.as.ter.y** ['mɔnəstəri] *n.* manastır; **mo.nas.tic, mo.nas.ti.cal** ◻ [mə'næstik(əl)] manastıra ait, manastır...; **mo'nas.ti.cism** [~sizəm] *n.* manastır hayatı (*veya* sistemi).

**mon.au.ral** [mɔn'ɔːrəl] *adj.* tek kulaklı; tek kulakla duymaya ait; mono...

**Mon.day** ['mʌndi] *n.* pazartesi.

**mon.e.tar.y** ['mʌnitəri] *adj.* paraya ait, parasal; ~ reform para reformu.

**mon.ey** ['mʌni] *n.* para, nakit; ready ~ nakit, peşin para; out of ~ parasız; ~ down peşin para; get one's ~'s worth parasının karşılığını almak; marry ~ zengin biriyle evlenmek; make ~ para kazanmak; **'~-box** *n.* kumbara; **'~-chang.er** *n.* sarraf; **mon.eyed** ['mʌnid] *adj.* paralı, para babası.

**mon.ey...:** **'~-grub.ber** *n.* para canlısı kimse; **'~-lend.er** *n.* tefeci, faizci; **'~-mar.ket** *n.* para piyasası, borsa; **'~-or.der** *n.* para havalesi; **'~-spin.ner** *n.* F iyi para getiren şey.

**mon.ger** ['mʌŋgə] *suffix* ...satıcısı; ...yapan.

**Mon.gol** ['mɔŋgɔl], **Mon.go.lian** [~'gəuljən] **1.** *adj.* Moğol ırkına *veya* Moğolcaya ait; **2.** *n.* Moğol(ca).

**mon.grel** ['mʌŋgrəl] **1.** *n.* melez köpek, bitki *veya* insan; **2.** *adj.* karışık soylu, melez...

**mo.ni.tion** [məu'niʃən] *n.* ikaz, ihtar; **mon.i.tor** ['mɔnitə] *n.* sınıf başkanı; ↓ ağır toplu savaş gemisi; *radyo:* dinleme servisi görevlisi; monitör; **'mon.i.to.ry** *adj.* uyarıcı, ikaz edici, öğüt veren.

**monk** [mʌŋk] *n.* rahip, keşiş; **'monk.er.y** *n. part. contp.* manastır (hayatı).

**mon.key** ['mʌŋki] **1.** *n.* maymun (*a. fig.*); ⊕ şahmerdan başı; *sl.* 500 pound *veya* dolar; put s.o.'s ~ up F *b-nin* tepesini attırmak; ~ business *Am. sl.* düzenbazlık; aşk ilişkisi; **2.** *v/i.* F oynamak; ~ about with kurcalamak *-i*, oynayıp durmak *ile*; **'~-en.gine** *n.* şahmerdan motoru; **'~-jack.et** *n.* ↓ gemici ceketi; **'~-nut** *n.* ♣ yerfıstığı; **'~-puz.zle** *n.* ♣ bir tür çam ağacı; **'~-wrench** *n.* ⊕ İngiliz anahtarı; throw a ~ in s.th. *Am. sl.* bşi bozmak, bşe çomak sokmak.

**monk.hood** ['mʌŋkhud] *n.* keşişlik, rahiplik; **'monk.ish** *adj. mst contp.* keşiş gibi.

**mono...** ['mɔnəu] *prefix* tek, bir, mono...; **mo.no.chrome** *paint.* ['mɔnəkrəum] **1.** *adj.* tek renkli; **2.** *n.* tek renkli resim; **mon.o.cle** ['mɔnəkl] *n.* tek gözlük, monokl; **mo.no.cot.y.le.don** ♣ ['mɔnəukɔti-'liːdən] *n.* tek çenekli bir bitki, monoko tiledon; **mo.noc.u.lar** [mɔ'nɔkjulə] *adj.* tek gözlü; **mo'nog.a.my** [~gəmi] *n.* tekeşlilik, monogami; **mon.o.gram** ['mɔnəgræm] *n.* monogram, bir ismin baş harflerinden oluşan desen; **mon.o.graph** ['~grɑːf] *n.* monografi, tekyazım; **mon.o.lith** ['mɔnəuliθ] *n.* yekpare taştan abide; **mon.o.logue** ['mɔnəlɔg] *n.* monolog; **mon.o.ma.ni.a** ['mɔnəu'meinjə] *n.* sabit fikir, saplantı; **'mon.o'ma.ni.ac** [~niæk] *n.* saplantılı kimse; **mon.o.plane** ♣ ['mɔnəuplein] *n.* tek kanatlı uçak; **mo.nop.o.list** [mə'nɔpəlist] *n.* tekelci; **mo'nop.o.lize** [~laiz] *v/t.* tekeline almak (*a. fig.*); **mo'nop.o.ly** *n.* tekel (maddesi); **mon.o.syl.lab.ic** ['mɔnəusi'læbik] *adj.* (~ally) tek heceli; **mon.o.syl.la.ble** ['mɔnəsiləbl] *n.* tek heceli kelime; **mon.o.the.ism** ['mɔnəuθiːzəm] *n.* tektanrıcılık, monoteizm; **mon.o.tone** ['mɔnətəun] **1.** *n.* düz ses; **2.** ~ yeknesak, monoton, düz sesle; **2.** *v/t.* tekdüze konuşmak (*veya* okumak *veya* şarkı söylemek); **mo-**

not.o.nous ☐ [mə'nɒtnəs] monoton, tekdüze, sıkıcı, yeknesak; mo'not.o.ny n. monotonluk, tekdüzelik, yeknesaklık; mon.o.type typ. ['mɒnəutaip] n. monotip; mon.ox.ide ⚛ [mɒ'nɒksaid] n. monoksit.

mon.sieur [mə'sjəː] n. bay, bey, efendi, mösyö.

mon.soon [mɒn'suːn] n. muson.

mon.ster ['mɒnstə] n. canavar, dev (a. fig.); attr. koskocaman..., dev gibi...

mon.strance eccl. ['mɒnstrəns] n. içinde okunmuş ekmek olan kap.

mon.stros.i.ty [mɒns'trɒsiti] n. canavar-(lık); çirkin şey; 'mon.strous ☐ canavar gibi; anormal; koskocaman; ürkünç, korkunç, inanılmaz, hayret verici; saçma sapan.

mon.tage [mɒn'taːʒ] n. fotomontaj.

month [mʌnθ] n. ay; this day ~ önümüzdeki ay bugün; 'month.ly 1. adj. & adv. aylık, ayda bir (olan); ~ season ticket aylık bilet; 2. n. aylık dergi.

mon.u.ment ['mɒnjumənt] n. anıt, abide; eser; tarihî yapı; mon.u.men.tal ☐ [~'mentl] anıtsal, abidevî...; muazzam, şahane; koskocaman.

moo [muː] 1. v/i. böğürmek; 2. n. böğürme.

mooch F [muːtʃ] v/i.: ~ about aylak aylak dolaşmak.

mood¹ gr. [muːd] n. kip.

mood² [~] n. mizaç, ruh haleti (veya durumu).

mood.i.ness ['muːdinis] n. karamsarlık; 'mood.y ☐ dargın, küskün; karamsar, umutsuz; sinirli, huysuz, aksi.

moon [muːn] 1. n. ay, kamer; uydu; mehtap; once in a blue ~ F kırk yılda bir; 2. v/i. mst ~ about dalgın dalgın gezinmek; v/t. ~ away boşa geçirmek (zaman); 'moon.beam n. ay ışını; 'moon.less adj. aysız, mehtapsız; 'moon.light n. mehtap; 'moon.lit adj. mehtaplı.

moon...: '~.shine n. mehtap; saçmalık; Am. kaçak içki; '~.shin.er n. Am. F içki kaçakçısı; '~.struck adj. aysar, deli; 'moon.y ☐ aya ait, ay...; hilâl şeklinde; F hayalperest, dalgın, düşünceli; sl. aylak.

Moor¹ [muə] n. Mağribî; Faslı.

moor² [~] n. kır, part. avlak; † veya prov. bataklık.

moor³ ⚓ [~] v/t. & v/i. palamarla bağla(n)mak; moor.age ['muəridʒ] n. demir atma; gemi bağlama yeri.

moor.fowl ['muəfaul], 'moor.game [~geim] n. ormantavuğu.

moor.ing-mast ['muəriŋmaːst] n. balon

bağlama direği.

moo.rings ['muəriŋz] n. pl. ⚓ palamar takımı; gemi bağlama yeri; ahlakî değerler.

Moor.ish ['muəriʃ] adj. Mağribî; Fas'a ait, Fas...

moor.land ['muələnd] n. (boz)kır.

moose zo. [muːs] n. a. ~-deer bir çeşit geyik.

moot [muːt] 1. n. ~ case, ~ point şüpheli (veya tartışmalı) mesele; 2. v/t. tartışmak.

mop [mɒp] 1. n. silme bezi; dağınık saç; 2. v/t. silip süpürmek, temizlemek; ~ up silmek; sl. silip süpürmek; sl. işini bitirmek; ~ the floor with s.o. b-ni alt etm., ezip geçmek, mat etm.

mope [məup] 1. n. sıkıcı kimse; üzüntü; the ~s pl. sıkıntı, bunaltı, hüzün; 2. v/i. hüzünlü (veya keyifsiz) olm.

mo.ped ['məuped] n. moped, motorlu bisiklet.

mop.ing ☐ ['məupiŋ], 'mop.ish hüzünlü, kasvetli.

mo.raine geol. [mɒ'rein] n. buzultaş, moren.

mor.al ['mɒrəl] 1. ☐ ahlâki..., törel...; erdemli, fazletli; manevî; doğru, dürüst; 2. n. ahlâk dersi; ~s pl. ahlâk; mo.rale [mə'raːl] n. part. ✕ maneviyat, manevî güç, moral; mor.al.ist ['mɒrəlist] n. ahlâkçı; mo.ral.i.ty [mə'ræliti] n. ahlâk (dersi); hist. thea. karakterlerin erdem ve kötülük gibi ahlâki değerleri simgelediği bir dram türü; mor.al.ize ['mɒrəlaiz] v/i. ahlâk dersi vermek (upon hususunda); v/t. ahlâki yönden değerlendirmek.

mo.rass [mə'ræs] n. batak(lık); engel, güçlük.

mor.bid ☐ ['mɒːbid] hastalıklı; bozuk, çarpık (fikir); mor'bid.i.ty, 'mor.bid.ness n. marazi konulara aşırı ilgi duyma; hastalık oranı, morbidite.

mor.dant ['mɒːdənt] 1. adj. iğneleyici, sert, keskin; 2. n. renkleri sabitleştiren madde, mordan.

more [mɒː] 1. adj. daha çok; daha fazla; biraz daha; 2. adv. daha; bir daha; once ~ bir (kez) daha; two ~ iki tane daha; so much ~, all the ~ haydi haydi; no ~ artık ...değil; ~ and ~ gittikçe; 3. n. fazlalık, çokluk.

mo.rel ⚘ [mɒ'rel] n. siyah mantar.

mo.rel.lo ⚘ [mɒ'reləu] n. a. ~ cherry vişne.

more.o.ver [mɒː'rəuvə] adv. bundan başka, ayrıca, üstelik.

Mo.resque [mɒ'resk] 1. adj. Fas mimarisi türünde; **2.** *n.* Fas· mimarisinde süs, arabesk.

**mor.ga.nat.ic** [mɔːgəˈnætik] *adj.* (~ally) yukarı ve aşağı tabakadan kişilerce yapılan *(evlilik).*

**morgue** [ˈmɔːg] *n.* morg.

**mor.i.bund** [ˈmɔːribʌnd] *adj.* ölüm döşeğinde, can çekişmekte *(a. fig.);* sonu gelmiş.

**Mor.mon** [ˈmɔːmən] *n.* Mormon.

**morn** *poet.* [mɔːn] *n.* sabah.

**morn.ing** [ˈmɔːniŋ] **1.** *n.* sabah, seher; *fig.* başlangıç; good ~! günaydın!, iyi sabahlar!; in the ~, during the ~ sabahleyin; .this ~ bu sabah; tomorrow ~ yarın sabah; **2.** *adj.* sabaha mahsus, sabah ...; ~ **coat** jaketatay; ~ **dress** frak, resmî sabah kıyafeti; ˈ~-ˈglo.ry *n.* ❦ gündüzsefası, kahkahaçiçeği; ~ **per.form.ance** matine, gündüz seansı.

**Mo.roc.can** [məˈrɔkən] *adj.* Fas'a ait, Fas...; Faslı...

**mo.roc.co** [məˈrɔkəu] *n. a.* ~ **leather** maroken.

**mo.ron** [ˈmɔːrɔn] *n.* doğuştan geri zekâlı kimse; F kuş beyinli kimse.

**mo.rose** ☐ [məˈrəus] somurtkan, suratsız, asık suratlı; **moˈrose.ness** *n.* suratsızlık.

**mor.phi.a** [ˈmɔːfjə], **mor.phine** [ˈmɔːfiːn] *n.* morfin.

**mor.pho.lo.gy** *biol., gr.* [mɔːˈfɔlədʒi] *n.* şekilbilim, morfoloji.

**mor.row** [ˈmɔrəu] *n. mst poet.* sabah; yarın, ertesi gün; the ~ of *-in* ertesi günü.

**Morse** [mɔːs] *n. a.* ~ **code** Mors alfabesi.

**mor.sel** [ˈmɔːsəl] *n.* lokma, parça.

**mor.tal** [ˈmɔːtl] **1.** ☐ ölümlü, fani, geçici; öldürücü, amansız; ölene dek süren; kin dolu; çok uzun *(süre);* F çok büyük, aşırı; F olası, mümkün; **2.** *n.* insan(oğlu); **mor.tal.i.ty** [mɔːˈtæliti] *n.* ölümlülük, fanilik; ölüm oranı; ölü sayısı, can kaybı.

**mor.tar** [ˈmɔːtə] **1.** *n.* harç; havan; ✕ havan topu; **2.** *v/t.* harç ile sıvamak; ˈ~-board *n.* harç tahtası; *univ.* kep.

**mort.gage** [ˈmɔːgidʒ] **1.** *n.* ipotek; *a.* ~-deed ipotekli borç senedi; **2.** *v/t.* rehine koymak; ipotek etm.; **mort.ga.gee** [mɔːgəˈdʒiː] *n.* ipotekli alacak sahibi; **mort.ga.gor** [~ˈdʒɔː] *n.* ipotek yapan borçlu.

**mor.tice** [ˈmɔːtis] = mortise.

**mor.ti.cian** *Am.* [mɔːˈtiʃən] *n.* cenaze işleri görevlisi.

**mor.ti.fi.ca.tion** [mɔːtifiˈkeiʃən] *n.* ❦ kangren; küçük düşme, rezil olma.

**mor.ti.fy** [ˈmɔːtifai] *v/t.* alçaltmak, rezil

etm., küçük düşürmek; *v/i.* ❦ kangren olm.

**mor.tise** ⊕ [ˈmɔːtis] **1.** *n.* zıvana, yuva; **2.** *v/t.* zıvana ile birleştirmek; *-e* zıvana açmak.

**mor.tu.ar.y** [ˈmɔːtjuəri] **1.** *adj.* ölüme ait, ölüm...; cenazeye ait, cenaze...; **2.** *n.* morg.

**mo.sa.ic¹** [məuˈzeiik] *n.* mozaik.

**Mo.sa.ic²** [~] *adj.* Musa'ya ait.

**mo.selle** [məuˈzel] *n.* beyaz Alman şarabı.

**Mos.lem** [ˈmɔzləm] **1.** *adj.* Müslüman; **2.** *n.* Müslüman, Müslim.

**mosque** [mɔsk] *n.* cami.

**mos.qui.to** *zo.* [məsˈkiːtəu] *n., pl.* **mosˈqui.toes** [~z] sivrisinek; **mosˈqui.to-craft** *n.* ⚓ küçük savaş gemileri; **mosˈqui.to-net** *n.* cibinlik.

**moss** [mɔs] *n.* ❦ yosun; a rolling stone gathers no ~ yuvarlanan taş yosun tutmaz; ˈmoss.i.ness *n.* yosunlu olma; ˈmoss.y *adj.* yosunlu, yosunumsu.

**most** [məust] **1.** ☐ en çok, en fazla; for the ~ part genellikle, çoğunlukla, tamamen; başlıca; **2.** *adv.* pek, en çok, son derecede; en çoğu; **3.** *n.* çoğunluk, çokluk, en çok miktar; at (the) ~ en fazla, olsa olsa; make the ~ of *-den* sonuna kadar yararlanmak.

...**most** [məust, məst] *suffix* en...

**most.ly** [ˈməustli] *adv.* ekseriya, çoğunlukla, çoğu kez.

**mote** [məut] *n.* zerre; the ~ In another's eye kendi yaptıklarına oranla önemsiz bir hata.

**mo.tel** [məuˈtel] *n.* motel.

**mo.tet** ♪ [məuˈtet] *n.* çok sesli kilise ilâhisi.

**moth** [mɔθ] *n.* güve; pervane; ˈ~-ball *n.* yuvarlak naftalin; In ~s *fig.* bir kenara kaldırılmış; ˈ~-eat.en *adj.* güve yemiş.

**moth.er** [ˈmʌðə] **1.** *n.* anne, ana, valide; **2.** *v/t.* bakmak, annelik etm.; doğurmak; himaye etm.; ~ **coun.try** anayurt, anavatan; **moth.er.hood** [ˈ~hud] *n.* analık, annelik; ˈmoth.er-in-law *n.* kaynana, kayınvalide; ˈmoth.er.less *adj.* anasız, öksüz; ˈmoth.er.li.ness *n.* anaya yakışırlık; ˈmoth.er.ly *adj.* ana gibi; anaya yakışır. **moth.er...:** ˈ~-of-ˈpearl *n.* sedef; ~ **ship** *(diğer gemilerin her türlü ihtiyacını sağlayan)* ana gemi; ~ **tongue** anadili.

**moth-proof** [ˈmɔθpruːf] **1.** *adj.* güve yemez; **2.** *v/t.* güve yemez hale getirmek; ˈmoth.y *adj.* güve dolu.

**mo.tif** [məuˈtiːf] *n.* motif.

**mo.tion** [ˈməuʃən] **1.** *n.* hareket, devinim

(a. ⊕ ); *parl.* teklif, talep, önerge; ⚡ dışkılama; bring forward a ~ teklif sunmak; agree upon a ~ önergeyi kabul etm.; go through the ~s *bşi* yapar görünmek, baştan savma yapmak; set in ~ harekete getirmek, çalıştırmak; **2.** *v/t.* el ile işaret etm. *-e;* **ˈmo.tion.less** *adj.* hareketsiz; **motion pic.ture** sinema filmi.

**mo.ti.vate** [ˈməutiveit] *v/t.* sevketmek, hareketle geçirmek; **mo.tiˈva.tion** *n.* sevketme; saik, güdü, dürtü.

**mo.tive** [ˈməutiv] **1.** *adj.* hareket yaratan, itici...; devindirici...; güdüsel; ~ power itici güç; **2.** *n.* saik, güdü, dürtü; sebep, neden; motif; **3.** *v/t.* harekete getirmek; **ˈmo.tive.less** *adj.* sebepsiz, nedensiz.

**mo.tiv.i.ty** [məuˈtiviti] *n.* hareket kuvveti.

**mot.ley** [ˈmɔtli] *adj.* rengârenk, alaca; ayrı cinsten.

**mo.tor** [ˈməutə] **1.** *n.* motor; makine; otomobil, araba; ⚡ adele, kas; **2.** *adj.* motorlu: devindirici; makine...; motor...; araba...; hareket kaslarına ait; ~ nerve motor sinir; **3.** *v/i.* otomobille gitmek; **ˈ~-as.sist.ed** *adj.* motor takviyeli; **ˈ~-bi.cy.cle,** **ˈ~-bike** = motor-cycle; **ˈ~-boat** *n.* deniz motoru, motorbot; **ˈ~-ˈbus** *n.* otobüs; **~.cade** *Am.* [ˈ~keid] *n.* araba korteji, konvoy; **ˈ~-car** *n.* otomobil; **ˈ~-coach** *n.* otobüs; **ˈ~-cy.çle** *n.* motosiklet; **ˈ~-cy.clist** *n.* motosiklet sürücüsü; **mo.to.ri.al** [məuˈtɔːriəl] *adj.* hareket ettiren, işleten; **mo.tor.ing** [ˈməutəriŋ] *n.* otomobilcilik; araba kullanma; **ˈmo.tor.ist** *n.* sürücü, otomobil kullanan; **mo.tor.i.za.tion** [~raiˈzeifən] *n.* motorize etme; **ˈmo.tor.ize** *v/t.* motorla donatmak, motörleştirmek, motorize etm.; **ˈmo.tor-launch** *n.* motorbot, çok küçük vapur; **ˈmo.tor.less** *adj.* motorsuz.

**mo.tor...:** **ˈ~-man** *n.* makinist; sürücü; vatman; **ˈ~-plough** *n.* motorlu saban; **ˈ~-road,** **ˈ~.way** *n.* karayolu, otoyolu.

**mot.tle** [mɔtl] *v/t.* beneklemek; **ˈmot.tled** *adj.* benekli.

**mot.to** [ˈmɔtəu] *n., pl.* **mot.toes** [ˈ~z] ve.cize; parola, ilke.

**mo(u)ld¹** [məuld] *n.* bahçıvan toprağı, gübreli toprak; küf.

**mo(u)ld²** [~] **1.** *n.* kalıp; *fig.* yapı, karakter; **2.** *v/t.* kalıba dökmek; şekillendirmek, şekil vermek (on, upon *-e*).

**mo(u)ld-board** [ˈməuldbɔːd] *n.* saban kulağı.

**mo(u)ld.er¹** [ˈməuldə] *n.* kalıpçı, dökmeci.

**mo(u)lder²** [~] *v/i.* a. ~ away ˈçürümek, çürüyüp gitmek.

**mo(u)ld.i.ness** [ˈməuldinis] *n.* küflülük.

**mo(u)ld.ing** [ˈməuldiŋ] *n.* kalıplama; ⚠ tiriz, silme, korniş, pervaz; *attr.* kalıplama...

**mo(u)ld.y** [ˈməuldi] *adj.* küflü.

**moult** [məult] **1.** *n.* tüyˈdökme; **2.** *v/i.* tüylerini dökmek.

**mound** [maund] *n.* höyük; tepecik, tümsek; burial-~ mezar tümseği.

**mount** [maunt] **1.** *n.* dağ, tepe; binek; dayanak; top arabası; **2.** *v/t. & v/i.* ata bin(dir)mek; çıkmak *-e,* tırmanmak *-e;* asmak; takmak; üzerine koymak, oturtmak; ⊕ kurmak, monte etm. *-i;* üzerine yapıştırmak, çerçeveye geçirmek; girişmek *-e;* *thea.* sahneye koymak; *mst* ~ up yükselmek, artmak, çoğalmak; çiftleşmek *(hayvan)*; ~ed atlı; binmiş; takılı, hazır; kakma; *s.* guard 1.

**moun.tain** [ˈmauntin] *n.* dağ, tepe; ~s *pl.* dağ silsilesi; *attr.* dağ...; ~ ash ꝗ üvez; ~ chain dağ silsilesi; ~ dew F İskoç viskisi; **moun.tain.eer** [~ˈtiˈniə] *n.* dağlı; dağcı; **moun.tainˈeer.ing** *n.* dağcılık; **moun.tainˈous** *adj.* dağlık; dağ gibi; **mountain sick.ness** dağ hastalığı.

**moun.te.bank** [ˈmauntibæŋk] *n.* şarlatan kimse.

**mount.ing** ⊕ [ˈmauntiŋ] *n.* montaj; dayanak, destek.

**mourn** [mɔːn] *v/i.* yas tutmak; *v/t.* *-in* matemini tutmak; **ˈmourn.er** *n.* yaslı kimse; ~'s bench. Am. = anxious bench; **mourn.ful** □ [ˈ~ful] yaslı, matemli; kederli, üzgün; acıklı; **ˈmourn.ful.ness** *n.* yaslılık; üzgünlük.

**mourn.ing** [ˈmɔːniŋ] **1.** □ yas..., matem...; **2.** *n.* matem, yas; kederlenme, ağıt; ~s *pl.* matem elbiseleri; **ˈ~-band** *n.* matem bandı; **ˈ~-bor.der,** **ˈ~-edge** *n.* siyah kenar; **ˈ~-pa.per** *n.* siyah kenarlı mektup kâğıdı.

**mouse** [maus] **1.** *n., pl.* **mice** [mais] fare, sıçan; **2.** [mauz] *vb.* fare yakalamak; **mous.er** [ˈmauzə] *n.* fare yakalayan kedi; **ˈmouse-trap** *n.* fare kapanı.

**mousse** [muːs] *n.* bir çeşit dondurma.

**mous.tache** [məsˈtaːʃ] *n.* bıyık.

**mouth 1.** [mauθ] *n., pl.* **mouths** [mauðz] ağız; haliç, boğaz; down in the ~ keyifsiz, karamsar; laugh on the wrong side of one's ~ gülerken ağlamak, hüsrana uğramak; **2.** [mauð] *v/t. & v/i.* mırıldanmak, ağzında gevelemek *(laf)*; söylemek; savurmak *(küfür)*; ağza almak, yemek; ağızla dokunmak; geme alıştırmak *(at)*; surat burusturmak; atıp tutmak: **mouth.ful** [ˈmauθful] *n.* ağız dolusu; lokma.

**mouth...:** **ˈ~-or.gan** *n.* ağız mızıkası, armonika; '~.piece *n.* ağızlık; ⊕ zıvana; *fig.* sözcü; '~-wash *n.* gargara, ağız çalkalamada kullanılan antiseptik sıvı.

mov(e).a.ble ['muːvəbl] 1. *adj.* taşınabilir; kımıldayabilir; ꝋꝋ menkul; 2. *n.* ~s *pl.* menkul eşya; 'mov(e).a.ble.ness *n.* hareketlilik, devingenlik.

move [muːv] 1. *v/t.* & *v/i. com.* hareket et(tir)mek, kımılda(t)mak, oyna(t)mak, harekete getirmek, yürütmek; tahrik etm.; önermek, teklif etm.; teşvik etm., gayretlendirmek; tesir etm., etkilemek; ☞ işletmek *(bağırsak);* ilerlemek; *a.* ~ house taşınmak; yürümek, gitmek; ~ for s.th. *bş* için öneride bulunmak; ~ heaven and earth her çareye baş vurmak; ~ in eve taşınmak; ~ on ileri gitmek, ilerlemek, yürümek; değiştirmek; ~ out evden çıkmak, taşınmak; 2. *n.* hareket, kımıldama; göç, nakil, taşınma; *fig.* tedbir; *satranç:* taş sürme, hamle; on the ~ hareket halinde, ilerlemekte; get a ~ on F acele etm., çabuk olm., işe girişmek; make a ~ gitmek; harekete geçmek; 'move.ment *n.* hareket, kımıldanma; ♪ tempo, usül, ölçü; ⊕ mekanizma; ☞ bağırsakların işlemesi; ✕ manevra; 'mover *n.* hareket eden kimse; teklif sunan kimse; nakliyeci.

mov.ie F ['muːvi] *n.* film; ~s *pl.* sinema.

mov.ing □ ['muːviŋ] oynar, hareketli; *fig.* dokunaklı, acıklı; ~ staircase yürüyen merdiven.

mow¹ [mau] *n.* ekin *(veya* ot) yığını.

mow² [məu] *(irr.) v/t.* biçmek; 'mow.er *n.* biçen kimse *veya* alet; 'mow.ing *n.* biçme; 'mow.ing-ma.chine *n.* ekin biçme makinesi; mown *p.p. of* mow².

much [mʌtʃ] *adj.* & *adv.* çok(ça), fazla(ca), hayli(ce); as ~ more, as ~ again bu kadar daha, bir misli daha; as ~ as ...ile aynı, ...kadar; not so ~ as ...bile değil, hatta; nothing ~ hiçbir şey; ~ less ...bırak, ...şöyle dursun; ~ as I would like sevmeme rağmen; I thought as ~ bunu bekliyordum, aklıma gelmedi de değil; make ~ of anlamak -i; önem vermek -e; I am not ~ of a dancer iyi bir dansöz değilimdir, ben kim dansöz olmak kim; (not) up to ~ iyi (değil); this *veya* that ~ bu *veya* şu kadar; 'much.ness *n.* F çokluk; much of a ~ hemen hemen aynı.

mu.ci.lage ['mjuːsilidʒ] *n.* zamk, yapışkan; mu.ci.lag.i.nous [~'lædʒinəs] *adj.* zamklı.

muck [mʌk] 1. *n.* gübre; F pislik *(a. fig.);* make a ~ of s.th. *bşi* kirletmek; *bşi* bozmak; 2. *v/t.* gübrelemek; *mst* ~ up kir-

letmek, pisletmek; bozmak; ~ s.th. up *bşi* kirletmek; *bşi* berbat etm., bozmak; ~ about *sl.* dalga geçmek; aylaklık etm.; 'muck.er *n. sl.* ayaktakımı, it; come *veya* go a ~ *part. fig.* batmak, başarısızlığa uğramak; muck-rake ['~reik] 1. *n.* gübre yabası; = ~r; 2. *vb.* çamur atmak, karalamak; 'muck.rak.er *n. Am.* skandal yaratan kimse *veya* şey; kötücül kimse; 'muck.y *adj.* kirli, pis.

mu.cous *physiol.* ['mjuːkəs] *adj.* sümüklü; sümüksü; sümük *(veya* balgam) salgılayan; ~ membrane mukoza, salgılı zar.

mu.cus ['mjuːkəs] *n.* sümük; balgam.

mud [mʌd] *n.* çamur; throw ~ at s.o. *b-ne* çamur atmak; 'mud-bath *n.* çamur banyosu; 'mud.di.ness *n.* çamurluluk; mud.dle ['mʌdl] 1. *v/t.* karıştırmak; *a.* ~ up. ~ together birbirine karıştırmak, karman çorman etm., birbirinden ayıramamak; F yüzüne gözüne bulaştırmak; *v/i.* kafası karışmak; ~ through F işin içinden başarıyla sıyrılmak; 2. *n.* karışıklık; şaşkınlık; F arapsaçı; get into a ~ belâya çatmak, işleri karışmak; 'mud.dle-head.ed *adj.* sersem, kalın kafalı; 'mud.dy 1. □ çamurlu; çamur gibi, bulanık; karışık; 2. *v/t.* çamurlamak, çamura bulamak.

mud...: '~.guard *n.* çamurluk; '~.lark *n.* F sokak çocuğu, afacan; '~-sling.ing *n.* F çamur atma, karalama.

muff¹ [mʌf] 1. *n.* F beceriksizlik; beceriksiz kimse; 2. *v/t.* yüzüne gözüne bulaştırmak; yakalayamamak *(top).*

muff² [~] *n.* manşon; ⊕ boru bileziği.

muf.fin ['mʌfin] *n.* yassı pide; muf.fin.eer [~'niə] *n.* tuzluk, şekerlik.

muf.fle ['mʌfl] 1. *n.* ⊕ mufla; 2. *v/t. oft.* ~ up sar(ın)mak; boğmak *(ses);* 'muffler *n.* boyun atkısı, fular; ♪ piyano yastığı; *mot.* susturucu.

muf.ti ['mʌfti] *n.* sivil elbise *(part.* ✕ *);* in ~ sivil elbiseli.

mug [mʌg] 1. *n.* maşrapa, bardak; ağız; *sl.* yüz, surat; budala, *(veya* avanak) kimse; gangster, eşkıya; kimlik fotoğrafı; a ~'s game boş iş; 2. *v/t.* saldırıp soymak; ~ up iyi bilmek; ineklemek.

mug.gy ['mʌgi] *adj.* kapalı, sıkıntılı, sıcak ve rutubetli *(hava).*

mug.wort ⚘ ['mʌgwəːt] *n.* pelin.

mug.wump *Am. iro.* ['mʌgwʌmp] *n.* kendini beğenmiş kimse; *pol.* bağımsız kimse.

mu.lat.to [mjuː'lætəu] *n.* beyaz ile zenci melezi kimse.

mul.ber.ry ['mʌlbəri] *n.* dut.

mulch [mʌltʃ] 1. *n.* bitki köklerini koruyucu tabaka; **2.** *v/t.* böyle tabakayla örtmek.

**mulct** [mʌlkt] **1.** *n.* ✳ para cezası; **2.** *v/t.* para cezasına çarptırmak; dolandırmak.

**mule** [mjuːl] *n.* katır; F katır gibi inatçı kimse; şıpıdık, arkalıksız terlik; as stubborn *veya* obstinate as a ~ katır gibi inatçı; = '~-jenny *n.* çıkrık makinesi; **mu.le.teer** [~liˈtiə] *n.* katırcı; '**mule-track** *n.* katır yolu, patika.

**mul.ish** ☐ ['mjuːliʃ] katır gibi inatçı.

**mull¹** ⸆ [mʌl] *n.* ince müslin kumaş.

**mull²** F [~] *v/t.*: ~ over düşünüp taşınmak.

**mulled** [mʌld] *adj.*: ~ ale sıcak bira; ~ wine şekerli ve baharatlı sıcak şarap.

**mul.le(i)n** ⸙ ['mʌlin] *n.* sığırkuyruğu.

**mul.let** *ichth.* ['mʌlit] *n.* dubar; red ~ barbunya.

**mul.li.gan** *Am.* F ['mʌligən] *n.* türlü, güveç; **mul.li.ga.taw.ny** [mʌligəˈtɔːni] *n. a.* ~ soup etli ve baharatlı çorba.

**mul.li.grubs** *sl.* ['mʌligrʌbz] *n. pl.* karın ağrısı.

**mul.lion** ⚠ ['mʌliən] **1.** *n.* pencere çerçevesinin dikey bölme tirizlerinden biri; **2.** *v/t.* tirizlerle ayırmak.

**mul.ti.far.i.ous** ☐ [mʌltiˈfɛəriəs] çeşitli, çeşit çeşit; **mul.ti.form** ['~fɔːm] *adj.* çok şekilli; **mul.ti.lat.er.al** ☐ ['~ˈlætərəl] çok yanlı, çok taraflı; **mul.ti-mil.lion.aire** ['~miljəˈnɛə] *n.* mültimilyoner; **mul.ti.ple** ['mʌltipl] **1.** *adj.* katmerli, çeşitli, çok yönlü, çok kısımlı; ~ choice çok seçenekli; ~ firm, ~ shop firma (*veya* mağaza) şubesi; ~ switchboard ⚡ çok hatlı santral; **2.** *n.* ⚡ çok safhalı akım; ⚓ katsayı; **mul.ti.plex** ['~pleks] *adj.* çok kısımlı, kat kat, katmerli; **mul.ti.pli.cand** ⚓ [~pliˈkænd] *n.* çarpılan; **mul.ti.pli.ca.tion** [~pliˈkeiʃən] *n.* çoğal(t)ma; ⚓ çarpma; compound (simple) ~ bileşik (âdi) çarpım; ~ table çarpım tablosu; **mul.ti.plic.i.ty** [~ˈplisiti] *n.* çokluk, fazlalık; çeşitlilik; **mul.ti.pli.er** [~ˈplaiə] *n.* çarpan; **mul.ti.ply** ['~plai] *v/t. & v/i.* çoğal(t)mak; art(tır)mak; çarpmak; üremek; **mul.ti.tude** ['~tjuːd] *n.* kalabalık, izdiham; çokluk; avam; **mul.ti.tu.di.nous** [~ˈtjuːdinəs] ☐ (pek) çok, bir sürü.

**mum¹** [mʌm] **1.** *n.* sessizlik; **2.** *int.* sus!; **3.** *v/i.* kılık değiştirip eğlenceye katılmak.

**mum²** F [~] *n.* anne.

**mum.ble** ['mʌmbl] *v/t. & v/i.* mırılda(n)mak, ağzında gevelemek (*laf*); kemirmek.

**Mum.bo Jum.bo** ['mʌmbəuˈdʒʌmbəu] *n.*

anlaşılmaz söz *veya* büyü.

**mum.mer** *contp.* ['mʌmə] *n.* maskeli aktör; '**mum.mer.y** *n. contp.* maskeli gösteri; anlamsız ayin.

**mum.mied** ['mʌmid] *adj.* mumyalı.

**mum.mi.fi.ca.tion** [mʌmifiˈkeiʃən] *n.* mumyalama; **mum.mi.fy** ['~fai] *v/t.* mumyalamak; kupkuru yapmak.

**mum.my¹** ['mʌmi] *n.* mumya; beat to a ~ F eşek sudan gelinceye kadar dövmek, pestilini çıkarmak.

**mum.my²** F [~] *n.* anneciğim.

**mump** [mʌmp] *v/i.* dilenmek; '**mump.ish** *adj.* asık suratlı, somurtkan; **mumps** [mʌmps] *n. sg.* ⚕ kabakulak.

**munch** [mʌntʃ] *v/t.* kıtır kıtır (*veya* katır kutur, şapır şupur, hapır hupur) yemek.

**mun.dane** ☐ ['mʌndein] günlük, olağan, dünyevî...; sıradan...

**mu.nic.i.pal** ☐ [mjuːˈnisipl] belediyeye ait, belediye...; şehre ait, şehir...; **mu.nic.i.pal.i.ty** [~ˈpæliti] *n.* belediye.

**mu.nif.i.cence** [mjuːˈnifisns] *n.* cömertlik; **muˈnif.i.cent** ☐ cömert, eli açık.

**mu.ni.ments** ['mjuːnimənts] *n. pl.* senet, belgit.

**mu.ni.tions** [mjuːˈniʃənz] *n. pl.* savaş gereçleri, cephane.

**mu.ral** ['mjuərəl] **1.** *adj.* duvara ait, duvar...; duvar gibi; duvara asılan; **2.** *n.* fresk, duvara yapılan resim.

**mur.der** ['məːdə] **1.** *n.* katil, adam öldürme, cinayet; **2.** *v/t.* öldürmek, katletmek (*a. fig.*); *fig.* berbat etm., rezil etm.; '**mur.der.er** *n.* katil, cani; '**mur.der.ess** *n.* kadın katil; '**mur.der.ous** ☐ öldürücü; kanlı; *fig.* sert, şiddetli.

**mure** [mjuə] *v/t.* mst ~ up hapsetmek.

**mu.ri.at.ic ac.id** 🜩 [mjuəriˈætikˈæsid] *n.* tuzruhu.

**murk.y** ☐ ['məːki] karanlık, kasvetli; yoğun (*sis*); utanç verici.

**mur.mur** ['məːmə] **1.** *n.* mırıltı, mırıldanma; söylenme; uğultu; **2.** *vb.* mırılda(n)mak; homurdanmak, söylenmek (*against*, at -e karşı); çağıldamak, uğuldamak; '**mur.mur.ous** ☐ mırıltılı, homurtulu.

**mur.phy** *sl.* ['məːfi] *n.* patates.

**mur.rain** ['mʌrin] *n.* hayvanlara özgü bulaşıcı bir hastalık.

**mus.ca.dine** ['mʌskədin], **mus.cat** ['~kət], **mus.ca.tel** [~kəˈtel] *n.* misket üzümü *veya* şarabı.

**mus.cle** ['mʌsl] **1.** *n.* adale, kas; **2.** *v/i.* ~ in Am. sl. kaba kuvvet kullanmak; '**~-bound** *adj.* adaleli; kas tutukluğu olan; **mus.cu.lar** ☐ ['~kjulə] adaleye ait,

adale...; adaleli; kuvvetli.
**Muse¹** [mjuːz] *n.* Müzlerden biri.
**muse²** [~] *v/i.* düşünceye dalmak, dalıp gitmek (on, upon -e); ¹**mus.er** *n.* dalgın kimse.
**mu.se.um** [mjuːˈziəm] *n.* müze.
**mush** [mʌʃ] *n.* mısır unu lapası.
**mush.room** [¹mʌʃrum] **1.** *n.* mantar; *fig.* türedi şey *veya* kimse; **2.** *adj.* mantarımsı...; *fig.* türedi...; *fig.* hızlı...; **3.** *v/i.* mantar gibi yerden bitmek, artmak, çoğalmak; ~ out hızla yayılmak; ~ up göklere yükselmek; go ~ing mantar toplamak.
**mu.sic** [¹mjuːzik] *n.* müzik, musiki; makam, nota; set to ~ bestelemek; face the ~ F güçlüklere *veya* eleştirilere göğüs germek; ¹**mu.si.cal 1.** ☐ müziğe ait, müzik...; müzikal; ahenkli, uyumlu; müziksever; ~ box müzik kutusu; ~ clock müzikli saat; ~ instrument müzik aleti (*veya* enstrumanı); **2.** *n. a.* ~ comedy müzikal komedi.
**mu.sic**...: ¹~-**book** *n.* nota kitabı; ¹~-**box** *n. Am.* müzik kutusu; ¹~-**hall** *n.* müzikhol; varyete.
**mu.si.cian** [mjuːˈziʃən] *n.* çalgıcı; müzisyen, bestekâr.
**mu.sic**...: ¹~-**pa.per** *n.* nota kâğıdı; ¹~-**stand** *n.* nota sehpası; ¹~-**stool** *n.* piyano taburesi.
**musk** [mʌsk] *n.* misk (kokusu); ⚘ amberçiçeği, miskotu; = ¹~-**deer** *n. zo.* misk geyiği.
**mus.ket** [¹mʌskit] *n.* asker tüfeği; **musket.eer** *hist.* [~¹tiə] *n.* tüfekli asker, silahşör; **mus.ket.ry** X [¹~ri] *n.* tüfek atışı; tüfekler.
**musk**...: ¹~-**rat** *n. zo.* misk sıçanı; ¹~-**rose** *n.* ⚘ misk gülü; ¹**musk.y** *adj.* misk kokulu.
**Mus.lim** [¹mʌslim] *s.* Moslem.
**mus.lin** † [¹mʌzlin] *n.* muslin.
**mus.quash** [¹mʌskwɔʃ] *n.* misk sıçanı kürkü.
**muss** *part. Am.* F [mʌs] **1.** *n.* karışıklık, arapsaçı; **2.** *v/t.* bozmak, dağıtmak, arapçasına çevirmek.
**mus.sel** [¹mʌsl] *n.* midye.
**Mus.sul.man** [¹mʌslmən] **1.** *n.* Müslüman; **2.** *adj.* Müslüman...
**must¹** [mʌst, məst] **1.** *v/aux. (irr.)* -meli, -malı; I ~ not ...mamalıyım, izinli değilim; **2.** *n.* zorunluluk, şart, gereklilik; this book is a ~ bu kitap mutlaka okunmalıdır.
**must²** [mʌst] *n.* şıra.
**must³** [~] *n.* küf (kokusu).

**mus.tache** *Am.* [məsˈtaːʃ], **mus.ta.chio** *Am.* [məsˈtaːʃiːəu] *s.* moustache.
**mus.tang** [¹mʌstæŋ] *n.* yabani at.
**mus.tard** [¹mʌstəd] *n.* hardal (bitkisi): ~ gas X iperit; ~ **plas.ter** ⚕ hardal yakısı.
**mus.ter** [¹mʌstə] **1.** *n.* X içtima, bir araya toplanma; yoklama; toplanan kimseler *veya* sayıları; *mst* ~ roll X yoklama defteri; pass ~ *fig.* yeterli (*veya* tatminkâr) olm., kabul olunmak; **2.** *v/t. & v/i.* X topla(n)mak; ~ in askere kaydetmek; *mst* ~ up *fig.* toplamak (*cesaret*).
**mus.ti.ness** [¹mʌstinis] *n.* küflülük; ¹**mus.ty** *adj.* küflü, küf kokulu; *fig.* demode, bayat, eski.
**mu.ta.bil.i.ty** [mjuːtəˈbiliti] *n.* değişebilirlik; ¹**mu.ta.ble** ☐ değişebilir, değişken; **mu.ta.tion** [~¹teiʃən] *n.* değişme, dönüşme; *gr.* bir ünlü *veya* ünsüzün değişmesi.
**mute** [mjuːt] **1.** ☐ sessiz, suskun; dilsiz; *gr.* okunmaz (*harf*); **2.** *n.* dilsiz kimse; ♪ surdin; *gr.* sağır ses, okunmayan harf; **3.** *v/t. part.* ♪ sesini kısmak.
**mu.ti.late** [¹mjuːtileit] *v/t.* kötürüm etm. (*a. fig.*); *fig.* bozmak, katletmek; **mu-ti¹la.tion** *n.* kötürüm etme; bozma.
**mu.ti.neer** [mjuːtiˈniə] *n.* isyan eden asker, isyancı, asi; ¹**mu.ti.nous** ☐ isyankâr, asi; ¹**mu.ti.ny** **1.** *n.* isyan, ayaklanma; **2.** *v/i.* ayaklanmak, isyan etm. (*against -e karşı*).
**mutt** *sl.* [mʌt] *n.* kuş beyinli kimse.
**mut.ter** [¹mʌtə] **1.** *n.* mırıltı; **2.** *v/i.* mırıldanmak, homurdanmak, söylenmek.
**mut.ton** [¹mʌtn] *n.* koyun eti; leg of ~ koyun budu; ¹~-¹**chop** *n.* koyun pirzolası.
**mu.tu.al** ☐ [¹mjuːtʃuəl] karşılıklı; ortak, müşterek; ~ insurance karşılıklı sigorta; **mu.tu.al.i.ty** [~tʃuˈæliti] *n.* karşılıklı olma.
**muz.zle** [¹mʌzl] **1.** *n.* hayvan burnu; burunsalık; top *veya* tüfek ağzı; **2.** *v/t.* burunsalık takmak -*e*; *fig.* susturmak; ¹~-**load.er** *n.* X ağızdan dolma top *veya* tüfek.
**muz.zy** ☐ [¹mʌzi] kafası karışmış; keyifsiz; sersem; bulanık.
**my** [mai] *pron.* benim.
**my.al.gi.a** ⚕ [maiˈældʒiə] *n.* kasınç, kas ağrısı.
**my.col.o.gy** [maiˈkɔlədʒi] *n.* mantarları inceleyen bilim dalı.
**my.ope** ⚕ [¹maiəup] *n.* miyop kimse; **my-o.pi.a** [maiˈəupjə] *n.* miyopluk; **my.op.ic** [~ˈɔpik] *adj.* (~ally) miyop.
**myr.i.ad** [¹miriəd] **1.** *n.* çok sayı; **2.** *adj.* çok, sayısız.

myr.mi.don [ˈməːmidən] n. contp. körü
körüne itaat eden kimse.
myrrh ⚕ [məː] n. mür(rüsafî).
myr.tle ⚕ [ˈməːtl] n. mersin.
my.self [maiˈself] pron. ben, kendim, bizzat.
mys.te.ri.ous □ [misˈtiəriəs] esrarengiz,
gizemli, garip; mysˈte.ri.ous.ness n. esrarengizlik, gizemlilik.
mys.ter.y [ˈmistəri] n. gizem, sır; anlaşılmaz şey; a. ~ play hist. dinî piyes; ˈ~-
-ship n. ✕ tuzak gemi.
mys.tic [ˈmistik] 1. a. ˈmys.ti.cal □ mistik, tasavvufa ait; gizemli; gizli; gizli
anlamlı, esrarlı; 2. n. gizemci, mutasav-

vıf; mys.ti.cism [ˈ~sizəm] n. gizemcilik,
mistisizm, tasavvuf; mys.ti.fi.ca.tion [~fi-
ˈkeiʃən] n. şaşırtma; mys.ti.fy [ˈ~fai]
v/t. şaşırtmak, hayrette bırakmak.
mys.tique [misˈtiːk] n. yetenek, marifet,
gizli güç; özellikler.
myth [miθ] n. efsane, mit; hayalî kimse
veya şey; myth.ic, myth.i.cal □ [ˈ~ik(əl)]
efsanevî, esatirî; hayalî.
myth.o.log.ic, myth.o.log.i.cal □ [miθə-
ˈlɔdʒik(əl)] mitolojik, esatirî; my.thol.o-
gy [miˈθɔlədʒi] n. mitoloji.
myx.o.ma.to.sis [miksəuməˈtəusis] n. öldürücü bir tavşan hastalığı.

# N

**nab** *sl.* [næb] *v/t.* yakalamak, enselemek, tutuklamak; almak.

**na.bob** [ˈneibɔb] *n.* ensesi kalın (*veya* çok varlıklı) kimse.

**na.celle** ⚓ [næˈsel] *n.* motor yeri.

**na.cre** [ˈneikə] *n.* sedef; **na.cre.ous** [ˈ~kriəs] *adj.* sedefli.

**na.dir** [ˈneidiə] *n. ast.* ayakucu; *fig.* en düşük nokta.

**nag¹** F [næg] *n.* yaşlı at.

**nag²** [~] *v/i.* dırlanmak, dırdır etm., söylenip durmak; ~ at *-in* başının etini yemek.

**Nai.ad** [ˈnaiæd] *n.* su perisi.

**nail** [neil] **1.** *n.* çivi, mıh; *anat. & zo.* tırnak; fight tooth and ~ çok şiddetli dövüşmek, dişe diş kavga etm.; on the ~ derhal, hemen; hit the (right) ~ on the head tam üstüne basmak, taşı gediğine koymak; as hard as ~s acımasız, sert; turp gibi; **2.** *v/t.* çivilemek, mıhlamak (to *-e*); F tutmak, yakalamak, esir almak; dikmek (*göz*); ~ down çivilemek; F garantiye almak; ~ s.o. down to *fig. b-ni* zorla konuşturmak; ~ to the counter teşhir etm., yalancı çıkarmak, yalanlamak; ˈ~brush *n.* tırnak fırçası; ˈnail.ing *adj. sl. oft.* ~ good şahane, emsalsiz; ˈnail-scis.sors. *n. pl.* tırnak makası; ˈnail-var.nish *n.* tırnak cilâsı, oje.

**nain.sook** [ˈneinsuk] *n.* nansuk, bir tür ince ve sık dokunmuş patiska.

**na.i.ve** □ [naːˈiːv] **na.ive** [neiv] saf, bön; deneyimsiz, toy; **na.ive.te** [naːˈiːvtei], **na.ive.ty** [ˈneivti] *n.* saflık, bönlük; toyluk.

**na.ked** □ [ˈneikid] çıplak; *fig.* yalın, açık; örtüsüz; silahsız; *poet.* korumasız, himayesiz; sade; salt (*gerçek*); ˈna.ked.ness *n.* çıplaklık.

**nam.by-pam.by** [ˈnæmbiˈpæmbi] **1.** *adj.* budalaca duygusal; kararsız; **2.** *n.* budalaca duygusal (*veya* sıkılgan) kimse.

**name** [neim] **1.** *n.* isim, ad; nam, şöhret, ün; ünvan; meşhur kimse; of *veya* by the ~ of... ...isiminde, ...adında; call s.o. ~s *b-ne* sövüp saymak; not have a penny to one's ~ meteliğe kurşun atmak, cebi

delik olm.; know s.o. by ~ *b-ni* ismen tanımak; **2.** *v/t.* adlandırmak, isim koymak *-e*; söylemek; vermek (*fiyat*); tayin etm., atamak; ˈ~day *n. eccl.* isim günü; ˈname.less □ isimsiz, adsız; bilinmeyen; bahsedilmeye değmez; tarifi olanaksız; ˈname.ly *adv.* yani, şöyle ki; ˈname-part *n.* başrol; ˈname-plate *n.* tabela; ˈname-sake *n.* adaş.

**nan.cy** *sl.* [ˈnænsi] *n.* çıtkırıldım, hanım evlâdı; homoseksüel.

**nan.keen** [nænˈkiːn] *n.* pamuklu kumaş; ~s *pl.* pamuklu kumaştan elbise.

**nan.ny** [ˈnæni] *n.* dadı; ˈ~goat *n.* dişi keçi.

**nap¹** [næp] *n.* tüylü yüz, hav.

**nap²** [~] **1.** *n.* şekerleme, kestirme, kısa uyku; have *veya* take a ~ şekerleme yapmak, kestirmek; **2.** *v/i.* şekerleme yapmak, kestirmek; catch s.o. ~ping *b-ni* gafil avlamak.

**nap³** [~] *n.:* go ~ *fig.* tek bir darbe ile başarıyı elde etmeğe çalışmak.

**na.palm** [ˈneipɑːm] *n.:* ~ bomb ✕ napalm bombası.

**nape** [neip] *n. mst* ~ of the neck ense.

**naph.tha** ⚗ [ˈnæfθə] *n.* neftyağı.

**nap.kin** [ˈnæpkin] *n.* peçete; kundak bezi; ˈ~ring *n.* peçete halkası.

**Na.po.le.on.ic** [nəpəuliˈɔnik] *adj.* Napolyon'a ait.

**nap.py** F [ˈnæpi] *n.* çocuk bezi.

**nar.cis.sism** *psych.* [naːˈsisizm] *n.* narkislik, narkisizm, kendi kendine aşık olma; **nar.ciss.us** ⚘ [~ˈsisəs] *n.* nergis, zerrin, fulya.

**nar.co.sis** ⚕ [naːˈkəusis] *n.* narkoz.

**nar.cot.ic** [naːˈkɔtik] **1.** *adj.* (~ally) narkotik, uyuşturucu; **2.** *n.* uyuşturucu ilâç, narkotik; uyuşturucu düşkünü kimse; **nar.co.tize** [ˈnaːkətaiz] *v/t.* ilâç ile uyuşturmak *veya* uyutmak.

**nard** [naːd] *n.* hintsümbülü.

**nark¹** *sl.* [naːk] *n.* ajan; narkotik ajanı.

**nark²** F [~] *v/t.* canını sıkmak, tepesini attırmak; *v/i.* sızlanmak, yakınmak.

**nar.rate** [nəˈreit] *v/t.* anlatmak, nakletmek; **nar.ra.tion** *n.* (hikâye) anlatma, anlatım; hikâye; **nar.ra.tive** [ˈnærətiv] **1.** □

hikâye türünde; hikâye anlatmaya ait;
**2.** *n.* rivayet, hikâye, anlatı (sanatı);
**nar.ra.tor** [nəˈreitə] *n.* hikâyeci; anlatan
kimse.

**nar.row** [ˈnærəu] **1.** ☐ dar, ensiz; kısıtlı;
késin; dàrlık içinde; dar fikirli; cimri,
pinti; *s.* escape; **2.** *n.* ~s *pl.* dar boğaz;
**3.** *v/t.* & *v/i.* daral(t)mak; kısmak (*göz*);
kısıtlamak; ˈ~-ˈchest.ed *adj.* dar göğüslü; ˈ~-gauge *n.* 🚉 dekovil; ˈ~-ˈmind.ed
☐ dar fikirli (*veya* görüşlü); ˈnar.row-
ness *n.* darlık (*a. fig.*).

**nar.whal** *zo.* [ˈnɑːwəl] *n.* denizgergedanı.

**nar.y** *Am.* [ˈnɛəri] *adj.* hiç bir.

**na.sal** [ˈneizəl] **1.** ☐ buruna ait, burun...;
genzel; **2.** *n.* genzel ses; **na.sal.i.ty** [~-
ˈzæliti] *n.* genzellik; **na.sal.ize** [ˈ~-zəlaiz]
*v/i.* genizden konuşmak; *v/t. gr.* genizden çıkarmak (*ses*).

**nas.cent** [ˈnæsnt] *adj.* oluşmaya (*veya* gelişmeye) başlayan, filizlenen.

**nas.ti.ness** [ˈnɑːstinis] *n.* iğrençlik; çirkinlik.

**nas.tur.tium** 🌼 [nəsˈtəːʃəm] *n.* lâtinçiçeği.

**nas.ty** [ˈnɑːsti] ☐ pis, kirli, fena kokulu,
iğrenç, berbat, tiksindirici, kötü, çirkin;
yaramaz; ayıp ,terbiyesiz, edepsiz, açık
saçık, ahlâksız; tehlikeli, korkutucu, ürkütücü, şiddetli.

**na.tal** [ˈneitl] *adj.* doğuşa ait, doğum...;
**na.tal.i.ty** [nəˈtæliti] *n.* doğum oranı.

**na.ta.tion** [nəˈteiʃən] *n.* yüzme (sanatı);
**na.ta.to.ri.al** [nætəˈtɔːriəl] *adj.* yüzmeye
ait, yüzme...

**na.tion** [ˈneiʃən] *n.* millet, ulus; budun.

**na.tion.al** [ˈnæʃənl] **1.** ☐ millete ait, ulusal..., milli...; **2.** *n.* vatandaş, yurttaş;
**na.tion.al.ism** [ˈnæʃnəlizəm] *n.* ulusçuluk,
milliyetçilik; ˈna.tion.al.ist **1.** *n.* milliyetçi; **2.** *adj.* = **na.tion.alˈis.tic** milliyetçili-
ğe ait, milliyetçilik...; **na.tion.al.i.ty** [næ-
ʃəˈnæliti] *n.* milliyet; millet; vatandaşlık;
uyrukluk, tabiiyet; **na.tion.al.i.za.tion**
[næʃnəlaiˈzeiʃən] *n.* millileştirme; ˈna-
tion.al.ize *v/t.* millileştirmek, kamulaştırmak, devletleştirmek.

**na.tion-wide** [ˈneiʃənwaid] *adj.* millet (*veya* ülke) çapında.

**na.tive** [ˈneitiv] **1.** ☐ yerli, doğal; doğma;
doğuştan; özgü (to -*e*); Tanrı vergisi (*yetenek*); saf(i) (*maden*); ~ land anavatan, anayurt; ~ language anadili; **2.** *n.*
yerli, yerli mal *veya* hayvan; a ~ of
Ireland İrlanda'nın yerlisi; ˈ~-born *adj.*
yerli, doğma büyüme.

**na.tiv.i.ty** [nəˈtiviti] *n.* doğuş, doğum; ♀
Play Hz. İsa'nın doğumunu anlatan oyun.

**na.tron** ⚗ [ˈneitrən] *n.* tabiî sodyum kar-

bonat.

**nat.ter** F [ˈnætə] *v/i.* çene çalmak, laklak
etm.

**nat.ty** ☐ [ˈnæti] şık, zarif.

**na.tu.ral** [ˈnætʃrəl] **1.** ☐ tabiî, doğal; doğuştan; sunî olmayan, normal; ♪ natü-
rel; gayri meşru (*çocuk*); ~ history tabiat bilgisi; ~ note ♪ tabiî nota; ~ philosopher tabiat bilgini; ~ philosophy tabiat bilgisi; ~ science tabiat bilgisi; **2.** *n.*
† doğuştan geri zekâlı kimse; ♪ bekar;
piyanonun beyaz tuşu; *bşe* tam uygun
kimse *veya* şey; ˈnat.u.ral.ism *n.* doğacı-
lık ,natüralizm; ˈnat.u.ral.ist *n.* natüralist, doğacı; tabiat bilgisi uzmanı; **nat-
u.ral.i.za.tion** [~lai'zeiʃən] *n.* vatandaşlığa kabul etme; ˈnat.u.ral.ize *v/t.* vatandaşlığa kabul etm.; lisana almak (*yabancı kelime*); ♀, *zo.* yerlileştirmek; ta-
biileştirmek; *v/i.* yerlisi gibi olm.; ˈnat-
u.ral.ness *n.* tabiilik; **na.tu.ral se.lec.tion**
*biol.* doğal ayıklanma.

**na.ture** [ˈneitʃə] *n.* tabiat, doğa; mizaç,
yaradılış, yapı; çeşit, tür, tip; kâinat,
dünya, evren; ˈna.tured *comb.* ...mizaç-
lı, ...huylu.

**naught** [nɔːt] *n.* sıfır; † hiç; come (bring)
to ~ boşa çık(ar)mak, suya düş(ür)mek;
set at ~ aldırmamak, önemsememek;
**naugh.ti.ness** [ˈ~tinis] *n.* yaramazlık,
haylazlık; ˈnaugh.ty ☐ yaramaz, haylaz,
haşarı; kötü; ahlâksız, açık saçık; münasebetsiz.

**nau.se.a** [ˈnɔːsjə] *n.* mide bulantısı; deniz tutması; *fig.* iğrenme, tiksinme; **nau-
se.ate** [ˈnɔːsieit] *v/t.* & *v/i.* midesi(ni)
bulan(dır)mak, iğren(dir)mek, tiksin-
(dir)mek; be ~d midesi bulanmak; iğrenmek; **nau.seous** ☐ [ˈnɔːsjəs] mide bulandırıcı, iğrenç.

**nau.ti.cal** [ˈnɔːtikəl] *adj.* gemiciliğe ait, gemicilik..., deniz(s)el...; ~ mile deniz mili.

**naut.i.lus** *zo.* [ˈnɔːtiləs] *n.* sedefli deniz helezonu.

**na.val** ☐ [ˈneivəl] bahriye ile ilgili, de-
niz(s)el; savaş gemilerine ait; ~ base
deniz üssü; ~ staff deniz kurmay subayları.

**nave**[1] 🔔 [neiv] *n.* kilisede halkın oturduğu orta kısım.

**nave**[2] [~] *n.* dingil başlığı, tekerlek poyrası.

**na.vel** [ˈneivəl] *n.* göbek; *fig.* merkez;
~ or.ange bir tür göbekli ve çekirdeksiz
portakal.

**nav.i.ga.ble** ☐ [ˈnævigəbl] gidiş gelişe elverişli; dümen kullanılabilir (*gemi*);
**nav.i.gate** [ˈ~geit] *v/i.* gemi ile gezmek,

gemi kullanmak, seyretmek; kaptanlık
*(veya* kılavuzluk) etm.; *v/t.* kullanmak
*(gemi, uçak);* **nav.i|ga.tion** *n.* denizcilik;
dümencilik, gemicilik; **ˈnav.i.ga.tor** *n.*
denizci, gemici, dümenci, ⚓ seyir subayı; ⚓ kaptan pilot.
**nav.vy** [ˈnævi] *n.* işçi, amele.
**na.vy** [ˈheivi] *n.* deniz kuvvetleri, donanma; deniz filosu; **ˈ⁓ˈblue** *adj.* lâcivert,
koyu mavi.
**nay** [nei] **1.** *adv.* † *veya prov.* hayır, yok;
hem de, hatta; **2.** *n.* ret oyu (veren kimse).
**Naz.a.rene** [næzəˈriːn] *n.* Nasıralı; Nas-
ranî.
**naze** [neiz] *n.* burun, sahil çıkıntısı.
**Na.zi** [ˈnɑːtsi] **1.** *n.* Nazi; **2.** *adj.* Nazi...
**neap** [niːp] *n. a.* ⁓tide alçalma ile yük-
selmenin en az olduğu gelgit; **ˈneaped**
*adj.:* be ⁓ ⚓ *(gelgit nedeniyle)* kara üzerinde kalmak *(gemi).*
**Ne.a.pol.i.tan** [niəˈpɔlitən] **1.** *adj.* Napoli'ye
ait, Napoli'ye özgü; **2.** *n.* Napolili.
**near** [niə] **1.** *adj.* yakın; bitişik; samimi,
içlidışlı; soldaki; cimri, eli sıkı; ⁓ at
hand el altında, yakın; a ⁓ thing ucu ucuna kazanma; darı darına *(veya* ucuz)
kurtulma; **2.** *adv.* yakın(da); hemen hemen, az daha, neredeyse; aşağı yukarı;
**3.** *prp.* bitişik, yakın; **4.** *v/i.* yaklaşmak
-e; **near.by** [ˈ⁓bai] *adj. & adv.* yakın(da);
**ˈnear.ly** *adv.* hemen hemen, âdeta, neredeyse; yakından; not ⁓ hiç te, katiyen;
**ˈnear.ness** *n.* yakınlık; **ˈnear-ˈsight.ed**
*adj.* miyop.
**neat¹** □ [niːt] temiz, düzenli, düzgün, zarif, zevkli; nefis, enfes; zekice, akıllıca; su katılmamış, saf, katışıksız *(içki).*
**neat²** ⚲, [⁓] *n.* büyükbaş hayvanlar.
**neat.ness** [ˈniːtnis] *n.* temizlik, düzgünlük.
**neat...:** **ˈ⁓ˈs-foot oil** sığır paçası yağı;
**ˈ⁓ˈs-leath.er** *n.* sığır derisi; **ˈ⁓ˈs-tongue**
*n.* sığır dili.
**neb.u.la** *ast.* [ˈnebjulə] *n.* nebula; **ˈneb.u-**
**lar** *adj.* nebulaya ait, nebula...; **neb.u.los-**
**i.ty** [⁓ˈlɔsiti] *n.* bulutluluk; **ˈneb.u.lous** □
bulutlu, dumanlı, bulanık *(a. fig.).*
**ne.ces.sa.ri.ly** [ˈnesisərili] *adv.* mutlaka,
muhakkak, illâ(ki); **ˈnec.es.sar.y 1.** □ gerekli, zorunlu, lüzumlu, zarurî, lâzım;
kaçınılmaz; **2.** *n. mst* necessaries *pl.* gerekli şey; levazım; **ne.ces.si.tate** [niˈse-
siteit] *v/t.* gerektirmek, zorunlu kılmak;
**neˈces.si.tous** *adj.* fakir, yoksul, muhtaç; elzem; **neˈces.si.ty** *n.* lüzum, zaruret, ihtiyaç, gerekseme, gereksinme;
*mst* necessities *pl.* gerekli şey; of ⁓ zo-

runlu olarak, mutlaka.
**neck** [nek] **1.** *n.* boyun, gerdan; şişe boğazı; kıstak, boğaz, dil; elbise yakası;
keman sapı; break the ⁓ of a task bir
işin hakkından gelmek; ⁓ and ⁓ başa
baş, at başı beraber; ⁓ and crop F tamamen; paldır küldür; pılı pırtıyı toplayarak; ⁓ or nothing F herşeyi göze alarak,
ya hep ya hiç; get it in the ⁓ *sl.* zılgıt
yemek, azar işitmek, canına okunmak;
**2.** *v/i. sl.* öpüşmek, cinsî münasebette
bulunmadan sevişmek; **ˈ⁓.band** *n.* dik
elbise yakası; **ˈ⁓.cloth** *n.* fular; **neck.er-**
**chief** [ˈnekətʃif] *n.* boyun atkısı; **neck-**
**lace** [ˈ⁓lis], **neck.let** [ˈ⁓lit] *n.* kolye,
gerdanlık; **ˈneck.tie** *n.* kravat; **ˈneck-**
**wear** *n.* † boyuna takılan şeyler.
**ne.cro.lo.gy** [neˈkrɔlədʒi] *n.* ölenlerin isim
listesi; bir ölü hakkında yazılmış yazı;
**nec.ro.man.cy** [ˈnekrəumænsi] *n.* ruh çağırma; büyücülük.
**nec.tar** [ˈnektə] *n.* nektar, abıhayat; **nec-**
**tar.ine** [ˈ⁓rin] *n.* tüysüz şeftali, durakı.
**née** [nei] *adj.* kızlık soyadıyle.
**need** [niːd] **1.** *n.* ihtiyaç, lüzum, gereklik,
zorunluluk, gereksinme, gerekseme (for
*için);* fakirlik, darlık, yokluk; one's own
⁓s *pl. b-nin* gereksinmeleri; if ⁓ be gerekirse; be *veya* stand in ⁓ of -e muhtaç olm., gereksinme duymak; **2.** *v/t.* ihtiyacı olm. -e, gereksemek -i, gereksinmek -e, istemek -i; gerektirmek -i; **need-**
**ful** [ˈ⁓ful] **1.** □ gerekli, lâzım; **2.** *n.* F
ihtiyaç *(part. para);* **ˈneed.i.ness** *n.* fakirlik, yoksulluk.
**nee.dle** [ˈniːdl] **1.** *n.* iğne; ibre; örgü şişi;
tığ; dikilitaş; **2.** *v/t.* iğne ile dikmek,
tutturmak, delmek; *part. Am.* kızdırmak; F artırmak *(alkol derecesini);* ⁓
one's way through yol bulup geçmek, arasından sıyrılmak; **ˈ⁓-case** *n.* iğne kutusu; **ˈ⁓-gun** *n.* iğneli tüfek.
**need.less** □ [ˈniːdlis] gereksiz, lüzumsuz;
**ˈneed.less.ly** *adv.* gereksizce, lüzumsuz-
ca; **ˈneed.less.ness** *n.* gereksizlik, lüzumsuzluk.
**nee.dle...:** **ˈ⁓.wom.an** *n.* dikişçi kadın;
**ˈ⁓.work** *n.* iğne işi, işleme.
**needs** [niːdz] *adv.* ister istemez, mutlaka; **ˈneed.y** □ muhtaç, fakir, yoksul.
**ne'er** [nɛə] = never; **⁓-do-well** [ˈ⁓duːwel]
*n.* bir işe yaramaz kimse.
**ne.far.i.ous** □ [niˈfɛəriəs] kötü, şeytansı;
kanunlara *veya* ahlâk prensiplerine aykırı.
**ne.gate** [niˈgeit] *v/t.* inkâr etm., reddetmek; etkisini yok etm.; **neˈga.tion** *n.* inkâr, ret; eksiklik; **neg.a.tive** [ˈnegətiv]

**1.** □ olumsuz; negatif; aksi, ters; **2.** *n.* olumsuz söz *veya* yanıt; ret yanıtı; *phot.* negatif; **3.** *v/t. a.* answer in the ~ olumsuz yanıt vermek; inkâr etm.; hükümsüz kılmak; çürütmek; tesirini yok etm.; menetmek.

**neg.lect** [ni'glekt] **1.** *n.* ihmal; **2.** *v/t.* ihmal etm., savsaklamak; bakmamak, yapmamak; **neg'lect.ful** □ [~ful] ihmalci, savsak, kayıtsız (of *-e karşı*).

**nég.li.gé, neg.li.gee** ['negli:ʒei] *n.* süslü gecelik.

**neg.li.gence** ['neglidʒəns] *n.* dikkatsizlik, kayıtsızlık; ᚱ ihmal; **'neg.li.gent** □ kayıtsız, ihmalci, savsak (of *-e karşı*).

**neg.li.gi.ble** ['neglidʒəbl] *adj.* önemsemeye değmez, az.

**ne.go.ti.a.bil.i.ty** [nigəuʃjə'biliti] *n.* satılabilme; akdolunma olanağı; **ne'go.ti.a.ble** □ tartışılabilir; akdolunabilir; tedavülü kolay, ciro edilebilir; devredilebilir; aşılabilir (*yol vs.*); not ~ geçerli değildir, takas (*veya* ciro) edilemez; **ne'go.ti.ate** [~ʃieit] *v/t.* müzakere etm.; ciro etm. (*çek, bono*); akdetmek; aşabilmek, geçebilmek; başarmak; tamamlamak; *v/i.* görüşme yapmak; **ne.go.ti'a.tion** *n.* müzakere, görüşme; tamamlama; ciro etme; under ~ görüşülmekte, halledilmekte; **ne'go.ti.a.tor** *n.* delege; arabulucu.

**ne.gress** ['ni:gris] *n.* zenci kadın; **ne.gro** ['ni:grəu] *n., pl.* **ne.groes** [~z] zenci; **ne.groid** ['ni:grɔid] *adj.* zencilere ait, zenci...; zenciye benzer.

**ne.gus** ['ni:gəs] *n.* baharatlı ve şekerli sıcak şarap.

**neigh** [nei] **1.** *n.* kişneme; **2.** *v/i.* kişnemek.

**neigh.bo(u)r** ['neibə] **1.** *n.* komşu; **2.** *v/t. & v/i.* yaklaş(tır)mak; komşu olm.; yakın olm.; **neigh.bo(u)r.hood** ['~hud] *n.* komşuluk, yakınlık; komşular; civar, semt, mahalle; in the ~ of *-in* havalisinde, *-in* civarında (*a. fig.* F); **'neigh.bo(u)r.ing** *adj.* yakın, civar; komşu, bitişik; **'neigh.bo(u)r.li.ness** *n.* komşuya yaraşır davranış; **'neigh.bo(u)r.ly** *adj.* dostça, arkadaşça, komşuya yaraşır; komşuluğa ait, komşuluk...

**nei.ther** ['naiðə] **1.** *adj. & pron.* hiç biri, ne bu ne öteki; ve ne de; **2.** *adv.:* ~ ...nor ne... ne de...; not... ~ bile değil.

**nem.e.sis** ['nemisis] *n.* hak edilen ceza; kuvvetli rakip *veya* düşman.

**ne.o.lith.ic** [ni:əu'liθik] *adj.* ikinci taş devrine ait, neolitik.

**ne.ol.o.gism** [ni:'ɔlədʒizəm] *n.* yeni kelimeler bulma *veya* kullanma; yeni kelime.

**ne.on** ['ni:ən] *n.* neon; ~ **light** neon ışığı; ~ **sign** ışıklı reklam.

**neph.ew** ['nevju:] *n.* erkek yeğen.

**ne.phri.tis** ᚱ [ne'fraitis] *n.* böbrek iltihabı, nefrit.

**nep.o.tism** ['nepətizəm] *n.* akraba kayırma.

**Nep.tune** ['neptju:n] *n.* Neptün gezegeni.

**Ne.re.id** ['niəriid] *n.* su perisi.

**nerve** [nə:v] **1.** *n.* sinir, asab; cesaret, soğukkanlılık; ~s *pl.* duyarlık; ᚱ damar; küstahlık, yüzsüzlük; get on s.o.'s ~s *b-nin* sinirine dokunmak; **2.** *v/t.* cesaret vermek *-e* (for *için*); **'~-cell** *n.* sinir hücresi; **'~-cen.tre** *n.*, *Am.* **'~-cen.ter** sinir merkezi; **nerved** *adj.* ᚱ damarlı; **'nerve.less** □ zayıf, cansız, güçsüz, dermansız; cesaretsiz; soğukkanlı; **'nerve-rack.ing** *adj.* sinir bozucu.

**nerv.ine** ᚱ ['nə:vi:n] **1.** *adj.* sinirleri yatıştırıcı; **2.** *n.* sinirleri yatıştırıcı ilâç.

**nerv.ous** □ ['nə:vəs] sinirli, asabi; çekingen, ürkek; sinirsel; **'nerv.ous.ness** *n.* sinirlilik.

**nerv.y** *sl.* ['nə:vi] *adj.* yüzsüz, küstah; sinirli.

**nes.ci.ence** ['nesiəns] *n.* bilgisizlik, cehalet; **'nes.ci.ent** *adj.* cahil, bilgisiz, habersiz (of *-den*).

**ness** [nes] *n.* burun, çıkıntı.

**nest** [nest] **1.** *n.* yuva (*a. fig.*); haydut yatağı; **2.** *v/t. & v/i.* iç içe yerleş(tir)mek; yuva yapmak; **'nest.ed** *adj.* iç içe; **'nest-egg** *n.* fol; *fig.* ilerisi için biriktirilen para, ihtiyat akçesi; **'nest.er** *n.* yuva yapan kuş; **'nes.tle** ['nesl] *v/i.* sokulmak (to *-e*); gömülmek; *v/t.* barındırmak, sığındırmak; yaslamak; bağrına basmak; **nest.ling** ['nestliŋ] *n.* yavru kuş.

**net**[1] [net] **1.** *n.* ağ, tuzak; şebeke; hile; **2.** *v/t.* ağ ile tutmak; ağ ile örtmek; *fig.* avlamak.

**net**[2] [~] **1.** *adj.* net, kesintisiz; halis, safi, katışıksız; **2.** *v/t.* kazanmak, kâr etm.

**net.ball** ['netbɔ:l] *n.* voleybol türünde bir oyun.

**neth.er** ['neðə] *adj.* alt(taki); **'~.most** *adj.* en alttaki.

**net.ting** ['netiŋ] *n.* ağ (örme); örgü.

**net.tle** ['netl] **1.** *n.* ᚱ ısırgan; **2.** *v/t.* ᚱ ısırganla yakmak; *fig.* kızdırmak, öfkelendirmek; **'~-rash** *n.* ᚱ kurdeşen, ürtiker.

**net.work** ['netwə:k] *n.* şebeke; ağ örgüsü; *radyo:* yayın istasyonları şebekesi.

**neu.ral** ᚱ ['njuərəl] *adj.* sinirlere ait, sinirsel.

neu.ral.gia 🐦 [njuə'rældʒə] n. nevralji; neu.ras.the.ni.a 🐦 [njuərəs'θiːnjə] n. nevrasteni; neu.ras.then.ic [~'θenik] 1. adj. nevrasteniye ait, nevrasteni...; 2. n. sinir hastası, nevrastenik kimse; neu.ri.tis 🐦 [njuə'raitis] n. sinir iltihabı; neu.rol.o.gist [~'rolədʒist] n. asabiyeci; neu'rol.o.gy n. nevroloji, sinirbilim; neu.ro.path.ic 🐦 [~rəu'pæθik] 1. adj. nevropatik; 2. n. nevropat kimse; neu.ro.sis 🐦 [~'rəusis] n. nevroz; neu.rot.ic [~'rɔtik] 1. adj. nevrozlu, sinir hastalığı olan; evhamlı; 2. n. nevrozlu kimse.

neu.ter ['njuːtə] 1. adj. ✚, zo. cinsiyetsiz; gr. cinssiz; geçişsiz (fiil); 2. n. cinsiyetsiz hayvan veya bitki; gr. cinsiyet belirtmeyen kelime.

neu.tral ['njuːtrəl] 1. ☐ yansız, tarafsız; 🔥 nötr; belirli bir özelliği olmayan; rengi belirsiz; tarafsız ülkeye ait; mot. boşta (vites); 2. n. tarafsız kimse veya ülke; boş vites; neu.tral.i.ty [~'træliti] n. tarafsızlık; neu.tral.i.za.tion [~trəlai-'zeiʃən] n. yansız kılma; 🔥 nötrleme; 'neu.tral.ize v/t. etkisiz bırakmak; yansız kılmak; 🔥 nötrlemek.

neu.tron phys. ['njuːtrɔn] n. nötron.

né.vé mount. ['nevei] n. kar; karlı alan.

nev.er ['nevə] adv. asla, hiç bir zaman, hiç, katiyen; ~ so hiç de öyle değil; on the ~-~ sl. taksitle; the ℮-℮ (Land) hayal beldesi; 'nev.er'more adv. asla, artık hiç, bundan böyle; nev.er.the.less [~ðə'les] adv. bununla beraber, mamafih, yine de.

new [njuː] adj. yeni; taze; acemi; yeni keşfedilmiş; görülmemiş, alışılmamış; '~.born 1. adj. yeni doğmuş; 2. n. yeni doğmuş bebek; 'new-'com.er n. yeni gelmiş kimse; New Eng.land.er kuzey Amerikalı; new.fan.gled ['~'fæŋgld] adj. yeni çıkmış, yeni model; new look yeni moda; 'new.ly adv. geçenlerde, yakınlarda, yeni; yeni bir şekilde; 'newly-weds n. pl. yeni evliler; 'new.ness n. yenilik.

news [njuːz] n. haber, havadis; what's the ~? ne haber?, ne var ne yok?; he is much in the ~ F herkesin diline düştü; '~.a.gen.cy n. haber ajansı; '~.a.gent n. gazeteci; '~.boy n. gazeteci çocuk; '~-butch.er n. Am. sl. seyyar gazeteci; '~.cast n. radyo: haber yayını; ~ cin.e.ma aktualite filmleri gösteren sinema; '~.let.ter n. sirküler, genelge; '~.mon.ger n. dedikoducu kimse; '~.pa.per n. gazete; attr. gazete...; '~.print n. gazete kâğıdı; '~.reel n. film; aktualite filmi; '~-room n. gazete bayii; Am. gazete: ha-

ber alma ve derleme bürosu; '~-stall, Am. '~.stand n. gazete tezgâhı; '~-ven-dor n. gazete satıcısı, gazeteci; news.y ['njuːzi] adj. F haber (veya havadis) dolu (mektup vs.).

newt zo. [njuːt] n. semender, su keleri.

New World ['njuː'wəːld] n. Yeni dünya, Amerika.

new year ['njuː'jəː] n. yılbaşı; ~'s day yılbaşı günü; ~'s eve yılbaşı arifesi; ~'s gift yılbaşı hediyesi.

next [nekst] 1. adj. en yakın, yanı başındaki; bitişik; bir sonraki; gelecek, önümüzdeki, ertesi; ~ but one bir evvelki; ~ door bitişik ev(deki); ~ door to fig. hemen hemen, neredeyse; the ~ of kin en yakın akraba; ~ to -e bitişik, -in yanın(d)a, -den sonra; F sıkı fıkı, içlidışlı; ~ to nothing hemen hemen hiç; what ~? başka?; 2. adv. (ondan) sonra, daha sonra.

nib [nib] n. kalem ucu.

nib.ble ['nibl] v/t. & v/i. azar azar ısırmak; a. ~ at kemirmek -i; fig. ilgi göstermek -e, iyice düşünmek -i.

nib.lick ['niblik] n. golf sopası.

nice ☐ [nais] güzel, hoş, sevimli; cazip; ince; iyi; kibar, nazik; titiz; iro. zor, güç, kötü; ~ and warm sıcacık, oldukça sıcak; 'nice.ly adv. F iyi bir şekilde, çok iyi, incelikle; 'nice.ness n. incelik; hoşluk, güzellik; nice.ty ['~siti] n. incelik, titizlik; doğruluk, kesinlik; güzellik, hoşluk; to a ~ tamı tamamına, tam karar; stand upon niceties ayrıntılar üzerinde durmak.

niche [nitʃ] n. duvarda hücre (veya oyuk); fig. uygun yer.

Nick¹ [nik] n.: Old ~ şeytan.

nick² [~] 1. n. çentik, kertik, diş; sl. durum, sağlık; in the (very) ~ of time tam zamanında; 2. v/t. çentmek; kesmek; sl. aşırmak, yürütmek; sl. enselemek.

nick.el ['nikl] 1. n. min. nikel; Am. beş sent; ~-in-the-slot machine Am. otomatik tevzi makinesi; 2. v/t. nikel ile kaplamak.

nick.el.o.de.on Am. [nikl'əudjən] n. eskiden beş sente film gösterilen sinema; eskiden para ile çalınan otomatik pikap.

nick-nack ['niknæk] = knickknack.

nick.name ['nikneim] 1. n. takma isim, lakap, takılmış ad; 2. v/t. lakap takmak -e.

nic.o.tine ['nikətiːn] n. nikotin.

nid-nod ['nidnɔd] v/i. başını eğmek.

niece [niːs] n. kız yeğen.

niff sl. [nif] n. leş gibi koku.

**niff.y** *sl.* [ˈnifi] *adj.* leş gibi kokan.
**nif.ty** *Am.* [ˈnifti] **1.** *adj.* şık; hoş; oturaklı *(darbe)*; *sl.* kokmuş, leş gibi kokan; **2.** *n.* şık *bş.*
**nig.gard** [ˈnigəd] **1.** *n.* cimri (*veya* eli sıkı) kimse; **2.** □ tamahkâr, cimri; **ˈnig.gard.li.ness** *n.* cimrilik; **ˈnig.gard.ly** *adj. & adv.* cimri(ce), tamahkâr(ca).
**nig.ger** F *mst contp.* [ˈnigə] *n.* zenci; that's the ~ in the woodpile *Am. sl.* işte güçlük orada, işin kazık tarafı bu.
**nig.gle** [ˈnigl] *v/i.* lüzumsuz ayrıntılarla zaman geçirmek, önemsiz şeylerle uğraşmak; **ˈnig.gling** *adj.* can sıkıcı; dikkat isteyen *(iş)*; gereksiz ayrıntılı.
**nigh** † *veya prov.* [nai] = near.
**night** [nait] *n.* gece; akşam; by ~, in the ~, at ~ geceleyin; ~ out izinli gece; make a ~ of it eğlenceli bir gece geçirmek; **ˈ~-bell** *n.* gece kullanılan kapı zili; **ˈ~-bird** *n.* gece kuşu *(a. fig.)*; **ˈ~.cap** *n.* yatarken giyilen bere; yatmadan önce içilen alkollü içki; **ˈ~-club** *n.* gece kulübü; **ˈ~-dress** *n.* gecelik; **ˈ~.fall** *n.* akşam vakti; **ˈ~-gown** = night-dress; **night.in.gale** *orn.* [ˈ~iŋgeil] *n.* bülbül; **ˈnight.ly** *adv. & adj.* geceleyin (olan), her gece (olan).
**night...:** **ˈ~.mare** *n.* karabasan, kâbus; **ˈ~-school** *n.* gece okulu; **ˈ~.shade** *n.* ⚘ itüzümü, köpeküzümü; deadly ~ güzelavratotu, belladon; **ˈ~-shirt** *n.* erkeklerin giydiği gecelik entarisi; **ˈ~.spot** *n.* *Am.* gece kulübü; **ˈ~.stop** *n.* geceleme, gece molası; **ˈ~-stop** *vb.* gecelemek; **ˈ~-time** *n.* gece vakti; **ˈ~-walk.er** *n.* gece dolaşan kimse, uyurgezer; **ˈ~-ˈwatch** *n.* gece nöbeti; gece bekçisi; **ˈ~-ˈwatch.man** *n.* gece bekçisi (*veya* nöbetçisi); **ˈ~.work** *n.* gece işi; **ˈnight.y** *n.* F gecelik.
**ni.hil.ism** [ˈnaiilizəm] *n.* hiçlik, nihilizm; **ˈni.hil.ist** *n.* nihilizm yanlısı.
**nil** [nil] *n. part. spor:* sıfır, hiç.
**nim.ble** □ [ˈnimbl] çevik, tez, atik; keskin *(zekâ)*; **ˈnim.ble.ness** *n.* çeviklik, çabukluk.
**nim.bus** [ˈnimbəs] *n.* ayla, hale; yağmur bulutu.
**nim.i.ny-pim.i.ny** [ˈniminiˈpimini] *adj.* titiz, kılı kırk yaran; çıtkırıldım; fazla resmî.
**Nim.rod** [ˈnimrɔd] *n.* Nemrud; usta avcı.
**nin.com.poop** F [ˈninkəmpu:p] *n.* geri zekâlı (*veya* ahmak) kimse.
**nine** [nain] **1.** *adj.* dokuz; ~ day's wonder kısa süre ilgi çekip sonra unutulan şey; **2.** *n.* dokuz sayısı; dressed up to the ~s F iki dirhem bir çekirdek; **ˈ~.fold** *adj. & adv.* dokuz misli; **ˈ~.pins** *n. pl.* kiy oyunu; **nine.teen** [ˈ~ˈti:n] *adj.* on dokuz; talk ~ to the dozen car car konuşmak; **ˈnine-ˈteenth** *adj.* on dokuzuncu; on dokuzda bir; **nine.tieth** [ˈ~tiiθ] **1.** *adj.* doksanıncı; doksanda bir; **2.** *n.* doksanda bir kısım; **ˈnine.ty** *adj.* doksan.
**nin.ny** F [ˈnini] *n.* ahmak (*veya* budala) kimse.
**ninth** [nainθ] **1.** *adj.* dokuzuncu; dokuzda bir; **2.** *n.* dokuzda bir kısım; **ˈninth.ly** *adv.* dokuzuncu olarak.
**nip¹** [nip] **1.** *n.* çimdik; ⚘ ayaz; **2.** *v/t.* çimdiklemek, kıstırmak; kesmek, budamak; dondurmak, sızlatmak *(soğuk)*; zarar vermek *-e*; *sl.* aşırmak, yürütmek; ~ in the bud dal budak salmadan yok etm., başlarken bastırmak; suya düşürmek *-i (plan vs.)*; *v/i.* hızlı gitmek.
**nip²** [~] **1.** *n.* azıcık içki; **2.** *v/t.* azıcık içmek, yudumlamak *(içki)*.
**nip.per** [ˈnipə] *n.* F kırpan *veya* kesen kimse *veya* şey; (a pair of) ~s *pl.* kıskaç; F küçük çocuk *(part. erkek)*.
**nip.ple** [ˈnipl] *n.* meme başı; şişe emziği; ⊕ nipel, emzik.
**nip.py** F [ˈnipi] *adj.* çevik, atik, çabuk; yakıcı, soğuk, dondurucu.
**nir.va.na** [niəˈvɑ:nə] *n. Budizm:* aşırı istek ve tutkulardan kurtularak erişilen mutluluk hali.
**Ni.sei** *Am.* [ˈniˈsei] *n. (a. pl.)* Amerika'da doğup büyüyen Japon asıllı kimse.
**Nis.sen hut** [ˈnisnˈhʌt] *n.* çelikten yapılmış yarım silindir biçiminde bina, baraka.
**nit** [nit] *n.* bit yumurtası, sirke.
**ni.trate** ⚗ [ˈnaitreit] *n.* nitrat.
**ni.tre, ni.ter** ⚗ [ˈnaitə] *n.* güherçile.
**ni.tric ac.id** ⚗ [ˈnaitrikˈæsid] *n.* nitrik asit, kezzap.
**ni.tro.chalk** [ˈnaitrəuˈtʃɔ:k] *n.* çim gübresi.
**ni.tro.gen** ⚗ [ˈnaitrədʒən] *n.* nitrojen, azot; **ni.trog.e.nous** [~ˈtrɔdʒinəs] *adj.* nitrojene ait, nitrojen...; azotlu.
**ni.tro.glyc.er.ine** ⚗ [ˈnaitrəuglisəˈri:n] *n.* nitrogliserin.
**ni.trous** ⚗ [ˈnaitrəs] *adj.* azota ait; azot gibi; azotlu.
**nit.wit** F [ˈnitwit] *n.* kuş beyinli kimse; **ˈnit.wit.ted** *adj.* F kuş beyinli.
**nix** [nıks] *n.* küçük su perisi; **nix.ie** [ˈ~i] *n.* dişi su perisi.
**no** [nəu] **1.** *adj.* hiç (bir); in ~ time çarçabuk, derhal, hemencecik; ~ man's land iki cephe arasındaki sahipsiz arazi; ~ one hiç kimse; **2.** *adv.* hayır, yok, olmaz, öyle değil; **3.** *n.* yok yanıtı, hayır kelimesi; noes *pl.* *bşe* karşı çıkanlar.

**nob¹** *sl.* [nɔb] *n.* baş, kafa; ⊕ topuz, tokmak.

**nob²** *sl.* [ˌ] *n.* asılzade, soylu.

**nob.ble** *sl.* [ˈnɔbl] *v/t.* kazanmasını önlemek *(yarış atı);* -*in* dikkatini çekmek; hile ile kazanmak.

**nob.by** *sl.* [ˈnɔbi] *adj.* fiyakalı, afili.

**no.bil.i.ar.y** [nəuˈbiliəri] *adj.* asılzadelere ait.

**no.bil.i.ty** [nəuˈbiliti] *n.* asalet, soyluluk, asılzadelik; asılzadeler sınıfı.

**no.ble** [ˈnəubl] **1.** ☐ asil, soylu; yüce gönüllü; heybetli, muhteşem, ulu, yüce; kimyasal değişiklik göstermeyen *(maden);* **2.** *n.* asılzade, soylu kimse; ˈˌman *n.* asılzade; ˈˌmind.ed *adj.* asil fikirli; ˈno.ble.ness *n.* asalet, soyluluk; ˈno.ble.wom.an *n.* soylu kadın.

**no.bod.y** [ˈnəubədi] **1.** *pron.* hiç kimse; **2.** *n.* bir hiç olan kimse.

**nock** [nɔk] *n.* okun arka ucundaki kertik.

**noc.tur.nal** [nɔkˈtəːnl] *adj.* geceye ait, gece...; geceleyin olan; geceleyin yapılan; geceleri gezen.

**noc.turne** [ˈnɔktəːn] *n .paint.* gece manzarası; ♪ tatlı ve duygulu parça.

**nod** [nɔd] *v/i.* başını sallamak *(kabul ifade etmek için);* uyuklamak; hata yapmak; sallanmak; ˌding *acquaintance az* tanıma *(veya* bilme*),* tanıdık(lık); pek tanımadık *(veya* sadece selamlaşılan*)* kimse; ˌ off uyuklamak; *v/t.* başını sallayarak belirtmek; ˌ out dışarıyı işaret etm.; **2.** *n.* baş sallama.

**nod.dle** F [ˈnɔdl] *n.* baş, kafa.

**node** [nəud] *n.* düğüm *(a. ♀ & ast.);* ⅋ yumru, şiş.

**nod.u.lar** [ˈnɔdjulə] *adj.* yumru *veya* düğüme ait; yumru, düğümlü.

**nod.ule** [ˈnɔdjuːl] *n.* yumru, düğüm, boğum; şiş, bezecik.

**No.el** [nəuˈel] *n.* Noel.

**nog** [nɔg] *n. (içinde yumurta bulunan)* alkollü içki; kuvvetli bira; takoz; **nog.gin** [ˈnɔgin] *n.* kafa, baş; ufak bir içki ölçüsü; ˈnog.ging *n.* ♀ duvar örme.

**no.how** F [ˈnəuhau] *adv.* asla, hiç bir suretle.

**noil** [nɔil] *n. dokumacılık:* tarak döküntüsü.

**noise** [nɔiz] **1.** *n.* gürültü, patırtı, ses, şamata, yaygara, velvele; parazit; big ˌ *part. Am.* F kodaman, önemli şahıs; **2.** *v/t.* ˌ abroad yaymak, duyurmak, söylemek.

**noise.less** ☐ [ˈnɔizlis] sessiz, gürültüsüz; ˈnoise.less.ness *n.* sessizlik.

**nois.i.ness** [ˈnɔizinis] *n.* gürültü.

**noi.some** [ˈnɔisəm] *adj.* iğrenç, berbat; can sıkıcı; zararlı; ˈnoi.some.ness *n.* iğrençlik; zararlılık.

**nois.y** ☐ [ˈnɔizi] gürültülü, sesli; gürültücü, yaygaracı.

**no.mad** [ˈnəumæd] *n.* göçebe kimse; **no.mad.ic** [ˌˈmædik] *adj. (ˌally)* göçebeye ait, göçebe...; göçebe gibi, yersiz yurtsuz; **no.mad.ize** [ˈˌmədaiz] *v/i.* göçebe lik etm.

**nom de plume** [ˈnɔːmdəˈpluːm] *n.* yazarın takma adı.

**no.men.cla.ture** [nəuˈmenklətʃə] *n.* terminoloji.

**nom.i.nal** ☐ [ˈnɔminl] sözde; itibarî, saymaca; önemsiz; değersiz; çok düşük *(fiyat);* gr. isimle ilgili; nominal; ˌ value itibarî kıymet, nominal değer; **nom.i.nate** [ˈˌneit] *v/t.* atamak, görevlendirmek; aday göstermek; **nom.iˈna.tion** *n.* aday gösterme; atama, tayin; in ˌ aday olarak; **nom.i.na.tive** *gr.* [ˈˌnətiv] *n. a.* ˌ case yalın hal; **nom.i.na.tor** [ˈˌneitə] *n.* atayan kimse; **nom.i.nee** [ˌˈniː] *n.* aday, namzet.

**non** [nɔn] *prefix* -siz, -sız, gayri-.

**non-ac.cept.ance** [ˈnɔnəkˈseptəns] *n.* ret, kabul etmeme.

**non.age** [ˈnəunidʒ] *n.* küçüklük, çocukluk, rüşte ermemiş olma.

**non.a.ge.nar.i.an** [nəunədʒiˈnɛəriən] *n.* doksanlık kimse.

**non-ag.gres.sion** [ˈnɔnəˈgreʃən] *n.:* ˌ pact saldırmazlık antlaşması.

**non-al.co.hol.ic** [ˈnɔnælkəˈhɔlik] *adj.* alkolsüz.

**non-a.lign.ment** *pol.* [nɔnəˈlainmənt] *n.* müttefik olmama.

**non-ap.pear.ance** ⚖ [ˈnɔnəˈpiərəns] *n.* hazır bulunmama, gıyap.

**non-at.tend.ance** ⚖ [ˈnɔnəˈtendəns] *n.* katılmama, gıyap.

**nonce** [nɔns] *n.:* for the ˌ şimdilik.

**non.cha.lance** [ˈnɔnʃələns] *n.* ilgisizlik, soğukkanlılık; ˈnon.cha.lant** ☐ ilgisiz, soğukkanlı, sakin.

**non.com** ✕ F [nɔnˈkɔm] *n.* erbaş.

**non-com.mis.sioned** [ˈnɔnkəˈmiʃənd] *adj.* resmen görevli olmayan; asteğmenden aşağı rütbesi olan; ˌ officer ✕ erbaş.

**non-com.mit.tal** [ˈnɔnkəˈmitl] *adj.* tarafsız, yansız; fikrini söylemeyen.

**non-com.pli.ance** [ˈnɔnkəmˈplaiəns] *n.* itaatsizlik (with *-e).*

**non com.pos men.tis** ⚖ [nɔnˈkɔmpɔsˈmentis] *adj.* aklî dengesi bozuk, mümeyyiz olmayan.

**non-con.duc.tor** ⚡ [ˈnɔnkəndʌktə] *n.* yalıtkan madde.

**non.con.form.ist** ['nɔnkən'fɔːmist] *n.* toplumua uymayan kimse; Anglikan kilisesine bağlı olmayan kimse; **non.con'form.i-ty** *n.* uymama, ayak uydurmama; *eccl.* kiliseye uymama.

**non-de.liv.er.y** ['nɔndi'livəri] *n.* ademiteslim, teslim etmeme.

**non-de.nom.i.na.tion.al school** ['nɔndinəmi-'neiʃənl'skuːl] *n.* mezhep farkı gözetmeyen okul.

**non.de.script** ['nɔndiskript] **1.** *adj.* kolay tanımlanamaz, alelade; **2.** *n.* tanımlanamayan (*veya* alelade, sıradan) kimse.

**none** [nʌn] **1.** *pron.* hiç biri, hiç kimse; **2.** *adv.* hiç, asla, hiç bir suretle; ~ **the less** yine de, bununla birlikte.

**non.en.ti.ty** [nɔ'nentiti] *n.* önemsiz kimse; var olmayan (*veya* hayali) şey; *fig.* hiçlik, yokluk.

**non-es.sen.tial** ['nɔni'senʃəl] **1.** *adj.* gereksiz, önemsiz; **2.** *n.* gereksizlik.

**non-ex.ist.ence** ['nɔnig'zistəns] *n.* yokluk, varolmayış; **'non.ex'ist.ent** *adj.* varolmayan.

**non-fic.tion** ['nɔn'fikʃən] *n.* kurgusal olmayan düzyazı.

**non-in.ter.fer.ence** ['nɔnintə'fiərəns], **non--in.ter.ven.tion** ['nɔnintə'venʃən] *n.* başka devletlerin işine karışmama politikası.

**non-lad.der.ing** ['nɔn'lædəriŋ] *adj.* kaçmaz (*çorap*).

**non-mem.ber** ['nɔn'membə] *n.* üye olmayan kimse.

**non-ob.serv.ance** ['nɔnəb'zɔːvəns] *n.* uymama, çiğneme (*kural vs.*).

**non.pa.reil** [nɔnpə'rel] *n.* eşsiz (*veya* emsalsiz) kimse *veya* şey; *typ.* altı puntoluk harf.

**non-par.ti.san** [nɔn'pɑːtizæn] *adj.* partizan olmayan; tarafsız.

**non-par.ty** *pol.* ['nɔn'pɑːti] *adj.* partisiz.

**non-pay.ment** ['nɔn'peimənt] *n.* ödememe.

**non-per.form.ance** ['nɔnpə'fɔːməns] *n.* yerine getirmeme, yapmama.

**non.plus** ['nɔn'plʌs] **1.** *n.* şaşkınlık, hayret; **at a** ~ şaşkınlık içinde; **2.** *v/t.* şaşırtmak; ~**sed** apışıp kalmış, şaşkın.

**non-pro.lif.er.a.tion** ['nɔnprəulifə'reiʃən] *n.* nükleer silahların artması ve yayılmasını önleme; istenmeyen şeylerin yayılmasını önleme.

**non-res.i.dent** ['nɔn'rezidənt] *adj.* görevli olduğu yerde oturmayan.

**non.sense** ['nɔnsəns] *n.* saçma, boş laf; aptalca davranış; **non.sen.si.cal** □ [~-'sensikəl] saçma, abuk sabuk, ipe sapa gelmez.

**non-skid** ['nɔn'skid] *adj.* kaymaz (*lastik*).

**non-smok.er** ['nɔn'sməukə] *n.* sigara içmeyen kimse; sigara içilmeyen kompartıman.

**non-stop** ['nɔn'stɔp] *adj.* 🚂, ✈ doğru giden, aktarmasız, direkt; aralıksız.

**non.such** ['nʌnsʌtʃ] *n.* eşsiz (*veya* emsalsiz) kimse *veya* şey.

**non.suit** ☼ ['nɔn'sjuːt] *n.* davanın reddi; davanın düşmesi.

**non-U** F ['nɔnjuː] *adj.* üst tabakaya ait olmayan.

**non-un.ion** [nɔn'juːnjən] *adj.* sendikaya ait olmayan, sendikasız; sendika kurallarına uymayan; sendikaları tanımayan.

**noo.dle¹** F ['nuːdl] *n.* ahmak (*veya* sersem) kimse.

**noo.dle²** [~] *n.* şehriye.

**nook** [nuk] *n.* bucak, köşe.

**noon** [nuːn] **1.** *n.* öğle (vakti); **2.** *adj.* öğle vaktinde olan, öğle...; **'~.day**, **'~.tide** = noon.

**noose** [nuːs] **1.** *n.* ilmik; **2.** *v/t.* ilmikle tutmak; ilmiklemek.

**nope** *Am.* F [nəup] *int.* yok!, hayır!, olmaz!

**nor** [nɔː] *cj.* ne de, ne; ~ **do I** ben de (*olumsuz anlamda*).

**Nor.folk jack.et** ['nɔːfək'dʒækit] *n.* bir çeşit kuşaklı erkek ceketi.

**norm** [nɔːm] *n.* kural, norm, örnek; ortalama; **'nor.mal 1.** □ normal; düzgün, doğal, uygun; düzgülü; A dikey; ~ **school** öğretmen okulu; **2.** *n.* normal, standart; A dikey; **'nor.mal.ize** *v/t.* & *v/i.* normalleş(tir)mek, normale dön(dür)mek.

**Nor.man** ['nɔːmən] **1.** *n.* Normandiyalı kimse; Normandiyalıların konuştuğu Fransızca lehçe; **2.** *adj.* Normandiya *veya* Normandiyalılara ait.

**Norse** [nɔːs] **1.** *adj.* İskandinavya'ya *veya* İskandinavya dillerine ait; **2.** *n.* İskandinavya dili; Norveç dili; **'Norse.man** *n.* İskandinavyalı; Norveçli.

**north** [nɔːθ] **1.** *n.* kuzey; **2.** *adj.* kuzey...; **~** kuzeye bakan; kuzeyden gelen *veya* esen; **'~-'east 1.** *n.* kuzeydoğu; **2.** *adj.* a. **~-'east.ern** kuzeydoğuda olan; kuzeydoğudan gelen; **north.er.ly** ['~-ðəli] *adj.* & *adv.* kuzeye doğru (olan); kuzeyden (esen); kuzeydeki; **north.ern** ['~ðən] *adj.* kuzeye ait, kuzey...; kuzeyde olan, kuzeyli; **'north.ern.er** *n.* kuzeyli kimse; 2 *Am.* kuzey eyaletlerinde oturan kimse; **'north.ern.most** *adj.* en kuzeydeki; **north-ing** ['~θiŋ] *n.* ⚓ kuzey rotası; kuzeye doğru katedilen mesafe; **'North.man** *n.* İskandinavyalı; **north.ward(.ly)** ['~wəd-

(li)] *adj.* & *adv.*, **north.wards** [¹˗wədz] *adv.* kuzeye doğru (olan), kuzeyden (esen).

**north...: ¹˗˗ˈwest** 1. *n.* kuzeybatı; 2. *adj. a.* ¹˗˗ˈwest.ern, ¹˗˗ˈwest.er.ly kuzeye ait, kuzey...; kuzeyden gelen; karayel yönünden.

**Nor.we.gian** [nɔːˈwiːdʒən] 1. *adj.* Norveçli, Norveç'e ait; 2. *n.* Norveçli; Norveç dili.

**nose** [nəuz] 1. *n.* burun; koklama duyusu; uç; ↓ pruva; cut off one's ~ to spite one's face nispet olsun diye kendi çıkarını zedelemek, gâvura kızıp oruç bozmak; pay through the ~ avuç dolusu para ödemek, ateş pahasına almak; poke *veya* push *veya* thrust one's ~ into s.th. bşe burnunu sokmak; turn one's ~ up at -i hor görmek, -e burun kıvırmak; put s.o.'s ~ out of joint b-nin pabucunu dama atmak; b-nin ayağını kaydırmak; 2. *v/t. a.* ~ out koklayarak bulmak, arayıp bulmak -i; -in kokusunu almak; burunla itmek; kıl payı kazanmak; ~ one's way dikkatle ilerlemek; *v/i.* koklamak (after, for -i); ¹˗bag *n.* atın yem torbası; ¹˗-band *n.* yuların atın burnu üzerinden geçen kısmı; nosed *comb.* ...burunlu.

**nose...: ¹˗-dive** *n.* ✈ pike; ¹˗.gay *n.* çiçek demeti; ¹˗-heav.y *adj.* ✈ pike yapmaya çalışan; ¹˗-o.ver *n.* ✈ burun üstüne çakılma; ¹˗.ring *n.* burun halkası.

**nos.ing** ⚠ [ˈnəuziŋ] *n.* basamak çıkıntısı.

**nos.tal.gi.a** [nɔsˈtældʒiə] *n.* özlem; vatan *(veya* sıla) hasreti; **nosˈtal.gic** [˗dʒik] *adj.* sıla hasreti kabilinden.

**nos.tril** [ˈnɔstril] *n.* burun deliği.

**nos.trum** [ˈnɔstrəm] *n.* kocakarı ilâcı; her derde deva.

**nos.y** [ˈnəuzi] 1. *adj.* meraklı; *b.s.* başkasının işine burnunu sokan; ♀ Parker = 2. *n.* başkasının işine burnunu sokan kimse.

**not** [nɔt] *adv.* değil, olmayan; ~ at all asla, hiç; birşey değil, rica ederim.

**no.ta.bil.i.ty** [nəutəˈbiliti] *n.* şöhret; şöhretli kimse; ¹no.ta.ble 1. □ dikkate değer; tanınmış, meşhur; göze çarpan; 2. *n.* tanınmış *(veya* meşhur) kimse; ¹no.ta.bly *adv.* dikkate değer şekilde; özellikle.

**no.tar.i.al** □ [nəuˈtɛəriəl] notere ait, noter...; **no.ta.ry** [ˈnəutəri] *n. oft.* public ~ noter.

**no.ta.tion** [nəuˈteiʃən] *n.* not; ♩ rakamlar ve işaretler sistemi; ♩ notalar ile işaretler sistemi; kayıt.

**notch** [nɔtʃ] 1. *n.* çentik, kertik; ⊕ diş, yiv; *Am.* dar dağ geçidi; derece, basamak; 2. *v/t.* çentmek, kertmek; ~ up kazanmak, kırmak *(rekor vs.).*

**note** [nəut] 1. *n.* not, işaret; ♩, *pol.* nota; ↑ senet, pusula; önem; şöhret, itibar; dikkat; banknot; take ~ of -e dikkat etm., önem vermek; strike the right ~ lafı gediğine oturtmak; strike *veya* sound a false ~ k-ni gözden düşürecek bş yapmak *veya* söylemek; 2. *v/t.* kaydetmek; *a.* ~ down deftere yazmak, not almak; dikkat etm., önem vermek; ¹˗.book *n.* not defteri, defter; ¹not.ed *adj.* ünlü, meşhur, tanınmış (for *ile*, as *olarak*); ~ly özellikle, bilhassa; ¹note-pa.per *n.* mektup kâğıdı; ¹note.wor.thy *adj.* önemli, dikkate değer.

**noth.ing** [ˈnʌθiŋ] 1. *n.* hiç bir şey; sıfır; önemsiz kimse *veya* şey; hiçlik, yokluk; for ~ ücretsiz, parasız, bedava; boş yere; good for ~ hayırsız, hiç bir işe yaramaz; come (bring) to ~ boşa çık(ar)mak, suya düş(ür)mek; go for ~ boşa gitmek; make ~ of -i önemsememek; -i anlayamamak; I can make ~ of it anlıyorsam arap olayım; ˈsay ~ of bile değil, şöyle dursun; think ~ of -i önemsememek; 2. *adv.* hiç (bir suretle), asla, katiyen; ¹noth.ing.ness *n.* yokluk, hiçlik; boşluk; anlamsızlık, önemsizlik.

**no.tice** [ˈnəutis] 1. *n.* haber; ilân, ihbarname; uyarı, ikaz, ihtar; önemseme, dikkat; eleştiri; saygı; at short ~ kısa ihbar süreli, kısa mühletli; give ~ that önceden haber vermek; give a week's ~ bir hafta önceden bildirmek; take ~ of -i dikkate almak, -e aldırış etm.; until further ~ yeni bir habere kadar; without ~ haber *(veya* mühlet) vermeden, müddetsiz; 2. *v/t.* farkına varmak -in, farketmek -i, görmek -i; dikkat etm. -e; önem vermek -e; saygı göstermek -e; eleştirmek *(kitap);* ¹no.tice.a.ble □ görülebilir, farkedilir; önemsenmeye değer; ¹no.tice-board *n.* ilân tahtası.

mek -e; saygı göstermek -e; eleştirmek *(kitap);* ¹no.tice.a.ble □ görülebilir, farkedilir; önemsenmeye değer; ¹no.tice-board *n.* ilân tahtası.

**no.ti.fi.a.ble** [ˈnəutifaiəbl] *adj.* bildirilmesi zorunlu; **no.ti.fi.ca.tion** [˗fiˈkeiʃən] *n.* bildirme; ihbar.

**no.ti.fy** [ˈnəutifai] *v/t.* ilân etm.; bildirmek.

**no.tion** [ˈnəuʃən] *n.* sanı, zan; fikir, düşünce, bilgi; inanç; ~s *pl. Am.* tuhafiye; have no ~ of ...hakkında bir fikri olmamak; ¹no.tion.al □ hayalî, soyut, kuramsal; itibarî *(değer).*

no.to.ri.e.ty [nəutə'raiəti] n. kötü şöhret; adı çıkmışlık; no.to.ri.ous ☐ [-'tɔːriəs] adı çıkmış, dile düşmüş (for -den dolayı, için).

not.with.stand.ing [nɔtwiθ'stændiŋ] 1. prp. -e rağmen, yine de; 2. adv. gerçi, her ne kadar, buna rağmen; 3. cj. ~ that ...rağmen, ...ise de.

nou.gat ['nuːgɑː] n. koz helvası.

nought part. Ḁ [nɔːt] n. sıfır; hiç.

noun gr. [naun] n. isim, ad.

nour.ish ['nʌriʃ] v/t. beslemek (a. fig.), yedirmek; gübrelemek (toprak); fig. desteklemek; 'nour.ish.ing adj. besleyici; 'nour.ish.ment n. yemek, gıda; besle(n)-me.

nous [naus] n. akıl, zekâ; sebep; sağduyu; idrak, anlayış.

nov.el ['nɔvəl] 1. adj. yeni, tuhaf, acayip, alışılmamış; 2. n. roman; short ~ = nov-el.ette [nɔvə'let] n. kısa roman; 'nov.el.ist n. romancı, roman yazarı; nov.el.ty ['nɔvəlti] n. yenilik; yeni bş.

No.vem.ber [nəu'vembə] n. kasım (ayı).

nov.ice ['nɔvis] n. çırak; acemi kimse; eccl. rahip veya rahibe adayı.

no.vi.ci.ate, no.vi.ti.ate [nəu'viʃiit] n. çıraklık (veya acemilik) devresi; papaz adaylığı devresi.

now [nau] 1. adv. şimdi, bu anda; işte; by ~ şimdiye dek; just ~ demin(cek), hemen şimdi; before ~ bundan önce; ~ and again, ~ and then arasıra, bazen, zaman zaman; 2. cj. a. ~ that mademki, artık; 3. n. şu an, şimdiki zaman.

now.a.day ['nauədei] adj. bugünkü, şimdiki; now.a.days ['~z] adv. bugünlerde, şimdi, günümüzde.

no.way(s) F ['nəuwei(z)] adv. hiç bir suretle, asla, olmaz.

no.where ['nəuweə] adv. hiçbir yer(d)e.

no.wise ['nəuwaiz] adv. hiç bir suretle, asla.

nox.ious ☐ ['nɔkʃəs] zararlı.

noz.zle ['nɔzl] n. ⊕ ağızlık, meme, burun; hortum başı.

nu.ance [njuː'ãːns] n. nüans, ince fark.

nub [nʌb] n. yumru, topak; Am. F öz, püf noktası.

nu.bile ['njuːbail] adj. evlenecek yaşa gelmiş, gelinlik (kız).

nu.cle.ar ['njuːkliə] adj. nükleer...; ~ disintegration çekirdek dağılması; ~ physics sg. nükleer fizik; ~ pile atom reaktörü; ~ power plant nükleer elektrik santralı; ~ research nükleer araştırma; ~ station nükleer elektrik santralı; nu.cle.on phys. ['~kliɔn] n. nükleon; nu.cle-

us ['~kliəs] n., pl. a. nu.cle.i ['~kliai] çekirdek, cevher, öz.

nude [njuːd] 1. adj. çıplak; 2. n. çıplak insan vücudu; paint. nüd; study from the ~ çıplak modelle çalışma.

nudge F [nʌdʒ] 1. v/t. dirsek ile dürtmek; 2. n. dürtme.

nud.ism ['njuːdizəm] n. çıplak dolaşma; 'nud.ist n. çıplak kimse; attr. çıplaklar... (kampı); 'nu.di.ty n. çıplaklık.

nu.ga.to.ry ['njuːgətəri] adj. önemsiz, değersiz ,ufak tefek, boş; geçersiz.

nug.get ['nʌgit] n. (part. altın) külçe.

nui.sance ['njuːsns] n. sıkıcı şey veya kimse; sıkıntı, baş belâsı, dert; fig. yük, külfet; what a ~! tüh be!, işe bak!, help Allah!; commit no ~! çöp dökmeyiniz!, işemek (veya pislemek) yasaktır!; make o.s. veya be a ~ can sıkıcı olm.

null [nʌl] adj. ⅋ & fig. etkisiz, değersiz; ~ and void hükümsüz, geçersiz; nul.li.fi-ca.tion [nʌlifi'keiʃən] n. hükümsüz kılma; nul.li.fy ['~fai] v/t. hükümsüz kılmak; etkisiz bırakmak; iptal; fig. hiç; 'nul.li.ty n. hükümsüzlük; iptal; fig. hiç.

numb [nʌm] 1. adj. uyuşuk, uyuşmuş (with -den); duygusuz, hissiz; 2. v/t. uyuşturmak; azaltmak (acı); ~ed uyuşmuş.

num.ber ['nʌmbə] 1. n. sayı, adet, numara, rakam; miktar; sayı; ~s pl. Ḁ aritmetik; ~s pl. poet. şiir; ♪ parça; your ~ is up işin bitik, suyun kaynadı, hapı yuttun, ayvayı yedin; without ~ sayısız, hesapsız; in ~ sayıca; 2. v/t. saymak; numara koymak -e, numaralamak; hesaplamak; kapsamak, katmak; ~ among, ~ in, ~ with katmak, saymak; 'num.ber.less adj. sayısız, pek çok; number one F insanın kendi çıkarı; bir numaralı kimse; en önemli; look after ~ kendi çıkarını düşünmek; 'num.ber-plate n. mot. plaka.

numb.ness ['nʌmnis] n. uyuşukluk, duygusuzluk.

nu.mer.a.ble ['njuːmərəbl] adj. sayılabilir; 'nu.mer.al 1. adj. sayıya ait, sayı...; sayı yerini tutan; 2. n. sayı, rakam, adet; nu.mer'a.tion n. numaralama, sayma; 'nu.mer.a.tor n. Ḁ pay; sayıcı.

nu.mer.i.cal ☐ [njuː'merikəl] sayıya ait, sayı...

nu.mer.ous ☐ ['njuːmərəs] birçok, sayısız, dünya kadar, bir hayli; 'nu.mer.ous-ness n. çokluk.

nu.mis.mat.ic [njuːmiz'mætik] adj. (~ally) paraya ait, para...; nu.mis'mat.ics n. mst sg. para ve madalya ilmi; nu'mis.ma.tist [~mətist] n. para uzmanı.

**num.skull** ⨍ [ˈnʌmskʌl] *n.* kalın kafalı (*veya* mankafa) kimse.

**nun** [nʌn] *n.* rahibe; *orn.* mavi iskete kuşu.

**nun.ci.a.ture** *eccl.* [ˈnʌnʃjətʃə] *n.* papalık elçisinin görev süresi; **nun.ci.o** *eccl.* [ˈ~ʃiəu] *n.* papalık elçisi.

**nun.ner.y** [ˈnʌnəri] *n.* rahibe manastırı.

**nup.tial** [ˈnʌpʃəl] **1.** *adj.* evlenmeye *veya* düğüne ait; **2.** *n.* ~s *pl.* düğün, nikâh.

**nurse** [nəːs] **1.** *n.* hemşire, hastabakıcı; *a.* wet ~ sütnine; dadı; at ~ bakılmakta; put out to ~ bakmak; emzirmek; **2.** *v/t.* & *v/i.* emzirmek; beslemek; bakmak *-e*; iyileştirmek; hastabakıcılık yapmak; ~ a cold soğukalgınlığını tedavi etm.; 'ₓ' -maid *n.* dadı.

**nurs.er.y** [ˈnəːsri] *n.* çocuk odası; ✓ fidanlık; ~ school anaokulu; 'ₓ'.man *n.* fidanlık bahçıvanı; 'ₓ'-rhymes *n. pl.* çocuk şiirleri *veya* şarkıları; ~ slopes *pl. kayak:* yeni öğrenenler için yamaçlar.

**nurs.ing** [ˈnəːsiŋ] *n.* hastabakıcılık, hemşirelik; 'ₓ'-bot.tle *n.* biberon; 'ₓ'-home *n.* özel sağlık yurdu.

**nurs.ling** [ˈnəːsliŋ] *n.* süt çocuğu.

**nur.ture** [ˈnəːtʃə] **1.** *n.* büyütme; terbiye; eğitim; **2.** *v/t. a.* ~ up büyütmek; yetiştirmek; *fig.* eğitmek, geliştirmek.

**nut** [nʌt] **1.** *n.* fındık, ceviz; ⊕ vida somunu; *sl.* baş, kafa; ~s *pl.* deli, çılgın,

kaçık; that is ~s to *veya* for him *sl.* onun için deli olur; be ~s on *sl. -e* abayı yakmak, *-in* delisi olm.; drive ~s *sl.* çıldırtmak; go ~s *sl.* keçileri kaçırmak; **2.** *v/i.* go ~ting fındık *veya* ceviz toplamak.

**nu.ta.tion** *ast.* [njuːˈteiʃən] *n.* nütasyon, üğrüm.

**nut.crack.er** [ˈnʌtkrækə] *n., mst* (a pair of) ~s *pl.* fındıkkıran; 'nut-gall *n.* meşe mazısı; 'nut-house *n. sl.* tımarhane; **nut.meg** [ˈ~meg] *n.* ufak hindistancevizi ağacı.

**nu.tri.a** [ˈnjuːtriə] *n.* kunduz (kürkü).

**nu.tri.ent** [ˈnjuːtriənt] **1.** *adj.* besleyici...; gıdalı...; **2.** *n.* besin, gıda; 'nu.tri.ment *n.* gıda, besin, yemek.

**nu.tri.tion** [njuːˈtriʃən] *n.* besle(n)me; yiyecek, gıda; **nu'tri.tious** ☐ besinli, besleyici...; **nu'tri.tious.ness** *n.* besleyicilik.

**nu.tri.tive** ☐ [ˈnjuːtritiv] ⊨ nutritious.

**nut.shell** [ˈnʌtʃel] *n.* fındık kabuğu; in a ~ kısaca, bir iki kelime ile; 'nut.ting *s.* nut 2.; **nut.ty** [ˈnʌti] *adj.* fındık *veya* ceviz tadında; cevizli *veya* fındıklı; *sl.* çatlak, kaçık, deli.

**nuz.zle** [ˈnʌzl] *vb.* burun ile itmek *veya* dokunmak, burun sürtmek; *a.* ~ o.s. sokulmak.

**ny.lon** [ˈnailɔn] *n.* naylon; ~s *pl.* naylon çorap.

**nymph** [nimf] *n.* peri.

# O

**o** [əu] **1.** *int.* o!, ya!; **2.** *n. teleph.* sıfır.

**oof** [əuf] *n.* budala (*veya* ahmak) kimse, kaba adam; **¹oaf.ish** *adj.* kaba, sersem, budala.

**oak** [əuk]·**1.** *n.* meşe ağacı; meşe odunu; *s.* sport; **2.** *adj.* meşe...; **¹~ap.ple**, **¹~gall** *n.* yaş mazı; **¹oak.en** *adj.* meşeden yapılmış, meşe...

**oa.kum** [¹əukəm] *n.* üstüpü.

**oar** [ɔː] **1.** *n.* kürek; F kürekçi; **pull a good ~** iyi bir kürekçi olm.; **put in one's ~** F burnunu sokmak; **rest on one's ~s** işleri yavaşlatmak, bir süre dinlenmek; **2.** *vb.* kürek çekmek; **oared** [ɔːd] *adj.* kürekli...; **oars.man** [¹ɔːzmən] *n.* kürekçi; **¹oars.man.ship** *n.* kürekçilik; **¹oars.woman** *n.* kadın kürekçi.

**o.a.sis** [əu¹eisis] *n.*, *pl.* **o¹a.ses** [~siːz] vaha.

**oast** [əust] *n.* şerbetçiotu kurutma fırını.

**oat** [əut] *n. mst* **~s** *pl.* yulaf (tanesi); **feel one's ~s** *Am.* F *k-ni* zinde hissetmek; *k-ni* beğenmek; **sow one's wild ~s** gençlikte çılgınlık yapmak; **¹oat.en** *adj.* yulaftan yapılmış, yulaf...

**oath** [əuθ] *n.*, *pl.* **oaths** [əuðz] yemin, ant; *b.s.* küfür, lânet; **administer** *veya* **tender an ~ to s.o.**, **put s.o. to** *veya* **on his ~** *b-ne* yemin ettirmek, ant içirmek; **bind by ~** yeminle bağlamak; **on ~** yeminli, yemin etmiş; **take** *veya* **make** *veya* **swear an ~** yemin etm., ant içmek (**on**, **to** *üzerine*).

**oat.meal** [¹əutmiːl] *n.* yulaf ezmesi, yulaf unu.

**ob.du.ra.cy** [¹ɔbdjurəsi] *n.* inatçılık, sertlik; **ob.du.rate** ☐ [¹~rit] inatçı, katı kalpli; sert, kırıcı.

**o.be.di.ence** [ə¹biːdjəns] *n.* itaat (etme), söz dinleme, boyun eğme; **in ~ to -e** itaat ederek; **o¹be.di.ent** ☐ itaatli, söz dinleyen, yumuşak başlı, uysal.

**o.bei.sance** [əu¹beisəns] *n.* hürmetle eğilme; hürmet, saygı; **do** *veya* **make** *veya* **pay ~** hürmet etm., saygı göstermek.

**ob.e.lisk** [¹ɔbilisk] *n.* dikilitaş, abide; *typ.* başvurma işareti.

**o.bese** ☐ [əu¹biːs] çok şişman, şişko;

**o¹bese.ness**, **o¹bes.i.ty** *n.* şişmanlık.

**o.bey** [ə¹bei] *v/t.* itaat etm. **-e**, boyun eğmek **-e**; yerine getirmek; *v/i.* denileni yapmak, söz dinlemek.

**ob.fus.cate** *fig.* [¹ɔbfʌskeit] *v/t.* şaşırtmak; karartmak.

**o.bit.u.ar.y** [ə¹bitjuəri] **1.** *n.* ölüm ilânı; anma yazısı; **2.** *adj.* **b-nin** ölümüne ait, ölüm...; **~ notice** ölüm ilânı.

**ob.ject 1.** [¹ɔbdʒikt] *n.* şey, madde, nesne, obje; *fig.* amaç, hedef, gaye; *gr.* nesne; komik *veya* acayip kimse *veya* şey; **what an ~ you look!** ne komik görünüyorsun!; **salary no ~** ücret söz konusu değildir; **2.** [əb¹dʒekt] *v/t.* itiraz etm. (**to -e**); *v/i.* razı olmamak, itiraz etm. (**to -e**), karşı gelmek (**to -e**); **~-glass** *opt.* [¹ɔbdʒiktglɑːs] *n.* objektif.

**ob.jec.tion** [əb¹dʒekʃən] *n.* itiraz; kusur, mahzur; **there is no ~ (to it) (ona)** itiraz yok; **ob¹jec.tion.a.ble** ☐ [~ʃnəbl] itiraz edilebilir; hoşa gitmeyen, tatsız (*söz*).

**ob.jec.tive** [əb¹dʒektiv] **1.** ☐ objektif; gerçek; tarafsız; nesnel; **2.** *n.* amaç, gaye, hedef (*a.* ✕); *opt.* mercek, objektif; *a.* **~ case** *gr.* ismin -i hali; **ob¹jec.tive.ness**, **ob.jec¹tiv.i.ty** *n.* tarafsızlık.

**ob.ject...;** **¹~-lens** *n.* *opt.* objektif, mercek; **¹~less** ☐ gayesiz, amaçsız; **¹~-les.son** *n.* uygulamalı ders; *fig.* ibret, ders; **¹~teach.ing** *n.* uygulamalı öğretim; **ob.jector** [əb¹dʒektə] *n.* itirazcı, aleyhtar, muhalif; *s.* conscientious.

**ob.jur.gate** [¹ɔbdʒəːgeit] *v/t.* azarlamak, paylamak; haşlamak; **ob.jur¹ga.tion** *n.* azarlama, paylama, haşlama; **ob¹jur.gato.ry** [~gətəri] *adj.* azarlayıcı, paylayıcı.

**ob.late** ☐ [¹ɔbleit] Å kutupları yassılaşmış; **¹ob.late.ness** *n.* yassılık.

**ob.la.tion** [əu¹bleiʃən] *n.* adak.

**ob.li.gate** ☐ *fig.* [¹ɔbligeit] *v/t.* zorlamak, mecbur etm., zorunda bırakmak; **ob.li¹ga.tion** *n.* mecburiyet, zorunluluk, yüküm, ödev, görev, vazife; senet, borç; **be under (an) ~ to s.o. b-ne** minnettar olm., müteşekkir olm.; **be under ~ to** *inf.* **-meğe** yükümlü olm.; **ob.lig.a.to.ry** ☐ [¹~gətəri] mecburî, gerekli, zorunlu (**on**

**için);**

**o.blige** [ə'blaidʒ] *v/t.* zorunlu kılmak, zorlamak, mecbur etm.; minnettar kılmak; memnun etm.; ~ s.o. *b-ni* memnun etm., *b-ne* iyilikte bulunmak; ~ the company with beraberindekilerin eğlencesine ...ile katkıda bulunmak; be ~d minnnettar olm., müteşekkir olm.; mecbur olm., zorunlu olm. (to *inf.* -*meğe*); much ~d çok minnettar, müteşekkir; *v/i.* ~ with a song F eğlenceye bir şarkı ile katkısı olm.; please ~ with an early reply erken vereceğiniz cevap bizi minnettar kılacaktır; **ob.li.gee** [ɔbli'dʒiː] *n.* alacaklı; **o.blig.ing** [ə'blaidʒiŋ] nazik, yardımsever, hoş, sevimli, tatlı; **o-'blig.ing.ness** *n.* yardımseverlik, nezaket; **ob.li.gor** [ɔbli'gɔ:] *n.* borçlu.

**ob.lique** [ə'bliːk] eğri, eğik, meyilli; dolaylı, ima yollu; *gr.* hal; ~ case ismin hitap ve yalın halinden başka herhangi bir hali; **ob'lique.ness, ob.liq.ui.ty** [ə'blikwiti] *n.* meyil, eğilim, eğiklik; ahlâksızlık, yoldan çıkma.

**ob.lit.er.ate** [ə'blitəreit] *v/t.* silmek, yok etm., bozmak, gidermek; *fig.* tahrip etm., mahvetmek, harap etm.; **ob.lit.er-'a.tion** *n.* yok etme, silme; mahvetme.

**ob.liv.i.on** [ə'blivən] *n.* unut(ul)ma; *pol.* af; bilinçsizlik, farkında olmama; **ob'liv-i.ous** □ unutkan; bilinçsiz, habersiz; be ~ of -*i* unutmak; -*den* haberi olmamak; be ~ to -*i* önemsememek, nazarı dikkate almamak.

**ob.long** ['ɔblɔŋ] **1.** *adj.* dikdörtgen şeklinde, boyu eninden fazla; **2.** *n.* dikdörtgen.

**ob.lo.quy** ['ɔbləkwi] *n.* kötüleme, kınama, iftira etme, yerme, küfretme.

**ob.nox.ious** □ [ɔb'nɔkʃəs] iğrenç, tiksindirici; **ob'nox.ious.ness** *n.* iğrençlik, çirkinlik, tiksindiricilik.

**o.boe** ♪ ['əubəu] *n.* obua.

**ob.scene** □ [əb'siːn] açık saçık, müstehcen; tiksindirici, iğrenç; ağıza alınmaz (*söz*); **ob'scen.i.ty** [~niti] *n.* açık saçıklık, müstehcenlik; açık saçık söz.

**ob.scu.ra.tion** [ɔbskjuə'reiʃən] *n.* karar(t)ma; **ob.scure** [əb'skjuə] **1.** □ çapraşık; *fig.* belirsiz, şüpheli, anlaşılmaz; karanlık, bulutlu; saklı, gizli; tanınmamış, bilinmeyen; **2.** *v/t.* karartmak; örtmek, saklamak, gizlemek; **ob'scu.ri.ty** *n.* çapraşıklık; *fig.* belirsizlik.

**ob.se.quies** ['ɔbsikwiz] *n. pl.* cenaze törenleri.

**ob.se.qui.ous** □ [əb'siːkwiəs] dalkavukluk eden, yağcılık eden, aşırı itaatli (to -*e*);

**ob'se.qui.ous.ness** *n.* dalkavukluk.

**ob.serv.a.ble** □ [əb'zəːvəbl] görünür, farkedilir; ölçülür; izlenebilir; izlenmeye değer, incelenmeye değer; **ob'serv.ance** *n.* yerine getirme, yapma; görenek; âdet; tören, usül; **ob'serv.ant** □ dikkatli, dikkat eden (of -*e*); itaatli, uyan, riayetkâr (of -*e*); be ~ of the rules kurallara uymak; **ob.ser.va.tion** [ɔbzə'veiʃən] *n.* gözetleme; dikkatli bakma, inceleme; gözlem, rasat; fikir, yorum; *attr.* gözetleme...; inceleme...; ~ car geniş pencereli vagon; ~ post topçu gözleme yeri; **ob.serv.a.to.ry** [əb'zəːvətri] *n.* rasathane, gözlemevi; **ob'serve** *v/t.* gözlemek; *fig.* yerine getirmek, uymak, itaat etm. (*kural*); incelemek; kutlamak; ileri sürmek, belirtmek; *v/i.* dikkat etm.; gözlem yapmak; fikrini söylemek (on *hakkında*); **ob'serv.er** *n.* gözleyen kimse, gözlemci, itaat eden kimse; toplantıya gözlemci olarak katılan temsilci.

**ob.sess** [əb'ses] *v/t.* musallat olm. -*e*, tedirgin etm. -*i*; meşgul etm. (*zihin*); ~ed by *veya* with musallat -*e*; tedirgin -*den*, endişeli -*den*; kafayı takmış -*e*; **ob.ses.sion** [əb'seʃən] *n.* kafayı meşgul eden düşünce; sürekli endişe; sabit fikir; musallat fikir.

**ob.sid.i.an** *min.* [ɔb'sidiən] *n.* koyu renkli volkanik cam.

**ob.so.les.cence** [ɔbsə'lesns] *n.* eskime, demode olma, kullanılmama; **ob.so'les-cent** *adj.* eskiyen, demode olan, modası geçmekte olan, az kullanılan.

**ob.so.lete** ['ɔbsəliːt] *adj.* eskimiş, kullanılmayan, modası geçmiş, demode; *biol.* eskilerine oranla az gelişmiş.

**ob.sta.cle** ['ɔbstəkl] *n.* engel, mâni; ~ race engelli yarış.

**ob.stet.ric** [ɔb'stetrik], **ob'stet.ri.cal** *adj.* ♀ doğum *veya* gebeliğe ait, çocuk doğum...; gebelik...; **ob.ste.tri.cian** [~'triʃən] *n.* doğum mütehassısı; **ob'stet.rics** [~triks] *n. mst sg.* gebelik *veya* doğumla uğraşan tıp dalı.

**ob.sti.na.cy** ['ɔbstinəsi] *n.* inatçılık, dik başlılık; **ob'sti.nate** □ ['~nit] inatçı, dik kafalı, söz dinlemez; yenmesi güç, direnci kırılmaz (*fig. hastalık*).

**ob.strep.er.ous** □ [əb'strepərəs] gürültücü, şamatacı, yaygaracı; ele avuca sığmaz, haylaz.

**ob.struct** [əb'strʌkt] *v/t.* tıkamak, kapamak -*i*; engel olm., mâni olm. -*e*; zorlaştırmak -*i*; **ob'struc.tion** *n.* engel, mâni(a), set; blokaj; *parl.* engelleme; **ob'struc.tive** □ [~tiv] engelleyici (of -*i*).

**ob.tain** [əbˈtein] *v/t.* bulmak, almak, ele geçirmek, elde etm.; *v/i.* geçerli olm., süregelmek, yerleşmiş olm. *(gelenek)*; **obˈtain.a.ble** *adj.* bulunabilir, elde edilebilir; † satın alınabilir; **obˈtain.ment** *n.* elde etme, bulma, alma.

**ob.trude** [əbˈtruːd] *v/t.* zorla kabul ettirmek (on -i); *v/i.* k-ni zorla kabul ettirmek; **obˈtru.sion** [~ʒən] *n.* k-ni zorla kabul ettirme; **obˈtru.sive** ☐ [~siv] k-ni zorla kabul ettiren, sokulup sıkıntı veren, yılışık.

**ob.tu.rate** [ˈɔbtjuəreit] *v/t.* engellemek, mâni olm., kapamak, tıkamak; **ˈob.tu.ra.tor** *n.* engelleyen kimse *veya* şey, tıkayıcı şey.

**ob.tuse** ☐ [əbˈtjuːs] keskin olmayan, kör, küt; A geniş *(açı)*; *fig.* kalın kafalı, aptal, bön; duygusuz; **obˈtuse.ness** *n.* duygusuzluk; *fig.* bönlük, aptallık.

**ob.verse** [ˈɔbvəːs] *n.* paranın yüz kısmı, tura; herhangi bir şeyin yüz tarafı; *fig.* eş, karşılık; ters önerme.

**ob.vi.ate** *fig.* [ˈɔbvieit] *v/t.* önlemek, gidermek, ortadan kaldırmak.

**ob.vi.ous** ☐ [ˈɔbviəs] (bes)belli, (ap)açık, aşikâr; **ˈob.vi.ous.ness** *n.* aşikârlık, açıklık, meydanda olma.

**oc.ca.sion** [əˈkeiʒən] **1.** *n.* fırsat, münasebet, vesile, durum, hal; sebep, neden, gereklilik, lüzum; F olay, hadise; iş; kutlama: on ~ ara sıra, fırsat düştükçe; gerektiğinde; on the ~ of dolayısıyla, vesilesiyle; **2.** *v/t.* vesile olm., sebep olm. -e; **ocˈca.sion.al** ☐ [~ʒən] ara sıra olan, fırsat düştükçe yapılan; **ocˈca.sion.al.ly** [~ʒnəli] *adv.* ara sıra, bazen.

**oc.ci.dent** *poet. & rhet.* [ˈɔksidənt] *n.* batı, batı yarıküresi; **oc.ci.den.tal** ☐ [~ˈdentl] batılı, batıya ait, batısal, batı...

**oc.cult** ☐ [ɔˈkʌlt] gizli, saklı, bilinmez, anlaşılmaz; doğaüstü, büyülü, esrarlı, sihirli; **oc.culˈta.tion** *n. ast.* karartma, gizleme; **oc.cult.ism** [ˈɔkəltizəm] *n.* gizli güçlere inanma; **ˈoc.cult.ist** *n.* gizli güçlere inanan kimse; **oc.cult.ness** [ɔˈkʌltnis] *n.* gizlilik.

**oc.cu.pan.cy** [ˈɔkjupənsi] *n.* işgal (of -i); **ˈoc.cu.pant** *n.* işgal eden kimse; **oc.cuˈpa.tion** *n.* meslek, iş, sanat, meşguliyet; X işgal; **oc.cuˈpa.tion.al** [~ʃən] *adj.* iş *(veya* meslek) ile ilgili, iş..., meslek...; işgal kuvvetleri; ~ therapy meşguliyetle tedavi, rehabilitasyon; **oc.cu.pi.er** [ˈɔkjupaiə] *s.* occupant; **oc.cu.py** [ˈ~pai] *v/t.* ...de oturmak, ...de yaşamak; X işgal etm., zaptetmek; meşgul etm., doldurmak *(süre)*; bulunmak *(görev)*; ~ o.s. *veya* be

occupied with *veya* in *ile* meşgul olm.

**oc.cur** [əˈkəː] *v/i.* olmak, meydana gelmek, yer bulmak; hatıra gelmek, akla gelmek; bulunmak; mevcut olm.; it ~red to me aklıma geldi; **oc.cur.rence** [əˈkʌrəns] *n.* olay, hadise, vaka; olma, meydana çıkma.

**o.cean** [ˈouʃən] *n.* okyanus, derya, deniz; ~ liner okyanus gemisi; ~s of time F dünya kadar vakit; ˈ~-go.ing *adj.* okyanus..., okyanuslarda işleyen...; **o.ce.an.ic** [ouʃiˈænik] *adj.* okyanusa ait, okyanus...; okyanusta bulunan...

**o.chre** *min.* [ˈoukə] *n.* toprak boya, aşı boyası; koyu sarı renk.

**o'clock** [əˈklɔk] *adv.* saate göre; five ~ saat beş.

**oc.ta.gon** [ˈɔktəgən] *n.* sekizgen; **oc.tag.o.nal** [ɔkˈtægənl] *adj.* sekiz kenarlı.

**oc.tane** ♫ [ˈɔktein] *n.* oktan; ~ rating *mot.* oktan sayısı.

**oc.tave** J [ˈɔktiv] *n.* oktav; sekiz notalık ara; bir sonenin sekiz mısraı; sekiz mısralı şiir; **oc.ta.vo** [ɔkˈteivou] *n.* yarım fasiküllük kâğıt tabakası *veya* kitap; **oc.tet(te)** [ɔkˈtet] *n.* J sekiz kişi tarafından söylenen *veya* çalınan müzik parçası.

**Oc.to.ber** [ɔkˈtoubə] *n.* ekim (ayı).

**oc.to.ge.nar.i.an** [ɔktəudʒiˈnɛəriən] **1.** *adj.* seksen yaşında, seksenlik, sekseninde; **2.** *n.* seksenlik kimse.

**oc.to.pus** *zo.* [ˈɔktəpəs] *n.* ahtapot; *fig.* yaygın ve yıkıcı örgüt.

**oc.to.roon** [ɔktəˈruːn] *n.* zenci karışımı beyaz kimse.

**oc.u.lar** ☐ [ˈɔkjulə] göze ait, göz...; gözle görülür; ~ demonstration, ~ proof kesin delil; **ˈoc.u.list** *n.* göz mütehassısı, göz doktoru.

**odd** ☐ [ɔd] tek, ikiye bölünmeyen *(sayı)*; tek *(ayakkabı, eldiven vs.)*; geriye kalan, küsur; düzensiz, seyrek, ara sıra olan; tuhaf, acayip, garip; 50 ~ 50 küsur; 14 pounds ~ 14 küsur pound; jobs *pl.* düzensiz işler, geçici işler; at ~ times boş vakitlerde, vakit buldukça; ~ man out garip adam, acayip herif; *s.* odds; **ˈodd.i.ty** *n.* tuhaflık, acayiplik, gariplik; F garip kimse; **ˈodd.ments** *n. pl.* ufak tefek şeyler, artık şeyler; † döküntüler, kırıntılar; **odds** [ɔdz] *n. pl. oft. sg.* eşitsizlik, fark, üstünlük; ihtimal *(veya* olabilirlik) oranı; ~s are against you ihtimaller aleyhinizdedir; the ~ are that ihtimali var ki, muhtemeldir ki; be at ~ aralarında açık olm.; ~ and ends *pl.* ufak tefek şeyler, eften püften şeyler; it makes no ~ zararı yok, farketmez; 'what's the ~? ne çıkar?, ne önemi var?

**ode** [əud] *n.* gazel; övgü, kaside.

**o.di.ous** ☐ ['əudjəs] tiksindirici, iğrenç, çirkin, nefret verici; **o.di.um** ['əudjəm] *n.* nefret, kin; yüz karası, ayıp; iğrençlik.

**o.dom.e.ter** *mot.* [ɔ'dɔmitə] *n.* kilometre sayacı, mesafe kaydedici, odometre.

**o.don.to.lo.gy** ❦ [ɔdɔn'tɔlədʒi] *n.* diş, diş gelişimi ve diş hastalıkları ile uğraşan ilim.

**o.dor.if.er.ous** ☐ [əudə'rifərəs] hoş kokulu, güzel koku yayan; **'o.dor.ous** ☐ (hoş) kokulu.

**o.do(u)r** ['əudə] *n.* koku; *fig.* şöhret, itibar; **'o.dor.less** *adj.* kokusuz.

**O.dys.sey** ['ɔdisi] *n.* Odise destanı; *fig.* maceralı uzun yolculuk.

**oe.col.o.gy** [i:'kɔlədʒi] *s.* ecology.

**oec.u.men.i.cal** *eccl.* ☐ [i:kju:'menikəl] kiliselerin birleşmesine ait; bütün Hıristiyanlarca kabul edilen.

**oe.de.ma** ❦ [i:'di:mə] *n.* ödem, vücutta su toplanması.

**o'er** [əuə] = over.

**oe.soph.a.gus** *anat.* [i:'sɔfəgəs] *n.* yemek borusu.

**of** [ɔv, əv, v] *prp. com.* -(n)in *(the works of Shakespeare: Shakespear'in eserleri);* -den *(proud / ashamed / afraid / glad/ tired of: -den gurur duyan / utanan/ korkan/ memnun olan/ bıkan);* -den yapılmış *(a table of wood: tahtadan yapılmış bir masa);* -li *(a man ~ honour: şerefli bir adam);* ~ o.s. kendiliğinden, kendi teşebbüsüyle; kendi hakkında; this world ~ ours bizim bu dünyamız; ~ an evening F akşamları.

**off** [ɔːf, ɔf] **1.** *adv.* uzakta, ileride, ötede; uzağa, ileriye, öteye *(3 miles ~: 3 mil ötede);* bitmiş, bozulmuş *(their engagement is ~: nişanları bozuldu);* kesik *(the water/electricity is ~: su/elektrik kesik);* görev dışında, izinli *(the manager gave the staff a day ~: müdür personele bir günlük izin verdi);* kopuk; ~ and on arasıra, bazen; be ~ ayrılmak, terketmek, gitmek; be ~ with s.o. *b-den* ayrı kalmak; right ~, straight ~ derhal, hemen; well etc. ~ hali vakti yerinde, zengin *vs.*; **2.** *prp.* -den, -dan *(fall ~ a ladder/ a tree/ a horse: merdivenden/ ağaçtan/ attan düşmek);* -den uzak *(a house ~ the main road: ana yoldan uzak bir ev);* ↓ açıklarında *(a ship anchored ~ the harbour entrance: liman girişi açıklarında demirlemiş gemi);* bırakmış

*(she's ~ smoking: sigarayı bıraktı);* a street ~ the Strand Strand'den ayrılan sokak; be ~ duty izinli olm.; be ~ smoking sigarayı bırakmak; ~ the point konudan uzak, konu dışı; be ~ one's feed *sl.* hiç iştahı olmamak;; ~ one's head *sl.* kafayı üşütmüş; **3.** *adj.* sağdaki *(the ~ front wheel: sağ ön tekerlek);* uzak; ↓ denize doğru açılan; bitmiş, ertenlemiş; çalışmayan, işlemeyen; yanlış, hatalı; normalden aşağı, âdi; izinli, görev dışında; cansız, hareketsiz, ölü *(mevsim, sezon);* solmuş, soluk; bitmiş, tükenmiş; ~ chance zayıf bir ihtimal; ~ shade ❀ rengi kaçmış, solmuş; **4.** *int.* defol!, çek arabanı!, yaylan!

**of.fal** ['ɔfəl] *n.* çerçöp, süprüntü; ~s *pl.* hayvanın yenemeyen iç kısımları; sakatat.

**off-beat** F ['ɔf'biːt] *adj.* olağandışı, alışılmamış, tuhaf.

**of.fence** [ə'fens] *n.* suç, kabahat, kusur; hakaret, incitme, gücendirme; hücum, tecavüz, saldırı; no ~! gücenmeyin!, darılmayın!; give ~ gücendirmek, darıltmak; take ~ gücenmek, darılmak *(at -e).*

**of.fend** [ə'fend] *v/t.* gücendirmek, darıltmak, hatırını kırmak; ihlâl etm., bozmak; kızdırmak; *v/i.* suç işlemek, kabahat işlemek *(against -e karşı);* **of'fend.er** *n.* suçlu; first ~ ilk kez suç işlemis kimse.

**of.fense** [ə'fens] = offence.

**of.fen.sive** [ə'fensiv] **1.** ☐ çirkin, iğrenç; yakışmaz; kötü...; saldırı..., hücum...; **2.** *n.* taarruz, saldırı, hücum.

**of.fer** ['ɔfə] **1.** *n.* teklif; sunu; ~ of marriage evlenme teklifi; on ~ satışa sunulmuş; **2.** *v/t.* teklif etm.; vermek *(fiyat);* takdim etm., arzetmek, sunmak; göstermek; *v/i.* meydana çıkmak, gözükmek, görünmek; **'of.fer.ing** *n.* teklif; sunu; kurban.

**of.fer.to.ry** *eccl.* ['ɔfətəri] *n.* kilisede ayin esnasında para toplama; para toplanırken çalınan müzik.

**off-hand** ['ɔːf'hænd] *adj.* düşünmeden yapılmış, rasgele yapılmış, hazırlıksız yapılmış; ters *(hareket, söz).*

**of.fice** ['ɔfis] *n.* büro, yazıhane, ofis; daire; bakanlık; hizmet, iş, memuriyet, vazife, görev; iktidar; ~s *pl.* yardım; booking ~, *thea.* box ~ bilet gişesi; Divine ♀ ibadet; dini ayin; '~-bear.er *n.* memur, görevli; '~-block *n.* iş hanı; '~-boy *n.* yazıhanede ayak işlerine bakan çocuk.

**of.fi.cer** ['ɔfisə] *n.* memur; polis memuru; ✕ subay; **'of.fi.cered:** ~ by -*in* kumandası altında.

**of.fi.cial** [ə'fiʃəl] **1.** □ resmî; memuriyete ait; memura yakışır; **☞** = officinal; **2.** *n.* memur; **of'fi.cial.dom** *n.* memur sınıfı, memurlar; **of.fi.cial.ese** [‿'li:z] *n.* resmî yazı üslubu; **of'fi.cial.ism** = officialdom.

**of.fi.ci.ate** [ə'fiʃieit] *v/i.* resmî bir görevi yerine getirmek.

**of.fic.i.nal** [ɔfi'sainl] *adj.* hazır *(ilâç)*; iyileştirici, tedavi edici.

**of.fi.cious** □ [ə'fiʃəs] her şeye karışan, el sokan, işgüzar, gereksiz yere yardım etmek isteyen.

**off.ing** ↓ ['ɔfiŋ] *n.* sahilden görülen açık deniz; in the ~ *fig.* olması yakın; **'off.ish** *adj.* F uzak duran, soğuk *(davranış)*.

**off...:** '~-li.cence *n.* içki satma ruhsatı; içki satılan dükkân; '~-print *n.* ayrı baskı; '~.scour.ings *pl.*, '~.scum *n.* çerçöp, süprüntü, pislik; '~.set **1.** *n.* △ düz çıkıntı; ⊕ dirsek; *typ.* ofset; *s.* offshoot: *s.* set-off; **2.** *v/t* dengelemek, denkleştirmek; ofset usulü basmak; '~.shoot *n.* dal *(a. fig.)*; '~-shore *adj.* kıyıdan uzak; kıyıdan esen *(rüzgâr)*; '~-'side *adj. spor:* ofsayt; '~.spring *n.* döl, evlât; ürün; '~--the-'rec.ord *adj.* kayda geçmeyecek, yayınlanmayacak, gizli; '~-time *n.* boş vakit.

**oft** *poet.* [ɔft] *adv.* çok kere, sık sık.

**of.ten** ['ɔfn] *adv.* çok defa, çoğu kez, sık sık; as ~ as her ne zaman, her; as ~ as not, more ~ than not ekseriya, çok sık; every so ~ arasıra, bazen; 'of.ten.times, 'oft-times *adv.* † sık sık.

**o.gee** △ ['əudʒiː] *n.* S şeklinde korniş *veya* köşebent, deve boynu.

**o.gi.val** [əu'dʒaivəl] *adj.* sivri kemer..., beyzî kemer...; 'o.give *n.* △ sivri tepeli kemer; grafikte bir eğri çeşidi.

**o.gle** ['əugl] *vb.* âşıkane bakmak, göz süzerek bakmak; âşıkane süzmek.

**o.gre** ['əugə] *n.* insan yiyen dev; **o.gress** ['əugris] *n.* insan yiyen dişi dev.

**oh** [əu] *int.* ya!, sahi!, öyle mi?

**ohm** ⚡ [əum] *n.* om, elektrik direnç birimi.

**o.ho** [əu'həu] *int.* ha!, çaktım!, anladım!, tamam!

**oil** [ɔil] **1.** *n.* yağ; petrol; zeytinyağı; yağlıboya (resim); F pohporhlama, yağ çekme; burn the midnight ~ geç vakte kadar çalışmak, gecesini gündüzüne katmak; smell of ~ gece geç vakte kadar çalıştığı belli olm.; pour ~ on the flame(s) kızıştırmak, yangına körükle gitmek; pour ~ on the (troubled) waters yatıştırmak; strike ~ petrol bulmak; *fig.* köşeyi dön-

mek; paint in ~s yağlıboya resim yapmak; **2.** *v/t.* yağlamak; *fig. b-ne* rüşvet vermek; yağ çekmek; ~ s.o.'s palm *b-ne* rüşvet vermek; '~-burn.er *n.* yağ brülörü, yağ memesi; '~-cake *n.* yağ küspesi; '~-can *n.* yağdanlık; '~.cloth *n.* muşamba; '~-col.o(u)r *n.* yağlıboya; 'oil.er = oil-can; oil tanker; 'oil-field *n.* petrol sahası; 'oil.i.ness *n.* yağlılık; *fig.'* kaypaklık, yağcılık, dalkavukluk; 'oil-man *n.* yağ *veya* yağlı boya üreticisi *veya* satıcısı; makine yağcısı; 'oil-paint.ing *n.* yağlıboya resim; 'oil-pa.per *n.* yağlı kâğıt; 'oil-skin *n.* çok ince muşamba; ~s *pl.* bu muşambadan yapılmış elbiseler; 'oil-tank.er *n.* tanker; 'oil-well *n.* petrol kuyusu; 'oil.y □ yağlı *(a. fig.)*; *fig.* yağcı, dalkavuk.

**oint.ment** ['ɔintmənt] *n.* merhem.

**O.K., o.kay** ['əu'kei] **1.** *adj. & adv.* peki; doğru; geçer; iyi, makbul; **2.** *v/t.* onaylamak, tasdik etm.

**old** [əuld] *adj.* köhne, eskimiş, aşınmış; ihtiyar, yaşlı; sabık, önceki; tecrübeli, deneyimli, pişkin; F sevgili *(dost)*; *sl.* çok; harika, fevkalâde; the ~ yaşlılar, ihtiyarlar; young and ~ herkes; ~ age yaşlılık, ihtiyarlık; the ~ man koca; baba; gemi kaptanı; ~ man yaşlı adam; the ~ woman karı, eş; the ~ country göçmenin eski vatanı; an ~ boy eski öğrenci; a high ~ time *sl.* eski güzel günler; the ~ one, the ~ gentleman, ~ Harry *veya* Scratch şeytan; days of ~ geçmiş günler, mazi; '~-age *adj.* yaşlılık...; '~--'clothes.man *n.* eskici; 'old.en *adj.* † *veya poet.* eski; in the ~ days eskiden, eski günlerde.

**old...:** '~-'fash.ioned **1.** *adj.* modası geçmiş, demode; eski kafalı; sitemkâr *(bakış)*; **2.** *n. Am.* viski ile yapılan bir çeşit kokteyl; '~-'fo.g(e)y.ish *adj.* eski kafalı; ♬ Glo.ry A.B.D.'nin bayrağı; 'old.ish *adj.* oldukça yaşlı *veya* eski; 'old-'maid.ish *adj.* titiz, düzenli, tertipli; old.ster ['~stə] *n.* yaşlı adam; 'old-time *adj.* eski; yaşlı; 'old-'tim.er *n.* kıdemli kimse; *esp. Am.* yaşlı adam; 'old-'wom.an.ish *adj.* titiz, müşkülpesent, kılı kırk yaran; 'old-world *adj.* eski, modası geçmiş.

**o.le.ag.i.nous** [əuli'ædʒinəs] *adj.* yağlı; yağ çıkaran; şişman; yağlı...

**o.le.an.der** ♣ [əuli'ændə] *n.* zakkum, ağı ağacı, gül defnesi.

**ol.fac.to.ry** *anat.* [ɔl'fæktəri] *adj.* koklamaya ait, koklama..., koku ...

**ol.i.garch.y** ['ɔligɑːki] *n.* oligarşi.

**ol.ive** ['ɔliv] *n.* ♣ zeytin; ♣ zeytin ağacı;

zeytin dalı *veya* çelengi; **¹.~-branch** *n.* barış sembolü olan zeytin dalı; **¹.~-tree** *n.* zeytin ağacı.

**O.lym.pi.ad** [əu'limpiæd] *n.* olimpiyat; **O¹lym.pi.an** [~piən] *adj.* tanrısal; harika, şahane; **O¹lym.pic games** *pl.* olimpiyat oyunları.

**om.e.let, om.e.lette** [¹ɔmlit] *n.* omlet, kaygana.

**o.men** [¹əumen] *n.* kehanet.

**om.i.nous** ☐ [¹ɔminəs] uğursuz; korkutucu; ~ of disaster uğursuz felâket.

**o.mis.si.ble** [əu'misibl] *adj.* atlanabilir, yapılmayabilir; **o.mis.sion** [ə'miʃən] *n.* atlama, bırakma, yapmama; ihmal; sin of ~ ihmal suçu.

**o.mit** [ə¹mit] *v/t.* bırakmak, atlamak, ihmal etm. *(a.* to *inf. -meği).*

**om.ni.bus** [¹ɔmnibəs] **1.** *n.* † otobüs; antoloji; **2.** *adj.* çok maddeli...; çok maksatlı...; ~ volume içinde birçok konu olan cilt.

**om.nip.o.tence** [ɔm'nipətəns] *n.* herşeye gücü yetme; sonsuz güç; **om¹nip.o.tent** ☐ her şeye kadir.

**om.ni.pres.ence** [¹ɔmni¹prezəns] *n.* her yerde bulunma; **¹om.ni¹pres.ent** ☐ her yerde ve her zaman hazır, her yerde hazır ve nazır.

**om.nis.cience** [ɔm¹nisiəns] *n.* her şeyi bilme; sonsuz bilgi; **om¹nis.cient** ☐ her şeyi bilen, âlim.

**om.niv.o.rous** [ɔm¹nivərəs] *adj.* her şeyi yiyen; *fig.* her çeşit kitabı okuyan.

**on** [ɔn] **1.** *prp. mst* üzerinde, üstünde *(~ the wall: duvarın üzerinde)*; esnasında, zarfında, sürecinde; hakkında, konusunda, hususunda *(talk ~ a subject: bir konu hakkında konuşmak)*; *-e* doğru *(march ~ London: Londra'ya doğru yürümek)*; *-e* yakın; kenarında *(a house ~ the main road: ana yolun kenarında bir ev)*; halinde; get ~ a train *part. Am.* trene binmek; turn one's back ~ *s.o. b-ne* sırt çevirmek; ~ these conditions bu şartlarda; ~ this model bu modele göre; ~ hearing it onu duyması üzerine; **2.** *adv.* üzerinde, üstünde; ileriye, ileride; aralıksız, durmadan; olmakta; ~ and ~ durmaksızın, ara vermeden, biteviye; ~ to... ...(y)e; from that day ~ o günden itibaren; be ~ olmak, vuku bulmak; *thea.* oynamak; what is ~ tonight? bu gece ne oynuyor?; be a bit ~ *sl.* çakırkeyf olm., kafayı bulmak; **3.** *int.* haydi!

**once** [wʌns] **1.** *adv.* bir defa, bir kez, kere; bir zamanlar, eskiden; hemen, derhal; at ~ derhal, hemen; aynı anda; all

at ~ aniden, birden(bire); ~ again bir kez daha; ~ for all (ilk ve) son olarak; for ~ bu seferlik, bir kerelik; ~ in a while arasıra, bazen; this ~ bu sefer; ~ more tekrar, bir kez daha; ~ upon a time there was... evvel zaman içinde bir ... varmış; **2.** *cj. a.* ~ that ...ir ...irmez.

**once-o.ver** *Am.* F [¹wʌnsəuvə]'*n.* hemen bakma, inceleme, tetkik.

**on-com.ing** [¹ɔnkʌmiŋ] **1.** *adj.* yaklaşmakta olan, yaklaşan, ilerleyen; **2.** *n.* yaklaşma.

**one** [wʌn] **1.** *adj. & pron.* bir, tek; biri(si); herhangi biri(si); his ~ care onun tek endişesi, üzüntüsü; ~ day bir gün, günün birinde; ~ of these days bu günlerde; ~ Mr. Miller Mr. Miller isminde bir zat; *s.* any, every, no; take ~'s walk yürüyerek gezmek; a large dog and a little ~ büyük bir köpek ve bir de küçük bir tane; for ~ thing sebeplerden biri, çünkü; ~ and the same tıpkısı, aynı; **2.** *n.* tane; biri(si); adam, kimse, kişi; bir rakamı; the little ~s *pl.* küçük çocuklar; ~ another birbir(ler)ini, birbir(ler)ine; at ~ beraber, birleşmiş, uyuşmuş; ~ by ~, ~ after another birer birer, birbiri ardına; it is all ~ (to me) (benim için) hava hoş, farketmez; I for ~ bana kalırsa, bence; ~ with another ortalama olarak; **¹.~-armed** *adj.* tek kollu; ~ bandit para ile çalışan oyun makinesi; **¹.~-¹eyed** *adj.* tek gözlü; *fig.* kısıtlı, az; **¹.~-¹horse** *adj.* tek atlı; *fig. sl.* ikinci derecede, adi; ~ town küçük ve can sıkıcı kasaba; **¹.~-¹ldea'd** *adj.* sabit fikirli; **¹one.ness** *n.* birlik, bir olma.

**on.er.ous** ☐ [¹ɔnərəs] ağır, zor, külfetli, sıkıntılı.

**one...:** ~¹self *pron.* kendisi, bizzat, kendi kendine; by ~ kendi kendine; **¹.~-¹sid.ed** ☐ tek taraflı; **¹.~-time** *adj.* sabık, eski; have a ~ mind tek bir şey düşünmek, ak- **¹.~-¹track** *adj.* tek yollu; ısrarcı, şaşmaz; lında tek bir şey olm.; **¹.~-way:** ~ street tek yönlü sokak; ~ ticket gidiş bileti.

**on.fall** [¹ɔnfɔ:l] *n.* hücum, taarruz.

**on.go.ings** [¹ɔngəuiŋz] *n. pl.* olay, hadise, vaka.

**on.ion** [¹ʌnjən] *n.* soğan; off one's ~ *sl.* kafayı üşütmüş.

**on.look.er** [¹ɔnlukə] *n.* seyirci.

**on.ly** [¹əunli] **1.** *adj.* (bir) tek, biricik, eşsiz; yegâne; **2.** *adv.* yalnız, ancak, sadece, yalnızca, başlı başına; ~ yesterday sadece dün; ~ just ancak, henüz; hemen hemen hiç; ~ think! düşün bir kere!; **3.** *cj.* ~ (that) ne var ki, ...mezse.

**on.o.mat.o.poe.ia** [ɔnəumætəuˈpiːə] *n.* doğal sesleri yansılayan kelimeleri kullanma.

**on.rush** [ˈɔnrʌʃ] *n.* üşüşme, saldırma.

**on.set** [ˈɔnset], **on.slaught** [ˈɔnslɔːt] *n.* başlama, başlangıç; *part. fig.* şiddetli saldırı, hücum.

**on.to** [ˈɔntu, ˈɔntə] *prep. -in* üstün(d)e.

**on.tol.o.gy** *phls.* [ɔnˈtɔlədʒi] *n.* ontoloji.

**o.nus** *fig.* [ˈɔunəs] *n.* yük, görev, sorumluluk, külfet.

**on.ward** [ˈɔnwəd] **1.** *adj.* ileriye doğru giden, ilerleyen; **2.** *a.* ~s *adv.* ileri, ileriye doğru, ileride.

**on.yx** *min.* [ˈɔniks] *n.* damarlı akik.

**oo.dles** *sl.* [ˈuːdlz] *n. pl.* büyük miktar (of).

**oof** *sl.* [uːf] *n.* mangır, mangiz.

**oomph** *sl.* [uːmf] *n.* azim, şevk, gayret; cinsî cazibe.

**ooze** [uːz] **1.** *n.* çamur, balçık; ⊕ sızıntı; **2.** *v/t. & v/i.* sız(dır)mak; dışarı sızmak, duyulmak *(sır, haber);* dışarı vermek, çıkarmak; ~ *away* azalmak, eksilmek.

**oo.zy** ☐ [ˈuːzi] sızıntılı; sızdıran; sulu çamur gibi.

**o.pac.i.ty** [əuˈpæsiti] *n.* donukluk, şeffaf olmama; *fig.* ahmaklık, mankafalık.

**o.pal** *min.* [ˈɔupəl] *n.* opal, panzehirtaşı;

**o.pal.es.cent** [~ˈlesnt] *adj.* yanardöner, şanjan.

**o.paque** ☐ [əuˈpeik] donuk, şeffaf olmayan, ışık geçirmez, kesif; *fig.* ahmak, mankafa.

**ope** *poet.* [əup] = open.

**o.pen** [ˈɔupən] **1.** ☐ *com.* açık, içine girilir, serbest; üstü açık; açık *(hava);* açmış *(çiçek);* aşikâr, meydanda, gizli olmayan; herkese açık, umumi; karar verilmemiş, halledilmemiş *(mesele);* korumasız, sipersiz; ödenmemiş *(borç);* kapanmamış *(hesap);* açık fikirli (to -e); with ~ *arms* samimiyetle; with ~ *hands* cömertçe; the ~ *door* serbest ticaret; keep ~ *house* evinin kapısı herkese açık olm.; *lay o.s.* ~ *to -e* maruz kalmak; ~ *letter* açık mektup; ~ *season hunt.* serbest sezon; **2.** *n.* in the ~ (air) açık havada; açıkta; *come out into the* ~ *fig.* açığa çıkmak; **3.** *v/t. & v/i.* aç(ıl)mak; umuma açmak; başla(t)mak -*e;* kesip açmak, yar(ıl)mak, deşmek; gevşe(t)mek; çöz(ül)mek; yay(ıl)mak, ser(il)mek; göz önüne çıkarmak; çatla(t)mak; göstermek, bildirmek; ~ *into* içeri doğru açılmak; ~ *on to -e* açılmak; ~ *out* yaymak; sermek; açılmak; ~ *up* açmak; başlamak; geliştirmek; **~-'air** *adj.* açık hava...; **~-armed** *adj.* candan, içten, sami-

mi; **o.pen.er** [ˈɔupnə] *n.* açacak; **o.pen-~eyed** *adj.* açıkgöz, dikkatli; şaşkın, afallamış; **o.pen-~hand.ed** *adj.* eli açık, cömert; **o.pen-~heart.ed** *adj.* açık kalpli, samimi; **o.pen.ing** [ˈɔupniŋ] **1.** *n.* açıklık, delik; başlangıç; açılış, açılma; fırsat; münhal görev; **2.** *adj.* ilk..., birinci...; **o.pen-~mind.ed** *adj. fig.* açık fikirli; **o.pen-~mouthed** *adj.* ağzı açık kalmış *(hayretten);* açgözlü, obur; **o.pen.ness** [ˈɔupnnis] *n.* açıklık.

lü, obur; **o.pen.ness** [ˈɔupnnis] *n.* açıklık.

**open...:** ~ *or.der* ✕ dağınık savaş düzeni; ~ *shop* sendikalı *veya* sendikasız herkesi çalıştıran kuruluş; ~ *vow.el* açık sesli harf; ~ *work* kafes halinde işlemeli süs.

**op.er.a** [ˈɔpərə] *n.* opera; opera müziği; opera binası; **'~-cloak** *n.* bayanların tuvaletle birlikte giydikleri pelerin; **'~-glass(es** *pl.)* *n.* opera dürbünü; **'~-hat** *n.* katlanabilen silindir erkek şapkası; **'~-house** *n.* opera binası.

**op.er.ate** [ˈɔpəreit] *v/t. & v/i.* işle(t)mek, çalış(tır)mak, kullanmak; iş görmek; etkilemek, çalıştırmak; be *operating* işler olm.; **op.er.at.ic** [~ˈrætik] *adj.* operaya ait, opera...; ~ *singer* opera şarkıcısı; **op.er.at.ing** [ˈɔpəreitiŋ] *adj.* ameliyat...; ~ *expenses pl.* işletme masrafları; ~ *instructions pl.* işletme talimatı; ~ *theatre* ameliyat odası; **op.er'a.tion** *n.* işle(t)me, çalışma (tarzı); iş, fiil; etki, hüküm; ↑ borsada alışveriş; ✗ ameliyat; ✕ harekât; be in ~ yürürlükte olm.; *come into* ~ yürürlüğe girmek; **op.er'a.tion.al** [~ʃənl] *adj.* işletme...; kullanıma hazır...; **op.er.a.tive** [ˈɔpərətiv] **1.** ☐ işleyen, faal, çalışan; etkin, etkili; geçerli, yürürlükte olan; ✗ ameliyata ait, ameliyat edilebilir; **2.** *n.* usta işçi, teknisyen; **op.er.a.tor** [~ˈreitə] *n.* ✗ cerrah, operatör; *film:* gösterici; santral memuru; ⊕ operatör, teknisyen; ↑ spekülatör.

**op.er.et.ta** [ɔpəˈretə] *n.* operet.

**oph.thal.mi.a** ✗ [ɔfˈθælmiə] *n.* göz iltihabı; **oph'thal.mic** *adj.* göze ait, göz...; ~ *hospital* göz hastalıkları hastanesi.

**o.pi.ate** *pharm.* [ˈɔupiit] **1.** *n.* afyonlu ilâç; **2.** *adj.* afyonlu...; uyuşturucu..., sersemletici...

**o.pine** [əuˈpain] *v/t.* yürütmek *(fikir);* zannetmek, düşünmek, farzetmek; **o.pin.ion** [əˈpinjən] *n.* fikir, düşünce; zan, tahmin, kanı, görüş; the (public) ~ kamuoyu; *I am of the* ~ *that* ...fikrindeyim, görüşündeyim; in my ~ bence, kanımca.

fikrimce, kanaatimce; **o¹pin.ion.at.ed** [~eitid] *adj.* inatçı, fikrinden dönmeyen, dik kafalı.

**o.pi.um** *pharm.* [¹əupjəm] *n.* afyon.

**o.pos.sum** *zo.* [ə¹pɔsəm] *n.* opossum, keselisıçangillerden Amerika'ya mahsus memeli bir hayvan.

**op.po.nent** [ə¹pəunənt] **1.** *n.* hasım, düşman, rakip, muhalif; **2.** *adj.* karşı(ki); karşıt, zıt.

**op.por.tune** ☐ [¹ɔpətjuːn] elverişli, uygun, münasip; tam vaktinde yapılan; **¹op.por.tun.ism** *n.* fırsatçılık; **¹op.por.tun.ist** *n.* fırsatçı kimse; **op.por¹tu.ni.ty** *n.* fırsat, uygun zaman, elverişli durum.

**op.pose** [ə¹pəuz] *v/t.* direnmek, engel olm., mâni olm., karşı koymak, karşı çıkmak -*e*; karşıla(ştır)mak -*i*; **op¹posed** *adj.* karşı; karşısında; zıt, aksi; be ~ to -*e* karşı olm.; **op.po.site** [¹ɔpəzit] **1.** ☐ karşı ([to] s.th. bşe); karşıdaki, karşıki; zıt, aksi, karşıt, ters; ~ number karşı taraftaki meslektaş, iş arkadaşı; **2.** *prp.* & *adv.* karşı karşıya; karşılıklı; karşıda; karşıya; **3.** *n.* zıt kelime *veya* şey; **op¹po¹si.tion** *n.* zıtlık, karşıtlık; muhalefet (to -*e*); mücadele; karşı durma, karşı koyma; † rekabet; *parl.* muhalif parti; *ast.* birbirinden 180° uzaklıktaki iki gökcisminin durumu.

**op.press** [ə¹pres] *v/t.* sık(ıştır)mak, baskı yapmak; zulmetmek -*e*, canını yakmak; canını sıkmak, üzerine yüklenmek; **op.pres.sion** [ə¹preʃən] *n.* baskı, zulüm, cefa; zulmetme; sıkıntı, güçlük; **op¹pres.sive** ☐ [~siv] ezici, zulmedici; sıkıcı, bunaltıcı; **op¹pres.sive.ness** *n.* gaddarlık; sıkıcılık; **op¹pres.sor** *n.* zalim (*veya* acımasız) kimse.

**op.pro.bri.ous** ☐ [ə¹prəubriəs] hakaret dolu, aşağılayıcı; utandırıcı; yüz kızartıcı; **op¹pro.bri.um** [~briəm] *n.* hakaret, aşağılama; rezalet, ayıp.

**op.pugn** [ɔ¹pjuːn] *v/t.* karşı koymak -*e*, karşı olm. -*e*.

**opt** [ɔpt] *vb.* seçmek; karar vermek (for -*e*); **op.ta.tive** *gr.* [¹ɔptətiv] *n.* istek kipi, dilek kipi.

**op.tic** [¹ɔptik] *adj.* görme duyusuna ait, göz...; = **¹op.ti.cal** ☐ optikle ilgili; **op¹ti.cian** [~ʃən] *n.* gözlükçü; **¹op.tics** *n. sg.* optik.

**op.ti.mism** [¹ɔptimizəm] *n.* iyimserlik; **¹op.ti.mist** *n.* iyimser kimse; **op.ti¹mis.tic** *adj.* (~ally) iyimser.

**op.ti.mum** [¹ɔptiməm] **1.** *n.* en uygun durum, en elverişli ortam; **2.** *adj.* en uygun..., en elverişli..., en ideal...

**op.tion** [¹ɔpʃən] *n.* seçme (hakkı), tercih (hakkı); seçme yetkisi; seçilen şey, şık, seçenek; † satma *veya* satın alma hakkı; **op.tion.al** ☐ [¹ɔpʃənl] isteğe bağlı, zorunlu olmayan, ihtiyarî, seçmeli.

**op.u.lence** [¹ɔpjuləns] *n.* servet, zenginlik; bolluk, bereket; **¹op.u.lent** ☐ zengin; bol, bereketli.

**o.pus** [¹əupəs] *n.* müzik parçası, opus; magnum ~ edebiyat *veya* sanatta şaheser.

**or** [ɔː] *cj.* veya, yahut; yoksa; ya; either ... ~ ya ... ya da...; ~ else yoksa, aksi takdirde; two ~ three iki veya üç; ~ so aşağı yukarı, tahminen, takriben.

**or.a.cle** [¹ɔrəkl] *n.* kehanet; eski Yunanistan'da gaipten haber veren kâhin; kehanette bulunulan kutsal yer; vahiy, ilham; work the ~ F başarı için kulis yapmak, torpil işletmek; **o.rac.u.lar** [ɔ¹rækjulə] *adj.* kehanetle ilgili, kehanet...; *fig.* gizli anlamlı.

**o.ral** ☐ [¹ɔːrəl] sözlü, ağızdan söylenen; ağızdan alınan...; ağız...

**o.rang** [¹ɔːrəŋ] = orang-outang.

**or.ange** [¹ɔrindʒ] **1.** *n.* portakal; portakal rengi, turuncu; **2.** *adj.* portakal rengindeki; **or.ange.ade** [¹~¹eid] *n.* portakal şurubu; **or.ange.ry** [¹~əri] *n.* iklimi soğuk olan yerlerde portakal yetiştirilen kapalı yer, limonluk.

**o.rang-ou.tang** *zo.* [ɔːrəŋ ¹uːtæŋ] *n.* orangutan.

**o.ra.tion** [ɔː¹reiʃən] *n.* nutuk, söylev, hitabe; **or.a.tor** [¹ɔrətə] *n.* hatip, söyleyici, güzel konuşan kimse; **or.a.tor.i.cal** ☐ [~¹tɔrikəl] hatipliğe ait, hatiplik...; hatibe yakışır; **or.a.to.ri.o** ♪ [~¹tɔːriəu] *n.* oratoryo; **or.a.to.ry** [¹~təri] *n.* hatiplik, hitabet, güzel konuşma sanatı; *eccl.* küçük mabet, özel tapınak.

**orb** [ɔːb] *n.* küre; daire; göz; gökcismi; *poet.* göz; **or.bic.u.lar** ☐ [ɔː¹bikjulə] küre şeklinde, küresel, yuvarlak, dairemsi; **or.bit** [¹ɔːbit] **1.** *n.* yörünge; çember; göz çukuru; **2.** *v/t.* & *v/i.* -*in* etrafında dön(dür)mek; yörüngeye sokmak; bir yörüngede dönmek.

**or.chard** [¹ɔːtʃəd] *n.* meyve bahçesi.

**or.ches.tra** ♪ [¹ɔːkistrə] *n.* orkestra; ~ pit *thea.* orkestranın bulunduğu yer, parter; **or.ches.tral** [ɔː¹kestrəl] *adj.* orkestraya ait, orkestra...; **or.ches.trate** ♪ [¹ɔːkistreit] *v/t.* orkestra için bestelemek.

**or.chid** ♀ [¹ɔːkid] *n.* orkide, salep; **or.chis** ♀ [¹ɔːkis] *n.* salepotu.

**or.dain** [ɔː¹dein] *v/t.* papazlığa atamak, papaz yapmak; mukadder kılmak, (ka-

derini) tayin etm.
or.deal [ɔːˈdiːl] *n.* işkence yaparak yargılama usulü; *fig.* büyük sıkıntı.
or.der [ˈɔːdə] 1. *n.* düzen, nizam, intizam; sıra, dizi; usül, yol, kural; emir; † sipariş, ısmarlama; havale; niyet, amaç, gaye; tabaka, sınıf; tarikat, mezhep; şeref rütbesi; mimari tarz; çeşit, cins, tür; by ~ emre göre, emir gereğince; ~ of the day gündem; X günlük emir; take (holy) ~s papaz olm.; put in ~ düzene koymak; in ~ to... -*mek* için; in ~ that ...diye; on the ~s of -*in* emrinde; on ~ † ısmarlama, sipariş üzerine; make to ~ sipariş üzerine yapmak, ısmarlama yapmak; standing ~s *pl. parl.* geçerliği süren emirler; 2. *v/t.* emretmek, buyurmak; † ısmarlamak, sipariş etm.; düzenlemek, intizama sokmak; ~ arms! tüfek çıkar!; ~ about emir yağdırmak; ~ down (up) getirmesini emretmek; ˈ~book *n.* † sipariş defteri; ˈor.dered *adj.* muntazam, tertipli, derli toplu; ˈor.der.li.ness *n.* intizam, düzenlilik, derli topluluk; ˈor.der.ly 1. *adj.* düzgün, düzenli, intizamlı, derli toplu; itaatkâr, uysal, uslu; X emre ait, emir...; ~ officer nöbetçi subayı; ~ room yazıhane, büro; 2. *n.* X emir eri; hastane hademesi.
or.di.nal [ˈɔːdinl] 1. *adj.* sıra *veya* derece gösteren...; 2. *n. a.* ~ number sıra sayısı.
or.di.nance [ˈɔːdinəns] *n.* emir; düzen, kural; kanun; alın yazısı, yazgı.
or.di.nar.y [ˈɔːdənri] 1. □ adi, bayağı, alışılmış, alelade; ~ debts *pl.* † adi borçlar; ~ seaman acemi denizci, gemici; *s.* share; 2. *n.* alışılmış şey; in ~ devamlı olarak, sürekli.
or.di.nate ≙ [ˈɔːdnit] *n.* ordinat.
or.di.na.tion [ɔːdiˈneiʃən] *n.* papaz atama töreni; papazlığa atama.
ord.nance X, ⤓ [ˈɔːdnəns] *n.* savaş gereçleri; ~ map kurmay haritası; ~ survey bir ülkenin resmî haritası; ~-survey map (1:25000) ölçekli harita.
or.dure [ˈɔːdjuə] *n.* pislik, gübre, dışkı.
ore [ɔː] *n.* maden cevheri; *poet.* maden, metal.
or.gan [ˈɔːgən] *n.* ♪ org, erganun; organ, örgen, uzuv; araç, vasıta, alet; haber organı.
or.gan.die, or.gan.dy [ˈɔːgəndi] *n.* ince ve yarı şeffaf muslin; organze.
or.gan-grind.er [ˈɔːgəngraində] *n.* latarna çalan kimse; or.gan.ic [ɔːˈgænik] *adj.* (~ally) organik, örgensel; yaşayan, canlı; yapısal; or.gan.ism [ˈɔːgənizəm] *n.* or-

ganizma, örgenlik; oluşum; ˈor.gan.ist *n.* org çalan kimse; or.gan.i.za.tion [~nai-ˈzeiʃən] *n.* teşkilât, örgüt, kurum, teşekkül, dernek; düzen(leme); organizma, yapı; ˈor.gan.ize *v/t.* düzenlemek, örgütlemek, kurmak, tertip etm., teşkil etm., teşkilâtlandırmak; ˈor.gan.iz.er *n.* düzenleyici, organizatör.
or.gy [ˈɔːdʒi] *n.* çılgınca eğlenme; içki âlemi; aşırı miktar.
o.ri.el ⌂ [ˈɔːriəl] *n.* cumba, çıkma.
o.ri.ent 1. [ˈɔːriənt] *adj.* doğuya özgü, doğu...; yükselen, doğan (*güneş*); 2. [~] *n.* doğu, şark; doğu memleketleri; 3. [ˈ~ent] *v/t.* doğuya yöneltmek; o.ri.en.tal [~ˈentl] 1. □ doğu ile ilgili, doğuya özgü, doğusal; 2. *n.* doğulu kimse; o.ri.en.tate [ˈɔːrienteit] *v/t.* doğuya yöneltmek; alıştırmak; o.ri.en.ta.tion *n.* yönel(t)me; çevreye uy(dur)ma, alış(tır)ma.
or.i.fice [ˈɔrifis] *n.* delik, ağız.
or.i.gin [ˈɔridʒin] *n.* asıl, köken, kaynak, başlangıç; nesil, soy, doğuş.
o.rig.i.nal [əˈridʒənl] 1. □ aslî, esasa ait, ilk, birinci; yeni, orijinal, yeni icat olunmuş; yaratıcı (*kimşe, zekâ*); † menşe...; *s.* share; ~ capital ilk sermaye, kuruluş sermayesi; ~ sin yaradılıştan olan günah; 2. *n.* asıl nüsha; asıl kaynak, köken, menşe; garip kimse; o.rig.i.nal.i.ty [~ˈnæliti] *n.* yaratıcılık; orijinallik, özgünlük; o.rig.i.nal.ly [əˈridʒnəli] *adv.* aslen, esasında, aslında; orijinal bir biçimde.
o.rig.i.nate [əˈridʒineit] *v/t.* meydana getirmek, sebep olm., çıkarmak, yaratmak, türetmek, icat etm.; *v/i.* meydana gelmek, çıkmak (from, in s.th. *bşden*; with, from s.o. *b-den*); o.rig.i.na.tion *n.* icat etme, icat edilme, meydana gelme; o-ˈrig.i.na.tive □ [~tiv] yaratıcı; oˈrig.i.na-tor *n.* yaratıcı kimse.
o.ri.ole *orn.* [ˈɔːriəul] *n.* sarı asma kuşu, sarıcık.
o.ri.son [ˈɔrizən] *n.* dua, yakarış.
or.mo.lu [ˈɔːməuluː] *n.* yaldızlı bronz, altın taklidi pirinç.
or.na.ment 1. [ˈɔːnəmənt] *n.* süs, ziynet; süsle(n)me; *fig.* şan, şeref; 2. [ˈ~ment] *v/t.* süslemek, donatmak; ˈor.naˈmen.tal □ süs kabilinden; or.na.men.ta.tion *n.* süs, ziynet; süsle(n)me.
or.nate □ [ɔːˈneit] çok süslü, şatafatlı, gösterişli; dili süslü (*yazı*).
or.ni.tho.log.i.cal □ [ɔːniθəˈlɔdʒikl] kuşlar bilgisine ait, ornitolojik; or.ni.thol.o.gist [~ˈθɔlədʒist] *n.* kuş uzmanı, ornitolog; or.niˈthol.o.gy *n.* zoolojinin kuşlarla ilgili

bölümü, ornitoloji.

**o.ro.tund** [ˈɔːrəutʌnd] *adj.* heybetli, muhteşem; dolgun sesli; süslü, tumturaklı.

**or.phan** [ˈɔːfən] 1. *n.* öksüz, yetim, kimsesiz *b-i*; 2. *adj. a.* '.-ed öksüz, yetim, kimsesiz; **ˈor.phan.age** *n.* öksüzler yurdu, yetimhane.

**or.rer.y** [ˈɔrəri] *n.* planetaryum, güneş ve gezegenlerin hareketlerini gösteren aygıt.

**or.tho.dox** ☐ [ˈɔːθədɔks] ortodoks; dinsel inançlarına sadık; geleneksel, göreneksel; **ˈor.tho.dox.y** *n.* ortodoksluk; inanç sağlamlığı.

**or.tho.graph.ic**, **or.tho.graph.i.cal** ☐ [ɔːθəuˈgræfik(əl)] imlâya ait, imlâ...; **or.thog.ra.phy** [ɔːˈθɔgrəfi] *n.* imlâ·(usulü).

**or.tho.pae.dic** [ɔːθəuˈpiːdik] *adj.* (.-ally) ortopedik; **or.thoˈpae.dist** *n.* ortopedi uzmanı, ortopedist; **ˈor.tho.pae.dy** *n.* ortopedi.

**or.to.lan** *orn.* [ˈɔːtələn] *n.* kirazkuşu.

**Os.car** [ˈɔskə] *n.* Oskar ödülü *(Amerikan sinemasında).*

**os.cil.late** [ˈɔsileit] *v/i.* sallanmak, sarsılmak; *fig.* tereddüt etm.; **os.cilˈla.tion** *n.* sallanma, salınma, titreşim; **os.cil.la.to.ry** [ˈ.-lətəri] *adj.* sallanan, salınan; **os.cil.lo.graph** [ɔˈsiləugraːf] *n.* osilograf, elektrik akımlarındaki titreşimi kaydeden alet.

**os.cu.late** *co.* [ˈɔskjuleit] *v/t.* öpmek.

**o.sier** ❧ [ˈəuʒə] *n.* sepetçi söğüdü.

**os.mo.sis** *phys.* [ɔzˈməusis] *n.* geçişme, osmos.

**os.prey** [ˈɔspri] *n.* balık kartalı, deniz tavşancılı; † şapka tüyü.

**os.se.ous** [ˈɔsiəs] *adj.* kemikli...; kemik gibi; iskeleti olan; **os.si.fi.ca.tion** [ɔsifiˈkeifən] *n.* kemikleşme; **os.si.fy** [ˈ.-fail] *v/t. & v/i.* kemikleş(tir)mek; kemik gibi sertleş(tir)mek; katılaş(tır)mak; **os.su.ar.y** [ˈɔsjuəri] *n.* kemikhane, kemik saklanan yer.

**os.ten.si.ble** ☐ [ɔsˈtensəbl] görünüşteki, görünen.

**os.ten.ta.tion** [ɔstenˈteifən] *n.* gösteriş, fiyaka, caka; **os.tenˈta.tious** ☐ gösterişli, fiyakalı, afili, cakalı.

**os.te.ol.o.gy** *anat.* [ɔstiˈɔlədʒi] *n.* osteoloji, kemikbilimi; **os.te.o.path** [ˈɔstiəpæθ] *n.* kemikleri ve kasları düzeltme yoluyla tedavi yapan uzman.

**ost.ler** [ˈɔslə] *n.* seyis.

**os.tra.cism** [ˈɔstrəsizəm] *n.* toplum dışında bırakma, ilişkiyi kesme; **os.tra.cize** [ˈ.-saiz] *v/t.* toplum dışında bırakmak, toplum dışına itmek.

**os.trich** *orn.* [ˈɔstritʃ] *n.* devekuşu.

**oth.er** [ˈʌðə] 1. *adj.* başka, diğer, gayrı, sair; 2. *pron.* başka birisi, başka kimse, başkası, diğeri; 3. *adv.* başka şekilde, başka türlü; the ~ day geçen gün; the ~ morning geçen sabah; every ~ day gün aşırı; each ~ birbirini, birbirine; somebody or ~ herhangi biri, şu veya bu kimse; '..wise *adv.* başka türlü, başka şekilde; yoksa, aksi takdirde; diğer taraftan.

**o.ti.ose** ☐ [ˈəuʃiəus] faydasız, yararsız, verimsiz, boş; aylak, tembel, başıboş.

**ot.ter** *zo.* [ˈɔtə] *n.* susamuru, sarı samur; samur kürk.

**Ot.to.man** [ˈɔtəmən] *n. & adj.* Osmanlı; ♀ divan.

**ought** [ɔːt] 1. = aught; 2. *v/aux.* (*irr.*) -meli, -malı; I ~ to do it onu yapmalıyım; you ~ to have done it onu yapmalıydın.

**ounce¹** [auns] *n.* ons (*28, 35 gram);* you wouldn't do that if you had an ~ of sense beş paralık aklın olsa bunu yapmazsın.

**ounce²** *zo.* [~] *n.* tekir, kar parsı.

**our** [ˈauə] *adj.* bizim; **ours** [ˈauəz] *pron.* bizimki; *pred.* bizim; **ourˈselves** *pron.* kendimiz, bizler.

**oust** [aust] *v/t.* yerinden çıkarmak, defetmek, kovmak, dışarı atmak.

**out** [aut] 1. *adv.* dışarı, dışarıda; dışarıya; dışında; yüksek sesle; bütün bütün, tamamen; meydana, ortaya; sonuna kadar; be ~ dışarıda olm.; grevde olm.; mevcut olmamak; alçalmış olm. *(gelgit)*; iktidarda olmamak *(parti);* modası geçmiş olm., demode olm.; sönmek *(yangın);* ortaya çıkmak *(sır);* açmak *(çiçek);* basılmak *(kitap);* süresi dolmak *(kontrat);* hatalı olm., yanlış yapmak; be ~ for s.th. *veya* to do s.th. *sl.* bşin *veya* bş yapmak peşinde olm.; she is not ~ yet henüz dışarı çıkmadı; be ~ with dargın olm. *ile;* ~ and ~ tam manasıyla, tamamen, her yönüyle; ~ and about kalkmış, iyileşmiş *(hasta);* ~ and away pek çok, büyük bir farkla, fersah fersah; *s.* elbow; have it ~ with s.o. bşi b-le tartışarak çözümlemek; voyage ~ gidiş, çıkış, gemiyle dışarı gitme; way ~ çıkış yolu; her day ~ günü boş, serbest; ~ with him! dışarı atın onu!, defedin gitsin!; 2. *n. typ.* atlanmış kelime; *Am.* F çıkar yol, çözüm yolu; the ~s *pl. parl.* muhalefet; *spor:* oyuncuyu çıkarma; çıkarılan oyuncu; 3. *adj.* dışarıdaki, dış...; uzakta bulunan; iktidarda olmayan, muhalif; modası geçmiş; imkânsız, olanaksız; † zararda olan; 4. *prp.* ~ of -*den* dışarı; -*in* dışında; -*den* dolayı; için; -*in* arasından;

-den yapılmış; -siz, -sız; -in açığında; s. date, drawing, laugh, money; 5. *v/t.* F kovmak, kapı dışarı etm.; *boks:* nakavt etm. **out...:** ~and~ ['autnd¹aut] *adj.* tam..., bütün...; '~-and-¹out.er *n. bşde* aşırıya kaçan kimse; '~.back 1. *adj. (Avustralya'da)* nüfusu seyrek olan yerlere ait; 2. *n.* nüfusu seyrek olan yerler; ~¹bal.ance *v/t.* geçmek, daha ağır gelmek *(tartı);* ~¹bıd *(irr.* bid) *v/t. (açık arttırmada)* artırmak *(fiyat);* '~.board *adj.* takma motorlu..., dıştan motorlu...; ~¹brave *v/t.* cesaretle karşı gelmek *-e,* karşı koymak *-e;* '~.break *n.* feveran, patlama, patlak verme; yükselme *(ateş);* fışkırma, çıkma; istilâ *(böcek);* isyan, ayaklanma, ihtilâl; '~.build.ing *n.* ek bina; '~.burst *n.* feveran, patlama, patlak verme, fışkırma, tufan *(kahkaha);* '~.cast 1. *adj.* toplumdan atılmış, serseri; 2. *n.* toplumdan atılmış kimse, serseri kimse; ~.caste *n. (Hindistan'da)* kast dışı olan kimse, parya; ~¹class *v/t. spor:* geçmek *-i,* üstün gelmek *-e;* be ~ed geri kalmak, geçilmek; '~.come *n.* sonuç; etki; '~.crop *n.* patlama, patlak verme; *geol.* yeryüzüne çıkmış kaya; kayanın yeryüzüne çıkması; '~.cry *n.* haykırma, çığlık, feryat, bağırma; açık arttırma; protesto; ~¹dat-ed *adj.* modası geçmiş, demode; ~¹dis-tance *v/t.* geçmek, arkada bırakmak; ~¹do *(irr.* do) *v/t.* üstün gelmek *-e,* geçmek *-i;* '~.door *adj.* dışarıda yapılan..., açık hava...; ~ dress açık hava giyisisi; '~.doors *adv.* açık havada, dışarıda. **out.er** ['autə] *adj.* dış(taki), dışarıdaki...; ~ garments *pl.* üste giyilen giysiler; ~ space yıldız ve gezegenlerin bulunduğu boşluk; '~.most *adj.* en dıştaki... **out...:** ~¹face *v/t.* karşı durmak *-e,* meydan okumak *-e;* bakışlarını kaçırıncaya kadar birine dik dik bakmak; *b-ni* utandırmak; '~.fall *n.* çıkış yeri, nehir ağzı; '~.fit 1. *n. pl.* gereçler, araç gereç, takım taklavat; *Am.* askeri birlik; 2. *v/t.* donatmak; '~.fit.ter *n.* giyim eşyası satan kimse; teçhizatçı; ~¹flank *v/t.* ✗ çevirmek *(düşman kanadını);* '~.flow *n.* akış, akma; gönderilme; ~¹gen.er.al *v/t. (daha iyi plan yaparak)* yenmek; ~¹go 1. *(irr.* go) *v/t.* geçmek, aşmak; *fig.* yenmek; 2. ['~] *n. pl.* masraf, gider; ~¹go.ing 1. *adj.* giden, çıkan, ayrılan; sempatik, arkadaş canlısı; 2. *n.* gidiş, çıkış, ayrılış; ~s *pl.* masraf, giderler, harcama; ~¹grow *(irr.* grow) *v/t. -den* daha çabuk büyümek; *fig.* zamanla bırakmak *(kötü alışkanlık vs.);* sığmamak *(elbiselerine);*

'~.growth *n.* büyüme, gelişme; sonuç, netice, akıbet; dal; '~.house *n. (sundurma, baraka, ahır gibi)* küçük ek bina; *Am.* dışarıda olan tuvalet. **out.ing** ['autin] *n.* tatil, gezinti. **out...:** ~¹land.ish *adj.* tuhaf, acayip, garip; yabancı, ecnebi; uzak, ırak; ~¹last *v/t. -den* daha çok dayanmak; *-den* daha çok sürmek; '~.law 1. *n.* kanun dışı adam; kanun kaçağı; 2. *v/t.* kanun dışı etm.; toplum dışı bırakmak; yasaklamak, men etm.; '~.law *n.* kanuna karşı gelme; kanun dışı bırakma; '~.lay *n.* masraf, giderler; harcama, masraf etme; '~.let *n.* çıkış (yeri), kapı; yol, ağız, delik; *fig.* açılma fırsatı; ✝ satış alanı, pazar, mahreç; ✗ çıkış, fiş; '~.line 1. *n.* taslak, plan; ~s *pl. (resim, harita vs.)* ana hat(lar); 2. *v/t. -in* taslağını çizmek; *-in* ana hatlarını göstermek; ~¹live *v/t. -den* fazla yaşamak; '~.look *n.* görünüş *(a. fig.);* manzara; bakış açısı, görüş açısı; *pol.* genel görünüş; '~.ly.ing *adj.* uzakta bulunan, ücra...; ~¹ma¹noeu.vre *v/t.* rakibinden daha etkili hareket etm., manevra yapmada yenmek; '~.march *v/t.* daha hızlı *veya* daha uzun yürüyerek geçmek *-i;* ~¹match *v/t.* üstün gelmek *-e,* geçmek *-i;* ~¹mod.ed *adj.* modası geçmiş, demode; '~.most *adj.* en dışarıdaki; ~¹num.ber *v/t.* sayıca üstün gelmek *-e;* '~.of-¹door(s) = outdoor(s); '~.of-the-¹way *adj.* uzak, sapa, ücra, ulaşılması güç; *fig.* garip, acayip; '~.of-¹work pay işsizlik tazminatı; ~¹pace *v/t.* ...den daha çabuk gitmek, geçmek *-i;* '~.pa.tient *n.* ayakta tedavi edilen hasta; ~¹play *v/t. -den* daha iyi oynamak, yenmek *-i;* '~.post *n.* ileri karakol; '~.pour.ing *n.* dökülme, taşma, akma *(a. fig.);* '~.put *n.* verim, randıman; güç, enerji; bilgisayardan alınan bilgi. **out.rage** ['autreidʒ] 1. *n.* zorbalık, zulüm (on *-e);* tecavüz (on *-e);* hakaret (on *-e);* rezalet; 2. *v/t.* kötü davranmak *-e;* hakaret etm. *-e,* sövüp saymak *-e;* tecavüz etm. *-e,* bozmak *-i;* **out¹ra.geous** □ gaddar, insafsız, zalim; çok çirkin, iğrenç, tiksindirici; terbiyesiz. **out...:** ~¹range *v/t. -den* daha iyi menzili olm.; ~¹rank *v/t. -den* daha yüksek rütbede olm. **ou.tré** [¹u:trei] *adj.* alışılagelmişin dışında, garip, acayip, tuhaf. **out...:** ~¹reach *vb.* aşmak *-i,* geçmek *-i, -den* fazla gelmek; '~.re.lief *n.* fakirlere evlerinde yapılan yardım; ~¹ride *(irr.* ride) *v/t. -den* daha hızlı sürmek; ↓ atlatmak *(fırtına);* '~.rid.er *n.* bir arabanın yanı sıra giden atlı *veya* motosiklet sürücüsü; **'~.rig.ger** *n.* ↓ avara demiri; **~.right 1.** ['autrait] *adj.* tam, bütün; açık, belli; karşılıksız; **2.** [aut'rait] *adv.* açıkça, açık açık; tamamen, bütün bütün; büsbütün; doğrudan doğruya; bir seferde; **~'ri.val** *v/t.* rekabette geçmek *-i*; **~'run** (*irr.* run) *v/t. -den* daha hızlı koşmak; aşmak *-i*; **'~.run.ner** *n.* bir arabanın yanı sıra koşan uşak; **'~.set** *n.* başlangıç; **~'shine** (*irr.* shine) *v/t. -den* daha çok parlamak; *fig.* gölgede bırakmak *-i*; **'~.side 1.** *n.* dış (taraf); *fig.* dış görünüş; at the **~** en fazla, taş çatlasa, olsa olsa; **2.** *adj.* dış...; azamî..., en fazla...; dıştan gelen..., haricî...; **~** right *spor:* sağaçık; **~** left solaçık; **3.** *adv.* dışarıda, dışarıya; **~** of = **4.** *prp. -in* dışında, *-den* başka; **'~.sid.er** *n.* bir grubun dışında olan kimse; kazanma ihtimali az olan yarışmacı *veya* at; **'~.size** *n.* † büyük boy; **'~.skirts** *n. pl.* kenar, civar, varoş, dış mahalleler; etek (*dağ*); **'~.smart** *v/t. Am.* F *-den* daha akıllı olup yenmek; **~'spoken** □ sözünü sakınmaz, açık sözlü, dobra dobra konuşan; **'~.spread** *adj.* açık, açılmış, yayılmış; **~'stand.ing** *adj.* göze çarpan, önemli; *fig.* çıkıntılı, fırlak, kepçe (*kulak*); kalmış (*borç*); **~'stay** *v/t. -den* fazla kalmak; **~** one's welcome ev sahibini bıktırıncaya kadar kalmak; **~'stretched** = outspread; **~'strip** *v/t.* yarışta geçmek *-i*; *fig. -den* üstün çıkmak; **'~.turn** *n.* verim, randıman; **~'vie** *v/t.* yarışta yenmek *-i*; **~'vote** *v/t. -den* daha çok oy toplamak.

**out.ward** ['autwəd] **1.** *adj.* dış, haricî; **2.** *adv. mst* **'out.wards** görünüşte; dışarıya doğru; **'out.ward.ly** *adv.* görünüşte; dışa doğru; **'out.ward.ness** *n.* haricî olma; dışa doğru olma.

**out...:** **~'wear** (*irr.* wear) *v/t. -den* daha uzun dayanmak; yıpratmak; tüketmek; **~'weigh** *v/t. -den* daha ağır gelmek; *fig.* daha ağır basmak; **~'wit** *v/t. -den* daha akıllıca davranarak atlatmak, *-den* daha kurnazca davranmak; **'~.work** *n.* ✕ haricî istihkâm; ⊕ evlerde yapılmak üzere verilen fabrika işi; **'~.work.er** *n.* eve iş getiren kimse; **'~.worn** *adj.* fazla eskimiş; *fig.* modası geçmiş, demode.

**ou.zel** *orn.* ['u:zl] *n.* karatavuk.

**o.val** ['əuvəl] **1.** *adj.* oval..., beyzî...; **2.** *n.* oval biçimde herhangi *bş.*

**o.va.ry** ['əuvəri] *n. anat.* yumurtalık; ⚘ yumurtalık, ovar.

**o.va.tion** [əu'veiʃən] *n.* coşkunca alkış.

**ov.en** ['ʌvən] *n.* fırın; **'~.bird** *n. orn. Am.*

bir tür ötleğen.

**o.ver** ['əuvə] **1.** *adv.* yukarıda; tamamen, baştan başa; tekrar, yine, gene, yeniden, bir daha; karşı taraf(t)a; fazla, artık; bitmiş; geçmiş (*fırtına*); **~** and above *-den* başka, *-den* fazla, *-e* ilâveten; (all) **~** again bir daha, tekrar; **~** against *-in* karşısın(d)a, *-e* karşı; all **~** her tarafında, büsbütün, tamamiyle; **~** and **~** again tekrar tekrar, defalarca; fifty times **~** elli defa daha; read **~** baştan başa okumak; **2.** *prp.* üzerin(d)e, üstün(d)e, yukarısın(d)a; karşıdan karşıya, karşı tarafa, öbür tarafına; boyunca; başında (*yönetimi*); bütün (*zaman*); *-den* fazla; sırasında, esnasında; all **~** the town tüm şehirde; **~** night tüm gece; **~** a glass of wine bir kadeh şaraptan fazla; **~** the way yolun karşısında, karşı tarafta.

**o.ver...:** **~'act** *v/t. & v/i.* abartmalı bir şekilde oynamak (*rol*); **~'all 1.** *n.* iş elbisesi; **~s** *pl.* iş tulumu; **2.** *adj.* baştan başa olan..., kapsamlı; **~'arch** *v/t. & v/i.* (*üstünde*) kemer oluşturmak; **~'awe** *v/t.* çok korkutmak; **~'bal.ance 1.** *n.* fazla ağırlık; **2.** *v/t.* dengesini bozmak, devirmek; *-den* fazla gelmek; *v/i.* tartıda ağır gelmek; dengesini kaybetmek; **~'bear** (*irr.* bear) *vb.* yenmek, *-den* üstün gelmek; *-den* ağır gelmek; fazla ürün vermek; **~'bear.ing** □ buyurucu, küstah, amirlik taslayıcı; zorba tavırlı; **~'bid** (*irr.* bid) *vb. -den* fazla fiyat vermek (*açık artırmada*); *-in* değerinden fazla fiyat vermek; *briç:* deklarasyon yapmak; **'~.blown** *adj.* tazeliğini kaybetmiş (*çiçek*); heybetli, cüsseli; abartmalı; **~.board** *adv.* ↓ gemiden denize; **'~.brim** *vb.* üstünden aşmak, taşmak; **'~.bur.den** *v/t.* fazla yük yüklemek *-e*; fazla sıkıntı vermek *-e*; **'~.cast 1.** *adj.* bulutlu (*hava*); *fig.* kasvetli, sıkıcı; **2.** *n.* bulutlu hava; **~'charge 1.** *v/t.* aşırı fiyat istemek *-den*, kazıklamak *-i*; fazla doldurmak *-i*; abartmak *-i*; **2.** *n.* fazla yük; fazla fiyat; **~'cloud** *vb.* bulutlarla kaplamak; *fig.* kederlendirmek, tatsızlaştırmak; **'~.coat** *n.* palto; **~'come** (*irr.* come) *vb.* yenmek, alt etm., kazanmakla gelmek; çaresini bulmak; **'~.con.fi.dent** □ kendine çok güvenen (*of hususunda*); **~'crowd** *v/t.* fazla kalabalık etm.; **~'do** (*irr.* do) *v/t.* abartmak, şişirmek; abartarak oynamak (*rol*); fazla özenmek *-e*; fazla pişirmek; çok yormak; **~.done** [~'dʌn] *adj.* abartmalı; çor yorgun, bitkin; [~'dʌn] çok pişmiş, bit-kin; **'~.draft** *n.* † hesaptan çekilen fazla para; hesaptan

fazla para çekme; açık itibar; **'~'draw**
(*irr.* draw) *vb.* abartmak; † *(bankada-
ki hesabından)* fazla para çekmek;
**'~'dress** *v/t.* aşırı süslü giydirmek; *v/i.*
aşırı süslü giyinmek; **'~.drive** *n. mot.* fazla sürat düzeni; **'~'due** *adj.* ▓▓ gecikmiş, rötarlı; † vadesi geçmiş; **'~'eat** (*irr.*
eat); ~ o.s. *v/i.* aşırı yemekten gına gelmek; **'~'es.ti.mate** *vb. -den* fazla tahmin
etm.; **'~.ex'pose** *v/t. phot.* fazla poz vermek *(filme)*; **'~-ex'po.sure** *n. phot.* filme
fazla poz verme; **'~.fa'tigue 1.** *adj.* bitkin,
çok yorgun; **2.** *n.* bitkinlik, aşırı yorgunluk; **'~'feed** (*irr.* feed) *v/t.* fazla yem
vermek; **~.flow 1.** [~'fləu] (*irr.* flow) *v/t.*
su basmak; *v/i.* taşmak; **2.** ['~'fləu] *n.*
taşma; sel; taşkın şey; çok bol şey;
**'~.freight** *n.* fazla yük; **'~.ground** *adj.* yer
üzerinde yükselen; **'~'grow** (*irr.* grow)
*vb. -den* daha çok büyümek; hızla büyümek; **'~.growth** *n.* aşırı büyüme; **'~.hand**
*adj. spor.* yukarıdan aşağıya inen...;
**~.hang 1.** ['~'hæŋ] (*irr.* hang) *vb. (üzerine)* sarkmak; *fig.* tehlikesi olm.; **2.**
['~'hæŋ] *n.* çıkıntı; **'~'haul** *v/t.* elden geçirmek, kontrol etm.; yetişmek *-e*; **~.head**
**1.** [~'hed] *adv.* yukarıda, tepede, üstte,
üst katta; **2.** ['~'hed] *adj.* † genel masraflarla ilgili; yukarıdan geçen; ~ railway asma demiryolu, havai demiryolu;
~ wire ⚡ havai hat; **3.** ['~'hed] *n.*:
~s *pl.* † genel masraflar; **'~'hear** (*irr.*
hear) *v/t.* rastlantılı olarak işitmek, kulak misafiri olm.; **'~'heat** *v/t.* fazla ısıtmak; *v/i.* fazla ısınmak; **'~'is.sue** *v/t.*
fazla basmak *(para)*; **~'joy** *v/t.* çok sevindirmek; **'~.land 1.** *adj.* kara yolu ile
yapılan...; **2.** *adv.* karada(n); **~'lap** *v/t.*
& *v/i.* üst üste kapla(n)mak; üst üste
getirmek *veya* gelmek; **~.lay 1.** [~'lei]
(*irr.* lay) *v/t.* kaplamak; ⊕ katlamak;
**2.** ['~.lei] *n.* kaplama; kaplayan şey; ~
mattress katlama yatak; **'~'leaf** *adv.* sayfanın öbür tarafında; **'~'leap** (*irr.* leap)
*v/t. -in* üstünden atlamak; ~ o.s. *fig.* haddini aşmak, ileri gitmek; **~.load 1.**
['~'ləud] *v/t.* fazla yüklemek *veya* doldurmak; **2.** ['~'ləud] *n.* fazla yük; **'~'look**
*v/t.* gözden kaçırmak, dikkate almamak;
göz yummak; muayene *veya* teftiş etm.;
yukarıdan bakmak *-e*; **'~'lord** *n.* lordlar
lordu; derebeyi; **'~.man.tel** *n.* ocak dav-
lumbazı; **'~'mas.ter** *v/t.* boyun eğdirmek,
hakkından gelmek; **~'match** *v/t.* yenmek; **'~.much** *adj.* & *adv.* pek çok, aşırı, gereğinden fazla; **'~'night 1.** *adv.* gece sırasında, geceleyin, bir gecede; dün
gece; **2.** *adj.* geceleyin olan...; bir gece

için, bir gecelik...; **'~.pass** *n.* üst geçit;
**'~'pay** (*irr.* pay) *v/t.* fazla ödemek;
**~'peo.pled** *adj.* aşırı kalabalık; **'~.plus**
*n.* fazlalık; **~'pow.er** *v/t.* zararsız hale
getirmek, yenmek; **'~'print** *vb. -in* üstüne yeniden basmak; **'~.pro'duc.tion** *n.*
fazla üretim; **'~'rate** *v/t.* fazla önem vermek *-e*, çok önemsemek *-i*; **'~'reach** *v/t.*
aldatmak, dolandırmak; yetişip geçmek;
~ o.s. kendi çıkarını zedelemek; **~'ride**
(*irr.* ride) *v/t. fig.* önem vermemek *-e*;
**~'rid.ing** *adj.* ağır basan; **'~'rule** *v/t.* yönetmek, etkili olm.; ⚖ geçersiz kılmak,
bozmak, nakzetmek; **'~'run** (*irr.* run) *v/t.*
kaplamak, istilâ etm.; geçmek *-i*, aşmak
*-i*; *typ.* yeniden dizmek; **'~'sea 1.** *adj. a.*
**~s** denizaşırı; **2.** *adv.* **~s** denizaşırı; yurt
dışında; **'~'see** (*irr.* see) *v/t.* yönetmek,
idare etm.; **'~.se.er** *n.* ustabaşı; müfettiş, yönetici, denetçi, idareci; **~'set** (*irr.*
set) *v/t.* devirmek; *fig.* perişan etm.,
sarsmak; **'~.sew** (*irr.* sew) *v/t.* teyellemek; **'~'shad.ow** *v/t.* gölgelemek, gölge
düşürmek, küçültmek; **'~.shoe** *n.* şoson,
lastik, kaloş; **'~'shoot** (*irr.* shoot) *vb.*
ötesine atmak, aşırmak; ~ o.s. aşırılığa
kaçmak; **'~'shot** *adj.* suyu üstten alan...;
**~.sight** *n.* kusur, yanlış; gözetim; **'~.sim-
plifi'ca.tion** *n.* anlamını yitirecek derecede basitleştirme; **'~'sleep** (*irr.* sleep)
*v/i. a.* ~ o.s. uyuya kalıp gecikmek, çok
uyumak; **'~.sleeve** *n.* kolluk; **'~.spill** *n.*
*(part. nüfus)* fazlalık; **'~'state** *v/t.* abartmak; **'~'state.ment** *n.* abartma, abartı;
**'~'step** *v/t.* aşmak, geçmek; **'~'stock** *vb.*
*(fazla mal ile)* doldurmak; **~.strain 1.**
['~'strein] *v/t.* fazla yormak; *fig.* aşırıya kaçırmak; **2.** ['~'strein] *n.* fazla yor-
ma; **~.strung** ['~'strʌŋ] *adj.* çok sinirli;
['~'strʌŋ] telleri üst üste gerilmiş *(piyano)*; **'~.sub'scribe** *v/t.* gereğinden fazlasını taahhüt etm.; **'~.sup'ply** *n.* talep fazlası.

**o.vert** ['əuvə:t] *adj.* açıkça yapılan.

**over...:** **'~'take** (*irr.* take) *v/t.* yetişmek
*-e*, yakalamak *-i*; **'~'tax** *v/t.* ağır vergi
koymak; *fig.* aşırı yüklenmek *-e*; **~.throw**
**1.** [~'θrəu] (*irr.* throw) *v/t.* devirmek,
yıkmak *(a. fig.)*; bozmak, yenmek; harap etm.; **2.** ['~θrəu] *n.* devirme, yıkma;
✕ bozgun, yenilgi; **'~.time** *n.* fazla çalışma süresi, mesai; **'~'tire** *v/t.* çok yormak; **'~.tone** *n.* ♪ armonik seslerden biri; **'~'top** *v/t. -in* tepesini aşmak; üstün
gelmek; **'~.trump** *vb. -den* daha yüksek
koz oynamak.

**over.ture** ['əuvətjuə] *n.* ♪ uvertür; teklif,
öneri.

**o.ver...: ~.turn 1.** [ˈ~təːn] *n.* devirme; devrilme; **2.** [~ˈtəːn] *v/t.* devirmek, altüst etm., bozmak; *v/i.* devrilmek; **ˈ~ˈval.ue** *v/t.* fazla kıymet takdir etm.; **~ˈween.ing** *adj.* kendinden çok emin, gururlu, kibirli; **~.weight 1.** [ˈ~weit] *n.* fazla ağırlık; **2.** [ˈ~ˈweit] *v/t.* fazla yük koymak *-e*; **~ˈwhelm** *v/t.* yenmek, alt etm.; *fig.* bunaltmak, garketmek, boğmak; **ˈ~ˈwise** □ ukalâ; **~.work 1.** [ˈ~wəːk] *n.* fazla çalışma; **2.** [~ˈwəːk] (*irr.* work) *v/t. & v/i.* fazla çalış(tır)mak; **ˈ~ˈwrought** *adj.* sinirleri bozuk; çok heyecanlı; aşırı süslü, cicili bicili.

**o.vi.duct** ⚥ [ˈəuvidʌkt] *n.* dölyatağı borusu; **o.vi.form** [ˈ~fɔːm] *adj.* oval, yumurta şeklindeki; **oˈvip.a.rous** *zo.* [~pərəs] *adj.* yumurtlayan; **o.vule** *biol.* [ˈəuvjuːl] *n.* yumurtacık; **o.vum** *biol.* [ˈəuvəm] *n.*, *pl.* **o.va** [ˈəuvə] yumurta(cık).

**owe** [əu] *vb.* borcu olm., borçlu olm. (s.o. s.th. *-e -den dolayı*); etkisinde olm.; minnettarı olm.; *spor:* avans vermek; ~ s.o. a grudge *b-ne* kin beslemek.

**ow.ing** [ˈəuiŋ] *adj.* borç olan; ~ to sebebiyle, yüzünden, ...den dolayı; be ~ to ...den dolayı olm.

**owl** *orn.* [aul] *n.* baykuş, puhu; **owl.et** [ˈaulit] *n.* baykuş yavrusu; **ˈowl.ish** □ baykuşa benzeyen, baykuş gibi...

**own** [əun] **1.** *adj.* kendi(nin), özel, kendine özgü; öz; my ~ self bizzat ben; ~ brother to s.o. *b-nin* öz kardeşi; she makes her ~ clothes kendi elbiselerini kendi diker; **2.** my ~ kendi malım, benim; a house of one's ~ *b-nin* kendi' evi; come into one's ~ lâyık olduğu yere erişmek, *k-ni* göstermek; get one's ~ back F öcünü almak; hold one's ~ dayanmak, karşı koymak, yerini korumak; on one's ~

F yalnız, tek başına; kendi hesabına, kendi başına; üstüne olmayan, bir eşi daha olmayan; **3.** *v/t.* sahip olm., malik olm. *-e*; kabul etm., tanımak, itiraf etm., doğrulamak *-i*; ~ up (to) F açıkça itiraf etm.

**own.er** [ˈəunə] *n.* sahip, mal sahibi; **ˈ~ˈdriv.er** *n.* kendi aracını kullanan şoför; **ˈ~.less** *adj.* sahipsiz; **ˈ~ˈoc.cu.pied** *adj.* sahibinin oturduğu (*ev*); **ˈown.er.ship** *n.* mülkiyet, sahiplik.

**ox** [ɔks] *n.*, *pl.* **ox.en** [ˈɔksən] öküz, sığır. **ox.al.ic ac.id** 🜍 [ɔkˈsælikˈæsid] *n.* oksalik asit.

**Ox.bridge** [ˈɔksbridʒ] *n.* Oxford *ve(ya)* Cambridge üniversitesi.

**ox.cart** [ˈɔkskɑːt] *n.* kağnı, öküz arabası; **ox.en** [ˈɔksən] *n. pl. of* ox; **ˈox-eye** *n.* ❦ sarı papatya.

**Ox.ford shoes** [ˈɔksfədˈʃuːz] *n. pl.* bağlı erkek ayakkabısı.

**ox.i.da.tion** 🜍 [ɔksiˈdeiʃən] *n.* oksitlenme, oksidasyon; **ox.ide** [ˈɔksaid] *n.* oksit; **ox.i.dize** [ˈɔksidaiz] *v/t. & v/i.* oksijen ile birleş(tir)mek; oksitle(n)mek.

**ox.lip** ❦ [ˈɔkslip] *n.* çuhaçiçeği.

**Ox.o.ni.an** [ɔkˈsəunjən] **1.** *adj.* Oxford Üniversiteli...; **2.** *n.* Oxford üniversitesi öğrencisi *veya* öğretim görevlisi.

**ox.y.gen** 🜍 [ˈɔksidʒən] *n.* oksijen; **ox.y.gen.ate** [ɔkˈsidʒineit] *v/t.* oksijen ile karıştırmak.

**ox.y.hy.dro.gen** 🜍 [ˈɔksiˈhaidridʒən] *n.* oksihidrojen gazı.

**o.yer** ⚖ [ˈɔiə] *n.* sorguya çekme, sorgu. **o.yez** [əuˈjes] *int.* dinleyin!

**oys.ter** [ˈɔistə] *n.* istiridye; *attr.* istiridye...; **ˈ~-bed** *n.* istiridye yatağı.

**o.zone** 🜍 [ˈəuzəun] *n.* ozon; **o.zon.ic** [əuˈzɔnik] *adj.* ozona ait, ozon...

# P

P [piː]: mind one's Ps and Qs hareketlerine dikkat etm.

**pa** F [paː] *n.* baba.

**pab.u.lum** [ˈpæbjuləm] *n.* yiyecek, gıda.

**pace** [peis] **1.** *n.* adım, yürüyüş (hızı); gidiş; rahvan yürüyüş (*at*); *fig.* gelişme, ilerleme hızı; keep ~ with ayak uydurmak *-e*; put s.o. through his ~s *b-nin* yeteneğini ölçmek; set the ~ sürati tayin etm., tempoyu ayarlamak; **2.** *v/t.* adımlamak; ayarlamak; *spor*: tayin etm. (*sürat*); *v/i.* yürümek, gezinmek; eşkin gitmek, rahvan gitmek (*at*); **paced** *adj.* adımlanmış...; rahvan yürüyüşlü...; **ˈpace-mak.er** *n.* *spor:* yarışta sürati ayarlayan binici *veya* koşucu; **ˈpac.er** *n.* yaya yürüyen (*veya* ölçülü adımlarla giden) kimse; = pace-maker.

**pach.y.derm** *zo.* [ˈpækidəːm] *n.* kalın derili ve dört ayaklı bir hayvan (*fil, suaygırı, gergedan v.b.*).

**pa.cif.ic** [pəˈsifik] **1.** *adj.* (~ally) barışçı, barışsever, sulhçu, sulhperver; sakin; the 2 Ocean = **2.** *n.* the 2 Büyük Okyanus, Pasifik Okyanusu; **pac.i.fi.ca.tion** [pæsifiˈkeiʃən] *n.* barış(tır)ma, uzlaş(tır)ma; barış anlaşması.

**pac.i.fi.er** [ˈpæsifaiə] *n.* barıştıran kimse; *Am.* emzik; **ˈpac.i.fism** *n.* barışseverlik, sulhperverlik; **ˈpac.i.fist** *n.* barışçı kimse.

**pac.i.fy** [ˈpæsifai] *v/t.* yatıştırmak, sakinleştirmek; barıştırmak, uzlaştırmak; boyun eğdirmek, baskı altında tutmak (*ülke*).

**pack** [pæk] **1.** *n.* bohça, çıkın; sürü, takım; köpek sürüsü; *iskambil:* deste; *Am.* paket (*sigara*); balya; denk; ⚡ kompres, buz torbası; *a.* ~-ice buz kütlesi; a ~ of nonsense bir sürü saçmalık; **2.** *v/t.* bohçalamak; denk etm.; ambalajlamak, paketlemek, sarmak (*a.* ⚡); istif etm.; tıkıştırmak, sıkıştırmak, tıka basa doldurmak; hazırlamak, toplamak (*bavul*); bavul, sandık *veya* kutuya koymak; *a.* ~ off defetmek, kovmak, postalamak; *Am.* F taşımak, nakletmek, götürmek; ⊕ kalafatlamak; *v/i.* a. ~ up gitmek, defolmak; birleşmek, bir araya gelmek, sıkışmak; send s.o. ~ing pılıyı pırtıyı toplatıp defetmek; ~ up F durmak; ~ up F durmak; ⊕ bohça; *part.* *Am.* paket; balya; koli; **ˈpack.age** *n.* ambalaj; bohça; *part.* grup turu; **ˈpack-an.i.mal** *n.* yük hayvanı; **ˈpack.er** *n.* ambalajcı, paket yapan kimse *veya* alet; **pack.et** [ˈpækit] *n.* paket, çıkın, bohça, deste; *sl.* dünya kadar para; *a.* ~-boat posta gemisi; catch a ~ *sl.* ağır yaralı olm.; **ˈpack-horse** *n.* yük beygiri.

**pack.ing** [ˈpækiŋ] *n.* bağlama, paketleme, ambalaj; ⊕ salmastıra, tıkaç, conta, tampon; *attr.* paket...; **ˈ~-box** *n.* ⚡ eşya sandığı; ~ house *Am.* büyük mezbaha.

**pack.thread** [ˈpækθred] *n.* sicim, kınnap.

**pact** [pækt] *n.* antlaşma, sözleşme, pakt.

**pad¹** *sl.* [pæd] *vb.* a. ~ it, ~ along yayan gitmek, taban tepmek.

**pad²** [~] **1.** *n.* yastık; kâğıt destesi; *spor:* tekmelik; ıstampa; ⊕ rampa; bazı hayvanların yumuşak tabanı; *sl.* yatak, oda, apartman dairesi; **2.** *v/t.* -in içini doldurmak; takviye etm.; şişirmek (*konuşma, yazı vs.*); ~ out *fig.* şişirmek (*konuşma, yazı vs.*); ~ded cell duvarları takviyeli hücre; **ˈpad.ding** *n.* vatka; kıtık; *fig.* abartma.

**pad.dle** [ˈpædl] **1.** *n.* tokaç; nehir vapurunun yan çarkı; ↓ kısa kürek, pala; **2.** *v/t. & v/i.* kısa kürekle yürü(t)mek; yavaş yavaş kürek çekmek; tokmakla dövmek (*çamaşır*); el ve ayakları suda oynatmak; sendeleyerek yürümek; suda oynamak; paddling pool sığ havuz; ~ one's own canoe kendi işini kendi görmek; **ˈ~-box** *n.* ↓ davlumbaz, yandan çark mahfazası; **ˈ~-steam.er** *n.* ↓ yandan çarklı gemi; **ˈ~-wheel** *n.* geminin yan çarkı.

**pad.dock** [ˈpædək] *n.* çayırlık, otlak; *spor:* pist; eyerleri tartma yeri; pözaj.

**pad.dy¹** [ˈpædi] ♉ *n.* kabuklu pirinç, çeltik; pirinç tarlası.

**pad.dy²** F [~] *n.* öfke, hiddet, köpürme.

**pad.lock** [ˈpædlɔk] **1.** *n.* asma kilit; **2.** *vb.* asma kilitle kilitlemek, asma kilit vurmak.

**pad.re** F ✗ [ˈpɑːdrei] *n.* papaz, rahip, vaiz.

**pae.an** [ˈpiːən] *n.* şükran *veya* zafer şarkısı.

**paed.er.as.ty** [ˈpedəræsti] *n.* oğlancılık, ibnelik, kulamparalık.

**pae.di.a.tri.cian** [piːdiəˈtriʃən] *n.* çocuk doktoru; **pae.di.at.rics** [~ˈætriks] *n. sg.* çocuk bakımı *veya* tedavisi ilmi.

**pa.gan** [ˈpeigən] **1.** *adj.* dinsiz, putperest, kâfir; **2.** *n.* putperest kimse; **ˈpa.gan.ism** *n.* putperestlik.

**page¹** [peidʒ] **1.** *n.* otel garsonu; iç oğlanı; *Am.* ulak, uşak; **2.** *v/t. Am.* hoparlör ile çağırmak.

**page²** [~] **1.** *n.* sayfa; *fig.* kayda değer olay; **2.** *v/t.* *-in* sayfalarını numaralamak *(gazete, kitap vs.).*

**pag.eant** [ˈpædʒənt] *n.* tarihi oyun; alay, tören; gösteri, temsil; **ˈpag.eant.ry** *n.* görkemli temsil *(veya gösteri).*

**pag.i.nate** [ˈpædʒineit] *s.* page² 2; **pag.i.na.tion** *n.* kitap sayfalarını numaralama.

**pa.go.da** [pəˈgəudə] *n.* pagoda, Uzak Doğu'da tapınak.

**paid** [peid] *pret. & p.p. of* pay 2.

**pail** [peil] *n.* kova.

**pail.lasse** [ˈpæliæs] *n.* ot minder.

**pain** [pein] **1.** *n.* ağrı, sızı, acı; dert, keder, elem, ıstırap, azap; **~s** *pl.* özen, itina, zahmet; doğum sancıları; on *veya* under ~ of death aksi takdirde cezası ölüm; be in ~ acı çekmek; bir yeri ağrımak; be at ~s, take ~s özen göstermek; özenmek, zahmete girmek; **2.** *v/t.* acı vermek *-e*, ağrı vermek *-e*; üzmek *-i*, eziyet etm. *-e*; **pain.ful** □ [ˈ~ful] acı veren, ıstırap çektiren; zahmetli, güç; üzücü; **ˈpain-kill.er** *n.* ağrı kesici ilâç; **ˈpain.less** □ acısız, ağrısız; **ˈpains.tak.ing** **1.** □ özenli, dikkatli; hamarat, çalışkan; **2.** *n.* özenme, itina etme.

**paint** [peint] **1.** *n.* boya; kozmetik; makyaj; wet ~! yeni boyanmıştır!; **2.** *v/t.* boyamak; boyayarak süslemek; boya ile resim yapmak; *fig.* tasvir etm., resmetmek; ~ out üzerine boya sürerek kapatmak *(veya* gidermek); *v/i.* yağlıboya resim yapmak; makyaj yapmak; **ˈ~-box** *n.* boya kutusu; **ˈ~-brush** *n.* boya fırçası.

**paint.er¹** [ˈpeintə] *n.* ressam; boyacı.

**paint.er²** ⬇ [~] *n.* pruva halatı.

**paint.ing** [ˈpeintiŋ] *n.* ressamlık; resim, tablo.

**pair** [peə] **1.** *n.* çift, iki adet; karı koca; karşı cinsten iki hayvan; a ~ of scissors makas; in ~s ikişer ikişer, çifter çifter; **2.** *v/t. & v/i.* çiftleş(tir)mek; a. ~ off

çiftlere ayırmak *veya* ayrılmak; ~ off with F evlenmek.

**pa.ja.mas** [pəˈdʒɑːməz] = pyjamas.

**Pa.kis.ta.ni** [pɑːkisˈtɑːni] *n. & adj.* Pakistanlı.

**pal** *sl.* [pæl] **1.** *n.* arkadaş, dost, ahbap; **2.** *v/i.* ~ up with s.o. *b-le* arkadaş *(veya* kafadar) olm.

**pal.ace** [ˈpælis] *n.* saray; saray gibi bina; lüks eğlence yeri.

**pal.ae.o.** [ˈpæliəu] *comb.* eski zaman...; **pal.ae.o.lith.ic** [~əuˈliθik] *adj.* taş devrine ait; **pal.ae.on.tol.o.gy** [~ɔnˈtɔlədʒi] *n.* paleontoloji.

**pal.at.a.ble** □ [ˈpælətəbl] lezzetli, leziz; *fig.* makûl, akla yatkın; **ˈpal.at.a.ble.ness** *n.* lezizlik.

**pal.a.tal** [ˈpælətl] **1.** *adj.* damağa ait; dilin damağa dokunmasıyla çıkarılan *(ses);* **2.** *n. gr.* dilin damağa dokunmasıyla çıkarılan ses, damak sessizi.

**pal.ate** [ˈpælit] *n.* damak; *fig.* ağız tadı, zevk, haz.

**pa.la.tial** □ [pəˈleiʃəl] saray gibi, görkemli.

**pa.lat.i.nate** [pəˈlætinit] *n.* palatinlik, kont *veya* dük'ün yönettiği ülke; the ♀ Palatina.

**pal.a.tine** [ˈpælətain] *adj.* Palatinalı, Palatinliğe ait, Palatina...; Count ♀ Palatinlik kontu.

**pa.lav.er** [pəˈlɑːvə] **1.** *n.* görüşme, konuşma; *sl.* boş laf, palavra; **2.** *v/i.* boş laf etm., palavra atmak, atıp tutmak.

**pale¹** [peil] **1.** □ soluk, solgun, renksiz, mat, donuk; ~ ale beyaz bira; **2.** *v/t. & v/i.* sarar(t)mak, sol(dur)mak, donuklaş(tır)mak, beti benzi atmak.

**pale²** [~] *n.* kazık; etrafı çevrili yer.

**pale-face** [ˈpeilfeis] *n.* soluk benizli.

**pale.ness** [ˈpeilnis] *n.* solgunluk, renksizlik, matlık.

**pa.le.o-** [ˈpæliəu] *s.* palaeo-.

**pal.ette** *paint.* [ˈpælit] *n.* palet; **ˈ~-knife** *n.* boya malası.

**pal.frey** [ˈpɔːlfri] *n.* binek atı.

**pal.imp.sest** [ˈpælimpsest] *n.* önceden yazıları silinerek üzerine yeniden başka yazı yazılmış parşömen.

**pal.ing** [ˈpeiliŋ] *n.* kazıklardan yapılmış çit.

**pal.i.sade** [pæliˈseid] **1.** *n.* parmaklık, çit; ~s *pl. Am.* kayalık uçurum; **2.** *v/t.* kazıklarla çevirmek *veya* sağlamlaştırmak.

**pall¹** [pɔːl] *n.* tabut örtüsü; *fig.* kasvetli hava.

**pall²** [~] *vb.* yavanlaşmak, tatsızlaşmak, tadı kaçmak; usandırmak, bıktırmak, gına getirmek (upon s.o. ḅ-ni).

**pal.la.di.um** [pə'leidjəm] *n.* himaye, koruma; koruyucu şey, güvenlik unsuru.

**pal.let** ['pælit] *n.* ot minder.

**pal.liasse** ['pæliæs] = palliasse.

**pal.li.ate** ['pælieit] *v/t.* hafifletmek (*ağrı, hastalık*), yatıştırmak; örtbas etm., mazur göstermek (*suç*); **pal.li.a.tion** *n.* hafifletme, yatıştırma; özür; **pal.li.a.tive** ['⸴ətiv] *adj. & n.* hafifletici (*şey*); *fig.* örtbas etme; geçici önlem.

**pal.lid** □ ['pælid] solgun, sararmış, beti benzi atmış, renksiz; **'pal.lid.ness, pal.lor** ['pælə] *n.* solgunluk.

**palm** [pɑːm] **1.** *n.* avuç içi, el ayası; hurma ağacı; palmiye; have an itching ~ anaforcu olm., para canlısı olm.; **2.** *v/t.* avuç içinde saklamak; avuç içi ile dokunmak *veya* vurmak; ~ s.th. off upon s.o. *b-ne bşi* yutturmak, sokuşturmak; **pal.mer** ['pɑːmə] *n.* Kudüs'ten hurma dalı ile dönen hacı; **'palm.ist** *n.* el falına bakan kimse; **'palm.is.try** *n.* el falı; **'palm-oil** *n.* hurma yağı; *co.* rüşvet; **'palm-tree** *n.* hurma ağacı; **'palm.y** *adj.* muhteşem, görkemli, refah içindeki.

**pal.pa.ble** ['pælpəbl] □ hissedilebilir, dokunulabilir; *fig.* açık (seçik), belli, belirgin, bariz.

**pal.pi.tate** ['pælpiteit] *v/i.* küt küt atmak (*kalp*); heyecandan titremek; **pal.pi'ta-tion** *n.* çarpıntı, küt küt atma (*kalp*).

**pal.sy** ['pɔːlzi] **1.** *n.* felç, inme; *fig.* aciz, kuvvetsizlik; **2.** *v/t. fig.* felce uğratmak, aksatmak.

**pal.ter** ['pɔːltə] *vb.* küçümsemek, yabana atmak, önemsememek (with *-i*).

**pal.tri.ness** ['pɔːltrinis] *n.* değersizlik, önemsizlik; **'pal.try** □ değersiz, önemsiz.

**pam.pas** ['pæmpəz] *n. pl.* Güney Amerika'daki ağaçsız geniş ovalar.

**pam.per** ['pæmpə] *v/t.* şımartmak, pohpohlamak, üstüne çok düşmek.

**pam.phlet** ['pæmflit] *n.* broşür, kitapçık, risale; **pam.phlet.eer** [~'tiə] *n.* broşür yazarı.

**pan** [pæn] **1.** *n.* tava; kefe, terazi gözü; eski tüfeklerde falya tavası; *sl.* yüz, surat; sert eleştiri; **2.** *v/t. & v/i.* toprağı yıkayarak çıkarmak (*altın*); tavada yıkamak; tavaya koymak; *Am.* F şiddetle eleştirmek; bir yandan öbür yana çevirmek (*kamera*); maden cevherini yıkamak; ~ out başarıya ulaşmak; sonuç vermek, değmek.

**pan...** [~] *prefix* bütün..., tüm...

**pan.a.ce.a** [pænə'siə] *n.* her derde deva.

**pan.cake** ['pænkeik] *n.* gözleme; ~ landing

**T** uçağın yere yatay durumda çarparak inişi.

**pan.cre.as** ♀ ['pæŋkriəs] *n.* pankreas.

**pan.de.mo.ni.um** *fig.* [pændi'məunjəm] *n.* karışıklık, kargaşa, şamata, kıyamet; cehennem.

**pan.der** ['pændə] **1.** *vb.* hoşnut etm. (to *-i*); pezevenklik etm.; **2.** *n.* pezevenk.

**pane** [pein] *n.* pencere camı; ⊕ levha, tabaka.

**pan.e.gyr.ic** [pæni'dʒirik] *n.* övgü, methiye, kaside; **pan.e'gyr.ist** *n.* kaside yazarı, methiyeci.

**pan.el** ['pænl] **1.** *n.* ♠ kapı aynası; pano; *paint.* resim tahtası; elbise eteğine konulan parça; ½ jüri heyeti (isim listesi); panel, açık oturum; heyet; **2.** *v/t.* tahta ile kaplamak; **'~-doc.tor** *n.* sigorta doktoru; **'pan.el.ist** *n.* açık oturumda konuşmacı; **'pan.el.(l)ing** *n.* tahta kaplama.

**pang** [pæŋ] *n.* ani ağrı, sancı; *fig.* ıstırap, sıkıntı.

**pan.ic** ['pænik] **1.** *adj.* yersiz, sebepsiz (*korku*); **2.** *n.* panik, korku; **3.** *v/t. & v/i. pret. & p.p.* **'pan.icked** paniğe uğratmak; korkmak, paniğe kapılmak; *sl.* coşturmak, kahkahadan kırıp geçirmek; **'pan.ick.y** *adj.* paniğe kapılmış; **'pan.ic-mon-ger** *n.* panik yaratan kimse; **'pan.ic-strick.en** *adj.* paniğe kapılmış, panik içinde.

**pan.nier** ['pæniə] *n.* küfe, sepet.

**pan.ni.kin** ['pænikin] *n.* küçük madeni kap.

**pan.o.ply** ['pænəpli] *n.* zırh takımı.

**pan.o.ra.ma** [pænə'rɑːmə] *n.* panorama, manzara; devamlı değişen şey; toplu bakış; **pan.o.ram.ic** [~'ræmik] *adj.* (~ally) panoramik.

**pan.sy** ['pænzi] *n.* ♀ alaca menekşe, hercai menekşe; *a.* ~-boy homoseksüel erkek.

**pant** [pænt] *v/i.* solumak, kalmak (for breath *nefes nefese*); nefesi kesilmek; özlem duymak (for, after *-e*); *v/t.* ~ out nefes nefese söylemek.

**pan.ta.loon** [pæntə'luːn] *n.* maskara, soytarı, palyaço; ~s *pl. co. veya Am.* pantolon.

**pan.tech.ni.con** [pæn'teknikən] *n. a.* ~ van eşya kamyonu.

**pan.the.ism** ['pænθiizm] *n.* panteizm, kamutanrıcılık; **pan.the'is.tic** *adj.* (~ally) panteizme ait, kamutanrısal.

**pan.ther** *zo.* ['pænθə] *n.* pars, panter, puma.

pant.les F ['pæntiz] *n. pl.* kadın külotu; kısa çocuk pantolonu.

pan.tile ['pæntail] *n.* kiremit.

pan.to F [pæntəu] = pantomime.

pan.to.graph ⊕ ['pæntəugrɑːf] *n.* pantograf.

pan.to.mime ['pæntəmaim] *n.* pandomima; pan.to.mim.ic [~'mimik] *adj.* (~ally) pandomima kabilinden.

pan.try ['pæntri] *n.* kiler; sofra takımının muhafaza edildiği yer; *(otel, gemi vs.)* soğuk yemeklerin hazırlandığı yer.

pants [pænts] *n. pl.* pantolon; † don, külot.

pant.y [pænti] hose *n.* külotlu çorap.

pap [pæp] *n.* lapa *veya* sulu yemek *(çocuklar veya hastalar için).*

pa.pa [pə'pɑː] *n.* baba *(çocuk dilinde).*

pa.pa.cy ['peipəsi] *n.* papalık (sistemi).

pa.pal □ ['peipəl] papa *veya* papalığa ait.

pa.per ['peipə] 1. *n.* kâğıt; gazete; *a.* ~ money kâğıt para, banknot; *sl.* paso; hüviyet kartı, kimlik belgesi; imtihan soruları; makale, yazı; duvar kâğıdı; ~s *pl.* evrak; send in one's ~s istifa etm.; 2. *v/t.* duvar kâğıdı ile kaplamak, kâğıtlamak; '~.back *n.* karton kapaklı kitap; ~ bag kesekâğıdı; '~.chase *n.* tavşan tazı oyunu; '~.clip *n.* raptiye; ~ cred.it † vadeli senet; '~.fast.en.er *n.* tel raptiye, ataş; '~.hang.er *n.* duvar kâğıdı yapıştıran kimse; '~.hang.ings *n. pl.* duvar kâğıdı yapıştırma; '~.mill *n.* kâğıt fabrikası; '~.weight *n.* uçmasını önlemek için kâğıt üzerine konan ağırlık, prespapye; 'pa.per.y *adj.* kâğıt gibi, ince.

pa.pier mâ.ché ['pæpjei'mɑːʃei] *n.* kartonpiyer.,

pa.pist *contp.* ['peipist] *n.* katolik.

pap.py ['pæpi] *n.* baba.

pap.ri.ka ['pæprikə] *n.* kırmızı biber.

pa.py.rus [pə'paiərəs] *n.* papirüs; papirüs üzerine yazılmış yazı.

par [pɑː] *n.* † itibari kıymet, nominal değer; eşitlik, parite; above (below) ~ itibari kıymetten *(veya* pariteden) fazla (düşük); at ~ paritede, başabaş; be on a ~ with ...ile eşit derece *veya* kıymette olm.

par.a.ble ['pærəbl] *n.* mesel, ibret alınacak öykü.

pa.rab.o.la Å [pə'ræbələ] *n.* parabol; par.a.bol.ic, par.a.bol.i.cal □ [pærə'bɔlik(əl)] benzetme *veya* kıyas yoluyla ifade edilen; Å parabolik.

par.a.chute ['pærəʃuːt] *n.* paraşüt; 'par.a-

chut.ist *n.* paraşütçü.

pa.rade [pə'reid] 1. *n.* ✕ geçit resmi, tören; gösteri, nümayiş; tören alanı; mesire yeri; *eccl.* dini alay; make a ~ of s.th. *bşle* hava atmak; 2. *v/t. & v/i.* ✕ sıraya diz(il)mek; ✕ saflar halinde yürü(t)mek; gösteriş yapmak; kibirle göstermek; pa'rade-ground *n.* ✕ tören alanı.

par.a.digm *gr.* ['pærədaim] *n.* çekim listesi.

par.a.dise ['pærədais] *n.* cennet; cennet bahçesi; cennet gibi yer; büyük mutluluk.

par.a.dis.i.ac [pærə'disiæk] *adj.* cennete ait, cennet gibi, cennet...

par.a.dox ['pærədɔks] *n.* paradoks, kökleşmiş düşüncelere aykırı olarak ileri sürülen düşünce; par.a'dox.i.cal □ mantığa aykırı görünen.

par.af.fin ⚗ ['pærəfin] *n.* mum, parafin; gazyağı.

par.a.gon ['pærəgən] *n.* fazilet örneği.

par.a.graph ['pærəgrɑːf] *n.* satırbaşı; paragraf, bent, fıkra; paragraf işareti.

par.a.keet *orn.* ['pærəkiːt] *n.* muhabbetkuşu, bir çeşit ufak papağan.

par.al.lel ['pærəlel] 1. *adj.* paralel, koşut; *fig.* aynı, benzer; 2. *n.* paralel doğru; *fig.* benzerlik; karşılaştırma, mukayese; ⚡ paralel bağlantı; without (a) ~ emsalsiz, eşsiz; 3. *v/t.* kıyaslamak, karşılaştırmak; paralel olm. -e; benzer olm. -e; ~ bars *pl.* spor: barfiks; 'par.al.lel.ism *n.* paralellik; benzerlik; par.al'lel.o.gram Å [~'lougræm] *n.* paralelkenar, paralelogram.

par.a.lyse ['pærəlaiz] *v/t.* felce uğratmak; *fig.* etkisiz bırakmak; pa.ral.y.sis ⚕ [pə'rælisis] *n.* felç, inme; par.a.lyt.ic [pærə'litik] 1. *adj.* (~ally) felçli, inmeli, kötürüm; 2. *n.* felçli kimse.

par.a.mil.i.tar.y ['pærə'militəri] *adj.* yarı askeri.

par.a.mount ['pærəmaunt] *adj.* üstün, en önemli, fevkalâde.

par.a.mour *rhet.* ['pærəmuə] *n.* gayri meşru karı *veya* koca, metres.

par.a.pet ['pærəpit] *n.* ✕ siper; korkuluk duvarı.

par.a.pher.na.li.a [pærəfə'neiljə] *n. pl.* özel eşya; F teçhizat, takım taklavat.

par.a.phrase ['pærəfreiz] 1. *n.* başka kelimelerle açıklama; 2. *v/t.* başka kelimelerle açıklamak.

par.a.site ['pærəsait] *n.* parazit, asalak *(a. fig.);* par.a.sit.ic, par.a.sit.i.cal □ [~'sitik-(əl)] asalak olarak yaşayan, parazit..., asalak...

**par.a.sol** [ˈpærəˌsɔl] *n.* güneş şemsiyesi, güneşlik.

**par.a.troop.er** [ˈpærətruːpə] *n.* ✕ paraşütçü; **ˈpar.a.troops** *n. pl.* paraşütçü kıtası.

**par.a.ty.phoid** ⚕ [ˈpærəˈtaifɔid] *n.* paratifo.

**par.boil** [ˈpɑːbɔil] *v/t.* yarı kaynatmak; *fig.* kavurmak.

**par.cel** [ˈpɑːsl] 1. *n.* paket, koli, bohça, çıkın; ⁎ parça, kısım, parsel; *contp.* küme, yığın; 2. *v/t.* ~ out bölme, taksim etm.; parsellemek *(arazi)*; ~ post paket postası.

**parch** [pɑːtʃ] *v/t. & v/i.* kavurup kurutmak, kavurmak, yakmak *(güneş)*; kavrulmak, kurumak; ~ing heat kavurucu sıcak

**parch.ment** [ˈpɑːtʃmənt] *n.* parşömen (kâğıdı), tirşe.

**pard** *sl.* [pɑːd] *n.* arkadaş, dost.

**par.don** [ˈpɑːdn] 1. *n.* af, bağışlama; ♫ özel af; *eccl.* günah çıkarma; I beg your ~! affedersiniz!; 2. *v/t.* affetmek, bağışlamak (s.o. *b-ni*; s.th. *bş için)*; **ˈpar.don.a.ble** □ affolunabilir, bağışlanabilir; **ˈpar.don.er** *n. hist.* Orta Çağda günahların affını satmaya yetkili kimse.

**pare** [pɛə] *v/t.* yontmak; *-in* kabuğunu soymak; ~ away, ~ down *fig.* azaltmak, kısmak *(masraf)*.

**par.ent** [ˈpɛərənt] *n.* baba; anne; ata, cet; *fig.* sebep, neden, kaynak; ~s *pl.* ana baba, ebeveyn; *attr. fig.* anne...; asıl...; **ˈpar.en.tage** *n.* soy, nesil, ebeveynlik; **pa.ren.tal** □ [pəˈrentl] ana babaya ait, ana baba...

**pa.ren.the.sis** [pəˈrenθisis] *n., pl.* **pa.ren.the.ses** [~siːz] parantez, ayraç; parantez cümlesi; *typ.* parantez işareti; **par.en.the.tic**, **par.en.thet.i.cal** □ [pærənˈθetik(əl)] parantez gibi; parantez...

**par.ent.hood** [ˈpɛərənthud] *n.* analık *veya* babalık; **ˈpar.ent.less** *adj.* anasız babasız.

**pa.ri.ah** [ˈpæriə] *n.* parya; *fig.* toplum dışı bırakılmış kimse.

**pa.ri.e.tal** [pəˈraiitl] *adj.* parietal...; ~ bone *anat.* kafatasının yan kemiği.

**par.ing** [ˈpɛəriŋ] *n.* kabuğunu soyma; soyulmuş kabuk; ~s *pl.* kabuk parçaları, kırpıntı; **ˈ~knife** *n.* ⊕ soyma bıçağı.

**par.ish** [ˈpæriʃ] *n.* cemaat; bir papazın idaresindeki bölge; go on the ~ kilise yardımıyla geçinmek; *attr.* kilise...; papaz...; ~ clerk kilise kâtibi; papaz muavini; ~ council kilise meclisi; ~ register kilise defteri; **pa.rish.ion.er** [pəˈriʃənə] *n.* kilise cemiyeti üyesi.

**Pa.ri.sian** [pəˈrizjən] 1. *adj.* Paris'e ait,

Paris...; 2. *n.* Parisli.

**par.i.ty** [ˈpæriti] *n.* eşitlik; *borsa:* fiyat birliği, değer eşitliği, parite.

**park** [pɑːk] 1. *n.* park; ✕ savaş gereçlerinin saklandığı yer; *mst* car-~ otopark; 2. *v/t. mot.* park etm.; F koymak, yerleştirmek.

**par.ka** [ˈpɑːkə] *n.* parka, anorak.

**park.ing** *mot.* [ˈpɑːkiŋ] *n.* park yapma; ~ lot araba park yeri; ~ me.ter otopark sayacı.

**par.ky** *sl.* [ˈpɑːki] *adj.* soğuk, buz gibi *(hava)*.

**par.lance** [ˈpɑːləns] *n.* konuşma şekli; tabir, deyiş, deyim.

**par.ley** [ˈpɑːli] 1. *n. (esp. düşman ile yapılan)* toplantı, görüşme; 2. *v/i.* barış görüşmeleri yapmak; *v/t.* müzakere etm.

**par.lia.ment** [ˈpɑːləmənt] *n.* parlamento, millet meclisi; **par.lia.men.tar.i.an** [~menˈtɛəriən] *n.* parlamenter; **par.lia.men.ta.ry** □ [~ˈmentəri] parlamentoya ait, parlamento...

**par.lo(u)r** [ˈpɑːlə] *n.* oturma odası, salon; makam; *beauty* ~ *part. Am.* güzellik salonu; ~ car 🚍 *Am.* lüks vagon; **ˈ~maid** *n.* sofra hizmetçisi kız.

**pa.ro.chi.al** □ [pəˈroukjəl] cemaate ait, cemaat...; *fig.* dar, sınırlı; ~ politics *pl.* dargörüşlülük siyaseti.

**par.o.dist** [ˈpærədist] *n.* hezel *(veya* parodi) yazarı; **ˈpar.o.dy** 1. *n.* parodi, edebi bir eserin gülünç biçimde taklidi; 2. *v/t.* gülünç biçimde taklit etm.

**pa.role** [pəˈroul] 1. *n.* ✕ parola, şeref sözü; mahkûmu şartlı olarak serbest bırakma; put on ~ = 3; 2. *adj.* ♫ sözlü, şifahi; 3. *v/t.* ♫ *part. Am.* şartlı olarak serbest bırakmak.

**par.ox.ysm** [ˈpærəksizəm] *n.* ani kriz *veya* boşalma.

**par.quet** [ˈpɑːkei] *n.* parke; *Am. thea.* orkestranın olduğu yer ile parter arasındaki kısım; **par.quet.ed** [ˈpɑːkitid] *adj.* parke...; **ˈpar.quet.ry** *n.* parke (döşeme).

**par.ri.cide** [ˈpærisaid] *n.* ana baba katili; kendi ana babasını öldürme.

**par.rot** [ˈpærət] 1. *n. orn.* papağan *(a. fig.)*; 2. *v/t.* papağan gibi tekrarla(t)mak.

**par.ry** *fenc.* [ˈpæri] 1. *n.* savuşturma, bertaraf etme *(darbe)*; 2. *v/t.* bertaraf etm. *(darbe)*; *fig.* kaçamak cevaplamak.

**parse** [pɑːz] *v/t.* dilbilgisi yönünden incelemek *(kelime, cümle)*.

**Par.see** [pɑːˈsi] *n.* Zerdüşt.

**par.si.mo.ni.ous** □ [pɑːsiˈmounjəs] aşırı tutumlu; *b.s.* cimri, pinti; **par.si.mo.ni-**

ous.ness, par.si.mo.ny [¹⁓məni] n. cimrilik, pintilik.

pars.ley ⁴ [¹pɑːsli] n. maydanoz.

pars.nip ⁴ [¹pɑːsnip] n. yabanî havuç.

par.son [¹pɑːsn] n. rahip, vaiz, papaz; ¹par.son.age n. papaz evi.

part [pɑːt] 1. n. parça, bölüm, kısım; thea. rol; ♪ fasıl, parti; ⁓s pl. bölge, semt; görev. vazife; katkı; taraf; pay, hisse; yedek parça; bşin esas kısmı; ⁓ of speech gr. sözbölüğü; ⁓ and parcel of -in esas kısmı; a man of ⁓s yetenekli (veya çok yönlü) adam; have neither ⁓ nor lot in hiç bir kârı olmamak; in foreign ⁓s dış ülkelerde; play a ⁓ fig. rol oynamak; take a ⁓ in s.th. katılmak -e. iştirak etm. -e; take in good (bad) ⁓ bşi iyi (kötü) yönünden almak; for my (own) ⁓ bence, bana kalırsa, kanımca; for the most ⁓ çoğunlukla, ekseriya; in ⁓ kısmen; do one's ⁓ kendine düşeni yapmak; on the ⁓ of ...nin tarafından; oh my ⁓ benim tarafımdan; 2. adv. kısmen; 3. v/t. (parçalara) ayırmak, bölmek, taksim etm.; ⁓ company ayrılmak, bırakmak, terketmek (with -den, -i); v/i. ayrılmak (from -den); ⁓ with bırakmak -i, ayrılmak -den.

par.take [pɑː¹teik] (irr. take) v/i. katılmak, iştirak etm. (in veya of s.th. bşe); ⁓ of ...niteliğinde olm.; yemeğe buyurmak; par¹tak.er n. iştirak eden, katılan kimse (of -e).

par.terre [pɑː¹tɛə] n. çiçek bahçesi; thea. parter.

Par.thian [¹pɑːθjən] adj. Partiya'ya veya Partlılara ait.

par.tial □ [¹pɑːʃl] eksik, tam olmayan; taraflı, taraf tutan; kısmî; düşkün (to -e); par.ti.al.i.ty [pɑːʃi¹æliti] n. tarafgirlik, taraf tutma; beğenme, düşkünlük (to, for -i, -e).

par.tic.i.pant [pɑː¹tisipənt] n. katılan kimse, iştirakçi; par¹tic.i.pate [⁓peit] v/i. katılmak, iştirak etm., ortak olm. (in -e); par.tic.i¹pa.tion n. katılma, iştirak; par.ti.cip.i.al [⁓¹sipiəl] gr. ortaç kabilinden; par.ti.ci.ple [¹⁓sipl] n. gr. ortaç, sıfat-fiil.

par.ti.cle [¹pɑːtikl] n. cüz, zerre, tanecik; fig. azıcık şey; gr. edat, takı, ek.

par.ti-col.oured [¹pɑːtikʌləd] adj. rengârenk, alaca.

par.tic.u.lar [pə¹tikjulə] 1. □ mst belirli, muayyen; özel, hususî, has, mahsus; şahsî, kişisel; dikkate lâyık; ayrıntılı, etraflı, detaylı; titiz, müşkülpesent (in, about, as to hususunda); 2. n. madde,

husus; ⁓s pl. ayrıntılar, detay; in ⁓ özellikle, bilhassa; par.tic.u.lar.i.ty [⁓¹læriti] n. özellik, hususiyet; titizlik; par¹tic.u.lar.ize [⁓ləraiz] v/t. ayrı ayrı söylemek; ayrıntıları ile anlatmak; v/i. ayrıntılara girmek; par¹tic.u.lar.ly adv. özellikle, bilhassa.

part.ing [¹pɑːtiŋ] 1. n. ayrılma; veda etme; saçı ayırma çizgisi; ⁓ of the ways part. fig. iki şıktan birini seçme; 2. adj. ayıran..., bölen...; ayrılırken yapılan...

par.ti.san [pɑː¹ti¹zæn] 1. n. taraftar, partizan; ✕ gerillacı, çeteci; 2. adj. partizanla ilgili, partizan...; par.ti¹san.ship n. partizanlık, taraftarlık.

par.ti.tion [pɑː¹tiʃən] 1. n. taksim; bölme, duvar, tahta perde; bölünme, ayrılma; ⁓ wall bölme duvar; 2. v/t. ⁓ off taksim etm., bölmek, ayırmak.

par.ti.tive □ [¹pɑːtitiv] kısımlara ayıran; bir bütünün parçasını belirten (kelime).

part.ly [¹pɑːtli] adv. kısmen, bir dereceye kadar.

part.ner [¹pɑːtnə] 1. n. eş, karı veya koca; dans (veya oyun) arkadaşı; ✝ ortak; 2. v/t. ortak etm.; v/i. ortak gibi davranmak; ortak olm.; ¹part.ner.ship n. ✝ ortaklık; enter into ⁓ with ...ile ortak olm.

part...: ¹⁓-own.er n. hissedar; ¹⁓-pay.ment n. kısmen ödeme; taksit; avans; kapa-ro.

par.tridge orn. [¹pɑːtridʒ] n. keklik.

part...: ¹⁓-song n. birkaç sesle söylenen şarkı; ¹⁓-time 1. adj. yarım günlük...; 2. adv. yarım gün olarak.

par.ty [¹pɑːti] n. grup; parti, toplantı, şölen, ziyafet, eğlence; pol. siyasal parti; ⚠ taraf; ✕ birlik; co. kimse, şahıs; s. line¹ 1.

par.ve.nu [¹pɑːvənjuː] n. sonradan görme kimse, türedi.

pas.chal [¹pɑːskəl] adj. Musevilerin Fısıh bayramına ait; paskalyaya ait.

pa.sha [¹pɑːʃə] n. paşa.

pass [pɑːs] 1. n. geçiş, geçme; paso, şebeke; futbol: pas; univ. sınavda geçme; hokkabazların kaybetme oyunu; fenc. hamle; boğaz, geçit; iskambil: pas; pasaport; hal, durum; sl. kur, flört; free ⁓ parasız giriş kartı; hold the ⁓ fig. bir fikri savunmak; 2. v/i. ileri gitmek, ilerlemek; gitmek, ayrılmak; geçmek (zaman); dönüşmek; karar vermek, hüküm vermek; intikal etm., miras kalmak; olmak, meydana gelmek; kabul edilmek; fenc. hamle yapmak; futbol: pas vermek, paslaşmak; iskambil: pas demek;

bitmek, sona ermek; sayılmak (as, for *olarak*); *a.* ~ away ölmek, vefat etm.; geçmek: ~ for ...olarak sayılmak, ...gözüyle bakılmak; ~ off bitmek, sona ermek; geçmek *(ağrı)*; meydana gelmek, olmak; ~ out F bayılmak, kendinden geçmek; come to ~ olmak, meydana gelmek; bring to ~ sonuçlandırmak; **3.** *v/t.* geçmek, aşmak; geçirmek, atlatmak; geçirmek *(zaman)*; kabul ve tasdik ettirmek; devretmek *(hak)*; tedavüle çıkarmak, sürmek *(para)*; vermek, uzatmak; gezdirmek, dolaştırmak; bildirmek, söylemek, açıklamak *(fikir, karar)*; boşaltmak, dışarı atmak; vurmak *(topa)*; ~ s.o. (s.th.) by *b-ni (bşi)* önemsememek; ~ off görmemezlikten gelmek, geçiştirmek, çevirmek *(dikkatini)*; ~ o.s. (s.th.) off as *k-ne* ...süsü vermek, *k-ni* ...diye satmak, ...tavrı takınmak; ~ over göz yummak, görmezlikten gelmek, ihmal etm.; it ~es my comprehension ona benim aklım ermiyor; ~ one's hand across one's forehead eliyle alnını silmek; ~ water işemek; ~ one's word söz vermek; **'pass.a.ble** □ geçilebilir, geçit verir *(yol)*; oldukça iyi, kabul edilir, geçerli.

**pas.sage** [ˈpæsidʒ] *n.* geçme, gitme; yol; geçit, boğaz; yolculuk, seyahat; pasaj; koridor, dehliz; bent, parça, paragraf, fıkra; tasarının kabul edilip kanunlaşması; ~s *pl.* tanışıklık, karşılıklı güven; ♪ geçiş; geçiş hakkı *(veya* ücreti); ~ of *veya* at arms mücadele, kavga, çekişme; bird of ~ göçmen kuş; **'~.way** *n.* pasaj, geçit; koridor.

**pass-book** ⸸ [ˈpɑːsbuk] *n.* hesap cüzdanı.

**pas.sé(e)** [ˈpɑːsei] *adj.* geçmiş, eski; modası geçmiş, demode.

**pas.sen.ger** [ˈpæsindʒə] *n.* yolcu, seyyah, gezgin.

**passe-par.tout** [ˈpæspɑːtuː] *n.* ana anahtar.

**pass.er-by**, *pl.* **pass.ers-by** [ˈpɑːsə(z)ˈbai] *n.* yoldan gelip geçen kimse.

**pas.sim** [ˈpæsim] *adv.* çeşitli yerlerde *(kitapta)*; sık sık.

**pass.ing** [ˈpɑːsiŋ] **1.** *n.* geçiş, gitme; göçme, ölüm; in ~ antrparantez, sırası gelmişken; geçerken; **2.** *adj.* geçen, geçici; rastgele, tesadüfi; olup biten; **'~-bell** *n.* matem canı.

**pas.sion** [ˈpæʃən] *n.* hırs, ihtiras, tutku; ask, cinsel istek, şehvet; hiddet, öfke; ıstırap, elem; aşırı heves; ♀ Hz. İsa'nın çarmıha gerilmesinde çektiği acı; be in a ~ son derece öfkelenmek; in ~ şid-

detli ve ani heyecan anında;; ♀ Week paskalyadan bir önceki hafta; **pas.sion.ate** □ [ˈ~ʃənit] heyecanlı, ateşli, şiddetli, hararetli; hiddetli; kara sevdalı; **'pas.sion-flow.er** *n.* ♀ çarkıfelek; **'pas.sion-less** □ soğukkanlı, heyecansız; **'pas.sion-play** *n.* Hz. İsa'nın çarmıha gerilmesini canlandıran piyes.

**pas.sive** □ [ˈpæsiv] pasif, hareketsiz, ilgisiz, uysal, eylemsiz, faaliyetsiz; *gr.* edilgen; **'pas.sive.ness, pas'siv.i.ty** *n.* pasiflik, ilgisizlik, uysallık; dirençsizlik.

**pass-key** [ˈpɑːskiː] *n.* ana anahtar; kapı anahtarı.

**Pass.o.ver** [ˈpɑːsəuvə] *n.* Musevilerin Fısıh bayramı.

**pass.port** [ˈpɑːspɔːt] *n.* pasaport.

**pass.word** ✕ [ˈpɑːswəːd] *n.* parola.

**past** [pɑːst] **1.** *adj.* geçmiş, geçen, bitmiş, olmuş, sabık; *gr.* geçmiş zaman...; ~ master usta kimse, erbap; for some time ~ bir süreden beri; **2.** *adv.* geçecek şekilde, -in yanından geçerek; rush ~ fırlayıp yanından geçmek; **3.** *prp.* -den daha ilerde *veya* ileriye; ötesinde; half ~ two iki buçuk; it is ~ comprehension akıl almaz; ~ cure tedavi edilemez; ~ endurance tahammül edilemez, dayanılmaz; ~ hope ümitsiz; **4.** *n.* geçmiş zaman; bir kimsenin geçmişi.

**paste** [peist] **1.** *n.* macun; çiriş, kola; hamur; lapa; elmas taklidi cam; **2.** *v/t.* (kola ile) yapıştırmak; **'~.board** *n.* mukavva; *sl.* kartvizit; iskambil kâğıdı; bilet; *attr.* mukavva...

**pas.tel** [pæsˈtel] *n.* *paint.* pastel kalemi (ile yapılmış resim); pastel renk; **pas.tel.(l)ist** [ˈ~təlist] *n.* pastel resim yapan kimse.

**pas.tern** *vet.* [ˈpæstəːn] *n.* atın ayağına bukağı takılan yer.

**pas.teur.ize** [ˈpæstʃəraiz] *v/t.* pastörize etm.

**pas.tille** [pæsˈtəl] *n.* pastil.

**pas.time** [ˈpɑːstaim] *n.* eğlence, oyun, meşgale.

**pas.tor** [ˈpɑːstə] *n.* papaz; **'pas.to.ral 1.** □ doğa güzelliklerini anlatan, pastoral...; papazlığa ait, papazlık...; ~ staff papazlık asası; **2.** *n.* idil; *paint.* pastoral resim; *eccl.* papazın kendi bölgesindeki kilise görevlilerine yazdığı resmî mektup.

**pas.try** [ˈpeistri] *n.* hamur işi, pasta; **'~-cook** *n.* pastacı.

**pas.tur.age** [ˈpɑːstjuridʒ] *n.* ot; otlak; otlatma hakkı.

**pas.ture** [ˈpɑːstʃə] **1.** *n.* çayır, otlak, mera; ~ ground otlak; **2.** *v/t.* & *v/i.* çayırda otla(t)mak.

**past.y 1.** [ˈpeisti] *adj.* hamur gibi; solgun; **2.** [ˈpæsti] *n.* etli börek.

**pat** [pæt] **1.** *n.* el ile hafif vuruş; 'pat' sesi; ufak kalıp *(tereyağ)*; **2.** *v/t.* hafifçe vurmak *-e*; *v/i.* hafif adımlarla koşmak; **3.** *adv.* hemen, anında, tam vaktinde; stand ~ alışkanlığını bozmamak; kararından dönmemek.

**patch** [pætʃ] **1.** *n.* yama; ⚕ yakı; ⚕ göz sargısı; benek, ben, leke; arazi parçası; strike a bad ~ şanssızlığa uğramak; ~ pocket yama cep; **2.** *v/t.* yamamak, yamalamak, yama vurmak; ~ up tamir etm.; *fig.* halletmek, yoluna koymak.

**patch.work** [ˈpætʃwəːk] *n.* yama işi; *fig.* uydurma iş; **ˈpatch.y** *adj.* yamalı; derme çatma yapılmış, uydurma; düzensiz.

**pate** F [peit] *n.* baş, kafa, kelle; beyin, akıl.

**pat.ent** [ˈpeitənt] **1.** *adj.* belli, açık, aşikâr, apaçık, meydanda olan...; patent almış, patentli...; letters ~ [ˈpætənt] *pl.* patent; ~ article patentli mal, tescilli mal; ~ leather güderi; **2.** *n.* patent, imtiyaz; patentli mal; ~ agent patent işleri uzmanı; ~ office patent dairesi; **3.** *v/t.* -*in* patentini almak; **pat.ent.ee** [peitənˈtiː] *n.* patent sahibi.

**pa.ter.nal** □ [pəˈtəːnl] babaya ait, babaya yakışır, baba...; babadan kalma; **paˈter.ni.ty** *n.* babalık; kaynak, köken.

**path** [paːθ] *n.*, *pl.* **paths** [paːðz] keçi yolu, patika; takip edilen yol, davranış; *spor:* pist.

**pa.thet.ic** [pəˈθetik] *adj.* (~ally) acıklı, dokunaklı, etkileyici, üzücü.

**path.less** [ˈpaːθlis] *adj.* patikasız, yolsuz.

**path.o.log.i.cal** □ [pæθəˈlɔdʒikəl] patolojik; **pa.thol.o.gy** [pəˈθɔlədʒi] *n.* patoloji, hastalıklar bilimi.

**pa.thos** [ˈpeiθɔs] *n.* merhamet ve sempati hissi uyandırma gücü.

**path.way** [ˈpaːθwei] *n.* patika.

**path.y** *Am.* ⚕ *contp.* [pæθi] *n.* tedavi.

**pa.tience** [ˈpeiʃəns] *n.* sabır, tahammül, dayanma; dişini sıkma; tek başına oynanılan iskambil oyunu; be out of ~ with, have no ~ with sabrı tükenmek; **ˈpa.tient 1.** □ sabırlı, tahammüllü, dayanıklı; be ~ of sabırlı olm. -*e karşı*; *fig.* bşe göz yummak; **2.** *n.* hasta.

**pa.ti.o** *Am.* [ˈpætiəu] *n.* avlu, teras, veranda.

**pa.tri.arch** [ˈpeitriaːk] *n.* patrik; yaşlı ve saygıdeğer adam; bir aile *veya* kabilenin başı; **pa.triˈar.chal** □ patriğe ait;

saygıdeğer.

**pa.tri.cian** [pəˈtriʃən] **1.** *adj.* soylulara ait, soylu...; **2.** *n.* soylu kimse, asılzade.

**pat.ri.mo.ny** [ˈpætriməni] *n.* babadan kalan miras; kilise vakfı.

**pa.tri.ot** [ˈpætriət] *n.* vatanperver *(veya* yurtsever) kimse; **pa.tri.ot.eer** [~əˈtiə] *n.* şoven, aşırı milliyetçi kimse; **pa.tri.ot.ic** [~ˈɔtik] *adj.* (~ally) yurtsever, vatanperver; **pa.tri.ot.ism** [ˈ~ətizəm] *n.* yurtseverlik, vatanperverlik.

**pa.trol** ✕ [pəˈtrəul] **1.** *n.* devriye, karakol; keşif kolu; devriye gezme; ~ wagon *Am.* polis devriye arabası; **2.** *v/i.* devriye gezmek; **~.man** [pəˈtrəulmən] *n.* (devriye) polis.

**pa.tron** [ˈpeitrən] *n.* veli, hami; patron, efendi; daimi müşteri, velinimet; **pa.tron.age** [ˈpætrənidʒ] *n.* himaye, koruma; *b-ni* göreve atama hakkı; müşteriler; hor görme; iş, ticaret; **pa.tron.ess** [ˈpeitrənis] *n.* koruyan azize *vs.* (*s.* patron); **pa.tron.ize** [ˈpætrənaiz] *v/t.* korumak, himaye etm.; kanatları altına almak; hor görmek; müşterisi olm.; **ˈpa.tron.iz.er** *n.* koruyucu, hami.

**pat.ter** [ˈpætə] *v/t.* & *v/i.* hızlı hızlı konuşmak; pıtırdamak; kısa ve süratli adımlarla yürümek; mırıldar gibi söylemek; **2.** *n.* konuşma tarzı; çok hızlı söylenen şarkı; pıtırtı, ses.

**pat.tern** [ˈpætən] **1.** *n.* model, örnek *(a. fig)*; numune, mostra; elbiselik kumaş; motif, süs; şablon; döküm kalıbı; elbise patronu; *fig.* şekil, düzen; by ~ post kıymetsiz numune; **2.** *v/t.* örneğe göre yapmak; örnek almak; motiflerle süslemek; 'ˈ~.mak.er *n.* ⊕ modelci.

**pat.ty** [ˈpæti] *n.* küçük börek.

**pau.ci.ty** [ˈpɔːsiti] *n.* azlık, kıtlık, yetersizlik.

**Paul.ine** [ˈpɔːlain] *adj.* apostol Paul'e ait.

**paunch** [pɔːntʃ] *n.* göbek; **ˈpaunch.y** *adj.* göbekli, şişko.

**pau.per** [ˈpɔːpə] *n.* sadaka ile geçinen fakir kimse, yoksul; *attr.* fakir, yoksul...; **ˈpau.per.ism** *n.* fakirlik, yoksulluk; **ˈpau.per.ize** *v/t.* sadakaya muhtaç hale getirmek, fakirleştirmek.

**pause** [pɔːz] **1.** *n.* ara(lık), fasıla, mola, teneffüs; durma; ♪ notanın üzerine *veya* altına konan uzatma işareti: give ~ to s.o. *b-ni* düşündürmek, tereddütte bırakmak; **2.** *v/i.* durmak, duraklamak; tereddüt etm., duraksamak (upon *hususunda*).

**pave** [peiv] *v/t.* kaldırım döşemek; *fig.* yolu açmak; **ˈpave.ment** *n.* kaldırım; ~

artist kaldırım ressamı.

**pa.vil.ion** [pə'viljən] *n.* büyük çadır; müzikhol; pavyon; köşk.

**pav.ing-stone** ['peiviŋstəun] *n.* kaldırım taşı.

**paw** [pɔ:] **1.** *n.* pençe; *co.* el; **2.** *v/t.* & *v/i.* pençelemek; ön ayaklarıyla eşelemek *(at)*; F kabaca ellemek; pençe atmak.

**pawn**[1] [pɔ:n] *n.* satranç: piyon, piyade, paytak; *fig.* maşa, bir işe alet edilen kimse, kukla.

**pawn**[2] [~] **1.** *n.* rehin; rehine koyma; in ~, at ~ rehinde; **2.** *v/t.* rehine koymak; *fig.* tehlikeye atmak; '~.bro.ker *n.* rehinci, tefeci; **pawn**[1]**ee** *n.* rehinli alacaklı, rehinle borç veren kimse; '**pawn.er** *n.* malını rehine veren kimse; '**pawn.shop** *n.* rehinci dükkânı; '**pawn-tick.et** *n.* rehin makbuzu.

**pay** [pei] **1.** *n.* maaş, ücret; ödeme; bedel, karşılık; *fig.* mükâfat; **2.** *(irr.) v/t.* ödemek, tediye etm.; karşılığını vermek; etmek; yarar sağlamak; getirmek *(kâr)*; ~ attention *veya* heed to dikkat etm. *-e*; ~ away, ~ out ↓ kaloma etm. *(halat, zincir)*; ~ down peşin ödemek; ~ off tamamen ödemek *(borç)*; ücretini verip kovmak; ~ s.o. out for s.th. misliyle mukabele etm., başın acısını b-den çıkarmak, başdan dolayı b-den öc almak; ~ up tamamını ödemek, kapatmak *(borç)*; ~ one's way borca girmemek; put paid to s.th. F halletmek, yoluna koymak; *v/i.* borcunu ödemek; masrafına *veya* çabasına değmek; ~ for bş için para vermek; *-in* cezasını çekmek; '**pay.a.ble** *adj.* ödenmesi gereken; ödenebilir; ⚒, ⊤ verimli, kârlı; '**pay-as-you-learn** *n.* gelir vergisinin gelirin kaynağından kesildiği sistem; '**pay-day** *n.* ücretlerin verildiği gün, aybaşı; **pay dirt** *Am.* içinde işletilebilecek kadar maden olan toprak; **pay**[1]**ee** *n.* ⊤ alacaklı kimse; '**pay-en.ve.lope** *n.* maaş zarfı; maaş miktarı; '**pay.er** *n.* ödeyen kimse; ⊤ muhatap, borçlu kimse; '**pay. ing** *adj.* kârlı, kazançlı, verimli; ~ concern kârlı *(veya* verimli) iş; '**pay-load** *n.* gelir getiren yük; füze içindeki bomba; uzay aracının mürettebatı *veya* teçhizatı; '**pay.mas.ter** *n.* ✕, ↓ maaş kâtibi, mutemet; '**pay.ment** *n.* ödeme, tediye; ücret maaş; *fig.* ödül; ceza; additional ~ ek ödeme; on ~ of ...ödemek üzere.

**pay...:** '~-off *n.* hesaplaşma *(a. fig.)*; *Am.* F doruk noktası; ödül, kâr; sonuç, netice; '~-of.fice *n.* kasa, gişe, vezne dairesi; '~-pack.et *n.* maaş zarfı; '~-roll *n.* ücret bordrosu; '~.station *n. Am.* umumi telefon.

**pea** 🌱 [pi:] *n.* bezelye.

**peace** [pi:s] *n.* barış, sulh; huzur, sükûn(et); asayiş; barış anlaşması; the (King's) ~ huzur, barış, asayiş; be at ~ barış halinde olm., huzur içinde olm.; break the ~ huzuru *(veya* asayişi) bozmak; keep the ~ barışı korumak, asayişi sağlamak; '**peace.a.ble** ☐ barışsever; sakin; '**peace-break.er** *n.* huzur bozucu kimse; **peace.ful** ☐ ['~ful] sakin, yumuşak başlı, uysal; barışsever; '**peace.mak.er** *n.* barıştırıcı kimse, arabulucu.

**peach**[1] [pi:tʃ] *n.* 🌱 şeftali (ağacı); şeftali rengi; *sl.* çekici kimse *veya* şey.

**peach**[2] *sl.* [~]: ~ (up)on *vb.* ihbar etm., ispiyon etm., ele vermek, gammazlamak; boşboğazlık etm.

**pea-chick** ['pi:tʃik] *n.* yavru tavus.

**peach.y** ['pi:tʃi] *adj.* şeftali gibi; *sl.* mükemmel.

**pea.cock** ['pi:kɔk] *n.* tavus; '**pea.fowl** *n.* tavus; '**pea**[1]**hen** *n.* dişi tavus.

**pea-jack.et** ↓ ['pi:dʒækit] *n.* gemici ceketi.

**peak** [pi:k] **1.** *n.* zirve, tepe, doruk; kasket siperi; *attr.* zirve..., tepe...; ~ hour sıkışık saat *(trafik)*; ~ load azamî yük; ~ power *etc.* azamî güç *vs.*; **2.** *v/i.* F zayıflamak, süzülmek; doruk noktasına ulaşmak; **peaked** [pi:kt] *adj.* zayıf düşmüş, bitkin durumda; siperli; ~ cap siperli şapka; '**peak.y** *adj.* sivri tepeli; bitkin durumda.

**peal** [pi:l] **1.** *n.* gürültü; gürültülü çan sesi; çan takımı; ~s *pl.* of laughter kahkaha tufanı; **2.** *v/t.* & *v/i.* gürültülü çal(ın)mak *(çan)*; ses vermek.

**pea.nut** ['pi:nʌt] *n.* Amerikan fıstığı, yerfıstığı; *fig.* önemsiz kimse.

**pear** 🌱 [pɛə] *n.* armut (ağacı).

**pearl** [pɔ:l] **1.** *n.* inci *(a. fig.)*; inci rengi; sedef; *typ.* beş puntoluk harf; *attr.* inci...; **2.** *v/i.* inci avlamak; *v/t.* incilerle süslemek; inciye benzetmek; '**pearl.y** *adj.* inci gibi; incilerle süslenmiş.

**pear-tree** ['pɛətri:] *n.* armut ağacı.

**peas.ant** ['pezənt] *n.* köylü, rençper; *attr.* köylü...; '**peas.ant.ry** *n.* köylüler, köylü sınıfı.

**pease** [pi:z] *n. pl.* bezelye.

**pea-shoot.er** ['pi:ʃu:tə] *n.* üfleyerek bezelye atılan oyuncak boru.

**pea soup** ['pi:'su:p] *n.* bezelye çorbası; '**pea**[1]**soup.er** *n.* F koyu sis.

**peat** [pi:t] *n.* turba, çürümüş bitkilerden elde edilen yakacak; '~-bog *n.* turbalık.

**peb.ble** ['pebl] *n.* çakıl taşı; '**peb.bly** *adj.*

çakıllı, çakıl döşeli.

**pe.can** ♀ [pi'kæn] *n.* cevize benzer bir ağaç.

**pec.ca.ble** ['pekəbl] *adj.* günah işleyebilir.

**peck¹** [pek] *n.* 9,087 litrelik bir hacim ölçü birimi; *fig.* büyük miktar.

**peck²** [~] *v/t. & v/i.* gaga ile vurmak (at -*e*); az yemek yemek; ~ at one's food yemeğin iştahsızca yemek; gagalamak; gagalayarak açmak (*delik*); **'peck.er** *n. sl.* büyük burun; keep one's ~ up neşesini kaybetmemek; **'peck.ish** *adj.* F karnı aç olan, karnı zil çalan.

**pec.tin** ['pektin] *n.* pektin.

**pec.to.ral** ['pektərəl] **1.** *adj.* göğüse ait, göğüs...; göğüse takılan...; **2.** *n.* göğüse takılan süs; göğüs hastalıklarına ait ilâç.

**pec.u.late** ['pekjuleit] *v/t.* zimmetine geçirmek; **pec.u'la.tion** *n.* zimmetine geçirme; **'pec.u.la.tor** *n.* zimmetine para geçiren kimse.

**pe.cul.iar** □ [pi'kju:ljə] özel, hususî; acayip, garip, tuhaf, alışılmamış; mahsus, özgü, kendine has; **pe.cu.li.ar.i.ty** [~li'æriti] *n.* özellik, hususiyet; gariplik, acayiplik.

**pe.cu.ni.ar.y** [pi'kju:njəri] *adj.* parayla ilgili, parasal..., maddî...

**ped.a.gog.ic**, **ped.a.gog.i.cal** □ [pedə'gɔdʒik(əl)] pedagojik; **ped.a'gog.ics** *n.* pedagoji ilmi; **ped.a.gogue** ['~gɔg] *n.* pedagog; F ukalâ (*veya* işgüzar) öğretmen; **ped.a.go.gy** ['~gɔdʒi] *n.* pedagoji.

**ped.al** ['pedl] **1.** *n.* pedal; **2.** *adj.* ayağa ait, ayak...; **3.** *v/t. & v/i.* ayakla işletmek; pedal kullanmak; bisiklete binmek.

**ped.ant** ['pedənt] *n.* ukalâ kimse; **pe.dan.tic** [pi'dæntik] *adj.* (~ally) ukalâ, bilgiçlik taslayan; **ped.ant.ry** ['pedəntri] *n.* ukalâlık.

**ped.dle** ['pedl] *v/t. & v/i.* seyyar satıcılık yapmak; önemsiz şeylerle ilgilenmek; ~ azar azar satmak; **'ped.dling** *adj.* önemsiz, ufak tefek; **'ped.dler** *Am.* = pedlar.

**ped.es.tal** ['pedistl] *n.* heykel *veya* sütun tabanı, kaide; *fig.* esas, temel; **pe.des'tri.an** [pi'destriən] **1.** *adj.* yürümeye ait, yürüme...; sıkıcı, ağır; **2.** *n.* yaya; ~ crossing yaya geçidi.

**ped.i.cab** ['pedikæb] *n.* üstü kapalı, üç tekerlekli ve bisiklete benzer bir tür yolcu taşıma aracı.

**ped.i.cure** ['pedikjuə] *n.* pedikür.

**ped.i.gree** ['pedigri:] **1.** *n.* soy, nesep, şecere, soy ağacı; **2.** ~d *adj.* soyu sopu belli olan.

**ped.i.ment** ⚠ ['pedimənt] *n.* alınlık.

**ped.lar** ['pedlə] *n.* seyyar satıcı; **'ped.lar.y** *n.* seyyar satıcılık.

**pe.dom.e.ter** [pi'dɔmitə] *n.* pedometre, adımölçer.

**peek** [pi:k] **1.** *v/i.* gizlice bakmak, dikizlemek; **2.** *n.* gizlice bakma, gözetleme, dikiz; **peek.a.boo** ['pi:kəbu:] *n.* çocuklara «ce» yapılan oyun.

**peel** [pi:l] **1.** *n.* (*meyve veya sebze*) kabuk; **2.** *a.* ~ off *v/t. -in* kabuğunu soymak; çıkarmak (*elbise*); *v/i.* soyulmak (*kabuk*); *sl.* soyunmak.

**peel.er** *sl.* † ['pi:lə] *n.* polis.

**peel.ing** ['pi:lin] *n.* soyulmuş kabuk.

**peep¹** [pi:p] **1.** *n.* civciv gibi ötme; civciv sesi; **2.** *v/i.* civciv gibi ötmek, «cik cik» etm.

**peep²** [~] **1.** *n.* azıcık bakış, kaçamak (*veya gizli*) bakış; **2.** *v/i.* gizlice bakmak (at -*e*); röntgencilik etm., dikiz geçmek; *a.* ~ out yavaş yavaş ortaya çıkmak (*a. fig*); ~ at gizlice bakmak -*e*; **'peep.er** *n.* röntgenci kimse; *sl.* göz; **'peep-hole** *n.* gözetleme deliği; **'peep-show** *n.* büyüteçle küçük bir delikten seyredilen resim *vs.*

**peer¹** [piə] *v/i.* dikkatle bakmak; ~ at yakından bakmak -*e.*

**peer²** [~] *n.* eş, akran, emsal; asılzade; **'peer.age** *n.* asalet, asılzadelik; **'peer.ess** *n.* kadın asılzade; asılzade karısı; **'peer.less** □ eşsiz, emsalsiz.

**peeved** F [pi:vd] *adj.* sinirli, hırçın, huysuz.

**pee.vish** □ ['pi:viʃ] titiz, huysuz, ters, aksi, hırçın, densiz; **'pee.vish.ness** *n.* huysuzluk, aksilik, hırçınlık, densizlik.

**pee.wit** ['pi:wit] = pewit.

**peg** [peg] **1.** *n.* ağaç çivi; askı, kanca; küçük kazık; ♪ yaylı çalgılarda akort anahtarı; *fig.* sebep, vesile, bahane; sodalı viski *veya* konyak; F tahta bacak; take s.o. down a ~ or two *b-ni* küçük düşürmek; be a square ~ in a round hole yeteneklerine uygun işte olmamak, bulunduğu mevkiye yakışmamak; **2.** *vb.* ağaç çivi ile mıhlamak; asmak (*çamaşır*); kısıtlamak, sınırlamak; † -*de* istikrar sağlamak; *a.* ~ out çiviler çakarak işaretlemek; fırlatmak, atmak; *a* ~ away, ~ along F istikrarlı bir şekilde çalışmak; koşuşturmak; ~ out *sl.* ölmek, gebermek.

**peg-top** ['pegtɔp] *n.* topaç.

**peign.oir** ['peinwa:] *n.* sabahlık.

**pe.jo.ra.tive** ['pi:dʒərətiv, pi'dʒɔrətiv] *adj.* küçük düşürücü, alçaltıcı.

**pelf** *contp.* [pelf] *n.* para, servet.

**pel.i.can** *orn.* [ˈpelikən] *n.* pelikan, kaşıkçıkuşu.

**pel.let** [ˈpelit] *n.* küçük topak; ufak kurşun, saçma; hap.

**pel.li.cle** [ˈpelikl] *n.* ince zar.

**pell-mell** [ˈpelˈmel] 1. *adv.* paldır küldür, apar topar, alelacele; karman çorman, allak bullak; 2. *n.* karmakarışıklık.

**pel.lu.cid** [peˈljuːsid] *adj.* açık seçik; yarı şeffaf.

**Pel.o.pon.ne.sian** [peləpəˈniːʃən] *adj.* Moralı, Mora'ya ait.

**pelt¹** [pelt] *n.* deri, post, kürk; † işlenmemiş deri.

**pelt²** [~] 1. *v/t.* & *v/i.* atmak, fırlatmak; taşlamak; boşanmak *(yağmur)*; koşuşturmak; 2. *n.* atma, fırlatma; boşanma *(yağmur)*; at full ~ son süratle (koşarak).

**pelt.ry** [ˈpeltri] *n.* hayvan deri *veya* postları.

**pel.vis** *anat.* [ˈpelvis] *n.* pelvis, leğen, havsala.

**pem.mi.can** [ˈpemikən] *n.* dövülüp çöreklere karıştırılan kurutulmuş et.

**pen¹** [pen] 1. *n.* yazı kalemi, tüy kalem; tükenmez kalem; dolmakalem; yazı üslubu; 2. *v/t.* mürekkepli kalemle yazmak.

**pen²** [~] 1. *n.* ağıl, kümes, kafes; ⚓ denizaltı doku; *a.* play-~ çocukların içinde oynadıkları portatif bahçe; 2. *(irr.)* *oft.* ~ up, ~ in *v/t.* kapatmak, ağıla koymak.

**pe.nal** □ [ˈpiːnl] cezaya ait, cezaî, ceza...; ~ code ceza kanunu; ~ servitude ağır hapis cezası; **pe.nal.ize** [ˈpiːnəlaiz] *v/t.* cezalandırmak *(a. fig.)*; **pen.al.ty** [ˈpenlti] *n.* ceza; *spor:* penaltı; ~ area *futbol:* ceza sahası; ~ kick penaltı atışı; under ~ of ...cezası ile.

**pen.ance** [ˈpenəns] *n.* ceza; pişmanlık; kefaret.

**pen...:** ˈ~-and-ˈink draw.ing *n.* mürekkepli kalemle çizilmiş resim.

**pence** [pens] *pl. of* penny.

**pen.cil** [ˈpensl] 1. *n.* kurşunkalem; makyaj kalemi; 2. *v/t.* kurşunkalem ile yazmak *veya* çizmek; ˈ~-sharp.en.er *n.* kalemtıraş.

**pend.ant** [ˈpendənt] *n.* asılı şey; pandantif; avize; flama.

**pend.ent** [~] *adj.* asılı, sarkık, sarkan; muallakta olan, karar verilmemiş.

**pend.ing** [ˈpendiŋ] 1. *adj.* 🌿 henüz karara bağlanmamış, askıda olan; 2. *prp.* zarfında, esnasında, -e kadar.

**pen.du.lous** [ˈpendjuləs] *adj.* sarkan, asılı, sallanan; **pen.du.lum** [ˈ~ləm] *n.* rak-

kas, sarkaç.

**pen.e.tra.bil.i.ty** [penitrəˈbiliti] *n.* içine nüfuz edilebilirlik; **ˈpen.e.trq.ble** □ delinebilir, nüfuz edilebilir; anlaşılır; **pen.e.tra.li.a** [~ˈtreiljə] *n.* bşin en iç kısmı; **pen.e.trate** [ˈ~treit] *v/t.* & *v/i.* delip girmek -*e*, -*in* içine girmek, nüfuz etm.; anlamak, idrak etm.; içeriye sızmak; **pen-eˈtra.tion** *n.* sokulma, nüfuz etme, içine işleme; etki, tesir; anlayış; **pen.eˈtra.tive** □ [ˈ~trətiv] delici, nüfuz edici *(a. fig.)*; ~ effect delme etkisi.

**pen-friend** [ˈpenfrend] *n.* mektup arkadaşı.

**pen.guin** *orn.* [ˈpeŋgwin] *n.* penguen.

**pen.hold.er** [ˈpenhəuldə] *n.* kalem sapı.

**pen.i.cil.lin** *pharm.* [peniˈsilin] *n.* penisilin.

**pen.in.su.la** [piˈninsjulə] *n.* yarımada; **penˈin.su.lar** *adj.* yarımadaya ait, yarımada...

**pen.i.tence** [ˈpenitəns] *n.* pişmanlık, tövbe; **ˈpen.i.tent** 1. □ pişman, tövbekâr; 2. *n.* tövbekâr kimse; **pen.i.ten.tial** □ [~ˈtenʃəl] pişmanlıkla ilgili; **pen.i.ten.tia.ry** [~ˈtenʃəri] *n. Am.* hapishane, cezaevi.

**pen.knife** [ˈpennaif] *n.* çakı.

**pen.man** [ˈpenmən] *n.* yazar; hattat; he is a poor ~ kötü bir elyazısı vardır; **ˈpen.man.ship** *n.* yazı yazma sanatı; hattatlık, el yazısı.

**pen-name** [ˈpenneim] *n.* yazarın takma adı.

**pen.nant** [ˈpenənt] *n.* ⚓ flama, flandra; *part. Am.* şampiyonluk forsu; *fig.* şampiyonluk.

**pen.ni.less** □ [ˈpenilis] (beş) parasız, meteliksiz, cebi delik.

**pen.non** [ˈpenən] *n.* ✗ bayrak, sancak; flama.

**pen.ny** [ˈpeni] *n.*, *pl.* **pence** [pens] pens, peni; *Am.* sent; a pretty ~ dünya kadar para; in for a ~, in for a pound ne pahasına olursa olsun bitirilmesi gerekir, battı balık yan gider; turn an honest ~ alın teri ile para kazanmak; ~ wise and pound foolish ufak şeylerde tutumlu, büyük şeylerde müsrif olan; ˈ~-a-ˈlin.er *n.* kalitesiz yazar; ˈ~-ˈdread.ful *n.* ucuz basılı tutulan polisiye roman; ˈ~.weight *n.* 1,56 gr. ağırlığında eczacı tartısı; ~.worth [ˈpenθ] *n.* bir penilik bş; a ~ of tobacco bir penilik tütün.

**pen.sion** [ˈpenʃən] 1. *n.* emekli aylığı; [ˈpäːŋsioː ŋ] pansiyon; 2. *oft.* ~ off *v/t.* emekli aylığı bağlamak; **ˈpen.sion.ar.y**, **ˈpen.sion.er** *n.* emekli (aylığı alan kimse)

**pen.sive** ☐ [ˈpensiv] dalgın, düşünceli, endişeli, kara kara düşünen; **ˈpen.sive.ness** n. dalgınlık, kara kara düşünme.

**pent** [pent] pret. & p.p. of pen² 2; ˈ~ˈup adj. bastırılmış; kapatılmış, hapsedilmiş.

**pen.ta.gon** [ˈpentəgən] n. beşgen; the ☉ Am. Milli Savunma Bakanlığı (binası); **pen.tag.o.nal** [~ˈtægənl] adj. beş köşeli, beşgen biçiminde.

**pen.tath.lon** [penˈtæθlɔn] n. spor: pentatlon.

**Pen.te.cost** [ˈpentikɔst] n. Şavuot; Hıristiyanların Hamsin yortusu; **pen.teˈcos.tal** adj. bu yortuya ait.

**pent.house** [ˈpenthaus] n. çatı katı, çekme kat.

**pe.num.bra** [piˈnʌmbrə] n. yarı gölge, yarı karanlık.

**pe.nu.ri.ous** ☐ [piˈnjuəriəs] fakir, yoksul; cimri, pinti; az, kıt; **peˈnu.ri.ous.ness** n. cimrilik, pintilik; fakirlik, yoksulluk.

**pen.u.ry** [ˈpenjuri] n. yoksulluk, fakirlik; eksiklik.

**pe.o.ny** ♀ [ˈpiəni] n. şakayık.

**peo.ple** [ˈpiːpl] 1. n. coll. halk, ahali; akrabalar; my ~ ailem; ulus, millet; ırk, kavim; the ~s pl. of Asia Asya milletleri; 2. v/t. insanla doldurmak.

**pep** sl. [pep] 1. n. kuvvet, enerji; azim, şevk; 2. ~ up v/t. canlandırmak, hareketlendirmek.

**pep.per** [ˈpepə] 1. n. biber; kırmızı biber; 2. v/t. biberlemek; -e yağdırmak (taş, soru, mermi); ˈ~-box n. biberlik; ˈ~.corn n. tane biber; ˈ~.mint n. ♀ nane; ˈpep.per.y ☐ biberli; fig. sert huylu, geçimsiz.

**per** [pɔː, pə] prp. vasıtasıyle, eliyle; tarafından.

**per.ad.ven.ture** rhet. [pəˈrədˈventʃə] 1. adv. belki, olabilir, şayet, kazara; 2. n. şüphe, belirsizlik; ihtimal; beyond ~, without ~ şüphesiz.

**per.am.bu.late** [pəˈræmbjuleit] v/t. (etrafını) gezmek; teftiş etm.; v/i. gezinmek, dolaşmak; **per.am.buˈla.tion** n. gez(in)me, dolaşma; **per.am.bu.la.tor** [ˈpræmbjuleitə] n. çocuk arabası.

**per.cale** [pəˈkeil] n. ince ve sık dokunmuş pamuklu bez.

**per cap.i.ta** [pəˈkæpitə] adv. nüfus başına, kişi başına.

**per.ceive** [pəˈsiːv] v/t. görmek, anlamak, idrak etm., farkına varmak.

**per cent,** a. **per.cent** [pəˈsent] n. yüzde; **perˈcent.age** n. yüzde(lik); oran, nispet; fig. hisse, pay, kâr.

**per.cep.ti.ble** ☐ [pəˈseptəbl] anlaşılabilir, idrak edilebilir, algılanabilir, duyulur, farkına varılır; **perˈcep.tion** n. idrak, algı, anlayış, seziş; **perˈcep.tive** ☐ [~tiv] idrak edebilen; idrak kabilinden; **perˈcep.tive.ness, per.cepˈtiv.i.ty** n. anlayış, idrak kabiliyeti.

**perch¹** ichth. [pəːtʃ] n. tatlı su levreği.

**perch²** [~] 1. n. 5,029 metrelik uzunluk ölçüsü; tünek; yüksekçe yer; F fig. yüksek mevki; 2. vb. tüne(kle)mek; yüksek bir yere oturmak; yüksekte olm.; ~ed fig. mevki sahibi.

**per.chance** [pəˈtʃɑːns] adv. muhtemelen, belki; şans eseri olarak.

**per.cip.i.ent** [pəˈsipiənt] 1. adj. anlayışlı, idraki keskin; 2. n. anlayışlı kimse, idraki kuvvetli kimse.

**per.co.late** [ˈpəːkəleit] v/t. & v/i. süz(ül)mek, sızmak, filtreden geçirmek; **ˈper.co.la.tor** n. süzgeçli kahve ibriği.

**per.cus.sion** [pəˈkʌʃən] n. vurma, çarpma (sesi); ♬ perküsyon; ~ cap tüfek kapsülü; ~ instruments pl. ♪ vurularak çalınan enstrümanlar; **perˈcus.sive** [~siv] adj. vuruş kabilinden.

**per.di.tion** [pəˈdiʃən] n. mahvolma, harap olma; cehennem azabı.

**per.e.gri.nate** [ˈperigrineit] v/t. & v/i. seyahat etm.; yürümek; katetmek, aşmak; **per.e.griˈna.tion** n. yolculuk, seyahat.

**per.emp.to.ri.ness** [pəˈremtərinis] n. katilik, kesinlik, mutlaklık; b.s. otoriterlik, despotluk; **perˈemp.to.ry** ☐ katî, kesin, mutlak; b.s. otoriter, despot.

**per.en.ni.al** [pəˈrenjəl] 1. ☐ bir yıl süren; daimi, uzun süren; ♀ iki yıldan fazla yaşayan (bitki); 2. n. ♀ iki yıldan fazla yaşayan bitki.

**per.fect** 1. [ˈpəːfikt] ☐ tam, kusursuz, mükemmel, fevkalâde; iyi öğrenilmiş; oldukça, tamamen; 2. [~] n. a. ~ tense gr. geçmiş zaman; 3. [pəˈfekt] v/t. tamamlamak, bitirmek; mükemmelleştirmek, geliştirmek; **perˈfec.tion** n. kusursuzluk, mükemmellik; bitirme, tamamlama, ikmal; fig. zirve, doruk.

**per.fid.i.ous** ☐ [pəˈfidiəs] hain, asî, sadakatsiz (to -e karşı); **perˈfid.i.ous.ness, ˈper.fi.dy** n. hainlik, hıyanet, sadakatsizlik.

**per.fo.rate** [ˈpəːfəreit] v/t. delmek; sıra sıra delmek (pul); **per.foˈra.tion** n. delme; delik; **ˈper.fo.ra.tor** n. delgi, zımba.

**per.force** [pəˈfɔːs] adv. mecburen, ister istemez.

**per.form** [pəˈfɔːm] v/t. & v/i. yapmak, yerine getirmek; ifa etm.; thea. oynamak, sunmak *(oyun)*; canlandırmak; ♪ çalmak, icra etm.; rol yapmak; **per'formance** *n.* yerine getirme, yapma, ifa, icra; *thea.* gösteri, temsil, oyun; ⊕ çalışma, işleme; **per'form.er** *n.* artist, oyuncu; icracı; yerine getiren kimse; **per'form.ing** *adj.* terbiye edilmiş *(hayvan).*

**per.fume 1.** ['pəːfjuːm] *n.* güzel koku, ıtır; parfüm, esans; **2.** [pə'fjuːm] *v/t.* lavanta sürmek, parfüm sürmek *-e*; **per'fum.er** *n.* parfüm yapan *veya* satan kimse; **per'fum.er.y** *n.* parfümeri, ıtriyat (dükkânı).

**per.func.to.ry** ☐ [pə'fʌŋktəri] baştan savma, dikkatsizce yapılan, yarımyamalak, iş olsun diye yapılan.

**per.haps** [pə'hæps, præps] *adv.* belki, muhtemelen.

**per.i.gee** *ast.* ['peridʒiː] *n.* bir gezegenin yeryüzüne en yakın olan noktası.

**per.il** ['peril] **1.** *n.* tehlike, risk; at my ~ benim sorumluluğumda; **2.** *v/t.* tehlikeye atmak; **'per.il.ous** ☐ tehlikeli, riskli.

**pe.ri.od** ['piəriəd] *n.* çağ, devir, devre, dönem, süre, müddet; nokta; *gr.* tam cümle; ~s *pl.* ¶ âdet, aybaşı; ~ furniture belli bir çağa ait mobilya; **pe.ri.od.ic** [~'ɔdik] *adj.* belirli aralıklarla yer bulan, peryodik; **pe.ri'od.i.cal 1.** ☐ belli zamanlarda çıkan; **2.** *n.* dergi, mecmua. **per.i.pa.tet.ic** [peripə'tetik] *adj.* *(~ally)* gezen, gezgin(ci).

**pe.riph.er.y** [pə'rifəri] *n.* dış sınır çizgisi *veya* yüzeyi.

**pe.riph.ra.sis** [pə'rifrəsis] *n., pl.* **pe'riphra.ses** [~siːz] dolaylı anlatım; **per.iphras.tic** [peri'fræstik] *adj.* *(~ally)* dolaylı anlatılmış.

**per.i.scope** ↓, ✕ ['periskəup] *n.* periskop.

**per.ish** ['periʃ] *v/t. & v/i.* ölmek; mahvolmak, yok olm.; yok etm.; be ~ed with *-den* mahvolmak, *-den* helâk olm.; **'perish.a.ble 1.** ☐ kolay bozulur *(yiyecek)*; **2.** *n.* ~s *pl.* kolay bozulabilen gıda maddeleri; **'per.ish.ing** ☐ mahvedici, yok edici; F çirkin, iğrenç.

**per.i.style** ['peristail] *n.* bir binayı çevreleyen sıra sütunlar; sütunlarla çevrili yer.

**per.i.wig** ['periwig] *n.* peruka, takma saç. **per.i.win.kle¹** ♣ ['periwiŋkl] *n.* Cezayir menekşesi.

**per.i.win.kle²** *zo.* [~] *n.* bir cins deniz salyangozu.

**per.jure** ['pəːdʒə] *v/t.:* ~ o.s. yalan yere yemin etm.; **'per.jured** *adj.* yalan yere yemin eden; **'per.jur.er** *n.* yalan yere yemin eden kimse; **'per.ju.ry** *n.* yalan yere yemin (etme).

**perk¹** F [pəːk] = percolate.

**perk²** F [~] **1.** *mst* ~ up *v/t. & v/i.* neşelen(dir)mek, canlan(dır)mak; kaldırmak *(başını)*; **2.** = ~y; **perk.i.ness** ['~inis] *n.* havailik, hoppalık; canlılık.

**perks** F [pəːks] *pl.* = perquisites.

**perk.y** ☐ ['pəːki] hoppa, havaî, canlı; kendinden emin.

**perm** F [pəːm] **1.** *n.* perma(nant); **2.** *v/t.* perma yapmak.

**per.ma.nence** ['pəːmənəns] *n.* süreklilik, devam, istikrar; **'per.ma.nen.cy** *s.* permanence; sürekli *bş*; **'per.ma.nent** ☐ sürekli, devamlı, daimî; ~ wave perma(nant); ~ way 🚇 demiryolu üst yapısı.

**per.me.a.bil.i.ty** [pəːmjə'biliti] *n.* geçirgenlik, nüfuz edilme kabiliyeti; **'perme.a.ble** ☐ geçirgen, nüfuz edilebilen (to *-e*); **per.me.ate** ['~mieit] *v/t. & v/i.* *-den* geçmek, sızmak; nüfuz etm. (into *-e*); yayılmak, yaygınlaşmak *(among arasında).*

**per.mis.si.ble** ☐ [pə'misəbl] izin verilebilir, hoş görülebilir, uygun; **per.mis.sion** [pə'miʃən] *n.* izin, müsaade; ruhsat; **per'mis.sive** [~siv] izin veren, müsaade eden; ⚙ ihtiyarî, istemli, keyfî.

**per.mit 1.** [pə'mit] *vb. a.* ~ of izin vermek, müsaade etm.; fırsat vermek, imkân tanımak; bırakmak; kabul etm.; weather ~ting müsait hava; **2.** ['pəːmit] *n.* permi, ruhsatname, izin kâğıdı.

**per.ni.cious** ☐ [pə'niʃəs] zararlı, tehlikeli; ¶ öldürücü, habis.

**per.nick.et.y** F [pə'nikiti] *adj.* kılı kırk yaran, titiz.

**per.o.ra.tion** [perə'reiʃən] *n.* konuşmanın özeti ve sonu.

**per.ox.ide** 🜍 [pə'rɔksaid] *n.:* ~ of hydrogen oksijenli su.

**per.pen.dic.u.lar** [pəːpən'dikjulə] **1.** ☐ dik(ey), düşey, amudî, şakulî; ~ style ▲ Gotik mimari tarzı; **2.** *n.* dikey çizgi, şakulî hat; dik duruş.

**per.pe.trate** ['pəːpitreit] *v/t.* işlemek *(suç, hata)*; F yapmak *(şaka)*; **per.pe'tra.tion** *n.* işleme *(suç, hata)*; yapma *(şaka)*; **'per.pe.tra.tor** *n.* fail, suçlu kimse.

**per.pet.u.al** ☐ [pə'petʃuəl] sürekli, daimî, ebedî, aralıksız, bitip tükenmez; **per'pet.u.ate** [~eit] *v/t.* ebedileştirmek, ölümsüzleştirmek, daimî kılmak; **per.pet.u'a.tion** *n.* sürdürme, devam (ettirme); **per.pe.tu.i.ty** [pəːpi'tjuːiti] *n.* ebediyet, daimîlik; daimî gelir; in ~ ebediyen, sonsuza kadar.

**per.plex** [pə'pleks] *v/t.* şaşırtmak, allak

bullak etm. *(zihin)*; anlaşılması güç hale getirmek, karıştırmak; **per¹plexed** □
zihni karışmış, şaşırmış; karışık; **per-
¹plex.i.ty** *n.* şaşkınlık; karışıklık; zihni
karıştıran şey.
**per.qui.sites** [¹pəːkwizits] *n. pl.* maaştan
ayrı gelir.
**per.se.cute** [¹pəːsikjuːt] *v/t.* sıkıştırmak,
zorlamak, baskı yapmak; zulmetmek *-e*,
eziyet etm. *-e*; **per.se¹cu.tion** *n.* zulüm,
gaddarlık; zulmetme; ~ **mania** zulmetme
hastalığı; **per.se.cu.tor** [¹~tə] *n.* gaddar
kimse, zalim.
**per.se.ver.ance** [pəːsi¹viərəns] *n.* sebat,
azim; **per.se.vere** [~¹viə] *v/i.* sebat göstermek, azimle devam etm. (at, in, with
*-de, -e)*; **per.se¹ver.ing** □ azimli, sebat
eden.
**Per.sian** [¹pəːʃən] **1.** *adj.* İranlı, İran'a
ait; Farsça'ya ait; **2.** *n.* İranlı; Farsça.
**per.sim.mon** ♀ [pə¹simən] *n.* hurma.
**per.sist** [pə¹sist] *v/i.* ısrar etm., üstelemek, sebat etm., inat etm. (in *-de)*; kalmak, devam etm.; **per¹sist.ence, per¹sist-
en.cy** *n.* sebat, ısrar, inat, devam etme;
**per¹sist.ent** □ ısrarlı, inatçı; devamlı.
**per.son** [¹pəːsn] *n.* kimse, adam, kişi, şahıs *(a. gr.)*, fert; şahsiyet, sıfat; *thea.*
rol; in ~ şahsen, bizzat; **¹per.son.a.ble**
*adj.* güzel görünümlü, yakışıklı, cana yakın; **¹per.son.age** *n.* şahsiyet, zat, önemli kişi; *thea.* karakter; **¹per.son.al 1.** □
özel, hususi, şahsi, zati; *gr.* üç şahıstan
birine ait; bedensel; ~ **property** *veya*
**estate** ☼ *s.* personalty; **2.** *n.* belirli bir
kişi hakkında çıkmış gazete yazısı; **per-
son.al.i.ty** [pəːsə¹næliti] *n.* şahsiyet, kişilik, ferdiyet; şahıs, zat, kimse; **persona-
lities** *n. pl.* kaba sözler; **per.son.al.ty**
[¹pəːsnlti] *n.* ☼ şahsi *veya* menkul *(veya*
taşınır) mal; **per.son.ate** [¹~səneit] *v/t.*
canlandırmak *(karakter)*; *k-ni* ...diye
satmak, *k-ne* ...süsü vermek; **per.son¹a-
tion** *n. k-ni* ...diye satma; canlandırma;
**per.son.i.fi.ca.tion** [pəːsɔnifi¹keiʃən] *n.* ci-
simlendirme; şahıslandırma, canlandır-
ma; **per.son.i.fy** [pəːsɔnifai] *v/t.* cisimlendirmek, şahıslandırmak, canlandırmak; **per.son.nel** [pəːsə¹nel] kadro, personel, takım.
**per.spec.tive** [pə¹spektiv] **1.** □ perspekti-
fe göre çizilmiş; **2.** *n.* perspektif (resim);
görüş açısı.
**per.spex** [¹pəːspeks] *n.* transparan plastik, mika.
**per.spi.ca.cious** □ [pəːspi¹keiʃəs] keskin
zekâlı, anlayışlı; **per.spi.cac.i.ty** [~¹kæsi-
ti] *n.* keskin zekâ, anlayış; **per.spi.cu.i.ty**

[~¹kjuiti] *n.* açıklık, anlaşılırlık; **per.spic-
u.ous** [pə¹spikjuəs] □ açık, anlaşılır.
**per.spi.ra.tion** [pəːspə¹reiʃən] *n.* ter(leme);
**per.spire** [pəs¹paiə] *v/i.* terlemek.
**per.suade** [pə¹sweid] *v/t.* kandırmak, ikna etm., razı etm. (to *inf. -meğe*, into
*-e)*; inandırmak (of *-e)*; **per¹suad.er** *n. sl.*
tabanca.
**per.sua.sion** [pə¹sweiʒən] *n.* ikna (kabiliyeti), inandırma, kandırma; inanç, kanaat, itikat; mezhep, din; F *co.* cins, nevi, tür.
**per.sua.sive** □ [pə¹sweisiv] kandırıcı, ikna edici; **per¹sua.sive.ness** *n.* ikna kabiliyeti.
**pert** □ [pəːt] sırnaşık, yılışık, arsız, yüzsüz, küstah, şımarık, lâubali.
**per.tain** [pə¹tein] *v/i.* ait olm.; ilgili olm.;
uygun olm. (to *-e)*.
**per.ti.na.cious** □ [pəːti¹neiʃəs] azimli, kararlı, sebatkâr; inatçı; **per.ti.nac.i.ty**
[~¹næsiti] *n.* azim, kararlılık, sebat, inatçılık.
**per.ti.nence, per.ti.nen.cy** [¹pəːtinəns(i)] *n.*
ilgi, alâka; uyum; **¹per.ti.nent** □ ilgili,
alâkalı; uygun, uyumlu; be ~ to ilgili
olm. *-e*.
**pert.ness** [¹pəːtnis] *n.* arsızlık, küstahlık,
lâubalilik.
**per.turb** [pə¹təːb] *v/t.* altüst etm., rahatsız etm., canını sıkmak; **per.tur.ba.tion**
[pəːtə¹beiʃən] *n.* huzursuzluk, rahatsızlık.
**pe.ruke** [pə¹ruːk] *n.* peruka, takma saç.
**pe.rus.al** [pə¹ruːzəl] *n.* dikkatle okuma;
**pe¹ruse** *v/t.* dikkatle okumak; *fig.* incelemek, tetkik etm.
**Pe.ru.vi.an** [pə¹ruːvjən] **1.** *adj.* Perulu; Peru'ya özgü; ~ **bark** ♀ kınakına kabuğu;
**2.** *n.* Perulu kimse.
**per.vade** [pə¹veid] *v/t.* kaplamak, istilâ
etm.; yayılmak *-e*; **per¹va.sion** [~ʒən] *n.*
kaplama, yayılma; **per¹va.sive** [~siv]
*adj.* yayılmış, kaplayan, geniş.
**per.verse** □ [pə¹vəːs] ters, aksi, zıt; ahlâksız, yoldan çıkmış; ⚕ sapık; **per¹verse-
ness** = perversity; **per¹ver.sion** *n.* (cinsel)
sapıklık; ayartma, yoldan çıkarma; ters
anlam verme; **per¹ver.si.ty** *n.* yoldan çıkma; ahlâksızlık; ⚕ sapıklık; **per¹ver.sive**
*adj.* yanıltıcı (of).
**per.vert 1.** [pə¹vəːt] *v/t.* (doğru yoldan)
saptırmak, ayartmak, baştan çıkarmak,
çelmek *(aklını)*, yanlış yola sürüklemek;
yanlış anlam vermek; **2.** [¹pəːvəːt] *n.* ⚕
cinsî sapık.
**per.vi.ous** [¹pəːvjəs] *adj.* yanına girilebilir, nüfuz edilebilir *(a. fig.)*; geçirgen
*(toprak vs.)*.

**pes.ky** ☐ *sl.* ['peski] baş belâsı, sıkıntı veren, sinir bozucu.

**pes.si.mism** ['pesimizəm] *n.* kötümserlik, karamsarlık; **'pes.si.mist** *n.* kötümser kimse; **pes.si'mis.tic** *adj.* (*~ally*) kötümser, karamsar.

**pest** [pest] *n. fig.* baş belâsı, sıkıcı şey *veya* kimse, zararlı şey *veya* kimse; ve.ba, taun; **'pes.ter** *v/t.* sıkmak, sinirlendirmek, sıkıntı vermek, usandırmak, bıktırmak, baş ağrıtmak.

**pest.i.cide** ['pestisaid] *n.* böcek zehiri; **pes'tif.er.ous** ☐ [*~fərəs*] bulaşıcı; zararlı; ahlâksız; baş belâsı; **pes.ti.lence** ['*~ləns*] *n.* salgın ve çok tehlikeli hastalık, *part.* veba, taun; **'pes.ti.lent** *adj.* bulaşıcı hastalık getiren; tehlikeli; öldürücü; ahlâk bozucu; baş belâsı; **pes.ti.len.tial** ☐ [*~'lenʃəl*] veba getiren; ahlâk bozucu; sıkıcı; tehlikeli.

**pes.tle** ['pesl] **1.** *n.* havan tokmağı; **2.** *v/t.* havanda dövmek.

**pet¹** [pet] *n.* öfke, hiddet, kızgınlık; **in a ~** kızgın.

**pet²** [*~*] **1.** *n.* evde beslenen hayvan; çok sevilen kimse *veya* şey, sevgili; **2.** *adj.* evcil...; gözde...; *~ dog* evcil köpek; *~ name* takma isim; *it is my ~ aversion* ondan nefret ederim, o benim sinirime dokunuyor; **3.** *v/t.* okşamak, sevmek; F sevişmek, öpüşmek.

**pet.al** ♀ ['petl] *n.* çiçek yaprağı, petal.

**pe.tard** [pe'taːd] *n.* † kapı, duvar *vs.* yıkmak için kullanılan bomba.

**pe.ter** ['piːtə] *v/i.:* *~ out* yavaş yavaş azalmak, tükenmek.

**pet.i.ole** ♀ ['petiəul] *n.* yaprak sapı, petiol.

**pet.it** ['peti] *adj.* küçük, ufak; **pe.tite** [pə'tiːt] *adj.* küçük, ince, narin.

**pe.ti.tion** [pi'tiʃən] **1.** *n.* dilekçe; rica, istirham, dilek, talep; *~ in bankruptcy* ∞ alacaklı *veya* borçlu tarafından yapılan iflas talebi; *~ for divorce* ∞ boşanma talebi; **2.** *vb.* dilekçe vermek *-e* (for *için*; to *inf.* *-mek için*); rica (*veya* istirham, talep) etm., dilemek (s.o. *b-ne;* for *için*); **pe'ti.tion.er** [*~ʃnə*] *n.* dilekçe (*veya* müracaat) sahibi.

**pet.rel** *orn.* ['petrəl] *n.* uzun kanatlı bir çeşit deniz kuşu.

**pet.ri.fac.tion** *geol.* [petri'fækʃən] *n.* taşlaşma, taş kesilme (*a. fig.*); fosil.

**pet.ri.fy** ['petrifai] *v/t. & v/i.* taşlaş(tır)mak; taş haline getirmek; taş haline gelmek; *fig.* aklını başından almak.

**pet.rol** *mot.* ['petrəl] *n.* benzin; *~ engine* benzin motoru; *~ station* benzin istasyonu; *~ tank* benzin deposu.

**pe.tro.le.um** [pi'trəuljəm] *n.* petrol; *~ jelly* vazelin, parafin.

**pe.trol.o.gy** *geol.* [pe'trɔlədʒi] *n.* kaya ilmi.

**pet.ti.coat** ['petikəut] *n.* iç etekliği, jüpon.

**pet.ti.fog.ger** ['petifɔgə] *n.* madrabaz avukat; kılı kırk yaran kimse; **'pet.ti.fog.ging** *adj.* kılı kırk yaran; gereksiz detaylı (*metod*).

**pet.ti.ness** ['petinis] *n.* önemsizlik; aşağılık, küçüklük.

**pet.tish** ☐ ['petiʃ] hırçın, huysuz; **'pet.tish.ness** *n.* hırçınlık, huysuzluk.

**pet.ty** ☐ ['peti] küçük; önemsiz, ehemmiyetsiz, adi, ufak tefek; dar kafalı; *~ cash* † küçük kasa; *~ officer* ⚓ assubay, erbaş; *~ sessions* *pl.* ∞ adi mahkeme.

**pet.u.lance** ['petjuləns] *s.* pettishness; **'pet.u.lant** *s.* pettish.

**pew** [pjuː] *n.* (*kilisede*) oturacak sıra.

**pe.wit** *orn.* ['piːwit] *n.* kızkuşu.

**pew.ter** ['pjuːtə] *n.* kurşun ve kalay alaşımı; bu alaşımdan yapılan kap; **'pew.ter.er** *n.* kurşun ve kalay alaşımı dökümcüsü.

**pha.e.ton** *hist.* ['feitn] *n.* fayton, payton.

**pha.lanx** ['fælæŋks] *n.* eski Yunanistan'da asker alayı.

**phan.tasm** ['fæntæzəm] *n.* hayalet; hayal, aldanış, fantezi; **phan.tas.ma.go.ri.a** [*~məˈgɔːriə*] *n.* rüyadaki gibi bir seri tutarsız hayal.

**phan.tom** ['fæntəm] **1.** *n.* hayal(et); aldanış, görüntü; **2.** *adj.* hayalet gibi...

**Phar.i.sa.ic,** **Phar.i.sa.i.cal** ☐ [færi'seiik(əl)] Ferisîlere ait; ikiyüzlü.

**Phar.i.see** ['færisiː] *n.* Ferisî; ikiyüzlü kimse.

**phar.ma.ceu.ti.cal** ☐ [faːməˈsjuːtikəl] eczacılığa ait, eczacılık...; ilâç...; **phar.ma.cist** ['*~*sist] *n.* eczacı; **phar.ma.col.o.gy** [*~'kɔlədʒi*] *n.* farmokoloji, eczacılık ilmi; **'phar.ma.cy** *n.* eczane; eczacılık.

**phar.ynx** *anat.* ['færiŋks] *n.* farinks, yutak.

**phase** [feiz] *n.* safha, faz, görünüş; **phased** *adj.* safhalı.

**pheas.ant** *orn.* ['feznt] *n.* sülün (eti).

**phe.nom.e.nal** ☐ [fi'nɔminl] algılanabilir; fenomen ile ilgili; olağanüstü, hayret verici; **phe'nom.e.non** [*~nən*] *n.*, *pl.* **phe'nom.e.na** [*~nə*] fenomen; *fig.* harika şey, kimse *veya* olay.

**phew** [fjuː] *int.* öf!, pöf!

**phi.al** ['faiəl] *n.* ufak şişe.

**Phi Be.ta Kap.pa** *Am.* ['fai'biːtəkæpə] *n.* çok eski üniversiteliler birliği.

**phi.lan.der** [fi'lændə] *v/i.* kur yapmak,

flört etm.

**phil.an.throp.ic** [filən'θrəpik] *adj.* (~ally) iyiliksever, yardımsever; insan sevgisine ait; **phi.lan.thro.pist** [fi'lænθrəpist] *n.* hayırsever, yardımsever; insancıl kimse; **phi'lan.thro.py** *n.* insanseverlik, insancıllık, hayırseverlik.

**phi.lat.e.list** [fi'lætəlist] *n.* pul meraklısı; **phi'lat.e.ly** *n.* pul koleksiyonculuğu.

**phi.lip.pic** [fi'lipik] *n.* tenkit niteliğinde sert konuşma.

**Phi.lis.tine** ['filistain] *n.* Filistinli; *fig.* kültürsüz (*veya* estetik anlayıştan yoksun) kimse.

**phil.o.log.i.cal** □ [filə'lɔdʒikəl] filolojik; **phi.lol.o.gist** [fi'lɔlədʒist] *n.* dilbilimci, filoloji uzmanı; **phi'lol.o.gy** *n.* filoloji, dilbilim.

**phi.los.o.pher** [fi'lɔsəfə] *n.* filozof, felsefeci; kendine hakim (*veya* dengeli, kalender) kimse; ~ s' stone herhangi bir madeni altına dönüştürdüğü farzolunan tılsımlı taş; **phil.o.soph.ic, phil.o.soph.i.cal** [filə'sɔfik(əl)] *adj.* felsefi, filozofça; akıllıca, düşünceli; **phi.los.o.phize** [fi'lɔsəfaiz] *v/i.* filozofça konuşmak *veya* düşünmek; **phi'los.o.phy** *n.* felsefe; ağır başlılık, kalenderlik.

**phil.tre, phil.ter** ['filtə] *n.* aşk iksiri.

**phiz** F *co.* [fiz] *n.* yüz (ifadesi).

**phle.bi.tis** ʒ̃ [fli'baitis] *n.* f(i)lebit.

**phlegm** [flem] *n.* balgam; kayıtsızlık; kaygısızlık; **phleg.mat.ic** [fleg'mætik] *adj.* (~ally) soğukkanlı, sakin.

**phoe.be** *orn.* ['fiːbi] *n.* bir çeşit sinekyutan.

**Phoe.ni.cian** [fi'niʃən] **1.** *adj.* Fenikeli, Fenike'ye ait; **2.** *n.* Fenike dili; Fenikeli kimse.

**phoe.nix** *myth.* ['fiːniks] *n.* Anka kuşu.

**phone¹** F [fəun] **1.** *n.* telefon; **2.** *v/t.* telefon etm. -*e*.

**phone²** [~] *n.* ses.

**pho.neme** ['fəuniːm] *n.* fonem; **pho'nem.ics** *n.* fonem bilimi; fonem sistemi.

**pho.net.ic** [fə'netik] *adj.* (~ally) fonetik, sesçil; ~ spelling fonetik imlâ; ~ transcription transkripsiyon fonetik; **pho.ne.ti.cian** [~niˈtiʃən] *n.* fonetik uzmanı, sesbilimci; **pho.net.ics** [~ˈnetiks] *n. sg.* fonetik, sesbilim.

**pho.ney** *sl.* ['fəuni] *adj.* sahte, düzme, kalp.

**pho.no.graph** *Am.* ['fəunəgraːf] *n.* pikap, fonograf.

**pho.nol.o.gy** [fə'nɔlədʒi] *n.* fonoloji.

**pho.ny** *Am. sl.* ['fəuni] **1.** *n.* sahtekâr kimse; **2.** = phoney.

**phos.phate** ʒ̃ ['fɔsfeit] *n.* fosfat.

**phos.pho.resce** [fɔsfə'res] *v/i.* fosfor gibi parlamak; **phos.pho'res.cent** *adj.* fosfor gibi parlayan, fosforlu; **phos.phor.ic** ʒ̃ [~'fɔrik] *adj.* fosforlu...; **phos.pho.rous** ʒ̃ ['~fərəs] *adj.* fosforlu; **phos.pho.rus** ʒ̃ ['~fərəs] *n.* fosfor.

**pho.to** F ['fəutəu] *n.* fotoğraf; ~-en'grav.ing *n.* fotoğraf vasıtasıyla klişe çıkarma işi; '~-'finish *n.* Am. fotofiniş; '~-'flash *n.* flaş; ~.gen.ic [fəutəu'dʒenik] *adj.* ışık üreten (*veya* yayan); fotojenik; ~.gram.me.try [~'græmitri] *n.* fotogrammetri.

**pho.to.graph** ['fəutəgraːf] **1.** *n.* fotoğraf; take a ~ fotoğraf çekmek; **2.** *v/t.* -*in* fotoğrafını çekmek; **pho.tog.ra.pher** [fə'tɔgrəfə] *n.* fotoğrafçı; **pho.to.graph.ic** [fəutə'græfik] *adj.* (~ally) fotoğraflarla ilgili; ~ print foto baskısı; **pho.tog.ra.phy** [fə'tɔgrəfi] *n.* fotoğrafçılık.

**pho.to.gra.vure** [fəutəgrə'vjuə] *n.* fotogravür; **pho.tom.e.ter** [~'tɔmitə] *n.* fotometre, ışıkölçer; **pho.to-play** ['~təplei] *n.* filme alınan piyes; **pho.to.stat** ['~təustæt] *n.* fotostat; fotokopi; **pho.to.te.leg.ra.phy** [~təti'legrəfi] *n.* telle resim gönderme usulü; **pho.to.type** ['~təutaip] *n.* fotoğraftan yapılan klişe.

**phrase** [freiz] **1.** *n.* ibare; deyim, tabir; ♪ cümle; **2.** *v/t.* kelimelerle ifade etm.; '~-mon.ger *n.* süslü konuşan kimse; **phra.se.ol.o.gy** [~ɔlədʒi] *n.* ifade tarzı, cümle dizimi, üslup; **'phras.ing** *n.* deyim kurma tarzı.

**phre.net.ic** [fri'netik] *adj.* (~ally) coşkun, çok heyecanlı.

**phre.nol.o.gy** [fri'nɔlədʒi] *n.* frenoloji.

**phthis.i.cal** ʒ̃ ['θaisikəl] *adj.* veremli; astımlı; **phthi.sis** ['~sis] *n.* verem.

**phut** *sl.* [fʌt] *n.:* go ~ suya düşmek (*plan*); hapı yutmak.

**phys.ic** F ['fizik] **1.** *n.* tıp ilmi, hekimlik; ilâç; **2.** *v/t.* amel vermek; iyileştirmek; **'phys.i.cal** □ fiziksel, fizikî; maddî; bedene ait, bedensel, cismanî ~ condition sağlık durumu; ~ culture vücut bakımı; ~ education, ~ training beden eğitimi; **phy.si.cian** [fi'ziʃən] *n.* doktor, hekim; **phys.i.cist** ['~sist] *n.* fizikçi; **phys.ics** ['fiziks] *n. sg.* fizik.

**phys.i.og.no.my** [fizi'ɔnəmi] *n.* fizyonomi; dış görünüş; **phys.i.o.log.i.cal** [~ə'lɔdʒikəl] *adj.* fizyolojik, diriksel; **phys.i.ol.o.gist** [~'ɔlədʒist] *n.* fizyolog; **phys.i'ol.o.gy** *n.* fizyoloji.

**phy.sique** [fi'ziːk] *n.* bünye, vücut, fizik, beden yapısı.

**pi.an.ist** ['piənist] *n.* piyanist.

**pi.a.no¹** ♪ [ˈpjɑːnəu] adj. & adv. hafif (sesle).

**pi.an.o²** [ˈpjænəu] n. a. **pi.an.o.for.te** [~-ˈfɔːti] piyano; grand piano kuyruklu piyano.

**pi.as.ter** [piˈæstə] n. kuruş.

**pi.az.za** [piˈætsə] n. (İtalya'da) şehir meydanı veya pazar yeri; Am. veranda, taraça.

**pi.broch** [ˈpiːbrɔk] n. gaydalarla çalınan askerî müzik.

**pic.a.resque** [pikəˈresk] adj. külhanbeyler veya sabıkalılarla ilgili; ~ novel külhanbeyleri veya sabıkalılarla ilgili roman.

**pic.a.yune** Am. [pikəˈjuːn] 1. n. mst fig. önemsiz kimse veya şey; 2. adj. önemsiz, küçük, değersiz.

**pic.ca.nin.ny** co. [ˈpikənini] 1. n. part. zenci çocuk; 2. adj. çocukça, çok küçük.

**pick** [pik] 1. n. seçme; = pickaxe; kürdan; sivri uçlu herhangi bir alet; 2. v/t. & v/i. delmek; kazmak; yolmak, koparmak, toplamak (meyve, çiçek); seçmek; aşırmak, çalmak, soymak; sebep olm.; parmaklarla çalmak (enstruman); gagalamak; anahtarsız açmak (kilit); azar azar yemek (yiyecek); kazma ile çalışmak; hırsızlık yapmak; azar azar yemek yemek; ~ s.o.'s pocket b-nin cebinden bş yürütmek; ~ one's way k-ne yol açmak; ~ one's words ağzından çıkanı kulağı duymak; ~ at iştahsızca yemek; Am. F rahat vermemek, dır dır etm.; ~ off koparmak, yolmak; silahla vurmak; ~ on seçmek; ~ out seçmek, ayırmak; anlamak; ~ over ayıklamak; ~ up kazmak; kaldırmak, toplamak; kulaktan öğrenmek (dil); hızlanmak; rasgele bulmak; iyileşmek; tanışmak; ayağa kalkmak; beraberinde götürmek; ~ o.s. up ayağa kalkmak; ~ up speed hızlanmak; ~ up with tanışmak, ayarlamak; ~-a-back [~ˈəbæk] adv. omuzda, sırtta; ˈ~-axe n. kazma; ˈpick.er n. toplayıcı şey veya kimse; pamuk atma makinesi.

**pick.er.el** ichth. [ˈpikərəl] n. yavru turnabalığı.

**pick.et** [ˈpikit] 1. n. kazık; ✕ ileri karakol; grev gözcüsü; 2. v/t. & v/i. kazıklarla etrafını çevirmek; ✕ nöbetçi veya karakol koymak; kazığa bağlamak (hayvan); nöbet beklemek, grev gözcülüğü yapmak.

**pick.ing** [ˈpikiŋ] n. toplama (s. pick); mst ~s pl. aşırma (mallar).

**pick.le** [ˈpikl] 1. n. turşu, hıyar turşusu, salamura; F haşarı çocuk; F sıkıntılı durum; s. mix; 2. v/t. -in turşusunu kurmak; ~d herring salamura ringa balığı.

**pick...:** ˈ~.lock n. maymuncuk; hırsız; ˈ~-me-up n. F canlandırıcı içki; ˈ~.pock.et n. yankecisi; ˈ~-up n. pikap (kolu); pikap, kamyonet; hızlanma; alıcı cihaz; radyoda mikrofon tertibatı; gelişme; a. ~ in prices ↑ borsadaki fiyatların yükselmesi; sl. rastgele tanışılan kimse.

**pic.nic** [ˈpiknik] n. piknik; fig. kolay veya hoşa giden şey; 2. v/i. piknik yapmak.

**pic.to.ri.al** [pikˈtɔːriəl] 1. ☐ resimli...; resimlerle ilgili; ~ advertising resimli ilan; 2. n. resimli dergi.

**pic.ture** [ˈpiktʃə] 1. n. resim, tablo; tasvir, suret, timsal; tanımlama; film; görüntü; ~s pl. F sinema; put s.o. in the ~ b-ni bşden haberdar etm.; 2. v/t. -in resmini yapmak, boyamak; tasavvur etm., hayal etm., canlandırmak; tanımlamak, tasvir etm.; ˈ~-book n. resim kitabı, resimli kitap; ˈ~-gal.ler.y n. resim galerisi; ˈ~-go.er n. sinema tutkunu; ~ post-card resimli kartpostal.

**pic.tur.esque** ☐ [piktʃəˈresk] pitoreks, resme elverişli; canlı, kuvvetli; etkili; güzel; **pic.tur'esque.ness** n. pitorekslik; güzellik, canlılık.

**pidg.in** [ˈpidʒin] n.: ~ English Uzak Doğu'da konuşulan İngilizceden bozma karışık dil; that's not my ~ F bu benim işim değil.

**pie¹** [pai] n. tart, börek, turta; s. finger 1.

**pie²** orn. [~] n. saksağan.

**pie.bald** [ˈpaibɔːld] adj. alaca, benekli (at).

**piece** [piːs] 1. n. parça, bölüm, kısım, tane; piyes, oyun; madenî para; numune, örnek; dama taşı; resim; heykel; silah; a ~ of advice bir nasihat; a ~ of news bir haber; ~ by ~ birer birer, parça parça; of a ~ aynı, tıpkısı, benzer; be of a ~ with uygun olm. -e, aynı olm. ile; give s.o. a ~ of one's mind b-nin hakkında ne düşündüğünü açıkça söylemek, b-ni paylamak, azarlamak; take to ~s parçalara ayırmak, sökmek; 2. v/t. a. ~ up parçalarını bir araya getirerek tamir etm., parça eklemek, yamamak; ~ together birleştirmek, bir araya getirmek; ~ out parça ekleyerek tamamlamak; ˈ~-goods n. pl. parça mal, metreyle satılan kumaş vs.; ˈ~-meal adv. & adj. parça parça (yapılmış); ˈ~-work n. parça başı iş.

**pied** [paid] adj. benekli, alaca.

**pie.plant** Am. [ˈpaiplɑːnt] n. ravent.

**pier** [piə] n. iskele, rıhtım; kemer veya

köprü payandası; iki pencere *veya* kapı arasındaki duvar; **¹pier.age** *n.* ⫞ rıhtım ücreti.

**pierce** [piəs] *v/t.* & *v/i.* delmek, delip geçmek, delik açmak; nüfuz etm. -*e*; içine işlemek; etkilemek, tesir etm.; bıçaklamak; zorla girmek; **¹pierc.ing** ☐ keskin, tiz (*ses*); içe işleyen (*soğuk*).

**pier-glass** [¹piəglɑːs] *n.* boy aynası.

**pi.e.tism** [¹paiətizəm] *n.* softalık; dindarlık.

**pi.e.ty** [¹paiəti] *n.* kendini Tanrıya adama; dindarlık.

**pif.fle** *sl.* [¹pifl] **1.** *n.* saçma söz; **2.** *v/i.* saçmalamak.

**pig** [pig] **1.** *n.* domuz (yavrusu); domuz eti; domuz derisi; domuz gibi herif; *metall.* pik (demiri); kötü yola düşmüş kadın; *sl.* polis, aynasız; buy a ~ in a poke *bşi* görmeden (*veya* körü körüne) almak; **2.** *v/i.* yavrulamak (*domuz*); F domuz gibi yaşamak, süfli bir hayat sürmek.

**pi.geon** [¹pidʒin] *n.* güvercin; *sl.* kolay aldanan kimse, safdil, aval; **¹~breast.ed** *adj.* çıkık göğüslü; **¹~hole 1.** *n.* (*yazı masasında vs.*) göz; **2.** *v/t.* göze yerleştirmek; bir yana atmak, hasıraltı etm.; tasnif etm.; **¹pi.geon.ry** *n.* güvercinlik.

**pig.ger.y** [¹pigəri] *n.* domuz ahırı (*veya* ağılı, çiftliği).

**pig.gish** ☐ [¹pigiʃ] domuz gibi; pis; obur, pisboğaz.

**pig.gy** [¹pigi] **1.** *n.* küçük domuz; ~ bank domuz şeklinde kumbara; **2.** *adj.* obur.

**pig.head.ed** [¹pig'hedid] *adj.* aksi, inatçı.

**pig-i.ron** [¹pigaiən] *n.* pik demiri.

**pig.ment** [¹pigmənt] *n.* boya (*veya* renk) maddesi, pigment.

**pig.my** [¹pigmi] = pygmy.

**pig...:** **¹~.nut** *n.* bir çeşit ceviz; **¹~.skin** *n.* domuz derisi; **~.sty** [¹~stai] *n.* domuz ağılı; **¹~.tail** *n.* saç örgüsü; **¹~.wash** *n.* domuza verilen yiyecek artığı.

**pike** [paik] *n.* ✕ kargı, mızrak; *ichth.* turnabalığı; ana yol, asfalt; paralı yol; **¹pik.er** *n.* Am. *sl.* az parayla oynayan kumarbaz; *fig.* cimri kimse; **¹pike.staff** *n.*: as plain as a ~ apaçık, meydanda.

**pil.chard** *ichth.* [¹piltʃəd] *n.* sardalya.

**pile¹** [pail] **1.** *n.* yığın, küme; büyük para; kocaman bina; ⨍ pil; atomic ~ atom reaktörü; **2.** *v/t.* & *v/i.* oft. ~ up, ~ on yığ(ıl)mak, birik(tir)mek; üşüşmek, doluşmak; çarpışmak; istif etm., kümelemek; çatmak (*silah*); doldurmak.

**pile²** [~] *n.* kazık, direk.

**pile³** [~] *n.* tüy, hav.

**pile-driv.er** ⊕ [¹paildraivə] *n.* kazık var-

yosu, şahmerdan; **¹pile-dwell.ing** *n.* kazık temelli ev.

**piles** ⁊ [pailz] *n. pl.* basur memesi, hemoroid.

**pil.fer** [¹pilfə] *v/t.* çalmak, aşırmak, yürütmek.

**pil.grim** [¹pilgrim] *n.* hacı; yolcu, seyyah; ♀ Fathers *pl.* 1620'de Amerika'ya göç edip «Plymouth» kolonisini kuran İngiliz Püriterleri; **¹pil.grim.age** *n.* hacca gitme, hac(ılık).

**pill** [pil] *n.* hap; the ~ doğum kontrol hapı.

**pil.lage** [¹pilidʒ] **1.** *n.* yağma, talan, çapulculuk; **2.** *v/t.* yağmalamak, talan etm.

**pil.lar** [¹pilə] *n.* direk, sütun; dikme (benzeri şey); destek (*a. fig.*); **¹~-box** *n.* posta kutusu; **¹pil.lared** *adj.* sütunlu, destekli.

**pil.lion** [¹piljən] *n.* binicinin arkasında oturana mahsus minder; *mot.* motosiklet arkalığı; ride ~ atın terkisine binmek.

**pil.lo.ry** [¹piləri] **1.** *n.* teşhir direği; in the ~ teşhir edilmekte; **2.** *v/t.* teşhir direğine bağlamak; *fig.* elâleme rezil etm., küçük düşürmek -*i*.

**pil.low** [¹piləu] **1.** *n.* yastık; ⊕ yatak kovanı; **2.** *v/t.* yastığa yatırmak; **¹~-case**, **¹~-slip** *n.* yastık yüzü.

**pi.lot** [¹pailət] **1.** *n.* ⫞ kılavuz; ✈ pilot; *fig.* rehber; ~ instructor öğretmen pilot; ~ officer havacı teğmen; ~ pupil öğrenci pilot; **2.** *adj.* pilot, deney...; ~ plant deney tertibatı; **3.** *v/t.* kılavuzluk etm. -*e*, yol göstermek -*e*; kullanmak (*uçak*); **¹pi.lot.age** *n.* kılavuzluk; kılavuz ücreti; **¹pi.lot-bal.loon** deney balonu; **¹pi.lot-light** *n.* gaz lambalarında *veya* şofbende devamlı yanan küçük alev.

**pi.men.to** [pi'mentəu] *n.* yenibahar.

**pimp** [pimp] **1.** *n.* pezevenk, kadın simsarı; **2.** *v/i.* pezevenklik etm.

**pim.ple** [¹pimpl] *n.* sivilce; **¹pim.pled**, **¹pim.ply** *adj.* sivilceli.

**pin** [pin] **1.** *n.* topluiğne; broş, iğne; askı çivisi; mil; lobut; değersiz şey; ♪ akort anahtarı; ~s *pl. sl.* bacaklar; **2.** *vb.* iğnelemek, iliştirmek, tutturmak; yüklemek (*sorumluluk*); hareketsiz kılmak; *a.* ~ down *sl. fig.* içyüzünü araştırmak; ~ one's hopes on bel bağlamak -*e*.

**pin.a.fore** [¹pinəfɔː] *n.* göğüslük, önlük.

**pin.cers** [¹pinsəz] *n. pl.* (a pair of ~) kerpeten, kıskaç.

**pinch** [pintʃ] **1.** *n.* çimdik; tutam; sıkıntı, ihtiyaç; hırsızlık; tutuklama; at a ~ gerektiğinde, icabında; **2.** *v/t.* çimdiklemek, kıstırmak, sıkıştırmak; sıkıştırıp acıtmak; sıkıntıya düşürmek; F aşırmak, çalmak, yürütmek; *sl.* enselemek, tutuklamak; be ~ed for money eli darda olm.; *v/i.* cimrilik etm.; ıstırap vermek; vurmak *(ayakkabı)*; pinched *adj.* az, kıt; *fig.* ince, zayıf.

pinch.beck ['pintʃbek] 1. *n.* ⊕ altın taklidi olarak kullanılan bakır ve çinko alaşımı; *fig.* taklit şey; 2. *adj.* taklit...

pinch-hit *Am.* ['pintʃhit] *(irr.* hit) *v/i. beysbol:* vuruş yapmak (for *-in yerine*).

pin.cush.ion ['pinkuʃən] *n.* iğne(den)lik.

pine¹ ⚙ [pain] *n.* çam (ağacı).

pine² [~] *v/i.* zayıflamak, bitkinleşmek; hasret çekmek, özlemek (for, after *-i*); ~ away eriyip gitmek, sararıp solmak.

pine...: '~.ap.ple *n.* ⚙ ananas; '~-cone *n.* çam kozalağı; 'pin.er.y *n.* ananas seri; '~-tree = pine¹.

pin-feath.er ['pinfeðə] *n.* yeni biten kuş tüyü.

ping [piŋ] *v/i.* «vız» diye ses çıkarmak *(kurşun)*.

ping-pong ['piŋ pɔŋ] *n.* masa tenisi, pingpong.

pin.ion ['pinjən] 1. *n.* kanat *(a. poet.); a.* ~-feather kanat tüyü; ⊕ dişli çark, pinyon; 2. *v/t.* uçmasını engellemek için ucunu kesmek *(kanat); fig.* elini kolunu bağlamak.

pink¹ [piŋk] 1. *n.* ⚙ karanfil; pembe renk; in the ~ *sl.* sapasağlam, demir *(veya* turp) gibi; 2. *adj.* pembe.

pink² [~] *v/t.* bıçaklamak; küçük delikler açmak; deliklerle süslemek.

pink³ *mot.* [~] *v/i.* vuruntu yapmak.

pink.ish ['piŋkiʃ] *adj.* pembemsi, pembemtırak.

pin.nace ⚓ ['pinis] *n.* büyük filika.

pin.na.cle ['pinəkl] *n.* ⚘ sivri tepeli kule; *fig.* zirve, tepe, doruk.

pin.nate ⚙ ['pineit] *adj.* tüysü.

pi.noc(h).le *Am.* ['pi:nʌkl] *n.* 48 kâğıtla oynanan bir iskambil oyunu.

pin...: '~.prick *n. fig.* iğne, taş, kinaye; '~-stripe *n.* çok ince çizgi *(kumaşta).*

pint [paint] *n.* galonun sekizde biri *(0,57 l, Am. 0,47 l).*

pin-up ['pinʌp] *n.* duvara asılan seksi kadın resmi.

pi.o.neer [paiə'niə] 1. *n.* öncü; ✕ istihkâm eri; 2. *v/t.* & *v/i.* öncülük etm.; açmak *(yol);* göstermek *(yeni metodlar).*

pi.ous ⬜ ['paiəs] dindar.

pip¹ [pip] *n. vet.* tavuklarda görülen dilaltı hastalığı, kurbağacık; *sl.* efkâr, öfke, hiddet; have the ~ canı sıkılmak, öfkelenmek; it gives me the ~ o benim ka-

famı bozuyor, tepemi attırıyor, sinirime dokunuyor.

pip² [~] *n.* meyve çekirdeği; zar üzerindeki nokta; ✕ teğmenlere takılan yıldız işareti.

pip³ *sl.* [~] *vb.* öl(dür)mek; yenmek; sınavda kalmak, sınavda çak(tır)mak; yumurtadan çıkmak için delmek *(kabuk);* ~ out ölmek, kuyruğu titretmek.

pip⁴ [~] *n.* radyoda saati belirten vuruşlardan biri.

pipe [paip] 1. *n.* boru; kaval, düdük; çubuk; pipo; ♪ gayda; ⚓ silistre; nefes borusu; künk; bir çubukluk tütün; 470 litrelik şarap fıçısı; 2. *v/t.* & *v/i.* düdük çalmak; düdük çalarak kumanda vermek; cırlak sesle konuşmak; silistre ile çağırmak; borularla iletmek; borularla donatmak; ~ one's eye F ağlamak; ~ down F sesini kesmek, susmak; ~ up F söze, şarkıya *veya* çalmaya başlamak; '~.clay 1. *n.* kil; 2. *v/t.* kil ile beyazlatmak *veya* temizlemek; '~-lay.er *n.* boru döşeyen kimse; *Am. pol.* elebaşı, öncü kimse; '~.line *n.* petrol borusu *(veya* hattı); 'pip.er *n.* kavalcı; gaydacı; pay the ~ F masrafı yüklenmek.

pip.ing ['paipiŋ] 1. *adj.* düdük gibi çıkaran; tiz, cırlak, kulak tırmalayıcı *(ses);* ~ hot çok sıcak, buram buram; dumanı üstünde; 2. *n.* borular; şerit şeklinde süs *(elbisede, pastada);* kaval çalma; kaval sesi.

pip.pin ⚙ ['pipin] *n.* birkaç çeşit elma.

pip-squeak *sl.* ['pipskwi:k] *n.* ciğeri beş para etmez kimse.

pi.quan.cy ['pi:kənsi] *n.* mayhoşluk; cazibe; 'pi.quant ⬜ mayhoş, iştah açıcı; etkileyici, merak uyandırıcı.

pique [pi:k] 1. *n.* gurur; incinme, darılma, içerleme; 2. *v/t.* gururunu kırmak, incitmek, darıltmak; kışkırtmak; ~ o.s. upon övünmek *ile.*

pi.ra.cy ['paiərəsi] *n.* korsanlık; izinsiz olarak yayımlama; pi.rate ['~rit] 1. *n.* korsan (gemisi); wireless ~, radio ~, ~ listener kaçak dinleyen kimse; 2. *vb.* izinsiz yayımlamak *(başkasının eserini);* korsanlık etm.; pi.rat.i.cal ⬜ [pai'rætikl] korsanca.

pis.ci.cul.ture ['pisikʌltʃə] *n.* balık üretimi.

pish [piʃ] *int.* öf!, püf!

piss *sl.* [pis] 1. *n.* çiş, sidik; 2. *vb.* işemek, çiş yapmak; ıslatmak *(altını, yatağı).*

pis.ta.chi.o [pis'sta:tʃiəu] *n.* şamfıstığı (ağacı); şamfıstığı yeşili.

pis.til ⚙ ['pistil] *n.* pistil, dişi organ; pis.til.late ⚙ ['~lit] *adj.* dişi organı olan.

**pis.tol** ['pistl] *n.* tabanca, pistol, revolver, piştov.

**pis.ton** ⊕ ['pistən] *n.* piston; '~-rod *n.* piston kolu; '~-stroke *n.* piston tulû (*veya* siası).

**pit** [pit] **1.** *n.* çukur (*a.* ✗); *anat.* koltuk altı; hendek şeklinde tuzak; çiçek hastalığından sonra vücutta kalan küçük çukur; *thea.* parter; parterde oturan seyirciler; *Am. bórsa:* bölüm; pilot kabini; etli meyve çekirdeği; the ~ cehennem; **2.** *vb.* çukurlaştırmak; çukurcuklarla doldurmak; çekirdeklerini çıkarmak; çukura yerleştirmek *veya* gömmek; yüzde çopur bırakmak; ~ against kapıştırmak; ~ted with smallpox çiçek hastalığından dolayı çukur çukur olmuş (*yüz*).

**pit-a-pat** ['pitə'pæt] *adv.* küt küt (*kalp*); pat pat (*ayak sesi*).

**pitch¹** [pitʃ] **1.** *n.* zift; **2.** *v/t.* ziftlemek; ↓ katranlamak.

**pitch²** [~] **1.** *n.* fırlatma, atış, atım; yükseklik; ♪ perde; derece; meyil, eğim, yokuş; ↓ baş kıç vurma; *spor:* saha; işportacının tezgâh yeri; F satıcı ağzı; **2.** *v/t.* kurmak (*çadır*); atmak, fırlatmak; *beysbol:* vurucuya atmak (*top*); ♪ tam perdesini vermek; aşağıya meyletmek; düşürmek; ~ed battle meydan savaşı; *v/i.* ✗ ordugâh kurmak; ↓ baş kıç vurmak; düşmek; *beysbol:* atıcı olarak oynamak; ~ upon rasgele seçmek; ~ into F saldırmak; girişmek.

**pitch...:** '~-and-'toss *n.* yazı tura atma oyunu; '~-'black, '~-'dark *adj.* simsiyah, kapkaranlık, zifiri karanlık.

**pitch.er** ['pitʃə] *n.* testi, sürahi, ibrik; maşrapa.

**pitch.fork** ['pitʃfɔːk] **1.** *n.* saman tırmığı, diren; ♪ diyapazon; **2.** *v/t.* saman tırmığı ile savurmak; zorla getirmek (into *bir mevkiye*).

**pitch-pine** ♀ [pitʃpain] *n.* çıra(lı çam).

**pitch.y** ['pitʃi] *adj.* ziftli, katranlı; simsiyah.

**pit-coal** ✗ ['pitkəul] *n.* taşkömür, maden kömürü.

**pit.e.ous** ☐ *rhet.* ['pitiəs] acınacak halde olan, hazin, yürekler acısı.

**pit.fall** ['pitfɔːl] *n.* tuzak (olarak kazılan çukur); gizli tehlike.

**pith** [piθ] *n.* yumuşak ve süngerimsi doku; ilik; *fig.* öz, cevher, ruh; güç, kuvvet, enerji.

**pith.y** ☐ ['piθi] özlü; kuvvetli, etkili, tesirli; anlamlı.

**pit.i.a.ble** ☐ ['pitiəbl] acınacak halde olan, acıklı.

**pit.i.ful** ☐ ['pitiful] acınacak halde olan, merhamet uyandıran; *contp.* değersiz, aşağılık; merhametli, şefkatli.

**pit.i.less** ☐ ['pitilis] merhametsiz, 'acımasız, kalpsiz.

**pit.man** ['pitmən] *n.* maden ocağı işçisi.

**pit.tance** ['pitəns] *n.* çok az ücret, az miktarda gelir.

**pi.tu.i.tar.y** [pi'tjuːitəri] *adj.* balgam salgılayan...; ~ gland hipofiz guddesi.

**pit.y** ['piti] **1.** *n.* merhamet, acıma, şefkat (on *-e*); for ~'s sake! Allah aşkına!; it is a ~ yazık, vah vah, tüh; it is a thousand pities aman ne yazık; **2.** *v/t.* acımak, merhamet etm.; I ~ him ona acıyorum.

**piv.ot** ['pivət] **1.** *n.* ⊕ mil, eksen, mihver; *fig.* önemli kimse *veya* şey; **2.** *v/i.* mil *veya* eksen üzerinde dönmek (on, upon); *v/t.* mil üzerine yerleştirmek; **piv.o.tal** ['~-tl] *adj.* mile ait; asıl, esas, en önemli.

**pix.i.lat.ed** *Am.* F ['piksəleitid] *adj.* kaçık, çatlak, delidolu, bir tahtası eksik.

**piz.za** [piːtsə] *n.* pizza.

**pla.ca.bil.i.ty** [plækə'biliti] *n.* kolay yatıştırılabilirlik; **pla.ca.ble** ☐ kolay yatışır, hoşgörülü, uysal.

**pla.card** ['plækaːd] **1.** *n.* afiş, levha, yafta, duvar ilanı, poster; **2.** *v/t.* afiş ile bildirmek; *-in* üzerine afiş yapıştırmak.

**pla.cate** [plə'keit] *v/t.* yatıştırmak, teskin etm.

**place** [pleis] **1.** *n.* yer, mevki, mahal, mekân, mevzi; semt, şehir, kasaba; alan, meydan; bina; ♣ basamak, hane; memuriyet, görev, vazife; arazi, toprak; ev, yuva; oturacak yer, koltuk; ~ of delivery teslim yeri; ~ of employment işyeri; give ~ to yer vermek; öncelik tanımak; in (out of) ~ yerli yerinde (yersiz); *fig.* uygun(suz); in ~ of *-in* yerine; in his ~ onun yerinde; in the first ~ ilk olarak, ilk etapta; **2.** *vb.* koymak, yerleştirmek; atamak, tayin etm.; bir mevkiye getirmek; yatırmak (*para*); vermek (*sipariş*); ✗ mevzilemek; be ~d *spor:* ilk üç arasında olm.; '~-name *n.* yer ismi; **plac.er** *n.* yerleştiren kimse; derece *veya* yer alan kimse *veya* şey; nehir sularının getirdiği kum, çakıl *vs.* birikintisi.

**plac.id** ☐ ['plæsid] sakin, halim, yumuşak, uysal; durgun; **pla'cid.i.ty** *n.* sükûnet, yumuşak başlılık, uysallık.

**plack.et** ['plækit] *n.* giyside fermuar yeri; eteklik cebi.

**pla.gi.a.rism** ['pleidʒjərizəm] *n.* çalıntı (eser); **'pla.gi.a.rist** *n.* başkasının eserini kendisininmiş gibi yayımlayan kimse:

**390**

¹pla.gi.a.rize *vb. (bir başkasının eserini)* kendisininmiş gibi yayımlamak, aşırmalar yapmak *-den.*

plague [pleig] 1. *n.* veba; belâ, musibet, dert; 2. *v/t.* bezdirmek *-i,* eziyet vermek *-e,* rahatsız etm. *-i,* canını sıkmak *-in,* belâsını vermek; ¹~-spot *n. mst fig.* kötülük kaynağı.

pla.guy [¹pleigi] *adj.* F sıkıcı, başa belâ olan.

plaice *ichth* [pleis] *n.* pisibalığı.

plaid [plæd] *n.* ekose kumaş; ekose desen; İskoçya dağlılarının giydiği ekose şal.

plain [plein] 1. ☐ düz, sade, basit, desensiz, süssüz; açık seçik, basit, kolay anlaşılır, net; sıradan, alelade; yavan, baharatsız *(yiyecek);* dobra dobra, dürüst; alımsız, çirkin; ~ fare orta hallilerin yedikleri yemek; ~ knitting düz örgü; ~ sewing düz dikiş; 2. *adv.* açıkça; tamamen; 3. *n.* ova, düzlük; *part. Am. attr.* çayır...; ¹~-clothes man sivil polis; ~ deal.ing dürüstlük; dürüst iş; ¹plain.ness *n.* düzlük; sadelik, basitlik, açıklık; plain sail.ing *fig.* kolay *(veya* basit) iş.

plains.man [¹pleinzmən] *n.* ovalı *(veya* ovada yaşayan) kimse; *Am.* çayırlıkta yaşayan kimse.

plaint [pleint] *n.* dava (dilekçesi), şikâyet. yakınma; feryat, figan; plain.tiff [¹~tif] *n.* ☯ davacı; ¹plain.tive ☐ iniltili, kederli, yakınan, sızlanan.

plait [plæt] 1. *n.* örgü; = pleat 1; 2. *v/t.* örmek *(saç vs.);* = pleat 2.

plan [plæn] 1. *n.* plan, taslak, kroki; niyet, maksat, fikir; yol, usül, tarz; 2. *v/t.* planını çizmek; tertiplemek, düzenlemek; *fig.* niyetlenmek, düşünmek, tasarlamak, planlamak; ~ned economy planlı ekonomi; ~ ning board planlama dairesi.

plane¹ [plein] 1. *adj.* düz, dümdüz; düzlem; yassı; 2. *n.* ☒ düzlem; düzey, seviye; ✝ uçak; *fig.* derece, kademe, basamak, sınıf; ⊕ planya, rende; elevating (depressing) ~s *pl.* ✝ yükselme (alçalma) dümeni; 3. *v/t. & v/i.* rendelemek, düzeltmek; ✝ uçmak; havada süzülmek.

plane² ❦ [~] *n. a.* ~-tree çınar (ağacı).

plan.et *ast.* [¹plænit] *n.* gezegen, seyyare.

plane-ta.ble *surv.* [¹pleinteibl] *n.* plançete.

plan.e.tar.i.um [plæni¹tɛəriəm] *n.* planetaryum; plan.e.tar.y [¹plæni¹təri] *adj.* gezegenlerle ilgili, gezegen gibi; *fig.* seyyar, gezginci.

pla.nim.e.try ⅄ [plæ¹nimitri] *n.* yüzölçümü ölçme şekli.

plan.ish ⊕ [¹plæniʃ] *v/t.* parlatmak, perdahlamak.

plank [plæŋk] 1. *n.* uzun tahta, kalas; *Am. parl.* parti programı ana maddesi; 2. *v/t.* tahta ile kaplamak; ~ down *veya* out *sl., Am.* F derhal ödemek; ~ bed kerevet; ¹plank.ing *n.* döşeme tahtası; kaplama.

plank.ton *biol.* [¹plæŋktən] *n.* plankton.

plant [plɑːnt] 1. *n.* bitki, nebat, ot; fabrika, atelye; demirbaş; teçhizat; *sl.* hile, oyun, dolap; 2. *vb.* dikmek, ekmek; kurmak, tesis etm.; *fig.* tohumlarını atmak *(fikir)*; koymak, yerleştirmek; ~ o.s. dikilmek; *sl.* yapıştırmak, aşketmek, indirmek *(tokat, yumruk)*; ~ s.th. on s.o. *b-ne bşi* yüklemek.

plan.tain¹ ❦ [¹plæntin] *n.* sinirotu.

plan.tain² ❦ [~] *n.* bir çeşit muz.

plan.ta.tion [plæn¹teiʃən] *n.* koru, fidanlık; büyük çiftlik, geniş tarla; plant.er [¹plɑːntə] *n.* ekici, ziraatçı; çiftlik sahibi; tohum serpme makinesi; ¹plant-louse *n.* yaprakbiti.

plaque [plɑːk] *n.* levha, plaket.

plash [plæʃ] 1. *n.* şıpırtı, su sıçratma sesi; 2. *int.* foş!; 3. *vb.* su sıçratmak. plash.y [¹plæʃi] *adj.* çamurlu, ıslak, bataklık.

plas.ma *biol.* [¹plæzmə] *n.* (proto)plazma.

plas.ter [¹plɑːstə] 1. *n. pharm.* yakı; plaster; ⊕ sıva; *mst* ~ of Paris alçı; ~ cast alçı; 2. *v/t.* sıvamak, sıva vurmak; yakı yapıştırmak *-e;* ¹plas.ter.er *n.* sıvacı; ¹plas.ter.ing *n.* sıva; alçı; F acı yenilgi.

plas.tic [¹plæstik] 1. *adj.* (~ally) plastik...; naylon...; şekil verilebilen...; ~ arts plastik sanatlar; 2. *n.* plastik; plas.ti.cine [¹~tisiːn] *n.* modelci çamuru; plas.tic.i.ty [~¹tisiti] *n.* istenilen şekle sokulabilme; ¹plas.tics = plastic 2.

plat [plæt] *s.* plait; *s.* plot¹.

plate [pleit] 1. *n. com.* tabak; levha; *phot.* fotoğraf camı; *typ.* klişe; plaka; *Am. beysbol:* kale işareti olan levha; kupa, şilt; altın *veya* gümüş sofra takımı; *a. dental* ~ damak, takma diş, protez; *radyo:* anot; ⊕ maden baskı kalıbı; 2. *v/t.* madenle kaplamak; ✗, ⬦ zırh levharla kaplamak.

pla.teau *geogr.* [¹plætəu] *n.* plato, yayla.

plate-bas.ket [¹pleitbɑːskit] *n.* sofra takımı sepeti; plate.ful [¹~ful] *n.* bir tabak dolusu.

plate...: ¹~-glass *n.* dökme cam; ¹~-lay.er *n.* 🚋 demiryolu işçisi.

plat.en [¹plætən] *n. typ.* daktilo merdanesi.

**plat.er** ['pleitə] *n.* ⊕ kaplamacı; *spor:* ikinci sınıf yarış atı.

**plat.form** ['plætfɔːm] *n.* sahanlık; platform; *geogr.* yayla, plato; 🚋 peron; *Am. part.* kürsü; podyum; *pol.* parti programı; *part. Am. pol.* çalışma programı.

**plat.i.num** *min.* ['plætinəm] *n.* platin.

**plat.i.tude** *fig.* ['plætitjuːd] *n.* yavan laf; adilik, bayağılık.

**pla.toon** ✕ [plə'tuːn] *n.* takım, müfreze.

**plat.ter** ['plætə] *n.* düz ve büyük tabak.

**plau.dit** ['plɔːdit] *n.* *mst* ~s *pl.* alkış, takdir, tezahürat.

**plau.si.bil.i.ty** [plɔːzə'biliti] *n.* akla yatkınlık, makûl olma; olasılık.

**plau.si.ble** □ ['plɔːzəbl] akla sığan, makûl, akla yatkın; olası.

**play** [plei] **1.** *n.* oyun, eğlence; *thea.* piyes; şaka; oynama; kumar; *fig.* hareket serbestliği; faaliyet (alanı); ⊕ işleme, çalışma; fair (foul) ~ doğru (hileli) oyun; ~ on words kelime oyunu, cinas; **bring into** ~ kullanmak, harekete geçirmek; **make great** ~ **with** vurgulamak, ısrar etm.; **2.** *v/i.* oyun oynamak; eğlenmek; hareket etm., kımıldamak, sallanmak; ♪ çalgı çalmak; rol yapmak; kumar oynamak; ⊕ çalışmak; ~ **fast and loose** with ikiyüzlü davranmak, oyun etm. *-e*; ~ **at** cards iskambil oynamak; ~ **for** time zaman kazanmaya çalışmak; ~ **up** gayretle oynamak; yaramazlık yapmak; ~ **upon** istismar etm. *-i*; *v/t.* oyna(t)mak; yapmak *(hile)*; *thea.* temsil etm., canlandırmak; çalmak *(enstruman)*; işletmek, kullanmak; ~ **off** *fig.* düşürmek *(against each other birbirine)*; ~**ed** out yorgun, bitkin; modası geçmiş, demode; **'~-act.ing** *n.* temsil etme; *fig.* gösterişçilik; **'~-bill** *n.* tiyatro afişi; oyun programı; **'~-book** *n.* *thea.* libretto; **'~--boy** *n.* zevk peşinde koşan zengin delikanlı; **'play.er** *n.* oyuncu; aktör; çalgıcı; kumarbaz; müzik çalmak için kullanılan alet; **'play.er-pi.an.o** *n.* otomatik piyano; **'play.fel.low** *n.* oyun arkadaşı; **play.ful** □ ['~ful] oyunbaz, şakacı, eğlenceli, şen; **'play.ful.ness** *n.* oyunbazlık; şakacılık.

**play...:** '~.**go.er** *n.* tiyatro meraklısı; '~-**ground** *n.* oyun sahası; '~.**house** *n.* tiyatro; *Am.* çocukların içinde oynadıkları küçük ev.

**play.ing...:** '~-**card** *n.* iskambil kâğıdı; '~.-**field** *n.* oyun sahası.

**play...:** '~.**mate** *s.* playfellow; '~.-**off** *n. spor:* rövanş maçı; '~.**thing** *n.* oyuncak *(a.*

*fig)*; '~.**wright** *n.* *thea.* piyes yazarı.

**pla.za** ['plɑːzə] *n.* (İspanya'da) meydan, pazar yeri.

**plea** [pliː] *n.* 🔒 müdafaa, savunma; dava; rica, yalvarma; itiraz; bahane, özür, mazeret; **make a** ~ itirazda bulunmak, reddetmek; **on the** ~ **of** *veya* **that ...** bahanesiyle.

**plead** [pliːd] *v/i.* yalvarmak, rica etm., istirham etm.; dava açmak; ~ **for** savunmak *-i*; *s.* guilty; *v/t.* ileri sürmek, iddia etm.; savunmak; suçlamak; mazeret olarak göstermek; **'plead.a.ble** *adj.* davada cevap, delil *veya* özür olarak gösterilebilir; **'plead.er** *n.* 🔒 avukat, dava vekili; **'plead.ing** *n.* 🔒 dava açma; ~s *pl.* 'lâyihalar, yazılı savunmalar.

**pleas.ant** □ ['pleznt] hoş, latif, güzel, tatlı, cana yakın; **'pleas.ant.ness** *n.* hoşluk, letafet; **'pleas.ant.ry** *n.* şaka(cılık), komiklik; neşe, hoşbeş.

**please** [pliːz] *v/i.* memnun edici olm.; **if you** ~ *iro.* ister misin...!; lütfen, rica ederim; **isterseniz;** ~ **come in!** lütfen girin!; *v/t.* sevindirmek, hoşnut etm., memnun etm., *-in* hoşuna gitmek; ~ **yourself** F nasıl isterseniz öyle yapın; **be** ~**d to do** seve seve yapmak, yapmaktan memnun ~ *b-ni* memnun etm.; **take** ~ **in ...***den* **pleased** *adj.* memnun, hoşnut.

**pleas.ing** □ ['pliːziŋ] hoş, sevimli, hoşa giden, memnuniyet verici, zevk veren.

**pleas.ur.a.ble** □ ['pleʒərəbl] zevk veren, hoşa giden; tatminkâr.

**pleas.ure** ['pleʒə] **1.** *n.* zevk, keyif, memnuniyet, sevinç, sefa, haz, lezzet; emir, irade, istek, arzu; *attr.* zevk veren...; **at** ~ arzuya göre, istenildiği kadar; **give s.o.** ~ *b-ni* memnun etm.; **take** ~ **in ...***den* zevk almak; **2.** *vb.* zevk almak; zevk vermek; **'~-ground** *n.* lunapark.

**pleat** [pliːt] **1.** *n.* pli, plise; **2.** *v/t.* pli yapmak.

**ple.be.ian** [pli'biːən] **1.** *adj.* *(eski Roma'da)* aşağı tabakadan olan; adi, bayağı; **2.** *n.* aşağı tabakadan kimse.

**pleb.i.scite** ['plebisit] *n.* plebisit.

**pledge** [pledʒ] **1.** *n.* rehin; söz, vaat, yemin, ant; güvence, teminat, taahhüt; **put in** ~ rehine koymak; **take out of** ~ rehinden kurtarmak; **2.** *v/t.* rehin olarak vermek, rehine koymak; taahhüt etm.; söz verdirmek; *-in* şerefine içmek; **he** ~**d himself** vaat etti; **pledg'ee** *n.* rehinli alacaklı; **'pledg.er** *n.* rehinli borçlu, rehin veren.

**Ple.iad** ['plaiəd] *n.,* *pl.* **Ple.ia.des** ['~diːz] Süreyya burcu, Ülker.

**ple.na.ry** [ˈpliːnəri] *adj.* tam *(yetki)*, sınırsız, sonsuz, bütün; tüm üyelerin katıldığı *(toplantı)*.

**plen.i.po.ten.ti.ar.y** [plenipəuˈtenʃəri] 1. *adj.* tam yetkili *(elçi vs.)*; 2. *n.* tam yetkili elçi.

**plen.i.tude** [ˈplenitjuːd] *n.* bolluk, çokluk, doluluk, bütünlük.

**plen.te.ous** □ *poet.* [ˈplentjəs] çok, bol, bereketli; **ˈplen.te.ous.ness** *n.* bolluk, çokluk, bereket.

**plen.ti.ful** □ [ˈplentiful] bol, çok, bereketli, verimli.

**plen.ty** [ˈplenti] 1. *n.* bolluk, çokluk, zenginlik; ~ of çok, bol; horn of ~ bolluk (sembolü); 2. *adj.* F pek çok, bol, bereketli.

**ple.o.nasm** [ˈpliːənæzəm] *n.* kelime fazlalığı, laf kalabalığı, söz uzatımı.

**pleth.o.ra** [ˈpleθərə] *n.* dolgunluk, fazlalık; ✷ kan fazlalığı; **ple.thor.ic** [pleˈθɔrik] *adj.* (~ally) pletorik; *fig.* şişman.

**pleu.ri.sy** ✷ [ˈpluərisi] *n.* zatülcenp.

**pli.a.bil.i.ty** [plaiəˈbiliti] *n.* esneklik, yumuşaklık; *fig.* uysallık.

**pli.a.ble** □ [ˈplaiəbl] bükülür, esnek, yumuşak; *fig.* uysal.

**pli.an.cy** [ˈplaiənsi] *n.* esneklik, bükülebilirlik.

**pli.ant** □ [ˈplaiənt] = pliable.

**pli.ers** [ˈplaiəz] *n. pl.* (a pair of *bir*) kıskaç, pens(e).

**plight¹** [plait] 1. *v/t.* söz vermek, güvence vermek; 2. *n.* söz, vaat.

**plight²** [~] *n.* kötü durum, çıkmaz.

**plim.solls** [ˈplimsəlz] *n. pl.* tenis ayakkabısı.

**plinth** ⌂ [plinθ] *n.* duvar etekliği, etek tahtası.

**plod** [plɔd] *vb. a.* ~ along, ~ on ağır ağır yürümek, çalışmak vs.; ‖**plod.ding** □ ağır, hantal.

**plop** [plɔp] 1. *int.* cup!; 2. *n.* ˈcup' sesi; 3. *v/i.* ˈcup' diye ses çıkarmak; ˈcup' diye düşmek.

**plot¹** [plɔt] *n.* arsa, parsel.

**plot²** [~] 1. *n.* entrika, suikast, fesat, gizli plan, kumpas, komplo, dolap; romanın konusu; 2. *v/t. a.* ~ down -in haritasını çıkarmak; plan *veya* haritada göstermek; *b.s.* -e karşı entrika çevirmek; *v/i.* kumpas kurmak, kötü niyetlerle plan yapmak; ‖**plot.ter** *n.* entrikacı, suikastçı, fesatçı.

**plough** [plau] 1. *n.* saban, pulluk; ⊕ sabana benzer alet; *univ. sl.* başarısızlık, çakma, kalma *(sınavda)*; the ♉ *ast.* Büyükayı; 2. *v/t.* sabanla işlemek; yarıp

geçmek; ~ back tekrar yatırmak *(para)*; be ~ed *univ. sl.* çakmak, kalmak *(sınavda)*; *v/i.* saban sürmek; ağır ağır ilerlemek; ‖~.man *n.* saban süren kimse; çiftçi, köylü; ‖~.share *n.* saban demiri, saban kulağı.

**plov.er** [ˈplʌvə] *n. orn.* yağmurkuşu.

**plow** [plau], **plow.man** *part.* Am. = plough *etc.*

**pluck** [plʌk] 1. *n.* cesaret, yiğitlik; koparma, yolma; çekme; 2. *v/t.* koparmak, yolmak; çekmek, çekip almak (from -den); *sl.* soyup soğana çevirmek, yolmak *(kumarda)*; parmakla çalmak *(telli saz)*; *univ. sl.* döndürmek, çaktırmak *(sınavda)*; ~ at tutup çekmek, çekiştirmek -i; ~ up courage cesaretini toplamak.

**pluck.y** F □ [ˈplʌki] cesur, yiğit, yürekli, yılmaz.

**plug** [plʌg] 1. *n.* tapa, tıkaç, tampon; ⚡ fiş; *mot.* buji; tütün parçası; Am. *radyo:* durmadan tekrarlanan reklam; F vuruş, vurma; değersiz şey; yaşlı at; yangın musluğu; ~ socket elektrik prizi; 2. *vb.* tıkamak; *sl.* tabanca ile vurmak; yumruklamak; Am. F durmadan reklamını yapmak; ~ in ⚡ prize sokmak; *sl.* eşek gibi çalışmak; ateş etm.; ‖**plug-ˈug.ly** *n.* Am. *sl.* gangster, eşkıya, katil.

**plum** [plʌm] *n.* erik (ağacı); kuru üzüm; arzulanacak şey; F en güzel lokma, kıyak şey; bonbon, şekerleme; *sl.* £ 100.000.

**plum.age** [ˈpluːmidʒ] *n.* kuşun tüyleri.

**plumb** [plʌm] 1. *adv.* düşey olarak, dimdik; tamamen, kesinlikle; 2. *n.* şakul, iskandil kurşunu; 3. *vb.* iskandil etm., şakule vurmak, şakullemek; ölçmek, tartmak; doğrultmak, düzeltmek; kurşunla kaplamak; *fig.* araştırmak, kökenine inmek; F tesisatçılık yapmak; **plum.ba.go** [~ˈbeigəu] *n.* kalem kurşunu, grafit; **plumb.er** *n.* lehimci, muslukçu, su tesisatçısı; **plumb.bic** [ˈplʌmbik] *adj.* 🜛 kurşun...; **plumb.ing** [ˈ~miŋ] *n.* boru tesisatçılığı, muslukçuluk; su tesisatı; **ˈplumb-line** *n.* ⊕ şakul (sicimi), çekül; **ˈplumb-rule** *n.* çekül.

**plume** [pluːm] 1. *n.* iri ve gösterişli tüy, sorguç; tüye benzer şey; şeref madalyası; nişan; 2. *vb.* (gaga ile) düzeltmek *(tüylerini)*; tüylerle süslemek; övünmek; ~ o.s. on ...ile övünmek, *k-ni* beğenmek.

**plum.met** [ˈplʌmit] *n.* şakul kurşunu, çekül; ağırlık.

**plum.my** F [ˈplʌmi] *adj.* iyi, güzel, hoş, çekici, cazip; sahte tavırlı, yapmacık.

**plump¹** [plʌmp] **1.** *adj.* dolgun, tombul, tıknaz, şişman, balık etinde; semiz *(hayvan)*; **2.** *v/t. & v/i.* şişmanla(t)mak, dolgunlaş(tır)mak.

**plump²** [~] **1.** *v/t. & v/i.* birden düş(ür)-mek; «pat» diye oturmak; *parl.* oy vermek (for *-e*); yardım etm. *-e*; **2.** *n.* ani düşüş; **3.** *adv.* F aniden, birden; açıkça, kabaca; **4.** □ F tam, kesin, direkt.

**plump.er** [ˈplʌmpə] *n. parl.* oy; *sl.* yalan.

**plump.ness** [ˈplʌmpnis] *n.* dolgunluk, tombulluk; F samimiyet, içtenlik, doğruluk.

**plum-pud.ding** [ˈplʌmˈpudiŋ] *n.* baharatlı Noel pudingi.

**plum.y** [ˈpluːmi] *adj.* tüylü, tüy gibi, tüylerle süslenmiş.

**plun.der** [ˈplʌndə] **1.** *n.* yağma(cılık), çapulculuk; **2.** *v/t. & v/i.* yağma etm., soymak, talan etm.; çapulculuk etm.; **plun.der.er** *n.* yağmacı, çapulcu.

**plunge** [plʌndʒ] **1.** *n.* dalış, dalma; yüzme; F tehlikeli girişim; make *veya* take the ~ tehlikeli bir işe girişmek; **2.** *v/t. & v/i.* dal(dır)mak, sokmak; at(ıl)mak (into *-e*); boğmak *(karanlığa)*; batırmak (into *-e*); gir(iş)mek; ileriye atılmak *(at)*; ↓ baş kıç vurmak; büyük kumar oynamak; borca girmek.

**plung.er** [ˈplʌndʒə] *n.* piston; dalgıç; *sl.* kumarbaz; vurguncu.

**plunk** [plʌŋk] *v/t. & v/i.* birden düş(ür)-mek.

**plu.per.fect** *gr.* [ˈpluːˈpəːfikt] *n.* geçmiş zamanın hikâye şekli.

**plu.ral** *gr.* [ˈpluərəl] *n.* çoğul; **plu.ral.i.ty** [~ˈræliti] *n.* çokluk, ekseriyet, çoğunluk; ~ of wives poligami, çokevlilik.

**plus** [plʌs] **1.** *prp.* fazlasıyle, ilavesiyle; ayrıca, ve; **2.** *adj.* fazla, ilave olan; pozitif; **3.** *n.* artı (işareti); pozitif miktar; fazlalık; ~-fours F [ˈ~ˈfɔːz] *n. pl.* golf pantolonu.

**plush** [plʌʃ] *n.* pelüş.

**plush.y** [ˈplʌʃi] *adj.* pelüş...; *sl.* süslü, gösterişli, lüks.

**plu.toc.ra.cy** [pluːˈtɔkrəsi] *n.* plütokrasi, zenginler hâkimiyeti; zenginerki; **plu.to.crat** [ˈ~təukræt] *n.* plütokrat.

**plu.to.ni.um** ⚗ [pluːˈtəunjəm] *n.* plutonyum.

**plu.vi.al** [ˈpluːviəl] *adj.*, **plu.vi.ous** yağmurlu, yağmurla ilgili; **plu.vi.om.e.ter** [~ˈɔmitə] *n.* yağmurölçer.

**ply** [plai] **1.** *n.* kat, katmer, tabaka; *fig.* meyil, eğilim; iplik teli; **2.** *v/t.* işletmek, kullanmak; etmek, yapmak; eğmek; durmadan vermek *(yiyecek, içki)*; tutmak *(soru yağmuruna)*; ~ a trade ticaret yap-

mak; *v/i.* çalışmak; düzenli seferler yapmak, gidip gelmek.

**ply-wood** [ˈplaiwud] *n.* kontrplak.

**pneu.mat.ic** [njuːˈmætik] **1.** *adj.* (~ally) hava basıncı ile ilgili; hava basıncı ile çalışan...; içinde sıkıştırılmış hava olan...; ~ hammer hava çekici; ~ tire şişirilmiş otomobil lastiği; **2.** *n.* şişirilmiş otomobil lastiği, iç lastik.

**pneu.mo.ni.a** ⚕ [njuːˈməunjə] *n.* zatürree.

**poach¹** [pəutʃ] *v/i.* bata çıka yürümek; cıvık cıvık olm. *(toprak)*; gizlice avlanmak, yasak bölgede avlanmak.

**poach²** [~] *vb. a.* ~ up kazıp karıştırmak.

**poach³** [~]: ~ed eggs *pl.* sıcak suya kırılıp pişirilmiş yumurtalar.

**poach.er** [ˈpəutʃə] *n.* ruhsatsız avlanan kimse, yasak bölgede avlanan kimse; yumurta haşlama kabı.

**po.chette** [pɔˈʃet] *n.* el torbası, poşet.

**pock** ⚕ [pɔk] *n.* çiçek hastalığı kabarcığı.

**pock.et** [ˈpɔkit] **1.** *n.* cep; *geol.* çukur, gedik; para, maddi olanak; ⚓ hava boşluğu; bölge, semt; **2.** *v/t.* cebe koymak, cebine atmak, *sl.* iç etmek; *Am. pol.* veto etm.; gizlemek, saklamak, bastırmak; **3.** *adj.* cebe sığan..., cep...; ~ lighter cep çakmağı; ~ lamp cep feneri; **¹~.book** *n.* cep kitabı; cüzdan; *Am.* kadın cüzdanı *veya* el çantası.

**pod** [pɔd] **1.** *n.* ♣ kabuk, zarf; hayvan sürüsü; **2.** *v/t. -in* kabuğunu soymak; *v/i.* tohum zarfı oluşturmak.

**po.dag.ra** ⚕ [ˈpɔdəgrə] *n.* ayakta görülen gut hastalığı.

**podg.y** F [ˈpɔdʒi] *adj.* bodur, tıfıl, tıknaz.

**po.di.um** [ˈpəudiəm] *n.* podyum, platform.

**po.em** [ˈpəuim] *n.* şiir, koşuk, manzume.

**po.e.sy** [ˈpəuizi] *n.* şairlik, şiir sanatı; şiirler.

**po.et** [ˈpəuit] *n.* şair, ozan; **po.et.as.ter** [ˈ~tæstə] *n.* şair bozuntusu, kalitesiz şair; **¹po.et.ess** *n.* kadın şair; **po-et.i.cal** □ [pəuˈetik(ə)l] şiire ait, şiir niteliğinde, manzum, şairane; **po¹et.ics** *n. pl.* vezin tekniği; koşuk kural ve usulü; **po-et.ize** [ˈ~itaiz] *vb.* şiir yazmak; **¹po.et.ry** *n.* şiir sanatı; *coll.* şiirler.

**poign.an.cy** [ˈpɔinənsi] *n.* keskinlik, acılık; *fig.* ıstırap; **¹poign.ant** □ acı, keskin; kuvvetli; tesirli, şiddetli; *fig.* dokunaklı.

**point** [pɔint] **1.** *n.* nokta (a. *gr,* ♪, *phys. etc.)*; uç, burun; puan; sayı; mesele, husus, özel bir durum; ↓ pusula taksimatından biri, kerte; mesele, ana fikir; punto; cihet, bakım; sebep, neden; özellik; ⚡ priz; etki, tesir; ~s *pl.* 🚂 makaslar; *s.* ~-lace; ~ of view görüş noktası, bakış açısı; the ~ is that... mesele şu ki...; there is no ~ in ger. ...mekte bir yarar yok, ...menin bir anlamı yok; make a ~ of s.th. bşe özen göstermek; make the ~ that ...dığını göstermek; stretch a ~ ödün vermek, göz yummak, izin vermek; in ~ of hususunda, bakımından; in ~ of fact hakikaten, gerçekten; off *veya* beyond the ~ konu dışında; differ on many ~s birçok noktada ayrılmak; he was on the ~ of coming gelmek üzereydi; win on ~s *boks:* sayı ile kazanmak; to the ~ isabetli, uygun; stick to the ~ konuya bağlı kalmak, konu dışına çıkmamak; 2. *v/t.* ucunu sivriltmek; doğrultmak, yöneltmek; çimento *veya* harç ile doldurmak; noktalamak; virgülle hanelere ayırmak; *oft.* ~ out göstermek, belirtmek, işaret etm.; ~ at yöneltmek *-e,* doğrultmak *-e,* çevirmek *-e; v/i.* göstermek; silahını doğrultmak *-e;* ferma etm. *(köpek);* yönelmek; ~ at göstermek *-i;* ~ to göstermek *-i,* delâlet etm. *-e;* '~-'blank *adj.* yatay olarak atılan; yakın menzilden yapılan *(atış);* açık, kesin, dolaysız; ~ shot yakın menzil atışı; '~-du.ty *n.* belli bir noktada yapılan görev *(part. trafik kontrolü):* 'point.ed □ sivri uçlu; *fig.* manalı, alamlı; keskin, tesirli; 'point.ed.ness *n.* sivri uçluluk; anlamlı olma; 'point.er *n.* işaret değneği; gösterge, ibre; F anlamlı söz, ima; zağar, bir cins av köpeği; 'point-'lace *n.* oya işi; 'point.less *adj.* uçsuz; anlamsız, manasız; gayesiz, amaçsız; puansız, sayısız *(oyun);* 'point--po'lice.man *n.* belli bir noktada görev yapan trafik polisi; 'points.man *n.* makasçı; 'point-to-'point race arazide iki nokta arasında yapılan at yarışı.

poise [pɔiz] 1. *n.* denge; istikrar; kendine güven; kendine hâkim olma; duruş, hal; 2. *v/t.* & *v/i.* dengele(n)mek; *-in* dengesini sağlamak; dik tutmak, kaldırmak, havada tutmak; dengeli olm.; asılı olm., sarkmak; havada durmak; be ~d dengede durmak.

poi.son ['pɔizn] 1. *n.* zehir; 2. *v/t.* zehirlemek *(a. fig.);* 'poi.son.er *n.* zehirleyici; zehirle adam öldüren kimse; 'poi.son-ous □ zehirli; *fig.* fesat; F iğrenç, tiksindirici.

poke [pəuk] 1. *n.* itme, dürtme; yumruk atma; 2. *v/t.* dürtmek; saplamak; atmak, vurmak *(yumruk);* uzatmak, çıkarmak; sokmak; *a.* ~ up karıştırmak; ~ fun at alay etm., dalga geçmek *ile;* ~ one's nose into s.th. bşe burnunu sokmak; *v/i.* dürtüklemek *(at -i);* araştır-

mak (into *-i);* oyalanmak, aylak aylak dolaşmak; çıkıntı yapmak.

pok.er¹ ['pəukə] *n.* ocak demiri.

po.ker² [~] *n.* poker oyunu; ~ face *fig.* ifadesiz yüz.

pok.er-work ['pəukəwəːk] *n.* pirogravür.

pok.y ['pəuki] *adj.* küçük, ufak; sıkıcı, kasvetli,. bunaltıcı; çok yavaş.

po.lar ['pəulə] *adj.* kutba ait, kutupsal; tamamen birbirine zıt; ~ bear kutup ayısı; po.lar.i.ty *phys.* [pəul'læriti] *n.* kutbiyet, polarite; po.lar.i.za.tion *phys.* [-ləri-'zeifən] *n.* polarma; 'po.lar.ize *v/t.* & *v/i. phys.* polarmak; iki zıt kutba ayırmak *(veya* ayrılmak).

Pole¹ [pəul] *n.* Polonyalı, Lehli.

pole² [~] *n.* kutup *(geogr., ast., phys., fig.).*

pole³ [~] 1. *n.* direk, kazık, sırık; 5,029 metrelik bir uzunluk; olta kamışı; 2. *v/t.* & *v/i.* sırıklamak, sırıklarla donatmak; sırıkla desteklemek; sırıkla itmek; sırıkla kayığı yüzdürmek; '~-ax(e) *n.* X uzun saplı balta; teber; kasap satırı; '~.cat *n.* zo. kokarca; *Am.* sansar; ~ jump = pole vault.

po.lem.ic [pɔ'lemik] 1. *a.* po'lem.i.cal □ tartışmalı, münakaşalı, polemiğe ait; 2. *n.* tartışma, münakaşa; tartışmacı, münakaşacı; po'lem.ics *n. pl.* tartışma sanatı, polemik.

pole-star ['pəulstaː] *n.* Kutupyıldızı; *fig.* önder, yönetici unsur.

pole-vault ['pəulvɔːlt] *n. spor:* sırıkla yüksek atlama.

po.lice [pɔ'liːs] 1. *n.* polis (teşkilâtı); two ~ iki polis; ~ dossier iyi hal belgesi; 2. *v/t.* polis kuvvetiyle sağlamak *(düzen ve asayişi);* idare etm., kontrol etm.; po-'lice.man *n.* polis memuru; po'lice-of.fice *n.* karakol; po'lice-of.fi.cer *n.* polis memuru; po'lice-sta.tion *n.* karakol; po'lice--sur'veil.lance *n.* polis gözetimi; po'lice--trap *n.* hız kontrol bölgesi; po'lice-wom.an *n.* kadın polis.

pol.i.cy¹ ['pɔlisi] *n.* siyaset, politika, idare, yönetim; takip edilen yol, hareket tarzı.

pol.i.cy² [~] *n.* poliçe; *Am.* bir çeşit lotarya.

po.li.o(.my.e.li.tis) ['pəuliəu(maiə'laitis)] *n.* çocuk felci; omurilikteki gri maddenin iltihabı.

Pol.ish¹ ['pəulif] *adj.* Leh, Polonya *veya* Polonyalılara ait.

pol.ish² ['pɔlif] 1. *n.* cilâ, perdah; boya; cilâlama; *fig.* incelik, zarafet, terbiye, nezaket; 2. *v/t.* & *v/i.* cilâla(n)mak, parla(t)mak; *fig.* terbiye etm., süslemek, zarifleştirmek; ~ off hemen bitirmek, silip süpürmek *(yemek)*; ~ up pırıl pırıl yapmak, iyice cilâlamak; **'pol.ish.ing 1.** *n.* cilâ(lama); **2.** *adj.* cilâlı..., parlak...

**po.lite** □ ['pə'lait] nazik, kibar, terbiyeli, ince; **po'lite.ness** *n.* nezaket, kibarlık, incelik.

**pol.i.tic** □ ['pɔlitik] siyasî, politik; basiretli, sağgörülü, tedbirli, akıllı; body ~ devlet teşekkülü; **po.lit.i.cal** □ [pə'litikəl] siyasî, siyasal, politik; devlet *veya* hükümete ait; **pol.i.ti.cian** [pɔli'tiʃən] *n.* politikacı, siyasetçi; *contp.* kendi çıkarına siyaset ile uğraşan kimse; **pol.i.tics** ['~tiks] *n. sg.* siyaset, politika; parti entrikaları.

**pol.i.ty** ['pɔliti] *n.* hükümet *veya* idare şekli; devlet, hükümet.

**pol.ka** ['pɔlkə] *n.* polka dansı *veya* müziği; ~ dot *Am.* puanlı, benekli *(kumaş)*.

**poll¹** ['pəul] *n.* seçim, oy verme; oy (sayısı); seçmen sayısı; seçim bürosu; anket; *co.* baş, kelle, kafa; go to the ~s oy vermek; **2.** *v/t.* kesmek, kırkmak, kırpmak; toplamak *(oy)*; seçim listesine kaydetmek; = pollard 2; *v/i.* oy vermek; ~ for oy vermek -*e*.

**poll²** [pɔl] *n.* papağan.

**pol.lard** ['pɔləd] **1.** *n.* boynuzsuz hayvan; budanmış ağaç; **2.** *v/t.* budamak *(ağaç)* -*in* boynuzlarını kesmek.

**poll-book** ['pəulbuk] *n.* seçmen kütüğü.

**pol.len** ⚕ ['pɔlin] *n.* çiçek tozu; **pol.li.na.tion** [pɔli'neiʃən] *n.* tozaklama.

**poll.ing...: '~-booth** *n.* .oy verme hücresi; **'~-dis.trict** *n.* seçim bölgesi; **'~-place** *n.* oy atılan yer; **'~-sta.tion** *n.* oy verme yeri.

**poll-tax** ['pəultæks] *n.* kişi başına düşen vergi; baş vergisi; oy kullanmak için ödenen vergi.

**pol.lute** [pə'luːt] *v/t.* pisletmek, kirletmek *(a. fig.)*; **pol'lu.tion** *n.* pisletme, kirletme; kirlilik.

**po.lo** ['pəuləu] *n. spor.* polo, çevgen; water ~ sutopu; **'~-neck** *adj.* balıkçı yaka...

**po.lo.ny** [pə'ləuni] *n.* domuz etinden yapılan sosis.

**pol.troon** [pɔl'truːn] *n.* korkak kimse; **pol'troon.er.y** *n.* korkaklık.

**po.lyg.a.my** [pɔ'ligəmi] *n.* çokkarılılık, poligami; **pol.y.glot** ['~glɔt] *adj.* birçok dilde yazılmış olan; birçok dil bilen; **pol.y.gon** ['~gən] *n.* poligon, çokgen; **po'lyg.o.nal** [~gənl] *adj.* çokköşeli, çokgen...; **pol.y.phon.ic** ♪ [~'fɔnik] *adj.* çok sesli,

polifonik; **pol.yp** *zo.* ['pɔlip] *n.*, **pol.y.pus** ⚕ ['~pəs] polip; **pol.y.syl.lab.ic** ['~si-'læbik] *adj.* çok heceli; **pol.y.syl.la.ble** ['~siləbl] *n.* üçten fazla heceli kelime; **pol.y.tech.nic** [~'teknik] *n.* sanat *veya* fen öğreten okul; **pol.y.the.ism** ['~θiː-izəm] *n.* çoktanrıcılık.

**po.made** [pə'mɑːd] *n.* briyantin, merhem, pomat.

**pome.gran.ate** ⚕ ['pɔmigrænit] *n.* nar.

**Pom.er.a.nian** [pɔmə'reinjən] **1.** *adj.* Pomeranya'ya ait; **2.** *n.* Pomeranyalı; *a.* ~ dog Pomeranya köpeği.

**pom.mel** ['pʌml] **1.** *n.* eyer kaşı; kılıç kabzasının başı; **2.** *v/t.* yumruklamak, yumrukla dövmek.

**pomp** [pɔmp] *n.* gösteriş, tantana, ihtişam, azamet, görkem.

**pom.pom** ['pɔmpɔm] *n.* otomatik uçaksavar top.

**pom.pos.i.ty** [pɔm'pɔsiti] *n.* tantana, ihtişam, görkem; **'pomp.ous** □ tantanalı, debdebeli, görkemli; azametli, gururlu; süslü.

**pon.cho** ['pɔntʃəu] *n.* baştan geçme kepenek, panço.

**pond** [pɔnd] *n.* havuz, gölcük.

**pon.der** ['pɔndə] *v/t.* zihninde tartmak, düşünmek; *v/i.* uzun boylu düşünmek (on, over -*i*); **pon.der.a.bil.i.ty** [~rə'biliti] *n.* ölçülebilirlik, tartılabilirlik; **'pon.der.a.ble** *adj.* ölçülebilir, tartılabilir; **pon.der.os.i.ty** [~'rɔsiti] *n.* ağırlık, sıklet; **'pon.der.ous** □ ağır, hantal, iri, cüsseli; can sıkıcı; **'pon.der.ous.ness** = ponderosity.

**pone** [pəun] *n.* mısır ekmeği.

**pon.iard** ['pɔnjəd] *n.* kama, hançer.

**pon.tiff** ['pɔntif] *n.* papa, piskopos; **pon-'tif.i.cal** □ papaya *veya* piskoposa ait; gururlu; amirane; **pon'tif.i.cate** [~kit] *n.* papanın makamı *veya* görev süresi, papalık.

**pon.toon** ✕ [pɔn'tuːn] *n.* duba, tombaz; **pon'toon-bridge** *n.* dubalar üstüne kurulan köprü, tombaz köprüsü.

**po.ny** ['pəuni] *n. zo.* midilli; *sl.* 25 İngiliz lirası; **'~-'en.gine** *n.* 🚂 manevra lokomotifi; **'~-tail** *n.* at kuyruğu *(saç)*.

**pooch** *Am. sl.* [puːtʃ] *n.* it, köpek.

**poo.dle** ['puːdl] *n.* kaniş köpeği.

**pooh** [puː] *int.* öf!

**pooh-pooh** [puː'puː] *v/t.* küçümsemek, alaya almak.

**pool¹** [puːl] *n.* gölcük, su birikintisi; herhangi bir sıvı birikintisi; havuz; bir nehrin derin ve durgun bölümü.

**pool²** [~] **1.** *n.* ortaya konulan para; toto; † tüccarlar birliği; bir çeşit bilar-

do oyunu; ~ room bilardo salonu; 2. *v/t.*
† ortaklaşa toplamak, birleştirmek.

**poop** ↓ [puːp] 1. *n.* pupa; 2. *v/t.* pupadan
yemek *(dalga)*.

**poor** ☐ [puə] fakir, yoksul, muhtaç; zavallı, biçare; fena, adi, bayağı, naçizane; az, biraz, kıt; zayıf, kuru, kuvvetsiz; the ~ yoksullar, fakir fukara; ~ me!
zavallı ben!; ~ health bozuk sıhhat; '~-
-box *n.* sadaka kutusu; '~-house *n.* darülaceze, düşkünler yurdu; '~-law *n.* ळ
fakirleri koruyan kanun; **'poor.ly** 1. *adj.*
*pred.* hasta, rahatsız; 2. *adv.* kötü bir şekilde, fena', başarısızlıkla; kusurlu olarak; he is ~ off meteliğe kurşun atıyor;
**'poor.ness** *n.* fakirlik, yoksulluk; **'poor-
-rate** *n.* zekât, halktan alınan fakirlere
yardım vergisi; **'poor-'spir.it.ed** korkak,
ödlek, yüreksiz; çekingen.

**pop**[1] [pɔp] 1. *n.* patlama sesi; F gazoz;
in ~ *sl.* rehinde; 2. *v/t. & v/i.* patla(t)-
mak, 'pat' diye ses çıkarmak; ateş etm.;
*sl.* rehine vermek; Am. patlatmak *(mısır)*; hemen sokuvermek; ~ in uğramak;
birden sokmak; ~ the question to a lady
bir kadına evlenme teklif etm.; ~ up birden gelmek, çıkıvermek; 3. *adv.* aniden,
birden; 4. *int.* pat!, çat!

**pop**[2] F [~] 1. *adj.* sevilen, tutulan, popüler; 2. *n.* pop müziği; pop şarkısı.

**pop**[3] Am. F [~] *n.* baba.

**pop-corn** *part.* Am. ['pɔpkɔːn] *n.* patlamış
mısır.

**pope** [pəup] *n.* papa; **'pope.dom** *n.* papalık; **'pop.er.y** *n. contp.* papalık sistemi.

**pop-eyed** ['pɔpaid] *adj.* patlak gözlü.

**pop.gun** ['pɔpgʌn] *n.* oyuncak mantarlı tüfek, patlangaç.

**pop.in.jay** ['pɔpindʒei] *n.* züppe kimse.

**pop.ish** ☐ ['pəupiʃ] Katolik kiliselerine
ait.

**pop.lar** ❦ ['pɔplə] *n.* kavak.

**pop.lin** ['pɔplin] *n.* poplin.

**pop.pet** ['pɔpit] *n.* ↓ kızak payandası; ⊕
başlıklı cıvata; *s.* puppet.

**pop.py** ❦ ['pɔpi] *n.* gelincik; haşhaş, afyon; '~.cock *n.* Am. F saçma, boş laf.

**pop.u.lace** ['pɔpjuləs] *n.* halk, avam, kitle.

**pop.u.lar** ☐ ['pɔpjulə] halka ait; herkesçe anlaşılabilen; halkın kesesine uygun;
herkesçe sevilen, popüler, revaçta olan;
genel, yaygın; ~ front faşizm ve gerici-
liğe karşı olan solcu koalisyonu; **pop.u-
lar.i.ty** [~'læriti] *n.* halk tarafından tutulma, rağbet, popülerlik; **pop.u.lar.ize**
['~ləraiz] *vb.* halkın beğeneceği şekle
sokmak; herkesin anlayacağı şekle sokmak; halka hitap etm.; **'pop.u.lar.ly** *adv.*

herkesçe sevilerek; halka hitap eder şekilde.

**pop.u.late** ['pɔpjuleit] *v/t.* şeneltmek, nü-
fuslandırmak; bayındırlaştırmak; **pop-
u'la.tion** *n.* nüfus, ahali.

**pop.u.lous** ☐ ['pɔpjuləs] nüfusu çok, kalabalık, yoğun nüfuslu.

**por.ce.lain** ['pɔːslin] *n.* porselen (eşya).

**porch** [pɔːtʃ] *n.* kapı önünde sundurma;
Am. veranda, taraça.

**por.cu.pine** *zo.* ['pɔːkjupain] *n.* oklukirpi.

**pore**[1] [pɔː] *n.* gözenek, mesane.

**pore**[2] [~] *v/i.* dikkatle bakmak (over -*e*);
derin derin düşünmek (over, on, upon -*i*).

**pork** [pɔːk] *n.* domuz eti; '~-bar.rel *n.' Am.
sl.* politik amaçlarla kullanılmak üzere
devlet hazinesinden ayrılan para; '~-
-butch.er *n.* domuz kasabı; **'pork.er** *n.*
besili domuz; **'pork.y** 1. *adj.* F yağlı, semiz, şişko; 2. Am. F = porcupine.

**por.nog.ra.phy** [pɔː'nɔgrəfi] *n.* pornografi,
müstehcen yazı *veya* resimler.

**po.ros.i.ty** [pɔː'rɔsiti] *n.*, **po.rous.ness**
['pɔːrəsnis] gözenekli olma.

**po.rous** ☐ ['pɔːrəs] gözenekli; su *veya*
hava geçiren.

**por.phy.ry** *min.* ['pɔːfiri] *n.* somaki, porfir.

**por.poise** *ichth.* ['pɔːpəs] *n.* yunusbalığı.

**por.ridge** ['pɔridʒ] *n.* yulaf lapası; **por.rin-
ger** ['pɔrindʒə] *n.* çorba *veya* lapa kâsesi.

**port**[1] [pɔːt] *n.* liman (şehri); ~ of call uğ-
ranılacak *(veya* ara) liman; ~ of destina-
tion gidilecek liman; ~ of trans-shipment
aktarma limanı.

**port**[2] ↓ [~] *n.* lombar (kapağı).

**port**[3] [~] 1. *v/t.* ✗ namlusu sol omuza doğru olmak üzere eğri tutmak *(tüfek)*; 2.
*n.* tüfek *veya* başka bir silahın omuzda-
ki duruşu.

**port**[4] ↓ [~] 1. *n.* geminin sol *veya* iskele
tarafı; 2. *v/t.* iskeleye kırmak *(dümen)*.

**port**[5] [~] *n.* porto şarabı.

**port.a.ble** ['pɔːtəbl] *adj.* taşınabilir, porta
tif; ~ radio set portatif radyo; ~ typewriter portatif daktilo.

**por.tage** ['pɔːtidʒ] *n.* taşıma, nakletme;
nakliyat yolu; *s.* porterage.

**por.tal** ['pɔːtl] *n.* görkemli kapı, giriş;
**'por.tal-to-'por.tal pay** işçinin işyerinde
harcadığı zamana göre ödenen para.

**port.cul.lis** ✗ [pɔːt'kʌlis] *n.* kaleye girişi
önlemek için indirilen demir parmaklık.

**por.tend** [pɔː'tend] *v/t.* yakında olacağına alâmet olm. *(kötü bir olay)*, delâlet
etm. -*e*.

**por.tent** ['pɔːtent] *n.* kehanet; alâmet, geleceği gösteren işaret; **por'ten.tous** ☐

[~təs] uğursuz; harikulâde, fevkalâde; olağanüstü.

**por.ter**[1] [ˈpɔːtə] n. kapıcı.

**por.ter**[2] [~] n. hamal; yataklı vagon görevlisi; siyah bira; **ˈpor.ter.age** n. hamallık (ücreti), hamaliye; **ˈpor.ter-house** n. birahane; a. ~ steak bir çeşit biftek.

**port.fire** [ˈpɔːtfaiə] n. barutlu fitil.

**port.fo.li.o** [pɔːtˈfəuljəu] n. evrak çantası; bakanlık (görevi); bir kimseye ait tüm tahviller; minister without ~ sandalyesiz bakan.

**port-hole** ↓ [ˈpɔːthəul] = port[2].

**por.ti.co** ⚠ [ˈpɔːtikəu] n. revak, kemeraltı, sütunlu giriş.

**por.tière** [ˈpɔːtiɛə] n. kapı gibi kullanılan kalın perde.

**por.tion** [ˈpɔːʃən] 1. n. hisse, pay; parça, kısım; porsiyon; kısmet, talih, kader; çeyiz; 2. v/t. ayırmak, bölmek, taksim etm.; kızına vermek (çeyiz); **ˈpor.tion.less** adj. çeyizsiz.

**port.li.ness** [ˈpɔːtlinis] n. şişmanlık, heybet, iriyarılık; **ˈport.ly** adj. iri yapılı, iriyarı, cüsseli, şişman; heybetli, gösterişli.

**port.man.teau** [pɔːtˈmæntəu] n. bavul; ~ word gr. birleşik (veya uydurma) sözcük, kelime.

**por.trait** [ˈpɔːtrit] n. portre, resim, tasvir; kelimelerle yapılan tanım; **ˈpor.trait.ist** n. portreci; **por.trai.ture** [ˈ~tʃə] = portrait; resim sanatı; tanımlama .

**por.tray** [pɔːˈtrei] v/t. resmetmek, -in resmini yapmak; tanımlamak, tasvir etm.; **porˈtray.al** n. resmetme; tanımlama, tasvir etme.

**Por.tu.guese** [pɔːtjuˈgiːz] 1. adj. Portekiz'le ilgili; 2. n. Portekizce; Portekizli.

**pose** [pəuz] 1. n. poz, duruş, vaziyet; tavır; yapmacık tavır, numara; 2. v/t. & v/i. yerleş(tir)mek; poz vermek; poz almak; ortaya atmak (soru), yaratmak (sorun); tavır takınmak; taslamak (as -i) **ˈpos.er** n. poz veren kimse; şaşırtıcı soru(n).

**posh** sl. [pɔʃ] adj. şık, modaya uygun; lüks, birinci sınıf, en iyi.

**po.si.tion** [pəˈziʃən] n. yer, mevki, mahal (a. fig.); durum, vaziyet; ✕ mevzi; ast., ↓ duruş, pozisyon; fig. sosyal durum; hal, tavır; iş, görev, vazife, memuriyet; fikir, iddia; tutum; ~ light seyir ışığı, pozisyon ışığı; be in a ~ to do bşi yapma yetki ve durumunda olm.

**pos.i.tive** [ˈpɔzətiv] 1. □ kesin, katî, mutlak; olumlu, müspet; emin; yapıcı; tam, gerçek; esaslı; gerekli; A, phls., phys., phot., ƒ pozitif; 2. n. olumlu derece;

**phot.** pozitif resim; gr. belgin sıfat; kesin şey; **ˈpos.i.tive.ness** n. kesinlik.

**pos.se** [ˈpɔsi] n. polis müfrezesi; heyet, takım, grup.

**pos.sess** [pəˈzes] v/t. malik•olm., sahip olm. -e; hükmetmek; meşgul etm.; kurcalamak (zihin); ~ed deli, çılgın; düşkün (with -e); ~ed of sahip olan -e, ...si olan; ~ o.s. of ele geçirmek -i, sahibi olm. -in; **pos.ses.sion** [pəˈzeʃən] n. iyelik, sahiplik, sahip olma; cinnet, delilik; sömürge, koloni; tasarruf, kullanma yetkisi; ~s pl. mal, mülk, servet; in ~ ol elinde, elde etmiş -i; **posˈses.sive** gr. [~siv] 1. □ iyelik gösteren, iyelik...; ~ case -in hali; 2. n. -in hali; **posˈses.sor** n. mal sahibi; **posˈses.so.ry** adj. sahipliğe ait.

**pos.set** [ˈpɔsit] n. bira veya şaraplı baharatlı sıcak süt.

**pos.si.bil.i.ty** [pɔsəˈbiliti] n. imkân, olanak; ihtimal, olabilirlik; **ˈpos.si.ble** 1. □ mümkün, olası, muhtemel, kabil; makûl, akla yatkın; 2. n. spor: rekor; olası bş, imkân; **ˈpos.si.bly** adv. belki, ihtimal, mümkündür ki, imkân dahilinde; if I ~ can olurda ...bilirsem; how can I ~ do it? onu nasıl yapabilirim acaba?; I cannot ~ do it onu yapmama imkân yok.

**pos.sum** F [ˈpɔsəm] = opossum; play ~ uyur veya ölü taklidi yapmak.

**post**[1] [pəust] 1. n. direk, kazık, destek; v/t. mst ~ up yapıştırmak, asmak (ilan).

**post**[2] [~] n. ✕ ordugâh, kışla, askeri menzil; ✝ alışveriş merkezi; ✕ kol, karakol, devriye; polis noktası; iş, görev, memuriyet; atama, tayin; ❤ posta (servisi); atlı postacı; posta arabası; posta kutusu; postane; at one's ~ ✕ nöbeti başında; by ~ posta ile; 2. v/t. yerleştirmek, koymak; görevlendirmek; postaya vermek, postalamak; ✝ defteri kebire işlemek; oft. ~ up ✝ yevmiye defterinden defteri kebire geçirmek; bildirmek, bilgi vermek; keep s.o. ~ed up b-ni haberdar etm.; v/i. posta atlarıyle seyahat etm.; acele gitmek.

**post**[3] ✕ [~] n. sinyal, boru; last ~ yat borusu.

**post.age** [ˈpəustidʒ] n. posta ücreti; ~ due eksik ödenmiş posta ücreti; ~ stamp posta pulu.

**post.al** [ˈpəustəl] 1. □ posta ile ilgili, posta...; ~ order posta havalesi; ℗ Union milletlerarası posta birliği; 2. n. a. ~ card Am. kartpostal.

**post.card** [ˈpəustkɑːd] n. kartpostal, posta kartı.

post.date ['pəust'deit] v/t. -in üzerine ileri bir tarih atmak.

post.er ['pəustə] n. yafta, afiş, poster; a. bill-~ afiş yapıştıran kimse.

poste res.tante ['pəust 'resta:nt] n. postrestant.

pos.te.ri.or F [pɔs'tiəriə] 1. □ sonra gelen, sonraki (to -den); gerideki; 2. n. a. ~s pl. kaba etler, insan kıçı.

pos.ter.i.ty [pɔs'teriti] n. gelecek nesiller; döl.

pos.tern ['pəustə:n] n. yan kapı, yan giriş; arka kapı.

post-free ['pəust'fri:] adj. posta ücretine tabi olmayan; posta ücreti ödenmiş.

post-grad.u.ate ['pəust'grædjuit] 1. adj. üniversite sonrası öğrenime ait; 2. n. üniversite mezunu, doktora talebesi.

post-haste ['pəust'heist] adv. büyük bir telaşla, apar topar, alelacele, ivedilikle.

post.hu.mous □ ['pɔstjuməs] ölümden sonra olan; yazarın ölümünden sonra yayınlanan (eser); babasının ölümünden sonra doğmuş (çocuk).

pos.til.(l)ion [pəs'tiljən] n. posta arabasını çeken atlardan birine binerek sürücülük eden kimse.

post...: '~.man n. postacı; '~.mark 1. n. posta damgası; 2. v/t. damgalamak; '~.mas.ter n. postane müdürü; ♀ General posta genel müdürü.

post me.rid.i.em ['pəust mə'ridiəm] adj. öğleden sonraya ait; post-mor.tem ['~'mɔ:tem] 1. adj. öldükten sonra yapılan; 2. n. a. ~ examination otopsi.

post...: '~-of.fice n., mst ~ of.fice postane; Am. öpücük oyunu; general ~ merkez postane; ~ box posta kutusu; ~ order posta havalesi; '~-paid adj. & adv. posta ücreti ödenmiş (olarak).

post.pone [pəus'pəun] v/t. ertelemek, sonraya bırakmak, tehir etm.; post'pone.ment n. erteleme, tehir.

post.pran.di.al □ co. [pəust'prændiəl] yemek sonrası.

post.script ['pəusskript] n. derkenar, (dip)not.

pos.tu.lant ['pɔstjulənt] n. namzet, aday; pos.tu.late 1. ['~lit] n. önerme; kabulü zorunlu olan esas; 2. ['~leit] v/t. istemek, talep etm., dilemek; öneri olarak kabul etm.; var saymak; pos.tu'la.tion n. talep, istek, dilek; öneri olarak kabul etme.

pos.ture ['pɔstʃə] 1. n. duruş, poz, vaziyet; hal, durum, gidişat; davranış, tutum; 2. v/t. & v/i. poz ver(dir)mek; ta-

vır takınmak.

post-war ['pəust'wɔ:] adj. savaş sonra-sı...

po.sy ['pəuzi] n. çiçek demeti.

pot [pɔt] 1. n. çömlek, kavanoz, kap; saksı; F spor: gümüş kupa; Am. sl. haşiş; büyük miktar; a ~ of money F dünya kadar para; big ~ F kodaman; 2. v/t. saksıya dikmek; kavanozda konserve etm.: rasgele vurmak, avlamak; lâzımlığa oturtmak (bebek); bilardo: çukura düşürmek (top); v/i. F rasgele ateş etm.

po.ta.ble ['pəutəbl] adj. içilebilir.

pot.ash ♈ ['pɔtæʃ] n. potas, kalya taşı, potasyum hidrat.

po.tas.si.um ♈ [pə'tæsjəm] n. potasyum.

po.ta.tion [pəu'teiʃən] n. mst ~s pl. içki (içme).

po.ta.to [pə'teitəu] n., pl. po'ta.toes [~z] patates; ~ bee.tle zo. patates böceği.

pot...: '~-bel.ly n. göbek; göbekli kimse; '~-boil.er n. sadece para kazanmak için yazılan kitap vs.; '~-boy n. meyhanede içki servisi yapan garson.

po.ten.cy ['pəutənsi] n. güç, kuvvet, kudret; potansiyel; erkeğin cinsi iktidarı; 'po.tent □ kuvvetli, güçlü, kudretli, etkili, tesirli, nüfuzlu; cinsi iktidarı olan (erkek); po.ten.tate ['~teit] n. nüfuzlu kimse; hükümdar, kral; po.ten.tial [pəu'tenʃəl] 1. adj. kuvvetli; muhtemel, olası; phys. potansiyel, gizil; 2. n. a. ~ mood gr. yeterlik kipi; ihtimal, olasılık; gizil, iktidar; ≠ potansiyel, gerilim; po.ten.ti.al.i.ty [~ʃi'æliti]n. imkân, ihtimal.

poth.er ['pɔðə]1. n. dert, sıkıntı; gürültü, karışıklık, şamata; 2. v/t. başını ağrıtmak, üzmek, sinirlendirmek; v/i. gürültü etm.

pot...: '~-herb n. yemeğe çeşni veren yeşillik; '~-hole n. mot. derin çukur; geol. kayalarda suyun açtığı çukur; '~-hook n. tencereyi ateş üstüne asmaya yarayan S şeklinde çengel; ~s pl. yazmayı öğrenenlerin S şeklindeki çizgileri; '~-house n. düşük kaliteli meyhane, birahane.

po.tion ['pəuʃən]n. ilâç dozu; iksir.

pot-luck ['pɔt'lʌk] n.: take ~ Allah ne verdiyse yemek.

pot.tage ['pɔtidʒ] n. koyu sebze çorbası.

pot.ter¹ ['pɔtə] vb.: ~ about oyalanmak; ~ away vakit geçirmek.

pot.ter² [~] n. çömlekçi; ~'s wheel çömlekçi çarkı; 'pot.ter.y n. çanak çömlek; çömlek imalâthanesi; çömlekçilik.

pot.ty ['pɔti] 1. adj. sl. önemsiz, ufak tefek; çılgın, deli; 2. n. çocuk lâzımlığı.

pouch [pautʃ] 1. n. torba, kese (a. zo);

göz altlarındaki şişlik; **2.** *vb.* torbaya koymak; torba gibi yapmak; **pouched** *adj.* keseli.

**poul.ter.er** ['pəʊltərə] *n.* tavukçu.

**poul.tice** 🌷 ['pəʊltis] *n.* yara lapası.

**poul.try** ['pəʊltri] *n.* kümes hayvanları.

**pounce** [paʊns] **1.** *n.* saldırma, atılma, hamle; **2.** *v/i.* atılmak (on, upon -in üzerine).

**pound¹** [paʊnd] *n.* libre (=453,6 g); ~ (sterling) sterlin, İngiliz lirası (*abbr.* £ = 100 pence).

**pound²** [~] **1.** *n.* sahipsiz araç veya hayvanların muhafaza edildiği yer; **2.** *v/t.* ağıla kapamak.

**pound³** [~] *v/t.* dövmek, vurmak, ezmek; yumruklamak; *sl.* borsa: indirmek *(fiyat); v/i.* küt küt atmak *(kalp);* ~ away ağır ağır yürümek.

**pound.age** ['paʊndidʒ] *n.* sterlin başına alınan komisyon.

**pound.er** ['paʊndə] *n.* ... librelik *bş.*

**pour** [pɔː] *v/t. & v/i.* ak(ıt)mak, dök(ül)-mek, boşal(t)mak; koymak *(çay vs.);* akın etm.; bardaktan boşanırcasına yağmak; ~ out boşaltmak, koymak; *fig.* içini dökmek; ~ with rain bardaktan boşanırcasına yağmak; it never rains but it ~s *fig.* aksilikler üst üste gelir.

**pout** [paʊt] **1.** *n.* somurtma, surat asma; **2.** *v/t.* sarkıtmak *(dudaklarını); v/i.* somurtmak, surat asmak; **'pout.er** *n.* zo. kursağını şişirebilen bir güvercin.

**pov.er.ty** ['pɔvəti] *n.* yoksulluk, fakirlik; yetersizlik, eksiklik; **'~-strick.en** *adj.* çok fakir, yoksul, muhtaç.

**pow.der** ['paʊdə] **1.** *n.* toz; pudra; barut; **2.** *v/t. & v/i.* toz veya pudra sürmek -e, pudralamak; pudra kullanmak; **'~-box** *n.* pudralık, pudriyer; **'~-puff** *n.* pudra ponponu; **'pow.der.y** *adj.* tozlu, toz gibi, toz halinde.

**pow.er** ['paʊə] *n.* kuvvet, kudret, güç *(a.* ⊕, *⚡);* yetki, salâhiyet; etki, tesir; hâkimiyet, nüfuz, sözü geçerlik; ⚡ vekâlet(name); etkili kişi, otorite, ꓥ üs; F çok miktar; yetenek, kabiliyet; devlet, hükümet; merceğin büyütme kabiliyeti; in ~ iktidarda; **'~-dive** *n.* 🛧 pike; **pow.er.ful** ['~ful] ☐ kuvvetli, güçlü, kudretli; etkili, tesirli; nüfuzlu, yetkili; **'pow.er-**-**house** = power-station; **'pow.er.less** *adj.* kuvvetsiz, güçsüz, kudretsiz; beceriksiz; **pow.er line** ⚡ elektrik hattı; **pow.er plant** = power-station; **pow.er pol.i.tics** *n. sg.* kuvvet politikası; **'pow.er-sta.tion** *n.* elektrik santralı.

**pow.wow** ['paʊwaʊ] *n.* toplantı; *Am.* Kızılderililerin yaptığı toplantı; F büyücü hekim.

**pox** *sl.* [pɔks] *n.* frengi.

**pra(a)m** ⚓ [prɑːm] *n.* altı düz bir çeşit kayık.

**prac.ti.ca.bil.i.ty** [præktikə'biliti] *n.* pratiklik, kullanışlılık; **'prac.ti.ca.ble** ☐ yapılabilir; elverişli, kullanışlı; **'prac.ti.cal** ☐ uygulamalı, pratik; kullanışlı, elverişli, uygulanabilir; gerçekçi; tecrübeli, deneyimli; işlek; ~ joke eşek şakası; ~ chemistry uygulamalı kimya; **prac.ti.cal-**-**i.ty** [~'kæliti] *n.* uygulanabilme, elverişlilik; **prac.ti.cal.ly** ['~kəli] *adv.* pratik olarak; hemen hemen, yaklaşık olarak; gerçekte. fiilen.

**prac.tice** ['præktis] **1.** *n.* uygulama, tatbikat; alışıklık, alışkanlık, âdet; pratik, egzersiz, idman; müşteriler; meslek icrası; doktorluk, avukatlık; işyeri; out of ~ körlenmiş, körelmiş; put into ~ uygulamaya koymak; sharp ~ dalavere; **2.** *Am.* = practise.

**prac.tise** [~] *v/t. & v/i.* yapmak; uygulamak, tatbik etm.; talim etm., eğitmek; çalışmak; k-ni alıştırmak; pratik yapmak, egzersiz yapmak; bir meslekte çalışmak; *spor:* idman *(veya* antrenman) yapmak; ♪ pratik yapmak; ~ upon k-ne yontmak; istifade etm. -den; **'prac.tised** *adj.* tecrübeli, deneyimli; alışık, talimli; hünerli.

**prac.ti.tion.er** [præk'tiʃnə] *n.* pratik yapan kimse; doktor; avukat; *a.* general ~ pratisyen doktor.

**prae.tor** ['priːtə] *n.* eski Roma'da hâkim.

**prag.mat.ic** [præg'mætik] *adj.* (~ally) pratik, ameli; pragmatizme ait.

**prai.rie** *Am.* ['prɛəri] *n.* bozkır, büyük çayırlık; ~ schooner üstü kapalı atlı araba.

**praise** [preiz] **1.** *n.* övgü; şükür; tapınma; **2.** *v/t.* övmek, methetmek; şükretmek.

**praise.wor.thy** ['preizwɔːði] ☐ övülmeye değer, takdire lâyık.

**pram** F [præm] *n.* çocuk arabası.

**prance** [prɑːns] *v/i.* fırlamak *(at);* caka satarak yürümek; zıp zıp zıplamak, zıplayan ata binmek; *v/t.* zıplatıp oynatmak *(at).*

**pran.di.al** ☐ ['prændiəl] yemekle ilgili, yemek...

**prang** *sl.* [præŋ] *n.* şiddetli bombardıman.

**prank** [præŋk] **1.** *n.* kaba şaka, eşek şakası; oyun; **2.** *vb.* ~ out telleyip pullamak, çok süslemek; caka satmak.

**prate** [preit] **1.** *n.* gevezelik; **2.** *vb.* geve-

zelik etm., çok konuşmak, boş laf etm.;
**'prat.er** n. geveze kimse.
**prat.tle** ['prætl] = prate.
**prawn** zo. [prɔːn] n. büyük karides, deniz
tekesi.
**pray** [prei] v/i. dua etm. (to -e; for için):
ibadet etm., namaz kılmak; yalvarmak
(to -e); v/t. çok rica etm. (for -i); ~ tell
me lütfen bana söyleyin.
**prayer** [prɛə] n. dua, niyaz; duacı, dua
eden kimse; ibadet, namaz; oft. ~s pl.
temenni, rica; Lord's ~ Hıristiyanların
fatihaya benzetilebilen duası; Book of
Common ♀ dua kitabı; '~-book n. dua kitabı; '~-rug n. seccade.
**pre...** [priː, pri] prefix önce, evvel, ön.
**preach** [priːtʃ] v/t. & v/i. va'zetmek, vaız
vermek (to -e); nasihat etm., öğüt vermek; ileri sürmek; telkin etm.; **'preacher** n. vaiz; **'preach.ing** n. vaız; öğüt;
**'preach.ment** n. vaız; va'zetme.
**pre.am.ble** [priːæmbl] n. önsöz, başlangıç.
**pre.ar.range** [priːə'reindʒ] v/t. önceden
düzenlemek.
**preb.end** eccl. ['prebənd] n. papaza bağlanan ödenek; **'pre.ben.dar.y** n. ödenek
alan papaz.
**pre.car.i.ous** □ [pri'kɛəriəs] kararsız, şüpheli; tehlikeli, rizikolu, nazik; güvenilmez, istikrarsız, asılsız; **pre'car.i.ous.ness**
n. riziko, tehlikeli durum.
**pre.cau.tion** [pri'kɔːʃən] n. tedbir, önlem,
ihtiyat; **pre'cau.tion.ar.y** [~ʃnəri] adj. önlem olarak, ihtiyati.
**pre.cede** [priː'siːd] vb. -den önce gelmek,
-den önde olm.; -in önünde yürümek;
fig. -den daha önemli (veya üstün) olm.;
**pre'ced.ence, pre'ced.en.cy** n. önce gelme,
öncelik, üstünlük; kıdem; **prec.e.dent**
['presidənt] n. emsal; örnek, numune;
**pre.ced.ing** [priː'siːdiŋ] adj. önceki, önde olan, takip edilen.
**pre.cen.tor** eccl. [priː'sentə] n. kilisede
müziği idare eden kimse.
**pre.cept** ['priːsept] n. emir, hüküm; ilke,
ahlâki kural; talimat, yönerge; ♂ mahkeme emri; **pre.cep.tor** [priː'septə] n. öğretmen, eğitmen; **pre'cep.tress** [~tris] n.
bayan öğretmen.
**pre.cinct** ['priːsiŋkt] n. mıntıka, bölge, yöre; part. Am. seçim bölgesi; ~s pl. havali, çevre; pedestrian ~ sadece yayala-
ra mahsus yol.
**pre.cious** ['preʃəs] 1. n. kıymetli, değerli;
çok sevilen, gözde; aşırı titiz, müşkülpesent; kibar, nazik; F kötü, rezil; 2. adv.
F pek, çok; **'pre.cious.ness** n. değer, kıymet; pahalılık; aşırı kibarlık.

**prec.i.pice** ['presipis] n. uçurum; sarp kayalık; **pre.cip.i.tance, pre.cip.i.tan.cy** [pri-
'sipitəns(i)] n. acele(cilik), telaş; **pre-
'cip.i.tate** 1. [~teit] v/i. & v/i. yüksek bir
yerden aşağı at(ıl)mak, düş(ür)mek;
zamanından önce meydana getirmek;
hızlandırmak; ♂ çökel(t)mek; yoğunlaştırmak (buhar); yoğunlaşıp yağmur
vs. şeklinde yağmak; 2. [~tit] □ aceleci; düşüncesiz; acele ile yapılmış; anî;
3. ♂ [~tit] n. tortu, çökelti; **pre.cip.i.ta-
tion** [~'teiʃən] n. yağış (miktarı); acelecilik, telaş; ♂ çökelme; **pre'cip.i.tous**
□ çok dik, sarp, uçurum gibi; aceleci,
atılgan; çok hızlı.
**pré.cis** ['preisiː] n. öz(et).
**pre.cise** □ [pri'sais] tam(am), katî, kesin; titiz, dakik; kusursuz; ~ly! elbette!;
**pre'cise.ness** n. kesinlik; dakiklik; açıklık, vuzuh.
**pre.ci.sion** [pri'siʒən] n. dikkat, kesinlik,
katilik; dakiklik; doğruluk; attr. dakik;
hassas (alet).
**pre.clude** [pri'kluːd] v/t. önlemek, engel
olm., meydan vermemek; ~ s.o. from ger.
b-ni bş yapmaktan alıkoymak.
**pre.co.cious** □ [pri'kəuʃəs] vaktinden önce gelişmiş, fig. büyümüş de küçülmüş;
**pre'co.cious.ness, pre.coc.i.ty** [pri'kɔsiti]
n. erken gelişmişlik.
**pre.con.ceive** [priːkən'siːv] vb. peşin hüküm vermek, önyargıda bulunmak; ~d
önyargılı.
**pre.con.cep.tion** ['priːkən'sepʃən] n. önyargı, peşin hüküm.
**pre.con.cert.ed** ['priːkən'səːtid] adj. önceden kararlaştırılmış.
**pre.cur.sor** [priː'kɔːsə] n. haberci, müjdeci; işaret, alâmet; **pre'cur.so.ry** adj. ön,
ilk; önceden haber veren.
**pre.date** ['priː'deit] vb. erken tarih atmak; daha önce gelmek.
**pred.a.to.ry** ['predətəri] adj. yağmacılıkla
geçinen, çapulcu, talancı; yırtıcı (hayvan).
**pre.de.cease** ['priːdi'siːs] v/t. -den önce ölmek.
**pre.de.ces.sor** ['priːdisesə] n. öncel, selef:
ata, cet.
**pre.des.ti.nate** [priː'destineit] v/t. önceden nasip etm., alnına yazmak -in, önceden mukadder kılmak; **pre.des.ti'na.tion**
n. takdir; eccl. yazgı, alın yazısı, kader,
nasip, kısmet; **pre'des.tined** adj. seçkin,
güzide.
**pre.de.ter.mine** ['priːdi'təːmin] v/t. önceden tayin etm.; önceden kararlaştırmak.
**pred.i.ca.ble** ['predikəbl] adj. iddia edile-

bilir.

**pre.dic.a.ment** [pri'dikəmənt] *n. phls.* kötü durum, çıkmaz.

**pred.i.cate** 1. ['predikeit] *v/t.* doğrulamak; belirtmek, ifade etm., göstermek; dayan(dır)mak (on -*e*); 2. ['‿kit] *n. gr.* yüklem; **pred.i.ca.tion** [‿'keiʃən] *n.* hüküm, yükleme; **pred.i.ca.tive** [pri'dikətiv] □ doğrulayıcı; *gr.* yüklemi oluşturan.

**pre.dict** [pri'dikt] *v/t.* önceden bildirmek, kehanette bulunmak; **pre.dic.tion** [‿'dikʃən] *n.* önceden haber verme, kehanet.

**pre.di.lec.tion** [pri:di'lekʃən] *n.* yeğleme, tercih (for -*i*).

**pre.dis.pose** ['pri:dis'pəuz] *v/t.* önceden hazırlamak (to -*e*); yetenekli kılmak; **pre.dis.po.si.tion** ['‿dispə'ziʃən] *n.* yatkınlık, yetenek, kabiliyet; *part.* ? eğilim (to -*e*).

**pre.dom.i.nance** [pri'dominəns] *n.* üstünlük, ağır basma; **pre'dom.i.nant** □ üstün, ağır basan, hâkim, galip; **pre'dom.i.nate** [‿neit] *v/i.* hâkim olm. (over -*e*); üstün olm., galip gelmek.

**pre-em.i.nence** [pri:'eminəns] *n.* üstünlük, seçkinlik; **pre'em.i.nent** □ üstün, seçkin.

**pre-emp.tion** [pri:'empʃən] *n.* başkalarından önce satın alma (hakkı).

**preen** [pri:n] *v/t.* gaga ile düzeltmek (*tüy*); *k-ne* çekidüzen vermek; ~ o.s. on *fig.* övünmek *ile.*

**pre-en.gage** [pri:in'geidʒ] *v/t.* önceden taahhüt etm.; önceden tutmak, peylemek; **pre-en'gage.ment** *n.* önceden taahhüt etme.

**pre-ex.ist** ['pri:ig'zist] *v/i.* daha önce var olm. *veya* yaşamak; **'pre-ex'ist.ence** *n.* daha önce var olma.; **'pre-ex'ist.ent** *adj.* daha önce var olan.

**pre.fab** ['pri:'fæb] 1. *adj.* prefabrik...; 2. *n.* prefabrik yapı; **'pre'fab.ri.cate** [‿rikeit] *v/t.* parçalarını önceden hazırlamak *veya* imal etm.

**pref.ace** ['prefis] 1. *n.* önsöz, başlangıç; 2. *v/t.* önsöz ile başlamak; -*in* önsözünü yazmak.

**pref.a.to.ry** □ ['prefətəri] önsözle ilgili, önsöz niteliğinde...

**pre.fect** ['pri:fekt] *n.* eski Roma'da vali, yüksek rütbeli memur; Paris polis şefi; *okul:* sınıf mümessili (*veya* başkanı).

**pre.fer** [pri'fə:] *v/t.* tercih etm., yeğlemek (to -*e*); daha çok beğenmek; sunmak, arzetmek; atamak; terfi ettirmek; *s.* share 1; I should ~ you not to go gitmemenizi yeğlerim, bence gitmeseniz daha iyi; **pref.er.a.ble** □ ['prefərəbl] daha iyi (to -*den*), tercih edilir (to -*e*); **'pref.er-**

a.bly *adv.* tercihen; **'pref.er.ence** *n.* yeğleme, yeğ tutma, tercih (hakkı); *part.* ? öncelik, üstünlük, rüçhan; *s.* share 1.; **pref.er.en.tial** □ [‿'renʃəl] tercihli; tercih ed(il)en...; **pref.er'en.tial.ly** *adv.* tercihen; **pre.fer.ment** [pri'fə:mənt] *n.* terfi, yükselme; öncelik.

**pre.fix** 1. ['pri:fiks] *n.* önek; ünvan; 2. [pri:'fiks] *v/t.* koymak (*önek*).

**preg.nan.cy** ['pregnənsi] *n.* gebelik, hamilelik; *fig.* dolgunluk; derinlik; anlam; **'preg.nant** □ hamile, gebe; *fig.* anlamlı, manalı; dolu, yüklü; verimli.

**pre-heat** ⊕ ['pri:'hi:t] *vb.* önceden ısıt mak.

**pre.hen.sile** [pri'hensail] *adj.* kavrayabilen, tutabilen.

**pre.his.tor.ic** ['pri:his'tɔrik] *adj.* tarih öncesine ait, tarihöncesi..., tarihten önceki...

**pre-ig.ni.tion** *mot.* ['pri:ig'niʃən] *n.* erken ateşleme.

**pre.judge** ['pri:'dʒʌdʒ] *v/t.* önceden hüküm vermek.

**prej.u.dice** ['predʒudis] 1. *n.* önyargı, peşin hüküm; haksız hüküm; tarafgirlik; without ~ to etki altında kalmadan, zarar vermeksizin -*e*; 2. *v/t.* haksız hüküm verdirmek -*e* (against -*e karşı*); haksız hüküm *veya* iş ile zarar vermek -*e*; ~**d** tarafgir; zarar görmüş.

**prej.u.di.cial** □ [predʒu'diʃəl] önyargılı; zararlı (to -*e*).

**prel.a.cy** ['preləsi] *n.* piskoposluk.

**prel.ate** ['prelit] *n.* piskopos.

**pre.lec.tion** [pri'lekʃən] *n.* konferans, ders; **pre'lec.tor** *n.* konferansçı.

**pre.lim** F [pri'lim] *n.* ön sınav, yeterlik sınavı.

**pre.lim.i.nar.y** [pri'liminəri] 1. □ hazırlayıcı, ilk, ön, başlangıç niteliğinde; 2. *n.* ön sınava, yeterlik sınavı; **pre'lim.i.na.ries** [‿riz] *n. pl.* ön hazırlık, başlangıç.

**prel.ude** ['prelju:d] 1. *n.* ♪ peşrev, fasıl, prelüd; başlangıç, giriş; 2. *vb.* ♪ peşrev'le açmak; bir başlangıçla açmak; peşrev çalmak.

**pre.ma.ture** □ [premə'tjuə] *fig.* zamanından evvel olan *veya* gelişen, erken...; erken doğan; vakitsiz, mevsimsiz; ~ delivery erken doğum; **pre.ma'ture.ness, pre-ma'tu.ri.ty** [‿riti] *n. fig.* zamanından evvel gelişme, mevsimsizlik.

**pre.med.i.tate** [pri:'mediteit] *v/t.* önceden düşünmek, tasarlamak, amaçlamak; ~**d** murder 🞠 taammüden cinayet; **pre.med-i'ta.tion** *n.* tasarlama, kasıt; önceden düşünme.

pre.mi.er ['premjə] 1. *adj.* baştaki, birinci, ilk, baş, asıl; 2. *n.* başbakan.

prem.ière ['premièə] *n.* gala.

pre.mi.er.ship ['premjəʃip] *n.* başbakanlık.

prem.ise 1. ['premis] *n.* terim, önerme, öncül; ~s *pl.* mülk, ev ve müştemilâtı; ana madde; licensed ~s *pl.* meyhane; on the ~s yerinde, mahallinde, bina müştemilâtı içinde; 2. pre.mise [pri'maiz] *v/t.* açıklayarak önceden belirtmek.

pre.mi.um ['pri:mjəm] *n.* prim; mükâfat, ödül; değer; ikramiye; hediye; ücret; ⚕ prim, acyo, kâr, temettü; at a ~ fazla fiyatla; çok rağbette, tutulan.

pre.mo.ni.tion [pri:mə'niʃən] *n.* önsezi; uyarma; pre.mon.i.to.ry □ [pri'mənitəri] önsezi kabilinden, haber verici, uyarıcı.

pre.na.tal ['pri:'neitl] *adj.* doğum öncesine ait.

pre.oc.cu.pan.cy *fig.* [pri:'ɔkjupənsi] *n.* dalgınlık (in -e); pre.oc.cu.pa.tion [~'pei-ʃən] *n.* zihin meşguliyeti (with *ile*); zihni meşgul eden şey, tasa, kaygı; değer; pre'oc.cu.pied [~paid] *adj.* zihni meşgul; pre'oc.cu.py [~pai] *v/t.* meşgul etm. (*zihin*); başkasından önce ele geçirmek.

pre.or.dain ['pri:ɔ:'dein] *v/t.* önceden takdir etm., önceden nasip etm.

prep F [prep] = preparation, preparatory school.

pre.paid ['pri:'peid] *adj.* önceden ödenmiş.

prep.a.ra.tion [prepə'reiʃən] *n.* hazırlama; hazırlık; hazırlanan şey; hazır ilâç; ev ödevi; pre.par.a.tive [pri'pærətiv] *n.* hazırlık, hazırlama; pre'par.a.to.ry [~təri] □ hazırlayıcı, hazırlık; ~ school üniversiteye hazırlayan özel okul; ~ to -den evvel, -meden önce.

pre.pare [pri'pɛə] *v/t. & v/i.* hazırla(n)-mak; düzenlemek; donatmak; pişirmek; yapmak; pre'pared □ hazır; ~ for hazır -e; pre'pared.ness *n.* hazırlık, hazır olma (for -e).

pre.pay ['pri:'pei] (*irr.* pay) *v/t.* peşin ödemek; 'pre'pay.ment *n.* peşin ödeme.

pre.pense [pri'pens] önceden düşünülmüş, tasarlanmış, kasıtlı; with malice ~ taammüden, kasten, kasıtlı.

pre.pon.der.ance [pri'pɔndərəns] *n.* çoğunluk, üstünlük, fazlalık; pre'pon.der.ant □ ağır basan, baskın gelen, hâkim, galip; pre'pon.der.ate [~reit] *v/i.* ağır basmak, baskın gelmek, galip gelmek; hâkim olm.; ağır çekmek.

prep.o.si.tion *gr.* [prepə'ziʃən] *n.* edat, ilgeç; prep.o'si.tion.al □ [~ʃənl] edat niteliğinde, edat...

pre.pos.sess [pri:pə'zes] *v/t.* lehinde fi-

kir hâsıl ettirmek, gönlünü çelmek, etkilemek; meşgul etm. (*zihin*); pre.pos-'sess.ing □ cazibeli, çekici, alımlı; pre.pos.ses.sion [~'zeʃən] *n.* tarafgirlik; zihin meşguliyeti.

pre.pos.ter.ous [pri'pɔstərəs] *adj.* akıl almaz, mantıksız, inanılmaz, saçma.

pre.puce *anat.* ['pri:pju:s] *n.* sünnet derisi.

pre.req.ui.site ['pri:'rekwizit] *n.* önceden gerekli olan şey.

pre.rog.a.tive [pri'rɔgətiv] *n.* ayrıcalık, yetki hak, imtiyaz.

pres.age ['presidʒ] 1. *n.* önsezi; geleceği bildiren belirti; 2. *v/t.* önceden bildirmek *veya* göstermek; kehanet etm.

pres.by.ter ['prezbitə] *n.* kilise ileri gelenlerinden biri; Pres.by.te.ri.an [~'tiəriən] 1. *adj.* İskoç Protestan kilisesine ait; 2. *n.* bu kiliseye ait üye; pres.by.ter.y *eccl.* ['~təri] *n.* kilisede sadece papazlara ait kapalı kısım; Presbiteryen kiliselerinde yönetim kurulu.

pre.sci.ence [presiəns] *n.* geleceği görme, önceden bilme, öngörü; pre.sci.ent *adj.* geleceği gören, önceden bilen, öngörülü.

pre.scribe [pris'kraib] *v/t. & v/i.* emretmek; ⚕ (salık) vermek (*ilâç*), reçete yazmak; nizam koymak (for *için*); zaman aşımına uğramak.

pre.script ['pri:skript] *n.* kanun, emir, yönerge, hüküm; pre.scrip.tion [pris'krip-ʃən] *n.* emir, talimat; ⚕ reçete; zaman aşımına dayanan hak; pre'scrip.tive □ [~tiv] emreden, buyuran; yetkili; yapılagelen.

pres.ence ['prezns] *n.* huzur, varlık, hazır bulunma; hal, tavır, davranış; hayal, görüntü; ~ of mind serinkanlılık, soğukkanlılık; '~-cham.ber *n.* kabul salonu.

pres.ent¹ ['preznt] 1. □ bulunan, hazır, mevcut; şimdiki, şu anki; ~ tense *gr.* şimdiki zaman; ~ company mevcut topluluk; ~ company excepted söz meclisten dışarı; ~ value şu anki değer; ~! burada!; 2. *n. gr. a.* şimdiki zaman; halihazır, şimdiki durum; by the ~ ⚕, by these ~s bu belge ile, ilişikte; at ~ şimdi, şu anda; for the ~ şimdilik, şu anda.

pre.sent² [pri'zent] *v/t.* sunmak, takdim etm., arzetmek; tanıştırmak; göstermek; doğrultmak (*silah*); ✕ selâm vaziyetinde tutmak (*tüfek*); sağlamak (with -i); ~ o.s. görünmek, meydana çıkmak, hazır bulunmak; ~ one's compliments to s.o. *b-ne* kompliman yapmak.

pres.ent³ ['preznt] *n.* hediye, armağan;

make s.o. a ~ of s.th. *b-ne bş* armağan etm.

**pre.sent.a.ble** [pri'zentəbl] *adj.* sunulabilir; düzgün görünüşlü, prezentabl; is this suit ~? bu elbise iyi görünüyor mu?

**pres.en.ta.tion** [prezən'teiʃən] *n.* sunma, takdim; hediye; temsil, oyun; gösterme; ⊤ ibraz; ~ copy hediyelik kopya *(kitap).*

**pres.ent-day** ['prezəntdei] *adj.* şimdiki, günümüz...

**pre.sen.ti.ment** [pri'zentimənt] *n.* önsezi, içe doğuş.

**pres.erit.ly** ['prezntli] *adv.* derhal, hemen; birazdan, yakında; *Am.* şimdi, şu anda.

**pre.sent.ment** [pri'zentmənt] *n. s.* presentation; ⅍ büyük jüri raporu; *thea.* temsil, oyun.

**pres.er.va.tion** [prezə'veiʃən] *n.* sakla(n)-ma, koru(n)ma, muhafaza; in good ~ iyi korunmuş; **pre.serv.a.tive** [pri'zə:vətiv] **1.** *adj.* saklayan, koruyan, koruyucu; **2.** *n.* koruyucu madde.

**pre.serve** [pri'zə:v] **1.** *v/t.* korumak, saklamak, esirgemek (from *-den*); *-in* konservesini yapmak; *-in* reçelini yapmak; dayandırmak, sağlam tutmak; **2.** *n. hunt. oft.* ~s *pl.* av hayvanları için ayrılmış koru; *fig.* alan, saha; *mst* ~s *pl.* reçel; **pre'ser.ver** *n.* koruyucu; konserveci.

**pre.side** [pri'zaid] *v/i.* başkanlık etm. (over *-e*); ~ over an assembly bir toplantıya başkanlık etm.

**pres.i.den.cy** ['prezidənsi] *n.* başkanlık (süresi); reislik; **'pres.i.dent** *n.* başkan; baş, reis; rektör; *Am. (şirket, banka)* müdür; **pres.i.den.tial** [~'denʃəl] *adj.* başkanlığa ait, başkanlık...

**press** [pres] **1.** *n.* baskı, sıkıştırma; basın (mensupları); matbaa, basımevi; pres, cendere, mengene; kalabalık, izdiham; elbise dolabı; ütü *(giyside); a.* printing~ matbaa makinesi; *fig.* sıkıntı, baskı; ~ of sail ⚓ yelkenlerin rüzgârın elverdiğince açılması; the freedom of the ~ basın özgürlüğü; **2.** *v/t.* sık(ıştır)mak *(a. ✕);* basmak; sıkıp suyunu çıkarmak; *fig.* zorlamak, baskı yapmak, sıkıştırmak; ütülemek; zorla kabul ettirmek (on *-e*); ısrar etm., üstelemek; ~ the button düğmeye basmak *(a. fig.);* ~ the point that ...konusunda ısrarla durmak; be ~ed for time sıkışmak, vakti dar olm., az vakti olm.; *v/i.* kitle halinde ilerlemek; üşüşmek; koşuşturmak; ~ for ısrarla istemek, sıkıştırmak **için**; ~ on zorla kabul **ettirmek** -*e*; ~ back basıya yapmak -*e*, **zorlamak** -*i*; **'~.a.gen.cy** *n.* basın sözcülü- **ğü;** ~ a.gent basın sözcüsü; **'~-but.ton** *n.*

çıtçıt; elektrik düğmesi; **'~-cor.rec.tor** *n. typ.* matbaa provasını düzelten kimse, düzeltmen; **'~-cut.ting** *n.* gazete kupürü; **'press.er** *n.* basımcı, matbaacı; gazeteci; ütücü; **'press.ing 1.** □ acele, âcil, ivedili; sık boğaz eden, sıkıcı; ısrarlı...; **2.** *n.* plak; **'press.man** *n.* basımcı, matbaacı; gazeteci; ütücü; **'press-mark** *n.* kütüphanede kitap numarası; **pres.sure** ['preʃə] *n.* basınç, tazyik; baskı *(a. fig.);* **pres.sure cook.er** *n.* düdüklü tencere; **'pres.sure-gauge** *n.* ⊕ basıölçer, manometre; **pres.sur.ize** ['~raiz] *v/t.* basınç altında tutmak; **'press-work** *n. typ.* basım işi, matbaa işi.

**pres.ti.dig.i.ta.tion** ['prestididʒi'teiʃən] *n.* el çabukluğu, hokkabazlık.

**pres.tige** [pres'ti:ʒ] *n.* ün, şöhret; nüfuz, itibar, prestij, saygınlık.

**pres.to** ['prestəu] *adj. & adv.* çabuk, hızlı; hızla, çabucak.

**pre-stressed** ['pri:'strest] *adj.:* ~ concrete öngerilimli beton.

**pre.sum.a.ble** □ [pri'zju:məbl] tahmin olunur, farz edilir; **pre'sume** *v/t. & v/i.* tahmin etm., farzetmek; ihtimal vermek; cesaret etm. *-e*; haddini aşmak, cüret etm. (to *-e);* ~ upon istismar etm. *-i;* **pre'sum.ed.ly** [~idli] *adv.* tahminen, galiba; **pre'sum.ing** □ haddini aşan, cüretkâr, kendini beğenmiş.

**pre.sump.tion** [pri'zʌmpʃən] *n.* farz, tahmin, varsayım, ipucu; küstahlık, cüret; **pre'sump.tive** □ [~tiv] muhtemel, olası; tahminî, varsayılı; **pre'sump.tu.ous** □ [~tjuəs] küstah, kibirli, kendine fazla güvenen.

**pre.sup.pose** [pri:sə'pəuz] *v/t.* önceden farzetmek; koşul olarak gerektirmek, belirtmek; **pre.sup.po.si.tion** [pri:sʌpə'ziʃən] *n.* önceden farzetme; önceden farzedilen şey, tahmin.

**pre.tence,** *Am.* **pre.tense** [pri'tens] *n.* hile, bahane; iddia; gösteriş; false ~ sahte tavır; make ~ yapar gibi görünmek, yalandan yapmak.

**pre.tend** [pri'tend] *v/t.* yalandan yapmak; *k-ne* ...süsü vermek; taslamak (to *inf. -meği);* taklit etm., benzetmek; ~ to be ill hasta numarası yapmak; *v/i.* yapar gibi görünmek; iddia etm. (to *-i);* **pre'tend.ed** □ yapmacık, sözde, sahte, yalan; **pre'tend.er** *n.* hak iddia eden kimse.

**pre.ten.sion** [pri'tenʃən] *n.* sav, iddia, hak iddiası (to *-e);* taslama; küstahlık; gösteriş.

**pre.ten.tious** □ [pri'tenʃəs] *adj.* gösterişçi, kurumlu; **pre'ten.tious.ness** *n.* gösterişçilik.

**pret.er.it(e)** *gr.* [ˈpretərit] *n.* geçmiş zaman kipi.

**pre.ter.mis.sion** [priːtəˈmiʃən] *n.* ihmal; vaz geçme, cayma.

**pre.ter.nat.u.ral** □ [priːtəˈnætʃrəl] olağandışı; doğaüstü.

**pre.text** [ˈpriːtekst] *n.* bahane, sudan sebep, kulp.

**pret.ti.fy** [ˈpritifai] *v/t.* güzelleştirmek.

**pret.ti.ness** [ˈpritinis] *n.* güzellik, sevimlilik.

**pret.ty** [ˈpriti] **1.** □ güzel, sevimli, hoş, latif; iyi, âlâ; F epey büyük, kocaman; α ~ penny F avuç dolusu para; my ~! canım!, tatlım! ;**2.** *adv.* oldukça, hayli, epeyce.

**pre.vail** [priˈveil] *v/t.* hâkim olm.; yürürlükte olm.; galip gelmek (over, against -e karşı); yaygın olm., âdet olm.; başarmak, etkili olm.; ~ (up)on s.o. to do *b-ni bş* yapmaya ikna etm.; **pre.vail.ing** □ en sık esen (rüzgâr); geçerli, yaygın; hâkim olan; galip gelen.

**prev.a.lence** [ˈprevələns] *n.* yaygınlık; hüküm sürme, hâkim (veya egemen) olma.; **ˈprev.a.lent** □ yaygın, olagelen, hüküm süren, etkili.

**pre.var.i.cate** [priˈværikeit] *v/i.* yalan söylemek, yalan ifade vermek, kaçamaklı cevap vermek; **pre.var.iˈca.tion** *n.* kaçamak söz, yalan.

**pre.vent** [priˈvent] *v/t.* önlemek, engellemek, durdurmak, alıkoymak (from *ger.* -mekten); **preˈvent.a.ble** *adj.* önlenebilir, durdurulabilir; **pre.vent.a.tive** [~tətiv] = preventive; **preˈven.tion** *n.* önleme, engelleme; **preˈven.tive 1.** □ önleyici, engelleyici (of); ~ detention tekrar suç işlemeleri için suçluların yargılanıncaya kadar hapsedilmesi; **2.** *n.* önleyici şey veya tedbir.

**pre.view** [ˈpriːvjuː] *n.* thea., film: gelecek programdan gösterilen parçalar; bir film, sanat eseri vs. nin halka gösterilmeden önce özel olarak gösterilmesi.

**pre.vi.ous** □ [ˈpriːvjəs] önceki, evvel(ki), eski, sabık; F vaktinden önce, mevsimsiz; ~ conviction sabıka; ~ to -den önce; **ˈpre.vi.ouˈs.ly** *adv.* önce(den), evvelce.

**pre.vi.sion** [priːˈviʒən] *n.* basiret, sağduyu; önsezi, öngörü.

**pre.war** [ˈpriːˈwɔː] *adj.* savaş öncesi...

**prey** [prei] *n.* av; *fig.* yem: beast (bird) of ~ yırtıcı hayvan (kuş); be a ~ to kurbanı olm. -in, av olm. -e, kapılmış olm. -e; **2.** *vb.* beslenmek (on ~); ~ on, ~ upon soymak, yağma etm. -i; *fig.* sıkıntı vermek, içine dert olm.

**price** [prais] **1.** *n.* fiyat, paha, bedel; değer, kıymet; ödül; rüşvet; at any ~ her ne pahasına olursa olsun; **2.** *v/t.* fiyat koymak -e, paha biçmek -e; fiyatını sormak -in; **ˈprice.less** *adj.* paha biçilmez; gülünç, komik, çok hoş, yaman.

**prick** [prik] *n.* iğne veya diken batması; iğnele(n)me; diken; *sl.* kalleş; *sl.* penis; **2.** *v/t.* (iğne, diken vs.) sokmak, delmek; vicdan azabı vermek; *a.* ~ out oymak, açmak (delik); ~ out ✓ toprağa dikmek (fide); ~ up one's ears (at, köpek) kulaklarını dikmek; *fig.* kulak kabartmak; *v/i.* batmak; batma acısı duymak; mahmuzla atı dürtmek; ~ up dikmek; **ˈprick.er** *n.* delen şey *veya* kimse; delgi; **prick.le** [ˈ~l] *n.* diken, sivri uç; karıncalanma; **ˈprick.ly** *adj.* dikenli; kirpi gibi; karıncalanan; huysuz, çabuk öfkelenen; ~ heat ❦ isilik; ~ pear ❦ hintinciri, frenkinciri, firavuninciri.

**pride** [praid] **1.** *n.* kibir, gurur, tafra, azamet, övünme, iftihar; küme, sürü; ~ of place en üstün mevki; take (α) ~ in gurur duymak -den, iftihar etm. ile; **2.** *vb.* ~ o.s. (up)on *bşle* övünmek, gurur duymak, iftihar etm.

**priest** [priːst] *n.* papaz, rahip; ˈ~.craft *n.* papazlık; **ˈpriest.ess** *n.* dinsel tören yöneten kadın; **priest.hood** [ˈ~hud] *n.* papazlık, rahiplik; **ˈpriest.ly** *adj.* papaz gibi; papaza ait, papaza yakışır; **ˈpriest-rid.den** *adj.* papaz (veya kilise) yönetimindeki...

**prig** [prig] *n.* kendini beğenmiş (veya ukalâ) kimse; **ˈprig.gish** □ kendini beğenmiş, ukalâ(ca).

**prim** □ [prim] düzgün, düzenli, tertipli; fazla resmî, biçimci, formaliteci, kurallara fazla bağlı.

**pri.ma.cy** [ˈpraiməsi] *n.* öncelik, üstünlük; başpikoposluk; **pri.mal** [ˈpraiməl] *adj.* esasî, aslı; baş(lıca)...; **pri.ma ri.ly** [ˈ~rili] *adv.* evvela, öncelikle; aslında; **ˈpri.ma.ry 1.** □ ilk. birinci, asıl, ana; başlıca, ileri gelen; ilk(s)el; ✠, ❦ primer; **2.** *n. a.* ~ meeting *Am.* parti aday seçimi; *s.* share; **ˈpri.ma ry school** ilkokul; **pri.mate** *eccl.* [ˈ~mit] *n.* başpiskopos.

**prime** [praim] **1.** □ birinci, ilk; baş(lıca), asıl, aslî; asal (sayı); en önemli; en iyi, birinci kalite; ~ cost maliyet; ♀ Minister başbakan; ~ number asal sayı; **2.** *n. fig.* en mükemmel devir, her şeyin en iyisi; olgunluk çağı; başlangıç; in the ~ of youth gençliğin baharında; **3.** *v/t.* kullanma hazırlamak; talimat vermek. (ne diyeceğini) öğretmek; F içirmek *veya* yedirmek; *paint.* astar vurmak.

**prim.er¹** [ˈpraimə] *n.* ilk okuma kitabı;
*typ.* [ˈprimə]: great ~ on sekiz puntoluk
harf; long ~ on puntoluk harf.

**prim.er²** [ˈpraimə] *n.* astar boya; falya barutu.

**pri.me.val** [praiˈmiːvəl] *adj.* ilk(s)el, çok
eski...

**prim.ing** [ˈpraimiŋ] *n. paint.* astar boya;
✕ falya barutu; *attr.* ateşleme...

**prim.i.tive** ˈ[ˈprimitiv] **1.** ☐ ilkel, iptidaî;
basit; kaba; demode; ilk, eski; **2.** *n. gr.*
kök kelime; **ˈprim.i.tive.ness** *n.* ilkellik;
basitlik.

**prim.ness** [ˈprimnis] *n.* ˙resmiyet; fazla
ciddiyet.

**pri.mo.gen.i.ture** [praiməuˈdʒenitʃə] *n.* ilk
evlât olma; en büyük erkek evlât önce-
liği.

**pri.mor.di.al** ☐ [praiˈmɔːdjəl] başlangıçta var olan, ilk; en eski...

**prim.rose** ❦ [ˈprimrəuz] *n.* çuhaçiçeği; ~
path *veya* way *fig.* zevk ve sefa yolu;
take the ~ path zevk ve sefa içinde yaşamak.

**prince** [prins] *n.* prens; kral, hükümdar,
emir; ♀ **Con.sort** kraliçenin kocası;
**ˈprince.ly** *adj.* prense ait; prense yakışır; cömert, asil, kibar; şahane; **princess** [prinˈses] *n.* prenses.

**prin.ci.pal** [ˈprinsəpəl] **1.** ☐ baş(lıca), en
önemli, ana, büyük, asıl; *gr.* ~ parts *pl.*
İngilizce fiillerin çekim şekilleri; **2.** *n.*
müdür, yönetici, başkan; *part. Am.* okul
müdürü; ✝ patron, şef; müvekkil; sermaye, anapara, anamal; asıl sorumlu;
**prin.ci.pal.i.ty** [prinsiˈpæliti] *n.* prenslik.

**prin.ci.ple** [ˈprinsəpl] *n.* prensip, ilke; kural; temel sebep, köken; dürüstlük, ahlâk; ⌐ tamamlayıcı unsur; in ~ genel
olarak, genelde; on ~ prensip olarak,
prensip yönünden, ilke olarak.

**prink** F [priŋk] *vb.* giydirip kuşatmak,
süslemek; ~ oneself (up) süslenip püslenmek.

**print** [print] **1.** *n.* bası, tabı; basılmış yazı, matbua; damga, kalıp; emprime, bas-
ma kumaş; iz; basılı resim; *phot.* negatiften yapılmış resim; *Am.* gazete, dergi; out of ~ baskısı tükenmiş; in cold ~
yazılmış, basılmış; **2.** *v/t.* basmak, yayımlamak; *phot.* negatiften çıkarmak
*(resim)*; matbaa harfleriyle yazmak;
*fig.* nakşetmek (on -e); ~ed form çizelge, cetvel; ~ed matter matbua, basma;
*v/i.* matbaacılık yapmak; **ˈprint.er** *n.* basımcı, matbaacı; ~'s devil matbaacı çı-
rağı; ~'s flower çiçek modelli süsleme;

~'s ink matbaa mürekkebi.

**print.ing** [ˈprintiŋ] *n.* matbaacılık, baskı-
cılık; *phot.* basma, tabetme; **ˈ~.frame** *n.*
*phot.* kopya şasisi; **ˈ~.ink.** *n.* matbaa (*veya* baskı) mürekkebi; **ˈ~.of.fice** *n.* basımevi, matbaa; **ˈ~.press** *n.* matbaa makinesi.

**pri.or** [ˈpraiə] **1.** *adj.* önce, evvel(ki) (to
-den); sabık; kıdemli; **2.** *adv.* ~ to -den
önce, -den evvel; **3.** *n. eccl.* manastır
başrahibi; **ˈpri.or.ess** *n. eccl.* başrahibe;
**pri.or.i.ty** [~ˈɔriti] *n.* öncelik, kıdem; üstünlük hakkı (to, over -de); *s.* share 1;
**pri.o.ry** *eccl.* [ˈ~əri] *n.* manastır.

**prism** [ˈprizəm] *n.* prizma, biçme; prizmatik şeffaf cisim; ~ binoculars *pl.* priz-
malı dürbün; **pris.mat.ic** [~ˈmætik] *adj.*
(~ally) prizma biçiminde, prizmatik, biç-
mesel; şeffaf prizmadan oluşan *(renk)*.

**pris.on** [ˈprizn] **1.** *n.* cezaevi, hapishane,
tutukevi; **2.** *v/t. poet.* hapsetmek; **ˈpris-
on.er** *n.* tutuklu, hükümlü, mahkûm;
esir; ⚥ mevkuf, sanık; be a ~ to *fig.*
esiri olm. -in, mahkûm olm. -e; take s.o.
~ b-ni esir almak; ~'s bars...~'s base köşe
kapmaca oyunu.

**pris.sy** *Am.* F [ˈprisi] *adj.* titiz, kılı kırk
yaran.

**pris.tine** [ˈpristain] *adj.* eski zamana ait,
eski...; bozulmamış; taze ve temiz.

**prith.ee** ✝ [ˈpriði:] *int.* lütfen, rica ederim.

**pri.va.cy** [ˈpraivəsi] *n.* özellik; gizlilik,
mahremiyet; kişisel dokunulmazlık.

**pri.vate** [ˈpraivit] **1.** ☐ özel, hususî, kişisel, şahsî; gizli, mahrem; gözden uzak,
yalnız, baş başa; gayri resmi; ~ company
özel şirket; ~ member milletvekili; ~
theatre özel tiyatro; ~ view özel açılış;
at ~ sale et altından; **2.** *n.* ✕ nefer, er,
asker; ~s *pl.*, mst ~ parts *pl.* edep yerleri; in ~ gizlice, özel olarak.

**pri.va.teer** [praivəˈtiə] *n.* özel korsan
gemisi (komutanı); **pri.va.teer.ing** *n.* korsanlık yapma; *attr.* korsan...

**pri.va.tion** [praiˈveiʃən] *n.* yoksunluk, sıkıntı, mahrumiyet, ihtiyaç.

**pri.va.tive** ☐ [ˈprivətiv] yok eden, mahrum eden, -den yoksun bırakan; olumsuz *(a. gr.)*.

**priv.et** ❦ [ˈprivit] *n.* kurtbağrı, kurt baharı

**priv.i.lege** [ˈprivilidʒ] **1.** *n.* ayrıcalık, imtiyaz; özel izin, müsaade, ruhsat; hak;
**2.** *v/t.* ayrıcalık vermek; ~d imtiyazlı,
ayrıcalıklı.

**priv.i.ty** [ˈpriviti] *n.* ortak çıkarlara dayanan ilişki; gizli bilgi.

**priv.y** [ˈprivi] **1.** ☐ ~ to sır ortağı olan

*-e;* 🕮 ortak, hissedar; gizli; özel, kişisel; ♀ Council İngiltere'de kralın danışma meclisi; özel meclis; ♀ Councillor kralın danışma meclisi üyesi; ~ parts *pl.* edep yerleri, cinsel organlar; ~ purse hazineden kralın şahsına ayrılan para; ♀ Seal resmî devlet mührü; Lord ♀ Seal ferman mührü emini; **2.** *n.* 🕮 ortak (to *-e*); tuvalet, helâ, ayakyolu.

**prize¹** [praiz] **1.** *n.* ödül, mükâfat, ikramiye; ⚓ ganimet; first ~ *piyango:* en büyük ikramiye; **2.** *adj.* ödül olarak verilen; mükâfata lâyık...; ödül kazanan...; mükemmel; ⚓ ganimet; ~ competition ödüllü yarışma; **3.** *v/t.* değer vermek *-e;* paha biçmek *-e;* ⚓ zaptetmek, el koymak.

**prize²** [~] **1.** *v/t. a.* ~ open zorla (*veya* manivela *vs.* ile) açmak; **2.** *n.* kaldıraç.

**prize...:** '~fight.er *n.* profesyonel boksör; '~list *n.* ödül listesi, kazananlar listesi; '~.man = prize-winner; '~-ring *n. boks:* ring; '~-winner *n.* ödül kazanan (*veya* birinci gelen) kimse.

**pro** [prəu] **1.** *prp.* için; *s.* con³; **2.** *adv.* lehinde, ...taraftarı; **3.** *n.* profesyonel oyuncu.

**prob.a.bil.i.ty** [prɔbə'biliti] *n.* ihtimal, olasılık; muhtemel şey; **'prob.a.ble** □ muhtemel, olasılı.

**pro.bate** 🕮 ['prəubit] *n.* vasiyetnamenin resmen onaylanması; vasiyetnamenin onaylı kopyası.

**pro.ba.tion** [prə'beiʃən] *n.* deneme süresi; *part.* 🕮 gözaltına tutma koşuluyle salıverme; 🕮 vasiyetnamenin onaylanması; ~ officer suçluyu gözaltında tutan memur; on ~ denenmekte; 🕮 gözaltında; **pro'ba.tion.ar.y** *adj.:* ~ period 🕮 gözaltında bulunma süresi; **pro'ba.tion.er** *n.* stajyer hemşire (*veya* doktor *vs.*); deneme devresinde olan kimse; 🕮 gözaltında olan kişi.

**pro.ba.tive** 🕮 ['prəubətiv] *adj.:* ~ force ispat kudreti.

**probe** [prəub] **1.** *n.* 🟊 cerrah mili, sonda; *fig.* araştırma; insansız uzay roketi; lunar ~ ay araştırması; **2.** *vb. a.* ~ into sonda ile yoklamak *-i,* sondaj yapmak *-e;* derinliğine araştırmak, incelemek; '~-scis.sors *n. pl.* yara makası.

**prob.i.ty** ['prəubiti] *n.* doğruluk, dürüstlük.

**prob.lem** ['prɔbləm] *n.* sorun, mesele; ♫ problem; do a ~ problem çözmek; **prob.lem.at.ic, prob.lem.at.i.cal** □ [~bli'mætik-(əl)] şüpheli, belli olmayan.

**pro.bos.cis** [prəu'bɔsis] *n.* fil hortumu; böcek hortumu.

**pro.ce.dur.al** [prə'si:dʒərəl] *adj.* yargılama usulüne ait; **pro'ce.dure** *n.* işlem, muamele; davaya bakma usulü, yargılama yöntemi; iş görme usulü.

**pro.ceed** [prə'si:d] *v/i.* ilerlemek (*a. fig*); girişimde bulunmak, başlamak *veya* devam etm. (with *-e*); gitmek; dava açmak (against *-e karşı*); *univ.* doktor ünvanını kazanmak; ~ from çıkmak *-den,* doğmak *-den;* ~ on one's journey seyahatine devam etm.; ~ to başlamak *-e,* geçmek *-e;* **pro'ceed.ing** *n.* usül, yöntem, muamele, işlem; hareket tarzı, tavır, davranış; ~s *pl.* 🕮 dava işlemleri, yargılama usülleri; ~s *pl.* tutanak, zabıt; take ~s against dava açmak *-e karşı;* **pro.ceeds** ['prəusi:dz] *n. pl.* kazanç, gelir, hâsılat (from *-den*).

**proc.ess** ['prəuses] **1.** *n.* yöntem, metod, işlem, yol, usül; gidiş, gelişme, ilerleme; 🕮 dava (muamelesi); çağrı kâğıdı, celpname; 🞌 işlem; *anat.,* ♣ yumru; süreç; in ~ yapılmakta; in ~ of construction inşa halinde; **2.** *v/t.* belli bir işleme tabi tutmak; muamelesini yapmak; ⊕ işlemek; tebliğ etm.; dava açmak; ~ into işlemek; **'proc.ess.ing** *n.* ⊕ işleme; **pro.ces.sion** [prə'seʃən] *n.* alay, tören alayı; geçit töreni; **pro'ces.sion.ar.y** [~ʃnəri] *adj.* alay kabilinden, alay...

**pro.claim** [prə'kleim] *v/t.* ilan etm.; beyan etm.; göstermek, ele vermek, açığa vurmak.

**proc.la.ma.tion** [prɔklə'meiʃən] *n.* ilan; bildiri, beyanname.

**pro.cliv.i.ty** [prə'kliviti] *n.* eğilim, meyil (to *-e*).

**pro.con.sul** [prəu'kɔnsəl] *n.* eski Roma'da vali, prokonsül.

**pro.cras.ti.nate** [prəu'kræstineit] *vb.* süruncemede bırakmak, geciktirmek, ağırdan almak; ertelemek; **pro.cras.ti'na.tion** *n.* geciktirme; erteleme.

**pro.cre.ate** ['prəukrieit] *vb.* döllemek; doğurmak, yaratmak; procre'a.tion *n.* dölleme; doğurma; **'pro.cre.a.tive** *adj.* dölleyici; doğurgan...

**proc.tor** ['prɔktə] *n.* 🕮 dava vekili, hukuk müşaviri; *univ.* disiplini sağlayan memur.

**pro.cum.bent** [prəu'kʌmbənt] *adj.* sürüngen (*sap*); yüzükoyun.

**pro.cur.a.ble** [prə'kjuərəbl] *adj.* bulunabilir, elde edilebilir.

**proc.u.ra.tion** [prɔkjuə'reiʃən] *n.* tedarik, elde etme, bulma; † vekillik, vekâlet-(name); pezevenklik; by ~ temsilen, vekâleten; **¹proc.u.ra.tor** *n.* vekil.

**pro.cure** [prə¹kjuə] *v/t.* elde etm., tedarik etm., sağlamak (s.o. s.th., s.th. for s.o. *b-ne bş*); edinmek; sebep olm. *-e*, neden olm. *-e*; *v/i.* pezevenklik etm.; **pro¹cure-ment** *n.* tedarik, elde etme; **pro¹cur.er** *n.* tedarik eden kimse; pezevenk; **pro¹cur-ess** *n.* pezevenk kadın.

**prod** [prɔd] 1. *n.* üvendire; dürtme, itme; *fig.* tahrik, teşvik; 2. *v/t.* dürtmek, itmek; *fig.* tahrik etm., kışkırtmak, özendirmek.

**prod.i.gal** [¹prɔdigəl] 1. ☐ savurgan, müsrif, tutumsuz, har vurup harman savuran (of *-i*); çok bol; the ~ son mirasyedi *(veya* savurgan) kimse; 2. *n.* müsrif *(veya* tutumsuz) kimse; **prod.i.gal.i.ty** [~¹gæliti] *n.* bolluk, bereket; müsriflik, savurganlık.

**pro.di.gious** ☐ [prə¹didʒəs] kocaman, çok büyük; şaşılacak, harika, müthiş; **prod-i.gy** [¹prɔdidʒi] *n.* olağanüstü şey, mucize, harika; dâhi *(a. fig.)*; *oft.* infant ~ harika çocuk.

**prod.uce¹** [¹prɔdjuːs] *n.* ürün, mahsül; sebze, zerzevat .

**pro.duce²** [prə¹djuːs] *vb.* üretmek, yapmak, imal etm.; yetiştirmek; meydana getirmek; (ortaya) çıkarmak, göstermek; doğurmak; sebep olm., neden olm., yaratmak; ↯ uzatmak *(doğru)*; *film:* sahneye koymak; **pro¹duc.er** *n.* üretici; *film:* prodükter, yapımcı; *thea.* rejisör; *radyo:* yayın direktörü; gaz jeneratörü; **pro¹duc.i.ble** *adj.* üretilebilir; sahneye konabilir; **pro¹duc.ing** *adj.* üretim...

**prod.uct** [¹prɔdʌkt] *n.* ürün, mahsül, hâsılat; sonuç, netice; ↯ çarpım; **pro.duc-tion** [prə¹dʌkʃən] *n.* üretim, imal(ât) ürün; eser, yapıt; *thea.* sahneye koyma; ~ line sürekli iş şeridi; **pro¹duc.tive** ☐ verimli, bereketli; yaratıcı (of *-i*); **pro¹duc.tive.ness, pro.duc.tiv.i.ty** [prɔdʌk-¹tiviti] *n.* verimlilik.

**prof** *Am.* F [prɔf] *n.* profesör.

**prof.a.na.tion** [prɔfə¹neiʃən] *n.* kutsiyetini bozma, kutsal şeylere karşı saygısızlık; **pro.fane** [prə¹fein] 1. ☐ dinle ilgisi olmayan, dünyevî, cismanî; kâfir; adî, bayağı; küfürlü; 2. *v/t.* kutsiyetini bozmak; suiistimal etm.; kirletmek; saygısızca kullanmak; **pro.fan.i.ty** [~¹fæniti] *n.* hürmetsizlik; ağız bozukluğu; küfür.

**pro.fess** [prə¹fes] *v/t.* & *v/i.* açıkça söylemek, itiraf etm.; ikrar etm. *(inancını);* iddia etm., taslamak; icra etm. *(meslek),* öğretmenlik yapmak; **pro-¹fessed** ☐ iddia edilen; açıklanmış, iti-

raf edilmiş; sözde, güya; **pro¹fess.ed.ly** [~sidli] *adv.* iddiaya göre; sözde, güya.

**pro.fes.sion** [prə¹feʃən] *n.* uğraş, iş, meslek, sanat; iddia, söz; itiraf; beyan, ikrar; **pro¹fes.sion.al** [~ʃənl] 1. ☐ mesleğe ait, meslekî; ustalıklı; meslek sahibi; profesyonel; ~ men *pl.* üniversite mezunu kimseler *(doktor, avukat vs.);* 2. *n.* mütehassıs, uzman; *part. spor:* profesyonel kimse; **pro¹fes.sion.al.ism** [~ʃnəlizm] *n. spor:* profesyonellik.

**pro.fes.sor** [prə¹fesə] *n.* profesör; **pro¹fes-sor.ship** *n.* profesörlük.

**prof.fer** [¹prɔfə] 1. *v/t.* teklif etm., önermek, sunmak, arzetmek; 2. *n.* teklif, öneri.

**pro.fi.cien.cy** [prə¹fiʃənsi] *n.* ehliyet, becerilik, ustalık, maharet; **pro¹fi.cient** 1. ☐ ehliyetli, usta, mahir, becerikli (in, at *-de*); 2. *n.* uzman, mütehassıs (in *-de*).

**pro.file** [¹prəufail] *n.* profil, kesit, yanal görünüş (a. ⌂); enine kesit; *fig.* kısa biyografi.

**prof.it** [¹prɔfit] 1. *n.* kâr, kazanç; menfaat, fayda, yarar; 2. *vb.* kazanç getirmek *-e*, kâr getirmek *-e*; ~ by (from) yararlanmak *-den*, istifade etm. *-den;* **¹prof.it-a.ble** ☐ kazançlı, kârlı; faydalı, yararlı; **¹prof.it.a.ble.ness** *n.* kazançlılık, faydalı; **prof.it.eer** [~¹tiə] 1. *v/i.* çok para kazanmak, vurgunculuk yapmak; 2. *n.* vurguncu *(veya* fırsatçı) kimse; war ~ savaş zengini; **prof.it¹eer.ing** *n.* vurgunculuk; **¹prof.it.less** ☐ kârsız; faydasız; **prof.it--shar.ing** [~¹ʃɛəriŋ] *n.* kârı bölüşme, kâra katılma.

**prof.li.ga.cy** [¹prɔfligəsi] *n.* ahlâksızlık; müsriflik, savurganlık; utanmazlık; hovardalık; **prof.li.gate** [~-git] 1. ☐ ahlâksız; müsrif, savurgan; utanmaz; hovarda, uçarı; 2. *n.* ahlâksız *(veya* edepsiz, savurgan) kimse.

**pro.found** ☐ [prə¹faund] derin; engin; esaslı, adamakıllı; çok büyük; çok bilgili; *fig.* şüpheli; **pro¹found.ness, pro.fun.di.ty** [~¹fʌnditi] *n.* derinlik *(a. fig.),* genişlik.

**pro.fuse** ☐ [prə¹fjuːs] çok, bol; savurgan, aşırı (in, of *-de*); cömert; verimli; **pro¹fuse.ness, pro.fu.sion** [~¹fjuːʒən] *n.* bolluk; *fig.* savurganlık, aşırılık.

**prog** *sl. univ.* [prɔg] *n.* disiplini sağlayan memur.

**pro.gen.i.tor** [prəu¹dʒenitə] *n.* ata, cet, dede; **pro¹gen.i.tress** [~tris] *n.* büyükanne, nine; **prog.e.ny** [¹prɔdʒini] *n.* soy, nesil, torunlar; *fig.* mahsül, ürün.

**prog.no.sis** ? [prɔg¹nəusis] *n., pl.* **prog¹no-ses** [~siːz] prognoz, tahmin.

prog.nos.tic [prəg'nɔstik] 1. adj. önceden gösteren (of -i); 2. n. belirti, alâmet; kehanet; prog'nos.ti.cate [~keit] v/t. önceden haber vermek, kehanette bulunmak; prog.nos.ti'ca.tion n. önceden haber verme, kehanet, belirti.

pro.gram, mst pro.gramme ['prəugræm] n. program; radyo: yayın; düzen.

prog.ress¹ ['prəugres] n. gelişme, ilerleme (a. ✕), yükselme; in ~ yapılmakta, ilerlemekte, gelişmekte.

pro.gress² ['prə'gres] v/i. ilerlemek, ileri gitmek, gelişmek, kalkınmak; iyiye gitmek, düzelmek; devam etm.; pro'gres.sion [~ʃən] n. ilerleme, devam; ✚ dizi; pro'gres.sion.ist [~ʃnist], pro'gress.ist [~sist] n. pol. ilerici, erkinci kimse; pro'gres.sive 1. ☐ ilerleyen, gelişen; genişleyen, artan; pol. ilerici, erkinci; ~ form gr. sürekli zaman şekli; 2. n. pol. ilerici, erkinci kimse.

pro.hib.it [prə'hibit] v/t. yasaklamak, yasak etm., menetmek (s.th. bşi; s.o. from ger. b-ni -mekten); mâni olm. -e, engel olm. -e; pro.hi.bi.tion [prəuhi'biʃən] n. yasak (emri); içki yasağı, içkilerin yasak olması; pro.hi'bi.tion.ist [~ʃnist] n. part. Am. içki yasağı taraftarı; pro.hib.i.tive ☐ [prə'hibitiv] yasaklayıcı; engelleyici; aşırı, fahiş (fiyat); ~ duty yasak gümrüğü.

proj.ect ['prɔdʒekt] n. plan, proje, tasarı.

pro.ject [prə'dʒekt] v/t. tasarlamak, düşünmek, tasavvur etm.; perdede göstermek (film, resim); -in planını çizmek; yansıtmak (gerçekleri); fırlatmak, atmak, savurmak; ✚ izdüşürmek; ~ o.s. into k-ni götürmek -e, k-ni ...de farz etm.; v/i. çıkık olm., çıkıntı oluşturmak; pro.jec.tile 1. ['prɔdʒiktail] n. mermi, top güllesi, fırlatılan taş veya mermi; 2. [prə'dʒektail] adj. fırlatıcı..., atıcı...; fırlatılan...; pro.jec.tion [prə'dʒekʃən] n. projeksiyon; gösterim; fırlatma, atma, atış; çıkıntı; proje, tasarı; ✚, ast., phot. izdüşüm; ~ room film: projeksiyon odası; pro'jec.tion.ist [~ʃnist] n. film makinisti (veya göstericisi); pro'jec.tor n. proje (veya plan) yapan kimse; ✝ kurucu; opt. sinema makinesi, projektör, ışıldak.

pro.le.tar.i.an [prəuli'tɛəriən] 1. adj. ücretle çalışan sınıftan; 2. n. proleter, emekçi; pro.le'tar.i.at, mst. pro.le'tar.i.ate [~riət] n. proletarya, işçi sınıfı.

pro.lif.ic [prəu'lifik] adj. (~ally) doğurgan; fig. bereketli, verimli, semereli·(of, in).

pro.lix ☐ ['prəuliks] sözü çok uzatan; yorucu, sıkıcı; uzun, ayrıntılı; pro'lix.i.ty n.

sözü boşuna uzatma, söz uzunluğu.

pro.logue, Am. a. pro.log ['prəulɔg] n. prolog, önsöz, başlangıç, giriş; ~ to fig -in başlangıcı.

pro.long [prə'lɔn] v/t. uzatmak, sürdürmek; ✝ temdit etm.; pro.lon.ga.tion [~ 'geiʃən] n. uzatma, sürdürme.

prom F [prɔm] = promenade concert.

prom.e.nade [prɔmi'naːd] 1. n. gezinti, gezme (yeri), mesire; büyük balo; 2. v/t. & v/i. gez(dir)mek, gezinmek; ~ concert ayakta dinlenilen konser.

prom.i.nence ['prɔminəns] n. ün, şöhret; önem; göze çarpan şey; çıkıntı; concr. tümsek, engebe; 'prom.i.nent ☐ çıkık, çıkıntılı, ileri fırlamış; önemli, mühim; meşhur, şöhretli; göze çarpan; fig. seçkin, güzide, ileri gelen.

prom.is.cu.i.ty [prɔmis'kjuːiti] n. (karma)karışıklık, (darma)dağınıklık; pro.mis.cu.ous ☐ [prə'miskjuəs] (karma)karışık, (darma)dağınık; farksız; rasgele; rasgele cinsel ilişkide bulunan.

prom.ise ['prɔmis] 1. n. söz, vaat, taahhüt, vaat edilen şey; fig. ümit verici şey (of); of great ~ çok ümit verici; 2. vb. söz vermek -e, vaat etm. -e; belirtisi olm. -in, göstermek; temin etm., garanti etm., ümit vermek; I ~ you F sana söz veriyorum; 'prom.is.ing ☐ ümit verici, geleceği parlak; prom.is.so.ry [~səri] adj. vaat (veya taahhüt) içeren; ~ note ✝ bono, emre yazılı senet.

prom.on.to.ry ['prɔmɔntri] n. dağlık burun.

pro.mote [prə'məut] v/t. ilerletmek; terfi ettirmek, rütbesini yükseltmek; part. Am. okul: sınıf geçirmek; parl. desteklemek; ✝ kurmak, tesis etmek; part. Am. reklâmını yaparak tanıtmak; pro'mot.er n. destekleyen kimse; ✝ girişim sahibi. kurucu; organizatör; pro'mo.tion n. terfi, yüksel(t)me; geçme; ✝ tesis; reklâm; mevki, rütbe; teşvik.

prompt [prɔmpt] 1. ☐ hemen, çabuk, acele, hazır, seri, tez; dakik; 2. adv. tam, dakikası dakikasına; 3. vb. tahrik etm., sevketmek, teşvik etm., harekete getirmek, kışkırtmak; thea. suflörlük etm.; 4. n. ✝ vade: thea. oyuncuya hatırlatılan söz, hatırlatma; '~-box n. thea. suflör hücresi; 'prompt.er n. thea. suflör; promp.ti.tude ['~titjuːid] n., 'prompt.ness sürat, çabukluk; harekete hazır olma.

pro.mul.gate ['prɔmʌlgeit] v/t. resmen ilân etm., duyurmak, bildirmek, neşretmek; yaymak (fikir); yürürlüğe koymak (kanun); pro.mul'ga.tion n. duyuru; resmen yürürlüğe koyma.

**prone** ☐ [proun] yüzükoyun (yatmış, yere uzanmış); eğilimli, meyilli; ~ to *fig.* eğimli *-e*; **'prone.ness** *n.* eğilim, meyil (to *-e*).

**prong** [prɔŋ] *n.* çatal dişi; sivri uç(lu alet); boynuz çatalı; **pronged** *adj.* dişli, sivri uçlu.

**pro.nom.i.nal** ☐ *gr.* [prəu'nɔminl] zamire ait, zamir kabilinden.

**pro.noun** *gr.* ['prəunaun] *n.* zamir, adıl.

**pro.nounce** [prə'nauns] *v/t. & v/i.* resmen bildirmek, beyan etm., ilan etm., açıklamak *(karar vs.)*; telaffuz etm., söylemek; fikrini söylemek (on *hakkında*); **pro'nounced** ☐ *[adv.* ~ıdli] kati, kesin; belli, belirgin, bariz; **pro'nounce.ment** *n.* bildiri, duyuru, beyan, tebliğ.

**pro.nounc.ing** [prə'naunsiŋ] *adj.* telaffuz...

**pron.to** *Am.* F ['prɔntəu] *adv.* hemen, derhal, çabuk.

**pro.nun.ci.a.tion** [prənʌnsi'eiʃən] *n.* telaffuz, söyleniş, söyleyiş.

**proof** [pru:f] **1.** *n.* delil, kanıt, tanıt, ispat; imtihan, tecrübe, deneme, test; *typ.* prova; *typ., phot.* ayar; Å sağlama; '~ alkol derecesi; in ~ of *-in* delili olarak; **2.** *adj.* dayanıklı, kuvvetli, dirençli (against, to *-e karşı*); geçirmez *(kurşun, su, ses vs.)*; *fig.* karşı çıkan (against *-e*); **3.** *v/t. (su, hava vs.)* geçirmez yapmak; '~-read.er *n. typ.* düzeltmen; '~-sheet *n. typ.* prova; '~-spir.it Å standart dereceli alkol.

**prop** [prɔp] **1.** *n.* destek *(a. fig.)*, ayak, payanda; çamaşır sırığı; destek olan kimse; *thea. sl.* sahne eşyası, dekor; pit-~s *pl.* maden ocağı direkleri; **2.** *v/t. a.* ~ up desteklemek; dayamak, yaslamak.

**prop.a.gan.da** [prɔpə'gændə] *n.* propaganda; **prop.a'gan.dist** *n.* propagandacı; **prop.a.gate** ['~geit] *v/t. & v/i.* üre(t)mek, çoğal(t)mak; çiftleştirmek; *fig.* yaymak, dağıtmak; geçirmek, bulaştırmak; nakletmek; yavrulamak, türemek; **prop.a'ga.tion** *n.* üreme, yavrulama; yayım, yay(ıl)ma; **'prop.a.ga.tor** *n.* üretici; yayıcı.

**pro.pel** [prə'pel] *v/t.* sevketmek, itmek, ileri doğru sürmek; **pro'pel.lant** *n.* ileriye sevkedici şey, muharrik kuvvet; kursun *veya* uzay gemisini iten kuvvet; yakıt; **pro'pel.lent** = propellant; **pro'pel.ler** *n.* pervane, uskur; ~ shaft kardan mili; **pro'pel.ling** *adj.* itici...; ~ pencil sürgülü kurşun kalem.

**prop.er** ☐ ['prɔpə] uygun, yakışır, münasip, layık (for *-e*); has, hususi, mahsus, ait (to *-e*); F doğru, gerçek, tam; hürmete layık, saygıdeğer; güzel, fevkalâde; F yakışıklı; ~ name özel isim; **'prop.er.ty** *n.* mal, mülk, emlâk, arazi; özellik; öö mülkiyet, sahiplik; properties *pl. thea.* sahne donanımı; **'prop.er.ty-man** *n. thea.* sahne donanımcısı; **'prop.er.ty-tax** *n.* emlâk vergisi.

**proph.e.cy** ['prɔfisi] *n.* önceden haber verme, kâhinlik, kehanet; **proph.e.sy** ['~sai] *v/t. & v/i.* önceden haber vermek, kehanette bulunmak; peygamberlik etm.; önceden tahmin etm.

**proph.et** ['prɔfit] *n.* peygamber; kâhin; taraftar; öncü; **'proph.et.ess** *n.* kadın peygamber; **pro.phet.ic, pro.phet.i.cal** ☐ [prə'fetik(əl)] peygamber *veya* peygamberliğe ait; kehanete ait, kehanet gibi.

**pro.phy.lac.tic** ♀ [prɔfi'læktik] (~ally) hastalıktan koruyan, koruyucu, önleyici.

**pro.pin.qui.ty** [prə'piŋkwiti] *n.* yakınlık; akrabalık; yakın benzerlik.

**pro.pi.ti.ate** [prə'piʃieit] *v/t.* yatıştırmak, sakinleştirmek; *-in* gönlünü almak; *-in* teveccühünü kazanmak; **pro.pi.ti'a.tion** *n.* yatıştırma; teveccühünü kazanma, telâfi etme *(suç vs.)*; **pro'pi.ti.a.to.ry** ☐ [~ʃiətəri] yatıştırıcı; gönül alan...

**pro.pi.tious** ☐ [prə'piʃəs] uygun, elverişli; bağışlayıcı, şefkatli; yardımsever; uğurlu, hayırlı; **pro'pi.tious.ness** *n.* elverişlilik *(hava)*; yardımseverlik; şefkat.

**pro.por.tion** [prə'pɔ:ʃən] **1.** *n.* oran(tı), nispet; hisse, pay; Å, Å orantı (kuralı); ~s *pl.* ebat, boyutlar; **2.** *v/t.* oranlamak (to *-e*); **pro'por.tion.al 1.** ☐ orantılı; *s.* proportionate; **2.** *n.* Å orantılı sayı; **pro'por.tion.ate** ☐ [~ʃnit] uygun, orantılı (to *-e*); **pro'por.tioned** *adj.* ... orantılı.

**pro.pos.al** [prə'pəuzəl] *n.* önerme, teklif, öneri; evlenme teklifi; **pro'pose** *v/t.* önermek, teklif etm.; sunmak, arzetmek; niyetlenmek; ~ to o.s. *bş* yapmaya niyetlenmek; ~ a motion bir teklifte bulunmak; *v/i.* evlenme teklif etm. (to *-e*); **pro'pos.er** *n.* teklifte bulunan kimse; **pro.po.si.tion** ☐ [prɔpə'ziʃən] *n.* teklif, öneri; mesele, sorun; ifade; *phls.,* Å teorem, sav, tez, dava; *sl.* uygunsuz teklif, sevişme teklifi.

**pro.pound** [prə'paund] *v/t.* ileri sürmek, ortaya atmak, arzetmek, önermek.

**pro.pri.e.tar.y** [prə'praiətəri] **1.** *adj.* sicilli, markalı, müseccel; sahipli, hususi; patentli, tescilli; mal sahipliğine ait; ~ name tescilli marka; **2.** *n.* mal sahibi;

mal sahipleri; pro'pri.e.tor *n.* mal sahibi, sahip; pro'pri.e.tress *n.* mal sahibi kadın; pro'pri.e.ty *n.* uygunluk, münasebet, yerindelik, mantıklılık; the proprieties *pl.* töre, adap, görgü kuralları.

props F *thea.* [prɔps] *n. pl.* sahne donanımı.

pro.pul.sion ⊕ [prə'pʌlʃən] *n.* itici güç; sevk, tahrik; pro'pul.sive [~siv] *adj.* yürütücü, çalıştırıcı, itici...; tahrik edici...

pro.rate *Am.* [prəu'reit] *v/t.* eşit olarak bölüp dağıtmak.

pro.ro.ga.tion *parl.* [prəurə'geiʃən] *n.* parlementoyu tatil etme; pro.rogue *parl.* [prə'rəug] *v/t.* tatil etm.

pro.sa.ic [prəu'zeiik] *adj.* (~ally) *fig.* sıkıcı; adi, bayağı, yavan.

pro.scribe [prəus'kraib] *v/t.* yasaklamak; yasal haklardan yoksun bırakmak.

pro.scrip.tion [prəus'kripʃən] *n.* yasakla(n)ma.

prose [prəuz] 1. *n.* nesir, düzyazı; 2. *adj.* nesir...; nesir şeklinde yazılmış; can sıkıcı, yavan 3. *vb.* nesir yazmak.

pros.e.cute ['prɔsikjuːt] *vb.* devam etm. -c, sürdürmek -i; ᵰ kovuşturmak, cezalandırmak, kanunî takibat yapmak (for için); pros.e'cu.tion *n.* devam, sürme; takibat, kovuşturma; ᵰ dava(cı); iddia makamı; witness for the ~ sanığın aleyhindeki tanık; 'pros.e.cu.tor *n.* ᵰ davacı; savcı; public ~ savcı.

pros.e.lyte *eccl.* ['prɔsilait] *n.* din değiştiren kimse, dönme; pros.e.lyt.ism ['~litizəm] *n.* başkalarını kendi dinine sokmaya çalışma; 'pros.e.lyt.ize *vb.* dininden çevirmek.

pros.er ['prəuzə] *n.* nesir yazarı; sıkıcı yazar *veya* konuşmacı.

pros.o.dy ['prɔsədi] *n.* vezin tekniği, prosodi, aruz.

pros.pect 1. ['prɔspekt] *n.* manzara, görünüş *(a. fig.)*; ümit, umut; gelecek; olasılık, ihtimal; † *part. Am.* muhtemel müşteri; have in ~ ümidi olm.; hold out a ~ of s.th. ümit vermek; 2. [prəs'pekt] *vb.* ᚷ araştırmak (for -i); pro'spec.tive □ beklenen, umulan, ümit edilen; müstakbel; muhtemel; ~ buyer muhtemel alıcı; pros'pec.tor *n.* ᚷ maden arayıcısı; pro'spec.tus [~təs] *n.* prospektüs; tarif(nam)e.

pros.per ['prɔspə] *v/i.* başarılı olm.; gelişmek, büyümek; zenginleşmek; *v/t.* başarısına yardımcı olm., korumak; pros.per.i.ty [~'periti] *n.* başarı; *fig.* refah, saadet, gönenç; pros.per.ous □ ['~pərəs] başarılı; bayındır; uygun, elverişli;

şanslı, talihli; *fig.* refah içinde.

pros.ti.tude ['prɔstitjuːt] 1. *n.* fahişe, orospu; 2. *v/t.* fahişeliğe sevketmek; *fig.* kötüye kullanmak; pros.ti'tu.tion *n.* fahişelik, fuhuş; *fig.* kötüye kullanma.

pros.trate 1. ['prɔstreit] *adj.* yüzükoyun yatmış, yere uzanmış; takati kesilmiş, dermansız; sarsılmış, yıkılmış *(üzüntüden)*; 2. [prɔs'treit] *v/t.* yıkmak, devirmek, yere sermek; *fig.* halsiz bırakmak; sarsmak *(üzüntü)*; pros'tra.tion *n.* yere atılma, kapanma; *fig.* takatsizlik, dermansızlık, bezginlik.

pros.y □ *fig.* ['prəuzi] sıkıcı, ağır, usandırıcı, yavan.

pro.tag.o.nist [prəu'tægənist] *n. thea.* başrol oyuncusu, kahraman; *fig.* öncü.

pro.tect [prə'tekt] *v/t.* korumak, muhafaza etm., saklamak (from *-den*); † yabancı mallara gümrük koyarak (yerli malları) korumak; pro'tec.tion *n.* koruma, muhafaza, himaye; yabancı mallara gümrük koyarak yerli malları koruma; koruyucu kimse *veya* şey; pro'tec.tion.ist 1. *n.* ithalât üzerine vergi koyarak yerli sanayii koruma taraftarı; 2. *adj.* koruyucu...; pro'tec.tive *adj.* koruyucu, himaye edici; savunucu; ~ custody koruyucu *(veya* ihtiyati) tevkif; ~ duty koruyucu gümrük resmi; pro'tec.tor *n.* koruyucu, hami; *hist.* kral vekili; pro-'tec.tor.ate [~tərit] *n.* başka devletin idaresinde olan küçük devlet; pro'tec.to.ry *n.* ıslahevi; pro'tec.tress *n.* kadın koruyucu.

pro.té.gé ['prəuteʒei] *n.* başkasının himayesinde olan kimse.

pro.te.in ᚷ ['prəutiːn] *n.* protein.

pro.test 1. ['prəutest] *n.* protesto, itiraz (beyannamesi); in ~ against protesto ederek -i; enter *veya* make a ~ itirazda bulunmak, protesto etm.; 2. [prə'test] *v/t.* & *v/i.* karşı çıkmak, itiraz etm. -e; iddia etm.; protesto etm. (against -i).

Prot.es.tant ['prɔtistənt] 1. *adj.* Protestanlara ait; 2. *n.* Protestan; 'Prot.es.tant.ism *n.* Protestanlık, Protestan mezhebi.

prot.es.ta.tion [prɔutes'teiʃən] *n.* protesto etme, itiraz.

pro.to.col ['prəutəkɔl] 1. *n.* tutanak; protokol; 2. *vb.* protokol yapmak.

pro.ton *phys.* ['prəutɔn] *n.* proton.

pro.to.plasm *biol.* ['prəutəuplæzəm] *n.* protoplazma.

pro.to.type ['prəutəutaip] *n.* esas model, ilk örnek, prototip.

pro.tract [prə'trækt] *v/t.* uzatmak; pro-'trac.tion *n.* uzatma; pro'trac.tor *n.* Ꜳ iletki, minkale.

**pro.trude** [prəˈtruːd] *v/t. & v/i.* dışarı çık(ar)mak, çıkıntı yapmak, pırtlamak; **proˈtru.sion** [-ʒən] *n.* çıkar(ıl)ma; çıkıntı.

**pro.tu.ber.ance** [prəˈtjuːbərəns] *n.* tümsek, şiş(kinlik), çıkıntı, bel verme; **proˈtu.ber.ant** *adj.* şiş, tümsek, çıkık, bel vermiş, pırtlak, dışarı uğramış.

**proud** □ [praud] kıvanç duyan, iftihar eden, gurur duyan (of *-den*; to *inf. -mek-ten*); kibirli, gururlu, mağrur; görkemli, muhteşem; ~ flesh ❓ yara etrafındaki şiş; do s.o. ~ F *b-ne* hürmet göstermek.

**prov.a.ble** □ [ˈpruːvəbl] tanıtlanabilir, ispatı mümkün, ispat edilebilir; **prove** *v/t.* tanıtlamak, ispatlamak, ispat etm, göstermek; denemek, sınamak; *v/i.* olmak, çıkmak; ~ true (false) doğru (yanlış) çıkmak; he has ~d to be the heir onun vâris olduğu ortaya çıktı; the exception ~s the rule istisnalar kaideyi bozmaz; **proven** [ˈ-vən] *adj.* ispatlanmış, tanıtlanmış; sınanmış, denenmiş.

**prov.e.nance** [ˈprɔvinəns] *n.* kaynak, köken, asıl, menşe.

**prov.en.der** [ˈprɔvində] *n.* hayvan yemi; F yiyecek.

**pro.verb** [ˈprɔvəːb] *n.* atasözü; be a ~ atasözü olm. *veya b.s.* adı çıkmış olm. (for *-den dolayı*); **pro.ver.bi.al** □ [prəˈvəːbjəl] atasözüne ait, atasözü gibi; ünlü, herkesçe bilinen.

**pro.vide** [prəˈvaid] *v/t.* tedarik etm., sağlamak, bulmak (with *-i*); donatmak; şart koşmak; *v/i.* sağlamak (for *-i*); önlem almak, hazırlıklı bulunmak (against *-e* karşı; for *için*); ~ for geçimini sağlamak; ~d (that) *-si, -mek* şartıyle, yeter ki. **prov.i.dence** [ˈprɔvidəns] *n.* ilahî takdir; basiret, sağgörü; ♀ Tanrı; **ˈprov.i.dent** □ tedbirli, basiretli; **prov.i.den.tial** □ [~-ˈdenʃəl] Allahtan, Tanrıdan gelen *veya* olan; talihli, kısmetli.

**pro.vid.er** [prəˈvaidə] *n.* tedarik eden kimse; aile geçindiren kimse.

**prov.ince** [ˈprɔvins] *n.* il, vilâyet; taşra; *fig.* yetki alanı.

**pro.vin.cial** [prəˈvinʃəl] **1.** *adj.* eyalete ait; taşraya ait, taşra...; taşralı, kaba, görgüsüz, dar düşünceli; **2.** *n.* taşralı kimse, köylü *(a. contp.)*; **proˈvin.cial.ism** *n.* taşralılık, köylülük; taşraya özgü âdet ve ağız.

**pro.vi.sion** [prəˈviʒən] **1.** *n.* tedarik (olunan şey); hazırlama, hazırlık; ♂♂ (kanuni) hüküm; şart, koşul; ~s *pl.* erzak, za-

hire; make ~ for *bş* için gerekli tedbiri almak; ~ merchant gıda maddeleri satıcısı; **2.** *v/t. -in* erzağını tedarik etm.; **proˈvi.sion.al** [~ʒənl] □ geçici, muvakkat.

**pro.vi.so** [prəˈvaizəu] *n.* kayıt, şart, koşul; **proˈvi.so.ry** [~zəri] *adj.* şartlı, koşullu.

**prov.o.ca.tion** [prɔvəˈkeiʃən] *n.* kızdırma, sinirlendirme, gücendirme; kışkırtma; kızılacak şey; **pro.voc.a.tive** [prəˈvɔkətiv] **1.** *adj.* sinirlendirici, kızdırıcı; kışkırtıcı; cazip, çekici; **2.** *n.* tahrik edici kimse *veya* şey.

**pro.voke** [prəˈvəuk] *v/t.* kızdırmak, sinirlendirmek, öfkelendirmek; kışkırtmak, tahrik etm., dürtmek; sebep olm. *-e*, neden olm. *-e*; **proˈvok.ing** □ sinirlendirici, can sıkıcı, sinir bozucu.

**prov.ost** [ˈprɔvəst] *n.* bazı üniversitelerde dekan; İskoçya'da belediye başkanı; ✗ [prəˈvəu] ~ marshal inzibat amiri, askerî subay.

**prow** ⚓ [prau] *n.* pruva.

**prow.ess** [ˈprauis] *n.* yiğitlik, cesaret, mertlik; cesaret isteyen iş.

**prowl** [praul] **1.** *v/t. & v/i.* gizli gizli gezinmek; etrafı kolaçan etm.; sinsi sinsi dolaşmak; **2.** *n.* sinsi sinsi dolaşma; ~ car *Am.* polis devriye arabası.

**prox.i.mate** □ [ˈprɔksimit] en yakın, hemen yanındaki; yaklaşık, takribi; **proxˈim.i.ty** *n.* yakınlık, civar; **prox.i.mo** [ˈ-məu] *adj.* ✝ gelecek ayın...

**prox.y** [ˈprɔksi] *n.* vekil(lik), vekâlet(name; by ~ vekâleten, adına.

**prude** [pruːd] *n.* fazilet taslayıcı.

**pru.dence** [ˈpruːdəns] *n.* ihtiyat, basiret, sağgörü; akıl, sağduyu; **ˈpru.dent** □ ihtiyatlı, tedbirli, basiretli, sağgörülü; tutumlu; **pru.den.tial** □ [~ˈdenʃəl] basiretli, sağgörülü, ihtiyatlı.

**prud.er.y** [ˈpruːdəri] *n.* aşırı erdem (*veya* iffet) taslama; erdem taslayıcı hareket *veya* söz; **ˈprud.ish** □ aşırı erdem taslayan.

**prune¹** [pruːn] *n.* kuru erik, çir.

**prune²** [~] *v/t.* budamak *(a. fig.)*; *a.* ~ away, ~ off fazla kısımları atmak.

**prun.ing...:** ˈ~-hook, ˈ~-knife *n.* budama bıçağı; ˈ~-saw *n.* budama testeresi.

**pru.ri.ence, pru.ri.en.cy** [ˈpruəriəns(i)] *n.* şehvet (düşkünlüğü); **ˈpru.ri.ent** □ şehvetli; şehvet düşkünü; ❓ çok üreyen.

**Prus.sian** [ˈprʌʃən] **1.** *adj.* Prusyalı, Prusya'ya ait; ~ blue koyu lâcivert; **2.** *n.* Prusyalı; Prusya dili.

**prus.sic ac.id** [ˈprʌsikˈæsid] *n.* asit prusik.

**pry¹** [prai] **1.** *v/t.* ~ open manivela ile açmak; ~ up kaldırmak; **2.** *n.* manivela, kaldıraç.

**pry²** [~] *vb.* merakla bakmak, gözetlemek; ~ into burnunu sokmak -e; **'pry.ing** ☐ meraklı.

**psalm** [saːm] *n.* ilâhi; **'psalm.ist** *n.* ilâhi yazarı; **psal.mo.dy** ['sælmədi] *n.* ilâhi okuma; ilâhiler kitabı.

**Psal.ter** ['ısɔːltə] *n.* ilâhiler kitabı.

**pseu.do...** ['sjuːdəu] *prefix* sahte..., yalancı..., takma...; **pseu.do.nym** ['~dənim] *n.* takma ad; **pseu.don.y.mous** ☐ [~'dɔniməs] takma ad altında yazılmış.

**pshaw** [pʃɔː] *int.* öf!

**pso.ri.a.sis** ⚕ [psɔ'raiəsis] *n.* sedef hastalığı.

**psy.che** ['saikiː] *n.* insan ruhu; can; akıl.

**psy.chi.a.trist** [sai'kaiətrist] *n.* ruh doktoru, psikiyatr; **psy'chi.a.try** *n.* psikiyatri, ruh hekimliği.

**psy.chic, psy.chi.cal** ☐ ['saikik(əl)] ruhsal, ruhî; zihnî; telepati ile ilgili; **'psy-chics** *n. sg.* psikoloji.

**psy.cho-a.nal.y.sis** [saikəuə'næləsis] *n.* psikanaliz; **psy.cho-an.a.lyst** [~'ænəlist] *n.* psikanalist, ruhsal çözümleme.

**psy.cho.log.i.cal** ☐ [saikə'lɔdʒikəl] psikolojik, ruhbilimsel; ruhî; **psy.chol.o.gist** [sai'kɔlədʒist] *n.* psikolog, ruh bilgini; **psy'chol.o.gy** *n.* psikoloji, ruhbilim.

**psy.cho.path** ['saikəupæθ] *n.* psikopat, ruh hastası.

**psy.cho.sis** [sai'kəusis] *n.* psikoz, akıl hastalığı, ruhsal bozukluklar.

**psy.cho.ther.a.py** ['saikəu'θerəpi] *n.* psikoterapi, ruhî tedavi.

**pto.maine** ⚕ ['təumein] *n.* bozulan yiyecekte bulunan bir çeşit zehir.

**pub** F [pʌb] *n.* birahane, meyhane.

**pu.ber.ty** ['pjuːbəti] *n.* ergenlik çağı, buluğ, rüşt, erinlik.

**pu.bes.cence** [pjuː'besns] *n.* erginleşme, buluğa erme; **pu'bes.cent** *adj.* ergin, erin, buluğa ermiş; ♀ tüylü.

**pub.lic** ['pʌblik] **1.** ☐ halka ait, umuma ait; umumî, genel; açık, aleni; herkese mahsus; devletle ilgili; ~ address system hoparlör tertibatı; ~ man halktan biri; ~ spirit yardımseverlik; *s.* utility; works; **2.** *n. sg. & pl.* halk, ahali, umum; seyirciler; in ~ açık açık, açıkça, alenen; **pub.li.can** ['~kən] *n.* meyhaneci, birahaneci; *hist.* vergi tahsildarı; **pub.li.ca.tion** [~'keiʃən] *n.* yayım(lama); yayın; monthly ~ aylık mecmua; **'pub.lic house** lokanta, birahane, meyhane; **pub.li.cist**

[~-sist] *n.* politika yazarı; reklamcı; **pub'lic.i.ty** [~siti] *n.* aleniyet, alenilik; şöhret; tanıtma, reklam; ~ agent reklamcı; **pub.li.cize** ['~saiz] *v/t.* reklamını yapmak; halka duyurmak. **pub.lic...:** ~ li.bra.ry halk kütüphanesi; '~-'pri.vate *adj.* karma *(ekonomi)*; ~ re.la.tions *pl.* halkla ilişkiler; ~ school özel okul; *Am.* parasız resmî okul; '~-'spir.it.ed ☐ yardımsever, umumun yararını düşünen.

**pub.lish** ['pʌbliʃ] *vb.* yayımlamak, neşretmek; bastırmak; ilan etm., söylemek, açığa vurmak; **'pub.lish.er** *n.* yayınlayıcı, yayımcı; *Am.* yayınevi; **'pub.lish.ing** *n.* yayın, basım; *attr.* yayın...; ~ house yayınevi.

**puce** [pjuːs] *n.* koyu mor renk, koyu kahverengi.

**puck** [pʌk] *n.* folklorda yaramaz peri; *hockey:* lastik disk.

**puck.a** ['pʌkə] *adj.* gerçek; kaliteli; üstün, lüks, birinci sınıf.

**puck.er** ['pʌkə] **1.** *n.* kırışık, buruşukluk; **2.** *v/t. & v/i. a.* ~ up buruş(tur)mak, kırış(tır)mak, büz(ül)mek.

**puck.ish** ☐ ['pʌkiʃ] yaramaz.

**pud.ding** ['pudiŋ] *n.* puding, muhallebi; black ~ kan, yulaf ezmesi *vs.* ile doldurulmuş domuz bağırsağı; '~-face *n.* tombul surat.

**pud.dle** ['pʌdl] **1.** *n.* su birikintisi, gölcük; ⊕ kumlu harç; **2.** *vb.* ⊕ ocakta tavlamak *(dökme demir)*; sıva haline sokmak *(çamur ve kumu karıştırarak)*; bulamaç yapmak; **'pud.dler** *n.* ⊕ dökme demirci; **'pud.dling-fur.nace** *n.* ⊕ tavlama fırını.

**pu.den.cy** ['pjuːdənsi] *n.* utangaçlık, sıkılganlık; **'pu.dent** *adj.* utangaç, sıkılgan.

**pudg.y** F ['pʌdʒi] *adj.* tıknaz, bodur, küt.

**pueb.lo** [pu'ebləu] *n.* kızılderili köyü.

**pu.er.ile** ☐ ['pjuərail] çocukça, çocuksu, aptalca; önemsiz; **pu.er.il.i.ty** [~'riliti] *n.* çocukluk; aptallık; çocukça davranış *ve ya* söz.

**puff** [pʌf] **1.** *n.* üfleme, püf; üfürük, soluk; hafif yumuşak börek, pufböreği; pudra ponponu; elbisenin büzülmüş ve kabarık yeri; aşırı övgü; yorgan; saç lülesi; abartmalı övgü; **2.** *v/t.* şişirmek; gururlandırmak; abartarak övmek; öve rek reklamını yapmak; *a.* at tüttürmek *(pipo vs.)*; *oft.* ~ out, ~ up üfleyerek söndürmek *(mum vs.)*; şişirmek; abartarak övmek; gururlandırmak; ~ up çıkmak *(duman vs.)*; ~ed up *fig.* kendini beğenmiş, kibirli; ~ed eyes *pl.* şişmiş gözler;

~ed sleeve büzgülü kol; v/i. üflemek; püflemek; solumak; püfür püfür esmek; **'~-box** n. pudra kutusu; **'puff.er** n. püfleyen şey *veya* kimse; F lokomotif; kirpi balığı; **'puff.er.y** n. aşırı övgü; **'puff.i.ness** n. kabartı, şişkinlik; **'puff.ing** n. aşırı övme; **puff paste** pufböreği hamuru; **'puff.y** *adj.* nefesi kesilmiş; şişkin, kabarık; abarţmalı, görkemli; püfür püfür esen (*rüzgâr*).

**pug** [pʌg] n., **'~-dog** buldoğa benzeyen bir cins köpek.

**pu.gil.ism** ['pjuːdʒilizəm] n. boksörlük; **'pu.gil.ist** n. boksör.

**pug.na.cious** [pʌg'neiʃəs] *adj.* kavgacı, hırçın, dövüşken; **pug.nac.i.ty** [~'næsiti] n. kavgacılık, dövüşkenlik.

**pug-nose** ['pʌgnəuz] n. basık burun.

**puis.ne** ♫ ['pjuːni] *adj.* ikinci gelen, küçük...

**pu.is.sant** ['pjuːisnt] *adj.* güçlü, kudretli, nüfuzlu.

**puke** *sl.* [pjuːk] v/t. & v/i. kus(tur)mak.

**pule** [pjuːl] v/i. ağlam(sam)ak.

**pull** [pul] 1. n. çekme, çekiş; yudum, fırt; *typ.* prova; cazibe (of); *sl.* torpil, iltimas (with *den*); gayret; tutamaç, sap; ~ at the bottle *sl.* şişeden alınan yudum, fırt; ~ fastener fermuar; 2. v/t. çekmek; koparmak; yolmak (*tüy*); sürüklemek; aşırı zorlamak; *typ.* çıkarmak (*prova*); ↓ çekmek (*kürek*); soymak; çalmak; çekmek (*diş, silah*); ~ one's weight gerekli gayreti göstermek; ~ about oraya buraya sürüklemek, çekiştirmek; ~ down yıkmak, indirmek; *fig.* çökertmek; ~ in içeriye çekmek; durdurmak (*at*); yakalamak, tevkif etm.; F kazanmak (*para*); ~ off kenara çekmek (*araç*); çıkarmak, soymak, kazanmak, başarmak; ~ round iyileştirmek, kendine getirmek; ~ through iyileştirmek; zorluktan kurtarmak; imtihanı kazandırmak; ~ o.s. together kendine gelmek, kendine hâkim olm.; ~ up durdurmak; azarlamak; v/i. gelmek; bir yudum içki içmek; ↓ kürek çekmek; bir nefes çekmek; silah çekmek; tezahürat yapmak (for *-e*); ~ in istasyona girmek (*tren*); ~ out ayrılmak, çıkmak; ~ round iyileşmek, kendine gelmek; ~ through iyileşmek, kendine gelmek; başarılı olm.; ~ together beraber çalışmak, işbirliği yapmak; ~ up durmak; ~ up with, ~ up to yetişmek *-e*; **'pull.er** n. çeken şey *veya* kimse, çekici.

**pul.let** ['pulit] n. piliç.

**pul.ley** ⊕ ['puli] n. makara; kasnak; *a.* set of ~s palanga.

**pull-in** ['pulin] = pull-up.

**Pull.man car** 🚃 ['pulmən'kaː] n. pulman vagon; yataklı vagon.

**pull...**: **'~-o.ver** n. kazak, süveter; **'~-up** n. mola yeri.

**pul.mo.nar.y** *anat.* ['pʌlmənəri] *adj.* akciğere ait, akciğer...

**pulp** [pʌlp] 1. n. meyve *veya* sebze eti; lapa; ⊕ kâğıt hamuru; *a.* ~ *magazine* *Am.* ucuz dergi; 2. v/t. & v/i. lapalaş(tır)mak; hamurlaş(tır)mak (*kâğıt*).

**pul.pit** ['pulpit] n. mimber, kürsü.

**pulp.y** □ ['pʌlpi] etli, özlü, yumuşak.

**pul.sate** [pʌl'seit] v/t. & v/i. nabız gibi atmak, yürek gibi çarpmak, nabız gibi kımıldamak, titre(t)mek, titreşmek; **pul.sa.tile** ♪ ['~sətail] *adj.* ritmik...; **pul.sa.tion** [~'seiʃən] n. nabız (atışı).

**pulse¹** [pʌls] 1. n. nabız (atışı); 2. v/i. nabız atmak, çarpmak.

**pulse²** [~] n. baklagiller, bakliyat.

**pul.ver.i.za.tion** [pʌlvərai'zeiʃən] n. ezme, toz haline getirme; **'pul.ver.ize** v/t. ezmek, toz haline getirmek; *fig.* mahvetmek; v/i. toz haline gelmek; **'pul.ver.iz.er** n. toz haline getiren kimse *veya* alet.

**pu.ma** *zo.* ['pjuːmə] n. puma.

**pum.ice** ['pʌmis] n., *a.* ~-stone süngertaşı.

**pum.mel** ['pʌml] v/t. yumruklamak, dövmek.

**pump¹** [pʌmp] 1. n. tulumba, pompa; *attr.* pompa...; 2. v/t. tulumba ile çekmek; pompa ile şişirmek (*lastik vs.*); pompa ile basmak (*hava*); F ağzını aramak; *sl.* zorla sokmak (*kafasına*); v/i. tulumba işletmek.

**pump²** [~] n. iskarpin.

**pump.kin** ♀ ['pʌmpkin] n. helvacıkabağı.

**pump-room** ['pʌmprum] n. kaplıcada şifalı suyun bulunduğu oda.

**pun** [pʌn] 1. n. kelime oyunu, söz oyunu, cinas; 2. v/i. kelime oyunu yapmak.

**Punch¹** [pʌntʃ] n. bodur ve kambur kukla; ~ and Judy show ['dʒuːdi] İngiltere'de kukla oyunu.

**punch²** [~] 1. n. ⊕ zımba, delgi, matkap, ıstampa; 2. v/t. zımbalamak, zımba ile açmak (*delik*), ıstampa ile basmak; biz ile delmek.

**punch³** [~] 1. n. yumruk, muşta; F etki, tesir; *fig.* enerji, kuvvet; 2. vb. yumruklamak; *Am.* gütmek (*sığır vs.*).

**punch⁴** [~] n. meşrubat, punç.

**pun.cheon** ['pʌntʃən] n. çatı direği; zımba; şarap fıçısı; 320 litrelik şarap ölçüsü.

**punch.er** ['pʌntʃə] n. zımba; F kavgacı kimse; *Am.* kovboy; **'punch.ing-ball** n.

boksörlerin antrenman için kullandıkları torba.

**punc.til.i.o** [pʌŋk'tiliəu] *n.* titizlik; formalite ve görgü kurallarına düşkünlük; = punctiliousness; **punc.til.i.ous** [~'tiliəs] *adj.* merasime (*veya* resmiyete) düşkün, titiz; **punc'til.i.ous.ness** *n.* titizlik.

**punc.tu.al** □ ['pʌŋktʃuəl] tam zamanında gelen, dakik; **punc.tu.al.i.ty** [~'æliti] *n.* dakiklik, şaşmazlık.

**punc.tu.ate** ['pʌŋktʃueit] *v/t.* noktalamak; *fig.* kesmek (*sözünü*); **punc.tu'a.tion** *n.* noktalama (kuralı).

**punc.ture** ['pʌŋktʃə] 1. *n.* delik (delme); *mot.* lastik patlaması; patlak; have a ~ lastiği patlamak 2. *v/t. & v/i.* patla(t)-mak. delmek.

**pun.dit** ['pʌndit] *n.* Hindu dini bilgini; bilgin, âlim, üstat; F bilgiç, ukalâ kimse.

**pun.gen.cy** ['pʌndʒənsi] *n.* keskinlik, acılık (*a. fig.*); **'pun.gent** *adj.* sert, acı, keskin, tesirli, iğneleyici (*fig.*).

**pun.ish** ['pʌniʃ] *v/t.* cezalandırmak; kötü dövmek, hırpalamak; yola getirmek; azarlamak; F silip süpürmek (*içki, yemek vs.*); **'pun.ish.a.ble** □ cezalandırılabilir; cezayı hak etmiş; **'pun.ish.er** *n.* cezalandıran kimse; **'pun.ish.ment** *n.* ceza(-landırma).

**pu.ni.tive** ['pjuːnitiv] *adj.* cezalandırıcı; ceza...; cezayı gerektirici.

**punk¹** *Am.* [pʌŋk] 1. *n.* çürük tahta; kav; F değersiz şey, boş laf, saçma; *sl.* ciğeri beş para etmez adam; 2. *adj. sl.* kalitesiz, değersiz; rahatsız, hasta.

**punk²** [~] *n.* «punk rock» hayranı kimse; it, kopuk, serseri; ~ **rock** *s.* pop music.

**pun.ster** ['pʌnstə] *n.* kelime oyunu yapan kimse.

**punt¹** ↓ [pʌnt] 1. *n.* altı düz kayık; 2. *v/t.* sırıkla yüzdürmek; kayık ile taşımak; *v/i.* sandalla gitmek.

**punt²** [~] *vb.* yere düşmeden vurmak (*topa*).

**pu.ny** □ ['pjuːni] çelimsiz, zayıf; önemsiz, ufak.

**pup** [pʌp] 1. = puppy; 2. *v/i.* yavrulamak (*köpek*).

**pu.pa** *zo.* ['pjuːpə] *n.* krizalit.

**pu.pil** ['pjuːpl] *n. anat.* gözbebeği; öğrenci, talebe; **pu.pil.(l)age** [~'pilidʒ] *n.* öğrencilik; küçüklük.

**pup.pet** ['pʌpit] *n.* kukla (*a. fig.*); **'~-show** *n.* kukla oyunu.

**pup.py** ['pʌpi] *n.* köpek yavrusu; *fig.* züppe genç.

**pur.blind** ['pəːblaind] *adj.* yarı kör; *fig.* mankafa, ahmak, gabi.

**pur.chase** ['pəːtʃəs] 1. *n.* satın alma, alım; satın alınan şey; sıkı tutma, kavrama; ⊕ makara; bedel; **make ~s** alışveriş yapmak, öteberi almak; **at twenty years' ~** yirmi yıllık gelirine bedel; **his life is not worth an hour's ~** bir saatlik ömrü kaldı; 2. *v/t.* satın almak; *fig.* gayretle elde etm., kazanmak; ⊕ manivela ile kaldırmak *veya* çekmek; **'pur.chas.er** *n.* alıcı, müşteri.

**pure** □ [pjuə] *com.* saf(i), halis, som, has, temiz; kusursuz, lekesiz; kuramsal, teorik; namuslu, masum; **'~-bred** *adj. Am.* saf kan; **pu.rée** ['pjuərei] *n.* püre, ezme; **'pure.ness** *n.* safilik, temizlik; iffet; nezaket.

**pur.ga.tion** [pəː'geiʃən] *n. mst fig.* temizleme, paklama, arındırma (*günahtan*); ℞ müshil ile bağırsakların temizlenmesi; **pur.ga.tive** ℞ ['~gətiv] 1. *adj.* müshil; 2. *n.* müshil, sürgün ilâcı; **'pur.ga.to.ry** *n. eccl.* Araf.

**purge** [pəːdʒ] 1. *n.* ℞ müshil ilâcı; *pol.* tasfiye; 2. *v/t. mst fig.* temizlemek, paklamak, arındırmak (**of, from** -*den*); *pol.* tasfiye etm.; ℞ ishal (*veya* amel) vermek.

**pu.ri.fi.ca.tion** [pjuərifi'keiʃən] *n.* temizleme; tasfiye; **pu.ri.fi.er** ['~faiə] *n.* temizleyici (*part. alet*); **pu.ri.fy** ['~fai] *v/t.* temizlemek, paklamak (**of, from** -*den*); ⊕ arıtmak; *fig.* ıslah etm.

**Pu.ri.tan** ['pjuəritən] 1. *n.* Püriten, mutaassıp Protestan; 2. *adj.* sofu, mutaassıp; **pu.ri.tan.ic** [~'tænik] *adj.* (~ally) sofu; **Pu.ri.tan.ism** ['~tənizəm] *n.* sofuluk.

**pu.ri.ty** ['pjuəriti] *n.* temizlik, haslık, saflık (*a. fig.*); iffet; nezaket.

**purl¹** [pəːl] *n.* dantela için sırma teli; yün örgüsünde ters iğne; pli.

**purl²** [~] 1. *n.* çağıltı, şırıltı; 2. *v/i.* çağıldayarak akmak.

**purl.er** F ['pəːlə] *n.* şiddetli düşüş; **come a ~** baş aşağı düşmek.

**pur.lieus** ['pəːljuːz] *n.* dış mahalleler, etraf, hudut, civar, çevre.

**pur.loin** [pəː'lɔin] *v/t.* çalmak, aşırmak; **pur'loin.er** *n.* hırsız.

**pur.ple** ['pəːpl] 1. *adj.* mor, erguvanî; ~ **passage** süslü yazı; 2. *n.* mor, erguvanî, eflatun renk; 3. *v/t.* mor renge boyamak; *v/i.* mor rengini almak; **'pur.plish** *adj.* morumsu, eflatuni.

**pur.port** ['pəːpət] 1. *n.* anlam, mana, kavram; 2. *v/t.* ...anlamında olm., delâlet etm. -*e*, göstermek; iddia etm.

**pur.pose** ['pəːpəs] 1. *n.* maksat, niyet, ideram, murat, amaç; karar; **for the ~ of**

...maksadıyle; on ~ isteyerek, kasten, mahsus, bile bile; to the ~ isabetli, yerinde, asıl konu ile ilgili; to no ~ faydasızca, boşuna, boş yere; **2.** *v/t.* niyet etm., tasarlamak; istemek; **pur.pose.ful** □ [¹~ful] maksatlı; önemli; anlamlı, manalı; ¹**pur.pose.less** □ manasız; amaçsız, maksatsız; ¹**pur.pose.ly** *adv.* bile bile, kasten, mahsus.

**purr** [pəː] **1.** *v/i.* mırlamak *(kedi)*; *v/t.* mırıldanmak; **2.** *n.* kedi mırlaması.

**purse** [pəːs] **1.** *n.* para kesesi; *Am.* el çantası; yardım parası, fon; hazine; public ~ devlet hazinesi; **2.** *v/t. oft.* ~ up büzmek, bükmek *(dudak)*; keseye koymak; ¹~**proud** *adj.* parasına güvenen; ¹**purs.er** *n.* ♩ gemi muhasebecisi *veya* veznedarı; ¹**purse-strings** *n.*: hold the ~ para işini idare etm.; loosen the ~ kesenin ağzını açmak.

**pur.si.ness** [¹pəːsinis] *n.* tıknefeslik; şişmanlık.

**purs.lane** ♧ [¹pəːslin] *n.* semizotu.

**pur.su.ance** [pə¹sjuːəns] *n.* takip etme; devam; ifa; tatbik; in ~ of ifa ederken, yaparken; **pur¹su.ant** □: ~ to uygun olarak -*e*, gereğince.

**pur.sue** [pə¹sjuː] *v/t.* & *v/i.* takip etm., izlemek, kovalamak, peşine düşmek; devam etm. -*e*, sürdürmek; aramak; *fig.* -*in* peşini bırakmamak *(talihsizlik vs.)*; ardı sıra gitmek; ~ after takip etm., izlemek; **pur¹su.er** *n.* takip eden kimse; ♂ davacı; **pur.suit** [pə¹sjuːt] *n.* kovalama, takip, izleme, arama *(of -i)*; *mst.* ~*s pl.* iş, meşguliyet, uğraş; ~ plane avcı uçağı; **pur.sui.vant** [¹pəːsivənt] *n.* izleyen kimse; refakatçi, teşrifatçı.

**pur.sy¹** [¹pəːsi] *adj.* şişman; tıknefes.

**pur.sy²** [~] *adj.* büzülmüş *(dudak vs.)*; buruşuk, kırışık; servetine güvenen.

**pu.ru.lent** □ [¹pjuərulənt] cerahatli, irinli.

**pur.vey** [pə¹vei] *v/t.* tedarik etm., sağlamak, temin etm.; *v/i.* ~ for erzak temin etm. -*e*; **pur¹vey.ance** *n.* sağlama, tedarik etme; **pur¹vey.or** *n.* satıcı, temin eden kimse *(part. erzak)*.

**pur.view** [¹pəːvjuː] *n.* konu; saha; faaliyet *(alanı)*.

**pus** [pʌs] *n.* irin, cerahat.

**push** [puʃ] **1.** *n.* itiş, kakış, dürtüş; girişkenlik, teşebbüs; çaba, güç, gayret; ilerleme, hücum, atak; azim; at a ~ gerekirse, gerektiğinde, icabında; when it comes to the ~ sıkışınca, iş esasa binince; get the ~ *sl.* kovulmak, sebeplenmek; give s.o. the ~ *sl. b-ne* yol vermek, kovmak, sepetlemek; **2.** *v/t.* itmek, dürt-

mek; sürmek, sevketmek, yürütmek; saldırmak; *fig.* sıkıştırmak; basmak *(düğmeye vs.)*; kanunsuz yoldan satmak *(uyuşturucu madde)*; a. ~ through çaba harcayarak kabul ettirmek, geçirmek, *(tasarı vs.)*; ~ s.th. on s.o. *bşi b-ne* zorla kabul ettirmek; ~ one's way başarılı olm., yükselmek; ite kaka ilerlemek; be ~ed for time (money) vakti (eli) dar olm.; she is ~ing thirty otuza merdiven dayadı; *v/i.* itişip kakışmak; hücum etm.; uğraşmak (for için); ~ along, ~ on, ~ forward devam etm., ileri sürmek; ~ off avara etm. *(kayık)*; F (çekip) gitmek; ¹~**ball** *n.* bir çeşit top oyunu; ¹~**bike** *n.* bisiklet; ¹~**but.ton** *n.* ⚡ pusbuton, elektrik düğmesi; ¹**push.er** *n.* fırsat düşkünü kimse; uyuşturucu madde satan kimse; *Am.* 🚂 itici lokomotif; **push.ful** □ [¹~ful], ¹**push.ing** □ girişken, enerjik; *b.s.* sırnaşık, küstah; ¹**push-off** *n.* baş(langıç); ¹~**o.ver** *n. part. Am.* çok kolay iş, çocuk oyuncağı; kolay aldanır kimse; ¹**push-up** *n.* şınav.

**pu.sil.la.nim.i.ty** [pjuːsiləˡnimiti] *n.* çekingenlik, ürkeklik, korkaklık; **pu.sil.lan.i.mous** □ [~ˡlæniməs] korkak, ürkek, yüreksiz, çekingen, pısırık.

**puss** [pus] *n.* kedi; *fig.* kız; *sl.* surat; ¹**puss.y** *n.* ♧ söğüt tırtılsısı; *a.* ~**-cat** kedi; ¹**puss.y.foot** *Am.* F **1.** *n.* sır küpü *(veya* fikrini belirtmeyen) kimse; **2.** *v/i.* F fikrini belirtmemek; kedi gibi sessizce yürümek; çok tedbirli davranmak.

**pus.tule** ⚕ [¹pʌstjuːl] *n.* sivilce, kabarcık, püstül.

**put** [put] *(irr.)* **1.** *v/t.* koymak, yerleştirmek, sokmak, takmak (on, to -*e*); maruz bırakmak; söylemek, öne sürmek; oya koymak; kelimelerle ifade etm.; tercüme etm.; uyarlamak; adamak; sevketmek, zorlamak; tahrik etm., kışkırtmak; yatırmak; tahmin etm. *(at olarak)*; yazmak; işaretlemek; avucu yukarı doğru tutarak atmak *(gülle)*; ~ about yaymak *(dedikodu)*; ♩ çevirmek *(geminin başını)*; ~ across *sl.* başarı ile yapmak; yutturmak; ~ away kaldırmak, yerine koymak; biriktirmek, bir kenara ayırmak *(para)*; vazgeçmek; *sl.* öldürmek; F tıkmarhaneye kapatmak; *sl.* silip süpürmek; ~ back *Ⴕ* geri dönmek; geri koymak, yerine koymak; geri almak *(saat)*; *fig.* geriletmek, sekte vurmak; ~ by biriktirmek, bir kenara ayırmak *(para)*; ~ down indirmek, yere koymak; yerleştirmek; bastırmak *(ayaklanma vs.)*; susturmak; yazmak, kaydetmek (for -*e*);

geçırmek (to -e); yüklemek, vermek (to
-e); koymak (as, for *yerine*); ~ forth ileri sürmek; çıkarmak, yayımlamak; sürmek (*tomurcuk*); ortaya koymak; ~
forward ileri sürmek, ortaya atmak; ileri almak *(saat)*; ~ o.s. forward *k-ni* öne
sürmek, sokulmak; adaylığını koymak;
~ in başvurmak (for *için*); sokmak; yerleştirmek; arzetmek, sunmak; vurmak
*(yumruk)*; söylemek *(söz)*; yapmak;
seçmek; F geçirmek *(vakit)*; ~ in an
hour's work bir saatlik iş yapmak; ~ off
sonraya bırakmak, tehir etm., ertelemek; çıkarmak *(elbise)*; engellemek;
vazgeçirmek; *fig.* bırakmak, üstünden
atmak *(korku, şüphe vs.)*; ~ on giymek
*(elbise)*; takınmak *(tavır)*; † eklemek
(to -e); açmak; artırmak; koymak *(ek
sefer vs.)*; *thea.* sahneye koymak
*(oyun)*; ileri almak *(saat)*; F aldatmak;
he is ~ting it on abartıyor; ~ it on thick
abartmak, izam etm.; ~ on airs hava atmak, caka satmak; ~ on weight kilo almak, şişmanlamak; ~ out söndürmek
*(ışık, ateş vs.)*; çıkarmak; faize vermek
*(para)*; üretmek; kovmak; yayınlamak
*(haber vs.)*; sinirlendirmek; şaşırtmak;
rahatsız etm.; ~ out of action faaliyet
dışı bırakmak, işe yaramaz hale sokmak;
~ over başarmak; ertelemek, tehir etm.;
~ o.s. over etkilemek; ~ right düzeltmek,
düzene koymak; ~ through *teleph.* bağlamak (to -e); tabi tutmak *(test vs.)*; F
gerçekleştirmek, yapmak, yürütmek
*(iş vs.)*; ~ s.o. through it F *b-nin* yeteneğini ölçmek; ~ to ilâve etm., birleştirmek; sunmak; arzusuna bırakmak; açıklamak; be (hard) ~ to it akla karayı seçmek, çok sıkıntı çekmek; ~ to expense
masrafa sokmak; ~ to death öldürmek;
~ to the rack *veya* torture eziyet etm.,
işkence etm.; ~ together birleştirmek,
biraraya getirmek, monte etm.; kafasın-
da toplamak *(fikir, düşünce vs.)*; ~ up
kaldırmak; çekmek *(bayrak vs.)*; kurmak *(çadır vs.)*; inşa etm.; asmak *(ilan
vs.)*; artırmak, yükseltmek; ortaya koymak; sağlamak, temin etm. *(para)*; kı-
nına sokmak *(kılıç)*; salıvermek *(hayvan)*; toplamak *(saç)*; misafir etm.;
aday göstermek (for *için*); ~ s.o. up to
s.th. *b-ni* bşe teşvik etm., kışkırtmak; 2.
*v/i.* acele gitmek; ↓ yol almak; ~ off, ~
out, ~ to sea ↓ denize açılmak; ~ in ↓
limana girmek; ~ up at konaklamak, gecelemek; ~ up for adaylığını koymak -e;
~ up with katlanmak -e, çekmek -i, tahammül etm. -e.

pu.ta.tive ['pjuːtətiv] *adj.* farzedilen, varsayılan.
put.log ⊕ ['pʌtlɔg] *n.* iskele kirişi.
pu.tre.fac.tion [pjuːtri'fækʃən] *n.* kokma,
çürüme, bozulma; çürümüş şey; pu.tre-
'fac.tive [~tiv] *adj.* çürütücü.
pu.tre.fy ['pjuːtrifai] *v/t.* & *v/i.* çürü(t)-
mek, kok(ut)mak, bozulmak, kokuşmak.
pu.tres.cence [pjuː'tresns] *n.* çürüklük,
bozukluk; pu'tres.cent *adj.* çürüyen, çürümekte olan.
pu.trid □ ['pjuːtrid] çürük, bozuk, kokmuş; *sl.* iğrenç; pu'trid.i.ty *n.* çürüklük;
çürük şey.
putt [pʌt] *golf:* 1. *vb.* deliğe sokmak için
topa hafifçe vurmak; 2. *n.* topu deliğe
sokmak için yapılan hafif vuruş.
put.tee ['pʌti] *n.* dolak.
putt.er ['pʌtə] *n. golf:* golf sopası.
put.ty ['pʌti] 1. *n. a.* glaziers' ~ camcı macunu; *a.* plasterers' ~ sıva, harç; 2. *vb.*
macunlamak.
put-up job ['putʌp'dʒɔb] *n.* hile(li iş).
puz.zle ['pʌzl] 1. *n.* bilmece, bulmaca; mesele, sorun; şaşkınlık, hayret; 2. *v/t.* &
*v/i.* şaşır(t)mak, hayrete düş(ür)mek;
düşündürmek; çok düşünmek (over -*i*);
~ one's brains kafa patlatmak, zihnini
yormak; ~ out kafa yorarak çözmek;
'~-head.ed *adj.* şaşırmış, kafası bulanık;
'puz.zler *n.* güç durum, karışık mesele;
anlaşılmaz kişi.
pyg.m(a)e.an [pig'miːən] *adj.* cüce...; pygmy ['pigmi] *n.* pigme; *fig.* cüce, bodur
kimse; *attr.* cüce...
py.ja.mas [pə'dʒɑːməz] *n. pl.* pijama.
py.lon ['pailən] *n.* pilon, çelik telgraf direği.
py.lo.rus *anat.* [pai'lɔːrəs] *n.* pilor, mide
kapısı.
py.or.rh(o)e.a ჳ [paiə'riə] *n.* piyore, dişeti
iltihabı.
pyr.a.mid ['pirəmid] *n.* piramit, ehram;
py.ram.i.dal □ [pi'ræmidl] piramit şeklinde.
pyre ['paiə] *n.* odun yığını *(part. ölüleri
yakmak için)*.
py.ri.tes [pai'raitiːz] *n.:* copper ~ bakır
sülfid; iron ~ demir sülfid, pirit.
py.ro... ['paiərəu] *prefix* ateş *veya* ısı ile
ilgili, ateş..., ısı...; py.rog.ra.phy [pai-
'rɔgrəfi] *n.* pirogravür; py.ro.tech.nic,
py.ro.tech.ni.cal [pairəu'teknik(əl)] *adj.*
fişeklere *veya* fişekçiliğe ait; py.ro'technics *n. pl.* fişekçilik; fişek eğlenceleri;
*fig.* ortalığı birbirine katan hareket; py-
ro'tech.nist *n.* fişekçi.
Pyr.rhic vic.to.ry ['pirik'viktəri] *n.* büyük

kayıp verilerek kazanılan başarı.

**Py.thag.o.re.an** [paiθægəˈriːən] **1.** *adj.* Pitagor'a ait; **2.** *n.* Pitagor taraftarı kimse.

**Pyth.i.an** [ˈpiθiən] *adj.* Apollon'a ait.

**py.thon** [ˈpaiθən] *n.* piton yılanı.

**pyx** [piks] *n. eccl.* Katolik kilisesinde kutsal ekmeğin konulduğu kutu.

# Q

**Q-boat** ⚓ [ˈkjuːbəut] *n.* düşman denizaltılarını tuzağa düşüren ticaret *veya* balıkçı gemisi görünümündeki gemi.

**quack¹** [kwæk] **1.** *n.* ördek sesi, vak vak; **2.** *v/i.* ördek gibi bağırmak, 'vak vak' etm.

**quack²** [~] **1.** *n.* doktor taslağı, şarlatan, yalancı doktor; **2.** *adj.* şarlatan...; **3.** *v/i.* şarlatanlık etm.; **quack.er.y** [ˈ~əri] *n.* şarlatanlık.

**quad** [kwɔd] = quadrangle, quadrat.

**quad.ra.ge.nar.i.an** [kwɔdrədʒiˈnɛəriən] **1.** *adj.* kırk ile elli yaşları arasında olan *(kimse)*; **2.** *n.* kırk ile elli yaşları arasındaki kimse.

**quad.ran.gle** [ˈkwɔdræŋgl] *n.* dörtgen; avlu, bahçe *(okul vs.)*.

**quad.rant** [ˈkwɔdrənt] *n.* oktant, yükseklik ölçme aleti; *part.* ✠ çeyrek daire.

**quad.rat** *typ.* [ˈkwɔdræt] *n.* katrat; **quad.rat.ic** ✠ [kwɔˈdrætik] **1.** *adj.* dörtgen gibi; ✠ ikinci dereceden; **2.** *n.:* ~ equation ikinci dereceden denklem; **quad.ra.ture** [ˈkwɔdrətʃə] *n.* kare yapma; ✠ alan hesabı; *ast.* dördün.

**quad.ren.ni.al** ☐ [kwɔˈdrenjəl] dört senede bir olan; dört sene süren.

**quad.ri.lat.er.al** ✠ [kwɔdriˈlætərəl] **1.** *adj.* dört kenarlı; **2.** *n.* dörtgen, dörtkenar.

**qua.drille** [kwɔˈdril] *n.* kadril dansı (müziği).

**quad.ri.par.tite** [kwɔdriˈpɑːtait] *adj.* dört taraflı, dört kısımlı.

**quad.ru.ped** [ˈkwɔdruped] **1.** *n.* dört ayaklı hayvan; **2.** *adj. a.* quad.ru.pe.dal [kwɔˈdruːpidl] dört ayaklı *(hayvan)*; **quad.ru.ple** [ˈkwɔdrupl] **1.** ☐ dört kısımlı; dört kişilik; *a.* ~ to, ~ of dört misli, dört katı *-in;* **2.** *n.* bşin dört misli; **3.** *v/t. & v/i.* dört misli çoğal(t)mak, art(ır)mak; **quad.ru.plet** [ˈkwɔdruplit] *n.* dördüzlerden biri; **quad.ru.pli.cate 1.** [kwɔˈdruːplikit] *adj.* dört kat, dört misli; **2.** [~keit] *v/t.* dörtle çarpmak; dört misli çoğaltmak.

**quaff** [kwɑːf] *vb.* (bir yudumda) içmek; ~ off kana kana içmek.

**quag** [kwæg] = ~mire; **¹quag.gy** *adj.* bataklık gibi; gevşek, yumuşak; **quag.mire** [ˈ~maiə] *n.* batak(lık).

**quail¹** *orn.* [kweil] *n.* bıldırcın.

**quail²** [~] *v/i.* yılmak, sinmek, ürkmek, korkmak.

**quaint** ☐ [kweint] tuhaf, acayip, antika, orijinal, garip ve hoş; **¹quaint.ness** *n.* tuhaflık, antikalık, garip hoşluk.

**quake** [kweik] **1.** *v/i.* sallanmak, sarsılmak; titremek (with, for *-den*); **2.** *n.* sallantı; zelzele, deprem; titreme, ürperme.

**Quak.er** [ˈkweikə] *n.* Kuveykır mezhebinin üyesi.

**qual.i.fi.ca.tion** [kwɔlifiˈkeiʃən] *n.* nitelik, vasıf, meziyet, ehliyet; şart; kayıt, kısıtlama; *gr.* niteleme; **qual.i.fied** [ˈ~faid] *adj.* ehliyetli, vasıflı, kalifiye; şartlı, kısıtlı, sınırlı; **qual.i.fy** [ˈ~fai] *v/t. & v/i.* hak kazan(dır)mak, ehliyetli kılmak; kısıtlamak, sınırla(ndır)mak; hafifletmek; nitelendirmek; tanımlamak, tasvir etm.; *gr.* nitelemek; ehliyet göstermek; qualifying examination eleme sınavı, yeterlilik imtihanı; **qual.i.ta.tive** ☐ [ˈ~tətiv] niteliğe ait, nitel(eyici); **¹qual.i.ty** *n.* kalite; nitelik, vasıf; özellik, hususiyet; üstünlük; çeşit, sınıf, nevi.

**qualm** [kwɑːm] *n.* vicdan azabı, pişmanlık; bulantı; şüphe, huzursuzluk, kuruntu, kuşku; **¹qualm.ish** ☐ mide bulandırıcı, tiksindirici; midesi çabuk bulanan; vicdanının sesini dinleyen.

**quan.da.ry** [ˈkwɔndəri] *n.* şüphe, tereddüt, hayret, şaşkınlık; müşkül durum, ikilem.

**quan.ti.ta.tive** ☐ [ˈkwɔntitətiv] nicel, niceliğe ait **¹quan.ti.ty** *n.* kemiyet, nicelik *(a.* ✠); miktar; ~s *pl.* bolluk, çokluk, çok miktar; ~ surveyor yapı malzeme tahmincisi.

**quan.tum** [ˈkwɔntəm] *n.* miktar, meblağ, tutar; pay, hisse; ~ theory *phys.* kuantum teorisi.

**quar.an.tine** [ˈkwɔrəntiːn] **1.** *n.* karantina; **2.** *v/t.* karantina altına almak.

**quar.rel** [ˈkwɔrəl] **1.** *n.* kavga, münakaşa, çekişme, bozuşma; **2.** *v/i.* kavga etm., münakaşa etm., çekişmek, bozuşmak; **quar.rel.some** [ˈ~səm] ☐ kavgacı, ters, huysuz.

quar.ry[1] [ˈkwɔri] 1. *n.* taş ocağı; *fig.* zengin kaynak, maden; 2. *vb.* taş ocağından kazıp çıkarmak; araştırmak (for *-i*).

quar.ry[2] [~] *n.* av (*a. fig.*).

quar.ry.man [ˈkwɔrimən] *n.* taş ocağı işçisi.

quart [kwɔːt] *n.* kuart, galonun dörtte biri (*1, 136 I, Am. 0,946 I*); *fenc.* [kaːt] bir duruş şekli.

quar.ter [ˈkwɔːtə] 1. *n.* dörtte bir, çeyrek; *part.* çeyrek saat; üç aylık süre; Am. 25 sent; ♪ kıç; ♪ gemide tayfanın görev yeri; ✕ aman, hayatını bağışlama; *fig.* hoşgörü, müsamaha; *fig.* yön, istikamet; taraf, civar, bölge, havali, semt, mahalle; ~s *pl.* ✕ kışla, ordugâh, konak; *fig.* kaynak; dördün; live in close ~s yakında oturmak; at close ~s yan yana, çok yakından; come to close ~s göğüs göğüse dövüşmek; 2. *v/t.* dörde ayırmak, bölmek; parçalara ayırmak; ✕ yerleştirmek (*asker*); '~.back *n.* Am. *spor:* oyunu idare eden oyuncu; '~.deck *n.* kıç güvertesi; savaş gemisi *veya* donanmanın subayları; 'quar.ter.ly 1. *adj.* & *adv.* üç aylık, üç ayda bir (olan); 2. *n.* üç ayda bir çıkan dergi; 'quar.ter.mas.ter *n.* ✕ levazım subayı; ♪ serdümen; quar.tern [ˈ~tən] *n.* bir ölçünün dörtte biri; *a.* ~-loaf dört librelik ekmek somunu; 'quar.ter.staff *n.* eskiden silah olarak kullanılan sopa.

quar.tet(te) ♪ [kwɔːˈtet] *n.* kuartet, dörtlü müzik topluluğu; dört ses *veya* çalgı ile yapılan müzik parçası.

quar.to [ˈkwɔːtəu] *n.* dört yapraklık forma.

quartz *min.* [kwɔːts] *n.* kuvars; quartz.ite [ˈ~ait] *n.* kuvarsit.

quash ʊ̌ [kwɔʃ] *v/t.* iptal etm., feshetmek, kaldırmak, bozmak.

qua.si [ˈkwɑːziː] *prefix* güya, sanki, sözümona.

qua.ter.na.ry [kwəˈtəːnəri] *adj.* dördüncü; dörtlü; *geol.* son zamana ait.

qua.ver [ˈkweivə] 1. *n.* titreme; ♪ ses titremesi; ♪ sekizlik; 2. *vb.* titremek (*ses*); titrek sesle söylemek (*şarkı vs.*); 'qua.ver.y *adj.* titrek.

quay [kiː] *n.* rıhtım, iskele; quay.age [ˈ~idʒ] *n.* iskele ücreti.

quea.si.ness [ˈkwiːzinis] *n.* bulantı, mide bulanması; 'quea.sy ☐ mide bulandırıcı (*yiyecek*); midesi kolayca bulanan; midesi bulanmış, kusacak durumda; titiz, müşkülpesent; kılı kırk yaran; I feel ~ midem bulanıyor.

queen [kwiːn] 1. *n.* kraliçe; *satranç:* vezir; *iskambil:* kız; *sl.* ibne; ~ bee arı beyi, ana arı; ~'s ware krem renginde bir tür İngiliz çömleği; 2. *v/t. satranç:* vezir çıkmak; kraliçe olarak saltanat sürmek; (*bir kadını*) kraliçe yapmak; ~ it çaka satmak, hava atmak (over *-e*); 'queen.like, 'queen.ly *adj.* kraliçe gibi; kraliçeye yaraşır; haşmetli, muhteşem.

queer [kwiə] 1. *adj.* acayip, tuhaf, garip, alışılmamış; şüpheli; F rahatsız, hasta; F deli, kaçık; F sarhoş; F sahte, kalp; F homoseksüel; 2. *v/t.* bozmak; ~ s.o.'s pitch *sl. b-nin* planını bozmak, işine engel olm.; 3. *n.* homoseksüel kimse.

quell *rhet.* [kwel] *v/t.* bastırmak (*ayaklanma vs.*), ezmek, boyun eğdirmek; yatıştırmak.

quench [kwentʃ] *v/t. fig.* gidermek (*susuzluk, hararet*); söndürmek (*ateş, yangın*); son vermek; bastırmak (*ayaklanma vs.*); su ile soğutmak (*çelik*); 'quench.er *n.* F içki; quench.less ☐ söndürülemeyen (*ateş, alev vs.*); giderilemez.

que.rist [ˈkwiərist] *n.* soruşturma yapan kimse.

quern [kwəːn] *n.* el değirmeni.

quer.u.lous ☐ [ˈkwerʊləs] yakınan, şikâyetçi, titiz, ters, aksi, huysuz.

que.ry [ˈkwiəri] 1. *n.* soru (işareti), sual, sorgu; şüphe, kuşku; 2. *v/t.* sormak *-e*, araştırmak; koymak (*soru işareti*); şüphelenmek, kuşku duymak *-den.*

quest [kwest]1. *n.* ara(ştır)ma; soruşturma; macera; in ~ of ...aramak için, aramaya, *-in* peşinde; 2. *vb.* ara(ştır)mak; av izini aramak (*köpek*).

ques.tion [ˈkwestʃən] 1. *n.* soru, sual; mesele, konu, sorun; şüphe, kuşku; teklif, öneri; ihtimal, imkân, şans; sorgu, soruşturma; ~! *parl.* konuya gelelim!, konu dışına çıkmayalım!; beyond (all) ~ elbette, şüphesiz; in ~ söz konusu olan; come into ~ konu olm., tartışılmak; call in ~ şüphe etm., itiraz etm.; beg the ~ söz konusu meseleyi etkin olarak cevaplandırmamak; the ~ is mesele şu ki; that is out of the ~ bu söz konusu olamaz, imkânsızdır, olanak yok; there is no ~ of *veya* of ger. söz konusu değil, sözü edilmez; 2. *v/t.* sual (*veya* soru) sormak *-e*; sorguya çekmek *-i*; şüphe etm. *-den*, kuşku duymak *-den*; 'ques.tion.a.ble ☐ şüpheli, kuşkulu; kesin olmayan; 'ques.tion.a.ble.ness *n.* şüpheli durum; 'ques.tion.er *n.* soru soran *veya* sorguya çeken kimse; ques.tion.naire [kwestʃəˈnɛə] *n.* anket; soru kâğıdı.

**queue** [kjuː] 1. *n.* kuyruk, sıra, bekleyen halk *veya* araba dizisi; saç kuyruğu; 2. *v/i.* mst ~ up kuyruğa girmek, kuyruk olm.

**quib.ble** [ˈkwibl] 1. *n.* kaçamaklı cevap *veya* söz, yanıltmaca; 2. *v/i.* kaçamaklı cevap vermek; önemsiz konu üzerinde durmak; **ˈquib.bler** *n.* safsatacı kimse.

**quick** [kwik] 1. *adj.* çabuk, hızlı, tez, süratli, seri; keskin, anlayışlı; işlek, faal; akıllı, zeki, titiz, çabuk kızan; canlı, parlak; ~ march X hızlı yürüyüş; 2. *n.* tırnak altındaki hassas et; can alıcı nokta; the ~ *pl.* canlılar; to the ~ tırnak altındaki hassas ete kadar; *fig.* en hassas noktaya kadar; cut s.o. to the ~ *b-ni* can evinden vurmak, duygularını incitmek; 3. *s.* ~ly; **ˈ~-change** ac.tor kostüm *veya* görünüşünü sık değiştiren aktör; **ˈquick.en** *v/t.* & *v/i.* hızlan(dır)mak, çabuklaş(tır)mak; canlan(dır)mak, diril(t)mek; neşelen(dir)mek, heveslen(dir)mek; rahimde hayat belirtisi göstermek *(çocuk);* **ˈquick-fir.ing** *adj.* X seri ateşli *(top);* **quick.ie** [ˈ~i] *n.* çok çabuk yapılan şey; F kısa metrajlı ucuz film; **ˈquick.lime** *n.* sönmemiş kireç; **ˈquick.ly** *adv.* çabuk-(ça), hızlı hızlı, acele; **ˈquick-match** *n.* ateşleme fitili; **ˈquick-mo.tion** pic.ture *film:* hızlı çekim film; **ˈquick.ness** *n.* çabukluk, sürat, hız.

**quick...:** **ˈ~.sand** *n.* bataklık kumu; **ˈ~.set** *n.* ✓ çit; *a.* ~ hedge köklü bitkilerden oluşan çit; **ˈ~-ˈsight.ed** *adj.* keskin gözlü; **ˈ~.sil.ver** *n. min.* civa; **ˈ~.step** *n.* hareketli dans; X hızlı askerî yürüyüş; **ˈ~-ˈwit.ted** *adj.* çabuk anlayan, zeki, hazırcevap.

**quid¹** [kwid] *n.* ağızda çiğnenen tütün parçası.

**quid²** *sl.* [~] *n.* bir sterlin.

**quid.di.ty** *phls.* [ˈkwiditi] *n.* nitelik, öz; önemsiz konu, safsata.

**quid pro quo** [ˈkwid prəu ˈkwəu] *n.* karşılık, bedel; ödün, taviz.

**qui.es.cence** [kwaiˈesns] *n.* sükûn(et), istirahat, hareketsizlik, pasiflik; **quiˈescent** ☐ hareketsiz, pasif, istirahatte, sakin: *fig.* uyuşuk.

**qui.et** [ˈkwaiət] 1. ☐ sessiz, sakin, durgun *(deniz vs.):* hareketsiz, rahat; nazik, yumuşak huylu, tatlı, uslu *(çocuk);* gösterişsiz, yumuşak *(renk);* on the ~ *(sl.:* on the q.t. [ˈkjuːˈtiː]) gizlice, çaktırmadan; 3. *v/i. a.* ~ down susmak, yatışmak, sakinleşmek; dinmek; *v/t.* susturmak, yatıştırmak, sakinleştirmek; **ˈqui.et.en** =

**quiet** 3; **qui.et.ism** [ˈkwaiitizəm] *n. eccl.* dünya olaylarından ilgiyi keserek Tanrı düşüncesine dalma felsefesi; **ˈqui.et.ist** *n.* bu felsefe taraftarı kimse; **qui.et.ness** [ˈkwaiətnis] *n.*, **qui.e.tude** [ˈkwaiitjuːd] sessizlik, sakinlik, durgunluk, sükûnet, rahat.

**qui.e.tus** [kwaiˈiːtəs] *n.* hesabın ödenip kapanması, aklama, ibra; öldürme; susturma, bastırma.

**quill** [kwil] 1. *n.* tüy (kalem); kirpi dikeni; tüy sapı; makara; ♩ mızrap; 2. *vb.* makaraya sarmak *(iplik);* fitilli dikmek *(elbise);* **ˈ~-driv.er** *n.* yazar; **ˈquill.ing** *n.* farbala, fırfır; **ˈquill-pen** *n.* tüy kalem.

**quilt** [kwilt] 1. *n.* yorgan; 2. *vb.* yorgan gibi dikmek; içine pamuk doldurup yorgan yapmak; **ˈquilt.ing** *n.* yorgancılık; yorgan yapma; yorganlık malzeme.

**quince** ♀ [kwins] *n.* ayva (ağacı).

**qui.nine** *pharm.* [kwiˈniːn, *part. Am.* ˈkwainain] *n.* kinin.

**quin.qua.ge.nar.i.an** [kwiŋkwədʒiˈneəriən] 1. *adj.* elli yaşlarında olan; 2. *n.* elli yaşlarındaki kimse.

**quin.quen.ni.al** ☐ [kwiŋˈkweniəl] beş yılda bir; beş yıl süren.

**quins** F [kwinz] *n. pl.* beşiz.

**quin.sy** ☞ [ˈkwinzi] *n.* anjin.

**quin.tal** [ˈkwintl] *n.* 100 kiloluk ağırlık, kental.

**quint.es.sence** [kwinˈtesns] *n.* öz, cevher, hulâsa, esas nokta.

**quin.tu.ple** [ˈkwintjupl] 1. *adj.* beş kat, beş misli; 2. *v/t.* & *v/i.* beş misli art(ır)mak; beş misli yapmak *veya* olm.; **quin.tu.plets** [ˈ~plits] *n. pl.* beşiz.

**quip** [kwip] *n.* alaylı şaka, hazır cevap, iğneli söz, saçma cevap.

**quire** [ˈkwaiə] *n.* 24 tabakalık kâğıt destesi.

**quirk** [kwəːk] *n.* tuhaflık, acayiplik; garip hareket, delilik; ⊿ kabartmalı süslemede aralık *veya* girinti.

**quis.ling** [ˈkwizliŋ] *n.* istilâcılarla işbirliği yapan vatan haini.

**quit** [kwit] 1. *v/t.* & *v/i.* terketmek, bırakmak, boşaltmak, çıkmak *(ev);* ayrılmak *(iş);* ödemek *(borç);* durmak, kesilmek, dinmek; gitmek; işten çıkmak; vaz geçmek; 2. *adj.* kurtulmuş, serbest (of *-den).*

**quite** [kwait] *adv.* tamamen, bütün bütün, tam tamına, tamamiyle, büsbütün, gerçekten, hakikaten; hayli, epey; ~ a lot epeyce; defalarca; ~ (so)!, ~ that! gerçekten öyle!, ya öyle!; ~ the thing F moda olmuş, modaya uygun.

**quits** [kwits] *adj.* ödeşmiş, fit olmuş, berabere, başabaş (with *ile*); cry ~ yeter artık demek.

**quit.tance** [ˈkwitəns] *n.* borçtan *veya* yükümden kurtuluş (belgesi); karşılık, bedel, ücret.

**quit.ter** *Am.* F [ˈkwitə] *n.* işi bırakan kimse; sözünden dönen kimse.

**quiv.er¹** [ˈkwivə] **1.** *n.* titreme; **2.** *v/t.* & *v/i.* titre(t)mek, titreş(tir)mek.

**quiv.er²** [~] *n.* ok kılıfı, sadak.

**quix.ot.ic** [kwikˈsɔtik] *adj.* donkişotvari, dünyâdan haberi olmayan, romaneks.

**quiz** [kwiz] **1.** *n.* küçük imtihan; sorgu, test; alay, eğlence; eşek şakası; garip kimse; **2.** *v/t.* sorguya çekmek; imtihan etm.; alay etm., takılmak; küstahça bakmak; ˈquiz.zi.cal □ tuhaf, garip, gülünç; şakacı, alaycı.

**quod** *sl.* [kwɔd] *n.* kodes, cezaevi.

**quoin** [kɔin] *n.* duvarın dış köşesi; köşe (taşı); *typ.* harf takozu.

**quoit** [kɔit] *n.* oyunda atılan çember, halka; ~s *pl.* halka oyunu.

**quon.dam** [ˈkwɔndæm] *adj.* eski, sabık.

**quon.set** *Am.* [ˈkwɔnsit] *n. a.* ~ hut çelik baraka.

**quo.rum** *parl.* [ˈkwɔːrəm] *n.* yetersayı, çoğunluk; have a ~, form a ~ yetersayıyı oluşturmak.

**quo.ta** [ˈkwəutə] *n.* hisse, pay, kota, kontenjan.

**quot.a.ble** [ˈkwəutəbl] *adj.* aktarılabilir, aktararak söylenebilir.

**quo.ta.tion** [kwəuˈteiʃən] *n.* aktarma; aktarılan söz; † fiyat, piyasa rayici, kur; familiar ~s *pl.* vecizeler; **quoˈta.tion-marks** *n. pl.* tırnaklar, tırnak işareti.

**quote** [kwəut] *vb.* (aktarma yolu ile) söylemek, aktarmak, tekrarlamak (*b-nin sözünü*); tekrar yazmak; † vermek (*fiyat*) (*at olarak*); tırnak işareti içine almak.

**quoth** † [kwəuθ] *v/t.:* ~ I, ~ he dedim, dedi.

**quo.tid.i.an** [kwɔˈtidiən] *adj.* her gün olan, günlük.

**quo.tient** Å [ˈkwəuʃənt] *n.* bölüm.

# R

**r** [a:]; the three R's (= reading, writing, arithmetic) okuma, yazma ve aritmetik.

**rab.bet** ⊕ ['ræbit] **1.** *n.* ek yeri, dişli yiv, lamba, zıvana yuvası; **2.** *v/t.* içiçe geçirmek, içine sokmak; yiv açmak.

**rab.bi** ['ræbai] *n.* haham, Musevi dinî lider.

**rab.bit** ['ræbit] *n. zo.* adatavşanı; F acemi oyuncu; '~-fe.ver *n.* bir tür veba, tularemi.

**rab.ble** ['ræbl] *n.* ayaktakımı, düzensiz kalabalık; '~-rous.er *n.* demagog, halk avcısı.

**rab.id** □ ['ræbid] kudurmuş *(hayvan)*; *fig.* aşırı, bağnaz; yabanî, vahşi; hiddetli, gazaplı, öfkeli; 'rab.id.ness *n.* kudurmuşluk, kuduzluk, cinnet, delilik, çılgınlık, kaçıklık.

**ra.bies** *vet.* ['reibi:z] *n.* kuduz (hastalığı).

**rac.coon** [rə'ku:n] = racoon.

**race**[1] [reis] *n.* ırk, soy; nesil, döl, tür, cins; familya, aile.

**race**[2] [~] **1.** *n.* yarış, koşu *(a. fig.)*, koşu yarışması; yaşam süresi; akıntı, cereyan; ~s *pl.* at yarışı; **2.** *v/i.* yarışmak, koşmak, seğirtmek; yıldırım kanunu çıkarmak; *mot.* hızlı çalışmak; *v/t.* yarıştırmak, koşuya sokmak; '~-course *n.* yarış pisti, koşu yolu, parkur.

**race-ha.tred** ['reis'heitrid] *n.* ırklar arasındaki kin ve nefret duygusu.

**race-horse** ['reisho:s] *n.* yarış atı.

**rac.er** ['reisə] *n.* yarış atı; yarış kayığı *(veya* teknesi); yarış otomobili; yarışçı, koşucu.

**ra.cial** ['reiʃəl] *adj.* ırka ait, ırksal...; 'ra.cial.ism *n.* ırkçılık, ırklar arasındaki kin ve nefret duygusu.

**rac.i.ness** ['reisinis] *n.* canlılık, neşe, coşkunluk, zindelik; müsehcenlik; orijinallik.

**rac.ing** ['reisiŋ] *n.* yarış(çılık); *attr.* yarış...; ~ car yarış otomobili.

**rack**[1] [ræk] **1.** *n.* parmaklık; raf; portmanto, askılık; eşya filesi *(araba, tren vs.'de)*; yemlik; ⊕ dişli çubuk; işkence sehpası; kerevet; **2.** *v/t.* yormak; germek, (gerip) işkence etm.; *fig.* azap ver-

mek; istismar etm., kendinden yana yontmak; *(fiyat vs.)* yükselterek sıkıntıya sokmak, eziyet etm.; ~ one's brains kafa yormak *(veya* patlatmak) -e.

**rack**[2] [~] **1.** *n.* sürüklenen hafif bulut; **2.** *v/i.* rüzgârda sürüklenmek *(bulut)*.

**rack**[3] [~] *n.* haraplık, yıkım; go to ~ and ruin tamamiyle mahvolmak, harabeye dönmek.

**rack**[4] [~] *v/t. a.* ~ off tortudan bira *veya* şarap çıkarmak, süzmek.

**rack.et**[1] ['rækit] *n. tenis vs.:* raket; ~s *pl.* dört duvarda sektirilerek oynanan bir tür tenis oyunu.

**rack.et**[2] [~] **1.** *n.* gürültü, patırdı, velvele, şamata; *fig.* hareket, faaliyet, telaş, heyecan; *Am.* F dolandırıcılık, şantaj, haraç(çılık); F iş, meslek; *sl.* rahat iş, beleş; stand the ~ sınavda başarılı olm.; suçu, masraf vs.'yi üstlenmek, sorumluluğu almak; **2.** *v/i.* gürültü patırtı etm., eğlenmek, şamata yapmak; **rack.et.eer** *n. esp. Am. sl.* şantajcı, haraççı; **rack.et'eer.ing** *n. esp. Am. sl.* şantaj yapma, haraç kesme; 'rack.et.y *adj.* haşarı, gürültücü, şamatacı; gürültülü, şamatalı.

**rack-rail.way** ['rækreilwei] *n.* dişli tren.

**rack-rent** [rækrent] **1.** *n.* fahiş kira; **2.** *vb.* fahiş kira talep etm. *-den.*

**ra.coon** *zo.* [rə'ku:n] *n.* Kuzey Amerika'da yaşayan et yiyici ve tilkiden büyücek bir tür hayvan, rakun.

**rac.y** □ ['reisi] canlı, dinç, zinde; çeşnili, baharlı, aromatik; açık saçık, orijinal.

**ra.dar** ['reidə] *n.* radar (aygıtı).

**rad.dle** ['rædl] **1.** *n.* kırmızı tebeşir, aşıboyası; **2.** *v/t.* kırmızıya boyamak.

**ra.di.al** □ ['reidjəl] merkezden çevreye doğru düzenlenmiş, yelpazevarî, radyal, yayılan ışın şeklinde; Ⓐ yarıçapa ait: ~ engine yıldız motor.

**ra.di.ance, ra.di.an.cy** ['reidjəns(i)] *n.* parlaklık, aydınlık; 'ra.di.ant □ parlak, parlayan, aydın; şaşaalı, muhteşem *(a. fig.)*: ışı yayan...; ışın yayan...

**ra.di.ate 1.** ['reidieit] *v/i.* ışın yaymak, neşretmek; yelpazevarî yayılmak; *v/t.*

yaymak, saçmak; **2.** [ˈ-it] *adj.* bir merkezden yayılan, yelpezevarî, ışın...; **radiˈa.tion** *n.* yayılma, ışık ve sıcaklık verme, radyasyon; **ra.di.a.tor** [ˈ-eitə] *n.* radyatör, kalorifer; *mot.* radyatör, soğutucu aygıt.

**rad.i.cal** [ˈrædikəl] **1.** □ kökten, köke ait, temel...; esaslı, kök salmış, yerleşmiş; radikal *(a. pol.)*; köksel; ~ sign Å kök işareti; **2.** *n. gr.* kök; 🔊 unsur, eleman, anamadde; *part. pol.* aşırılar, müfritler; **ˈrad.i.cal.ism** *n.* radikalizm, köktencilik; radikalizm ilkeleri.

**ra.di.o** [ˈreidiəu] **1.** *n.* radyo; telsiz telgraf; radyogram, telsiz haberi; radyo alıcı *veya* vericisi, *telsiz* telgraf aygıtı; ~ car telsizli polis arabası; ~ drama, ~ play radyo tiyatrosu, radyofonik piyes; ~ engineering radyo *(veya* telsiz*)* mühendisliği; ~ set radyo makinesi; **2.** *v/t.* & *v/i.* yayımlamak, telsizle göndermek; telsiz *veya* telgrafla haberleşmek; **ˈ-ˈac.tive** *adj.* radyoaktif; **ˈ-acˈtiv.i.ty** *n.* radyoaktivite; radyo etkinliği; **ra.di.o.gram** [ˈ-græm] *n.* radyogram, radyo telgraf; = **ra.di.o-gram.o.phone** [ˈ-ˈgræməfəun] *n.* pikaplı *(veya* gramofonlu*)* radyo; **ra.di.o-graph** [ˈ-grɑːf] **1.** *n.* radyografi; röntgen (filmi); **2.** *v/t.* röntgenini almak; radyografisini çıkarmak; **ra.di.o-loˈca.tion** *n.* radarla yerini saptama; **ra.di.ol.o.gy** *phys.* [reidiˈɔlədʒi] *n.* radyoloji; **ra.di.o-tel.e.gram** [ˈreidiəuˈteligræm] *n.* radyogram, telsiz telgraf; **ˈra.di.o-ˈther.a.py** *n.* radyoterapi, röntgen ile tedavi.

**rad.ish** ⱱ [ˈrædiʃ] *n.* bayır turpu; red ~ kırmızı turp.

**ra.di.um** [ˈreidjəm] *n.* radyum.

**ra.di.us** [ˈreidjəs] *n., pl.* **ra.di.i** [ˈ-diai] yarıçap; *anat.* radyus, önkol kemiği; ⊕ tekerlek parmağı; *fig.* çevre, muhit, alan.

**raff.ish** [ˈræfiʃ] *adj.* ihmalkâr; sefaperest, rezil, hovarda.

**raf.fle** [ˈræfl] **1.** *n.* piyango, kur'a, çekiliş; **2.** *v/t.* bşi piyangoya koymak, piyango çekmek.

**raft** [rɑːft] **1.** *n.* sal; **2.** *v/t.* salla taşımak; salla karşıya geçmek; sal yapmak -i; *v/i.* sal kullanmak; **ˈraft.er** *n.* ⊕ çatı kirişi, kiriş; **ˈrafts.man** *n.* salcı.

**rag¹** [ræg] *n.* paçavra, bez parçası; *cntp.* değersiz gazete, değersiz şey.

**rag²** *sl.* [~] **1.** *v/t.* & *v/i.* b-ni kızdırmak, takılmak; muziplik yapmak, kaba şaka yapmak; gürültü ve şamata yapmak, ortalığı velveleye vermek, etrafı gürültüye boğmak; **2.** *n.* muziplik, kaba şaka; gü-

rültü patırdı, yaygara, şamata.

**rag.a.muf.fin** [ˈrægəmʌfin] *n.* üstü başı perişan sokak *(veya* mahalle*)* çocuğu.

**rag**...; **ˈ-bag** *n.* paçavra, ufak tefek bez parçaları torbası; **ˈ-book** *n.* yırtılmaz resimli kitap.

**rage** [reidʒ] **1.** *n.* öfke, hiddet, gazap; ihtiras, hırs, düşkünlük (for *-e*); heyecan, coşkunluk, cezbe; it is all the ~ çok rağbet görüyor, moda oldu, alıp yürüdü; **2.** *v/i.* hiddetlenmek, kudurmak, azmak, küplere binmek, köpürmek.

**rag-fair** [ˈrægfɛə] *n.* bitpazarı.

**rag.ged** □ [ˈrægid] pürüzlü, düzgün olmayan; düzensiz; yırtık pırtık, lime lime.

**rag.man** [ˈrægmən] *n.* paçavracı, eskici.

**ra.gout** [ˈræguː] *n.* yahni.

**rag**...: **ˈ-tag** *n. mst* ~ and bobtail ayaktakımı, avam, olur olmaz adamlar; **ˈ-time** *n.* ♪ cazda olduğu gibi kesik tempo, kesik tempolu parça.

**raid** [reid] **1.** *n.* akın, baskın; polis ve gümrük memurları baskını; *(hava)* akın, taarruz; **2.** *vb.* baskın yapmak *-e*; yağma etm., çapulculuk etm.; akın etm.; **ˈraid.er** *n.* akıncı, baskıncı.

**rail¹** [reil] **1.** *n. a.* ~s *pl.* parmaklık, korkuluk, tırabzan; 🚉 ray, *fig.* demiryolu; off the ~s yoldan *(veya* raydan*)* çıkmış; *fig.* yoldan *(veya* çığrından*)* çıkmış, düzensiz; by ~ demiryolu ile; **2.** *v/t.* *a.* ~ in, ~ off parmaklıkla çevirmek.

**rail²** [~] *v/i.* küfretmek, sövüp saymak (at, against *b-ne, bşe*).

**rail³** *orn.* [~] *n.* sutavuğu.

**rail-car** [ˈreilkɑː] *n.* otomotris.

**rail.ing** [ˈreiliŋ] *n. a.* ~s *pl.* parmaklık, korkuluk, tırabzan, lata ile yapılan çit.

**rail.ler.y** [ˈreiləri] *n.* alay, istihza, şaka (cılık).

**rail.road** *Am.* [ˈreilrəud] **1.** *n.* demiryolu; **2.** *v/t.* yıldırım kanunu çıkarmak; demiryolu ile göndermek; aceleye getirmek; **rail.way** [ˈreilwei] *n.* demiryolu; **ˈ-.man** *n.* demiryolcu.

**rai.ment** *rhet.* [ˈreimənt] *n.* elbise, giysi.

**rain** [rein] **1.** *n.* yağmur; **2.** *v/t.* & *v/i.* (yağmur) yağmak; yağmur gibi yağdırmak *(bomba, ok vs.)*; **~.bow** [ˈ-bəu] *n.* alkım, gökkuşağı; **ˈ-.coat** *n. Am.* yağmurluk; **ˈ-.drop** *n.* yağmur damlası; **ˈ-.fall** *n.* yağış miktarı; sağanak; **~.ga(u)ge** [ˈ-geidʒ] *n.* yağış ölçer, yağmur ölçeği; **ˈ-.proof** **1.** *adj.* su *(veya* yağmur*)* geçirmez; **ˈrain.y** □ yağmurlu, yağmur...: *a.* ~ day *fig.* sıkıntılı *(veya* darda kalınan*)* zaman, kara gün.

**raise** [reiz] v/t. oft. ~ up kaldırmak, yükseltmek; bina etm., dikmek; artırmak, çoğaltmak (a. fig.); sağlamak, ödünç almak (para); toplamak, mevzilemek (ordu); ayağa kaldırmak; yerden kaldırmak; büyütmek, yetiştirmek (çocuk, hayvan, tahıl); ses yükseltmek; öldükten sonra diriltmek; ileri sürmek (soru vs.); neden olm. -e, uyandırmak; teşvik etm., harekete getirmek; son vermek -e, kaldırmak (kuşatma); **'rais.er** n. hayvan veya bitki yetiştiren b-i; kurucu.

**rai.sin** ['reizn] n. kuru üzüm.

**ra.ja(h)** ['rɑːdʒə] n. raca (Hindistan Prensi).

**rake¹** [reik] 1. n. saplı tarak, tırmık; 2. v/t. taramak, tırmıklamak; a. ~ up, ~ over fig. köşe bucak aramak, araştırmak, taramak; ✕, ⚓ ateşle taramak; kuşbakışı taramak; ~ off, ~ away ortadan kaldırmak, toparlayıp kaldırmak; v/i. taraklamak, tırmıklamak; ara(ştır)-mak (for); '~-off n. Am. sl. anafor, pay komisyon, kârdan hisse.

**rake²** ⚓ [~] 1. n. meyil, baca ve direğin kıça doğru meyli; 2. vb. meyletmek, yan yatmak.

**rake³** [~] n. sefih (veya hovarda) adam, safa pezevengi.

**rak.ish** ['reikiʃ] 1. adj. şık, zarif, modaya uygun; 2. ⬜ sefih, ahlâksız, çapkın.

**ral.ly¹** ['ræli] 1. n. toplama, toplantı, miting; istirahat; tenis: karşılıklı arka arkaya birkaç vuruş; mot. ralli; 2. v/i. düzene girmek; toplanmak; iyileşmek; v/t. düzeltmek; toplamak, canlandırmak.

**ral.ly²** [~] v/t. b-ne takılmak, şakalaşmak.

**ram** [ræm] 1. n. zo. koç; ast. Koç takımyıldızı; ✕ hist. mancınık; ⊕, ⚓ şahmerdan; harp gemisi mahmuzu; su terazisi; 2. v/t. vurmak, vurarak yerleştirmek; ⚓ bindirerek batırmak; ~ up barikatlamak.

**ram.ble** ['ræmbl] 1. n. gezinme, gezinti; 2. v/i. boş gezinmek; konuyu dağıtmak; enine boyuna gelişip büyümek (bitki); **'ram.bler** n. yaya gezen, dolaşan kimse; ✿ çardak gülü; **'ram.bling** 1. ⬜ avare, dolaşan; sabit olmayan, değişken, kararsız; dağınık; 2. n. avare (veya boş gezinen) kimse.

**ram.i.fi.ca.tion** [ræmifi'keiʃən] n. dallanıp budaklanma; **ram.i.fy** ['~fai] v/i. çatallaşmak, dallanıp budaklanmak; v/t. kollara, şubelere ayırmak.

**ram.jet** ['ræmdʒet] n. a. ~ engine dina-

mik basınçlı jet motoru.

**ram.mer** ⊕ ['ræmə] n. şahmerdan.

**ramp¹** sl. [ræmp] n. dolandırıcılık, kazık atma.

**ramp²** [~] 1. n. rampa; 2. v/i. şahlanmak, şaha kalkmak, kudurmak; **ram.page** co. [ræm'peidʒ] 1. v/i. kudurmak, sağa sola saldırmak; 2. be on the ~ heyheyleri tutmak, çılgınca davranışlarda bulunmak; **ramp.an.cy** ['~pənsi] n. şaha kalkma, şahlanma, azma; **'ramp.ant** ⬜ şahlanmış; fig. dizginlerini koparmış, azgın, başıboş kalmış; ♠ yukarı çıkan, rampa.

**ram.part** ['ræmpɑːt] n. sur, kale duvarı, siper.

**ram.rod** ['ræmrɔd] n. tüfek harbisi; top tomarı.

**ram.shack.le** ['ræmʃækl] adj. viran, yıkılmaya yüz tutan, harap; cılız, sıska.

**ran** [ræn] pret. of run 1.

**ranch** [rɑːntʃ] n. hayvan çiftliği, büyük çiftlik; **'ranch.er, 'ranch.man** n. çiftlik sahibi, çiftçi; kovboy.

**ran.cid** ⬜ ['rænsid] acılaşmış, ağırlaşmış, kokmuş, küflü, ekşimiş (yağlı yemek vs.); **ran'cid.i.ty, 'ran.cid.ness** n. acılık, ekşilik, küflülük.

**ran.cor.ous** ⬜ ['ræŋkərəs] kinci, garazkâr.

**ran.cor** ['ræŋkə] n. kin, hınç, garaz.

**ran.dom** ['rændəm] 1. at ~ rasgele, tesadüfi, körükörüne, gelişigüzel; 2. adj. rasgele, gelişigüzel, ince eleyip sık dokumaksızın.

**rang** [ræŋ] pret. of ring² 2.

**range** [reindʒ] 1. n. sıra, dizi, seri, ⊤ seçme mal, koleksiyon; mutfak ocağı; alan, saha; erim, menzil, tesir sahası; hareket serbestliği; uzaklık; atış yeri; Am. otlak; take the ~ mesafeyi tahmin etm.; 2. v/t. dizmek, sıralamak; dolaşmak, gezmek; ⚓ ...boyunca seyretmek; otlatmak; sınıflandırmak; menzile ulaşabilmek, menzili ... olm.; v/i. bir sırada olm., sıralanmak, dizilmek; dolaşmak, gezinmek (through); uzanmak, yetişmek (over); ~ along ...boyunca gitmek; '~-find.er n. telemetre; **'rang.er** n. korucu, orman memuru; ✕ komando; **'rang.y** adj. dağlık; ince, fidan gibi.

**rank¹** [ræŋk] 1. n. sıra, dizi, saf; ✕ rütbe, derece, sınıf, paye, aşama, mevki; sat ranç: yatay kareler; the ~s pl., the ~ and file erat, erler; üyeler, fertler; fig. aşağı tabaka, büyük kitle; join the ~s orduya katılmak; rise from the ~s erlikten subaylığa yükselmek; 2. v/t. sıralamak, tasnif etm.; saymak, addetmek (with -*i*); *v/i.* sıralanmak, dizilmek; katılmak (among, with -*e*), addolunmak, sayılmak, dahil olm. -*e*; daha yüksek rütbede olm, rütbece -*den* üstün olmak, derecelenmek (above; next to); ~ as sayılmak, addedilmek ,telâkki edilmek .

**rank**² □ [~] uzun büyümüş, dolgun üreyen; verimli, mümbit *(toprak)*; bozulmuş, kokmuş, bozuk.

**rank.er** [ˈræŋkə] *n.* alaylı, erbaş.

**ran.kle** *fig.* [ˈræŋkl] *v/i.* için için yemek, yiyip bitirmek, kemirmek, acısı unutulmak; kaçırımak *(kız).*

**rank.ness** [ˈræŋknis] *n.* uzun ve dolgun büyüme; verimlilik; kokmuşluk, bozulmuşluk.

**ran.sack** [ˈrænsæk] *v/t.* araştırmak, altını üstüne getirmek, üstünü yoklamak; yağma *(veya* talan) etm.

**ran.som** [ˈrænsəm] **1.** *n.* fidye, kurtulmalık; *eccl.* kefaret; kurtuluş; **2.** *v/t.* fidye ile kurtarmak; halâs etm.

**rant** [rænt] **1.** *n.* lâf kalabalığı *(veya* bolluğu), tumturak, farfaralık, ağız kalabalığı; **2.** *vb.* lâf kalabalığı etm., yüksekten atmak; yüksek sesle ve aktör gibi mimikler yaparak konuşmak, va'zetmek; ˈ**rant.er** *n.* ağız kalabalığı eden, tumturaklı konuşan kimse, palavracı.

**ra.nun.cu.lus** ♀ [rəˈnʌŋkjuləs] *n.* düğünçiçeği.

**rap**¹ [ræp] **1.** *n.* hafif vuruş *veya* darbe; **2.** *v/t.* hafifçe vurmak, çalmak, çarpmak (at -*e*); ~ s.o.'s fingers *veya* knuckles *fig. b-nin* parmaklarına vurmak; *b-ne* haddini bildirmek; ~ out şiddetle söylemek *veya* vurmak; ağızdan kaçırmak.

**rap**² *fig.* [~] *n.* mangır, metelik.

**ra.pa.cious** □ [rəˈpeiʃəs] haris, açgözlü, doymak bilmez, tamahkâr; yırtıcı, zorba; **ra.pac.i.ty** [rəˈpæsiti] *n.* yırtıcılık hırsı, zorbalık; hırs, açgözlülük.

**rape**¹ [reip] **1.** *n.* kız kaçırma, dağa kaldırma; ♀ zorla ırza geçme; ~ ond murder ırza saldırı ve öldürme; **2.** *v/t.* -*in* ırzına geçmek; yağma etm., zorla elinden almak; kaçırmak *(kız).*

**rape**² ♀ [~] *n.* kolza, küçük şalgam; ˈ~-**oil** *n.* kolza yağı; ˈ~.**seed** *n.* kolza tohumu.

**rap.id** [ˈræpid] **1.** □ çabuk, hızlı, tez, seri, süratli, ani(den); *phot.* aydınlık *(nesne);* hassas *(film);* ~ fire seri ateş eden *(silah);* **2.** *n.* ~s *pl. geo.* ivinti yeri, şiddetli nehir akıntısı; **ra.pid.i.ty** [rəˈpiditi] *n.* sürat, hız.

**ra.pi.er** *fenc.* [ˈreipjə] *n.* dar ve uzun kı-

lıç, meç.

**rap.ine** *rhet.* [ˈræpain] *n.* yağma(cılık), çapulculuk.

**rap.proche.ment** *pol.* [ræˈprɔʃmɑːŋ] *n.* uzlaşma.

**rapt** [ræpt] *adj. fig.* dalgın, esri(k) (in -*e*); meftun, baygın (with -*e*).

**rap.ture** [ˈræptʃə] *n. a.* ~s *pl.* kendinden geçme, esrilik, vecit, mest olma; in ~s etekleri zil çalan, coşku içinde, mest olmuş; go into ~s *b-e* delice sevinmek, sevinçten deliye dönmek; ˈ**rap.tur.ous** □ *k-den* geçmiş, sevinç içinde, vecit halinde; *k-den* geçiren, çok sevindirici, coşku veren.

**rare** □ [rɛə] seyrek, nadir *(a. fig. harikulâde);* az bulunur, tek tük; *phys. etc.* az oksijenli, yoğun olmayan *(hava).*

**rare.bit** [ˈrɛəbit] *n.:* Welsh ~ kızarmış ekmeğe sürülen peynir.

**rar.e.fac.tion** *phys.* [rɛəriˈfækʃən] *n.* basıncı azaltma; **rar.e.fy** [ˈ~fai] *v/t. & v/i.* seyrekleş(tir)mek, azal(t)mak; incel(t)mek; ˈ**rare.ness,** ˈ**rar.i.ty** *n.* nadirlik; en-der rastlanan şey, kıymetli şey; seyreklik; değerlilik.

**ras.cal** [ˈrɑːskəl] *n.* çapkın, serseri; hain, alçak herif, pezevenk, teres; yaramaz, haşarı kimse; **ras.cal.i.ty** [~ˈkæliti] *n.* alçaklık, hainlik; serserilik, çapkınlık, pezevenklik; **ras.cal.ly** *adj. & adv.* [ˈ~kəli] alçak(ça), hain(ce); yaramaz, müzevir.

**rash**¹ □ [ræʃ] aceleci, sabırsız, düşüncesiz, ihtiyatsız; gözünü budaktan sakınmaz.

**rash**² ☞ [~] isilik, egzama.

**rash.er** [ˈræʃə] *n.* ince kesilmiş jambon vs. dilimi.

**rash.ness** [ˈræʃnis] *n.* acelecilik, düşüncesizlik, tedbirsizlik.

**rasp** [rɑːsp] **1.** *n.* raspa, kaba törpü; **2.** *v/t.* törpülemek, rendelemek; *b-nin* canını acıtmak, ıstırap vermek; *v/i.* cızırdamak, törpü gibi ses çıkarmak.

**rasp.ber.ry** ♀ [ˈrɑːzbəri] *n.* ahududu.

**rasp.er** [ˈrɑːspə] *n.* çamurluk demiri; törpü.

**rasp.ing** [ˈrɑːspiŋ] *n.* törpüleme; cızırdayan şey; ~s *pl.* törpü, rende artığı, yonga, talaş.

**rat** [ræt] **1.** *n. zo.* sıçan, iri fare; *pol.* karşı tarafa geçen milletvekili; *sl.* grev bozucu; smell a ~ ortalıkta bir tehlike sezmek; ~s! *sl.* boş lâkırdı!, saçmasapan söz!, zırva!; **2.** *v/i.* fare tutmak; *pol.* karşı tarafa geçmek.

**rat.a.ble** □ [ˈreitəbl] vergiye tabi, vergi ile yükümlü.

**ratch** ⊕ [rætʃ] *n.* dişli çark mandalı.

**ratch.et** ⊕ [ˈrætʃit] *n.* tevkif mandalı, dişli çark mandalı, kastanyola; '**.-wheel** *n.* kilit çarkı, mandallı çark.

**rate**[1] [reit] **1.** *n.* nispet, oran, ölçü; fiyat, paha, eder; belediye vergisi, mülk vergisi; sınıf, çeşit, derece, *part.* ↓ mevki; hız, sürat; ücret; at the ~ of oranında, miktarında; hızında; at a cheap ~ ↑ ucuza; at any ~ herhalde, her nasılsa; ~ of exchange ↓ kambiyo rayici (*veya* sürümdeğeri), döviz kuru; ~ of interest faiz oranı; ~ of taxation vergi oranı; **2.** *vb.* tahmin etm., (kıymet) takdir etm. (at); vergi koymak.

**rate**[2] [~] *v/t.* azarlamak, haşlamak (for, about); *v/i. b-ni* azarlamak (at).

**rate-pay.er** [ˈreitpeiə] *n.* vergi mükellefi (*veya* yükümlüsü).

**rath.er** [ˈrɑːðə] *adv.* oldukça, bir hayli, epeyce; daha çok, tercihan, *-e* kalırsa, *-den* ziyade; daha doğrusu; tersine, aksine; ~! [*a.* ˈrɑːˈðɔː] *int.* F hem de nasıl!, sorulur mu!; I had *veya* would ~ do yapmayı yeğlerim; I ~ expected it doğrusu bunu umuyordum; ~ than *-den* ziyade.

**rat.i.fi.ca.tion** [rætifiˈkeiʃən] *n.* onay, tasdik; **rat.i.fy** [ˈ~fai] *v/t.* tasdik etm., onaylamak.

**rat.ing**[1] [ˈreitiŋ] *n.* değerlendirme, tahmin, takdir; vergi oranı; ↓ rütbe, hizmet derecesi; ↓ deniz eri, tayfa.

**rat.ing**[2] [~] *n.* tekdir, azar(lama).

**ra.tio** [ˈreiʃiəu] *n.* oran, nispet.

**ra.tion** [ˈræʃən] **1.** *n.* pay, hisse; tayın; miktar; ~ card (book) (*gıda maddeleri*) vesika, karne; **2.** *v/t.* karneye bağlamak; *b-nin* tayın miktarını saptamak.

**ra.tion.al** □ [ˈræʃənl] akıl sahibi; akıllı, mantıklı, anlayışlı, rasyonel (*a.* Å); **ration.al.ism** [ˈræʃnəlizəm] *n.* usçuluk, akılcılık, rasyonalizm; **ˈra.tion.al.ist** *n.* rasyonalist, akılcı, usçu; **ra.tion.al.i.ty** [ræʃəˈnæliti] akıl, us, aklıselim; **ra.tional.i.za.tion** [ræʃnəlaiˈzeiʃən] *n.* akla uydurma; rasyonalizasyon; modernleşme; ˈra.tion.al.ize *v/t.* akla uydurmak, mantıklı kılmak; ölçülü şekle sokmak, modernleştirmek.

**rat race** [ˈrætreis] *n.* anlamsız mücadele, koşuşturma, hengame.

**rat-tat** [ˈrætˈtæt] *n.* kapı çalınma sesi.

**rat.ten** [ˈrætn] *v/t.* sabote etm., baltalamak *-i;* *v/i.* sabotaj yapmak; ˈ**rat.ten.ing** *n.* sabotaj, baltalama.

**rat.tle** [ˈrætl] **1.** *n.* takırtı, çıtırtı; boş lâf, gevezelik; zırıltı; bebek çıngırağı; hırıltı; can çekişme (*veya* hırıltısı); **2.** *v/i.*

takırdamak; gevezelik etm.; hırıldamak; *v/t.* takırdatmak; F sinirlendirmek *-i;* ~ off *veya* out ezbere çabucak okumak *-i;* '**.-brain**, '**.-pate** *n.* zihni darmadağınık, çalçene, geveze kimse; '**.-brained**, '**.-pat.ed** *adj.* çalçene, geveze; ˈ**rat.tler** *n.* geveze, boşboğaz, lâkırdıcı kimse; *sl.* yaman herif, şeytanın art bacağı; *Am.* F = ˈ**rat.tle.snake** *n. zo.* çıngıraklı yılan; ˈ**rat.tle.trap** **1.** *adj.* cılız, mecalsiz; **2.** *n.* kırık dökük hurda şey (*araba vs.*).

**rat.tling** □ [ˈrætliŋ] F canlı, vızır vızır işleyen, çalışan; *adv.* çok, gayet; at a ~ pace delice bir süratle.

**rat.ty** *sl.* [ˈræti] *adj.* sinirli, hiddetli, huysuz.

**rau.cous** □ [ˈrɔːkəs] boğuk. kısık.

**rav.age** [ˈrævidʒ] **1.** *n.* tahribat, harap etme; **2.** *v/t.* tahrip etm., harabetmek, kırıp geçirmek, yakıp yıkmak; *v/i.* tahribat yapmak.

**rave** [reiv] *v/i.* çıldırmak, kudurmak, küplere binmek; hezeyan etm., sayıklamak; bayılmak (about, of *-e*).

**rav.el** [ˈrævəl] *v/t.* dolaştırmak, karıştırmak; *a.* ~ out sökmek, ayırmak (*teyelleri*); *v/i. a.* ~ out açılmak, çözülmek, tel tel olm., sökülmek.

**ra.ven**[1] [ˈreivn] **1.** *n. zo.* kuzgun; **2.** *adj.* kuzguni (*renk*).

**rav.en**[2] [ˈrævn] **1.** *s.* ravin; **2.** *vb.* yağmacılık, çapulculuk etm.; hırslı, açgözlü olm.; oburca yutmak, tıkıştırmak; **raven.ous** □ [ˈrævənəs] obur, pisboğaz, hasis, doymak bilmez; ˈ**rav.en.ous.ness** *n.* hırslılık; oburluk, pisboğazlık; şiddetli açlık.

**rav.in** *rhet.* [ˈrævin] *n.* yırtıcılık hırsı; yağma; av.

**ra.vine** [rəˈviːn] *n.* boğaz, dağ geçidi, çukur, koyak.

**rav.ings** [ˈreiviŋz] *n. pl.* deli saçması söz(ler).

**rav.ish** [ˈræviʃ] *v/t.* esritmek, mest etm., çok sevindirmek, coşturmak; *b-nin* ırzına geçmek; *rhet. b-den bşi* gaspetmek, zorla almak; ˈ**rav.ish.er** *n.* ırza geçen, alçak kimse; ˈ**rav.ish.ing** □ cazip, cazibeli, coşturan, alımlı; ˈ**rav.ish.ment** *n.* esrime, kendinden geçme; ırza tecavüz.

**raw** □ [rɔː] **1.** çiğ, pişmemiş; ham, işlenmemiş; yaralı, bereli, derisi soyulmuş; soğuk ve yağışlı (*hava*); *fig.* acemi, tecrübesiz; ~ material hammadde; he got *o* ~ deal *sl.* haksızlığa uğradı; **2.** *n.* yara; hassas nokta, bam teli (*part. fig.*); '**.-boned** *adj.* zayıf, kuru, çelimsiz, bir deri bir kemik, kemikleri sayılan; '**.-hide**

*n.* ham deri; **'~raw.ness** *n.* kabalık, hayvanca davranış; çiğlik; acemilik.

**ray¹** [rei] **1.** *n.* şua, ışın; *fig.* iz, eser, zerre; **2.** *v/i.* şua (*veya* ışın) salmak, ışımak.

**ray²** *ichth.* [~] *n.* vatoz; tırpana.

**ray.less** ['reilis] *n.* şuasız, ışınsız.

**ray.on** ['reiɔn] *n.* suni ipek.

**raze** [reiz] *v/t.* temelinden yıkmak (*ev vs.*); ~ to the ground yerle bir etm.

**ra.zor** ['reizə] *n.* ustura; tıraş makinesi; **'~-blade** *n.* ustura ağzı; jilet; **'~-'edge** *n.* *fig.* bıçak ağzı; zor, kritik durum; **'~.strop** *n.* bileği kayışı.

**razz** *Am. sl.* [ræz] *v/t.* alay etm. *ile,* alaya almak *-i.*

**raz.zi.a** ['ræziə] *n.* çapul(culuk), yağma-(cılık), akın(cılık).

**raz.zle-daz.zle** *sl.* ['ræzldæzl] *n.* karmakarışıklık, şamata, gürültü patırtı, cümbüş, alem.

**re** 𝄞, 🎵 [riː] *prep.* hakkında, dair, *-e* ait.

**re...** [~] *prefix* geri(ye); yeniden, tekrar.

**reach** [riːtʃ] **1.** *n.* uzatma; uzanma, yetişme; menzil, erim; ufuk, görüş sahası; alan, bölge; beyond ~, out of ~ erişilmez, yetişilmez; within easy ~ kolay erişilebilir; **2.** *v/t.* & *v/i.* *a.* ~ out uzanmak, erişmek (to, for *-e*); uzamak, yetişmek; ⚓ rüzgâr yönünde seyretmek; uzatmak, *bşi* elden ele geçirmek, *bşi* almak için elini uzatmak; *oft.* ~ out *bşi* uzatmak; vasıl olm., varmak, gelmek; görüşebilmek, temas kurmak.

**reach-me-downs** F ['riːtʃmiˈdaunz] *n.* *pl.* kalitesiz, ucuz hazır elbise.

**re.act** [riˈækt] *v/i.* tepkimek, tepki göstermek, karşılık vermek; etkilemek (to), etki etm. (on, upon *-e*); isyan etm., ayaklanmak (against *-e*).

**re.ac.tion** [riˈækʃən] *n.* tepki(me) (to *-e*); aksi tesir, reaksiyon (upon *-e*); *pol.* gericilik, irtica; **reˈac.tion.ar.y** *part. pol.* [~ʃnəri] **1.** *adj.* gerici; **2.** *n.* gerici, eski kafalı kimse.

**re.ac.tive** □ [riːˈæktiv] tepkisel, aksi tesir yaratan; **reˈac.tor** *n.* *phys.* reaktör; kimyasal reaksiyonda kullanılan kap.

**read** **1.** [riːd] (*irr.*) *v/t.* okumak (*a .fig.*), anlam vermek, yorumlamak; göstermek, işaret etm., kaydetmek (*termometre vs.*); ~ off bir yerden (*veya* bir sayfadan) okumak; ~ out yüksek sesle okumak; sonuna dek okumak; ~ to s o. *b-ne bşi* okumak; *v/i.* okumak, anlamak; okunmak; *üniv.* bir konu üzerinde çalışmak; ~ between the lines gizli anlamını keşfetmek; **2.** [red] *pret.* & *p.p. of* 1; **3.** [red] *adj.*

okumuş, bilgili (in).

**read.a.ble** □ ['riːdəbl] okunaklı; oku(n)-mağa değer.

**re-ad.dress** ['riːəˈdres] *v/t.* değişik bir adres yazmak, değişik bir adresle göndermek.

**read.er** ['riːdə] *n.* okuyucu, okur; *typ.* düzeltmen, musahhih; *üniv.* doçent (in); okuma kitabı; **'read.er.ship** *n.* okur sayısı; doçentlik, okutmanlık.

**read.i.ly** ['redili] *adv.* seve seve, gönüllü olarak; kolayca; **'read.i.ness** *n.* hazır olma; rıza, muvafakat; tezlik, çabukluk, sürat; ~ of mind *veya* wit hazırcevaplık, şaşırmazlık.

**read.ing** ['riːdiŋ] *n.* oku(n)ma (*a. parl.*); göstergenin kaydettiği ölçüm (*termometre vs.*); bilgi, edebi araştırma; kıraat, okuma (tarzı); anlayış, fikir; **'~-room** *n.* okuma odası.

**re.ad.just** ['riːəˈdʒʌst] *v/t.* & *v/i.* tekrar düzenlemek, yeniden ayarlamak, uydurmak; *pol.* yeni bilgi vermek; **'re.adˈjust.ment** *n.* yeni koşullara alış(tır)ma; yeniden düzenleme, reorganizasyon.

**re.ad.mis.sion** ['riːədˈmiʃən] *n.* yeniden kabul edilme (*üyelik, öğrencilik vs.*).

**re.ad.mit** ['riːədˈmit] *v/t.* yeniden kabul etm.; **'re.adˈmit.tance** *n.* yeniden kabul edilme.

**read.y** ['redi] **1.** *adj.* □ hazır, amade (to do sth. *-i yapmağa*); istekli, razı; hazır, elde bulunan; *-mak* üzere olan (to *-e*); serî, çabuk, çevik, atik (at, in *-de*); kolay, külfetsiz; yakında, hemen alınıverecek; 🎵 nakit (*para*); ⚓ hazır; ~ reckoner hesap cetveli; barem; ~ for action muharebeye hazır; ~ for take-off 🛫 uçuşa hazır; ~ for use kullanılmaya hazır; ~ to serve sofra servisine hazırlanmış; make *veya* get ~ hazırla(n)mak; ~ money hazır para, nakit; **2.** *adv.* önceden hazır(lanmış) (to *-e*); **3.** *su.* at the ~ atışa hazır; **'~-'made** *adj.* hazır, konfeksiyon...; *fig.* klişeleşmiş, gündelik, hergünkü; **'~-to-'wear** *adj.* konfeksiyon (*elbise*).

**re.af.firm** ['riːəˈfəːm] *v/t.* yeniden onaylamak, teyit etm.

**re.a.gent** 🜂 [riːˈeidʒənt] *n.* miyar, belirteç.

**re.al** □ [riəl] gerçek, hakiki; asıl; samimi, içten; ~ es.tate gayrimenkul (*veya* taşınmaz) mal, mülk.

**re.a.lign** ['riːəˈlain] *v/t.* siyasal reorganizasyon yapmak, yeni gruplar oluşturmak; **'re.aˈlign.ment** *n.* siyasal reorganizasyon.

**re.a.lism** ['riəlizəm] *n.* gerçekçilik, realizm; **'re.al.ist 1.** *n.* gerçekçi, realist kimse; **2.** = **re.al'is.tic** *adj.* (~ally) gerçekçi, realist; gerçeğe uygun; **re.al.i.ty** [ri'æliti] *n.* gerçeklik, realite, hakikat; **re.al.iz.a-ble** [] ['riəlaizəbl] gerçekleştirilebilir, realize edilebilir; **re.al.i'za.tion** *n.* gerçekleştirme; farketme, anlama, idrak; ♀ paraya çevirme; **'re.al.ize** *v/t.* anlamak, farkına varmak *-in*; gerçekleştirmek *-i*; † paraya çevirmek, satmak *-i*; kâr etmek; **'re.al.ly** *adv.* gerçekten, sahiden, hakikati halde, aslında.

**realm** [relm] *n.* kırallık; *fig.* alan, saha, ülke; Peer of the ~ Lordlar Kamarası üyesi

**re.al.tor** *Am.* ['riəltə] *n.* emlâkçı; **'re.al.ty** *n.* ♣ gayrimenkul (*veya* taşınmaz) mal, mülk.

**ream¹** [ri:m] *n.* 480 *veya* 500 tabakalık kâğıt topu.

**ream²** ⊕ [~] *v/t.* genişletmek (*çukur*); *mst.* ~ out delik açmak, delmek, burgulamak; **'ream.er** *n.* bıçırgan, rayma; limon sıkacağı.

**re.an.i.mate** ['ri:'ænimeit] *v/t.* yeniden canlandırmak, taze hayat vermek, canlılık kazandırmak; **'re.an.i'ma.tion** *n.* yeniden hayata kazandırma, diriltme.

**reap** [ri:p] *vb.* biçmek, hasat etm., oraklamak, tırpanlamak; *fig.* kazanmak, semeresini almak; **'reap.er** *n.* orakçı, tırpancı; biçerdöver; **'reap.ing** *n.* hasat; **'reap.ing-hook** *n.* orak; **'reap.ing-ma.chine** *n.* biçerdöver.

**re.ap.pear** ['ri:ə'piə] *v/i.* tekrar görünmek, ortaya çıkmak; **'re.ap'pear.ance** *n.* yeniden görünme.

**re.ap.pli.ca.tion** ['ri:æpli'keifən] *n.* yeniden uygulama, tatbik etme.

**re.ap.point** ['ri:ə'pɔint] *v/t.* yeniden tayin etm.

**re.ap.prais.al** ['ri:ə'preizəl] *n.* yeniden gözden geçirme, inceleme.

**rear¹** [riə] *v/t.* yetiştirmek, büyütmek; *rhet.* dikmek, inşa etm.; *v/i.* yükselmek, şahlanmak.

**rear²** [~] **1.** *n.* arka, geri (taraf); *mot.* ♣ kıç, kupa; ✕ artçı, dümdar ,arkadan gelen kıta; kıç, popo; at the ~ of, in (the) ~ of *-in* arkasın(d)a, gerisinde; from the ~ geriden, arkadan; **2.** *adj.* arkadaki, en geri, arka.... geri...; ~ wheel drive *mot.* arkadan itişli; **'~-'ad.mi.ral** *n.* ♣ tuğamiral; **'~-'guard** *n.* ✕ artçı, dümdar; **'~-lamp**, **'~-light** *n. mot.* arka lambası (*veya* feneri).

**re-arm** ['ri:'a:m] *v/t.* & *v/i.* yeniden silahlan(dır)mak; **'re-'ar.ma.ment** *n.* yeniden silahlan(dır)ma.

**rear.most** ['riə'məust] *adj.* en arkadaki.

**re.ar.range** ['ri:ə'reind3] *v/t.* yeniden düzenlemek.

**rear.ward** ['riəwəd] **1.** *adj.* arkada bulunan; **2.** *adv. a; ~s* arkaya doğru.

**re.as.cend** ['ri:ə'send] *v/i.* yeniden yükselmek, çıkmak, tırmanmak.

**rea.son** ['ri:zn] **1.** *n.* akıl, idrak, muhakeme; sebep, neden, illet; insaf, itidal, hak; delil, tanıt; by ~ of nedeniyle, sebebiyle, *-den* dolayı; for this ~ bu nedenle, bu sebeple, bundan dolayı; listen to ~ lâf anlamak; it stands to ~ that... aşikârdır ki..., apaçıktır ki...; **2.** *v/i.* makûl (*veya* mantıklı) olm., anlamak, sonuç çıkarmak, müzakere etm.; kandırmağa çalışmak (with *-e*); *v/t. a.* ~ out düşünmek; hesabetmek kitabetmek, uslamlamak, muhakeme etm.; ~ away münakaşada (*veya* münazarada) bulunmak; ~ so. into (out of) s.th. *b-ne* bşi kanıtlar göstererek inandırmak, vazgeçirmek; ~ed *adj.* üzerinde düşünülmüş, mantıklı, akla dayanan; **'rea.son.a.ble** [] akla uygun, makûl, mantıklı; orta, vasat; **'rea.son.a.bly** *adv.* oldukça, epeyce; makûlce; **'rea.son.er** *n.* fikir adamı, mantıklı kimse; **'rea.son.ing** *n.* muhakeme, uslamlama, usa vurma, kıyaslama; *attr.* düşünme..., muhakeme...

**re.as.sem.ble** ['ri:ə'sembl] *v/t.* & *v/i.* yeniden birleş(tir)mek, topla(n)mak.

**re.as.sert** ['ri:ə'sə:t] *v/t.* yeniden iddia etm., ileri sürmek.

**re.as.sur.ance** [ri:ə'fuərəns] *n.* yeniden temin etme, güven ver(il)me; güven veren şey; **re.as'sure** *v/t.* tekrar güven vermek *-e*, temin etm. *-i*.

**re.a.wak.en** [ri:ə'weikən] *v/t.* & *v/i.* yeniden uyan(dır)mak.

**re.bap.tize** ['ri:bæp'taiz] *v/t.* yeniden vaftiz etm.

**re.bate¹** † ['ri:beit] *n.* iskonto, tenzilat, indirim.

**re.bate²** ⊖ ['ræbit] **1.** *n.* dişili yiv, oluk; **2.** *v/t.* içiçe geçirmek; yiv açmak.

**reb.el 1.** ['rebl] *n.* asi, ihtilâlci; **2.** [~] *adj.* isyan eden, ayaklanan; *fig.* itaatsiz, serkeş, marazacı; **3.** [ri'bel] *v/i.* isyan etm., ayaklanmak; **re'bel.lion** [~jən] *n.* isyan, ayaklanma; **re'bel.lious** = rebel 2.

**re.birth** ['ri:'bə:θ] *n.* yeniden doğma, dünyaya gelme; yeniden uyanış, canlanma, rönesans.

**re.bound** [ri'baund] **1.** *v/i.* (çarpıp) geri tepmek, sıçramak; **2.** *n.* geri tepme, sıçrama.

**re.buff** [ri'bʌf] **1.** *n.* ret; ters cevap, azarlama; **2.** *v/t.* reddetmek; ters cevap vermek, azarlamak.

**re.build** ['ri:'bild] (*irr.* build) *v/t.* yeniden inşa etm., kurmak.

**re.buke** [ri'bju:k] **1.** *n.* azar, paylama; **2.** *v/t.* azarlamak, paylamak.

**re.bus** ['ri:bəs] *n.* resimli bilmece, sorulan sözcük *ya da* tümcenin kısımlarını ayrı resim *ya da* harflerle göstererek oynanan bir tür bulmaca (*örneğin bir çanak ve bir kale resmi Çanakkale okunacak*).

**re.but** [ri'bʌt] *v/t.* yanlışlığını kanıtlamak; **re!but.tal** *n.* yanlışlığını kanıtlama *veya* kanıtlayan şey.

**re.cal.ci.trant** [ri'kælsitrənt] *adj.* serkeş, aksi, dikkafalı.

**re.call** [ri'kɔ:l] **1.** *n.* geri çağırma; anımsama, hatırlama; geri çağırma işareti *veya* emri; beyond ~, past ~ geri alınamaz, dönülemez; hatırlanamaz; **2.** *v/t.* geri çağırmak; *fig.* (to s.o.'s mind) bşi b-nin hatırına getirmek, hatırlatmak; gönderilmesini emretmek (*mal*); bşi hatırlamak, anımsamak; uyandırmak (*duygu, his*); feshetmek, geri almak; ⊤ geri çekmek (*kapital*); ~ that -i (b-ne) hatırlat ki; until ~ed geri çağrılana kadar.

**re.cant** ['rikænt] *vb.* sözünden dönmek, caymak; **re.can.ta.tion** [ri:kæn'teiʃən] *n.* sözünden dönme, cayma.

**re.cap¹** F ['ri:'kæp] = recapitulate; recapitulation.

**re.cap²** *Am.* ['ri:'kæp] *v/t.* taban geçirmek, kaplamak (*lastik tekerlek*).

**re.ca.pit.u.late** [ri:kə'pitjuleit] *vb.* kısaca yeniden özetlemek; **!re.ca.pit.u!la.tion** *n.* kısa özet.

**re.cap.ture** ['ri:'kæptʃə] **1.** *n.* yeniden ele geçirme (*veya* zaptetme); **2.** *v/t.* yeniden elde etm., geri almak.

**re.cast** ['ri:'ka:st] **1.** (*irr.* cast) *v/t.* ⊕ eriterek başka bir kalıba dökmek, kaptan kaba nakletmek; şeklini değiştirmek; *thea.* oyuncuları değiştirmek; **2.** *n.* yeni şekil verme -e.

**re cede** [ri:'si:d] *v/i.* geri çekilmek, gerilemek; ⊤ düşmek (*fiyat*); receding *adj.* basık, içeri kaçık (*alın, çene*).

**re.ceipt** [ri'si:t] **1.** *n.* alındı, tesellüm, makbuz; giriş (*mal*); ⊤ alındı makbuzu; reçete; yemek tarifi; ~s *pl.* gelir; **2.** *v/t.* makbuz vermek, alındığına dair imza etm.

**re.ceiv.a.ble** [ri'si:vəbl] *adj.* kabul edilebilir, alınabilir, elverişli; ⊤ tahsil edilecek; **re!ceive** *v/t.* almak (*haber, mek-*

*tup vs.*); kabul etm., misafir etm.; maruz kalmak; almak (*radyo, TV yayını*); teslim almak; *v/i.* ev sahipliği yapmak; **re!ceived** *adj.* teslim alınmış; kabul edilmiş; **re!ceiv.er** *n.* alıcı (*a. tel. & radyo*); *teleph.* ahize; *a.* ~ of stolen•goods çalıntı malı bilerek satın alan şahıs; yatakçı; *a.* official ~ ⵝⵝ iflâs masası görevlisi; *phys.* hava boşaltma tulumbasının cam kavanozu; ⵝ distilasyonda toplama kabı; **re!ceiv.er.ship** *n.* ⵝⵝ davalı malların idaresi; **re!ceiv.ing** *n.* kabul, teslim; *radyo:* alma, ahiz; yataklık; ~ set radyo *veya* TV alıcısı.

**re.cen.cy** ['ri:snsi] *n.* yenilik, yeni vuku bulma.

**re.cen.sion** [ri'senʃən] *n.* düzeltme, tashih; düzeltilmiş metin.

**re.cent** ☐ ['ri:snt] yeni (olmuş), yakın geçmişte olan; in ~ years son yıllarda; **!re.cent.ly** *adv.* son zamanlarda, geçenlerde, yakın zamanda; **!re.cent.ness** *n.* yeni vuku bulma.

**re.cep.ta.cle** [ri'septəkl] *n.* kap, zarf; depo vs.; *a.* floral ~ ❀ çiçek tablası.

**re.cep.tion** [ri'sepʃən] *n.* kabul (*a. fig.*); al(ın)ma (*a. radyo*); kabul merasimi; resepsiyon (*otel*); **re!cep.tion.ist** *n.* resepsiyon memuru; **re!cep.tion-room** *n.* kabul odası.

**re.cep.tive** ☐ [ri'septiv] çabuk kavrayan, anlayışlı (of); alıcı, kabul eden; **re.cep!tiv.i.ty** *n.* çabuk kavrayış; alma yeteneği (*radyo vs.*).

**re.cess** [ri'ses] **1.** *n.* paydos, fasıla verme, teneffüs, ara; *part. parl.* tatil; *arch.* girinti, boşluk (*duvarda dolap vs. için*); ~es *pl. fig.* iç taraf; **2.** *vb.* girintiye yerleştirmek; girinti yapmak, oymak; ara vermek, paydos yapmak.

**re.ces.sion** [ri'seʃən] *n.* geri çekilme, gerileme; ⊻ fiyat düşüşü; durgunluk; **re!ces.sion.al** [~ʃənl] **1.** *adj.* eccl. son...; *parl.* tatil...; **2.** *n. eccl.* dini tören sonunda okunan ilâhi: **re!ces.sive** [~siv] *adj.* geri çekilme eğiliminde olan; *biol.* resesif.

**re.chris.ten** ['ri:'krisn] *v/t.* b-nin adını değiştirmek.

**re.cid.i.vist** [ri'sidivist] *n.* sabıkalı, tövbesini bozan kimse, mükerrir, mutat suçlu.

**rec.ipe** ['resipi] *n.* reçete; yemek tarifi.

**re.cip.i.ent** [ri'sipiənt] *n.* alıcı, verilen *veya* gönderilen bşi alan kimse.

**re.cip.ro.cal** [ri'siprəkəl] **1.** *adj.* karşılıklı, mütekabil: A, gr., phls. ortak, karşılıklı: **2.** *n.* A karsıt, ortak değer; **re!cip.ro.cate** [~keit] *v/t. & v/i.* bşin acısını çıkarmak, misillemede bulunmak, öcünü almak; bir iyiliğin karşılığını vermek; ⊕ bir düzlem içinde ileri geri çalışmak *(piston vs.)*; karşılıklı iyi dileklerini iletmek, değişmek, mukabele etm.; reciprocating engine pistonlu motor; **re.cip.ro-ca.tion** *n.* ileri geri çalışma; karşılık, tekabül, değişme, mübadele; karşılıklı etki; **rec.i.proc.i.ty** [resi¹prɔsiti] *n.* karşılıklı durum, karşılıklık.

**re.cit.al** [ri¹saitl] *n.* beyan, ifade, birer birer anlatma; hikâye; ezberden okuma; ♪♪ ifade, takrir, gerçekleri sergileme; ♪ solist konseri, resital; **rec.i.ta.tion** [resi-¹teiʃən] *n.* ezberden okuma; ezberden okunan parça, bölüm; *Am.* dersle ilgili soruları yanıtlayarak ders anlatma; **rec.i.ta.tive** ♪ [⁓təⁱti:v] 1. *adj.* resital şeklinde, ezber şeklinde; 2. *n.* konuşur gibi okunan güfte *veya* makam; **re.cite** [ri¹sait] *v/t.* & *v/i.* ezberden okumak; nakletmek, ileri sürmek; yüksek sesle ve yakışır bir tavırla okumak; *Am.* ders anlatmak, soruyu yanıtlamak **re¹cit.er** *n.* ezberden okuyan *(veya* nakleden, ileri süren) kimse.

**reck** *poet.* [rek] *vb.* önemsemek, ehemmiyet vermek, *bşe* aldırış etm., *bşin* önemi olm. (of).

**reck.less** □ [¹reklis] pervasız, dikkatsiz, lâkayt (of), saygısız, düşüncesiz; **¹reck-less.ness** *n.* pervasızlık, dikkatsizlik, lâkaytlık; saygısızlık.

**reck.on** [¹rekən] *v/t.* hesap etm., saymak; *a.* ⁓ for, ⁓ as tahmin etm., takdir etm., farzetmek, sanmak; ⁓ up saymak, *bşin* hesabını yapmak; *v/i.* sayı saymak; zannetmek, tahmin etm.; ⁓ (up)on *b-ne, bşe* güvenmek, bel bağlamak; ⁓ with hesaba katmak *-i;* **reck.on.er** [¹reknə] *n.* sayan, hesap eden kimse; **¹reck.on.ing** *n.* hesap(lama); hesap görme; be out in *veya* of one's ⁓ *fig. b-nin* hesabında yanılmak; tahmininde aldanmak.

**re.claim** [ri¹kleim] *v/t.* geri istemek, tekrar elde etm.; elverişli hale koymak, iyileştirmek, yoluna koymak; ıslah etm.; ehlileştirmek, alıştırmak *(hayvan);* medenileştirmek; toprağı temizleyerek tarla haline getirmek; ⊕ hurdadan yararlanmak; iadesini talep etm., hak iddia etm.; **re¹claim.a.ble** *adj.* ıslah edilebilir, yararlanılabilir.

**rec.la.ma.tion** [rekl㘱¹meiʃən] *n.* ıslah; geri isteme; tarıma elverişli kılma *(toprak);* hurdadan yararlanma.

**re.cline** [ri¹klain] *vb.* uzanmak (against, on -e); dayanmak, istinat etm. (against,

on); ⁓ upon *fig. b-ne* sırtını dayamak; **re-clin.ing chair** koltuk.

**re.cluse** [ri¹klu:s] 1. *adj.* dünyadan elini eteğini çekmiş, münzevi, insanlardan kaçan; 2. *n.* münzevi kimse; keşiş.

**rec.og.ni.tion** [rekəg¹niʃən] *n.* tanı(n)ma; itiraf, ona(n)ma, kabul, tasdik; **rec.og-niz.a.ble** *adj.* [¹⁓naizəbl] tanınabilir, tanı(n)ması olası, farkedilebilir; **re.cog.ni-zance** ♪♪ [ri¹kɔgnizəns] *n.* taahhütname, kefalet, teminat; tanıma; **rec.og.nize** [¹rekəgnaiz] *v/t.* tanımak; onaylamak, kabul etm., teslim ve itiraf etm., itibar etm., takdir etm.; selâm vermek *(sokakta).*

**re.coil** [ri¹kɔil] 1. *v/i.* geri çekilmek; geri tepmek; 2. *n.* geri tepme; geri çekilme; iğrenme.

**rec.ol.lect¹** [rekə¹lekt] *v/t.* hatırlamak *-i.*
**re.col.lect²** [¹ri:kə¹lekt] *v/t.* yeniden toplamak, yığmak; ⁓ o.s. *k-ni* toplamak.
**rec.ol.lec.tion** [rekə¹lekʃən] *n.* hatıra (of -in), anı, hatırlanan şey.

**re.com.mence** [¹ri:kə¹mens] *v/t.* & *v/i.* yeniden başla(t)mak.

**rec.om.mend** [rekə¹mend] *v/t.* tavsiye etm., salık vermek; çekici kılmak; **rec-om¹mend.a.ble** *adj.* tavsiye etmeğe değer, salık verilir; **rec.om.men¹da.tion** *n.* tavsiye, salık, referans, bonservis; **rec-om¹mend.a.to.ry** [⁓dətəri] *adj.* tavsiye kabilinden, tavsiye ...

**re.com.mis.sion** [¹ri:kə¹miʃən] *v/t.* yeniden yerleştirmek, tekrar hizmete almak.
**re.com.mit** [¹ri:kə¹mit] *v/t. parl.* yeniden görüşülmek için *b-ne* havale etm.; ⁓ to prison yeniden tutuklamak.

**rec.om.pense** [¹rekəmpens] 1. *n.* mükâfat, karşılık, ikramiye, ödül; ceza; misilleme; 2. *v/t.* mükâfatlandırmak *veya* cezalandırmak *-i,* zarar ve ziyanı ödetmek, telâfi etm., tazminat vermek.

**re.com.pose** [¹ri:kəm¹pəuz] *v/t.* yeniden oluşturmak *(veya* düzenlemek).

**rec.on.cil.a.ble** [¹rekənsailəbl] *adj.* uzlaşma sağlanabilir, barıştırılabilir, teklif edilebilir, birleşmeleri sağlanabilir; **¹rec.on.cile** *v/t.* barıştırmak, uzlaştırmak; mutabık kılmak, bağdaştırmak, uydurmak (with, to *ile);* arabuluculuk etm. *(kavga vs.'de);* ⁓ o.s. to razı olm. *-e; b-le* barışmak, uzlaşmak; alışmak *-e;* **¹rec.on.cil.er** *n.* uzlaştırıcı, ara bulan kimse; **rec.on.cil.i.a.tion** [⁓sili¹eiʃən] *n.* uzlaşma, barışma.

**re.con.dite** □ *fig.* [ri¹kɔndait] derin; muğlak, kapalı, anlaşılmaz *(konu, fikir vs.).*

**re.con.di.tion** [¹ri:kən¹diʃən] *v/t.* tamir

edip yenilemek; revizyon yapmak; ⊕ rektifiye etm.

**re.con.nais.sance** [ˈriˈkɔnisəns] *n.* ✕ keşif, yoklama, istikşaf; *fig.* kavrama, anlayış; ~ **car** ✕ zırhlı keşif arabası.

**rec.on.noi.ter, rec.on.noi.tre** ✕ [rekəˈnɔitə] *vb.* keşif yapmak, keşfetmek; incelemek, araştırma yapmak.

**re.con.quer** [ˈriːkɔŋkə] *v/t.* yeniden fethetmek, zaptetmek; ˈreˈcon.quest [~kwest] *n.* yeniden fetih, zapt.

**re.con.sid.er** [ˈriːkənˈsidə] *vb.* tekrar düşünmek, muhakeme etm.; ˈre.con.sid.er.ˈa.tion *n.* tekrar düşünme (*veya* tetkik).

**re.con.sti.tute** [ˈriːˈkɔnstitjuːt] *v/t.* yeniden oluşturma (*veya* kurmak); eski haline getirmek; ˈre.con.stiˈtu.tion *n.* yeniden oluşturma (*veya* kurma).

**re.con.struct** [ˈriːkənsˈtrʌkt] *v/t.* yeniden inşa etm., kurmak; yinelemek; ˈre.conˈstruc.tion *n.* tekrar inşa; yeniden kalkınma.

**re.con.ver.sion** [ˈriːkənˈvəːʃən] *n.* yeniden düzenle(n)me, reorganizasyon (*part. savaş sonrası*); reorganizasyon süreci; ˈre.conˈvert *v/t.* yeniden düzenlemek, reorganize etm.

**rec.ord¹** [ˈrekɔːd] *n.* kayıt, not; ∞ zabıt, tutanak, tutulga, mazbata; belge, vesika (*a. fig.*); sicil, dosya; şan, şöhret (*part. pol.*); liste, cetvel, katalog; plâk, disk; *spor:* rekor; ~ time rekor süresi; it is on ~ ...gerçekten olmuştur, ...dığı vakidir; place on ~ kaydetmek; beat *veya* break the ~ rekoru kırmak; set up *veya* establish a ~ rekor kırmak (*veya* tesis etm.); ~ Office devlet arşivi; off the ~ gayriresmî; gizli, yayınlanmamak koşuluyla.

**re.cord²** [ˈriˈkɔːd] *v/t.* kaydetmek, yazmak, not etm.; yazıya dökmek; plağa almak, banda almak, kaydetmek; reˈcord.er *n.* kayıt (*veya sicil*) memuru; hâkim, yargıç; kayıt aygıtı, teyp; ♪ blokflüt; reˈcord.ing *n.* radyo: plak; bant; kayıt, plağa al(ın)ma; ˈrec.ord-play.er *n.* pikap.

**re.count¹** [riˈkaunt] *v/t.* anlatmak, hikâye etm., nakletmek.

**re-count²** [ˈriːˈkaunt] **1.** *v/t.* yeniden saymak (*oy vs.*); **2.** *n.* yeniden sayım.

**re.coup** [riˈkuːp] *v/t.* *b-nin* zarar ve ziyanını ödemek, telâfi etm., karşılamak.

**re.course** [riˈkɔːs] *n.* yardım dileme, başvurma; have ~ to başvurmak -e, *bşden* çare aramak.

**re.cov.er¹** [riˈkʌvə] *v/t.* yeniden elde etm., ele geçirmek; telâfi etm.; tahsil etm.

(*alacak*); be ~ed eski sağlığına kavuşmak; *v/i.* iyileşmek, şifa bulmak; *k-ne* gelmek; *a.* ~ o.s. *k-ni* toplamak, silkinmek, *k-ne* gelmek; ∞ (in one's suit) kazanmak (*dava*).

**re-cov.er²** [ˈriːˈkʌvə] *v/t.* yeniden kaplamak, döşemesini yenilemek.

**re.cov.er.a.ble** [riˈkʌvərəbl] *adj.* geri alınabilir; tahsil edilebilir; iyileştirilebilir; reˈcov.er.y *n.* geri alma; iyileşme; *k-ne* gelme.

**rec.re.ant** [ˈrekriənt] **1.** □ korkak, ödlek; hain, sadakatsiz, sadık olmayan; **2.** *n.* korkak (*veya* sadakatsiz, hain) kimse.

**rec.re.ate** [ˈrekrieit] *v/t.* yenilemek, tazelemek (*anı vs.*); canlandırmak, neşelendirmek, dinlendirmek; *v/i. a.* ~ o.s. dinlenmek, istirahat etm.; **rec.reˈa.tion** *n.* dinlenme, istirahat; eğlence, neşelenme; ~ **ground** spor sahası, oyun sahası; ˈrec.re.a.tive *adj.* canlandırıcı, dinlendirici, neşelendirici, eğlendirici.

**re.crim.i.nate** [riˈkrimineit] *v/t.* şikâyete karşı şikâyet *veya* iftiraya karşı iftirada bulunmak; re.crim.iˈna.tion *n.* karşılıklı birbirini suçlama, şikâyet etme.

**re.cross** [ˈriːˈkrɔs] *v/t.* yeniden geçmek (*nehir vs.*).

**re.cru.desce** [riːkruːˈdes] *v/i.* nüksetmek (*hastalık vs.*); tekrar şiddetlenmek; açılmak (*yara vs.*) re.cruˈdes.cence *n.* nüksetme, yenilenme.

**re.cruit** [riˈkruːt] **1.** *n.* acemi er; *fig.* acemi, deneyimsiz; **2.** *v/t.* toplamak, oluşturmak (*grup, asker vs.*); ikmal etm., bütünlemek; iyileştirmek (*hasta*); ✕ silah altına çağırmak; *v/i.* iyileşmek; reˈcruit.ment *n.* acemi erleri silah altına toplama; iyileş(tir)me.

**rec.tan.gle** [ˈrektæŋgl] *n.* dik dörtgen; recˈtan.gu.lar □ [~gjulə] dik dörtgen şeklinde; dik açılı.

**rec.ti.fi.a.ble** [ˈrektifaiəbl] *adj.* düzeltilebilir; rec.ti.fi.ca.tion [~fiˈkeiʃən] *n.* düzelt(il)me, tashih; tasfiye; ♁ eğri uzunluğunu ölçme; ∿ sürekli distilasyonla saflaştırma; **rec.ti.fi.er** [ˈ~faiə] *n.* düzelten *b-i veya bş;* radyo: redresör, doğrultmaç; **rec.ti.fy** [ˈ~fai] *v/t.* düzeltmek, tashih etm., doğrultmak; ♁ uzunluğunu ölçmek (*eğri*); ∿ saflaştırmak; ♪, *radyo:* doğru akıma çevirmek; **rec.ti.lin.e.al** [rektiˈlinjəl], **rec.tiˈlin.e.ar** □ [~njə] doğrusal, doğrulu, düz çizgili; **rec.ti.tude** [ˈrektitjuːd] *n.* doğruluk, düzlük; dürüstlük, samimiyet.

**rec.tor** [ˈrektə] *n.* papaz; *univ.* rektör; (*okul*) müdür; **rec.tor.ate** [ˈ~rit], ˈrector.ship *n.* rektörlük, müdürlük; **¹rec.to-ry** *n.* papaz ikâmetgâhı (*veya* konutu).

rec.tum *anat.* [ˈrektəm] *n.* rektum, kalın barsağın son kısmı.

re.cum.bent □ [riˈkʌmbənt] uzanan, yatan, dayanmış.

re.cu.per.ate [riˈkjuːpəreit] *v/i.* iyileşmek, sağlığına kavuşmak; re.cu.perˈa.tion *n.* iyileşme; **reˈcu.per.a.tive** [~rətiv] *adj.* sıhhatini yeniden kazandıran.

re.cur [riˈkəː] *v/i.* tekrar dönmek (to -e); tekrar olm., tekrarlamak (*olay, hastalık vs.*); ~ to s.o.'s mind *b-nin* hatırına gelmek; ~ring decimal devirli ondalık kesir; re.cur.rence [riˈkʌrəns] *n.* dönüş; tekrarlanma, tekerrür, nüksetme; ~ to tekrar bahis konusu olma; reˈcur.rent □ tekrar olan; *anat.* tersyöne giden; ~ fever tekrar tekrar gelen nöbet.

re.curve [riːkəːv] *v/t.* & *v/i.* geriye *veya* içe doğru eğ(il)mek.

rec.u.sant [ˈrekjuzənt] *adj.* özellikle kilise kurallarına uymayı reddeden; dikkafalı, serkeş.

red [red] 1. *adj.* kırmızı, kızıl, al; ♀ Crescent Kızılay; ♀ Cross Kızılhaç; currant (*kırmızı veya siyah*) frenküzümü; ~ deer kırmızı derili bir tür geyik; ~ ensign İngiltere'de ticaret gemileri bayrağı; ~ heat tav (*metal*); ~ herring ilgiyi başka yöne çekmek için ortaya atılan konu; draw a ~ herring across the trail dikkati başka yöne çevirmek, oyalamak; ~ lead süliğen; paint the town ~ *sl.* sarhoş olup ortalığı velveleye vermek, gürültü çıkarmak; 2. *n.* kırmızı renk; *part. pol.* kızıl, komünist; see ~ birden öfkelenmek; be in the ~ *Am.* F borç içinde olm.

re.dact [riˈdækt] *v/t.* telif etm., kaleme almak, neşretmek; reˈdac.tion *n.* redaksiyon, düzeltilmiş ve düzenlenmiş nüsha, metin; yeni bası.

red.breast [ˈredbrest] *n. a.* robin ~ *zo.* kızıl gerdan, nar bülbülü; kızıl göğüslü kuş; **¹Red.brick** *n.* Londra dışında kurulmuş üniversite(ler); **¹red.cap** *n.* askerî polis; *Am.* bagaj hamalı; red.den [ˈredn] *v/t.* & *v/i.* kırmızılaş(tır)mak. kızıllaş-(tır)mak, kızarmak; **¹red.dish** *adj.* kırmızımtırak, kızılımsı, kızılca; **red.dle** [~l] *n.* kırmızı tebeşir (*veya* boya).

re.dec.o.rate [ˈriːˈdekəreit] *vb.* yenileştirmek, yeniden dekore etm.; **¹re.dec.oˈra-tion** *n.* yeniden dekore etme, redekorasyon.

re.deem [riˈdiːm] *v/t.* fidye vererek kurtarmak, rehinden kurtarmak, bedelini verip geri almak; ♰ amortize etm.; nakit olarak ödemek, tazminat vermek, borçtan kurtarmak; telâfi etm. (*zaman*); korumak (from -*den*); **reˈdeem.a-ble** *adj.* ♰ paraya çevrilir (*senet*); fidye ile kurtarılabilir; amorti edilebilir; **Re-ˈdeem.er** *n.* Kurtarıcı, Halâskâr; *rel.* Hazreti İsa.

re.de.liv.er [ˈriːdiˈlivə] *v/t.* yeniden teslim etm., dağıtmak; yeniden kurtarmak, halâs etm.

re.demp.tion [riˈdempʃən] *n.* halâs, kurtar(ıl)ma; ♰ amortisman; paraya çevrilme; tazminat; reˈdemp.tion.er *n. hist.* Amerika göçmeni; reˈdemp.tive *adj.* kurtarıcı, kurtaran.

re.de.ploy [ˈriːdiˈplɔi] *v/t.* daha etken olacak şekilde yeniden düzenlemek (*asker, işçi vs.*).

red...: **¹~ˈfaced** *adj.* kırmızı yüzlü; **¹~.haired** *adj.* kızıl saçlı; **¹~-ˈhand.ed** *adj.*: catch s.o. ~ *b-ni* suçüstü yakalamak; **¹~.head** *n.* kızıl saçlı kimse; **¹~-ˈhead.ed** *adj.* kızıl saçlı; **¹~-ˈhot** *adj.* kızgın (*metal*); *fig.* canı tez, kabına sığmayan; kızgın, çok öfkeli; en yeni (*veya* son) (*haber vs.*).

re.dif.fu.sion [ˈriːdiˈfjuːʒən] *n.* merkezî bir alıcı aygıttan diğer umumî yerlerdeki alıcılara yapılan ses ve televizyon yayım sistemi.

Red In.di.an [reˈdindjən] *n.* Kızılderili.

red.in.te.grate [reˈdintigreit] *v/t.* yeniden eski haline getirmek, iyi hale koymak, yenilemek, tamir etm.; red.in.teˈgra.tion *n.* yenileme.

re.di.rect [ˈriːdiˈrekt] *v/t.* düzeltilmiş adresi yazmak (*mektup*); yeni adresine göndermek.

re.dis.count [riːˈdiskaunt] 1. *vb.* reeskont etm., senet kır(dır)mak; 2. *n.* reeskont.

re.dis.cov.er [ˈriːdisˈkʌə] *v/t.* yeniden keşfetmek (*veya* bulmak).

re.dis.trib.ute [ˈriːdisˈtribjuːt] *v/t.* yeniden dağıtmak (*veya* hisselere bölmek).

red-let.ter day [ˈredˈletəˈdei] *n.* yortu günü; *fig.* önemli gün, mutlu bir gün.

red-light dis.trict [ˈredlaitˈdistrikt] *n.* genelev mahallesi.

red.ness [ˈrednis] *n.* kırmızılık, kızıllık.

re.do [ˈriːˈduː] (*irr.* do) *vb.* yeniden yapmak.

red.o.lence [ˈredəuləns] *n.* güzel koku, ıtır, rayiha; **¹red.o.lent** *adj.* güzel kokulu (of); be ~ of *fig.* hatırlatmak, akla getirmek.

re.dou.ble [riˈdʌbl] *v/t.* tekrarlamak, iki misli yapmak -*i*; *v/i.* iki misli olm.

**re.doubt** ✕ [ri'daut] *n.* tabya, palanka, ağaç ve toprakla yapılıp hendekle çevrilmiş küçük hisar; **re'doubt.a.ble** *adj. rhet.* müthiş, dehşetli.

**re.dound** [ri'daund] *v/t.*: ～ to artırmak, yükseltmek, bahşetmek *(şan, şeref vs.)*; ～ (up)on gözden düşmek, gerilemek *(şeref, şan vs.).*

**re.draft** ['ri:'dra:ft] 1. *n.* yeni müsvedde; † protesto olan bir senedin masraflarla beraber yeni şekli; 2. *vb.* yeni müsvedde yapmak.

**re.dress** [ri'dres] 1. *n.* çare, düzeltme, telâfi; ☆ tazminat; legal ～ adlî yardım; 2. *v/t.* düzeltmek; telâfi etm.

**red...**: '～.skin *n.* kızılderili; '～.start *n. orn.* kızılkuyruk; ～ tape, ～-tap.ism ['～'teipizəm] *n.* kırtasiyecilik, bürokrasi; '～-'tap-ist *n.* bürokrat, kırtasiyeci, evrak adamı.

**re.duce** [ri'dju:s] *v/t. fig.* geri getirmek (to -e), azaltmak, indirmek, küçültmek (to -e); düşürmek *(fiyat)*; ✕ fethetmek; *fig.* zayıflatmak, kuvvetten düşürmek; zorlamak, mecbur etm. (to -e); Å, ☍ indirgemek, redüklemek; *phot.* zayıflatmak; ⚡ *(çıkık, kol vs.)* yerine koymak; † bakıyeyi eşitlemek; Ⅎ bir deri bir kemik bırakmak; *v/i.* perhiz *vs.* ile zayıflamak; ～ to writing yaz(dır)mak, kaleme almak, kaydetmek; **re'duc.i.ble** *adj.* indirilir, azaltılabilir (to -e); zayıflatılabilir; indirgenebilir; **re.duc.tion** [ri'dΛk-ʃən] *n.* azaltma, indirme, küçültme; azaltılmış şey; indirim, tenzilat, ıskonto; küçültülmüş harita, resim *vs.*; zaptetme, galibiyet; ⚡ çıkık kol vs.'yi yerine koyma.

**re.dun.dance, re.dun.dan.cy** [ri'dΛndəns-(i)] *n.* fazlalık, bolluk, çokluk; bol bol mevcut olma; işsizlik (oranı), işten çıkarılma; ağdalı ifade; **re'dun.dant** ☐ gerekenden fazla, bol bol, kesretli, artakalan; işsiz, işten çıkarılmış; fazla sözle ifade edilmiş, ağdalı, fazla detaylı, uzun uzadıya.

**re.du.pli.cate** [ri'dju:plikeit] *v/t.* iki kat yapmak, ikilemek, tekrarlamak, duble etm., iki misline çıkarmak; **re.du.pli'ca-tion** *n.* iki misline çık(ar)ma, tekrarlama.

**red.wood** ['redwud] *n.* kırmızı kereste veren bir tür ağaç; bu ağacın kerestesi.

**re.dye** ['ri:'dai] *v/t.* yeniden boyamak -i.

**re-ech.o** [ri:'ekəu] *vb.* aksiseda vermek, tekrar akset(tir)mek, yankıla(n)mak.

**reed** [ri:d] *n.* saz, kamış (sapı); sazlık; kamış düdük *(zurna vs.nin ucuna takılan)*; the ～s *pl.* ♪ ağzında bulunan ince

maden *veya* kamış vasıtasiyle ses çıkaran müzik aletleri *(obua, klarnet zurna vs.).*

**re.ed.it** ['ri:'edit] *v/t.* yeniden basmak, yayımlamak.

**re-ed.u.ca.tion** ['ri:edju'keiʃən] *n.* yeniden eğitme.

**reed.y** ['ri:di] *adj.* kamış *(veya* saz) dolu; kamış düdük gibi tiz ses çıkaran.

**reef¹** [ri:f] *n.* resif, kayalık.

**reef²** [～] ⚓ 1. *n.* yelkenin bir kat camadanı; yelkeni camadan ile küçültme; 2. *v/t.* yelken camadanını bağlayarak küçültmek; cıvadıra bastonunu mayna etm.

**reef.er¹** ['ri:fə] *n.* denizci ceketi.

**reef.er²** *Am. sl.* [～] *n.* esrarlı sigara.

**reek** [ri:k] 1. *n.* duman, buhar, sis; fena koku; 2. *v/i.* duman çıkmak, tütmek; buğulanmak (with *ile*); kokusunu yaymak (of, with *-in*); '**reek.y** *adj.* dumanlı; fena kokulu.

**reel** [ri:l] 1. *n.* makara, iplik çıkrığı; bobin, masura; film makarası; bant makarası *(teyp)*; olta çubuğunun alt ucuna takılan makara; makaraya sarılmış ip, tel, bant *vs.*; 2. *v/t.* makaraya sarmak, çile (veya tura) yapmak, dolamak; ～ off çıkrıktan geçirmek; ezberden çabucak söylemek, sayıp dökmek; *v/i.* sendelemek, sallanmak; başı dönmek.

**re-e.lect** ['ri:i'lekt] *v/t. pol.* yeniden seçmek; '**re-e'lec.tion** *n.* yeniden seç(il)me.

**re-el.i.gi.ble** ['ri:'elidʒəbl] *adj.* yeniden seçilebilir.

**re-en.act** ['ri:i'nækt] *v/t.* yeniden kararlaştırmak; *thea.* yeniden sahneye koymak.

**re-en.force** ['ri:in'fɔ:s] *etc.* = reinforce *etc.*

**re-en.gage** ['ri:in'geidʒ] *v/t.* yeniden hizmete almak (veya tutmak).

**re-en.list** ['ri:in'list] *v/t.* yeniden askere almak.

**re-en.ter** ['ri:i'entə] *vb.* yeniden girmek -e *(veya* kaydetmek, kaydolmak, katılmak); girişmek; '**re-'ent.er.ing, re.en-trant** [ri:'entrənt] *adj.* girintili *(köşe).*

**re-es.tab.lish** ['ri:is'tæbliʃ] *v/t.* yeniden kurmak, tesis etm., eski haline getirmek, iyileştirmek.

**reeve¹** ↓ [ri:v] *v/t.* halatın ucunu bir delik *veya* makaradan geçirmek.

**reeve²** [～] *n. hist.* İngiltere'de vali, idareci, hakim *vs.*

**re-ex.am.i.na.tion** ['ri:igzæmi'neiʃən] *n.* yenilenen sınav; yeniden değerlendirme; '**re-ex'am.ine** *v/t.* yeniden sorguya çekmek.

**re-ex.change** [¹riːiksˈtʃəindʒ] *n.* yeniden değiştirme, trampa etme; † protestolu senedi masrafları ekleyerek yenileme; retret.

**re.fec.tion** [riˈfekʃən] *n.* serinlik; hafif yemek (*veya* kahvaltı); hafif yemek *veya* içki ile ferahla(t)ma, serinle(t)me; **reˈfec.to.ry** [~təri] *n.* yemekhane (*okul vs.de*).

**re.fer** [riˈfəː] *v/t.*: ~ to göndermek, havale etm. -*e*, *b-ni b-ne* göndermek; müracaat etm., başvurmak, danışmak; *v/i.* ima etm., zikretmek, işaret etm., göstermek (to -*i*); *bşi* içermek, kapsamak, ilgili olm. *ile*; isnat etm., bir nedene bağlamak; **reˈfer.a.ble** *adj.*: ~ to havale edilebilir -*e*, isnat edilebilir -*e*; başvurulabilir -*e*; **ref.er.ee** [refəˈriː] *n.* hakem; *boks:* ring hakemi; *parl.* raportör, eksper; bilirkişi; **ref.er.ence** [¹refrəns] *n.* referans, tavsiye; başvuruş; ilgi, münasebet; havale etme *veya* olunma; ima, kinaye; isnat etme (to -*e*); bilgi, malûmat (veren *b-i veya bş*); in *veya* with ~ to ...*e* gelince, ...le ilgili olarak, ...hakkında, ait, ... e nispetle; terms *pl.* of ~ direktif, talimat; yetki alanı; work of ~, ~ book başvuru kitabı; ~ library araştırmada yararlanılan fakat dışarı kitap alınmayan kütüphane; ~ number dosya (*veya* evrak) numarası; make a ~ to zikretmek -*i*; başvurmak *a*, bakmak -*e*. **ref.er.en.dum** [refəˈrendəm] *n.* referandum, halk oyuna başvurma.

**re.fill** [¹riˈfil] **1.** *n.* yedek takım, eksilen, biten maddenin yerine konan yedek; yedek kalem içi; yedek kâğıt; **2.** *v/t.* tekrar doldurmak.

**re.fine** [riˈfain] *v/t.* tasfiye etm., saflaştırmak, arıtmak; inceltmek (*a.* ⊕ & *fig.*); ⊕ rafine etm.; *fig.* ıslah etm.; *v/i.* incelmek, zarifleşmek; saflaşmak, temizlenmek; kılı kırk yarmak, titizlik etm. (on, upon); ~ (up)on arılaştırmak, ıslah etm., geliştirmek (*yöntem, plan vs.*); **re.fine.ment** *n.* arıtma, saflaştırma; saflık, halislik, tasfiye; incelik, kibarlık; nezaket, zariflik; **reˈfin.er** *n.* tasfiye eden, arıtan *b-i veya bş*; **reˈfin.er.y** *n.* ⊕ rafineri; şeker fabrikası; *metall.* dökümhane, izabehane.

**re.fit** ⤓ [¹riˈfit] **1.** *v/t.* & *v/i.* yeniden donatmak, yenilemek; yeniden donatılıp sefer için hazır olm.; **2.** *n.* tamir, yeniden donatma.

**re.flect** [riˈflekt] *v/t.* & *v/i.* aksettirmek (*ısı, ışık, ses vs.*) (*a. fig*); ifade etm.,

beyan etm., açıklamak; ~ (up)on düşünmek -*i*, ölçüp biçmek, düşünüp taşınmak -*i*; suçlayarak düşüncesini söylemek; *b-nin, bşin* kötü yanını göstermek, kusurunu göstermek; şeref kazandırmak; **reˈflec.tion** *n.* yansıma, aksetme; yansıyan (*veya* akseden) şey; düşünme, düşünce, fikir; ayıplama, kınama; leke, kusur, şaibe; **reˈflec.tive** ☐ yansıtan, aksettiren; yansıyan, akseden; düşünceli, derin düşüncelere dalmış; **reˈflec.tor** *n.* yansıtan yüzey; projektör, ışıldak; yansıtaç (*karayolunda*); reflektör; aynalı teleskop.

**re.flex** [¹riːfleks] **1.** *adj.* yansımalı, geri çevrilmiş, tepkimiş, refleks...; **2.** *n.* refleks, tepke, yansı (*a. physiol.*); akis, yansımış şekil; **reˈflex.ion** [riˈflekʃən] = reflection; **re.flex.ive** ☐ [riˈfleksiv] üzerinde tepki yapan; *gr.* dönüşlü (*veya* eylem gösteren).

**ref.lu.ent** [¹reflluənt] *adj.* dönüp geri akan.

**re.flux** [¹riːflʌks] *n.* geri(ye) akış, cezir haline geliş.

**re.for.est.a.tion** [¹riːfɔrisˈteiʃən] *n.* yeniden orman haline getirme, ağaçlandırma.

**re.form¹** [riˈfɔːm] **1.** *n.* reform, ıslah(at), düzeltme, yenilik; **2.** *v/t.* ıslah etm., düzeltmek, iyileştirmek, geliştirmek; *v/i.* iyileşmek, düzelmek, ıslah olm.

**re-form²** [¹riːˈfɔːm] *vb.* yeniden şekil vermek (*veya* teşkil etm.), düzenle(n)mek; ✕ yeniden dizmek, oluşturmak.

**ref.or.ma.tion** [refəˈmeiʃən] *n.* gelişme, yenileşme, nefis ıslahı, ıslahat, ıslah olma *veya* etme; ♀ *eccl.* Reformasyon, dinsel devrim; **re.form.a.to.ry** [riˈfɔːmətəri] **1.** *adj.* düzeltici, ıslah edici; ıslahat gerektiren; **2.** *n.* ıslahhane, ıslahevi; **reˈformed** *adj.* ıslah edilmiş, ıslah olmuş; *eccl.* Kalvinist, protestan; **reˈform·er** *n.* ıslahatçı, reformcu; **reˈform·ist** *adj.* reform (*veya* ıslahat) taraftarı olan, reformist.

**re.found** [¹riːfaund] *v/t.* kaptan kaba nakletmek, eriterek başka bir kalıba (*veya* bir daha) dökmek.

**re.fract** [riˈfrækt] *v/t.* kırmak (*ışınları*); ~ing telescope mercekli teleskop; **reˈfrac.tion** *n.* kırılma; **reˈfrac.tive** *adj. opt.* kır(ıl)an...; **reˈfrac.tor** *n. opt.* mercekli teleskop; **reˈfrac.to.ri.ness** *n.* inatçılık, dikkafalılık; ⚗ ısıya dayanıklılık, kolay ergimezlik; **reˈfrac.to.ry** **1.** ☐ inatçı, dikkafalı, serkeş; ⊕ ısıya dayanıklı, işlenemez; ⚗ erimez; **2.** *n.* ⊕ ısıya dayanıklı malzeme.

**re.frain¹** [riˈfrein] *v/i.* çekinmek, sakın-

mak (from -*den*), yapmaktan vazgeçmek, *k-ni* tutmak (from -*den*).

re.frain² [~] *n.* ♪ nakarat, şarkı nakaratı.

re.fran.gi.ble *phys.* [ri'frændʒəbl] *adj.* kırılabilir.

re.fresh [ri'freʃ] *v/t.* & *v/i.* canlan(dır)-
mak, serinlet(t)mek, dinlen(dir)mek;
hayat vermek, tazelemek; kuvvetlendirmek *(anı)*; re'fresh.er *n.* F içki, serinletici *(veya* canlandırıcı) şey; 👁 uzayan
celse için avukata ödenen ek ücret; ~
course eski bilgileri hatırlayıp yenilikle-
ri öğrenmek için yapılan eğitim çalışması; re'fresh.ment *n.* canlan(dır)ma; canlandırıcı şey; ~ room büfe, büvet *(istasyonda).*

re.frig.er.ant [ri'fridʒərənt] 1. *adj.* soğutucu, serinletici; 2. *n.* soğutucu *veya* dondurucu şey *(kimyasal madde)*; re'frig.er-
ate [~reit] *v/t.* soğutmak, serinletmek,
dondurmak; re'frig.er.at.ing *adj.* soğutan,
buz...; re.frig.er'a.tion *n.* soğutma, dondurma, serin tutma; re'frig.er.a.tor *n.*
buzdolabı, soğutucu; soğuk hava deposu; ~ lorry frigorifik kamyon, soğuk hava vagonu.

re.fu.el [ri:'fjuəl] *vb.* yakıt almak *(veya*
ikmal etm.).

ref.uge ['refju:dʒ] *n.* sığınak, barınak,
melce; çare; *a.* street-~ refüj; *mount.*
sığınak, kulübe, barınacak yer; take ~ in
sığınmak, barınacak yer bulmak; ref.u-
gee [~'dʒi] *n.* mülteci, başka ülkeye sı-
ğınan kimse, sığınık; ~ camp mülteci
kampı.

re.ful.gence [ri'fʌldʒəns] *n.* parlaklık, parıltı; re'ful.gent □ parlak, parlıyan, ışın
saçan, ışıl ışıl; görkemli.

re.fund 1. [ri'fʌnd] *v/t.* parayı geri vermek; 2. ['ri:fʌnd] *n.* geri ödeme; geri
ödenen meblağ.

re.fur.bish ['ri:'fə:biʃ] *v/t.* yeniden cilâlamak, perdahlamak, parlatmak *(a. fig.).*

re.fur.nish ['ri:fə:niʃ] *v/t.* yeniden döşemek *(veya* tefriş etm.).

re.fus.al [ri'fju:zəl] *n.* ret, kabul etmeyiş
*veya* olunmayış, ret cevabı; kabul *veya*
reddetme hakkı.

re.fuse¹ [ri'fju:z] *v/t.* & *v/i.* reddetmek,
kabul etmemek, istememek; vazgeçmek;
ürkmek, hendek *vs.*'den atlamayı istememek *(at).*

ref.use² ['refju:s] *n.* süprüntü, döküntü,
çöp; *fig.* ayaktakımı.

ref.u.ta.ble □ ['refjutəbl] çürütülebilir,
cerhedilebilir, yalanlanabilir; ref.uta-
tion [refju:'teiʃən] *n.* yalanlama, çürütme, tekzip; re.fute [ri'fju:t] *v/t.* yalan-

lamak, çürütmek, cerhetmek, tekzip etm.

re.gain [ri'gein] *v/t.* tekrar ele geçirmek
*(veya* kazanmak).

re.gal □ ['ri:gəl] krala ait, krala yakışır, şahane.

re.gale [ri'geil] *v/t.* ağırlama ve ikram-
da bulunmak, ağırlamak, yedirip içirmek; eğlendirmek, hoşça vakit geçirtmek; *v/i.* zevk ve safa içinde yaşamak
(on).

re.ga.li.a [ri'geiljə] *n. pl.* kral tacı ve süsü; nişan ve rütbe alâmetleri.

re.gard [ri'ga:d] 1. *n.* bakış, nazar; saygı, hürmet, takdir; itibar, sayma; fikir;
dikkat, önem; ilişki; ~s *pl.* selâm; have
~ to bşe riayet etm., nazarı itibara almak -*i*; with ~ to bakımından, karşısında, nazaran, -*e* gelince; with kind ~s saygılar, selâmlar; 2. *vb.* dikkatle bakmak -*e*; nazarı dikkate almak, -*i*, hesaba
katmak -*i*; itibar etm. -*e*, saymak -*i*; hürmet etm., riayet etm., uymak; ...naza-
riyle bakmak, ...gibi telâkki etm.; ait
olm.; as ~s hakkında, hususunda, -*e*
gelince; re'gard.ful □ [~ful] saygılı, hürmet eden, göz önünde bulunduran, düşünüp hatırlayan (of); re'gard.ing *adj.*
hakkında, hususunda, -*e* gelince; re-
'gard.less □ pervasız, lâkayt, aldırış etmeyen, dikkatsiz, saygısız; ~ of -*e* bak-
mayarak, ne olursa olsun, aldırmaya-
rak.

re.gat.ta [ri'gætə] *n.* kürek *veya* yelken
yarışı.

re.gen.cy ['ri:dʒənsi] *n.* hükümdarlık, saltanat (süresi); kral naipliği; naipler kurulu; naiplik süresi.

re.gen.er.ate 1. [ri'dʒenəreit] *v/t.* & *v/i.*
yeniden hayat vermek, yeniden teşkil
etm., canlandırmak; ıslah etm. *veya*
olm., iyileş(tir)mek; ahlâkî yönden ge-
liş(tir)mek; 2. *adj.* ahlâk ve davranışları ıslah olmuş; yeniden doğmuş; re-
gen.er.a.tion [~'reiʃən] *n.* yenileme; *fig.*
yeniden hayat verme, doğma; iyileşme,
ıslah olma; *part. biol.* yeniden oluşma;
re'gen.er.a.tive [~rətiv] *adj. radyo:* reaksiyonu harekete geçirici, reaktif.

re.gent ['ri:dʒənt] 1. *adj.* hükümdarın yokluğu *veya* hastalığında vekillik eden; 2.
*n.* saltanat vekili, kral naibi; 're.gent-
ship *n.* hükümdarlık; saltanat vekilliği.

reg.i.cide ['redʒisaid] *n.* hükümdarı öldürme; hükümdar katili.

ré.gime, re.gime [rei'ʒi:m] *n.* rejim, sistem, idare (şekli), hükümet şekli; =
regimen.

reg.i.men ['redʒimen] *n.* perhiz, rejim; *gr.*

bir sözcüğün kendisiyle ilgili başka bir sözcüğü biçimsel olarak etkilemesi; = régime.

**reg.i.ment** ['redʒimənt] **1.** *n.* X alay; *fig.* insan sürüsü, kalabalık; **2.** ['~ment] *v/t.* alay oluşturmak; sistematik şekle koymak, organize etm., *(insanları)* kontrol altına almak; **reg.i.men.tal** [~'mentl] *adj.* X alaya ait, alay...; **reg.i.men.tal.ly** [~'mentəli] *adv.* alay gibi; **reg.i'men.tals** *n. pl.* X askeri üniforma; **reg.i.men'ta-tion** *n.* sistematik şekle koyma, organize etme, kontrol etme.

**re.gion** ['riːdʒən] *n.* bölge, mıntıka, semt, taraf, yer, çevre, havali, saha; *fig.* muhit, çevre; olasılık alanı; **re.gion.al** ['~dʒənl] **1.** □ bölgesel, mıntıkaya ait, mahalli, lokal, yöresel; *radyo:* ~ station mahalli radyo istasyonu.

**reg.is.ter** ['redʒistə] **1.** *n.* sicil; kayıt, liste, katalog, fihrist, cetvel; kütük, resmî kayıt defteri; ⊕ valf, subap, sürgü; regülatör; ♪ ses perdesi; *cash* ~ otomatik yazar kasa; *parish* ~ kilise cemaati sicil kütüğü; **2.** *v/t.* kaydetmek, deftere geçirmek, tescil etm., kütüğe geçirmek; göstermek *(termometre vs.)*; ifade etm. *(yüz ifadesi)*; taahhütlü olarak göndermek *(mektup vs.)*; *v/i.* kaydolunmak, adını sicil *vs.*'ye geçirtmek; **'reg.is.tered** *adj.* taahhütlü; kaydolunmuş, kayıtlı; ~ *design* kullan(ıl)ma kılavuzu.

**reg.is.trar** [redʒis'traː] *n.* kayıt tescil memuru, sicil memuru; nüfus memuru; **reg.is.tra.tion** [~'treiʃən] *n.* kayıt, tescil; ~ *fee* kayıt ücreti; **'reg.is.try** *n.* kayıt; sicil; sicil dairesi, evrak kalemi; ~ *office* evlen(dir)me dairesi, nikâh memurluğu; *servants'* ~ iş bulma bürosu.

**reg.nant** ['regnənt] *adj.* hükmeden, tahtta olan, saltanat süren n*(part. kraliçe)*.

**re.gress** ['riːgres] *n.* geri dönüş, avdet, eskiye dönüş; *fig.* azalma, düşüş; **re.gres.sion** [ri'greʃən] *n.* dönüş, avdet; *psych.* gerileme; **re'gres.sive** □ [~siv] geri giden, tersyön, gerileyen, tepki oluşturan.

**re.gret** [ri'gret] **1.** *n.* teessüf (at); üzüntü, keder (for); pişmanlık; **2.** *v/t.* teessüf etm., üzülmek -e, müteessir olm., kederlenmek; pişman olm. -e; özlemini çekmek -in, yokluğunu hissetmek -in, bşin kaybolduğunu farketmek; **re'gret.ful** □ [~ful] kederli, üzüntülü, esef dolu; ~ly esefle, acınarak, teessüfle; **re'gret.ta.ble** □ acınacak, şayanı teessüf, üzücü.

**reg.u.lar** ['regjulə] **1.** □ muntazam, düzgün; düzenli, kurallı; aynı zamanda olan; değişken olmayan; X muvazzaf; *eccl.* manastır sistemine bağlı, tarikat...; **2.** *n. eccl.* bir tarikat *veya* manastır sistemine bağlı imam *veya* papaz; X muvazzaf asker; F müdavim; devamlı *(veya* gedikli) müşteri; **reg.u.lar.i.ty** [~'læriti] *n.* düzen, intizam, nizam, tertip.

**reg.u.late** ['regjuleit] *v/t.* düzenlemek; yoluna koymak; kurala bağlamak, düzeltmek; ayar etm., tesviye etm., tanzim etm., uydurmak; **'reg.u.lat.ing** *adj.* ⊕ ayar..., tanzim...; **reg.u'la.tion 1.** *n.* düzen, intizam, nizam; hüküm, kural, emir, karar; ~s *pl.* tüzük; kurallar; *contrary to* ~s nizama aykırı; **2.** *adj.* talim(at)nameye uygun; X askerlik...; **reg.u.la.tive** □ ['~lətiv] düzenleyici, ayarlayıcı; **reg.u.la.tor** ['~leitə] *n.* düzenleyici *b-i veya bş*; ⊕ regülatör, düzengeç; saat rakkası.

**re.gur.gi.tate** [ri'gəːdʒiteit] *v/t.* kusturmak, istifrağ ettirmek; geri dökmek, akıtmak, fışkırtmak, çıkartmak; *v/i.* kusmak; geri akmak, fışkırmak *(su, gaz vs.).*

**re.ha.bil.i.tate** [riːə'biliteit] *v/t.* yenileştirmek, tamir etm., onarmak *(ev)*; bir hastalıktan, özellikle sıtmadan kurtarmak *(mahalleyi)*; yeniden dahil etm., koordine etm. *(meslek)*; eski hakları iade etm.; yeniden eğiterek eski yaşantılarına kavuşturmak *(savaş malülleri vs.)*; **'re.ha.bil.i'ta.tion** *n.* eski hakların iadesi; eski hale gelme, eski yaşama kavuşma; yenileme, onarım.

**re.hash** *fig.* ['riː'hæʃ] **1.** *v/t.* aynı şeyi *veya* konuyu tekrar gündeme getirmek, tekrar açmak, temcit pilavı gibi sunmak; **2.** *n.* tekrarlama, aynısını sunma; tekrarlanan konu *veya* şey.

**re.hears.al** [ri'həːsəl] *n. thea.,* ♪ prova; tekrarlama; **re'hearse** *vb. thea.* prova etm.; tekrarlamak; ezberden okumak, sayıp dökmek; alıştırmak *(oyuncu)*.

**re.heat** [riː'hiːt] *v/t.* yeniden ısıtmak.

**reign** [rein] **1.** *n.* hükümet, hükümdarlık, saltanat (devri); *fig.* nüfuz, otorite; **2.** *v/i.* hüküm sürmek, hâkim olm., hükümet etm.

**re.im.burse** [riːim'bəːs] *v/t.* masrafı geri ödemek; *b-ne* tazminat vermek; parasını geri vermek; † masraflarını kapatmak; **re.im'burse.ment** *n.* geri ödeme, masrafını iade; tazmin etme.

**rein** [rein] **1.** *n.* dizgin; yönetim, idare; *give* ~ *to* yularını salıvermek, başıboş bırakmak; **2.** *v/t.:* ~ *in,* ~ *up,* ~ *back* bir atın dizginlerini çekmek; *fig.* bşe gem vurmak, *bşi* frenlemek.

**rein.deer** *zo.* ['reindiə] *n.* rengeyiği.

**re.in.force** [riːinˈfɔːs] **1.** *v/t.* kuvvetlendirmek, takviye etm., sağlamlaştırmak; asker *veya* kuvvet göndererek takviye etm.; ~ed concrete ⊕ betonarme; **2.** *n.* ˈforce.ment *n.* takviye (etme), kuvvetlendirme; tahkim *(beton)*; ~s *pl.* ✗ takviye birliği.

**re.in.stall** ['riːinˈstɔːl] *v/t.* yeniden yerleştirmek, kurmak, eski haline getirmek; ˈre.inˈstal(l).ment *n.* yeniden yerleş(tir)me.

**re.in.state** ['riːinˈsteit] *v/t.* eski görevine iade etm.; eski haline getirmek; tamir etm., onarmak; ˈre.inˈstate.ment *n.* eski görevine iade edilme; restore etme, onarım.

**re.in.sur.ance** ['riːinˈʃuərəns] *n.* reasürans, yinelenmiş *(veya* mükerrer) sigorta; **re.in.sure** [ˈˌ~ˈʃuə] *v/t.* yeniden sigorta etm.

**re.in.vest** ['riːinˈvest] *v/t.* yeniden yatırmak *(veya* yatırım yapmak).

**re.is.sue** ['riːˈisjuː] **1.** *v/t.* tekrar çıkarmak *(veya* neşretmek, yayımlamak); **2.** *n.* yeni baskı.

**re.it.er.ate** [riːˈtəreit] *v/t.* tekrarlamak; **re.it.erˈa.tion** *n.* tekrarlama.

**re.ject** [riˈdʒekt] *v/t.* reddetmek, kabul etmemek, tanımamak; işe yaramaz diye atmak; reˈjec.tion *n.* ret, reddedilme; seçip atma; ~s *pl.* özürlü *(veya* sakat) eşya, mezat malı; re.jec.tor cir.cuit *radyo:* kısma devresi.

**re.jig** ['riːˈdʒig] *v/t. (fabrika)* yeni makinelerle donatmak.

**re.joice** [riˈdʒɔis] *v/t.* sevindirmek, hoşlandırmak, memnun etm.; rejoiced at *veya* by memnun, sevinçli, neşeli *-den*; *v/i.* *bşden* dolayı sevinmek, memnun olm. *(at.* in); reˈjoic.ing **1.** □ sevinçli, mutlu; sevindiren; **2.** *n. oft.* ~s *pl.* sevinç, neşe, hoşnutluk; şenlik, eğlence.

**re.join¹** ['riːˈdʒɔin] *v/t. & v/i.* tekrar kavuş(tur)mak, birleş(tir)mek *(to.* with *-e, ile).*

**re.join²** [riˈdʒɔin] *v/t.* cevap vermek *-e,* yanıtlamak *-i,* karşılık vermek *-e;* reˈjoin.der *n.* yanıt, cevap karşılık.

**re.ju.ve.nate** [riˈdʒuːvineit] *v/t. & v/i.* yeniden gençleş(tir)mek; canlan(dır)mak; re.ju.veˈna.tion *n.* gençleş(tir)me, canlan(dır)ma.

**re.kin.dle** ['riːˈkindl] *v/t. & v/i.* yeniden tutuş(tur)mak, yakmak, yanmak, alevlen(dir)mek *(a. fig.).*

**re.lapse** [riˈlæps] **1.** *n.* eski hale dönme; nüksetme, yinelenme *(hastalık vs.);* te-

kerrür; **2.** *v/i.* tekrar fenalaşmak, nüksetmek *(hastalık);* tekrar *(kötü yola)* sapmak (into *-e),* aynı hataya tekrar düşmek.

**re.late** [riˈleit] *v/t.* anlatmak, hikâye etm., nakletmek, söylemek, bildirmek; ilişki *(veya* bağlantı) kurmak (to, with *-(l)e); v/i.* ilgili olm. (to *ile),* ait olm., bağlı olm. (to *-e);* reˈlat.ed *adj.* akraba olan (to *-in);* ilgili, ilişik, ilgisi olan; anlatılmış; reˈlat.er *n.* anlatan, hikâye eden kimse.

**re.la.tion** [riˈleiʃən] *n.* ilişki; ilgi, alâka (with *ile);* nispet, oran (to *-e);* akraba(lık), hısım(lık); hikâye (etme), nakil, anlatma; in ~ to hakkında, *-e ilişkin, -e* dair, *-e* gelince; *-e* nispetle; reˈla.tion.ship *n.* akrabalık; ilgi, alâka, ilişki.

**rel.a.tive** ['relətiv] **1.** □ göreli, nispî, bağıntılı, izafî; bağlı, ait, ilişkin (to *-e); gr.* nispî, izafî; **2.** *n. gr.* ilgi adılı *(veya* zamiri); akraba, hısım; ˈrel.a.tive.ly *adv.* nispeten, oldukça; rel.aˈtiv.i.ty *n.* izafyet, görelik, nispilik; mensubiyet, ilişkili olma, görelilik.

**re.lax** [riˈlæks] *v/t. & v/i.* gevşe(t)mek, hafifle(t)mek, rahatla(t)mak, yumuşa(t)mak, dinlen(dir)mek, gerginliğini gidermek *veya* kaybetmek; re.laxˈa.tion *n.* gevşeme, rahatlama, dinlenme, rahavet; reˈlaxed *adj.* gevşek; rahat, dinlenmiş; teklifsiz, lâubali.

**re.lay¹** [riˈlei] **1.** *n.* değiştirme atı, nöbetleşe iş gören hayvan *veya* insan(lar) *veya* şey; ⚡ düzenleyici, röle; *radyo:* naklen yayın; ~ race *spor:* bayrak koşusu; **2.** *v/t. radyo:* nakletmek, yaymak.

**re.lay²** ['riːˈlei] *(irr.* lay) *v/t. (kablo, halı vs.)* yeniden döşemek *(veya* sermek).

**re.lease** ['riˈliːs] **1.** *n.* kurtarma, salıverme; *fig.* azadetme, azat olunma; serbest bırak(ıl)ma; *film: oft.* first ~ ilk temsil, ilk gece, vizyona sokma, gösterme; 💿 vazgeçme, ferağat; ⊕, *phot.* deklanşör; ilk basım *(hikâye vs.);* **2.** *v/t.* affetmek, kurtarmak; serbest bırakmak, salıvermek *(from -den);* vazgeçmek, ferağat etm., devir ve ferağ etm., ibra etm.; *film:* gösterilmesine izin vermek, ilk kez göstermek; yayınlanmasına izin vermek *(kitap, plak vs.);* ⊕ harekete geçirmek; *phot.* deklanşöre basmak.

**rel.e.gate** ['religeit] *v/t.* göndermek, sürmek, *b-ni veya bşi* daha aşağı sınıf *(veya* sıraya, yere) indirmek; havale etm. (to *-e);* rel.eˈga.tion *n.* sürgün; daha alt seviyeye indirme; havale etme.

**re.lent** [riˈlent] *v/i.* yumuşamak, acıyıp

merhamete gelmek; şiddetini azaltmak *(rüzgâr)*; re**l**lent.less ☐ merhametsiz, acımayan, şefkatsiz, amansız, zalim.
rel.e.vance, rel.e.van.cy ['relivəns(i)] *n.* ilgi, alâka; uygunluk (to *-e*); **l**rel.e.vant *adj.* (amaca) uygun, ilgili, alâkalı (to *-e*).
re.ll.a.bil.l.ty [rilaiə**l**biliti] *n.* güvenilir olma; re**l**ll.a.ble ☐ güvenilir, emin.
re.ll.ance [ri**l**laiəns] *n.* güven, itimat, emniyet, inanç (on); *fig.* destek, istinat; re**l**ll.ant *adj.* güvenen, inanan, itimat eden, bel bağlayan.
rel.ic ['relik] *n.* kalıntı, bakıye, döküntü, artık; *eccl.* kutsal emanet; anı, yadigâr; ~s *pl.* bir azizin kemikleri; rel.ict ['relikt] *n.* dul *(kadın)*; türü tükenmekte olan bir hayvan *veya* bitki.
re.lief [ri**l**li:f] *n.* ferahlama, iç rahatlaması; teselli, avuntu; ara verme, fasıla; yardım, imdat, bağış; ✕ nöbet değiştirme; ✕ kurtarmaya gelen kuvvetler; ǒǒ mağduriyetin giderilmesi, çare, düzeltme; △ kabartma (iş), rölyef; be on ~ yardım almak *(para vs.)*; poor ~ fakirlere yardım (kuruluşu); ~ work sosyal yardım; ~ works *pl.* işsizlere iş sağlamak amacıyla yapılan yol, köprü *vs.*; stand out in ~ against kontrast teşkil etm., iyice belirmek, göze çarpmak.
re.lieve [ri**l**li:v] *v/t.* hafifletmek, ferahlatmak, yumuşatmak, teskin etm., yatıştırmak, azaltmak; yardım etm. *-e*; ✕ nöbet değiştirmek; ✕ imdada yetişerek kuşatmadan kurtarmak; ǒǒ çare bulmak; hariç tutmak, muaf kılmak (of *-den*), *b-ni bşden* kurtarmak, esirgemek (of); çeşni katmak, renklendirmek *(parti vs.)*; ~ nature, ~ o.s. def'i hacet etm., aptes bozmak, dışarı çıkmak.
re.lie.vo [ri**l**li:vəu] *n.* kabartma, rölyef.
re.ll.gion [ri**l**lidʒən] *n.* din, iman; din duygusu, dindarlık; *fig.* onur meselesi; tapma; ilke edinilen şey.
re.ll.gious ☐ [ri**l**lidʒəs] dinî, dinsel, din...; dindar; *eccl.* tarikat..., mezhep...; dikkatli, itinalı, vicdanlı, sadakatli; re**l**ll.gious.ness *n.* dindarlık.
re.lin.quish [ri**l**liŋkwiʃ] *v/t.* terketmek, bırakmak; vazgeçmek; *-den*, feragat etm., davasından vazgeçmek; re**l**lin.quish.ment *n.* terk, cayma, vazgeçme, feragat (of).
rel.i.quar.y ['relikwəri] *n.* kutsal emanetler mahfazası.
rel.ish ['reliʃ] 1. *n.* tat, lezzet, çeşni; lezlet veren şey *(hardal, salça, v.b.)*; *fig.* tadımlık, örnek, mostra; haz, zevk, sevinç, hoşnutluk; 2. *v/t. & v/i.* severek,

ağız tadıyla yemek; *bşden* hoşlanmak, zevk almak; lezzet vermek, çeşni katmak; beğenmek; lezzetli olm., çeşnisi olm.; *bş* hoşuna gitmek, *bşi* beğenmek (of); did you ~ your dinner? yemek hoşunuza gitti mi?
re.load ['ri:**l**ləud] *v/t.* yeniden yüklemek, doldurmak.
re.lo.ca.tion ['ri:ləu**l**keiʃən] *n.* yeni bir bölgeye yerleştirme *(veya* taşıma, sevketme).
re.luc.tance [ri**l**lʌktəns] *n.* isteksizlik, gönülsüzlük, rızasızlık; *part. phys.* manyetik mukavemet *(veya* direnç); re**l**luc.tant ☐ gönülsüz (olarak), isteksiz(ce), zoraki, istemeyerek; be ~ to do *bşi* yapmak için isteksiz olm., ~ diye *bşi* yapmayacağım diye dayatmak.
re.ly [ri**l**lai] *v/t.:* ~ (up)on *b-ne, bşe* güvenmek, bel bağlamak, itimat etm.
re.main [ri**l**mein] 1. *v/i.* kalmak(ta devam etm.); geri kalmak; (arta) kalmak; durmak; 2. *n.* ~s *pl.* kalıntılar *(yemek artığı, posa, harabe vs.)*; cenaze, ceset; re**l**main.der [~də] *n.* bakıye, artan, geri kalan miktar, kalıntı; *kitapçılık: b-nin* ölümünden sonra basılan eserleri; ǒǒ tekrar intikal.
re.mand [ri**l**ma:nd] 1. *v/t.* (ǒǒ *tutuklu)* tutukvine geri göndermek; iade etm., geri göndermek; be on ~ tutuklu olm.; *prisoner* on ~ tutuklu; ~ home tutukevi *(çocuklar için)*.
re.mark [ri**l**ma:k] 1. *n.* söz, fikir ve mütalâa beyanı; mülâhaza, düşünce; dikkat (etme), farketme; pass a ~ *b-i veya bş* hakkında fikir beyan etm.; 2. *v/t.* farkına varmak, farketmek *-i;* söylemek, demek; *v/i.* fikir beyan etm., düşüncesini söylemek (upon); re**l**mark.a.ble ☐ dikkate değer; olağanüstü, harikulâde; re**l**mark.a.ble.ness *n.* fevkalâdelik, olağanüstü olma; tuhaflık.
re.mar.riage ['ri:**l**mæridʒ] *n.* yeniden evlenme *(veya izdivaç)*; **l**re**l**mar.ry *v/t. & v/i.* yeniden evlenmek.
re.me.di.able ☐ [ri**l**mi:djəbl] çaresi bulunur, iyileştirilebilen; re.me.di.al ☐ [ri**l**mi:djəl] iyileştiren; çare kabilinden.
rem.e.dy ['remidi] *n.* çare, vasıta, düzeltme; ilaç, panzehir; yasal yollar; 2. *v/t.* düzeltmek; çaresini bulmak *-in,* iyileştirmek.
re.mem.ber [ri**l**membə] *v/t.* *bşi* hatırlamak, anımsamak; unutmamak, hatırda tutmak; saygılarını sunmak *(mektupta)*; *(bahşiş, hediye vs.)* vermeyi unutma-

mak; anmak, yâdetmek; ~ me to hlm! ona benden selâm söyleyin!, ona saygılarımı iletin!; re!mem.brance *n.* hatırlama; andaç, yadigâr, hatıra; ~s *pl.* selâm, saygı(lar).

re.mil.i.ta.rize ['ri:'militəraiz] *v/t.* yeniden ordu *veya* silahla donatmak (*ulus vs.'yi*).

re.mind [ri'maind] *v/t. b-ne bşi* hatırlatmak (of), hatırına getirmek; ~ me to answer that letter bana o mektubu yanıtlamayı hatırlat; re!mind.er *n.* hatırlatma; hatırlatan *b-i veya bş*, tekit, üsteleme.

rem.i.nis.cence [remi'nisns] *n.* anımsama, hatırlama (*geçmişi*); hatıra, hatırlanan şey; rem.i!nis.cent ☐ hatırlatan, anımsatan, andıran (of *-i*); hatırlayan; hatıra...; be ~ of *b-ne bşi* hatırlatmak, anımsatmak.

re.miss [ri'mis] ☐ üşengeç, miskin, tembel; ihmalkâr, gevşek, kayıtsız; re!mis.si.ble *adj.* affedilebilir; re!mis.sion *n.* af, bağışlama (*borç vs.*); günah çıkarma; hafifle(t)me (*humma hastalığı vs.*); cezasını azaltma; ~ of fees ücretleri eksiltme (*veya* azaltma); re!miss.ness *n.* ihmal, kusur, kabahat, özensizlik.

re.mit [ri'mit] *v/t. & v/i.* affetmek, bağışlamak; *b-nin* borcunu silmek; *b-ni* bir cezadan affetmek; ara vermek, vazgeçmek *-den; bb* yeniden görüşülmek üzere *b-ne* havale etm., yollamak, göndermek, havale etm. (*para*); azalmak, eksilmek, inmek, dinmek; re!mit.tance *n.* (*part. para*) gönderme, havale etme; gönderilen para; ✝ poliçe, römiz; re.mit!tee *n.* alıcı, adına gönderilen; re!mit.tent *adj.* artıp eksilen, azalıp çoğalan; bir iyileşip bir kötüleşen (*humma vs.*); re!mit.ter *n.* (*para*) gönderen; affeden *veya* bağışlayan; *bb b-ni* eski makamına iade etme kararı; ✝ poliçe eden (*veya* gönderen).

rem.nant ['remnənt] *n.* bakıye, artık, döküntü, kalıntı; kumaş parçası; ~ sale parça *veya* kilo ile kumaş satışı.

re.mod.el ['ri:'mɔdl] *v/t.* değişiklikler yapmak *-de*, şeklini değiştirmek *-in*, yeni şekline koymak *-i*.

re.mon.strance [ri'mɔnstrəns] *n.* itiraz, protesto, çıkış, şikâyet, sitem; re!mon.strant *n.* itiraz eden kimse; re.mon.strate ['remənstreit] *v/i.* protesto etm. (against, on, with *-i*); *v/t.* itiraz etm. (that *-e*).

re.morse [ri'mɔ:s] *n.* vicdan azabı, pişmanlık, nedamet; re!morse.ful ☐ [~ful] pişman, tövbeli, nadim; re!morse.less ☐ merhametsiz, katı yürekli, amansız, gad-

dar, acımayan.

re.mote ☐ [ri'məut] uzak(ta), ırak; **bambaşka, büyük farklılıklar gösteren** (*teori vs.*); çok seyrek olan; pek az (*olasılık vs.*); ~ control uzaktan kontrol (*cihazı*); re!mote.ness *n.* uzaklık.

re.mount 1. [ri:'maunt] *vb.* tekrar **binmek** (*at vs.*); tırmanmak (*merdiven, tepe vs.*); dinlenmiş at vermek (*b-ne, orduya*); çerçevelemek (*resim vs.*); 2. ['ri:-maunt] *n.* yedek at; ✗ yedek süvari atları dairesi.

re.mov.a.ble [ri'mu:vəbl] *adj.* kaldırılabilir, uzaklaştırılabilir, nakledilebilir; **adledilebilir; temizlenebilir;** re!mov.al [~vəl] *n.* kaldır(ıl)ma; taşınma, nakil; yol verme, ihraç etme (from office *görevden*); ~ van nakliye kamyonu; re!move 1. *v/t.* kaldırmak, uzaklaştırmak, ortadan kaldırmak, toparlayıp kaldırmak; yerini değiştirmek, başka yere nakletmek; yol vermek, azletmek (from office); temizlemek, izale etm.; *v/i.* taşınmak; başka yere naklolmak, gitmek; 2. *n.* uzaklaş(tır)ma; ayrılıp gitme, yer değiştirme; derece, kademe; get one's ~ ara sınıfa alınmak (*İngiltere'de*); re!mov.er *n.* leke *vs.* giderici; nakliyeci.

re.mu.ner.ate [ri'mju:nəreit] *v/t.* ödüllendirmek, mükâfatını vermek; hakkını vermek, emeğinin karşılığını vermek; re.mu.ner!a.tion *n.* ödül, mükâfat; karşılık, hak, ücret; re!mu.ner.a.tive ☐ [~rətiv] kârlı, kazançlı.

Ren.ais.sance [ri'neisəns] *n.* Rönesans.

re.nal *anat.* ['ri:nl] *adj.* böbreklere ait.

re.name ['ri:'neim] *v/t.* yeni bir ad vermek *-e*.

re.nas.cence [ri'næsns] *n.* yeniden doğma, canlanma, uyanma, yenilenme; the ♀ Rönesans; re!nas.cent *adj.* yeniden doğan, canlanan.

rend [rend] (*irr.*) *v/t. & v/i.* yırt(ıl)mak, parçala(n)mak.

ren.der ['rendə] *v/t.* kılmak, yapmak, etmek; iade etm., geri vermek; göstermek (*iyi muamele, teveccüh vs.*), şükranlarını sunmak (*esp. Tanrıya*); tercüme etm., çevirmek (into *-e*); teslim etm.; ♪ çalmak, icra etm.; anlatmak, anlamını açıklamak; ✝ tevdi etm., görmek, vermek (*hesap*); eritmek (*yağ*); birinci katını sürmek (*sıva*); !ren.der.ing *n.* iade, tediye, ödeme, tercüme, açıklama; ♪ icra; *theat.* temsil, oynama.

ren.dez.vous ['rɔndivu:] *n.* randevu (yeri), buluşma (yeri).

ren.di.tion [ren'diʃən] *n.* tercüme, tefsir;

icra, temsil; teslim, ödeme.

**ren.e.gade** ['renigeid] *n.* mürtet, dinden dönen kimse; ülkesinden kaçan kimse, firarî.

**re.new** [ri'njuː] *v/t.* yenile(ştir)mek, yenisi ile değiştirmek; **re'new.al** *n.* yenile(n)me; yenilenen şey.

**ren.net** ['renit] *n.* yoğurt (*veya* peynir) mayası.

**re.nom.i.nate** [riː'nɔmineit] *v/t.* yeniden atamak (*veya* görevlendirmek).

**re.nounce** [ri'nauns] *v/t.* terketmek *-i*; vazgeçmek *-den*, reddetmek *-i*, tanımamak, yadsımak *-i*; *v/i. iskambil:* başka renkten kâğıt atmak.

**ren.o.vate** ['renəuveit] *v/t.* yenileştirmek, tazele(ştir)mek; **ren.o'va.tion** *n.* yenileme, onarım; **'ren.o.va.tor** *n.* yenileştiren kimse.

**re.nown** [ri'naun] *n.* şöhret, ün; **re'nowned** *adj.* ünlü, meşhur.

**rent¹** [rent] **1.** *rent* & *p.p.* of rend; **2.** *n.* yırtık, yarık, çatlak; bölünme (*a. fig.*).

**rent²** [~] **1.** *n.* kira (bedeli); **2.** *vb.* kiralamak, kira ile vermek *veya* tutmak; kira getirmek; **'rent.a.ble** *adj.* kiralanabilir; kira getirebilir; **'rent.al** *n.* kira bedeli; ~ value kira değeri (*veya* ederi); **'rent- -charge** *n.* kira üzerinden alınan vergi; **'rent.er** *n.* kiracı; film kiraya veren kimse; **'rent-'free** *adj.* kirasız, bedava.

**re.nun.ci.a.tion** [rinʌnsi'eiʃən] *n.* vazgeçme, feragat, terk (of).

**re.o.pen** ['riː'əupən] *v/t.* & *v/i.* yeniden aç(ıl)mak, yeniden başla(t)mak.

**re.or.ga.ni.za.tion** ['riːɔːgənai'zeiʃən] *n.* reorganizasyon, yeniden örgütle(n)me (*veya* düzenleme); † ıslah; **'re'or.gan.ize** *v/t.* düzenlemek, reorganize etm.; † ıslah ederek sağlamlaştırmak.

**rep¹** [rep] *n.* koltuk, sandalye döşemesinde kullanılan kalın kumaş.

**rep²** *sl.* [~] *n.* hovarda, çapkın; ün, şöhret, nam.

**rep³** F [~] *n.* repertuvarındaki piyesleri birbiri ardına değişik günlerde oynayan tiyatro topluluğu.

**re.pack** ['riː'pæk] *v/t.* yeniden denk yapmak, ambalajını değiştirmek.

**re.paint** ['riː'peint] *v/t.* yeniden boyamak, badana etm.

**re.pair¹** [ri'pɛə] **1.** *n.* tamir, onarma; ~s *pl.* tamirat, onarım; ~ shop tamir evi; in good ~ iyi durumda, iyi halde bulunan; out of ~ yıkılmağa yüz tutan, kötü durumda; **2.** *v/t.* tamir etm., onarmak, düzeltmek, restore etm., yenilemek; telâfi etm., tazminat vermek *-e*.

**re.pair²** [~] *v/i.*: ~ to gitmek, çekilmek.

**rep.a.ra.ble** ['repərəbl] *adj.* tamir edilebilir; **rep.a'ra.tion** *n.* onar(ıl)ma, onarım; özür dileme, tarziye; ~s *pl. pol.* tazminat; make ~s *pol.* (*harp*) tazminat vermek.

**rep.ar.tee** [repaː'tiː] *n.* hazırcevap sözlerle konuşma, hazırcevaplık; be good at ~ hazırcevap olm.

**re.par.ti.tion** ['riːpaː'tiʃən] *n.* yeniden dağıtım (*veya* bölme).

**re.pass** ['riːpaːs] *v/i.* geri gitmek, dönmek; *v/t.* yeniden *b-nin* yanından geçmek.

**re.past** [ri'paːst] *n.* yemek (vakti), öğün.

**re.pa.tri.ate** **1.** [riː'pætrieit] *v/t. b-ni* kendi vatanına göndermek *veya* getirtmek; **2.** [~it] *n.* evine (*veya* yurduna) dönen kimse; **re.pa.tri.a.tion** ['~'eiʃən] *n.* kendi vatanına dönme.

**re.pay** (*irr.* pay) [riː'pei] *v/t.* geri ödemek; *fig.* karşılık vermek, misilleme yapmak; tazminat vermek; ödüllendirmek, *-in* karşılığını verrmek; **re'pay.a.ble** *adj.* geri ödenebilir, karşılığı verilir; **re'pay.ment** *n.* geri ödeme, tediye; karşılık, mukabele.

**re.peal** [ri'piːl] **1.** *n.* iptal, ilga, fesih, yürürlükten kaldırma (*yasa*); **2.** *v/t.* yürürlükten kaldırmak, feshetmek, iptal etm. (*yasa*).

**re.peat** [ri'piːt] **1.** *v/t.* & *v/i.* tekrarlamak, bir daha yapmak; bir daha söylemek, yinelemek; ezberden okumak; aynını söylemek *veya* yapmak; yasaya aykırı olarak ikinci kez *oy* vermek; (*silah*) kesintisiz ateş etm.; tekrarlanmak, yinelenmek; ~ an order for s.th. tekrar ısmarlamak; **2.** *n.* tekrarla(n)ma; tekrarlanan şey; *oft.* ~ an order tekrar sipariş verme; ♪ tekrar (işareti); **re'peat.ed** □ mükerrer, tekrarlanan; **re'peat.er** *n.* tekrarlayan *b-i veya bş;* tekrarlanan ondalık kesir; makineli tüfek; sabıkalı, bir kaç kez hapse girip çıkmış *b-i;* *tel.* bir mesajı zayıf devreden kuvvetli devreye nakleden otomatik röle; çalar saat.

**re.pel** [ri'pel] *v/t.* püskürtmek, defetmek; reddetmek; *fig.* tiksindirmek, nefret ettirmek; **re'pel.lent** *adj.* uzaklaştırıcı; tiksindirici, iğrenç.

**re.pent** [ri'pent] *v/t. a.* ~ of pişman olm. *-e*, tövbe etm. *-e.*

**re.pent.ance** [ri'pentəns] *n.* pişmanlık, nedamet, tövbe; **re'pent.ant** *adj.* pişman (olan). nadim, tövbekâr.

**re.peo.ple** ['riː'piːpl] *v/t.* nüfusu artırmak; yeni insanlar yerleştirmek.

**re.per.cus.sion** [riːpəˈkʌʃən] *n.* geri tepme; akis, yankı; *fig.* ters tepki, reaksiyon.

**rep.er.toire** *thea. etc.* [ˈrepətwɑː] *n.* repertuvar.

**rep.er.to.ry** [ˈrepətəri] *n. thea.* temsile hazır oyunlar, repertuvar; *fig.* zengin kaynak.

**rep.e.ti.tion** [repiˈtiʃən] *n.* tekrarla(n)ma; ezberden okuma; ezbere okunan parça; ～ order ʈ tekrar sipariş (etme).

**re.pine** [riˈpain] *v/i.* yakınmak, hoşnut olmamak, şikâyet etm. *-den*, homurdanmak, mırıldanmak, üzülmek (at *-e*); **re-ˈpin.ing** □ somurtkan, homurdanan, asık suratlı, hoşnutsuz, memnun olmayan.

**re.place** [riˈpleis] *v/t.* tekrar yerine koymak; *-in* yerini almak; *b-nin* yerine geçmek; ödemek; **reˈplace.ment** *n.* yerine geçen şey *-in*; tekrar yerine koyma; *b-nin* yerine geçen kimse; yedek kuvvet.

**re.plant** [ˈriːˈplɑːnt] *v/t.* etrafına bitki (*veya* ağaç vs.) dikmek.

**re.plen.ish** [riˈpleniʃ] *v/t.* tekrar doldurmak; **reˈplen.ish.ment** *n.* tekrar doldur(ul)ma ,ikmal.

**re.plete** [riˈpliːt] *adj.* dolu, dolmuş (with *ile*), ikmal edilmiş, depolanmış; **reˈpletion** *n.* çokluk, bolluk, bol bol mevcut olma.

**rep.li.ca** [ˈreplikə] *n. paint. etc.* kopya, suret; *fig.* tam benzeri, örnek, numune.

**rep.li.ca.tion** [repliˈkeiʃən] *n.* ٥ davacının mahkemeye verdiği yanıt; eko, akis; kopya, suret.

**re.ply** [riˈplai] **1.** *vb.* cevap vermek, yanıtlamak (to *-e*, *-i*); karşılık vermek, mukabele etm.; **2.** *n.* cevap, yanıt, karşılık; ～ postcard yanıtlı kartpostal.

**re.port** [riˈpɔːt] **1.** *n.* rapor (on); haber, gazete haberi; bilgi; bildiri; söylenti, rivayet, şayia; (iyi) ün, şöhret; patlama (sesi), infilâk (sesi); not karnesi, diploma; **2.** *v/t.* bildirmek, haber vermek; anlatmak; söylemek; (rapor) vermek *veya* yazmak; raportörlük etm. (on, upon); geldiğini haber vermek (to *-e*); **reˈport.er** *n.* muhabir; raportör; muhbir.

**re.pose** [riˈpəuz] **1.** *n. com.* rahat, huzur (*a. fig.*), istirahat, sükûn; ahenk; **2.** *v/t.* yatırmak, dinlendirmek, rahat (*veya* huzur) sağlamak; ～ trust *etc.* in güvenmek *-e*, itimat etm. *-e*; *v/i. a.* ～ o.s. istirahat etm., yatmak, dinlenmek, uyumak; dayanmak (on *-e*); **re.pos.i.to.ry** [riˈpɔzitəri] *n.* mahfaza (*kutu, dolap, oda vs.*), depo, antrepo; *fig.* zengin kaynak; sırdaş.

**rep.re.hend** [repriˈhend] *v/t.* azarlamak,

tekdir etm.; **rep.reˈhen.si.ble** □ [～səbl] azarlanmayı hakeden, kınanacak, kötü; **rep.reˈhen.sion** *n.* ihtar, kınama, azar tekdir.

**rep.re.sent** [repriˈzent] *vb.* göstermek; cisimlendirmek, şahıslandırmak; *thea.* (*piyes*) oynamak, rolünü yapmak; anlatmak, tasvir etm.; temsil etm; olduğunu *veya* olacağını söylemek, belirtmek, ifade etm. (as); *b-ni veya bşi* temsil etm., *b-ne* vekâlet etm.; **rep.re.senˈta.tion** *n.* temsil (edilme); göster(il)me; tasvir, anlatım; *thea.* oyun, temsil, piyes; fikir, düşünce; ٥, *pol.* vekillik, vekâlet; önerme; simge, işaret; **rep.reˈsent.a.tive** □ [～tətiv] **1.** temsil eden, numune olan, örnek..., tipik, karakteristik (of *-in*); ～ government seçimle iş başına gelen (*veya* temsile dayanan, temsili) hükümet; **2.** *n.* vekil; mümessil, temsilci; milletvekili; House of ٤s *Am. parl.* Temsilciler Meclisi.

**re.press** [riˈpres] *v/t.* bastırmak, baskı altında tutmak; *psych.* ihtibas etm., bilinçdışına itmek (*duygu, istek vs.*); kontrol altına almak; **reˈpres.sion** *n.* bastır(ıl)ma, baskı altında tut(ul)ma; tutma, zaptetme, ihtibas, ket vurma (*duygu*); **reˈpres.sive** □ bastırıcı, baskı altında tutan, engelleyici, sıkı.

**re.prieve** [riˈpriːv] **1.** *n.* geçici olarak erteleme, tehir, (ölüm cezasının infazını) geciktirme; **2.** *v/t.* geçici olarak ertelemek, tehir etm., süre tanımak, (ölüm cezasının infazını) geciktirmek.

**rep.ri.mand** [ˈreprimɑːnd] **1.** *n.* azar, paylama, tekdir; **2.** *v/t.* azarlamak, paylamak *-i*; resmen kınamak *-i*.

**re.print** [ˈriːˈprint] **1.** *v/t.* yeni baskısını yapmak, tekrar basmak; **2.** *n.* yeni baskı.

**re.pris.al** [riˈpraizəl] *n.* misilleme, karşılık, zorunlu önlem.

**re.proach** [riˈprəutʃ] **1.** *n.* ayıp(lama), serzeniş, tekdir, azar; yüz karası (olan *b-i veya bş*); **2.** *v/t.* ayıplamak, serzenişte bulunmak, *b-ni bşden* dolayı kınamak (with); azarlamak (for *için*, *-den dolayı*); **reˈproach.ful** □ [～ful] sitem dolu, serzenişkâr, ayıplayan; yüz kızartıcı, utanılacak.

**rep.ro.bate** [ˈreprəubeit] **1.** *adj.* ahlâkı bozuk, sefih, serseri; **2.** *n.* ahlâkı bozuk (*veya* serseri) kimse; **3.** *v/t.* ayıplamak, uygun görmemek, tel'in etm., lânetlemek; **rep.roˈba.tion** *n.* ayıplama, lânet (leme); mahkûmiyet, reddolunma.

**re.pro.duce** [riːprəˈdjuːs] *v/t.* yeniden meydana getirmek, yaratmak; çoğaltmak; kopya etm., taklit etm., reprodüksiyon yapmak *(resim vs.)*; *thea. (piyes)* yeniden oynamak; *v/i.* çoğalmak, üremek; **re.pro.duc.tion** [~ˈdʌkʃən] *n.* çoğalma, üreme, yayılma *(a. physiol.)*; kopya, reprodüksiyon; **re.proˈduc.tive** □ üretken, üreyen, çoğalan; kopya etme ile ilgili, reprodüksiyon...

**re.proof¹** [riˈpruːf] *n.* azar, paylama, serzeniş.

**re.proof²** [ˈriːˈpruːf] *v/t.* yeniden emprenye etm., su geçirmez yapmak *(yağmurluk, çadır vs.)*.

**re.prov.al** [riˈpruːvəl] *n.* azar(lama), sitem, paylama, tekdir; **reˈprove** *v/t.* ayıplamak, azarlamak, tekdir etm.

**rep.tile** [ˈreptail] **1.** *n.* sürüngen *(yılan, timsah vs.)*; *fig.* aşağılık kimse, dalkavuk; **2.** *adj.* sürüngenlerle ilgili, sürünen; *fig.* alçak, sefil.

**re.pub.lic** [riˈpʌblik] *n.* cumhuriyet; **reˈpub.li.can 1.** *adj.* cumhuriyete ait; **2.** *n.* cumhuriyetçi; **reˈpub.li.can.ism** *n.* cumhuriyetçilik, cumhuriyet idaresi.

**re.pub.li.ca.tion** [ˈriːpʌbliˈkeiʃən] *n.* yeniden yayınlama *(veya* basma, neşretme); yeni bası.

**re.pub.lish** [ˈriːˈpʌbliʃ] *v/t.* yeniden yayınlamak *(veya* neşretmek).

**re.pu.di.ate** [riˈpjuːdieit] *v/t.* tanımamak, reddetmek, kabul etmemek; yadsımak *(çocuğunu, borcunu vs.)*; **re.pu.diˈa.tion** *n.* ret, yadsıma, tanımama.

**re.pug.nance** [riˈpʌgnəns] *n.* nefret, tiksinme, isteksizlik, antipati (to *-e*); **reˈpug.nant** □ iğrenç, çirkin, tiksinti veren, hoş olmayan, can sıkıcı.

**re.pulse** [riˈpʌls] **1.** *n.* püskürtme, bozguna uğratma; *fig.* ret, kabul etmeme, defetme; **2.** *v/t.* püskürtmek, kovmak; *fig.* reddetmek, defetmek; **reˈpul.sion** *n. phys.* iteleme; *fig.* nefret, tiksinme, tiksinti ve korku (of *-den)*; **reˈpul.sive** □ *fig.* iğrenç, tiksindirici, mide bulandıran; *phys.* uzaklaştıran, geri itici, defedici.

**re.pur.chase** [riˈpəːtʃəs] **1.** *n.* tekrar satın alma; **2.** *v/t.* geri satın almak.

**rep.u.ta.ble** □ [ˈrepjutəbl] saygıdeğer, muhterem; şerefli, namuslu; **rep.u.ta.tion** [repjuˈteiʃən] *n. (part. iyi)* şöhret, ün, itibar, şeref; **re.pute** [riˈpjuːt] **1.** *n.* ün, şöhret, itibar; by ~ ismen, ününden *(tanımak)*; **2.** *v/t.* saymak, kabul etm., farzetmek, itibar etm.; be ~d to be *veya* as ...sayılmak, farzedilmek, addedilmek; be well (ill) ~d iyi (kötü) sanılmak, farzedilmek, bilinmek; **reˈput.ed** *adj.* ünlü,

namlı, şöhretli; ...sayılan, farzedilen, sözüm ona, denen, diye; **reˈput.ed.ly** *adv.* sözde, söylenenlere göre, güya.

**re.quest** [riˈkwest] **1.** *n.* rica, dilek, istek; ⊤ talep, rağbet; at s.o.'s ~ *b-nin* ricası üzerine; by ~, on ~ arzu edilirse, istenildiği zaman, rica üzerine; in (great) ~ (çok) aranılan, rağbet gören; ~ stop ihtiyarî durak; *(musical)* ~ programme dinleyici isteklerinden oluşan (müzik) program(ı); **2.** *v/t.* rica etm., dilemek (from *-den)*.

**re.qui.em** [ˈrekwiem] *n.* ölünün ruhu için okunan dua *(hıristiyanlıkta)*; bu tören için yazılan dinsel müzik.

**re.quire** [riˈkwaiə] *v/t.* gerektirmek, istemek, talep etm. (of *-i)*; muhtaç olm., gereksinimi olm. (of *-e)*; ~ (of) s.o. to *b-ne* ...nı emretmek, istemek; **reˈquired** *adj.* gerekli, lüzumlu; **reˈquire.ment** *n.* gereksinim, ihtiyaç; lüzum, koşul; *fig.* talep.

**req.ui.site** [ˈrekwizit] **1.** *adj.* gerekli, elzem (for); **2.** *n.* gerekli şey, elzem şey; toilet ~s *pl.* tuvalet eşyası; **req.uiˈsi.tion** **1.** *n.* rica, talep, başvuru; ✗ elkoyma; **2.** *v/t.* ✗ el koymak, zaptetmek *(resmî olarak)*; istemek, talep etm.

**re.quit.al** [riˈkwaitl] *n.* misilleme, karşılık; mukabele, bedel.

**re.quite** [riˈkwait] *v/t. b-ni* ödüllendirmek, mükâfatlandırmak, -in karşılığını vermek, misilleme yapmak; hak edilen ödül *veya* cezayı vermek.

**re-read** [ˈriːˈriːd] *(irr.* read) *v/t.* yeniden okumak.

**re.scind** [riˈsind] *v/t.* feshetmek, iptal etm.; vazgeçmek.

**re.scis.sion** [riˈsiʒən] *n.* fesih, iptal, ilga, yürürlükten kaldırma.

**re.script** [ˈriːskript] *n.* emir, karar(name), tamim.

**res.cue** [ˈreskjuː] **1.** *n.* kurtuluş, kurtarış; *(♂ yasal gözetimden)* kurtulma, kurtarılma; **2.** *v/t.* kurtarmak; *(♂ yasal gözetimden)* bağışık kılmak, muaf tutmak; **ˈres.cu.er** *n.* kurtarıcı, halâskâr.

**re.search** [riˈsəːtʃ] **1.** *n.* araştırma, tetkik, inceleme; **2.** *v/i.* araştırma yapmak (into, on *-da)*; **reˈsearch.er** *n.* araştırıcı, araştırmacı.

**re.seat** [ˈriːˈsiːt] *v/t.* yeni sandalye koymak, oturacak yeni yer sağlamak; yeniden oturtmak.

**re.se.da** [ˈriːsidə] *n.* ✿ muhabbetçiçeği.

**re.sell** [ˈriːsel] *(irr.* sell) *v/t.* yeniden satmak; **reˈsell.er** *n.* yeniden satan.

**re.sem.blance** [riˈzembləns] *n.* benzeyiş, benzerlik (to *-e)*; bear ~ to ile benzerliği olm.; re'sem.ble [~bl] *v/t.* benzemek *-e,* andırmak *-i.*

re.sent [ri'zent] *v/t. bşden* dolayı *b-ne* gücenmek, darılmak, içerlemek; alınmak *-den;* re'sent.ful □ [~ful] gücenik, dargın, alıngan; ~ of darılmış, gücenmiş *-e;* re'sent.ment *n.* gücenme, darılma, içerleme, kızma.

res.er.va.tion [rezə'veiʃən] *n.* 𝄢 ihtiraz kaydı, çekince; *Am. pol.* yerlilere ayrılmış bölge; yer ayırtma, rezervasyon; ayrılmış yer *(oda vs.);* kuşku, şüphe.

re.serve [ri'zə:v] **1.** *n.* yedek olarak saklanan şey, stok; ♀ fon, karşılık, ihtiyat ( *veya* yedek) akçesi; yedek, ihtiyat *(a.* ✕); çekingenlik, ağırbaşlılık, açılamama; ağız sıkılığı; ✝ ihtiraz kaydı, çekince, rezerv; *spor:* yedek *(oyuncu);* bir amaç için ayrılmış arazi; in ~ yedek olarak elde mevcut; with certain ~s belli koşullarla, belli ihtiraz kaydıyla; **2.** *v/t.* saklamak, tasarruf etm., rezerve etm.; ayırtmak, rezerve ettirmek *(yer vs.); (hakkını)* muhafaza etm., sonraya bırakmak *-i;* re'served □ *fig.* ağzı sıkı; sesi çıkmaz, çekingen; saklı tutulmuş, mahfuz.

re.serv.ist ✕ [ri'zə:vist] *n.* yedek, ihtiyat.

res.er.voir [ˈrezəvwa] *n.* su haznesi, rezervuar; havza; *fig.* hazne.

re.set [ˈriːˈset] *(irr.* set) *v/t.* yeniden yerine koymak, yerleştirmek; bilemek, keskinleştirmek *(testere vs.); typ.* yeniden dizmek; ayarlamak *(saat).*

re.set.tle [ˈriːˈsetl] *v/t.* & *v/i.* yeni bir ülkeye yerleş(tir)mek, iskân et(tir)mek; re'set.tle.ment *n.* yeni bir ülkeye yerleşme, iskân.

re.ship [ˈriːˈʃip] *v/t.* yeniden gemi ile nakletmek *(veya* gemiye yüklemek).

re.shuf.fle [ˈriːˈʃʌfl] **1.** *v/t.* & *v/i.* değişiklikler yapmak, değiştirmek; *(oyun kâğıtlarını)* yeniden karıştırmak; **2.** *n.* değişiklikler yapma, yeniden kurma.

re.side [ri'zaid] *v/i.* oturmak, ikamet etm.; ~ in *-de* bulunmak; ait olm. *-e (güç, hak vs.);* res.i.dence [ˈrezidəns] *n.* ikamet(gâh), ev, mesken; bir yerde oturma; ~ permit ikamet tezkeresi; ˈres.i.dent **1.** *adj.* oturan, yerleşmiş, sakin, mukim; **2.** *n.* bir yerde oturan kimse, yerli; *(sömürgede)* devlet temsilcisi, genel vali; res.i.den.tial [~ˈdenʃəl] *adj.* ikametgâh...; içinde oturulur, oturmaya ayrılmış.

re.sid.u.al [ri'zidjuəl] *adj.* artan, kalan; tortu niteliğinde; re'sid.u.ar.y *adj.* artan, geri kalan; res.i.due [ˈrezidjuː] *n.* artan miktar, artık; 𝄢 ölen *b-nin* borç ve va-

siyetinden artan tereke; re.sid.u.um [riˈzidjuəm] *n. part.* 𝄢 tortu, posa; çöküntü, *(a. fig.);* ♀ kalan bakiye.

re.sign [ri'zain] *v/t.* bırakmak, terketmek; vazgeçmek *-den;* (görevden) istifa etm., çekilmek; ~ o.s. to baş eğmek *-e; bşle* yetinmek; *v/i.* istifa etm., çekilmek; tevekkül göstermek; res.ig.na.tion [rezigˈneiʃən] *n.* istifa, çekilme; tevekkül, uysallık; re.signed □ [riˈzaind] baş eğmiş, uysal, teslimiyet göstermiş, mütevekkil, işi oluruna bırakmış; istifa etmiş.

re.sil.i.ence [riˈziliəns] *n.* elâstikiyet, esneklik, geri fırlama; *fig.* kabiliyet, kuvvet, iktidar; re'sil.i.ent *adj.* elâstiki, esnek; *k-ni* çabuk toparlayan *(insan); fig.* kabiliyetli, kuvvetli, takatlı.

res.in [ˈrezin] **1.** *n.* sakız, reçine; **2.** *v/t.* reçinelemek *-i;* ˈres.in.ous *adj.* reçineli, sakızlı.

re.sist [riˈzist] *v/t.* karşı koymak, direnmek, mukavemet etm. *-e;* dayanmak, tahammül etm. *-e;* re.sist.ance *n.* direniş, mukavemet, karşı koyma, .rezistans, direnç *(a. phys., ≠;* to *-e);* line of least ~ en kolay yol, çözüm; *attr.* mukavemet...; re'sist.ant *adj.* karşı koyan, direnen, dayanıklı, mukavemetli, dirençli (to *-e);* re'sis.tor *n. ≠* rezistan(s), direnç.

re.sole [ˈriːˈsoul] *v/t.* yeni pençe *(veya* taban) geçirmek.

res.o.lute □ [ˈrezəluːt] kararlı, azimli, sebatlı, tereddütsüz; cesur, yiğit; ˈres.o.lute.ness *n.* azim(kârlık), sebat, kararlılık, metanet; cesaret, yiğitlik.

res.o.lu.tion [rezəˈluːʃən] *n. phys.,* ♀, ♪ ayrışma, çözme, çözüm; kararlılık, azim; *parl.* önerge; karar; çözüm, açıklama.

re.solv.a.ble [riˈzɔvəbl] *adj.* çözümlenebilir, halledilebilir.

re.solve [riˈzɔlv] **1.** *v/t.* çözmek, ayırmak (into *-e; a.* ♀, ♀, ♪); *fig.* halletmek *(soru);* ortadan kaldırmak *(sorun);* kararlaştırmak (to *-i);* ~ o.s. (itself) into *-e* dönüşmek, halini almak; ayrışmak; *v/i. a.* ~ o.s. karar vermek, kararlaştırma, tasarlamak; ~ (up)on azmetmek, *bşe* kesin karar vermek, karara varmak; **2.** *n.* karar, hüküm, tasarlama; *lit.* azim(kârlık); re'solved □ azimli, kararlı, tereddütsüz.

res.o.nance [ˈreznəns] *n.* yankılama, aksiseda, rezonans; ˈres.o.nant □ yankılayan, *(sesi)* aksettiren; tanınan; tok sesli.

re.sorp.tion *physiol.* [riˈsɔːpʃən] *n.* em(il)me.

re.sort [riˈzɔːt] **1.** *n.* dinlenme yeri, mesire; sık sık gidilen, uğranılan yer; barınak, sığınacak yer; çare; yardımına başvurulan kişi *veya* şey; health ~ kaplıca, ılıcalar; seaside ~ plâj (kenti); summer ~ sayfiye, yazlık; in the last ~ son çare olarak; 2. *v/i.* ~ to sık sık gitmek *-e*, ziyaret etm. *-i (yer)*; başvurmak *-e*, *bşden* çare aramak.

re.sound [ri'zaund] *v/i.* çınlamak, yankılamak (with *ile*).

re.source [ri'sɔ:s] *n. (doğal)* kaynak, zenginlik; çare, yardım kaynağı, vasıta; halletme yeteneği, kafalılık, iş bilme, beceriklilik; oyalanma; oyalayan, vakit geçirten şey, dinlendiren meşgale; ~s *pl.* olanaklar, imkânlar; re'source.ful □ [~ful] becerikli, hünerli, mahir; zengin kaynaklı; re'source.ful.ness *n.* zenginlik, servet; beceriklilik.

re.spect [ris'pekt] 1. *n.* saygı, hürmet, itibar (to, of *-e*); münasebet, ilgi, alâka, oran, nispet, husus, cihet; takdir, hürmet (for *-e*); ~s *pl.* selâmlar, saygılar, hürmetler; with ~ to *-e* gelince, ... hakkında, ait, nispetle, göre; in ~ of ...bakımından, ...gözönüne alındığında; pay one's ~s on s.o. *b-ne* nezaket ziyaretinde bulunmak, saygılarını sunmak; 2. *v/t. b-ne* saygı göstermek, hürmet etm.; *bşe* riayet etm.; *k-ne* özsaygısı olm.; re.spect.a'bil.i.ty *n.* saygınlık, itibar, saygıdeğer olma; *†* ekonomik açıdan güçlü, güvenilir olma; respectabilities *pl.* âdabı muaşeret, görgü kuralları; re'spect.a.ble □ namuslu, iffetli, saygın; epeyce, haylı, kayda değer; *part. †* ekonomik itibarı sağlam; re'spect.ful □ [~ful] saygılı, hürmet eden, nazik, terbiyeli; Yours ~ly derin saygıyla sunarım *(mektupta)*; re'spect.ful.ness *n.* saygılı olma, hürmetkârlık; re'spect.ing *prep. -e* bakımından, *-c* gelince, *-e* ilişkin; re'spec.tive □ ayrı ayrı, her biri *k-nin* olan; we went to our ~ places her birimiz kendi evimize gittik; re'spec.tive.ly *adv.* sırası ile, biri birine ve diğeri ötekine ait olmak üzere, biri ... öteki...

res.pi.ra.tion [respə'reiʃən] *n.* nefes (alma), soluma, teneffüs; soluk.

res.pi.ra.tor ['respəreitə] *n.* gaz maskesi, nefes filtresi, respirator; *†* solunum cihazı; re.spir.a.to.ry [ris'paiərətəri] *adj.* solunumla ilgili, solunum...

re.spire [ris'paiə] *v/i.* teneffüs etm., nefes almak, soluk almak; *fig.* ferahlamak, soluk almak.

res.pite ['respait] 1. *n.* ♂ mühlet, mehil, tecil, vâde, süre, geçici erteleme; pay dos, ara, fasıla; 2. *v/t.* ertelemek, tehir etm.; mühlet vermek *-e*.

re.splend.ence, re.splend.en.cy [ris'plendəns(i)] *n.* parlaklık, parıltı; *fig.* şaşaa, ihtişam, debdebe, lüks; re'splend.ent □ parlak, göz alıcı; şaşaalı, ihtişamlı.

re.spond [ri'spɔnd] *v/i.* cevap vermek, karşılık vermek, mukabelede bulunmak (to *-e*); re'spond.ent 1. *adj.* ♂♂ savunan, dâvalı; ~ to karşılık veren, cevap veren *-e*; 2. *n.* ♂♂ savunan, dâvalı kimse.

re.sponse [ris'pɔns] *n.* cevap (verme), yanıt, karşılık; *fig.* tepki, reaksiyon (to *-e*). re.spon.si.bil.i.ty [rispɔnsi'biliti] *n.* sorumluluk (for, of *-in*); güvenilirlik; *†* ödeme gücü, sağlamlık; re'spon.si.ble *adj.* sorumlu, mesul (for *-den*, to *-e*); güvenilir; *†* ödeme gücü olan; be ~ for *bşde* suçu olm., kabahati olm., *bşin* nedeni olm., sorumlusu olm.; re'spon.sive □ cevap veren, karşılık...; *bş* karşısında duygulu, duyarlı, hassas, uyumlu (to *-e*).

rest¹ [rest] 1. *n.* rahat, huzur, sükûnet, sessizlik; istirahat, dinlenme; uyku; *fig.* ölüm; mesnet, dayanak, destek; ♪ es, fasıla, durak işareti; at ~ hareketsiz; rahatta; ölmüş; 2. *v/i.* dinlenmek, istirahat etm., mola vermek; uyumak; dayanmak, yaslanmak, istinat etm. *(a. fig.)* (on, upon *-e*); ~ (up)on *fig. bşden* ileri gelmek, *bşe* bağlı olm.; it ~s with you bu sizin elinizdedir, size bağlıdır; *v/t.* dinlendirmek, dayamak, yaslamak, koymak (on *-e*); dayandırmak, bir nedene bağlamak *(sav)*; *(gözlerini)* bir yöne dikmek, sabit bakmak; durdurmak *(makine vs.)*.

rest² [~] 1. *n.* artan, geri kalan miktar, artık, bakiye; diğerleri, ötekileri, devamı; üst yanı; diğer şeyleri; *†* ihtiyat akçesi; for the ~ belirtilenin dışında, zaten, esasen, herşeyin ötesinde; 2. *v/i.* olmağa devam etm.; kalmak; ~ assured emin olm., kesinlikle inanmak.

re.state ['ri:'steit] *v/t.* yeniden belirtmek, söylemek, sekillendirmek.

re.stau.rant ['restrɔnt] *n.* restoran, lokanta; '~-car *n.* yemekli vagon, vagon-restoran

rest-cure *♂* ['restkjuə] *n.* dinlenme tedavisi.

rest.ful ['restful] *adj.* sakin, rahat (verici), huzurlu, dinlendirici.

res.ting-place ['restiŋpleis] *n.* dinlenme yeri, konak yeri; mezar.

res.ti.tu.tion [resti'tju:ʃən] *n.* çalınan *veya* kaybolan *bşi* sahibine geri verme; zararı ödeme; tazminat; onarma, restore et me, eski haline getirme; make ~ tazmin etm., zararı ödemek (of -i).

**res.tive** □ ['restiv] inatçı, dikkafalı, aksi, rahat durmaz; **'res.tive.ness** n. inatçılık, dikkafalılık.

**rest.less** ['restlis] adj. yerinde durmaz; huzursuz, rahatsız; dalgalı, hareketli (deniz vs.); uykusuz; durup dinlenmeyen, kıpır kıpır; tezcanlı, vesveseli; **'rest.less.ness** n. huzursuzluk, rahatsızlık; tezcanlılık; yerinde duramama.

**re.stock** ['ri:'stɔk] v/t. & v/i. doldurmak, eksikleri tamamlamak; yeniden stok etm. (with ile).

**res.to.ra.tion** [restə'reiʃən] n. yenileme, restore etme, eski haline getirme; eski görevini iade etme (to -e); bşi geri verme, iade; bşin aslını gösteren model; **re.stor.a.tive** □ [ris'tɔrətiv] güçlendiren, düzelten, canlandıran; ayıltan (ilaç vs.).

**re.store** [ris'tɔ:] v/t. yenilemek, eski haline getirmek, restore etm.; iade etm., geri vermek; eski yerine koymak; zarar ve ziyanı ödemek, telâfi etm.; yeniden canlandırmak; ~ s.o. to liberty b-ne özgürlüğünü geri vermek; ~ to health veya life iyileştirmek, sağlığına kavuşturmak, hayata döndürmek; **re'stor.er** n. yenileyen, eski haline getiren, restore eden kimse; hair ~ saç gürleştiren ilaç.

**re.strain** [ris'trein] v/t. geri tutmak, alıkoymak, tutmak (from -den), zaptetmek; bastırmak, sınırlamak, yasaklamak; **re'strained** adj. kontrollu, zaptedilmiş; **re'straint** [~'treint] n. k-ni tutma, sinirlerine hâkim olma; sınırlılık, tahdit, engel; zorunluluk; baskı, tazyik; tutukluluk; çekinme, sıkılma.

**re.strict** [ris'trikt] v/t. kısıtlamak, sınırlamak -i, tahdit koymak -e; **re'stric.tion** n. sınırlama, kısıtlama, tahdit (of, on); koşul, kayıt, sınır; **re'stric.tive** □ sınırlayıcı, kısıtlayıcı, bağlayıcı.

**rest room** Am. tuvalet, helâ.

**re.sult** [ri'zʌlt] 1. n. sonuç, netice; son; 2. v/i. meydana gelmek, çıkmak (from -den); ~ in bşle sonuçlanmak, son bulmak; **re'sult.ant** 1. adj. meydana gelen, çıkan; 2. n. ⊕ sonuç, netice.

**ré.su.mé** ['rezju:mei] n. özet, hulâsa; özgeçmiş.

**re.sume** [ri'zju:m] vb. yeniden başlamak, kalan yerden devam etm. -e; geri almak, yeniden elde etm. -i; **re.sump.tion** [ri-'zʌmpʃən] n. yeniden başlama, devam etme; geri alma.

**re.sur.face** ['ri:'sə:fis] v/t. yüzeyi yeniden kaplamak (yol vs.); v/i. suyun yüzüne

çıkmak (denizaltı).

**re.sur.gence** [ri'sə:dʒəns] n. yeniden yükselme, sivrilme, doğma, dirilme, taraftar bulma, canlanma (fikir, inanış vs.); **re'sur.gent** adj. yeniden canlanan, doğan, dirilen, yükselen.

**res.ur.rect** [rezə'rekt] v/t. yeniden canlandırmak, moda etm., ortaya çıkarmak; F arayıp bulmak, keşfetmek; yeniden kazmak, hafriyat yapmak; yeniden diriltmek, hortlatmak; **res.ur'rec.tion** n. yeniden diril(t)me, basübadelmevt; yeniden canlanma, ortaya çıkma; **res.ur'rec.tion.ist** [~ʃnist], **res.ur'rec.tion.man** [~ʃənmən] n. ceset hırsızı.

**re.sus.ci.tate** [ri'sʌsiteit] v/t. & v/i. yeniden diril(t)mek, canlan(dır)mak; **re.sus.ci'ta.tion** n. yeniden diril(t)me.

**re.tail** 1. ['ri:teil] n. perakende satış, perakendecilik; by ~ perakende; ~ price perakende fiyat(ı); 2. [~] adj. perakende...; 3. [~] adv. s. by ~; 4. [ri:'teil] v/t. perakende olarak satmak; ayrıntılariyle anlatmak; v/i. perakende olarak satılmak (at -e); **re'tail.er** n. perakendeci.

**re.tain** [ri'tein] v/t. alıkoymak, zaptetmek; hatırda tutmak, unutmamak; tutmak, elinde bulundurmak; hizmetine almak, ücretle tutmak (avukat); **re'tain.er** n. hist. hizmetkâr, uşak; old ~ yaşlı uşak, kâhya; **re'tain.ing fee** avans olarak (avukata) verilen para.

**re.take** [ri:'teik] (irr. take) v/t. geri almak (savaşta kaybedilen yeri); tekrar fotoğrafını çekmek.

**re.tal.i.ate** [ri'tælieit] v/t. dengiyle karşılamak, misillemek; v/i. öcünü almak, intikam almak (on, upon -den); **re.tal.i'a.tion** n. misilleme, kısas, misliyle karşılık verme; **re'tal.i.a.to.ry** [~ətəri] adj. misilleme kabilinden, misilleme...

**re.tard** [ri'ta:d] v/t. geciktirmek, sürüncemede bırakmak, tecil, talik etm., alıkoymak; ~ed ignition mot. geç ateşleme; mentally ~ed zihni gelişmesi yavaş olan, geri zekâlı; **re.tar.da.tion** [ri:ta:'deiʃən] n. gecik(tir)me, alıkoyma; geciktiren şey, engel.

**retch** [retʃ] v/i. öğürmek, kusmağa çalışmak.

**re.tell** ['ri:'tel] (irr. tell) v/t. tekrar anlatmak, başka bir yol veya dilde anlatmak.

**re.ten.tion** [ri'tenʃən] n. alıkoyma, tutma; hatırda tutma; ℛ idrar tutulması, vücuttan atılamaması; muhafaza etme (ana.ne, ahlâk vs.); **re'ten.tive** □ alıkoyan, tutan, salıvermeyen; hatırda iyi tutan, hafızası kuvvetli olan.

**re.think** ['ri:θiŋk] (*irr.* think) *vb.* yeniden etraflıca düşünmek, hesabetmek kitabetmek.

**ret.i.cence** ['retisəns] *n.* ağız sıkılığı, sır saklama, susma, ketumiyet (of); **ret.i.cent** *adj.* ağzısıkı, ketum, suskun, sesi çıkmaz.

**ret.i.cle** ['retikl] *n.* optik cihazlarda göz merceğine yerleştirilen ve görüşü kolaylaştıran çizgiler *veya* küçük bir ağ sistemi.

**re.tic.u.late** ['ri'tikjulit], **re'tic.u.lat.ed** □ [~leitid] ağ gibi, ağ şeklinde, ağ..., şebekeli; **ret.i.cule** ['retikju:l] *n.* küçük bayan elçantası; = reticle.

**ret.i.na** *anat.* ['retinə] *n.* ağtabaka, retina.

**ret.i.nue** ['retinju:] *n.* maiyet, heyet.

**re.tire** [ri'taiə] *v/t.* geri çekmek; emekliye ayırmak; *v/i.* geri çekilmek (*a.* X); *(bir köşeye)* çekilmek; emekliye ayrılmak; *a.* ~ to bed yatağa yatmak; **re'tired** □ emekli; münzevi, dünyadan elini eteğini çekmiş; ıssız, uzaklarda *(yer)*; ~ pay emekli maaşı; **re'tire.ment** *n.* emeklilik; inziva; **re'tir.ing** □ çekingen, sıkılgan, utangaç, mahcup, sesi çıkmaz; ~ pension emekli maaşı.

**re.tort** [ri'tɔːt] **1.** *n.* cevap, karşılık; sert, hazır ve çoğu zaman eğlendirici cevap; `⌒` (boynuzlu) imbik; **2.** *v/t.* & *v/i.* *(hakaret vs.)* karşılık vermek, cevap vermek (on, upon -e); sert cevap vermek.

**re.touch** ['ri:'tʌtʃ] *v/t.* gözden geçirmek, revizyon yapmak; *phot.* rötuş yapmak.

**re.trace** [ri'treis] *v/t.* (*-in izini)* takip ederek kaynağına gitmek; ~ one's steps geldiği yönden geri gitmek.

**re.tract** [ri'trækt] *v/t.* & *v/i.* geri çek(il)-mek, geri al(ın)mak; ⊕ içeri *veya* geri çekmek; sözünü geri almak; caymak, sözünden dönmek; **re'tract.a.ble** *adj.* geri çekilebilir, alınabilir (*`✝` tekerlekler)*; **re.trac'ta.tion** *n.* cayma, sözünden dönme; sözünü geri alma; **re'trac.tion** *n.* geri çek(il)me, geri alma; cayma, vazgeçme.

**re.trans.late** ['ri:træns'leit] *v/t.* yeniden tercüme etm.; **'re.trans'la.tion** *n.* yeniden tercüme.

**re.tread** ['ri:'tred] **1.** *v/t.* *(lastik tekerlek)* dışını kaplamak; **2.** *n.* kaplanmış lastik *(tekerlek)*.

**re.treat** [ri'tri:t] **1.** *n.* geri çek(il)me; geri çekilme işareti; sığınak, inziva köşesi, emniyette ve huzur içinde olunacak yer, tenha yer; X ricat borusu; beat a ~ *fig.* geri çekilmek, hoş olmayan bir durumla karşılaşmamak için kaçmak; **2.** *v/i.* geri

çekilmek; *fig.* gerilemek, vazgeçmek.

**re.trench** [ri'trentʃ] *v/t.* & *v/i.* azaltmak, kısmak, indirmek, küçültmek; çizmek, iptal etm. *(sözcük vs.)*; X tahkim etm.; azalmak, küçülmek, masrafları azaltmak; **re'trench.ment** *n.* azaltma, kısma, tasarruf, idare; X savunma hattı.

**re.tri.al** `⅓` ['ri:traiəl] *n.* yeniden dava açma.

**re.tri.bu.tion** [retri'bju:ʃən] *n.* karşılıkta bulunma, misilleme; ceza, günahların bedeli; **re.trib.u.tive** □ [ri'tribjutiv] karşılık olarak, misilleme..., cezalandırıcı, ödüllendirici.

**re.triev.a.ble** [ri'tri:vəbl] *adj.* tekrar ele geçirilebilir, düzeltilebilir, telâfi edilebilir, geri getirilebilir; **re'triev.al** *n.* geri alma, geri getirme, düzeltme, telâfi; beyond ~, past ~ geri getirilemez, düzeltilemez, telâfi edilemez.

**re.trieve** [ri'tri:v] *vb.* tekrar ele geçirmek; düzeltmek, iyileştirmek, telâfi etm., tazminat vermek; *hunt.* bulup getirmek; **re'triev.er** *n. hunt.* kapıp getiren av köpeği.

**ret.ro...** ['retrəu] *prefix* geriye doğru, geri(ye), arkada, arkaya...; **~'ac.tive** *adj.* geriye dönük, evvelce olanı kapsayan *(part. yasa)*; **~'cede** *v/i.* geri gitmek, çekilmek, dönmek; geri vermek; **~'ces.sion** *n.* geri çekilme, gerileme; geri verme, iade; **~.gra'da.tion** *n. ast.* doğudan batıya doğru geri gitme; gerileme, geri çekilme; *fig.* gerileme, düşüş; **'~.grade 1.** *adj.* gerileyen, geri giden, ters yönde giden; giderek kötüleşen; **2.** *v/i.* gerilemek; bozulmak, kötüye gitmek *(a. fig.)*. **ret.ro.gres.sion** [retrəu'greʃən] *n.* gerileme, geriye gitme; bozulma, yozlaşma; **ret.ro.spect** ['~spekt] *n.* geçmişe bakış, in ~ geçmişe bakıldığında; **ret.ro'spec.tion** *n.* geçmişe bakış, geçmişi anma; **ret.ro'spec.tive** □ geçmişle ilgili, geçmişi hatırlayan; geriye dönük, önceyi kapsayan; ~ view geçmişe bakış.

**re.trous.sé** [rə'tru:sei] *n.*: ~ nose yukarı kalkık kısa burun.

**re.try** `⅓` ['ri:'trai] *v/t.* yeniden yargılamak.

**re.turn** [ri'tə:n] **1.** *n.* (geri) dönüş; *parl.* seçim; seçim mazbatası; seçilme; *oft.* ~s *pl.* kazanç, kâr; `⅌` nüksetme, tekrar olma; iade, geri ver(il)me; ödeme, tediye; misilleme, karşılık, cevap; şükran, teşekkür; resmi rapor, banka raporu; vergi beyanı, beyanname; Δ bir binanın yan kısmı; F dönüş bileti; ~s *pl.* istatistik cetveli; many happy ~s of the day!

nice mutlu -yıllara! (*b-nin isim gününde söylenir*); election ~s pl. seçim mazbataları, seçim sonuçları; in ~ karşılık olarak; in ~ for -e karşılık, -in karşılığında; by ~ (of post) ilk posta ile, hemen, acele; ~ match rövanş maçı; ~ ticket gidiş dönüş bileti; Am. dönüş bileti; ~ visit iadei ziyaret; **2.** *vb.* geri dönmek; tekrar olm.; ~ to *fig.* bir konuya geri dönmek; eski alışıkanlıklarına dönmek; yeniden *b-nin* eline geçmek; geri vermek, iade etm., geri göndermek; cevap vermek, yanıtlamak; geri ödemek; iadei ziyarette bulunmak, şükranlarını sunmak; ᇮ yargılamak, hüküm vermek; resmî rapor vermek; *parl.* seçmek; kâr bırakmak; ~ guilty ᇮ suçlu olduğuna karar vermek; **re!turn.a.ble** *adj.* geri verilmesi *veya* gönderilmesi gereken; geri verilebilir *veya* gönderilebilir; **re!turn.er** *n.* geri ödeyen, geri gönderen; **re!turn.ing-of.fi.cer** *n.* seçim memuru.

**re.u.ni.fi.ca.tion** ['riːjuːnifi'keiʃən] *n.* yeniden birleşme, uzlaşma.

**re.un.ion** ['riːjuːnjən] *n.* tekrar birleşme, bir araya gelme; **re.u.nite** ['riːjuːˈnait] *v/t.* & *v/i.* yeniden birleş(tir)mek, bir araya gelmek, getirmek.

**rev** *mot.* F [rev] **1.** *n.* devir, dönme; **2.** *v/t.* & *v/i.* dön(dür)mek; ~ up motorun hızını artırmak.

**re.val.or.i.za.tion** ['riːvælərai'zeiʃən], **re.val.u.a.tion** ['riːvæljuei'ʃən] *n.* yeniden değerlendirme; **!re!val.or.ize** [~əraiz], **re.val.ue** ['riːˈvæljuː] *v/t.* yeniden değerlendirmek, kıymetlendirmek.

**re.vamp** ⊕ ['riːˈvæmp] *v/t.* tamir etm., yenilemek; Am. döşemesini değiştirmek (*koltuk vs.*).

**re.veal** [riˈviːl] *v/t.* açığa vurmak, ifşa etm.; göstermek, ortaya koymak; **re!veal.ing** *adj.* anlamlı, manidar; bir kısmını gösteren (*elbise vs.*).

**re.veil.le** X [riˈvæli] *n.* kalk borusu.

**rev.el** ['revl] **1.** *n.* eğlence, şenlik, eğlenti, cümbüş, içki alemi; **2.** *v/i.* eğlenmek, cümbüş yapmak; mest olm. (in -de); keyiflenmek, zevk almak (in -den).

**rev.e.la.tion** [revi'leiʃən] *n.* açığa vurma, ifşa; *rel.* ilham, vahiy.

**rev.el.(l)er** ['revlə] *n.* eğlenen, şenlik yapan kimse, sabahçı, sabaha dek eğlenen, akşamcı, eğlence düşkünü kimse; **!rev.el.ry** *n.* gürültülü eğlenti, cümbüşlü eğlence, sefahat taşkınlıkları, âlem, şenlik.

**re.venge** [riˈvendʒ] **1.** *n.* öç, intikam, hınç; rövanş (*oyun*); **2.** *v/t.* intikam almak,

hıncını çıkarmak (on, upon -*den*); ~ o.s. on, be ~d on *b-den* intikamını almak, öcünü almak, *b-şin* acısını çıkarmak; **re!venge.full** □ [~ful] kinci, kin tutan; **re!venge.ful.ness** *n.* intikam hırsı, kincilik; **re!veng.er** *n.* intikam alıcı kimse.

**rev.e.nue** ['revinjuː] *n.* gelir, irat, varidat; ~s *pl.* devletin vergi gelir(ler)i; ~ board, ~ office defterdarlık, maliye tahsilât şubesi; ~ cutter gümrük muhafaza gemisi; ~ officer gümrük memuru; ~ stamp damga pulu, bandırol.

**re.ver.ber.ate** [riˈvəːbəreit] *v/t.* & *v/i.* akset(tir)mek, yankıla(n)mak, yansı(t)mak; **re.ver.ber!a.tion** *n.* yankıla(n)ma, akset(tir)me; **re!ver.ber.a.tor** *n.* yansıtaç, ışıldak.

**re.vere** [riˈviə] *v/t.* saymak, saygı göstermek -e, yüceltmek, ululamak -i; **rev.er.ence** ['revərəns] **1.** *n.* derin saygı, hürmet; saygı ile eğilme, reverans; Your ℨ † *veya* co. saygıdeğer efendim; **2.** *v/t.* saygı göstermek -e, yüceltmek -i; **!rev.er.end 1.** *adj.* saygıdeğer, muhterem, sayın; Right ℨ muhterem, aziz (*papaz*); **2.** *n.* muhterem (*papazın lakabı*).

**rev.er.ent** □ ['revərənt], **rev.er.en.tial** □ [~'renʃəl] saygılı, hürmetkâr, saygıdan ileri gelen.

**rev.er.ie** ['revəri] *n.* dalgınlık, sayıklama, derin düşünüş; hayal.

**re.ver.sal** [riˈvəːsəl] *n.* evirtim, tersine çevirme, akis, ani değişiklik; ᇮ iptal, fesih, geri alma; ⊕ geri dönme, çevirme; **re!verse 1.** *n.* arka, ters taraf, arka yüz; aksi, zıt, ters olan şey; aksilik, başarısızlık; geri tepme; in ~ tersine, sondan başa doğru; X arkadan hücum; **2.** □ ters, aksi, arka, geriye, gerisin geriye; ~ gear *mot.* geri vites; ~ side ters taraf (*kumaşta arka yüz*); **3.** *vb.* ters(ine) çevirmek; tersine dönmek; (*iş*) feshetmek, lağvetmek, kapatmak; ⊕ geri hareket ettirmek; ᇮ iptal etm., hükmü değiştirmek; **re!vers.i.ble** *adj.* tersine çevrilebilir; geri çalıştırılabilir, döndürülebilir; iki taraflı, ters yüz edilebilir (*kumaş, pardesü vs.*); **re!vers.ing** *adj.* ⊕ geri dönebilen...

**re.ver.sion** [riˈvəːʃən] *n.* eski konu, durum *veya* alışkanlıklarına dönme, dönüş; ᇮ tekrar intikal, mülkün sahibine geçmesi; veraset hakkı (of -*in*); biol. çok uzun süredir görülmemiş ilkel özelliklerin yeniden belirmesi; **re!ver.sion.ar.y** [~ʃnəri] *adj.* intikal ile ilgili; **re!ver.sion.er** ᇮ [~ʃənə] *n.* aslî zilyet.

**re.vert** [riˈvəːt] *vb.* eski durumuna (*veya*

alışkanlıklarına) dönmek, geri gitmek (to -e); *fig.* gerilemek, geri kalmak; eski konuya dönmek; **⇗** intikal etm., mülk sahibine geçmek; çevirmek *(bakış).*
**rev.er.y** [ˈreveri] = reverie.
**re.vet.ment** ⊕ [riˈvetmənt] *n.* kaplama duvarı.
**re.view** [riˈvjuː] 1. *n.* gözden geçirme, tetkik, resmî teftiş, inceleme; ✕, ⬇ geçit töreni; eleştiri, tenkit; mecmua, dergi; ders tekrarı; pass s.th. in ⁓ geçit töreni yapmak; year under ⁓ denetim yılı; 2. *v/t.* yeniden incelemek, gözden geçirmek; ✕, ⬇ teftiş, denetim yapmak; eleştirmek; *v/i.* eleştiri yazısı yazmak; **re-ˈview.er** *n.* eleştirmen, eleştirici; ⁓'s copy eleştiri yazısı nüshası.
**re.vile** [riˈvail] *v/t.* küfretmek, hakaret etm., yermek, sövmek (for -e).
**re.vis.al** [riˈvaizl] *n.* yeniden inceleme, tetkik, teftiş, revizyon.
**re.vise** [riˈvaiz] 1. *v/t.* tekrar gözden geçirip düzeltmek, provaları tashih etm. *(kitap)*; değiştirmek; tekrar çalışmak *(ders)*; 2. *n. typ.* tashih provası, ikinci prova; = revision; **reˈvis.er** *n. bşi* gözden geçirip düzelten, inceleyen kimse; *typ.* tashih eden, düzeltmen, musahhih.
**re.vi.sion** [riˈviʒən] *n.* yeniden inceleyip düzeltme, gözden geçirme, tetkik, teftiş; tashih, düzelt(il)me, revizyon.
**re.vis.it** [ˈriːˈvizit] *v/t.* tekrar ziyaret etm.
**re.vi.so.ry** [riˈvaizəri] *adj.* düzeltici; tashih...
**re.vi.tal.ize** [ˈriːˈvaitəlaiz] *v/t.* yeniden canlandırmak, güç katmak, teşvik etm., tazelemek.
**re.viv.al** [riˈvaivəl] *n.* yeniden canlan(dır)-ma, taze hayat bulma, diril(t)me, revaç bulma; yıllar sonra yeniden oynanma *(piyes vs.)*; *fig.* uyanma, uyanış; **re.vive** *v/t.* (yeniden) canlandırmak, ihya etm., diriltmek, taze hayat vermek; yeniden kurmak, tesis etm.; yenilemek; yeniden ilgi gördürmek; yıllar sonra yeniden sahneye koymak *(piyes vs.)*; *v/i.* yeniden canlanmak; yeniden ilgi görmek, revaç bulmak; **reˈviv.er** *n.* yeniden canlandıran, dirilten, ihya eden kimse; canlandıran, kuvvetlendiren ilaç, serinleten *bş;* **re.viv.i.fy** [riːˈvivifai] *v/t.* yeni bir hayat ve sağlık vermek -e, canlandırmak.
**rev.o.ca.ble** ☐ [ˈrevəkəbl] geri alınabilir, feshedilebilir; **⁎** kabili rücu, iptal edilebilir; **rev.o.ca.tion** *n.* geri alınma, iptal, fesih, hükümsüz kılma.
**re.voke** [riˈvəuk] *v/t.* geri almak, iptal

etm.; sözünden dönmek; *v/i. iskambil:* aynı renkten kâğıt atmamak.
**re.volt** [riˈvəult] 1. *n.* isyan, ayaklanma, ihtilâl, kıyam; 2. *v/i.* isyan etm., ayaklanmak; *fig.* tiksinmek (at, against -den); *v/t. fig.* tiksindirmek, nefret hissi vermek; **reˈvolt.ing** *adj.* tiksindirici, iğrenç, menfur.
**rev.o.lu.tion** [revəˈluːʃən] *n.* devrim, yeni bir dönem, ihtilâl; devir, dönme; *pol.* devrim, inkılâp; ⁓s per minute *mot.* dakikada devir sayısı; **rev.oˈlu.tion.ary** [⁓ʃnəri] 1. *adj.* devrimci; ihtilâlci; 2. *a.* **rev.oˈlu.tion.ist** *n.* devrimci, ihtilâlci kimse; **rev.oˈlu.tion.ize** *v/t.* tamamen değiştirmek; ayaklandırmak, isyan ettirmek; devirmek, devrim yapmak.
**re.volve** [riˈvɔlv] *v/t. & v/i.* dön(dür)mek (about, on, round); *fig.* düşünüp taşınmak -i; **reˈvolv.er** *n.* revolver, altıpatlar, tabanca; **reˈvolv.ing** *adj.* dönen..., döner...
**re.vue** *thea.* [riˈvyuː] *n.* revü, kabare, dans ve şarkılı sahne gösterisi.
**re.vul.sion** [riˈvʌlʃən] *n. fig.* nefret, tiksinme, ânî reaksiyon, tiksinti; düşünce *veya* duyguda ani değişiklik; **⁎** başka yöne çevirme; **reˈvul.sive ⁎** [⁓siv] 1. ☐ ters etki yapan; 2. *n.* ters etki yapan ilaç.
**re.ward** [riˈwɔːd] 1. *n.* ödül, ikramiye, mükâfat, karşılık; 2. *v/t.* ödüllendirmek, mükâfat vermek.
**re.word** [ˈriːˈwɔːd] *v/t.* yeni sözcüklerle söylemek *veya* yazmak.
**re.write** [ˈriːˈrait] *(irr.* write) *v/t.* yeniden değişik ve daha uygun şekilde yazmak.
**rhap.so.dist** [ˈræpsədist] *n.* eski Yunan'da profesyonel destan anlatıcı; **ˈrhap.so.dize** *v/i. bşi* öve öve bitirememek, *bşden* fazla heyecanla bahsetmek; **ˈrhap.so.dy** *n. fig.* coşkunluk, heyecan, esrime; rapsodi, değişik parçalardan düzenlenmiş eser; heyecanlı konuşma *veya* yazı.
**rhe.o.stat ⁑** [ˈriːəustæt] *n.* direnç aygıtı, reosta.
**rhet.o.ric** [ˈretərik] *n.* hitabet; beyan ve belâgat sanatı; **rhe.tor.i.cal** ☐ [riˈtɔrikəl] retorik, güzel söz söylemeye (*veya* sanatına) ait; **rhet.o.ri.cian** [retəˈriʃən] *n.* güzel konuşma ustası, iyi hatip.
**rheu.mat.ic ⁑** [ruːˈmætik] 1. *adj.* (ally) romatizma ile ilgili, romatizmalı; ⁓ fever eklem romatizması; 2. *n.* romatizmalı kimse; ⁓s F *pl.* = **rheu.ma.tism ⁑** [ˈruːmətizəm] *n.* romatizma.
**rhi.no¹** *sl.* [ˈrainəu] *n.* mangır, mangiz.
**rhi.no²** F [⁓] = **rhi.noc.er.os** *zo.* [raiˈnɔsərəs] *n.* gergedan.

rhomb, rhom.bus.凡 ['rɔm(bəs] *n.* eşkenar dörtgen, main.

rhu.barb ¥ [ru:ba:b] *n.* ravent.

rhyme [raim] 1. *n.* kafiye, uyak (to -*e*); kafiyeli yazma; beyit, şiir; without ~ or reason mantıksız olarak, anlamsız, saçma, ipsiz sapsız; 2. *vb.* kafiyeli olarak yazmak; kafiyeli sona ermek; **'rhyme.less** □ kafiyesiz, uyaksız; **'rhym.er, rhyme.ster** ['~stə] *n.* şair taslağı (*veya* bozuntusu).

rhythm ['riðəm] *n.* ritim, kadans, müzikte ahenk, uyum, düzün, düzenlilik, ahenkli hareket; vezin; **rhyth.mic, rhyth.mi.cal** □ ['riðmik(əl)] ritmik, ahenkli, uyumlu, düzünlü.

Ri.al.to *Am.* [ri'æltəu] *n.* tiyatroların çok olduğu bölge.

rib [rib] 1. *n. anat.* kaburga (kemiği); pirzola; ¥ yaprak damarı; şemsiye teli; gemi iskeleti; 2. *v/t.* damarlı, yivli desende örnek (*çorap vs.); Am. sl.* takılmak, alaya almak -*i*.

rib.ald ['ribəld] 1. *adj.* ağzı bozuk, kaba, sağa sola sataşan, etrafı rahatsız eden; açık saçık, müstehcen; 2. *n.* ağzı bozuk, küfürbaz kimse; dedikoducu kimse; **'rib-ald.ry** *n.* soğuk şaka, küstahça alay etme; kaba dil.

rib.and ⊕ ['ribənd] *n.* şerit, seri imalatta kullanılan döner bant.

ribbed [ribd] *adj.* yivli, girintili, çıkıntılı, çizgili.

rib.bon ['ribən] *n.* kurdele, şerit, bant; madalya kurdelesi; daktilo şeridi; çizgi, çubuk (*kumaş*); ~s *pl.* bez parçası, paçavra; dizgin (*at*); ~ building, ~ development şehir imarının anayol boyunca şehir dışına doğru gelişmesi.

rice [rais] *n.* ¥ pirinç.

rich [ritʃ] □ [ritʃ] zengin, servet sahibi; bol, fazla, külliyetli (in -*de*); mükellef, muhteşem, değerli, kıymetli; verimli, bereketli; gür, tok, dolgun (*ses*); yağlı, ağır, hazmı güç (*yemek*); koyu, canlı, parlak (*renk*); besleyici, vitaminli; F mükemmel, enfes, şahane (*şaka, nükte*); the ~ *pl.* zenginler, servet sahipleri; **rich.es** ['~iz] *n .pl.* zenginlik, servet; **'rich.ness** *n.* zenginlik, bolluk, verim, bereket; yağlılık; gürlük (*ses*); parlaklık (*renk*).

rick¹ ✓ [rik] 1. *n.* kuru ot yığını, tınaz; 2. *v/t.* kuru ot yığını yapmak, yığmak.

rick² [~] = wrick.

rick.ets ⌘ ['rikits] *n. sg. veya pl.* raşitizm; **'rick.et.y** *adj.* raşitizm hastalığına tutulmuş, raşitik; sakat, hastalıklı, sarsık sursuk; çürük, köhne.

rick.shaw ['rikʃɔ:] *n.* bir *veya* iki kişilik olup insan tarafından çekilen hafif bir Doğu Asya faytonu.

rid [rid] (*irr.) v/t.* kurtarmak (of -*den*); get ~ of başından atmak, defetmek, savmak -*i*; **'rid.dance** *n.* kurtuluş, kurtulma, başından atma; he is a good ~ ondan kurtulduğumuz iyi oldu, iyi ki çekip gitti.

rid.den ['ridn] *p.p. of* ride 2; *comb.* ...ile dolu; ... in istilâsına uğramış.

rid.dle¹ ['ridl] 1. *n.* bilmece, bulmaca, muamma; 2. *vb.* anlamını çıkarmak; bilmece çözmek, bilmece ile söylemek; ~ me F tahmin etsene!

rid.dle² [~] 1. *n.* kalbur; 2. *v/t.* kalburdan geçirmek, elemek; delik deşik etm., kalbura çevirmek.

rid.dling □ ['ridliŋ] akıl ermez, muammalı, şaşırtıcı.

ride [raid] 1. *n.* atla gezinti; gezinti yeri *veya* yolu, ağaçsız orman yolu; binme, biniş; go for a ~ bir araçla gezmeğe çıkmak, atla gezintiye çıkmak; 2. (*irr.) v/i.* ata binmek, atla gitmek; ata biner gibi oturmak; *part.* bisiklet *veya* araçla gitmek; *fig.* muallâkta kalmak, sürüklenmek; rahat gitmek (*araba); ~* at anchor demirli yatmak (*gemi); ~* for a fall *fig.* körükörüne bir felâkete sürüklenmek, akılsızca davranmak; *v/t.* binmek -*e*, sürmek -*i (at, bisiklet vs.);* (bir yeri) atla dolaşmak, gezmek; binip gitmek -*e*; su üstünde gitmek, yüzmek (*gemi*); bindirmek -*e;* ~ s.o. down *b-ni* atla yetişip yakalamak; *b-ni* atla çiğnemek; ~ (on) a bicycle bisiklete binmek; ~ out ↓ su yüzünde kalmak (*fırtınada*), kazasız belâsız atlatmak (*a. fig.); 'rid.er n.* atlı, binici, süvari; ek, ilâve, özel hüküm; ⊕ değişebilen, hareket edebilen ağırlık (*veya* parça).

rid.ge [ridʒ] 1. *n.* sırt, bayır, dağ sırtı, dağ sırası; ∆ çatı sırtı; ✓ tarla kenarı; 2. *v/t.* evlek açmak, iz bırakmak; kırıştırmak (*alın); '~.pole n.* çatının yatay direği.

rid.i.cule ['ridikju:l] 1. *n.* alay, istihza, eğlenme, saraka; hold s.o. up to ~ *b-ni* elâleme rezil etm., herkesin alay konusu etm.; 2. *v/t. b-le* alay etm., zevklenmek, *b-ni* alay konusu etm.; **ri'dic.u.lous** [~juləs] *adj.* gülünç, gülünecek, alay edilecek, tuhaf, saçma; **ri'dic.u.lous.ness** *n.* maskaralık, soytarılık, gülünçlük, tuhaflık.

rid.ing ['raidiŋ] 1. *n.* biniş; binicilik; 2. *adj.* binek...; '~**breech.es** *n. pl.* süvari pantolonu; '~**hab.it** *n.* kadın için binici elbisesi.

**rife** ☐ [raif] yaygın, bol, sık sık olan; dolu olan (with *ile*); ~ with *ile* dolu.

**riff-raff** [ˈrifræf] *n.* ayak takımı, avam, aşağı sınıf.

**ri.fle¹** [ˈraifl] *v/t.* yağma etm., soyup soğana çevirmek.

**ri.fle²** [~] 1. *n.* tüfek, karabina; ~s *pl.* ✕ avcı erleri; 2. *v/t.* yiv açmak; '~man *n.* ✕ avcı eri; '~-range *n.* poligon, atış alanı; atış menzili.

**ri.fling** ⊕ [ˈraiflɪŋ] *n.* yiv helezonu *(tüfek).*

**rift** [rift] *n.* yarık, açıklık, çatlak.

**rig¹** [rig] 1. *v/t. (pazar, piyasa vs.)* hile karıştırmak *-e,* hileli şekilde kurmak; 2. *n.* (hile)kârlık, dalavere.

**rig²** [~] 1. *n.* ⬇ donanım, arma; *fig.* süs, şatafat; elbise; 2. *vb.* donatmak, teçhiz etm., armasını takmak; ~ s.o. out *b-ne bşi* sağlamak, temin etm.; *b-ni* telleyip pullamak (with *ile*), hazırlamak, giydirmek; ~ s.th. up hemen uydurmak, acele ile geçici olarak *bş* yapmak; '**rig.ger** *n.* ⬇ armador; ✝ makinist, mekanisyen; '**rig.ging** *n.* ⬇ donanım, geminin arması.

**right** [rait] 1. ☐ doğru, dürüst, hatasız, kusursuz; âdil, insaflı; doğru, sahih; sağlam, sıhhatli; en uygun, münasip; haklı; gereken, aranan; sağ *(taraf);* ~ angle ⅄ dik açı; be ~ haklı olm.; be ~ to *-mekle* iyi etm.; *-mak* üzere olm.; all ~! herşey yolunda!; münasip, uygun, kusursuz; pekalâ, tamam!; peki, hay hay!; on the ~ side of 30 yaşı otuz yoktur; get s.th. ~ *bşi* düzeltmek, yoluna koymak; put *veya* set ~ düzeltmek, ayarlamak, yoluna koymak; 2. *adv.* sağa doğru; doğru (olarak); hemen; doğruca, dosdoğru; uygun şekilde; tamamiyle; pek, çok, ziyade; ~ away derhal, hemen; haydi!, yürü!; ~ on doğruca; 3. *n.* sağ (taraf); hak, selâhiyet, yetki (to, of *-e);* *parl.* sağ kanat; *boks:* sağ; the ~s of man insan hakları; in ~ of his mother annesinin tarafında, annesini haklı bulan; in one's own ~ *k-si* hak sahibi olarak; the ~s and wrongs doğru ile eğri; haklı ile haksız, işin doğrusu, gerçeği; by ~(s) usulen, yasal olarak; by ~ of nedeniyle, hak *veya* yetkisiyle; set *veya* put to ~s yeniden düzeltmek, yoluna koymak; on *veya* to the ~ sağ taraf(t)a; 4. *v/t.* düzeltmek; ⬇ doğrultmak; ayarlamak; ~-an.gled ⅄ [ˈ~læŋgld] *adj.* dik açılı; '~-down *adj.* uygun, muntazam, tam, sapına kadar; olumlu; **right.eous** ☐ [ˈ~ʃəs] dürüst, adil, erdemli, namuslu; '**right.eous.ness** *n.* dü-

rüstlük; **right.ful** ☐ [ˈ~ful] haklı; yasal; gerçek; '**right-hand** *adj.* sağdaki, sağdan; sağ elle yapılan; sağa doğru...; güvenilir; '**right-ˈhand.ed** *adj.* sağ elini kullanan; sağ elle kullanmak için yapılmış *(makas vs.);* '**right.ly** *adv.* doğru, gerçek olarak; haklı olarak; emin olarak; '**right¹mind.ed** *adj.* dürüst, adil, sağduyu sahibi; '**right.ness** *n.* doğruluk, adalete uygunluk; **right of way** önden geçme hakkı, geçiş hakkı.

**rig.id** ☐ [ˈridʒid] eğilmez, bükülmez, dimdik, kaskatı; *fig.* sert, haşin, boyun eğmez; **ri¹git.i.ty** *n.* sertlik, bükülmezlik, diklik.

**rig.ma.role** [ˈrigmərəul] *n.* boş lâf, gevezelik, saçma konuşma.

**rig.or** [ˈraigɔː] *n.* sertlik, katılık, eğilmezlik; insafsızlık; ✚ titreme, ürperme; ~ mortis ölümden sonra kasların katılaşması; **rig.or.ous** ☐ [ˈrigərəs] sert, şiddetli.

**rig.o.(u)r** [ˈrigə] *n.* sertlik, şiddet; ~s kötü koşullar.

**rile** F [rail] *v/t.* kızdırmak, sinirlendirmek.

**rill** *poet.* [ril] *n.* küçük dere.

**rim** [rim] 1. *n.* kenar; jant, ispit; 2. *v/t.* kenar çevirmek *(veya* yapmak).

**rime¹** [raim] *n.* kafiye, uyak.

**rime²** *poet.* [~] *n.* kırç, kırağı; '**rim.y** *adj.* kırağı ile örtülü; kırağı gibi.

**rind** [raind] *n.* kabuk, kışır; herhangi *bşin* dış yüzeyi.

**ring¹** [riŋ] 1. *n.* halka, çember; *boks:* ring; kartel, tröst; daire; yüzük; sirk çadırı vs.; at yarışı acentası *(veya* tezgâhı); make ~s round s.o. F *bşi b-den* daha iyi ve daha hızlı yapmak; 2. *vb.* daire *(veya* yuvarlak) içine almak *-i,* halka takmak *(hayvanın burnuna, ayağına vs);* halka atmak *(oyunda);* mst ~ in, ~ round, ~ about etrafını sarmak, ortaya almak *-i.*

**ring²** [~] 1. *n.* zil sesi, çan sesi, çınlama; zil çalma; give s.o. a ~ *b-ne* telefon etm.; 2. *(irr.) v/i.* çan, zil, saat çal(ın)mak; çınlamak, tınlamak; *oft.* ~ out çınlamak (with *ile*); ~ again yankılanmak; ~ off *teleph.* telefonu kapamak; the bell ~s zil çalıyor; *v/t.* çalmak, çınlatmak; *fig.* tesir bırakmak, çalkanmak *(şöhret);* ~ the bell zile basmak, çıngırağı çekmek; F başarmak, muvaffak olm.; ~ a bell F *b-ne bş* hatırlatmak, çağrışım yapmak; yabancı gelmemek; s.o. ~ up *b-ne* telefon etm.; '**ring.er** *n.* çan çalan cihaz; çancı, zangoç; *sl. b-nin* tıpatıp benzeri; ¹ring.ing ☐ çalan, çınlayan; ¹ring.lead.er *n.* çete başı, elebaşı; ringlet [¹-lit] *n.* saç lülesi; ¹ring.worm *n.* ⚥ mantar hastalığı.

rink [rıŋk] *n.* patinaj alanı; buz sahası.

rinse [rins] 1. *v/t. oft.* ~ out çalka(la)mak; 2. = ¹rins.ing *n.* çalkalama, sudan geçirme; ~s *pl.* bulaşık suyu.

ri.ot [¹raiət] 1. *n.* kargaşalık, gürültü, patırtı, velvele; cümbüş, eğlenti; taşkınlık *(a. fig.)*; F çok komik ve başarılı kimse *veya bş*; isyan, ayaklanma, baş kaldırma; run ~ gemi azıya almak, kontroldan çıkmak, kıyameti koparmak; 2. *v/i.* kargaşalık yaratmak, gürültü patırtı çıkarmak, azmak, kudurmak; ayaklanmak, isyan etm.; *fig.* mest olm. (in *-de*); ¹riot.er *n.* asi, ayaklanan; gürültücü kimse; ¹ri.ot.ous ☐ gürültülü, karışıklık yaratan, gürültücü; sefih, maceraperest.

rip¹ [rip] 1. *n.* yırtık, yarık; sökük dikiş; 2. *v/t.* sökmek, teyelleri ayırmak; ~ up yırtmak, yarmak, çatlatmak *(kereste vs.)*; *v/i.* yırtılmak, yarılmak, dikişleri açılmak; çok hızlı geçip gitmek.

rip² F [~] *n.* uçarı, yaramaz, haylaz, çapkın.

rip-cord [¹ripkɔːd] *n.* paraşüt *(veya* balon vs.*)* ipi.

ripe ☐ [raip] olgun(laşmış); kemale ermiş, yetişmiş; ¹rip.en *v/t. & v/i.* olgunlaş(tır)mak; yetişmek, erginleşmek; ¹ripe.ness *n.* olgunluk, kemal, erginlik.

ri.poste [ri¹pəust] 1. *n. fenc.* karşı darbe, hücum, atak; *fig.* çabuk ve zekice verilen yanıt; 2. *v/i.* çabuk karşı darbe *(veya* atak*)* yapmak; çabuk ve zekice yanıt vermek.

rip.per [¹ripə] *n.* kesici *b-i veya bş*; *sl.* yaman adam; müstesna bir parça; ¹ripping ☐ *sl.* fevkalâde, harikulâde, yaman, muhteşem.

rip.ple [¹ripl] 1. *n.* ufacık dalga, dalgacık; 2. *v/t. & v/i.* hafifçe dalgalan(dır)mak, çağıldamak, şırıldamak, kırış(tır)mak.

rise [raiz] 1. *n.* yükseliş, artış, çıkış, çoğalış *(ses, fiyat, su vs.)*; bayır, tepe, yokuş; *fig.* yükselme; ⚥ doğma, çıkış *(güneş vs.)*; başlangıç noktası, kaynak; give ~ to *bşe* neden olm., sebebiyet vermek; take (one's) ~ kaynağından çıkmak, ortaya çıkmak, doğmak; 2. *(irr.) v/i.* kalkmak, yükselmek, artmak, çıkmak *(fiyat vs.)*; kabarmak, yükselmek *(nehir vs.)*; ayağa kalkmak; doğmak, yükselmek *(güneş vs.)*; toplantıyı bitirmek; kızmak, sinirlenmek (against, on *-e*); doğmak, ortaya çıkmak, hasıl olm. *(nehir vs.)*;

ayaklanmak, baş kaldırmak; su yüzüne çıkmak *(balık vs.)*; yukarı doğru meyillenmek *(bayır vs.)*; ~ to *b-nin veya bşin* hakkından gelmek; ~ to the bait yemi ağzıyla kapmaya çalışmak; ris.en [¹rizn] *p.p. of.* rise 2; ¹ris.er *n.* merdiven basamağının dik olan kısmı; yokuş; early ~ sabah erken kalkan.

ris.i.bil.i.ty [rizi¹biliti] *n.* gülme eğilimi *(veya* isteği)*; ris.i.ble ☐ [¹-ibl] gülme..., gülmeye eğilimi olan; gülünç, komik.

ris.ing [¹raiziŋ] 1. *n.* yükselme, yükseliş; kalkma; artma, çoğalma; doğma, çıkış; ayaklanma, isyan; 2. *adj.* yükselen, artan, çoğalan; yetişen, büyüyen.

risk [risk] 1. *n.* tehlike, tehlikeli girişim; ⚔ risk, riziko; at the ~ of riski göze alarak, tehlikeye atarak; run the ~ zararı göze almak, rizikolu bir işe girişmek; 2. *v/t.* tehlikeye atmak, göze almak; ¹risk.y ☐ tehlikeli, riskli.

ris.sole [¹risəul] *n. (patates, yumurta vs. ile kızgın yağda pişirilen)* bir tür et *veya* balık yemeği.

rite [rait] *n. rel.* ayin, tören; rit.u.al [¹ritjuəl] 1. ☐ törensel, merasimle yapılan; ayine ait; 2. *n.* dinî ayin ve merasim (kuralları).

ri.val [¹raivəl] 1. *n.* rakip, müsabık; 2. *adj.* rekabet eden, çekişen, yarışan ile; ⚔ rakip...; 3. *v/t.* rekabet etm., yarışmak, çekişmek ile; ¹ri.val.ry *n.* rekabet, rakip olma.

rive [raiv] *(irr.) vb,* çatla(t)mak, yar(ıl)mak, yarık açmak.

riv.en [¹rivn] *p.p. of* rive.

riv.er [¹rivə] *n.* nehir, ırmak, akıntı *(a. fig.)*; sell s.o. down the ~ *b-ne* ihanet etm.; ¹~-horse *n.* suaygırı; ¹~.side *n.* ırmak *(veya* su) kenarı; *attr.* nehir kıyısı.

riv.et [¹rivit] 1. *n.* ⊕ perçin; 2. *v/t.* perçinlemek; *b-nin* ilgisini çekmek; *b-ne* gözünü dikmek (on, upon).

riv.u.let [¹rivjulit] *n.* dere, çay.

roach icht. [rəutʃ] *n.* çamça balığı.

road [rəud] *n.* yol, sokak, cadde, şose; Am. = railroad; *mst* ~s *pl.* ⚓ demirleme sahası, liman ağzı; take the ~ yola düzülmek; main ~ ana cadde, kalabalık yol; ¹~.bed *n.* yol yapı temeli; 🚍 sürekli *(veya* bozulmayan) hat; ¹~-block *n.* barikat, yol maniası; ¹~-hog *n. mot.* süratli, bencil ve dikkatsiz şoför *(veya* sürücü); ¹~-mend.er *n.* yol amelesi; ¹~-race *n.* sokak yarışı; ¹~-sense *n. mot.* trafikte yürür *veya* araba kullanırken kazadan sakınma duyusu; ¹~.side *n.* yol kenarı; ¹~.sign trafik işareti; ¹~.stead *n.*

roadster

↓ liman ağzı, demirleme yeri; **road.ster** [ˈ~stə] *n.* iki kişilik üstü açık araba; ˈ**road.way** *n.* araba yolu.

**roam** [rəum] *v/i.* dolaşmak, gezinmek, başıboş *(veya* amaçsız*)* gezinmek; *v/t.* gezmek, dolaşmak; ˈ**roam.er** *n.* yaya gezen; turist; kaldırımları eskiten kimse, serseri, aylak, boş gezen kimse.

**roan** [rəun] **1.** *adj.* demir kırı donlu *(at, inek vs.);* **2.** *n.* demir kırı donlu at; ⊕ güderi, koyun derisi.

**roar** [rɔː] **1.** *vb.* gürlemek *(a. fig. konuşma, gülme),* gümbürdemek; gök gürlemek; kükremek *(aslan);* kızıp bağırmak; gürleyerek akıp gitmek; **2.** *n.* gürleme, gümbürdeme, kükreme; çatırdama; kahkaha; **roar.ing** [ˈ~riŋ] **1.** = roar 2; **2.** ☐ gürleyen, gümbürdeyen, kükreyen; gittikçe artan; be in ~ health sıhhati çok yerinde olm.

**roast** [rəust] **1.** *vb.* kızartmak; kavurmak; *sl. b-ne* takılmak, *b-ni* alaya almak; **2.** *adj.* kızar(tıl)mış; kavrulmuş; ~ beef sığır orstosu *(veya* kızartması*),* rozbif; ~ meat kebap, kızartma *(et);* **3.** *n.* kebap kızartma; rule the ~ idare etm., dizginleri elinde tutmak; ˈ**roast.er** *n.* kızartma fırını *(kahve)* kavurma makinesi; henüz süt emen domuz yavrusu; ˈ**roast.ing-jack** *n.* döner yapma cihazı.

**rob** [rɔb] *vb.* soymak, yağma etm., çalmak, *b-nin* para ve eşyasını alıp soymak; *b-den* bşi gaspetmek; ˈ**rob.ber** *n.* hırsız; soyguncu haydut, karmanyolacı; ˈ**rob.ber.y** *n.* yol kesme, soygun, adam soyma, karmanyolacılık, haydutluk.

**robe** [rəub] **1.** *n.* rop, cübbe, kisve, biniş; *poet.* üstlük giysi, urba; *Am.* penyuvar, ropdöşambr, sabahlık; ~s *pl.* resmî *veya* tören elbisesi; gentlemen of the ~ hukukçular; **2.** *v/t. & v/i.* giyinmek, giydirmek, kaftan vs. giydirmek; *fig.* süsle(n)mek.

**rob.in** *orn.* [ˈrɔbin] *n.* kızıl gerdan (kuşu).

**ro bot** [ˈrəubɔt] *n.* makine adam, robot *(a. fig.);* otomat; *attr.* otomatik..., mekanik..., robot...

**ro.bust** ☐ [rəuˈbʌst] dinç, sağlam, güçlü kuvvetli, dayanıklı; **ro**ˈ**bust.ness** *n.* sağlamlık, dinçlik, güçlülük, dayanıklılık.

**rock**[1] [rɔk] *n.* kaya(lık), büyük taş parçası; *sl.* kıymetli taş; naneli çubuk şekeri; get down to ~ bottom bir konuyu inceden inceye araştırmak; ~ crystal necef taşı; ~ salt kayatuzu.

**rock**[2] [~] *v/t. & v/i.* salla(n)mak, tartmak, sars(ıl)mak, silkmek; *fig.* müteessir etm., sarsmak.

**rock-bottom** F [ˈrɔkˈbɔtəm] *adj.* en düşük *(fiyat).*

**rock.er** [ˈrɔkə] *n.* beşik vs.'nin altındaki kavisli ayak; *Am.* salıncaklı koltuk; *sl.* çatlak *(veya* deli*)* kimse.

**rock.er.y** [ˈrɔkəri] *n.* kayalık bahçe, taş yığınından yapılmış çiçeklik.

**rock.et**[1] [ˈrɔkit] **1.** *n.* roket, füze; havaî fişek; F azarlama, haşlama; ~ plane füze uçağı; ~ propulsion roket tahriki; **2.** *v/i.* F aniden yükselmek, fırlamak *(fiyat);* rüzgâr gibi gitmek.

**rock.et**[2] ♀ [~] *n.* roka.

**rock.et-pow.ered** [ˈrɔkitpauəd] *adj.* roket tahrikli; **rock.et.ry** [ˈ~ri] *n.* roket kullanma tekniği.

**rock...** ˈ~.**fall** *n.* kaya yığını; ˈ~-**gar.den** *n.* kayalık bahçe.

**rock.ing...** [ˈrɔkiŋ]: ˈ~-**chair** *n.* salıncaklı koltuk; ˈ~-**horse** *n.* salıncaklı oyuncak at.

**rock.y** [ˈrɔki] *adj.* kayalık; kaya gibi; F sallantılı, titrek.

**ro.co.co** [rəuˈkəukəu] *n.* mimarîde rokoko tarzı.

**rod** [rɔd] *n.* çubuk, değnek; falaka değneği; baston; olta kamışı; ⊕ rot; beş metrelik uzunluk ölçüsü (= 5 ½ *yards);* ˌ *Am. sl.* revolver, tabanca; **have a ~ in** pickle for s.o. *b-le* paylaşılacak kozu olm.

**rode** [rəud] *pret. of* ride 2.

**ro.dent** [ˈrəudənt] *n.* kemirgen hayvan.

**ro.de.o** *Am.* [rəuˈdeiəu] *n.* rodeo.

**rod.o.mon.tade** [rɔdəmɔnˈteid] *n.* övünme, yüksekten atma.

**roe**[1] [rəu] *n. a.* hard ~ balık yumurtası; soft ~ balık menisi.

**roe**[2] [~] *n.* karaca; ˈ~.**buck** *n.* erkek karaca.

**ro.ga.tion** *eccl.* [rəuˈgeiʃən] *n.* yakarış, yalvarma; ~ Sunday Miraçtan önceki pazar.

**rogue** [rəug] *n.* çapkın *(veya* derbeder, sefil*)* kimse; dolandırıcı *(veya* düzenbaz*)* kimse; yaramaz kimse; azgın fil; ~s' gallery sabıkalıların resimlerini olduğu koleksiyon; ˈ**ro.guer.y** *n.* derbederlik, çapkınlık; düzenbazlık; yaramazlık; ˈ**ro.guish** ☐ çapkın, derbeder; kurnaz; yaramaz; düzenbaz.

**roist.er** [ˈrɔistə] *v/i.* şamata *(veya* âlem, cümbüs*)* yapmak; ˈ**roist.er.er** *n.* şamatacı, cümbüşçü.

**role, rôle** *thea.* [rəul] *n.* rol *(a. fig.).*

**roll** [rəul] **1.** *n.* yuvarla(n)ma; top, rulo; sicil, kayıt, liste, defter; ⊕ silindir, merdane, makara; tomar; küçük ekmek; ↓ yalpa; gümbürtü, gürleme; **2.** *v/t. & v/i.* yuvarla(n)mak, tekerle(n)mek; sar(ıl)-

mak; silindirle düzletmek; *sl.* soymak; atmak *(zar)*; çevirmek, devirmek *(göz)*; kalın sesle söylemek; açmak; dolaşmak, dönmek; inişli yokuşlu uzanıp gitmek; dalgalanmak; gürlemek *(gök)*; geçip gitmek *(zaman)*; gülmekten katılmak; yalpalamak; ↓ yalpa vurmak; ~ed gold altın kaplama; be ~ing in money para içinde yüzmek; ~ up tomar yapmak, dürmek, sarmak, sıvamak *(kol)*; birikmek, yığılmak, art(tır)mak; gelmek, varmak; durmak *(araç)*; **ˈ~-call** *n.* yoklama *(a.* X*)*; **ˈroll.er** *n.* silindir; merdane; büyük dalga; bigudi; *mst ~ bandage* sargı; ~ coaster *Am. (Lunaparklarda)* keskin viraj ve iniş-çıkışları olan tren; ~ skate tekerlekli paten; ~ towel uçları birbirine dikili bir makaraya asılarak kullanılan havlu; **ˈroll-film** *n. phot.* makaralı film.
**rol.lick.ing** [ˈrolikiŋ] *adj.* gürültülü, şamatalı, eğlenceli.
**roll.ing** [ˈrɔuliŋ] **1.** *adj.* inişli yokuşlu *(arazi)*; çok zengin, para babası; **2.** *n.* yuvarlanma; ~ mill ⊕ haddehane; ~ press *typ.* rotatif; **ˈ~-stock** *n.* 🚂 lokomotif ve vagonlar.
**roll-on** [ˈrɔulɔn] *n. a.* ~ belt korse.
**roll-top desk** [ˈrɔultɔpˈdeks] *n.* kapağı kıvrılarak açılıp kapanan yazı masası.
**ro.ly-po.ly** [ˈrɔuliˈpɔuli] **1.** *n.* marmelatlı kek; **2.** *adj.* tıknaz, tombul.
**Ro.man** [ˈrɔumən] **1.** *adj.* Roma'ya *veya* Romalılara ait; Roma mimarisine ait; **2.** *n.* Romalı; *mst* ♀ *typ.* Latin harfleri.
**ro.mance**[1] [rɔuˈmæns] **1.** *n.* macera; aşk macerası; macera romanı; romantiklik; *fig.* martaval, palavra; **2.** *v/i. fig.* atıp tutmak, tıraş etm., palavra atmak.
**Ro.mance**[2] [rɔuˈmæns] *adj.:* ~ languages *pl.* Latince kökenli diller.
**ro.manc.er** [rɔuˈmænsə] *n.* roman yazarı; palavracı kimse.
**Ro.man.esque** [rɔuməˈnesk] *n.* 11. ve 12. yüzyıl Roma mimari tarzı.
**Ro.man.ic** [rɔuˈmænik] *adj.* Latince kökenli; *part.* ~ people *pl.* Latin Milletleri.
**ro.man.tic** [rɔuˈmæntik] **1.** *adj.* (~ally) roman gibi; hayalperest, romantik; düşsel, gerçek dışı, hayali; **2.** = **roˈman.ti.cist** [~tisist] *n.* romantik kimse; **roˈman.ti.cism** *n.* romantizm.
**Rom.ish** *mst contp.* [ˈrɔumiʃ] *adj.* Katolik.
**romp** [rɔmp] **1.** *n.* ele avuca sığmaz *(veya* haşarı) çocuk; boğuşma; **2.** *v/i.* gürültü ile oynamak, boğuşmak, azmak, kudurmak *(çocuk)*; **ˈromp.er(s** *pl.)* *n.* çocuk tulumu.
**ron.do** ♪ [ˈrɔndəu] *n.* rondo.

**rood** [ruːd] *n.* haç; bir uzunluk ölçüsü *(10, 117 ar)*; **ˈ-loft** *n.* △ *(kilise)* balkon.
**roof** [ruːf] **1.** *n.* dam, çatı; ~ of the mouth damak; **2.** *v/t. a.* ~ over çatı ile örtmek; **ˈroof.ing** **1.** *n.* çatı malzemesi; **2.** *adj.* çatı...; ~ felt katranlı mukavva, tavan keçesi; **ˈroof-tree** *n.* çatı kirişi.
**rook**[1] [ruk] **1.** *n. orn.* ekinkargası; *fig.* düzenbaz kimse; **2.** *v/t.* dolandırmak, kazıklamak.
**rook**[2] [~] *n.* satranç: kale.
**rook.er.y** [ˈrukəri] ekinkargalarının yuvalarının olduğu yer; ayıbalığı *veya* penguen barınağı; *fig.* çok sefil insanların oturduğu kalabalık ev.
**rook.ie** *sl.* [ˈruki] *n.* X acemi asker; *fig.* acemi çaylak.
**room** [rum] *n.* oda; yer, meydan; şans; neden; sebep; ~s *pl.* apartman dairesi; make ~ yer açmak (for *-e*); **...room.ed** *comb.* ...odalı; **ˈroom.er** *n. part. Am.* pansiyoner; **ˈroom.ing-house** *n. part. Am.* pansiyon; **ˈroom-mate** *n.* oda arkadaşı; **ˈroom.y** ☐ geniş, ferah; bol *(elbise)*.
**roost** [ruːst] **1.** *n.* tünek; **2.** *v/i.* tünemek; *fig.* gecelemek, konaklamak; **ˈroost.er** *n.* horoz.
**root**[1] [ruːt] **1.** *n.* kök *(a. fig., anat.,* Å, *gr.)*; ~ and branch kökünden, tamamen; take *veya* strike ~ kök salmak; kökleşmek *(fikir)*; ~ idea ana fikir; **2.** *v/t.* & *v/i.* kökleş(tir)mek, tut(tur)mak; ~ out kökünden sökmek; kökünü kazımak; **ˈroot.ed** *adj.* mıhlanmış; kökleşmiş, sabit *(fikir)*.
**root**[2] [~] *v/t. a.* ~ up karmakarışık *(veya* altüst) etm.; ~ out *veya* up arayıp bulmak; *v/i.* bşi karıştırmak, eşelemek; ~ for *Am. sl.* tezahürat yapmak -e, desteklemek *-i*; **ˈroot.er** *n. Am. sl.* koyu taraftar.
**root.let** [ˈruːtlit] *n.* kökcük.
**rope** [rɔup] **1.** *n.* halat; ip; ipe çekme, idam; on the ~ birbirine bağlı; be at the end of one's ~ F çaresiz kalmak; know the ~s bir işin yolunu yordamını bilmek; learn the ~s çalışarak öğrenmek; **2.** *v/t.* halatla bağlamak; kemontle yakalamak; *mst* ~ in, ~ off, ~ out ip çevirerek sınırlamak, iple çevirmek; *mount.* iple bağlamak; ~ down iple bağlamak; *v/i.* ip haline gelmek; **ˈ~-danc.er** *n.* ip cambazı; **ˈ~-lad.der** *n.* ip merdiven; **ˈ~-mak.er** *n.* ipçi, halatçı, urgancı; **ˈrop.er.y** *n.* ipçilik, halatçılık, urgancılık; **ˈrope-walk** *n.* halat bükme yeri; **ˈrope-way** *n.* asma hat, teleferik.
**rop.i.ness** [ˈrɔupinis] *n.* kalitesizlik, ber-

batlık.

**rop.y** ['rəupi] *adj.* kalitesiz, berbat; ip gibi; yapışkan, cıvık; adaleli, kuvvetli.

**ro.sa.ry** ['rəuzəri] *n. eccl.* tespih; dua kitabı; tespih ile okunan dualar; gül bahçesi.

**rose[1]** [rəuz] *n.* ❧ gül (rengi); hortum süzgeci.

**rose[2]** [~] *pret. of* rise 2.

**rose...:** '~.bud *n.* gül goncası; *Am.* güzel kız; '~-col.o(u)red *adj.* gül renginde; *fig.* ümit verici.

**ro.se.ate** ['rəuziit] *adj.* gül renginde, kırmızı; ümit verici.

**rose.mar.y** ❧ ['rəuzməri] *n.* biberiye.

**ro.se.ry** ['rəuzəri] *n.* gül tarhı.

**ro.sette** [rəu'zet] *n.* gül şeklinde rozet.

**rose.wood** ['rəuzwud] *n.* koyu kırmızı sert bir odun.

**ros.in** ['rɔzin] **1.** *n.* reçine; **2.** *v/t.* reçine sürmek *-e.*

**ros.ter** ✕ ['rəustə] *n.* nöbet listesi.

**ros.trum** ['rɔstrəm] *n.* kürsü.

**ros.y** ☐ ['rəuzi] gül gibi; kırmızı, al; *fig.* ümit verici.

**rot** [rɔt] **1.** *n.* çürüme, bozulma; çürük; çürüme hastalığı; *sl.* saçma(lık), zırva; **2.** *v/t. & v/i.* çürü(t)mek, boz(ul)mak; *sl.* bozmak *(plan vs.)*.

**ro.ta.ry** ['rəutəri] *adj.* dönen, dönel, döner...; ~ press *typ.* rotatif; **ro.tate** [rəu'teit] *v/t. & v/i.* dön(dür)mek; sıra ile çalış(tır)mak; **ro'ta.tion** *n.* dönme, deveran, tur; ~ of crops ✓ her yıl sıra ile değişik ekinler ekme; **ro.ta.to.ry** ['~tətəri] *s.* rotary; nöbetleşe, sıra ile.

**rote** [rəut] *n.:* by ~ ezbere.

**ro.tor** ['rəutə] *n.* ⊕ rotor, döneç; ✈ helikopter pervanesi.

**rot.ten** ☐ ['rɔtn] çürük, bozuk; *sl.* berbat, rezalet; 'rot.ten.ness *n.* çürüklük; berbatlık.

**rot.ter** *sl.* ['rɔtə] *n.* ciğeri beş para etmez kimse.

**ro.tund** ☐ [rəu'tʌnd] yuvarlak, toparlak; dolgun *(ses)*; tumturaklı *(söz, yazı)*; **ro'tun.da** △ [~də] *n.* kubbeli bina *veya* oda; **ro'tun.di.ty** *n.* yuvarlaklık; dolgunluk *(ses)*.

**rouge** [ru:ʒ] **1.** *n.* allık; ruj; **2.** *vb.* allık sürmek.

**rough** [rʌf] **1.** ☐ pürüzlü; sert; *fig.* kaba, yontulmamış; engebeli; inişli yokuşlu *(yol)*; zor, çetin *(hayat vs.)*; kabataslak; fırtınalı *(hava, deniz)*; müsveddelik *(kâğıt)*; talihsiz, şanssız; belâlı *(yer)*; yaramaz, haşarı *(çocuk)*; ahenksiz *(ses)*; ~ and ready konforsuz,

basit; çetin; *fig.* eğreti, geçici *(yöntem vs.)*; şöyle böyle; ~ copy taslak, müsvedde; cut up ~ F tepesi atmak, sinirlenmek; **2.** *n.* engebeli arazi; pürüzlü yüzey; zorluk, güçlük; nahoşluk; taslak; sokak serserisi, külhanbeyi; kaba herif; **3.** *v/t.* hırpalamak, dövmek, saldırmak; pürüzlendirmek; *-in* taslağını yapmak; dağıtmak *(saç)*; bozmak; ~ it sefalet çekmek, sürünmek; 'rough.age *n.* selülozu bol yiyecek; kaba madde; 'rough-and--'tum.ble **1.** *adj.* düzensiz, kuralsız; şiddetli *(kavga, mücadele)*; **2.** *n.* düzensiz durum; 'rough.cast **1.** *n.* △ kaba sıva; **2.** *adj.* bitmemiş, eksik; **3.** *v/t.* △ kaba sıva vurmak; 'rough.en *v/t. & v/i.* pürüzlen(dir)mek; kabar(t)mak.

**rough...:** ~'hewn *adj.* kabaca kesilmiş; kaba; '~-house *sl.* **1.** *n.* kavga, boğuşma; gürültü patırtı; **2.** *v/i.* boğuşmak; gürültü patırtı çıkarmak; '~-neck *n. Am. sl.* serseri, külhanbeyi; kaba saba herif; 'rough.ness *n.* kabalık, sertlik; 'rough--rid.er *n.* at terbiyecisi; azgın ata binebilen kimse; 'rough.shod; ride ~ over kaba davranmak *-e*; başkasının hakkını yemek; aldırmamak *-e*, önemsememek *-i.*

**rou.lette** [ru:'let] *n.* rulet.

**Rou.ma.nian** [ru:'meinjən] = Rumanian.

**round** [raund] **1.** ☐ yuvarlak, toparlak, küresel, top; tam; dolgun *(ses)*; hayli, çok; yuvarlak *(rakam)*; süratli, hızlı, atik; okkalı *(küfür)*; ~ hand okunaklı el yazısı; ~ table yuvarlak masa toplantısı; ~ trip gidiş dönüş, tur; **2.** *adv.* etrafa, etrafında, civarında; *a.* ~ about civarda; all ~ çepeçevre; *fig.* fark gözetmeksizin, ayırmaksızın; all the year ~ tüm yıl boyunca; 40 inches ~ çevresi kırk inç; **3.** *prp. -in* etrafın(d)a, *-in* çevresin(d)e; go ~ the house evi gezmek; ~ about 8 o'clock saat 8 sularında; **4.** *n.* yuvarlak, daire; devir, sefer, posta; sıra; ♪ kanon; ✕ devriye; *boks:* ravnt; dönem; parti; ✕ tek atış, bir el; 100 ~s ✕ yüz el atış; **5.** *v/t. & v/i.* yuvarlaklaş(tır)mak ,yuvarlak hale getirmek; büzmek *(dudak)*; dönmek *-den*, dolaşmak; ~ off yuvarlak yapmak *(sayı)*; bitirmek, tamamlamak; ~ up bir araya toplamak; yakalamak *(suçlu)*; yuvarlak yapmak *(sayı)*.

**round.a.bout** ['raundəbaut] **1.** *adj.* dolambaçlı; dolaylı; **2.** *n.* atlıkarınca, dönme dolap; *mot.* yuvarlak kavşak, döner ada.

**roun.del** ['raundl] *n:* daire içinde kabartma *veya* resim gibi süs; askeri uçağın hangi millete ait olduğunu gösteren yuvarlak levha; **roun.de.ly** [¹~dilei] *n.* nakaratlı basit ve kısa şarkı.

**round.ers** [¹raundəz] *n. pl.* beysbola benzer bir oyun; ¹**round.head** *n. hist.* İngiltere iç savaşında cumhuriyetçi; ¹**round-ish** *adj.* yuvarlakça; ¹**round.ness** *n.* yuvarlaklık, toparlaklık; dolgunluk; **rounds-man** † [¹~zmən] *n.* dağıtıcı; ¹**round-the-clock** *adj.* gece gündüz, devamlı, 24 saat; ¹**round-ta.ble con.fer.ence** yuvarlak masa konferansı; ¹**round-up** *n.* bir araya toplama; toparlama.

**roup** *vet.* [ru:p] *n.* bir çeşit tavuk nezlesi.

**rouse** [rauz] *v/t. & v/i.* uyan(dır)mak; canlandırmak; tahrik etm., kışkırtmak; ~ o.s. bütün gücünü toplamak, canlanmak; ¹**rous.ing** *adj.* heyecan verici; büyük, eşsiz; faal, canlı.

**roust.a.bout** *Am.* [¹raustə¹baut] *n.* gemi *veya* rıhtım işçisi, iskele hamalı; vasıfsız işçi.

**rout¹** [raut] *n.* ayaktakımı, izdiham, halk yığını; † serseri takımı; parti, eğlence.

**rout²** [~] 1. *n.* bozgun; put to ~ = 2. *v/t.* bozguna uğratmak.

**rout³** [~] = root².

**route** [ru:t, ✕ *a.* raut] *n.* yol; rota; ✕ yürüyüş yolu; en ~ yolda; ¹~-**march** *n.* adi adım yürüyüş, uzun talim yürüyüşü.

**rou.tine** [ru:¹ti:n] 1. *n.* usül, iş programı; 2. *adj.* alışılmış, her zamanki; düzenli.

**rove** [rəuv] *vb.* dolaşmak, gezinmek; ¹**rov-er** *n.* gezen (*veya* avare) kimse.

**row¹** [rəu] *n.* dizi, saf, sıra *a.* (*thea.*); a hard ~ to hoe güç iş, zorluklarla dolu hayat.

**row²** [~] 1. *v/i.* kürek çekmek; *v/t.* kürek çekerek götürmek; 2. *n.* kürek çekme; sandal gezintisi.

**row³** F [rau] 1. *n.* kavga, patırtı, münakaşa, kargaşa, gürültü; what's the ~? ne oluyor yahu?; 2. *vb.* azarlamak, haşlamak; kavga (*veya* münakaşa) etm. (with *ile*).

**row.an** ♣ [¹rauən] *n.* üvez.

**row-boat** [¹rəubout] *n.* sandal, kayık.

**row.dy** [¹raudi] 1. *n.* külhanbeyi; 2. *adj.* zorba, kaba, terbiyesiz.

**row.el** [¹rauəl] 1. *n.* mahmuz; 2. *v/t.* mahmuzlamak.

**row.er** [¹rəuə] *n.* kürekçi, kayıkçı, sandalcı.

**row.ing-boat** [¹rəuiŋbəut] *n.* kayık, sandal.

**row.lock** [¹rɔlək] *n.* ıskarmoz.

**roy.al** [¹rɔiəl] 1. □ krala (*veya* krallığa) ait; krala yaraşır; şahane, muhteşem, görkemli 2. *n.* ↓ kontra babafingo; ¹**roy-**

**al.ism** *n.* kralcılık; ¹**roy.al.ist** 1. *n.* kralcı; 2. *adj.* kralcı...; ¹**roy.al.ty** *n.* hükümdarlık, krallık; saltanat; kâr hissesi, işletme payı.

**rub** [rʌb] 1. *n.* ovalama, sürt(ün)me; *fig.* güçlük, engel; there is the ~ işin güç yanı asıl bu, işte sorun da orada; 2. *v/t. & v/i.* sürt(ün)mek, ov(ala)mak; ovarak cilâlamak; ovuşturmak; sürmek; sürtüşmek; ~ along, ~ on, ~ through *fig.* geçinip gitmek; ~ down aşındırmak; zımparalayarak düzeltmek; kurulamak; ~ in ovarak yedirmek (*krem vs.*); *fig.* üzerinde ısrarla durmak; tekrar tekrar söylemek; ~ off çık(ar)mak, .dökülmek; sil(in)mek; ~ out sili(n)mek, çık(ar)mak; *Am. sl.* gebertmek, temizlemek; ~ up ovarak cilâlamak, silip parlatmak; tazelemek (*bilgi*).

**rub.ber** [¹rʌbə] *n.* lastik, kauçuk; silgi; ⊕ sürtünme levhası; ovan kimse *veya* alet; *Am.* prezervatif, kaput; ~s *pl.* lastik ayakkabı; *attr.* lastik..., kauçuk...; ~ check *Am. sl.* karşılıksız (*veya* sahte) çek; ~ solution lastik solüsyon; ¹~.**neck** *Am. sl.* 1. *n.* meraklı kimse, herkese *veya* herşeye dönüp dönüp bakan kimse; turla gezen turist; 2. *v/i.* merakla bakmak, dönüp dönüp bakmak; geziye çıkmak; ~ stamp lastik mühür, ıstampa; *Am.* F *fig.* taklitçi (*veya* kişiliksiz) kimse; ¹~-¹**stamp** *v/t.* düşünmeden onaylamak.

**rub.bish** [¹rʌbiʃ] *n.* süprüntü, çöp; *fig.* saçma; ¹**rub.bish.y** *adj. fig.* beş para etmez, tapon.

**rub.ble** [¹rʌbl] *n.* moloz (taşı), yapı döküntüsü.

**rube** *Am. sl.* [ru:b] *n.* yontulmamış (*veya* hödük) kimse.

**ru.be.fa.cient** ⚕ [ru:bi¹feiʃjənt] *adj.* deriyi kızartan.

**ru.bi.cund** [¹ru:bikənd] *adj.* kırmızı, al; yüzünden kan damlayan, sağlıklı.

**ru.bric** [¹ru:brik] *n.* kırmızı bölüm başlığı; kural, açıklama, direktif; *eccl.* dini bir kitapta bölüm başı; **ru.bri.cate** [¹~keit] *v/t.* kırmızı renkle yazmak.

**ru.by** [¹ru:bi] 1. *n. min.* yakut (rengi); lâl; *typ.* 5 ½ puntoluk harf; 2. *adj.* kırmızı, al.

**ruck** [rʌk] *n.:* the ~ kalabalık, izdiham, insan yığını; *at* yarışı: geri kalan atların oluşturduğu grup; the (common) ~ *fig.* normal yaşam düzeyi.

**ruck(.le)** [¹rʌk(l)] *v/t. & v/i. a.* ~ up buruş(tur)mak, kırış(tır)mak.

**ruck.sack** [¹rʌksæk] *n.* sırt çantası.

**ruc.tion** *sl.* [¹rʌkʃən] *n.* kargaşa, karışıklık, kıyamet.

**rud.der** ⚓, ⚓ [ˈrʌdə] *n.* dümen.

**rud.di.ness** [ˈrʌdinis] *n.* kırmızılık; **'rud-dy** *adj.* kırmızı, al; kırmızı yanaklı; *sl.* kahrolası.

**rude** □ [ruːd] **kaba**; terbiyesiz; edepsiz; sert, şiddetli; yontulmamış, kaba saba; ilkel; basit; dinç, kuvvetli, gürbüz; işlenmemiş, ham; vahşî; ayıp; **'rude.ness** *n.* kabalık; terbiyesizlik.

**ru.di.ment** *biol.* [ˈruːdimənt] *n.* gelişmemiş kısım (of *bir organın; a. fig.);* ~s *pl.* ilke, ilk adım; **ru.di.men.ta.ry** [~ˈmentəri] *adj.* temel; gelişmemiş, eksik.

**rue**[1] ¥ [ruː] *n.* sedefotu.

**rue**[2] [~] *v/t.* pişmanlık duymak *-den.*

**rue.ful** □ [ˈruːful] pişman; acıklı; **'rue-ful.ness** *n.* pişmanlık.

**ruff**[1] [rʌf]*n.* kırmalı yakalık.

**ruff**[2] [~] *iskambil:* **1.** *n.* kozla alma; **2.** *v/t.* kozla almak.

**ruf.fi.an** [ˈrʌfjən] *n.* kavgacı (*veya* gaddar, zalim) kimse; **'ruf.fi.an.ly** *adj.* zalimce, gaddarca, canavarca.

**ruf.fle** [ˈrʌfl] **1.** *n.* kırma, farbala, fırfır; hafifçe dalgalandırma (*su vs.); fig.* kargaşa, patırtı, gürültü; ~ collar kırmalı yaka; **2.** *v/t.* & *v/i.* kabartmak (*saç, tüy);* buruşturmak; büzmek, kırma yapmak; *fig.* rahatsız etm.; kız(dır)mak, öfkelen-(dir)mek; hafifçe dalgalandırmak, çırpıntılı yapmak (*göl vs.).*

**rug** [rʌg] *n.* halı, kilim; örtü.

**Rug.by** [ˈrʌgbi] *n. a.* ~ football Amerikan futbolu.

**rug.ged** □ [ˈrʌgid] engebeli, pürüzlü, arızalı; düzensiz; *fig.* sert, haşin; bakımsız; kaba, terbiyesiz; kırışık, buruşuk; kulak tırmalayıcı; sıhhatli, zinde; sağlam, dayanıklı; fırtınalı; **'rug.ged.ness** *n.* sertlik; kabalık; zindelik.

**rug.ger** F [ˈrʌgə] = Rugby.

**ru.in** [ˈruːin] **1.** *n.* yıkım, yıkılma, harabiyet; tahrip; perişanlık; iflâs; *mst* ~s *pl.* yıkıntı, kalıntı, harabe; lay in ~s harap etm., tahrip etm.; **2.** *v/t.* yıkmak, tahrip etm., harap etm., viraneye çevirmek; perişan etm., mahvetmek, altüst etm.; batırmak, iflâs ettirmek; bozmak; **ru.in'a-tion** *n.* yık(ıl)ma, yıkım, harabiyet; F felâket; **'ru.in.ous** □ yıkıcı, felâkete götüren; yıkık, harap, viran.

**rule** [ruːl] **1.** *n.* yönetim; idare; âdet; alışkanlık; yol, usül; *eccl.* kaide, kural; ☼ kanun, hüküm; *a.* standing ~ statü, tüzük; ⊕ cetvel, metre; as a ~ genellikle, çoğunlukla; ~(s) of court mahkeme hükümleri; ~(s) of the road yol nizamname-

si, trafik kuralları; ~ of three ♈ üçlü kuralı; ~ of thumb göz kararı, pratik usul; make it a ~ alışkanlık haline getirmek, âdet (*veya* prensip) edinmek; work to ~ kurallara uygun çalışmak; **2.** *v/t.* idare etm., yönetmek; *a.* ~ over hükmetmek; (cetvelle) çizmek (*kâğıt vs.);* dizginlemek, hâkim olm.; buyurmak, emretmek; çok etkilemek; ~ out çıkarmak, silmek; bir kenara bırakmak; önlemek, engellemek; *v/i.* üstün olm.; hüküm (*veya* saltanat) sürmek; † belli bir seviyede olm. (*fiyat);* **'rul.er** *n.* cetvel; hükümdar, yönetici; **'rul.ing** *n. part.* ☼ yargı, hüküm; çizme; çizgi; yönetim, hükümdarlık; ~ price † piyasada günlük fiyat, cari fiyat.

**rum**[1] [rʌm] *n.* rom; *Am.* alkollü içki.

**rum**[2] *sl.* □ [~] garip, tuhaf, acayip.

**Ru.ma.nian** [ruːˈmeinjən] **1.** *adj.* Romen; **2.** *n.* Romanyalı; Romen(ce).

**rum.ble**[1] [ˈrʌmbl] **1.** *n.* gürleme, gümbürtü, gürültü; guruldama, gurultu; *Am. a.* ~-seat *mot.* arka koltuk; *Am.* F dalaş, sokak kavgası; **2.** *v/i.* gümbürdemek, gürlemek (*gök);* guruldamak, gurlamak (*mide).*

**rum.ble**[2] *sl.* [~] *v/t. b-nin* içini okumak.

**ru.mi.nant** [ˈruːminənt] **1.** *adj.* gevişgetiren; **2.** *n.* gevişgetiren hayvan; **ru.mi-nate** [ˈ~neit] *v/i.* geviş getirmek; *fig.* derin derin düşünmek; **ru.mi'na.tion** *n.* geviş getirme; derin derin düşünme.

**rum.mage** [ˈrʌmidʒ] **1.** *n.* adamakıllı arama, araştırma; ~ sale fakirlerin yararına yapılan eşya satışı; **2.** *v/t.* araştırmak; didik didik aramak; *v/i.* araştırma yapmak.

**rum.mer** [ˈrʌmə] *n.* ayaklı içki bardağı.

**rum.my**[1] *sl.* □ [ˈrʌmi] = rum[2].

**rum.my**[2] [~] *n.* bir tür iskambil oyunu.

**ru.mo(u)r** [ˈruːmə] **1.** *n.* söylenti, şayia; dedikodu; **2.** *v/t.* yaymak, çıkarmak (*dedikodu);* it is ~ed söylentiye göre; **'~-mon.ger** *n.* dedikoducu kimse.

**rump** [rʌmp] *n. anat.* but; *orn.* kıç; *co.* popo, kıç; artan parça, bakiye.

**rum.ple** [ˈrʌmpl] *v/t.* buruşturmak; karmakarışık etm., bozmak.

**rump.steak** [ˈrʌmpsteik] *n.* biftek.

**rum.pus** F [ˈrʌmpəs] *n.* gürültü, şamata; kavga, münakaşa.

**rum-run.ner** *Am.* [ˈrʌmrʌnə] *n.* içki kaçakçısı.

**run** [rʌn] **1.** (*irr.) v/i. com.* koşmak; akmak, dökülmek (*nehir, su vs.):* gitmek; uzanmak; işlemek, çalışmak; adaylığını koymak (for *için);* dörtnala gitmek (*at);*

kaçmak, tüymek; arkadaşlık etm. (with *ile*); yarışmak; yuvarlanmak; kaçmak *(çorap)*; dönmek; göç etm. *(balık)*; erimek; irin akıtmak; yönelmek *-e*; devam etm.; oynanmak *(piyes)*; geçmek; yayılmak; ~ across s.o. *b-ne* rast gelmek, rastlamak; ~ after *-in* peşinden koşmak; ~ away kaçmak *(a. fig.)*; akıp gitmek; ~ down bitmek; durmak *(saat)*; çarpmak *-e*; *fig.* kuvvetten düşmek; ~ dry kurumak;.~ for koşmak *-e*; *parl.* adaylığını koymak *-e*; ~ high kabarmak, çok dalgalı olm. *(deniz)*; şiddetli olm. *(his, duygu)*; yükselmek, artmak *(fiyat)*; ~ in akınak *(su vs.)*; *b-ni* arabasıyla bırakmak; yarışmak; that ~s in the blood (family) aile içinde kalıtsal olm., aileden gelmek, kanında olm.; ~ into girmek *-e*; karşılaşmak *ile (güçlük)*; akmak, dökülmek *-e*; *b-ni* arabasıyla bırakmak; çarpmak *-e*; ulaşmak *-e*; ~ into s.o. *b-ne* rast gelmek, rastlamak; ~ low azalmak; ~ mad delirmek; ~ off kaçmak; gitmek; akmak; kaymak; ~ on konuşup durmak; geçmek *(vakit)*; ~ out sona ermek *(süre)*, bitmek, tükenmek; akmak; uzanmak; I have ~ out of tobacco tütünüm bitti; ~ over bir koşu gitmek; *b-ni* arabasıyla götürmek; taşmak; gezinmek; ~ short tükenmek, bitmek, kıtlaşmak; ~ through akmak; dolaşmak *(haber vs.)*; ~ to akmak, dökülmek *-e (nehir)*; *b-ni* arabasıyla götürmek; devam etm. *-e kadar*; uzanmak *-e doğru*; ulaşmak *-e*; F kesesi müsaade etm. *-e*; ~ up artmak, fırlamak *(fiyat)*; birikmek *(borç)*; ~ up to yanaşmak, yaklaşmak *-e*; ulaşmak *-e*; ~ (up)on *ile* meşgul olm. *(zihin)*; çarpmak, bindirmek *-e (gemi)*; ~ with yarışmak *ile*; arkadaşlık *etm. ile*; 2. *(irr.) v/t.* sürmek, kullanmak; yarıştırmak; aday göstermek; gütmek *(davar)*; *hunt.* kovalamak, takip etm.; yarmak *(abluka)*; batırmak, saplamak; geçirmek; çarpmak; kaçırmak *(mal)*; gezdirmek *(göz)*; işletmek, çalıştırmak; yönetmek, idare etm.; doldurmak; dökmek, akıtmak; tasfiye etm. *(petrol)*; girmek *(riske)*; çizmek; basmak *(kitap vs.)*; taşımak, nakletmek, götürmek; ~ the blockade ablukayı yarmak; ~ down arayıp bulmak; kovalayıp yakalamak; yormak, bitkin düşürmek; gezdirmek *(göz vs.)*; *fig.* yermek, kötülemek; be ~ down bitkin *(veya* yorgun) olm.; ~ errands haber götürmek *veya* bir iş için bir yere gitmek; ~ hard sıkıştırmak *(rakip)*; ~ in *mot.* alıştırmak, açmak; ge-

çirmek *(iplik vs.)*; batırmak, saplamak *(kılıç)*; eklemek, katmak; yarıştırmak; F içeri atmak, hapsetmek; ~ into batırmak, saplamak *(iğne, kılıç)*; sokmak *-e (borç vs.)*; ~ off akıtmak, boşaltmak; kaçırtmak *(davar)*; yazıverhek; basmak; ezbere okumak; etkilememek *-i*, tesir etmemek *-e*; ~ out uzatmak; salıvermek *(ip vs.)*; kovmak, sepetlemek; ~ over ezmek, çiğnemek; göz gezdirmek *-e*, gözden geçirmek *-i*; tekrarlamak *-i*, *-in* üzerinden geçmek; ~ s.o. through *b-ne* kılıç saplamak, *b-ni* süngülemek; ~ up çekmek *(bayrak)*; artırmak, yükseltmek *(borç vs.)*; yapıvermek; toplamak *(sayı)*; denemek *(motor)*; 3. *n.* koşma, koşuş; koşu *(part. sporda)*; gezi(nti); gidilen mesafe; yol, rota; seri, sıra; oynama *(veya* gösterim) süresi; süre; kümes bahçesi; akış, seyir; gidişat, eğilim; *spor:* sayı; kayma yokuşu; balık sürüsü; ✝ talep, rağbet (on, upon *-e)*; *Am.* çay, dere, ırmak; *part. Am.* çorap kaçığı; ♪ sesgeçidi, nağmeleme; ✝ cins, nevi, çeşit, tür; the common ~ alışılmış türden, sıradan; have a ~ of 25 nights *thea.* 25 gece oynamak; have the ~ of s.th. bşi serbestçe kullanabilmek; be in the ~ *veya* ~ing kazanma şansı olm.; in the long ~ eninde sonunda, zamanla; in the short ~ kısa vadede; on the ~ kaçmakta; telâş içinde, koşuşturmakta.

**run.a.bout** *mot.* [ˈrʌnəbaut] *n.* küçük araba.

**run.a.way** [ˈrʌnəwei] 1. *n.* kaçak, kaçgın, firarî; 2. *v/i.* kaçmak; 3. *adj.* kontrolden çıkmış; kaçak...

**rune** [ruːn] *n.* eski Germen alfabesinin bir harfi.

**rung**[1] [rʌŋ] *p.p. of* ring[2] 2.

**rung**[2] [~] *n.* portatif merdiven basamağı; sandalyenin basamak çubuğu; *fig.* kademe.

**run.ic** [ˈruːnik] *adj.* eski Germen alfabesi harfleriyle yazılmış.

**run-in** [ˈrʌnˈin] *n. spor:* hız alma mesafesi; F çatışma, anlaşmazlık.

**run.let** [ˈrʌnlit], **run.nel** [ˈrʌnl] *n.* çay, dere; su oluğu.

**run.ner** [ˈrʌnə] *n.* koşucu, atlet; ✕ haberci, ulak; kızak ayağı; kaçakçı; ⚘ yan filiz; uzun masa örtüsü; yol halısı, yolluk; ˈ~-ˈup *n. spor:* ikinci gelen yarışmacı *veya* takım.

**run.ning** [ˈrʌniŋ] 1. *adj.* koşan; akan; koşarak yapılan; sürekli, devamlı, aralıksız; işlek, bitişik *(elyazısı)*; koşuyla ilgili, koşu...; genel; içinde bulunulan *(ay,* yıl *vs.)*; arka arkaya, peş peşe; cera-hatli, akıntılı, sızıntılı; two days ~ peş peşe iki gün; ~ hand bitişik elyazısı; ~ start *spor:* hızlı başlangıç, iyi çıkış; ~ stitch düz dikiş; 2. *n.* koşu; koşma; '~-board *n. mot.,* 🚗 *etc.* marşpiye, basamak.

runt [rʌnt] *n. zo.* çelimsiz hayvan; *fig.* bücür kimse, beberuhi.

run.way ['rʌnwei] *n.* 🛫 pist; *hunt.* geçit.

ru.pee [ruːˈpiː] *n.* rupi.

rup.ture ['rʌptʃə] 1. *n.* kopma, kır(ıl)ma; kesilme; 🩺 fıtık; *fig.* dostça ilişkilerin sona ermesi; 2. *v/t.* & *v/i.* kop(ar)mak, kır(ıl)mak; ilişkisini kesmek; fıtık olm.

ru.ral □ ['ruərəl] köye ait, kırsal; tarımsal, ziraî; köy yaşamına ait; 'ru.ral.ize *vb.* köylüleştirmek; köyde yaşamak.

ruse [ruːz] *n.* hile, tuzak, oyun.

rush[1] 🎵 [rʌʃ] *n.* saz, hasırotu; *fig.* ıvır zıvır, fasa fiso.

rush[2] [~] 1. *n.* hamle, saldırış, hücum; koş(uştur)ma; telâş; üşüşme; sıkışıklık; hengâme; 🏃 büyük talep (for -*e*); ⚡ akım artışı; ~ hour(s *pl.*) işin *veya* trafiğin en yoğun olduğu zaman, kalabalık saatler; ~ order 🏃 acele sipariş; 2. *v/i.* koş(uştur)mak, acele etm.; fırlamak; ~ at saldırmak -*e*; ~ into extremes aşırıya kaçmak; ~ into print yayımlamakta acele etm.; *v/t.* acele ettirmek, koşturmak; püskürtmek; ✗ & *fig.* hücum etm. -*e*; acele ile yapmak; ~ s.o. off his feet *b-nin* iki ayağını bir pabuca sokmak; ~ through *parl.* acele ile meclisten geçirmek; 'rush.ing □ hararetli.

rusk [rʌsk] *n.* gevrek, peksimet.

rus.set ['rʌsit] 1. *adj.* koyu kırmızı; 2. *n.* koyu kırmızı renk; kış elması.

Rus.sia (leath.er) ['rʌʃə('leðə] *n.* Rus me-

şini, sahtiyan; 'Rus.sian 1. *adj.* Rus, Rusya *veya* Rusçaya ait; 2. *n.* Rus(yalı); Rusça.

rust [rʌst] 1. *n.* pas (rengi); 🌾 pas hastalığı; zehirli mantar; 2. *v/t.* & *v/i.* paslan(dır)mak (a. *fig.*).

rus.tic ['rʌstik] 1. *adj.* (~ally) köye ait, kırsal; *fig.* kaba saba, yontulmamış; 2. *n.* köylü; basit ve kaba kimse; rus.ti.cate ['~keit] *v/t.* & *v/i. univ.* geçici uzaklaştırma cezası vermek; kaba işçilikle yapmak; köyde yaşamak; rus.ti.ca.tion *n.* köyde yaşama; *univ.* geçici olarak uzaklaştırma; rus.tic.i.ty [~ˈtisiti] *n.* köylülük; köy yaşamı; kabalık.

rus.tle ['rʌsl] 1. *v/t.* & *v/i.* hışırda(t)mak; hışırtı çıkararak ilerlemek; *Am.* F davar çalmak; ~ up bulmak, bulup buluşturmak; 2. *n.* davar *veya* at hırsızı.

rust...: '~.less *adj.* paslanmaz; '~-'proof, '~.re'sist.ant *adj.* pas tutmaz; 'rust.y *adj.* paslı, paslanmış (a. *fig.*); *fig.* unutulmuş, ham, körelmiş; rengi atmış (*siyah kumaş).*

rut[1] *hunt.* [rʌt] 1. *n.* azgınlık dönemi, kösnüme; 2. *v/i.* kösnümek.

rut[2] [~] *n.* tekerlek izi; *part. fig.* alışkı, âdet.

ruth.less □ ['ruːθlis] merhametsiz, acımasız, zalim, insafsız; 'ruth.less.ness *n.* acımasızlık, merhametsizlik.

rut.ted ['rʌtid] *adj.* tekerlek izleriyle dolu (*yol).*

rut.ting *hunt.* ['rʌtiŋ] *adj.* kösnüme ile ilgili, kösnüme...; ~ season kösnüme mevsimi.

rut.ty ['rʌti] *adj.* tekerlek izleriyle dolu (*yol).*

rye 🌾 [rai] *n.* çavdar.

# S

**Sab.bath** [ˈsæbəθ] *n.* sebt günü, kutsal dinlenme günü *(Yahudilerin cumartesi, Hıristiyanların pazar günü).*

**sab.bat.i.cal** □ [səˈbætikəl] sebt gününe ait, tatil...; ~ year *üniv.* yedi yılda bir gelen tatil yılı *(öğretim üyesi için).*

**sa.ble** [ˈseibl] 1. *n. zo.* samur (kürkü); samur rengi, siyah renk; 2. *adj. lit.* siyah, çok koyu.

**sab.o.tage** [ˈsæbətɑːʒ] 1. *n.* sabotaj, baltalama; 2. *v/t.* baltalamak, sabote etm.

**sa.bre** [ˈseibə] 1. *n.* kılıç, suvari kılıcı; 2. *v/t.* kılıçtan geçirmek, katletmek.

**sac** *anat., zo* [sæk] *n.* kese, küçük torba.

**sac.cha.rin** ⚗ [ˈsækərin] *n.* sakarin; **sac.cha.rine** [ˈ~-rain] *adj.* çok tatlı..., şeker...; *fig.* şeker gibi, bal gibi; suni, yapay, yapmacık, doğal olmayan.

**sac.er.do.tal** □ [sæsəˈdəutl] papazlığa ait, papaz...

**sack¹** [sæk] 1. *n.* çuval, torba, *Am.* kese kâğıdı; bir çuval (dolusu); bol gelen ceket, kadın ceketi; **give (get)** the ~ *F* işinden çıkar(ıl)mak, tezkeresini eline vermek, sepetlemek; 2. *v/t.* torba vs'ye koymak; *F* işinden çıkarmak, atmak, kovmak.

**sack²** [~] 1. *n.* yağma, çapul; 2. *v/t.* yağma etm.

**sack³** [~] *n.* Güney Avrupa'ya mahsus beyaz şarap.

**sack.cloth** [ˈsækklɔːθ], **sack.ing** *n.* çuval bezi, çul.

**sac.ra.ment** *eccl.* [ˈsækrəmənt] *n. (Hıristiyanlıkta)* kutsal ayin; **sac.ra.men.tal** □ [~ˈmentl] dinî ayine ait, ayin niteliğinde.

**sa.cred** □ [ˈseikrid] kutsî, kutsal, mukaddes; dinî, dinsel *(şiir, müz·k)*; saygıdeğer, aziz, mübarek; **ˈsa.cred.ness** *n.* kutsiyet, kutsallık, azizlik.

**sac.ri.fice** [ˈsækrifais] 1. *n.* kurban; fedakârlık, özveri; **at** a ~ † zararına, pahasına; 2. *v/t. & v/i.* kurban etm.; feda etm., gözden çıkarmak; † zararına satmak.

**sac.ri.fi.cial** [sækriˈfiʃəl] *adj.* kurbanlık, kurbanla ilgili; † zararına, çok ucuza...

**sac.ri.lege** [ˈsækrilidʒ] *n.* kutsal bir yere *veya* şeye saygısızlık; tecavüz etme;

**sac.ri.le.gious** □ [~ˈlidʒəs] kutsal şeye saygısız, şerir, günahkâr; tecavüzkârane.

**sa.crist, sac.ris.tan** *eccl.* [sækrist(ən)] *n.* zangoç, kilise kayyumu, kilisede hizmet eden kimse.

**sac.ris.ty** *eccl.* [ˈsækristi] *n.* kilisede kutsal eşyaların muhafaza edildiği oda.

**sad** □ [sæd] kederli, üzgün; acıklı; acınacak, endişe verici; donuk, karanlık, kasvetli *(renk).*

**sad.den** [ˈsædn] *v/t. & v/i.* kederlen(dir)mek, acınmak, müteessir etm. *veya* olm., üz(ül)mek.

**sad.dle** [ˈsædl] 1. *n.* eyer; sırt; **break** to the ~ talim ve terbiye etm. *(at);* 2. *v/t.* eyerlemek; *fig.* ağırlık vermek, ağır gelmek, sıkıntı vermek; yüklemek *(upon),* **ˈ~-bag** *n.* heybe, hurç, eyer çantası; **ˈ~-cloth** *n.* haşa, çul, teğelti, eyer altına konan çul, **ˈsad.dler** *n.* saraç; **ˈsad.dler.y** *n.* saraçhane; saraçlık; saraciye.

**sad.ism** [ˈseidizəm] *n.* sadizm.

**sad.ness** [ˈsædnis] *n.* keder, üzgünlük, hüzün, üzüntü, mahzunluk, melânkoli, karasevda.

**sa.fa.ri** [səˈfɑːri] *n.* safari, *(part.* Afrika'da) av partisi.

**safe** [seif] 1. □ *com.* emin (from *-den),* güvenilir, emniyetli, sağlam; tehlikesiz, salim; **to be on the** ~ side ihtiyatlı davranmak, sonuçtan emin olm.; 2. *n.* kasa; yemek dolabı, teldolap; ~ deposit kasa dairesi; **ˈ~-blow.er** *n.* kasa hırsızı; ~ con.duct geçiş izni, himaye *veya* seyahat belgesi *(savaşta);* **ˈ~.guard** 1. *n.* koruma, himaye, koruyucu şey; muhafız; 2. *v/t.* korumak, emniyet altına almak (against *-e karşı);* ~ing duty koruyucu gümrük vergisi; **ˈsafe.ness** *n.* emniyet, güvenlik.

**safe.ty** [ˈseifti] *n.* güvenlik, asayiş, emniyet; ~ belt *mot.* emniyet kemeri; ~ **cur.tain** *thea.* yanmaz perde; ~ **is.land** trafik adası, refüj; **ˈ~-lock** *n.* emniyet kilidi: **ˈ~-pin** *n.* çengelli iğne; ~ **ra.zor** traş makinesi.

**saf.fron** [ˈsæfrən] 1. *n.* ⚘ safran; bu çiçegin boya maddesi *veya* baharat olarak kullanılan tohumları; koyu sarı renk; **2.** *adj.* safran renginde, koyu sarı.

**sag** [sæg] **1.** *v/i.* eğilmek, sarkmak, çökmek; ⊕ bel vermek; ↓ batmak *(a. fig.)*; rüzgâr altına sürüklenmek; düşmek *(fiyat)*; kaybolmak, kaçmak *(neşe, heves)*; **2.** *n.* çöküntü, eğilme; ⊕ bel verme; düşüş *(fiyat)*.

**sa.ga** [ˈsɑːgə] *n.* eski İskandinav hikâyesi, saga, efsane; destan.

**sa.ga.cious** ☐ [səˈgeiʃəs] akıllı, sağgörülü, zeki, anlayışlı, keskin görüşlü.

**sa.gac.i.ty** [səˈgæsiti] *n.* akıllılık, zekâ, anlayış, anlak, sağgörü.

**sag.a.more** [ˈsægəmɔː] *n.* kızılderili kabile reisi.

**sage**[1] [seidʒ] **1.** ☐ akıllı; hikmet sahibi, ağırbaşlı, hakim; **2.** *n.* hikmet sahibi kimse, yaşını başını almış akıllı kimse, filozof, bilge.

**sage**[2] ⚘ [~] *n.* adaçayı.

**sage.brush** ⚘ [ˈseidʒbrʌʃ] *n.* A.B.D.'de bir tür kokulu çalı.

**sa.go** [ˈseigəu] *n.* sagu, bir kaç tür hurma ağacından alınan bir tür nişasta.

**sa.hib** [ˈsɑːhib] *n.* Hindistan'da Avrupalılara verilen ünvan; efendi.

**said** [sed] *pret. & p.p. of* say 1.

**sail** [seil] **1.** *n.* yelken; deniz yolculuğu; yel değirmeni yelpazesi; yelkenli; set ~ yelken açıp denize açılmak; **2.** *v/t. & v/i.* yelkenliyle *(veya* gemiyle) gitmek; (gemi ile) yola çıkmak, ayrılmak; üzerinde seyretmek *(veya* gitmek); uç(ur)mak, süzülmek; yönetmek *(yelkenli)*; **ı~-boat** *n.* yelkenli gemi; **ı~-cloth** *n.* yelken bezi; **ısail.er** *n.* yelkenli gemi; **ısail.ing-ship,** **ısail.ing-ves.sel** *n.* yelkenli, yelken gemisi; **ısail.or** *n.* gemici, denizci; tayfa, deniz eri; ~'s knot gemici düğümü; be a good (bad) ~ k-ni deniz tut(ma)mak; **ısail-plane** *n.* planör.

**saint** [seint] **1.** *n. & adj.* kutsal, aziz, evliya, eren; *(özel ismin önünde:* S., St.) Ermiş. Aziz; **2.** *v/t.* azizler mertebesine çıkarmak; **ısaint.ed** *adj.* aziz; aziz mertebesine ulaşmış, cennete giden, merhum; mukaddes, kutsal; **ısaint.li.ness** *n.* azizlik. evliyalık; kutsiyet; **ısaint.ly** *adj.* evliya gibi, azizlere yakışır, mübarek.

**saith** † *veya poet.* [seθ] *3rd sg. person of* say

**sake** [seik] *n.*: for the ~ of *-in* uğruna, *-in* aşkına, *-in* hatırı için; for my ~ hatırım için, benim için; for God's ~ Allah aşkına.

**sal** ⚗ [sæl] *n.* tuz: ~ ammoniac nişadır;

~ volatile karbonat amonyum ruhu.

**sal.a.ble** [ˈseiləbl] *adj.* satılabilir, geçer.

**sa.la.cious** ☐ [səˈleijəs] şehvani, şehvetli; müstehcen, açık saçık.

**sal.ad** [ˈsæləd] *n.* salata.

**sal.a.man.der** [ˈsæləmændə] *n. zo.* semender; ateşte yanmayan efsanevi bir tür hayvan: ocak demiri; salamandra.

**sa.la.mi** [səˈlɑːmiː] *n.* salam.

**sal.a.ried** [ˈsælərid] *adj.* maaşlı, ücretli; maaşlı...; **ısal.a.ry** **1.** *n.* maaş, ücret, aylık; **2.** *v/t.* maaş *(veya* aylık, ücret) vermek; **ısal.a.ry.earn.er** maaş *(veya* aylık ücret) alan kimse.

**sale** [seil] *n.* satış, satım, satma, satılış; mezat; talep, revaç; indirimli satış; for ~, on ~ satılık; by private ~ el altından satış; **ısale.a.ble** *adj.* satılabilir.

**sales**... [seilz]: **ı~.man** *n.* satıcı, tezgâhtar; **ı~.man.ship** *n.* satıcılık, satma yeteneği, işin adamı *(veya* eri) olma; ~ re-**sist.ance** alıcının isteksizliği *veya* satıcıyı geri çevirebilmesi; **ı~.wom.an** *n.* satıcı kadın.

**sa.li.ence** [ˈseiljəns] *n.* çıkıntı, çıkma, cumba; göze çarpan şey; dikkati çekme; **ısa.li.ent** **1.** ☐ belirgin, çarpıcı, göze çarpan, dikkati çeken; çıkıntılı, çıkık; *fig.* mükemmel, mümtaz, frapan, birinci kalitede; **2.** *n.* çıkıntı, cumba; ✕ *(cephe, siper)* dış açı.

**sa.line** **1.** [ˈseilain] *adj.* tuzlu; tuz gibi, tuz...; **2.** [səˈlain] *n.* madensel tuz; tuzla; 🜊 tuzlu eriyik.

**sa.li.va** *physiol.* [səˈlaivə] *n.* salya, tükürük; **sal.i.var.y** [ˈsæliverı] *adj.* salya ile ilgili; tükürük salgılayan; **sal.iˈva.tion** *n.* tükürük çıkarma *(veya* salgılama).

**sal.low**[1] ⚘ [ˈsæləu] *n.* bodur söğüt ağacı.

**sal.low**[2] ⚘ [~] *adj.* soluk yüzlü, benzi sararmış; **ısal.low.ness** *n.* solgunluk, sarılık, solukluk.

**sal.ly** [ˈsæli] **1.** *n.* ✕ çıkış, çemberi yarma, huruç hareketi; nükteli çıkış, espri; **2.** *v/i.* ✕ *a.* ~ out dışarı fırlamak, çemberi yarmak; ~ forth, ~ out yola düzülmek, toplu harde çıkmak.

**sal.ma.gun.di** [sælməˈgʌndi] *n. (kıyılmış et, ançüez, yumurta ve sebze karışımı)* bir tür salata; *fig.* karmakarışık şey.

**salm.on** [ˈsæmən] *n.* som balığı (rengi); **2.** *adj.* som balığı renginde, sarımsı pembe.

**sal.on** [ˈsælɔn] *n.* ressam ve yazarlar topluluğu; sergi salonu, galeri; güzel sanatlar sergisi; salon, misafir odası.

**sa.loon** [səˈluːn] *n.* büyük salon; birinci mevki salon *(gemide)*; bar; *Am.* meyhane; = **sa¹loon-car** 🚗 *n.* vagon-salon; *mot.* üstü kapalı 4-7 kişilik otomobil, limozin.

**salt** [sɔːlt] **1.** *n.* tuz; *fig.* tat, tat tuz, lezzet, çeşni; tuzluk; *old ~ fig.* eski deniz kurtlarından; with a grain of ~ hakları kullanabilme koşuluyla; kuşkuyla, ihtiyatla; **2.** *adj.* tuzlu; tuzlanmış; **3.** *v/t.* tuzlamak *-i*, salamura yapmak *-i*; *fig.* heyecan katmak, ilginç göstermek; **¹~-cel.lar** *n.* tuzluk; **¹salt.ed** *adj.* tuzlu; *sl.* bağışık, pişkin; **salt.pe.tre** [¹~piːtə] *n.* güherçile; **¹salt-wa.ter** *adj.* tuzlu su(da) ...; **¹salt.works** *n. sg.* tuzla, tuz fabrikası; **¹salt.y** *adj.* tuzlu; denizi hatırlatan; keskin, nükteli, müstehcene kaçan.

**sa.lu.bri.ous** ☐ [sə¹luːbriəs] sağlam, salim, sıhhatli, sıhhî; **sa.lu.bri.ty** [sə¹luːbriti], **sal.u.tar.i.ness** [¹sæljutərinis] *n.* sıhhatlilik, yararlılık, sıhhî oluş; **sal.u.tar.y** ☐ [¹sæljutəri] = salubrious.

**sal.u.ta.tion** [sælju:¹teiʃən] *n.* selâm (verme), hatır sorma; hitap, seslenme; **sa.lu.ta.to.ry** [sɔl¹juːtətəri] *adj.* selâm niteliğinde; selâm veren; **sa.lute** [sə¹luːt] **1.** *n.* selâm (verme); *co.* öpücük, buse; X selâmlama; **2.** *vb.* selâmlamak, selâm vermek; X selâm çakmak; resmî saygıda bulunmak, karşılamak.

**sal.vage** [¹sælvidʒ] **1.** *n.* tahlisiye (ücreti), kurtarma ve yardım (ücreti); kurtarılan mal; **2.** *v/t.* kurtarmak, çıkarmak, emniyet altına almak (*eşya*).

**sal.va.tion** [sæl¹veiʃən] *n.* kurtuluş, kurtar(ıl)ma, kurtarış, selâmet; *fig.* kurtuluş; **2** Army selâmet ordusu, fakirler için para toplayan bir Protestan grubu; **sal-¹va.tion.ist** *n.* selâmet ordusu üyesi.

**salve¹** [sælv] *v/t.* (*kaza, deniz veya yangından*) kurtarmak.

**salve²** [saɑːv] **1.** *n.* merhem, pomat; *fig.* teselli; **2.** *v/t.* mst *fig.* merhem sürmek; acısını dindirmek, teskin etm.

**sal.ver** [¹sælvə] *n.* tepsi.

**sal.vo** [¹sælvəu] *n., pl.* **sal.voes** [¹~z] X salvo, yaylım ateşi; selâm topu; *fig.* alkış, kahkaha vs. tufanı; ~ release 🎯 bombardıman; **sal.vor** ⚓ [¹~və] *n.* kurtarma gemisi.

**Sa.mar.i.tan** [sə¹mæritn] **1.** *adj.* Samiriye ile ilgili; **2.** *n.* Samiriyeli, Samiriye dili.

**same** [seim]: the ~ aynı, tıpkı(sı); eşit; adı geçen; all the ~ bununla beraber, mamafih, yine, hal böyle iken; it is all the ~ to me bence hepsi bir, benim için hava hoş; **¹same.ness** *n.* ayrılık, monotonluk, tekdüzelik; benzerlik.

**samp** *Am.* [sæmp] *n.* iri taneli öğütülmüş

mısır unu.

**sam.ple** [¹saːmpl] **1.** *n. part.* † numune, örnek, eşəntiyon; mostra; model, tip; **2.** *v/t.* örnek olarak denemek, numune almak; çeşnisine bakmak, kalitesini saptamak; **¹sam.pler** *n.* el işi örneği; örnekleri deneyen kimse, çeşnici.

**san.a.tive** [¹sænətiv] *adj.* iyileştiren, şifa verici; sıhhi, yararlı; **san.a.to.ri.um** [~¹tɔːriəm] *n.* (*part. akciğer*) sanatoryum, sağlık yurdu; temiz havalı yer; **san.a.to.ry** [¹~təri] *adj.* şifa verici; yararlı.

**sanc.ti.fi.ca.tion** [sæŋktifi¹keiʃən] *n.* kutsama, takdis, tasvip; resmen ibadete tahsis; **sanc.ti.fy** [¹~fai] *v/t.* kutsallaştırmak, takdis etm.; tasvip etm., onaylamak; günahlardan arındırmak; **sanc.ti-mo.ni.ous** ☐ [~¹məunjəs] kaba sofu, iki yüzlü, riyakâr; **sanc.tion** [¹sæŋkʃən] **1.** *n.* onay, tasdik, tasvip; yaptırım, zorunlu önlem; **2.** *v/t.* uygun bulmak, onaylamak; **sanc.ti.ty** [¹~titi] *n.* kutsallık, mukaddes olma; **sanc.tu.ar.y** [¹~tjuəri] *n.* kutsal yer; tapınak, mabet; sığınak; **sanc.tum** [¹~təm] *n.* kutsal yer; inziva yeri, *b-nin* sessiz ve yalnız olabileceği yer.

**sand** [sænd] **1.** *n.* kum; ~s *pl.* kumluk, kumsal, kum çölü; his ~s are running out ömrünün sonuna geldi, ömrü kısalıyor; **2.** *v/t.* üstüne kum serpmek, içine kum atmak, kumla örtmek.

**san.dal¹** [¹sændl] *n.* çarık, sandal.

**san.dal²** [~], **¹~.wood** *n.* sandal ağacı, sandal tahtası.

**sand...**: **¹~.bag** *n.* kum torbası; **¹~.bank** *n.* kumsal sığlık, kum bankı (*su altında*); **¹~.blast** ⊕ *n.* kum fışkırtma aleti; **¹~.boy** *n.*: as jolly as a ~ çok keyifli; **¹~.glass** *n.* kum saati; **¹~.hill** *n.* kumul, kum tepesi; **¹~.pa.per 1.** *n.* zımpara kâğıdı; **2.** *v/t.* zımparalamak *-i*; **¹~.pip.er** *n. orn.* kum çulluğu; **¹~.shoes** *n.* plaj ayakkabısı, lastik tabanlı bez ayakkabı; **¹~.stone** *n.* kumtaşı, gre.

**sand.wich** [¹sænwidʒ] **1.** *n.* sandviç; **2.** *v/t.* *a.* ~ in *-in* arasına yerleştirmek, sıkıştırmak; **¹~.man** *n.* önünde ve arkasında reklam yaftaları asılı gezen adam.

**sand.y** [¹sændi] *adj.* kumlu; kum...; kumsal; kum rengine çalan, saman sarısı (*saç*).

**sane** [sein] *adj.* aklı başında, akıllı; makûl; mantıklı (*cevap vs.*).

**San.for.ize** [¹sænfəraiz] *vb.* çekmesini önlemek üzere özel bir işleme tabi tutmak (*kumaş*).

**sang** [sæŋ] *pret. of* sing.

**san.gui.nary** ☐ ['sæŋgwinəri] kana susamış, kan dökücü, zalim; kanlı; **san.guine** ['~gwin] adj. neşeli, kanı sıcak (mizaçlı); iyimser, ümitli, emin; gayretli; kan gibi kırmızı (cilt); **san.guin.e.ous** [~ 'giwiniəs] adj. kan...; = s. sanguine.

**san.i.tari.an** [sæni'tɛəriən] n. sağlık uzmanı, sıhhiyeci; **san.i.ta.ri.um** [sæni'tɛəriəm] n. Am. of sanatorium; **san.i.tar.y** ☐ ['~təri] sağlıkla ilgili, ⊕ sıhhî...; ~ towel âdet bezi.

**san.i.ta.tion** [sæni'teiʃən] n. sağlık koruma, hıfzısıhha; sağlık işleri (örgütü); sıhhî tertibat; **'san.i.ty** n. akıl sağlığı, akıllılık, aklı başında olma.

**sank** [sæŋk] pret. of sink 1.

**sans** lit. [sænz] prp. -siz.

**San.skrit** ['sænskrit] n. Sanskrit dili, Sanskritçe.

**San.ta Claus** [sæntə'klɔːz] n. Noel baba.

**sap**[1] [sæp] n. ♀ özsu, usare; fig. canlılık, dirilik, hayatiyet, öz, ruh; sl. alık, öküz aleyhisselâm; pısırık, sünepe.

**sap**[2] [~] 1. n. ✗ lağım, siper, hendek, sıçanyolu; inek, çok çalışan, hafızlayan kimse; 2. v/i. siper kazmak; sl. ineklemek, hafızlamak; v/t. altından sıçanyolu kazarak yıkmak -i, lağım açmak; kuvvetten düşürmek -i, takatini kesmek -in. **sap.id** ['sæpid] adj. lezzetli, tadı tuzu yerinde; **sa.pid.i.ty** [sə'piditi] n. lezzet, çeşni, tat.

**sa.pi.ence** mst iro. ['seipjəns] n. akıl, hikmet, dirayet; **'sa.pi.ent** mst iro. ☐ akıllı, hikmetli, dirayetli.

**sap.less** ['sæplis] adj. kuvvetsiz, kudretsiz, mecalsiz, takatsiz.

**sap.ling** ['sæpliŋ] n. fidan, körpe ağaç; fig. delikanlı, genç çocuk.

**sap.o.na.ceous** ⌐ veya co. [sæpəu'neiʃəs] adj. sabunlu, sabun gibi.

**sap.per** ✗ ['sæpə] n. istihkâm eri, sıçanyolu kazan.

**sap.phire** min. ['sæfaiə] n. safir, gökyakut.

**sap.pi.ness** ['sæpinis] n. canlılık, hayatiyet; özlü oluş; toyluk.

**sap.py** ['sæpi] adj. özlü; canlı; fig. dinç, kuvvetli; sl. ahmak, sünepe, alık.

**Sar.a.cen** ['særəsn] n. Haçlı seferleri zamanında müslümanlara verilen ad.

**sar.casm** ['sɑːkæzəm] n. dokunaklı alay, acı istihza, şaraka; **sar.cas.tic, sar.cas.ti.cal** ☐ [sɑː'kæstik(əl)] iğneleyici, istihzalı, alaylı, dokunaklı, müstehzi, tahkiramiz, sarkastik.

**sar.coph.a.gus** n., pl. **sar.coph.a.gi** [sɑː-'kɔfəgəs, gai] lahit, sanduka.

**sar.dine** ichth. [sɑː'diːn] n. sardalya, ateş balığı.

**Sar.din.i.an** [sɑː'dinjən] 1. adj. Sardinya ile ilgili; 2. n. Sardinyalı.

**sar.don.ic** [sɑː'dɔnik] adj. (~ally) alaycı, hor gören, acı, hakaret dolu, sinik, kelbi.

**sar.to.ri.al** [sɑː'tɔːriəl] adj. terzi veya terziliğe ait.

**sash**[1] [sæʃ] n. pencere çerçevesi.

**sash**[2] [~] n. geniş kuşak, omuz atkısı.

**sash-window** ['sæʃwindəu] n. sürme pencere.

**sas.sa.fras** ♀ ['sæsəfræs] n. kuzey Amerika ve Asya'da yetişen bir tür küçük ağaç.

**sat** [sæt] pret. & p.p. of sit.

**Sa.tan** ['seitən] n. eccl. Şeytan, İblis.

**sa.tan.ic** [sə'tænik] adj. (~ally) şeytani, şeytanca, ibliskârane, hınzırca.

**satch.el** ['sætʃəl] n. okul çantası, el çantası.

**sate** [seit] = satiate.

**sa.teen** [sæ'tiːn] n. satene benzer pamuklu kumaş.

**sat.el.lite** ['sætəlait] n. (a. suni, yapma) uydu, peyk, satelit, bir gezegenin uydusu; uydu devlet.

**sa.ti.ate** ['seiʃieit] v/t. doyurmak, kandırmak, tok hale getirmek, tıka basa yedirmek, b-nin açlığını gidermek; **sa.ti.a.tion** n. doy(ur)ma; **sa.ti.e.ty** [sə'taiəti] n. doymuşluk, usanç, gına, tokluk.

**sat.in** ['sætin] n. saten, atlas; **sat.i.net(te)** [~'net] n. ince saten veya saten taklidi kumaş.

**sat.ire** ['sætaiə] n. hiciv, yergi, taşlama; **sa.tir.ic, sa.tir.i.cal** ☐ [sə'tirik(əl)] yergili, hicivli, satirik; **sat.i.rist** ['sætərist] n. hicivci, taşlama yazarı; **'sat.i.rize** v/t. alay etm., istihza etm. hicvetmek.

**sat.is.fac.tion** [sætis'fækʃən] n. hoşnutluk, memnuniyet; tarziye, hoşnut etme, tatmin; ödeme, tazmin.

**sat.is.fac.to.ri.ness** [sætis'fæktərinis] n. memnuniyet verici durum, yeterlik; **sat.is'fac.to.ry** ☐ memnuniyet verici, hoşnut kılan; doyurucu, tatminkâr, kâfi, yeterli.

**sat.is.fied** ☐ ['sætisfaid] memnun, hoşnut, tatmin olmuş, ikna olmuş, inanmış; **sat.is.fy** ['~fai] vb. com. memnun etm. -i, hoşnut etm. -i; tazmin etm., zararı ödemek; yetmek, kâfi gelmek; koşulları yerine getirmek; b-ni bşe inandırmak, ikna etm. (of); doyurmak; ortadan kaldırmak (şüphe).

**sa.trap** ['sætrəp] n. eski İran'da vali.

**sat.u.rate** ⌐ & fig. ['sætʃəreit] v/t. doyurmak, doymuş hale getirmek, içirmek, iş-

ba haline getirmek; **sat.u'ra.tion** *n.* do-
y(ur)ma, işba.
**Sat.ur.day** ['sætədi] *n.* cumartesi.
**Sat.urn** ['sætən] *n.* Satürn, zühal; *myth.*
Satürn, ziraat tanrısı; **sat.ur.nine** ['~na-
in] *adj.* melânkolik, asık yüzlü, sıkıcı,
kasvetli.
**sat.yr** ['sætə] *n.* yarı insan yarı keçi şeklinde bir yarıtanrı; şehvet düşkünü kimse.
**sauce** [sɔːs] **1.** *n.* (*oft. soğuk*) salça, sos;
*Am.* komposto; *fig.* tat, lezzet, çeşni; F
yüzsüzlük, küstahlık; **2.** *v/t.* sos ilâve
etm., lezzet, çeşni katmak; F *b-nin* tepesine çıkmak, küstahlık etm.; '**~boat** *n.*
salçalık; '**~.pan** *n.* uzun saplı tencere,
kaçarula; **'sauc.er** *n.* fincan tabağı.
**sau.ci.ness** F ['sɔːsinis] *n.* arsızlık, saygısızlık, küstahlık.
**sau.cy** □ F ['sɔːsi] küstah, cüretli, arsız,
saygısız, yüzsüz, utanmaz, pişkin.
**saun.ter** ['sɔːntə] **1.** *n.* ağır ağır ve amaçsız yapılan yürüyüş, dolaşma, gezinti,
gezme; **2.** *v/i.* yavaş yavaş dolaşmak, gezinmek; **'saun.ter.er** *n.* avare, kaldırım
mühendisi.
**sau.ri.an** *zo.* ['sɔːriən] *n.* kertenkele ve
timsah türünden eski çağ hayvanı, sor-
yen.
**sau.sage** ['sɔsidʒ] *n.* sucuk, salam, sosis.
**sau.té** ['səutei] *adj.* tavada hafif kızartılmış, sote (*az yağda*).
**sav.age** ['sævidʒ] **1.** □ vahşi, yabanî, medeniyetsiz; yırtıcı, gaddar, merhametsiz,
zalim; işlenmemiş, yontulmamış; F gazaplı, şiddetli, hiddetli; **2.** *n.* vahşi, barbar, zalim kimse; medeniyetsiz kimse;
**3.** *v/t.* vahşice saldırmak (*hayvan*);
**'sav.age.ness, 'sav.age.ry** *n.* yabanilik,
barbarlık, vahşet, gaddarlık, vandalizm.
**sa.van.na(h)** [sə'vænə] *n.* savana, ağaçsız
ova, kır.
**sav.ant** ['sævənt] *n.* âlim, bilgin, hakim.
**save** [seiv] **1.** *v/t.* & *v/i.* kurtarmak; (*gemi vs*) çıkarmak, kurtarmak; korumak,
saklamak, muhafaza etm. (from *-den*);
biriktirmek, tasarruf etm.; sakınmak,
esirgemek; kaybını önlemek, kazandırmak; para biriktirmek, tutumlu olm.; **2.**
*prp.* & *cj. a.* ~ that *-den* başka, maada,
müstesna, yalnız.
**sav.e.loy** ['sæviloi] *n.* bir tür yağsız pişirilmiş sosis.
**sav.er** ['seivə] *n.* kurtarıcı; para birikti-
ren kimse; para ve zaman kazandıran
alet.
**sav.ing** ['seiviŋ] **1.** □ tasarrufkâr, tutumlu, idareli; **2.** *n.* kurtarma; ~s *pl.* birik-

tirilen paralar, tasarruf, iktisat.
**sav.ings...** ['seiviŋz]: '**~bank** *n.* tasarruf
sandığı *veya* bankası; '**~de.pos.it** *n.* tasarruf.
**sav.io(u)r** ['seivjə] *n.* kurtarıcı, halâskâr,
Saviour Hazreti İsa.
**sa.vo(u)r** ['seivə] **1.** *n.* tat, lezzet, çeşni;
*fig.* lezzet, tat tuz; **2.** *v/i.* tadı olm., andırmak (of *-i*), kokmak; *v/t.* tadına bakmak, kokusunu almak *-in*; tadını (*veya*
zevkini) çıkarmak *-in*; **sa.vo(u)r.i.ness**
['~rinis] *n.* lezzetlilik, hoş tat; **'sa.vo(u)r-
less** *adj.* tatsız (tuzsuz), kokusuz.
**sa.vo(u)r.y¹** □ ['seivəri] lezzetli, tadı tuzu
yerinde, iştah açıcı; güzel kokulu; baharatlı.
**sa.vo(u)r.y²** ♀ [~] *n.* kekiğe benzer bir tür
kokulu ot.
**sa.voy** [sə'vɔi] *n.* bir tür kıvırcık kış lahanası.
**sav.vy** *sl.* ['sævi] **1.** *v/i.* anlamak, idrak
etm., kavramak; **2.** *n.* kavrayış, anlayış,
anlak, idrak, kafa.
**saw¹** [sɔː] *pret. of* see.
**saw²** [~] *n.* vecize, atasözü, özdeyiş, darbımesel.
**saw³** [~] **1.** *n.* testere, bıçkı, hızar; **2.** *vb.*
testere ile kesmek, bıçkılamak; '**~.dust**
*n.* testere talaşı, bıçkı tozu; '**~-horse** *n.*
tahta biçmeye mahsus sehpa; '**~-mill** *n.*
kereste fabrikası, hızarhane; **saw** [sɔːn]
*p.p. of* saw³ **2.**; **saw.yer** ['~jə] *n.* bıçkıcı,
hızarcı.
**Sax.on** [sæksn] **1.** *adj.* Saksonya ile ilgili; Sakson...; Cermen...; **2.** *n.* Saksonyalı.
**sax.o.phone** ♪ ['sæksəfəun] *n.* saksafon.
**say** [sei] **1.** (*irr.*) *v/t.* söylemek, demek;
ezberden söylemek; beyan etm.; bildir-
mek, haber vermek; ~ grace yemekten
önce ve sonra dua etm.; ~ mass kuddas
ayini yapmak; that is to ~ yani, demek
ki; do you ~ so? sahi mi (diyorsun)?;
you don't ~ so! yok canım!, deme!; I ~!
(*bir tümce başında dikkati çekmek için
kullanılan deyim*) bana bak!, beni dinle!, yaa!; he is said to be... onun -diği
söyleniyor; no sooner said than done demesiyle yapması bir oldu; **2.** *n.* söz, denilen şey, kelam, kelime; söz sırası; it
is my ~ now şimdi söz sırası benim; let
him have his ~ bırak söyleyeceğini söylesin; have a *veya* some (no) ~ in s.th.
bir meselede söz sahibi ol(ma)mak; '**saying** *n.* söz; atasözü, özdeyiş; it goes
without ~ hiş kuşku yok ki, elbette.
**scab** [skæb] *n.* yara kabuğu; uyuz illeti;
*sl.* grev bozan.
**scab.bard** ['skæbəd] *n.* (*kılıç vs.*) kın.

scabby

464

scab.by □ [ˈskæbi] yara gibi kabuk kabuk olan, kabuk bağlamış; uyuz, uyuza tutulmuş.

sca.bi.es ⚑ [ˈskeibiːz] n. uyuz illeti.

sca.bi.ous ⚑ [ˈskeibjəs] n. uyuzotu.

sca.brous [ˈskeibrəs] adj. pul pul, kabuk bağlamış, kepekli, pürtüklü; pürüzlü, çapraşık; açık saçık, edepsizce, yakışıksız.

scaf.fold [ˈskæfəld] n. yapı iskelesi, darağacı platformu; ˈscaf.fold.ing n. yapı iskelesi kerestesi.

scald [skɔːld] 1. n. haşlama, haşlayıp yakma; kaynar sudan ileri gelen yanık veya yara; 2. vb. kaynar su ile haşlamak; a. ~ out iyice kaynatmak; (süt) kaynatmak.

scale¹ [skeil] 1. n. balık pulu; kazan çeperine yapışan kefeki (taşı); diş pası, kefeki, pesek; remove the ~s from s.o.'s eyes b-nin gözünü açmak, gerçekleri görmesini sağlamak; 2. v/t. pullarını çıkarmak, derisini yüzmek; üst kısmını kazımak; ⊕ (kazandaki kefeki taşı) vurarak düşürmek; (diş pası) temizlemek; v/i. oft. ~ off pul pul dökülmek.

scale² [~] 1. n. terazi gözü, kefe; (a pair of) ~s pl. terazi; ~s pl. ast. Mizan, Terazi; 2. v/t. tartmak, ağırlığını ölçmek.

scale³ [~] 1. n. ölçek; dereceli cetvel; ♪ ıskala, gam; derece taksimatı, derece; fig. ölçü, mikyas; on a large ~ geniş ölçüde (veya çapta); 2. v/t. bşe tırmanmak, çıkmak; ~ up (down) belli oranda büyütmek (küçültmek).

scaled [skeild] adj. pullu; kepekli.

scale.less [ˈskeillis] adj. pulsuz; kepeksiz.

scal.ing-lad.der [ˈskeiliŋlædə] n. ✕ tırmanma merdiveni; yangın merdiveni.

scal.lion ⚑ [ˈskæljən] n. yeşil soğan; pırasa.

scal.lop [ˈskɔləp] 1. n. zo. tarak; tarak kabuğu şeklinde tabak veya tava; tarak kabuğu şeklinde işlenmiş oya, fisto; 2. v/t. tarak kabuğ şeklinde kesmek veya yapmak; yemeğin üstüne sos katarak fırında pişirmek; fisto yapmak.

scalp [skælp] 1. n. kafatasını kaplayan deri; zafer alâmeti; 2. v/t. -in başının derisini yüzmek; karaborsa sinema, tiyatro vs. bileti satmak.

scal.pel ⚑ [ˈskælpəl] n. ufak ve düz bıçak, tesrih bıçağı.

scal.y [ˈskeili] adj. pul pul, pullarla kaplı; kabukları pul pul soyulan.

scamp [skæmp] 1. n. yaramaz (veya haylaz, çapkın) kimse; 2. v/t. kötü iş görmek, acele ile yüzüne gözüne bulaştır-

mak; ˈscamp.er 1. v/i. acele ve neşeli koşuşturmak, seyirtmek; 2. n. fig. acele kaçış, tüyme, dört nala kaçış.

scan [skæn] v/t. incelemek, tetkik etm.; gözden geçirmek; fig. göz gezdirmek; televizyon: bir resmin tüm noktalarından sıra ile geçmek; v/i. vezne göre okumak, vezin analizi yapmak.

scan.dal [ˈskændl] n. rezalet, skandal, ayıp, kepazelik, rüsvaylık; dedikodu, iftira; ˈscan.dal.ize v/t. rezalet çıkararak b-ni utandırmak; be ~d at veya by bşi mahzurlu bulmak, hoş görmemek, ˈscandal-mon.ger n. geveze (veya dedikoducu) kimse; scan.dal.ous □ [ˈ~dələs] rezil, iftiralı, dokunaklı, kepaze, ayıp; dedikoducu, boşboğaz; ˈscan.dal.ous.ness n. rezalet, kepazelik.

Scan.di.na.vi.an [skændiˈneivjən] 1. adj. İskandinavyalı; İskandinavya'ya ait; 2. n. İskandinavyalı; İskandinav dili.

scant lit. [skænt] 1. adj. kıt, eksik, az, dar; yetersiz; sınırlı; 2. v/t. cimrilik etm., kısmak, sınırlamak.

scant.i.ness [ˈskæntinis] n. kıtlık, eksiklik, yetmezlik, darlık.

scant.ling [ˈskæntliŋ] n. çatı kirişi; kereste kalınlığı; eşantiyon, numune.

scant.y □ [ˈskænti] az, kıt, noksan, eksik, dar, yetersiz.

scape.goat [ˈskeipgəut] n. başkalarının suçlarını yüklenen kimse; fig. şamar oğlanı.

scape.grace [ˈskeipgreis] n. hiç bir işe yaramayan değersiz ve güvenilmez kimse, hayırsız, yaramaz.

scap.u.lar [ˈskæpjulə] 1. adj. anat. kürek kemiğine ait; 2. n. eccl. bazı keşişlerin giydiği kolsuz gömlek.

scar¹ [skaː] 1. n. yara izi; tırmık, yırtık, yara; fig. namus lekesi; leke, kusur, şaibe; tahrip izi; 2. v/t. -in üstünde yara izi bırakmak; hafifçe sıyırmak, tırmıklamak; v/i. yara izi oluşmak, kapanmak (yara).

scar² [~] n. kayalık, çıplak kaya; dik yamaç, sarp yokuş.

scar.ab zo. [ˈskærəb] n. bokböceği; eski Mısırlıların kutsal böceği.

scarce [skɛəs] adj. az bulunur, nadir, seyrek; kıt; make o.s. ~ F ortadan kaybolmak, sıvışmak; ˈscarce.ly adv. pek az, hemen hemen hiç; güçlükle; ˈscar.ci.ty n. azlık, kıtlık, eksiklik (of); pahalılık, fiyat yüksekliği.

scare [skɛə] 1. v/t. korkutmak; a. ~ away ürkütmek, kovmak; be ~d korkmak, ürkmek (of -den); 2. n. panik, bozgun, ani (*veya* sebepsiz) korku; '~.crow *n.* bostan korkuluğu; '~.head *n. Am.* büyük harf manşet, heyecan yaratıcı başlık *(gazetede)*; '~.mon.ger *n.* şom ağızlı, bedbin, korkulu söylentiler yayan kimse.

**scarf**[1] [skɑːf] *n., pl. a.* **scarves** [skɑːvz] boyun atkısı; şal; eşarp, kaşkol; fular, boyunbağı.

**scarf**[2] ⊕ [~] 1. *n.* geçme ek yeri, oyuk yer, yuva; süyek, cebire; 2. *v/t.* iki kereste, metal *vs.*'nin ucunu birbirine geçirerek eklemek.

**scarf**...: '~-pin *n.* kravat iğnesi; '~-skin *n.* üstderi, epiderm.

**scar.i.fi.ca.tion** [skɛərifiˈkeiʃən] *n.* ⚑ tarama, hacamat; gücendirme *(kırıcı eleştiri)*; **scar.i.fy** ['~fai] *v/t.* hacamat etm., deriyi kazımak ve yer yer hafifçe kesmek; ✓ taramak, sürgü ile eşmek; gücendirmek; incitmek, şiddetle eleştirmek.

**scar.la.ti.na** ⚑ [skɑːləˈtiːnə] *n.* kızıl.

**scar.let** ['skɑːlit] 1. *n.* al, kırmızı, erguvanî (renk); 2. *adj.* al, kırmızı, erguvanî; ~ fever ⚑ kızıl hastalığı; ~ runner ⚘ çalıfasulyesi; ~ woman fahişe.

**scarp** [skɑːp] 1. *vb.* dikine kesmek; ~ed *adj. dik, sarp;* 2. *n.* uçurum, dik yamaçlar silsilesi.

**scarred** [skɑːd] *adj.* yara izi olan.

**scarves** [skɑːvz] *pl. of* scarf[1]

**scar.y** F ['skɛəri] *adj.* korku veren; korkak.

**scath.ing** *fig.* ['skeiðiŋ] *adj.* sert, kırıcı; yakıcı.

**scat.ter** ['skætə] *v/t. & v/i.* saç(ıl)mak, dağıtmak, dağılmak, serpmek, yay(ıl)mak; ~ed dağınık, aralıklı, seyrek; '~-brain *n.* zihni darmadağınık kimse; '~-brained *adj.* şaşırmış, aklı fikri perişan.

**scav.enge** ['skævindʒ] *v/t. & v/i.* süpürmek, temizlemek *(sokak),* çöpçülük etm.; çöplükten işe yarar şey aramak; silindirden egzos boşaltmak; **'scav.enger** *n.* leş yiyen hayvan; çöpleri karıştırarak işe yarar şeyleri arayan kimse; çöpçü.

**sce.nar.i.o** [siˈnɑːriəu] *n. film:* senaryo, bir film *veya* tiyatro eserinin konusunun ana hatları; **sce.nar.ist** ['siːnərist] *n.* senaryo yazarı, senarist.

**scene** [siːn] *n.* sahne; olayın geçtiği yer ve koşullar; *thea.* sahne, tablo; sahne dekoru, mizansen; manzara, peysaj; ~s *pl.* kulis; behind the ~s perde arkasından, gizlice; '~-paint.er *n.* sahne dekoru, ressamı; **scen.er.y** ['~əri] *n.* doğal man-

zara; *thea.* sahne dekoru, dekor.

**sce.nic, sce.ni.cal** □ ['siːnik(əl)] manzara ile ilgili, pitoresk, manzara kabilinden; sahneye *(veya* tiyatroya) ait; scenic railway minyatür tren *(veya* demiryolu).

**scent** [sent] 1. *n.* güzel koku, rayiha, parfüm, ıtır; *hunt.* koku alma (hassası); *hunt.* iz (kokusu); yol; 2. *v/t. -in* kokusunu almak, sezmek; koku ile doldurmak *-i;* güzel koku saçmak; koklayarak iz sürmek; **'scent.ed** *adj.* güzel kokulu, ıtırlı; **'scent.less** *adj.* kokusuz.

**scep.tic** ['skeptik] *n.* şüpheci kimse; **'scep.ti.cal** □ şüpheci, septik (about); **scep.ti.cism** ['~sizəm] *n.* kuşkuculuk, şüphecilik.

**scep.tre** ['septə] *n.* hükümdarlık asası, asa.

**sched.ule** ['ʃedjuːl, *Am.* 'skedjul] 1. *n.* liste, program; ✝ envanter, bilanço; ♫ ek, zeyil, ilâve; *part. Am.* hareket cetveli, tarife; on ~ planlandığı zamanda, dakik; 2. *v/t. -in* listesini yapmak; kararlaştırmak, program yapmak; tarifeye geçirmek *-i;* ♫ eklemek, ilâve etm. (to -e); ~d for programlanmış *-e,* tarifeye göre.

**scheme** [skiːm] 1. *n.* plân, proje, tasarı; entrika; 2. *v/t & v/i.* tasarlamak, plânlamak; *b.s.* entrika çevirmek (for, against -e karşı); plân yapmak; **'schem.er** *n.* plân yapan kimse; dolap *(veya* entrika) çeviren kimse.

**schism** ['sizəm] *n.* hizip(leşme), bölüntü, bölünme; *fig.* ayrılık, bozuşma; **schis-mat.ic** [sizˈmætik] 1. *a.* schisˈmat.i.cal □ hizip yaratan, ayrılık çıkaran, bölücü; 2. *n.* hizipçi, ayrılıkçı, bölücü.

**schist** *min.* [ʃist] *n.* tabaka halinde kaya, kayağantaş, şist.

**schi.zo.phre.nia** *psych.* [skitsəuˈfriːnjə] *n.* şizofreni, kişiliğin ikiye bölünmesi belirtilerini gösteren hastalık.

**schol.ar** ['skɔlə] *n.* alim, bilgin; *univ.* burslu öğrenci; ✝ öğrenci; he is an opt ~ yetenekli bir öğrencidir; **'schol.ar.ly** *adj.* alimce, bilgince; çok bilgili; ilmî; **'schol-ar.ship** *n.* alimlik, bilginlik; bilim; *univ.* burs.

**scho.las.tic** [skəˈlæstik] 1. *adj.* (~ally) okul ve öğretime ait, eğitimsel; alimane; ortaçağda felsefe *veya* din okullarına ait, iskolastik; kuru, cansız; 2. *n.* ortaçağda alim adam; felsefe *veya* dinî konularda ilmi metodlarla çalışan kimse; **scho.las-ti.cism** [skəˈlæstizəm] *n.* iskolastik felsefe.

**school**[1] [skuːl] = shoal[1] 1.

**school²** [~] **1.** *n.* okul, mektep *(a. fig.);* *univ.* fakülte, yüksek okul, ilim şubesi; ekol, aynı tarz, üslup ve düşüncede olan kişilerin oluşturduğu grup *(güzel sanıt-larda);* okul binası; at ~ okulda; put to ~ okula yaz(dır)mak; **2.** *v/t.* alıştırmak, terbiye etm., eğitmek, öğretmek, okutmak; **'~.boy** *n.* erkek öğrenci; **'~.fel.low** *n.* okul arkadaşı; **'~.girl** *n.* kız öğrenci; **'~.house** *n.* okul binası; **'school.ing** *n.* eğitim, öğretim, terbiye; okul ücreti.

**school...:** **'~-leav.ing age** zorunlu olarak öğrenim görülmesi gereken yaş sınırı; **'~.man** *n.* ortaçağda bilgin; **'~.mate** *n.* okul arkadaşı; **'~.mis.tress** *n.* kadın öğretmen; **'~.teach.er** *n.* öğretmen.

**schoon.er** ['sku:nə] *n.* ♩ ıskuna, golet, iki *veya* üç direkli ve yelkenleri yandan olan gemi; *Am.* büyük bira bardağı; = **prairie-~**

**sci.at.i.ca** ♗ [sai'ætikə] *n.* siyatik.

**sci.ence** ['saiəns] *n.* ilim, bilgi, bilim; fen, teknik.

**sci.en.tif.ic** [saiən'tifik] *adj.* (~ally) ilmî; bilimsel, fennî; *spor:* profesyonel(ce).

**sci.en.tist** ['saiəntist] *n.* ilim adamı; fen adamı.

**scim.i.tar** ['simitə] *n.* enli kılıç, pala.

**scin.til.late** ['sintileit] *v/t.* & *v/i.* parlamak, pırıldamak, ışıldamak, çıkarmak *(ışık);* saçmak *(kıvılcım);* **scin.til'la.tion** *n.* parıldama, ışıldama.

**sci.on** ['saiən] *n.* ✓ aşılanacak *veya* daldırılacak filiz, fidan; *fig.* oğul, evlât.

**scis.sion** ['siʒən] *n.* kes(il)me, biçme; çatlama, böl(ün)me; **scis.sors** ['sizəz] *n. pl.* (a pair of ~) makas.

**scle.ro.sis** ♗ [skliə'rəusis] *n.* doku sertleşmesi, skleroz.

**scoff** [skɔf] **1.** *n.* alay, istihza; küçümseme; **2.** *v/i.* alay etm., tahkir etm., eğlenmek, zevklenmek *(at ile);* *v/t.* açgözlü gibi çabucak yemek, silip süpürmek; **'scoff.er** *n.* alaycı, müstehzi.

**scold** [skəuld] **1.** *n.* huysuz *(veya* kavgacı) kadın; **2.** *v/t. b-ni* azarlamak, tekdir etm., ayıplamak, paylamak, *b-ne* çıkışmak; *bşe, b-ne* sövüp saymak; **scold.ing** *n.* azar, tekdir, paylama.

**scol.lop** ['skɔləp] = **scallop.**

**sconce¹** [skɔns] *n.* aplik, duvar şamdanı.

**sconce²** *univ. sl.* [~] *v/t.* cezalandırmak; para cezasına çarpmak.

**scon(e)** [skɔn] *n.* küçük francala, pötipen.

**scoop** [sku:p] **1.** *n.* kepçe, kürek, kova; ♗ spatül; F vurgun, büyük kazanç; *gazete:* atlatma *(haber);* **2.** *vb. mst* ~ **out** kep-

çe ile çıkarmak, oymak, kazmak, çukurlaştırmak; *sl.* vurgun vurmak, para kesmek; *gazete:* atlatmak *(haber).*

**scoot** ['sku:t] *v/i.* F kaçmak, tüymek, fırlamak.

**scoot.er** ['sku:tə] *n.* trotinet; skuler, küçük motosiklet; süratli motor.

**scope** [skəup] *n.* saha, alan; faaliyet alanı; konu, mevzu; ufuk, fırsat, olanak; çevre, genişlik; have free ~ hareket serbestliği olm.

**scorch** [skɔ:tʃ] *v/t.* kavurmak, yakmak, alazlamak, ütülemek; *v/i.* kavrulmak, yanmak; F küplere binmek, kudurmak; **'scorch.er** *n.* F kavurucu sıcak gün; delice sürtte giden şoför.

**score** [skɔ:] **1.** *n.* çentik, kertik, sıyrık; hesap, masraf, fatura; 20 sayısı; *spor:* puan sayısı; neden, vesile; ♪ partisyon, hınç, hesap; *sl.* hazırcevap karşılık; ~s of pek çok kalabalık; four ~ seksen; run up ~s borçlanmak; on the ~ of *-dan, -dan* dolayı, nedeniyle, yüzünden, için; **2.** *v/t.* & *v/i.* çentmek; çetele tutmak, *(puanları)* saymak; hesap etm.; *spor: (puan)* kazanmak, sayı yapmak; kazanmak; ♪ partisyon yazmak, orkestralamak; *Am.* F bşi eleştirmek; kaydetmek, not etm.; başarı kazanmak; *fig.* iyi not almak; *futbol:* gol atmak; *spor:* sayı yapmak, puan kazandırmak; *iskambil:* sayı almak; *sl.* şansı yaver gitmek, şanslı olm.; ~ off s.o. F *b-ni* baştan savmak, atlatmak; *b-ni* mat etm., yenmek; **'scor.er** *n.* puanları kaydeden kimse; *futbol:* gol atan futbolcu.

**sco.ri.a** *n., pl.* **sco.ri.ae** ⊕ ['skɔ:riə, '~rii:] cüruf, dışık.

**scorn** [skɔ:n] **1.** *n.* küçümseme, hor görme; tahkir; laugh s.o. to ~ *b-le* alay etm., *b-nin* küçümsenmesine neden olm.; **2.** *v/t.* küçümsemek, bşe hor bakarak tenezzül etmemek, reddetmek; **'scorn.er** *n.* alaycı, müstehzi; **scorn.ful** □ ['~ful] tahkir edici, hakaret dolu; hor gören, küçümseyen.

**scor.pl.on** *zo.* ['skɔ:pjən] *n.* akrep.

**Scot¹** [skɔt] *n.* İskoçyalı.

**scot²** [~] *n.:* pay ~ and lot tamamen ödemek.

**Scotch¹** [skɔtʃ] **1.** *adj.* İskoçya ile ilgili; **2.** *n.* İskoçyalı; İskoçyalı lehçesi; İskoç viskisi; the ~ *pl.* İskoçyalı.

**scotch²** [~] *v/t.* incitmek, hafifçe yaralamak; yalanlamak *-i,* son vermek *-e.*

**Scotch.man** ['skɔtʃmən] *n.* İskoçyalı.

**scot-free** ['skɔt'fri:] *adj.* vergiden muaf.

**Scots** [skɔts] = scotch¹; **Scots.man** =

scotchman.

**Scot.tish** ['skɔtiʃ] *adj.* İskoçya halkı ve diliné ait; İskoçyalı.

**scoun.drel** ['skaundrəl] *n.* alçak herif, hain, kötü adam, teres; **'scoun.drel.ly** *adj.* alçak, hain.

**scour¹** ['skauə] *v/t.* oyalayarak temizlemek, silmek; su yatağı açmak.

**scour²** [~] *v/i.* acele etm., seğirtmek, koşuşturmak; ~ about *bşin* peşinden koşuşturup aramak; *v/t.* araştırmak, köşe bucak aramak.

**scourge** [skəːdʒ] **1.** *n.* kırbaç, kamçı; *fig.* felâket, musibet, afet; **2.** *v/t.* kamçılamak, kırbaçlamak; *fig.* teşhir etm., şiddetle eleştirmek.

**scout¹** [skaut] **1.** *n.* casus, keşif eri, gözcü, öncü; ⚓ keşif gemisi; ✈ keşif uçağı; *univ.* hademe; (Boy) ♀ (erkek) izci; ~ party ✗ keşif kolu; **2.** *vb.* keşfetmek, taramak; gözetlemek; keşfe çıkmak.

**scout²** [~] *vb.* hor görerek reddetmek; hor görmek.

**scout.mas.ter** ['skautmɑːstə] *n.* izcibaşı, oymak beyi.

**scow** ⚓ [skau] *n.* salapurya, mavnanın küçüğü.

**scowl** [skaul] **1.** *n.* kaş çatma, tehditkâr bakış; **2.** *vb.* kaşlarını çatıp bakmak, sert sert bakmak, surat asmak.

**scrab.ble** ['skræbl] *vb.* sıyırmak, kazımak; hafifçe kaşımak; acele ile yazmak, kargacık burgacık yazmak, karalamak.

**scrag** [skræg] **1.** *n. fig.* iskelet, çok zayıf (*veya* kuru kemikli) kimse; *a.* ~-end (of mutton) koyun etinin kemikli gerdan tarafı; **2.** *v/t. sl.* boğmak, boğarak öldürmek; boğazını sıkmak; **'scrag.gi.ness** *n.* sıskalık, cılızlık; **'scrag.gy** ☐ kuru, cılız, zayıf, bir deri bir kemik.

**scram** *sl.* [skræm] *v/t.* sıvışmak, kaçmak, tüymek.

**scram.ble** ['skræmbl] **1.** *vb.* tırmanmak -*e*; itişip kakışmak (for *için*); karıştırmak -*i*; sinyal *veya* dalgayı değiştirmek (*radyo, telefon vs.*); ~d eggs *pl.* karıştırılıp yağda pişirilmiş yumurtalar; **2.** *n.* tırmanış; itişip kakışma, mücadele; motokros yarışı.

**scrap** [skræp] **1.** *n.* parça, döküntü, hurda, kırıntı, kırpıntı; kupür; ~s *pl.* artık; erimiş yağdan arta kalan kıkırdak; tortu; ~ of paper kâğıt paçavrası; **2.** *vb.* hurda olarak kullanmak; hurdaya (*veya* çürüğe, açığa) çıkarmak; parçalamak, kırıntı haline getirmek; **'~-book** *n.* albüm, kolleksiyon defteri.

**scrape** [skreip] **1.** ⚓. kazıma, sıyırma;

güçlük, varta, sıkıntı, dert; sürtme; **2.** *vb.* kazımak, sıyırmak; raspa etm.; tırmalamak; sıyırtmak; sürtmek (*ayak*); güçlükle biriktirmek, çok tutumlu olm.; hafifçe dokunmak, sürtünmek; gıcırda(t)mak; ~ away, ~ off kazıyarak silmek, kazıyıp çıkarmak; ~ together, ~ up güçlükle biriktirmek, azar azar toplamak, dişinden tırnağından artırmak; ~ acquaintance with -*in* yanına sokulup tanışmaya gayret etm.; **'scrap.er** *n.* raspa, sistre; demir çamurluk (*kapıda*); kazıma aleti; greyder; **'scrap.ing** *n.* kazıma, sıyırma; ~s *pl.* kazıntılar; *fig.* zar zor bir kenara biriktirilen para.

**scrap...:** '~-heap *n.* hurda, çöp yığını; '~-i.ron *n.* hurda demir; **'scrap.py** ☐ kırıntı ve parçalardan ibaret, bölük pörçük, yarım yamalak; kavgacı.

**scratch** [skrætʃ] **1.** *n.* çizik, sıyrık, tırmık, çizgi; cızırtı (sesi); *spor:* başlama çizgisi; karalama; come up to ~ tam zamanında hazır bulunmak; beklenilen sonucu vermek; formda olm.; sonuna kadar dayanmak; up to ~ iyi durumda; start from ~ *fig.* bşe sıfırdan başlamak; **2.** *adj. yarışçılık:* avanssız, handikapsız; gelişigüzel, rastgele, tesadüfî; **3.** *v/t.* kaşımak, tırmalamak, tırnaklamak, tahriş etm.; *parl. & spor:* iptal etm., listeden çıkarmak; ~ out kazıyarak çıkarmak; karalamak, çizmek; ~ the surface *fig.* ilk adımı atmak; *v/i.* kaşınmak; eşelenmek; cızırdamak; *spor:* yarıştan çekilmek; **'scratch.y** *adj.* kaşıntı veren, kaşındıran; gıcırtılı, cızırtılı; karalanmış, çok kötü yazılmış; derme çatma; *spor:* denk olmayan, uyumsuz.

**scrawl** [skrɔːl] **1.** *v/t.* acele ile yazmak, karalamak, kargacık burgacık yazı ile yazmak; **2.** *n.* dikkatsiz yazı.

**scraw.ny** *Am.* F ['skrɔːni] *adj.* zayıf, cılız, kemikleri sayılan.

**scream** [skriːm] **1.** *n.* feryat, çığlık, haykırış; he is a ~ F amma da komik kimse; **2.** *vb.* feryat etm., haykırmak, çığlık atmak, bağırmak; **'scream.ing** ☐ haykıran, çığlık atan; göze çarpan; gülmekten kırıp geçiren, çok komik.

**scree** [skriː] *n.* dağ yamacında yassı çakıl, kayşak.

**screech** [skriːtʃ] = scream. '~-owl *n.* orn. cüce baykuş.

**screed** [skriːd] *n.* uzun ve bıktırıcı konuşma *veya* yazı.

**screen** [skriːn] **1.** *n.* paravana, bölme, soba paravanı; ⚔ perde, örtü; *fig.* maske; *film:* beyaz perde, ekran, sinema; kalbur, elek; parmaklık, kafes; **2.** *v/t.* gizlemek, korumak, saklamak; elemek, kalburdan geçirmek, seçmek; ✕ örtmek, maskelemek, gizlemek, kamuflâj yapmak; perdeye aksettirmek *(film)*; filme almak; *fig.* araştırmayı derinleştirmek; ~ play senaryo *(film)*; TV filmi.

**sceev.er** ['skri:və] *n.* kaldırım ressamı.

**screw** [skru:] **1.** *n.* vida; ⤓ pervane, uskur; ✝ pervane; F *(tütün vs.)* küçük paket; *sl.* gardiyan; *sl.* maaş, ücret; yaşlı ve zayıf at; hebas a ~ loose F tahtası eksik, kaçık; **2.** *vb.* vidalamak, sıkıştırmak, sıkmak; döndürmek, çevirmek, burmak; tehdit ve hile ile almak, sızdırmak, dolandırmak; *sl.* cinsel ilişkide bulunmak -*le*; ~ round tamamen çevirmek; ~ up vidalamak, sıkıştırıp düzeltmek; *sl.* düzensizliğe itmek; ~ up one's courage cesaretlenmek; '~.ball *n. Am. sl.* garip herif, deli, kaçık; '~.driv.er *n.* tornavida; '~.jack *n.* kriko; '~.pro'pel.ler *n.* uskur, gemi pervanesi.

**scrib.ble** ['skribl] **1.** *n.* dikkatsiz yazı; **2.** *vb.* dikkatsiz yazmak, karalamak, kargacık burgacık yazı ile yazmak; ~ over çızıktırmak, çizmek; '**scrib.bler** *n.* çalakalem yazan kimse; ikinci sınıf yazar, yazar taslağı.

**scribe** [skraib] *n.* yazan, yazıcı, kâtip, yazman; kopye eden; *İncil:* İsa öncesinde ve zamanında papaz olmayan dini öğretmen ve hakim.

**scrim** [skrim] *n.* hafif keten bezi.

**scrim.mage** ['skrimid3] *n.* göğüs göğüse çarpışma, saç saça baş başa dövüşme; karışıklık, dağdağa, gürütü; *rugby:* topu ilerletmek için hücum, saldırı.

**scrimp** [skrimp], '**scrimp.y** = skimp etc.

**scrip** ✝ [skrip] *n.* geçici senet.

**script** [skript] *n.* yazı, yazış; el yazısı, müsvedde; *thea. & film:* senaryo; ~s *pl.* sınav kâğıdı; ~-writer *n.* radyo ve TV oyun yazarı.

**Scrip.tur.al** ['skriptʃərəl] *adj.* Tevrat ve İncille ilgili; **Scrip.ture** ['~tʃə] *mst* the Holy ~s Kutsal kitap.

**scrof.u.la** 𝄐 ['skrɔfjulə] *n.* sıraca illeti; '**scrof.u.lous** ☐ sıracalı, sıracası olan.

**scroll** [skrəul] *n.* tomar *(kâğıt)*; liste, cetvel; △ helezoni kıvrım *(sütun, kolon)*; süslü püslü harf, girift yazı.

**scro.tum** *anat.* ['skrəutəm] *n.* haya torbası, safen.

**scrounge** F [skraund3] *v/t. & v/i. k-ne* mal etm., gaspetmek, benimsemek, aşırmak, yürütmek.

**scrub**[1] [skrʌb] *n.* çalılık, fundalık; cü-

ce, bodur bacaksız, beberuhi.

**scrub**[2] [~] **1.** *v/t.* fırçalayarak yıkamak, temizlemek, silmek; iptal etm.; **2.** *n. spor:* B takımı (oyuncusu).

**scrub.bing-brush** ['skrʌbiŋbrʌʃ] *n.* tahta fırçası.

**scrub.by** [skrʌbi] *adj.* dik duran *(saç)*; karışık; kaba kıllı, fırça gibi sert; yırtık pırtık, lime lime; sefil, perişan, acınacak.

**scruff** [skrʌf] *n.:* ~ of the neck ense, boyun.

**scrum** [skrʌm], '**scrum.mage** = scrimmage.

**scrump.tious** *sl.* ['skrʌmpʃəs] *adj.* fevkalâde, harikulâde, emsalsiz, yaman, enfes, mükemmel.

**scrunch** [skrʌntʃ] *v/t.* ezmek, hurdahaş etm., pestilini çıkarmak; *v/i.* gıcırdamak, çatırdamak.

**scru.ple** ['skru:pl] **1.** *n.* şüphe, tereddüt, kararsızlık; vicdan; endişe; az miktar; 1296 gr.'lık eczane tartısı; make no ~ to do bşi yapmakta tereddüt etmemek; **2.** *vb.* tereddüt etm.; vicdan elvermemek; **scru.pu.lous** ☐ ['~pjuləs] dikkatli, titiz, düşünceli (about). vicdanlı, dürüst.

**scru.ti.neer** [skru:ti'niə] *n.* seçimde oyları sayan *veya* gözcülük eden resmi görevli; '**scru.ti.nize** *v/t.* incelemek, tahkik etm.; '**scru.ti.ny** *n.* tetkik, inceleme; seçimde oyların yeniden sayımı.

**scud** [skʌd] **1.** *n.* hızla gitme, sürüklenme; kısa süren şiddetli rüzgâr; rüzgârda sürüklenen hafif bulutlar; **2.** *v/i.* hızla sürüklenmek, hızla hareket etm.; ⤓ rüzgârın önüne düşüp seyretmek.

**scuff** [skʌf] *v/t. & v/i.* yürürken *(ayakları)* sürümek; sürüyerek aşındırmak; ayağı sürüyerek yürümek; yürürken aşınmak; şıp şıp yürümek.

**scuf.fle** ['skʌfl] **1.** *n.* dövüşme, boğuşma, itişme; **2.** *v/i.* itişip kakışmak, saç saça baş başa gelmek, çekişmek, dövüşmek.

**scull** ⤓ [skʌl] **1.** *n.* kısa kürek, boyna küreği; bu kürekle çekilen küçük sandal; **2.** *vb.* kürek çekmek, boyna etm.

**scul.ler.y** ['skʌləri] *n. (büyük veya eski evlerde mutfak yanındaki bulaşık kapların yıkanıp muhafaza edildiği)* küçük oda; ~ maid ortalık hizmetçisi; **scul.lion** ✝ ['skʌljən] *n.* bulaşıkçı.

**sculp.tor** ['skʌlptə] *n.* heykeltıraş.

**sculp.ture** ['skʌlptʃə] **1.** *n.* heykel(tıraşlık), plastik sanat; **2.** *vb.* oymak. hakketmek; şekil vermek; kalıplamak; heykelini yapmak -*in*.

**scum** [skʌm] *n.* pis köpük; kir tabakası;

cürüf; *fig.* ayaktakımı.

**scup.per** ↓ [ˈskʌpə] *n.* frengi deliği, geminin güvertesinden suyun denize akmasına mahsus delik.

**scurf** [skəːf] *n.* kepek, konak *(başta)*; **ˈscurf.y** □ kepekli, pullu, kabuklu.

**scur.ril.i.ty** [skʌˈriliti] *n.* küfür, ağız bozukluğu, kabalık, bayağılık; müstehcenlik; **ˈscur.ril.ous** *adj.* iğrenç, pis, kaba, bayağı, küfürlü; ağzı bozuk, küfürbaz.

**scur.ry** ˈ[ˈskʌri] **1.** *vb.* acele etm., hızlı olm., seğirtmek; kovalamak, takip etm.; **2.** *n.* acele kaçış *(veya* gidiş), seğirtme; kısa at yarışı.

**scur.vy¹** ⚕ [ˈskəːvi] *n.* iskorbüt.

**scur.vy²** [ˌ] *adj.* alçak, adi, bayağı, iğrenç.

**scut** [skʌt] *n.* kısa kuyruk *(tavşan v.b.).*

**scutch.eon** [ˈskʌtʃən] = escutcheon.

**scut.tle¹** [ˈskʌtl] *n.* kömür kovası.

**scut.tle²** [ˌ] **1.** *n.* ↓ lomboz, ambar kapağı; **2.** *v/t.* (*gemi)* dibini delerek batırmak.

**scut.tle³** [ˌ] **1.** *n.* seğirtme, sıvışma, tabanları yağlama; **2.** *vb.* seğirtmek, sıvışmak; *fig.* kaçmak *(tehlike, güçlük vs.'den).*

**scythe** ✓ [saið] **1.** *n.* tırpan; **2.** *vb.* orak *veya* tırpanla biçmek.

**sea** [siː] *n.* deniz, okyanus, derya *(a. fig.)*; yüksek dalga; at ~ denizde, gemide; *fig.* şaşkın, çaresiz, ne yapacağını bilmeyen; by the ~ deniz kenarında; go to ~ denizci olm.; deniz yolculuğuna çıkmak, açılmak; *s.* put 2.; **ˈ~.board** *n.* deniz kıyısı, kıyı (bölgesi); ~ **cap.tain** kaptan, süvari; ~ **coast** deniz kıyısı, sahil; **ˈ~-dog** *n.* eski gemici, deniz kurdu, deniz kahramanı, büyük denizci; = seaˈ¹; **ˈ~.far.ing** *adj.* denizcilikle uğraşan; **~.food** *n. Am.* yenebilen deniz ürünü; **ˈ~.go.ing** *adj.* açık denizlerde kullanmaya elverişli, açık deniz..., okyanus...; **ˈ~-gull** *n. zo.* martı.

**seal¹** *zo.* [siːl] *n.* fok, ayıbalığı.

**seal²** [ˌ] **1.** *n.* mühür, damga; teyit, onay, taahhüt, teminat; great ~, broad ~ devlet mühürü; **2.** *v/t.* mühürlemek, damgalamak; *fig.* mühürünü basmak; onaylamak; ~ off *fig.* son vermek; kapatmak, kilitlemek, tıkamak; ~ up sıkıca kapamak; ⊕ contalamak.

**seal.er** [ˈsiːlə] *n.* fok balığı avcısı *veya* av gemisi.

**sea-lev.el** [ˈsiːlevl] *n.* deniz seviyesi.

**seal.ing** [ˈsiːliŋ] *n.* fok balığı avı.

**seal.ing-wax** [ˈsiːliŋwæks] *n.* mühür mumu.

**seal.skin** [ˈsiːlskin] *n.* fok balığı derisi.

**seam** [siːm] **1.** *n.* dikiş (yeri); ⊕ ek yeri; *geol.* tabaka, damar, yatak; yara izi; ⚕ dikiş yeri; burst at the ~s çok dolu, dopdolu *(a. fig.)*; **2.** *vb.* hafifçe yaralamak, sıyırmak, tırmıklamak; evlek açmak; birbirine dikmek *(kumaş).*

**sea.man** [ˈsiːmən] *n.* denizci, gemici; bahriyeli, deniz eri; **ˈsea.man.ship** *n.* gemicilik.

**sea.mew** [ˈsiːmjuː] *n.* martı.

**seam.less** □ [ˈsiːmlis] dikişsiz; kaynaksız; eksiz.

**seam.stress** [ˈsemstris] *n.* dikişçi kadın.

**seam.y** [ˈsiːmi] *adj.* yara izi, çirkin görünüşlü; dikişli; ~ side *fig.* madalyonun tersi.

**sea...:** **ˈ~-piece** *n. paint.* deniz manzaralı tablo; **ˈ~.plane** *n.* deniz uçağı; **ˈ~.port** *n.* liman, liman şehir; **ˈ~-pow.er** *n.* deniz kuvveti, donanma.

**sear** [siə] **1.** *adj.* kurumuş, solgun, solmuş, pörsümüş, kuru; **2.** *v/t.* kurutmak; hafifçe yakmak, alazlamak, dağlamak; ⚕ koterize etm.; *fig.* katılaştırmak, sertleştirmek, körletmek.

**search** [səːtʃ] **1.** *n.* arama, araştırma (for), tetkik, sondaj; in ~ of ara(ştır)makta, peşinde; **2.** *v/t.* ara(ştır)mak, yoklamak, tetkik etm.; ⚕ sondalamak; gedik açmak *(mermi vs.)*; ~ out keşfetmek, ortaya çıkarmak, arayıp bulmak; *v/i.* araştırmak, soruşturmak (for); ~ into iyice incelemek -*i*, içyüzünü araştırmak -*in*; **ˈsearch.er** *n.* arayan, arayıcı, arayıcı, kâşif; **ˈsearc.ing** □ araştırıcı, inceden inceye araştıran; araştırıcı, sıkı, tetkik edici *(bakış)*; **ˈsearch-light** *n.* ışıldak, projektör; **ˈsearch-war.rant** *n.* ☒ arama emri.

**sea...:** **ˈ~-rov.er** *n.* deniz haydutu, korsan (gemisi); **~-scape** [ˈsiːskeip] *n.* deniz manzaralı tablo; **ˈ~-ser.pent** *n.* deniz yılanı; **ˈ~-shore** *n.* sahil; **ˈ~.sick** *adj.* deniz tutmuş; **ˈ~.sick.ness** *n.* deniz tutması; **ˈ~.side** *n.* deniz kıyısı, sahil; ~ place, ~ resort plaj; go to the ~ deniz kıyısına gitmek.

**sea.son** [ˈsiːzn] **1.** *n.* mevsim; zaman; dönem, devre, sezon; F = ~-ticket; height of the ~ mevsimin en civcivli zamanları; in (good *veya* due) ~ uygun bir zamanda, tam zamanında; cherries are in ~ şimdi kirazın tam mevsimidir *(ucuz, olgun)*; out of ~ vakitli vakitsiz, yersiz; for a ~ mevsimlik, bir süre; with the compliments of the ~ yeni yıl *(veya* bayram vs.) için en iyi dileklerimle; **2.** *v/t.*

& *v/i.* çeşnilendirmek; yumuşatmak; alış(tır)mak *(to -e)*; kuru(t)mak *(yapı kerestesi v.b.)*; **'sea.son.a.ble** □ tam vaktinde olan, uygun, zamana uygun; **season.al** □ mevsimlik; mevsime uygun; ✝ mevsimlik, mevsime bağlı; **'sea.son.ing** *n.* çeşni veren şey, bahar(at); **'sea.son-tick.et** *n.* 🔲 abone kartı, karne; *thea.* abone (bileti).

**seat** [si:t] **1.** *n.* oturulacak yer, iskemle, sandalye, tabure, peyke, kanepe; ikâmetgâh, mesken, köşk, yalı, çiftlik; *pol.* koltuk, mevki; kaba et, makat, kıç; sahne, saha, yer, merkez; mahal; *thea.* koltuk; **2.** *vb.* oturtmak, yerleştirmek *(rütbe veya makama)*; mevki sahibi olm.; oturacak yer temin etm.; yerine oturtmak *(makine parçası vs.)*; ~ o.s. oturmak; be ~ed! oturunuz!; **'~-belt** *n.* ✝ emniyet kemeri; **'seat.ed** *adj.* oturmuş, yerleşmiş; **'seat.er** *comb. part. mot.*, ✝ belirli sayıda oturacak yeri olan; ...kişilik.

**sea-ur.chin** ['si:ˈləːtʃin] *n.* denizkestanesi; **sea.ward** ['~wəd] *adj.* denize doğru giden; *adv. a.* **sea.wards** ['~wədz] denize doğru.

**sea...:** '~.weed *n.* ♀ yosun, deniz sazı; '~.wor.thy *adj.* denize elverişli *(veya* dayanıklı).

**se.ba.ceous** *physiol.* [siˈbeiʃəs] *adj.* yağlı..., yağ içeren.

**se.cant** ♫ ['si:kənt] **1.** *adj.* birbirini kateden *(veya* kesen); **2.** *n.* sekant.

**sec.a.teur** ✓ [sekəˈtəː] *n.* mst (a pair of) ~s *pl.* bahçıvan makası.

**se.cede** [si'si:d] *v/i.* çekilmek, ayrılmak *(örgüt, üyelik vs.'den)*; b'den vazgeçmek; **se'ced.er** *n.* sadakatsiz, asi; mürtet, dininden dönmüş.

**se.ces.sion** [si'seʃən] *n.* ayrılma, vazgeçme, bölünme; **se'ces.sion.ist** [~ʃnist] *n.* ayrılma taraftarı.

**se.clude** [si'klu:d] *v/t.* ayırmak, tecrit etm., uzaklaştırmak; **se'clud.ed** *adj.* tecrit edilmiş; kuytu, tenha, ıssız; dünyadan el çekmiş; **se'clu.sion** [~ʒən] *n.* inziva, yalnızlık, köşeye çekilme.

**sec.ond¹** ['sekənd] **1.** □ ikinci (derecede), *-den* sonraki, diğer, öteki; he is ~ to none kimseden aşağı kalmaz, o en iyisidir; on ~thoughts iyice düşündükten sonra; **2.** *n.* ikinci kimse *veya* şey; düello şahidi; yardımcı, muavin; saniye; ~s *pl.* ✝ ikinci kalite mal, tapon mal; ~ of exchange ✝ poliçenin ikinci nüshası; **3.** *v/t.* b-ne yardım etm., b-ni desteklemek, b-nin lehinde olm.; düello-

da *b-ne* şahitlik etm. **se.cond²** ✗ [si'kɔnd] *v/t.* bir işe, vazifeye tayin etm., atamak *(usu. belirli bir süre için)*.

**sec.ond.ar.i.ness** ['sekəndərinis] *n.* ikincil *(veya* tali) olma; **sec.ond.ar.y** □ ikincil, tali, ikinci derecede; ...yanında; ast, alt aşamada bulunan; **sec.ond.ar.y school** orta dereceli okul; **'sec.ond-'best** *adj.* ikinci (kalite); en iyiden hemen sonra gelen; come off ~ F başkası tarafından mağlûp edilmiş, alt edilmek; **'sec.ond-'class** *adj.* ikinci derece, ikinci kalite (li); 🔲 ikinci mevki; **'sec.ond.er** *n.* destekleyen kimse *(part. parl.)*; **sec.ond-hand 1.** ['sekənd'hænd] *adj.* kullanılmış, elden düşme; başkasından öğrenilmiş, ikinci elden; ~ bookseller sahaf; ~ bookshop ikinci elden kitapların satıldığı kitapçı; **2.** ['sekəndhænd] *n.* saat kadranında saniyeleri gösteren ibre; **'sec.ond.ly** *adv.* ikinci olarak, saniyen; **'sec.ond-'rate** *adj.* ikinci derecede; ✝ ~ quality ikinci kalite.

**se.cre.cy** ['si:krisi] *n.* sır saklama; gizlilik, ketumiyet, saklılık; **se.cret** [si:krit] **1.** □ gizli, mahrem, saklı; ~ agent gizli ajan; **2.** *n.* sır, gizli şey; in ~ gizlice; be in the ~, be taken into the ~ sırra ortak olm.

**sec.re.tar.i.at(e)** [sekrəˈtɛəriət] *n.* kalem odası; kâtiplik; müdüriyet (personeli). **sec.re.tar.y** ['sekrətri] *n.* zabıt kâtibi, sekreter, kâtip, yazman; yazı masası; ♀ of State bakan; *Am.* Dışişleri Bakanı; **'secre.tar.y.ship** *n.* kâtiplik, sekreterlik, yazmanlık.

**se.crete** [si'kri:t] *v/t.* gizlemek, saklamak, örtmek; *physiol.* salgılamak, ifraz etm.; **se'cre.tion** *n. physiol.* salgı, ifraz(at); **se'cre.tive** *adj. fig.* kapalı kutu, ağzı sıkı; salgılayan.

**sect** [sekt] *n. rel.* tarikat, mezhep; **sectar.i.an** [~ˈtɛəriən] **1.** *adj.* mezhebe ait; bağnaz, darkafalı; **2.** *n.* mezhep yanlısı; bağnaz yandaş, darkafalı kimse.

**sec.tion** ['sekʃən] *n.* ♀ operasyon; kesme, kesiş; kesilmiş şey; ♫ kesit; ♦ profil; kısım, parça; *typ.* paragraf, fıkra, fasıl; s. ~-mark: grup, dal, kol, şube, daire; bölge, kesim; shopping (residental) ~ alış veriş (yerleşim) bölgesi; **sec.tional** ['~fənl] *adi* bir bölüme ait, bir bölgeye ait, bölgesel, mahalli; kesit, parça halinde; **'sec'tion.al.ism** *n.* bölgecilik, grupçuluk; **'sec-tion-mark** *n.* paragraf işareti.

**sec.tor** ['sektə] *n.* daire kesmesi, daire dilimi; ✗ bölge, mıntıka; sektör, kesim.

**sec.u.lar** [ˈsekjulə] layik; dünyevî, cismanî; manastır *veya* tarikat sistemine bağlı olmayan; yüz yıllık, yüz yılda bir olan; **sec.u.lar.i.ty** [ˌ~ˈlæriti] *n.* layiklik; dünyevilik, cismanilik; **sec.u.lar.ize** [ˈ~ləraiz] *v/t.* layikleştirmek; dünyevileştirmek.

**se.cure** [siˈkjuə] **1.** ☐ güvenli, emin, emniyetli, sağlam (of, against, from -e karşı); **2.** *v/t.* sağlamak, temin etm., elde etm.; bağlamak; güven altına almak (from, against); saklamak, muhafaza etm.

**se.cu.ri.ty** [siˈkjuəriti] *n.* emniyet, güven(lik); sağlam (*veya* kesin) bilgi; rehin, teminat (akçesi), emanet, kefalet, depozito; **se¹cu.ri.ties** *pl.* kıymetli evrak, tahviller, senetler, menkul kıymetler.

**se.dan** [siˈdæn] *n.* limuzin, kapalı büyük otomobil; *a.* ~-chair *n.* sedye; tahtırevan.

**se.date** ☐ [siˈdeit] temkinli, ağırbaşlı, sakin, vakarlı, ciddî, **¹se¹date.ness** *n.* temkin, ağırbaşlılık, sükûn(et), sessizlik.

**sed.a.tive** *mst* ℱ [ˈsedətiv] **1.** *adj.* teskin edici, rahatlatıcı, yatıştırıcı, hafifletici; **2.** *n.* müsekkin, yatıştırıcı ilaç.

**sed.en.tar.i.ness** [ˈsedntərinis] *n.* yerleşik, oturgan oluş; **¹sed.en.tar.y** ☐ yerleşmiş, mukim, daimi ikametgâhı olan, temelli oturmuş; oturmaya alışmış, evden dışarı çıkmayan; oturularak yapılan.

**sedge** ♀ [sedʒ] *n.* saz, kamış, ayakotu.

**sed.i.ment** [ˈsedimənt] *n.* tortu, telve, posa, rüsup; *geol.* çöküntü, suyun dibinde biriken şey; **sed.i.men.ta.ry** [ˌ~ˈmentəri] *adj. geol.* tortul, tortudan oluşmuş; tortulu.

**se.di.tion** [siˈdiʃən] *n.* ayaklanma(ya teşvik), isyan; kargaşalık; fesat, fitne.

**se.di.tious** ☐ [siˈdiʃəs] fesatkârane; arabozucu; fitneci; ayaklandıran.

**se.duce** [siˈdjuːs] *v/t.* baştan çıkarmak, ayartmak; iğfal etm.; **se¹duc.er** *n.* ayartan (*veya* baştan çıkaran) kimse; iğfal eden kimse; **se.duc.tion** [ˌ~ˈdʌkʃən] *n.* baştan çıkarma, ayartma; iğfal; baştan çıkaran şey; **se¹duc.tive** ☐ ayartıcı, kandırıcı: cazip, çekici.

**sed.u.lous** ☐ [ˈsedjuləs] faal, aktif, gayretli. sebatlı, çalışkan.

**see¹** [siː] (*irr.*) *v/i.* görmek; icabına bakmak; *fig.* anlamak, kavramak; I ~ anlıyorum, anladım; ~ about s.th. bşe karışmak, bsi düşünmek, bşle meşgul olm., icabına bakmak -*in*; ~ through s.o. *veya* s.th. bnin *veya* bsin içini okumak, arasından *veya* içinden bakmak *veya* gör-

mek; ~ to bakmak -*e*, dikkat etm. -*e*, meşgul olm. *ile*; ~ for o.s. bşi kendi gözüyle görmek; *v/t.* görmek -*i*, bakmak -*e*; göz(et)mek, anlamak, kavramak; (*hasta*) ziyaret etm., vizita yapmak; ~ s.th. done bşin yapılmasını sağlamak; go to ~ s.o. b-nin ziyaretine gitmek; ~ s.o. home b-ni evine götürmek, eşlik etm.; ~ off uğurlamak; ~ out kapıya kadar geçirmek; bitirmek; sonuna kadar beklemek; ~ over s.th. bşi gözden geçir-mek, incelemek; ~ s.th. through sonuna kadar sabretmek, dayanmak, muradına ermek, bir işi başarmak; ~ s.o. through b-ne bşi yapması için sonuna kadar yardım etm.; live to ~ yaşayıp görmek.

**see²** [~] *n.* piskoposluk; Holy ♀ Papalık (makamı).

**seed** [siːd] **1.** *n.* tohum, tohumluk hububat; (*meyve*) çekirdek; döl, evlât; kaynak, menşe; sperma, meni, bel suyu; go *veya* run to ~ tohuma kaçmak; *fig.* kuvvetten düşmek; **2.** *v/t.* tohum ekmek; (*meyve*) çekirdek çıkarmak; *spor:* (*oyuncu*) b-ni b-nin yerine geçirmek; *v/i.* filizlenip tohum vermek; **¹~.bed** = seed--plot; **¹seed.i.ness** *n.* tohuma kaçma; F (*sarhoşluktan gelen*) mahmurluk; **¹seed.less** *adj.* çekirdeksiz (*meyve*); **¹seed.ling** *n.* ✓ fide; **¹seed-plot** *n.* ✓ fidelik; *fig.* menba, ocak, kaynak; **seeds.man** [ˈ~zmən] *n.* tohumcu, tohum satıcısı; **¹seed.y** *adj.* tohumlu, tohuma kaçmış; havı dökülmüş, lime lime olmuş, yırtık pırtık; F rahatsız, yoksul, sefil.

**see.ing** [ˈsiːiŋ] **1.** *n.* görme, bakma; worth ~ gör(ül)meğe değer; **2.** *cj.* ~ that madem(ki), -dığı için; ...e göre, ...karşısında.

**seek** [siːk] (*irr.*) *v/t. & v/i. a.* ~ after, ~ for aramak -*i*; araştırmak; istemek, bşi çok arzu etm., elde etmeğe çalışmak; **¹seek.er** *n.* arayıcı kimse *veya* şey.

**seem** [siːm] *v/i.* görünmek, gözükmek, gelmek (*like gibi*), benzemek; **¹seem.ing** **1.** ☐ görünüşte, zahirî, gûya, yalandan; **2.** *n.* görünüş, zevahir, dış (*veya* aldatıcı) görünüş; **¹seem.li.ness** *n.* uygunluk, yakışık alma, münasebet, edep ve ahlâka uygun olma, terbiye; **¹seem.ly** *adj.* yakışık alır, uygun, münasip.

**seen** [siːn] *p.p. of* see¹.

**seep** [siːp] *v/i.* sızmak, sızıntı yapmak, damlaya damlaya akmak; **¹seep.age** *n.* sızıntı.

**seer** [ˈsiːə] *n.* seyirci; resul, peygamber; kâhin.

**see.saw** [ˈsiːsɔː] **1.** *n.* tahterevalli; ileri

geri hareket, iniş çıkış; **2.** *v/i.* ileri geri
*veya* aşağı yukarı hareket etm.; tahte-
revalliye binmek; *fig.* tereddüt etm., ne
yapacağını bilmemek, kararsız olm.
**seethe** [si:ð] *v/t.* & *v/i.* kayna(t)mak,
haşla(n)mak, piş(ir)mek, öfkelenmek,
küplere binmek.
**seg.ment** [ˈsegmənt] *n.* parça, kısım; *part.*
Ⱥ daire kesmesi.
**seg.re.gate** [ˈsegrigeit] *vb.* ayırmak, tecrit etm.; bir bütünden ayrılmak; **seg.re-**
**ˈga.tion** *n.* ayırım, fark gözetme, ırk ayırımı.
**seine** [sein] *n.* balıkçılık: iğrip ağı, büyük ağ.
**sei.sin** 𝕏 [ˈsi:zin] *n.* temellük, tasarruf,
mülkiyeti elinde bulundurma.
**seis.mo.graph** [ˈsaizməgrɑːf] *n.* deprem-
ölçer. sismograf.
**seize** [si:z] *v/t.* yakalamak, tutmak, kavramak; gaspetmek, zaptetmek, ele geçirmek; haczetmek, el koymak, müsadere etm.; *fikir:* kavramak; etkisi altına almak; ⅃ sicim sarıp bağlamak; *v/i.*
⊕ sıkışıp çalışmamak, takılmak, yapışmak; ~ upon *b-ni veya* *bşi* emri altına
almak, hükmü altına almak; **ˈseiz.ing** *n.*
tutma, kavrama, yakalama; *mst* ~s *pl.*
⅃ halat; **sei.zure** [ˈ~ʒə] *n.* yakalama,
zapt; 𝕏 müsadere, el koyma, haciz; ⅃
anî nöbet, tut(ul)ma, felç.
**sel.dom** [ˈseldəm] *adv.* nadiren, seyrek.
**se.lect** [siˈlekt] **1.** *v/t.* seçmek, ayırmak,
içinden beğenip almak; **2.** *adj.* seçkin,
seçilmiş, güzide, elit, seçme, ilik gibi;
**seˈlec.tion** *n.* seçme (şeyler); seçme,
ayırma, beğenme; *zo.*, ⚘ doğal ayıklanma; *a. musical* ~ seçme parçalar, potpuri; **seˈlec.tive** ⬜ ayıran, seçici, seçim-
li; seçme...; *radyo:* selektif, seçici, yayını parazitsiz alan; **se.lecˈtiv.i.ty** *n.* rad-
*yo:* selektivite, seçicilik, yayını parazitsiz alma; **seˈlec.tor** *n.* Am. belediye
meclisi üyesi; **seˈlec.tor** *n.* seçen kimse
*veya* aygıt, seçici kimse; *radyo:* selektör, seçici, dalga ayırıcı.
**self** [self] **1.** *pron.* bizzat, kendi(si), kendi kendine; ⸸ *veya* F = *myself etc.*; **2.**
*adj.* şahsî; ⚘ düz renkli, üni; **3.** *n. pl.*
**selves** [selvz] zat, kişi, kendi; karakter,
kişilik, şahsiyet, benlik; kişisel çıkar,
bencillik; *my poor* ~ âcizleri, âciz kulla-
rı; **ˈ~ˈabase.ment** *n.* k-ni alçaltma, aşa-
ğılanma, bayağılanma, yalvarıp yakar-
ma; **ˈ~ˈact.ing** *adj.* otomatik, mekanik,
kendi *k-ne* hakaret eden; **ˈ~ˈcen.tred,**
*Am.* **ˈ~ˈcen.tered** *adj.* hodperest, hodpesent, heᴏ *k-ni* düşünen, bencil; **~ˈcol.o-**

(u)red *adj.* düz renkli, boyanmamış;
**ˈ~com.mand** *n.* k-ni tutma, nefsini yenme; **ˈ~conˈceit** *n.* k-ni beğenmişlik, azamet; **ˈ~conˈceit.ed** *adj.* kibirli, mağrur,
kurumlu, azametli, hodperest; **ˈ~ˈcon.fi-**
**dence** *n.* k-ne güven, nefse güven;
**ˈ~ˈcon.scious** *adj.* utangaç, sıkılgan; ne
yaptığını bilen; **ˈ~ˈcon.scious.ness** *n.*
utangaçlık, mahcupluk, sıkılganlık;
**ˈ~conˈtained** *adj.* kendi *k-ne* yeter; kendi içinde bir bütün oluşturan; az konuşur, çekingen, ağzı sıkı, düşüncelerini
başkalarına rahat söyleyemeyen; ~
*country* kendi *k-ne* yeten ülke; ~ *house*
bir ailelik ev, müstakil daire; **ˈ~conˈtrol**
*n.* k-ne hakim olma, k-ni yenme, nefsini
zaptetme; **ˈ~deˈfence** *n.* nefis müdafaası, nefsini koruma, k-ni savunma; in ~
meşru müdafaa; **ˈ~deˈni.al** *n.* feragat,
özveri. k-ni tutma; **ˈ~de.ter.miˈna.tion** *n.*
bir ulusun kendi yönetim şeklini *k-nin* ka-
rarlaştırması, hür irade; **ˈ~emˈployed**
*adj.* müstakil, bağımsız, serbest çalışan;
**ˈ~ˈev.i.dent** *adj.* aşikâr, belli; **ˈ~ˈgov-**
**ern.ment** *n.* kendi *k-ni* yönetme, özerklik,
muhtariyet, otonomi; **ˈ~inˈdul.gent** *adj.*
kendi isteklerine düşkün; lâkayt, tembel,
istifini bozmayan; **ˈ~ˈin.ter.est** *n.* kişisel
çıkar, bencillik, hodbinlik; **ˈself.ish** ⬜
egoist, bencil, hodbin; **ˈself.ish.ness** *n.*
bencillik, egoizm, hodkâmlık.
**self...**: **ˈ~ˈmade** *adj.* k-ni yetiştirmiş; ~
man kendi *k-ni* yetiştirmiş kişi; **ˈ~pos-**
**ˈses.sion** *n.* k-ne hakim olma, itidal, soğukkanlılık, nefsini yenme; **ˈ~pre.serˈva-**
**tion** *n.* nefsini idame, mevcudiyetini koruma; **ˈ~reˈgard** *n.* k-ni önemseme;
**ˈ~reˈli.ance** *n.* k-ne güven, öz güven;
**ˈ~reˈli.ant** *adj.* k-ne güvenir; **ˈ~reˈspect**
*n.* izzetinefis, onur, öz saygısı; **ˈ~re-**
**ˈspect.ing**: *every* ~ *nation* onurlu ve dimdik ayakta olan her ulus; **ˈ~ˈright.eous**
*adj.* k-ni beğenmiş, hodpesent; **ˈ~ˈsacri.fice** *n.* özveri, fedakârlık; **ˈ~same** *adj.*
*lit.* tıpkı, aynı; **ˈ~ˈseek.ing** *adj.* bencil,
menfaatperest, çıkarcı, egoist; **ˈ~ˈserv-**
**ice res.tau.rant** selfservis lokanta; **ˈ~-**
**ˈstart.er** *n.* mot. hareket tertibatı, starter, marş; **ˈ~sufˈfi.cien.cy** *n.* kendi *k-ne*
yetme, başkasına muhtaç olmama;
**ˈ~supˈpli.er** *n.* tüketim mallarını *k-si* üre-
~en: ˈ ~supˈport.ing *adi.* kendi *k-ne.* başkasının yardımı olmadan; (ekonomik
açıdan) bağımsız; **ˈ~ˈwill** *n.* dikkafalılık, inatçılık; **ˈ~ˈwilled** *adj.* inatçı, dikkafalı.
**sell** [sel] **1.** *(irr.)* *v/t.* satmak *(a. fig.);*
*Am.* F önermek, tavsiye etm, methetmek,

beğendirmek; ~ (out) F aldatmak, kazıklamak; ~ off ↑ hepsini satmak, satıp kurtulmak; ~ up *b-nin* malını satmaya zorlamak; *v/i.* ticaret yapmak; alıcı bulmak, satılmak; revaç bulmak *(mal)*; ~ off, ~ out ↑ bütün stoku satmak, elden çıkarmak; **2.** *n.* F dolandırıcılık, hilekârlık, dalavere; hayal kırıklığı, fiyasko; **'sell.er** *n.* satıcı, bayi; good *etc.* ~ çok *vs.* satılan mal.

**selt.zer** ['seltsə] *n. a.* ~ water soda, maden suyu.

**sel.vage, sel.vedge** ⊕ ['selvidʒ] *n.* kumaş kenarı.

**selves** [selvz] *pl. of* self 3.

**se.man.tics** [si'mæntiks] *n. sg.* semantik, anlambilim.

**sem.a.phore** ['seməfɔː] **1.** *n.* semafor, taşıtlara yolun açık olduğunu göstermek için renkli levha *veya* ışıkla işaret veren dikme *(tren vs.)*; ✗ işaretçi, flamacı; 📧 işaret direği; **2.** *vb.* işaretlerle bildirmek, haberleşmek, semaforla haberleşmek.

**sem.blance** ['sembləns] *n.* benzerlik; biçim, dış görünüş.

**se.mes.ter** *univ.* [si'mestə] *n.* sömestr, ders yılı yarısı.

**sem.i...** ['semi] *prefix* yarı, yarım, buçuk, yarı...; **'~.breve** *n.* ♩ dörtlük nota, tam nota; **'~.cir.cle** *n.* yarım daire; **'~'cir.cu.lar** *adj.* yarım daire şeklinde; **'~'co.lon** *n.* noktalı virgül; **'~-de'tached house** ortak duvarlı iki daireyi içeren ev; **'~-'fi.nal** *n. spor:* yarı final, finalden bir önceki müsabaka; **'~.man.u'fac.tured** *adj.* yarı mamul; yarıda kalmış.

**sem.i.nal** ['siːminl] *adj.* sonraki gelişmenin tohumlarını içeren; başkalarına yeniliklerle etki eden, yeni ufuklar açan; sperma ile ilgili, meni içeren, spermalı.

**sem.i.nar.y** ['seminəri] *n.* seminer; *fig.* okul; papaz okulu.

**sem.i-of.fi.cial** ['semiə'fiʃəl] *adj.* yarı resmî.

**sem.i.qua.ver** ♩ ['semikweivə] *n.* onaltılık nota.

**Sem.ite** ['siːmait] *n.* Samî ırkından olan kimse; **Se.mit.ic** [si'mitik] *adj.* Samî.

**sem.i.tone** ♩ ['semitəun] *n.* yarım ton.

**sem.i.vow.el** ['semivauəl] *n.* yarı ünlü ses.

**sem.o.li.na** [seməˈliːnə] *n.* irmik.

**semp'stress** ['sempstris] *n.* dikişçi kadın.

**sen** [sen] *n.* sen *(Japon madeni parası)*.

**sen.ate** ['senit] *n.* senato.

**sen.a.tor** ['senətə] *n.* senatör; **sen.a.to.ri.al** ☐ [~'tɔːriəl] senatörlük *veya* senatör ile

---

ilgili; senatörlerden oluşan.

**send** [send] *(irr.) vb.* yollamak, göndermek; fırlatmak, atmak, savurmak *(top vs.)*; atış yapmak *(kurşun vs.)*; **s.** pack **2;** ~ for çağırmak *-i;* getirtmek *-i,* ayağına davet etm. *-i,* celbetmek; ısmarlamak; ~ forth neşretmek, yaymak, salmak *(ışık, koku vs.)*; kamuoyuna bildirmek; ~ in sunmak, arzetmek, takdim etm.; ~ in one's name *b-nin* geldiğini haber vermek; ~ off göndermek, uğurlamak, yolcu etm.; ~ up yukarı göndermek; *fig.* yükseltmek *(fiyat);* ~ word haber yollamak; *b-ne* bş hakkında bilgi vermek; **'send.er** *n.* gönderen; *tel.* radyo. istasyonu, verici; **'send-'off** *n.* yolcu etme, veda, uğurlama (töreni).

**sen.e.schal** ['seniʃəl] *n.* ortaçağda asilzadelerin en güvendikleri yardımcısı *(veya* mutemedi *veya* teşrifatçısı).

**se.nile** ['siːnail] *adj.* ihtiyarlıkla ilgili; eli ayağı tutmaz olmuş; bunak; **se.nil.i.ty** [si'niliti] *n.* ihtiyarlık; güçsüzlük; bunaklık.

**sen.ior** ['siːnjə] **1.** *adj.* yaşça büyük (to); kıdemli; son sınıfa ait; üst...; ~ partner ↑ patron, baş; **2.** *n.* yaşça büyük kimse; kıdemli kimse; son sınıf öğrencisi; oğula nisbetle baba; he is a year my ~ by a year, he is a year my ~ o benden bir yaş büyüktür; **sen.ior.i.ty** [siːni'ɔriti] *n.* yaşça büyüklük; kıdem(lilik).

**sen.sa.tion** [sen'seiʃən] *n.* his, duygu, izlenim; heyecan, merak; heyecan uyandıran olay, sansasyon; **sen'sa.tion.al** ☐ [~ʃənl] duygusal, hissî, sansasyonal, heyecan verici, müthiş, heyecanlı; **sen'sa.tion.al.ism** [~ʃnəlizəm] *n.* göze girmeye çalışma, heyecan uyandırıcı yollara baş vurma, sansasyon hevesi, sansasyonalizm, duyumculuk.

**sense** [sens] **1.** *n.* duyu, his (of); duyum, duyarlık; akıl; zekâ, anlayış; mana, anlam; fikir, düşünce, kanı; in (out of) one's ~s aklı başında(n gitmiş, deli); bring s.o. to his ~s *b-nin* aklını başına getirmek; make ~ anlamı olm., akla uygun gelmek; talk ~ akıllıca konuşmak; saçmalamamak; **2.** *v/t.* hissetmek, duymak, sezmek; anlamak.

**sense.less** ☐ ['senslis] baygın; duygusuz hissiz, donuk; anlamsız, manasız, abuk sabuk, saçma; **'sense.less.ness** *n.* baygınlık, şuursuzluk; hissizlik, duygusuzluk, saçmalık.

**sen.si.bil.i.ty** [sensi'biliti] *n.* duyarlık, duygunluk, duygululuk, hassasiyet (to, *a.* of); seziş inceliği; **sensibilities** *pl.* anlayış, hassasiyet, nezaket.

**sen.si.ble** ☐ ['sensəbl] aklı başında, makûl, mantıklı; farkedilir, hissedilir; akla uygun, yerinde; *bş* karşısında pek hassas, duyarlı (of); be *~* of *bşi* iyice bilmek, sezmek *-i*, farkına varmak *-in*; **ˈsen.si.ble.ness** *n.* akıllılık, makûl olma; şuurlu olma; hassasiyet.

**sen.si.tive** ☐ ['sensitiv] hassas, içli, duygulu (to), alıngan; *phot.* ışığa duyarlı; **ˈsen.si.tive.ness, sen.si.tiv.i.ty** *n.* duyarlık, hassasiyet, hassaslık; alınganlık.

**sen.si.tize** *phot.* ['sensitaiz] *v/t.* ışığa duyarlı hale getirmek (*kâğıt, film*).

**sen.so.ri.al** [sen'sɔːriəl], *adj.* **sen.so.ry** ['~səri] duygu ile ilgili, duyusal...

**sen.su.al** ☐ ['sensjuəl] şehvani, şehvetli; tensel, duyusal; **ˈsen.su.al.ism** *n.* duyumculuk; şehevilik, şehvet (düşkünlüğü); **ˈsen.su.al.ist** *n.* şehvet düşkünü (*veya* zevkine düşkün) kimse; **sen.su.al.i.ty** [~'æliti] *n.* şehvet (düşkünlüğü), kösnü; duyarlık.

**sen.su.ous** ☐ ['sensjuəs] duyumsal, hissi, hislere ait.

**sent** [sent] *pret. & p.p. of* **send.**

**sen.tence** ['sentəns] **1.** *n.* 𝄐 hâkim kararı, hüküm, yargı; *gr.* tümce, cümle; serve one's *~* ceza süresini (hapiste) doldurmak; *s.* life; **2.** *v/t.* mahkûm etm., hüküm giydirmek (to).

**sen.ten.tious** ☐ [sen'tenʃəs] aşırı tatlı dilli, şatafatlı; veciz, anlamlı; anlamlı sözlerle dolu olan.

**sen.tient** ['senʃənt] *adj.* hisseden, sezgili; duygulu.

**sen.ti.ment** ['sentimənt] *n.* his, duygu, seziş; düşünce, fikir, kanaat, hüküm; *s.* ~ality; **sen.ti.men.tal** ☐ [~'mentl] hisli, duygusal, yanık, içli, duygulara kapılarak yapılan; **sen.ti.men.tal.ist** [~'mentəlist] *n.* duygularına aşırı kapılan kimse; **sen.ti.men.tal.i.ty** [~men'tæliti] *n.* aşırı duygusallık (*veya* duyarlık), içlilik.

**sen.ti.nel** ['sentinl], **sen.try** ['sentri] *n.* ✕ nöbetçi, gözcü.

**sen.try...:** '~.box *n.* nöbetçi kulübesi; '~.go *n.* nöbet.

**se.pal** ♀ ['sepəl] *n.* çanak yaprağı, sepal.

**sep.a.ra.bil.i.ty** [sepərə'biliti] *n.* ayrılabilir olma **ˈsep.a.ra.ble** ☐ ayrılabilir; **sep.a.rate 1.** ☐ ['seprit] ayrı(lmış), müstakil; *~* property 𝄐 karı *veya* kocanın şahsi malları; **2.** ['~əreit] *v/t. & v/i.* ayırmak; bölmek; ayrılmak; **sep.a.ra.tion** *n.* ayırma, ayrılma, ayrılış; **sep.a.ra.tist** ['~ərətist] *n. eccl.* tarikat yanlısı; *pol.* parti-

den ayrılma taraftarı, ayrılık çıkaran; **sep.a.ra.tor** ⊕ ['~əreitə] *n.* ayırıcı, santrifüjör; krema makinesi (*süt*).

**se.pi.a** *paint.* ['siːpjə] *n.* sepya, mürekkep balığı salgısından yapılan boya *veya* mürekkep; bu rengin hâkim olduğu fotoğraf *veya* resim.

**sep.sis** 𝄐 ['sepsis] *n.* septisemi, kana mikrop ve toksin karışması.

**Sep.tem.ber** [sep'tembə] *n.* eylül.

**sep.ten.ni.al** ☐ [sep'tenjəl] yedi yıl süren, yedi senelik, yedi yılda bir olan.

**sep.tic** 𝄐 ['septik] *adj.* bulaşık, mikroplu.

**sep.tu.a.ge.nar.i.an** [septjuedʒi'nɛəriən] *n.* yetmişle yetmişdokuz yaşlar arasında olan kimse.

**se.pul.chral** [si'pʌlkrəl] *adj.* mezara ait; ölü...; *fig.* loş, kasvetli, hüzünlü; **sep.ul.chre** ['sepəlkə] **1.** *n.* mezar, kabir; **2.** *v/t.* gömmek, defnetmek; **sep.ul.ture** ['~tʃə] *n.* gömme, defin.

**se.quel** ['siːkwəl] *n. bşin* devamı, arkası; son, sonuç, netice; in the *~* sonradan.

**se.quence** ['siːkwəns] *n.* art arda gelme, sürüp gitme, ardıllık; sıra; *film:* sahne; *~* of tenses *gr.* zaman uyumu.

**se.ques.ter** [si'kwestə] *v.* sequestrate; *~* o.s. geri çekilmek (from *-den*), tenha bir yere çekilmek; *~ed* dünyadan el çekmiş, münzevî, tek başına.

**se.ques.trate** 𝄐 [si'kwestreit] *v/t.* (*mal, mülk*) el koymak, haczetmek; **se.ques.tra.tion** [si:kwes'treiʃən] *n.* ayırma, bir köşeye çekilme; 𝄐 el koyma, müsadere; **ˈse.ques.tra.tor** 𝄐 yediemin, yasaca güvenilir kimse olarak seçilen kimse.

**se.quol.a** ♀ [si'kwoiə] mamut ağacı, sekoya.

**se.ragl.io** [se'raːliəu] *n.* sultan sarayı; harem dairesi.

**ser.aph** ['serəf] *n., pl. a.* **ser.a.phim** ['~fim] melâikeden *b-i*; **se.raph.ic** [se'ræfik] *adj.* (~ally) melek gibi, meleğe ait; çok güzel ve masum.

**Serb, Ser.bi.an** ['sɜːb(jən)] **1.** *adj.* sırp, Sırbistan'a ait; **2.** *n.* sırp(lı); Sırp dili, Sırpça.

**sere** *poet.* [siə] *adj.* kuru, solgun.

**ser.e.nade** [seri'neid] **1.** *n.* ♪ serenat; **2.** *vb. b-nin* penceresi önünde serenat çalmak.

**se.rene** ☐ [si'riːn] açık, berrak, belli, aşikâr; sakin, hareketsiz; **se.ren.i.ty** [si'reniti] *n.* sükunet, sessizlik, durgunluk; huzur.

**serf** [sɜːf] *n.* serf, köle; *fig.* kul, esir; **ˈserf.age, ˈserf.dom** *n.* kölelik, serflik.

**serge** [sɜːdʒ] *n.* serj, yünlü kumaş.

**ser.geant** ✕ ['sɑ:dʒənt] *n.* çavuş; *(polis)* komiser muavini; '.-'ma.jor *n.* ✕ başçavuş.

**se.ri.al** □ ['siəriəl] **1.** seri halinde olan, tefrika halinde yayımlanan; sıra takibeden, seri...; .ly tefrika halinde, seri olarak; **2.** *n.* tefrika *(roman vs.).*

**se.ries** ['siəri:z] *n. sg. & pl.* sıra, dizi *(a.* ⨍*),* seri; *biol.* grup; . in ⨍ seri bağlama.

**se.ri.ous** □ ['siəriəs] ciddi, ağırbaşlı, vakarlı; önemli; ağır, tehlikeli; gerçek, içten; be . ciddiye almak, ciddi söylemek; '**se.ri.ous.ness** *n.* ciddiyet, ağırbaşlılık, vakar.

**ser.jeant** *parl.* ['sɑ:dʒənt] *n.*: 2-at-arms oturumlarda güvenlik görevlisi.

**ser.mon** ['sə:mən] *n.* dinsel konuşma, vaiz; *iro.* şiddetli kınama, ihtar, yüzleme; '**ser.mon.ize** *vb.* vazetmek, nasihat etm., uzun ve sıkıcı öğütler vermek; azarlamak, haddini bildirmek.

**se.rol.o.gy** ⅋ [siə'rɔlədʒi] *n.* seroloji, serom ve etkilerinden bahseden ilim.

**se.rous** ['siərəs] *adj.* seromla ilgili; ince ve sulu *(sıvı).*

**ser.pent** ['sə:pənt] *n.* yılan; iblis; hain adam; **ser.pen.tine** ['.-tain] **1.** *adj.* yılankavî, yılan gibi kıvrılan, dolambaçlı; **2.** *n. min.* yılantaşı.

**ser.rate** ['serit], **ser.rat.ed** [se'reitid] *adj.* girintili çıkıntılı, testere dişli *(yaprak),* serrat; **ser'ra.tion** *n.* testere gibi dişli oluş.

**ser.ried** ['serid] *adj.* sıkışık, sıkı sıra halinde.

**se.rum** ['siərəm] *n.* serom *(⅋ aşı maddesi; physiol.* özsu).

**serv.ant** ['sə:vənt] *n.* hizmetçi, uşak; *a.* domestic . hizmetçi; '.-girl *n.* hizmetçi kız.

**serve 1.** [sə:v] *v/t.* hizmet etm. -e; yardım etm., yardımcı olm. -e; servis yapmak, sofraya koymak -i; yararı dokunmak, yaramak -e; sağlamak, vermek, ...olarak kullanılmak (with); *(müşteriye)* istediği şeyleri vermek; *(sofraya)* bakmak; *bşden* yararlanmak; idare etm, işlerini çevirmek; a. up *(yemek)* sofraya koymak -i; amacına uymak -in; muamele etm., davranmak -e; *tenis:* servis atmak; (it) .s him right! oh olsun!, bunu hak etti!, yapmasaydı!, söz dinleseydi!; *s.* sentence 1; . out dağıtmak, taksim etm.; F hizmetini tamamlamak; . a writ on s.o., . s.o. with a writ ⅋⅋ *b-ne* bir mahkeme emrini tebliğ etm.; *v/i.* hizmette bulunmak *(a.* ✕ ), işini görmek, hizmetçi

olm.; yetişmek, elvermek; amaca uymak; yaramak, faydası dokunmak *(as,* for -e); . at table sofrada hizmet etm.; **2.** *n. tenis:* servis (yapma sırası); '**serv-er** *n. tenis:* servis atan oyuncu; *eccl.* papaz cömezi; tepsi.

**serv.ice** ['sə:vis] **1.** *n.* hizmet; servis; askerlik; görev, iş; hizmetçilik; ⅋ müşteriye hizmet; *a.* divine . ibadet, ayin, tören; yarar, fayda, istifade; servis takımı; ⅃ palamar kaplama; ⅋⅋ tebliğ, tebligat; *tenis:* servis; be at s.o.'s . *b-nin* hizmetinde olm.; **2.** *vb.* candan bakmak; *b-ne* pervane olm., *b-ne* yardım etm., omuz vermek; ⊕ *bşe* bakmak, işleyecek hale koymak; '**serv.ice.a.ble** □ işe yarar, faydalı, elverişli; dayanıklı, çok kullanılabilen; '**serv.ice.a.ble.ness** *n.* yarar, elverişli olma; dayanıklılık.

**serv.ice...:** '.-ball *n. tenis:* servis topu; . flat hizmetçili apartman dairesi; '.-line *n. tenis:* servis çizgisi; . pipe ⊕ bağlantı borusu; . station benzin istasyonu.

**ser.vile** □ ['sə:vail] kölelere ait, kölelere özgü; köle gibi, gurursuz, hakir, aşağılık; **ser.vil.i.ty** [.-'viliti] *n.* kölelik; aşağılık, gurursuzluk.

**serv.ing** ['sə:viŋ] *n.* tabak, porsiyon.

**ser.vi.tude** ['sə:vitju:d] *n.* serflik, esaret, kölelik, kulluk, uşaklık; ⅋⅋ irtifak hakkı, başkasının mal *veya* mülkünden belirli bir yolla yararlanma hakkı; *s.* penal.

**ser.vo-brake** *mot.* ['sə:vəubreik] *n.* servo fren.

**ses.a.me** ⅋ ['sesəmi] *n.* susam.

**ses.sion** ['seʃən] *n.* oturum, celse; toplantı (hali); toplanma süresi, dönem; be in . toplantı halinde olm.; **ses.sion.al** ['seʃənl] *adj.* oturum..., celse..., oturumla ilgili.

**set** [set] **1.** *(irr.) v/t.* koymak, yerleştirmek, yerli yerine koymak; dikmek *(bitki);* kurmak *(çalar saat);* düzeltmek, tanzim etm.; üzerine saldırtmak *(köpek)* (at, on -e); bilemek *(bıçak vs.);* yerleştirmek, oturtmak *(mücevher);* tespit etm., kararlaştırmak *(zaman);* katılaştırmak, pıhtılaştırmak; ⅋ yerine koymak, yerleştirmek *(kırık, çıkık);* kuluçkaya yatırmak; . s.o. laughing *b-ni* güldürmek; . an example örnek vermek; . the fashion moda çıkarmak; . sail rüzgâra yelken açmak; . one's teeth azmetmek, dişini sıkmak; karar vermek; . against karşısına koymak, karşı koymak; dayamak -e; *s.* apart; . aside bir kenara koymak, rezerve etm.; lağvetmek, feshetmek; *fig.* reddetmek, tanımamak; ~ at defiance *b-ne* karşı durmak, meydan okumak; ~ at ease teskin etm., rahatlatmak *-i*; ~ at liberty tahliye etm.; ~ at rest rahatlatmak *-i*; karara bağlamak *(soru)*; ~ store by çok değerli saymak; ~ down indirmek *(yolcu)*; kaydetmek; tespit etm., koymak *(kural, yöntem)*; bir arada yazmak (to s.o. *b-ne)*; ~ forth göstermek, bildirmek, izah etm.; ~ off yola çıkmak; belirtmek; hesaba katmak, göz önüne almak (against *-e karşı)*; eşitlemek, denklemek; ~ on tahrik etm., teşvik etm., ayartmak; ~ out teşhir etm., yaymak, göstermek; anlatmak, izah etm.; daldırmak, dikmek *(bitki)*; ~ up dikmek, kurmak, tesis etm.; koymak, va'zetmek *(fikir)*; çıkarmak *(nida, haykırış)*; yoluna koymak; girişmek, teşebbüs etm. *(iş)*; ~ up in type *typ.* dizmek, tertip etm.; **2.** *(irr.) v/i.* batmak *(güneş vs.)*; pıhtılaşmak, koyulaşmak; akmak *(elektrik akımı, seyelan)*; *hunt.* av grubuna başkanlık etm.; vücuda iyi oturtmak, yakışmak *(elbise)*; ~ about s.th. bir işe koyulmak; ~ about s.o. F *b-nin* üzerine atılmak; ~ forth açılmak, yola düzülmek; ~ forward ilerletmek, yol açmak; ~ in başlamak *(kış, hastalık vs.)*; ~ off yola düzülmek; araba *vs.* ile gitmek (for); ~ (up)on üzerine saldır(t)mak; *fig.* başlamak, azmetmek; ~ to başlamak *-e*, girişmek *e-*; ~ up bir yere konmak, yerleşmek (as); ~ up for sarfolunmak *(para), k-ne* ... süsü vermek, *k-ni* ... diye tanıtmak; **3.** *adj.* sabit, değişmez, hareketsiz; muayyen, belirli; düzenli; ~ up(on) *bşe* düşkün, haris; azimli; ~ with meşgul *ile*; ~ fair *barometre:* sabit, devamlı açık hava; hard ~ büyük ihtiyaç *(veya* güçlük *vs.)*; ~ piece sanat eseri; ~ speech klişe nutuk, iyi düşünülüp hazırlanmış konuşma; **4.** *n.* sıra, dizi, seri; grup, zümre, takım; sofra takımı; TV, radyo alıcısı; koleksiyon; şirket; cemaat, topluluk, grup, klik; ✓ fide, fidan; *tenis:* set; meyil, eğilim, temayül; heves, istek; yön, yol; kesim, biçim, makas *(elbise); poet.* batma, sukut; *thea.* dekor, mizansen; *(güneş)* batma, gurup; *sinema:* set; make a dead ~ *fig.* üzerine atılmak *-in*, kancayı takmak *-e*, tavlamaya çalışmak *-i*.

**set.back** ['setbæk] *n. fig.* geri tepme, aksilik; kötüleşme, nüksetme; ◬ belli bir noktadan geride inşa etme; **'set-down** *n.* indirme, azaltma; hiçe sayma, hakir gör-

me; **'set-'off** *n.* kontrast, tezat, ayrılık; süs, dekor; † & ♫ mahsup, karşılık, mukabil talep.

**set.tee** [se'ti:] *n.* kanepe.

**set.ter** [setə] *n.* dizici, mürettip; *hunt.* seter *(av köpeği)*.

**set the.o.ry** ♣ *n.* dizi teorisi.

**set.ting** ['setin] *n.* yuva *(s.* set 1 & 2); katılaşma, pıhtılaşma; bir defada kuluçkaya yatırılan yumurtalar; *ast.* batma, gurup; yön, seyir *(rüzgâr)*; yerleştirme, oturtma; ortam, çevre, koşullar; *thea.* dekor, mizansen; *fig.* kuşatma; ♪ beste, kompozisyon; sofra takımı; '~-lo.tion *n. (saç)* fiksatif, sprey.

**set.tle** ['setl] **1.** *n.* tahta kanepe, peyke, sıra; **2.** *v/t.* kararlaştırmak; bakmak *(çocuk)*; yerleştirmek, iskân etm.; düzeltmek; halletmek, çözmek; bitirmek, sona erdirmek *(iş)*; bir karara bağlamak *(soru)*; görmek, ödemek *(hesap)*; teskin etm., rahatlatmak; yatıştırmak *(kavga)*; maaş bağlamak (on s.o. *b-ne)*; insan yerleştirmek, iskân etm.; yerine getirmek; *v/i. oft.* ~ down, *a.* ~ o.s. oturmak, yerleşmek; *a.* ~ in evini döşeyip yerleşmek; konmak, tünemek; ↓ dibe çökmek, batmak; hafiflemek, inmek, yatışmak *(hiddet vs.)*; durulmak *(hava)*; azmetmek, kararlı olm. (on); yetinmek, kanaat etm. (with *ile)*; it is settling for a frost don olacak gibi; ~ down to *k-ni b-şe* vakfetmek, adamak.

**set.tled** ['setld] *adj.* sabit; devamlı, muntazam; muayyen; katî, kesin; sakin, durgun, değişmez *(rüzgâr)*; ödenmiş *(hesap)*; ~ in life evli (barklı), iş güç sahibi; meskûn, şenelmiş.

**set.tle.ment** ['setlmənt] *n.* yerleş(tir)me, bir yerde oturma; anlaşma, uzlaşma; yeni koloni; ♫ ferağ, gelir bağlama; † hesap görme, tasfiye; halletme; yeni iskân edilmiş yer; mülk *(veya* para, hediye *vs.)* verme; misyon, sosyal faaliyetlerde bulunan cemiyet; ev, mesken: temelin oturması *(bina)*.

**set.tler** ['setlə] *n.* yeni yerleşen göçmen; *sl.* nihaî darbe, susturucu cevap.

**set.tling** ['setlin] *n.* yerleşme, iskân *(s.* settle 2); † hesaplaşma, tasfiye.

**set...: '~-'to** *n.* kavga, dövüş, çarpışma; tartışma, dalaşma; '~-up *n.* F durum, vaziyet; yapı, organizasyon; F kazanılması plânlanmış maç; F kolay iş; *Am.* F içki için ikram edilen bardak, buz ve soda.

**sev.en** ['sevn] **1.** *adj.* yedi; **2.** *n.* yedi sayısı; **'sev.en.fold** *adj.* yedi kat, yedi misli; **sev.en.teen** [ˈ~ˈtiːn] *adj.* on yedi; **seventh** [ˈsevnθ] 1. ☐ yedinci; 2. *n.* yedide bir; ♪ yedili; **se.ven.ti.eth** [ˈ~tiiθ] *adj.* yetmişinci; **ˈsev.en.ty** 1. *adj.* yetmiş; 2. *n.* yetmiş sayısı.

**sev.er** [ˈsevə] *v/t.* & *v/i.* ayırmak, ayrılmak, kop(ar)mak; çöz(ül)mek; parçala(n)mak.

**sev.er.al** ☐ [ˈsevrəl] birçok, muhtelif, birkaç; çeşitli, bazı; ayrı, başka; joint *and* ~ *tt* müteselsil, müştereken ve münferiden, zincirleme; **ˈsev.er.al.ly** *adv.* birer birer,'ayrı ayrı, teker teker.

**sev.er.ance** [ˈsevərəns] *n.* ayrılma, ayrılık, ilişik kesme.

**se.vere** ☐ [siˈviə] sert, şiddetli, haşin; sert, kasvetli *(hava, kış)*; sert, acı *(eleştiri)*; ciddi; şiddetli *(ağrı)*; keskin, sert *(üslup, güzellik)*; kötü, berbat *(kaza, yara)*; **se.ver.i.ty** [siˈveriti] *n.* sertlik, şiddet; ciddiyet.

**sow** [səu] *(irr.) vb.* dikiş dikmek; dikmek, ciltlemek *(kitap)*; ~ up dikmek, dikerek kapamak.

**sew.age** [ˈsjuːidʒ] *n.* pis su, lağım suyu; ~ farm lağım sularıyla sulanan tarla.

**sew.er¹** [ˈsəuə] *n.* dikici, dikişçi.

**sew.er²** [ˈsjuə] *n.* lağım; **ˈsew.er.age** *n.* lağım, kanalizasyon.

**sew.ing** [ˈsəuiŋ] 1. *n.* dikiş, iğne işi; 2. *adj.* dikiş...

**sewn** [səun] *p.p. of* sew.

**sex** [seks] *n.* cins; cinsiyet, seks, eşey; cinsel ilişki; *attr.* cinsî...; ~ appeal cinsî cazibe, seksapel; ~ education üreme konusunda aydınlatma, seks eğitimi.

**sex.a.ge.nar.i.an** [seksədʒiˈnɛəriən] *n.* altmış ile yetmiş yaşları arasındaki kimse;

**sex.en.ni.al** ☐ [sekˈsenjəl] altı senede bir olan, altı sene süren, altı senelik; **sextant** [ˈsekstənt] *n.* sekstant, gemilerde yıldızlar arasındaki açıyı ölçmeye yarayan alet.

**sex.ton** [ˈsekstən] *n.* zangoç, kilise kayyumu.

**sex.tu.ple** [ˈsekstjupl] *adj.* altı misli, altı kat.

**sex.u.al** ☐ [ˈseksjuəl] cinsî, seksüel, cinsel, eşeysel, cinsî...; ~ desire cinsel arzu; ~ intercourse cinsel ilişki; **sex.u.al.i.ty** [~ˈæliti] *n.* cinsiyet, cinsellik.

**shab.bi.ness** [ˈʃæbinis] *n.* kılıksızlık, alçaklık, haksızlık; **ˈshab.by** ☐ kılıksız, pejmürde, yırtık pırtık, sefil; alçak, adi; cimri, hasis.

**shack** part. *Am.* [ˈʃæk] *n.* baraka, kulübe, salaş.

**shack.le** [ˈʃækl] 1. *n.* zincir, pranga, bo-

yunduruk *(fig. mst ~s pl.)*; engel, mania; ⚓, ⊕ bağlantı demiri *(veya zincir baklası)*, kelepçe; 2. *v/t.* bağlamak, zincire vurmak, kelepçe takmak; köstekle-mek, engel olm.

**shad** *ichth.* [ʃæd] *n.* tirsi balığı *(ringa türü)*.

**shade** [ʃeid] 1. *n.* gölge; karanlık, zulmet *(a. fig.)*; abajur, karpuz *(lamba)*; gölgelik *(yer)*, siper; *Am.* bir tür perde; *fig.* kolay iş, çocuk oyuncağı; renk tonu; nüans, ayırtı, çok hafif fark; himaye, koruma; hayalet; tayf; 2. *vb.* ışıktan korumak (from *-den*); gölgelemek *(a. fig.)*; örtmek, maskelemek *(ışık)*; muhafaza etm.; *paint.* resme gölge vermek; ~ away, ~ off yavaş yavaş değişmek *(renk, durum vs.)* (into *-e*); **ˈshad.ing** *paint.* resimde gölgeleme; *fig.* nüans, ayırtı.

**shad.ow** [ˈʃædəu] 1. *n.* gölge, karanlık *(a. fig.)*; hayal, karaltı; eser, iz, alâmet; koruma,' himaye; *b-nin* peşinden ayrılmayan *(b-i, köpek)*; rahatsız eden duygu; 2. *v/t.* gölgelemek, karartmak *(a. fig.)*; örtmek, gizlemek; *mst ~* forth, ~ out ima etm., sezdirmek; sembolize etm.; gizlice gözetlemek, peşini bırakmamak; **ˈshad.ow.y** *adj.* gölgeli, karanlık, loş; müphem, şüpheli; belirsiz, hayal gibi.

**shad.y** [ˈʃeidi] *adj.* gölgeli, karanlık; F şüpheli, kötü, namussuz; on the ~ side of forty kırkını aşmış.

**shaft** [ʃɑːft] *n.* sap, kol; sütun, dayak, payanda, destek *(a. fig.)*; *poet.* aydınlık, parıltı, ışın; ⊕ şaft, mil, araba oku; ✕ kuyu; aydınlık, hava bacası.

**shag** [ʃæg] *n.* ince kıyılmış sert tütün.

**shag.gy** [ˈʃægi] *adj.* kaba tüylü.

**sha.green** [ʃæˈgriːn] *n.* sağrı; köpekbalığı derisi.

**Shah** [ʃɑː] *n.* İran şahı.

**shake** [ʃeik] 1. *(irr.) v/t.* silkmek, silkelemek, sallamak, sarsmak, çalka(la)-mak; titretmek; ~ down sarsarak yere düşürmek; küme halinde yığmak *(buğday)*; *sl.* sızdırmak (*para*); ~ hands el sıkısmak, tokalaşmak; ~ up sallayarak silkerek gevşetmek, sertliğini gidermek *(yatak vs.)*; *fig.* sarsarak uyandırmak; *v/i.* titremek, sarsılmak, sallanmak (with *ile*); ♪ titreşim halinde olm.; ~ down arkadaşlık, ahbaplık oluşturmak; 2. *n.* sarsıntı, titreme; ♪ sesi titretme, rulat; çalkalanmış şey; F an, lâhza; *Am.* F deprem; ~ of the hand el sıkma; no great ~s F adî, sıradan, şöyle böyle, pek o kadar değil; **ˈ~ˈdown** *n.* yer yatağı; *Am.*

*sl.* şantaj, para sızdırma; *Am.* son deneme, tecrübe; ~ cruise ⚓ deney seferi; **~-hands** *n.* el sıkışma; **¹shak.en 1.** *p.p. of* shake 1; **2.** *adj.* sarsılmış; müteessir, etkilenmiş; **¹shak.er** *n.* karıştırıcı, içinde *bş* çalkalanan kap; tuzluk vs.

**shake-up** F [¹ʃeik¹ʌp] *n.* yeniden düzenleme, personelde değişiklik yapma.

**shak.i.ness** [¹ʃeikinis] *n.* titreklik, sarsaklık; zayıflık, sakatlık; **¹s.hak.y** □ *mst* titrek, sarsak, sarsıntılı; zayıf, sakat; şüpheli, sallantıda.

**shale** *geol.* [ʃeil] *n.* tortulu şist.

**shall** [ʃæl] *(irr.) v/aux* -ecek; -meli.

**shal.lot** ⚘ [ʃə¹lɔt] *n.* bir tür yabanî sarmısak *veya* ufak soğan.

**shal.low** [¹ʃælou] **1.** *adj.* sığ, yalpık; *fig.* üstünkörü; **2.** *n.* sığ yer, kumsal; **3.** *v/t. & v/i.* sığlaş(tır)mak, düzle(n)mek; **¹shal.low.ness** *n.* sığlık, sığ olma; *fig.* yavan *(veya* tatsız) olma.

**shalt** † [ʃælt] *v/aux.* -eceksin, *s.* shall.

**sham** [ʃæm] **1.** *adj.* yapma, taklit, sahte, suni, yapay; **2.** *n.* taklit, yalan, hile, dolap, aldat(ıl)ma; dolandırıcı, hilekâr, dubaracı; **3.** *vb.* yalandan yapmak, yapar gibi görünmek; *b-ne* karşı sahte tavır takınmak; sayrımsamak; ~ III *k-ni* yalandan hasta göstermek.

**sham.ble** [¹ʃæmbl] *vb.* badi badi *(veya* paytak paytak) yürümek.

**sham.bles** *fig.* [¹ʃæmblz] *n.* harp yeri; yıkıntı, moloz.

**sham.bling** □ [¹ʃæmbliŋ] sallanan, oynayan, gevşek, sarsak.

**shame** [ʃeim] **1.** *n.* utanç, ar; ayıp, rezalet; ~!, for ~, ~ on you! tuu!, ayıp!, pöf!, yazıklar olsun!, utan!; cry ~ upon s.o. *b-nin* yüzüne «utan!» diye bağırmak; put to ~ utandırmak, mahcup etm., rezil etm.; **2.** *vb.* utandırmak -i, mahcup etm. -i; *b-nin* namusuna tecavüz etm., lekelemek, namussuzluk etm.

**shame.faced** □ [¹ʃeimfeist] mahcup, utangaç, sıkılgan; **¹shame.faced.ness** *n.* utangaçlık, mahcubiyet.

**shame.ful** □ [¹ʃeimful] utandırıcı, ayıp, yüzkarası, utanç verici; alçak, kepaze; **¹shame.ful.ness** *n.* utanç verici durum, namussuzluk, alçaklık.

**shame.less** □, [¹ʃeimlis] utanmaz, arsız, edepsiz; **¹shame.less.ness** *n.* arsızlık, hayâsızlık, edepsizlik.

**sham.my** [¹ʃæmi] *n.* süet, podösüet, güderi.

**sham.poo** [ʃæm¹puː] **1.** *n.* şampuan; saçı şampuanla yıkama; **2.** *v/t.* şampuanla yıkamak *(saç).*

**sham.rock** [¹ʃæmrɔk] *n.* ⚘ yonca; tirfil yaprağı *(İrlanda'nın ulusal sembolü).*

**shang.hai** ⚓ *sl.* [ʃæŋ¹hai] *v/t. b-ni* sersemletip *veya* sarhoş edip kaçırarak gemide çalışmaya zorlamak.

**shank** [ʃæŋk] *n.* incik, baldır; ⚘ sap; ⚓ çapa gövdesi; go on 2's mare *veya* pony F tabanvayla gitmek; **shanked** *comb.* ... baldırlı.

**shan't** [ʃɑːnt] = shall not.

**shan.tung** [ʃæn¹tʌŋ] *n.* şantug *(bir tür ipek).*

**shan.ty** [¹ʃænti] *n.* kulübe, baraka; = chanty.

**shape** [ʃeip] **1.** *n.* şekil, biçim, tarz, suret, düzen; hal, durum; in bad ~ kötü durumda; **2.** *v/t.* şekil vermek -e, teşkil etm. -i; düzenlemek -i; uydurmak (to -e); ~ one's course for *b-nin* geleceğini yönlendirmek; *v/i.* gelişmek, ortaya çıkmak, şekillenmek; gibi görünmek, manzara arzetmek; **shaped** *adj.* ... şeklinde; şekilli, biçimli; **¹shape.less** *adj.* biçimsiz, şekilsiz; **¹shape.ly** *adj.* biçimli, endamlı, yakışıklı.

**share¹** [ʃɛə] *n.* saban demiri.

**share²** [~] **1.** *n.* pay, hisse, parça, kısım; kontenjan; † hisse senedi, aksiyon; ✗ itibarî değeri olmayan madencilik hisse senedi; original ~, ordinary ~, primary ~ † adi hisse senedi; preference ~, preferred ~, priority ~ † imtiyazlı hisse senedi; have a ~ in *bşe* iştirak etm.; go ~s paylaşmak, bölüşmek (with s.o.; in s.th.); ~ and ~ alike eşit paylarla; **2.** *v/t.* paylaşmak (among, with *arasında, ile);* *bşe* katılmak, *bşe* iştirak etm.; *v/i. b-ne bşden* pay çıkmak, hissesi olm.; ortaklaşa kullanmak; **¹~.crop.per** *n. Am.* ortakçı, tarla kiracısı; **¹~.hold.er** *n.* † hissedar; **¹shar.er** *n.* hissedar, ortak.

**shark** [ʃɑːk] *n. ichth.* köpekbalığı; *fig.* hilebaz, dolandırıcı; *Am. sl.* bir işin ehli, otorite.

**sharp** [ʃɑːp] **1.** □ bilenmiş, keskin *(a. fig.);* sivri; zeki; sert, şiddetli *(ağrı vs.);* sek, ekşi, buruk *(şarap vs.);* tiz, kulakları tırmalayan *(ses);* canı tez, kabına sığmayan *(mizaç);* tez, acele, ani; kurnaz, hilekâr, şeytanı şişeye sokan; ♪ yarım ton ince, diyez; **2.** *adv.* ♪ yarım ton ince; F dakikası dakikasına, tam; look ~! haydi çabuk!; **3.** *n.* ♪ diyez, yarım ton ince nota; hilebaz, dolandırıcı; **¹sharp.en** *vb.* bilemek, keskinleştirmek, sivriltmek, yontmak; iştah açmak, teşvik etm., hırslandırmak; şiddetlendirmek, güçlendirmek; acılaştırmak, ekşileştirmek; **ˈsharp.en.er** *n.* kalemtıraş; biley taşı, zağ taşı; **ˈsharp.er** *n.* hilekâr, dolandırıcı; **ˈsharp.ness** *n.* keskinlik *(a. fig.)*; şiddet, sertlik; *fig.* şiddetli oluş *(ağrı)*; zeki oluş; hilekârlık.

**sharp**...: **ˈ~ˈset** *adj.* karnı aç; bşe düşkün, haris (on); **ˈ~ˈshoot.er** *n.* keskin nişancı; **ˈ~ˈsight.ed** *adj.* keskin bakışlı, keskin görüşlü; **ˈ~ˈwit.ted** *adj.* zeki.

**shat.ter** [ˈʃætə] *v/t. & v/i.* kır(ıl)mak, parçala(n)mak, tahrip etm., yok etm. *(a. fig.)*; bozmak *(sinir)*, şirazesinden çıkarmak.

**shave** [ʃeiv] **1.** *(irr.) v/t.* tıraş etm., kazımak; *(part. ağaç)* soymak, yüzmek, rendelemek; çok yakınından sürtünür gibi geçmek; *v/i.* tıraş olm.; ~ through maharetle bir engelden geçmek, *fig.* bşden ucuz kurtulmak; **2.** *n.* tıraş; rende; have a ~ tıraş olm.; by a ~ az kaldı, kıl payı; a close ~, a narrow ~ güçbelâ *(veya* daradar, kılpayı) kurtuluş; **ˈshav.en** *p.p. of* shave **1;** a ~ head ustura ile kazınmış kafa; **ˈshav.er** *n.* berber; tıraş makinesi; young ~ F acemi çaylak.

**shav.ing** [ˈʃeivin] *n.* tıraş; ~s *pl. (part. (rende, planya)* yonga, talaş, kırpıntı; *attr.* tıraş..., berber...; **ˈ~-brush** *n.* tıraş fırçası.

**shawl** [ʃɔ:l] *n.* omuz atkısı, şal.

**shawm** ♪ [ʃɔ:m] *n.* çoban kavalı.

**shay** † *veya* F [ʃei] *n.* hafif gezinti arabası.

**she** [ʃi:, ʃi] **1.** *pron.* o *(dişil);* **2.** *n.* kadın, dişi; **she-...** dişi *(hayvanlar için)*.

**sheaf** [ʃi:f] *n., pl.* **sheaves** [ʃi:vz] demet, deste, bağlam.

**shear** [ʃiə] **1.** *(irr.) v/t.* kırkmak, kesmek, makaslamak; F soymak, yolunmuş tavuğa döndürmek; **2.** *n.* (a pair of) ~s *pl.* büyük makas; **ˈshear.er** *n.* kesen kimse, orakçı, tırpancı; **ˈshear.ing** *n.* kırkım, kırpma, makaslama; ~s *pl.* yapağı, yün.

**sheath** [ʃi:θ] *n., pl.* **sheaths** [ʃi:ðz] kın, kılıf *(a. ♀ & anat.);* zo. mahfaza, zarf **sheathe** [ʃi:ð] *v/t.* içine koymak, sokmak, örtmek; ⊕ kaplamak, donatmak; **ˈsheath.ing** *n.* ⊕ kaplama (malzemesi), zırh, örtü.

**sheave** ⊕ [ʃi:v] *n.* makara, bobin; yuvarlak levha, disk.

**sheaves** [ʃi:vz] *pl. of* sheaf.

**she.bang** *Am. sl.* [ʃəˈbæŋ] *n.* yıkılmak üzere olan, virane baraka; the whole ~ hepsi, tümü.

**shed¹** [ʃed] *(irr.) vb.* dökmek, akıtmak, boşaltmak *(kan, gözyaşı vs.);* yaymak, neşretmek *(ışık, fikir vs.)* (upon) dök-

mek, değiştirmek *(kıl, deri vs.);* çıkarıp atmak, kurtulmak *-den.*

**shed²** [~] *n.* baraka, kulübe, sundurma, odunluk; uçak hangarı.

**sheen** [ʃi:n] *n.* parlaklık, parıltı *(kumaş)*; **ˈsheen.y** *adj.* parlak.

**sheep** [ʃi:p] *n.* koyun(lar *pl.*) koyun derisi, meşin; *fig.* safdil, budala kimse; **ˈ~-cot** = sheep-fold; **ˈ~-dog** *n.* çoban köpeği; **ˈ~-fold** *n.* koyun ağılı; **ˈsheep.ish** ☐ sıkılgan, utangaç; sersem, budala; koyun gibi; **ˈsheep.ish.ness** *n.* aptallık, budalalık; mahcubiyet, sıkılganlık.

**sheep**...: **ˈ~.man** *n. Am.* koyun yetiştiren kimse; **ˈ~-run** = sheep-walk; **ˈ~.skin** *n.* pösteki, koyun postu; *Am.* diploma; **ˈ~-walk** *n.* koyun otlağı.

**sheer¹** [ʃiə] *adj. & adv.* halis, saf, katışıksız, hakiki; (büs)bütün, tam(amiyle); dik, sarp, dikey; doğru(dan), vasıtasız; çok ince, hafif ve şeffaf *(kumaş)*.

**sheer²** [~] **1.** *vb.* ↓ rotadan sapmak, yolundan ayrılmak; ~ off *fig.* tüymek, sıvışmak; **2.** *n.* ↓ borda kavsi; yoldan sapma.

**sheet** [ʃi:t] **1.** *n.* yatak çarşafı; yaprak, tabaka *(kâğıt);* levha *(cam, metal vs.);* geniş yüzey *(su vs.);* ↓ ıskota, büyük yelkenleri yönetmek için kullanılan ip; the rain came down in ~s yağmur sağanak halinde indi; ~ iron saç *(demir);* **2.** *v/t.* çarşaf vs. ile örtmek; **ˈ~-an.chor** *n.* ↓ ocaklık demiri, çapa; *fig.* kurtuluş ümidi; **ˈsheet.ing** *n.* çarşaflık keten bezi, **ˈsheet-light.ning** *n.* ufukta şimşek çakması.

**sheik(h)** [ʃeik] *n.* şeyh, kabile reisi.

**shelf** [ʃelf] *n. pl.* **shelves** [ʃelvz] raf, etajer, pervaz; *geol.* resif, şelf, sığlık, kum bankı; on the ~ *fig.* rafa kaldırılmış, kadro dışı; get on the ~ *fig.* dansa davet edilmemek *(kız).*

**shell** [ʃel] **1.** *n.* kabuk; kaplumbağa kabuğu, bağa; istiridye *(veya* midye) kabuğu; ⊕ iskelet *(bina);* ✕ top mermisi, obüs, bomba; ince uzun yarış kayığı; **2.** *v/t. & v/i.* kabuğunu çıkarmak *(veya* soymak, kırmak); koçandan ayırmak *(mısır);* başaktan ayırmak *(buğday);* ✕ bombardıman etm.; kabuktan ayrılmak, sıyrılmak, soyulmak; ~ out *sl.* mangizleri sökülmek, hesabı ödemek.

**shel.lac** [ʃəˈlæk] *n.* gomalaka, şelak, cilâ yapmakta kullanılan bir tür reçine.

**shell-cra.ter** [ˈʃəlkreitə] *n.* mermi hunisi; **shelled** [ʃeld] *comb.* ... kabuklu.

**shell**...: **ˈ~-fire** *n.* top ateşi; **ˈ~-fish** *n. zo.* kabuklu hayvan; **ˈ~-proof** *adj.* mermi (*veya* bomba) işlemez; **'~-shock** *n.* savaş yorgunluğu, savaşın neden olduğu ruhsal çöküntü.

**shel.ter** ['ʃeltə] **1.** *n.* sığınak, barınak, siper, sundurma, saçak; *fig.* himaye, koru(n)ma; **2.** *v/t.* & *v/i.* barın(dır)mak, koru(n)mak, muhafaza etm.; **'shel.ter·less** *n.* himayeden yoksun, korunmasız; desteksiz, arkasız.

**shelve¹** [ʃelv] *v/t.* (içine) raflar yapmak; rafa koymak; *fig.* rafa kaldırmak, ertelemek, bir kenara koymak; emekliye ayırmak, kadro dışı bırakmak; F *b-ne,* *bşe* aldırış etmemek.

**shelve²** [~] *v/i.* (yavaş yavaş) meyletmek.

**shelves** [ʃelvz] *pl. of* shelf.

**shelv.ing** ['ʃelviŋ] **1.** *n.* raf (malzemesi); **2.** *adj.* eğik, meyilli.

**she.nan.i.gan** *Am.* F [ʃi'nænigən] *n.* açıkgözlük, dolandırıcılık, dalaverecilik, maskaralık.

**shep.herd** ['ʃepəd] **1.** *n.* çoban; **2.** *vb.* otlatmak, çobanlık etm.; rehberlik etm., sevk ve idare etm.; **'shep.herd.ess** *n.* kadın çoban.

**sher.bet** ['ʃɔ:bət] *n.* şerbet; karbonatlı limonata, gazoz; dondurma.

**sher.iff** ['ʃerif] *n.* şerif; (*ilçe veya bucakta*) polis müdürü.

**sher.ry** ['ʃeri] *n.* beyaz İspanyol şarabı.

**shew** ↖ [ʃəu] = show.

**shib.bo.leth** ['ʃibəleθ] *n.* tanıtma işareti, parola; artık fazla anlamı olmayan eski deyim *veya* âdet.

**shield** [ʃi:ld] **1.** *n.* kalkan; siper, koruyucu şey; **2.** *v/t.* korumak, himaye etm. (from *-den*); **'shield.less** *adj.* korumasız, himayesiz.

**shift** [ʃift] **1.** *n.* değiş(tir)me; nöbet; geçici çare; önlem; hile, desise; çalışma grubu, iş devresi, vardiya, posta; taşınma; make ~ çaresini bulmak (to *-e*); işin içinden sıyrılmak (with; without); **2.** *v/t.* yerini değiştirmek; ↓ dümen kırmak; bir yerden başka bir yere aktarmak; başka yere nakletmek (*yer, sahne*), yerini değiştirmek; *mot.* vites değiştirmek; (*işletme*) başka işler için ayarlamak (to *-e*); *v/i.* değişmek, başkalaşmak; (*rüzgâr*) dönmek; ↓ (safra) fazla gelmek; işin içinden sıyrılmak, çare bulmak; ~ for o.s. başının çaresine bakmak, *k-ni* geçindirmek, kendi işine bakmak; **'shift.ing** □ değişken, değişir; ~ sands *pl.* bataklık kumu; **'shift.less** □ biçare, çaresiz; *fig.* beceriksiz, uyuşuk, sünepe; **'shift.y** □ hilekâr, kurnaz, pişkin.

**shil.ling** ['ʃiliŋ] *n.* şilin, eski İngiliz gümüş parası; cut off with a ~ mirastan yoksun bırakmak.

**shil.ly-shal.ly** ['ʃiliʃæli] *adj.* kararsız, mütereddit.

**shim.mer** ['ʃimə] *v/i.* parıldamak, pırıldamak, hafif ışık salmak.

**shin** [ʃin] **1.** *a.* ~-bone *n.* incik kemiği; **2.** *vb.* ~ up tırmanmak.

**shin.dy** F ['ʃindi] *n.* gürültü, patırdı, şamata, arbede, yaygara.

**shine** [ʃain] **1.** *n.* parlaklık, ışık, ziya; cilâ(lama); give one's shoes a ~ *b-nin* ayakkabılarını boyayıp cilâlamak; rain or ~ hava nasıl olursa olsun; **2.** *v/i.* parıldamak, ışık vermek; *fig.* parlamak, mükemmel olm.; *v/t.* cilâlamak, parlatmak.

**shin.gle¹** ['ʃiŋgl] **1.** *n.* çatı padavrası, ince tahta, tahta kiremit; *Am.* F levha, tabela; **2.** *v/t.* çatıyı padavra ile kaplamak; kısa kesmek (*saç*).

**shin.gle²** *coll.* [~] *n.* çakıl(lı sahil).

**shin.gles** ⚕ ['ʃiŋglz] *n. pl.* zona (hastalığı).

**shin.gly** ['ʃiŋgli] *adj.* çakıllı, çakıl...

**shin.y** □ ['ʃaini] parlak, cilâlı; açık, berrak.

**ship** [ʃip] **1.** *n.* gemi, vapur; *Am.* F uçak; ~'s company gemi mürettebatı; **2.** *v/t.* gemiye yüklemek; gemiyle sevketmek, yollamak; yandan su almak (*gemi*); the oars kürekleri yerine takmak; ~ a sea dalga yemek (*gemi*); *v/i.* gemi hizmetine yazılmak; gemiye binmek; **'~-board:** on ~ ↓ gemide **'~-brok.er** *n.* gemi simsarı; deniz sigortası acentası; **'~-build.er** *n.* gemi yapıcısı; **'~-build.ing** *n.* gemi yapımı, gemi inşaatı; **'~-ca.nal** *n.* yapay gemi kanalı; **'~-chan.dler** *n.* gemi levazımatı satan' kimse; **'~-chan.dler.y** *n.* gemi levazımatı *veya* kumanyası; **'~.load** *n.* kargo, gemi hamulesi *veya* gemi yükü; **'ship.ment** *n.* gemiye yükleme; yüklenen eşya, yük, kargo, hamule; **'ship.own.er** *n.* armatör, gemi sahibi; **'ship.per** *n.* gemiye yüklenen *veya* yükleten kimse, ihracatçı.

**ship.ping** ['ʃipiŋ] **1.** *n.* gemiye yükleme; filo, donanma; tonaj; gemicilik, gemi trafiği; gemi ile mal taşımacılığı, deniz nakliyesi; **2.** *adj.* gemilere *veya* denizciliğe ait, gemi...; deniz...; **'~-a.gent** *n.* deniz nakliyecisi, gemicilik şirketi (*veya* temsilciliği); **'~-of.fice** *n.* sevkiyat bürosu, nakliye şirketi, deniz taşımacılığı bürosu.

**ship...:** **'~.shape** *adj.* temiz ve düzenli; **'~-way** *n.* gemi yapı kızağı; **'~.wreck 1.**

*n.* deniz kazası; gemi enkazı; **2.** *v/t.* karaya oturmak; be ~ed kazaya uğramak; **'~.wrecked** *adj.* kazazede; batık; **'~-.wright** *n.* tersane işçisi; **'~.yard** *n.* tersane.

**shire** ['ʃaiə, *in compound word* ...ʃiə] *n.* kontluk; ~ horse bir tür İngiliz kadanası.

**shirk** [ʃəːk] *vb.* kaçınmak -*den,* yan çizmek, kaytarmak, atlatmak; **'shirk.er** *n.* atlatan, yan çizen kimse, kaytarıcı.

**shirt** [ʃəːt] *n.* gömlek; *a.* ~-waist *Am.* gömlek şeklinde blûz; keep one's ~ on *sl.* soğukkanlılığını kaybetmemek; **'shirt.ing** *n.* ✝ gömleklik (*kumaş*); **'shirt-sleeve 1.** *n.* gömlek kolu; **2.** *adj.* kollu; ~ diplomacy *part. Am.* açık diplomasi; **'shirt.y** *adj. sl.* hiddetli, şiddetli, kızgın ve kaba.

**shiv.er¹** ['ʃivə] **1.** *n.* ufak parça, kıymık; break to ~s = **2.** *v/t. & v/i.* ufak parçalara böl(ün)mek.

**shiv.er²** [~] **1.** *n.* titreme, heyecan; the ~s *pl.* hararet, humma; ürperme; it gives me the ~s tüylerimi ürpertiyor; **2.** *v/t.* titremek, (tüyleri) ürpermek; soğuktan titremek; ~ing fit nöbet titremesi; **'shiv.er.y** *adj.* titrek; tüyler ürpertici.

**shoal¹** [ʃəul] **1.** *n.* oğul, küme, kalabalık, sürü (*balık; a. fig.*); **2.** *vb.* bir araya toplanmak, sürü oluşturmak (*balık*).

**shoal²** [~] **1.** *n.* sığlık yer, resif; **2.** *vb.* sığlaş(tır)mak; **3.** = **'shoal.y** *adj.* sığ, kumsal.

**shock¹** ✓ [ʃɔk] *n.* ekin yığını, dokurcun.

**shock²** [~] **1.** *n.* sars(ıl)ma, sarsıntı, darbe, vuruş; rezalet, kepazelik, skandal; ⚡ şok, sinir buhranı; elektrik çarpması; **2.** *v/t. & v/i. fig.* ka!bi kır(ıl)mak, darıl(t)mak, hatırlı b-ni gücendirmek; sars(ıl)mak; iğrendirmek.

**shock³** [~] *n.* (of hair *saç*) demet, perçem; kabarık, kıtık gibi saç.

**shock...:** **'~-ab.sorb.er** *n. mot.* amortisör; **'~-bri.gade** *n.* çarpışma, hücum tugayı; **'~-proof** *adj.* sarsıntıya dayanır; ~ **ther.a.py**, ~ **treat.ment** elektroterapi, elektro sokla tedavi.

**shock.er** *sl.* ['ʃɔkə] *n.* heyecanlı roman.

**shock.ing** ▢ ['ʃɔkiŋ] korkunç şok etkisi yapan; yakışıksız, müstehcen, iğrenç; kızdırıcı, incitici, gönül kırıcı; tüyler ürpertici.

**shod** [ʃɔd] *pret. & p.p. of* shoe 2.

**shod.dy** ['ʃɔdi] **1.** *n.* kullanılmamış fakat bir kez örülüp sökülerek yeniden örülmüş yün, kumaş tiftiği; *fig.* değersiz şeyler, değersiz eser; **2.** *adj.* sahte, taklit, yapay, suni; bavağı, değersiz, fena.

**shoe** [ʃuː] **1.** *n.* kundura, ayakkabı; nal;

tekerlek çarığı; fren balatası; **2.** (*irr.*) *vb.* ayakkabı giydirmek; nallamak, nal çakmak; **'~.black** *n.* lostracı, ayakkabı boyacısı; **'~.black.ing** *n.* boyama, parlatma (*ayakkabı*); **'~.horn** *n.* ayakkabı çekeceği, kerata; **'~-lace** *n.* ayakkabı bağı; **'~.mak.er** *n.* kunduracı, ayakkabıcı; **'~-string** *n.* ayakkabı bağı; on a ~ F çok az parayla.

**shone** [ʃɔn] *pret. & p.p. of* shine 2.

**shoo** [ʃuː] *vb.* korkutmak, ürkütmek, kışkışlamak (*kuş, çocuk vs.*).

**shook** [ʃuk] *pret. of* shake 1.

**shoot** [ʃuːt] **1.** *n. fig.* atım, atış; av (partisi); av alanı; ✓ filiz, sürgün; **2.** (*irr.*) *v/t.* ateş etm., atış yapmak, ateşlemek; atmak, fırlatmak; silahla vurmak, öldürmek; *film:* filme almak; (*resim*) çekmek; kurşunla delmek; şut çekmek; *golf:* vuruş yapmak; ⚓ sürmek, filizlenmek; sürmek (*sürgü, mandal*); boşaltmak, dökmek (*çöp, kamyon*); yuvarlamak (*fıçı vs.*); ⚡ enjekte etm.; *v/i.* ateş etm. (at -*e*); zonklamak, sancımak (*uzuv*); bir yerden fırlamak; *a.* ~ forth filizlenmek, sürmek; ⬇ fazla gelmek (*safra*); ~ .ahead ok gibi fırlamak, atılmak; ~ ahead of mesafeyi açmak; ~ down düşürmek; ~ up hızla büyümek, yükselmek; **'shoot.er** *n.* nişancı; avcı.

**shoot.ing** ['ʃuːtiŋ] **1.** *n.* atış; avcılık (hukuku), düzensiz silah atma; *film:* filme alma; **2.** *adj.* zonklayan (*uzuv*); **'~-box** *n.* avcı kulübesi; **'~-brake** *n.* kaptıkaçtı, pikap (*araba*); **'~-gal.ler.y** *n.* poligon, atış meydanı; (*lunapark*) atış barakası; **'~-range** *n.* poligon; ~ **star** akanyıldız, göktaşı; **'~-war** *n.* sıcak savaş.

**shop** [ʃɔp] **1.** *n.* dükkân, mağaza; atelye, iş yeri, fabrika; set up ~ dükkân açmak, yeni bir iş kurmak; talk ~ iş konusunda konuşmak; **2.** *vb. mst* go ~ping alış-veriş yapmak, satın almak; **'~-as.sist.ant** *n.* satıcı tezgâhtar; **'~-keep.er** *n.* dükkâncı, mağaza sahibi; **'~-lift.er** *n.* dükkân hırsızı; **'~-man** *n.* tezgâhtar; **'shop.per** *n.* alıcı, müşteri; **'shop.ping** *n.* alışveriş (etme); ~ centre *Am.* ~ center alış-veriş merkezi, büyük çarşı.

**shop...:** **'~-soiled** *adj.* uzun süre dükkânda kalıp ellenmekten hasar görmüş *veya* kirlenmiş *veya* vitrinde bekletilmiş (*mal*); **'~-stew.ard** *n.* işyeri temsilcisi; **'~-walk.er** *n.* mağazada çalışanlara ve alıcılara yardım eden görevli; **'~-win.dow** *n.* vitrin.

**shore¹** [ʃɔː] *n.* sahil, kıyı, yaka; on ~ karada.

**shore²** [~] 1. *n*. destek, istinat, payanda; 2. *vb*.: ~ up payanda vurmak, desteklemek.

**shore...**: '~.line *n*. kıyı şeridi; '~.ward ['~wəd] *adv*. kıyıya doğru.

**shorn** [ʃɔːn] *p.p. of* shear 1.; ~ of yoksun -*den*.

**short** [ʃɔːt] 1. *adj*. kısa; bodur, kısa boylu; az, eksik, yetersiz; iyi pişmiş, gevrek, yumuşak (*çörek, pasta vs.*); çapaklı, karıncalı (*metal*); kaba, nezaketsiz (*cevap*); † kısa vadeli; *s*. circult; ~ wave *radyo*: kısa dalga; In ~ sözün kısası, kısaca; ~ of -*si* eksik; nothing ~ of -*den* başka bir şey değil; sırf, hepsi; doğrudan doğruya; ~ of London Londra'ya varmadan az önce; come *veya* fall ~ of yetmemek, erişememek, ulaşamamak; cut ~ birden kesmek, bşe ara vermek; kısa kesmek; fall *veya* run ~ yetmemek, tükenmek, kıtlaşmak; stop ~ of bşe ara vermek; 2. *n. gr*. yarı sesli, kısa hece; kısa metrajlı film; ≠ kontak, kısa devre; *s*. shorts; ~ circult; '**short.age** *n*. yokluk, kıtlık, eksiklik.

**short...**: '~.cake *n*. üstüne ezilmiş meyve dökülmüş kek; '✓.'clr.cult *n*. ≠ kısa devre; '~-'com.ing *n*. kusur; noksan, eksiklik; ~ cut kestirme yol; '~-'dated *adj*. † kısa vadeli; '**short.en** *v/t. & v/i*. kısal(t)mak; '**short.en.ing** *n*. unla karıştırılan yağ.

**short...**: '~.fall *n*. açık, eksik; '~.hand *n*. stnenografi; ~ typlst steno daktilo; '~-'hand.ed *adj*. yardımcısı az; '~-'lived *adj*. kısa ömürlü; '**short.ly** *adv*. kısaca, sözün kısası; birazdan, yakında; '**short.ness** *n*. kısalık, eksiklik.

**shorts** [ʃɔːts] *n. pl*. şort, kısa pantolon, dizlik, külot, kispet.

**short...** '~-'sight.ed *adj*. miyop; *fig*. kısa görüşlü; '~-'tem.pered *adj*. çabuk kızan, öfkeli; '~-'term *adj*. kısa vadeli; '~-wave *adj. radyo*: kısa dalga...; '~-'wind.ed *adj*. tık nefes, nefes darlığı olan.

**shot¹** [ʃɔt] 1. *pret. & p.p. of* shoot 2; 2. *adj*. şanjan, yanardöner (*kumaş*).

**shot²** [~] *n*. atış, atım; gülle, küre, top; erim, menzil; girişim; tahmin; *a*. small ~ av saçması; *pl. mst* ~ saçma tanesi; nişancı, avcı; *spor*: • vuruş (*bilardo*); şut; *phot., film*: fotoğraf, resim, film; ≸ şırınga, iğne; *sl*. bir yudum içki; *sl*. cinsel birleşme, boşalma; have a ~ at bşi bir kez denemek, şansını denemek; not by a long ~ katiyen, hiç; within (out of) ~ atış menzili içinde (dışında); like a ~ F mermi gibi; blg ~ F önemli şahıs, ko-

daman, nüfuzlu kimse, make a bad ~ hedefi kaçırmak; *fig*. yanlış tahmin etm.; '~.gun *n*. av tüfeği, çifte; ~ marriage *Am*. F zorunlu evlilik; '~-proof *adj*. mermi işlemez.

**shot.ten her.ring** ['ʃɔtn'heriŋ] *n*. yumurtlamış ringa balığı.

**should** [ʃud] *pret. of* shall.

**shoul.der** ['ʃəuldə] 1. *n*. omuz (*a. hayvanların*); *fig*. destek; omuza benzer çıkıntı; dağ kolu (*veya* yamacı); kürek eti; give s.o. the cold ~ bne soğuk davranmak; put one's ~ to the wheel çok çaba göstermek, omuz vermek; rub ~s with arkadaşlık etm., temas etm. ile; ~ to ~ omuz omuza, birlikte; 2. *vb*. omuzlamak; X omuz vurmak, yüklenmek; ~ one's way yol açmak; '~-blade *n. anat*. kürek kemiği; '~-strap *n*. X apolet; omuz askısı (*elbise*).

**shout** [ʃaut] 1. *n*: bağırma, nida, seslenme, çığlık; 2. *v/t. & v/i*. bağırmak, seslenmek, haykırmak, çağırmak, sevinç nidaları çıkarmak, yaygara koparmak.

**shove** [ʃʌv] 1. *n*. itme, kakma, dürtme; 2. *vb*. itmek, dürtmek, sürmek, itip kakmak.

**shov.el** ['ʃʌvl] 1. *n*. kürek, faraş; 2. *vb*. kürelemek, kürekle alıp atmak; '~-board *n*. gemide oynanan bir tür oyun.

**show** [ʃəu] 1. (*irr.*) *v/t*. göstermek; işaret etm.; sergilemek; göstermek (*lûtuf, tenezzül*); tanıtlamak; kanıtlamak; anlatmak; öğretmek; seyrettirmek; ~ forth göstermek, teşhir etm.; ~ in içeri sokmak; ~ out uğurlamak, kapıya kadar geçirmek; ~ round dolaştırmak, gezdirmek; ~ up meydana çıkarmak, maskesini düşürmek; *v/i. a*. ~ up görünmek, gözükmek; ~ off göstermek; övünmek, palavracılık etm., *k-ni* ... gibi göstermek; 2. *n*. gösteriş, gösterme; görünüş; sergi, teşhir; *thea*. temsil, oyun, gösteri; *sl*. iş, konu, girişim; ~ of hands el kaldırarak yapılan oylama; ~ dumb ~ pandomima; on ~ sergilenmekte; run the ~ *sl*. dükkân, iş *vs*. işletmek, idare etm.; ~ busi.ness eğlence sanayii, tiyatroculuk *vs*.; '~-card *n*. ticarî ilân, afiş, pankart; '~-case *n*. küçük vitrin; '~-down *n*. iskambilde eldeki kâğıtları açma, kozları ortaya koyma (*a. fig.*); *fig*. güç denemesi.

**show.er** ['ʃauə] 1. *n*. sağanak; duş; *fig*. dolgunluk, bolluk, çokluk; 2. *v/i*. sağanak halinde yağmak (*a. fig.*), dökülmek, akmak; *v/t*. bol vermek, yağdırmak; dökmek, üstünden aşağı akıtmak; ~-bath ['~baːθ] *n*. duş; '**show.er.y** *adj*. yağmurlu; yağmur...

**show.i.ness** ['ʃəuinis] *n.* gösteriş, debdebe, tantana. saltanat; **ᶦshow.man** *n.* oyun, müzikal vs. hazırlayan kimse; şovmen, seyirciyi eğlendiren, oyalayan kimse; sirk, eğlence yeri vs. müdürü; **ᶦshow-man.ship** *n.* seyircinin ilgisini çekme sanatı; **shown** [ʃɔun] *p.p. of* show 1; **ᶦshow-place** *n.* görülmeye değer olan yer; **ᶦshow-room** *n.* sergi salonu; **ᶦshow-window** *n.* vitrin; **ᶦshow.y** □ gösterişli, mükemmel, göze çarpan, göz alıcı.

**shrank** [ʃræŋk] *pret. of* shrink.

**shrap.nel** ✕ [ˈʃræpnl] *n.* şarapnel.

**shred** [ʃred] 1. *n.* dilim, ufak kesilmiş *veya* yırtılmış parça, kırpıntı; paçavra (*a. fig.*); 2. (*irr.*) *v/t.* parçalamak, çekip yırtmak, tarazlamak.

**shrew** [ʃruː] *n.* kavgacı, şirret kadın; *a.* ~-mouse *zo.* sivri burunlu fare, soreks.

**shrewd** □ [ʃruːd] kurnaz, becerikli, zeki; **ᶦshrewd.ness** *n.* kurnazlık, açıkgözlük, cin fikirlilik.

**shrew.ish** □ [ˈʃruːiʃ] kavgacı, huysuz, şirret.

**shriek** [ʃriːk] 1. *n.* feryat, yaygara, çığlık; 2. *vb.* çığlık koparmak, cıyaklamak, haykırmak.

**shrike** *orn.* [ʃraik] *n.* örümcekkuşu.

**shrill** [ʃril] 1. □ keskin sesli, kulakları tırmalayan; 2. *vb.* acı ve tiz sesle haykırmak.

**shrimp** *zo.* [ʃrimp] *n.* karides, deniz tekesi; *fig.* bücür, cüce, çelimsiz kimse.

**shrine** [ʃrain] *n.* kutsal emanetler mahfazası; türbe.

**shrink** [ʃriŋk] (*irr.*) *v/i.* küçülmek, büzülmek, çekmek, daralmak (*kumaş*); geri çekilmek; *a.* ~ back ürkerek gerilemek (from, at -*den*); *v/t.* daraltmak, büzmek; ⊕ çektirmek; **ᶦshrink.age** *n.* çekme payı, fire, daralma; *fig.* kıymetten düşme, inme, düşüş.

**shriv.el** [ˈʃrivl] *vb. a.* ~ up büzülmek, buruşmak, pörsümek; *fig.* içi geçmek; âciz duruma düşmek.

**shroud¹** [ʃraud] 1. *n.* kefen; tabut örtüsü; *fig.* örtü. 2. *v/t.* kefenlemek, kefene sarmak; *fig.* sarmak, örtmek.

**shroud²** ⚓ [~] *n.* çarmık, ana direkleri ve gabya çubuklarını tutan halatlar; *mst* ~s *pl.* çarmıklar.

**Shrove.tide** [ˈʃrəuvtaid] *n.* Hıristiyanlarda büyük perhizden önce gelen süre, et kesimi, apukurya; **Shrove Tues.day** büyük perhizin arife günü.

**shrub** [ʃrʌb] *n.* çalı, küçük ağaç, funda; **ᶦshrub.ber.y** *n.* çalılık, fundalık; **ᶦshrub.by** 

*adj.* çalı gibi; çalılık...

**shrug** [ʃrʌg] 1. *vb.* omuz silkmek; ~ s.th. off *b*şe aldırmamak, boşvermek; 2. *n.* omuz silkme.

**shrunk** [ʃrʌŋk] *p.p. of* shrink; **ᶦshrunk.en** *adj.* daral(tıl)mış, çekmiş; çökmüş (*yanak*).

**shuck** *Am.* [ʃʌk] 1. *n.* kabuk, kılıf, zarf; ~s! F boş lâf!, saçma!, zırva!; 2. *vb.* kabuğunu vs. çıkarmak, soymak.

**shud.der** [ˈʃʌdə] 1. *v/i.* ürpermek, titremek (at); 2. *n.* titreme, ürperti.

**shuf.fle** [ˈʃʌfl] 1. *v/t. & v/i.* karıştırmak, karman çorman etm.; karıştırmak, karmak (*oyun kâğıdı*); yer değiştirmek, elden ele dolaştırmak; kaçamaklı cevap vermek, sözü değiştirmek, ağız yapmak; ayak sürümek; başından atmak, defetmek; ~ away güçlükle ve acemice ilerlemek; ~ off üstünden atmak (*sorumluluk*); ~ through one's work kötü iş görmek; 2. *n.* kırıştırma (*oyun kâğıdı*); ayak sürüme; bu tür bir dans; *pol.* düzenleme (*kabinede*); **ᶦshuffler** *n.* karıştıran kimse (*kâğıt*); ağız değiştiren kimse, dubaracı; **ᶦshuf.fling** □ kaçamaklı; hilekâr.

**shun** [ʃʌn] *v/t.* b*ş*den sakınmak, kaçınmak.

**shunt** [ʃʌnt] 1. *n.* 🚂 manevra; 🚂 makas; ⚡ paralel devre; 2. *vb.* 🚂 yan yola geçirmek, manevra yapmak, makas değiştirmek, yolunu değiştirmek; ⚡ paralel bağlamak, akımın bir kısmını başka kablodan geçirmek; *fig.* b-ni yerinden oynatmak, b-nin yerini değiştirmek; **ᶦshunt.er** *n.* 🚂 manevracı; **ᶦshunt.ing sta.tion** *n.* 🚂 manevra istasyonu.

**shut** [ʃʌt] (*irr.*) *v/t.* kapa(t)mak; ~ one's eyes göz yummak, müsamaha etm. -*e*; ~ down tatil etm., faaliyeti durdurmak, kapamak (*iş yeri*); ~ in kapamak, kilitlemek; sıkıştırmak (*parmak*); ~ out dışarıda bırakmak; ~ up kapamak, kilitlemek; ~ up shop dükkânı kapamak, işten vazgeçmek; *v/i.* kapanmak; ~ up! F sus!; kapat çaneni!; **ᶦ~.down** *n.* işin tatil olması, faaliyetin durması; **ᶦ~.out** *n.* *spor:* sayı vermeden mağlûp etme; **ᶦshut.ter** *n.* kepenk, panjur; *phot.* obtüratör, kapak; put up the ~s kepenkleri indirmek, dükkânı kapatmak; rolling ~ kepenk.

**shut.tle** [ˈʃʌtl] 1. *n.* mekik (*a. dikiş makinesinde*); 🚂 kısa mesafede mekik dokuyan tren servisi; ~ train karşılıklı sefer yapan tren; 2. *vb.* mekik dokumak, mekik gibi işlemek; karşılıklı sefer yapmak; **ᶦ~.cock** *n.* raketle oynanan ucu tüylü mantar banminton topu *veya* bu topla oynanan oyun.

**shy¹** [ʃai] **1.** □ korkak, ürkek, çekingen, mahçup, utangaç; be *veya* fight ~ of ürkmek, çekinmek -*den veya* sakınmak -*den*; **2.** *v/i.* bşden, bden çekinmek, korkmak, ürkmek (at).

**shy²** F [~] **1.** *v/t.* fırlatmak, atmak; **2.** *n.* atış, fırlatma; have a ~ at bş üzerinde tecrübe yapmak, bir denemek.

**shy.ness** [ˈʃainis] *n.* çekingenlik, ürkeklik, korkaklık.

**shy.ster** *part Am. sl.* [ˈʃaistə] *n.* iyi şöhreti olmayan avukat, hileli iş yürüten kimse.

**Si.a.mese** [saiəˈmiːz] **1.** *adj.* Siyamlı; Siyam diline ait; **2.** *n.* Siyam halkı *veya* dili.

**Si.be.ri.an** [saiˈbiəriən] **1.** *adj.* Sibiryalı; **2.** *n.* Sibiryalı kimse.

**sib.i.lant** [ˈsibilənt] **1.** □ ıslık gibi, vızıltılı; **2.** *n. gr.* ıslık gibi ses veren harf *(s, z, ş, j)*.

**sib.yl** [ˈsibil] *n.* eski zamanda falcı, kâhin kadın; **sib.yl.line** [~lain] *adj.* fala, kehanete ait.

**Si.cil.ian** [siˈsiljən] **1.** *adj.* Sicilyalı; **2.** *n.* Sicilyalı kimse.

**sick** [sik] *adj.* hasta, keyfisiz (of, with); midesi bulanmış; bıkmış, bezmiş (of -*den*); be ~ for bşin hasretini çekmek, bş için yanıp tutuşmak; be ~ of bıkmak, tiksinmek, usanmak; go ~, report ~ *k-ni* hasta diye bildirmek; **ˈ~-bed** *n.* hasta yatağı; **ˈ~-ben.e.fit** *n.* hastalık parası; **ˈsick.en** *v/i.* hastalanmak, hastalıklı (*veya* dertli) olm.; ~ at bşden tiksinmek, nefret etm.; ~ of bıkıp usanmak, gına gelmek -*den*; *v/t.* hasta etm.; bıktırmak, usandırmak.

**sick.le** [ˈsikl] *n.* orak.

**sick-leave** [ˈsikliːv] *n.* hastalık izni; **ˈsick.ly** *adj.* hastalıklı, dertli; zayıf bünyeli, hassas; solgun; gayrisıhhi *(iklim)*; tiksindirici, iğrenç *(koku vs.)*; bitkin, yorgun; **ˈsick.ness** *n.* hastalık; kusma, mide bulantısı.

**side** [said] **1.** *n. com.* yan, taraf; sahil, kıvı, kenar; *spor:* takım, taraf; grup. hizin; yön: ~ by ~ yan yana: *fig.* yanıbaşında; by one's ~ *b-nin* tarafında; ~ by ~ with yanında -*in*, ... ile beraber; at *veya* by s.o.'s ~ *b-nin* yanında; put on ~ F çaka satmak, tafra satmak; **2.** *adj.* yan..., ikinci derecede, ... den başka; **3.** *vb.* taraf tutmak, desteklemek (with, against); **ˈ~-arms** *n. pl.* X kasatura, kılıç vs. gibi yana takılan silahlar; **ˈ~.board** *n.*

büfe; **ˈ~-car** *n. mot.* motosiklet yan arabası, sepet; **ˈsid.ed** *comb.* ... taraflı, cepheli; çevrili.

**side...: ˈ~-face** *n.* yandan görünüş, profil; ~ **is.sue** önemsiz, ikincil soru *veya* konu; **ˈ~-light** *n.* borda feneri; yan pencere; sinyal lambaları; *fig.* önemsiz fakat bir konuyu aydınlatan açıklama; **ˈ~-line** *n.* 🏷 tali hat; ek görev; *spor:* kenar çizgisi; **ˈ~.long** **1.** *adv.* yan (tarafa), yandan; **2.** *adj.* yan, kenardan, meyilli; *fig.* gizli, saklı.

**si.de.re.al** *ast.* [saiˈdiəriəl] *adj.* yıldızlarla ilgili, yıldızlarla hesaplanan.

**side...: ˈ~-sad.dle** *n.* kadın eyeri; **ˈ~-slip** *v/i.* 🛬 yan inişi yapmak; *mot.* patinaj yapmak; **ˈsides.man** [ˈ~zmən] *n.* Anglikan kilisesinde mütevelli yardımcısı.

**side...: ˈ~-split.ting** *adj.* kahkahaya boğan, çok komik; **ˈ~-step 1.** *n.* yana atılan adım; kaçınma, yan çizme; **2.** *vb.* yana kaçmak, yan çizmek, sorumluluktan kaçmak; **ˈ~-stroke** *n.* yan yüzme; **ˈ~-track 1.** *n.* 🏷 yan hat; **2.** *v/t.* yan hatta geçirmek; *part. Am. fig.* önemli ve faydalı bir şeyi geri bıraktırıp önemsiz bir şeyle uğraştırmak; **ˈ~-walk** *n. part. Am.* yaya kaldırımı; **ˈside.ward** [ˈ~wəd] **1.** *adj.* yana doğru olan, yan; **2.** *adv.* = **side.wards** [ˈ~wədz], **ˈside.ways**, **ˈside.wise** yan tarafa, yana doğru.

**sid.ing** 🏷 [ˈsaidiŋ] *n.* yan hat, içtinap durağı.

**si.dle** [ˈsaidl] *vb.* yan yan gitmek.

**siege** [siːdʒ] *n.* kuşatma, muhasara; lay ~ to kuşatmak, sarmak, ele geçirmeye çalışmak.

**si.er.ra** [ˈsiərə] *n.* zirveli dağ silsilesi.

**sieve** [siv] **1.** *n.* kalbur, elek; **2.** *v/t.* elemek, kalburdan geçirmek.

**sift** [sift] *v/t.* kalburdan geçirmek, elemek; *fig.* incelemek; ayırmak.

**sift.er** [ˈsiftə] *n.* üstü delikli un, şeker vs. kabı *(tuzluk, şekerlik vs.)*.

**sigh** [sai] **1.** *n.* iç çekme; **2.** *v/i.* iç çekmek; bş için yanıp tutuşmak, hasret kalmak (for, after -*e*).

**sight** [sait] **1.** *n.* görme, görüm, görüş; *fig.* bakış, nazar; manzara, görünüş, temasa; nişangâh; F büyük miktar, birçok; çokluk; **~s** *pl.* gezip görülecek yerler; second ~ gaipten haber verme, kehanet; at *veya* on ~ görür görmez, derhal, görü(lü)nce; ♪ notaya bakarak; †ibrazında, gösterilince; catch ~ of görüvermek, gözüne ilişmek; lose ~ of gözden kaybetmek, unutmak; within ~ göz önünde, gözle görünür; out of ~ gözden uzak; çok yüksek, fahiş; take ~ nişan almak; not by a long ~ asla, hiç; know by ~ yüzünden tanımak, göz aşinalığı olm.; 2. *vb.* görmek; nişan almak (along); **¹sight.ed** *adj.* görebilen, ... görülen; **¹sight.ing-line** *n.* nişan hattı; **¹sight.less** *adj.* kör, göremeyen; **¹sight.li.ness** *adj.* güzellik, yakışıklılık, göze hitap etme; **¹sight.ly** *adj.* güzel, yüzüne bakılır, kayda değer.

**sight...:** **¹~.see.ing** *n.* seyredecek yerleri görmeğe gitme, gezme; **¹~.se.er** *n.* turist; **¹~.sing.ing** *n.* ♪ notaya bakarak şarkı söyleme.

**sign** [sain] **1.** *n.* işaret, ikaz, ima, alâmet; iz, belirti; levha, trafik işaret levhası; *ast.* on iki burçtan biri; **in ~ of** ... işareti olarak; **2.** *v/i.* işaret vermek; ~ **on** (off) *radyo:* yayına başlamak *veya* yayını bitirmek; *v/t.* imzalamak; işaret etm. `~-e`; ~ **on** mukavele ile taahhüt altına al(ın)mak.

**sig.nal** [¹signl] **1.** *n.* işaret, sinyal; ihtar, ikaz; **~s** *pl.* ✕ parola; **busy ~** *teleph.* meşgul işareti; **2.** ☐ kayda değer, dikkate değer, fevkalâde, harikulâde; **3.** *vb.* işaretle bildirmek, işaret etm.; *b-ne bşi* bildirmek, haber vermek; **¹~-box** *n.* 🏠 manevra tertibatı *veya* merkezi; **sig.nal.ize** [¹~nəlaiz] *v/t.* dikkati çekerek bildirmek; şöhret kazandırmak, nişan vermek; = **signal** 3.

**sig.na.to.ry** [¹signətəri] **1.** *n.* imza sahibi, imza eden kimse; **2.** *adj.* imzalayan; **powers ~** to an agreement devletler arası anlaşmaları imzalayanlar.

**sig.na.ture** [¹signitʃə] *n.* imza; marka, damga, işaret (*a. typ.*, ♪, ✝); ~ **tune** *radyo:* tanıtma müziği.

**sign.board** [¹sainbɔːd] *n.* tabela, afiş, yafta; **¹sign.er** *n.* imza sahibi.

**sig.net** [¹signit] *n.* mühür, damga; **¹~-ring** *n.* mühür yüzüğü.

**sig.nif.i.cance,    sig.nif.i.can.cy** [sig¹nifikəns(i)] *n.* mana, anlam; önem; **sig¹nif.i.cant** ☐ anlamlı, manidar; önemli; karakteristik (of); **sig.ni.fi¹ca.tion** *n.* anlam, mana; **sig¹nif.i.ca.tive** [~kətiv] *adj.* anlamlı, karakteristik (of). manidar, *bş* anlatan, ifade eden.

**sig.ni.fy** [¹signifai] *vb.* belirtmek, ifade etm., işaretle anlatmak; delâlet etm. `-e`, ... anlamına gelmek; it does not ~ önemi yok, farketmez.

**si.gnor** [¹siːnjɔː] *n.* bay, efendi, İtalyanların kullandığı bir ünvan; **si¹gnor.a** [~rə] *n.* bayan, hanım (*evli*); **si.gno.ri.na** [~¹riːnə] *n.* matmazel, bayan, genç kız-

lara verilen unvan.

**sign...:** **¹~-paint.er** *n.* tabelacı, levhacı; **¹~.post** *n.* yol gösteren levha, işaret direği.

**si.lage** [¹sailidʒ] *n.* siloda muhafaza olunan hayvan yemi, ot vs.

**si.lence** [¹sailəns] **1.** *n.* sessizlik, sükut, durgunluk, huzur; susma, *bşden* bahsetmeme; ~! sus(unuz)!; put *veya* reduce to ~ = **2.** *v/t.* susturmak, sesini kesmek; **¹si.lenc.er** *n.* ⊕ ses azaltıcı, susturucu; *mot.* egzoz borusuna takılan susturucu; **si.lent** ☐ [¹sailənt] sessiz, sakin; suskun, susan, sesi çıkmaz; sessiz (*harf*); ~ **film** sessiz film; ~ **partner** *part:* Am. ✝ hususi şerik, komanditer.

**Si.le.sian** [sai¹liːzjən] **1.** *adj.* Silezyalı; **2.** *n.* Silezyalı kimse.

**sil.hou.ette** [silu¹et] **1.** *n.* siluet, gölge (resim); **2.** be `~d` against iyice belirmek, kontrast teşkil etm.

**sil.i.ca** [¹silikə] *n.* silis(li toprak); **sil.i.cat.ed** [¹~keitid] *adj.* silisit asitli; **sil.i.ceous** [~ʃəs] *adj.* silisli; **sil.i.con** [¹~kən] *n.* silisyum; **sil.i.cone** [¹~kəun] *n.* silikon; **sil.i.co.sis** 🏥 [~¹kəusis] *n.* silis tozu tenefffüs etmekten oluşan bir tür akciğer hastalığı.

**silk** [silk] **1.** *n.* ipek; *b̃s* ipek cüppe; kral(içe) avukatı; ipeğe benzer mısır püskülü; **take ~** kral(içe) avukatı olm.; **2.** *adj.* ipekli, ipek...; **silk.en** ☐ ipekli; *s.* silky: **¹silk.i.ness** *n.* ipek gibi oluş; yumuşak oluş; **¹silk.¹stock.ing** *n.* Am. kibar, aristokrat, soylu, asil; **¹~.worm** *n.* ipekböceği; **¹silk.y** ☐ ipek gibi; yumuşacık.

**sill** [sil] *n.* eşik, pencere tahtası; denizlik.

**sil.li.ness** [¹silinis] *n.* ahmaklık; saçma şey, herze.

**sil.ly** ☐ [¹sili] ahmak, budala, aptal, bön; saçma, gülünç; ~ **season** (*gazete*) haber bakımından kısır dönem.

**si.lo** [¹sailəu] *n.* silo.

**silt** [silt] **1.** *n.* çamur, balçık, mil; **2.** *vb. mst* ~ **up** çamur *veya* mille dol(dur)mak.

**sil.ver** [¹silvə] **1.** *n.* gümüş (*para, sofra takımı vs.*); **2.** *adj.* gümüşten, gümüş kaplı; gümüş gibi; gümüş...; **3.** *vb.* gümüş kaplamak `-e`; gümüş gibi parla(t)mak; **¹~¹plate** *n.* ⊕ gümüş kaplama; **¹~.ware** *n.* Am. gümüş eşya, gümüş sofra takımı; **¹sil.ver.y** *adj.* gümüş gibi, parlak; *zo.* & ♀ gümüş gibi parlak...; yumuşak ve berrak (*ses*).

**sim.i.lar** ☐ [¹similə] benzer (to `-e`), gibi, ... vari; **sim.i.lar.i.ty** [~¹læriti] *n.* benzerlik, benzeşlik.

**sim.i.le** ['simili] *n.* mecaz, teşbih, kıyas, benzetme.

**si.mil.i.tude** [si'militju:d] *n.* benzerlik, benzeşme; tam benzeri; kıyas, teşbih, mecaz, benzetme.

**sim.mer** ['simə] *v/t. & v/i.* yavaş yavaş kayna(t)mak; *fig.* galeyana getirmek *veya* gelmek *(duygu);* ~ down yatışmak, sakinleşmek.

**Si.mon** ['saimən] *n.* on iki havariden biri; the real ~ Pure F hakikisi; simple ~ F budala, ahmak; **si.mo.ny** ['~ni] *n.* kilise görev *veya* donatımının alım satımı.

**si.moom** *meteor.* [si'mu:m] *n.* samyeli.

**sim.per** ['simpə] 1. *n.* aptalca sırıtma; 2. *v/i.* aptal aptal sırıtmak.

**sim.ple** □ ['simpl] basit, sade, gösterişsiz, alçak gönüllü; kolay; bölünmeyen, tek; katışıksız, saf; doğal, yapmacıksız; aptal, budala, safdil; önemsiz, basit *(rütbe, sınıf);* **'~-'heart.ed, '~-'mind.ed** *adj.* safdil, temiz yürekli, kolay kanan; **sim.ple.ton** ['~tən] *n.* ahmak, budala.

**sim.plic.i.ty** [sim'plisiti] *n.* sadelik, berraklık, açıklık; saflık, budalalık; temiz yüreklilik, safdillik; **sim.pli.fi.ca.tion** [~fi'keiʃən] *n.* basitleştirme, sadeleştirme; basitleşme; **sim.pli.fy** ['~fai] *v/t.* kolaylaştırmak, sadeleştirmek.

**sim.ply** ['simpli] *adv.* basit olarak *(s.* simple*);* sadece, sırf, ancak; doğrusu, gerçekten.

**sim.u.late** ['simjuleit] *v/t.* yalandan yapmak, ... gibi görünmek; taklit etm., benzetmek; ... taslamak; sim.u'la.tion *n.* taklit; sahte tavır, yapmacık; **'sim.u.la.tor** *n.* herhangi bir eğitimde o ortamın koşullarını hissettiren cihaz.

**si.mul.ta.ne.i.ty** [siməltə'ni:iti] *n.* aynı zamanda olma, eşzamanlık.

**si.mul.ta.ne.ous** □ [siməl'teinjəs] aynı zamanda olan, eşzamanlı; **si.mul'ta.ne.ous.ness** *n.* eşzamanlılık, aynı zamanda olma.

**sin** [sin] 1. *n.* günah; suç, kabahat; 2. *v/i.* günah işlemek.

**since** [sins] 1. *prp.* -den beri, -den itibaren, olalı, edeli; 2. *adv.* o zamandan beri; önce, evvel; long ~ uzun zamandan beri, çok zaman oluyor; how long ~? ne zamandan beri?; a short time ~ geçenlerde; 3. *cj.* -diğinden beri, olalı, yapalı; madem ki, çünkü, zira.

**sin.cere** □ [sin'siə] samimi, içten, yalansız, doğru; Yours ~ly saygılarımla *(mektup sonunda);* **sin.cer.i.ty** [~'seriti] *n.* samimiyet, içtenlik, doğruluk.

**sine** Ą [sain] *n.* sinüs.

**si.ne.cure** ['sainikjuə] *n.* kolay ve iyi maaşlı iş, arpalık.

**sin.ew** ['sinju:] *n.* kiriş, veter; sinir; *mst* ~s *pl.* güç, enerji; güçlü kılan şey; **'sin.ew.y** *adj.* kiriş gibi; *fig.* güçlü, dinç, kuvvetli.

**sin.ful** □ ['sinful] günahkâr; utanç verici, çok kötü; şerir, fena; **'sin.ful.ness** *n.* günahkâr olma, günah(kârlık).

**sing** [siŋ] *(irr.) v/i.* şarkı söylemek; ötmek, şakımak; uğuldamak *(rüzgâr);* çınlamak *(kulak); v/t.* söylemek, okumak; ~ out bağırmak, seslenmek; ~ small, ~ another song *veya* tune süt dökmüş kedi gibi olm., yelkenleri suya indirmek, aşağıdan almak.

**singe** [sindʒ] *v/t.* yakmak, ütülemek, alazlamak.

**sing.er** ['siŋə] *n.* şarkıcı.

**sing.ing** ['siŋiŋ] *n.* şarkı söyleme, şakıma, ırlama; ~ bird ötücü kuş.

**sin.gle** [siŋgl] 1. □ tek, bir, yalnız, ayrı; tek kişilik, özel; münferit...; bekâr; sade, basit, saf; ~ bill † bono; ~ combat teke tek kavga, düello, vuruşma; book-keeping by ~ entry basit *(veya* tek taraflı) defter tutma usulü; ~ file tek sıra, birbiri ardına; 2. *n.* tenis: tekler; tek kişilik oda; gidiş bileti; 3. ~ out seçmek, ayırmak; **'~-'breast.ed** *adj.* tek sıra düğmeli *(ceket vs.);* **'~-'en.gin.ed** *adj.* † tek motorlu; **'~-'hand.ed** *adj.* tek başına; **'~-'heart.ed** □, **'~-'mind.ed** □ samimî, içten, doğru dürüst; yolundan şaşmayan, tuttuğunu koparan, azimli; **'~-'line** *adj.* tek hatlı; **'sin.gle-'seat.er** *n.* tek kişilik *(uçak);* **'sin.gle.stick** *n.* eskrim değneği; kısa kalın sopa; **sin.glet** ['singlit] *n.* fanila, iç gömleği; **sin.gle.ton** ['~tən] *n.* iskambil: oyun başında oyuncunun elindeki bir renkten tek kâğıt; **'sin.gle-'track** *adj.* tek yönlü; **'sin.gly** *adv.* yalnız, tek başına; tek tek, birer birer.

**sing.song** ['siŋsɔŋ] *n.* aynı tonda ve can sıkıcı şarkı söyleme *veya* konuşma.

**sin.gu.lar** ['singjulə] 1. □ yalnız, tek, ayrı; eşsiz, müstesna, fevkalâde; acayip, garip, tuhaf; *gr.* tekil 2. *n. gr. a.* ~ number tek sayı; tekil sözcük; **sin.gu.lar.i.ty** [~'læriti] *n.* özellik, hususiyet; tuhaflık; eşsizlik, görülmemişlik.

**Sin.ha.lese** [sinhə'li:z] 1. *adj.* Sri Lankalı, Sri Lanka diline ait; 2. *n.* Sri Lankalı kimse; Sri Lanka dili.

**sin.is.ter** □ ['sinistə] uğursuz, meşum; endişe verici; tekin olmayan *(yer);* fesat, kötü.

**sink** [siŋk] **1.** *(irr.) vb.* batmak *(gemi, güneş vs.)*; ağır ağır inmek; çökmek; çukurlaşmak; alçalmak, azalmak; dalmak *(uyku)*; düşmek *(fiyat)*; kötüleşmek, ölüme yaklaşmak *(hasta)*; batırmak; daldırmak ,gömmek (into -e); ⚔ kazmak, açmak *(kuyu)*; yatırmak *(para)*; yavaş yavaş ödemek *(borç)*; uzlaşmak, yatıştırmak, unutmak *(kavga)*; **2.** *n.* fosseptik, lağım çukuru; musluk taşı, bulaşık oluğu; *fig.* bataklık; **'sink.er** *n.* ⚔ kuyucu, maden işçisi; iskandil, olta *veya* ağ kurşunu; **'sink.ing** *n.* düşüş, batış; ⚓ dermansızlık, zayıflık, halsizlik; ~ fund bir borcu ödemek için oluşturulan fon, itfa fonu, amortisman sandığı.

**sin.less** ['sinlis] *adj.* günahsız, masum, saf.

**sin.ner** ['sinə] *n.* günahkâr kimse.

**Sinn Fein** ['ʃin'fein] *n.* bir İrlanda milliyetçi teşkilâtı.

**Sin.o...** ['sinəu] *comb.* Çin ile ilgili, Çinli; Çin...

**sin.u.os.i.ty** [sinju'ositi] *n.* yılankavilik, dolaşıklık, eğilip bükülme; kavis, viraj, dönemeç; **'sin.u.ous** ☐ yılankavi, dolaşık, eğri, çarpık *(a. fig.)*, dolambaçlı.

**si.nus** *anat.* ['sainəs] *n.* sinüs; **si.nus.i.tis** [~'saitis] *n.* sinüzit, sinüs iltihabı.

**Sioux** [su:] *n., pl.* ~ [su:z] Siyu *(Kuzey Amerika kızılderilileri).*

**sip** [sip] **1.** *n.* yudum; yudumlama; **2.** *vb.* yudumlamak, azar azar içmek.

**si.phon** ['saifən] **1.** *n.* sifon, pipet; **2.** *vb.* sifonla su çekmek (out); emmek, içine çekmek.

**sir** [sə:] *n.* bay; beyefendi; efendim; ♀ sör *(bir asalet ünvanı)*.

**sire** ['saiə] *n.* *mst poet.* baba, peder; cet, ata; *zo.* bir at, köpek vs.'nin babası; † haşmetmeap, efendimiz.

**si.ren** ['saiərən] *n.* canavar düdüğü, siren.

**sir.loin** ['sə:lɔin] *n.* sığır filetosu.

**sir.rah** *contp.* † ['sirə] herif, adam.

**sir.up** ['sirəp] *n.* şurup; melâs.

**sis** F [sis] *n.* sister'ın kısaltılmış şekli.

**sis.al** ['saisəl] *n.* sisal keneviri, dayanıklı bir tür kenevir.

**sis.kin** *orn.* ['siskin] *n.* karabaşlı iskete.

**sis.sy** *Am.* ['sisi] *n.* çıtkırıldım, muhallebi çocuğu, hanım evlâdı.

**sis.ter** ['sistə] *n.* kızkardeş, hemşire; hastabakıcı, hemşire; rahibe; ~ of charity *veya* mercy hayırsever rahibeler birliği üyesi; **sis.ter.hood** [~'hud] *n.* kızkardeşlik; rahibeler birliği; **'sis.ter-in-law** *n.* görümce, baldız, yenge, elti; **'sis.ter.ly**

*adj.* kızkardeş gibi, kızkardeşe yakışır; müşfik.

**sit** [sit] *(irr.) v/i.* oturmak; toplanmak, toplantı yapmak ,müzakerede bulunmak *(meclis)*; kuluçkaya yatmak *(tavuk)*; ~ down (yerine) oturmak; tünemek, konmak; ~ (up)on araştırmak, incelemek; F susturmak, yola getirmek; ~ up dik oturmak; yatmamak; doğrulmak; make s.o. ~ up b-ni sarsarak uyandırmak; b-ne kulak kesilmek, dikkatli dinlemek; *v/t.* oturtmak; *(at vs.'ye)* oturmak, binmek; ~ a horse well ata iyi binmek; ~ s.th. out bşin sonuna kadar oturmak; ~ s.o. out b-ne uzun süre tahammül etm.; ~-down strike oturma grevi.

**site** [sait] **1.** *n.* yer, mahal, mevki, nokta, alan; **2.** *v/t.* yaymak, açmak.

**sit.ter** ['sitə] *n.* oturan *b-i veya* bş; poz veren kimse; kuluçka; *sl.* kolay av, kolay iş, avanta; **'~-in** *n.* anne ve babası evde yokken ücretle çocuğa bakan kimse.

**sit.ting** ['sitin] *n.* oturma, oturuş; oturum, toplantı, celse; at one ~ bir defada; **'~-room** *n.* oturma odası.

**sit.u.ate** ['sitjueit] *vb.* başka bir yere koymak, yerleştirmek; yerini tayin etm. *-in*; **'sit.u.at.ed** *adj.* bulunan, olan, vaki; be ~ bulunmak (in *-de*); thus ~ bu *(veya* şu, o) durumda; **sit.u.a.tion** *n.* yer, mevki; durum, koşullar.

**six** [siks] **1.** *adj.* altı; **2.** *n.* altı sayısı; be at ~es and sevens tam bir karışıklık ve şaşkınlık içinde olm.; **'~.fold** *adj.* altı kat, altı misli; **'~.pence** *n.* altı peni(lik para); **six.teen** ['~'tiːn] *adj.* on altı; **six.teenth** ['~'tiːnθ] **1.** *adj.* on altıncı; **2.** *n.* on altıda bir; **sixth** [~θ] **1.** *adj.* altıncı; **2.** *n.* altıda bir; **sixth.ly** *adv.* altıncı olarak; **six.ti.eth** ['~tiəθ] *adj.* altmışıncı; **'six.ty** **1.** *adj.* altmış; **2.** *n.* altmış sayısı.

**siz.a.ble** ☐ ['saizəbl] oldukça büyük, büyücek, oylumlu.

**size**[1] [saiz] **1.** *n.* hacim, oylum; büyüklük, ebat; beden *(elbise)*; numara *(ayakkabı)*; **2.** *vb.* büyüklüğüne göre düzenlemek; ~ up F *b-ni veya* bşi tartmak, değerlendirmek, takdir, tahmin etm.; **sized** *comb.* ... büyüklüğünde, ... genişliğinde, ... ölçüsünde.

**size**[2] [~] **1.** *n.* çiriş, tutkal; **2.** *adj.* çirişli, tutkallı.

**size.a.ble** ☐ ['saizəbl] = sizable.

**siz.zle** ['sizl] *v/i.* tıslamak, cızırdamak, hışıldamak *(kâğıt, yaprak vs.)*, çıtır çıtır yanmak *(ateş)*; **sizzling hot** bunaltıcı sıcak.

**skate** [skeit] 1. *n.* paten; roller-~ tekerlekli paten; 2. *v/i.* patinaj yapmak, patenle kaymak; **ˈskat.er** *n.* patinajcı; **ˈskat.ing-** **-rink** *n.* patinuvar, patinaj sahası.

**ˈske.dad.dle** F [skiˈdædl] *v/i.* sıvışmak, tüymek, tabanları yağlamak.

**skein** [skein] *n.* yumak, çile.

**skel.e.ton** [ˈskelitn] 1. *n.* iskelet; insan kurusu, çok zayıf kimse; çatı, iskelet, karkas *(bina)*; taslak, müsvedde; ✗ kadro, çekirdek birlik; 2. *adj.* iskelete benzer; kaba taslak..., iskelet...; ✗ kadro..., esas...; ~ key maymuncuk, her kilidi açan anahtar.

**skep.tic** [ˈskeptik] = sceptic.

**sketch** [sketʃ] 1. *n.* taslak, kroki; küçük hikâye, skeç; 2. *vb.* taslak yapmak, krokisini almak, kabataslak tarif etm.; *-in* taslağını çizmek; **ˈsketch.y** □ kabataslak; noksan, yarım yamalak, yüzeysel.

**skew** [skjuː] *adj.* meyilli, inişli; eğri, çarpık, eğri büğrü.

**skew.er** [ˈskjuə] 1. *n.* kebap şişi; şişe benzer bş; 2. *vb.* kebap şişine geçirmek, şişe dizmek.

**ski** [skiː] 1. *n. pl. a.* ~ kayak, ski; 2. *v/i.* kayak yapmak.

**skid** [skid] 1. *n.* takoz, köstek, fren çarığı; ⚓ kayma kızağı; *mot.* patinaj; (yana) kayma; 2. *vb.* takoz koymak, kösteklemek; yana kaymak; süzülmek; aşağı kaymak; *mot.* patinaj yapmak.

**ski.er** [ˈskiːə] *n.* kayakçı.

**skiff** ⚓ [skif] *n.* hafif yelkenli, filika, kik *(yarış kayığı).*

**ski.ing** [ˈskiːiŋ] *n.* kayakçılık, kayak yapma; **ˈski-jump** *n.* kayakçının yaptığı sıçrama *veya* atlama; atlama tepesi; **ˈski-** **-jump.ing** *n.* kayakla atlama.

**skil.ful** □ [ˈskilful] hünerli, mahir, becerikli, eli yatkın; **ˈskil.ful.ness, skill** [skil] *n.* hüner, ustalık, becerililik, maharet.

**skilled** [skild] *adj.* deneyimli, usta, hünerli; kalifiye; ~ worker kalifiye işçi, vasıflı işçi.

**skil.let** [ˈskilit] *n.* tava.

**skill.ful** [ˈskilful] *Am. of* skilful.

**skim** [skim] 1. *vb. a.* ~ off kaymağını, yağını almak *(süt)*; bş üzerinden kaymak, süzülmek, sıyırıp geçmek; *fig.* göz gezdirmek *-e;* üstünkörü incelemek *-i; -den* uçarak geçmek *(uçak);* su üstünde sektirmek *(taş);* köpüğünü *(veya* istenmeyen maddeleri) almak *-in;* ~ through kitabın sayfalarını birer birer çevirmek, üstünkörü göz gezdirmek; 2. *n.* ~ milk kaymağı alınmış süt; **ˈskim.mer** *n.* kevgir, köpük kepçesi.

**skimp** [skimp] *v/t. & v/i.* cimri davranmak, cimrilik etm., kıt vermek, hesaplı davranmak; **ˈskimp.y** □ kıt, az, eksik, yetersiz; yarım yamalak.

**skin** [skin] 1. *n.* cilt, deri; post, pösteki; kabuk; ⚓ dış kaplama; *(balon)* kılıf; *(şarap)* tulum; *by veya* with the ~ of one's teeth güç belâ, daradar, ancak; have a thick *(thin)* ~ vurdumduymaz (hassas) olm.; 2. *v/t.* yüzmek, *-in* kabuğunu soymak; F dolandırmak, soyup soğana çevirmek *(of);* ~ off F *(çorap vs.)* çıkarmak; keep one's eyes ~ned F dikkat etm., gözünü dört açmak; *v/i. a.* ~ over kapanmak *(yara vs.);* **ˈ~ˈdeep** *adj.* sathî, yüzeysel; **ˈ~-div.ing** *n. (aletsiz)* suya dalma sporu; **ˈ~.flint** *n.* cimri kimse; **ˈ~-graft.ing** *n.* 乎 deri transplantasyonu; **ˈskin.ner** *n.* derici, kürkçü; **ˈskin.ny** *adj.* sıska, çelimsiz, bir deri bir kemik; F berbat.

**skip** [skip] 1. *n.* sekme, zıplama, sıçrayış; ✗ kafes; 2. *vb.* zıplamak, sekmek, sıçramak; ip atlamak; *a.* ~ over atlamak, sıçrayarak geçmek *-i;* **ˈ~-jack** *n.* suyun yüzünde sıçrayan herhangi bir tür balık; *zo.* sıçrayan bir tür böcek.

**skip.per¹** [ˈskipə] *n.* sıçrayan *b-i veya* bş.

**skip.per²** [~] *n.* ⚓ kaptan, süvari; F *spor:* takım kaptanı.

**skip.ping-rope** [ˈskipiŋrəup] *n.* atlama ipi.

**skir.mish** ✗ [ˈskəːmiʃ] 1. *n.* çatışma, hafif çarpışma; 2. *v/i.* çatışmak, çekişmek; **ˈskir.mish.er** *n.* avcı, gözcü.

**skirt** [skəːt] 1. *n.* etek(lik); *oft.* ~s *pl.* kenar *(kumaş);* kenar, sınır *(bölge),* varoş; *sl.* kız, kadın; 2. *vb.* bşin kenarından geçmek, bastırmak; ana konuya temas etmemek, kaytarmak; *a.* ~ along bşin kenarı boyunca gitmek *veya* uzanmak; **ˈskirt.ing-board** *n.* süpürgelik.

**skit¹** [skit] *n.* dokunaklı söz, iğneleme, hiciv, kinaye (on, upon).

**skit²** [~] *n.* kalabalık, sürü, yığın.

**skit.tish** □ [ˈskitiʃ] azgın, serkeş, ürkek *(part. at);* haşarı, şamatacı, muzip.

**skit.tle** [ˈskitl] *n.* dokuz kuka, kiy oyunu; *play (at)* ~s kiy oyunu oynamak; **ˈ~-al.ley** *n.* kiy oyunu sahası.

**skiv.vy** F *contp.* [ˈskivi] *n.* karı, hizmetçi kız.

**skul.dug.er.y** *Am.* F [skʌlˈdʌgəri] *n.* dalavere, hilekârlık oyunları.

**skulk** [skʌlk] *v/i.* sessizce yaklaşmak, gizlice sokulmak; gizlenmek, saklanmak, pusuda beklemek; *b-ne* pusu kurmak; sıvışmak, yan çizmek, kaytarmak; **ˈskulk-** **er** *n.* gizlenen kimse.

**skull** [skʌl] *n.* kafatası, kafa, beyin; ~ and cross-bones *(tehlike işareti)* kuru kafa; have a thick ~ kalın kafalı, aptal olm.

**skunk** [skʌŋk] *n. zo.* kokarca (kürkü); F alçak, hain, teres, köpeoğlu köpek kimse.

**sky** [skai] *oft.* **skies** *n. pl.* gök(yüzü), sema, gök kubbe; praise to the skies *fig.* göklere çıkarmak, öve öve bitirememek; '~-¹blue *adj.* gök mavisi; '~-ˌjack *v/t.* kaçırmak *(uçak)*; '~-ˌlark 1. *n. orn.* tarlakuşu; 2. *v/i.* cümbüş yapmak, eğlenmek *(about)*; '~-ˌlight *n.* dam penceresi, kaporta, vazistas; '~-ˌline *n.* ufuk çizgisi; silûet; '~-ˌrock.et *v/i.* aniden ve dikine yüksɪlmek; kabarmak; '~-ˌscrap.er *n.* gökdeleɪ; **sky.ward(s)** [¹~wəd(z)] *adv.* göğe doğru; **ˈsky-writ.ing** *n.* uçakla havada yazılan yazı.

**slab** [slæb] *n.* kalın, dilim, tabaka, levha, plâka, tabla; fayans, çini, tuğla; ⊕ kaplama tahtası.

**slack** [slæk] 1. *adj.* gevşek, gerilmemiş, sarkık; kayıtsız, miskin, üşengeç, tembel; ⅋ durgun; ~ water ⅊ durgun su; 2. *n.* ⅊ halat vs.'nin sarkık, çözük kısmı; ⅊ durgunluk, kesat; kömür tozu; *s.* ~s; 3. *vb.* = ~en; = slake; F tembel davranmak, bşi yapmağa üşenmek; **ˈslack.en** *vb.* tembellik etm., miskin olm.; gevşe(t)mek *(halat vs.)*; hafifle(t)mek, şiddetini kaybet(tir)mek; yavaşla(t)mak; **ˈslack.er** *n.* F tembel, haylaz kimse; **ˈslack.ness** *n.* gevşeklik; üşengeçlik, tembellik; **slacks** *n. pl.* bol pantolon *(kadın)*.

**slag** [slæg] *n.* cüruf, dışık, mucur; **ˈslag.gy** *adj.* cüruflu; **ˈslag-heap** *n.* cüruf yığını.

**slain** [slein] *p.p. of* slay.

**slake** [sleik] *vb.* gidermek *(susuzluk, hasret vs.)*; söndürmek *(kireç)*.

**sla.lom** [¹sleiləm] *n. spor:* slalom.

**slam** [slæm] 1. *n.* patlama, infilâk sesi; hızla ve gürültülü vurma, çarpma; *iskambil:* kaput; mars; şilem; 2. *vb.* kapıyı hızla ve gürültülü çarpıp kapamak; yere vurmak; sözle saldırmak, kalaylamak.

**slan.der** [¹slɑːndə] 1. *n.* iftira, karacılık; 2. *v/t.* b-ne iftira etm., karalamak; **ˈslan.der.ous** □ iftira niteliğinde; karalayıcı havadis yayan.

**slang** [slæŋ] 1. *n.* argo, külhanbeyi dili, laubali konuşma dili; 2. *v/t.* argo konuşmak, sövüp saymak; **ˈslang.y** □ argo...; bayağı; argo konuşan.

**slant** [slɑːnt] 1. *n.* eğim, meyil; meyilli

düzey; *Am.* F yan bakış; görüş noktası, tutum; 2. *v/t.* & *v/i.* eğ(il)mek, meyletmek; **ˈslant.ing** □ *adj.*, **ˈslant.wise** *adv.* meyilli (olarak), verev.

**slap** [slæp] 1. *n.* şamar, tokat, hafif sille; ~ in the face hakaret, tokat *(a. fig.)*; 2. *v/t.* avuçla vurmak -e, b-ne tokat aşketmek, şaklatmak; 3. *adv.* doğrudan (doğruya), hemen, birdenbire; '~-¹bang *n.* apansızın, pattadak; '~-ˌdash *adj.* aceleci, atılgan, alelacele yapılmış, baştan savma; *adv. a.* dikkatsizce, düşünmeyerek; '~-ˌjack *n. Am.* tatlı omlet, krep konfitür; '~-ˌstick *n. thea.* güldürü, hokkabaz oyunu; *a.* ~ comedy kaba komedi, maskara; '~-up F *adj.* kıyak, iki dirhem bir çekirdek, fevkalâde.

**slash** [slæʃ] 1. *n.* uzun yara; yarık; kamçı vuruşu; yırtmaç *(elbise)*; 2. *v/t.* & *v/i.* uzunluğuna açmak, yarmak; kamçılamak; *fig.* teşhir etm., şiddetle eleştirmek; F çok indirmek *(fiyat)*; çalakılıç yürümek, yol açmak *(at)*; **ˈslash.ing** □ keskin, şiddetli, tahripkâr *(eleştiri)*.

**slat** [slæt] *n.* tiriz, lata, ince varak, levha *(pancur için)*.

**slate** [sleit] 1. *n.* kayağantaş, arduvaz; taş tahta, kara tahta; *part. Am.* aday listesi; start with a clean ~ yeni bir hayata başlamak; 2. *v/t.* arduvazla kaplamak; şiddetle eleştirmek, kınamak; *Am.* F bir görev *veya* amaç için tayin etm.; '~-¹pencil *n.* taş kalem; **ˈslat.er** *n.* arduvaz kaplama; **ˈslat.ing** *n.* sert eleştiri.

**slat.tern** [¹slætəːn] *n.* pasaklı kadın; **ˈslat.tern.ly** *adj.* pasaklı, şapşal, hırpani, pis.

**slat.y** □ [¹sleiti] aduvazlı *veya* arduvaza benzer.

**slaugh.ter** [¹slɔːtə] 1. *n.* kesim *(hayvan)*, kan dökme, katliam; *fig.* katil, katletme; 2. *v/t.* kesmek, boğazlamak, katletmek, kılıçtan geçirmek; **ˈslaugh.ter.er** *n.* kasap; katil; **ˈslaugh.ter-house** *n.* mezbaha, salhane, kesimevi; **ˈslaugh.ter.ous** □ *rhet.* öldürücü, korkunç; katil, kırıp geçiren.

**Slav** [slɑːv] 1. *n.* İslav ırkından kimse; İslav dili; 2. *adj.* İslav diline ait.

**slave** [sleiv] 1. *n.* köle, esir, kul, halayık, cariye; *fig.* köle gibi çalışan kimse; 2. *v/i.* köle gibi çalışmak, eşek gibi çalışmak *(away)*.

**slav.er**[1] [¹sleivə] *n.* esir tüccarı *veya* gemisi.

**slav.er**[2] [¹slævə] 1. *n.* salya; 2. *v/i.* salya akıtmak, salyası akmak *(a. fig.)*.

**slav.er.y** [¹sleivəri] *n.* kölelik, esirlik, esaret.

slav.ey *sl.* ['slævi] *n.* kâhya, orta hizmetçisi.

Slav.ic ['slɑːvik] 1. *adj.* İslav; İslav diline ait; 2. *n.* İslav ırkından olan kimse.

slav.ish □ ['sleiviʃ] dalkavuk, aşağılık, köle gibi, köpek gibi sadık; 'slav.ish.ness *n.* dalkavukluk, körü körüne itaat.

slaw [slɔː] *n.* lahana salatası.

slay *rhet.* [slei] (*irr.*) *v/t.* öldürmek, katletmek; 'slay.er *n.* katil.

sled [sled] = sledge¹.

sledge¹ [sledʒ] 1. *n.* kızak, yük kızağı; 2. *v/i.* kızakla gitmek *veya* yük taşımak.

sledge² [~] *n. a.* ~-hammer balyoz.

sleek [sliːk] 1. □ düzgün, parlak (*saç vs.*, *a. fig.*); 2. *v/t.* düzlemek, düzeltmek; 'sleek.ness *n.* düzgünlük, parlaklık.

sleep [sliːp] 1. (*irr.*) *v/i.* uyumak; ayakta (*veya* hareketsiz) durmak (*topaç*); ~ up-(on) *veya* over bir işin sonucu için istihareye yatmak; bşi ertesi güne bırakmak (*daha fazla düşünebilmek için*); *v/t. b-ne* yatacak yer sağlamak; ~ away geç uyanmak; ~ off uyuyarak geçirmek (*sarhoşluk vs.*); 2. *n.* uyku; go to ~ yatağa yatmak; 'sleep.er *n.* uyuyan kimse; 🔛 yataklı vagon; travers; be a light (fast) ~ uykusu hafif (derin) olm.; 'sleep.i.ness *n.* uykulu olma, uyuklama.

sleep.ing ['sliːpiŋ] *adj.* uyuyan, uykuda, uyku...; '~-bag *n.* uyku tulumu; 2 Beauty Uyuyan Güzel; '~-car, '~-'car.riage *n.* 🔛 yataklı vagon; '~-draught *n.* yatmadan önce içilen uyku getirici madde; ~ part-ner † özel ortak, komanditer; '~-'sick-ness *n.* uyku hastalığı.

sleep.less □ ['sliːplis] uykusuz; 'sleep-less.ness *n.* uykusuzluk.

sleep.walk.er ['sliːpwɔːkə] *n.* uyurgezer.

sleep.y □ ['sliːpi] uykusu gelmiş, uyku basmış, uyku gözünden akan; '~.head *n.* F *fig.* uykucu, miskin, üşengeç.

sleet [sliːt] 1. *n.* sulusepken kar; 2. *v/i.* sulusepken yağmak; 'sleet.y *adj.* sulusepken gibi.

sleeve [sliːv] 1. *n.* yen, elbise kolu; ⊕ manşon, rakor, kol, bilezik; have something up one's ~ bir sırrı gelecekte koz olarak kullanmak üzere saklamak; 2. *vb.* kol takmak; sleeved *com.* ...kollu; 'sleeve.less *adj.* kolsuz, yensiz; 'sleeve--link *n.* kol düğmesi.

sleigh [slei] 1. *n.* kızak (*atlı*); 2. *v/i.* kızakla gitmek.

sleight [slait] *n.*: ~ of hand elçabukluğu, hokkabazlık, hüner, marifet.

slen.der □ ['slendə] ince (belli), narin, fidan gibi; küçük, ufak, kıt, az; zayıf, der-

mansız; 'slen.der.ness *n.* incelik, zayıflık; dermansızlık.

slept [slept] *pret. & p.p. of* sleep 1.

sleuth [sluːθ] *n.* '~-hound bir tür av köpeği; *fig.* hafiye.

slew¹ [sluː] *pret. of* slay.

slew² [~] *v/t. & v/i. a.* ~ round dön(dür)-mek, çevirmek, devret(tir)mek.

slice [sl isː] 1. *n.* dilim, parça, kısım; hisse; balık bıçağı; 2. *vb.* dilimlemek; bıçakla kesmek; topu keserek atmak (*golf*).

slick F [slik] 1. *adj.* düz(gün), parlak, kaygan; *fig.* yapmacık kibar, kurnaz, hilekâr, şeytan gibi; 2. *adv.* ustalıkla, kurnazca; 3. *n. a.* ~ paper *Am. sl.* klâs mecmua; 'slick.er *n.* muşamba yağmurluk; kurnaz, hilekâr kimse.

slid [slid] *pret. & p.p. of* slide 1.

slide [slaid] 1. (*irr.*) *v/t. & v/i.* kay(dır)-mak, süzülmek; sessizce ortadan kaybolmak, savuşmak; let things ~ işleri oluruna bırakmak, sermek; 2. *n.* kayma; ⊕ sürme, sürgü; diyapozitif slayt; *a.* land ~ heyelân, kayşa; 'slid.er *n.* sürgü, sürme; 'slide-rule *n.* hesap cetveli.

slid.ing ['slaidiŋ] 1. *n.* kayma; 2. *adj.* sürme..., kayıcı; ~ roof açılır kapanır tavan; ~ rule sürgülü hesap cetveli; ~ scale değiştebilen değerlendirme oranı; ~ seat (*yarış kayığı*) kızaklı kürekçi oturma yeri.

slight [slait] 1. □ zayıf, ince, narin, hafif; önemsiz, değersiz, cüzi; 2. *n.* saygısızlık, küçümseme; 3. *v/t.* önem vermemek -e, hesaba katmamak, küçümsemek -i; 'slight.ing □ küçümseyen, hafifseyen; 'slight.ly *adv.* biraz, bir parça; 'slight-ness *n.* zayıflık; önemsizlik.

slim [slim] 1. □ ince, zayıf, narin, fidan gibi; az, kıt, eksik; *sl.* kurnaz, şeytana çarığı ters giydiren; 2. *v/i.* incelmek, zayıflamak.

slime [slaim] *n.* sümük, balgam; balçık, çamur.

slim.i.ness ['slaiminis] *n.* kayganlık, yapışkanlık; çamurlu ve sümüksel olma.

slim.ness ['slimnis] *n.* incelik, narinlik.

slim.y □ ['slaimi] çamurlu, balçıklı; sümüksü, pis.

sling [sliŋ] 1. *n.* sapan, mancınık; (kayış) asma; † bocurgat, yük kaldırmakta kullanılan mekanik aygıt; 2. (*irr.*) *v/t.* sapanla atmak; askı ile kaldırmak; *a.* ~ up yukarı kaldırmak.

slink [sliŋk] (*irr.*) *vb.* sinsi sinsi yürümek, gizlice sokulmak; sıvışmak; vakitsiz yavrulamak, (*hayvan*) yavrusunu düşürmek.

**slip** [slip] **1.** *v/t.* & *v/i.* kay(dır)mak; ayağı kaymak; kaç(ır)mak; hataya düşmek, yanılmak; salıvermek; *(hayvan)* yavrusunu düşürmek; *oft.* ~ away kaçmak, sıvışmak; geçip gitmek *(zaman)*; ~ in arasına girmek *(lâf)*; ~ into içine koymak, sokmak, tutuşturmak -*e*; ~ on giyivermek, üzerine geçirmek *(elbise vs.)*; **2.** *n.* kayma; yanlış adım *(a. fig.)*, hata, kusur; sürçme, söz kaçırma, dikkatsizlik; *a.* ~ paper pusula, kâğıt; ✓ daldırma, çelik; *fig.* evlât, döl; jüpon, kombinezon; ~s *pl. veya* ~ way ⏚ geminin suya indirildiği *veya* sudan çekildiği kızak; yastık yüzü; ~s *pl.* deniz donu; a ~ of a girl ince, narin bir kız; ~ of a pen yazı hatası; it was a ~ of the tongue dil sürçmesiydi; give s.o. the ~ b-nin elinden kurtulmak, sıvışmak; **¹~-knot** *n.* ilmik, fiyonk; **¹~-on** *n.* kolay giyilip çıkarılan *(elbise vs.)*; **¹slip.per** *n.* terlik; **¹slip.per.y** ☐ kaygan; *fig.* kaypak; **¹slip-road** *n.* otoyola çıkan yol; **slip.shod** [¹~ʃɔd] *adj.* dikkatsiz, kayıtsız, düzensiz, pasaklı, kötü; **slip.slop** [¹~ˈslɔp] *n.* dil hatası; **¹slip-stream** *n.* ✈ motorun arkaya ittiği hava akıntısı; **¹slip-up** *n.* F hata, kabahat, sürçme.

**slit** [slit] **1.** *n.* kesik, yarık, çatlak; **2.** *(irr.)* *v/t.* yarmak, uzunluğuna açmak, kesmek.

**slob.ber** [¹slɔbə] **1.** *n.* salya; **2.** *vb.* salya akıtmak, üzerine salya bulaştırmak; abartmalı söz söylemek, gevezelik etm. (over); **¹slob.ber.y** *adj.* ıslak, cıvık; salyalı.

**sloe** ✿ [sləu] *n.* çakaleriği; kara diken.

**slog** F [slɔg] **1.** *vb.* dövmek, rasgele vurmak; didinmek, ağır ve zahmetli iş görmek, eşek gibi çalışmak; **2.** *n.* vuruş, darbe; uzun gayret.

**slo.gan** [¹sləugən] *n. fig.* parola, slogan.

**sloop** ⏚ [sluːp] *n.* şalopa, büyük sandal.

**slop¹** [slɔp] **1.** *n.* sulu çamur, pis su birikintisi; ~s *pl.* bulaşık suyu; hasta çorbası, kalitesiz sulu yemek; **2.** *v/t. a.* ~ over beceriksizce dökmek; *v/i.* dökülmek, taşmak; *fig.* taşkınlık yapmak.

**slop²** [~] *n.:* ~s *pl.* ucuz konfeksiyon elbise; ⏚ elbise ve yatak takımı.

**slop-ba.sin** [¹slɔpbeisn] *n.* tabağa dökülen çay *veya* kahveyi dökmek için kullanılan kap.

**slope** [sləup] **1.** *n.* bayır, iniş, yokuş; meyilli düzey; **2.** *v/t.* meyillendirmek, meyilli kılmak, eğmek; ⊕ meyilli, şevli kesmek; ~ arms! ✕ tüfek omuza!; *v/i.* mey-

letmek, meyilli olm., eğilmek; ~ off, *a.* do a ~ *sl.* sıvışmak, tüymek; **¹slop.ing** ☐ eğik, eğri, mail.

**slop-pail** [¹slɔppeil] *n.* çöp kovası, bulaşık kabı; **¹slop.py** ☐ çamurlu, balçıklı, nemli; kirli, pasaklı, pis; sulu, çorba gibi.

**slop-shop** [¹slɔpʃɔp] *n.* ucuz konfeksiyon malları satılan mağaza.

**slosh** [slɔʃ] *vb.* suda *veya* çamurda yürümek; suda çalkalamak; su sıçratmak; *sl.* dayak atmak -*e*.

**slot** [slɔt] *n. hunt.* iz, yol; delik, kertik, uzun ensiz yarık *(mektup vs. atmak için)*; ⊕ dişili yiv.

**sloth** [sləuθ] *n.* tembellik, haylazlık; *zo.* Amerika'da ağaçlara tırmanan ve yavaş hareket eden bir kaç tür hayvan; **slothful** ☐ [¹~ful] tembel, yavaştan alan.

**slot-ma.chine** [¹slɔtməʃiːn] *n. (mal veya oyun için)* otomatik makine.

**slouch** [slautʃ] **1.** *v/i.* yorgun, omuzlar düşük, ayakları sürüyerek yürümek; **2.** *n.* yorgun, bitap yürüyüş; tembel, düzensiz kimse; ~ hat geniş ve sarkık kenarlı şapka.

**slough¹** [slau] *n.* bataklık.

**slough²** [slʌf] **1.** *n. zo.* değiştirilip atılan deri *(yılan vs.)*; ⚕ kabuk, ruhya; **2.** *v/t.* & *v/i.* pul pul olm. *(kabuk vs.)*, derisi soyulmak, gömlek değiştirmek; dökmek, değiştirmek *(deri)*.

**slough.y** [¹slaui] *adj.* batak, çamurlu.

**Slo.vak** [¹sləuvæk] **1.** *n.* Slovakyalı kimse, Slovak; Slovak dili; **2.** = **Slo¹va.ki.an** *adj.* Slovakyalı; Slovak diline ait.

**slov.en** [¹slʌvn] *n.* hırpani, şapşal giyinen kimse; **¹slov.en.li.ness** *n.* hırpanilik, şapşallık; **¹slov.en.ly** *adj.* hırpani, yırtık pırtık, şapşal.

**slow** [sləu] **1.** ☐ ağır, yavaş *(of)*; vakit alan; geri *(kalmış) (saat)*; hantal, üşengeç; yavaş etki eden *(ateş)*; can sıkıcı, monoton; aptal, kalın kafalı; *spor:* yorucu; be ~ to do s.th. bşi yaparken yavaş davranmak; my watch is ten minutes ~ saatim 10 dakika geri kalmış; **2.** *adv.* yavaş yavaş, ağır ağır, tembelce; **3.** *v/t.* & *v/i. oft.* ~ down, ~ up, ~ off yavaşla(t)mak; yavaş gitmek, ağırlaşmak; **¹~-coach** *n.* hareketleri ağır kimse; eski kafalı kimse; **¹~.match** *n.* funya, barutlu fitil; **¹~·mo.tion film** yavaşlatılmış, ağır çekim film; **¹slow.ness** *n.* yavaşlık, ağırlık; **¹slow.worm** *n. zo.* köryılan.

**sludge** [slʌdʒ] *n.* sulu çamur, balçık.

**slue** [sluː] = **slew²**.

**slug¹** [slʌg] *n.* işlenmemiş metal parça; *typ.* linotip makinesinin döktüğü bir satır yazı.

**slug²** *zo.* [~] *n.* kabuksuz sümüklü böcek.

**slug³** [~] *Am. of* slog¹.

**slug.gard** [ˈslʌɡəd] *n.* tembel, haylaz kimse; **ˈslug.gish** ☐ tembel, haylaz, cansız.

**sluice** [sluːs] **1.** *n.* savak, kapaklı su bendi; **2.** *v/t.* (out, down) yıkayarak temizlemek, çalkalamak; **ˈ~ˈgate** *n.* savak kapağı; **ˈ~ˈway** *n.* savak yatağı.

**slum** [slʌm] *n. a.* ~s *pl.* teneke mahallesi, şehrin fakir mahallesi, kenar mahalle, fukara yatağı, gecekondu bölgesi.

**slum.ber** [ˈslʌmbə] **1.** *n. a.* ~s *pl.* uyku, uyuklama; **2.** *v/i.* uyumak, uyuklamak. **slum.brous, slum.ber.ous** ☐ [ˈslʌmbrəs, ˈ~bərəs] uykusu gelmiş, uyku gözünden akan; uyku getiren.

**slump** [slʌmp] *borsa:* **1.** *v/i.* düşmek, değer kaybetmek; **2.** *n.* düşme, ekonomik bunalım, durgunluk.

**slung** [slʌn] *pret. & p.p. of* sling 2.

**slunk** [slʌŋk] *pret. & p.p. of* slink.

**slur** [sləː] **1.** *n.* leke, ayıp; *fig.* serzeniş, eleştiri; ♪ bağ işareti; **2.** *v/t. oft.* ~ over dikkate almamak, *b-ne, bşe* itibar etmemek; ♪ bağlama işaretini koymak; birbirine bağlayarak telâffuz etm. *(hece vs.).*

**slush** [slʌʃ] *n.* eriyen kar; çamur, balçık; F değersiz eser; **ˈslush.y** *adj.* çamurlu, batak; F zevksiz, zevke hitap etmeyen.

**slut** [slʌt] *n.* pasaklı kadın; **ˈslut.tish** *adj.* pasaklı, düzensiz, hırpani, ihmalkâr.

**sly** ☐ [slai] kurnaz, şeytan gibi, sinsi; on the ~ gizli(den), sezdirmeden, sinsice; **ˈ~.boots** *n.* F akıl kumkuması; **ˈsly.ness** *n.* hile, kurnazlık, sinsilik, şeytanlık.

**smack¹** [smæk] **1.** *n.* tat, lezzet, hafif çeşni; tutam *(tuz vs.)*; *fig.* zerre, nebze; **2.** *vb.* çeşnisi olm. (of *-in*).

**smack²** [~] **1.** *n.* şapırtı *(öpücük, ağız)*; şaklayış *(kırbaç)*; şamar, tokat; **2.** *vb.* şaplatmak, patlatmak; ağzını şapırdatmak; şapır şupur öpmek; *b-ne* tokat aşketmek; **3.** *int.* şaklama, şakırdama.

**smack³** ⚓ [~] *n.* büyük balıkçı teknesi.

**smack.er** *Am. sl.* [ˈsmækə] *n.* bir dolar *veya* sterlin; şapırtılı öpücük.

**small** [smɔːl] **1.** *adj. com.* küçük, ufak; az; önemsiz; *fig.* hasis (ruhlu); alçak, soysuz; ~ eater az yiyen, boğazsız; feel ~, look ~ utanmak, küçük düşmek; the ~ hours *pl.* gece yarısından sonraki saatler; in a ~ way mütevazi şekilde, alçak gönüllü; **2.** *n.* ufak şey; az miktar; ~s *pl.* F iç çamaşırı, mendil vs. gibi ufak çamaşırlar; ~ of the back *anat.* sağrı kemiği, kuyruk sokumu; **ˈ~.arms** *n. pl.* ta-

banca vs. gibi el silahları; ~ **beer** hafif bira; think no ~ of o.s. F *k-ne* toz kondurmamak; be ~ önemsiz olm.; ~ **change** bozuk para; *fig.* önemsiz söz; **ˈ~ˈhold.er** *n.* küçük çiftçi; **ˈ~ˈhold.ing** *n.* küçük çiftlik; **ˈsmall.ish** *adj.* küçükçe, ufakça; **ˈsmall.ness** *n.* ufaklık, küçüklük; azlık. **small:** **ˈ~.pox** *n. pl.* ❀ çiçek hastalığı; ~ **talk** boş lâflar, önemsiz sohbet; havadan sudan konuşma; **ˈ~.time** *adj. Am.* F önemsiz, ikinci derecede.

**smalt** ⊕ [smɔːlt] *n.* potas, silis ve kobalt karışımından yapılan mavi cam; bu camdan elde edilen koyu mavi boya maddesi.

**smarm.y** F [ˈsmɑːmi] *adj.* sırnaşık, sulu, dalkavuk.

**smart** [smɑːt] **1.** ☐ şık, zarif, temiz, pak; yakışıklı, gösterişli; yeni, pırıl pırıl; şiddetli, sert *(savaş vs.)*; çevik, canlı; kurnaz; becerikli, eli yatık; ~ aleck *Am.* ukalâ dümbeleği; **2.** *n.* sızı; acı, elem, keder; **3.** *vb.* ağrımak, sızlamak, sancımak, dert çekmek; you shall ~ for it bunun cezasını çekeceksin; **ˈsmart.en** *vb.* mst ~ up üstünü başını düzeltmek, canlandırmak, telleyip pullamak; **ˈsmart-mon.ey** *n.* manevi zarar için tazminat; **ˈsmart.ness** *n.* şıklık; açıkgözlük; ustalık, beceri.

**smash** [smæʃ] **1.** *v/t. oft.* ~ up ezmek, parçalamak; ~ in vurup kırmak; *fig.* yok etm., mahvetmek, tahrip etm.; hiddetle yere atmak; *v/i.* ezilmek, parçalanmak; *fig.* kırılmak; düşüp kırılmak; *oft.* ~ up iflâs etm., mahvolmak; **2.** *n.* parçalanma, şangırtı ile kırılma, ezilme; çarpışma, kaza; mahvolma, iflâs; *tenis:* küt inme; **ˈ~-and-ˈgrab raid** camekânı kırarak teşhir malını çalma; **ˈsmash.er** *n. sl.* müthiş *b-i veya* bş; kırıcı eleştiri; **ˈsmash.ing** *adj. fig.* çok güzel; **ˈsmash-up** *n.* şiddetli çarpışma; parçalanma.

**smat.ter.ing** [ˈsmætərin] *n.* çat pat bilgi; az buçuk bilme.

**smear** [smiə] **1.** *vb.* bulandırmak, lekelemek, karalamak *(yazı)*; sürmek, yağlamak (on); *fig.* karalamak, pislemek; ~(ing) campaign iftira kampanyası; **2.** *n.* yağlı *veya* yapışkan madde, pislik, (bula-şık) leke; iftira.

**smell** [smel] **1.** *n.* (fena) koku; koklama; ima; **2.** *(irr.)* *v/t. -in* kokusunu almak, *bşi* koklamak; *v/i.* kokmak *(a.* ~ at; of); **ˈsmell.ing-salt** *n.* amonyak ruhu; **ˈsmell.y** *adj.* (fena) kokulu, pis kokan.

**smelt¹** [smelt] *pret. & p.p. of* smell 2.

**smelt²** *ichth.* [~] *n.* çamuka.

**smelt³** [~] *v/t.* eritmek *(maden filizi)*; **'smelt.er** *n.* dökümcü, dökmeci; **'smelt-ing-ıfur.nace** *n.* izabe fırını, yüksek fırın.

**smile** [smail] **1.** *n.* gülümseme, tebessüm; **2.** *vb.* gülümsemek (at *-e*); ~ on, ~ at *b-ne* gülümsemek.

**smirch** *rhet.* [sməːtʃ] *v/t.* leke sürmek, kirletmek; *fig.* karalamak.

**smirk** [sməːk] **1.** *v/t.* (pişmiş kelle gibi) sırıtmak; **2.** *n.* budalaca sırıtma, yapmacık gülümseyiş.

**smite** [smait] *(irr.) vb. poet. veya co.* darbe indirmek, vurmak, çarpmak, kırıp geçirmek; belâ kesilmek; çok etkilemek; pişman etm.; üzmek, rahatsız etm. *(vicdan)*; ~ upon *part. fig.* (kulağında) şaklamak.

**smith** [smiθ] *n.* demirci, nalbant.

**smith.er.eens** F [ˈsmiðəˈriːnz] *n. pl.* ufak parçalar; mermi parçaları; paçavra; kıymık; smash to ~ paramparça etm.

**smith.y** [ˈsmiði] *n.* nalbant dükkânı; demirhane.

**smit.ten** [ˈsmitn] **1.** *p.p. of* smite; **2.** *adj.* çarpılmış, etkilenmiş, şaşkın; *fig.* âşık, vurgun (with *-e*).

**smock** [smɔk] **1.** *v/t.* plise yapmak *(elbise)*; **2.** *n. a.* ~ frock iş kıyafeti, gömlek, önlük; **'smock.ing** *n.* bal peteği şeklinde iğne işi.

**smog** [smɔg] *n.* dumanlı sis.

**smoke** [sməuk] **1.** *n.* duman; X kamuflaj sisi; F içme *(sigara vs.)*; F tütün, sigara; have a ~ sigara içmek; **2.** *v/i.* tütmek, duman çıkarmak; *v/t.* tütsülemek; içmek, kullanmak *(sigara vs.)*; X sisle karartmak *(hava)*; **'~-bomb** *n.* sis bombası; **'~-dried** *adj.* tütsülenmiş; **'smoke.less** □ dumansız; **'smok.er** *n.* tütün içen; 🚬 tütün içenlere mahsus vagon; **'smoke-screen** *n.* X sis perdesi; **'smoke-stack** *n.* 🚬 & ⚓ baca.

**smok.ing** [ˈsməukiŋ] **1.** *n.* tütün içme; no ~! sigara içilmez!; **2.** *comb.* tüten...; tütün içen...; **'~-com.part.ment** *n.* 🚬 tütün içenlere mahsus vagon; **'~-room** *n.* tütün içenlere mahsus salon.

**smok.y** □ [ˈsməuki] dumanlı, tüten; duman renginde koyu füme.

**smol.der** *Am.* [ˈsməuldə] = smoulder.

**smooth** [smuːð] **1.** □ düz(gün), pürüzsüz; *fig.* engelsiz; sakin, yumuşak, halim; tatlı dilli, yüze gülen; akıcı, kaygan; sert olmayan *(içki, sigara vs.)*; **2.** *v/t. oft.* ~ out, ~ down düzlemek, düzeltmek; kolaylaştırmak *(a. fig.)*; inceltmek, tesviye etm.; *a.* ~ down yatıştırmak, teskin etm.; *a.* ~ over, ~

away ortadan kaldırmak, kurtulmak *(üzüntü, güç durum vs.)*; ~ down düzlenmek; **'smooth.ing 1.** *n.* ˌdüzle(n)me; **2.** *adj.* düz..., düzgün...; ~ iron ütü; ~ plane plânya; **'smooth.ness** *n.* düzlük, pürüzsüzlük; kayganlık; sokulganlık, tatlılık.

**smote** [sməut] *pret. of* smite.

**smoth.er** [ˈsmʌðə] **1.** *n.* kesif duman; boğucu madde; baskı altında kalma; **2.** *v/t.* & *v/i. a.* ~ up boğ(ul)mak *(a. fig.)*.

**smoul.der** [ˈsməuldə] *v/i.* dumansız yanmak, için için yanmak.

**smudge** [smʌdʒ] **1.** *v/t.* kirletmek, pislemek, bulaştırmak; *v/i.* kirlenmek, pislenmek, is bulaşmak; **2.** *n.* leke, kir *(veya* pislik, çamur) lekesi; **'smudg.y** □ lekeli, isli, kirli, pis.

**smug** [smʌg] *adj. k-ni* beğenmiş, hodpe-rest, *k-ni* dev aynasında gören; şıklık merakhsı.

**smug.gle** [ˈsmʌgl] *vb.* kaçırmak *(gümrükten)*, yurda kaçak mal sokmak *veya* çıkarmak; **'smug.gler** *n.* kaçakçı; **'smug-gling** *n.* kaçakçılık.

**smut** [smʌt] **1.** *n.* is, kurum, kir, pislik; pis laf, yakası açılmadık söz; ✿ buğday pası, sürme, bir tür buğday mantar hastalığı; **2.** *v/t.* kirletmek, pisletmek, lekelemek; ✿ buğday pası ile lekelemek.

**smutch** [smʌtʃ] **1.** *v/t.* kirletmek, pislemek, lekelemek; **2.** *n.* koyu leke.

**smut.ty** □ [ˈsmʌti] isli, kirli; müstehcen; ✿ mantarlı, sürmeli.

**snack** [snæk] *n.* hafif yemek, kahvaltı, çerez; **'~-bar,** **'~-coun.ter** *n.* hafif yemek yenen lokanta vs.

**snaf.fle¹** [snæfl] *n.* bir tür gem.

**snaf.fle²** sl. [~] *v/t.* aşırmak, çalmak.

**snaf.fle-bit** [ˈsnæflbit] *n.* gem ağızlığı.

**sna.fu** *Am. sl.* X [snæˈfuː] **1.** *adj.* karmakarışık, allak bullak, talan olmuş; **2.** *n.* karmakarışıklık, dağınıklık.

**snag** [snæg] *n.* kırık dal; kırık diş; *fig.* pürüzlü nokta, müşkül taraf; *Am.* ağaç gövdesi *(nehirde)*; **snag.ged** [ˈ~gid], **'snag.gy** *adj.* budaklı, çıkıntılı.

**snail** *zo.* [sneil] *n.* sümüklüböcek, salyangoz.

**snake** *zo.* [sneik] *n.* yılan *(a. fig.)*; **'~-charm.er** *n.* yılan oynatan; **'~-weed** *n.* ✿ yılan kökü, kurt pençesi.

**snak.y** □ [ˈsneiki] yılankavi, yılan gibi kıvrılan, kıvrak; *fig.* hain, kurnaz.

**snap** [snæp] **1.** *n.* ısırma, ağzıyla kapn.a; çatırtı, çatlama, şıkırtı, şaklama; *fig.* hamle, coşkunluk; kopça, çıtçıt; *phot.* enstantane; bisküvit, pötibör; cold ~ soğuk dalgası; **2.** *v/i.* aniden ısırmak, dişlemek (at *-i*); kopmak; çatırdayıp kırılmak; birdenbire kapanmak *(kilit)*; terslemek, veriştirmek, çıkışmak (at s.o. *-i, -e*); ~ **into** it *Am. sl.* haydi gayret!, çabuk ol!; ~ **out** of it *Am. sl.* kendine gelmek; *v/t.* kırmak; şaklatmak *(kamçı, parmak vs.); phot.* enstantane fotoğraf çekmek; ~ one's fingers at s.o. *b-ni* umursamamak, hiçe saymak; ~ **out** birdenbire söyleyivermek *(söz);* ~ **up** kapmak, yakalamak; *b-ne* çıkışmak, veriştirmek; *b-nin* sözünü kesmek; **3.** *int.* iki aynı şey görüldüğünde söylenen söz; **'~-drag.on** *n.* ♥ aslanağzı; **'~-fas.ten.er** *n.* çıtçıt *(elbisede);* **'snap.pish** □ huysuz, kavgacı, aksi; alaycı, müstehzi; *k-ni* beğenmiş, laübali; **'snap.pish.ness** *n.* huysuzluk, aksilik, *k-ni* beğenmişlik; **'snap.py** = snappish; F atılgan, yaman, çevik, tez, atik; make it ~! elini çabuk tut!, sallanma!; **'snap.shot 1.** *n.* enstantane fotoğraf; **2.** *vb.* enstantane fotoğraf çekmek.

**snare** [snɛə] **1.** *n.* tuzak, kapan; **2.** *v/t.* tuzağa düşürmek, yakalamak; *fig.* ele geçirmek.

**snarl** [snɑːl] **1.** *v/i.* hırlamak; homurdanmak, söylenmek; **2.** *n.* hırlama; homurdanma, ters laf.

**snatch** [snætʃ] **1.** *n.* kapma, kapış, yakalama, anî hareket, birdenbire çekme; an, lahza; *sl.* adam kaçırma; by ~es kesik kesik hareket ederek, hamle ile; **2.** *v/t.* kapmak, koparmak, yakalamak; *k-ne* doğru çekmek; eline geçirmek; ~ at *bşe* el uzatmak, kapmaya çalışmak; ~ from s.o. *bşi b-nin* elinden zorla almak.

**sneak** [sniːk] **1.** *v/i.* sinsi sinsi dolaşmak, gizlice sokulmak; F ihbar etm., ispiyon etm. *(okulda); v/t.* F aşırmak, çalmak; **2.** *n.* sır küpü, yere bakan yürek yakan, sinsi kimse; F gammaz, ispiyoncu; **'sneak.ers** *n. pl.* F hafif lastik tenis ayakkabısı; **'sneak.ing** □ sinsi, gizli *(duygu),* şüpheli.

**sneer** [sniə] **1.** *n.* alay, istihza; hakaret; **2.** *v/i.* küçümsemek (at *-i*), zevklenmek, alay etm. *ile,* alaycı gülmek; **'sneer.er** *n.* alaycı, müstehzi kimse; **'sneer.ing** □ alaycı.

**sneeze** [sniːz] **1.** *v/i.* aksırmak, hapşırmak; not to be ~d at F hiç de fena değil, yabana atılmaz; **2.** *n.* aksırma, aksırık.

**snick.er** [ˈsnikə] *v/i.* kıs kıs gülmek; kişnemek *(at).*

**sniff** [snif] **1.** *v/i.* burnuna hava çekmek; *bşe* burun kıvırmak (at); *v/t. bşi* koklamak; **2.** *n.* koklama; burun kıvırma; **'sniff.y** *adj.* F burnu havada, *k-ni* beğenmiş, kibirli; pis kokan, fena kokulu.

**snig.ger** [ˈsnigə] *v/i.* kıs kıs gülmek, alaylı gülmek (at *-e).*

**snip** [snip] **1.** *n.* kesme, biçme; kesilmiş parça; **2.** *v/t.* makasla kesmek (off); zımbalamak *(bilet).*

**snipe** [snaip] **1.** *n. orn.* çulluk; bekasin, su çulluğu; **2.** *v/i.* ✗ pusuya yatarak düşmanı vurmak *(çete savaşı),* pusudan ateş etm.; **'snip.er** *n.* ✗ pusuya yatan nişancı; çeteci, partizan.

**snip.pets** [ˈsnipits] *n. pl.* kısa, küçük parçalar *(yazı, konuşma vs.); fig.* parça, fragman.

**snitch** *sl.* [snitʃ] *v/i.:* ~ **on** s.o. *b-ni* ihbar etm., gammazlamak.

**sniv.el** [ˈsnivl] *v/i.* burnu akmak; ağlayıp sızlamak, burnunu çekerek ağlamak; **'sniv.el.(l)ing** *adj.* çıtkırıldım, ağlayıp sızlayan; çabuk ağlayan; acınacak durumda; sırılsıklam.

**snob** [snɔb] *n.* snop, züppe, farfara kimse; **'snob.ber.y** *n.* züppelik; **'snob.bish** □ snop, züppe tavırlı, kibarlık taslayan.

**snook.er** [ˈsnuːkə] **1.** *n.* yirmi bir topla altı delikli masada oynanan bir tür tür bilardo oyunu; **2.** *v/t.* be ~ed F sıkıştırılmak, zor duruma sokulmak.

**snoop** *Am. sl.* [snuːp] **1.** *vb. fig.* burnunu sokmak (upon *-e);* **2.** *n.* her işe burnunu sokan kimse; casus, ajan.

**snoot.y** F [ˈsnuːti] *adj.* züppe, *k-ni* beğenmiş.

**snooze** F [snuːz] **1.** *n.* şekerleme, uyuklama; **2.** *v/i.* şekerleme yapmak, kısaca uyumak.

**snore** [snɔː] **1.** *n.* horlama, horultu; **2.** *v/i.* horlamak.

**snor.kel** ↓ [ˈsnɔːkəl] *n.* şnorkel.

**snort** [snɔːt] **1.** *n.* horuldama, öfke ile belirtme, hızlı hızlı nefes alma, soluma; **2.** *v/i.* at gibi horuldamak, burnundan solumak.

**snot** F [snɔt] *n.* mankafa, alçak herif; sümük; **'snot.ty** *adj.* sümüklü; *fig.* alçak, küstah, kibirli.

**snout** [snaut] *n. zo.* hortum, burun.

**snow** [snəu] **1.** *n.* kar (yağışı); *sl.* kokain; **2.** *v/i.* kar yağmak; be ~ed under with *fig.* işe boğulmak; ~ed up *veya* up karla kapanmak, kardan mahsur kalmak; **'~.ball 1.** *n.* kar topu; **2.** *v/i.* çığ gibi büyümek; **'~-bound** *adj.* kardan mahsur kalmış; **'~-capped, '~-clad, '~-covered** *adj.* karla örtülü, karlı; **'~-drift** *n.* kar yığıntısı; **'~.drop** *n.* ♥ kardelen;

ǀ~.fall *n.* kar yağışı; ǀ~.flake *n.* kar lapası, kar tanesi, kuşbaşı; ǀ~-gog-gles *n. pl.* (a pair of) kar gözlüğü; ǀ~-line *n.* toktağan (*veya* hiç erimeyen) karların hududu; ǀ~-plough, *Am.* ǀ~.plow *n.* kar temizleme makinesi; ǀ~-shoe *n.* kar ayakkabısı; ǀ~.storm *n.* kar fırtınası, tipi; ǀ~-ǀwhlte *adj.* bembeyaz, kar gibi; ǀsnow.y ☐ karlı; kar gibi, beyaz.

**snub** [snʌb] 1. *v/t.* hor davranmak, terslemek, küçümsemek, hiçe saymak; 2. *n.* hiçe sayma, küçümseme; ǀsnub nose ucu kalkık kısa burun; ǀsnub-nosed *adj.* kısa ve kalkık burunlu.

**snuff** [snʌf] 1. *n.* fitilin yanmış yeri (*mum*); enfiye; up to ~ F keyfi yerinde; kurnaz, açıkgöz, uyanık; 2. *vb. a.* take ~ enfiye çekmek, buruna çekmek; fitilin yanık ucunu kesmek (*mum*); ǀ~-box enfiye kutusu; ǀsnuff.ers *n. pl.* mum makası; snuf.fle [ǀ~fl] *v/i.* burnunu çekmek, solumak; genizden konuşmak; ǀsnuff.y *adj.* enfiye gibi, enfiyeli; pis kokan; *fig.* rencide olan, dargın, öfkeli, ters.

**snug** ☐ [snʌg] rahat, konforlu; kuytu; ëmniyetli; iyi oturmuş (*elbise*); ǀsnug.ger.y *n.* konforlu yer, sıcak yuva; ǀsnug.gle [ǀ~gl] *v/i. a.* ~ up yerleşmek, sokulmak (to, in -e).

**so** [səu] 1. *adv.* böyle, öyle, şöyle; bu derece, bu kadar; onun için, bu nedenle, bu münasebetle: o derece, ... kadar; çok, pek; pek çok; dahi, de, da; 2. *conj.* şartı ile, -ması için, -sin diye; müddetçe; *int.* ya!, Öyle mi?, Tamam!; demek ki; yeter; 3. *adj.* doğru; I hope ~ umarım öyledir; you are tired, ~ am I yorgunsunuz, ben de; a mile or ~ bir mil kadar; ~ as to ...mak için, ...cek şekilde, maksadiyle; ~ far şimdiye kadar; ~ far as I know bildiğim kadariyle.

**soak** [səuk] 1. *v/t.* ıslatmak, suya batırmak, sırsıklam etm.; *sl.* para sızdırmak, kazıklamak; ~ up *veya* in emmek, içine çekmek; *v/i.* (suda) ıslanmak, yumuşamak, içine geçmek (into, in); F içkiyi fazla kaçırmak; 2. *n.* ıslanma, ıslatma, emme; = ǀsoak.er F ayyaş kimse.

**so-and-so** [ǀsəuənsəu] *n.* filanca; Mr. ♀ falanca zat.

**soap** [səup] 1. *n.* sabun; soft ~ arap sabunu; F dalkavukluk, yağcılık; 2. *v/t.* sabunlamak, sabun sürmek; ǀ~-box *n.* sabun sandığı; *fig.* sokakta nutuk çekenlerin üstüne çıktığı sandık; ~ orator sokak konuşmacısı, sokakta nutuk atan kimse; ~ race çocukların kendi yaptığı sandık arabalarla yaptıkları yokuş aşağı yarış;

ǀ~-dish *n.* sabun tası; ǀ~-bub.bǀe *n.* sabun köpüğü; ǀ~-op.er.a *n. Am.* radyo *veya* televizyonda yayınlanan dizi melodram; ǀ~-suds *n. pl., a. sg.* sabun köpüğü; ǀsoap-y ☐ sabunlu, sabun gibi; *fig.* yağcı, boyun eğen.

**soar** [sɔ:] *v/i.* yükselmek, yücelmek, havalanmak (*a. fig.*); ✝ havada süzülmek; aynı yükseklikte uçmak; artmak, fırlamak (*fiyat vs.*).

**sob** [sɔb] 1. *n.* hıçkırık, hıçkırma; 2. *v/i.* hıçkıra hıçkıra ağlamak, hüngür hüngür ağlamak.

**so.ber** [ǀsəubə] 1. ☐ ayık; temkinli, kendine hakim; makûl, ölçülü, ılımlı; ciddi, ağırbaşlı; sade, gösterişsiz; 2. *v/t. & v/i. oft.* ~ down ciddileş(tir)mek, aklını başına getirmek, ayıl(t)mak; ǀso.ber.ness, so.bri.e.ty [~ǀbraiəti] *n.* ayıklık; ağırbaşlılık, ciddiyet; ılımlılık.

**sob-stuff** F [ǀsɔbstʌf] *n.* santimantalizm, duygusallık.

**so-called** [ǀsəuǀkɔːld] *adj.* diye anılan, sözde, güya.

**soc.cer** F [ǀsɔkə] *n.* futbol (oyunu).

**so.cia.bil.i.ty** [səuʃəǀbiliti] *n.* hoşsohbetlik, toplumsal olma, girişkenlik; ǀso.cia.ble ☐ 1. girgin, arkadaş canlısı; nazik, tatlı dilli, sempatik; 2. *n.* sohbet toplantısı.

**so.cial** [ǀsəuʃəl] 1. ☐ hoş sohbet, girgin; sosyal, toplumsal, topluma ait; ~ activities *pl.* sosyal faaliyetler; ~ insurance sosyal sigorta; ~ services *pl.* sosyal hizmetler; 2. *n.* sohbetli toplantı (meclisi); ǀso.cial.ism *n.* sosyalizm, toplumculuk; ǀso.cial.ist 1. *n.* sosyalist, toplumcu; 2. *adj. a.* so.cialǀis.tic sosyalizme ait, toplumcu; so.cial.ite F [ǀ~lait] *n.* tüm modaya uygun partilere katılan; ǀso.cial.ize *vb.* kamulaştırmak, topluma mal etm.; sosyalleştirmek.

**so.ci.e.ty** [səǀsaiəti] *n.* kurum, şirket, ortaklık; cemiyet, toplum, topluluk; kulüp, dernek; sosyete; arkadaşlık, dostluk; secret ~ gizli cemiyet.

**so.ci.o.log.i.cal** ☐ [sousjəǀlɔdʒikəl] sosyolojik, toplumbilimsel, sosyolojiye ait; so.ci.ol.o.gist [~siǀɔlədʒist] *n.* sosyolog, toplumbilimci; so.ciǀol.o.gy *n.* sosyoloji, toplumbilim.

**sock**[1] [sɔk] *n.* kısa çorap, şoset; mantar taban.

**sock**[2] *sl.* [~] 1. *n.* dayak, kötek; give s.o. ~s = 2. *v/t. b-ne* dayak atmak, pataklamak.

**sock.er** F [ǀsɔkə] = soccer.

**sock.et** [ǀsɔkit] *n.* sap deliği, yuva, oyuk

*(göz, diş)*; mafsal oyuğu; ♪ duy, priz.

**so.cle** [ˈsɔkl] *n.* kaide, ayaklık, kürsü, temel, destek, taban.

**sod** [sɔd] 1. *n.* çimen (parçası), çim; 2. *vb.* çimen parçaları ile kaplamak.

**so.da** ⚗ [ˈsɔudə] *n.* soda; karbonat, sodyum bikarbonat; ˈ~-foun.tain *n.* sifon; büfe, büvet, dondurma salonu; ˈ~-wa.ter *n.* maden sodası; gazoz.

**sod.den** [ˈsɔdn] *adj.* sırsıklam; iyice ıslanmış; hamurumsu *(ekmek)*; ayyaş suratlı.

**so.di.um** ⚗ [ˈsəudjəm] *n.* sodyum, sut.

**so.ev.er** [səuˈevə] *adv.* her ne, herhangi, her.

**so.fa** [ˈsəufə] *n.* kanepe, sedir.

**sof.fit** ⚠ [ˈsɔfit] *n.* kemer, taban, balkon *veya* merdivenin alt yüzü.

**soft** [sɔft] 1. □ *com.* yumuşak; yumuşak başlı, mülayim, uysal; ılık, tatlı *(iklim)*; zayıf, gevşek; ince, narin; hafif, kolay, rahat; F aklı kıt, budala; ~ drink F alkolsüz içki, içecek; a ~ thing *sl.* kolay ve paralı iş; *s.* soap 1; 2. *adv.* yavaşça; 3. *n.* yumuşak şey; F ahmak, öküz aleyhisselâm, sünepe; ˈ~-ˈboiled *adj.* rafadan *(yumurta)*.

**soft.en** [ˈsɔfn] *v/t. & v/i.* yumuşa(t)mak *(a. fig.)*; yatış(tır)mak, teskin etm.; kısmak *(ses)*; sindirmek *(boya)*; ⊕ tavlayıp yavaş yavaş soğutarak sertleştirmek *(metal)*; ˈsoft.en.er *n.* yumuşatıcı *(madde)*; **soft-head.ed** [ˈsɔftˈhedid] *adj.* bunak, budala, ebleh; ˈsoft-ˈheart.ed *adj.* yumuşak kalpli, yufka yürekli; ˈsoft.ness *n.* yumuşaklık, uysallık; ˈsoft-ˈped.al *v/t.* ♪ pianoyu pedalla çalmak; *fig.* basitleştirmek, önemsememek, hafifletmek, gevşetmek; ˈsoft-ˈsaw.der *n.* 1. *v/i.* tatlı dil dökmek, pohpohlamak; 2. *n.* tatlı dil, yüze gülüş, pohpohlama; ˈsoft-ˈsoap *vb.* yağ çekmek, ayartmak, yaltaklanmak; ˈsoft-ware *n.* kompütere verilen program; ˈsoft.y *n.* F ahmak. sünepe.

**sog.gy** [ˈsɔgi] *adj.* sırsıklam, iyice ıslanmış, yaş, ıslak.

**so.ho** [səuˈhəu] *int.* hey!

**soil¹** [sɔil] *n.* toprak, yer; arazi, memleket. ülke.

**soil²** [~] 1. *n.* kir, leke, pislik, çöp; gübre. dışkı; 2. *v/t.* kirletmek, lekelemek; namusuna leke sürmek; *v/i.* kirlenmek, pislenmek. lekelenmek; ˈsoil-pipe *n.* künk, boşaltma borusu.

**so.journ** [ˈsɔdʒəːn] 1. *n.* konukluk, misafirlik; 2. *v/i.* kalmak, konaklamak, misafir olarak kalmak; ˈso.journ.er *n.* konuk, misafir.

**sol** ♪ [sɔl] *n.* sol, gamda beşinci nota.

**sol.ace** [ˈsɔləs] 1. *n.* avuntu, teselli; 2. *v/t.* teselli etm., avutmak.

**so.lar** [ˈsəulə] *adj.* güneşe ait, güneş...

**sold** [səuld] *pret. & p.p. of* sell 1.

**sol.der** ⊕ [ˈsɔldə] 1. *n.* lehim; 2. *v/t.* lehimlemek (up); ˈsol.der.ing-i.ron *n.* havya.

**sol.dier** [ˈsɔuldʒə] 1. *n.* asker, er; 2. *v/i.* askerlik yapmak; go ~ing asker olm.; ˈsol.dier.like, ˈsol.dier.ly *adj.* askerî, askerce, asker gibi; ˈsol.dier.ship *n.* askerlik; ˈsol.dier.y *n.* askerler, ordu, asker sınıfı; *contp.* düzensiz asker topluluğu.

**sole¹** □ [səul] tek, yalnız, biricik, yegâne; ~ agent tek mümessil.

**sole²** [~] 1. *n.* taban, pençe; 2. *v/t.* pençe vurmak -e.

**sole³** *ichth.* [~] *n.* dilbalığı.

**sol.e.cism** [ˈsɔlisizəm] *n.* dilbilgisi kurallarının dışına çıkma, deyim hatası; aykırı davranış ve tutum.

**sol.emn** □ [ˈsɔləm] törenli, merasimle yapılan; ağırbaşlı ,vakur; kutsal; heybetli; **so.lem.ni.ty** [səˈlemniti] *n.* tantanalı tören, kutlama; ağırbaşlılık, vakar; **sol-em.ni.za.tion** [ˈsɔləmnaiˈzeifən] *n.* kutla(n)ma, ayin, tören; ˈsol.em.nize *vb.* kutlamak, resmi ayin yapmak.

**so.lic.it** [səˈlisit] *vb.* istemek, rica etm. (s.o.; s.th.; s.o. for s.th. *veya* s.th of s.o.), dilemek; rahatsız etm., huzurunu kaçırmak, balta elm.; **so.lic.i¹ta.tion** *n.* rica, talep, müracaat, istek; tahrik, davet; **so¹lic.i.tor** *n.* ⚖ müşavir avukat, dava vekili; *Am.* acenta, propagandist, reklamcı; ⚖ General başsavcı, müddei umumi; **so¹lic.it.ous** □ endişeli, meraklı, vesveseli (about, for için); ~ of istekli, arzulu -e; ~ to dikkatli, gayretli; **so¹lic.i.tude** [~tjuːd] *n.* endişe, kaygı, sıkıntı, korku, vesvese; gayret, çaba(lama), ilgi.

**sol.id** [ˈsɔlid] 1. □ katı; sağlam, dayanıklı; som, masif, yekpare; ⚖ cisimsel; *fig.* güvenilir, emin; *part.* † ekonomik saygınlığı tam; dayanışık, aralarında dayanışma olan; a ~ hour tam bir saat; ~ geometry ⚖ uzay geometri; ~ leather köselenin en iyi kısmı; 2. *n.* katı madde; üç boyutluluk; **sol.i.dar.i.ty** [~ˈdæriti] *n.* dayanışma, omuzdaşlık. tesanüt; **so¹lid.i.fy** [~difai] *vb.* katı¹as(tır)mak, sertleş(tir)mek, kuvvetlendirmek; **so¹lid.i.ty** *n.* katılık; uyuşum, tesanüt; sağlamlık, dayanıklılık; güvenirlik, emniyet.

**so.lil.o.quize** [səˈliləkwaiz] *vb.* kendi k-ne konuşmak; **so¹lil.o.quy** *n.* monolog. kendi k-ne konuşma.

**so¹.l.taire** [sɔliˈtɛə] *n.* mücevherde tek

taş; tek kişilik kâğıt oyunu. **sol.i.tar.y** □ [ˈ-təri] tek, yalnız; tenha, ıssız; tek başına; ~ confinement münferit hapis, hücre hapsi; **sol.i.tude** [ˈ-tjuːd] *n*. yalnızlık; ıssızlık, boşluk.

**so.lo** [ˈsəuləu] *n*. ♪ & *iskambil:* solo; iki *veya* üç kişiye karşı tek oynanan oyun; ✝ tek başına uçuş; **'so.lo.ist** *n*. solist.

**sol.stice** [ˈsɔlstis] *n. astr.* gündönümü.

**sol.u.bil.i.ty** [sɔljuˈbiliti] *n*. eriyebilme yeteneği; **sol.u.ble** [ˈ-bl] *adj*. eriyebilir, çözülebilir.

**so.lu.tion** [səˈluːʃən] *n.* erime, çözünme; çöz(ül)me, çözüm *(a.* ♈ & ♏ *)*, çare; ⊕ kauçuk eriyik.

**solv.a.ble** [ˈsɔlvəbl] *adj*. çözülür, halledilir; **solve** *v/t.* halletmek, çözmek, yanıt bulmak; **sol.ven.cy** ✝ [ˈ-vənsi] *n*. ödeme gücü; **'sol.vent 1.** *adj.* ✝ borcunu ödeyebilir, ödeme gücü olan; eritici, çözücü; **2.** *n.* eritici sıvı, eritken.

**som.bre,** *Am.* **som.ber** □ [ˈsɔmbə] loş, karanlık *(a. fig.);* bulanık, mat.

**some** [sʌm, səm] **1.** *pron.* & *adj.* bazı; bir, herhangi bir; biraz, bir parça, birkaç, birçok; hayli, epey; bazısı, kimi(si); ~ bread bir parça ekmek; ~ few oldukça; ~ 30 miles yaklaşık 30 mil; in ~ degree, to ~ extent kısmen, bir dereceye kadar; this is ~ speech! konuşma diye buna denir!, öyle bir konuşma ki!; **2.** *adv.* yaklaşık (olarak), biraz; *Am.* klâs, şık; **'~.body** *pron.* biri(si); **'~.day** *adv.* bir gün *(gelecekte);* **'~.one** *pron.* biri(si); **'~.how** *adv.* her nasılsa, bir yolunu bulup, herhangi bir şekilde; ~ or other her nasıl olursa olsun.

**som.er.sault** [ˈsʌməsɔːlt] *n*. taklak, perende; turn a ~ takla atmak.

**some...:** ~.**thing** [ˈsʌmθiŋ] *pron.* bir şey; ~ like daha çok ... e benzeyen; yaklaşık; **'~.time 1.** *adv.* günün birinde, gelecekte; **2.** *adj.* eski. sabık; **'~.times** *adv.* bazen. arasıra: **'~.what** *adv.* bir dereceye kadar; **'~.where** *adv.* bir yer(d)e; **'~.while** *adv.* bir süre, arasıra yapılan.

**som.nam.bu.lism** [sɔmˈnæmbjulizəm] *n*. uyurgezerlik; **som'nam.bu.list** *n*. uyurgezer.

**som nif.er ous** □ [sɔmˈnifərəs] uyutucu, uyku getirici; uyuşturucu.

**som.no.lence** [ˈsɔmnələns] *n*. uyku basması, uyuklama, uykulu hal; **'som.no.lent** *adi*. uykusu gelmiş, uyku basmış, uyuklayan.

**son** [sʌn] *n*. oğul, erkek evlât.

**so.na.ta** ♪ [səˈnɑːtə] *n*. sonat.

**song** [sɔŋ] *n*. şarkı, türkü, kanto, şan;

şiir, manzume; ötme; for a mere *veya* an old ~ yok pahasına, çok ucuza; nothing to make a ~ about F pek o kadar değil, mesele yapmağa değmez; **'~.bird** *n*. ötücü kuş; **'~.book** *n*. şarkı kitabı; **'~.hit** *n*. günün şarkısı; **songs.ter** [ˈ-stə] *n*. şantör, şarkıcı; ötücü kuş; **song.stress** [ˈ-stris] *n*. şantöz, hanende, kantocu.

**son.ic** [ˈsɔnik] *adj*. ses hızı *veya* dalgalarıyle ilgili; ~ bang ses duvarını aşan bir uçağın neden olduğu patlama sesi; ~ barri.er ses duvarı.

**son-in-law** *n., pl.* **sons-in-law** [ˈsʌn(z)inlɔː] damat.

**son.net** [ˈsɔnit] *n*. sone, on dört dizeli bir batı koşuk türü.

**son.ny** [ˈsʌni] *n*. oğlum, yavrum, evlâdım.

**so.no.rous** □ [səˈnɔːrəs] tınlayan, yankılı, ses çıkaran, sesli; **so'no.rous.ness** *n*. ses bolluğu, dolgun seslilik.

**soon** [suːn] *adv*. birazdan, biraz sonra; hemen, şimdi, derhal; erken; seve seve, memnuniyetle; as *veya* so ~ as -ince, olur olmaz, yapar yapmaz; **'soon.er** *adv*. daha önce, daha erken; daha çok *(veya* fazla), tercihan; no ~ ... than -ir -mez, olur olmaz; no ~ said than done demesiyle yapması bir oldu.

**soot** [sut] **1.** *n*. is, kurum; **2.** *v/t.* is(e) bulaştırmak (up).

**sooth** [suːθ] *n*.: in ~ gerçekte, hakikatte; **soothe** [suːð] *v/t.* yatıştırmak, teskin etm., rahatlatmak; **sooth.say.er** [ˈsuː-θseiə] *n*. falcı (kadın), geleceği söyleyen, kâhin.

**soot.y** □ [ˈsuti] isli, kurumlu.

**sop** [sɔp] **1.** *n.* sıvıda yumuşatılmış şey, tirit; *fig.* yumuşatıcı şey, rüşvet, sus payı; **2.** *v/t.* etsuyuna banmak, batırmak; ıslatarak yumuşatmak; ~ up suyu emmek: kurulamak, silmek.

**soph.ism** [ˈsɔfizəm] *n.* sofizm, bilgicilik, safsata, mantığa uymazlık.

**soph.ist** [ˈsɔfist] *n*. safsatacı kimse, sofist: so.phis.tic, so.phis.ti.cal □ [sɔˈfistik(əl)] safsatalı, sofistçe; so'phis.ti.cate [-keit] *vb*. safsata karıştırmak; hile ile saflığını bozmak; deneyim kazandırmak; so'phis.ti.cat.ed *adj*. hayata alışmış, kasarlanmış, kurnaz, pişkin; çağdaş, kültürlü. entelektüel; karışık. komplike: yapmacık: **so.phis.ti'ca.tion** *n.* safsata(cılık); çokbilmişlik, kurnazlık, komplike *veya* karışık olma; **soph.ist.ry** [ˈsɔfistri] *n.* safsata(cılık), sofistlik.

**soph.o.more** *Am.* [ˈsɔfəmɔː] *n.* kolej *veya* üniversitede ikinci sınıf öğrencisi.

**so.po.rif.ic** [sɔpəˈrifik] **1.** *adj.* (~ally) uyu-

tucu; uyuşturucu; 2. *n.* uyutucu ilaç.
**sop.ping** ['sɔpiŋ] *adj. a.* ~ wet sırsıklam;
**'sop.py** *adj.* çok ıslanmış, sırsıklam; F
aptal; duygusal, sentimental *(hikâye
vs.).*
**so.pran.o** ♪ [sə'prɑːnəu] *n.* soprano.
**sor.cer.er** ['sɔːsərə] *n.* büyücü, sihirbaz;
**'sor.cer.ess** *n.* büyücü kadın, cadı; **'sor-
cer.y** *n.* büyü(cülük), afsun.
**sor.did** □ ['sɔːdid] alçak, sefil, adi, bayağı *(a. fig.)*; kirli, pis, pasaklı; pinti, hasis, çıkarcı; **'sor.did.ness** *n.* alçaklık, se-
fillik; pintilik, cimrilik.
**sore** [sɔː] 1. □ acı veren, azmış *(yara)*,
ıstırap veren, ağrıyan, sızlayan; iltihaplı, yaralı; şiddetli, sert; *fig.* vahim, endişe verici; kırgın, küskün; ~ throat boğaz ağrısı; 2. *n.* ağrıyan yer; yara *(a.
fig.)*, bere **'sore.head** *n. Am.* F hayal kırıklığına uğramış *veya* asık suratlı, çabuk sinirlenen kimse; **'sore.ly** *adv.* şiddetle, pek çok; **'sore.ness** *n.* elem, acı(lık).
**so.ror.i.ty** [sə'rɔriti] *n. Am. univ.* kız öğrenciler birliği *(veya* yurdu).
**sor.rel¹** ['sɔrəl] 1. *adj.* kırmızımsı kahverengi *(part. at)*; 2. *n.* al don, kızıl doru,
kula (at).
**sor.rel²** ♀ [~] *n.* kuzukulağı.
**sor.row** ['sɔrəu] 1. *n.* keder, acı, dert, tasa, elem, gam, üzüntü; 2. *v/i.* kederlenmek, esef etm., kasvet çekmek; **sor.row-
ful** □ ['sɔrəful] kederli, elemli; keder veren, üzüntülü.
**sor.ry** □ ['sɔri] üzgün, kederli, gamlı,
mahzun; acınacak, pişman; (I am) (so)
~! üzgünüm!, maalesef!, pardon!, affedersiniz!; I am ~ for him ona acıyorum,
onun için üzülüyorum; we are ~ to say
üzülerek söylemek zorundayız, maalesef
söylemek zorundayız.
**sort** [sɔːt] 1. *n.* çeşit, nevi, tür; uᵘ'ül, tarz
yol; what ~ of nasıl bir; of a ~, of ~s sözüm ona, sıradan; out of ~s F rahatsız,
keyifsiz; canı sıkılmış, neşesiz; a good
~ çok iyi bir adam; (a) ~ of peace sözüm
ona *(veya* iyi kötü) huzur, barış; 2. *vb.*
sınıflandırmak, ayıklamak; † tasnif
etm.; ~ out seçmek, seçip ayırmak, ayıklamak.
**sor.tie** ✕ ['sɔːtiː] *n.* huruç, çıkış hareketi; ✈ bombardıman uçuşu.
**sot** [sɔt] *n.* ayyaş kimse, bekri.
**sot.tish** □ ['sɔtiʃ] ayyaş, küfelik.
**sou** [suː] *n.* eski bir ufak Fransız parası; *fig.* mangır, metelik.
**souf.flé** ['suːfleı] *n.* sufle.
**sough** [sau] 1. *n.* vızıltı, uğultu; 2. *v/i.*
uğuldamak, hışıldamak *(part. rüzgâr).*

**sought** [sɔːt] *pret. & p.p. of* seek; **'~-'after** *adj.* revaçta olan, çok rağbet gören.
**soul** [səul] *n.* ruh, can *(a fig.)*; **'~-de-
stroy.ing** *adj.* can sıkıcı, monoton; **'soul-
less** □ ruhsuz, cansız, duygusuz.
**sound¹** □ [saund] *com.* sağlam, esen, salim *(a. fig.)*; mükemmel, inceden inceye, tamamen; akıllı, mantıklı, anlayışlı; derin *(uyku)*; şiddetli *(vuruş, darbe)*; † emin, güvenilir; ♫ yasal, meşru,
muteber, geçerli.
**sound²** [~] 1. *n.* ses, sada; ima, anlam;
gürültü; ses erimi; 2. *v/i.* ses çıkarmak,
ses vermek, duyulmak, aksetmek; gelmek, görünmek (lıke gibi); *v/t. (ses)* çıkartmak, çalmak -i, öttürmek -i; sesle
ilân etm.; açıkça övmek; ~ the charge
✕ hücum borusu çalmak.
**sound³** [~] *n. geol.* boğaz; balığın yüzme
kesesi, solungaç.
**sound⁴** [~] 1. *n.* ♪ sonda; 2. *v/t.* ♪ sondalamak *(a. fig.)*; ⬇ iskandil etm.; ♪ kulaklık ile muayene etm.; ~ s.o. out *b-nin*
ağzını aramak, düşüncesini öğrenmeğe
çalışmak.
**sound...:** '~-box *n.* gramofon, pikap; diyafram; ~ broad.cast.ing sesli radyo yayını; ~ ef.fects *pl. (radyo, tiyatro)* efekt,
konuşmaların dışındaki sesler; '~-film *n.*
sesli film.
**sound.ing** ⬇ ['saundıŋ] *n.* iskandil etme;
~s *pl.* iskandil edilen suyun derinliği.
**sound.ing-board** ['saundıŋbɔːd] *n.* ses yan-
sıtıcısı; rezonans gövdesi *(keman vs.'-
de).*
**sound.less** □ ['saundlıs] sessiz, sedasız.
**sound.ness** ['saundnıs] *n.* sıhhat, sağ-
(lam)lık, esenlik; doğruluk; metanet.
**sound...:** '~-proof, '~-tight *adj.* ses geçirmez; '~-track *n. film:* ses yolu; '~-wave
*n. phys.* ses dalgası.
**soup¹** [suːp] *n.* çorba, elvziye.
**soup²** *Am. sl.* [~] 1. *n.* beygir gücü; 2. *vb.*
~ up *(motor)* gücünü artırmak.
**sour** ['sauə] 1. □ ekşi(miş); *fig.* acı, dokunaklı; *fig.* somurtkan, asık suratlı,
huysuz; 2. *v/t.* ekşitmek; asitlendirmek;
*fig. b-nin* hayatını zehir etm.; *v/i.* ekşimek, kesilmek *(süt)*; *fig.* somurtkan, surat asmak.
**source** [sɔːs] *n.* kaynak, memba, pınar;
menşe, köken.
**sour.ish** □ ['sauərıʃ] ekşi(ce), mayhoş;
**'sour.ness** *n.* ekşilik; *fig.* huysuzluk, somurtkanlık, terslik.
**souse** [saus] 1. *v/t.* batırmak, banmak,
daldırmak, ıslatmak; tuzlamak, salamura yapmak, turşu yapmak; 2. *n.* güm di-

ye düşme, gümbürtü, «plof» diye ses çıkararak düşme; salamura; **soused** *adj. sl.* sarhoş, ayyaş.

**sou.tane** *eccl.* [su:ˈtɑ:n] *n.* papaz cüppesi.

**south** [sauθ] **1.** *n.* güney, cenup; to the ~ of *-in* güneyinde; **2.** *adj.* güney...; cenubi, güneye doğru; güneyden gelen.

**south-east** [ˈsauθiːst] **1.** *n.* güney doğu; **2.** *adj. a.* **south-ˈeast.ern** *-in* güneydoğusunda.

**south.er.ly** [ˈsʌðəli], **south.ern** [ˈ~ən] *adj.* güneye doğru, güney...; **ˈsouth.ern.er** *n. Am.* A.B.D.'nin güneydoğu eyaletlerinden olan kimse, güneyli.

**south.ern.most** [ˈsʌðənməust] *adj.* en güneyde olan.

**south.ing** [ˈsauðiŋ] *n.* ↓ güneye doğru rota.

**south...:** ˈ~.land *n.* güney bölgesi; ˈ~.paw *n. Am. beysbol:* solak oyuncu; ♀ Pole Güney Kutbu.

**south.ward(s)** [ˈsauθwəd(z)] *adv.* güneye doğru.

**south...:** ˈ~.ˈwest **1.** *n.* güney batı; **2.** *adj. a.* ~.ˈwest.er.ly ~.ˈwest.ern güney(d)e; güneyden esen *(rüzgâr),* lodos(tan); ~.ˈwest.er *n.* güney rüzgârı, lodos; = **souˈwest.er** ↓ [sauˈwəstə] *n.* gemicilerin muşamba başlığı.

**sou.ve.nir** [ˈsuːvəniə] *n.* hatıra, andaç (of).

**sov.er.eign** [ˈsɔvrin] **1.** □ en yüksek, yüce; mükemmel, şahane; etkili *(ilâç);* mutlak, bağımsız; hükümran; **2.** *n.* hükümdar, kral(içe); eski altın İngiliz lirası; **sov.er.eign.ty** [ˈ~rənti] *n.* hükümranlık, hâkimiyet, egemenlik; bağımsızlık.

**so.vi.et** [ˈsɔuviət] *n.* Sovyet; idare meclisi.

**sow¹** [sau] *n. zo.* dişi domuz; ⊕ erimiş maden oluğu; bu olukta yapılan maden külçesi.

**sow²** [səu] *(irr.) vb.* ekmek, serpmek, yaymak *(tohum);* yaymak, neşretmek; ˈsower *n. tohum;* tohum ekme makinesi; çiftçi; **sown** [səun] *p.p. of* sow².

**so.ya** ♀ [ˈsɔiə] *n.* soya; ~ bean soya fasulyesi.

**soz.zled** *sl.* [ˈsɔzld] *adj.* sarhoş, ayyaş.

**spa** [spɑ:] *n.* kaplıca, içmeler, ılıca *(yeri).*

**space** [speis] **1.** *n.* feza, uzay; alan, yer, mevki; aralık, açıklık, mesafe; müddet, süre; *typ.* espas, iki sözcük arasına açmak için kullanılan maden parçası; **2.** *vb. a.* ~ out aralık koymak, fasıla bırakmak; *typ.* aralıklı dizmek; ˈ~.craft, ˈ~.ship *n.* uzay gemisi; ˈ~.sult *n.* uzay elbisesi; ˈ~.ˈtime *n.* yer-zaman ilintisi.

**spa.cious** □ [ˈspeiʃəs] geniş, engin, bol, pek büyük; ferah, havadar; ˈspa.ciousness *n.* genişlik, enginlik, açıklık.

**spade** [speid] **1.** *n.* bahçıvan beli, kazma; call a ~ a ~ açıkça, isim vererek söylemek; *mst* ~s *pl. iskambil:* maça, pik; **2.** *vb.* bellemek, bel ile kazmak; ˈ~.work *n.* bel işi; bir iş için zahmetli hazırlık.

**spa.ghet.ti** [spəˈgeti] *n.* çubuk makarna, spageti.

**spake** † *veya poet.* [speik] *pret. of* speak.

**span¹** [spæn] **1.** *n.* karış; süre, aralık; ♠ kemer *veya* köprü ayakları arasındaki açıklık; *Am.* çift koşum; **2.** *v/t.* ölçmek, karışlamak; boydan boya uzatmak.

**span²** [~] *pret. of* spin.

**span.gle** [ˈspæŋgl] **1.** *n.* pul, payet, pul gibi pırıldayan süs; **2.** *v/t.* pullarla süslemek.

**Span.iard** [ˈspænjəd] *n.* İspanyol.

**span.iel** [ˈspænjəl] *n.* uzun tüylü ve uzun sarkık kulaklı bir tür köpek, spanyel.

**Span.ish** [ˈspæniʃ] **1.** *adj.* İspanyol, İspanyalı; İspanya *veya* İspanyolca'ya ait; **2.** *n.* İspanyalı; İspanyolca; the ~ *pl.* İspanya halkı.

**spank** F [spæŋk] **1.** *v/t. -in* kıçına şaplak vurmak; ~ along hızlı gitmek *veya* denizde seyretmek; **2.** *n.* şaplak, hafif vurma; ˈspank.er *n.* ↓ randa yelkeni; ˈspanking **1.** □ şiddetli, kuvvetli *(rüzgâr);* tez, çabuk koşan; F inanılmayacak kadar büyük; **2.** *n.* F iyi bir dayak; şaplak atma.

**span.ner** ⊕ [ˈspænə] *n.* somun anahtarı; throw a ~ into the works *fig.* işe çomak sokmak.

**spar¹** [spɑ:] *n.* ↓ seren, direk; ⚓ kanat ana kirişi.

**spar²** [~] *v/i. boks:* hafif boks yapmak (with *ile); fig.* ağız kavgası etm. (at), horoz gibi dövüşmek; ~ring partner *boks:* idman arkadaşı.

**spar³** *min.* [~] *n.* ispat *(bir tür taş).*

**spare** [spɛə] **1.** □ az, yetersiz, seyrek, kıt, dar; pinti, eli sıkı; boş, serbest; fazla, artakalan, kullanılmayan; yedek..., ihtiyat; sıska, zayıf; ~ hours *pl.* boş zaman; ~ room misafir için yatak odası; ~ time boş vakit; **2.** *n.* ⊕ yedek parça; **3.** *v/t.* canını bağışlamak; biriktirmek *(para);* kazanmak *(vakit);* zahmetten kurtulmak; esirgemek; tutumlu kullanmak *-i;* vazgeçmek *-den;* enough and to ~ yeter de artar; *v/i.* idareli olm., tutumlu olm.; esirgemek; ˈspare.ness *n.* azlık, kıtlık; zayıflık; **spare part** yedek parça; ˈsparerib *n.* az etli domuz pirzolası.

**spar.ing** □ [ˈspɛəriŋ] tutumlu, idareli (**in**,

of); az kullanan; **ˈspar.ing.ness** *n.* tutum, tasarruf.

**spark¹** [ˈspɑːk] **1.** *n.* kıvılcım *(a, fig.)*; **2.** *v/i.* kıvılcım saçmak; *v/t.* ~ s.th. off bşi harekete geçirmek; *b-ni* teşvik etm., kışkırtmak

**spark²** [~] *n.* şık ve yakışıklı delikanlı, kavalye.

**spark.ing-plug** *mot.* [ˈspɑːkiŋplʌg] *n.* buji.

**spar.kle** [ˈspɑːkl] **1.** *n.* kıvılcım; parlayış, parıltı; parıldayan şey; **2.** *v/i.* parıldamak; kıvılcım saçmak *(zekâ)*; köpürmek *(şarap)*; köpüklenmek; sparkling wine köpüklü şarap; **spar.klet** [ˈ~klit] *n.* küçük kıvılcım, zerre *(a. fig.).*

**spark-plug** *mot.* [ˈspɑːkplʌg] *n.* buji.

**spar.row** *orn.* [ˈspærəu] *n.* serçe; ˈ~-hawk *n. orn.* atmaca.

**sparse** [spɑːs] seyrek, sık olmayan.

**Spar.tan** [ˈspɑːtən] **1.** *adj.* Spartalı; Sparta ile ilgili; güçlüklere dayanan, yılmaz; **2.** *n.* Spartalı kimse.

**spasm** ⚕ [ˈspæzəm] *n.* kramp, ıspazmoz, sinir kasılması; **spas.mod.ic, spas.mod.i-cal** □ [~ˈmɔdik(əl)] kasılımlı, ıspazmoz kabilinden; sürekli olmayan, düzensiz; *fig.* daldan dala konan.

**spat¹** [spæt] *n.* istiridye yumurtası.

**spat²** [~] *n.* kısa tozluk, dolak.

**spat³** [~] *pret. & p.p. of* spit² 2.

**spatch-cock** [ˈspætʃkɔk] *vb.* serpiştirmek, içine katmak *(konuşma, not).*

**spate** [speit] *n.* sel, su baskını; *fig.* akın, kütle, kalabalık; be in ~ sele kapılmak.

**spa.tial** □ [ˈspeiʃəl] mekân, hacim vs. itibariyle, uzaysal.

**spat.ter** [ˈspætə] **1.** *v/t. & v/i.* serpmek, sıçratmak *(su vs.)*; damlalar halinde dökülmek; **2.** *n.* kısa süren sağanak, serpinti; serpme, sıçratma *(a. fig.).*

**spat.u.la** [ˈspætjulə] *n.* spatüla, macun malası.

**spav.in** *vet.* [ˈspævin] *n.* at ayağının oynak yerinin şişmesi.

**spawn** [spɔːn] **1.** *n.* balık yumurtası; *fig. mst contp.* döl, evlât; **2.** *vb.* yumurta dökmek; üretmek, *fig.* meydana getirmek, yumurtlamak; ˈ**spawn.er** *n.* yumurtlayan *(balık)*; ˈ**spawn.ing 1.** *n.* yumurtlama; **2.** *adj.* yumurtlayan...

**speak** [spiːk] *(irr.) v/i.* konuşmak (to *ile)*; bahsetmek (about, of *-den)*; nutuk söyleme yapmak; ♪ tınlamak; ~ing! *teleph.* evet!; Brown ~ing! ben Bay Brown'ım; ~ out yüksek sesle söylemek; açıkça söylemek; ~ to *b-le* konuşmak, *b-ne* söylemek; ~ up çekinmeden açıkça söylemek; ~ up! yüksek sesle konuş!; ~ up against

aleyhinde konuşmak, karşısında olm.; that ~s well for him bu onun iyi olduğunu kanıtlar; *v/t.* söylemek, beyan etm. *(düşünce)*, bildirmek; ˈ~-eas.y *n. Am. sl.* gizli içki satılan yer; ˈ**speak.er** *n.* konuşan *veya* söyleyen kimse, konuşmacı, sözcü, spiker.

**speak.ing** [ˈspiːkiŋ] *adj.* konuşan; canlı; açık ve düzgün *(ifade)*; dokunaklı *(tablo, bakış)*; be on ~ terms with selâm vermekten öteye gitmeyen düzeyde tanışıyor olm.; ˈ~-trum.pet *n.* ses nakil borusu; megafon.

**spear** [spiə] **1.** *n.* mızrak, kargı; **2.** *v/t.* mızrakla vurmak -*e*; saplamak; ˈ~.head **1.** *n.* mızrak ucu; *fig.* baş, öncü öncüsü; **2.** *v/t.* öncülük etm., önayak olm. -*e*.

**spec** ⑰ *sl.* [spek] *n.* spekülasyon, vurgun.

**spe.cial** [ˈspeʃəl] **1.** □ özel, hususi, fevkalâde; *k-ne* mahsus, ayrı; **2.** *n. a.* ~ constable yardımcı polis; *a.* ~ edition özel baskı; *a.* ~ train özel tren; *Am.* özel teklif *(iş)*; *Am.* günün özel yemeği *(lokanta)*; ˈ**spe.cial.ist** *n.* uzman, mütehassıs; ⚕ mütehassıs hekim; **spe.ci.al.i.ty** [speʃiˈæliti] *n.* özellik, hususiyet; ⸆ ihtisas; **spe.cial.i.za.tion** [speʃəlaiˈzeiʃən] *n.* ihtisas sahibi olma; ˈ**spe.cial.ize** *vb.* ihtisas yapmak; tek bir konu üzerinde çalışmak; ihtisas sahibi olm. (in -*in*), mütehassıs olm.; ˈ**spe.cial.ty** [ˈ~ti] *n. s.* speciality; ⚼ mühürlü sözleşme.

**spe.cie** [ˈspiːʃiː] *n.* madeni para, sikke; ˈ**spe.cies** *n. pl. & sg.* tür, çeşit, cins.

**spe.cif.ic** [spiˈsifik] **1.** *adj.* (~ally) özgü, *k-ne* has, özel, spesifik, hususi, mahsus; belirli, muayyen; kati, kesin; ~ gravity *phys.* özgül ağırlık; **2.** *n.* ⚕ belirli tedavide kullanılan ilâç.

**spec.i.fi.ca.tion** [spesifiˈkeiʃən] *n.* tayin, belirtme; ⚼ şartname; ~s *pl* ayrıntılı tanımlama; *(teknik)* tarifname; **spec.i.fy** [ˈ~fai] *v/t.* belirtmek, ayrı ayrı göstermek *veya* söylemek.

**spec.i.men** [ˈspesimin] *n.* örnek, numune, model.

**spe.cious** □ [ˈspiːʃəs] aldatıcı yanıltıcı *(dış görünüş olarak)*, sahte; samimiyetsiz, güvenilmez; ˈ**spe.cious.ness** *n.* dış görünüşün aldatıcı olması.

**speck** [spek] **1.** *n.* nokta, benek, ufak leke; küçük parça, parçacık; **2.** *vb.* lekelemek; **speck.le** [ˈ~kl] **1.** *n.* ufak benek *veya* leke, çil; **2.** *vb. s.* speck 2.

**specs** F [speks] *n. pl.* gözlük.

**spec.ta.cle** [ˈspektəkl] *n.* manzara, görülecek şey, görünüş; (a pair of) ~s *pl.* gözlük; ˈ**spec.ta.cled** *adj.* gözlüklü.

**spec.tac.u.lar** □ [spek¹tækjulə] **1.** görülmeye değer,·göz alıcı, olağanüstü, göze çarpan; **2.** *n. Am.* F hayret verici manzara.

**spec.ta.tor** [spek¹teitə] *n.* seyirci.

**spec.tral** □ [¹spektrəl] hayalet kabilinden; hayal gücüne dayanan; hayalî; *opt.* tayfi, ışık dağılımına ait; **spec.tre** [¹-tə] *n.* hayal(et); **spec.tro.scope** *opt.* [¹-trəskəup] *n.* spektroskop, ışığı yedi renge ayıran alet; **spec.trum** [¹-trəm] *n.* tayf.

**spec.u.late** [¹spekjuleit] *vb.* zihnini kurcalamak, (kuramsal olarak) düşünmek, mütalâa etm. (on, upon -i); † borsada oynamak, spekülasyon yapmak; **spec-u¹la.tion** *n.* kurgu, vehim, işkil; † spekülasyon; **spec.u.la.tive** □ [¹-lətiv] spekülatif; kuruntulu, vesveseli; kuramsal, nazari, teorik; † borsa oyunuyla ilgili, spekülatif; rizikolu, tehlikeli; **spec.u.la.tor** [¹-leitə] *n.* † spekülatör, kapatçı, vurguncu.

**spec.u.lum** ⚥, *opt.* [¹spekjuləm] *n.* (metal) ayna, spekülom.

**sped** [sped] *pret. & p.p. of* speed 2.

**speech** [spiːtʃ] *n.* konuşma yeteneği, düzgün ve iyi konuşma yetisi; söz, nutuk, söylev; dil; make a ~ söylev vermek, konuşma yapmak, nutuk çekmek; ¹-.day *n. (okul)* diploma töreni; **speech.i.fy** *contp.* [¹-ifai] *v/i.* fazla konuşmak, nutuk çekmek, kafa şişirmek; ¹speech.less □ dili tutulmuş, dilsiz; sessiz; sözle anlatılamaz.

**speed** [spiːd] **1.** *n.* hız, sürat, çabukluk, acele; ⊕ devir sayısı; *phot.* ışığa karşı duyarlık; **2.** *(irr.)* *v/i.* hızla gitmek, acele etm, çabuk gitmek; ~ up *(pret. & p.p. ~ed)* hızlanmak; *v/t.* hızlandırmak; uğur getirmek; ~ up *(pret. & p.p. ~ed)* hızını arttırmak; ¹-.boat *n.* sürat motoru, yarış kayığı; ¹-.cop *n.* motorlu trafik polisi; ¹-.in.di.ca.tor = speedometer; ¹-.lim.it *n.* azami sürat; **speed.om.e.ter** *n. mot.* hızölçer; ¹speed.way *n.* sürat yolu, hız yolu; ¹speed.well *n.* ⚥ yavşanotu; ¹speed.y □ çabuk, hızlı.

**spell¹** [spel] **1.** *n.* nöbet, süre; ⊕ vardiya, posta; **2.** *vb.* nöbeti devralarak b-ni serbest kılmak (at), nöbetini almak -in.

**spell²** [~] **1.** *n.* büyü, sihir, tılsım; **2.** *(irr.)* *vb.* büyülemek; bir sözcüğün hecelerini ayrı ayrı söylemek, hecelemek; ifade etm., belirtmek, söylemek; ~ out heceleyerek okumak *veya* yazmak, deşifre etm.; detaylı açıklamak; ¹-.bind.er *n. Am.* büyüleyici konuşan hatip; ¹-.bound

*adj. fig.* büyülenmiş; ¹spell.er: he is a bad ~ doğru yazamaz.

**spell.ing** [¹spelin] *n.* imlâ, yazım; ¹-.book *n.* yazım kılavuzu.

**spelt¹** [spelt] *pret. & p.p. of* spell² 2.

**spelt²** ⚥ [~] *n.* kaplıca buğday.

**spel.ter** [¹speltə] *n.* çinko. ˚

**spen.cer** [¹spensə] *n.* kısa ceket.

**spend** [spend] *(irr.)* *v/t.* harcamak (on, upon -e), sarfetmek *(para)* (on); israf etm., havaya savurmak; geçirmek *(zaman)*; *(part.* ~ o.s.) *k-ni* tüketmek; ~ the night gecelemek, konaklamak; *v/i.* kuvveti azalmak; sarfolunmak; ¹spend.er *n.* müsrif, mirasyedi.

**spend-thrift** [¹spendθrift] **1.** *n.* müsrif, mirasyedi kimse; **2.** *adj.* müsrif(ce), mirasyedi.

**spent** [spɛnt] **1.** *pret. & p.p. of* spend; **2.** *adj.* tükenmiş, bitkin, yorgun; harcanmış, sarfedilmiş.

**sperm** [spəːm] *n.* sperma, belsuyu, meni; **sper.ma.ce.ti** [~məˡseti] *n.* ispermeçet, balinadan çıkarılan bir tür yağ; **sper.ma.to.zo.on** *biol.* [~ətəuˡzəuɔn] *n.* sperma hayvancığı.

**spew** [spjuː] *vb.* kus(tur)mak, istifrağ et(tir)mek.

**sphere** [sfiə] *n.* küre, yuvarlak, yerküre, arzküre; *fig.* muhit, çevre; alan, arazi, saha; sınıf, derece; **spher.i.cal** □ [¹sferikəl] küresel, yusyuvarlak.

**sphinc.ter** *anat.* [¹sfiŋktə] *n.* büzgen kas.

**sphinx** [sfiŋks] *n.* (i)sfenks; *fig.* anlaşılması güç ve konuşmayan kimse, esrarengiz adam.

**spice** [spais] **1.** *n.* bahar(at); *fig.* tat, çeşni; **2.** *v/t.* baharat koymak, çeşni vermek -e; ¹spic.er.y *n.* baharat.

**spic.i.ness** [¹spaisinis] *n.* çeşnili, aromatik oluş; *fig.* açık saçık oluş.

**spick and span** [¹spikənˡspæn] *adj.* yeni ve temiz, pırıl pırıl.

**spic.y** □ [¹spaisi] baharatlı, çeşnili; *fig.* açık saçık.

**spi.der** *zo.* [¹spaidə] *n.* örümcek; ¹spi.der.y *adj.* örümcek gibi; örümcekli; zarif, çok ince.

**spiel** *Am. sl.* [spiːl] *n.* konuşma, lafazanlık.

**spiff.y** *sl.* [¹spifi] *adj.* güzel, şık.

**spig.ot** [¹spigət] *n. (fıçı, varil)* tıpa, tıkaç, musluk.

**spike** [spaik] **1.** *n.* ince başsız çivi, uçlu demir, sivri uçlu şey; *spor.:* ayakkabı altına çakılan çivi parçaları, kabara; *mot.* ekser, enser; ⚥ başak; **2.** *v/t.* çivi ile tutturmak, ekserlemek; ✕ topu körletmek için falya deliğini çivi ile tıkamak; çivi ile delmek; **spike.nard** [ˈ~nɑːd] *n.* sümbül yağı; Hint sümbülü; **ˈspik.y** □ sivri uçlu, çivili.

**spill¹** [spil] 1. *(irr.) v/t.* dökmek, döküp saçmak; akıtmak *(kan)*; F üstünden atmak, düşürmek, fırlatmak *(süvari)*; F açığa vurmak, ifşa etm.; *v/i.* dökülmek, saçılmak; 2. *n.* dökme; F düşüş, düşme *(at vs.'den).*

**spill²** [~] *n.* lamba, pipo vs. yakmağa yarıyan kâğıt *veya* tahta parçası.

**spill.o.ver** [ˈspiləuvə] *n.* taşan şey; nüfus fazlalığı.

**spill.way** [ˈspilwei] *n.* taşma savağı.

**spilt** [spilt] *pret. & p.p. of* **spill¹** 1.; cry over ~ milk boşuna üzülmek, iş işten geçtikten sonra dövünmek.

**spin** [spin] 1. *(irr.) v/t.* eğirmek, bükmek *(a. fig.)*; döndürmek, çevirmek; tasarlayıp uydurmak; ~ s.th. out *bşi* uzatmak; *v/i.* iplik vs.'yi eğirmek; *a.* ~ round dönmek; ☈ dikine düşmek, vril yapmak; ~ along hızla geçip gitmek; send s.o. (ѕ.th.) ~ning *b-ni (bşi)* fırlatıp yere atmak; 2. *n.* (fırıl fırıl) dönme, devir; kısa gezinti; ☈ dikine düşüş.

**spin.ach** ☈ [ˈspinidʒ] *n.* ıspanak.

**spi.nal** [ˈspainl] *adj. anat.* belkemiğine ait, omurga...; ~ column belkemiği, omurga; ~ cord, ~ marrow omurilik; ~ curvature kamburluk, omurga eğriliği.

**spin.dle** [ˈspindl] *n.* iğ, eğirmen; mil, dingil; **ˈspin.dly** *adj.* uzun, ince ve zayıf görünüşlü, leylek bacaklı.

**spin-dri.er** [ˈspindraiə] *n.* santrifüjlü çamaşır kurutma makinesi.

**spin-drift** [ˈspindrift] *n.* dalga serpintisi.

**spine** [spain] *n. anat.* omurga, belkemiği; diken; sırt *(dağ, kitap)*; **ˈspine.less** *adj.* omurgasız *(hayvan)*; *fig.* cesaretsiz, yüreksiz.

**spin.et** ♪ [spiˈnet] *n.* spinet, bir tür küçük piyano.

**spin.na.ker** ⚓ [ˈspinəkə] *n.* üç köşe büyük yarış yelkeni.

**spin.ner** [ˈspinə] *n.* eğiren, iplikçi kimse; eğirme *veya* bükme makinesi; **spin.ner.et** *zo.* [ˈspinərət] *n.* örümcek ve ipekböceğinin iplik salan uzvundaki memeciklerden her biri.

**spin.ning...:** ~**-jenny** ⊕ [ˈspininˈdʒəni] *n.* iplik eğirme makinesi, çıkrık makinesi; **ˈ~-mill** *n.* iplikhane; **ˈ~-wheel** *n.* çıkrık.

**spin.ster** [ˈspinstə] *n.* kalık, yaşı geçmiş kız, evde kalmış, evlenmemiş kız.

**spin.y** [ˈspaini] *adj.* dikenli, iğneli; güçlüklerle dolu.

**spi.ra.cle** [ˈspaiərəkl] *n.* nefes alıp verme deliği.

**spi.rae.a** ⚘ [spaiˈriə] *n.* çayırmelikesi, erkeçsakalı.

**spi.ral** [ˈspaiərəl] 1. □ helezonî, burmalı, sarmal; 2. *n.* helis, helezon; *fig.* karışıklık, hercümerç; sarmal hareket; ⚘ spiral; 3. *vb.* helezon teşkil etm., dönmek.

**spire** [ˈspaiə] *n.* tepe *(kule, dağ, ağaç).*

**spir.it** [ˈspirit] 1. *n. com.* ruh, can; his, duyarlık; canlılık; cesaret; peri, cin; ◌̃ ispirto; alkol; ~s *pl.* huy, karakter; alkollü içkiler; ~ of wine şarap ruhu; in (high) ~s keyifli, neşeli; In low ~s kederli, üzgün; 2. *vb.* ~ away, ~ off gizlice götürmek *veya* göndermek, ortadan yok etm.; ~ up canlandırmak, şenlendirmek; cesaretlendirmek.

**spir.it.ed** □ [ˈspiritid] cesur, faal, canlı, esprili, nüktedan; **ˈspir.it.ed.ness** *n.* canlılık, şevk, cesaret.

**spir.it.ism** [ˈspiritizəm] *n.* ispritizma; **ˈspir.it.ist** *n.* ispiritizmaya inanan ve onunla ilgilenen kimse.

**spir.it.less** □ [ˈspiritlis] ruhsuz, cansız, hevessiz, sıkıcı; üzgün, neşesiz; korkak, yüreksiz.

**spir.it-lev.el** [ˈspiritlevl] *n.* tesviye ruhu, su terazisi.

**spir.it.u.al** [ˈspiritjuəl] 1. □ ruhanî, manevi, ruhî, ruhsal; dinî, kutsal; 2. *n.* Amerikan zencilerine özgü ilâhi; **ˈspir.it.u.al.ism** *n.* ispritizma, ruhanilik, ruhlara inanma; **spir.it.u.al.i.ty** [~ˈæliti] *n.* ruhanilik, manevilik, tinsellik, dua, ibadet vs. gibi dinî şeylere düşkünlük; **spir.it.u.al.ize** [ˈ~əlaiz] *v/t.* ruhanileştirmek, manevi değer kazandırmak.

**spir.it.u.el(le)** [spiritjuˈel] *adj.* zeki, akıllı, nüktedan, espri sahibi.

**spir.it.u.ous** [ˈspiritjuəs] *adj.* alkollü, ispirtolu.

**spirt** [spəːt] 1. *v/t. & v/i.* sıçra(t)mak, fışkır(t)mak *(su)*; anî hamle yapmak; 2. *n.* anî hamle; fışkır(t)ma *(su).*

**spit¹** [spit] 1. *n.* kebap şişi; *geogr.* dil; 2. *v/t.* şiş saplamak, şişlemek.

**spit²** [~] 1. *n.* tükürük, salya; be the very ~ of s.o. *b-ne* tıpatıp benzemek, ırak değip burnundan düşmüş olm.; 2. *(irr.) v/i.* tükürmek (on -*e*); tükürük saçarak konuşmak; *(kedi)* tıslamak; çiselemek, serpiştirmek; ~ at *(yüzüne)* tükürmek, hakaret etm.; ~ upon *(üstüne)* tükürmek; *v/t. (mst* ~ out) *bşi* tükürmek, tükürük gibi saçmak; ~ it out! F açıkla!, söyle!

**spit³** [~] *n.* bir bel boyu derinlik *(toprak).*

**spite** [spait] 1. *n.* kin, garaz, şer, kötülük; in ~ of -e rağmen; 2. *v/t.* kindarlık etm. -e, inadına yapmak -i, üzmek; kahretmek -i.

**spite.ful** □ ['spaitful] garazkâr, kinci; **'spite.ful.ness** *n.* kötülük, şer, garazkârlık.

**spit.fire** ['spitfaiǝ] *n.* çabuk öfkelenen, ateş püsküren kimse.

**spit.tle** ['spitl] *n.* tükürük, salya.

**spit.toon** [spi'tuːn] *n.* tükürük hokkası.

**spiv** *sl.* [spiv] *n.* karaborsacı, vurguncu, adi soyguncu.

**splash** [splæʃ] 1. *n.* zifos, sıçratılmış çamur *veya* su; su sıçratma (sesi); make a ~ F sükse yapmak, sansasyon yaratmak, dikkat çekmek; 2. *v/t. & v/i.* zifos atmak, su sıçratmak -e; etrafa sıçratarak suya dalmak, suya çarpmak; kötü resim yapmak; *sl.* reklamını yapmak; ~ one's money about *sl.* parasını saçıp savurmak; **'~.board** *n.* çamurluk, siper; **'~.down** *n.* denize inme (*uzay gemisi*); **'splash.y** □ ıslak, çamurlu, lekeli; F gösterişli.

**splay** [splei] 1. *n.* yayvanlık; meyilli kısım (*kapı, pencere vs.*), eğik kesilmiş kenar; 2. *vb.* dışa doğru meyletmek; yayılmak. genişlemek; 3. *adj.* geniş ve yayvan; eğik kesilmiş; **'~-foot** *n.* düztaban.

**spleen** [spliːn] *n. anat.* dalak; huysuzluk, terslik, kızgınlık, öfke, kin; **spleen.ful** ['~ful], **spleen.y** *adj.* kızgın, aksi, ters, huysuz, somurtkan.

**splen.did** □ ['splendid] parlak, gösterişli; mükemmel, fevkalâde, enfes; **splen.dif.er.ous** F [~'difǝrǝs] = splendid; **'splen.do(u)r** *n.* parlaklık, parıltı, şaşaa, ihtişam, debdebe, heybet, tantana.

**sple.net.ic** [spli'netik] 1. *a.* **sple'net.i.cal** □ aksi, ters, kızgın, öfkeli; 2. *n.* hipokondriyak, titiz, merak hastalığı olan kimse.

**splice** [splais] 1. *n.* iki ucu birbirine ekleme, dikiş; ⅃ fazla içki alma; 2. *vb.* iki ucu örerek birbirine eklemek; iki tahtayı birbirine çivileyerek tutturmak; yapıştırarak eklemek (*band, film*); ⅃ fazla içki hakkını vermek; ⊕ eklemek; *sl.* evlen(dir)mek.

**splint** ⸮ [splint] 1. *n.* cebire, süyek, kırık tahtası; 2. *vb.* kırık tahtası ile çıkık (*veya* kırık) bağlamak; **'~-bone** *n. anat.* incik kemiği.

**splin.ter** ['splintǝ] 1. *n.* kıymık; küçük parça; 2. *v/t. & v/i.* parçala(n)mak, parça parça olm. *veya* etm.; yar(ıl)mak; **'splin-ter-proof** *adj.* mermi parçalarını geçir-

meyen; çatlamaz, dağılmaz.

**split** [split] 1. *n.* yarık, çatlak; *fig.* bölünme, ikiye ayrılma, hizipleşme; ~s *pl.* ayaklar ayrıkken elleri yere değdirme hareketi; 2. *adj.* yarılmış, çatlamış, ayrılmış; 3. *v/t.* yarmak, bölmek; ayırmak, dağıtmak; *v/i.* yarılmak, ayrılmak, çatlamak; ~ hairs kılı kırk yarmak; ~ one's sides with laughter *b-nin* gülmekten kasıkları çatlamak; ~ up bölünmek, taksim olm.; bölüştürmek; *fig.* araları açılmak, bozuşmak; ~ on *sl.* ispiyon etm., *b-ni* ele vermek; **'split.ting** *adj.* şiddetli, keskin; F delice, çılgınca (*sürat*).

**splotch** [splɔtʃ] *n.* leke, benek.

**splurge** [splǝːdʒ] *n.* gösteriş, fiyaka; savurganlık.

**splut.ter** ['splʌtǝ] *s.* sputter; *vb.* ↑ cızırdamak, boğulmak (*motor*).

**spoil** [spɔil] 1. *n. oft.* ~s *pl.* yağma, çapul, ganimet, karmanyola; *fig.* hasılat; moloz, süprüntü; 2. (*irr.*) *v/t.* zorla elinden almak, *b-den* bşi gaspetmek, yağma etm.; bozmak, mahvetmek; yüz vermek, nazlı alıştırmak (*çocuk*), şımartmak; *v/i.* bozulmak, çürümek, telef olm.; ~ing for a fight kavgacı, kavga arayan; **'spoil.er** *n.* eşkiya, haydut, korsan, karmanyolacı; *bşi* yüzüne gözüne bulaştıran, bozan kimse; **spoils.man** Am. *pol.* ['~zmǝn] *n.* koltuk avcısı; **'spoil-sport** *n.* oyunbozan, mızıkçı; **spoils system** Am. *pol.* çıkar sağlamak için kurulan rüşvet verme sistemi.

**spoilt** [spɔilt] *pret. & p.p. of* spoil 2.

**spoke**[1] [spǝuk] *pret. of* speak.

**spoke**[2] [~] *n.* tekerlek parmağı, basamak; ⅃ dümen dolabı parmaklığı.

**spo.ken** ['spǝukǝn] *p.p. of* speak.

**spokes.man** ['spǝuksmǝn] *n.* sözcü, başkası adına konuşan kimse.

**spo.li.a.tion** [spǝuli'eiʃǝn] *n.* yağma, çapul, soygun, talan.

**spon.dee** ['spɔndiː] *n.* iki uzun heceli sözcük.

**sponge** [spʌndʒ] 1. *n.* sünger; throw up the ~ *boks & fig.* havlu atmak, mücadeleden vazgeçmek; 2. *v/t.* süngerle silmek *veya* suyunu almak (*away, off*); ~ up emmek, suyu massetmek; *v/i.* tufeylilik (*veya* otlakçılık) etm. (on, from), başkasının kesesinden geçinmek; **'~-cake** *n.* pandispanya; **'spong.er** *n.* asalak, tufeyli, *fig.* otlakçı.

**spon.gi.ness** ['spʌndʒinis] *n.* sünger gibi oluş; **'spon.gy** *adj.* sünger gibi, mesameli, gözenekli.

**spon.sor** ['spɔnsǝ] 1. *n.* vaftiz babası; kefil; hami, koruyucu; reklâm giderlerini üstlenen firma; **2.** *v/t.* desteklemek *-i;* kefil olm. *-e;* korumak, himaye etm. *-i;* **'spon.sor.ship** *n.* kefalet, kefillik; destek. **spon.ta.ne.i.ty** [spɔntə'niːiti] *n.* kendiliğinden, ihtiyari olarak yapma *veya* olma, doğrudan doğruya, vasıtasız olma; **spon-ta.ne.ous** □ [~'teinjəs] kendiliğinden olan, ihtiyari, içten gelen; ⚹ hızlı büyüyen; ~ combustion içten yanma, kendiliğinden yanma; ~ generation cansızdan canlı oluşumu.

**spoof** *sl.* [spuːf] **1.** *v/t.* b-ni alaya almak, *b-ne* yalan yutturmak; **2.** *n.* süprüntü; ʂaçma; yalan, hilekârlık.

**spook** [spuːk] *n.* hayalet, hortlak; *Am. sl.* casus; **'spook.y** *adj.* hayalet gibi; tekin olmayan.

**spool** [spuːl] **1.** *n.* makara, bobin; **2.** *v/t.* makaraya sarmak.

**spoon** [spuːn] **1.** *n.* kaşık, kaşık şeklindeki şey; *sl.* deli divane, vurgun kimse; be ~s on *sl. b-ne* abayı yakmak; **2.** *vb.* kaşıklamak; *sl.* zevzeklik etm., oynaşmak *ile;* '~-drift *n.* rüzgârın denizden getirdiği su serpintisi; **'spoon.er.ism** *n.* ses *veya* heceleri konuşurken şaka olsun diye *veya* yanlışlıkla karıştırma *(örnek: 'gözünü aç' yerine 'açını göz');* **'spoon-fed** *adj. fig.* nazlı yetişmiş, şımarık; kaşıkla beslenmiş *(bebek);* **spoon.ful** [!~ful] *adj.* kaşık dolusu; **'spoon-meat** *n. (çocuk, hasta için)* lapa, bulamaç; **'spoon.y** □ F abayı yakmış (on).

**spoor** *hunt.* [spuə] *n.* vahşî hayvan izi. **spo.rad.ic** [spə'rædik] *adj.* (~ally) tektük, münferit, seyrek.

**spore** ⚹ [spɔː] *n.* spor.

**sport** [spɔːt] **1.** *n.* spor; oyun *(a. fig.);* eğlence, eğlenti; alay, şaka, latife; ~s *pl com.* atletik sporlar; spor bayramı, şöleni; *a.* good ~ iyi bir kimse; make ~ of *b-le* alay etm., *b-ni* alaya almak; **2.** *v/i.* takılmak (at, over *-e)*; oynamak; şaka söylemek; eğlenmek; *v/t.* övünmek *ile;* ~ one's oak F rahatsız edilmemek için kapıyı kapamak; **'sport.ing** □ spor-la ilgili. av... spor... sportmence, sportif; ~ chance kazanma olasılığı tanıma; **'spor.tive** □ eğlendirici; neşeli; oyun oynamayı seven; **'sports-car** *n. mot.* spor araba; **'sports-jack.et** *n.* spor ceket; **'sports-man** *n.* sporcu, sportmen; avcı; profesyonel kumarbaz; **'sports.man.like** *adj.* sportmence, sporcuya yakışır; **'sports.man.ship** *n.* sportmenlik, sporculuk; **'sports-wear** *n.* spor giysi; **'sports-wom.an** *n.* sporcu kadın.

**spot** [spɔt] **1.** *n. com.* nokta, benek, leke; kusur, şaibe, ayıp; yer, mevki; insan vücudunda leke, ben; sivilce, ergenlik; ~s *pl.* peşin parayla satılan mallar; ~ of F biraz, bir parça; on the ~ yerinde; derhal, hemen, doğrudan doğruya; be on the ~ hazır bulunmak; **2.** *adj.* peşin; rasgele; **3.** *v/t.* lekelemek *(a. fig.),* beneklemek; bulmak, keşfetmek, görmek; *v/i.* lekelenmek, benek benek olm.; F yağmur yağmak; **'spot.less** □ lekesiz, temiz; **'spot.less.ness** *n.* lekesizlik, temizlik; **'spot.light** *n. thea.* sahne projektörü; *mot.* müteharrik projektör; in the ~ *fig.* ön planda, dikkati çeken; **'spot.ted** *adj.* noktalı, lekeli, benekli; ~ fever ⚹ lekeli humma, tifüs; **'spot.ter** *n.* gözcü, gözetleyici, rasat eden kimse *veya* şey *(özellikle düşman uçaklarını);* Am. kontrolör, murakıp, müfettiş; **'spot.ti.ness** *n.* lekelilik; **'spot.ty** *adj.* lekeli, benekli, noktalı.

**spouse** [spauz] *n.* eş, koca, karı.

**spout** [spaut] **1.** *n.* bir kabın ağzı, ağız; emzik; jet borusu; △ oluk ağzı; fışkıran su; *v/t. & v/i.* fışkır(t)mak; F tumturaklı konuşmak.

**sprain** [sprein] **1.** *n.* burkulma *(mafsal);* *v/t.* burkmak.

**sprang** [spræŋ] *pret. of* spring 2.

**sprat** *ichth.* [spræt] *n.* çaçabalığı.

**sprawl** [sprɔːl] *v/i.* yerde uzanmak, *fig.* maça beyi gibi kurulmak, terbiyesizce uzanmak; ⚹ üremek, azmak, yayılmak; *v/t.* ~ out uzatmak, germek.

**spray**[1] [sprei] *n.* yapraklı ve çiçekli ufak dal *(süs için).*

**spray**[2] [~] **1.** *n.* (toz halinde) serpinti, sprey; çise, çisinti; püskürgeç; = ~er; **2.** *vb.* (toz halinde) serpmek, püskürtmek; **'spray.er** *n.* püskürteç, vaporizatör, pülverizatör, sprey.

**spread** [spred] **1.** *(irr.) v/t. a.* ~ out yaymak, sermek, açmak, genişletmek, uzatmak; neşretmek, yaymak *(söylenti, hastalık vs.);* sürmek *(yağ);* ~ the table sofrayı kurmak; *v/i.* yayılmak *(a. fig.),* genişlemek; **2.** *adj.* ~ eagle kanat ve ayakları gerilmiş durumda, uçan *(arma kartalı);* **3.** *n.* yayılma; genişlik, vüsat, enginlik; saha; kanatların yayılımı; Am. örtü, yorgan, çarşaf, sofra örtüsü; F ziyafet; '~-ea.gle *adj.* F gösterişçi; şoven; **'spread.er** *n.* yayan *veya* süren kimse *veya* şey; **'spread.ing** *adj.* geniş, yaygın, engin.

**spree** F [spriː] *n.* eğlence, cümbüş, âlem; go on a ~ âlem yapmak.

**sprig** [sprig] 1. *n.* ince dal, fışkın, sürgün; *fig.* delikanlı; ⊕ başsız çivi; 2. *vb.* başsız çivi ile sağlamlaştırmak; budamak; ince dallarla süslemek; ~ged *adj.* çiçekli, dallı, çiçek işlemeli.

**spright.li.ness** [ˈspraitlinis] *n.* canlılık, neşeli olma; **ˈspright.ly** *adj.* canlı, pürhayat, neşeli, şen.

**spring** [spriŋ] 1. *n.* sıçrayış, hamle, fırlama; helezoni yay; yay elastikiyeti; *tech.* yay, zemberek; kaynak, memba, pınar; *fig.* köken, menşe; (ilk)bahar; 2. *(irr.)* *v/t.* fırlatmak; parçalamak; birdenbire ortaya çıkarmak; av hayvanını yerinden çıkarmak; ~ a leak ⌄ su etmeğe başlamak; ~ s.th. on s.o. *b-ne* sürpriz yapmak; *v/i.* sıçramak, fırlamak; çıkmak (from -*den*); ✢ çimlenmek, filiz sürmek; ~ up fırlayıp ayağa kalkmak; doğmak *(fikir)*; baş göstermek; ~ into existence birdenbire doğmak, çıkmak; ˈ~ˈbal.ance *n.* yaylı terazi, kantar; ˈ~ˈboard *n.* tramplen, sıçrama tahtası.

**springe** *hunt.* [sprindʒ] *n.* ilmekli tuzak, kuş kapancası.

**spring gun** [ˈspriŋgʌn] *n.* kendiliğinden boşanan atım; **ˈspring.l.ness** *n.* elastikiyet, yaylılık; **spring mat.tress yaylı** somya; **spring tide** şiddetli met hareketi; **ˈspring.tide**, **ˈspring.time** *n.* **ilkbahar**; **ˈspring.y** □ yaylı, elastiki, esnek.

**sprin.kle** [ˈspriŋkl] *vb.* serpmek, ekmek, saçmak; sulamak; çiselemek *(yağmur)*; **ˈsprin.kler** *n.* sulama tesisatı, püskürgeç, pülverizatör; **ˈsprin.kling** *n.* az miktar, serpinti, çise; a ~ of *fig.* bir tutam, bir parça.

**sprint** [sprint] *spor:* 1. *v/i.* (tabana kuvvet) koşmak; 2. *n.* kısa koşu; sürat koşusu; **ˈsprint.er** *n.* kısa mesafe koşucusu.

**sprit** ⌄ [sprit] *n.* yan yelkenin sereni.

**sprite** [sprait] *n.* hayal(et); peri, cin.

**sprit.sail** ⌄ [ˈspritsl] *n.* yan yelken serenine açılan yelken.

**sprock.et-wheel** ⊕ [ˈsprɔkitwiːl] *n.* zincir dişlisi.

**sprout** [spraut] 1. *v/t.* & *v/i.* filizlenmek, tomurcuklanmak, bitmek; filiz sürdürmek; 2. *n.* ✢ filiz, fidan, tomurcuk; *a.* Brussels ~s Brüksel lahanası.

**spruce¹** □ [spruːs] 1. *adj.* şık, zarif; temiz, pak; 2. *vb.* (up) temiz ve şık giyinmek, çekidüzen vermek, derleyip toplamak.

**spruce²** ✢ [~] *n. a.* ~ fir ladin ağacı, alaçam.

**sprung** [sprʌŋ] *pret.* (◥) & *p.p. of* spring 2.

**spry** [sprai] *adj.* canlı, çevik, faal.

**spud** [spʌd] *n.* **çapa**, tirpidin, bahçe malası; F patates.

**spume** *lit.* [spjuːm] *n.* köpük; **ˈspu.mous**, **ˈspum.y** □ köpüklü.

**spun** [spʌn] *pret.* & *p.p. of* spin 1.

**spunk** [spʌŋk] *n.* kav, mantar kavı; alev, kıvılcım; F cesaret, yüreklilik; **ˈspunk.y** □ cesur, yiğit, mert.

**spur** [spəː] 1. *n.* mahmuz *(a. zo.)*; ✢ bazı çiçeklerde mahmuz şeklindeki çıkıntı; *fig.* güdü; saik, teşvik eden şey; çıkıntı, çıkma, cumba; dağ kolu; on the ~ of the moment anında, derhal, hemen; put *veya* set ~s to mahmuzlamak; *fig.* teşvik etm.; win one's ~s liyâkatini kanıtlamak; ~ gear ⊕ alın dişlisi, düz dişli çark; 2. *vb.* *a.* ~ on kışkırtmak (into -*e*); mahmuzlamak, dürtmek *(a. fig.)*; *poet.* atını dört nala koşturmak.

**spurge** ✢ [spəːdʒ] *n.* sütleğenotu.

**spu.ri.ous** □ [ˈspjuəriəs] sahte, taklit, yapma, suni; **ˈspu.ri.ous.ness** *n.* taklidi, benzeri olma.

**spurn** [spəːn] *v/t.* hor bakarak *bşe* tenezzül etmemek, hakaretle reddetmek, **hiçe** saymak.

**spurt** [spəːt] 1. *v/i.* ani hamle yapmak, davranmak; son derece artmak *(satış vs.)*; *spor:* finişe kalkmak; *s.* spirt; 2. *n.* ani hamle, kısa süre için gösterilen gayret; *spor:* finiş, ani hamle; *s.* spirt.

**sput.nik** [ˈsputnik] *n.* Sovyetler Birliği'nin uzaya gönderdiği ilk uydunun adı, sputnik.

**sput.ter** [ˈspʌtə] 1. *n.* tükürük saçma; kuru gürültü; 2. *vb.* tükürük saçmak; tükürük saçarak konuşmak (at s.o.); *a.* ~ out alelâcele ve anlaşılmaz söylemek; saçmak.

**spy** [spai] 1. *n.* casus, hafiye, ajan; 2. *v/i.* gözetlemek; casusluk etm.; ~ (up)on s.o. *b-ni* gizlice gözetlemek; ˈ~.glass *n.* küçük teleskop; ˈ~.hole *n.* gözetleme deliği.

**squab** [skwɔb] *n.* yavru güvercin.

**squab.ble** [ˈskwɔbl] 1. *n.* ağız kavgası, çekişme, hırgür; 2. *v/i.* kavga etm., çekişmek, dalaşmak; **ˈsquab.bler** *n.* kavgacı.

**squad** [skwɔd] *n.* takım, ekip, grup; **squad.ron** [ˈ~rən] *n.* ✕ suvari bölüğü; ◈ uçak bölüğü, uçak filosu; ⌄ filo.

**squal.id** □ [ˈskwɔlid] kirli, pis, bakımsız, sefil, perişan.

**squall¹** [skwɔːl] 1. *n.* yaygara, feryat, haykırış; ~s *pl.* bağrışma; 2. *v/i.* yaygara koparmak, bağrışmak, feryat etm.

**squall²** □ [~] *n.* bora, kasırga, az süren şiddetli rüzgâr; **ˈsquall.y** *adj.* ⌄ fırtınalı, boralı.

**squa.lor** ['skwɔlə] *n.* kir, pislik, sefalet, bakımsızlık.

**squa.mous** ['skweiməs] *adj.* pullu, kepekli, pul pul.

**squan.der** ['skwɔndə] *v/t.* boş yere harcamak, çarçur etm., israf etm., savurmak; **'~'ma.ni.a** *n.* savurganlık tutkunluğu.

**square** [skweə] **1.** □ dördül, kare şeklinde, dört köşeli; dikey, dik açılı (to, with -*e*, *ile*); uygun, münasip; düzenli; direkt, kesin, açık; tam, eşit (with *ile*); F namuslu, şerefli, dürüst; özlü, doyurucu; *Am.* F modası geçmiş, eski kafalı; ~ measure yüzey ölçü birimi; ~ mile mil kare *(259 hektar)*; (take a) ~ root *A* kare kök (almak); ~ sail ♣ dört köşe seren yelkeni; **2.** *n.* dördül, kare; gönye; *A* bir sayının ikinci kuvveti, kare; F bol ve doyurucu yemek; satranç tahtası; *A* sütun kaidesi; *X* kale *(veya* kare) nizamı; meydan, alan, saha; *Am.* F darkafalı adam; **3.** *v/t.* dört köşeli yapmak; *A -in* karesini almak; doğrultmak, düzlemek (with *ile*); *†* ödemek, tediye etm. -*i*; rüşvet vermek, para yedirmek -*e*; *v/i.* (with) uymak, muvafık gelmek; **'~-'built** *adj.* iri yapılı, kaba saba; ~ dance dört çiftle yapılan bir tür dans; **'~-'rigged** *adj.* ♣ dört köşe seren yelkeni olan, kabasorto; **'~-toed** *adj.* küt burunlu *(ayakkabı)*; eskiye düşkün, tutucu.

**squash¹** [skwɔf] **1.** *n.* ezme; şerbet, meyve suyu; ağır ve yumuşak bir şeyin düşmesi; raketle oynanan bir tür oyun; *mst* ~-hat geniş kenarlı şapka; **2.** *vb.* ezmek, sıkmak, bastırmak, son vermek -*e*; *fig.* bunaltmak; F *b-nin* ağzını tıkamak, susturmak -*i*, haddini bildirmek -*e*.

**squash²** ♣ [~] *n.* kabak.

**squat** [skwɔt] **1.** *adj.* çömelmiş; bodur, tıknaz; çok alçak *(bina)*; **2.** *v/i.* çömelmek; boş topraklara yerleşmek; **'squat-ter** *n.* boş bir mülkü işgal eden kimse; sahipsiz bir araziyi işgal eden kimse, gecekonduda oturan kimse; koyun yetiştirici *(Avustralyalı)*.

**squaw** [skwɔː] *n.* kızılderili kadın.

**squawk** [skwɔːk] **1.** *v/i.* cıyaklamak, acı acı bağırmak *(ördek vs.)*; **2.** *n.* cıyaklama, yaygara.

**squeak** [skwiːk] **1.** *v/i.* cırlamak; gıcırdamak *(kapı, yay vs.)*; *sl.* ihbar etm.; ele vermek; **2.** *n.* cırlama; gıcırtı; a narrow ~ F paçayı güçbelâ kurtarma; **'squeak.y** □ cızırtılı, gıcırtılı.

**squeal** [skwiːl] *v/i.* domuz gibi ses çıkarmak; vak vak etm., acı acı feryat etm.; *s.* squeak.

**squeam.ish** □ ['skwiːmiʃ] titiz, hassas, çabuk gücenen, müşkülpesent; çabuk tiksinen, midesi hemen bulanan; **'squeam-ish.ness** *n.* aşırı duyu, tiksinti.

**squee.gee** ['skwiːˈdʒiː] *n.* araba cam sileceğine benzer kısa saplı cam, tahta vs. silicisi; *phot.* lastik silindir.

**squeez.a.ble** ['skwiːzəbl] *adj.* uysal, uslu, munis.

**squeeze** [skwiːz] **1.** *v/t.* sık(ıştır)mak; *fig.* rahatsız etm., baskı yapmak; **2.** *n.* tazyik, baskı *(a. fig.)*, sıkıştırma; kuvvetli el sıkma; kalabalık, izdiham; **'squeez.er** *n.* sıkıştırma aygıtı, pres *(part. meyve)*.

**squelch** F [skweltʃ] *vb.* susturmak, bastırmak, son vermek -*e*; pestilini çıkarmak, hurdahaş etm.

**squib** [skwib] *n.* fişek, kestane fişeği, maytap; hiciv, yergi.

**squid** *zo.* [skwid] *n.* mürekkepbalığı.

**squif.fy** *sl.* ['skwifi] *adj.* çakırkeyf.

**squill** ♣ [skwil] *n.* adasoğanı.

**squint** [skwint] **1.** *v/i.* şaşı bakmak; yan bakmak; gözleri kısarak bakmak; **2.** *n.* şaşılık, şaşı bakma; F yan bakış; **'~-eyed** *adj.* şaşı; *fig.* kötü(cül), şerir.

**squire** ['skwaiə] **1.** *n.* asılzade; geniş arazi sahibi, bey, köy ağası; *Am.* F avukatlık *veya* yargıçlık ünvanı; *hist.* silahtar; *co.* kavalye; **2.** *v/t. (bir bayana)* refakat etm.

**squir(e).arch.y** ['skwaiəraːki] *n.* geniş arazi sahiplerinin hükümranlığı.

**squirm** F [skwəːm] *v/i.* kıvranmak.

**squir.rel** *zo.* ['skwirəl] *n.* sincap.

**squirt** [skwəːt] **1.** *n.* fışkıran su, fıskiye; fışkır(t)ma; F nanemolla, *k-ni* beğenmiş genç; **2.** *v/t. & v/i.* fışkır(t)mak.

**squish** F [skwiʃ] *n.* marmelat.

**stab** [stæb] **1.** *n.* bıçak yarası; bıçakla yaralama; F deneme; ~ in the back *fig.* arkadan vurma; **2.** *vb.* bıçaklamak; saplamak (at).

**sta.bil.i.ty** [stəˈbiliti] *n.* sağlamlık; istikrar, kararlılık, sebat; *♈* dinamik denge.

**sta.bi.li.za.tion** [steibilaiˈzeifən] *n.* dengede tutma, istikrar, stabilizasyon, sabit kılma *veya* olma; sağlamlaştırma.

**sta.bi.lize** ['steibilaiz] *v/t.* dengelemek, sağlamlaştırmak, sabit kılmak, istikrar kazandırmak, stabilize etm.; *♈* dengeyi sağlamak; **'sta.bi.liz.er** *n. ♈, ♣* dengeyi sağlayan aygıt.

**sta.ble¹** □ ['steibl] sağlam, dayanıklı, muhkem; sabit, sarsılmaz, devrilmez, değişmez; sürekli, kalıcı.

**sta.ble²** [~] **1.** *n.* ahır; *Am.* F ekip; **2.** *v/t.*

ahıra bağlamak, ahırda tutmak.
**sta.bling** ['steibliŋ] *n.* ahır ve ahır malzemesi.
**stac.ca.to** ♪ [stə'ka:təu] *adj.* her ses ayrı ve kesik kesik olarak.
**stack** [stæk] 1. *n.* ✓ saman, ot *vs.* yığını, tınaz, istif; baca; ✕ tüfek çatısı; raf *(büyük kütüphanelerde)*; ~s *pl part. Am.* kütüphanede kitap deposu; F bolluk, kalabalık, sürü; 2. *v/t.* yığmak, istif etm.
**sta.di.um** ['steidjəm] *n. spor:* stadyum, spor sahası, arena.
**staff** [sta:f] 1. *n.* değnek, asa, sopa; direk, gönder *(bayrak)*; destek, dayak, payanda; ✕ erkânıharbiye, kurmay; personel, kadro, bir kurumun çalışanları; öğretim kurulu; ♪ *pl.* staves [steivz] *n.* porte; 2. *vb.* personel, kadro *vs.'yi* sağlamak.
**stag** [stæg] *n. zo.* erkek geyik; F *(bir toplantı vs.'de)* bayansız erkek; † piyasaya yeni çıkan hisse senetleri üzerine borsa oynayan kimse.
**stage** [steidʒ] 1. *n.* sahne, meydan, saha; tiyatro; tiyatro sahnesi; safha, aşama, merhale; yapı iskelesi; konak; go on the ~ sahne hayatına atılmak; 2. *vb.* sahneye koymak; sahneye konmaya elverişli olm.; '~-coach *n.* posta arabası; '~-craft *n.* piyes yazma *veya* sahneye koyma sanatı; ~ di.rec.tion senaryo; ~ fright seyirci önünde korku, heyecan hali; ~ man.a.ger rejisör, sahne âmiri; 'stag.er: old ~ çok deneyimli kimse; 'stage.y = stagy.
**stag.ger** ['stægə] 1. *v/i.* sallanmak, sendelemek, sersemlemek; *fig.* tereddüt etm., kuşkulanmak; *v/t.* şaşırtmak, sersemletmek, hayrete düşürmek; ⊕ derecelere ayırmak, kademelendirmek; 2. *n.* sendeleme, sallanma, bocalama, kuşku; ⊕ derecelendirme, kademe; ~s *pl. vet. (at)* beyin hastalığı.
**stag.nan.cy** ['stægnənsi] *n.* durgunluk; kesatlık; 'stog.nant □ durgun *(su)*; atıl; † durgun, kesat; stag.nate [~'neit] *v/i.* durgunlaşmak, durgun olm., kesat gitmek; stag.na.tion *n.* durgunluk.
**stag-par.ty** F ['stægpα:ti] *n.* yalnız erkeklere mahsus toplantı, eğlence.
**stag.y** □ ['steidʒi] gösterişli, sahte tavırlı; aktör gibi, aktörce.
**staid** □ [steid] sakin, heyecansız, temkinli, ağırbaşlı, ciddi; 'staid.ness *n.* ağırbaşlılık, ciddiyet, sakin olma.
**stain** [stein] 1. *n.* leke *(a fig.)*; boya, vernik; benek; 2. *v/t.* lekelemek *(a. fig.)*, kirletmek, pisletmek; ⊕ abanoz renginde boyamak, *bşe* renk vermek; *v/i.* kir-

lenmek, lekelenmek, rengi kararmak; ~ed glass renkli cam; 'stain.less □ lekesiz; tertemiz; ⊕ paslanmaz.
**stair** [stɛə] *n.* basamak; ~s *pl.* merdiven; '~-car.pet *n.* merdiven halısı; '~.case *n.* merdiven, binanın merdiven bölümü; '~.rod *n.* merdiven halısı çubuğu; '~.way = staircase.
**stake** [steik] 1. *n.* kazık, direk; işkence direği; işkence direğinde ölüm cezası; kumarda ortaya konan para; çıkar, menfaat; ~s *pl. (at yarışı)* ödül; koşu, yarış; pull up ~s *Am.* F defolup gitmek; be at ~ tehlikede olm.; place one's ~ on varını yoğunu *bşe* bağlamak; 2. *v/t.* tehlikeye koymak, riske sokmak; kumarda para koymak; ~ out, ~ off sınırını kazıklarla işaretlemek.
**stal.ac.tite** ['stæləktait] *n.* sarkıt, iskalaktit; **stal.ag.mite** ['stæləgmait] *n.* dikit; iskalagmit.
**stale**[1] □ [steil] taze olmayan, dura dura bozulmuş, tatsız, bozuk *(su, haber vs.)*, bayat *(ekmek)*; bitkin, yorgun, tükenmiş *(güç, hava vs.)*; eski, bayat *(espri)*.
**stale**[2] [~] 1. *v/i.* kaşanmak, işemek *(at)*; 2. *n.* idrar, sidik *(at, sığır)*.
**stale.mate** ['steil'meit] 1. *n. satranç:* pata; *fig.* açmaz, çıkmaz, kitlenme; 2. *v/t.* satranç: pata duruma getirmek; *fig.* durdurmak, çıkmaza sokmak.
**stalk**[1] [stɔ:k] *n.* sap, bitki sapı.
**stalk**[2] [~] 1. *v/i.* azametle yürümek; *hunt.* sezdirmeden ava yaklaşmak; *v/t.* sinsice takip etm.; 2. *n. hunt.* sezdirmeden ava yaklaşma; 'stalk.er *n.* iz üstündeki avcı; 'stalk.ing-horse *n. fig.* bahane, ardına gizlenilen şey.
**stall** [stɔ:l] 1. *n.* ahır *(bölmesi)*; sergi, satış yeri, tezgâh, büfe *(gazete vs.)*; soyunma kabini; *thea.* koltuk; *eccl.* kısmen kapalı koro sandalyeleri; 2. *v/t.* ahıra kapamak; † hızını düşürmek; *mot.* durdurmak, stop etm.; *v/i. mot.* durmak; † hız kaybedip düşmek; *fig.* oyalamak, ağız yapmak, estek köstek etm.; '~-feed.ing *n.* ahırda besleme.
**stal.lion** ['stæljən] *n.* aygır, damızlık at.
**stal.wart** ['stɔ:lwət] 1. □ kuvvetli, iri yapılı; cesur, gözüpek; güvenilir; 2. *n. pol.* sadık, tuttuğu yoldan ayrılmayan kimse, güvenilir taraftar.
**sta.men** ♀ ['steimen] *n.* ercik, stamen, erkeklik uzvu; **stam.i.na** ['stæminə] *n.* dayanıklılık, güç, canlılık, tahammül; **stam.i.nate** ♀ ['~-nit] *adj.* ercikli, erkeklik uzvu olan *veya* üreten.
**stam.mer** ['stæmə] 1. *v/i.* kekelemek, pe-

pelemek; **2.** *n.* kekemelik; **¹stam.mer.er** *n.* kekeme.

**stamp** [stæmp] **1.** *n.* tepinme, ayağını yere vurma; ⊕ tokmak, şahmerdan; damga, mühür, alâmeti farika; ıstampa; zımba; *fig.* alâmet, iz; pul, posta pulu; kabartma şekil; cins, nitelik, tür; **2.** *v/t.* tepinmek, ayağıyle yere vurmak; şekil vermek, kalıba sokmak; zımbalamak; damgalamak, mühürlemek -i; pul yapıştırmak -e; ~ on the memory hafızasına yerleştirmek; ~ out ayağiyle ezmek, çiğnemek; *fig.* kökünü kurutmak; *v/i.* ayağiyle yere vurup ses çıkarmak; **¹~-al.bum** *n.* pul albümü; **¹~-col.lec.tor** *n.* filatelist, pul koleksiyoncusu; **¹~-deal.er** *n.* pul satıcısı; **¹~-du.ty** *n.* damga resmi.

**stam.pede** [stæm¹piːd] **1.** *n.* panik, bozgun, izdiham; **2.** *v/t. & v/i.* panik halinde kaç(ır)mak

**stamp.er** [¹stæmpə] *n.* tokmak, tokaç; damga, mühür, ıstampa, zımba; **¹stamp-(.ing)-mill** *n. metall.* maden filizi kırma makinesi.

**stance** [stæns] *n. golf:* topa vururken bacakların duruş şekli.

**stanch** [staːntʃ] **1.** *v/t.* durdurmak *(kan)*, alıkoymak; **2.** *adj.* = staunch 1; **stan.chion** [¹staːnʃən] *n.* destek, dayak, payanda, kazık.

**stand** [stænd] **1.** *(irr.) v/i. com.* durmak, olmak, bulunmak, mevcut olm.; sebat etm.; *mst* ~ still yerinde durmak, kımıldamamak, (ayakta) durmak; ~ against karşı koymak, kafa' tutmak -e; ~ aside bir kenara çekilmek; ~ back, ~ clear geri çekilmek, gerilemek; ~ by yanında durmak, hazır beklemek; *fig.* ilgisiz kalmak, arka çıkmamak; ~ for manası olm.; talip olm., istemek; *Am. parl.* aday olm.; *b-ne* sahip çıkmak, kayırmak; *b-ni* temsil etm.; F hoşgörmek, nazını çekmek; ~ in dublörlük yapmak, *b-nin* yerine iş görmek (for); ⟂ karaya yanaşmak; ~ in with araları iyi olm.; ~ off uzak durmak, gerilemek; ⟂ denize doğru açılmak; ~ off! çekil oradan!; ~ on ısrar etm. -de; ~ out fırlamak; *fig.* göze çarpmak; iyice belirmek, kontras teşkil etm. (against); *k-ni* uzak(ta) tutmak; karşı koymak, dayanmak (against); bildiğinden şaşmamak (for); ⟂ denize açılmak; ~ over olduğu yerde hareketsiz kalmak; ertelenmek; ~ pat *Am.* F dikkafalılık etm., düşüncesinde ısrar etm.; ~ to -in üzerinde ısrar etm.; *s.* reason; ~ to! × tüfek as!; ~ up ayağa kalkmak; *fig.* yükselmek; ~ up for taraftarı olm. -in,

*b-ne* sahip çıkmak; ~ up to cesaretle karşılamak, dayanmak; ~ upon -in üzerinde ısrar etm.; *-in* tarafını tutmak; *v/t.* bir yere koymak, dikmek; dayanmak, tahammül etm., katlanmak *-e; s.* ground; ~ s.o. a dinner F *b-ne* yemek ikram etm.; *s.* treat; **2.** *n.* durma, duruş; ayaklık, sehpa, askı; satış sergisi; tezgâh; durak; direnme; vaziyet, durum; durma; seyirci tribünü; hatip kürsüsü; *part. Am.* mahkemede tanık yeri; make a *veya* one's ~ against dayanmak, mukavemet etm. *-e*, karşı koymak *-e*.

**stan.dard** [¹stændəd] **1.** *n.* sancak, flama, bayrak; standart, model, tekbiçim, norm(a); mikyas, ölçü; düzey, seviye, derece; *(ilkokul)* sınıf; para ayarı; direk, çubuk; ♀ gövdesi ağaç gibi büyüyen bir tür çalı; ~ lamp ayaklı lamba; ~ of living hayat standardı; **2.** *adj.* standart, genel, herkesçe kabul edilen, normal..., ölçü olarak kabul edilmiş; **¹~-bear.er** *n. part. fig.* bayraktar, sancaktar; parti vs. lideri; **¹~-ga(u)ge** *adj.* 🚇 standart ray aralığı *(1,435 m);* **stand.ard.i.za.tion** [~ai¹zeiʃən] *n.* standartlaştırma, standardizasyon, ayarlama, tek tipe indirme; normalleştirme; **¹stand.ard.ize** *v/t.* belirli bir ölçüye uydurmak, standardize etm., tek tipe indirmek, ayarlamak, kararlaştırmak.

**stand-by** [¹stændbai] *n.* yardım, destek, himaye; yedek, hazır bekleyen *b-i veya bş.*

**stand.ee** [¹stæn¹diː] *n.* ayakta kalan kimse *(yer olmadığı için).*

**stand.er-by** [¹stændə¹bai] *n.* yanında duran kimse; seyirci.

**stand-in** [¹stænd¹in] *n. film:* dublör.

**stand.ing** [¹stændin] **1.** ☐ ayakta (duran); sabit, devamlı, değişmez; dayanıklı; ~ committee *pol.* daimi encümen; ~ jump ayakta sıçrayış, atlama; ~ orders *pl. parl.* iç tüzük; **2.** *n.* ayakta durma; durum, vaziyet; mevki, şöhret, şan; süreklilik, devam; of long ~ çoktan beri devam eden, eski; **¹~-room** *n.* ayakta duracak yer.

**stand...;** **¹~-off** *n. Am.* karşı kuvvet, etkisiz bırakma; ilgisizlik; erteleme; *(oyun)* denklik, beraberlik; **¹~-off.ish** *adj.* ilgisiz; soğukneva; ~¹pat.ter *n. Am.* F *pol.* tutucu, değişikliğe karşı olan kimse; **¹~-pipe** *n.* dikme boru; yangın musluğu; **¹~.point** *n.* bakım, görüş *(noktası);* **¹~.still** *n.* durma, duraklama; be at a ~ yerinden kımıldanmamak, durgun halde olm.; come to a ~ duraklamak, sekteye uğramak; **¹~-up** *adj.;* ~ collar dik yaka;

**~ fight** kurallara uygun mücadele, müsabaka; **~ supper** ayakta yenen soğuk yemekler.

**stank** [stæŋk] *pret. of* stink 2.

**stan.nic** ʔ ['stænik] *adj.* kalay cinsinden, kalaya ait.

**stan.za** ['stænzə] *n.* şiirde stans denilen kıta şekli, kıta, kesim.

**sta.ple¹** ['steipl] **1.** *n.* başlıca ürün; *fig.* başlıca konu, esas; hammadde; elyaf, lif; **2.** *adj.* başlıca, esas, temel...

**sta.ple²** [~] *n.* U şeklindeki kanca; iki başlı çivi; tel raptiye, zımba.

**sta.pler** ['steiplə] *n.* zımba.

**star** [staː] **1.** *n.* yıldız; yıldız işareti; *fig.* talih, kader; *thea.* sahne yıldızı; ²s and Stripes *pl.* Am. A.B.D.'nin bayrağı; **2.** *v/t.* yıldızla işaret koymak; *v/i. thea.* başrolde oynamak; *fig.* birinci rolü oynamak; **~** (it) parlamak; *thea.* misafir sanatçı olarak oynamak; **~ring** başrolde...

**star.board** ⚓ ['staːbəd] **1.** *n.* sancak, geminin sancak tarafı; **2.** *adj.* sancak tarafında olan *(dümen)*.

**starch** [staːt∫] **1.** *n.* nişasta; kola; *fig.* katılık, sertlik; **~ flour** nişasta; **2.** *v/i.* kolalamak; **~ed** *adj. fig.* sert, katı; **'starch-i.ness** *n.* sertlik, katılık; **'starch.y** □ nişastalı; kolalı; sert, katı, soğuk tavırlı.

**stare** [stɛə] **1.** *n.* sabit bakış, bakışların bir noktaya takılıp kalması; **2.** *v/i.* dik bakmak (at -e), uzun uzun bakmak, bakakalmak, hayretle bakmak (at -e).

**star.fish** *zo.* ['staːfi∫] *n.* denizyıldızı.

**star.ing** □ ['stɛərin] sabit, hareketsiz *(bakış)*; göze çarpan, göz kamaştırıcı, çok parlak.

**stark** [staːk] *adj.* sert, kaskatı, dik; bütün bütün, tam; sade; *adv.* büsbütün, tamamen; **~ naked** çırılçıplak.

**star.light** ['staːlait] *n.* yıldız ışığı.

**star.ling¹** *orn.* ['staːliŋ] *n.* sığırcık.

**star.ling²** [~] *n.* buzkıran *(köprü)*.

**star.lit** ['staːlit] *adj.* yıldızlarla aydınlanmış.

**star.ry** ['staːri] *adj.* yıldızlı, yıldızlarla dolu.

**star-span.gled** ['staːspæŋgld] *adj.* yıldızlarla süslü; Star-Spangled Banner Am. A.B.D.'nin bayrağı.

**start** [staːt] **1.** *n.* başlangıç, başlama; anî hareket; irkilme; start, çıkış; yola koyulma; kalkış; sıçrama; *fig.* avans, avantaj; get the **~** of s.o. *b-den* önce başlamak; give a **~** ürküp yerinden fırlamak; *(yarış)* avans vermek; *s.* fit²; **2.** *v/i.* ürkmek, sıçramak; ani bir hareket yapmak

(at); *spor:* start yapmak, çıkmak; hareket etm., yola çıkmak; yola düzülmek (for -e); *fig. (düşünce vs.)* -den yola çıkmak, başlamak (on -e; doing -meğe) to **~** with her şeyden önce, ilk iş olarak; *v/t.* harekete geçirmek, çalıştırmak -i, işletmek *(makine)*; *spor:* başlatmak; vahşi av hayvanını yerinden çıkarmak; *fig.* teşebbüs etm. -e; bşe teşvik etm., sevketmek (doing); kurmak, tesis etm. *(iş)*; ortaya atmak, yöneltmek *(soru)*.

**start.er** ['staːtə] *n.* *spor:* starter, çıkış işareti veren; koşucu, müsabık; *mot.* marş.

**start.ing-point** ['staːtiŋpɔint] *n.* başlama noktası, hareket noktası.

**star.tle** ['staːtl] *v/t.* ürkütmek, korkutmak; **'star.tling** □ şaşırtıcı, sansasyonel; ürkütücü.

**star.va.tion** [staːˈvei∫ən] *n.* açlık(tan ölme); **starve** *v/t. & v/i.* açlıktan öl(dür)mek; *fig.* mahrum olm., özlemini çekmek (for, of -den, -in); **starve.ling** ['~liŋ] **1.** *n.* dilenci, açlıktan ölecek durumda olan *b-i* veya *bş*; *fig.* cılız, kavruk kimse; **2.** *adj.* açlıktan ölecek durumda, çok zayıf; *fig.* perişan, yoksul, sefil.

**state** [steit] **1.** *n.* hal, durum; görkem, ihtişam, debdebe; devlet; *pol. mst* ² hükümet; eyalet; **~** of life sosyal mevki; in **~** merasimle yapılan, debdebeli; get into a **~** F heyecanlanmak, sinirlenmek; **2.** *v/t.* beyan etm., belirtmek; tayin etm., saptamak, tesbit etm.; **~ a.part.ment** gösterişli salon; **~ coach** büyük merasim arabası; **'~.craft** *n. pol.* devlet idaresi, devletçilik; ² De.part.ment Am. pol. Dışişleri Bakanlığı; **'state.less** *adj.* vatansız, tabiyetsiz; **'state.li.ness** *n.* haşmetli olma; ihtişam, lüks; **'state.ly** *adj.* haşmetli, heybetli; görkemli; **'state.ment** *n.* ifade; demeç; rapor; ⊤ (of account) hesap raporu, hesap hülâsası; ⊕, ⊤ tarife, cetvel; **'state room** *n.* ⬇ tek kişilik kamara; yataklı vagon kompartmanı; merasim odası; **'state.side** *adj.* Am. F A.B.D.'de olan, A.B.D...; go **~** *(eve, yurda)* dönmek.

**states.man** ['steitsmən] *n.* devlet adamı; **'states.man.like** *adj.* devlet adamına yakışır, akıllı ve tedbirli; **'states.man.ship** *n.* siyaset, devlet idaresi sanatı.

**stat.ic** ['stætik] *adj. phys.* statik, değişmeyen, duruk: sakin...; **'stat.ics** *n. pl. veya sg.* nesneler arasında dengeyi sağlayan güçleri inceleyen bilim, statik ilmi; *radyo:* parazit.

**sta.tion** ['stei∫ən] **1.** *n.* durak; yer, mevki; ✕, ⬇, ⬛ istasyon, gar; radyo, TV istasyonu; makam, rütbe; sosyal durum, derece; ✻ meslek, iş; *(TV)* kanal; ✗, ⬦ özel görev yeri, karakol; **2.** *v/t.* yerleştirmek, bir yere tayin etm.; **sta.tion.ar.y** ☐ [ˡ~ʃnəri] sabit, hareketsiz; ~ engine sabit makine; **ˡsta.tion.er** *n.* kırtasiyeci; ℒsˡ Holl İngiltere'de bir kitabın telif hakkını almak üzere kaydedilen daire; **ˡsta.tion.er.y** *n.* kırtasiye, yazı malzemesi; **sta.tion-mas.ter** [ˡ~ʃənmɑːstə] *n.* 🏠 istasyon müdürü; **sta.tion wag.on** *Am. mot.* pikap, kaptıkaçtı.

**sta.tis.ti.cal** ☐ [stəˡtistikəl] istatistikî, istatistikle ilgili, istatistiğe dayanan; **siat.is.ti.cian** [stætisˡtiʃən] *n.* istatistik uzmanı; **statˡis.tics** *n. pl.* istatistik (bilimi); vital ~ nüfus istatistiği.

**stat.u.ar.y** [ˡstætjuəri] **1.** *adj.* heykeltraşlıkla ilgili, heykel...; **2.** *n.* heykeltraşlık; heykeller; heykeltraş; **stat.ue** [ˡ~tʃuː] *n.* heykel; **stat.u.esque** ☐ [~tjuˡesk] heykel gibi; **stat.u.ette** [~tjuˡet] *n.* küçük heykel, heykelcik.

**stat.ure** [ˡstætʃə] *n.* boy bos, endam, şekil; kişilik.

**sta.tus** [ˡsteitəs] *n.* durum, hal, vaziyet; sosyal durum, sınıf; medeni hal.

**stat.ute** [ˡstætjuːt] *n.* kanun, yasa; kural, nizamname, statü; emir, hüküm; ˡ~-book *n.* yasalar kitabı, kanunname; ~ law yazılı hukuk; ~ mile bir mil *(1,609 km.)*. **stat.u.to.ry** ☐ [ˡstætjutəri] yasal, meşru.

**staunch** [stɔːntʃ] **1.** ☐ sağlam, kuvvetli; güvenilir, sadık; **2.** *v/t.* durdurmak, akmasını önlemek *(part. kan)*.

**stave** [steiv] **1.** *n.* fıçı tahtası; değnek, çubuk; *poet.* kıta, beyit; **2.** *(irr.) vb. mst* ~ in döşeme vs.'yi kırmak, delmek; ~ off defetmek, savmak, uzaklaştırmak; geciktirmek.

**staves** ♪ [steivz] *pl. of* staff 1.

**stay** [stei] **1.** *n.* ⬦ istralya; *fig.* destek, payanda; kalma, ikamet, kalış, durma; oturma, ziyaret; tehir, erteleme; ~s *pl.* † korse; **2.** *v/t. & v/i.* dur(dur)mak, alıkoymak; tehir etm., ertelemek; kalmak; beklemek; dayanmak, devam etm. *-e*; desteklemek; geçici olarak gidermek, bastırmak *(açlık)*; ~ away gelmemek; ~ in evde kalmak, dışarı çıkmamak; ~ for b-ne bakmak; ~ (for) supper akşam yemeğine kalmak; ~ put F yerinden kımıldamamak; ~ up uyatmamak; ~ the course sonuna kadar dayanmak, sabretmek; ~ing power dayanma gücü, metanet; ˡ~-at-home *n.* evinden dışarı çıkmayan kimse, kül kedisi; ˡ~-ˡdown strike oturma grevi; **ˡstay.er** *n.* spor: yarışı tamam-

layan koşucu *veya* at; be a good ~ sonuna kadar dayanmak, yarışı tamamlamak.

**stead** [sted] *n.* başkasının yeri; yer, mevki; in his ~ onun yerine; stand s.o. in good ~ b-ne yararlı olm., b-ne faydası dokunmak.

**stead.fast** ☐ [ˡstedfəst] sabit, sarsılmaz. metin; sabırlı; sadık; **ˡstead.fast.ness** *n.* sebat.

**stead.i.ness** [ˡstedinis] *n.* sebat, metanet.

**stead.y** [ˡstedi] **1.** ☐ devamlı, düzenli, sürekli; sabit, sarsılmaz; sakin, sessiz, ağırbaşlı; † sağlam, sarsılmaz, güvenilir; **2.** *v/t. & v/i.* sabit kılmak; sağlamlaş(tır)mak; yatış(tır)mak, teskin etm. *veya* olm.; **3.** *n. Am.* devamlı çıkılan karşı cinsten arkadaş.

**steak** [steik] *n.* biftek, fileto, kontrfile.

**steal** [stiːl] **1.** *(irr.) v/t.* çalmak, aşırmak *(a. fig.)*; ~ a march on s.o. *b-den* önce davranmak; *v/i.* gizlice hareket etm.; ~ into sokulmak, gizlice girmek; **2.** *n. Am.* çalıntı mal; hırsızlık; *sl.* kelepir.

**stealth** [stelθ] *n.* gizlilik; gizli iş *veya* girişim; by ~ gizlice; **ˡstealth.i.ness** *n.* gizlilik; sinsilik; **ˡstealth.y** ☐ gizli, hırsızlama; sinsi.

**steam** [stiːm] **1.** *n.* buhar, istim; buğu; F güç, enerji; F öfke, hiddet; let off ~ ⊕ buhar salıvermek, istim boşaltmak; *fig.* içini döküp rahatlamak; **2.** *attr.* buharlı, buhar...; **3.** *v/i.* buhar salıvermek; buharla hareket etm.; ~ up buğulanmak *(cam)*; *v/t.* buharda pişirmek, buğulamak; ˡ~.boat *n.* buharlı vapur; ˡ~-boil.er *n.* buhar kazanı; **steamed** *adj.* buğulu *(pencere)*; **ˡsteam-en.gine** *n.* buhar makinesi; **steam.er** *n.* ⬦ vapur; ⊕ buharla yemek pişirmeye *(veya* eşya yıkamaya) yarayan kap; **ˡsteam.i.ness** *n.* buharlılık. **steam...:** ˡ~-roller **1.** *n.* buharlı yol silindiri; *fig.* ezici güç; **2.** *v/t. fig.* zorla elde etm., ezmek; ˡ~.ship *n.* = steamboat; ~ tug ⬦ şilep, romorkör; **ˡsteam.y** ☐ buharlı; buğulu, sisli.

**ste.a.rin** 🜂 [ˡstiərin] *n.* stearin.

**steed** *rhet.* [stiːd] *n.* at.

**steel** [stiːl] **1.** *n.* çelik; çelik bileği, masat; büyük güç; **2.** *adj.* çelik gibi sağlam, çelikten; **3.** *v/t.* çelik gibi sertleştirmek, çelik gibi yapmak, katılaştırmak; ˡ~-clad *adj.* çelik zırh giymiş; ~ en-grav.ing *n.* çelik levha üzerine gravür; ˡ~-ˡplat.ed *adj.* çelik zırhlı; ˡ~-works *n.* çelik fabrikası; **ˡsteel.y** *adj. mst fig.* sert, çelik gibi, çelikten; **ˡsteel.yard** *n.* kollu el kantarı.

**steep¹** [sti:p] **1.** *adj.* dik, sarp, yalçın; F aşırı, yüksek *(fiyat);* **2.** *n. poet.* dik yokuş.

**steep²** [~] *vb.* suya batırmak, ıslatmak; *fig.* içine dalmak, *bşin* içine gömülmek (in).

**steep.en** [ˈsti:pən] *v/t.* & *v/i.* dikleş(tir)mek.

**stee.ple** [ˈsti:pl] *n.* kilise kulesi, çan kulesi; '~-chase *n.* engelli yarış; '~-jack *n.* kule *veya* baca işçisi.

**steep.ness** [ˈsti:pnis] *n.* diklik, sarplık.

**steer¹** [stiə] *n.* boğa; öküz.

**steer²** [~] *v/t.* (dümenle) idare etm., yönetmek; ~ clear of *fig.* sakınmak, uzak durmak; '~steer.a.ble *adj.* yönetilebilir, idare edilebilir.

**steer.age** ⊥ [ˈstiəridʒ] *n.* dümen kullanma; ara güverte; '~-way *n.* ⊥ geminin dümen dinlemesi için gerekli asgari hız.

**steer.ing...** [ˈstiəriŋ]: ~ col.umn *mot.* direksiyon mili; '~-gear *n.* ⊥ dümen donanımı, '~-wheel *n.* direksiyon.

**steers.man** ⊥ [ˈstiəzmən] *n.* dümenci, serdümen.

**stein** [stain] *n.* büyük bira bardağı *(1 lt. 'lik).*

**stel.lar** [ˈstelə] *adj.* yıldızlarla ilgili.

**stem¹** [stem] **1.** *n.* ağaç gövdesi; sap, kol; sözcük kökü; pipo sapı; **2.** *vb.* saplarını koparmak; *Am.* gelmek, çıkmak (from -den), *b-nin* neslinden olm.

**stem²** [~] **1.** *n.* ⊥ geminin baş bodoslaması; pruva; **2.** *vb.* karşı durmak, dayanmak, mücadele etm.; *(kayak)* göğüs verip ilerlemek; ~(ming) turn eğri duruş.

**stench** [stentʃ] *n.* pis koku.

**sten.cil** [ˈstensl] **1.** *n.* kalıp, klişe, şablon, model, patron, matris; mumlu kâğıt, stensil; **2.** *vb.* kalıpla örneğini çıkarmak; teksir makinesiyle çoğaltmak.

**ste.nog.ra.pher** [steˈnɔgrəfə] *n.* **stenograf; sten.o.graph.ic** [~nɔˈgræfik] *adj.* (~ally) stenografik; **ste.nog.ra.phy** [~nɔgrəfi] *n.* stenografi.

**step** [step] **1.** *n.* adım; basamak, eşik; *fig.* kısa yol; ayak sesi; ayak izi; kademe, derece; girişim, eylem; (a pair of) ~s *pl.* evin dışındaki taş merdiven; in ~ with ayak uydurarak *ile;* take ~s bşe önlem almak, girişmek, yapmağa kalkmak; **2.** *v/i.* adım atmak, girmek (into -e), ayak basmak (on -e); ~ in *fig.* bşe karışmak, müdahale etm.; ~ on it! *sl.* çabuk ol!; ~ out geniş adımlarla hızlanmak; acele etm.; *v/t.* ~ out, ~ off adımla ölçmek, adımlamak; ~ up arttırmak, hızlandırmak; *fig.* canlandırmak.

**step²** [~] *prefix* üvey...; '~.fa.ther *n.* üvey baba; '~.moth.er *n.* üvey ana.

**steppe** [step] *n.* bozkır, step.

**step.ping-stone** [ˈstepiŋstəun] *n.* atlama taşı; *fig.* basamak,

**ster.e.o** [ˈstiəriəu] **1.** *n. typ.* klişe; **2.** *adj.* ♪ stereo...

**ster.e.o...** [ˈstiəriə]: ~.phon.ic [~ˈfɔnik] *adj.* stereofonik, iki ayrı sesli, stereo...; '~.scope *n.* stereoskop; '~.type **1.** *n.* stereotip, sayfa halinde baskı klişesi; *fig.* basmakalıp söz; **2.** *vb.* bir kalıba sokmak; stereotipten basmak; ~d stereotip, basmakalıp, klişe.

**ster.ile** [ˈsterail] *adj.* kısır, ürün vermeyen; verimsiz; mikropsuz; **ste.ril.i.ty** [~ˈriliti] *n.* kısırlık, verimsizlik; **ster.il.i.za.tion** [sterilaiˈzeiʃən] *n.* kısırlaştırma; mikroptan arındırma, sterilize etme; **'ster.i.lize** *v/t.* kısırlaştırmak; sterilize etm., mikroptan arındırmak.

**ster.ling** [ˈstə:liŋ] *adj.* kıymetli, değerli; halis, gerçek, hakiki, esaslı; ✝ sterlinle ödenebilen; pound ~ İngiliz lirası; sterlin; ~ a.re.a İngiliz lirası kullanılan ülkeler bloku.

**stern¹** □ [stə:n] *adj.* ciddî, ağırbaşlı; acımasız, sert, haşin, katı; şiddetli.

**stern²** ⊥ [~] *n.* kıç, pupa.

**stern.ness** [ˈstə:nnis] *n.* sertlik, katılık, haşinlik.

**stern-post** ⊥ [ˈstə:npəust] *n.* kıç bodoslaması.

**ster.num** *anat.* [ˈstə:nəm] *n.* göğüs kemiği.

**steth.o.scope** ✝ [ˈsteθəskəup] *n.* stetoskop, göğüs dinleme aleti.

**ste.ve.dore** ⊥ [ˈsti:vidɔ:] *n.* yükleme ve boşaltma işçisi, istifçi.

**stew** [stju:] **1.** *v/t.* & *v/i.* hafif ateşte kayna(t)mak; **2.** *n.* güveç, yahni; F heyecan, telaş, üzüntü.

**stew.ard** [ˈstjuəd] *n.* kâhya, vekilharç; ⊥ kamarot; ambar memuru, idare memuru; **stew.ard.ess** *n.* ⊥ kadın kamarot; ✝ hostes.

**stew...:** '~-pan, '~-pot *n.* güveç, türlü tencresi.

**stick¹** [stik] **1.** *n.* değnek, sopa, çubuk; sap *(süpürge vs.);* baston; F çam yarması, hantal, kaba kimse; ~s *pl.* ufak odun; the ~s *pl. Am.* F taşra; **2.** *vb.* ✔ (kazığa) saplamak, kazıklamak.

**stick²** [~] *(irr.) v/i.* saplanıp kalmak; yapışmak, takılmak (to -e); *fig.* ayağını, başını vs.'yi bir yere çarpmak (at); ~ at nothing hiç *bşden* çekinmemek, korkmamak; ~ out, ~ up çıkıntılı olm., ucu dışarı çıkmak; F dayanmak, karşı koymak; F ısrar etm. (for); ~ to *bş* üzerinde ısrar etm., ayrılmamak *-den*; ~ up for s.o. *b-nin* tarafını tutmak; *v/t.* saplamak; bıçaklamak; iğneyle tutturmak; yapıştırmak; yafta asmak; F tahammül etm., dayanmak *-e*; ~ it on *sl.* fahiş fiyat istemek; ~ out dışarı çıkarmak, uzatmak; ~ it out F dayanmak, katlanmak *-e*; ~ up *sl. (banka vs.)* soymak; yolunu kesmek; **¹stick.er** *n.* yapışan etiket; etiket yapıştıran kimse; **¹stick.i.ness** *n.* yapışkanlık; **¹stick.ing-plas.ter** *n.* yara bandı; **¹stick-in-the-mud 1.** *adj.* tutucu, gerici; uyuşuk; **2.** *n.* gerici, darkafalı adam, mıymıntı.

**stick.le** [¹stikl] *vb.* titiz davranmak, pürüz çıkarmak, tereddüt etm.; **¹stick.le-back** *n. ichth.* dikence balığı; **¹stick.ler** *n.* mutaassıp, titizlenen kimse (for).

**stick-up** [¹stikʌp] *n. a.* ~ collar F dik yaka; *sl.* yol kesme.

**stick.y** □ [¹stiki] yapışkan; çamurlu, ağdalı, üstüne başına bulanan; güç, berbat; aksi, huysuz; come to a ~ end *sl.* kötü akıbete uğramak; be ~ about doing F *bşi* yapmakta gönülsüz, isteksiz olm.

**stiff** □ [stif] katı, sert; bükülmez, eğilmez; inatçı, serkeş; yorucu, zahmetli, zor; tutulmuş *(adele vs.)*; resmî, soğuk *(gülümseme vs.)*; sert, alkolü çok *(içki vs.)*; be bored ~ F uzun sıkıcı konuşmadan bıkmak, bezmek; keep a ~ upper lip cesaretini kaybetmemek; **¹stiff.en** *v/t. & v/i.* katılaş(tır)mak, sertleş(tir)mek; *fig.* desteklemek, takviye etm.; **¹stiff.en-er** *n.* sertleştirici parça; destekleyici şey; **¹stiff-¹necked** *adj.* dikkafalı, serkeş.

**sti.fle¹** *vet.* [¹staifl] *n.* diz eklemi.

**sti.fle²** [~] *v/t. & v/i.* boğ(ul)mak, nefesi tıka(n)mak.

**stig.ma** [¹stigmə] *n.* cilde vurulan kızgın damga; kötülük izi *(veya* eseri), leke, ar; ♀ tepecik; ♀ araz, belirti, alâmet; **stig.ma.tize** [¹-taiz] *v/t. fig.* damga vurmak, leke sürmek.

**stile** [stail] *n.* çit *veya* duvar basamağı; ⊕ kenar tahtalarından biri *(kapı, pencere vs.).*

**sti.let.to** [sti¹letəu] *n.* ufak hançer; biz.

**still¹** [stil] **1.** *adj.* sessiz; sakin; durgun, sütlüman, hareketsiz; ~ wine köpüksüz şarap; **2.** *n. (sinema filmi tanıtan)* fotoğraf; sessizlik; **3.** *adv.* hâlâ, henüz; yine, her şeye rağmen; daha (da); **4.** *cj.* bununla beraber, mamafih, yine de, (olduğu) halde; **5.** *vb.* durdurmak; yatış(tır)mak, teskin etm.

**still²** [~] *n.* imbik, damıtma aleti.

**still...:** **¹~-born** *adj.* ölü doğmuş; **¹~-hunt** *vb.* sessizce ve gizlenerek avlamak; **¹~-hunt.ing** *n.* sessizce ve gizlice avlama; ~ **life** natürmort, çiçek ve meyve resmetme; **¹still.ness** *n.* durgunluk, sessizlik, huzur.

**still-room** [¹stilrum] *n.* kiler, depo; imbik odası.

**still.y** *poet.* [¹stili] *adj.* sakin, durgun, hareketsiz.

**stilt** [stilt] *n.* yere basmadan yürümeye yarayan tek basamaklı sırık, ayaklık; **¹stilt.ed** *adj.* tumturaklı, tantanalı; suni, zorlayışlı.

**stim.u.lant** [¹stimjulənt] **1.** *adj.* ♀ uya(ndı)rıcı; **2.** *n.* ♀ uya(ndı)rıcı ilaç; F alkollü içki; **stim.u.late** [¹~-leit] *v/t.* uyarmak, canlandırmak, teşvik etm., tahrik etm., gayrete getirmek; **stim.u.la.tion** *n.* uyarım, teşvik; **stim.u.la.tive** [¹-lətiv] *adj.* uyandırıcı, canlandırıcı, muharrik; **stim.u.lus** [¹-ləs] *n.* dürtü (to *-e*), uyarıcı şey.

**sting** [stiŋ] **1.** *n.* iğne *(arı vs.)*; sokma, ısırma; *fig.* iğneleyici söz; acı, sızı; yakıp kavurma; **2.** *(irr.) v/t.* sokmak, yakmak *-i*, batmak *-e*; *fig.* incitmek, gücendirmek; işkence, eziyet etm.; yakmak, kavurmak; *v/i.* acımak, canı yanmak; yanmak, kavrulmak; be stung *sl.* kazıklanmak (for); **¹sting.er** *n.* F acıtıcı darbe vs.

**stin.gi.ness** [¹stindʒinis] *n.* pintilik, cimrilik.

**sting(.ing)-net.tle** ♀ [¹stiŋ(iŋ)netl] *n.* ısırgan.

**stin.gy** □ [¹stindʒi] pinti, cimri; kıt, az.

**stink** [stiŋk] **1.** *n.* pis koku; **2.** *(irr.) v/i.* pis kokmak, kokusunu çıkarmak (of *-in*; *sl. a. fig.*); *v/t.* kokutmak.

**stint** [stint] **1.** *n.* had, sınır, kayıt, limit; belirli bir süre için yapılan görev, iş *(as-kerlik vs.)*; **2.** *vb. bşi* esirgemek, cimrilik etm., *b-ne* az para *veya* yemek vermek; sınırlamak, kayıtlamak, azaltmak, kısmak *(masraf).*

**sti.pend** [¹staipend] *n.* ücret, maaş *(part. papazlara)*; **sti¹pen.di.ar.y** [~dʒəri] **1.** *adj.* ücretli, maaşlı; **2.** *n.* ücretli sulh yargıcı.

**stip.ple** *paint.* [¹stipl] *vb.* noktalayarak resmetmek.

**stip.u.late** [¹stipjuleit] *vb. a.* ~ for şart koymak; kararlaştırmak, anlaşmak *-de*; **stip.u.la.tion** *n.* şart (koyma).

**stir¹** [stə:] **1.** *n.* karıştırma; hareket, kımıldanma; canlılık, heyecan, telâş; gürültü, patırtı; 2. *v/t.* karıştırmak; harekete geçirmek, tahrik etm.; yerini değiştirmek; ~ up karıştırmak *(sıvı)*; kışkırtmak; *v/i.* kımılda(n)mak, yerinden oynamak.

**stir²** *sl.* [~] *n.* hapishane, kodes.

**stir.ring** [ˈstəːriŋ] *adj.* heyecan verici, canlandırıcı, canlı, heyecanlı.

**stir.rup** [ˈstirəp] *n.* üzengi.

**stitch** [stitʃ] 1. *n.* dikiş; ilmik; böğür sancısı; not have a dry ~ on one sırılsıklam, çok ıslanmış olm.; a ~ in time saves nine vaktinde yapılan küçük bir iş insanı büyük zahmetten kurtarır; 2. *vb.* dikmek, dikiş dikmek; ciltlemek *(kitap)*.

**stoat** *zo.* [stəut] *n.* kakım, as.

**stock** [stɔk] 1. *n.* ağaç gövdesi, kütük; sap, kabza, dipçik; soy, nesil, aile; hammadde; çorba malzemesi *(et, sebze vs.)*; mevcut mal, stok, depo mevcudu; *a.* live ~ hayvan mevcudu, çiftlik hayvanları; *hist.* boyunbağı; ♀ üzerine aşı yapılan dal; † esas sermaye, kapital; ~s *pl.* menkul değerler, sermaye hisseleri; hisse senetleri; ~s *pl.* ⇓ yapı kızağı; ~s *pl. hist.* tomruk *(ceza)*; in (out of) ~ mevcut (-du tükenmiş); take ~ † mal mevcudunu sayarak kontrol etm.; take ~ of *fig.* farkına varmak *-in,* tahmin etm.; 2. *adj.* stok olarak bulundurulan, stok...; *part. thea.* devamlı; standart...; basmakalıp, alelâde; ~ play repertuvardan seçilen oyun; 3. *vb.* yığmak, stok etm., mal ile doldurmak; filiz sürmek.

**stock.ade** [stɔˈkeid] 1. *n.* lata ile yapılan çit, hatıllı çit, şarampol; 2. *vb.* şarampolla çevirmek, korumak.

**stock...:** ˈ~-breed.er *n.* büyükbaş yetiştiren çiftçi; ˈ~-brok.er *n.* borsacı; ˈ~-car *n.* hayvan vagonu; ~ com.pa.ny *thea.* daimî tiyatro grubu; ~ ex.change borsa; ˈ~-farm.er *n.* hayvan yetiştiricisi; ˈ~.hold.er *n.* hissedar, hisse senedi sahibi.

**stock.i.net** [stɔkiˈnet] *n.* triko, jarse.

**stock.ing** [ˈstɔkiŋ] *n.* uzun çorap.

**stock.ist** † [ˈstɔkist] *n.* stokçu.

**stock...:** ˈ~-in-ˈtrade *n.* mevcut mal, sermaye, malzeme, teçhizat, alet ve edevat; ˈ~.job.ber *n.* borsa acentası, borsacı; ~ mar.ket borsa; ˈ~-pil.ing *n.* stok etme; ˈ~-ˈstill *adv.* kımıldamadan, hareketsiz; ˈ~.tak.ing *n.* stok sayımı, envanter yapma.

**stock.y** [ˈstɔki] *adj.* bodur, tıknaz.

**stock.yard** [ˈstɔkjɑːd] *n.* hayvanın geçici muhafaza edildiği yer, ağıl.

**stodge** *sl.* [stɔdʒ] *v/t.* & *v/i.* tıkabasa ye-(dir)mek; ˈstodg.y □ hazmı güç olan, ağır; *fig.* hantal, can sıkıcı, monoton.

**sto.gy, sto.gie** *Am.* [ˈstəugi] *n.* ucuz, kalitesiz puro.

**sto.ic** [ˈstəuik] 1. *adj.* heyecan, sevinç, üzüntü duygularını göstermeyen, revaki, stoik; 2. *n.* sevinç, keder duygularını belli etmeyen kimse; ˈsto.i.cal □ *fig.* revaki, stoik, metin; **sto.i.cism** [ˈ~sizəm] *n.* stoacılık, stoik felsefe; sevinç ve kedere karşı kayıtsızlık, soğukkanlılık.

**stoke** [stəuk] *vb.* ateşe kömür atmak; ateş yakmak, ısıtmak; ˈ~.hold, ˈ~.hole *n.* ⇓ külhan ağzı; ˈstok.er *n.* ateşçi.

**stole¹** [stəul] *n.* uzun cüppe.

**stole²** [~] *pret.,* ˈsto.len *p.p. of* steal 1.

**stol.id** [ˈstɔlid] duygusuz, vurdumduymaz, kayıtsız, duygularını belli etmez; **stoˈlid.i.ty** *n.* duygusuzluk, vurdumduymazlık.

**stom.ach** [ˈstʌmək] 1. *n.* mide; karın; *fig.* heves, istek (for *-e);* 2. *v/t.* hazmetmek, sindirmek; *fig.* b*şe* tahammül etm.; ˈ~-ache *n.* mide ağrısı; **sto.mach.ic** [stəuˈmækik] 1. *adj.* (~ally) mide ile ilgili, mide..., hazmı kolaylaştıran; 2. *n.* hazmı kolaylaştıran ilaç.

**stomp** *Am.* [stɔmp] *vb.* tepinmek, ayağını yere vura vura yürümek *veya* dansetmek.

**stone** [stəun] 1. *n.* taş; çekirdek *(meyve);* mesane taşı; *a.* precious ~ kıymetli taş, mücevher; 6.35 kg.'lık bir ağırlık ölçüsü; 2. *adj.* taştan yapılmış, taş...; 3. *vb.* taşlamak, taş atmak; -in çekirdeğini çıkarmak *(meyve);* ♀ Age taş devri, ˈ~-ˈblind *adj.* tamamen kör; ˈ~-ˈcold *adj.* buz gibi soğuk; ˈ~.crop *n.* ♀ damkoruğu, kayakoruğu; ˈ~-ˈdead *adj.* ölmüş gitmiş; ˈ~-ˈdeaf *adj.* tamamen sağır, duvar gibi sağır; ˈ~-ˈfruit *n.* ♀ çekirdekli meyve; ˈ~-ma.son *n.* taşçı, duvarcı; ˈ~-pit *n.* taş ocağı; ˈ~.wall.ing *n. spor:* kazanmaktansa kaybetmemek için oynama, müdafaa yapma; *pol.* mecliste engelleme ile görüşmeleri yavaşlatma; ˈ~.ware *n.* bir tür sert taş içeren topraktan yapılmış çanak çömlek; ˈ~.work *n.* taşçı işi.

**ston.i.ness** [ˈstəuninis] *n.* sertlik, taş gibi oluş.

**ston.y** [ˈstəuni] *adj.* taşlı(k); *fig.* taş gibi; katı; *a.* ~-broke *sl.* meteliksiz, beş parasız, tırıl, züğürt.

**stood** [stud] *pret.* & *p.p. of* stand.

**stooge** *sl.* [stuːdʒ] 1. *n. thea.* ikili komedyenlerden kendisine gülüneni; *fig.* el ulağı, yamak, yardakçı; 2. v/i. sahnede aptal, k-ne gülünen kimse olm.; sarsak sursak yürümek.

**stool** [stu:l] *n.* tabure, arkalıksız iskemle; ℣ dışkı, büyük aptes; ❧ filiz veren kök *veya* kütük; ❧ kök sürgünü; '~-pigeon *n. part. Am.* çığırtkan güvercin; *sl.* polisin kullandığı muhbir, gammaz.

**stoop** [stu:p] 1. *v/i.* eğilmek; alçalmak, tenezzül etm.; ikibüklüm yürümek; *v/t.* eğmek *(baş)*; 2. *n.* kambur duruş; *Am.* veranda.

**stop** [stɔp] 1. *v/t.* durdurmak, önlemek, kesmek, engellemek (from -*den*); son vermek *-e; a.* ~ up tıkamak, kapa(t)mak; doldurmak *(diş)*; kapa(t)mak, kesmek *(yol)*; bloke etm., durdurmak *(çek)*; kesmek *(ödeme)*; alıkoymak *(ücret, kira vs.)*; ♪ dokunmak *(ses, tel)*; *v/i.* durmak, kesilmek, hareket etmemek; bitmek, sonu olm.; F kısa süre için kalmak; ~ dead, ~ short aniden durmak; ~ at home F evde kalmak; ~ over yolculukta mola vermek; ~ up late F yatmamak; 2. *n.* dur(dur)ma; durak, mola, ara; ⊕ vurma, çarpma; sonuç; durak yeri, istasyon; *mst* full ~ *gr.* nokta; ♪ org düğmesi; ♪ flavta anahtarı, kle; *gr.* patlama sesi; '~.cock *n.* ⊕ valf, vana; '~.gap *n.* geçici önlem *veya* çare; '~.o.ver *n.* mola, konaklama; ⌁ ara iniş; 'stoppage *n.* tıkama, durdurma, kes(il)me; maaşa haciz koyma; stopaj; ⊕ işletme arızası; tıkanıklık *(trafik)*; 'stop.per 1. *n.* tıkaç, tapa; spor: top kesici; ~ circuit ⚡ kapalı devre; 2. *vb. (tapa, tıkaç vs. ile)* tıkamak; 'stop.ping *n.* ℣ dolgu; 'stop-press *n.* baskı bitmek üzereyken gazeteye eklenen son haber(ler); 'stop-watch *n.* kronometre, saniye ölçer saat.

**stor.age** ['stɔ:ridʒ] *n.* depoya koyma, saklama, depolama; ardiye (ücreti); ~ battery akümülatör.

**store** [stɔ:] 1. *n.* stok, depo mevcudu; *a.* ~s *pl. fig.* bolluk; ambar, depo, antrepo; *Am.* dükkân, mağaza; ~s *pl.* bonmarşe; ~s *pl.* X, ❧ mühimmat, savaş gereçleri, levazım, kumanya; in ~ elde, mevcut, depoda; be in ~ for *b-ni*, bşi beklemek; have in ~ for rezerve etm., temin etmiş olm., hazırlamak *-e*; set *veya* put great ~ by bşe çok değer vermek; 2. *v/t. a.* ~ up ambara koymak, yığmak, koymak, istif etm., yerleştirmek, depo etm.; saklamak; biriktirmek; doldurmak *(with ile)*; '~.house *n.* ambar, depo; *mst fig.* hazine; '~.keep.er *n.* ambar memu-

ru; *Am.* mağazacı; '~-room *n.* ambar, kiler, depo.

**sto.rey(ed)** ['stɔ:ri(d)] *s.* story[2], storied[2].

**sto.ried** ['stɔ:rid] *adj.* pek çok hikâyeye konu olmuş.

**sto.ried[2]** [~] *adj.* ...katlı.

**stork** [stɔ:k] *n.* leylek.

**storm** [stɔ:m] 1. *n.* fırtına, kasırga, bora; X hücum; *(alkış vs.)* tufan; şiddetli öfke; take by ~ hücum ederek almak; 2. *v/t.* hücumla zaptetmek *(a. X); v/i.* fırtına patlamak, fırtınalı geçmek; hiddetlenmek, kudurmak (at -*e)*; 'storm.y ☐ fırtınalı.

**sto.ry[1]** ['stɔ:ri] *n.* hikâye, öykü, masal, roman, efsane; tarih; konu, makale; F yalan, palavra; short ~ kısa hikâye, fıkra.

**sto.ry[2]** [~] *n.* bina katı.

**sto.ry-tell.er** ['stɔ:ritelə] *n.* öykü anlatan, masalcı; F yalancı kimse.

**stout** [staut] 1. ☐ sağlam, kuvvetli, sıhhatli; şişman, göbekli; cesur, yiğit; 2. *n.* sert bira, siyah bira; '~'heart.ed *adj.* yiğit, cesur, yürekli; 'stout.ness *n.* cesaret, yiğitlik, mertlik; şişmanlık; *spor:* sebat, azim, metanet.

**stove** [stəuv] 1. *n.* soba; fırın, ocak; ✓ ser, limonluk; 2. *vb.* kurutmak; dezenfekte etm. *(ısı ile)*; 3. *pret. & p.p. of* stove 2; '~.pipe *n.* soba borusu; *Am.* F silindir şapka.

**stow** [stəu] *v/t.* saklamak, istif etm., paketlemek; 'stow.age *n.* istifleme, yerleştirme; istif yeri; ↓ istif ücreti; istif olunan şey; 'stow.a.way *n.* ↓ kaçak yolcu.

**stra.bis.mus** ℣ ['strə'bizməs] *n.* şaşılık.

**strad.dle** ['strædl] *v/t. & v/i.* apış(tır)mak, bacaklar açık oturmak, durmak *veya* yürümek, ata biner gibi oturmak; X hedefin önüne hem arkasına ateş ederek hedefi ayarlamak; *Am. fig.* iki tarafı birden idare etm.; ne yapacağını bilmemek.

**strafe** [stra:f] *v/t.* F cezalandırmak; X borbardıman etm.; ⌁ ağır makineli ile hücum etm.

**strag.gle** ['strægl] *vb.* yoldan sapmak; sürü *veya* grubun gerisinde kalıp dağınık gitmek, dağınık olm.; dağınık büyümek; *fig.* konu dışına çıkmak; ❧ üremek, türemek; 'strag.gler *n.* arkada kalan; X döküntü er(ler); 'strag.gling ☐ dağınık, seyrek.

**straight** [streit] 1. *adj.* doğru, müstakim, (düm)düz; *fig.* dürüst, samimi, namuslu; düz *(saç); Am.* saf, halis *(içki); Am.*

**pol.** sabit yüzdeli; F güvenilir, doğru; ciddi; **put ~** düzeltmek, yoluna koymak; **2. n.** yarışçılık; yarış çizgisi, düz hat; **3. adv.** doğrudan doğruya, doğruca, sapmaksızın; derhal, hemen; açıkça, dobra dobra; **~** away, **~** off hemen, derhal; **~** out açıkça, dobra dobra; **¹straight.en** v/t. & v/i. doğrul(t)mak, düzel(t)mek; **~** out yoluna koymak; düzeltmek; **straight¹for.ward** ☐ doğru sözlü, dürüst, samimi; **¹straight.way** adv. derhal, hemen.

**strain¹** [strein] **1. n.** ⊕ gerginlik, ger(il)me; aşırı zihinsel ve duygusal gerginlik; zorlama, baskı, tazyik (on); ⚇ burkulup incinme, bir veterin fazla gerilmesi; mst **~s** pl. ♪ melodi, makam, nağme; soydan gelen nitelik (of) (delilik vs.); **put a great ~** on yük olmak, yük getirmek; **2. v/t.** germek, zorlamak (a. fig.); zarar vermek, zayıflatmak (vücut); ⊕ zorlamak; işletmek; ⚇ (zorla, hırpalayarak) çekmek; süzgeçten geçirmek, süzmek; v/i. gerilmek, zorlanmak; nefsine eziyet etm. (after); çabalamak; süzülmek; çekmek (at); burkulup incinmek.

**strain²** [~] n. nesil, soy, kan, menşe, nesep, soy sop.

**strain.er** [¹streinə] n. süzgeç, filtre; elek, kalbur.

**strait** [streit] **1. n.** geogr. boğaz (özel isimlerle ²s pl.), dar geçit; **~s** pl. sıkıntı, zorluk, darlık; **2. adj.** dar, sıkı; **~** jacket deli gömleği; **¹strait.en** v/t. sıkıştırmak, daraltmak; **~ed** adj. sıkıntıda, darlık içinde, çaresiz (for); **strait-laced** [¹-leist] adj. tutucu, dargörüşlü; **¹strait.ness** n. darlık, sıkışıklık, eksiklik.

**strand¹** [strænd] **1. n.** sahil, plaj, deniz kıyısı; **2. v/t. & v/i.** karaya otur(t)mak (gemi); fig. başarısızlığa uğra(t)mak; **~ed** adj. zor durumda, sıkıntıda; mot. bir yere saplanıp kalmış.

**strand²** [~] n. halat bükümü, kablo örgüsü; iplik, tel (saç).

**strange** ☐ [streindʒ] yabancı, elâlem (a. fig.); tuhaf, garip, acayip; yeni, acemi; **¹strange.ness** n. tuhaflık, acayiplik; yabancılık; **¹stran.ger** n. yabancı, el, tanınmayan kimse; yeni gelen kimse (to -e).

**stran.gle** [¹stræŋgl] vb. boğ(ul)mak, boğazlamak; fig. bastırmak, zulmetmek; **¹~.hold** n. boğazı sıkma vaziyeti.

**stran.gu.late** ⚇ [¹stræŋgjuleit] vb. boğ(ul)mak, düğümle(n)mek (bağırsak vs.), sıkıştırmak (damar vs.); **stran.gu¹la.tion** n. boğ(ul)ma; ⚇ düğümlenme.

**strap** [stræp] **1. n.** kayış, sırım; şerit, bant,

atkı; kayışla döverek cezalandırma; tutunma kayışı (otobüs, tren vs.'de); **2. v/t.** kayışla bağlamak; kayışla dövmek, kamçılamak; bantlamak; **¹~.hang.er** n. F ayakta kayışa tutunan yolcu (otobüste); **¹strap.less** adj. atkısız (bayan elbisesi); **¹strap.ping 1.** adj. dolgun (bayan); kuvvetli, iriyapılı; **2. n.** ⚇ bant, yapışkan şerit, plaster.

**stra.ta** [¹strɑːtə] pl. of stratum.

**strat.a.gem** [¹strætidʒəm] n. harp hilesi; desise, kurnazlık.

**stra.te.gic** [strə¹tiːdʒik] adj. (**~ally**) stratejik; **strat.e.gist** [¹strætidʒist], n. stratej, strateji uzmanı; **¹strat.e.gy** n. strateji, bir amaca varmak için eylem birliği sağlama ve düzenleme sanatı.

**strat.i.fy** [¹strætifai] vb. tabakalar halinde düzenlemek.

**stra.to.cruis.er** ✈ [¹strætəukruːzə] n. stratosfer uçağı.

**strat.o.sphere** phys. [¹strætəusfiə] n. stratosfer.

**stra.tum** geol. [¹strɑːtəm] n., pl. **stra.ta** [¹-tə] kat, tabaka, katman, zümre (a. fig.).

**straw** [strɔː] **1. n.** saman, saman çöpü; fig. önemsiz şey, hiç; **I don't care a ~** bu bana vız gelir; **a man of ~** fig. kukla adam; **2. adj.** saman...; **~** vote Am. pol. genel seçimden önceki nabız yoklaması (veya kamuoyu araştırması) **¹~.ber.ry** n. çilek; **¹straw.y** adj. samanlı, saman gibi.

**stray** [strei] **1. v/i.** yoldan sapmak, yolunu şaşırmak, sapmak (from -den; a. fig.); dolaşmak, gezinmek, avarelik etm.; **2. adj. a. ~ed** yoldan sapmış; başıboş, dağınık; tesadüfî; **3. n.** sürüden ayrılmış hayvan; başıboş kimse; ayrı düşmüş b-i veya bş; **~s** pl. ⚡ yıldırım yüzünden oluşan parazitler.

**streak** [striːk] **1. n.** çizgi, hat; fig. damar; iz, eser; kısa süre; **~** of lightning yıldırım; **2. vb.** çizgilemek, çizgilerle süslemek; acele etm., çok hızlı hareket etm.; çırılçıplak durumda herkesin önünden hızla geçmek; **¹streak.y** ☐ çizgili, çubuklu, yollu.

**stream** [striːm] **1. n.** ırmak, çay, dere; akıntı; akım, cereyan; sel; (okulda) başarı derecesi; **go with the ~** fig. ayak uydurmak -e; **2. v/i.** (çağlayarak) akmak, sel gibi akmak; dalgalanmak (saç, bayrak vs); taşmak; v/t. akıtmak; **stream.er** n. flama, fors; serpantin, renkli kâğıt tekerleği; göğe doğru yükselen ışık sütunu (kuzey veya güneyde); gazete: manşet; **stream.let** [¹-lit] n. küçük çay *veya* dere.

**strear line** ['stri:mlain] **1.** *n.* aerodinamik şekil. lüzenli akıntı; **2.** *v/t.* aerodinamik şekil vermek, su *veya* hava içinde kolay hareket edebilir hale koymak; kolay ve elverişli duruma getirmek; *fig.* modernleştirmek.

**street** [stri:t] *n.* sokak, cadde, yol; not in the same ~ with F ...ile kıyaslanamaz; '~-car *n. part. Am.* tramvay; '~walk.er *n.* sokak kadını, fahişe, adi orospu.

**strength** [streŋθ] *n.* kuvvet, güç *(a. fig.);* ✕, ⚓ kadro, askeri güç; on the ~ of -e uyarınca, -e dayanarak, güvenerek; **'strength.en** *v/t.* kuvvetlendirmek; desteklemek; *v/i.* kuvvetlenmek, güçlenmek.

**stren.u.ous** ☐ ['strenjuəs] faal, gayretli, çalışkan, istekli; **'stren.u.ous.ness** *n.* gayret, çaba, canlılık, çalışkanlık.

**stress** [stres] **1.** *n.* baskı, tazyik, şiddet; *gr.* vurgu, aksan; ⊕ gerilme, zorlama; önem; *psych.* sıkıntı, gerginlik; lay ~ (up)on *bşi* önemle belirtmek, üzerinde ısrarla durmak -*in;* **2.** *v/t.* üzerinde durmak, vurgulamak; ⊕ tazyik etm., germek, baskı yapmak, zorlamak; üzerine basmak, vurgu koymak.

**stretch** [stretʃ] **1.** *v/t.* germek, uzatmak; sermek, yaymak; *mst* ~ out uzatmak *(kol vs.);* kurmak *(yay); fig.* abartmak, aşırıya kaçırmak; *v/i.* uzanmak, gerilmek, genişlemek (into -*e); a.* ~ one's powers tüm gücünü kullanmak; **2.** *n.* uzanma, gerilme; gerginlik; abartma; geniş yer, yüzey; süre; at a ~ aralıksız, hiç durmadan, ara vermeden; on the ~ gergin, sıkı; **'stretch.er** *n.* sedye, teskere; ayakkabı kalıbı; *(kayık)* yarım oturak; **'stretch.er-bear.er** *n.* sedye taşıyan hastabakıcı.

**strew** [stru:] *(irr.) v/t.* serpmek, dağıtmak, yayılarak kaplamak; **strewn** [stru:n] *p.p. of* strew.

**stri.ate** ['straiit], **stri.at.ed** [~'eitid] *adj.* dar çizgili, çizgili.

**strick.en** ['strikən] *adj.* müteessir, başına gelmiş, uğramış (with -*e)*; yaralı, yaralanmış: ~ in age yaşlı, kocamış.

**strict** [strikt] *adj.* sıkı, sert, şiddetli; kesin; titiz; tam, harfi harfine olan, mutlak: ~ly speaking doğrusunu söylemek gerekirse; **'strict ness** *n.* sıkılık, sertlik, disiplin; kesinlik; **stric.ture** [~tʃə] *n.* oft. ~s *pl.* kınama, yerme, şiddetli eleştiri; ⚕ kanal daralması.

**strid.den** ['stridn] *p.p. of* stride 1.

**stride** [straid] **1.** *(irr.) v/t.* yürüyerek bir

yerden geçmek, bir yeri aşmak; *v/i. a.* ~ out geniş adımlar atmak; **2.** *n.* (geniş) adım; get into one's ~ harekete gelmek, tam yoluna girmek.

**stri.dent** ☐ ['straidənt] gıcırtılı, cıyak cıyak, keskin, tiz *(ses).*

**strife** *lit.* [straif] *n.* çekişme, didişme, mücadele, ihtilâf.

**strike** [straik] **1.** *n.* grev; bulma *(maden filizi, petrol vs.);* vurma, çarpma; *fig.* beklenmedik başarı, isabet, büyük vurgun; ✕ hava hücumu *(tek hedefe); Am. beysbol:* topa vuramama; be on ~ grevde olm.; go on ~ greve gitmek, grev yapmak; **2.** *(irr.) v/t.* vurmak, çarpmak, darbe indirmek; beklenmedik bir anda yapmak; çalmak *(saat, nota vs.);* etkilemek; dehşet salmak; indirmek *(bayrak, yelken vs.);* yıkmak *(çadır vs.);* çınlatmak *(ses);* birden aklına gelmek; bulmak, keşfetmek; kök salmak; akdetmek, anlaşmak *(pazarlık vs.);* yakmak, tutuşturmak *(ateş,˸ışık); s.* attitude; ~ a balance hesapları dengelemek, hesap bakiyesini saptamak; ~ oil petrole rastlamak, petrol bulmak; F vurgun vurmak, bahtı açık olm.; ~ off listeden çıkarmak, çizip silmek; ~ out *plan:* taslağını çizmek; çıkarmak, silmek -*den;* ~ through çizmek, karalamak; ~ up şarkı söylemeğe başlamak; başlatmak *(arkadaşlık); v/i.* çarpmak (at); ⚓ karaya oturmak; ✕, ✕ fors indirmek; grev yapmak; çalmak *(saat);* çakmak *(şimşek);* ateş almak *(kibrit);* kök tutmak; ~ home etkilemek, tesirli olm.; ~ in vurup saplamak; lâfa karışmak; ~ into *bşe* düşmek; ~ up çalmaya başlamak *(orkestra);* ~ upon the ear kulağına çalınmak; '~-bound *adj.* grev yüzünden felce uğramış; '~-break.er *n.* grev kırıcı işçi; '~-pay *n.* grevdeyken işçilere ödenen para; **'strik.er** *n.* grevci; ⊕ müsademe *(veya* çarpışma) iğnesi, zil çekici.

**string** [striŋ] **1.** *n.* ip, sicim; kordon, şerit, bağ; *Am.* F koşul, şart, pürüz; veter, kiriş; ♀ lif, yaprak damarı; ♪ tel. kiriş; sıra, dizi, kol; ~s *pl.* ♪ telli çalgı(lar). yaylı sazlar; harp on the same ~ aynı konuyu tekrarlayıp durmak, diline dolamak; have two ~s to one's bow *b-nin* elinde iki olanak bulunmak; pull the ~s iltimas yaptırmak; there are ~s attached to it F işin altından bir çapanoğlu çıktı;˙ **2.** *(irr.)* vb. dizmek, ipe geçirmek; tel takmak -*e (keman vs.);* kılçıklarını çıkarmak *(taze fasulye)*; Am. sl. b-ne yalan yutturmak; *b-ni* alaya almak; ~ up F ipe çekmek, asmak; be strung up çok heyecanlı, sinirli, endişeli vs. olm; ~ **bag** file; ~ **band** ♪ yaylı sazlar orkestrası; ~ **bean** çalı fasulyesi; **stringed** *adj.* ♪ telli...; ...telli.

**strin.gen.cy** ['strindʒənsi] *n.* sıkılık, sertlık, şiddet; ✝ para darlığı; **'strin.gent** ☐ sert, şiddetli, zorlu; sıkı; para darlığında olan.

**string.y** ['striŋi] *adj.* lifli; telli, tel tel olan; kılçıklı.

**strip** [strip] 1. *v/t.* soymak (off), *fig.* soyup soğana çevirmek, yağma etm. (off); sıyırmak, soymak *(kabuk vs.)*; ⊕ sökmek, parçalara ayırmak; ⚓ armasını soymak; *a.* ~ off çıkarmak *(elbise vs.)*; *v/i.* F soyunmak; 2. *n.* şerit, uzun ve dar parça; ~ **car.toon** = comics.

**stripe** [straip] 1. *n.* çubuk, kumaş yolu, çizgi; ✕ sırma, şerit; 2. *v/t.* çizgilemek, çizgilerle süslemek; **striped** *adj.* çizgili, yollu.

**strip-light.ing** ['striplaitiŋ] *n.* neon ışığı ile aydınlatma.

**strip.ling** ['stripliŋ] *n.* delikanlı, genç adam.

**strip-tease** ['striptiːz] *n.* striptiz.

**strive** [straiv] *(irr.)* *vb.* uğraşmak, çalışmak (for, after -*meğe*); zahmet etm., yorulmak; mücadele etm. (against, for -e *karşı, için*); **striv.en** *p.p.* of strive 1.

**strode** [strəud] *pret.* of stride 1.

**stroke** [strəuk] 1. *n.* vuruş, çarpma, darbe (etkisi); sars(ıl)ma, şok; ✞ inme, felç; ⊕ piston siası; fırça darbesi; vuruş sesi *(saat)*; hamlacı; yüzme tarzı, kulaç; okşama; ~ of genius dahiyane bir davranış; ~ of luck şans, iyi tesadüf; 2. *v/t.* okşamak; *(kürek)* hareket işareti vermek.

**stroll** [strəul] 1. *v/i.* gezinmek, dolaşmak; 2. *n.* gezme; **'stroll.er** *n.* gezinen kimse, avare; Am. açılır kapanır çocuk arabası.

**strong** ☐ [strɔŋ] *com.* kuvvetli, güçlü, dinç; *fig.* yetenekli, ehil; enerjik. istekli, gayretli; sağlam, dayanıklı; başa vuran, sert *(icki, koku vs.)*; şiddetli; *gr.* mastarın ünlü harfinin değişmesi ile geçmiş zamanlarını oluşturan *(örnek: sing, sang, sung)*; *s.* language; feel ~(ly) about bse sinirlenmek, hevecanlanmak; bş hakkında *k-ne* has düşüncesi olm.; be going ~ F yaşına göre sağlam, güçlü olm.; **'~-box** *n.* çelik kasa; **'~.hold** *n.* kale, müstahkem yer; *fig.* merkez; **'~-'mind.ed** *adj.* azimli, bildiğinden şaş-

maz, kararlı; **'~-room** *n.* hazine odası; **'~-'willed** *adj.* inatçı, iradeli, kararlı.

**strop** [strɔp] 1. *n.* bileği kayışı, ustra kayışı; ⚓ direk sapanı; 2. *v/t.* kayışa sürterek bilemek *(ustra vs.)*.

**stro.phe** ['strəufi] *n. (özellikle eski Yunan'da)* koronun okuduğu kıta, bent.

**strove** [strəuv] *pret.* of strive.

**struck** [strʌk] *pret. & p.p.* of strike 2.

**struc.tur.al** ☐ ['strʌktʃərəl] bina *veya* yapıya ait, yapı...; organik, yapısal; **'struc.ture** *n.* bina, yapı; yapılış, bünye; teşekkül, çatı.

**strug.gle** ['strʌgl] 1. *v/i.* çabalamak, mücadele etm., uğraşmak (for, against *ile*); *k-ni* çok yormak, yapmayacağım diye datyatmak, çırpınmak; 2. *n.* savaş, mücadele (for *için*); çaba, uğraş, gayret; zorluk, zahmet; **'strug.gler** *n.* savaşan, mücadele eden kimse.

**strum** [strʌm] 1. *v/t. & v/i.* tıngırda(t)mak *(müzik aleti vs.)*; 2. *n.* yaylı sazları tıngırdatma.

**strum.pet** ✝ ['strʌmpit] *n.* fahişe, orospu.

**strung** [strʌŋ] *pret. & p.p.* of string 2.

**strut** [strʌt] *v/i.* baba hindi gibi gezmek, azametle yürümek; *v/t.* ⊕ payanda vurmak, desteklemek; 2. *n.* azametli yürüyüş; ⊕ bağlama kirişi, destek, payanda.

**strych.nine** ⚗ ['strikniːn] *n.* striknin, kargabüken özü.

**stub** [stʌb] 1. *n.* kütük, kesilmiş ağaç gövdesi; sigara izmariti; Am. koçan, kontrol kuponu; 2. *vb. mst* ~ up kökleri temizlemek, köklemek; ayağını bir yere çarpmak; ~ **out** söndürmek *(sigara)*.

**stub.ble** ['stʌbl] *n.* ekin anızı; uzamış tı raş.

**stub.bly** ['stʌbli] *adj.* anızlı; sert kıllı.

**stub.born** ☐ ['stʌbən] inatçı, dikkafalı, aksi, sert, serkeş; azimli, sebatlı; sıkışmış, oynamayan *(kilit vs.)*; **'stub.born.ness** *n.* dikkafalılık ,inatçılık.

**stub.by** ['stʌbi] *adj.* kısa ve kalın, küt, güdük.

**stuc.co** ['stʌkəu] 1. *n.* dış duvar sıvası, alçı vs. 2. *vb.* karışımla sıvamak, süslemek.

**stuck** [stʌk] *pret. & p.p.* of stick²; ~ on Am. F *b-ne* abayı yakmış, tutkun, âşık; **'~-'up** *adj.* F burnu havada, hodpesent.

**stud¹** [stʌd] 1. *n.* duvar çivisi, iri başlı çivi; topuz; yaka düğmesi; saplama; 2. *v/t.* iri başlı çiviler çakmak, çivilerle donatmak, süslemek.

**stud²** [~] *n.* hara; damızlık at, aygır; **'~-book** *n.* özellikle yarış atlarının soy defteri.

**stud.ding** Δ [ˈstʌdiŋ] *n.* iskelet, çatı.

**stu.dent** [ˈstjuːdənt] *n.* öğrenci; araştırıcı, uzman; **ˈstu.dent.ship** *n.* öğrencilik; burs.

**stud.ied** □ [ˈstʌdid] prova edilmiş, hazırlanmış *(rol)*; sahte, yapmacık, zoraki; kasıtlı, maksatlı.

**stu.di.o** [ˈstjuːdiəu] *n.* stüdyo, atelye; yayın odası *(radyo, TV).*

**stu.di.ous** □ [ˈstjuːdjəs] çalışkan, gayretli; dikkatli (of); çabalayan (to -e); kasıtlı, bilerek; **ˈstu.di.ous.ness** *n.* çalışkanlık, gayret, çaba.

**stud.y** [ˈstʌdi] **1.** *n.* tahsil, öğrenim; tetkik, araştırma; çalışma (odası); taslak *(resim vsk.)*; be in a brown ~ çok dalgın, zihni karmakarışık olm.; **2.** *v/i.* incelemek, araştırma yapmak (for); *v/t.* incelemek, araştırmak; öğrenim görmek, tahsil etm.; gayret etm.; hazırlamak.

**stuff** [stʌf] **1.** *n.* madde; malzeme; kumaş; † yün(lü kumaş); eşya, şey; ilaç; *fig.* zırva, saçma; **2.** *v/t.* doldurmak, tıkıştırmak (into -e); ~ up kapa(t)mak, tıkamak; ~ed shirt *Am. sl. k-ni bş* sanan kimse, ukalâ; *v/i.* tıkınmak, çok yemek; **ˈstuff.ing** *n.* dolma (içi); doldurma, şişirme; dolgu; ⊕ fodra, elbisede kumaşı dik tutan kolalı bez; **ˈstuffy** □ havasız, küf kokulu; F alıngan, dargın, öfkeli; F kibirli, soğuk; tıkalı.

**stul.ti.fi.ca.tion** [stʌltifiˈkeiʃən] *n.* aptallaştırma; ket vurma; **stul.ti.fy** [ˈ~fai] *v/t.* aptallaştırmak; faydasız *veya* aptalca göstermek, maskaraya çevirmek, rezil kepaze etm.

**stum.ble** [ˈstʌmbl] **1.** *n.* sürçme, sendeleme, tökezleme; hata, yanılgı; **2.** *v/i.* ayağı dolaşmak, sendelemek, sürçmek; kekelemek, dili sürçmek; ~ across, ~ upon rastlamak -e; **ˈstum.bling-block** *n. fig.* engel, ket.

**stump** [stʌmp] **1.** *n.* kütük; kesilen bir şeyin geri kalan parçası; kırık diş kökü; *(sigara)* izmarit; *kriket oyunu:* üç hedef sopasından her biri; F seçim propagandası *veya* propagandanın yapıldığı yer; ~s *pl.* F bacaklar; stir one's ~s F hızlı yürümek, pergelleri açmak; **2.** *v/t. kriket:* hedefi vurarak *b-ni* oyun dışı etm.; F şaşırtmak, afallatmak; *Am.* F *b-ne* meydan okumak; ~ up *sl.* ödemek; ~ the country ülkeyi dolaşarak seçim propagandası *veya* ~ed for çekingen, mahcup; *v/i.* ağır basarak yürümek, tahta ayaklı gibi yürümek; **ˈ~ˈor.a.tor** *n.* sokak hatibi, halk hatibi; **ˈstump.y** □ kısa, bodur, tıknaz; küt; güdük.

**stun** [stʌn] *v/t.* sersemletmek *(a. fig.)*; ~ned *fig.* şaşkın, afallamış, sersem, ağzı açık kalmış.

**stung** [stʌŋ] *pret. & p.p. of* sting 2.

**stunk** [stʌŋk] *pret. & p.p. of* stink 2.

**stun.ner** F [ˈstʌnə] *n.* yaman kimse *veya* şey; çok çekici kimse *(part. kadın)*; **ˈstun.ning** □ F enfes, fevkalâde.

**stunt**[1] F [stʌnt] **1.** *n.* hüner, ustalık, marifet, dikkati çekmek *veya* reklâm yapmak için yapılan davranış; † akrobasi uçuşu; **2.** *vb.* akrobasi uçuşu *(veya* gösterisi) yapmak.

**stunt**[2] [~] *v/t.* büyümesini önlemek *-in*, bodur bırakmak *-i*; **ˈstunt.ed** *adj.* bodur kalmış.

**stupe** ፠ [stjuːp] **1.** *n.* sıcak kompres; **2.** *vb.* kompres yapmak.

**stu.pe.fac.tion** [stjuːpiˈfækʃən] *n.* şaşkınlık, hayret; sersemlik; duyumsuzluk; **stu.pe.fy** [ˈ~fai] *v/t. fig.* sersemletmek, şaşırtmak, afallatmak; aptallaştırmak.

**stu.pen.dous** □ [stjuːˈpendəs] şaşılacak, hayret edilecek, muazzam.

**stu.pid** □ [ˈstjuːpid] budala, aptal, akılsız, alık; saçma; **stuˈpid.i.ty** *n.* aptallık, budalalık.

**stu.por** [ˈstjuːpə] *n.* uyuşukluk, sersemlik.

**stur.di.ness** [ˈstəːdinis] *n.* sağlamlık, güçlülük, dayanıklılık; metanet; **ˈstur.dy** *adj.* kuvvetli, güçlü, dayanıklı; metanetli; azimli, sebatlı.

**stur.geon** *ichth.* [ˈstəːdʒən] *n.* mersin balığı.

**stut.ter** [stʌtə] **1.** *v/i.* kekelemek, pepelemek; **2.** *n.* kekeleme, kekemelik; **ˈstut.ter.er** *n.* kekeme.

**sty**[1] [stai] *n.* domuz ahırı.

**sty**[2] [~] *n. (göz)* arpacık, itdirseği.

**style** [stail] **1.** *n.* taş kalem; ♀ pistil, boyuncak; tarz, üslup, usul; çeşit, tip, stil; giyimde moda; takvim usulü; in ~ klas. birinci sınıf; under the ~ of... ♀ ...ticaret ünvanı altında; **2.** *vb.* ad vermek, demek.

**styl.ish** □ [ˈstailiʃ] şık, modaya uygun, zarif; üsluba uygun; **ˈstyl.ish.ness** *n.* modaya uygunluk, şıklık.

**styl.ist** [ˈstailist] *n.* üslupçu; modacı, desinatör.

**sty.lo** F [ˈstailəu], **sty.lo.graph** [ˈ~grɑːf] *n.* dolmakalem, stilo.

**styp.tic** [ˈstiptik] *adj.* kan durdurucu *veya* dindirici *(ilaç).*

**sua.sion** [ˈsweiʒən] *n.* ikna etme, razı etme.

**suave** ☐ [swaːv] nazik, hoş tavırlı; tatlı (*şarap vs.*); **ˈsuav.i.ty** *n.* tatlı dillilik, hoş tavır, nezaket.

**sub** F [sʌb] *abbr. of* subordinate 2; subscription; substitude 2; submarine 2.

**sub...** [~] *prefix* mst ast-, alt, aşağı; ikincil; yan; biraz (daha)..., hemen hemen...

**sub.ac.id** [ˈsʌbˈæsid] *adj.* ekşimtrak, mayhoş, buruk; *fig.* hırçın, kavgacı, sert.

**sub.al.tern** [ˈsʌbltən] *n.* ikincil, ast; X astsubay.

**sub.a.tom.ic** [ˈsʌbəˈtɔmik] *adj.* atomdan küçük, atom içindeki.

**sub.com.mit.tee** [ˈsʌbkəmiti] *n.* alt komisyon.

**sub.con.scious** ☐ [ˈsʌbˈkɔnʃəs] bilinçaltındaki.

**sub.con.tract** [sʌbˈkɔntrækt] *n.* yan mukavele, alt sözleşme.

**sub.cu.ta.ne.ous** ☐ [ˈsʌbkjuːteinjəs] deri altındaki, deri altına şırınga edilen.

**sub.deb** *Am.* F [sʌbˈdeb] *n.* ondört ile onyedi yaş arasındaki genç kız.

**sub.di.vide** [sʌbdiˈvaid] *v/t. & v/i.* kısımlara ayırmak, parsellemek; **sub.di.vi.sion** [ˈ~viʒən] *n.* parselleme; parsellenmiş toprak; alt bölüm.

**sub.due** [səbˈdjuː] *v/t.* zaptetmek, boyunduruk altına almak, zorlamak; azaltmak, hafiflemek (*ışık vs.*).

**sub.head(.ing)** [ˈsʌbhed(iŋ)] *n.* tâli (*veya* ikincil) başlık; bölüm başlığı.

**sub.ja.cent** [sʌbˈdʒeisənt] *adj.* altındaki, alttaki.

**sub.ject** [ˈsʌbdʒikt] **1.** *adj.* bağımlı olan (to -e), *b-nin* emri altında olan; maruz, karşı karşıya olan *ile*; be ~ to *bşe* meyletmek, temayül göstermek; ~ to a fee *veya* duty vergiye tabi; **2.** *adv.* ~ to *bşin* kaydı ihtirazisi altında, ...koşulu ile; ~ to change without notice ihbarsız değiştirilebilir; **3.** *n.* tebaa, vatandaş, uyruk; *phls., gr.* özne, fail; *a.* ~ matter esas fikir, konu, mevzu; ♪ tem, esas makam; *paint.* süje, resme konu olan şey; ders (konusu); denek; vesile, neden; **4.** *v/t.* boyunduruk altına almak; ~ to maruz kılmak -e; **sub.jec.tion** *n.* hüküm altına alma; boyun eğme, itaat; **sub.jec.tive** ☐ sübjektif; öznel; kişisel.

**sub.join** [ˈsʌbˈdʒɔin] *v/t.* ilâve etm., katmak, eklemek.

**sub.ju.gate** [ˈsʌbdʒugeit] *v/t.* zaptetmek, boyunduruk altına almak; **sub.ju.ga.tion** *n.* boyunduruk altına alma.

**sub.junc.tive** *gr.* [səbˈdʒʌŋktiv] *n. a.* ~ mood şart kipi.

**sub.lease** [ˈsʌbˈliːs], **sub.let** [ˈ~ˈlet] (*irr.* let) *vb.* kiracının kiracısı olm.; kiralananı kira ile başkasına devretmek.

**sub.II. mate** ⚗ **1.** [ˈsʌblimit] *n.* süblime, aksülümen; **2.** [ˈ~meit] *v/t.* süblimleştirmek; arıtmak; **sub.li¹ma.tion** *n.* süblimleş(tir)me; arıtma; **sub.lime** [səˈblaim] **1.** ☐ ulu, yüce, asil; **2.** *n.* the ~ ulviyet; **3.** *v/t.* ⚗ süblimleştirmek; *fig.* yüceleştirmek; **sub.lim.i.ty** [səˈblimiti] *n.* yücelik, asillik, ululuk.

**sub-ma.chine gun** [ˈsʌbməˈʃiːngʌn] *n.* hafif makineli tüfek.

**sub.ma.rine** [sʌbməˈriːn] **1.** *adj.* denizaltı...; denizaltında yetişen; **2.** *n.* ⚓ denizaltı.

**sub.merge** [səbˈməːdʒ] *v/t. & v/i.* bat(ır)mak; (*bir yeri*) su basmak; **sub.mers.i-bil.i.ty** [~səˈbiliti] *n.* su altında kalabilme; **sub¹mer.sion** *n.* dal(dır)ma; bat(ır)ma; su baskını.

**sub.mis.sion** [səbˈmiʃən] *n.* boyun eğme, itaat, teslim olma (to -e); alçak gönüllülük, uysallık; arz, sunuş; **sub¹mis.sive** ☐ boyun eğen, itaatkâr, alçakgönüllü.

**sub.mit** [səbˈmit] *v/t.* teslim etm. (to -e); takdirine bırakmak, sunmak -e; *part. parl.* ileri sürmek; *v/i. a.* ~ o.s. boyun eğmek, itaat etm. (to -e); *fig. k-ni bşe* hasretmek, adamak (to).

**sub.or.di.nate** **1.** ☐ [səˈbɔːdnit] ikincil, alt, ast; tabi, bağlı; ~ clause *gr.* yan cümle, bağımlı cümlecik; **2.** *n.* ikinci derecede, ast memur; **sub.or.di¹na.tion** *n.* ikincil olma (to -e); itaat, boyun eğme.

**sub.orn** ♫ [sʌˈbɔːn] *v/t.* yalancı tanıklığa teşvik etm., kışkırtmak, ayartmak (to -e); **sub.or¹na.tion** *n.* yalancı tanıklığa teşvik.

**sub.p(o)e.na** ♫ [səbˈpiːnə] **1.** *n.* çağrı kâğıdı, celp, mahkemeye davet; **2.** *v/t.* mahkemeye davet etm. -i.

**sub.scribe** [səbˈskraib] *v/t.* bağış olarak vermek, bağışlamak (*para*) (to -e); imzalamak; altına adını yazmak (to -e); *v/i.* (*gazete, dergi vs.*) abone olm. (to -e); imzalayarak onaylamak; **sub¹scrib.er** *n.* bağış veren (for, to -e); abone (*a. teleph.*) olan.

**sub.scrip.tion** [səbˈskripʃən] *n.* imza; abone; üye aidatı.

**sub.sec.tion** [ˈsʌbsekʃən] *n.* şube, kol, dal.

**sub.se.quence** [ˈsʌbsikwəns] *n.* sonradan gelme, arkası gelme; **sub.se.quent** ☐ sonra gelen, sonraki (to); ~ly sonradan, arkadan.

**sub.serve** [səbˈsəːv] *vb.* hizmette bulunmak, işe yaramak, ilerlemesine yardım etm.; **subˈser.vi.ence** [˵-vjəns] *n.* yararlılık; boyun eğme, itaatkârlık; **subˈser.vi.ent** ☐ boyun eğen, itaatkâr; faydalı, yararlı.

**sub.side** [səbˈsaid] *v/i.* inmek, alçalmak; düşmek *(ateş)*; *(toprağa)* yerleşmek, çökmek *(ev)*; yatışmak, sakinleşmek; ˵ into *bşe* düşmek, gömülmek *(koltuğa)*; çekilmek, hafiflemek *(sel, rüzgâr vs.)*; **sub.sid.ence** [ˈsʌbsidəns] *n.* çökme; yatışma, hafifleme *(rüzgâr vs.)*; **sub.sid.i-ar.y** [səbˈsidjəri] **1.** ☐ yardımcı..., ek; bağlı, tabi, yardımcı olarak kullanılan (to -e); be ˵ to yardımcı olm., bütünleyici olm.; **2.** *n.* bayi, şube; muavin, yardımcı; *a.* ˵ company bağımlı ortaklık, yan kuruluş; **sub.si.dize** [ˈsʌbsidaiz] *v/t.* para vermek *-e*, tahsisat bağlamak *-e*, sübvansiyone etm. *-i*; **ˈsub.si.dy** *n.* devlet yardımı, tahsisat, sübvansiyon.

**sub.sist** [səbˈsist] *v/i.* yaşamak, geçinmek, beslenmek (on *ile*; by *ile*); *v/t. bşe.* bakmak, beslemek; **subˈsist.ence** *n.* geçinim, rızk, nafaka; ˵ wage en düşük geçinme ücreti.

**sub.soil** [ˈsʌbsɔil] *n.* toprakaltı.

**sub.son.ic** [sʌbˈsɔnik] *adj.* ses hızından yavaş.

**sub.stance** [ˈsʌbstəns] *n.* madde, cevher, cisim; öz; *fig.* asıl mesele; içerik, esas; realite, gerçeklik; unsur; varlık, servet. **sub.stan.tial** ☐ [səbˈstænʃəl] gerçek; önemli, esaslı; dayanıklı, mukavim; zengin, varlıklı; **sub.stan.ti.al.i.ty** [˵-ʃiˈæliti] *n.* gerçek varlık, öz, realite; dayanıklılık.

**sub.stan.ti.ate** [səbˈstænʃieit] *v/t.* kanıtlamak, neden göstermek.

**sub.stan.ti.val** ☐ *gr.* [sʌbstənˈtaivəl] isim, ad olarak kullanılan, isim niteliğinde; **sub.stan.tive** [ˈ˵-tiv] **1.** ☐ bağımsız, müstakil; *gr.* isim olarak kullanılan; dayanıklı; tözel; **2.** *n.* isim, ad.

**sub.sti.tute** [ˈsʌbstitjuːt] **1.** *v/i.* yerine geçmek (for -*in*); *v/t.* yerine koymak (for -*in*); **2.** *n.* vekil, mümessil; bedel; **sub.sti**ˈ**tu.tion** *n.* ikame, yerine koyma, başka *bşin* yerine kullanma.

**sub.stra.tum** [ˈsʌbˈstɑːtəm] *n.* esas, temel; ⊕, *geol.* alt tabaka; cevher, madde, töz.

**sub.struc.ture** [ˈsʌbstrʌktʃə] *n.* yapı temeli, toprak alt yapı.

**sub.ten.ant** [ˈsʌbˈtenənt] *n.* kiracının kiracısı, ikinci kiracı.

**sub.ter.fuge** [ˈsʌbtəfjuːdʒ] *n.* kaçamak, kaçamaklı söz, bahane.

**sub.ter.ra.ne.an** ☐ [sʌbtəˈreinjən] yeraltı; gizli.

**sub.til.ize** [ˈsʌtilaiz] *v/t.* inceltmek, düzeltmek; *v/i.* incelikle, ustalıkla kullanmak.

**sub.ti.tle** [ˈsʌbtaitl] *n.* ikincil başlık.

**sub.tle** ☐ [ˈsʌtl] ince (ruhlu); esrarengiz; çözümü zor, karışık; kurnaz, hilekâr; kılı kırk yaran; mahir, usta; **ˈsub.tle.ty** *n.* incelik, naziklik; kurnazlık, cin fikirlilik.

**sub.to.pia** [sʌbˈtəupiə] *n.* şehir dışında geniş yerleşim bölgesi.

**sub.tract** [səbˈtrækt] *v/t.* ⅍ çıkarmak, hesaptan düşmek **subˈtrac.tion** *n.* çıkarma, tarh.

**sub.trop.i.cal** [ˈsʌbˈtrɔpikəl] *adj.* astropikal.

**sub.urb** [ˈsʌbəːb] *n.* varoş, banliyö, dış mahalle; **sub.ur.ban** [səˈbəːbən] *adj.* kenar mahallede oturan; banliyö..., banliyö ile ilgili; **subˈur.bia** [˵-bjə] *n.* dış mahalleler ve buralarda oturanların yaşamı.

**sub.ven.tion** [səbˈvenʃən] *n.* para yardımı, tahsisat, sübvansiyon, yardım.

**sub.ver.sion** [sʌbˈvəːʃən] *n.* devirme, devrilme; yık(ıl)ma, tahrip; **subˈver.sive** *adj.* yıkıcı, devirmeyi amaçlayan, tahripkâr (of).

**sub.vert** [sʌbˈvəːt] *v/t.* devirmeye çalışmak *(hükümeti)*; sarsmak, harap etm.; bozmak, ifsat etm.

**sub.way** [ˈsʌbwei] *n.* (*part. yaya*) tünel, yeraltı geçidi; *Am.* yeraltı metro, tünel. **suc.ceed** [səkˈsiːd] *vb.* muvaffak olm.; başarmak (in -*i*); vâris olm. (to -*e*); -*in* yerine geçmek *(taht vs.)*; başarıyla sonuçlanmak; izlemek, sonra gelmek -*den*; he ˵s in -*de* başarılı oluyor.

**suc.cess** [səkˈses] *n.* başarı(lı sonuç), muvaffakiyet; başarılı kimse; he was a great ˵ çok başarılıydı; **sucˈcess.ful** ☐ [˵-ful] başarılı, muvaffakiyetli; be ˵ başarılı olm.; **suc.ces.sion** [˵ˈseʃən] *n.* ardıllık, silsile, sıra, seri; kalıtım; döl, zürriyet; ˵ to the throne tahta geçme hakkı, veliaht olma; in ˵ ardı ardına; ˵ duty veraset ve intikal vergisi; **sucˈces.sive** ☐ ardıl, müteakip, birbirini izleyen; **sucˈces.sor** *n.* halef, ardıl, vâris; ˵ to the throne veliaht.

**suc.cinct** ☐ [səkˈsiŋkt] az ve özlü, kısa ve açık olarak.

**suc.co.ry** ⚕ [ˈsʌkəri] hindiba.

**suc.co(u)r** [ˈsʌkə] **1.** *n.* yardım, imdat; ✕ kurtarmaya gelen kuvvetler; **2.** *v/t.* yardım etm. -*e*; ✕ imdada yetişerek kuşat

suitor

madan kurtarmak.

**suc.cu.lence** [ˈsʌkjuləns] *n.* körpelik, sulu olma, özlülük; **ˈsuc.cu.lent** □ sulu, özlü; lezzetli; dolgun *(meyve)*, etli, kalın *(bitki)*.

**suc.cumb** [səˈkʌm] *v/i.* dayanamamak (to -e); yenik düşmek (to -e).

**such** [sʌtʃ] **1.** *adj.* böyle, şöyle, öyle, bu gibi; bu kadar, o kadar; ~ a man böyle bir adam, öyle biri ki; *s.* another; no ~ thing böyle bir şey yoktur; ~ as gibi, örneğin; ~ and ~ falan filân; ~ is life hayat bu; **2.** *pron.* bu, şu, o gibi; **ˈsuch.like** *adj. & pron.* bu gibi, buna benzer, benzeri, böylesi.

**suck** [sʌk] **1.** *vb.* emmek, içine çekmek; meme emmek; ~ up to *sl. b-ne* çanak yalayıcılığı, yaltaklık etm.; ~ s.o.'s brains *b-nin* ağzını aramak, bilgi almaya çalışmak; **2.** *n.* emme, emiş, mas; give ~ emzirmek; **ˈsuck.er** *n.* emen *b-i veya bş;* ⊕ tulumba pistonu; *Am.* F saplı şeker; ♀ kök filizi, fışkın; *Am.* budala, ahmak; **ˈsuck.ing** *adj.* emici; ~ pig henüz süt emen domuz yavrusu; **suck.le** [ˈ~l] *vb.* emzirmek, çocuğa meme vermek; **ˈsuck.ling** *n.* memede çocuk, süt çocuğu.

**suc.tion** [ˈsʌkʃən] *n.* emme; *attr.* emici...; ~ cleaner, ~ sweeper aspiratör.

**sud.den** □ [ˈsʌdn] ani, beklenilmeyen, birden; on a ~, (all) of a ~ ansızın, birdenbire; **ˈsud.den.ness** *n.* birdenbire olma.

**su.dor.if.ic** [sjuːdəˈrifik] *adj.* terletici *(ilâç).*

**suds** [sʌdz] *n. pl.* alkalik sıvı, sabun köpüğü; **ˈsuds.y** *adj. Am.* köpüklü, sabunlu.

**sue** [sjuː] *v/t. b-nin* aleyhine dava açmak; ~ out mahkemeden hüküm çıkartmak; *v/i.* istemek, talep etm. (for -i), dava açmak (for).

**suède** [sweid] *n.* (podü)süet.

**su.et** [ˈsjuit] *n.* içyağı, donyağı; **ˈsu.et.y** *adj.* içyağlı.

**suf.fer** [ˈsʌfə] *v/i.* tutulmuş olm. (from -e), dert çekmek (from -den); *v/t.* katlanmak -e, dayanmak, sabretmek; **ˈsuf.fer.ance** *n.* müsamaha, göz yumma; on ~ müsamaha yüzünden *(veya* dolayısiyle); **ˈsuf.fer.er** *n.* dertli, ıstırap çeken kimse; hasta; kazazede; **suf.fer.ing** *n.* acı, ıstırap.

**suf.fice** [səˈfais] *vb.* kâfi gelmek, yet(iş)mek; ~ it to say yalnız şu kadarını söyleyeyim ki.

**suf.fi.cien.cy** [səˈfiʃənsi] *n.* yeterlilik, kifayet; geçinecek kadar gelir; a ~ of money yeterli miktar para; **sufˈfi.ci.ent** □ kâfi, yeterli; be ~ kâfi gelmek, yetmek.

**suf.fix** *gr.* [ˈsʌfiks] **1.** *v/t.* bir sözcüğün

sonuna ek koymak; **2.** *n.* sonek, sontakı.

**suf.fo.cate** [ˈsʌfəkeit] *v/t. & v/i.* boğ(ul)-mak; tıka(n)mak; sön(dür)mek; **suf.fo-ˈca.tion** *n.* boğ(ul)ma; sön(dür)me; **suf-fo.ca.tive** □ [ˈ~kətiv] boğucu.

**suf.fra.gan** *eccl.* [ˈsʌfrəgən] *n.* piskopos yardımcısı; **ˈsuf.frage** *n.* oy kullanma (hakkı); onay, tasvip (oyu); **suf.fra.gette** [~ə-ˈdʒet] *n.* kadınların oy kullanma haklarını savunan kadın.

**suf.fuse** [səˈfjuːz] *v/t.* dökmek, yayılıp örtmek, kaplamak *(renk, sıvı vs.);* **suf-ˈfu.sion** [~ʒən] *n.* yay(ıl)ma; kızartı.

**sug.ar** [ˈʃugə] **1.** *n.* şeker; *fig.* tatlı söz; **2.** *v/t.* şeker katmak -e; tatlı sözle yumuşatmak -i; **ˈ~.ba.sin** *n.* şekerlik, şeker kutusu; **ˈ~.beet** *n.* şeker pancarı; **ˈ~.bowl** *n. Am.* şekerlik, şeker kâsesi; **ˈ~.cane** *n.* şekerkamışı; **ˈ~.coat** *v/t.* şekerle kaplamak; tatlılaştırmak; **ˈ~.loaf** *n.* kelle şekeri; **ˈ~.plum** *n.* bonbon, şekerleme; **ˈ~.tongs** *n. pl.* (a pair of) şeker maşası; **sug.ar.y** *adj.* şekerli, şekere benzer, şeker gibi, bal gibi; yüze gülücü.

**sug.gest** [səˈdʒest] *v/t.* telkin etm.; teklif etm., önermek, sunmak; ileri sürmek, ortaya koymak; ima etm., sezdirmek; **sugˈges.tion** *n.* fikir, teklif; öneri, tavsiye; ima, işaret; telkin, ilham.

**sug.ges.tive** □ [səˈdʒestiv] manalı, telkin edici, imalı, fikir verici, manidar (of); açık saçık, müstehcen; **sugˈges.tive.ness** *n.* anlamlılık, manalılık; müstehcenlik.

**su.i.cid.al** □ [sjuiˈsaidl] intiharla ilgili, intihar etme isteğiyle igili, intihara sürükleyen; **su.i.cide** [ˈ~said] **1.** *n.* intihar; kendini öldüren kimse; **2.** *v/i. Am.* intihar etm.

**suit** [sjuːt] **1.** *n.* takım; erkek elbisesi; tayyör, kostüm; dilek, istek; evlenme teklifi; *iskambil:* takım; ♂ dava; follow ~ *iskambil:* takıma uymak; *fig.* aynı şeyi yapmak, taklit etm.; **2.** *v/t.* uygun gelmek, yaramak, iyi gelmek, uygun düşürmek, uydurmak; *b-ne* yakışmak, açmak, uymak *(elbise, renk vs.);* ~ oneself kendi rahatını, gereksinimini, isteklerini sağlamak; ~ s.th. to *bşi* uydurmak, intibak ettirmek; be ~ed uygun olm. (for, to -e); *v/i.* uymak, olmak; işine gelmek; **suit-aˈbil.i.ty** *n.* uygunluk, elverişlilik; **ˈsuit.a-ble** □ uygun, elverişli (for, to -e); **ˈsuit-a.ble.ness** = suitability; **ˈsuit.case** *n.* bavul, valiz; **suite** [swiːt] *n.* maiyet; takım; ♪ suit; *a.* ~ of rooms daire, takım odalar *(otelde);* suit.ing *n.* kumaş *(bir kanepe, iki koltuk);* **suit.ing** † [ˈsjuːtiŋ] *n.* takım elbiselik kumaş; **ˈsuit.or** *n.* âşık, bir kıza talip erkek; öö davacı.

**sulk** [sʌlk] **1.** v/i. a. be in the ~s somurtmak, gücenmek, surat asmak; **2.** n. **sulks**
pl., **'sulk.i.ness** asık suratlılık, somurtkanlık; **'sulk.y 1.** ☐ somurtkan, asık suratlı, aksi, huysuz; **2.** n. spor: iki tekerlekli tek kişilik hafif atlı araba.

**sul.len** ☐ ['sʌlən] can sıkıcı, sinirlendirici, asık yüzlü. somurtkan; kapanık; **'sul-
len.ness** n. somurtkanlık.

**sul.ly** mst fig. ['sʌli] v/t. kirletmek, lekelemek.

**sul.pha** ['sʌlfə] pl. = sulphonamides.

**sul.phate** ﾑ ['sʌlfeit] n. asit sülfirik tuzu,
sülfat; **sul.phide** ﾑ ['~faid] n. sülfirik
karışımı, sülfit.

**sul.pho.na.mides** ﾠ [sʌl'fɔnəmaidz] n. pl.
sülfonamid.

**sul.phur** ﾑ ['sʌlfə] **1.** n. kükürt; **2.** v/t. kükürtlemek; **sul.phu.re.ous** [sʌl'fjuəriəs]
adj. kükürtlü, kükürt gibi; **sul.phu.ret-
ted hy.dro.gen** ['~fjuretid'haidridʒən] n.
sülfit hidrik; **sul.phu.ric** [~'fjuərik] adj.
kükürtlü; ~ acid sülfirik asit, zaçyağı;
**'sul.phu.rize** v/t. ⊕ kükürtlemek; kükürt
katmak, vulkanize etm.; **sul.phur.ous**
['~fərəs] adj. kükürtlü, kükürt gibi.

**sul.tan** ['sʌltən] n. sultan, padişah; **sul-
tan.a** [sʌl'tɑːnə] n. sultan karısı, annesi
veya kızı.

**sul.tri.ness** ['sʌltrinis] n. sıcak ve rutubetli oluş, boğucu oluş; **'sul.try** ☐ boğucu,
bunaltıcı, sıkıntılı; fig. ateşli, hararetli,
heyecanlı.

**sum** [sʌm] **1.** n. tutar, hesap; toplam, yekûn; miktar, meblağ; özet, hülâsa; fig.
örnek; aritmetik problemi; do ~s bşin
hesabını yapmak, saymak; in ~ özetle,
kısaca; **2.** vb. mst ~ up özetlemek; b-i
hakkında hüküm vermek; yekûn toplamak.

**su.mac(h)** ﾠ ['suːmæk] n. sumak, somak.

**sum.ma.rize** ['sʌməraiz] v/t. özetlemek;
**sum.mar.y 1.** ☐ kısa, özet halinde; öö
seri, basit ve kısa...; jürisiz; **2.** n. özet,
hülâsa.

**sum.mer¹** ['sʌmə] **1.** n. yaz (mevsimi); ~
resort sayfiye; **2.** v/t. & v/i. yazı geçirmek; yazın beslemek; **'~.house** n. kameriye, çardak.

**sum.mer²** ﾑ [~] n. tabanın ana kirişi, ta
şıyıcı kiriş.

**sum.mer.like** ['sʌməlaik], **'sum.mer.ly** adj.
yazlık, yaza ait, yaz gibi.

**summer...:** '~**-school** n. yaz okulu; '**.time**
n. yaz mevsimi; '~'time n. yaz saati (bir
saat ileri); **'sum.mer.y** adj. yaza ait, yaz
gibi.

**sum.mit** ['sʌmit] n. tepe, zirve, doruk, en
üst derece (a. fig.).

**sum.mon** ['sʌmən] v/t. çağır(t)mak, emir-
le davet etm.; öö celp etm.; fig. mst ~ up
toplamak (güç); **'sum.mon.er** n. haberci,
kurye, ulak; **sum.mons** ['~z] n. pl. öö
celpname, çağrı; ✗ teslim ol çağrısı.

**sump** mot. [sʌmp] n. çirkef çukuru (ma-
dende); ⊕ yağ haznesi.

**sump.ter** ['sʌmptə] n. a. '~**-horse,**
'~**-mule** † yük beygiri.

**sump.ter** ['sʌmptjuəri] adj. sarfiyata ait,
**sump.tu.ar.y** ['sʌmptjuəri] adj. sarfiyata
ait, masrafla ilgili; masrafları sınırla-
yan; lüks...

**sump.tu.ous** ☐ ['sʌmptjuəs] kıymetli, mükellef, tantanalı, çok konforlu, muhteşem; **'sump.tu.ous.ness** n. görkem, ihtişam, tantana, lüks.

**sun** [sʌn] **1.** n. güneş; **2.** v/t. & v/i. güneş-
len(dir)mek; güneşe sermek; güneş ban-
yosu yapmak; '~**.baked** adj. güneşte ku-
rutulup sertleştirilmiş; '~**-bath** n. güneş
banyosu; '~**-bathe** v/i. güneşlenmek, güneş banyosu yapmak; '~**.beam** n. güneş
ışını; '~**-blind** n. güneşlik, güneş tentesi; '~**.burn** n. güneşten yanma; güneş yanığı; '~**.burnt** adj. güneşten esmerleşmiş.

**sun.dae** ['sʌndi] n. üstü ceviz meyve ve
şurupla kaplanmış dondurma, peşmelba.

**Sun.day** ['sʌndi] n. pazar (günü); ~ **school**
kilisede pazar günleri din dersleri verilen okul.

**sun.der** poet. ['sʌndə] vb. birbirinden ayırmak, ayrılmak; kop(ar)mak.

**sun-di.al** ['sʌndaiəl] n. güneş saati.

**sun.down** ['sʌndaun] n. güneş batması,
gurup.

**sun.dry** ['sʌndri] **1.** adj. çeşitli (şeyler);
**2. sun.dries** n. pl. part. † ['~driz] ufak
tefek şeyler, muhtelif parça mallar.

**sun.flow.er** ﾠ ['sʌnflauə] n. ayçiçeği.

**sung** [sʌŋ] pret. & p.p. of sing.

**sun...:** '~**-glass.es** n. pl. (a. pair of) güneş
gözlüğü; '~**-god** n. güneş tanrısı; '~**-hel-
met** n. tropik güneş ışınından koruyan
şapka, kolonyal şapka.

**sun-lamp** ['sʌnlæmp] n. ﾠ ültraviyole lam
bası; film: jüpiter lambası.

**sun.less** ['sʌnlis] adj. güneş ışığı almə
yan, karanlık, kasvetli; **'sun.light** n. güneş ışığı; **'sun.lit** adj. güneşle aydınlan
mış.

523 **supplant**

sun.ni.ness ['sʌninis] *n.* güneşlilik, güneşli olma, parlak olma *(a. fig.);* **'sun.ny** ☐
güneşli, aydınlık *(a. fig.);* neşeli.
sun...: '~.rise *n.* gün doğuşu, tulu; '~.room
*n.* camekânlı taraça; '~.set *n.* güneş batması; '~.shade *n.* güneş şemsiyesi, parasol; '~.shine *n.* güneş ışığı; ~ roof *mot.*
açılır kapanır tavan; '~.shin.y *adj.* güneşli, açık, bulutsuz; neşeli, keyifli; '~-spot
*n. ast.* güneş lekesi; '~-stroke *n.* ⚡ güneş
çarpması; '~-up *n.* gündoğumu.
sup¹ [sʌp] *v/i.* akşam yemeğini yemek
(off *veya* on s.th.).
sup² [~] *v/t.* & *v/i.* yudum yudum içmek,
yudumlamak; kaşık kaşık içmek.
su.per¹ ['sjuːpə] 1. *n. thea. sl.* figüran; 2.
*adj.* F birinci sınıf, süper, mükemmel;
büyük boyda.
su.per² [~] *prefix* üst, üstün(de); fazla.
su.per...: ~.a'buond *vb.* fazlasiyle bulunmak, *bş* çok bol miktarda bulunmak (in,
with); ~.a'bun.dant ☐ bol bol, pek çok, bitmez tükenmez; '~.'add *v/t.* daha da ilâve etm., eklemek; ~.an.nu.ate [~'ræn-
jueit] *v/t.* emekliye ayırmak; ~d emekli,
yaşlılık nedeniyle çalışamaz olmuş; eski kafalı; eskimiş, modası geçmiş; ~.an-
nu'a.tion *n.* emeklilik; emekli maaşı; ~
fund emekli sandığı.
su.perb ☐ muhteşem, görkemli, harikulâde, enfes. .
su.per...: '~.car.go *n.* ⚓ geminin yük memuru *veya* armatör vekili; '~.charg.er *n.*
*mot.* kompresör, üfleç; su.per.cil..i.ous
☐ [~'siliəs] kibirli, gururlu; su.per'cil.i-
ous.ness *n.* kibir, gurur; su.per-'dreadnought *n.* ağır toplu deniz zırhlısı; su-
per.er.o.ga.tion [~rero'geiʃən] *n.* vazife-
nin gereğinden fazla iş görme; su.per.e-
rog.a.to.ry ☐ [~re'rogətəri] vazifesinden
fazla olarak; su.per.fi.cial ☐ [~'fiʃəl]
sathî, üstünkörü. yüzeysel; su.per.fi.ci.al-
i.ty [~fiʃi'æliti] *n.* sathilik, üstünkörü
oluş; su.per.fi.ci.es [~'fiʃiːz] *n.* satıh,
yüz(ey); 'su.per'fine *adj.* fevkalâde güzel; çok zarif; pek ince; su.per.flu.i.ty
[~'fluːiti] *n.* bolluk, fazlalık, çokluk (of);
su'per.flu.ous ☐ [~fluəs] fazla, lüzumsuz,
bol bol; su.per'heat *v/t.* ⊕ fazla ısıtmak;
su.per.het ['~'het] *n. radyo:* gelen sinyali aynı sinyale karıştıran alıcı, cihaz.
su.per...: ~.'high.way *n. Am.* oto yolu, otoban: ~'hu.man ☐ insanüstü; ~.im.pose
['~rim'pəuz] *v/t. bşin* üzerine koymak
*veya* birbiri üzerine koymak; ~.in.duce
['~rin'djuːs] *v/t.* eklemek, eklemek (on,
upon -e); ~.in.tend [~rin'tend] *v/t.* kontrol etm.. gözetmek; ~.in'tend.ence *n.*

kontrol, gözetim; ~.in'tend.ent 1. *n.* müfettiş; müdür; 2. *adj.* yönetimsel, idarî;
yöneten.
su.pe.ri.or [sjuː'piəriə] 1. ☐ üstün (to), daha yüksek,.daha iyi; mükemmel, fevkalâde, olağanüstü; kibirli, üstünlük taslayan; ~ officer üst subay *veya* memur; 2.
*n.* üst, amir; *eccl.* baş rahip; *mst* lady ~
başrahibe; su.pe.ri.or.i.ty [~'ɔriti] *n.* üstünlük.
su.per.la.tive [sjuː'pəːlətiv] 1. ☐ en yüksek; mükemmel, eşsiz; fazla; *gr.* enüs-
tün *(sıfat ve zarfların);* 2. *n. a.* ~ degree
*gr.* enüstünlük (derecesi); su.per.man
['sjuːpæmən] *n.* üst insan, fevkalbeşer;
'su.per.mar.ket *n.* büyük mağaza, süpermarket; su.per.nal [sjuː'pəːnl] *adj.* göksel, semavî; ulu, yüce; ilâhi; su.per.nat-
u.ral ☐ [sjuːpə'nætʃrəl] doğaüstü, sürna-
türel, harikulâde; su.per.nu.mer.ar.y
[~'njuːmərəri] 1. *adj.* fazla, artakalan;
2. *n.* fazla *b-i veya bş; thea.* figüran;
'su.per'pose *vb.* başka *bşin* üstüne koymak; birbiri üzerine koymak; su.per.po-
'si.tion *n.* üstüste koyma; *geol.* katmanlaşma, tabakalaşma; 'su.per'scribe *vb.*
üstüne yazmak, başlığını koymak; adres
yazmak, koymak; su.per.scrip.tion *n.* yazıt; adres; başlık; su.per.sede [~'siːd]
*v/t.* yerine geçmek, yerine başka *bşi (veya b-ni)* geçirmek, *b-nin* ayağını kaydı-
rarak yerine geçmek; *fig. b-ni* geçmek,
geride bırakmak; su.per'ses.sion *n.* yerine geçme; su.per.son.ic *phys.* [~'sɔnik]
*adj.* sesten hızlı; su.per.sti.tion [~'stiʃən]
*n.* bâtıl itikat, boş inan; hurafe; su.per-
sti.tious ☐ [~'stiʃəs] boş şeylere inanan;
su.per.struc.ture [~'strʌktʃə] *n.* üst yapı;
temel üzerine yapılan bina; su.per.vene
[~'viːn] *v/i. b-ne* iltihak etm., katılmak;
eklenmek, ilâve olunmak (on, upon -e),
ummadık anda dahil olm., katılmak; su-
per.ven.tion [~'venʃən] *n.* iltihak, dahil
olma, eklenme; su.per.vise ['~'vaiz] *v/t.*
nezaret etm. -e, denetlemek -i; gözetmek
-i; idare etm. -i; su.per.vi.sion [~'viʒən]
*n.* nezaret, denetim, gözetim; idare, kontrol; su.per.vi.sor ['~vaizə] *n.* murakıp,
denetçi, müfettiş; *univ.* danışman.
su.pine 1. *gr.* ['sjuːpain] *n.* Latince'de *-i
veya* -den halindeki isim-fiil; 2. ☐ [~
'pain] sırtüstü yatan, yüz yukarı duran,
yatay (duran); kaygısız, üşengeç, miskin. lâkayt; su'pine.ness *n.* lâkaytlık,
miskinlik.
sup.per ['sʌpə] *n.* akşam yemeği; the
(Lord's) ♀ *eccl.* Kudas.
sup.plant [sə'plaːnt] *v/t. b-nin* ayağını

kaydırıp yerine geçmek; *fig.* gölgede bırakmak, üstün gelmek.

**sup.ple** [ˈsʌpl] **1.** □ kolayca eğilir, yumuşak, elâstiki; uysal, muti; **2.** *vb.* yumuşatmak, kolay eğilir hale getirmek.

**sup.ple.ment 1.** [ˈsʌplimənt] *n.* ek, zeyil, ilâve *(gazete vs.)*; **2.** *v/t.* [ˈ~ment] ilâve etm., eklemek, tamamlamak (by, with *ile*) **sup.ple'men.tal** □, **sup.ple'men.ta.ry** *adj.* eklenen, ilâve...; bütünleyici, tamamlayıcı; ~ order ek sipariş.

**sup.ple.ness** [ˈsʌplnis] *n.* yumuşaklık, esneklik; *fig.* uysallık.

**sup.pli.ant** [ˈsʌpliənt] **1.** □ yalvarıp yakaran, rica eden; **2.** *n.* dilekçe sahibi; ricacı kimse.

**sup.pli.cate** [ˈsʌplikeit] *vb. b-ne* yalvarmak, rica etm.; yakarmak; **sup.pli'ca.tion** *n.* yalvarış, niyaz; **sup.pli.ca.to.ry** [ˈ~kətəri] *adj.* yalvarış kabilinden; niyaz eden.

**sup.pli.er** [səˈplaiə] *n.* gereksinimleri karşılayan kimse *veya* firma *(a. ↑)*.

**sup.ply** [səˈplai] **1.** *v/t.* bşi *b-ne* sağlamak, temin etm., ihtiyacı karşılamak (with *ile)*; çare bulmak; tamin etm., görevini yerine getirmek; *b-nin* yerini tutmak, telâfi etm.; teçhiz etm.; ikmal etm.; **2.** *n.* gereç, malzeme; tedarik, temin; stok, depo mevcudu; ↑ arz, sunu; mümessil, acenta; *mst* supplies *pl.* ↑ erzak, gereçler, levazım; *parl.* bütçe, tahsisat, ödenek; ✕ ikmal; in short ~ yetersiz, kıt, az; on ~ *b-ne* vekâleten, *b-nin* yerine; Committee of ~ *parl.* bütçe komisyonu.

**sup.port** [səˈpɔːt] **1.** *n.* dayanak, destek *(a. fig.)*; ⊕ mesnet, dayak, istinatgâh; destekleme, yardım, geçim; **2.** *v/t.* desteklemek *(a. fig.)*; beslemek *-i*, bakmak, yardım etm. *-e (aile vs.)*; ısrar etm., durmak *(münakaşa)*; arka olm. *-e*, savunmak, müdafaa etm.; ileri sürmek, iddia etm. *(düşünce)*; tahammül etm., dayanmak, katlanmak *-e*; ~ing actor yardımcı oyuncu; ~ing programme *film*: esas filmden başka gösterilen (küçük) film(ler); **sup'port.a.ble** □ katlanılabilir, çekilir, tahammül edilebilir; dayanıklı; **sup'port.er** *n.* taraftar; yardımcı, muavin; jartiyer, askı, korse.

**sup.pose** [səˈpəuz] *v/t.* farzetmek, zannetmek; he is ~d to do yapması gerekir; ~ *veya* supposing (that)... faraza, farzedelim ki...; ~ we go gitsek nasıl olur?; he is rich, I ~ sanırım zengindir.

**sup.posed** □ [səˈpəuzd] sözde, sözüm ona, farzedilen, denen; **sup'pos.ed.ly** [~idli] *adv.* güya, muhtemel.

**sup.pos.ing** [səˈpəuziŋ] *conj.* şayet, faraza.

**sup.po.si.tion** [sʌpəˈziʃən] *n.* farz, zan, tahmin; varsayım, ipotez, farazîye; **sup.pos.i.ti.tious** □. [səpɔziˈtiʃəs] değiştirilmiş, sahte; varsayılı, ipotetik, **sup'pos.i.to.ry** [~təri] fitil, supozituvar.

**sup.press** [səˈpres] *v/t.* bastırmak, sindirmek; zaptetmek; basılıp yayınlanmasını önlemek; **sup.pres.sion** [səˈpreʃən] *n.* bastırma, sindirme; baskı, tutma, önleme; örtbas etme; **sup'pres.sive** □ [~siv] bastıran, sindiren; tutan, zapteden; **sup'pres.sor** *n.* ↯ paraziti önleyici cihaz.

**sup.pu.rate** [ˈsʌpjuəreit] *v/i.* cerahat toplamak, irin:enmek; işlemek *(yara)*; **sup'pu'ra.tion** *n.* cerahat, irin.

**su.pra-na.tion.al** [ˈsjuːprəˈnæʃənl] *adj.* devletlerüstü.

**su.prem.a.cy** [sjuˈpreməsi] *n.* üstünlük, yücelik, ululuk; egemenlik; **su.preme** □ [sjuːˈpriːm] en yüksek; en yüksek derecede; en yüksek mertebede; kritik; ☰ Court Anayasa Mahkemesi; Yargıtay.

**sur.charge** [sɔːˈtʃɑːdʒ] **1.** *v/t.* fazla yüklemek, fazla doldurmak; sürşarj basmak *-e*; posta pulunun üzerine yeni fiyat bastırmak; **2.** *n.* sürşarj; fazla ağır yük; fazla navlun alma, sürtaks.

**surd** ♮ [səːd] *adj.* asam, tamsayı ile ifade edilemeyen, irrasyonel *(sayı)*.

**sure** □ [ʃuə] *com.* güvenilir, emin (of *-den*); kesin; sağlam; şüphesiz, muhakkak; to be ~! F ~ enough!, *Am.* ~! elbette, muhakkak; I'm ~ I don't know vallahi bilmiyorum; he is ~ to return muhakkak geri gelir; make ~ kanaat getirmek (of); temin, tasdik etm. (of); **'~-foot.ed** *adj.* ayağını sıkı basan, düşmez, kaymaz; **'sure'ly** *adv.* elbette, şüphesiz; emniyetle olarak, tehlikesizce; **'sure.ness** *n.* kesinlik; emin olma, güven; **'sure.ty** *n.* emniyet, güvenlik; güvence; kefil, rehine.

**surf** [səːf] *n.* çatlayan dalgalar; dalgaların kıyıya *veya* kayalara vurup çatlaması.

**sur.face** [ˈsəːfis] **1.** *n.* yüz, düzey, satıh, dış görünüş, yüzey; görünüş; ✈ kanatlar; control ~ ✈ kontrol dümeni; below the ~ ✕ yeraltında; **2.** *v/i.* suyun üstüne çıkmak *(denizaltı)*; kaplamak *(yol)*; düz yapmak; **'~.man** *n.* ◉ hat amelesi.

**surf...**: **'~-board** *n. surfing*: kayak; **'~-boat** *n.* dalgaları aşabilen hafif kayık.

**sur.feit** [ˈsəːfit] **1.** *n.* aşırı doyma; yemekte aşırılık, şişkinlik, tiksinti; **2.** *v/t.* & *v/i.* tıka basa dol(dur)mak; fazlasiyle doy(ur)mak (on, with); *fig.* bıktırmak.

çatlayacak derecede ye(dir)mek.

**surf-rid.ing** [ˈsəːfraidiŋ] *n. spor:* dalgalar üzerinde tahta ile kayarak yapılan bir tür su kayağı.

**surge** [səːdʒ] **1.** *n.* büyük dalga; dalgaların çatlaması; dalga gibi sürüklenme; **2.** *vb.* dalgalanmak; kabarmak; sahile veya kayalara vurup parçalanmak.

**sur.geon** [səːdʒən] *n.* cerrah, operatör; ✕ askerî doktor; ⚓ gemi doktoru; **sur.ger.y** [ˈsəːdʒəri] *n.* cerrahlık (ilmi), operatörlük; muayene(hane); ameliyat(hane); ~ hours *pl.* hasta kabul saati.

**sur.gi.cal** [ˈsəːdʒikəl] cerrahî, cerrahlığa ait, ameliyat...

**sur.li.ness** [ˈsəːlinis] *n.* aksilik, huysuzluk, somurtkanlık; **ˈsur.ly** gülmez, ters, aksi, huysuz; sert *(arazi).*

**sur.mise 1.** [ˈsəːmaiz] *n.* sanı, zan; kuşku, vesvese; **2.** [səˈmaiz] *vb.* sanmak, zannetmek, kuşkulanmak; vesvese beslemek, şüphe etm.

**sur.mount** [səˈmaunt] *v/t.* üstün gelmek -*e*, üstesinden gelmek -*in (güçlük vs.)*; *b-ni* yenmek, galip gelmek; ~ed by veya with *bşin* üstünde olan, üstü ...ile örtülen; **surˈmount.a.ble** *adj.* üstesinden gelinebilir.

**sur.name** [ˈsəːneim] **1.** *n.* soyadı, aile adı; lakap; **2.** *v/t.* soyadı vermek -*e*; ~d soyadlı.

**sur.pass** *fig.* [səːˈpɑːs] *v/t.* geçmek, aşmak; üstün olm. -*e*; **surˈpass.ing** eşsiz, fevkalâde, harikulâde.

**sur.plice** *eccl.* [ˈsəːpləs] katolik papazların kilisede giydikleri beyaz cüppe.

**sur.plus** [ˈsəːpləs] **1.** *n.* fazla kısım, artan miktar; **2.** *adj.* artık, fazla(lık); ~ population nüfus fazlalığı; **ˈsur.plus.age** = surplus 1; gerektiğinden fazla olan şey.

**sur.prise** [səˈpraiz] **1.** *n.* sürpiz, hayret, şaşkınlık; baskın; beklenmedik olay; ✕ baskınla ele geçirme; take by ~ gafil avlamak; *attr.* sürpriz..., beklenmedik...; **2.** *v/t.* hayrete düşürmek, şaşırtmak; ✕ baskın yapmak; **surˈpris.ing** hayret verici, şaşırtıcı.

**sur.re.al.ism** [səˈriəlizəm] *n. sanat:* sürrealizm, gerçeküstücülük; **surˈre.al.ist** *n.* sürrealist, gerçeküstücü kimse.

**sur.ren.der** [səˈrendə] **1.** *n.* teslim(iyet), feragat; bırakma, terk; **2.** *v/t.* teslim etm.; terk etm. *(mülkiyet);* feragat etm., vermek; *v/i. a.* ~ o.s. teslim olm. (to -*e*); bir duygu ve fikrin esiri olm., kapılmak -*e*.

**sur.rep.ti.tious** [sʌrəpˈtiʃəs] gizli, saklı, el altından.

**sur.ro.gate** [ˈsʌrogit] *n.* vekil, mümessil *(part. papaz),* yerine geçen *b-i veya bş*.

**sur.round** [səˈraund] *v/t.* etrafını sarmak, çevirmek; ✕ kuşatmak, çember içine almak; **surˈround.ing** *adj.* civarında bulunan; **surˈround.ings** *n. pl.* çevre, muhit, etraf.

**sur.tax** [ˈsəːtæks] *n.* munzam vergi, ek vergi, katma vergi.

**sur.veil.lance** [səːˈveiləns] *n.* gözetim, gözaltı(nda tutma).

**sur.vey 1.** [səːˈvei] *v/t.* teftiş, tetkik etm.; yoklamak, gözden geçirmek; mesaha etm., haritasını çıkarmak; dikkatle *bşin* tümüne göz gezdirmek; **2.** [ˈ~] *n.* teftiş, tetkik; gözden geçirme; *bşe* genel bakış; mesaha, yüzölçümü, yer ölçmesi; rapor, ekspertiz; **surˈvey.or** *n.* sürveyan; mesaha memuru, arazi mühendisi; müfettiş, bilirkişi.

**sur.viv.al** [səˈvaivəl] *n.* kalım, beka, hayatta kalma, artakalma; **surˈvive** *v/t.* fazla yaşamak -*den,* daha uzun ömürlü olm. -*den; v/i.* hayatta kalmak; **surˈvi.vor** *n.* hayatta kalan, kurtulan kimse.

**sus.cep.ti.bil.i.ty** [səseptəˈbiliti] *n.* alınganlık, hassasiyet (to -*e); oft.* susceptibilities *pl.* hassas nokta(lar); **susˈcep.ti.ble** ◻, **susˈcep.tive** hassas, alıngan (to -*e*); duygulu; be ~ of elverişli -*e,* kaldırır.

**sus.pect 1.** [səsˈpekt] *v/t. b-den, bşden* şüphelenmek, kuşkulanmak, *bşe* ihtimal vermek, endişe etm., vesveselenmek; **2.** [ˈsʌspket] *n.* şüpheli, kuşkulu, zanlı *b-i veya bş,* sanık; **3.** = susˈpect.ed *adj.* şüpheli, kuşkulu, zanlı, güvenilmez.

**sus.pend** [səsˈpend] *vb.* asmak; havada asılmış gibi durmak; ertelemek, tehir etm., askıya almak; tatil etm., geçici olarak durdurmak *(iş);* ertelemek, tecil etm. *(hüküm);* bir memura geçici işten el çektirmek; boykot etm. *(sporcu);* ~ed asılı, muallak; ~ed animation zâhiri ölüm, geçici olarak canlılığını kaybetme; **susˈpend.er** *n.* çorap askısı, jartiyer; ~s *pl. Am.* pantolon askısı.

**sus.pense** [səsˈpens] *n.* muallak kalma, askıda kalış, şüpheli olma, kararsızlık, tereddüt; merak, heyecan; ~ account ⊤ geçici, muvakkat hesap; **sus.pen.sion** [~ˈpenʃən] *n.* as(ıl)ma; erteleme, sonraya bırakma, tehir, tatil; geçici tatil, durdurma; geçici olarak memuriyetten ihraç; boykot *(spor vs.);* ödemeleri geçici durdurma; **sus.pen.sion bridge** *n.* asma köprü; **susˈpen.sive** ◻ erteleme kabilinden, geçici...; **sus.pen.so.ry** [~ˈpensəri] *adj.* asmaya yarayan; muallakta bırakan; ~ bandage **℣** kasık bağı, suspensuvar; asıcı bağ.

**sus.pi.cion** [səs'piʃən] *n.* şüphe(lenme), kuşku(lanma), vehim; *fig.* iz, belirti;

**sus¹pi.cious** □ şüphelenen, şüpheci; şüphe verici, kuşkulu, vesveseli; şüpheli, güvenilmez; **sus¹pi.cious.ness** *n.* şüpheli, kuşkulu oluş; vesveseli duygu *veya* karakter.

**sus.tain** [səs'tein] *v/t.* desteklemek, payanda vurmak; beslemek; dayanmak, katlanmak -*e*; ♪ uzatmak; ♋ teslim ve itiraf etm.; *thea.* b-nin oyun gücünü takdir etm., hakkını teslim etm.; kuvvet vermek -*e*; **sus¹tain.a.ble** *adj.* dayanıklı; onaylanabilir, kanıtlanabilir; **sus¹tained** *adj.* sürekli, devamlı, aralıksız.

**sus.te.nance** [¹sʌstinəns] *n.* besleme; gıda, yiyecek, içecek.

**sut.ler** ✕ [¹sʌtlə] *n.* kantinci, orduya gıda maddesi satan seyyar satıcı.

**su.ture** [¹suːtʃə] 1. *n.* ♋, *anat.*, **℣** dikiş (yeri), sutur, derz; 2. *vb.* dikişle birleştirmek, dikmek.

**su.ze.rain** [¹suːzərein] *n.* k-ne uyruk olunan b-i *veya* devlet; hükümdar.

**svelte** [svelt] *adj.* narin, ince yapılı, fidan gibi.

**swab** [swɔb] 1. *n.* temizleme bezi, tahta bezi; ⚓ denizci, tayfa; **℣** ilaçlı bez, tampon; 2. *v/t* a. ~ down silmek, temizlemek.

**Swa.bi.an** [¹sweibjən] 1. *n.* Suebyalı (kadın); 2. *adj.* Suebyalı, Suebya ile ilgili.

**swad.dle** [¹swɔdl] *v/t.* kundaklamak, kundağa sarmak *(bebek);* **¹swad.dling--clothes** *n. pl.* kundak (takımı); *fig.* bebeklik çağı.

**swag.ger** [¹swægə] 1. *v/i.* caka satmak, azametle yürümek, horozlanmak; *bşle* övünmek, atıp tutmak; 2. *adj.* F şık, modaya uygun; 3. *n.* caka, kurum; kabadayılık, farfaralık; **¹~-cane** *n.* ✕ süs için taşınan kamçı vs.

**swain** *poet. veya* † [swein] *n.* genç köylü, çoban; *co.* âşık.

**swale** *Am.* [sweil] *n.* çukur (yer); vadi, ova.

**swal.low¹** *orn.* [swɔləu] *n.* kırlangıç.

**swal.low²** [~] 1. *n.* yutma, yutuş; yudum; 2. *v/t.* yutmak; içine çekmek, emmek; *(fig. mst ~ up)* yutmak; tükürdüğünü yalamak, sözünü geri almak; sineye çekmek, tahammül etm.; *v/i.* yutkunmak.

**swam** [swæm] *pret. of* swim 1.

**swamp** [swɔmp] 1. *n.* batak(lık); 2. *vb.* batırmak *(a. fig.);* ⚓ içine su doldurup batırmak; *fig.* başını kaşıyacak vakti olmamak; **¹swamp.y** *adj.* bataklık.

**swan** [swɔn] *n. zo.* kuğu.

**swank** *sl.* [swæŋk] 1. *n.* caka, fiyaka, gösteriş; 2. *v/i.* caka satmak, gösteriş yapmak; **¹swank.y** *adj.* çalımlı, gösterişli, övünen.

**swan-neck** [¹swɔnnek] *n.* kuğu boynu; **¹swan.ner.y** *n.* kuğuların beslenip muhafaza edildiği yer; **¹swan-song** *n.* efsaneye göre kuğunun ölmeden önceki son ötüşü; bir sanatçının son eseri.

**swap** F [swɔp] *vb.* değiş tokuş etm., trampa etm.

**sward** [swɔːd] *n.* çim, çimen(lik).

**sware** † [sweə] *pret. of* swear.

**swarm¹** [swɔːm] 1. *n.* arı kümesi, oğul; *fig.* sürü, küme, kalabalık, kütle; 2. *v/i.* toplanmak; *(oğul arıları)* kovanı terketmek; kaynaşmak (with *ile).*

**swarm²** [~] *v/t.:* ~ up tırmanmak *(ip. ağaç vs.'ye).*

**swarth.i.ness** [¹swɔːθinis] *n.* esmerlik, karalık; **¹swarth.y** □ siyahımsı, siyahımtırak; esmer, yağız.

**swash** [swɔʃ] 1. *v/i.* çalkalanmak; övünmek, caka satmak; *v/t.* su sıçratmak, çalkalamak; 2. *n.* çalkantı (sesi), çalkalama *(su);* **~.buck.ler** *n.* atılgan, cesur, dövüşken kimse *(part. film ve hikâyelerde).*

**swas.ti.ka** [¹swɔstikə] *n.* gamalı haç, Nazilerin sembolü olan haç.

**swat** [swɔt] 1. *v/t.* ezmek, şaklatmak *(sinek vs.);* 2. *n.* vuruş, darbe, ezme.

**swath** ✓ [swɔːθ] *n.* orakla biçilip yere serilmiş ekin.

**swathe** [sweið] 1. *n.* kundak bağı; sargı; *s.* swath; 2. *vb.* sarmak, çevrelemek, bürümek.

**sway** [swei] 1. *n.* sallanma, dalgalanma; nüfuz, tesir, etki; makam, güç, otorite; 2. *v/t.* sallamak; nüfuz ve etki altında bulundurmak; hükmetmek; *v/i.* sallanmak, sarsılmak.

**swear** [sweə] 1. *(irr.) v/t.* yemin etm., andıçmek (by F b-ne *veya* bşe), yeminle onaylamak (to s.th.); küfretmek, lânet etm. (at -*e);* *v/t.* yeminle işe başlatmak; ~ s.o. b-ne yemin ettirmek; 2. *n. a.* ~-**word** F küfür, sövüp sayma; lânet.

**sweat** [swet] 1. *n.* ter(leme); terletici iş, angarya; old ~ *sl.* eski kurt; by the ~ of one's brow alnının teriyle; 2. *(irr.) v/t. & v/i.* terle(t)mek; çok sıkı çalış(tır)mak, ağır iş gör(dür)mek; düşük ücretle çalıştırmak, sömürmek; sızıntı yapmak; ⊕ kaynak yapmak *(kablo vs.),* **¹sweat.ed** *adj.* az ücretle uzun süre çalışmaya zorlanan; **¹sweat.er** *n.* kazak, süveter, pulover; işçilerini sömüren işveren; **ˈsweat-shop** *n.* az ücretle işçi çalıştıran işyeri; **sweat suit** antrenman elbisesi, eşofman; **ˈsweat.y** *adj.* terli, terlemiş, ter gibi; terletici, güç, ağır *(iş).*

**Swede** [swiːd] *n.* İsveçli; **Swed.ish** [ˈswiːdiʃ] 1. *adj.* İsveçli, İsveç ile ilgili; 2. *n.* İsveç dili, İsveççe.

**sweep** [swiːp] 1. *(irr.) v/t.* süpürmek, temizlemek; *fig.* (*mst* with *adv.*) silip süpürmek, ezici çoğunlukla kazanmak; taramak *(a.* X*);* sürüklemek; temizlemek, yok etm. *(suç vs.); v/i.* geçmek, çok hızla geçip gitmek, azametle geçip gitmek; kavis yaparak dönmek; şiddetle esmek *(rüzgâr);* sürmek, uzanmak; be swept off one's feet *fig.* üstüne fazla düşmek -*in;* heyecana kapılmak; 2. *n.* süpürme; hızlı hareket, savlet; ♪ farfar, üflemeli bakır çalgılardan kurulu mızıka takımı; bütün ödülleri kazanma; muhteşem zafer; kavis, dönemeç; alan, saha; etki alanı, hareket serbestliği; ocakçı, baca temizleyicisi; uzun kürek; tulumba kolu; make a clean ~ of bütün bütün temizlemek, ortadan kaldırmak; *(masayı)* silip süpürmek; *b-ni* kapı dışarı etm.; **ˈsweep.er** *n.* sokak süpürücüsü, çöpçü; **ˈsweep.ing** □ şümullü, geniş bir alanı kapsayan; umumî, genel *(iddia vs.);* **ˈsweep.ings** *n. pl.* süprüntü; **sweep.stakes** [ˈ~-steiks] *n. pl.* bahsimüşterek *(part. at yarışı).*

**sweet** [swiːt] 1. □ tatlı, şekerli; sevimli, şirin, hoş; kolay, rahat; güzel kokulu; ⊕ sessiz, gürültüsüz; verimli *(toprak);* have a ~ tooth tatlı şeyleri sevmek; 2. *n.* tatlı (şey); sevgili, gözde; tatlılık; ~s *pl.* bonbon, şekerleme; **ˈ~.bread** *n. (part. dana)* uykuluk; **ˈ~.ˈbri.ar** *n.* ♀ yaban gülü; **ˈsweet.en** *v/t. & v/i.* tatlılaş(tır)mak; *fig.* cazip hale getirmek *veya* gelmek; **ˈsweet.heart** *n.* sevgili, gözde; **ˈsweet.ish** *adj.* tatlımsı; aşırı tatlı; **ˈsweet.meat** *n.* şekerleme, bonbon; reçel; **ˈsweet.ness** *n.* tatlılık; sevimlilik, hoşluk; **sweet pea** ♀ kokulu bezelye çiçeği; **ˈsweet.shop** *n.* şekerci dükkânı; pastane; **ˈsweet-ˈwil.liam** *n.* ♀ hüsnüyusuf çiçeği.

**swell** [swel] 1. *(irr.) v/i.* şişmek, kabarmak (into -e) *(a. fig. & yelken vs.); v/t.* şişirmek, kabartmak; büyütmek, yükseltmek; 2. *adj.* F şık, züppe; *Am. sl.* fevkalâde, güzel. a*lâ*, birinci sınıf; 3. *n. part.* ♪ kreşendo ve ardından diminuendo; şiddetlenme; şişme, kabarış; ⬦ ölü dalga; yükseklik; tatlı meyil, tümseklik; F züppe, şık kimse; **ˈswell.ing** 1. *n.* kabarma, şişlik; 2. □ şiş, kabarık; fazla süs-

lü *(üslup vs.).*

**swel.ter** [ˈsweltə] *v/i.* sıcaktan bunalmak, çok terlemek.

**swept** [swept] *pret. & p.p. of* sweep 1.

**swerve** [swɔːv] *v/i.* yoldan sapmak; aniden direksiyonu kırmak, çevirmek; *v/t.* yolundan çevirmek, saptırmak; *spor:* kesmek, çelmek *(top).*

**swift** [swift] 1. □ çabuk, hızlı, süratli, çevik, atik; 2. *n. orn.* bir tür kırlangıç; **ˈswift.ness** *n.* sürat, hız, çeviklik, çabukluk.

**swig** F [swig] 1. *n.* yudum; içme; 2. *vb.* yutmak, bir dikişte içmek; *sl.* kafayı çekmek, çakıştırmak.

**swill** [swil] 1. *n.* bulaşık suyu *(a. fig.);* sulu domuz yemi; *sl.* bir dikişte içilen içki; 2. *vb.* sudan geçirmek, bol su ile yıkamak, çalkalamak -i; fazla içmek, kafayı çekmek.

**swim** [swim] 1. *(irr.) v/i.* yüzmek, batmamak, su yüzünde durmak; dönmek; my head ~s başım dönüyor; *v/t.* yüzerek boydan boya geçmek -i; sürükleyip götürmek, yüzdürmek; 2. *n.* yüzme (hareketi); be in the ~ hayatta olup bitenden haberdar olm.; **ˈswim.mer** *n.* yüzücü.

**swim.ming** [ˈswimiŋ] 1. *n.* yüzme; yüzücülük; baş dönmesi; 2. *adj.* yüzmeye ait *veya* uygun; yüzme...; dönen *(baş);* **ˈ~-bath** *n.* yüzme yeri, üstü kapalı yüzme havuzu; **ˈ~-cos.tume** *n.* mayo; **ˈswim-ming.ly** *adv.* kolaylıkla, rahatlıkla; **ˈswim.ming-pool** *n.* yüzme havuzu; **ˈswim-suit** *n.* mayo.

**swin.dle** [ˈswindl] 1. *v/t.* dolandırmak, aldatmak (out of); *v/i.* dolandırıcılık etm., yalan söylemek, uydurmak; **ˈswin.dler** *n.* dolandırıcı.

**swine** *only rhet., zo. veya fig. contp.* [swain] *n., pl.* ~ domuz; **ˈswine.herd** *n.* domuz çobanı.

**swing** [swiŋ] 1. *(irr.) v/i.* sallanmak, salınmak; sendelemek; F darağacına çekilmiş olm.; sallana sallana yürümek; dönmek, deveran etm., devretmek *(eksen üzerinde);* ~ into motion harekete geçmek, işlemeğe başlamak; *v/t.* sallamak; asmak, sallandırmak; idare etm., işletmek; 2. *n.* salla(n)ma; salıncak; rakkasın bir sallanma mesafesi; hareket sahası *(a. fig.);* ♪ hızlı ritim; 1930'larda kuvvetli ritimli bir tür caz müziği; *boks:* sving; in full ~ en civcivli anında, tam faaliyette; go with a ~ herşey yolunda gitmek; *attr.* salla(n)ma..., sallanan...; **~ bridge** açılır kapanır köprü; **~ door** iki tarafa açılır kapanır kapı.

swinge.ing ☐ F ['swindʒiŋ] çok, pek, gayet, muazzam.

swing.ing ☐ [s'wiŋiŋ] neşeli, canlı; ileri görüşlü, modern (part. seks konusunda).

swin.gle ⊕ ['swiŋgl] 1. v/t. tokmakla döverek temizlemek (keten); 2. n. keten bıçağı;ı '~.tree n. araba falakası.

swin.ish ☐ ['swainiʃ] domuz gibi, kaba.

swipe [swaip] 1. vb. koluyla hızla vurmak, kuvvetli bir darbe indirmek; sl. aşırmak, çalmak; 2. n. kuvvetli darbe; ~s pl. hafif bira.·

swirl [swəːl] 1. vb. şiddetle dön(dür)mek, girdap gibi dön(dür)mek; 2. n. girdap.

swish [swiʃ] 1. vb. vız diye geçip gitmek; havada hareket ederken ıslık gibi ses çıkarmak, vızlamak, tıslamak (tırpan); hışırdamak; kırbaçlamak; 2. n. hışırtı vs.; 3. adj. F cazip, çekici.

Swiss [swis] 1. adj. İsviçreli, İsviçre ile ilgili; 2. n. İsviçreli; the ~ pl. İsviçre halkı.

switch [switʃ] 1. n. ince ağaç dalı, değnek, çubuk; 🔚 makas; ∮ şalter, düğme, anahtar; takma saç örgüsü; 2. vb. değnekle vurmak, dövmek; sallamak, savurmak; 🔚 makastan geçirmek; ∮ elektrik düğmesini çevirmek; (rüzgâr) yön değiştirmek; fig. değiş tokuş etm.; ~ on (off) ∮ elektrik düğmesini açmak (kapatmak); '~.back n. iniş çıkışlı tren yolu (part. lunaparkta); '~.board n. ∮ telefon santralı; anahtar tablosu, tevzi tablosu; ~ box ∮ anahtar kutusu, tablo.

swiv.el ⊕ ['swivl] n. fırdöndülü zincir halkası, fırdöndü; attr. döner...; ~ chair döner iskemle.

swol.len ['swəulən] p.p. of swell 1.

swoon [swuːn] 1. n. bayılma, baygınlık; 2. v/i. bayılmak.

swoop [swuːp] 1. v/i. = down on veya upon üzerine atılmak, çullanmak; 2. n. üstüne çullanma. ani saldırış.

swop F [swɔp] vb. değiş tokuş etm., trampa etm.

sword F [sɔːd] n. kılıç, pala; '~-cane n. kılıçlı baston; '~-play n. eskrim kılıç oyunu; fig. söz düellosu.

swords.man ['sɔːdzmən] n. eskrimci, kılıcı ustalıkla kullanan kimse; 'swords.man.ship n. eskrimcilik, kılıç kullanmada ustalık.

swore [swɔː] pret. of swear 1.

sworn [swɔːn] 1. p.p. of swear 1.; 2. adj. 🜂 yeminli; ~ expert 🜂 yeminli bilirkişi.

swot okul sl. [swɔt] 1. n. inekleme; inekleyen öğrenci; 2. v/i. ineklemek.

swum [swʌm] p.p. of swim 1.

swung [swʌŋ] pret. & p.p. of swing 1.

syb.a.rite ['sibərait] n. lüks ve rahatlık içinde yaşayan kimse, muhallebi çocuğu.

syc.a.more ⨂ ['sikəmɔː] n. firavuninciri; Am. çınar ağacı.

syc.o.phant ['sikəfənt] n. dalkavuk, yaltakçı, parazit, asalak kimse; syc.o.phan.tic [~'fæntik] adj. (~ally) dalkavukluk kabilinden.

syl.lab.ic [si'læbik] adj. (~ally) hece itibariyle, hecelere ait, hecelerden ibaret, hece...; syl.la.ble ['siləbl] n. hece.

syl.la.bus ['siləbəs] n. müfredat programı, plan; hulasa, özet; liste, cetvel.

syl.lo.gism phls. ['silədʒizəm] n. tasım, kıyas.

sylph [silf] n. havada yaşadığı farzedilen peri; ince ve zarif kadın.

sly.van ['silvən] adj. ormanlık; ormana ait, orman...

sym.bi.o.sis biol. [simbi'əusis] n. birbirinden farklı canlıların ortak yaşayışı, ortak yaşama, sembiyoz.

sym.bol ['simbəl] n. sembol, simge, işaret, belirti, nişan, timsel, amblem; sym.bol.ic, sym.bol.i.cal ☐ [~'bɔlik(l)] sembolik, simgesel; sym.bol.ism ['~bəlizəm] n. simgecilik, sembolizm; ısym.bol.ize vb. temsil etm., sembolize etm.; sembolü olm.

sym.met.ri.cal ☐ [si'metrikəl] simetrik, bakışık; uygun, mütenasip; sym.me.try ['simitri] n. simetri, bakışım.

sym.pa.thet.ic [simpə'θetik] adj. (~ally) sempatik, sevimli, karşısındakinin duygularına katılan, sevgi ve acıma gösteren; uygun, ahenkli; anat. sempatik; ~ strike dayanışma grevi; 'sym.pa.thize v/i. sempatizan olm., yakınlık duymak (with -e); 'sym.pa.thiz.er n. sempatizan, yandaş, taraftar; sym.pa.thy ['~θi] n. sempati; dert ortaklığı, aynı duyguları paylaşma, duygudaşlık, şefkat.

sym.phon.ic ♪ [sim'fɔnik] adj. senfonik; sym.pho.ny ♪ ['~fəni] n. senfoni.

sym.po.sium [sim'pəuzjəm] n. sempozyum, belirli bir konunun tartışıldığı bilimsel toplantı; aynı konuda yazılmış bilimsel yazılar serisi.

symp.tom ['simptəm] n. araz, belirti, alâmet; symp.to.mat.ic [~'mætik] adj. (~ally) arazî; bşe delâlet eden, belirti niteliğinde, araz olan (of).

syn.a.gogue ['sinəgɔg] n. havra, sinagog.

Syn.chro.flash phot. ['siŋkrəuflæʃ] n. senkronize mağnezyum ışığı.

syn.chro-mesh gear mot. ['siŋkrəumeʃ'giə] n. dişlilerin kolay ve sessizce birleşmesini sağlayan vites tertibatı.

**syn.chro.nism** [ˈsiŋkrənizəm] *n.* aynı anda olma, eşzamanlılık, zamandaşlık; **ˈsyn.chro.nize** *v/i.* aynı zamana uymak, aynı zamanda olm.; *v/t.* aynı zamana uydurmak; ayarlarını birbirine uydurmak *(saatler)*; aynı tarihe tesadüf ettirmek; **ˈsyn.chro.nous** □ aynı zamanda olan, zamandaş, eşzaman, senkronize; aynı frekansta olan.

**syn.chro.tron** *phys.* [ˈsiŋkrəutrɔn] *n.* sinkrotron, elektronları çok hızlı hareket ettiren aygıt.

**syn.co.pate** [ˈsiŋkəpeit] *v/t.* kısaltmak, sözcüğün ortasında bulunan bir fonemi düşürmek; ♪ senkope etm.; **syn.co.pe** [ˈ⁓pi] *n.* senkop, sözcüğün ortasında bulunan bir fonemin *(özellikle bir ünlünün)* düşmesi; ♥ beyine kan gitmemesinden olan baygınlık.

**syn.dic** [ˈsindik] *n.* mutemet, müşavir, vekil, savunucu; **syn.di.cate 1.** [ˈ⁓kit] *n.* sendika; ticarî firmalar birliği, kartel; yazıları gazetelere satan kurum; **2.** [ˈ⁓keit] *vb.* sendika oluşturmak; şirket *veya* kartel oluşturmak; şirket vasıtasiyle üretmek *(mal)*; kurum aracılığı ile üretmek *veya* satmak *(yazı, seri vs.)*; **ˈsyn.di.cat.ed** *adj.* pek çok gazetede birden yayımlanan.

**syn.od** *eccl.* [ˈsinəd] *n.* kilise meclisi; **syn.od.al** [ˈ⁓dəl], **syn.od.ic**, **syn.od.i.cal** □ *eccl.* [siˈnɔdik(l)] kilise meclisine ait.

**syn.o.nym** [ˈsinənim] *n. gr.* eşanlam, anlamdaş sözcük; **syn.on.y.mous** □ [siˈnɔniməs] anlamdaş, eş anlamlı.

**syn.op.sis** [siˈnɔpsis] *n., pl.* **synˈop.ses** [⁓siːz] özet, hulasa.

**syn.op.tic**, **syn.op.ti.cal** □ [siˈnɔptik(əl)] özet halinde olan.

**syn.tac.tic**, **syn.tac.ti.cal** □ *gr.* [sinˈtæktik(əl)] sentaksik, sözdizimi kuralları ile ilgili; **syn.tax** *gr.* [ˈsintæks] *n.* sözdizimi, sentaks.

**syn.the.sis** [ˈsinθisis] *n., pl.* **syn.the.ses** [ˈ⁓siːz] bireşim, sentez; **syn.the.size** ⊕ [ˈ⁓saiz] *v/t.* bireşim haline getirmek, sentez yapmak, sentez yoluyla ortaya çıkarmak.

**syn.thet.ic**, **syn.thet.i.cal** □ [sinˈθetik(əl)] sentetik, yapay, suni.

**syn.to.nize** [ˈsintənaiz] *vb. radyo:* birbirine uydurmak *(frekans)*; **ˈsyn.to.ny** *n.* birbirine uyma, seselim, rezonans.

**syph.i.lis** ♥ [ˈsifilis] *n.* frengi, sifilis.

**syph.i.lit.ic** ♥ [sifiˈlitik] *adj.* sifilitik, frengili.

**sy.phon** [ˈsaifən] = siphon.

**Syr.i.an** [ˈsiriən] **1.** *adj.* Suriyeli; **2.** *n.* Suriyeli kimse.

**sy.rin.ga** ♣ [siˈriŋgə] *n.* leylâk.

**syr.inge** [ˈsirindʒ] **1.** *n.* şırınga; **2.** *v/t.* şırınga etm. *-i.*

**syr.up** [ˈsirəp] *n.* şekerli sos, şurup.

**sys.tem** [ˈsistim] *n.* sistem, usul, düzen, kural, yol, kaide; bünye, organizma; evren, âlem, kâinat; **sys.tem.at.ic** [⁓ˈmætik] *adj.* (⁓ally) sistematik, sistemli, usul ve kurala göre *veya* uygun, planlı.

# T

**T** [tiː]: to a ~ F aynen, tıpatıp, tıpkı; mükemmel olarak.

**tab** [tæb] *n.* askı, brit; kayış, şerit, kaytan; etiket, yafta; ayakkabı bağındaki madenî parça; F hesap; keep a ~ on, keep ~s on hesabını tutmak *-in; fig.* kontrol etm. *-i.*

**tab.ard** [ˈtæbəd] *n.* şövalyelerin zırh üzerine giydikleri kolsuz ve kısa cüppe.

**tab.by** [ˈtæbi] *n., a.* '~-cat tekir kedi.

**tab.er.nac.le** [ˈtæbəːnækl] *n.* (taşınabilen) tapınak.

**ta.ble** [ˈteibl] **1.** *n.* masa; sofra, sofraya konan yemek; masada oturanların hepsi; liste, cetvel, tablo, çizelge; tarife; *incil:* tablet, yazılı taş; *s.* ~-land; at ~ sofrada; lay s.th. on the ~ *parl.* bşi süresiz ertelemek; turn the ~s durumu aleyhine çevirmek (on *-in*); **2.** *v/t.* listeye geçirmek; masaya koymak; *parl.* tehir etm., ertelemek; müzakereye sunmak *(tasarı, teklif vs.).*

**tab.leau** [ˈtæbləu] *n., pl.* **tab.leaux** [ˈtæbləuz] canlı tablo.

**ta.ble...:** '~-cloth *n.* masa örtüsü, sofra bezi; '~-land *n.* plato, yayla; '~-lin.en *n.* masa örtüsü takımı; '~-spoon *n.* yemek kaşığı; '~-spoon.ful *n.* bir yemek kaşığı dolusu miktar.

**tab.let** [ˈtæblit] *n.* levha, kitabe, yazıt; yazı kâğıdı destesi, bloknot; *pharm.* tablet, komprime.

**ta.ble...:** '~-talk *n.* sofra sohbeti; '~-ten.nis *n.* masa tenisi, pingpong; '~-top *n.* masa üstü.

**tab.loid** [ˈtæbloid] *n.* resimli küçük gazete.

**ta.boo** [təˈbuː] **1.** *adj.* yasak, tabu, dokunulmaz; **2.** *n.* tabu olan şey; **3.** *v/t.* yasaklamak.

**ta.bor** ♪ [ˈteibə] *n.* dümbelek; zilli tef.

**tab.u.lar** □ [ˈtæbjulə] cetvel *(veya* çizelge) şeklindeki; masa şeklindeki; cetvele göre hesaplanmış; **tab.u.late** [ˈ~leit] *v/t.* cetvel haline koymak; **tab.uˈla.tion** *n.* cetvel haline koyma.

**tac.it** □ [ˈtæsit] söylenmeden anlaşılan, kapalı ifade olunan, zımnî; kontratsız yapılan; **tac.i.turn** □ [ˈ~təːn] az konuşur, sessiz, ağzı var dili yok; **tac.iˈtur.ni.ty** *n.* sessizlik, suskunluk.

**tack** [tæk] **1.** *n.* ufak çivi, pünez; teyel (dikişi); ↓ kuntra; *fig.* yol, usül; ↓ yelken durumuna göre gidilen yol; ↓ yiyecek, gıda; on the wrong ~ yanlış yolda; **2.** *v/t.* çivi ile iliştirmek; teyellemek; *fig.* eklemek (to, on *-e); v/i.* ↓ orsa etm.; *fig.* bşi iyi kötü yoluna koymak.

**tack.le** [ˈtækl] **1.** *n.* tutma, zaptetme; ↓ halat takımı; ↓ palanga; ⊕ takım, cihaz; **2.** *v/t.* uğraşmak (s.th. *ile),* çaresine bakmak, üstesinden gelmek; tutmak, zaptetmek; *v/i.* Am. futbol: topu taşıyan rakibini tutup durdurmak.

**tack.y** [ˈtæki] *adj.* yapışkan, yapış yapış, henüz kurumamış *(boya vs.);* Am. F yırtık pırtık, pejmürde.

**tact** [tækt] *n.* incelik, nezaket, zarafet; **tact.ful** [ˈ~ful] *adj.* ince(likli), nazik, zarif.

**tac.ti.cal** □ ╳ [ˈtæktikəl] taktiğe ait, taktik...; **tac.ti.cian** [~ˈtiʃən] *n.* taktik veren kimse, tabiyeci; **tac.tics** [ˈ~iks] *n. pl., a. sg.* taktik, manevra, tabiye.

**tac.tile** [ˈtæktail] *adj.* dokunma duyusuna ait, dokunma...

**tact.less** □ [ˈtæktlis] nezaketsiz, kaba, patavatsız.

**tad.pole** *zo.* [ˈtædpəul] *n.* iribaş, tetari.

**taf.fe.ta** [ˈtæfitə] *n.* tafta.

**taf.fy** Am. [ˈtæfi] = toffee; F dalkavukluk, yağcılık.

**tag** [tæg] **1.** *n.* etiket, fiş; ayakkabı bağı demiri; meşhur söz; sarkık uç; «elim sende» oyunu; **2.** *v/t.* etiketlemek, etiket yapıştırmak (to, onto *-e);* ~ after takılmak *-e,* peşinden gitmek *-in;* ~ together birleştirmek, biraraya getirmek.

**tail** [teil] **1.** *n.* kuyruk; kuyruğa benzer şey; arka; son; maiyet; *sl.* kıç, popo; *sl.* cinsel ilişki; *sl.* b-nin peşine salınan kimse; sayfa altındaki boşluk; saç örgüsü; ~s *pl.* paranın resimsiz tarafı, yazı; F frak; from the ~ of one's eye göz ucuyla; turn ~ gerisin geriye kaçmak; ~s up keyfi yerinde, keyfi kekâ; **2.** *v/t.* ~ after s.o. b-ni izlemek, takip etm.; ~

s.o. *Am. b-nin* peşini bırakmamak; *v/i.*
~ off, ~ away azalmak, küçülmek; geride kalmak, geride kalarak dağılmak; **'~-board** *n. mot.* arka kapak; **'~-coat** *n.* frak; **tailed** *comb.* ...kuyruklu; **'~-'end** *n.* arka kısım, kıç; son; **'tail.less** *adj.* kuyruksuz; **'tail-light** *n.* stop lambası, kuyruk lambası.

**tai.lor** ['teilə] **1.** *n.* terzi; **2.** *vb.* terzilik yapmak; biçip dikmek; uydurmak, uyarlamak; ~ed suit ısmarlama elbise; '~--made *adj.* terzi elinden çıkmış, iyi dikilmiş; *fig.* uygun; ~ costume ısmarlama kostüm.

**tail**...: '~.piece *n. typ.* kitap sonundaki süslü şekil; '~-spin *n.* ✈ kuyruk çevrintisi.

**taint** [teint] **1.** *n.* leke, nokta, iz, eser; ayıp, kusur; sirayet, bulaşma; çürüme, bozulma; **2.** *v/t. & v/i.* boz(ul)mak; lekelemek; 🜚 bulaştırmak; ahlâkını bozmak.

**take** [teik] **1.** *(irr.) v/t.* almak; tutmak, yakalamak, kapmak; zaptetmek; esir etm.; kazanmak *(ödül vs.)*; kullanmak; çalmak; yararlanmak *-den*; götürmek; tuzağa düşürmek; yapmak; kiralamak; içmek *(çay vs.)*; yemek; satın almak; kabul etm.; getirmek *(kazanç)*; *phot.* çekmek *(resim)*; F kavramak, anlamak; sanmak, zannetmek (for); üstlenmek, yüklenmek *(sorumluluk, görev vs.)*; seçmek; uymak *(tavsiyeye vs.)*; çıkarmak; *sl.* aldatmak, kandırmak; sürmek; uğramak *-e*; ihtiyacı olm. *-e*; the devil ~ it! Allah kahretsin!, kör şeytan!; I ~ it that sanıyorum ki; ~ breath nefes almak; ~ comfort teselli bulmak, avunmak; ~ compassion on acımak *-e*; *s.* consideration; ~ counsel danışmak; *s.* decision; ~ a drive araba ile gezmek; *s.* effect; *s.* exercise; ~ fire ateş almak; ~ in hand avucunun içine almak, idaresini ele almak; *s.* heart; ~ hold of tutmak, kapmak, yakalamak; ~ it F anlamak; katlanmak; *s.* liberty; *s.* note; *s.* notice; ~ pity on acımak *-e*; ~ place olmak, vuku bulmak; ~ s.o.'s place *b-nin* yerine geçmek, yerini almak; ~ a rest dinlenmek; *s.* rise; ~ a seat oturmak; ~ a walk yürüyüşe çıkmak; ~ my word for it bana inanın, sizi temin ederim; ~ about gezdirmek, dolaştırmak; ~ along beraberinde götürmek; ~ down yazmak, kaydetmek, dikte almak; indirmek; sökmek, parçalara ayırmak; yıkmak; ~ for sanmak, zannetmek; ~ from alıp götürmek; çekip almak, çıkarmak; küçültmek, azaltmak; ~ in (içeriye) almak; daraltmak *(elbise vs.)*; sarmak *(yelken)*; kap-

samak; zimmetine geçirmek; talep etm. *(hak)*; anlamak, kavramak; görmek; heyecanla dinlemek *veya* izlemek; kabul etm.; F aldatmak, yutturmak; ~ off çıkarmak *(elbise vs.)*; kesmek *(sakal, bıyık vs.)*; seferden almak, kaldırmak *(tren, uçak vs.)*; çekmek; indirmek *(fiyat)*; götürmek, yol göstermek; kurtarmak; F taklit etm.; be ~n off 🜚 servisten kalkmak; ~ on üstüne almak, üstlenmek, yüklenmek; işe almak; almak *(yolcu)*; ~ out çıkar(t)mak; götürmek, eşlik etm., çekmek *(diş)*; ~ it out of s.o. *fig.* bitkin düşürmek, halsiz bırakmak, perişan etm.; ~ over götürmek, taşımak; devralmak, *-in* idaresini ele almak; ~ to alışmak *-e*; başlamak *-e*; çare olarak kullanmak; sevmek, hoşlanmak; ~ to pieces sökmek, parçalara ayırmak, dağıtmak *(a. fig.)*; ~ up kaldırmak; almak *(yolcu)*; emmek *(sıvı)*; eritmek; başlamak; işgal etm., kaplamak *(yer)*; tutmak, almak *(zaman)*; kabul etm.; arz etm., sunmak (with *-e*); be ~n up with *fig.* ilgilenmek *ile*, yakınlık duymak *-e*; çok hoşuna gitmek; ~ upon o.s. üzerine almak, yüklenmek; **2.** *(irr.) v/i.* yola çıkmak, gitmek; işe yaramak; olmak; yakalanmak *(hastalığa vs.)*; yapışmak; büyüleyici olm.; etkili olm.; ateş almak, tutuşmak; resim çektirmek; ~ after benzemek *-e*; ~ from itibarını bozmak, lekelemek; ~ off yola çıkmak, ayrılmak; ✈ havalanmak, kalkmak; ~ on F rol yapmak; ~ over idareyi ele almak, yönetici olm.; ~ to bşe alışmak; bşe müracaat etm.; *fig. k-ni* bşe vermek; hoşuna gitmek; ~ to ger. bşe yapmaya başlamak; ~ up F açılmak, düzelmek *(hava)*; çekmek, küçülmek, kısalmak; ~ up with arkadaş olm. *ile*; that won't ~ with me o beni etkilemiyor; **3.** *n.* hâsilat; *film:* çekim; alma, alış; tutma, tutuş; bir seferlik av miktarı; tutma *(aşı)*.

**take**...: '~-home pay net maaş; '~-'in *n.* F aldatmaca, yutturmaca; 'tak.en *p.p. of* take; be ~ ele geçmek; be ~ with bşe hayran olm., bayılmak; etkilenmek *-den*; be ~ ill! hastalanmak; 'take-off *n.* taklit; karikatür; ✈ kalkış, havalanma; başlama *veya* hareket noktası; 'tak.er *n.* bahse giren kimse.

**tak.ing** ['teikiŋ] **1.** ☐ F cazip, çekici, büyüleyici; **2.** *n.* alma, alış; kötü durum; F heyecan, telâş; ~s *pl.* 🜚 hâsilat, gelir.

**talc** *min.* [tælk] *n.* talk; **tal.cum** ['~kəm] = talc.

**tale** [teil] *n.* masal, hikâye; rapor; dedi-

kodu; yalan; sayı, adet, toplam; it tells
its own ~ kendini bizzat açıklıyor, başka *bş* söylemeğe gerek yok '~.bear.er *n.*
dedikoducu kimse.

tal.ent ['tælənt] *n.* kabiliyet, yetenek, hüner, Allah vergisi; ltal.ent.ed *adj.* kabiliyetli, hünerli, yetenekli.

ta.les ŏ̃ ['teiliːz] *n. pl.* yedek jüri üyeleri.

tal.is.man ['tælizmən] *n.* tılsım.

talk [tɔːk] 1. *n.* konuşma; laf, söz, lakırdı; görüşme, müzakere; boş laf; konuşma şekli, ağız; dedikodu, söylenti; konferans; give a ~ konuşma yapmak; have
a ~ konuşmak, görüşmek; 2. *v/t.* konuşmak, söylemek; görüşmek, tartışmak,
müzakere etm.; konuşarak etkilemek;
*v/i.* konuşmak, laf (*veya* lakırdı) etm.;
dedikodu etm.; ~ to s.o. F *b-ni* terslemek,
azarlamak, haşlamak; talk.a.tive □
['~ətiv] konuşkan, çenesi düşük, geveze;
talk.ee-talk.ee F ['tɔːki'tɔːki] *n.* gevezelik, boş laf; ltalk.er *n.* konuşkan, geveze,
boşboğaz kimse; konuşan kimse; he is a
good ~ iyi konuşur, iyi bir konuşmacı-
dır; talk.ie F ['~i] *n.* sesli film; ıtalk.ing
*n.* konuşma; talk.ing-to F ['~tuː] *n.* azar-
(lama), paylama, haşlama.

tall [tɔːl] *adj.* uzun (boylu); yüksek; F
abartmalı; büyük, fahiş, fazla; that's a
~ order F yerine getirilmesi güç bir istek; ltall.boy *n.* şifoniyer, konsol; ltall-
ness *n.* uzunluk, uzun boyluluk; yükseklik.

tal.low ['tæləu] *n.* donyağı; mum yağı;
ltal.low.y *adj.* yağlı.

tal.ly ['tæli] 1. *n.* çetele; karşılık, denk
(of *-in*); etiket, fiş; çentik, kertik; hesap
(tutma); 2. *v/t. & v/i.* uy(dur)mak; çe-
teleye yazmak; sayı(m) yapmak.

tal.ly-ho ['tæli'həu] 1. *int.* haydi!, yallah!;
2. *n. hunt.* köpekleri ileri sürmek için av-
cının seslenmesi; 3. *vb.* «Haydi!» diyerek köpekleri koşturmak.

tal.on *orn.* ['tælən] *n.* pençe.

ta.lus¹ ['teiləs] *n.* meyil; *geol.* tepe *veya*
uçurum dibinde biriken kaya parçaları;
kayşat.

ta.lus² *anat.* [~] *n.* aşık kemiği.

tam.a.b!e ['teiməbl] *adj.* evcilleştirilebilir,
ehlileştirilebilir.

tam.a.rind ŷ ['tæmərind] *n.* demirhindi(nin
meyvesi).

tam.a.risk ŷ ['tæmərisk] *n.* ılgın.

tam.bour ['tæmbuə] 1. *n.* kasnak, gergef;
trampet, ufak davul; ♧ kasnak işi; 2.
*v/t.* kasnağa gerip işlemek; tam.bou.rine
♪ [~bə'riːn] *n.* tef.

tame [teim] 1. □ evcil, ehlî; uysal,
yumuşak başlı; tatsız, yavan, sıkıcı; zararsız; 2. *v/t.* evcilleştirmek, ehlileştirmek, alıştırmak; uysallaştırmak; yumuşatmak; ltame.ness *n.* evcillik; uysallık;
boyun eğme; ltam.er *n.* terbiyeci.

Tam.ma.ny *Am.* ['tæməni] *n.* New York'-
taki demokratik parti merkez kuruluşu.

tam-o'-shan.ter [tæmə'ʃæntə] *n.* İskoç beresi.

tamp [tæmp] *v/t.* ✕, ⊕ bastırıp sıkıştırmak.

tam.per ['tæmpə] *v/t. & v/i.:* ~ with ka-
rış(tır)mak, kurcalamak, oynamak; dokunmak; değiştirip bozmak,

tam.pon ⚕ ['tæmpən] *n.* tampon.

tan [tæn] 1. *n.* güneş yanığı; tanen, mazı tozu: 2. *adj.* açık kahverengi; 3. *v/t.*
& *v/i.* karar(t)mak. esmerleş(tir)mek;
tabaklamak (*deri*); F kamçılamak. dövmek.

tan.dem ['tændəm] *n.* iki kişilik bisiklet;
~ connexion ✄ seri bağlantı.

tang¹ [tæŋ] *n.* pırazvana, berazban, bıçağın sapa giren kuyruğu; *fig.* ağızda kalan tat *veya* koku.

tang² [~] 1. *n.* madenî ses, tangırtı; 2. *v/i.*
madeni ses çıkarmak, tangırdamak.

tan.gent A ['tændʒənt] *n.* teğet; tanjant;
go (*a.* fly) off at a ~ birden fikir *veya* konu değiştirmek, daldan dala konmak;
tan.gen.tial □ A [~'dʒenʃəl] teğet şeklinde, teğet halindeki...

tan.ger.ine ŷ [tændʒə'riːn] *n.* mandalina.

tan.gi.bil.i.ty [tændʒi'biliti] *n.* tutulabilme;
tan.gi.ble □ ['~dʒəbl] dokunulur, tutu-
lur; anlaşılır, açık; *fig.* gerçek; maddî;
duyulur, hissedilir.

tan.gle ['tæŋgl] 1. *n.* karışıklık; karmakarışık şey, arapsaçı; düğüm; 2. *v/t. & v/i.*
karış(tır)mak, dolaş(tır)mak, karmakarışık etm., arapsaçına çevirmek; tartışmak, münakaşa etm. (with *ile*).

tan.go ['tæŋgəu] *n.* tango.

tank [tæŋk] 1. *n.* depo, sarnıç, tank; havuz, gölcük; ⊕, ✕ tank; 2. *v/t.* depo *veya* sarnıca koymak; ~ up arabanın de-
posunu doldurmak, yakıt almak; ltank-
age *n.* havuz *veya* depo istiap hacmi; havuz *veya* depoya doldurma; havuz doldurma ücreti.

tank.ard ['tæŋkəd] *n.* içki maşrapası.

tank-car ⛟ ['tæŋkkaː] *n.* tanklı vagon;
ltank.er *n.* tanker.

tan.ner¹ ['tænə] *n.* sepici, tabak.

tan.ner² *sl.* [~] *n.* altı penilik para.

tan.ner.y ['tænəri] *n.* tabakhane.

tan.nic ac.id ⚗ ['tænik'æsid] *n.* tanen asidi.

**tan.nin** ⌢ [ˈtænin] *n.* tanen, mazı tozu.

**tan.ta.lize** [ˈtæntəlaiz] *v/t.* hayal kırıklığına uğratmak, boşuna ümit vermek, *bşi* gösterip vermemek, eziyet etm.

**tan.ta.mount** [ˈtæntəmaunt] *adj.* eşit, aynı (to -*e, ile*).

**tan.trum** F [ˈtæntrəm] *n.* hiddet (nöbeti), aksilik, terslik.

**tap¹** [tæp] **1.** *n.* hafif vuruş; **2.** *v/t.* hafifçe vurmak -*e*.

**tap²** [~] **1.** *n.* musluk; fıçı tapası, tıkaç; F fıçıdan alınmış içki; ⊕ kılavuz, burgu; F *s.* ~-room; ⨍ bağlantı; on ~ fıçıdan alınıp satılmaya hazır *(içki); fig.* hazır; **2.** *v/t.* akıtmak -*i*; delerek akıtmak *(kauçuk)*; sızdırmak *(para, bilgi vs.)*; ~ the wire(s) ⨍ gizli bağlantı kurmak; *teleph.* gizlice dinlemek.

**tap-dance** [ˈtæpdɑːns] ayakları yere vurarak yapılan bir çeşit dans.

**tape** [teip] *n.* şerit, bant, kurdele; metre şeridi; *spor:* varış ipi; *tel.* kâğıt şerit; red ~ bürokrasi, gereksiz resmî muamele, kırtasiyecilik; **'~-meas.ure** *n.* mezûr, mezura, metre şeridi; **tape re.cord.er** *n.* teyp; **tape re.cord.ing** teybe alma.

**ta.per** [teipə] **1.** *n.* çok ince mum; **2.** *adj.* gittikçe incelen; **3.** *v/t. & v/i.* gittikçe incel(t)mek, sivril(t)mek; azalmak, eksilmek; ~ing = ~ **2.**

**tap.es.tried** [ˈtæpistrid] *adj.* goblenle kaplı; **'tap.es.try** *n.* goblen, resim dokumalı duvar örtüsü.

**tape.worm** [ˈteipwəːm] *n.* bağırsak kurdu, şerit, tenya.

**tap.i.o.ca** [tæpiˈəukə] *n.* tapyoka.

**ta.pir** *zo.* [ˈteipə] *n.* tapir.

**tap.pet** ⊕ [ˈtæpit] *n.* kol, manivela.

**tap-room** [ˈtæprum] *n.* meyhane, bar.

**tap-root** ♀ [ˈtæpruːt] *n.* ana kök.

**taps** *Am.* ✗ [tæps] *n. pl.* yat borusu.

**tap.ster** [ˈtæpstə] *n.* barmen.

**tar** [tɑː] **1.** *n.* katran; Jack ♀ F deniz kurdu, denizci, gemici; **2.** *v/t.* katranlamak.

**ta.ran.tu.la** *zo.* [təˈræntjulə] *n.* büyük örümcek.

**tar-board** [ˈtɑːbɔːd] *n.* katranlı mukavva.

**tar.di.ness** [ˈtɑːdinis] *n.* gecikme; yavaşlık, ağırlık; **'tar.dy** ☐ yavaş, ağır; geç kalan *veya* gelen, geciken.

**tare¹** ♀ [tɛə] *n. mst* ~*s pl.* delice.

**tare²** ⊤ [~] **1.** *n.* dara; **2.** *v/t.* -*in* darasını düşmek.

**tar.get** [ˈtɑːgit] *n.* hedef, nişangâh; *fig.* eleştiriye hedef olan *bş veya b-i*; ulaşılmak istenilen miktar; amaç, gaye; ~ practice atış talimi.

**tar.iff** [ˈtærif] *n.* gümrük tarifesi; fiyat listesi.

**tar.mac** [ˈtɑːmæk] *n.* ˌasfalt *(yol veya uçak iniş alanı).*

**tarn** [tɑːn] *n.* dağ gölü.

**tar.nish** [ˈtɑːniʃ] **1.** *v/t. & v/i.* ⊕ donuklaş(tır)mak, matlaş(tır)mak, karar(t)mak; *fig.* lekelemek, kirletmek *(şöhret vs.);* **2.** *n.* donukluk, matlık; leke, kir.

**tar.pau.lin** [tɑːˈpɔːlin] *n.* ↓ gemici, denizci; su geçirmez muşamba *veya* örtü.

**tar.ry¹** *lit.* [ˈtæri] *v/i.* kalmak, durmak; gecikmek, oyalanmak.

**tar.ry²** [ˈtɑːri] *adj.* katranlı.

**tart** [tɑːt] **1.** ☐ ekşi, mayhoş; keskin, acı; *fig.* ters, sert *(davranış, huy vs.);* **2.** *n.* turta; *sl.* fahişe, orospu.

**tar.tan** [ˈtɑːtən] *n.* kareli ve yünlü İskoç kumaşı; ~ plaid İskoç şalı.

**Tar.tar¹** [ˈtɑːtə] *n.* Tatar; *fig.* düzenbaz kimse, baş belâsı kimse; catch a ~ belâya çatmak, daha belâlısına çatmak.

**tar.tar²** [~] *n.* ⌢ kefeki, pesek; şarap tortusu.

**task** [tɑːsk] **1.** *n.* ödev; iş, görev, vazife; hizmet; külfet; take to ~ (for) azarlamak, paylamak, haşlamak *(-den dolayı);* **2.** *v/t.* külfet yüklemek -*e*; görevlendirmek, vazifelendirmek; **task force** ✗ geçici işbirliği; **'task.mas.ter** *n.* angaryacı.

**tas.sel** [ˈtæsəl] **1.** *n.* püskül; **2.** *v/t.* püsküllerle süslemek.

**taste** [teist] **1.** *n.* tat, lezzet, çeşni; tat alma duyusu; yudumluk, tadımlık miktar (of -*in*); hoşlanma, zevk, beğeni (for -*e karşı*); there is no accounting for ~*s* zevkler ve renkler tartışılmaz; to ~ zevkine uygun; **2.** *v/t.* -*in* tadına bakmak, tatmak; denemek -*i*; *v/i.* tadı olm., tat vermek (of); **'taste.ful** ☐ [~ˈful] lezzetli; zevkli; uyumlu, zarif.

**taste.less** ☐ [ˈteistlis] tatsız, yavan; zevksiz; uygunsuz; **'taste.less.ness** *n.* tatsızlık; uygunsuzluk.ˌ-

**tas.ter** [ˈteistə] *n.* çeşnici *(şarap, çay vs.).*

**tast.y** ☐ F [ˈteisti] tatlı, lezzetli, leziz; zevkli.

**tat¹** [tæt] *s.* tit¹.

**tat²** [~] *v/i.* mekik oyası yapmak.

**ta-ta** [ˈtæˈtɑː] *int.* F *(çocuk dilinde veya co.)* Allaha ısmarladık; güle güle.

**tat.ter** [ˈtætə] **1.** *v/t. & v/i.* parçala(n)mak, parçalayıp paçavra yapmak; **2.** *n.* ~*s pl.* paçavra, çaput; **tat.ter.de.mal.ion** [~dəˈmeiljən] *n.* pejmürde kimse, üstübaşı döküke kimse.

**tat.tle** [ˈtætl] **1.** *v/i.* gevezelik etm., çene çalmak, boşboğazlık etm.; *v/t. b.s.* fitlemek, gammazlamak; **2.** *n.* boşboğaz-

lık, dedikodu, zevzeklik; *b.s.* fitnecilik, gammazlık; **tat.tler** *n.* boşboğaz *(veya* zevzek, fitneci, gammaz) kimse.
**tat.too¹** [təˈtuː] 1. *n.* ✕ koğuş borusu; beat
the devil's ~ *fig.* parmakları bir yere tıkır tıkır vurmak; 2. *vb. fig.* tıkır tıkır
vurmak, tıkırdatmak.
**tat.too²** [~] 1. *v/t.* dövme yapmak *-e;* 2.
*n.* dövme.
**taught** [tɔːt] *prep & p.p. of* teach.
**taunt** [tɔːnt] 1. *n.* hakaret, alay; iğneli
söz; 2. *v/t.* alay etm. *ile,* sataşmak *-e;*
~ s.o. with s.th. *b-le* bş yüzünden alay
etm., başına kakmak *-i;* **taunt.ing** ☐
alaylı; iğneli *(söz).*
**taut** [tɔːt] *adj.* ⬇ sıkı, gergin *(ip, halat
vs.); fig.* gergin *(sinir);* **taut.en** *v/t. &
v/i.* gerginleş(tir)mek, sıkılaş(tır)mak;
⬇ aganta etm.
**tau.tol.o.gy** [tɔːˈtɔlədʒi] *n.* gereksiz tekrar-
(lanan ifade).
**tav.ern** [ˈtævən] *n.* meyhane, taverna;
han.
**taw¹** ⊕ [tɔː] *v/t.* şaplamak.
**taw²** [~] *n.* bilye (oyunu).
**taw.dri.ness** [ˈtɔːdrinis] *n.* zevksizlik, bayağılık; **taw.dry** ☐ ucuz ve gösterişli,
bayağı, zevksiz.
**taw.ny** [ˈtɔːni] *adj.* sarımsı kahverengi,
esmer, koyu kumral.
**tax** [tæks] 1. *n.* vergi, resim (on *üzerine); fig.* külfet, yük (on, upon *-e);* ~ evasion
vergi kaçırma; 2. *vb.* vergi koymak *-e; fig.* külfet olm., yük olm., tüketmek *(sabır);* 🕸 mahkeme masrafını belirle-
mek; suçlamak; ~ s.o. with s.th. *b-ni
bşden* dolayı suçlamak; **tax.a.ble** ☐ vergiye tabi; **tax.a.tion** *n.* vergi (tarhı); ver-
gilendirme; *part.* 🕸 mahkeme masrafı;
**tax-col.lec.tor** *n.* vergici, tahsildar; **tax-
-free** *adj.* vergiden muaf.
**tax.i** F [ˈtæksi] 1. *n.* = ~-cab taksi; 2. *v/t.
& v/i.* taksi ile gitmek *veya* taşımak; ⫟
taksile(t)mek; **~-danc.er** *n.* dansetmek
için tutulan kız; **~-driv.er** *n.* taksi şoförü; **~.me.ter** *n.* taksimetre.
**tax.pay.er** [ˈtækspeiə] *n.* vergi mükellefi.
**tea** [tiː] *n.* çay (fidanı); çay ziyafeti;
akşam kahvaltısı; high ~, meat ~ ikindi
kahvaltısı, beş çayı; **~-cad.dy** *n.* çay kutusu.
**teach** [tiːtʃ] *(irr.) v/t.* öğretmek, okutmak, eğitmek, yetiştirmek; ders vermek
*-e;* göstermek; I'll ~ you to come home
late! eve geç gelmeyi ben sana gösteri-
rim!; *v/i.* öğretmenlik yapmak; **teach-
a.ble** ☐ çabuk öğrenen, öğrenmeye hevesli; **teach.er** *n.* öğretmen, hoca;

**teach.er-train.ing col.lege** eğitim fakültesi; **teach-in** *n.* tartışma, münazara;
**teach.ing** *n.* öğretme, öğretim; öğretmenlik; ~s *pl.* telkin, talim, öğretilen
şey.
**tea...:** **~-co.sy** *n.* çaydanlık külâhı; **~.cup**
*n.* çay fincanı; storm in a ~ *fig.* bir bardak suda fırtına; **~-gown** *n.* ikindide giyilen elbise.
**teak** ♀ [tiːk] *n.* tik ağacı (kerestesi).
**tea-ket.tle** [ˈtiːketl] *n.* çaydanlık.
**team** [tiːm] *n.* ekip, grup; çift hayvan takımı; *part. spor:* takım; ~ **spir.it** ekip
halinde çalışma ruhu; **team.ster** [~stə]
*n.* çift hayvan süren kimse; *Am.* kamyon
şoförü; **team-work** *n.* takım halinde çalışma, ekip çalışması *(a. spor); thea.* piyesteki oyuncuların hepsi.
**tea.pot** [ˈtiːpɔt] *n.* demlik, çaydanlık.
**tear¹** [tɛə] 1. *(irr.) v/t. & v/i.* yırt(ıl)mak,
kop(ar)mak, yar(ıl)mak, çok hırpala(n)-
mak; açmak *(delik);* yolmak; F çılgın
gibi koşmak; 2. *n.* yırtık; *s.* wear.
**tear²** [tiə] *n.* gözyaşı.
**tear.ful** ☐ [ˈtiəful] gözleri yaşlı, ağlayan.
**tear-gas** [ˈtiəgæs] *n.* göz yaşartıcı gaz.
**tear.ing** *fig.* [ˈtɛəriŋ] *adj.* çılgınca, müthiş.
**tear.less** ☐ [ˈtiəlis] gözyaşsız, gözleri kurumuş.
**tea.room** [ˈtiːrum] *n.* kafeterya.
**tease** [tiːz] 1. *v/t.* tedirgin etm., rahatsız etm., kızdırmak; *fig.* takılmak *-e,*
alay etm. *ile;* liflere ayırmak; kabartmak *(saç);* 2. *n.* takılmayı seven kimse,
şakacı kimse; **tea.sel** ♀ [ˈtiːzl] *n.* tarakotu; ⊕ hav kabartma tarağı; **teas.er** *n.*
F *fig.* zor mesele, güç iş.
**tea...:** **~-spoon** *n.* çay kaşığı; **~.spoon.ful**
*n.* çay kaşığı dolusu; **~.strain.er** *n.* çay
süzgeci.
**teat** [tiːt] *n.* meme, emcik.
**tea...:** **~-things** *n. pl.* çay takımı; **~-urn**
*n.* semaver.
**tech.nic** [ˈteknik] *n. a.* ~s *pl. veya sg.* =
technique; **tech.ni.cal** ☐ teknik..., mesleki..., ilmî; resmî; kurallara uygun;
**tech.ni.cal.i.ty** [~ˈkæliti] *n.* teknik ayrıntı, incelik, ilmî nitelik; **tech.ni.cian**
[~ʃən] *n.* teknisyen, teknikçi, tekniker.
**tech.ni.col.or** [ˈteknikalə] 1. *adj.* renkli
film...; 2. *n.* renkli film.
**tech.nique** [tekˈniːk] *n.* teknik, yöntem,
yordam, metod, yapma usulü.
**tech.no.cra.cy** [tekˈnɔkrəsi] *n.* teknokrasi.
**tech.nol.o.gy** [tekˈnɔlədʒi] *n.* teknoloji;
school of ~ teknik üniversite.
**tech.y** [ˈtetʃi] = testy.

**ted.der** *Am.* [ˈtedə] *n.* yaş otu harman makinesi.

**ted.dy boy** F [ˈtedibɔi] *n.* asi genç.

**te.di.ous** ☐ [ˈtiːdjəs] usandırıcı, can sıkıcı, yorucu; **ˈte.di.ous.ness** *n.* sıkıcılık, usandırıcılık; can sıkıntısı; monotonluk.

**te.di.um** [ˈtiːdjəm] *n.* sıkıcılık; can sıkıntısı, bezginlik.

**tee** [tiː] **1.** *n. spor:* hedef; *golf:* topun konulduğu küçük kum yığını *veya* tahta çubuk; **2.** *vb.* ~ off topa kum yığınının üstünden vurarak oyuna başlamak.

**teem** [tiːm] *v/i.* dolu olm., kaynamak (with *ile*); boşanmak, çok yağmak *(yağmur)*.

**teen-ag.er** [ˈtiːneidʒə] *n.* on üç on dokuz yaşlar arasındaki kimse, genç, delikanlı.

**teens** [tiːnz] *n. pl.* on üç ile on dokuz arasındaki yaşlar; in one's ~ 13-19 yaşları arasında.

**tee.ny** F [ˈtiːni] *adj.* ufak, ufacık, küçük, mini mini.

**tee.ter** F [ˈtiːtə] *v/i.* sendeleyerek yürümek, sallanmak, bocalamak.

**teeth** [tiːθ] *pl. of* tooth.

**teethe** [tiːð] *v/i.* diş çıkarmak; **teething troubles** *pl.* diş çıkardığı için bebeğin huysuzluğu.

**tee.to.tal** [tiːˈtəutl] *adj.* içki içmemeye ait; yeşilaycı; **tee¹to.tal.(l)er** *n.* alkollü içki içmeyen kimse.

**tee.to.tum** [ˈtiːtəuˈtʌm] *n.* el ile çevrilen topaç.

**tel.e.cast** [ˈtelikɑːst] **1.** *n.* televizyon yayını; **2.** *v/t.* televizyonla yayınlamak.

**tel.e.course** *Am.* F [ˈtelikɔːs] *n.* televizyonla öğretim.

**tel.e.gram** [ˈteligræm] *n.* telgraf(name).

**tel.e.graph** [ˈteligrɑːf] **1.** *n.* telgraf (makinesi); *attr.* telgraf...; **2.** *v/i.* telgraf çekmek; *v/t.* tellemek; **tel.e.graph.ic** [~ˈgræfik] *adj.* (~ally) telgrafla ilgili, telgraf...; **te.leg.ra.phist** [tiˈlegrəfist] *n.* telgrafçı; **teˈleg.ra.phy** *n.* telgraf sistemi, telgrafçılık.

**te.lep.a.thy** [tiˈlepəθi] *n.* telepati, uzaduyum.

**tel.e.phone** [ˈtelifəun] **1.** *n.* telefon; by ~ telefonla; be on the ~ telefonda olm.; **2.** *v/t.* telefon etm. *-e;* ~ **booth** telefon kulübesi; **ˈtel.e.phon.ic** [~ˈfɔnik] *adj.* (~ally) telefona ait, telefon...; **te.leph.o.nist** [tiˈlefənist] *n.* santral memuru, telefoncu; **teˈleph.o.ny** *n.* telefonculuk.

**tel.e.pho.to** *phot.* [ˈteliˈfəutəu] *n. a.* ~ **lens** teleobjektif, teleskopik mercek; telefotografik resim.

**tel.e.print.er** [ˈteliprintə] *n.* teleks.

**tel.e.scope** [ˈteliskəup] **1.** *n. opt.* teleskop, ırakgörür; **2.** *v/t. & v/i.* iç içe geç(ir)mek; kısal(t)mak; iç içe girmek; **tel.e.scop.ic** [~ˈkɔpik] *adj.* teleskopa ait; teleskopik; teleskopla görülebilen; ~ **sight** nişan dürbünü *(tüfekte).*

**tel.e.typ.er** [ˈteliˈtaipə] *n.* teleks.

**tel.e.vise** [ˈtelivaiz] *v/t.* televizyonla yayınlamak; **tel.e.vi.sion** [ˈ~viʒən] *n.* televizyon, uzagörüm; *attr.* televizyon...; watch ~ televizyon seyretmek; ~ **set** televizyon cihazı; **tel.e.vi.sor** [ˈ~vaizə] *n.* televizyon alıcısı.

**telex** [ˈteleks] *n.* teleks.

**tell** [tel] *(irr.) v/t.* söylemek *-e*, anlatmak *-e*, bildirmek *-e*, nakletmek *-e*; ifade etm., belirtmek; emretmek; anlamak; keşfetmek; haber vermek; temin etm.; itiraf etm.; ~ s.o. to do s.th. *b-ne bş* yapmasını söylemek; I have been told bana söylendi; ~ off sayıp ayırmak (for s.th. *bş için;* to do *bş* yapmak için); F paylamak, haşlamak; ~ the world *sl.* yedi mahalleye duyurmak; *v/i.* bahsetmek (about *-den*); gammazlamak, ispiyonlamak (on *i-);* ifşa etm., yaymak (on, of *-i);* tesiri olm., tesir etm. *(darbe vs.);* **ˈtell.er** *n.* veznedar; anlatan kimse; mecliste oyları sayan kimse, sayıcı; **ˈtell.ing** ☐ etkili, tesirli; **tell.tale** [ˈ~teil] **1.** *adj.* dedikoducu; belli eden; *fig.* ağzında bakla ıslanmayan; **2.** *n.* gammaz kimse, dedikoducu kimse; ⊕ sayaç; ~ **clock** çalışanların işe gelip gitme zamanını kaydeden saat.

**tel.ly** F [ˈteli] *n.* televizyon.

**tel.pher** [ˈtelfə] *n.* teleferik.

**te.mer.i.ty** [tiˈmeriti] *n.* gözüpeklik, delice cesaret; aşırı cüret, küstahlık.

**tem.per** [ˈtempə] **1.** *v/t.* yumuşatmak, hafifletmek; ayarlamak; kıvama getirmek; su ile yoğurmak *(balçık);* ⊕ tavlamak, su vermek *(çelik); ♪* gam dizisine göre akort etm.; sertleştirmek; **2.** *n.* ⊕ kıvam, karar, terkip; tabiat, huy, mizaç; öfke, terslik, aksilik; hot ~ öfkelenme, köpürme; lose one's ~ hiddetlenmek, tepesi atmak; **tem.per.a.ment** [ˈ~rəmənt] *n.* mizaç, tabiat, huy, yaradılış; *♪* akort; **tem.per.a.men.tal** ☐ [~ˈmentl] mizaca bağlı; limoni tabiatlı, değişken mizaçlı; çabuk kızan, öfkesi burnunda, **ˈtem.per.ance 1.** *n.* ölçülülük, ılımlılık; içkiden kaçınma; **2.** *adj.* içkiden kaçınan...; alkolsüz...; **tem.per.ate** ☐ [ˈ~rit] ılımlı, mutedil; ılıman, ılık; içkiden kaçınan; ~ **zone** ılıman bölge; **tem.per.a.ture** [ˈtempritʃə] *n.* sıcaklık, ısı, hararet; ısı derecesi; **ʔ**

ateş; have *veya* run a ~ ateşi olm.; **tempered** [ˈtempəd] *comb.* ... mizaçlı,... huylu; hot-~ sinirli, öfkeli.

**tem.pest** [ˈtempist] *n.* fırtına, bora; **tempes.tu.ous** ☐ [~ˈpestjuəs] fırtınalı; şiddetli, zorlu.

**Tem.plar** [ˈtemplə] *n. hist.* şövalye; 2 *univ.* Londra'da Temple'de oturan hukuk öğrencisi.

**tem.ple¹** [ˈtempl] *n.* mabet, tapınak.

**tem.ple²** *anat.* [~] *n.* şakak.

**tem.po** [ˈtempəu] *n.* tempo; gidiş(at), tarz.

**tem.po.ral** ☐ [ˈtempərəl] geçici; (şimdiki) zamana ait; dünyevî; cismanî; *gr.* zaman belirten; **tem.po.ral.i.ties** [~ˈrælitiz] *n. pl.* dünyevî mülk; **tem.po.ra.ri.ness** [ˈ~rərinis] *n.* geçicilik; **tem.po.rar.y** ☐ geçici, muvakkat; ~ bridge geçici köprü; ~ work geçici iş; **tem.po.rize** *v/i.* zamana ayak uydurmak; uzlaşmak; vakit kazanmaya çalışmak.

**tempt** [tempt] *v/t.* baştan çıkarmak, ayartmak, kandırmak; çekmek, cezbetmek; teşvik etm.; sinirlendirmek; be ~ed baştan çıkarılmak; **temp¡ta.tion** *n.* günaha teşvik; ayartma, baştan çıkarma; cezbedici şey; **tempt.er** *n.* ayartan kimse, baştan çıkaran kimse; şeytan; **tempt-ing** ☐ cezbedici, çekici; **tempt-ress** *n.* baştan çıkaran kadın.

**ten** [ten] 1. *adj.* on; 2. *n.* on sayısı *veya* rakamı.

**ten.a.ble** [ˈtenəbl] *adj.* savunması kolay; elde tutulabilen; makûl.

**te.na.cious** ☐ [tiˈneiʃəs] yapışkan; tutan, bırakmayan, vazgeçmez (of -*den*); kuvvetli (*hafıza*); inatçı, direngen; **te.nac.i.ty** [tiˈnæsiti] *n.* yapışkanlık; sebat, direnme; bırakmama, vazgeçmeme (of -*den*); sağlamlık.

**ten.an.cy** [ˈtenənsi] *n.* kiracılık, kullanım; kira süresi.

**ten.ant** [ˈtenənt] 1. *n.* kiracı; *fig.* bir yerde oturan kimse, sakin; ~ right kiracının kirayı ödedikçe kullanma hakkı; 2. *v/t.* kiralamak; **ten.ant.ry** *n.* kiracılar; kiracılık.

**tench** *ichth.* [tentʃ] *n.* kilizbalığı.

**tend¹** [tend] 1. *v/i.* meyletmek, yönelmek, eğinmek (to, towards -*e*); ~ from uzaklaşmaya çalışmak -*den*; ~ upwards yükselmek (*fiyat*).

**tend²** [~] *v/t.* bakmak -*e*, dikkat etm. -*e*, göz kulak olm. -*e*; kullanmak (*makine*); **tend.ance** *n.* bakım, bakma, göz kulak olma.

**tend.en.cy** [ˈtendənsi] *n.* meyil, eğilim,

eğinme; yönseme; **ten.den.tious** [~ˈdenʃəs] *adj.* belli bir amaç güden, davalı, tezli; meyilli, eğik.

**ten.der¹** ☐ [ˈtendə] nazik, hassas, kolay incinir; müşfik, şefkatli, merhametli; inœ, narin, cılız; olgunlaşmamış; sevecen; körpe, gevrek.

**ten.der²** [~] 1. *n.* teklif, arz; † teklif; ihale; legal ~ geçerli para; 2. *v/t.* sunmak, teklif etm; *v/i.* teklif vermek.

**ten.der³** [~] *n.* bakıcı; 🚂, ⚓ tender.

**ten.der.foot** *Am.* F [ˈtendəfut] *n.* güçlüklere alışık olmayan kimse, acemi; **ten.der.loin** [ˈ~lɔin] *n. part. Am.* fileto; *Am.* her türlü karanlık işin yapıldığı bölge; **tender.ness** *n.* şefkat, yufka yüreklilik.

**ten.don** *anat.* [ˈtendən] *n.* veter, kiriş, tendon.

**ten.dril** ⚘ [ˈtendril] *n.* asma *veya* sarmaşık filizi.

**ten.e.ment** [ˈtenimənt] *n.* çok kiracılı ucuz apartman; (kiralık) daire; 🏠 mülk olabilen herhangi *bş*; konut, mesken; ~ house ucuz apartman.

**ten.et** [ˈtiːnet] *n.* inan, doktrin, akide, prensip, ilke, görüş.

**ten.fold** [ˈtenfəuld] *adv.* on kat, on misli.

**ten.nis** [ˈtenis] *n.* tenis; ~-court *n.* tenis kortu.

**ten.on** ⊕ [ˈtenən] *n.* erkek geçme parçası; ~-saw *n.* ⊕ zıvana testeresi.

**ten.or** [ˈtenə] *n.* gidiş(at), akış; yön: anlam, mana; ♪ tenor (sesi), tenor çalgı.

**tense¹** *gr.* [tens] *n.* fiil zamanı.

**tense²** ☐ [~] gergili, gergin (a. fig.); sinirli; nazik; **tense.ness** gerginlik; **tensile** [ˈtensail] *adj.* geril(ebil)ir; gerilme...; ~ strength gerilme direnci; **tension** [ˈ~ʃən] *n.* gerginlik; ger(il)me; ⚡ gerilim: high ~ ⚡ yüksek gerilim; ~ test germe deneyi.

**tent¹** [tent] *n.* çadır, otağ, oba; pitch one's ~s çadır kurmak; *fig.* bir yere yerleşmek.

**tent²** [~] *n.* bir çeşit siyah şarap.

**ten.ta.cle** *zo.* [ˈtentəkl] *n.* kavrama uzvu; dokunaç.

**ten.ta.tive** [ˈtentətiv] 1. ☐ deneme..., tecrübe olarak yapılan; ~ly deneme kabilinden; 2. *n.* deneme, tecrübe.

**ten.ter** [ˈtentə] *n.* gergef, gergi; ~-hook *n.* gergi kancası; be on ~s *fig.* endişe içinde olm.

**tenth** [tenθ] 1. *adj.* onuncu; onda bir; 2. *n.* onda bir kısım; onuncu gelen şey; onda lık; **tenth.ly** *adv.* onuncu olarak.

**tent-peg** [ˈtentpeg] *n.* çadır kazığı.

**ten.u.ous** ☐ [ˈtenjuəs] ince, narin; seyrek, hafif.

**ten.ure** ['tenjuǝ] *n.* tasarruf (hakkı); görev süresi; kullanım süresi; işinde kalabilme hakkı; ~ of office hizmet süresi.

**te.pee** ['ti:pi:] *n.* kızılderili çadırı.

**tep.id** □ ['tepid] ılık; **te'pid.i.ty, 'tep.idness** *n.* ılıklık.

**ter.cen.te.nar.y** [tǝːsen'tiːnǝri], **ter.cen.tenni.al** [~'tenjǝl] **1.** *adj.* üç yüzyıla ait; **2.** *n.* üç yüzüncü yıldönümü.

**ter.gi.ver.sa.tion** [tǝːdʒivǝː'seifǝn] *n.* döneklik, değişkenlik.

**term** [tǝːm] **1.** *n.* süre, müddet, vade; sömestr; dönem; Ⱥ, *phls.* had, terim; ȡ toplantı devresi; anlatım, dil, söz, terim; ~s *pl.* koşullar, şartlar; ~s *pl.* ilişkiler; in ~s of praise överek, övgü ile; be on good (bad) ~s with *b-le* arası iyi (kötü) olm.; come to ~s, make ~s anlaşmak, uzlaşmak; **2.** *v/t.* isim vermek, adlandırmak, demek.

**ter.ma.gant** ['tǝːmǝgǝnt] **1.** □ yaygaracı, şirret, cadaloz *(kadın)*; **2.** *n.* şirret kadın, cadaloz kadın.

**ter.mi.na.ble** □ ['tǝːminǝbl] sınırlan(dırıl)abilir, süresi tayin edilebilir; **ter.mi.nal** ['~nl] **1.** □ uçta bulunan, uç, son; döneme ait, dönem...; ölümcül, ölümle sonuçlanan; ᵠ dal *veya* sapın ucunda olan; ~ly ölümcül derecede; **2.** *n.* son, uç, nihayet; ᵠ kutup, terminal; 🚌 *etc.* terminal; **ter.mi.nate** ['~neit] *v/t.* & *v/i.* bit(ir)mek, son vermek; sınırlamak; sona ermek; **ter.mi'na.tion** *n.* son, bit(ir)me; sonuç, netice; sınır; *gr.* sonek, çekim eki.

**ter.mi.nol.o.gy** [tǝːmi'nɔlǝdʒi] *n.* terminoloji; özel anlamlı terimler.

**ter.mi.nus** ['tǝːminǝs] *n.*, *pl.* **ter.mi.ni** ['~nai] son, nihayet, hudut, sınır; 🚌 son istasyon; son durak; terminal.

**ter.mite** *zo.* ['tǝːmait] *n.* beyaz karınca, divik.

**tern** *orn.* [tǝːn] *n.* balıkçın, deniz kırlangıcı.

**ter.na.ry** ['tǝːnǝri] *adj.* üçlü; üçer üçer giden; üç madenden oluşmuş *(alaşım)*.

**ter.race** ['terǝs] *n.* taraça, teras; set; sıra evler; **ter.raced** *adj.* teraslı..., taraçalı...; ~ house sıra ev.

**ter.ra-cot.ta** ['terǝ'kɔtǝ] *n.* pişirilmiş tuğla *veya* çömlek.

**ter.rain** ['terein] *n.* arazi, alan, arsa, yer.

**ter.res.tri.al** □ [ti'restriǝl] dünya ile ilgili, dünyasal; kara ile ilgili, karasal; karadan oluşan; *part. zo.*, ᵠ karada yaşayan.

**ter.ri.ble** □ ['terǝbl] korkunç, dehşetli; aşırı, çok, pek; berbat; **'ter.ri.ble.ness**

*n.* korkunçluk; aşırılık; berbatlık.

**ter.ri.er** *zo.* ['teriǝ] *n.* teriyer.

**ter.rif.ic** [tǝ'rifik] *adj.* (~ally) korkunç, dehşetli, dehşet verici; aşırı, çok, pek; F fevkalâde, harika, çok güzel; **ter.ri.fy** ['terifai] *v/t.* korkutmak, dehşete düşürmek.

**ter.ri.to.ri.al** [teri'tɔːriǝl] **1.** □ karaya ait; belirli bir bölgeye ait; *Am.* devlet teşkilâtına girmemiş bölgelere ait; ~ waters *pl.* kara suları; 🇬 Army, 🇬 Force yedek gönüllü ordusu, ana vatan ordusu; **2.** *n.* ✕ ana vatan ordusu üyesi; **ter.ri.to.ry** ['~tǝri] *n.* toprak, arazi; memleket, ülke; bölge.

**ter.ror** ['terǝ] *n.* terör, tedhiş; korku, dehşet; baş belâsı kimse; çok yaramaz çocuk; **'ter.ror.ism** *n.* tedhişçilik, terörizm; **'ter.ror.ist** *n.* tedhişçi, terörist; **'ter.ror.ize** *v/t.* tedhiş etm., yıldırmak.

**terse** □ [tǝːs] kısa ve öz, veciz *(söz, konuşma)*; **'terse.ness** *n.* kısa ve özlülük.

**ter.tian** ᵠ ['tǝːfǝn] *adj.* & *n.* günaşırı tutan (nöbet); **'ter.ti.ar.y** *adj.* üçüncü (dereceye ait); *geol.* üçüncü zamana ait.

**Ter.y.lene** ['terǝliːn] *n.* terilen.

**tes.sel.late** ['tesilet] *v/t.* mozaik taş *veya* parçalarla donatmak; ~d pavement mozaik döşeli kaldırım.

**test** [test] **1.** *n.* test, imtihan; tecrübe, deney; test, muayene; *fig.* deneme; ᵓₙ analiz, çözümleme, tahlil; ölçü, ayar; maden potası; put to the ~ denemeye tabi tutmak, sınamak, tecrübe etm.; **2.** *v/t.* denemek, prova etm.; imtihan etm., tecrübe etm.; çözümlemek, tahlil etm.; kontrol etm.

**tes.ta.ceous** *zo.* [tes'teifǝs] *adj.* kabuklu...

**tes.ta.ment** *Mukaddes Kitap*, ȡ ['testǝmǝnt] *n.* ahit; vasiyetname; **tes.ta.men.ta.ry** [~'mentǝri] *adj.* vasiyet kabilinden; vasiyetnamede olan.

**tes.ta.tor** [tes'teitǝ] *n.* vasiyetname sahibi, vasiyetçi.

**tes.ta.trix** [tes'teitriks] *n.* vasiyetname yapan kadın.

**test case** ['test'keis] *n.* deneme davası.

**tes.ter¹** ['testǝ] *n.* yatak tentesi.

**test.er²** [~] *n.* muayene eden kimse *veya* alet.

**tes.ti.cle** *anat.* ['testikl] *n.* testis, erbezi, husye, haya, taşak.

**tes.ti.fi.er** ['testifaiǝ] *n.* şahit, tanık (to -e); **tes.ti.fy** ['~fai] *v/t.* kanıtlamak, ispatlamak; açığa vurmak; *v/i.* şehadette bulunmak (on *üzerine*); şahitlik etm. (for *lehte*).

**tes.ti.mo.ni.al** [testi'mǝunjǝl] *n.* bonservis,

tavsiye mektubu; belge; takdirname;
**tes.ti.mo.ny** [ˈ~məni] *n.* tanıklık, şahadet, şahitlik (to *-e*); ifade.
**tes.ti.ness** [ˈtestinis] *n.* terslik, hırçınlık.
**test...**: ˈ~-match *n. kriket: uluslararası
kriket turnuva maçı; ˈ~-pa.per *n.* ᚛ turnusol kâğıdı; ˈ~-pi.lot *n.* ᚛ deney pilotu; ˈ~-print *n. phot.* prova; ˈ~-tube *n.* ᚛ deney tüpü.
**tes.ty** □ [ˈtesti], **tetch.y** □ [ˈtetʃi] ters, hırçın, huysuz, sinirli, alıngan.
**teth.er** [ˈteðə] 1. *n.* hayvanı bağlama ipi; *fig.* sınır, had; at the end of one's ~ *fig.* kuvvet *veya* sabrının son haddinde; 2. *v/t.* iple bir yere bağlamak *(at vs.).*
**tet.ra.gon** Ⱥ [ˈtetrəgən] *n.* dörtgen, dörtkenar; **te.trag.o.nal** [~ˈtrægənl] *adj.* dört açılı.
**tet.ter** ᚛ [ˈtetə] *n.* temriye.
**Teu.ton** [ˈtjuːtən] *n.* Germen kabile üyesi; **Teu.ton.ic** [~ˈtɔnik] *adj.* Germen halkına ait.
**text** [tekst] *n.* metin, parça; konu; asıl kitap *veya* yazı; ˈ~book *n.* ders kitabı.
**tex.tile** [ˈtekstail] 1. *adj.* dokumacılıkla ilgili, dokuma...; 2. *n.* dokuma kumaş; ~s *pl.* mensucat.
**tex.tu.al** □ [ˈtekstjuəl] metne ait, metin...
**tex.ture** [ˈtekstʃə] *n.* doku; dokum, dokunuş; bünye, yapı, teşekkül.
**than** [ðæn, ðən] *cj.* -den (daha), -dan, -e göre; -den başka, -den hariç.
**thane** *hist.* [θein] *n.* krala hizmet eden asilzade.
**thank** [θæŋk] 1. *v/t.* teşekkür etm. *-e;* şükretmek *-e;* ~ you teşekkür ederim; no, ~ you hayır, teşekkür ederim; I will thank you for ... için size minnettar kalırım; ~ you for nothing *iro.* yine de sağol; 2. *n.* ~s *pl.* teşekkür, şükran, şükür; ~s! teşekkürler!; give ~s şükretmek; ~s to *-in* sayesinde; **thank.ful** □ [ˈ~ful] minnettar, müteşekkir, memnun; ˈthank**less** □ nankör, iyilik bilmez; değeri bilinmemiş; **thanks.giv.ing** [ˈ~sgiviŋ] *n.* teşekkür, minnet; şükran duası; ♀ *(Day) part. Am.* şükran yortusu; ˈthank.wor**thy** *adj.* teşekküre lâyık.
**that** [ðæt, ðət] 1. *pron.* (*pl.* those) o, şu; ki o; so ~'s ~! hepsi bu kadar!, işte o kadar!; ... and ~ ve bu da; at ~ bundan başka, hem de, artık; 2. *cj.* ki; -sin diye; -si için; böylece.
**thatch** [θætʃ] 1. *n.* dam örtüsü olarak kullanılan saman *veya* saz; 2. *v/t.* sazla kaplamak *(dam vs.).*
**thaw** [θɔː] 1. *n.* erime, çözülme; ısınma; samimileşme; 2. *v/t. & v/i.* eri(t)mek,

buzları çözülmek; ısınmak, samimileşmek, kaynaşmak, açılmak.
**the** [ðə; ðiː] 1. *definite article, determiner (belirtme edatı)* bu, şu, o; 2. *adv.* ~ ... ~ ne kadar... o kadar.
**the.a.tre, Am. the.a.ter** [ˈθiətə] *n.* tiyatro (binası); amfi(teatr); *fig.* olay yeri, alan, sahne, meydan; ˈ~-go.er *n.* tiyatro meraklısı; **the.at.ric, the.at.ri.cal** □ [θiˈætrik(əl)] tiyatroya ait, tiyatro...; yapmacık, sahte *(tavır vs.);* **theˈat.ri.cals** *n. pl.* amatörlerce oynanan piyesler.
**thee** † *veya lit.* [ðiː] *pron.* sen(i), sana.
**theft** [θeft] *n.* hırsızlık.
**their** [ðɛə] *adj.* onların; **theirs** [~z] *pron.* onların(ki).
**the.ism** [ˈθiːizəm] *n.* Allaha inanma; tektanrıcılık, monoteizm.
**them** [ðem, ðəm] *pron.* onları, onlara.
**theme** [θiːm] *n.* konu, mevzu, tema *(a. ♪);* ♪ vazife, ödev, görev; kompozisyon ödevi; *gr.* kök, gövde; ~ **song** müzikal oyunda sık tekrarlanan müzik parçası; film müziği.
**them.selves** [ðəmˈselvz] *pron.* kendileri (ni, -ne, -nde), bizzat.
**then** [ðen] 1. *adv.* o zaman, o vakit; o zamanın; (ondan) sonra, daha sonra; demek (ki); ayrıca, bundan başka; bunun için; sonuç olarak; by ~ o zamana kadar; every now and ~ bazen, arada bir, ara sıra; there and ~ derhal, hemen; now ~ şu halde, öyle ise; 2. *cj.* öyle ise, o halde, şu halde; 3. *adj.* o zaman olan.
**thence** *lit.* [ðens] *adv.* oradan; bundan dolayı; o zamandan.
**thence.forth** [ˈðensˈfɔːθ] *adv.*, **thence.for**ward [ˈ~ˈfɔːwəd] o zamandan beri.
**the.oc.ra.cy** [θiˈɔkrəsi] *n.* teokrasi, dincierki (ülke); papazlar idaresi; **the.o.crat**ic [θiəˈkrætik] *adj.* (~ally) teokratik, dinerkine dayalı.
**the.o.lo.gi.an** [θiəˈləudʒjən] *n.* ilahiyatçı, tanrıbilimci; **the.o.log.i.cal** □ [~ˈlɔdʒikəl] ilahiyata ait, tanrıbilimle ilgili; **the.ol.o**gy [θiˈɔlədʒi] *n.* ilahiyat, tanrıbilim, teoloji.
**the.o.rem** [ˈθiərəm] *n.* teorem; **the.o.ret.ic, the.o.ret.i.cal** □ [~ˈretik(əl)] kuramsal, nazari; ˈthe.o.rist *n.* nazariyeci, kuramcı; ˈthe.o.rize *v/i.* teori kurmak, nazariye yürütmek; ˈthe.o.ry *n.* teori, kuram. ˈ~.os.o.phy [θiˈɔsəfi] *n.* teosofi.
**ther.a.peu.tic** [θerəˈpjuːtik] 1. *adj.* tedavi edici, iyileştirici, şifa verici; 2. *n.* ~s *mst sg.* terapi ilmi; ˈther.a.py *n.* tedavi, terapi; ˈther.a.pist *n.* terapist; **mental** ~ pisikoterapist.

**there** [ðɛə] **1.** *adv.* ora(sı); orada; oraya; o noktada, o hususta, o konuda; ~ is, ~ are [ðə'riz, ðə'rɑː] var; ~ you are! demedim mi!, buyurun!; **2.** *int.* gördün mü?, işte!, haydi! **there...:** '~.a.bout(s) *adv.* o civarda, oralarda, o sularda; ~'aft.er *adv.* (ondan) sonra; '~'by *adv.* o suretle, o münasebetle; ~'for *adv.* onun için, ona; '~.fore *adv.* onun için, bundan dolayı, bu yüzden; ~'from *adv.* ondan, oradan; ~'in *adv.* orada, onda, o hususta; ~'of *adv.* ondan; bundan dolayı; ~'on *adv.* onun üzerine; ~'to *adv.* ona, oraya; ilâveten, ayrıca; '~.up'on *adv.* onun üzerin(d)e; bundan dolayı; hemen, derhal; ~'with *adv.* onunla; ~.with'al *adv.* ayrıca, bundan başka.

**ther.mal** [ˈθəːməl] **1.** ☐ termal, kaplıca kabilinden; *phys.* sıcağa ait; ~ value ısı değeri; **2.** *n.* yükselen sıcak hava kitlesi; 'ther.mic *adj.* (~ally) ısıya ilişkin, termik...; therm.i.on.ic [~'ɔnik] *adj.* radyo: ~ valve termiyonik lamba.

**ther.mo-e.lec.tric cou.ple** *phys.* [ˈθəː-məuˈlektrikˈkʌpl] *n.* termoelektrik kuplesi; **ther.mom.e.ter** [θəˈmɔmitə] *n.* termometre, sıcakölçer; **ther.mo.met.ric, ther.mo.met.ri.cal** ☐ [θəˈməuˈmetrik(əl)] termometreye ait, termometre...; **ther.mo.pile** *phys.* [ˈ~məupail] *n.* termopil; **Ther.mos** [ˈ~mɔs] *n. a.* ~ flask, ~ bottle termos; **ther.mo.stat** [ˈ~məstæt] *n.* termostat.

**the.sau.rus** [θiˈsɔːrəs] *n.* kavramlar dizini; kelime kitabı; hazine, ambar.

**these** [ðiːz] *adj. & pron.* (*pl. of* this) bunlar; ~ three years bu üç yıl.

**the.sis** [ˈθiːsis] *n., pl.* **the.ses** [ˈ~siːz] sav, dava, önerme, iddia; tez, inceleme, araştırma.

**they** [ðei] *pron.* onlar.

**thick** [θik] **1.** ☐ *com.* kalın; sık (*saç vs.*); çok; kesif (*hava vs.*); koyu (*sis, çorba vs.*); boğuk, kısık (*ses*); ahmak, kalın kafalı; samimî, senli benli; aşırı; *oft.* as ~ as thieves F *pred.* aralarından su sızmaz; ~ with kesif, yoğun, dolu *ile*; that's a bit ~! *sl.* bu kadarı da fazla!; **2.** *n.* en kalabalık yer; bşin kalın kısmı; *fig.* bşin en yoğun yeri *veya* zamanı; in the ~ of ortasında, en şiddetli anında; 'thick.en *v/t. & v/i.* kalınlas(tır)mak; koyulas(tır)mak; bulan(dır)mak; sıklaş(tır)mak; yoğunlaş(tır)mak; **thick.et** [ˈθikit] *n.* çalılık, ağaçlık; 'thick-head.ed *adj.* kalın kafalı; 'thick.ness *n.* kalınlık; sıklık; ⊕, ⊤ kat, tabaka; 'thick-'set *adj.* tıknaz; sık dikilmiş *(bitkiler)*; 'thick-

'skinned *adj. fig.* vurdumduymaz, duygusuz.

**thief** [θiːf] *n., pl.* **thieves** [θiːvz] hırsız; **thieve** [θiːv] *v/i.* hırsızlık yapmak; *v/t.* çalmak; 'thiev.er.y *n.* hırsızlık.

**thiev.ish** ☐ [ˈθiːviʃ] hırsızlığa alışmış; hırsız gibi; 'thiev.ish.ness *n.* hırsızlık alışkanlığı.

**thigh** [θai] *n.* uyluk, but.

**thim.ble** [ˈθimbl] *n.* yüksük; **thim.ble.ful** [ˈ~ful] *n.* yüksük dolusu miktar; azıcık şey.

**thin** [θin] **1.** ☐ *com.* ince, zayıf; seyrek; az; cılız, çelimsiz, kuvvetsiz; sulu, hafif (*içki vs.*); sudan (*bahane*); soğuk (*espri*); soluk, cansız; eksik, yetersiz; he had a ~ time F çok eziyet çekti, berbat vakit geçirdi; **2.** *v/t. & v/i.* incel(t)mek; seyrekleş(tir)mek, seyrelmek; zayıfla(t)mak; dağılmak *(sis)*.

**thine** † *veya poet.* [ðain] *pron.* senin(ki).

**thing** [θiŋ] *n.* şey, nesne; mesele, mevzu, konu; şart, durum; olay; mahlûk, yaratık; ~s *pl.* giyecekler, eşya; such a ~ böyle bir şey; the ~ F doğru (*veya* moda, uygun, gerekli) olan şey; the ~ is mesele şu ki ,önemli olan; know a ~ or two F çok iyi bilmek; of all ~s her şeyden evvel, evvelemirde; ~s are going better durum iyiye gidiyor; I don't feel quite the ~ F biraz keyifsizim.

**thing.um(.a).bob** F [ˈθiŋəm(i)bɔb] *n.*, **thing.um.my** F [ˈ~əmi] şey, zımbırtı, zırıltı.

**think** [θiŋk] (*irr.*) *v/i.* düşünmek (of, about -i; to inf. ...meyi); düşünüp taşınmak (about, over üzerinde); hatırlamak, ileri sürmek, tavsiye etm. (of -i); *v/t.* düşünmek; zannetmek, sanmak; niyet etm., tasarlamak; hatırlamak; tasavvur etm., farz etm.; addetmek; ummak; ~ much etc. of çok kıymet vermek -e, değer vermek -e, sevmek -i; ~ out düşünüp çıkarmak; tasarlamak; ~ s.th. over -in üzerinde düşünmek; 'think.a.ble *adj.* düşünülebilir, akla uygun; 'think.er *n.* düşünür, filozof; 'think.ing *adj.* düşünceli; akıllı; mantıklı...

**thin.ness** [ˈθinnis] *n.* incelik; zayıflık.

**third** [θəːd] **1.** *adj.* üçüncü; ~ degree işkence ile yapılan sorgu; **2.** *n.* üçte bir; ♪ üçlü; 'third.ly *adv.* üçüncü olarak; 'third-'rate *adj.* kalitesiz, adi.

**thirst** [θəːst] **1.** *n.* susuzluk; *fig.* özlem, tutku; **2.** *v/i.* susamak (for, after -e); 'thirst.y ☐ susuz, susamış; *fig.* çok istekli; F kurak (*toprak vs.*).

**thir.teen** [ˈθəːˈtiːn] *adj. & n.* on üç (sayı sı); 'thir'teenth [~θ] **1.** *adj.* on üçüncü;

**2.** *n.* on üçte bir; **thir.ti.eth** [ˈθəːtiiθ] **1.** *adj.* otuzuncu; **2.** *n.* otuzda bir; **ˈthir.ty** *adj.* & *n.* otuz (sayısı); the thirties *pl.* 30-39 yaşları arası.

**this** [ðis] *adj.* & *pron.* (*pl.* these) bu; ✝ cari; in ~ country bu ülkede; ~ morning bu sabah; ~ day week haftaya bugün. **this.tle** ✦ [ˈθisl] *n.* devedikeni; **ι~-down** *n.* diken pamuğu.

**thith.er**(**.ward**) ✝ *veya* poet. [ˈðiðə(wəd)] *adv.* oraya; o yöne.

**tho'** [ðəu] = though.

**thole** ↓ [θəul] *n.* kürek ıskarmozu; **ι~-pin** *n.* *fig.* eksen.

**thong** [θɔŋ] *n.* sırım.

**tho.rax** *anat.* [ˈθɔːræks] *n.* göğüs, toraks.

**thorn** ✦ [θɔːn] *n.* diken; *fig.* üzüntü, cefa; **ˈthorn.y** *adj.* dikenli; *fig.* sıkıntılı, cefalı.

**thor.ough** ☐ [ˈθʌrə] tam, mükemmel; çok dikkatli, titiz; baştan başa; ayrıntılı; **~ly** tamamen, adamakıllı; **ι~.bred** **1.** *adj.* saf kan; soylu; tam...; **2.** *n.* saf kan hayvan; *fig.* kültürlü kimse; **ι~.fare** *n.* cadde, yol, geçit; **ι~.go.ing** *adj.* tam, adamakıllı; **ˈthor.ough.ness** *n.* kusursuzluk; dikkatlilik; **ˈthor.ough.paced** *adj.* her türlü yürüyüşe alışkın (*at*); tam, mükemmel.

**those** [ðəuz] *adj.* & *pron.* (*pl. of* that **1.**) şunlar; onlar; are ~ your parents? şunlar senin ebeveynin mi?

**thou** ✝ *İncil, poet.* [ðau] *pron.* sen.

**though** [ðəu] *cj.* gerçi, her ne kadar, ise de; -diği halde, olsa da; as ~ -miş gibi, sanki, güya.

**thought** [θɔːt] **1.** *pret.* & *p.p. of* think; **2.** *n.* düşünme; düşünce, fikir, görüş, kanaat; düşünce tarzı; endişe; niyet; ümit; give ~ to üzerinde enine boyuna düşünmek; on second ~s yeniden düşününce; take ~ for -i düşünmek, tartmak. **thought.ful** ☐ [ˈθɔːtful] dalgın, düşünceli (of); saygılı, nazik (of); dikkatli; **ˈthought-ful.ness** *n.* düşüncelilik; saygı.

**thought.less** ☐ [ˈθɔːtlis] düşüncesiz (of), saygısız; dikkatsiz, pervasız; bencil; **ˈthought.less.ness** *n.* düşüncesizlik; dikkatsizlik.

**thought-read.ing** [ˈθɔːtriːdiŋ] *n.* düşünceleri okuma.

**thou.sand** [ˈθauzənd] **1.** *adj.* bin; **2.** *n.* bin sayısı; **thou.sandth** [ˈ~zəntθ] **1.** *adj.* bininci; **2.** *n.* binde bir.

**Thra.cian** [ˈθreiʃən] **1.** *n.* Trakyalı; **2.** *adj.* Trakya'ya özgü.

**thral**(**l**)**.dom** [ˈθrɔːldəm] *n.* kölelik, esaret.

**thrall** [θrɔːl] *n.* esir, köle(lik), esaret.

**thrash** [θræʃ] *v/t.* dövmek, dayak atmak; kamçılamak, kırbaçlamak; F yenmek; tartışarak halletmek (*sorun*); tartışarak varmak (*karara, çözüme*); yapmak (*plan vs.*); *v/i.* *b-ni* pataklamak; kıvranmak (*acıdan vs.*); ↓ denize karşı seyretmek; = thresh; **ιthrash.er** = thresher; **ιthrash.ing** *n.* dayak, kötek; yenilgi; = threshing.

**thread** [θred] **1.** *n.* iplik, tire; tel, lif; ince çizgi; çok ince bş; ⊕ yiv; sıra, silsile; **2.** *v/t.* *-de* iplik geçirmek; ipliğe dizmek; yol bulup geçmek; arasına serpmek; takmak (*film vs.*); **ι~.bare** *adj.* eskimiş, yıpranmış, pejmürde (*giyecek*); *fig.* bayatlamış (*espri vs.*); **ˈthread.y** *adj.* iplik gibi; tel tel.

**threat** [θret] *n.* tehdit, gözdağı; tehlike; **ˈthreat.en** *v/t.* tehdit etm., gözdağı vermek, korkutmak; yıldırmak; *v/i.* kötü bşe işaret olm.; **ˈthreat.en.ing** *adj.* tehdit edici; endişe verici

**three** [θriː] **1.** *adj.* üç; **2.** *n.* üç rakamı; **ι~-ˈcol.our** *adj.* üç renkli...; **ι~.fold** *adv.* üç misli; **~.pence** [ˈθrepəns] *n.* üç peni; **ι~.pen.ny** *adj.* üç penilik...; *fig.* değersiz; **~-phase cur.rent** ⚡ [ˈθriːfeizˈkʌrənt] *n.* trifaz akım; **ι~ˈscore** *adj.* & *n.* altmış (sayısı).

**thresh** [θreʃ] *v/t.* dövmek (*harman*); ~ out *fig.* inceden inceye görüşmek (*iş, mesele*). **thresh.er** [ˈθreʃə] *n.* harman dövme makinesi; harmancı; sapanbalığı. **thresh.ing** [ˈθreʃiŋ] *n.* harman dövme; **ι~-floor** *n.* harman yeri; **ι~-ma.chine** *n.* harman dövme makinesi. **thresh.old** [ˈθreʃhəuld] *n.* eşik; *fig.* başlangıç.

**threw** [θruː] *pret. of* throw **1.**

**thrice** ✦ [θrais] *adv.* üç kez, üç kere.

**thrift** [θrift], **thrift.i.ness** [θrift, ˈ~inis] *n.* idare. tutum, tasarruf, ekonomi; verimlilik; **ˈthrift.less** ☐ müsrif, idaresiz, tutumsuz, savurgan; **ˈthrift.y** ☐ tutumlu, idareli; *poet.* verimli, başarılı, hızla büyüyen.

**thrill** [θril] **1.** *v/t.* & *v/i.* (heyecanla) titremek (with *ile*); heyecanlan(dır)mak; tesir etm., etkile(n)mek; **2.** *n.* titreme; titreşim; heyecan; **ˈthrill.er** *n.* F heyecanlı kitap *veya* piyes.

**thrive** [θraiv] (*irr.*) *v/i.* iyi gitmek, gelişmek, başarılı olm.; *fig.* zenginleşmek, refaha ermek; büyümek; **thriv.en** [ˈθrivn] *p.p. of* thrive; **thriv.ing** ☐ [ˈθraiviŋ] başarılı, gelişen, büyüyen.

**thro'** [θruː] *abbr. of* through.

**throat** [θrəut] *n. com.* boğaz, gırtlak; clear one's ~ hafifçe öksürmek. «öhö öhö» de mek; **'throat.y** ☐ gırtlaktan çıkan *(ses).*

**throb** [θrɔb] **1.** *v/i.* vurmak, çarpmak, atmak *(nabız, kalp);* zonklamak *(baş);* titreşmek; **2.** *n.* nabız artması, kalp çarpması; çarpıntı; titreşme.

**throe** [θrəu] *n.* sancı, ağrı; elem, dert; ~s *pl.* doğum *veya* ölüm sancısı.

**throm.bo.sis** ⚥ [θrɔm'bəusis] *n.* tromboz.

**throne** [θrəun] **1.** *n.* taht; hâkimiyet, saltanat; kral, hükümdar; **2.** *v/t. & v/i.* tahta geç(ir)mek.

**throng** [θrɔŋ] **1.** *n.* kalabalık, izdiham; **2.** *v/t.* üşüşmek *-e; v/i.* toplanmak, kalabalık etm.

**thros.tle** *orn.* [θrɔsl] *n.* ardıçkuşu.

**throt.tle** [θrɔtl] **1.** *v/t.* boğmak; bastırmak; ⊕ kısmak; **2.** *n.* = '~-valve ⊕ kısma valfı, kelebek.

**through** [θruː] **1.** *prp.* içinden, bir yandan diğer yana, bir başından diğer başına; başından sonuna kadar; sayesinde; -den (geçerek); her tarafına; her yerin(d)e; -den dolayı, yüzünden; **2.** *adv.* (başından) sonuna kadar; baştan başa; tamamen; **3.** *adj.* engelsiz, direkt *(yol);* aktarmasız *(tren),* ekspres; işi bitik; bitirmiş; ~'out **1.** *prp.* baştan başa, boyunca, *-in* her tarafında, her hususta; ~ the year yıl boyunca; **2.** *adv.* baştan başa, baştan aşağı.

**throve** [θrəuv] *pret. of* thrive.

**throw** [θrəu] **1.** *(irr.) v/t. com,* atmak, fırlatmak; üstünden atmak *(at);* kullanmak *(güç, nüfuz);* inşa etm., yapmak; şekillendirmek *(çömlek);* ⊕ büküp ibrişim yapmak *(ipek);* atmak, savurmak *(yumruk);* atmak *(zar); Am.* F yere sermek, düşürmek *(rakibini);* bırakmak, terketmek; giyivermek *(elbise);* meydana getirmek; şike yaparak kaybetmek *(oyun);* vermek *(parti);* çekmek *(ziyafet); (yılan)* değiştirmek *(deri);* yavrulamak *(hayvan);* sarsmak, perişan etm.; ~ at fırlatmak, savurmak *-e;* dikkatini vermek *-e;* ~ away kaçırmak *(fırsat);* ziyan etm., çarçur etm.; vaz geçmek; atmak; ~ in fazladan eklemek, parasız olarak ilâve etm.; birbirine geçirmek *(dişli);* katmak *(söze);* oyuna dahil etm. *(top);* ~ off çıkarmak, üstünden atmak; -den kurtulmak; atlatmak; başka tarafa savurmak, yöneltmek; saçmak, yaymak; çabucak yapıvermek; ~ out söylemek *(söz);* savurmak *(tehdit); part. parl.* reddetmek, kabul etmemek *(tasarı);* inşa etm., yapmak; şaşırtmak, kafasını karıştırmak; dışarı atmak; işten kovmak; geçmek, geride bırakmak; yaymak, saç-

mak *(ışık, koku vs.);* altüst etm. *(plan);* ⊕ ayırmak, debreye etm. *(motor);* ~ over terketmek, (yüzüstü) bırakmak, vaz geçmek; ~ up yukarı'atmak; kusmak; -den istifa etm., bırakmak *(işini);* ortaya çıkarmak; acele inşa etm.; yığıvermek; *s.* sponge; *v/i.* fırlatıp atmak, savurmak; ~ off ava başlamak; **2.** *n.* atış, atma; atım; ⊕ sia uzunluğu; risk, tehlike; örtü; atkı, eşarp; birim; '~-back *n. part. biol.* atavizm, atacılık; **thrown** [θrəun] *p.p. of* throw; **'throw-'off** *n.* ava başlama; başlangıç.

**thru** *Am.* [θruː] = through.

**thrum¹** [θrʌm] *n. dokumacılık:* kırpıntı; iplik saçağı *veya* püskülü.

**thrum²** [~] *v/t.* tıngırdatmak *(çalgı);* monoton bir şekilde söylemek.

**thrush¹** *orn.* [θrʌʃ] *n.* ardıçkuşu.

**thrush²** [~] *n.* ⚥ pamukçuk.

**thrust** [θrʌst] **1.** *n.* itme, itiş, dürtme; hamle; × taarrüz, hücum; *fig.* çıkışma, sert çıkma; ⊕ itme kuvveti; **2.** *(irr.) v/t.* itmek, dürtmek; saplamak *(bıçak, süngü vs.);* ite kaka sürmek; zorla getirmek *(bir mevkiye);* yüklemek *(sorumluluk vs.);* ~ o.s. into *k-ni* zorla kabul ettirmek *-e,* davetsiz olarak girmek *-e;* ~ out savurmak; uzatmak *(dil);* ~ upon s.o. *b-ne* zorla kabul ettirmek; *v/i.* saldırmak *(at -e).*

**thud** [θʌd] **1.** *v/i.* güm diye ses çıkarmak; **2.** *n.* gümbürtü.

**thug** [θʌg] *n.* katil, cani, eşkiya.

**thumb** [θʌm] **1.** *n.* başparmak; Tom 2 parmak çocuk; **2.** *vb.* çevirmek *(sayfa);* başparmakla tuta tuta aşındırmak *veya* kirletmek *(sayfa);* ~ one's nose at s.o. *b-ne* nanik yapmak; ~ a lift otostop yapmak; '~-print *n.* parmak izi; '~ screw *n.* parmakla döndürülen vida; ⊕ kelébek başlı civata; '~-stall *n.* başparmak kılıfı; '~.tack *n. Am.* pünez, raptiye.

**thump** [θʌmp] **1.** *n.* vuruş; yumruk (sesi), darbe (sesi). güm; ağır düşüş (sesi); **2.** *v/t.* güm güm vurmak *-e;* yumruklamak, dövmek; *v/i.* küt küt atmak *(kalp);* gümbürdemek; 'thump.er *sl.* vurucu, katil; 'thump.ing *adj. sl.* iri, kocaman.

**thun.der** [θʌndə] **1.** *n.* gök gürlemesi; *fig.* oft. ~s *pl.* gürültü, gümbürtü, tufan *(alkış vs.);* **2.** *v/i.* gürlemek, gümbürdemek; *v/t.* şiddetle söylemek; '~.bolt *n.* yıldırım; *fig.* beklenmedik olay; '~.clap *n.* gök gürlemesi; *fig.* kötü olay *veya* haber; '~.cloud *n.* fırtına bulutu. **thun.der...:** '~.head *n.* fırtına bulutu *(a. fig.);* 'thun.der.ing *adj. sl.* (kos)kocaman, muazzam; **'thun.der.ous** ☐ *fig.* gürleyen; ~ applause alkış tufanı; **'thun.der.storm** *n.* gök gürültülü yağmur fırtınası; **'thun.der.struck** *adj.* hayrete düşmüş, yıldırımla vurulmuşa dönmüş; **'thun.der.y** *adj.* gök gürültülü *(hava).*

**Thurs.day** ['θəːzdi] *n.* perşembe.

**thus** [ðʌs] *adv.* böyle(ce), bu suretle, bunun için, bu nedenle, nitekim.

**thwack** [θwæk] = whack.

**thwart** [θwɔːt] 1. *v/t.* bozmak *(işini vs.),* önlemek, engellemek; hüsrana uğratmak; 2. *n.* kürekçinin oturduğu tahta.

**thy** *Kutsal Kitap, poet.* [ðai] *adj.* senin.

**thyme** ♀ [taim] *n.* kekik.

**thy.roid** *anat.* ['θairɔid] 1. *adj.* kalkansı... tiroid...; ~ extract kalkanbezi özü; gland = 2. *n.* tiroid, kalkanbezi.

**thy.self** *Kutsal Kitap, poet.* [ðai'self] *pron.* bizzat kendin.

**ti.ar.a** [ti'ɑːrə] *n.* papanın üç katlı tacı; taç.

**tib.i.a** *anat.* ['tibiə] *n.* kaval kemiği; incik kemiği.

**tic** ♯ [tik] *n.* tik.

**tick¹** *zo.* [~] *n.* kene, sakırga.

**tick²** [~] *n.* kılıf.

**tick³** F [~]: on ~ veresiye.

**tick⁴** [~] 1. *n.* tıkırtı; saatin tik tak sesi; doğru işareti (√); F an; to the ~ saatin çalması ile; 2. *v/i.* tıkırdamak, tıklamak, tik tak etm. *(saat);* ~ over *mot.* rölantide çalışmak; *v/t.* işaret koymak, çetele çekmek; ~ off işaret koymak, işaretleyerek saymak; *sl.* azarlamak, haşlamak, paylamak.

**tick.er** ['tikə] *n.* özellikle borsa fiyatlarını şeride kaydeden alet; F saat; *sl.* kalp; *sl.* yürek, cesaret; **'~.tape** *n. coll.* eğlencelerde fırlatılan renkli kâğıt şerit.

**tick.et** ['tikit] 1. *n.* bilet; etiket; *pol.* aday listesi; *(trafik)* para cezası, karakol davetiyesi; ehliyet (kâğıdı); the ~ F doğru olan, münasip şey; ~ of leave ♂ tahliye izni; 2. *v/t.* etiketlemek; **'~.col.lec.tor** *n.* biletçi, kondüktör; **'~.in.spec.tor** *n.* bilet kontrolörü; **'~.ma.chine** *n.* bilet makinesi; **'~.of.fice**, **'~.win.dow** *n. part. Am.* bilet gişesi; **'~.punch** *n.* bilet zımbası.

**tick.ing** ['tikiŋ] *n.* kılıflık kumaş.

**tick.le** ['tikl] *v/t. & v/i.* gıdıkla(n)mak; *fig.* eğlendirmek; **'tick.ler** *n.* güç durum; *a.* ~ coil reaksiyon bobini; **'tick.lish** ☐ gıdıklanır; nazik, tehlikeli *(durum, so-run vs.).*

**tid.al** ☐ ['taidl] gelgite bağlı; ~ wave met dalgası; *fig.* galeyan.

**tid.bit** ['tidbit] = titbit.

**tid.dly-winks** ['tidliwiŋks] *n.* parmak gücüyle disk atma oyunu.

**tide** [taid] 1. *n.* gelgit, meddücezir, (low ~) met ve (high ~) cezir; *fig.* akış, cereyan, eğilim, meyil; mevsim; zaman, vakit; turn of the ~ *fig.* durumun lehe dönmesi, şansın dönmesi; 2. *v/t. & v/i.* akıntı ile yüz(dür)mek; ~ over *fig.* çıkarmak *(kışı vs.),* atlatmak *(krizi),* üstesinden gelmek.

**ti.di.ness** ['taidinis] *n.* düzen, tertip, intizam.

**ti.dings** ['taidiŋz] *n. pl. veya sg.* haber. havadis.

**ti.dy** ['taidi] 1. *adj.* temiz, düzenli, tertipli, derli toplu, muntazam; F oldukça, epey *(para);* 2. *n.* kap; 3. *vb. a.* ~ up düzeltmek, derleyip toplamak, çekidüzen vermek.

**tie** [tai] 1. *n.* bağ *(a. fig.),* düğüm; fiyonk; kravat, boyunbağı; bağlantı; ♪ bağlı nota işareti; △ kiriş, lata; *fig.* ayak bağı; *spor:* beraberlik, berabere kalma; *parl.* oy eşitliği; 🚉 *Am.* travers; 2. *v/t. com.* bağlamak *(a. ♪),* raptetmek; düğümlemek; △ tespit etm.; ~ down *fig.* bağlamak (to -e); ~ up bağlamak *(para vs.);* şarta bağlamak; *v/i. spor:* berabere kalmak (with *ile).*

**tier** [tiə] *n. thea.* sıra, kat, dizi.

**tierce** [tiəs] *n. fenc.* bir vaziyet şekli; *is-kambil:* üçlü seri.

**tie-up** ['taiʌp] *n.* bağ(lantı); † ortaklık; *part. Am.* işin durması, grev; birleşme; tıkanıklık *(trafik);* kesatlık, durgunluk *(iş);* ahır.

**tiff** F [tif] 1. *n.* münakaşa, hafif tartışma; 2. *v/i.* münakaşa etm., gücenmek, darılmak.

**tif.fin** ['tifin] *n.* hafif öğle yemeği.

**ti.ger** ['taigə] *n.* kaplan; *Am.* F kana susamış adam; **'ti.ger.ish** ☐ *fig.* vahşî, yırtıcı; kaplan gibi.

**tight** ☐ [tait] sıkı, gergin; su geçirmez, akmaz, sızmaz; zor, müşkül; dar, sıkışık; cimri, eli sıkı; tıkalı; ucu ucuna; kesat; F sarhoş, küfelik; be in a ~ place *veya* corner F zor *veya* tehlikeli durumda olm.; hold ~ sık tut(un)mak; it is a ~ fit dar, sıkı; **'tight.en** *v/t. & v/i. a.* ~ up sıkış(tır)mak; ger(ginleş)mek; **'~-'fist-ed** *adj.* eli sıkı, cimri; **'~-laced** *adj.* sofu; **'~-lipped** *adj.* ağzı sıkı, ağzı pek; **'tight.ness** *n.* sıkılık, gerginlik; **'tight-rope** *n.* sıkı gerilmiş ip; **tights** [~s] *n. pl.* sıkı giysi; külotlu çorap; **'tight.wad** *n. sl.* cimri, pinti kimse.

**ti.gress** [ˈtaigris] *n.* dişi kaplan.

**tile** [tail] **1.** *n.* kiremit; tuğla; çini; *sl.* silindir şapka; he has a ~ loose *sl.* kaçık, bir tahtası noksan; **2.** *v/t.* kiremit kaplamak *-e*; ˈ~-lay.er, **ˈtil.er** *n.* kiremitçi.

**till¹** [til] *n.* para çekmecesi, kasa.

**till²** [~] *prp.* & *cj.* -e kadar, -e değin, -e gelinceye kadar, zamana kadar.

**till³** ✓ [~] *v/t.* işlemek *(toprak)*; **ˈtill.age** *n.* toprağı işleme, çiftçilik, ziraat; işlenmiş toprak.

**till.er¹** [ˈtilə] *n.* çiftçi.

**till.er²** ↓ [~] *n.* dümen yekesi.

**tilt¹** [tilt] *n.* tente.

**tilt²** [~] **1.** *n.* eğim, meyil, eğiklik; eğilme; *fig.* çekişme, kavga, atışma; hız; at üstünde yapılan mızrak oyunu; on the ~ meyilli, eğri, devrilmekte; (at) full ~ son süratle, bütün hızı ile; have a ~ at s.o. *b-ne* saldırmak, itiraz etm.; **2.** *v/t.* & *v/i.* eğ(il)mek, devirmek; devrilmek; at üzerinde mızrakla saldırmak (at *-e*); ~ against koşarken çarpmak *e*; **ˈtilt.ing** *adj.* eğik..., meyilli...

**tilth** [tilθ] *n.* ziraat, çiftçilik, tarım; işlenmiş toprak.

**tim.bal** ♪ [ˈtimbəl] *n.* dümbelek.

**tim.ber** [ˈtimbə] **1.** *n.* kereste(lik orman); ↓ gemi kaburgası *(veya* postası); **2.** *v/t.* kereste ile kaplamak *veya* desteklemek; ~ed kerestelik, ağaçlık; ahşap *(ev)*; ˈ~-line *n.* orman sınırı; ˈ~-work *n.* ahşap yapı; ˈ~-yard *n.* kereste deposu.

**time** [taim] **1.** *n.* vakit, zaman; süre, müddet; kere, defa, kez; ♪ tempo; saat, dakika; çağ, devir, devre; vade, mühlet; ecel; kat, misil; ~! *parl.* paydos!; ~ and again tekrar tekrar, defalarca; at ~s ara sıra, bazen, zaman zaman; at a ~, at the same ~ aynı zamanda; yine de, bununla birlikte; at one ~ bir zamanlar, vaktiyle, eskiden; before one's ~ vakitsiz; behind one's ~ gecikmiş, geç kalmış; behind the ~s eski kafalı, zamana ayak uyduramayan; çok eski; by that ~ o zamana kadar; do ~ F hapse girmek; for the ~ being şimdilik; have a good ~ iyi vakit geçirmek, eğlenmek; in (good) ~ tam zamanında, vaktinde; in no ~ bir an evvel; in a month's ~ bir ay sonra; *s.* mean² 1; on ~ tam zamanında, vaktinde; out of ~ mevsimsiz; beat the ~ tempo tutmak; *s.* keep; **2.** *v/t.* ayarlamak; uydurmak; ölçmek; *a.* take the ~ of saat tutmak *için;* the train is ~d to leave at 7 tren saat 7'de hareket edecektir; *v/i.* ♪ tempo tutmak (to *-e*); ˈ~-bar.gain *n.* vadeli alışveriş, alivre satış; ˈ~-ex.po.sure

*n. phot.* poz; uzun pozlu resim; ˈ~-hon.o(u)red *adj.* eskiliğinden dolayı saygı duyulan; ˈ~-keep.er *n.* çalışma saatlerini tutan kimse *veya* gösterge; saat hakemi; *part.* saat, kronometre; ˈ~-lag *n.* ara; ˈ~-lim.it *n.* sınırlı zaman; zaman sınırı; **ˈtime.ly** *adj.* yerinde olan, uygun; vakitli; **ˈtime.piece** *n.* saat, kronometre; **ˈtim.er** *n. spor:* kronometre (tutan kimse), saat hakemi; *phot.* deklanşör.

**time...**: ~-serv.er [ˈtaimsəːvə] *n.* eyyamcı, zaman adamı, çıkarcı; ˈ~-sheet *n.* yoklama cetveli; ˈ~-sig.nal *n. part. radyo:* saat ayarı; ˈ~-ta.ble *n.* 🚂 tarife; *okul:* ders programı.

**tim.id** ☐ [ˈtimid] sıkılgan, ürkek, çekingen, mahçup, utangaç; **tiˈmid.i.ty** *n.* utangaçlık, çekingenlik.

**tim.ing** [ˈtaimiŋ] *n.* ayarlama, zamanlama.

**tim.or.ous** ☐ [ˈtimərəs] = timid.

**tin** [tin] **1.** *n.* teneke (kutu); kalay; *sl.* mangır, mangiz; **2.** *adj.* tenekeden yapılmış, teneke...; kalay...; ~ solder kalay lehimi; **3.** *v/t.* kalaylamak; teneke kutulara doldurmak; ~ned meat konserve et.

**tinc.ture** [ˈtiŋktʃə] **1.** *n.* hafif renk; *fig.* görünüş, sahte tavır; *pharm.* ispirto eriyiği, ruh, mahlul; **2.** *v/t.* hafifçe boyamak; içine katmak; hafifçe etkilemek.

**tin.der** [ˈtində] *n.* kav.

**tine** [tain] *n.* çatal dişi; geyik boynuzunun çatalı.

**tin.foil** [ˈtinˈfɔil] *n.* stanyol, kalay yaprağı.

**ting** F [tin] = tinkle.

**tinge** [tindʒ] **1.** *n.* hafif renk, boya; *fig.* az miktar, nebze, cüz; iz, belirti; **2.** *v/t.* hafifçe boyamak; içine katmak; *fig.* hafifçe etkilemek.

**tin.gle** [ˈtiŋgl] *v/i.* sızlamak; karıncalanmak; çınlamak.

**tin...**: ~ god F put, sanem; ~ hat *sl.* miğfer, çelik asker başlığı.

**tink.er** [ˈtiŋkə] **1.** *n.* tenekeci; lehimci; tamirci(lik); **2.** *v/t.* tamir etm.; *v/i.* üstünkörü çalışmak (at *üzerinde*); ~ up amatörce çalışmak; kabaca tamir etm.

**tin.kle** [ˈtiŋkl] **1.** *v/t.* & *v/i.* çıngırda(t)mak, çınlamak; **2.** *n.* çıngırtı.

**tin.man** [ˈtinmən] *n.* tenekeci; **ˈtin.ny** *adj.* teneke gibi, teneke sesli; teneke tadı veren; **ˈtin.o.pen.er** *n.* konserve açacağı; **ˈtin.plate** *n.* saç, demir levha.

**tin.sel** [ˈtinsl] **1.** *n.* gelin teli; *fig.* aldatıcı parlaklık, cicili bicili şey; **2.** *adj.* gösterişli fakat değersiz, cicili bicili...; aslı astarı olmayan; **3.** *v/t.* gelin teli ile süslemek; cicili bicili yapmak.

**tint** [tint] **1.** *n.* hafif renk; renk tonu; **2.** *v/t.* hafifçe boyamak, hafif renk vermek; ~ed paper renkli kâğıt.

**tin.tin.nab.u.la.tion** [ˈtintinæbjuˈleiʃən] *n.* çıngırdama; çan çalınması; çan sesi.

**tin.ware** [ˈtinwɛə] *n.* teneke kaplar.

**ti.ny** □- [ˈtaini] küçücük, ufacık, minicik, ufak tefek.

**tip** [tip] **1.** *n.* uç, burun; tepe, doruk; ağızlık; bahşiş, sadaka; tavsiye; tiyo; hafif vuruş; çöplük *(a .fig.)*; give s.th. a. ~ bşi devirmek; **2.** *v/t. & v/i.* eğ(il)mek, bir yana yat(ır)mak; devirmek; devrilmek; ucuna bş takmak; dökmek, boşaltmak; hafifçe vurmak; bahşiş vermek -e; a. ~ off imada bulunmak -e; sır vermek -e; uyarmak -i; 'ı~cart *n.* atlı yük arabası; 'ı~off *n.* ima, ikaz, ihtar, uyarı.

**tip.pet** [ˈtipit] *n.* boyun atkısı.

**tip.ple** [ˈtipl] **1.** *vb.* içkiye düşkün olm.; **2.** *n.* içki; 'tip.pler *n.* akşamcı, ayyaş.

**tip.si.ness** [ˈtipsinis] *n.* çakırkeyflik.

**tip.staff** [ˈtipstɑ:f] *n.* şerif vekili; mübaşir, kavas.

**tip.ster** [ˈtipstə] *n.* yarış öncesi gizli bilgi veren kimse, tiyocu.

**tip.sy** [ˈtipsi] *adj.* çakırkeyf.

**tip.toe** [ˈtiptəu] **1.** *v/i.* ayaklarının ucuna basa basa yürümek; **2.** *n.* on ~ ayaklarının ucuna basarak.

**tip.top** F [ˈtipˈtɔp] **1.** *n.* en iyi kalite; **2.** *adj.* birinci sınıf, en âlâ.

**tip-up seat** *thea.* [ˈtipʌpˈsi:t] *n.* açılır kapanır koltuk.

**ti.rade** [taiˈreid] *n.* tirad; azarlayıcı sert söz.

**tire¹** [ˈtaiə] *n.* dış lastik.

**tire²** [~] *v/t. & v/i.* yor(ul)mak; usan(dır)mak, bık(tır)mak (of *-den*).

**tired** □ [ˈtaiəd] yorgun, bitkin, bitap; usanmış, bıkmış (of *-den*); 'tired.ness *n.* yorgunluk.

**tire.less** □ [ˈtaiəlis] dur durak bilmez, yorulmak bilmez, yorulmaz; bitmez tükenmez.

**tire.some** □ [ˈtaiəsəm] yorucu, sıkıcı.

**ti.ro** [ˈtaiərəu] *n.* acemi *(veya* yeni başlayan) kimse.

**'tis** [tiz] = it is.

**tis.sue** [ˈtiʃu:] *n.* doku; (ince tül) kumaş; kâğıt mendil; ince kâğıt; *fig.* ağ, şebeke; seri, silsile; † dokuma; 'ı~ˈpa.per *n.* ince (ipek) kâğıt.

**tit¹** [tit] *n.*: ~ for tat yumruğa yumruk; *fig.* kısasa kısas.

**tit²** *Am.* [~] = teat.

**tit³** *orn.* [~] *n.* baştankara.

**Ti.tan** [ˈtaitən] *n.* Titan; 'Ti.tan.ess *n.* sü-

per güçleri olan kadın; **ti.ta.nic** [~ˈtænik] *adj.* (~ally) muazzam, koskocaman.

**ti.ta.ni.um** 🔊 [taiˈteinjəm] *n.* titan.

**tit.bit** [ˈtitbit] *n.* lezzetli lokma, cazip kısım.

**tithe** [taið] *n.* ondalık, öşür; aşar vergisi; *mst fig.* onda bir.

**tit.il.late** [ˈtitileit] *v/t.* gıcıklamak, gıdıklamak; **tit.il·la.tion** *n.* gıdıkla(n)ma, gıcıkla(n)ma.

**tit.i.vate** F [ˈtitiveit] *v/t. & v/i.* süsle(n)mek, şıklaş(tır)mak.

**ti.tle** [ˈtaitl] **1.** *n.* başlık; ünvan, isim, lakap; hak (to *-e*); senet, tapu; **2.** *v/t.* lakap *veya* ünvan vermek; isimlendirmek; ~d *part.* asil, asılzade; 'ı~deed *n.* 🔊 tapu senedi; 'ı~hold.er *n. part. spor:* ünvan sahibi kimse; 'ı~page *n.* baş sayfa; 'ı~role *n.* başrol.

**tit.mouse** *orn.* [ˈtitmaus] *n., pl.* **tit.mice** [ˈ~mais] baştankara.

**ti.trate** 🔊 [ˈtitreit] *vb.* titre etm., derecesini saptamak; **tiˈtra.tion** *n.* titre, titrasyon.

**tit.ter** [ˈtitə] **1.** *v/i.* kıkır kıkır gülmek, kıkırdamak; **2.** *n.* kıkırdama.

**tit.tle** [ˈtitl] *n.* nokta; *fig.* zerre, cüz, nebze; 'ı~tat.tle **1.** *n.* dedikodu; **2.** *v/i.* dedikodu yapmak.

**tit.u.lar** □ [ˈtitjulə] hak olarak elde tutulan; ismi var cismi yok; lakaba ait; ünvandan dolayı olan.

**to** [tu:; tə] **1.** *particle* -mek (için), -mak (için); **2.** *prp.* -e -a, -ye, -ya; -e doğru *(a. adv.)*, yönüne doğru, tarafına; -e kadar, -e değin; ile; -e nispetle, -e nazaran, -e göre; -e dair, hakkında; için, maksadıyla; ~ me, ~ you bana, sana; he di; it happened ~ me başıma geldi; alive ~ s.th. bşin farkında, bilincinde; cousin ~ -in kuzeni; heir ~ -in vârisi, mirasçısı; secretary to -in sekreteri; ( weep ~ think of it onu düşününce ağlarım; here's ~ you! şerefinize!, sıhhatinize!; ~ and fro öteye beriye, öne ve arkaya.

**toad** *zo.* [təud] *n.* kara kurbağa; 'ı~.stool *n.* zehirli *(veya* şapkalı) mantar.

**toad.y** [ˈtəudi] **1.** *n.* dalkavuk, yağcı; **2.** *v/i.* dalkavukluk etm., yağ çekmek. yaltaklanmak (to *-e*); 'toad.y.ism *n.* dalkavukluk, yağcılık.

**toast** [təust] *n.* **1.** kızartılmış ekmek; sıhhatine içme; sıhhatine içilen kimse; **2.** *v/t. & v/i.* kızar(t)mak *(ekmek); fig.* ateşe tutup ısıtmak; çok ısınmak, yanmak; sıhhatine içmek -in; 'toast.er ekmek kızartma makinesi.

**to.bac.co** [tə'bækəu] *n.* tütün; **to'bac.co.nist** [~kənist] *n.* tütüncü.

**to.bog.gan** [tə'bɔgən] **1.** *n.* kızak; **2.** *v/i.* kızakla kaymak.

**toc.sin** ['tɔksin] *n.* alarm zili; *fig.* tehlike işareti.

**to.day** [tə'dei] *n. & adv.* bugün; günümüz; bu günlerde, şimdi.

**tod.dle** ['tɔdl] *v/i.* sendeleyerek yürümek, tıpış tıpış yürümek; gitmek; **'tod.dler** *n.* yeni yürümeye başlayan çocuk.

**tod.dy** ['tɔdi] *n.* sıcak su ile karıştırılmış içki; bazı hurma ağaçlarından çıkarılan öz.

**to-do** F [tə'duː] *n.* gürültü, patırtı, telâş, kıyamet.

**toe** [təu] **1.** *n.* ayak parmağı; ayak ucu; uç; ayakkabı *veya* çorap burnu; from top to ~ tepeden tırnağa; on one's ~s *fig.* uyanık, tetikte, dikkatli; **2.** *v/t.* ayak parmakları ile vurmak, dokunmak *veya* ulaşmak; ~ the line *spor:* başlama çizgisinde dizilmek; *pol.* söyleneni yapmak, verilen emirlere uymak.

**toed** [təud] *adj.* ... parmaklı.

**toff** P [tɔf] *n.* iyi giyimli, şık kimse.

**tof.fee, tof.fy** ['tɔfi] *n.* bonbon, şekerleme.

**tog** F [tɔg] **1.** *v/t.* giydirmek; **2.** *s.* togs.

**to.ga** ['təugə] *n.* toga.

**to.geth.er** [tə'geðə] *adv.* beraber(ce), birlikte, hep bir yerde, hep bir arada; aralıksız, durmadan, devamlı.

**tog.gle** ⌁ & ⊕ ['tɔgl] **1.** *n.* kasa çeliği; **2.** *v/t.* kasa çeliği ile bağlamak.

**togs** F [tɔgz] *n. pl.* elbise, giysi.

**toil** [tɔil] **1.** *n.* zahmet, emek, yorgunluk; uğraş; **2.** *v/i.* zahmet çekmek, didinmek, çalışmak, yorulmak; zar zor ilerlemek.

**toil.er** *fig.* ['tɔilə] *n.* ağır işçi.

**toi.let** ['tɔilit] *n.* tuvalet, apteshane; tuvalet, makyaj, giyinip kuşanma, süslenme; *Am.* banyo odası; make one's ~ giyinip kuşanmak; **'~.pa.per** *n.* tuvalet kâğıdı; **'~.set** *n.* tuvalet takımı; **'~.ta.ble** *n.* tuvalet masası.

**toils** [tɔilz] *n. pl.* tuzak, ağ *(a. fig.).*

**toil.some** □ ['tɔilsəm] zahmetli, yorucu, ağır *(iş vs.).*

**toil-worn** ['tɔilwɔːn] *adj.* bitkin, yorgun.

**to ken** ['təukən] *n.* belirti, iz, işaret, nişan; hatıra. yadigâr, andaç; özellik, hususiyet; jeton; ~ money itibarî para; in ~ of -in belirtisi olarak.

**told** [təuld] *pret. & p.p. of* tell; all ~ toplam olarak, tümü.

**tol.er.a.ble** □ ['tɔlərəbl] dayanılabilir, çekilebilir, hoşgörülebilir, katlanılabilir; orta, ne iyi ne kötü, iyice; **'tol.er.ance** *n.*

müsamaha, hoşgörü, tolerans, tahammül; **'tol.er.ant** □ müsamahakâr, hoşgörülü, toleranslı, hoşgörücü; hoşgörü sahibi, tahammüllü, sabırlı (of -e *karşı*); **tol.er.ate** ['~-reit] *v/t.* müsamaha etm. -e, hoş görmek -i, tolerans göstermek -e; katlanmak -e, tahammül etm. -e; **tol.er.a.tion** *n.* müsamaha, hoşgörü, tolerans; müsaade; sabır, tahammül.

**toll[1]** [təul] *n.* yol *veya* köprü parası, resim, geçiş ücreti; giriş ücreti; şehirlerarası telefon ücreti; *fig.* haraç; ~ call *teleph.* şehirlerarası telefon konuşması; ~ of the road trafik kazalarında ölen *veya* yaralananlar; **'~-bar, ~-gate** *n.* bariyer, paralı köprü *veya* yol girişi.

**toll[2]** [~] *v/t. & v/i.* çalmak *(çan vs.).*

**tom.a.hawk** ['tɔməhɔːk] **1.** *n.* kızılderili baltası; **2.** *v/t.* bu balta ile vurmak, kesmek *veya* öldürmek.

**to.ma.to** ♀ [tə'mɑːtəu, *Am.* tə'meitəu] *n.,* *pl.* **to'ma.toes** domates (fidanı).

**tomb** [tuːm] *n.* kabir, mezar, gömüt, sin; türbe.

**tom.boy** ['tɔmbɔi] *n.* erkek tavırlı kız, erkek Fatma.

**tomb.stone** ['tuːmstəun] *n.* mezar taşı.

**tom.cat** ['tɔm'kæt] *n.* erkek kedi.

**tome** [təum] *n.* cilt, büyük kitap.

**tom.fool** ['tɔm'fuːl] **1.** *n.* aptal kimse; **2.** *adj.* aptal; **tom'fool.er.y** *n.* aptallık; aptalca şaka, saçmalık.

**tom.my** *sl.* ['tɔmi] *n.* İngiliz eri, askeri; ~ gun hafif makineli tüfek; ~ rot saçma.

**to.mor.row** [tə'mɔrəu] *n. & adv.* yarın.

**tom.tom** ['tɔmtɔm] *n.* tamtam.

**ton** [tʌn] ton *(1016 kilo, Am. 907 kilo);* ~s *pl.* F yığın, dünya kadar *(para vs.).*

**to.nal.i.ty** [təu'næliti] *n.* tonalite, tonculuk; *paint.* renk uyumu.

**tone** [təun] **1.** *n.* ses, nitelik; ♪ ton, perde; ♣ beden kuvveti; *paint.* renk tonu; *fig.* tarz, tavır, hal, hava; out of ~ akortsuz, akordu bozuk; **2.** *v/t.* belirli bir ses *(veya* özellik) vermek; *paint.* renk vermek; *phot.* nüanslamak; ~ down tonunu hafifletmek -in, yumuşatmak; donuklaştırmak; *v/i.* uymak (with -e) *(part. renk);* ~ down yumuşamak; donuklaşmak.

**tongs** [tɔŋz] *n. pl.* (a pair of *bir)* maşa.

**tongue** [tʌŋ] *n. com.* dil; lisan; dil şeklinde bş; söz, konuşma (tarzı); broş iğnesi; araba oku; *geogr.* dil; hold one's ~ çenesini tutmak, susmak; speak with one's ~ in one's cheek alaylı ve gerçek niyetini aksettirmeyen türde konuşmak; yarım ağızla söylemek; **'tongue.less** *adj.* dilsiz; *fig.* sessiz, suskun; **'tongue-tied**

*adj.* dili tutulmuş; *fig.* ağzı var dili yok; **tongue-twist.er** *n.* tekerleme.

**ton.ic** ['tɔnik] 1. *adj.* (~ally) ♪ sese ait; ♣ kuvvet verici; *gr.* vurgulu; ~ chord ♪ ses akordu; 2. *n.* ♪ ana *veya* baş nota; ♣ kuvvet ilacı, tonik; soda; *gr.* vurgulu ses.

**to.night** [tə'nait] *n.* & *adv.* bu gece, bu akşam.

**ton.ing so.lu.tion** *phot.* ['təuniŋ səˈluːʃən] *n.* viraj (*veya* ton tespit) banyosu.

**ton.nage** ↓ ['tʌnidʒ] *n.* tonilato, tonaj, taşıma kapasitesi; bir memleketin tüm gemilerinin tonajı; tonaj ücreti.

**ton.sil** *anat.* ['tɔnsl] *n.* bademcik; **ton.sil.li.tis** [~siˈlaitis] *n.* bademcik iltihabı.

**ton.sure** ['tɔnʃə] 1. *n.* başın tepesini traş etme; başın traş edilmiş tepe kısmı; 2. *v/t. -in* tepesini traş etm.

**ton.y** *Am. sl.* ['təuni] *adj.* yüksek zümreye ait, lüks.

**too** [tuː] *adv.* dahi, keza, de, da, ilâveten, ek olarak, hem de, üstelik; (haddinden) fazla, çok.

**took** [tuk] *pret. of* take.

**tool** [tuːl] 1. *n.* alet (*a. fig.*); 2. *v/t.* aletle süslemek *veya* şekillendirmek; **~-bag**, **~-kit** *n.* takım çantası.

**toot** [tuːt] 1. *v/t.* & *v/i.* öt(tür)mek, çalmak (*düdük, korna vs.*); 2. *n.* düdük (*veya* boru) sesi.

**tooth** [tuːθ] *n., pl.* **teeth** [tiːθ] diş; dişe benzer *bş*; etkin güç; ~ and nail canını dişine takarak, var gücüyle; cast s.th. in s.o.'s teeth *bşi b-nin* yüzüne vurmak, yüzüne karşı söylemek; **~.ache** *n.* diş ağrısı; **~-brush** *n.* diş fırçası; **toothed** *comb.* ...dişli; **tooth.ing** *n.* ⊕ diş açma, dişleme; **tooth.less** □ dişsiz; **tooth-paste** *n.* diş macunu; **tooth.pick** *n.* kürdan.

**tooth.some** □ ['tuːθsəm] lezzetli, leziz, tadı güzel (*yiyecek*).

**too.tle** ['tuːtl] *vb.* yavaş *veya* sürekli çalmak (*nefesli çalgı*).

**top**[1] [tɔp] 1. *n.* üst, zirve, tepe, doruk; baş; *fig.* en yüksek nokta, yer *veya* derece; *mot. Am.* kapak; ↓ çanaklık; at the ~ üstünde, tepesinde, başında, zirvesinde; at the ~ of *-in* üstünde, tepesinde, başında, zirvesinde; at the ~ of one's speed âzami sürati ile; at the ~ of one's voice avazı çıktığı kadar, bar bar; on ~ tepede, üstte; on ~ of *-in* üstün(d)e; *-e* ilâveten, üstelik, hem de, ...yetmiyormuş gibi; 2. *adj.* en yüksek, en üst; en iyi, birinci sınıf; önde gelen; the ~ right corner sağ üst köşe; 3. *v/t.* kapamak, üstünü örtmek; *fig.* üstün gelmek *-den*, geçmek

*-i*, üstesinden gelmek; *-in* birincisi olm., *-in* zirvesinde olm.; ✓ tepesini kesmek; *-in* tepesine çıkmak; ~ up doldurmak, tamamlamak.

**top**[2] [~] *n.* topaç; sleep like a ~ kütük gibi uyumak, horul horul uyumak.

**to.paz** *min.* ['təupæz] *n.* topaz.

**top...:** **~-boots** *n. pl.* uzun çizme; ~ **dog** *sl.* galip, üstün gelen, fatih; efendi, lider, patron.

**to.pee** ['təupiː] *n.* güneş başlığı, kolonyal şapka.

**top.er** ['təupə] *n.* akşamcı, ayyaş kimse.

**top...:** **~-flight** *adj.* F birinci sınıf, üstün, seçkin; **~.gal.lant** ↓ [~ˈgælənt, ↓ təˈgælənt] 1. *adj.* babafingo...; 2. *n. a.* ~ sail babafingo; ~ hat silindir şapka; **~-heav.y** *adj.* havaleli, üstü çok yüklü; **~-hole** *adj. sl.* birinci sınıf, en iyi kalite, şahane.

**top.ic** ['tɔpik] *n.* konu, mevzu; **top.i.cal** □ güncel, aktüel; konuya ait; tartışmalı; yöresel; ♣ lokal.

**top...:** **~-knot** *n.* saç topuzu; *orn.* sorguç, tepe, ibik; **~.most** *n.* ↓ gabya çubuğu; **~-most** *adj.* en üstteki, en tepedeki; **~-notch** *adj.* F birinci sınıf, en iyi kalite, seçkin.

**to.pog.ra.pher** [təˈpɔgrəfə] *n.* topografya uzmanı; **top.o.graph.ic**, **top.o.graph.i.cal** □ [təpəˈgræfik(əl)] topografik; **to.pog.ra.phy** [təˈpɔgrəfi] *n.* topografya.

**top.per** F ['tɔpə] *n.* silindir şapka; **top.ping** *adj.* F birinci sınıf, şahane, fevkalâde.

**top.ple** ['tɔpl] *v/t.* & *v/i.* mst ~ over, ~ down düş(ür)mek; devirmek; devrilmek; yık(ıl)mak.

**top.sail** ↓ ['tɔpsl] *n.* gabya yelkeni.

**top.sy.tur.vy** □ ['tɔpsiˈtəːvi] altüst, baş aşağı; karmakarışık, karman çorman.

**toque** [təuk] *n.* sıkı ve kenarsız bir çeşit kadın şapkası.

**tor** [tɔː] *n.* kayalık tepe (*veya* burun).

**torch** [tɔːtʃ] *n.* meşale; *a.* electric ~ cep feneri; *Am.* asetilen lambası; **~-light** *n.* meşale ışığı; ~ procession fener alayı.

**tore** [tɔː] *pret of* tear[1] 1.

**tor.ment** 1. ['tɔːment] *n.* cefa, eziyet, işkence, elem, azap, dert; 2. [tɔːˈment] *v/t.* eziyet etm. *-e*, işkence etm. *-e*, azap çektirmek *-e*; *-in* canını sıkmak, *-in* başını ağrıtmak; **tor.men.tor** *n.* eziyetçi kimse *veya* şey.

**torn** [tɔːn] *p.p. of* tear[1] 1.

**tor.na.do** [tɔːˈneidəu] *n., pl.* **tor.na.does** [~z] kasırga, hortum.

**tor.pe.do** [tɔːˈpiːdəu] *n., pl.* **tor.pe.does**

[~z] **1.** *n.* ↓, ⊤ torpil; *a.* toy ~ eğlence fişeği; *a.* ~-fish *ichth.* torpilbalığı, uyuşturanbalığı; **2.** *v/t.* ↓ torpillemek; *fig.* baltalamak, kösteklemek; ~-**boat** *n.* ↓ torpido(bot); ~-**tube** *n.* torpil kovanı.

**tor.pid** □ ['tɔːpid] uyuşuk, uyuşmuş; ölü gibi; duygusuz; *fig.* durgun, hareketsiz, atıl; **tor'pid.i.ty**, **ltor.pid.ness**, **tor.por** ['tɔːpə] *n.* uyuşukluk, hareketsizlik, cansızlık.

**torque** ⊕ [tɔːk] *n.* dönme momenti, tork; burma madenden gerdanlık.

**tor.rent** ['tɔrənt] *n.* sel (*a. fig.*); **tor.rential** □ [tɔ'renʃəl] sel gibi; selden oluşan; *fig.* sert, şiddetli.

**tor.rid** ['tɔrid] *adj.* çok sıcak, kızgın, yakıcı; tropikal; ~ **zone** tropikal kuşak, tropika, sıcak bölge.

**tor.sion** ['tɔːʃən] *n.* bur(ul)ma, bük(ül)me, kıvırma, kıvrılma; **tor.sion.al** ['~ʃənl] *adj.* bükülmeye ait, bükülme..., burulma...

**tor.so** ['tɔːsəu] *n.* insan *veya* heykel gövdesi.

**tort** ⟂⟂ [tɔːt] *n.* haksız muamele (*veya* fiil), haksızlık.

**tor.toise** *zo.* ['tɔːtəs] *n.* kaplumbağa; ~-**shell** ['tɔːtəʃel] *n.* bağa, kaplumbağa kabuğu.

**tor.tu.os.i.ty** [tɔːtjuˈɔsiti] *n.* eğri büğrülük, yılankavilik; **ltor.tu.ous** □ eğri büğrü, yılankavi, dolambaçlı (*a. fig.*); *fig.* çapraşık, hileli.

**tor.ture** ['tɔːtʃə] **1.** *n.* işkence, eziyet, elem, azap; **2.** *v/t.* işkence etm. -*e*, eziyet etm. -*e*, azap çektirmek -*e*; **ltor.tur.er** *n.* işkence (*veya* eziyet) eden kimse.

**To.ry** ['tɔːri] **1.** *n.* tutucu (*veya* muhafazakâr) parti üyesi; **2.** *adj.* tutucu..., muhafazakâr...; **lTo.ry.ism** *n.* tutuculuk.

**tosh** *sl.* [tɔʃ] *n.* saçma.

**toss** [tɔs] **1.** *n.* atma, fırlatma; yazı tura için para atma; **win the** ~ yazı turada kazanmak; **2.** *v/t. a.* ~ **about** atmak, fırlatmak, savurmak, çalkalamak; hafifçe karıştırmak; rahatsız etm.; *a.* ~ **up** yazı tura için atmak (*para*); ~ **off** bir dikişte içmek, yuvarlamak (*içki*); yapıvermek, kolayca yapmak; *v/i.* yatakta dönüp durmak; oraya buraya çarpmak; çalkalanmak; çalkanmak; silkinmek, sarsılmak; *a.* ~ **up** yazı tura atmak (for *için*); '~-**up** *n.* yazı tura için para atma; *fig.* şüpheli durum, düşeş, şans işi; **lt's a** ~ şüphelidir.

**tot¹** F [tɔt] *n.* minimini yavru, yavrucak, minicik çocuk; bir yudum içki.

**tot²** F [~] **1.** *n.* toplam, yekûn; **2.** *v/t.* ~ **up**

toplamak; *v/i.* tutmak, bulmak (to -*i*).

**to.tal** ['təutl] **1.** □ bütün, tam(am), tüm; top yekûn (*savaş*); **2.** *n.* toplam, tutar, yekûn; top, hepsi; **3.** *vb.* toplamak, hesaplamak, yekûnunu bulmak; tutmak, etmek; hurdahış etm. (*araba*); **to.tal.itar.i.an** [~tæli'tɛəriən] *adj.* totaliter, bütüncül; **to.tal.i'tar.i.an.ism** *n.* totalitercilik; **to'tal.i.ty** *n.* bütünlük, tümlük; **to.tali.zator** ['~təlaizeitə] *n.* at yarışlarında müşterek bahisleri hesaplayan makine; **to.tal.ize** ['~təlaiz] *v/t.* toplamak; özetlemek.

**tote** F [təut] *v/t.* taşımak (*part. silah*).

**to.tem** ['təutəm] *n.* totem (heykeli), ongun; '~-**pole** *n.* totem heykeli.

**tot.ter** ['tɔtə] *v/i.* sendelemek, yalpalamak; sendeleyerek kalkmak; sallanmak; **ltot.ter.ing** □, **ltot.ter.y** sarsak (sursak) sallantıdıa olan.

**touch** [tʌtʃ] **1.** *v/t.* dokunmak -*e* (*a. fig.*), ellemek -*i*, el sürmek -*e*; koparmak, sızdırmak (*para*); bitiştirmek; erişmek -*e*, ulaşmak -*e*; teğet geçmek -*e*, değmek -*e*; etkilemek, tesir etm. -*e*; bozmak; *fig.* incitmek, kalbini kırmak; ~ **one's hat to** s.o. şapkasına dokunarak *b-ni* selamlamak; ~ **bottom** dibe değmek; çok düşmek (*fiyat*); *fig.* suya düşmek (*ümit*); ~ **the spot** F makbule geçmek; ~ s.o. for sl. *b-den* para dilenmek; a bit ~ed *fig.* kaçık, kafadan çatlak; ~ **off** ateşlemek (*top vs.*); *fig.* başlatmak; ~ **up** yenilemek; *phot.* rötuş yapmak; *v/i.* temas etm.; ~ **at** ↓ uğramak; ~ (up)on *fig.* değinmek (*bir konuya*); **2.** *n.* dokunma, dokunuş, temas, değme; iz; dokunma hissi, dokunum; üslûp; rötuş; ♪ tuşlayış; *spor:* taç; *k-den* kolayca para sızdırılan kimse; **get in**(to) ~ **with** temas kurmak *ile*, temasa geçmek *ile*; '~-**and-ıgo 1.** *n.* şüpheli durum; **lt is** ~ şüphelidir, belli değil; **2.** *adj.* tehlikeli, riskli, nazik, şüpheli; **ltouch.i.ness** *n.* alınganlık; titizlik; **ltouch.ing 1.** □ dokunaklı, acıklı; **2.** *prp.* ...*e* dair, ...hususunda, ilgili olarak; **ltouch-line** *n.* *futbol:* taç çizgisi; **ltouchstone** *n.* mihenk taşı, denektaşı (*a. fig.*); **ltouch.y** □ alıngan; = testy.

**tough** [tʌf] **1.** *adj.* sert; kopmaz, kırılmaz, dayanıklı; kart; çetin, zor, güç; kuvvetli, dirfrom, dirençli; sağlam; inatçı, boyun eğmez; a ~ **customer** F baş belâsı kimse; **2.** *n.* külhanbeyi, bıçkın, kabadayı; **ltough.en** *v/t. & v/i.* sertleş(tir)mek, katılaş(tır)mak; **ltough.le** F ['tʌfi] = tough 2; **ltough.ness** *n.* dayanıklılık, sertlik; zorluk.

tour 548

tour [tuə] 1. *n.* gezi, tur, seyahat; devir; dolaşma; nöbet; turne; conducted ~ rehberli gezi; 2. *v/t. & v/i.* gezmek, seyahat etm.; turneye çıkmak; **'tour.ing** *adj.* gezi..., tur..., seyahat...; ~ car *mot.* büyük otomobil; **'tour.ist** *n.* turist; ~ agency, ~ office, ~ bureau seyahat acentesi; ~ industry turizm sanayii; ~ season turizm mevsimi; ~ ticket tur bileti.

tour.ma.line *min.* ['tuəməlin] *n.* turmalin.

tour.na.ment ['tɔːnəmənt] *n.*, tour.ney ['~ni] turnuva, yarışma; ortaçağda mızrak oyunu.

tour.ni.quet ⚕ ['tuənikei] *n.* sıkı sargı.

tou.sle ['tauzl] *v/t.* karıştırmak *(saç)*, karmakarışık etm., arap saçına çevirmek.

tout [taut] 1. *n.* tiyocu, karaborsacı, simsar; 2. *v/i.* müşteri aramak, çığırtkanlık etm., simsarlık etm.; tiyo vermek.

tow¹ ↓ [təu] 1. *n.* yedekte çek(il)me; take in ~ yedekte çekmek, yedeğe almak; 2. *v/t.* (yedekte) çekmek.

tow² [~] *n.* kıtık.

tow.age ↓ ['təuidʒ] *n.* yedekte çekme (ücreti).

to.ward(s) [təˈwɔːd(z), tɔːd(z)] *prp.* -e doğru, doğrultusunda, tarafına doğru, yönün(d)e; -e karşı, -e yakın; için.

tow.el ['tauəl] 1. *n.* havlu; 2. *v/t.* havlu ile kurulamak *veya* silmek; **'~-horse** *n.* havlu asacağı; **'~-rock** = ~-horse.

tow.er ['tauə] 1. *n.* kule, burç; kale, hisar; *fig.* himaye, sığınak, siper; 2. *v/i.* yükselmek; ~ above *mst fig. b-den* daha üstün olm.; **'tow.er.ing** ☐ çok yüksek; *fig.* şiddetli *(öfke).*

tow(.ing)... ['təu(iŋ)]: **'~-line** *n.* çekme halatı; **'~-path** *n.* kanal *veya* nehir kıyısında gemi çeken atlara ait yol.

town [taun] *n.* şehir (merkezi), kasaba; kasaba halkı; man about ~ sosyete adamı, hovarda kimse; *attr.* şehir..., kasaba...; ~ cen.tre, *Am.* ~ cen.ter şehir merkezi; ~ clerk kasaba sicil memuru; ~ coun.cil belediye meclisi; ~ coun.cil.lor belediye meclis üyesi; ~ cri.er şehir tellâlı; ~ hall belediye binası; **'~-'plan.ning** *n.* şehir planlaması; **~.scape** ['~skeip] *n.* şehir manzarası.

towns.folk ['taunzfəuk] *n.* şehir halkı.

town.ship ['taunʃip] *n.* kaza, ilçe.

towns.man ['taunzmən] *n.* şehirli, hemşeri; fellow ~ hemşeri; **'towns.people** = townsfolk.

tow...: **'~-path** *n.* kanal *veya* nehir kıyısında gemi çeken atlara ait yol; **'~-rope** *n.* ↓ çekme *(veya* yedek) halatı.

tox.ic, tox.i.cal ☐ ['tɔksik(əl)] zehirli, ze-

hirden oluşmuş; tox.in ['tɔksin] *n.* toksin.

toy [tɔi] 1. *n.* oyuncak; değersiz şey; ~s *pl.* oyuncak eşya; 2. *adj.* oyuncak gibi, oyuncak...; küçük..., ufak...; 3. *v/i.* oynamak *(mst fig.),* eğlenmek; önemsememek; **'~-book** *n.* resimli kitap; **'~-box** *n.* oyuncak kutusu; **'~.shop** *n.* oyuncakçı dükkânı.

trace¹ [treis] 1. *n.* iz *(a. fig.),* eser, nişan; zerre, azıcık miktar; işaret; kalıntı; 2. *v/t.* izlemek; kopya etm.; çizmek; dikkatle yazmak; keşfetmek; ~ back uzanmak, dayanmak (to -e); ~ out planını, krokisini yapmak, yolunu çizmek.

trace² [~] *n.* koşum kayışı; kick over the ~s *fig.* gemi azıya almak, serkeşlik etm.

trace.a.ble ☐ ['treisəbl] izlenebilir, izi bulunabilir; **'trac.er** *n. a.* ~ ammunition havada iz bırakan mermi; *a.* ~ element *(teşhiste kullanılan)* radyoaktif izotop; **'trac.er.y** *n.* ✦ ağ şeklinde süs.

tra.che.a *anat.* [trəˈkiːə] *n.* nefes *(veya* soluk*)* borusu.

trac.ing ['treisiŋ] *n.* kopya (etme); **'~-pa**per *n.* kopya *(veya* aydinger*)* kâğıdı.

track [træk] 1. *n.* iz *(a. hunt.),* eser, nişan; 🚂 ray, hat; dümen suyu; keçi yolu, patika; *part. spor:* pist; ⊕ palet, tırtıl; yol; dizi, seri; yörünge; ~ events *pl. (koşu pistinde yapılan)* atletizm karşılaşmaları; 2. *v/t.* izlemek, takip etm., *-in* izini aramak; geçmek *(çöl vs.);* ayakla içeri taşımak *(çamur vs.);* ~ down, ~ out izleyerek bulmak; *v/i.* iz bırakmak *veya* yapmak; **'track.er** *n. part. hunt.* iz süren kimse; **'track.less** *adj.* izsiz; yolsuz; ⊕ raysız giden.

tract¹ [trækt] *n.* saha, alan, arazi, toprak; *anat.* bölge, nahiye, sistem.

tract² [~] *n.* risale, broşür.

trac.ta.bil.i.ty [træktəˈbiliti] *n.*, **'trac.ta.ble**ness uysallık, yumuşaklık; **'trac.ta.ble** ☐ uysal, yumuşak başlı, söz dinler; kolay işlenir.

trac.tion ['trækʃən] *n.* çek(il)me, çekiş gücü; ~ engine yük çekme makinesi; **'trac**tive *adj.* çekici...; **'trac.tor** *n.* ⊕ traktör.

trade [treid] 1. *n.* ticaret; alışveriş; meslek, iş, sanat; esnaf; müşteriler; değiş tokuş, takas, trampa; Board of 2 Ticaret Bakanlığı; the 2s *pl.* ↓ alize rüzgârları; 2. *v/i.* ticaret yapmak (with *ile;* in *-de);* alışveriş etm.; iş yapmak; ~ on *-den* faydalanmak, istifade etm.; *v/t.* takas etm., değiş tokuş etm. (for *ile);* ~ s.th. in fiyat farkı vererek eskisini yenisi ile değiştirmek; ~ cy.cle ticaret çarkı; **'~-fair** *n.* ☨ ticaret fuarı; ~ mark alâmeti farika, marka; ~ **name** ticaret ünvanı; ~ **price** ticari (*veya* toptan) fiyat; **¹trad.er** *n.* tüccar, tacir; ticaret gemisi; **trade school** sanat okulu; **trades.man** [¹~zmən] *n.* dükkâncı, esnaf kimse; **¹trades.peo.ple** *n.* esnaf; **trade uni.on** sendika; **trade-¹un.ion.ism** *n.* sendikacılık; **trade-¹un.ion.ist** 1. *n.* sendikacı; 2. *adj.* sendika..., sendikal.

**trade wind** ⭥ [¹treid¹wind] *n.* alize rüzgârı.

**trad.ing** [¹treidiŋ] *adj.* ticaretle ilgili, ticari, alışveriş...

**tra.di.tion** [trə¹diʃən] *n.* gelenek, anane, görenek, âdet; **tra¹di.tion.al** □ [~ʃənl], **tra¹di.tion.ar.y** [~ʃnəri] geleneksel, ananevi, göreneksel.

**traf.fic** [¹træfik] 1. *n.* trafik, gidişgeliş; ticaret, trampa, alışveriş, değiş tokuş; yük; yolcu sayısı; iş, muamele; 2. *v/i.* ticaret yapmak (in *ile*); **traf.fi.ca.tor** [¹~keitə] *n. mot* sinyal; **¹traf.fick.er** *n.* tüccar; *b.s.* kaçakçı; **traf.fic jam** trafik tıkanıklığı; **traf.fic light** trafik lambası (*veya* ışığı).

**tra.ge.di.an** [trə¹dʒiːdjən] *n.* trajedi yazarı *veya* aktörü; **trag.e.dy** [¹trædʒidi] *n.* trajedi (*a. fig.*); facia, felâket.

**trag.ic, trag.i.cal** □ [t¹rædʒik(əl)] trajik (*a. fig.*); feci, korkunç, müthiş, hüzünlü, acıklı.

**trag.i.com.e.dy** [¹trædʒikɔmidi] *n.* trajikomedi, güldürülü trajedi; **¹trag.i.¹com.ic** *adj.* (~ally) hem ağlatıcı hem güldürücü.

**trail** [treil] 1. *n. fig.* kuyruk; iz (*a. hunt*); yol, patika, keçiyolu; (bir) süre, (bir) yığın; ~ of smoke havada uzanan duman; 2. *v/t. & v/i.* peşinden sürükle(n)mek; izlemek, takip etm.; yerde sürünmek (*a.* ♥); geri kalmak; iz bırakmak; ~ **blaz.er** *Am.* yol açan kimse; öncü; **¹trail.er** *n.* römork; treyler; ♥ sürüngen bitki; *film:* fragman, (gelecek programla ilgili) reklâm filmi.

**train** [trein] 1. *n. com.* tren, katar; maiyet, refakatçiler; sıra, silsile, dizi, zincir (*olaylar*); yerde sürünen uzun etek; barut serpintisi; 2. *v/t. & v/i.* öğretmek, alıştırmak, talim et(tir)mek, yetiştirmek, eğitmek; ehlileştirmek; *spor:* antrenman (*veya* idman) yapmak; doğrultmak (*top vs.*); *a.* ~ **it** F trenle gitmek; **¹~-ac.ci.dent, ¹~-dis.as.ter** *n.* tren kazası (*veya* faciası); **train¹ee** *n.* stajyer; **¹train.er** *n.* eğitici, antrenör; eğitim uçağı; **¹train-¹fer.ry** *n.* tren feribotu.

**train.ing** [¹treiniŋ] *n.* talim; *spor:* antrenman, idman; physical ~ beden eğitimi; **¹~-col.lege** *n.* öğretmen okulu, eğitim fa-

kültesi; **¹~-ship** *n.* okul gemisi.

**train-oil** [¹treinɔil] *n.* balina yağı.

**trait** [treit] *n.* özellik.

**trai.tor** [¹treitə] *n.* hain, vatan haini (to -e karşı); **¹trai.tor.ous** □ haince.

**trai.tress** [¹treitris] *n.* hain kadın.

**tra.jec.to.ry** *phys.* [¹trædʒiktəri] *n.* mermi yolu; yörünge.

**tram** [træm] *n.* ⚔ maden ocağı arabası, dekovil; = ~-car, ~way; **¹~-car** *n.* tramvay (vagonu); **¹~-line** *n.* tramvay hattı.

**tram.mel** [¹træməl] 1. *n.* ağ; ⊕ elipsograf; ~s *pl. fig.* engel, mânia; 2. *v/t.* engellemek; güçleştirmek; ağa düşürmek.

**tramp** [træmp] 1. *n.* serseri, derbeder, avare (gezme); ağır adım ve sesi; uzun yürüyüş; sürtük; *a.* ~ sıeamer ⭥ tarifesiz işleyen yük gemisi; on the ~ serserilik etmekte; 2. *v/i.* avare (*veya* serserice) dolaşmak; ağır adımlarla yürümek; taban tepmek, yayan gitmek; *v/t.* ayak altında çiğnemek, **tram.ple** [¹~l] *v/t.* ayak altında çiğnemek, ezmek.

**tram.way** [¹træmwei] *n.* tramvay (hattı).

**trance** [trɑːns] *n.* dalınç, kendinden geçme, esrime, vecit; (h)ipnotizma.

**tran.quil** □ [¹træŋkwil] sakin, rahat, asude, sessiz, durgun; **tran¹quil.(l)i.ty** *n.* sükûn, sessizlik; **tran.quil.i.za.tion** [~lai-¹zeiʃən] *n.* yatıştırma, sakinleştirme; **¹tran.quil.(l)ize** *v/t. & v/i.* sakinleş(tir)mek, yatış(tır)mak; **¹tran.quil.(l)i.zer** *n.* yatıştırıcı (ilaç), müsekkin.

**trans.act** [træn¹zækt] *v/t.* bitirmek, görmek (*iş*); ~ business iş yapmak; **trans¹ac.tion** *n.* iş (görme), muamele; ~s *pl.* bir kurumun tüm işlemlerini gösteren rapor *veya* kayıtlar.

**trans.al.pine** [¹trænz¹ælpain] *n. & adj.* Alplerin ötesinde yaşayan (kimse).

**trans.at.lan.tic** [¹trænzət¹læntik] *adj.* Atlantik aşırı coğrafi, transatlantik...

**tran.scend** [træn¹send] *v/t.* geçmek, aşmak, -in ötesinde olm.; üstün gelmek; **tran¹scend.ence, tran¹scend.en.cy** *n.* üstünlük; *phls.* deneyüstülük; **tran¹scend.ent** □ üstün, âlâ; *a.* = tran.scen.den.tal □ [~¹dentl] A üstün (*fonksiyon*); *phls.* deneyüstü; P şüpheli, bellisiz, anlaşılması güç; doğaüstü.

**trans.con.ti.nen.tal** [¹trænzkɔnti¹nentl] *adj.* kıtayı katenden.

**tran.scribe** [træns¹kraib] *v/t.* kopya etm., suret çıkarmak; ♪ uyarlamak; *radyo:* kaydetmek.

**tran.script** [¹trænskript] *n.* ikinci nüsha, kopya, suret; **tran¹scrip.tion** *n.* kopya etme; transkripsiyon; ♪ uyarlama; *radyo:*

kaydetme, kayıt.
**tran.sept** ⚠ ['trænsept] *n.* haç şeklindeki kilisenin iki kanadı.
**trans.fer 1.** [træns'fɔː] *v/t.* nakletmek, geçirmek (to, in, into -e); devretmek *(part.* 🕱, to -e); havale etm.; baskı ile kopya etm.; *v/i.* aktarma yapmak; **2.** ['~] *n.* taşıma, nakil, havale, geçirme, devir *(part.* 🕱); ✝ transfer; aktarma bileti; *spor:* kulüp değiştirme, transfer; **trans-'fer.a.ble** *adj.* devredilebilir, nakli mümkün, havale edilebilir; **trans.fer.ee** 🕱 [~fəˈriː] *n. k-ne bş* devredilen kimse; **trans.fer.ence** ['~fərəns] *n.* nakletme, nakledilme; **¹trans.fer.or** *n.* 🕱 devreden kimse; **trans.fer-pic.ture** ['~fəːpiktʃə] *n.* çıkartma.
**trans.fig.u.ra.tion** [trænsfigjuəˈreiʃən] *n.* şekil değişimi; **trans.fig.ure** [~ˈfigə] *v/t.* şeklini değiştirmek, başkalaştırmak; yüceltmek.
**trans.fix** [træns'fiks] *v/t.* mıhlamak, delmek; kazığa oturtmak, kazıklamak; hareketsiz bırakmak; ~əd *fig.* donakalmış (with *-den).*
**trans.form** [træns'fɔːm] *v/t.* başka kalıba sokmak; *-in* şeklini değiştirmek, dönüştürmek; tahvil etm. *-i;* **trans.for.ma.tion** [~fəˈmeiʃən] *n.* dönüş(tür)üm, şekil değişmesi; **trans.form.er** ⚡ [~ˈfɔːmə] *n.* transformatör, trafo.
**trans.fuse** [træns'fjuːz] *v/t.* ⚡ aktarmak, nakletmek *(kan vs.)* (into *-e); fig.* ilham etm., esinlemek (with *ile);* **trans'fu.sion** [~ʒən] *n. (part.* ⚡ *kan)* nakil, aktarma.
**trans.gress** [træns'gres] *v/t.* bozmak, ihlâl etm., çiğnemek, karşı gelmek *(kanun vs.);* aşmak; *v/i.* günah işlemek; sınırı aşmak; **trans'gres.sion** *n.* sınırı aşma; suç, günah; ihlâl, karşı gelme; **trans-'gres.sor** [~sə] *n.* tecavüz eden kimse, günahkâr kimse.
**tran.sience, tran.sien.cy** ['trænziəns(i)] *n.* geçicilik.
**tran.sient** ['trænziənt] **1.** *adj.* geçici, süreksiz, kısa; fani; kalımsız; **2.** *n. Am.* kısa zaman kalan misafir.
**tran.sis.tor** [træn'zistə] *n.* ✄ transistor.
**trans.it** ['trænsit] *n.* geçme; geçiş; taşı(n)ma, nakil; transit; **in** ~ nakledilirken; transit olarak; ~ **camp** transit kampı.
**tran.si.tion** [træn'siʒən] *n.* geçiş, intikal, değişim; **tran'si.tion.al** 🗆 [~ʒənl] geçişe ait, geçiş..., değişme...
**tran.si.tive** 🗆 *gr.* ['trænsitiv] geçişli, nesneli *(fiil).*
**tran.si.to.ri.ness** ['trænsitərinis] *n.* geçici-

lik; fanilik; **¹tran.si.to.ry** 🗆 geçici, süreksiz; fani, kalımsız.
**trans.lat.a.ble** [træns'leitəbl] *adj.* tercüme edilebilir, çevrilebilir; **trans'late** *v/t.* çevirmek, tercüme etm.; ölmeden cennete göndermek; nakletmek; *fig.* dönüştürmek, değiştirmek (into *-e);* (başka kelimelerle) açıklamak; *v/i.* tercüme edilmek; tercümanlık yapmak; **trans'la.tion** *n.* çeviri, tercüme; nakil; **trans'la.tor** *n.* çevir(m)en, tercüman, mütercim.
**trans.lu.cence, trans.lu.cen.cy** [trænz'luː-sns(i)] *n.* yarı şeffaflık; **trans'lu.cent** *adj.* yarı şeffaf; *fig.* açık, belli.
**trans.ma.rine** [trænzməˈriːn] *adj.* denizaşırı.
**trans.mi.grant** ['trænzmigrənt] *n.* göçmen; **trans.mi.grate** ['trænzmaiˈgreit] *v/t.* & *v/i.* göç et(tir)mek, hicret et(tir)mek; *fig.* göçmek *(ruh);* **trans.mi'gra.tion** *n.* göç, hicret; ~ **of souls** ruh göçü, başka bir varlığa geçme *(ruh).*
**trans.mis.si.ble** [trænz'misəbl] *adj.* geçirilebilir, nakledilebilir, gönderilebilir; **trans'mis.sion** *n.* geçirme, nakil, intikal, gönderme; *biol.* kalıtım; *phys.* iletme, taşıma; ⊕ transmisyon; *mot.* vites; *radyo:* yayım.
**trans.mit** [trænz'mit] *v/t.* geçirmek; *tel., radyo:* yayımlamak, göndermek, nakletmek; *biol.* kalıtımla geçirmek; *phys.* iletmek *(ısı vs.);* **trans'mit.ter** *n.* yayım *(veya* verici) istasyonu; *tel. etc.* nakledici alet; **trans'mit.ting** *adj. radyo:* verici...; ~ **station** verici istasyonu.
**trans.mog.ri.fy** F [trænz'mɔgrifai] *v/t.* şeklini değiştirmek, garip şekle sokmak.
**trans.mut.a.ble** 🗆 [trænz'mjuːtəbl] değiştirilebilir; **trans.mu'ta.tion** *n.* değiştir(il)me; **trans'mute** *v/t.* şeklini değiştirmek, dönüştürmek (into *-e).*
**trans.o.ce.an.ic** ['trænzəuʃi'ænik] *adj.* okyanus aşırı *(veya* ötesi).
**tran.som** ⚠ ['trænsəm] *n.* vasistas; çapraz kiriş; travers.
**trans.par.en.cy** [træns'pɛərənsi] *n.* şeffaflık, saydamlık; slayt; **trans'par.ent** 🗆 şeffaf, saydam, berrak; *fig.* açık (seçik), apaçık, kolay anlaşılır.
**tran.spi.ra.tion** [trænspiˈreiʃən] *n.* terleme; **tran.spire** [~ˈpaiə] *v/i.* terlemek; *fig.* duyulmak, sızmak *(haber, sır vs.); sl.* olmak, meydana gelmek.
**trans.plant** [træns'plɑːnt] *v/t.* başka bir yere dikmek *veya* yerleştirmek; nakletmek *(organ vs.);* **trans.plan'ta.tion** *n.* nakil.
**trans.port 1.** [træns'pɔːt] *v/t.* götürmek,

nakletmek, taşımak; *fig.* coşturmak, heyecanlandırmak; *hist.* sürgüne göndermek; **2.** [ˈ~] *n.* nakil; taşı(n)ma; (askeri) araç, taşıt; ulaştırma, ulaşım; coşku; Minister of ♀ Ulaştırma Bakanı; **in ~s** coşku içinde; **transˈport.a.ble** *adj.* nakledilebilir, taşınabilir; **trans.porˈta.tion** *n.* nakil, ulaştırma; ulaşım; taşıt, araç; sürgün cezası.

**trans.pose** [trænsˈpəuz] *v/t.* sırasını (*veya* yerlerini) değiştirmek; ♪ aktarmak, perdesini değiştirmek; **trans.po.si.tion** [~pəˈˈziʃən] *n.* yerlerini değiştirme; ♪ aktarma.

**trans-ship** ⬇, 🚢 [trænsˈʃip] *v/t.* aktarmak; *v/i.* aktarma yapmak.

**tran.sub.stan.ti.ate** [trænsəbˈstænʃieit] *v/t.* başka bir cisme dönüştürmek; *eccl.* Hz. İsa'nın et ve kanına değiştirmek (*ekmek ve şarabı*); **ˈtran.sub.stan.tiˈa.tion** *n.* başka bir cisme dönüştürme; *eccl.* ekmek ve şarabın Hz. İsa'nın et ve kanına değiştirilmesi.

**trans.ver.sal** [trænzˈvəːsəl] **1.** □ yanal, çaprazvari, enine; **2.** *n.* Å doğru çizgi; **ˈtrans.verse** □ .karşıdan karşıya, enine, çaprazvari...; **~ section** enine (*veya* profil) kesit; **~ strength** ⊕ çapraz kuvvet.

**trap¹** [træp] **1.** *n.* tuzak (*a. fig.*), kapan(ca); hile, oyun, dolap; küçük at arabası; *sl.* ağız, gaga; ⊕ boruda U şeklindeki kısım; **~ door;** **2.** *v/t.* tuzağa düşürmek (*a. fig.*), yakalamak, tutmak.

**trap²** *min.* [~] *n.* bir çeşit volkanik siyah taş.

**trap.door** [ˈtræpˈdɔː] *n.* kapak şeklinde kapı; *thea.* sahne kapısı.

**trapes** F [treips] *v/i.* sürtmek, taban tepmek.

**tra.peze** [trəˈpiːz] *n.* sirk: trapez; **traˈpe.zi.um** Å [~zjəm] *n.* yamuk; **trap.e.zoid** Å [ˈtræpizɔid] *n.* ikizkenar yamuk.

**trap.per** [ˈtræpə] *n.* tuzakçı, avcı.

**trap.pings** [ˈtræpiŋz] *n. pl.* süslü koşum takımı; *fig.* süs, ziynet.

**Trap.pist** *eccl.* [ˈtræpist] *n.* konuşmanın bile yasak olduğu Katolik manastırda rahip.

**traps** F [træps] *n. pl.* eşya, pılı pırtı.

**trash** [træʃ] *n.* çerçöp, süprüntü; *fig.* değersiz (*veya* eski püskü) şey, pılı pırtı; değersiz, ciğeri beş para etmez adam; ayaktakımı, avam; artık; saçma; **ˈtrash.y** □ adi, değersiz, beş para etmez.

**trav.ail** † [ˈtræveil] *n. pl.* doğum sancıları; zahmet.

**trav.el** [ˈtrævl] **1.** *v/i.* seyahat etm., yolculuk etm. (*a.* †); yol almak, gitmek; *v/t.* (gezip) dolaşmak; **2.** *n.* yolculuk, seyahat; ⊕ işleme; **~s** *pl.* yolculuk, seyahat; **ˈtrav.el(l)ed** *adj.* çok seyahat etmiş; işlek; **ˈtrav.el.(l)er** *n.* yolcu, seyyah; † satış elemanı, pazarlamacı; ⊕ transbordör; **~'s cheque** seyahat çeki; **ˈtrav.el-(l)ing** *adj.* seyahat..., yolculuk...; ⊕ hareketli...; **~ rug** yol battaniyesi.

**trav.e.log(ue)** [ˈtrævəlɔg] *n.* bir seyahati anlatan film *veya* konferans.

**trav.erse** [ˈtrævəːs] **1.** *n.* çapraz (*veya* kateden) kısım; travers; galeri; engel, mâni(a); çapraz çizgi; *mount.* çapraz geçiş (yeri); ♂♂ resmi red; ✕ top yönünü değiştirme; ⊕ yanal hareket sahası; **2.** *v/t. & v/i.* karşıdan karşıya geç(ir)mek; taramak; geçmek, aşmak, katetmek; *fig.* karşı gelmek, engel olm.; resmen reddetmek (*iddia*); incelemek; sağa sola dön(dür)mek; *mount.* çaprazlama geçmek.

**trav.es.ty** [ˈtrævisti] **1.** *n.* alay, hiciv, karikatür, hezel; **2.** *v/t.* taklit etm.; hicvetmek.

**trawl** [trɔːl] **1.** *n.* tarak ağı; sürtme ağı; **2.** *v/t. & v/i.* tarak ağı ile (balık) tutmak; **ˈtrawl.er** *n.* tarak ağlı balıkçı (gemisi).

**tray** [trei] *n.* tepsi, sini; tabla; **pen-~** kalemlik.

**treach.er.ous** □ [ˈtretʃərəs] hain, güvenilmez, emniyetsiz; aldatıcı; tehlikeli; **ˈtreach.er.ous.ness, ˈtreach.er.y** *n.* hainlik, ihanet.

**trea.cle** [ˈtriːkl] *n.* şeker pekmezi; **ˈtreac.ly** *adj.* şeker pekmezi gibi ağdalı; *fig.* çok hoş.

**tread** [tred] **1.** (*irr.*) *v/i.* (ayakla) basmak (on, upon -*e*); yürümek; çiftleşmek; *v/t.* çiğnemek -*i*, ezmek -*i*; çiftleştirmek; yürüyerek yapmak (*yol vs.*); **2.** *n.* ayak basışı; yürüyüş; merdiven basamağı; ayak sesi; lastik tırtılı; tread **ˈdle** [ˈ~dl] **1.** *n.* pedal, basarak, ayaklık; **2.** *v/t. & v/i.* pedalla çalış(tır)mak; **ˈtread.mill** *n.* ayak değirmeni; *fig.* sıkıcı iş.

**trea.son** [ˈtriːzn] *n.* hainlik, hıyanet, ihanet; **ˈtrea.son.a.ble** □ hainlik kabilinden (*part. devlete*).

**treas.ure** [ˈtreʒə] **1.** *n.* hazine (*a. fig.*); **~s of the soil** yeraltı zenginlikleri; **~-house** hazine dairesi; **~ trove** define, gömü, hazine; **2.** *v/t. oft.* **~ up** biriktirmek; aklında tutmak; *fig.* değerli tutmak, çok değer vermek -*e*; **ˈtreas.ur.er** *n.* haznedar, veznedar, kesedar.

**treas.ur.y** ['treʒəri] *n.* hazine; maliye dairesi; fon; bilgi hazinesi *(kimse, kitap vs.);* ♀ (Board), *Am.* ♀ Department Maliye Bakanlığı; ♀ **Bench** *parl.* Avam Kamarası'nda bakanların oturduğu sıra; ~ **bill** hazine bonosu; ~ **note** hazinece çıkarılan kâğıt para, banknot.

**treat** [tri:t] **1.** *v/t.* davranmak *-e,* muamele etm. *-e;* sunmak, *-e,* ikram etm. *-e;* ele almak; kullanmak; tedavi etm. *-i;* işlemden geçirmek; dikkate almak, düşünmek; ~ s.o. to s.th. *b-ne bş* ısmarlamak, ikram etm.; ~ o.s. to s.th *k-ne bş* almak; *v/i.* ~.of bahsetmek *-den.* söz etm. *-den;* ~ with müzakereye girişmek (for *için);* **2.** *n.* zevk (verici şey); ikram; it is my ~ F bu benden, benim ikramım; stand ~ F ısmarlamak, ikram etm.; **trea.tise** ['~tiz] *n.* risale; bilimsel inceleme, tez; **!treat.ment** *n.* muamele, davranış; tedavi; **!trea.ty** *n.* antlaşma; be in ~ with anlaşmak *ile;* ~ port antlaşma şartı ile dış ticarete açık olan liman, serbest liman.

**tre.ble** ['trebl] **1.** ☐ üç kat. üç misli; ♪ tiz...; **2.** *n.* ♪ soprano ses(li çalgı *veya* kimse); **3.** *v/t.* & *v/i.* üç misli art(ır)mak, üç kat etm.

**tree** [tri:] **1.** *n.* ağaç; *s.* family; at the top of the ~ *fig.* mesleğinin zirvesinde; up a ~ F çıkmaza girmiş, şaşkın halde; **2.** *v/t.* ağaca çıkarmak; *fig.* çıkmaza sokmak; **!tree.less** *adj.* ağaçsız; **!tree.top** *n.* ağaç tepesi.

**tre.foil** [ıtrefɔil] *n.* ♣ yonca; ♣ yonca şeklinde süs.

**trek** [trek] *Güney Afrika:* **1.** *v/i.* kağnı ile seyahat *veya* göç etm.; **2.** *n.* kağnı ile seyahat *veya* göç.

**trel.lis** ['trelis] **1.** *n.* ✓ kafes işi; **2.** *v/t.* birbirine geçirmek; ✓ dallarını kafese sarmak.

**trem.ble** ['trembl] **1.** *v/i.* titremek (with *-den),* sallanmak; ürpermek; endişe etm. (for *-den);* **2.** *n.* titreme; ürperme; he was all of a ~ tir tir titriyordu.

**tre.men.dous** ☐ [tri'mendəs] (kos)kocaman, çok büyük, muazzam; heybetli; F şahane, görkemli, olağanüstü.

**trem.or** ['tremə] *n.* titreme; ürperme; sarsıntı.

**trem.u.lous** ☐ ['tremjuləs] titrek; ürkek, ödlek; sinirli; **!trem.u.lous.ness** *n.* titreklik; ödleklik.

**trench** [trentʃ] **1.** *n.* hendek, çukur; ✕ siper; ~ warfare siper savaşı; **2.** *v/t.* hendekle çevirmek; ✓ bellemek; *v/i.* ✕ siper kazmak; ~ (up)on tecavüz etm. *-e;*

*fig.* yakın gelmek; **!trench.ant** ☐ kuvvetli, tesirli, etkin, acı, şiddetli, keskin *(dil vs.);* **trench coat** trençkot, yağmurluk.

**trench.er** ['trentʃə] *n.* hendek kazıcısı; *hist.* büyük tahta tabak; ~ cap üniversite öğrencilerinin giydiği dört köşeli kasket.

**trend** [trend] **1.** *n.* yön; *fig.* eğilim, meyil (towards *-e);* **2.** *v/i.* yönelmek, meyletmek (towards *-e).*

**tre.pan** [tri'pæn] **1.** ⚕ *hist.* yuvarlak, kafatası delme testeresi; **2.** *v/t.* ⚕ cerrah testeresi ile delmek *(kafatası);* ⊕ burgu ile delmek.

**trep.i.da.tion** [trepi'deiʃən] *n.* korku, dehşet; titreme; ürperme.

**tres.pass** ['trespəs] **1.** *n.* günah, suç; başkasının arazisine izinsiz girme; ihlâl; **2.** *v/i.* başkasının arazisine izinsiz girmek; tecavüz etm. (on, upon *-e);* ihlâl etm. *-i,* bozmak *-i,* çiğnemek *-i;* günah işlemek; **!tres.pass.er** *n.* başkasının arazisine izinsiz giren kimse; ~s will be prosecuted bu araziye girenler cezalandırılacaklardır.

**tress** [tres] *n.* saç (örgüsü), bukle, lüle.

**tres.tle** ['tresl] *n.* sehpa; ~ bridge sehpa köprü.

**trey** [trei] *n.* iskambil *veya* zar üçlüsü.

**tri.ad** ['traiəd] *n.* üçlü takım.

**tri.al** ['traiəl] *n.* tecrübe, deneme (of *-i); fig.* test, imtihan; ☆☆ muhakeme, duruşma, yargılama; baş belâsı kimse *veya* şey, dert; ~ match hazırlık maçı; on ~ deneme için; denenince; imtihan üzerine; yargılanmakta; prisoner on ~ yargılanan mahkûm, hükümlü; ~ of strength kuvvet denemesi; bring to ~ mahkemelik etm., mahkemeye vermek, dava etm. *-i;* give s.o. *veya* s.th. a ~ *b-ni veya bşi* bir denemek; send for ~ duruşmaya çağırmak; he is a ~ to his family ailesi için bir baş belasıdır; ~ run deneme, tecrübe yapmak.

**tri.an.gle** ['traiæŋgl] *n.* üçgen; üçlü grup; ♪ üçköşe, triangle; **tri.an.gu.lar** ☐ [~'æŋgjulə] üçgen şeklinde, üç köşeli; üçlü; **tri.an.gu.late** *surv.* [~leit] *v/t.* nirengi yapmak; üçgenlere bölmek.

**trib.al** ☐ ['traibəl] kabileye ait, kabile...;

**tribe** *n.* kabile, aşiret, boy, oymak, soy; *part. contp.* grup; ♣, *zo.* takım, familya; **tribes.man** ['~zmən] *n.* kabile üyesi.

**trib.u.la.tion** [tribju'leiʃən] *n.* dert, keder, sıkıntı.

**tri.bu.nal** [tri'bju:nl] *n.* mahkeme; hâkimler kurulu; hâkim kürsüsü; **!trib.une** *n.* halkı savunan kimse, halkın koruyucusu; kürsü, platform, tribün.

**trib.u.tar.y** ['tribjutəri] **1.** □ vergi veren; haraç olarak verilen; bağımlı; bir ırmağa karışan *(akarsu)*; **2.** *n.* haraç veren hükümet *veya* hükümdar; ırmak ayağı; **trib.ute** ['–bju:t] *n.* haraç, vergi; takdir, övme; hediye; saygı.
**trice¹** [trais] *n.:* in a ~ bir anda, bir çırpıda.
**trice²** [~] *v/t.:* ~ up kaldırıp bağlamak, hisa etm.
**tri.chi.na** *zo.* [tri'kainə] *n.* trişin.
**trick** [trik] **1.** *n.* oyun, hile, düzen, dolap, entrika; şeytanlık, yaramazlık, eşek şakası; marifet, hüner; hokkabazlık, el çabukluğu; garip huy; özellik; *iskambil:* el; ↓ nöbet; F şirin çocuk; güzel kadın; ~ film miki filmi; **2.** *v/t.* aldatmak, kandırmak, dolandırmak, aldatarak almak (out of *-i);* faka bastırmak; ayartmak, kafeslemek (into *için);* ~ out, ~ up süslemek, telleyip pullamak; **ltrick.er, trick.ster** ['–stə] *n.* hilekâr, düzenbaz, üçkâğıtçı kimse; **ltrick.er.y** *n.* hile(kârlık), düzenbazlık, üçkâğıtçılık; **ltrick.ish** □ hile kabilinden.
**trick.le** ['trikl] **1.** *v/t.* & *v/i.* damla damla ak(ıt)mak, damla(t)mak; F *fig.* yavaş yavaş çıkmak, gelmek; yavaş yavaş kaybolmak; **2.** *n.* damla(ma).
**trick.si.ness** ['triksinis] *n.* muziplik, yaramazlık; **ltrick.sy** □ muzip, yaramaz, haşarı; = **ltrick.y** □ hileli, aldatıcı, üçkâğıtçı; F beceri isteyen *(iş vs.);* güç, zor; tehlikeli.
**tri.col.o(u)r** ['trikələ] *n.* üç renkli bayrak; the ♀ Fransız bayrağı.
**tri.cy.cle** ['traisikl] *n.* üç tekerlekli bisiklet.
**tri.dent** ['traidənt] *n.* üç çatallı mızrak.
**tri.en.ni.al** □ [trai'enjəl] üç yılda bir olan; üç yıl süren, üç yıllık.
**tri.er** ['traiə] *n.* deneyen kimse; elinden geleni yapan kimse; yargılayan kimse.
**tri.fle** ['traifl] **1.** *n.* önemsiz şey; az miktar, az para; bir çeşit tatlı; a ~ biraz, azıcık; **2.** *v/i.* oynamak; oyalanmak, vakit öldürmek; boş boş konuşmak; *v/t.* önemsememek, yabana atmak, hafife almak; ~ *away* harcamak *(güç vs.),* öldürmek *(vakit),* çarçur etm. *(para vs.);* **ltri.fler** *n.* işini ciddiye almayan kimse.
**tri.fling** ['traiflin] □ önemsiz, değersiz, ufak tefek, az; saçma, manasız *(konuşma vs.);* yüzeysel, üstünkörü.
**trig¹** [trig] **1.** *v/t.* takozlayarak hareketini engellemek; up düzeltmek, çekidüzen vermek, güzelleştirmek, şıklaştırmak; **2.** *n.* takoz, köstek.

**trig²** [~] *adj.* şık, temiz giyimli; sağlam, dayanıklı, sıkı; emin; canlı, cıvıl cıvıl.
**trig.ger** ['trigə] **1.** *n.* tetik; *phot.* deklanşör; **2.** *v/t.* ~ off *fig.* başlatmak, sebep olm.
**trig.o.no.met.ric, trig.o.no.met.ri.cal** ᐱ [trigənə'metrik(əl)] trigonometrik; **trig.o.nom.e.try** ᐱ [~'nɔmitri] *n.* trigonometri.
**tri.lat.er.al** □ ᐱ ['trai'lætərəl] üç yönlü, üç kenarlı, üç taraflı.
**tril.by** F ['trilbi] *n.* yumuşak keçeli erkek şapkası.
**tri.lin.gual** ['trai'lingwəl] üç dil konuşan; üç dilli; üç dilde söylenen.
**trill** [tril] **1.** *n.* ses titremesi; titrek ses: 'r' sesinin titretilerek söylenmesi; **2.** *v/t.* & *v/i.* sesi titre(t)mek, titrek sesle söylemek *veya* çalmak; titrek sesle ötmek, şakımak *(kuş).*
**tril.lion** ['triljən] *n.* trilyon; *Am.* bilyon.
**trim** [trim] **1.** □ biçimli, şık; düzenli, tertipli, derli toplu; **2.** *n.* nizam, intizam, düzen, tertip; hal, durum, vaziyet; süs; kıyafet; kılık; ↓ geminin dengesi; in (out of) ~ iyi (kötü) durumda; dengeli (dengesiz) *(gemi);* idmanlı (idmansız); **3.** *v/t.* düzeltmek, budamak, kırkmak; süslemek; kısaltmak; ᐱᐱ, ↓ denkleştirmek, ayar etm.; rüzgâra göre ayarlamak *(yelken);* azarlamak, paylamak; yenmek; aldatmak, kandırmak; *v/i. fig.* iki parti arasında her ikisine de taraftar görünmek; **ltrim.mer** *n.* süslemeci, düzenleyici kimse; ↓ gemiyi dengeleyen kimse; *pol.* çıkarcı politikacı; **ltrim.ming** *n.* süsleme; dayak, yenilgi; *mst* ~s *pl.* süs, garnitür, kırpıntı; **ltrim.ness** *n.* düzgünlük, derli topluluk.
**tri.mo.tor** ['taiməutə] *n.* üç motorlu uçak; **ltri.mo.tored** *adj.* üç motorlu...
**Trin.i.ty** ['triniti] *n.* teslis.
**trin.ket** ['trinkit] *n.* değersiz süs, biblo; ~s *pl.* cici bici.
**tri.o** ♪ ['tri:əu] *n.* üçlü, triyo.
**trip** [trip] **1.** *n.* gezi(nti), kısa seyahat; tur; takılma, tökezlenme; hata, yanlış; *sl.* uyuşturucu madde etkisi, keyif hali, dalga; *fig.* sürçme; ~ of the tongue dil sürçmesi; **2.** *v/i.* sürçmek *(dil);* tökezlenmek, takılmak (over -*e);* seke seke yürümek, koşmak *veya* dans etm.; *fig.* hata yapmak, yanılmak; sekmek, sıçramak; seyahat etm.; uyuşturucu madde etkisinde olm.; catch s.o. ~ing b-nin hatasını yakalamak; *v/t. a.* ~ up çelme takmak, düşürmek; *fig.* yalanını yakalamak.
**tri.par.tite** ['trai'pɑ:tait] *adj.* üçlü; üç par-

tripe 554

tili; üç taraf arasında yapılmış *(antlaş- ma vs.).*

**tripe** [ˈtraip] *n.* işkembe; *sl.* saçma.

**tri.phase** [ˈtraiˈfeiz] *adj.* üç fazlı; ~ current ≠ üç fazlı, trifaze akım.

**tri.plane** ⚓ [ˈtraiplein] *n.* üst üste üç kanatlı uçak.

**tri.ple** □ [ˈtripl] üç misli, üç kat, üçlü.

**tri.plet** [ˈtriplit] *n.* üçlü takım; *poet.* üç mısralı şiir parçası; ♪ triolet, üçlem; üçüzlerden biri, üçüz; ~s *pl.* üçüzler.

**tri.plex** [ˈtripleks] *adj.* üç kısımlı, üç katlı; üç kez; ~ glass tripleks, mikalı cam.

**trip.li.cate** 1. [ˈtriplikit] *adj.* üç kopyadan oluşan; üç kat, üç misli; 2. [ˈ~keit] *v/t.* üç kopyasını çıkarmak; üç kat yapmak.

**tri.pod** [ˈtraipɔd] *n.* üç ayaklı sehpa *(a. phot.).*

**tri.pos** [ˈtraipɔs] *n.* Cambridge Üniversitesinde şeref payesi imtihanı.

**trip.per** F [ˈtripə] *n.* gezenti. seyahat eden kimse; **ˈtrip.ping** 1. □ çevik, kıvrak; 2. *n.* seke seke yürüme.

**trip.tych** [ˈtriptik] *n.* üç kez katlanan resim.

**tri.sect** [ˈtraiˈsekt] *v/t.* üç (eşit) kısma bölmek.

**tris.yl.lab.ic** [ˈtraisiˈlæbik] *adj.* (~ally) üç heceden ibaret, üç heceli...; **ˈtriˈsyl.la.ble** *n.* üç heceli kelime.

**trite** □ [trait] basmakalıp, herkesçe bilinen; adi, bayağı; bayat, eski.

**trit.u.rate** [ˈtritjureit] *v/t.* ezip toz etm., öğütmek, ezmek; dövmek.

**tri.umph** [ˈtraiəmf] 1. *n.* zafer, başarı, galebe, yengi (over -e karşı); zafer alayı; 2. *v/i.* yenmek, zafer kazanmak, galip gelmek (over -i, -e karşı) *(a. fig.);* **tri.um.phal** [~ˈʌmfəl] *adj.* zafere ait, zafer...; ~ arch zafer takı; ~ procession zafer alayı; **triˈum.phant** □ muzaffer, galip, utkulu.

**tri.um.vi.rate** [traiˈʌmvirit] *n.* triumvirlik, üç kişiden oluşan yönetim şekli; üçlü grup.

**tri.une** [ˈtraijuːn] *adj.* birde üç olan.

**triv.et** [ˈtrivit] *n.* ayaklı destek; nihale, sahan altlığı; as right as a ~ iyi bir durumda, sağlığı yerinde.

**triv.i.al** □ [ˈtriviəl] ufak tefek, önemsiz; yavan, monoton; bayağı, sıradan, alelade, olağan; üstünkörü, yarımyamalak; değersiz, işe yaramaz; saçma, abes; **triv.i.al.i.ty** [~ˈæliti] *n.* önemsizlik; alela delik; saçmalık.

**tro.chee** [ˈtrouki:] *n.* biri uzun ve biri kısa iki heceli vezin.

**trod** [trɔd], *pret.,* **ˈtrod.den** *p.p. of* tread 1.

**trog.lo.dyte** [ˈtrɔglədait] *n.* mağarada yaşayan kimse.

**Tro.jan** [ˈtrəudʒən] 1. *adj.* Truva şehrine *veya* halkına ait; 2. *n.* Truvalı; work like a ~ çok çalışmak.

**troll¹** [trəul] *v/t. & v/i.* suda oltayı çekerek (balık) tutmak; bağıra bağıra (şarkı) okumak; döndürmek; gezinmek.

**troll²** [~] *n.* efsanevî cüce *veya* dev.

**trol.l(e)y** [ˈtrɔli] *n.* el arabası, yük arabası; *a.* tea-~ tekerlekli servis masası; *Am.* tramvay (arabası); **ˈ~bus** *n.* troleybüs.

**trol.lop** *contp.* [ˈtrɔləp] *n.* pasaklı kadın; fahişe, orospu, sürtük.

**trom.bone** ♪ [trɔmˈbəun] *n.* trombon.

**troop** [tru:p] 1. *n.* takım, sürü, küme. grup; cemaat; süvari bölüğü; erkek izci grubu; ✕ bölük, tabur, alay; ~s *pl.* askerler, askerî kuvvetler; 2. *v/t. & v/i.* bir araya topla(n)mak; ~ away, ~ off yürüyüş yapmak, ilerlemek, gitmek, gidivermek; ~ing the colour(s) ✕ bayrak taşıma töreni; ˈ~carri.er *n.* ↓, ⚓ asker taşıyan uçak *veya* gemi; **ˈtroop.er** *n.* süvari askeri; atlı polis; F polis; swear like a ~ ağzına geleni söylemek.

**trope** [trəup] *n.* mecaz, kinaye.

**tro.phy** [ˈtrəufi] *n.* ganimet; hatıra, andaç, yadigâr; ödül, kupa.

**trop.ic** [ˈtrɔpik] *n.* tropika, dönence; ~s *pl.* sıcak ülkeler, tropical kuşak; **ˈtrop.ic, ˈtrop.i.cal** □ tropikal.

**trot** [trɔt] 1. *n.* tırıs; hızlı gitme, koşuş; be on the ~ *fig.* koşuşturmak, koşturup durmak; *sl.* ishal olm.; 2. *v/i.* tırıs gitmek; koşmak; yürümek, gitmek; ~ out F teşhir etm., göstermek; ~ s.o. round b-ni gezdirmek, dolaştırmak; b-ni beraberinde götürmek.

**troth** † [trəuθ] *n.* sadakat, bağlılık; gerçek, hakikat; plight one's ~ yemin etm.; evlenmeye söz vermek.

**trot.ter** [ˈtrɔtə] *n.* tırıs giden koşu atı; ~s *pl.* paça.

**trou.ble** [ˈtrʌbl] 1. *n.* sıkıntı, zahmet, üzüntü, ıstırap; dert, keder, belâ; rahatsızlık, hastalık; endişe; mutsuzluk; mesele; ~s *pl. pol.* huzursuzluk, asayişsizlik, kargaşalık; be in ~ başı belâda *veya* dertte olm.; ask *veya* look for ~ belâ aramak, kaşınmak; take (the) ~ zahmete katlanmak, zahmet etm.; 2. *v/t.* rahatsız etm., tedirgin etm., zahmet vermek, canını sıkmak; endişelendirmek; zahmet etm.; başını ağrıtmak, üzmek, eziyet vermek; ~ s.o. for b-ne zahmet vermek; *v/i.* F zahmet çekmek, üzülmek, telâşlanmak; **ˈ~.man, ˈ~shoot.er** *n. Am.* F arabulucu, aracı, uzlaştırıcı kimse; makine bakımcısı; **trou.ble.some** [ˈ~səm] *adj.* zahmetli, sıkıntılı, belâlı, üzüntülü; baş belâsı, can sıkıcı; **ˈtroub.lous** *adj.* karışık, kargaşalı, güç, sıkıntılı.

**trough** [trɔf] *n.* tekne, yalak; oluk; uçurum; ~ of the sea iki dalga arasındaki çukur.

**trounce** F [trauns] *v/t.* dövmek, pataklamak, dayak atmak; yenmek; azarlamak, haşlamak.

**troupe** [truːp] *n.* trup, oyuncu grubu.

**trou.sered** [ˈtrauzəd] *adj.* pantolonlu; **trou.sers** [ˈ~z] *n. pl.* (a pair of *bir*) pantolon.

**trous.seau** [ˈtruːsəu] *n.* çeyiz.

**trout** *ichth.* [traut] *n.* alabalık.

**tro.ver** ⚖ [ˈtrəuvə] *n.* istirdat (*veya* istihkak) davası.

**trow** † *veya co.* [trau] *vb.* inanmak; sanmak, zannetmek.

**trow.el** [ˈtrauəl] *n.* mala.

**troy (weight)** [ˈtrɔi(weit)] *n.* kuyumcu tartısı.

**tru.an.cy** [ˈtruːənsi] *n.* dersi asma, okulu kırma; **ˈtru.ant** 1. *adj.* kaçak, firarî; aylak; 2. *n.* dersi asan, okulu kıran çocuk; *fig.* işten kaytaran kimse; avare, başıboş kimse; play ~ dersi asmak, okulu kırmak.

**truce** [truːs] *n.* ateşkes, mütareke, anlaşma; political ~ siyasi anlaşma.

**truck¹** [trʌk] *n.* kamyon; el arabası; üstü açık yük vagonu.

**truck²** [~] 1. *v/t.* değiş tokuş etm., takas etm., trampa etm.; 2. *n.* değiş tokuş, takas, trampa; *mst* ~ system ücretlerin para yerine mal olarak ödenmesi sistemi; garden ~ *Am.* sebze ve meyve.

**truck.le¹** [ˈtrʌkl] *v/i.* boyun eğmek, yaltaklanmak (to -*e*).

**truck.le²** [~] *n. mst* ~-bed karyolanın altına itilebilen tekerlekli portatif yatak.

**truck.man** [ˈtrʌkmən] *n.* kamyon şoförü, kamyoncu.

**truc.u.lence, truc.u.len.cy** [ˈtrʌkjuləns(i)] *n.* kavgacılık, saldırganlık, vahşîlik; **ˈtruc.u.lent** □ kavgacı, saldırgan, vahşi, haşin, zalim, gaddar, insafsız.

**trudge** [trʌdʒ] *v/i.* zahmetle yürümek, yorgun argın yürümek.

**true** [truː] *adj.* (*adv.* truly) doğru, gerçek, sahi, hakikî; halis, som, katkısız, safi; sadık, vefakâr, samimî, içten; tam, aynı; iyi yerleştirilmiş; be ~ of gerçek, doğru olm.; it is ~ doğrudur, gerçektir; come ~ gerçekleşmek *(ümit, hayal vs.)*; ~ to life (nature) gerçek hayatta olduğu gibi; prove ~ doğru çıkmak; **ˈ~-ˈblue** *fig.* 1. *adj.* çok sadık, sözünün eri; 2. *n.* sözünün eri kimse; **ˈ~-bred** *adj.* soylu; safkan; **ˈ~-love** *n.* sevgili, âşık; **ˈtrue.ness** *n.* doğruluk, hakikat, gerçeklik; bağlılık, sadakat, vefa; saflık.

**truf.fle** ⚘ [ˈtrʌfl] *n.* yermantarı, domalan.

**tru.ism** [ˈtruːizəm] *n.* su götürmez gerçek, apaçıklık, bellilik.

**tru.ly** [ˈtruːli] *adv.* gerçekten, hakikaten, doğrulukla, sadakatle, içtenlikle, samimi olarak; tamamen, doğru olarak; Yours ~ saygılarımla.

**trump** [trʌmp] 1. *n. iskambil:* koz; F yaman adam, iyi adam; 2. *v/i.* koz çıkarmak, koz oynamak; ~ up uydurmak *(bahane, yalan vs.)*; **ˈtrump.er.y** 1. *n.* gösterişli fakat adi şey, pılı pırtı; saçma; 2. *adj.* gösterişli fakat değersiz; uydurma, sudan *(bahane)*.

**trum.pet** [ˈtrʌmpit] 1. *n.* ♪ boru (sesi); borazan; blow one's own ~ *fig. k-ni* methetmek, övünmek; *s.* ear-~, speaking-~; 2. *v/t.* (boru çalarak) ilan etm., bildirmek, yaymak; ~ forth *fig.* yedi mahalleye davul zurna ile duyurmak; *v/i.* boru çalmak; boru gibi ses çıkarmak; **ˈtrum-pet.er** *n.* boru çalan kimse, borazan; tellal.

**trun.cate** [ˈtrʌŋkeit] *v/t.* kısaltmak, budamak, ucunu *veya* tepesini kesmek; **trunˈca.tion** *n.* ucunu *veya* tepesini kesme, kısaltma.

**trun.cheon** [ˈtrʌntʃən] *n.* sopa, çomak; cop.

**trun.dle** [ˈtrʌndl] 1. *n.* çember; 2. *v/t.* yuvarlamak, çevirmek *(çember)*.

**trunk** [trʌŋk] *n.* bavul; gövde, beden; hortum *(fil)*; ağaç gövdesi; otomobil bagajı; *Am.* kısa don; *s.* ~-line; **ˈ~-call** *n. teleph.* şehirlerarası telefon; **ˈ~-exchange** *n. teleph.* şehirlerarası telefon santralı; **ˈ~-line** *n.* 🚂 demiryolu ana hattı; *teleph.* şehirlerarası telefon hattı; **trunks** *n. pl.* erkek mayosu.

**trun.nion** ⊕ [ˈtrʌnjən] *n.* top muylusu, mil, aks, şaft.

**truss** [trʌs] 1. *n.* saman demeti; ⚕ kasık bağı; ⚠ kiriş, destek, makas, dayak 2. *v/t.* sımsıkı bağlamak; ⚠ kirişle desteklemek; **ˈ~-bridge** *n.* çatkılı köprü.

**trust** [trʌst] 1. *n.* güven, itimat, inanç (in -*e*); sorumluluk, mesuliyet; emanet; ⚖ mutemetlik; ⚖ vakıf, tesis; † tröst; ~ company tröst şirketi; in ~ himayesinde, gözetiminde; on ~ güvenerek, güvenle, emniyetle; † kredi ile, veresiye; position of ~ sorumluluk mevkii; 2. *v/t.* güven-

mek -e, itimat etm. -e; emanet etm., teslim etm., güvenerek vermek (s.o. with s.th., s.th. to s.o. bşi b-ne); inanmak; ~ s.o. to do s.th. b-nin bşi yapacağına güvenmek; ümit etm., ummak; kredi vermek; v/i. inancı, güveni olm. (in, to -e).
**trus.tee** [trʌsˈtiː] n. ʊ̃ mutemet, vekil, yediemin, mütevelli; ~ security, ~ stock mütevelli senedi (veya tahvili); **trusˈtee-ship** n. vekillik, mütemetlik.
**trust.ful** ☐ [ˈtrʌstful], **ˈtrust.ing** ☐ güvenen.
**trust.wor.thi.ness** [ˈtrʌstwəːðinis] n. güvenilirlik; **ˈtrust.wor.thy** adj. güvenilir, güvene lâyık; **ˈtrust.y** adj. güvenilir, emniyetli.
**truth** [truːθ] n., pl. **truths** [truːðz] doğruluk, hakikat, gerçek(lik); sadakat, vefa; samimiyet, içtenlik; dürüstlük; Tanrı; ~ to life hayata bağlılık; to tell the ~ doğruyu söylemek gerekirse, doğrusunu isterseniz.
**truth.ful** ☐ [ˈtruːθful] doğru, gerçek; doğru sözlü, doğrucu, içten; **ˈtruth.ful.ness** n. doğru(cu)luk, gerçeklik.
**try** [trai] 1. v/t. denemek (a. fig.), tecrübe etm., imtihan etm., sınamak; teşebbüs etm., kalkışmak; ʊ̃ yargılamak, muhakeme etm. (for -den); elde etmeye çalışmak (for -i); yormak; taşırmak (sabrını); göstermek, ispatlamak; arıtmak, tasfiye etm.; eritmek (yağ); araştırmak, tetkik etm.; ~ on prova etm. (elbise); ~ it on with s.o. F bşi b-de cüretle denemeye kalkışmak; ~ one's hand at bşe el atmak, bşi denemek; ~ out denemek; v/i. uğraşmak, çalışmak (at -e); 2. n. F deneme, tecrübe; çalışma, uğraşma; have a ~ bir deneyivermek; **ˈtry.ing** ☐ yorucu, sıkıcı, sinirlendirici, sabır tüketici; **ˈtry-lon** n. prova; F cüretkâr teşebbüs; **ˈtry-lout** n. deneme; spor: yetenek denemesi; **try.sail** ↓ [ˈtraisl] n. yan yelken.
**tryst** [traist] 1. n. randevu, buluşma (yeri); 2. vb. randevulaşmak.
**Tsar** [zɑː] n. çar.
**T-shirt** [ˈtiːʃəːt] n. tişört.
**T-square** [ˈtiːskwɛə] n. T cetveli.
**tub** [tʌb] 1. n. tekne (dolusu), yayık, fıçı. leğen; banyo; F küvet; F co. tekne; sl. külüstür otomobil; 2. v/t. & v/i. teknede yıkamak; fıçıya dikmek veya koymak; F yıka(n)mak, banyo yap(tır)mak; **ˈtub.by** adj. fıçı gibi; bıdık, tıknaz; boğuk sesli.
**tube** [tjuːb] n. boru, tüp; mot. iç lastik; F metro (part. Londra'da); sl. televiz-

yon; radyo lambası.
**tu.ber** ♀ [ˈtjuːbə] n. yumru kök; **tu.ber.cle** [ˈ~bəːkl] n. anat., zo. yumrucuk, tümsecik, türberkül; ☀ küçük ur, kabarcık, şiş; **tu.ber.cu.lo.sis** ☀ [~bəːkjuˈləusis] n. tüberküloz, verem; **tuˈber.cu.lous** adj. ☀ veremli, tüberkülozlu; **tu.ber.ous** ♀ [ˈ~bərəs] adj. yumrulu.
**tub.ing** [ˈtjuːbiŋ] n. boru şeklinde dokuma; boru takımı.
**tu.bu.lar** ☐ [ˈtjuːbjulə] boru şeklinde; borulu...
**tuck** [tʌk] 1. n. elbise kırması, pli; sl. yemek, börek çörek; 2. v/t. katlamak, (içine) sokmak, (içine) tıkmak, altına kıvırmak; sıkıştırmak; ~ in iştahla yemek, tıkınmak; içeri sokmak; ~ up sıvamak, katlamak.
**tuck.er** hist. [ˈtʌkə] n. dantel şal.
**tuck...**: **ˈ~-in** n. sl. yemek; **ˈ~-shop** n. sl. pastane, kantin.
**Tues.day** [ˈtjuːzdi] n. salı.
**tu.fa** min. [ˈtjuːfə] n., **tuff** [tʌf] süngertaşı.
**tuft** [tʌft] n. küme, öbek, top; tepe, sorguç; püskül; **ˈ~-hunt.er** n. otlakçı, bedavacı, asalak kimse; **ˈtuft.y** ☐ öbek öbek, püsküllü, küme küme.
**tug** [tʌg] 1. n. kuvvetli çekiş; ↓ römorkör; fig. büyük güçlük, zorluk; ~ of war spor: halat çekme oyunu; fig. şiddetli rekabet; 2. v/t. (şiddetle) çekmek, çekelemek (at -i); ↓ römorkörle çekmek; sıkıntı çekmek (for -den).
**tu.i.tion** [tjuːˈiʃən] n. eğitim, öğretim, ders; okul taksidi.
**tu.lip** ♀ [ˈtjuːlip] n. lale.
**tulle** [tjuːl] n. tül.
**tum.ble** [ˈtʌmbl] 1. v/t. & v/i. düş(ür)mek, yık(ıl)mak, yuvarla(n)mak, devirmek; devrilmek; karıştırmak, karman çorman etm., altüst etm.; rastlamak, rast gelmek; ~ to F anlamak, kavramak; 2. n. düşüş, yuvarlanma; karman çorman durum. karmakarışıklık; **ˈ~.down** adj. yıkılacak gibi, yıkılmak üzere; **ˈtumbler** n. bardak; ⊕ kilidin hareketli kısmı; orn. taklakçı güvercin; akrobat, cambaz.
**tum.brel** [ˈtʌmbrəl] n., **tum.bril** [ˈ~bril] suçluları idama götürmek için kullanılan araba.
**tu.mid** [ˈtjuːmid] adj. şişmiş, şişkin, kabarmış, kabarık; fig. abartmalı, şişirilmiş, tumturaklı; **tuˈmid.i.ty** n. şişkinlik, kabarıklık.
**tum.my** F [ˈtʌmi] n. mide, karın, göbek.
**tu.mo(u)r** ☀ [ˈtjuːmə] n. tümör, ur, şiş, yumru.

**tu.mult** ['tjuːmʌlt] *n.* kargaşa(lık), gürültü, karışıklık; isyan, ayaklanma; *fig.* heyecan; **tu'mul.tu.ous** ☐ [~tjuəs] gürültülü, kargaşalı, patırdılı; düzensiz.

**tu.mu.lus** ['tjuːmjuləs] *n.* höyük; mezar üzerindeki toprak yığını.

**tun** [tʌn] *n.* büyük fıçı, varil; 950 litrelik sıvı ölçüsü.

**tu.na** *ichth.* ['tuːnə] *n.* tonbalığı, orkinos.

**tun.dra** ['tʌndrə] *n.* tundura.

**tune** [tjuːn] **1.** *n.* nağme, melodi, beste, hava; mizaç, huy; ♪ akort; *fig.* ahenk, düzen, uyum; in ~ akortlu; *fig.* uyumlu (with *ile*); out of ~ akortsuz; *fig.* uyumsuz, ahenksiz, düzensiz; to the ~ of $ 200 $ 200'a kadar; change one's ~ *fig.* ağız değiştirmek; **2.** *v/t.* akort etm.; *fig.* ahenk vermek; ~ in *radyo:* frekansı ayarlamak (to -*e*); ~ out *radyo:* istasyonu düzeltmek; ~ up çalgıları akort etm.; *fig.* forma girmek; *mot.* ayarlamak; ♪ şarkı söylemeye başlamak; **tune.ful** ☐ ['~ful] ahenkli, hoş sesli; **'tune.less** ☐ ahenksiz, makamsız; sessiz, müziksiz; **'tun.er** *n.* ♪ akortçu; *radyo:* amplifikatör ve hoparlörsüz radyo.

**tung.sten** ☌ ['tʌŋstən] *n.* tungsten, volfram.

**tu.nic** ['tjuːnik] *n.* tünik; ✕ asker ceketi; *anat.* tabaka, kılıf; ♀ gömlek, zar, kılıf. **tun.ing...:** '~-coil *n. radyo:* ayar bobini; '~-fork *n.* ♪ diyapazon.

**tun.nel** ['tʌnl] **1.** *n.* tünel; ✕ yatay yol; **2.** *vb.* tünel açmak.

**tun.ny** *ichth.* ['tʌni] *n.* tonbalığı, orkinos.

**tun.y** F ['tjuːni] *adj.* ahenkli, hoş sesli.

**tur.ban** ['təːbən] *n.* sarık, turban.

**tur.bid** ['təːbid] *adj.* koyu, yoğun; çamurlu, bulanık; karmakarışık, allak bullak; **'tur.bid.ness** *n.* bulanıklık; koyuluk; karmakarışıklık.

**tur.bine** ⊕ ['təːbin] *n.* türbin; '~-'**pow.ered** *adj.* türbinle işleyen; **tur.bo-jet** ['təːbəu'dʒet] *n.* türbinli jet motoru ile işleyen uçak; **tur.bo-prop** ['~'prɔp] *n.* türbin pervaneli uçak.

**tur.bot** *ichth.* ['təːbət] *n.* kalkan balığı.

**tur.bu.lence** ['təːbjuləns] *n.* karışıklık, kargaşal.k, düzensizlik; **'tur.bu.lent** ☐ çalkantılı, dalgalı; serkeş, kavgacı, hır çıkaran; sert, şiddetli; karışık, düzensiz.

**tu.reen** [tjuˈriːn] *n.* derin çorba kâsesi.

**turf** [təːf] **1.** *n.* çimen(lik), çim; kesek; turba; the ~ hipodrom; at yarışçılığı; **2.** *v/t.* çimen dösemek -*e*, çimlendirmek; ~ out *sl.* kovmak, dışarı atmak; **turf.ite** ['~ait] *n.* at yarış meraklısı; '**turf.y** *adj.* kesekle kaplı, çimli; at yarışına ait.

**tur.gid** ☐ ['təːdʒid] şişkin, şiş(miş); *fig.* tumturaklı, şatafatlı; **tur'gid.i.ty** *n.* şişkinlik.

**Turk** [təːk] *n.* Türk.

**tur.key** ['təːki] **1.** *n.* ♀ carpet Türk halısı; **2.** *n. orn.* hindi; *Am. sl. thea., film:* fiyasko.

**Turk.ish** ['təːkiʃ] *adj.* Türk...; Türkçe...; ~ bath Türk hamamı; ~ delight lokum; ~ towel havlu.

**tur.moil** ['təːmɔil] *n.* kargaşa, gürültü, karışıklık.

**turn** [təːn] **1.** *v/t.* döndürmek, çevirmek; altüst etm., bozmak, bulandırmak, ekşitmek; erişmek, ulaşmak, gelmek; torna tezgâhında şekillendirmek; tersyüz etm. (*elbise*); burkmak; kıvırmak; doğrultmak, yöneltmek; püskürtmek (*düşman vs.*); yönünü değiştirmek; adamak, vakfetmek; göndermek, nakletmek; takas etm., değiş tokuş etm.; körletmek (*bıçak vs.*); dönüştürmek (into -*e*); geri döndürmek, caydırmak (from -*den*); tercüme etm., çevirmek (into English İngilizce-*ye*); he has ~ed 50, he is ~ed (of) 50 ellisini aştı; ~ s.o.'s brain kafasını allak bullak etm., beynini bulandırmak; ~ colour renk değiştirmek; ~ the corner buhranı (*veya* krizi, tehlikeyi) atlatmak; he can ~ his hand to anything elinden herşey gelir, on parmağında on marifet; ~ tail F sıvışmak, tüymek, tabanları yağlamak; ~ s.o. against b-ni -*e* karşı kışkırtmak, düşman etm.; ~ aside bir tarafa çevirmek; ~ away döndürmek, geri çevirmek; kovmak; ~ down kıvırmak, bükmek, katlamak; kısmak; indirmek; reddetmek, geri çevirmek; ~ in içine kıvırmak; teslim etm. (*polise*); F geri vermek, iade etm.; ~ off kapatmak, kesmek, söndürmek; ~ on açmak; çevirmek; heyecanlandırmak, etkilemek; bağlı olm.; ~ out dışarı doğru döndürmek; söndürmek, kapatmak; boşaltmak; yapmak, üretmek, imal etm., meydana getirmek; toplamak, biraraya getirmek; yataktan kaldırmak; kovmak, defetmek; tersyüz etm.; ~ over çevirmek, devirmek; devretmek, bırakmak; teslim etm.; *fig.* altüst etm.; † alıp satmak; üzerinde düşünmek; ~ over a new leaf yeni bir hayata başlamak; ~ round çevirmek, döndürmek; ~ up yukarı çevirmek. sıvamak; açmak, çevirmek; ortaya çıkarmak; ✓ altüst etm. (*toprağı*); F kusturmak, iğrendirmek; *v/i.* dönmek; olmak; sersemlemek, başı dönmek; sapmak, yönelmek (to -*e*); bulanmak; başvurmak (to -*e*); *k-ni* adamak

(to -e); değişmek, dönüşmek (into -e); a.
~ sour ekşimek, bozulmak; solmak, renk
atmak; eğilmek, yamulmak; körelmek,
körlenmek, körleşmek; ~ about diğer tarafa dönmek; X geriye dönmek; ~ away
başka tarafa yönelmek; çekip gitmek;
~ back geri dönmek; ~ in içeri kıvrılmak; F yatmak; ~ off sapmak; ~ on zevk
almak, heyecan duymak; düşman olm.;
saldırmak; ~ out meydana çıkmak, olmak; yukarı doğru bakmak; toplanmak,
biraraya gelmek; F yataktan kalkmak;
X yola çıkmak, hareket etm.; ~ over devrilmek, dönmek, altüst olm.; ~ round
dönmek, çevrilmek; ~ to işe koyulmak;
başvurmak, müracaat etm., danışmak;
koşmak; ~ up bulunmak, ortaya çıkmak;
olmak; gelmek, görünmek; ~ upon saldırmak; 2. n. dönme, dönüş, devir, deveran; sapma, yön değiştirme, yönelme;
dönemeç, viraj; sıra; değişiklik, değişim; kabiliyet, yetenek; eğilim, meyil;
amaç, gaye, maksat; gezme, dolaşma;
nöbet; tarz, nevi; kısa piyes; F sarsıntı,
şok; işlem, muamele; büklüm, kıvrım;
at every ~ her defasında, her keresinde;
by veya in ~s nöbetleşe, sıra ile, arka arkaya; do s.o. a good (bad) ~ b-ne iyilik
(kötülük) etm., b-ne yardım et(me)mek;
in ~ sıra ile, arka arkaya; in my ~ tarafımdan; it is my ~ sıra bende, sıra benim; take a ~ değişmek; tur atmak; take
a ~ at. s.th. payına düşeni yapmak; take
a few ~s gezinmek, dolaşmak; take one's
~ sırası gelmek; take ~s nöbetleşerek,
sıra ile yapmak (at -i); to a ~ tam kararında, kıvamında; does it serve your ~?
o işinizi görür mü?; '~.a.bout n. atlıkarınca; '~-buck.le n. ⊕ germe donanımı;
'~.coat n. dönek adam; 'turn.down collar devrik yaka; 'turn.er n. tornacı; be-
deneğitimi uzmanı; 'turn.er.y n. tornacılık; tornacı dükkânı.

turn.ing ['tə:niŋ] n. dönüş, dönme; dönen;
dönemeç; take a ~ dönmek; '~-lathe n.
⊕ torna tezgâhı; '~-point n. fig. dönüm
noktası.

tur.nip ⚘ ['tə:nip] n. şalgam.

turn.key ['tə:nki:] n. zindancı, gardiyan;
'turn-lout n. † ürün, verim, mahsül; katılanlar, toplantı mevcudu; ⚙, ↓ yan
hat; grev(ci); sapak, dönemeç; malzeme, teçhizat; temizlik; giysi; 'turn.o.ver
n. † satış; sermaye devri, ciro; devrilme; meyveli turta; 'turn.pike n. bariyer;
Am. geçiş parası alınan yol; 'turn-screw
n. tornavida; 'turn.spit n. kebapçı, dö-
nerci; 'turn.stile n. turnike; 'turn-ta.ble

n. 🛤 döner levha; 'turn-lup 1. adj. katlı;
kalkık (burun, yaka vs.); 2. n. duble
paça.

tur.pen.tine ⚘ ['tə:pəntain] n. terebentin.
neftyağı.

tur.pi.tude lit. ['tə:pidju:d] n. ahlaksızlık,
günahkârlık, kötücülük.

tur.quoise min. ['tə:kwa:z] n. firuze, türkuvaz.

tur.ret ['tʌrit] n. küçük kule; X, ↓ taret;
🗼 uçağın baştarafı; ~ lathe ⊕ torna
tezgâhı; 'tur.ret.ed adj. kuleli, taretli; kule şeklindeki.

tur.tle¹ zo. ['tə:tl] n. kaplumbağa; turn ~
alabora olm., devrilmek.

tur.tle² orn. [~] n. mst ~-dove kumru.

Tus.can ['tʌskən] 1. adj. Toskana'ya ait;
2. n. Toskanalı; Toskana lehçesi.

tush [tʌʃ] int. sus!, boş ver!

tusk [tʌsk] n. fildişi; azıdişi.

tus.sle ['tʌsl] 1. n. itişip kakışma, çekişme, çetin mücadele, kavga; 2. v/i. mücadele etm., uğraşmak, kavga etm.

tus.sock ['tʌsək] n. ot öbeği, çalı demeti.

tut [tʌt] int. yetti be!, kes sesini!, adam
sen de!

tu.te.lage ['tju:tilidʒ] n. vasilik, vesayet.

tu.te.lar.y ['tju:tiləri] adj. vasi olan; vasiye ait, vasi...

tu.tor ['tju:tə] 1. n. özel öğretmen; univ.
öğretmen; Am. univ. asistan öğretmen;
öö vasi, veli; 2. v/t. -e özel ders vermek;
fig. hükmetmek -e, hâkim olm. -e; tu.to-
ri.al [~'tɔ:riəl] 1. adj. özel öğretmene veya vasiye ait; özel öğretmenli...; özel öğretmen...; 2. n. univ. özel ders; tu.tor.ship
['~təʃip] n. özel öğretmenlik; öö vesayet.

tux.e.do Am. [tʌk'si:dəu] n. smokin.

TV ['ti:'vi:] n. televizyon.

twad.dle ['twɔdl] 1. n. saçma, boş laf; 2.
v/i. saçmalamak, boş boş konuşmak.

twain † [twein] n. iki.

twang [twæŋ] 1. n. tıngırtı; mst nasal ~
genizden çıkan ses, genzel ses; 2. v/t. &
v/i. tıngırda(t)mak; genizden konuşmak.

'twas [twɔz, twəs] = it was.

tweak [twi:k] v/t. çimdikleyip çekmek,
bükmek.

tweed [twi:d] n. tüvit.

'tween [twi:n] = between.

tween.y ['twi:ni] n. hizmetçi kız.

tweet [twi:t] v/i. cıvıldamak (kuş);
'tweet.er n. radyo: tiz sesler için küçük
hoparlör.

tweez.ers ['twi:zəs] n. pl. (a pair of bir)
cımbız.

twelfth [twelfθ] 1. adj. on ikinci; 2. n. on
ikide bir; '2-night n. Noelden on iki gün

sonraki gece.

**twelve** [twelv] *n.* & *adj.* on iki; ~fold
[ˈ~fəuld] *adj.* on iki misli; ˈ~month *n.*
yıl, sene.

**twen.ti.eth** [ˈtwentiiθ] **1.** *adj.* yirminci; **2.**
*n.* yirmide bir.

**twen.ty** [ˈtwenti] *n.* & *adj.* yirmi; ~fold
[ˈ~fəuld] *adj.* yirmi misli.

'**twere** [twəː] = It were.

**twerp** *sl.* [twəːp] *n.* hergele, herifçioğlu.

**twice** [twais] *adv.* iki kere, iki defa, iki
kez; ~ the sum iki misli miktar; ~ as
much iki misli, iki katı.

**twid.dle** [ˈtwidl] **1.** *v/t.* döndürmek, dön-
dürüp durmak; *v/i.* oynayıp durmak; **2.**
*n.* hafifçe döndürme.

**twig**[1] [twig] *n.* ince dal, sürgün, çubuk.

**twig**[2] F [~] *v/t.* anlamak, farkına varmak,
kavramak, çakmak.

**twi.light** [ˈtwailait] *n.* alaca karanlık; *fig.*
karanlık devre; ~ of the gods tanrılarla
devlerin birbirlerini mahvettikleri savaş;
*attr.* alaca karanlık...; ~ sleep ₮ ağrıyı
kesmek için yapılan hafif anestezi.

**twill** [twil] **1.** *n.* kabarık ve çapraz dokunmuş kumaş; **2.** *vb.* böyle kumaş dokumak.

'**twill** [~] = It will.

**twin** [twin] **1.** *adj.* çift(e)...; **2.** *n.* ikiz;
~en.gined ₮ [ˈ~end3ind] *adj.* çift mo-
torlu.

**twine** [twain] **1.** *n.* sicim; sarma, bükme;
**2.** *v/t.* & *v/i.* sar(ıl)mak, dola(n)mak,
kıvrılmak; bükmek; *fig. b-ni* bir işe bulaştırmak; ~ o.s. sarılmak, çöreklenmek,
kıvrılmak.

**twinge** [twind3] *n.* ani ve şiddetli ağrı,
sancı.

**twin.kle** [ˈtwiŋkl] **1.** *v/i.* pırıldamak, parlamak; göz kırpıştırmak; in the twinkling
of an eye göz açıp kapayıncaya kadar;
**2.** *n.* pırıltı, parıltı; göz kırpıştırma; in a
~ kaşla göz arasında.

**twirl** [twəːl] **1.** *n.* dönüş, kıvrılış; kıvrım,
büklüm; **2.** *v/t.* & *v/i.* dön(dür)mek; çevirmek; fırıldatmak; fırıldanmak; burmak, kıvırmak.

**twirp** [twəːp] = twerp.

**twist** [twist] **1.** *n.* bük(ül)me, bur(kul)-
ma, sar(ıl)ma; sicim, ibrişim; dönüş;
dönme; düğüm; kötülüğe eğilim, meyil;
**2.** *v/t.* & *v/i.* bük(ül)mek, bur(ul)mak,
sar(ıl)mak; dolamak; burkmak; döndürmek, çevirmek; kıvırmak; ters anlam
vermek, saptırmak, çarpıtmak; kıvrılmak; bozmak; ˈtwist.er *n.* büken şey *veya*
kimse; *spor.* yuvarlanarak giden top; F
sahtekâr kimse; F zor iş *veya* sorun;

*Am.* kasırga, hortum.

**twit** *fig.* [twit] *v/t.* takılmak, kızdırmak,
alaya almak (with *hakkında*).

**twitch** [twitʃ] **1.** *v/t.* & *v/i.* seğir(t)mek;
birden çekmek, kapıvermek; **2.** *n.* seğir-
me, tik; birden çekme, kapıverme; *vet.*
yavaşa; = twinge.

**twit.ter** [ˈtwitə] **1.** *v/i.* cıvıldamak; kıkırdamak, kıs kıs gülmek; titrek bir sesle
konuşmak; **2.** *n.* cıvıltı; kıkırdama; heyecan; be in a ~ titremek, heyecan içinde olm.

'**twixt** [twikst] = betwixt.

**two** [tuː] **1.** *adj.* iki, çift; in ~ iki kısma,
ikiye; put ~ and ~ together doğru tahmin
etm., bağdaştırarak sonuç çıkarmak; **2.**
*n.* iki rakamı; in ~s ikişer ikişer; ˈ~bit
*adj.* 25 sentlik...; *fig.* ucuz, değersiz,
önemsiz, ufak tefek...; ˈ~edged *adj.* iki
yüzü de keskin (*kılıç*); iki anlamlı; ˈ~
-faced *adj.* ikiyüzlü, riyakâr; ~fold
[ˈ~fəuld] *adj.* & *adv.* iki kat, iki misli;
ˈ~hand.ed *adj.* iki elle kullanılan (*kılıç*);
iki kişi ile kullanılan (*testere vs.*);
~.pence [ˈtʌpəns] *n.* iki peni; ~.pen.ny
[ˈtʌpəni] *adj.* iki penilik...; ˈ~phase *adj.*
⅀ çift fazlı; ˈ~piece *n.* iki parçalı giysi; ˈ~ply *adj.* katmerli, iki katlı; ˈ~seat-
er *n. mot.* iki kişilik araba; ˈ~sid.ed *adj.*
iki taraflı, iki yanlı; ˈ~step *n.* bir çeşit
dans; bu dansın müziği; ˈ~stro.ke *adj.*
iki katlı; ˈ~stroke *adj. mot.* iki zamanlı...; ˈ~thirds *adj.* üçte iki...; ˈ~way
*adj.* ⊕ çift taraflı; ~ adapter ₮ çiftli
adaptör; ~ traffic iki yönlü *veya* yollu
trafik.

'**twould** [twud] = It would.

**ty.coon** *Am.* F [taiˈkuːn] *n.* büyük işadamı, sermayedar; kodaman.

**tyke** [taik] *n.* it, sokak köpeği; kaba saba
adam, hödük.

**tym.pa.num** [ˈtimpənəm] *n. anat.* timpan,
kulak davulu, orta kulak; ◬ alın.

**type** [taip] **1.** *n.* çeşit, tip, cins, nevi, tür,
kategori, sınıf; örnek, numune; ⊕ mo-
del; *typ.* basma harf, hurufat; in ~ baskıya hazır; ~ area tertip dizisinin boyu;
true to ~ tipine uygun; set in ~ dizmek;
**2.** ~ write; ˈ~found.er *n.* dizmen, diz-
(g)ici; ˈ~script *n.* daktilo ile yazılmış
yazı; ˈ~set.ter *n.* diz(g)ici, dizmen; dizgi
makinesi; ~ write (*irr.* write) *v/t.* daktilo etm., daktilo ile yazmak; *v/i.* daktilo
yazmak; ˈ~writer *n.* daktilo, yazı makinesi; ~ face daktilo yazısı; ~ ribbon daktilo şeridi; ˈ~writ.ten *adj.* daktilo edilmiş,
daktiloda yazılmış.

**ty.phoid** ₮ [ˈtaifɔid] **1.** *adj.* tifoya benzer;

~ fever = 2. *n.* tifo.

**ty.phoon** *meteor.* [tai'fuːn] *n.* tayfun.

**ty.phus** ⚓ ['taifəs] *n.* tifüs.

**typ.i.cal** ☐ ['tipikəl] tipik; simgesel, sembolik (of); **typ.i.fy** ['~fai] *v/t.* -*in* simgesi, sembolü olm.; simgesel olarak göstermek; **typ.ist** ['taipist] *n.* daktilo(graf); shorthand ~ stenograf.

**ty.pog.ra.pher** [tai'pogrəfə] *n.* matbaacı, basımcı; **ty.po.graph.ic**, **ty.po.graph.i.cal** ☐ [~pə'græfik(əl)] matbaacılığa ait; basımcılık...; **ty.pog.ra.phy** [~'pogrəfi] *n.* matbaacılık, basımcılık, tipografya.

**ty.ran.nic**, **ty.ran.ni.cal** ☐ [ti'rænik(əl)] zalim(ce), gaddar(ca); **ty'ran.ni.cide**

[~said] *n.* zalimi öldürme; zalimi öldüren kimse; **tyr.an.nize** ['tirənaiz] *vb.* eziyet etm. -*e*, işkence etm. -*e*; ~ over zulmetmek -*e*; **'tyr.an.nous** ☐ zalim(ce), gaddar(ca); **'tyr.an.ny** *n.* zulüm, gaddarlık, istibdat; zorba hükümet (devresi).

**ty.rant** ['taiərənt] *n.* zalim, zorba, gaddar, acımasız, yıkıcı; zorba hükümdar, tiran.

**tyre** ['taiə] *s.* tire[1].

**ty.ro** ['taiərəu] *s.* tiro.

**Tyr.o.lese** [tirə'liːz] **1.** *n.* Tirol halkı; Tirollü; **2.** *adj.* Tirol eyalet *veya* halkına ait.

**Tzar** [zaː] *n.* çar.

# U

**u.biq.ui.tous** □ [juː'bikwitəs] aynı anda her yerde olan, hazır ve nazır; **u'biq.ui.ty** *n.* hazır ve nazırlık, aynı anda her yerde hazır olma.

**U-boat** ⚓ ['juːbəut] *n.* Alman denizaltısı.

**ud.der** ['ʌdə] *n.* inek memesi.

**ugh** [ʌx, uh, əːh] *int.* of!, öf!, ö!

**ug.li.fy** ['ʌglifai] *v/t.* çirkinleştirmek.

**ug.li.ness** ['ʌglinis] *n.* çirkinlik, iğrençlik.

**ug.ly** □ ['ʌgli] çirkin, iğrenç; korkunç, berbat; ters, huysuz; nahoş; fırtınalı; tehlikeli.

**U.krain.i.an** [juː'kreinjən] **1.** *adj.* Ukrayna *veya* Ukraynacaya ait; **2.** *n.* Ukraynalı; Ukraynaca, Rutenca.

**u.ku.le.le** ♪ [juːkə'leili] *n.* Hawaii adalarına ait dört telli gitar, kitara.

**ul.cer** ⚕ ['ʌlsə] *n.* ülser, karha; **ul.cer.ate** ['ʌreit] *v/t.* & *v/i.* ülsere dönüş(tür)-mek, ülser olm.; ülsere sebep olm.; **ul-cer'a.tion** *n.* ülser(leşme); **'ul.cer.ous** *adj.* ülserli, ülserleşmiş.

**ul.lage** ⚓ ['ʌlidʒ] *n.* fıçıda boş kalan kısım; fire.

**ul.na** *anat.* ['ʌlnə] *n.*, *pl.* **ul.nae** ['ʌniː] ulna, dirsek kemiği.

**ul.ster** ['ʌlstə] *n.* bol ve uzun palto.

**ul.te.ri.or** □ [ʌl'tiəriə] ötedeki, öteyandaki, uzaktaki; *fig.* gizli; sonraki; ~ motive gizli maksat, art niyet.

**ul.ti.mate** □ ['ʌltimit] (en) son, nihai, en uzak; esas, temel, asıl; en yüksek, en büyük; aşırı; çözümlenemeyen; **'ul.ti-mate.ly** *adv.* (eninde) sonunda.

**ul.ti.ma.tum** ['ʌlti'meitəm] *n.*, *pl. a.* **ul.ti'ma-ta** [~tə] ültimatom.

**ul.ti.mo** ⚓ ['ʌltiməu] *adj.* geçen ayın..., geçen ayki, geçen ayda.

**ul.tra** ['ʌltrə] *adj.* aşırı, son derece, fazla; **'~'fash.ion.a.ble** *adj.* son derece modaya uygun; **~.ma'rine 1.** *adj.* denizaşırı; **2.** *n.* ⚗, *paint.* lâcivert (boya); **'~'mod.ern** *adj.* çok modern; **~.mon.tane** *eccl.*, *pol.* [~'mɔntein] **1.** *adj.* Papanın mutlak yetkisinden yana olan; **2.** *n.* Papanın mutlak yetkisinden yana kimse; **'~.'red** *adj.* kızılötesi, enfraruj; **'~.'short wave** çok kısa dalga; **'~.'son.ic** *adj.* ses-

ötesi, yüksek frekanslı *(titreşim, ses)*; **'~.'vi.o.let** *adj.* ültraviyole, morötesi.

**ul.u.late** ['juːljuleit] *v/i.* ulumak; feryat, figan etm.

**um.bel** ⚘ ['ʌmbəl] *n.* umbel, şemsiye şeklinde çiçek durumu.

**um.ber** *min.*, *paint.* ['ʌmbə] *n.* ombra, aşıboyası.

**um.bil.i.cal** □ [ʌm'bilikəl, ⚕ ~'laikəl] göbeğe ait, göbek...; ~ cord göbek kordonu.

**um.brage** ['ʌmbridʒ] *n.* gücenme, alınma, içerleme; *poet.* gölge; kuşku, şüphe; ima; **um.bra.geous** □ [~'breidʒəs] gölgeli; *fig.* alıngan.

**um.brel.la** [ʌm'brelə] *n.* şemsiye; *fig.* himaye, koruma; ✈ koruyucu avcı uçakları; **um'brel.la-stand** *n.* şemsiyelik.

**um.pire** ['ʌmpaiə] **1.** *n.* hakem; **2.** *v/t.* yönetmek *(maç vs.)*; *v/i.* hakemlik yapmak.

**ump.teen** ['ʌmptiːn] *adj.*, **'ump.ty** *sl.* pek çok, bir sürü, sayısız.

**un...** [ʌn] *prefix* -siz, -sız, gayri.

**'un** F [ʌn, ən] = one.

**un.a.bashed** [ʌnə'bæʃt] *adj.* küstah, arsız, utanmaz, yüzsüz.

**un.a.bat.ed** [ʌnə'beitid] *adj.* şiddeti azalmayan, dinmemiş, şiddetini sürdüren *(fırtına vs.)*.

**un.a.ble** ['ʌn'eibl] *adj.* gücü yetmez, yapamaz (to *inf. -meyi*), iktidarsız, âciz; beceriksiz.

**un.a.bridged** ['ʌnə'bridʒd] *adj.* kısaltılmamış, orijinal, tam.

**un.ac.cept.a.ble** ['ʌnək'septəbl] *adj.* kabul edilemez.

**un.ac.com.mo.dat.ing** ['ʌnə'kɔmədeitiŋ] *adj.* rahatına düşkün.

**un.ac.count.a.ble** □ ['ʌnə'kauntəbl] anlatılmaz, açıklanamaz, garip; olağanüstü; sorumsuz.

**un.ac.cus.tomed** ['ʌnə'kʌstəmd] *adj.* alışılmamış, garip, tuhaf; ~ to alışmamış -*e*, alışık olmayan -*e*.

**un.ac.knowl.edged** ['ʌnək'nɔlidʒd] *adj.* kabul edilmemiş, onaylanmamış, cevaplandırılmamış.

**un.ac.quaint.ed** ['ʌnə'kweintid] *adj.*; ~

with tanışmayan *ile*, tanışık olmayan *ile*, bilmez.

**un.a.dorned** [ˈʌnəˈdɔːnd] *adj.* süslenmemiş, süssüz, sade, donatılmamış.

**un.a.dul.ter.at.ed** □ [ˈʌnəˈdʌltəreitid] saf(i), halis, katıksız.

**un.ad.vis.a.ble** □ [ˈʌnədˈvaizəbl] tavsiye edilmez; **ˈun.adˈvised** □ [ˌʌzd, *adv*. ˌzidli] danışmamış, nasihat almamış; düşüncesiz, patavatsız.

**un.af.fect.ed** □ [ˈʌnəˈfektid] etkilenmemiş, değişmemiş; *fig.* samimî, içten.

**un.a.fraid** [ˈʌnəˈfreid] *adj.* korkusuz, cesur, gözü pek.

**un.aid.ed** [ˈʌnˈeidid] *adj.* yardım görmemiş, yardım edilmemiş, yardımsız.

**un.al.ien.a.ble** [ˈʌnˈeiljənəbl] *adj.* alınamaz, ayrılamaz, devredilemez.

**un.al.loyed** [ˈʌnəˈlɔid] *adj.* saf(i), halis, katışıksız; *fig.* tam.

**un.al.ter.a.ble** □ [ʌnˈɔːltərəbl] değiş(tirile)mez, sabit; **unˈal.tered** *adj.* değiştirilmemiş.

**un.am.big.u.ous** □ [ˈʌnæmˈbigjuəs] tam, kesin, açık, belli.

**un.am.bi.tious** □ [ˈʌnæmˈbiʃəs] kanaatkâr, kanık, ihtirası olmayan, yetingen.

**un.a.me.na.ble** [ˈʌnəˈmiːnəbl] *adj.* dik başlı, asi; sorumsuz.

**un-A.mer.i.can** [ˈʌnəˈmerikən] *adj.* Amerikan(vari) olmayan.

**un.a.mi.a.ble** □ [ˈʌnˈeimjəbl] sevimsiz, nahoş.

**u.na.nim.i.ty** [juːnəˈnimiti] *n.* oy birliği, ittifak; **u.nan.i.mous** □ [juːˈnæniməs] aynı fikirde, hemfikir, oydaş.

**un.an.nounced** [ˈʌnəˈnaunst] *adj.* duyurulmamış, anons edilmemiş, habersiz (gelen).

**un.an.swer.a.ble** □ [ʌnˈɑːnsərəbl] cevaplandırılamaz, reddedilemez; **ˈunˈanswered** *adj.* cevaplandırılmamış *(mektup vs.)*; karşılıksız *(aşk)*.

**un.ap.palled** [ˈʌnəˈpɔːld] *adj.* korkusuz, pervasız.

**un.ap.peal.a.ble** ⚡ [ˈʌnəˈpiːləbl] *adj.* temyiz edilemez.

**un.ap.peas.a.ble** □ [ˈʌnəˈpiːzəbl] yatıştırılamaz, amansız.

**un.ap.proach.a.ble** □ [ˈʌnəˈprəutʃəbl] yanına varılamaz, yaklaşılmaz; uzak; çok üstün, eşsiz.

**un.ap.pro.pri.at.ed** [ˈʌnəˈprəuprieitid] *adj.* sahipsiz.

**un.apt** □ [ˈʌnˈæpt] uygunsuz; kalın kafalı; ˌ to *inf*. ˈmeyi yapacağa benzemeyen; **bə** ˌ to **learn** çarçabuk öğrenememek.

**un.armed** [ˈʌnˈɑːmd] *adj.* silahsız.

**un.a.shamed** □ [ˈʌnəˈʃeimd] utanmaz, arsız, yüzsüz.

**un.asked** [ˈʌnˈɑːskt] *adj.* sorulmamış; davetsiz; istenmemiş.

**un.as.sail.a.ble** □ [ˈʌnəˈseiləbl] katî, kesin, muhakkak; saldırılamaz.

**un.as.sist.ed** □ [ˈʌnəˈsistid] yardım(cı)sız.

**un.as.sum.ing** [ˈʌnəˈsjuːmiŋ] *adj.* gösterişsiz, mütevazı, alçak gönüllü.

**un.at.tached** [ˈʌnəˈtætʃt] *adj.* bağımsız, bekâr.

**un.at.tain.a.ble** □ [ˈʌnəˈteinəbl] elde edilemez; ulaşılamaz.

**un.at.tend.ed** [ˈʌnəˈtendid] *adj.* yalnız, arkadaşsız; yapılmamış, bakılmamış *(iş vs.)*; sahipsiz.

**un.at.trac.tive** □ [ʌnəˈtræktiv] gösterişsiz, sade, şatafatsız, cazibesiz, sevimsiz.

**un.au.thor.ized** [ˈʌnˈɔːθəraizd] *adj.* yetkisiz; gayri resmi.

**un.a.vail.a.ble** [ˈʌnəˈveiləbl] *adj.* mevcut olmayan; kullanılmaz, işe yaramaz; **ˈun.aˈvail.ing** *adj.* boşuna; başarısız; tesirsiz, faydasız.

**un.a.void.a.ble** □ [ʌnəˈvɔidəbl] kaçınılmaz, çaresiz.

**un.a.ware** [ˈʌnəˈwɛə] *adj.* habersiz, farkında olmayan; önemsemeyen; **bə** ˌ **of** *-in* farkında olmamak, *-den* habersiz olm.; **ˈun.aˈwares** *adv.* beklenmedik bir anda, ansızın; farkında olmadan, bilinçsizce.

**un.backed** [ˈʌnˈbækt] *adj.* desteklenmeyen; üzerine bahse girilmemiş; arkasız; ˌ **horse** üzerine binilmemiş at.

**un.bal.ance** [ˈʌnˈbæləns] *n.* dengesizlik; **ˈunˈbal.anced** *adj.* dengesiz; akli dengesi bozuk; birbirini tutmayan.

**un.bap.tized** [ˈʌnbæpˈtaizd] *adj.* vaftiz edilmemiş.

**un.bar** [ˈʌnˈbɑː] *v/t.* *-in* sürgüsünü açmak.

**un.bear.a.ble** □ [ʌnˈbɛərəbl] dayanılmaz, çekilmez, hoşgörülmez.

**un.beat.en** [ˈʌnˈbiːtn] *adj.* kırılmamış *(rekor vs.)*; yenilmemiş *(takım vs.)*; dövülmemiş; ayak basılmamış.

**un.be.com.ing** □ [ˈʌnbiˈkʌmiŋ] yakışmamış, yakışıksız, uygunsuz, münasip olmayan (**to** *veya* **for** s.o. *b-i için*).

**un.be.friend.ed** [ˈʌnbiˈfrendid] *adj.* arkadaşsız, dostsuz.

**un.be.known** [ˈʌnbiˈnəun] *adj.* meçhul; habersiz; ˌ **to** s.o. *b-nin* haberi olmadan.

**un.be.lief** [ˈʌnbiˈliːf] *n.* imansızlık, inançsızlık; **un.beˈliev.a.ble** □ inanılmaz; **ˈunbeˈliev.er** *n.* imansız, dinsiz, kâfir; **ˈun-**

be**llev.ing** ☐ imansız; şüpheci.

un.be.loved ['ʌnbi'lʌvd] *adj.* sevilmeyen.

un.bend ['ʌn'bend] *(irr.* bend) *v/t.* & *v/i.* gevşe(t)mek *(a. fig.),* yumuşa(t)mak; dinlen(dir)mek; ⊕ düzel(t)mek, doğrul(t)mak; **un'bend.ing** ☐ eğilmez; *fig.* kararlı, sabit, kararından dönmez; boyun eğmez.

un.be.seem.ing ☐ ['ʌnbi'si:miŋ] yakışıksız, uygunsuz.

un.bi.as(s)ed ☐ ['ʌn'baiəst] tarafsız, yansız, bitaraf.

un.bid(.den) ['ʌn'bid(n)] *adj.* davetsiz; kendiliğinden gelen.

un.bind ['ʌn'baind] *(irr.* bind) *v/t.* çözmek; gevşetmek; serbest bırakmak, salıvermek.

un.bleached ['ʌn'bli:tʃt] *adj.* ağartılmamış.

un.blem.ished [ʌn'blemiʃt] *adj.* lekesiz; hatasız, kusursuz.

un.blush.ing ☐ [ʌn'blʌʃiŋ] utanmaz, arsız, yüzsüz.

un.bolt ['ʌn'bəult] *v/t.* -*in* sürgüsünü açmak; **un'bolt.ed** *adj.* sürgülenmemiş; elenmemiş *(un vs.).*

un.born ['ʌn'bɔ:n] *adj.* henüz doğmamış; gelecek, müstakbel.

un.bos.om [ʌn'buzəm] *v/t.* açığa vurmak, ortaya dökmek; ~ o.s. içini dökmek (to s.o. *b·ne).*

un.bound ['ʌn'baund] *adj.* çözük, bağlı olmayan; ciltsiz *(kitap).*

un.bound.ed ☐ [ʌn'baundid] sınırsız, hudutsuz; sonsuz, ölçüsüz.

un.brace ['ʌn'breis] *v/t.* çözmek; gevşetmek; zayıflatmak.

un.break.a.ble ☐ ['ʌn'breikəbl] *adj.* kırılamaz.

un.bri.dled [ʌn'braidld] *adj.* gem vurulmamış *(at); fig.* azgın, dizginlenemeyen, önüne geçilmez *(hırs vs.).*

un.bro.ken ['ʌn'brəukən] *adj.* kırılmamış *(rekor vs.);* sürekli, aralıksız; ehlileştirilmemiş, alıştırılmamış *(at);* bütün, tam; bozulmamış; sürülmemiş *(toprak).*

un.buck.le ['ʌn'bʌkl] *v/t.* -*in* tokasını çözmek.

un.bur.den ['ʌn'bə:dn] *v/t. mst fig.* açığa vurmak, dökmek *(içini, derdini).*

un.bur.led ['ʌn'berid] *adj.* gömülmemiş.

un.burned ['ʌn'bə:nd] *adj.,* un.burnt ['ʌ·'bə:nt] yanmamış.

un.busi.ness.like [ʌn'biznislaik] *adj.* iş düzenine aykırı.

un.but.ton ['ʌn'bʌtn] *v/t.* -*in* düğmelerini çözmek.

un.called ['ʌn'kɔ:ld] *adj.* çağrılmamış, da-

vetsiz; † talep edilmemiş; **un'called-for** *adj.* lüzumsuz, gereksiz, yersiz.

un.can.did ☐ ['ʌn'kændid] ikiyüzlü, dürüst olmayan.

un.can.ny ☐ [ʌn'kæni] tekin olmayan; esrarengiz, acayip, anlaşılmaz.

un.cared-for ['ʌn'kɛədfɔ:] *adj.* bakımsız, ihmal edilmiş.

un.case ['ʌn'keis] *v/t.* açmak, çözmek.

un.ceas.ing ☐ [ʌn'si:siŋ] durmayan, aralıksız, sürekli, devamlı; sonsuz, ebedî.

un.cer.e.mo.ni.ous ☐ ['ʌnseri'məunjəs] gayri resmî; teklifsiz, lâubali; kaba, nezaketsiz.

un.cer.tain ☐ [ʌn'sə:tn] *com.* şüpheli; kararsız, belirsiz; güvenilmez; değişken, dönek; be ~ of -*den* emin olmamak; **un'cer.tain.ty** *n.* şüphe, tereddüt, kesin olmayış.

un.chain ['ʌn'tʃein] *v/t.* serbest bırakmak, salıvermek.

un.chal.lenge.a.ble ['ʌn'tʃælindʒəbl] *adj.* su götürmez, tartışılmaz; **un'chal.lenged** *adj.* itiraz kabul etmez, tartışılmaz.

un.change.a.ble ☐ [ʌn'tʃeindʒəbl], **un'chang.ing** değişmez; **un'changed** *adj.* değişmemiş, eskisi gibi.

un.char.i.ta.ble ☐ [ʌn'tʃæritəbl] merhametsiz, katı, sert.

un.chart.ed ['ʌn'tʃa:tid] *adj.* haritada olmayan; meçhul, bilinmeyen, keşfedilmemiş.

un.chaste ☐ ['ʌn'tʃeist] namussuz, iffetsiz; **un.chas.ti.ty** ['ʌn'tʃæstiti] *n.* namussuzluk.

un.checked ['ʌn'tʃekt] *adj.* durdurulmamış, serbest, kontrolsüz, dizginsiz.

un.chris.tian ['ʌn'kristjən] Hıristiyan olmayan; Hıristiyanlığa aykırı; medeniyetsiz; yersiz, uygunsuz.

un.civ.il ☐ ['ʌn'sivl] nezaketsiz, kaba; **un'civ.i.lized** [~vilaizd] *adj.* medeniyetsiz, medenileşmemiş.

un.claimed ['ʌn'kleimd] *adj.* sahibi çıkmamış.

un.clasp ['ʌn'kla:sp] *v/t.* bırakmak *(sıkılan el vs.),* açmak *(toka vs.).*

un.cle ['ʌŋkl] *n.* amca, dayı, enişte; *sl.* tefeci.

un.clean ☐ ['ʌn'kli:n] pis, kirli; *fig.* ahlâksız.

un.clench ['ʌn'klentʃ] *v/t.* & *v/i.* aç(tır)mak.

un.cloak ['ʌn'kləuk] *v/t.* -*in* örtüsünü kaldırmak; *fig.* açığa vurmak, ortaya dökmek.

un.close ['ʌn'kləuz] *v/t.* & *v/i.* aç(ıl)mak; açığa vurmak.

**un.clothe** [ˈʌnˈkləuð] *v/t.* *-in* elbisesini çıkarmak, soymak.

**un.cloud.ed** [ˈʌnˈklaudid] *adj.* bulutsuz; berrak, parlak *(a. fig.)*.

**un.coil** [ˈʌnˈkɔil] *v/t.* & *v/i.* çöz(ül)mek, aç(ıl)mak.

**un.col.lect.ed** [ˈʌnkəˈlektid] *adj.* toplanmamış; *fig.* kendine hâkim olmayan.

**un.col.o(u)red** [ˈʌnˈkʌləd] *adj.* boyasız; *fig.* abartmasız.

**un-come-at-a.ble** F [ˈʌnkʌmˈætəbl] *adj.* yanına varılmaz, erişilmez.

**un.come.ly** [ˈʌnˈkʌmli] *adj.* yakışık almaz, yersiz, uygunsuz.

**un.com.fort.a.ble** □ [ʌnˈkʌmfətəbl] rahatsız (edici).

**un.com.mit.ted** [ʌnkəˈmitid] *adj.* taahhüt altına girmemiş; *pol.* bağımsız, hür.

**un.com.mon** □ [ʌnˈkɔmən] *(a.* F *adv.)* olağanüstü, görülmedik; nadir, seyrek.

**un.com.mu.ni.ca.tive** [ˈʌnkəˈmjuːnikətiv] *adj.* az konuşur, ağzı sıkı.

**un.com.plain.ing** □ [ˈʌnkəmˈpleiniŋ] şikâyet etmeyen, sabırlı.

**un.com.pro.mis.ing** □ [ʌnˈkɔmprəmaiziŋ] uzlaşmaz, uyuşmaz; *fig.* eğilmez, sert.

**un.con.cern** [ˈʌnkənˈsəːn] *n.* ilgisizlik, kayıtsızlık; **ˈun.con.ˈcerned** □ *[adv.* ~idli] endişesiz, kayıtsız, ilgisiz *(about hususunda)*; duygusuz, hissiz (with *-e karşı)*; ilgisi olmayan, karışmamış (in *-e)*.

**un.con.di.tion.al** □ [ˈʌnkənˈdiʃənl] (kayıtsız) şartsız.

**un.con.fined** □ [ˈʌnkənˈfaind] kuşatılmamış; sınırsız, hudutsuz, serbest.

**un.con.firmed** [ˈʌnkənˈfəːmd] *adj.* doğrulanmamış; ✝ teyitsiz.

**un.con.gen.ial** [ˈʌnkənˈdʒiːnjəl] *adj.* sıkıcı; uygun olmayan.

**un.con.nect.ed** □ [ˈʌnkəˈnektid] ilgisiz, alâkasız, birbirini tutmaz.

**un.con.quer.a.ble** □ [ʌnˈkɔŋkərəbl] zaptedilemez, fethedilemez; **ˈun.ˈcon.quered** *adj.* fethedilmemiş.

**un.con.sci.en.tious** □ [ˈʌnkɔnʃiˈenʃəs] vicdansız; mantıksız; aşırı, fazla.

**un.con.scion.a.ble** □ [ʌnˈkɔnʃnəbl] mantıksız; vicdansız; prensipsiz; F fahiş *(fiyat)*.

**un.con.scious** [ʌnˈkɔnʃəs] **1.** □ şuursuz, bilinçsiz; baygın; be ~ of *-in* bilincinde olmamak; **2.** *n.* the ~ *psych.* bilinçaltı; **unˈcon.scious.ness** *n.* şuursuzluk, bilinçsizlik.

**un.con.se.crat.ed** [ˈʌnˈkɔnsikreitid] *adj.* adanmamış; kutsanmamış.

**un.con.sid.ered** [ˈʌnkənˈsidəd] *adj.* düşüncesizce söylenmiş *(söz)*; önemsenmemiş.

**un.con.sti.tu.tion.al** □ [ˈʌnkɔnstiˈtjuːʃənl] anayasaya aykırı.

**un.con.strained** □ [ˈʌnkənˈstreind] serbest, kolay.

**un.con.test.ed** □ [ˈʌnkənˈtestid] itiraza uğramamış.

**un.con.tra.dict.ed** [ˈʌnkɔntrəˈdiktid] *adj.* yalanlanmamış.

**un.con.trol.la.ble** □ [ʌnkənˈtrəuləbl] idare edilemez, yönetilemez; önlenemez; **ˈun.conˈtrolled** *adj.* kontrolsüz, başıboş, idaresiz; *fig. k-ne* hâkim olamayan, dizginsiz.

**un.con.ven.tion.al** □ [ˈʌnkənˈvenʃənl] göreneklere uymayan; garip, acayip; lâubali.

**un.con.vert.ed** [ˈʌnkənˈvəːtid] *adj.* değiştirilmemiş; ✝ paraya çevrilmemiş.

**un.con.vinced** [ˈʌnkənˈvinst] *adj.* emin olmayan, inanmamış; **ˈun.conˈvinc.ing** *adj.* inandırıcı olmayan, inanılmaz.

**un.cooked** [ˈʌnˈkukt] *adj.* piş(iril)memiş.

**un.cord** [ˈʌnˈkɔːd] *v/t. -in* ipini çözmek.

**un.cork** [ˈʌnˈkɔːk] *v/t. -in* tapasını çıkarmak.

**un.cor.rupt.ed** □ [ˈʌnkəˈrʌptid] bozulmamış.

**un.count.a.ble** [ˈʌnˈkauntəbl] *adj.* sayılamayan; **ˈun.ˈcount.ed** *adj.* sayılmamış; hesapsız, sayılamayacak kadar çok.

**un.cou.ple** [ˈʌnˈkʌpl] *v/t.* çözmek, ayırmak.

**un.couth** □ [ʌnˈkuːθ] kaba, nezaketsiz, kültürsüz; garip, acayip.

**un.cov.er** [ʌnˈkʌvə] *v/t. -in* örtüsünü kaldırmak, açmak; ortaya, açığa çıkarmak; saldırmak; *v/i.* şapkasını çıkarmak.

**un.crit.i.cal** □ [ˈʌnˈkritikəl] eleştirmeyen, tenkit etmeyen.

**un.crowned** [ˈʌnˈkraund] *adj.* taç giymemiş; resmî sıfatı olmayan.

**unc.tion** [ˈʌŋkʃən] *n.* yağ (sürme); *fig.* aşırı tatlı dillilik, yalancı nezaket; extreme ~ *eccl.* Katoliklerde ölmekte olan birine yağ sürme ayini; **unc.tu.ous** [ˈʌŋktjuəs] yağlı; *fig.* aşırı tatlı dilli, yalandan heyecanlı görünen.

**un.cul.ti.vat.ed** [ˈʌnˈkʌltiveitid] *adj.* işlenmemiş *(toprak)*; *fig.* kültürsüz, yontulmamış.

**un.cured** [ˈʌnˈkjuəd] *adj.* iyileşmemiş; tedavi edilmemiş.

**un.curl** [ˈʌnˈkəːl] *v/t.* & *v/i.* aç(ıl)mak *(kıvrım)*.

**un.cut** [ˈʌnˈkʌt] *adj.* kesilmemiş, makaslanmamış *(film)*, kısaltılmamış *(kitap)*; sayfa kenarları açılmamış *(kitap)*; yontulmamış *(kıymetli taş)*.

**un.dam.aged** [ˈʌnˈdæmidʒd] *adj.* zarar gör-

memiş, sağlam.
**un.damped** [ˈʌnˈdæmpt] *adj.* sindirilmemiş; gücenmemiş, kırılmamış.
**un.dat.ed** [ˈʌnˈdeitid] *adj.* tarihsiz.
**un.daunt.ed** □ [ʌnˈdɔːntid] korkusuz, gözü pek, yılmaz.
**un.de.ceive** [ˈʌndiˈsiːv] *v/t.* aldatılmaktan kurtarmak, gözünü açmak (of).
**un.de.cid.ed** □ [ˈʌndiˈsaidid] kararsız; kararlaştırılmamış; as(k)ıda, sallantıda.
**un.de.ci.pher.a.ble** [ˈʌndiˈsaifərəbl] *adj.* okunamaz, çözülemez.
**un.de.fend.ed** [ˈʌndiˈfendid] *adj.* korunmamış, savunulmamış.
**un.de.filed** [ˈʌndiˈfaild] *adj.* lekelenmemiş, kirlenmemiş, tertemiz.
**un.de.fined** □ [ˈʌndiˈfaind, *adv.* ˷nidli] tarif edilmemiş; bellisiz, belirsiz.
**un.de.mon.stra.tive** □ [ˈʌndiˈmɔnstrətiv] ağzı sıkı; duygularını belli etmeyen.
**un.de.ni.a.ble** □ [ʌndiˈnaiəbl] inkâr olunamaz; mükemmel.
**un.de.nom.i.na.tion.al** □ [ˈʌndinɔmiˈneiʃənl] mezhepsiz, din ayrımı gözetmeyen.
**un.der** [ˈʌndə] **1.** *adv.* -*in* altın(d)a, dibe; -*den* aşağı(da), altta; alt mevkide, daha aşağı derecede; **2.** *prp.* -*in* altın(d)a; -*in* altı; -*in* altından; -*in* aşağısın(d)a; -*den* eksik, -*den* düşük; -*den* küçük; -*in* himayesinde; -*in* kumandasında, emrinde; -*in* yetkisinde; from ˷ ... -*in* altından; ˷ sentence of ... öö ...hükmü altında, ...e mahkûm olmuş; **3.** *adj.* alt...; alt(taki), az...; yardımcı, ikinci; iç; ˈ˷ˈact *v/t.* & *v/i. thea.* (rolü) cansız, isteksiz oynamak; ˈ˷ˈbid (*irr.* bid) *v/t.* -*den* daha düşük fiyat vermek; ˈ˷ˈbred *adj.* terbiyesiz, kaba; saf kan olmayan; ˈ˷.brush *n.* çalılık; ˈ˷.car.riage *n.* 🛧 iniş takımı; *mot.* şasi; ˈ˷ˈcharge *v/t.* -*den* az ücret istemek; ˈ˷.clothes *n. pl.,* ˈ˷.cloth.ing iç çamaşır; ˈ˷.cov.er *adj.* gizli...; ˈ˷.cur.rent *n.* dip akıntısı; *fig.* gizli eğilim; ˈ˷ˈcut *v/t.* -*den* daha ucuza fiyat teklif etm., kırmak (*fiyat*); -*in* altını kesmek; ˈ˷ˈdog *n.* ezilen kişi, haksızlığa uğramış zavallı kimse, biçare; ˈ˷ˈdone *adj.* iyi piş(iril)memiş, az pişmiş; ˈ˷ˈdress *v/t.* -*in* altına giydirmek; *v/i.* -*in* altına giyinmek; ˈ˷ˈes.ti.mate *v/t.* gereğinden az değer vermek -*e*, küçümsemek -*i*; ˈ˷ˈexˈpose *v/t. phot.* karanlık çıkarmak, düşük poza tutmak; ˈ˷ˈfed *adj.* gıdasız; ˈ˷ˈfeed.ing *n.* yetersiz beslenme; ˷ˈfoot *adv.* ayak altında; yerde, yolda; ˷ˈgo (*irr.* go) *v/t.* katlanmak, uğramak -*e*, çekmek -*i*; geçirmek -*i*; ˷ˈgrad.u.ate *n. univ.* üniversite öğrencisi; ˈ˷.ground **1.** *adj.* yeraltında

olan, yeraltı...; gizli...; ˷ movement yeraltı örgütü; go ˷ saklanmak; **2.** *n. a.* ˷ railway metro; yeraltı geçidi; ˈ˷ˈgrowth *n.* çalılık; ˈ˷.hand *adj.* & *adv.* el altından, gizlice, sinsi sinsi, kurnazca, alçakça; *spor:* aşağıdan atılan (*veya* vurulan); ˈ˷ˈhung *adj.* alt çenesi çıkık; ˷.lay **1.** [ʌndəˈlei] (*irr.* lay) *v/t.* -*in* altını kaplamak; -*in* altına koymak, beslemek; **2.** [ˈ˷] *n.* besleme maddesi (*keçe, lastik vs.*); ˈ˷ˈlet (*irr.* let) *v/t.* düşük fiyata kiraya vermek; ˷ˈlie (*irr.* lie) *vb.* -*in* altında olma.; *fig.* -*in* esasını oluşturmak; ˷.line **1.** [ʌndəˈlain] *v/t.* -*in* altını çizmek; -*in* önemini belirtmek; **2.** [ˈ˷] *n.* alt çizgi; ˈ˷.lin.en *n.* iç çamaşır.
**un.der.ling** [ˈʌndəliŋ] *n.* ast, başkasının emrinde olan kimse; **un.derˈly.ing** *adj.* alttaki; temel, esas; **un.der.manned** [ˈ˷ˈmænd] *adj.* personeli yetersiz olan; **un.derˈmine** *v/t.* -*in* altını kazmak (*veya* oymak); *fig.* -*in* temelini çürütmek, zayıflatmak, sarsmak (*otorite vs.*); ˈun.dermost *adj.* & *adv.* en alttaki; **un.derˈneath** [˷ˈniːθ] *prp.* & *adv.* -*in* altın(d)a; ˈun.derˈnour.ished *adj.* iyi beslenmemiş, gıdasız kalmış.
**un.der...:** ˈ˷.pass *n.* alt geçit; ˈ˷ˈpay (*irr.* pay) *v/t.* hakkından az ücret vermek -*e*; ˷ˈpin *v/t.* ⊕ -*in* altını desteklemek, beslemek; *fig.* desteklemek, arka çıkmak; ˷ˈpin.ning *n.* ⊕ destek, ayak; yapı temeli; ˈ˷.plot *n.* yan aksiyon; ˈ˷ˈprint *v/t. phot.* az basmak; ˈ˷ˈpriv.i.leged *adj.* temel imkânları kıt olan; ˷ˈrate *v/t.* gereğinden az değer vermek -*e*, küçümsemek -*i*; ˷ˈscore *v/t.* -*in* altını çizmek; -*in* üstünde durmak; ˈ˷ˈsec.re.tar.y *n.* müsteşar. müşavir; ˈ˷ˈsell † (*irr.* sell) *v/t.* fiyat kırarak satmak; ˈ˷ˈshoot (*irr.* shoot) *v/t.:* ˷ the runway 🛧 uçağı inişten önce piste değdirerek yeniden havalandırmak; ˈ˷.shot *adj.* alt dişleri çıkıntılı olan; alttan geçen su ile işleyen; ˈ˷.side *n.* alt kısım; ˷ˈsigned *adj.* imza sahibi; ˈ˷ˈsized *adj.* normalden küçük; bodur, cücemsi; ˈ˷ˈslung *adj. mot.* dingile alttan bağlı...; ˷ frame alçak şasi; ˈ˷ˈstaffed *adj.* personeli az olan; ˷ˈstand (*irr.* stand) *v/t. com.* anlamak, kavramak, bilmek; öğrenmek; kestirmek; farz etm.; tahmin etm.; *v/i.* anlayışlı olm.; *b-nin* duygularını paylaşmak; make o.s. understood derdini anlatabilmek; it is understood demek (oluyor ki), anlaşılıyor ki; that is understood anlaşıldı; an understood thing anlaşılmış bş; ˷ˈstand.a.ble *adj.* anlaşılır, kavranılır; ˷ˈstand.ing **1.** *n.* anlayış,

kavrama; anlaşma; açıklama, yorum; duygudaşlık, sempati; on the ~ that ...koşuluyla, ...şartıyla; **2.** *adj.* anlayışlı; **'~'state** *v/t.* olduğundan az *veya* hafif göstermek, küçültmek; **'~'state.ment** *n.* olduğundan hafif gösteren ifade, az gösterme.

**un.der...:** **'~.strap.per** = underling; **'~.study** *thea.* **1.** *n.* yedek oyuncu, yardımcı oyuncu; **2.** *vb.* başka oyuncunun yerine geçebilmek için onun rolünü ezberlemek; **~'take** (*irr.* take) *v/t.* üzerine almak, yüklenmek, üstlenmek (to *inf. -meyi*); girişmek, başlamak; ~ that ...meyi garanti etm., ...meye söz vermek; **'~.tak.er** *n.* cenaze işleri görevlisi, ölü kaldırıcısı; **~'tak.ing** *n.* iş, teşebbüs, girişim; garanti, vaat, söz; cenaze işi; **'~'ten.ant** *n.* ikinci kiracı, kiracının kiracısı; **'~.tone** *n.* alçak ses tonu, fısıltı; donuk *veya* mat renk; in an ~ alçak sesle; **'~'val.ue** *v/t.* kıymetinden az değer vermek *-e*; küçümsemek, hafife almak; **'~.wear** *n.* iç çamaşır; **'~-weight** *n.* normalden hafif olan ağırlık; **'~.wood** *n.* çalılık; **'~.world** *n.* ölüler diyarı; kanunsuzlar âlemi, yeraltı dünyası; **'~.write** † (*irr.* write) *v/t. -in* masrafını ödemeyi taahhüt etm.; sigorta etm.; imzalamak; **'~.wri.ter** *n.* sigortacı.

**un.de.served** □ [ˈʌndiˈzɜːvd] lâyık olmayan, hak edilmemiş; **'un.deˈserv.ing** *adj.* hak etmeyen.

**un.de.signed** □ [ˈʌndiˈzaind] kasıtsız; önceden tasarlanmamış; önceden bilinmeyen.

**un.de.sir.a.ble** [ˈʌndiˈzaiərəbl] **1.** □ hoşa gitmeyen, istenilmeyen; itiraz edilebilir, hoş karşılanmayan; **2.** *n.* istenilmeyen kimse.

**un.de.terred** [ˈʌndiˈtɜːd] *adj.* azimli, yılmayan.

**un.de.vel.oped** [ˈʌndiˈveləpt] *adj.* gelişmemiş; işlenmemiş *(toprak)*.

**un.de.vi.at.ing** □ [ʌnˈdiːvieitiŋ] yolunu şaşmayan.

**un.dies** F [ˈʌndiz] *n. pl.* kadın iç çamaşırı.

**un.di.gest.ed** [ˈʌndiˈdʒestid] *adj.* hazmedilmemiş.

**un.dig.ni.fied** □ [ʌnˈdignifaid] onursuz; haysiyetsiz; beceriksiz, sakar.

**un.di.min.ished** [ˈʌndiˈminiʃt] *adj.* azalmamış, eksilmemiş.

**un.di.rect.ed** [ˈʌndiˈrektid] *adj.* idare altında olmayan; yönlendirilmemiş; adressiz *(mektup)*.

**un.dis.cerned** □ [ˈʌndiˈsɜːnd] ayırt edilmemiş; **'un.disˈcern.ing** *adj.* anlayışsız.

**un.dis.charged** [ˈʌndisˈtʃɑːdʒd] *adj.* boşaltılmamış *(yük)*; ödenmemiş *(borç)*.

**un.dis.ci.plined** [ʌnˈdisiplind] *adj.* disiplinsiz, terbiye edilmemiş; afacan.

**un.dis.cov.ered** [ˈʌndisˈkʌvəd] *adj.* keşfedilmemiş, meçhul.

**un.dis.crim.i.nat.ing** □ [ˈʌndisˈkrimineitiŋ] farkı ayırt edemeyen.

**un.dis.guised** □ [ˈʌndisˈgaizd] kılığını değiştirmemiş, gizlenmemiş; açık, içten.

**un.dis.posed** [ˈʌndisˈpəuzd] *adj.* isteksiz, gönülsüz (to *-e*); † satılmamış, elde kalmış.

**un.dis.put.ed** □ [ˈʌndisˈpjuːtid] karşı gelinmeyen, tartışılmaz.

**un.dis.tin.guished** [ˈʌndisˈtiŋgwiʃt] *adj.* alelade, silik, önemsiz, hiçten; kaba.

**un.dis.tort.ed** [ˈʌndisˈtɔːtid] *adj.* bozulmamış, çarpıtılmamış.

**un.dis.turbed** □ [ˈʌndisˈtəːbd] karıştırılmamış, rahatsız edilmemiş; rahat.

**un.di.vid.ed** □ [ˈʌndiˈvaidid] bölünmemiş; bütün; devamlı.

**un.do** [ˈʌnˈduː] (*irr.* do) *v/t.* açmak, çözmek, sökmek, gevşetmek; ✎ bozmak, mahvetmek; telâfi etm.; **'unˈdo.ing** *n.* çözme, açma; yıkım, felâket; feshetme.

**un.do.mes.ti.cat.ed** [ˈʌndəˈmestikeitid] *adj.* ev işlerine alıştırılmamış, ev işlerine ilgi duymayan.

**un.done** [ˈʌnˈdʌn] *adj.* açık, bağı çözülmüş; bitirilmemiş, yapılmamış; mahvolmuş, perişan; he is ~ hapı yuttu, yandı; come ~ açılmak, çözülmek.

**un.doubt.ed** □ [ʌnˈdautid] kesin, şüphesiz.

**un.dreamt** [ʌnˈdremt] *adj.* ~-of akla hayale gelmez.

**un.dress** [ˈʌnˈdres] **1.** *v/t. & v/i.* soy(un)mak, elbiselerini çıkarmak; **2.** *n.* çıplaklık; ✗ sivil elbise; **'unˈdressed** *adj.* çıplak; işlenmemiş *(deri vs.)*; bakımsız.

**un.due** [ˈʌnˈdjuː] *adj.* uygunsuz, yakışık almaz; aşırı; kanunsuz; gereksiz, yersiz; † vadesi gelmemiş.

**un.du.late** [ˈʌndjuleit] *v/t. & v/i.* dalgalan(dır)mak; dalga dalga olm., inişli çıkışlı olm.; **'un.du.lat.ing** □ dalgalı; inişli çıkışlı; **un.duˈla.tion** *n.* dalga(lanma); **un.du.la.to.ry** [ˈ~lətəri] *adj.* dalgalanmaya ait; dalgalı...

**un.du.ly** [ˈʌnˈdjuːli] *adv. of* undue.

**un.du.ti.ful** □ [ˈʌnˈdjuːtiful] itaatsiz, saygısız; görevine bağlı olmayan, sorumluluk duygusu taşımayan.

**un.dy.ing** □ [ʌnˈdaiiŋ] ölmez, ölümsüz, sonsuz, ebedî.

**un.earned** [ˈʌnˈəːnd] *adj.* çalışarak kaza

nılmamış; *fig.* hak edilmemiş; ~ income havadan gelen gelir.

**un.earth** [ˈʌnˈɔːθ] *v/t.* topraktan çıkarmak; *fig.* ortaya çıkarmak, keşfetmek; **unˈearth.ly** *adj.* doğaüstü; esrarengiz, korkunç, müthiş; F uygunsuz.

**un.eas.i.ness** [ʌnˈiːzinis] *n.* huzursuzluk, rahatsızlık; endişe; **unˈeas.y** ⬜ huzursuz, rahatsız; üzgün; gergin; endişeli (about -den); rahatsız edici.

**un.eat.a.ble** [ˈʌnˈiːtəbl] *adj.* yen(il)mez.

**un.e.co.nom.ic,** **un.e.co.nom.i.cal** ⬜ [ˈʌniːkəˈnɔmik(əl)] ekonomik olmayan; savurgan.

**un.ed.i.fy.ing** ⬜ [ˈʌnˈedifaiɳ] eğitici olmayan.

**un.ed.u.cat.ed** [ˈʌnˈedjukeitid] *adj.* okumamış, cahil.

**un.em.bar.rassed** [ˈʌnimˈbærəst] *adj.* utanmaz, sıkılmaz.

**un.e.mo.tion.al** ⬜ [ˈʌniˈməuʃənl] hissiz, duygusuz.

**un.em.ployed** [ˈʌnimˈplɔid] **1.** *adj.* işsiz (güçsüz); kullanılmayan; **2.** *n.* the ~ *pl.* işsizler; **ˈun.emˈploy.ment** *n.* işsizlik; ~ benefit, ~ pay işsizlik tazminatı.

**un.en.cum.bered** [ˈʌninˈkʌmbəd] *adj.* ipoteksiz; yüksüz; engelsiz.

**un.end.ing** ⬜ [ʌnˈendiɳ] sonsuz, bitmez tükenmez.

**un.en.dowed** [ˈʌninˈdaud] *adj.* bağışlanmamış; doğuştan yeteneksiz (with).

**un.en.dur.a.ble** [ˈʌninˈdjuərəbl] *adj.* dayanılmaz, çekilmez.

**un.en.gaged** [ˈʌninˈgeidʒd] *adj.* serbest, hür.

**un-Eng.lish** [ˈʌnˈiɳgliʃ] *adj.* İngiliz'e yakışmaz *veya* benzemez.

**un.en.light.ened** [ˈʌninˈlaitnd] *adj. fig.* okumamış; önyargılı; batıl inançlı.

**un.en.ter.pris.ing** [ˈʌnˈentəpraiziɳ] *adj.* uyanık olmayan, girişken olmayan.

**un.en.vi.a.ble** ⬜ [ˈʌnˈenviəbl] kıskanılmaya değmez.

**un.e.qual** ⬜ [ˈʌnˈiːkwəl] eşit olmayan; düzensiz; aynı nitelikte olmayan; haksız, adaletsiz; yetersiz (to -e); **ˈun.e.qual(l)ed** *adj.* eşsiz, eşi bulunmaz; üstün, rakipsiz.

**un.e.quiv.o.cal** ⬜ [ˈʌniˈkwivəkəl] kesin, şüphesiz; tek anlamlı.

**un.err.ing** ⬜ [ˈʌnˈɔːriɳ] tam isabetli, doğru, kesin; yanılmaz, emin.

**un.es.sen.tial** ⬜ [ˈʌniˈsenʃəl] gereksiz, önemsiz (to -e).

**un.e.ven** ⬜ [ˈʌnˈiːvən] düz olmayan, eğri büğrü, çarpık çurpuk; Å tek *(sayı)*; gayri muntazam, düzensiz, gelişigüzel; eşit olmayan, eşitsiz; değişken, dengesiz

*(karakter vs.).*

**un.e.vent.ful** ⬜ [ˈʌniˈventful] olaysız, sakin; be ~ olaysız geçmek.

**un.ex.am.pled** [ʌnigˈzɑːmpld] *adj.* misli *(veya* eşi) görülmemiş, eşsiz.

**un.ex.cep.tion.a.ble** ⬜ [ʌnikˈsepʃnəbl] karşı çıkılmaz, itiraz kabul etmez; kusursuz.

**un.ex.pect.ed** ⬜ [ˈʌniksˈpektid] beklenilmedik, umulmadık.

**un.ex.pired** [ˈʌniksˈpaiəd] *adj.* süresi dolmamış, vadesi gelmemiş, günü geçmemiş.

**un.ex.plained** [ˈʌniksˈpleind] *adj.* açıklanmamış, anlaşılmamış.

**un.ex.posed** *phot.* [ˈʌniksˈpəuzd] *adj.* poz verilmemiş.

**un.ex.plored** [ˈʌniksˈplɔːd] *adj.* keşfedilmemiş.

**un.ex.pressed** [ˈʌniksˈprest] *adj.* açıklanmamış.

**un.fad.ing** ⬜ [ʌnˈfeidiɳ] solmaz, solmayan.

**un.fail.ing** ⬜ [ʌnˈfeliɳ] (bitmez) tükenmez, sonu gelmez; şaşmaz, doğru, güvenilir; yorulmaz; *fig.* sadık, vefalı.

**un.fair** ⬜ [ˈʌnˈfɛə] haksız, adaletsiz; hileli; **ˈunˈfair.ness** *n.* haksızlık.

**un.faith.ful** ⬜ [ˈʌnˈfeiθful] sadakatsiz, vefasız; güvenilmez; yanlış, hatalı; **ˈunˈfaith.ful.ness** *n.* sadakatsizlik.

**un.fal.ter.ing** ⬜ [ʌnˈfɔːltəriɳ] kararlı, azimli.

**un.fa.mil.iar** [ˈʌnfəˈmiljə] *adj.* iyi bilmeyen, yabancı (with -i, -e); alışılmamış, garip.

**un.fash.ion.a.ble** ⬜ [ˈʌnˈfæʃnəbl] modaya uymayan; eski moda.

**un.fas.ten** [ˈʌnˈfɑːsn] *v/t.* açmak, çözmek, gevşetmek.

**un.fath.om.a.ble** ⬜ [ʌnˈfæðəməbl] dibine ulaşılamaz; *fig.* anlaşılmaz, kavranılamaz, akıl ermez.

**un.fa.vo(u)r.a.ble** ⬜ [ˈʌnˈfeivərəbl] müsait olmayan; elverişsiz; zıt, ters, aksi; olumsuz; zararlı, sakıncalı.

**un.feel.ing** ⬜ [ʌnˈfiːliɳ] hissiz, duygusuz; katı yürekli, acımasız, merhametsiz.

**un.feigned** ⬜ [ʌnˈfeind, *adv.* ~nidli] yapmacıksız, samimî, içten; hakiki.

**un.felt** [ˈʌnˈfelt] *adj.* hissedilmemiş.

**un.fer.ment.ed** [ˈʌnfɔːˈmentid] *adj.* mayalandırılmamış.

**un.fet.ter** [ˈʌnˈfetə] *v/t.* kurtarmak, özgür kılmak; **ˈunˈfet.tered** *adj. fig.* serbest, özgür.

**un.fil.i.al** ⬜ [ˈʌnˈfiljəl] evlada yakışmaz, saygısız.

un.fin.ished [ˈʌnˈfiniʃt] *adj.* bitmemiş, tamamlanmamış.

un.fit 1. □ [ˈʌnˈfit] uymaz, uygunsuz (for s.th. bşe; to *inf.* -meye); yetersiz, ehliyetsiz; **2.** [ʌnˈfit] *v/t.* işe yaramaz hale getirmek, kuvvetten düşürmek; ˈunˈfitness *n.* uygunsuzluk; unˈfit.ted *adj.* ehliyetsiz, uygun nitelikleri olmayan.

un.fix [ˈʌnˈfiks] *v/t.* çözmek, açmak, sökmek; kararsız kılmak; ˈunˈfixed *adj.* kararlaştırılmamış.

un.flag.ging □. [ʌnˈflægiŋ] yorulmaz; bitmez tükenmez.

un.flat.ter.ing □ [ˈʌnˈflætəriŋ] yerici, zemmedici.

un.fledged [ˈʌnˈfledʒd] *adj.* tüyleri bitmemiş, uçamayan (kuş); *fig.* toy, acemi çaylak, olgunlaşmamış.

un.flick.er.ing [ˈʌnˈflikəriŋ] *adj.* titrek yanmayan; *fig.* sabit.

un.flinch.ing □ [ʌnˈflintʃiŋ] korkusuz, yiğit, cesur, yılmaz.

un.fly.a.ble [ˈʌnˈflaiəbl] *adj.*: ~ weather ᵴ uçuşa elverişli olmayan hava.

un.fold [ˈʌnˈfəuld] *v/t.* & *v/i.* aç(ıl)mak, yaymak; açıklamak, bildirmek, göz önüne ser(il)mek; gelişmek (hikâye vs.).

un.forced □ [ˈʌnˈfɔːst, *adv.* ~sidli] tabiî.

un.fore.seen [ˈʌnfɔːˈsiːn] *adj.* beklenmedik, umulmadık.

un.for.get.ta.ble □ [ˈʌnfəˈgetəbl] unutulmaz.

un.for.giv.ing [ˈʌnfəˈgiviŋ] *adj.* uzlaşmaz; affetmez, bağışlamaz, acımasız.

un.for.got, un.for.got.ten [ˈʌnfəˈgɔt(n)] *adj.* unutulmamış.

un.for.ti.fied [ˈʌnfɔːˈtifaid] *adj.* kuvvetlendirilmemiş.

un.for.tu.nate [ʌnˈfɔːtʃnit] **1.** □ talihsiz, bahtsız, şanssız, bedbaht, biçare, kimsesiz; pişmanlık duyulan; isabetsiz, uygunsuz; **2.** *n.* şanssız kimse; unˈfor.tu.nate.ly *adv.* maalesef, (ne) yazık ki.

un.found.ed □ [ˈʌnˈfaundid] temelsiz, asılsız, boş, yalan.

un.fre.quent [ʌnˈfriːkwənt] *adj.* nadir, ender, seyrek.

un.fre.quent.ed [ˈʌnfriˈkwentid] *adj.* seyrek ziyaret edilen, sık sık gidilmeyen; ıssız, tenha.

un.friend.ed [ˈʌnˈfrendid] *adj.* arkadaşsız, dostsuz; unˈfriend.ly *adj.* dostça olmayan, samimiyetsiz, düşmanca; soğuk.

un.frock [ˈʌnˈfrɔk] *v/t.* papazlıktan çıkarmak.

un.fruit.ful □ [ˈʌnˈfruːtful] verimsiz, mahsulsüz; semeresiz, başarısız; kısır, dölsüz.

un.ful.filled [ˈʌnfulˈfild] *adj.* yerine getirilmemiş.

un.furl [ˈʌnˈfəːl] *v/t.* açmak, yaymak, sermek.

un.fur.nished [ˈʌnˈfəːniʃt] *adj.* mobilyasız, döşenmemiş; ~ with *ile* donatılmamış.

un.gain.li.ness [ʌnˈgeinlinis] *n.* hantallık, biçimsizlik; sakarlık; kabalık; unˈgain.ly *adj.* hantal, biçimsiz; sakar; kaba, inceliksiz.

un.gal.lant □ [ˈʌnˈgælənt] kaba, nezaketsiz (to -e karşı).

un.gear ⊕ [ˈʌnˈgiə] *v/t.* birbirinden ayırmak, avaraya almak; boşa almak (vites).

un.gen.er.ous □ [ˈʌnˈdʒenərəs] cömert olmayan, cimri, pinti; merhametsiz, gönlü yüce olmayan.

un.gen.ial □ [ˈʌnˈdʒiːnjəl] suratsız, soğuk, nezaketsiz.

un.gen.tle □ [ˈʌnˈdʒentl] sert, haşin, gaddar, kaba.

un.gen.tle.man.ly [ʌnˈdʒentlmənli] *adj.* nezaketsiz, kaba.

un.get-at-able [ˈʌngetˈætəbl] *adj.* erişilmez, yanına yaklaşılmaz.

un.glazed [ˈʌnˈgleizd] *adj.* sırlanmamış, perdahsız.

un.god.li.ness [ʌnˈgɔdlinis] *n.* dinsizlik, günahkârlık, Allahsızlık; unˈgod.ly □ Allahsız, dinsiz, günahkâr; F Allahın cezası, berbat, uygunsuz; F can sıkıcı.

un.gov.ern.a.ble □ [ʌnˈgʌvənəbl] yönetilemez, hâkim olunmaz, asi; unˈgov.erned *adj.* k-ne hâkim olamayan.

un.grace.ful □ [ˈʌnˈgreisful] inceliksiz, kaba, nezaketsiz; beceriksiz, hantal.

un.gra.cious □ [ˈʌnˈgreiʃəs] nezaketsiz, kaba; hoşa gitmeyen, kaba.

un.gram.mat.i.cal □ [ˈʌngrəˈmætikəl] dil bilgisi kurallarına aykırı olan.

un.grate.ful □ [ʌnˈgreitful] nankör; nahoş, tatsız (iş).

un.ground.ed [ʌnˈgraundid] *adj.* asılsız, yersiz, boş; ≴ topraklanmamış.

un.grudg.ing □ [ˈʌnˈgrʌdʒiŋ] isteyerek, seve seve yapan; istekli.

un.gual *anat.* [ˈʌŋgwəl] *adj.* toynak..., pençe..., tırnak...

un.guard.ed □ [ˈʌnˈgɑːdid] koruyucusuz; dikkatsiz, tedbirsiz, gafil; ⊕ muhafazasız.

un.guent [ˈʌŋgwənt] *n.* merhem, yağ.

un.guid.ed □ [ˈʌnˈgaidid] rehbersiz.

un.gu.late [ˈʌŋgjuleit] *n. a.* ~ animal toynaklılar familyasından bir hayvan.

un.hal.lowed [ʌnˈhæləud] *adj.* takdis edilmemiş, kutsanmamış; kötü, hayırsız; kâfir; ahlâksız, edepsiz.

**un.ham.pered** [ˈʌnˈhæmpəd] *adj.* engellenmemiş, serbest.

**un.hand.some** ☐ [ʌnˈhænsəm] yakışıklı olmayan, çirkin *(a. fig.)*; uygunsuz, yakışıksız; kaba, nezaketsiz.

**un.hand.y** ☐ [ʌnˈhændi] kullanışsız, elverişsiz; acemi, sakar, eli işe yakışmaz.

**un.hap.pi.ness** [ʌnˈhæpinis] *n.* mutsuzluk, keder; **unˈhap.py** ☐ mutsuz, kederli, üzüntülü; uygunsuz, münasebetsiz; şanssız, talihsiz; uğursuz.

**un.harmed** [ʌˈnˈhɑːmd] *adj.* zararsız, sağsalim.

**un.har.mo.ni.ous** ☐ [ˈʌnhɑːˈməunjəs] ahenksiz, uyumsuz.

**un.har.ness** [ˈʌnˈhɑːnis] *v/t.* -*den* koşum takımını çıkarmak.

**un.health.y** ☐. [ʌnˈhelθi] sıhhate zararlı; sıhhati bozuk, keyifsiz; tehlikeli; ahlâkı bozan.

**un.heard** [ˈʌnˈhəːd] *adj.* duyulmamış, işitilmemiş; duyulmayan; **un.heard-of** [ʌnˈhəːdəv] *adj.* misli görülmemiş, olağanüstü.

**un.heed.ed** [ˈʌnˈhiːdid] *adj.* önemsenmeyen, aldırış edilmeyen; **ˈunˈheed.ing** *adj.* dikkat etmeyen, önemsemeyen, kayıtsız.

**un.hes.i.tat.ing** ☐ [ʌnˈheziteitiŋ] tereddüt etmeyen; ~ly tereddüt etmeyerek.

**un.hin.dered** [ˈʌnˈhindəd] *adj.* engellenmeyen.

**un.hinge** [ʌnˈhindʒ] *v/t.* menteşelerden çıkarmak *(kapı vs.)*; *fig.* dengesini bozmak, oynatmak *(akıl)*.

**un.his.tor.ic, un.his.tor.i.cal** ☐ [ˈʌnhisˈtɔrik(əl)] tarihî olmayan.

**un.hitch** [ˈʌnˈhitʃ] *v/t.* çözmek, açmak.

**un.ho.ly** [ʌnˈhəuli] *adj.* kutsal olmayan; kötücül, günahkâr; F berbat, iğrenç.

**un.hon.o(u)red** [ˈʌnˈɔnəd] *adj.* şereflendirilmemiş; ödenmemiş *(çek vs.)*.

**un.hook** [ˈʌnˈhuk] *v/t.* -*in* çengellerini çıkarmak; çengelden çıkarmak.

**un.hoped-for** [ʌnˈhəuptfɔː] *adj.* beklenmedik, umulmadık.

**un.horse** [ˈʌnˈhɔːs] *v/t.* attan düşürmek; üstünden atmak.

**un.house** [ˈʌnˈhauz] *v/t.* evden atmak, evsiz barksız bırakmak.

**un.hung** [ʌnˈhʌŋ] *adj.* asılmamış.

**un.hurt** [ˈʌnˈhəːt] *adj.* zarar görmemiş, incinmemiş, sağlam.

**u.ni.corn** [ˈjuːnikɔːn] *n.* tek boynuzlu ata benzer hayali bir hayvan.

**u.ni.fi.ca.tion** [juːnifiˈkeiʃən] *n.* birleş(tir)me.

**u.ni.form** [ˈjuːnifɔːm] **1.** ☐ aynı, değiş-

mez; düzenli; tekdüzen, yeknesak; ~ price tek fiyat; **2.** *n.* üniforma, resmî elbise; **3.** *v/t.* üniforma giydirmek; aynı şekle sokmak, standartlaştırmak; **u.niˈform.i.ty** *n.* aynılık, değişmezlik; düzen; tekdüzenlik, monotonluk.

**u.ni.fy** [ˈjuːnifai] *v/t.* birleştirmek.

**u.ni.lat.er.al** [ˈjuːniˈlætərəl] *adj.* tek taraflı, tek yanlı.

**un.im.ag.i.na.ble** ☐ [ʌniˈmædʒinəbl] tasavvur edilemez; **ˈun.imˈag.i.na.tive** ☐ [~nətiv] yaratma kabiliyeti olmayan, hayal gücü dar.

**un.im.paired** [ˈʌnimˈpɛəd] *adj.* zarar görmemiş, bozulmamış.

**un.im.peach.a.ble** ☐ [ʌnimˈpiːtʃəbl] şüphe götürmez, güvenilir; kusursuz, suçsuz; çürütülemez.

**un.im.ped.ed** ☐ [ˈʌnimˈpiːdid] engellenmemiş.

**un.im.por.tant** ☐ [ˈʌnimˈpɔːtənt] önemsiz.

**un.im.proved** [ˈʌnimˈpruːvd] *adj.* geliştirilmemiş; değerlendirilmemiş *(fırsat vs.)*; sürülmemiş *(toprak)*; iyileşmemiş.

**un.in.flu.enced** [ˈʌnˈinfluənst] *adj.* etkilenmemiş.

**un.in.formed** [ˈʌninˈfɔːmd] *adj.* haberdar edilmemiş.

**un.in.hab.it.a.ble** [ˈʌninˈhæbitəbl] *adj.* oturulamaz, yaşanılmaz; **ˈun.inˈhab.it.ed** *adj.* oturulmamış; ıssız, tenha, boş.

**un.in.jured** [ˈʌninˈindʒəd] *adj.* yaralanmamış, incinmemiş.

**un.in.struct.ed** [ˈʌninˈstrʌktid] *adj.* talimat verilmemiş.

**un.in.sured** [ˈʌninˈʃuəd] *adj.* sigorta edilmemiş.

**un.in.tel.li.gi.bil.i.ty** [ˈʌnintelidʒəˈbiliti] *n.* anlaşılmazlık; **ˈun.inˈtel.li.gi.ble** ☐ anlaşılmaz.

**un.in.tend.ed** ☐ [ˈʌninˈtendid] kasıtsız; niyet edilmemiş.

**un.in.ten.tion.al** ☐ [ˈʌninˈtenʃənl] isteneyerek yapılan, kasıtsız.

**un.in.ter.est.ing** ☐ [ˈʌnˈintristiŋ] ilginç olmayan.

**un.in.ter.rupt.ed** ☐ [ˈʌnintəˈrʌptid] aralıksız, kesilmemiş, devamlı; ~ working hours *pl.* devamlı çalışma saatleri.

**un.in.vit.ed** [ˈʌninˈvaitid] *adj.* davet edilmemiş; **ˈun.inˈvit.ing** ☐ davet edilmeyen.

**un.ion** [ˈjuːnjən] *n.* birleş(tir)me; anlaşma; *pol.* birlik, ittifak; dernek, sendika; dariülaceze, güçsüzler yurdu; evlilik; ⊕ rakor, bilezik; **ˈun.ion.ism** *n. pol. etc.* birlik taraftarı olma; sendikacılık; **ˈun.ion.ist** *n. pol. etc.* birlik taraftarı; sendika yanlısı, sendikacı; **ˈun.ion.ize** *v/t.* birlik haline getirmek; sendikalaştırmak.

**un.ion...:** ♀ **Jack** İngiliz bayrağı; ~ **suit** *Am.* kombinezon.

**u.nique** [juːˈniːk] ☐ tek, biricik, yegâne; eşsiz.

**u.ni.son** ♪ & *fig.* [ˈjuːnizn] *n.* birlik, ahenk, uyum; **in** ~ hep bir ağızdan, hep beraber; **u.nis.o.nous** ♪ [juːˈnisənəs] *adj.* aynı perdeden; birlikte.

**u.nit** [ˈjuːnit] *n.* birlik (*a.* ✕); A, ⊕ birim, ünite; ~ furniture mobilya ünitesi; **U.ni-tar.i.an** [~ˈtɛəriən] **1.** *n.* teslis doktrinini reddeden bir Hıristiyan mezhebi üyesi; **2.** *adj.* bu Hristiyan mezhebine ait; **u.ni-tar.y** [ˈ~təri] *adj.* üniteye ait, birimsel..., ünite...; A bölünmez..., tek...; **u.nite** [juːˈnait] *v/t.* & *v/i.* birleş(tir)mek, bağlamak; bitişmek.

**u.nit.ed** [juːˈnaitid] *adj.* birleşmiş, birleşik; ahenkli, uyumlu; ♀ **King.dom** Britanya Krallığı; ♀ **Na.tions** *pl.* Birleşmiş Milletler; ♀ **States** *pl.* **of America** Amerika Birleşik Devletleri.

**u.ni.ty** [ˈjuːniti] *n.* birlik, ittifak; birleşme; A bir sayısı.

**u.ni.ver.sal** ☐ [juːniˈvəːsəl] genel, umumî; evrensel, dünya çapında; külli, tümel; ⊕ üniversal; ~ heir tek vâris; ~ joint ⊕ üniversal kavrama; ~ language evrensel dil; ♀ *Postal* Union Milletlerarası Posta Birliği; ~ suffrage genel oy hakkı; **u.ni.ver.sal.i.ty** [~ˈsæliti] *n.* genellik, evrensellik; **u.ni.verse** [ˈjuːnivəːs] *n.* evren, kâinat, âlem; **u.niˈver.si.ty** *n.* üniversite.

**un.just** ☐ [ˈʌnˈdʒʌst] haksız, adaletsiz; **unˈjus.ti.fi.a.ble** ☐ [~tifaiəbl] gereksiz, yersiz.

**un.kempt** [ˈʌnˈkempt] *adj.* taranmamış (saç); *fig.* dağınık, düzensiz, derbeder, hırpani.

**un.kind** ☐ [ʌnˈkaind] dostça olmayan, sert, zalim, kalp kırıcı.

**un.knit** *part. fig.* [ˈʌnˈnit] (*irr.* knit) *v/t.* sökmek, çözmek.

**un.knot** [ˈʌnˈnɔt] *v/t.* -*in* düğümünü çözmek.

**un.know.ing** ☐ [ˈʌnˈnəuiŋ] habersiz; **ˈun-ˈknown 1.** *adj.* bilinmez, meçhul, yabancı; **2.** *adv.* ~ to me bana yabancı, benim bilmediğim; **3.** *n.* yabancı, meçhul kimse; A bilinmeyen.

**un.lace** [ˈʌnˈleis] *v/t.* -*in* bağlarını gevşetmek, çözmek, açmak.

**un.lade** [ˈʌnˈleid] (*irr.* lade) *v/t.* boşaltmak; *v/i.* ⚓ yükünü boşaltmak.

**un.la.dy.like** [ˈʌnˈleidilaik] *adj.* hanıma yakışmaz.

**un.laid** [ˈʌnˈleid] *adj.* ipleri ayrılmış, örgüsü açılmış.

**un.la.ment.ed** [ˈʌnləˈmentid] *adj.* yası tutulmayan.

**un.latch** [ˈʌnˈlætʃ] *v/t.* -*in* mandalını açmak; *v/i.* açılmak.

**un.law.ful** ☐ [ˈʌnˈlɔːful] kanunsuz, gayri meşru, kanuna aykırı.

**un.learn** [ˈʌnˈləːn] (*irr.* learn) *v/t.* unutmak (öğrendiğini), bırakmak, vazgeçmek (alışkanlık vs.); **ˈunˈlearn.ed** ☐ [~nid] okuma yazma bilmez, cahil, bilgisiz; çalışarak öğrenilmeyen.

**un.leash** [ˈʌnˈliːʃ] *v/t.* tasmasını çıkarmak (köpek); *fig.* serbest bırakmak, koyvermek.

**un.leav.ened** [ˈʌnˈlevnd] *adj.* mayasız (ekmek).

**un.less** [ənˈles] *cj.* -medikçe, -mezse, meğerki.

**un.let.tered** [ˈʌnˈletəd] *adj.* okuma yazma bilmez, cahil, okumamış.

**un.li.censed** [ˈʌnˈlaisənst] *adj.* ehliyetsiz, ruhsatsız.

**un.licked** *mst fig.* [ˈʌnˈlikt] *adj.* şekilsiz, biçimsiz, yontulmamış; ~ cub acemi çaylak, ağzı süt kokan genç.

**un.like** ☐ [ˈʌnˈlaik] -*e* benzemeyen, farklı (s.o. b-den); **unˈlike.li.hood** [~lihud] *n.* olasısızlık; **unˈlike.ly** *adj.* umulmaz, olasısız, muhtemel olmayan.

**un.lim.it.ed** [ʌnˈlimitid] *adj.* sınırsız, sonsuz, sayısız; *fig.* kısıtsız, kayıtsız, şartsız.

**un.lined** [ˈʌnˈlaind] *adj.* çizgisiz.

**un.liq.ui.dat.ed** [ˈʌnˈlikwideitid] *adj.* tasfiye edilmemiş, ödenmemiş.

**un.load** [ˈʌnˈləud] *vb.* boşaltmak (yük, silah); başından savmak; dökmek (derdini); kurtarmak -*den*; rahatlatmak.

**un.lock** [ˈʌnˈlɔk] *v/t.* -*in* kilidini açmak; açmak (kapı); *fig.* çözmek, ortaya çıkarmak; **ˈunˈlocked** *adj.* açık.

**un.looked-for** [ʌnˈluktfɔː] *adj.* beklenmedik, umulmadık.

**un.loose, un.loos.en** [ˈʌnˈluːs(n)] *v/t.* çözmek; salıvermek, serbest bırakmak.

**un.lov.a.ble** [ˈʌnˈlʌvəbl] *adj.* sevilmeyen; **ˈunˈlove.ly** *adj.* sevimsiz; hoşa gitmeyen; **ˈunˈlov.ing** ☐ hissiz, sevgisiz.

**un.lucky** ☐ [ʌnˈlʌki] talihsiz, şanssız, bahtsız; uğursuz.

**un.made** [ˈʌnˈmeid] *adj.* yapılmamış.

**un.make** [ˈʌnˈmeik] (*irr.* make) *v/t.* bozmak; harap etm.; parçalamak; değiş tirmek.

**un.man** [ˈʌnˈmæn] *v/t.* cesaretini kırmak; yumuşatmak; gevşetmek; kısırlaştırmak; adamsız bırakmak.

un.man.age.a.ble □ [ʌnˈmænidʒəbl] idare edilemez.

un.man.ly [ˈʌnˈmænli] adj. zayıf, korkak, ödlek; erkeğe yaraşmaz, kadınımsı, erkekçe olmayan.

un.manned [ˈʌnˈmænd] adj. insansız; mürettebatsız.

un.man.ner.ly [ʌnˈmænəli] adj. kaba, terbiyesiz, saygısız.

un.marked [ˈʌnˈmɑːkt] adj. işaretsiz; çizgisiz; not verilmemiş.

un.mar.ried [ˈʌnˈmærid] adj. evlenmemiş, bekâr.

un.mask [ˈʌnˈmɑːsk] v/t. maskesini çıkartmak; fig. ortaya çıkarmak, maskesini düşürmek.

un.matched [ˈʌnˈmætʃt] adj. eşsiz, emsalsiz.

un.mean.ing □ [ʌnˈmiːniŋ] anlamsız; ifadesiz; un.meant [ˈʌnˈment] adj. kasıtsız.

un.meas.ured [ʌnˈmeʒəd] adj. sonsuz, sınırsız.

un.meet [ˈʌnˈmiːt] adj. uygunsuz, yakışıksız.

un.men.tion.a.ble [ʌnˈmenʃnəbl] 1. adj. sözü edilmez, ağıza alınmaz; 2. n. ~s pl. F iç çamaşırları.

un.mer.ci.ful □ [ʌnˈməːsiful] insafsız, merhametsiz, zalim.

un.mer.it.ed [ʌnˈmeritid] adj. haksız.

un.me.thod.i.cal [ˈʌnmiˈθɔdikəl] adj. sistemsiz, yöntemsiz.

un.mil.i.tar.y [ˈʌnˈmilitəri] adj. askerî olmayan.

un.mind.ful □ [ʌnˈmaindful] unutkan; dikkatsiz, düşüncesiz, kayıtsız, aldırmaz (of -e).

un.mis.tak.a.ble □ [ˈʌnmisˈteikəbl] açık, belli.

un.mit.i.gat.ed [ʌnˈmitigeitid] adj. tam; fig. dinmeyen...

un.mixed [ˈʌnˈmikst] adj. karış(tırıl)mamış, saf, halis.

un.mod.i.fied [ˈʌnˈmɔdifaid] adj. değiştirilmemiş.

un.mo.lest.ed [ˈʌnməuˈlestid] adj. rahatsız edilmemiş, rahat bırakılmış.

un.moor [ˈʌnˈmuə] v/i. lenger çekmek.

un.mor.al [ˈʌnˈmɔrəl] adj. ahlâki değerleri olmayan.

un.mort.gaged [ˈʌnˈmɔːgidʒd] adj. ipoteksiz.

un.mount.ed [ˈʌnˈmauntid] adj. atsız; çerçevelenmemiş; oturtulmamış; monte edilmemiş.

un.mourned [ˈʌnˈmɔːnd] adj. yas tutulmamış.

un.moved □ [ˈʌnˈmuːvd] mst fig. hissiz, duygusuz; sarsılmaz; kayıtsız, lâkayt; unˈmov.ing adj. hareketsiz.

un.mu.si.cal □ [ˈʌnˈmjuːzikəl] ahenksiz, uyumsuz.

un.muz.zle [ˈʌnˈmʌzl] v/t. -in burunsalığını çıkarmak; ~d burunsalıksız.

un.named [ˈʌnˈneimd] adj. isimsiz; bahsedilmeyen.

un.nat.u.ral □ [ʌnˈnætʃrəl] tuhaf, garip, anormal; tabiata aykırı.

un.nav.i.ga.ble [ˈʌnˈnævigəbl] adj. gidişe elverişsiz.

un.nec.es.sar.y □ [ʌnˈnesisəri] lüzumsuz, gereksiz; faydasız.

un.neigh.bo(u)r.ly [ˈʌnˈneibəli] adj. komşuya yakışmaz.

un.nerve [ˈʌnˈnəːv] v/t. cesaretini kırmak, güvenini sarsmak, sinirlendirmek.

un.not.ed [ˈʌnˈnəutid] adj. dikkate alınmamış.

un.no.ticed [ˈʌnˈnəutist] adj. gözden kaçmış.

un.num.bered [ˈʌnˈnʌmbəd] adj. numarasız; sayılamaz; sayılmamış; poet. sayısız.

un.ob.jec.tion.a.ble □ [ˈʌnəbˈdʒekʃnəbl] itiraz edilemez, kusursuz.

un.ob.serv.ant □ [ˈʌnəbˈzəːvənt] dikkatsiz, dikkat etmeyen (of -e); ˈun.obˈserved □ dikkat edilmemiş, gözden kaçmış.

un.ob.tain.a.ble [ˈʌnəbˈteinəbl] adj. elde edilemez, bulunamaz.

un.ob.tru.sive □ [ˈʌnəbˈtruːsiv] göze çarpmaz; alçak gönüllü.

un.oc.cu.pied [ˈʌnˈɔkjupaid] adj. boş, serbest; işsiz, boşta gezen.

un.of.fend.ing [ˈʌnəˈfendiŋ] adj. karıncayı ezmez, zararsız, kusursuz.

un.of.fi.cial □ [ˈʌnəˈfiʃəl] resmi olmayan, gayri resmî.

un.o.pened [ˈʌnˈəupənd] adj. açılmamış.

un.op.posed [ˈʌnəˈpəuzd] adj. karşı çıkılmamış; rakipsiz.

un.or.gan.ized [ˈʌnˈɔːgənaizd] adj. örgütlenmemiş, düzenlenmemiş, organize edilmemiş; inorganik; sendikalaşmamış.

un.os.ten.ta.tious □ [ˈʌnɔstenˈteiʃəs] gösterişsiz, dikkati çekmeyen, sade.

un.owned [ˈʌnˈəund] adj. sahipsiz.

un.pack [ˈʌnˈpæk] v/t. boşaltmak; açmak (bavul vs.).

un.paid [ˈʌnˈpeid] adj. ödenmemiş; alacaklı; ücretsiz; ☞ pulsuz.

un.pal.at.a.ble [ʌnˈpælətəbl] adj. tatsız, yavan; fig. hoşa gitmeyen.

un.par.al.leled [ʌnˈpærəleld] adj. eşsiz, emsalsiz.

un.par.don.a.ble ☐ [ʌnˈpɑːdnəbl] affedilemez.

un.par.lia.men.ta.ry ☐ [ˈʌnpɑːləˈmentəri]
parlamento kaidelerine aykırı.

un.pat.ent.ed [ˈʌnˈpeitəntid] adj. patentsiz

un.pa.tri.ot.ic [ˈʌnpætriˈɔtik] adj. (~ally)
vatanperver olmayan.

un.paved [ˈʌnˈpeivd] adj. asfaltlanmamış.

un.per.ceived ☐ [ˈʌnpəˈsiːvd] kavranılma-
mış.

un.per.formed [ˈʌnpəˈfɔːmd] adj. yerine
getirilmemiş.

un.per.plexed [ˈʌnpəˈplekst] adj. şaşırma-
mış, zihni karışmamış.

un.per.turbed [ˈʌnpəˈtəːbd] adj. sakin, soğukkanlı, tasasız.

un.phil.o.soph.i.cal ☐ [ˈʌnfiləˈsɔfikəl] felsefi olmayan.

un.pick [ˈʌnˈpik] v/t. sökmek.

un.pin [ˈʌnˈpin] v/t. -in iğnelerini çıkarmak; açmak, çözmek.

un.placed [ˈʌnˈpleist] adj. yarışma: ilk üçe
girememiş.

un.pleas.ant ☐ [ʌnˈpleznt] nahoş, hoşa gitmeyen; unˈpleas.ant.ness n. nahoşluk,
tatsızlık.

un.plumbed [ˈʌnˈplʌmd] adj. derinliği öl-
çülmemiş; su boruları tesisatı olmayan.

un.po.et.ic, un.po.et.i.cal ☐ [ˈʌnpəuˈetik-
(əl)] şiirsel olmayan.

un.po.lished [ˈʌnˈpɔliʃt] adj. parlatılma-
mış; fig. kaba.

un.polled [ˈʌnˈpəuld] adj. seçmen olarak
kaydedilmemiş.

un.pol.lut.ed [ˈʌnpəˈluːtid] adj. kirletilme-
miş.

un.pop.u.lar [ˈʌnˈpɔpjulə] rağbet görmeyen, benimsenmeyen, tutulmayan;
gözden düşmüş; un.pop.u.lar.i.ty [ˈ~ˈlæri-
ti] n. tutulmama; gözden düşmüş olma.

un.pos.sessed [ˈʌnpəˈzest] adj.: ~ of s.th.
bşi olmayan.

un.prac.ti.cal ☐ [ˈʌnˈpræktikəl] elverişli
(veya kullanışlı) olmayan; ˈunˈprac.ticed,
ˈunˈprac.tised [~tist] adj. acemi, deneyimsiz.

un.prec.e.dent.ed ☐ [ʌnˈpresidəntid] emsali görülmemiş, eşsiz, yeni.

un.prej.u.diced ☐ [ʌnˈpredʒudist] önyargısız, peşin hükümsüz, tarafsız, yansız.

un.pre.med.i.tat.ed ☐ [ˈʌnpriˈmediteitid]
kasıtsız; önceden tasarlanmamış.

un.pre.pared ☐ [ˈʌnpriˈpɛəd, adv. ~ridli]
hazırlıksız, tedbirsiz.

un.pre.pos.sess.ing [ˈʌnpriːpəˈzesiŋ] adj.
cazibesiz, albenisiz, alımsız.

un.pre.sent.a.ble [ˈʌnpriˈzentəbl] adj. su-
nulamaz, insan içine çıkarılamaz.

un.pre.tend.ing [ˈʌnpriˈtəndiŋ], ˈun.pre-
ˈten.tious ☐ alçak gönüllü, mütevazı.

un.prin.ci.pled [ʌnˈprinsəpld] adj. karaktersiz, ahlâksız, prensipsiz.

un.print.a.ble [ˈʌnˈprintəbl] adj. basılma-
ya elverişsiz.

un.priv.il.eged Am. [ʌnˈprivilidʒd] adj. ay-
rılacalıksız.

un.pro.duc.tive ☐ [ˈʌnprəˈdʌktiv] bereketsiz, kısır (of); † verimsiz, randımansız,
kâr getirmeyen.

un.pro.fes.sion.al ☐ [ˈʌnprəˈfeʃənl] meslek kurallarına aykırı, mesleğine yakışmaz.

un.prof.it.a.ble ☐ [ʌnˈprɔfitəbl] kârsız, kazançsız, verimsiz; boş, nafile; unˈprof-
it.a.ble.ness n. kârsızlık, verimsizlik.

un.prom.is.ing ☐ [ˈʌnˈprɔmisiŋ] ümit vermeyen.

un.prompt.ed [ʌnˈprɔmptid] adj. ihtiyari,
istemli.

un.pro.nounce.a.ble ☐ [ˈʌnprəˈnaunsəbl]
telaffuz edilemeyen.

un.pro.pi.tious ☐ [ˈʌnprəˈpiʃəs] elverişsiz,
uygunsuz.

un.pro.tect.ed ☐ [ˈʌnprəˈtektid] korunmamış, korunmasız; himaye görmeyen.

un.proved [ˈʌnˈpruːvd] adj. ispatlanma-
mış.

un.pro.vid.ed [ˈʌnprəˈvaidid] adj. yoksun
(with -den); ~ for ihtiyacı karşılanmamış.

un.pro.voked ☐ [ˈʌnprəˈvəukt] kışkırtılma-
mış, tahrik edilmemiş.

un.pub.lished [ˈʌnˈpʌbliʃt] adj. basılmamış, yayımlanmamış.

un.punc.tu.al ☐ [ˈʌnˈpʌŋktjuəl] dakik olmayan, tam zamanında gelmeyen; un-
punc.tu.al.i.ty [ˈ~ˈæliti] n. dakik olmayış.

un.pun.ished [ʌnˈpʌniʃt] adj. cezalandı-
rılmamış; go ~ cezasız kalmak.

un.qual.i.fied [ʌnˈkwɔlifaid] ehliyetsiz,
yetersiz; şartsız; sınırsız; F tam, kesin,
müthiş.

un.quench.a.ble ☐ [ʌnˈkwentʃəbl] söndürülemez, bastırılamaz (a. fig.).

un.ques.tion.a.ble ☐ [ʌnˈkwestʃənəbl] şüphe götürmez, kesin, muhakkak; unˈques-
tioned adj. kesin, şüphesiz; sorgusuz;
unˈques.tion.ing ☐ kayıtsız şartsız.

un.qui.et [ʌnˈkwaiət] adj. rahatsız, huzursuz, endişeli.

un.quote [ˈʌnˈkwəut] vb. tırnak işaretini
kapamak; unˈquot.ed adj. borsa: kayıtlı
olmayan.

un.rav.el [ʌnˈrævəl] v/t. & v/i. sök(ül)-
mek, çöz(ül)mek.

un.read [ˈʌnˈred] adj. okunmamış; cahil;
un.read.a.ble [ˈʌnˈriːdəbl] adj. okunmaz.

okunaksız.

**un.read.i.ness** ['ʌn'redinis] *n.* hazırlıksızlık; **'un'read.y** ☐ hazırlıksız, hazır olmayan; yavaş, ağır.

**un.re.al** ☐ ['ʌn'riəl] gerçek olmayan, gerçek dışı, hayalî, asılsız; **un.re.al.is.tic** ['ʌnriə'listik] *adj.* gerçekçi olmayan; gerçeğe uymayan; **un.re.al.i.ty** ['~'æliti] *n.* gerçeksizlik; **'un're.al.iz.a.ble** [~əlaizəbl] *adj.* gerçekleştirilemez; † satılmaz.

**un.rea.son** ['ʌn'riːzn] *n.* mantıksızlık; saçmalık; **un'rea.son.a.ble** ☐ makûl olmayan, mantıksız; aşırı.

**un.re.claimed** ['ʌnri'kleimd] *adj.* yeniden talep edilmemiş; işlenmemiş *(toprak).*

**un.rec.og.niz.a.ble** ☐ ['ʌn'rekəgnaizəbl] tanınmaz; **'un'rec.og.nized** ☐ tanınmamış.

**un.rec.om.pensed** ['ʌn'rekəmpenst] *adj.* mükâfatlandırılmamış.

**un.rec.on.ciled** ['ʌn'rekənsaild] *adj.* uzlaşmamış, barışmamış.

**un.re.cord.ed** ['ʌnri'kɔːdid] *adj.* kaydedilmemiş.

**un.re.dee.med** ☐ ['ʌnri'diːmd] rehinden kurtarılmamış; *fig.* yerine getirilmemiş, tutulmamış *(söz vs.).*

**un.re.dressed** ['ʌnri'drest] *adj.* düzeltilmemiş.

**un.reel** ['ʌn'riːl] *v/t.* & *v/i.* makaradan çöz(ül)mek.

**un.re.fined** ['ʌnri'faind]' *adj.* tasfiye edilmemiş, ham; *fig.* inceliksiz, kaba.

**un.re.flect.ing** ☐ ['ʌnri'flektiŋ] yansımasız, aksetmeyen.

**un.re.formed** ['ʌnri'fɔːmd] *adj.* düzeltilmemiş; yola gelmemiş.

**un.re.gard.ed** ['ʌnri'gɑːdid] *adj.* önemsenmemiş; **'un.re'gard.ful** [~ful] *adj.* dikkatsiz (of *-e karşı).*

**un.reg.is.tered** ['ʌn'redʒistəd] *adj.* kaydedilmemiş; taahhütlü gönderilmemiş *(mektup).*

**un.re.lat.ed** ['ʌnri'leitid] *adj.* ilgisiz, alâkasız (to *-e karşı).*

**un.re.lent.ing** ☐ ['ʌnri'lentiŋ] acımasız, amansız, sert, şiddetli; gevşemeyen.

**un.re.li.a.ble** ['ʌnri'laiəbl] *adj.* güvenilmez, inanılmaz.

**un.re.lieved** ☐ ['ʌnri'liːvd] hafiflememiş, dinmemiş, rahatlamamış; monoton, tekdüzen.

**un.re.mit.ting** ☐ [ʌnri'mitiŋ] sürekli, devamlı, aralıksız.

**un.re.mu.ner.a.tive** ☐ ['ʌnri'mjuːnərətiv] kârsız, kazançsız.

**un.re.pealed** ['ʌnri'piːld] *adj.* feshedilmemiş.

**un.re.pent.ed** ['ʌnri'pentid] *adj.* pişmanlık

duymamış.

**un.re.pin.ing** ☐ ['ʌnri'painiŋ] halinden memnun.

**un.re.quit.ed** ☐ ['ʌnri'kwaitid] karşılıksız, karşılık görmeyen; ödüllendirilmemiş.

**un.re.served** ☐ ['ʌnri'zəːvd, *adv.* ~vidli] sınırlanmamış; samimî, açık sözlü, serbest.

**un.re.sist.ing** ☐ ['ʌnri'zistiŋ] karşı koymayan, dirençsiz.

**un.re.spon.sive** ['ʌnris'pɔnsiv] *adj.* tepki göstermeyen (to *-e).*

**un.rest** ['ʌn'rest] *n.* kargaşa, huzursuzluk; rahatsızlık; **'un'rest.ing** ☐ dur durak bilmeyen.

**un.re.strained** ☐ ['ʌnris'treind] frenlenmemiş, denetsiz, serbest.

**un.re.strict.ed** ☐ ['ʌnris'triktid] sınırsız, kısıtsız; hız sınırı olmayan *(yol).*

**un.re.vealed** ['ʌnri'viːld] *adj.* açıklanmamış.

**un.re.ward.ed** ['ʌnri'wɔːdid] *adj.* ödüllendirilmemiş.

**un.rhymed** ['ʌn'raimd] *adj.* kafiyesiz.

**un.rid.dle** ['ʌn'ridl] *v/t.* çözmek, halletmek.

**un.rig** ↓ ['ʌn'rig] *v/t. -den* donanımı çıkarmak.

**un.right.eous** ☐ [ʌn'raitʃəs] haksız, adaletsiz; günahkâr, kötü.

**un.rip** ['ʌn'rip] *v/t.* dikişlerini sökmek; parçalamak.

**un.ripe** ['ʌn'raip] *adj.* ham; erken gelişmiş; hazırlıksız.

**un.ri.val(l)ed** [ʌn'raivəld] *adj.* eşsiz, emsalsiz; rakipsiz.

**un.roll** ['ʌn'rəul] *v/t.* & *v/i.* aç(ıl)mak, yay(ıl)mak; göz önüne sermek.

**un.roof** ['ʌn'ruːf] *v/t. -in* çatısını *veya* üstünü açmak.

**un.rope** mount. ['ʌn'rəup] *v/t.* & *v/i.* çöz(ül)mek.

**un.ruf.fled** ['ʌn'rʌfld] *adj.* sakin, soğukkanlı.

**un.ruled** ['ʌn'ruːld] *adj. k-ne* hâkim olamayan; çizgisiz *(kâğıt).*

**un.rul.y** [ʌn'ruːli] *adj.* azılı; itaatsiz, asi; ele avuca sığmaz.

**un.sad.dle** ['ʌn'sædl] *v/t. -in* eyerini çıkarmak; eyerden düşürmek.

**un.safe** ☐ ['ʌn'seif] emniyetsiz, güvensiz, tehlikeli.

**un.said** ['ʌn'sed] *adj.* söylenmemiş, bahsedilmemiş.

**un.sal(e).a.ble** ['ʌn'seiləbl] *adj.* satılamaz.

**un.salt.ed** ['ʌn'sɔːltid] *adj.* tuzlanmamış.

**un.sanc.tioned** ['ʌn'sæŋkʃənd] *adj.* onaylanmamış.

**un.san.i.tar.y** ['ʌn'sænitəri] *adj.* sağlıkla ilgili olmayan.

**un.sat.is.fac.to.ry** □ [ˌʌnsætisˈfæktəri] memnuniyet vermeyen; yetersiz, tatmin etmeyen; **ˈunˈsat.is.fled** [-faid] *adj.* giderilmemiş; hoşnut kalmamış; **ˈunˈsat-is.fy.ing** □ [-faiiŋ] = unsatisfactory.

**un.sa.vo(u)r.y** □ [ˈʌnˈseivəri] tatsız, lezzetsiz, yavan; *fig.* çirkin, kötü, rezil.

**un.say** [ˈʌnˈsei] (*irr.* say) *v/t.* geri almak *(sözünü).*

**un.scathed** [ˈʌnˈskeiðd] *adj.* yaralanmamış, incinmemiş.

**un.schooled** [ˈʌnˈskuːld] *adj.* cahil, tahsilsiz; doğal.

**un.sci.en.tif.ic** [ˈʌnsaiənˈtifik] *adj.* (-ally) bilimsel olmayan; bilime aykırı.

**un.screw** [ˈʌnˈskruː] *v/t.* -*in* vidalarını sökmek; çevirerek açmak -*i.*

**un.script.ur.al** □ [ˈʌnˈskriptʃərəl] Kitabı Mukaddes'e aykırı.

**un.scru.pu.lous** □ [ʌnˈskruːpjuləs] vicdansız; prensipsiz.

**un.seal** [ˈʌnˈsiːl] *v/t.* -*in* mührünü bozmak *veya* açmak.

**un.search.a.ble** □ [ʌnˈsəːtʃəbl] anlaşılmaz; keşfedilmez.

**un.sea.son.a.ble** □ [ʌnˈsiːznəbl] mevsimsiz; *fig.* zamansız, vakitsiz; **ˈunˈsea-soned** *adj.* yaş *(tahta); fig.* olgunlaşmamış; baharatsız *(yemek).*

**un.seat** [ˈʌnˈsiːt] *v/t.* görevden almak, azletmek; binicisini düşürmek *(at);* be -ed görevden alınmak.

**un.sea.wor.thy** ↓ [ˈʌnˈsiːwəːði] *adj.* denize çıkmaya elverişsiz.

**un.seem.li.ness** [ʌnˈsiːmlinis] *n.* uygunsuzluk; **unˈseem.ly** *adj.* uygunsuz, yakışıksız, yakışık almaz *(davranış vs.).*

**un.seen** [ˈʌnˈsiːn] **1.** *adj.* görülmemiş; görünmez, gizli; **2.** *n. okul:* tercüme, çeviri; the - ahret, öbür dünya.

**un.self.ish** □ [ˈʌnˈselfiʃ] kendini düşünmeyen, bencil olmayan, özverili; **ˈunˈself.ish.ness** *n.* kendini düşünmeme, özveri.

**un.sen.ti.men.tal** [ˈʌnsentiˈmentl] *adj.* hissi olmayan, hissiz, duygusuz.

**un.serv.ice.a.ble** □ [ˈʌnˈsəːvisəbl] işe yaramaz.

**un.set.tle** [ˈʌnˈsetl] *v/t.* & *v/i.* yerinden çık(ar)mak; tedirgin etm.; düzenini bozmak; tedirgin olm.; **ˈunˈset.tled** *adj.* kararlaştırılmamış; henüz yerleş(il)memiş; belirsiz; boş; değişken, dönek *(hava);* † ödenmemiş, kapanmamış *(borç);* kararsız; düzensiz.

**un.sex** [ˈʌnˈseks] *v/t.* cinsiyetinden yoksun kılmak.

**un.shack.le** [ˈʌnˈʃækl] *v/t.* -*in* zincirlerini çıkarmak.

**un.shak.en** [ˈʌnˈʃeikən] *adj.* sarsılmaz, metin; sabit.

**un.shape.ly** [ˈʌnˈʃeipli] *adj.* biçimsiz, şekilsiz.

**un.shav.en** [ˈʌnˈʃeivn] *adj.* tıraşı uzamış.

**un.sheathe** [ˈʌnˈʃiːð] *v/t.* kınından çıkarmak.

**un.shell** [ˈʌnˈʃel] *v/t.* -*in* kabuğunu soymak.

**un.ship** [ˈʌnˈʃip] *v/t.* gemiden çıkarmak, boşaltmak; fora etm. *(kürek);* F *fig.* -*den* kurtulmak.

**un.shod** [ˈʌnˈʃɔd] *adj.* yalınayak; nalsız.

**un.shorn** [ˈʌnˈʃɔːn] *adj.* saçı kesilmemiş.

**un.shrink.a.ble** [ˈʌnˈʃriŋkəbl] *adj.* çekmez, büzülmez; **ˈunˈshrink.ing** □ çekinmesiz, sarsılmaz; çekmeyen.

**un.sight.ed** [ʌnˈsaitid] *adj.* nişangâhsız, **unˈsight.ly** *adj.* çirkin, göz zevkini bozan, göze batan.

**un.signed** [ˈʌnˈsaind] *adj.* imzalanmamış.

**un.skil(l).ful** □ [ˈʌnˈskilful] beceriksiz, hünersiz, acemi; **ˈunˈskilled** *adj.* beceriksiz, maharetsiz, ehliyetsiz; hüner gerektirmeyen *(iş).*

**un.skimmed** [ˈʌnˈskimd] *adj.* kaymağı alınmamış.

**un.sleep.ing** [ˈʌnˈsliːpiŋ] *adj.* uykusuz.

**un.so.cia.ble** [ʌnˈsəuʃəbl] *adj.* çekingen, konuşmayan, kaçınık ,çekilgen; **unˈso-cial** *adj.* insandan kaçan, kaçınık, yabani.

**un.sold** [ˈʌnˈsəuld] *adj.* satılmamış.

**un.sol.der** [ˈʌnˈsɔldə] *v/t.* -*in* lehimini çıkarmak.

**un.sol.dier.ly** [ˈʌnˈsəuldʒəli] *adj.* askere yakışmaz.

**un.so.lic.it.ed** [ˈʌnsəˈlisitid] *adj.* istenilmemiş; davetsiz.

**un.solv.a.ble** [ˈʌnˈsɔlvəbl] *adj.* çözülemez, halledilemez; **ˈunˈsolved** *adj.* çözülemiş, halledilmemiş.

**un.so.phis.ti.cat.ed** [ˈʌnsəˈfistikeitid] *adj.* saf, bön, acemi, tecrübesiz; basit, sade; halis, katkısız.

**un.sought** [ˈʌnˈsɔːt] *adj.* araştırılmamış.

**un.sound** □ [ˈʌnˈsaund] sağlam olmayan, çürük, derme çatma; hastalıklı, sıhhatsiz; hafif *(uyku);* gerçeksiz; geçersiz; of - mind şuuru bozuk.

**un.spar.ing** □ [ˈʌnˈspɛəriŋ] esirgemeyen (of, in -*i*); bol, çok (of -*i*), acımasız, zalim.

**un.speak.a.ble** □ [ʌnˈspiːkəbl] kelimelerle anlatılamaz, tarife sığmaz; yakışıksız, ağıza alınmaz.

**un.spec.i.fied** [ˈʌnˈspesifaid] *adj.* kesinlikle belirtilmemiş.

**un.spent** [ˈʌnˈspent] *adj.* sarfedilmemiş, harcanmamış.

**un.spoiled** [ˈʌnˈspɔild] *adj.*, **ˈunˈspoilt** [˷t] bozulmamış; şımarmamış.

**un.spo.ken** [ˈʌnˈspəukən] *adj.* açığa vurulmamış, söylenmemiş.

**un.sport.ing** [ˈʌnˈspɔːtiŋ] *adj.*, **un.sportsman.like** [ˈʌnˈspɔːtsmənlaik] sportmence olmayan.

**un.spot.ted** [ˈʌnˈspɔtid] *adj.* lekesiz, beneksiz; *fig.* temiz, pak, arı.

**un.sta.ble** □ [ˈʌnˈsteibl] sağlam olmayan; kararsız, dönek, gelgeç; düzensiz, değişken.

**un.stained** *fig.* [ˈʌnˈsteind] *adj.* lekesiz, kusursuz.

**un.stamped** [ˈʌnˈstæmpt] *adj.* damgalanmamış; ♦ pulsuz.

**un.states.man.like** [ˈʌnˈsteitsmənlaik] *adj.* devlet adamına yakışmaz.

**un.stead.y** □ [ˈʌnˈstedi] sallanan, oynak; titrek; düzensiz; değişken, kararsız, güvenilmez.

**un.stint.ed** [ʌnˈstintid] *adj.* kayıtsız şartsız, sınırsız.

**un.stitch** [ˈʌnˈstitʃ] *v/t.* -in dikişlerini sökmek.

**un.stop** [ˈʌnˈstɔp] *v/t.* açmak; -in tıkacını çıkarmak.

**un.strained** [ˈʌnˈstreind] *adj.* süzülmemiş; *fig.* tabii.

**un.strap** [ˈʌnˈstræp] *v/t.* -in kayışını çıkarmak *veya* gevşetmek.

**un.stressed** [ˈʌnˈstrest] *adj.* vurgusuz.

**un.string** [ˈʌnˈstriŋ] (*irr.* string) *v/t.* -in tellerini çıkarmak *veya* gevşetmek; zayıflatmak, bozmak (*sinir*); **un.strung** [ˈʌnˈstrʌŋ] *adj.* gevşek; *fig.* sinirleri bozuk, sinirli.

**un.stuck** [ˈʌnˈstʌk] *adj.*: come ˷ açılmak, ayrılmak; *sl.* başarısız olm.; suya düşmek (*plan vs.*).

**un.stud.ied** [ˈʌnˈstʌdid] *adj.* tabii, doğal; çalışılmamış; çalışma ile öğrenilmemiş, plansız.

**un.sub.dued** [ˈʌnsəbˈdjuːd] *adj.* boyun eğmemiş.

**un.sub.mis.sive** □ [ˈʌnsəbˈmisiv] itaatsiz, boyun eğmez, serkeş, dik kafalı.

**un.sub.stan.tial** □ [ˈʌnsəbˈstænʃəl] cisimsiz; hayali; asılsız.

**un.suc.cess.ful** □ [ˈʌnsəkˈsesful] başarısız; **ˈun.sucˈcess.ful.ness** *n.* başarısızlık.

**un.suit.a.ble** □ [ˈʌnˈsjuːtəbl] uygunsuz, yakışıksız; **ˈunˈsuit.ed** *adj.* uymamış, yakışmamış (for, to -e).

**un.sul.lied** [ˈʌnˈsʌlid] *adj.* lekesiz, (ter)temiz.

**un.sup.port.ed** [ˈʌnsəˈpɔːtid] *adj.* desteksiz.

**un.sure** [ˈʌnˈʃuə] *adj.* emin olmayan; emniyetsiz.

**un.sur.passed** [ˈʌnsəˈpɑːst] *adj.* geçilemez, üstün, eşsiz.

**un.sus.pect.ed** [ˈʌnsəsˈpektid] *adj.* şüphelenilmeyen; **ˈun.susˈpect.ing** *adj.* masum, saf; *pred.* kuşkulanmayan (of -den).

**un.sus.pi.cious** □ [ˈʌnsəsˈpiʃəs] şüpheci olmayan, kalbi temiz, kuşkusuz.

**un.swear** [ˈʌnˈsweə] (*irr.* swear) *v/i.* sözünden *veya* yemininden dönmek.

**un.swerv.ing** □ [ˈʌnˈswəːviŋ] değişmez; sapmaz.

**un.sworn** [ˈʌnˈswɔːn] *adj.* yeminli olmayan (*tanık*).

**un.tack** [ˈʌnˈtæk] *v/t.* çıkarmak, sökmek.

**un.taint.ed** □ [ˈʌnˈteintid] lekesiz; *fig.* namuslu.

**un.tam(e).a.ble** [ˈʌnˈteiməbl] *adj.* evcilleştirilemez; **ˈunˈtamed** *adj.* evcilleştirilemiş, yabani.

**un.tan.gle** [ˈʌnˈtæŋgl] *v/t.* açmak, çözmek.

**un.tanned** [ˈʌnˈtænd] *adj.* tabaklanmamış.

**un.tar.nished** [ˈʌnˈtɑːniʃt] *adj.* lekesiz, kararmamış.

**un.tast.ed** [ˈʌnˈteistid] *adj.* tadılmamış.

**un.taught** [ˈʌnˈtɔːt] *adj.* cahil, tahsilsiz; doğal, doğuştan olan.

**un.taxed** [ˈʌnˈtækst] *adj.* vergilendirilmemiş.

**un.teach.a.ble** [ˈʌnˈtiːtʃəbl] *adj.* söz dinlemez (*kimse*); öğretilemez.

**un.tem.per.a.men.tal** [ˈʌntempərəˈmentl] *adj.* cansız, ruhsuz.

**un.tem.pered** [ˈʌnˈtempəd] *adj.* ⊕ tavlanmamış, su verilmemiş.

**un.ten.a.ble** [ˈʌnˈtenəbl] *adj.* savunulamaz.

**un.ten.ant.ed** [ˈʌnˈtenəntid] *adj.* kiralanmamış, şenelmemiş, kiracısız, boş.

**un.thank.ful** □ [ˈʌnˈθæŋkful] nankör; istenmeyen, hoş karşılanmayan.

**un.think.a.ble** [ˈʌnˈθiŋkəbl] *adj.* düşünülemez, akla gelmez, olanaksız; **ˈunˈthinking** □ düşüncesiz; düşüncesizce yapılan.

**un.thought** [ˈʌnˈθɔːt] *adj.* düşünülmemiş; ˷-of beklenmedik, akla hayale gelmedik.

**un.thread** [ˈʌnˈθred] *v/t.* -in ipliğini çıkarmak; *fig.* yolunu bulmak, k-ne yol açmak.

**un.thrift.y** □ [ˈʌnˈθrifti] savurgan, tutumsuz.

**un.ti.dy** □ [ʌnˈtaidi] düzensiz, tertipsiz, dağınık, şapşal.

**un.tie** [ˈʌnˈtai] *v/t. & v/i.* çöz(ül)mek.

aç(ıl)mak; halletmek.

**un.til** [ənˈtil] *prp. & cj.* -e kadar, -e değin, e- dek; not ~ -den önce değil.

**un.tilled** [ˈʌnˈtild] *adj.* işlenmemiş *(toprak).*

**un.time.ly** [ʌnˈtaimli] *adj.* vakitsiz, zamansız, mevsimsiz; uygunsuz, yersiz.

**un.tir.ing** □ [ʌnˈtaiəriŋ] yorulmak bilmez.

**un.to** [ˈʌntu] = to.

**un.told** [ˈʌnˈtəuld] *adj.* anlatılmamış; hesapsız, sayısız, haddi hesabı olmayan, muazzam.

**un.touched** [ˈʌnˈtʌtʃt] *adj.* dokunulmamış; *fig.* etkilenmemiş; *phot.* rötuşsuz.

**un.to.ward** [ʌnˈtəuəd] *adj.* uygunsuz, münasebetsiz; bahtsız, şanssız; aksi, ters, huysuz.

**un.trained** [ˈʌnˈtreind] *adj.* eğitilmemiş; tecrübesiz, acemi.

**un.tram.mel(l)ed** [ʌnˈtræməld] *adj.* engellenmemiş, serbest.

**un.trans.fer.a.ble** [ˈʌntrænsˈfəːrəbl] *adj.* nakledilemez; devredilemez.

**un.trans.lat.a.ble** [ˈʌntrænsˈleitəbl] *adj.* tercüme edilemez, çevrilemez.

**un.trav.el(l)ed** [ˈʌnˈtrævld] *adj.* kullanılmayan *(yol)*; dar kafalı *(kimse)*.

**un.tried** [ˈʌnˈtraid] *adj.* denenmemiş; ☼ yargılanmamış.

**un.trimmed** [ˈʌnˈtrimd] *adj.* budanmamış; kesilip düzeltilmemiş *(saç vs.)*.

**un.trod, un.trod.den** [ˈʌnˈtrɔd(n)] *adj.* ayak basılmamış, bakir.

**un.trou.bled** [ˈʌnˈtrʌbld] *adj.* sıkıntısız, dertsiz; durgun, sakin.

**un.true** □ [ˈʌnˈtruː] yalan, sahte, yanlış; sadakatsiz, hakikatsiz, vefasız.

**un.trust.wor.thy** □ [ˈʌnˈtrʌstwəːði] güvenilmez, dönek.

**un.truth** [ˈʌnˈtruːθ] *n.* yalan; sahtelik; vefasızlık.

**un.tu.tored** [ˈʌnˈtjuːtəd] *adj.* eğitilmemiş, cahil, tahsilsiz, saf, bön.

**un.twine** [ˈʌnˈtwain], **un.twist** [ˈʌnˈtwist] *v/t. & v/i.* aç(ıl)mak, çöz(ül)mek.

**un.used** [ˈʌnˈjuːzd] *adj.* kullanılmamış; [ˈʌnˈjuːst] alışık olmayan *(to -e)*; **un.u.su.al** □ [ʌnˈjuːʒuəl] görülmedik, nadir; olağandışı, garip, acayip.

**un.ut.ter.a.ble** □ [ʌnˈʌtərəbl] ağıza alınmaz, söylenmez, anlatılamaz.

**un.val.ued** [ˈʌnˈvæljuːd] *adj.* değer verilmemiş, önemsenmemiş; paha biçilmemiş.

**un.var.ied** [ʌnˈvɛərid] *adj.* değişmemiş.

**un.var.nished** [ˈʌnˈvɑːniʃt] *adj.* cilasız; *fig.* sade, süssüz; dürüst; salt *(gerçek)*.

**un.var.y.ing** □ [ʌnˈvɛəriiŋ] değişmez.

**un.veil** [ʌnˈveil] *v/t.* -in örtüsünü *(veya* peçesini) açmak; açığa vurmak, ortaya çıkarmak.

**un.versed** [ˈʌnˈvəːst] *adj.* deneyimsiz, acemi (in -de).

**un.voiced** [ˈʌnˈvɔist] *adj.* açıklanmamış, söylenmemiş; *gr.* ünsüz, sessiz.

**un.vouched** [ˈʌnˈvautʃt] *adj. a.* ~-for doğrulanmamış.

**un.want.ed** [ˈʌnˈwɔntid] *adj.* istenilmez, istenmeyen.

**un.war.i.ness** [ʌnˈwɛərinis] *n.* gaflet, tedbirsizlik.

**un.war.like** [ˈʌnˈwɔːlaik] *adj.* barışçı, barışsever.

**un.war.rant.a.ble** □ [ʌnˈwɔrəntəbl] affedilemez, haklı sayılmaz; özürsüz; **ˈunˈwar.rant.ed** *adj.* haksız, özürsüz.

**un.war.y** □ [ˈʌnˈwɛəri] gafil, dikkatsiz, tedbirsiz.

**un.washed** [ˈʌnˈwɔʃt] *adj.* yıkanmamış.

**un.wa.tered** [ˈʌnˈwɔːtəd] *adj.* sulanmamış.

**un.wa.ver.ing** [ʌnˈweivəriŋ] *adj.* değişmez, sabit, kararlı.

**un.wea.ried** [ʌnˈwiərid], **un.wea.ry.ing** □ [ʌnˈwiəriiŋ] yorulmak bilmez, usanmaz; yorulmamış.

**un.wel.come** [ʌnˈwelkəm] *adj.* hoş karşılanmayan, istenilmeyen; hoşa gitmeyen, tatsız.

**un.well** [ˈʌnˈwel] *adj.* rahatsız, keyifsiz, hasta.

**un.whole.some** [ˈʌnˈhəulsəm] *adj.* sıhhate zararlı; sakat, sıhhatsiz; bozuk; iğrenç.

**un.wield.y** □ [ʌnˈwiːldi] hantal, kaba, kocaman; ❧ havaleli.

**un.will.ing** □ [ˈʌnˈwiliŋ] isteksiz, gönülsüz; istemeyerek yapılan *veya* verilen; be ~ to do bş yapmaya isteksiz olm.; be ~ for s.th. to be done bşin yapılmasına isteksiz olm.

**un.wind** [ˈʌnˈwaind] *(irr.* wind) *v/t. & v/i.* çöz(ül)mek, aç(ıl)mak, gevşe(t)mek; rahatla(t)mak.

**un.wis.dom** [ˈʌnˈwizdəm] *n.* akılsızlık; **un.wise** □ [ˈʌnˈwaiz] akılsız; makûl olmayan.

**un.wished** [ʌnˈwiʃt] *adj.* dileğinden vaz geçmiş; ~-for arzu edilmemiş.

**un.wit.ting** □ [ʌnˈwitiŋ] farkında olmayan, habersiz; kasıtsız.

**un.wom.an.ly** [ʌnˈwumənli] *adj.* kadına yakışmaz, kadınca olmayan.

**un.wont.ed** □ [ʌnˈwəuntid] alışılmamış *(to -e)*; nadir, olağandışı.

**un.work.a.ble** [ˈʌnˈwəːkəbl] *adj.* kullanışsız; ⊕ işlenemez.

**un.world.ly** [ˈʌnˈwəːldli] *adj.* tinsel, ruhanî, manevî.

**un.wor.thy** □ [ʌnˈwəːði] değmez; yakışmaz, uygunsuz; lâyık olmayan (of -e); değersiz.

**un.wrap** [ˈʌnˈræp] v/t. & v/i. aç(ıl)mak, çöz(ül)mek.

**un.wrin.kle** [ˈʌnˈriŋkl] v/t. -in kırışıklarını gidermek.

**un.writ.ten** [ˈʌnˈritn] adj. yazılmamış; geleneksel; yazısız, boş.

**un.wrought** [ˈʌnˈrɔːt] adj. işlenmemiş, ham...

**un.yield.ing** □ [ʌnˈjiːldiŋ] boyun eğmez, direngen; sert.

**un.yoke** [ˈʌnˈjəuk] v/t. boyunduruktan kurtarmak; ayırmak; v/i. boyunduruktan kurtulmak.

**up** [ʌp] **1.** adv. yukarı(ya); yukarıda; yükseğe; yüksek mevkiye; öne, ileri(ye); ♪ tize doğru; -e kadar; tamamen; kuzeye doğru; come ~ to s.o. b-ne yaklaşmak; ~ and about hastalıktan kurtulmuş, ayağa kalkmış; be hard ~ eli darda olm.; ~ against a task bir işle karşı karşıya olm.; ~ to -e kadar; s. date² 1; be ~ to s.th. bşe eşit olm.; fig. dolap çevirmek, halt karıştırmak; it is ~ to me to do yapması bana kalmış; s. mark 1; the time is ~ vakit doldu; what are you ~ to there? orada ne halt ˌkarıştırıyorsun?; what's ~ sl. ne oluyor?, ne var?; ~ with ile aynı hizada; it's all ~ with him hapı yuttu, yandı, ayvayı yedi; **2.** int. kalk!; yukarı(ya)!; **3.** prp. yukarıya, yukarıda; ileride; içeride; -e, -a; ~ the hill tepeye; **4.** adj. yükselmiş; yataktan kalkmış; ayakta; yüksek, kabarık; üstün; hazır, yapılmış; ata binmiş; haberdar; yargılanmakta; ~ train şehir treni; **5.** n. the ~s and downs pl. iniş çıkışlar, iyi ve kötü günler; **6.** v/t. & v/i. F yüksel(t)mek; artırmak; ayağa kalkmak; kaldırmak.

**up-and-com.ing** Am. F [ˈʌpənˈkʌmiŋ] adj. ümit verici; başarı vadeden, girişken.

**up.braid** [ʌpˈbreid] v/t. azarlamak, paylamak, haşlamak (s.o. with veya for s.th. b-ni bşden dolayı).

**up.bring.ing** [ˈʌpbriŋiŋ] n. yetiş(tir)me, terbiye.

**up.build** [ˈʌpˈbild] (irr. build) v/t. inşa (veya bina) etm.

**up.cast** [ˈʌpkɑːst] n. yukarıya at(ıl)ma, yukarıya çevirme veya çevrilme; a. ~ shaft ✕ hava bacası.

**up-coun.try** [ˈʌpˈkʌntri] **1.** adj. sahilden uzak, iç taraftaki, iç kesimdeki; **2.** adv. iç kesimlere doğru.

**up-cur.rent** ⚓ [ˈʌpkʌrənt] yükselen hava akımı.

**up.grade** **1.** [ˈʌpgreid] n. yokuş; artış; on the ~ fig. iyileşmekte; gelişmekte; artmakta; **2.** [ʌpˈgreid]v/t. -in kalitesini artırmak; -in rütbesini yükseltmek.

**up.heav.al** [ʌpˈhiːvəl] n. geol. yer kabuğunun kabarması; fig. karışıklık, ayaklanma, devrim.

**up.hill** [ˈʌpˈhil] adj. & adv. yokuş yukarı (giden); yükselen; fig. zor, güç, çetin.

**up.hold** [ʌpˈhəuld] (irr. hold) v/t. kaldırmak; tutmak, desteklemek; onaylamak; onamak, uygun bulmak; **up¹hold.er** n. fig. destek, savunucu kimse, arka.

**up.hol.ster** [ʌpˈhəulstə] v/t. döşemek, kaplamak (koltuk vs.); **up¹hol.ster.er** n. döşemeci; **up¹hol.ster.y** n. döşemecili⁻; döşemelik eşya, mefruşat.

**up.keep** [ˈʌpkiːp] n. bakım (masrafı).

**up.land** [ˈʌplənd] **1.** n. oft. ~s pl. yüksek arazi, yayla; **2.** adj. yüksek.

**up.lift 1.** [ʌpˈlift] v/t. fig. yüceltmek; **2.** [ˈ~] n. arazi çıkıntısı; sütyen; fig. yüceltme.

**up.most** [ˈʌpməust] = uppermost.

**up.on** [əˈpɔn] = on.

**up.per** [ˈʌpə] **1.** adj. üst(teki); yukarıdaki; the ~ ten (thousand) onbinden fazlası; **2.** n. mst ~s pl. saya, ayakkabı yüzü; be (down) on one's ~s F meteliğe kurşun atmak, cebi delik (veya züğürt) olm.; **¹~.cut** n. boks: aparküt, aperkat; **¹~.most** adj. en üst, en yukarıdaki; akla ilk gelen, başlıca.

**up.pish** □ F [ˈʌpiʃ] kibirli, kendini beğenmiş.

**up.pi.ty** F [ˈʌpiti] adj. kibirli, kendini beğenmiş.

**up.raise** [ʌpˈreiz] v/t. yükseltmek, kaldırmak.

**up.rear** [ʌpˈriə] v/t. & v/i. yüksel(t)mek; dikmek.

**up.right 1.** □ [ˈʌpˈrait] dik(ey); fig. [ˈ~] dürüst, namuslu, âdil; **2.** [ˈ~] n. direk; dik duran şey; = ~ pia.no ♪ dik (veya düz) piyano.

**up.ris.ing** [ʌpˈraiziŋ] n. ayaklanma, isyan.

**up.roar** fig. [ˈʌprɔː] n. şamata, gürültü; kargaşa; **up¹roar.i.ous** □ gürültülü; kahkahadan kırıp geçiren.

**up.root** [ʌpˈruːt] v/t. kökünden sökmek; yerini değiştirme, uzaklaştırma; kökünü kazıma, yok etm.

**up.set** [ʌpˈset] **1.** (irr. set) v/t. devirmek, altüst etm. (a. fig.); bozmak; sinirlendirmek; hükümsüz kılmak; bozguna uğratmak; düzenini bozmak, karıştırmak;

⊕ döverek kısaltıp kalınlaştırmak; be ~ keyfi kaçmak; *v/i.* devrilmek, altüst olm.; **2.** *n.* devrilme, altüst olma; *spor:* bozguh, sürprizli yenilgi; bozukluk, bozulma; stomach ~ mide bozulması; sarsıntı, şok; ~ **price** açık arttırmada satıcının koyduğu en düşük fiyat.

**up.shot** [ˈʌpʃɔt] *n.* netice, sonuç, son; **in the ~** sonunda.

**up.side** *adv.* [ˈʌpsaid]: ~ **down** tepetaklak, tepesi üstü, ters; *fig.* altüst; turn ~ down altüst etm., altını üstüne getirmek.

**up.stage** F *fig.* [ˈʌpˈsteidʒ] *adj.* kibirli, kendini beğenmiş.

**up.stairs** [ˈʌpˈstɛəz] **1.** *adj.* üst kattaki, yukarıdaki; **2.** *adv.* üst kat(t)a, yukarıya, yukarıda; **3.** *n.* üst kat.

**up.stand.ing** [ʌpˈstændiŋ] *adj.* dik; gürbüz, sağlıklı; dürüst.

**up.start** [ˈʌpstɑːt] **1.** *n.* birden zengin olan kimse; **2.** *adj.* türedi, sonradan görme.

**up.state** *Am.* [ˈʌpˈsteit] *n.* taşra.

**up.stream** [ˈʌpˈstriːm] *adv.* akıntıya karşı; nehrin yukarısına doğru.

**up.stroke** [ˈʌpstrəuk] *n. (yazı)* yukarı doğru çekilen kuyruk.

**up.surge** [ˈʌpsəːdʒ] *n.* kabarma, hızlı artış.

**up.swing** [ˈʌpswiŋ] *n.* yukarıya sallanma; ilerleme, yükselme, iyileşme.

**up.take** [ˈʌpteik] *n.* kavrama, anlama; be slow (quick) in *veya* on the ~ F yavaş (çabuk) kavramak, anlamak.

**up.throw** [ˈʌpθrəu] *n.* yukarıya fırlatma.

**up-to-date** [ˈʌptəˈdeit] *adj.* modern, asrî, çağcıl, güncel, çağdaş.

**up-town** [ˈʌpˈtəun] *adj. & adv.* şehir merkezinin dışında(ki).

**up.turn** [ʌpˈtəːn] *v/t. & v/i.* yukarı dön(dür)mek.

**up.ward** [ˈʌpwəd] **1.** *adj.* yükselen, yukarı doğru giden; **2.** *adv.* = **up.wards** [~z] yukarıya doğru, yukarı; ~ of -den fazla.

**u.ra.ni.um** [juəˈreinjəm] *n.* uranyum.

**ur.ban** [ˈəːbən] *adj.* şehre ait, şehir...; **ur.bane** [əːˈbein] görgülü, nazik, kibar; **ur.ban.i.ty** [əːˈbæniti] *n.* nezaket, kibarlık; **ur.ban.i.za.tion** [əːbənaiˈzeiʃən] *n.* kentleşme, şehirleşme; **ur.ban.ize** *v/t.* kentleştirmek, şehirleştirmek.

**ur.chin** [ˈəːtʃin] *n.* afacan, haşarı çocuk.

**urge** [əːdʒ] **1.** *v/t. oft.* ~ on ileri sürmek, sevketmek, harekete geçirmek; *fig.* kışkırtmak (to -e); zorlamak (to *inf.* -meye); dürtmek; sıkıştırmak; ~ s.th. on s.o. *b-ne bşi* ısrarla anlatmak; **2.** *n.* dürtü; zorlama; kışkırtma; özlem, arzu; **ur.gen.cy** [ˈəːdʒənsi] *n.* acele; ısrar; sıkıştırma;

zorunluluk; **ur.gent** □ acele olan, âcil; zorunlu, kaçınılmaz; ısrar eden; be ~ with s.o. to *inf. b-ni bş* yapmaya zorlamak.

**u.ric** [ˈjuərik] *adj.* idrara ait, idrar..., ürik...

**u.ri.nal** [ˈjuərinl] *n.* idrar kabı, sürgü, ördek; pisuar; **u.ri.nar.y** *adj.* idrara ait, sidik...; **u.ri.nate** [~neit] *v/i.* işemek; **u.rine** *n.* idrar, sidik.

**urn** [əːn] *n.* kap; büyük kavanoz; sema ver.

**us** [ʌs, əs] *pron.* bizi, bize; all of ~ hepimiz.

**us.a.ble** [ˈjuːzəbl] *adj.* kullanışlı, elverişli, kullanılabilir.

**us.age** [ˈjuːzidʒ] *n.* kullanış, kullanım; işlem; usül; âdet, gelenek.

**us.ance** † [ˈjuːzəns] *n.* yabancı tahvillerin ödenme vadesi; **bill at ~** vadeli senet.

**use 1.** [juːs] *n.* fayda, yarar; kullanma, kullanım; alışıklık, âdet; amaç, gaye; kullanma hakkı; be of ~ yararlı olm.; it is (of) no ~ *ger. veya* to *inf.* ...menin yararı yok, ...mek bir işe yaramaz; have no ~ for -*e* hiç tahammülü olmamak; artık ihtiyacı olmamak; *Am.* F -*den* hiç hoslanmamak; put to ~ kullanmak; **2.** [juːz] *v/t.* kullanmak; yararlanmak -*den*; davranmak -*e*; ~ up tüketmek, sarfetmek, harcamak; I ~d [ˈjuːs(t)] to do eskiden yapardım; used [ˈjuːzd] kullanılmış; [ˈjuːst] alışık, alışkın (to -*e*); **use.ful** □ [ˈjuːsful] faydalı, yararlı; ⊕ işe yarar; **use.ful.ness** *n.* fayda, yarar, kullanışlılık; **use.less** □ faydasız, yararsız. boş, nafile; bir işe yaramaz; **use.less.ness** *n.* faydasızlık, yararsızlık; **us.er** [ˈjuːzə] *n.* kullanan.

**ush.er** [ˈʌʃə] **1.** *n.* mübaşir; kapıcı; *thea.* yer gösteren kimse; *contp.* yardımcı öğretmen; **2.** *v/t.* yer göstermek -*e*; *mst* ~ in bildirmek, haber vermek; *fig.* açmak, başlatmak *(yeni bir devir)*; **ush.er.ette** [~ˈret] *n.* yer gösteren kadın.

**u.su.al** □ [ˈjuːʒuəl] her zamanki, olağan, alışılagelmiş; as ~ her zamanki gibi; **u.su.al.ly** *adv.* çoğunlukla, ekseriya, çoğu kere.

**u.su.fruct** [ˈjuːsjuːfrʌkt] *n.* yararlanma hakkı, intifa hakkı; **u.su.fruc.tu.ar.y** [~tjuəri] *n.* intifa hakkı olan kimse.

**u.su.rer** [ˈjuːʒərə] *n.* tefeci; **u.su.ri.ous** □ [juːˈʒuəriəs] tefecilik kabilinden, aşırı faizli...

**u.surp** [juːˈzəːp] *v/t.* gaspetmek -*i*, zorla almak -*i*, el koymak -*e*; **u.sur.pa.tion** *n.*

gasp, zorla alma, el koyma; **u'surp.er** *n*.
gasp, zorla alan kimse.

**u.su.ry** ['juːʒuri] *n*. tefecilik; aşırı faiz.

**u.ten.sil** [juː'tensl] *n*. kap; alet; ~s *pl*.
malzeme; alet edavat; kap kacak, mutfak takımı.

**u.ter.ine** ['juːtərain] *adj*. rahme ait, rahim...; anası bir babası ayrı; ~ brother üvey kardeş; **u.ter.us** *anat*. ['~rəs] *n*. rahim, dölyatağı.

**u.til.i.tar.i.an** [juːtili'tɛəriən] **1.** *n*. faydacıl kimse; **2.** *adj*. faydacıl; **u'til.i.ty 1.** *n*. yarar(lık), fayda; işe yarar şey; kamu hizmeti yapan kuruluş; *a*. public ~ kamu hizmeti; public utilities kamu kuruluşları; **2.** *adj*. kullanışlı.

**u.ti.li.za.tion** [juːtilai'zeiʃən] *n*. kullanım, yararlanma; **'u.ti.lize** *v/t*. kullanmak; faydalanmak -den.

**ut.most** ['ʌtməust] *adj*. en uzak, en son; en büyük, olanca, en yüksek, en fazla; azamî, son derece.

**U.to.pi.an** [juː'təupjən] **1.** *adj*. ülküsel, ideal, hayalî, ütopik; **2.** *n*. ütopyacı kimse.

**ut.ter** ['ʌtə] **1.** *fig*. tam(amen), bütün bütün; kesin, son; sapına kadar, su katılmadık; **2.** *v/t*. ağza almak, söylemek; ağızdan çıkarmak *(ses)*; piyasaya sürmek *(sahte para vs.)*; **'ut.ter.ance** *n*. ifade; konuşma şekli; söz; söyleme; give ~ to dile getirmek, kelimelerle ifade etm.; **'ut.ter.er** *n*. konuşan kimse; **'ut.ter.most** *adj*. azamî; en son, en uzak.

**u.vu.la** *anat*. ['juːvjulə] *n*. küçükdil; **'u.vu.lar** *adj*. küçükdile ait.

**ux.ori.ous** [ʌk'sɔːriəs] *adj*. karısına çok düşkün.

# V

**vac** F [væk]' = vacation.

**va.can.cy** ['veikənsi] *n.* boşluk *(a. fig.)*; açık kadro; boş yer, aralık; gaze into ~ boşluğa dalıp bakmak; **¹va.cant** □ boş *(a. fig.)*; açık; münhal; bön, aptal; ifadesiz; terkedilmiş, sahipsiz; vârissiz.

**va.cate** [vəˈkeit, *Am.* ¹veikeit] *v/t.* tahliye etm., boşaltmak; boş bırakmak, terketmek; bırakmak; kalkmak *(yerinden)*; lağvetmek, feshetmek; **vaˈca.tion 1.** *n.* tatil; **2.** *v/t. Am.* tatilini geçirmek (at, in -de); **vaˈca.tion.ist** *n. Am.* tatile çıkan kimse.

**vac.ci.nate** ['væksineit] *v/t.* aşılamak, aşı yapmak; **vac.ciˈna.tion** *n.* aşı(lama); **¹vac.ci.na.tor** *n.* aşıcı; **vac.cine** ['~si:n] *n.* aşı (maddesi).

**vac.il.late** ['væsileit] *v/i.* tereddüt etm., kararsız olm.; sallanmak, sendelemek; **vac.ilˈla.tion** *n.* tereddüt; sendeleme.

**va.cu.i.ty** [Aæ¹kju:iti] *n.* boşluk *(mst fig.)*; aptallık; düşüncesizlik; budalaca konuşma; işsizlik; **vac.u.ous** □ ['vækjuəs] *fig.* boş, anlamsız; aptal; işsiz; **vac.u.um** ['~əm] **1.** *n. phys.* boşluk, vakum; ~ brake vakum freni; ~ cleaner elektrik süpürgesi; ~ flask, ~ bottle termos; ~ tube radyo lambası; **2.** *v/i.* elektrik süpürgesi kullanmak.

**va.de-me.cum** ['veidi¹mi:kəm] *n.* her zaman yanda taşınılan elkitabı.

**vag.a.bond** ['vægəbənd] **1.** *adj.* serseri, avare; *⚡* kararsız (akım); **2.** *n.* serseri kimse, avare kimse; **¹vag.a.bond.age** *n.* serserilik.

**va.gar.y** ['veigəri] *n.* garip davranış veya fikir; kapris; delilik, çılgınlık.

**va.gran.cy** ['veigrənsi] *n.* serserilik; göçebelik; **¹va.grant 1.** *adj.* serseri, avare; *fig.* göçebe, yersiz yurtsuz; **2.** = vagabond 2.

**vague** □ [veig] belirsiz, müphem, bulanık, şüpheli, anlaşılmaz; **¹vague.ness** *n.* belirsizlik, anlaşılmazlık.

**vail** † *veya poet.* [veil] *v/t.* indirmek *(bayrak)*; çıkarmak *(şapka)*.

**vain** □ [vein] boş, nafile; *fig.* kendini beğenmiş, kibirli, gururlu; değersiz, verimsiz; faydasız, anlamsız; in ~ (boşu) boşuna, beyhude (yere); **~.glo.ri.ous** □ [~¹glɔ:riəs] mağrur, gururlu; **~¹glo.ry** *n.* kendini beğenmişlik, gurur.

**val.ance** ['væləns] *n.* saçak, farbala, fırfır.

**vale** [veil] *n. poet.* vadi, dere.

**val.e.dic.tion** [væli¹dikʃən] *n.* veda; **val.e-¹dic.to.ry** [~təri] **1.** *adj.* veda...; **2.** *n.* veda konuşması.

**va.lence** *⚛* ['veiləns] *n.* valans, değerlik.

**val.en.tine** ['væləntain] *n.* 14 Şubat Valentine gününde seçilen sevgili(ye gönderilen kart).

**va.le.ri.an** *⚹* [vəˈliəriən] *n.* kediotu.

**val.et** ['vælit] **1.** *n.* uşak, erkek oda hizmetçisi; **2.** *v/t.* oda hizmetçiliği yapmak -e.

**val.e.tu.di.nar.i.an** ['vælitju:di¹nɛəriən] **1.** *adj.* sıhhatsiz, sağlığı bozuk; sağlığına çok düşkün; **2.** *n.* hasta kimse; sağlığına çok düşkün kimse.

**val.iant** □ ['væljənt] yiğit, cesur, yürekli.

**val.id** □ ['vælid] geçerli, yürürlükte olan; doğru, sağlam; kanuni, yasal; be ~ geçerli olm.; **val.i.date** ['~deit] *v/t.* geçerli kılmak; onaylamak; **va.lid.i.ty** [vəˈliditi] *n.* geçerlik; yürürlük; sağlamlık, doğruluk.

**va.lise** [vəˈli:z] *n.* valiz, küçük bavul; ✗ sırt çantası.

**val.ley** ['væli] *n.* vadi, dere.

**val.or.i.za.tion** [vælərai¹zeiʃən] *n.* hükümetçe fiyat tespiti; **¹val.or.ize** *vb.* hükümetçe fiyat tespit etm.

**val.or.ous** □ ['vælərəs] cesur, yiğit.

**val.o(u)r** ['vælə] *n.* yiğitlik, cesaret, kahramanlık.

**val.u.a.ble** □ ['væljuəbl] **1.** □ değerli, kıymetli, pahalı; aziz; **2.** *n.* ~s *pl.* değerli şey, mücevherat.

**val.u.a.tion** [vælju¹eiʃən] *n.* değer (biçme); kıymet; **¹val.u.a.tor** *n.* istimator, tahminci.

**val.ue** ['vælju:] **1.** *n.* değer, kıymet *(a. fig.)*; önem, itibar; gerçek değer; *♪* değer; *paint.* renk tonu; anlam, mana; mal; give (get) good ~ (for one's money)

**†** parasının tam karşılığını vermek (almak); ~-added tax katma değer vergisi; **2.** *v/t.* takdir etm., saymak, paha biçmek; *fig.* değer vermek *-e;* **ıval.ued** *adj.* değerlendirilmiş, değerli; **ıval.ue.less** *adj.* değersiz, beş para etmez.

**valve** [vælv] *n.* valf, supap, ventil; **♀** çenet; *anat.* kapacık; *radyo:* radyo lambası.

**va.moose** *Am. sl.* [væ'muːs] *v/i.* defolmak, çekip gitmek, tüymek.

**vamp¹** [væmp] **1.** *n.* saya; **2.** *v/t. -e* saya takmak; uydurmak *(bahane);* **♪** eşlik etm.

**vamp²** F [~] **1.** *n.* şuh kadın, fındıkçı kadın; **2.** *v/t.* ayartmak *(erkeği),* baştan çıkarmak.

**vam.pire** [ıvæmpaiə] *n.* vampir, hortlak.

**van¹** [væn] *n.* üstü kapalı yük arabası, karavan; **🚃** furgon.

**van²** ✕ *veya fig.* [~] *n.* keşif kolu, öncü.

**Van.dal** [ıvændəl] *n. hist.* vandal; **2** *fig.* barbar, yıkıcı, vahşi kimse; **ıvan.dal.ism** *n.* yıkıcılık, vandalizm.

**van.dyke** [væn'daik] *n.* geniş oymalı yaka; keçisakal; *attr.* **2** Van Dyck...

**vane** [vein] *n.* rüzgârgülü; fırıldak, yelkovan; pervane kanadı; yeldeğirmeni kanadı.

**van.guard** ✕ [ıvænguːd] *n.* ileri kol, öncü kolu.

**va.nil.la** **♀** [və'nilə] *n.* vanilya.

**van.ish** [ıvæniʃ] *v/i.* gözden kaybolmak, yok olmak, uçup gitmek; ~ into thin air yer yarılıp içine girmek.

**van.i.ty** [ıvæniti] *n.* kendini beğenmişlik, kibirlilik; nafilelik; değersizlik; gösteriş, caka; ~ bag, ~ case makyaj çantası.

**van.quish** [ıvæŋkwif] *v/t.* yenmek, altetmek, hakkından gelmek.

**van.tage** [ıvaːntidʒ] *n.* üstünlük; *tenis:* düsten sonra gelen puan, avantaj; ı~-ground *n.* avantajlı alan.

**vap.id** □ [ıvæpid] sıkıcı; yavan; tatsız, sönük, cansız.

**va.po(u)r.ize** [ıveipəraiz] *v/t. & v/i.* buharlaş(tır)mak; **ıva.po(u)r.iz.er** *n.* ⊕ püskürteç, vaporizatör *(a.* **♀** *).*

**va.por.ous** □ [ıveipərəs] buharlı, dumanlı; *fig.* hayalperest; boş, asılsız.

**va.po(u)r** [ıveipə] *n.* buhar, buğu, duman; *fig.* hayali şey, kuruntu; ~ bath buhar banyosu; ıva.po(u)r.y = vaporous.

**var.i.a.bil.i.ty** [vɛəriə'biliti] *n.* değişkenlik; **ıvar.i.a.ble** □ değişken; kararsız; **ıvar.i.ance** *n.* değişiklik; uyuşmazlık, çelişki, ayrılık; be at ~ aykırı olm.. araları bozuk olm., uyuşamamak (with *ile);* set

at ~ aralarını bozmak; **ıvar.i.ant 1.** *adj.* farklı, değişik; **2.** *n.* varyant; değişik biçim; **var.iᵗa.tion** *n.* değişme, dönme, dönüşme; değişiklik; **♪** çeşitleme, varyasyon.

**var.i.cose** **♀** [ıværikəus] *adj.* genişlemiş, varisli...; ~ vein varisli damar.

**var.ied** □ [ıvɛərid] çeşitli, farklı, türlü, değişik; **var.i.e.gate** [ı~rigeit] *v/t.* renklendirmek; çeşitlemek; **ıvar.i.eᵗga.ted** *adj.* alaca(lı), rengârenk; **var.i.eᵗga.tion** *n.* renklilik, alacalık; çeşitlilik; **va.ri.e.ty** [vəᵗraiəti] *n.* değişiklik, farklılık; karışım; *part.* **†** çeşit *(a. biol.);* cins, nevi, tür; ~ show varyete; ~ theatre varyete tiyatrosu.

**va.ri.o.la** **♀** [vəᵗraiələ] *n.* çiçek hastalığı.

**var.i.ous** □ [ıvɛəriəs] çeşitli, birkaç, muhtelif; değişik, farklı.

**var.let †** [ıvaːlit] *n.* alçak adam; şövalye uşağı.

**var.mint** *sl., co.* [ıvaːmint] *n.* sefil adam, alçak adam.

**var.nish** [ıvaːniʃ] **1.** *n.* vernik, cila; *fig.* yapmacıklık, dış güzellik; **2.** *v/t.* verniklemek, cilalamak; *fig.* içyüzünü gizlemek, görünüşte süslemek.

**var.si.ty** F [ıvaːsiti] *n.* üniversite.

**var.y** [ıvɛəri] *v/t. & v/i.* değiş(tir)mek; farklı olm. (from *-den);* *part.* **♪** çeşitlemek; değişime uğramak.

**vas.cu.lar** **♀**, *anat.* [ıvæskjulə] *adj.* damara ait, damar(lı)...

**vase** [vaːz, *Am.* veiz] *n.* vazo.

**vas.sal** [ıvæsəl] *n.* vasal; uyruk; köle, hizmetli; *attr.* vasal...; **ıvas.sal.age** *n.* vasallık; kölelik, kulluk (to *-e).*

**vast** □ [vaːst] engin, geniş, vâsi; çok, dünya kadar; koskocaman; muazzam; enginlik; büyüklük; çokluk.

**vat** [væt] **1.** *n.* tekne, fıçı; sarnıç; **2.** *v/t.* fıçıya koymak, fıçılamak.

**vat.ted** [ıvætid] *adj.* fıçılanmış *(şarap vs.).*

**vaude.ville** [ıvəudəvil] *n. Am.* vodvil, varyete.

**vault¹** [vɔːlt] **1.** *n.* tonoz, kemer; mahzen; yeraltı mezarı; *(banka)* kasa dairesi; gök, sema; **2.** *v/t.* üstünü kemerle çevirmek.

**vault²** [~] **1.** *v/t.* atlamak, sıçramak; **2.** *n.* atlayış, atlama.

**vault.ing** **△** [ıvɔːltiŋ] *n.* tonozlu *(veya* kemerli) yapı.

**vault.ing-horse** [ıvɔːltiŋhɔːs] *n. jimnastik:* kasa, atlama beygiri.

**vaunt** *lit.* [vɔːnt] **1.** *v/t. & v/i.* öv(ün)mek; **2.** *n.* övünme; **ıvaunt.ing** □ övün-

gen, farfara.
**veal** [viːl] *n.* dana eti; roast ~ dana rostosu.
**veer** [viə] **1.** *v/t. & v/i.* dön(dür)mek, yön(ünü) değiştirmek; *fig.* caymak, fikrini değiştirmek; **2.** *n.* dönüş, dönme.
**veg.e.ta.ble** [ˈvedʒitəbl] **1.** *adj.* bitkilere ait, bitkisel...; **2.** *n.* bitki; *mst* ~s *pl.* sebze, zerzevat; **veg.e.tar.i.an** [~ˈtɛəriən] **1.** *n.* et yemez kimse, otobur; **2.** *adj.* etyemez; yalnız sebzeden oluşan, sebze...; **veg.e.tate** [ˈ~teit] *v/i. fig.* ot gibi yaşamak; **veg.e'ta.tion** *n.* bitkiler, bitki örtüsü; **veg.e.ta.tive** □ [ˈ~tətiv] bitkisel; bitek; ot gibi yaşayan, hareketsiz.
**ve.he.mence** [ˈviːiməns] *n.* şiddet, hiddet, ateşlilik; **'ve.he.ment** □ şiddetli, hiddetli, ateşli.
**ve.hi.cle** [ˈviːikl] *n.* taşıt, araç, vasıta (*a. fig.*); *pharm.* vehikül, vasıta; **ve.hic.u.lar** □ [viˈhikjulə] taşıtlara ait, taşıt...
**veil** [veil] **1.** *n.* peçe, yaşmak, perde (*a. phot.*); örtü, tül; *fig.* bahane, maske; **2.** *v/t. & v/i.* ört(ün)mek; *fig.* gizlemek, saklamak; **'veil.ing** *n.* peçelik ince kumaş (*a. ↑*); *phot.* donukluk, vual.
**vein** [vein] *n.* damar (*a. fig.*); huy, mizaç; oluk, oyuk; **veined** *adj.* damarlı; **'vein.ing** *n.* damar sistemi.
**vel.le.i.ty** [veˈliːiti] *n.* hafif heves, eğilim.
**vel.lum** [ˈveləm] *n.* parşömen, tirşe; *a.* ~ paper parşömen kâğıdı.
**ve.loc.i.pede** [viˈlɔsipiːd] *n. Am.* üç tekerlekli çocuk bisikleti, velespit; *hist.* ön tekerlekten pedallı bisiklet.
**ve.loc.i.ty** [viˈlɔsiti] *n.* hız, sürat (derecesi).
**ve.lour(s)** [vəˈluə] *n.* kadife taklidi.
**vel.vet** [ˈvelvit] **1.** *n.* kadife, velur; *hunt.* kadifemsi deri; *sl.* kolay kazanç; **2.** *adj.* kadife...; kadife gibi; yumuşak; **vel.vet.een** [~ˈtiːn] *n.* pamuklu kadife; **'vel.vet.y** *adj.* kadife gibi; yumuşak.
**ve.nal** [ˈviːnl] *adj.* satın alınır, rüşvetle kandırılır, rüşvet alan, yiyici; **ve.nal.i.ty** [viːˈnæliti] *n.* rüşvet yeme.
**vend** [vend] *v/t.* satmak; **'vend.er, 'vend.or** *n.* satıcı, işportacı; **'vend.i.ble** *adj.* satılabilir; **'vend.ing ma.chine** para ile çalışan satıcı makine.
**ven.det.ta** [venˈdetə] *n.* kan davası.
**ve.neer** [viˈniə] *n.* kaplama tahtası; *fig.* yapma tavır, gösteriş; **2.** *v/t.* kaplamak; *fig.* cilalamak, yaldızlamak.
**ven.er.a.ble** □ [ˈvenərəbl] muhterem, saygıdeğer; **ven.er.ate** [ˈ~reit] *v/t.* saygı göstermek -*e*, hürmet etm. -*e*; tapmak -*e*; **ven.er'a.tion** *n.* hürmet, saygı; **'ven-**

**er.a.tor** *n.* hürmet eden (*veya* tapınan) kimse.
**ve.ne.re.al** [viˈniəriəl] *adj.* cinsel ilişkiye ait; *a.* ⚥ zührevi; ~ disease zührevi hastalık.
**Ve.ne.tian** [viˈniːʃən] **1.** *adj.* Venedik'e ait; ~ blind jaluzi; **2.** *n.* Venedikli.
**venge.ance** [ˈvendʒəns] *n.* öç, intikam; with a ~ F son derecede, alabildiğine, şiddetle; **venge.ful** □ [ˈ~ful] intikamcı, kinci.
**ve.ni.al** □ [ˈviːnjəl] affedilir, önemsiz.
**ven.i.son** [ˈvenzn] *n.* geyik *veya* karaca eti.
**ven.om** [ˈvenəm] *n.* yılan *vs.* zehiri; *fig.* düşmanlık, kin, garez; **'ven.om.ous** □ zehirli; kinci, garezkâr, düşman.
**ve.nous** [ˈviːnəs] *adj.* toplardamara ait, toplardamar...; ⚥ damarlı...
**vent** [vent] **1.** *n.* delik, menfez, ağız; kıç; yırtmaç; yarık, çıkak, çıkıt; give ~ to -*i* açığa vurmak, *k-ni* tutamamak; **2.** *v/t.* dışarı salıvermek; *fig.* göstermek, ifade etm., çıkarmak (*öfkesini*) (on -*den*); '~-hole *n.* hava deliği.
**ven.ti.late** [ˈventileit] *v/t.* havalandırmak; *fig.* açığa vurmak, tartışmak; **ven.ti'la.tion** *n.* havalandırma (*a.* ✕); *fig.* açığa vurma; **'ven.ti.la.tor** *n.* ventilatör.
**ven.tral** [ˈventrəl] *adj.* karına ait, karın...
**ven.tri.cle** *anat.* [ˈventrikl] *n.* karıncık; beden *veya* organda boşluk.
**ven.tril.o.quist** [venˈtriləkwist] *n.* vantrlok; **ven'tril.o.quize** *v/i.* vantrlokluk yapmak.
**ven.ture** [ˈventʃə] **1.** *n.* tehlikeli iş, şans işi; risk, riziko; at a ~ rasgele; **2.** *v/t. & v/i.* tehlikeye atmak; göze almak (to *inf.* -*meyi*); şansa bırakmak; riske girmek; ~ (up)on girişmek -*e*, atılmak -*e*; cesaret etm.; I ~ to say diyebilirim ki; **ven.ture.some** □ [ˈ~səm], **'ven.tur.ous** □ atılgan, cesur, atak; tehlikeli, riskli.
**ven.ue** [ˈvenjuː] *n.* olay yeri; yetki dairesi; *fig.* yarışma yeri; F buluşma yeri.
**ve.ra.cious** □ [vəˈreiʃəs] doğru (sözlü); gerçeğe sadık; **ve.rac.i.ty** [vəˈræsiti] *n.* gerçek(lik); dürüstlük.
**ve.ran.da(h)** [vəˈrændə] *n.* veranda, camlı taraça.
**verb** *gr.* [vəːb] *n.* fiil; **'ver.bal** □ fiile ait, fiil...; sözlü; kelimesi kelimesine, harfiyen; **ver.ba.tim** [~ˈbeitim] *adj.* kelimesi kelimesine; **ver.bi.age** [ˈ~biidʒ] *n.* laf kalabalığı; **ver.bose** □ [~ˈbəus] ağzı kalabalık; gereksiz sözlerle dolu; **ver.bos.i.ty** [~ˈbɔsiti] *n.* laf kalabalığı.
**ver.dan.cy** [ˈvəːdənsi] *n.* yeşillik, tazelik;

*fig.* toyluk; **'ver.dant** □ yeşil, taze; *fig* toy, deneyimsiz.

**ver.dict** ['vəːdikt] *n.* ʤʤ jüri kurulu hükmü; karar, hüküm; *fig.* fikir, kanaat (on *-de*); bring in *veya* return a ~ of guilty suçlu olduğu kararına varmak.

**ver.di.gris** ['vəːdigris] *n.* jengâr, zencar, bakır pası.

**ver.dure** ['vəːdʒə] *n.* yeşillik, çimen.

**verge¹** [vəːdʒ] *n.* değnek, sopa, asa.

**verge²** [~] 1. *n. mst fig.* kenar, hudut, sınır, eşik; on the ~ of eşiğinde, üzere; 2. *v/i.* yönelmek; ~ (up)on yaklaşmak *-e.*

**ver.ger** ['vəːdʒə] *n.* piskopos hizmetlisi; zangoç.

**ver.i.fi.a.ble** ['verifaiəbl] *adj.* doğrulanabilir; tetkik edilebilir; **ver.i.fi.ca.tion** [~fi'keiʃən] *n.* tahkik, tetkik; doğrulama; **ver.i.fy** ['~fai] *v/t.* doğrulamak, gerçeklemek; tahkik etm., tetkik etm.; **'ver.i.ly** *adv.* † gerçekten, doğrusu; **ver.i.si.mil.i.tude** [~si'militjuːd] *n.* gerçeğe benzeme; olasılık; **ver.i.ta.ble** □ ['~təbl] gerçek, hakikî; **'ver.i.ty** *n.* doğru(luk), gerçek(lik).

**ver.mi.cel.li** [vəːmi'seli] *n.* tel şehriye; **ver.mi.cide** *pharm.* ['~said] *n.* solucan ilacı; **ver.mic.u.lar** [~kjulə] *adj.* solucana benzer; **ver.mi.form** ['~fɔːm] *adj.* solucan şeklindeki, kurda benzer; **ver.mi.fuge** *pharm.* ['~fjuːdʒ] *n.* solucan ilacı.

**ver.mil.ion** [vəˈmiljən] 1. *n.* parlak kırmızı; sülügen; 2. *adj.* zincifre kırmızısı, al.

**ver.min** [vəːmin] *n.* haşarat; *hunt.* zararlı hayvanlar; *fig.* mikrop, ayaktakımı; **'ver.min.ous** *adj.* haşaratlı; haşarattan olan; alçak, pis.

**ver.m(o)uth** ['vəːməθ] *n.* vermut.

**ver.nac.u.lar** [vəˈnækjulə] 1. □ bölgesel; ana diline ait; argoyla ilgili; yaygın; 2. *n.* günlük dil; anadil; lehçe; argo.

**ver.nal** ['vəːnl] *adj.* ilkbaharda olan; ilkbahar...; *fig.* gençliğe ait, taze.

**ver.ni.er** ['vəːnjə] *n.* Ʌ, ⊕ verniye.

**ver.sa.tile** □ ['vəːsətail] çok iş bilen, çok yönlü; çok kullanımlı; **ver.sa.til.i.ty** [~'tiliti] *n.* çok yönlülüਣ; becerililik.

**verse** [vəːs] *n.* dize, mısra; şiir, koşuk, nazım; beyit, kıta; ayet; **versed** *adj.* bilgili, becerikli, usta (in *-de*).

**ver.si.fi.ca.tion** [vəːsifiˈkeiʃən] *n.* şiir yazma sanatı; şiir vezni; **ver.si.fy** ['~fai] *v/t.* şiir haline koymak; *v/i.* şiir yazmak.

**ver.sion** ['vəːʃən] *n.* tercüme, çeviri; okunuş tarzı; yorum.

**ver.sus** *part.* ʤʤ ['vəːsəs] *prp.* -e karşı, *-in* aleyhinde.

**vert** F *eccl.* [vəːt] *vb.* din değiştirmek.

**ver.te.bra** *anat.* ['vəːtibrə] *n., pl.* **ver.te.brae** ['~briː] omur(ga kemiği), vertebra; **ver.te.bral** ['~brəl] *adj.* vertebral, omur...; **ver.te.brate** ['~brit] 1. *adj.* omurgalı...; ~ animal = 2. *n.* omurgalı hayvan.

**ver.tex** ['vəːteks] *n., pl.* **mst ver.ti.ces** ['~tisiːz] zirve, doruk, tepe; **'ver.ti.cal** □ dikey, düşey...

**ver.tig.i.nous** □ [vəːˈtidʒinəs] baş döndürücü; **ver.ti.go** ['~tigəu] *n.* baş dönmesi.

**verve** [vəːv] *n.* şevk, gayret, heves.

**ver.y** ['veri] 1. *adv.* çok, pek, gayet, ziyadesiyle; gerçekten; tam(amen); 2. *adj.* tam, ta kendisi; aynı, tıpkısı; bile, hatta; en; kati; belirli; the ~ same tıpkı tıpkısına; in the ~ act suçüstü; to the ~ bone ta iliklerine kadar; the ~ thing biçilmiş kaftan; the ~ thought düşüncesi bile; the ~ stones taşlar bile; the veriest baby bebekler bile; the veriest rascal alçakların alçağı, köpoğlu köpek.

**ves.i.ca** ['vesikə] *n.* torba; mesane, sidik torbası; **ves.i.cle** ['~kl] *n.* kabarcık, kese, kist.

**ves.per** ['vespə] *n. poet.* akşam; ~s *pl. eccl.* akşam duası.

**ves.sel** ['vesl] *n.* kap, tas, leğen; ⏚ gemi, tekne; *anat.* damar.

**vest** [vest] 1. *n.* iç gömleği, fanila; † yelek; 2. *v/t. mst fig. b-ne* vermek (with *-i*); hak vermek (in *-e*); yetki vermek (in s.o. *b-ne*); giydirmek (*cüppe*); *v/i.* hakkı olm. (in s.o. *b-nin*); ~ed rights *pl.* kazanılmış haklar.

**ves.tal** ['vestl] 1. *adj.* ocak tanrıçasına ait; namuslu; 2. *n.* ocak tanrıçasının rahibesi.

**ves.ti.bule** ['vestibjuːl] *n.* giriş, antre; part. Am. vagonlar arasındaki kapalı geçit.

**ves.tige** ['vestidʒ] *n.* iz, eser, işaret; **ves.tig.i.al** [~dʒiəl] *adj.* iz bırakmış; artakalan.

**vest.ment** ['vestmənt] *n.* giysi, resmî elbise; cüppe.

**vest-pock.et** ['vest'pɔkit] *adj.* cebe sığacak kadar küçük, küçücük...

**ves.try** ['vestri] *n. eccl.* giyinme odası; yönetim kurulu; '~.man *n.* kilise yönetim kurulu üyesi.

**ves.ture** *poet.* ['vestʃə] 1. *n.* giysi, kılık kıyafet; örtü; 2. *v/t.* giydirmek.

**vet** F [vet] 1. *n.* veteriner, baytar; *Am.* ✗ kıdemli asker; 2. *v/t.* muayene etm.; *fig.* dikkatle incelemek.

**vetch** ❦ [vetʃ] *n.* baklagillerden herhangi bir bitki.

**vet.er.an** [ˈvetərən] **1.** *adj.* kıdemli, deneyimli; emekli; **2.** *n.* kıdemli asker; emekli asker; deneyimli kimse.

**vet.er.i.nar.y** [ˈvetərinəri] **1.** *adj.* veterinerliğe ait; **2.** *n. a.* ~ surgeon veteriner, baytar.

**ve.to** [ˈviːtəu] **1.** *n., pl.* **ve.toes** [ˈ~z] veto; put a *veya* one's ~ (up)on = **2.** *v/t.* veto etm., reddetmek.

**vex** [veks] *v/t.* kızdırmak, canını sıkmak, sinirlendirmek; darıltmak; incitmek; rahatsız etm.; tartışmak; *part.* öő eziyet etm.; **vexˈa.tion** *n.* kızma, sinirlenme; sıkıntı, üzüntü; **vexˈa.tious** ☐ gücendirici, üzücü, sinirlendirici, can sıkıcı; **vexed** ☐ dargın, kızgın, canı sıkkın (at s.th. *bşe*, with s.o. *b-ne*); ~ question tartışmalı mesele; **ˈvex.ing** ☐ üzücü, can sıkıcı.

**vi.a** [ˈvaiə] *prp.* yolu ile, *-den* geçerek.

**vi.a.ble** [ˈvaiəbl] *adj.* yaşayabilir; uygulanabilir.

**vi.a.duct** [ˈvaiədʌkt] *n.* köprü, viyadük.

**vi.al** [ˈvaiəl] *n.* küçük şişe.

**vi.and** [ˈvaiənd] *n. mst* ~s *pl.* yemek, yiyecek.

**vi.at.i.cum** *eccl.* [vaiˈætikəm]*n.* ölüm döşeğindeki kimseye verilen Aşai Rabbani.

**vi.brant** [ˈvaibrənt] *adj.* titrek, titreşimli; canlı; coşkun; gür, tok, yankılı *(ses)*.

**vi.brate** [vaiˈbreit] *v/t. & v/i.* titre(t)mek, sallan(dır)mak; titreşmek; **viˈbra.tion** *n.* titreşim; titreme, sallanma; **viˈbra.tor** *n.* titreten şey; titreşimli masaj aleti; elektrik zilinin dili; **vi.bra.to.ry** [ˈ~brətəri] *adj.* titretici; titreşimli.

**vic.ar** *eccl.* [ˈvikə] *n.* papaz; vekil; ~ general piskopos yardımcısı; **ˈvic.ar.age** *n.* papazın evi; **vi.car.i.ous** ☐ [vaiˈkɛəriəs] başkasının yerine yapılmış; vekâleten yapılan.

**vice¹** [vais] *n.* kötü huy, ayıp, kusur, leke.

**vice²** ⊕ [~] *n.* mengene, sıkmaç.

**vice³** [ˈvaisi] *prp. -in* yerine.

**vice⁴** [vais] **1.** *adj.* muavin, yardımcı, ikinci; **2.** *n.* F vekil, muavin; **ˈ~-ˈad.mi.ral** *n.* koramiral; **ˈ~-ˈchair.man** *n.* başkan yardımcısı; **ˈ~-ˈchan.cel.lor** *n.* başhâkim yardımcısı; *univ.* rektör yardımcısı; **ˈ~-ˈcon.sul** *n.* viskonsül, konsolos yardımcısı; **~.ge.rent** [ˈ~ˈdʒerənt] *n.* vekil; **ˈ~-ˈpres.i.dent** *n.* ikinci başkan, başkan yardımcısı; **ˈ~-ˈre.gal** *adj.* genel valiye ait; **~.reine** [ˈ~ˈrein] *n.* genel vali karısı; kadın genel vali; **~.roy** [ˈ~ˈrɔi] *n.* genel vali.

**vi.ce ver.sa** [ˈvaisiˈvəːsə] *adv.* tersine;

karşılıklı olarak.

**vic.i.nage** [ˈvisinidʒ] *n.*, **viˈcin.i.ty** civar, çevre, havali, yöre, semt, mahalle; yakınlık (to *-e*); in the ~ of 50 50 civarında, 50 kadar.

**vi.cious** ☐ [ˈviʃəs] kötü; kinci, haince; ahlâkı bozuk; huysuz, hırçın *(hayvan)*; kusurlu, bozuk; çirkin; şiddetli, sert; ~ **cir.cle** kısır döngü.

**vi.cis.si.tude** [viˈsisitjuːd] *n.* değişiklik; ~s *pl.* olaylar.

**vic.tim** [ˈviktim] *n.* kurban; mağdur kimse; **ˈvic.tim.ize** *v/t.* cezalandırmak; *fig.* aldatmak, faka bastırmak.

**vic.tor** [ˈviktə] *n.* galip, fatih; **Vic.to.ri.an** *hist.* [vikˈtɔːriən] *adj.* Kraliçe Viktorya zamanına ait; **vicˈto.ri.ous** ☐ galip, muzaffer; **vic.to.ry** [ˈ~təri] *n.* zafer, yengi, utku, başarı.

**vict.ual** [ˈvitl] **1.** *v/t. -e* erzak tedarik etm.; *v/i.* erzak almak; yemek yemek; **2.** *n. mst* ~s *pl.* yemek, erzak; **vict.ual.(l)er** [ˈvitlə] *n.* erzakçı; lokantacı; erzak gemisi; licensed ~ meyhaneci, ruhsatlı içki satıcısı.

**vi.de** [ˈvaidiː] *vb.* bakınız!

**vi.de.li.cet** [viˈdiːliset] *adv.* (*abbr.* viz.) yani, demek oluyor ki.

**vid.e.o** [ˈvidiəu] *adj.* televizyonla resim nakline ait, video...

**vie** [vai] *v/i.* yarışmak, çekişmek, rekabet etm. (with *ile*).

**Vi.en.nese** [vieˈniːz] **1.** *n.* Viyanalı; **2.** *adj.* Viyana'ya ait.

**view** [vjuː] **1.** *n.* bakış, nazar; fikir, görüş (alanı); manzara, görünüm *(a. paint., phot.)*; görme fırsatı; amaç, maksat, gaye, emel; at first ~ ilk bakışta; In ~ görünürde; beklenen, umulan; in ~ of *-in* karşısında,... göz önüne alındığında; *-den* dolayı, ...yüzünden; in my ~ kanımca, bence; on ~ sergilenmekte; out of ~ görünmez; with a ~ to *ger.*, with the ~ of *ger.* amacıyle; ümidiyle, umarak; come into ~ görünmek, ortaya çıkmak; have (keep) in ~ gözü önünde olm. *(veya* tutmak); **2.** *v/t.* bakmak *-e*, görmek *-i*; tetkik etm. *-i*, incelemek *-i*; düşünmek *-i*; **ˈview.er** *n.* seyirci; **ˈview-find.er** *n. phot.* vizör; **ˈview.less** *adj.* fikirsiz; manzarasız; *poet.* görünmez; **ˈ~.point** *n.* görüş noktası, bakış açısı; **ˈview.y** ☐ F gösterişli; garip fikirli.

**vig.il** *part. eccl.* [ˈvidʒil] *n.* yortu arifesi; uyanıklık; gece nöbet tutma; **ˈvig.i.lance** *n.* uyanıklık, uyumama; ~ **committee** *Am. hist.* güvenliği sağlamak için kurulan yasadışı örgüt; **ˈvig.i.lant** ☐ uyanık, tetikte, tedbirli; **vig.i.lan.te** Am. [~'lænti] n. «vigil committee» üyesi.

**vi.gnette** typ., phot. [vi'njet] 1. n. süs; 2. v/t. süslemek.

**vig.or.ous** ☐ ['vigərəs] dinç, kuvvetli, etkin; fig. gayretli, enerjik; **'vig.o(u)r** n. kuvvet, dinçlik; fig. gayret, enerji.

**vi.king** ['vaikiŋ] n. viking; korsan.

**vile** ☐ [vail] kötü, iğrenç, berbat, çirkin, pis, utanç verici; aşağılık, değersiz; alçak, rezil.

**vil.i.fi.ca.tion** [vilifi'keiʃən] n. iftira, yerme; **vil.i.fy** ['~fai] v/i. iftira etm.; alçaltmak, kötülemek, yermek.

**vil.la** ['vilə] n. villa, köşk.

**vil.lage** ['vilidʒ] n. köy; ~ green köy merası; **'vil.lag.er** n. köylü.

**vil.lain** ['vilən] n. alçak veya çapkın adam (a. co.); **'vil.lain.ous** ☐ çirkin, bozuk, habis; F çok fena, kötü; **'vil.lain.y** n. kötülük, rezalet, alçaklık.

**vil.lein** hist. ['vilin] n. derebeyi idaresindeki köylü.

**vim** F [vim] n. enerji; gayret.

**vin.di.cate** ['vindikeit] v/t. -in doğruluğunu ispat etm., haklı çıkarmak; korumak -i, savunmak -i (from -den); **vin.di'ca.tion** n. koruma, doğrulama; **vin.di.ca.to.ry** ☐ ['~təri] koruma kabilinden.

**vin.dic.tive** ☐ [vin'diktiv] kinci; affetmeyen.

**vine** ⚘ [vain] n. asma (çubuğu); sarılgan herhangi bir bitki; '~-dress.er n. bağcı; **vin.e.gar** ['vinigə] n. sirke; hırçınlık, suratsızlık; gayret, enerji; **'vin.e.gar.y** adj. mst fig. suratsız, asık suratlı; vine--grow.er ['vaingrəuə] n. bağcı; **'vine--grow.ing** n. bağcılık; **'vine-louse** n. asma biti; **vine.yard** ['vinjəd] n. bağ.

**vi.nous** ['vainəs] adj. şaraba ait, şarap...; şarap gibi.

**vin.tage** ['vintidʒ] 1. n. bağ bozumu; bir mevsimin bağ ürünü; kaliteli şarap; 2. adj. kaliteli...; eski, klasik, seçkin; demode; ~ car mot. eski araba; **'vin.tag.er** n. üzüm toplayıcısı; **vint.ner** ['vintnə] n. şarap tüccarı.

**vi.ol** ♪ ['vaiəl] n. viyol.

**vi.o.la** 1. ♪ ['vi'əulə] n. viyola; 2. ⚘ ['vaiələ] n. bir tür hercai menekşe.

**vi.o.la.ble** ☐ ['vaiələbl] bozulabilir, ihlal edilebilir.

**vi.o.late** ['vaiəleit] v/t. bozmak, ihlal etm., çiğnemek, karşı gelmek; tecavüz etm. -e (a. fig.), ırzına geçmek; **vi.o'la.tion** n. ihlal; tecavüz; **'vi.o.la.tor** n. tecavüz veya ihlal eden kimse.

**vi.o.lence** ['vaiələns] n. zor(lama), şiddet,

tecavüz; zorbalık; bozma; iğfal; do veya offer ~ to aykırı olm. -e, zorlamak -i; **'vi.o.lent** ☐ şiddetli, sert, zorlu, kuvvetli; berbat.

**vi.o.let** ['vaiəlit] 1. n. ⚘ menekşe; 2. adj. mor.

**vi.o.lin** ♪ [vaiə'lin] n. keman; **'vi.o.lin.ist** n. kemancı.

**vi.o.lon.cel.list** ♪ [vaiələn'tʃelist] n. viyolonsel çalan kimse; **vi.o.lon'cel.lo** [~ləu] n. viyolonsel.

**VIP** sl. ['vi:ai'pi:] n. kodamanlar.

**vi.per** zo. ['vaipə] n. engerek; fig. yılan; **vi.per.ine** ['~rain], **'vi.per.ous** ☐ mst fig. zehirli, yılan..., hain...

**vi.ra.go** [vi'ra:gəu] n. şirret kadın, eli maşalı kadın, cadaloz kadın.

**vir.gin** ['və:dʒin] 1. n. kız, bakire; 2. ☐ bakire...; bakir, el değmemiş, balta girmemiş (orman); bozulmamış, doğal; kullanılmamış; fig. & ⊕ işlenmemiş; **'vir.gin.al** ['və:dʒinl] 1. ☐ bakireye yaraşır; bakireye ait, bakire...; 2. n. ♪ virginal; **Vir.gin.ia** [və'dʒinjə] n. a. ~ tobacco Virjinya tütürü; ~ creeper frenk asması; **Vir'gin.i.an** adj. Virjinya...; Virjinyalı; **vir.gin.i.ty** [və:'dʒiniti] n. kızlık, bakirelik, bekâret.

**vir.ile** ['virail] adj. erkekçe, yiğit, kuvvetli, enerjik; iktidarlı (erkek); **vi.ril.i.ty** [vi'riliti] n. erkeklik, cinsel güç; yiğitlik.

**vir.tu** [və:'tu:] n.: article of ~ ince sanat eseri; **vir.tu.al** ☐ ['~tjuəl] gerçek kuvveti olan; fiilî, esas, asıl; **'vir.tu.al.ly** adv. aslında; gerçekte; fiilen; **vir.tue** ['~tju:] n. fazilet, iffet, erdem, namus; etki, tesir, yarar, fayda; avantaj, üstünlük; in veya by ~ of -e dayanarak, -den dolayı, ...sebebiyle; make a ~ of necessity zorunlu bir durumdan fazilet hissesi çıkarmak; **vir.tu.os.i.ty** [və:tju'ɔsiti] n. virtüözlük, büyük ustalık; **vir.tu.o.so** [~'ləuzəu] n. part. ♪ virtüöz; güzel sanatlardan anlayan kimse; **vir.tu.ous** ☐ iffetli, erdemli; dürüst.

**vir.u.lence** ['viruləns] n. zehirlilik, tehlikelilik, öldürücülük; aşırı sertlik; fig. kötülük; **'vir.u.lent** ☐ kuvvetli (zehir); öldürücü; zehirli (hastalık vs.); fig. kötücül; şiddetli.

**vi.rus** ⚕ ['vaiərəs] n. virüs; fig. zehir.

**vi.sa** ['vi:zə] 1. n. vize; 2. v/t. pret. & p.p. **'vi.saed** vize etm.

**vis.age** lit. ['vizidʒ] n. yüz, surat, sima, çehre.

**vis.cer.a** anat. ['visərə] n. iç organlar.

**vis.cid** ☐ ['visid] = viscous.

**vis.cose** ⚗ ['viskəus] n. viskoz; ~ silk selüloz ipeği; **vis.cos.i.ty** [-'kɔsiti] *n.* yapışkanlık; yarı sıvılık, viskozite.

**vis.count** ['vaikaunt] *n.* vikont; **'vis.countess** *n.* vikontes.

**vis.cous** ☐ ['viskəs] yapışkan; yarı sıvı, lüzuci.

**vise** [vais] *Am. for* vice².

**vi.sé** ['vi:zei] = visa.

**vis.i.bil.i.ty** [vizi'biliti] *n.* görüş mesafesi *(veya* derecesi); görünürlük, görme olanağı; **'vis.i.ble** ☐ görünebilir, görülür; *fig.* belli, açık.

**vi.sion** ['viʒən] *n.* görme (gücü); görüş; önsezi; *fig.* hayal, kuruntu, evham; **vision.ar.y** [-nəri] **1.** *adj.* hayali; merakli, kuruntulu; düşsel; **2.** *n.* hayalperest kimse.

**vis.it** ['vizit] **1.** *v/t.* ziyaret etm., görmeğe gitmek, uğramak; teftiş etm.; cezalandırmak, çektirmek (upon -i, -e); *v/i.* ziyarette bulunmak; ~ with *Am. ile* çene çalmak; kalmak; **2.** *n.* ziyaret, uğrama (to -e), görüşmeye gitme; *(doktor)* vizite; misafirlik; **'vis.it.ant** *n.* ziyaretçi; *orn.* göçmen kuş; **vis.it'a.tion** *n.* (resmi) ziyaret; *fig.* felâket; **vis.it.a.to.ri.al** [-təˈtɔ:riəl] *adj.* teftişe ait, teftiş...; **'vis.it.ing** *n.* & *adj.* ziyaret (eden); ~ card kartvizit; **'vis.i.tor** *n.* ziyaretçi, misafir konuk (to -e); müfettiş; turist; ~s' book ziyaretçi defteri.

**vi.sor** ['vaizə] *n.* miğfer siperliği; *mot.* güneşlik.

**vis.ta** ['vistə] *n.* manzara; *fig.* olaylar serisi.

**vis.u.al** ☐ ['vizjuəl] görmekle ilgili, görme...; görülebilir; optik; **'vis.u.al.ize** *v/t.* & *v/i.* gözünde canlan(dır)mak.

**vi.tal** ☐ ['vaitl] hayati...; yaşam için gerekli; canlı, yaşayan, dirimsel; esaslı, zaruri, önemli, elzem (to *için*); öldürücü, amansız; ~s *pl.*, ~ parts *pl.* yaşam için gerekli olan organlar *(kalp, ciğer, beyin vs.);* s. statistics; **vi.tal.i.ty** [-ˈtæliti] *n.* dirilik, hayatiyet, canlılık; dayanma gücü; **vi.tal.ize** ['-təlaiz] *v/t.* hayat vermek, canlandırmak *(a. fig.),* diriltmek.

**vi.ta.min(e)** ['vitəmin] *n.* vitamin; **vi.ta.minized** ['-naizd] *adj.* vitaminli.

**vi.ti.ate** ['viʃieit] *v/t.* kirletmek; (tesirini) bozmak, etkisini azaltmak; iptal etm.; ☒ hükümsüz kılmak.

**vit.i.cul.ture** ['vitikʌltʃə] *n.* bağcılık.

**vit.re.ous** ☐ ['vitriəs] camdan yapılma, cam...; cam gibi, camlı...

**vit.ri.fac.tion** [vitri'fækʃən] *n.* camlaştırma; **vit.ri.fy** ['-fai] *v/t.* & *v/i.* camlaş-

(tır)mak.

**vit.ri.ol** ☒ ['vitriəl] *n.* sülfürik asit, zaç yağı, karaboya.

**vi.tu.per.ate** [vi'tjuːpəreit] *vb.* küfretmek, sövmek; **vi.tu.per'a.tion** *n.* sövüp sayma, küfretme, hakaret etme; **vi'tu.per.a.tive** ☐ [-rətiv] küfürbaz.

**vi.va** (vo.ce) ['vaivə('vəusi] **1.** *adj.* sözlü; **2.** *n.* sözlü imtihan.

**vi.va.cious** ☐ [vi'veiʃəs] canlı, neşeli, hayat dolu; **vi.vac.i.ty** [vi'væsiti] *n.* canlılık, neşelilik.

**viv.id** ☐ ['vivid] canlı, berrak; parlak; açık, belli; kuvvetli; hayat dolu; **'viv.idness** *n.* canlılık, parlaklık.

**viv.i.fy** ['vivifai] *v/t.* canlandırmak, canlılık vermek; **vi'vip.a.rous** ☐ [-pərəs] doğurucu; **viv.i.sec.tion** [-'sekʃən] *n.* bilimsel araştırma için canlı hayvanlar üzerinde yapılan deney.

**vix.en** ['viksn] *n.* dişi tilki; cadaloz kadın.

**viz.** [viz] = videlicet.

**vi.zier** [viˈziə] *n.* vezir.

**vi.zor** ['vaizə] = visor.

**vo.cab.u.lar.y** [vəuˈkæbjuləri] *n.* kısa sözlük; kelime bilgisi *(veya* haznesi).

**vo.cal** ☐ ['vəukəl] sesle ilgili; ses...; sesli; ses gibi, sesle söylenen; kelimelerle açıklanmış; konuşkan, sözünü sakınmaz; ♪ vokal...; *gr.* ünlü, sesli; ~ c(h)ord ses teli; **'vo.cal.ist** *n.* şarkıcı, vokalist; **vo.cal.ize** *v/t.* seslendirmek; söylemek; ♪ vokallemek; **'vo.cal.ly** *adv.* sesli olarak.

**vo.ca.tion** [vəuˈkeiʃən] *n.* davet, çağrılma; iş, meslek; yetenek, kabiliyet; **vo'ca.tional** ☐ [-ʃənl] meslekle ilgili, mesleki...; ~ guidance meslek seçiminde rehberlik.

**voc.a.tive** *gr.* ['vɔkətiv] *n.* bir ismin hitap şekli.

**vo.cif.er.ate** [vəuˈsifəreit] *v/t.* bağıra bağıra söylemek; *v/i.* bağırmak, haykırmak; **vo.cif.er'a.tion** *n. a.* ~s *pl.* bağırma, haykırma, feryat; **vo'cif.er.ous** ☐ gürültülü, bağırtkan, şamatalı.

**vogue** [vəug] *n.* moda; rağbet, itibar; in ~ moda halinde; rağbette.

**voice** [vɔis] **1.** *n.* ses; fikir; active *(passive)* ~ *gr.* etken (edilgen) çatı; in (good) ~ şarkı söyleyebilir *veya* konuşabilir durumda; give ~ to -i ifade etm.; **2.** *v/t.* söylemek, ifade etm., belirtmek; *gr.* telaf fuz etm.; ♪ akort etm.; **voiced** *comb. gr.* ...sesli; **'voice.less** ☐ *part. gr.* sessiz.

**void** [vɔid] **1.** *adj.* boş, ıssız; faydasız, yararsız; ☒ hükümsüz; ~ of -den mahrum. -den yoksun, -siz, -sız; **2.** *n.* boşluk *(a. fig.);* **3.** *v/t.* hükümsüz kılmak; boşalt-

**mak;** çıkarmak; **ˈvoid.ness** *n.* boşluk.
**voile** [vɔil] *n.* ince kumaş, vual.
**vol.a.tile** [ˈvɔlətail] *adj.* buharlaşabilen, uçucu; *fig.* havaî; dönek; **vol.a.til.i-ty** [~ˈtiliti] *n.* uçuculuk; **vol.a.til.ize** [vɔ-ˈlætilaiz] *v/t.* & *v/i.* buharlaş(tır)mak.
**vol.can.ic** [vɔlˈkænik] *adj.* (~ally) volkanik; **vol.ca.no** [vɔlˈkeinəu] *n., pl.* **vol¹ca-noes** [~z] yanardağ, volkan.
**vo.li.tion** [vəuˈliʃən] *n.* irade; on one's own ~ kendi iradesiyle.
**vol.ley** [ˈvɔli] 1. *n.* yaylım ateş; *fig.* yağmur; *tenis:* topa yere değmeden geri vurma; vole; 2. *v/t. mst* ~ out (*soru vs.*) yağmuruna tutmak; yere değmeden geri vurmak (*top*); *v/i.* yaylım ateş etm.; **ˈvol.ley.ball** *n. spor:* voleybol.
**vol.plane** ⚓ [ˈvɔlplein] 1. *n.* süzülme uçuş; 2. *v/i.* süzülerek uçmak.
**volt** ⚡ [vɔult] *n.* volt; **ˈvolt.age** *n.* ⚡ voltaj, gerilim; **vol.ta.ic** ⚡ [vɔlˈteiik] *adj.* galvanik.
**volte-face** *fig.* [ˈvɔltˈfɑːs] *n.* tamamen geriye dönüş.
**volt.me.ter** ⚡ [ˈvəultmiːtə] *n.* voltmetre.
**vol.u.bil.i.ty** [vɔljuˈbiliti] *n.* dillilik, konuşkanlık; **vol.u.ble** □ [ˈ~bl] dilli, konuşkan, çenebaz.
**vol.ume** [ˈvɔljum] *n.* cilt; miktar; *phys. etc.* hacim, oylum; ses şiddeti; ~ of sound *radyo:* ses şiddeti; ~ control, ~ regulator potansiyometre, ses (yükseltme) regülatörü; **vo.lu.mi.nous** □ [vəˈljuːminəs] büyük, hacimli, koskocaman; ciltler doldurur; çok kitap yazan, verimli (*yazar*).
**vol.un.tar.y** [ˈvɔləntəri] 1. □ gönüllü, ihtiyarî, istemli; *physiol.* iradeli; iradeye bağlı, iradî; ~ death intihar; 2. *n.* istemli hareket; ♪ org solosu; **vol.un.teer** [~ˈtiə] 1. *n.* gönüllü (asker); *attr.* gönüllü...; 2. *v/i.* gönüllü yazılmak (for -e); *v/t.* kendi isteği ile teklif etm. *veya* vermek.
**vo.lup.tu.ar.y** [vəˈlʌptjuəri] *n.* şehvet düşkünü, şehvestperest kimse.
**vo.lup.tu.ous** □ [vəˈlʌptjuəs] şehvetli; duygusal; zevk düşkünü: **vo¹lup.tu.ous-ness** *n.* şehvete düşkünlük.
**vo.lute** ⌂ [vəˈljuːt] *n.* kıvrım, sarmal süs; **vo¹lut.ed** *adj.* sarmal.
**vom.it** [ˈvɔmit] 1. *v/t.* & *v/i.* kus(tur)mak; *fig.* çıkarmak; (*yanardağ*) ağzından fışkırtmak (*lav*); 2. *n.* kusmuk; kusma; kusturucu ilaç.
**voo.doo** [ˈvuːduː] 1. *n.* zenci büyücü *veya* büyüsü; 2. *vb.* büyülemek, büyü yapmak.
**vo.ra.cious** □ [vəˈreiʃəs] doymak bilmez,

açgözlü, obur; çok istekli; **vo¹ra.cious-ness, vo.rac.i.ty** [vəˈræsiti] *n.* açgözlülük; hırs (of).
**vor.tex** [ˈvɔːteks] *n., pl.* **mst vor.ti.ces** [ˈ~tisiːz] girdap (*mst fig.*).
**vo.ta.ry** [ˈvəutəri] *n.* kendini *bşe* adamış kimse, *bşe* düşkün kimse; hararetli taraftar.
**vote** [vəut] 1. *n.* oy (hakkı), rey; oy toplamı; ~ of no confidence güvensizlik oyu; cast a ~ oy vermek; put to the ~ oya sunmak; take a ~ on s.th. *bşe* oy vermek; 2. *v/t.* seçmek; önermek; F söylemek, bildirmek; *v/i.* oy vermek; ~ for -*in* lehine oy vermek; **ˈvot.er** *n.* seçmen.
**vot.ing...:** ~**booth** [ˈvəutinbuːð] *n.* oy verme kulübesi; ˈ~**box** *n.* oy sandığı; ˈ~**pa-per** *n.* oy pusulası.
**vo.tive** [ˈvəutiv] *adj.* adak olarak verilen, adak...
**vouch** [vautʃ] *v/t.* temin etm., garanti etm.; doğrulamak (for -*i*); *v/i.* ~ for -*e* kefil olm.; **ˈvouch.er** *n.* belgit, tanıt, vesika, senet, alındı, makbuz; kefil; **vouch-ˈsafe** *vb.* lütfetmek, vermek; tenezzül etm.
**vow** [vau] 1. *n.* adak, yemin, söz; 2. *v/t.* yemin etm. -*e*; adamak, nezretmek -*i*; ahdetmek.
**vow.el** [ˈvauəl] *n.* sesli, ünlü harf, vokal.
**voy.age** [ˈvɔiidʒ] 1. *n.* yolculuk, seyahat; 2. *v/i.* yolculuk etm.; **voy.ag.er** [ˈvɔiədʒə] *n.* yolcu, gezmen.
**vul.can.ite** [ˈvʌlkənait] *n.* ebonit; vulkanit; **vul.can.i¹za.tion** *n.* ⊕ ebonitleştirme, vulkanizasyon; **ˈvul.can.ize** *v/t.* ⊕ ebonitleştirmek, vulkanize etm.; ~d fibre vulkanize lif.
**vul.gar** [ˈvʌlgə] 1. □ kaba, terbiyesiz; aşağılık; bayağı, adi; halka ait, halka özgü; ~ tongue halk dili; 2. *n.* the ~ avam; ayaktakımı; **ˈvul.gar.ism** *n.* kabalık, adilik; argo; **vul.gar.i.ty** [~ˈgæriti] *n.* kabalık, terbiyesizlik; **vul.gar.ize** [ˈ~gəraiz] *v/t.* adileştirmek; genelleştirmek, herkesin anlayacağı şekle sokmak.
**vul.ner.a.bil.i.ty** [vʌlnərəˈbiliti] *n.* yaralanma olasılığı; **ˈvul.ner.a.ble** □ kolayca yaralanır, zedelenir, incinebilir; *fig.* zayıf (*nokta*); **ˈvul.ner.ar.y** 1. *adj.* şifalı, yarayı iyileştiren; 2. *n.* yarayı iyileştiren ilaç.
**vul.pine** [ˈvʌlpain] *adj.* tilki gibi (a. *fig.*): *fig.* kurnaz.
**vul.ture** *orn.* [ˈvʌltʃə] *n.* akbaba; *fig.* aç gözlü kimse; **vul.tur.ine** [ˈ~tʃurain] *adj.* akbaba familyasından.
**vy.ing** [ˈvaiiŋ] *adj.* rekabet eden.

# W

**wab.ble** [ˈwɔbl] = wobble.

**wack.y** *Am. sl.* [ˈwæki] *adj.* kaçık, sapık, manyak.

**wad** [wɔd] 1. *n.* tıkaç, tampon; tutam, tomar, deste; çok miktar; bir tomar para; 2. *v/t.* pamukla beslemek; tıkamak; **ˈwad.ding** *n.* tıkaç, tampon; pamuk vatkası.

**wad.dle** [ˈwɔdl] *v/i.* badi badi yürümek, paytak paytak yürümek.

**wade** [weid] *v/i.* su *veya* çamur içinde yürümek; *fig.* zorla bitirmek, güçlükle ilerlemek; *v/t.* yürüyerek geçmek; **ˈwad.er** *n.* su *veya* çamurda yürüyen kimse; ~s *pl.* su geçirmez uzun çizme.

**wa.fer** [ˈweifə] *n.* bisküvi, kâğıt helvası; *a.* consecrated ~ *eccl.* mayasız ince ekmek.

**waf.fle** [ˈwɔfl] 1. *n.* boş laf, saçma; 2. *v/i.* F saçmalamak.

**waft** [wɑːft] 1. *v/t.* sürüklemek, yavaşça götürmek; 2. *n.* hafif koku, esinti; sürükleme.

**wag¹** [wæg] 1. *v/t.* & *v/i.* salla(n)mak; 2. *n.* salla(n)ma.

**wag²** [~] *n.* şakacı kimse; play ~ *sl.* okulu kırmak.

**wage** [weidʒ] 1. *v/t.* sürdürmek, yürütmek; 2. *n.* *mst* ~s *pl.* ücret, maaş, haftalık; ~-earn.er [ˈ~əːnə] *n.* ücretli kimse, haftalıkçı kimse; ˈ~-sheet, ˈ~.es-sheet *n.* ücret bordrosu.

**wa.ger** *lit.* [ˈweidʒə] 1. *n.* bahis; 2. *v/i.* bahis tutuşmak (on *üzerine*).

**wag.ger.y** [ˈwægəri] *n.* şaka(cılık); **ˈwag-gish** ☐ şakacı; şaka yollu yapılan.

**wag.gle** F [ˈwægl] = wag¹ 1; ˈwag.gly *adj.* F sallanan.

**wag.(g)on** [ˈwægən] *n.* yük arabası; yük vagonu, katar; devriye arabası; tekerlekli servis arabası; be *veya* go on the (water) ~ F artık ağzına içki koymamak; ˈwag.(g)on.er *n.* arabacı.

**wag.tail** *orn.* [ˈwægteil] *n.* kuyruksallayan.

**waif** [weif] *n.* kimsesiz çocuk; başıboş hayvan; ~s and strays *pl.* evsiz barksız çocuklar.

**wail** [weil] 1. *n.* çığlık, figan, feryat; 2. *v/t.* feryat etm., figan etm.; *v/i.* hayıflanmak (over -*e*).

**wain** *poet.* [wein] *n.* yük arabası; Charles's ♌, the ♌ *ast.* Büyükayı.

**wain.scot** [ˈweinskət] 1. *n.* tahta kaplama, lambri; 2. *v/t.* lambri kaplamak.

**waist** [weist] *n.* bel (*a.* ↧); korsaj; bluz; ˈ~-band *n.* bel kuşağı; ~.coat [ˈweiskəut] *n.* yelek; ~-deep [ˈweistˈdiːp] *adj.* & *adv.* yarı beline kadar (çıkan).

**wait** [weit] 1. *v/i.* beklemek; *a.* ~ at (*Am.* on) table -*e* hizmetçilik (*veya* servis) yapmak; ~ for -*i* beklemek; ~ (up)on s.o. *b-ne* hizmet etm.; *b-ni* ziyaret etm.; keep ~ing bekletmek; ~ and see bekleyip görmek; ~ in line kuyrukta beklemek; *v/t.* ertelemek, bekletmek; 2. *n.* bekleme (süresi); gecikme; pusu; ~s *pl.* Noel'de sokaklarda ilâhiler söyleyen grup; have a long ~ uzun süre beklemek; lie in ~ for s.o. *b-i* için pusuya yatmak; ˈwait.er *n.* garson.

**wait.ing** [ˈweitiŋ] *n.* bekleme; in ~ refakat eden; no ~ bekleme yapılmaz; ˈ~-maid *n.* hizmetçi kız; ˈ~-room *n.* bekleme salonu.

**wait.ress** [ˈweitris] *n.* kadın garson.

**waive** [weiv] *v/t.* vazgeçmek -*den*, feragat etm. -*den* (*a.* ⚖); ertelemek; ˈwaiv.er *n.* ⚖ feragat(name).

**wake¹** [weik] *n.* ↧ dümen suyu; ⚓ hava çevrisi; *fig.* iz, eser; in the ~ of -*in* peşi sıra; -*in* sonucu olarak.

**wake²** [~] 1. (*irr.*) *v/t.* & *v/i.* a. ~ up uyan-(dır)mak; *fig.* canlan(dır)mak; hareke-te getirmek; ölü başında beklemek; 2. *n.* ölüyü bekleme; ölüyü bekleme merasimi sırasında verilen ziyafet; **wake.ful** ☐ [ˈ~ful] uyanık; uykusuz; ˈwak.en *v/t.* & *v/i.* uyan(dır)mak; *fig.* uyarmak.

**wale** [weil] *part. Am. for* weal².

**walk** [wɔːk] 1. *v/t.* & *v/i.* yürü(t)mek, gez-(dir)mek; yürüyerek (*veya* yaya) gitmek; yürüyüşe çık(ar)mak; hareket etm., davranmak; yürüyerek eşlik etm.; adımlamak; ~ about dolaşmak; ~ into *sl.* saldırmak; paylamak, haşlamak, azarlamak; açgözlülükle yemek; ~ out F grev yapmak; ~ out on *sl.* terketmek; ~ the hospitals *(tıp öğrencisi)* hastane stajı yapmak; **2.** *n.* yürüyüş; gezme, yürüme; davranış, hareket, gidiş; yürüyüş yeri, kaldırım, yol; go for a ~ yürüyüşe çıkmak, dolaşmak, gezinmek; ~ of life sosyal durum, hayat yolu; meslek; ıwalk·er *n.* gezen, yürüyen, yaya; *spor.* yürüyücü; be a good ~ ayağına sıkı olm.; ıwalk.er-on *n. thea.* figüran.

walk.ie-talk.ie × [ˈwɔːkiˈtɔːki] *n.* portatif telsiz telefon.

walk.ing [ˈwɔːkiŋ] *n.* gezme, yürüme; *attr.* yürüme..., yürüyüş...; ~ pa.pers *pl. Am.* F işten atılma kâğıdı; ˈ~-stick *n.* baston, asa; ˈ~-tour *n.* gezinti.

walk...: ˈ~-out *n. Am.* grev; *(toplantı vs.- 'yi)* terketme; ı~-over *n.* kolay yengi; ˈ~-up *adj.* asansörsüz *(bina)*.

wall [wɔːl] **1.** *n.* duvar; sur; give s.o. the ~ *b-ne* kibarca yol göstermek; go to the ~ *fig.* iflâs etm.; çıkmaza girmek; **2.** *v/t.* duvarla çevirmek; *fig.* kapatmak, ayırmak; ~ up duvarla kapamak.

wal.la.by *zo.* [ˈwɔləbi] *n.* küçük kanguru.

wal.let [ˈwɔlit] *n.* cüzdan; † sırt çantası.

wall...: ˈ~-eye *n. vet.* akçıl gözbebeği; ı~.flow.er *n.* ⚘ bahçe şebboyu; *fig.* damsız olduğu için dans edemeyen kimse; ˈ~-fruit *n.* espalye ağacının meyvesi; ˈ~-map *n.* duvar haritası.

Wal.loon [wɔˈluːn] **1.** *n.* Valon (dili), Valonca; **2.** *adj.* Valon'a ait.

wal.lop F [ˈwɔləp] **1.** *v/i.* bata çıka yürümek; ses çıkararak kaynamak; *v/t.* eşek sudan gelinceye kadar dövmek; **2.** *n.* ağır darbe; *sl.* bira; ˈwal.lop.ing *adj.* F koskocaman; kuyruklu *(yalan)*.

wal.low [ˈwɔləu] **1.** *v/i.* çamur içinde yuvarlanmak; *fig.* büyük zevk almak (in -den); **2.** *n.* hayvanın yuvarlandığı çamurlu yer; çamurda yuvarlanma.

wall...: ˈ~-pa.per *n.* duvar kâğıdı; ˈ~-sock-et *n.* ∮ duvar prizi.

wal.nut ⚘ [ˈwɔːlnʌt] *n.* ceviz (ağacı).

wal.rus *zo.* [ˈwɔːlrəs] *n.* mors.

waltz [wɔːls] **1.** *n.* vals; **2.** *v/t. & v/i.* vals yap(tır)mak.

wam.pum [ˈwɔmpəm] *n.* para *veya* süs olarak Amerikan kızılderililerince kullanılan boncuklar; *sl.* mangır, mangiz.

wan □ [wɔn] solgun, soluk, beti benzi atmış, bitkin.

wand [wɔnd] *n.* değnek, çubuk; asa.

wan.der [ˈwɔndə] *v/i.* dolaşmak, gezmek; *a.* ~ about aylak aylak dolanıp durmak; *fig.* ayrılmak (from -den); abuk sabuk

konuşmak, sayıklamak; ˈwan.der.er *n.* gayesizce dolaşan kimse, avare; ˈwan.der.ing **1.** □ dolaşan, gezginci; *fig.* daldan dala konan; **2.** *n.* ~s *pl.* seyahatler; sayıklama.

wane [wein] **1.** *v/i.* küçülmek *(ay)*; *fig.* azalmak, zayıflamak; solmak; **2.** *n.* azalma; on the ~ azalmakta.

wan.gle *sl.* [ˈwæŋgl] *v/t.* sızdırmak, dalavereyle koparmak; ˈwan.gler *n.* hilekâr kimse.

want [wɔnt] **1.** *n.* yokluk, azlık, kıtlık (of), sıkıntı, zaruret, fakirlik; ihtiyaç, lüzum, gerek, hacet; arzu, istek; for ~ of ...bulunmadığından,... yokluğundan; **2.** *v/i.* be ~ing eksik olm.; be ~ing in *-den* yoksun olm.; he does not ~ for *-e* ihtiyaç duymuyor, *-e* gereksinmesi yok; it ~s lâzım, gerek; *v/t.* istemek, arzulamak; gereksemek; gerektirmek; it ~s s.th. *bş* gerektiriyor; he ~s energy gayrete gereksinmesi var; you ~ to be careful dikkatli olmanız gerekir; ~ s.o. to do *b-den bş* yapmasını istemek; ~ed aranan, istenen; ˈ~-ad *n.* küçük ilan.

wan.ton [ˈwɔntən] **1.** □ zevk düşkünü; şehvet düşkünün, ahlâksız; amaçsız, gayesiz, nedensiz; acımasız, insanlık dışı; sorumsuz, başıboş; **2.** *n.* ahlâksız kadın; **3.** *v/i.* ⚘ çok gelişmek; ˈwan.ton.ness *n.* şehvet.

war [wɔː] **1.** *n.* savaş, harp *(a. fig.)*; *attr.* savaş...; at ~ savaşmakta, savaş halinde; make ~ savaşmak (upon *ile*); ~ criminal savaş suçlusu; **2.** *v/i. lit.* savaşmak; *fig.* mücadele etm.

war.ble [ˈwɔːbl] **1.** *v/i.* ötmek, şakımak; **2.** *n.* ötme, şakıma; ˈwar.bler *n.* ötücü kuş; şarkıcı.

war...: ˈ~-cry *n.* savaş narası; *fig.* parola.

ward [wɔːd] **1.** *n.* vesayet (altında bulunan kimse); *(hastane, hapishane vs.)* koğuş; bölge, mıntıka; *fenc.* çelme, parad; ⊕ kilit dili; in ~ vesayet altında; **2.** *v/t.* ~ off savuşturmak, geçiştirmek; ˈward.en *n.* bekçi, koruyucu; müdür; *univ.* rektör; ˈward.er *n.* bekçi, koruyucu; gardiyan; ˈward.robe *n.* giysi dolabı, gardırop; elbiseler; *thea.* kostümler; ~ dealer elbiseci; ~ trunk gardırop bavul; ˈward-room *n.* ↓ oyun salonu ve yemekhane; ˈward.ship *n.* koruyuculuk; vasilik, vesayet.

ware [ wɛə] *n.* mal, emtia, eşya.

ware.house **1.** [ˈwɛəhaus] *n.* ambar; ant repo; eşya deposu; mağaza; **2.** [ˈ~hauz] *v/t.* ambarda saklamak; **~.man** [ˈ~hausmən] *n.* ambarcı; antrepocu; mağaza sahibi.

**war...: ˈ~.fare** *n.* savaş(ma); mücadele; ˈ~.grave *n.* asker mezarı; ˈ~.head *n.* merminin patlayıcı kısmı, harp başlığı.

**war.i.ness** [ˈwɛərinis] *n.* uyanıklık, ihtiyat.

**war.like** [ˈwɔːlaik] *adj.* savaşçı; savaşla ilgili, savaş...; askerî.

**war-loan** [ˈwɔːləun] *n.* savaş borçlanması.

**warm** [wɔːm] **.1.** ☐ sıcak *(a. fig.)*, hararetli, ılık; sıcak tutan, ısıtan; *fig.* gayretli, şevkli; *fig.* içten, candan; *fig.* sevimli, sempatik; yeni, taze; make things ~ for s.o. *b-nin* anasının emdiğini burnundan getirmek; **2.** *n.* F ısınma; **3.** *v/t. & v/i. a.* ~ up ısıtmak; ısınmak; kız(dır)mak; *sl.* coş(tur)mak; şevkle sarılmak (to *-e)*; **ˈwarm.ing** *n. sl.* pataklama.

**war-mon.ger** [ˈwɔːmʌŋgə] *n.* savaş kışkırtıcısı; **ˈwar-mon.ger.ing, ˈwar.mon.ger.y** *n.* savaş kışkırtıcılığı.

**warmth** [wɔːmθ] *n.* sıcaklık, ılıklık; coşkunluk; içtenlik.

**warn** [wɔːn] *v/t.* ikaz etm., uyarmak (of, against *-e karşı)*; tembihlemek (to *inf. -meyi)*; ihtar etm. *-e* (of *-i)*; öğütlemek (of *-i)*; **ˈwarn.ing** *n.* ihtar, ikaz, uyarı; ihbar; give ~ uyarmak, ikaz etm.; take ~ from *-den* ibret almak.

**War Of.fice** [ˈwɔːrɔfis] *n.* Millî Savunma Bakanlığı.

**warp** [wɔːp] **1.** *n.* çözgü, arış; ⚓ palamar; *fig.* eğrilik, çarpıklık; **2.** *v/t. & v/i.* eğril(t)mek, yamul(t)mak; ⚓ palamarı çekerek yürütmek; ⚓ yesarilenmek; saptırmak (from *-den)*.

**war-paint** [ˈwɔːpeint] *n.* savaş işareti olarak vücuda sürülen boya; *fig.* resmî kıyafet; *sl.* kozmetik; in full ~ resmî kıyafetli.

**warp.ing** ⚓ [ˈwɔːpiŋ] *n.* yesarilenme.

**war...: ˈ~.plane** *n.* savaş uçağı; **ˈ~-profit.eer** *n.* savaş zengini.

**war.rant** [ˈwɔrənt] **1.** *n.* yetki; ruhsat; makbuz; teminat, garanti, kefalet; arama kâğıdı; ♘ müzekkere; *a.* ~ of apprehension *veya* ~ of arrest tevkif müzekkeresi; **2.** *v/t.* temin etm.; izin *(veya* ruhsat) vermek *-e;* kefil olm. *-e; part.* ✝ garanti etm., teminat vermek; **ˈwar.ranta.ble** ☐ garanti edilebilir; *hunt.* avlanabilir; **ˈwar.rant.a.bly** *adv.* uygun bir şekilde; **ˈwar.rant.ed** *adj.* garantili; **war.ranˈtee** *n.* ♘ *k-ne* teminat verilen kimse; **ˈwar.rant-offi.cer** *n.* ⬇ güverte subayı; ✗ gedikli, erbaş; **war.ran.tor** ♘ [ˈ~tɔː] *n.* kefil; **ˈwar.ran.ty** *n.* kefalet(name), ga

ranti, teminat; yetki.

**war.ren** [ˈwɔrən] *n.* tavşanın bol olduğu yer.

**war.ri.or** [ˈwɔriə] *n.* savaşçı, cenkçi, asker.

**war.ship** [ˈwɔːʃip] *n.* savaş gemisi.

**wart** [wɔːt] *n.* siğil; *part.* ✿ yumru, şiş; **ˈwart.y** *adj.* siğilli.

**war.time** [ˈwɔːtaim] **1.** *n.* savaş zamanı; **2.** *adj.* savaştan doğan, savaş...

**war.y** ☐ [ˈwɛəri] uyanık, ihtiyatlı, açıkgöz.

**was** [wɔz, wəz] *pret. of* be; he ~ to have come gelmiş olmalıydı.

**wash** [wɔʃ] **1.** *v/t. & v/i.* yıka(n)mak, ıslatmak; yıkanmaya gelmek *(kumaş)*; yalamak *(dalga)*; aşındırarak açmak; ~ed out yağmur nedeniyle ertelenmiş *veya* kapanmış; solgun, soluk; F bitkin, yorgun; ~ up bulaşık yıkamak; elini yüzünü yıkamak; **2.** *n.* yıka(n)ma; çamaşır(hane); çalkantı; dalga sesi; losyon, şampuan; sulu mutfak artığı; ⬇ dümen suyu; *contp.* saçmalık; mouth-~ gargara; *s.* white~; **ˈwash.a.ble** *adj.* yıkanabilir; **ˈwash-ba.sin** *n.* lavabo; **ˈwash-cloth** *n.* sabun bezi, havlu; **ˈwash-draw.ing** *n.* sulu boya resim.

**wash.er** [ˈwɔʃə] *n.* yıkama makinesi; yıkayıcı; ⊕ pul, rondela; **ˈ~-wom.an** *n.* çamaşırcı kadın.

**wash.ing** [ˈwɔʃiŋ] *n.* yıka(n)ma; ~s *pl.* çamaşır; *attr.* çamaşır...; **ˈ~-ma.chine** *n.* çamaşır makinesi; ~ pow.der çamaşır tozu.

**wash.ing-up** [ˈwɔʃiˈnʌp] *n.* bulaşık yıkama.

**wash...: ˈ~-ˈout** *n. sl.* başarısız kimse; fiyasko; ˈ~.rag *n. part. Am.* sabun bezi, havlu; **ˈ~-stand** *n.* lavabo; **ˈ~-tub** *n.* leğen; **ˈwash.y** *adj.* sulu; soluk, solgun; cansız, sönük.

**was.n't** [wɔznt] = was not.

**wasp** [wɔsp] *n.* yabanarısı; **ˈwasp.ish** ☐ hırçın, huysuz, dik kafalı.

**was.sail** † [ˈwɔseil] *n.* içki âlemi; baharlı içki.

**wast.age** [ˈweistidʒ] *n.* israf, sarfiyat.

**waste** [weist] **1.** *adj.* boş, ıssız; çorak, kıraç; artık, işe yaramaz, atılmış; viran, harap; ⊕ kullanılmaz; lay ~ harap etm., viraneye çevirmek; ~ paper kullanılmış kâğıt; **2.** *n.* israf, çarçur, savurma, sarfiyat; artık, çöp, süprüntü; boş arazi, ıssız yer; yıkım; go *veya* run to ~ israf olm., ziyan olm., boşa gitmek; **3.** *v/t.* boşuna sarfetmek; israf etm., çarçur etm.; harap etm., viraneye çevirmek; aşındır

mak; *v/i.* heba olm.; aşınmak; ~ away eriyip gitmek, günden güne zayıflamak; **waste.ful** ☐ ['~ful] savurgan, ziyankâr; **'waste-pa.per** bas.ket *n.* kâğıt sepeti; **'waste-pipe** *n.* künk; **'wast.er** *n.* savurgan kimse; = wastrel.
**wast.rel** ['weistrəl] *n.* savurgan kimse; bir işe yaramaz kimse.
**watch** [wɔtʃ] **1.** *n.* gözetleme, bekçilik; nöbet (*a.* ↓); nöbetçi, bekçi; nöbetçilik; devriye; cep *veya* kol saati; uyanıklık; be on the ~ for *-i* gözlemek, yolunu beklemek; *-e* dikkat etm., *için* tetikte olm.; **2.** *v/i.* dikkat etm., göz kulak olm. (with, over *-e*); ~ for *-i* beklemek, gözlemek; ~ out F dikkat etm.; *v/t.* gözetlemek, seyretmek; ~ one's time uygun zamanı beklemek; '~.boat *n.* ↓ devriye botu; '~-brace.let *n.* saat bileziği; '~-case *n.* saat kutusu; '~.dog *n.* bekçi köpeği; **'watch.er** *n.* muhafız, bekçi; bakıcı; gözlemci; **watch.ful** ☐ ['~ful] uyanık, tetik. **watch**...: '~-mak.er *n.* saatçi; '~.man *n.* bekçi; '~-tow.er *n.* gözetleme kulesi; '~.word *n.* parola.
**wa.ter** ['wɔːtə] **1.** *n.* su; ~s *pl.* sular; ~s *pl.* kara suları; gölcük, gölet; gözyaşı; salya; (*kumaş*) hare, şanjan; ~ supply su rezervi: su kaynakları; high ~ met, kabarma; low ~ cezir, inme; by ~ deniz yoluyla; drink *veya* take the ~s kaplıcalara gidip şifalı su içmek; of the first ~ en iyi kalite, birinci sınıf; be in hot ~ F başı dertte olm., ayvayı yemiş olm., hapı yutmuş olm.; be in low ~ F meteliğe kurşun atmak, eli darda olm.; hold ~ *fig.* su kaldırmak, tutacak yanı olm.; make ~ su dökmek, işemek; **2.** *v/t. & v/i.* sulamak; sulan(dır)mak; suvar(ıl)mak; *oft.* ~ down sulandırmak; *fig.* hafifletmek, yumuşatmak; ⊕ harelemek (*ipek*); 𝄞 denize inmek; make s.o.'s mouth ~ *b-nin* ağzını sulandırmak; '~-blis.ter *n.* 𝄞 su kabarcığı; '~-borne *adj.* deniz yoluyla nakledilen (*mal*); '~-bot.tle *n.* su şişesi; matara; '~-buf.fa.lo *n.* manda; '~-cart *n.* su arabası; '~-clos.et *n.* hela, tuvalet, apteshane; '~-col.o(u)r *n.* suluboya (resim); '~-cool.ing *n.* suyla soğutma; '~.course *n.* dere, çay; kanal; nehir yatağı; '~.cress *n.* 𝄞 suteresi; '~.fall *n.* çağlayan, şelale; '~.fowl *n. pl.* su kuşu, su kuşları; '~-front *n.* sahil arsası; *part. Am.* liman bölgesi; '~.ga(u)ge *n.* ⊕ derinlik göstergesi; '~-glass *n.* 𝄞 sodyum silikat; '~-hose *n.* su hortumu; 'wa.ter.i.ness *n.* sululuk; lezzetsizlik; solgunluk. **wa.ter.ing** ['wɔːtəriŋ] *n.* sulama; '~-can,

'~-pot *n.* emzikli kova, sulama ibriği; '~-place *n.* içmeler; plaj; kaplıca; suvarma yeri. **water**...: '~-jack.et *n.* ⊕ su soğutma gömleği; '~-lev.el *n.* su seviyesi; ⊕ tesviye ruhu; '~-lil.y 𝄞 nilüfer; '~.logged *adj.* içi su dolu; '~-main *n.* yeraltı su borusu; '~.man *n.* kayıkçı; '~-mark *n.* filigran; '~-mel.on *n.* 𝄞 karpuz; '~-pipe *n.* su borusu; '~-plane *n.* deniz uçağı; '~-po.lo *n.* su topu; '~-pow.er *n.* su gücü; ~ station hidroelektrik santralı; '~.proof **1.** *adj.* sugeçirmez; **2.** *n.* yağmurluk, muşamba; **3.** *v/t.* sugeçirmez hale koymak; '~-re'pel·lent *adj.* su çekmez; '~.shed *n.* iki nehir havzası arasındaki set; sınır; '~.side **1.** *n.* sahil, kıyı; **2.** *adj.* sahilde olan; sahilde çalışan; sahile özgü, sahil...; '~-ski *n.* su kayağı; '~.spout *n.* oluk; deniz hortumu; '~-ta.ble *n.* yağmur etekliği; su tabakası (seviyesi); '~.tight *adj.* sugeçirmez, sızmaz, akmaz; *fig.* hata kabul etmez, göz açtırmaz; '~-wave **1.** *n.* ondüle; **2.** *vb.* ondüle yapmak; '~-way *n.* su yolu, kanal; '~.works *n. pl., a. sg.* su dağıtım tesisatı; gözyaşı; 'wa.ter.y *adj.* sulu (*a. fig.*); su gibi; soluk (*renk*); sudan, zayıf.
**watt** ≠ [wɔt] *n.* vat.
**wat.tle** ['wɔtl] **1.** *n.* dal *veya* çubuklardan örülmüş yapı; *orn.* sarkık gerdan; 𝄞 akasya; **2.** *vb.* ince çubuklarla çit örmek.
**waul** [wɔːl] *v/i.* miyavlamak.
**wave** [weiv] **1.** *n.* dalga (*a. phys. & saç*); el sallama; dalgalanma; hare; **2.** *v/t. & v/i.* dalgalan(dır)mak; salla(n)mak; harelemek; el sallamak (to s.o. *b-ne*); elle işaret etm.; ondüle yapmak (*saç*); ~ aside bir kenara bırakmak; reddetmek; '~-length *n.* ≠ dalga boyu (*veya* uzunluğu).
**wa.ver** ['weivə] *v/i.* kararsızlık göstermek, tereddüt etm., duraksamak; sallanmak; sendelemek; titrek yanmak.
**wave**...: '~-range *n. radyo:* dalga gamı; '~-trap *n. radyo:* süzme (*veya* süzgeç) devresi.
**wav.y** ['weivi] *adj.* dalgalı, dalga dalga; titreyen, titreşen.
**wax¹** [wæks] **1.** *n.* balmumu, mum; parafin; kulak kiri; cila; kızgınlık; ~ candle mum; ~ doll balmumundan bebek; **2.** *v/t.* mum sürmek *-e*, mumlamak; cilalamak.
**wax²** [~] (*irr.*) *v/i.* büyümek, artmak, yükselmek; † olmak.
**wax.en** ['wæksn] *adj.* mumdan yapılmış; mum gibi; *fig.* beti benzi atmış, solgun; **'wax.work** *n.* balmumu işi; balmumundan

yapılmış heykel; ~s *pl.*, ~ show balmumundan yapılmış heykeller (müzesi); **¹wax.y** ☐ mum gibi; mumlu; solgun; öfkeli.

**way** [wei] **1.** *n. mst* yol; F yön, istikamet, taraf, yan, cihet; ↓ rota; *fig.* hal, durum, gidiş(at); mesafe; tarz, usül; şekil; çare, vasıta; yer; tutum, davranış, huy, âdet; ~ in giriş; ~ out çıkış; *fig.* çıkar yol; ~s and means para bulma (yolları); right of ~ ₫♭ irtifak hakkı; *part. mot.* yol hakkı; ~ of life yaşam biçimi; yaşama tarzı; this ~ bu taraftan, buraya; the wrong ~ yanlış yol; in some ~, in a ~ bir bakıma; in no ~ hiç bir suretle, asla, katiyen; go a great ~ towards *ger.*, go a long (some) ~ to *inf.* büyük katkıda bulunmak -e; by the ~ aklıma gelmişken, sırası gelmişken; by ~ of ...yolu ile, ...üzerinden; ...niyetiyle; by ~ of excuse özür mahiyetinde; on the ~, on one's ~ yol üstünde, yol(un)da, yoluna; out of the ~ alışılmışın dışında; sapa; yerinde olmayan; under ~ devam etmekte, hareket halinde, ilerlemekte; ↓ rotasında; give ~ geri çekilmek; kopmak; kırılmak; çökmek, yol vermek (to -e); öncelik vermek (to -e); *k-ni* vermek (to -e); küreklere asılmak; have one's ~ arzusuna kavuşmak, muradına ermek; if I had my ~ istediğim olsa; have a ~ with ikna kabiliyeti olm.; lead the ~ yol göstermek (*a. fig.*); *s.* make; pay one's ~ kendi masrafını ödemek; kimseye borcu olmamak; see one's ~ to *ger. veya inf.* ...ceğini sanmak; ...i mümkün görmek; **2.** *adv.* uzak; yakın; **'~-bill** *n.* manifesto, nakliye senedi; **'~.far.er** *n.* yaya yolcu; **~'lay** (*irr.* lay) *v/t.* -in yolunu kesmek, pusuya yatıp beklemek -i; **'~-leave** *n.* geçit hakkı; **'~.side 1.** *n.* yol kenarı; by the ~ yol kenarında; **2.** *adj.* yol kenarındaki; ~ **sta.tion** *Am.* ara istasyon; ~ **train** *Am.* dilenci postası, her istasyona uğrayan tren.

**way.ward** ☐ ['weiwəd] ters, inatçı, aksi, dik başlı; **'way.ward.ness** *n.* inatçılık, dik başlılık.

**we** [wi:, wi] *pron.* biz.

**weak** ☐ [wi:k] *com.* zayıf, kuvvetsiz, halsiz, takatsiz; dayanıksız; sulu, yavan (*çorba vs.*); *gr.* vurgusuz; **'weak.en** *v/t. & v/i.* zayıfla(t)mak, kuvvetten düş(ür)mek, hafifle(t)mek; **'weak.ling** *n.* zayıf kimse *veya* hayvan; karaktersiz kimse; **'weak.ly 1.** *adv.* zayıf bir şekilde; **2.** *adj.* hastalıklı; **'weak-¹mind.ed** *adj.* zayıf iradeli; **'weak.ness** *n.* zayıflık, kuvvetsizlik; zaaf; hata, kusur.

**weal¹** [wi:l] *n.* refah, saadet.

**weal²** [~] *n.* iz, bere.

**wealth** [welθ] *n.* servet, zenginlik, varlık, para, mal; *fig.* bolluk; **'wealth.y** ☐ zengin, varlıklı.

**wean** [wi:n] *v/t.* sütten (*veya* memeden) kesmek; *fig.* ~ s.o. from *veya* of s.th. *b-ne bşi* bıraktırmak, *b-ni bşden* vazgeçirmek.

**weap.on** ['wepən] *n.* silah; **'weap.on.less** *adj.* silahsız.

**wear** [wɛə] **1.** (*irr.*) *v/t. & v/i.* giymek, tak(ın)mak; yıpratmak, yemek; taşımak; dayanmak -e; açmak (*delik, yol*); kabul etm., uygun görmek; kullanmak; yormak; yıpranmak; tükenmek; *a.* ~ away, ~ down, ~ off, ~ out aşın(dır)mak, eski(t)mek; ~ away azaltmak (*direnç*); tüketmek; tükenmek (*sabır*); zayıfla(t)mak; geç(ir)mek (*zaman*); ~ off yavaş yavaş yok olm.; yavaş yavaş geçmek (*ağrı*); ~ on yavaş geçmek (*zaman*); ~ out düzelmek (*kıvrım, kırışıklık*); yormak, tüketmek, yıpratmak; sıkıcı bir şekilde geç(ir)mek (*zaman*); tükenmek (*sabır*); giyip eskitmek (*elbise*); dövmek, pataklamak; kullanmak (*eski bir giyim*); **2.** *n.* giysi, elbise; aşınma, yıpranma, eskime; dayanıklılık; gentlemen's ~ erkek elbiseleri; for hard ~ çok dayanaklı; *s.* worse 1; there is plenty of ~ in it yet daha giyilebilir, bu daha çok dayanır; **'wear.a.ble** *adj.* giyilebilir; **wear and tear** aşınma, yıpranma: zararlı etkiler; **'wear.er** *n. bş* giyen (*veya* takan) kimse.

**wea.ri.ness** ['wiərinis] *n.* yorgunluk, bezginlik; *fig.* usanç, bıkkınlık.

**wea.ri.some** ☐ ['wiərisəm] usandırıcı, sıkıcı, yorucu, bıktırıcı.

**wea.ry** ['wiəri] **1.** ☐ yorgun, bitkin (with); yorucu, bıkkınlık verici, sıkıcı, usandırıcı; *fig.* bıkmış, usanmış (of s.th. *bşden*); **2.** *v/t. & v/i.* yor(ul)mak; bık(tır)mak, usan(dır)mak, bez(dir)mek.

**wea.sel** *zo.* ['wi:zl] *n.* gelincik, samur.

**weath.er** ['weðə] **1.** *n.* hava; *s.* permit; **2.** *adj.* ↓ rüzgâr yönündeki...; ₫♭ havaya göstermek; ↓ -in rüzgâr yönünden geçmek; *a.* ~ out geçiştirmek, savuşturmak (*fırtına*); *fig.* atlatmak (*güçlük*); **~ed** yıpranmış; meyilli; *v/i.* aşınmak; solmak; **'~-beat.en** ['~bi:tn] *adj.* fırtına yemiş; yanık (*yüz, cilt*); **'~-board** *n.* bindirme, siper tahtası; **'~-board.ing** = ~-board; **'~.bound** *adj.* kötü hava yüzünden evde kalmış *veya* gecikmiş; **'~-bureau** *n.* meteoroloji bürosu; **'~.chart** *n.* meteoroloji (*veya* hava) haritası; **'~.cock** *n.* rüzgârgülü, fırıldak, yelkovan **'~-fore-**

**cast** *n.* hava raporu; '~-proof, '~-tight *adj.* rüzgâr *(veya* yağmur) geçirmez; '~-sta.tion *n.* meteoroloji istasyonu; '~- -strip *n.* pencere bandı; '~-vane *n.* rüzgârgülü, fırıldak; '~-worn *adj.* hava etkisiyle bozulmuş *veya* aşınmış.

**weave** [wiːv] 1. *(irr.) v/t.* dokumak; örmek *(sepet); fig.* yapmak, kurmak; *v/i.* zikzak yapmak; 2. *n.* dokuma; örme; 'weav.er *n.* dokumacı, çulha; 'weav.ing *n.* dokuma; *attr.* dokuma...

**wea.zen** ['wiːzn] *adj.* buruşuk, kırışık.

**web** [web] *n.* ağ; örümcek ağı; dokuma; *orn.* perde; *anat.* zar; doku; örgü; tomar; **webbed** *adj.* perde ayaklı; 'web.bing *n.* kalın dokuma kayış; 'web.foot.ed *adj.* perde ayaklı.

**wed** [wed] *vb.* evlenmek *ile,* kocaya varmak, dünya evine girmek; *fig.* bağlanmak, birleşmek (to *-e*).

**we'd** F [wiːd] = we had; we should; we would.

**wed.ded** ['wedid] *adj.* evli; ~ to *fig.* bağlı *-e*, kendini adamış *-e;* 'wed.ding *n.* evlenme, düğün, nikâh; *attr.* nikâh..., evlilik...; ~ ring nikâh yüzüğü.

**wedge** [wedʒ] 1. *n.* kıskı, kama, takoz, çivi; the thin end of the ~ *fig.* büyük değişikliklerin ilk adımı, atılan ilk sağlam adım; ~ heel sivri topuk; 2. *v/t.* kıskı ile sıkıştırmak; *a.* ~ in sık(ıştır)mak; '~- -shaped *adj.* kama şeklinde.

**wed.lock** ['wedlɔk] *n.* evlilik; out of ~ evlilik dışı, gayri meşru.

**Wednes.day** ['wenzdi] *n.* çarşamba.

**wee** [wiː] *adj.* küçücük, minnacık, minimini, azıcık; a ~ bit biraz, oldukça.

**weed** [wiːd] 1. *n.* yabani ot, zararlı ot; F tütün, sigara, puro; *sl.* haşiş; bir deri bir kemik kimse; 2. *v/t.* *-den* yabani otları temizlemek; ~ out ayıklamak, temizlemek, başından savmak; 'weed.er *n.* yabanî ot temizleyen kimse *veya* alet; 'weed-kill.er *n.* yabanî otları öldürmekte kullanılan madde.

**weeds** [wiːdz] *n. pl. mst* widow's ~ matem elbisesi.

**weed.y** ['wiːdi] *adj.* yabani otlarla dolu; *fig.* çiroz gibi, kara kuru, çelimsiz.

**week** [wiːk] *n.* hafta; this day ~ haftaya bugün; '~-day *n.* iş günü, sair gün, hafta günü; '~-end 1. *n.* hafta sonu; ~ ticket hafta sonu bileti; 2. *v/i.* hafta sonunu geçirmek; '~-'end.er *n.* hafta sonunu evinden uzakta geçiren kimse; 'week.ly 1. *adj.* haftalık; 2. *adv.* haftada bir, her hafta; 3. *n. a.* ~ paper haftalık gazete *veya* dergi.

**weep** [wiːp] *(irr.) vb.* ağlamak, göz yaşı dökmek (for *için);* sızmak, damlamak; 'weep.er *n.* ağlayan kimse, ağıtçı; ~s *pl.* uzun favori; 'weep.ing 1. *adj.* gözleri yaşlı; yağmurlu; sarkık dallı; ~ willow ↓ salkımsöğüt; 2. *n.* ağlama.

**wee.vil** ['wiːvil] *n.* buğday biti; pamuk kurdu.

**weft** [weft] *n.* kumaş atkısı, argaç; *poet.* dokuma, örgü.

**weigh** [wei] 1. *v/t.* tartmak; *a.* ~ up *fig.* ölçünmek, hesap etm.; anlamak; ~ anchor ↓ demir almak, vira etm.; ~ down yüklemek; üzmek, kederlendirmek; ~ed down yere eğilmiş; üzgün; yüklü; *v/i.* ...ağırlığında olm., ...gelmek; *fig.* önem taşımak, etkilemek (with *-e göre, -i);* ~ in (out) tartılmak; ~ in with ileri sürmek, ortaya koymak; ~ (up)on üzmek ,kurcalamak *(zihin);* 2. *n.* get under ~ (= way) ↓ yola çıkmak; 'weigh.a.ble *adj.* tartılabilir; 'weigh.bridge *n.* kantar; 'weigh.er *n.* tartan kimse; 'weigh.ing-ma.chine *n.* kantar, baskül.

**weight** [weit] 1. *n.* ağırlık *(a. fig.),* siklet; tartı; dirhem; ağır cisim; *fig.* önem, nüfuz, itibar, etki; *fig.* endişe, sıkıntı, yük; carry great ~ *fig.* büyük önem taşımak; give short ~ eksik gelmek; putting the ~ gülle atma; 2. *v/t.* ağırlaştırmak; *fig.* yüklemek; eklemek; 'weight.i.ness *n.* ağırlık; önemlilik; 'weight.y □ ağır; yüklü; sıkıntılı; önemli, etkili, nüfuzlu.

**weir** [wiə] *n.* su seddi, bent, büğet, bağlağı.

**weird** [wiəd] *adj.* anlaşılmaz, esrarengiz, tekinsiz; F garip, acayip, olağandışı.

**wel.come** ['welkəm] 1. □ sevindirici, istenilen, hoşa giden, makbule geçen; hoş karşılanan; you are ~ to *inf.* kuşkusuz ...ebilirsiniz; you are ~ to it buyurun, alın, denemesi bedava, buyurunuz; (you are) ~! bir şey değil!, rica ederim!; 2. *n.* karşılama; 3. *v/t.* hoş karşılamak; hoş geldiniz demek *-e; fig.* karşılamak.

**weld** ⊕ [weld] 1. *v/t.* & *v/i.* kayna(t)mak (into *-e),* kaynak yaparak birleştirmek; 2. *n. a.* ~ing seam kaynak yeri; 'weld.ing *n.* ⊕ kaynak yapma; *attr.* kaynak...

**wel.fare** ['welfɛə] *n.* refah, sıhhat, afiyet; (yoksullara) yardım; ~ cen.tre yardım merkezi; ~ state refah devleti; ~ work sosyal yardım; ~ work.er sosyal yardım uzmanı.

**well¹** [wel] 1. *n.* kuyu; memba, pınar; *fig.* kaynak; ⊕ boru; ⊕ merdiven boşluğu; 2. *v/i.* kaynamak, fışkırmak.

**well²** [~] 1. *adv.* iyi(ce), tamamiyle, oldukça, hayli; güzel, hoş; hakkıyle; çok, pek; *s. as;* ~ off zengin, hali vakti yerinde; şanslı, talihli; ~ past fifty ellisini hayli geçmiş; **2.** *pred. adj.* iyi, güzel; sıhhatli, sağlıklı; uygun, yerinde; elverişli; I am not ~ rahatsızım, keyfim yok; that's ~ iyi; **3.** *int.* iyi!; şey!; F pekâlâ!; işte!; neyse!

**we'll** F [wi:l] = we will; we shall.

**well**...: '~-ad'vised *adj.* akıllı, sağgörülü; inceden inceye düşünülmüş; '~-'bal.anced *adj.* dengeli; '~-'be.ing *n.* saadet, refah, iyilik; '~-'born *adj.* kibar, soylu, iyi bir aileden gelmiş; '~-'bred *adj.* terbiyeli, kibar; '~-de'fined *adj.* açık seçik görülen, belirgin; '~-dis'posed *adj.* kibar, yardımsever (to, towards *-e karşı);* '~-'fa.vo(u)red *adj.* güzel, yakışıklı; '~-in'formed *adj.* çok bilgili, her şeyden haberi olan.

**Wel.ling.tons** ['weliŋtənz] *n. pl.* lastik çizme.

**well**...: '~-in'ten.tioned *adj.* iyi niyetli; '~-'knit *adj.* adaleli, kuvvetli; ~ known, '~-'known *adj.* tanınmış, meşhur, ünlü, bilinen; ~ made endamlı, boyu bosu yerinde; '~-'man.nered *adj.* terbiyeli; '~-'marked *adj.* açık, belirgin; '~-'nigh *adv.* hemen hemen; '~-'or.dered *adj.* derli toplu, düzenli; '~-'sea.soned *adj.* baharatlı; ~-timed *adj.* uygun, zamanlı; '~-to-'do *adj.* hali vakti yerinde, zengin; '~-'trained *adj.* iyi eğitilmiş; ~ turned *fig.* güzel ifade edilmiş; '~-'wish.er *n.* iyiliksever kimse; '~-'worn *adj.* eskimiş; *fig.* bayatlamış, sıradan.

**Welsh¹** [welʃ] **1.** *adj.* Gal eyaletine ait; Gallilere özgü; **2.** *n.* Gal dili; the ~ *pl.* Gallier.

**welsh²** [~] *v/i.* borcunu ödememek; sözünü tutmamak; 'welsh.er *n.* borcunu ödemeyen, sözünü tutmayan kimse.

**Welsh**...: '~.man *n.* Galli; ~ rab.bit kızarmış ekmeğe sürülen peynir; '~.wom.an *n.* Galli kadın.

**welt** [welt] **1.** *n.* ⊕ kösele şerit; elbisenin kenar şeridi; kamçı izi; **2.** *v/t.* şerit koymak; F vurup iz bırakmak; ~ed kösele şeritli *(ayakkabı).*

**wel.ter** ['weltə] **1.** *v/i.* yatıp yuvarlanmak, ağnamak; ~ in *fig.* içinde yüzmek *(kan vs.);* **2.** *n.* karışıklık, kargaşa; '~-'weight *n. boks:* 62-67 kilo arasındaki boksör.

**wen** [wen] *n.* ℱ yağ kisti; *fig.* çok büyük şehir.

**wench** [wentʃ] *n.* kız, genç kadın; fahişe.

**wend** [wend] *v/t.:* ~ one's way yönelmek, gitmek (t^ ~ -e).

**went** [went] *pret. of* go 1.

**wept** [wept] *pret. & p.p. of* weep.

**were** [wə:, wə] *pret. of* be.

**we're** F [wiə] = we are.

**weren't** F [wə:nt] = were not.

**west** [west] **1.** *n.* batı; **2.** *adj.* batı..., batıdaki...; batıya doğru olan; batıdan gelen *(rüzgâr);* go ~ *sl.* ölmek, gebermek; mahvolmak, bozulmak.

**west.er.ly** ['westəli] *adj.* batıya doğru olan; batıdaki; batıdan gelen *(rüzgâr).*

**west.ern** ['westən] **1.** *adj.* batıya ait, batı...; **2.** *n.* kovboy filmi *veya* romanı; = 'west.ern.er *n.* batılı; *Am.* batı Amerikalı; 'west.ern.most *adj.* en batıdaki.

**West In.dian** ['west'indjən] **1.** *adj.* Batı Hint adalarına ait; **2.** *n.* Batı Hint adalarında yaşayan kimse.

**west.ing** ⬇ ['westiŋ] *n.* batı rotası; batıya yönelme.

**west.ward(s)** ['westwəd(z)] *adv.* batıya doğru.

**wet** [wet] **1.** *adj.* ıslak, yaş, rutubetli; yağmurlu, yağışlı; *Am.* içki yasağı olmayan *(yer); sl.* isteksiz *(kimse); s.* blanket 1.; ~ through sır(ıl)sıklam; **2.** *n.* yağmur(lu hava); ıslak yer; yaşlık, nem, rutubet; *sl.* içki; **3.** *(irr.) v/t.* ıslatmak; F içki içerek kutlamak; *v/i.* ıslanmak;/~ through sır(ıl)sıklam etm.

**wet.back** *Am. sl.* ['wetbæk] *n.* Amerika'ya kaçak giren Meksikalı.

**weth.er** ['weðə] *n.* iğdiş edilmiş koç.

**wet-nurse** ['wetnə:s] *n.* sütnine.

**we've** F [wi:v] = we have.

**whack** F [wæk] **1.** *v/t.* dövmek, pataklamak; küt diye vurmak; **2.** *n.* şaklama; deneme, tecrübe; *sl.* hisse, pay; have *veya* take a ~ at denemek -i; 'whack.er *n.* F koskocaman şey; kuyruklu yalan; 'whack.ing F **1.** *n.* dayak; **2.** *adj.* koskocaman; kuyruklu *(yalan).*

**whale** [weil] *n.* balina; a ~ of oldukça, hayli, büyük, çok; a ~ at F bir işin ehli, otorite; '~.bone *n.* balina *(elbisede);* '~-'fish.er, '~.man, *mst* 'whal.er *n.* balina avcısı; balina avlama gemisi; 'whale-oil *n.* balina yağı.

**whal.ing** ['weiliŋ] *n.* balina avı.

**whang** F [wæŋ] **1.** *n.* şaplak; **2.** *v/t.* dövmek, şak diye vurmak.

**wharf** [wɔ:f] **1.** *n., pl. a.* wharves [wɔ:vz] iskele, rıhtım; **2.** *v/t.* rıhtıma boşaltmak; 'wharf.age *n.* iskele ücreti; wharf.in.ger ['~-indʒə] *n.* rıhtım müdürü.

**what** [wɔt] **1.** *pron.* ne, hangi şey; -dığı şey; know ~'s ~ neyin ne olduğunu bilmek; ~ money I had ne kadar param var-

**whip**

sa, bendeki para; ... and ~ not ve saire,
falan filan; 2. *int.* ne?, vay!; ~ about ...?
...den ne haber?, ya ...?, ...e ne dersin?;
~ for? niçin?; ~ of it? bana ne!, ne çıkar?, ne olmuş yani?; ~ if ...? ya ...ise?;
~ though ...? ...ise ne olmuş?; what-
-d'you-call-him, ~'s-his-name adı her neyse, falanca; ~ next? başka?; *iro.* daha
neler!, yok canım!; ~ a blessing! ne iyi!,
çok şükür!; ~ impudence! bu ne lâubalilik!; 3. *adv.* ~ with ... ~ with... ... ve ... yüzünden; what.e'er *poet.* [wɔt¹cə], what¹ev-
er = whatsoever; ¹what.not *n.* biblo rafı;
falan; what.so.e'er *poet.* [wɔtsəu¹cə],
what.so'ever 1. *pron.* her ne, her hangi;
2. *adj.* ne, hangi.
wheat ⚘ [wiːt] *n.* buğday; ¹wheat.en *adj.*
buğdaydan yapılmış, buğday...
whee.dle [¹wiːdl] *vb.* tatlılıkla ikna etm.
(into -e); kandırıp elinden almak; ~ s.th.
out of s.o. tatlı sözlerle *b-den bş* almak.
wheel [wiːl] 1. *n.* tekerlek; deveran, dönme; *part.* Am. F bisiklet; X çark; *mot.*
direksiyon; 2. *v/t. & v/i.* dön(dür)mek;
sür(ül)mek ;tekerlekli bir taşıtla götürmek; X çark etm.; ¹~.bar.row *n.* tekerlekli el arabası; ~ base *mot.* dingil mesafesi; ~ chair tekerlekli sandalye;
¹wheeled *adj.* tekerlekli; ¹wheel.wright *n.*
tekerlekçi, tekerlek tamircisi.
wheeze [wiːz] 1. *v/i.* hırıltıyla solumak;
2. *n.* hırıltılı ses; *thea. sl.* espri; parlak
fikir; ¹wheez.y □ hırıltılı.
whelk *zo.* [welk] *n.* bir tür deniz salyangozu.
whelp *rhet.* [welp] 1. *n.* yırtıcı hayvan
yavrusu, en(c)ik; *com.* genç kız *veya* delikanlı; terbiyesiz genç; 2. *v/i.* eniklemek, enciklemek.
when [wen] 1. *adv.* ne zaman?; 2. *cj. -diği*
zaman; iken; sırasında; *-mesine* rağmen ;eğer, şayet.
whence [wens] *adv.* nereden.
when.e'er *poet.* [wen¹cə], when.(so.)ev.er
[wen(səu)¹evə] *adv. & cj.* her ne zaman.
where [wɛə] 1. *adv.* nerede?; nereye?; 2.
*cj. -diği* yer(d)e; ~.a.bout, *mst* ~.a.bouts
1. [¹wɛərə¹baut(s)] *adv.* nereler(d)e; 2.
[¹~] *n.* olduğu (*veya* bulunduğu) yer;
~¹as *cj.* halbuki, oysa; ☒ mademki, ...
dayanarak; ~¹at 1. *adv.* neye; 2. *cj.* bunun üzerine; ~¹by *adv.* vasıtasiyle; mademki; ¹~.fore *adv.* niçin, neden; ~¹in
*adv.* nerede, neyin için(d)e; hangi hususta; ~¹of *adv.* -den; ~¹on *adv.* üstünde; bunun üzerine; ~.so'ev.er *adv.* her
nerede, her nereye; ~.up¹on *adv. & cj.*
bunun üzerine; wher¹ev.er *adv. & cj.* her

nereye; her nerede; where¹with *adv.* (ne)
ile, nasıl; where.with.al 1. [wɛəwi¹ðɔːl]
*adv.* ne ile, nasıl; 2. F [¹~] *n.* araçlar,
gereçler; para.
wher.ry [¹weri] *n.* küçük kayık.
whet [wet] 1. *v/t.* bilemek; açmak (*iştah*); 2. *n.* bile(n)me; iştah açıcı şey.
wheth.er [¹weðə] *cj.* -ip -mediğini, -mi
acaba; ~ or no olsa da olmasa da.
whet.stone [¹wetstəun] *n.* bileğitaşı.
whew [hwuː] *int.* pöf!, püf!, ya! vay be!
whey [wei] *n.* kesilmiş sütün suyu.
which [witʃ] 1. *adj.* hangi(si) 2. *pron.* han-
gisin(i); ki o, ki; ki onu, -dığım; ~¹ev.er
1. *pron.* her hangi(si); 2. *adj.* (her)han-
gi, hangisi olursa olsun.
whiff [wif] 1. *n.* esinti; koku; püf; küçük
puro; 2. *v/t.* ağızdan çıkarmak (*tütün
dumanı*); *v/i.* kötü kokmak.
Whig [wig] 1. *n.* İngiliz liberal partisi üyesi; 2. *adj.* İngiliz liberal partisine ait.
while [wail] 1. *n.* müddet, zaman, süre,
vakit; for a ~ bir süre; worth ~ değer; 2.
*v/t. mst* ~ away geçirmek (*vakit*); 3. *cj.
a.* whilst [wailst] iken; -*diği* halde, -*e*
rağmen; süresince.
whim [wim] = whimsy.
whim.per [¹wimpə] 1. *v/i.* ağlamak, inlemek, sızlanmak; 2. *n.* inleme, sızlanma.
whim.si.cal □ [¹wimzikəl] tuhaf, acayip,
kaprisli, saçma; garip fikirli; havaî;
whim.si.cal.i.ty [~¹kæliti], whim.si.cal.ness
[¹~.kəlnis] *n.* tuhaflık, saçmalık; kapris.
whim.s(e)y [¹wimzi] *n.* saçma arzu, kapris; tuhaflık; mizah.
whin ⚘ [win] *n.* katırtırnağına benzer bir
bitki.
whine [wain] 1. *v/i.* sızlanmak, mırıldanmak, zırıldamak; ağlamsamak, mızmızlanmak; 2. *n.* sızlanma; mızmızlanma;
zırıltı.
whin.ny [¹wini] *v/i.* kişnemek.
whip [wip] 1. *v/t.* kamçılamak; F dövmek;
pataklamak; çalkamak, çırpmak (*yumurta*); yenmek; çalmak, aşırmak,
araklamak; çıkarıvermek; sokuvermek;
bastırmak (*kumaş*); döndürmek, çevirmek (*topaç*); fırlatmak; ~ away aniden
çekmek, çıkarmak; götürmek; ~ in *parl.*
bir araya toplamak (*parti üyesi*); ~ off
çıkarmak; uçurmak (*çatı vs.*); götürmek; gitmek; ~ on yürütmek, kamçı ile
dürtmek; ~ up kışkırtmak; yapıvermek;
çırpmak (*yumurta vs.*); kapmak; arttırmak, toplamak; *v/i.* hızla hareket etm.,
fırlamak; 2. *n.* kırbaç, kamçı; *hunt.* köpekleri idare eden kimse; *parl.* parti denetçisi; çırpılmış yumurta ile yapılan yi-

yecek; **'~.cord** *n.* sırım; kalın kumaş; **'~-'hand** *n.* üstünlük, idare; have the ~ of s.o. *b-ne* oranla üstünlüğü olm.

**whip.per...** ['wipə]: **'~-'in** *n. hunt.* köpekleri idare eden kimse; *parl.* parti denetçisi; **'~-snap.per** *n. k-ni bş* zanneden genç.

**whip.pet** *zo.* ['wipit] *n.* tazı.

**whip.ping** ['wipiŋ] *n.* kamçılama, dövme; dayak; **'~-boy** *n.* başkalarının cezasını yüklenen kimse, şamar oğlanı; *hist.* bir soylunun çocuğunun yerine cezalandırılan çocuk; **'~-post** *n. hist.* kamçılamak üzere suçluların bağlandığı direk; **'~-top** *n.* topaç.

**whip.poor.will** *orn.* ['wippuəwil] *n.* çobanaldatana benzer bir kuş.

**whip-saw** ⊕ ['wipsɔ:] *n.* tomruk testeresi.

**whir** [wə:] = whirr.

**whirl** [wə:l] **1.** *v/t.* & *v/i.* hızla dön(dür)mek; hızla götürmek; hızla geçmek; kafası karışmak; başı dönmek; **2.** *n.* hızla dönme; koşuşturma; **whirl.l.gig** ['~ligig] *n.* topaç; fırıldak; atlıkarınca; *fig.* devir, dönüş; **'whirl.pool** *n.* girdap, burgaç; **'whirl.wind** *n.* kasırga, hortum.

**whirr** [wə:] **1.** *v/i.* vızlamak, pırlamak; **2.** *n.* vızıltı, pırlama sesi; zırıltı.

**whisk** [wisk] **1.** *n.* yumurta teli; tüy süpürge; **2.** *v/t.* & *v/i.* çalkamak; fırla(t)mak; çırpmak *(yumurta)*; hafifçe süpürmek; sallamak; götürmek; ~ away ortadan kaldırmak; **'whis.ker** *n. zo.* hayvan bıyığı; *mst* (a pair of) ~s *pl.* favori, bıyık; **'whis.kered** *adj.* favorili.

**whis.k(e)y** ['wiski] *n.* viski.

**whis.per** ['wispə] **1.** *v/i.* fısıldamak; hışırdamak; *v/t.* gizlice söylemek; **'whis.per.er** *n.* dedikoducu kimse; **whis.per.ing cam.paign** *b-nin* aleyhinde dedikodu veya iftira yayma.

**whist¹** [wist] *int.* sus!

**whist²** [~] *n.* vist, bir çeşit iskambil oyunu.

**whis.tle** ['wisl] **1.** *v/i.* ıslık çalmak; düdük çalmak; *v/t.* ıslıkla çalmak; ıslıkla çağırmak; **2.** *n.* ıslık; düdük; ~ **stop** *Am.* işaret verildiğinde trenin durduğu istasyon; *pol.* seçim gezisi.

**whit¹** [wit] *n.:* not a ~ hiç, asla.

**Whit²** [~] *n.* pantekot yortusunun pazar günü; ~ week pantekot haftası.

**white** [wait] **1.** *adj. com.* beyaz, ak; soluk, solgun; sütlü *(kahve)*; saf, lekesiz; F edepli, terbiyeli; boş, yazısız; **2.** *n.* beyaz renk; yumurta akı; beyaz tenli kimse; gözün beyaz kısmı; *typ.* beyaz aralık; ~ **ant** *zo.* beyaz karınca, divik; **'~.bait** *n. ichth.* bir çeşit küçük balık; ~ **book** *pol.* resmî hükümet raporu; **'~-caps** *n. pl.* kö-

püklü dalgalar; **'white-col.lar(ed)** *adj.* dairede çalışan, büro...; ~ workers *pl.* masa başında çalışanlar, memur sınıfı; **'~-'faced** *adj.* beti benzi atmış; **'~-'haired** *adj.* ak saçlı; ~ **heat** akkor; **'~'hot** *adj.* kızgın, akkor; ~ **lie** zararsız yalan; **'~-'liv.ered** *adj.* ödlek, korkak; ~ **man** beyaz tenli adam; **'whit.en** *v/t.* & *v/i.* ağar(t)mak, beyazlatmak; beyazlanmak; **'whit.en.er** *n.* beyazlatıcı madde; **'white.ness** *n.* beyazlık; saflık; **'whit.en.ing** *n.* beyazlatıcı madde.

**white...:** ~ **pa.per** *pol.* resmî hükümet raporu; **'~.smith** *n.* tenekeci; kalaycı; **'~.wash 1.** *n.* badana; örtbas etme; **2.** *v/t.* badana etm., badanalamak; *fig.* örtbas etm., temize çıkarmak; **'~.wash.er** *n.* badanacı.

**whith.er** *lit.* ['wiðə] *adv.* nereye; **whith.er.so'ev.er** *adv.* her nereye.

**whit.ing** ['waitiŋ] *n.* arıtılmış tebeşir tozu; *ichth.* merlanos.

**whit.ish** ['waitiʃ] *adj.* beyazımsı, beyazımtırak, akça.

**whit.low** ⌀ ['witləu] *n.* dolama.

**Whit.sun** ['witsn] *adj.* pantekot yortusuna ait; **~.day** ['wit'sʌndi] *n.* pantekot yortusunun pazar günü; **~.tide** ['witsntaid] *n.* pantekot.

**whit.tle** ['witl] *v/t.* yontmak; ~ away eksiltmek, azaltmak; ~ down zayıflatmak; kesmek.

**whit.y** ['waiti] *adj.* beyazımsı...

**whiz(z)** [wiz] **1.** *v/i.* vızıldamak, vızlamak; yıldırım gibi gitmek; **2.** *n.* vızıltı.

**who** [hu:] **1.** *cj.* o ki, onlar ki; **2.** *pron.* kim?; Who's Who? Kim Kimdir, ünlülerin kimliğini açıklayan yıllık ansiklopedi.

**whoa** [wəu] *int.* çüş!, dur!

**who.dun.(n)it** *sl.* [hu:'dʌnit] *n.* dedektif romanı.

**who.ev.er** [hu:'evə] *pron.* kim olursa olsun, her kim.

**whole** [həul] **1.** □ bütün, tam, tüm; † sağlıklı; iyi, sağlam; made out of ~ cloth *Am.* F uydurmasyon yapılmış; **2.** *n.* tam şey; toplam; tüm, bütün; the ~ of London Londra'nın tümü; the ~ of them onların hepsi; (up)on the ~ genellikle; çoğunlukla; **'~-'heart.ed** □ samimî, içten, candan; **'~-'hog.ger** *n. sl.* bir işi sonuna kadar götüren kimse; **'~-'meal bread** kepekli buğday ekmeği; **'~.sale 1.** *n. mst* ~ trade toptan satış; **2.** *adj.* toptan...; *fig.* çok sayıda; ~ **dealer** = **'~.sal.er** *n.* toptancı; **whole.some** □ ['~səm] sıhhate yararlı; sıhhatli; yarar-

lı; **ʰwhole.time** *adj.* tüm vakti alan...;
**ʰwhole.wheat** *adj.* kepekli buğdaydan yapılmış.
**who'll** F [huːl] = who will; who shall.
**whol.ly** [ʰhəulli] *adv.* tamamen, büsbütün, sırf.
**whom** [huːm, hum] *acc. of* who.
**whoop** [huːp] **1.** *n.* bağırma, çığlık; boğmaca öksürüğü sesi; **2.** *v/i.* bağırmak, haykırmak, çığlık atmak; ~ it up *Am. sl.* çılgınlar gibi eğlenmek; **whoop.ee** *Am.* F [ʰwupiː] *n.* şamata; make ~ şamata yapmak; **whoop.ing-cough** 🕈 [ʰhuːpiŋkɔf] *n.* boğmaca öksürüğü.
**whop** *sl.* [wɔp] *v/t.* vurmak, dövmek; yenmek; **ʰwhop.per** *n. sl.* kocaman şey; *part.* kuyruklu yalan; **ʰwhop.ping** *adj.* koskocaman; kuyruklu *(yalan).*
**whore** [hɔː] *n.* fahişe, orospu.
**whorl** [wəːl] *n.* ⊕ ağırşak; 🕈 halkadizilişli yapraklar; *zo., anat.* helezoni kabuğun bir halkası.
**whor.tle.ber.ry** 🕈 [ʰwəːtlberi] *n.* çayüzümü; red ~ kırmızı yabanmersini.
**who's** F [huːz] = who is.
**whose** [huːz] *gen. of* who; **who.so.(-ev.er)** [ʰhuːsəu; huːsəuʰevə] *pron.* her kim.
**why** [wai] **1.** *adv.* niçin?, niye?, neden?; ~ so? neden böyle?; that is ~ işte bu yüzden; **2.** *int.* demek öyle!, ya!, bak sen!
**wick** [wik] *n.* fitil.
**wick.ed** ☐ [ʰwikid] fena, kötü(cül), günahkâr; hayırsız; aşağılık; tehlikeli, şeytansı; kinci, hain; yaramaz; ahlâksız; **ʰwick.ed.ness** *n.* kötülük; günahkârlık.
**wick.er** [ʰwikə] *adj.* hasır...; ~ basket hasır sepet; ~ chair hasır koltuk; ~ furniture hasır mobilya; ʰ~.work **1.** *n.* sepet işi; **2.** = wicker.
**wick.et** [ʰwikit] *n.* ufak kapı; *kriket:* kale; ʰ~-keep.er *n.* top hedefinin arkasında duran oyuncu.
**wide** [waid] *a.* ☐ & *adv.* geniş, enli; açık, engin; ferah; uzak; *sl.* üçkâğıtçı; ~ awake tamamen uyanık; 3 feet ~ 3 ayak genişliğinde; ~ difference büyük fark; ʰ~.an.gle *adj. phot.* geniş açılı...; ʰ~awake [ʰwaidəʰweik] *adj.* tamamen uyanık; F zeki, açıkgöz; ʰ~-ʰeyed *adj.* gözleri faltaşı gibi açılmış; saf, masum; ʰwid.en *v/t.* & *v/i.* genişle(t)mek, aç(ıl)mak, bollaş(tır)mak; ʰwide.ness *n.* genişlik; ʰwide-ʰo.pen *adj.* ardına kadar açık; *Am. sl.* kanun yönünden gevşek *(şehir);* ʰwide.spread *adj.* yaygın.
**wid.ow** [ʰwidəu] *n.* dul kadın; *attr.* dul...; ʰwid.owed *adj.* dul kalmış; *fig.* boş, tenha; ʰwid.ow.er *n.* dul erkek; **wid.ow.hood**

[ʰ~hud] *n.* dulluk.
**width** [widθ] *n.* genişlik, en(lilik).
**wield** *lit.* [wiːld] *v/t.* kullanmak.
**wife** [waif] *n., pl.* wives [waivz] karı, eş, hanım; ʰwife.ly *adj.* eşe yaraşır.
**wig** [wig] *n.* peruka, takma saç; **wigged** *adj.* perukalı, takma saçlı; ʰwig.ging *n.* F azar, haşlama.
**wig.gle** [ʰwigl] *v/t.* & *v/i.* kıpırda(t)mak, kımılda(t)mak, kıpır kıpır oynamak.
**wight** † *veya co.* [wait] *n.* insan, kimse.
**wig.wag** F [ʰwigwæg] *vb.* işaretle (haber) vermek.
**wig.wam** [ʰwigwæm] *n.* Kuzey Amerika yerlilerinin çadır *veya* kulübesi.
**wild** [waild] **1.** ☐ *com.* yabanî, vahşî; şiddetli; sert, fırtınalı; hiddetli, öfkeli; çılgın, deli gibi; düzensiz, dağınık; rasgele; terbiyesiz, arsız; çok hevesli, meraklı; zırzop; dönek; serseri *(kurşun);* iyi, hoş; kaba *(tahmin);* run ~ başıboş kalmak; 🕈 yabanîleşmek; talk ~ saçma sapan konuşmak; be ~ for *veya* about s.th. bşe bayılmak, bş için deli olm.; **2.** *n. mst* the ~s *pl.* çorak ve ıssız yer; ʰwild.cat **1.** *n. zo.* yaban kedisi; yasak; *Am.* huysuz kimse; *part. Am.* verimsiz bir bölgede petrol veren kuyu; **2.** *adj. fig.* düzensiz; rizikolu, çürük *(iş);* kanun dışı; **wil.der.ness** [ʰwildənis] *n.* kır, sahra; el değmemiş bölge; boşluk; **wild.fire** [ʰwaildfaiə] *n.:* like ~ hızla, süratle, çarçabuk; ʰwild-goose chase *fig.* boş iş, aptalca girişim; ʰwild.ing *n.* 🕈 yabani bitki; ʰwild.ness *n.* yabanîlik, vahşet.
**wile** [wail] **1.** *n. mst* ~s *pl.* oyun, hile, kurnazlık; **2.** *v/t.* ayartmak, baştan çıkarmak, cezbetmek; ~ away = while 2.
**wil.ful** ☐ [ʰwilful] inatçı; kasıtlı.
**wil.i.ness** [ʰwailinis] *n.* düzenbazlık.
**will** [wil] **1.** *n.* istek, arzu, dilek, murat; vasiyet(name), maksat, amaç; at ~ istediği zaman, canı nasıl isterse; of one's own free ~ kendi isteğiyle; **2.** *(irr.)* *v/aux.:* he ~ come gelecek; I ~ do it onu yapacağım; **3.** *v/t.* vasiyetle bırakmak; amaçlamak; niyet etm., karar vermek; arzulamak; emretmek, buyurmak *(Tanrı);* willed *comb.* ...iradeli.
**will.ing** ☐ [ʰwilin] gönüllü; içten; *pred.* razı, istekli, hazır (to *inf. -meğe);* I am ~ to believe inanmak istiyorum; ʰwill.ing.ly *adv.* isteyerek, seve seve; ʰwill.ing.ness *n.* gönüllülük, isteyerek yapma.
**will-o'-the-wisp** [ʰwiləðəwisp] *n.* bataklık yakamozu.
**wil.low** [ʰwiləu] *n.* 🕈 söğüt; ⊕ hallaç makinesi; *attr.* söğüt...; ʰ~-herb *n.* 🕈 yakı

otu; **¹wil.low.y** *adj.* söğüdü çok; *fig.* narin, zarif.

**wil.ly-nil.ly** [¹wili¹nili] *adv.* ister istemez, istense de istenmese de.

**wilt¹** † [wilt] *vb.* -eceksin.

**wilt²** [~] *v/t.* & *v/i.* sol(dur)mak; *fig.* bitkin düşmek.

**Wil.ton car.pet** [¹wiltən¹ka:pit] *n.* bir çeşit halı.

**wil.y** ☐ [¹waili] düzenbaz, hilekâr, kurnaz.

**wim.ple** [¹wimpl] *n.* rahibe başörtüsü.

**win** [win] **1.** (*irr.*) *v/t.* kazanmak, yenmek; elde etm., ele geçirmek; doğru tahmin etm.; erişmek, ulaşmak, varmak; çıkarmak (*maden, kömür*); ✕ *sl.* organize etm.; ikna etm. (to *inf.* -*meğe*); ~ s.o. over *b-ni* ikna etm., kandırmak; *v/i.* haklı çıkmak; başarılı olm.; ~ through to tüm güçlükleri yenmek; **2.** *n. spor:* yengi, galibiyet, zafer, başarı.

**wince** [wins] **1.** *v/i.* birdenbire ürkmek, ürküp çekinmek; **2.** *n.* ürkme, çekinme.

**winch** [wintʃ] *n.* vinç, bocurgat.

**wind¹** [wind, *poet. a.* waind] **1.** *n.* rüzgâr, yel; hava; *fig.* nefes, soluk; 🎵 osuruk; ♪ nefesli çalgılar; koku; boş laf, saçmalık; be in the ~ ortalıkta bir şeyler dönmek; have a long ~ nefesi kuvvetli olm.; throw to the ~s *fig.* bşe kulak asmamak, aldırış etmemek; saçıp dağıtmak; raise the ~ *sl.* gerekli parayı sağlamak; get *veya* have the ~ up *sl.* korkmak, endişelenmek; **2.** *v/t. hunt.* koklayarak bulmak; nefes nefese bırakmak; nefesini kesmek; be ~ed nefesi kesilmek, nefes nefese kalmak.

**wind²** [waind] (*irr.*) *v/t.* & *v/i.* çevirmek, dola(ş)mak; döndürmek; sar(ıl)mak; eğrilmek, bükülmek, kıvrılmak; sokulmak; *a.* ~ o.s. sarınmak; ~ one's way kıvrıla kıvrıla uzanmak; ~ up çıkarmak, kaldırmak, açmak (*araba camı*); kurmak (*saat*); sarmak (*ip*); bitirmek, bağlamak (*konuşma vs.*); † tasfiye (*veya* likide) etm.; olmak; gitmek, varmak; boylamak (*hapsi*); almak (*ödül vs.*).

**wind...** [wind]: **¹~.bag** *n. contp.* geveze (*veya* çenesi düşük) kimse; **¹~-break** *n.* rüzgâr çiti; **¹~-cheat.er** *n.* parka, anorak; **¹~.fall** *n.* ağaçtan düşmüş meyve; beklenmedik yerden gelen para *vs.*; **¹~-ga(u)ge** *n.* rüzgârın gücünü ölçen alet; **¹wind.i.ness** *n.* rüzgârlılık; gevezelik.

**wind.ing** [¹waindiŋ] **1.** *n.* dön(dür)me; sarmal sargı; ⊕ bobin; dönemeç; dolambaç; **2.** ☐ dolambaçlı; sarmal; ~ staircase, ~ stairs *pl.* döner merdiven; **¹~-sheet** *n.* kefen; **¹~-¹up** *n.* bit(ir)me, son,

kapanış; † tasfiye.

**wind-in.stru.ment** ♪ [¹windinstrumənt] *n.* nefesli çalgı.

**wind-jam.mer** ⚓ F [¹winddʒæmə] *n.* yelkenli gemi; *Am.* geveze kimse.

**wind.lass** ⊕ [¹windləs] *n.* ırgat, bocurgat.

**wind.mill** [¹windmil] *n.* yeldeğirmeni.

**win.dow** [¹windəu] *n.* pencere; vitrin; **¹~-dress.ing** *n.* vitrin dekorasyonu; *fig.* göz boyama; **¹win.dowed** *adj.* pencereli.

**win.dow...:** ~ **en.ve.lope** adresin görüneceği kısmı şeffaf olan zarf, pencereli zarf; **¹~-frame** *n.* pencere çerçevesi; **¹~-ledge** *n.* pencere eşiği; **¹~-pane** *n.* pencere camı; **¹~-shade** *n. Am.* güneşlik; **¹~-shop-ping** *n.* vitrin gezme; **¹~-shut.ter** *n.* pancur, kepenk; **¹~.sill** *n.* pencere eşiği.

**wind...** [wind]: **¹~.pipe** *n.* nefes borusu; **¹~.screen,** *Am.* **¹~-shield** *n. mot.* ön cam; ~ wiper silecek, silgiç; **¹~-tun.nel** *n.* ✈ hava deneme tüneli.

**wind.ward** [¹windwəd] **1.** *adj.* rüzgâr üstü yönündeki; **2.** *n.* rüzgâr üstü.

**wind.y** ☐ [¹windi] rüzgârlı; fırtınalı; *fig.* geveze; *sl.* korkmuş; 🎵 gaz yapan.

**wine** [wain] *n.* şarap; **¹~-grow.er** *n.* bağcı; **¹~-mer.chant** *n.* şarap tüccarı; **¹~.press** *n.* üzüm cenderesi; **¹~-vault** *n.* şarap mahzeni.

**wing** [wiŋ] **1.** *n.* kanat (*a.* ✕, ♣); F *co.* kol; *mot.* çamurluk; ✈ kanat; uçuş; ✈, ✕ kol; *futbol:* kanat (oyuncusu); ~s *pl. thea.* kulis; ♣ ek bina; take ~ uçup gitmek; kanatlanmak; be on the ~ uçuyor olm.; *fig.* ayağı üzengide olm.; **2.** *v/t.* & *v/i.* uç(ur)mak; kanat takmak; kanadından *veya* kolundan yaralamak; kanatlanmak; **¹~-case, ¹~-sheath** *n. zo.* böcek kanadının kabuğu; **¹~-chair** *n.* koltuk; **winged** *adj.* kanatlı...

**wink** [wiŋk] **1.** *n.* göz kırpma; an; not get a ~ of sleep gözünü kırpmamak, hiç uyumamak; tip s.o. the ~ *sl. b-ni* gizlice uyarmak, haber vermek; ~ forty; **2.** *v/i.* göz kırpmak; gözle işaret vermek (at -e); *fig.* pırıldamak; ~ at göz yummak -e, görmezlikten gelmek -i; **¹wink.ing light** *mot.* yanıp sönen ışık.

**win.ner** [¹winə] *n.* kazanan; *spor:* galip.

**win.ning** [¹winiŋ] **1.** ☐ kazanan; cazip; dostça, sevimli; **2.** *n.* ~s *pl.* kazanç; **¹~-post** *n. spor:* bitiş direği.

**win.now** [¹winəu] *v/t.* savurup tanelerini ayırmak (*buğday*); *fig.* ayırmak.

**win.some** [¹winsəm] *adj.* güzel, çekici, alımlı; hoş, sevimli; neşeli, şen.

**win.ter** [¹wintə] **1.** *n.* kış; ~ sports kış sporları; **2.** *v/i.* kışlamak, kışı geçirmek.

win.try ['wintri] adj. kış gibi; fig. pek soğuk, buz gibi.

wipe [waip] 1. v/t. silmek, silip kurutmak; ~ off silip gidermek, temizlemek, silmek; ~ out silip yok etm., silmek, temizlemek; fig. ortadan kaldırmak; 2. n. silme, temizleme; F darbe, kötek; alay; 'wip.er n. silecek.

wire ['waiǝ] 1. n. tel; F telgraf; attr. tel...; pull the ~s fig. torpil patlatmak; s. live 2; 2. v/t. telle bağlamak; ⨍ elektrik tesisatı döşemek -e; v/i. telgraf çekmek -e; '~.drawn adj. kılı kırk yaran; '~-ga(u)ge n. ⊕ tel mastarı; '~.haired adj. tel gibi tüyleri olan (köpek); 'wire-less 1. □ telsiz; 2. n. a. ~ set radyo; on the ~ radyoda; ~ station radyo istasyonu; 3. v/t. telsizle göndermek; 'wireınetting n. tel örgü; 'wire-pull.er n. fig. torpil patlatan kimse; 'wire-wove adj. kaliteli...

wir.ing ['waiǝrin] n. tel çekmè; ⨍ tel bağlantı sistemi; ~ diagram ⨍ tel bağlantı şeması, şebeke planı; 'wir.y □ tel gibi; sırım gibi.

wis.dom ['wizdǝm] n. akıl(lılık), hikmet; bilgece söz; ~ tooth akıl dişi, yirmi yaş dişi.

wise¹ □ [waiz] akıllı; tedbirli; tecrübeli, deneyimli; bilgili; mahir, usta; ~ guy Am. sl. ukalâ dümbeleği; put s.o. ~ b-ne bilgi vermek (to, on hakkında).

wise² † [~] n. usül, tarz, suret.

wise.a.cre ['waizeikǝ] n. ukalâ; 'wise-crack F 1. n. espri; 2. v/i. espri yapmak.

wish [wiʃ] 1. v/t. istemek, arzu etm., dilemek, temenni etm.; ~ s.o. joy (of) b-ne bşden dolayı başarılar dilemek; ~ for -i çok arzulamak, -e can atmak; ~ well (till) iyi şans dile(me)mek (to -e); 2. n. istek, arzu, dilek, emel; good ~es pl. tebrikler; wish.ful □ ['~ful] arzulu, istekli (to inf. -meğe); ~ thinking hüsnükuruntu; 'wish-(.ing)-bone n. lades kemiği.

wish-wash F ['wiʃwɔʃ] n. yavan içki; saçmalık; 'wish.y-wash.y adj. F yavan, sulu, hafif; karaktersiz; boş (fikir).

wisp [wisp] n. tutam; demet, deste.

wist.ful □ ['wistful] hasretli, arzulu, istekli, dalgın.

wit [wit] 1. n. akıl; a. ~s pl. zekâ, anlayış; nükte(ci); be at one's ~'s end apışıp kalmak, tamamen şaşırmak, ne yapacağını bilememek; have veya keep one's ~s about one paniğe kapılmamak, tetikte olm.; live by one's ~s açıkgözlülükle geçimini sağlamak; out of one's ~s çileden çıkmış; 2. vb. to ~ yani, demek

ki.

witch [witʃ] n. büyücü kadın; cadı, kocakarı; büyüleyici güzellikte kadın; '~-craft, ıwitch.er.y n. büyü(cülük); witch hunt Am. düzene baş kaldıranları sindirme avı.

with [wið] prp. ile; -den; -e karşı; -e rağmen; -den dolayı; -in yanında, ile birlikte; it is just so ~ me benim için öyle; ~ it sl. zamane, modern.

with.al † [wi'ðɔːl] 1. adv. bununla beraber; ayrıca; 2. prp. ile.

with.draw [wið'drɔː] (irr. draw) v/t. & v/i. geri çek(il)mek; geri almak; çekmek (para); with'draw.al n. geri alma; part. ✕ geri çek(il)me.

withe [wiθ] n. söğüt çubuğu, saz.

with.er ['wiðǝ] v/t. & v/i. a. ~ up, ~ away kuru(t)mak, sol(dur)mak; çürü(t)mek, boz(ul)mak; utandırmak, susturmak; fig. kaybolmak, yıkılmak (umut).

with.ers ['wiðǝz] n. pl. cıdağı, cıdağu, atın iki omuzunun arası.

with.hold [wið'hǝuld] (irr. hold) v/t. tutmak, saklamak (s.th. from s.o. b-den bşi); vermemek; bırakmamak; kısıtlamak; with'in 1. lit. adv. içeride(n), içeriye; from ~ içeriden; 2. prp. -in içinde, zarfında, dahilinde; ~ doors evde; ~ a mile of -e bir mil kala; ~ call, ~ sight, ~ hearing çağrılabilecek, görülebilecek, duyulabilecek uzaklıkta; with'out 1. lit. adv. dışarıda; from ~ dışarıdan; 2. prp. -siz, -sız, -meyerek, -meden, -meksizin; lit. hariç, -in dışında; with'stand (irr. stand) v/t. dayanmak -e, karşı koymak -e.

with.y ['wiði] = withe.

wit.less □ ['witlis] akılsız, kafasız, düşüncesiz.

wit.ness ['witnis] 1. n. tanık, şahit; delil, tanıt; şahitlik, tanıklık; bear ~ tanıklık etm.; kanıtlamak (to -i); in ~ of -in kanıtı olarak; marriage ~ nikâh şahidi; 2. v/t. şahit olm. -e, görmek -i; şehadet etm. -e; v/i. şahitlik (veya tanıklık) etm. (for, to lehte; against aleyhte); '~-box, Am. ~ stand tanık kürsüsü.

wit.ti.cism ['witisizǝm] n. espri, şaka; 'wit.ti.ness n. espri yeteneği, hazırcevaplık; 'wit.ting.ly adv. bile bile, kasten; 'wit.ty □ nükteli, esprili, hazırcevap; nükteci, zeki.

wives [waivz] pl. of wife.

wiz Am. sl. [wiz] n. deha; wiz.ard ['~ǝd] 1. n. büyücü, sihirbaz; fig. deha; financial ~ çok kolay para kazanan kimse; 2. adj. sl. mükemmel, şahane.

wiz.en(.ed) ['wizn(d)] adj. pörsümüş, pör

sük.

**wo(a)** [wəu] *int. atları durdurmak için kullanılan bir ünlem.*

**woad** ✍, ⊕ [wəud] *n.* çivitotu.

**wob.ble** [ˈwɔbl] *v/t. & v/i.* salla(n)mak; titremek; tereddüt etm., bocalamak; sendelemek; ⊕ yalpalamak, yalpa vurmak.

**wo(e)** *rhet. veya co.* [wəu] *n.* keder, dert, elem, acı; ~ is me! vah başıma gelenlere!, eyvahlar olsun; ˈ~be.gone *adj.* kederli, gamlı; **wo(e).ful** □ *rhet. veya co.* [ˈ~ful] kederli, hüzünlü; üzücü; ˈwo(e).ful.ness *n.* hüzün, keder.

**woke** [wəuk] *pret. & p.p. of* woke[2] 1.

**wold** [wəuld] *n.* yayla, bozkır.

**wolf** [wulf] *n., pl.* **wolves** [wulvz] 1. *n. zo.* kurt; *sl.* zampara, çapkın; cry ~ yalan yere tehlike işareti vermek; 2. *v/t.* F aç kurt gibi yemek, silip süpürmek *(yemek);* ˈwolf.ish □ kurt gibi; F *fig.* aç kurt gibi. 1

**wolf.ram** *min.* [ˈwulfrəm] *n.* tungsten, volfram.

**wolves** [wulvz] *pl. of* wolf.

**wom.an** [ˈwumən] *n., pl.* **wom.en** [ˈwimin] *n.* kadın; eş, karı; sevgili, metres; kadınlık; kadın cinsi; ~'s rights *pl.* kadın hakları; *attr.* kadın...; ~ doctor kadın doktor; ~ student kız öğrenci; ~ suffrage kadınların oy kullanma hakkı; ˈwom.an--hat.er *n.* kadın düşmanı; **wom.an.hood** [ˈ~hud] *n.* kadınlık; kadınlar; reach ~ kadın olm.; ˈwom.an.ish □ kadın gibi, kadınsı; ˈwom.an.kind *n.* kadınlar; ˈwom.an.like *adj.* kadın gibi; ˈwom.an.ly *adj.* kadına yakışır; kadın gibi.

**womb** [wuːm] *n. anat.* rahim, dölyatağı; *fig.* menşe.

**wom.en** [ˈwimin] *pl. of* woman; ~'s rights kadın hakları; ~'s team *spor:* bayan takımı; **wom.en.folk(s)** [ˈ~fəuk(s)], ˈwom.en.kind *n.* kadınlar, kadın kısmı; kadın akrabalar.

**won** [wʌn] *pret. & p.p. of* win 1.

**won.der** [ˈwʌndə] 1. *n.* harika, şaşılacak şey, mucize; hayret; şaşkınlık; for a ~ hayret; 2. *vb.* şaşmak, hayret etm. *(at -e);* hayrette kalmak, hayran olm.; merak etm. *(whether, if -ip -mediğini);* düşünmek; şüphe etm.; **won.der.ful** □ [ˈ~ful] hayret verici, harika, fevkalâde, şahane; şaşılacak, tuhaf; ˈwon.der.ing 1. □ şaşkın, şaşırmış; 2. *n.* hayret, şaşkınlık; ˈwon.der.land *n.* harikalar diyarı; ˈwon.der.ment *n.* hayret, şaşkınlık; merak; ˈwon.der-struck *adj.* hayretler içinde kalmış; ˈwon.der-work.er *n.* harikalar

yaratan kimse.

**won.drous** □ *lit.* [ˈwʌndrəs] harikulade, olağanüstü.

**won.ky** *sl.* [ˈwɔŋki] *adj.* çürük *(a. fig.);* halsiz, bitkin, zayıf.

**won't** [wəunt] = will not.

**wont** [wəunt] 1. *pred.* alışmış, alışkanlık haline getirmiş; be ~ to do bşi yapmak âdetinde olm.; 2. *n.* âdet, alışkanlık; ˈwont.ed *adj.* alışılmış, her zamanki.

**woo** [wuː] *v/t.* kur yapmak -e; kazanmaya çalışmak; kendine çekmek.

**wood** [wud] *n.* orman, koru; odun, tahta, kereste, ağaç; ♪ tahtadan yapılmış nefesli sazlar; ~s *pl.* orman, koru; touch ~! şeytan kulağına kurşun!, nazar değmesin!; out of the ~ *fig.* tehlikeden uzak, güçlükleri yenmiş; from the ~ fıçıdan; ~.bine, *a.* ~.bind ♀ [ˈ~bain(d)] *n.* hanımeli, ˈ~carv.ing *n.* oymacılık; tahta oyma işi; ˈ~chuck *n. zo.* bir çeşit dağ sıçanı; ˈ~cock *n. orn.* çulluk; ˈ~craft *n.* ormancılık; oymacılık; ˈ~cut *n.* tahta basma kalıbı (ile basılmış desen *veya* resim); ˈ~cut.ter *n.* baltacı, oduncu; ˈwood.ed *adj.* ağaçlı; ormanla kaplı; ˈwood.en tahtadan yapılmış, tahta..., ahşap...; *fig.* odun gibi, sert; ˈwood-en.grav.er *n.* tahta oymacısı *(veya* hakkâkı); ˈwood-en.grav.ing *n.* ağaç oymacılığı; ˈwood.i.ness *n.* ağaçlık *(veya* ormanlık) olma; orman bolluğu. **wood**...; ˈ~.land 1. *n.* ormanlık, ağaçlık; 2. *adj.* ormanlık...; orman...; ˈ~.lark *n. orn.* ağaççıl tarlakuşu; ˈ~louse *n. zo.* tespihböceği ˈ~.man *n.* oduncu, baltacı; orman adamı; ˈ~.peck.er *n. orn.* ağaçkakan; ˈ~.pile *n.* odun yığını; ˈ~pulp *n.* kâğıt hamuru; ˈ~.ruff *n.* ♀ ince otu; ˈ~.shav.ings *n. pl.* talaş; ˈ~.shed *n.* odunluk; ˈwoods.man *Am. for* woodman; ˈwood--wind *n., a.* ~ instruments *pl.* ♪ tahtadan yapılmış nefesli sazlar; ˈ~.work *n.* doğrama(cılık), dülgerlik *(part.* ⚙); ˈ~--work.ing *ma.chine* marangoz tezgâhı; ˈwood.y *adj.* ormanlık, ağaçlık; ağaç cinsinden, ağaçsıl; ˈwood.yard *n.* kereste deposu.

**woo.er** [ˈwuːə] *n.* âşık, kur yapan kimse.

**woof** [wuːf] *s.* weft.

**woof.er** ✍ [ˈwuːfə] *n.* alçak titreşimli ses hoparlörü.

**wool** [wul] *n.* yün, yapağı; kıvırcık saç; dyed in the ~ dokunmadan önce boyanmış; *fig.* tam, halis muhlis; koyu; pull the ~ over s o.'s eyes b-ni aldatmak, b-nin gözünü boyamak; lose one's ~ F tepesi atmak, kızmak, sinirlenmek; ˈ~gath.er.ing 1. *n.* aklı başka yerde olma, dalgınlık; go ~ aklı başka yerde olm., dalgın olm.; **2.** *adj.* dalgın, aklı başka yerde olan; **'wool.(l)en 1.** *adj.* yünden yapılmış, yünlü, yün...; **2.** *n.* ~s *pl.* yünlüler; **'wool-(l)y 1.** *adj.* yünlü; yün gibi; yumuşak; *paint.* & *fig.* bulanık, dağınık; flu; **2.** *n.* woollies *pl.* F yünlü giyecek, *part.* kazak. **wool**...: **'~.sack** *n.* Lortlar Kamarası başkanının meclisteki yün minderi; **'~-sta-pler** *n.* yün tüccarı; **'~-work** *n.* yün işi. **Wop** *Am. sl.* [wɔp] *n.* İtalyan.

**word** [wɜ:d] **1.** *n.* mst kelime, söz(cük); laf; haber, bilgi; vaat, söz; emir, kumanda; ✗ parola; ~s *pl.* konuşma; *fig.* ağız kavgası, münakaşa; by ~ of mouth ağızdan, sözlü olarak, şifahen; eat one's ~s tükürdüğünü yalamak, sözünü geri almek; have ~s ağız kavgası (*veya* münakaşa) etm. (with *ile*); leave ~ haber bırakmak; send (bring) ~ haber göndermek (getirmek); be as good as one's ~ sözü nün eri olm.; take s.o. at his ~ b-nin sözüne inanmak; **2.** *v/t.* ifade etm., söylemek; ~ed as follows şöyle denilmiştir; **'~-book** *n.* sözlük; libretto; **'word.l.ness** *n.* çok kelimelilik; **'word.ing** *n.* yazılış tarzı, üslup; **'word.less** *adj.* kelimesiz, sessiz, suskun; **'word-'per.fect** *adj. thea.* ezbere bilen; **'word-split.ting** *n.* bilgicilik, sofizm. **word.y** ☐ [·wɜ:di] çok kelimeli; kelimeye ait, kelime...

**wore** [wɔ:] *pret. of* wear 1.

**work** [wɜ:k] **1.** *n.* iş, çalışma; emek; vazife, görev; eser; ~s *sg.* fabrika, tesis; ~s *pl.* ⊕ mekanizma; ✗ istihkâm; public ~s *pl.* bayındırlık; ~ of art sanat eseri; at ~ iş başında, işte; be in ~ bir işi olm.; be out of ~ işsiz, boşta olm.; make sad ~ of yüzüne gözüne bulaştırmak; make short ~ of çabucak bitirivermek, kısa kesmek; put out of ~ işsiz bırakmak; set to ~, set *veya* go about one's ~ işe koyulmak, başlamak; ~s council yönetim kurulu; **2.** (*irr.*) *v/t.* & *v/i.* çalış(tır)mak; işle(t)mek; oyna(t)mak; çözmek, halletmek; etkilemek; yaratmak, yapmak; zorlamak (into -*e*); uğraşmak, emek sarf etm.; görevli olm.; yürümek; başarılı olm., iyi sonuç vermek; mayalanmak; ~ one's way k-*ne* yol açmak; he is ~ing his way through college hem okuyup hem çalışıyor; ~ one's will istediğini yaptırmak (upon -*e*); ~ it *sl.* becermek, halletmek; ~ at çalışmak, çabalamak; ~ off çık(ar)mak; geç(ir)mek; bitirmek; ↑ çalışarak ödemek (*borç*); ~ out çık(ar)mak; hesaplamak; halletmek, çöz(ül)-mek, çözüm yolu bulmak; anlamak, kes-

tirmek; sonuçlanmak; geliş(tir)mek; başarılı olm., başarı kazanmak; bitirmek (*maden damarı*); idman yapmak; geçirmek (*vakit*); çalışarak ödemek (*borç*); gitmek; bulmak, keşfetmek; ~ up geliş-(tir)mek, ilerle(t)mek; artırmak; heyecanlandırmak, kamçılamak, körüklemek; beslemek (*ümit*); bitirmek, tamamlamak, düzenlemek; sokmak (into ... *haline*).

**work.a.ble** ☐ ['wɜ:kəbl] işlenebilir; pratik, elverişli; işletilebilir; **'work.a.day** *adj.* sıradan, alelade, sıkıcı; **'work.day** *n.* işgünü; **'work.er** *n.* işçi, amele; ~s *pl.* işçi sınıfı; **'work.house** *n.* darülaceze; *Am.* ıslahevi.

**work.ing** ['wɜ:kiŋ] **1.** *n.* çalışma; **2.** *adj.* iş gören, çalışan; işleyen; işe ait, iş...; ~ knowledge yeterli bilgi; in ~ order çalışır vaziyette, işler durumda; ~ **cap.i.tal** döner sermaye; **'~-class** *adj.* işçi sınıfı...; ~ **day** işgünü; ~ **draw.ing** △ çalışma projesi; ~ **hours** *pl.* iş saatleri; ~ **man** işçi; **'~-out** *n.* uygulama, tatbik; hesaplama; ~ **plan** △ çalışma planı. **work.man** ['wɜ:kmən] *n.* işçi; **'~.like** *adj.* ustaya yakışır; **'work.man.ship** *n.* ustalık; usta işi; zanaat. **work**...: **'~.out** *n. Am.* F mst spor: idman, antrenman; **'~.room** *n.* çalışma odası; **'~.shop** *n.* atelye; **'~-shy** *adj.* tembel, işten kaçan; **'~.wom.an.** *n.* kadın işçi.

**world** [wɜ:ld] *n. com.* dünya, cihan, âlem; evren; uzay; yer(yüzü); gezegen; hayat, ömür; toplum; a ~ of dünya kadar, pek çok; in the ~ dünyada; yahu, Allah aşkına; what in the ~ are you doing? ne yapıyorsun sen Allah aşkına?; bring (come) into the ~ dünyaya getirmek (gelmek). doğ(ur)mak; for all the ~ like *veya* as if *ile* tıpatıp aynı, hık demiş burnundan düşmüş; a ~ too wide çok geniş; think the ~ of hayran olm. -*e*, çok sevmek -*i*; man of the ~ dünya (*veya* hayat) adamı; **world.li.ness** ['-linis] *n.* dünyevilik, maddecilik; **'world.ling** *n.* dünyaperest kimse. **world.ly** ['wɜ:ldli] *adj.* dünyevî; maddî; ~ innocence dünyadan haberi olmama; ~ wisdom görmüş geçirmişlik; **'~-wise** *adj.* görmüş geçirmiş, pişkin. **world**...: **'~.pow.er** *n. pol.* önemli devlet; **'~-wear.y** *adj.* dünyadan bezmiş; **'~-wide** *adj.* dünya çapında, dünyaya yaygın, âlemşümul.

**worm** [wɜ:m] **1.** *n.* kurt, solucan; *fig.* aşağılık (*veya* pısırık) kimse; ⊕ vidanın helezoni kısmı; ⊕ sonsuz vida; **2.** *v/t.* ~ a secret out of s.o. b-nin ağzından us-

talıkla laf almak; ~ o.s. sokulmak; *fig.*
girmek (into -*e*); ɪ~-**drive** *n.* ⊕ helezonî
dişli; ɪ~-**eat.en** *adj.* kurt yemiş; *fig.* eski,
demode; ɪ~-**gear** *n.* ⊕ sonsuz dişli; =
'~-**wheel** *n.* ⊕ helezonî tekerlek; ɪ~-**wood**
*n.* pelin; *fig.* acılık; acı veren şey;
ɪ**worm.y** *adj.* kurtlu; kurt yemiş; kurt
gibi.
**worn** [wɔːn] *p.p. of* wear 1; '~-'**out** *adj.*
bitkin, çok yorgun; eskimiş, aşınmış,
yıpranmış.
**wor.ri.ment** F ['wʌrimənt] *n.* üzüntü, endişe; **wor.rit** *sl.* [ɪwʌrit] *vb.* canını sıkmak;
'**wor.ry** 1. *v/t.* & *v/i.* üz(ül)mek, endişe-
len(dir)mek; rahatsız etm., canını sıkmak; ısırmak (*köpek*); merak etm., kaygılanmak, tasalanmak (about -*e*); 2. *n.*
üzüntü, endişe, merak, tasa, kaygı, sıkıntı; baş belâsı.
**worse** [wəːs] 1. *adj.* daha fena, daha kötü, beter; ⚕ daha hasta; ~ luck! maale-
scf!, ne yazık ki!; he is none the ~ for it
ondan ona bir zarar gelmez; the ~ for
wear giyile giyile eskimiş; bitkin, çok
yorgun; 2. *n.* daha kötü şey, beteri; from
bad to ~ daha kötüye; ɪ**wor.sen** *v/t.* & *v/i.*
fenalaş(tır)mak, kötüleş(tir)mek.
**wor.ship** ['wəːʃip] 1. *n.* tapınma, ibadet;
hayranlık, tapma; Your ♀ zatıaliniz;
place of ~ ibadethane; 2. *v/t.* tapmak, tapınmak, hayranlık duymak -*e*; *v/i.* ibadet etm.; **wor.ship.ful** □ ['~-ful] saygıdeğer, muhterem; '**wor.ship.(p)er** *n.* tapan,
ibadct eden kimse.
**worst** [wəːst] 1. *adj.* en fena, en kötü; 2.
*n.* en kötü şey *veya* durum; at (the) ~
en kötü olasılıkla; do your ~! elinden geleni ardına koyma!; get the ~ of it yenilmek; if the ~ comes to the ~ başka çıkar
yol kalmazsa, durum daha da kötü olursa; 3. *v/t.* yenmek, mağlûp etm.
**wor.sted** ['wustid] *n.* bükme ün, yün ipliği; bükme yünden dokunmuş kumaş.
**wort**¹ ♀ [wəːt] *n.* bitki, sebze, ot.
**wort**² [~] *n.* bira mayası.
**worth** [wəːθ] 1. *adj.* değer, lâyık;... değe-
rinde, -lik, ...sahibi; he is ~ a million bir
milyonu var; ~ reading okumaya değer;
2. *n.* değer, kıymet; servet, varlık; bedel. -lik; **wor.thi.ness** ['wəːðinis] *n.* değer-
(lilik); **worth.less** □ [ɪwəːθlis] değersiz,
işe yaramaz; karaktersiz, ciğeri beş para etmez; '**worth-'while** *adj.* (zahmetine)
değer, yapmaya değer; faydalı; **wor.thy**
[ɪwəːði] 1. □ değerli; layık (of -*e*), reva,
müstahak; uygun, yaraşır; *oft. co.* saygıdeğer, muhterem; ~ of s.th. *bşe* lâyık,
*bşe* değer; 2. *n.* değerli kimse.

**would** [wud, wəd] *pret. of* will; -ecek(ti);
istedi.
**would-be** ['wudbiː] *adj.* sözde, güya, sözümona; ~ aggressor güya saldırgan; ~
buyer sözümona müşteri; ~ painter sözde ressam; ~ poet şair müsveddesi; ~
politician sözümona politikacı.
**wouldn't** ['wudnt] = would not.
**wound**¹ [wuːnd] 1. *n.* yara, bere; *fig.* gönül yarası; 2. *v/t.* yaralamak; *fig. -in*
gönlünü kırmak, incitmek.
**wound**² [waund] *pret.* & *p.p. of* winʻd².
**wove** *pret.*, **wo.ven** ['wəuv(ən) *p.p. of*
weave 1.
**wow** *Am.* [wau] 1. *int.* hayret!, deme!; 2.
*n. thea. sl.* büyük başarı.
**wrack**¹ ♀ [ræk] *n.* deniz yosunu.
**wrack**² [~] = rack³.
**wraith** [reiθ] *n.* bir kimsenin ölümünden
az önce görülen hayali, tayf; sıska kimse.
**wran.gle** ['ræŋgl] 1. *v/i.* kavga etm., çekişmek; ağız dalaşı yapmak, münakaşa
etm.; 2. *n.* kavga, ağız dalaşı.
**wrap** [ræp] 1. *v/t.* & *v/i.* ört(ün)mek; *oft.*
~ up sar(ıl)mak, sarmalamak, paketle-
mek; bürü(n)mek; bükmek, katlamak;
*fig.* bitirmek, bağlamak (*iş*); be ~ped up
in -*e* sarılmış, bürünmüş olm.; -*de* gizli,
saklı olm.; *fig.* -*e* dört elle sarılmış, kendini vermiş, dalmış olm.; 2. *n.* örtü; atkı; giysi; '**wrap.per** *n.* sargı; sabahlık;
a postal ~ kitap kabı; '**wrap.ping** *n.* ambalaj; sargı; ~ paper paket (*veya* ambalaj) kâğıdı.
**wrath** *lit.* [rɔθ] *n.* öfke, hiddet, gazap;
**wrath.ful** □ ['~-ful] öfkeli, küplere binmiş.
**wreak** [riːk] *v/t.* yapmak, çıkarmak (*hınç,
öfke vs.*) (upon -*den*).
**wreath** [riːθ] *n., pl.* **wreaths** [riːðz] çelenk; **wreathe** [riːð] *v/t.* & *v/i.* sar(ıl)-
mak; kaplamak; çelenk yapmak; çörek
lenmek (*yılan*); daireler halinde hareket etm. (*duman vs.*).
**wreck** [rek] 1. *n.* ⊥ gemi enkazı; harabe,
virane, yıkıntı, enkaz (*oft. fig.*); kazaya
uğrama; harabiyet, tahribat; *fig.* harap
olmuş kimse; 2. *v/t.* kazaya uğratmak;
yıkmak, altüst etm.; be ~ed ⊥ karaya
oturmak; kazaya uğramak; '**wreck.age**
*n.* enkaz, yıkıntı; **wrecked** *adj.* kazaya
uğramış; karaya oturmuş; yıkılmış, *fig.*
**'wreck.er** *n.* ⊥ enkaz temizleyen kimse;
*fig.* sabotajcı; *Am.* bina yıkıcısı; *mot.*
kurtarıcı, çekici; '**wreck.ing** *n.* enkaz hır-
sızlığı; ~ company eski binaları yıkan
şirket; ~ service *mot.* kurtarma (*veya*

yedeğe alma) servisi.
**wren** *orn.* [ren] *n.* çalıkuşu.
**wrench** [rentʃ] **1.** *v/t.* burkmak; burkarak koparmak; zorla almak (from s.o. *b-den*); *fig.* çarpıtmak *(anlam)*; ~ open çekip açmak; ~ out çekip çıkarmak; **2.** *n.* burk(ul)ma; bük(ül)me; *fig.* ayrılık acısı; ⊕ İngiliz anahtarı.
**wrest** [rest] *v/t.* zorla elde etm., zorla almak (from s.o. *b-den*); çarpıtmak *(anlam, gerçek).*
**wres.tle** [ˈresl] **1.** *v/i.* güreşmek; *fig.* uğraşmak, mücadele etm.; **2.** = wrestling; ˈwres.tler *n.* pehlivan, güreşçi; ˈwrestling *n.* güreş(me).
**wretch** [retʃ] *n.* sefil, biçare, zavallı kimse; *co.* herif, alçak adam; poor ~ adamcağız.
**wretch.ed** □ [ˈretʃid] alçak, sefil; bitkin, bezgin, üzgün; perişan, acınacak halde; acıklı; kötü, berbat; ˈwretch.ed.ness *n.* sefalet, perişanlık; bitkinlik.
**wrick** [rik] **1.** *v/t.* burkmak; **2.** *n.* burk(ul)ma.
**wrig.gle** [ˈrigl] *v/t. & v/i.* kımılda(t)mak; sıyrılmak, sıyrılıp çıkmak; kıvranmak, sallanmak; kıpır kıpır kıpırdanmak; kıvrılmak; ~ out of *-den* sıyrılıp çıkmak; *-den* yakayı sıyırmak *(güçlük vs.).*
**wright** [rait] *n.* işçi; yapımcı; yazar; marangoz.
**wring** [riŋ] **1.** *(irr.) v/t.* burup sıkmak; burmak, bükmek, sıkmak; ~ s.th. from s.o. *b-den* bşi zorla almak; ~ s.o.'s heart *b-nin* yüreğine işlemek; ~ing wet sırılsıklam; **2.** *n.* burma, sıkma; ˈwring.er, ˈwring.ing-ma.chine *n.* çamaşır merdanesi.
**wrin.kle**¹ [ˈriŋkl] **1.** *n.* kırışık, buruşuk; yöntem, teknik; **2.** *v/t. & v/i.* kırış(tır)mak, buruş(tur)mak; ~d kırışık, buruşuk.
**wrin.kle²** F [~] *n.* fikir, öğüt, çıtlatma.
**wrist** [rist] *n.* bilek; ~ watch kol saati; ˈwrist.band *n.* kol ağzı, manşet; = wristlet [ˈ~lit] *n.* kayış *(part. saat)*; *spor:* bileklik.
**writ** [rit] *n.* yazı; ferman, ilâm, mahkeme emri; davetiye; Holy 2 İncil; ~ of attachment ṣ̌̌ haciz belgesi; ~ of execution ṣ̌̌ icra emri.
**write** [rait] *(irr.) v/t.* yazmak; kaleme almak; ifade etm.; kaydetmek; doldurmak *(form vs.)*; ~ down yazmak, kaydetmek; ~ in full tam olarak *(veya* ayrıntıla-

rıyla) yazmak; ~ off derhal yazmak, yazıvermek; kapatmak, ödemek *(borç)*; iptal etm.; hurdahaş etm.; † zarara geçmek; ~ out yazıya dökmek; yazmak *(çek vs.)*; ~ up yazıp tamamlamak; değerini yüksek göstermek *(hisse vs.)*; *fig. -den* övgüyle bahsetmek; *v/i.* yazı yazmak; yazarlık yapmak; ~ for ...hesabına yazı yazmak; beste yapmak; mektupla bş ısmarlamak; ~ home about *fig.* bahsetmeye değer; ˈ~-off *n.* † zarar olarak kabul edilen miktar; a complete ~ F hurdahaş olmuş şey.
**writ.er** [ˈraitə] *n.* yazar; kâtip; ~ to the signet *(İskoçya'da)* noter; ~'s cramp, ~'s palsy çok yazı yazmaktan ele giren kramp.
**write-up** [ˈraitʌp] *n.* makale; övücü yazı.
**writhe** [raið] *v/i.* kıvranmak; *fig.* acı çekmek.
**writ.ing** [ˈraitiŋ] *n.* yazı; el yazısı; yazı yaz(ıl)ma; yazarlık; ~s *pl.* eser, kitap; *attr.* yazı...; in ~ yazılı; ˈ~-block *n.* bloknot; ˈ~-case *n.* sumen; ˈ~-desk *n.* yazı masası; ˈ~-pa.per *n.* yazı kâğıdı.
**writ.ten** [ˈritn] **1.** *p.p. of* write; **2.** *adj.* yazılı.
**wrong** [rɔŋ] **1.** □ yanlış, hatalı; ters; haksız; uygunsuz, yakışık almaz; bozuk; be ~ yanılmak; hatalı, yanlış olm.; uygunsuz olm.; bozuk olm.; yanlış gitmek *(saat)*; go ~ yanılmak; kötü sonuçlanmak; bozulmak; *fig.* doğru yoldan sapmak; there is something ~ bir bozukluk var; what's ~ with...? F *-in* nesi var?; on the ~ side of sixty altmış yaşını geçmiş; **2.** *n.* hata, kusur; haksızlık; günah; yalan; be in the ~ hatalı, haksız olm.; put s.o. in the ~ *b-ni* haksız çıkarmak; **3.** *v/t.* haksız muamele etm. *-e*, haksızlık etm. *-e*; *-in* hakkını yemek; ˈ~-ˈdo.er *n.* haksızlık eden *(veya* günahkâr) kimse; ˈ~ˈdo.ing *n.* haksızlık; günah; **wrong.ful** □ [ˈ~ful] haksız; kanunsuz; gayri meşru; ˈwrongˈhead.ed *adj.* inatçı, ters; yanlış; ˈwrong.ness *n.* haksızlık, yanlışlık.
**wrote** [rəut] *pret. of* write.
**wroth** *poet. veya co.* [rəuθ] *adj.* öfkeli, hiddetli.
**wrought** *lit.* [rɔːt] *pret. & p.p. of* work 2; ˈ~-ˈi.ron **1.** *n.* dövme demir; **2.** *adj.* dövme demirden yapılmış; ˈ~-up *adj.* çok heyecanlı, sinirli.
**wrung** [rʌŋ] *pret. & p.p. of* wring 1.
**wry** □ [rai] eğri, çarpık.

# Y

**yacht** ↓ [jɔt] **1.** *n.* yat; **2.** *v/i.* yat ile gezmek *veya* yarışmak; **¹~-club** *n.* yat kulübü; **¹yacht.er, yachts.man** [¹~smən] *n.* yat sahibi *veya* yat kullanan kimse; **¹yacht.ing** *n.* yatçılık, kotracılık; *attr.* yat...

**yah** [jɑː] ah!, ya!

**ya.hoo** [jə¹huː] *n.* hayvan gibi herif.

**yam** ❦ [jæm] *n.* Hint yerelması.

**yank¹** [jæŋk] **1.** *v/t.* birden çekmek; **2.** *n.* birden çekiş .

**Yank²** *sl.* [~] = Yankee.

**Yan.kee** F [¹jæŋki] *n.* Amerikalı; ABD:'-nin kuzey eyaletlerinde oturan kimse; ~ Doodle Amerikan halk şarkısı.

**yap** [jæp] **1.** *v/i.* havlamak; F gevezelik etm.; **2.** *n.* havlama; F gevezelik.

**yard¹** [jɑːd] *n.* yarda *(0,914 m)*; ↓ seren.

**yard²** [~] *n.* avlu; *Am.* bahçe; the ♀ Londra Emniyet Müdürlüğü; *marshalling ~.* *railway ~* manevra istasyonu.

**yard...:** **¹~-arm** *n.* ↓ seren cundası; **¹~.man** *n.* 🚂 manevracı; **¹~-meas.ure,** **¹~.stick** *n.* bir yardalık ölçü (çubuğu).

**yarn** [jɑːn] **1.** *n.* iplik; ↓ gemici masalı; F masal, hikâye; spin a ~ hikâye anlatmak; **2.** *v/i.* F hikâye anlatmak.

**yar.row** ❦ [¹jærəu] *n.* civanperçemi.

**yaw** ↓, ✈ [jɔː] *v/i.* rotadan çıkmak.

**yawl** ↓ [jɔːl] *n.* filika; iki yelkenli gemi.

**yawn** [jɔːn] **1.** *v/i.* esnemek; açılmak, yarılmak; **2.** *n.* esneme.

**ye** † *veya poet. veya co.* [jiː, ji] *pron.* siz(ler).

**yea** † *veya prov.* [jei] **1.** *adv.* evet; **2.** *n.* olumlu oy (veren kimse).

**year** [jiə, jɔː] *n.* yıl, sene; yaş; ~ of *arace* milâdî yıl; he bears his ~s well yaşına göre çok dinç; **¹year.ling** *n.* bir yaşında hayvan yavrusu; **¹year-long** *adj.* bir yıllık, bir yıl süren; **¹year.ly** *adj. & adv.* yıllık, senelik, yılda bir (olan).

**yearn** [jəːn] arzulamak, çok istemek (for, after *-i; to inf. -meği);* **¹yearn.ing 1.** *n.* arzu, hasret, özlem; **2.** ☐ hasretli, özlemli.

**yeast** [jiːst] *n.* maya; **¹yeast.y** ☐ mayalı, maya gibi; köpüklü; *fig.* önemsiz, boş, anlamsız.

**yegg(.man)** *Am. sl.* [¹jeg(mən)] *n.* hırsız, kasa hırsızı.

**yell** [jel] **1.** *v/i.* çığlık koparmak, bağırmak, haykırmak, feryat etm.; **2.** *n.* çığlık, bağırma, haykırma.

**yel.low** [¹jeləu] **1.** *adj.* sarı; F ödlek, korkak; *sl.* şoven; heyecan yaratan *(gazete);* **2.** *n.* sarı renk; yumurta sarısı; **3.** *v/t. & v/i.* sarar(t)mak; ~ed sararmış, solmuş; **¹~.back** *n.* değersiz eski kitap; ~ **fe.ver** ♀ sarıhumma; **¹~-ham.mer** *n.* *orn.* sarıcık; **¹yel.low.ish** *adj.* sarımsı, sarımtırak; **¹yel.low press** olayları heyecanlı bir biçimde veren gazeteler.

**yelp** [jelp] **1.** *n.* kesik kesik havlama; **2.** *v/i.* kesik hesik havlamak.

**yen** *Am. sl.* [jen] *n.* hasret, özlem, arzu.

**yeo.man** [¹jəumən] *n.* toprak sahibi; ~ of the guard hassa askeri; **¹yeo.man.ry** *n.* küçük toprak sahipleri; ✗ çiftçilerden oluşan gönüllü süvari alayı.

**yep** *Am.* F [jep] *adv.* evet.

**yes** [jes] **1.** *adv.* evet, hay hay; **2.** *n.* olumlu yanıt; olumlu oy (veren kimse); **~-man** *sl.* [¹~mæn] *n.* evet efendimci.

**yes.ter.day** [¹jestədi] *n. & adv.* dün; **yes.ter¹year** *n. & adv.* geçen yıl.

**yet** [jet] **1.** *adv.* henüz, daha, hâlâ; bile; yine, nihayet; as ~ şimdiye kadar; not ~ henüz değil; **2.** *cj.* ancak; yine de, bununla birlikte, buna rağmen.

**yew** ❦ [juː] *n.* porsukağacı.

**Yid.dish** [¹jidiʃ] *n.* Eskenazi dili.

**yield** [jiːld] **1.** *v/t.* vermek, meydana çıkarmak; getirmek *(kâr);* sağlamak; ~ up the ghost ruhunu teslim etm., ölmek; *v/i. part.* ✓ mahsül vermek; razı olm., teslim olm., boyun eğmek (to *-e);* çökmek, kırılmak; **2.** *n.* mahsül, ürün. rekolte, hâsılat, gelir; **¹yield.ing** ☐ bükülebilir, eğrilebilir; verimli, bereketli; *fig.* yumuşak, uysal.

**yip** *Am.* F [jip] *v/i.* acı acı havlamak.

**yo.del, yo.dle** [¹jəudl] **1.** *n.* pesten tize anî geçişlerle söylenen şarkı; **2.** *vb.* böyle şarkı söylemek.

**yo.gi** [¹jəugi] *n.* yogacı.

**yo.gurt, yo.ghurt, yo.ghourt** [¹jɔgət] *n.* yogurt.

**yoicks** *hunt.* [jɔiks] *int.* haydi!

**yoke** [jəuk] **1.** *n.* boyunduruk *(a. fig.)*; çift; omuz sırığı; bağ; **2.** *v/t.* & *v/i.* boyunduruğa koşmak; boyunduruk vurmak; bağla(n)mak; *fig.* evlendirmek (to *ile*); **'~-fel.low** *n.* arkadaş, *part.* hayat arkadaşı, eş.

**yo.kel** F ['jəukəl] *n.* hödük, cahil taşralı.

**yolk** [jəuk] *n.* yumurta sarısı.

**yon** † *veya poet.* [jɔn], **yon.der** *lit.* ['jɔndə] **1.** *adj.* ötedeki, oradaki, şuradaki; **2.** *adv.* orada, şurada, ötede.

**yore** [jɔː] *n.:* of ~ eskiden olan.

**you** [juː, ju] *pron.* sen; siz(ler); sana, seni; size, sizi.

**you'd** F [juːd] = you had; you would; **you'll** F [juːl] = you will; you shall.

**young** [jʌŋ] **1.** □ genç, küçük; taze, körpe, yeni; toy; **2.** *n.* yavru(lar); with ~

hamile, gebe; **'young.ish** *adj.* gepegenç, oldukça genç; **young.ster** ['~stə] *n.* çocuk, yavru, *part.* delikanlı.

**your** [jɔː, jə] *adj.* senin; sizin; **you're** F [juə] = you are; **yours** [jɔːz] *pron.* seninki; sizinki; **your'self,** *pl.* **your.selves** [~'selvz] *pron.* kendin(iz); kendi kendinize.

**youth** [juːθ] *n., pl.* **youths** [juːðz] genç, delikanlı; gençlik; ~ hostel gençlik yurdu, hostel; go ~-hostelling hostellerde gecelemek.

**youth.ful** □ ['juːθful] genç, dinç, taze; **'youth.ful.ness** *n.* gençlik, dinçlik.

**you've** F [juːv, juv] = you have.

**yuc.ca** ⚶ ['jʌkə] *n.* avizeağacı.

**Yu.go-Slav** [ˌjuːgəuˈslɑːv] *n.* & *adj.* Yugoslav(yalı).

**Yule** *lit.* [juːl] *n.* Noel; ~ log Noel gecesi yakılan kütük.

# Z

**za.ny** [ˈzeini] *n.* soytarı, palyaço, maskara.

**zeal** [ziːl] *n.* gayret, heves, istek, azim; **zeal.ot** [ˈzelət] *n.* gayretli kimse; *part. eccl.* fanatik kimse; **ˈzeal.ot.ry** *n.* fanatizm; **ˈzeal.ous** ☐ şevkli, gayretli (for *-e;* to *inf. -meğe*).

**ze.bra** *zo.* [ˈziːbrə] *n.* zebra, zebir; **~ cross-ing** çizgili yaya geçidi.

**ze.bu** *zo.* [ˈziːbuː] *n.* hörgüçlü Hint sığırı.

**ze.nith** [ˈzeniθ] *n.* başucu; *fig.* zirve, doruk.

**zeph.yr** [ˈzefə] *n.* esinti, meltem; ♱ zefir (kumaş).

**zep.pe.lin** [ˈzepəlin] *n.* zeplin.

**ze.ro** [ˈziərəu] *n.* sıfır; *fig.* hiç; **~ hour** ✕ saldırı saati.

**zest** [zest] **1.** *n.* tat, lezzet, çeşni; *fig.* zevk, haz, heyecan (for *için*); **~ for life** yaşama coşkusu; **2.** *vb.* çeşni vermek.

**zig.zag** [ˈzigzæg] **1.** *n.* zikzak yol; *attr.* zigzag..., dolambaçlı, yılankavî; **2.** *v/i.* zikzak yapmak.

**zinc** [ziŋk] **1.** *n.* *min.* çinko, tutya; **2.** *v/t.* çinko kaplamak, galvanizlemek.

**Zi.on** [ˈzaiən] *n.* İsrail kavmi; cennet; **ˈZi.on.ism** *n.* siyonizm; **ˈZi.on.ist** *n.* & *adj.* siyonist.

**zip** [zip] **1.** *n.* vızıltı; F gayret, enerji; **2.** *vb.* fermuarı kapatmak; vızıldayarak geçmek (*kurşun*); **zip code** *Am.* posta bölgesi numarası; **ˈ~-fas.ten.er** = zipper 1; **ˈzip.per 1.** *n.* fermuar; **2.** *vb.* fermuarlamak; **ˈzip.py** *adj.* F hareketli, enerjik.

**zith.er** ♪ [ˈziθə] *n.* kanuna benzer bir çalgı aleti.

**zo.di.ac** *ast.* [ˈzəudiæk] *n.* zodyak; burçlar kuşağı; **zo.di.a.cal** [zəuˈdaiəkəl] *adj.* zodyaka ait, zodyak...

**zon.al** ☐ [ˈzəunl] kuşağa ait, kuşak...; **zone** *n.* kuşak; *fig.* bölge, mıntıka, yöre.

**zoo** F [zuː] *n.* hayvanat bahçesi.

**zo.o.log.i.cal** ☐ [zəuəˈlɔdʒikəl] zoolojik; **~ garden(s** *pl.*) hayvanat bahçesi; **zo.ol.o.gist** [~ˈlɔlədʒist] *n.* zoolog; **zoˈol.o.gy** *n.* zooloji, hayvanlar bilimi.

**zoom** [zuːm] **1.** *v/i.* ♱ *sl.* dikine yükselmek; *fig.* fırlamak (*fiyat*); rüzgâr gibi gitmek (*araba*); *phot.* zum yapmak, mesafeyi ayarlamak; **2.** *n.* dikine yükselme; **~ lens** *phot.* mesafeyi ayarlayan mercek.

**Zu.lu** [ˈzuːluː] *n.* Zulu (dili).

**zy.mot.ic** [zaiˈmɔtik] *adj.* ♻ mayalamaya ait, mayalanmadan ileri gelen; ♱ bulaşıcı hastalığa ait.

# Countries of the World
## Dünya Ülkeleri

**Af.ghan.i.stan** [æf'gænistaːn] Afganistan
**Al.ba.ni.a** [æl'beinjə] Arnavutluk
**Al.ge.ri.a** [æl'dʒiəriə] Cezayir
**An.dor.ra** [æn'dɔrə] Andorra
**Ar.gen.ti.na** [ɑːdʒən'tiːnə] Arjantin
**Aus.tra.lia** [ɔs'treiljə] Avusturalya
**Aus.tri.a** ['ɔstriə] Avusturya
**Ba.ha.mas** [bə'hɑːməz] Bahama Adaları
**Bah.rain** [baː'rein] Bahreyn
**Ban.gla.desh** [bæŋglə'deʃ] Bangaldeş
**Bar.ba.dos** [baː'beidəs] Barbados
**Bel.gium** ['beldʒəm] Belçika
**Ber.mu.da** [bə'mjuːdə] Bermuda
**Bo.liv.i.a** [bə'liviə] Bolivya
**Bra.zil** [brə'zil] Brezilya
**Bul.gar.i.a** [bʌl'gɛəriə] Bulgaristan
**Bur.ma** ['bəːmə] Birmanya
**Cam.er.oon** [kæmə'ruːn] Kamerun
**Can.a.da** ['kænədə] Kanada
**Chad** [tʃæd] Çad
**Chil.e** ['tʃili] Şili
**Chi.na** ['tʃainə] Çin
**Co.lom.bia** [kə'lɔmbiə] Kolombiya
**Cos.ta Ri.ca** [kɔstə'riːkə] Kostarika
**Cu.ba** ['kjuːbə] Küba
**Cy.prus** ['saiprəs] Kıbrıs
**Den.mark** ['denmaːk] Danimarka
**Ec.ua.dor** ['ekwədɔː] Ekvador
**E.gypt** ['iːdʒipt] Mısır
**El Sal.va.dor** [el'sælvədɔː] El Salvador
**E.thi.o.pi.a** [iːθi'əupjə] Habeşistan
**Fin.land** ['finlənd] Finlandiya
**France** [frɑːns] Fransa
**Gam.bi.a** ['gæmbiə] Gambia
**Ger.ma.ny** ['dʒəːməni] Almanya
**Gha.na** ['gɑːnə] Gana
**Gi.bral.tar** [dʒi'brɔːltə] Cebelitarık
**Great Brit.ain** ['greit'britn] Büyük Britanya
**Greece** [griːs] Yunanistan
**Gua.te.ma.la** [gwɑːtə'mɑːlə] Guatemala
**Hai.ti** ['heiti] Haiti

610

**Hol.land** [ˈhɔlənd] Hollanda
**Hon.du.ras** [hɔnˈdjuərəs] Honduras
**Hun.ga.ry** [ˈhʌŋgəri] Macaristan
**Ice.land** [ˈaislənd] İslanda adası
**In.dia** [ˈindjə] Hindistan
**In.do.ne.sia** [indəˈniːzjə] Endonezya
**I.ran** [iˈrɑn] Iran
**I.raq** [iˈrɑːk] Irak
**Ire.land** [ˈaiələnd] İrlanda
**Is.ra.el** [ˈizreil] Israil
**It.a.ly** [ˈitəli] İtalya
**Ja.mai.ca** [dʒəˈmeikə] Jamaika
**Ja.pan** [dʒəˈpæn] Japonya
**Jor.dan** [ˈdʒɔːdn] Ürdün
**Ken.ya** [ˈkenjə] Kenya
**Ko.re.a** [kəˈriə] Kore
**Ku.weit** [kuˈweit] Kuveyt
**Leb.a.non** [ˈlebənən] Lübnan
**Lib.ya** [ˈlibiə] Libya
**Lux.em.b(o)urg** [ˈlʌksəmbəːg] Lüksemburg
**Mad.a.gas.car** [mædəˈgæskə] Madagaskar Adası
**Mal.ta** [ˈmɔːltə] Malta
**Mex.i.co** [ˈmeksikou] Meksika
**Mo.na.co** [ˈmɔnəkou] Monako
**Mo.roc.co** [məˈrɔkou] Fas
**Mo.zam.bique** [mouzæmˈbiːk] Mozambik
**Neth.er.lands** [ˈneðələndz] Hollanda
**New Zea.land** [njuːˈziːlənd] Yeni Zeland
**Nic.a.ra.gua** [nikəˈrægjuə] Nikaragua
**Ni.ge.ri.a** [naiˈdʒiəriə] Nijerya
**Nor.way** [ˈnɔːwei] Norveç
**Pak.i.stan** [pɑːkisˈtɑːn] Pakistan
**Pan.a.ma** [pænəˈmɑː] Panama
**Par.a.guay** [ˈpærəgwai] Paraguay
**Pe.ru** [pəˈruː] Peru
**Phil.ip.pines** [ˈfilipiːnz] Filipinler
**Po.land** [ˈpoulənd] Polonya
**Por.tu.gal** [ˈpɔːtʃugl] Portekiz
**Oa'tar** [ˈkʌtɑː] Katar
**Rho.de.sia** [rouˈdiːʒə] Rodezya
**Ro.ma.nia** [rəˈmeinjə] Romanya
**Rus.sia** [ˈrʌʃə] Rusya
**Sa.u.di A.ra.bi.a** [saudiəˈreibiə] Saudi Arabistan
**Sen.e.gal** [seniˈgɔːl] Senegal
**Sin.ga.pore** [siŋgəˈpɔː] Singapur
**Spain** [spein] Ispanya
**Sri Lan.ka** [sriˈlæŋkə] Sri Lanka
**Su.dan** [suːˈdɑːn] Sudan
**Swe.den** [ˈswiːdn] Isveç
**Swit.zer.land** [ˈswitsələnd] İsviçre
**Syr.i.a** [ˈsiriə] Suriye
**Tai.wan** [taiˈwɑːn] Tayvan

**Tan.za.ni.a** [tænzə'niə] Tanzanya
**Thai.land** ['tailænd] Tayland
**Trin.i.dad** ['trinidæd] Trinidad
**Tu.ni.sia** [tju:'niziə] Tunus
**Tur.key** ['tə:ki] Türkiye
**U.gan.da** [ju:'gændə] Uganda
**U.nit.ed States of A.mer.i.ca** [ju:'naitid steits əv ə'merikə] Amerika Birleşik Devletleri
**U.ru.guay** ['juərəgwai] Uruguay
**Ven.e.zue.la** [veni'zweilə] Venezuela
**Vi.et.nam** [vjet'næm] Vietnam
**Yem.en** ['jemən] Yemen
**Za.i.re** [za:'iə] Zaire
**Zam.bi.a** ['zæmbiə] Zambia

# The Most Common Forenames in English

### İngilizce'de En Yaygın İsimler

**Men**
**Erkek**

Abraham ['eibrəhæm]
Adam ['ædəm]
Adrian ['eidriən]
Alan, Allan, Allen ['ælən]
Albert ['ælbət]
Alexander [ælig'za:ndə]
Alex ['æliks]
Alfred ['ælfrid]
Andrew ['ændru:]
Anthony, Antony ['æntəni]
Arnold ['a:nld]
Arthur ['a:θə]
Benjamin ['bendʒəmin]
Bernard ['bə:nəd]
Bill [bil]
Bob [bɔb]
Bruce [bru:s]
Carl [ka:l]
Charles [tʃa:lz]
Christian ['kristʃən]
Christopher ['kristəfə]
Clement ['klemənt]
Clifford ['klifəd]
Colin ['kɔlin]
Cyril ['sirəl]
Daniel ['dæniəl]
David ['deivid]
Dean [di:n]
Dennis, Denis ['denis]
Derek ['derik]
Desmond ['dezmənd]
Dick [dik]
Dominic ['dɔminik]
Douglas ['dʌgləs]
Edmund ['edmənd]
Edward ['edwəd]
Eric ['erik]
Ernest ['ə:nist]
Felix ['fi:liks]
Francis ['fra:nsis]
Frank [fræŋk]
Frederick ['fredrik]

Gary ['gæri]
Geoffrey ['dʒefri]
George [dʒɔ:dʒ]
Gerald ['dʒerəld]
Gerard ['dʒerəd]
Gilbert ['gilbət]
Godfrey ['gɔdfri]
Gordon ['gɔ:dn]
Graham ['greiəm]
Gregory ['gregəri]
Harold ['hærəld]
Harry ['hæri]
Harvey ['ha:vi]
Henry ['henri]
Hilary ['hiləri]
Howard ['hauəd]
Humphrey ['hʌmfri]
Isaac ['aizək]
Jack [dʒæk]
James [dʒeimz]
Jason ['dʒeisn]
Jeffrey ['dʒefri]
Jeremy ['dʒerəmi]
Jerry ['dʒeri]
Jim [dʒim]
Jo, Joe [dʒou]
John [dʒɔn]
Jonathan ['dʒɔnəθən]
Joseph ['dʒəuzif]
Julian ['dʒu:liən]
Keith [ki:θ]
Ken [ken]
Kevin ['kevin]
Larry ['læri]
Laurence ['lɔrəns]
Leo ['li:əu]
Leonard ['lenəd]
Lewis ['lu:is]
Malcolm ['mælkəm]
Mark [ma:k]
Martin ['ma:tin]
Matthew ['mæθju:]

Max [mæks]
Michael ['maikl]
Mick [mik]
Mike [maik]
Nicholas ['nikələs]
Nick [nik]
Noel ['nəuəl]
Norman ['nɔːmən]
Oliver ['ɔlivə]
Oscar ['ɔskə]
Oswald ['czwɔld]
Patrick ['pætrik]
Paul [pɔːl]
Peter ['piːtə]
Philip ['filip]
Ralph [rælf]
Raymond ['reimənd]
Rex [reks]
Richard ['ritʃəd]
Robert ['rɔbət]
Robin ['rɔbin]

Roger ['rɔdʒə]
Ronald ['rɔnld]
Roy [rɔi]
Rudolf ['ruːdɔlf]
Sam [sæm]
Samuel ['sæmjuəl]
Sandy ['sændi]
Sidney ['sidni]
Simon ['saimən]
Stanley ['stænli]
Steve [stiːv]
Stewart ['stjuːət]
Ted [ted]
Thomas ['tɔməs]
Timothy ['timəθi]
Tom [tɔm]
Tony ['təuni]
Victor ['viktə]
Walter ['wɔːltə]
Wayne [wein]
William ['wiliəm]

## Women
### Kadın

Agatha ['ægəθə]
Alexandra [ælig'zaːndrə]
Alice ['ælis]
Amanda [ə'mændə]
Angela ['ændʒələ]
Ann, Anne [æn]
Barbara ['baːbrə]
Belinda [bə'lində]
Bella ['belə]
Betsy ['betsi]
Betty ['beti]
Brenda ['brendə]
Carol, Carole ['kærəl]
Caroline ['kærəlain]
Carolyn ['kærəlin]
Catherine ['kæθrin]
Celia ['siːliə]
Christine ['kristiːn]
Clare [kleə]
Constance ['kɔnstəns]
Deborah ['debərə]
Diana [dai'ænə]
Doris ['dɔris]
Dorothy ['dɔrəθi]
Elizabeth [i'lizəbəθ]
Emily ['eməli]
Emma ['emə]
Erica ['erikə]
Eve [iːv]
Flora ['flɔːrə]
Florence ['flɔrəns]
Frances ['fraːnsis]
Gloria ['glɔːriə]

Grace [greis]
Harriet ['hæriət]
Helen ['helən]
İngrid ['ingrid]
Isabel ['izəbel]
Isabella [izə'belə]
Jane [dʒein]
Janet ['dʒænit]
Jacqueline ['dʒækəlin]
Jennifer ['dʒenifə]
Jenny ['dʒeni]
Jessica ['dʒesikə]
Jill [dʒil]
Joan [dʒəun]
Joanna [dʒəu'ænə]
Josephine ['dʒəuzəfiːn]
Julia ['dʒuːliə]
Julie ['dʒuːli]
Juliet ['dʒuːliət]
Karen ['kærən]
Kate [keit]
Katherine ['kæθrin]
Kay [kei]
Laura ['lɔːrə]
Lily ['lili]
Linda ['lində]
Lisa ['liːsə]
Liz [liz]
Liza ['laizə]
Louise [luː'iːz]
Lucy ['luːsi]
Maggie ['mægi]
Margaret ['maːgrit]

Martha ['mɑːθə]
Maria [mə'riə]
Marilyn ['mærəlin]
Mary ['mɛəri]
Monica ['mɔnikə]
Nancy ['nænsi]
Natalie ['nætəli]
Nelly ['neli]
Olive ['bliv]
Pamela ['pæmələ]
Patricia [pə'triʃə]
Paula ['pɔːlə]
Rebecca [rə'bekə]
Rita ['riːtə]
Rose [rəuz]
Rosemary ['rəuzməri]
Sally ['sæli]

Samantha [sə'mænθə]
Sandra ['saːndrə]
Sarah ['sɛərə]
Shirley ['ʃəːli]
Sheila ['ʃiːlə]
Stella ['stələ]
Stephanie ['stefəni]
Susan ['suːzn]
Susie ['suːzi]
Suzanne [suːˈzæn]
Sylvia, Silvia ['silviə]
Tracy ['treisi]
Ursula ['əːsjulə]
Veronica [və'rɔnikə]
Victoria [vik'tɔːriə]
Virginia [və'dʒiniə]

# The Most Common Abbreviations in English

## İngilizce'de En Yaygın Kısaltmalar

**A**

**A-bomb** atomic bomb atom bombası
**A.A.** Automobile Association Otomobil Kurumu
**A.A.A.** Amateur Athletics Association Amatör Atletizm Kurumu; *Am.* American Automobile Association Amerikan Otomobil Kurumu.
**A.B.** Able Seaman Gemici; *Am.* Bachelor of Arts Edebiyat Fakültesi Mezunu.
**A.B.C.** Australian Broadcasting Commission Avustralya Radyo, Televizyon Kurumu.
**a.c.** alternating current alternatif akım.
**a/c** account hesap.
**acc(t)** account hesap.
**ad(vt)** advertisement reklam.
**A.D.** Anno Domini *(Lat.* = in the year of the Lord) M.S., milattan sonra.
**A.D.C.** Aide-de-camp emir subayı, yaver.
**add(r)** address adres.
**A.G.M.** Annual General Meeting Yıllık Genel Kurul.
**a.m.** ante meridiem *(Lat.* = before noon) öğleden önce.
**amp.** ampere(s) amper.
**anon.** anonymous isimsiz.
**appro.** approval onaylama.
**approx.** approximately yaklaşık olarak, takriben.
**Apr.** April Nisan.
**arr.** arrival varış, geliş.
**asap.** as soon as possible mümkün olduğunca çabuk.
**asst.** assistant asistan, yardımcı
**Aug.** August Ağustos.
**A.V.** Audio-Visual Görsel-Işitsel.
**Av(e).** Avenue Cadde, Bulvar.
**A.W.O.L.** absent without leave izinsiz kaçan.

**B**

**b** born doğmuş, doğumlu.
**b & b** bed and breakfast yatak ve kahvaltı.
**B.A.** Bachelor of Arts Edebiyat Fakültesi mezunu; British Airways Ingiliz Hava Yolları.
**Barr.** Barrister avukat.
**B.B.C.** British Broadcasting Corporation Ingiliz Radyo, Televizyon Kurumu.
**B.C.** Before Christ M.Ö., milattan önce; British Council İngiliz Konseyi.
**B.D.** Bachelor of Divinity Ilahiyat Fakültesi mezunu.
**bk.** book kitap.

616

**B.M.** British Museum Ingiliz Müzesi.
**B.M.A.** British Medical Association İngiliz Tıp Kurumu.
**Br.** Brother erkek kardeş.
**Brit.** Britain Britanya; British Ingiliz.
**Bro(s).** brother(s) kardeş(ler).
**B.S.** *Am.* Bachelor of Science Fen Fakültesi mezunu.
**B.Sc.** Bachelor of Science Fen Fakültesi mezunu.

**C**

**C** Centigrade santigrat.
**c** cent(s) sent; century yüzyıl; circa aşağı yukarı, takriben; cubic kübik.
**C.A.** Chartered Accountant ayrıcalıklı muhasebeci.
**Capt.** Captain kaptan.
**Cath.** Catholic Katolik.
**C.B.C.** Canadian Broadcasting Corporation Kanada Radyo, Televizyon Kurumu.
**c.c.** cubic centimetre(s) kübik santimetre.
**Cdr.** Commander komutan.
**Cdre.** Commodore komodor.
**cert.** certificate sertifika, belge; certified onaylı.
**c.f.** confer karşılaştırınız.
**cg.** centigram santigram.
**c.h.** central heating kalorifer.
**ch(ap).** chapter bölüm, kısım.
**C.I.A.** *Am.* Central Intelligence Agency Amerikan Merkezi Haberalma Orgütü.
**C.I.D.** Criminal Investigation Department Cinayet Araştırma Dairesi.
**c.i.f.** cost, insurance, freight fiyat, sigorta, navlun.
**C-in-C** Commander-in-Chief Başkomutan.
**cl.** class sınıf; centilitre(s) santilitre.
**cm.** centimetre(s) santimetre.
**Co.** Company şirket.
**c/o** care of eliyle.
**C.O.D.** Cash on Delivery ödemeli, teslimde ödeme.
**Col.** Colonel Albay.
**Coll.** College Üniversite, Yüksekokul.
**Cons.** Conservative Muhafazakâr Parti.
**Corp.** Corporation anonim şirket.
**c.p.** compare karşılaştırınız.
**Cpl.** Corporal onbaşı.
**C.S.** Civil Servant devlet memuru; Civil Service devlet hizmeti.
**C.S.E.** Certificate of Secondary Éducation ortaokul diploması.
**cu.** cubic kübik.

**D**

**d** penny *(Lat.* = denarius) peni; died ölmüş, merhum.
**dbl** double çift.
**d.c.** direct current doğru akım.
**D.D.** Doctor of Divinity ilahiyat doktoru.
**D.D.T.** dichloro-diphenyl-trichloroethane D.D.T.
**Dec.** December Aralık.
**dec.** deceased merhum, rahmetli.
**deg.** degree(s) derece.
**Dem.** Democrat Demokrat.

**dep.** departure kalkış, hareket; **deputy** vekil, yardımcı.

**Dept.** Department kısım, bölüm, şube.

**diag.** diagram diyagram.

**diff.** difference fark; **different** farklı.

**Dip.** Diploma diploma.

**Dir.** Director müdür.

**D.J.** dinner jacket smokin; **disc jockey** diskcokey.

**DM.** Deutschmark Alman Markı.

**dol.** dollar(s) dolar.

**doz.** dozen düzine.

**Dr.** Debtor borçlu; **Doctor** doktor.

**dr.** dram(s) dirhem.

**dupl.** duplicate suret, kopya.

**D.V.** Deo Volente *(Lat.* = God being willing) inşallah, Allah'ın emriyle.

**E**

E east doğu.

**Ed.** editor editör; **edition** baskı; **education** eğitim.

**E.E.C.** European Economic Community A.E.T., Avrupa Ekonomik Topluluğu.

**E.F.T.A.** European Free Trade Association Avrupa Serbest Ticaret Birliği.

**e.g.** exempli gratia *(Lat.* = for example, for instance) örneğin.

**enc(l).** enclosed ilişikte.

**Eng.** Engineer(ing) mühendis(lik); **England** İngiltere; **English** İngiliz.

**Esq.** Esquire bay, bey, efendi.

**etc.** et cetera vs., ve saire.

**eve.** evening akşam.

**F**

F Fahrenheit fahrenhayt; **Fellow** akademi üyesi.

**f.** foot (feet) ayak *(30, 48 cm.);* female dişil.

**F.A.** Football Association Futbol Birliği.

**F.A.O.** Food and Agricultural Organisation Birleşmiş Milletler Gıda ve Tarım Örgütü.

**F.B.I.** *Am.* Federal Bureau of Investigation Federal Araştırma Bürosu.

**Feb.** February Şubat.

**Fed.** Federal federal; **Federated** federe; **Federation** federasyon.

**fem.** female dişil; **feminine** dişil.

**fig.** figurative mecazi; **figure** rakam.

**fl.** fluid sıvı; **floor** kat.

**fm.** fathom(s) kulaç *(1,83 m.).*

**F.M.** Frequency Modulation frekans modülasyonu.

**F.O.** Foreign Office Dışişleri Bakanlığı.

**f.o.b.** free on board gemide teslim.

**for.** foreign yabancı.

**Fr.** Father baba; **Franc** frank; **France** Fransa; **French** Fransız.

**Fri.** Friday Cuma.

**ft.** foot (feet) ayak *(30,48 cm.).*

**furn.** furnished mobilyalı.

**G**

**g.** gram(s) gram.

**gal(l).** gallon(s) galon.

**GATT** General Agreement on Tariffs and Trade Gümrük Tarifeleri ve Ticaret Genel Antlaşması.

618

**G.B.** Great Britain Büyük Britanya.
**Gen.** General general.
**G.H.Q.** General Headquarters genel merkez.
**Gk.** Greek Yunanlı.
**gm.** gram(s) gram.
**G.M.** General Manager genel müdür.
**G.M.T.** Greenwich Mean Time Greenwich saat ayarı.
**gov(t).** government hükümet.
**Gov.** Governor vali.
**G.P.** General Practitioner pratisyen doktor.
**G.P.O.** General Post Office merkez postanesi.
**gr.** grain bir eczacı tartısı *(0,0648 g.)*; gross brüt; group grup.

## H

**h** height yükseklik; hour saat.
**ha.** hectare(s) hektar.
**H-bomb** Hydrogen bomb hidrojen bombası.
**H.E.** high explosive kuvvetli patlayıcı madde; His/Her Excellency Ekselansları.
**H.F.** High Frequency Yüksek frekans.
**H.M.** His/Her Majesty Majesteleri, Haşmetmeapları.
**Hon.** Honorary fahri.
**hosp.** hospital hastane.
**H.P.** Horse Power beygir gücü.
**H.Q.** Headquarters karargâh, merkez.
**H.R.H.** His/Her Royal Highness Ekselansları.

## I

**I** Island ada.
**ib(id).** ibidem *(Lat.* = in the same place) aynı yerde.
**I.C.B.M.** Inter-continental Ballistic Missile kıtalararası balistik mermi.
**i.e.** id est *(Lat.* = which is to say, in other words) yani.
**I.L.O.** International Labo(u)r Organisation Uluslararası Çalışma Örgütü.
**I.M.F.** International Monetary Fund Uluslararası Para Fonu.
**in.** inch(es) inç *(2,54 cm.)*.
**Inc.** Incorporated anonim.
**incl.** including dahil.
**info.** information bilgi.
**Inst.** Institute kuruluş, müessese, enstitü.
**int.** interior dahili; internal dahili; international uluslararası.
**I.O.U.** I owe you size olan borcum.
**I.R.A.** Irish Republican Army Irlanda Cumhuriyetçi Ordusu.

## J

**Jan.** January Ocak.
**J.C.** Jesus Christ Isa Mesih.
**J.P.** Justice of the Peace sulh hâkimi.
**Jul.** July Temmuz.
**Jun.** June Haziran.

## K

**kg.** kilogram(s) kg., kilogram.
**km.** kilometre(s) km., kilometre.

**K.O.** knock-out nakavt.
**kw.** kilowatt(s) kilovat.

**L**

**L** lake göl; little küçük; *pol.* Liberal Liberal Parti.
**l** left sol; length uzunluk; line yol, hat.
**L.A.** Legislative Assembly Yasama Meclisi; Los Angeles Los Angeles.
**Lab.** Labour İşçi Partisi.
**lang.** language dil, lisan.
**lat.** latitude enlem.
**lb.** pound(s) libre.
**L.C.** letter of credit akreditif.
**Ld.** Lord Lord.
**lit.** literal kelimesi kelimesine; literature edebiyat, yazın.
**loc. cit.** loco citato *(Lat.* = in the place mentioned) yukarıda belirtilen yerde.
**long.** longitude boylam.
**L.P.** long-playing (record) uzunçalar.
**Lt.** Lieutenant teğmen.
**Ltd.** Limited limitet.
**lux.** luxury lüks.

**M**

**M** Member üye.
**m** male erkek; married evli; metre(s) metre; mile(s) mil; million milyon.
**M.A.** Master of Arts Edebiyat Fakültesi Lisansüstü Derecesi.
**Maj.** Major binbaşı.
**Mar.** March Mart.
**masc.** masculine eril.
**math(s)** mathematics matematik.
**max.** maximum maksimum.
**M.C.** Master of Ceremonies protokol görevlisi, teşrifatçı; *Am.* Member of Congress kongre üyesi.
**M.D.** Doctor of Medicine tıp doktoru.
**mg.** milligram(s) miligram.
**min.** minimum minimum.
**ml.** mile(s) mil; millilitre(s) mililitre.
**mm.** millimetre(s) milimetre.
**M.O.** Medical Officer sağlık memuru; Money Order para havalesi.
**Mon.** Monday Pazartesi.
**M.P.** Member of Parliament milletvekili; Military Police askeri inzibat.
**m.p.h.** miles per hour saat mil.
**Mr.** Mister bay.
**Mrs.** Mistress bayan.
**Ms.** Miss bayan.
**MS(S)** manuscript(s) el yazması.
**Mt.** Mount dağ, tepe.

**N**

**N** north kuzey.
**N.A.A.F.I.** Navy, Army and Air Force Institute Deniz, Kara ve Hava Kuvvetleri Kurumu.

**NATO** North Atlantic Treaty Organisation Kuzey Atlantik Paktı Teşkilatı.
**N.C.O.** Non-Commissioned Officer assubay.
**NE** northeast kuzeydoğu.
**no** number numara, no.
**Nov.** November Kasım.
**nr.** near yakın.
**N.T.** New Testament Yeni Ahit, Incil.
**NW.** northwest kuzeybatı.
**N.Z.** New Zealand Yeni Zeland.

**O**

**ob** obiit *(Lat.* = died) ölmüş, merhum.
**Oct.** October Ekim.
**OECD** Organisation for Economic Co-operation and Development Ekonomik İşbirliği ve Kalkınma Teşkilatı.
**OPEC** Organisation of Petroleum Exporting Countries Petrol İhraç Eden Ulkeler Teşkilatı.
**orch.** orchestra orkestra.
**O.T.** Old Testament Eski Ahit.
**oz.** ounce(s) ons *(28,35 g.).*

**P**

**P** page sayfa; penny peni; pence pens; per herbiri için, başına.
**p.a.** per annum *(Lat.* = per year) yıllık.
**P.A.Y.E.** pay as you earn 'kazandıkça öde' sistemi, işverenin personel ücretlerini öderken gelir vergisini kestiği sistem.
**pd.** paid ödendi.
**P.E.** physical education beden eğitimi.
**PEN** International Association of Writers Uluslararası Yazarlar Birliği.
**Pk** Park park.
**pkt** packet paket.
**P.M.** Prime Minister başbakan.
**p.m.** post meridien *(Lat.* = after noon) öğleden sonra.
**P.O.** Post Office postane; Postal Order posta havalesi.
**P.O. Box** Post Office Box posta kutusu.
**P.O.W.** Prisoner of War savaş esiri.
**p.p.** per procurationem *(Lat.* = on behalf) adına.
**pr.** pair çift; price fiyat.
**Pres.** President cumhurbaşkanı.
**Prof.** Professor profesör.
**P.S.** Postscript ek not, dipnot.
**pt.** part kısım; payment ödeme; point nokta.
**Pte.** Private asker, er.
**P.T.O.** Please turn over lütfen sayfayı çeviriniz.
**Pvt.** Private *Am.* asker, er.
**p.w.** per week haftalık.
**P.X.** post exchange *Am.* ordu pazarı.

**Q**

**qt.** quart kuart.
**Qu.** queen kraliçe; question soru.

**R**

**R.** River ırmak, nehir.
**r.** radius yarıçap; right sağ.
**R.A.** Rear-Admiral tuğamiral; Royal Academy Kraliyet Akademisi.
**R.A.F.** Royal Air Force İngiliz Hava Kuvvetleri.
**R.C.** Red Cross Kızılhaç.
**Rd.** Road yol, cadde.
**rec(d).** received alındı.
**ref.** referee hakem; reference referans.
**resp.** respectively sırasıyla.
**ret(d).** retired emekli.
**Rev(d).** Reverend sayın, muhterem.
**RIP** requiescat in pace (Lat. = may he rest in peace) huzur içinde yatsın.
**rly.** railway demiryolu.
**rm.** room oda.
**R.N.** Royal Navy İngiliz Donanması.
**R.S.V.P.** repondez s'il vous plait (Fr. = please reply) lütfen cevap verin.
**rt.** right sağ.

**S**

**S** south güney.
**s** second(s) saniye; shilling(s) şilin.
**SALT** Strategic Arms Limitation Talks Stratejik Silahların Sınırlandırılması Görüşmeleri.
**Sat.** Saturday Cumartesi.
**s/c** self-contained müstakil.
**Sch.** School okul.
**SE** southeast güneydoğu.
**sec.** second ikinci; secretary sekreter.
**Sen.** Senate senato; Senator senatör; Senior büyük.
**Sept.** September Eylül.
**Sgt.** Sergeant çavuş.
**Sn(r).** Senior büyük.
**Sol.** Solicitor avukat.
**sp. gr.** specific gravity özgül ağırlık.
**Sq.** Square meydan, alan.
**S.S.** Steamship vapur.
**St.** Street sokak, cadde.
**Sta.** Station istasyon.
**Str.** Strait boğaz; Street sokak, cadde.
**Sun.** Sunday Pazar.
**SW.** southwest güneybatı.

**T**

**T** temperature ısı, sıcaklık.
**t.** ton(s) ton.
**T.B.** Tuberculosis tüberküloz, verem.
**tel.** telephone telefon.
**Thurs.** Thursday Perşembe.
**TIR** Transport International Routier Uluslararası karayolu taşımacılığı.

**T.K.O.** technical knock-out teknik nakavt.
**T.U.** Trade Union işçi sendikası.
**Tues.** Tuesday Salı.
**T.V.** television TV, televizyon.

## U

**U.F.O.** unidentified flying object uçan daire.
**U.H.F.** ultra high frequency çok yüksek frekans.
**U.K.** United Kingdom Büyük Britanya.
**U.N.** United Nations Birleşmiş Milletler.
**UNESCO** United Nations Educational, Scientific and Cultural Organisation Birleşmiş Milletler Eğitim, Bilim ve Kültür Örgütü.
**UNICEF** United Nations Children's Emergency Fund Birleşmiş Milletler Uluslararası Çocuklara Acil Yardım Fonu.
**UNIDO** United Nations Industrial Development Organization Birleşmiş Milletler Sınai Kalkınma Örgütü.
**Univ.** University üniversite.
**UNO** United Nations Organisation Birleşmiş Milletler Teşkilatı.
**U.S.A.** United States of America Amerika Birleşik Devletleri.
**USAF** United States Air Force Amerika Birleşik Devletleri Hava Kuvvetleri.

## V

**V** Volt volt.
**v** very çok; verse mısra, beyit, kıta; versus karşı; vide *(Lat.* = see) bakınız.
**V.A.** Vice-Admiral koramiral.
**V.A.T.** Value Added Tax K.D.V., katma değer vergisi.
**V.D.** Venereal Disease zührevi hastalık.
**V.H.F.** very high frequency çok yüksek frekans.
**V.I.P.** very important person çok önemli kişi.
**vol.** volume cilt.
**vs.** versus karşı.

## W

**W** west batı.
**w** watt(s) vat; week hafta; width genişlik, en.
**w.c.** water closet tuvalet.
**wk.** week hafta.
**wt.** weight ağırlık.

## X

**Xmas** Christmas Noel.

## Y

**YMCA** Young Men's Christian Association Genç Hıristiyan Erkekler Birliği.
**yr.** year yıl; your senin, sizin.
**YWCA** Young Women's Christian Association Genç Hıristiyan Kadınlar Birliği.